ISBN 978-0-282-21416-6
PIBN 10844625

FB &c Ltd, Dalton House, 60 Windsor Avenue, London, SW19 2RR.
Company number 08720141. Registered in England and Wales.

For support please visit www.forgottenbooks.com

A

DICTIONARY

OF THE

WELSH LANGUAGE,

EXPLAINED IN ENGLISH;

WITH

NUMEROUS ILLUSTRATIONS, FROM THE LITERARY REMAINS AND FROM THE LIVING SPEECH OF THE

Cymmry.

TO WHICH IS PREFIXED,

A WELSH GRAMMAR.

THE SECOND EDITION.

By W. OWEN PUGHE, D.C.L. F.A.S.

VOL. II.

DENBIGH:

PRINTED AND PUBLISHED BY THOMAS GEE;

AND MAY BE HAD OF LONGMAN, REES, ORME, AND GREEN, PATERNOSTER-ROW; AND J. JONES, 3, DUKE-STREET, WEST SMITHFIELD, LONDON.

1832.

GEIRIADUR CYMMRAEG A SAESONEG.

WELSH-ENGLISH DICTIONARY.

E, *A prefix in composition.* It implies aptness to act, or to move.

E, standing alone, as a word, implies action going on, and when it accompanies a verb it is the agent performing the action described without the discrimination of a person. The pronoun *it*; but the particular character is generally marked by the context; except in the *Silurian Dialect*, where it implies he, and his. It is appropriately the sign of the active participle, making actions of the present tense, which without it would be otherwise. It has also the form, in many expressions, of what would be termed an adverb. Examples, *gwelir*, there will be seen; *e welir*, seeing takes place, or, it is seen; *e'm gwelir*, the seeing of me takes place, or, I am seen; *e dyngai*, the agent swearing was, or he (she, or it) swore; *e dyngai y dyn*, the man swore, *nag e*, not it, or it not.

> E fynai y gath bysgod, ond ni fynai wlychu ei throed.
>
> The cat would have fish, but she would not have to wet her foot. *Adage.*

Eang, *a.* (ang) Ample, large, wide, loose, free. *Gwr ëang*, a free man.

> Eang yw y byd i bawb.
>
> The world is *spacious* for all. *Adage.*

Eangawl, *a.* (ëang) Tending to make spacious.

Eangder, *s. m.* (ëang) Spaciousness, capacity.

Eangiad, *s. m.* (ëang) A making capacious.

Eangrwydd, *s. m.* (ëang) Spaciousness, capacity.

Eangu, *v. a.* (ëang) To make ample or spacious.

Eawg, *s. m.—pl.* ëogiaid (awg) A salmon.

> Nid mwynaidd ond ëawg.
>
> There is nothing so pleasing as the *salmon*. *Adage.*

Eawn, *a.* (awn) Bold, daring, intrepid, brave.

Eaws, *s. f.—pl.* ëosau (aws) A nightingale.

> Nid serchawg ond ëaws.
>
> There is nothing so loving as the *nightingale*. *Adage.*

EB, *s. m. r.—pl. t.* ion. A going; a going from, a proceeding out of; a sending from; utterance; in a state abstracted from.

Eb, *v. n.* (*for* ebu) To go, or proceed from; to send from; to utter; to say. *Eb fi, eb y fi, ebwyf fi, ebof fi*, quoth I; *eb di*, quoth thou; *eb efe*, saith he; *eb y ni*, quoth we.

Ebach, *s. f.—pl. t.* au (eb—ach) A nook, a corner, a cove, a bay.

> Ac yna yr ai Collen i fynydd Glesynfre, ac yno i gwnai efe guddigl dan ebach careg mewn lle dirgel.
>
> And then Collen went to the mountain of Glastonbery, and there he made a hermitage under the *corner* of a stone in a secret place. *Buchedd Collen.*

Ebachawg, *a.* (ebach) Full of nooks, or coves.

Ebaeth, *s. m.* (eb—aeth) A nook, or corner.

Eban, *s. m.—pl.* ebyn (eb) A passing on; a going by, or through. *v. a.* To go; to pass.

> Fy march Melyngan
> Cyfred a gwylan
> My han nid eban
> Cyfrwng mor a glan.
>
> My steed Melyngan is swift as the sea mew which *will not pass* me between the sea and the shore. *Taliesin.*

> Pan wnel Duw dangaws ei faran
> Dyddwyre dy daered arnan;
> Dychryn twrf torfoedd yn eban
> Dychyrch hynt——
>
> When God shall reveal his countenance, the boss of earth will raise itself over us; terror, with the tumultuous noise of armies *in passing*, will take his course. *Casnodyn.*

Ebargof, *s. m.—pl. t.* ion (argof) A forgetting.

Ebargofi, *v. n.* (ebargof) To forget, to let out of mind; to have short memory.

Ebargofiad, *s.m.* (ebargof) A forgetting, oblivion.

Ebawl, *s. m.—pl.* ebolion (eb—awl) A colt, a foal, a young horse. *Mae efe yn un ebawl*, he is quite a colt, or full of life.

> Hir y bydd march bach yn ebawl.
>
> Long will a little horse be a *colt*. *Adage.*
>
> Ni thelir saeth i ebawl.
>
> An arrow will not be paid to a *colt*. *Adage.*

Ebediw, *s. m.—pl. t.* iau (eb—ediw) A heriot.

Ebestawl, *s.m.—pl.* ebestolion (eb—est) An apostle

Ebiaith, *s. f.—pl.* ebieithion (eb—iaith) A part or division of a sentence.

> Gwelwch osawd y gair llais dair gwaith yn nechreuad yr ebiaith wahannodawl.
>
> You see the word *llais* placed three times in the beginning of the semicolon *division of the sentence*. *H. Perri.*

Ebill, *s. m.—pl. t.* ion (pill) A piercer; a pin, or peg; an auger; a gimblet; the key of a musical instrument. *Ebillion telyn*, the keys, or pins of a harp.

> ——Dy gi
> A'i ebillion gwynion ar gau
> Yn union yn ei enau.
>
> Thy dog with his white pegs on the close straightly set in his jaws. *T. Prys.*

Ebilldaradr, *s. m.—pl.* ebillderydr (ebill—taradr) A small auger.

> Ebilldaradr dimai a dal.
>
> A *small auger* its value is a half-penny. *Welsh Laws.*

Ebillen, *s. f. dim.* (ebill) A small peg; a gimblet.

Ebilliad, *s. m.* (ebill) A pegging; a boaring.

Ebilliaw, *v. a.* (ebill) To peg, to pierce; to bore.

Ebilliawg, *a.* (ebill) Having pegs or pins.

Ebod, *s. pl. aggr.* (eb) What is voided, dung.

Ebodn, *s. m.* (ebod) The dung of a horse.

Ebodni, *v. a.* (ebodn) To void dung, as a horse.

Ebolaidd, *a.* (ebawl) Like a colt, or coltish.

Eboles, *s. f.—pl. t.* au (ebawl) A young mare.

> Ni chaf un man, achwyn man,
> Heb lais fy eboleseu—
> I cwyn edwyn cennadwr,
> Achwyn yw am na chan' wr.

I get not a single spot, it is my complaint, free from the noise of my fillies; their craving is known to the messenger; it is grief because they can not get a husband. *R. Pyngiwyd, i ofyn caseg.*

Ebolgarn, *s. m.—pl. t.* au (ebawl—carn) Colts foot, a herb, also called *alan bychan; ebolgarn y gerddi*, asarrabacca; *ebolgarn y mor*, sea-bindweed.

Eboli, *v. n.* (ebawl) To become as a colt.

Ebolawg, *a.* (ebawl) Fit for foaling, or breeding.

Teithi caseg yw tynu car yn allt ac yn ngwaered, a dwyn pwn trawn, a bod yn eboliawg.

The qualities of a mare are to draw a drag up hill and down hill, and to carry a cross load, and to be *with foal*. *Welsh Laws.*

Eboludd, *adv.* (eb—goludd) Without let, or hinderance, without delay, forthwith, presently.

Ebran, *s.m.—pl.t.* au (eb—rhan) Horse provender

Y distain a ddyly ddau ebran i'w farch, a phedair pedol, ac eu to a hoelion unwaith yn y flwyddyn i gan y gofiyn.

The steward of the household is entitled to two *baits* for his horse, and four shoes with their sets of nails once in a year from the smith of the court. *Welsh Laws.*

Ebraniad, *s. m.* (ebran) A baiting, a foddering.

Ebranu, *v. a.* (ebran) To bait; to fodder. *Ebranu meirch*, to bait horses.

Ebranwr, *s. m.—pl.* ebranwyr (ebran—gwr) One who gives provender for horses.

Ebrawl, *a.* (ebr) Having a tendency to go.

Ebreidiad, *s. m.* (abred) A passing onward.

Ebreidiawg, *a.* (abred) Abounding with motion.

Ebri, *s. m.* (ebr) A going, egress, passage, utterance, a passing a word, surety.

> Ac yssi iddi dirgel ddiarael ebri;
> Ac am i mynwent mynawc heli;
> Ynys Fair firain.

And it has a sequestered place not worn by *travelling*, and around its cemetery is the bosom of the sea; the beautiful island of Mary. *Meilyr, i Enlli.*

Ebriad, *s. m.* (ebr) A going from or out of.

Ebrifed, *a.* (eb—rhifed) Without number.

> Cad ar wy cyrchwd
> Gwaewawr ebrifed.

To the conflict there resorted spears *innumerable*. *Taliesin.*

Ebrill, *s. m.* (eb—rhill) The month of April.

Ebrilliaidd, *a.* (ebrill) Like April; springing.

Ebru, *a.* (ebr) To move, to go from; to utter.

Ebrwydd, *a.* (eb—rhwydd) Quick, hasty, soon.

> A esgyno yn hwyr ebrwydd y disgyn.

He that climbs up late soon he will descend. *Adage.*

> Breuddwyd yw ebrwydded oes.

It is a dream *how swift* is life. *D. ab Gwilym.*

Ebrwyddaw, *v. a.* (ebrwydd) To hasten, to hie.

> Ef a ebrwyddodd ei hynt.

He *has quickened* his course. *H. Cw. Mag.—Mabinogion.*

Ebrwyddawl, *a.* (ebrwydd) Hastening, accelerating

Ebrwyddedig, *a.* (ebrwydd) Accelerated.

Ebrwyddiad, *s. m.* (ebrwydd) An acceleration.

Ebrydig, *a.* (abred) Having power to move.

Ebrydu, *v. a.* (abred) To move, pass onward.

Ebryfygawl, *a.* (rhyfygawl) Apt to neglect.

Ebryfygedig, *a.* (rhyfygedig) That is neglected. *Dadl ebryfygedig*, a neglected cause.

Ebryfygiad, *s. m.* (rhyfygiad) A neglecting.

Ebryfygu, *v. a.* (rhyfygu) To desist from having to do with; to neglect.

> Ebryfygais fwyta fy mara.

I neglected to eat my bread. *Dafydd Ddu.*

Ebu, *v. a.* (eb) To proceed out; to utter; to speak, to say.

Ebustl, *s. m.* (bustl) Gall bitter. *a.* Bitter.

Ebwch, *s. m.* (eb—wch) A gasp; a groan, a sigh.

Ebwr, *s. m.* (bwr) That hems in. *a.* Causing dread.

Ebwystl, *s. m.—pl. t.* ion (eb—gwystl) An embryo.

Ebychawl, *a.* (ebwch) Gasping, sighing, groaning.

Ebychedig, *a.* (ebwch) That is made to sigh.

Dywawd Braint Hir—Mae cenedl y Brytaniaid heb gaffael un tywysawg a allai ei dwyn ar eu hen ddylyedawd, a heddyw ebychedig a oedd o ymgynnal cerbydodd dy fod tithau yn dyoddef hefyd hyny ac ei golli.

Braint Hir said—The nation of the Britons is without obtaining one prince that could restore them to their ancient dignity, and this day it is *distressing* in endeavouring to preserve that honour that thou shouldest also suffer it to be diminished and lost. *Gr. ab Arthur.*

Ebychiad, *s. m.—pl. t.* au (ebwch) A gasping.

Ebychiawl, *a.* (ebwch) Gasping; sighing.

Ebychu, *v. a.* (ebwch) To gasp; to clamour.

Ebyd, *s. m.* (eb) A going from, a passing off.

Ebyri, *s. m.* (ebwr) That causes dread or fear.

Ebyrn, *s. m.—pl. t.* i (byrn) A brook bank.

> Gain cyniwyre tarthawg byrn;
> Esgudsaid ceirw tros ebyrn;
> Gnawd naid ei nangwyd trachwyrn.

Splendid the uprising of the foggy brook; of nimble leap the harts over the *bank*: the over hasty is accustomed to frequent tumbles. *E. C. Cynnwyre.*

Ecraidd, *a.* (egr) Of a harsh or severe nature.

Ecrawl, *a.* (egr) Of a harsh or severe nature.

Ecriad, *s. m.* (egr) A becoming harsh or sharp.

Ecrwr, *s. m.—pl.* ecrwyr (egr—gwr) A sharp dealing person, a sharper, an extortioner.

ECH, *s. f. r.* What is still; what pervades. It is seldom used except when compounded with other words. Also a portion of arable land; an acre.

> Tudfwlch Hir ech o dir a'i dirwydd.

Tudfwlch the tall, a *spot* of earth reduces him to corruption. *Aneurin.*

Echaeth, *s. m.* (ech) A seclusion; retirement.

Echain, *v. n.* (ech) To become secluded; to retire aside; to rest; to repose; to sleep.

Echawl, *a.* (ech) Secluded, retired; reposing.

Echdoe, *s. m.* (ech—doe) The day before yesterday. *adv.* On the day before yesterday.

> Echdoe a doe y deuwn
> I'r byd da, a'r bywyd hwn;
> Heddyw ni'th omeddaf Dafydd,
> Yn fore deuaf ar y dydd.

The day before yesterday and yesterday I would to come the good state and this living; to-day, Dafydd, I will not disappoint thee, early on the day I will come. *Gut. Owain.*

Echdoeawl, *a.* (echdoe) Of two days ago.

Echdywyn, *s. m.* (dywyn) Splendour, brightness.

Echdywynawl, *a.* (echdywyn) Glittering, luminous

Echdywynedig, *a.* (echdywyn) Resplendent, glittering, shining.

Y forwyn Eryla hono, nid oedd hawdd caffael dyn cun decach â hi yn yr holl fyd; canys gwynach oedd ei chnawd nag echdywynedig asgwrn morfil.

Eryla that same maid, it was not easy to find a person so fair as she in the whole world: for her body was whiter than the *polished* bone of the sea animal. *Gr. ab Arthur.*

Echdywynedigrwydd, *s. m.* (echdywynedig) Glitteringness, or resplendency.

Arthur a welai freuddwyd—sef, draig yn ehedeg o wrth y gorllewin ac echdywynedigrwydd ei llygaid yn goleuaw y wlad.

Arthur beheld a dream; namely, a dragon flying from out of the west, and the *brightness* of her eyes illuminating the country. *Gr. ab Arthur.*

Echdywyniad, *s. m.* (echdywyn) A glittering.

Echdywynu, *v. a.* (echdywyn) To cast a light.

Echdywynyg, *s. m.* (echdywyn) A diffusing of light. *v. a.* To cast a lustre; to glitter.

Echdywynygawl, *a.* (echdywynyg) Resplendent.

Echdywynygiad, *s. m.* (echdywynyg) A glittering.
Echdywynygu, *v. a.* (echdywynyg) To cast a splendour, to glitter, to shine.
Echeiniad, *s. m.* (echen) A giving origin to.

> Na'm didawl o'th fedd, udd echeiniad,
> Na'm gwellyg yn mhlyg yn mhlaid irad.

Deprive me not of thy blessing, Lord of the *creation*, leave me not neglected and confined with the hideous crew. *Cynddelw.*

Echel, *s. f.—pl.* echyl (ech—el) Axis; axle-tree.

> Mawr fwy y credaf no chrair cred neirthiad
> Echel cad cad aduair.

Much more than the gospel of the faith I believe the supporter and the *pillar* of battle; the scatterer of treasure. *Phylip Brydydd.*

Echen, *s. f.—pl.* echyn (ech—en) A source, or origin; a stock, tribe, family, or nation.

> Gwr hydr i'n hoedran a ddel,
> Gwawr echen gwryd Echel!

May a gallant hero come in our time, the luminary of the *tribe* having the courage of Echel! *Ll. P. Moch.*

> I'm peryf digardd bwyf dygen geiniad;
> I'r Mab, i'r Mawr-dad roddiad fy Rheen,
> I'r Ysbryd uchel o'r un echen.

To my pure great cause may I be a conspicuous singer; to the Son, to the great Father, the giver of my Lord, to the supreme Spirit from the one *source*. *Cynddelw, m. R. Fleidd.*

Echenawg, *a.* (echen) Having an origin or stock.
Echenawl, *a.* (echen) Belonging to a tribe.
Eching, *s. m.* (ech—ing) A confined state.
Eching, *a.* (ech—ing) Straitened, restrained.

> Eching ynof cof, neu'm cafas edlid
> Am edliu teyrnas!

Oppressed is memory within me, am I not assailed by affliction after the heir of a kingdom! *Ll. P. Moch, m. H. ab Gr. ab Cynan.*

Echlur, *s. m.* (ech—llur) What causes paleness. *a.* Of a pale hue, livid.
Echlys, *s. m.—pl. t.* ion (ech—llys) Cause, motive; occasion; opportunity.
Echlysawl, *a.* (echlys) Occasional; opportune.
Echlysiad, *s. m.—pl. t.* au (echlys) An occasioning
Echlysu, *v. a.* (echlys) To occasion; to cause.

> Am gydfrawd Medrawd Myrddin darogan;
> Am orwyr Cynan cerdd echlysu.

Of the joint brother of Medrod Myrddin predicteth: *of* the great grandson of Cynan the song *is called forth. Gw. Brycheiniawg.*

Echlysur, *s. m.—pl. t.* ion (echlys) A cause, a motive.
Echlysuraw, *v. v.* (echlysur) To make an occasion.
Echlysurawl, *a.* (echlysur) Occasional; causing.
Echlysuriad, *s. m.—pl. t.* au (echlysur) A causing.
Echnos, *s. f.—pl. t.* au (ech—nos) The night before last. *a.* Of the night before last.
Echre, *adv.* (ech—rhe) Rather, yea rather.
Echrestr, *s. f.—pl.* echrestrau (rhestr) What is registered or entered for a deposit; a register.

> Echrestr yr ammod.

The *registered copy* of the covenant. *Cer. o Langerforn.*

Echrestrawl, *a.* (echrestr) Belonging to registering
Echrestriad, *s. m.* (echrestr) A registering.
Echrestru, *v. a.* (echrestr) To put in a register.
Echryd, *s. m.—pl. t.* au (cryd) Abashment, affright; a trembling, or shivering.
Echrydiad, *s. m.—pl. t.* au (echryd) A shivering.
Echrydu, *v. a.* (echryd) To shiver or tremble.
Echrydus, *a.* (echryd) Shocking, terrible, horrid.
Echryn, *s. m.* (cryn) A trembling, a quaking, or shivering; terror, horror, dread.
Echrynadwy, *a.* (echryn) Capable of agitating.
Echrynawl, *a.* (echryn) Shivering, trembling.
Echrynedig, *a.* (echryn) Made to quake.
Echryniad, *s. m.—pl. t.* au (echryn) Trepidation.
Echrynu, *v. a.* (echryn) To quake, to tremble.

Echrys, *s. m.* (ech—rhys) What causes a starting, hurt, mischief; terror. *a.* Dire, horrid.
Echrysawl, *a.* (echrys) Tending to frighten.
Echrysder, *s. m.* (echrys) What causes a sudden shock; direfulness.
Echryshaint, *s. m.* (echrys—haint) A blast; or malignant distemper; a benumbing stroke.
Echrysiad, *s. m.* (echrys) A striking with a shock.
Echryslawn, *a.* (echrys) Direful, or horrible.
Echryslondeb, *s. m.* (echryslawn) Direfulness.
Echryslonder, *s. m.* (echryslawn) Direfulness.
Echryslonedd, *s. m.* (echryslawn) Direfulness.
Echrysloni, *v. n.* (echryslawn) To become direful.
Echryslonrwydd, *s. m.* (echryslawn) Direfulness; heinousness, cursedness.
Echrysu, *v. n.* (echrys) To become malignant.
Echu, *v. n.* (ech) To be not acted upon; to go aside, to retire; to be reposing.
Echudd, *s. m.* (cudd) A hiding, a hiding place.

> Mynaches wyd mewn echudd.

Thou art a nun in *seclusion*. *D. Llwyd.*

Echuddiad, *s. m.* (echudd) A hiding, or secluding
Echuddiaw, *v. a.* (echudd) To hide, or to seclude
Echur, *s. m.* (cur) Anguish, pain; disorder.
Echw, *s. m.* (ech) What has motion; a horse.

> Hy byddai y'nghyfrain Present mab Pel;
> Ar ei echw byddai oni fai atre.

Present the son of Pel would be bold in the conflict; on his *horse* he would be if he should not be on the return. *Aneurin.*

Echwa, *v. n.* (echw) To be on horseback; to ride.

> ——Y wrthyd ni'm pella;
> Pell ydwyf o nwyf yn echwa;
> Ar ni fo pwyllawg ni's pwylla.

Drive me not far from thee; because of lust far *I am riding away;* he that is not circumspect will not use discretion. *Cynddelw.*

Echwaint, *s. m.* (echw) A being riding.

> Meifod——
> A'i balch-wawr yn awr yn newaint,
> A'i balchgor heb achor echwaint.

Meifod with its proud illumination in the matin hour, and its proud choir without a *circle of progression*. *Cynddelw.*

Echweg, *a.* (chweg) Luscious to the taste, sweet.
Echwith, *a.* (chwith) Adverse, contrary; awkward
Echwng, *a.* (ech—wng) Closed upon. *v. a.* To close upon, to envelope, to close to.

> Hiraeth a'm gwalaeth gweled arnaw fwng
> Hirbebrwng echwng; o'ch o'r cuddlawl!

Sorrow oppresses me, to see upon him the gloom of the *closed* long separation; alas, this covering over!

> Gwaith blwng oedd echwng, och, Wenhwyfar deg
> Dygn ynof dy alar!

It was gloomy work *to close in*, ah, fair Gwenhwyvar severe is my grief for thee! *Gr. ab M. ab Dafydd.*

Echwraint, *s. m.* (ech—gwraint) A quiescent quality, or nature.
Echwydd, *s. m.* (echw) A state of stillness, rest, or quiescence, a cessation; a cleared region, or a place cleared of its wild state; but the common meaning of the word is the evening; and in some places it is the term for autumn.

> Tan yn nhai cyn dydd
> Rhag udd yr echwydd;
> Yr echwydd tecaf,
> A'i dynion haelaf;
> Gnawd Eingl heb waesaf
> Am deyrn glewaf.

Fire in houses ere the day appears before the sovereign of the *cultivated plain*; the fairest *cultivated plain*, and its most generous men; the Angles are without homage from the most energetic prince. *Taliesin, i Urien.*

> Cyfranc allt a gallt ac echwydd.

The junction o cliff with cliff and the *cultivated plain*. *Taliesin.*

> Aeth i gym'ryd bedydd———
> Dlau Fab Duw nef yn nwfr echwydd.

The true Son of God of heaven went to take baptism in the water of *stillness*. *Gwalchmai.*

Echwyddaw, *v.* (echwydd) To be still or at rest.

> *Ffrewer wen brodyr a'th fu,*
> *Pan glywynt gyfrwng llu,*
> *Ni echwyddai oy gantho.*

Fair Frewer thou hadst brothers, when they heard the clashing together of spears, *there would be no still abode with them.* *Llywarch Hen.*

Echwyn, *s. m.—pl. t.* ion (cwyn) What is taken or given for use; a loan.

> Echwyn yw nag.

A denial is what *is upon trust.* *Adage.*

> Ni chyngain cwyn am echwyn.

An action will not accord for *what is upon return.* *Adage.*

> Cas dyn a ddyco yn echwyn mwy nag allo dalu byth.

Odious is the man that shall take upon *trust* more than he can ever pay. *Adage.*

Echwyna, *v. a.* (echwyn) To take upon use; to borrow, to take a loan; to lend. *Echwyna ganddo*, to borrow of him; *echwyna iddo*, to lend to him.

> Chwannawg wyf i echwyna——
> A dwyn pann y dyn pennaf.

I am ambitious for *to take upon trust*, and to take the peacock of the chief of men. *D. ab Ieu. Ddu.*

Echwynaw, *v. a.* (echwyn) To borrow, to take a loan; to lend, or give upon trust.

> Cas a echwyno cymaint ag na bo ganddo a'i talo.

Odious is he *that shall borrow* so much as not to have wherewithal to pay it. *Adage.*

Echwynawl, *a.* (echwyn) Relating to borrowing.

Echwyniad, *s. m.* (echwyn) A giving or taking upon trust; a borrowing.

Echwynwr, *s. m.—pl.* echwynwyr (echwyn—gwr) A lender, or giver upon trust; a creditor.

> Dau ddyledwr oedd i'r un echwynwr.

There were two debtors for the one *creditor.* *Luc vii. 41.*

Echwynydd, *s. m.—pl. t.* ion (echwyn) A creditor

Echwyrth, *a.* (ech—gwyrth) Dull, sottish, foolish.

Echyngawl, *a.* (echwng) Having aptness to close

Echyngiad, *s. m.* (echwng) An approximating.

Echyngu, *v. a.* (echwng) To approximate.

> Echyngodd deigr bardd ech i rudd;
> Och anhawdd yn ddig gyda chwynion!

The tear of a bard *has approached* to his cheek; ah, it is difficult to be angry with complaints! *Gr. ab M. ab Dafydd.*

Echyr, *s. m.* (cyr) A reach, or attainment.

Ed, *s. m. r.* What has aptness to act, or velocity. It is doubtful whether it is used in its simple form. Compounded with other words it is very generally used, both as a prefix and affix; it is particularly the termination of many verbs

Edaf, *s. f.—pl. t.* edd (ed—af) A thread, or yarn.

Edafedd, *s. m aggr.* (edaf) Thread, or yarn.

> Aur a dyf ar edafedd.

Gold doth grow upon the *threads.* *D. ab Gwilym, I'r haul.*

> Hyd yr edafedd yr oedd oriau, diwrnodau, a blynyddoedd; a thynged wrth ei lyfr yn torri edafedd einioes, ac yn agor drysau y wal derfyn rhwng y ddau fyd.

Along the *threads* there were hours, days, and years; and fate by his book was cutting the *threads* of life, and opening the doors of the boundary wall between the two worlds. *Elis Wyn, B. Cwsg.*

Edafeddawg, *a.* (edafedd) Full of thread; ropy. *Yr edafeddawg*, cudweed; *edafeddawg llwyd, llwyd y ffordd, llwydyn y ffordd, llwyd bonheddig*, common cudweed.

Edafeddu, *v. n.* (edafedd) To form into thread; to become thread; to grow ropy.

Edau, *s. f.* (ed—au) Thread, or yarn. *Edau wlan*, woollen yarn; *edau sidan*, silk thread; *edau lin*, flaxen thread; *edau gywarch*, hempen thread.

> Ni ddodwyd ynddi edau
> Na llewion bras, na llin brau.

There was not put in it *thread* of crude hemp, nor rotten flax. *I. Llwyd, Brydydd, i wasgod.*

Edefyn, *s. m. dim.* (edaf) A single thread.

Edeifniad, *s. m.—pl.* edeifniaid (deifniad) One that is trained up, educated, or civilised.

> Pan orug Coll cuddfyddiaid daiar,
> Dyniadon edeifniaid,
> Ef goreu un gwreu yn nhlaid
> Cymmry.

When the Mysterious One created the superior ones in knowledge of the earth, the *polished ones* of mankind, he formed one worthy to support the Welsh. *Ll. P. Moch, i Rodri.*

Eden, *s. f.—pl.* ednod (ed) A flying creature, a fowl, or a bird.

> Adar â gaid âr y gwynt,
> O'i ddwy angor ni ddiangynt,
> Ehillion edeinion yn cau
> Eden y bwn dan i bawn.

Birds that should be found upon the wind, from his two grapples they would not escape, that were crooked pegs clutching a *winged animal* the bittern under his nails. *T. Aled, i Walch.*

> Dof yw'r adar wrth fara,
> Diod yr ednod yw'r ia.

Tame are the fowls to the bread, the drink of the birds is the ice. *D. ab Ieuan ddu, i alarch.*

Edenawg, *a.* (eden) Having winged motion. *s. f.* A hearse, or bier.

> Cenyn cenid aer;
> Aer edrchiawg,
> Aer edenawg.

With us was there not a battle; a harnessed battle, a battle of the *bier.* *Aneurin.*

> Heddyw hawdd y gallaf wylaw;
> Cudd-fedd (wartheiwar wedd) wrthaw,
> Ac edenawg y danaw!

To-day I can easily weep; the gloomy grave (precious the countenance) near him, and the *bier* under him. *Gr. ab Gwrgenau.*

Edfryd, *s. m.* (ed—bryd) The act of restoring.

> Gorwyr Bleddyn——
> Heb edfryd y'ngweryd wely!

The great grandson of Bleddyn without *return* in the bed of earth he lies! *Gwalchmai.*

Edfryd, *v. a.* (ed—bryd) To restore, to return.

> Os o log, neu o adneu, neu o fenthyg, yr holi dy dda, rhaid iti fynegi y dydd y dylid ei edfryd.

If with respect to interest, or pledge, or a loan thou dost claim thy property, it is necessary for thee to declare the day on which it ought *to be restored.* *Welsh Laws.*

Edfrydawl, *a.* (edfryd) Tending to restore.

Edfrydiad, *s. m.—pl. t.* au (edfryd) A restoration.

Edfrydwr, *s. m.* (edfryd—gwr) A restorer.

Edfrydydd, *s. m.—pl. t.* ion (edfryd) A restorer.

Edfudd, *s. m.—pl. t.* ion (ed—budd) Interest.

Edfuddiaw, *v. a.* (edfudd) To make advantage of

Edfuddiawl, *a.* (edfudd) Advantageous.

Edfyn, *s. m.—pl. t.* oedd (ed—myn) Rejection; the act of going from, a departure.

> All llam an edfyn
> Yw lladd Llywelyn.

Like the step *of departure* is the killing of Llywelyn. *Gwalchmai.*

Edfyn, *v. a.* (ed—myn) To refrain from, to go from, to depart.

> Ei angerdd nis edfyn.

His ardency *will not depart.* *Cynddelw.*

> A'th gyfarchaf naf ni edfyn beirdd
> Megys Bardd ar drwnyn.

Chief, I will greet thee, whom bards *will not depart from*, being a bard on a journey. *Ll. P. Moch.*

> Melys yw pechawd pan i herlyn digrifaid;
> Mor drwm yr enaid yn ye[illegible] edfyn.

Sweet is sin when the mischievous pursues it; how sad the soul that *refrains not from* it. *Meilyr ab Gwalchmai.*

Edfynt, *s. m.* (edfyn) The act of refraining, or going from, a departure.

> Am orwyr Bleddyn
> Ym gorhoedd llodgynt,
> Aml edfynt am dyfu,
> Am ddifod arth arfod arf hei!

For the grandson of Bleddyn indignation assails me, frequent the *departure* homeward because of the nonexistence of the bear of conflict with the bold weapon. *Gwalchmai.*

Hil Meredudd drawe hawdd drostaw lodgynt;
Hil edfynt Bleddynt blaidd ymwriaw.

The offspring of the haughty Meredudd, it is easy to be indignant for his loss; the *departed* offspring of Bleddynt the wolf of conflict. *Bleddyn Fardd, m. O. Goch.*

Edgyllaeth, *s. m.* (ed—cyllaeth) Separation; grief, sorrow, wailing.

Gwae fi, o'i golli drwy edgyllaeth hydr,
Hidl fydd deigr o hiraeth!

Woe to me from losing him, by the awful *separation* flowing will be tears from sorrowful longing! *Prydydd Bychan.*

Edifar, *a.* (difar) Penitent, Repenting, sorry. *Edifar genyf hyny*, I am sorry for that.

Cas a wnel ddrwg ac ni bo edifar ganddo.

Odious is he that doth evil, and is not *sorry* for it. *Adage.*

Edifarâad, *s. m.* (edifar) A repenting; contrition.
Edifarâawl, *a.* (edifar) Penitential, repenting.
Edifarâu, *v. n.* (edifar) To repent; to relent.
Edifarâwr, *s. m.—pl.* edifarâwyr (edifar—gwr) One who is penitent, or that repents.
Edifaru, *v. n.* (edifar) To repent, to be sorry.
Edifarus, *a.* (edifar) Penitent, contrite, sorry.
Edifarwch, *s. m.* (edifar) Penitence, contrition.
Edifaw, *v. a.* (tifaw) To succeed to; to possess.
Edifedd, *s. m.—pl. t.* ion (tifedd) A successor, or heir; issue, or offspring; an inheritor.
Edifeddawl, *a.* (edifedd) That comes in succession
Edifeddiad, *s. m.—pl. t.* au (edifedd) A succeeding
Edifeddu, *v. a.* (edifedd) To succeed to, to inherit.
Edifeiriad, *s. m.—pl. t.* au (edifar) A repenting.
Edifeiriant, *s. m.* (edifar) Penitence, contrition.
Edifeiriaw, *v. n.* (edifar) To repent, to be sorry.
Edifeiriawg, *a.* (edifar) Repentant, contrite.

Edifeiriawg da Duw a'i ceinmyn;
Ef ceiff carennydd o'i ffydd fechyn.

The good *penitent*, God will honour him; he shall have favour on account of his little faith. *Meilyr ab Gwalchmai.*

Edifeiriawl, *a.* (edifar) Penitent, or contrite.
Edifeirwch, *s. m.* (edifar) Repentance, contrition.

Gorea edifeirwch edifeirwch gwerthu.

The best *repentance* is the *repentance* for selling. *Adage.*

Eding, *s. m.* (ed—ing) Freedom from restraint.
Edlaes, *a.* (ed—llaes) Slack, or trailing.
Edlid, *s. m.—pl. t.* ion (ed—llid) Irritation.

Dymdoddyw edliw ac edlid
Am haelon haelder cynenid!

There are come to me reproach and *vexation* for the generous ones of the stock of generosity. *Ll. P. Moch.*

Mwyfwy yn tramwy tramawr edlid—
Lliw ar fy wyneb ni liwyr edid!

More and more my travelling with extreme *vexation*; not the least colour has been left on my face! *Ior. Fychan.*

Edlin, *s. m.* (ed—llin) One in the line of succession; a grandson; an heir; an heir apparent.

Anrhydeddusaf wedi y brenin ac y frenines yw edlin braint neu eni.

The most honourable after the king and the queen is the *heir apparent* by privilege, or birth. *Welsh Laws.*

Edliw, *s. m.* (ed—lliw) Reproach, upbraiding.
Edliw, *v. a.* (ed—lliw) To upbraid, to reproach.
Edliwgar, *a.* (edliw) Reproachful; contumelious.
Edliwgarwch, *s. m.* (edliwgar) Contumeliousness.
Edliwiad, *s. m.* (edliw) A reproaching, a twiting.
Edliwiant, *s. m.* (edliw) Reproach, contumely.
Edliwiaw, *v. a.* (edliw) To upbraid, to reproach.

Edliwiaist, lle gwelaist gur,
I'm daim o'm clwyf a'm dolur.

Thou hast reproached, where thou hast seen affliction, to me much of my disease and pain. *G. ab H. ab Tudur.*

Edliwiawl, *a.* (edliw) Upbraiding, contumelious.
Edliwied, *v. a.* (edliw) To upbraid, to reproach.
Edliwiwr, *s. m.—pl.* edliwiwyr (edliw—gwr) An upbraider, or reproacher.

Edlwg, *s. m.—pl.* edlygon (ed—llwg) A review, or observation. *Bwrw edlwg*, to cast a look.
Edlygawl, *a.* (edlwg) Reviewed, observing.
Edlygiad, *s. m.—pl. t.* au (edlwg) A reviewing.
Edlygu, *v. a.* (edlwg) To review, to observe.
Edlym, *a.* (ed—llym) Pungent, piercing, acute.

Mewn hanesgerdd—bydded yr adroddiad yn edlym a nwyfus.

In narrative poetry let the description be *acute* and vigorous. *Barddas.*

Gwae fardd ofer-ddysg edlym
Afrwydded fu'r dynged ym!

Woe to the bard of *acute* learning that is useless, that fate should have been so adverse to me! *D. ab Gwilym.*

Edlymawl, *a.* (edlym) Tending to make sharp.
Edlymiad, *s. m.* (edlym) A making acute.
Edlymu, *v. a.* (edlym) To make acute or sharp.
Edlynawl, *a.* (ed—glynawl) Besmeared, daubed.
Edlyniad, *s. m.—pl. t.* au (ed—glyniad) A smearing
Edlynu, *v. a.* (ed—glynu) To besmear, or bedaub

Ac efe a edlynai ei lygaid â gweryd y bedd.

And *he was wont to besmear* his eyes with the dust of the grave. *H. Peredur—Mabinogion.*

Edmyg, *s. m.—pl. t.* ion (ed—myg) Honour, reverence. *Clod ac edmyg*, fame and honour. *a.* Honoured, revered.

Henbych well penteyrnedd;—Boed cyflawn dy rad dithau, a'th glod, a'th edmyg yn yr ynys hon.

All health to you supreme of kings!—Be thy favour also perfect, and thy fame, and thy honour in this island. *H. Culhwch—Mabinogion.*

Edmygawl, *a.* (edmyg) Honouring, reverential.
Edmygedd, *s. m.* (edmyg) Honourableness, reverence, solemnity.
Edmygiad, *s. m.* (edmyg) A honouring, revering.
Edmygu, *v. a.* (edmyg) To honour, to reverence.

Edmygir ei fab Tegfan,
Wrth rif, ac wyth ran,
Wyr Calfan graid.

Honoured will be his son Tegvan, at numbering, and at partition, the grandson of the fiery Calvan. *Taliesin.*

Edmygaf radau rhian rhadlawn,
Rhad wehyn——

I will honour the endowments of gracious lords, dispensing happiness. *Cynddelw, m. Cad. ab Madawg.*

Edn, *s. m.—pl.* ednod (ed) A flying creature, a bird.

Hoff gan bob edn ei lais.

Every *bird* loves his own voice. *Adage.*

Edn eiddig, wyd anaddwyn;
Adref! drwg ei llef o'r llwyn.

Jealous bird, thou art disagreeable; go home! with thy ugly noise, out of the grove. *D. ab Gwilym.*

Ednain, *s. pl. aggr.* (ednan) The winged tribe.
Ednaint, *s. pl. aggr.* (ednain) The winged tribe.

Y gwr a oreu awyrawl ednaint,
Ac adneu daiarawl——Ef molaf.

The being that formed the ærial *winged tribe*, and the terrestrial flocks——Him I sing. *Elidr Sais.*

Ednan, *s. f. dim.* (edyn) One of the winged tribe.

Carafi yr ednan a'i llaryan llais,
Cathl-foddawg coed cadr ei hethais.

I love the *little winged one* with her mildly soothing voice, that solaces the wood with hymns, whose spreading seat is strong. *Gwalchmai.*

Ednarmes, *s. m.* (edn—armes) Augury.
Ednarmu, *v. a.* (edyn—armu) To augurize.
Ednawg, *a.* (edyn) Having the power to fly; elated. *s. pl.* Ednogion, winged ones.
Ednawl, *a.* (edyn) Relating to birds or fowls.
Ednid, *s. m.* (nid) Entanglement.
Ednogaeth, *s. m.* (ednawg) Ornithology, a description of winged creatures.
Ednogyn, *s. m. dim.* (ednawg) A fly; a gnat.

Ni ddeil yr eryr ednogyn.

The eagle will not catch the *fly*. *Adage.*

> Lladd a wnai oni lludd nos
> Ednogyn, o dae'n agos.

He would kill, except hindered by the night, a fly, if it came near. *Ll. ab Gwilym, i'r Ci.*

Ednydd, *s. m.—pl. t.* ion (ed—nydd) The withe by which a rustic gate is swung to the post.

Ednyddawl, *a.* (ednydd) Wreathing backward and forward, retortive.

Ednyddiad, *s. m.—pl. t.* au (ednydd) A writhing back, a retortion.

Ednyddu, *v. a.* (ednydd) To wreathe back.

Ednyfed, *s. m.* (nyfed) What is repurified, what is very pure, or bright; essence.

Ednyfedawg, *a.* (ednyfed) Full of purity, or essence; spirited, vigorous, animated.

> Tri gwydd ellyll Ynys Prydain: yr ellyll banawg, ellyll ednyfedawg drythyll, ac yr ellyll melyn.

The three wild monsters of the Isle of Britain: the spotted monster, the *high spirited* wanton monster, and the yellow monster. *Trioedd.*

Ednyw, *s. f.—pl. t.* iau (ed—nyw) Essence, spirit, purity, vigour, life.

> Rhaid bod hyn oll o gampau, a theithi, ac ednywiau, a rhinweddau ar y Gymraeg.

There must be all these excellencies, and qualities, and essences, and virtues in the Welsh language. *Barddas.*

Ednywed, *s. m.* (ednyw) The state of being repurified, the essential, pure, or spiritual state.

> Gwyn i fyd a fydd o frodded
> Mon y trig gwledig gwlad ednywed.

Happy his state who shall be partaking the joy of the place where dwells the sovereign of the region of regeneration. *Llywelyn Fardd, i Gadfan.*

Edrif, *s. m.—pl. t.* ion (ed—rhif) A reckoning.

Edrifaw, *v. a.* (edrif) To recount, to reckon.

> Edfynt edryfynt wrth edrifaw rhodd
> A gefais o'i fodd o fodd gnadaw.

A sigh they would return in *recounting* the gift which I received with his good will and of profit from him. *Cynddelw.*

Edrifawl, *a.* (edrif) Relating to reckoning.

Edrifiad, *s. m.—pl. t.* au (edrif) A recounting.

Edrin, *s. m.—pl. t.* ion (ed—rhin) A remurmur.

> Prythwch gauaf garw—
> Brwydr edrin brenin breiniog naf.

Like the tumult of blustering winter the *clashing* of the conflict of the king our mighty sovereign. *Cynddelw.*

Edrinaw, *v. a.* (edrin) To reverberate, to echo.

> Twr Cynfael yn cwyddaw,
> A fflamau edrum yn edrinaw,
> Ac angerdd ac angyr yn llaw.

The tower of Cynvel falling, and fiercely rising flames *murmuring echoes*, and violence and spears in hand. *Cynddelw.*

> Edrychaf Geraint Carnwys a'i fyddin yn dawed, a Bane o Rydychain; ac yn ddiannod eu tylin, ac o hyny allan ni allai na rapl arnaddynt, namyn ymffust yn greulawn, oni glywid eu sain yn edrinaw yn yr awyr.

Behold Geraint Carnwys with his host coming, and Bane of Rhydychain; and immediately breaking through them; and from that time forward not the least order could be kept amongst them, whereupon a furious combating took place, so that their noise was heard *echoing* in the sky. *Gr. ab Arthur.*

Edrinawl, *a.* (edrin) Reverberating, echoing.

Edriniad, *s. m.—pl. t.* au (edrin) Reverberation, a climbing.

Edring, *s. f.—pl. t.* au (dring) A lease; also called *goresgyn Gwent.*

Edrith, *s. m.—pl. t.* ion (ed—rhith) A simulation.

Edrithiad, *s. m.—pl. t.* au (edrith) An appearing

Edrithiaw, *v. a.* (edrith) To put on appearance.

Edrithiawl, *a.* (edrith) Under an appearance.

Edrwyth, *s. m.* (trwyth) A resolvent, a solvent.

Edrybod, *s. m.* (rhybod) A history, or a story.

Edrych, *s. m.—pl. t.* ion (ed—rhych) The appearance.

> Pa raid i rai hert drych
> A'th ddiwydrwydd i'th edrych.

What necessity is there that some should procure a mirror whilst thy sincerity is on thy countenance. *T. Aled.*

Edrych, *v. a.* (ed—rhych) To look, to behold, to see, to view.

Edrychator, *ger.* (edrych) Being in the act of looking.

Edrychedig, *a.* (edrych) That is viewed or observed.

Edrychedigaeth, *s. m.—pl. t.* au (edrychedig) The act or state of seeing; appearance. *Dwyfawl edrychedigaeth*, divine appearance.

Edrychgar, *a.* (edrych) Speculative, observant.

Edrychiad, *s. m.—pl. t.* au (edrych) A seeing, or beholding, vision, appearance, or sight. *Dyn ag edrychiad drwg*, a man of a bad aspect.

> Ei hedrychiad oedd rwyfus ac anwadal, ac yr oedd yn troi ei golygon o bob ffordd.

Her *appearance* was presumptuous and volatile, and she was turning her eyes every way. *Marchawg Crwydrad.*

Edrychiawl, *a.* (edrych) Observing or looking.

Edryd, *s. f.—pl. t.* au (ed—rhyd) A resource, what has the power to restore, or to renew; a source, or origin; a stock, family, or kindred.

> Uchdryd, un o'ch edryd oedd.

Uchdryd, one of your *tribe* was he. *T. Aled.*

> A gyr y sarff, a'i gwres oedd
> A'r un edryd a'r nadroedd.

And the motion of the serpent and her heat were of the same origin as the snakes. *T. Aled.*

Edryd, *v. a.* (ed—rhyd) To restore, to return.

> Dynion anghyfieithus a fwrier o long i dir, hyd yn nhen tair nos a thridiau, yn i wybod cyfraith y wlad, ni ddylyir arnynt am eu lledrad amgen nag edryd i'r colledig yr eiddaw.

Men of strange language that shall be cast from a ship on land, to the end of three nights and three days, so as to know the law of the country, nothing shall be required of them because of their theft, otherwise than *to restore* to the loser the goods. *Welsh Laws.*

Edrydawl, *a.* (edryd) Restoring, restorative.

Edrydiad, *s. m.—pl. t.* au (edryd) A restoration.

Edrydu, *v. a.* (edryd) To restore, or to return.

Edryf, *s. f.—pl. t.* au (ed—rhyf) A resource, a source, or origin; a stock, a tribe.

Edryfawl, *a.* (edryf) Tending to reassume.

Edryfiad, *s. m.—pl. t.* au (edryf) A reassuming.

Edryfu, *v. a.* (edryf) To reassume, to assume.

Edrysedd, *s. m.* (ed—rhysedd) Superfluity, excess, abundance.

> Cyfoethawg torfawg, nyw terfir i gledd,
> Cyfedd edrysedd ef ni dreisir.

Wealthy and of a numerous train, his sword will not be made to run away, feasting in *abundance* he will not be oppressed. *Ll. Brydydd Hodnant.*

Edryw, *s. m.—pl. t.* ion (tryw) Instinct, perceptions, knowledge by the sense of smelling.

Edrywan, *s. m.—pl. t.* au (edryw) What is found out or followed by scent; a scent.

> Ar gnawd y cyglyn adnau adnain,
> Ar edrywan gwan gwaew yn adain,
> Ar edrywedd gwaed gwaeddid gygfrain
> Marchogynt feirw ar fil frain.

On a corpse was beheld the flocking of birds, on the *scent of* the wound of the spear in the wing, on the sources of blood the ravens were calling out, the dead were riding on a thousand crows. *Cynddelw, i O. Gwynedd.*

Edrywant, *s. m.* (edrywan) A scent, a trace.

Edrywedd, *s. m.* (trywedd) Knowledge or intimation obtained by the scent; a scent.

> Gorddyar adar ar edrywedd,
> Uan llef cwn yn niffaith,
> Gorddyar adar eilwaith.

Clamorous the birds on a *scent*, loud the cry of dogs in a desert; again clamorous the birds. *Llywarch Hen.*

Edryweddawl, *a.* (edrywedd) Tracing by scent.

Edryweddiad, *s. m.—pl. t.* au (edrywedd) A tracing by the scent; a smelling out.

Edryweddu, *v. a.* (edrywedd) To trace by scent.

Edw, *a.* (ed) Dying away; faded; withered.

Edwad, *s. m.* (edw) A fading, a decaying, a passing away, a consuming.

Edwaint, *s. m.* (edw) Decay, a passing away.

Edwedd, *s. f.* (edw) What is in a state of decay.

O edwedd Morial,
A gwedy Rhys mawr y sonial.

Of the *faded remains* of Morial, and after Rhys great is the talking. *Llywarch Hen.*

Edwi, *v. n.* (edw) To pass away; to consume, to decay; to grow faint; to turn stale; to wither, to fade.

Dyn fal corbedw yn edwi.

Man like the tender birch *decaying*. *D. ab Gwilym.*

Calan hyddfref tymp dydd yn edwi.

The beginning of October is the time of the day's *dying away*. *Ll. P. Moch.*

Edwica, *v. a.* (gwica) To extort; to forestall.

Ni ddaw i'r cybydd o'i dda
Ond ocr ac i edwica.

There will not come to the miser from his wealth but usury, and to *forestall*. *Gr. Gryg.*

Edwicwr, *s. m.—pl.* edwicwyr (gwicwr) A regrator; a forestaller, a monopolizer; an extortioner; an itinerant dealer.

Edwin, *a.* (edw) Fading; withering; faded; faint

Edwiniad, *s. m.* (edwin) A fading, a withering.

Edwinaw, *v. n.* (edwin) To fade, or wither; to waste away; to decay, to consume.

Edwinawl, *a.* (edwin) Fading, or withering.

Edyl, *a.* (ed) Symmetrical, shapely.

Edyrn, *s. m.* (ed—gyrn) Sovereignty, supremacy

O freithell Cattraeth pan adroddir,
Maon dychuriant eu hoed bu hir,
Edyrn diedyrn, a mygu dir.

Of the conflict of Cattraeth when it shall be related, the multitude shall bewail, their grief long has been, a *government* without a sovereign, and a murky land. *Aneurin.*

Edd, *s. m. r.—pl. t.* ion. A moment; a present time of motion; a going, or moving; a glide; a tranquil state. It is used as a prefix in composition; it is also the termination of nouns, as *gwirionedd*, *caredd*, or the like; and it forms the plural of some others, as *teyrnedd*, *rhianedd* and *gwreigedd*.

Eddain, *s. m.* (edd) A moving or gliding onward.

Orig a merin
O derfyn chwefrin
Ieithoedd eddain.

Fickle and dissolving from the mazy boundary are the *flowing* languages. *Taliesin.*

Bid dysgethrin drud,
A bid eddain alltud.

Let the daring be blustering, and let the exile be *wandering*. *Llywarch Hen.*

Eddain, *v. a.* (edd) To move, glide, or pass on.

Moch gwelwyf, a'm nwyf yn eddain i wrthaw,
Ac i'm llaw fy llain
Lleuer glaer.

Soon may I see him and my vigour *in motion* on his account, and my blade in my hand, a bright gleam. *H. ab Owain.*

Eddaint, *s. m.* (eddain) A motion, a passing on.

Eddestl, *s. m.—pl. t.* on (edd—estl) A quick mover, or fleet runner, a steed.

Blaen eddestlawr pasg a'i gwaredai.

The van of the fattened steeds would deliver him. *Aneurin.*

Eddeifniad, *s. m.—pl.* eddeifniaid (deifniad) He that imbibes, or sucks, a sucker.

Eddestr, *s. m.—pl. t.* od (estr) A steed; a draft horse, a chariot horse.

Rym a fai biw blith yr haf,
Rym a fai eddystrod y gauaf.

To me might there be milch kine in summer, to me might there be *steeds* in winter. *Taliesin.*

Addwyn eddestr y'nghebystr lledrin.

Beautiful the *steed* in a leathern halter. *Taliesin.*

Pedestr o eddestr addwyn

A pacer that is a gentle *steed*. *Guto'r Glyn.*

Eddëu, *v. a.* (edd) To give impulse to, to impel.

Eddewid, *s. f.—pl. t.* ion (addaw) A promise.

Eddewidiaw, *v. a.* (eddewid) To make a promise

Eddewidiawl, *a.* (eddewid) Promissory.

Eddi, *s. pl. aggr.* (edd) Thrums, or the ends of weaver's threads; fringe.

Mal yr eddi am y garfan.

Like the *thrums* about the loom. *Adage.*

Eddïawg, *a.* (eddi) Having thrums, fringed.

Eddrin, *s. m.—pl. t.* ion (edd—rhin) A whispering. *a.* Secretly whispering or gossiping.

Gwylain yn gware ar wely lliant,
Lleithrion eu pluawr, Pleidiau eddrin.

Sea mews playing on a bed of torrent, polished their plumage the *secret gossiping* groups. *Gwalchmai.*

Eddrin, *v. a.* (edd—rhin) To whisper together.

Eddrith, *s. m.—pl. t.* ion (edd—rhith) A moving or variable appearance.

Tudwedd töydd eddrith fyth fydd Cymmru
A Chymmru a chymmrwyn.

A land with aspect of *varied appearance* Wales shall ever be, and the Welsh united in affliction. *Gwalchmai.*

Eddu, *v. a.* (edd) To go. *Eddwyd*, thou art gone; *o un i un eddynt oll*, one by one they are all gone; *y dydd eddyw*, the day going on, or this day.

Eddw, *a.* (edd) That is become cause of motion.

Eddwll, *a.* (dwll) Covered over; submissive.

Eddyl, *s. m.—pl. t.* au (dyl) Duty, incumbency; intention; purpose; attribute.

Hyn a oeda gyfraith yn ddiodor: angeu, clefyd gorweiddiawg, na bo hydrym iddo ei wlad nag i'w genad, neu fod mordwy gweilgi rhyngtho a'i eddyl.

The following shall delay law proceedings always: death, illness so as to keep the bed, that is hindered from entering his country, or sending his messenger, or that there should be an overflow of the sea between him and his *duty*. *Welsh Laws.*

Cyll dyn dref ei dad o rybuddiaw gorwlad rhag eddyl arglwydd ei genedl.

A person shall lose his patrimony by warning another country of the *purpose* of the sovereign of his own nation. *Welsh Laws.*

Tri angen eddyl beirdd Ynys Prydain: amlygu gwir a'i ddosbarth, cynnal cof mawl am a fo ddaionus a rhagor, a gyru heddwch ar ddifrawd ac aurhaith.

The three necessary *duties* of the bards of the isle of Britain: to make truth manifest and to diffuse it, to perpetuate the praise of all that is good and excellent, and with peace to prevail over the lawless and depredatory. *Barddas.*

Cyfarch dydd da gwae a'i gwyl,
Iddyn', ddifeitl iaf eddyl.

Woe to him that shall see a good day greeted to them, the most worthless *duty*. *T. Prys.*

———Pa obaith
A ddel i mi, eddyl maith.

What hope shall come to me, extensive the *duty*. *Ras. ab Robert.*

Eddyllder, *s. m.* (eddwll) Humility, submission.

Oeraf maith farw-daith fu ar fyrder:
Arwydd yw na'm llwyr llwydd eddyllder.

The most sad and long death journey suddenly took place; it is a sign that perfect submission will not avail to me. *Gr. ab M. ab Dafydd.*

Eddyllu, *v. a.* (eddwll) To cover over; to be covered over, to be submissive, or humble.

Eddyrn, *a.* (edd—gyrn) Supreme, pre-eminent.

Neud eddyrn teyrn hyd lan Tuedd.

Is not the prince *supreme* as far as the bank of Tuedd. *Gr. ab M. ab Dafydd.*

Eddyw, *part.* (edd—yw) That is going on, going or passing. *Y dydd eddyw*, the day passing on.

EF, *s. m. r.* It is often used for *E*, the pronomial agent governing the action of a verb, without the discrimination of person; *pron.* him.

Nid ef euir pawb yn ddoeth.

Every body will not be born wise. *Llefoed.*

Ef a ddaw haf i gi.

Summer *it* will come to a dog. *Adage*

Pob llais diwael yn ar' nant,
A gan ef o gu awyrfant.

Every masterly note, on the side of the brook, *he* doth sing from ardent love. *D. ab Gwilym, i'r frwfraith.*

Gyd ag ef y cartrefaf,
Nef yn ei gartref a gaf.

With *him* I will dwell, heaven in his dwelling I shall obtain. *L. G. Cothi.*

Efa, *v. a.* (ef) To cause motion; to agitate.
Efain, *v. a.* (ef) To move about; to be moving.
Efan, *s. m.* (ef) A motion; a course, a career.

Eryr Pengwern pengam llwyd,
Aruchel ei efan,
Eiddig am gig Cynddylan.

The eagle of Pengwern with the grey wry head, very high his *flight*, jealous for the flesh of Cynddylan. *Llywarch Hen.*

Efe, *pron.* (ef—e) He. *Efe a biau*, he doth own.

Efe a ymsynai o'i chwant hi, canys mwy rhagorawl oedd hi nog y clywsai efe son am dani gan y beirddorion.

He burnt with a desire to obtain her, for more excellent was she than the report *he* had heard of her from the bards. *Car. o Langarfan.*

Efel, *a.* (e—mal) That is like, or similar.
Efelwch, *s. m.* (efel) Similitude, or likeness.
Efelychadwy, *a.* (efelwch) Imitable; comparable.
Efelychiad, *s. m.—pl. t.* au (efelwch) Imitation.
Efelychu, *v. a.* (efelwch) To imitate, to do the like; to resemble.

Gwedi marw Elidyr War y daeth Rhys fab Gorfynion yn frenin; a'i ewythr a *efelychws* ef o synwyr, a phradd-der a doethineb.

After the death of Elidyr the mild, came Rhys the son of Gorfynion to be king; and *he resembled* his uncle in sense, and discretion, and wisdom. *Gr. ab Arthur.*

Efelly, *adv.* (efel) In that wise or form; so.

Ac fal yd oedd Arthur yn eu gwarchae *efelly* euychaf Gillamwri, brenin Ywerddon, yn dyfod a llynges ganddo, ac amlder o bobloedd anghyfieith.

And as Arthur was besieging them *in that wise*, behold Gillamwri, king of Ireland, coming, having a fleet with him, and a multitude of people of strange language. *Gr. ab Arthur.*

Efengyl, *s. f.—pl. t.* au (ef—eng—yl) What is spread abroad, manifested or declared; the gospel.

Da yw y maen gyd a'r efengyl.

The touchstone is good with the *gospel*. *Adage.*

Efengylaidd, *a.* (efengyl) Evangelical.
Efengyles, *s. f.—pl. t.* au (efengyl) A female preacher of good tidings.

Dring rhagot, yr *efengyles* Sion, i fynydd uchel; dyrchafa dy lef trwy nerth, O *efengyles* Ierusalem, dyrchafa, nag ofna!

O Zion, *that bringest good tidings*, get thee up into the high mountain, lift up thy voice with strength, O Jerusalem *that bringest good tidings* lift it up; be not afraid. *Isaiah* xl. 9.

Efengylu, *v. a.* (efengyl) To preach the gospel.
Efengylwr, *s. m.—pl.* efengylwyr (efengyl—gwr) An evangelist, or preacher of the gospel.
Efengylydd, *s. m.—pl. t.* ion (efengyl) An evangelist; one who brings good tidings.
Efnys, *s. pl. aggr.* (afn) That comes forward, or in opposition; foes, or enemies.

Brenin brwydr, efnys gwrys gwallyniawg,
Pen rhiau paran anoleithiawg.

King of conflict, the correction of the *foes*, chief of princes with spears not sparing of havoc. *Meilyr, i Gr. ab Cynan.*

Ni thraws ei gefn ar efnys.

He turned not his back upon the *foe*. *I. ab H. Burdwel.*

Efo, *pron.* (e—mo) He, or him. *Dos gyd ag efo*, go along with him.

A fyno efo a fydd yn ei fro,
A'r hyn a fyno na bo ni bydd.

What *he* willeth will be in his country, and what he willeth that it be not will not be. *L. G. Cothi.*

Efo, *conj.* (ef) With. *Dos efo fo*, go with him; *af efo ag ef*, I will go with him.
Efory, *s. m.* (mory) To-morrow. *adv.* To-morrow, or on the morrow.

Efr, *s. m.—pl. t.* au (ef) A tare, among corn.
Efrad, *s. m.* (brad) Crime, or transgression.
Efrais, *a.* (brais) Powerful of body; muscular.

Gwr efrais yn abrais, yn abroedd,
Gwr afraid i farw naid i fedd.

A man *powerful* in oppression, and in transgression; a man whose dying course to the grave was premature. *Cynddelw, m. O. Gwynedd.*

Efras, *s. m.* (bras) Plumpness or growth of youth.

Y dref wen yn mron y coed,
Ys ef yw i hefras erioed
Ar wyneb gwellt y gwaed.

The white town in the bosom of the wood, the blood of its *youth* at all times has been running over the grass. *Llywarch Hen.*

Y dref wen e hefras e glas fyfyr.

The white town its *youth* its blue tone of contemplation. *Llywarch Hen.*

Efras, *a.* (bras) Plump, in a state of growing.

Maranwyn, tra fum i efras,
Gwnawn weithred gwr tra byddwn gwas.

Maranwyn, whilst I was young *and sleek* I would perform the feats of a man whilst I was but a youth. *Llywarch Hen.*

Arddwyreaf glew, llew lluch efras.

I will extol the brave, the sprightly young lion. *Gwalchmai.*

Efrefiad, *s. m.* (brefiad) A lowing, a bleating.
Efrefu, *v. a.* (brefu) To low, or to bleat.
Efrëu, *v. a.* (brëu) To low, or to bleat; to cry.

Pan ymchoelwys
Nid efrewys buch wrth ei llo.

When he returned the cow *did* not *low* to her calf. *Taliesin.*

Efrilid, *s. m.—pl. t.* au (afr—llid) Merit.

Ebai Oswallt, plygwn ein gliniau, a gweddiwn—ein rhyddhau y gan syberw lu y Prydeiniaid—Ac efelly pan ddoai y dydd y cyrchynt eu gelynion; a herwydd efrilid eu ffydd hwynt, a gafynt y fuddygoliaeth.

Oswallt said, let us bend our knees, and let us pray to be delivered from the haughty army of the Britons; and so when the day came they attacked their enemies; and because of the *merit* of their faith they obtained the victory. *Gr. ab Arthur.*

Mynych ydd ymladdynt a mi o'm ieuenctid, dyweded Israel yr awr hon yn eu hefrilid.

Many times have they fought against me from my youth, let Israel say at this hour in their *meritoriousness*. *D. Ddu, Ps.* cxxix. 1.

Efryd, *s. m.—pl. t.* iau (bryd) Study, meditation.
Efrydiaw, *v. a.* (efryd) To purpose; to study.

Ei saethau——
Selwodd, efrydiodd i'th frad,
Bol-ddig hir, saiw duw cariad.

His arrows he pointed, *he meditated* treachery to me, with a long angry look, the puny god of love. *S. Tudur.*

Efrydiawl, *a.* (efryd) Studious; meditating.
Efrydd, *a.* (brydd) Maimed, lame; defective in any limb. *Efrydd gwyllt*, out of all order.

Aeth un yn rhydd, a'r llall yn efrydd yn y ffynon.

One became perfect, and the other *disabled* in the spring. *D. Jones, o Lanfair.*

Efryddawl, *a.* (efrydd) Tending to maim or hurt.
Efryddiad, *s. m.—pl. t.* au (efrydd) A maiming.
Efryddlawn, *a.* (efrydd) Full of maims or defects
Efryddu, *v. a.* (efrydd) To maim, to disable.

Henaint a ddaw fal hoenyn
A'i dwyll i efryddu dyn.

Old age will come like a snare with its deceit *to disable* man. *D. ab Gwilym.*

Efwr, *s. m.* (bwr) The cow-parsnep. It grows profusely about Dinevwr, where it is the name of the plant.

Melyn eithin, crin efwr.

The furze is yellow, the *cow-parsnep* is dry. *Llywarch Hen.*

Osglawg blaen derw, chwerw chwaeth on,
Cwag efwr, chwerthiniad ton.
Ni chel grudd cystudd calon.

Full of branches the top of the oak, bitter the taste of the ash, sweet the *cow parsnep*, the wave is blundering, the cheek conceals not the affliction of the heart. *Llywarch Hen.*

Efwrn, *s. m.* (bwrn) A swell, or spreading out.

Efydd, *s. m.* (mydd) Copper; tempered copper.

Ymofal am waew efydd,
Am nad gwiw meined y gwŷdd.

Solicitous for a spear of *brass*, for it was of no moment how slender the wood. *Ieuan Deulwyn.*

Efyddaid, *a.* (efydd) Done with copper.

Ffrwynau efyddaid, pedair ceiniawg a dal.

Bridles *done with copper*, the value four-pence. *Welsh Laws.*

Efyddaidd, *a.* (efydd) Of the nature of copper.
Efyddawg, *a.* (efydd) Having copper, coppery.
Efyddawl, *a.* (efydd) Of copper, coppery; brassy.
Efydden, *s. f.—pl. t.* au (efydd) A copper pan.
Efyddu, *v. a.* (efydd) To do with copper.
Efyddwaith, *s. m.* (efydd—gwaith) Copper-work.
Efyddyn, *s. m.—pl. t.* au (efydd) A copper vessel.
Efyntau, *pron.* (ef—yntau) He also; and him.
Efyrnig, *s. f. dim.* (efwrn) A young goat, or that is with young the first time.

Trithi efyrnig ceiniawg a dimai—canys hanner cerdded gafr yw yr eiddi.

The qualities of the *yearling goat* are valued at one penny and halfpenny; for hers be half of that of the goat. *Welsh Laws.*

Efyrllys, *s. m.* (efwr—llys) Cow-parsnep.
Effaith, *s. f.—pl.* effeithiau (ffaith) An effect.
Effeithiad, *s. m.—pl. t.* au (effaith) Effectuation.
Effeithiadwy, *a.* (effeithiad) Effectible, or feasible
Effeithiaw, *v. a.* (effaith) To effect, to effectuate.
Effeithiawl, *a.* (effaith) Effectual, or efficient.
Effeithiedig, *a.* (effaith) Efficient, effectuated.
Effeithiolaeth, *s. m.* (effeithiawl) Effectuation.

Pa beth a ddichon gynnal yr ysbryd, namyn anadl Duw, trwy ddylanwad gyson awl, ac effeithiolaeth ddibaid a bythawl!

What is there that can support the spirit, except the breath of God, by an agreeable replenishing, and incessant and ever *effectuation!* *I. er. Owain.*

Effeithioldeb, *s. m.* (effeithiawl) Efficaciousness.
Effeithioli, *v. a.* (effeithiawl) To make effectual.
Effeithiolrwydd, *s. m.* (effeithiawl) Efficaciousness
Effeithiwr, *s. m.—pl.* effeithwyr (effaith—gwr) One who effects, or brings to pass.
Efflan, *a.* (plan) Splendid, bright, or glittering.
Efflanawl, *a.* (efflan) Resplendent, coruscant.
Efflaniad, *s. m.—pl. t.* au (efflan) A coruscation.
Efflanu, *v. a.* (efflan) To coruscate, to glitter.
Efforth, *s. m.—pl. t.* au (porth) An effort to aid.
Efforthawl, *a.* (efforth) Tending to help or aid.
Efforthi, *v. a.* (efforth) To make effort to aid.
Efforthiad, *s. m.—pl. t.* au (efforth) Exertion.
Effraw, *a.* (ffraw) In motion; awake, or wakeful.

Newydd roi fy mhen i lawr: ac yn lled effraw, mi a glywn bwys mawr yn dawed arnaf yn lledradaidd.

Having just laid my head down, and being partly *awake*, I could feel a great weight coming slily upon me. *Elis Wyn, B. Cwsg.*

Effröad, *s. m.* (effraw) A stirring about; a waking
Effröi, *v. a.* (effraw) To stir up; to awake.
Effrom, *a.* (ffrom) Swelling up; towering; stiff, sturdy; haughty, stubborn, pertinacious.
Effros, *s. pl. aggr.* (ffros) The herb eye-bright.
EG, *s. m. r.* What is open, plain, or clear; what is opened; what is discriminated; the quantity of land ploughed, or opened in a day; an acre.
Egain, *s. m.* (cain) That is splendid; a lord.
Egalen, *s. f.—pl. t.* au (galen) A whetstone.
Egawr, *v. a.* (eg) To open, to expand; to widen; to display.

Gwell egawr no chyunwys.

It is better *to open* than to contain. *Adage.*

Egel, *s. f.* (eg—el) The sow-bread.
Egfaen, *s. m.—pl.* egfain (eg—maen) The haw, or white-thorn berry.

Egfaenrwydd, *s. m.* (egfaen—gwydd) Hawthorn.
Egin, *s. pl. aggr.* (cin) A crop, or what covers the surface, the first shoots, or blades of vegetation.

Ni chel dryg-dir ei egin.

Bad land will not conceal its *vegetation*. *Adage.*

Eginad, *s. m.* (egin) Germination, springing.
Eginaw, *v. a.* (egin) To germinate, to spring, to sprout forth, or to shoot up.

Ac un llygriad â hadyd
Yw dynion beilchion y byd;
Ag egino gogoniant,
Yn da nerth, drwy Grist a wnant.

And of the same corruption as the seed corn are the proud men of the world; and if the soil is good, they will, through Christ, *shoot forth* glory. *T. Aled.*

Eginawl, *a.* (egin) Germinant, shooting, sprouting
Eginyn, *s. f. dim.* (egin) A germe, a sprout.
Eglan, *s. f.—pl. t.* oedd (eg—glan) An opening shore, or bank, a gulf.

Addfwyn gaer y sydd yn yr eglan,
Addfwyn y rhoddir i bawb ei ran.

A pleasant fort there is in the *gulf*, there pleasantly is given to every one his share. *Taliesin.*

Eglawg, *a.* (eg—llawg) Widely gaping, yawning.

Er yfais o win o gawg,
Gan rian ryfel eglawg,
Myrddin yw fy enw amhelawg.

For what I have drank of wine from a goblet, from lords *of devouring* war, Myrddin is my prudent name. *Myrddin.*

Eglur, *a.* (eg—llur) Bright, clear, plain, visible.
Eglurâad, *s. m.* (eglur) Explanation, illustration.
Eglurâawl, *a.* (eglurâu) Exegetical, explanatory.
Egluradwy, *a.* (eglur) Demonstrable, explicable.
Eglurain, *a.* (eglur) Illustrious, conspicuous.
Egluraint, *s. m.* (eglurain) Illustriousness, glory.

Meifod———
A'i balch-lwys eglwys egluraint.

Meivod with its proudly solemn temple of *splendour*. *Cynddelw.*

Eglurâu, *v. a.* (eglur) To make clear, or plain.
Egluraw, *v. a.* (eglur) To make clear, or apparent, to manifest, to discover, to explain.

Morgan fab Arthal—o ddysg ei rieni a wnai iawnder, ac a eglurwr genedl Prydain o weithredoedd da.

Morgan the son of Arthal, from the instruction of his parents, did equity, and *he rendered conspicuous* the people of Britain for good actions. *Gr. ab Arthur.*

Eglurawl, *a.* (eglur) Explanatory, illustrative.
Eglurdeb, *s. m.* (eglur) Clearness, perspicuity.

Tair colofn eglurdeb; y gair a fo raid, y maint a fo raid, ac y ddull a fo raid.

The three bases of *perspicuity*; the word that is necessary, the quantum that is necessary, and the form that is necessary. *Barddas.*

Egluredig, *a.* (eglur) Exemplified, demonstrated.
Egluriad, *s. m.—pl. t.* au (eglur) Illustration, explanation, exemplification, manifestation.
Egluriadawl, *a.* (egluriad) Explanatory, demonstrative, exemplifying.
Eglurwr, *s. m.—pl.* eglurwyr (eglur—gwr) An illustrator, exemplifier, or explainer.
Egluryn, *s. m.* (eglur) An exemplar, an exemplifier; a manifesto.
Eglwg, *a.* (eg—llwg) Bright, clear, manifest.

Llemais i lam o lam eglwg;
Heusid da ul'r gao ddrwg;
Mygedorth Rhun ys ef ddlwg.

I have leaped a leap, a *clear* leap; good has been dispersed abroad if a person finds no evil; the funeral pile of Rhun it is an expiation. *Taliesin.*

Eglwys, *s. f.—pl. t.* au, i, ydd (eg—glwys) That is hallowed or sanctified; a church.
Eglwys, *a.* (glwys) Hallowed, solemn, fair.
Eglwysaidd, *a.* (eglwys) Of a hallowed nature; like the church; of the church.

Eglwysaw, *v. a.* (eglwys) To hallow, to sanctify, to purify; to church.

Eglwysawl, *a.* (eglwys) Tending to holiness; belonging to the church.

Eglwysiad, *s. m.* (eglwys) A hallowing; sanctification, or purification; a churching.

Eglwysig, *a.* (eglwys) Hallowed, sanctified; solemn; belonging to, or of, the church. *Gwr eglwysig*, a man of the church, a clergyman.

Eglwyswr, *s. m.—pl.* eglwyswyr (eglwys—gwr) A churchman, a church minister.

> A iechawdwriaeth, medd Duw naf,
> Y gwisgaf ei heglwyswr.
>
> With salvation, saith God the Lord, I will clothe her minister. *E. Prys.*

Eglyd, *a.* (eg—glyd) Hovering over, wavering.

Eglygder, *s. m.* (eglwg) Brightness, clearness.

Eglyn, *s. m.* (eg—glyn) The golden saxifrage.

Egni, *s. m.—pl. t.* on (eg—gni) Strength, force, vigour, effort: *A'i holl egni*, with all his might.

> Dwys gred, nid oes greadur—
> Gymmaint a'th wnel yn elyn,
> Egni dost, ag i gwna dyn!
>
> Momentous the thought, there is not a creature that so greatly makes thee a foe as doth man, afflicting is the impulse. *Gr. Ll. ab D. ab Einion.*

Egnïad, *s. m.—pl. t.* au (egni) A making effort.

Egnïaw, *v. a.* (egni) To make an effort, to use exertion, to endeavour.

Egnïawl, *a.* (egni) Forcible, vigorous, impetuous.

Egnïus, *a.* (egni) Vehement, impetuous, forcible.

Egnïwr, *s. m.—pl.* egnïwyr (egni—gwr) One that makes an effort, or endeavour.

Egored, *a.* (egawr) Open, expanded, exposed.

> Eid ei i gell egored.
>
> Let the dog go to an open chamber. *Adage.*

Egoredig, *a.* (egawr) Opened, spread out, displayed.

Egoredigaeth, *s. m.* (egoredig) The act of opening

Egori, *v. a.* (egawr) To open, to disclose.

Egoriad, *s. m.—pl. t.* au (egawr) A making an aperture; an opening; a key.

Egoriadawl, *a.* (egoriad) Aperient, apt to open.

Egorwr, *s. m.—pl.* egorwyr (egawr—gwr) An opener, or one who opens.

Egr, *a.* (eg) Sharp, sour, tarting, biting, severe, poignant, eager.

> Llyn gwin egr, llanw gwinengach.
>
> A puddle of stale wine, a flood of murky red. *D. ab Gwilym, i'r meanwbwll.*

Egraidd, *a.* (egr) Tending to be hard, or stale.

Egrawl, *a.* (egr) Tending to harden or make stale.

Egredig, *a.* (egr) That is hardened, or made stale.

Egredd, *s. m.* (egr) Hardness, flatness, staleness.

Egri, *s. m.* (egr) Hardness, staleness, sharpness.

Egriad, *s. m.* (egr) A making, or becoming stale.

Egrifft, *s. m.* (eg—grifft) The spawn of frogs; a tadpole; also a fabulous animal the griffon.

Egroes, *s. pl. aggr.* (egr) Hips, or berries of the dog-rose; called also *Aeron mieri Mair*.

Egroeswydd, *s. m.* (egroes—gwydd) The dog-rose.

> Minnau wnaf, o byddaf hen,
> Dy goroni, bryd egroesen.
>
> And I will crown thee, if I shall be old, thou of the hue of the eglantine berry. *D. ab Gwilym, i'r corw.*

Egrwydd, *s. m.* (egr) Sourness, sharpness, acidity.

Egru, *v. n.* (egr) To become sharp, sour, or stale; to turn to acid. *Diawd wedi egru*, stale drink

Egryd, *s. m.* (cryd) Tremulation. *a.* Trembling.

Egrygi, *s. m.* (crygi) Hoarseness, roughness.

> Archaf yn Arglwydd cetwydd cêl,
> Nid af a archaf arch egrygi.
>
> I will intreat of my Lord, the love-prospering mysterious one, I will not crave of him a petition of roughness. *Ein. ab Gwalchmai.*
>
> Gwelais feirdd yn gryg, nid egrygi,
> Gal fawdd, yn adrawdd dy wrhydri.
>
> I have seen a throng of bards, not with the roughness of the hostile shout, recounting thy gallantry. *Ll. P. Moch, bygwth D. ab Owain.*

Egryn, *s. m.* (cryn) Fear, trembling. *a.* Trembling

Egrynedig, *a.* (egryn) Trembling. *Egrynedigion gamau*, trembling steps.

Egwal, *s. m.—pl. t.* au (gwal) A cot, or hut.

Egwan, *a.* (gwan) Feeble, drooping, or flagging.

> Rhon' iddo—
> Wileged ef'n wael egwan.
>
> They will give to him, jades that are poor and flagging. *T. Prys.*
>
> Un wedd egwan, un ddygwydd,
> Ydyw gwr a blodau gwydd.
>
> Of the same feeble appearance, of the same end, is man as the blossoms of trees. *Ifan Llwyd Sieffre.*

Egwanaeth, *s. m.* (egwan) Feebleness, imbecility.

> Gwyn eu byd, bellach darfu'r achwyn,
> A phob egwanaeth, a phob gwenwyn!
>
> Happy their state, at length complaining is ended, and every frailty, and every malevolence. *Llywelyn, o Langewydd.*

Egwander, *s. m.* (egwan) Feebleness, or debility.

Egweddi, *s. m.—pl. t.* au (gweddi) A portion, a dowery, what is given by the husband for a wife, a settlement, or jointure.

> Egweddi yw y da a roddo gwr i'r wraig y bore cyn cyfodi o'i gwely.
>
> The jointure is the goods which the husband shall give to the wife the morning before rising from her bed. *Welsh Laws.*
>
> Os gwr a gwraig a ysgarant cyn pen y saith mlynedd, talwr iddi ei hegweddi, a'i hargyfreu, a'i chowyll, os yn forwyn y daeth; ac os cyn y saith mlynedd yr ymad hi a'i gwr, hi a gyll y cwbl ond ei chowyll.
>
> If a man and woman shall separate before the end of seven years, let there be restored to her her portion, and her paraphernalia, and her maiden fee if she came a virgin; but if before the end of seven years she shall part from her husband, she shall lose the whole except her maiden fee. *Welsh Laws.*
>
> A thrannoeth y bore ydd erchis y forwyn ei hegweddi, am ei chaffael yn wyryf.
>
> And the next day morning the maid demanded her jointure for finding her a virgin. *Br. M. Wledig—Mabinogion.*

Egweddïawl, *a.* (egweddi) Relating to a jointure.

Egwy, *s. m.* (eg—gwy) Watery eruption; a plague.

Egwya, *v. a.* (egwy) To break out in blotches.

Egwyd, *s. m.—pl. t.* ydd (eg—gwyd) The small of the leg, the fetlock.

> Milgi gwiw rhwng rhiw a rhyd,
> Main egwyd-isel, min gwaedlyd.
>
> A greyhound that is masterly between the ascent and the ford, with a small low fetlock, and bloody lip. *H. ab Rhenallt.*

Egwydled, *s. m.* (egwyd—lled) The small of the leg.

Egwyddawr, *s. f.—pl.* egwyddorion (eg—gwyddawr) A first principle, a rudiment; an alphabet. *Egwyddorion crefydd*, the first principles of religion.

Egwyddorawl, *a.* (egwyddawr) Elementary, elemental; initiating; intuitive; alphabetical.

Egwyddoredig, *a.* (egwyddawr) Grounded upon rudiments; initiated, instructed in the alphabet

Egwyddori, *v. a.* (egwyddawr) To instruct in rudiments, or elements; to initiate.

Egwyddoriad, *s. m.—pl. t.* au (egwyddawr) The initiating in rudiments; initiation.

Egwyddorig, *a.* (egwyddawr) Having rudiments, or elements; grounded upon an alphabet. *s. c.* A learner of the alphabet, an Abecedarian.

Egwyl, *s. m.—pl. t.* ion (e—gwyl) Convenience, fit time, opportunity. *Egwyl dda*, a good season.

Egyllt, *s. m.* (eg) The herb crowfoot.
Egyr, *s. m.* (eg) An acre; also called *erw*.
Ehagr, *a.* (hagr) Ugly, unsightly, deformed.
Ehagrawl, *a.* (ehagr) Tending to render ugly.
Ehagriad, *s. m.* (ehagr) A making unsightly.
Ehagru, *v. a.* (ehagr) To make ugly, to deform.
Ehagrwch, *s. m.* (ehagr) Ugliness, unsightliness.
Ehed, *s. f.—pl. t.* ion (hed) A flight. *a.* Flying. *Maen ehed*, neu *ehedfaen*, a loadstone.
Ehed, *v. a.* (hed) To fly. *Ehed fry*, fly upward.

Mygedawg farchawg feirch yn ehed.

An honourable rider of *steeds a flying*. *Cynddelw.*

Ehedawg, *a.* (ehed) Having flight; flying.
Ehedawl, *a.* (ehed) Relating to flight; flying.
Ehedbysg, *s. pl. aggr.* (ehed—pysg) Flying-fish.
Ehedeg, *v. a.* (ehed) To fly. *Ehedeg trwy yr awyr*, to fly through the air.
Ehedfaen, *s. m.—pl.* ehedfain (ehed—maen) A loadstone, or magnet.

Llawn o hud llun ehedfaen,——
Yw'r drych.

Full of deception, of the form of a *magnet*, is the mirror. *D. ab Gwilym.*

Ehedfan, *v. a.* (ehed) To fly about, to hover.
Ehediad, *s. m.—pl. t.* au (ehed) A flying, a flight,
Ehediad, *s. m.—pl.* ehediaid (ehed) What flies.

Llywodraeth dyn—holl dda maes,
A'r adar llaes eu hesgyll,
Ehediad nef, a'r pysg o'r don
Sy'n tramwy'r eigion archyll.

Under the dominion of man are all the beasts of the field; and birds of extending wings; the *flight* of heaven, and the fish of the wave that travel the awful ocean. *E. Prys.*

Ehedion, *s. pl. aggr.* (ehed) The refuse of corn.
Ehedwr, *s. m.—pl.* ehedwyr (ehed—gwr) A man that flies, a flyer.
Ehedydd, *s. m.—pl. t.* ion (ehed) A flyer; the lark. *Ehedydd y coed*, neu *esgudogyll*, a wood-lark; *ehedydd coch*, red-lark; *ehedydd cribawg*, neu *gwich*, grasshopper-lark; *ehedydd yr helyg*, willow-lark; *coeg ehedydd*, neu *cor ehedydd*, titlark.
Ehedyn, *s. m. dim.* (ehed) A winged creature.

Ehedaist, mor hy ydwyd,
Hyd y nef, ehedyn wyd.

Thou hast flown, so daring thou art, up to heaven, thou art a *flyer*. *Iolo Goch, i Edward III.*

Ehegr, *s. m.—pl. t.* on (hegr) The staggers.

Ni phella'r ehegr neb tlawd.

Precipitation will not drive any poor one far. *Adage.*

A dan dri haint y dylyir bod am deithi march; rhag yr ehegr, dri gwlith, rhag yr ysgyfaint, dair lloer; rhag y llynmeirch, flwyddyn

Against three diseases there ought to be warranted the qualities of a horse, against the *staggers*, three dews; against the glanders, three moons; and against the spavin, a year. *Welsh Laws.*

Ehegrawl, *a.* (ehegr) Tending to be swift.
Ehegriad, *s. m.* (ehegr) A becoming quick.
Ehegru, *v. a.* (ehegr) To go rapidly or wildly.
Ehegyr, *a.* (hegyr) Swift, speedy; abrupt; wild. *adv.* Quickly, forthwith.

Aer gyniaid cyrchiad coch eu hongyr,
Trais erwyr yn ffwyr ffaw ehegyr.

The first ones in the onset of slaughter with reddened spears, of darting violence in the pursuit of rapid course. *O. Cyfeiliawg.*

Ni wyddost pa bryd y bydd hyny, ai yn hwyr ai yn ehegr.

Thou knowest not what time that will be, whether late or *speedily*. *Ll. G. Hergest.*

Ehelaeth, *a.* (helaeth) Extensive; expansive; spacious, large, wide; abundant.

Ni baidd llwfr llaw ehelaeth.

The coward will not dare the *extended* hand. *Adage.*

Ehelaethawl, *a.* (ehelaeth) Tending to amplify.
Ehelaethiad, *s. m.* (ehelaeth) A making spacious.
Ehelaethrwydd, *s. m.* (ehelaeth) Speciousness.
Ehelaethu, *v. a.* (ehelaeth) To amplify, to enlarge.
Ehelaethwr, *s. m.—pl.* ehelaethwyr (ehelaeth—gwr) An amplifier, or enlarger.
Ehöeg, *s. m.* (höeg) Green colour. *a.* Green.

Nid ymddug ddillad, na glas, na gwrr,
Na choch, nag ehöeg——

He will not bear cloaths, nor of blue, nor brown, nor red, nor *green*. *Taliesin.*

Addwyn grug pan fo ehöeg,
Arall addwyn morfa i wartheg.

Pleasant is the heath when it is *green*, again pleasant is the sea beach for cattle. *Taliesin.*

Ehofn, *a.* (hofn) Daring, gallant, intrepid.

Mynw ehofn colofn cyfwyrain;
Mir meddgyrn mychedyrn Mechain.

A *gallant* person like a towering column; fair the mead-horns of the potent prince of Mechain. *Cynddelw, i O. Cyfeiliawg.*

Ef yw'r ehofnaf o'r gwyr ehofnion.

He is the *most gallant* of the *gallant ones*. *Einion Offeiriad.*

Ehofnawl, *a.* (ehofn) Intrepid, daring, bold.
Ehofnder, *s. m.* (ehofn) Intrepidity, boldness.
Ehofnedd, *s. m.* (ehofn) Intrepidity, prowess.
Ehofni, *v. a.* (ehofn) To act daringly; to be bold.
Ehorth, *a.* (horth) Diligent, assiduous, attentive.
Ehorthedd, *s. m.* (ehorth) Diligence, assiduity.
Ehud, *a.* (hud) Easy to be deceived, rash, unadvised, foolhardy; heedless.

Buan barn pob ehud.

The judgement of every one *rash* is hasty. *Adage.*

Anwadal ehud.

The heedless is inconstant. *Adage.*

Ehudrwydd, *s. m.* (ehud) Rashness, heedlessness.
Ehydr, *a.* (hydr) Magnanimous, brave, great.
Ehydriad, *s. m.* (ehydr) A making, or becoming great, grand, or magnanimous.
Ei, *pron.* (e) His, her, its. It strictly implies possession by the third person without denoting the gender, which is shewn by form of construction. *Ei dad*, his father; *ei thad*, her father.

Deubarth cerdd ei gwrandaw.

Two parts of a song the hearing *it*. *Adage.*

Cas dyn a fygythio bawb, ac ni bo ar neb ei ofn.

Odious is the person that threatens every body, and whom no body is under *his* dread. *Adage.*

Eich, *pron.* (ach) Your; you. *Eich lle*, your place; *eich dau*, you two, *m. eich dwy*, you two, *f.*
Eichiad, *s. m.* (aich) A crying out loudly.
Eichiaw, *v. a.* (aich) To sound, to utter noise.
Eichiawg, *a.* (aich) Abounding with noise; loud. *s. c.* What is loudly uttered; loud fame.

Cog lafar a gan gan ddydd,
Cyfrau eichiawg yn nolydd.

The loquacious cuckoo sings with the day, the *noisy* jewel in the dales. *Llywarch Hen.*

Cyn golo gweryd ar y grudd hael edfynt,
Doeth dygyrched e ged, a'i glod, a'i eichiawg.

Before the earth was covered over the cheek of the generous departed one, wisely collected was his treasure, and his praise, and his *high sounding fame*. *Aneurin.*

Eichiawl, *a.* (aich) Tending to be noisy or loud.
Eidiaw, *v. a.* (aid) To give life, or briskness.
Eidiawg, *a.* (aid) Full of life, lively; vigorous, mettlesome, brisk; wanton.

Bywiawg ac eidiawg ydyw——
Y march.

Lively and *vigorous* is the steed. *T. Aled.*

Eidiawl, *a.* (aid) Lively, animated, vigorous.

Os doeth wyd, ystwyth, eidiol,
'Y ngharw ffyrf, gwna gyngor ffol.

If thou art wise, my lusty stag supple and *vigorous*, do according to the advise of the simple. *W. Cynwal.*

Eidiogi, *v. a.* (eidiawg) To invigorate; to wanton

Eidiogrwydd, *s. m.* (eidiawg) Liveliness, briskness

Eidion, *s. m.—pl. t.* au (aid) A beast; a neat; a bullock; a beef; a steer. *Eidion moel*, a beast without horns.

> Nid gwar ond ych, nid talawg ond eidion.
>
> Nothing so gentle as an ox, nothing so surly as a *steer*. *Adage.*

Eidionyn, *s. m. dim.* (eidion) A beast, one of the horned cattle.

> Yn hael ni bu yn hilliaw nob
> Eidionyn an addfwyn.
>
> Liberally there has not been procreating a *beast of* so much wantonness. *D. ab Ieuan Ddu, i darw.*

Eidral, *s. m. aggr.* (eidr) Ground-ivy; called also, *eiddew y ddaiar*, and *y feidiawg las.*

> Eidral, ac iegoll nadroedd, a lleiaw
> A llysiau mynyddoedd———
> Yw cwrw Dinbych.
>
> *Ground-ivy*, and viper broth, and urine, and mountain herbs make Denbigh ale. *S. Tudur.*

Eidr, *s. m.* (aid) What has a tendency to creep.

Eidran, *s. m.* (eidr) The marjoram.

Eiddaw, *s. m.* (aidd) One's own; possession; chattels. *Eiddof*, my property, or mine; *eiddot*, thine; *eiddo*, his property; *eiddi*, hers; *eiddom*, ours; *eiddoch*, yours; *eiddont*, *eiddynt*, *eiddudd*, theirs.

> Hirlas nai Bedwyr, yn gyffroedig o angau ei ewythr, a gymyrth y gyd ag ef tri-chanwr o'r rhai eiddaw; a megys baedd coed yn mhlith torf o'r cwn, efelly y cerddws ef trwy y gelynawl fyddinoedd.
>
> Hirlas the nephew of Bedwyr, being agitated for the death of his uncle, took with him three hundred men of those who were *his own*; and like a wild boar amongst a pack of dogs, so he passed through the hostile legions. *Gr. ab Arthur.*
>
> I afyrnig y mae teithi; canys hanner cerdded gafr yw yr eiddiorf un geiniawg am ei llaeth, a dimai am ei myn.
>
> To the young goat there are legal qualities; for half of what is upon the goat is *hers*, namely one penny on account of her milk and a halfpenny for her kid. *Welsh Laws.*

Eiddawl, *s. f.—pl.* eiddolon (addawl) An idol.

Eiddew, *s. m. aggr.* (aidd) Ivy; called also, *eiddiorwg.* *Eiddew y ddaiar*, ground-ivy.

Eiddiad, *s. m.* (aidd) A taking to; a possessing.

Eiddiar, *s. m. aggr.* (aidd) Heath, ling, or hether.

Eiddiaw, *v. a.* (aidd) To take to one; to possess.

> Duw ni eiddiodd (dawn iddi)
> Merch i'th oes mor wych a thi.
>
> God *possessed* not (grace be to her) a maid in thy time so fair as thee. *D. ab Gwilym.*
>
> Gwraig y bo marw ei gwr, hi a ddyly fod yno uwch ben ei aelwyd hyd yn mhen y nawfed dydd; ac yno ar ol y geiniawg ddiweddaf o'r a eiddiai.
>
> A wife whose husband shall die, she ought to be there over his hearth until the end of the ninth day; and then till after the last penny that *she should have possession of*. *Welsh Laws.*
>
> Brenin tir rhywir, rhyfedd ydd eiddiw
> Nad eiddio fo Wynedd.
>
> The undoubted king of the land, it is wonderful that *he doth not possess* Gwynedd. *Einion Wan.*

Eiddiawg, *a.* (aidd) That is possessed. *s. m.* One that is possessed, a slave.

> Da angeu ar eiddiawg.
>
> Death is a blessing to a *slave*. *Adage.*

Eiddiawl, *a.* (aidd) Relating to possession.

Eiddiawr, *s. m.* (aidd) That adheres, or closes to.

Eiddig, *a.* (aidd) Jealous. *s. m.* A jealous one.

> Dewin pob eiddig.
>
> Every *jealous one* is a conjurer. *Adage.*

Eiddigawl, *a.* (eiddig) Apt to incite jealousy.

Eiddigedd, *s. m.* (eiddig) Jealousy; zeal; solicitude. *O ddirfawr eiddigedd daioni*, from extreme zeal for goodness.

Eiddigeddawl, *a.* (eiddigedd) Tending to create jealousy.

Eiddigeddiad, *s. m.* (eiddigedd) A being jealous.

Eiddigeddu, *v. n.* (eiddigedd) To be jealous; to be zealous, to have zeal.

Eiddigeddus, *a.* (eiddigedd) Apt to be jealous.

Eiddigeddwr, *s. m.—pl.* eiddigeddwyr (eiddigedd—gwr) One who is jealous.

Eiddiges, *s. f.—pl. t.* au (eiddig) A jealous female

Eiddigiad, *s. m.* (eiddig) A becoming jealous.

Eiddigor, *s. m.* (eiddig) One that is a possessor, or guarding; a lord, or master.

Eiddigus, *a.* (eiddig) Jealous; cautious; zealous.

Eiddigyn, *s. m. dim.* (eiddig) A jealous person.

Eiddil, *a.* (aidd—ll) Slender; small, dimunitive.

> Clwm eiddil moch ellwng.
>
> A *weak* knot will soon loosen. *Adage.*
>
> Ni bu eiddil hen yn was.
>
> The aged was not *slender* when a youth. *Adage.*
>
> Lluddedig eiddigion;
> Gnawd ar eiddil ofalon.
>
> Wearied the jealous ones; the *enfeebled* is used to cares. *Llywarch Hen.*

Eiddilâad, *s. m.* (eiddil) A lessening, a making slender: extenuation; enervation.

Eiddilâawl, *a.* (eiddil) Tending to reduce small.

Eiddilâu, *v. n.* (eiddil) To reduce, or make slender; to become reduced, or feeble.

Eiddilaw, *v. a.* (eiddil) To make slender, to lessen; to extenuate; to become small.

Eiddileb, *s. f.* (eiddil) Diminution, or extenuation; the *Meiosis*, in rhetoric, in which a thing is spoken of in slighter terms than it deserves.

Eiddiliad, *s. m.—pl. t.* au (eiddil) A making slender; extenuation, diminution.

Eiddilwas, *s. m.—pl.* eiddilweis (eiddil—gwas) A slender, or emaciated youth; a fribble.

Eiddilwch, *s. m.* (eiddil) Slenderness, smallness.

Eiddilwr, *s. m.* (eiddil—gwr) A slender-man.

> Pian y bedd yn y clydwr,
> Tra fu ni bu eiddilwr:
> Bedd Ebediw ab Maelwr.
>
> He whose grave is in the sheltering slope, whilst he was he was no *slender person*, it is the grave of Ebediw the son of Maelwr. *E. Beddau Milwyr.*

Eiddion, *s. pl. aggr.* (aidd) Personal property.

Eiddionydd, *s. m.* (eiddion) An estate which a man holds in his own right, a demesne.

Eiddiorwg, *s. m.* (eiddiawr) What clasps round; ivy.

> Neus endewais'i gog ar eiddiorwg bren,
> Neur laesawys fy nghylchwyd;
> Eiddig a gerais, neud mwy!
>
> Heard I not a cuckoo on the tree *that is bound with ivy*, which made me trail my shield, begone whom I loved, hence it shall be no more! *Llywarch Hen.*
>
> Yr oedd yn berwi (wb o'r berwau)
> Saith gan mil peiriaid o eneidiau,
> A bargen hir-ddrwg, a phob eiddiorwg,
> A phawb heb olwg ar ei bolfau.
>
> There were boiling (horrid the boilings!) seven hundred thousand cauldrons-full of souls, and long wicked spite, and every *clinging thing*, and every one without sight and crawling. *Gr. ab Rhydderch Goch.*
>
> Llafnau dur o gur, ac eiddiorwg a'i caffo,
> Lleidr ceffyl dieddrwg.
>
> May steel blades of pain, and *grapple* lay hold of him, the thief of the harmless nag. *S. Mefrum.*

Eiddo, *s. m.* (aidd) One's own; possession; chattels. *Eiddof*, my property, or mine; *eiddot*, thine; *eiddo*, his; *eiddi*, hers; *eiddom*, ours; *eiddoch*, yours; *eiddynt*, *eiddont*, *eiddudd*, theirs. —*Eiddo Duw i Dduw*, the things that are God's to God.

> Y da nid eiddo'r cybydd,
> Yr hael a'i rho piau fydd.
>
> Wealth is not the *property* of the miser, the generous that gives it is the one who owns it. *Adage.*

Eiddoed, *s. m.* (aidd—oed) A point of meeting; a banner, or a standard.

Atorelwis Urien, ydd yr-echwydd,
O bydd ymgyfarfod, am garennydd,
Derchafwn eiddoed odduch mynydd.

Urien answered again if there should be a meeting because of kindred, we will lift up a *banner* above the mountain. *Taliesin.*

A weles Llwyfenydd ufydd cyngryn
Yn eiddoed cyhoedd, yn ail meyn,
Cad yn Rhyd Alclyd, cad yn Ynfer.

Humble and trembling that saw Llwyvenydd, a conspicuous *banner*, in the second place, a battle in the ford of Alclyd, a battle in the confluence. *Taliesin.*

Eiddolfa, *s. f.—pl. t.* on (eiddawl) A temple, a place of worship.

Eiddoli, *v. a.* (eiddawl) To worship, or to adore.

Eiddun, *a.* (aidd—un) Tending to raise a desire.

Ysgodig rhag cerdd cerdd orun deyrn,
Cledr cedeirn cad eiddun.

Sheltering from disgrace the loud of song of the prince, the stay of the mighty ones *fond* of battle. *Cynddelw, i O. Cyfeiliawg.*

Eiddunadwy, *a.* (eiddun) That may be wished.

Eiddunaw, *v. a.* (eiddun) To desire, or to wish.

Eiddunaf na fwyf ganmlwydd.

I pray that I be not a hundred years old. *Llywarch Hen.*

Eiddunawd, *s. m.* (eiddun) The act of wishing.

Eiddunawl, *a.* (eiddun) Having a wish, delectable

Eidduned, *s. f.—pl. t.* au (eiddun) A wish; a desire, an option, or choice.

Eidduned berwr hir-nos.

The *desire* of one on the scout is a long night. *Adage.*

Eiddunedig, *a.* (eiddun) That is wished.

Eiddunedigaeth, *s. m.—pl. t.* au (eiddunedig) The act of wishing, or desiring.

Eiddunedigawl, *a.* (eiddunedig) Optative, optional.

Eidduneda, *v. a.* (eidduned) To wish, or to desire.

Eiddunfryd, *s. m.—pl. t.* au (eiddun—bryd) A longed for purpose, or intention.

Am urddas addas eiddunfryd Cymmry,
Daeth cymmraw a thristyd!

Upon the appropriate honour of the *choice reliance* of the Welsh, there came dejection and sorrow. *Bleddyn Fardd.*

Eidduniad, *s. m.—pl. t.* au (eiddun) A desiring, wishing, or longing.

Eiddunwr, *s. m.—pl.* eiddunwyr (eiddun—gwr) One who wishes, or desires; an intreater.

Eiddunydd, *s. m.—pl. t.* ion (eiddun) A desirer.

Eiddwch, *s. m.* (aidd) The state of being near, or within reach; proximity.

Eiddwg, *s. m.* (aidd) Nearness. *a.* Contiguous.

Y dydd hwnw, nid eiddwg,
Coffa dioer, i caiff y dwg.

On that day, which is not *near*, the memorial is certain, he shall obtain the benefit. *Ieuan Tew.*

Eiddwng, *a.* (aidd—wng) Hard by, near, contiguous. *s. m.* A neighbour.

Ef yw———
Un heb eiddwng neb iddo.

He is one without any body a *neighbour* to him. *Cad. Dafydd.*

Eiddygan, *v. a.* (eiddwg) To approximate.

Eiddyganawl, *a.* (eiddygan) Approximating.

Eiddyganiad, *s. m.* (eiddygan) Approximation, a drawing near, or approaching.

Eiddyganu, *v. a.* (eiddygan) To approximate.

Yr aelwyd hon, neus cladd cywen,
Ni's eiddyganai anghen
Yn myw Owain ac Urien.

This hearth, is it not scratched up by the fowl, want *would* not *approach* towards it in the life of Owain and Urien. *Llywarch Hen.*

Eiddyn, *s. m.* (aidd) The state of being close to, or set upon, or against.

Bum geiliawg rhedyn
Ar ieir yn eiddyn.

I have been a cock grasshopper upon the hens in a *contact state*. *Taliesin.*

Eigiad, *s. m.—pl. t.* au (aig) A bringing forth.

Eigiaeth, *s. m.* (aig) The state of teeming, fullness.

Eigian, *s. m.* (aig) A bringing forth, or producing; a forcing out; force. *Mae yn gweiddi o eigian ei ben*, he is calling with all the force of his head; *gweithia o nerth eigian dy freichiau*, work with the power of the force of thy arms.

Eigian, *v. a.* (aig) To bring forth; to force out; to sob.

Eigiaw, *v. a.* (aig) To bring forth, to generate.

Eigiodd llyffaint haint egwan.

Frogs *generated* an enfeebling contagion. *W. Middleton.*

Eigiawl, *a.* (aig) Generative, prolific, teeming.

Eigiawn, *s. m.* (aig) The great source; the middle; the abyss, or the ocean.

Oeddynt yn mwynâu rhyddid—wrth eu bod mewn eigiawn oddieithr y byd yn preswyliaw.

They were enjoying liberty, by being in an *ocean* dwelling separated from the world. *Gr. ab Arthur.*

Eigion, *s. m.—pl. t.* ydd (aig) The great source; the middle; the abyss, or great deep; the ocean. *Naw ton eigion*, the nine waves of the ocean.

Trwy eigion byd trig yn ben.

Through the *midst* of the world he will continue the thief. *Iaco Brydydd.*

Eigr, *s. f.—pl. t.* ion (aig) A maid, a virgin.

Gwell eigr ddoeth yn ofni Duw,
A 'chydig bach o fodd i fyw,
No'r—— oludawg ffol.

Better a discreet *maid* that feareth God, with a very little means to live, than the silly one with wealth. *R. Pritchard, o Lanymddyfri*

Eigraeth, *s. m.* (eigr) The state of a virgin.

Eigraidd, *a.* (eigr) Like a virgin, maidenly.

Eigrau, *s. pl.* (eigr) Stockings without feet. *s.* Eigren. They are otherwise called *bacsau*, and *hosanau pen geist*.

Eigraw, *v. a.* (eigr) To make fit, to generate.

Eigrawl, *a.* (eigr) Proper for generating.

Eigriad, *s. m.* (eigr) A forming for generation.

Eigryn, *s. m.* (eigr) Quaking grass.

Eil, *s. c.* (ail) A second, or next in succession; a successor; a son; as, *Morfran eil Tegid*, *Dylan eil Ton*, and others.

Eilar, *s. m.* (ail—âr) A second ploughing.

Eilaru, *v. a.* (eilar) To plough a second time.

Eilchwaith, *s. f.* (ail—chwaith) The second time. *adv.* A second time, or once more.

Eilchwyl, *s. f.* (ail—chwyl) The second turn. *adv.* A second time, once more, again.

Eilewydd, *s. m.* (alaw) A musician; a minstrel.

Can yw y daethant,
Can eilewydd gant,
Ef a'u darogant.

Since it is they are come, a hundred with the *master of harmony*, he will foretell of them. *Taliesin.*

Eilewydd celfydd
Pyr na'm dywêyd?

The ingenious *minstrel* why doth he not inform me? *Taliesin.*

Eilfaint, *s. m.* (ail—maint) Second rate. *a.* Second rate, of the second magnitude.

Eilfam, *s. f.* (ail—mam) A second mother.

Eilfam modryb dda.

A good aunt is a *second mother*. *Adage.*

Eilfydd, *a.* (ail—bydd) Being second to or like.

Eilfyddu, *v. a.* (eilfydd) To imitate, to resemble.

Eiliad, *s. m.—pl. t.* au (ail) A placing alternately, or putting together in order, a constructing.

Eilio'r iaith fal Iolo'r oedd,
Eiliad awdl Aled ydoedd,
Awen ddofn o'r un ddefnydd
A'r gawod fel ar goed fydd.

He was harmonising the language like Iolo, it was the ode construction of Aled, it was a profound gift of the same matter as memory dew which on trees is found.
Gr. ab I. ab Llywelyn Fychan.

Eiliant, *s. m.* (ail) Constructure, concordance.

Eilias, *s. f.* — *pl. t.* au (al—ias) Harmonic influence or power.

Eiliasaf, *s. m.* (eilias) The flow of harmonious influence or power.

> Urien yd gyrchaf—
> Cynnwys a gaffaf
> O'th parth goreuaf,
> Ydan eiliasaf.

To Urien I will resort, reception I will meet with, in the best of attentions under the *flow of sweet music.* *Taliesin.*

> Dinas ei dias ar led eithaf,
> Dor angor byddin budd eiliasaf.

A city whose fame extends to the remotest parts, the straying shelter of the host, the benefit of the *flow of pervading melody.* *Aneurin.*

> Dygoglawdd ton bebr benerin
> Men ydynt eiliasaf elain.

The bright wave on her pilgrimage rolls down where the young deer are in *full melody.* *Aneurin.*

Eiliaw, *v. a.* (ail) To put in succession, or order; to harmonize; to construct; to build, or to erect; to plait; to wattle.

> Eiliais erod glod, ghwa-deg Wenlliant;
> Lliaws dy foliant fil ychwaneg.

I have constructed a panegyric for thy sake, Gwenlliant brightly fair, a thousand more *have constructed* thy praise
Casnodyn.

Eiliawd, *s. m.* (ail) The act of placing alternately, or constructing.

Eiliawg, *a.* (ail) Placed together, or constructed.

Eilier, *s. m.*—*pl. t.* au (ail) What makes, or undergoes, changes; the butterfly. It is also called, *eilir*, *ilir*, *pila*, *pilai*, and *gloyn byw.*

Eilig, *a.* (al) Having aptness to glide or flow.

> Gorwyn blaen helig, eilig Pysg yn llyn,
> Gochwiban gwynt uch blaen gwrysg man,
> Trech anian noc addysg.

Glittering the tops of the willows, *playful* the fish in the pool; whistling the wind over the small branches, nature is more powerful than precept. *Llywarch Hen.*

Eilir, *s. m.*—*pl. t.* ion (ail—ir) Regeneration, reanimation, a return of moisture; a butterfly. *Alban eilir*, the vernal equinox.

> Mwy na'r eilir yn min drych
> Ni wnaent ond edrych arno.

Like the *butterfly* on the side of the mirror they will do nothing but gaze upon him. *H. Llwyd.*

Eiliw, *s. m.*—*pl. t.* oedd (ail) Appearance, colour, pretence, form, or figure.

Dwyn eu heiliw eu hun oddiarnynt, a dodi eiliw arall arnynt, fal na adnapid, a orug.

He took away their own *form* from them, and gave another *form* to them, so that they were not known.
H. P. P. Dyfed—Mabinogion.

Eiliwed, *s. m.* (eiliw) Reproach, or disgrace.

> Crefydd y Creawdr a gyfrifed
> I Ruffudd, gloyw ri'd a'i cudd tudwed,
> Hyd na'n gwnel pechawd pell eiliwed,
> Pedryddawg deyrn uch cyrn cowrd.

Faith in the Creator is attributed to Gruffudd, the exalted chief, who is concealed in earth, so that sin shall not cause distant reproach, be that is a powerful prince over the horns of exhilaration.
Meilyr.

Eiloes, *s. f.* (ail—oes) A second age, or life; a second time. *adv.* Again.

Eilon, *s. m.* (al—on) Music, harmony, melody; also the hart, or roebuck. *Eilon mynydd*, a wild roebuck.

> Yr ydwyf yn gynt—i dal'r ddau—
> Na'r eilon i'r bán, na'r elain i'r coed,
> Nag a droed a roed i aradain.

I am swifter to the *houses of the two*, than the roebuck to the heath, than the hind to the wood, or than the speed that is given to the swiftest wing. *L. G. Cothi.*

> Oian parchellan, andaw di'r eilon
> A gread adar cwr Caer Rheon.

Listen, little pig, hear thou the *melody* which the feathered tribes are making by Caer Rheon. *Myrddin.*

> Carafi eaws fal forwhun hudd,
> A golygon hwyr hir-wyn i gnudd;
> Caraf eilon mygr maith arueddudd,
> Eiliwed noeth, a serch cystudd.

I love the nightingale the obstruction of the morning sleep in May, with downcast locks, and long white-sided head; I love the sweet *melody*, heavy upon her the reproach of shining in solitude, with the trappings of affliction. *Gwalchmai.*

Eilpai, *adv.* (ail—pe) As if.

Eilsaig, *s. m.*—*pl.* eilseigiau (ail—saig) Second course, or portion of victuals.

Eilun, *s. m.* (ail—un) A copy, image, or resemblance; a representation, picture, or portrait, an idol.

> Y mae delw ac eilun Duw mewn dyn.

There be the form and *image* of God in man.
Ll. G. Hergest.

Eilunaddolaidd, *a.* (eilun—addolaidd) Idolatrous.

Eilunaddolgar, *a.* (eilun—addolgar) Idolatrous.

Eilunaddoli, *v. a.* (eilun—addoli) To worship images, or idols, to commit idolatry.

Eilunaddoliad, *s. m.* (eilun—addoliad) A worshipping of images; idolatry.

Eilunaddoliaeth, *s. m.* (eilun—addoliaeth) Idolatry.

Eilunaddoliant, *s. m.* (eilun—addoliant) Idolatry.

Eilunaddolwr, *s. m.*—*pl.* eilunaddolwyr (eilun—addolwr) A worshipper of images.

Eiluniad, *s. m.* (eilun) A copying, a portraying.

Eiluniaeth, *s. m.* (eilun) A copy, or resemblance.

Eiluniant, *s. m.* (eilun) A portraiture, a picture.

Eiluniaw, *v. a.* (eilun) To copy, or to represent.

> Eilunid Dunawd Deheuwint.
> Aer ei enw, ei arfau o Ffrainc.

Dunawd *let him resemble* Deheuwint, whose name is slaughter, and his arms from France. *Meigant, m. Cynddylan.*

Eiluniawl, *a.* (eilun) Having a resemblance.

Eiluniwr, *s. m.*—*pl.* eilunwyr (eilun—gwr) One who makes a copy, or resemblance.

Eilw, *s. m.* (al) Melody, harmony. *a.* Melodious.

Eilwaith, *s. f.* (ail—gwaith) A second time, or turn. *a.* Second time, or again.

> Pryn hen, pryn eilwaith.

Buy what is old, and buy a *second time.* *Adage.*

Eilwy, *s. m.*—*pl. t.* on (al) That makes melody, or harmony; a musician; a minstrel.

> Agorai ei lys i les eilwyon byd;
> Rhoddi i ebyd ei ysborthion.

He opened his court for the benefit of the *minstrels* of the world; to the guests are given his provisions.
Cynddelw, i Gadwallawn.

> I geiddawr am breiddiawr, am brain;
> I eilwyon am eirchion arbfain,
> I dawdd rhodd i orddaw budd i frain;
> I feirdd dwfn dyfyd a gofiain.

To a songster looking for the *fruit of the chase*, and for a delicacy, to the *sons of melody* for slender bodied gifts; to a ruddy wolf to prepare a treasure for ravens, to the profound bards will come what will be kept in memory.
Cynddelw, m. O. Gwynedd.

Eilwydd, *s. m.* (al—gwydd) Harmonic presence, a love meeting, or assignation.

> Ebrwydd—ydd af,
> Lle fym llwydd eilwydd arwydd araf.

Quickly I will go where I shall prosper in a *meeting of harmony*, a gentle sign. *Ll. P. Moch, i ferch.*

> —Gwneuthum
> Dydd Llun oed a bun lle bum,
> Lle gwelais hwn gwiw trais trai;
> Ddywedai y bi oddiwrthai
> Ddyfod i eilwydd ofyn,
> Lle ni ddaeth llawen o ddyn.

I made on Monday an assignation with the fair where I have been, where I have seen her of the hue of the foamy waves of the straining ebb, on Monday she had promised to come to seek an *assignation* where the blithesome nymph never came.
D. ab Gwilym, i Forfudd.

Eilwys, *s. pl.* (al—gwys) Powers of harmony.

> Y a wnaeth eilwys,
> Yn llys paradwys,
> O aeen aswys
> Iesu Ffemon.

The *powers of harmony*, in the court of paradise, did form, out of a left rib, a beauteous female. *Anell fraith.*

Eilydd, *s. m.—pl. t.* ion (al) One who produces harmony; a musician.

Rhyfeddaf dincler nad yw,
Yn ol eilydd celfydd clyw.

I wonder that he is not a meer poetaster, following a *musician* of correct ear. *Llywarch Hen.*

Mab cadr Cadwaladr ceidw eilydd hael.

The mighty son of Cadwaladr he keeps a liberal *minstrel*. *Sypyn Cyfeilliawg.*

Eilyg, *s. m.* (al) Harmony, melody, delight.

Gwynedd, argynan, aer gynnygn rebydd,
Gwystl bedydd, byd eilyg.

The famed one of Gwynedd, the battle supporting leader, the pledge of the faith, the *delight* of the world. *Cynddelw, m. O. Gwynedd.*

Eilyrth, *s. m.—pl. t.* ion (al—yrth) The touch or impulse of melody.

Llef a glywaf, gloew eilyrth;
Llef eilon yn eilwydd ferth!
Llef ban corn blaen cad ehorth,
Llais garw, a llef tarw Talgarth.

I hear a sound, the clear *touch of melody*; the sound of music in hallowed harmonic presence; the loud sound of the horn before the mighty battle; an awful voice, the call of the bull of Talgarth. *Cynddelw.*

Eilyw, *s. m.* (al) Harmony; melody; music.

Eilywiant, *s. m.* (eilyw) The profession of music.

Arnaf ernlwaf ernlwed a'm clwyf;
Am gleddyf-rudd rwyf ym rhygodded;
Coddiant eilywiant rhag eiliwed;
Eiliw a'm doddyw, Duw ym gwared!

I am afflicted with affliction that wounds me; for the chief with the ruddy sword I have been over anxious; the anxiety of *minstrelsy* for fear of disgrace; disgrace is come to me, may God save me! *Cynddelw, m. Cad. ab Madawg.*

Eill, *pron.* (ill) They, those. *Eill dau*, they two.

Eilldu, *s. m.* (aill—tu) The outward side.

Eilldy, *s. m.* (aill—ty) A shaving house.

Eilliad, *s. m.* (ell) A cutting close, a shaving.

Eilliaeth, *s. m.* (ell) The act of putting out; the state of being out, excommunicated.

Eilliaw, *v. a.* (ell) To part from, to sever; to cut off from, to exterminate; to shave.

Gwedi caffael o Gaswallawn y fuddygoliaeth, cerdded a orug trwy wladoedd y Saeson;—ac nid arbedis nag i wr, nag i wraig, nag i fab; canys ef a fynai yn llwyr eilliaw cenedl y Saeson o'r ynys.

After obtaining the victory of Caswallon, he went through the countries of the Saxons, and he spared neither man, nor woman, nor a youth, nor a boy; for he was determined utterly *to exterminate* the nation of the Saxons out of the island. *Gr. ab Arthur.*

Eilliedig, *a.* (ell) That is cut off, or shorn.

Eilliedydd, *s. m.—pl. t.* ion (eilliad) A shaver; a razor; a plough for cutting paper.

Eilliwr, *s. m.—pl.* eillwyr (ell—gwr) A shaver.

Eillwraig, *s. f.—pl.* eillwreigedd (ell—gwraig) A shaving woman.

Ein, *pron.* (ei) A sign of possession; property of; our property, ours; our. *Einof*, *einwyf*, mine *einot*, *einod*, *einwyd*, thine, *eino*, his property, *eini*, hers, *ein*, *einom*, *einym*, ours, *einoch*, yours, *einont*, *einynt*, theirs.

Medd y ddwy Wynedd einym;
Da yw a gatwo Duw ym.

The mead of the two Gwynedds is *ours*, it is good what God preserves for me. *Iolo Goch.*

Einawr, *s. m.* (ein—awr) The hour that is ours, the present time, or now. *adv.* Now, at present.

Einioes, *s. f.* (ein—oes) One's life; the whole time of a man's life; life. *Diwedd einioes*, the end of life; *hir einioes*, long life; "*Einioes dyn yn estynu*," the life of man drawing onward.

Einioes fyth i ynys Fon,
A dwy einioes i'w dynion.

Everlasting *existence* be to the isle of Mon, and two *ages* to its people. *L. G. Cothi.*

Tair merched, tair tynged ton,
Y sy'n dwyn einioes y dynion

Three females, three cutting destinies, there be taking away the *life* of men. *Guto y Glyn.*

Eingiaw, *v. a.* (ang) To cause to expand or dilate.

Eingion, *s. f.* (ang) An anvil, a forging utensil.

Eira, *s. m.* (air) Snow. *Caseg eira*, a snow-ball.

All i'r alarch ar y don
Lliw'r eira ar fron fynyddig;
Llawer gwaith, cyn canu'r gog,
Y rhois ym clog am dana',
Ac a'm telyn gyd a mi,
I ganu i ti, lliw'r eira.

Like the swan upon the wave is she of the hue *of snow* on the mountain side; many a time before the singing of the cuckoo have I wrapt my cloke around me, and my harp along with me, to sing to thee who art of the colour of *snow*. *Pennill.*

Eiras, *s. m.* (air—as) What glows, or gives light; burning matter, a fiery body; burning cinder.

Eirchiad, *s. m.—pl.* eirchiaid (arch) A demander.

Eirchiawl, *a.* (arch) Mandatory, commanding.

Eirfydd, *s. m.—pl. t.* ion (arf) A blazoner of arms.

Arfer yr hen eirfyddion Cymmreig yw cyfrif dysg yn gydradd ag y bonedd uchaf.

The custom of the old Welsh *heralds* is to reckon learning of equal dignity with the noblest descent. *Traeth. Arwyddion.*

Eiriach, *v. a.* (air) To deprecate, to avert.

Eiriach law, nag eiriach droed.

Deprecate a hand, *do* not *deprecate* a foot. *Adage.*

Eiriachawl, *a.* (eiriach) Deprecatory, averting.

Eiriachiad, *s. m.* (eiriach) A deprecating.

Eiriachu, *v. a.* (eiriach) To deprecate, to avert.

Maxen a Cynan—ag eu gwelai hwynt, ag eu clywai, ffo a wnaeynt rhagddynt y ffordd y tebygynt caffael nodded o eu heneidiau; ac nid eiriechynt hwyntau neb ar a gyfarfai ag hwynt na's dienyddynt onid gwreigedd.

Maxen and Cynan, whosoever beheld them, and heard them, suddenly would fly from them, the way they should think of obtaining refuge for their souls; and on their part *they would spare* not any body who should come in their way that they would not put to death, except women. *Gr. ab Arthur.*

Eiriachus, *a.* (eiriach) Deprecatory, tending to save

Eiriachydd, *s. m.—pl. t.* ion (eiriach) A deprecator

Eirian, *a.* (air) Bright, splendid; fair, beautiful.

Yn Dad——
Ac yn Fab arab eirian,
Ac yn Ysbryd gloew-bryd glan.

Being a Father, and a Son blessed and *fair*, and a spirit of bright appearance and pure. *S. Cert.*

Eirianaidd, *a.* (eirian) Of a splendid appearance.

Eirianawl, *a.* (eirian) Tending to make fair.

Eirianedd, *s. m.* (eirian) Splendour; beauty.

Eirianiad, *s. m.* (eirian) A making fine or gay.

Eirianrod, *s. f.* (eirian—rhod) The galaxy.

Mi fum dri chyfnod
Yn nghaer eirianrod.

I have been for three seasons in the borders of the *milky way*. *Taliesin.*

Eirianu, *v. a.* (eirian) To make splendid.

Eirias, *s. m.—pl. t.* au (eirias) Burning matter, or the body of fire, in opposition to the flame; burning cinders; a burning log.

Nid tan heb eirias.

There is no fire without a *burning body*. *Adage.*

Wyt chwyrn, wyt teyrn, wyt eirias cadau, wyt cadarn fal dinas.

Thou art ardent, thou art a prince, thou art the *fire* of battles, thou art strong like a rampart. *Ll. P. Moch, i Lywelyn I.*

Eiriasawl, *a.* (eirias) Of a glowing nature.

Eiriasdan, *s. m.* (eirias—tân) A glowing fire.

Eiriasedd, *s. m.* (eirias) Glowingness; fieriness.

Eiriasu, *v. n.* (eirias) To burn vehemently.

Eiriaw, *v. a.* (air) To brighten; to become bright.

Eiriawg, *a.* (air) Abounding with brightness.

Eiriawl, *a.* (air) Splendid, bright; beautiful; the snowdrop; also called *cloch maban*.

Priaf brenin Troea gwr mawr oedd, a theg, ac ymadrawdd hynaws, a chorph eiriawl.

Priam king of Troy, he was a big man, and fair, and he was of a pleasing conversation, and he had a *beautiful* form. *H. Dared—Mabinogion.*

Eiriawl, *v. a.* (air—iawl) To intreat; to intercede; to use persuasion, to persuade.

> Hawdd eiriawl ar y garer.
>
> It is easy *to persuade* one that is beloved. *Adage.*
>
> Eiriawl ni charer ni chynghan.
>
> It is not meet *to intreat* one that is not loved. *Adage.*

Eiriachaeth, *s. m.* (eiriach) Deprecation; intreaty
Eiriesyn, *s. m. dim.* (eirias) A glowing cinder.
Eirif, *s. m.—pl. t.* ion (rhif) A number; a counting; a numbering.

> Ni ddodai eirif ar ei ddillad.
>
> He would not fix a *number* on scarlet garments. *D. Benfras.*

Eirifaw, *v. a.* (eirif) To number, to enumerate.
Eirifawl, *a.* (eirif) Relating to number.
Eirifiad, *s. m.* (eirif) A numbering, enumeration
Eirig, *a.* (air) Splendid, shining; gay, or fine.

> Eirig ei reiawr rieddawg.
>
> *Splendid* his princely spear. *Taliesin.*

Eirioes, *s. f.* (air—oes) Pure, or holy life.

> Goreuyn blaen egrwn; ald moes caledi,
> Cadwed bawb ei eirioes
> Gwaethaf anaf anfoes.
>
> Glittering the tops of the haws: hardship is not mannerly; let every one preserve his *purity of life*: the worst of blemish is want of manners. *Llywarch Hen.*

Eiriolad, *s. m.* (eiriawl) A using persuasion.
Eiriolaeth, *s. m.—pl. t.* au (eiriawl) Intercession.
Eirioled, *s. m.* (eiriawl) Intreaty; intercession.
Eirioledd, *s. m.* (eiriawl) Intreaty, persuasion.
Eirioleddus, *a.* (eirioledd) Of persuading nature.
Eirioli, *v. a.* (eiriawl) To intreat; to persuade, or to use persuasion; to intercede.
Eiriolus, *a.* (eiriawl) Persuasive; intercessory.
Eiriolusrwydd, *s. m.* (eiriolus) Persuasiveness.
Eiriolwch, *s. m.* (eiriawl) Intreaty, intercession.
Eiriolwr, *s. m.—pl.* eiriolwyr (eiriawl—gwr) One who uses persuasion; an intercessor, or mediator
Eiriolydd, *s. m.—pl. t.* ion (eiriawl) A paraclete; an advocate, a mediator, or intercessor.
Eiriolyddiaeth, *s. m.* (eiriolydd) A mediatorship.
Eirion, *s. pl. aggr.* (air) What gives splendour, or lustre, ornaments.
Eirionawl, *a.* (eirion) Ornamental; adorning.
Eirioni, *v. a.* (eirion) To ornament, to adorn.
Eirionyn, *s. m.—pl. t.* au (eirion) A border, the list of cloth; the edge, or selvage, any border set on for ornament; a ruffle. *Dau eirionyn tir*, the two borders, or cross ridges of a field. *Welsh Laws.*
Eirionynawg, *a.* (eirionyn) Having a border.
Eirionynawl, *a.* (eirionyn) Having trimmings.
Eirionynu, *v. a.* (eirionyn) To border, to edge; to fringe, to ruffle.
Eirllyd, *a.* (eiry) Apt to snow, apt to be snowy.
Eirllydrwydd, *s. m.* (eirllyd) A snowiness.
Eirthiad, *s. m.—pl. t.* au (arth) A growling as a bear; a baiting, or attacking as a bear.
Eirthiaw, *v. a.* (arth) A baiting, a setting upon.

> A'i cwyn a'm treisyn treisid eiddiaw,
> Ail gwr gwrdd gorddew arthan eirthiaw.
>
> Another woe about a foe from retirement of him, a second mighty hero that *toils like a bear* in the combat.
> *Cynddelw, m. R. Flaidd.*

Eirthiawl, *a.* (arth) Buffetting, or baiting.
Eirw, *s. m.—pl. t.* on (air) A foaming place, a cataract, or waterfall.
Eirwlaw, *s. m.—pl. t.* ion (eiry—gwlaw) Sleet.
Eirwlawiaw, *v. a.* (eirwlaw) To fall in sleet.
Eirwlawiawg, *a.* (eirwlaw) Abounding with sleet.
Eirwlawiogrwydd, *s. m.* (eirwlawiawg) Sleetiness.
Eirwy, *s. m.—pl. t.* on (eirw) A foaming cataract
Eirwynt, *s. m.—pl. t.* oedd (eiry—gwynt) Snowy wind, or wind that brings snow.
Eiry, *s. m.* (air) Snow. *Adar yr eiry*, starlings.
Eiryaid, *s. m.* (eiry) Summer snowflake.
Eiryaidd, *a.* (eiry) Like snow, or snowy.
Eiryawg, *a.* (eiry) Abounding with snow, snowy.

> A Gruffudd yntau o gynnefindra a brwydr a luestwys yn ei erbyn yn mreichiau Eryri eiryawg.
>
> And Gruffudd also from a familiarity with war pitched his tent against him in the ridges of the *snowy* Eryri.
> *Buchedd G. ab Cynan.*

Eiryawl, *a.* (eiry) Tending to snow, snowy.
Eiryn, *s. pl. aggr.* (aren) Glands; testicles; a plumb. *Eiryn duon*, common black plumbs; *eiryn hirion*, damascenes; *eiryn cochion*, Orlean plumbs; *eiryn gwyrddion*, green gage plumbs; *eiryn gwlanawg*, peaches; *eiryn surion*, *eiryn perthi*, *eiryn tagu*, bullace; *eiryn Mai*, *eiryn perth eurddrain*, gooseberries; *eiryn gwion*, the briony berries; *eiryn y ci*, cullions.
Eirynbren, *s. m.* (eiryn—pren) A plumb-tree.
Eirynen, *s. f.* (eiryn) One plumb, a plumb.
Eirynllys, *s. m. aggr.* (eiryn—llys) The Saint John's wort.

> Rhag man cymer yr eirynllys a doda wrtho pan arganfer gyntaf.
>
> Against a mole take the *St. John's wort*, and apply to it when first observed. *Meddygon Myddfai.*

Eirynwydd, *s. pl.* (eiryn—gwydd) Plumb trees.

> Eirynwydd yn prin,
> Anchwant o ddynin.
>
> *Plumb trees*, that are scarce, unambitious heroism. *Taliesin.*

Eirys, *s. m.—pl. t.* od (air) A coal, an ember.
Eisawl, *a.* (ais) Costal, belonging to the ribs.
Eisen, *s. f.* (ais) A lath; also a rib.
Eisgiad, *s. m.* (asg) A parting off, or cleaving.
Eisgiaw, *v. a.* (asg) To part from; to cleave; to be destitute, to be in want.
Eisglwyf, *s. m.—pl. t.* on (ais—clwyf) A pleurisy.
Eisglwyfaw, *v. n.* (eisglwyf) To become pleuritic.
Eisglwyfawl, *a.* (eisglwyf) Pleuritic, pleuritical.
Eisiaw, *v. a.* (ais) To lathe, to lay laths; to make lattice-work.
Eisieu, *s. m.* (es) Want, necessity, need, lack.

> Gwell benthyg nag eisieu.
>
> Borrowing is better than *want*. *Adage.*

Eisieuedig, *a.* (eisieu) Necessitated; indigent.
Eisin, *s. m. aggr.* (sin) Bran, or husks of corn.
Eisina, *v. a.* (eisin) To gather bran or husks.
Eisinaw, *v. a.* (eisin) To produce bran or husks.
Eisinaidd, *a.* (eisin) Branny, husky; like bran.
Eisinawg, *a.* (eisin) Branny, full of bran.
Eisinawl, *a.* (eisin) Made of bran; like bran.
Eisingrug, *s. m.* (eisin—crug) A heap of bran.
Eisinllyd, *a.* (eisin) Branny, full of bran; husky.
Eisiw, *s. m.—pl. t.* on (es) Want, need; poverty.
Eisiwaw, *v. n.* (eisiw) To become destitute.
Eisiwawl, *a.* (eisiw) Tending to neediness.
Eisiwed, *s. m.—pl. t.* au (eisiw) A destitute state, want, need, or lack; indigence.

> Heb nebawd eisiwed.
>
> Without any kind of *want*. *Cynddelw.*
>
> Mae gwyrda Gwynedd, gwae ni yr eisiwed, ysywaeth yn trengi!
>
> Woe to us because of the *lack*, the worthy men of Gwynedd, also, are dying! *Bleddyn Fardd.*

Eisiwedig, *a.* (eisiwed) That is destitute, needy, in want; indigent, poor.

> Treet yd gwyn pob cwledig,
> Ffest yd hawl eisiwedig.
>
> Piteously doth every condemned one complain; with alacrity the *needy* makes his claim. *Taliesin.*

Eisiwedd, *s. m.* (eisiw) A state of want; neediness

Eisiwiad, *s. m.* (eisiw) A rendering destitute.
Eisiwyd, *s. m.* (eisiw) Want; indigence, poverty.

Cysefin i'm byd
A fu eisiwyd;
Myuaich alaid
Pyr na'm dywaid.

Generally through my life *poverty* hath been; the wealthy monk will hardly speak to me. *Taliesin.*

Eisoes, *adv.* (es—oes) Nevertheless, however; moreover; likewise; already.
Eisor, *a.* (es—or) Equal; of the same sort, like.
Eisorawd, *s. m.* (eisor) What is like; a counterpart.
Eisorawl, *a.* (eisor) Tending to make equal.
Eisori, *v. a.* (eisor) To make equal, or like.
Eisoriad, *s. m.—pl. t.* au (eisor) An equalizing.
Eisorig, *a.* (eisor) Tending to assimilate.
Eissill, *s. f.* (essill) What is parted from.
Eissilledd, *s. m.* (eissill) Offspring, or progeny.

Trwy for llithrant eu heisilledd.

Their *offspring* will glide through a sea. *Taliesin.*

Eissillid, *s. m.* (eissill) Offspring, or progeny.
Eissillyd, *s. m.* (eissill) Offspring, or progeny.
Eissillydd, *s. m.* (eissill) Offspring, or progeny.

Ni bu edifar y dydd y cyrchodd,
Cyrch ehofn eissillydd;
Gwelai wawr âr wyr lluosydd,
Fal gwr yn gwrthladd cywilydd.

There was no repentance for the day he attacked, it was the onset of a brave *race*, he perceived a hue on the men of battle, like a man opposing reproach. *Llygad Gwr, i Lywelyn II.*

Eiste, *s. m.* (aes—te) A sitting, the act of sitting.
Eiste, *v. a.* (aes—te) To sit; to be seated.

Pwy bynag a eistôo ynddi.

Whosoever that *shall sit* in it. *Breinlau Arfon.*

Eistedd, *s. m.* (eiste) A sitting, the act of sitting.
Eistedd, *v. a.* (eiste) To sit. *Eistedd ar wyau*, to sit upon eggs; *eistedd wrth*, to sit down by, to lay siege to.

A chan y fuddygoliaeth hono y doel Beli hyd at Fran ei frawd â oedd yn eistedd wrth Rufain.

And in consequence of that victory Beli came to Bran his brother that was *sitting* before Rome. *Gr. ab Arthur.*

Eisteddawg, *a.* (eistedd) Sedentary, or that sits.
Eisteddawl, *a.* (eistedd) Relating to sitting.
Eisteddfa, *s. f.—pl. t.* on (eistedd—ma) A sitting place; also a station.
Eisteddfod, *s. f.—pl. t.* au (eistedd—bod) A being sitting, a sitting; a meeting, or assembly; a session. *Eisteddfod y beirdd*, a congress of the bards.
Eisteddiad, *s. m.—pl. t.* au (eistedd) A sitting.
Eisteddial, *v. a.* (eistedd) To sit often.
Eisteddig, *a.* (eistedd) Apt to be sitting.
Eisteddle, *s. m.—pl. t.* oedd (eistedd—lle) A sitting place; a station.
Eisteddogrwydd, *s. m.* (eistedd) Sedentariness.
Eisteddolrwydd, *s. m.* (eistedd) Sedentariness.
Eisteddwr, *s. m.—pl.* eisteddwyr (eistedd—gwr) A sitter, a sedentary person.
Eistydd, *s. m.* (eistedd) The act of seating.
Eistyddiad, *s. m.—pl. t.* au (eistydd) A seating.
Eistyddiaw, *v. a.* (eistydd) To place in a seat.
Eiswng, *s. m.—pl.* eisyngion (ais—wng) Deprivation; imminent want; a sigh.

Uffern—a'i hir eisyngion a'i hersangau.

Hell, with its lasting *sighs*, and its tramplings. *G. ab M. ab Dafydd.*

Eiswys, *adv.* (eisys) Likewise, besides; already.
Eisyddyn, *s. m.—pl. t.* au (syddyn) A tenement.
Eisys, *adv.* (es—ys) Likewise, besides; already.

Bod yn hir yn glaf a marw eisys.

To be long sick and to die *besides*. *Adage.*

Eithaf, *s. m.—pl. t.* on (aith) The acme, the uttermost, the outermost, the farthest, the ultimate. *a.* Ultimate; farthest, most distant. *Eithafon byd*, the uttermost parts of the world.

Dymchwel y rhyfel——
Hyd eithafion pella'.

Return the war to the most distant *extremities*. *W. Middleton.*

Eithafed, *s. m.—pl. t.* oedd (eithaf) The utmost limit, or extremity.
Eithafig, *a.* (eithaf) Extreme, or ultimate. *s. pl.* *Eithafigion*, borderers, or the inhabitants of the marches. Also a sward.
Eithafnod, *s. m.—pl. t.* au (eithaf—nod) Nonplus.
Eithen, *s. f. dim.* (aith) A prickle, a sharp point.
Eithin, *s. pl. aggr.* (aith) Furze, whins, or gorse. *Eithin ffreinig*, common furze; *eithin merwlas*, *eithin man*, whin; *eithin yr ieir*, *crach eithin*, needle furze, or petty whin.
Eithin, *a.* (aith) Prickly, or full of prickles.

Ag eiddew ar ei bryd,
Mor eithin, i'r gryd
Sirian senyzid.

With ivy on his front, so bristled, the cherry tree was provoked to the combat. *Taliesin.*

Eithinawg, *a.* (eithin) Overgrown with furze. *Tir eithinawg*, furzy land: *yr eithinawg fawr*, the greater furze bush.
Eithinen, *s. f.* (eithin) A furze, a furze bush. *Eithinen ber*, or *eithinen y cwrw*, juniper.
Eithinfyw, *s. m.* (eithin—byw) The savine.
Eithiw, *a.* (aith) Prickly, or full of points.
Eithiwaw, *v. a.* (eithiw) To make prickly.
Eithiwawg, *a.* (eithiw) Having prickles or points.
Eithr, *adv.* (aith) Except, without; besides; but.

Eithr gallu nid oes dim.

Besides power there is nothing. *Adage.*

Eithrad, *s. m.—pl.* eithraid (eithr) An excepted, or excluded one, a stranger.
Eithradwy, *a.* (eithr) Exceptionable, that may be excluded, or estranged.
Eithraw, *v. a.* (eithr) To except, to exclude.
Eithrawl, *a.* (eithr) Exceptive; exclusive.
Eithriad, *s. m.—pl. t.* au (eithr) Exception.

Rhys rwysg chwel rhyfel— -
Eithriad brad bron eiliasaf,
Eithr cenyd cynnelw ni wnaf.

Rhys, whose sway is like the course of war, a *stranger* to treachery his breast that flows with harmony, except of thee no dependance will I seek. *Phylip Brydydd, i Rys Ieuanc.*

EL, *s. m. r.—pl. t.* od. What has in itself the power of motion, a moving principle; an intelligence; a spirit; an angel. *Tywysoges yr elod*, the queen of the fairies.
Elaeth, *s. m.* (el) The act, or power, of self-motion; intelligence, or the state of angelic existence.
Elaidd, *a.* (el) Intelligential, of angelic nature.
Elaig, *s. m.* (llaig) A secluded one; a hermit.

Nid wyd ti ysgolaig,
Nid wyd elaig,
Unben ni'th elwir yn nydd rhaid;
Och Cynddilig na buost gwraig!

Thou art not a scholar, thou art not a *minstrel*, a monarch thou wilt not be called in the day of necessity. O Cynddilig, why wert thou not a woman! *Llywarch Hen.*

Elain, *s. f.—pl.* eleinod (el—ain) A fawn.
Elanedd, *s. pl. aggr.* (llanedd) The intestines.
Elawch, *s. m.* (llawch) Indulgence, tenderness.
Elawr, *s. f.—pl.* elorau (llawr) A bier. *Elawr feirch*, a hearse.

Yn Llongborth gwelais drydar,
Ac elorawr yn ngwyar,
A gwyr rhudd rhag rhuthr esgar.

In Llongborth I saw a tumult, and *biers* in blood, and ruddy men from the onset of the foe. *Llywarch Hen.*

Elcys, *s. pl. aggr.* (el—cws) Wild geese, ganzas.
Elcysen, *s. f.* (elcys) A wild goose, or ganza.
Elech, *s. f.—pl. t.* au (llech) A slate, stone.

Joseph a drosra elech fawr ar ddrws bedd Crist.

Joseph rolled a great *flat stone* upon the door of the grave of Christ.

Aelwyd rhwng pedair elech.

A hearth between four *flat stones*. *L. G. Cothi.*

Eleigiad, *s. m.—pl. t.* au (elaig) A becoming solitary, or secluded.
Eleigiaw, *v. a.* (elaig) To seclude; to conceal.
Eleigiawl, *a.* (elaig) Tending to make solitary.
Elen, *s. f.* (el) An intelligence, an angel.
Eleni, *s. f.* (elen) The present year. *adv.* This year, the year now going on.
Elenid, *s. f.* (elen) Present year. *adv.* This year.
Elest, *s. m. aggr.* (el—est) Flags, sedges; rushes.
Elestr, *s. m.—pl. t.* on (elest) The iris, flag, or sedge. *Ystrail elestr*, a mat of sedges.
Elestraidd, *a.* (elestr) Like flags; like lillies.
Elestrawg, *a.* (elestr) Having lillies.
Elestren, *s. f.* (elestr) A flag or sedge leaf.

Nid hawdd blingaw ag elestren.

It is not easy to flay with a *flag leaf*. *Adage.*

Elf, *s. m.—pl. t.* odd (el) A moving principle.
Elfaeth, *s. m.* (elf) Elementation; elementarity.
Elfed, *s. m.* (el—med) Autumn. *Alban elfed*, the autumnal equinox.
Elfen, *s. f.—pl. t.* au (elf) An operative cause; a particle, or constituent part; an element. *Elfen tân*, a particle, or spark of fire.
Elfenawl, *a.* (elfen) Elemental, elementary.
Elfeniad, *s. m.* (elfen) An elementation.
Elfenu, *v. a.* (elfen) To element, to constitute.
Elfod, *s. m.—pl. t.* au (el—bôd) Intellectual existence, or the state of spirits.
Elfyd, *s. m.—pl. t.* oedd (el—byd) Intellectual world, or spiritual existence.
Elfydd, *s. m.—pl. t.* au (elf) The state of simple self-motion; an element, or first principle, earth, land.

Tri phrif elfydd y sydd daiar, dwfr, a thân.

There are three primary *elements* earth, water, and fire. *Trioedd.*

Iolwn ni a grewys
Nef ac elfydd.

We will adore him that created heaven and the *elementary world*. *Taliesin.*

Yn amwyn Elfael pan wnai Elfed,
Elfyddon greulawn, elfydd greuled.

In defending Elfael when Elfed, a fierce region, made a blood-stained land. *Cynddelw, i Gadwallawn.*

Neu'm bu dydd, cer elfydd Elwy
Elfwn wawd— —

Have I not enjoyed a day, by the *region* of Elwy, when I composed a panegyric. *Ll. P. Moch.*

Ni'm dawr, can del dros elfydd
Llanw o fôr, a lli o fynydd

I shall not be concerned, if there shall come over the *country* a tide from the sea, and a flood from the mountain. *D. Llwgwrn Mew.*

Elfyddaid, *s. m.* (elfydd) An elementation.
Elfyddan, *s. f.—pl. t.* au (elfydd) That is formed of elements; the earth, the world.

All i foddi elfyddan.
Yw llosgi eleni'n lan.

Like to the drowning of *the world* is the complete burning this year. *T. Prys.*

Elfyddawl, *a.* (elfydd) Elemental, elementary.
Elfydden, *s. m.—pl. t.* au (elfydd) What is formed of the elements; earth, or land; a region.

Mab Llywelyn hael hylwydd berchen
Ar wyneb Prydain, prif elfydden.

The son of the generous Llywelyn, a prosperous proprietor on the face of Britain, the chief *region*. *Ll. P. Moch, i Ruf ab Llywelyn.*

Elfyddiad, *s. m.—pl. t.* au (elfydd) Elementation.
Elfyddnewidiad, *s. m.—pl. t.* au (elfydd—newidiad) Trans-elementation.
Elfyddu, *v. a.* (elfydd) To form element; to constitute.
Elff, *s. m.—pl.* eilff (el) What moves in a simple, or pure, state; a spirit; a demon.
Elgain, *a.* (el—cain) Supremely fair or elegant.
Elgeth, *s. f.—pl. t.* i (el—ceth) The jawbone.
Eli, *s. m.—pl. t.* on (el) A salve, a remedy.
Eliad, *s.* (eli) The applying a salve or plaster.
Eliaw, *v. a.* (eli) To anoint with salve.
Eliawl, *a.* (eli) Of the nature of salve, emplastic.
Elin, *s. m.—pl. t.* au (glin) An angle, an elbow. *Penelin*, the elbow point, the elbow.

I'r milwr y mae elin
A wnai drwst â'i waew'n y drin.

To the warrior there is an *elbow* that would make a tumult with his spear in the conflict. *L. G. Cothi.*

Elinad, *s. m.* (elin) A making an angle;—a cubit.
Elinaw, *v. a.* (elin) To describe an angle; to elbow.
Elinawg, *a.* (elin) Abounding with angles, angular, jointy, elbow-wise. *Yr elinawg*, woody nightshade, *elinawg goch*, arsmart; called also, *y bengoch*, *y benboeth*, *llawagor*, *llysiau y dîn*.
Elindys, *s. pl. aggr.* (elin—tâs) The aurelia; the caterpillar; the volvox, or vinefretter.
Elorawg, *a.* (elawr) Having a bier, put on a bier.
Elorwydd, *s. m.* (elawr—gwydd) A hearse.
Elu, *v. a.* (el) To move onward; to go. *Elsynt yno*, they went there; *elid*, let the goer (of any gender) go; *mal yr elwyf*, so that I may be going; *er nad elo*, though he may not go.

Eli i ryw ar barth ba yw.

Let sex go upon the part of which it is. *Adage.*

Elid llaw gan droed.

Let the hand go with the foot. *Adage.*

Maddeu'n beiau i'n bywyd,
Er bar, cyn eliom o'r byd

Forgive the faults of our lives, because of wrath, before we shall go out of the world. *T. Ll. D. ab Hywel.*

Elus, *a.* (al) Benevolent, bounteous, charitable.
Elusen, *s. f.* (elus) Benevolence, charity, alms.

Nid oes gwyl rhag elusen.

There is no pretence against *charity*. *Adage.*

Elusen tam o garw.

Even a morsel out of a stag is *alms*. *Adage.*

Elusenaidd, *a.* (elusen) Of a charitable turn.
Elusenawl, *a.* (elusen) Eleemosynary, bounteous.
Elusendawd, *s. m.* (elusen) Benevolence, charity
Elusendy, *s. m.* (elusen—ty) Almshouse.
Elusengar, *a.* (elusen) Charitable, benevolent.
Elusengarwch, *s. m.* (elusengar) Charitableness.
Elusengist, *s. f.* (elusen—cist) A charity box.
Eluseni, *s. m.* (elusen) Benevolence, charity.

A son am eluseni,
Deilynged, hardded oedd hi.

And discoursing of *benevolence*, how meritorious, how fair she is. *Parch. Evan Evans.*

Elusenwr, *s. m.—pl.* elusenwyr (elusen—gwr) An almsgiver, an almoner.
Elw, *s. m.—pl. t.* oedd (el) What is past motion, or become stationary; property, goods, or chattels; profit, advantage, lucre, gain.

Ni wnaed arwid ni cheiff elw.

He makes no good bargain that gets no *gain*. *Adage*

Elwa, *v. a.* (elw) To get wealth; to make profit.

Holl ofal dyn, cerlyn caeth,
Yw elwa am fywioliaeth.

All the care of man, a slavish toiler, is *to traffick* for a livelihood. *L. Hopcin.*

Elwâad, *s. m.* (elwa) A making advantageous.
Elwant, *s. m.* (elw) Advantage, profit, gain.
Elwâu, *v. a.* (elwa) To enrich; to make profit.
Elwawd, *s. m.* (elw) The act of enriching.

Dygychwyn olwyn elwawd fangre.

Wheel, begin thy course to the place of *profit*. *Ll. P. Moch.*

Elwawg, *a.* (elw) Having property, or profit.
Elwch, *s. m.* (al) Acclamation, joy, gladness.

Llaryedd hedd boddiaw,
Lle gwyl hwyl heiliaw,
Llawr nef dref dreiddiaw,
Alaw elwch.

The mildness of peace diffusing, where the course of the festive service is seen; the confine of heaven's mansions resound with the music of *gladness*. *Casnodyn.*

Elwi, *v. a.* (elw) To get wealth; to turn to gain.

Gwyth ysgor tra mor, tra Menai,
Gwlydd elfydd elwais o honai,
Tra fu Owain mawr a'i meddai,
Medd a gwin a'n gwirawd fyddai.

The channel of the village beyond the sea, beyond Menai, a mild region out of which *I have profited*; whilst Owain the great was, who owned it, mead and wine were wont to be our beverage. *Cynddelw, m. O. Gwynedd.*

Elwig, *a.* (elw) Being inherent, as a principle. *Hydr elwig*, boldness that is inherent.

Neud adwen ar fy ngwen;
Yn hanfod cun achen,
Tri gwyddorig elwig awen.

Doth he not recognise upon my mien, shewing a descent from a royal line, the three principles of *inventive* genius. *Llywarch Hen.*

Elwl, *s. pl. aggr.* (el—gwl) The reins, or kidneys.
Elwlen, *s. f.—pl. t.* au (elwl) One of the reins.
Elwydd, *s. m.* (el—gwydd) Beatific presence.

Credaf i Beryf nef yn elwydd,
A'm gwnaeth o berawr yn brydydd.

I believe in the Creator of heaven in the *supernal light*, who made me from a minstrel to be a poet. *Cynddelw.*

Elwysen, *s. f.* (alwysen) A donation, or alms.

Elwysen tam o garw.

Even a morsel out of a stag is *alms*. *Adage.*

Elyd, *s. m.* (al) What is fused or run to metal.
Elydn, *s. m.* (elyd) A mixed metal; brass.

Corff elydn, cas-wydn, cels-wer—
Sydd i fadyn.

A body of *brass*, hatefully tough, seeking tallow, has reynard got. *R. Goch Eryri.*

Elydnaidd, *a.* (elydn) Of the nature of brass.
Elydnawl, *a.* (elydn) Consisting of brass; brassy.
Elydr, *s. m.—pl. t.* on (elyd) A compound metal; bell-metal; brass.

Gwiail elydr, goleu-liw,
A geidw ei gorff, yn goed gwiw.

Rods of *brass*, of bright hue, guard his body, like fair trees. *Cynfrig ab Dafydd Goch, i bawn.*

Elydraidd, *a.* (elydr) Of a brassy nature.
Elydrawl, *a.* (elydr) Consisting of brass; brassy.
Elyf, *s. m.* (al) What flows, or glides. *a.* Smooth, or polished; delicate.

Rhodri——
Yn ardwy y beirdd, dwfyn dyfnaid i alaf,
I elyf feirch cunaid,
Yn erch lyfn, yn erch-liw gleisiaid,
Yn erfawr ffroen-fawr, ffriw euraid.

Rhodri regulating the bards, deep the attraction of his treasure, his *delicate* shining steeds, highly sleek, and of the high colour of the salmon, with mighty distended nostrils and golden front. *Ll. P. Moch, i R. ab Owain.*

Elyfflu, *s. m.* (llwff—llu) A ravaging host; annoyance, or grievance.

Cyd delai Gymmru, ac elyfflu o Loegr,
A llawer o bobtu,
Dangosais Pyll bwyll iddu.

Should Wales come forward, and *oppression* from England, and many on both sides, Pyll would shew them a feat. *Llywarch Hen.*

Elyffwl, *s. m.* (llwff) Annoyance, grievance, plague
Elyw, *s. m.* (al) The aloes, the juice of aloes.

A glud, ac ystor,
Ac elyw tramor.

And frankincense, and myrrh, and transmarine *aloes*. *Taliesin*

ELL, *s. f. r.—pl. t.* au. What is outward, separated, or divided. *a.* Outward, prominent, conspicuous. *adv.* Extremely, very.
Ellael, *s. f.—pl. t.* iau (ell—ael) The eyebrow.

Ni mynwn, pe gallwn gael,
Dy dwyllaw, du dy ellael.

If I could have the opportunity, I would not deceive thee, thou whose *eyebrow* is black. *D. ab Gwilym.*

Ellaig, *s. f.—pl.* elleigion (ell—aig) A pear.
Ellain, *a.* (ell) Radiating, casting rays, splendid.
Ellast, *s. m.* (ell—ast) The common line thistle.
Ellbwyd, *s. m.* (ell—bwyd) Famine, foodless.
Ellmyn, *s. pl. aggr.* (allman) Foreigners; the Allemanni, or Germans.

Dos a chymhell yr Ellmyn.

Go and drive away the *Germans*. *I. ab R. ab I. Llwyd.*

Ellt, *s. m.* (ell) What is of a separating quality.
Elltrewen, *s. f.—pl. t.* au (alltraw) A tutoress that is not of the family; a sponsor; a gossip; a step-mother.

Ni garo ei fam cared ei elltrewen.

Let him that loves not his mother love his *step-mother*. *Adage.*

Y naill flwyddyn a fydd mam i ddyn, ac y llall fydd ei elltrewen.

One year will be a mother to a man, and the other will be his step-mother. *Adage.*

Ellwedd, *s. f.* (ell—gwedd) An outward appearance. *Teg ei hellwedd*, the fair of outward form.
Ellwen, *s. f.* (ell—gwen) Otwardly fair. *Yr ellwen*, the fair one. *Silurian.*
Ellydd, *s. m.* (ell) A cutting off, extermination.
Ellyll, *s. m.—pl. t.* on (ell—yll) A wandering spirit, an elf, a demon; a phantom; a goblin. *Bwyd ellyllon*, mushrooms; *menyg ellyllon*, fox-gloves.

Tri tharw ellyll ynys Prydain: ellyll Gwydawl, ellyll Llyr Merini, ac ellyll Gwrthmwl wledig.

The three *monster* bulls of the isle of Britain: the *monster* of Gwydawl, the *monster* of Llyr Merini, and the *monster* of Gwrthmwl wledig. *Trioedd.*

Ellyllaidd, *a.* (ellyll) Like a demon; selfish.
Ellylldan, *s. m.* (ellyll—tan) Ignis fatuus, Will-with-the-whisp, or Jack-with-the-lanthorn.

Mwg ellylldan o annwn.

The smoke of *demon-fire* from the great abyss. *D. ab Gwilym.*

Ellylles, *s. f.—pl. t.* au (ellyll) A she demon.

A'i gwedd wynebpryd dyn gwar,
A'i nud ellylles adar.

And the form of her visage like a sedate man, and her condition the *scarecrow* of the feathered tribe. *D. ab Gwilym, i'r ddylluan.*

Ellyllyn, *s. m. dim.* (ellyll) A little devil; an elf.
Ellyn, *s. m.—pl. t.* au (ell) An exterminator; a razor.

Mal y gwalch dros fin yr ellyn.

Like the hawk over the edge of the *razor*. *Adage.*

Ellynedd, *s. m.* (llynedd) The last year, or the year gone by. *adv.* Last year.
EM, *s. f. r.—pl. t.* au. A rarity; a jewel, a gem.

Bychan, em eirian, i mi
——Dy sori.

It is a small thing, my fair *jewel*, to me that thou shouldest be affronted. *D. ab Gwilym.*

Emano, *adv.* (eman) Three days since.
Emenydd, *s. m.* —*pl. t.* au (em—enydd) The brain
Emid, *s. m.* (em) What is precious or unique.
Emig, *s. f. dim.* (em) A little jewel or toy.
Eminiawg, *s. f.*—*pl. t.* au (miniawg) A door-post.
Emwydd, *s. m.* (em—gwydd) A covered presence
Emyl, *s. m.*—*pl. t.* on (byl) A border, or edge.
Emyn, *s. m.*—*pl. t.* au (em) A hymn, a chaunt.

> Cyfiawn mewn glyn d' emyn di.
>
> Chaste, in the dale, is thy *hymn*. *D. ab Gwilym.*

EN, *s. m. r.*—*pl. t.* oedd. The source of life; a living principle, or what is immortal; a being; a deity; a soul; a spirit, essence, or *ens*. *a.* Pure, essential; self-movement; quick; noble. *adv.* Very. It is used as a prefix, and postfix in composition.
Enad, *s. m.* (en) That has soul! animation.

> Dysgweyd ceiniaid cyfa enaid eu rhwyf,
> Eu rhwydd fodd yn amhad.
>
> The songsters relate of the full *animation* of their leader, their free will in variation. *Cynddelw.*

Enaele, *s. m.* (en—aele) A maim, hurt, or wound.
Enaele, *a.* (en—aele) Painful, smarting; piteous.
Enaelen, *s. m.* (enaele) A maim, hurt, or wound.
Enaid, *s. m.*—*pl.* eneidiau (en—aid) A soul; life. *Perchen enaid*, endued with a soul; *enaid ych*, the life of an ox.

> Rhyfeddaf yn llyfrau
> Na's gwyddant yn ddiau
> Enaid pwy ei hadnau,
> Pwy bryd ei haelodau.
>
> I wonder that in books, they know not with certainty, where the seat of the *soul* is, what the appearance of its members. *Taliesin.*

Enain, *a.* (en) Abounding with essence, essential *Enain-gyffaith*, a medical bath. *Medd. Myddfai.*
Enaint, *s. m.*—*pl.* eneiniau (enain) An ointment.

> Bleiddyd a adeilwys Gaer Baddon, ac a wnai yno yr enaint twymyn.
>
> Bleiddyd built Caer Baddon, and he made there the warm *bath*. *Gr. ab Arthur.*

Enawel, *s. f.* (en—awel) A tempest, a hurricane.
Enawr, *s. m.* (en) An intelligence; a soul.
Enbyd, *a.* (en—pyd) Dangerous, or perilous.
Enbydawl, *a.* (enbyd) Tending to endanger.
Enbydiad, *s. m.* (enbyd) A making dangerous.
Enbydrwydd, *s. m.* (enbyd) Perilousness; peril.
Enbydu, *v. a.* (enbyd) To endanger; to hazard.
Enbydus, *a.* (enbyd) Perilous, or dangerous. *Dyn diniwed enbydus*, a very harmless person. *Dyfed.*

> Gwae a ro ei fryd, er byd rhon,
> Ar ein byd mawr enbydus.
>
> Woe to him that shall give his mind, but for a moment, upon our greatly *perilous* world. *Gr. Gwyfyn.*

Encil, *s. m.*—*pl. t.* ion (en—cil) A retreat, a fall back; a flight. *Myned ar encil*, to go upon a retreat, or to abscond.
Enciliad, *s. m.*—*pl. t.* au (encil) A retreating; an absconding; desertion, secession.
Enciliaw, *v. a.* (encil) To retreat, to retire, to step aside, to withdraw; to fly away, to desert.
Enciliedig, *a.* (encil) Withdrawn; deserted.
Enciliwr, *s. m.*—*pl.* encilwyr (encil—gwr) Deserter
Encilydd, *s. m.*—*pl. t.* ion (encil) A retreater; a seceder, or one who separates himself.
Encudd, *s. m.* (cudd) A concealment; a hoard.

> Hir o amser, a thros oesoedd, y bu y pethau hyn ar encudd, a choll yn eigion y tywyllwch.
>
> A long time, and for ages, have these things been in *concealment* and lost in the midst of darkness. *Ed. Dafydd.*

Encuddiad, *s. m.*—*pl. t.* au (encudd) An envelope.
Encuddiaw, *v. a.* (encudd) To envelope, to cover.
Encuddiawl, *a.* (encudd) Tending to envelope.
Encuddiedig, *a.* (encudd) Enveloped, covered.
Encyd, *s. m.* (en—cyd) A space, a while. *Tros encyd*, for a while; *encyd o ffordd*, a good way off.

> Mal yr oeddwn——
> Yn coeliaw 'mun yn cael modd,
> Encyd awr yn cydorwedd.
>
> As I was giving credit to my nymph, and receiving enjoyment, and mutually reclining for the *space* of an hour. *D. ab Gwilym.*

Enchwardd, *s. m.* (chwardd) A laughter; joy.
Enchwarddawl, *a.* (enchwardd) Exulting, joyous.
Enchwarddiad, *s. m.* (enchwardd) Exultation.
Enchwarddu, *v. a.* (enchwardd) To exult.

> Ni enchwardd ei alon
> O Ysyr wystlon.
>
> His foes will not *exult* because of the hostages of Ysyr. *Taliesin.*

Enderig, *s. m.*—*pl. t.* edd (terig) A young ox.

> Rhuthr enderig o'r allt.
>
> The run of the *steer* from the hill. *Adage.*
>
> Hir y bydd enderig ych drygwr.
>
> The ox of a wicked man will long be a steer. *Adage.*
>
> Gwas ystafell a gaiff yr anneiredd ac yr enderigedd o anrhaith a ddyccer o orwlad.
>
> The chamberlain shall have the heifers and the *steers* of the spoil that shall be taken from another country. *Welsh Laws.*

Endid, *s. m.*—*pl. t.* au (en) State of being; entity.

> ——Dy enw mawr santeiddier
> Hyd eithaf holl endid, lle treigla'th haelioni.
>
> Thy great name, be it hallowed to the utmost of all *entity* where thy benevolence spreads about. *Coleg.*

Enddawd, *s. m.* (en—dawd) A placing as a mark. *a.* Conspicuous, remarkable.
Enddigonawd, *s. m.* (digon) A making sufficient.
Enddodawl, *a.* (enddawd) Conspicuous, notable.
Enddodi, *v. a.* (enddawd) To place conspicuously.
Enddodiad, *s. m.*—*pl. t.* au (enddawd) A denoting
Enddodiant, *s. m.* (enddawd) Distinction.
Enddwl, *s. m.*—*pl.* enddylon (en—dwl) The flow of the soul, or mind; the will, or affection.
Enddylu, *v. a.* (enddwl) To shew the affection.
Eneidfaddeu, *s. m.* (enaid—maddeu) One whose soul is remitted; a condemned criminal. *a.* Soul-remitted; or cast for death.

> Tri dyn y sydd eneidfaddeu, ac ni ellir eu prynu: bradwr ei arglwydd, a dyn a laddo arall yn fwrdrig, a lleidr cyfaddef am werth mwy no phedair ceiniawg.
>
> Three persons that are *worthy of death*, and they cannot be bought off; a traitor to the lord, and a man who kills another maliciously, and a confessed thief for the value of more than four pence. *Welsh Laws.*

Eneidiad, *s. m.* (enaid) An enduing with soul.
Eneidiaw, *v. a.* (enaid) To endue with a soul.
Eneidiawg, *a.* (enaid) Having a soul, or life.
Eneidiawl, *a.* (enaid) Endued with a soul; living.

> Mi brydydd brydest anianawl;
> Ti arwr orwu eneidiawl.
>
> Me a poet of natural genius; thou a hero most excellent and *animated*. *Ll. P. Moch, i D. ab Owain.*

Eneidioli, *v. a.* (eneidiawl) To make animated.
Eneidiolrwydd, *s. m.* (eneidiawl) Animality.
Eneidrwydd, *s. m.*—*pl. t.* au (enaid) The temples

> Ni roddaf—orphwys i'm eneidrwyddau.
>
> I will give no rest to my *temples*. *Dafydd Ddu, Ps.* cxxxii. 4.

Eneiniad, *s. m.*—*pl. t.* au (enain) An anointing.
Eneiniaw, *v. a.* (enain) To anoint, to apply unction.
Eneiniawg, *a.* (enain) That is anointed. *s. m.* An anointed one: a Messiah.
Eneiniwr, *s. m.*—*pl.* eneinwyr (enain—gwr) Anointer; one who applies unction.
Eneirchiad, *s. m.* (arch) A covering with armour.

Eneirchiaw, *v. a.* (arch) To cover with armour.
Eneirchiawg, *a.* (eirchiawg) Of complete armour.

> Pan ddyfon dros for, gwyr eneirchiawg,
> Cadfeirch y danynt deuwynebawg;
> Deufaen ar eu gwaew naoleithiawg,
> Erddi heb fedi yu myd dibeddawg.
>
> When they shall come over sea, the men *completely covered with armour*, with double-faced war steeds under them; two points on their spears not sparing of havoc. *Myrddin.*

Ener, *s. m.* (en) An agent of intelligence. *Rhwydd ener*, a liberal soul.

> Cerdd waban Cadfan cad-walch nifer;
> Cerdd weddawl gedawl Gadell ener.
>
> The appropriate song of Cadvan the hawk of battle of the multitude; the moderate song for gifts from the *living representative* of Cadell. *Cynddelw, i'r argl. Rhys.*

Enfawr, *a.* (en—mawr) Very great, vast or huge.
Enfil, *s. m.—pl. t.* od (en—mil) An animal.
Enfilaidd, *a.* (enfil) Of the nature of an animal.
Enfyged, *s. f.* (en—myged) Worship, honour.
Enfys, *s. f.—pl. t.* au (en—bys) A rainbow.
Enfysg, *s. f.—pl. t.* au (enfys) A rainbow.
Enhudd, *s. m.—pl. t.* ion (en—hudd) A covered, shaddowed, or darkened state.
Enhuddaw, *v. a.* (enhudd) To shadow, to darken. *Enhuddaw y tan*, to cover the fire with ashes.
Enhuddawl, *a.* (enhudd) Of a covering quality.
Enhudded, *s. f.—pl. t.* au (enhudd) A covering.

> Doe'n argiwydd cenedl-rwydd ced
> Heddyw dan yr enhudded.
>
> Our lord of a race liberal of treasure comes to day under the *covering*. *Gr. ab Gwegyn.*

Enhuddedig, *a.* (enhudded) Covered, enveloped.
Enhuddiad, *s. m.—pl. t.* au (enhudd) A covering.
Enhuddiant, *s. m.* (enhudd) The act of covering.
Enhued, *s. m.* (hued) One who follows the chase.

> Nid wyf enhued, miled ni chadwaf;
> Ni allaf ddarymred:
> Tra fo da gan gog caned!
>
> I am not a *hunter*, animals I do not keep: I cannot move along: as long as it seemeth good let the cuckoo sing! *Llywarch Hen.*

Eni, *v. a.* (en) To exert the mind or soul.

> Pan wasgar beleirn, pan bêir;
> Pan wesgryn cammawn camp enir;
> Yn llachar yd fernir.
>
> When troos shall be scattered, or when strewed; when the combat shall be agitated the feat *will be toiled for*, he will be judged splendid. *Cynddelw, i H. ab Owain.*
>
> Am arch-fain riain rhaid i'm eni,
> Trwy ddiwyd eirawl deddfawl Dewi.
>
> For a slender bodied lady I must *use exertion* by closely interceding with pious Dewi. *Ein. ab Gwalchmai.*

Eniad, *s. m.—pl. t.* au (eni) A content, or area.
Eniain, *s. m.* (iain) State of the weather, or temperature. *a.* Very clear, pure, or intense. *Garw yw ei heniain heddy*, severe is its temperatnre to day; *mae yn eniain oer*, it is intensely cold.
Enid, *s. f.—pl. t.* iau (en) The wood-lark.

> A glywesti chwedl yr enid,
> Yn y gwyddel rhag ymlid—
> Drwg pechawd o'i hir erlid!
>
> Hast thou heard the saying of the *wood-lark*, in the brake avoiding pursuit—bad is sin from long following it! *Englynion y Clywed.*

Enig, *a.* (en) Full of soul, or animation.
Eniwaid, *s. m.* (niwaid) Damage, harm, hurt.
Eniwaw, *v. a.* (niwaw) To endamage, to hurt.

> Ysaid i'm eniwed eniwaw wrthaw.
>
> There is harm to my lot for *to be hurt* at him. *Llywelyn Fardd.*

Eniwawl, *a.* (niwawl) Tending to damage.
Eniwed, *s. m.—pl. t.* au (niwed) Damage, hurt, harm; wrong, prejudice. *Twrf ac eniwed*, disturbance and harm, the manner of disturbing quiet possession to prevent a title.

> Sef yw twrf ac eniwed llosgi tai a thori ereidr.
>
> Disturbance and *harm* is to burn houses and to break ploughs. *Welsh Laws.*

Eniwedu, *v. a.* (eniwed) To damage, to harm.
Eniweidiad, *s. m.—pl. t.* au (eniwed) A hurting.

> Na nodwch eniweidiad,
> A chynnyg yw'ch iawn a gwad.
>
> Notice not an *injury*, when amends and acknowledgement are offered to you. *T. Aled.*

Eniweidiaw, *v. a.* (eniwed) To hurt, to harm.
Eniweidiawl, *a.* (eniwed) Apt to damage, hurtful.
Enllib, *s. m.—pl. t.* ion (en—llib) Slander, calumny, or libel; a reproach.

> Elid gwraig yn ol ei henllib.
>
> Let a woman go after her *reproach*. *Adage.*

Enllibiad, *s. m.—pl. t.* au (enllib) A slandering, calumniating, or disparaging; detraction.
Enllibiaidd, *a.* (enllib) Calumnious, detractive.
Enllibiaw, *v. a.* (enllib) To calumniate, to detract.
Enllibiawl, *a.* (enllib) Contumelious, detracting.
Enllibiedig, *a.* (enllib) Slandered, calumniated.
Enllibieiddrwydd, *s. m.* (enllibiaidd) Contumeliousness, slanderousness.
Enllibiwr, *s. m.—pl.* enllibwyr (enllib—gwr) A slanderer, a defamer, or a libeller.
Enllibus, *a.* (enllib) Slanderous, calumnious.
Enllibusrwydd, *s. m.* (enllibus) Slanderousness.
Enllyn, *s. m.—pl. t.* oedd (llyn) Victuals, anything eaten with bread, as butter, or cheese. *Bara ac enllyn*, bread and sool. *North of England.*
Enllyniad, *s. m.* (enllyn) A moistening for food.
Enllynu, *v. a.* (enllyn) To moisten a bit of food.

> Hwnw yw ef yr un y rhoddwy fi iddo dam wedy yr i mi ei enllynu; ac ef a enllynai damaid, ac ei rhoddes i Iudas.
>
> That one is he to whom I shall give a morsel after I shall have done *to moisten* it, and *he moistened* a bit, and gave it to Judas. *W. Salisbury.*

Enmynedd, *s. m.* (mynedd) Patience, forbearance.
Enmyneddgar, *a.* (enmynedd) Patient, forbearing
Enmyneddgarweh, *s. m.* (enmynedd) Patientness.
Enmyneddus, *a.* (enmynedd) Patient, passive.

> Enmyneddus fum, fur cadeithi,
> Enwawg orthowys, o'm gorthewi.
>
> I have been *patient*, thou bulwark of the war and famed leader, because of my being made silent. *Ll. P. Moch, bygwth D. ab Owain.*

Ennill, *s. m.* (en—nill) Advantage, gain, profit.
Ennill, *v. a.* (en—nill) To get advantage, to gain.
Ennilladwy, *a.* (ennill) Capable of giving profit.
Ennilleg, *s. f.* (ennill) What causes advantage. *Bwyall ennilleg*, a battle-axe.
Ennillgar, *a.* (ennill) Advantageous, gainful.
Ennyn, *s. m.* (en—yn) A kindling, ignition.
Ennyn, *v. a.* (en—yn) To kindle, to set on fire; to inflame; to excite, to be inflamed, or incensed. *Ennyn o lid*, to burn with anger.
Ennynawl, *a.* (ennyn) Apt to kindle, ignitible.
Ennynfa, *s. m.—pl. t.* oedd (ennyn—ma) A kindling, what is set on fire; a burning heat.
Ennyniad, *s. m.—pl. t.* au (ennyn) A kindling.
Ennynu, *v. a.* (ennyn) To kindle; to set on fire; to inflame; to be inflamed. *Ennyni o'i chwant hi*, thou wilt be inflamed with her love.

> O derfydd ennynu ty yn mhlith tref, taled y ddau dŷ nesaf a ennyno ganto, un o bob parth iddo.
>
> If a house shall be *set on fire* in the midst of a town, let it pay for the two adjoining houses that *shall kindle* from it, one on each side of it. *Welsh Laws.*

Enraith, *s. m.—pl.* enreithi (rhaith) A friend.

Enrhy, *s. m.—pl. t.* on (en—rhy) An abundance. *a.* Very much, very abundant.

Enrhyal, *s. m.* (rhyal) The increase of cattle.

> Tri anifei sy fwy gwerth eu teithi nog eu gwerth cyfraith; ystalwyn, a tharw trefgordd, a baedd cenfaint; canys yr enrhyal a gollir o colli wyntau.
>
> There are three animals the value of whose perfection is greater than their law value: a stallion, and a bull of a township, and a boar of a herd of swine; for the breed will be lost if they shall be lost. *Welsh Laws.*

Enrhydedd, *s. m.* (rhydedd) Honour, reverence.

Enrhydeddawl, *a.* (enrhydedd) Apt to honour.

Enrhydeddu, *v. a.* (enrhydedd) To honour.

Enrhydeddus, *a.* (enrhydedd) Honourable.

Enrhydeddwr, *s. m.—pl.* enrhydeddwyr (enrhydedd—gwr) One who honoureth.

Enrhyfedd, *a.* (rhyfedd) Wonderful, marvellous.

Enrhyfeddawd, *s. f.* (enrhyfedd) A great wonder

> Ni's cyfrif nebawd
> O'r holl fedysawd,
> Ac fyth ni's traetha,
> A wnaeth i'n rhiau
> O enrhyfeddodau
> Tra fu yma.
>
> No body can recount, of all the world, and never can he relate what he hath done for our princes, of wonders, whilst he was here. *Taliesin.*

Enrhyfeddawl, *a.* (enrhyfedd) Wondrous.

Enrhyfeddig, *a.* (enrhyfedd) Of a wonderful nature.

> Efe a adnewyddwys muroedd Llundain, ac o enrhyfeddig dyrroedd ai damgylchynwys.
>
> He built anew the walls of London, and with *wonderful towers* he surrounded it. *Gr. ab Arthur.*

Enrhyfeddu, *v. a.* (enrhyfedd) To be wondering, to be marvelling; to be amazed.

Enserth, *s. m.* (serth) A lax, or falling state. *a.* Of a slippery, or falling nature.

Enserthawl, *a.* (enserth) Debasing, apt to fall.

Enserthu, *v. a.* (enserth) To make abject.

Enserthus, *a.* (enserth) Debasing, apt to be vile. *Merch ddrwg enserthus*, an evil and debased woman.

Entraw, *s. m.—pl.* entrawon (en—traw) Master.

Entrew, *s. m.—pl. t.* au (trew) A sneeze. *Turo entrew*, to give a sneeze.

Entrewi, *v. a.* (entrew) To sneeze, to sternutate.

> Cofia dy din pan entrewych.
>
> Remember thy posterior when *thou dost sneeze.* *Adage.*

Entrewiad, *s. m.—pl. t.* au (entrew) A sternutation

Entrych, *s. m.* (trych) The great scope, or expanse, the firmament.

Entyrch, *s. m.* (tyrch) The firmament, the vault or canopy of the heavens.

> Yn myned, mewn lluddied llwyr,
> A chowydd i entrych awyr.
>
> Going, in extreme toil, with a hymn to the *vault of the sky.* *D. ab Gwilym, i'r hedydd.*

Enw, *s. m.—pl. t.* au (nw) A name, appellation.

> Goreu enw ei hinu.
>
> The best name is I own it. *Adage.*
>
> Y dyn a gaffo enw da
> A gaiff gan bawb ei goffa.
>
> The man who shall acquire a good name will get to be remembered by every body. *L. G. Cothi.*

Enwad, *s. m.—pl. t.* au (enw) A nomination.

Enwadawl, *a.* (enwad) Denominative, appellative.

Enwaered, *s. m.* (gwaered) Very low, or prone.

Enwai, *s. m.—pl.* enweion (enw) Nominative case.

Enwaid, *a.* (enw) Having a name or title.

Enwaidedig, *a.* (enwaid) Named, circumcised.

Enwaidiad, *s. m.—pl. t.* au (enwaid) Circumcision

Enwaidiaw, *v. a.* (enwaid) To give a name; to circumcise.

Enwair, *a.* (gwair) Full of energy or vigour.

> Rhyddyrllid fy ngherdd——
> Yn Aber mener Menaidon,
> Yn enwair yn ddiwair ddibon.
>
> My song will obtain its mead in Aber, where dwells the pillar of the people of Menai, an *energetic* and continent sovereign. *Cynddelw, i H. ab Owain.*

Enwaisg, *a.* (gwaisg) Very brisk, merry, or gay.

> Bum enwaisg, a phawb i'm annerch,
> Yn garwr bun fwyn mewn llwyn a llannerch.
>
> I have been blithesome, and every body greeting me, a lover of the kind maid in the grove and in the lawn. *T. Hywel Sion.*

Enwawd, *s. m.* (enw) Nomination, name, title.

> Perchen cor——
> Llech faran, llech fan i folawd;
> Arfoliant eddiant urdd enwawd.
>
> Possessing a choir of splendid appearance, a splendid place for praise, the adoration of the dignity of a great name. *Cynddelw, i Dysilio.*

Enwawg, *a.* (enw) Having a name; renowned.

Enwawl, *a.* (enw) Nominal; having a name.

Enwedig, *a.* (enw) Nominated, specified, specific. particular, especial. *Yn enwedig*, especially.

Enwedigaeth, *s. m.* (enwedig) Nomination.

Enwedigaethydd, *s. m.* (enwedigaeth) Nominative case, in grammar.

Enwedigaw, *v. a.* (enwedig) To denominate.

Enwedigawl, *a.* (enwedig) Nominative.

Enwedydd, *s. m.—pl. t.* ion (enwad) Denominator

Enweirus, *a.* (enwair) Energetic; vigorous.

> Marw Rhys, draig enweirus drud
> A'm gwnaeth drwy hiraeth driistyd!
>
> The dying of Rhys, a dragon energetic and brave, both through longing caused to me sadness! *Prydydd Bychan.*

Enwi, *v. a.* (enw) To name, to term, to entitle.

Enwig, *a.* (enw) Having a name; famed.

> Derchafawd gwledig
> Am derfyn hen enwig.
>
> The sovereign is exalted round the old and *famous boundary.* *Taliesin.*

Enwir, *a.* (en—gwir) Very true, or perfect.

> Enwir yth elwir o'th gywir weithred—
> Angor dewr darn,
> Sarff safwy raen.
>
> *Perfect* art thou called from thy just deed, thou brave and wide extending stay with a spear like a serpent. *Taliesin.*

Enwogi, *v. a.* (enwawg) To make renowned.

Enwogiad, *s. m.* (enwawg) A making renowned.

Enwogrwydd, *s. m.* (enwawg) Renownedness.

Enwyllt, *a.* (gwyllt) Very wild, furious, or raging.

> Ni bydd unawr, baedd enwyllt,
> Heb ewyn gwyn o'i ben gwyllt.
>
> He is not at any time, the *furious* boar, without a white foam out of his fierce head. *E. Meirion.*

Enwyn, *a.* (gwyn) Very white. *Llaeth enwyn*, butter-milk. *s. m.* Butter-milk.

Enycha, *v. imper.* (nycha) Behold, lo; look there.

> Mal yd oeddynt y llongau yn caffael y tir, enycha Caswallawn a holl gadernyd ynys Prydain canddo yn dawed i Gastell Dolobel yn erbyn Caesar.
>
> As the ships were making to the land, *behold* Caswallon, with all the strength of the island of Britain with him, coming to the castle of Dolobel against Caesar. *Gr. ab Arthur.*

Enyd, *s. m.* (en—yd) Space, while, time, leisure. *Tros enyd*, for a while; *cael enyd*, to get leisure.

Enydd, *s. m.* (en) The seat of intellect or soul.

Enyfed, *s. m.* (nyfed) Animation, or vigour.

ENG, *s. m. r.—pl. t.* ion. Space, amplitude. *a.* Large, specious; loose, at large, free.

Engfod, *s. m.* (eng—bod) Unconnected, or loose existence; a fallible state.

Engherdded, *s. m.—pl. t.* ion (cerdded) A tedious travelling or sojourning.

> Hir y bu efe yn yr engherdded hwnw.
>
> Long has he been in that *sojourning.* *H. Peredur—Mabinogion.*

Engi, *v. a.* (ang) To set at large; to deliver, to loosen, to extricate; to be delivered.

> Dadleu mawr mynych ac engi ar lygoden.
>
> Long and frequent disputing and to be delivered of a mouse. *Adage.*
>
> O derfydd beichiogi gweinyddiawg o gaeth, y neb a'i beichiogo a ddyly roddi gwraig arall cystal a hi i wasanaethu yn ei lle yn i engo.
>
> If a female slave shall be made pregnant, he that shall make her pregnant is obliged to furnish another woman as good as she is to serve in her stead until *she shall deliver.* *Welsh Laws.*

Englyn, *s. m.—pl. t.* ion (glyn) A term in prosody for one of the three primary metres, being a flowing combination of accordant sounds, as it were chained together; a stanza of such kind of metre; an epigram. There are many varieties of the *englyn;* as, the *union, cyrch, crwca, cyfnewidiawg, cudwynawg,* and *triban milwr.*

Englynaidd, *a.* (englyn) Having the character of an *englyn;* an epigrammatic.

Englynawl, *a.* (englyn) Relating to the *englyn* metre; epigrammatic.

Englynydd, *s. m.—pl. t.* ion (englyn) A maker of an *englyn;* an epigrammatist.

Engu, *v. a.* (ang) To set at large, to deliver out; to render ample, or loose; to be freed.

> Engwn bryd rhag angen bro;
> Duw o ing a'n diengo!
>
> *We will be ample* against the necessity of a country: may God deliver us from trouble! *Rhys Penarth.*

Engur, *a.* (eng—ur) Awful, marvellous; amazing.

Enguriaw, *v. a.* (engur) To marvel, to wonder.

Enguriawl, *a.* (engur) Tending to amaze; awful.

Engwarth, *s. m.—pl.* engweirth (eng—gwarth) A spreading surface; a beach.

> Bum lli yn eirth;
> Bum ton yn engweirth.
>
> I have been a torrent on the slope; I have been a wave on the *extended shore.* *Taliesin.*

Engwawd, *s. m.* (eng—gwawd) A free panegyric.

Engwth, *s. m.* (gwth) A quick push. *a.* Sudden.

Engyl, *s. m.* (eng—yl) An expanding principle; fire. *Rhwng y ddau engyl,* between the two fires

> Cyllell——
> I dynu y ceir, diweir-chwaen,
> I mi, yr engyl o'r maen.
>
> A knife, it will be had to draw, (a fortunate lot for me) the *fire* out of the stone. *Rhys Goch Bryri.*

Engyn, *s. m. dim.* (eng) An unconnected one, or a frail one.

> Ni wel dyn, engyn anghall,
> Y llam y syrthiodd y llall.
>
> Man, as imprudent *wretch,* sees not the way another fell. *Ieuan Tew.*

Engyniawg, *a.* (engyn) Full of laxity; fallible.

Engyr, *s. m.* (eng—gyr) A pervading impulse; a shock. *a.* Impulsive; awful, marvellous, amazing

> Brenin Powys, pobl ddêt yn engyr,
> Yn ongyr gorfoost.
>
> King of Powys, a people severe in the *shock,* in the conflict of spears thou didst overcome. *Ll. P. Moch.*

Engyriawl, *a.* (engyr) Amazing, or wonderful.

Engyriolaeth, *s. m.* (engyriawl) Fierceness; terribleness.

> Parhau a wnai gwyr Rhufain trwy engyriolaeth yn eu herbyn.
>
> The men of Rome persevered with *fierceness* against them *Gr. ab Arthur.*

Engyrth, *a.* (eng—gyrth) Terrible, or awful.

> Angeu pob rhian diau y daw
> Engyrth rhy gymyrth ei gam rhagddaw.
>
> The death of all great ones certainly will come, *awfully* he prepares to take his step onward! *Bleddyn Fardd.*

Engyrthawl, *a.* (engyrth) Tending to terrify.

> Cyn goddef angeu engyrtholion
> A'm bwyf gan deu-haelcael cyfeillion
>
> Before *suffering* the death of *terrors* may I be with two generous ones to obtain friends. *Gr. ab yr Ynad Coch.*

Eoca, *v. a.* (ëawg) To fish for, or catch salmon.

Eofn, *a.* (ofn) Dauntless, causing dread; bold; daring, adventurous, confident, courageous.

Eofnder, *s. m.* (ëofn) Confidence, assurance.

Eofndra, *s. m.* (ëofn) Daringness, boldness.

Eofneg, *s. f.* (ëofn) The parrhesia; boldness, or liberty of speech.

Eofni, *v. a.* (ëofn) To cause dread; to be bold.

Eofniad, *s. m.* (ëofn) A causing dread; a daring.

Eogfrithyll, *s. m.—pl. t.* iaid (ëawg—brithyll) A salmon-trout.

Eogyn, *s. m. dim.* (eawg) A samlet, a little salmon.

Eon, *a.* (on) Bold, forward, daring, presuming.

> I'th weini——
> Dy weision ëon ynt.
>
> To serve thee, thy minions are *bold.* *D. ab Gwilym.*

Eonder, *s. m.* (ëon) Boldness, or forwardness.

> Tair ffynnon deall; ëonder, awyf ac ymgais.
>
> The three springs of the understanding; *boldness,* vigour, and exertion. *Barddas.*

Eondra, *s. m.* (ëon) Boldness, or forwardness.

Eonfalch, *a.* (ëon—balch) Boldly-aspiring.

Eonfalchedd, *s. m.* (ëonfalch) Aspiring pride.

> Bu i'r arglwydd ei geryddu am ei ëonfalchedd.
>
> It came that the Lord chastised him for his *presumption.* *Marchawg Crwydrad.*

Eoni, *v. n.* (ëon) To become bold or daring.

Eoniad, *s. m.* (ëon) A becoming bold or daring.

Eorth, *a.* (gorth) Diligent, assiduous, studious.

> Gweddiaw Duw, gwedd ëorth,
> Y bum; canaf gerdd am borth.
>
> Praying to God in a *diligent* manner, I have been ' I will sing a song for aid. *Iolo Goch.*

Eorthawl, *a.* (ëorth) Of a diligent disposition.

Eorthedd, *s. m.* (ëorth) Studiousness; meditation.

Eosaidd, *a.* (ëaws) Like a nightingale; melodious

> Yn araf ydd wyd——
> O dalu aur dros gerdd ëosaidd.
>
> With gentleness thou didst distribute gold for the *philomelian* song. *L. G. Cothi.*

Eosig, *a.* (ëaws) Of the nature of a nightingale.

Epa, *s. m.—pl. t.* od (ab) An ape, a monkey.

Epäaidd, *a.* (epa) Like an ape, or apish.

Eples, *s. m.* (eb—lles) Leaven, a ferment.

Eppil, *s. f. aggr.—pl. t.* oedd (eb—hil) Offspring, issue, prosperity, progeny, or descendants

Eppiledd, *s. pl. aggr.* (eppil) Progeny, descendants

Eppilgar, *a.* (eppil) Tending to procreate.

Eppilgarwch, *s. m.* (eppilgar) Aptness to generate

Eppiliad, *s. m.* (eppil) A bringing forth issue.

Eppiliaeth, *s. m.* (eppil) The act of bringing forth.

Eppiliaw, *v. a.* (eppil) To procreate; to generate, to bring forth, or multiply, to beget issue.

Eppiliawd, *s. m.* (eppil) The act of bringing forth

Eppiliawg, *a* (eppil) Having issue or progeny.

Eppiliwr, *s. m.—pl.* eppilwyr (eppil—gwr) One who generates, or begets issue.

Eppilwraig, *s. f.—pl.* eppilwreigedd (eppil—gwraig) One who brings forth.

Epynt, *s. m.* (eb—ynt) An ascent, rise or slope.

> Na'm casa pwyllaw, pwylliawg edfynt Rys,
> Y rhwng rhos ac epynt,
> Bardd fum it' trymud tremynt,
> A chydymaith canwaith cynt
>
> Hate me not, consider, Rhys of impelling course between the plain and the *sweeping slope.* I have been a bard to thee of wary watchfulness, and a companion a hundred times formerly. *Phylip Brydydd, i R. Gryg.*
>
> Cyfleuer gwawr ddydd pan ddwyre hynt;
> Cyfliw eiry gorwyn gorwydd epynt.
>
> Splendid as the dawn of day when it rises on its course; of the same hue as the purely white snow drifting on the *slope.* *Cynddelw, i Rys f. Madawg.*

ER, *s. m. r.* A motion, or impulse forward; a progress, or course. It is prefixed in composition to enhance the meaning of words.

Er, *prep.* For, because of, with respect to, in the place of, in order; towards; to; for the sake of, on account of, through, notwithstanding; from; since, ever since.—*Erddwyf, erof*, for my sake; *erod, erot*, for thy sake; *ero*, for him; *eri*, for her; *erom*, for our sake; *eroch*, for your sake; *eront, erynt*, for their sake.—*Nid er dim*, not for any thing; *er dechreuad y byd*, from the beginning of the world; *er dywedyd o hono*, notwithstanding its being said by him; *er ys blwyddyn*, for a year; *er doe*, since yesterday; *er ys talm byd*, for a long while since; *er swllt y dydd*, for a shilling a day; *er hyn i gyd*, notwithstanding all this; *er hyny*, notwithstanding that; *er amled*, though ever so numerous; *er lleied y bo*, though it be ever so small.

> Ni chred eiddig er a dynger.
>
> The jealous one will not believe *for* all that is sworn. *Adage.*
>
> Bid chwd drud er chwerthin.
>
> Let the jealous be fickle *though* he laughs. *Adage.*
>
> Er ammheu o rai ymo,
> Er hyn Duw sy'n rhanu da.
>
> *Though* some here may doubt, *notwithstanding* this God is dispensing good. *T. Aled.*

Eraill, *s. pl.* (arall) Others. *pron.* Those others.

Erain, *a.* (er) Abounding with impulse; what may be impelled.

Eraint, *s. f.* (erain) A round body; a ball; a bowl, or cup; a pear.

Erbarch, *s. m.* (parch) Reverence, deference.

> Neu'r orfydd dy ofn nad ant i'th erbyn,
> I'th erbarch teithiawl;
> Neu'r orfydd yn ngorenw Morgant
> Ar filwyr Prydain pedryfant!
>
> Will not thy dread cause that they shall not go against thee, to thy enjoyment of *honour*, will it not overcome in the high title of Morgant the warriors of Britain in all its bounds! *Ll. P. Moch, i Lywelyn I.*

Erbarchawl, *a.* (erbarch) Reverential, revering.

Erbarchiad, *s. m.* (erbarch) A reverencing.

Erbarchu, *v. a.* (erbarch) To reverence.

Erbin, *s. m.* (pin) The common calamint.

Erbwl, *a.* (pwl) Blunting, tending to blunt.

Erbyliad, *s. m.* (erbwl) A making blunt.

Erbylu, *v. a.* (erbwl) To blunt, to make dull.

> Ar ol erbylu cerdd nid cwlfaid ei ddwyn
> Oddyman hyd Rufain.
>
> After *discarding of* all the songs it is no good sense that he should be carried from here to Rome. *Seisyll Bryffwrch.*

Erbyn, *s. m.—pl. t.* ion (pyn) Contrast, opposition. *prep.* Against, over against, opposite; towards; by.

> Tri pheth nid oes a el yn eu herbyn: defawd gorsedd, cân gorsedd, a llafar gorsedd.
>
> Three things to which nothing can go in *opposition*: custom of the convention, song of the convention, and voice of the convention. *Barddas.*

Erbyn, *v. a.* (pyn) To take to, to take, to receive, to accept; to give reception, or to entertain.

Erbynddywedyd, *s. m.* (erbyn—dywedyd) A gainsaying, or contradiction.

Erbyniad, *s. m.—pl. t.* au (erbyn) A receiving; reception, acceptation, or adoption.

Erbyniaw, *v. a.* (erbyn) To receive, to accept.

Erbyniawd, *s. m.* (erbyn) Reception, acceptation.

Erbyniawl, *a.* (erbyn) Receiving, adoptive.

Erbynied, *v. a.* (erbyn) To take; to receive.

Erbyniwr, *s. m.—pl.* erbynwyr (erbyn—gwr) A receiver, or accepter.

Erbynydd, *s. m.—pl. t.* ion (erbyn) An accepter.

Erch, *s. m.* (er) A dark colour, a dark brown.

> E'm rhydd feirch—
> Llawer llwyd, a llai,
> Llawer erch arfai.
>
> He will give me of steeds, many a grey, and roan, many a dun there would be for me. *Gwalchmai.*

Erch, *a.* (er) Of a dark hue, darkish brown, dun; dismal, dreadful, terrible, dire.

Erchi, *v. a.* (arch) To ask, to demand.

> Erchi a orug Emrys iddo dywedyd y darogenau a ddelai rhag llaw: ac yna y dywawd Myrddin, 'Arglwydd, nid iawn draethu o'r rhyw bethau hyny onnyd pan y cymhello anghenraid. Pei a'u dywetwn ni yn amser ni bai raid wrthynt, ysbryd yn dysgu imau; a phan fai raid wrtho y ffoai rhagof.'
>
> Ambrosius *requested of him* to declare the predictions that should come in future, and Myrddin thereupon said, 'My lord, it is not right to treat of those kind of things, except when necessity compelleth. If I were to speak at a time when there should be no call for them, the spirit would come to teach me then; and when he should be wanted he would go away from me. *Gr. ab Arthur.*
>
> Arch i Ddafydd a archaf;
> Arch cyn ei herchi a gaf.
>
> A request of Dafydd *I will ask*; the request before *it is asked* I shall have. *L. G. Cothi.*

Erchlais, *s. m.—pl.* erchleisiau (arch—llais) A frightful voice, or scream.

> Fy nghalon a gryn rhag erchlais y fran.
>
> My heart doth tremble because of the *ugly croak* of the raven. *Peryf ab Cedifor.*

Erchlas, *s. m.* (erch—glas) A dusky blue; a grey.

Erchliw, *s. m.* (erch—lliw) A dusky or dun colour.

> Fi elyf leirch cannaid,
> Yn erchlyfn, yn erchliw gleisiaid.
>
> His valuable cloak stands so very smooth, of the *dusky hue* of salmons. *Ll. P. Moch, i Rodri.*

Erchryn, *a.* (cryn) Agitating, trembling, quaking.

Erchrynawl, *a.* (erchryn) Tending to agitate.

Erchryniad, *s. m.—pl. t.* au (erchryn) Agitation.

Erchrynu, *v. a.* (erchryn) To agitate; to tremble.

Erchwyn, *s. m.—pl. t.* au (cwyn) A pass over; a side. *Erchwyn gwely*, a side, or stead of a bed, the outer side of a bed.

> Mab Llywelyn hael hawl gyfa eirchiaid,
> Erchwyn graidd grym tyrfa.
>
> The son of the generous Llywelyn is the entire claim of the petitioners, the fiery motion and strength of a host. *Ll. P. Moch, i Rufydd.*
>
> Graidd eryr milwyr Maelawr a archaf
> I erchwyn nef a llawr;
> Udd dinag dinas gwriawr,
> Un dinam, un mab mam mawr.
>
> The fiery eagle of the warriors of Maelor I ask of the *support* of heaven and earth; the never refusing chief of the city of heroism, a spotless one, the one great son of a mother. *Ll. P. Moch, i Fadawg ab Gruffudd.*

Erchwynedig, *a.* (erchwyn) That has a passage over.

> Gorair erchwynedig hon a fo weithddrych peth arall o'i hol; megis—Gwelaf.
>
> A *verb transitive* is this that is the object of something else following it, such as—I see.

Erchwynedigaeth, *s. m.—pl. t.* au (erchwynedig) The act of passing over; transition.

> O erchwynedigaeth Babilon hyd enedigaeth Crist i bu oesoedd gwyr pedair ar ddeg.
>
> From the *captivity* of Babilon to the birth of Christ there were of the ages of men fourteen. *Ll. G. Hergest.*

Erchwyniad, *s. m.* (erchwyn) Transition.

Erchwyniaw, *v.* (erchwyn) To cause to pass over.

Erchwyniawg, *a.* (erchwyn) Having cause of motion. *s. m.* A place to pass over, or to range.

> Edyrn trin feddgyrn trydar erchwyniawg.
>
> The sovereign of the battle of meadhorns, a *briskly moving* tumult. *Llywelyn Fardd.*
>
> Morhanat diwarchwant erchwyniawg gwlading
> Gwlad Frochfael Ysgithrawg.
>
> Morhanat the truly delectable *range* of the sovereign of the country of Brochwael Ysgithrawg. *Cynddelw, m. O. ab Madawg.*
>
> Erchwyniawg trylew trylwyn uch gwin.
>
> The *career* of the most gallant one most complaisant over the banquet. *Cynddelw.*

Erchwyniawl, *a.* (erchwyn) Apt to pass over.
Erchwyrn, *a.* (chwyrn) Rapidly moving.
Erchwys, *s. f.* (erch—gwys) A pack of hounds.
Erchyll, *a.* (erch) Ghastly, horrible, or dreadful.

Nid chwarea a fo erchyll.

It is no play that is *terrifying.* *Adage.*

Erchylldawd, *s. m.* (erchyll) Horribleness.
Erchylldra, *s. m.* (erchyll) Horribleness, frightfulness.
Erchyllfa, *s. f.*—*pl. t.* on (erchyll) Hideous place.

Tynais fyrddiwn o honochwi, fy engyllion duon gyd a'm cynffon i'r erchyllfa anesgor hon.

I have drawn a million of you, my black angels, with my tail to this never to be left *place of horror.* *Elis Wyn, B. Cwsg.*

Erchyllrwydd, *s. m.* (erchyll) Frightfulness.
Erchyllu, *v. a.* (erchyll) To look ghastly.
Erchynawl, *a.* (cynawl) Apt to exalt or lift.
Erchyniad, *s. m.*—*pl. t.* au (cyniad) Elevation.
Erchynu, *v. a.* (cynu) To elevate, to exalt.
Erchywyn, *s. m.*—*pl. t.* au (cywyn) A pass over.
Erchywynedig, *a.* (erchywyn) Transmigratory.
Erchywynedigaeth, *s. m.*—*pl. t.* au (erchywynedig) Transmigration, or a passing over.
Erchywyniad, *s. m.*—*pl. t.* au (erchywyn) A transmigrating, a passing over.
Erchywynu, *v. a.* (erchywyn) To transmigrate.
Erdolwg, *v. a.* (dolwg) To beseech, to intreat. *Erdolwg, dywed pwy oedd yno,* I pray thee, tell me who was there.
Erdd, *s. m.* (er) Impulse forward, or course. It is prefixed in composition, to enhance the meaning of words.
Erdd, *prep.* For, because, for the sake of. *Erddwyf, erddof,* for my sake; *erddod, erddot,* for thy sake; *erddo,* for his sake; *erddi,* for her; *erddom,* for us; *erddoch,* for your sake; *erddynt,* for their sake, or for them.
Erddrwng, *a.* (erdd—rhwng) Confused, huddled.

Gwnaeth drallif gwyar uch Trallwng Elfael,
Pan fu ymdrafael drud ac erddrwng.

He caused a torrent of blood above Trallwng Elvael, when the fierce and confused conflict took place. *E. ab M. Rhahawd.*

Erddrym, *s. m.* (erdd—grym) Potency, strength.
Erddrym, *a.* (erdd—grym) Potent, robust, lusty.

Grym erddrym aer ddraig afael——
Gruffudd hil Meredudd hael.

Powerful of body, with the grasp of the dragon of slaughter, is Graffudd the descendant of the generous Meredudd. *Bleddyn Fardd.*

Oni'th gaf er cerdd erddrym——
Yn iach i'r byd!

If I obtain thee not through the potent song, farewell to the world! *D. ab Gwilym.*

Erddrymawl, *a.* (erddrym) Having robustness.
Erddrymedd, *s. m.* (erddrym) Robustness.
Erddwyn, *v. a.* (dwyn) To bear away; to get.
Erddygan, *s. f.*—*pl. t.* au (dygan) Euphony.

Yr hen feirdd a ganant yn foel-awdl; sef yn ddigynghanedd; a rhoddi pwys y ganiadaeth ar yr erddygan.

The old bards sing in bare rhyme, that is, without concatenation; and laying the stress of the harmony upon the *accentation.* *Barddas.*

Beirdd dysgedigion a fasant yn well yr hen drefn ar acanu y gerdd; sef amrafaelion acenion ac erddyganau blith tra phlith.

Bards that are learned ones relish better the ancient order of accenting the composition; that is, varieties of accents and *emphatic sounds* promiscuously. *Barddas.*

Hoew erddygan a ganai.

Sprightly *harmony* he was wont to sing. *D. ab Gwilym, i'r aderyn.*

Un don yw'r erddygan dau
Ag anal y meginau.

Of the same tone is thy *harmony* as the blast of the bellows. *M. ab Rhys, i'r gwynt.*

Erddyganawl, *a.* (erddygan) Euphonical.

Erddyganu, *v. a.* (erddygan) To yield euphony.
Erddygnawd, *s. m.* (dygnawd) A belabouring.

Ni wyr neb, pan ruddir
Ei bron huan,
Py ddyddwg glain,
O erddygnawd fain.

No body knows when the bosom of the pervading orb is reddened, what *brings out* the sparkle from *hard working* of the stones. *Taliesin.*

Erddygnawl, *a.* (dygnawl) Very toilsome.
Erddygniad, *s. m.*—*pl. t.* au (dygniad) A toiling.
Erddygnu, *v. a.* (dygnu) To toil, to labour hard.
Erddygyd, *v. a.* (dygyd) To bear from; to get.

Gwyr Powys——
Pedair cynneddf, cadw cadr urdden,
Ar ddeg erddygant o Feigen.

The men of Powys, fourteen superior distinctions, honoured for powerful defence, *they acquired* from Meigen. *Cynddelw.*

Erechwydd, *s. m.* (echwydd) A fixed state; purpose, or resolution. *a.* Intent, resolved.

Ar erechwydd ethyw gwall,
O fraw marchawg ysgnall:
A fydd wrth Urien arall?

Upon the resolution there came a failing from the dread of a furious knight; will there be another compared with Urien? *Llywarch Hen.*

Pwyllai Dunawd, farchawg gwain,
Erechwydd gwneuthur celain,
Yn erbyn cryssaid Owain.

Dunawd the leading knight would drive onward, *intent* on making a corpse, against the onset of Owain. *Llywarch Hen.*

Erefain, *v. a.* (efain) To impel, or move onward.
Ereill, *s. pl.* (arall) Others. *pron.* Others.
Ereinnwg, *s. f.* (eraint) A pear orchard. The old name of Herefordshire.
Eres, *a.* (er—es) Marvellous, wonderful, strange. *Eres yw genyf,* it is strange to me.
Eresi, *s. m.* (eres) Amazement, or wonder.
Erestyn, *s. m.* (erestyn) A hurdy-gurdy; buffoon. *Pwnc erestyn,* a hurdy-gurdy strain.

Erestyn hi's car ef a'i graedant——
Cler y dom, eroû heb warant amlwg,
Ei gwech a'i olwg a ochelant.

A hurdy-gurdy he loves not with his harsh string; the vagabond minstrels, that come before us without a clear licence, his frown and his look they will avoid. *L. G. Cothi.*

Eresu, *v. a.* (eres) To wonder, or to marvel.
Erf, *s. m.* (er) What has motion, or briskness. *a.* Brisk, or full of motion.
Erfai, *a.* (erf) Brisk, or lively; animated.

Erbyned erfai eur-falch-wawd Walchmai,
Yn awr ddifai yn urddedig;
Yn synwyr yn llwyr yn llunedig,
Yn faith ferth, yn gerth yn goethedig.

Let him receive the *animated* and exalted golden panegyric of Gwalchmai, dignified in a happy hour; in sense completely formed, beautifully aspiring, nervous and pure. *Gwalchmai i Rodri.*

Addoli mun dan ddail Mai,
A dirfaint cariad erfai.

Worshipping my fair under the leaves of May, with excess of animated love. *D. ab Gwilym.*

Erfawr, *a.* (mawr) Very great; magnificent.
Erfid, *s. m.* (er—mid) That produces a meeting; a junction, or meeting; a conflict, or rencounter. *Aethant ben yn erfid,* they are gone to loggerheads. *Sil.*

Ton tyrfid, toid erfid;
Pan ant cyfrain y'nghofid,
Gwen, gwae rhy hen o'th edlid.

Let the wave bluster, let it cover the *coast*, when the mutual spears go into toil, Gwen, woe to him that is too old, because of thy fury. *Llywarch Hen.*

Erfid a drychid rhag ei drachwres.

The *union* was wont to be broken from his violent passion. *Cynddelw.*

Wedi cad dramawr, ac awr dremid,
A chyfarfod pobl pen yn erfid
——Cyrn a genid.

After the tremendous conflict, and the hour of awful sight, and the meeting of men with heads in contact, horns were blown. *Phylip Brydydd.*

Erfid, *v. a.* (er—mid) To come in contact.

> Piau y bedd hwn, nid arall,
> Gwyddhwch wrth erfid,
> Trathiathau: chwarthai wrthid.
>
> The owner of this grave, not another, a wild bear when coming in contact, Trathiathau: he would smile over thee. *Engl. Beddau Milwyr.*

Erfin, *s. pl. aggr.* (erf) Turnips. *Erfin y coed*, *neu maip bendiged*, briony roots.

Erfinen, *s. f.* (erfin) A turnip, or one turnip. *Erfinen yr yd*, rape, or cole seed.

Erflawdd, *a.* (blawdd) Causing a tumult.

Erfyn, *s. m. dim.* (arf) A weapon, a tool.

Erfyn, *s. m.—pl. t.* ion (myn) A request, a petition, prayer, or intreaty.

Erfyn, *v. a.* (myn) To request, to beseech, to intreat, or beg; to expect, or look for.

Erfyniad, *s. m.—pl. t.* au (erfyn) A requesting; a petition, a request, or intreaty.

Erfyniaw, *v. a.* (erfyn) To request; to beseech.

> Eidol esgob Caerloyw, brawd Eidol iarll, pan welys Hingestr i dywed, pe erfyniai pawb rhyddau Hingestr, mi a'i lladdwn *fy* hun.
>
> Eidol bishop of Gloucester, brother to Eidol the earl, when he saw Hingestr, said, If every one *should solicit* to liberate Hingestr I would myself slay him. *Gr. ab Arthur.*

Erfyniawl, *a.* (erfyn) Supplicatory, petitionary.

Erfynied, *v. a.* (erfyn) To request; or to intreat.

Erfyniedig, *a.* (erfyn) Supplicated, implored.

Erfyniedydd, *s. m.—pl. t.* ion (erfyniad) A beseecher, solicitor, or one who intreats.

Erfyniwr, *s. m.—pl.* erfynwyr (erfyn—gwr) One who solicits, or begs, an intreater.

Erganiad, *s. m.—pl. t.* au (caniad) A singing of.

Ergann, *v. a.* (canu) To sing of, to celebrate.

> Derwyddon doethur,
> Daroganwch i Arthur,
> Yssid y sy gynt
> Neu'r mi erganynt.
>
> Ye intelligent druids, declare to Arthur, what is there more early than me *that they sing of*. *Taliesin.*

Erglyw, *s. m.* (clyw) A listening, or attention.

Erglywed, *s. m.* (erglyw) A hearing, a listening.

Erglywed, *v. a.* (erglyw) To hear; to attend to.

> Yth edrydd yth adrawdd is nef;
> Par eur-glawr, *erglyw fy* mardd-ief!
>
> Thy relatives make mention of thee as first under heaven; thou gold-arrayed chief, *hear my* bardic lore! *Cynddelw, i'r argl. Rhys.*

Erglywiad, *s. m.* (erglyw) A hearing, a listening.

Ergryd, *s. m.* (cryd) Trembling, horror, dread.

> Gorug Maxen y ffordd i cerddai yni ytoedd ei ofn, a'i ergryd ar bob tywysawg, a phob brenin o'r a'i clywai.
>
> Maxentius conquered the way he went, so that his fear and dread was upon every prince, and every king that heard of him. *Gr. ab Arthur.*

Ergryd, *v. a.* (cryd) To cause to tremble, to agitate; to terrify; to tremble, to be terrified.

> Gwelant glyw Powys i hell oesydd,
> A hawdd i ergryd——
>
> They shall see the sovereign of Powys to distant ages, and aptly *causing fear*. *Meilyr.*

Ergrydiad, *s. m.—pl. t.* au (ergryd) A causing to tremble; agitation; a terrifying.

Ergrydiaw, *v. a.* (egryd) To cause to quake; to agitate; to terrify, to be terrified.

> Gwan yn aer rain
> Gwyr yn ergrain
> Yn ergrydiaw.
>
> Spears in the slaughter will wound men wallowing in death and trembling. *Brwydr Bryffwrch.*

Ergrydiawl, *a.* (ergryd) Tending to agitate.

Ergryf, *a.* (cryf) Productive of strength; strong.

> Aer alyf gwaeddyf, ergryf ergrawn.
>
> A sword glutted with slaughter, *endued with strength* to collect a heap. *Einion Offeiriad.*

Ergryn, *s. m.* (cryn) Terror, horror, dread.

Ergrynawd, *s. m.* (ergryn) Trepidation, agitation.

Ergrynawl, *a.* (ergryn) Tending to agitate.

Ergrynedig, *a.* (ergryn) Made to tremble.

> Pa beth y ffowch, chwi ofnogion ergrynedig?
> Ymchwelwch! ymchwelwch, ac ymladdwch!
>
> Why do you flee, ye trembling timid ones! return! return, and fight. *Gr. ab Arthur.*

Ergrynedigaeth, *s. m.—pl. t.* au (ergrynedig) A causing to tremble; agitation, tremulation.

Ergryniad, *s. m.—pl. t.* au (ergryn) A trembling.

Ergrynig, *a.* (ergryn) Apt to tremble, timid.

> Rhyddadolwyfai, rhychanaf i wledig,
> Yn y wlad ydd oedd ergrynig,
> Ni'm gwnel ni's gwnel anawig.
>
> I will earnestly intreat, I will greatly sing to a sovereign in the region where he was *agitated with frailty*, that he cause me not to be unable to form the lay. *Taliesin.*

Ergrynu, *v. n.* (ergryn) To be quaking, to tremble.

> Ergryn llwfr llawer abddoed.
>
> A great many banners will *terrify* a coward. *Adage.*
>
> Ergrynai fy mhwyll o hell gerddaed.
>
> My faculty would *be agitated* with exploring far. *Meilyr.*

Ergwydd, *s. m.—pl. t.* au (cwydd) A tumble.

Ergwyddaw, *v. a.* (ergwydd) To cause a fall.

Ergwyddawl, *a.* (ergwydd) Tending to fall down.

Ergwyddiad, *s. m.—pl. t.* au (ergwydd) A falling

Ergwyn, *s. f.—pl. t.* ion (cwyn) Cause or ground of complaint.

Ergwynaw, *v. a.* (ergwyn) To make to complain.

Ergwynawl, *a.* (ergwyn) Plaintive, doleful.

Ergwyniad, *s. m.—pl. t.* au (ergwyn) A complaining, or lamenting.

Ergyd, *s. m.—pl. t.* ion (cyd) A propulsion, a throw, a cast, a hurl, a shot; a charge; a stroke

> Ergyd ar gais.
>
> A *throw* at a venture. *Adage.*
>
> Ergyd yn llwyn cyssul heb erchi.
>
> An advice unasked is like a shot into a wood. *Adage.*

Ergydiad, *s. m.—pl. t.* au (ergyd) A propelling, a forcing, or effecting; a shooting; a striking; projection, or ejection; a cast, or throw.

Ergydiaw, *v. a.* (ergyd) To propel, or cast forward; to throw, to hurl, to fling; to push forward; to dart, to shoot; to charge.

Ergydiawl, *a.* (ergyd) Propulsive, impelling; missive, that is thrown, cast, or ejected.

Ergydiwr, *s. m.—pl.* ergydwyr (ergyd—gwr) A thrower, a caster, a flinger, a hurler; a shooter

Ergyr, *s. m.—pl. t.* ion (er—cyr) An impulse, a thrust, or push forward; an instigation.

Ergyrch, *s. m.* (cyrch) An onset, or attack.

Ergyrchawl, *a.* (ergyrch) Tending to come upon.

Ergyrchiad, *s. m.—pl. t.* au (ergyrch) An attacking

> Gwr didramgwydd——
> Goreu ergyrchiad faiddiad fyddai.
>
> A man free from errors, the best adventurer in the enterprise he was used to be. *Philyp, i Ieuan Llwyd.*

Ergyrchu, *v. a.* (ergyrch) To make an onset.

Ergyriad, *s. m.—pl. t.* au (ergyr) An impelling, or pushing forward; impulsion; instigation.

Ergyriaw, *v. a.* (ergyr) To impel, to thrust, or push violently; to instigate.

Ergyriawl, *a.* (ergyr) Impulsive; instigatory.

Ergyrwaew, *s. m.* (ergyr—gwaew) A thrusting spear; an impelled, or flying spear.

> Ergyrwaew tyllew tra ei darian.
>
> A vehemently *thrusting spear* before his shield. *O. Cyfeiliawg.*

Erhelfa, *s. f.—pl. t.* au (helfa) A hunt, or hunting expedition, a hunting party.

A rhanu yr erhelfiau: ac ar ail ystum i doal y carw i erhelfa Arthur.

And dividing the *hunting parties*: and upon the second turn the stag came into the *chase* of Arthur. *H. Geraint—Mabinogion.*

Erioed, *adv.* (er—oed) From the beginning; ever, the past; never, the past.

Ni las cenad erioed.

A messenger has not *ever* been slain. *Adage.*

Llygaid!
Ag erioed ni las gwr iach
Digardd ag arfau degach.

The eyes!—There has not been *ever slain* a hale innocent man with fairer weapons. *Sypyn Cyfeiliawg.*

Eriw, *s. m.—pl. t.* ion (er) A progress, a course.

Dyddaw y'nghyntefin cain hin dydd,
Araf eriw haf hyfryd dedwydd.

In June there will come the day of fair weather; in the gentle *progress* of summer happy is the man of observation. *Gwalchmai.*

Erlewyn, *s. m.—pl. t.* oedd (llewyn) What causes light, or splendour, a meteor.

Erlid, *s. f.—pl. t.* iau (eryl) A pursuit; a driving.

Erlid, *v. a.* (eryl) To follow after, to pursue; to prosecute; to persecute; to chase, to drive.

Gwanhau a wnaeynt, a ffo trachefn hyd pan gyfarfuant a byddin Hywel ab Emyr Llydaw a Gwalchmai. Ac y fyddin hono megis flam yn ennynu goddaith, can alw y rhai a ffoynt cyrchu eu gelynion. Ac y rhai a oeddynt cynno hyny yn erlid y rhai hyny a gymhellynt trach eu cefn ar ffo.

They became exhausted, and retreated back until they met with the division of Hywel the son of Emyr of Llydaw, and Gwalchmai. And that host was like a flame burning the wilderness, calling upon those who were retreating to attack their enemies. Whereupon those that were before then *pursuing* those they compelled to retreat back in turn. *Gr. ab Arthur.*

Erlidedig, *a.* (erlid) Pursued, chased, persecuted.

Erlidedigaeth, *s. m.—pl. t.* au (erlidedig) The act of pursuing; persecution.

Erlidfa, *s. f.—pl. t.* au (erlid) A chase, a pursuit.

Erlidiad, *s. m.—pl. t.* au (erlid) A pursuing.

Erlidiaw, *v. a.* (erlid) To follow; to pursue.

Erlidiawl, *a.* (erlid) Pursuing, or chasing.

Erlidig, *a.* (erlid) Apt to pursue, or chase.

Erlidigaeth, *s. m.—pl. t.* au (erlidig) The act of pursuing, or chasing; persecution.

Erlidiwr, *s. m.—pl.* erlidwyr (erlid—gwr) A pursuer, a chaser, a persecutor.

Erlidydd, *s. m.—pl. t.* ion (erlid) A pursuer.

Erlif, *s. m.—pl. t.* ion (llif) A great torrent.

Erlifaw, *v. a.* (erlif) To flow in a torrent.

Erlifiad, *s. m.—pl. t.* au (erlif) A deluging.

Trydar aer lafar erlifiad gwaedffreu,
Trefnau clod oleu, clau adeiliad.

The tumult of the noisy conflict, and the *streaming* of gore, are themes of splendid fame in fine-wrought structure. *Rhuierdyn.*

Erlifiant, *s. m.* (erlif) A violent torrent.

Erlyn, *s. m.—pl. t.* ion (eryl) A pursuit, a chase.

Erlyn, *v. a.* (eryl) To pursue, to follow after.

Ysef a'i herly arlwy garthan dyn
Llywelyn gwawd-wyn gwan.

That is to say he *that pursues* it by providing a severe conflict is Llywelyn whose course is incited by praise. *Llywarch Llaety.*

Erlynad, *s. m.—pl. t.* au (erlyn) A following after, a proceeding. *Erlynadau cyfraith*, law proceedings.

Erlynadwy, *a.* (erlyn) That may be pursued.

Erlynawl, *a* (erlyn) Pursuing, chasing, persecuting

Erlynedig, *a.* (erlyn) Pursued; persecuted.

Erlynedigaeth, *s. m.* (erlynedig) Persecution.

Erlynedigawl, *a.* (erlynedig) Of a persecuting nature; being apt to pursue.

Erlyniad, *s. m.—pl.* erlyniaid (erlyn) A pursuer.

Gnawd serchawg erlyniad.

A *pursuer* is generally one in love. *Adage.*

Erlyniaeth, *s. m.—pl. t.* au (erlyn) The act of pursuing; persecution.

Erlyniedydd, *s. m.—pl. t.* ion (erlynad) One who pursues; a persecutor.

Erlyniwr, *s. m.—pl.* erlynwyr (erlyn—gwr) A pursuer, a chaser, a persecutor.

Erlynydd, *s. m.—pl. t.* ion (erlyn) A pursuer.

Erllen, *s. f.—pl. t.* au (er—llën) A lamp.

Erllusg, *s. m.* (llusg) Lesser periwinkle.

Erllyfasawl, *a.* (llyfasawl) Of a daring disposition.

Erllyfasiad, *s. m.* (llyfasiad) An adventuring.

Erllyfasu, *v. a.* (llyfasu) To adventure, to dare.

Nid arlluddiaw rhi rhyellir;
Nid er lles nid erllyfesir.

To cause obstructions to the prince it cannot be done; to advantage he *will not be dared.* *Cynddelw, i H. ab Owain.*

Erllynedd, *adv.* (llynedd) Since last year.

Erllyriad, *s. m.—pl.* erllyriaid (llyriad) The plantain, a herb; also called *Llydan y ffordd.*

Ermaes, *a.* (maes) External, exterior, outward.

Ermid, *s. m.* (mid) A cause of meeting; contact, or junction; a conflict.

Ermid ei greu-law ar ei greulan.

The *conflict* of his bloody hand upon his gory plain. *Cynddelw.*

Ermidedd, *s. pl. aggr.* (ermid) Rencounters.

Llywelyn—
Lloegr wrthryn tra llyn Llwmynnwy;
Wyr Madawg ermidedd fwyfwy.

Llywelyn the adversary of Lloegr beyond the lake of Llwmynnwy, the grandson of Madog inured to conflicts. *Ll. P. Mech.*

Ermideddawg, *a.* (ermidedd) Having conflicts.

Ermig, *s. m.—pl. t.* ion (er—mig) An instrument.

Ermilus, *a.* (milus) Prowling, hunting about.

Ermoed, *adv.* (er—my—oed) In all my life.

Ni thewais ermoed o'i moli mal drud.

I have not in *all my life time* ceased from praising her like one distracted. *Cynddelw.*

Ermyg, *s. m.—pl. t.* ion (myg) What claims reverence, respect, or honour.

Ermygawl, *a.* (ermyg) Tending to honour.

Ermygiad, *s. m.—pl. t.* au (ermyg) A worshipping, a hallowing, or honouring; adoration.

Ermygu, *v. a.* (ermyg) To adore, to honour.

Er ammod arfod arfaethai;
Ermygai gelanedd,
O wyr gwychr gwnedd,
Yn mlaen Gwynedd gwanai.

For the agreement of combat he would be preparing; *he would honour* the corpses of brave and powerful men, which in the upper part of Gwynedd he should thrust through. *Aneurin.*

Hyfaidd Hir ermygir tra fo cerddawr.

Hyfaidd Hir, he *will be celebrated* as long as there shall be a minstrel. *Aneurin.*

Ern, *s. m.* (er) What serves to drive on; earnest, earnest money, or what is given to settle a bargain.

Mae i'm llaw, o daw i dir,
Geiniawg ern, ag oen gorn-hir.

There is in my hand, should he come to land, a penny of *earnest* with a long-horned ewe. *Gyto y Glyn.*

Ernaw, *v. a.* (ern) To give earnest money.

Ernes, *s. f.—pl. t.* au (ern) Earnest, or pledge.

Erniw, *s. m.—pl. t.* ion (niw) Harm, or hurt.

Erniwaid, *s. m.* (erniw) Harm, or damage.

Erniwaw, *v. a.* (erniw) To hurt, or to harm; to be afflicted, or hurt.

Nid angeu Ffreuer a erniwaf heno,
Namyn my hun mi wan-giaf;
Fym brodyr a'm tymyr a gwynaf!

It is not the death of Freuer that *I am afflicted* with this night, but that myself am feebly sick; my associates and my country I mourn! *Llywarch Hen.*

Hwn—
A'm erniw er na ddaw.

This one *doth hurt* me though he doth not come. *Cynddelw.*

Erniwawl, *a.* (erniw) Detrimental, hurtful.

Erniwed, *s. m.* (erniw) Detriment, or harm.

Erniwiad, *s. m.—pl. t.* au (erniw) A doing harm.
Erniwiant, *s. m.* (erniw) Detriment, or hurt.
Ernwy, *s. m.* (nwy) Briskness, or vivacity.
Ernych, *s. m.* (nych) What causes anguish.
Ernychawl, *a.* (ernych) Tormenting, afflicting.
Ernychiad, *s. m.—pl. t.* au (ernych) A tormenting.
Ernychu, *v. a.* (ernych) To torment, or to afflict.

Os dyn llonydd y fydd fo,
Fo ernych hwn iwch arno.

If a quiet man he shall be, this one for you *will tyrannize* over him. *F. Prys.*

Ernyd, *s. m.* (ern) A precipice, or a slope.
Errith, *s. m.—pl. t.* ion (rhith) A passing form.

Rhag deuwr yn nentur y tiran',
Rhag errith a chyrrith i ar welwgan.

Before two men they will land in the heaven; before a *passing object* and a phantom over the pale clear fluid. *Myrddin.*

Ertrai, *s. m.—pl.* ertreion (trai) The ebbing, or the ebb tide; also the high-water mark, or where the tide begins to turn.

Syllai, can gerdded yr eingwarth—celain yn dyfod gyd a'r ertrai.

He beheld, in walking the strand, a corpse coming with the *tide*. *H. P. P. Dyfed—Mabinogion.*

Gwyddfeirch ton toryn yn ertrai.

The wooden wafters a wave broke them in the *ebb tide*. *Cynddelw.*

Rhwng Menai a'i hertrai hi.

Between Menai and its *ebbing tide*. *Rhys Goch Eryri.*

Erth, *s. m.—pl. t.* au (er) An effort; a puff.
Erthawl, *a.* (erth) Forcible, violent; puffing.
Erthi, *s. m.* (erth) An effort; a puff.
Erthiad, *s. m.—pl. t.* au (erth) A making an effort
Erthrwch, *s. m.—pl.* erthrychion (trwch) A tear, a rent.
Erthrychawl, *a.* (erthrwch) Tending to mangle.
Erthrychiad, *s. m.—pl. t.* au (erthrwch) A tearing.
Erthrychu, *v. a.* (erthrwch) To tear, or to mangle.
Erthu, *v. a.* (erth) To make an effort; to puff.
Erthwch, *s. m.—pl.* erthychion (erth) A puffing, or difficulty of breathing; a groan. *Gwedd erthwch*, a countenance of distress.
Erthychain, *v. a.* (erthwch) To puff, or breathe with difficulty; to breathe fast and thick; to puff; to utter groans; to roar.
Erthychiad, *s. m.—pl. t.* au (erthwch) A puffing.
Erthychlyd, *a.* (erthwch) Short-breathed.
Erthychu, *v. a.* (erthwch) To breathe hard.
Erthyl, *s. m.—pl. t.* od (erth—yl) That is born untimely, an untimely birth, a miscarriage.
Erthylaidd, *a.* (erthyl) Of an untimely birth.
Erthylawg, *a.* (erthyl) Having miscarriages, that miscarries; abortive. *Croth erthylawg*, a miscarrying womb.
Erthyliad, *s. m.—pl. t.* au (erthyl) Abortion.
Erthylu, *v. a.* (erthyl) To bring forth before the time, to miscarry.
Erthylyn, *s. m. dim.* (erthyl) An abortive birth.
Erthyst, *s. m.* (tyst) Testimony, evidence.

Rhybu erthyst yn; rhybu Arthur gynt;
Rhybu anngyfrwng, gwynt gwan tra messur.

There had been *evidence* for us; there had been Arthur of yore; there had been the impulse of wind brushing through above measure. *Ll. P. Moch.*

Erw, *s. f.—pl. t.* i (er) A drive, or a day's ploughing; a slang of arable land, a ridge; an acre. *Erw gymreig*, a Welsh acre, being 160 square perches of 20 feet each.—*Erw ddiffoddedig*, an extinguished acre, or escheat; *erw yr ych du*, the acre of the black ox, or land allotted to one who had a beast hurt by ploughing in conjunction; *erw y gwydd*, the acre of the wood or plough.

Messur erw gyfreithlawn; pedair troedfedd yn hyd y fferiau; wyth yn y fer-iau; deuddeg yn y gesyliau, unarbymtheg yn yr hirian, a gwialen gyhyd a hono yn llaw y geilwad; ac y llaw arall iddo ar y fer perfedd yr iau hono; a hyd y cyrhaeddo hono o bobtu iddo yw lled yr erw; a'i deg ar ugaint yw ei hyd.

The measure of a lawful *acre*, four feet in the length of the short yoke, eight in the close yoke; twelve in the lateral yoke, sixteen in the long yoke, and a rod of equal length with that in the hand of the driver, with his other hand upon the middle knob of that yoke, and as far as that reaches on each side of him is the breadth of the acre, and thirty times that is its length. *Welsh Laws.*

Un droedfedd ar bymtheg a fydd yn hyd yr hirian; ac un iau ar bymtheg a wnant hyd yr erw; a dwy fydd ei lled.

Sixteen feet are in the length of the yoke, and sixteen yokes make the length of the *acre*, and two make its breadth. *Welsh Laws.*

O bydd marw ych o dra aredig, ei berchenawg a gaiff erw; a elwir erw yr ych du.

If an ox shall die from excessive ploughing, his owner shall have an *acre*, and that is called the *acre* of the black ox. *Welsh Laws.*

Erwain, *s. pl. aggr.* (erw) The meadow sweet, also called, *chwys Arthur*, and *llysiau y gwenyn*.

Pan yw per erwain.

When the goat's beard be sweet. *Taliesin.*

Erwaint, *s. pl. aggr.* (erwain) The goat's beard.

Ni mwy gorenai aur neg erwaint flawd.

He would no more hoard gold than blossoms of the goat's beard. *Gwalchmai.*

Erwan, *s. m.—pl. t.* au (gwan) A stab, pricking, or stinging.

A garw ddyagyr gwyr a gwyth erwan.

And horrid shrieks of men with agony of wound. *O. Cyfeiliawg.*

Erwan, *a.* (gwan) Debilitating, feeble, weak.
Erwanawl, *a.* (erwân) Stabbing, or thrusting.
Erwaniad, *s. m.* (erwân) A running through.
Erwanu, *v. a.* (erwân) To run through; to stab.

Dug Ywain wyn-fain, ni wn ban ai hood;
Neud i hoedl a'm erwan!

He has taken Owain, the fair and slender one, I know not whether to proceed or stay; his life being at an end *it doth wound me*! *Ll. P. Moch, i Mad. ab Gruffudd.*

O'i golli——
Erwan dolur mil mil-cant.

From losing him, pain *will sting* a thousand thousands of hundreds. *Prydydd Bychan.*

Erwas, *s. m.—pl.* erweision (gwas) A hero.

Oian, parchellan; y parchell dedwydd,
Na chladd dy redgyr yn mhen mynydd,
Yn lle argel yn argoedydd,
Rhag erwein Rhydderch hael rwyfiadur ffydd.

Listen, little pig, thou discreet pig, bury not thy snout on the mountain top, in a secluded place in forests, for fear of the *heroes* of Rhydderch the generous, the leader of christendom. *Myrddin.*

Erwawd, *s. m.* (gwawd) Panegyric, encomiast.
Erwch, *s. m.* (er) Impulse, drive, or push.
Erwig, *s. f. dim.* (erw) A small piece of ground.

Mab Rhys aeth o'i lys i lawr yr erwig:
Mewn gro a cherrig mae'n garcharawr.

The son of Rhys, he is gone from his mansion to the bottom of the *small plot*; under gravel and stones he is a prisoner. *D. Nanmor.*

Erwyd, *s. f.—pl. t.* oedd (erw) A pole, or perch.

Hil Cynan erwan erwyddeu——
Mwyniant cerdd, nid cerdd ei ddiwedd.

The offspring of Cynan, he is transfixed with *pikes*, the enjoyment of the song, his end was no disgrace. *Gr. ab Gurgenau.*

Erwydd, *s. f.—pl. t.* au (erw) A pole, a rod.
Erwydd, *s. pl. aggr.* (gwydd) Staves, or split wood, used in coopery.
Erwydd, *s. m.* (gwydd) Presence. *conj.* Because, in regard to.
Erwyddaid, *s. m.—pl.* erwyddeidiau (erwydd) The length of a perch, or a pole.
Erwydden, *s. f. dim.* (erwydd) A rod; a perch.

Erwyll, *a.* (gwyll) That casts a gloom; gloomy.

Pan safai yn nrws pebyll
I ar orwydd erwyll
Arddelwai o wr wraig Pyll.

When he should stand in the door of a tent upon a *dark grey* steed, the wife of a hero. *Llywarch Hen.*

Erwyn, *a.* (gwyn) Very white, or splendid.

Hanbych well Dafydd, dawn gaffael,
O Ddnw deon archafael,
Ac o ddyn, bawl erwyn hael.

Be thou more blest, David, obtaining grace, of God the supreme distributor, and of man, a *splendid* and liberal claim. *G. Ryfel, i D. ab Owain.*

Erŵyr, *a.* (gŵyr) Tending to be oblique, or awry.

Erydd, *s. m.—pl. t.* on (er—ydd) An eagle. *Sil.*

Eryf, *s. m.—pl. t.* oedd (er—yf) Impulsion, violent exertion.

Llaw ar lafn, a'r llafn ar lu Nortmain,
Ac eryfoedd trwm rhag tremid angeu
Fyned crau ag eryfain.

A hand on the blade, and the blade on the host of Normandy, and heavy *exertions* against the signal of death from the running of gore with toiling. *Cynddelw, i O. Gwynedd.*

Arf eryf eryr Nanhoenain,
Araf yw arwydd i dichwain.

The weapon of *exertion* of the eagle of Nanhoenain, gentle is the token of its fate. *Cynddelw, m. O. Gwynedd.*

Eryfain, *v. a.* (eryf) To use exertion.

Eryfed, *s. m.* (yfed) A quaffing; a carousal.

Eryfed, *v. a.* (yfed) To drink much, to quaff.

Eryfais dy win o'th wen adaf; diwedd,
Eryfaf dy fedd; dy fodd a wnaf;
Eryfant anant
O aur ac ariant.

I have drunk to excess of thy wine from thy fair hand, having done, *I will deeply quaff* thy mead; thy pleasure I will do; minstrels *will deeply quaff* out of gold and silver. *Llywelyn Fardd, i O. Gwynedd.*

Eryl, *s. f.—pl. t.* oedd (er—yl) A look out.

Y lle y gosoter cwn yn eryl, y cyntaf o honynt a gymero iwrch, neu gadno, neu ysgyfarnawg, ei berchen bieufydd.

Where dogs are placed on the *watch*, the first of them that shall take a buck, or a fox, or a hare, his owner shall possess whichever it be. *Welsh Laws.*

Eryl, *v. a.* (er—yl) To watch, to look after.

Brenin a'i werin yn ei eryl.

A king with his commonalty *guarding* him. *L. G. Cothi.*

Eryr, *s. m.—pl. t.* od (er—yr) An eagle. *Eryr melyn*, neu *eryr euraid*, golden eagle; *eryr tinwyn*, ring tail eagle; *eryr y mor*, *eryr y dwfr*, neu *pysg-eryr*, the osprey.

Nerth eryr yn ei ylfin.

The strength of an *eagle* in his beak. *Adage.*

Eryrai, *s. f.* (eryr) The eagle stone, or œtitis.

Eryraidd, *a.* (eryr) Aquiline, like an eagle.

Eryran, *s. m.* (eryr) A young eagle, or eaglet.

Eryrawl, *a.* (eryr) Aquiline, like an eagle.

Eryres, *s. f.—pl. t.* au (eryr) A female eagle.

Eryri, *s. f.* (eryr) What is precipitated, or thrown out violently, an irruption; the shingles; called also, *eryr* and *eryrod*. It is the appellation of the mountainous part of Arvon, called in former times by the English, the forest of Snowdon

Eryron, *s. pl. aggr.* (eryr) Eagles; heroes.

Dywawd derwyddon
Dadeni haelon
O hil eryron o Eryri.

Druids do sing of generous ones being born again of the race of *heroes* out of Eryri. *Ll. P. Moch.*

Erysdyddiau, *adv.* (dydd) Days ago; a good while ago, some time since.

Erysgwyddiad, *s. m.—pl. t.* au (ysgwyddiad) Supportation; a shouldering, or propping up.

Dryll cadr cad,
Cain erysgwyddiad.

The powerful instrument of battle, a fair *support*. *Taliesin.*

Erysi, *s. m.* (eres) Marvellousness; a wonder.

Lle chwery awen o erysi bryd;
Lle chwery esbyd byd heb oedi.

Where the bright genius will play his mind being filled with *amazement*, where the guests of all the world will play without one missing. *D. ab Gwilym.*

Erysmeityn, *adv.* (ysmeityn) Some moments ago; sometime since; a while ago.

Erystalm, *adv.* (ystalm) Since a while ago, some time since, a good while ago.

Erysu, *v. a.* (eres) To wonder, or to marvel.

Canynt cerddorion;
Erysynt cadfion;
Dadwyrain i Frython
A oreu Gwydion.

Minstrels have sung; men of conflict have wondered at the renewed glory to Britons which Gwydion accomplished. *Taliesin.*

ES, *s. m. r.* Motion from, or a divergency; separation, division, or parting from; a shoot, or dart from. It is used as a prefix in composition, being of the same force and origin with the latin *ex*. It is also a termination of feminine personal nouns, and of the third person of verbs in the preterit.

Ni wddant cwdd ant rhy coddes
Yn dyrlid moliant, mal ydd es.

They know not where they shall go whom he afflicted, meriting praise as *he went*. *Ll. P. Moch, i Rodri.*

Esbyd, *s. pl. aggr.* (es—pyd) Guests, strangers.

Goronwy, gwr—
Dewr-goeth, lluddfawr yn llu arallwlad,
Dinidr gad gynnyddu;
Dinas esbyd gyd gyrchu;
Dinag goelfain faneg fu.

Goronwy, a man nobly brave, warlike in the host of a foreign country, not to be opposed in making the battle to prosper; the strong hold where *guests* mutually approach; a token of unfailing happiness he has been. *Bleddyn Fardd.*

Esg, *s. m.* (es) What diverges or shoots out.

Esgaeth, *a.* (es—caeth) Void of restraint, divested of bondage; liberty, or free.

Esgaethu, *v. a.* (esgaeth) To free of bondage.

Esgaidd, *a.* (esg) Nimble, brisk; smart, gay. *Troi yn esgaidd iawn*, to turn very smartly. *Sil.*

Esgair, *s. f.—pl.* esgeiriau (esg) A shank, a leg, a limb; a long ridge, a hill, or mountain that stretches out, whence it is the appellation of several places; as, *Esgair Weddar*, *Esgair-yn-eira*, *Esgair Geiliawg*, *Esgair Hir*, and *Esgair Galed*.

Esgair dda i llun i'm bun bach;
Od unnos nid yw wynach.

A well-formed *limb* my little fair one has got, the one night's snow is not whiter than it. *S. ab Hywel.*

Lle cerddo lleg i hesgair
Ni chyfyd nag yd na gwair.

Where she with feeble *shank* happens to walk there will not grow nor corn nor hay. *Goronwy Owain, i gengen.*

Esgar, *s. m.—pl. t.* ion (es—car) A separation, a divided state; a divorce, an adversary, or enemy. *Un gar un esgar*, common friend and common foe.

Cant car a fydd i ddyn a chant esgar.

A man shall have a hundred friends and a hundred *enemies*. *Adage.*

Esgar, *v. a.* (es—car) To separate, to part; to cast off; to divorce.

Esgarant, *s. m.—pl.* esgeraint (esgar) An adversary

Nis medd trais, nis traidd esgeraint.

Oppression has no hold of him, *enemies* come not in to him. *Cynddelw.*

Esgard, *s. m.—pl. t.* ion (esgar) A cleft, or chap.

Esgardiaw, *v. a.* (esgard) To cause to chap.

Esgardd, *s. m.—pl. t.* ion (esgar) A rupture.

Esgarddawl, *a.* (esgardd) Tending to disperse.

Esgardde, *s. f.* (esgardd) A dispersion, a scattering

> Dyfuwyd fy ysgwyd yn esgardde;
> Dyfusnt esgarant gwaew o'i hangre.
>
> My shield has been used to dispersion, foes will be accustomed to pass from its shelter. *Ll. P. Moch.*

Esgaredd, *s. m.* (esgar) Separation, or schism.
Esgaredig, *a.* (esgar) Separated, parted; divorced
Esgaredigaeth, *s. m.* (esgaredig) Separation.
Esgariad, *s. m.—pl. t.* au (esgar) A separating.
Esgariaeth, *s. m.—pl. t.* au (esgar) A separation.
Esgariaw, *v. a.* (esgar) To separate, to part.
Esgarllys, *s. m. aggr.* (esgar—llys) Birthwort, hart-wort. *Esgarllys gron*, round birthwort; *esgarllys hir*, long birthwort; *esgarllys bychan*, periwinkles, or climbers.
Esgaru, *v. a.* (esgar) To separate, to disjoin.
Esgeiddig, *a.* (esgaidd) Smart, nimble; moving with ease. *Cerddediad esgeiddig*, a smart walk; *dyn esgeiddig*, a graceful person.

> Yr hardd esgeiddig wen-fun sy'n bort ei llun a'i lliw,
> Clyw achwyn mab serchogaidd——
>
> The comely and graceful fair one, beauteous of form and complexion, hear the complaint of a lovesick youth. *Ifan Bin.*

Esgeirca, *v. a.* (esgair—ca) To move the shanks.
Esgeircawraig, *s. f.—pl.* esgeircawreigedd (esgeirca—gwraig) A walking woman, a walker.

> Tebyg oedd Elen iddynt hwythau; a theg, a gwreigiaidd, a hynaws oedd; ac esgeircawraig dda; a man oedd rhwng ei dwyael.
>
> Elen was similar to them also; and fair, and effeminate, and kind was she, and a good walking woman, and there was a mark between her eyebrows. *H. Dared—Mabinogion.*

Esgeiriawg, *a.* (esgair) Having shanks, or legs.
Esgeirnoeth, *a.* (esgair—noeth) Bare-legged.
Esgemydd, *s. f.—pl. t.* au (es—cam) A bench.
Esgeraint, *s. pl. aggr.* (esgarant) Adversaries.

> Teyrnas i'th law, lid Geraint, nid chwith,
> Er chwydiad esgeraint,
> Nid hath llath yn llaw ysgeraint;
> Ni bydd byth bydawl ei gymmaint.
>
> Thou who art in wrath like Geraint, a kingdom in thy hand is not awkward, notwithstanding the vomiting of *adversaries*; very different the shaft in the hands of the relatives; there will never be another worldling to match with him. *Ll. P. Moch, i Rodri.*

Esgeulus, *a.* (cael) Negligent, careless, heedless.

> Nid esgeulus ond gwasanaethwg;
> Nid cywir ond ci.
>
> The most *careless* is a servant; the most faithful is a dog. *Adage.*

Esgeulusaw, *v. a.* (esgeulus) To disregard.
Esgeulusawl, *a.* (esgeulus) Disregarding.
Esgeulusdawd, *s. m.* (esgeulus) Negligence.
Esgeulusder, *s. m.* (esgeulus) Negligence.
Esgeulusdra, *s. m.* (esgeulus) Negligence.
Esgeulusedig, *a.* (esgeulus) Neglected.
Esgeulusiad, *s. m.* (esgeulus) A neglecting, or disregarding; a carelessly acting.
Esgeulusiant, *s. m.* (esgeulus) Indifference.
Esgeuluswydd, *s. m.* (esgeulus) Heedlessness, negligence, or neglectfulness.
Esgeuluswr, *s. m.—pl.* esgeuluswyr (esgeulus—gwr) A neglecter; a heedless person.
Esgid, *s. f.—pl. t.* iau (es—cid) A shoe. *Esgidiau y gog*, blue bells; *esgid Mair*, lady's slipper; *esgid morforwyn*, mermaid's shoe, a species of sea-weed.
Esgidiedig, *a.* (esgid) Furnished with shoes; shod
Esgidiwr, *s. m.—pl.* esgidwyr (esgid—gwr) A shoe man, or dealer in shoes.
Esglyw, *s. m.* (es—llyw) Protection; defence.
Esglywiad, *s. m.—pl. t.* au (esglyw) A defending.
Esglywn, *v. a.* (esglyw) To protect, to defend.

> Esgud at esgud i esglywn gwlad.
>
> Nimble is his hand *to defend* a country. *Gwalchmai.*

Esglywyn, *v. a.* (esglyw) To protect, to defend.

> Esgud esgud i esglywyn gwlad.
>
> A nimble hand for *defending* a country. *Meilyr.*

Esgob, *s. m.—pl. t.* ion (cob) A bishop. *Esgob gwyn*, white bishop, or bellis major, a herb.

> Cas esgob heb ddysg.
>
> Odious is a *bishop* without learning. *Adage.*

Esgobaeth, *s. f.—pl. t.* au (esgob) A bishopric.
Esgobawd, *s. f.* (esgob) A bishopric; a diocess.
Esgobawl, *a.* (esgob) Diocesan, or episcopal.
Esgobdy, *s. m.—pl. t.* au (esgob—tŷ) A bishop's palace; a bishopric.
Esgor, *s. m.—pl. t.* au (es—cor) A partage.
Esgor, *v. a.* (es—cor) To separate; to dismiss; to quit, to leave off; to bring forth.
Esgoradwy, *a.* (esgor) Separable, that may be parted, or divided; that may be left off.
Esgordd, *s. pl. aggr.* (cordd) Such as be out of the circle; *esgorddion*, strangers.
Esgored, *s. f.* (esgor) What is parted from.
Esgoredfa, *s. f.—pl. t.* au (esgored) A place of breaking forth, or separation.
Esgoredig, *a.* (esgor) Separated; delivered.
Esgoredigaeth, *s. m.—pl. t.* au (esgoredig) A separation; a quitting; a deliverance.
Esgoredigawl, *a.* (esgoredig) Parturient.
Esgorfa, *s. f.—pl. t.* au (esgor) A parturition; a deliverance; a place of deliverance.
Esgorfaich, *a.* (esgor—baich) Delivered of a load

> Ni bu esgorfaich Brynaich brain.
>
> The crows of the Highlands have not been *free from a burden*. *Cynddelw.*

Esgori, *v. a.* (esgor) To separate; to dismiss; to quit, to be delivered, to bring forth.
Esgoriad, *s. m.—pl. t.* au (esgor) A separating; a delivering; a being delivered; parturition.
Esgoriant, *s. m.* (esgor) Separation; deliverance.
Esgorlys, *s. pl. aggr.* (esgor—llys) Birth-wort; called also, *llysiau y galon*; *esgorlys bychan*, climbing birthwort; *esgorlys crwn*, round birthwort; *esgorlys hir*, long birthwort.
Esgorwraig, *s. f.—pl.* esgorwreigedd (esgor—gwraig) A midwife.
Esgoryd, *v. a.* (esgor) To part from; to deliver.

> Cyn esgar, wrth esgoryd
> Morwyn wen addfwyn oeddyd.
>
> Before separation, in *bringing forth* a fair kind maid thou wert. *H. ab Rhys ab Gwilym.*

Esgorydd, *s. m.—pl. t.* ion (esgor) One who takes from, or divides; a deliverer; an accoucheur.
Esgud, *a.* (cud) Swift, quick; nimble; skittish; flippant; active, diligent.

> Mam esgud a wna merch ddiawg.
>
> A lazy daughter makes a *brisk* mother. *Adage.*
>
> Un esgud i'w dud ydwyf;
> O'i dai a'i gyfch diawg wyf.
>
> A *nimble* one am I to his ground; going out of his houses and his neighbourhood I am a lazy one. *L. G. Cothi.*

Esgudawg, *a.* (esgud) Abounding with activity.
Esgudfryd, *s. m.* (esgud—bryd) Of quick mind.
Esgudfrys, *s. m.* (esgud—brys) Quick bustle.
Esgudogyll, *s. m.* (esgudawg) The wood-lark.
Esgudwal, *s. f.* (esgud—gwal) A quickly-moving shelter.

> Pieu yr ysgwyd, esgudwal cynnwan
> A'r cant waew am ei thal!
> Ysgwyd Llywelyn.
>
> Who owns the shield, the quickly-moving shelter of the foremost course with the hundred spears around its front?—It is the shield of Llywelyn. *Llywarch Llaety, i G. ab Madawg.*

Esgudwan, *s. f.* (esgud—gwan) A swift career; *Esgudwan garthan*, the swift course of conflict.
Esgus, *s. m.—pl. t.* ion (es—cus) A receding from, a refraining; an excuse; an apology.
Esgusaw, *v. a.* (esgus) To recede; excuse.
Esgusawd, *s. m.—pl.* esgusodion (esgus) A refraining, or flinching from; an excusation.
Esgusawl, *a.* (esgus) Excusatory; apologetic.
Esgusedig, *a.* (esgus) Excused; palliated.
Esgusiad, *s. m.—pl. t.* au (esgus) An excusing.
Esgusodai, *s. m.—pl.* esgusodeion (esgusawd) One that is excused; one apologized to.
Esgusodawl, *a.* (esgusawd) Tending to excuse; excusatory; palliative.
Esgusodedig, *a.* (esgusawd) Excused; remitted.
Esgusodedigaeth, *s. m.* (esgusodedig) Excusation, the act of excusing.
Esgusodedigawl, *a.* (esgusodedig) Palliative.
Esgusodi, *v. a.* (esgusawd) To apologize.
Esgusodiad, *s. m.—pl. t.* au (esgusawd) Excusation; an excusing, or apologizing.
Esgusodwr, *s. m.—pl.* esgusodwyr (esgusawd—gwr) One who excuses, an excuser.
Esgusodydd, *s. m.—pl. t.* ion (esgusawd) An excuser; an apologist.
Esgutwyth, *a.* (esgud—gwyth) Quickly provoked. *Dyn esgutwyth*, a person easily provoked. *Dyfed.*
Esgymawl, *a.* (cym) Unassociating; unsociable.
Esgymiad, *s. m.—pl. t.* au (cym) A dissolving or separating a society.
Esgymun, *a.* (cymun) Excommunicate; accursed, execrable; detestable.
Esgymunaw, *v. a.* (esgymun) To excommunicate, to exclude from society.
Esgymunawd, *s. m.* (esgymun) Excommunication, exclusion from society.
Esgymunawl, *a.* (esgymun) Excommunicate.
Esgymuniad, *s. m.—pl. t.* au (esgymun) An excommunicating; excommunication.
Esgymunrwydd, *s. m.* (esgymun) An excommunicated state; accursedness.
Esgymu, *v. a.* (cym) To disconnect, to break off from associating.
Esgymus, *a.* (cym) Separated from society.
Esgyn, *s. m.* (cyn) The act of ascending up.
Esgyn, *v. a.* (cyn) To ascend, to mount, to rise.
Esgynadwy, *a.* (esgyn) Ascendable, that may be ascended, or mounted.
Esgynawl, *a.* (esgyn) Ascendant; ascending.
Esgynedig, *a.* (esgyn) Mounted up, ascended.
Esgynedigaeth, *s. m.—pl. t.* au (esgynedig) The act of ascending; ascension.
Esgynfa, *s. f.—pl. t.* au (esgyn) An ascent, rise, or acclivity; a getting up; a horse-block.
Esgynfaen, *s. m.—pl.* esgynfain (esgyn—maen) A mounting stone, a horse-block.

> Minnau fyddaf ar ben yr esgynfaen acw i'th aros di.
>
> And I shall be on the top of yonder *horse-block* to stay for thee. *H. O. ab Urien—Mabinogion.*

Esgynglwm, *s. m.—pl.* esgynglymau (esgyn—clwm) An ascending node, in astronomy.
Esgyniad, *s. m. —pl. t.* au (esgyn) A rising, or ascending; ascension; acclivity.
Esgyniadawl, *a.* (esgyniad) Ascensive, rising.
Esgyniaith, *s. f.* (esgyn—iaith) A climax.
Esgynlawr, *s. m.—pl.* esgynloriau (esgyn—llawr) A scaffold; a raised platform.
Esgynwr, *s. m.—pl.* esgynwyr (esgyn—gwr) One who mounts up; an ascender.
Esgynydd, *s. m—pl. t.* ion (esgyn) An ascender.

Esgyr, *s. f.—pl. t.* oedd (es—gyr) A day's ploughing with one yoke; an acre. *Esgyr Gwyngu, Esgyr Milwyr*; places so called.
Esgyrnawl, *a.* (asgwrn) Ossific; of bony nature.
Esgyrndy, *s. m.—pl. t.* au (esgwrn—ty) A bone-house or a charnel house.
Esgyrniad, *s. m.* (asgwrn) Ossification; a boning.
Esgyrniawg, *a.* (asgwrn) Having bones, bony.
Esgyrnle, *s. f.—pl. t.* oedd (asgwrn—lle) A charnel-house, or ossuary.
Esgyrnllyd, *a.* (asgwrn) Of a bony nature, osseous.
Esgyrnllym, *a.* (asgwrn—llym) Sharp-boned.
Esgyrnllymedd, *s. m.* (esgyrnllym) Scragginess.
Esgyrnwg, *s. m.* (asgwrn) Fullness of bones.
Esgyrnygawl, *a.* (esgyrnwg) Grinning, gnashing.
Esgyrnygfa, *s. f.—pl. t.* au (esgyrnwg) A place of grinning, or gnashing of teeth.
Esgyrnygiad, *s. m.—pl. t.* au (esgyrnwg) A grinning; a gnashing the teeth.
Esgyrnygu, *v. a.* (esgyrnwg) To grin, to gnash the teeth: to chop bones, to bone.
Esill, *s. m.—pl. t.* ion (sill) A member; offspring.
Esillt, *s. m.—pl. t.* ion (esill) Offspring, issue.
Esilltydd, *s. pl. aggr.* (esillt) Offspring, progeny.
Esillydd, *s. pl. aggr.* (esill) Offspring, progeny.
Esin, *a.* (es) Apt to fly out, or burst; perturbed.
Esing, *s. m.* (esin) The act of breaking out. *Yr oeddwn i yn esing gwyllt ganddo*, I was in a wild tumult with it, or I could hardly contain myself on account of it. *Sil.*

> Trais dwyn glyw aesawyn, glew esing ofal,
> Ofynaig Maelgyning;
> Mab Owain caeifain coeling,
> Mawr rad gwallofiad gwelling.
>
> It was oppression to take away the guardian chief, the brave *dispeller* of care, the hope of the country of Maelgwn; the son of Owain, the portended treasure, the great gift of the distributor of blessings. *Gw. Ryfel, i D. ab Owain.*

Esiw, *a.* (es) In a state of privation, or destitute.
Esiwaw, *v. a.* (esiw) To cause privation.
Esiwydd, *s. m.* (esiw) A state of privation.
Esiwyddawl, *a.* (esiwydd) Necessitous, needy.
Esiwyddiad, *s. m.—pl. t.* au (esiwydd) A feeling want: privation, or destitution.
Esiwyddu, *v. n.* (esiwydd) To experience want.
Esmwyth, *a.* (mwyth) Soft, or smooth to the feel; easy; quiet; agreeable, comfortable.

> Esmwythaf gwaith yw methu.
>
> The *easiest* work is to fail. *Adage.*
>
> Mi fum esmwyth a llawn dawn,
> A balch lle bawn, a brywus,
> A llawenaf dyn i'm plwy',
> A heddyw 'dd wy'n ofalus!
>
> I have been *comfortable*, and full of enjoyment, and proud wherever I was, and wanton, and the merriest man in my community, and to day I am oppressed with care! *Hyw. T. Phylip.*

Esmwythâad, *s. m.* (esmwyth) A softening; quieting; a mollifying, or assuaging.
Esmwythâawl, *a.* (esmwyth) Mollificative.
Esmwythator, *ger.* (esmwyth) Making easy.
Esmwythâu, *v. a.* (esmwyth) To soften, to mollify; to become easy or composed.
Esmwythaw, *v. a.* (esmwyth) To soften, to make soft and easy; to ease, to emollify; to assuage; to quiet; to be easy, or quiet.
Esmwythawl, *a.* (esmwyth) Mollient, assuasive.
Esmwythder, *s. m.* (esmwyth) Softness; easiness; quietness; tranquillity; ease, rest.

> Tri dyn ni charant eu gwlad: a garo ei fol, a garo gyfoeth, ac a garo esmwythder.
>
> Three persons who have no regard for their country; that loves his belly, that loves wealth, and that loves *ease*. *Bardd. s.*

Esmwythdra, *s. m.* (esmwyth) Softness to the feel, easiness; quietness, stillness, rest.
Esmwythedig, *a.* (esmwyth) Softened, mollified.

Esmwythedigaeth, *s. m.* (esmwythedig) The act of giving ease, or quietness; mollification.
Esmwythiad, *s. m.* (esmwyth) A softening; a quieting; mollification.
Esmwythiant, *s. m.* (esmwyth) A state of ease.
Esmwythid, *s. m.* (esmwyth) A state of ease, rest.
Esmwythitor, *sup.* (esmwythid) To be easing.
Esmwythyd, *s. m.* (esmwyth) A state of ease.
Esogryn, *s. f.* (gogryn) An inflammation about the jaws, or the mumps.
Esplydd, *a.* (plydd) Delicate, tender, or soft.

Afallen beren blodau esplydd—
A dyf yn argel yn argoedydd.

Sweet apple tree with *delicate* blossoms—that grows a shelter in the forests. *Myrddin.*

Esplydden, *s. f.—pl. t.* au (esplydd) A pippin.
Esill, *s. m.—pl. t.* ion (sill) Offspring, issue.
Esilliad, *s. m.—pl. t.* au (esill) A generation.
Esilliaw, *v. a.* (esill) To beget offspring.
Esilling, *s. m.* (esill) An origin, or source.

O'r cedeirn cedawl hawl hirddifing;
O Gadell corr o gadelling,
O'r glan esillid glew esilling;
O'r glyw glew dywal ni dal ni ding

Of the munificent mighty ones of far extending claim; of Cadell's stock of Cadellian power, of the pure offspring of the splendid source; of the chief brave and fierce that will not conceale, that will not flinch. *Cynddelw, i Kiryd Fleidd.*

Esillt, *s. m.—pl. t.* ion (esill) Offspring, issue.
Esilltydd, *s. pl. aggr.* (esill) Offspring, progeny.
Esillyd, *s. pl. aggr.* (esill) Offspring, issue.
Esillydd, *s. pl. aggr.* (esill) Offspring, progeny.

Pedwaredd welygordd, pedwerydd molawd.
Molafi lyw ai dyrllydd,
Mawr dorf darf gylarf gyweithydd,
Madogion Madawg esillydd.

The fourth community, a fourth panegyric, I will praise him who deserves it, a mighty host striking terror when an auxilliary with the mutual weapon, Madogion, the *offspring* of Madog. *Cynddelw.*

Est, *s. m.* (es) A partition, or parting from.
Estawl, *a.* (est) Tending to separate or part.
Estrawn, *s. m.—pl.* estronion (trawn) One of a separate community; a stranger, a foreigner.

Dal llid, gofid, ac afar,
A chas wrth estrawn a char.

Holding malice, pain and vexation, and hatred to *stranger* and friend. *Gw. ab Sefnyn.*

Estriciad, *s. m.* (estrig) A hastening, a bustling.
Estriciaw, *v. a.* (estrig) To bustle, to brush away, to make haste; to be active.
Estrig, *a.* (estr) Apt to dart away; quick.
Estronaidd, *a.* (estrawn) Strange, extraneous.
Estronawg, *a.* (estrawn) Extraneous; strange.

A'th folaf, filwr pedrydawg,
A'th folant pymthegcant cadeiriawg,
Rhythfawl ar yn sydd estronawg

I will praise thee, warrior of swift career, fifteen hundred presiding bards will extol thee, thou wilt be greatly praised by such as are *strange*. *Ll. P. Moch, i Lywelyn I.*

Estronawl, *a.* (estrawn) Tending to estrange; foreign; extraneous.

Carawn a erchis gwarchadw ynys Prydain ar longau ar y moroedd yn i chylch rhag gormesoedd y gan estronion genedloedd.

Caraw demanded permission to guard the Isle of Britain with ships, upon the seas surrounding it, against the depredations of *foreign nations.* *Gr. ab Arthur.*

Estronedig, *a.* (estrawn) Estranged, alienated.
Estroneiddiad, *s. m.* (estronaidd) An estranging.
Estroneiddiaw, *v. a.* (estronaidd) To be estranged, to render estranged.
Estroneiddiawl, *a.* (estronaidd) Apt to estrange.
Estrones, *s. f.—pl. t.* au (estrawn) A strange female, or a strange woman.

Onid yn estronesau y cyfrifai efe nyni?

Did he not consider us to be strangers? *Genesis xxxi. 15.*

Estroni, *v. a.* (estrawn) To estrange, to alienate.

Ni ellid ei wahanu i wrtho, na'i estroni er a ddywetai neb.

He could not be separated from him, nor could he *be alienated* for what any body could say. *H. Bown o Hamtwn—Mabinogion.*

Estroniad, *s. m.—pl. t.* au (estrawn) An estranging; estrangement, alienation.
Estroniaeth, *s. m.* (estrawn) An estrangement.
Estl, *s. m.—pl.* estlon (est—yl) What ranges.
Estyll, *s. pl. aggr.—pl. t.* od (astell) Slit boards, or shingles; laths, or staves. *Estyll dyrwyn*, winding blades.
Estyllawg, *a.* (estyll) Having shingles or boards.
Estylledig, *a.* (estyll) Being done with boards.
Estyllen, *s. f. dim.—pl. t.* au (estyll) A shingle, or thin split board, a board, a close-stool.
Estyllfa, *s. f.—pl. t.* au (estyll) A board yard.
Estyllodi, *v. a.* (estyll) To slit into boards.
Estyllu, *v. a.* (estyll) To do with shingles.
Estyn, *s. m.—pl. t.* ion (es—tyn) Extent; in law, a grant, or investiture; the act of investing with possession when seisin is given of an estate.
Estyn, *v. a.* (es—tyn) To extend, to stretch out, to enlarge; to stretch, to reach, to hold out; to invest, or make a grant of.

Dyn wyf o glwyf yn dwyn gloes,
Os dyn fwyn estyn f'einioes.

I am one bearing the smart of a wound, if thou art a kind maid *lengthen* my life. *D. ab Gwilym.*

Estynadwy, *a.* (estyn) Extensible, ductile; that may be extended, stretched, or reached out.
Estynawl, *a.* (estyn) Extensive, extending; stretching, or reaching out; invested, or having seisin

Os derfydd i'r arglwydd geisiaw cymhell o lüydd y rhai ni bont estynolion o dir o fewn ei gyfoeth ef, ni ddylyir lüydd iddynt o gyfraith.

If the prince should attempt to compel *those* that are not *invested with seisin* of land within his jurisdiction to serve in the army, the law says they ought not to be obliged to serve. *Welsh Laws.*

Estynedig, *a.* (estyn) Extended, stretched out.
Estynedigaeth, *s. m.* (estynedig) An extension.
Estynedigawl, *a.* (estynedig) Of an extending, enlarging, or stretching quality.
Estyniad, *s. m.—pl. t.* au (estyn) A reaching out, stretching, or extending; extension, continuation; a giving possession, investiture.
Estyniawg, *a.* (estyn) Having extension, extended
Estynu, *v. a.* (estyn) To extend, to stretch.
Estynwefl, *s. f.—pl. t.* au (estyn—gwefl) A pouting lip; a long snout.
Estynwr, *s. m.—pl.* estynwyr (estyn—gwr) An extender, one who stretches, a reacher out.
Estynydd, *s. m.—pl. t.* ion (estyn) An extender.
Estyr, *s. m.—pl.* estrod (est—yr) That darts away
Esu, *v. a.* (es) To push away; to range out.
Eswrn, *s. m.—pl.* esyrnau (swrn) The joint next to the foot of animals, the fet-lock joint.
Esyddyn, *s. m.—pl. t.* au (syddyn) A mansion, a dwelling place.

Tri pheth teg arbenig sydd i dri mychdeyrn dyledawg Cymmru yn esyddynau breiniawl iddynt, sef yw Aberffraw yn Ngwynedd, Dinefwr yn y Deheu, a Mathrafal Wynfa yn Mhowys.

There are three appropriate courts for the three supreme princes of Wales as privileged *mansions* for them; one is Aberffraw in Gwynedd, Dinefwr in the South, and Mathrafal Gwynfa in Powys. *Trioedd.*

Esyddynawg, *a.* (esyddyn) Having a dwelling.
Esyddynawl, *a.* (esyddyn) Relating to a dwelling.
Esyddyniad, *s. m.* (esyddyn) A fixing a dwelling.
Esyddynu, *v. a.* (esyddyn) To settle a habitation.
Esyllt, *s. f.* (syllt) That is fair, or open to view. The name of several famous women.
Esyllwg, *s. f.* (syllwg) That abounds with prospects. It is the name of a part of South Wales,

latinized *Siluria*, and was of considerable extent in ancient times. It was also called *Gwent*.
Esyth, *s. pl. aggr.* (aseth) Sharp sticks, waggets.
Esythu, *v. a.* (esyth) To drive a stake through.
Etewyn, *s. m.—pl. t.* ion (tewyn) A firebrand.

Gwell y llysg dau etewyn nog un.

Two *firebrands* will burn better than one! *Adage.*

Etifaw, *v. a.* (tifaw) To inherit, to possess.
Etifawg, *a.* (tifawg) Having an inheritance.
Etifawl, *a.* (tifawl) Hereditary, hereditable.
Etifedd, *s. m.—pl. t.* ion (tifedd) A birth; an infant; an heir.

Nid boffder ond etifedd.

The supreme pleasure is an *heir*. *Adage.*

Etifeddawg, *a.* (etifedd) Having a child, or lying in childbed.
Etifeddawl, *a.* (etifedd) Hereditary, hereditable.

Nid etifeddawl neb i dalu dylyed dros ei rieni.

No body is *hereditary* to pay a debt on account of his parents. *Welsh Laws.*

Etifeddedig, *a.* (etifedd) Made hereditary.
Etifeddes, *s. f.—pl. t.* au (etifedd) A female inheritor, an heiress.
Etifeddiad, *s. m.* (etifedd) An inheriting; possession.
Etifeddiaeth, *s. m.—pl. t.* au (etifedd) An inheritance, or heritage.
Etifeddiant, *s. m.* (etifedd) An inheritance.
Etifeddu, *v. a.* (etifedd) To inherit, to possess by hereditary right.
Etifeddwely, *s. m.* (etifedd—gwely) A child-bed.
Etifeddwr, *s. m.—pl.* etifeddwyr (etifedd—gwr) An inheritor, or one who holds by heirship.
Etifiad, *s. m.* (tifiad) A getting Inheritance.
Etifiant, *s. m.* (tifiant) Heirship, heritage.
Etto, *conj.* (ed—to) Yet, still, also; however; nevertheless. *adj.* Yet, again, once more, another time, still; hitherto.

Gwrach a fydd marw etto yn Rhiw Fabon.

An old woman will die *again* in Rhiw Vabon. *Adage.*

Etton, *conj.* (ed—ton) Yet, still. *adv.* Again.

A chaf——
Y gan hon etton atteb?

Shall I obtain from this female *yet* an answer. *G. ab D. ab Tudur.*

Etwa, *conj.* (ed—gwa) Yet, still. *adv.* Yet, again.
Etwaeth, *conj.* (ed—gwaeth) Yet, still. *adv.* Yet.
ETH, *s. m.* r. That is in motion, or progression; a pervading quality.
Ethais, *s. m.* (tais) What is spread or laid out.

Carafi yr ednan a'i llarian llais,
Cathlfoddawg coed, cadr i hethais.

I love the little bird with her mild voice, filling the woods with song, firm is her *seat*. *Gwalchmai.*

Ethol, *s. m.* (tol) Choice, election. *a.* Select.
Ethol, *v. a.* (tol) To elect, to select, to choose.
Etholadwy, *a.* (ethol) That may be chosen.
Etholedig, *a.* (ethol) Elected, elect, chosen. *Etholedigion i ddidranc boenau*, chosen as objects of endless torments.
Etholedigaeth, *s. m.—pl. t.* au (etholedig) The act of choosing, or electing, selection.
Etholi, *v. a.* (ethol) To elect, to choose, to select.
Etholiad, *s. m.—pl. t.* au (ethol) An election.
Etholiadawl, *a.* (etholiad) Elective, selecting.
Etholiant, *s. m.* (ethol) Election, or choice.
Etholwr, *s. m.—pl.* etholwyr (ethol—gwr) One who elects, an elector.
Etholydd, *s. m.—pl. t.* ion (ethol) An elector.
Etholyddiaeth, *s. m.* (etholydd) Electorship.

Ethrefiad, *s. m.—pl. t.* au (trefiad) Domestication.
Ethrefig, *a.* (trefig) Domestical, homely.
Ethrefigaw, *v. a.* (ethrefig) To domesticate.

Ni'm ethrefig Duw a dig-fryd oseb;
Ni loddiwn i neb newid breuddwyd.

God *will not domesticate* me with an angry-minded guest: I would not obstruct any one to change a dream. *Gwalchmai.*

Ethrefigawl, *a.* (ethrefig) Apt to domesticate.
Ethrefu, *v. a.* (trefu) To domesticate.
Ethrewyn, *v. a.* (trewyn) To conciliate, to pacify.
Ethrin, *s. m.* (trin) A conflict, a toil.

Castell Mathrafal, mwyth werin wythawg,
Du pelthiawg poeth ethrin.

The castle of Mathraval where there is a pampered furious throng, is black and open from fiery *conflict*. *Ll. P. Moch.*

Ethrinaw, *v. a.* (ethrin) To conflict; to toil.
Ethriniad, *s. m.* (ethrin) A conflicting.
Ethriniawl, *a.* (ethrin) Conflicting, toiling.
Ethryb, *s. m.—pl. t.* oedd (tryb) Cause, or occasion. *O ethryb*, because, on account of.

Penllynig fy nghof ynghyntefin,
Yn ethryb caru Carwys febin.

Distracted is my memory in the spring season, on *account* of loving a young fair one of Caerwys. *Gwalchmai.*

Ethrychwil, *s. f.—pl. t.* od (try—chwil) A lizard.
Ethrylith, *s. m.—pl. t.* au (trylith) Intuition.
Ethrylithawg, *a.* (ethrylith) That is instructed.
Ethrywyllt, *a.* (trywyllt) Ferocious, furious.
Ethrywyn, *v. a.* (trywyn) To conciliate.

Byth nid ethrywyn, heb wg,
Y ddwy-wlad i ddau olwg.

Never will the two countries *draw the attention* of his eyes so as to take away the frown. *Bedo Aurdrem.*

Pan ddel angeu——
Ni ddichon neb atteb yn
Daith rywyr, nag ethrewyn.

When death comes, no body will be able to answer to us a long journey, nor *to pacify*. *Dr. S. Cent.*

Ethu, *v. a.* (eth) To go, to proceed, to move off.

Can ethyw dy bwyll gan wyllion mynydd,
A thy hun yn agro,
Pwy wledych gwedy Iago?

Since thy intellect *is gone* with the dark spirits of the mountain, and thyself dejected, who shall reign after Iago? *Cyfoesi Myrddin.*

Ethwyf o wiw-nwyf yn iach.

I am become well from excess of passion. *D. ab Gwilym.*

Ethw, *a.* (eth) Of a pervading quality.
Ethy, *s. f.—pl. t.* au (eth) A sharp point; a spur

Greddf gwr, oed gwas,
Gwychr un dias——
Cleddyfawr glas glan,
Ethy aur a phan.

The perfection of a man, the age of a youth had the gallant one of tumult, a gashing sword blue and bright, golden *spur* and ermine. *Aneurin.*

Eu, *pron. pl.* (ei) Their, them. *Eu tadau*, their fathers; *eu hunain*, themselves; *eu lladd a wnai*, kill them he would; *garw eu bod yma*, their being here is terrible.
Euad, *s. f.—pl.* euaid (au) The pink. It is also the veronica, or speedwell, also called *gwrnerth, dail duon da, craith unnos*, and *llysiau llywelyn, euad ddu*, black yles; *euad goch*, red yles.
Euain, *v. a.* (au) To be moving, or wandering.

Bid euain alltud·
Bid ddysgethrin drud;
Bid chwannawg ynfyd i chwerthin.

Let the exile *be wandering*, let the furious be raving; let the silly be fond of laughing. *Llywarch Hen.*

Euawg, *a.* (au) Guilty, false, imperfect.
Euddon, *s. pl. aggr.* (au) Acarus, or mites.
Euddonawg, *a.* (euddon) Abounding with mites.
Euddoni, *v. a.* (euddon) To breed mites; to be-

come mity. *Blawd wedi euddoni*, meal having become mity.

Eugi, *v. a.* (aeg) To bowl, to cry out, to shriek.

Euloa, *s. pl. aggr.* (aal) Excrements, dung. *Eulon geifr*, goat's dung.

Euloni, *v. a.* (eulon) To void excrements.

Eulun, *s. m.—pl. t.* od (au—llun) A false image.

Euocâad, *s. m.* (euawg) A making guilty; a becoming guilty, or wicked.

Euocâawl, *a.* (euawg) Tending to make guilty.

Euocâu, *v. a.* (euawg) To make guilty; to become guilty.

> Euocâu a wnaethoch, a lladd y cyfiawn, yr hwn nis gwrthwynebodd chwi.
>
> You have *become guilty* in slaying the righteous, the one who has not opposed you. *W. Salisbury, Iago* 5.

Euod, *s. pl. aggr.* (au) Worms in a sheep's liver.

Euogâad, *s. m.* (euawg) A making guilty, or condemning; a becoming guilty.

Euogâu, *v. a.* (euawg) To make guilty; to condemn; to become guilty.

> Ni ddanfonodd Duw i Fab i'r byd i euogâu y byd.
>
> God did not send his Son into the world *to condemn* the world. *Marchawg Crwydrad.*

Euogfarn, *s. f.—pl. t.* au (euawg—barn) A sentence of guilt; condemnation.

Euogfarniad, *s. m.* (euogfarn) Condemnation.

Euogfarnu, *v. a.* (euogfarn) To judge guilty.

Euogi, *v. a.* (euawg) To make guilty, to condemn

Euogrwydd, *s. m.* (euawg) Guiltiness, guilt.

Euon, *s. pl. aggr.* (au) Bots, a species of worms in the entrails of horses.

Eurafal, *s. m.—pl. t.* au (aur—afal) An orange.

Eurafallach, *s. f.* (aur—afallach) An orangery.

Euraid, *a.* (aur) Golden, of gold, or like gold.

Euraidd, *a.* (aur) Of the nature of gold, golden.

Euraint, *s. m.* (aur) What is made of gold.

Euraw, *v. a.* (aur) To do with gold; to gild; to make splendid, to embellish.

> Eurodd Iorwerth, gwin-werth gan,
> Ertlynodd gwir gyfedd gwin,
> Arawd teg o eron [illegible];
> O rodd Duw, a eurodd dyn.
>
> Iorwerth, of high-prized song, [illegible] at a true banquet of wine, *embellished* a fair oration of [illegible] account, the gift of God, and which man hath *embellished*. *Sefnyn.*
>
> Swyddau a gafas sydd gyfion;
> Swydd i law eurow i gwddiorion.
>
> He obtained offices that are just; the office of his hand his [illegible] *to supply with gold*. *L. G. Cothi.*

Eurawd, *s. m.* (aur) The act of doing with gold.

Eurawg, *a.* (aur) Abounding with gold.

Eurawl, *a.* (aur) Belonging to gold; auriate.

Eurben, *s. m.—pl. t.* au (aur—pen) The gilthead, a fish; called also *benures*.

Eurbiben, *s. pl. aggr.* (aur—pib) Orpiment.

Eurdafawd, *s. m.* (aur—tafawd) A golden tongue

Eurdafodiawg, *a.* (eurdafawd) Golden tongued.

Eurdalaeth, *s. f.—pl.* eurdaleithiau (aur—talaeth) A gold fillet, or coronet.

Eurdaleithiawg, *a.* (eurdalaeth) Golden-crowned

Eurdo, *s. m.* (aur—to) A gold covering. *a.* Covered, or plated, with gold. *Llurig eurdo*, gold-covered corslet.

Eurddonen, *s. f.* (aur—dawn) The gold-gifted; an appellation for the river Jordan.

> Bood ef y talwyf [illegible],
> Ar lan Eurddonen, [illegible].
>
> Be it that I repay the bounteous Lord of lords, on the banks of Jordan, for the sake of his merits. *Ein. ab Gwalchmai.*

Eurdorch, *s. f.—pl. t.* au (aur—torch) A golden wreathe; being an ornament of distinction worn by the ancient warriors.

Eurdorchawg, *a.* (eurdorch) Having a gold wreathe

> Or a aeth Gatraeth o eurdorchogion,
> Ar neges Mynyddawg mynawg meon,
> Ni ddorth yn addwyrth o barth Brython
> Ododin wr bell well no Cynon.
>
> Of all that went to Cattraeth of *those wearing the golden torques* on the errand of Mynyddawg gentle leader of the throng, there came not void of shame on the part of the Britons of Gododin, a mighty man better than Cynon. *Aneurin.*

Eurdreth, *s. f.* (aur—treth) Gold tribute.

Eurdywod, *s. m. aggr.* (aur—tywod) Gold dust.

Eurddail, *s. pl. aggr.* (aur—dail) Gold leaves.

Eurddalen, *s. f.* (aur—dalen) Gold leaf.

Eurddalenydd, *s. m.* (eurddalen) A gold-beater.

Eurdde, *a.* (aur—de) Covered with gold, gilt.

Eurddraenen, *s. f.* (eurddrain) The barberry tree. It is also called *pren melyn*.

Eurddrain, *s. pl.* (aur—drain) Barberry trees.

Euredig, *a.* (aur) Done with gold; auriate.

Eurem, *s. f.* (aur—em) A golden jewel.

Eurenau, *s. pl. aggr.* (aur—genau) Golden lips. *a.* Golden-mouthed; eloquent.

Eurfaen, *s. m.—pl.* eurfain (aur—maen) A chrysolite.

Eurfail, *s. f.—pl.* eurfeiliau (aur—mail) A golden goblet.

Eurfal, *s. m.—pl. t.* au (aur—bal) An orange.

Eurfanadl, *s. pl. aggr.* (aur—banadl) Dyer's greenweed; also called *corfanadl*, *gruglwyn*, and *banadlos*.

Eurflawd, *s. m.* (aur—blawd) Gold powder. *Eurflawd ei ysgwyd*, his gold-powdered shield.

Eurfodrwy, *s. f.* (aur—modrwy) A gold ring.

Eurfodrwyawg, *a.* (eurfodrwy) Goldringed.

Eurfrodiad, *s. m.—pl. t.* au (aur—brodiad) Gold embroidery; gold brocade.

Eurfrodiaw, *v. a.* (aur—brodiaw) To embroider with gold; to brocade.

Eurfrodiawg, *a.* (aur—brodiawg) Embroidered with gold; brocaded with gold.

Eurgaen, *s. f.* (aur—caen) A golden surface. *a.* Covered, or sprinkled over with gold.

Eurgain, *a.* (aur—cain) Of golden brightness.

> Eurgain, merch Maelgwn Gwynedd, a [illegible] y ganwyll wrth yr adar gwylltion i ddangaws y ffordd i'w chariad.
>
> EURGAIN, the daughter of Maelgwn Gwynedd, fastened a torch to the wild fowls to shew the way to her lover. *Mabinogion.*

Eurgalch, *s. m.* (aur—calch) Gold enamel. *a.* Gold-enamelled.

> Glyw glew——
> Gwalch yn eurgalch, yn eurgaen.
>
> A brave leader, a hawk in *gold enamel*, in gold armour. *Cynddelw, i O. ab Madawg.*

Eurged, *s. f.—pl. t.* ion (aur—ced) A gold treasure

> Rhed eurged ergyd tros Wynedd;
> Rhyd gwynfyd gwan-fardd Arllechwedd.
>
> The *gold treasure* will take a course over Gwynedd; the poor bard's road to happiness in Arllechwedd. *Sefnyn.*

Eurglawr, *s. m.—pl.* eurgloriau (aur—clawr) A cover or flat surface of gold.

> Oedd ongledr gwir dir ddiys
> Ar eurglawr yr arglwydd Rhys.
>
> He was truly and doubtless the trusty protection of the *golden plate* of the lord Rhys. *Prydydd Bychan.*

Eurgoron, *s. f.* (aur—coron) Gold crown.

Eurgoronawg, *a.* (eurgoron) Golden crowned.

Eurgrawn, *s. f.* (aur—crawn) A collection of gold; a treasure.

> Or cladd dyn dir dyn arall er cuddiaw peth ynddo, [illegible] cyfraith a gaiff perchennog y tir am agori daiar, ac y guddfa; eithr eurgrawn fydd, canys brenin biau bob eurgrawn.
>
> If a person shall dig the land of another person for the purpose of hiding something in it, the owner of the land shall have fourpence in law for opening the earth, and the hoard; except it shall be a *treasure of gold*, for the king owns every *hoard of gold*. *Welsh Laws.*

Eurgrwydr, *a.* (aur—crwydr) Strewed with gold, scattered over with gold.

> Tal ysgwyd eurgrwydr torynt yn fuan.

> The front of the *gold-bespangled* shield they quickly broke.
> *O. Cyfeiliawg.*

Euriad, *s. m.—pl. t.* au (aur) A doing with gold.

Eurin, *a.* (aur) Of gold, like gold, golden.

> Ar llaw Owain hael, hawl ddilis
> Gwrhaich, y mae gorfwch eurin.

> Upon the hand of generous Owain, the pure claim of heroic pride, there is the *golden* casket. *Cynddelw.*

Eurinaw, *v. a.* (eurin) To make like gold.

Eurinawg, *a.* (eurin) Having the nature of gold.

Eurinawl, *a.* (eurin) Of the nature of gold.

> Ti eryr ongyr angerddawl,
> Tau yth lys lestri eurinawl.

> Thou eagle of the vehement spear, thine the court with *golden* vessels. *Ll. P. Moch, i D. ab Owain.*

Eurinllys, *s. m.* (eurin—llys) St. John's wort.

Eurlaw, *a.* (aur—llaw) Gold handed; munificent.

Eurlen, *s. f.—pl. t.* i (aur—llen) Arras.

Eurlin, *s. m.* (aur—llin) The raw silk.

Eurliw, *s. m.* (aur—lliw) Gold colour. *a.* Of the colour of gold; yellow-hued.

Eurliliw, *s. m.* (aur—lliw) That is of golden colour; orpiment, or yellow arsenic.

Eurllys, *s. m. aggr.* (aur—llys) Orache. It is also called, *y llew gwyn.*

Eurmydeddawg, *a.* (aur—mydeddawg) Abounding with golden circles or arches.

> Eurmydeddawg lyn erbyn eurban—
> Eurgyrn buelin; buelgyrn ban,
> Erioed y porthaist parth ag attan.

> The *gold-circling* beverage the golden flagon receives; the golden horns of the buffalo; the high horns of the ox, thou hast ever directed towards us. *Cynddelw, i Mad. ab Meredydd.*

Euron, *s. f.* (aur—on) The bean-trefoil tree.

> Euron delis bryd,
> Allmyr eich gillryd.

> The *laburnum* held in mind that your wild nature was foreign.
> *Taliesin, Cad. Goddeu.*

Eurrwy, *s. m.—pl. t.* ion (aur—rhwy) A gold ring

Eurrwyawg, *a.* (eurrwy) Wearing a gold ring.

Eursiderawg, *a.* (aur—siderawg) Laced with gold

Eurwaith, *s. m.* (aur-gwaith) A gold work.

Eurwallt, *s. m.* (aur—gwallt) Golden hair. *Eurwallt y forwyn*, common hair-moss.

Eurwawd, *s. m.* (aur—gwawd) Golden panegyric

Eurwawn, *a.* (aur—gwawn) Golden gossamer.

> Teifi, dwfr tyfiad eurwawn,
> Gad i'r dyn gadeiriaw dawn.

> Teifi, whose water is the source of *golden flying circles*, let the fair person establish grace. *D. ab Gwilym.*

Eurwawr, *s. f.* (aur—gwawr) A golden dawn.

Eurwch, *s. m.* (aur) What is made of gold.

Eurwedd, *s. f.* (aur—gwedd) A golden, or fine appearance. *a.* Golden-hued, yellow-hued.

Eurwernen, *s. f.* (aur—gwern) Lime tree.

Eurwialen, *s. f.* (aur-gwiail) Golden-rod.

Eurych, *s. m.—pl. t.* od (aur) A goldfiner, a worker in gold; a goldsmith; a worker of metal; a tinker.

> Mal dau eurych.

> Like two *tinkers*. *Adage.*

Eurychaeth, *s. m.* (eurych) The trade, or art, of a goldsmith; the art of working metals.

> Er achub creft eurychaeth,
> I efail o ddail ydd aeth.

> To preserve the trade of *jewelry* she went to a smithy of leaves.
> *D. ab Gwilym, i Forfudd.*

Eurychawl, *a.* (eurych) Of a goldsmith's trade.

Eurychwaith, *s. m.* (gwaith) Goldsmith's work.

Eurydd, *s. m.—pl. t.* ion (aur) A goldsmith.

Euryll, *s. m. dim.* (aur) A golden jewel or toy.

Euryn, *s. m. dim.* (aur) A golden trinket.

Eurysgwyd, *s. f.* (aur—ysgwyd) A gold shield. *a.* Having a golden shield.

EW, *s. m. r.* What has aptness to glide; what is clear, smooth, or sleek.

Ewa, *s. m. dim.* (ewythr) An uncle, in fond speech

Ewach, *s. m.* (gwach) A weakling, or a fribble.

Ewaint, *s. pl.* (gwaint) Youth, young people.

> Bid anhygar diriad, bid fer pob ewaint,
> Bid hanaint i dylodedd,
> Bid addfwyn yn ancwyn medd.

> Let the mischievous be disgusting, let all *young people* be strong, to poverty let old age come, let mead be pleasant in the feast.
> *Llywarch Hen.*

Ewerddon, *s. f.* (gwerddon) A green spot of ground; the Welsh name of Ireland.

Ewerddonig, *a.* (ewerddon) Like green Erin.

Ewi, *v. a.* (ew) To listen, to hear, to attend. *Ewais er lais adar*, I have listened to the song of birds.

Ewiar, *a.* (ew) Smooth; clear; sleek, glossy.

> Nis car——
> Meirch mawrthig, frwythig, ffraeth, anwar,
> Ffrawddus, a pharciddiau ewiar.

> He loves not thy magnificent steeds, prolific, noisy, unruly, and wanton, nor the *sleek herds*. *Ll. P. Moch, i Lywelyn I.*

Ewig, *s. f.—pl. t.* od (ew—ig) A hind; a deer.

> Ewigod sy yn rhodiaw,
> Yn weddwon ry drymion draw;
> Rhedant, a neidiant yn wyllt,
> Eisiau gwr anna gorwyllt.

> *Hinds* are wandering about yonder, in widowhood and very heavy; they run, they wildly skip about for want of a wanton bodied husband. *T. Prys, i afyn torw.*

Ewin, *s. f.—pl. t.* edd (ew—in) A nail of the fingers, or toes; a talon, or claw, of birds; a division of the horny substance of the foot of any animal, that is divided, or cloven. *Ewin ebill*, the screw, or edge of an auger.

Ewinallt, *s. f.* (ewin—allt) A steep cliff.

Ewinaw, *v. a.* (ewin) To use the nails, to claw.

> Da i gwyddost, yd i gweddyn,
> Yn i dop ewinaw dyn.

> Well thou knowest they suit thee, *to claw* a person's head.
> *Rhis. Iorwerth.*

Ewinawg, *a.* (ewin) Having nails, or claws.

> Clywn wrach——
> Ewinawg, grafangawg gref.

> I could hear a hag, *furnished with claws* and strong of grasp.
> *D. ab Gwilym.*

Ewinbren, *s. m.—pl. t.* i (ewin—pren) A girder, or binder, in carpentry.

Ewinfedd, *s. f.—pl. t.* i (ewin—bedd) A nail's measure, a nail.

> Ni chai——
> 'Winfedd oll o'i anfodd wr.

> Thou wilt not, man, get a *nail's breadth* against his will.
> *E. Brwynllys.*

Ewingraff, *a.* (ewin—craff) That is sharp clawed. *s. f.* A grimalkin.

Ewingrwn, *a.* (ewin—crwn) That is turned as a nail. *s. m.* German text writing.

Ewinor, *s. f.* (ewin—gor) A whitlow.

Ewinrew, *s. f.* (ewin—rhew) Nipping frost; numbness of the fingers, or toes, from a cold. *a.* Frostbitten.

Ewinwasg, *s. f.* (ewin—gwasg) An agnail.

Ewn, *a.* (gwn) Powerful; impetuous; bold.

Ewnder, *s. m.* (ewn) Impetuosity; boldness.

Ewni, *v. n.* (ewn) To become impetuous.

Ewybr, *s. f.* (gwybr) What abounds with velocity; the firmament; the atmosphere.

Ewybr, *a.* (gwybr) Having velocity, full of motion; quick; nimble. *Yn ewybr*, quickly.

——Gwir mai dihiraf,
Rhag ei ddarfod, ddyfod yr haf
A llednais wybr ewybraf
A llewych haul.—

Truly it is vexatious, lest it should have an end, that ever the summer should come, and the gairish *swiftest* moving welkin, and the smiling sun. *D. ab Gwilym.*

Ewybraidd, *a.* (ewybr) Of a swift nature.

Ewybraw, *v. a.* (ewybr) To move with velocity, to brandish; to vibrate; to glitter, to shine with a trembling light; to dart.

Ewybrawl, *a.* (ewybr) Apt to be swift.

Ewybrddrud, *a.* (ewybr—drud) Swiftly-fierce.

Ymlithraw a oreg Arthur y gantho, a'i guraw yn ewybrddrud.

Arthur slided out of his hold, beating him with blows *swiftly-fierce.* *Gr. ab Arthur.*

Ewybredd, *s. m.* (ewybr) Velocity, swiftness.

Ewybren, *s. f.* (ewybr) Firmament, atmosphere.

Ewybrenawl, *a.* (ewybren) Atmospherical.

Ewybriad, *s. m.* (ewybr) A moving with velocity.

Ewydn, *a.* (gwydn) Tough, clammy, viscous.

Ewydnaw, *v. n.* (ewydn) To become viscous.

Ewydnedd, *s. m.* (ewydn) Toughness.

Ewydnu, *v. n.* (ewydn) To become viscous.

Yn barawd ei waed ewydn.

Ready in his clammy blood. *D. ab Gwilym.*

Ewydd, *s. m.* (gwydd) Presence.

Ewyll, *s. m.* (ew—yll) The will, the action, or determination of the mind.

Ewylliad, *s. m.—pl. t.* au (ewyll) A volition.

Ewylliaw, *v. a.* (ewyll) To exert the will.

Ewyllu, *v. a.* (ewyll) To exert the will, to will.

Dafod ye talau,
Huddid ewyllai,
Cyn bu clawr glas
Bedd Gwrfoling frang.

If he did requite there is no disgrace, Huddid *willed* it, before the grave of the gigantic Gwrfoling became a green sward.

Ewyllys, *s. m.—pl. t.* ion (ewyll) Will, inclination, desire.

Dwyparth rhodd yw ewyllys.

Two parts of a gift is the *will.* *Adage.*

Y genedl noeth ddiarfau a ymchwelynt ar ffo i'r lle y ceffynt wnawd ac amddiffyn, ac ni bu un gohir, yn y lle daly Gillamwri a wneuthbwyd, a'i gymhell wrth ewyllys Arthur.

The naked and unarmed nation returned back flying to the place where they could obtain shelter and protection; and there was no delay, for immediately Gillamwri was laid hold of, and dealt with according to the *will* of Arthur. *Gr. ab Arthur.*

Ewyllysgar, *a.* (ewyllys) Willing, complying.

Ewyllysgarwch, *s. m.* (ewyllysgar) Willingness.

Ewyllysiad, *s. m.—pl. t.* au (ewyllys) A willing, or wishing; volition.

Ewyllysiaw, *v. a.* (ewyllys) To will, to desire.

Ewyllysiawl, *a.* (ewyllys) Voluntary, willing.

Ewyllysiolrwydd, *s. m.* (ewyllysiawl) Voluntariness, willingness.

Ewyllysiwr, *s. m.—pl.* ewyllysiwyr (ewyllys—gwr) A willer, a desirer. *Ewyllysiwr da*, a well-wisher.

Ewyn, *s. m.—pl. t.* oedd (ew—yn) Foam, spume, froth. *Malu ewyn*, to foam, to scatter foam about.

Ewyn dwfr addewid gwas.

A youth's promise is like the *froth of water.* *Adage.*

Ewynawg, *a.* (ewyn) Foamy, full of froth.

Ewynawl, *a.* (ewyn) Foaming, or apt to foam.

Ewynedd, *s. m.* (ewyn) Foaminess, frothiness.

Ewynfriw, *s. m.* (ewyn—briw) The spraying of foam. *a.* Foam-spraying.

Ewyngaen, *s. f.* (ewyn—caen) A surface of foam, a covering of foam. *Hoen ewyngaen*, the briskness of the foamy surface.

Ewyngant, *s. m.—pl.* ewyngaint (ewyn—cant) A circle of foam, or foamy circle; the breakers on the sea shore.

Ei gwallt melyn——
Gorllaw y wen-gern gorthaw ewyngant.

Her yellow hair around the white chin, passing the hue of the *foamy circle.* *D. ab Gwilym.*

Ewyniad, *s. m.—pl. t.* au (ewyn) A foaming.

Ewynllyd, *a.* (ewyn) Apt to produce foam.

Ewynllydrwydd, *s. m.* (ewynllyd) Foaminess.

Ewynriw, *s. m.* (ewyn—rhiw) The fall of foam.

Molaf iawn i dawn, gur gwawn gwawd chwarg;
Fliw ewynriw gwyn-friw gweneg —
Gloew-deg Wenllian.

I will praise her of perfect accomplishment, of the hue of the sweet flowing gossamer, like the passing white *falling foam* of the wave: Gwenllian brightly fair. *Cynddelw.*

Ewynu, *v. a.* (ewyn) To foam, to froth; to gather into foam, froth, or scum; to despumate.

Ewythr, *s. m.—pl.* ewythredd (gwythr) An uncle; also a term of respect to an elderly man. *Ewythr a modryb*, uncle and aunt; familiarly used in the same sense as *master and dame*, or *gaffer and gammer*, in English.

Ewythr yw brawd tad, neu fam, neu hendad, neu henfam, neu orhendad, neu orhenfam.

An *uncle* is a brother of a father, or mother, or grand father, or grand mother, or great grand father, or great grand mother. *Welsh Laws.*

FF.

FFA, *s. m. r.* What is enveloped, or covered over. *s. pl. aggr.* Beans. *Ffa ffreinig*, French beans; *ffa cochion*, scarlet beans; *ffa y gors*, buck beans, or marsh trefoil; *ffa y moch*, henbane.

Ffaced, *s. m.* (ffag) Curd; posset curds.

Ffad, *s. f.—pl. t.* au (ffa—ad) That is disguised or masked.

Ffo a wna'r Bedo o'r badell; drew oen,
Ffad gwesteion ffiaidd gywaith;
Ffagl o wellt, fal ffagl o wellt;
Ffiaidd ffwyn,
Ffagiodd fydd ffosyddyn,
Ffad anghlod englyn.

That Bedo will run away out of the pan, disgusting is the conduct of the youths of hidden connection, his work is all wind, like a blaze of straw, the babbling of the lowest of the ditches is stave of the scandal verse of the dirty fellow. *Bedo Brwynllys, i B. Brwynllys.*

Ffadu, *v. n.* (ffad) To be disguised; to be covered over.

Ffadw, *a.* (ffad) Of a dark bay colour; dusky.

Ffael, *s. f.—pl. t.* ion (ael) A failing; a fault.

Ffaeledig, *a.* (ffael) Failed, miscarried; fallible.

Ffaeliad, *s. m.—pl. t.* au (ffael) A failing.

Ffaelu, *v. a.* (ffael) To fail, to miss, to miscarry.

Ffaen, *s. f. dim.* (ffa) A bean, a single bean.

Ffaeth, *a.* (ffy—aeth) Luxuriant, fruitful, rich, fecund; mellow, ripe. *Tir gwydd a thir ffaeth*, wild land and cultivated land.
Ffaethawl, *a.* (ffaeth) Tending to make mellow.
Ffaethder, *s. m.* (ffaeth) Luxuriancy, richness, fecundity; mellowness, uberosity.
Ffaethedig, *a.* (ffaeth) Fecundated, mellowed.
Ffaethedd, *s. m* (ffaeth) Luxuriance, mellowness
Ffaethiad, *s. m.—pl. t.* au (ffaeth) A mellowing, a ripening; fecundation.
Ffaethiant, *s. m.* (ffaeth) Uberosity, fecundity.
Ffaethu, *v. a.* (ffaeth) To make rich, mellow, or fruitful, to ameliorate; to become luxuriant; to ripen; to fecundate.
Ffaethus, *a.* (ffaeth) Luxuriant, of a rich quality.
Ffaethusrwydd, *s. m.* (ffaethus) Mellowness.
Ffag, *s. f.—pl. t.* oedd (ffa) What unites together, or meets, in a point.
Ffagiad, *s. m.—pl. t.* au (ffag) A gathering round to a point.
Ffagl, *s. f.—pl.* ffaglau (ffag) A blaze, a flame.
Ffaglawg, *a.* (ffagl) Blazing, or flaming.
Ffaglawr, *s. m.—pl.* ffaglorion (ffagl) A conflagrator, a blazer.
Ffagliad, *s. m.—pl. t.* au (ffagl) A blazing.
Ffaglu, *v. a.* (ffagl) To blaze, to flame, to conflagrate; to be all in a flame.
Ffaglwr, *s.m.—pl.* ffaglwyr (ffagl—gwr) A blazer, one who bears a blaze; one who sets on fire.
Ffaglydd, *s. m.—pl. t.* ion (ffagl) A blazer.
Ffagod, *s. f.—pl. t.* au (ffag) A faggot, a bundle of sticks, or twigs.

> Coed mawr yn ffagodau man.
>
> Great trees in small *faggots*. *H. Dafi.*

Ffagoden, *s. f. dim.—pl. t.* i (ffagod) A faggot.
Ffagodi, *v. a.* (ffagod) To faggot, to bundle.
Ffai, *s. m.* (ffa) An extreme; a stop; a cessation; forgetfulness, or a cessation of memory.
Ffaig, *s. f.—pl.* ffeigiau (ffai) An extremity, or farthest point; a stop; a turn: a nonplus, or embarrassment. *Mae e mewn ffaig yn awr*, he is under an embarrassment at present; *pa fodd y daetho'r ffaig hyn?* How did he come out of this difficulty?

> Rhaff gadarn, ryw ffaig ydoedd,
> Duw yn dost, am danad oedd!
>
> A strong rope, severely, O God! the kind of *restraint* that was round thee. *I. ab H. Cae Llwyd, i Grist.*
>
> Ffrawd-grych fal rhaiadr ffryd-graig
> O ffrydiau ffynnoniau ffaig.
>
> A boiling agitation, like the cataract of the rock of torrents, from the streams or the springs of *extremity*. *R. Goch Eryri.*
>
> ——Boneddigion medrus
> Sydd a'u gweddi yn mhob ffaig
> I gysuro'i wraig wylofus.
>
> Gentlefolks of information are, with their prayers, in every *embarrassment*, ready to comfort the mourning widow. *S. Morgan.*

Ffain, *s. m.* (ffai) What rises round as a cone.
Ffair, *s. f.—pl.* ffeiriau (ffai) An eminence; a public place; a forum; a fair.

> Ef a gyfyd ffair rhwng pedair ffynnon.
>
> There will arise an *eminence* between four springs. *Taliesin.*
>
> O daw i'r ffair, difa i'r dydd.
>
> If he comes to the *public spot*, may the day determine it. *D. ab Gwilym.*
>
> Pawb o'r ffair
> A ddengys a bys dy boen.
>
> Every body of the *fair* will with the finger point at thy torture. *D. ab Gwilym, i'r pawl haf.*

Ffaith, *s. m.—pl.* ffeithiau (ffai) A fact, an act.
Ffal, *s. m.—pl. t.* au (ffa) What goes round, a closure; the heel of a shoe.

Ffald, *s. f.—pl. t.* iau (ffal) A fold; a pinfold.

> Uchel
> Ei leferydd with fugeilydd, gwylwyr ffaldau.
>
> Loud his voice to the shepherds, the watchmen of the *folds*. *Bleddyn Fardd.*

Ffaling, *s. f.—pl. t.* au (ffal) A mantle, a cloak.

> Mal y Gwyddyl am y ffaling.
>
> Like the Irishman for the *cloak*. *Adage.*
>
> Guto wnaeth ffaling gotwm.
>
> Guto has made a shaggy *cloak*. *Guto y Glyn.*

Ffalingaw, *v. a.* (ffaling) To cloak, or to robe.
Ffalingiad, *s. m.* (ffaling) A cloaking, a robing.
Ffalm, *a.* (ffal) Turning round; whirling.—*Gwynt ffalm*, a whirlwind; a gust of wind.
Ffals, *a.* (ffal) Covered, or masked; false, deceitful; unfaithful.

> Yr oriais—cabler ei bryd,
> Coluddyn ffals celwyddawg,
> Cnyciau ci yn cnecciau cawg.
>
> The clock—cursed be its face, with its *false* guts full of lies and its dog-joints knocking against a bowl. *D. ab Gwilym.*

Ffalsder, *s. m.* (ffals) Falseness, or deceitfulness.
Ffalsedd, *s. m.* (ffals) Falseness, deceitfulness.
Ffalst, *a.* (ffals) Masked, false, deceitful, wily.
Ffalstedd, *s. m.* (ffalst) Dissimulation, falsity.

> O achaws trais, a bradiad, anwiredd, ac amryw ffalstedd.
>
> On account of oppression, and treachery, and injustice, and a variety of *deceit*. *Car. o Langarfan.*

Ffalsu, *v. a.* (ffals) To use falsity, to deceive.
Ffall, *s. f.* (ffy—all) What spreads out, what is squabby, bulky, or thick. *a.* Broadset.
Ffallach, *s. c.—pl. t.* au (ffall) A short punch, one that walks waddlingly. *Dos y ffallach front!* Begone, thou nasty squab! *Y fath ffallach yw efe!* What a punch he is!

> Llawer cell yn bon ddiffaith bellach,
> Llawer ffau ellyll, llawer ffallach,
> Llawer cyw wyth-ryw cyfathrach dan lwyn,
> Llawer twyn o frwyn a chyfrinach.
>
> Many a chamber in ruins at length will be in her, many a monster's den, many a *squabby spright*, many a brat from the connexion of eight breeds under a hedge, many a tump of rushes and sacred haunts. *L. G. Cothi, i Gaerlleon*

Ffallachawg, *a.* (ffallach) Of a squabby form.
Ffan, *s. m.* (ffa) A covering, or surface.
Ffaner, *s. m.* (ffan) A supreme, a sovereign.
Ffanwg, *s. m.* (ffan) Coveredness, shelter.
Ffanygl, *s. m.* (ffanwg) What covereth; protection; safety.

> Ni phoened neb wrth ffenestr,
> Rhwng ffanygl nos a rhos rhestr,
> Heb huno, fal i'm poenwyd.
>
> No body has been tormented under a window, what with the *covering* of night, and a pane of lattice work, divested of sleep, as I have been tormented. *D. ab Gwilym.*

Ffaon, *s. pl. aggr.* (ffa) Pod fruit, beans.
Ffaonwydd, *s pl.* (ffaon—gwydd) Bean trees.
Ffar, *s. m.* (ffa) That extends out, or over.
Ffaraon, *s. pl. aggr.* (ffar) The higher powers.
Ffargod, *s f.—pl. t.* au (ffar—cod) A big paunch.
Ffas, *s. m.—pl. t.* au (ffy—as) A ligature, a band.
Ffasg, *s. f.—pl. t.* au (ffas) A tie, a bundle, a faggot, or any things bound together.
Ffasgawl, *a.* (ffasg) Being bundled, or tied up.
Ffasgedig, *a.* (ffasg) Bundled, fagotted, tied up.
Ffasgell, *s. f. dim.—pl. t.* au (ffasg) A bundle.

> Cynghawau a gydymgydiant y naill yn y llall, oni byddont yn un ffasgell.
>
> The combined rhymes are connected one with the other, so that they become as one *tissue*. *Barddas.*

Ffasgellawg, *a.* (ffasgell) In bundles, or bunches.
Ffasgelliad, *s. m.—pl. t.* au (ffasgell) A bundling.
Ffasgellu, *v. a.* (ffasgell) To tie up in a bundle.

Ffagiad, *s. m.—pl. t.* au (ffag) A ligation, a tying in a bundle; a bundling.
Ffagu, *v. a.* (ffag) To bind, tie in a bundle.
Ffat, *s. m.—pl. t.* iau (ffy—at) A smart blow, a pat.
Ffatiad, *s. m.—pl. t.* au (ffat) A patting, a striking smartly and lightly.
Ffatiaw, *v. a.* (ffat) To strike lightly, to pat.
Ffatiwr, *s. m.—pl.* ffatiwyr (ffat—gwr) A patter.
Ffau, *s. f.—pl.* ffenau (ffa) A den, or cave, a hole; a lurking-place of wild beasts.

Nid cau ffau ar lwynawg.

Not to shut a *den* on a fox. *Adage.*

Tywyllodd wybr fantrline
Y ffordd, fel petwn mewn ffau.

The mantle of the firmament darkened the way as if I were in a dungeon. *D. ab Gwilym, i'r niwl.*

Ffaw, *s. m.* (ffy—aw) A flowing from; radiancy; glory; pre-eminence; honour.

Canys Rhydderch biau ffaw,
A Chymmru oll y danaw.

For Rhydderch enjoys the *honour*, and all Wales subject to him. *Myrddin.*

Brodyr a'm bwyad a ddyg Duw rhagof;
Fy anffawd a'u gorug!
Ni obrynynt ffaw er ffug.

Brothers to me there were whom God hath taken from me; my misfortune was the cause! they did not acquire *glory* through deceit. *Llywarch Hen.*

Caraf i meusydd a'u man feillion arnaw,
Man yd gafas ffaw ffyrf orfoledd.

I love its fields and their delicate trefoils its covering, where I obtained *glory* of lasting celebrity. *H. ab Owain Gwynedd.*

Per eisor aesawr weiniflad,
Pand rhagdaw bu ffaw, bu ffyagtad!

The guardian chief and manager of the shield, preceding him what *glory* was there seen, and what haste! *Ll. P. Moch.*

Gwr a obryn ffaw heb ffo un droedfedd;
Nid mawr o'i drawedd nab ni dreisia.

A man who merits *fame* without ever retreating a foot; he is not great in transgression who doth not oppress. *Llygad Gwr, i R. ab Madawg.*

Ffaw, *a.* (ffy—aw) Radiant, glorious, honourable.

Llwyddid fy nghywydd y'nghywir grad;
Y'nghrefydd, yn ffydd, yn ffaw gnawd.

Prosperous be my muse in perfect orthodoxy; in religion, in faith, in a *glorious* pursuit. *Gwalchmai.*

Duw' wyd——
Brenin pob ffin, pob ffaw dynged.

God' thou art the sovereign of every extremity, and every *glorious* destiny. *Ll. P. Moch.*

Ffawd, *s. m.—pl.* ffodiau (ffaw) Fortune, luck; fate; prosperity; happiness.

Ni ladd anmraint ffawd.

Want of privilege will not hinder *good fortune*. *Adage.*

Gwrtai ffawd hyd frawd yn dir.

Fortune must be *followed* till doomsday. *Adage.*

Da fu ffawd ei wawd i Wiwon ddewin;
Da Fyrddin, a'i lin o lwyth Meirchiawn.

Good was the *fortune* of the praise of Gwion the divine; and good to Myrddin, with his descent from the tribe of Meirchion. *Befwyn.*

Ffawdus, *a.* (ffawd) Fortunate, or prosperous.
Ffawdd, *s. m.* (ffaw) Radiation, splendour.
Ffawg, *s. m.* (ffaw) Delight, pleasure. *a.* Delightful, glorious, pleasing.

Dy rad a'th gariad——
A gaffwyf, perffeith-nwyf ffawg,
Trwy gur Brenin trugarawg.

Thy grace and thy love may I obtain, a perfect state of *pleasure*, through the suffering of the merciful king. *D. ab Gwilym.*

Gwr a oedd un ffydd, a ffawg,
A'r tri gwir lwr trugarawg.

A man that is one in faith and *delight* with the three truly merciful divine Persons. *H. ab D. ab I. ab Rhys.*

Merch a gawsant, ffyniant ffawg'
Mair oedd hon.——

A woman they found, *delightful* fortune' this was Mary. *T. Derllys.*

Ffawliw, *s. m.* (ffaw—lliw) A splendid yellow hue. *a.* Of a yellow hue.

Rhag Madawg—o feirch——
Lliaws coch cain-wiw,
Cynrau ffordd ffawliw,
Ffrwing rhi rededdwys.

Before Madog, there are of steeds, numbers of bay truly fair, white-fronted of the gold-coloured road, and on the king's horses running led by hand. *Gwalchmai.*

Ffawr, *s. m.—pl.* fforiau (ffaw) A running from.

Mawr yw i'm draig, wawr ffawr ffaw ffwyr ffyagtad,
Ffyng lew cad, cad wallaw,
Bood addef nef yn eiddiaw,
A'r byd achan y danaw.

It is great to my sovereign, the light of the *course of glory* in the vehement pursuit, the active lion of battle distributing treasure, that the mansion of heaven should be his, and all the world submitting to him. *Phylip Brydydd, i Rys Ieuanc.*

Ffawwydd, *s. m. aggr.* (ffaw—gwydd) Pines, firs, *Coed ffawwydd*, fir trees; *byrddau ffawwydd*, deal boards.

Morawg a Moryd,
Ffawwydd ryniewyd.

Morawg and Moryd were made prosperous in *pines*. *Taliesin.*

Ffawwyddawg, *a.* (ffawwydd) Abounding with pines.
Ffawwydden, *s. f. dim.* (ffawwydd) A pine, or fir-tree.
Ffawydd, *s. pl. aggr.* (ffa—gwydd) Beech wood.

Mal y moch am y ffawydd.

Like the swine after the beech *trees*. *Adage.*

Ffawydden, *s. f.* (ffawydd) A beech tree.
FFE, *s. m. r.* What is outward or exterior.
Ffed, *s. f.—pl. t.* ion (ffe) An outside, appearance, or presence; demeanour, carriage, manner, or behaviour. *a.* Exposed; outward.

Truth noeth! traethu a wnaethost,
Na chaent hwy (gwn arhwyn tost,
Groen du ffol, groen yw dy ffed)
Gwrydd nef yn agored.

Manifest ribaldry' thou hast declared that they shall not obtain (I know of sad complaint, thou foolish black skin of rough outside) the portals of heaven open. *Dr. S. Cent, i'r llyfr.*

Pwy a wnai, pe annuwiol,
Niwed i ddyn di ffed ffol.

Who would, even if ungodly, do harm to a foolish person void of demeanour. *Edm. Prys.*

Gwr annuwiol ffol ei ffed,
Huw Machno cono carned.

An ungodly man of foolish conduct, Huw Machno a brazen chap. *R. Wyn ab Cadwaladr.*

Yr henddyn o'r cornel, wrth wrando'r ei chwedl
A'i 'tebai e'n uchel, yn dra ffel ei ffed.
Mi'th ddysgaf.——

The old man at the fireside, listening to his narrative, answered him aloud, with a most impressive *demeanour*, I will instruct thee. *H. ab Ieu. ab Robert.*

Ffedawg, *a.* (ffed) Covering over, or before. *s. f.—pl.* ffedogau, What is put on, before, or to appear in, a covering; an apron.
Ffedawnen, *s f.* (ffed) A neck-cloth, or cravat.
Ffedel, *s. f.—pl. t.* au (ffed) The lap. *Gosoda hwn yn dy ffedel*, Place this in thy lap.
Ffedegaid, *s. f. pl.* ffedogeidiau (ffedawg) An apron-full.
Ffedogi, *v. a.* (ffedawg) To put into the apron.
Ffedon, *s. f.* (ffed) What is put before; a screen.
Ffedonas, *s. f.* (ffedon) What screens; a fan.
Ffedu, *v. a.* (ffed) To place forward, or outward; to expose, to make manifest.
Ffedus, *a.* (ffed) Apparent, manifest, plain.

Ffedus wad——
Ffei! galw a Duw' ffagio'dd wyd.

A manifest denial: fie' calling upon God' thou art dissembling. *Edm. Prys, i W. Cynwal.*

Ffei, *interj.* (ffe) Begone! off! shame! fie!

Ffei o trwarctyd am ffe;
Ni ffy hanaid; ffei hono'

Fie that youth should run away; old age will not flee; *fie* upon him! *W. Cynwal.*

Ffei bono ganwaith! ni bu i ddiffeithiach;
Ffei o'i lis-olwg! a phwy sy waeiach!

Shame on it a hundred times! there never was its worse; *shame* of his sneaking look! and who can be more vile! *T. Prys.*

Ffeiad, *s. m.* (ffei) A shaming away; a fying.
Ffeiaw, *v. a.* (ffei) To put to shame; to hoot.
Ffeigiad, *s. m.* (ffaig) A driving to extremity.
Ffeigiaw, *v. a.* (ffaig) To drive to extremity; to embarrass, to puzzle, to nonplus.
Ffeigiawl, *a.* (ffaig) Ultimate, extreme; embarrassing, or puzzling.
Ffeinid, *s. m.* (ffain) A rising into a point.
Ffeinidwydd, *s. pl.* (ffeinid—gwydd) Pine trees.

Ffeinidwydd y'nghyntedd,
Cadair gyngwrysedd.

Pine trees in the porch, a seat of disputation. *Taliesin.*

Ffeiriad, *s. m.* (ffair) An exposing in a mart; a trafficking; a changing.
Ffeiriaw, *v. a.* (ffair) To exchange, to change.

Saffir faen ni's ffeiriaf fi
Sy'n Mhenal dros fy mhoeni.

The sapphire stone, that is in Penal, I will not *exchange* though I were to be tortured. *S. Fychan.*

Ffeiriawl, *a.* (ffair) Commercial; trading.
Ffeiriwr, *s. m.—pl.* ffeirwyr (ffair—gwr) A chapman, a trafficker; a changer.
Ffeithiad, *s. m.—pl. t.* au (ffaith) An effectuating.
Ffeithiant, *s. m.* (ffaith) Effectuation; operation.
Ffeithiaw, *v. a.* (ffaith) To effectuate; to make.

Hyn nid ffaith yn ffaeth pob sarug;
Gwr gorfawr gorffwng pan amug.

This will not *render* pliant every stubborn one; a great man is irritable in the extreme when put on the defence. *Ll. P. Moch.*

Ffeithiawl, *a.* (ffaith) Effectuating; operative.
Ffeithiedig, *a.* (ffaith) Effectuated; performed.
Ffèl, *a.* (ffy—el) Subtile, fine; cunning, wily. *Ffèl cadno,* wily is the fox.

Phylip ab Rhys gyff hael-wych,
Ffèl yw i gorff.——

Phylip the son of Rhys of a generous and brave stock, *fine* is his body. *L. G. Cothi.*

Gwiliwch, mae'n ffèl y gelyn,
A'i dwyll yn bradychu dyn.

Take heed, the enemy is *crafty,* with his deception deluding man. *Parch. E. Evans.*

Ffèlaidd, *a.* (ffèl) Of a subtile nature; sly.
Ffelaig, *s. m.* (ffel—aig) Preceptive source; a sovereign, or governor.

Cyflafan taer-dan rhag teyrnon,
Cain ffelaig, pen draig, a phen dragon.

The devastation of fierce fire precedes the prince, a splendid *source of knowledge,* chief dragon, a chief leader. *Gwalchmai.*

Ffelaig, *a.* (ffel—aig) Preceptive; governing.

A dwy ddraig ffelaig ffaw gyman,
Fal deu-lew ny'n dylochasan'.

And the two *leading* dragons of glorious onset, like two lions they were protecting us. *Ll. P. Moch.*

Greddfawl Lywelyn, grym geir-bar torf,
Terfynwyd ei amser!
Ysgrud fud draig ffelaig ffer,
Ysgwn ysgwyd rhwydd rhagder.

The accomplished Llywelyn, the theme of the sweetly-speaking host, his time is closed! The dragon *foremost,* and mighty, with the uplifted shield ready in resisting, is now a dumb corpse. *Ll. P. Moch, i Lywelyn I.*

Ffelder, *s. m.* (ffèl) Subtlety; craftiness, wiliness.
Ffeldra, *s. m.* (ffèl) Subtileness; craftiness.
Ffeliant, *s. m.* (ffèl) Subtlety; cunning, crafft.
Ffelrwydd, *s. m.* (ffèl) Subtileness; craftiness.
Ffelu, *v. a.* (ffèl) To act subtlely; to become subtile, wily, or discreet.
Ffen, *s. f.* (ffy—en) Flowing principle; air.
Ffenestr, *s. f.—pl.* ffenestri (ffen—estr) An opening, or passage; an air hole; a window. It is also figuratively used, the same as *gwerddyr* and *ffwrch,* for the vagina, in speaking of animals; as *ffenestr buwch; ffenestr pob benyw.*

Rhieingerdd Efa a fawreynt;
Tremyn y treiddwni trefyn a gedwynt,
Treiddie glyw Powys, pei a'm gelynt;
Pan dreiddwn yno yn ydd oeddynt,
Trwy ffenestri gwydr ydd ym gwelynt.

The epithalamium of Eva they were used to extol; in the scene I was used to pass through they were used to keep order, should they bear with me in the place of audience of the sovereign of Powys; when I appeared there as they were present, through glass *windows* they beheld me. *Cynddelw.*

Ffenestrawg, *a.* (ffenestr) Having windows.
Ffenestrawl, *a.* (ffenestr) Fenestral; windowed.

Tored diawl, ffenestrawl ffau,
A phwl arf ar ei phileriau.

The windowed den, may the devil with a blunt weapon, break its pillars. *D. ab Gwilym, i'r ffenestr dderw.*

Ffenestru, *v. a.* (ffenestr) To make an opening; to make a window.
Ffenigl, *s. m.* (ffen) Fennel. *Ffenigl helen lwyddawg,* spignel, or baldmoney; *ffenigl y mor,* samphire.
Ffer, *s. f.—pl. t.* au (ffy—er) What is hard, or solid, what is congealed, or fixed with cold; a severe cold; also the ankle, or ankle-bone.
Ffer, *a.* (ffy—er) Dense, solid; fixed; strong.

Nid muner na ffer na ffynedig;
Nis difeirn cadeirn cad arglodig.

Not a placid one either the strong or the prosperous, the mighty ones will not condemn a splendid battle. *Gwalchmai, i Rodri.*

Ni thechai ner ffer ffrawddus;
Mab Owain bro goelfain brys.

The sovereign *strong* and active would not flee: the son of Owain the quick omen of the happiness of a country. *Prydydd Bychan.*

Llywelyn——
I ddylif cynnif cynhebyceir;
I ddylan am lan, am leisiaid ffer,
Tersfysg ton dylyag dyleiaw aber.

Llywelyn—to the progress of tumult he is compared; to the flood covering the shore, covering the *strong* salmons, or the raging of the wave that fills the bay with wreck. *Ein. ab Gwgawn.*

Fferadwy, *a.* (ffer) Congealable, that may be fixed with cold, or that may be concreted.
Fferawl, *a.* (ffer) Concretive, or coagulative.
Fferdawd, *s. m.* (ffer) Concreteness; coagulation; a numbness with a cold; a freezing.
Fferder, *s. m.* (ffer) Concreteness, congealedness
Fferdra, *s. m.* (ffer) Concreteness, congealedness.
Fferdd, *a.* (ffer) Substantial; solid, firm; thick.

Aeth yn wan darn o'r deyrnas;
Clidro ail Iago a las!
Ai gwir yw lladd y gwr llon?
Os gwir, Duw groeso Garon!
Mae eisiau pynciau pen-cerdd,
A gwn ffwrw, ac awen fferdd.

A part of the kingdom is become feeble; Clidro, like Iago, has been slain! Is it true that the pleasant man is cut off! If true, God prosper Caron! there is the lack of the notes of a chief of song, and the fur gown, and the *strong* genius. *S. Tudur.*

Fferedig, *a.* (ffer) Congealed, fixed with cold.
Fferedigaeth, *s. m.* (fferedig) Congealment.
Fferf, *a.* (ffer) Substantial; solid; firm; thick.
Fferiad, *s. m.—pl. t.* au (ffer) A congelation.
Fferiant, *s. m.* (ffer) Concreture, congealment.
Fferis, *s. f.* (ffer) Hard metal; steel. *Fferis dan,* a steel to strike fire with.
Fferllyd, *a.* (ffer) Apt to congeal, or fix with cold; benumbing, chilling
Fferllydrwydd, *s. m.* (fferllyd) Aptness to congeal, or fix with cold; freeziness; numbedness.
Ffern, *s. f.—pl. t.* au (ffer) The ankle-bone.
Fferu, *v. a.* (ffer) To concrete, to congeal, to fix with cold; to freeze; to numb, to be numbed with cold, to be chilled; to be very cold.
Fferyll, *s. m.—pl. t.* ion (ffer) A metallurgist, or one skilled in working metals; also one skilled in any handicrafft; an artist in any branch.

> Llygyrn clyr, llygaid gwyr gynt,
> Lleuadau llewadau pdyrst——
> Drychau o ffeirian fferyll.
>
> The lamps of the minstrels; eyes of men of yore, forms of moons they seem, or mirrors from the fairs of a *metallist*.
> *G. ab Gwilym, i blu paun.*
>
> Os mynni wybod ardymheru tir, a'i ddiwylliadraeth, dysg lyfr fferyllt yr hwn a elwir Virgil.
>
> If thou wouldest know the ameliorating of land, and its cultivation, learn the book of *Georgics*, the which is called Virgil.
> *Gate Gymmroeg.*
>
> A'i fur yn debyg, wrth fwriad fferyll,
> I drio gestyll ar dir gwastad.
>
> With its wall similar, after the designation of an artist, to three castles on level land.
> *L. G. Cothi.*
>
> Gweithiaw i maent, rhag wythwynt,
> Gwaith fferyll ar gestyll gynt.
>
> They are working, to make secure against eight winds, the work of a *metallist* on castles in former times.
> *Gute y Glyn.*

Fferyllawl, *a.* (fferyll) Relating to metallurgy.

Fferylliad, *s. m.—pl.* fferylliaid (fferyll) A metallist; one skilled in metallurgy.

Fferyllineth, *s. m.* (fferyll) Chymistry; metallurgy

Fferyllt, *s. m.—pl. t.* iau (fferyll) A worker of metals; a metallist; an artisan.

> Ei chwr y sydd, nid gwydd gwyllt,
> O ffyrf gelfyddyd fferyllt.
>
> The top of its angle is, not of splitting wood, but of the firm work of the *metallist*.
> *D. ab Gwilym, i'r delyn.*
>
> Mae'r dager o waith fferyllt;
> Gythrel o hil Gwyddel gwyllt.
>
> The dagger is of the work of a *cutler*, an imp of the offspring of a wild Irishman.
> *R. Goch Eryri, i Wil. Ormes.*

Fferylltaeth, *s. m.* (fferyllt) Mechanical art.

Fferylltiad, *s. m.— pl.* fferylltiaid (fferyll) A worker of metals; a hardwareman; a metallist.

> Fferylltiaid oedd yn trigaw yn Rhydychain cyn gwneuthur o Alfred ysgol ynddi.
>
> *Hardwaremen* were dwelling in Oxford before Alfred had erected a school in it.
> *Hen Hanesion.*

Fferylltiaeth, *s. m.* (fferyllt) Mechanical art.

Ffes, *s. m.* (ffy—es) What penetrates; subtlety.

Ffesawd, *s. m.* (ffes) Knowledge; subtlety.

Ffesawg, *a.* (ffes) Full of subtlety, or knowing.

Ffesawl, *a.* (ffes) Of a subtile nature; clever.

Ffesig, *a.* (ffes) Having subtlety; clever; cunning

Ffest, *a.* (ffes) Fast, speedy, hasty, or quick; adroit, clever. *Cerdded yn ffest*, to walk fast; *gwlawio yn ffest*, to rain fast.

> Tost yd gwyn pob colledig;
> Ffest yd hawl eiddwedig.
>
> Piteously doth every condemned one complain; every [illegible] one claims *with speed.*
> *Adage.*
>
> Ffest a giro y maen'n rhewi.
>
> *Fast* and severe it is freezing.
> *D. ab Gwilym.*

Ffestin, *a.* (ffest) Of an active nature; hasty.

Ffestiniad, *s. m.* (ffest) A hastening; festination.

Ffestiniaw, *v. a.* (ffestin) To festinate, to hasten.

> Tarf ar ysgwydau, terwyniaw a ddysg
> Tarfyng ffysg ffestiniaw.
>
> Shields being scattered, a becoming enraged will teach the tumult of quickly *hastening.*
> *Cynddelw.*

Ffestiniawl, *a.* (ffestin) Hastening, hurrying.

Ffestiniawr, *s. m.—pl.* ffestinorion (ffestin) A hastener, or one who accelerates.

Ffestrwydd, *s. m.* (ffest) Speediness; adroitness.

Ffestu, *v. a.* (ffest) To make speed, to hurry.

Ffesu, *v. a.* (ffes) To penetrate, to pervade; to have perception, or knowledge.

Ffetan, *s. f.—pl. t.* au (ffed) A budget, a bag; a saucy girl.

> Ni phrynaf gath yn ffetan.
>
> I will not buy a cat in a *bag*.
> *Adage.*
>
> Gwell i'r gwr a aeth â maneg i ymofyn yd, nag â ffetan.
>
> Better for the man that has gone with a glove to beg for corn, than with a *bag*.
> *Adage.*

Ffetaniad, *s. m.* (ffetan) A budgeting, a bagging.

Ffetanu, *v. a.* (ffetan) To budget, or to bag.

Ffetanwr, *s. m.—pl.* ffetanwyr (ffetan—gwr) One who sacks; a bag-man, a budget man.

Ffetur, *s. m.* (ffed) What is all outside, wild oats

Ffetus, *a.* (ffed) What is under cover; subtile.

FFI, *s. m. r.* The act of casting off, or loathing. *interj.* Fie!

Ffiaidd, *a.* (ffi) Loathsome, abominable, odious.

> Ffiaidd ni charer.
>
> What is not loved is *detestable.*
> *Adage.*

Ffiawg, *a.* (ffi) Having aptness to recede.

Ffieidd-dra, *s. m.* (ffiaidd) Loathsomeness, abomination; disgust; disdain.

Ffieiddiad, *s. m.* (ffiaidd) A loathing, or detesting; detestation, abhorrence.

Ffieiddiaw, *v. a.* (ffiaidd) To loathe, to abominate

Ffieiddiawl, *a.* (ffiaidd) Abhorrent, abominable.

Ffieiddiwr, *s. m.—pl.* ffieiddwyr (ffiaidd—gwr) A loather, a detester, an abhorrer.

Ffieiddrwydd, *s. m.* (ffiaidd) Abhorrence, disgust

Ffil, *s. f.—pl. t.* au (ffy—il) That is ejected, or thrown from; a scud, a quick dart.

Ffilawg, *a.* (ffil) That scuds, or darts. *s. f.—pl.* ffilogod, A wing; also a young mare, or filly; a wanton girl.

> Gan faint trwst-gwrydr ar lwydrew
> Dwy ffilawg y talawg tew,
> Tybiais—mai trwst eiddig.
>
> From the greatness of the noisy course on the hoar frost of the two wings of the fat rogue, methought it was the blustering of the jealous churl.
> *D. ab Gwilym, i'r cyffylog.*

Ffilcas, *s. pl. aggr.* (ffil) Offcasts, old rags.

Ffiloges, *s. f.—pl. t.* au (ffilawg) A flirting female

Ffilor, *s. m.—pl. t.* ion (ffil) A minstrel, a fiddler.

Ffiloreg, *s. f.* (ffilor) Vain babbling, idle talk.

Ffilores, *s. f.—pl. t.* au (ffilor) A female minstrel

Ffill, *s. f.—pl. t.* ion (ffy—ill) A writhe, a turn.

Ffilliad, *s. m.—pl. t.* au (ffill) A writhing, a wreathing, or turning about.

Ffilliaw, *v. a.* (ffill) To writhe, to twirl about.

Ffilliawg, *a.* (ffill) Having a writhing motion.

Ffin, *s. m.—pl. t.* iau (ffy—in) A bound, a limit.

> Gorwyliais nos yn achadw ffin
> Gorlifo rydiau dwfr Dygen Freiddin.
>
> I anxiously watched the night guarding the *boundary* of the murmuring fords of the water of Dygen Vreiddin.
> *Gwalchmai.*

Ffinedd, *s. m.* (ffin) A confinity a boundary.

> Arllechwedd, Arfon, Eiddionydd,
> O ffinedd eu hannedd i'r mynydd——
> A glyw.
>
> Arllechwedd, Arvon and Eiddionydd, from the *vicinity* of their habitation in the mountains, will hear.
> *Brigant.*

Ffinfa, *s. f.—pl.* ffinfeydd (ffin) A boundary.

Ffinfaen, *s. m.—pl.* ffinfeini (ffin—maen) A boundary stone; a landmark.

Ffiniad, *s. m.—pl. t.* au (ffin) A bounding; a setting a boundary, or limit.

Ffiniaw, *v. a.* (ffin) To set a boundary; to border.

Ffiniawl, *a.* (ffin) Limitaneous; bounding.

Ffiniedig, *a.* (ffin) Terminated, bounded, limited.

Ffiogen, *s. f. dim.* (ffiawg) A coney, a rabbit.

Ffion, *s. m.* (ffi) The foxglove, or digitalis; a crimson, or ruddy hue. *a.* Crimson; ruddy; blushing. *Gruddiau ffion*, ruddy cheeks. *dail ffion ffrwyth*, the leaves of the digitalis; *ffion y ffridd*, purple foxglove.

> Duw mawr amherawdr dynion,
> Dillwng dy walch terwyn-falch tirion:
> Dewr Owain deurudd liw ffion.
>
> Great God the sovereign of the sons of men, liberate thy mild and ardently towering hawk the brave Owain with cheeks of the colour of crimson.
> *H. Foel ab Griffri.*
>
> Ystola goi o ffion.
>
> A new robe of crimson.
> *R. Goch, i'r gwregys.*

Ffith, *s. m.* (ffy—ith) A gliding motion.
Ffithell, *s. f. dim.*—*pl. t.* od (ffith) Young salmon
Ffithelliad, *s. m.* (ffithell) A platting or laying the upper row of rods in hedging.
Ffithellu, *v. a.* (ffithell) To plat the top row in hedging.
Ffithl, *s. m.* (ffith) A glide, a dart forward.
Ffithlen, *s. f.*—*pl. t.* i (ffithl) A darter, or what moves forward by gliding.

Ffithlen fain, a phoethlawn fo——
Y neidr.

A slender *glider*, and that is full of heat is the snake. *W. Lleyn.*

Ffithlen geg-fain goegfalch——
Yw'r ddyn.

A narrow—mouthed *eel* pertly proud is the fair one. *T. d'r Nant.*

Ffithliad, *s. m.*—*pl. t.* au (ffithl) A gliding.
Ffithliaw, *v. a.* (ffithl) To glide, to dart forward.
Ffithys, *s. pl. aggr.* (ffith) The bindweed.
Ffla, *s. m.* (ffy—lla) A parting off, or from.
Fflaced, *s. f.*—*pl. t.* au (fflag) A mass; a flock.

Ffacedau a phlu coedydd.

Flocks and plumage of trees. *D. ab Gwilym, i'r cnau.*

Ffiad, *s. m.* (ffla) What throws, or gives out.
Ffladr, *a.* (fflad) Doting, oafish, foolish; fondling; using fair words, flattering.

Y ddylluan——
Wyll fladr a gan i'r lladron.

The owl gloomy and *stupid* that sings to the thieves. *D. ab Gwilym.*

Ffladraidd, *a.* (ffladr) Doting; oafish; fondling.
Ffladrawl, *a.* (ffladr) Apt to be complying.
Ffladriad, *s. m.* (ffladr) An acting dotingly.
Fladru, *v. a.* (ffladr) To act the dotard.
Fflag, *s. f.*—*pl. t.* iau (ffla) What parts from; what is separated, or rifted; a flag.
Fflaim, *s. f.*—*pl.* ffleimiau (ffla) A lancet, a fleam.
Fflair, *s. f.*—*pl.* ffleiriau (ffla) A feist.
Fflais, *s. m.*—*pl.* ffleisiau (ffla) A break, opening, or rent; a ravage. *a.* Open; exposed.
Fflam, *s. f.*—*pl. t.* au (ffla) A flame; a blaze.

Duryn fflam y daran flwch,
Dug warwyfa'n digrifwch.

The *flame* bolt of the pervading thunder it took away the pleasure of our play. *D. ab Gwilym.*

Gwasgwyn o fflam a haiarn à anrheithiws, a'i thywysogion à ddarostyngwys i Arthur.

Gascogne with *flame* and iron he devastated, and her princes became subjected to Arthur. *Gr. ab Arthur.*

Fflamaidd, *a.* (fflam) Like a flame, flaming.
Fflamboer, *s. m.* (fflam—poer) A vomiting of fire. *a.* Vomiting a flame, flammivomous.
Fflamdan, *s. m.* (fflam—tan) A blazing fire.

Gnawd yd gyrch——
Mal pan gyrch fflamdan fflamdo ysbwng.

He is used to assault as when the *flaming fire* pervades the perforated vault of fire. *Bin. ab M. Rhahawd.*

Fflamdo, *s. m.* (fflam—tô) A covering of fire.
Fflamdrais, *s. m.* (fflam—trais) Ravage of flames
Fflamddwyn, *a.* (fflam—dwyn) Flammiferous.

Ffwyr ffysgiad mal ffleimiad fflamddwyn.

A hastening tumult like a *flame-bearing* conflagrator. *Cynddelw.*

Fflameg, *s. f.* (fflam) Inflammation; blearedness.
Fflamgoed, *s. f.* (fflam—coed) Spurge, also called *dalen dda.*
Fflamgyrch, *s. m.*—*pl. t.* au (fflam—cyrch) An attack with flames; a carrying flames. *a.* Flammiferous.

Hirbell, fal Fflamddwyn, ei fflamgyrchau.

Far-extending, like Fflamddwyn, were his *fire-attacks*. *Llygad Gwr.*

Fflamiad, *s. m.*—*pl. t.* au (fflam) Flammation.
Fflamiaw, *v. a.* (fflam) To flame, or to blaze; to inflame; to be inflamed.
Fflamiawg, *a.* (fflam) Abounding with flames.
Fflamiawl, *a.* (fflam) Flaming, or blazing.
Fflamliw, *s. m.* (fflam—lliw) A flame colour. *a.* Flamecoloured.
Fflamlyd, *a.* (fflam) Flammeous, flamy.
Fflamlydrwydd, *s. m.* (fflamlyd) Flammability.
Fflamwch, *s. m.* (fflam) A flaming state.
Fflamychadwy, *a.* (fflamwch) Inflammable.
Fflamychawl, *a.* (fflamwch) Inflammative.
Fflamychu, *v. a.* (fflamwch) To emit flames.

Pan ruddam rudd-fflam fflamychai hyd nef,
Yn addef ni noddai.

When we would kindle the ruddy flame *it would blaze* up to heaven, a dwelling would yield no safety. *H. ab Owain.*

Fflasg, *s. f.*—*pl. t.* au (ffla—asg) A vessel made with wicker; or straw work; a basket. *Fflasg ddillad*, a clothes basket.
Fflasgaid, *s. f.*—*pl. t.* iau (fflasg) A flasket-full.
Fflasged, *s. f.*—*pl. t.* i (fflasg) A vessel of straw, or wicker work; a large vessel of straw bound with briars, like the work of a beehive. *Fflasged flawd*, a meal receptacle.
Fflasgu, *v. a.* (fflasg) To put in a basket.
Fflau, *s. f.* (ffla) A spreading out; radiation.
Fflaw, *s. f.*—*pl.* ffloion (ffla) A piece shivered off; a ray; a dart; a banner; a shiver, a splinter.

Fflaw claer, o bob aer caffael gwystlon.

A bright *ray*, from every battle obtaining hostages. *Cywrysedd Gwynedd a Dehau.*

Ffle, *s. m.* (ffal) A hem round; a closure.
Fflech, *s. f.*—*pl. t.* au (ffle) A shrill utterance.

Nid tebyg, enyd tybiais,
Ei fflech lom i fflwch lais.

Not at all like (long have I thought) is his naked *squeak* to a prompt voice. *D. ab Gwilym, i'r bwa bach.*

Ffled, *s. f.*—*pl. t.* ion (ffle) Restraint; refusal. *Rhag ofn ffled*, for fear of refusal.

Taled, gwrthoded ffled i Ellmyn.

Let him pay, let him refrain from a *refusal* to Germans. *Taliesin.*

Pan brynasant Daned, drwy ffed calledd,
Gan Hors a Hengys, oedd yn eu rhysedd;
Eu cynnydd bu i wrthym yn anfonedd.

When they have bargained for Thanet, through *lack* of discretion, with Hors and Hengys, who were in their career; their prosperity has been derived from us without honour. *Taliesin.*

Ffled, *a.* (ffle) Restricted, or stinted; scarce.

Yssym aur ac ariant nid ffled.

I am possessed of gold and silver not *scanty*. *Ll. P. Moch.*

Ac o'r pryd y profaf nad ffed,
Ne'th adws Iesu eisiwed.

And from the time I shall prove that it was not *scarce*, that Jesus left thee not to want. *Ll. P. Moch.*

Ffleg, *s. f.*—*pl. t.* au (ffle) Confined utterance.
Fflegain, *a.* (ffleg) Squeaking; chuckling. *Iar fflegain*, a chuckling hen.
Ffleisawr, *s. m.*—*pl.* ffleisorion (fflais) A ravager.
Ffleisiad, *s. m.*—*pl. t.* au (fflais) A ravaging.
Ffleisiaw, *v. a.* (fflais) To break out; to ravage.
Ffleimgoed, *s. pl. aggr.* (fflaim—coed) Spurge.
Ffleimiad, *s. m.*—*pl.* ffleimiaid (fflam) A bearer of flames, a conflagrator.

Pan gychwynws——
Oedd ffysgiad ffleimiad fflam gan ucher.

When he arose he was the quick *blazer* of the flame at evening. *Cynddelw, i'r ergl. Rhys.*

Ffleimiaw, *v. a.* (fflaim) To lance, to use a fleam.
Ffleirgi, *s. m.*—*pl. t.* on (fflair—ci) A feisting dog
Ffleiriad, *s. m.*—*pl. t.* au (fflair) A feisting.
Ffleiriast, *s. f.* (fflair—gast) A feisting bitch.
Ffleiriaw, *v. a.* (fflair) To feist, to make a stink.

Ffleiriawg, *a.* (fflair) Apt to feist, or to stink.
Ffleiryn, *s. m. dim.* (fflair) A feister, a stinkard.
Fflemawr, *s. m.—pl.* fflemorion (fflam) A burner, or conflagrator; a fugitive. *Welsh Laws.*

> All dyn anrhaithodder y fydd fflemawr.
>
> The next person liable to be outlawed is a *burner*. *Welsh Laws.*

Ffles, *s. m.—pl.* fflesion (ffy—lles) The dregs.
Fflew, *s. f.—pl. t.* ion (ffle) That keeps in.

> Llew a fflew, glew ei glod;
> Llew Einion Eitil bynod.
>
> A lion and a *guardian*, of fair fame; the lion of the famed Einion the Twin. *Gr. Hiraethawg.*

Fflicìad, *s. m.—pl. t.* au (fflig) A darkening.
Fflicìaw, *v. n.* (fflig) To become overcast.
Fflicws, *s. m. dim.* (fflig) That is dripping with rain, or dew. *a.* Drizzling.
Fflich, *s. f.—pl. t.* iau (ffal—ich) A squeal.
Fflichiaw, *v. a.* (ffich) To squeak, or to squeal.
Fflichiawg, *a.* (ffich) Squeaking, or squealing.

> Dymunai——
> Dair gwiliog wedi'r gwyliau,
> Fflichiawg lanceul flychion,
> Ffromedig ar frig y fron.
>
> He would desire three fillies after the holidays, *squealing* and fleet prancers, proud on the brow of the hill. *T. Prys.*

Fflig, *a.* (ffal—ig) Tending to overcast.
Fflöad, *s. m.* (fflaw) A darting; radiation.
Ffloch, *a.* (fflwch) Flying about; rise; abrupt.

> Cyd el y dywarchen ffloch
> Yn bridd hagr y brawd dugoch
> Nid a llewych cnawd mirain,
> Pryd balch, ond yn lliw'r calch cain.
>
> Though the transient clod turns to ugly mould, thou friar in black, the appearance of the delicate flesh of dignified aspect will only turn to the colour of the splendid chalk. *D. ab Gwilym.*

Fflochen, *s. f.—pl. t.* au (ffloch) A splinter, a rift.
Fflochenawl, *a.* (fflochen) Splintered, or shivered
Fflocheniad, *s. m.* (fflochen) A splintering.
Fflochenu, *v. a.* (fflochen) To splinter, to shiver.
Fflochi, *v. a.* (ffloch) To dart suddenly from.
Fflochiad, *s. m.—pl. t.* au (ffloch) A darting out.
Ffloew, *a.* (fflaw) Radiant, lucid, bright, dazzling

> Y ddraig goch——
> Ffloew ei mynwair fflam unwedd.
>
> The red dragon with *radiant* collar like a flame *R. Goch Eryri.*

Ffloi, *v. a.* (flaw) To diverge, to radiate; to ray.
Fflöyn, *s. m. dim.* (fflaw) A shiver; a splinter; a shred. *Ni thal a fflöyn*, it is not worth a straw. *Fflöyn!* nonsense! *Sil.*
Fflu, *s. m.—pl. t.* on (ffy—llu) A breaking out.
Fflur, *s. m.—pl. t.* oedd (fflu) Bright hue; bloom

> Rhybu Ul Cesar cyrchiant fflur
> Y gan udd Prydain, prid bongur.
> Rhybu Bran ab Llyr, llu rwyfiadur mad
> Yn nghamp, yn nghyvlad, yn nghad, yn nghur.
>
> There has been Julius Cæsar who went to obtain the *bright gem* from the sovereign of Britain, of meritorious course; there has been Bran the son of Llyr, a leader of a host good in the feast, in society, in battle, and in toil. *Ll. P. Moch.*

> Digon i'r byd o degwch
> Eigr bryd fflur, a bryd fflwch.
>
> Enough of beauty for the world is the *blooming* countenance of the nymph of ruddy deceit. *D. ab Gwilym.*

> Casglaf——
> Meirw faillion, dillynion llawr,
> A glwys bert fflur y glaswawr——
> Ar fedd Ifor.
>
> I will collect the sprightly trefoils, the jewels of the ground, and the purely gay bloom of the green pasture, upon the grave of Ivor. *D. ab Gwilym.*

Ffluraidd, *a.* (fflur) Of a blooming nature.
Ffluraw, *v. n.* (fflur) To seem bright; to bloom.
Fflureg, *s. f.* (fflur) A ship's prow; forecastle.
Ffluw, *s. m.* (fflu) A diverging, a running out.
Ffluwch, *s. m.* (ffluw) A full or bushy hair.
Ffluwchaidd, *a.* (ffluwch) Of a bushy nature.
Ffluwchawg, *a.* (ffluwch) Waving about.

Fflw, *s. m.* (ffy—llw) A tendency to spread out.
Fflwch, *a.* (fflw) Prevalent, rife, abundant; full; flush; brisk, lusty.

> Cyw ar hoff lef cywair fflwch;
> Cyfeilydd can cof elwch.
>
> The bird with the lovely voice correct and *flush*, the inventor of the song of the memorial of joy. *D. ab Gwilym, i'r furyalch.*

> Llesteiriodd brif ddigrifwch,
> Llais ei ffo a'i llefau fflwch.
>
> She hindered supreme delight, she with her trailing plumage and *prompt* cries. *D. ab Gwilym, i'r fran.*

> Daryn fflam y daran fflwch
> Dug wareyfa'n digrifwch.
>
> The flaming point of the *abrupt* thunder, it took away the pleasure of our diversion. *D. ab Gwilym.*

Fflychiad, *s. m.—pl. t.* au (fflwch) A breaking out abruptly; a prevailing.
Fflychiaw, *v. a.* (fflwch) To break out abruptly.
Fflychiawl, *a.* (fflwch) Breaking out suddenly.
FFO, *s. m. r.* A going from; a flight, or a retreat

> Rhag angeu ni thycia ffo.
>
> From death *flight* will not avail. *Adage.*

Ffo, *v. a.* (ffo) To flee, to retreat, to run away.

> Trwst taran——
> Gwylltiodd forwyn fwyn feinwen,
> Gwasgu a ffo gwyng ei phen;
> Ffynnu'n deg, ffoes ninnau'n dau,
> E ffoes hon, a ffois innau!
>
> The rumbling of the thunder it scared the kind and delicate maid, who wrapping herself close ran *off* head foremost, fairly prospering we both *fled away*! she fled, and I fled too. *D. ab Gwilym.*

Ffoad, *s. m.* (ffo) A running away, a fleeing.
Ffoadur, *s. m.—pl. t.* ion (ffoad) A fugitive.
Ffoaduriad, *s. m.—pl.* ffoaduriaid (ffoadur) A fugitive, a retreater, or one who takes flight.
Ffoadurus, *s. m.* (ffoadur) Fugitive, fugacious.
Ffoadwy, *a.* (ffoad) Capable of retreating.
Ffoawd, *s. m.* (ffo) The act of retreating.
Ffoawdr, *s. m.—pl.* ffoodron (ffoawd) Fugitive.

> Ffoodron rhag holion.
>
> *Fugitives* from claims. *L. G. Cothi, Dedd Rhuddlan.*

Ffoawl, *a.* (ffo) Fugitive, retreating, or fleeing.
Ffoc, *s. f.—pl. t.* au (ffy—oc) A focus; a fireplace, a furnace.

> Mal dal i gel brodoll i'm tostes yr haiarn dur! Pied emendigaid y ffoc y berwid ynddi, ac y gof a'i dygawdd! Mor drwg yw!
>
> Like laying hold of an open leech has the tempered steel pained me! Let the *furnace* wherein it was melted be accursed, and the smith who made it! How severe it is! *H. Culhwch—Mabinogion.*

Ffod, *s. m.—pl. t.* au (ffy—od) A shank, a leg.

> Yr aradr——
> A'i fod, bellach bach di bwl,
> A'i gebystr a'i glust yn gubwl.
>
> The plough with its small sharp *shank*, with its band, and lastly its loop. *L. G. Cothi.*

Ffodawg, *a.* (ffod) Having thick shanks; squabby. *Dyna burtan ffodawg*, see there a thick-legged runt. *Mon.*
Ffodiant, *s. m.* (ffawd) Prosperity, good luck.
Ffodiaw, *v. n.* (ffawd) To prosper, to be lucky.
Ffodiawg, *a.* (ffawd) Prosperous, fortunate.

> Bedd Meilyr Melwynawg, milwr ffodiawg ynawyr,
> Ffyngiad arfawr ffodiawg,
> Mab i Brwyn o Frycheiniawg.
>
> This is the grave of Meilyr Melwynog, of freshly furnished armour, the bestower of a *fortunate* career, son to Brwyn of Brecheiniog. *E. Beddau Milwyr.*

> Yn llys Aberffraw, er ffaw ffodiawg,
> Bum o du gwledig yn lleithiawg.
>
> In the court of Aberffraw, for the honour of the *fortunate*, I have been seated by the side of a sovereign. *Meilyr.*

Ffodiawl, *a.* (ffawd) Tending to luck, prospering
Ffodiogrwydd, *s. m.* (ffodiawg) Fortunateness.
Ffoddadwy, *a.* (ffawdd) That may be lighted.
Ffoddawl, *a.* (ffawdd) Of a shining quality.

Ffoddi, *v. a.* (ffawdd) To cast a splendour.
Ffoddiad, *s. m.—pl. t.* au (ffawdd) An illumining.
Ffoddiain, *a.* (ffawdd) Phosphoric.
Ffoddiaint, *s. m.* (ffoddiain) Phosphorus.
Fföedig, *a.* (ffo) Fugitive, fleeing, retreating.
Fföedigaeth, *s. m.—pl. t.* au (fföedig) Fugation.
Fföedigrwydd, *s. m.* (fföedig) Fugacity, flightiness.
Ffoi, *v. a.* (ffo) To run away, to flee, to retreat.

Ni cheiff ei ddewis gam a ffôo.

He will not get his choice of step that flies. *Adage.*

Ffoai ddiawl hawl wrth holl
I'r tan rhag ofn dy bryd ti.

From disputing a claim the devil himself *would fly* into the fire for fear of thy countenance. *T. Prys.*

Ffol, *a.* (ffy—ol) Round, blunt, silly, simple, foolish, vain. *Gwaith ffol*, useless labour; *dyn ffol*, a foolish man; *ffol geni*, an ideot.

Ffol pob tylawd.

Foolish is every poor one. *Adage.*

Ymryson a ffol ti a fyddi ffolach.

Dispute with the *foolish* and thou wilt be *more foolish*. *Adage.*

Tri chwerthin ffol; am ben y da, am ben y drwg, ac am ben na's gŵyr pa beth.

The three laughters of the *silly*: at what is good, at what is evil, and at what he knows not. *Barddas.*

Ffoledd, *s. m.* (ffol) Foolishness, silliness, folly.

Yn mhob pechawd y mae ffoledd.

In every sin there is *folly*. *Adage.*

Ffolen, *s. f.—pl. t.* au (ffol) A buttock, a haunch.

Pa beth—dros gamwedd a roddwn iddo? A hwy a ddywedynt pump o ffolenau aur, a phump o lygod aur.

What shall we render him for transgression? And they said, five *haunches* of gold, and five mice of gold. *I. Samuel* vi. 4.

Ffolenawg, *a.* (ffolen) Having buttocks; having large buttocks; squabby.
Ffolenig, *s. f. dim.* (ffolen) A little buttock.
Ffolenu, *v. n.* (ffolen) To become rotund.
Ffoles, *s. f.—pl. t.* au (ffol) A foolish female.
Ffoli, *v. a.* (ffol) To condemn as foolish, to deride. *Maent yn fy ffoli*, they accuse me of folly.
Ffolineb, *s. m.* (ffol) Silliness, foolishness, folly.

Nid ffolineb ond meddwdawd.

There is no *folly* except drunkenness. *Adage.*

Ffolog, *s. f.—pl. t.* od (ffol) A silly female.
Ffoll, *s. m.—pl. t.* au (ffy—oll) A broad mass.

Gorwyn blaen coll geir Digyll bre;
Diawg fydd pob ffoll
Gweithred cadarn cadw arfoll.

Glittering the top of the hazel by the hill of Digoll; every *squabby one* will be lazy. It is the action of the mighty to keep a treaty. *Llywarch Hen.*

Ffollach, *s. f.—pl. t.* au (ffoll) A squabby body.

Y fran wyd——
Ffollach wegil-grach gul-greg.

Thou crow art a scabby necked *waddler* with a straitened hoarseness. D. *ab Gwilym.*

Ffollachawg, *a.* (ffollach) Having a bulky form; thick set. *Ei cherdded yn ffollachawg*, her walk is waddling.
Ffon, *s. f.—pl.* ffyn (ffy—on) A staff, or stick; a cudgel. *Ffyn car*, the sticks of a drag-frame, *ffyn rhesel*, the sticks of a crib; *ffon dan*, a tube used in blowing the fire; *ffon ddwybig*, a quarter staff. *Ffon y bugail*, a shepherd's rod, *ffynwewyr ellyllon*, *ffynwewyr y plant*, cat's tail, or reed mace.

Trydydd troed i hen ei ffon.

The third foot of the aged is his *staff*. *Adage.*

Cystal ar draed a marchogaeth ffon.

As good on his feet as the riding of a *stick*. *Adage.*

Ffonawd, *s. f.—pl.* ffonodiau (ffon) A stroke with a stick.
Ffondoriad, *s. m.* (ffon—toriad) A striking with a stick; a breaking a stick on one.
Ffondoriaw, *v. a.* (ffon—toriaw) To beat with a stick, a cudgelling.
Ffonodiad, *s. m.—pl. t.* au (ffonawd) A cudgelling.
Ffonodiaw, *v. a.* (ffonawd) To beat with a stick.
Ffonwaew, *s. f.—pl.* ffynwewyr (ffon—gwaew) A javelin. *Ffynwewyr ellyllon*, reed mace.
Ffor, *s. f.—pl. t.* iau (ffy—or) An opening; a pass.
Fforch, *s. f.—pl.* (ffor) A fork, a parting into two blades, or shanks.
Fforchaid, *s. f.—pl.* fforcheidiau (fforch) What is taken upon a fork.
Fforchawdl, *s. f.—pl.* fforchodlau (fforch—awdl) A kind of alternate rhime, in prosody.
Fforchawg, *a.* (fforch) Forked, pronged, straddling.
Fforchawl, *a.* (fforch) Tending to part into two; forked, divaricating.
Fforchdroed, *s. m.—pl.* fforchdraed (fforch—troed) A divided or cloven foot. *a.* Bisulcous.
Fforchi, *v. a.* (fforch) To fork, to part into two.
Fforchiad, *s. m.* (fforch) A forking, a parting.
Fforchogi, *v. n.* (fforchawg) To divaricate, or become forked; to cleave the hoof; to straddle.
Fforchogiad, *s. m.* (fforchawg) Forking, a straddle
Fforchwain, *s. f.—pl.* fforchweiniau (fforch—gwain) A small rustic cart, contrived to be drawn either by hand or by horses; it is made of a forked tree, the car that holds the load being built upon the fork, which rests upon the axletree.
Ffordd, *s. f.—pl.* ffyrdd (ffor) A passage, a road, a way. *Ffordd fawr*, a high way; *ffordd draed*, a foot way; *myned i ffordd*, *myned i ffwrdd*, *myned i faes*, *myned i bant*, *myned ymaith*, *myned hwnt*, to go away.

Deuparth ffordd ei gwybod.

Two parts of a *road* is to know it. *Adage.*

Adfyd Ffranc ar ffo ffordd ni ofyn.

The tribulation of a Frank on the retreat the *way* he doth not seek. *Myrddin.*

Fforddawl, *a.* (ffordd) Relating to passage; travelling, wayfaring. *s. pl.* Fforddolion, travellers.

Maith o'th rad, heb raid eu heiriawl,
Mythion feirch ffwyr tyweirch fforddawl.

Abundantly of thy grace, without the necessity of interceding for them, fleet steeds throw up the *way* clods.
Ll. P. Moch, i D. ab Owain.

Ei gaeau i gyd——
Yr holl fforddolion a'u rhed
Drwy yspail a gormail gwyd.

His fields entirely will be run over by all the *travellers* intent on spoil and mischievous trespass. *W. Middleton, Ps.* 89.

Fforddiad, *s. m.* (ffordd) A making out, or exploring the way; a directing the way.
Fforddiaw, *v. a.* (ffordd) To explore the way; to direct the way.
Fforddoli, *v. a.* (fforddawl) To direct in the way.
Fforddoliad, *s. m.—pl.* fforddoliaid (fforddawl) One who shows the way; a guide.

Mae i ni fforddoliad trwy ffydd at y rhad hyn; yn yr hwn ydd ym yn sefyll, ac yn ymlawenychu dan obaith y gogoniant.

There is a *guide* for us through faith to this grace; in whom we stand, and rejoice under the hope of glory.
W. Salusbury, Rom. 5.

Fforddrych, *a.* (ffor—drych) Having sight of the way, acquainted with the road; wayfaring.

——Dwyn dyn gwawd-air,
A gado Bleddyn gidwm,
Fforddrych druan cryman crwm.

Taking away a man of good word, and leaving Bleddyn the rapacious one, a *vagabond*, miserable, and bent like a sickle.
Gr. Gryg, i D. ab Gwilym.

Ffordd yr arch yn fforddrych iawn.

The way that ye would go very readily. *Adage.*

Fforddwr, *s. m.—pl.* fforddwyr (ffordd—gwr) A wayfaring man, a traveller.

Fforddwydd, *s. m.* (ffordd—gwydd) A wayfare.

Gwell yw y march a fo yn ei fforddwydd, nag a fo yn ei breseb.

Better is the horse that shall be on his way, than that shall be in his stall. *Adage.*

Fforest, *s. m.—pl. t.* ydd (ffor—est) An impassable place; a forest.

Fforestawl, *a.* (fforest) Relating to a forest.

Fforestiad, *s. m.* (fforest) A making into a forest.

Fforestu, *v. a.* (fforest) To make void of ways; to make into a forest; to forest.

Y gweirgladdau a fforestir rhag y moch bob amser o'r flwyddyn; canys llygru y tir a wnant.

The meadows *shall be shut* up from the swine at all times of the year; for they will hurt the land. *Welsh Laws.*

Fforestwr, *s. m.—pl.* fforestwyr (fforest—gwr) A forester, or keeper of a forest.

Myn Llonddad! O daw dy wr
Ar ffrwst ar ben fforestwr—
Ni'n gwel.

By Saint Llonddad! should thy husband come in a hurry upon the *forester*, he will not see us. *D. ab Gwilym.*

Fforffed, *s. f.—pl. t.* ion (ffor—ffed) A forfeit.

Gwell enwed fforffed ffug
Na sarf'n wiedaidd sarug.

Better is the harm of a false *demand* than to be boorishly affronted. *D. ab Gwilym.*

Rhoes ei gorff, heb ddim fforffed,
Ar bren croes i brynu cred.

He resigned his body, without any *obligation*, on a cross, to redeem the believing world. *D. ab Gwilym.*

Fforiad, *s. m.—pl. t.* au (ffor) Exploration.

Fforiaw, *v. a.* (ffor) To explore a way; to scout.

Fforiawl, *a.* (ffor) Exploratory; shewing the way.

Fforiwr, *s. m.—pl.* fforwyr (ffor—gwr) One who explores a way; a scout.

Ffos, *s. f.—pl. t.* ydd (ffy—os) A ditch, a trench.

Yr eiry man—
Somiant bryn, a phant, a ffos.

The driven snow is the deception of the hill, the hollow, and the ditch. *D. ab Gwilym.*

Ffosawd, *s. m.—pl.* ffosodau (ffos) A gash; a stroke, or cut with a sword.

Er perygl preiddwyr peri ffosawd.

To cause a *gashing* that shall be a peril to the ravagers. *Meilyr.*

Bwlch ei lafn o lafur ffosawd.

His blade is notched from the toil of *gashing*. *Cynddelw, i'r argl. Rhys.*

Ffosawg, *a.* (ffos) Abounding with trenches.

Ffosi, *v. a.* (ffos) To make a trench or dyke.

Ffosiad, *s. m.* (ffos) A making a trench.

Ffosodiad, *s. m.* (ffosawd) A gashing, a slashing.

Ffosodiaw, *v. a.* (ffosawd) To gash, to slash.

Ffosb, *s. m.* (ffos) A breach, gap, or entrance.

Ef yw'r—cynghorawr ffosb.

He is the vanguard of the *breach*. *Gwalchmai.*

Ffoswn, *s. m.* (ffos) A gasher; a sword.

Ffoth, *s. f.—pl. t.* au (ffy—oth) A round vessel.

Ffothell, *s. f.—pl. t.* au (ffoth) A wheal, a blister.

Ffothellawg, *a.* (ffothell) Having blisters.

Ffothelliad, *s. m.—pl. t.* au (ffothell) A blistering.

Ffothellu, *v. a.* (ffothell) To raise blisters.

Ffra, *s. m.* (ffy—rha) A state of readiness, promptitude, or activity.

Ffraeth, *a.* (ffra) Prompt; ready; fluent; articulate; clear of speech, eloquent.

Gnawd ffo ar ffraeth.

The *loquacious* is wont to fly. *Adage.*

Ffraethach yw hon mewn hoenallt
Y nos no'r eos.

More loquacious is she in the towering cliff, at night, than the nightingale. *D. ab Gwilym, i'r ddylluan.*

Ffraethaidd, *a.* (ffraeth) Of fluent utterance.

Ffraethair, *s. m.—pl.* ffraetheiriau (ffraeth—gair) An eloquent expression; a repartee.

Ffraethawg, *a.* (ffraeth) Having free utterance.

Ffraethawl, *a.* (ffraeth) Freely uttering; fluent.

Ffraethder, *s. m.* (ffraeth) Fluency of speech.

Ffraetheb, *s. f.* (ffraeth) An oration; oratory.

Ffraethebawl, *a.* (ffraetheb) Oratorial.

Fraethebiad, *s. m.* (ffraetheb) The act of haranguing.

Ffraethebu, *v. a.* (ffraetheb) To harangue.

Mae ffraethineb yn ffraethebu, ac areithiaw yn hyawdl.

The science of elocution teaches *to harangue* and to discourse fluently. *H. Perri.*

Ffraethedig, *a.* (ffraeth) Endued with fluency.

Ffraethodd, *s. m.* (ffraeth) Fluency; eloquence.

Ffraethineb, *s. m.* (ffraeth) Fluency; eloquence.

Ffraethogi, *v. a.* (ffraethawg) To make eloquent; to become eloquent, or of fluent speech.

Ffraethoneg, *s. f.* (ffraeth) Art of elocution.

Ffrain, *a.* (ffra) Abounding with promptitude, frankness, or freedom of action.

Ffrainc, *s. f.* (ffrain) France. *Ffrinc ddwyreiniawl*, Franconia.

Ffràl, *s. m.—pl. t.* oedd (ffra) A skipper. *Rhyw ffràl o ddyn*, a hair-brained person. *Sil.*

Ffranc, *s. m.—pl. t.* od (ffra) An active one; a youth; a freeman; a Frenchman. Different tribes of Celts went under the appellation of Franks. The people about the Seine were so called before the Franks of Germany settled in Gaul.

Ffranc, *a.* (ffra) Prompt; active; free or frank.

Ffrancon, *s. pl. aggr.* (ffranc) The beaver.

Ffrantr, *s. m.—pl. t.* au (ffra) Pewter.

Ffrau, *s. m.* (ffra) A flux, a stream, a torrent. *a.* Flowing, streaming, or gushing.

Llawer twr twn-friw,
A gwaed-ffrau ar friw.

Many a mouldering tower, and *streaming* blood on a visage. *Gwalchmai.*

Oedd trabludd gwyr
A llif crau a lliw ffrau ar ffrwyn.

There was the anguish of men, with the flowing of blood and the colour of a *stream* on the bridle. *Cynddelw.*

Ffraul, *s. m.—pl.* ffreulon (ffra) A rippling.

Ffraw, *s. m.* (ffra) Promptness to move; agitation; activity. *a.* Agitated, full of motion. *Awel ffraw*, a brisk gale; *llys ffraw*, a court full of bustle; *udd ffraw*, an alert leader. *Aberffraw*, in Mon, the fall of the river *Ffraw* into the sea; a place celebrated for being the chief residence of the princes of North Wales.

Terfysg yn rhwng-ffysg yn rhagder a wnaeth,
Twrf ton ffraeth Ffraw Aber.

In forwardly hurrying in opposing he raised a tumult, like the noise of a sonorous wave of the efflux of the *Ffraw*. *Cynddelw, m. Rhi. ab M. ab Iddon.*

Ywain fab Gruffudd—
Eryr ffraw, ni ddaw i'w ddaioni neb,
Am glod ac wyneb, Gwynedd lochi.

Owain the son of Gruffudd, the active eagle, not one will come up to his goodness, for fame and candour, the protector of Gwynedd. *Bleddyn Fardd.*

Ffrawd, *s. m.—pl.* ffrodiau (ffraw) Commotion, or bustle. *Ni wnai fawr o ffrawd*, he made no great bustle.

Ni warth cor ffraeth lle cair ffrawd
Na Samson os â i ymnawd.

A pert dwarf is as good where a *tumult* takes place as Samson, if he should go to engage. *T. Prys, i'r gwn.*

Ffrawdd, *s. m.* (ffraw) Promptness of action; agitation, tumult, or confusion.

Dar a dyfwys ar y clawdd
Gwedi gwaedffrau, gwedi ffrawdd:
Gwae wrth win ymdrin ymdrawdd.

An oak hath grown upon the dyke after the spilling of blood, after *tumult*: woe from the dispute and contention over wine.
Rhobert Tywysawg Norddmandi.

Duw a'n gwnel gochel ffrawdd oerfel ffrau,
Ffrwd uffern astrus ffrawddus ffrydiau.

God make us to escape the *tumult* of the streaming cold, the torrent of confused hell of tumultuous torrents.
Ein. ab Gwalchmai.

Ffrawdd, *a.* (ffraw) Prompt or ready to move; tumultuous, agitated.

Emys ffraeth yn ffrwynfawr a'm daw
O ffrawdd fodd udd heb luddiaw.
Caffwn i radau;
Caffwd an gwawdau;
Cathlau clau cardddau rau.

The ready steeds highly trained to the bridle will come to me, from the *prompt* good will of the sovereign, without obstruction. We obtain his gifts; he shall obtain our praises: unceasing strains of well-combined songs.
Cynddelw, i O. Gwynedd.

Ffrawddawl, *a.* (ffrawdd) Of an active tendency.
Ffrawdden, *s. f.* (ffrawdd) Emotion, humour.
Ffrawddenus, *a.* (ffrawdden) Humoursome.
Ffrawddged, *a.* (ffrawdd—ced) Prompt of gift; profuse, liberal.
Ffrawddiain, *a.* (ffrawdd) Having activity.

Llywelyn, fab Iorwerth——
Fab Owain ffrawddiain ffrwyth cynnar,
Ef dyfu draig llu yn llasar ddillad.

Llewelyn the son of Iorwerth, the son of Owain, the *animated* early fruit, he has been the leader of a host in blue garments.
Ll. P. Moch.

Ffrawddiaint, *s. m.* (ffrawddiain) Plenitude of motion; agility, or nimbleness.
Ffrawddu, *v. a.* (ffrawdd) To move promptly; to be active, or full of bustle.
Ffrawddun, *s. m.* (ffrawdd) A commotion.
Ffrawddunniad, *s. m.* (ffrawddun) A putting in a state of motion; a making a bustle.
Ffrawdduniaw, *v. a.* (ffrawddun) To put in a state of motion; to agitate; to be bustling.

Ebai Culhwch; ni ddeuthym i yma er ffrawdduniaw bwyd a llyn, namyn or caffaf fy nghyfarws.

Saith Culhwch; I did not come here for the sake of *consuming* meat and drink, but that I may obtain my boon.
H. Culhwch—Mabinogion.

Ffrawdduniawl, *a.* (ffrawddun) Apt to agitate.
Ffrawddus, *a.* (ffrawdd) Tumultuous, agitated.

Rodri Mael, ei hafal ni gwnaid,
O ddwfr ac awyr, ac enaid a phridd,
A ffrawddus dan ni phaid.

Rodri the generous, his fellow has not been formed, of water and air, soul and matter, and *active* fire that ceaseth not.
Ll. P. Moch.

Tranc ar bob Ffranc ffrawddus gylch.

An end to every Frank of *tumultuous* career.
Prydydd Bychan.

Ffrawddusrwydd, *s. m.* (ffrawddus) Tumultuousness; a state of activity, or bustle.
Ffre, *s. f.* (ffy—rhe) A quick or sharp noise; a clack.
Ffrec, *s. f.* (ffre) A chatter, or chattering.

Uchel ei ffrec mewn teg-coed.

Loud is her *chatter* in the fair wood.
D. ab Gwilym, i'r ddylluan.

Ffreg, *s. f.* (ffre) A chatter, a babbling; chat.
Ffregawd, *s. f.—pl.* ffregodau (ffreg) A preachment.

Och it, ond teg dy ffregawd!

The deuce take thee, how fair thy *preachment!*
D. Llwyd Gorlech.

Ffregodi, *v. a.* (ffregawd) To chatter, or to talk gibberish; to speak affectedly.
Ffreinig, *a.* (ffrain) Of a prompt, free nature; of a free, or full growth. *Dyn ffreinig*, a gigantic person; *collen ffreinig*, a walnut tree; *cnau ffreinig*, walnuts; *eithin ffreinig*, the greater furze; *berwr ffreinig*, garden cresses; *ffa ffreinig*, French beans; *y frech ffreinig*, venereal pox; *llygod ffreinig*, rats; *ceiliawg ffreinig*, a turkey cock.
Ffrengig, *a.* (ffranc) Promp, frank, free; of a prompt, active, or free nature; of a free, or full growth; French.

Nid oedd debig, ffrengig ffriw,
Dyhuddiant doe i heddyw.

The pleasure of yesterday, of Frenchified face, was nothing like that of to-day.
D. ab Gwilym.

Ffres, *a.* (ffre) Active, vigorous, pure, fresh.

Ffres twf blagur a bywull, mal tardd dail a glaswellt, a balant blodau.

Fresh the growth of shoots and germs, like the breaking out of leaves, and green grass, and the buds of flowers.
Beirdd.

Ffresg, *a.* (ffres) Active, pure, or fresh.
Ffresgaidd, *a.* (ffresg) Of a fresh nature.
Ffresgawl, *a.* (ffresg) Tending to make fresh.
Ffresgiad, *s. m.—pl. t.* au (ffresg) A freshening.
Ffresgu, *v. a.* (ffresg) To freshen, to grow fresh.
Ffresiad, *s. m.* (ffres) A freshening, a briskening.
Ffresiaw, *v. a.* (ffres) To freshen; to grow fresh.
Ffresiawl, *a.* (ffres) Freshening, refreshing.
Ffreuad, *s. m.* (ffrau) A spouting, a gushing out.
Ffreuaw, *v. a.* (ffrau) To gush, to spout out, to spurt; to flow, to stream. *Gwaed yn ffreuaw*, blood spouting out.
Ffreuawl, *a.* (ffrau) Gushing, spouting, spurting.
Ffreulad, *s. m.* (ffraul) A purling; a rippling.
Ffreulaw, *v. a.* (ffraul) To purl; to ripple.
Ffreulawg, *a.* (ffraul) Purling, rippling, gurgling.
Ffrewi, *v. a.* (ffraw) To interpose in an affray: to make up a quarrel, or to pacify.
Ffrewiad, *s. m.* (ffrew) An interposition in an affray or quarrel.
Ffrewyll, *s. f.—pl. t.* (ffraw) A scourge, a whip.
Ffrewylliad, *s. m.—pl. t.* au (ffrewyll) A scourging, whipping, or flagellation.
Ffrewylliaw, *v. a.* (ffrewyll) To scourge, to whip.
Ffrewylliedig, *a.* (ffrewyll) Scourged, whipped.
Ffrewylliwr, *s. m.—pl.* ffrewyllwyr (ffrewyll—gwr) A scourger, or a whipper.
Ffrewyllydd, *s. m.—pl. t.* ion (ffrewyll) Scourger.
Ffrewyn, *v. a.* (ffraw) To allay an affray.
Ffrewynawl, *a.* (ffrewyn) Tending to stop an affray
Ffrewyniad, *s. m.* (ffrewyn) A stopping an affray
Ffrewynu, *v. a.* (ffrewyn) To stop a quarrel.
Ffrewynydd, *s. m.—pl. t.* ion (ffrewyn) One who interposes to put an end to an affray.
Ffrid, *s. m.—pl. t.* iau (ffy—rhid) Sudden start.
Ffridd, *s. f.—pl. t.* oedd (ffy—rhidd) A forest; a plantation; a track of ground inclosed from the mountains; a sheep-walk; a track inclosed on the side of hills to turn cattle into at all times. In the extent of Anglesey, it signifies a tenantless farm or land. *Ffridd Celyddon*, the forest of Caledonia.

Mae'r ffridd o wydd Moreiddig
Wedi bwrw oll hyd y brig;
Etto hefyd i tyfant
O egin coed ugain cant.

The *park* of the wood of Moreiddig has shed its leaves quite to the top, again nevertheless they will grow in thousands of young trees.
L. G. Cothi, i orgl. Bleddfoch.

Ffriddlys, *s. m.* (ffridd—llys) Wood anemone, also called *ffriddogen*.
Ffril, *s. m.—pl. t.* ion (ffy—rhil) A fickle one; mean thing. *Ffril o ddyn*, a fribble of a man.
Ffrill, *s. m.—pl. t.* ion (ffy—rhill) A twitter, a chatter. *Ffrill adar*, twittering of birds.

Ffrin, *s. m.—pl. t.* iau (ffy—rhin) The brow, edge, or ledge of a cliff. *Sil.*

Ffring, *s. m.—pl. t.* au (ffy—rhing) The brow of a cliff or precipice.

Ydd wy'n darfod—
Mal pres rhwng y maen a'i fling,
Neu'r lluwch ar ffring y llethri.

I am consuming like brass on the stone that grinds it, or the drift of snow upon the brow of cliffs. *Gufodau.*

Ffris, *s. m.—pl. t.* iau (ffy—rhis) What is raised up; a nap, or friese, as of cloth.

Ffrist, *s. m.—pl. t.* iau (ffris) What is formed into sides; a dice.

Ffristial, *s. m.—pl. t.* au (ffrist) A dice-box.

Ffristialu, *v. a.* (ffristial) To throw the dice.

Ffristiol, *s. m.—pl. t.* au (ffrist) A dice-box.

Gweris ffristiol a thalbwrdd,
Chwr eu gwaith, clawr awyr gwrdd;
Nodwyddau, ai a'u diddawr
Gwisg pen y ffurfafen fawr;—
Mrillion ar wynebion wybr.

They are the men of the chessboard; elegant their workmanship, on the vast surface of the sky; for what concerns us they may be the pins of the head-dress of the grand firmament; or trefoils strewed on the aspects of the revolving space. *D. ab Gwilym.*

Ffrit, *s. m.—pl. t.* iau (ffrid) A sudden start, a jerk; refuse of corn.

Ffriten, *s. f. dim.* (ffrit) A flighty little pert girl.

Ffrityn, *s. m. dim.* (ffrid) A little flighty fellow—*Ffrityn o ddyn*, a fribble of a person.

Ffrith, *s. f.—pl. t.* oedd (ffy—rhith) A forest; a plantation; woodland; a track inclosed from the mountain; the same as *ffridd*.

Rho'th gnwd, mal ffrwd, ar bob ffrith,
A'r gweunydd, a'r tir gwenith.

Send thy produce, like a stream, upon every lawn, and the meadows, and the wheat land. *D. ab Gwilym.*

Ffriw, *s. f.* (ffy—rhiw) A mien, or a countenance.

Meirch enaid—
Yn erfawr ffroen-fawr ffriw euraid.

Splendid steeds, great of growth, nostril wide, and golden front. *Ll. P. Moch.*

Udo'n ffrwyth; adwaen ei ffriw;
Edn Gwyn ab Nudd.

She howls loudly; I know her phiz; she is the bird of Gwyn the son of Nudd. *D. ab Gwilym, i'r Ddylluan.*

Ffro, *s. m.* (ffy—rho) A violent motion, or impulse. *a.* Ardent, fierce.

Ffroch, *s. f.—pl. t.* ion (ffro) Fury, violence. *a.* Furious, fierce, ardent.

Ffrochwyllt, *a.* (ffroch—wyllt) Furiously wild.

Ffroell, *s. m.* (ffraw—ell) Inflamed flesh, or the part that looks angry, in a wound.

Ffroen, *s. f.—pl. t.* au (ffraw) A nostril.

Emys—
Ffrwsth brision leisiaid cynhebig
Ffriw eurdo, ffrwyn-gnu, ffroen ddyfrig.

The noisy gray stallions like salmons with gold-covered front, gnawing the bridle and with snorting nostrils. *Cynddelw.*

Ffroenfoll, *a.* (ffroen—moll) Having a distended nostril, as in snorting or snuffling.

Ffroengraff, *a.* (ffroen—craff) Sharp-scented.

Ffroengraffder, *s. m.* (ffroengraff) Sharpness of scent.

Ffroengraffu, *v. a.* (ffroengraff) To scent sharply.

Ffroeni, *v. a.* (ffroen) To work the nostrils, to snort; to smell to a thing.

Ffroeni byth, ffrwynaw ei ben
I'th ydoedd at i ddiben.

He is ever snorting and bridling his head towards his pop. *T. Prolliyn, i bigedd.*

Ffroeniad, *s. m.—pl. t.* au (ffroen) A snorting.

Ffroeniaw, *v. a.* (ffroen) To blow, or breathe out of the nostrils, to snort; to snuffle.

Ffroeniawg, *a.* (ffroen) Having nostrils, of large nostrils.

Ffroeniawl, *a.* (ffroen) Relating to the nostrils.

Ffroeniwr, *s. m.—pl.* ffroenwyr (ffroen—gwr) One who snorts, or exerts the nostrils.

Ffroenllif, *s. m.—pl. t.* ion (ffroen—llif) Snivel.

Ffroenllifaw, *v. a.* (ffroenllif) To run at the nose.

Ffroenllifawg, *a.* (ffroenllif) Having snivel.

Ffroenllym, *a.* (ffroen—llym) Sharp of scent.

Ffroenllymder, *s. m.* (ffroenllym) Keenness of scent.

Ffroenllymedd, *s. m.* (ffroenllym) Sharpness of scent.

Ffroenllymu, *v. a.* (ffroenllym) To use the sense of smelling; to snuffle.

Ffroenuchel, *a.* (ffroen—uchel) Of high gait.

Ffroenwawd, *s. m.* (ffroen—gwawd) A disdainful scoff, a sarcasm; mycterismus, in rhetoric.

Ffroenydd, *s. m.—pl. t.* ion (ffroen) A snorter.

Ffroes, *s. f.* (ffraw—es) A dish of flesh and eggs fried; an omelet.

Ffrom, *a.* (ffro) Fuming, in a chase, violent.

Taro a wnaeth,—
Trwst taran trwy y tiroedd,
A ffrydiaw crasw-wlaw crwnlawn
A phoeri mellt yn ffrom iawn.

The rumbling of the outrageous thunder reverberated over the lands, and the fast blustering rain strummed, and the lightnings spit most violently. *D. ab Gwilym.*

Ffromaidd, *a.* (ffrom) Of a haughty nature.

Ffromawl, *a.* (ffrom) Apt to be touchy or testy.

Ffromder, *s. m.* (ffrom) Testiness, touchiness.

Gwrthod draw ddigtow, dda agwedd a gwyrth;
Gwrthod lid a ffromedd.

Refrain there to be angry, commendable the condition and holy; refrain thee from wrath and passion. *W. Middleton.*

Ffromi, *v. n.* (ffrom) To chafe, to fume; to be in a fume; to grow angry, to be in a pet.

Gwyn fyd y Cymry—
Pan ddel llynges i Aberdaugleddau,
Ac Englisiaid yn ffo ar ddyw Iau,
A'r meirch yn ffromi yn eu ffrwynau,
Gan weled i chywent eu cyfrwyau.

Happy the state of the Welsh, when a fleet shall come to Aberdaugleddau, and the Englishmen retreating on a Wednesday, and the steeds chafing in their bridles from feeling their saddles so light. *Grono Ddu.*

Ffromiad, *s. m.—pl. t.* au (ffrom) A becoming testy, a taking fire at, a becoming angry.

Ffromllys, *s. m.* (ffrom—llys) The yellow balsam, or touch me not.

Ffromwr, *s. m.—pl.* ffromwyr (ffrom—gwr) An irritable man, one that is testy.

Ffromwyllt, *a.* (ffrom—gwyllt) Haughtily fierce.

Ffromyn, *s. m. dim.* (ffrom) A testy person.

Ffronc, *s. m.—pl. t.* au (ffro) A shelter; a cage; a hut. *a.* Sheltered, or covered over.

Ffros, *s. m.* (ffro) An abrupt rise or toss.

Ffrost, *s. m.* (ffros) A strong emotion, a swell, a brag, a vaunt; pomp, ostentation.

Etto ddyn yn ei ddyrog.
Pan ddel a'i ffrost ar antug,
Rhag d'euaid dywaid yn deg.

Again, my fair, there is instruction for thee: when he comes openly with his swaggering, for thy life speak fairly. *D. ab Gwilym, cyngor i wraig.*

Ffrostiad, *s. m.—pl. t.* au (ffrost) A swaggering.

Ffrostiaw, *v. a.* (ffrost) To vaunt, to brag.

Ffrostiawl, *a.* (ffrost) Vaunting, bragging.

Ffrostiwr, *s. m.—pl.* ffrostwyr (ffrost—gwr) A vaunter, a bragger, a braggadocio.

Ffrowyll, *s. m.* (ffro—gwyll) A quickly moving violence; outrage; commotion, or tumult.

Ac am ddwylan Ffraw ffrowyll.

And on both banks of Ffraw there was violence. *Llywarch Hen.*

Ffrowyllaidd, *a.* (ffrowyll) Of a violent nature.

Ffrowyllaw, *v. a.* (ffrowyll) To act furiously; to move violently; to brandish.

> Pwyliais i pan las Elgno;
> Ffrowyllai lafn a reiddio Pyll,
> A phebyllaw o'i fro.
>
> I pushed onward when Elgno fell; the blade which *Pyll* should hurl *would gleam with wrath*, if tents were pitched in his country. *Llywarch Hen.*

Ffrowyllawg, *a.* (ffrowyll) Abounding with violence, or fierceness.

Ffrowylliad, *s. m.—pl. t.* au (ffrowyll) A moving violently; a swelling with fury; a raging.

Ffrowys, *a.* (ffro—gwys) Of a violent course; turbulent, outrageous.

> Cwymp ffrowys ar yr eglwys.
>
> A *terrible* fall on the church. *Cyfoesi Myrddin.*
>
> Ffrom olwg, oed drwg y tro,
> Ffrowys yn mynych ffraeo.
>
> Was not the time accursed: haughty look, and *turbulent*, frequently quarrelling. *T. Prys.*

Ffrw, *s. m.* (ffy—rhw) A strong effort or impulse.

Ffrwch, *s. m.—pl.* ffrychion (ffrw) A violent breaking out; a ruption, a burst.

Ffrwd, *s. f.—pl.* ffrydiau (ffrw) Stream, torrent.

> Rhodio'r wyf ffrwd yr afon,
> A dyn a'i daith dan y don;
> A llyma'r modd y boddaf,
> Elipai'n ffrydiau tonau Taf.
>
> I am travelling the *stream* of the river; I am a person whose journey is under the waves, and thus behold the way I shall be drowned, as if in the *torrents* of the waves of the Taf. D. *ab Gwilym.*
>
> Gwanar ffrwd, gwenwyna'r ffriw;
> Gwen galchaidd-len gylchaidd-liw.
>
> An extensive *torrent*, it will blight the countenance; a veil white like chalk, of a surrounding appearance. *Gynwelyn Gach.*

Ffrwg, *s. m.* (ffrw) Violence; outrage, tumult.

Ffrwgwd, *s. f.* (ffrwg) A squabble; a fray, a brawl

Ffrwm, *a.* (ffrw) Displaying vigour; luxuriant. *Tyfu yn ffrwm*, to grow luxuriantly.

Ffrws, *s. m.—pl.* ffrysoedd (ffrw) Sudden emotion

Ffrwst, *s. m.* (ffrws) Quick motion; hurry, bustle

> Ffwyr dra ffwyr dra llwyr dra Lloegr fethia;
> Ffrawdd dra ffrawdd dra chawdd drachymhenu;
> Ffrwst dra ffrwst dra thrwst trethau o Lundain;
> Traethadur Prydain wyf yn prydu.
>
> Force upon force to the entire discomfiting of Lloegria; tumult upon tumult towards curbing of too much bickering; bustle upon bustle from the din of bringing tributes from London; I, the historian of Britain, in song record it. *Gw. Brycheiniawg, i'r argl. Rhys.*

Ffrwt, *s. m.—pl.* ffrytiau (ffrw) A quick impulse; or jet; a toss.

Ffrwy, *s. m.* (ffrw) A strong effort or impulse.

Ffrwyd, *s. m.—pl. t.* au (ffrwy) Pulsion; impulse

Ffrwydr, *s. m.—pl.* ffrwydrau (ffrwyd) A violent expulsion; an explosion, or blast.

Ffrwydraw, *v. a.* (ffrwydr) To make an explosion

Ffrwydrawl, *a.* (ffrwydr) Blasting, exploding.

Ffrwydriad, *s. m.—pl. t.* au (ffrwydr) An exploding, or blasting; explosion.

Ffrwyl, *s. m.* (ffrwy) Drizzling rain, mist.

Ffrwylaidd, *a.* (ffrwyl) Drizzly, apt to drizzle.

Ffrwylaw, *v. n.* (ffrwyl) To drizzle, to be misty.

Ffrwyliad, *s. m.* (ffrwyl) A falling in small drops.

Ffrwyn, *s. f.—pl. t.* i (ffrwy) A bridle; also a curb or a restraint.

> Defin-fab——
> Dywed, dan gron ffynnon ffeif,
> Pa fodd y llithrodd llathr-wynt
> Y gerdd a fu anwyl gynt?
> Ti a wyddost, tau addaw,
> Tori ffrwyn marchawg tir Ffraw.
>
> Son of Prophecy, below the round and potent fountain, tell me, how has the song of gentle air thus stolen away. Thou knowest well; 'tis owned by thee, broken is the *bridle* of the knight of the land of Ffraw. *Gr. ab Gronw Gethin.*

Ffrwynadwy, *a.* (ffrwyn) That may be bridled.

Ffrwynaw, *v. a.* (ffrwyn) To bridle; or to curb.

Ffrwynawl, *a.* (ffrwyn) Bridling, restraining.

Ffrwynddof, *a.* (ffrwyn—dof) Used to the bridle.

Ffrwynedig, *a.* (ffrwyn) Having a bridle, bridled.

Ffrwynfawr, *a.* (ffrwyn) Easily restrained.

Ffrwyniad, *s. m.—pl. t.* au (ffrwyn) A bridling.

Ffrwynwr, *s. m.* (ffrwyn—gwr) One who bridles.

Ffrwynydd, *s. m.—pl. t.* ion (ffrwyn) A bridler.

Ffrwys, *s. m.—pl. t.* au (ffrwy) Vehemency.

Ffrwys, *a.* (ffrwy) Of a violent quality; violent.

Ffrwysaw, *v. a.* (ffrwys) To act violently.

Ffrwysawl, *a.* (ffrwys) Tending to be vehement.

Ffrwysiad, *s. m.—pl. t.* au (ffrwys) An acting violently; a becoming vehement.

Ffrwyth, *s. m.—pl. t.* au (ffrwy) Fruit; vigour, strength. *Nid oes dim ffrwyth ar y pren*, there is no fruit on the tree; *collais ffrwyth fy mraich*, I have lost the use of my arm; *nid oes dim ffrwyth ynddo*, there is no strength in it.

> Minnau——o gnau——
> A dalaf bwyth ffrwyth y ffridd.
>
> And I, with nuts, will return the kindness of the *fruit* of the grove. *D. ab Gwilym.*

Ffrwythadwy, *a.* (ffrwyth) Fruitful, prolific.

Ffrwythaw, *v. a.* (ffrwyth) To invigorate; to fructify, to be fruitful, to bear fruit.

> Can rhydd Duw Dofydd dawn ehalaeth,
> Can ran goleu-ddawn ffrwythaw ffraeth.
>
> As the Lord God will confer ample talent, for a distinguished and energetic portion to *invigorate* an eloquent one. *Cynddelw.*

Ffrwythawl, *a.* (ffrwyth) Fructuous; fertile.

Ffrwythedig, *a.* (ffrwyth) Fructified; fertilized.

Ffrwythiad, *s. m.* (ffrwyth) A making powerful; a making productive; fructification.

Ffrwythiannawl, *a.* (ffrwythiant) Tending to fertilize.

Ffrwythiannu, *v. a.* (ffrwythiant) To fructify; to make fruitful, to fertilize.

Ffrwythiannus, *a.* (ffrwythiant) Fructiferous; producing fruit; tending to make fruitful.

Ffrwythiant, *s. m.* (ffrwyth) Fructification.

Ffrwythig, *s. m.* (ffrwyth) Capable of producing; powerful; fruitful, prolific.

> F'm donia h——
> Meirch mawrthig, ffrwythig, ffraeth, anwar.
>
> He bestows on me amply grown steeds, *vigorous*, noisy, and untractable. *Ll. P. Moch.*

Ffrwythineb, *s. m.* (ffrwyth) Fructuosity.

Ffrwythlawch, *a.* (ffrwyth—llawch) Fructiferous; congenial to fruit.

> Gwnaethost for tawch
> A thir ffrwythlawch,
> Awch ochelfawdr
>
> Thou didst form the exhaling sea and the *fruit-preserving* land, of high-tending growth. *Dafydd y Coed.*

Ffrwythlawn, *a.* (ffrwyth) Fruitful, luxuriant.

Ffrwythlondeb, *s. m.* (ffrwythlawn) Fruitfulness.

Ffrwythlonder, *s. m.* (ffrwythlawn) Fruitfulness.

Ffrwythlonedd, *s. m.* (ffrwythlawn) Fruitfulness.

Ffrwythloni, *v. a.* (ffrwythlawn) To make fruitful; to become fruitful, or prolific.

> Duw Hollalluawg a'th ffrwythlono.
>
> May the Almighty God *make* thee *fruitful*. *Gen.* xxviii. 3.
>
> Tri pheth a ffrwythlona yr awen: dyddanwch meddwl, coleddu daionus feddwl, a phorthi cof.
>
> Three things *that enrich* genius: placidness of mind, the cherishing a good mind, and the strengthening the memory. *Barddas.*

Frwythloniad, *s. m.* (ffrwythlawn) A becoming fruitful; a rendering fruitful.

Ffrwythlonrwydd, *s. m.* (ffrwythlawn) Fruitfulness

Ffrwythlonus, *a.* (ffrwythlawn) Tending to render fruitful; tending to enrich.

Ffrwythus, *a.* (ffrwyth) Of a fruitful nature.

Ffrychwyllt, *a.* (ffrwch—gwyllt) Outrageously wild.

Ffrydan, *s. f. dim.* (ffrwd) A streamlet, a stream.

Ffrydiad, *s. m.* (ffrwd) A streaming; a flowing.

Ffrydiaw, *v. a.* (ffrwd) To stream; to run out.

Ffrydiawl, *a.* (ffrwd) Streaming; gushing.

Ffrydioledd, *s. m.* (ffrydiawl) Flowingness, fluidity

Ffrydiolrwydd, *s. m.* (ffrydiawl) Fluidity; fluency.

Ffrymaidd, *a.* (ffrwm) Vigorous; luxuriant.

Ffrymiad, *s. m.* (ffrwm) A rendering vigorous; a becoming vigorous or luxuriant.

Ffrymiaw, *v. a.* (ffrwm) To make prolific or luxuriant; to become vigorous or luxuriant.

Ffrymiawl, *a.* (ffrwm) Of vigorous quality.

Ffryn, *s. m.* (ffy—rhyn) A quiver, a shudder.

Ffrysiad, *s. m.—pl. t.* au (ffrws) A briskly driving.

Ffrysiaw, *v. a.* (ffrws) To impel briskly; to be hurrying or hastening.

> Yr wylan——
> Ferch bown lan ar farch heli,
> Yn ffrydiaw tou, ffrwo wyd ti.
>
> The sea-mew, like a brisk fair lady on a steed of brine hurrying on the wave, thou art pure. *D. Llwyd, ab Ll. ab Gruffudd.*

Ffrysiawl, *a.* (ffrws) Briskly impelling; hurrying

Ffrystell, *s. m.—pl. t.* oedd (ffrwst) Hurly burly.

Ffrystellach, *s. m.* (ffrystell) Hurly burly, bustle. *v. a.* To bustle, or to be all in motion.

Ffrystelliad, *s. m.* (ffrystell) A bustling, or hurrying about; a being in a hurly burly.

Ffrystellu, *v. a.* (ffrystell) To bustle, to hurry.

Ffrystiad, *s. m.—pl. t.* au (ffrwst) Ffestination.

> Gwae a gar, na gwar, na gwyllt ffrystiad
> Gwawt tref, dyrithr nef tangnef eia Tad!
>
> Woe to him that loves any thing, either what is gentle or wild commotion of a town scene, instead of Heaven the blest abode of our father! *Llywelyn Ddu.*

Ffrystiaw, *v. a.* (ffrwst) To bustle, to hurry; to make haste; to accelerate.

> Dechreuais, ffrystiais yn ffraeth,
> Gwneuthur awdl i'r genedlaeth.
>
> I did begin, *I hurried* fluently, to compose an ode to the tribe. *T. Prallyn, s'r Saeson.*

Ffrystiawl, *a.* (ffrwst) Bustling, full of hurry.

Ffrystiedig, *a.* (ffrwst) Accelerated, or hastened.

Ffrystiwr, *s. m.—pl.* ffrystwyr (ffrwst—gwr) One who is full of haste, a bustler.

FFU, *s. m. r.—pl. t.* on. A fleeting state; a passing, or vanishing nature; a veiled state.

Ffuannaidd, *a.* (ffuant) Apt to dissemble; feigned

Ffuannawl, *a.* (ffuant) Feigning, dissembling, counterfeiting, canting, hypocritical.

Ffuanniad, *s. m.—pl. t.* au (ffuant) Dissimulation.

Ffuannu, *v. a.* (ffuant) To feign, to dissemble.

Ffuant, *s. m.—pl.* ffuannoedd (ffu) A feint, disguise, colour, pretence, or hypocrisy.

Ffuantiad, *s. m.* (ffuant) A feigning; a disguising.

Ffuantu, *v. a.* (ffuant) To feign, to make a feint, To dissemble, to counterfeit; to cant.

Ffuantus, *a.* (ffuant) Dissembling; canting.

Ffuantwr, *s. m.—pl.* ffuantwyr (ffuant—gwr) A feigner, a dissembler, a hypocrite.

Ffug, *s. m.—pl. t.* ion (ffu) Delusion; a feint, disguise; guile, deception, or dissimulation.

> Hawdd talu ffug i ffol
>
> It is easy to retaliate a *trick* on the silly *Adage.*
>
> Rhuthr a ddug, nid ffug ffoyr ddilyn,
> Brynaich, braw iddynt a dychryn.
>
> An assault he will make, and a *feint* of the attack in the pursuit, the Highlanders, dismay to them and terror. *Gwgawn.*

Ffugiad, *s. m.—pl. t.* au (ffug) A deluding; a feigning, a dissembling; dissimulation.

Ffugiaw, *v. a.* (ffug) To delude; to feign, to dissemble, to deceive; to deal hypocritically.

Ffugiawl, *a.* (ffug) Deluding, illusive; obscure, deceiving; dissembling; apt to counterfeit.

Ffugiedig, *a.* (ffug) Glossed over, dissembled.

Ffugiedydd, *s. m.—pl. t.* ion (ffugiad) A feigner.

Ffugiwr, *s. m.—pl.* ffugwyr (ffug—gwr) A deluder; a dissembler, a deceiver, a falsifier.

Ffugl, *s. m.—pl.* ffuglion (ffug) A puff of wind.

Ffugliad, *s. m.—pl. t.* au (ffugl) An inflating, a puffing; an inflation.

Ffugliaw, *v. a.* (ffugl) To inflate, or to puff wind.

Ffugliawg, *a.* (ffugl) Inflated, flatuous, puffed.

Ffugliogrwydd, *s. m.* (ffugliawg) Flatulentness.

Ffugliw, *s. m.—pl. t.* iau (ffug—lliw) A feigned colour; a false colour.

Ffugr, *s. m.—pl. t.* au (ffug) A type; a figure.

Ffugyrn, *s. m. dim.* (ffugr) Type, figure.

Ffull, *s. f.—pl. t.* ion (ffu) Haste, speed, celerity.

> Ni char ffull na charw ffest,
> Na chan dwrn a chaid ornest.
>
> He loves not *bustle*, nor much fighting, nor of clenching the fist should a strife take place. *Gronwy Owain.*
>
> Llamais a mawr ffull ymaith
> Yn brudd wedi difudd daith.
>
> I bounded away with great *haste*, pensively after a fruitless journey. *Gronwy Owain.*

Ffulliad, *s. m.—pl. t.* au (ffull) Festination.

Ffulliaw, *v. a.* (ffull) To hasten, to make haste.

> Y rhodd——
> Archaf, a ffulliaf, yn na phalled.
>
> I will ask, I will be impatient, let not the gift fail to come to me. *Gw. Tew.*

Ffulliawg, *a.* (ffull) Full of bustle, hurrying.

Ffulliawl, *a.* (ffull) Tending to produce bustle.

Ffulliwr, *s. m.—pl.* ffullwyr (ffull—gwr) One who hurries, a bustler.

Ffun, *s. f.—pl. t.* oedd (ffy—un) What is united, or combined together; a bundle.

> A phan oedd yn ffunodd yd.
>
> And when there were to me *sheaves* of corn. *Bedo Brwynllys.*

Ffunell, *s. f.—pl. t.* au (ffun) A little bundle.

Ffunen, *s. f.—pl. t.* au (ffun) A band, a lace, a riband; a head-band; a fishing line.

> Drwy ffenestr dyro ffunen
> Dy fam hael i dod fy mhen.
>
> Through the window give thy generous mother's *head-band* to cover my head. *D. ab Edmwnd.*

Ffuneniad, *s. m.* (ffunen) A binding with a lace, or with a riband.

Ffunenig, *s. f. dim.* (ffunen) A bandlet, or a lace.

Ffunenu, *v. a.* (ffunen) To bind with a riband or with a lace, to tie in a bundle.

Ffuniad, *s. m.—pl. t.* au (ffun) A tying together, a banding round.

Ffunud, *s. m.* (ffun) Figure, form, manner. *Mae y ddau yn union yr un ffunud a'u gilydd*, the two are exactly of the same form with one another.

> Sef a oruc Hengist yna meddylaw o bob moddol twyllodrus pa ffunud y gallai ef ddyfod i'r tir.
>
> What did Hengist then do was to devise by every deceitful means in what *wise* he should be able to come to the land. *Gr. ab Arthur.*

Ffüon, *s. m. aggr.* (ffu) That is of a blushing, blooming, or red nature.

> Cochach oedd ei deurudd no'r ffion cochaf.
>
> Her two cheeks were more red than the reddest roses. *H. Culhwch—Mabinogion.*

Ffur, *a.* (ffy—ur) Of a penetrating, or subtle nature; cunning, wary, wily, crafty; wise.

> Ffur ici lolaf
> Buddig o Feli,
> Ab Manogan ri;
> Rhygeidw ei deithi
> Ynys fel Beli,
> Teithiawg oedd iti.
>
> Cunningly I will give thee praise, having pre-eminence from Beli, the son of Manogan the prince, thou wilt uphold the honours of the honey island of Beli. *Taliesin.*

Ffuraw, *v. a.* (ffur) To act warily; to be cunning, wary, or crafty; to be wise.
Ffurawl, *a.* (ffur) Of a subtile nature.
Ffured, *s. f.—pl. t.* au (ffur) That is subtle, crafty, or cunning; a ferret.

Fo eiff i rodiaw yn fwy ffuredach
Na chi, na baili.

He will go to take his range *more craftily* than a dog, or a bailiff. *T. Prys, i glerwr.*

Ffuredaidd, *a.* (ffured) Of the nature of a ferret.
Ffurediad, *s. m.* (ffured) An acting craftily.
Ffuredu, *v. a.* (ffured) To act subtilely; to ferret.
Ffuredwr, *s. m.* (ffured—gwr) A ferreter.
Ffurf, *s. f.—pl. t.* iau (ffur) What is designed, or contrived; shape; form; order; manner.
Ffurfafen, *s. f.* (ffurf—men) The firmament.

Ni phrofais dan ffurfafen
Gwe mor gaeth a'r Gymmraeg wen.

I have not tried under *heaven* a structure so exact as the fair Welsh tongue. *Edm. Prys.*

Ffurfaidd, *a.* (ffurf) Shapely; orderly; formal.
Ffurfeiddiad, *s. m.* (ffurfaidd) A making orderly.
Ffurfeiddiaw, *v. a.* (ffurfaidd) To frame, to form.
Ffurfeiddiawl, *a.* (ffurfaidd) Tending to make orderly, or formal.
Ffurfeiddrwydd, *s. m.* (ffurfaidd) Shapeliness.
Ffurfiaw, *v. a.* (ffurf) To form, to shape.
Ffust, *s. f.—pl. t.* iau (ffu) A flail; a thresher.
Ffustfa, *s. f.—pl.* ffustfëydd (ffust) A beating, a boxing match.
Ffustiaw, *v. a.* (ffust) To thresh, to beat, to bang.
Ffustiad, *s. m.* (ffust) A banging, a thumping.
FFW, *s. m. r.* Volatility, or quickness of motion.
Ffwd, *s. m.* (ffw) An abruptness; a quick motion
Ffwdan, *s. f.—pl. t.* au (ffwd) Bustle, or flurry.

Gresyn oedd na 'mgroesai ef,
A pheidiaw, annoeth ffwdan
Taith gwael, a'i lesteiriaeth gwan.

It were a pity that he should not take warning, and cease with his feeble pimping, a silly *toil*, and a vile journey. *T. Prys.*

Och, o'r ffwdan i'm anerch;
Yn tori trwyn er mwyn merch!

Dear, what *trouble* am I assailed with, breaking my nose for the sake of a girl! *D. ab Gwilym.*

Ffwdanllyd, *a.* (ffwdan) Full of bustle, or flurry; fidgety, restless.
Ffwdanu, *v. a.* (ffwdan) To bustle, or toil hard; to be in agitation, to fidget, to be restless.
Ffwdanus, *a.* (ffwdan) Full of business, or hurry.
Ffwg, *s. m.* (ffw) What is volatile; dry grass.
Ffwgws, *s. m.* (ffwg) Dry leaves; tobacco.
Ffwl, *s. m.* (ffw) What is light, wasted, or dry.
Ffwl, *s. m.—pl.* ffyliaid (ffy—wl) A blunt one, a stupid one, a dolt, a fool.

A chymwl yw ffwl y fair.——
I'w chuddio.

And the *fool* of the fair is a cloud to hide her. *S. Tudur.*

Ffwlach, *s. m. aggr.* (ffwl) Refuse; light corn.
Ffwlbri, *s. m.* (ffwl) Refuse, trash, or dregs.
Ffwlbriaidd, *a.* (ffwlbri) Of the nature of trash.
Ffwn, *s. m.* (ffw) A state of proceeding from, or originating; a source; the breadth, or respiration; a puff of breath expelled; a sigh.
Ffwnt, *s. m.* (ffwn) A produce, or what is generated or made to spring out.
Ffwr, *s. m.* (ffw) A divergency, or going away. *prep.* Off. *v. imp.* Away, off, begone.
Ffwrch, *s. m.—pl.* ffyrchod (ffwr) An angle from which any thing branches out; the fork, or inside of the junction of the thighs.

Gwelwn—llwynog coch——
Yn eiste fal dinas-dwrch
Ger ei ffau ar gwr ei ffwrch.

I could see a red fox, sitting like a city hog, by the side of his den, on the bottom of his *haunch*. *D. ab Gwilym.*

Ffwrdd, *s. m.* (ffwr) A divergency, a going away. *prep.* Off, from. *adv.* Away. *v. imp.* Hence, be gone. *Dos i ffwrdd*, get thee away; *ffwrdd!* avaunt! begone!
Ffwrn, *s. m.* (ffwr) A point of divergency; a focus; a furnace, an oven.
Ffwrw, *s. m.* (ffwr) What is apt to diverge or fly about; fur.

Ffriw sad mewn ffwrw sidan
Ffrwd mor uwch offeiriaid man.

A firm aspect in silken *fur*, like the torrent of the sea above little parsons. *T. Aled.*

Ffwrwr, *s. m.* (ffwrw) Fur, soft hair of animals.

Broch a'i fol atoch fal twr
Brawn ffyrf mewn brwyn a ffwrwr.

A badger with his belly towards you, like a heap of solid brawn in rushes and fur. *Rhys Nanmor.*

Ffwtiar, *s. m.* (ffwd) A short person, or a squab.
Ffwtog, *s. f.—pl. t.* au (ffwd) A scut, a short tail.
Ffwy, *s. m.* (ffw) Volatility, aptness of motion.
Ffwyl, *s. m.—pl. t.* au (ffwy) A drive, or impulsion, a stroke upon; a foil.

Ei hwch anwyl——
Hi gafodd yn dren ar ei phen y ffwyl;
Hyll oedd Martha am ei lladd a mwrthwyl.

Her beloved sow, woefully has she received the *foil* on her head; furious was Martha, to kill her with a hammer. *C. Daf. Meredydd.*

Ffwyn, *s. m.—pl. t.* au (ffwy) What is produced, or thrown out; hay; hay newly cut given to cattle when it is green.
Ffwynen, *s. f.—pl. t.* au (ffwyn) A band of hay.
Ffwynog, *s. f.—pl. t.* ydd (ffwyn) Meadow land.
Ffwyr, *s. f.—pl. t.* au (ffwy) A vehement propulsion, or drive; an onset, or assault.

Mor gyfran gyfred y donion
Mur mawr-gor, Morgant arwyddion;
Mor gadarn i ffwyr ar ffarsoo Ffrainc,
Ac ar ffrawdd o wystlon!

How complete and accordant the endowments of the far-extending bulwark with the banners of Morgant; how mighty his *onset* on the heroes of France, and on the tumult of hostages. *Cynddelw, i'r O. Gwynedd.*

Gwr creulawn, creulan a'i cyffry,
Cyffraw cad cadelling wely;
Gwr a wyr yn nydd ffwyr na ffy.

A furious man, who will be agitated by the bloody plain; the terror of the battle of the Cadellian tribe; a hero who knows in the day of *onset* not to flee. *Cynddelw, i argl. Rhys.*

Arthur gynt, ffwyr luchynt ffam,
A'i ceisiai fal y cawsam.

Arthur of yore, whose *course* was the darting of flame, made effort to obtain it as we have done. *Ll. P. Moch.*

Gnawd Ffranc rhag ffwyr dranc a ffo arno.

It will be common to see a Ffranc on flight, for fear of the deadly *assault*. *D. Benfras.*

Ffwyrad, *s. m.* (ffwyr) Impulsion; an assaulting. *Ffwyrad Awel*, a gust of wind. *Arm.*
Ffwyraw, *v. a.* (ffwyr) To impel, expel or drive violently; to assault.
Ffwyrawl, *a.* (ffwyr) Violently driving, or impelling; assaulting.
FFY, *s. m. r.* Aptness to move, or impel. It is used as a prefix in the composition of words, denoting agency, or cause.
Ffyd, *s. pl. aggr.* (ffed) Coverings, or garments.

Dig hefyd, a'i ffyd i ffordd,
Yw'r esgob; gwael yw'r ysgordd.

Envious also, divested of his *robes*, is the bishop; miserable is the reflection. *Dr. S. Cent.*

Ffydd, *s. f.* (ffy—ydd) Faith, or confidence; reliance, dependance.

Deuparth ffydd y'nghalon.

Two parts of *faith* lie in the heart. *Adage.*

Gobaith nid oes ond gwibio
Y dydd, ar fy ffydd, a ffo!

Hope there is not lost of wandering through the day, upon my *faith*, and fleeing away ! *D. ab Gwilym.*

> Gwir ffydd——
> Duw, cynnal fy amcanion
> O wres hardd yr eirias hon !

True *faith*——God support my endeavours by the rising heat of this fire ! *H. D. ab Ifan.*

Ffyddfrawd, *s. m.*—*pl.* ffyddfrodyr (ffydd—brawd) A brother in the faith.

Ffyddiad, *s. m.* (ffydd) The having faith or reliance.

Ffyddiaw, *v. a.* (ffydd) To have faith; to confide.

Ffyddiawg, *a.* (ffydd) Having faith, or faithful.

> Ys imi udd——
> Ffyddiawg ffodiawg i ymdro.

I have a *faithful* sovereign of prosperous course. *Phylip Brydydd, i R. Gryg.*

Ffyddiawl, *a.* (ffydd) Relating to faith; faithful.

> Truenaidd gwetiaidd gwynion a'u gobaith,
> Ni ddiffydd eilwaith i ffyddolion.

Feeble miserable ones blessed with their hope, which again will not be extinguished to the *faithful* ones. *W. Middleton.*

Ffyddlawn, *a.* (ffydd) Faithful. *Ffyddloniaid*, faithful ones, or believers.

Ffyddlondeb, *s. m.* (ffyddlawn) Faithfulness.

Ffyddlonder, *s. m.* (ffyddlawn) Faithfulness.

Ffyddloni, *v. n.* (ffyddlawn) To become faithful.

Ffyddloniad, *s. m.*—*pl.* ffyddloniaid (ffyddlawn) A faithful one, or a believer.

Ffyll, *s. m.*—*pl. t.* on (ffy—yll) That shades, or covers over. *a.* Overgrown; gloomy.

Ffylliad, *s. m.*—*pl. t.* au (ffyll) A shading over; a becoming overgrown.

Ffylliaw, *v. a.* (ffyll) To overshade, to grow over; to become gloomy, or dusky.

Ffylliawg, *a.* (ffyll) Shading over; abounding with dark coverts, or brakes.

Ffyllog, *s. f.*—*pl. t.* od (ffyll) A place that is overgrown, wild, or uncultivated. *Y Ffyllog*, a low plain so called in Glamorganshire.

Ffyllon, *s. pl. aggr.* (ffyll) Gloomy recesses, or brakes. *Nant Ffyllon*, a place so called in Montgomeryshire.

Ffyllwyllt, *a.* (ffyll—gwyllt) Darkly wild.

Ffynadwy, *a.* (ffwn) Productive, prosperous.

Ffyned, *s. f.* (ffwn) The act of generating, or expelling air; a breathing.

Ffynedig, *a.* (ffwnt) Prosperous, fortunate.

> Gwellwell pob ffynedig.

Better and better every *prosperous one*. *Adage.*

Ffynedigrwydd, *s. m.* (ffynedig) Prosperousness.

Ffyneg, *s. f.*—*pl. t.* au (ffwn) What generates.

Ffynegl, *s. f.*—*pl.* ffyneglau (ffyneg) A furrow.

Ffynegliad, *s. m.* (ffynegl) A furrowing.

Ffyneglu, *v. a.* (ffynegl) To make into furrows.

Ffynel, *s. f.*—*pl. t.* oedd (ffwn) An air-hole, or funnel; a chimney.

Ffynell, *s. f.*—*pl. t.* au (ffwn) An air-hole.

Ffynetr, *s. f.*—*pl.* ffynetri (ffyned) A chimney.

Ffyniant, *s. m.* (ffwn) Production, generation; abundance, prosperity.

Ffyniaw, *v. a.* (ffwn) To produce; to generate.

> ——Ffynwyd o gened!
> Y Gwinau Dewfreuddwyd.

He was produced from the family of Gwinau Dewfreuddwyd. D. ab Gwilym.

Ffynadwy, *a.* (ffwnt) Capable of prospering.

Ffynnawn, *s. f.*—*pl.* ffynonau (ffwnt) A fountain, a spring, a source. *Ffynonydd oerion*, cold springs.

Ffynnedig, *a.* (ffwnt) Made lucky: prosperous.

Ffynnedigrwydd, *s. m.* (ffynnedig) Prosperousness

Ffyniannawl, *a.* (ffyniant) Prospering.

Ffyniannus, *a.* (ffyniant) Prospering.

Ffynniant, *s. m.* (ffwnt) Prosperity; luck, fortune

> Wyrda! ymogyfanniannwn ninnau yn ffyniant a glewder; ac ymogelwn rhag anahyngedfan gywilyddus, ebai Beno.

Good fellows! let us exalt ourselves also in good *fortune* and bravery; and let us guard against shameful ill luck, said Beno. *Gr. ab Arthur.*

Ffynnon, *s. f.*—*pl. t.* au (ffwnt) A fountain.

> Ni wyddis eisieu y ffynnon oni el yn hesb.

The want of the *spring* is not known until it becomes dry. *Adage.*

Ffynnonawg, *a.* (ffynnon) Abounding with springs

Ffynnonell, *s. f. dim.* (ffynnawn) A small spring, or fountain; an issue.

Ffynnoni, *v. a.* (ffynnon) To rise up in springs.

Ffynnonwa, *s. m.* (ffynnon) A place full of springs

> Y berwr gwynion a dyf y'ngoder ffynnonwa.

The white cresses grow in the outlet of *springs*. *Llyfr Meddyg.*

Ffynnonwys, *s. m.* (ffynnon) Place full of springs

Ffynnu, *v. n.* (ffwnt) To be productive; to prosper, to be fortunate.

> Ffyniant i'w gorff, a'i wanëg,
> Ffynnon dysg yn ffynnu'n deg.

Success to him, and to his ways, the fountain of learning fairly *prospering*. *E. Prys.*

Ffynnon, *s. f.*—*pl. t.* ydd (ffwn) A spring, a well. *Ffynnon Las*, *Ffynnon Felen*, *Ffynnon Frech*, lakes so called in Eryri.

Ffynu, *v. a.* (ffwn) To produce, or to generate.

Ffynus, *a.* (ffwn) Productive or abundant.

Ffyr, *s. m.* (ffy—yr) A substantial or firm state.

Ffyrf, *a.* (ffyr) Substantial, thick; firm, strong.

> Rhym gelwir yn ffyrf, yn ffyng, arab beryl,
> Yn arab hawl dartyng,
> Yn ffyrdd cynnid cerdd dyfawdlyng,
> Yn brydydd, yn brifardd dysg.

I am denominated powerful, impetuous, of joyous course, of joyous claim of tumult in the ways of songs of the soothing muse, a poet, and a primary bard of instruction. *Cynddelw.*

Ffyrfhad, *s. m.* (ffyrf) A rendering thick, or firm, a becoming thick, or firm.

Ffyrfhawl, *a.* (ffyrf) Of a tendency to thicken.

Ffyrfaidd, *a.* (ffyrf) Of a solid or firm nature.

Ffyrfhau, *v. a.* (ffyrf) To make substantial; to strengthen; to establish; to become substantial, to grow thick; to become firm.

Ffyrfawl, *a.* (ffyrf) Tending to make solid or thick

Ffyrfder, *s. m.* (ffyrf) Substantialness, thickness; firmness; steadiness.

> ——Cyfrifant
> Ffwyr ffyrfder ffer ffyniant.

They reckon the impulse of *firmness* great prosperity. *Cynddelw.*

Ffyrfeiddiad, *s. m.* (ffyrfaidd) A rendering substantial, or firm; a becoming substantial.

Ffurfeiddiaw, *v. n.* (ffyrfaidd) To render substantial; to become thick or firm.

Ffyrfeiddiawl, *a.* (ffyrfaidd) Tending to make substantial, solid, or thick.

Ffyrfeiddrwydd, *s. m.* (ffyrfaidd) Substantialness; bulkiness; thickness.

Ffyrfiad, *s. m.*—*pl. t.* au (ffyrf) A rendering, or becoming firm; a thickening.

Ffyrfiant, *s. m.* (ffyrf) Substance; firmness; thickness.

Ffyrnaid, *s. f.*—*pl.* ffyrneidiau (ffwrn) A furnace-full; an oven-full.

Ffyrnaidd, *a.* (ffwrn) Focale; violent; pungent.

Ffyrnawl, *a.* (ffwrn) Focale; of a sharp, or violent quality.

Ffyrnig, *a.* (ffwrn) Penetrating; wily, cunning; violent; outrageous; fierce.

Moddion chwith! meddwon ni chant
Etifeddu at feddiant
Teyrnas Duw trwy nawsei ddig,
Can' ffwrn sy'n cynneu'n ffyrnig.

Sad matters! drunkards, they shall not get to attain the possession of the kingdom of God; through the force of his wrath they shall have the furnace that burns *furiously*. *Ed. Morus.*

Nid ffyrnig ond ci.

Nothing so *fierce* as a dog. *Adage.*

Ffyrnigaidd, *a.* (ffyrnig) Violent; ferocious.

Ffyrnigaw, *v. a.* (ffyrnig) To act violently; to act subtilely, or cunning; to become violent, outrageous, or fierce.

——Pan ryfelodd
Poen uffern agaws pan ffyrnigodd——
Daiar yn gynnar pan gwnodd ddyrnawd
Gan ei arfawd a gynhyrfodd.

When he warred, he was nearly the torment of hell when *he became outrageous:* when he uplifted a stroke soon the earth did tremble from the motion of his weapon. *S. Tudur.*

Ffyrnigawl, *a.* (ffyrnig) Of a violent tendency.

Ffyrnigiad, *s. m.* (ffyrnig) A becoming fierce.

Ffyrnigrwydd, *s. m.* (ffyrnig) Aptness to penetrate through; subtlety, craftiness, violence, outrageousness, fierceness.

Sef yw ffyrnigrwydd difwynaw y da iddo ei hun, ac i'r neb bieufo.

Outrageousness consists in the spoiling of property to himself, and to him that is the owner. *Welsh Laws.*

Sef yw ffyrnigrwydd mernaw dyn, a lladd dyn, heb well, neu â gwenwyn; a difwynaw da iddo ei hun, ac i'w berchenawg.

Outrageousness consists in setting upon a man, and killing a man without a wound, or with poison; and to spoil property to himself, and to its owner. *Welsh Laws.*

Ffyrnigwr, *s. m.—pl.* ffyrnigwyr (ffyrnig—gwr) A violent or outrageous man.

Ffysg, *s. m.—pl. t.* ion (ffy—ysg) A quick course; impetuosity.

Cyfaillt grym ysy m——
Cedawl wirawd wawd wahawdd;
Cadr ffysg rwydd byddysg, rodd hawdd.

I have a powerful friend, profuse of beverage and inviting praise; of mighty, free, and well-trained *course*, and frank of gift. *Llywelyn Brydydd Hodnant.*

Ffysg, *a.* (ffy—ysg) Of a quick motion; sudden; abrupt, quick, hasty; or impetuous.

Udd ysym eddyw ar geir,
Nis arfaidd llew a dan lloer;
Gwaew crwm yn nydd trwm, trwy ffwyr;
Gwan ffysg yn eur-wrysg yn aer.

To me there is a sovereign this day on the cars, there is not a lion beneath the moon that would dare him; he couched the spear on the sad day, with violence; *impetuous* his course, wearing golden branches in the battle. *Cynddelw, i O. Cyfeiliawg.*

Ffrawdd ystryw estronion hual,
Ffysg dyfysg diffwys-gad ardal.

The ready device of the fetters of strangers *impetuously* he hastens over the embattled plain. *Cynddelw, i O. Gwynedd.*

Y gefnach——
Crair hy bron a ffy ar ffysg.

The hare, a bold jewel of the lawn that on a *sudden* squds away. *D. ab Gwilym.*

Angharad fein-llun!
Hoen ffysg dda ddysg, nid oedd un,
Huan 'wybr, a hi nebun.

Angharad of slender form! The *brisk* whirl of the wave, of goodly instruction, there was not one and she not one, luminary of the firmament. *D. ab Gwilym.*

Ffysgiad, *s. m.—pl. t.* au (ffysg) A moving with celerity, a going rapidly; a hastening.

Dyfrydedd Gwynedd! gwae ni, ryalled
Gwalch ffysgiad, roddiad rudd a phali!

The mourning of Gwynedd! Woe to us the being deprived of the hawk of *impetuosity*, the bestower of crimson and velvet. *Bleddyn Fardd.*

Gwae Fon, ac Arfon, gorfod colli rhwyf
Rwysg angerdd Elifri;
Gwaew gwaed ffysgiad gad gyni,
Gwawr detfeinawg; ruddfoawg ri.

Woe to Mon and Arfon, to be fated to lose a prince of the violent course of Elivri: with a spear of blood, the hastening of the anguish of battle; the accomplished luminary, and red-stained chief. *Bleddyn Fardd, m. D. ab G. ab Llywelyn.*

Ffysgiaw, *v. a.* (ffysg) To move suddenly, to hurry; to go impetuously.

Gwryd diogel, diogan ffysgiad,
Yn ffysgiaw biw garthan;
Aerfa fawr aer-wawr eur-wan,
Eur-walch balch bolch ei darian.

Of secure manhood, and unblemished impulsion, *hastening away* the kine of the depredation, of golden course gleaming death in the great slaughter; a towering golden hawk with broken shield. *Cynddelw, i Wenwynwyn.*

Ffysgiawd, *s. m.* (ffysg) The act of moving quickly, or impetuously.

Mawr-bysg mirain ffysg ffysgiawd eigion.

The fair great fishes of the *impetuous motion* of the ocean. *Einion Offeiriad.*

Ffysgiawl, *a.* (ffysg) Of a quick or hasty nature.

Ffysgiolin, *a.* (ffysgiawl) Of a quick, vehement, or impetuous course.

Bid Gymmry ni gnaws yng ngnawd feithrin bar,
Ac ym cyfaillt car corf ffysgiolin.

Let the Welsh be not fond of being accustomed to cherish wrath respecting my associate, the friend with the *brisk* body. *Gwalchmai, i Rodri.*

Ffysgiolyn, *s. m.* (ffysgiawl) One of a quick, or impetuous course; a hero.

Ffysgiolyn byddin, budd achref cerddau;
Cerddwys hael yn nhangnef
Carno, fro freiniawl addef,
A gwedi Carno caer Nef.

The *hero* of the army, the treasure of benevolence of songs; the generous one is gone to the tranquillity of Carno, the resting place of a privileged country, and after Carno, the mansion of heaven. *Ll. P. Moch, m. Ior. ab Rhospert.*

G.

GA, *s. m. r.* A throw, or jut out; a divaricating, or parting from: whether it be used in its simple form, or uncompounded, is not certain.

Gad, *s. m.* (ga) A parting from; quitting; leaving, or desisting; quit; leave. *v. imp.* Quit; let, leave, suffer. *Gad lonydd,* let me alone; *gad iddo,* let it be so; *gad i hyny fod,* let that be; *gad imi beth,* leave some for me; *na ato nef,* may heaven prevent.

Gadael, *v. n.* (gad) To part from, to quit, to leave, to relinquish; to forsake, to abandon, to give over; to suffer.

Cas ni wnel dda, ac nis gato i arall.

Odious is he that will do no good himself, and *that will suffer* no one else. *Adage.*

Gadaw, *v. n.* (gad) To quit, to leave, to relinquish; to permit, to suffer. *Gadaw y maes,* to quit the field.

Ni ad diriad ei garu.

The mischievous *will* not *permit* himself to be loved. *Adage.*

Gadawedig, *a.* (gadaw) Relinquished, permitted.

Gadawedigaeth, *s. m.—pl. t.* au (gadawedig) The act of leaving, or relinquishing; abandonment, permission.

Gadawiad, *s. m.* (gadaw) A quitting, leaving, or relinquishing; permission, or suffering.

Gadu, *v. n.* (gad) To quit, to leave; to abandon; to permit; to resign.

> Gadu gwraig ag un fefl, ac ei chymmeryd a dwy.
>
> *To leave a wife with one disgrace and to take her with two.* *Adage.*

> Ni adan' berllan, o bydd,—
> Heb ei noethi.
>
> *They will leave not an orchard, if there should be one, without making it bare.* *G. ab T. ab Hywel, i ofr.*

Gadwr, *s. m.—pl.* gadwyr (gad—gwr) One who quits, or leaves; a relinquisher.

Gadyd, *s. m.* (gad) A leaving, or remainder.

Gaddaw, *s. m.* (addaw) A promise, a threat.

Gaddaw, *v. a.* (addaw) To promise, or to assure.

Gaddewid, *s. f.—pl. t.* ion (gaddaw) A promise.

Gaf, *s. m.* (ga) A reaching out, or divaricating.

Gafael, *s. m.—pl. t.* ion (gaf—ael) A hold, a grasp, a holding; a fastening. *Gafael srynawg*, a sheriff's arrest; *gafael cyfreithiawl*, a lawful deposit; *gafael cenedl*, the hold or tenure of a family; *gafael ty*, the gable of a house; *gafael o dir*, a hold of land; a division so called.

> Pedair rhandir yn mhob gafael.
>
> *Four shares of land in every tenure.* *Welsh Laws.*

Gafaeldrin, *s. m.* (gafael—trin) A close combat, or grapple. *v. a.* To fight grapplingly.

Gafaelfach, *s m.—pl t.* au (gafael—bach) A grappling-hook, or a grappler; a holdfast.

Gafaelgar, *a.* (gafael) Apt to hold, or tenacious.

Gafaelgarwch, *s. m.* (gafaelgar) Tenaciousness.

Gafaelgi, *s. m.—pl. t.* on (gafael—ci) A mastiff.

> Gwelynt heusawr a rhuchen o grwyn am dano, a gafaelgi cedenawg arn ei law.
>
> *They could see a herdsman with a coat of skins about him, and a shaggy mastiff close at his hand.* *H. Culhwch—Mabinogion.*

Gafaeliad, *s. m.—pl. t.* au (gafael) A holding, or laying hold of; a grasping, a caption.

Gafaeliaw, *v. a.* (gafael) To lay hold; to grasp; to grapple.

Gafaeliawg, *a.* (gafael) Having hold; grasping.

Gafaelu, *v. a.* (gafael) To hold, to lay hold of; to grasp, to grapple; to arrest.

> Gafael griw y'nghad,
> Gafaelid wlad;
> Gafaelant feirdd ei gad.
>
> *With the grasp of a hero in the conflict let him hold his country; the bards will lay hold of his treasure.* *Cynddelw, i O. Cyfeiliawg.*

Gafaelus, *a.* (gafael) Apt to hold, that holdeth fast, tenacious, clinging, adhering.

Gafaelwr, *s. m.—pl.* gafaelwyr (gafael—gwr) A holder, a grasper, a grappler; a distrainer.

Gafaelydd, *s. m.—pl. t.* ion (gafael) A holder.

Gafl, *s. m.—pl. t.* au (gaf) A fork or angle; the share, or inside of the thighs.

Gaflach, *s. m.—pl. t.* au (gafl) A fork, or angle; a barbed or bearded spear; a kind of hunting-pole; the stride, fork, or inside of the thighs. *Taflu gaflachau*, to throw darts.

Gaflaidd, *a.* (gafl) In the form of a fork.

Gaflachawg, *a.* (gaflach) Furcated, carrying a bearded dart; wide between the legs.

> Dechreu ffo a orugant y brenhinoedd [illegible] pan welynt y torfoedd buddygawl amryfel, a byddinoedd Gruffudd frenin; ac ei arwyddion yn eu herbyn, a gwyr Denmarc ag eu bwyeill deufiniawg, a'r Gwyddyl gaflachawg, ag eu pelau haiarnawl cyllellawg, a'r Gwyndyd gleddawg tariannawg.
>
> *The kings began therefore to retreat when they beheld the multitude of victorious bands, and the ranks of king Gruffudd; and his banners set against them; and the men of Denmark with their two-edged axes; and the dart-bearing Gwyddelians, with their iron balls full of spikes; and the Gwyneddians with swords and shields.* *Buch. Gr. ab Cynan.*

Gaflachiad, *s. m.* (gaflach) A dividing into forks, a forking; a becoming forked.

Gaflachu, *v. a.* (gaflach) To divide into two, or to fork; to become forked; to beard.

Gaflaw, *s. m.—pl. t.* on (gafl) A salmon-peel, a young salmon, or suin.

Gaflaweg, *s. f.* (gaflaw) A salmon, or suin net.

> Gaflaweg, deuddeg ceiniawg a dal.
>
> *The suin net its value is twelve pence.* *Welsh Laws.*

Gaflawg, *a.* (gafl) Having a fork or barb.

Gaflgam, *a.* (gafl—cam) Having the thighs bent outward; crooked thighs.

Gafr, *s. f.—pl.* geifr or gafrod (gaf) A goat. *Gafr ddan*, *gafr ddanas*, a hind; *gafr y dwr*, a water-spider.

> Mwy no'r afr er dangaws ei thin.
>
> *No more than the goat after showing her tail.* *Adage.*

Gafraidd, *a.* (gafr) Like a goat, goatish.

Gafren, *s. f. dim.* (gafr) A little she-goat.

Gafriad, *s. m.* (gafr) A harvesting of grain in heaps smaller than the stack.

Gafriaw, *v. a.* (gafr) To tie in little whisps, or bundles. *Gafriaw yd*, to rear up corn in small whisps; *gafriaw ffa*, to tie beans; a method of harvesting sometimes used.

Gafriam, *s. m.—pl. t.* au (gafr—llam) A capriole.

Gag, *s. f.—pl. t.* au (gag) An aperture, or opening

Gagen, *s. f.—pl. t.* au (gag) A cleft, a chink, a rift, a slit; a chap.

Gagenaidd, *a.* (gagen) Apt to rift, slit, or chap.

Gagenawg, *a.* (gagen) Full of chinks, or rifts.

Gagenawl, *a.* (gagen) Tending to slit, or chap.

Gagendor, *s. m.* (gagen—tor) A yawning gulf.

> Pan fo dy enaid am y clo
> A myn'd i'r fawr dragwyddawl fro,
> Oes brid wrth agor cil y ddôr,
> Pa du i'r agendor fyddo?
>
> *When thy soul is on the instant of going into the vast eternal region, is there no regard when the door begins to open, on which side of the gulf it may be?* *Elis Wyn, B. Cwsg.*

Gageniad, *s. m.* (gagen) A rifting, or chapping.

Gagenu, *v. a.* (gagen) To cleft, to rift; to slit; to chap; to gape, or to open.

Gai, *s. m.* (ga) What is thrown out; foam, spray.

Gail, *s. m.—pl.* geiliau (ga—il) The eye-lid.

Gaing, *s. m.—pl.* geingau (ainc) A wedge.

> Pob yn ddryll ydd â'r aing yn y pren.
>
> *By little and little the wedge goes into the timber.* *Adage.*

Gair, *s. m.—pl.* geiriau (ga—ir) A word; a saying; a report, or fame. *Gair da*, good report; *mae iti air bod yn meddwi*, there is a report of thee that thou dost get drunk; *ar fy ngair*, upon my word.

> Nid gair gair alltud ar Gymmro.
>
> *The word of a stranger is not a word over a Welshman.* *Adage.*

> O bedwar gair a'u perthynasau yr holir, ac o dri gair yr atebir.
>
> *Of four sayings and their relations there shall be questioning, and of three sayings there shall be answering.* *Welsh Laws.*

> A gair yw ei air ef ar bawb.
>
> *And his word is a word over every body.* *Welsh Laws.*

> Ni chollaist—
> Na'th air da, na'th wir di.
>
> *Thou hast not lost nor thy good word, nor thy right.* *Ior. Fynglwyd.*

Gaith, *s. f.—pl.* geithoedd (ga—ith) Utterance; perspicuity, clearness. *a.* Open, clear.

Gal, *s. m.—pl.* geli (ga—al) What is uttered, ejected, spread out, or cleared; an epithet for milk; a cleared or fair spot; a plain; a goal, or conspicuous station; also what breaks out, or makes an irruption; an enemy. The Cymmry, though they were generally careful of preserving their patronymic name, were often called after names characteristic of the countries they inhabited; the two most universal of which being the open plains and the woods; hence originated the two grand distinctions of *Gal* and *Celt*, or the *open plain* and the *covert*, with others of similar import. Of the same meaning with *Gal* and its derivatives are *Gwal*, *Prydain*, *Peithyw*, *Gwynedd*, *Gwent*, and *Syllwg*, fair or clear regions. With *Ceiltiaid*, may be classed the *Gwyddyl* or *Gwyddelod*; the *Ysgotiaid*, or *Ysgodogion*, and *Celyddon*,—the people of the coverts; of whom it is remarkable to observe, that not one became so powerful and stationary as to confer its name on the country. These two classes subsisted by different means, the result of which must of necessity have been a state of warfare; hence with the *Celt* the appellation of *Gal* came to be synonymous with Enemy; for as the *Gal* or cleared region, became too fully peopled, it sent out colonies in search of other settlements, to occupy which war must frequently have been the consequence

Eryr Gal ynhwch glew hael,
Rhyfel goddig, boddig fael;
Urien grudiawl gafael.

The eagle of *Gal* of violent thrust, brave and generous, vexed by war, precious treasure! Urien of ardent grasp.
Llywarch Hen.

Gwalchmai ym gelwir, gal Edwin ac Eingl——
O eisillydd Cynan.

Gwalchmai am I called, the *foe* of Edwin and the Angles, of the progeny of Cynan. *Gwalchmai.*

Tyllon ei alon ei al a gedwis
O gadwent ac ynial.

Overwhelmed are his foes, his *station* he has preserved from conflict and from tumult. *Ll. P. Moch.*

Cyn esgar llew llachar llachwres
A'i alon, a'i al anghymes,
Cynniflaid bleiniaid bleiddiau armes cad,
Bleiddiaa coed a'u llewes.

Ere the furious lion of gleaming heat separated from his foes, from his matchless *station*, the forward combatants, parties of the ominous conflict, the wolves of the wood devoured them.
Ll. P. Moch.

Gal, *a.* (ga—al) Uttered; spread out; cleared; clear; fair.

Llysoedd hardd——
A thir gal heb anialwch.

Noble mansions, and *fair* land without a wilderness.
Ieuan Tew, i Lyn Taf.

Afon reawg——
A'i hynt hir mewn gweundir gal.

A flowing river with its long course in *fair* meadow-land.
Ieuan Tew, i Lyn Taf.

Galaeth, *s. f.* (gal) The galaxy, or milky way.

Galaf, *s. m.* (gal) The green sward.

Galan, *s. f.—pl. t.* oedd (gal—an) That is deprived of being; a corpse, or dead body.

Galanas, *s. f.—pl. t.* au (galan) A massacre, or murder; also, in the laws, satisfaction for murder.

Y mae galanas y lladdedigion eto heb ddial.

The *murder* of the slaughtered ones is yet unrevenged.
H. Car. Mag.—Mabinogion.

Galanas boneddig cannwynawl, ac alltud brenin, tair buw a thriugain muw.

The *murder retribution* of a native gentlemen, and a king's foreign attendant is sixty three cows. *Welsh Laws.*

Galanas wasgarawg. Mal hyn y telir gwasgar alanas; punt fydd rhan brawd, chweugaint rhan cefnderw, triugaint rhan cyfyrderw, deg-arugaint rhan ceifn, pymtheg yw rhan gorcheifn, saith a dimai rhan gorchaw.

A divided *murder retribution*. In this manner shall be paid a divisible *murder retribution*, the share of a brother shall be a pound; the share of a cousin six score pence; the share of a second cousin three score pence, the share of a third cousin thirty pence the share of a fourth cousin fifteen pence, and the share of one of the fifth degree seven pence halfpenny. *Welsh Laws.*

Galanasawl, *a.* (galanas) Murderous, slaughtering

Galanasdra, *s. f.* (galanas) A massacre, general slaughter, or murder. *Rhoes ei alanasdra arnynt*, he laid his murder upon them.

Galanasiad, *s. m.* (galanas) A massacreing.

Galanasu, *v. a.* (galanas) To massacre, to murder.

Galar, *s. m.—pl. t.* au (gal—ar) Lamentation.

Tri achaws cyffredin sydd i alar: serch, coll, a gwrthwyneb.

There are three general causes of *lamentation*: love, loss, and repulse. *Barddas.*

Galareb, *s. f.—pl. t.* ion (galar) The voice of mourning; threnody; monody.

Galargan, *s. f.* (galar—can) A monody, an elegy.

Galargerdd, *s. f.—pl. t.* i (galar—cerdd) A monody, a song of lamentation.

Galargerdd yw can gwynfanus, hiraethlawn; a'i phrif achaws ac amcan yw galar.

The *monody* is a plaintive and mournful song; and its leading cause and intention is lamentation. *Barddas.*

Galargorn, *s. m.—pl.* galargyrn (galar—corn) The horn of lamentation.

Galargwyn, *s. f.—pl. t.* ion (galar—cwyn) The complaint of mourning; a monody.

Galargwynaw, *v. a.* (galargwyn) To mourn.

Galariad, *s. m.* (galar) A sorrowing, a mourning.

Galarloes, *s. f.—pl. t.* au (galar—gloes) The pang of mourning or lamentation.

Galarnad, *s. f.—pl. t.* au (galar—nâd) The cry of mourning, lamentation.

Galarnadu, *v. a.* (galarnad) To utter lamentation.

Galarnwyf, *s. m.—pl. t.* au (galar—nwyf) The passion of grief, or mourning.

Galaru, *v. a.* (galar) To mourn, or to lament.

Galarus, *a.* (galar) Mournful, lamentable.

Bid trist pob galarus.

Let every *mourning* one be dejected. *Adage.*

Ni chwsg gofalus, ac e gwsg galarus.

The one oppressed with care will not sleep, but the *sorrowful* will sleep. *Adage.*

Galarusrwydd, *s. m.* (galarus) Mournfulness, sorrowfulness, dolefulness, lamentableness.

Galarwawd, *s. m.* (galar—gwawd) A dirge.

Galarwisg, *s. f.—pl. t.* oedd (galar—gwisg) A mourning apparel, or weeds.

Galarwr, *s. m.* (galar—gwr) A mourner.

Galarydd, *s. m.—pl. t.* ion (galar) A mourner.

Galawnt, *a.* (gal) Brave, gallant; fair.

F' anwylyd, wyd fun alawnt.

My dear, thou art a *fair* damsel. *Ieuan Dyfi.*

Galeg, *s. f.* (gal) The language of the people of Gal; the Gaulish tongue.

Galeu, *s. f.—pl. t.* i (gal) A whet stone.

Galiod, *s. pl. aggr* (gal) The people of Gal; the people of Galloway.

Galofydd, *s. m.—pl. t.* ion (gal—ofydd) An architect; a fine artist.

Tri galofydd Ynys Prydain. Greidiawl, Trystan mab Tallwch, a Gwgon Gwron.

The three *architects* of the isle of Britain Greidiol, Trystan the son of Tallwch, and Gwgon Gwron. *Trioedd.*

Llywelyn gelyn galofydd,
Llwyr gyrch darogan cyman celfydd.

Llywelyn that is a foe *that builds castles*, that is exactly pointed at by the accurate prophecy. *Llygad Gwr, i Lywelyn II.*

Galofyddiaeth, *s. m.* (galofydd) The fine or higher arts; architecture.

Galon, *s. pl. aggr.* (gal) Enemies, hostile ones.

Rhyddyrllid fy ngherdd——
Pan wnaeth pen dragon pendrychion o wyr
Pan drychws ei alon.

Greatly incumbent was my song when the sovereign leader made broken headed men, when he hewed his *foes*.
Cynddelw, i O. Gwynedd.

Galw, *s. m.* (gal) A call; an invocation; a naming. *Bod wrth alw*, to be at a call.

Galw, *v. a.* (gal) To call, to invoke; to appeal to; to name. *Galw arno*, call upon him; *pwy sy'n galw*, who is calling, or who calls; *un a eilw*, one that calls; *galw ar y dosbarth*, to appeal against the decision; *galw barn*, to appeal for judgement; *galw ychain*, to drive oxen in drawing. *galw at arfau*, to call to arms.

Galwad, *s. m.—pl. t.* au (galw) A calling; an appeal. a vocation.

Galwadawl, *a.* (galwad) Relating to a calling.

Galwai, *s. m.—pl.* galweion (galw) A caller; an invoker; the vocative case; a driver of oxen.

Galwedig, *a.* (galw) Called; nominated, named.

Galwedigaeth, *s. m.—pl. t.* au (galwedig) A calling; an invocation; an appealing; a vocation, profession, or occupation.

Gwneuthur galwedigaeth am gamfarn.

To make an *appeal* respecting a wrong verdict. *Welsh Laws.*

Galwedigaethawl, *a.* (galwedigaeth) Professional.

Galwedigaethydd, *s. m.—pl. t.* ion (galwedigaeth) The nominative case, in grammar.

Galwedigawl, *a.* (galwedig) Vocative; belonging to a calling: denominative; nominative.

Galwys, *s. pl. aggr.* (gal—gwys) The men of Gal, or the Gauls.

Galwyth, *s. m.* (gal—gwyth) The rage of war.

Galwythaint, *s. m.* (galwyth) The wrath of war.

Pedwar meib ar ugaint yn nghenfaint Llywarch,
O wyr glew galwythaint;
Twll eu dyfod clod trameint.

Four and twenty sons in the family of Llywarch, of brave men of *warring wrath*, their coming is observed, whose fame was above measure. *Llywarch Hen.*

Gall, *s. m.* (ga—all) Energy; power; ability, capability; possibility; an eventual state, or when it is possible to be.

Gallad, *s. m.* (gall) A being able; ability.

Gallael, *v. n.* (gall) To be able, to have power; to be possible; may, or can.

Galldwymyn, *s. m.* (gall—twymyn) Tertian ague.

Galldwyn, *s. m.* (gall—twyn) The plague.

Galledig, *a.* (gall) Having power, potential.

Galledigaeth, *s. m.—pl. t.* au (galledig) Energy; possibility.

Tri pheth nis gellir darfod byth arnynt gan angen eu galledigaeth: dull hanfod, ansawdd hanfod, a lles hanfod, gan hyn byddant hyd byth yn eu hanawg, ai byw ai marw ydynt, yn amrytel harddu a daioni cylch y gwynfyd.

Three things can never be annihilated from the unavoidableness of their *possibility*: mode of existence, essentiality of existence, and utility of existence; these will, divested of their evil, endure for ever, animate or inanimate, as varieties of the beautiful and good in the circle of felicity. *Barddas.*

Gallel, *v. n.* (gall) To be of power, or ability, to be able: to effectuate; to have power to; to be possible.

I dai drwg onid ai draw,
Odid allel dy dwyllaw.

If to bad houses thou dost not yonder stray, seldom *will it be possible* to deceive thee. *G. ab I. ab Ll. Fychan.*

Gallmarw, *a.* (gall—marw) Under the possibility of dying, ready to die, half dead.

Yr awr i llewes yr ast y bara i bu allmarw, ac i syrthiai ei blew oll yn yr encyd.

And the instant the bitch devoured the bread she was *half dead*, and her hair fell off at the time. *Buchedd Dewi.*

Ef ei curei, ac ei gadawai yn allmarw.

He beat him, and he left him *nearly dead*. *Mabinogion.*

Gallt, *s. m.—pl. t.* oedd (gall) Energy, power.

Cymerai Adda ac Efa—
I gysgod i bei gwisgoedd,
A gwybod eu bod heb allt,
Rhyw ddyn'n anghywallt.

He took Adam and Eve to a shelter to procure garments; and knowing them to be void of *help*, a certain condition of nakedness. *Dr. S. Cent.*

Y mae gwared imi o'i gerydd,
A gallt i'w ado, a gwell diodydd.

There is deliverance for me from his severity, and means to leave him, and for better liquors. *D. ab Edmwnd.*

Gallt, *s. f.—pl.* gelltydd (gall) An ascent; a cliff; a woody cliff, or steep. *Yn allt ac yn ngwaered*, on the ascent and on the descent. *Welsh Laws.* It forms the names of several places; as *Gallt Fadawg*, *Gallt y Crib*, *Gallt y Mor*, *Pen yr Allt*, *Yr Allt Goch*, *Yr Allt Rudd*, *Yr Allt Wen*, *Y Wenallt*, *Y Dduallt*, *Y Felallt*, *Y Goedallt*.

Galltofydd, *s. m.—pl. t.* ion (gallt—ofydd) An artist of power; a mechanic.

Gallu, *s. m.—pl. t.* oedd (gall) Energy, power, might, ability; puissance.

Ni eill neb namyn ei allu.

Nobody can do beyond his *ability*. *Adage.*

Gallu, *v. n.* (gall) To be of power, or ability, to be able; to effectuate; to have power to, to be possible; may, or can.

Ni eill Duw dda i ddiriad.

God *can do* no good to the wicked. *Adage.*

Tri pheth nis gellir bardd hebddynt: awen wrth gerdd, gwybod cyfrinach barddas, a chynneddfau da.

Three things without which no one *can be* a bard; genius for poetry, knowledge in the mystery of bardism, and good morals. *Barddas.*

Ni allan' hyn a allych;
Nid hyfryd byd ond lle bych.

They can not what thou canst do; there is no *pleasure of life* but where thou art. *Huw Cowrys.*

Gallnad, *s. m.* (gallu) A making able, or enabling; a becoming enabled.

Galluadwy, *a.* (gallnad) Possible, effectible.

Galluaidd, *a.* (gallu) Of a powerful nature.

Gallnaw, *v. a.* (gallu) To endue with power.

Gallnawg, *a.* (gallu) Powerful, mighty, puissant.

Gallnawl, *a.* (gallu) Energetic, potent; possible.

Galluedig, *a.* (gallu) Endued with power.

Galluedigaeth, *s. m.—pl. t.* au (galluedig) A rendering able, or powerful.

Galluedigaw, *v. a.* (galluedig) To endue with power, to make mighty; to become able.

Galluedigawl, *a.* (galluedig) Potential.

Galluedd, *s. m.* (gallu) Puissance, ability; faculty, or power of acting.

Gallueiddrwydd, *s. m.* (galluaidd) Possibility.

Gallnogawl, *a.* (galluawg) Potential.

Gallnogedd, *s. m.* (galluawg) Potentiality.

Gallnogi, *v. a.* (galluawg) To empower.

Galluogrwydd, *s. m.* (galluawg) Powerfulness.

Gallnolrwydd, *s. m.* (gallnawl) Potentiality.

Gallus, *a.* (gall) Powerful, mighty; able.

Coronawg faban, medd Eraigen,
Hen ddewin yr Alban, a fydd allus.

A crowned infant, says Eraigen, an old prophet of Alban, will be *mighty*. *E. Nanmor, A. C. Faban.*

Gallusrwydd, *s. m.* (gallus) Potentialness.

Galliüs, *a.* (gallu) Potential; potent; able.

Galliüsrwydd, *s. m.* (galliüs) Potentialness.

Gallwyddel, *s. m.—pl.* gallwyddyl (gall—gwyddel) A name sometimes used for *Gwyddel*, woodman, an Irishman; but more appropriately to certain tribes, who partly lived in the woods and partly cultivated land.

Gan, *s. f.* (ga—an) A bringing forth; a birth. *Yr an wen*, the white thrush; *yr an goch*, the red thrush, diseases so called.

Gân, *s. m.—pl. t.* oedd (an) Capacity, or what has the power to contain; a mortise.

Gàn, *prep.* (càn) With; in company; in connection; in consequence of. *Genyf nid oes mor arian*, in my possession there is no money; *pa beth sy genyd?* what hast thou got? *mae ganddo olud*, he has got wealth; *bod ganddi*, to be with her; *mae ganom obaith*, we have hope; *nid oes ganoch ddim*, you have got nothing; *caf les ganddynt*, I shall obtain benefit from them; *aeth gàn y bad*, he went with the boat.

Adneu cybyryn gan gath.

To pawn a piece of flesh *with* a cat. *Adage.*

O'r dyrnawd hwnw dygwyddaw a wnai Ffrollo, ac a'i sodlau, maeddu y ddaiar, ac ellwng i enaid gan yr awel.

From that blow Frollo fel down, and with his heels he tore the ground, and let his soul pass away *with* the gale. *Gr. ab Arthur.*

Gàn, *conj.* (càn) In consequence of, because of, because; whereas, for as much; since. *Gan wneuthur o honot hyn o beth*, forasmuch as thou hast done this thing.

Ganawl, *a.* (gàn) Relating to capacity.

Ganiad, *s. m.* (gàn) A containing, a holding.

Ganu, *v. n.* (gan) To be of capacity; to contain. *Càn llawned ag y ganant*, as full as they can contain; *mal yr ano lawer*, so that it shall hold much.

Ganid ym wys yn nhy Duw.

There was room made for my call in the house of God. *Adage.*

Os adaw y llys a wna dyn yn anghyfreithiawl, ei ddyfarnu a wneir yn oes yr arglwydd biewfo yr orsedd hono; can ni ein yn mro ni rodda wir.

If a man shall quit the court unlawfully, he shall be held condemned during the life of the lord to whom that bench belongs; for he that will not yield justice, *can* not be received in a country. *Welsh Laws.*

Teulu Owain hael——
A ganir wedi hirdaith:
A ganwn yn Rhos noswaith!

The family of Owain the generous *will find reception* after a long journey; *shall we take up our abode* in Rhos for a night! *T. O. Cyfeiliawg.*

Gàr, *s. m.—pl. t.* au (ga) The shank; the ham, or lower part of the thigh. *Camedd gar*, the bend of the knee, or the ham; *afal y gàr*, the knee pan.

Tyfid ebawl o byd gar.

Let the colt grow from the *ham.* *Adage.*

Gàr, *prep.* (gèr) At, by, nigh, near, hard by. *Gàr llaw*, at hand; *gàr bron*, in presence.

Gàran, *s. m.—pl. t.* od (gàr) A shank; a shaft; a crane, or heron. *Garan grychydd*, the little crane; *garan hwyad*, the common wild duck.

Nid anferth ond garan.

Nothing so disproportioned as a *heron.* *Adage.*

Mal y garan am ei ddwygoes.

Like the *heron* for his two legs. *Adage.*

Garanawg, *a.* (garan) Branching out into shafts; greatly limbed, long shanked.

Os ciaf modur mur mawredd garanawg
Goronwy grair goreedd.——
Boed gwared.

The leading chief, the bulwark of *far-branching greatness*, Goronwy the hallowed one of the judgement-seat, if he is sick, be deliverance near. *G. ab M. ab Dafydd, i O. ab Tudur.*

Garanhir, *a.* (garan—hir) Long shanked.

Garanu, *v. a.* (garan) To furnish with a shank.

Llawer o brif orchestion sydd arnaf——
Garanu troell-faen breuanllif.

There are many first-rate excellencies belonging to me,—as the *putting a spindle* in the whirl-stone of a grinder. *G. ab I. ab Ll. Fychan.*

Gardas, *s. m.—pl.* gardysau (gàr—tas) A garter.

Gardys, *s. m.—pl. t.* au (gàr—tys) A garter.

Gardd, *s. f.—pl.* gerddi (gar) An enclosure; a garden. *Gardd yd*, corn-yard; *gardd wair*, hay garth; *gardd fagai*, a nursery.

Iddo fo mae neuadd falch,
Ac yn wengaer gan wyn-galch,
Ac o gylch ogylch i hon
Naw o arddau yn wyrddion.

To him belongs a gay hall, being white walled with fair lime and round about this nine *gardens* that are green. *L. G. Cothi.*

Gardden, *s. f. dim.* (gardd) A little garden.

Garddiad, *s. m.* (gardd) A making a garden; a gardening, or cultivating a garden.

Garddu, *v. a.* (gardd) To make a garden; to garden, or to cultivate a garden.

Garddwr, *s. m.—pl.* garddwyr (gardd) Gardener.

Garddwriaeth, *s. m.* (garddwr) Horticulture.

Garddwy, *s. m. aggr.* (gardd) Caraway, or carui.

Garfwch, *s. m.—pl.* garfychau (gàr—bwch) A flat-bottomed boat; a punt.

Gàrgam, *s. m.* (gar—cam) A bandy-legged person; a cripple. *a.* Knock-kneed.

Garhir, *a.* (gàr—hir) Having a long shank. *Englyn garhir*, a metre having one long verse, and the others shorter.

Oedd re redaint dan forddwyd Geraint,
Garhirion grawn foloeb, .
Rhuddion ruthr eryron coch.

Under the thigh of Geraint were fleet runners, *long-legged* and throwing about the grain, ruddy ones with the assault of the red eagles. *Llywarch Hen.*

Garllaes, *a.* (gàr-llaes) Limping, halting. *Englyn garllaes*, a metre so called, ending with a long verse.

Garlleg, *s. pl. aggr.* (gàr—lleg) The garlick.

Garllegan, *s. f. dim.* (garlleg) A head of garlick.

Garllegawg, *a.* (garlleg) Abounding with garlick. *Yr allegawg*, the snake's garlick.

Garm, *s. f.—pl. t.* oedd (ga—arm) An out-cry.

Rhegain garm rhyw gwn gormes;
Rhugl groen yn rhoi gwlaw a gwres.

The echoing of the cry of some depredating dogs; a noisy rambler that gives both rain and heat. *D. ab Gwilym, i'r daran.*

Garmiad, *s. m.* (garm) A shouting, or hallooing.

Garmiaw, *v. a.* (garm) To shout, to raise a cry.

Dafydd—mae i erchi rhodd;
Gormes a wyddiad garmio;
Garw flewyn a fyn fo.

Dafydd is come to crave a gift; a troublesome one who knows *to bawl*, a rough-haired one he would like to have. *W. Cynwal, i afyn bwch.*

Garmiawl, *a.* (garm) Shouting, or bawling.

Garmwyn, *s. m.—pl. t.* ion (garm) One of the shout; an epithet for a warrior.

Garsyth, *a.* (gàr—syth) Being stiff in the hams.

Garth, *s. f.—pl. t.* au (gar) A buttres, or rampart; a fort; a fold; a cape; a ridge; such a mountain ridge as forms a bend or cove. It forms the appellation of several places; as, *Garth Anarawd*, *Garth Beibio*, *Penarth*, *Gogarth*, *Garth Au*, and *Llwydiarth*.

Garthan, *s. f.* (garth) A camp, an encampment; battle array; battle.

A rhagod, pen clod claer vegwydawg,
E gud-wan garthan is Garthyuiawg.
Gwaed am draed.——

And before thee, who art foremost in fame, surrounded with bright shields, swiftly breaking through the *battle* below Garthyuiawg, and blood flowing round the feet. *Ll. P. Moch, i Lywelyn I.*

Ymcf a'i herly arlwy garthan dyn,
Llywelyn gwawd-wyn gwan.

He that pursues it, the provision of the firm *camp*, is Llywelyn of fair famed course. *Llywarch Llaety, i L. ab Madawg.*

Garthâu, *v. a.* (garth) To fortify; to defend.

Garthen, *s. f.—pl. t.* au (garth) An encampment.

Gartheniad, *s. m.—pl.* gartheniaid (garthen) A defender; a striver, or contender.

Ieuan——
Gwrthwyneb galon, gartheniad gydbar,
Gwrddgar, gwingar ior.

Ieuan the vexer of the foes, the *champion* with the mutual spear, a powerful and wine-enjoying chief. *D. ab Gwilym.*

Garthon, *s. m.* (garth) A rod to drive oxen with.

Garw, *s. m.—pl.* geirw (gàr) What is rough, or rugged; a torrent. *Y garw*, the after-birth; *tori y garw*, to break the rough; to break a great craving, to stay the stomach.

Garw, *a.* (gàr) Rough, rugged, uneven, harsh, sharp, severe. *Tywydd garw*, severe weather; *mor garw*, a rough sea; *mae yn arw iddo fod yno*, it is terrible for him to be there; *mae yn arw genyf am dano*, I am grieved for him.

Angeu garw drud a'i heirch.

Bold is he that chooses a *violent* death. *Adage.*

Mae ein meddyliau ni ynghylch y ddaear yn arwon ac yn anfanwl, o'r fath ag sydd yn gweddu i'n cyflwr.

Our ideas with respect to the earth are rough and inaccurate, of the sort that are consonant to our condition. *Ier. Owain.*

Garwhad, *s. m.* (garw) A making rough; a becoming rough, or rugged; a roughening.

Garwhawl, *a.* (garw) Tending to roughen.

Garwaidd, *a.* (garw) Of a rough, or severe nature.

Garwain, *a.* (garw) Abounding with roughness.

Garwâu, *v. a.* (garw) To roughen; to become rough, or rugged; to become severe.

Garwedd, *s. m.* (garw) Roughness, ruggedness.

Garwen, *s. f.* (garw) A rough female; a virago.

Gast, *s. f.—pl.* geist (ga—ast) A bitch. *Gast dòrarg*, a bitch big with young.

Gasten, *s. f. dim.* (gast) A little bitch.

Gau, *s. m.* (ga—au) What is covered, hidden, or masked; a falsehood, a lie.

Goreu pedestr yw gau.

The best traveller is a *lie*. *Adage.*

Pan farno Dofydd, dydd hir,
Tywyll fydd gau, goleu gwir.

When the Lord shall judge, long the day, *falsehood* shall be dark, and truth illumined. *Llywarch Hen.*

Gau, *a.* (ga) Hidden, masked; false, lying.

Rhys Fychan ei galwant, yn gau,
Rhys fawr falch yn'ngh...ch y 'nghadau.

Rhys the little they call him, it is *false*, he is Rhys the greatly towering in glittering armour in the battles. *Ll. P. Moch.*

Gauaf, *s. m.—pl. t.* oedd (gau—af) Winter. *Eidion tri gauaf*, a beast of three winters old.

Gauafaidd, *a.* (gauaf) Wintery, winter-like.

Gauafar, *s. m.* (gauaf—âr) Winter ploughing.

Gauafawl, *a.* (gauaf) Brumal, or wintery.

Py ddyg Herod—
Awyd gauafawl.

What brought on Herod the *wintery* blast. *Taliesin.*

Gauafawr, *a.* (gauaf) Brumal, or wintery.

Cynhwrf yn aber, llyr yn llanw,
Cynghyd gauafawr hwyliawr heli.

A tumult in the frith, the tide rising high, the *wintery* season raging in the course of the ocean. *Ll. P. Moch.*

Gauafdy, *s. m.—pl. t.* au (gauaf—ty) A winter house, a winter cot.

Gauafle, *s. m.—pl. t.* oedd (gauaf—lle) Winter quarter, or a winter place.

Gauafnos, *s. f.* (gauaf—nos) A winter night.

Gauafrawd, *s. m.* (gauaf—rhawd) The course or sway of winter.

Oer gauafrawd, tawd morfa.

Cold the *reign of winter*, naked is the sea-shore. *Llefard.*

Gauafu, *v. a.* (gauaf) To winter, to pass a winter.

Aethym i'r mor mewn llong o Alexandria, yr hon a fuasai yn gauafu yn yr ynys.

We went to sea in a ship of Alexandria, the which had been *wintering* in the island. *W. Salisbury.*

Gaulid, *s. m.* (gau—llid) Shame.

Gaw, *s. m.* (ga) What stretches, or extends; a sinew, tendon, or muscle.

Gawl, *s. m.—pl.* gwlau (awl) A light; a dawn. *a.* Holy, pure. *Tyle y Gawl*, the station of the light; a place so called in Glamorganshire.

Gawn, *a.* (awn) Direct; right, or just.

Gawr, *s. f.—pl.* gorian (awr) A shout, an outcry; a tumult, a conflict; a gray colour.

Gwelais wyr gorfawr
A ddygyrchynt awr.

I have seen gigantic men hastening to the *shout*. *Taliesin.*

Llas Morgan mur gawr, llafar wawr waner,
Llary, llarbar, llawch ceraddawr.

Slain is Morgant the bulwark of the *shout*, the leader shining in blue, mild and furious, the refuge of the minstrel.
Cynddelw, m. trais O. Gwynedd.

Gawri, *v. a.* (gawr) To shout, to cry aloud.

Gawriad, *s. m.* (gawr) A shouting, or bawling.

Gawy, *a.* (gaw) Muscular; nervous; strong.

GE, *s. m. r.* Aptitude. It is doubtful whether it is used except as a prefix in composition.

Gefail, *s. f.—pl.* gefeiliau (gaf—ail) Tongs, pincers, or nippers; a smithery, or smithy. *Gefail gnau*, nut-crackers.

Ymryson a'r gof yn ei efail.

To contend with the smith in his *smithy*. *Adage.*

Mae main ar bob adain hol,
Man gwynion, fal main gwenol;
Gwlith y gof, gloew, a theg ynt;
Gwiw flodau gefail ydynt.

There are stones set on each smooth wing; small and white, like those on a shuttle; the dew-drops of the smith, so clear and fair; they are the finest flowers of the *smithy*.
Gut. Owain, i davian.

Gefeiliad, *s. m.* (gefail) A holding with pincers, a pinching, or nipping.

Gefeiliaw, *v. a.* (gefail) To hold with tongs, or pincers; to use pincers, or nippers.

Gefeiliawg, *a.* (gefail) Pinching, or nipping.

Gefeiliaist fal drud, gefeiliawg yth law,
Gafaelus draig frwy fraw cymynawg.

Thou didst take hold like a fury, *of firm grasp* in thy hand, thou tenacious and active leader of the torrent of wounding.
Ll. P. Moch, i Lywelyn I.

Gefeilydd, *s. m.—pl. t.* ion (gefail) One who takes hold, one who holds with pincers.

Gefell, *s. c.—pl. t.* od (gav—ell) A twin. *Dau efell*, two twins.

Am Fadawg, fardd-ful efell—
Uthr yw gwnaw!

For Madawg, twin of the bardic song, terrible is the pang!
D. ab Gwilym.

Gefyn, *s. m.—pl. t.* au (gaf) A fetter, a gyve; a manicle, a shackle.

Gefynawg, *a.* (gefyn) Fettered, or shackled.

Gefyniad, *s. m.* (gefyn) A fettering, a shackling.

Gefyniaeth, *s. m.* (gefyn) A fettered condition.

Hon a roes haen i'm poeni;
Hiraeth gefyniaeth, gwae fi!

She has given a bond to torment me; it is the mourning of *bondage*, ah me! *D. ab Gwilym.*

Gefynu, *v. a.* (gafyn) To fetter, or to shackle.

Gefynwr, *s. m.—pl.* gefynwyr (gefyn—gwr) One who puts on fetters.

Geian, *s. m.* (gai) Spray, froth, or foam.

Geifawr, *a.* (gai—mawr) Greatly foaming.

Y mor ddygyfor, geifawr, a gyfyd
O'i ogofau trisdfawr.

The surge of the sea, greatly foaming, will rise out of his cells vast and awful. *D. Kanmer.*

Geilig, *a.* (gai) Apt to explore, or to hunt out.

Llawer ci geilig, a hebawg wyrenig
A lithiwyd ar ei llawr,
Cyn bu Erlleon llawedrawr.

Many a *hunting* dog, and aerial hawk have been trained on its floor, ere that Erlleon was desolate. *Llywarch Hen.*

Geilwad, *s. m.—pl.* geilwaid (galw) A caller, or crier. *Geilwad ychain*, a driver of oxen.

Geilyg, *s. m.* (gal) The state of being made clear.

Geingiad, *s. m.* (gaing) A driving in a wedge.

Geingiaw, *v. a.* (gaing) To drive in a wedge.

Geirber, *a.* (gair—per) Sweetly-speaking.

Geirda, *s. m.* (gair—da) A good word; fame.

> Melys geirda am y garer.
>
> The *praise* of what one loves is sweet. *Adage.*
>
> Gwell i ddyn golli ei dda,
> Ofer-daith, efo ei eirda.
>
> It is folly for a man to lose his property, and useless, with his *character*. *Ed. Morus.*

Geirdardd, *s. m.* (gair—tardd) Etymology.

Geirdarddawl, *a.* (geirdardd) Etymological.

Geirdro, *s. m.—pl. t.* ion (gair—tro) A pun.

Geirdröad, *s. m.* (geirdro) A punning.

Geirdröedydd, *s. m.—pl. t.* ion (geirdröad) A punster, a player upon words.

Geirddadl, *s. f.—pl.* geirddadlau (gair—dadl) A captious argument, or cavil about words.

Geirddadliad, *s. m.* (geirddadl) A cavilling about words; a quibbling.

Geirddadlu, *v. a.* (geirddadl) To cavil about words; to quibble.

Geirddadlus, *a.* (geirddadl) Apt to quibble.

Geirddadlydd, *s. m.—pl. t.* ion (geirddadl) A caviller about words; a quibbler.

Geirddoeth, *a.* (gair—doeth) Of discreet words.

Geirfrith, *a.* (gair—brith) Of probable word.

> Neu'r dierfais i rin—
> Yn geirfrith cyfreain
> Bran bore ddewin!
>
> Have I not exposed a mystery! If the omen of the diviner by the mourning raven be *of probable words*. *Taliesin.*

Geirgall, *a.* (gair—call) Of discreet words.

Geirgar, *a.* (gair—car) Verbose, fond of words.

Geirgarwch, *s. m.* (geirgar) Verbosity, prolixity.

Geiriad, *s. m.—pl. t.* au (gair) A wording.

Geiriadu, *v. a.* (geiriad) To word, to phrase.

Geiriadur, *s. m.—pl. t.* on (geiriad) A vocabulary.

Geiriaw, *v. a.* (gair) To word, or to phrase.

> Nycha, clywn gog, liosog lais,
> Yn geiriaw can a garais.
>
> Lo, I could hear the cuckoo, of full voice, *dictating* a song I loved. *D. ab Gwilym.*

Geiriawg, *a.* (gair) Wordy, verbose, full of words, or talkative. *s. m.—pl.* Geiriogion. A verbose person; an orator, or speaker.

Geiriawl, *a.* (gair) Verbal, garrulous; wordy.

> Yr aelwyd hon a'i gogiud gawr,
> Mwy gorddyfnasai ar i llawr
> Medd a meddwon geiriawl.
>
> This hearth that is forsaken by the shout, more congenial on its floor would have been the mead and *talkative* drunken ones. *Llywarch Hen.*

Geiriolaeth, *s. m.* (geiriawl) Phraseology.

> Mi osodais bob peth o'r athrawiaethau ar ddosbarth, yn y wedd, a'r drefn, a'r modd, herwydd iaith a geiriolaeth ymadrawdd ag y cefais hwynt yn yr hen lyfrau.
>
> I have laid down every thing of the instructions in regimen, in the way, order and mode, with respect to language, and *phraseology* of diction, as I have found them in the old books. *E. Dafydd.*

Geirioli, *v. a.* (geiriawl) To phrase; to verbalize.

> Tri iawnder y sydd ar iaith: iawn eirioli, iawn ymddwyn, ac iawn lefervdd.
>
> There are three just things appertaining to language: just phrasing, just construction, and just enunciation. *Barddas.*

Geiriolus, *a.* (geiriawl) Verbose, garrulous.

Geirlyfr, *s. m.—pl.* geirlyfrau (gair—llyfr) A vocabulary; a dictionary.

Geirllaes, *a.* (gair—llaes) Of drawling words.

Geirllaesrwydd, *s.* (geirllaes) Slowness of speech.

Geirllwydd, *a.* (llwydd) Of prosperous words.

> Fynawg riain fain funed,
> Fun arlludd hun, eirllwydd hud.
>
> She is a polite lady of delicate air, a fair one obstructing sleep, *of word prospering* allurement. *H. ab Einion Llygliw.*

Geirswyn, *s. m.* (gair—swyn) The charm, or power of words.

Geirw, *s. pl. aggr.* (garw) Roughs; surges, or billows; cataracts, or falls.

> Llif eirw o wir llif oer oedd.
> Llai fu eirw'r holl foroedd.
>
> The flowing *of cataracts* from the sky, a cold flood it was, less were the *surges* of all the seas. *Ior. Fynglwyd.*

Geirweddiad, *s. m.* (gair—gweddiad) Phraseology

> Y pethau a berant egler Gymmraeg yw perffaith leithyddiaeth, a chyflawn eirweddiad.
>
> The things that are conducive to perspecuity in the Welsh, are perfect construction, and just *phraseology*. *Barddas.*

Geirwir, *a.* (gair—gwir) Of true words; true.

> Geirwir fywyd a garoedd,
> All Homer, ddysg hyddysg, oedd.
>
> A life of *sincere conversation* he loved, like Homer, profound in learning was he. *Ios. Thomas, o Fergenny.*

Geirydd, *s. m.—pl t.* ion (gair) A worder; a philologist; a speaker.

> Ni elwir yn euawg onis geirydd.
>
> He will not be called lying if he is not a *speaker*. *Adage.*

Gel, *s. f.—pl. t.* od (ge—el) Aptness to flow, or to ooze; a leech. *Gel y meirch*, neu *gel bendoll*, the horse-leech.

Gelach, *s. m.—pl. t.* od (gel) A languid one; a little sorry fellow, a fribble.

Gelawr, *s. f.—pl* geloran (elawr) A bier.

Gele, *s. f.—pl. t.* od (gel) A slow rill; a leech.

> I'r gele y mae dwy ferch yn llefain, moes, moes.
>
> To the *leech* there are two daughters calling, give, give. *Prov.* xxx. 15.

Gelen, *s. f. dim.* (gel) A leech. *Gelen bendoll*, the horse leech.

Geleu, *s. f.—pl. t.* od (gel) That flows imperceptibly, that oozes; a leech.

> Edewis terwyn teyrn feibion,
> A edeu geleu yn eu galon.
>
> The violent one has left behind him royal sons who would leave *gushing of blood* in their foes. *Cynddelw, m. Cadwallon.*

Geleuan, *s. f. dim.* (geleu) A small leech.

Geleurudd, *s. m.* (geleu—rhudd) A flow, or oozing of red. *a.* Red oozing; crimson-stained.

> Geleurudd ein gwyr gwedi lludded trwm,
> Tremid gofwy mur Maelawr drefred.
>
> The *crimson-stain* of our men after heavy toil, be it seen by the visitant of the wall of Maelor Drefred. *O. Cyfeiliawg.*
>
> Bardd Llywelyn hael byd ym gelwir,
> Geleurudd gelyn i bob anwir.
>
> The bard of Llywelyn the generous, though I may be called *stained with blood*, a foe to every unjust one. *Cynddelw.*

Geleuruddiad, *s. m.* (geleurudd) A crimson-stained one; a blood-stained warrior.

> Ef gogwydd galon geleuruddiaid aer
> I orfod ei ysbaid.
>
> He will bring down the foes, *red-stained men* of slaughter to submit to his terms. *L. P. Moch, i Rodri.*

Geleuruddiaw, *v. a.* (geleurudd) To cause a crimson fluid; to stain with blood.

Gelfryd, *s. m.* (gel—bryd) A breaking out of the mind.

> Gwelais Rys yn llys Elasidio,
> Gelfryd gelyn yn allfro.
>
> I have seen Rhys in the hall of Elasidio, with the *raging mind* of an enemy in a foreign country. *Phylip Brydydd, i R. Gryg.*

Geli, *s. m.—pl. t.* on (gel) A shooting out.

> Dyddfawl baladr deddf ail Beli,
> Dawn Duw weli dan dy seilwydd;
> Dwg yn waladr deg iawn eli,
> Donian Celi, dinag hylwydd.
>
> With couched shaft following the example of Beli, the grace of God thou wilt see to support thy undertaking; the gifts of the mysterious one, infallibly prosperous, will produce a leader, a *branch* supremely fair. *Meir. Dafydd.*

Gelin, *s. m.—pl. t.* au (gel) What springs out.

> O lwyth Elystan, a'i lin
> Euraid wal yr wyd elin;
> O gynan, loew lydan wledd,
> Wyd o iawn-waed dwy Wynedd.

Of the tribe of Elystan, and his race of golden heritage, thou art a shoot, by Cynan, of the splendid and ample feast, thou art of the true blood of each Gwynedd. Meir. Dafydd.

Geloer, *a.* (gel—oer) Temperately cold, rather cold; fresh, enlivening, wholesome. *Bore gel-oer teg*, a fair and temperately cold morning. *Diawd eloer iawn*, very refreshing drink. *Gwent*

Geloer, *s m.* (gel—oer) A temperate, or refreshing coldness. *Sefyll yn y geloer*, to stand in a cool place, in warm weather. *Gwent.*

Gelwain, *v. a.* (galw) To cry out frequently.

Gelwig, *s. f.—pl. t.* oedd (gel—gwig) Small wood, brushwood, or underwood. *Sil.*

Gelyn, *s. m.—pl. t.* ion (gal) A foe, or enemy. *Gelyn yr ieir*, a buzzard.

Hoedl dyn nid gelyn a'i rhan.

The life of a man, it is not an *enemy* that has the disposal of it. *Adage.*

Tri chosb cristion ar ei elyn: maddeu iddo, tewi arno, a gwneuthur daioni iddo hyd eithaf gallu.

The three punishments of a christian on his *foe*, to forgive him, to be silent of him, and to do good to him to the utmost of his power. *Barddas.*

Gelynaidd, *a.* (gelyn) Of a hostile nature.

Gelynes, *s. f.—pl. t.* au (gelyn) A female foe.

Gelyniaeth, *s. m.—pl. t.* au (gelyn) Hostility.

Gelyniaethawl, *a.* (gelyniaeth) Relating to a state of warfare.

Gelyniaethu, *v. a.* (gelyniaeth) To create hostility, or warfare; to render hostile.

Gelyniaethus, *a.* (gelyniaeth) Suitable to hostility, or warfare; of hostile disposition.

Nid oes un cenedl mor ddigariad, a mor elyniaethus i'w iaith ei hunan ag ydyw y Cymmro.

There is not one nation so void of affection, and so *hostile* to its own language, as the Welshman is. *S. Trefredyn.*

Gelyniawl, *a.* (gelyn) Hostile, or adverse.

Yna trwy elyniawl drais y gwyntoedd, gwedi ei fod ar fawdd trwy yspaid pum nywyrnawd, y bwriwid y brenin Denmarc ygyd a'i forwyn, can ergrynedig ofn i'r gogledd i'r tir.

Then through the *hostile* power of the winds, after being on the brink of drowning, through the space of five days, the king of Denmark was cast on shore in the north, together with his damsel, trembling with fear. *Gr. ab Arthur.*

Gelynioldeb, *s. m.* (gelyniawl) A state of war.

Gelyniolrwydd, *s. m.* (gelyniawl) A hostile state.

Gelynus, *a.* (gelyn) Hostile, suitable to a foe.

Gelyst, *s. pl. aggr.* (gel—yst) Sedges, or flags.

Gell, *s. m.—pl. t.* oedd (ge—ell) A dun, or bay colour. *a.* Dun, or gloomy.

Gell y baladr, gell,
Gellach o bell

Dark is the shaft, *dark*,
Darker from afar. *Aneurin.*

Gellaig, *s. pl. aggr.* (gell) Pears. They are also called *Rhswyn* and *peranau*.

March Rhydderch ryddig
Llwyd liw ellaig,
Llamrai llawn elwig,
Ffroenfoll gwyrenig.

The steed of Rhydderch over-mottled, brown of the colour of *pears*, and Llamrai full of vigour, rearing the snorting nostril. *Taliesin.*

Gellast, *s. f.—pl.* gelleist (gell—gast) A buck-hound bitch.

Gelleigbren, *s. m.* (gellaig—pren) A pear tree.

Gelleigen, *s. f.* (gellaig) A pear, or one pear.

Gelleiglys, *s. m.* (gellaig—llys) Winter green.

Gelleigwydd, *s. pl.* (gellaig—gwydd) Pear trees.

Gelleigwydden, *s. f.* (gelleigwydd) A pear tree.

Gellgarw, *s. m.—pl.* gellgeirw (gell—carw) A reindeer; it is also called algar.

Gellgi, *s. m.—pl. t.* on (gell—ci) A kind of large hunting dog, of a dun colour; a buck-hound.

Yn y coed gyferbyn ag ef y clywai ellgwn yn cyfodi hyddgant.

In the wood facing him, he could hear the *hounds* starting a stag. *H. Peredur—Mabinogion.*

Gellhesg, *s. m.* (gell—hesg) Water flower-de-luce. *Gellhesgen yr yd*, corn-flag; *gellhesgen ber*, sweet flag.

Gellwng, *v. a.* (ge—llwng) To loosen, to let go; to discharge, to drop; to disband.

Gellyngawl, *a.* (gellwng) Laxative, relaxing.

Gellyngiad, *s. m.* (gellwng) A loosening; a dropping; a disbanding, or discharging.

Gem, *s. f.—pl. t.* au (em) A gem, a jewel.

Gwaeg sy 'ngem ei wregys.

There is a broche in the *jewel* of his girdle.

Gemawg, *a.* (gem) Abounding with gems.

Gemawl, *a.* (gem) Relating to gems; jewelled.

Gemiad, *s. m.* (gem) A setting with gems.

Gemu, *v. a.* (gem) To adorn with gems.

Gemwaith, *s. m.* (gem—gwaith) Work studded with gems; needle-work studded with gems.

Gemydd, *s. m.—pl. t.* ion (gem) A jeweller.

Gen, *s. m.—pl. t.* oedd (ge—en) The intellect, or soul. *Ar dy en na ddos yno*, on thy life go not there; *cei dalu, er gwaetha'n d'en*, thou shalt pay, do what thou wilt; *gwaetha'n d'en*, in spite of thee; *gwaetha' d'en*, maugre thee.

Gwr dirfing, gwryd oerfel,
Ein gelyn ni'n gelain el;
A gen y gwr gan ei gi,
A'i gorff el i Gaerdydd.

The severe man of cold constitution, a foe to us, may he become a corpse; and the *soul* of the fellow let it go into his dog, and his body let it go to Caerdiff. *D. ab Gwilym.*

Gen, *s. f.—pl. t.* au (ge—en) An opening, or mouth; a jaw; a chin. *Clicied gen*, a jawbone. *Mi'th lusgaf gerfydd dy ddwy en*, I will drag thee by thy two jaws.

Y corn a'th roddes di Urien,
A'r aswyd aur am ei en,
Chwyth ynddo o'th daw anghen.

The horn which was given to thee by Urien, with the golden chain round its *brim*, blow in it if danger comes to thee. *Llywarch Hen.*

Genau, *s. pl.* (gen) The jaws, the lips, the mouth; outlets or inlets. *Aur enau*, golden lips.—The double plural *Geneuau*, is often used. *Genau y Glyn*; places so called in Glamorganshire and Cardiganshire.

A fo doeth efe a dau;
Annoeth ni reol enau.

He that is wise will be silent, the unwise will not govern the *lips*. *G. ab Ieuan Hen.*

Genawg, *a.* (gen) Having a long jaw.

Genawl, *a.* (gan) Relating to birth, natural.

Genedig, *a.* (gan) Brought forth, or born.

Genedigaeth, *s. m.—pl. t.* au (genedig) A nativity.

Genedigawl, *a.* (genedig) Native, or natural.

Geneth, *s f.—pl. t.* od (gan) A damsel, a maid, a girl, a daughter.

Genethaidd, *a.* (geneth) Maidish, or girlish.

Genethan, *s. f. dim.* (geneth) A little maid.

Genethig, *s. f. dim.* (geneth) A little maid.

Geneuaid, *s. m.—pl.* geneueidiau (genau) A mouthful, or a chopful.

Geneuawl, *a.* (genau) By mouth, oral.

Geneugoeg, *s. f.—pl. t.* ion (genau—coeg) A lizard, an eft.

Ni fyn dyn weled y carnlladron o bechodau sydd yn llechu ynddo, mwy y gwelir y geneugoegion ac y pryfed mewn pwll drewllyd.

A person will not chuse to see the arrant deceivers of sins that lurk within him, just as thou canst the *efts* and other worms in a stinking pit. *Morgan Llwyd.*

Genfa, *s. f.—pl. t.* au (gen) A snaffle, or bit of a bridle; also a barnacle, a farrier's instrument.

Genffrwyn, *s. f.—pl. t.* au (gen—ffrwyn) The chinstay of a bridle.

Geni, *v. n.* (gan) To appear, to be brought forth, to be born.

Pob byw a eair i eagar.

Every living thing is *born* to separate. *Adage.*

Nid rhaid i ddedwydd namyn ei eni.

The discreet wants only *to be born*. *Adage.*

A'r drydedd gymyredd ced,
I Wynedd wiw a aned.

And the third, greeting with treasure, to fair Gwynedd *has been brought forth.* *Iolo Goch, i'r Seren.*

Gèni, *v. n.* (gàn) To be held, or contained.

Genid, *s. m.* (gan) Nativity, or birth; the state of being brought forth.

Genill, *s. m.—pl. t.* ion (gan—ill) A progeny, an offspring.

Genilles, *s. f. dim.* (genill) A young nymph.

Genilles, a'm lliw cyd a'm lladdwy ar air.

A *nymph* reproaches me, whilst with a word she kills me. *Gwalchmai.*

Genillyn, *s. m. dim.* (genill) One begotten.

Genogl, *s. f.—pl.* genoglau (genawg) The mandible, or jaw.

Genolaeth, *s. m.* (genawl) A bringing forth.

Genwair, *s. f.—pl.* genweiriau (gen—gwair) A fishing rod.

Rhaid iddo, cillo i cair,
Droi'n gyanil wrth drwyn genwair.

He will be found to draw back, he must turn with exactness at the end of the *angling rod*. *H. D. Llwyd.*

Genweiriad, *s. m.* (genwair) An angling, fishing.

Genweiriaw, *v. a.* (genwair) To angle, to fish.

Genweiriwr, *s. m.—pl.* genweirwyr (genwair—gwr) An angler, or a fisher with a rod and line.

Gëol, *s. f.—pl. t.* ydd (ge—ol) A gaol, a prison.

Ban yd ran ei rad——
Ban orch ëol cad cadawl wron.

Conspicuously he distributes his bounty; conspicuous the bound of the battle *prison* of the treasure-giving hero. *Gwalchmai.*

Ger, *s. m.—pl. t.* au (ge—er) Utterance, a cry.

Dymhunis ton wyrdd wrth Aber Dau:
Dychyrch glan glaswyn, glwys y ffrydau;
Diysig yd gan ednan enau,
Addawd ym gwrthrawd gwrthred gerau.

A green wave at Aber Dau gave me a lullaby: it embraces the pale green bank, pure are the streams; free from pain sings the mouth of the little bird, stationed to oppose me with contrary *notes*. *Gwalchmai.*

Gèr, *prep.* (cèr) By, or at; near to, hard by. *Ger wyneb â mi*, face to face with me. *Sil.*

Tri angen Duw: anfeidrawl ger ei hun, meidrawl ger meidrawl, a chyfun â phob cyflwr bywydolion yn nghylch y gwynfyd.

The three necessary essentials of God: *infinite by himself*, finite *to finite* comprehensions, and counting with every mode of existence in the circle of the world of intellect. *Barddas.*

Gerag, *prep.* (gèr) Toward, in a direction to.

Gerain, *v. a.* (ger) To squeal, to squeak, to cry.

Geran, *v. a.* (ger) To squeal, to squeak, to cry.

Ai byw ai marw garw ei gan,
Ai gwr a glywai'n geran!

Alive or dead, whence that sad moan; is it a man whom I hear *wailing!* *D. ab Gwilym, i'r Ysbryd.*

Geranllyd, *a.* (geran) Squealing, or squeaking.

Gerbron, *prep.* (ger—bron) In presence.

Gereinllyd, *a.* (gerain) Squeaking, squealing.

Gerfydd, *prep.* (gèr) In contact with, by. *Gerfydd dy law*, by thy hand; *llusgaf di gerfydd dy walli*, I will drag thee by thy hair.

Geri, *s. m.* (ger) The choler, bile, or gall.

Can chwerwed a'r geri.

As bitter as the gall. *Adage.*

Hebddi——
Geri yw i mi fy mod.

Without her it is *gall* for me to exist. *D. ab Gwilym.*

——Cewch gyhoeddi
Fal i medrwyf, yn ych plith,
A digon chwith, fal geri,
Gan ieuenctyd glywed hwn;
Ni ddysgwn fawr ddaioni.

You shall have it published, as well as I can, amongst you, and bitter enough, like *gall*, will it be with youths to hear this; we shall not teach much good. *T. ab Ieuan Madawg.*

Geriaidd, *a.* (geri) Choleric, or bilious, like bile.

Geriawg, *a.* (geri) Abounding with bile, bilious.

Geriawl, *a.* (geri) Relating to the choler, or bile.

Gerllaw, *prep.* (ger—llaw) At hand, by, near.

Germain, *v. a.* (garm) To cry often, to wail.

Pan eisteddo ar fainc y frawd
Fe glyw y tlawd yn germain.

When he shall sit on the throne of judgement, he will hear the poor *complaining*. *Edm. Prys.*

Gern, *s. m.—pl. t.* au (ger) That extends far; depth, or profundity; collateral; a fifth relative, or cousin.

Gerni, *s. pl. aggr.* (gern) Collateral kindred in the fifth degree. They are also called *Ceifyn* and *Ysgiwion*. *Gwrth gerni*, the same with *Gwrtherni*, relations in the sixth degree. See *Tras*.

Sef yw rhieni gwr, ei dad, ei hendad, ac ei orhendad; ac o hyny hyd y nawfed ach ac edryd, gerni en gelwir.

The parentage of a man implies, his father, his grandfather, and his great grandfather; and onwards unto the ninth degree and descent, they are called *cousins*. *Welsh Laws.*

Gerwin, *a.* (garw) Rough, severe, rigorous.

Gerwinad, *s. m.* (gerwin) A making rough; a becoming harsh, or severe.

Gerwinaw, *v. a.* (gerwin) To make rough, or harsh; to become rough or rigorous.

Gerwinawl, *a.* (gerwin) of a rough or harsh nature. *Mae yn gyru arno yn erwinawl*, he is driving upon him terribly.

Gerwindeb, *s. m.* (gerwin) Roughness, ruggedness, harshness, severity, or inclemency.

Gerwydd, *prep.* (ger—gwydd) In presence. *Gerwydd ei wyneb*, before his face; *gerwydd y ty*, before the house. *Sil.*

Gerwyneb, *prep.* (ger—gwyneb) In presence.

Gerwynebawl, *a.* (gerwyneb) Opposite. *Yn erwynebawl*, being present.

Gerwynebu, *v. a.* (gerwyneb) To place opposite.

Geryn, *s. m.—pl. t.* od (gar) One that utters a shrill cry. *Geryn hwyad*, a mallard.

Gestwng, *v. a.* (ystwng) To incline, bend, or bow down, to lower, to abase.

Drud i ddala, doeth i estwng.

A furious one to catch, a wise one to *subject*. *Adage.*

Gestyngawl, *a.* (gestwng) Tending to lower.

Gestyngiad, *s. m.* (gestwng) A lowering, a bowing, or inclining down; subjection.

Gestyngu, *v. a.* (gestwng) To lower, to bow down.

Geuaddoli, *v. a.* (gau—addoli) To worship falsely.

Geuaddoliad, *s. m.* (gau—addoliad) A false worshipping, idolatrous worship.

Geuaddoliaeth, *s. m.* (gau—addoliaeth) False worship; idolatry.

Geuaddolwr, *s. m.—pl.* geuaddolwyr (gau—addolwr) A false worshipper; an idolater.

Geuain, *a.* (gau) Full of falsity; lying; false.

Geuaw, *v. a.* (gau) To falsify, to make false.

Geuawd, *s. m.* (gau) A falsifying, deception.

Geuawg, *a.* (gau) Fallacious, lying, deceiving.

Nesau a orug Merddin at y dewinion, a gofyn iddynt: Dywedwch i mi, dwyllwyr geuawg, pa beth y sydd yn ngwaelawd y llyn.

Merddin drew near to the magicians, asking them: tell me, ye *false* deceivers, what is there in the bottom of the lake. *Gr. ab Arthur.*

Geuawl, *a.* (gau) Fallacious; deceiving.

Geublant, *s. pl. aggr.* (gau—plant) False children.

Crin calaf, a llif yn nant,
Cyfnewid Sais a'i ariant:
Digu enaid mam geublant.

A brittle reed, or a flood in the ravine, is the dealing of the Saxon with his money void of affection the soul of the mother of *false children*. *Llywarch Hen.*

Geubwyll, *s. m.—pl. t.* oedd (gau—pwyll) A false reason, false sense.

Geudeb, *s. m.* (gau) Falsehood, or deceit.

Geudy, *s. m.—pl. t.* au (gau—ty) A privy house.

Geuddadl, *s. f.—pl.* geuddadlau (gau—dadl) Paralogy, or sophistical argument.

Geuddadledd, *s. m.* (geuddadl) A paralogism.

Geuddadliad, *s. m.* (geuddadl) Arguing falsely.

Geuddadlu, *v. a.* (geuddadl) To paralogise.

Geudduw, *s. m.—pl. t.* iau (gau—duw) False god.

> Ei saeth, y geudduw syth-wan,
> A'i fwa loes a fo yn tan.
>
> May the arrow and the severe bow of his strutting, feeble, deceiving godship be in the fire. *S. Tudur, i'r Cariad.*

Geudduwiaeth, *s. m.* (geudduw) False theology.

Geuedd, *s. m.* (gau) Falsehood, falsity, fallacy.

Geufardd, *s. m.—pl* geufeirdd (bardd) False bard

Geuffydd, *s f.—pl. t.* ion (gau—ffydd) Heresy

Geuffyddiawg, *a.* (geu—ffydd) Having false faith

Geugred, *s. f.—pl. t.* ion (gau—cred) False belief, superstition.

Geugrediniaeth, *s. m.* (geugred) False belief.

Geugrefydd, *s. f.—pl. t.* au (gau—crefydd) A false religion, heresy.

Geugrefyddawl, *a.* (geugrefydd) Heretical in faith

Geulith, *s. m.—pl. t.* iau (gau—llith) Heterodoxy, or false doctrine, false teaching.

Geulithiad, *s. m.* (geulith) A teaching falsely.

Geulithiaw, *v. a.* (geulith) To misinstruct.

Geulithiawg, *a.* (geulith) Falsely instructed.

Geulun, *s. m.—pl. t.* iau (gau—llun) A chimera.

Geulunaidd, *a.* (geulun) Chimerical.

Geuogrwydd, *s. m.* (geuawg) Fallaciousness.

Geurith, *s. m.—pl. t.* iau (gau—rhith) A false appearance; illusion.

> I'w balchedd, unwedd anair,
> Melldith a geurith a gair.
>
> To her pride, of similar reproach, there will come a curse and delusion. *W. Middleton.*

Geuwedd, *s. m.* (gau—gwedd) A false appearance

Geuwr, *s. m.—pl.* geuwyr (gau—gwr) A false man, a deceiver, an impostor.

Gewach, *s. m.* (gaw) A lean one; a greedygut.

Gewai, *s. m.—pl.* geweiod (gaw) A lean person; a greedygut, a glutton.

Gewyn, *s. m.—pl. t.* au (gaw) A sinew, or tendon.

Gewynaidd, *a.* (gewyn) Of a sinewy nature.

Gewynawg, *a.* (gewyn) Sinewy, having tendons.

Gewynawl, *a.* (gewyn) Relating to the sinews.

Gewynllys, *s. m.* (gewyn—llys) Butcher's broom: also called *gwiolys*.

Gewynogrwydd, *s. m.* (gewynawg) Sinewness.

Gi, *s. f. r.—pl. t.* oedd. A slender fibre, a nerve.

Giach, *s. f.—pl. t.* ed (gi) A snipe. It is also called *Ysnid* and *Ysniten*.

Giau, *s. pl. aggr.* (gi) Nerves; nervous system.

> Anaf yn ngiau, angeu yn ngwythi.
>
> Disease in the nerves, death in the veins. *Adage.*
>
> Y mae gwewyr i'm giau
> A allai hon ei iachau.
>
> There is a disease in my nerves, which she could assuage. *H. Heilyn.*

Gid, *s. f.—pl. t.* au (gi—id) A she-goat, a goat.

Giden, *s. f. dim.* (gid) A young she-goat, a kid.

Gieuawg, *a.* (giau) Having nerves, nervous.

Gieuawl, *a.* (giau) Relating to the nerves, nervous

Gieuedd, *s. m.* (giau) The nervous system.

Gieulyd, *a.* (giau) Affecting the nerves, nervous.

Gieuyn, *s. m. dim.* (giau) A nerve, a sinew.

Gil, *s. f.—pl. t.* ion (gi—il) A yielding, or producing; work, or action; fermentation.

Gild, *s. m.—pl. t.* iau (gil) What is produced.

> Gwnaethan' les o'u hanes hwyr,
> Gild y rhew, goldwyr awyr.
>
> They have done good by their evening tale, the work of the frost, marigold of the sky. *D. ab Gwilym, i'r ser.*

Gildiad, *s. m.* (gild) A producing, bringing out.

Gildiaw, *v. a.* (gild) To produce, to yield, to concede, to contribute.

Gildiwr, *s. m.—pl.* gildwyr (gild—gwr) A producer; one who brings to effect; a yielder, a conceder; a contributor.

Gilydd, *s. pl.* (cil) Mutual efficients, mutual selves, or other selves. *pron.* One another, each other.

> Gwahoddion y'nghwlad Fon fydd
> Gwedi gwyl i dai 'gilydd.
>
> There will be invitations to the island of Mon after the holiday, to the houses of each other. *L. G. Cothi.*

Gin, *s. m.—pl. t* ion (gi—in) A pelt. *Gwlan gin*, pelt wool, plucked wool.

Gingroen, *s. f.* (gin—croen) The toadflax, a kind of stinking mushroom.

Giniad, *s. m.* (gin) A stripping off the skin.

Giniaw, *v. a.* (gin) To strip, to take off the skin, to pluck off the wool.

Giniawl, *a.* (gin) Stripping, or flaying.

Giniedig, *a.* (gin) Skinned, stript of covering.

Giniwr, *s. m.—pl.* ginwyr (gin—gwr) A flayer.

Girad, *s. m.* (irad) Mourning, lamentation. *a.* Piteous, lamentable, terrible.

> Craddwn hon Ruffudd, rudd ei rhod,
> Ac ni ryganai dyn dim mor irad.
>
> I sang this of Gruffudd, of ruddy course, a man had not sung any thing so mournful. *D. Benfras.*
>
> I ti cyffesaf—
> Gorwag feddyliau,
> Coelwrion gredau,
> Ofer lyfau,
> Geiriau girad!
>
> To thee will I confess—very vain thoughts, fanciful creeds, and useless oaths, dreadful words! *D. ab Gwilym.*

Giten, *s. f. dim.* (gid) A she goat, a young goat.

Gith, *s. m. aggr.* (gi—ith) Corn cockle. It is also called *ydig*. *Sil.*

Githran, *s. m.* (gith—rhan) Honewort: also called *githrag*.

Gla, *s. m.* (lla) A brightness, or glistening.

Glaf, *s. m.* (gla) That is glistening, or smooth.

Glafr, *s. m.* (glaf) What produces a glistening, flattery, or false praise.

Glafriad, *s. m.* (glafr) A making fair, or glistening; a flattering.

Glafru, *v. a.* (glafr) To glaver, to flatter.

Glai, *s. m.* (gla) That is glistening, or smooth. *a.* Glistening, glittering, dazzling.

Glaif, *s. m.—pl.* gleifiau (llaif) A bill-hook, a crooked sword, a scimitar, a glaive. *Gleifrudd*, ruddy-glaived, *gleif ruthr*, the assault of a glaive

> Gnawd it rudd a glaw glaif gan fawg gorwydd;
> Gnawd gochlyd rudwydd rawd enwawg.
>
> Usual to thee to have the red and dashing *glaive* over the mane of the steed; habitual the ruddy plain of conflict echoing of shouts. *E. ab Mad. Rhaeadr.*
>
> Da oedd ei gof mewn gofid,
> A'i laif yn gyflawn o lid.
>
> Collected was his mind in trouble, and his *glaive* teeming with wrath. *Iolo Goch.*

Glain, *s. m.—pl.* gleiniau (glai) What is pure, or holy; a pure one, an angel, a saint; what is bright, clear, or transparent; a gem, or jewel; a bead. *Glain nod*, a prime jewel; *glain cefn*, *gleiniau cefn*, the back bone, the joints of the back: *glain cawod*, *maen cawod*, or *maen gwlaw*, the rain stone, which was rolled to procure rain; *glain neidr*, *glain nadroedd*, *gleiniau nadroedd* *maen glain*, or *maen magl*, snake stones, adder stones, or adder beads. The *main glain*, transparent stones, or adder stones, were worn by the different orders of bards, each having its appropriate colour; the blue ones belonged to the presiding bards, the white to the druids, the green to the ovates, and the three colours blended, to the disciples. There is no certainty that they were worn from superstition originally; perhaps that was the circumstance which gave rise to it. Whatever might have been the cause, the notion of their rare virtues was universal in all places where the bardic religion was taught.—It may still be questioned whether they are the production of nature or art. Be that as it may, they are always to be found in great numbers; and there are people who may be aptly called hunters, from whom they are to be had; but they insist on being credited, that the *Gleiniau* are only to be had at one season of the year; and that they are blown by a knot of snakes. *Ai chwythu y glain y maent?* what, are they blowing the *gem?* (applied to people laying their heads together in conversation.)

Can diffyrth Trindawd tri macwy o dan,
Tri meib glan glain ofwy——
Hyderwn.

As the Trinity preserved the three children from the fire, three *angel*-visited comely youths, let us confide. *Cynddelw.*

Dyfo mab Cynan——
Gan y glain gloew adef yn nef drefred!

May the son of Cynan be with the gloriously dwelling angel in the region of heaven! *Meilyr, i R. ab Cynan.*

Enlli——
Ynys glan y glain.
Gwrthddrych dadwyrain
Yn cain ynddi.

Enlli, the holy island of the saint, where there is a splendid picture of the resurrection. *Meilyr.*

Glain, *a.* (glai) Pure, holy;—clear, bright, or transparent. *Gleinion seintiau*, holy saints; *gleinion radau*, pure virtues.

Glàn, *s. f.—pl.* glènydd (llan) The brink, side, or bank of a river, or any water. *Glan y mor*, the sea shore; *glan yr afon*, the river side; *glan y dwfr*, the water side; *ar y lan*, on the shore. *Hala hi i'r lan*, send her up. *Dyfed.*

Cynt y cwrdd dau ddyn no dwy lan.

Sooner will two men meet than two *banks.* *Adage.*

Glan, *a.* (gla) Pure, holy, fair, clean, complete, entire. *Yr Ysbryd Glan*, the Holy Spirit; *dynes lan*, a handsome woman; *dillad glan*, clean clothes; *mae wedi darfod yn lan*, it is entirely gone; *dyna fyw yn lan*, there is fine living; *dyna hi allan yn lan*, that is very fine indeed.

Llaw lan, diogel ei pherchen.

The owner of a *clean* hand is safe. *Adage.*

Cydymddyddan a'm hanwyl——
Newidiaw glan gusanau;
Cydchwerthin yn y min mau.

Mutually discoursing with my love; exchanging *pure* kisses; mutually smiling lip to lip. *D. ab Gwilym.*

Glanâad, *s. m.* (glan) A purifying; a cleansing.
Glanâawl, *a.* (glan) Abstergent, cleansing.
Glanâu, *v. a.* (glan) To purify, to hallow, to clear, to cleanse, to make clean, to clean.
Glandeg, *a.* (glan—teg) Comely and fair.

Ar bob twr yr oedd merch landeg arothr yn sefyll.

Upon every tower there was a *very fair and comely* woman standing. *Elis Wyn, B. Cwsg.*

Glaniad, *s. m.* (glan) A landing, or a going ashore.
Glaniaw, *v. a.* (glan) To land, to go ashore.
Glanwaith, *a.* (glan—gwaith) Clean and neat; complete. *Lle glanwaith*, a tidy place.

Glanweithdra, *s. m.* (glan—weith) Cleanliness.
Glanweithiad, *s. m.* (glanwaith) A cleansing.
Glanweithiaw, *v. a.* (glanwaith) To make clean.
Glanweithiawl, *a.* (glanwaith) Abstergent.
Glanweithus, *a.* (glanwaith) Abstergent.
Glas, *s. m.—pl.* gleision (llas) A blue colour; a verdancy; a green, a green plat. *Glas y dorlan*, the king's-fisher; *glas y llwyn*, wild hyacinth.

Dar a dyfwys ar y glas,
Gwedi gwaedffrau gwyr a las;
Gwae wr wrth y bo a'i cas!

An oak hath grown upon the *green*, after the blood stream of men who were slain; woe to the man of whom there shall be cause of hate. *Robert tywysawg Norddmandi.*

Pan ddelo hon i'r bronydd,
I leisiaw dim ar las dydd,
Yr adar, yn llwyr odiaeth,
A gan yn ffres gwynion fraeth.

When she comes to the lawns, to tune a lay at the *dawn* of morn, the birds most charmingly will briskly sing their eloquent complaints. *T. Prys, i'r gog.*

Glas, *a.* (llas) Blue, or azure; pale; gray; verdant, green; fresh, or young. *Brethyn glas*, blue cloth; *lliw glas*, blue colour; *wybren las*, a blue sky; *blodau gleision*, blue flowers; *arian gleision*, pale money, or silver; *wyneb glas*, a palid complexion; *maidd glas*, milky whey;—*march glas*, a gray horse; *caseg las*, a gray mare;—*gwellt glas*, green grass; *derwen las*, a green oak.—*Mae efe ar ei orau glas*, he is as busy as he can be.

Am ar y garaf ceu ni'm carwy,
Neud lluddedig glan rhag glas fordwy,
Neud llawen awen, awel neud mwy!

Since I am doomed to love one that will not my love return, are not the shores oppressed before the *blue* torrent, is not the muse animated, is not the gale increased! *Cynddelw, i Efa f. Madawg.*

Glasaidd, *a.* (glas) Bluish, or rather blue.
Glasar, *s. m.* (glas—ar) Land newly turned up.
Glasawg, *a.* (glas) That is blue, livid, or pale.
Glasbaill, *s. m.* (glas—paill) The bloom of fruit.
Glaschwerthin, *s. m.* (glas—chwerthin) A half laugh, a simper, or smirk.
Glaschwerthin, *v. a.* (glas—chwerthin) To simper, to smile, to smirk.
Glaschwerthiniad, *s. m.* (glaschwerthin) A making a half laugh, a smirking.
Glasdonen, *s. f.* (glas—tonen) The scarlet oak.
Glasdorch, *s. f.—pl.* glasdyrch (glas—torch) A leveret, or young hare; a young wolf.
Glasdwr, *s. m.* (glas—dwr) Milk and water drink.
Glasddydd, *s. m.* (glas—dydd) The dawning day.
Glasfaen, *s. m.* (glas—maen) Blue stone, vitriol.
Glasfaran, *s. m.—pl. t.* edd (glas—maran) A samlet, a young salmon.
Glasfedd, *s. m.* (glas—medd) Green metheglin.

Glasfedd eu hancwyn, a'u gwenwyn fu.

Green mead was their dainty and their poison. *Aneurin.*

Glasfor, *s. m.* (glas—mor) The blue sea.
Glasfyr, *s. m.* (glas—myr) The blue ocean.

Gorfu gwynt gwaeddfan uch glan glasfyr.

The loud-voiced wind raged on the shore of the *blue ocean.* *O. Cyfeiliawg.*

Glasgaen, *s. f.—pl. t.* au (glas—caen) A blue covering, or armour.
Glasgangen, *s. f.—pl. t.* od (glas—cangen) A fish called a greyling.
Glasgoch, *s. m.* (glas—coch) Bluish red, or purple. *a.* Of a purple tinge, of a purple red.
Glasgoed, *s. pl. aggr.* (glas—coed) Green trees; young trees.
Glasgoludd, *s. pl. aggr.* (glas—colydd) The small guts or entrails.
Glasgroen, *s. m.* (glas—croen) A thin cuticle.

Glasgyffaith, *s. m.* (glas—cyffaith) Blue electuary; some kind of compound medicine.

> Bolwst gohaddi o cyfyd, a glasgyffaith y meddygyr.
>
> If a cholic in the bowels should arise, with *blue electuary* it is to be cured. *Medd. Myddfai.*

Glasbaid, *s. f.*—*pl.* glasbeidiau (glas—baid) A young swarm.

Glasiad, *s. m.*—*pl. t.* au (glas) A tingeing with blue. *Glasiad y dydd*, the dawning of the day.

Glaslan, *s. f.*—*pl. t.* au (glas—llan) A green plat.

Glaslanc, *s. m.*—*pl. t.* iau (glas—llanc) A youth nearly grown up, a springal.

Glaslanerch, *s. m.*—*pl. t.* au (glas—llanerch) A green plat, or paddock.

Glasloew, *a.* (glas—gloew) Bluishly bright.

Glaslwyn, *s. m.*—*pl. t.* i (glas—llwyn) A green or verdant grove.

Glaslyn, *s. m.*—*pl. t.* au (glas—llyn) A blue pool.

Glaslys, *s. f.* (glas—llys) Woad. It is also called *y glas, y glaslys*, and *glasddur*.

Glasnoden, *s. f.* (glas—nod) Grass wrack; also called *gwellt y gamlas*.

Glasog, *s. f.*—*pl. t.* au (glas) An epithet for several internal vessels of animals; the liver; the kidney; the gizzard of a bird.

Glasogo, *s. f.* (glas—gogo) The flower of the flax plant.

Glassan, *s. f.*—*pl. t.* au (glas—san) A greyling.

Glassanen, *s. f. dim.* (glassan) A greyling.

Glasresaw, *s. m.* (glas—gresaw) A cold, or half welcome.

Glasresawiad, *s. m.* (glasresaw) A receiving coldly, or with a half welcome.

Glasresawu, *v. a.* (glasresaw) To receive, or entertain coldly.

> Glasresawu a wnaynt ar y gwyt, a chynneu tan gwryng iddynt.
>
> They looked with *affected commiseration* on the men, lighting for them fire with dry sticks. *Br. Rhonabwy—Mabinogion.*

Glasresawus, *a.* (glasresaw) Giving a ceremonious or half welcome.

Glasrew, *s. m.* (glas—rhew) A grey frost.

Glasu, *v. a.* (glas) To make blue; to become blue, to grow pale, or livid; to dawn; to become verdant, or green.

> Gwelais waed ar llawr;
> Rhag rhuthr cleddyfawr
> Glasynt engyll gwawr.
>
> I have seen blood on the ground; from the assault of the swords they tinged with *blue* the wings of the dawn. *Taliesin.*

Glaswawd, *s. m.* (glas—gwawd) Affected praise.

> Dygwelwi lesni o laswawd efrydd
> Wrth a gwedd ei gwnelawd.
>
> Thou wilt be calling forth paleness from the currency *of affected praise*, to such as is upprward in heart. *Taliesin.*

Glasweiw, *s. m.* (glas—gwelw) A bluish paleness; pale blue. *a.* Of a bluish paleness; pale.

Glaswelwder, *s. m.* (glaswelw) A bluish paleness.

Glaswelwi, *v. n.* (glaswelw) To become pale.

Glaswellt, *s. m.* (glas—gwellt) Green grass. *Glaswellt y cwn, llygad y ci*, couch-grass.

Glaswelltawg, *a.* (glaswellt) Herbous, grassy.

Glaswelltyn, *s. m.* (glaswellt) A blade of grass.

Glaswen, *s. f.* (glas—gwên) A simper, a smirk.

Glaswenawl, *a.* (glaswen) Simpering, smirking.

Glasweniad, *s. m.* (glaswen) A simpering.

Glaswenu, *v. a.* (glaswen) To simper, to smirk.

Glaswenwyn, *s. m.* (glas—gwenwyn) Devil's bit.

Glaswst, *s. f.* (glas—gwst) The chlorosis. It is also called *Y glesni*.

Glaswydd, *s. pl. aggr.* (glas—gwydd) Green wood

Glaswydden, *s. f. dim.* (glaswydd) A green tree, a sapling.

Glaswyn, *s. m.* (glas—gwyn) A bluish white. *a.* Of a bluish white.

Glaswynl, *s. m.* (glaswyn) A bluish whiteness.

Glaswynu, *v. a.* (glaswyn) To make of a bluish white; to become of a blue white.

Glaswyrdd, *s. m.* (glas—gwyrdd) A bluish green. *a.* Of a bluish green.

Glawdd, *s. m.* (glaw) A lustre, glow, or splendour

Gledd, *s. m.*—*pl. t.* au (lledd) The face of the earth.

> Pond oeddych yn wych dy wedd,
> Por glwys-law'n porio glas-ledd!
>
> Wert thou not of splendid appearance, covering with herbage the green sod, thou pure-coloured land! *D. ab Gwilym, i'r haf.*

Gleiad, *s. f.*—*pl.* gleiaid (glai) A cake of dried cow dung for fuel; a blake.

Gleiaden, *s. f.* (gleiad) A blake, or casing.

Gleifiad, *s. m.* (glaif) The using a scimitar.

Gleifiaw, *v. a.* (glaif) To use the scimitar.

Gleifiawg, *a.* (glaif) Having a scimitar.

Gleifiwr, *s. m.*—*pl.* gleifwyr (glaif—gwr) One who uses a scimitar.

Gleindid, *s. m.* (glain) Purity, holiness, brightness

> Achaws y dathoant y grawys, wrth ddylyu o bawb fod yn lan yn yr amser gleindid hwnw.
>
> The reason they came to lent was, that every body should be clean in that time of *purity*. *Welsh Laws.*

Gleindorch, *s. f.*—*pl.* gleindyrch (glain—torch) A circlet of beads; a bead necklace.

Gleinfaen, *s. m.*—*pl.* gleinfeini (glain—maen) Alabaster.

Gleiniad, *s. m.* (glain) A purifying; a hallowing, a brightening.

Gleiniadur, *s. m.* (gleiniad) A pair of snuffers.

Gleiniaw, *v. a.* (glain) To purify, to hallow, or to brighten.

Gleiniawg, *a.* (glain) Abounding with purity; full of brightness, or splendour.

Gleiniawl, *a.* (glain) Purifying, hallowing.

Gleisiad, *s. m.*—*pl.* gleisiaid, gleisiadau (glas) A salmon. The varieties are *maran, eawg, penllwyd, adfwlch, gwfaw, gwyniad y gog, gwyniad haf, brithyll y mor, brithyll du, brithyll brych*; the names for the fry are, *silod brithion, sil y gro*, and *brith y gro*.—*Gleisiad*, is a term also used for a draught of fishes.

Gleisiadeg, *s. f.* (gleisiad) A salmon net.

> Gleisiadeg pedair ar ugaint a dal.
>
> A salmon net its value is twenty-four pence. *Welsh Laws.*

Gleisiedyn, *s. m. dim.* (gleisiad) A salmon.

Gleision, *s. pl. aggr.* (glas) Whey cleared of the curd; any bluish liquid.

Glendid, *s. m.* (glan) Purity, holiness; fairness, comeliness, neatness, cleanliness.

Glendyd, *s. m.* (glan) Purity, holiness, fairness.

> Mae'r gair drwy Gymru i gyd
> Hyd Lundain am dy lendyd.
>
> Thy fame is over all Wales, and as far as London, for thy beauty. *E. Deio.*

Glesid, *s. m.* (glas) Blueness, azure, paleness.

Glesin, *s. m.* (glas) What is blue; what is verdant; a greensward.

> Yr aelwyd hon neus cudd glesin?
> Yn myw Owain ac Elffin
> Berwasai ei phair breiddin.
>
> This hearth is it not covered by the *greensward*? In the life time of Owain and Elphin, its cauldron boiled the prey. *Llywarch Hen.*

Glesni, *s. m.* (glas) Blueness, paleness, verdancy; bloom of fruit, the chlorosis.

Gleswg, *s. m.* (glas) Blueness, verdancy.

Glesygen, *s. f. dim.* (gleswg) A verdant spot.

Glesyn, *s. m. dim.* (glas) What is blue. *Glesyn y gauaf*, or *coedwyrdd*, the winter green; *glesyn y morlan*, sea lungwort; *glesyn y mynydd*, mountain bugle; *glesyn y wiber*, viper's bugloss; *glesyn y coed*, *yr elchenid*, bruise-wort, or bugle; borage.

Glew, *s. m.—pl. t.* ion (llew) A resolute, or persevering man; a hero.

> Yn mhob gwlad y magir glew.
>
> In every country a *hero* will be produced. *Adage.*
>
> Caledach glew no maen.
>
> A *resolute* man is harder than a stone. *Adage.*
>
> Tri glew Ynys Prydain: Grudneu, Henben, ac Aedenaw; eu cynneddfau oedd, nad eynt o gad namyn ar eu beloreu.
>
> The three *resolute ones* of the Isle of Britain: Greudnes, Henbeu, and Aedenaw; their principles were, that they would not go from battle except upon their biers. *Trioedd.*

Glew, *a.* (llew) Persevering, indefatigable; resolute, stout, brave, valiant; having penetration, sharp, acute. *Mae efe yn ddyn glew iawn*, he is a very provident man; *yr wyd ti yn o lew*, thou art pretty sharp, *a wyd ti yn o lew?* art thou pretty well?

> Bid drud glew, a bid rew bre.
>
> Let the *resolute* be daring, let the hill be icy. *Llywarch Hen.*
>
> Glew a fydd llew hyd yn llwyd.
>
> A lion will be *brave*, until he is gray. *Adage.*

Glewa, *v. a.* (glew) To make expedients, to shift; to acquire by sharp means. *Maent yn glewa pethau felly*, they scrape things together by that means.

Glewai, *s. c.* (glew) One who is sharp or greedy after any thing.

Glewdaer, *a.* (glew—taer) Resolutely ardent, or importunate.

Glewder, *s. m.* (glew) Perseverance; resolution, fortitude, stoutness, bravery, valour; sharpness, or cunning.

Glewdid, *s. m.* (glew) Perseverance; resolution, bravery, or valour; acuteness, or collectedness of mind.

Glewdraws, *a.* (glew—traws) Stoutly perverse.

Glewddrud, *a.* (glew—drud) Resolutely daring.

Glewineb, *s. m.* (glew) Bravery, resolution.

> Nid glewineb oud gloewineb.
>
> There is no *resolution* without perspicuity. *Catwg.*

Glewyd, *s. m.* (glew) Perseverance, bravery.

> Dychyfyd glewyd glew hyder.
>
> *Resolution* will produce valorous confidence. *Cynddelw.*

Glin, *s. m.—pl. t.* iau (gal—in) A knee. It is also called *pen lin* and *pen glin*. *Dos ar dy liniau*, go upon thy knees.

Glinbraff, *s. m. pl.* glinbreiffion (glin—praff) A Norfolk plover, a bird so called.

Glingam, *a.* (glin—cam) Having crooked knees, knock-kneed.

Gliniad, *s. m.* (glin) A kneeing, a kneeling.

Gliniaw, *v. a.* (glin) To kneel; to beat with the knee, to use the knees.

Gliniawg, *a.* (glin) Geniculated; having knees.

Gliniogai, *s. m.* (gliniawg) The cow-wheat.

GLO, *s. m. r.* What is black or glistening; coal. *Glo careg*, stone coal; *glo cwlm*, small coal, or culm; *glo rhinc*, or simply *rhinc*, the common coal; *glo spagog*, flaky coal.

Glöaidd, *a.* (glo) Of the nature of, or like coal.

Globwll, *s. m.—pl.* globyllau (glo—pwll) Coal pit

Gloddest, *s. f.—pl. t.* au (glawdd) A revel, carousal, or riotous living.

Gloddest, *v. a.* (glawdd) To revel, to carouse.

Gloddesta, *v. a.* (gloddest) To revel, to carouse.

Gloddestawl, *a.* (gloddest) Revelling, carousing.

Gloddestgar, *a.* (gloddest) Disposed to revel.

Gloddestgarwch, *s. m.* (gloddestgar) Fondness for revelling; riotousness of living.

Gloddestiad, *s. m.* (gloddest) A revelling, rioting.

Gloddestrwydd, *s. m.* (gloddest) Riotous living.

Gloddestu, *v. a.* (gloddest) To revel, to carouse.

Gloddestwr, *s. m.—pl.* gloddestwyr (gloddest—gwr) A reveller, a carouser.

Gloe, *s. m.* (glo) The state of being black or dark.

Glöen, *s. f.—pl. t.* au (glo) What shines. *Glöen byw*, a butterfly; a glow-worm.

Gloes, *s. f.—pl. t.* au (lloes) A pang, pain, or anguish; a swoon, or fainting fit; a qualm. *Gloesion angeu*, the pangs of death.

> Gloew oddef gloes lef a glas lain ar glun
> A glywir yn Mhrydain.
>
> A resolute suffering of the cry of *anguish*, with the blue blade on the thigh, will be heard in Britain. *Cynddelw.*
>
> Porthaist er pum oes gloes glas ferau;
> Pum weli Celi celfyddodau.
>
> For the sake of five ages thou didst bear the *pang* of blue shafts; the five wounds of the mysterious one are mysteries. *Ein. ab Gwalchmai.*

Gloesawd, *s. m.* (gloes) The act of tormenting, or paining; a state of pain.

Gloesi, *v. a.* (gloes) To pain, to cause a pang, or anguish; to swoon, to faint.

Gloesiad, *s. m.—pl. t.* au (gloes) A causing a pang, or anguish; a fainting, or swooning.

Gloesiaw, *v. a.* (gloes) To pain, to cause a pang; to suffer a pang; to swoon; to be in a qualm; to vomit.

> Wyron Llalson a lowsoedd,
> Marw fu'r un mwyaf eiroedd!
>
> The grand-children of Llalson *fainted*, the greatest that has been has died! *Ieu. Deulwyn.*

Gloesiawg, *a.* (gloes) Suffering anguish; having fainting fits or qualms.

Gloesineb, *s. m.* (gloes) A state of anguish.

Gloesion, *s. pl. aggr.* (gloes) Pangs; qualms; vomitings. *Y gloesion*, *y gloesion mawr*, *y gloesion llewyg*, *gloesion bwrw*, the falling sickness.

Gloeswg, *s. m.* (gloes) A state of anguish or pain.

Gloesygdawd, *s. m.* (gloeswg) A state of pain.

Gloesygiad, *s. m.—pl. t.* au (gloeswg) A paining; a fainting, or swooning.

Gloesygu, *v. a.* (gloeswg) To cause pain; to pain; to be in pain, to ache; to swoon, or to faint.

Gloesyn, *s. m. dim.* (gloes) A pang, or smart; a fainting; a qualm.

Gloesyndawd, *s. m.* (gloesyn) Anguish, or aching; a fainting; a loathing.

Gloesyni, *s. m.* (gloesyn) Anguish; fainting.

Gloesynu, *v. a.* (gloesyn) To cause pain; to be in pain, to ache; to swoon, or to faint.

Gloew, *a.* (gloe) Bright, clear, transparent.

> Crefydd y Creawdyr a gyfrifed
> I Ruffudd, gloew udd a'i cudd tudwed.
>
> Belief in the Creator was accounted to Gruffudd a *splendid* sovereign whom the earth doth cover. *Meilyr.*
>
> Rhodded——
> I Fadawg fad gynnwys,
> Gan lain ynglan baradwys,
> Gan engyllon gloewon glwys.
>
> To Madog has been given a happy reception, with saints in a hallowed paradise, with angels *bright* and pure. *Gwalchmai.*

Gloewaidd, *a.* (gloew) Of a bright, clear, or transparent nature.

Gloewawl, *a.* (gloew) Tending to brighten or to clear.

Gloewdeg, *a.* (gloew—teg) Brightly fair.

Gloewder, *s. m.* (gloew) Brightness, clearness, limpidness, transparency.

> Yn nghynnwys rhyddid gloewder,
> Yn ngoleuad rhad rhyddmawer.
>
> That be be receiving the freedom of the purity of brightness, in the illumination of grace, will be ardently prayed.
> *Cynddelw, i'r argl. Rhys.*

Gloewddu, *s. m.* (gloew—du) Bright-black, coal-black. *a.* Of a bright black.

Gloewedd, *s. m.* (gloew) Brightness, transparency

Gloewgain, *a.* (gloew—cain) Brightly fair.

Gloewgoch, *s. m.* (gloew—coch) Bright red, flame colour. *a.* Of a bright red, flame-coloured.

> Y brenin angeu yn ei frenhinawl gloewgoch, ac ar hyd-ddi lunlun gwreigedd a phlant yn wylaw, a gwyr yn ochneidio.
>
> The king death, in his royal attire of *bright red*, having over it the representation of women and children weeping, and men uttering sighs.
> *Elis Wyn, B. Cwsg.*

Gloewi, *v. a.* (gloew) To make clear, bright, or transparent; to become clear, to brighten.

Gloewiad, *s. m.* (gloew) A brightening, or clearing; a making transparent.

Gloewineb, *s. m.* (gloew) Lucidity, lucidness.

> Tri gloewineb cerdd: gloew iaith, gloew ystyr, a gloew ddyben.
>
> The three *perspicuities* of song: perspicuous language, perspicuous meaning and perspicuous design.
> *Barddas.*

Gloewliw, *s. m.* (gloew—lliw) A bright colour. *a.* Of a bright colour.

Gloewlys, *s. m.—pl. t.* iau (gloew—llys) The euphrasy, or eye-bright.

Gloewon, *s. pl. aggr.* (gloew) The clear of liquid.

Gloth, *a.* (*f. of* glwth) Voluptuous, gluttonous.

Glothineb, *s. m.* (gloth) Voluptuousness; riotous living; gluttony.

Glöwr, *s. m.—pl.* glowyr (glo—gwr) A collier.

Glöyn, *s. m. dim.* (glo) A lump of burning coal.

Glöyn, *s. m.—pl. t.* au (glo) A glow-worm. *Gloyn byw, pilai, eilir, ilir,* the butterfly.

> Gloynnau duw gleision dail.
>
> The *butterflies* are the gems of the leaves. *D. ab Gwilym.*

Glud, *s. m.—pl. t.* ion (llud) That is the essence or power; that is the point of attraction; a chief.

> Drud a glud gwledarddi ysgwndaw,
> Dewth a chwelh cyfoeth cylannaw,
> Dwys aer-gwys Powys gnawd amdaw.
> *Llygad Gwr, i Ruff. Maelawr.*

Glw, *s. m.* (llw) That is clear, bright, or pure.

Glwf, *s. m.* (glw) That is clear, or transparent.

Glwth, *s. m.—pl.* glythion (llwth) A voluptuous one, a voluptuary; a glutton;—a couch.

> Tri glwth byd: mor, dinas, ac arglwydd.
>
> The three *insatiable* ones of the world; the sea, a city, and a lord.
> *Adage.*
>
> Y maent—yn ymestyn ar eu glythau.
>
> They are stretching on their couches. *Amos vi. 4.*

Glwth, *a.* (llwth) Voluptuous, sensual; gluttonous, greedy.

> March i ddiawg, ci i lwth.
>
> A horse for the lazy, a dog for the voluptuous. *Adage.*
>
> Dau bryd newynawg a wna'r trydydd yn lwth.
>
> Two starving meals will make the third gluttonous. *Adage.*

Glwyd, *s. m.* (glw) That is of a bright or light hue. *a.* Of fair appearance; pure; venerable.

> Bardd Elffin, Dalhesin lwyd,
> O donnau mor a dynnwyd.
>
> The bard of Elphin, the venerable Taliesin, from the waves of the sea was drawn.
> *D. ab Ieuan Ddu.*

Glwys, *s. m.—pl. t.* au (glw) A hallowed place; a fair spot; a delectable spot.

> Gwenwyn yn amwyn am dir breiniawl Powys,
> A'i diffwys, a'i glwys a glyw ei hawl.
>
> Gwenwyn guarding round the privileged land of Powys, and its wilderness, and its *fair region* will hear his claim.
> *Ein. ab Gwgawn, i Lywelyn I.*

Glwys, *a.* (glw) Pure; holy; pleasant; fair; abounding with love; delectable.

> Llywelyn llew glwys, Lloegrwys lugyrn;
> Llary gyrg leithelyg llwng ei thafyrn,
> Twrwf tordwyat mawr mis Chwefrawr chwyrn.
>
> Llywelyn the *amiable* lion, the torch of the Lloegrians; the mild heavenly speaking out that burns its taverns, with the tumult of the great whirlwind of the severe month of February.
> *Ein. ab Gwalchmai.*
>
> Awn—
> I eglwys Duw ein glwys Dad.
>
> We will go to the temple of God, our *holy* Father. *Iolo Goch.*

Glwysaidd, *a.* (glwys) Of a pure nature.

Glwysaw, *v. a.* (glwys) To purify; to sanctify; to make delectable; to make fair, or beauteous

Glwysawg, *a.* (glwys) Having purity; hallowed; delectable, pleasant.

Glwysawl, *a.* (glwys) Of a pure nature; sanctified, or hallowed; delectable.

Glwysdeb, *s. m.* (glwys) Pureness; holiness.

Glwysder, *s. m.* (glwys) Purity; holiness; pleasantness; beauteousness.

Glwysedd, *s. m.* (glwys) Purity; sanctitude; delectableness.

Glwysiad, *s. m.* (glwys) A purifying; a hallowing; a rendering delectable.

Glwysle, *s. m.—pl. t.* oedd (glwys—lle) A holy place; a pleasant place, a region of delight.

Gly, *s. m.* (lly) Plastic principle; what keeps or connects together.

Glyd, *s. m.—pl. t.* ion (llyd) Viscous matter; glue; birdlime; paste.

Glyd, *a.* (llyd) Viscous, tenacious; that holds fast; patient, diligent.

Glydai, *s. m.—pl.* glydeion (glyd) One that sticks fast; an adherent.

Glydaidd, *a.* (glyd) Of a viscid or sticky nature.

Glydaw, *v. a.* (glyd) To stick together with any cement; to glue.

Glydedd, *s. m.* (glyd) Viscidity; clamminess.

Glydiad, *s. m.* (glyd) A cementing, or glueing.

Glydiaw, *v. a.* (glyd) To stick together, to glue.

> Rhwymer, glydier y gwledydd,
> Rhoed Duw rhwng pob rhai ood dydd.
>
> The countries be they bound, *be they cemented together,* let God give concord amongst every body. *H. ab D. ab I. ab Rhys.*

Glydiawg, *a.* (glyd) Viscous, viscid, glutinous.

Glydiawl, *a.* (glyd) Viscous, glutinous, sticky.

Glydiogi, *v. a.* (glydiawg) To make viscid, or ropy; to become ropy.

Glydiogrwydd, *s. m.* (glydiawg) Viscidity, glueiness, clamminess, ropiness.

Glydioli, *v. a.* (glydiawl) To make viscid, clammy, or sticky; to become viscid.

Glydiolrwydd, *s. m.* (glydiawl) Glueiness.

Glydlys, *s. m.* (glyd—llys) The catch-fly.

Glydrwydd, *s. m.* (glyd) Viscidity; clamminess.

Glydwydd, *s. pl. aggr.* (glyd—gwydd) Lime-twigs

Glyf, *s. m.—pl. t.* ion (glwf) The mallow.

Glyfoer, *s. m.—pl. t.* ion (glwf—goer) Drivel, slaver, or slabber.

Glyfoeriad, *s. m.* (glyfoer) A slavering.

Glyfoeriaw, *v. a.* (glyfoer) To drivel, to slaver.

Glyfoeriedig, *a.* (glyfoer) Drivelled, slavered.

Glyfoeriwr, *s. m.—pl.* glyfoerwyr (glyfoer—gwr) A driveller, a slaverer.

Glyfoerllyd, *a.* (glyfoer) Salivous; drivelling.

Glyn, *s. m.—pl. t.* oedd (llyn) A deep vale through which a river flows; a glen.

> Y gwr a fuasai anorchfygedic cyn no hyny, yr awr hon a edewid y mywn glynnau diffeithon.
>
> The man who had been theretofore invincible, now was left in the vales of desolation.
> *B. y Tywysogion.*

Glyn, *s. m.* (gly) Adhesion. *a.* Adhering, sticking

Glynawl, *a.* (glyn) Adhering, or sticking.

Glynedig, *a.* (glyn) Made to adhere; sticking.

Glyniad, *s. m.—pl. t.* au (glyn) Adhesion; a clinging, or sticking to.

Glynu, *v. a.* (glyn) To adhere, to stick, to cleave, to cling, to stick close to.

Glynwr, *s. m.—pl.* glynwyr (glyn—gwr) One who clings; an adherent, a stickler.

Glys, *s. m. aggr* (llys) The yellow stone-crop.

Glythaidd, *a.* (glwth) Apt to be voluptuous, gluttonous, or greedy.

Glythawg, *a.* (glwth) Voluptuous; gluttonous.

Glythawl, *a.* (glwth) Voluptuous; gluttonous.

Glythedd, *s. m.* (glwth) Voluptuousness, gluttony

Glythfin, *s. m.* (glwth—min) A voluptuous lip; a gluttonous mouth.

Glythi, *s. m.* (glwth) Voluptuousness, gluttony.

Glythig, *a.* (glwth) Voluptuous; gluttonous.

> Megis y mae—y twrch yn ymdrol mewn corsydd a thomydd, yn yr un modd y mae y rhai glythig meddwon yn ymdrol, ac yn ymgreinlaw mewn meddwdawd a glothineb.
>
> As a swine walloweth in bogs and dunghills, in the same manner do the *voluptuous* drunken ones wallow and grovel in drunkenness and gluttony. *Marchawg Crwydrad.*

Glythineb, *s. m.* (glwth) Voluptuousness; riotous living; gluttony.

> Glythineb yw cymeryd o ddyn, o achaws digrifwch cnawdawl, bwyd neu lyn mwy no digawn.
>
> *Gluttony* is when a person, for the sake of carnal sensuality, takes of meat or drink more than sufficient. *Ll. G. Hergest.*

Glythinebgar, *a.* (glythineb) Voluptuous; greedy

Glythinebgarwch, *s. m.* (glythinebgar) Voluptuousness; fondness, or greediness for eating and drinking.

Glythinebu, *v. a.* (glythineb) To live voluptuously; to live riotously, to revel; to gormandize

> Ereill a lythinebant ei dda ef.
>
> Others shall *riotously enjoy* his wealth. *Eccles.* xiv. 4.

Glythinebwr, *s. m.—pl.* glythinebwyr (glythineb—gwr) A voluptuous man; a greedygut.

Glythlyd, *a.* (glwth) Apt to be voluptuous; of a gluttonous disposition.

Glythni, *s. m.* (glwth) Voluptuousness; revelry; gluttony, gormandizing.

Glythu, *v. a.* (glwth) To indulge in voluptuousness; to gluttonize, to gormandize.

Glythwr, *s. m.—pl.* glythwyr (glwth—gwr) A voluptuous man, a gormandizer.

Glythyn, *s. m. dim.* (glwth) A voluptuous thing; a small couch.

Glyw, *s. m.—pl. t.* ion (llyw) A governor, or ruler

> Bu cyfrysedd—
> Rhwng glyw Powys a glwys Wynedd.
>
> There was contention between the *governor* of Powys and fair Gwynedd. *O. Cyfeiliawg.*
>
> Llywelyn, llyw Prydain a'i phâr;
> Llew, a glew, a glyw gyfarwar.
>
> Llywelyn the director of Britain and its spear; a lion, a hero, and a tranquillizing *governor*. *Ll. P. Moch, i Lywelyn I.*
>
> Tri pheth nid iawn y naill heb y lleill: glyw, glew, a gwlad.
>
> Three things wherein one is not right without the other: a *ruler*, a hero, and a country. *Trioedd Gwladoldeb.*

Glyw, *a.* (llyw) Regulating, commanding, puissant

> Llyw glyw glew anhangnefedd,
> Llywelyn gelyn Gwynedd.
>
> A leader *commanding* and persevering, a stranger to peace, Llywelyn the enemy of Gwynedd. *Llywarch Llaety, i L. ab Madawg.*
>
> Glew lew o lin Cadwallawn,
> Glyw lyw gan yd byw ba wnawn!
>
> A heroic lion of the line of Cadwallon, a *regulating* leader, since he is not alive, what shall we do! *Bleddyn Fardd, i O. Goch.*

Gnaw, *s. m.* (naw) Habit, custom, instinct.

Gnawd, *s. m.—pl.* gnodau (nawd) A thing accustomed; a habit, custom, or use.

> Doddyw am Owain, doeth-wawr o'i golled
> Gnawd gollwng deigr hyd lawr.
>
> There is come for Owain, the intelligent light, because of his loss the *habit* of letting the tears trickle to the ground. *Bleddyn Fardd, i O. Goch.*

Gnawd, *a.* (nawd) Accustomed, habitual, usual, common, fashionable. *Hwn yw y gnotaf*, this is the most fashionable.

> Gnawd ar eiddil ofalon.
>
> Cares are *habitual* with the feeble. *Adage.*
>
> Gnawd o'l ganmawl canmoladwy.
>
> It is usual for one being praised to become praiseworthy. *Adage.*
>
> I dref wen rhwng Tren a Throdwydd,
> Oedd gnodach ysgwyd ton
> Yn dawed o gad nog ydd ych i echwydd.
>
> To the white town between Tren and Trodwydd, *more usual* was the broken shield coming from battle than the ox to his evening rest. *Llywarch Hen.*

Gnaws, *s. m.* (gnaw) Nature or quality.

> Gloes, eisioes esgar,
> A'm cur mal carchar,
> Ac angerdd anwar,
> Gnaws dar dan las.
>
> A pang, already departed, afflicts me like a prison, and the fierce violence of the *state* of the oak under the beat. *Gwalchmai.*
>
> A berthyn am ddyn a ddywedaf;
> A bortho gofid bid bwyllocaf;
> A fo gnaws achaws uchaf i feddiant
> I feddwl bid leiaf.
>
> What appertains to man I will speak of; he that undergoes affliction, let him be the most patient; he that is of the highest possession from the cause of *nature*, let his mind be the feeblest. *Bleddyn Fardd.*

Gnaws, *a.* (gnaw) Natural, temperamental.

Gne, *s. m.* (ne) A hue, or tint; a complexion. *Gne gwyn*, a white hue; *gne gwin*, the hue of wine; *gne seren*, the brightness of a star; *gne caregryd nant*, the hue of the stony ford of the brook; *gne gwawn*, gossamer hue.

> Lliw geirw rhyd o bryd a wnaeth brad i'm gne,
> Gnawd serchawg ymlyniad.
>
> She that is of the colour of the rippling of the ford hath dealt treacherously to my *complexion*, the enamoured is habituated to be a pursuer. *Gr. ab M. ab Dafydd.*
>
> Curiais—
> Er's blwyddyn am ne llenydd.
>
> I have pined for a year for the *splendour* of the dales. *Ior. Fynglwyd.*
>
> A'th lun gwych wythliw ne gwawn.
>
> And thy elegant form eight times the colour of the *brightness* of the gossamer. *D. ab Gwilym.*

Gnes, *s. m.* (gne) A state of fluctuation; a flutter

Gni, *s. m—pl. t.* on (ni) What pervades; what overruns; shock, pain.

Gnif, *s. m.—pl. t.* ion (gni) Pain, anxiety, trouble, toil, conflict.

> Nid ofer gnif ym hogi maen.
>
> It is not useless *toil* for me to whet a stone. *Llywarch Hen.*
>
> Yn llafur dy ddwylaw, a gnif dy galon y bydd dy ymborth.
>
> In the labour of thine hands, and *anxiety* of thy heart, shall be thy provision. *H. Car. Mag.—Mabinogion.*
>
> Oedd cleu-daer, oedd claer cleddyf uch gwain,
> A llinon yngnif a llafnau llain.
>
> Incessantly ardent and bright was the sword out of the sheath, and the spear in the *toil* with the broad blades. *Cynddelw, i O. Gwynedd.*

Gnif, *s. m.—pl. t.* ion (gni) Pain, anxiety, trouble, toil, conflict.

Gnis, *s. m.—pl. t.* iau (gni) A brandishing, a flourish.

Gnisiad, *s. m.—pl. t.* au (gnis) A brandishing.

Gnisiaw, *v. a.* (gnis) To brandish, to flourish.

> Arddwyre Reged rysedd rïau,
> Gnisynt cad lafnawr
> Y dan gylchwy awr,
> Lleeu goleu gwyn gelain.

[illegible] in [illegible] of warlike chiefs; they brandished the blade of conflict under the round shield of the chest; whose light display-ed a white corpse. *Taliesin.*

Gnisiawl, *a.* (gnis) Brandishing, flourishing.

Gnodawl, *a.* (gnawd) Customary, common, universal; accustomed, fashionable. *Hyn sy gnodawl*, this is customary.

> Ergiyw ddig llawd gnawd yn gnodawl archi!
>
> [illegible] the [illegible] troubled one habituated in the *accustomed* petition! *Gwalchmai.*

Gnodi, *v. a.* (gnawd) To make common, to habituate, to become common.

> Gnawd o'i ryw gnwd ar ei ol.
>
> *There will be had of his sort a crop after him.* *T. Aled.*

Gnodig, *a.* (gnawd) Habitual, or common.

Gnodus, *a.* (gnawd) Habitual, customary.

Gnotâad, *s. m.* (gnawd) An accustoming, or habituating; a making or becoming common.

Gnotâawl, *a.* (gnawd) Accustoming, habitual.

Gnotäedig, *a.* (gnawd) Accustomed, or usual.

> Ai chwi! chwi yr analwedigion dyngheditmau, pa le i cerddwch chwi draw ych gnotaedigion hyntiau?
>
> Ha! you uncalled fates, where are you proceeding to over your *accustomed* courses! *Gr. ab Arthur.*

Gnotäedigaeth, *s. m.* (gnotäedig) The act of making habitual, or common.

Gnotai, *s. f.—pl.* gnoteion (gnawd) A circle about the sun, moon, or star; a halo.

Gnotâu, *v. a.* (gnawd) To accustom, to habituate, to make common, or general; to grow into custom, to become habitual; to become fashionable. *Canys gnotâai*, in regard it would be usual; *Gnotasai fod fal hyn*, it had been customary to be this wise.

> Megis y dywawd Gildas, nid amgen y pechawd hwnw, namyn yr holl bechodau a [illegible] dynawl anian eu gwneuthur.
>
> As Gildas has said, not excepting that sin, but all the sins which human nature is *accustomed* to commit. *Gr. ab Arthur.*

Gnotâus, *a.* (gnawd) Habitual, customary, usual.

Gnwth, *s. m.—pl.* gnythau (awth) Voracity.

Gnythawd, *s. m.* (gnwth) A devouring; voracity.

> Gwr, gwrthaw gwrthddrych yn dodawd,
> Gwrth ochyr gwrthddrychiaid yn gnawd;
> Gwrth aur-dro aur-drull gne gnythawd.
>
> A man, whose law is resistance to the opposing object, he will oppose the fates themselves should they become opponents; he will oppose the golden turn of the gleaming cutter with the bite of voracity. *Cynddelw, i'r argl. Rhys.*

Gnythawl, *a.* (gnwth) Voracious, devouring.

Gnythiad, *s. m.—pl. t.* au (gnwth) A devouring.

Gnythu, *v. a.* (gnwth) To eat greedily.

GO, *s. m. r.* A progress towards; that is gone, or going, approach. It is used as an inceptive preposition, denoting approach, or that the idea is somewhat of, or near to its absolute state. Therefore, when it is prefixed to *nouns* they are diminutives, the *verbs* are in a degree, or short of the absolute action, and the *adjectives* are partly the quality they describe, and they take the forms of adverbs, like those having the termination *ly* in English. *Gobant*, a little hollow; *gofron*, a little hill, or hillock, *gofiew*, tender hair, or down; *goderau*, partly to strike, or to pat gently; *godrigaw*, partly to tarry, or to linger;—*godenau*, in a degree thin, or thinnish; *goddrwg*, pretty bad, or baddish.

Go, *adv.* (go, *s.*) Somewhat in some degree, pretty. *Mae hi yn ddynes go dlws*, she is a tolerably handsome woman; *a wyt ti yn o dda?* art thou pretty well? *mae yn hin go arw*, it is rather rough weather.

Goachub, *v. a.* (achub) To save in some degree.

Goachubiad, *s. m.* (goachub) A partly saving.

Goachul, *a.* (achul) Somewhat puny, or ill.

Goadgas, *a.* (adgas) Somewhat vexatious.

Goafael, *s. m.* (gafael) A slight hold, or grasp.

> Cyfaill grym [illegible], nid oes gafael [illegible],
> O [illegible] hyder goafael.
>
> I have a friend of might, not a hero, that will take a disappointment, of the heroes of confidence of *feeble hold.* *Meilyr, i Ieu. Llwyd.*

Goafaeliad, *s. m.* (goafael) A holding slightly.

Goafaelu, *v. a.* (goafael) To hold slightly.

Goair, *s. m.* (gair) A half word, or expression.

> Nid oes er mawredd ane llefaryat,
> Goair anhebgor ane cymmodiyat.
>
> There was not for greatness but they would speak, except the indispensable *half* word but they would be reconciled. *Taliesin.*

Goammod, *s. f.—pl. t.* au (ammod) A promise in part, a half promise.

Goammodawl, *a.* (goammod) Partly promising.

Goammodi, *v. a.* (goammod) To promise partly.

Goaml, *a.* (aml) Somewhat frequent, or rife.

Goanesmwyth, *a.* (anesmwyth) Rather uneasy.

Goanesmwythaw, *v. n.* (goanesmwyth) To be somewhat uneasy, or troubled.

Goanesmwythyd, *s. m.* (goanesmwyth) A somewhat of an uneasiness.

Goanhyfryd, *a.* (anhyfryd) Rather unpleasant.

Goanhynaws, *a.* (anhynaws) Rather unkind.

Goanniddig, *a.* (anniddig) Rather uncomposed.

Goannyddan, *a.* (annyddan) Rather comfortless.

Goarfoel, *a.* (arfoel) Somewhat bald.

> Nycha y dynion yn dawed wr [illegible] goarfoel gogrygin a baich o gwryng.
>
> The men behold coming a red man *rather bald*, and rather decrepid, with a load of sticks. *Br. Rhonabwy,—Mabinogion.*

Goarfoeledd, *s. m.* (goarfoel) A somewhat of a baldness.

Goarfoeli, *v. a.* (goarfoel) To make somewhat bald, or bare.

Goarogl, *s. m.* (arogl) Some degree of smell.

Goarswyd, *s. f.—pl. t.* ion (arswyd) A little dread.

Goarswydaw, *v. n.* (goarswyd) To become somewhat frightened.

Goarswydiad, *s.* (goarswyd) A partly terrifying.

Goarswydus, *a.* (goarswyd) Somewhat timorous.

Goathraw, *s. m.—pl. t.* on (athraw) A smatterer in learning.

Goathrawd, *s. f.—pl.* goathrodion (athrawd) A slight reproach.

Goathrist, *a.* (athrist) Somewhat pensive.

Goathrodawl, *a.* (goathrawd) Somewhat reproachful, or detracting.

Goathrodi, *v. a.* (goathrawd) To detract slightly.

Gob, *s. f.—pl. t.* au (ob) A heap, a mound; what stays, or bears up; a pad, a cushion, froth.

Gobaill, *s. m.* (paill) A coarse kind of flour.

Gobaith, *s. m.—pl.* gobeithion (paith) A seeing darkly, a partly seeing, hope; a common or an open wild. *Meini gobaith*, stones of exploration, set up on mountains to direct the way.

> Gwlad a chenedl yn gyffredin biaufynt bob gwyllt a gobaith: heb gennad arglwydd, ni ddylid adeiliad yn [illegible], aredig yn ngobaith, a digoedlaw tir gwyllt yn [illegible].
>
> The country and nation in common own every wild and desert: without permission of the lord, there ought to be no building on a common, ploughing on a common, or the clearing wild land of wood on a common. *Trioedd Dyfnwal.*
>
> Gwell Duw no drwg obaith.
>
> God is better than we should lack *hope.* *Adage.*
>
> Y trydydd gloew-ddydd, rhyg[illegible] obaith,
> I bu fyw [illegible] heb [illegible].
>
> The third bright day, the *hope* of blessings, he was again alive void of [illegible]. *Gr. ab I. ab Ll. Fychan.*

Gobant, *s. m.—pl.* gobentydd (pant) A little dingle or hollow.

> Arthyn——
> Lle'r ydoedd yn mhob gobant
> Ellyllon mingeimion gant.

I traversed where in every *small dingle* there were hundreds of wry-mouthed goblins. *D. ab Gwilym, i'r niwl.*

Gobed, *s. m.—pl. t.* au (ped) A cobiron, or andiron.

Gobeilliad, *s. m.* (gobaill) A coarse kind of flour.

Gobeilliaw, *v. a.* (gobaill) To make into coarse flour.

Gobeithfawr, *a.* (gobaith) Full of hope.

Gobeithgar, *a.* (gobaith) Full of hope; expectant.

Gobeithiad, *s. m.—pl. t.* au (gobaith) A hoping.

Gobeithiadwy, *a.* (gobeithiad) That may be hoped or expected.

Gobeithiaw, *v. a.* (gobaith) To hope; to be in hopes. *s. m.* Hope; expectation.

> Goreu gwaith yw gobeithiaw;
> Gwybydd mai dy ddydd a ddaw.

The best employ is *to hope*, know that thy day will come. *Meredydd Brydydd.*

> Y mae'n well, pe ddeallyn',
> Byth Duw na gobeithiaw dyn.

If they would but understand, God is always better than the *expectation* of man. *Gw. Tew.*

Gobeithiawg, *a.* (gobaith) Having hope, hopeful.

Gobeithiawl, *a.* (gobaith) Hoping, looking for. *Carcharorion gobeithiawl*, prisoners of hope.

Gobeithioldeb, *s. m.* (gobeithiawl) Hopefulness.

Gobeithiolrwydd, *s.* (gobeithiawl) Hopefulness.

Gobeithiwr, *s. m.—pl.* gobeithwyr (gobaith—gwr) One who hopes.

Gobeithlawn, *a.* (gobaith) Full of hope, hopeful.

Gobeithus, *a.* (gobaith) Hoping; relying.

Pan glywwn yr ariwyddes Coffadigaeth yn darllain y geiriau hyn, mi a gymerwn galon obeithus.

When I heard the princess Remembrance reading these words, I took a *confident* heart. *Marchawg Crwydrad.*

Gobeithusrwydd, *s. m.* (gobeithus) Hopefulness.

Gobell, *s. f.—pl. t.* au (gob) A pad; a saddle.

> Mad ddodes ei forddwyd dros obell
> Ei orwydd o wng ac o bell.

Well he placed his thigh over the *saddle* of his steed, of the near and farther side. *Llywarch Hen.*

> Myn dy gael, rhyw afael rheg,
> Yn ngobant, yn ngobell mwg.

He will strive to get thee, by some fatal hold, in a dingle, in a *cloud* of smoke. *I. Deulwyn.*

Gobellawg, *a.* (gobell) Having a pad; saddled.

Gobellu, *v. a.* (gobell) To pad, to put on a pad; to saddle.

Goben, *s. m.—pl. t.* au (pen) A penultima.

Gobenawl, *a.* (goben) Penultimate, next to the termination.

Gobeniad, *s. m.—pl. t.* au (goben) A being nearly the head, or end; a placing in the penultima.

Gobenu, *v. a.* (goben) To conclude nearly; to place in the penultima.

Gobenydd, *s. m.—pl. t.* au (goben) An end, or headstead; a bolster; a cushion.

Y gwas ystafell â geiff—y gobenydd a ddoter dano yn ei gader.

The groom of the chamber shall have the *cushion* that shall be put under him in the chair. *Welsh Laws.*

> Lle bwyf a'm pen ar obenydd
> Ysgawen fon-wen â fydd.

Where I shall be with my head on a *pillow*, a white stemmed alder tree shall grow. *R. Ddu.*

Gobenyddiad, *s. m.—pl. t.* au (gobenydd) A fixing or supporting the head, or end; a bolstering; a bracketing; a bracket; a penultima.

Y pedwerydd treigliad a dderbyn yr henwau a font wedi estyn eu gobenyddiad, a'u terfyn yn y rhif lliosawg.

The fourth declension receives those names that have their *penultima extended*, and their termination in the plural number. *Gr. Roberts.*

Gobenyddiaw, *v. a.* (gobenydd) To fix up the end, to support the head, to bolster, to bracket.

Gobenyddu, *v. a.* (gobenydd) To bolster up.

Gober, *s. m.—pl. t.* oedd (per) Operation, deed.

> Berwid brad anfad ober.

Let treachery produce a graceless *deed*. *Llywarch Hen.*

> Treiglyd an cywyd, a'n cam ober.

May he turn away our wickedness, and our wrong *doing*. *Llywelyn Fardd.*

Goberaidd, *a.* (peraidd) Somewhat luscious.

Goberawl, *a.* (gober) Operative, or effective.

Goberiad, *s. m.—pl. t.* au (gober) An operating.

Goberu, *v. a.* (gober) To operate, to work.

Gobetrus, *a.* (petrus) Somewhat doubtful.

Gobetrusaw, *v. a.* (gobetrus) To hesitate a little; to be somewhat doubtful.

Gobetrusiad, *s. m.* (gobetrus) A partly hesitating, a being somewhat doubtful.

Gobisaw, *s. m.* (pisaw) The diabetes.

Gobisaw, *v. a.* (pisaw) To discharge urine dribblingly.

Gobisiad, *s. m.* (pisiad) A discharging of water drop by drop.

Goblyg, *s. m.—pl. t.* ion (plyg) A half double.

> Myg'r wenyg, a blyg am oblygion main
> Man y mae' fy ngheddon.

Fair waves embrace the *recesses* of the stones in the spot where my thoughts abide. *Gr. ab M. ab Dafydd.*

Goblygawl, *a.* (goblyg) Half doubled, partly doubled, or folded.

Goblygiad, *s. m.—pl. t.* au (goblyg) A partly doubling, or folding.

Goblygu, *v. a.* (goblyg) To make partly double.

Goborth, *s. m.* (porth) Sustenance, victuals.

Goborthiad, *s. m.—pl.* goborthiaid (goborth) A purveyor, a provider of food.

> Cynfelyn gasnar,
> Ysgwn bryfwn bar,
> Goborthiad adar.

Cynfelyn the hostile chief, the exalted source of wrath, the *preparer of food* for birds. *Taliesin.*

Goborthiant, *s. m.* (goborth) Sustenance. *Brain goborthiant*, food of ravens.

Gobr, *s. m.—pl. t.* au (gob) A recompense, or reward, price, wages, or hire; fee; bribe. *Gobr cyfraith*, law fee, due to the judge from the party gaining the cause; *gobr gwarchadw*, protection fee, being a hundred and twentypence, paid by a returning exile to his relations for preserving his title to his land, and restoring to him quiet possession; *Gobr mynawg*, fee for information;—*Gobr estyn*, extent, or seisin fee; *Gobr merch*, maiden fee. *Welsh Laws.*

Mynagwr a geiff obr mynag, sef yw, y degfed geiniawg a dalo y peth a fynaco.

An informer shall have an informing *reward*, which is, the tenth penny of the value of the thing he shall inform of. *Welsh Laws.*

Gobrawl, *a.* (gobr) Compensative, rewarded, hired, having a fee.

Gobriad, *s. m.* (gobr) A recompensing, a paying of wages, a feeing.

Gobrid, *s. m.* (prid) What is somewhat dear. *a.* Somewhat dear, pretty dear.

> Gorfynawg drythyll, gorddyfn ariwy,
> Ariwyaw erlidd gobrid gobrwy.

Of the height of complaisance is the fickle one, one of profound preparation, preparing the pursuit of the *slender attachment* of recompense. *Cynddelw, i Efa f. Madawg.*

> Morwyn a welais mor drybelid
> Yn eurllen, yn wen, yn wan obrid.

A maid have I seen so supremely gay in a golden veil, delicate and of small *degree of attachment*. *Ior. Fychan.*

Gobridiad, *s. m.—pl. t.* au (gobrid) A rendering somewhat dear, partly expiating; a rendering some consideration.

Gobridiaw, *v. a.* (gobrid) To render dear, to expiate partly; to give or pledge some value.

Gobru, *v. a.* (gobr) To compensate; to fee.

Gobrudd, *a.* (prudd) Somewhat sedate, or sad.

Gobruddâad, *s. m.* (gobrudd) A making sad, a becoming dejected.

Gobruddâu, *v. n.* (gobrudd) To become pensive.

Gobrwy, *s. m.—pl. t.* on (prwy) Recompense, reward, price, wages, hire, fee, bribe.

> Yn mhob daioni y mae gobrwy;
> Yn mhob drygioni y mae pechawd.
>
> In every good there is a *reward*, in every misdoing there is sin. *Adage.*

Gobrwyad, *s. m.—pl. t.* au (gobrwy) A recompensing, or rewarding; a giving a value, or price, a paying wages.

Gobrwyadwy, *a.* (gobrwyad) Remunerable.

Gobrwyaeth, *s. m.—pl. t.* au (gobrwy) A rewarding; a hiring, a feeing.

Gobrwyaw, *v. a.* (gobrwy) To recompense, to reward, to requite, to give value, or price; to pay wages, or hire; to fee, to bribe.

Gobrwyawg, *a.* (gobrwy) Having recompense, reward, or requital; having pay, or hire.

Gobrwyawl, *a.* (gobrwy) Rewarding, feeing.

Gobrwyedig, *a.* (gobrwy) Recompensed, rewarded, or requited; hired, or feed.

Gobrwyedigaeth, *s. m.—pl. t.* au (gobrwyedig) Remuneration; the act of hiring.

Gobrwyedigawl, *a.* (gobrwyedig) Remunerative.

Gobrwyedydd, *s. m.—pl. t.* ion (gobrwyad) A rewarder; one who gives hire, or fee.

Gobrwywr, *s. m.—pl.* gobrwywyr (gobrwy—gwr) A rewarder, a payer of wages, or fees.

Gobrwyydd, *s. m.—pl. t.* ion (gobrwy) A rewarder

Gobrydd, *s. m.—pl. t.* ion (gobr) A rewarder.

Gobryn, *s. m.—pl. t.* au (pryn) Desert, or merit.

> O dri pheth y syrthier yn abred gan angen, er ymlyno yn mhob peth arall wrth y da; o falchder hyd annwn, o anwiredd hyd obryn, ac o annhrugaredd hyd gyfdeb, a thrwyddo yn ol at ddyndawd, fal o'r blaen.
>
> For three reasons there will be a fall into the circle of inchoation through necessity, though there be an attachment to good in every thing else: for pride to the lowest point of existence, for falsehood to a *corresponding state*; and for cruelty to a corresponding brutality, whence to return to humanity, as before. *Barddas.*

Gobrynawg, *a.* (gobryn) Having merit, deserving.

Gobrynawl, *a.* (gobryn) Meriting; deserving.

Gobryniad, *s. m.* (gobryn) A meriting.

Gobrynu, *v. n.* (gobryn) To deserve, to merit.

> A dil goelio eidwyllwr a obryn ei dwyllaw.
>
> He that believes his deceiver a second time *deserves* to be deceived. *M. Cav. Mag.—Mabinogion.*

Gobwyll, *s. m.—pl. t.* oedd (pwyll) Indecision of the mind; consideration; meditation.

Gobwyllaw, *v. a.* (gobwyll) To take into consideration, to consider; to meditate.

> Enaid Owain ab Urien,
> Gobwyllid ei Ren ei raid.
>
> The soul of Owain the son of Urien, may his Lord *consider* its necessity. *Taliesin.*
>
> Ni chysgaf, gobwyllaf o'm diwedd.
>
> I will not sleep, *I will meditate* on my end. *Taliesin.*

Gobwyllawg, *a.* (gobwyll) Having consideration; considerate, thoughtful.

Gobwylliad, *s. m.—pl. t.* au (gobwyll) A considering, a meditating; consideration.

Gobwyllus, *a.* (gobwyll) Considerate, thoughtful.

Gobwys, *s. m.—pl. t.* au (pwys) A tendency to press to; gravity.

Gobwysaw, *v. a.* (gobwys) To gravitate.

Gobwysawl, *a.* (gobwys) Tending to press.

Gobwysiad, *s. m.—pl. t.* au (gobwys) Gravitation.

Gochan, *s. f.* (can) Equivocal song; irony.

Gochanu, *v. a.* (gochan) To sing equivocally; to sing ironically; to disparage.

> Gochanant ei feirdd—
> A minnau o'm rhodau rym anant
> Yn rhudd-aur yn rhwydd ardduniant.
>
> His bards *will lampoon*, whilst I, with my gifts of the power of harmony, am arrayed in ruddy gold prospering in honour. *Ll. P. Moch, i Lywelyn I.*

Gochel, *s. m.—pl. t.* oedd (cel) Act of avoiding.

> Tair dedd ochel y sydd ar fardd: gochel diogi, can mai gwr wrth ynnill ydyw; gochel cynnen, can mai gwr wrth heddwch ydyw; a gochel ffolineb, can mai gwr wrth bwyll ydyw.
>
> There are three injunctions of *refraining* on a bard: to avoid sloth, as being a man of exertion; to avoid contention, as being a man of peace; and to avoid folly, as being a man of reason. *Barddas.*

Gochel, *v. a.* (cel) To avoid, to eschew, to shun; to beware, to take heed.

> Gorug Lelius Galius, cydymdaith Alectus, cynnullaw y rhai ar ddiangasynt o'r Rhufeinwyr atto i Lundain,—a meddyliaw ceisiaw gwrthwynebu oddyno y Prydeiniaid, neu ynte gochel y cynddrychawl angeu oedd yn eu herbyn.
>
> Lelius Galius, the companion of Alectus, collected together those who had fled of the Romans to him to London; thinking to devise means from thence to withstand the Britons, or else *to avoid* the death that was present before them. *Gr. ab Arthur.*

Gocheladwy, *a.* (gochel) That may be avoided, avoidable, eludible.

Gochelawg, *a.* (gochel) Apt to shun, or avoid; wary, or shy.

Gocheledig, *a.* (gochel) Shunned, avoided.

Gocheledigaeth, *s. m.—pl. t.* au (gocheledig) The act or state of shunning.

Gochelffordd, *s. f.* (gochel—ffordd) A byeway.

Gochelgar, *a.* (gochel) Ready to avoid.

Gochelgarwch, *s. m.* (gochelgar) Circumspection

Gocheliad, *s. m.—pl. t.* au (gochel) A shunning.

Gochelus, *a.* (gochel) Apt to avoid; reserved.

Gochelwr, *s. m.—pl.* gochelwyr (gochel—gwr) One who avoids, or takes care, a shunner.

Gochelyd, *v. a.* (gochel) To avoid; to beware.

> Yno'r oeddwn—
> Yn goch'lyd tywyn-bryd tes.
>
> There I was, *avoiding* the glowing presence of the sunshine. *G. ab A. ab Dafydd.*

Gochlyw, *s. m.* (clyw) A hearing imperfectly.

Gochlywed, *v. a.* (gochlyw) To hear partly.

Gochrwm, *a.* (crwm) Somewhat crooked.

Gochrymawl, *a.* (gochrwm) Somewhat bending.

Gochrymiad, *s. m.* (gochrwm) A partly inclining.

Gochrymu, *v. a.* (gochrwm) To bend a little; to become somewhat crooked; to crouch a little.

Gochryn, *a.* (cryn) Somewhat shaking.

Gochrynawl, *a.* (gochryn) Somewhat trembling.

Gochryniad, *s. m.—pl. t.* au (gochryn) A making partly to tremble; a partly quaking.

Gochrynu, *v. a.* (gochryn) To shake somewhat.

Gochwaeth, *s. m.* (chwaeth) Degree of taste.

Gochwaethawl, *a.* (gochwaeth) Somewhat sapid, tasteful, or palatable.

Gochwaethiad, *s. m.* (gochwaeth) A partly tasting

Gochwaethu, *v. a.* (gochwaeth) To taste slightly.

Gochwareu, *s. —pl. t.* on (chwareu) Amusement.

Gochwareu, *v. a.* (chwareu) To act somewhat playfully.

Gochwerw, *a.* (chwerw) Somewhat harsh.

> Bu ddoeth, a chaeth, a sybarw;
> Nid oedd ef wrth gyfedd gochwerw.
>
> He was wise, and sincere, and majestic, he was not *harsh* to the social feast. *Aneurin.*

Gochwerwad, *s. m.* (gochwerw) A being bitterish.

Gochwerwawg, *a.* (gochwerw) Somewhat harsh.

> Rhieu, rhyfelgar gochwerwawg,
> Ef diddyrth addfwyn Llan Lleenawg.
>
> Chieftains warlike and *abounding with harshness*, are borne to fair Llan Lleenog. *Taliesin.*

Gochwerwawl, *a.* (gochwerw) Apt to be somewhat harsh, or bitter.

Gochwerwi, *v. n.* (gochwerw) To become bitterish

Gochwiban, *a.* (chwiban) Partly whistling.

> Hir nos, gorddyar mynydd,
> Gochwiban gwynt uch blaen gwydd:
> Ni thwyll drygnaws dedwydd.
>
> Long the night, blustering the mountain, *whistling* the wind over the top of the wood: ill nature will not deceive the discreet. *Llywarch Hen.*

Gochwibl, *a.* (chwibl) Somewhat sharp; sourish.

Gochwibliad, *s. m.* (gochwibl) A making or becoming tart, or sourish.

Gochwiblaw, *v. a.* (gochwibl) To make sourish; to become somewhat sour.

Gochwidr, *a.* (chwidr) Somewhat giddy, or wild.

Gochwidraw, *v. a.* (gochwidr) To make somewhat giddy; to become rather giddy.

Gochwidriad, *s. m.* (gochwidr) A making or becoming somewhat giddy.

Gochwil, *s. m.* (chwil) A slight turn about; a slight search.

Gochwiliad, *s. m.* (gochwil) A slightly searching.

Gochwiliaw, *v. a.* (gochwil) To search slightly.

Gochwimiad, *s. m.* (chwimiad) A partly moving; a slight motion.

Gochwimiaw, *v. a.* (chwimiaw) To move slightly.

Gochwimiawl, *a.* (chwimiawl) Somewhat moving.

Gochwith, *a.* (chwith) Somewhat awkward.

Gochwithaw, *v. n.* (gochwith) To become somewhat awkward.

Gochwithedd, *s. m.* (gochwith) An awkwardness.

Gochwydd, *s. m.* (chwydd) Somewhat of a swelling

Gochwyddaw, *v. n.* (gochwydd) To swell a little.

Gochwyddawl, *a.* (gochwydd) Tending to swell.

Gochwyddiad, *s. m.* (gochwydd) A partly swelling

Gochwys, *s. m.* (chwys) A degree of sweat; sweat

> Twrf marchogion meirch gochwys,
> Mal twrf toredwynt am brys.
>
> The tumult of knights with *foaming* steeds, like the tumult of a whirlwind about the brushwood. *Cynddelw.*

Gochwysawl, *a.* (gochwys) Somewhat sweating.

Gochwysiad, *s. m.* (gochwys) A sweating partly.

Gochwysu, *v. a.* (gochwys) To sweat partly.

Gochwyth, *s. m.* (chwyth) A slight puff, or blast.

Gochwythawl, *a.* (gochwyth) Somewhat blowing.

Gochwythiad, *s. m.* (gochwyth) A blowing gently.

Gochwythu, *v. a.* (gochwyth) To blow gently.

God, *s. m.* (go) A swerve from; incontinence.

Godaer, *a.* (taer) Somewhat ardent, or violent.

Godaerawl, *a.* (godaer) Somewhat contentious.

Godaeriad, *s. m.* (godaer) A slightly contending.

Godaeru, *v. a.* (godaer) To contend a little.

Godaiawg, *a.* (taiawg) Somewhat boorish.

> Mal hyn y dyly brodyr rann tir y rhyngddynt; pedair erw wrth bob tyddyn. A gwedy hyny y symudwys Bleddyn ab Cynfyn ddeuddeg erw i fab uchelwr, ac wyth i'r mab aillt, a phedair i'r godaiawg.
>
> In this wise should brothers divide land between them; four acres to every tenement. And after that Bleddyn the son of Cynvyn altered it to twelve acres to the son of a gentleman, and eight to the yeoman, and four to the *next to the villain*. *Welsh Laws.*

Godaran, *s. f.—pl. t.* au (taran) A murmur, or rumbling, somewhat like thunder.

> Celain a sych o du tan
> Pan glywyf godwrf godaran
> Llu Llemenig mab Mahawan.
>
> A corpse parches by the side of the fire when I hear the rumbling of the *thundering din* of the host of Llemenig the son of Mahawan. *Llywarch Hen.*

Godaraniad, *s. m.* (godaran) A slight rumbling.

Godaranu, *v.* (godaran) To rumble, to murmur.

Godardd, *s. m.* (tardd) A soft flow or oozing.

Godarddawl, *a.* (godardd) Oozing, softly springing

Godarddiad, *s. m.—pl. t.* au (godardd) An oozing.

Godarddu, *v. a.* (godardd) To flow out slowly.

Godarth, *s. m.—pl. t.* au (tarth) A gentle exhalation, or fog.

Godarthawl, *a.* (godarth) Gently exhaling.

Godarthiad, *s. m.* (godarth) A gently exhaling.

Godarthu, *v. a.* (godarth) To exhale gently.

Godaw, *s. m.* (taw) A half silence, a whisper.

Godawdd, *s. m.—pl.* gododdion (tawdd) What is partly melted, or dissolved.

Godawedawg, *a.* (godaw) Somewhat silent.

Godawel, *a.* (tawel) Somewhat calm, or still.

Godawelawg, *a.* (godawel) Somewhat calm.

Godaweliad, *s. m.* (godawel) A silencing partly.

Godawelu, *v. n.* (godawel) To be partly calm.

Godeb, *s. m.* (god) Incontinence; adultery.

Godebawg, *a.* (godeb) Incontinent; adulterate.

Godebu, *v. a.* (godeb) To act incontinently.

Godebyg, *a.* (tebyg) Somewhat similar, or like.

Godebygawl, *a.* (godebyg) Tending to be somewhat similar.

Godebygiad, *s. m.* (godebyg) A making partly like, or similar.

Godebygu, *v. a.* (godebyg) To make partly similar; to become something like.

Godech, *s. m.* (tech) A lurk, a sculk: a lounge.

Godech, *v. a.* (tech) To sculk, to lurk; to lie hid.

Godechawl, *a.* (godech) Apt to lurk, or to sculk.

Godechfa, *s. f.—pl. t.* oedd (godech) A lurking place.

Godechiad, *s. m.* (godech) A sculking, or lurking.

Godechial, *v. a.* (godech) To sculk, or lurk about.

Godechu, *v. a.* (godech) To sculk, to lurk about.

Godechwr, *s. m.—pl.* godechwyr (godech—gwr) A sculker, or lurker.

Godeimlad, *s. m.* (teimlad) A gently feeling.

Godeimlaw, *v. a.* (teimlaw) To feel gently.

Godemles, *s. m.* (temles) Serenity; temperature. *a.* That is of a serene nature.

> Cychwenychwy Enlli weles,
> A lenwis mican mar edles
> Ar ystre gan fore godemles.
>
> I may mutually wish for the repose of Enlli, which the shroud of the evil of mortality has filled, borne by the swift glider on a *serene* morn. *Taliesin.*

Godeneu, *a.* (teneu) Somewhat thin, or lean.

Godew, *a.* (tew) Somewhat thick, gross, or fat.

Godid, *s. m.* (god) The state of being out of the way, or extraordinary.

Godidawg, *a.* (godid) Extraordinary, excellent.

> Gwerthfawr pob godidawg.
>
> Every thing *rare* is precious. *Adage.*

Godidogi, *v. a.* (godidawg) To make rare, excellent, or preeminent.

Godidogiad, *s. m.* (godidawg) A making rare, excellent, or preeminent.

Godidogrwydd, *s. m.* (godidawg) What is rare, unusual, or excellent; excellence; simplicity.

> Godidogrwydd yw prif ragoriaeth pob peth; can nis gellir cynnal goleuder synwyr ban fo ry gymhleth yr amcan.
>
> *Simplicity* is the primary excellence of every thing; for the perspicuity of the sense cannot be supported when the design is too complicated. *Llywelyn o Langewydd.*

Godineb, *s. m.* (god) Incontinence; adultery, fornication.

> Godineb yw gweithred cydgnawd y rhwng gwr a gwraig adiad.
>
> *Adultery* is the act of carnal copulation between a strange man and woman. *Ll. G. Hergest.*
>
> Ni liwir y' ngolewad
> I neb odineb ei dad.
>
> Nobody will be reproached in public with the *adultery* of his father. *Iolo Goch.*

Godinebawl, *a.* (godineb) Adulterous, adulterate.

Godinebiad, *s. m.* (godineb) A committing adultery; fornication.

Godinebu, *v. a.* (godineb) To commit adultery.

Godinebus, *a.* (godineb) Adulterous, addicted to adultery or fornication.

Godinebwr, *s. m.—pl.* godinebwyr (godineb—gwr) An adulterer, a fornicator.

Godinebydd, *s. m.—pl. t.* ion (godineb) Adulterant

Godirion, *a.* (tirion) Somewhat agreeable.

Godirioni, *v. n.* (godirion) To become somewhat kind, or engaging.

Godlawd, *a.* (tlawd) Somewhat poor, or destitute

> Godlawd ni byddaf o'th gyfreithau.
>
> I shall not be *wanting* of thy laws. *Ein ab Gwalchmai.*

Godlodedd, *s. m.* (godlawd) A degree of poverty.

Godlodi, *s. m.* (godlawd) A degree of poverty.

Godo, *s. m.* (to) That partly covers; typha, or water orchis.

> Caerlleon, llyw Mon, myn Pabo, a'th dug,
> Ef a'th dug y'ngodo.
>
> Caerlleon, by Saint Pabo, hath taken thee away, governor of Mona, and will bear thee to the *extremity.* *Ll. P. Moch.*
>
> Gnawd rhegwydd rhygais ni allo;
> Gnawd gwael ud y'ngodo.
>
> He that cannot attempt much is habituated to frequent falling; meet is it, in winter, for the store to be under cover. *Phylip Brydydd.*

Gododdawl, *a.* (godawdd) Somewhat melting.

Gododdi, *v. a.* (godawdd) To dissolve partly.

Gododdiad, *s. m.* (godawdd) A half dissolving.

Godòni, *v. a.* (tòni) To strip the surface partly.

Godòniad, *s. m.* (tòniad) A paring slightly.

Godor, *s. m.—pl. t.* au (tor) A rupture; an interruption, discontinuance; a stop, let, hinderance, or delay.

> Os cyttirogion a holo dir o gydundeb, a chymeryd cydoed iddynt, o bydd un heb ddawed i'r oed, ac nas lluddio angen gyfreithiawl, godor yw hyny ar ei gymdeithion.
>
> If joint land holders shall prosecute a claim for land in conjunction, and take to themselves a joint term, if one shall be without coming to the term, and not hindered by lawful necessity, that is a *delay* on his companions. *Welsh Laws.*

Godoran, *s. m.* (godor) A tumult, a din.

> Cad yn ngwlad Brachan,
> Cadlan godoran,
> Teyrnedd truan
> Crynyd rhag Cynan.
>
> A battle in the country of Brachan, a warring scene of *tumult*, miserable chieftains were made to tremble before Cynan. *Taliesin.*

Godori, *v. a.* (godor) To make an interruption, discontinuance, or rupture; to prorogue: to stop, to hinder, to delay.

Godoriad, *s. m.* (godor) An interrupting, a discontinuing, a breaking off; a stopping, hindering, or delaying.

Godoriant, *s. m.* (godor) Interruption, discontinuance, ruption; stoppage, hinderance, delay.

Godorin, *s. m.* (godor) A tumultuous noise.

> Oedd brwing waing ei fodrio;
> Oedd brwysg rwysg rhag y godorin.
>
> Powerfully active was his host; awful was his course in front of the *tumult.* *D. Benfras, i Lewelyn I.*

Godorun, *s. m.* (godor) A tumultuous noise.

> Clywed godorun gwyr yn dawed.
>
> Hearing the *din* of men coming. *H. P. P. Dyfed—Mabinogion.*
>
> Godorun dan bared yr ystafell—a glywid.
>
> A *noise* was heard by the wall of the chamber. *H. Math. ab Mathonwy—Mabinogion.*

Godowydd, *s. m.* (godo—gwydd) The yellow water-lilly.

Godr, *s. m.* (god) An extremity, or girt.

Godrais, *s. m.—pl.* godreisiau (trais) A slight oppression.

Godramwy, *s. m.—pl. t.* on (tramwy) A slow travelling; a loitering peregrination.

Godramwy, *v. a.* (tramwy) To travel slowly.

Godramwyad, *s. m.* (godramwy) A travelling slowly, or loiteringly, a perambulation.

Godraws, *a.* (traws) Somewhat perverse, or cross.

Godre, *s. m.—pl. t.* on (god—rhe) A skirt, border, or edge; the lower edge. *Godrëon y llen*, the skirts of the veil; *godre y mynydd*, the skirt of the mountain.

> Gwedy seirch a meirch melyn,
> A gwyr a gwaewawr gwrthryn,
> Am ddiwes rhych bych dros odrëon
> Pen bardd Lleon llaw ysgyn.
>
> After the trappings, and yellow steeds, and shout, and opposing spears, for making the gutter to trickle, be you over the *skirts*, chief bard of Lleon with the uplifted hand. *Taliesin.*
>
> Ni bydd arodrydd ar odre Prydain
> Prydyddion arwyre.
>
> On the *border* of Britain the dignified poets will not be eloquent. *Ll. P. Moch.*

Godrëad, *s. m.* (godre) A bordering, or skirting.

Godrëawl, *a.* (godre) Bordered, or skirted.

Godref, *s. m.—pl. t.* i (tref) A lodge, or lodgement.

> O fynud pysgawd,
> Maint y godref
> Graian mor heli,
> Y dan dywawd.
>
> The fishes might shew the capacity of the *lodgements* of the gravel of the briny sea, beneath the sand. *Taliesin.*

Godreigl, *s. m.* (treigl) Somewhat of a turn.

Godreiglaw, *v. a.* (godreigl) To revolve partly.

Godreigliad, *s. m.* (godreigl) A partly revolving.

Godreisiad, *s. m.* (godrais) A using some force, a slightly oppressing.

Godreisiaw, *v. a.* (godrais) To act somewhat oppressively.

Godreisiawl, *a.* (godrais) Somewhat oppressive.

Godrem, *s. f.—pl. t.* ion (trem) A slight look, a glance; a glimmer.

Godremiad, *s. m.* (godrem) A slightly looking, a glancing; a glimmering.

Godremiaw, *v. a.* (godrem) To look slightly.

Godremiawl, *a.* (godrem) Slightly looking, or glancing; glimmering.

Godremydd, *s. m.—pl. t.* ion (godrem) A glancer.

> Godremydd gwyr ar dri-meirch.
>
> A *spectator* of men on three horses. *Dbel Ddu.*

Godrëon, *s. pl. aggr.* (godre) Skirtings, skirts; dag-locks.

Godricawr, *s. m.—pl.* godricorion (godrig) A lingerer; a sojourner.

> Ni aid af yna yn awr;
> Gelwn gwaith y godricawr.
>
> I will not go there at present; conspicuous the art of a *sojourner.* *Taliesin.*

Godrig, *s. m.—pl. t.* ion (trig) A delay, staying, or tarrying; an abode, dwelling. *Mae godrig ar y lleuad*, the moon is in the wane.

Godrigaw, *v. a.* (godrig) To delay, to tarry.

Godrigiad, *s. m.* (godrig) A delaying, a tarrying.

Godrigiaw, *v. a.* (godrig) To delay; to abide.

Godrigiawl, *a.* (godrig) Dilatory, apt to stay.

> Byddai ei had ef yn odrigiawl mewn tir estrawn.
>
> His seed would be *sojourning* in a strange land. *W. Salisbury.*

Godrin, *s. m.* (trin) Somewhat of a bustle.

> Oedd clwyd clwyf yn mhob elin;
> Oedd briw rhaw yn mhryshladd odrin.
>
> In every elbow a pain was felt, the shield was broken in the *confusion* of conflict. *D. Benfras, i Lywelyn I.*

Godriniad, *s. m.* (godrin) A bustling a little.

Godriniaw, *v. a.* (godrin) To bustle a little.

Godriniawl, *a.* (godrin) Somewhat bustling.

Godro, *s. m.* (godr) A milking. *Gwartheg godro,* or *Da blithion,* milch kine.

Godro, *v. a.* (godr) To milk. *Dos i odro,* go to milk.

> Godrodd buwch o'i pheh.
>
> The cow was *milked* from her head. *Adage.*

Godröad, *s. m.* (godro) A milking, the act of milking.

Godröawl, *a.* (godro) Relating to milking.

Godrom, *a.* (trom) Somewhat heavy, or weighty.

Godrosedd, *s. m.* (trosedd) A slight transgression.

Godrosi, *v. a.* (trosi) To drive out of the way partly.

> Nid oedd ef drabig ydd odrosi,
> Namyn i draisiaw dros a welai.
>
> He was not tyrannically inclined to *persecute in the least,* except to tyrannize over what he should see.
> *Cynddelw, i Gadwallawn.*

Godrosiad, *s. m.* (trosiad) A driving off a little.

Godröydd, *s. m.—pl. t.* ion (godro) A milker.

Godru, *a.* (tru) Somewhat miserable.

Godruan, *a.* (godru) Rather miserable.

Godruanaidd, *a.* (godruan) Somewhat of a miserable, or wretched condition.

Godruanu, *v. n.* (godruan) To become rather miserable, or wretched.

Godrudd, *a.* (trudd) Somewhat agitated.

> Llwrw llwyr-glod wawd rod odrudd.
>
> Towards the *summit* of fame the *agitated* course of praise.
> *Phylip Brydydd.*
>
> Rhod bydr am hoedlwydr odrudd.
>
> Anxious longing for an *agitated* life of frailty. *Cynddelw.*
>
> Pan wnaeth balch odrudd bytchu Flemisiaid,
> Fleimiaid graid gryd lofrudd:
> Brwysg aned o gad oedd gnotbudd.
>
> When the *active* towering hero hewed the Flemings, flames kindled from the ardency of the red-hand of carnage; a headlong running from battle they were used to.
> *Cynddelw, m. O. Gwynedd.*

Godruddaw, *v. a.* (godrudd) To agitate.

Godruddawl, *a.* (godrudd) Agitating, turbulent.

Godruddiad, *s. m.* (godrudd) Perturbation.

Godruth, *s. m.—pl. t.* iau (truth) A little flattery.

Godruthiad, *s. m.* (godruth) A partly flattering.

Godruthiaw, *v. a.* (godruth) To act rather fawningly, partly to flatter.

Godruthiawl, *a.* (godruth) Somewhat fawning

Godrwm, *a.* (trwm) Somewhat heavy, or weighty.

> O Dduw gwyn! i briddyn brych
> Ond oedd odrwm dy edrych!
>
> O blessed God! to a frail mortal was it not *melancholy* to behold thee! *D. ab Rhys, i Grist.*

Godrwsgl, *a.* (trwsgl) Somewhat awkward.

Godrwy, *s. m.—pl. t.* on (trwy) A wreathe, a chain.

Godrwyad, *s. m.—pl. t.* au (godrwy) A wreathing.

Godrwyaw, *v. a.* (godrwy) To wreathe.

Godrwyawg, *a.* (godrwy) Having wreathes.

Godrwyawl, *a.* (godrwy) Wreathing; entwined.

Godrwyawr, *a.* (godrwy) Of a wreathed form.

> Caeawg cynhorawg bleiddo moran,
> Gwefrawr godrwyawr torchawr am ran.
>
> Caeog with a countenance foremost in the rank, with amber *twined wreaths* round his temples. *Aneurin.*

Godrwyth, *s. m.—pl. t.* au (trwyth) Wild beet; melilot; otherwise called *pys y ceirw.*

> Gwynach oedd ei ddwylaw no chenawon godrwyth.
>
> Whiter were her hands than the blossoms of the *briony.*
> *H. P. P. Dyfed—Mabinogion.*

Godrymu, *v. n.* (godrwm) To grow somewhat heavy.

Godrysglaidd, *a.* (godrwsgl) Somewhat clumsy.

Godrythyll, *a.* (trythyll) Somewhat fickle, or wild.

Goduth, *s. m.—pl. t.* iau (tuth) A jog trot.

Goduthiad, *s. m.* (goduth) A trotting slowly.

Goduthiaw, *v. a.* (goduth) To trot slowly, to jog.

Goduthiawg, *a.* (goduth) Jogging; ambling.

Goduthiawl, *a.* (goduth) Jogging; ambling.

Godwll, *s. m.* (go—twll) An imperfect hole.

Godwllon, *s. f.* (godwll) Imperforate; St. John's wort.

Godwrdd, *s. m.—pl.* godyrddau (twrdd) A rumbling noise; a murmur; a din.

> Oian, parchellan, ni hawdd cysgaf,
> Rhag godwrdd y galar ysydd arnaf;
> Deg mlynedd a deugain yd borthais i boen;
> Ys drwg o orhoen y sydd arnaf.
>
> Listen, little pig, I cannot easily sleep, because of the *tumult* of the *grief* with which I am oppressed; fifty years have I endured pain; therefore the transport of joy now upon me is but an evil.
> *Myrddin.*
>
> Yn eu cylch hwynt gweirgloddiau gwastad boneddigaidd, cyflawn o flodau, trwy y rhai y cerdda dwfr y ffynnonau yn ffrydiau gan lithraw o araf odwrdd.
>
> Surrounding them there were level and noble meadows teeming with flowers, through which the water of the springs ran in streams by gliding in gentle *murmurs.* *Gr. ab Arthur.*

Godwrf, *s. m.—pl.* godyrfau (twrf) A rustling noise; a bustle, or stir; a murmur.

> Godwrf a glywaf am glawr Maelienydd,
> Mur elfydd Elfan gawr
> Teulu Madawg——
>
> I hear a *murmur* over the face of Maelienydd, the bulwark of the region of the mighty Elvan, the groan of the family of Madog.
> *Cynddelw, m. M. ab Meredudd.*

Godwyll, *s. m.* (twyll) A slight deception.

Godwyllaw, *v. a.* (godwyll) To deceive slightly.

Godwys, *s. m.* (twys) That is somewhat elevated. *a.* Somewhat raised, or heaped.

> Diffwys baith odwys,
> Beithyniad glud giwys.
>
> A steep plane *somewhat high,* a fair commanding prospect.
> *Taliesin.*

Godwysaw, *v. a.* (godwys) To raise, to elevate, or make preeminent in a degree.

Godwysawl, *a.* (godwys) Somewhat elevated.

Godwysiad, *s. m.* (godwys) A raising somewhat.

Godwyth, *s. m.* (twyth) Somewhat of a spring.

Godwythaw, *v. a.* (godwyth) To spring a little.

Godwythawl, *a.* (godwyth) Apt to spring.

Godwythiad, *s. m.* (godwyth) A springing a little.

Godŷ, *s. m.—pl. t.* au (tŷ) A shed or outhouse.

> Godai mab aillt yw a'i gell, a'i feudy, a'i ysgubawr, a'i odyn, a'r cail, a'r crau moch, a'i hafdŷ, a'i gynhauafdŷ.
>
> The *outhouses* of a yeoman are his buttery, and his cowhouse, and his barn, and his kiln, and the sheep cote, and the pigstye, and his summer-house, and his harvest house. *Welsh Laws.*

Godyn, *a.* (tyn) Somewhat tight, or pressed.

Godyner, *a.* (tyner) Somewhat tender, or soft.

Godyneru, *v. a.* (godyner) To emollify gently.

Godyniad, *s. m.* (godyn) A pulling gently.

Godynu, *v. a.* (godyn) To pull or draw gently.

Godyrddain, *v. a.* (godwrdd) To make a murmuring noise, to murmur.

Godyrddawl, *a.* (godwrdd) Rumbling, murmuring

Godyrddiad, *s. m.* (godwrdd) A rumbling.

Godyrddu, *v. a.* (godwrdd) To rumble, to murmur

Godyrfawl, *a.* (godwrf) Rumbling, tumultuous.

Godyrfiad, *s. m.* (godwrf) A making a tumult.

Godyrfu, *v. a.* (godwrf) To rumble, to murmur.

Godywyll, *a.* (tywyll) Somewhat dark, or gloomy.

> Aeron gynt a fu'n arall
> Dan bebyll godywyll dail.
>
> In days of yore Aeron used to watch beneath the *gloomy* tents of leaves. *D. ab Gwilym.*

Godywylliad, *s. m.* (godywyll) A making gloomy.

Godywyllu, *v. a.* (godywyll) To make gloomy.

Godywyllwch, *s. m.* (godywyll) A gloominess.

Godywyn, *s. m.* (tywyn) A glance, or gleam of light, a glimmer.

Godywyniad, *s. m.—pl. t.* au (godywyn) A throwing a gleam of light, a glimmering.

Godywynu, *v. a.* (godywyn) To cast a gleam of light; to shine faintly, to glimmer.

Godd, *s. m.—pl. t.* au (odd) That breaks out, or appears partially; a small plant, or shrub.

Goddail, *s. pl. aggr.* (dail) Leaves not fully spread, or grown, young leaves.

Goddaith, *s. m.—pl.* goddeithiau (daith) A smothering fire; a burning of a wild, or a place overgrown with brushwood, furze, or heath, and the like. *Llosgi goddeithiau*, to burn clearing fires.

> Oedd re rodaint dan forddwyd Geraint,
> Garhirion grawn bydd,
> Rhuthr goddaith ar ddiffaith fynydd.

> There were swift runners under the thigh of Geraint, long legged ones flinging the corn about, whose assault was like the *conflagration* on the wild mountain. *Llywarch Hen.*

Goddau, *s. pl. aggr.* (godd) Shrubs, shrubbery.

> A'm croe——
> O frialu, blodau bre:
> O flawd gwydd, a goddau.

> And importuning me for primroses, the flowers of the hill: for the blossoms of trees, and *shrubs*. *Taliesin.*

> Gogyfarch ——
> A brialu a briwddail,
> A blaen gwydd a goddau.

> Make the first greeting with primroses and the half-formed leaves, and the tops of the trees of the *shrubbery*. *Taliesin.*

> Cad Goddeu, un o dair ofer-gad Ynys Prydain—o achaws yr ast, a'r iwrch farbwys, a chornicyll.

> The battle of the *shrubbery*, one of the three foolish battles of the Isle of Britain—on account of the bitch, and the doe big with young, and the lapwing. *Trioedd.*

Goddawed, *v. a.* (dawed) To come gradually.

> Bryttaw a oruc Gwrtrydd yntau, ac eu herlid hwynt o le pwy gilydd, hyd pan i goddawed hwynt ar lan y mor.

> What Gwrtrydd then did was to pursue them from one place to another, until they were come to the sea shore. *Gr. ab Arthur.*

Goddawedawl, *a.* (goddawed) Adventitious.

Goddawediad, *s. m.* (goddawed) A partly coming.

Goddawl, *a.* (godd) A growing, or arising from; vegetative.

Godde, *s. m.—pl. t.* on (de) Design, purpose. *Godde gwrych*, a cormorant.

> Neidiodd gwas——
> Cul hig, ar odde caei bwyd.

> The long beaked rogue leaped with the *intent* to obtain food. *T. Prys.*

Godde, *v. a.* (de) To purpose, or to intend.

> Odde'r wyd o ddiriaid.
> Addail tir i ddiawl wyd ti.

> Thou dost design mischief: a leaf of the devil's land art thou. *Iolo Goch. i'r tafoed.*

Goddeall, *s. m.* (deall) Imperfect apprehension.

Goddeall, *v. n.* (deall) To apprehend partly.

Goddeallus, *a.* (goddeall) Somewhat discreet.

Goddëau, *a.* (deau) Nearly right; southerly.

> O niwl a blodau,
> A gwynt goddeau——
> Y digonir.

> Of mist and flowers, and *southerly* wind, there will be enough. *Taliesin.*

Goddef, *s. m.—pl. t.* ion (def) Sufferance; subjection; permission. *Bod yn arglwydd-oddef*, being under fealty to the lord.

> Gwell goddef na gofal.

> *Suffering* is preferable to care. *Adage.*

> O dripheth y mae doethineb: gwirionedd, ystyr, a goddef.

> Wisdom is from three causes: truth, thought, and *suffering*. *Barddas.*

Goddef, *v. n.* (def) To suffer, to bear, to endure, to acquiesce. *Goddef brawd*, to acquiesce in a verdict.

> A oddef a rydau.

> He that *endures* will be quickly altered. *Adage.*

> Trwy oddef ydd a cogail yn arwdiad paladr.

> Through *sufferance* the distaff becomes will rise to the privilege of a shaft. *Welsh Laws.*

> Er goddeu'r awr y gweddai,
> Ar oddef fyth yr oedd fai.

> Though there is propriety in *suffering* at times, but in *suffering* always there was a fault. *T. Aled.*

Goddefadwy, *a.* (goddef) That may be endured, sufferable, tolerable.

Goddefai, *s. m.* (goddef) That suffers; the passive, in grammar.

Goddefaint, *s. m.* (goddef) Suffering; sufferance.

Goddefawd, *s. m.* (goddef) Sufferance.

Goddefawl, *a.* (goddef) Passive, or suffering.

Goddefedig, *a.* (goddef) Passive; suffered, permitted. *Llef goddefedig*, passive voice.

Goddefedigaeth, *s. m.—pl. t.* au (goddefedig) Suffering; forbearance; permission.

Goddefedigaethydd, *s. m.* (goddefedigaeth) That undergoes the act of suffering.

Goddefedigawl, *a.* (goddefedig) Passible, passive

Goddefedd, *s. m.* (goddef) Sufferance, endurance, forbearance, patience.

Goddefgar, *a.* (goddef) Forbearing, patient.

Goddefgarwch, *s. m.* (goddefgar) Forbearance, endurance, tolerance, patience.

Goddefiad, *s. m.—pl. t.* au (goddef) A suffering; toleration; permission; indulgence.

Goddefiaeth, *s. m.* (goddef) Sufferance.

> A pha ddewlawl oddefiaeth,
> A pha les i neb a wnaeth!

> And what divine *forbearance*, and what good to any one did he do! *S. Phylip.*

Goddefiant, *s. m.* (goddef) Sufferance; forbearance; connivance.

Goddefoldeb, *s. m.* (goddefawl) Endurance.

Goddefus, *a.* (goddef) Patient; forbearing.

Goddefusrwydd, *s. m.* (goddefus) Passiveness.

Goddefwr, *s. m.—pl.* goddefwyr (goddef—gwr) One who bears, or suffers; a permitter.

Goddeg, *s. f.—pl. t.* au (godd—eg) Utterance, or speech. *Mae gwedi colli ei oddeg*, he has lost his utterance.

> Mynach bras gyfeillach brwg;
> Iddew heb gael ei oddeg.

> A rotten monk of faithless friendship, a Jew that hath not obtained his *speech*. *H. Cae Llwyd.*

Goddegawl, *a.* (goddeg) Relating to utterance.

Goddegiad, *s. m.* (goddeg) An enunciation.

Goddeheu, *s. m.* (deheu) That is pretty dexterous; that is partly south. *a.* Partly right, or dexterous; partly south.

Goddeiliad, *s. m.* (goddail) A covering with small leaves; a foliation.

Goddeiliaw, *v. a.* (goddail) To cover with leaves, to foliate; to adorn with leaves.

> Murch urbol a ddel i oddeiliaw ei ddl;
> Aed yn ei warth udon wrtho.

> May there come a lofty prop his front to *adorn with leaves*; from the top of it let him be suspended by a wythe. *S. Mrirlan.*

Goddeiliawg, *a.* (goddail) Having small leaves.

Goddeintiad, *s. m* (deintiad) A using the teeth slightly; a nibbling.

Goddeintiaw, *v. a.* (deintiaw) To use the teeth slightly; to nibble.

Goddeintiawl, *a.* (deintiawl) Apt to be nibbling.

Goddeithiad, *s. m.* (goddaith) A clearing of wilds by fire, a consuming with fire.

Goddeithiaw, *v. a.* (goddaith) To consume with fire; to burn heath, or any other wild growth.

> Y fflam a oddeithiodd holl brennau y maes.

> The flame *consumed* all the trees of the field. *Joel* i. 19.

> Mal y goddeithia fflam fynyddoedd.

> As the flame *consumes* the mountains. *Psalm* lxxxiii. 14.

Goddeithiawg, *a.* (goddaith) Consumed, or cleared by fire.
Goddeithiawl, *a.* (goddaith) Consuming.
Goddenawl, *a.* (denawl) Somewhat alluring.
Goddeniad, *s. m.* (deniad) A gently alluring.
Goddenu, *v. a.* (denu) To allure, or entice gently.
Goddeu, *s. m.—pl. t.* on (godde) Intent, purpose, design; resolution; aim, end. *Yr wyf ar oddeu gwneuthur hyny*, I am upon the intention of doing that; *O wir gwaith oddeu*, of downright act, or purpose, or on purpose.

Ni ddylyir dirwy am ddim ar goddeu heb weithred.

No fine is due on any account for the *intention* without the deed. *Welsh Laws.*

Ni ddaw o'i oddeu
Rr ofn un angau.

He will not come from his *purpose* through the dread of any death. *Taliesin.*

Dyniadon dedwyddiaint i'th oddeu.

Mankind thou hast formed to thy *purpose*. *Ein. ab Gwalchmai.*

Goddeu, *v. n.* (godde) To intend, to purpose.
Goddiff, *s. m.—pl. t.* ion (diff) A fling, or cast.
Goddiff, *v. a.* (diff) To fling, to cast; to dart.

Cymeryd a oreg ynhun yr ail llechwaew, a'i oddiff ar eu hol.

What did he do then was to take the second javelin and *throw* it after them. *H. Culhwch—Mabinogion.*

Goddiffaeth, *a.* (diffaeth) Somewhat ungenial.
Goddiffaw, *v. a.* (goddiff) To fling, to cast.
Goddiffawl, *a.* (goddiff) Ejecting, flinging, darting
Goddiffiad, *s. m.—pl. t.* au (goddiff) A flinging.
Goddig, *a.* (dig) Somewhat angry, or displeased.
Goddigiad, *s. m.* (goddig) A partly displeasing.
Goddigiaw, *v. a.* (goddig) To make a little angry.
Goddigiawl, *a.* (goddig) Of a displeasing tendency.
Goddirnad, *s. m.* (dirnad) A slight perception.
Goddirnad, *v. a.* (dirnad) To intimate; to have a slight idea of, or to perceive a little.
Goddirnadawl, *a.* (goddirnad) Intimating.
Goddirnadu, *v. a.* (goddirnad) To perceive slightly; to intimate; to have a faint idea.
Goddiw, *s. m.* (diw) That is partly complete.
Goddiwawd, *s. m.* (goddiw) The act of overtaking
Goddiwedydd, *s. m.* (diwedydd) The day of doom.

Cad Geredigiawn, gyfiawn gywydd,
Crefynt wreigedd gweddw goddiwedydd.

The battle of Ceredigion, worthy of the song, the widowed wives were wont to cry for the final day. *Meilyr.*

Goddiwedd, *s. m.—pl. t.* ion (goddiw) A coming to the end; a coming up to, an overtaking.
Goddiwedd, *v. a.* (goddiw) To come up with.
Goddiweddawl, *a.* (goddiwedd) Coming up with.
Goddiweddiad, *s. m.* (goddiwedd) An overtaking.
Goddiweddu, *v. a.* (goddiwedd) To come up with.
Goddiweddwr, *s. m.—pl.* goddiweddwyr (goddiwedd—gwr) One who overtakes.
Goddiweddyd, *v. a.* (goddiwedd) To come up with
Goddiwes, *v. a.* (goddiw) To overtake. *Cei oddiwes gwneuthur hyny*, thou shalt do that at thy leisure.
Goddiwesedig, *a.* (goddiwes) That is overtaken.
Goddiwesiad, *s. m.* (goddiwes) An overtaking.
Goddiwesu, *v. a.* (goddiwes) To come up with.
Goddiweswr, *s. m.—pl.* goddiweswyr (goddiwes—gwr) One who overtakes.
Goddiwesydd, *s. m.—pl. t.* ion (goddiwes) One who comes upon, or overtakes.
Goddolawg, *a.* (goddawl) Endowed, enriched.
Goddolef, *v. a.* (dolef) To make a clamour.

Senyllt a'i lestri llawn medd;
Goddolef ei gleddyf i gawdd.

An elder with his vessels of mead; his sword *rings* to the adversary. *Aneurin.*

Goddoli, *v. a.* (goddawl) To enrich, to endow.

O fychod goddolir.

Of bucks *he will be endowed*. *Llyfred.*

Madawg maddeuai goddoli;
Mwy gwnaeth fy modd no'm coddi.

Madog *that confers* bounties; more did he do my will than offend me. *Gwalchmai, i F. ab Owain.*

Goddoliad, *s. m.* (goddawl) An enriching, a gifting
Goddrud, *a.* (drud) Somewhat bold, or daring.

Rhwd amug Ododin o win a medd
Yn ddiedig yn nghystrang ystre,
Ac a dan cafoeeu cochre
Feirch marchawg goddrud yn more.

Illusive the defence of Gododin by wine and mead, without lacking in the council of the town, when beneath the spots of conflict flowing with red there be the steeds that were ridden *boldly* in the morn. *Aneurin.*

Godduned, *s. f.—pl. t.* au (duned) A vow; a pledge.

Llesgedd yw tori godduned.

It is a weakness to break a *vow*. *Ll. G. Hergest.*

Godduw, *s. m.—pl. t.* iau (duw) A demigod.
Godduwies, *s. f.—pl. t.* au (godduw) Demigoddess
Goddwfn, *a.* (dwfn) Somewhat profound.
Goddwr, *s. m.—pl.* goddwyr (godd—gwr) A counsellor, or adviser.

Chweched yw bod yn oddwr i'r lleidr.

The sixth is to be an *adviser* to the thief. *Welsh Laws.*

Goddyar, *a.* (dyar) Somewhat noisy, murmuring.
Goddyarad, *s. m.* (goddyar) A murmuring.
Goddyarawl, *a.* (goddyar) Murmuring, humming.
Goddyaru, *v. a.* (goddyar) To make a murmur.
Goddygn, *a.* (dygn) Somewhat toilsome.
Goddygnawd, *s. m.* (goddygn) A degree of severity
Goddygnawl, *a.* (goddygn) Somewhat painful.
Goddygniad, *s. m.* (goddygn) A toiling gently.
Goddygnu, *v. a.* (goddygn) To toil gently.
Goddyn, *s. m.—pl. t.* au (godd) An axis, or pivot.

Eigion y dyfn-for ymegorodd,
A goddyn y byd ddadymgnuddiodd.

The profundity of the vast sea did open itself; and the *axis* of the world became developed. *W. Middleton.*

Goddysg, *s. m.* (dysg) Smatter, half learning.
Goddysgawl, *a.* (goddysg) Superficially learned.
Goddysgiad, *s. m.* (goddysg) A smattering.
Goddysgu, *v. a.* (goddysg) To learn superficially.
Goddystaw, *a.* (dystaw) Somewhat silent or calm.
Goddystawiad, *s. m.* (dystaw) A partly silencing.
Goddystawu, *v. a.* (goddystaw) To hush partly.
Goed, *s. m.* (gwed) A saying; speech, utterance.
Goedawl, *a.* (goed) Speaking, or verbal.
Goediad, *s. m.* (goed) A speaking, a saying.
Goedyd, *v. a.* (goed) To speak, to say, to utter.
Göen, *s. m.* (en) Influence, or bias.
Goer, *s. m.* (gwer) A freshness. *a.* Fresh.

Lle ger dwfr, lle goer difwg.

A spot by the water, a spot *fresh* and without smoke. *D. ab Gwilym.*

Gof, *s. m.—pl. t.* au (of) An artist; a metallurgist; a smith. *Gof du*, a blacksmith; *gof gwyn*, a whitesmith; *gof aur*, a goldsmith; *gof arian*, a silversmith. In former times the smith prepared his own metal from the ore. Tradition relates of the last, who used to do so in Wales, that he blew up his forge by letting out too much metal to produce a report, in rejoicing for the revolution in 1688.—The *Gof* was reckoned in the Welsh Laws one of the three professors of liberal sciences.

Da mab y gof.

The son of the smith is good. *Adage.*

Ymryson a'r gof yn ei efail.

To contend with the smith in his smithy. *Adage.*

Ni ellir neb gof fod yn un cymmwd a'r gof llys heb ei ganiad.

No smith can be in the same bailiwick with the smith of the court without his permission. *Welsh Laws.*

Gofail, *s. f.*—*pl.* gofeiliau (gof) A smithy.

Gofal, *s. m.*—*pl. t.* on (mal) Care, anxiety, solicitude, regard, charge; thought.

Gofal dyn Duw ai gweryd.

The *anxiety* of man God will do away. *Adage.*

Tri gofal Cristion: rhag digiaw Duw; rhag tramgwyddaw dyn, a rhag ymwanaeu o'i gariadolaeb at bob daioni.

The three cares of a Christian: against offending God, against causing man to stumble; and against slackening in his affection towards every good. *Barddas.*

Gofalâad, *s. m.* (gofal) A becoming anxious.

Gofalâawl, *a.* (gofal) Tending to be anxious.

Gofalâu, *v. n.* (gofal) To become anxious.

Gofaledd, *s. m.* (gofal) Solicitude, carefulness.

Gofalfawr, *a.* (gofal) Full of anxiety, or care.

Dolurus calon ofalfawr

Aching is the heart *full of care.* *Adage.*

Gofaliad, *s. m.* (gofal) A caring, a being anxious.

Gofalrwydd, *s. m.* (gofal) Anxiousness, anxiety.

Gofalu, *v. a.* (gofal) To use care or solicitude; to take care of, to attend, to mind; to be careful.

Sef a wnaeth Gwrthefyr eu damgylchynu, ac o longawl ymladd beunydd eu gofalu.

What did Gwerthefyr do, was to surround them, and with naval war daily to *harrass* them. *Gr. ab Arthur.*

Gofalus, *a.* (gofal) Careful; solicitous; anxious.

Gofalusrwydd, *s. m.* (gofalus) Carefulness.

Gofalwr, *s. m.*—*pl.* gofalwyr (gofal—gwr) A caretaker; one who takes care of.

Gofan, *s. m.*—*pl.* gofain (gof) A smith.

Gofanineth, *s. m.* (gofan) Metallurgy; the craft or trade of a smith.

Gofant, *s. m.*—*pl.* gofaint (gof) A smith.

Gofar, *s. m.* (bar) Wrath, ire, fury, anger.

Gwr oedd mwyngaeâ eagar a'i ganiad;
Gwr a'm gwnaeth oddid gofid gofar.

A man who was so slight one as a foe; a man who has caused me the passion of affliction of *wrath.* *Bleddyn Fardd.*

Gofaran, *a.* (baran) Apt to be forward.

Diannod ei glôd—
Diachyr eryr gwyr gofaran.

Undisputed is his fame, the bold eagle of the *forward* heroes. *Aneurin.*

Gofardd, *s. m.*—*pl.* gofeirdd (bardd) A poetaster

A'r gofeirdd a'r beirdd yn cywryssedd;
Er pan fu Elffin y' nhywrysedd Maelgwn
Neda porthes pawb gnif dyfrydedd?

And the *poetasters* and the bards disputing; since the time that Elphin was in the contention of Maelgwn, has not the obstinacy spread extensive woe? *Phylip Brydydd.*

Cadair Maelgwn hir a hybarid i feirdd,
Ac nid i'r gofeirdd yd gyfarchëid.

The chair of the tall Maelgwn had been freely produced for the bards, and not to the *poetasters* was it granted. *Phylip Brydydd.*

Gofas, *a.* (bas) Somewhat shallow, or low.

Gofasw, *a.* (masw) Somewhat wanton.

Gofaswedd, *s. m.* (gofasw) A degree of levity.

Gofeddal, *a.* (meddal) Somewhat soft or tender.

Gofeddalu, *v. a.* (gofeddal) To make somewhat tender; to emollify.

Gofeddw, *a.* (meddw) Somewhat inebriated.

Gofeddwi, *v. n.* (gofeddw) To get rather drunk.

Gofeg, *s. f.*—*pl. t.* au (meg) The mind; thought; will; affection.

Fy negea oedd fynegi
Fy ngofeg, ddyn teg, i ti.

My business was to disclose my *mind* to thee, fair maid. *Bedo Brwynllys.*

Gofegawl, *a.* (gofeg) Relating to the will, mental

Gofeiliant, *s. m.*—*pl.* gofeiliaint (gofal) Solicitude, anxiety.

Gofelys, *a.* (melys) Somewhat sweet, sweetish.

Gofer, *s. m.*—*pl. t.* oedd (mer) A small current, or rivulet; a stream that runs out of a spring.

A red y dwfr—
O'r fanoel ar i fyny dd;
A'r gofer fryd ofer dadl,
Yn ol i'r ffynnon ailwaith.

Will the water run upwards from the vale; and the rivulet back, useless would be the stream, to the spring again. *Tomâ ab Ieân. Prys.*

Goferawl, *a.* (gofer) Drippling, or purling.

Goferedig, *a.* (gofer) That is made to dripple.

Goferedigaeth, *s. m.*—*pl. t.* au (goferedig) A drippling, or purling.

Goferedigawl, *a.* (goferedig) Apt to flow, or proceed out; apt to dripple.

Pob gair sydd on o ddwy ffurf; naill ai cysefinawl, ai goferedigawl.

Every word is of one of the two forms; either primitive or derivative. *Gr. Roberts.*

Goferen, *s. f. dim.* (gofer) A rivulet, or brook.

Goferiad, *s. m.*—*pl. t.* au (gofer) Effusion, effluxion; emanation.

Goferini, *s. m.* (gofer) The brooklime.

Goferllys, *s. m.* (gofer—llys) Common livergreen.

Goferu, *v. a.* (gofer) To effuse, to run out.

Rhagddo—
Gwaed gwyr goferai, gwyrai ouwydd.

Before him the blood of men would *stream*, when shafts would bend. *Meilyr.*

Goferw, *a.* (berw) Somewhat boiling.

Goferwad, *s. m.* (goferw) A partly boiling, or bubbling; a parboiling.

Goferwi, *v. a.* (goferw) To boil partly; to parboil, or to half boil.

Gofid, *s. m.*—*pl. t.* ion (mid) Affliction, trouble.

Gwell goluith na gofid.

Better is death than affliction. *Adage.*

Gofidiad, *s. m.*—*pl. t.* au (gofid) A grieving, a vexing, troubling, or afflicting,

Gofidiaw, *v. a.* (gofid) To afflict; to grieve, to wail, to lament; to be grieved.

Gofidiawg, *a.* (gofid) Afflicting, grievous.

Gofidiawl, *a.* (gofid) Afflicting, grievous.

Gofidiwr, *s. m.*—*pl.* gofidwyr (gofid—gwr) One who grieves, or is sorrowful.

Gofidus, *a.* (gofid) Grievous, vexatious; miserable, wretched, distressed.

Goflaen, *s. m.* (blaen) The foremost point.

Myned â orug Arthur i'r goflaen, ac erchi iddynt na ddelynt ato oni welynt angheu arno.

What Arthur did was to go to the *front*, and desire of them that they should not come to him, except they should see him in danger. *Gr. ab Arthur.*

Dodaf fy ffon—
Ar flaen ei goflaen hi gwymp.

I will set my stick on the point of its *end* and it will fall. *Goronwy Owain.*

Goflaenu, *v. a.* (goflaen) To set foremost.

Goflawd, *s. m.* (blawd) That is partly meal; the mill dust; meal over and above in baking.

Goflew, *s. pl. aggr.* (blew) Down, or soft hair.

Goflewawg, *a.* (goflew) Pappous, in botany.

Goflewiach, *s. pl. aggr.* (goflew) Down hair.

Goflin, *a.* (blin) Somewhat tiresome, or painful.

Goflinaw, *v. a.* (goflin) To tire a little; to become rather tired.

Goflodi, *v. a.* (goflawd) To make partly meal; to sprinkle meal, or flour; to dredge.

Goflodiad, *s. m.* (goflawd) A sprinkling of meal.

Goflodiaw, *v. a.* (goflawd) To make partly meal; to sprinkle meal; to dredge.

Goflodydd, *s. m.*—*pl. t.* ion (goflawd) A dredger.

Goflwch, *s. m.*—*pl.* goflychau (blwch) A small box.

Gofod, *s. m.—pl. t.* au (mod) Space. *Gofod undydd*, the space of one day.

Nead llai dy ofod, nead dy ofid ced?
Cadwgawn ry ddaid!

Is not thy space less, is not liberality thy affliction! Ah, were but Cadwgan come! *Ll. P. Moch, bygwth Gr. ab Cynan.*

Wyd balch——
A'th breiddin a'th braf dy ofod.

Thou art elate, with thy booty and the amplitude of thy *space*. *Ll. P. Moch.*

Gofoes, *s. f.—pl. t.* au (moes) Ceremoniousness.
Gofoesawg, *a.* (gofoes) Somewhat polite.
Gofoesawl, *a.* (gofoes) Ceremonious.
Gofoesgar, *a.* (gofoes) Apt to be ceremonious.
Gofram, *s. m.—pl. t.* au (bram) A feist; a jeer.

A'r geiniawg a roddyd i'r clerwr, er mwyn ei fod yn arddel ei hanfod (megis chwyn) o wyr wrth gerdd, a gofram a roddyd iddo, er mwyn dirmygu y cythraul a'i tynai mywn diogi.

And the penny was given to the strolling minstrel, on account of his asserting his descent (like a weed) from masters of song; and he had a *jeer* out of ridicule to the devil who enticed him to idleness. *Gosod. y Prydyddion.*

Goframawl, *a.* (gofram) Feisting; jeering.
Goframu, *v. a.* (gofram) To feist; to jeer.

Gyr——
Gafyr ymwan i'm goframu.

He sends a butting goat *to jeer me*. *H. ab Hywel.*

Gofras, *v.* (bras) Somewhat coarse; mean, base.
Gofreg, *s. m.* (breg) Frolick, or gambol.
Gofregedd, *s. m.* (gofreg) Frolicksomeness.
Gofregus, *a.* (gofreg) Frolicksome; fickle.
Gofri, *s. m.—pl. t.* on (bri) Attribute; glory.

Rhun ei enw, ryfel ofri,
A oganaf fi dyddarbi,
Gwenddydd: gwlad yn angad Beli.

Rhun his name, the *glory* of the war: what I predict surely will come to pass Gwenddydd—A sceptre in the hand of Beli. *Cyfoesi Myrddin.*

Un dra drugaredd anwedd ofri,
Un deg dair person
Uch archengylion.

One of infinite mercy, whose *glory* is too great for sight; one fair three persons above archangels. *Gwalchmai.*

Gofrïad, *s. m.* (gofri) An attribution.
Gofrïaw, *v. a.* (gofri) To endow with an attribute, or peculiar preeminence.
Gofrïawl, *a.* (gofri) Conferring dignity.
Gofron, *s. f.—pl. t.* ydd (bron) A gently rising hill.
Gofrwnt, *a.* (brwnt) Somewhat dirty, or filthy.

Gofrwnt y rhoes y gyfraith
Da a dyn i'r gelyn gaith.

Meanly did the law consign the chattels and the fair to the open foe. *D. ab Gwilym, i'r B. Bach.*

Gofrwy, *s. m.—pl. t.* oedd (brwy) What pervades or becomes universal.

Duw differ nefwy
Rhag llanw lled gofrwy.

God preserve the heavens from a flood of wide *spreading*. *Taliesin.*

I edryd fy lledfryd ai lled ofrwy;
I edryd llywy lliw ton dylan.

To renew my listlessness and its prevailing *influence*: to restore the nymph, fair as the ocean wave. *H. ab Owain.*

Gofrwyd, *s. m.—pl. t.* au (brwyd) An intricacy, maze, or quirk.

Dywed—ei ladd yn y ffrwgwd, a diangc rhag gofrwyd y gyfraith.

Say he was killed in the squabble, and flee for fear of the quirk of the law. *H. ab Ieu. ab Robert.*

Gofrwysg, *a.* (brwysg) Half drunk, maudlin.
Gofrwysgaw, *v. n.* (gofrwysg) To get half drunk.
Gofrwysgawl, *a.* (gofrwysg) Somewhat inebriating, or intoxicating.
Gofrwysgiad, *s. m.* (gofrwysg) A partly intoxicating.
Gofryd, *s. m.* (bryd) Design, purpose, intention. *Dyn gau ofryd*, a man of bad intention.
Gofrydawl, *a.* (gofryd) Designable, intentional.
Gofrydu, *v. a.* (gofryd) To purpose, to intend.
Gofryn, *s. m.—pl. t.* iau (bryn) A hillock.
Gofrys, *s. m.* (brys) Some degree of haste.
Gofrysiad, *s. m.* (gofrys) A hastening a little.
Gofrysiaw, *v. a.* (gofrys) To make some haste.
Gofrysiawl, *a.* (gofrys) Somewhat hasty.
Gofudr, *a.* (budr) Somewhat dirty, or foul.
Gofudredd, *s. m.* (gofudr) Squalidness, foulness.
Goful, *a.* (mul) Somewhat bashful; diffident.
Gofuldra, *s. m.* (goful) Diffidence, modesty.
Gofunad, *s. f.—pl.* gofunaid (munad) A resignation of the will; a solemn vow; a wish.

Gofunaid hualid yw hi,
Gwlm cydgerdd, gelyn coedgi.

She is the *desire* of the bounds of accordant note, the foe of the dog of the wood. *D. ab Gwilym. i geinach.*

Gofunaw, *v. a.* (munaw) To make a solemn engagement, to vow; to wish.
Gofuned, *s. f.—pl. t.* au (muned) A vow; a promise, or engagement; a petition. *Rhoddi gofuned*, to make a vow.
Gofunedawl, *a.* (gofuned) Devoted; devout.
Gofunediad, *s. m.* (gofuned) A making a solemn engagement; a vowing; a volition.
Gofunedig, *a.* (gofuned) Devoted; consecrated.
Gofunedu, *v. a.* (gofuned) To make a vow; to consecrate.
Gofunedus, *a.* (gofuned) Devoted; consecrated.
Gofunedwr, *s. m.—pl.* gofunedwyr (gofuned—gwr) A devotee.
Gofurthiach, *s. m.* (burthiach) A slight skirmishing or bickering. *a.* Bickering.

Tyllai Ylfach gwryd gofurthiach.

Gylfach would pierce *bickering* manhood. *Taliesin.*

Gofwr, *s. m.—pl.* gofyrau (bwr) A mound.

Yn amwyn Gwenystrad y gwelid gofwr.

In the defence of Gwenystrad there was seen a *mound*. *Taliesin.*

Gofwy, *s. m.—pl. t.* ion (mwy) A visit; an intercourse; a sending good or evil.
Gofwy, *v. a.* (mwy) To visit, to go to see.

Tra wyf ym gofwy gofal gogyweg,
Am fab teg Tudawel.

Whilst I am racking anxiety *will visit* me, after the fair son of Tydawel. *Cynddelw m. teulu Owain.*

Gofwyad, *s. m.—pl. t.* au (gofwy) A visitation.
Gofwyaeth, *s. m.—pl t.* au (gofwy) Visitation.
Gofwyaw, *v. a.* (gofwy) To visit; to keep up intercourse; to send good or evil.

Gwae a gawdd gwirion;
Gwae na ddyddan y cleifion;
A charcharorion nis gofwya.

Woe to him that shall distress the innocent: woe to him that shall not comfort the sick ones; and who *doth* not *visit* prisoners. *Ion. Mynyw.*

Gofwyawg, *a.* (gofwy) Having visits.
Gofwyawl, *a.* (gofwy) Visiting, relating to visits.
Gofwyedig, *a.* (gofwy) Visited. *Gofwyedigion*, those that are visited.
Gofwyedigaeth, *s. m.—pl. t.* au (gofwyedig) A visitation, or the act of visiting.
Gofychan, *a.* (bychan) Smallish, rather little.
Gofychanu, *v. a.* (gofychan) To make somewhat little; to disparage.
Gofydd, *s. m.—pl. t.* ion (ofydd) An artist.
Gofyddar, *a.* (byddar) Deafish, dull of hearing.
Gofyddeb, *s. f.—pl. t.* au (gofydd) A canon; that is scientific; a connection, or correspondence. *Cyfathrach a gofyddeb*, affinity and correspondence.

O bydd priawd arwyddocâad y geiriau yn yr Ysgrythyr Lan, yn anghydweddol a gofyddeb y ffydd, ynte ag y manau eglur o'r Ysgrythyr Lan, yno rhaid yw ceisiaw synwyr a deall arall, yn ei ansoddion y geiriau.

Should the appropriate signification of the words in the Holy Scripture be incompatible, whether with the *doctrine* of the faith or with the explicit texts of the Holy Scriptures, then it is necessary to seek for some other sense and meaning according to the properties of the words. *H. Perri.*

Gofyddebawl, *a.* (gofyddeb) Scientific; canonical
Gofyddiad, *s. m.—pl. t.* au (gofydd) A rendering scientific, correspondent, or regular.
Gofyddu, *v. a.* (gofydd) To render scientific.
Gofyddus, *a.* (gofydd) Canonical; accordant.

Rhaid i ddihareb fod yn synwyrawl, ac yn ofyddus, i gael ei hadnabod yn hylwydd.

It is requisite that a proverb should be rational, and *applicable*, so as to be easily recognized. *H. Perri.*

Gofyged, *s. f.—pl. t.* au (myged) What contributes to dignity, or to honour. *a.* Dignified.

Rhun gymmrawdd, Cymmry ofyged.

Convertible like Rhun, the *glory* of the Welsh. *Ll. P. Moch, i Rys Gryg.*

Nerad wy ai gofwy! nerad gofyged,
Gofalon ailon aelwyd Rheged!

Shall they not visit him! are not the afflictions of the *more dignified* on the hearth of Rheged! *Cynddelw, i O. ab Madawg.*

Gofygedigawl, *a.* (gofyged) Tending to honour.
Gofygedu, *v. a.* (gofyged) To render dignified.
Gofyn, *s. m.—pl. t.* ion (myn) A demand, a question; a petition, or request. *Heb ofyn, heb gênad*, without asking, and without leave.

Tri phrif ofynion Duw: cariad, cyfiawnder, ac ufydd-dawd.

The three primary *requisitions* of God: love, equity, and obedience. *Barddas.*

Gofyn, *v. a.* (myn) To ask, or to enquire.

Gododin, gofynaf o'th blegyd,
Y'ngwydd cant yn arial yr ennyd!

Gododin, on thy behalf *I will enquire*, in the presence of a hundred atchieving heroic deeds would thou not be seen! *Aneurin.*

Gofynadwy, *a.* (gofyn) That may be asked, or demanded, requirable.
Gofynag, *s. f.—pl.* gofynegion (gofyn) Desire; affiance; confidence, trust.

Ef a osodes ei obaith a'i ofynag y'nghynnorthwy Duw.

He placed his hope and his *confidence* in the assistance of God. *Mabinogion.*

Gofynaig, *s. f.—pl.* gofyneigion (gofyn) A request; a desire.

A Gwladus weddus wyl fabin fab-wraig,
Gofynaig y gwerin,
Achenaf ochenaid gyfrin;
Mi ai mawl â melyn eithin.

And for the handsome Gwladus the bashful nymph and bonny woman, the *desire* of the throng, I will utter the private sigh; I will greet her with the yellow blossom of the furze. *H. ab Owain Gwynedd.*

Gwladeiddd ei ofynaig, draig Gwynedodydd;
Gwr a roddai gad cyn dyllu y dydd.

He is the *desire* of nations, the dragon of the men of North Wales; a man that would give battle before the darkening of the day. *Meilyr.*

Gofynawg, *a.* (gofyn) That is asked, questioned, or inquired about.
Gofynawl, *a.* (gofyn) Inquisitive, asking.

O bydd neb gofynawl
Pwy gwnaeth hyn.

If any body should be *inquisitive* who composed this. *Hywel Swrdwal.*

Gofynedig, *a.* (gofyn) That is asked; questioned
Gofynedigaeth, *s. m.—pl. t.* au (gofynedig) The act of asking; enquiry; inquisition.
Gofynedigawl, *a.* (gofynedig) Inquisitorial.
Gofyniad, *s. m.—pl. t.* au (gofyn) The act of asking; a question; a demand.
Gofynnod, *s. m.—pl. t.* au (gofyn—nod) Note of interrogation.
Gofynydd, *s. m.—pl. t.* au (go—mynydd) A slope, a side of a hill. *Yr oedd yr hen fordd ar hyd y gofynydd hwn*, the old road was along this slope. *Dyfed.*

Gofyr, *a.* (byr) Somewhat short; curtailed.
Gofyrawl, *a.* (gofyr) Abbreviative.
Gofyriad, *s. m.—pl. t.* au (gofyr) A curtailing.
Gofyru, *v. a.* (gofyr) To curtail, to abbreviate.
Gofysiad, *s. m.* (bysiad) A fingering slightly.
Gofysiaw, *v. a.* (bysiaw) To finger gently.
Gofysiawl, *a.* (bysiawl) Slightly fingering.
Gofysiedig, *a.* (bysiedig) That is slightly fingered
Gofysiwr, *s. m.—pl.* gofyswyr (bysiwr) One who fingers gently.
Goffaig, *s. m.—pl.* goffeigiau (ffaig) What is somewhat embarrassing.
Goffeigiad, *s. m.—pl. t.* au (goffaig) A making rather puzzling.
Goffeigiaw, *v. a.* (goffaig) To embarrass slightly.
Goffeigiawl, *a.* (goffaig) Somewhat embarrassing.
Goffelaig, *a.* (ffelaig) Of a preceptive, or commanding nature.

Gwall gwall fu arfoll ar Cynon;
Graid graig goffelaig ddragon,
O Eryri fraith fron.

It was a fault of faults to receive Cynon; ardent and doubly ardent is the *high-commanding* leader from Snowdon of variegated hills. *Meigant, m. Cynddylan.*

Goffol, *v. a.* (ffol) Somewhat silly, or simple.

Nid hawdd i dlawd ffawd a'i phen goffol
Hwyr, goffaol hirwen.

It is not easy for the indigent to prosper in trying to possess the tall fair one with her *giddy* head. *D. ab Gwilym.*

Goffoledd, *s. m.* (goffol) A degree of silliness.
Goffoli, *v. a.* (goffol) To condemn as silly.
Goffreuad, *s. m.* (ffreuad) A small effusion.
Goffreuaw, *v. a.* (ffreuaw) To effuse a little.
Goffreuawl, *a.* (ffreuawl) Somewhat effusive.
Goffrom, *a.* (ffrom) Somewhat pert, or stiff.
Goffromawl, *a.* (goffrom) Tending to be pertish.
Goffromiad, *s. m.* (goffrom) A pertly acting.
Goffrost, *s. m.* (ffrost) Somewhat of a boast.
Goffrostiad, *s. m.* (goffrost) A swaggering partly.
Goffrostiaw, *v. a.* (goffrost) To swagger a little.
Goffrostiawl, *a.* (goffrost) Somewhat swaggering.
Goffrwd, *s. f.—pl.* goffrydiau (ffrwd) A streamlet.
Goffrydiad, *s. m.—pl. t.* au (goffrwd) A flowing in small streams.
Goffrydiaw, *v. a.* (goffrwd) To flow gently.

Ni wyddem dyfodydd
Am offrydiaw awenydd.

I had not known thy equal for *effusing* of the song. *Pervh. Evan Evans.*

Goffrydiawl, *a.* (goffrwd) Effusive, gently flowing
Gog, *s. m.—pl. t.* ion (og) Abundance, plenty.
Gogaled, *a.* (caled) Somewhat hard, or severe.
Gogaledawl, *a.* (gogaled) Of a hard tendency.
Gogalediad, *s. m.* (gogaled) A making somewhat hard or obdurate.
Gogaledu, *v. a.* (gogaled) To render somewhat hard, or obdurate.
Gogall, *a.* (call) Somewhat discreet, or prudent.
Gogalledd, *s. m.* (gogall) Half discretion.
Gogallu, *v. n.* (gogall) To become half-witted.
Gogam, *a.* (cam) Somewhat crooked, or bent.
Gogamawl, *a.* (gogam) Of a bending tendency.
Gogamawl, *a.* (gogam) A little bending.
Gogamiad, *s. m.* (gogam) A bending a little.
Gogamp, *s. f.—pl. t.* au (camp) An inferior feat, or game. *Y gogampau*, the minor games.

Un o'r pedair gogamp yw cyweiriaw telyn.

One of the four *inferior games* is the tuning of the harp. *Welsh Laws.*

Gogampus, *a.* (gogamp) Somewhat clever.
Gogamu, *v. a.* (gogam) To bend a little.

Gogan, *s. f.—pl. t.* ion (can) An ambiguous song; a presage, or prophecy; a satire; a lampoon.

> Wi! A Wenddydd wèn! Mawr andrastl gogan
> A chwedlau chanbiclau.

> Ho, fair Gwenddydd! awful the promised ills of the *oracle*, and the rumours of the maid of the circle. *Cyfoesi Myrddin.*

Goganair, *s. m.—pl.* goganeiriau (gogan—gair) An equivocal word; slander.

Goganawl, *a.* (gogan) Satirical, detracting.

Gogandryll, *a.* (candryll) Somewhat shattered.

Goganddyn, *s. m.—pl. t.* ion (gogan—dyn) A slandered person.

Gogangerdd, *s. f.—pl. t.* i (gogan—cerdd) A satirical song, a satire; a lampoon; an invective.

Goganiad, *s. m.—pl. t.* au (gogan) Equivocation.

Gogann, *v. a.* (gogan) To speak ambiguously; to presage; to satirize; to lampoon, to disparage, to inveigh.

> A ogano a ogenir.

> He that *disparages* will be *disparaged*. *Adage.*

> Ni fawrelr tra oganer.

> It will not be magnified that is *disparaged*. *Adage.*

Goganus, *a.* (gogan) Satirical; slanderous.

Goganwaith, *s. m.* (gogan—gwaith) The act of detracting, or finding fault.

> Madden——
> Ein goganwaith,
> A'n cyfrwyswaith,
> A'n cyfrysedd.

> Forgive our *detraction* and our cunning work, and our contention. *Gr. Gryg.*

Goganwawd, *s. m.* (gogan—gwawd) Equivocal praise; irony.

Gogarth, *s. m.—pl. t.* ion (carth) That has a cleansing quality. *Pridd gogarth*, fuller's earth.

Gogarthawl, *a.* (gogarth) Purifying, purgative.

Gogarthiad, *s. m.* (gogarth) A purifying.

Gogarthu, *v. a.* (gogarth) To purify; to purge.

Gogas, *a.* (cas) Somewhat odious, or hateful.

Gogasedd, *s. m.* (gogas) A degree of hatred.

Gogawn, *s. m.* (cawn) Capability; energy; fullness, plenitude. *a.* Capable; plenary.

Gogawn, *v. a.* (cawn) To endue with power; to render plenary.

> Ef gogawn glyw cammawn celniaid.

> The prince of conflict *will give energy* to the minstrels. *Cynddelw.*

Gogawr, *s. m.—pl.* gogorion (gog) Crop; food for cattle, fodder.

> Gogawr yw yd wedi y cychwyner o iar y tir y tyfo arno, a gwair sych a bresych, a tho ty.

> By *crop* is implied corn, when it is moved off the land, dry hay, cabbage, and thatch of a house. *Welsh Laws.*

Gogel, *a.* (cel) Somewhat concealed, or hidden.

Gogelawg, *a.* (gogel) Apt to shun, or avoid.

> Bid amlwg marchawg, bid ogelawg lleidr,
> Twyllid gwraig goludawg:
> Cyfaillt blaidd bugail diawg.

> Let a knight be conspicuous, let a thief be *sculking*, let the wife of the wealthy be deceived; a lazy shepherd is the wolf's friend. *Llywarch Hen.*

Gogeliad, *s. m.—pl. t.* au (gogel) A shunning.

Gogelrwydd, *s. m.* (gogel) Wariness; shyness.

Gogelu, *v. a.* (gogel) To eschew, to avoid; also to shelter, to cover over, to protect.

> Selyf diarswyd orsaf Gwygyr,
> Gogeled a'i cawdd, calon eryr.

> Selyf, with the heart of an eagle, dauntless at the post of Gwygyr, let whoever insults him *beware*. *O. Cyfeiliawg.*

Gogelus, *a.* (gogel) Apt to shun; very careful.

Gogelyd, *v. a.* (gogel) To shun, to eschew.

> Llaw ar gledd, arall ar groes,
> Gogeled pawb ei einioes;
> Gan Gyndaf cymmod nid oes.

> A hand on a sword, another on a cross, let every one *take care* for his life; with Cyndaf there is no reconciliation. *Cyfoesi Myrddin.*

Gogellwair, *s. m.* (cellwair) A half yoke.

Gogellweiriad, *s. m.* (gogellwair) A joking partly; an acting jocularly.

Gogellweiriaw, *v. a.* (gogellwair) To joke partly.

Gogellweirus, *a.* (gogellwair) A little jocose.

Gogerdd, *s. f.—pl. t.* au (cerdd) A burlesque.

Gogerddawl, *a.* (gogerdd) Burlesque, ludicrous.

Gogerdded, *s. m.* (cerdded) A gentle idle pace.

Gogerdded, *v. a.* (cerdded) To walk gently.

Gogerddediad, *s. m.—pl. t.* au (gogerdded) A walking gently.

Gogern, *s. m.—pl. t.* au (cern) Partly a side position of the face; a leer.

Gogerniad, *s. m.* (gogern) A leering turn.

Gogernu, *v. a.* (gogern) To half turn the face.

Gogerth, *a.* (certh) Somewhat imminent.

Gogerthawl, *a.* (gogerth) Tending to impend.

Gogerthu, *v. a.* (gogerth) To make rather imminent; to become somewhat impending.

Gogerydd, *s. m.* (cerydd) Slight chastisement.

Gogeryddu, *v. a.* (gogerydd) To chastise gently.

Gogest, *s. f.—pl. t.* au (cest) A small paunch.

Gogestu, *v. a.* (gogest) To gorge a little.

Gogethin, *a.* (cethin) Somewhat ugly.

Gogethinaw, *v. a.* (gogethin) To make rather unsightly; to become ugly.

Gogi, *v. a.* (gog) To shake, to agitate, to quake.

> Gwawd-feirdd a ogon a ogaf—
> Ac ereill a refon a rifaf,
> Rhyfeddawr yn erfawdd a naw cant gorwydd,
> Cyn cymun Cuneddaf.

> Bards of praise that shall exalt themselves, *I will agitate*, and others that shall enlarge, I will reckon wonderful, raising a tumult with nine hundred steeds before communion with Cuneddaf. *Taliesin.*

Gogiad, *s. m.—pl. t.* au (gog) An agitating.

Gogigawg, *a.* (cigawg) Somewhat fleshy.

Gogil, *s. m.* (cil) A small decline, or recession.

> Lleuad——
> Ar ogil heno ogawn:
> Diwedd lloer fal y dydd llawn.

> A moon on the *wane* this night was full; the end of the moon is like the complete day. *D. ab Gwilym.*

Gogiliad, *s. m.—pl. t.* au (gogil) A light retreating, or recession.

Gogiliaw, *v. a.* (gogil) To recede slightly.

Gogis, *s. m.—pl. t.* ion (cis) A slight flap.

Gogladd, *s. m.* (cladd) A burying, a depositing in, a penetrating into.

Gogladdawl, *a.* (gogladd) Tending to bury.

Gogladdiad, *s. m.—pl. t.* au (gogladd) Inhumation

Gogladdu, *v. a.* (gogladd) To inhumate, to bury, to trench up the ground.

Goglaiar, *a.* (claiar) Temperately warm.

Goglaiaru, *v. a.* (goglaiar) To make lukewarm.

Goglais, *s. m.—pl.* gogleisiau (clais) A faint stain, mark, or impression; a tickling.

Goglawd, *s. m.* (clawd) A murmur, a hum.

Goglawdd, *s. m.—pl.* gogloddiau (clawdd) A small trench, or embankment.

Gogledd, *s. m.* (cledd) A state of inaction; the north. *Gogledd-ddwyrain*, north east; *gogledd-ddwyreiniawl*, north easterly; *gogledd-ddwyreinwynt*, north-east wind; *gogledd-ogledd-ddwyrain*, north-north-east; *gogledd-ogledd-orllewin*, north-north west; *gogledd-orllewin*, north-west; *gogledd-orllewinawl*, north-westerly.

> Trwy fodd Duw——
> Elffinawg farchawg medd
> Hwyr dy ogledd.

> By the will of God, Elphinian Knight of mead, may it be long before thy *period of rest*. *Taliesin.*

Gogleddawl, a. (gogledd) Northern, northerly.
Gogleddiad, s. m. (gogledd) A veering northward
Gogleddig, a. (gogledd) Northern, northerly.
Gogleddu, v. a. (gogledd) To veer northward.
Gogleddwawr, s. f. (gogledd—gwawr) Aurora borealis, or northern lights.
Gogleddwynt, s. m.—pl. t. oedd (gogledd—gwynt) North wind.
Gogleddwr, s. m.—pl. gogleddwyr (gogledd—gwr) A man of the north; a Norman.

> Llu——
> A yr gogleddwyr o'n gwlad.
>
> A host which shall drive Normans from our country.
> *D. Llwyd Gorlech.*

Gogleisiad, s. m.—pl. t. au (goglais) A making a faint impression; a tickling.
Gogleisiaw, v. a. (goglais) To touch, or strike lightly; to tickle.

> Llywelyn——
> Ni lyfasai Sais ei ogleisiaw.
>
> Llywelyn, a Saxon would not dare to touch him.
> *Gr. ab yr Ynad Coch.*

Gogleisiawl, a. (goglais) Apt to touch, or tickle.
Gogleisiwr, s. m.—pl. gogleiswyr (goglais—gwr) A tickler, one who gently touches.
Gogloddiad, s. m.—pl. t. au (goglawdd) An embanking; an entrenchment.
Gogloddiaw, v. a. (goglawdd) To embank.

> Gorun morgymmlawdd ai goglawdd glan.
>
> The rage of the sea tumult, the shore doth close in. *Cynddelw.*

Gogloddiawl, a. (goglawdd) Having a tendency to trench, or throw up the ground.
Gogloff, a. (cloff) Somewhat limping, or lame.

> Swyddau gwlad sy heddyw gloff,
> A swydd eglwys sydd ogloff;
> A phob cyfraith ansathrawl,
> A llw dyn aeth yn llaw diawl.
>
> All public offices are lame this day, and the office of the church is rather limping; and every salutary law, and the oath of man, are gone into the devil's hand. *Ior. Fynglwyd.*

Gogloffi, v. a. (gogloff) To cause to limp; to become limping; to limp.
Gogloffiad, s. m. (gogloff) A causing to go limpingly; a limping.
Goglud, s. m. (clud) Dependence, trust, confidence, affiance.
Goglud, v. a. (clud) To adhere, to depend; to confide.

> Goglud a oruc Cai yn wybren o'r glasdowlir.
>
> What Cai did was to lay hold to a billet out of the pile.
> *H. Geraint—Mabinogion*

Gogludawl, a. (goglud) Adherent, dependent.
Goglysur, s. m.—pl. t. on (clysur) A small motion, impulse, or motive.
Goglyw, s. m. (clyw) An over-hearing; a hearing
Goglywed, v. a. (goglyw) To overhear; to hear.

> A fo glew goglywir i glod;
> O fychod goddolir.
>
> He that is brave, his fame will be heard abroad, from a little he will be enriched. *Llyfrad.*

Goglywiant, s. m. (goglyw) An over-hearing.
Gognaw, s. m. (ognaw) Activity, or ertness. a. Active, or full of motion.

> Carousawl cynnwedd ognaw,
> Mab Cynddylan clod artlaw,
> Nid ynad cyd mynad o honaw.
>
> Carousawl intimate with exertion, the son of Cynddylan of superior fame, is not a judge, though he would wish to be.
> *Llywarch Hen.*
>
> Ni phallai ced——
> Yn mywyd Rhyd wryd ognaw.
>
> The giving of treasure would not fail in the life of Rhyd of active manhood. *Cynddelw.*

Gognawd, a. (gnawd) Usual, or customary.
Gognöad, s. m.—pl. t. au (cnöad) A slightly gnawing, or biting.
Gognöawl, a. (cnöawl) Slightly gnawing.
Gognöi, v. a. (cnoi) To gnaw, or bite slightly.
Gogoch, a. (coch) Somewhat red, reddish.
Gogochi, v. a. (gogoch) To give a red tinge.
Gogof, s. f.—pl. t. au (ogof) A cave, a cavern.

> A gwedy gweled o'r cawri hwynt yn damgylchynu yr ynys, ffo a orugant i'r gogofau ac i'r mynyddoedd.
>
> And when the giants had seen them surrounding the island, they fled into the caves, and into the mountains. *Gr. ab Arthur.*

Gogofawg, a. (gogof) Cavernous; full of caves.
Gogofawl, a. (gogof) Like a cavern.
Gogofiad, s. m. (cofiad) A partly remembering.
Gogofiaw, v. n. (cofiaw) To call to mind.
Gogolofn, s. f.—pl. t. au (colofn) A secondary column; a secondary article.

> Y gogolofnau, sef o honynt y mae pymtheg, ac a elwir gan rai yr eilradd golofnau.
>
> Of the minor colons there are fifteen, and are called by some the secondary colons. *Barddas.*

Gogonawl, a. (conawl) Glorious, exalted.
Gogoned, s. m. (coned) That is exalted. a. Glorious.

> Tra da agwedd; tri digoll,
> Ag un Duw gogoned oll.
>
> A most goodly form; three without a failing, and one God altogether glorious. *Dr. S. Cent.*

Gogonedd, s. m.—pl. t. au (conedd) Glory.
Gogoneddawg, a. (gogonedd) Illustrious, glorious
Gogoneddawl, a. (gogonedd) Glorious, illustrious
Gogoneddiad, s. m.—pl. t. au (gogonedd) Glorification, a rendering illustrious.
Gogoneddrwydd, s. m. (gogonedd) Gloriousness.
Gogoneddu, v. a. (gogonedd) To glorify; to exalt
Gogoneddus, a. (gogonedd) Glorious, illustrious.
Gogoneddusrwydd, s. m. (gogoneddus) Gloriousness; splendour; magnificence.
Gogoni, v. a. (coni) To make illustrious, or glorious; to glorify; to assume consequence.
Gogoniad, s. m. (coniad) A glorification.
Gogoniaeth, s. m.—pl. t. au (coniaeth) A making exalted: glorification.
Gogoniannawl, a. (gogoniant) Glorious.
Gogoniannu, v. a. (gogoniant) To glorify.
Gogoniannus, a. (gogoniant) Illustrious.
Gogoniannusrwydd, s. m. (gogoniannus) Gloriousness.
Gogoniant, s. m.—pl. gogoniannau (coniant) An exalted state; glory.
Gogorawl, a. (gogawr) Of the nature of fodder.
Gogordy, s. m.—pl. t. au (gogawr—ty) A foddering house.
Gogorfa, s. f.—pl. t. oedd (gogawr—ma) Livery-stable.
Gogoriad, s. m. (gogawr) A foddering.
Gogoriaw, v. a. (gogawr) To supply with sustenance; to fodder.
Gogoriawg, a. (gogawr) Having fodder.

> Gogoriawg, goriawg gorwaar.
>
> Abounding with fodder, most verdant the cancelled spot.
> *Taliesin.*

Gogoriawl, a. (gogawr) Relating to fodder.
Gogr, s. m.—pl. t. au (gog) A sieve, a sierce. *Gogr bras*, coarse sieve; *gogr man*, fine sieve; *gogr deilt*, a sieve made of split wood; *gogr rhawn*, hair sieve; *gogr sidan*, silk sieve; *gogr rhwyll*, *gogr rhwrch*, *gogr dwlldi*, coarse sieves, so called, made of wooden lattice work; *gogr dirwrwn*, a cribble.

> Myned a gogr i'r afon.
>
> To go with a sieve to fetch water. *Adage.*

Gograid, s. m.—pl. gogreidiau (gogr) Sieve-full.
Gograwg, a. (gogr) Having a sieve, or sierce.

Gograwl, *a.* (gogr) Relating to sifting.
Gogrin, *a.* (crin) Somewhat brittle, or dry.
Gogrinaw, *v. n.* (gogrin) To become somewhat crisp, or brittle.
Gogrinawl, *a.* (gogrin) Apt to be rather brittle.
Gogrisbin, *a.* (crisbin) Somewhat crinkled.
Gogrisbiniaw, *v. a.* (gogrisbin) To render somewhat crinkled.
Gogrwm, *a.* (crwm) Somewhat bent, or hunchy.
Gogrwr, *s. m.—pl.* gogrwyr (gogr—gwr) A sifter, or one who sifteth.
Gogrwraig, *s. f.—pl.* gogrwreigedd (gogr—gwraig) A female sifter.
Gogrwydr, *s. m.* (crwydr) A saunter, a ramble.
Gogrwydraw, *v. a.* (gogrwydr) To saunter about.
Gogrwydrawl, *a.* (gogrwydr) Sauntering.
Gogrwydriad, *s. m.—pl. t.* au (gogrwydr) A sauntering about.
Gogrych, *a.* (crych) Somewhat curled, or rough.
Gogrychawl, *a.* (gogrych) Apt to curl a little.
Gogrychiad, *s. m.—pl. t.* au (gogrych) A curling a little.
Gogrychu, *v. a.* (gogrych) To curl a little.
Gogrydd, *s. m.—pl. t.* ion (gogr) A sifter.
Gogryddes, *s. f.—pl. t.* au (gogrydd) A sifter.
Gogryf, *a.* (cryf) Somewhat strong, or potent.
Gogryg, *a.* (cryg) Somewhat hoarse, or rough.
Gogrygu, *v. a.* (gogryg) To make somewhat hoarse; to become a little hoarse.
Gogryn, *v. a.* (gogr) To sift, to sierce, to bolt.
Gogrynedig, *a.* (gogryn) Sifted, or bolted.
Gogryniad, *s. m.* (gogryn) A sifting, a bolting.
Gogryniedydd, *s. m.—pl. t.* ion (gogryniad) Sifter.
Gogrynu, *v. a.* (gogryn) To sift, to sierce; to bolt, or to range meal.
Gogrynwr, *s. m.—pl.* gogrynwyr (gogryn—gwr) A sifter, or siercer.
Gogrynydd, *s. m.—pl. t.* ion (gogryn) A sifter.
Goguddl, *a.* (cudd) Somewhat obscure, or dark.
Goguddiad, *s. m.—pl. t.* au (gogudd) A partly hiding.
Goguddiaw, *v. a.* (gogudd) To hide partly.
Goguddiawg, *a.* (gogudd) Apt to be sculking.
Gogus, *s. m.—pl. t.* ion (cus) A dalliance.
Gogusa, *v. a.* (gogus) To follow pastime; to trifle, to dally, to act ludicrously.

> Gwag wy', golaiaw gogusa
> Eithr o'th waith athrawiaeth dda.
>
> I am vain to attempt *to trifle*, except of thy performance there is no good instruction. *G. ab Ieu. Hen.*

Gogusaw, *v. a.* (gogus) To trifle, to dally.
Gogusawl, *a.* (gogus) Apt to trifle, or dally.
Gogusiad, *s. m.* (gogus) A trifling, a dallying.
Gogwrf, *s. m.—pl.* gogyrf (cwrf) That is partly a body; a body that is purer than earthly.
Gogwy, *a.* (gog) Full of motion, active.

> Gogwy—trais aneryn——
> Pan aeth gwr gormes ufelyn
> Gwaith gogwy gwyth-gad ymosgryn.
>
> Active is the poison of oppression; when the hero went, whose ravage is like a conflagration, it was *active* work to move in the wrathful conflict. *Cynddelw.*

Gogwydd, *s. m.—pl. t.* ion (cwydd) Obliquity, inclination, a bowing downward, a bending; a tendency. *a.* Inclined, recumbent, fallen.

> Cyn glasu fy ngwedd; cyn glaswedd gwydd,
> Glesin deierin werin ogwydd,
> Rhydalwyf iawn!
>
> Before the growing pale of my visage; before the green appearance of trees and verdant earth, where lies the *fallen* multitude, may I make perfect restitution. *Ein. ab Gwalchmai.*

Gogwyddad, *s. m.* (gogwydd) A bending.
Gogwyddadwy, *a.* (gogwydd) Inclinable.
Gogwyddaw, *v. a.* (gogwydd) To incline, to bend, to lean; to decline, to give a tendency to; to become oblique, to incline, to bend, to tend.

> Gogwydda olwg addas,
> Duw'r hedd ar wasiedd dy was.
>
> *Incline* an appropriate look, God of peace on the abjectness of thy servant. *D. Richard.*

Gogwyddawg, *a.* (gogwydd) Having a bias.
Gogwyddawl, *a.* (gogwydd) Inclining, tending.
Gogwyddedig, *a.* (gogwydd) Biassed, inclined.
Gogwyddedigaeth, *s. m.—pl. t.* au (gogwyddedig) An inclination, a declination.
Gogwyddiad, *s. m.—pl. t.* au (gogwydd) Inclination, or bending downward; propensity.
Gogwymp, *s. m.* (cwymp) A partial fall.
Gogwympaw, *v. a.* (gogwymp) To fall partially.
Gogwympawl, *a.* (gogwymp) Partly falling.
Gogwympiad, *s. m.—pl. t.* au (gogwymp) A partially falling.
Gogyd, *s. m.* (cyd) A partial junction or union.
Gogydbwyll, *a.* (cydbwyll) Partly assenting.
Gogydgerdded, *v. a.* (cydgerdded) Partly to be concomitant.
Gogydiad, *s. m.—pl. t.* au (gogyd) A partially conjoining; an imperfect conjunction.
Gogydiaw, *v. a.* (gogyd) Partially to conjoin.
Gogydiawl, *a.* (gogyd) Partially conjunctive.
Gogydlais, *s. m.* (gogyd—llais) A jingling.
Gogydnaws, *s. m.* (cydnaws) A mean equality of nature. *a.* Homogeneous.
Gogydradd, *s. f.* (cydradd) A mean eqality of degrees, homolomery. *a.* Homolomerical.
Gogydryw, *s. m.* (cydryw) Homogeny. *a.* Homogeneal.

> Mae pethau gogydryw yn ymlucosogi yn ol ffrwythlondeb eu hachosion.
>
> *Homogeneous things* do multiply according to the energy of their causes. *E. Samuel—H. Grotius.*

Gogydrywiad, *s. m.* (gogydryw) A rendering partly homogeneous.
Gogydrywiaw, *v. a.* (gogydryw) To render partly homogeneous.
Gogydrywiawl, *a.* (gogydryw) Tending to make nearly homogeneous.
Gogydsain, *s. f.—pl.* gogydseiniau (gogyd—sain) A mean equality of sound. *a.* Homotonous.
Gogydseinedd, *s. m.* (gogydsain) Homotony.
Gogyfaddaw, *s. m.* (cyfaddaw) A threatening.

> Ni ladd gogyfaddaw.
>
> *Threatening* will not kill. *Adage.*

Gogyfaddaw, *v. a.* (cyfaddaw) To half promise; to threaten.

> Y llew a egores ei enau i ogyfaddaw ei lyncu.
>
> The lion opened his jaws to *threaten* to swallow him. *Mabinogion.*
>
> Cyflychwr yn gogyfaddaw nos yn ddiannod.
>
> The twilight *threatening* the night incontinently. *H. Cor. Mag.—Mabinogion.*

Gogyfaddöawl, *a.* (gogyfaddaw) Threatening.
Gogyfal, *a.* (cyfal) Somewhat alike.
Gogyfarch, *s. m.* (cyfarch) Easy notice. *a.* Easy to be noticed; conspicuous. *Cyfraith ogyfarch*, a conspicuous scar.
Gogyfarch, *v. a.* (cyfarch) To notice easily; to greet with ease; to welcome.

> Gogyfeirch pawb ar ni wypo.
>
> Every body will *greet* though he may not be acquainted. *Adage.*
>
> Dy farddar dy farch
> Wyf i'th ogyfarch.
>
> Thy bard on thy steed, am I *to greet* thee *freely*. *L. G. Cothi.*

Gogyfarchawl, *a.* (gogyfarch) Easily greeting.

Gogyfarchedig, *a.* (gogyfarch) Easily greeted.

Gogyfarchiad, *s. m.—pl. t.* au (gogyfarch) A greeting easily.

Gogyfarchu, *v. a.* (gogyfarch) To greet easily.

Gogyfartal, *a.* (cyfartal) Coequal, similar.

Gogyfartaledig, *a.* (gogyfartal) Partly proportioned.

Gogyfartaledigaeth, *s. m.—pl. t.* au (gogyfartaledig) A mean equality of proportion.

Gogyfartaledd, *s. m.* (gogyfartal) Parallelism.

Gogyfartaliad, *s. m.—pl. t.* au (gogyfartal) A partly proportioning, or making parallel.

Gogyfartalrwydd, *s. m.* (gogyfartal) A partial equality of proportion.

Gogyfartalu, *v. a.* (gogyfartal) To render partly proportionate, or parallel.

Gogyfartalus, *a.* (gogyfartal) Partly tending to proportion, or parallel.

Gogyfartalwch, *s. m.* (gogyfartal) Mean proportion

Gogyfer, *a.* (cyfer) Partly meeting, or aiming.

Gogyfeiriad, *s. m.* (gogyfer) Insinuation.

Gogyfeiriaw, *v. a.* (gogyfer) To insinuate.

Gogyferchydd, *s. m.—pl. t.* ion (gogyfarch) One who greets familiarly.

> Gogyfarchais, gogyfarchaf gogyferchydd.
>
> I have freely greeted, I will freely greet the *familiar greeter*. *Taliesin.*

Gogyfiad, *s. m.—pl. t.* au (cyfiad) A rendering coequal, a making a mean equation.

Gogyfiaw, *v. a.* (cyfiaw) To make co-equal.

> Gogyfarch teyrn gogwyr teyrn-fardd,
> Gogyfardd torment gogyfiaw torfoedd.
>
> A laureat bard knows how to greet a prince; the champion of conflict how to *arrange* his legion. *Ll. P. Moch, i D. ab Owain.*

Gogyfiawg, *a.* (cyfiaw) Having a mean equality.

Gogyfiawl, *a.* (cyfiawl) Tending to be coequal.

Gogyfing, *a.* (cyfing) Somewhat constrained.

Gogyfiwr, *s. m.—pl.* gogyfwyr (cyfiwr) One who makes coequal.

Gogyflawn, *a.* (cyflawn) Partially complete.

Gogyflawnder, *s. m.* (gogyflawn) A partial completeness.

Gogyflawnedig, *a.* (gogyflawn) Partly accomplished. *Amser gogyflawnedig*, preter-imperfect tense.

Gogyflawnedd, *s. m.* (gogyflawn) Completeness in a degree.

Gogyflawni, *v. a.* (gogyflawn) Partly to complete, or to accomplish.

Gogyflawniad, *s. m.* (gogyflawn) A partially, or imperfectly completing.

Gogyfled, *s. m.* (cyfled) Mean equality of breadth. *a.* Of one mean breadth.

Gogyfledawl, *a.* (gogyfled) Partly of uniform breadth.

Gogyfledìad, *s. m.—pl. t.* au (gogyfled) A rendering partly of uniform breadth.

Gogyfledu, *v. a.* (gogyfled) To render partly of uniform breadth.

Gogyfles, *s. m.* (cyfles) A mean equality of benefit

Gogyflesawl, *a.* (gogyfles) Of coequal good.

Gogyflesiad, *s. m.* (gogyfles) A rendering equally beneficial.

Gogyflesrwydd, *s. m.* (gogyfles) A mean equality of benefit.

Gogyflesu, *v. a.* (gogyfles) To render uniformly beneficial.

Gogyflid, *s. m.* (cyflid) A mutual animosity.

Gogyflidiad, *s. m.* (gogyflid) A becoming mutually inflamed, or enraged.

Gogyflidiaw, *v. a.* (gogyflid) To inflame mutually; to become mutually inflamed.

Gogyflidiawg, *a.* (gogyflid) Mutually inflaming.

Gogyflith, *s. m.—pl. t.* iau (cyflith) A mean equality of induction.

Gogyflithiad, *s. m.* (gogyflith) A reducing to a mean equality of induction.

Gogyflithiaw, *v. a.* (gogyflith) Partly to induce mutually.

Gogyflithiawl, *a.* (gogyflith) Coequally inductive, having a degree of mutual tendency to persuade.

Gogyfliw, *s. m.—pl. t.* iau (cyfliw) A mean equality of colour.

Gogyfliwiad, *s. m.* (gogyfliw) A rendering alike in colour.

Gogyfliwiaw, *v. a.* (gogyfliw) To reduce to a mean equality of colour.

Gogyfliwiawl, *a.* (gogyfliw) Of a mean uniformity of colour.

Gogyflog, *s. m.—pl. t.* au (cyflog) A partial covenant

Gogyflogawl, *a.* (gogyflog) Partially covenanted.

Gogyflogi, *v. a.* (gogyflawg) To covenant partially

Gogyflogiad, *s. m.* (gogyflog) Partially covenanting

Gogyflun, *s. m.—pl. t.* iau (cyflun) A mean equiformity. *a.* Of a mean conformity.

Gogyflunedd, *s. m.* (gogyflun) A mean conformity

Gogyfluniad, *s. m.—pl. t.* au (gogyflun) A reducing to a mean conformity.

Gogyfluniaw, *v. a.* (gogyflun) To configurate.

Gogyflwydd, *s. m.* (cyflwydd) A degree of mutual prosperity. *a.* Mutually prosperous in a degree.

Gogyflwyddaw, *v. n.* (gogyflwydd) To prosper mutually in a degree.

Gogyflwyddawl, *a.* (gogyflwydd) Mutually prosperous in a degree.

Gogyflwyddiad, *s. m.* (gogyflwydd) A prospering mutually in a degree.

Gogyflwyth, *s. m.—pl. t.* au (cyflwyth) A mean equality of burden.

Gogyflwythaw, *v. a.* (gogyflwyth) To burden mutually in a degree.

Gogyflwythawg, *a.* (gogyflwyth) Having a mean equality of burden.

Gogyflwythiad, *s. m.* (gogyflwyth) A burdening mutually in a degree.

Gogyflym, *a.* (cyflym) Somewhat nimble.

Gogyflymawl, *a.* (gogyflym) Of a quick tendency.

Gogyflymiad, *s. m.* (gogyflym) A rendering somewhat quick.

Gogyflymu, *v. a.* (gogyflym) To render somewhat quick.

Gogyfnaws, *s. m.* (cyfnaws) A mean equality of nature, or quality. *a.* Partially homogeneous.

Gogyfnawsiad, *s. m.* (gogyfnaws) A rendering homogeneous in a degree.

Gogyfnawsiaw, *v. a.* (gogyfnaws) To render partly homogeneous.

Gogyfnawsiawl, *a.* (gogyfnaws) Having a tendency to be partly homogeneous.

Gogyfnerth, *s. m.* (cyfnerth) A partial corroboration. *a.* Partially corroborative.

Gogyfnerthawl, *a.* (gogyfnerth) Tending to corroborate partially.

Gogyfnerthiad, *s. m.* (gogyfnerth) A partially corroborating; a partial confortation.

Gogyfnerthrwydd, *s. m.* (gogyfnerth) A partial conjunction of power.

Gogyfnerthu, *v. a.* (gogyfnerth) To corroborate partially.

Gogyfnes, *a.* (cyfnes) Partly approximate.

Gogyfnesawl, *a.* (gogyfnes) Partially co-approximating.

Gogyfnesiad, *s. m.—pl. t.* au (gogyfnes) A co-approximating partially.

Gogyfnesu, *v. a.* (gogyfnes) Mutually to approximate somewhat.

Gogyfnewid, *s. m.—pl. t.* iau (cyfnewid) A partial commutation.

Gogyfnewidiad, *s. m.—pl. t.* au (gogyfnewid) A partially commutating.

Gogyfnewidiaw, *v. a.* (gogyfnewid) To commutate partially.

Gogyfnewidiawl, *a.* (gogyfnewid) Partially commutable, or interchanging.

Gogyfnod, *s. m.—pl. t.* au (cyfnod) A mean conjuncture.

Gogyfnodawl, *a.* (gogyfnod) Having a partial conjuncture.

Gogyfnodi, *v. a.* (gogyfnod) To fix a partial conjuncture.

Gogyfnodiad, *s. m.* (gogyfnod) A fixing a partial conjuncture.

Gogyfnos, *s. m.—pl. t.* au (cyfnos) A partial approach of night, a twilight.

Gogyfnosawl, *a.* (gogyfnos) Relating to the twilight

Gogyfnosi, *v. a.* (gogyfnos) To become partially night, to produce a twilight.

Gogyfnosiad, *s. m.* (gogyfnos) A producing the twilight.

Gogyfochr, *s. m.—pl. t.* au (cyfochr) That is partly equilateral. *a.* Equilateral.

Gogyfochrawl, *a.* (gogyfochr) Partially equilateral, or parallel.

Gogyfochri, *v. a.* (gogyfochr) To render partially equilateral.

Gogyfochriad, *s. m.—pl. t.* au (gogyfochr) A making partially equilateral.

Gogyfoed, *a.* (cyfoed) Partly coetaneous, or of the same age. *s. pl.* ***Gogyfoedion***, those that are partly coetaneous.

Gogyfran, *s. f.—pl. t.* au (cyfran) A partial participation.

Gogyfranawl, *a.* (gogyfran) Partially participating

Gogyfraniad, *s. m.—pl. t.* au (gogyfran) A participating partially.

Gogyfranu, *v. a.* (gogyfran) To participate partially

Gogyfred, *s. f.* (cyfred) A partial concurrence. *a.* Partly running together, or of one course.

> Rhwydd ym rhodded——
> Cyfliwion gwellwon gweilch ogyfred;
> ——Feirch yn ebed.
>
> Freely to me were given high-metled ones, uniform in colour and pale ones of *one common course*, steeds that fly. *Cynddelw.*

Gogyfredawl, *a.* (gogyfred) Partly concurrent.

Gogyfredeg, *v. a.* (gogyfred) To run the same course nearly

Gogyfrediad, *s. m.* (gogyfred) A partly running together.

Gogyfres, *s. f.—pl. t.* au (cyfres) A partially uniform rank. *a.* Partly of an uniform range.

> Yn enw gwledig nef gorchorddion
> Rhygenant, rhychwynant i ddragon:
> Gwrthodes gogyfres gwelyddon
> Lliaws Rhun, a Nudd, a Nwython.
>
> In the name of the governor of the high powers of heaven they shall chiefly sing, shall chiefly complain to the prince; he who rejects the *uniform column* of the tribes of the numbers of Rhun, and Nudd, and Nwython. *Taliesin.*

Gogyfresawl, *a.* (gogyfres) Having a partial uniformity of rank.

Gogyfuch, *a.* (cyfuch) Partly of equal height.

Gogyfuchiad, *s. m.* (gogyfuch) A making partly of uniform height.

Gogyfuchiaw, *v. a.* (gogyfuch) To make nearly of uniform altitude.

Gogyfuchiawl, *a.* (gogyfuch) Tending to a partial equality of height.

Gogyfun, *a.* (cyfun) Partially united or agreed.

Gogyfunaw, *v. a.* (gogyfun) To unite partly.

Gogyfunawl, *a.* (gogyfun) Tending to partial union or agreement.

Gogyfundeb, *s. m.* (gogyfun) Partial union.

Gogyfunder, *s. m.* (gogyfun) Partial union.

Gogyfuniad, *s. m.—pl. t.* au (gogyfun) A uniting together partially.

Gogyfurdd, *s. m.—pl. t.* ion (cyfurdd) That is of equal dignity; a compeer. *a.* Coequal in dignity

> Yna ffoes Gofar Ffichti, ac y diengis o'i wyr hyd ar ddeuddeg gogyfurdd Ffrainc.
>
> Thereupon Gofar Picti retreated, and his men escaped to the twelve *compeers* of France. *Gr. ab Arthur.*

Gogyfurddas, *s. f.* (gogyfurdd) A partially equal dignity.

Gogyfurddasawl, *a.* (gogyfurddas) Partly co-equal in dignity.

Gogyfurddasiad, *s. m.* (gogyfurddas) A rendering partly coequal in dignity.

Gogyfurddasu, *v. a.* (gogyfurddas) To render partly of equal dignity.

Gogyfurddaw, *v. a.* (gogyfurdd) To compeer.

Gogyfurddawl, *a.* (gogyfurdd) Coequal in dignity. ***Gogyfurddolion***, those that are coequal in rank.

Gogyfurddawr, *s. m.—pl.* gogyfurddorion (gogyfurdd) That is partly equal in dignity.

Gogyfurddoriaeth, *s. m.—pl. t.* au (gogyfurddawr) Compeerage.

Gogyfuwch, *a.* (cyfuwch) Partly of equal height.

Gogyfwng, *a.* (cyfwng) Somewhat confined.

Gogyfyngder, *s. m.* (gogyfwng) A degree of straitness, or confinement.

Gogyfyngu, *v. a.* (gogyfwng) To confine a little.

Gogyfystlys, *a.* (cyfystlys) Partly collateral.

Gogyfystlysu, *v. a.* (gogyfystlys) To render partly collateral, or parallel.

Gogyffelyb, *a.* (cyffelyb) Somewhat similar.

Gogyffelybu, *v. a.* (gogyffelyb) To compare partly; to render somewhat similar.

Gogyffiniad, *s. m.* (cyffiniad) A terminating, or bounding together nearly.

Gogyffiniaw, *v.* (cyffiniaw) To conterminate nearly

Gogyffraw, *s. m.* (cyffraw) A degree of agitation.

Gogyffrawd, *s. m.* (cyffrawd) A slight impulse. *v. a.* To impel in a degree.

> O ryned present periglawd an gwaith;
> Anrhaith gwyth gogyffrawd.
>
> In this transitory world our action is danger; a *slight impulse* of wrath is destruction. *Taliesin.*

Gogyffred, *s. m.* (cyffred) A slight comprehension; a general or slight idea.

> Addwyn nyfed nwy gomedd gogyffred.
>
> Pleasing is the aspect that hinders not *some comprehension*. *Taliesin.*

Gogyffredawl, *a* (gogyffred) Partly comprehending

Gogyffrediad, *s. m.* (gogyffred) A partly comprehending.

Gogyffredin, *a.* (cyffredin) Rather common.

Gogyffredinaw, *v. a.* (gogyffredin) To render rather common, or general.

Gogyffredinawl, *a.* (gogyffredin) Tending to be rather common.

Gogyffrediniad, *s. m.* (gogyffredin) A rendering rather common.

Gogyffredu, *v. a.* (gogyffred) Partly to comprehend; partly to comprise.

> Y seirph a ogyffredynt gyrn tanollon yn ffestaw y gwragedd.
>
> The serpents were *wont to throw out* fiery horns to beat the women. *Breuddwyd Pawl.*

Gogyffröad, *s. m.* (gogyffraw) A partly agitating.
Gogyffröawl, *a.* (gogyffraw) Partly agitating.
Gogyffröi, *v. a.* (gogyffraw) To agitate a little.
Gogyhwrdd, *s. m.—pl.* gogyhyrdd (chwrdd) A partly coming in contact.
Gogyhyd, *s. m.* (cyhyd) That is of a mean equality of length. *a.* Of a mean equality of length.
Gogyhydawl, *a.* (gogyhyd) Of a mean equality of length.
Gogyhydedd, *s. m.* (gogyhyd) A mean equality of length.
Gogyhydeddawl, *a.* (gogyhydedd) Equatorial.
Gogyhydiad, *s. m.—pl. t.* au (gogyhyd) A rendering of mean equality of length.
Gogyhydu, *v. a.* (gogyhyd) To render generally of equal length; to become of equal length.
Gogyhyrddawl, *a.* (gogyhwrdd) Partly in contact
Gogyhyrddiad, *s. m.—pl. t.* au (gogyhwrdd) A coming partly in contact.
Gogyhyrddu, *v. a.* (gogyhwrdd) To become partly together, or in contact.
Gogylch, *s. m.—pl. t.* au (cylch) A circumference
Gogylchawl, *a.* (gogylch) Circumferential.
Gogylchedd, *s. m.* (gogylch) A circumference.
Gogylchiad, *s. m.—pl. t.* au (gogylch) A making a circumference.
Gogylchiadawl, *a.* (gogylchiad) Circumferential.
Gogylchiadu, *v.* (gogylchiad) To circumference.
Gogylchiaeth, *s. m.* (gogylch) A circumference.
Gogylchiaith, *s. f.* (gogylch—iaith) Periphrasis.
Gogylchu, *v. a.* (gogylch) To circumference.
Gogymaint, *a.* (cymaint) Partly of equal magnitude, or quantity.
Gogymeiniad, *s. m.* (gogymaint) A reducing to a mean magnitude.
Gogymeiniaw, *v. a.* (gogymaint) To reduce to a mean magnitude.
Gogymeiniawl, *a.* (gogymaint) Tending to a mean magnitude.
Gogymeradwy, *a.* (cymeradwy) Acceptable in a degree.
Gogymeradwyad, *s. m.* (gogymeradwy) A rendering of a mean equality of acceptation.
Gogymeradwyaw, *v. a.* (gogymeradwy) To render coequal in acceptation.
Gogymeradwyawl, *a.* (gogymeradwy) Of a mean equality of acceptableness.
Gogymeriad, *s. m.—pl. t.* au (cymeriad) Coequality of acceptation, or authority. *a.* Of equal acceptation, authority, rank or condition.

> Cyd bwed dau briodawr ogymeiriaid, a chyhyd eu gwarchadw ac amryw briodorion, ac ni wypo henafiaid gwlad bawn derfyn rhyngddynt, rhaid yn ddau hanner a ddylid.
>
> Should there be two proprietors, coequal ones in *authority*, and whose possession is equal in duration to any proprietors, with respect to whom, the elders of the country know not the exact boundary between them, it is then necessary to divide into two equal parts. *Welsh Laws.*

Gogymharawl, *a.* (cymharawl) Tending to a general comparison.
Gogymhariad, *s. m.—pl. t.* au (cymhariad) A making a general comparison.
Gogymhen, *a.* (cymhen) Somewhat florid; a little pert.
Gogymhenawl, *a.* (gogymhen) Apt to be pert.
Gogymheniad, *s. m.* (gogymhen) A being rather pert or saucy.
Gogymhenu, *v. a.* (gogymhen) To act a little pertly
Gogymhraff, *a.* (cymhraff) Of a mean thickness.
Gogymhwys, *a.* (cymhwys) Of a mean equality of weight; somewhat meet, or convenient.
Gogymhwysaw, *v. a.* (gogymhwys) To make tolerably correspondent, or suitable.
Gogymhwysawl, *a.* (gogymhwys) Partly of a benefiting tendency; partly corresponding.
Gogymhwysder, *s. m.* (gogymhwys) A mean fitness, or correspondence.
Gogymhwysiad, *s. m.—pl. t.* au (gogymhwys) A rendering of a mean fitness.
Gogymmraint, *s. m.* (cymmraint) A mean coequality of privilege. *a.* Partly coequal in privilege.
Gogymmreinniad, *s. m.* (gogymmraint) A reducing to a mean equality of privilege.
Gogymmreinniaw, *v. a.* (gogymmraint) To reduce to a mean equality of privilege.
Gogymmreinniawl, *a.* (gogymmraint) Tending to a coequality of privilege.
Gogymwyd, *s. m.* (cymwyd) Of a mean equality of pravity.

> Yn tyfrwyd prifdir, pelaidr gogymwyd.
>
> In the confusion of spears, spears all equally destructive. *Aneurin.*

Gogynhes, *a.* (cynhes) Somewhat warm.
Gogynhesawl, *a.* (gogynhes) Partly of a warming tendency.
Gogynhesiad, *s. m.* (gogynhes) A partly warming, a making somewhat warm.
Gogynhesu, *v. a.* (gogynhes) To warm gently.

> Fy nghyssair, o'r pair pan lleferid,
> O anadl naw morwyn gochynhessid.
>
> My leading word, when out of the cauldron it should be uttered, from the breath of nine damsels would it be gently warmed. *Taliesin.*

Gogyniannawl, *a.* (gogyniant) Partly preceding.
Gogyniannu, *v. a.* (gogyniant) To precede partly.
Gogyniant, *s. m.* (cyniant) A little priority.
Gogynnal, *v. a.* (cynnal) To uphold coequally.

> Gogwn hyn—
> Neu'r byd, pei syrthiei
> Py ar pei gwyddei;
> Pwy ai gogynnaliai.
>
> I have some idea of this; or of the world, should it fall, upon what it would come; who would *coequally uphold it.* *Taliesin, canu y byd bychan.*

Gogynnaliad, *s. m.* (gogynnal) A partly upholding; a general supportation.
Gogynnil, *a.* (cynnil) Somewhat exact, or accurate; rather near, or sparing.
Gogynnilaw, *v. a.* (gogynnil) To act rather exactly; to act a little sparingly.
Gogynniliad, *s. m.* (gogynnil) A using some accuracy; the acting somewhat niggardly.
Gogynnydd, *s. m.* (cynnydd) A little increase.
Gogynnyddawl, *a.* (gogynnydd) Apt to increase.
Gogynnyddiad, *s. m.* (gogynnydd) An increasing in a degree.
Gogynnyddu, *v. a.* (gogynnydd) To increase a little.
Gogyrch, *s. m.—pl. t.* au (cyrch) A tendency to a centre; a partly coming in contact.

> Gwawdodyn byr a fydd a dau fraich o naw sillaf ynddynt, a phedair englyn unodl union yn eu canlyn, ond bod yn y gogyrch naw sillaf.
>
> The short encomiastic ought to consist of two verses, with nine syllables in each and the stave of the monorhyme direct following the *a*, excepting that there are nine syllables in the *half recurved verse.* *Gr. Roberts.*

Gogyrchadwy, *a.* (gogyrch) Partly accessible.
Gogyrchawl, *a.* (gogyrch) Apt to approximate; partly coming in contact.

> Mae cingyrnach a deufraich o wyth sillaf, deufraich o chwech, a llosgwrn gogyrchawl o chwe sillaf.
>
> The rugged metre has two verses of eight syllables, two of six and a *half recurved* tail of six syllables. *Gr. Roberts.*

Gogyrchiad, *s. m.—pl. t.* au (gogyrch) A tending towards a centre; a coming partly in contact.

Gogyrchu, *v. a.* (gogyrch) To approach in a degree; to tend towards a centre; to come nearly in contact.

Gogyrfan, *s. m.—pl.* gogyrfyn (gogwrf) That is embodied in pure matter; an angelic form; a personified idea. There have been men called by this name: *Gogyrfan Gawr*, a chieftain of North Wales, was the father of *Gwenhwyfar*, one of the wives of king Arthur.

Gogyrfen, *s. f.—pl.* gogyrfyn (gogwrf) That is partly embodied, or enveloped in pure matter; a spiritual being, or form; a personified idea; a prosopœia.

> Nawdd ammag y'nghadair o bair Cyrridwen,
> Handid rydd fy nhafawd yn addawd gwawd Ogyrfen.
>
> Shall not my chair be protected by the spell of Cyrridwen? Let my tongue be eloquent in the store of praise to the *angelic form*.
> *Taliesin.*
>
> Saith ugain ogyrfen
> Y sydd yn awen.
>
> Seven score *personifications* are there in the flow of the mind.
> *Taliesin.*

Gogyrhaedd, *v. a.* (cyrhaedd) To reach partly.

Gogyrhaeddawl, *a.* (gogyrhaedd) Having partly a tendency to reach.

Gogyrhaeddiad, *s. m.* (gogyrhaedd) A reaching nearly; a partly extending to.

Gogyrhaeddyd, *v. a.* (gogyrhaedd) To reach partly

Gogyrrith, *a.* (cyrrith) Rather niggardly.

Gogysbell, *a.* (cysbell) Equidistant; parallel.

Gogysdadl, *a.* (cysdadl) Partly coequal; nearly of the same value, nearly on a par.

Gogysdadledd, *s. m.* (gogysdadl) Coequality.

Gogysdadliad, *s. m.* (gogysdadl) A rendering partly coequal.

Gogysdadlrwydd, *s. m.* (gogysdadl) The state of a mean equality.

Gogysdadlu, *v. a.* (gogysdadl) To partly equal.

Gogysgawd, *s. m.—pl.* gogysgodion (cysgawd) A phantom; a shadow.

> Mae y dwfr yn wrthwyneb i'r tân; a megis y dwfr y tân, felly i diffydd y bedydd y pechawd. A pheth arall yw dwfr ef a wlych bob peth budr, ac a welir y gwasgawd ynddo; felly i gwlych rhad yr Ysbryd Glan budredd y pechodau drwy y bedydd, a dilëu syched yr enaid a wna o eiriau Duw; a gogysgawd Duw yw, a'i ddelw a welir ynddo pan ymadawer a'r pechodau.
>
> The water is adverse to the fire; and as the water quenches the fire, so does the baptism extinguish the sin; And, the water has another quality, it washes every thing that is dirty; and what darkness is seen in it; so does the gift of the Holy Ghost wash the pollution of sins, through the baptism; and quenches the thirst of the soul from the words of God; and his image is seen in it, on forsaking the sins.
> *Elucidarius.*

Gogywed, *s. m.* (cywed) That is partly congenerous. *a.* Partly of the same breed.

Gogyweg, *a.* (cyweg) Partly tottering, or yielding

> Eir-gall, diwall, gall, bwyll ogyweg;
> Erioed yn difoed hoed gyhydreg.
>
> She is discreet in word, without a fault, and of nice judgment *apt to fluctuate*; always destroying the hope of contention.
> *Casnodyn.*

Gogyweg, *v. a.* (cyweg) To totter partly.

> Gwelygordd——
> Cymmhaid cynnygn ogyweg,
> Cyndrwyn, Cynddelw a'i hanreg.
>
> The tribe of Cyndrwyn, producing combatants *who cause* the opponents *to totter*; Cynddelw greets it.
> *Cynddelw.*

Gohallt, *a.* (hallt) Somewhat salt, saltish.

Gohanawl, *a.* (hanawl) Distinct, discriminate.

Gohaniad, *s. m.—pl. t.* au (haniad) A separation, discrimination, distinction.

Gohanred, *s. m.—pl. t.* ion (hanred) That proceeds from; discriminateness.

Gohanredawl, *a.* (gohanred) Discriminating.

Gohanrediad, *s. m.—pl. t.* au (gohanred) A proceeding, or separating from; discrimination.

Gohanredu, *v. a.* (gohanred) To discriminate.

Gohanu, *v. a.* (hânu) To make to proceed from; to separate; to discriminate.

Goheb, *s. m.—pl. t.* ion (heb) A soft or indistinct utterance; a whisper; conversation; correspondence.

Goheb, *v. a.* (heb) To utter indistinctly; to speak gently; to converse; to correspond.

Gohebawd, *s. m.* (goheb) Correspondence.

Gohebawl, *a.* (goheb) Conversing; corresponding

Gohebiad, *s. m.—pl. t.* au (goheb) A corresponding; a conversing in a whisper.

Gohebiaeth, *s. m.* (goheb) A correspondence.

Gohebu, *v. a.* (goheb) To correspond.

> Ni'th glyw neb yn gohebu;
> Ni'th wyl llwfr yn y dwfr du.
>
> No one hears thee *conversing*; the coward sees thee not, in the dark water.
> *D. ab Gwilym, i'r gleisiad.*

Gohebwr, *s. m.—pl.* gohebwyr (goheb—gwr) A person who corresponds; a correspondent.

Gohebydd, *s. m.—pl. t.* ion (goheb) A correspondent; a whisperer.

Gohed, *s. f.* (hed) A motion between a flight and a walk. *a.* Partly flying.

Gohedawl, *a.* (gohed) Tending to fly partly.

Gohedeg, *v. a.* (gohed) To fly partly; to go between flying and walking.

Gohediad, *s. m.—pl. t.* au (gohed) A flying, or going between flying and walking

Gohen, *s. m.* (hên) That puts forward; that influences; that gives a bias, or inclination; bias, inclination; influence.

> Y gof llys a ddyly amobrau merched y gofaint ereill â fwynt y dano ac wrth ei ohen.
>
> The smith of the palace is entitled to the maiden fee of the daughters of the other smiths who shall be under him, and at his *command*.
> *Welsh Laws.*
>
> Arddwyreaf ddraig, dragon nen Prydain:
> Llawer bardd prydfawr yn ei ohen.
>
> I will exalt the dragon, the leader of the sovereignty of Britain. many dignified bards are under his *influence*.
> *Ll. P. Moch, i R. ab Llywelyn.*
>
> Carws Duw dy fod fyd ohen Gymmro;
> Ar Gymmry ydd wyd nen.
>
> God took delight that thou a Welshman, shouldest be the *example* of the world; over Wales thou art supreme.
> *Ll. P. Moch, i Rodri ab Hywel.*

Gohil, *s. m.* (hil) That is but half produce, or breed; degenerate production.

Gohilion, *s. m. aggr.* (gohil) The small corn amongst grain; refuse of corn, refuse, or outcasts. *Ys gohilion hyn*, this is mere trash.

> Mae gohilion i'r gwenith.
>
> There is a *refuse* amongst the wheat.
> *Adage.*

Gohir, *s. m.—pl. t.* iau (hir) A linger, a delay, or stop; a put off. *Gohir dadl*, a demur in an action at law.

Gohiriad, *s. m.—pl. t.* au (gohir) A lingering, or delaying; a loitering; a staying; a putting off; a demurring; a prolation, or cunctation; a prolonging, or adjourning.

Gohiriadawl, *a.* (gohiriad) Tending to delay.

Gohiriadu, *v. a.* (gohiriad) To render lingering.

Gohiriannawl, *a.* (gohiriant) Tending to be lingering; of a loitering disposition.

Gohirianniad, *s. m.* (gohiriant) A prolongation, a creating a delay.

Gohiriannu, *v. a.* (gohiriant) To create delay; to cause to linger; to prolong.

Gohiriant, *s. m.—pl. t.* au (gohir) A prolongation, a prolation; delay.

Gohiriaw, *v. a.* (gohir) To prolong; to put off, to stay; to adjourn; to protract; to demur; to linger, to delay, to loiter.

Gohiriawg, *a.* (gohir) Full of delay, or full of hinderance.

Gohiriawl, *a.* (gohir) Prolonging, protractive.

Gohiriedig, *a.* (gohir) Prolonged, protracted.

Gohiriedigaeth, *s. m.* (gohiriedig) Prolongation.

Gohiriedigawl, *a.* (gohiriedig) Protractive.

Gohiriogrwydd, *s. m.* (gohiriawg) Protractiveness

Gohiriwr, *s. m.—pl.* gohirwyr (gohir—gwr) A prolonger, or protractor; a lingerer.

Gohoed, *s. m.—pl. t.* ion (hoed) Somewhat of a longing.

Gohoetial, *v. a.* (gohoed) To loiter, or to linger.

Gohoetiawl, *a.* (gohoed) Of a lingering nature.

Gohoew, *a.* (hoew) Somewhat active; sprightly.

> Tair gyhoew riain Ynys Prydain: Angharad Tonfelen, merch Rhydderch Hael, ac Anna, merch Maig Mygytwas; a Pherwyr merch Rhun Rhyfeddfawr.
>
> The three *sprightly* ladies of the isle of Britain; Angharad Yellow-skin, the daughter of Rhydderch the generous; and Anna, daughter of Maig Mygytwas; and Ferwyr, daughter of Rhun the admirable. *Trioedd.*

Gohoewi, *v. a.* (gohoew) To act smartly; to become sprightly, or active.

Gohor, *s. m.* (hor) Somewhat of a sloth. *a.* Rather inactive, or slothful.

Gohoriad, *s. m.* (gohor) An acting sluggishly.

Gohorian, *v. a.* (gohor) To act rather sluggishly.

Gohwrdd, *s. m.—pl.* gohyrddau (hwrdd) A small push or impulse.

Gohwyr, *s. m.—pl. t.* au (hwyr) The evening. *a.* Somewhat late.

Gohwyraw, *v. n.* (gohwyr) To grow latish.

Gohwyrawl, *a.* (gohwyr) Tending to grow late.

Gohyb, *s. m.—pl. t.* ion (hyb) A rising up, a coming out.

Gohybawl, *a.* (gohyb) Tending to rise up; tending to recover; convalescent.

Gohybiad, *s. m.—pl. t.* au (gohyb) Convalescence

Gohybu, *v. a.* (gohyb) To rise up, or come out; to be on the recovery.

Gohyd, *s. m.—pl. t.* oedd (hyd) A mean length.

Gohydawl, *a.* (gohyd) Of a mean length.

Gohydiad, *s. m.* (gohyd) A reducing to a mean length.

Gohydu, *v. a.* (gohyd) To make of a mean length.

Gohyll, *a.* (hyll) That causes some dread.

Gohylliad, *s. m.* (gohyll) A startling a little.

Gohyllu, *v. a.* (gohyll) To cause some dread, to startle a little.

Gohyrddawl, *a.* (gohwrdd) Apt to push a little.

Gohyrddiad, *s. m.—pl. t.* au (gohwrdd) A pushing a little; a small degree of impulsion.

Gohyrddu, *v. a.* (gohwrdd) To push gently.

Gohytian, *v. a.* (gohyd) To linger, to loiter.

Goiaen, *s. m.* (iaen) That covers universally; the omnipresent.

> Goiaen a wel y'nghyfyng.
>
> The *Supreme Being* sees in the difficulty. *Adage.*

Goisel, *a.* (isel) Somewhat low, or humble.

Gol, *s. m.—pl. t.* oedd (ol) That is outward, or as a surface; that goes round; or that envelops; a covering.

> Dygwrtheb gwrthrawd, gwrthrod i hael.
> Nawr yw Rhodri, rhwydd ar olodd.
>
> The opposing party reply, a contrary turn to expense, that one is Rodri, liberal of *garments.* *Gwalchmai.*

Golachar, *a.* (llachar) Somewhat refulgent, gleaming, or glittering.

> Gollycha dy fur feirddion westi:
> Gollachar i fur o feirddoni.
>
> The visiting bards will deprecate thy wrath; his wrath is rendered splendid by bardism. *Ll. P. Moch, i Ll. ab Owain.*

Golaeth, *s. m.* (gawl) Adoration, worship.

Golaith, *s. m.—pl. t.* iau (llaith) Dissolution.

> Dywal dir fydd ei olaith.
>
> The *death* of the fierce is certain. *Adage.*

Golaith, *v. a.* (llaith) To cause a dissolution.

> Gwr a wnai ar Loegr lwyr anrraith,
> A dwyn ei dynion yn gaith;
> A chwyddaw rhagddaw rif saith rhiallu,
> Ni ellid ei olaith.
>
> He was a man who would bring utter destruction upon England, and carry her men into bondage; and before him the number of seven myriads would fall; he could not be slain. *Dav. ab Llwyarch Hen.*

Golam, *s. m.—pl. t.* au (llam) A hop, a skip.

Golamsach, *s. m.* (llamsach) A prancing about.

Golamsach, *v. a.* (llamsach) To prance, to skip.

Golamu, *v. a.* (golam) To hop, to skip.

Golas, *s. m.* (glas) Pale blue, faint blue. *a.* Of a faint blue, bluish.

> Gwen yw hon gwn ei hannerch;
> Golas wyf, yn gul o'i serch.
>
> She is fair; I keep in my mind when I greeted her; I am *pale*, consuming with her love. *D. ab Gwilym.*
>
> Galwer yn Emrys, mewn golas wydrin,
> A minnau'n Feirddin union ei Feirddin.
>
> He shall be called Emrys, in a glass of bluish hue, and I shall be Merddin of accurate song. *L. G. Cothi.*

Golasiad, *s. m.* (golas) A making bluish, or pale.

Golast, *s. m.—pl.* golesti (llast) A hoop that is put under a beehive to enlarge its capacity.

Golasu, *v. a.* (golas) To make bluish or pale.

Golath, *s. f.—pl. t.* au (llath) A small lath.

Golathen, *s. f.—pl. t.* i (golath) A lath.

Golau, *s. m.—pl.* goleuon (gawl) Light.

Golau, *a.* (gawl) Light, bright, clear; manifest, evident; lightsome.

Golawch, *s. m.* (llawch) Ordinary protection.

Golch, *s. m.—pl. t.* ion (gol) An immersion; a wash, a washing; lye; urine. *Golch sur*, stale urine, or chamber lye; *golch enid*, bugle.

Golchbren, *s. m.—pl. t.* i (golch—pren) A wash beetle, a spattle, or battoon, used to beat cloaths in washing.

Golched, *s. m.* (golch) That is washed, or cleaned.

> Sais cyngryn, cyngryd,
> A brigwr wen olched;
> Ar elor ei dygud,
> A gran gwyarlled.
>
> A Saxon shivering and trembling, with white hair *washed*; on a bier he was borne, with a bloody visage. *Taliesin.*

Golchedig, *a.* (golched) That is washed.

Golchenid, *s. f.* (golch—genid) The bruise-wort, or bugle. It is also called *Glesyn y coed*, and *Llysiau y cwlwm*.

Golcheuraid, *s. f.* (golch—euraid) Wood sanicle. It is otherwise named *Golchwraidd*, *gorchwyraid*, *golchyddes*, and *Clust yr arth*.

Golchfa, *s. f.—pl. t.* au (golch—ma) A washing place; a bathing place, a bath; a washing.

Golchffon, *s. f.—pl.* golchffyn (golch—ffon) A washing beetle, or batting-staff.

Golchi, *v. a.* (golch) To wash, to cleanse, to rinse

Golchiad, *s. m.* (golch) A washing, a cleansing.

Golchion, *s. m. aggr.* (golch) Washes, slops, or suds from washing; water that hath been used in washing any thing; dish-water.

Golchionach, *s. m. aggr. dim.* (golchion) Slipslops

> Cymer—lower o lysiau;
> Rhai o'r maes, rhai o'r gerddau,
> A'u berwi mewn golchionach,
> Fal pair Cyridwen, yr hen wrach.
>
> Take a variety of herbs some from the field, some from the gardens, and boil them in *slipslops*, like the cauldron of Cyridwen, the old hag. *D. Ll. Dio Powel.*

Golchioni, *v. a.* (golchion) To make slipslops.

Golchur, *s. m.* (golch) A washer, or a cleanser.

Golchuries, *s. f.—pl. t.* au (golchur) A washer-woman. She had the twelfth place in the second class, in the royal household.

> Golchuries—ei nawdd yw hyd y gallo fwrw a'i golchbren.
>
> The washer-woman: her protection extends as far as she can fling her washing-beetle. *Welsh Laws.*

Golchwr, *s. m.—pl.* golchwyr (golch—gwr) A washer, or cleanser.

Golchwraidd, *s. f.* (golch—gwraidd) Butterwort.

Golchwraig, *s. f.—pl.* golchwreigedd (golch—gwraig) A washer-woman.

Golchydd, *s. m.—pl. t.* ion (golch) A washer.

Golchyddes, *s. f.—pl. t.* au (golchydd) A washer-woman.

Gold, *s. m.* (gol) The marigold flower.

Goldwyr, *s. m.* (gold—gwyr) The marigold.

Gole, *s. m.—pl. t.* au (gawl) Splendour, light. *Uchel ole*, a hill in Glamorgan, so called.

Golëad, *s. m.—pl. t.* on (gole) An illumination.

Goleâu, *v. a.* (gole) To illumine, to illume.

Golech, *s. m.* (llech) That is partly a hide.

Golechiad, *s. m.—pl. t.* au (golech) A being partly hidden, or private; a sculking.

Golechu, *v. a.* (golech) To hide partly; to sculk, or to lark.

Goled, *s. m.* (llêd) That is partly expanded.

Golediad, *s. m.—pl. t.* au (goled) A partly expanding.

Goledrad, *s. m.* (lledrad) That is partly by stealth

> Gorau modd, â geiriau mâd,
> Gael adrawdd serch goledrad.
>
> It is the best way, with choice words, to get to describe a lurking passion. *D. ab Gwilym.*

Goledradaidd, *a.* (goledrad) That is somewhat sly

Goledrata, *v. a.* (goledrad) To steal slightly, to pilfer.

Goledu, *v. a.* (goled) To expand a little.

Goledd, *s. m.* (lledd) A small obliquity. *Myned ar oledd*, to go obliquely. *Sil.*

Goleddf, *a.* (lleddf) Oblique in a degree.

Goleddfiad, *s. m.—pl. t.* au (goleddf) A rendering somewhat oblique.

Goleddfu, *v. a.* (goleddf) To make rather oblique; to render diagonal.

Golef, *s. m.* (llef) A faint voice, or cry.

Golefain, *v. a.* (golef) To cry out faintly.

Goleichiawg, *a.* (golech) Apt to shun, or sculk.

> Saith gynneddf ynghad: mud a byddar, drud a llafar, ufudd, ofnawg a goleichiawg.
>
> The seven qualities of a judge: dumb and deaf, bold and fluent, humble, fearful and *retired*. *Welsh Laws.*

Goleithiad, *s. m.* (golaith) A dissolution.

Goleithiaw, *v. a.* (golaith) To cause dissolution.

> Dos was, na oludd, na olaith dy lwrw;
> Dy luddiaw nid hawdd-waith!
>
> Go, young man, do not loiter, *consume* not thy share; to obstruct thee is no easy task. *O. Cyfeiliawg.*
>
> Yd oleithiid gwr, gwrdd i weled,
> Rhag ced elfwng llwng blaidd cynnyred.
>
> A man *has been slain*, of mighty aspect, who was like the devouring wolf on his course to prevent his being spoiled of treasure. *Cynddelw, m. Cadwallon.*

Goleithiawg, *a.* (golaith) Tending to dissolution.

Goleithiawl, *a.* (golaith) Tending to dissolution.

Goleithiawr, *a.* (golaith) Causing dissolution.

Goleithig, *a.* (golaith) Liable to dissolution.

Goleithwch, *s. m.* (golaith) State of dissolution.

Goleithychu, *v. a.* (goleithwch) To bring to a state of dissolution.

> Dy wyr di er Gwendir goleithychir, bonaf:
> Byddinoedd gorfelyn eu bongyr.
>
> Thy men, for the sake of the happy land, *will be slain*, I do assert; the hosts with yellow pointed spears. *Gwalchmai.*

Golemain, *v. a.* (golam) To hobble, or to hop.

Golesg, *a.* (llesg) Somewhat feeble, or weak.

Golesgiad, *s. m.* (golesg) An enfeebling.

Golesgu, *v. a.* (golesg) To enfeeble, to enervate.

Goleu, *s. m.—pl. t.* on (gawl) Light. *a.* Light.

Goleuâad, *s. m.* (goleu) An illumination.

Goleuâawl, *a.* (goleu) Illuminative.

Goleuad, *s. m.—pl. t.* au (goleu) Illumination, a lighting; a light, a luminary.

> Ef—
> O Fangor, fangaibr oleuad,
> Hyd orwydd Meirionydd meidriad.
>
> From Bangor, a sanctuary of illumination, to the summit of Meirionydd he is a man of knowledge. *Gwalchmai.*

Goleuadawl, *a.* (goleuad) Illuminative.

Goleuadwy, *a.* (goleuad) That may be lighted.

Goleuannawl, *a.* (goleuant) Illuminative.

Goleuanniad, *s. m.* (goleuant) Illumination.

Goleuannu, *v. a.* (goleuant) To illumine; to illustrate, to shed a light over.

Goleuant, *s. m.* (golau) An illumination.

Goleuâu, *v. a.* (golau) To illuminate.

Goleuaw, *v. a.* (golau) To enlighten, to illuminate, to give light, to shine; to reveal.

Goleuawd, *s. m.* (golau) Illumination.

Goleuawdr, *s. m.—pl.* goleuodron (goleuawd) An illuminator.

Goleuawg, *a.* (golau) Having light.

Goleuawl, *a.* (golau) Productive of light.

Goleuder, *s. m.* (golau) Light; brightness.

> Goleuder haul gwyl ydyw.
>
> She that is fair as the *brightness* of the sun is bashful. *D. ab Gwilym, i Forfudd.*

Goleuddal, *s. m.* (goleu—dal) A chandelier.

Goleuddydd, *s. m.* (goleu—dydd) Splendid day.

Goleuedig, *a.* (golau) Illumined, enlightened.

Goleuedigaeth, *s. m.—pl. t.* au (goleuedig) The act of enlightening, or illuming.

Goleuen, *s. f.—pl. t.* od (goleu) A glow-worm.

Goleufawr, *a.* (golau—mawr) Refulgent.

Goleufer, *s. m.* (lleufer) Light, splendour.

Goleuferu, *v. a.* (goleufer) To make luminous.

Goleufynag, *s. m.* (golau—mynag) An explanation, or demonstration.

Goleulawn, *a.* (golau—llawn) Refulgent.

Goleuliw, *s. m.—pl. t.* iau (golau—lliw) A light, or bright hue. *a.* Of a light hue.

> Golwg dof, dewis gan ai syllwy,
> Goleuliw golwg yr ai gwelwy.
>
> A gentle look, the desire of such as beholds her, *illumined* is the countenance of the one that sees her. *Cynddelw, i Efa f. Madawg.*

Goleuliwiad, *s. m.* (goleuliw) A making of a light or faint colour

Goleuliwiaw, *v. a.* (goleuliw) To make of a light or indistinct colour.

Goleuliwiawg, *a.* (goleuliw) Of a light hue.

Goleulon, *a.* (golau—llon) Lightsome.

Goleulonder, *s. m.* (goleulon) Lightsomeness.

Goleulònedd, *s. m.* (goleulon) Lightsomeness.

Goleulosg, *s. m.* (golau—llosg) A bright burning; a flammation.

> Hawdd gweled goleulosg arnei.
>
> It is easy to perceive a *flame* upon her. *H. ab O Gwynedd.*

Goleulosgi, *v. a.* (goleulosg) To burn brightly, or in a flame.

Goleune, *s. m.* (goleu—gne) A light tint.

> Oleune dyfr, neu Luned,
> Elynes gwedd ail Enid.
>
> The *bright colour* of water, or like Cynthia, the spoiler of the countenance like Enid. *Gr. ab M. ab Dafydd.*

Goleuni, *s. m.* (golau) Light; illustration.

Goleuod, *s. pl. aggr.* (goleu) Glow-worms.

M

Goleurwydd, *s. m.* (golau) Illustriousness.

> Treul gorddrud gulad goleurwydd;
> Cwl calan cymun cymhenrwydd.
>
> The lavish consumption of the wealth of *splendour*, the omen of the festival of universal wit. *Cynddelw.*

Goleuthiawg, *a.* (golaeth) Religious, pious.

> Ynghylch a dayly fod yn fud a byddar, drud a llafar, ofnadd ac ofnawg, a goleuthiawg.
>
> A judge is to be mute and deaf, bold and eloquent, humble and fearful, and *religious*. *Welsh Laws.*

Goleuwel, *s. m.* (golau—gwel) Perspicuity.

> Gwnaeth drefn a dosparth ar fesurau cerdd—gan roddi goleuwel athrawiaeth arnynt
>
> He brought the metres of song to order and discrimination, by giving to them the *perspicuity* of learning. *E. Lluyd.*

Goleüwr, *s. m.—pl.* goleüwyr (golau—gwr) A lighter, or one that makes a light.

Goleüydd, *s. m.—pl. t.* ion (golau) A lighter.

Goleüyn, *s. m. dim.* (golau) A small light.

> Griddfanais ryw ocheneid tuag i fyny: a chynted y meddyliwn, gwelwn ryw oleüyn o hirbell yn torri allan.
>
> I uttered a confused sigh towards heaven; and as soon as I began to think, I could perceive a kind of *small light*, breaking out at a great distance. *E. Wyn. B. Cwsg.*

Golewych, *s. m.* (llewych) A faint reflection.

Golewychawl, *a.* (golewych) Faintly shining.

Golewychiad, *s. m.—pl. t.* au (golewych) A faintly shining, a throwing a dim light.

Golewychu, *v. a.* (golewych) To shine faintly, to throw a dim light.

Golf, *s. m.—pl. t.* au (gwlf) What envelopes, or takes in; a swallow; a gulf.

Golfan, *s. f.—pl. t.* od (golf) A sparrow. *Golfan y mynydd*, a mountain sparrow; *golfan y gors*, the red sparrow; *golfan yr eira*, the greater brambling; *yr olfan leiaf*, the lesser brambling.

Goliannawl, *a.* (goliant) Illuminative.

Golianniad, *s. m.* (goliant) Illumination.

Golianno, *v. a.* (goliant) To illuminate.

> Y bore dranoeth, pan oedd pelydr yr haul yn harddu, ac yn goliannu yr ystafell—gwnelder a ddaeth i mewn attaf, ac a gyfarchai gwell i'm, drwy ofyn a gunnwn i fynydd.
>
> The next morning, when the rays of the sun were beautifying and *illumining* the chamber, frailty came in to me, and greeted me, at the same time asking if I would rise up. *Marchawg Crwydrad.*

Goliant, *s. m.* (gawl) Illumination, light.

Goliniad, *s. m.* (gliniad) A pushing with the knee.

Goliniaw, *v. a.* (gliniaw) To push with the knee; to push with the elbow.

> Goliniaw rhiain——
> A wnai a'i benelin oer.
>
> The fair one he would *push* with his cold elbow. *D. ab Gwilym.*

Goliniawg, *a.* (gliniawg) Having the joints projecting a little.

Golith, *s. m.—pl. t.* iau (llith) A gradual training; a gentle enticement.

Golithiad, *s. m.—pl. t.* au (golith) A training, or drawing on gradually; a gently alluring.

Golithiaw, *v. a.* (golith) To allure gently.

Golithiawg, *a.* (golith) That is gently allured.

Golithiawl, *a.* (golith) Tending to train, or entice gently.

Golithr, *s. m.* (llithr) A gradual slip or glide.

Golithraw, *v. a.* (golithr) To slip gradually.

> Teyrnedd——
> [illegible]
> [illegible] Cynan y cyndynawg.
>
> Princes—they would look abashed, they would *slip away* privately for fear of the only son of Cynan the stubborn one. *Meilyr.*

Golithrawl, *a.* (golithr) Tending to slip gradually.

Golithriad, *s. m.—pl. t.* au (golithr) A slipping gradually.

Golithrig, *a.* (golithr) Somewhat slippery.

Goliw, *s. m.—pl. t.* iau (lliw) A faint colour, a glimpse, a transitory lustre.

> Ymdrwsiaf——
> [illegible]
> [illegible], Ddafydd,
> Goliw ar Ddyn fal gwawr dydd.
>
> I will adorn myself, in order to obtain the smith's fair daughter; there, David, I shall perceive a *glimpse* of the maid like the dawn of day. *Gutto y Glyn.*

Goliwiad, *s. m.—pl. t.* au (goliw) A colouring faintly, a giving a slight tint.

Goliwiaw, *v. a.* (goliw) To colour slightly.

Goliwiawg, *a.* (goliw) Having a faint tint.

Goliwiawl, *a.* (goliw) Tending to tint slightly.

Golo, *s. m.—pl. t.* edd (gol) What encompasses; a covering; protection.

> [illegible]
> Golo Nest, goleu direidi!
> [illegible]
> [illegible]
> Gwynedd [illegible].
>
> She is deposited in the churchyard's vault of stone; a frail mansion; the closing up of Nest is a mournful cover! With eyes of a hawk, lively and dignified, and of the most illustrious race was she; fair as the gossamer, with her grace flowing from her goodness: the glory of Gwynedd, she was necessary for us. *Gwalchmai.*

Golo, *v. a.* (gol) To encompass round; to envelope, to cover; to protect.

> Gwedy golo dydd o dywyllawr;
> Gwedy [illegible] gwawr—
> Dy gâr fo dy gerddawr!
>
> After *mantling over* of the day by darkness; after the treacherous aspect of dusky light, be thou a friend to thy songster! *Ll. P. Moch.*

Golöad, *s. m.* (golo) A covering, or enveloping.

Golöawd, *s. m.* (golo) Envelopement, covering.

Golöawl, *a.* (golo) Tending to cover over.

Golochawl, *a.* (llochawl) Giving some protection.

Golochi, *v. a.* (golawch) To protect partly.

Golochiad, *s. m.* (golawch) A giving some protection; a partly defending.

Golochwyd, *s. m.* (golawch) A sequestered spot, a hiding place, a retreat.

> Y cariad——
> Ni lecha y'ngolochwyd.
>
> Love will not lurk under cover long. *D. ab Gwilym.*

Golochwyd, *v. a.* (golawch) To take refuge; to hide, to go to retreat.

> Cyd lawnach difyrach fo
> Coed olochwyd cyd lecha.
>
> So more complete, and more amusing was the wood *retreat* of our hiding together. *D. ab Gwilym.*

Golochwyda, *v. a.* (golochwyd) To lead the life of a hermit.

Golochwydawg, *a.* (golochwyd) Living as a hermit

Golochwydawl, *a.* (golochwyd) Eremitical.

Golochwydus, *a.* (golochwyd) Religiously solitary.

Golochwydwr, *s. m.—pl.* golochwydwyr (golochwyd—gwr) An hermit, or recluse, a religiously solitary man.

Golochwyta, *v. a.* (golochwyd) To live solitarily.

Golöed, *s. m.* (gole) A covering; a vestment. *v. a.* To envelope, to cover.

> Gruffudd greff [illegible],
> A grym hy Hywel, a hywydd olöed,
> A hwyaf arnaf [illegible].
>
> Gruffudd, of a fiery disposition, and the bold frame of Hywel, with a conspicuous *vestment*, and after whom I bear the longest affection. *Gwalchmai.*
>
> Gwae Gymmry, gymmarl gyfagar,
> Golöed grudd hyged hygar.
>
> Woe to Wales, sympathising in honours, that the liberal and amiable countenance *should be covered*. *Gwalchmai, m. Mab Meredudd.*

Golöedig, *a.* (golöed) Enveloped; covered.

Golöedigaeth, *s. m.—pl. t.* au (golöedig) The act of enveloping, or covering.

Goloew, *a.* (gloew) Partly bright, clear, or transparent; brightish.

Goloewad, *s. m.* (goloew) A brightening a little.

Goloewder, *s m.* (goloew) A degree of brightness.

Goloewi, *v. a.* (goloew) To brighten a little.

Golof, *s. f.—pl. t.* oedd (gol) A shelter; protection. *Golof a diebryd*, covert and frustration.

Golofaidd, *a.* (golof) Tending to cover over.

Cai dithau, wen haulwen ha',
Olofaidd wisg, fal Efa.

Thou, who art bright as the summer sunshine, shalt also have, like Eve, a robe *spreading round*. *D. ab Gwilym, i Forfudd.*

Golofawl, *a.* (golof) Tending to cover.

Golofi, *v. a.* (golof) To make a covering.

Golofydd, *s. m.—pl. t.* ion (golof) One who makes a covering; a manufacturer of covering, or wearing apparel.

Golofyddiaeth, *s. m.—pl. t.* au (golofydd) Manufacture of apparel, or cloths.

Golofyddiant, *s. m.* (golofydd) The making of covering, or apparel.

Golofrudd, *a.* (llofrudd) Ferocious, fierce.

Ex eyrchu à orug y cristianogion, ac ni chawsant nawdd ganddynt, namyn eu lladd yn olofrudd.

And the christians came upon them, and they received no quarters from them, but were slain *without mercy*. *H. Car. Mag.—Mabinogion.*

Golofruddiad, *s. m.* (golofrudd) A committing a ferocious, or bloody deed.

Golofruddiaw, *v. a.* (golofrudd) To act fiercely.

Golöi, *v. a.* (golo) To envelope, to protect.

Y gelain fainwen à olöir heddyw
A dan bridd a main;
Gwae fy llaw, lladd Owain!

The fair white corpse *is buried* this day under earth and stones, woe my hand, that Owain should be slain! *Llywarch Hen.*

Ni'm gwna o neb tra troed
Trosol i'r gof argiwyddi.
Mor yw gwael eu golöi!

Nobody could so endure for me the sad remembrance of chieftains; so miserable is it *to bury* them! *Gwalchmai.*

Golon, *a.* (llon) Somewhat chearful.

Golonawl, *a.* (golon) Of a chearful tendency.

Golòni, *v. a.* (golon) To make a little chearful.

Golòniad, *s. m.* (golon) A cheering a little.

Golosg, *s. m.—pl. t.* ion (llosg) Coke. *a.* That is partly burnt. *Glo golosg*, coked coal.

Golosgawl, *a.* (golosg) Tending to half burn.

Golosged, *s. m.* (golosg) What is half burnt, or charred; char; the snuff of a candle; tinder.

Cenfigen sydd yn grin lawn—
Ac a lysg fal golosged.

Envy is very withered, and burns like *tinder*. *L. G. Cothi.*

Golosgedig, *a.* (golosged) Half-burnt.

Golosgi, *v. a.* (golosg) To burn partly; to char; to singe; to blight, or to blast.

Yn llysoedd Dêau
Lliaws twr golau;
Yn Lloegr addodau
Yn golosgi.

In the palaces of the South are many lighted towers; in England stores *a burning*. *Ll. P. Moch.*

Golosgiad, *s. m.—pl. t.* au (golosg) A half burning, a charring, a reducing to tinder, a singeing; a blighting; adustion.

Golosgydd, *s. m.—pl. t.* ion (golosg) One who makes char; a charcoal burner.

Golt, *s. m. aggr.* (gold) Marigold. *Golt yd*, corn marigold; *golt y morfa*, marsh marigold; *golt mair*, marigold.

Goluch, *s. m.—pl. t.* ion (gawl) Adoration, worship, praise. *Dyffryn Goluch*, a valley in Glamorgan, where there are remarkable remains of ancient religious sanctuaries.

Eur-ddraig Eryri, eryron fyhyr,
Eryr gwyr goluchon,
Dangosed gweithred gwaith Fadon;
Yn nydd gwyth gweithfuddig dragon.

The golden dragon of Eryri, the foremost of eagles, the eagle of men that are *worshippers*; let him show a feat like the battle of Badon, in the day of wrath he is a victorious leader. *Cynddelw, m. O. Gwynedd.*

Goluchad, *s.* (goluch) A worshipping, or adoring.

Goluchaw, *v. a.* (goluch) To worship, to adore.

Dymgoluch Gogledd gweglyd luoedd;
Dymgeddeu Deheu dybynt breiddloedd.

The North, of feeble hosts, *will be giving me honour*; the South will be suffering me to have an open road for spoils. *Gwalchmai.*

Goluched, *s. m.—pl. t.* au (goluch) An act of worship; adoration.

Goluchedig, *a.* (goluched) That is worshipped.

Golud, *s. m.—pl. t.* oedd (llud) Wealth, or riches.

Hud yw golud, a gelyn
Brwydr dost yw, a bradwr dyn.

Wealth is delusion, and a fiercely warring foe, and the betrayer of man. *D. ab Gwilym.*

Rhai a ry serch ar ferched;
Ereill ar gyfaill, aur ged—
Rhai ar olud.

Some place their affection on women; others on a friend, a golden treasure; some on *wealth*. *Dr. S. Cent.*

Mae'n lled olud y Bedo,
A'i glod ef, no golud Io.

More extensive is the *wealth* of Bedo, and his fame, than the *wealth* of Job. *L. G. Cothi.*

Goludawg, *a.* (golud) Wealthy, rich, monied.

Goludiad, *s. m.* (golud) A making wealthy.

Goludiaeth, *s. m.* (golud) A rich condition.

Goludogi, *v. a.* (goludawg) To make wealthy.

Goludd, *s. m.—pl. t.* ion (lludd) A little hinderance, or obstruction; discouragement.

Mi af at fy naf yn ufudd,
Ac ni ddeuaf heb oludd.

I will go to my Lord submissively, and I will not return without *staying*. *Ieuan Tew.*

Goluddiad, *s. m.—pl. t.* au (goludd) A slightly obstructing; a causing hesitation.

Goluddias, *s. m.* (goludd) Slight obstruction.

Neum rhoddes o'i fudd, heb oluddias,
Gorwyddawd ffyrf, gwawd ffaw gymwynas.

Has he not given me from his revenue, without *hesitation*, powerful steed, the accustomed compliment of royalty. *Gwalchmai.*

Goluddiaw, *v. a.* (goludd) To hinder a little; to retard; to discourage; to cause hesitation.

Goluddiai wagiaith, gwyl ddiwygiad.

She *would discourage* vain talk, the modest reformers. *D. ab Gwilym, i Angharad.*

Goluddiawg, *a.* (goludd) Slightly obstructed.

Goluddiawl, *a.* (goludd) Slightly obstructive.

Goluddiwr, *s. m.—pl.* goluddwyr (goludd—gwr) One who obstructs a little.

Golwch, *s. m.—pl.* golychion (gawl) The act of illuminating, or lighting; the act of coming together in the light; the bardic worship; adoration.

Golwg, *s. m.—pl.* golygon (gawl) Sight, look, aspect, view, appearance. *Golwg-wasanaeth*, eye-service.

Carafi eos Fai, forehun ludd
A golygon swyr, hirwyn ei grudd.

I love the nightingale of May, that hinders the morning sleep, with languid *eyes*, and long white cheek. *Gwalchmai.*

Er ei gelu, i'r golwg
Y daw a ddaw, draw, a drwg.

Notwithstanding its being concealed, to the *view* the good will come by and by, and the evil. *L. Hopcin.*

Golwm, *a.* (llwm) Rather bare, or exposed.

Golyrch, *s. m.—pl.* golyrch (gol—gwrch) A box.

Golwst, *s. m.—pl.* golyst (gawl) An elucidator; an interpreter.

Golwth, *s. m.—pl.* golythau (clwth) A couch.

Golwybr, *s. m.—pl. t.* au (llwybr) A slight trace, or vestige.

Mae yntau yn gwrthawd ladd i wrtho tyb a golwybr brad.

He also is refusing to put from him the suspicion and *appearance* of treachery. *H. Car. Mag.—Mabinogion.*

Golwybraidd, *a.* (golwybr) Tending to produce a slight trace.

Golwybraw, *v. a.* (golwybr) To make a slight track or path.

Golwybrawl, *a.* (golwybr) Slightly tracing.

Golwybriad, *s. m.—pl. t.* au (golwybr) A faintly tracing; a forming a slight path.

Golwyd, *s. m.* (llwyd) Greyish tinge. *a.* Greyish.

Golwydaidd, *a.* (golwyd) Tending to be greyish.

Golwydaw, *v. a.* (golwyd) To make greyish.

Golwyth, *s. m.—pl. t.* ion (gawl—gwyth) Pure, or consecrated piece of flesh; choice viands: a piece, collop, or rasher of flesh.—*Golwythion cyfreithiawl*, lawful pieces, which were the twelve pieces into which a *Cyllaig*, or stag in season, was divided. *Golwyth y fren*, the milt.

Da gweddai y bêr i'r golwyth.

The spit is well suited for the *joint of meat*. *Adage.*

Ni bydd golwyth cyfreithlawn yn bydd y brenin gwedy calan Rhagfyr.

There will be no lawful *pieces* in the king's stag after the first of December. *Welsh Laws.*

Golwythaw, *v. a.* (golwyth) To cut into pieces.

Golwythiad, *s. m.* (golwyth) A cutting of flesh into pieces, cutlets, or collops.

Golybod, *s. m.* (gol) The sight, or vision.

Golychadwy, *a.* (golwch) That may be adored.

Golychator, *ger.* (golwch) Being adoring.

Ni'm gwlo Gymmro, gwr diober;
Ni'm gwladd golud golychator.

I shall not be protected by a Welshman, a man void of cloth; wealth shall not hinder me from *being worshipping*. *Cynddelw.*

Golychawd, *s. m.* (golwch) Act of worshipping.

Golychedig, *a.* (golwch) That is worshipped.

Golychiad, *s. m.* (golwch) A worshipping.

Golychitor, *sup.* (golwch) To be worshipped.

Golychu, *v. a.* (golwch) To worship, to adore.

Lliaws a'm golwch ni'm gwelsant er m'oed
O riaedd Gwent.—

Numbers *will praise* me who have never seen me, of the ladies of Gwent. *Gwalchmai.*

Goruchel Dduw golychir yn mhob lle.

The most high God *will be adored* in every place. *Ion. Mynyw.*

Golychwyd, *s. m.* (golwch) Worship, adoration.

Amser i fwyd, ac amser i olychwyd.

There is time for meat, and time for worship. *Adage.*

Golychwydaw, *v. a.* (golychwyd) To worship.

Golychwydawl, *a.* (golychwyd) Supplicant; given to prayer; devout; religious.

Golychwydus, *a.* (golychwyd) Given to worship.

Golychwydwr, *s. m.—pl.* golychwydwyr (golychwyd—gwr) A worshipper, one who adores.

Golygawd, *s. m.* (golwg) Prospect, view; sight; perspective.

Caer Rufain, ryfedd olygawd,
Caer uchaf, uchel ei dedwd.

The city of Rome, of wonderful *prospect*, the supreme city, of high usage. *Cynddelw.*

Golygawl, *a.* (golwg) Relating to vision; ocular; perspective.

Golygdwll, *s. m.—pl.* golygdyllau (golwg—twll) A peep-hole; the sight-hole of any instrument; the sight-hole of a cross bow.

Golygedig, *a.* (golwg) Endowed with sight.

Golygedigawl, *a.* (golygedig) Speculative.

Golygfa, *s. f.—pl.* golygfeydd (golwg) A place of vision; scenery.

Golygiad, *s. m.—pl. t.* au (golwg) The act of looking; vision; speculation; an object.

Golygiadawl, *a.* (golygiad) Relating to vision; prospective; speculative.

Golygiadu, *v. a.* (golygiad) To superintend.

Golygiannawl, *a.* (golygiant) Prospective.

Golygiannu, *v. a.* (golygiant) To speculate.

Golygiant, *s. m.—pl.* golygiannau (golwg) Scenery; scene.

Golygle, *s. m.—pl. t.* oedd (golwg—lle) A prospect place.

Golyglon, *a.* (golwg—llon) Of a cheerful look.

Golyglys, *s. m.* (golwg—llys) Eye-bright.

Golygu, *v. a.* (golwg) To look upon; to behold, to view; to oversee, to review.

Golygus, *a.* (golwg) Sightly; of good aspect.

Golygusrwydd, *s. m.* (golygus) Sightliness.

Golygwel, *s. m.* (golwg—gwel) Specimen.

Nid oedd hanner digon o benillion cynarych a golygwel er dysgu y mesurau.

There were not half enough of stanzas of example and specimen, for learning of the metres. *E. Dafydd.*

Golygwr, *s. m.—pl.* golygwyr (golwg—gwr) A spectator; an overseer.

Golygwriaeth, *s. m.—pl. t.* au (golygwr) The office of an overseer.

Golygydd, *s. m.—pl. t.* ion (golwg) A looker on, a spectator; an overseer, or intendant.

Golygyddiaeth, *s. m.—pl. t.* au (golygydd) The office of an overseer.

Golygyn, *s. m.* (golwg) A specimen, a sample.

Golym, *a.* (llym) Somewhat sharpish.

Golymaidd, *a.* (golym) Tending to be sharp.

Golymiad, *s. m.* (golym) A making sharpish.

Golyn, *s. m.—pl. t.* au (gol) The guard of a sword.

Golyth, *s. m.—pl. t.* ion (llyth) Rather feeble.

Cyfym golyth bon han yn d'uadrch o heil.

I was worn away when the fair one came and greeted from afar. *Gwalchmai.*

Golythiad, *s. m.—pl. t.* au (golyth) Enervation.

Golythiaw, *v. a.* (golyth) To enfeeble.

Golythiawl, *a.* (golyth) Tending to enervate.

Golyrchaid, *s. m.—pl.* golyrchaidiau (golwrch) A box-full.

Golyrchaid o ail gwerthfawr a dywalltodd Mair Magdalen am ben Crist.

A box-full of precious ointment did Mary Magdalen pour on Christ. *Hom. Gyfieithiad.*

Gollewin, *s. m.* (llewin) The hind part, the rear, the west.

Penaf oll yn y gollewin,
O byrth Caer hyd borth Ysgewin,
Un yw'r fun a fydd cynnfin folliant,
Gwenllian liw hinfa.

The first of all in the west, from the gates of Chester to the port of Ysgewin, is the fair one whose praise will be universal, Gwenllian blooming as the summer season. *H. ab Owain.*

Gollewin wledig, wlad tafdawg.

Sovereign of the west, a country perfect in good qualities. *Gwalchmai.*

Gollwng, *s. m.* (llwng) A loosening, or dropping, a brewing. *Brecon.*

Arddwyrcaf hael, hwyl-gled ollwng:
Addoniant torfoedd tyrfa ddidwng.

I will exalt the generous one, the *departing point* of the course of fame; the glory of armies, the attraction of the multitude. *Ein. ab Mad. ab Rhahawd.*

Gollwng, *v. a.* (llwng) To loosen, to let go; to slacken; to drop; to absolve, to release, to acquit, to free; to redeem; to brew.—*Gollwng gwaed*, to let blood; *gollwng diawd*, to draw drink; *gollwng ergyd*, to let off a gun; *gollwng tafawd*, to let the tongue run, or to scold: *gollwng ychain*, to unyoke oxen; *gollwng gwraig*, to church a woman.

Gwell mab Gwestai, y dydd y byddai drist y gollyngai y mall wedi iddo i waered hyd at ei fogel.

Blubber-mouth the son of Swallflout, the day when he happened to be sad, he would drop his under lip down to his navel. *H. Culhwch—Mabinogion.*

Gollyngadwy, *a.* (gollwng) That may be loosened, or let go; redeemable; repleviable.

Gollyngawl, *a.* (gollwng) Loosening, tending to slacken, or to drop; absolving.

Gollyngdawd, *s. m.* (gollwng) The act of loosening, or setting at large; release, acquittal, discharge, dismission, deliverance; absolution.

Gollyngdedawl, *a.* (gollyngdawd) Absolutory.

Gollyngedig, *a.* (gollwng) Loosened, absolved.

> Gwelynt—os bod yn ollyngedig o'r arfoll à roddesynt i Emrys Wledig.
>
> They perceived that they were *absolved*, from the oath, which they had given to Ambrosius the king. *Gr. ab Arthur.*

Gollyngedigaeth, *s. m.*—*pl.* *t.* au (gollyngedig) The act of loosening, absolving, or discharging.

Gollyngedigawl, *a.* (gollyngedig) Absolutory.

Gollyngiad, *s. m.*—*pl.* *t.* au (gollwng) A loosening, a letting go; remission, absolution.

Gollyngwr, *s. m.*—*pl.* gollyngwyr (gollwng—gwr) A loosener, absolver, or liberator.

Gom, *s. f.* (om) What turns adversely.

Gomach, *s. f.*—*pl.* *t.* au (gom) A shank; a shin.

> Claf yw'r troed,
> Clafach yw'r omach ind
>
> The foot is diseased, the shin I find more diseased. *Rhys Lloyd.*
>
> Edn bywiawg bach,
> Wyd imi, main yw d'omach.
>
> A little lively bird thou art to me, slender is thy *shank*. *D. ab Gwilym, i'r bioleyn.*

Gommedd, *s. m.* (gom—medd) An adverse saying; a refusal; a denial.

Gommedd, *v. a.* (gom—medd) To say adversely; to refuse; to deny.

> Trystan, aboneat ti y pwyllwn,
> Onid gommeddai'r arddwrn;
> Minnau a wnawn goreu a gallwn.
>
> Trystan, on thy account I would push onward, except my arm, *should refuse me*; and I would act as well as I could. *Ymdd. Trystan a Gwalchmai.*

Gommeddawl, *a.* (gommedd) Negative refusing.

Gommeddiad, *s. m.*—*pl.* *t.* au (gommedd) A refusing; a negation.

Gommeddu, *v. a.* (gommedd) To refuse; to deny.

Gommeddwr, *s. m.*—*pl.* gommeddwyr (gommedd—gwr) A refuser; a denyer.

Gonadd, *s. m.*—*pl.* *t.* ion (nadd) A thin shaving.

Gonaddiad, *s. m.* (gonadd) A shaving a planing.

Gonaddu, *v. a.* (gonadd) To shave with a plane.

Gonaid, *s. f.*—*pl.* goneidiau (naid) A hop.

Gonawdd, *s. m.*—*pl.* gonoddau (nawdd) A small degree of protection.

Gonawf, *s. m.* (nawf) A partly swimming.

Goneges, *s. m.*—*pl.* *t.* au (neges) A petty errand, a trifling business.

Gonegesa, *v. a.* (goneges) To do petty errands.

Goneidiad, *s. m.* (gonaid) A hopping, a skipping.

Goneidiaw, *v. a.* (gonaid) To hop, to skip.

Gonesiad, *s. m.* (nesiad) A gently approaching.

Gonest, *a.* (gawn) Honest, or sincere.

Gonestrwydd, *s. m.* (gonest) Honesty, sincerity.

Gonestu, *v. a.* (gonest) To make honest; to become honest, or sincere.

Gonesu, *v. a.* (nesu) To approximate a little.

Gonoddawl, *a.* (gonawdd) Tending to protect.

Gonoddi, *v. a.* (gonawdd) To protect a little.

Gonofiad, *s. m.* (gonawf) A partly swimming.

Gonofiaw, *v. a.* (gonawf) To swim partly.

Gonwyf, *s. m.*—*pl.* *t.* au (nwyf) A little briskness, or liveliness.

Gonwyfaw, *v. a.* (gonwyf) To render a little lively; to become somewhat animated.

Gonwyfawl, *a.* (gonwyf) A little animated.

Gonwyfiad, *s. m.* (gonwyf) A making, or becoming a little animated.

Göoer, *a.* (oer) Somewhat cool, or fresh.

Göoeraidd, *a.* (göoer) Tending to be coolish.

Göoeraiddrwydd, *s. m.* (göoeraidd) Freshness.

Göoerfa, *s. f.*—*pl.* göoerfëydd (göoer—ma) A cool place, an arbour.

Göoeri, *v. a.* (göoer) To make rather cool.

Gor, *s. m.*—*pl.* *t.* oedd (or) What is superior, uppermost, or extreme; an origin, or source; an opening; a rim; a border; congealed blood, gore; matter from a wound, pus; a brood. *a.* Superior, extreme, high; broody. *adv.* In the extreme, above, exceedingly, very.—It is used as a prefix in composition.

> Ef laddai offwydd a llafn llymaf,
> Mal brwyn yd gwyddynt rhag i adaf;
> Mab Clydno clod-hir canaf i ti,
> O'r clod heb or, heb eithaf.
>
> He would slay the foes with keenest blade, like rushes would fall before his arm: the son of Clydno of immortal fame I will sing to thee, of praise without *beginning*, without end. *Aneurin.*
>
> Owain arwyrain yr oroedd, ar bawb
> O bybyr genedloedd.
>
> Owain the exalted of the *boundaries*, over all the mighty nations. *Cynddelw, i O. ab Madawg.*
>
> Gwerth gwydd or, cydmaint a gwerth ei nyth: sef a ddyly fod yn ei nyth, pedwar cyw arugaint.
>
> The value of a *hatching* goose is as much as the value of her nest: there ought to be in her nest twenty-four young ones. *Welsh Laws.*

Gorad, *s. m.* (gor—ad) Superior activity.

Goradain, *a.* (gorad) Great velocity. *a.* Very quick, or nimble. *Gwalch goradain*, a swift hawk.

> Yn rhith llew rhag llyw goradain.
>
> Having the appearance of a lion before the quick-moving leader. *Cynddelw.*
>
> Gwr goradain gwir a gredai.
>
> The *active* man that confided in the truth. *L. G. Cothi.*
>
> Cynt wyf—no'r gwylain;
> No'r ewig i'r lan; no'r elain i'r coed;
> Nog o droed a roed i oradain.
>
> I am swifter than the sea-mews: than the hind to the plain; than the doe to the grove; than of the foot that is given to the *swift of motion*. *L. G. Cothi.*

Goraddaw, *v. a.* (addaw) To promise too much.

Goraddfed, *a.* (addfed) Over mellow, too ripe.

Goraddfedu, *v. n.* (goraddfed) To grow too ripe.

Goraddfwyn, *a.* (addfwyn) Over-friendly, kind to excess; very benevolent.

Goraddfwyn, *a.* (addfwyn) Supremely blessed.

Goraddwynaw, *v. a.* (goraddwyn) To render supremely blessed.

Goraddwynder, *s. m.* (goraddwyn) Excess of bliss.

Goraeth, *s. m.*—*pl.* *t.* au (gor) A tent for a wound.

Goraethawg, *a.* (goraeth) Tented, in surgery.

Goraethiad, *s. m.* (goraeth) A tenting a wound.

Goraethu, *v. a.* (goraeth) To tent a wound.

Goraf, *s. m.* (gor) Superlative degree of, or the most excellent. *a.* Superlative, best.

Gorafun, *s. m.*—*pl.* *t.* ion (grafyn) A grudge.

Gorafunaw, *v. a.* (gorafyn) To grudge, to grumble; to envy; to give or take reluctantly.

Gorafunawl, *a.* (gorafun) Grudging, envious.

Gorafuniad, *s. m.*—*pl.* *t.* au (gorafyn) A grudging, grumbling, or envying; a murmuring, a being unwilling.

Goraig, *s. f.*—*pl.* goreigiau (aig) A superior source of production.

Gorair, *s. m.*—*pl.* goreirian (gair) An adverb.

Goraith, *s. f.*—*pl.* goreithiau (rhaith) What is partly a rule, or law.

Goralw, *s. m.* (galw) A calling out aloud.

Goralw, *v. a.* (galw) To call aloud, to hollow.

Eryr Eli, gorelwi heno'
Am waed gwyr gwynedd;
Ef y'ngoed, trwm hoed imi!

Eagle of Eli, *thou dost call aloud* this night; thou dost meditate for the blood of men. He is enclosed in wood, and is the thought to me! *Llywarch Hen.*

Sef a orug Hirlas, goralw ar ei gydymdeithion; a chan eu hannog gyrchu eu gelynion.

What did Hirlas do was *to call aloud* after his friends, and by encouraging them to attack their enemies. *Gr. ab Arthur.*

Goralwad, *s. m.* (goralw) A calling out aloud.
Gorall, *s. m.* (gall) Superior power, or might.
Gorallt, *s. f.—pl.* gorelltydd (gallt) An overlooking cliff, a steep precipice.
Goralla, *s. m.—pl. t.* oedd (gorall) Superior power
Gorallu, *v. n.* (gorall) To be more than able.
Goralliad, *s. m.* (gorallu) A becoming, or rendering more than able.
Goralliaw, *v. n.* (gorallu) To be more than able; to render more than adequate.
Goralliawg, *a.* (gorallu) That is more than able.
Gorallüedd, *s. m.* (gorallu) Super-capability.
Goraml, *a.* (aml) Very frequent, superabundant.
Goramlâad, *s. m.* (goraml) A superabounding.
Goramledd, *s. m.* (goraml) Superabundance.
Goramlu, *v. a.* (goraml) To render very abundant; to superabound.
Goramlwg, *a.* (amlwg) Very conspicuous.
Goramlygawl, *a.* (goramlwg) Tending to make very manifest.
Goramlygiad, *s. m.* (goramlwg) A making very manifest.
Goramlygu, *v. a.* (goramlwg) To make very manifest, or conspicuous.
Gorambau, *s. m.* (ambau) Excess of doubt.
Gorambau, *v. a.* (ambau) To doubt overmuch; to hesitate to excess.
Gorambeuaeth, *s. m.* (gorambau) Excess of doubting, or hesitation.
Goranian, *s. m.* (anian) The highest or superior nature. *a.* Supernatural.
Goranianawl, *a.* (goranian) Supernatural.
Goraniander, *s. m.* (goranian) Supernaturalness.
Goranianu, *v. a.* (goranian) To render supernatural; to become supernatural.
Gorarianaid, *a.* (arianaid) Silvered over.
Gorarianiad, *s. m.* (arianiad) Argentation.
Gorarianu, *v. a.* (arianu) To silver over.
Gorarw, *a.* (garw) Very rough; too rough.
Gorarwedd, *s. m.* (gorarw) Over-roughness.
Gorasglod, *s. pl. aggr.* (asglod) Fine shavings.
Gorasgwn, *s. m.* (asgwn) An excrescence; an excrescence in the eye, a haw.
Gorastud, *a.* (astud) Over-studious, or busy.
Gorastudiaw, *v. a.* (gorastud) To over study.
Gorastudiwr, *s. m.—pl.* gorastudwyr (gorastud—gwr) One who studies too much.
Goreu, *s. m.—pl.* goreuon (gor) The superlative, the superlative degree. *a.* Superlative, best. *Pa beth sydd oreu?* what is best? *goreu wyt ti,* thou art the best; *o'r goreu,* very well, excellent; *goreu gan i py yr un gyntaf yr elo,* the sooner he goes the best, is my opinion.
Gorawen, *s. f.* (awen) A transport, or extatic flow of spirits; joy. *Nid oedd na gwen na gorawen arno,* there was not a smile, nor joy on his countenance.

Ni'm daw dydd llawen,
Na gair gorawen,
Na gwen, na gwyngen,
Am lee gwinger'

No glad day will come to me, nor word of joy, nor smile, nor tranquil face, after the wine loving chief! *D. ab Maredydd ab Dafydd.*

Gorawenawl, *a.* (gorawen) Of a joyous flow of spirits; blithesome.
Gorawenu, *v. n.* (gorawen) To be joyous.
Gorawenus, *a.* (gorawen) Extatic, transporting.

Gorawenus glyw rhag glew argiwydd.

A general is *full of joy* in the presence of a brave lord. *H. ab Owain.*

Gorawl, *a.* (gor) Effectual, effective, successful.

Eiriawl nid gorawl ni gynghain.

An entreaty that is not *effectual* will not be agreeable. *Llywarch Hen.*

Gorbaid, *a.* (paid) Totally ceased, or at rest.
Gorbais, *s. f.—pl.* gorbeisiau (pais) Upper coat.
Gorbarch, *s. m.* (parch) Excess of respect.
Gorbarchu, *v. a.* (gorbarch) To respect overmuch, to overprize, to overvalue.
Gorbeidrwydd, *s. m.* (gorbaid) Perfect cessation.
Gorbell, *a.* (pell) Very far, or distant.
Gorbellig, *a.* (gorbell) That is very distant.
Gorbellu, *v. a.* (gorbell) To send very distant.
Gorben, *s. m.—pl. t.* au (pen) Preeminence, superiority. *a.* Superior; forward.

Arddwyrêaf hael o hil—Einiawn Yrth,
O arth orben aerbeul cadgun.

I will exalt the generous one of the race of Einion Yrth, of the bear of *preeminence*, the piercer of the battle with the shaft of slaughter. *Gwalchmai, i O. Gwynedd.*

Gorbicrwydd, *s. m.* (gorbig) Excessive stinging, or pricking; remorse. *Gorbicrwydd cydwybod,* remorse of conscience.
Gorbig, *s. f.—pl. t.* ion (pig) A sharp point.
Gorbigaw, *v. a.* (gorbig) To prick severely.
Gorboeth, *a.* (poeth) Intensely hot; ardent.
Gorboethi, *v. a.* (gorboeth) To heat intensely.
Gorborth, *s. m.* (porth) A carrying off.

Lle bo cad fraged friw-goch ryfedd,
Llwyr orborth dyborth heb gymmodedd—
Gnawd iddaw bryddiaw trwyddi hwyfedd.

Where there is the battle's rage with onsets of wound red, and complete *carrying off* of moveables, without a jest, he is wont to tear through the midst of it. *Llygad Gwr, i Lywelyn II.*

Gorborthawl, *a.* (gorborth) Plundering.
Gorborthi, *v. a.* (gorborth) To carry away rapaciously, to plunder.
Gorborthiad, *s. m.—pl. t.* au (gorborth) A pillaging or plundering.
Gorbwyll, *s. m.—pl. t.* ion (pwyll) Intimation, a first impression of idea.
Gorbwylliaw, *v. a.* (gorbwyll) To give a hint or intimation; to have a slight idea, or notion. *Aeth hi ato heb ei orbwylliaw,* she went to him without giving him notice, or unexpectedly.
Gorbwylliawg, *a.* (gorbwyll) Having a hint.
Gorbwylliad, *s. m.—pl. t.* au (gorbwyll) An intimating, or hinting; intimation.
Gorbwyllig, *a.* (gorbwyll) Tending to impress an idea, or to intimate.
Gorbwys, *s. m.* (pwys) A dependence, reliance.

A bwrw'n gorbwys dwys ar Dduw,
Drwy hyn fe'n clyw.—

And placing our serious *dependence* upon God, through this he will hear us. *Hop. T. Phylip.*

Gorbwysaw, *v. a.* (gorbwys) To rest upon, to depend, to rely. *Gorbwysaw ar ddaioni,* to depend upon goodness.

Gwna fe'n gleirch—
A'i hirffon onnen i'w law,
A'r beswch i orbwysaw.

Make him an old man, with his pointed staff of ash in his hand *to rest upon* during a fit of coughing. *T. Ll. Deio ab Ieuan.*

Gorbwysawl, *a.* (gorbwys) Resting upon, dependent, relying.
Gorbwysiad, *s. m.—pl. t.* au (gorbwys) A resting upon, a depending.

Gorch, *s. f.*—*pl. t.* au (gor) What raises, or is raised round; what encompasses; a fence.

> Bun yd ran i rad i rodolion byd—
> Bun orch eol cad cadawl wson.
>
> Conspicuously he distributes his bounty to the sojourners of the world; conspicuous the mound of the fort of battle of the liberal hero. *Gwalchmai, i Rodri.*

Gorchadw, *v. a.* (cadw) To keep very strictly.

Gorchaeth, *a.* (caeth) Greatly confined, or bound.

> Duw a'm rhaid, rwydd fodd feddyliaid,
> Rhan dyddan gorchlan gorchaith-laid.
>
> God will grant me (liberal the manner of thinking) the happy portion of the high-fenced class of the *strongly imprisoning* clay. *Cynddelw.*

Gorchafarwy, *s. m.* (gorch—afarwy) A surrounding gloom; the evening.

Gorchafedig, *a.* (gorchaf) Obtained, or raised by superiority; that is made supreme.

Gorchafedd, *s. m.* (gorchaf) Superiority; supremacy, a state of advancement.

Gorchafiad, *s. m.* (gorchaf) A raising superior; an exalting; a making victorious; a rising over; a becoming superior; an overcoming.

Gorchafiaeth, *s. m.*—*pl. t.* au (gorchaf) Advancement over; superiority; conquest.

> Pan ydd oedd Julian yn rhoi ei ysbryd gwael i fyny, fe gwnaI ei law tua'r nefoedd, yn erbyn Duw, ac a ddywed: Yr awr hon, O tydi y Galilead, ti a gefaist y gorchafiaeth!
>
> When Julian was giving up his miserable ghost, he raised his hands towards the heavens, against God, and said,—at length, O thou Galilean, thou hast obtained the *victory*! *Marchawg Crwydrad.*

Gorchafu, *v. a.* (gorchaf) To raise superior; to make eminent, to exalt; to be exalted; to be superior; to be victorious; to overcome.

> Gorwiredd yw areitheb yn gorchafu gwirionedd, er mwyn chwanegu, neu ymlaw leiau y peth adroddedig.
>
> A hyperbole is a part of rhetoric *raising beyond* the truth, for the sake of increasing or diminishing the thing in relation. *H. Perri.*

Gorchafus, *a.* (gorcháf) Tending to superiority.

Gorchafusrwydd, *s. m.* (gorchafus) Superiority.

Gorchaled, *a.* (caled) Very hard, or severe.

> Ni lleflir gair gochaled,
> Ac ni lludd cadwosudd ced.
>
> He will not speak a *severe* word, and the planner of battle will not withhold his bounty. *Einion Wan, i Rodri.*

Gorchaledu, *v. a.* (gorchaled) To make over hard.

Gorchall, *a.* (call) Tending to be overwise

Gorchalledd, *s. m.* (gorchall) Conceitedness.

Gorcham, *s. m.*—*pl. t.* au (cam) An overstride; over-reach of a horse, in pacing.

Gorchamawg, *a.* (gorcham) Over-striding. *March gorchamawg*, an over-reaching horse.

Gorchamu, *v. a.* (gorcham) To over-stride; to over-reach the feet.

Gorchan, *s. f.*—*pl. t.* au (cân) The canon, or fundamental part of song; an incantation; an enchantment.

> Yr adlawiaid a ddawant oll o golofnau y naw gorchan; ac am hyny y gelwir y gorchanau yn ddyledogion gogyfurdd, am fod yr adlawiaid fal gweision dyled iddynt.
>
> The derivatives all come from the verses of the nine *canons*; and therefore the *canons* are called superiors co-equal in rank, on account of the derivatives being like servants dependent upon them. *Barddas.*

Gorchanawg, *a.* (gorchan) Having a canon, or fundamental rule; under incantation.

Gorchanawl, *a.* (gorchan) Fundamental, with respect to song; relating to incantation.

Gorchanu, *v. a.* (gorchan) To incantate; to charm.

Gorcharfan, *s. f.*—*pl. t.* au (gorch—ar—man) The roof of the mouth, the palate; the upper jaw.

Gorcharfanedd, *s. pl.* (gorcharfan) The upper part of the mouth; the palate.

Gorchaw, *s. m.*—*pl. t.* on (caw) A great great great grandchild, or a child in the fifth degree. *See* Tras.

Gorchawdd, *s. m.*—*pl.* gorchoddion (cawdd) A superior restraint, that keeps in subjection.

Gorchawn, *s. m.*—*pl.* gorchonau (gorch) What rises superior. *a.* Towering; majestic.

> Gorchawn cyrdd cainmyn
> Yw gwarchan Cynfelyn;
> Gorchan Cynfelyn cyfwy wylad.
>
> The *majesty* of the songs of imprecation is the charm of Cynfelyn; the incantation of Cynfelyn perceptive of love. *Taliesin.*

Gorchegin, *s. pl. aggr.* (gorch—egin) High-grown seed.

> Pei mi brydwn,
> Pei mi ganwn,
> Tarddai warchan gorchegin.
>
> Should I, enrapt, in mystic numbers sing,
> The *potent buds* of magic spells would spring. *Taliesin.*

Gorcheidwad, *s. m.*—*pl. t.* on (ceidwad) A guardian; a keeper.

Gorcheifn, *s. m.*—*pl. t.* aint (ceifn) Collateral relationship in the seventh degree. *See* Tras.

Gorcheiniad, *s. m.*—*pl.* gorcheiniaid (gorchan) An inchanter; a charmer; a magician.

Gorcheiniaeth, *s. m.*—*pl. t.* au (gorchan) Incantation; enchantment; necromancy.

Gorcheithiw, *a.* (gorchaeth) Greatly confined.

Gorchest, *s. f.*—*pl. t.* ion (cest) That is above comprehension; an enigma; a question; a great exploit, a feat, an extraordinary thing; excellency. *Careg orchest*, a feat stone, or a stone that is thrown to display strength. *Ni ofynaf iti orchest*, I will not ask of thee an enigma. *Dyna iti orchest*, there is a feat for thee!

Gorchestawl, *a.* (gorchest) Uncomprehended; extraordinary; questionable, or unexplained; enigmatical; excellent.

Gorchestwawd, *s. m.* (gorchest—gwawd) An enigmatic expression; an enigma.

Gorchestedd, *s. m.* (gorchest) What is not clearly comprehensible; an exploit.

Gorchestiad, *s. m.* (gorchest) A making enigmatical; a performing an exploit.

Gorchestu, *v. a.* (gorchest) To make an enigma; to perform an exploit.

Gorchfannad, *s. m.* (gorchfant) The upper jaw.

Gorchfanedd, *s. m.* (gorchfan) Upper jaw.

Gorchfant, *s. m.*—*pl.* gorchfannau (gorch—mant) The upper jaw.

Gorchfyg, *s. m.*—*pl. t.* au (gorch—myg) The act of getting the better, or subduing.

Gorchfygadwy, *a.* (gorchfyg) Vincible.

Gorchfygawl, *a.* (gorchfyg) Vanquishing.

Gorchfygedig, *a.* (gorchfyg) Vanquished.

> Rhoddes Meurig ran o'r Alban i'r bobl orchfygedig, a ddoboedd ygyd a Rodric, i breswyliaw ynddi.
>
> Meurig gave a part of Scotland to the *vanquished* people who came with Rodric to dwell therein. *Gr. ab Arthur.*

Gorchfygiad, *s. m.*—*pl. t.* au (gorchfyg) A vanquishing, or overcoming; a discomfiture.

Gorchfygu, *v. a.* (gorchfyg) To overcome, to vanquish, to conquer.

> Tri pheth a orchfygodd Loegr: cynnwys dyeithriaid, rhyddhau carcharorion, ac anrheg y gwr moel.
>
> Three things *subdued* England · receiving strangers, liberating prisoners, and giving presents to the bald person. *Trioedd.*

Gorchfygwr, *s. m.*—*pl.* gorchfygwyr (gorchfyg—gwr) A vanquisher, a subduer.

Gorchoddion, *s. pl. aggr.* (gorchawdd) Superior powers; potentates.

Gorcherdd, *s. m.*—*pl. t.* ion (cerdd) A superior circle; a high, or splendid retinue.

> Ef goreu gwron—
> Hyd Eifael, eilfa Gwenhwyseon;
> Hyd weryd wryd orchorddon.

He is the best of heroes as far as Elfael, the station of the sons of Gwent; as far as the region of the patriots of virtue.
Cynddelw, m. Cadwallon.

> Agored i lys i les effeyon—
> Yn muchedd gwledig gwlad orcherddion.

Open is his court for the benefit of the sons of harmony, through the whole life of the sovereign of the country of exalted patriots.
Cynddelw, m. Cadwallon.

> Rhyddyrllid fy ngherdd—
> Yn nghynghawl gorchrwt gorcherddion.

My muse will glow in the meeting for the exploit amongst defenders of the country. *Cynddelw.*

Gorchrain, *s. m.* (crain) That is placed very low, or prostrate. *a.* Very low, or prostrate.

> Oeddynt—
> Argledig arglwyddi orchrain.

They were high-famed lords that are lowly laid. *Cynddelw.*

Gorchrawn, *s. m.* (crawn) A great collection, or accumulation.

Gorchreiniad, *s. m.*—*pl. t.* au (gorchrain) A being very low, or prostrate.

Gorchreiniaw, *v. a.* (gorchrain) To prostrate, or lay very low.

Gorchreiniawl, *a.* (gorchrain) Placed very low.

Gorchronawl, *a.* (gorchrawn) Greatly collecting.

Gorchroni, *v. a.* (gorchrawn) To aggregate much.

Gorchroniad, *s. m.*—*pl. t.* au (gorchrawn) A collecting greatly; a vast aggregation.

Gorchrwm, *a.* (crwm) That bends, or bows much.

Gorchryd, *s. m.*—*pl. t.* iau (cryd) Great shivering.

Gorchrydawl, *a.* (gorchryd) Apt to quake much.

Gorchrydiad, *s. m.*—*pl. t.* au (gorchryd) A shivering excessively; a great trepidation.

Gorchrydu, *v. a.* (gorchryd) To shiver greatly.

Gorchrymawl, *a.* (gorchrwm) Bowing greatly.

Gorchrymiad, *s. m.*—*pl. t.* au (gorchrwm) A bowing, or bending greatly.

Gorchrymu, *v. a.* (gorchrwm) To bow greatly.

Gorchryn, *s. m.* (cryn) Excess of trembling.

Gorchrynawl, *a.* (gorchryn) Greatly agitated.

Gorchryniad, *s. m.*—*pl. t.* au (gorchryn) A trembling excessively.

Gorchrynu, *v. a.* (gorchryn) To tremble much; to be greatly agitated.

Gorchu, *v. a.* (gorch) To rise round; to raise round; to fence round.

Gorchudd, *s. m.*—*pl. t.* ion (cudd) An envelope, a covering, a cover.

Gorchuddiad, *s. m.*—*pl. t.* au (gorchudd) A covering over, or enveloping; a disguising.

Gorchuddiaw, *v. a.* (gorchudd) To envelope, to cover over, to cover, to disguise.

Gorchuddiawg, *a.* (gorchudd) Enveloped, covered over; disguised.

Gorchuddiawl, *a.* (gorchudd) Tending to envelope, or to cover over; disguising.

Gorchuddiedig, *a.* (gorchudd) Enveloped.

Gorchuddiedigaeth, *s. m.*—*pl. t.* au (gorchuddiedig) The state of being covered over.

Gorchuddiedigawl, *a.* (gorchuddiedig) Tending to become enveloped.

Gorchuddiwr, *s. m.*—*pl.* gorchuddwyr (gorchudd—gwr) One who covers over; a disguiser.

Gorchwai, *a.* (chwai) Very brisk, or nimble.

Gorchwant, *s. m.*—*pl. t.* au (chwant) Excess of desire, lust.

Gorchweiad, *s. m.*—*pl. t.* au (gorchwai) A making, or becoming very brisk.

Gorchweiaw, *v. a.* (gorchwai) To endue with great briskness; to become very nimble.

Gorchweiawl, *a.* (gorchwai) Tending to make, or become very brisk.

Gorchwidr, *a.* (chwidr) Very giddy, or fickle.

Gorchwidrad, *s. m.* (gorchwidr) A making to move wildly; a becoming very giddy.

Gorchwidraw, *v. a.* (gorchwidr) To make very giddy; to become very giddy.

Gorchwidrawl, *a.* (gorchwidr) Tending to be very giddy.

Gorchwidredd, *s. m.* (gorchwidr) Excess of giddiness, or fickle motion.

Gorchwil, *s. f.* (chwil) A cautious glance.

Gorchwiliad, *s. m.*—*pl. t.* au (gorchwil) A looking about with earnestness, or caution.

Gorchwiliaw, *v. a.* (gorchwil) To look about continually.

Gorchwiliawg, *a.* (gorchwil) To glance cautiously; to look about much.

Gorchwiliwr, *s. m.*—*pl.* gorchwilwyr (gorchwil—gwr) One who looks about cautiously.

Gorchwim, *s. m.*—*pl. t.* iau (chwim) A quick motion, a sudden emotion.

Gorchwimiad, *s. m.*—*pl. t.* au (gorchwim) A moving quickly; a starting suddenly.

Gorchwimiaw, *v. a.* (gorchwim) To move suddenly, to be all in motion.

Gorchwimiawl, *a.* (gorchwim) Full of motion.

Gorchwimiwr, *s. m.*—*pl.* gorchwimwyr (gorchwim—gwr) One full of motion.

Gorchwir, *s. m.* (gorch—gwir) An explicit truth.

Gorchwiriad, *s. m.*—*pl. t.* au (gorchwir) An attesting, asserting; attestation.

Gorchwiriaw, *v. a.* (gorchwir) To attest, to verify.

Gorchwiriawl, *a.* (gorchwir) Tending to verify.

Gorchwiriedig, *a.* (gorchwiriad) Attested, verified.

Gorchwiriwr, *s. m.*—*pl.* gorchwiriwyr (gorchwir—gwr) A verifier, an attester.

Gorchwith, *a.* (chwith) Very awkward, clumsy, or untoward.

Gorchwithaw, *v. a.* (gorchwith) To make very awkward, or untoward.

Gorchwithawl, *a.* (gorchwith) Tending to make very awkward.

Gorchwithiad, *s. m.* (gorchwith) A making, or becoming very awkward.

Gorchwithig, *a.* (gorchwith) Very untoward.

Gorchwiw, *s. f.*—*pl. t.* iau (chwiw) A quick turn, or whirl.

Gorchwiwiad, *s. m.* (gorchwiw) A turning, or whirling rapidly.

Gorchwiwiaw, *v. a.* (gorchwiw) To whirl quickly.

Gorchwiwiawl, *a.* (gorchwiw) Whirling rapidly, of a quick circular motion.

Gorchwsg, *s. m.* (cwsg) A dead or heavy sleep.

Gorchwy, *s. m.*—*pl. t.* oedd (gorch) An overwhelm

> Nid gorchwy elw medelwr.

The profit of a reaper is not over-much. *D. ab Gwilym.*

Gorchwy, *v. a.* (gorch) To overwhelm.

> Neud bedd dewr-walch gwledd daiar
> Dywarchen, ner'n gorchwy rhwy trugar

Is not the grave of the brave hawk the banquet of the earth clod, for the chief of tumult am I not overwhelmed!
Prydydd Bychan.

Gorchwyad, *s. m.* (gorchwy) An overwhelming.

Gorchwyaw, *v. a.* (gorchwy) To overwhelm.

Gorchwyawl, *a.* (gorchwy) Overwhelming.

Gorchwyd, *s. m.*—*pl. t.* oedd (chwyd) A vomit.

Gorchwydawl, *a.* (gorchwyd) Tending to vomit excessively.

Gorchwydiad, *s. m.* (gorchwyd) A vomiting much.

Gorchwydu, *v. a.* (gorchwyd) To vomit severely.
Gorchwydd, *s. m.—pl. t.* au (chwydd) A great fall.
Gorchwydd, *a.* (chwydd) Greatly fallen.

> Hil Tewdwr, diwoddwr Deau,
> Brwydr orchwydd, ni orchudd tlysau,
> Nac ariant, nac aur yn adnau!
>
> The descendant of Tewdwr, the last man of the south, *greatly fallen* in battle, no jewels cover him, nor silver, nor gold in the tomb! *Cynddelw, i'r arglwydd Rhys.*

Gorchŵydd, *s. m.* (chŵydd) A great swelling.
Gorchwyddaw, *v. n.* (gorchwydd) To fall greatly.
Gorchŵyddaw, *v. n.* (gorchŵydd) To swell much.
Gorchwyddawl, *a.* (gorchwydd) Apt to fall greatly
Gorchŵyddawl, *a.* (gorchŵydd) Apt to swell much
Gorchwyddiad, *s. m.* (gorchwydd) A falling greatly
Gorchŵyddiad, *s. m.* (gorchŵydd) A swelling much
Gorchwyf, *s. m.—pl. t.* au (chwyf) A great motion; a revolving swiftly.
Gorchwyfaw, *v. a.* (gorchwyf) To make a great motion, to revolve rapidly.
Gorchwyfawl, *a.* (gorchwyf) Swiftly moving.
Gorchwyfiad, *s. m.—pl. t.* au (gorchwyf) A moving or revolving swiftly.
Gorchŵyl, *s. f.—pl. t.* ion (chwyl) A superior turn, course, or revolution; what is more particularly going on; a concern, business, or employment; work or labour. *Yr orchwyl*, the superior revolution, or circle; the year.

> Y ferch, o'r fynachlog faen,
> Wiwdda orchwyl ddiweir-chwaen.
>
> The fair one of the stone nunnery, of happy *employ* and chaste condition. *D. ab Gwilym.*

Gorchŵyl, *a.* (gorch—gwyl) Very bashful.
Gorchwylaw, *v. a.* (gorchŵyl) To move in rotation; to be engaged in business.
Gorchwylawg, *a.* (gorchwyl) That is supremely revolving; that is more immediately going on; much engaged in business.
Gorchwyldy, *s. m.—pl. t.* au (gorchwyl—ty) A house for the transaction of business.
Gorchŵyledd, *s. m.* (gorch—gŵyl) Great bashfulness, shamefacedness, or modesty; a look expressing great veneration.
Gorchŵylfa, *s. f.—pl.* gorchwylfeydd (gorchwyl—ma) A place of business.
Gorchwylgar, *a.* (gorchwyl) Bustling, or busy.
Gorchwylgarwch, *s. m.* (gorchwyl) Bustlingness.
Gorchwyliad, *s. m.—pl. t.* au (gorchwyl) An executing a business, or concern.
Gorchwyliaeth, *s. m.* (gorchwyl) A transaction.
Gorchwyliaw, *v. a.* (gorchwyl) To revolve above; to negociate, to transact business, to operate.
Gorchwyliwr, *s. m.—pl.* gorchwyliwyr (gorchwyl—gwr) One who transacts business.
Gorchwylus, *a.* (gorchŵyl) Apt to be bashful.
Gorchwylusrwydd, *s. m.* (gorchwylus) Great bashfulness, shamefacedness.
Gorchwylydd, *s. m.—pl. t.* ion (gorchwyl) One that is in the act of turning; one that is doing, or in action; a gerund, in grammar.
Gorchwylyddiaeth, *s. m.* (gorchwylydd) Factorship
Gorchwyraid, *s. m.* (cwyr) Wild English clary; also called *gorchwyrydd*.
Gorchwyth, *s. m.—pl. t.* au (chwyth) Violent gust
Gorchwythawl, *a.* (gorchwyth) Hard-blowing.
Gorchwythiad, *s. m.—pl. t.* au (gorchwyth) A blowing violently, or in gusts.
Gorchwythu, *v. a.* (gorchwyth) To blow much.
Gorchyfant, *s. m.—pl. t.* au (cy—mant) Palate.
Gorchyfarwy, *s. m.* (gorchafarwy) The dusk of the evening, the twilight.
Gorchyferwy, *s. m.* (gorchafarwy) Twilight.
Gorchyflym, *a.* (cyflym) Very nimble or agile.
Gorchyflymder, *s. m.* (gorchyflym) Great nimbleness, or activity.
Gorchyflymiad, *s. m.* (gorchyflym) A making, or becoming very nimble.
Gorchyflymu, *v. a.* (gorchyflym) To make very quick, or nimble; to become very quick.
Gorchyfnai, *s. m.—pl.* gorchyfneiaint (cyfnai) A relation in the eighth degree of descent. *See* Tras.
Gorchyfran, *s. m.—pl. t.* au (cyfran) Super-proportion; that is over a share.
Gorchyfranawl, *a.* (gorchyfran) Super-proportioned.
Gorchyfraniad, *s. m.* (gorchyfran) The alloting an over-proportion.
Gorchyfranu, *v. a.* (gorchyfran) To over-proportion; to allot what is over a share.
Gorchyfrif, *s. m.—pl. t.* on (cyfrif) An over-reckoning.
Gorchyfrif, *v. a.* (cyfrif) To over-reckon.
Gorchyfrifiad, *s. m.* (gorchyfrif) The act of over-reckoning.
Gorchymaint, *adv.* (cymaint) So very great.
Gorchymmyn, *s. m.—pl. t.* ion (cymmyn) An injunction, a precept, a command, a commandment.

> Gnawd as tyr gant orchymmyn.
>
> He is used to it who breaks a hundred *commandments. Adage.*
>
> Cas a wypo gyfraith Duw, a'i orchymmynion, ac a ddadleu yn eu herbyn er gwobr.
>
> Odious is he who knows the law of God, and his commandments, and who will argue against them for a reward. *Adage.*

Gorchymmyn, *v. a.* (cymmyn) To command.
Gorchymmynawl, *a.* (gorchymmyn) Mandatory, imperative; preceptive.
Gorchymmynedig, *a.* (gorchymmyn) Commanded
Gorchymmynedigaeth, *s. m.—pl. t.* au (gorchymmynedig) The act of commanding.
Gorchymmynedigawl, *a.* (gorchymmynedig) Peremptory, mandatory.
Gorchymmyngar, *a.* (gorchymmyn) Peremptory.
Gorchymmyngarwch, *s. m.* (gorchymmyngar) Peremptoriness, dogmaticalness.
Gorchymmyniad, *s. m.—pl. t.* au (gorchymmyn) A commanding, or enjoining.
Gorchymmynwr, *s. m.—pl.* gorchymmynwyr (gorchymmyn—gwr) One who commands.
Gorchynan, *s. m.* (cynan) Great loquacity.

> Clywer—
> Gorchynan gosgordd gwaegawd calchdöed.
>
> There will be heard the *loud loquacity* of a train clad in painted armour. *Cynddelw.*

Gorchynanawl, *a.* (gorchynan) Over-loquacious.
Gorchynaniad, *s. m.* (gorchynan) A being over-loquacious; a talking over-much.
Gorchynanu, *v. a.* (gorchynan) To talk over-much
Gorchysgawl, *a.* (gorchwsg) Apt to sleep heavily.
Gorchysgiad, *s. m.—pl. t.* au (gorchwsg) An over-sleeping; a sleeping heavily.
Gorchysgu, *v. a.* (gorchwsg) To cause a dead sleep; to sleep very heavily; to be lethargic.
Gorchythrudd, *s. m.—pl. t.* au (cythrudd) Excess of affliction, or agitation.
Gorchythruddaw, *v. a.* (gorchythrudd) To afflict, or disturb to excess.
Gorchythruddawl, *a.* (gorchythrudd) Greatly agitating, tending to disturb excessively.
Gorchythruddiad, *s. m.—pl. t.* au (gorchythrudd) A disturbing excessively.
Gorchywrain, *a.* (cywrain) Very accurate.

Gorchywreiniad, *s. m.* (gorchywrain) A making very accurate, a being very ingenious.
Gorchywreiniaw, *v. a.* (gorchywrain) To render very accurate, or correct.
Gorchywreiniawl, *a.* (gorchywrain) Very accurate
Gordaen, *s. m.* (taen) A spread, or sprinkle over.
Gordaenawl, *a.* (gordaen) Tending to overspread.
Gordaeniad, *s. m.—pl. t.* au (gordaen) An overspreading.
Gordaenu, *v. a.* (gordaen) To overspread.
Gordaith, *s. f.—pl.* gordeithiau (taith) A great or tedious journey.
Gordal, *s. m.—pl. t.* ion (tal) A making satisfaction over, or before; an overpaying; an ordeal.

> Cystal am ordal i mi
> Dwywaith fyned at Dewi,
> A phe delwn—i Rufain.
>
> Equally good for me, for an *ordeal*, is to go twice to Dewi, as if I were to come to Rome. *I. ab R. ab Ieuan Llwyd.*

Gordaledig, *a.* (gordal) Being over-paid, or paid in advance; put to the ordeal.
Gordaliad, *s. m.—pl. t.* au (gordal) An over-paying; a paying before; a putting to the ordeal.
Gordalu, *v. a.* (gordal) To overpay; to satisfy before; to try by the ordeal.
Gordalydd, *s. m.—pl. t.* ion (gordal) One who overpays; one who pays in advance; one who takes the ordeal.
Gordardd, *s. m.* (tardd) A springing or breaking out to excess.
Gordarddawl, *a.* (gordardd) Tending to spring, or shoot out to excess.
Gordarddiad, *s. m.* (gordardd) A springing, or breaking out overmuch.
Gordarddu, *v. a.* (gordardd) To spring greatly.
Gordasg, *a* (tasg) An excessive task, an overtask.
Gordasgawl, *a.* (gordasg) Being too great a task.
Gordasgiad, *s. m.* (gordasg) A tasking overmuch.
Gordasgu, *v. a.* (gordasg) To task excessively.
Gordaw, *s. m.* (taw) That is over-silent, or tacit.
Gordawel, *a.* (tawel) Very calm, or serene.
Gordawelawg, *a.* (gordawel) Abounding with calmness in a great degree.
Gordaweliad, *s. m.* (gordawel) A becoming very calm, or serene.
Gordawelu, *v. a.* (gordawel) To make very calm; to become very serene.
Gordawiad, *s. m.* (gordaw) A being very silent.
Gordeithiad, *s m.* (gordaith) A journeying to excess, a travelling over-much.
Gordeithiaw, *v. a.* (gordaith) To travel over-much, to travel to excess.
Gordeithiawl, *a.* (gordaith) Travelling to excess.
Gordew, *a.* (tew) Over-thick, thick to excess.
Gordewi, *v. n.* (gordaw) To be over-silent.
Gordirion, *a.* (tirion) Over-kind; very pleasant.
Gordirionawl, *a.* (gordirion) Tending to be over-kind; tending to be very pleasant.
Gordirioni, *v. n.* (gordirion) To become over-kind; to be very pleasant.
Gordirioniad, *s. m.* (gordirion) A becoming over-kind; a becoming very pleasant.
Gordirionwch, *s. m.* (gordirion) Over-kindness.
Gordon, *s. f.* (ton) An outer coat, or skin; the epidermis, or scarf-skin.
Gordònawl, *a.* (gordon) Relating to the outer skin, or epidermis.
Gordoni, *v. a.* (gordon) To take off the upper skin, to peel the surface.
Gordòniad, *s. m.* (gordon) A peeling the surface
Gordreth, *s. f.—pl. t.* i (treth) An over-tax.
Gordrethawl, *a.* (gordreth) Taxed to excess.
Gordrethiad, *s. m.* (gordreth) An overtaxing.
Gordrethu, *v. a.* (gordreth) To overtax.
Gordrin, *s. m.* (trin) Excess of business.
Gordriniad, *s. m.* (gordrin) A being engaged to excess; a bustling overmuch.
Gordriniaw, *v. a.* (gordrin) To toil to excess.
Gordriniawl, *a.* (gordrin) Over-toiling, overbusy.
Gordrist, *a.* (trist) Over-sad; very pensive.
Gordristâad, *s. m.* (gordrist) A becoming very pensive; a rendering very sad.
Gordristâawl, *a.* (gordrist) Tending to make, or become, very dejected.
Gordristâu, *v. a.* (gordrist) To make very sad; to become very dejected.
Gordristwch, *s. m.* (gordrist) Sadness to excess.
Gordro, *s. m.—pl. t.* ion (tro) An excessive turn.
Gordröad, *s. m.—pl. t.* au (gordro) A turning excessively.
Gordröawl, *a.* (gordro) Turning excessively.
Gordröi, *v. a.* (gordro) To turn to excess.
Gordrom, *a.* (*f. of* gordrwm) Very heavy.
Gordroawl, *a.* (trosawl) Chasing greatly.
Gordroi, *v. a.* (trosi) To drive, or chase excessively, to over-drive.
Gordrosiad, *s. m.* (trosiad) A chasing much.
Gordruth, *s. m.* (truth) Excess of adulation.
Gordruthiad, *s. m.—pl. t.* au (gordruth) A fawning to excess, an overweening.
Gordruthiaw, *v. a.* (gordruth) To flatter overmuch to fawn excessively.
Gordruthiawl, *a.* (gordruth) Overweening.
Gordruthiwr, *s. m.—pl.* gordruthwyr (gordruth—gwr) A great flatterer.
Gordrwm, *a.* (trwm) Very heavy, very sad.
Gordrymâad, *s. m.* (gordrwm) A rendering very heavy; a becoming very heavy.
Gordrymâawl, *a.* (gordrwm) Tending to be very heavy or weighty.
Gordrymâu, *v. a.* (gordrwm) To make very heavy; to become very heavy.
Gordrymder, *s. m.* (gordrwm) Excess of heaviness
Gordudd, *s. m.* (tudd) An outer covering or case.
Gorduddaw, *v. a.* (gordudd) To cover over.
Gorduddawl, *a.* (gordudd) Overcovering.
Gorduddedd, *s. f.—pl t.* au (gordudd) An overcover
Gorduddiad, *s. m.—pl. t.* au (gordudd) An overcovering, a covering over.
Gordwf, *s. m.* (twf) An overgrowth; a super-excresence.
Gordwy, *s. m.—pl. t.* au (twy) Strict order.
Gordwyad, *s. m.—pl. t.* au (gordwy) An over-ruling, an ordering strictly.
Gordwyaw, *v. a.* (gordwy) To over-rule.
Gordwyawl, *a.* (gordwy) Over-ruling.
Gordwyll, *s. m.* (twyll) Great deception.
Gordwyllaw, *v. a.* (gordwyll) To deceive greatly.
Gordwylliad, *s. m.—pl. t.* au (gordwyll) A deceiving greatly.
Gordwyth, *s. m.—pl. t.* au (twyth) Excess of spring, or elasticity.
Gordwythaw, *v. a.* (gordwyth) To make too elastic, or springing.
Gordwythawl, *a.* (gordwyth) Over-elastic.
Gordwythiad, *s. m.—pl. t.* au (gordwyth) A rendering over-elastic.
Gordyfawl, *a.* (gordwf) Tending to overgrow.
Gordyfiad, *s. m.* (gordwf) An overgrowing.
Gordyfu, *v. n.* (gordwf) To overgrow, to become overgrown.
Gordyn, *s. m.* (tyn) A smart pluck, or pull.

Gordynawl, *a.* (gordyn) Drawing excessively.
Gordynfa, *s. f.—pl.* gordynfëydd (gordyn) An over-tension; excess of draught.
Gordyniad, *s. m.—pl. t.* au (gordyn) A plucking, a pulling smartly.
Gordynu, *v. a.* (gordyn) To pluck smartly.
Gordynwr, *s. m.—pl.* gordynwyr (gordyn—gwr) One who pulls smartly, a plucker.
Gordywyll, *a.* (tywyll) Excessively dark.
Gordywylliad, *s. m.* (gordywyll) A darkening overmuch.
Gordywyllu, *v. a.* (gordywyll) To over-darken.
Gordd, *s. f.—pl. t.* au (gor) An impetus; a beetle; a mallet; a churn-staff.
Gordd, *a.* (gor) Impetuous, ardent; earnest.
Gorddail, *s. pl. aggr.* (dail) Exterior leaves.
Gorddal, *s. m.* (dàl) An upholding.
Gorddal, *v. a.* (dàl) To uphold, to sustain.

—Argiwydd,
Onid gorddali awyr a ser!

The Lord, doth he not *uphold* the sky and the stars! *Meigant, i Gadwallon.*

Gorddalgar, *a.* (gorddal) Tending to uphold.
Gorddaliad, *s. m.—pl. t.* au (gorddal) An upholding.
Gorddaliedig, *a.* (gorddal) Upholden, supported.
Gorddaly, *v. a.* (gorddal) To uphold, to sustain.
Gorddan, *s. f.—pl. t.* au (gordd) A little mallet.
Gorddarn, *s. m.—pl. t.* au (darn) An exterior piece.
Gorddawd, *s. m.—pl.* gorddodau (gordd) An impulse; an effect; a stroke of a beetle, or mallet.

Tair llys gwlad a chyfraith amryfal eu cynnal, parth gorddawd ac ansawdd gwyr llys ac ei swyddwyr: un Powys; un Caer lleon ar Wysg, sef, un Morganwg a Deheubarth; ac un Gwynedd.

There are three courts of the country and law variously constituted, in respect to *effect* and character of the functionaries of court and its officers: the one of Powys; the one of Caerlleon upon Usk, or Morganwg and South Wales; and that of Gwynedd. *Trioedd Dyfnwal.*

Gorddawl, *a.* (gordd) Impulsive, propellant.
Gorddawn, *s. m.—pl.* gorddoniau (dawn) A superior gift, or endowment; herb of grace, or rue.
Gordd-dorch, *s. f.—pl.* gordd-dyrch (gordd—torch) A collar, a chain, or torque for the neck.

Gwisg o bali coch oedd am dano, a gordd-dorch aur am ei fwnwgl.

A garment of red velvet was upon him, and a golden *wreath* round his neck. *Br. M. Wledig—Mabinogion.*

Gorddeiliad, *s. m.—pl. t.* au (gorddail) A producing the outer leaves.
Gorddeiliaw, *v. a.* (gorddail) To produce the outer leaves.
Gorddeiliawg, *a.* (gorddail) Having outer leaves.
Gordden, *s. f.—pl. t.* au (gordd—en) Impulse of necessity; destiny.

Yn wir dymbi dyn dra Hafren,
Wrth efeddu Prydain brenin gordden,
Llary lywydd lluydd, lliaws ei echen.

Truly a man shall come from beyond Havren, by inheriting Britain a *king of destiny*, a mild ruler of armies, of numerous progeny. *Taliesin, ym. Ludd.*

Mad gwas gwledig
Mawr ei ordden;
Mawr Ddew rëen,
Rhan gogoned o hil Adda!

Blest the patriot youth of mighty *destiny*; great God the moving principle! a glorious portion of the race of Adam. *Taliesin, Llurig Alexander.*

Gordden, *a.* (gordd) Impulsive of necessity, or impelling as a principle. *Cyfraith ordden*, law of necessity.

O Ddew gordden,
A Duw rëen,
Rex meneifion,
Herod gystig
Ni bu goddig
Yn ngeleadon.

O *fate-impelling* God, and God the moving principle, king of the states of progression, the cruel Herod was not oppressive in the shroud of death. *Taliesin, Llath Moesen.*

Trais ormail ormaut ormes lofrudd gawr;
Gorddwy llawr gordden udd!

Ravaging force of the excess of molestation of the slayer in the shout; the burden of the ground is the *victorious* chief! *Cynddelw, m. O. Gwynedd.*

Gwyr y buam ygyd am gyd ordden;
Nid ym gyd am fudd am feddu gwen.

We are men who have been unanimous for *necessary* treasure; we are not unanimous for the benefit of possessing the fair one. *Cynddelw, m. Rhiryd Flaidd.*

Gorddenawl, *a.* (gordden) Necessitating.
Gorddeniad, *s.—pl. t.* au (gordden) Necessitation.
Gorddenu, *v. a.* (gordden) To impel by necessity, or instinct, to necessitate.

Nid cymmhwys i'r nef na bo trech ar a'i gorddenu.

He is not meet for heaven that is not master of what allures him. *Cyngogion Catwg.*

Gordderch, *s. c.—pl. t.* ion (gordd—erch) A paramour; an adulterer; a concubine. *Mab gordderch*, a bastard son.

O derfydd geni mab i wraig o'i gwr priawd, a geni mab arall o'i gordderch.

If a child should be born to a woman by her married husband, and another child born by her *paramour.* *Welsh Laws.*

Ni chawn fod yn ordderch yt.

I could not get to be the *object of thy love.* *D. ab Gwilym.*

Gordderchad, *s. m.—pl. t.* on (gordderch) One making love, or wooing; a fornicator.
Gordderchawl, *a.* (gordderch) Wooing, adulterous
Gordderchferch, *s. f.—pl. t.* ed (gordderch—merch) A concubine.
Gordderchfun, *s. f.* (gordderch—bun) A concubine.
Gordderchiad, *s. m.* (gordderch) A wooing; a committing the act of concubinage or of adultery.

Gwedy hwnw y gwledychai Elystan ei fab yntau, yr hwn a gawsai o ordderchiad.

After that Elystan his son also reigned, whom he begat by *concubinage.* *Brut y Saeson.*

Gordderchu, *v. a.* (gordderch) To seek one's love and affection; to woo; to play the wanton.

Prid swydd gordderchu pryd ser;
Pridach wedi y prioder.

A meritorious office *to woo* the image of the stars; more meritorious when marriage has taken place. *G. Tew.*

Mi a af i ordderchu drosod ti, ebai y forwyn wrth yr iarlles.

I will go to *make overtures* for thee, said the maiden to the lady. *H. O. ab Urien—Mabinogion.*

Gordderchwas, *s. m.—pl.* gordderchweis (gordderch—gwas) A paramour.

Llengel merch a'i gordderchwas,
Llawn o glod, ydyw'r llwyn glas.

The sheltering veil of a maid and her *lover* is the green grove abounding with praise. *D. ab Gwilym, i'r Bedw.*

Gordderchwawd, *s. m.* (gordderch—gwawd) Love encomiastic, love-song.
Gordderchwr, *s. m.—pl.* gordderchwyr (gordderch—gwr) A paramour; one who courts.
Gordderchwraig, *s. f.—pl.* gordderchwreigedd (gordderch—gwraig) A concubine.
Gorddestl, *a.* (destl) Over-trim, over-neat.
Gorddestledd, *s. m.* (gorddestl) The state of being over-trimmed.
Gorddestliad, *s. m.* (gorddestl) A trimming out to excess.
Gorddestlu, *v. a.* (gorddestl) To trim overmuch.
Gorddestlus, *a.* (gorddestl) Decked overmuch.
Gorddethawl, *a.* (dethawl) Very select.
Gorddethawl, *v. a.* (dethawl) To select.
Gorddetholi, *v. a.* (gorddethawl) To select.
Gorddetholiad, *s. m.* (gorddethawl) A selecting in a superior degree.

Gorddetholrwydd, *s. m.* (gorddethawl) A selectedness in a superior degree.

Gorddetholwr, *s. m.—pl.* gorddetholwyr (gorddethawl—gwr) The choicest man.

Gorddewis, *s. m.* (dewis) Nice selection.

Gorddewisaw, *v. a.* (gorddewis) To select over-nicely.

Gorddewisawl, *a.* (gorddewis) Very select.

Gorddewisiad, *s. m.* (gorddewis) A selecting over-nicely.

Gorddewr, *a.* (dewr) Brave or bold to excess.

Gorddewredd, *s. m.* (gorddewr) Excess of bravery.

Gorddewri, *v. n.* (gorddewr) To be over brave.

Gorddi, *v. a.* (gordd) To impel, to propel.

Gorddiad, *s. m.—pl. t.* au (gordd) An impelling.

Gorddïal, *s. m.—pl. t.* au (dïal) Excess of revenge.

Gorddïal, *v. a.* (dïal) To revenge to excess.

Gorddïaledd, *s. m.* (gorddïal) Excess of revenge.

Gorddïaleddgar, *a.* (gorddïaledd) Apt to be too revengeful.

Gorddïaleddiad, *s. m.* (gorddïaledd) A revenging to excess.

Gorddïaleddu, *v. a.* (gorddïaledd) To revenge to excess.

Gorddïaliad, *s. m.* (gorddïal) An over revenging.

Gorddïalu, *v. a.* (gorddïal) To revenge to excess.

Gorddiant, *s. m.—pl.* gorddiannau (gordd) An impulsion, or propulsion.

Gorddiawg, *a.* (diawg) Over idle, or slothful. *Gorddiogion*, slothful ones.

Gorddibed, *s. m.* (dib) An outskirt, or extremity.

> Pan fai arf am fwrdd a fwrwyd,
> Yn nghoedd gorfynwn yn gorddibed Lloegr.
> A llygru ei threfred.
>
> When there should be a weapon thrown round the board conspicuously I would strive to be in skirting the bound of Lloegr, and ruining its habitation. *Hywel ab Owain.*

Gorddiberth, *s. m.* (dib—erth) What blasts the extremity. *a.* Blasting the extremities.

> Bu——
> Gwynt gorddiberth
> Ar ddail a gwydd.
>
> There was wind *blasting the tops*, upon leaves and trees. *Taliesin, Pla yr Aifft.*

Gorddibl, *s. m.—pl. t.* au (dibl) An outskirt.

> Henwas mab Aflawn a sodes ei wala ar Arthur yn i gyfarws, trydydd gorddiblau Cernyw.
>
> Henwas the son of Aflawn fixt his sufficiency of recompence upon Arthur to be the third of the *outskirts* of Cornwall. *H. Culhwch—Mabinogion.*

Gorddiblaw, *v. a.* (gorddibl) To make outskirts.

Gorddiblawg, *a.* (gorddibl) Having outskirts.

Gorddibliad, *s. m.—pl. t.* au (gorddibl) A making an outskirt.

Gorddibyn, *s. m.—pl. t.* ion (dibyn) What overhangs; an overhanging precipice.

Gorddibynawl, *a.* (gorddibyn) Overhanging.

Gorddibyniad, *s. m.—pl. t.* au (gorddibyn) An overhanging, or over-impending.

Gorddibynu, *v. a.* (gorddibyn) To overhang.

Gorddichell, *s. f.—pl. t.* ion (dichell) A superior stratagem, or cunning.

Gorddichellgar, *a.* (gorddichell) Over-cunning.

Gorddichelliad, *s. c.—pl. t.* au (gorddichell) An acting over craftily; a being very wily.

Gorddichellu, *v. a.* (gorddichell) To act over-cunningly, to be crafty overmuch.

Gorddichlyn, *a.* (dichlyn) Assiduous to excess.

Gorddichlynedd, *s. m.* (gorddichlyn) Over-assiduousness, diligence to excess.

Gorddichlynu, *v. n.* (gorddichlyn) To be over assiduous, to be industrious to excess.

Gorddichon, *v. n.* (dichon) To be more than able; to be over adequate.

Gorddichonawl, *a.* (gorddichon) Being more than able; over-adequate.

Gorddichoni, *v. n.* (gorddichon) To be more than able; to be over-adequate.

Gorddichwant, *a.* (dichwant) Unambitious to excess; extremely void of desire.

Gorddifant, *s. m.—pl.* gorddifannau (difant) Utter deletion, or annihilation. *a.* Utterly delected.

Gorddifannawl, *a.* (gorddifant) Tending to delete, or to obliterate utterly.

Gorddifanniad, *s. m.* (gorddifant) Utter deletion, or obliteration; a vanishing entirely.

Gorddifanw, *a.* (difanw) Being beyond an evanescent or fleeting state.

> Neud gorddifanw bern hoedl, aber lledgynt;
> Neud gorddifynt hynt gwynt gwrth donnar!
>
> How beyond a *fleeting state* is the flush of life, like the passing gust; doth not the course of the wind annihilate the opposing wave? *Cynddelw, m. Rhyd Flaidd.*

Gorddifenwad, *s. m.—pl. t.* au (gorddifanw) A being beyond vanishing; utter annihilation.

Gorddifenwawl, *a.* (gorddifanw) Annihilating.

Gorddifenwi, *v. a.* (gorddifanw) To delete utterly.

Gorddifwng, *s. m.* (difwng) Superior constancy. *a.* Very free from wavering; very stedfast.

> Ysym arglwydd gwrdd gorddifwng ei far
> Gorddwy heb ayw hydwng.
>
> To me there is an ardent lord, whose wrath is *ever constant*, who will not be silenced by the violence of any one. *Cynddelw, i Wenwynwyn.*
>
> Trydedd welygordd, trydar orddifwng,
> Iorwerthiawn, i farthaw eugur.
>
> The third family stock, a *constant* tumult, the men of Iorwerth, to chase the foe. *Cynddelw, i Wel. Powys.*

Gorddig, *a.* (dig) Excessively angry; very irritable. *Gwraig orddig*, an outrageous woman.

> Al y brenin Harri y pedwerydd yn orddig wrthynt, ac yn erthrymmwr creulawn arnynt.
>
> King Henry the Fourth became *greatly enraged* against them, and a cruel oppressor over them. *C. Edwards, Hanes y Ffydd.*

Gorddigawn, *s. m.* (digawn) A redundance. *a.* Redundant; overmuch.

Gorddigiad, *s. m.* (gorddig) A making extremely angry; excess of irritation.

Gorddigiaw, *v. a.* (gorddig) To irritate to excess.

Gorddigiawl, *a.* (gorddig) Extremely irritating.

Gorddigonedd, *s. m.* (gorddigawn) Superfluity.

Gorddigoni, *v. a.* (gorddigawn) To over-satiate.

Gorddigor, *s. m.—pl. t.* au (digor) Prevailing passion, habit, condition.

Gorddillyn, *a.* (dillyn) Over neat, or over prim.

Gorddillynawl, *a.* (gorddillyn) Tending to be over smart, or nice.

Gorddillyniad, *s. m.* (gorddillyn) A making extremely prim, a decking out to excess.

Gorddillynu, *v. a.* (gorddillyn) To deck out overmuch; to become extremely smart.

Gorddin, *s. m.—pl. t.* au (gordd) What impels, or drives forward; what is posterior, ultimate, or following; the rear.

> Lleucu glaer fy chwaer yn chwerthin'
> Ac ni chwerddi ei gwr hi rhag gorddin:
> Gorddin mawr a'm dawr, a'm daerawd,
> A hiraeth ymywaeth ymy nawd,
> Am Nest deg.
>
> The splendid Lleucu, my sister laughs; but her husband laughs not from the *impulse*: a great *impulse* makes me concerned, makes me involved, and longing, to my sorrow, is become habitual, for fair Nest. *Hywel ab Owain.*
>
> Mi ydwyf eur dderddif, ddifreidn yn nhrin;
> Mi ydwyf llew rhag llu, llach fy ngorddin.
>
> I am a golden law, fearless in the conflict; I am a lion before a host, with my *rear* scattered. *Gwalchmai.*

Gorddiniad, *s. m.* (gorddin) An impelling.

Gorddinâawl, *a.* (gorddin) Tending to impel.
Gorddinâu, *v. n.* (gorddin) To become impulsive.
Gorddinaw, *v. a.* (gorddin) To impel, to propel.

> Ac yn y diwedd llidiaw a oreg Geraint a gorddinaw ei farch a'i gyrchu.
>
> And at length Geraint became enraged, and *gave the reins* to his steed, and attacked him. *H. Geraint—Mabinogion.*

Gorddinawl, *a.* (gorddin) Impelling, impulsive.
Gorddiniad, *s. m.* (gorddin) An impelling.
Gorddïogi, *v. n.* (gorddïawg) To become very lazy.

> Ni gwna eryr gwyr gorddïogi;
> Am ddadl udd trwyadl yn ddedd trol.
>
> The eagle of men *will not become* inactive, in debates chief that is smart in the law of turning a point. *Ll. P. Moch, i D. ab Owain.*

Gorddirwy, *s. f.—pl. t.* on (dirwy) Excessive fine.
Gorddirwyad, *s. m.* (gorddirwy) A fining to excess.
Gorddirwyaw, *v. a.* (gorddirwy) To over-fine.
Gorddirwyawg, *a.* (gorddirwy) That is over-fined.
Gorddirwyawl, *a.* (gorddirwy) Tending to fine to excess.
Gorddisgyn, *s. m.—pl. t.* oedd (disgyn) An extreme descent; the pitch of a hill.
Gorddisgyn, *v. a.* (disgyn) To descend over, to descend extremely.
Gorddisgynawl, *a.* (gorddisgyn) Extremely steep
Gorddisgyniad, *s. m.—pl. t.* au (gorddisgyn) A descending extremely; a pitching over.
Gorddiwedd, *v. a.* (diw) To come up with.
Gorddiwedd, *s. m.—pl. t.* ion (gorddiwedd) The extreme end, the upper end.
Gorddiweddu, *v. a.* (gorddiwedd) To come upon, to overtake.

> Gorddiweddid hwyr fuan.
>
> A quick closing of the day *would be overtaken.* *Adage.*

Gorddiwes, *s. m.* (diwes) An overtaking.
Gorddiwes, *v. a.* (diwes) To overtake, to come up.
Gorddiwesawg, *a.* (gorddiwes) That is overtaken.
Gorddiwesawl, *a.* (gorddiwes) Apt to overtake.
Gorddiwesedig, *a.* (gorddiwes) Overtaken.
Gorddiwesiad, *s. m.* (gorddiwes) An overtaking.
Gorddiwesu, *v. a.* (gorddiwes) To overtake.
Gorddiwyd, *a.* (diwyd) Extremely diligent.
Gorddiwydiad, *s. m.* (gorddiwyd) A being extremely diligent.
Gorddiwydiaw, *v. a.* (gorddiwyd) To act over-diligently; to be over-diligent.
Gorddiwydiawl, *a.* (gorddiwyd) Tending to be over-diligent.
Gorddodawl, *a.* (dodawl) Being placed over.
Gorddodi, *v. a.* (dodi) To place over, or above.
Gorddodiad, *s. m.—pl. t.* au (dodiad) Superinstitution.
Gorddodo, *s. m.* (gordd—godo) A forcing forward under cover; a burrowing.

> Coll mab Collfrewi a gedwis hwch Dallwair a ai yn ngorddodo hyd yn mhenryn Awstin yn Nghernyw, ac yna ydd ai yn y môr.
>
> Coll the son of Collvrewi guarded the sow of Dallwair, which went by *penetrating under ground* as far as the promontory of Awstin in Cornwall, and then she went into the sea. *Trioedd.*

Gorddodyn, *s. m.* (gorddodo) That burrows. *Twrch gorddodyn*, a burrowing pig, a mole.
Gorddoeth, *a.* (doeth) Over-wise, over-sapient.
Gorddor, *s. f.—pl. t.* au (dôr) Hatch, or wicket.
Gorddrud, *a.* (drud) Bold to excess, over-bold, over-daring.

> Drud wr gwrdd gorddrud i las-fer
> Drud rwyf torf trwyf llanw yn aber.
>
> A daring man whose blue shaft is *over-bold*, a daring leader of the multitude who is the tumult of the flood in the conflux. *Cynddelw, i O. Cyfeiliawg.*

Gorddrws, *s. m.—pl.* gorddrysau (drws) A wicket.

Gorddrych, *s. m.—pl. t.* au (drych) Similitude.

> Rhudd ongyr angerdd alawy;
> Rhudd lwybr gwaed, gwae lwfr a'i gwelwy,
> Rhun afael afwy rhugl orddwy orddrud,
> Ar orddrych Afarwy.
>
> With a ruddy lance ardent for the slaughter; a ruddy path of blood, woe to the coward who hath seen him; like Rhun with a hard grasp well inured in the over-daring violence, after the *example* of Afarwy. *Cynddelw, i O. Cyfeiliawg.*

Gorddrychawl, *a.* (gorddrych) Overlooking.
Gorddrychiad, *s. m.—pl. t.* au (gorddrych) An overlooking; a supervising.
Gorddrychu, *v. a.* (gorddrych) To overlook.
Gorddryn, *a.* (gordd—rhyn) Terror that scares.

> Gwr gorddryn, golud gelorau.
>
> A man of *flight-impelling terror*, the wealth of biers. *Cynddelw.*

Gorddryniad, *s. m.* (gorddryn) A driving by fear.
Gorddryniaw, *v. a.* (gorddryn) To drive away through fear.
Gorddryniawl, *a.* (gorddryn) Fear-impelling.
Gorddu, *s. m.* (du) A blackish surface, a blackish tinge. *a.* Of a blackish tinge.

> Gorddu yw brig Iwerddon
> Gan fwg ceginau o Fon.
>
> *Tinged with black* are the heights of Ireland from the smoke of the kitchens of Anglesey. *L. G. Cothi.*

Gordduad, *s. m.* (gorddu) A blacking the surface.
Gordduaw, *v. a.* (gorddu) To blacken a surface.
Gordduawg, *a.* (gorddu) Having a black tinge.
Gordduawl, *a.* (gorddu) Apt to blacken over.
Gordduedig, *a.* (gorddu) Tinged with black.
Gorddwfn, *s. m.* (dwfn) A profundity; an abyss. *a.* Profound.

> O'r gorddwfn rhyddwfn rhoddais lef, erglyw
> Arglwydd, clyw fy adlais.
>
> From the vastly-deep *abyss* I sent a cry; listen O Lord, and hear my iterated voice. *H. D. ab Ifan.*

Gorddwfr, *s. m.—pl.* gorddyfroedd (dwfr) The extremity of the water; a water brink.

> Nid rhaid tra dilyn pell ofyn pwy;
> Py geidw y gorddwfr rhag pob gorddwy
> Llywelyn a'i ceidw, llew yn adwy;
> Llyw Gwynedd a'i medd hyd yn Mawddwy.
>
> It is needless to follow too far in being inquisitive who it is; who guards the *boundary water* against every violence; Llywelyn guards it, the lion in the breach; the governor who owns Gwynedd as far as Mawddwy. *Ll. P. Moch.*

Gorddwr, *s. m.—pl.* gorddwyr (gordd—gwr) An impeller; one who uses a beetle, or mallet.
Gorddwy, *s. m.—pl. t.* oedd (gordd) A pressing; an impulsion; oppression; violence. *Porth orddwy*, assistance to impel, or to oppress. *Bod yn borth orddwy*, to be an accessary. The men of Powys were exempt from the *Gorddwy* and the *Gorddin*, or the van and the rear. *Rhyd Orddwy*, the name of a place in Flintshire.
Gorddwyad, *s. m.—pl. t.* au (gorddwy) A pressing, or impelling; instigation; oppression.
Gorddwyar, *s. f.* (gorddwy—ar) Din of violence.

> Trist wyf, mura-glwyf mawr trin erwin aer-wawr;
> Rhoi glew llew dan llawr, gawr gorddwyar.
>
> I am sad with an ardent hidden wound, the severe activity of the gleam of slaughter; from putting the intrepid lion under the sod there is the cry of the *din of violence.* *G. ab M. ab Dafydd, i D. ab Goronwy.*

Gorddwyaw, *v. a.* (gorddwy) To press greatly; to impel, to oppress; to trespass; to curb.

> Diriad cad cedeirn orddwyaw.
>
> The mischievous one of conflict *oppressing* the mighty. *Llygad Gwr.*
>
> Gorddwyai Duw y gerdd dant.
>
> God *would oppress* the music of the string. *W. Lleyn.*

Gorddwyawg, *a.* (gorddwy) Impelled; vexed.
Gorddwyawl, *a.* (gorddwy) Apt to press greatly.
Gorddwyedig, *a.* (gorddwy) Impelled; impressed.

Gorddwyedigaeth, *s. m.—pl. t.* au (gorddwyedig) The act of impelling; oppression.

Gorddwyn, *s. m.—pl. t.* au (gordd) A beetle, a rammer.

Gorddwyrain, *s. m.* (dwyrain) Great exaltation.

Gorddwyrain, *v. a.* (dwyrain) To exalt highly.

Gorddwyraw, *v. a.* (dwyraw) To exalt highly.

Gorddwyrawl, *a.* (dwyrawl) Highly exalted.

Gorddwyre, *s. m.* (dwyre) A rising superior. *a.* Highly exalted.

> Gorddyar gorddlawg, gorlasawg gorlanr;
> A gwaly a gorddwyre pob rhai;
> Song dilew du merwydd y Mordai.
>
> Tumultuous the slothful one, brightly shines the blue of the enamelled covering; prolific and *highly exalted* are all, without gallantry the step by the side of the watery fronts of the sea habitations. *Taliesin.*

Gorddwyrëad, *s. m.* (gorddwyre) A rising over, or superior; a becoming highly exalted.

Gorddwyrëain, *v. a.* (gorddwyre) To rise over, or superior; to become greatly exalted.

Gorddwyrëawg, *a.* (gorddwyre) Having a tendency to rise over, or superior.

Gorddwyrëawl, *a.* (gorddwyre) Tending to rise over; rising over.

Gorddwys, *a.* (dwys) Extremely dense, or close.

Gorddwysaw, *v. a.* (gorddwys) To make very dense.

Gorddwysawl, *a.* (gorddwys) Tending to make extremely dense, or compact.

Gorddwysedig, *a.* (gorddwys) Greatly condensed.

Gorddwysedigaeth, *s. m.* (gorddwysedig) The act of condensing to excess.

Gorddwysiad, *s. m.—pl. t.* au (gorddwys) A greatly condensing; a condensation in the extreme.

Gorddwywr, *s. m.—pl.* gorddwywyr (gorddwy—gwr) One who impels, or drives, overmuch; an oppressor; a trespasser.

Gorddyar, *s. m.—pl. t.* oedd (dyar) A roaring noise, a roaring, a bellowing. *a.* Roaring.

> Ef mud a llafar;
> Ef yn orddyar.
>
> He is dumb and vocal; he is *blustering*. *Taliesin i'r Gwynt.*
>
> Hir-nos gorddyar mynydd.
>
> On the long night *boisterous* is the mountain. *Llywarch Hen.*
>
> Gorddyar adar gwlyb gro;
> Dail cwyddid, difryd difro;
> Ni wadaf, wyf claf heno.
>
> Clamorous are the birds, the beach is wet; the leaves let them fall, unconcerned the exile: I do not deny it, I am disordered this night. *Llywarch Hen.*

Gorddyarad, *s. m.* (gorddyar) A making a great din, or tumult.

Gorddyarawl, *a.* (gorddyar) Tending to raise a great din, or tumult.

Gorddyaru, *v. a.* (gorddyar) To make a great din.

> Yna y bu y llefain a'r gorddyaru, yna y bu newidiaw mwyach ddyrnodau o bob parth.
>
> And then there was the shouting and the *making a great tumult*; then there was the exchanging of frequent blows on every side. *Gr. ab Arthur.*

Gorddybenawl, *a.* (dyben) Primarily descending.

Gorddybendawd, *s. m.* (dybendawd) Superconsequence; an over descent.

Gorddyeithraw, *v. a.* (gorddyeithr) To estrange greatly; to become very strange.

Gorddyeithrawl, *a.* (gorddyeithr) Greatly estranged.

Gorddyeithriad, *s. m.* (gorddyeithr) A greatly estranging.

Gorddyeithr, *a.* (dyeithr) Over-strange, too strange.

Gorddyfn, *s. m.—pl.* gorddyfnoedd (dyfn) Custom, use, habit, fashion, manner.

Gorddyfnad, *s. m.* (gorddyfn) An habituating, familiarising, or accustoming.

Gorddyfnaid, *v. a.* (gorddyfn) To habituate, to familiarize, to inure, to practise; to become accustomed.

> Mwy poen yw cofio pryddfawrwch a chyfoeth gwedi i golli, noc oedd dyoddef anghenoctyd heb orddyfnaid amwyniant cyn no hyny.
>
> It is more painful to remember magnificence and power after it is lost, than it was to suffer necessity without *experiencing* indulgence before that. *Gr. ab Arthur.*
>
> Ymwng uchenaid a ddyoaid arnaf
> Yn ol fy ngorddyfnaid,
> Ni ad Duw dda i ddiriaid.
>
> An oppressive sigh bespeaks upon me, after making me *habituated*, God will not suffer good to the mischievous. *Llywarch Hen.*
>
> Gwyr gorddyfnaid trais.
>
> Men *familiarizing* violence. *O. Cyfeiliawg.*

Gorddyfnawl, *a.* (gorddyfn) Tending to habituate, familiarize, or inure.

Gorddyfnder, *s. m.—pl. t.* au (gorddwfn) Profundity, depth. *Gorddyfnder barn Duw*, the depth of the judgment of God. *Gorddyfnderau y ddaiar*, the deep places of the earth.

Gorddyfnedig, *a.* (gorddyfn) Familiarised.

> Digoned ei lys—
> A llif gwirodau,
> A llafar gerddau,
> A llef gan dannau,
> Gorddyfnedig.
>
> His court was replenished with an overflow of liquors, and joyous songs, and voice according with the strings *familiarised*. *D. ab Ieuan Ddu.*

Gorddyfnedigaeth, *s. m.—pl. t.* au (gorddyfnedig) The act of familiarizing.

Gorddyfnedigawl, *a.* (gorddyfnedig) Having a tendency to habituate.

Gorddyfnedigrwydd, *s. m.* (gorddyfnedig) The state of being habituated, or inured.

Gorddyfniad, *s. m.—pl.* gorddyfniaid (gorddyfn) One who habituates, or makes familiar; one that is accustomed, or inured.

> Breuder wrdd, orddrud orddyfniad cnudoedd,
> Uch cnawd meirw ar ystrad.
>
> An ardent breast-plate, the ever-daring *one that habituates* the packs of wolves to be over dead carcases upon the plain. *Cynddelw, i O. Cyfeiliawg.*
>
> Ymyni glew, a llew, a lleiddiad,
> Yn rhyfel orun orddyfniad.
>
> To me there is a hero, and a lion, and a slayer, *one familiarised* in the tumult of war. *Ein. ab Gwgon.*

Gorddyfnu, *v. a.* (gorddyfn) To accustom, or to habituate; to become accustomed.

> Ni char gwaith nis gorddyfno.
>
> He loves not work *that is not accustomed to it*. *Adage.*
>
> Yr aelwyd hon neus cladd hwch;
> Mwy gorddyfnasai elwch gwyr,
> Ac amgyrn cyfeddwch!
>
> This hearth will it not be turned up by the swine; more *congenial to it would have been* the clamour of men, and the circling horns of the banquet. *Llywarch Hen.*
>
> Oedd tew peleidr crau, cräynt eigfrain;
> Celanedd gorwedd gorddyfnasain.
>
> Thick were the gory shafts; the ravens called aloud, *they become habituated* with fallen carcases. *Ein. ab Gwgon.*

Gorddyfnus, *a.* (gorddyfn) Habituated, inured.

Gorddyfnwr, *s. m.—pl.* gorddyfnwyr (gorddyfn—gwr) One who familiarizes.

Gorddyfnydd, *s. m.—pl. t.* ion (gorddyfn) One who familiarises, or makes habitual.

Gorddyfod, *v. a.* (dyfod) To be upon, or over.

> Gorddyfwy gallu gallaei rhoi'n ddiddig;
> Gwn ymo ryüg gwin ymrodiad.
>
> *Upon me may be* the power to be able to give without discontent! I experience the excess of the wine of contentation. *G. ab Ieuan Hen.*

Gorddyfodawl, *a.* (gorddyfod) Tending to be over or upon; superadvenient.

Gorddyfodi, *v. a.* (gorddyfod) To be upon, to supervene.

Gorddyfodiad, *s. m.* (gorddyfod) A being upon, a supervention.
Gorddyg, *s. m.* (dyg) A bringing over, or upon.
Gorddygadwy, *a.* (gorddyg) That may be brought over, or upon.
Gorddygai, *s. m.—pl.* gorddygeion (gorddyg) An abductor.
Gorddygan, *s. f.—pl. t.* au (dygan) A singing upon, or in harmony.

Un dôn yw'r orddygan dau
Ag anadl y meginau.

Thy *harmony* is of the same tone as the wind of the bellows. *Mr. ab Rhys, i'r gwynt.*

Gorddyganawl, *a.* (gorddygan) Harmonious.
Gorddyganiad, *s. m.* (gorddygan) A harmonizing, a singing in harmony.
Gorddyganu, *v. a.* (gorddygan) To harmonize.
Gorddygawl, *a.* (gorddyg) Bringing over.
Gorddygiad, *s. m.—pl. t.* au (gorddyg) Abduction
Gorddygn, *a.* (dygn) Very severe, or hard.
Gorddygnawd, *s. m.* (gorddygn) Over-exertion.

Cefais saith, ac of gwaith gorddygnawd;
Cefais wyth yn nhal pwyth peth or gwawd yr gaint:
Yn da dannedd rhag tafawd.

I obtained seven, and it was work of *over-exertion*; I obtained eight in recompence for some of the praise that was sung; but the teeth are good against the tongue. *H. ab Owain.*

Gorddygnawl, *a.* (gorddygn) Greatly toiling.
Gorddygniad, *s. m.—pl. t.* au (gorddygn) A toiling to excess; extreme exertion.
Gorddygnu, *v. a.* (gorddygn) To toil overmuch.
Gorddygyd, *v. a.* (gorddyg) To superinduce.
Gorddylif, *s. m.—pl. t.* oedd (dylif) An overflow.
Gorddylifaw, *v. a.* (gorddylif) To overflow.
Gorddylifawl, *a.* (gorddylif) Overflowing.
Gorddylifiad, *s. m.—pl. t.* au (gorddylif) An overflowing; a defluxion.
Gorddyllwng, *s. m.* (dyllwng) A dropping over; a shedding over. *v. a.* To drop over.
Gorddyllyngawl, *a.* (gorddyllwng) Dropping, or shedding over.
Gorddyn, *s. m.—pl. t.* au (gordd) What impels, or keeps off; a boundary.
Gorddynëad, *s. m.—pl. t.* au (dynëad) A pouring, or letting out, an effusion; a shedding.
Gorddynëawl, *a.* (dynëawl) Effusive, shedding.
Gorddynëu, *v. a.* (dynëu) To pour out, to effuse; to shed; to cast. *Gorddynëu gwaed*, to let blood; *gorddynëu delw*, to cast an image.
Gorddyrchad, *s. m.* (dyrchad) An exalting over.
Gorddyrchafawl, *a.* (dyrchafawl) Tending to exalt over; over-elevating.
Gorddyrchafiad, *s. m.—pl. t.* au (dyrchafiad) An exalting over.
Gorddyrchafu, *v. a.* (dyrchafu) To raise over. *Gorddyrchafu llais*, to over-strain the voice.
Gorddysg, *s. m.* (dysg) Superior instruction.
Gorddysgwyl, *s. m.—pl. t.* ion (dysgwyl) Earnest expectation.
Gorddysgwyl, *v. a.* (dysgwyl) To expect much.
Gorddysgwylgar, *a.* (gorddysgwyl) Apt to look forward, or expect earnestly.
Gorddysgwyliad, *s. m.—pl. t.* au (gorddysgwyl) A looking forward, or expecting; expectancy, abeyance.
Gorddysgwyliaw, *v. a.* (gorddysgwyl) To expect earnestly.
Gorddywal, *a.* (dywal) Extremely fierce.
Gorddywalder, *s. m.* (gorddywal) Excess of fierceness, or ferocity.
Gorddywalu, *v. n.* (gorddywal) To become fierce to excess.

Goreb, *s. m.—pl. t.* ion (eb) A response.
Gorebawl, *a.* (goreb) Responsive, colloquial.
Gorebiad, *s. m.—pl. t.* au (goreb) A responding.
Gorebu, *v. a.* (goreb) To response, to answer.
Gorebr, *s. m.—pl. t.* od (goreb) A night-raven.
Gored, *s. m.—pl. t.* au (gor) A wear, a place for catching fish.
Goredawg, *a.* (gored) Having a wear.
Grediad, *s. m.* (gored) A setting a wear.
Goredu, *v. a.* (gored) To make or set a wear.
Goredwr, *s. m.—pl.* goredwyr (gored—gwr) One who looks after a wear.
Gorefras, *s. m.—pl. t.* au (efras) That is greatly nourished, or fattened. *a.* Greatly plumped up, or nourished.

Tri gorefras direidi: glythineb, ymladd, ac anwadalwch.

The three *encouragements* of mischief: voluptuousness, fighting, and inconstancy. *Trioedd.*

Gwr gorefras, gwas gwanwyn,
Gwawr gwanar, hygar hygwyn.

A man *full of vigour*, a languid youth, the dawn of preeminence, amiable, and much lamented. *Cynddelw, m. meibion Dwywg.*

Gorefrasawl, *a.* (gorefras) Tending to nourish greatly, of a very fattening quality.
Gorefrasu, *v. a.* (gorefras) To nourish greatly.
Goregni, *s. m.—pl. t.* on (egni) Over-exertion.
Goregnïad, *s. m.* (goregni) An over-exerting.
Goregnïaw, *v. a.* (goregni) To over-exert.
Goregnïawl, *a.* (goregni) Tending to over-exert.
Goregnïwr, *s. m.—pl.* goregnïwyr (goregni—gwr) One who over-exerts.
Goreigiad, *s. m.* (goraig) A teeming greatly; superfetation, superimpregnation.
Goreigiaw, *v. a.* (goraig) To teem abundantly; to superfetate.
Goreigiawl, *a.* (goraig) Teeming over.
Goreiliad, *s. m.—pl. t.* au (eiliad) Superstruction.
Goreiliaw, *v. a.* (eiliaw) To raise a superstructure, to superstruct; to respire.

Tri pheth nid ydynt yn gorphwys un amser mewn dyn: y galon yn gweithiaw; yr anadl yn goreiliaw; ac yr enaid yn meddwl.

Three things which are never at rest in a man the heart beating; the breath in *respiring*, and the thought in thinking. *Trioedd Doethineb.*

Goreiliawg, *a.* (eiliawg) Superstructive.
Goreilid, *s. m.—pl. t.* au (eilid) What is laid upon, a pressure; a grievance.

Bwrw oddiwrthyd oreilid y cnawd.

Cast from thee the *burden* of the flesh. *Buch. Beuno.*

Boed i'm rad——
Gwr y sy'n goddef y goreilid.

May I receive the grace of him that is bearing the burden. *Ph. Brydydd.*

Goreilidiad, *s. m.* (goreilid) A violent bearing down, a pressing heavily; a grieving.
Goreilidiaw, *v. a.* (goreilid) To bear upon heavily; to burden; to be a burden, or grievance; to vex, to trespass.

Cas fydd a oreilidio.

Odious will be *him that trespasses*. *Adage.*

Goreilidiawg, *a.* (goreilid) That is burdened.
Goreilidiwr, *s. m.—pl.* goreilidwyr (goreilid—gwr) One that is cumbersome, or vexing.

Tri mad-oreilidiwr Ynys Prydain: Rhita Gawr yn goreilid gormes ac anrhaith y brenhinoedd annosbarthus.

The three good *harrassers* of the Isle of Britain: one was Rhita the giant, harrassing the molestation and tyranny of unruly kings. *Trioedd.*

Goreilidus, *a.* (goreilid) Burdensome, cumbersome
Goreiliedig, *a.* (goreiliad) That is superstructed.
Goreiliwr, *s. m.—pl.* goreilwyr (eiliwr) One who raises a superstructure.

Goreilydd, *s. m.—pl. t.* ion (eilydd) One who makes supremely uniform, or harmonious.
Goreilliad, *s. m.* (eilliad) A shaving the top.
Goreilliaw, *v. a.* (eilliaw) To shave the top.
Goreilliawg, *a.* (eilliawg) Having the top shaved.
Goreiriad, *s. m.* (gorair) A forming an adverb.
Goreirian, *a.* (eirian) Supremely splendid.
Goreiriaw, *v. a.* (gorair) To form an adverb.
Goreiriawg, *a.* (gorair) Having an adverb.
Goreiriawl, *a.* (gorair) Adverbial, as an adverb.
Goreisiau, *s. m.* (eisiau) Extreme want.
Goreisiwed, *s. m.* (eisiwed) Extreme indigence.
Goreiste, *s. m.* (eiste) A sitting aloft; a presiding
Goreiste, *v. a.* (eiste) To sit aloft; to preside.

> Goreiste ar fryn aerfrwyn fy mryd,
> A hefyd ni'm cychwyn
> Byr fy nhaith, diffaith fy nhyddyn.
>
> Sitting high upon a hill, my mind is brooding upon war, and yet it doth not impel me onward. short is my journey, and my dwelling wretched! *Llywarch Hen.*

Goreistedd, *s. m.* (eistedd) A presiding.

> Hir oreistedd i ogan.
>
> May scandal have a long *presiding*. *Adage.*

Goreistedd, *v. a.* (eistedd) To sit over; to preside
Goreisteddawg, *a.* (goreistedd) Presiding.
Goreisteddawl, *a.* (goreistedd) Presiding.
Goreisteddgar, *a.* (goreistedd) Having an aptness, or fondness, to preside.

> Na fydd oreisteddgar yn ystafell.
>
> Be not *fond of presiding* in a room. *Adage.*

Goreisteddgarwch, *s. m.* (goreisteddgar) Fondness for presiding.
Goreisteddiad, *s. m.* (goreistedd) A presiding.
Goreisteddwr, *s. m.—pl.* goreisteddwyr (goreistedd—gwr) One who sits above; a president.
Goreisteddwraig, *s. f.—pl.* goreisteddwreigedd (goreistedd—gwraig) A presiding woman.

> Ni lwydd cell goreisteddwraig.
>
> The household of the *presiding woman* will not prosper. *Adage.*

Gorel, *s. m.—pl. t.* au (gor) An aperture.
Gorelawg, *a.* (gorel) Abounding with apertures.
Goreliad, *s. m.* (gorel) A making an opening.
Gorelu, *v. a.* (gorel) To make an aperture.
Gorelwain, *v. a.* (goralw) To cry out violently.
Gorentrych, *a.* (entrych) Placed above the firmament, super-celestial.
Gorenw, *s. m.—pl. t.* au (enw) A surname.

> Neu'r orfenwyd, yn orenw Morgant,
> Ar filwyr Prydain pedryddant
> Dy gynnygn!
>
> In the superior name of Morgant, were not the warriors of Britain, from all parts, obliged to recognize thee! *Ll. P. Moch, i Llywelyn.*

Gorenwad, *s. m.—pl. t.* au (gorenw) A surnaming; a giving a name of distinction.
Gorenwawd, *s. m.* (gorenw) Great renown.
Gorenwawg, *a.* (gorenw) Having a great name.
Gorenwawl, *a.* (gorenw) Of great renown.
Gorenwi, *v. a.* (gorenw) To surname.
Gorergyd, *s. m.—pl. t.* ion (ergyd) An overshot.
Gorergydiad, *s. m.—pl. t.* au (gorergyd) An overshooting.
Gorergydiaw, *v. a.* (gorergyd) To overshoot.
Gorergydiawl, *a.* (gorergyd) Overshooting.
Gorerlid, *s. m.—pl. t.* iau (erlid) an eager pursuit, a violent persecution.
Gorerlid, *v. a.* (erlid) To pursue eagerly.
Gorerlidiad, *s. m.—pl. t.* au (gorerlid) A pursuing violently; a violent persecution.
Gorerlidiaw, *v. a.* (gorerlid) To pursue vehemently; to persecute greatly.
Gorerlidiawg, *a.* (gorerlid) Eagerly pursuing.
Gorerlidiawl, *a.* (gorerlid) Eagerly pursuing.
Gorerlidiwr, *s. m.—pl.* gorerlidwyr (gorerlid—gwr) A violent persecutor.
Gorerlyn, *s. m.—pl. t.* au (erlyn) A following eagerly; to persecute greatly.
Gorerlyn, *v. a.* (erlyn) To follow eagerly.
Gorerlynawl, *a.* (gorerlyn) Eagerly following.
Gorerlyniad, *s. m.—pl. t.* au (gorerlyn) A following, or pursuing eagerly.
Gorerlynwr, *s. m.—pl.* gorerlynwyr (gorerlyn—gwr) An eager follower.
Gorerwin, *a.* (gerwin) Over-severe; very rough.
Gorerwinad, *s. m.* (gorerwin) A making very rough; a becoming very rough.
Gorerwinaw, *v. a.* (gorerwin) To make very rough or severe; to become very rough.
Gorerwinawl, *a.* (gorerwin) Tending to make rough; of a severe tendency.
Gores, *s. f.—pl. t.* au (es) What lies open, or waste. *a.* Open, uninclosed, waste.

> Tri pheth ni ddygant wr i gymmeriad mawr; ei wraig yn feistres, ei geffyl yn llymen, ac ei dir yn ores.
>
> Three things which will not bring a man to great reputation; his wife the mistress, his horse lean, and his land *lying open*. *Triads.*

Goresawg, *a.* (gores) Lying open, or waste.
Goresawl, *a.* (gores) Laying open, or waste.
Goresgyn, *s. m.—pl. t.* oedd (esgyn) An advance, coming upon, or entry upon; a subduing, a taking possession, or conquest; an entail; a lease, also called *dring*. *Cyrchu goresgyn*, to dock an entail.
Goresgyn, *v. a.* (esgyn) To super ascend; to come upon, to enter upon; to take possession; to overrun, to subdue, to conquer.

> Sarffes gadwynawg,
> Falch anhrugarawg,
> A'i hasgyll yn arfawg,
> O Germania;
> Hono a oresgyn
> Holl Loegr a Phrydain,
> O lan mor Llychlyn
> Hyd Safrina.
>
> A coiling serpent, merciless and proud, with armed wings from Germany shall come; that one shall conquer all of England and of Scotland, from the shore of the Lochlin sea to the Severn. *Myr. T. Phyrip.*

Goresgynadwy, *a.* (goresgyn) That may be come upon; that may be possessed; conquerable.
Goresgynaeth, *s. m.* (gor—esgyn) Possession. *Goresgynaeth gynnwynawl*, native primary occupancy.
Goresgynawl, *a.* (goresgyn) Tending to come upon, or to possess; possessed; prevailing, prevalent, conquering.

> Mae ffydd am bethau heb eu gweled; yn yr un modd y mae gobaith hefyd; canys—gobaith yr hyn a welir nid gobaith ydyw, am ein bod yn oresgynawl o hyny yn barod.
>
> Faith is with respect to things not seen; of the same nature is hope likewise; for hope as to what is seen is not hope, because we are *possessed* of that already. *Marchawg Crwydrad.*

Goresgynawr, *s. m.—pl.* goresgynorion (goresgyn) An occupant; a vanquisher.
Goresgynedig, *a.* (goresgyn) That is come upon, entered, or possessed; overcome, subdued.
Goresgynedigaeth, *s. m.—pl. t.* au (goresgynedig) Super-ascendancy; the act of coming upon; a subjugation.
Goresgynedigawl, *a.* (goresgynedig) Tending to come upon, or to possess; subjective.
Goresgyniad, *s. m.—pl. t.* au (goresgyn) A coming upon; a possessing; possession, occupancy, a subduing, or overrunning, a conquering.
Goresgyniadawl, *a.* (goresgyniad) Tending to give possession; tending to subjection.

Goresgyniadu, *v. a.* (goresgyniad) To cause to come upon; to give possession, to subjugate.

Goresgyniaeth, *s. m.—pl. t.* au (goresgyn) Superascendancy; the act of coming upon; possession; subjugation.

Goresgynu, *v. a.* (goresgyn) To come upon, to enter upon; to possess; to subdue.

Goresgynwr, *s. m.—pl.* goresgynwyr (goresgyn—gwr) One who comes upon; a possessor, or occupant; a vanquisher, a conqueror.

Goresgynydd, *s. m.—pl. t.* ion (goresgyn) One who ascends, or comes upon; a primary occupant; a vanquisher; a child in the fifth degree, or a grandchild's grandson.

Goresiad, *s. m.* (gores) A laying out, or open, an exposing; a divesting of fence.

Gorest, *s. f.—pl. t.* au (gores) What lays open or waste. *a.* Open, uninclosed, waste. *Tir gorest*, waste land.

Gorestawl, *a.* (gorest) Laying open, or waste.

Gorestiad, *s. m.* (gorest) A laying open, or waste.

Gorestu, *v. a.* (gorest) To lay open; to lie waste.

Gorestwng, *v. a.* (estwng) To yield homage.

> I'r tywysawg hyny mi orestyngais; yntau, yr un modd, a'm mawrhodd innau.
>
> To that Prince *I submitted;* and he, in the same manner, aggrandized me likewise. *Marchawg Crwydrad.*

Gorestyn, *s. m.* (estyn) Extension over.

Gorestyn, *v. a.* (estyn) To extend over; to extend in continuity.

Gorestynawl, *a.* (gorestyn) Extending over.

Gorestynedig, *a.* (gorestyn) Extended over.

Gorestyniad, *s. m.—pl. t.* au (gorestyn) A stretching, or extending over.

Gorestyngad, *s. m.* (gorestwng) A yielding homage; humiliation, submission.

Gorestyngawl, *a.* (gorestwng) Humiliating.

Gorestyngder, *s. m.* (gorestwng) Condescension.

Gorestyngedig, *a.* (gorestwng) Become subject.

Gorestyngedigaeth, *s. m.—pl. t.* au (gorestwng) Humiliation, submission, condescension.

Gorestyngiad, *s. m.—pl.* gorestyngiaid (gorestwng) One who submits; a subject.

> Cefais wybod mai efe oedd Lucifer, tad yr halogrwydd—y bydolion sydd yn ei wasanaethu megys ei orestyngiaid.
>
> I received information that he was Lucifer, the father of pollution; the worldlings serve him as his *subjects.* *Marchawg Crwydrad.*

Gorestyngrwydd, *s. m.* (gorestwng) A state of subjection, humility.

Gorestyngu, *v. a.* (gorestwng) To submit.

Gorestyngwr, *s. m.—pl.* gorestyngwyr (gorestwng—gwr) One who yields homage or submits.

Gorestyngydd, *s. m.—pl. t.* ion (gorestwng) One who does homage, one who submits.

Goresu, *v. a.* (gores) To lay open; to lie waste.

Goresymiad, *s. m.* (rhesymiad) A partly arguing; a talking familiarly.

Goresymu, *v. a.* (rhesymu) To talk familiarly.

> Gwrndeyrn Prydain priodawr udd,
> Goresymed glyw a'i glywed yno,
> Rhag gorwyr Iago, gwyar drabludd.
>
> The blest lord of Britain, a proprietor supreme, *let it be mentioned* by a chief of his hearing him there, in the presence of the great grandson of Iago, that toils in blood. *Gwalchmai.*

Gorethboli, *v. a.* (gorethawl) To select nicely.

Gorethboliad, *s. m.* (gorethawl) A selecting nicely

Goreu, *s. m.—pl. t.* on (gor) A superior; what is best; excerption. *a.* Best. *adv.* Best, or in the highest degree of goodness. *O'r goreu*, of the best, or very well; *goreu iti beidio*, thou hadst best be quiet.

> Dirmad a gabla ei oreu.
>
> The worthless contemns his *better.* *Adage.*
>
> A fu goreu i ryfel goreu fydd i heddwch.
>
> What is *best* for war, will be the *best* for peace. *Adage*
>
> Cynnwys a gaffaf
> O'r parth goreuaf.
>
> I shall obtain reception in the *choicest* place. *Taliesin.*

Gorëu, *v. a.* (gore) To make, to create.

> Iawn yw moli——
> Y gwr a'n goreu ac a'n gweryd.
>
> It is right to praise him that did *form* us, and that will deliver us. *Elidr Sais.*

Goreuad, *s. m.—pl. t.* on (goreu) A bettering; surpassing.

Goreuaeth, *s. m.—pl. t.* au (goreu) Optimity.

Goreuant, *s. m.—pl.* goreuannau (goreu) A superior state; optimacy.

Goreuaw, *v. a.* (goreu) To better; to become better; to surpass.

Goreuawl, *a.* (goreu) Bettering; surpassing.

Goreugwr, *s. m.—pl.* goreugwyr (goreu—gwr) An optimate, or select man.

Goreurad, *s. m.* (eurad) A gilding with gold.

Goreuraid, *a.* (euraid) Done over with gold; gilt.

Goreuraw, *v. a.* (euraw) To cover over with gold; to gild.

Goreurawg, *a.* (eurawg) That is gilt with gold.

> Hael farchawg oreurawg wrfydd——
> Oedd ef.
>
> A generous knight of *golden* stem, was he. *R. Penurth.*

Goreurawl, *a.* (eurawl) Covered with gold.

Goreuredig, *a.* (euredig) Gilt with gold.

Goreurin, *a.* (eurin) Overlaid with gold, gilt.

Goreurwr, *s. m.—pl.* goreurwyr (eurwr) One who covers with gold; a gilder.

Goreurydd, *s. m.—pl. t.* ion (eurydd) A gilder.

Goreuryn, *s. m.—pl. t.* au (euryn) What is covered with gold; what is gilt.

Gorew, *s. m.* (rhew) A slight frost: thin ice.

Gorewi, *v. a.* (gorew) To freeze slightly.

> Mae tew glog hyd teiau'r glyn; gwe'r awyr
> Yn gorewi'r dyfryn.
>
> There is a thick mantle over the houses of the vale; the web of the sky *half-freezing* the globe. *H. Morys.*

Gorewlyd, *a.* (gorew) Somewhat frosty.

Gorewydd, *s. m.* (rhewydd) Bodily vigour.

> Diaspad mererid a'm gorfydd heno,
> Ac ni'm hawdd gorewydd:
> Gnawd gwedi traha tramgwydd.
>
> The tumult of the ocean oppresses me to night, but gives me no *vigour* it is usual for miscarriage to follow a great attempt. *Taliesin.*
>
> Neud euwawg farchawg feirch gorewydd!
>
> Is not he a distinguished knight with *vigorous* steeds! *Llygad Gwr.*

Gorewyddawl, *a.* (gorewydd) Invigorative.

Gorewyddiad, *s. m.* (gorewydd) An invigorating.

Gorewyddu, *v. a.* (gorewydd) To invigorate.

Gorewyn, *s. m.—pl. t.* oedd (ewyn) A high, or covering foam. *a.* High-foaming. *Medd gorewyn*, high-mantling mead.

Gorewynawd, *s. m.* (gorewyn) A foaming over.

Gorewynawg, *a.* (gorewyn) Covered with foam.

> Toresid gormes yn llyngesawg,
> Gwedi tonau gwyrdd gorewynawg.
>
> The invasion was broken in naval array, after the *high-foaming* green waves. *Meilir.*

Gorewynawl, *a.* (gorewyn) Tending to foam over

Gorewyniad, *s. m.* (gorewyn) A foaming over.

Gorewynu, *v. a.* (gorewyn) To foam over.

Gorfaidd, *s. m.* (baidd) A great venture.

Gorfain, *a.* (main) Extremely fine, or slender.

Gorfainc, *s. f.—pl.* gorfeinciau (mainc) A superior seat, or throne.

Gorfaint, *s. m.* (maint) An oversize.

Gorfaith, *a.* (maith) Extremely tedious;

Gorfalch, *a.* (balch) Highly towering; very proud, or stately; supercilious.
Gorfan, *a.* (ban) Extremely lofty, or high.
Gorfanadl, *s. m.* (banadl) Broom-rape.
Gorfanal, *s. m.* (banal) The broom-rape.
Gorfanc, *s. m.—pl. t.* ou (gor—banc) A stage; a cut of hay, in the rick.
Gorfaniad, *s. m.* (gorfan) A raising very lofty.
Gorfanson, *s. m.* (manson) A muttering.
Gorfanson, *v. a.* (manson) To mutter extremely.
Gorfant, *s. m.—pl. t.* au (mant) Upper mandible.
Gorfantawl, *s. m.* (mantawl) Over-balance, preponderance.
Gorfantoledig, *a.* (gorfantawl) Over-balanced.
Gorfantoli, *v. a.* (gorfantawl) To over-balance, to overpoise, to outweigh.
Gorfantoliad, *s. m.—pl. t.* au (gorfantawl) An over-balancing.
Gorfanu, *v. a.* (gorfan) To make very lofty.
Gorfanwl, *a.* (manwl) Extremely accurate.
Gorfanyliad, *s. m.* (gorfanwl) A scrutinizing over-much; a being over-nice.
Gorfanylu, *v. a.* (gorfanwl) To over-scrutinize.
Gorfaran, *s. m.* (baran) That spreads out extremely; that presents a vast front. *a.* Of a grand front; magnificent.

> Nead garw hin— —
> Pan yw gorfaran twrf tonau wrth lan.
>
> *Is not the weather rough when the tumult of the waves is of magnificent front against the shore.* — Taliesin.

Gorfaranawl, *a.* (gorfaran) Having a magnificent appearance.
Gorfaraniad, *s. m.* (gorfaran) A presenting a grand aspect.
Gorfaranu, *v. n.* (gorfaran) To appear extremely grand; to display a grand front.
Gorfas, *a.* (bas) Extremely shallow, or flat.
Gorfasiad, *s. m.* (gorfas) A making very shallow.
Gorfasu, *v. a.* (gorfas) To make very shallow; to become too shallow.
Gorfawdd, *s. m.* (bawdd) A great immersion.
Gorfawl, *s. f.* (mawl) Extreme praise.
Gorfawr, *a.* (mawr) Very great, immense.
Gorfawrâad, *s. m.* (gorfawr) A magnifying extremely.
Gorfawrâawl, *a.* (gorfawr) Tending to magnify greatly.
Gorfawrau, *v. a.* (gorfawr) To magnify much.
Gorfawredd, *s. m.* (gorfawr) Vast magnificence, extreme greatness.
Gorfeddiad, *s. m.* (meddiad) A possessing overmuch
Gorfeddiannawl, *a.* (gorfeddiant) Tending to possess overmuch.
Gorfeddianniad, *s. m.* (gorfeddiant) A possessing overmuch.
Gorfeddiannu, *v. a* (gorfeddiant) To over-possess
Gorfeddiant, *s. m.—pl.* gorfeddiannau (meddiant) Excess of possession.
Gorfeddu, *v. a* (meddu) To possess most securely; to possess overmuch.

> Na ba drwg newid a'm gorfeddo.
>
> *I pray that no bad wish may get too sure hold of me.* — Meilyr ab Gwalchmai.

Gorfeddw, *a.* (meddw) Extremely intoxicated.
Gorfeddwi, *v.* (gorfeddw) To intoxicate to excess
Gorfeiddiad, *s. m.* (gorfaidd) An over-daring.
Gorfeiddiaw, *v. a.* (gorfaidd) To over-dare.
Gorfeiddiawl, *a.* (gorfaidd) Over-daring.
Gorfeithder, *s. m.* (gorfaith) Extreme tediousness
Gorfeithdra, *s. m.* (gorfaith) Over tediousness.
Gorfeithedd, *s. m.* (gorfaith) Extreme tedium.
Gorfeithiad, *s. m.* (gorfaith) A rendering extremely tedious; a becoming very long.
Gorfeithiaw, *v. a.* (gorfaith) To make extremely tedious; to become very long.
Gorfeithiawl, *a.* (gorfaith) Over-tedious.
Gorfelyn, *s. m.* (melyn) Yellow exterior, yellow tip. *a.* Having a yellow extremity; tipped with yellow; very yellow. *Gorfelyn eu hengyr*, yellow-tipped their spears.

> Gorwyn blaen banadl, gynnadl serchawg;
> Gorfelyn cangau bagwyawg;
> Bas rhyd; gnawd hyfryd yn hunawg.
>
> *Glittering the tops of the broom, the lover's place of assignation: of splendid yellow the clustered branches; shallow the ford; contented has easy sleep.* — Llywarch Hen.

Gorfelynawg, *a.* (gorfelyn) Having a yellow extremity, or surface; of very bright yellow.
Gorfelyniad, *s. m.* (gorfelyn) A tipping with yellow; a making of very bright yellow.
Gorfelynu, *v. a.* (gorfelyn) To tip with yellow; to make of very bright yellow.
Goferw, *s. m.* (berw) What is thrown up by boiling; froth, or scum; the refuse of metal in melting of it.

> Cyd bwyf eiddil a bychan,
> Ar lan gorferw mor dylan,
> Mi a wnaf, yn nydd cyfrdan,
> Bu well no thrichan morau.
>
> *Though I may be feeble and small, on the shore of foam of the overwhelming sea, I shall, in the day of trial, yield thee more good than three hundred of the finny tribe.* — Taliesin.

Gorferwad, *s. m.* (gorferw) A throwing up by boiling; ebullition; an over-boiling.
Gorferwawl, *a.* (gorferw) Over-boiling; tending to throw up by boiling.
Gorferwedig, *a.* (gorferw) That is over-boiled; that is thrown up by boiling.
Gorferwi, *v. a.* (gorferw) To over-boil; to boil over; to throw up a scum; to bubble up.
Gorfeth, *s. m.* (meth) An extreme failing.
Gorfethedig, *a.* (gorfeth) Greatly enfeebled.
Gorfethiad, *s. m.* (gorfeth) A failing greatly; a being greatly enfeebled.
Gorfethiannawl, *a.* (gorfethiant) Tending to enfeeble excessively.
Gorfethianniad, *s. m.* (gorfethiant) An enfeebling to excess; a being greatly enfeebled.
Gorfethiannu, *v. a.* (gorfethiant) To enfeeble excessively; to become greatly enfeebled.
Gorfethiant, *s. m.* (gorfeth) Extreme debility.
Gorfethiantrwydd, *s. m.* (gorfethiant) Extreme feebleness; or failure.
Gorfin, *s. m.—pl. t.* ion (min) The outer edge; extreme edge.
Gorfiniad, *s. m.* (gorfin) A sharpening extremely.
Gorfiniaw, *v. a.* (gorfin) To make an extreme edge; to sharpen extremely.
Gorfiniawl, *a.* (gorfin) On the extreme edge.
Gorflawdd, *s. f.* (blawdd) Extreme uproar.
Gorflin, *a.* (blin) Extremely tiresome.
Gorfliniaw, *v. a.* (gorflin) To tire extremely, to overfatigue.
Gorflinder, *s. m.—pl. t.* au (gorflin) Over-fatigue.
Gorflinedig, *a.* (gorflin) Over-tired.
Gorfloddest, *s. f.—pl. t.* au (gorflawdd) A riotous festivity.
Gorfloddestgar, *a.* (gorfloddest) Apt to be very riotous, fond of loose festivity.
Gorfloddestiad, *s. m.* (gorfloddest) A raising a great riot; a becoming very riotous.
Gorfloddestu, *v. a.* (gorfloddest) To act very riotously, to be very uproarious.

Gorfloddi, *v. a.* (gorflawdd) To make extreme uprear; to make an uproar.

> Am orwyr Bleddyut
> 'Ym gorflowdd llidgyat.

> For the great grandson of Bleddyut indignation *outrages me in the extreme.* *Gwalchmai.*

Gorfloddiad, *s. m.—pl. t.* au (gorflawdd) A making an extreme uproar.

> O gadwyd Prydain rhag pryder gorwlad,
> Gorfloddiad, gorfyngder,
> Boed llewenydd, boed lloafer,
> Boed cyfoddiaf nef I'm ner.

> From securing Britain from the dread of a neighbouring country, dire-uproar and excess of discontent, let there be joy, let there be glory, let heaven be the portion of my sovereign! *Cynddelw, m. O. Gwynedd.*

Gorfloedd, *s. f.—pl. t.* au (bloedd) An outcry.

Gorfloeddawg, *a.* (gorfloedd) That makes an extreme outcry.

> Pan ddel ei rhydd
> Gorfloeddawg elfydd;
> Mawyd yn dragywydd;
> Yn tydi a fedydd
> Dyllf dewaint a dydd.

> When his powers come, *extremely noisy* the elements; for ever will thy impulse be; thou dost pervade the tide of darkness and of day. *Taliesin, I'r gwynt.*

Gorfloeddgar, *a.* (gorfloedd) Apt to make an extreme outcry.

Gorfloeddiad, *s. m.* (gorfloedd) A raising an extreme outcry.

Gorfloeddiaw, *v. a.* (gorfloedd) To cry out extremely; to make a great outcry.

Gorfloeddiwr, *s. m.—pl.* gorfloeddwyr (gorfloedd—gwr) One who makes a great outcry.

Gorflwch, *s. m.—pl.* gorflychau (blwch) Goblet.

> Gnawd i'th lys lyswledd gyangred,
> Gorflychau gan falch gylyfed.

> Familiar to thy hall the courtly resort, *goblets* with magnificent conviviality. *Llygad Gwr, i R. ab Madawg.*

Gorflwng, *a.* (blwng) Very sullen, or morose.

Gorflychaid, *s. m.—pl.* gorflycheidiau (gorflwch) A goblet-full, a cup-full.

Gorflychiad, *s. m.* (gorflwch) A filling a cup.

Gorflychu, *v. a.* (gorflwch) To fill a goblet.

Gorflyngder, *s. m.—pl. t.* au (gorflwng) Moroseness.

Gorflyngiad, *s. m.* (gorflwng) A rendering sullen, or sour; a becoming cross; exasperation.

Gorflyngu, *v. a.* (gorflwng) To make sour; to exasperate; to become morose.

Gorfod, *s. m.—pl. t.* au (gor—bod) The state which impels obligation, or submission; obligation, impulsion, necessity; cogency; the upper hand, or mastery; victory. *Bod a gorfod*, being and impulse.

> Tri sail gwybodaeth: pwyll, anianawdd a gorfod; neu Pwyll, anian, a thyst.

> The three foundations of knowledge: reason, peculiar quality, and *impulse;* or sense, nature, and evidence. *Barddas.*

Gorfod, *v. a.* (gor—bod) To get superior, or above; to cause obligation, or submission; to oblige, or necessitate; to vanquish, or to overcome;—to be fain, obliged, or forced to do, to be impelled;—to answer for, to warrant, to satisfy.—*Gorfod ciliaw*, to be obliged to retreat; *gorfu arno wadu*, he was obliged to deny; *gorfod gweithred*, to make satisfaction for an act; *gorfod anifel rhag clefyd*, to warrant a beast free from disease.

> Llafur a orfydd ar bob peth.

> Labour *will get the better* over every thing. *Adage.*

> Ni ad annoeth ei orfod.

> The unwise will not suffer himself *to be convinced.* *Adage.*

> Gwedi gorfod o'r Prydeiniaid, ffo a wnaelynt y Llychlynwyr—i eu llongau.

> After *overcoming* of the Britons, the men of Llochlin fled to their ships. *Gr. ab Arthur.*

Gorfodadwy, *a.* (gorfod) That may be overcome, surmountable; vincible; that may be obliged, or compelled.

Gorfodaeth, *s. m.—pl. t.* au (gorfod) The act of overcoming, or compelling; a vanquishing; victory, conquest; a making obligatory.

Gorfodai, *s. c.—pl.* gorfodeion (gorfod) A surmounter; a victor; an obligeor.

Gorfodawg, *a.* (gorfod) Having an obligation; able to constrain. *s. c.—pl.* gorfodogion. One who overcomes; an obligee; an umpire; a constrainant. *Mach gorfodawg*, a surety who answers for another's appearance.

> Y neb a fo gorfodawg dros arall, oni ellir ei ddwyn wrth gyfraith, dygwydded y gorfodawg yn ngbyfraith y neb ydd aeth efe drosto yn ngorfodogaeth.

> Any one who is an *obligee* for another, if he cannot bring him according to law, let the *obligee* to be cast in the action of him for whom he shall have entered into an obligation. *Welsh Laws.*

Gorfodawl, *a.* (gorfod) Tending to surmount, or to overcome; predominant; compulsive.

Gorfod-dref, *s. f.—pl. t.* i (gorfod—tref) The thirteenth part of a manor; being a supernumerary township.

> Gorfod-dref yw rhandiredd a gynullir o drefi uchelwyr a gyfarfyddont eu terfynau a therfyn y dref y bo y ddadl ynddi.

> The *hamlet of wardenship* consists of portions of land joined together out of the townships of freeholders, whose boundaries meet the boundary of the township wherein the cause of dispute lies. *Welsh Laws.*

Gorfod-dreth, *s. f.—pl. t.* i (gorfod—treth) A tax of compulsion, a tax levied by an enemy.

Gorfodedig, *a.* (gorfod) Surmounted, overcome.

Gorfodedigaeth, *s. m.—pl. t.* au (gorfodedig) The act of overcoming.

Gorfodedd, *s. m.* (gorfod) Predominancy.

Gorfodiad, *s. m.* (gorfod) An overcoming.

Gorfodocâad, *s. m.* (gorfodawg) A rendering obligatory, a putting under a controul.

Gorfodocâawl, *a.* (gorfodawg) Tending to render, or become obligatory.

Gorfodocâu, *v. a.* (gorfodawg) To put under obligation; to become cognizable.

Gorfodogaeth, *s. m.—pl. t.* au (gorfodawg) The act of taking upon one's self; an obligation, or injunction; a recognizance; a wardenship, management, or custody; the party, or what is under guarantee; the office of a surety, or guardian; the act, or office of arbitration; constrainance.

> Pwy bynag a gymero arall ar ei orfodogaeth, dygwydded efe yn mhob cerydd o'r a oedd ar y dyn a gymeres ato.

> Whosoever that shall take another upon his *recognizance*, let him fall in every condemnation, which was due to the person whom he attached to himself. *Welsh Laws.*

Gorfodogawl, *a.* (gorfodawg) Tending to render obligatory; under obligation.

Gorfodogi, *v. n.* (gorfodawg) To lay under an injunction, or obligation; to render obligatory; to put under management, or wardship.

> Gorfodocer y tir hyd y dydd a'r dydd.

> The land, *let it be put under safeguard* until a certain day. *Statute of Rhuddlan.*

Gorfodogiad, *s. m.* (gorfodawg) A rendering obligatory; a becoming liable to controul; a becoming obliged.

Gorfodogwr, *s. m.—pl.* gorfodogwyr (gorfodawg—gwr) One under obligation, or recognizance.

Gorfoddawg, *a.* (boddawg) Above being pleased, or contented; bad tempered, surly.

Gorfoledd, *s. m.—pl. t.* au (gorfawl) Great rejoicing; triumph; gladness.
Gorfoleddawg, *a.* (gorfoledd) Having triumph.
Gorfoleddiad, *s. m.* (gorfoledd) A triumphing.
Gorfoleddiant, *s. m.* (gorfoledd) A jubilation.
Gorfoleddu, *v. n.* (gorfoledd) To give great praise; to rejoice greatly; to triumph.
Gorfoleddus, *a.* (gorfoledd) Full of praise and gladness, triumphant.
Gorfoleddwr, *s. m.—pl.* gorfoleddwyr (gorfoledd—gwr) One who rejoices, or triumphs.
Gorfoli, *v. a.* (gorfawl) To praise to excess; to praise greatly, to compliment highly; to flatter.

> Fraidd entwng ardwng a orfolir;
> Meuvedr na'm dawel ni'm didolir.
>
> *The miles subjection of the herd will be flattered to excess, [illegible] neglect me not, I will not be neglected.* O. Cyfeiliawg.

Gorfoliannawl, *a.* (gorfoliant) Extremely commending, adulatory.
Gorfolianniad, *s. m.* (gorfoliant) A commending extremely; adulation.
Gorfoliannu, *v. a.* (gorfoliant) To commend extremely; to praise over-much.
Gorfoliannus, *a.* (gorfoliant) Extremely commending; adulatory.
Gorfoliant, *s. m.* (gorfawl) Excess of praise.
Gorfor, *a.* (mor) Upon the sea, that is on the sea.

> A pan font gorforion meibion Eidwng,
> Y bydd bore taer rhng Caer Ballawg.
>
> And when the sons of Eidwng shall be *travellers upon the sea*, there will be a severe morning before the castle of Ballawg. *Merddin, Hoianau.*

Gorforiaw, *v. a.* (gorfor) To go upon the sea.
Gorfras, *a.* (bras) Over-bulky, over-gross; over-fat; over-rank; too luxuriant.
Gorfrasder, *s. m.* (gorfras) Excess of bulkiness, excess of fatness, or rankness.
Gorfrasedd, *s. m.* (gorfras) Excess of bulkiness.
Gorfraint, *s. m.—pl.* gorfreintiau (braint) Superior privilege; prerogative.
Gorfrau, *a.* (brau) Extremely fragile, or brittle.
Gorfraw, *s. m* (braw) Extreme panic.
Gorfrawu, *v. a.* (gorfraw) To terrify extremely.
Gorfrawwch, *s. m.* (gorfraw) Extreme panic.
Gorfrawychawl, *a* (gorfrawwch) Extremely terrified, or intimidated.
Gorfrawychiad, *s. m.* (gorfrawwch) A terrifying or scaring extremely.
Gorfrawychu, *v. a.* (gorfrawwch) To terrify extremely; to be greatly scared.
Gorfreinniad, *s. m.* (gorfraint) A conferring a prerogative, or privilege.
Gorfreinniaw, *v. a.* (gorfraint) To confer superior privilege, or prerogative.
Gorfreinniawl, *a.* (gorfraint) Greatly privileged.
Gorfreuad, *s. m.* (gorfrau) A rendering very brittle; a becoming very fragile.
Gorfreuaw, *v. a.* (gorfrau) To make brittle in the extreme, to become very brittle.
Gorfreuawl, *a.* (gorfrau) Extremely fragile.
Gorfreuolder, *s. m.* (gorfreuawl) Over-brittleness
Gorfreuoledd, *s. m.* (gorfreuawl) Extreme brittleness, or fragility.
Gorfreuoli, *v. a.* (gorfreuawl) To make extremely brittle, or fragile.
Gorfrith, *a.* (brith) Variegated on the surface.
Gorfrithiaw, *v. a.* (gorfrith) To over variegate; to variegate over.
Gorfrithawl, *a.* (gorfrith) Apt to variegate over.
Gorfrithder, *s. m.* (gorfrith) Variegation of the surface.
Gorfrithedd, *s. m.* (gorfrith) Variegation of the surface.
Gorfrithiad, *s. m.* (gorfrith) An over-variegating.
Gorfrwd, *a.* (brwd) Extremely ardent or hot.
Gorfrwth, *s. m.—pl.* gorfrythau (brwth) A great tumult or uproar.
Gorfrwysg, *a.* (brwysg) Extremely unwieldy.
Gorfrwysgaw, *v. a.* (gorfrwysg) To make extremely unwieldy; to become very unwieldy.
Gorfrwysgawl, *a.* (gorfrwysg) Tending to become very unwieldy.
Gorfrwysgedd, *s. m.* (gorfrwysg) Unwieldiness in the extreme.
Gorfrwysgiad, *s. m.* (gorfrwysg) A making, or becoming extremely unwieldy.
Gorfryd, *s. m.—pl. t.* au (bryd) A superior mind,
Gorfrydawl, *a.* (gorfryd) Of a superior mind.
Gorfrydedd, *s. m.* (gorfryd) Magnanimity.
Gorfrydiad, *s. m.* (gorfrwd) A rendering extremely hot, a heating intensely; inflammation
Gorfrydiannawl, *a.* (gorfrydiant) Extremely inflammative.
Gorfrydiannu, *v. a.* (gorfrydiant) To heat, or inflame intensely; to be greatly inflamed.
Gorfrydiant, *s. m.* (gorfrwd) Extreme heat; the height of inflammation; a paroxism.
Gorfrydiaw, *v. a.* (gorfrwd) To overheat; to inflame greatly; to become much inflamed.
Gorfrydiawl, *a.* (gorfrwd) Overheating.
Gorfrydu, *v. a.* (gorfryd) To endow with magnanimity; to become high-minded.
Gorfrys, *s. m.* (brys) Extreme haste, or hurry.
Gorfrysiad, *s. m.* (gorfrys) A hurrying much.
Gorfrysiaw, *v. a.* (gorfrys) To over-hasten.
Gorfrysiawl, *a.* (gorfrys) Over-hastening.
Gorfrythawl, *a.* (gorfrwth) Outrageous.
Gorfrythiad, *s. m.* (gorfrwth) A making a great tumult; a becoming outrageous.
Gorfrythu, *v. a.* (gorfrwth) To act very tumultuously; to become outrageous.
Gorfuan, *a.* (buan) Overquick; oversoon.
Gorfuander, *s. m.* (gorfuan) Overquickness.
Gorfuchedd, *s. f.—pl. t.* au (buchedd) Superior life; survivance.
Gorfucheddawl, *a.* (gorfuchedd) An outliving.
Gorfucheddiaeth, *s m.* (gorfuchedd) Survivorship.
Gorfucheddu, *v. a.* (gorfuchedd) To survive, to overlive, to outlive.
Gorfucheddwr, *s. m.—pl.* gorfucheddwyr (gorfuchedd—gwr) An outliver, a survivor.
Gorfudd, *s. f.—pl. t.* ion (budd) Superior benefit.
Gorfuddiad, *s. m.* (gorfudd) A rendering a superior advantage.
Gorfuddiaw, *v. a.* (gorfudd) To afford superior advantage, or gain.
Gorfuddiawl, *a.* (gorfudd) Very advantageous.
Gorfurth, *s. m.* (burth) A very violent thrust.
Gorfurthi, *s. m.* (gorfurth) Extreme impulsion.

> Cadr breyngynt orfynt orfurthi Tewdwr;
> Cadr ysgor arfor arfod yddi.
>
> *Mightily then would oppose the ambition of the most zealous assault of Tewdwr; mighty the maritime bulwark when an attack is made upon her.* Llywarch Fardd, i Dyngu.

Gorfurthiad, *s. m.* (gorfurth) A thrusting very violently; a chasing extremely.
Gorfurthiaw, *v. a.* (gorfurth) To repel extremely; to drive, or chase, very violently.
Gorfurthiawl, *a.* (gorfurth) Very repellant.
Gorfyd, *s. m. -pl. t.* oedd (byd) Superior world; a superior state, or existence.
Gorfydiad, *s. m.* (gorfyd) A living in a superior state or world.

Gorfydiaw, *v. a.* (gorfyd) To live in a superior world, or state.
Gorfydiawg, *a.* (gorfyd) Of a superior state of existence.

> Un gorfydiawg
> Ammhrugarawg
> Ef a orfydd.
>
> The unmerciful one *of a higher state* he will vanquish. *Taliesin.*

Gorfyg, *s. f.—pl. t.* ion (myg) What spreads round; what is uppermost by its lightness.
Gorfygadwy, *a.* (gorfyg) Superable.
Gorfygawl, *a.* (gorfyg) Tending to overcome.
Gorfyged, *s. f.—pl. t.* au (gorfyg) Supreme glory, or honour.
Gorfygedawl, *a.* (gorfyged) Supremely glorious.
Gorfygedu, *v. a.* (gorfyged) To render supremely glorious, solemn, or grand.
Gorfygiad, *s. m.* (gorfyg) A surmounting, overcoming, or vanquishing.
Gorfygu, *v. a.* (gorfyg) To subdue, to vanquish, to overcome.
Gorfyn, *s. m.—pl. t.* au (myn) Rivalship, emulation; envy.
Gorfynawg, *a.* (gorfyn) Having an excessive desire to obtain; emulous; envious.

> Gorfynawg drythyll, gorfynt a ddygaf
> Wrth ar a folaf, a folaf gynt.
>
> *Ambitious* playful one, envy I bear towards whom I praise, and that I have praised before. *Cynddelw, i Efa, f. Madawg.*

Gorfynawl, *a.* (gorfyn) Having an extreme desire to obtain; ambitious; envious.
Gorfyndawd, *s. m.* (gorfyn) A state of rivalship; emulation; ambition; envy.
Gorfyniad, *s. m.—pl. t.* au (gorfyn) An aspiring after extremely; an envying.
Gorfynig, *a.* (gorfyn) Ambitious; emulous; envious.

> Gorfynig fy mhwyll yn mhell amgant beddyw,
> Wrth athreiddiaw tir tu Efyrnwy.
>
> *Ambitious* is my mind on the distant boundary this day, in perambulating the land on the side of Evyrnwy. *Gwalchmai.*

Gorfynnawl, *a.* (gorfynt) Extremely aspiring; ambitious, emulous; envious.
Gorfynniad, *s. m.—pl. t.* au (gorfynt) An aspiring after extremely; an envying.
Gorfynnu, *v. a.* (gorfynt) To aspire after extremely, to emulate, to envy, to be ambitious; to be envious.
Gorfynt, *s. m.—pl.* gorfynnau (gorfyn) Extreme mind, or desire; ambition; envy.

> Gwr gorfynt, gwr edfynt, gwr llawr,
> Ef rhwygai, a chethrai a chethrawr.
>
> The *envious man*, the fickle man, the base man he would tear, and would strive with the striver. *Ancurin.*

Gorfynu, *v. a.* (gorfyn) To aspire after extremely; to envy; to be ambitious; to be envious.
Gorfyny, *s. m.* (myny) An ascent, or up-hill.
Gorfynydd, *s. m.* (gorfyny) An ascent, or up-hill.

> Hydd gorfynydd rewydd redaint.
>
> The stag of the *upland* of wanton course. *G. Brycheiniawg.*

Gorfyr, *a.* (byr) Very short, brief, or abrupt.
Gorfys, *s. m.—pl. t.* edd (bys) The first finger.
Gorfyw, *a.* (byw) Living beyond; supervivant.
Gorfywdawd, *s. m.* (gorfyw) Extreme vivacity.

> Llys lleufer ynys, gwrys gorfywdawd,
> Pe dawant anant na pharydant wawd.
>
> The court that is the splendour of the isle full of *extreme animation* in debate, should the minstrels there resort let them sing no irony. *Meilyr.*

Gorfywiad, *s. m.* (gorfyw) An animating extremely; a becoming over-lively.
Gorfywiaw, *v. a.* (gorfyw) To animate to excess.
Gorfywiawg, *a.* (gorfyw) Extremely animated.
Gorfywiawl, *a.* (gorfyw) Extremely animating.
Gorfywyd, *s. m.* (gorfyw) Superior state of life.
Gorffaig, *s. f.—pl.* gorffeigiau (ffaig) Extreme embarrassment, or difficulty.
Gorffawd, *s. f.—pl.* gorffodiau (ffawd) Extraordinary luck, or good fortune.
Gorffawg, *s. m.* (ffawg) Extreme delight, or bliss.

> Ys ceffych, ys cyffuryf enwawg,
> Wrth dy fodd fod yn gyfoethawg,
> Ac yn y gorphen, gorffawg enrhydedd—
> Trugaredd gan Dduw trugarawg.
>
> Mayest thou, who art of renowned character, be according to thy desire, possessing wealth, and in the conclusion, *extreme bliss* the honour, mayest thou receive mercy from God the compassionate. *Llygad Gwr, i L. ab G. Maelor.*

Gorffeigiad, *s. m.* (gorffaig) An embarrassing extremely, a becoming greatly puzzled.
Gorffeigiaw, *v. a.* (gorffaig) To embarrass or to puzzle extremely.

> Gorffeigiodd trymgawdd tragwydd ym dwyn;
> Ni'm gorffeirch morwyn mor wyf ufudd.
>
> Sad affliction *has caused extreme embarrassment* as to my being taken to eternity: no distinguished regard will a maid bestow on me, being so very abject. *Ior. Fychan.*

Gorffeigiawl, *a.* (gorffaig) Very embarrassing.
Gorffel, *a.* (ffel) Extremely subtile, or cunning.
Gorffèldra, *s. m.* (gorffel) Extreme subtilty.
Gorfflam, *s. m.—pl. t.* au (fflam) Intense flame.
Gorfflamawl, *a.* (gorfflam) Intensely flammeous.
Gorfflamiad, *s. m.—pl. t.* au (gorfflam) Intense flammation; a flaming extremely.
Gorfflamliw, *s. m.* (gorfflam—lliw) A bright flame colour. *a.* Of a bright flame colour.
Gorfflwch, *a.* (fflwch) Very prevalent, or rife.
Gorfflychawl, *a.* (gorfflwch) Superabundant.
Gorfflychiad, *s. m.* (gorfflwch) A superabounding.
Gorfflychu, *v. n.* (gorfflwch) To superabound.
Gorfflemwch, *s. m.* (gorfflam) Great flammability.
Gorfflemychawl, *a.* (gorfflemwch) Extremely flammeous.
Gorfflemychiad, *s. m.* (gorfflemwch) A flaming extremely; extreme flammation.
Gorfflemychu, *v. a.* (gorfflemwch) To flame extremely.

> Gorfflemych llewych llen afallwydd can,
> Gorphowys am y gran a'i ban ni'm bydd.
>
> The glare of the white veil of the apple tree *flames brightly*, resting on the brow with me its down will not be. *Ior. Fychan.*

Gorffodiad, *s. m.* (gorffawd) A prospering much.
Gorffodiaw, *v. n.* (gorffawd) To prosper much.
Gorffodiawg, *a.* (gorffawd) Very prosperous.
Gorffraw, *a.* (ffraw) Extremely active, volatile, or agitated; full of briskness.
Gorffrawdd, *s. m.* (ffrawdd) Extreme bustle.
Gorffrom, *a.* (ffrom) Very irritable, or touchy.
Gorffromi, *v. n.* (gorffrom) To become very irritable, or testy.
Gorffromiad, *s. m.* (gorffrom) A becoming very irritable, or testy.
Gorffrwd, *s. f.—pl.* gorffrydau (ffrwd) A violent stream, or torrent.

> Gwelid——
> Gorffrydau cad orllawes orllawen.
>
> There were seen the *violent torrents* of the conflict full of alertness and exultation. *Cynddelw.*

Gorffrydiad, *s. m.* (gorffrwd) A streaming excessively; an overflowing.
Gorffrydiaw, *v. n.* (gorffrwd) To stream greatly.
Gorffrydiawl, *a.* (gorffrwd) Overflowing.
Gorffull, *s. f.—pl. t.* iau (ffull) Extreme celerity.
Gorffulldid, *s. m.* (gorffull) A hastening greatly.
Gorffulliaw, *v. n.* (gorffull) To move extremely brisk; to be extremely brisk.

Gorffalliawg, *a.* (gorffall) Extremely alert.
Gorffwdan, *s. f.* (ffwdan) Extreme bustle.
Gorffwdaniad, *s. m.* (gorffwdan) A bustling much.
Gorffwdanu, *v. a.* (gorffwdan) To bustle much.
Gorffwyr, *s. f.* (ffwyr) A very violent impulse. *a.* Extremely impetuous.

> Gwan gwairfforch gwanec orffwyr,
> Gwae ni ei marw fil mor fwyr.
>
> Dividing like a hay-fork with a gait most *impetuous*, woe to us that she should have died so late. *Iolo Goch.*
>
> Dy gwyaid, diaur, yn llwyr
> Be darfid yt, byd orffwyr.
>
> Certainly, thou wouldest be lamented if entirely exterminated, that are most repulsive to the world. *D. ab Gwilym, i'r celyn.*

Gorffwyrad, *s. m.* (gorffwyr) A greatly impelling.
Gorffwyraw, *v. a.* (gorffwyr) To impel extremely.
Gorffwyrawl, *a.* (gorffwyr) Extremely impulsive.
Gorffynawl, *a.* (ffynawl) Tending to great prosperity; extremely fortunate.
Gorffyniad, *s. m.* (ffyniad) A prospering greatly.
Gorffyniannawl, *a.* (gorffyniant) Tending to be very prosperous, or fortunate.
Gorffyniannu, *v. n.* (gorffyniant) To prosper extremely, to be very fortunate.
Gorffyniannus, *a.* (gorffyniant) Tending to be very prosperous, or fortunate.
Gorffyniant, *s. m.* (ffyniant) Excess of prosperity.

> Gorffyniant Ilfant lle Gwyndodydd,
> Gorphorawd i pharif wawd gan i pharydydd.
>
> The *supreme fortune* of the host of Gwyndod; most ready with her bard to her eulogy. *Ior. Fychan.*

Gorffyniaw, *v. n.* (ffyniaw) To be very fortunate.
Gorffyniawl, *a.* (ffyniawl) Very prosperous.
Gorffynu, *v. n.* (ffynu) To prosper extremely.
Gorffysg, *s. m.* (ffysg) Extreme celerity.
Gorffysgiad, *s. m.* (gorffysg) A moving with extreme celerity or swiftness.
Gorffysgiaw, *v.* (gorffysg) To move very quickly.
Gorffysgiawl, *a.* (gorffysg) Of extreme speed.
Gorgadw, *s. m.* (cadw) A supercharge.
Gorgadw, *v. a.* (cadw) To keep, or watch over, to superintend.
Gorgaddug, *s. m.* (caddug) Superior darkness, or a gloom that covers over.
Gorgaddugaw, *v. a.* (gorgaddug) To darken over.
Gorgaddugawl, *a.* (gorgaddug) Tending to darken over, or to become overcast.
Gorgaddugiad, *s. m.* (gorgaddug) A darkening over; an overcasting.
Gorgaeth, *a.* (caeth) Excessively confined.
Gorgaethawl, *a.* (gorgaeth) Tending to confine, or restrain extremely.
Gorgaethiad, *s. m.* (gorgaeth) A confining extremely; extreme restriction.
Gorgaethu, *v. a.* (gorgaeth) To confine greatly.
Gorgaffad, *s. m.* (caffad) Superior attainment.
Gorgaffael, *v. a.* (caffael) To attain supremely.
Gorgaffaeliad, *s. m.* (gorgaffael) An attaining supremely; a getting overmuch.
Gorgais, *s. m.* (cais) A superior attempt.
Gorgaled, *a.* (caled) Extremely hard, or severe.
Gorgaledu, *v. a.* (gorgaled) To harden extremely; to overharden.
Gorgall, *a.* (call) Extremely discreet, or crafty.
Gorgalledd, *s. m.* (gorgall) Extreme discretion; excess of cunning.
Gorgallus, *a.* (gorgall) Overwise, very crafty.
Gorgam, *a.* (cam) Extremely distorted.
Gorgamawl, *a.* (gorgam) Tending to bend, or distort extremely.
Gorgamiad, *s. m.* (gorgam) A bending much.
Gorgamu, *v. a.* (gorgam) To bend overmuch.
Gorgan, *a.* (can) Extremely white, or bright.
Gorganiad, *s. m.* (gorgan) A making very white.
Gorganu, *v. a.* (gorgan) To make very white.
Gorgas, *a.* (cas) Extremely disagreeable.
Gorgasâad, *s. m.* (gorgas) A hating to excess; a rendering extremely hateful; a becoming very disagreeable.
Gorgasau, *v. a.* (gorgas) To hate extremely.
Gorgawdd, *s. m.* (cawdd) Extreme vexation.
Gorged, *s. f.—pl. t.* oedd (ced) Superior treasure
Gorgedu, *v. a.* (gorged) To hoard extremely.
Gorgeidwad, *s. m.—pl. t.* on (gorgadw) One who guards, or watches over; a supercargo.
Gorgeisiad, *s. m.* (gorgais) A making a superior attempt, an over-attempting.
Gorgeisiaw, *v. a.* (gorgais) To make a superior attempt.
Gorglawdd, *s. m.—pl.* gorgloddiau (clawdd) The bank of a dike, a mound; a wall that is open.
Gorgoch, *a.* (coch) Extremely red; red on the extremity; tipt with red.

> Gorfoledd i Loegr gorgoch lafnau.
>
> The triumph of Lloegria the blades *tipt with red.* *Myrddin.*

Gorgoched, *s. m.* (gorgoch) A reddening over.
Gorgochi, *v. a.* (gorgoch) To make very red; to colour over with red; to tip with red.
Gorgodawl, *a.* (codawl) Supereminent.
Gorgodi, *v. a.* (codi) To rise superior.
Gorgodiad, *s. m.* (codiad) A rising superior.
Gorgoddawl, *a.* (gorgawdd) Very overbearing.
Gorgoddi, *v. a.* (gorgawdd) To vex extremely.
Gorgoddiad, *s. m.* (gorgawdd) A vexing extremely
Gorgoddiant, *s. m.* (gorgawdd) Extreme vexation
Gorgoeth, *a.* (coeth) Extremely pure, or refined.
Gorgoethawl, *a.* (gorgoeth) Tending to render very pure, of a very pure nature.
Gorgoethedd, *s. m.* (gorgoeth) Extreme purity.
Gorgoethi, *v. a.* (gorgoeth) To purify extremely.
Gorgoethiad, *s. m.* (gorgoeth) A purifying extremely.
Gorgosp, *s. f.—pl. t.* au (cosp) Extreme punishment, or correction
Gorgospawl, *a.* (gorgosp) Tending to excess of punishment.
Gorgospi, *v. a.* (gorgosp) To punish extremely.
Gorgospiad, *s. m.* (gorgosp) A punishing extremely
Gorgrafawl, *a.* (crafawl) Tending to scratch the surface.
Gorgrafiad, *s. m.* (crafiad) A scratching over.
Gorgrafu, *v. a.* (crafu) To scratch the surface.
Gorgraff, *a.* (craff) Very sharp of perception.
Gorgraffawl, *a.* (gorgraff) Very penetrating; very impressive.
Gorgraffedd, *s. m.* (gorgraff) Extreme penetration
Gorgraffiad, *s. m.* (gorgraff) A penetrating very quickly; a quickly perceiving.
Gorgraffu, *v. a.* (gorgraff) To penetrate very quickly, to perceive quickly.
Gorgraid, *a.* (craid) Extremely vehement.
Gorgras, *a.* (cras) Extremely parched, or arid.
Gorgrasiad, *s. m.* (gorgras) An over-parching.
Gorgrasu, *v. a.* (gorgras) To parch overmuch.
Gorgrawd, *s. m.* (crawd) A supercrescence.
Gorgrawn, *s. m.* (crawn) An over-collection.
Gorgred, *s. f.* (cred) Implicit belief; superstition

> Dwyn y corn ar cyfyfed—
> A dyddwg o fragawd, wirawd orgred,
> Ar law Gwgan Drawn.
>
> Bring thou the horn, for conviviality, and of bragget, a liquor of *confidence*, give into the hand of the stubborn Gwgan. *O. Cyfeiliawg.*

Gorgredawl, *a.* (gorgred) Superstitious.

Gorgredu, *v. n.* (gorgred) To believe implicitly; to be superstitious; to confide.

Gorgrin, *a.* (crin) Extremely crisp, or brittle.

Gorgrinaw, *v. n.* (gorgrin) To become extremely crisp, dry, or brittle.

Gorgrinawl, *a.* (gorgrin) Tending to render, or become brittle in the extreme.

Gorgrònawl, *a.* (gorgrawn) Tending to collect, or aggregate, overmuch.

Gorgròni, *v. a.* (gorgrawn) To collect overmuch.

Gorgròniad, *s. m.* (gorgrawn) An over-collecting.

Gorgroth, *s. f.—pl. t.* au (croth) A very great belly, or protuberance.

Gorgrothawl, *a.* (gorgroth) Bulging out extremely

Gorgrothi, *v. a.* (gorgroth) To bulge, or swell out extremely.

Gorgrothiad, *s. m.* (gorgroth) A bellying out excessively.

Gorgrwm, *a.* (crwm) Very much bent.

Gorgrwth, *s. m.* (crwth) A very great rotundity.

Gorgrwydr, *s. m.* (crwydr) Extreme wandering.

Gorgrwydrad, *s. m.* (gorgrwydr) A wandering excessively; extreme deviation.

Gorgrwydraw, *v. a.* (gorgrwydr) To wander overmuch.

Gorgrwydrawl, *a.* (gorgrwydr) Extremely devious or wandering.

Gorgryd, *s. m.* (cryd) Extreme agitation.

Gorgrydawl, *a.* (gorgryd) Very agitating.

Gorgrydiad, *s. m.* (gorgryd) A greatly agitating.

Gorgrydu, *v. a.* (gorgryd) To agitate extremely.

Gorgrymawl, *a.* (gorgrwm) That bends extremely

Gorgrymiad, *s. m.—pl. t.* au (gorgrwm) A bending extremely, a crouching.

Gorgrymu, *v. a.* (gorgrwm) To bend, or crouch extremely.

Gorgryn, *a.* (cryn) Extremely tremulous.

Gorgrynawl, *a.* (gorgryn) Tending to tremble exceedingly.

Gorgryndawd, *s. m.* (gorgryn) Great trembling.

Gorgryniad, *s. m.—pl. t.* au (gorgryn) A trembling excessively.

Gorgryno, *a.* (cryno) Very compact, or tidy.

Gorgrynòad, *s. m.* (gorgryno) A making very compact; an overstocking.

Gorgrynòawl, *a.* (gorgryno) Tending to make very compact.

Gorgrynòi, *v. a.* (gorgryno) To make very compact; to overstock.

Gorgrynu, *v. n.* (gorgryn) To shake or quake extremely.

Gorgrythawl, *a.* (gorgrwth) Tending to bulge out extremely.

Gorgrythiad, *s. m.* (gorgrwth) A bellying out extremely.

Gorgrythu, *v. a.* (gorgrwth) To bulge, or swell out, overmuch.

Gorgudd, *s. m.* (cudd) What covers over.

Gorguddiad, *s. m.* (gorgudd) A covering over.

Gorguddiaw, *v. a.* (gorgudd) To cover over.

Gorguddiawl, *a.* (gorgudd) Tending to hide, or to cover over.

Gorgwydd, *s. m.* (cwydd) A fall over.

Gorgwyddaw, *v. a.* (gorgwydd) To fall over.

Gorgwyddawl, *a.* (gorgwydd) Apt to fall over.

Gorgwyddiad, *s. m.* (gorgwydd) A falling over.

Gorgwyn, *s. f.—pl. t.* ion (cwyn) Extreme complaint or wailing.

Gorgwynaw, *v. a.* (gorgwyn) To complain extremely; to wail.

Gorgwynawl, *a.* (gorgwyn) Very plaintive.

Gorgwyniad, *s. m.* (gorgwyn) A complaining extremely; a greatly bewailing.

Gorgydgam, *s. m.—pl. t.* au (cydgam) Climax.

Gorgyflawn, *a.* (cyflawn) More than complete.

Gorgyflawnedd, *s. m.* (gorgyflawn) Superabundance; superfluity; surplus.

Gorgyflawni, *v. a.* (gorgyflawn) To render more than complete.

Gorgyfuwch, *v. a.* (cyfuwch) Surpassing in height

> Nid ynt gorgyfuwch a chyfraith.
>
> They are not *superior* to the law. — *Welsh Laws.*

Gorgyffraw, *s. m.* (cyffraw) Extreme agitation.

Gorgyffred, *s. m.—pl. t.* ion (cyffred) A surmise.

Gorgyffredawl, *a.* (gorgyffred) Imaginary.

Gorgyffrediad, *s. m.* (gorgyffred) A surmising.

Gorgyffredu, *v. n.* gorgyffred) To surmise.

Gorgyffröad, *s. m.* (gorgyffraw) An agitating extremely; excess of agitation.

Gorgyffröawl, *a.* (gorgyffraw) Greatly agitating.

Gorgyffröi, *v. a.* (gorgyffraw) To agitate extremely.

Gorgylch, *s. m.—pl. t.* au (cylch) A superior circle; an outer circle; that surrounds.

Gorgylchawl, *a.* (gorgylch) Surrounding.

Gorgylchedd, *s. m.* (gorgylch) What surrounds.

Gorgylchiad, *s. m.* (gorgylch) A surrounding.

Gorgylchu, *v. a.* (gorgylch) To surround.

Gorgylchyn, *s. m.—pl. t.* au (gorgylch) A surrounding circle.

Gorgylchynawl, *a.* (gorgylchyn) Surrounding.

Gorgylchyniad, *s. m.—pl. t.* au (gorgylchyn) A surrounding, a circumscribing.

Gorgylchynu, *v. a.* (gorgylchyn) To surround.

> Annogynt hwyntau iddo ef gerdded rhagddo o'r coel da hwnw i oresgyn Mon, ac Arfon, a Lleyn, ar y cantrefoedd cyffinydd i Loegr, a chymeryd gwrogaeth gan y werin, a cherdded y ffordd a gorgylchynu holl Wynedd.
>
> They importuned him that he would proceed forward, from that good omen, to subdue Mon, and Arfon, and Lleyn, and the provinces bordering on Lloegria; and to take homage from the people, and to proceed in that way, and *surround* all Gwynedd. — *Buch. Gr. ab Cynan.*

Gorgymhell, *s. m.—pl. t.* ion (cymhell) Extreme compulsion; excessive importunity.

Gorgymhell, *v. a.* (cymhell) To impel overmuch; to excite extremely.

Gorgymhellawl, *a.* (gorgymhell) Extremely compulsive; very urgent.

Gorgymhelliad, *s. m.—pl. t.* au (gorgymhell) A compelling, or urging extremely.

Gorgyrch, *s. m.—pl. t.* au (cyrch) Excess of resort.

Gorgyrchawl, *a.* (gorgyrch) Of excessive resort.

Gorgyrchiad, *s. m.* (gorgyrch) A resorting overmuch.

Gorgyrchu, *v. a.* (gorgyrch) To resort overmuch.

Gorhadawg, *s. m.* (had) The herb all-seed.

Gorhaedd, *s. m.* (haedd) An overreach; an overstretch.

Gorhaeddawl, *a.* (gorhaedd) Overreaching.

Gorhaeddiad, *s. m.* (gorhaedd) An overreaching.

Gorhaeddu, *v. a.* (gorhaedd) To overreach.

Gorhael, *a.* (hael) Extremely liberal; prodigal.

Gorhallt, *a.* (hallt) Extremely salt, or briny.

Gorhalltiad, *s. m.* (gorhallt) A salting overmuch.

Gorhalltu, *v. a.* (gorhallt) To salt overmuch.

Gorhardd, *a.* (hardd) Extremely towering.

Gorharddiad, *s. m.* (gorhardd) A towering greatly

Gorharddu, *v. n.* (gorhardd) To tower very high; To make very shewy.

Gorhawl, *s. f.—pl.* gorholion (hawl) A superior claim; an over-claim.

Gorheb, *s. m.—pl. t.* ion (heb) A response.

Gorhebawl, *a.* (gorheb) Responsive.

Gorhedawl, *a.* (hedawl) Flying above.

Gorhedeg, *v. a.* (hedeg) To fly above.

Gorhedlad, *s. m.—pl. t.* au (hedlad) A

Gorhelaeth, *a.* (helaeth) Over-ample ated; amplified.

Gorhelaethawl, *a.* (gorhelaeth) Tending to amplify to excess; exaggerating.

Gorhelaethiad, *s. m.—pl. t.* au (gorhelaeth) An over-amplifying; exaggeration; amplification.

Gorhelaethrwydd, *s. m.* (gorhelaeth) The state of being over ample, or exaggerated.

Gorhelaethu, *v. a.* (gorhelaeth) To make very ample; to amplify extremely; to exaggerate.

Gorhen, *a.* (hen) Extremely old, or ancient.

Gorhenaidd, *a.* (gorhen) Somewhat antiquated; superannuated.

Gorhenaint, *s. m.* (gorhen) Extreme age.

Gorhenedd, *s. m.* (gorhen) Extreme antiquity.

Gorhendad, *s. m.—pl. t.* au (hendad) A great grandfather.

Gorhendaid, *s. m.—pl.* gorhendeidian (hendaid) A great great grandfather.

Gorheneiddiaw, *v. n.* (gorhenaidd) To become superannuated.

Gorhenfam, *s. f.—pl. t.* au (gorhen—mam) A great grandmother.

Gorhengaw, *s. m.* (hengaw) A great great great grandfather.

> Y cyfryw geraint a dalwyet, alanas y gyd a'r llofrudd, y cyffelybion o blaid y dyn a laddwyd a'i derbyniant, o'r gorhengaw hyd y gorchaw.
>
> Such relatives as shall pay compensation for murder in conjunction with the murderer, those on the same degree on the part of the person slain shall receive it, from the great great great grandfather to the great great great grandchild. *Welsh Laws.*

Gorhennain, *s. f.—pl.* gorhenneinian (gorhen—nain) A great great grandmother.

Gorhenw, *s. m.—pl. t.* au (henw) A surname.

Gorhenwad, *s. m.* (gorhenw) A surnaming.

Gorhenwawl, *a.* (gorhenw) Relating to a surname.

Gorhenwi, *v. a.* (gorhenw) To surname.

Gorhesg, *s. pl. aggr.* (hesg) Large reeds.

> Cwrsa tan cul arlwng,
> Cadeon haidd, celyn a hesg.
>
> A bare tail of slender reeds, the beards of barley, holly, and sedges. *Iolo Goch, i'w farf.*

Gorhëwg, *a.* (hëwg) Full of assurance; saucy.

> Gorhëwg yn dwg deg orsedd gau,
> Gywair-fwch ni phalla,
> All y Cathau—
>
> Pertly shall I be carried to the fair sheltered station; the sure footed steed will not falter, no more than the Cathau. *Gr. ab Meredydd.*

Gorhëwgdra, *s. m.* (gorhëwg) Malapertness.

Gorhewgi, *v. n.* (gorhëwg) To be malapert.

Gorhiliad, *s. m.—pl. t.* au (hiliad) A bringing forth abundantly.

Gorhiliaw, *v. a.* (hiliaw) To increase the species, to propagate; to multiply; to enlarge.

Gorhiliawg, *a.* (hiliawg) Very prolific.

Gorhilig, *s. m.* (hil) Four-leaved allseed.

Gorhiniawg, *s. f.—pl.* gorhiniogau (hiniawg) The lintel, or top of a door-frame.

Gorhir, *a.* (hir) Overlong; extremely long.

Gorhiriad, *s. m.—pl. t.* au (gorhir) A lingering; a being very dilatory.

Gorhiriaw, *v. a.* (gorhir) To linger; to be very dilatory.

Gorhiriawl, *a.* (gorhir) Very lingering or slow.

Gorhoen, *s. f.* (hoen) Extreme flow; vivacity, or chearfulness.

> Duw a garai deg orhoen,
> A drwes [illegible] o'u poen.
>
> God, who delights in fair chearfulness, delivered the five ages out of their torment. [illegible] *Tew.*

Gorhoeni, *v. a.* (gorhoen) To exhilarate, to be exhilarated, to become chearful.

Gorhoenus, *a.* (gorhoen) Full of vivacity.

> Yr athraw doeth—a'm cynghorai i lawenychu yn yr Arglwydd, a byw yn orhoenus.
>
> The wise instructor would advise me to rejoice in the Lord, and to live *chearfully*. *E. Trefredyn.*

Gorhoenusrwydd, *s. m.* (gorhoenus) Chearfulness.

Gorhoff, *a.* (hoff) Very delectable, or lovely. *Gorhoffion*, most desirable things.

Gorhoffaidd, *a.* (gorhoff) Of a very delectable, or amiable nature.

Gorhoffedd, *s. f.* (gorhoff) That which extremely delights; what is a favourite. *Gorhoffedd Gwalchmai*, and *Gorhoffedd Hywel*, the titles of poems by those bards.

Gorhoffi, *v. a.* (gorhoff) To desire, or delight in, extremely; to love to excess; to overprize.

Gorhoffiad, *s. m.* (gorhoff) A desiring, or delighting in extremely.

Gorhoffiant, *s. m.* (gorhoff) Extreme fondness.

Gorholi, *v. a.* (gorhawl) To pursue a claim overmuch; to question overmuch.

Gorholiad, *s. m.* (gorhawl) A pursuing a claim overmuch; a questioning too closely.

Gorhonawl, *a.* (honawl) Asserted overmuch.

Gorhoni, *v. a.* (honi) To assert over-violently.

Gorhoniad, *s. m.* (honiad) An insisting to excess.

Gorhud, *s. m.* (hud) Extreme fascination.

Gorhudaw, *v. a.* (gorhud) To allure extremely.

Gorhudawl, *a.* (gorhud) Extremely alluring.

Gorhudiad, *s. m.—pl. t.* au (gorhud) A fascinating extremely; a greatly enticing.

Gorhudwr, *s. m.—pl.* gorhudwyr (gorhud—gwr) One who entices, or deceives, extremely.

Gorhudd, *s. m.—pl. t.* ion (hudd) An over cover; an upper covering, or envelope.

Gorhuddaw, *v. a.* (gorhudd) To cover over; to overcast, to overcloud; to overveil.

Gorhuddawl, *a.* (gorhudd) That is overcovering.

Gorhuddiad, *s. m.—pl. t.* au (gorhudd) A covering over; an overcasting.

Gorhul, *s. m.—pl. t.* iou (hul) An overcover.

Gorhuliad, *s. m.—pl. t.* au (gorhul) An overcovering.

Gorhuliaw, *v. a.* (gorhul) To overcover.

Gorhuliawg, *a.* (gorhul) That overcovers.

Gorhun, *s. f.* (hun) Excess of sleep; lethargy.

Gorhunaw, *v. a.* (gorhun) To oversleep.

Gorhunawg, *a.* (gorhun) Oversleepy.

Gorhunawl, *a.* (gorhun) Tending to oversleep.

Gorhuniad, *s. m.* (gorhun) An oversleeping.

Gorhydr, *s. m.* (hydr) Overboldness; arrogance.

Gorhydrawl, *a.* (gorhydr) Overconfident.

Gorhydri, *s. m.* (gorhydr) Overconfidence; arrogancy; pomp.

Gorhydriad, *s. m.* (gorhydr) An assuming overconfidence; an arrogating.

Gorhydru, *v. a.* (gorhydr) To assume overconfidence; to be overbold.

Gorhynawl, *a.* (gorhen) Extremely ancient.

Gorhynod, *a.* (hynod) Extremely notable.

Gorhynodawl, *a.* (gorhynod) Tending to render, or become very remarkable.

Gorhynodi, *v. a.* (gorhynod) To make very remarkable; to become very distinguished.

Gorhynodiad, *s. m.* (gorhynod) A rendering very remarkable, or conspicuous.

Gorhynt, *s. f.—pl. t.* iau (hynt) A superior course; that is upon the way; a sojourner.

Gori, *s. m.* (gor) The act of brooding, or breeding; suppuration.

Gori, *v. a.* (gor) To brood; to breed matter; to supparate. *Iar yn gori*, a hen hatching.

> Teithi pob aderyn benyw yw dodwy a gori.
>
> The perfections of every female bird are to lay eggs and *to brood*.
> *Welsh Laws.*

> Cyw iar, hyd na ddodwo, cywen, hyd na oro.
>
> A hen is a chick until she lays, and a pullet until she *broods*.
> *Welsh Laws.*

Goriad, *s. m.—pl. t.* au (gor) A brooding; suppuration.

Goriai, *s. c.—pl.* gorieion (gor) A brooder.

Gorisin, *s. m.* (gawr) A frequent crying out.

Gorisin, *v. a.* (gawr) To cry out frequently.

Gorian, *v. a.* (gawr) To cry out frequently; to moan, to complain.

Goriaw, *v. a.* (gawr) To utter moans, or cries; to be querulous.

Goriawl, *a.* (gawr) Apt to moan; querulous.

Gorifyny, *s. m.* (ifyny) An ascent, or acclivity.

Gorifynydd, *s. m.* (gorifyny) An ascent.

Gorimyn, *s. m.—pl. t.* au (rhimyn) A small chink

Gorior, *a.* (gawr) Apt to moan; querulous.

> Daeth canu teg—
> I yru Padrig orior
> Er mawl i Dduw i'r mor.
>
> There came pleasant singing to send the *querulous* Patrick into the sea for the honour of God. *I. ab R. ab Ieuan Llwyd.*

Gorir, *a.* (ir) Extremely fresh, or green.

Gorirsidd, *a.* (gorir) That is of a very fresh nature, or full of sap, or very green.

Goris, *prep.* (is) Greatly beneath, below, under, inferior to. *adv.* Beneath, in a lower place.

Gorisel, *a.* (goris) Very low, inferior.

Goriseledd, *s. m.* (gorisel) Extreme inferiority.

Goriseliad, *s. m.* (gorisel) A rendering, or becoming extremely low.

Goriselrwydd, *s. m.* (gorisel) Inferiorness.

Goriselu, *v. a.* (gorisel) To render very low; or inferior; to become extremely low.

Goriselwr, *s. m.—pl.* goriselwyr (gorisel—gwr) An inferior person, an inferior.

Gorisgell, *s. m.* (isgell) The froth of liquor.

Gorisgellawg, *a.* (gorisgell) Over-foaming.

> Bydd gwin gorisgellawg, a dyddan gerddau rhagot; a bwyd degwyr-arugaint a ddaw atat i'r yspytty: yno y bwyta y pellenigion.
>
> There will be *froth-mantled* wine, and amusing songs before thee; and provision for thirty persons shall come to thee into the lodging house: there the strangers eat.
> *H. Culhwch—Mabinogion.*

Gorisgelliad, *s. m.* (gorisgell) A mantling over with froth; a foaming over.

Gorisgellu, *v. n.* (gorisgell) To foam on the top.

> Debre genyw i'm tyno,
> A thwyd gwin gorisgello:
> Ugnach yw fy henw, mab Mydno.
>
> Come along with me to my dwelling, where there is gone wine that *will mantle over*; Ugnach is my name, the son of Mydno.
> *Ymddi. Ugnach a Thaliesin.*

Gorith, *s. m.* (rhith) A faint appearance; a phantom, or illusion. *a.* That partly appears; illusive

> Ef—
> Gorith gyfarchawr.
>
> He is an *illusive* greeter. *Taliesin.*

Gorithiad, *s. m.* (gorith) A faintly appearing; deception of appearance, illusion.

Gorithiaw, *v. a.* (gorith) To appear indistinctly.

Gorithiawl, *a.* (gorith) Tending to appear indistinctly; like a phantom.

Gorithiwr, *s. m.—pl.* gorithwyr (gorith—gwr) One who appears indistinctly.

Goriw, *s. f.—pl. t.* iau (rhiw) A gentle ascent.

Gorlad, *s. m.—pl. t.* au (llad) Supreme blessing.

Gorladawl, *a.* (gorlad) Supremely gracious.

Gorladiad, *s. m.* (gorlad) A blessing supremely.

Gorladu, *v. a.* (gorlad) To bless supremely.

Gorlaes, *a.* (llaes) That is very low, or trailing.

Gorlaesiad, *s. m.* (gorlaes) A trailing extremely.

Gorlaesu, *v. n.* (gorlaes) To trail overmuch.

Gorlais, *s. m.—pl.* gorleisiau (llais) A very shrill voice, an acute tone.

Gorlaith, *a.* (llaith) Humid, or moist, to excess.

Gorlam, *s. m.—pl. t.* au (llam) An overskip.

Gorlamawl, *a.* (gorlam) Supersalient.

Gorlamiad, *s. m.* (gorlam) Supersaliency.

Gorlamu, *v. a.* (gorlam) To overstep, to overskip; to leap upon, or over.

Gorlan, *a.* (glan) Extremely clean, or pure.

Gorlanâad, *s. m.* (gorlan) A making very clean, or pure; superpurgation.

Gorlanâawl, *a.* (gorlan) Tending to make very clean, or pure.

Gorlanastr, *s. m.—pl. t.* au (llanastr) An uppermost layer.

Gorlanastrawl, *a.* (gorlanastr) Being strewed over, or overspread.

Gorlanastriad, *s. m.* (gorlanastr) A strewing, or spreading over.

Gorlanastru, *v. a.* (gorlanastr) To strew over, to spread over.

Gorlanâu, *v. a.* (gorlan) To make very clean.

Gorlanw, *s. m.* (llanw) The state of being overfull; repletion; high-water, or high tide.

Gorlas, *s. m.* (glas) The blue which the intermediate air gives to distant objects; "*Nature's universal robe.*" *a.* Covered with superior blue, covered with a general verdancy, as it appears in a landscape, approaching to a blue.

> Gorlas gwellt didryf; dwfr neud lesin;
> Gorddyar eaws awdl gynnefin.
>
> Of *finest green* the untrodden grass; the water is it not of freshness, most vocal the nightingale of well-known song.
> *Gwalchmai.*

Gorlassaidd, *a.* (gorlas) Tending to be of a bluish hue; between a fine blue and green.

Gorlasar, *s. m.* (llasar) A fine blue enamel, or coatring. *a.* Of a fine blue enamel.

> Neu fi lluawg yn trydar;
> Ni pheidiwn rhwng deulu heb wyar;
> Neu fi a elwir gorlasar.
>
> Am I not powerful in the din of tumult; between two hosts I would not desist without blood; am I not called the one *clad in finest blue.* *Taliesin.*

Gorlasawg, *a.* (gorlas) Having a fine blue tint.

Gorlasawl, *a.* (gorlas) Tending to render, or become, of a fine blue.

Gorlasiad, *s. m.* (gorlas) A rendering, or becoming, of a superior blue; a doing over with blue, a covering with verdancy.

Gorlasu, *v. a.* (gorlas) To make of a fine blue; to colour very blue; to colour over with fine blue; to become very blue, to cover with verdancy.

Gorlawen, *a.* (llawen) Extremely joyful or glad.

Gorlawenu, *v. a.* (gorlawen) To overjoy; to be overjoyed.

Gorlawenydd, *s. m.* (gorlawen) Excess of joy.

Gorlawn, *a.* (llawn) Overfull, redundant.

Gorlawndid, *s. m.* (gorlawn) Redundancy.

Gorlawnedd, *s. m.* (gorlawn) Redundancy.

Gorlawniad, *s. m.* (gorlawn) An overfilling, a making redundant; repletion.

Gorlech, *s. f.—pl. t.* i (llech) What is above slate, a kind of stone;—also a flat stone roof, or cover

Gorlechiad, *s. m.—pl. t.* au (llechiad) A sculking extremely.

Gorlechu, *v. a.* (llechu) To sculk extremely.

Gorled, *s. m.* (lled) Extreme breadth, or width.

Goriedawl, *a.* (goried) Extremely expansive.
Goriediad, *s. m.* (gorled) An expanding extremely; extreme expansion.
Goriedrad, *s. m.* (lledrad) A heinous theft.
Goriedrata, *v. a.* (goriedrad) To steal heinously.
Goriedu, *v. a.* (gorled) To expand extremely.
Gorlef, *s. m.* (llef) A very loud voice; an outcry.
Gorlefain, *v. a.* (gorlef) To cry out loudly.
Gorlefawl, *a.* (gorlef) Extremely noisy.
Gorleisiad, *s. m.* (gorlais) A squeaking.
Gorleisiaw, *v. a.* (gorlais) To squeak, to squeal.
Gorleithiad, *s. m.* (gorlaith) A making, or becoming very humid.
Gorleithiaw, *v. n.* (gorlaith) To become very humid; to moisten extremely.
Gorleithiawl, *a.* (gorlaith) Very humific.
Gorlendid, *s. m.* (gorlan) Extreme purity, or clearness; extreme comeliness.
Gorlenwad, *s. m.* (gorlanw) An overfilling.
Gorlenwi, *v. a.* (gorlanw) To overfill.
Gorles, *s. m.* (llês) Supreme benefit, or good.
Gorlesawl, *a.* (gorles) Extremely beneficial.
Gorlesu, *v. a.* (gorles) To benefit extremely.
Gorlethawl, *a.* (llethawl) Very depressive.
Gorlethiad, *s. m.—pl. t.* au (llethiad) A depressing extremely; a smothering.
Gorlethu, *v. a.* (llethu) To depress extremely.
Gorlewin, *s. m.* (llewin) The extreme of light; point of radiation; ultimate point; the west.
Gorlewinaw, *v. n.* (gorlewin) To diverge; to tend westward.
Gorlewinawl, *a.* (gorlewin) Occidental.
Gorlid, *s. m.* (llid) Extreme rage, or wrath.
Gorlidiad, *s. m.* (gorlid) A raging extremely; a fuming excessively.
Gorlidiaw, *v. n.* (gorlid) To be very wrathful.
Gorlidiawg, *a.* (gorlid) Extremely enraged.
Gorlif, *s. m.—pl. t.* ion (llif) A great current; an upper current.
Gorlifaw, *v. n.* (gorlif) To flow very strongly; to flow above.
Gorlifawl, *a.* (gorlif) Superfluitant, overflowing.
Gorlifiad, *s. m.—pl. t.* au (gorlif) A flowing in a strong current; a flowing above; a current.
Gorlifiant, *s. m.* (gorlif) Superfluitance.
Gorlithr, *s. m.* (llithr) An overslip; extreme glibness; very slippery.
Gorlithraw, *v. a.* (gorlithr) To overslip.
Gorlithrawl, *a.* (gorlithr) Tending to overslip.
Gorlithriad, *s. m.* (gorlithr) An overslipping.
Gorlithrig, *a.* (gorlithr) Extremely slippery.
Gorliw, *s. m.—pl. t.* iau (lliw) Exterior colour; apparent hue; resemblance.
Gorliwiad, *s. m.* (gorliw) A colouring over; a giving an apparent hue; a giving a resemblance
Gorliwiaw, *v. a.* (gorliw) To colour over; to give an apparent hue; to give a resemblance.
Gorliwiawl, *a.* (gorliw) Tending to colour over, or to give an apparent hue; resembling.
Gorlochawl, *a.* (gorlawch) Tending to protect extremely; greatly cherishing.
Gorlochi, *v. a.* (gorlawch) To protect extremely.
Gorlochiad, *s. m.* (gorlawch) A protecting much.
Gorlog, *s. m.—pl. t.* au (llog) Extreme hire; excess of interest; usury.
Gorlogawl, *a.* (gorlog) Of extravagant hire; usurious.
Gorlogi, *v. a.* (gorlog) To hire at an extravagant price; to commit usury.
Gorlogiad, *s. m.* (gorlog) A hiring at an excessive price; a committing usury.

Gorloes, *s. f.—pl. t.* au (gloes) Extreme utterance; a murmuring sound; also an organ. *a.* Of a murmuring sound.

> Gorwyliais nos yn achadw fin
> Gorloes rydau dwfr Dygen Freiddin.

I anxiously watched guarding the bound of the loudly murmuring fords of the water of the towering Breiddin. *Gwalchmai.*

> Rhoes hidl bob rhyw wryddon;
> Rhogi folant o'r moddiant mau;
> Gwrdd lef telyn ac orloes:
> Gormodd rhodd gwr meddw a'i rhoes.

I bestowed every kind of assiduity upon her; flowing praise of my appropriate store; the powerful note of the harp and organ. too great a gift. it was a drunken man who gave it. *D. ab Gwilym.*

Gorloesi, *v. a.* (lloesi) To pour excessively; to pour over; to supereffuse.
Gorloesiad, *s. m.—pl. t.* au (lloesiad) Supereffusion
Gorlon, *a.* (llon) Extremely chearful.
Gorlonaid, *s. m.* (gorlon) An overfill.
Gorlonedd, *s. m.* (gorlon) Extreme chearfulness.
Gorloni, *v. a.* (gorlon) To make extremely chearful; to become overjoyed.
Gorlosg, *s. m.* (llosg) Extreme burning; the burning of the surface.
Gorlosgawl, *a.* (gorlosg) Tending to overburn.
Gorlosgi, *v. a.* (gorlosg) To overburn; to burn the surface.
Gorlosgiad, *s. m.* (gorlosg) An overburning.
Gorlosten, *s. f.—pl. t.* i (llosten) An earwig.
Gorludd, *s. m.* (lludd) Extreme depression, or hinderance.
Gorluddaw, *v. a.* (gorludd) To depress extremely; to hinder, or oppose, extremely.
Gorluddawl, *a.* (gorludd) Extremely depressive.
Gorludded, *s. f.* (gorludd) Extreme depression; an overburden.
Gorluddedig, *a.* (gorludded) Overfatigued.
Gorluddiad, *s. m.* (gorludd) An overfatiguing.
Gorlwg, *s. m.* (llwg) Superior brightness.
Gorlwm, *a.* (llwm) Extremely bare, or naked.
Gorlwnc, *s. m.* (llwnc) An excessive indraught.
Gorlwng, *s. m.* (llwng) An excessive indraught.
Gorlwybr, *s. m.—pl. t.* au (llwybr) A trace over, or along the surface.
Gorlwybraidd, *a.* (gorlwybr) Tending to overtrace, or to make a track.
Gorlwybraw, *v. a.* (gorlwybr) To over-trace.
Gorlwybrawl, *a.* (gorlwybr) Over-tracing.
Gorlwybriad, *s. m.* (gorlwybr) An over-tracing.
Gorlwydd, *s. m.* (llwydd) A helping onward.
Gorlwyddaw, *v. a.* (gorlwydd) To help on; to give success; to prosper greatly.
Gorlwyn, *s. m.* (llwyn) An escort, a convoy.
Gorlwyn, *v. a.* (llwyn) To escort, to convoy.
Gorlwynaw, *v. a.* (gorlwyn) To convoy.
Gorlwynawl, *a.* (gorlwyn) That convoys.
Gorlwyniad, *s. m.* (gorlwyn) A convoying.
Gorlwyth, *s. m.—pl. t.* au (llwyth) An overload, or surcharge.
Gorlwythaw, *v. a.* (gorlwyth) To overburden.
Gorlwythawg, *a.* (gorlwyth) Surcharged.
Gorlyd, *a.* (gor) Bloody; teeming, full of matter.
Gorlyfawl, *a.* (llyfawl) Apt to lick over.
Gorlyfiad, *s. m.* (llyfiad) A licking over.
Gorlyfn, *a.* (llyfn) Extremely smooth.
Gorlyfnawl, *a.* (gorlyfn) Tending to make very smooth; coaxing.
Gorlyfniad, *s. m.* (gorlyfn) A smoothing the surface; a coaxing; a harrowing.
Gorlyfnu, *v. a.* (gorlyfn) To smooth the surface; to make very smooth; to coax; to harrow.
Gorlyfu, *v. a.* (llyfu) To lick the surface.
Gorlygawl, *a.* (gorlwg) Extremely splendid.

Gorlygiad, *s. m.* (gorlwg) A casting a great glare.
Gorlygu, *v. a.* (gorlwg) To cast a great light.
Gorlymdra, *s. m.* (gorlwm) Extreme sharpness.
Gorlymedd, *s. m.* (gorlym) Extreme poignancy.
Gorlymu, *v. a.* (gorlwm) To sharpen extremely.
Gorlyna, *v. a.* (llyna) To tipple excessively.
Gorlyncawl, *a.* (gorlwnc) That swallows extremely
Gorlynciad, *s. m.* (gorlwnc) A swallowing greatly.
Gorlyngcu, *v. a.* (gorlwnc) To gorge; to gulp.
Gorlyngawl, *a.* (gorlwng) Having an indraught.
Gorlyngiad, *s. m.* (gorlwng) A swallowing in.
Gorlyngu, *v. a.* (gorlwng) To swallow in.
Gorlyw, *s. m.* (llyw) A superior director.
Gorlywiad, *s. m.* (gorlyw) A guiding over.
Gorlywiaw, *v. a.* (gorlyw) To guide over.
Gorlywydd, *s. m.—pl. t.* au (gorlyw) A superior governor, or president.
Gorllad, *s. m.—pl. t.* au (llad) Benediction.

Morwyn—
Yn orlliw eiry rhiw rhetid ym pwyllad,
Yn orllad cariad man y carid.

A maid of the superior brightness of the snow of the cliff, runs in my mind, the *supreme blessing* of love where she is wooed. *Ior. Fychan.*

Gorlladawl, *a.* (gorllad) Supremely gracious; consecrated.
Gorlladedd, *s. m.* (gorllad) Supreme grace.
Gorlladen, *s. f.—pl. t.* au (gorllad) The consecrated bread in the eucharist.

Mae'r mab rhad yn orlladen.

The son of grace is in the *host*. *Ieu. Dewlwyn.*

Gorlladiad, *s. m.* (gorllad) A blessing supremely; a conferring supreme grace; consecration.
Gorlladu, *v. a.* (gorllad) To consecrate.
Gorllaes, *a.* (llaes) That hangs very low; trailing.
Gorllaesawl, *a.* (gorllaes) Tending to hang down very much; trailing.
Gorllaesder, *s. m.* (gorllaes) The state of hanging down, trailing, or drooping.

Mewn hanesgerdd rhaid—gochel gormod gorllaesder o barth iaith a myfyrdawd.

In historical poetry too much *depression* must be avoided, with respect to language and thought. *Barddas.*

Gorllaesedd, *s. m.* (gorllaes) Extreme tendency downwards.
Gorllaesiad, *s. m.* (gorllaes) A hanging down very much; a drooping.
Gorllaesu, *v. a.* (gorllaes) To hang very low; to droop; to trail; to drawl.
Gorllaith, *s. m.* (llaith) Extreme moistness; slaughter. *a.* Extremely moist.

Ysgor ddigyfor, ddig afar obaith;
Oesgawdd ei orllaith, gwaith gwythlongar!

A hamlet without fullness, offensive and mournful prospect; his *death* is the grief of life, a wrathful deed! *Bleddyn Fardd, i D. ab Gruffudd.*

Gorllanw, *s. m.* (llanw) High-water, or full tide. *Pen gorllanw*, high-water mark.
Gorllawen, *a.* (llawen) Overjoyed; enraptnred.
Gorllawenâad, *s. m.* (gorllawen) An over-joying; a rejoicing extremely.
Gorllawenâawl, *a.* (gorllawen) Tending to make overjoyed.
Gorllawenâu, *v. n.* (gorllawen) To be overjoyed.
Gorllawenu, *v. a.* (gorllawen) To render overjoyed; to become overjoyed.
Gorllawenwch, *s. m.* (gorllawen) Extreme joy.
Gorllawenychawl, *a.* (gorllawenwch) Tending to make overjoyed.
Gorllawenychiad, *s. m.* (gorllawenwch) A rendering, or becoming, overjoyed.
Gorllawenychu, *v. a.* (gorllawenwch) To render overjoyed; to be enraptured.

Gorllawenydd, *s. m.* (gorllawen) Extreme joy; rapture, transport of joy.
Gorllawes, *a.* (llawes) Extremely expert.

Neud gwar gwawr trydar trin orllawes!

Is he not mild, the dawn of the tumult of the *extremely active* conflict! *Cynddelw.*

Gwyr Powys pobl diegywen
Cad orllawes, orllawen,
Pedair cynneddf, cadw cadr urdden,
Ar ddeg yr ddygant o Feigen.

The men of Powys a glorious people of the *most active* battle extremely merry, fourteen distinguished customs, strongly preserved and honoured, they acquired in Meigen. *Cynddelw.*

Gorllawn, *a.* (llawn) Over-full; replete.
Gorllawnawl, *a.* (gorllawn) Tending to be over-full; plethoric.
Gorllawndid, *s. m.* (gorllawn) Repletion; exuberancy, luxuriance.
Gorllawnedig, *a.* (gorllawn) Being over-filled.
Gorllawnedd, *s. m.* (gorllawn) Over-fill; plethora.
Gorllawniad, *s. m.* (gorllawn) An over-filling.
Gorllawnu, *v. a.* (gorllawn) To over-fill.
Gorllech, *s. f.—pl. t.* i (llech) What is above slate; a kind of fossil stone.
Gorllechawl, *a.* (llechawl) Very sculking.
Gorllechiad, *s. m.* (llechiad) A sculking much.
Gorllechu, *v. a.* (llechu) To sculk extremely.

Pebylliawnt ar Tren a Tharannon;
Gorllechynt, gorddyfynt i geisiaw Mon.

They would pitch tents upon Tren and Tarannon; *they would lie in ambush*, they would come to take Mon. *Taliesin.*

Gorlled, *s. m.* (llêd) Extreme breadth.
Gorlledawl, *a.* (gorlled) Extremely expansive.
Gorllediad, *s. m.* (gorlled) A widening greatly.
Gorlledu, *v. a.* (gorlled) To expand extremely.
Gorlleithiad, *s. m.* (gorllaith) A moistening extremely; a becoming very humid.
Gorlleithiaw, *v. a.* (gorllaith) To moisten extremely; to make very humid.
Gorlleithiawg, *a.* (gorllaith) Very humific.
Gorlleithiawg, *a.* (gorllaith) Tending to make very moist.
Gorllenwad, *s. m.* (gorllanw) Appletion, afflux.
Gorllenwi, *v. a.* (gorllanw) To over-fill; to flow over; to flow to the high-water mark.

Gorllenwi gwaed am draed a ymdrychant.

Blood *will overflow* round the feet of them that mangle one another. *Ll. P. Moch.*

Gorllewin, *s. m.* (llewin) The extreme of light; the point of radiation; the ultimate, rear, or posterior point; the west. *Mae y gorllewin yn tòri*, the dawn is breaking. *Gorllewin bon y gwynt*, the radiating point of the base of the wind, or that part of the sky where it begins to brighten. *Sil.*

Nid oes Arglwydd ond Iesu,
Na brenin gorllewin llu.

There is no Lord except Jesus, nor a king that is the *directing light* of men. *Iolo Goch.*

Lliwiawg yw fy ngorllewin,
Lliw oedd dda roes llew o ddyn.

Gaily coloured is my *back*, a goodly colour given by a lion-like man. *Ieuan Ddu, i'r gwn coch.*

Rhedi—
O ddwyrain wybr, hardd-lwybr hin,
Goreu lliw, i'r gorllewin.

Thou dost run from the eastern sky, the exalted path of the weather of choicest colour, to the *west*. *D. ab Gwilym, i'r haul.*

Gorllewinaw, *v. n.* (gorllewin) To diverge; tend westward; to go westward.
Gorllewinawl, *a.* (gorllewin) Occidental.
Gorllewiniad, *s. m.* (gorllewin) A rendering, or being, westerly.
Gorllewndid, *s. m.* (gorllawn) A repletion.
Gorllewychu, *v. a.* (llewychu) To reflect a light.

Gorllewydd, *s. m.* (llewydd) The extreme of light, or point of radiation; the west.

> Gyda'r llew o'r gorllewydd,
> Yn llu ydd [illegible] ei ddydd.
>
> With the Lion from the west, wherever he goes he will gain the day. *H. ab D. ab Tudur.*

Gorllewyddawl, *a.* (gorllewydd) Occidental.
Gorllewyn, *s. m.* (llewyn) The extreme of light, or point of radiation.
Gorllif, *s. m.—pl. t.* ion (llif) A superflux.
Gorllifaw, *v. a.* (gorllif) To flow above.
Gorllifawl, *a.* (gorllif) Flowing to excess; superfluitant.
Gorllifiad, *s. m.—pl. t.* au (gorllif) A flowing above; a flowing to excess; superfluitance; a flowing in current; a current.
Gorllifiannawl, *a.* (gorllifiant) Superfluitant.
Gorllifiannlad, *s. m.* (gorllifiant) A flowing above.
Gorllifiannu, *v. a.* (gorllif) To flow above.
Gorllifiant, *s. m.—pl.* gorllifiannau (gorllif) Superfluitance; a strong current.

> ———Gruddl dodid rhag poen
> Yn orllifiant heen hwn ni geisid.
>
> A disposition was given to guard against pain, an overflow of spirits, which was not sought for. *Ior. Fychan.*

Gorllin, *s. m.* (llin) A supreme of a race, or line. *a.* Being superior of a lineage.

> Teyrnedd orddwy, orddyfnied gorllin,
> Yn gorllwyn dwy gawad,
> Y'nghyfarf tarf torf amwad
> Y'nghyfarfod cyfoed cad.
>
> The curber of princes, the well-accomplished one *chief of a race*, following between two showers, in the meeting of weapons of the scattering of the fickle crowd, and in the rencounter of the appointed combat. *Cynddelw.*

Gorlliw, *s. m.—pl. t.* iau (lliw) Exterior colour; superior hue; a resemblance.

> Gorllwyn ydd wyf ddyn gairllaes,
> Gorlliw eiry man marian maes.
>
> I am pursuing after a person of complaisant word, of the *superior hue* of the driven snow of the plain of the field. *D. ab Gwilym.*

Gorlliwiad, *s. m.* (gorlliw) A giving an exterior colour; a making to resemble.
Gorlliwiaw, *v. a.* (gorlliw) To colour over, to colour the surface, to give a fine hue, to make to resemble.
Gorlliwiawl, *a.* (gorlliw) Being tinted over; resembling.
Gorllon, *a.* (llon) Overjoyed, enraptured.
Gorllonaid, *s. m.* (gorllawn) Surcharge; overflow.
Gorllònawl, *a.* (gorllon) Tending to make very cheerful; rapturous, ravishing.
Gorllòni, *v. a.* (gorllon) To give extreme delight, to be full of joy; to be transported with pleasure.
Gorllòniad, *s. m.* (gorllon) An overjoying.
Gorlludd, *s. m.—pl. t.* ion (lludd) An extreme depression, an over-pressure; extreme fatigue.
Gorlluddaw, *v. a.* (gorlludd) To depress overmuch; to over-fatigue.
Gorlluddawl, *a.* (gorlludd) Extremely depressive.
Gorlludded, *s. f.—pl. t.* au (gorlludd) Extreme depression; fatigue.
Gorlluddedig, *a.* (gorlludded) Over-fatigued, extremely depressed.
Gorlluddedu, *v. a.* (gorlludded) To over-fatigue.
Gorlluddiad, *s. m.—pl. t.* au (gorlludd) A depressing extremely, an over-fatiguing.
Gorllwg, *s. m.—pl.* gorllygion (llwg) The having an eye upon, an escort, a protection.
Gorllwm, *a.* (llwm) Extremely bare, or naked.
Gorllwnc, *s. m.* (llwnc) An excessive swallow.
Gorllwng, *s. m.* (llwng) An excessive indraught.

Gorllwybr, *s. m.—pl. t.* au (llwybr) A trace, or track, over; the mark of a footstep; an impression of a foot.

> Gorllwybr llo llanwis cwyngant.
>
> The *track* of the boat the circle of foam did fill. *Ll. P. Moch.*

Gorllwybrad, *s. m.* (gorllwybr) An overtracing.
Gorllwybraw, *v. a.* (gorllwybr) To overtrace.
Gorllwybrawl, *a.* (gorllwybr) An over-training.
Gorllwydd, *s. m.* (llwydd) A leading over; success, prosperity.
Gorllwyddaw, *v. a.* (gorllwydd) To prosper, to give success; to succeed.

> Ni orllwyddwys na llysau nag tyfer arall yno wedi hyny.
>
> Neither herbs or other growth *did prosper* there after that. *Buchedd Addaf.*

Gorllwyddawl, *a.* (gorllwydd) Being prosperous.
Gorllwyddiad, *s. m.* (gorllwydd) A prospering.
Gorllwyn, *s. m.—pl. t.* au (llwyn) An escort.
Gorllwyn, *v. a.* (llwyn) To escort, to convoy.

> Gad imi— —
> D' orllwyn tua dy eur-llys.
>
> Suffer me to escort thee towards thy splendid mansion. *D. ab Gwilym.*

Gorllwynaw, *v. a.* (gorllwyn) To escort, to convoy; to be a safeguard.
Gorllwynawl, *a.* (gorllwyn) Being an escort.
Gorllwyniad, *s. m.—pl. t.* au (gorllwyn) An escorting, or convoying.
Gorllwynydd, *s. m.—pl. t.* ion (gorllwyn) One who convoys, or conducts safely.
Gorllwyth, *s. m.—pl. t.* au (llwyth) An overburden; a surcharge.
Gorllwythaw, *v. a.* (gorllwyth) To surcharge.
Gorllwythawg, *a.* (gorllwyth) Overburdened.
Gorllwythawl, *a.* (gorllwyth) Overburdening.
Gorllwythedig, *a.* (gorllwyth) Over-burdened.
Gorllyd, *a.* (gor) Broody, teeming; full of matter; suppurative. *Iar orllyd*, a brood hen; *wy gorllyd*, a hatching egg; *pluf gorllyd*, moulting feathers.
Gorllydrwydd, *s. m.* (gorllyd) Broodiness; aptness to teem; a tendency to suppurate.
Gorllydd, *s. m.—pl. t.* ion (llydd) An embryo.

> Yn orllydd cynnydd cyn ei [illegible];
> Yn orllwybr ar [illegible] [illegible] [illegible].
>
> An *embryo* of increase was the fair one though yet unborn; a form that was to wear the coralline stone. *Ior. Fychan.*

Gorllyddawl, *a.* (gorllydd) Belonging to an embryo.
Gorllyddiad, *s. m.* (gorllydd) A forming an embryo.
Gorllyfawl, *a.* (llyfawl) That is licked over.
Gorllyfiad, *s. m.* (llyfiad) A licking the surface.
Gorllyfn, *a.* (llyfn) Extremely smooth.
Gorllyfnawl, *a.* (gorllyfn) Tending to smooth.
Gorllyfniad, *s. m.—pl. t.* au (gorllyfn) A smoothing the surface; a coaxing; a harrowing.
Gorllyfnu, *v. a.* (gorllyfn) To smooth the surface, to make smooth, to stroke, or to coax; to harrow.

> Gorllyfnu pen ci tra eler heibio.
>
> Stroking a dog's head whilst going by. *Adage.*

> Og yn gorllyfnu eigiawn,
> Ewig y mor [illegible] [illegible].
>
> A harrow *smoothing* the ocean, the doe of the sea full of [illegible]. *Iolo Goch, i'r Llong.*

Gorllyfu, *v. a.* (llyfu) To lick the surface.
Gorllygawl, *a.* (gorllwg) Being escorting.
Gorllygiad, *s. m.—pl. t.* au (gorllwg) An escorting, a convoying; a protecting.
Gorllygu, *v. a.* (gorllwg) To escort; to protect. *Pwy a'n gorllyg?* Who will protect us?

> Gwyddam a'n gorllwg, gwr llwydwg [illegible];
> Gwr hydrfer angeu y'nghynghellawr.
>
> We know who protects us, a man of hoary aspect [illegible] [illegible], a man at whom death aims his dart in the private chamber. *Ll. P. Moch.*

Or a fag daiar hi a'i dwg i'w phlant,
A'i phlu oedd i'm gorllwg.

Of what the earth produces she takes to her children, and her feathers *protect* me. *Elidr Sais.*

Gorllygydd, *s. m.—pl. t.* ion (gorllwg) An escorter, a convoyer; a protector.

Gorllym, *a.* (llym) Extremely sharp, or acute.

Gorllymawl, *a.* (gorllym) Tending to sharpen extremely; very poignant.

Gorllymiad, *s. m.—pl. t.* au (gorllym) A making extremely sharp.

Gorllymu, *v. a.* (gorllym) To sharpen extremely.

Gogan sydd yn—gorllymu cerydd a gwarth ar bob drwg.

Satire does make the rebuke and shame of every thing bad *extremely poignant.* *Barddas.*

Gorllymwr, *s. m.—pl.* gorllymwyr (gorllym—gwr) One who makes extremely sharp.

Gorllymydd, *s. m.—pl. t.* ion (gorllym) One who sharpens extremely.

Gorm, *s. m.* (gor) What has a tendency to force in, or to fill; a plenum.

Gormail, *s. m.—pl.* gormeilion (gorm) The act of overwhelming; the act of overcoming; oppression; distress.

Gormant, *s. m.—pl.* gormaint (gorm) That tends to run in, or to over-fill, a plenitude.

Mabsant syw gormant gormes haint ni fid.

The patron saint with *plenitude* of health, the intrusion of infection he will not suffer. *Gw. Brycheiniawg.*

Ef oedd——
Ar bob sant gormant gwagant gwned.

He was over every saint in the *plenitude* of true glory. *Gw. Brycheiniawg.*

Gormawd, *s. m.—pl.* gormodion (gorm) Plenitude, exuberance, excess. *a.* Overmuch.

Gormawl, *a.* (gorm) Tending to fill in; plenary.

Gormedd, *s. f.—pl. t.* ion (gorm) An overrunning, intrusion, or encroachment; invasion; grievance; molestation.

Tair gormedd a ddaeth i'r ynys hon, ac nid aeth yr un drachefn; cyntaf y Coraniaid, a ddaethynt yma yn oes Lludd mab Beli; ail gormes y Gwyddyl Ffichti; trydydd, gormes y Saeson.

Three *intruders* came to this island, and not one departed again. the nation of the Coranl, who came in the time of Lludd, son of Beli; secondly, the invasion of the Gwyddyl Ffichti; thirdly, the invasion of the Saxons. *Trioedd.*

Gormeiliad, *s. m.—pl. t.* au (gormail) An oppressing, a domineering, oppression.

Gormeiliaidd, *a.* (gormail) Of an oppressive tendency; tending to overwhelm.

Gormeiliaw, *v. a.* (gormail) To overwhelm; to overcome, to prevail, to predominate; to oppress; to become predominant.

Os gormail un o'r pedwar defnydd eu gilydd, yna y bydd clefyd.

If one of the four elements *shall predominate* over the others, then disease will ensue. *Meddygon Myddfai.*

Gormeiliawg, *a.* (gormail) Being overwhelmed; oppressed, afflicted.

Gormeiliedig, *a.* (gormail) Being overwhelmed.

Gormeilieidd-dra, *s. m.* (gormeiliaidd) Oppressiveness, burdensomeness.

Gormeiliwr, *s. m.—pl.* gormeilwyr (gormail—gwr) An oppressor, or a tyrant.

Gormeilus, *a.* (gormail) Oppressive, tyrannical.

Gormeisiad, *s. m.—pl.* gormeisiaid (gormes) An encroacher, or intruder.

Am Forgant gormant, gormes Beulli,
Gormeisiad, blaeniad, blaen dyfysgi—
Mae galar.——

After Morgant the *bold*, encroaching as Beulli, an *intruder* and foremost one of the front of tumult, there is mourning. *Cynddelw, i Gadwallon.*

Gormes, *s. f.—pl. t.* ion (gorm) Intrusion, or encroachment; invasion, grievance. *Lleuad ormes*, an intruding moon, or the thirteenth moon in the course of one year; *gwenynen ormes*, a drone bee; *bod yn ormes*, to be an encroachment.

Gormes y taiawg ar ei gilydd.

The *intrusion* of the clown upon his fellow. *Adage.*

Gormes oedd y Saeson ar wir ddylyed y Brydeiniaid.

The Saxons were an *encroachment* upon the just right of the Britons. *Gr. ab Arthur.*

Gormesawl, *a.* (gormes) Intruding, trespassing, usurping; oppressive, troublesome.

Gormesdeyrn, *s. m.—pl. t.* edd (gormes—teyrn) An usurping prince, an intruding tyrant.

Gormesedig, *a.* (gormes) Molested; usurped.

Gormesgylch, *s. m.—pl. t.* au (gormes—cylch) A circle, or circuit, of grievance; an oppressive circuit.

Ail gwerth gwarth gwrthodes cywrain;
Ail gormail gormesgylch rhiain.

A second compensation for shame the first of people rejected; a second oppression the *vexatious circuit* of the maidens. *Cynddelw, Breiniau Powys.*

Gormesiad, *s. m.—pl. t.* au (gormes) An intruding; a molesting, intrusion, molestation.

Gormeslyn, *s. m.—pl. t.* oedd (gormes—llyn) A redundant humour; a plethora.

Gormeslynawg, *a.* (gormeslyn) Having a redundant humour.

Gormesoldeb, *s. m.* (gormesawl) Intrusiveness; oppressiveness; burdensomeness.

Gormesu, *v. a.* (gormes) To intrude, to encroach, to molest; to trouble, to usurp, to oppress, to be burdensome.

Gormeswr, *s. m.—pl.* gormeswyr (gormes—gwr) An intruder, or encroacher, a molester; an usurper; a troublesome person.

Gormesydd, *s. m.—pl. t.* ion (gormes) Intruder.

Gormiad, *s. m.—pl. t.* au (gorm) A forcing in.

Gormod, *s. m.—pl. t.* oedd (gorm) Redundance, superfluity, excess. *a.* Redundant, superfluous. *a.* Too much, overmuch, too great.

Gormodawl, *a.* (gormod) Superabundant.

Gormodedd, *s. m.* (gormod) Superabundance.

Gormodi, *v. n.* (gormod) To superabound.

Gormodiad, *s. m.* (gormod) A rendering, or becoming redundant; a superabounding.

Gormodoldeb, *s. m.* (gormodawl) Excessiveness.

Gormodolrwydd, *s.* (gormodawl) Excessiveness.

Gormodd, *s. m.—pl. t.* ion (gorm) Excess; superabundance. *a.* Overmuch, too much.

Gwedi darfod iddynt gyflawni eu enrhydedd i'r dwywau, o'r gweddillion a'r gormoddion, hwyntau eu hunain a fwytaynt, megys y gweddid yn y rhyw aberthau.

After they had fulfilled their devotion to the gods, of the remains and *superfluities* they themselves then did eat, as it was meet in those sacrifices. *Gr. ab Arthur.*

Gormoddawl, *a.* (gormodd) Redundant.

Gormoddi, *v. a.* (gormodd) To make redundant.

Gormoddiad, *s. m.* (gormodd) A making redundant

Gormoddiaeth, *s. m.* (gormodd) A redundance.

Ni bydd ef byth yn wr da
Ag na wypo gwahaniaeth
Rhwng digon a gormoddiaeth.

He will never be a good man who knows no difference between enough and *excess.* *T. Ll. D. ab Hywel.*

Gormoddoldeb, *s.* (gormoddawl) Excessiveness.

Gormoddolrwydd, *s. m.* (gormoddawl) Excessiveness, superfluity, abundance.

Gormu, *v. a.* (gorm) To tend to force in; to intrude; to pervade.

Gormus, *a.* (gorm) Tending to force in, or to overrun; intrusive, pervading.

Gormwyth, *s. m.—pl. t.* oedd (gorm—gwyth) A rheum.

Gormwythaidd, *a.* (gormwyth) Rheumatic.

Gormwythaw, *v. a.* (gormwyth) To generate rheum.

Gormwythawg, *a.* (gormwyth) Rheumy.

Gormwythawl, *a.* (gormwyth) Catarrhous.

Gormwythiad, *s.m.—pl. t.* au (gormwyth) A flowing of rheum, a defluxion.

Gormwythig, *a.* (gormwyth) Rheumy.

Gormwythus, *a.* (gormwyth) Catarrhous.

Gormwythusrwydd, *s. m.* (gormwythus) The state of being rheumy, or catarrhous.

Gornawf, *s. m.* (nawf) A swim on the surface.

Gorne, *s. m.—pl. t.* oedd (ne) A superior hue; an exterior tint; a blush.

> Gwell gofne golchi nag on glythai.
>
> The *exterior hue* of washing is better than any soaking.
> *Adage.*

> Gwery [illegible] fanwl gwar [illegible] faith,
> Gorne gawr fore ar [illegible] [illegible].
>
> Chaste and perfect queen, of mind gentle and profound, with the *passing hue* of the dawn of morning on a raging sea.
> *Cynddelw, i Efa f. Madawg.*

Gornerth, *s. m.—pl. t.* oedd (nerth) Superior power, or impulse; also the knotty-rooted figwort, otherwise called *y ddeilen ddu, dail duon du, craith unnos*, and *goreunerth*.

Gornerthawl, *a.* (gornerth) Very powerful.

Gornerthiad, *s. m.—pl. t.* au (gornerth) A giving, or attaining, superior power.

Gornerthrwydd, *s.m.* (gornerth) Superior power, or force.

Gornerthu, *v. a.* (gornerth) To endow with superior power; to attain superior power, to attain superiority.

> Dy wybodaeth di sy ryfeddach nag y gallwyf ei threyllaw: mor hi yn arbenawg, ni allai mo'i gornerthu.
>
> Thy knowledge is more wonderful than that I should be able to deceive it. It is excellent, I cannot *surmount* it.
> *W. Perri, Psalm cxxxix. 6.*

Gornidr, *s. m.—pl. t.* au (nidr) Extreme intricacy or entanglement.

Gornidraw, *v. a.* (gornidr) To entangle extremely; to be bewildered extremely.

Gornidrawl, *a.* (gornidr) Very intricate.

Gornidriad, *s.m.* (gornidr) An entangling, or embarrassing extremely.

Gornod, *s. m.—pl. t.* au (nod) Conspicuous mark.

Gornodawl, *a.* (gornod) Conspicuously marked.

Gornodi, *v. a.* (gornod) To mark conspicuously.

Gornodiad, *s. m.—pl. t.* au (gornod) A marking conspicuously.

Gornofiad, *s. m.—pl. t.* au (gornawf) A swimming above, supernatation.

Gornofiaw, *v. a.* (gornawf) To swim above.

Gornofiawl, *a.* (gornawf) Supernatant.

Gorawyf, *s. m.—pl. t.* au (nwyf) Superior, or extreme briskness.

Gorawyfaw, *v. a.* (gorawyf) To endow with extreme briskness, or vivacity; to wanton.

Gorawyfawl, *a.* (gorawyf) Tending to make extremely brisk, or lively.

Gorawyfiad, *s. m.* (gorawyf) A making, or becoming, extremely brisk.

Gorawyfus, *a.* (gorawyf) Extremely brisk.

Gorober, *s. m.* (gober) An over-work; a seat.

> Rhy [illegible] [illegible] [illegible] cymer;
> Rhy [illegible] i wir, i orober.
>
> The minstrels will greatly praise, in concordant melody; his justice will be highly praised, and his supererogation.
> *Ein. ab Gwgon, i Lywelyn I.*

> [illegible] haul didawl, [illegible] fyrder darfyn;
> Yn hoedl dyn [illegible] trwm orober.
>
> Uniform the incessant sun, deceiving the abruptness of his career; to the life of momentary man, with heavy *load*.
> *Gr. ab M. ab Dafydd.*

> Golud mawr yw gweled modd
> Y gorober a grifiodd.
>
> It is a great profit to see the manner in which she carried the *extraordinary task*.
> *Dafydd Nez, i'r wenfon.*

Gorofal, *s. m.—pl. t.* on (gofal) Extreme care.

Gorofalus, *a.* (gorofal) Overcareful, overcautious.

Gorofer, *a.* (ofer) Extremely trifling.

Goroferedd, *s. m.* (gorofer) Extreme triflingness.

Gorofn, *s.m.—pl. t.* au (ofn) Extreme fear, or dread

> Gorofn y sydd arnaf hyd nas gwared dyn,
> Wedi Llywelyn, llywiawdr Gwynedd.
>
> *Extreme dread* afflicts me lest no man shall deliver me, after Llywelyn, the governor of the Land of Felicity.
> *D. Benfras.*

Gorofnawg, *a.* (gorofn) Over fearful.

Gorofnawl, *a.* (gorofn) Extremely awful.

Gorofni, *v. n.* (gorofn) To fear extremely; to be timid overmuch.

Gorofniad, *s. m.* (gorofn) A fearing extremely; a being over-timed

Gorofnus, *a.* (gorofn) Extremely timid.

Gorolch, *s. m.* (golch) An over-wash, a washing of the surface.

Gorolchaid, *a.* (gorolch) That is washed over.

Gorolchi, *v. a.* (gorolch) To over-wash.

> A chyn i ein dan elorch,
> Un ytoedd wryd yn i eirch,
> Gorolchas o greu i seirch:
> Buddfan fab Bleiddfan ddiaflarch.
>
> And before he was covered under the swans, one who would appear a hero in his shrine, *gore did over-wash* his harness: Buddfan the son of Bleiddfan the dauntless.
> *Aneurin.*

> Gwyar gorgolchir gwarthaf iad.
>
> The top of the head *will be over-washed* with blood.
> *Taliesin.*

Gorolchiad, *s. m.—pl. t.* au (gorolch) A washing over; ablution.

Gorolygawl, *a.* (golygawl) Being overlooking.

Gorolygiad, *s. m.* (golygiad) A supervision.

Gorolygu, *v. a.* (golygu) To supervise.

Goror, *s. f.—pl. t.* au (gor—or) An exterior border, coast, or region; a clime, the upper region; a confine, or border.

Gororawl, *a.* (goror) Boundary, bordering.

Gororeu, *s. m.—pl. t.* on (goreu) The very best. *a.* Superlative.

Gororwy, *s. m.—pl. t.* on (gorwy) The extreme verge, or rim.

Gorpharawd, *a.* (parawd) Being over-ready.

Gorphell, *a.* (pell) Very distant, very far.

Gorphelledd, *s. m.* (gorphell) Extreme remoteness; great distance.

Gorphelliad, *s. m.* (gorphell) A making very distant.

Gorphellu, *v. a.* (gorphell) To put very remote.

Gorphen, *s. m.—pl. t.* ion (pen) Extreme head, or end, a conclusion, the end, or termination.

> Pawb yn y gorphen.
>
> Every body in the conclusion.
> *Adage.*

Gorphen, *v. a.* (pen) To complete, to conclude, to finish, to end, to terminate.

Gorphenawl, *a.* (gorphen) Concluding, finishing.

Gorphenedig, *a.* (gorphen) That is concluded.

Gorphenhaf, *s. m.* (gorphen—haf) July.

Gorpheniad, *s.m.—pl. t.* au (gorphen) A finishing.

Gorphenu, *v. a.* (gorphen) To complete, to finish.

Gorphenwr, *s. m.—pl.* gorphenwyr (gorphen—gwr) A finisher, one who concludes, or ends.

Gorpherchi, *v. a.* (perchi) To reverence greatly, to adore.

Gorphowys, *s. m.—pl. t.* au (powys) Rest, repose, cessation from motion. *Nid oes na rheol na gorphowys arno*, there is neither rule nor rest in him. *Sil.*

Gorphowys, *v. n.* (powys) To rest, to repose.
Gorphowysaw, *v. a.* (gorphowys) To repose.
Gorphowysdra, *s. m.* (gorphowys) Reposedness.
Gorphwyll, *s. m.—pl. t.* oedd(pwyll) Loss of reason, distraction, madness, rage, folly.
Gorphwyllaw, *v. n.* (gorphwyll) To become distracted, to go mad, to lose the senses.
Gorphwyllawg, *a.* (gorphwyll) Being distracted, insane, or mad; being out of reason.
Gorphwylliad, *s. m.* (gorphwyll) A distracting; a becoming distracted; distraction.
Gorphwyllus, *a.* (gorphwyll) Tending to distract.
Gorphwys, *s. m.* (pwys) Rest, or repose.
Gorphwys, *v. n.* (pwys) To rest, to repose.
Gorphwysaw, *v. a.* (gorphwys) To go to rest, to rest; to take rest, to repose, to be at rest; to leave off, to cease, to desist.
Gorphwysawl, *a.* (gorphwys) Resting; quiescent.
Gorphwysdra, *s. m.* (gorphwys) Reposedness.
Gorphwysfa, *s. f.—pl. t.* au (gorphwys) A resting place, a rest.
Gorphwysiawn, *a.* (gorphwys) Restful, apt to rest.
Gorphwysle, *s. m.—pl. t.* oedd (gorphwys—lle) A resting place.
Gorphwyswr, *s. m.—pl.* gorphwyswyr (gorphwys—gwr) One who takes rest, a reposer.
Gorphwysydd, *s. m.—pl. t.* ion (gorphwys) A quietist.
Gorphwysyddiaeth, *s. m.* (gorphwysydd) Quietism
Gorrif, *s. m.—pl. t.* ion (rhif) An extra number.
Gorrifawl, *a.* (gorrif) Supernumerary.
Gorsaf, *s. f.—pl. t.* oedd (saf) A station, a stand, a standing place. *Gorsaf arf*, a magazine of arms; *gorsaf cyfraith*, a demur, or exception of law; *gorsaf gyfreithiawl*, a lawful exception.

Nid rhaid gwad dros orsaf: arddelw cyfreithiawl y sy gennyf fi, gorsafedig yn y gyfraith.

No denial is necessary for an *exception*: a lawful voucher I am possessed of, excepted in the law. *Welsh Laws.*

Gorsafawl, *a.* (gorsaf) Stationary, positional, standing. *Brwydr orsafawl*, a pitched battle.
Gorsafedig, *a.* (gorsaf) Being stationed, or pitched; excepted, demurred.
Gorsafiad, *s. m.—pl. t.* au (gorsaf) A stationing, a taking a station; a putting to a stand; a stopping, or halting; a withstanding, an opposition.
Gorsafoldeb, *s. m.* (gorsafawl) Stationariness.
Gorsafolrwydd, *s. m.* (gorsafawl) Stationariness.
Gorsafu, *v. a.* (gorsaf) To station, to settle, to stand in opposition, to withstand; to demur.
Gorsafwr, *s. m.—pl.* gorsafwyr (gorsaf—gwr) One who stations, or settles; an opposer.
Gorsaig, *s. m.—pl.* gorseigiau (saig) A superior mess, or course of meat.
Gorsang, *s. f.—pl. t.* au (sang) An over-tread.
Gorsangawl, *a.* (gorsang) Over-treading.
Gorsangedig, *a.* (gorsang) Over-trodden.
Gorsangiad, *s. m.—pl. t.* au (gorsang) A treading above, an over-treading.
Gorsangu, *v. a.* (gorsang) To over-tread.

Na orsang dy len, dy les wyf fi;
Na orsaf arnaf er neb ynl.

Over-tread not thy veil, I am thy gain; withstand me not, on account of any incitement. *Ll. P. Moch, i D. ab Owain.*

Gorsangwr, *s. m.—pl.* gorsangwyr (gorsang—gwr) one who over-treads.
Gorsedd, *s. f.—pl. t.* au (sedd) A supreme seat; a throne; a raised mound, tumulus, or place of presidency; a tribune, a tribunal, or court of judicature. *Gorsedd freinniawg*, a privileged session; *gorsedd gwlad ac arglwydd*, a session of the king and country, or of civil judicature; *Gorsedd ddygynnull*, a conventional session, an extraordinary tribunal; *gorsedd beirdd*, the session of the bards; *gorsedd daleithiawg*, a provincial assembly; *gorsedd gyfallwy*, the session of competency, being the third meeting, wherein what had been so many times recited was either ratified or rejected, by the bards; *Gorsedd cyngyd cynnal*, a session of confederate support; *gorsedd cyclad*, a federate country session; *gorsedd benbaladr*, a supreme, or special, session, or *rhaith Cymmry benbaladr*, the supreme voice of the Cymmry.

Tripheth nid oes a el yn eu herbyn: defawd gorsedd, cân gorsedd, a llafar gorsedd.

Three things which cannot be controverted: the usage of the *convention*, the song of the *convention*, and the voice of the *convention*. *Barddas.*

Gorseddawg, *a.* (gorsedd) Having a supreme seat; presiding. *s. c.—pl.* Gorseddogion, that has a presidency; a president; a magistrate.

Tri-dyn gorseddawg ynt, brenin, esgob, ac abad.

Three persons of *presidency* are, a king, a bishop, and an abbot. *Welsh Laws.*

Gorseddawl, *a.* (gorsedd) Relating to a supreme seat; presiding. *Crug gorseddawl*, the hill of judicature.
Gorseddedig, *a.* (gorsedd) Made presidential.
Gorseddfa, *s. f.—pl.* gorseddfeydd (gorsedd) A place of presidency; a seat of judicature.
Gorseddfaawl, *a.* (gorseddfa) Relating to presidency; judicatory.
Gorseddfainc, *s. f.—pl.* gorseddfeinciau (gorsedd—mainc) A seat of presidency; a throne.

A fydd cymdeithas i ti a gorseddfainc anwiredd?

Shall the *throne* of iniquity have fellowship with thee? *Psalm* xciv. 20.

Gorseddiad, *s. m.—pl. t.* au (gorsedd) A presiding, a sitting in judgement; a gossipping, or tattling
Gorseddogaeth, *s. m.—pl. t.* au (gorseddawg) The office of a president.
Gorseddogawl, *a.* (gorseddawg) Belonging to a presidency.
Gorseddogi, *v. a.* (gorseddawg) To endow with presidency; to become president.
Gorseddu, *v. a.* (gorsedd) To preside; to sit in judgement; to tattle; to establish one's self.
Gorseddwr, *s. m.—pl.* gorseddwyr (gorsedd—gwr) One who sits in judgement; a president.
Gorseddwraig, *s. f.—pl.* gorseddwreigedd (gorsedd—gwraig) A woman who presides, a tattling gossip
Gorsefyll, *v. a.* (gorsaf) To stand over; to take a station; to stand; to insist; to withstand.

Nid ef gwledig a orsafer.

He is not a sovereign who *shall be opposed*. *Cynddelw.*

Na'th orsaif na moel na myngawg.

Thou wilt not be opposed by a bald one nor one with flowing hair. *Ll. P. Moch.*

Gorsefylliad, *s. m.—pl. t.* au (gorsefyll) A taking a station, a stationing; a subsisting; an insisting; a withstanding.

Tebyg—bod y fath beth a dylanwad ac effaith uniongyrch, digyfrwng, a pharhaus yn llifeiriaw o allu Duw tuagat ein gorsefylliad, neu ein cynnaliad ni.

It is likely enough that there is such a thing as a direct influx and effect, immediate and continual, flowing from the power of God towards our *subsistence* or our support. *Ier. Owain.*

Gorsefylliawg, *a.* (gorsefyll) Being placed, or stationed; being insisting, or opposing.
Gorsefyllrwydd, *s. m.* (gorsefyll) The state of being stationed, or placed; opposedness.
Gorseiddiawg, *a.* (gorsedd) Having presidency.
Gorselawg, *a.* (selawg) Having an earnest look.

Gorsellad, *s. m.*—*pl. t.* au (sellad) A looking earnestly; a gazing.
Gorsela, *v. a.* (sellu) To look very stedfastly.
Gorsangi, *v. a.* (gorsang) To over-tread.
Gorserth, *a.* (serth) Extremely precipitate.
Gorserthawl, *a.* (gorserth) Very precipitous.
Gorserthiad, *s. m.* (gorserth) A rendering extremely precipitous; a becoming very steep.
Gorserthu, *v. n.* (gorserth) To become extremely precipitous; to make very steep; to be very loose, or obscene.
Gorsin, *s. m.*—*pl. t.* au (sin) A door-post.

Adwaen bob gorsin y'ngogof gorllewin.

I know every *pillar* in the cave of the west. *Taliesin.*

Taro gapan y drws fel y siglo y gorsingau.

Strike the lintel of the door so as to shake the *door posts.* *Amos* ix. 1.

Gorsor, *s. m.* (sor) Extreme offence, or pet.
Gorsori, *v. n.* (gorsor) To take extreme umbrage.
Gorsoriad, *s. m.* (gorsor) A being extremely offended; a being in a violent pet.
Gorsych, *a.* (sych) Extremely dry, or parched.
Gorsychawl, *a.* (gorsych) Extremely drying.
Gorsychiad, *s. m.* (gorsych) A drying extremely.
Gorsychu, *v. a.* (gorsych) To dry extremely.
Gorsylw, *s. m.*—*pl. t.* au (sylw) Earnest notice.
Gorsylwad, *s. m.*—*pl. t.* au (gorsylw) A regarding very earnestly.
Gorsylwawl, *a.* (gorsylw) Earnestly beholding.
Gorsylwi, *v. a.* (gorsylw) To regard earnestly.
Gorsylliad, *s. m.*—*pl. t.* au (sylliad) A beholding very earnestly; a gazing.
Gorsyllu, *v. a.* (syllu) To behold stedfastly.
Gorsŷn, *a.* (sŷn) Being extremely astonished.
Gorsynawl, *a.* (gorsyn) Tending to astonish, or stupify the senses, extremely.
Gorsyndawd, *s. m.* (gorsŷn) Great astonishment.
Gorsynu, *v. a.* (gorsŷn) To astonish extremely; to be extremely astonished, or amazed.
Gorsyth, *a.* (syth) Extremely erect; very stiff.
Gorsythawl, *a.* (gorsyth) Apt to be very erect.
Gorsythder, *s. m.* (gorsyth) Extreme erectness.
Gorsythdra, *s. m.* (gorsyth) Extreme erectness.
Gorsythedd, *s. m.* (gorsyth) Extreme erectness.
Gorsythiad, *s. m.*—*pl. t.* au (gorsyth) A rendering very erect, or stiff; a becoming very erect.
Gorsythu, *v. n.* (gorsyth) To become very erect, or stiff; to make very erect, or stiff.
Gort, *s. m.* (gor) A sharp spring, or impulse.
Gortain, *v. a.* (gort) To spring, or impel quickly.
Gortawl, *a.* (gort) Having a sharp impulse.
Gortiad, *s. m.*—*pl. t.* au (gort) An impelling, or uttering out sharply.
Gortiaw, *v. a.* (gort) To impel, or push sharply.
Gorth, *s. m.* (gor) That abuts, or stands opposite
Gorthasg, *s. f.*—*pl. t.* au (tasg) An over-task.
Gorthasgawl, *a.* (gorthasg) Being over-tasked.
Gorthasgiad, *s. m.*—*pl. t.* au (gorthasg) A giving an over-task.
Gorthasgu, *v. a.* (gorthasg) To give an over task.
Gorthaw, *s. m.* (taw) Extreme taciturnity, or silence; endurance without complaint; patience. *Gwr da ei orthaw*, a man of good forbearance, or a patient man.
Gorthawl, *s. m.*—*pl.* gortholion (tawl) An overbalance, a preponderance.
Gorthenau, *s. pl.* (gorth—genau) Opposing lips. *a.* Of opposing lips.

Yfwys bualin, bruiet ariant am ariant,
A'i gortho oed gorthenau.

The Bison of buffalo horn, highly enriched with ancient silver, he that covers it is not *of opposing lips.* *O. Cyfeiliawg.*

Gorthew, *a.* (tew) Extremely thick, or gross.

Bleidd bydd orthew yn aerva blyngawd.

The wolf of the *thickest* is gone in the sullen scene of sorrow. *Meilyr.*

Hywerth feirch orthew.

The worth sought for steeds most *sleek.* *Gwalchmai.*

Gorthewi, *v. n.* (gorthaw) To become very silent, or calm; to make very silent.

Gorthewis hi wrthyf, gwerth fy hirglwyf;
Nid gorthaw a wnaf fi wrth a garwyf.

She remained most *silent* to me, a cause of my tedious illness; *to be very silent* will not be what I shall do to the one I love. *Cynddelw, i Efa f. Madawg.*

Menestr a'm gorthaw na'm adawed.

The cup-bearer *tranquillizes* me, let him not leave me. *O. Cyfeiliawg.*

Gorthir, *s. m.*—*pl. t.* oedd (tir) The higher part of a country, the upper country, the highland.

Saith randir sydd yn mhob maenawl yn nro gyfannedd, a thair tref ar ddeg yn maenawl orthir.

There are seven portions of land in every manor of an inhabited region, and thirteen townships in an upland manor. *Welsh Laws.*

Gorthirawl, *a.* (gorthir) Being upland.
Gortho, *s. m.* (to) The upper covering, the roof; an envelope. *Gortho tir*, brush-wood.

Y bardd ni'm gostego,
Gostegf ni's caffo,
Oni el mewn gortho,
O ddaiar a gro.

The bard who shall not silence me, no silence may he obtain, until he goes into a *covering* of earth and gravel. *Taliesin.*

Gorthöad, *s. m.* (gortho) A covering over, or enveloping; an overcasting.
Gorthoawl, *a.* (gortho) Tending to envelope.
Gorthöedig, *a.* (gortho) Covered over, enveloped
Gorthöi, *v. a.* (gortho) To cover above, to cover over; to envelope; to overcast.

Pall, gwylfan gwylain,
Gwyl-falch wrth gerddawr
O ruddaur gwrthfawr
Y gorthöir.

A couch, the modest retreat of her who is like the sea-mew, diffidently proud of the minstrel, with precious ruddy gold is it covered. *Cynddelw, i Efa f. Madawg.*

Gorthorawl, *a.* (torawl) Being broken over.
Gorthorch, *s. f.*—*pl.* gorthyrch (torch) A superior wreath, a torque, a collar.

Ac yn ngwaith Arderydd oedd aur fy ngorthorch.

And in the action of Arderydd of gold was my *collar.* *Myrddin.*

A gorthorch aur am ei fwnwgl.

With a golden *collar* round his neck. *B. M. Wledig—Maddington.*

Gorthorch ni wnaf ei gwrthod.

A collar which I will not refuse. *Iolo Goch.*

Gorthorchawl, *a.* (gorthorch) Over-wreathing.
Gorthorchi, *v. a.* (gorthorch) To wreath round.
Gorthorchiad, *s. m.* (gorthorch) An over-wreathing
Gorthordd, *s. m.*—*pl. t.* ion (gorth—gordd) That is abutting, or external; that is out of jurisdiction; a banished one.

A'm rhodd fy ngwledig gwleddiadon,
Drefred gwlad wared orthorddion.

I am gifted by my sovereign of banqueters with the inheritance of a country, the refuge of the *exiles.* *Cynddelw.*

Gorthorddawl, *a.* (gorthordd) Being banished.
Gorthorddi, *v. a.* (gorthordd) To banish, to exile.
Gorthorddiad, *s. m.* (gorthordd) A banishing.
Gorthòri, *v. a.* (tòri) To cut over, to score; to make an incision.
Gorthòriad, *s. m.*—*pl. t.* au (tòriad) An incision; a cutting over; a scoring.
Gorthòriant, *s. m.* (tòriant) Incision; infraction.

Nid oeth trais dros Emrais a'i blant;
O'i amarswdd gwarthfawdd gorthoriant.

No violence was brooked by Emrais and his race, his misery was the *breaking* of the rage of scandal. *Cynddelw, i O. Gwynedd.*

A Dinbych wrthddrych orthoriant ar fil,
Ar Forfan, a Gronant.

The example of Denbigh was a *destruction* to a thousand on Morfan, and Gronant. *Ll. P. Moch, i Lywelyn I.*

Gorthrain, *s. m.* (train) Extreme scattering, prodigality. *a.* Very lavish, or prodigal.

Arglodig argiwyddi orthrain,
Arglwydd llawr, argiwydd mawr madiain.

The superior in fame of prodigal chiefs, the grounded bulwark, great lord of blessings. *Cynddelw, i O. Gwynedd.*

Gorthrais, *s. m.—pl.* gorthreisian (trais) Excessive rapacity, violence, or outrage.

Gorthrech, *s. m.—pl. t.* ion (trech) Mastery; victory; a keeping under by force.

Tri gorthrech ar ddrwg a chythraul y sydd: gwybodaeth, cariad, a gallu: gan y gwyr, y myn, ac y dichon y rhai hyn yn eu cynghyd y pethau a fynont; ac yng nghyflwr dyn eu dechre, a'u parau dros byth.

There are three *victories* over evil and the devil: knowledge, love, and power: for these know, will, and can perform what they list, in their connection; and in the state of humanity they originate, and they continue to eternity. *Barddas.*

Gorthrechadwy, *a.* (gorthrech) That may be mastered; conquerable; oppressible.

Gorthrechawl, *a.* (gorthrech) Domineering.

Gorthrechiad, *s. m.—pl. t.* au (gorthrech) A mastering, a conquering; oppression.

Gorthrechiannawl, *a.* (gorthrechiant) Dominative, tending to become oppressive.

Gorthrechianniad, *s. m.* (gorthrechiant) Domination, a becoming oppressive.

Gorthrechiannu, *v. a.* (gorthrechiant) To cause oppression; to become overbearing.

Gorthrechiannus, *a.* (gorthrechiant) Dominative.

Gorthrechiant, *s. m.* (gorthrech) Domination.

Gorthrechu, *v. a.* (gorthrech) To get the mastery, to master; to overcome, to get the better.

Gorthrechus, *a.* (gorthrech) Domineering.

Gorthrechwr, *s. m.—pl.* gorthrechwyr (gorthrech—gwr) One who gets the mastery; an oppressor

Gorthreiniad, *s. m.* (gorthrain) A scattering profusely; a lavishing to excess.

Gorthreiniaw, *v. a.* (gorthrain) To scatter profusely; to lavish to excess.

Gorthreiniawl, *a.* (gorthrain) Very lavishing.

Gorthreisiad, *s. m.* (gorthrais) An acting very rapaciously, or violently.

Gorthreisiaw, *v. a.* (gorthrais) To act very rapaciously; to do great violence.

Gorthreisiawl, *a.* (gorthrais) Very violent.

Gorthrin, *s. m.—pl. t.* ion (trin) An extreme toil.

Gwalchmai,——
O bae arnat ti orthrin,
Mi a wnawn waed hyd ddeulin.

Gwalchmai—shouldst thou be in *difficulty*, I will cause blood to flow to the knees. *Ymdd. G. a Thrystan.*

Gorthriniad, *s. m.* (gorthrin) A toiling extremely.

Gorthriniaw, *v. a.* (gorthrin) To toil extremely.

Gorthriniawl, *a.* (gorthrin) Very toilsome.

Gorthro, *s. m.—pl. t.* ion (tro) A turn over.

Gorthröad, *s. m.—pl. t.* au (gorthro) A turning over; a twisting over.

Gorthröawl, *a.* (gorthro) Turning over.

Gorthröi, *v. a.* (gorthro) To turn, or twist over.

Gorthrwch, *s. m.—pl.* gorthrychion (trwch) A groove, a groove in the stave of a cask, for holding the headpiece.

Gorthrwm, *a.* (trwm) Very heavy, or depressive.

Gorthrychawl, *a.* (gorthrwch) Being cut over.

Gorthrychiad, *s. m.—pl. t.* au (gorthrwch) A cutting over; a grooving.

Gorthrychu, *v. a.* (gorthrwch) To make a groove.

Gorthrymadwy, *a.* (gorthrwm) That may be greatly depressed, or oppressed.

Gorthrymawl, *a.* (gorthrwm) Very depressive.

Gorthrymder, *s. m.—pl. t.* au (gorthrwm) Great depression; heaviness; oppression; affliction.

Gorthrymdreth, *s. f.—pl. t.* i (gorthrwm—treth) An oppressive tax, or exaction.

Gorthrymedig, *a.* (gorthrwm) Being oppressed.

Gorthrymedigaeth, *s. m.—pl. t.* au (gorthrymedig) Depression, oppression.

Gorthrymedigawl, *a.* (gorthrymedig) Tending to be depressed; depressive, oppressive.

Gorthrymedd, *s. m.* (gorthrwm) Oppressiveness.

Gorthrymgaeth, *a.* (gorthrwm—caeth) Oppressively straitened.

Yna eu gwared hwynt a wnaeth
O'u holl orthrymgaeth foddion.

Then did he deliver them out of all their *heavily confined* conditions. *E. Prys, Ps. cvii.*

Gorthrymiad, *s. m.—pl. t.* au (gorthrwm) A greatly depressing; an oppressing.

Gorthrymiannawl, *a.* (gorthrymiant) Tending to depression; depressive, oppressive.

Gorthrymianniad, *s. m.* (gorthrymiant) A causing depression, or oppression.

Gorthrymiannu, *v. a.* (gorthrymiant) To cause an oppression; to become an oppression.

Gorthrymiant, *s. m.* (gorthrwm) Oppression.

Gorthrymig, *a.* (gorthrwm) Oppressive.

Gorthrymu, *v. a.* (gorthrwm) To depress greatly, to oppress; to burden; to afflict.

Gorthrymus, *a.* (gorthrwm) Oppressive; vexing.

Gorthrymwr, *s. m.—pl.* gorthrymwyr (gorthrwm—gwr) An oppressor.

Gorthrymydd, *s. m.—pl. t.* ion (gorthrwm) An oppressor.

Gorthur, *s. m.* (gorth) A repulse, or repulsion.

Gorthwf, *s. m.* (twf) An overgrowth; an excrescence; luxuriance.

Gorthwy, *s. m.—pl. t.* on (twy) A stretch over.

Gorthwym, *a.* (twym) Overwarm, overhot.

Gorthwymnaw, *v. a.* (gorthwymyn) To overheat.

Gorthwymniad, *s. m.* (gorthwym) An overheating

Gorthwymyn, *a.* (gorthwym) Overhot, very hot.

Gorthyfail, *s. m.* (gorthwf) The chervil.

Gorthyfawl, *a.* (gorthwf) Overgrown, excrescent.

Gorthyfiad, *s. m.—pl. t.* au (gorthwf) An overgrowing, a growing upon; excrescence.

Gorthyfiannawl, *a.* (gorthyfiant) Tending to overgrow, or to become overgrown.

Gorthyfianniad, *s. m.* (gorthyfiant) A rendering overgrown; a becoming overgrown.

Gorthyfiannu, *v. a.* (gorthyfiant) To cause to overgrow; to become overgrown.

Gorthyfiant, *s. m.* (gorthwf) An overgrowth.

Gorthyfu, *v. a.* (gorthwf) To overgrow; to grow as an excrescence; to luxuriate.

Gorthyn, *s. m.—pl. t.* ion (tyn) An overstrain. *a.* Overtight, overstrained.

Gorthynawl, *a.* (gorthyn) Over-straining.

Gorthyndra, *s. m.* (gorthyn) Overtightness.

Gorthynedig, *a.* (gorthyn) Overstrained.

Gorthyniad, *s. m.—pl. t.* au (gorthyn) An overstraining, an overdrawing.

Gorthynu, *v. a.* (gorthyn) To overstrain.

Gorthywys, *s. pl. aggr.* (tywys) That leads supremely; a generalissimo.

Wrth fy Nuw na fyn fy nidawl;
Ac wrthyd orthywys greidiawl
Na'm dod, udd mandoedd, yn mantawl ac aur.

From my God, do not wish to separate me; and with thyself, thou ardent *leader supreme*, and chief of fair-rooted mansions, place me not in the balance with gold. *Ll. P. Moch, i D. ab Owain.*

Amyneddus fym, fer cadeithi,
Euwawg orthywys, o'm gorthewl.

Patient have I been, bulwark of the conflicts, noble and supreme leader, in being constrained to be silent.
Ll. P. Moch, i D. ab Owain.

Gorthywysaw, *v. a.* (gorthywys) To lead supremely
Gorthywysawl, *a.* (gorthywys) Supremely leading
Gorthywysiad, *s. m.* (gorthywys) A leading supremely.
Goru, *v. a.* (gor) To cause; to accomplish.

Yn meddu meddgwd i oru eirchiawn.
Possessing a store of mead to indure the suitors.
Gwalchmai.

Goruch, *s. m.—pl. t.* ion (uch) That is above, or over; supremacy, sovereignty. *a.* Upper, uppermost, sovereign.

Efa—ti a fyddi tan oruch gwr.
Eve, thou wilt be under the dominion of man.
Ll. G. Hergest.

Goruch, *prep.* (uch) Above, superior to, over. *adv.* Above, over.
Goruchadail, *s. f.* (goruch—adail) Superstructure
Goruchadeilad, *s. m.* (goruchadail) Superstructure
Goruchadeilaw, *v. a.* (goruchadail) To superstruct
Goruchaf, *a.* (goruch) Most high, supreme, upper, uppermost. *s. m.* The Most High.
Goruchafaidd, *a.* (goruchaf) Tending to become supreme; predominant.

Cenfigen sydd oruchafaidd yn y rhai drwg, megys cariad perffaith yn y rhai da.
Envy is *predominant* in the wicked ones, as charity is in those that are good.
Marchawg Crwydrad.

Goruchafawd, *s. m.* (goruchaf) A rendering, or becoming supreme.
Goruchafawl, *a.* (goruchaf) Tending to render supreme; supereminent.
Goruchafiad, *s. m.* (goruchaf) A rendering, or becoming, supreme.
Goruchafiaeth, *s. m.—pl. t.* au (goruchaf) Supremacy, sovereignty; promotion; acquisition; victory, triumph.
Goruchafiaethawl, *a.* (goruchafiaeth) Relating to supremacy, or sovereignty.
Goruchafiaethu, *v. a.* (goruchafiaeth) To render supreme; to become sovereign.
Goruchafle, *s. m.—pl. t.* oedd (goruchaf—lle) A supreme place or station.
Goruchafu, *v. a.* (goruchaf) To exalt over.
Goruchalwad, *s. m.* (goruch—galwad) A superior calling; a supreme vocation.
Goruchanian, *s. f.—pl. t.* oedd (goruch—anian) That is supernatural; metaphysics. *a.* Supernatural.
Goruchanianawl, *a.* (goruchanian) Supernatural.
Goruchaniander, *s. m.* (goruchanian) Supernaturalness.
Goruchanianolaeth, *s. m.* (goruchanianawl) The science of metaphysics.
Goruchanianoldeb, *s. m.* (goruchanianawl) Supernaturalness, preternaturalness.
Goruchanianolder, *s. m.* (goruchanianawl) Supernaturalness, preternaturalness.
Goruchanianoli, *v. a.* (goruchanianawl) To render supernatural; to become supernatural.
Goruchanianrwydd, *s. m.* (goruchanian) Supernaturalness, preternaturalness.
Goruchanianu, *v. a.* (goruchanian) To render supernatural; to become supernatural.
Goruchanianydd, *s. m.—pl. t.* ion (goruchanian) A metaphysician.
Goruchder, *s. m.* (goruch) Superiority, supremacy
Goruchdeyrn, *s. m.—pl. t.* edd (goruch—teyrn) A lord paramount.
Goruchdderchafawl, *a.* (goruch—derchafawl) Tending to raise superior.
Goruchdderchafu, *v. a.* (goruch—derchafu) To exalt above; to render superexcellent.
Goruchedigawl, *a.* (goruchedig) Superlative.
Goruchedd, *s. m.* (goruch) Superiority; supremacy.
Goruchel, *s. m.—pl. t.* ion (goruch) That is sovereign. *a.* Sovereign, supreme; supernal; transcendant; very high; lofty.

Er mai un brenin oedd ben ar yr holl deyrnas, eto yr oedd amryw dywysogion ac arglwyddi, a llywodraeth oruchel yn eu dwylaw.
Though that one king was chief over all the kingdom, yet there were several princes and lords with *supreme* jurisdiction in their hands.
Theo. Evans.

Goruchelder, *s. m.—p. t.* au (goruchel) Supremacy; highness, loftiness; summit.

Cerrig y mynydd a'i oruchelder a oedd amddiffyn i'r Prydeiniaid, a llestair i'r gelynion.
The stones of the mountain and its *extreme loftiness* were a defence to the Britons, and an obstruction to their foes.
Gr. ab Arthur.

Goruchelfa, *s. f.—pl t.* oedd (goruchel—man) A supereminent station.
Gorucheliad, *s. m.* (goruchel) A rendering, or becoming supereminent.
Goruchelion, *s. pl. aggr.* (goruchel) Appearances in the heavens, meteors.
Goruchelradd, *s. f.—pl. t.* au (goruchel—gradd) Supreme rank, or order.
Goruchelrwydd, *s. m.* (goruchel) Superior height.
Goruchelu, *v. a.* (goruchel) To render supremely high; to raise very high.
Goruchiad, *s. m.—pl. t.* au (goruch) That moves above; a planet.

Syrthiodd, t'wnodd pentewynion o'r haul
Ar ei het fal gwreichion;
A'r lleuad goruchiad gron,
O fawr ysig yn friwsion.

From the sun the fiery cinders fell, and glowed, like sparks, upon his hat; and that round *luminary*, the moon, with great extremes to pieces flew.
T. Prys, i Ellis Pyrhon.

Goruchiannawl, *a.* (goruchiant) Tending to make supereminent.
Goruchiannu, *v. a.* (goruchiant) To render supereminent; to render most high.
Goruchiant, *s. m.* (goruch) Supereminence.
Goruchiaw, *v. a.* (goruch) To raise supreme.
Goruchiawl, *a.* (goruch) Supereminent.
Goruchiolaf, *a.* (goruchiawl) Most highest.
Goruchioli, *v. a.* (goruchiawl) To make supereminent; to raise supremely.
Goruchion, *s. pl. aggr.* (goruch) Appearances in the air, meteors.
Goruchionawl, *a.* (goruchion) Meteorous.
Goruchionen, *s. f. dim* (goruchion) A meteor.
Goruchiongraff, *s. m.* (goruchion—craff) Meteorology.
Goruchiongraffydd, *s. m.—pl. t.* ion (goruchiongraff) A meteorologist.
Goruchioni, *v. a.* (goruchion) To generate meteors; to become meteors.
Goruchionllyd, *a.* (goruchion) Abounding with meteors, generating meteors.
Goruchlyw, *s. m.* (goruch-llyw) A lord paramount.
Goruchlywiad, *s. m.* (goruchlyw) A governing supremely.
Goruchlywiaw, *v. a.* (goruchlyw) To exercise sovereign authority.
Goruchlywiawl, *a.* (goruchlyw) Supremely governing.
Goruchlywydd, *s. m.* (goruchlyw) Lord paramount
Goruchragor, *s. m.* (goruch—rhagor) Superexcellence.

Goruchragorawl, *a.* (goruchragor) Superexcellent

Goruchragori, *v. n.* (goruchragor) To excel in the highest degree; to become superexcellent.

Goruchragoriad, *s. m.* (goruchragor) A rendering or becoming, superexcellent.

Goruchragoriaeth, *s. m.* (goruchragor) Superexcellence; supereminence.

Goruchrif, *s. m.—pl. t.* ion (goruch—rhif) An extra, or superior number.

Goruchrifawl, *a.* (goruchrif) Supernumerary.

Goruchudd, *s. m.—pl. t.* ion (goruch—udd) A profound mystery.

Goruchwyl, *s. m.* (goruch—gwyl) A looking over.

Goruchwyliad, *s. m.* (goruchwyl) A superintending

Goruchwyliaeth, *s. m.—pl. t.* au (goruchwyl) A superintendence, or stewardship.

Goruchwylied, *v. a.* (goruchwyl) To superintend.

Goruchwyliwr, *s. m.—pl.* goruchwyliwyr (goruchwyl—gwr) A superintender.

Goruchysgrif, *s. f.—pl. t.* ion (goruch—ysgrif) A superscription.

Goruchysgrifen, *s. f.* (goruchysgrif) A superscription.

Gorudd, *a.* (rhudd) Somewhat ruddy, of a reddish brown; the herb red bartsia.

Goruddgoch, *a.* (gorudd—coch) Of reddish crimson

Goruddiaw, *v. a.* (gorudd) To make rather of a crimson colour; to become a little ruddy.

Gorug, *v. a.* (*preter. of* goru) Did, did perform, did act; he did, he made. It is frequently used as an auxiliary, answering to *Did*. *Ef a orug ddaioni imi*, he *did* good to me; *gorug iddo goron*, he made him a crown.

> Annelu ei fwa a orug y mab; ac yn ceisiaw medru y carw, sef y medrai ei dad y dan ei fron yn y golles enaid.
>
> Stretch his bow was what the youth *did*, and in attempting to shoot the stag, he shot his father below his breast, so that he lost a soul. *Gr. ab Arthur.*
>
> Yssef a orugant gwyr Rhufain eisioes cyd rhygyfarfai perigl a hwynt ar yr afon, ygyd ag y cawsant y tir yn wrawl gwrthwynebu y Prydeiniaid,—a dirfawr aerfa a orugbwyd o'r Prydeiniaid.
>
> Thus *did they* the men of Rome then, though danger met them upon the river, that no sooner had they attained the land, but they manfully opposed the Britons,—and an immense slaughter was made of the Britons. *Gr. ab Arthur.*
>
> Gorugost rydost rediad.
>
> *Thou didst accomplish* a course most severe. *D. ab Gwilym.*

Gorugaw, *v. a.* (gorug) To surmount, to accomplish, to do; to overcome.

Gorugawl, *a.* (gorug) Tending to accomplish.

Gorugiad, *s. m.* (gorug) An accomplishing.

Gorun, *s. m.* (gor) What is up in agitation; foam.

> Ef hybar——
> Y'ngwythlid, y'ngwythlawn orun.
>
> He ready with the spear in the rage of wrath, in the wrathful *tumult*. *Cynddelw.*
>
> Gorun morgymmlawdd ai goglawdd glan
> Par-goch glyw, glewdrawa, mawr mab Cadfan.
>
> The *surge* of the raging of the sea which the shore barely stems is the red-speared chief, bravely stubborn, the amiable son of Cadvan. *Cynddelw, i Fad. ab Meredydd.*
>
> Aer orun fal Rhun rudd ei onen.
>
> The *tumult* of the slaughter, like Rhun with the crimson lance. *Ll. P. Moch.*

Gorun, *a.* (gor) That foams; foamy; mantling.

> Bid wyn twr, bid orun seirch.
>
> Let the tower be white, let the harness be *foamy*. *Llywarch Hen.*

Gorurdd, *s. f.—pl. t.* au (urdd) Supremacy.

Gorurddas, *s. f.—pl. t.* au (gorurdd) Supreme rank

Gorurddasawl, *a.* (gorurddas) Of supreme rank.

Gorurddasiad, *s. m.* (gorurddas) A rendering of supreme rank.

Gorurddasu, *v. a.* (gorurddas) To make of superior, or supreme rank.

Goruthr, *a.* (uthr) Extremely amazing.

> Cleddyfau goruthr cleddyfal ar wyr
> A orug yn ddywal.
>
> He fiercely caused the most *terrible* blades to inflict wounds on men. *Cynddelw, i H. ab Owain.*

Goruthraw, *v. a.* (goruthr) To astonish extremely; to wonder extremely.

Goruthrawl, *a.* (goruthr) Very amazing.

Goruthredd, *s. m.* (goruthr) Extreme amazement

> Cynrain brain breiddfawr gawr goruthredd;
> Cedawl yw fy llyw llaw ddiommedd.
>
> His the foremost lance of the ravens amply glutted with food, that croak *extreme astonishment*, liberal is my chief with unrefusing hand. *Gr. ab M. ab Dafydd.*

Goruthriad, *s. m.* (goruthr) A causing extreme amazement.

Goruwch, *prep.* (uwch) Above, over, superior to.

Gorwaedd, *s. f.* (gwaedd) An extreme cry.

Gorwaeddawl, *a.* (gorwaedd) Of very loud cry.

Gorwaeddi, *v. a.* (gorwaedd) To cry out loudly.

Gorwaeddiad, *s. m.* (gorwaedd) A crying very loudly.

Gorwael, *a.* (gwael) Extremely abject, or low.

Gorwaelder, *s. m.* (gorwael) Extreme abjectness.

Gorwaeldra, *s. m.* (gorwael) Extreme abjectness.

Gorwaeledd, *s. m.* (gorwael) Extreme abjectness.

Gorwaeliad, *s. m.* (gorwael) A rendering extremely abject, or wretched.

Gorwaelu, *v. a.* (gorwael) To render very wretched; to become very abject.

Gorwaered, *a.* (gwaered) A descent, declivity.

Gorwag, *a.* (gwag) Supremely void; vain, empty; frivolous; pompous, vain glorious.

> Na chymmer enw Duw yn orwag.
>
> Take thou not the name of God in *vain*. *Ll. G. Hergest.*
>
> Gwelais wely hardd wedi ei drymo yn orwag; a hwnw a ganmolais yn fawr y pryd hynny: Gwaelder a ddywed mai hi oedd geidwad ar yr ystafell hono.
>
> I saw a splendid bed *pompously* decked out; and that I praised greatly at the time: Frailty then said that she was the guardian of that chamber. *Marchawg Crwydrad.*

Gorwagder, *s. m.* (gorwag) Extreme void; vanity, emptiness, futility; vain glory.

Gorwagedd, *s. m.* (gorwag) Vanity, emptiness; vain glory, pomposity.

> Pan fych fwyaf oll dy rwyf,
> Yn llawn o nwyf gorwagedd,
> Henaint, methiant ddaw i ti,
> A hyny'n ddigymmhedd.
>
> When thou art greatest in thy strength, full of the wantonness of *vanity*, old age and decrepitude will come to thee, and that without ceremony. *S. S. Hywel.*

Gorwagglod, *s. m.* (gorwag—clod) Empty praise.

Gorwagu, *v. a.* (gorwag) To render extremely empty, or vain; to become very vain.

Gorwain, *s. m.* (gwain) The horizon, the extreme verge.

Gorwall, *s. m.* (gwall) Extreme failing, neglect.

Gorwallder, *s. m.* (gorwall) Extreme, remissness.

Gorwallgof, *s. m.* (gorwall—cof) Extreme failure of memory; distraction.

Gorwallgofi, *v. n.* (gorwallgof) To fail extremely in memory; to become distracted.

Gorwallgofiad, *s. m.* (gorwallgof) A failing extremely in memory.

Gorwallgofus, *a.* (gorwallgof) Very forgetful.

Gorwalliad, *s. m.* (gorwall) A becoming extremely remiss, or neglectful.

Gorwallu, *v. n.* (gorwall) To become extremely remiss, or careless.

Gorwan, *a.* (gwan) Extremely weak, or feeble.

Gorwanâad, *s. m.* (gorwan) A rendering or becoming very feeble.

Gorwanâawl, *a.* (gorwan) Very debilitating.

Gorwanau, v. a. (gorwan) To enfeeble extremely

Gorwanc, s. f. (gwanc) A craving appetite; over-digestion.

Gorwanciad, s. m. (gorwanc) A gorging, or devouring extremely.

Gorwanciaw, v. a. (gorwanc) To overgorge.

Gorwancu, v. a. (gorwanc) To overgorge.

Gorwancus, a. (gorwanc) Overgreedy; voracious.

Gorwander, s. m. (gorwan) Extreme weakness.

Gorwar, a. (gwar) Extremely tame, or still.

> Brenin mawr llin, mab gwlad a gwyr,
> Wyf gorwar am danad.
>
> King of eminent race, the son of the country and of men, I am *extremely depressed* for thee. *Ll. P. Moch, i R. ab H. ab Owain.*

Gorwarâad, s. m. (gorwar) A rendering, or becoming, very tame.

Gorwarâawl, a. (gorwar) Tending to make extremely tame.

Gorwarâu, v. a. (gorwar) To make very tame; to become extremely docile.

Gorwarder, s. m. (gorwar) Extreme docility.

Gorwas, s. m.—pl. gorwais (gwas) A hero.

> Clod orwas ddifas ddadganant.
>
> Insipid *hero's* fame they sing. *Taliesin*

Gorwasg, s. f. (gwasg) Extreme pressure.

Gorwasgawl, a. (gorwasg) Of extreme pressure

Gorwasgiad, s. m. (gorwasg) An overpressing.

Gorwasgu, v. a. (gorwasg) To overpress.

Gorwastad, a. (gwastad) Very level, or even.

Gorwastata, v. n. (gorwastad) To become very even; to become very still.

Gorwastatâad, s. m. (gorwastad) A becoming very even; a becoming very still.

Gorwastatâawl, a. (gorwastata) Tending to make very even, or smooth.

Gorwastatân, v. a. (gorwastata) To make very level, or even; to become very even.

Gorwawd, s. f. (gwawd) Extreme praise; flattery

Gorwawdiad, s. m. (gorwawd) A praising extremely; a flattering.

Gorwawdiaw, v. a. (gorwawd) To praise extremely; to flatter.

Gorwawdus, a. (gorwawd) Very flattering.

Gorwedd, s. m. (gwedd) Recumbence, the posture of lying; repose.

Gorwedd, v. a. (gwedd) To lie down; to recline.

> Bran a gre yn y gyfarthfa,
> Ni ddarogan i'm ddim da.
> Bod mab brenin gwyn Gwynedd
> Yn gorwedd yn yr aerfa.
>
> The raven that croaks in the defile, it bodes to me no good: that the son of the blessed king of Gwynedd *is lying* in the field of slaughter. *Periv ab Cedifor.*

Gorweddawd, s. m. (gorwedd) Recumbency.

Gorweddawg, a. (gorwedd) Recumbent; clinic.

Gorweddawl, a. (gorwedd) Recumbent, lying.

Gorweddiad, s. m.—pl. t. au (gorwedd) A lying down, a couching; a reclining.

Gorweddial, s. m. (gorwedd) Concubinage.

Gorweddial, v. a. (gorwedd) To lie down frequently; to be in a state of concubinage.

Gorweddwr, s. m.—pl. gorweddwyr (gorwedd—gwr) One who lies down, or reclines.

Gorwegi, s. m. (gorwag) Extreme vanity.

Gorweiddiawg, a. (gorwedd) Being in a lying posture, clinical; bedridden.

> Gwyr a ddygawn golddai gwarthegawg,
> Hacarnddor, a Hyfaidd, a Gwallawg,
> Ac Owain Mon, maelgynig ddefawd,
> A wnaw peithwyr gorweiddiawg.
>
> Men who can obtain a store of cattle, Hacarnddor, and Hyfaidd, and Gwallog, and Owain of Mon, of Maelgynian maxim, who would bring the ravagers *prostrate*. *Taliesin.*

Gorwel, s. m. (gwel) The extreme of vision; the horizon.

Gorweled, v. n. (gorwel) To see in the extreme, to see over; to see in the horizon.

Gorwen, a. (f. of gorwyn) Extremely white, or fair; white-topt.

> Gorwen ton tuedd Porth Wyddno;
> Garw ei llef, a granwen y gro.
>
> *White the top* of the wave towards the port of Gwyddno; rough is its voice, and white-skirted is the beach. *Phylip Brydydd.*

Gorwen, s. f. (gwen) An extreme smile; a grin.

Gorwenad, s. m. (gorwen) A grinning.

Gorwenawl, a. (gorwen) Over-smiling, grinning.

Gorwenu, v. a. (gorwen) To over-smile; to grin.

> Gnawd i wraig anwadalu,
> Wylo, ac yr awr gorwenu.
>
> It is natural for a woman to be fickle, to weep, and in a moment after to *laugh*. *Araeth [illegible].*

Gorwenwr, s. m.—pl. gorwenwyr (gorwen—gwr) A grinner.

Gorwenydd, s. m.—pl. t. ion (gorwen) A grinner.

Gorwerth, s. m. (gwerth) Extreme price.

Gorwerthawl, a. (gorwerth) Overvalued.

Gorwerthedd, s. m. (gorwerth) An overvalue.

Gorwerthiad, s. m. (gorwerth) An overvaluing; an overselling.

Gorwerthu, v. a. (gorwerth) To oversell.

Gorwir, s. m. (gwir) That is very true. a. Very true.

Gorwireb, s. f.—pl. t. ion (gorwir) A hyperbole.

Gorwiriad, s. m. (gorwir) An asserting as true in the extreme.

Gorwiriaw, v. a. (gorwir) To assert as true overmuch.

Gorwisg, s. f.—pl. t. oedd (gwisg) An outer covering, an outer garment.

Gorwisgaw, v. a. (gorwisg) To clothe over; to become clothed over.

> Llym awel; llwm benyd er byw,
> Pan orwisg coed teglyw haf;
> Tarydd glaf wyf heddyw!
>
> Intense the gale; it is bare punishment to live, though the trees *array themselves* in a summer robe; severely ill am I this day! *Llywarch Hen.*
>
> Gorewynawg ton; tynhegl ebrwydd;
> Gorwisgwys afall arall arwydd.
>
> The wave is crowned with foam; tight-limbed the fleet one; the apple-tree *has put on* another hue. *H. ab Owain.*

Gorwisgawl, a. (gorwisg) Tending to cover over.

Gorwisgiad, s. m. (gorwisg) A clothing over.

Gorwiw, a. (gwiw) Superexcellent.

Gorwiwdeb, s. m. (gorwiw) Superexcellence.

Gorwlad, s. f.—pl. gorwledydd (gwlad) An exterior region; a bordering country; a foreign country.

> Y dystain a ddyly gadw rhan y brenin o'r anrhaith a ddel o orwlad yni fyno y brenin ei defnyddiaw.
>
> The steward of the household ought to keep the king's share of the spoil which shall come from a *foreign country* until the king wishes to make use of it. *Welsh Laws.*

Gorwladawl, a. (gorwlad) Relating to an exterior region, or foreign country; extraprovincial.

Gorwladu, v. a. (gorwlad) To render a foreign country or to become foreign.

Gorwledd, s. f.—pl. t. au (gwledd) Supreme banquet, a high feast.

Gorwledda, v. a. (gorwledd) To partake of a supreme banquet; to over-feast.

Gorwleddawl, a. (gorwledd) Over-feasting.

Gorwleddiad, s. m. (gorwledd) An over-feasting.

Gorwlyb, a. (gwlyb) Over-wet; very wet.

Gorwlych, a. (gwlych) Over-soaked, over-drenched

Gorwlychiad, s. m. (gorwlych) An over-drenching

Gorwlychu, *v. a.* (gorwlych) To over-drench.

> Ton wen orewyn a orwlych bedd
> Rhufon——

> The white wave crowned with foam *doth drench over* the grave of Rhufon. *H. ab Owain.*

Gorwr, *s. m.—pl.* gorwyr (gwr) A worthy.

Gorwraidd, *a.* (gorwr) Superhuman; heroic.

> Llys rybys a gwyst nid gwyd gair Aeron,
> Gorwraidd gymhlegyd;
> Lloegrwys dechwedd urieddyd,
> Llafn awchlym a grym y gryd.

> A conspicuous court of general invitation; not false the saying of Aeron, more than human that owns it, accustomed to put the Loegrians to silence, with a sharp-edged blade, and the energy of the conflict. *Heilyn.*

Gorwrawl, *a.* (gorwr) Supremely manful.

Gorwregys, *s. m.—pl. t.* au (gwregys) A bracing girdle.

Gorwy, *s. m.—pl. t.* on (gor) A margin, or rim.

Gorwych, *a.* (gwych) Extremely brave, or grand.

Gorwychder, *s. m.* (gorwych) Extreme bravery; magnificence, ostentation.

Gorwychedd, *s. m.* (gorwych) Pageantry, grandeur

Gorwychu, *v. a.* (gorwych) To make very brave; to make very gay, to overtrim.

Gorwydn, *a.* (gwydn) Extremely tough.

Gorwydnaw, *v. n.* (gorwydn) To become very tough or tenacious.

Gorwydr, *s. m.* (gwydr) A hoar frost.

Gorwydd, *s. m.—pl. t.* ion (gwydd) The superior or supreme aspect; the supreme presence; the summit.

> Cyd boed fychan, yn celfydd
> Ydd adail adar y'ngorwydd coed:
> Cyfoed fydd da a dedwydd.

> Though it may be small, accurately the birds do build in the *summit* of the wood: coeval will be the good and the diligent. *Llywarch Hen.*

> Tair aflawr gwyrthfawr, gwyrthau glywed,
> Yn sy rhwng mor, a gorwydd a gwrdd lanwed.

> Three hallowed altars, where miracles are heard, there are between the sea and the *summit* and a strongly-flowing frith. *Llywelyn Fardd.*

Gorwydd, *s. m.—pl. t.* au (rhwydd) That proceeds with ease; a trained, or managed horse; a steed, or courser.

> Mvned a orug y mab ar orwydd penlluchlwyd pedwar gauaf, gafgyfing, carngragen—pedair tywarchen a laddai bedwar carn y gorwydd, mal pedair gwenol yn yr awyr.

> What the youth did was to go upon a *steed* with a head dappled with gray, of four winters old, close between the legs and hoof like a shell.—four sods were the four hoofs of the *steed* wont to throw, like four swallows, into the air. *H. Culhwch Mabinogion.*

Gorwydd, *a.* (rhwydd) Of easy progress, or going pretty freely; moving without exertion.

> Arglwydd ein gorwydd gariad—
> Maddeu'n beiau i'n bywyd,
> Er bar, cyn elon o'r byd!

> Lord of our *unimpassioned* affection, forgive our crimes in our existence, to ward off wrath, before we go out of the world! *T. Ll. D. Hywel.*

Gorwyddaw, *v. a.* (gorwydd) To give easy progress

Gorwyddawd, *s. m.—pl.* gorwyddodion (gorwydd) That is in the state of managed progress.

> Rhys——
> Mur mawr-darf mawr-dwrf gorwyddawd.

> Rhys the bulwark of the greatly-dreaded great tumult of the *cavalry*. *Gwalchmai.*

> Ar orwyddawd barth ydd ymborthaf.

> Upon fine *cavalcade* I get myself conveyed. *Llywelyn Fardd.*

Gorwyddawg, *a.* (gorwydd) Having managed steeds

> Gruffudd grym cyhoedd, nid oedd gaddiawg,
> A ddyffyrth ei wyr yn orwyddawg.

> Gruffydd of conspicuous power, who was not sculking, that conveys his men *mounted on steeds*. *Meilyr.*

Gorwyddfarch, *s. m.—pl.* gorwyddfeirch (gorwydd—march) A managed horse.

Gorwyfaw, *v. a.* (rhwyfaw) To impel, or direct forward slightly; to row gently.

Gorwyfawl, *a.* (rhwyfawl) Slightly impelling.

Gorwyfiad, *s. m.* (rhwyfiad) A slightly impelling; or directing forward; a rowing gently.

Gorwyg, *s. m.* (rhwyg) A small rent, or tear.

Gorwygaw, *v. a.* (gorwyg) To tear a little.

Gorwygiad, *s. m.* (gorwyg) A tearing a little.

Gorŵyl, *a.* (gwyl) Very bashful, or modest.

Gorŵyldra, *s. m.* (gorŵyl) Extreme bashfulness.

Gorŵyledd, *s. m.* (gorŵyl) Excess of diffidence.

Gorwyliad, *s. m.* (gorwyl) An overwatching.

Gorwyliaw, *v. a.* (gorwyl) To watch carefully, to overwatch.

> Gorwyliais nos yn achadw ffin.

> *I anxiously watched* the night guarding the bound. *Gwalchmai.*

Gorwyll, *a.* (gwyll) Extremely dark, or gloomy.

> Gwisgawd coed cain gorwyll.

> The robe of the wood is a fine *enveloping gloom*. *Llevoed.*

Gorwylldra, *s. m.* (gorwyll) Extreme gloominess.

Gorwylliad, *s. m.* (gorwyll) A darkening greatly.

Gorwylliaw, *v. a.* (gorwyll) To make very gloomy

Gorwyllt, *a.* (gwyllt) Extremely wild; frantic.

> Dieiddil, a da oeddwn,
> A chryf a gorwyllt a chrwn.

> Unemaciated and goodly I was, and strong, and *very wild*, and robust. *D. ab Gwilym.*

Gorwylltedd, *s. m.* (gorwyllt) Extreme wildness; savageness; giddiness; wantonness.

Gorwylltiad, *s. m.* (gorwyllt) A rendering extremely wild; a becoming very wild.

Gorwylltiaw, *v. a.* (gorwyllt) To make very wild; to become very wild.

Gorwylltineb, *s. m.* (gorwyllt) Extreme wildness.

Gorwym, *s. m.—pl. t.* au (rhwym) A slight bandage

Gorwymaw, *v. a.* (gorwym) To bind slackly.

Gorwymawl, *a.* (gorwym) Slightly binding.

Gorwymiad, *s. m.* (gorwym) A binding slightly.

Gorwymp, *a.* (gwymp) Very fair, or gay.

> Hawdd fu i charu o'i chaer newydd,
> Hwyl orne beulfre ar froydd glas-for,
> Pan fydd gloew goror gorwymp lethrydd.

> Tempting was it to love her, coming from her new mansion, whose course was like the reflection of the sunny hill upon the regions of the blue sea, when the part near the *magnificent* cliffs is clear.) *Ior. Fychan.*

Gorwympaw, *v. a.* (gorwymp) To make extremely fair, or splendid.

Gorwympdra, *s. m.* (gorwymp) Extreme showyness, or beauty.

Gorwympedd, *s. m.* (gorwymp) Supreme beauty.

Gorwymyn, *s. m.—pl. t.* au (gorwym) A slight bandage.

Gorwyn, *a.* (gwyn) Over-white, white-topt.

Gorwyn, *s. m.—pl. t.* iau (gwyn) Extreme craving

Gorwynawg, *a.* (gorwyn) Having excessive craving or desire.

Gorwynbysg, *s. m.—pl. t.* od (gorwyn—pysg) A fish called a bleak.

Gorŵynder, *s. m.* (gorwyn) Extreme whiteness.

Gorŵyndra, *s. m.* (gorwyn) Extreme whiteness.

Gorwyniaw, *v. n.* (gorwyn) To have strong impulses of desire.

Gorŵynu, *v. a.* (gorwyn) To make over-white; to make very white; to tip with white; to become very white.

Gorwyr, *s. m.—pl. t.* ion (wyr) A great grandson.

Gorwyrain, *s. f.* (gwyrain) Supreme subject of praise.

> Ef yn llwyr a'n gwyr; ef gorfu;
> Ef goreu gorwyrain a fu;
> Ef gwnaeth daiar gynnyddu rhag ei fron,
> Fry o nef yn canfu.

> He altogether knows us; he created; he the best *theme of praise* that hath been! he made the earth to increase in his presence, above from heaven beholding. *Elidyr Sais.*

Gorwyres, *s. f.—pl. t.* au (wyres) A great grand-daughter.

Gorwys, *s. m.—pl. t.* ion (gwys) A public call.

Gorwysaw, *v. a.* (gorwys) To cite publickly.

Gorwysawl, *a.* (gorwys) Publickly cited.

Gorwysiad, *s. m.* (gorwys) A publickly summoning

Gorwyth, *s. m.—pl. t.* au (gwyth) Extreme ire.

> Gorwyth meddw meddwdawd.
>
> *The provocative of the drunkard is drunkenness.* *Taliesin.*

Gorwythaw, *v. n.* (gorwyth) To become extremely incensed, or irritated.

Gorwythawg, *a.* (gorwyth) Very ireful, or angry.

Gorwythawl, *a.* (gorwyth) Very irritating.

Gorwythdra, *s. m.* (gorwyth) Extreme irritability

Gorwythiad, *s. m.* (gorwyth) An irritating extremely; a becoming extremely angry.

Gorwythlawn, *a.* (gorwyth) Very wrathful.

Gorydd, *a.* (rhydd) Somewhat loose, or free.

Goryddâad, *s. m.* (gorydd) A partly loosening.

Goryddâu, *v. a.* (gorydd) To loosen a little.

Goryfyg, *s. m.* (rhyfyg) A little arrogance.

Goryfygawl, *a.* (goryfyg) Somewhat arrogant.

Goryfygu, *v. n.* (goryfyg) To assume a little boldness, or confidence.

Goryfygus, *a.* (goryfyg) Rather arrogant.

Gorymaddaw, *v. n.* (ymaddaw) To over-promise one's self.

Gorymbleidiad, *s. m.—pl. t.* au (ymbleidiad) An espousing a party to excess.

Gorymbleidiaw, *v. a.* (ymbleidiaw) To act factiously in the extreme.

Gorymbleidiawl, *a.* (ymbleidiawl) Apt to be extremely factious.

Gorymboeni, *v. n.* (ymboeni) To over-fatigue one's self.

Gorymborth, *s. m.* (ymborth) Excess of food.

Gorymborthawl, *a.* (gorymborth) Being overfed.

Gorymborthi, *v. a.* (gorymborth) To overfeed one's self.

Gorymborthiad, *s. m.* (gorymborth) An overfeeding of one's self.

Gorymchwal, *s. m.* (ymchwal) An overspreading of one's self; a becoming scattered over.

Gorymchwaliad, *s. m.* (gorymchwal) The act of overspreading of one's self.

Gorymchwalu, *v. a.* (gorymchwal) To overspread one's self; to become scattered over.

Gorymchwel, *s. m.—pl. t.* ion (ymchwel) An overturn; a conversion.

Gorymchweliad, *s. m.—pl. t.* au (gorymchwel) A turning over of one's self; a being converted.

Gorymchwelyd, *v. a.* (gorymchwel) To overturn one's self; to become converted.

Gorymchwyl, *s. f.—pl. t.* ion (ymchwyl) A subversion of one's self.

Gorymchwylaw, *v. a.* (gorymchwyl) To turn one's self over; to become subverted.

Gorymchwylawg, *a.* (gorymchwyl) Being overturned, or subverted.

Gorymchwyliad, *s. m.* (gorymchwyl) An overturning of one's self; a becoming overturned.

Gorymdaenu, *v. a.* (ymdaenu) To overspread one's self; to become overspread.

Gorymdaith, *s. f.—pl.* gorymdeithiau (ymdaith) A perambulation, a walk abroad. *v. a.* To perambulate, to walk abroad; to sojourn.

> Rhaid i mi orymdeithio heddyw, ac yfory, a thradwydd: canys ni all fod y collir prophwyd allan o Gaerusalem.
>
> *It is necessary for me to go about to-day, and to-morrow, and the following day: for it cannot be that a prophet shall be lost out of Jerusalem.* *W. Salesbury, Luc 13.*

Gorymdeithiad, *s. m.—pl. t.* au (gorymdaith) A perambulating, or walking abroad; a sojourning

Gorymdeithiaw, *v. a.* (gorymdaith) To travel overmuch; to be always travelling.

Gorymdeithiwr, *s. m.—pl.* gorymdeithwyr (gorymdaith—gwr) One who travels much.

Gorymdeithydd, *s. m.—pl. t.* ion (gorymdaith) One who travels much; a wayfaring man.

Gorymdriu, *s. m.—pl. t.* iau (ymdriu) A being busy overmuch.

Gorymdro, *s. m.—pl. t.* ion (ymdro) A turning about of one's self; extreme delay.

Gorymdröad, *s. m.* (gorymdro) An over-delaying.

Gorymdröawl, *a.* (gorymdro) Over-dilatory.

Gorymdröi, *v. a.* (gorymdro) To delay overmuch; to be over-dilatory.

Gorymdŷnawl, *a.* (ymdŷnawl) Over-tenacious.

Gorymdŷniad, *s. m.* (ymdŷniad) A contending overmuch, a being too tenacious.

Gorymdŷnu, *v. a.* (ymdŷnu) To contend overmuch; to be over-tenacious.

Gorymddadliad, *s. m.* (ymddadliad) A disputing overmuch.

Gorymddadlu, *v. a.* (ymddadlu) To dispute to excess; to be cavilling overmuch.

Gorymddal, *v. a.* (ymddal) To contain, or bear one's self extremely.

Gorymddwyn, *s. m.* (ymddwyn) A being brought over; an embolism, or insertion; comprehension. *Dyddiau gorymddwyn*, intercalatory days.

Gorymddwyn, *v. n.* (ymddwyn) To be brought over; to bring one's self over; to comprehend.

Gorymddygawl, *a.* (gorymddwyn) Being brought over; abducent, apagogical; embolismical.

Gorymddygiad, *s. m.—pl. t.* au (gorymddwyn) A being brought over; an abduction.

Gorymegniad, *s. m.* (ymegnïad) Over-exertion.

Gorymegnïaw, *v. a.* (ymegnïaw) To over-exert one's self.

Gorymegnïawl, *a.* (ymegnïawl) Tending to over-exert one's self.

Gorymestyn, *v. a.* (ymestyn) To overstretch one's self; to over-extend one's self.

Gorymestynawl, *a.* (gorymestyn) Self-extending in the extreme.

Gorymestyniad, *s. m.* (gorymestyn) An extending of one's self extremely.

Gorymwneuthur, *v. n.* (ymwneuthur) To exert one's self overmuch.

Gorymyl, *s. m.—pl. t.* ion (ymyl) The extreme edge, or margin.

> Am bob un cyssain sydd yn y gorymyl deau, un cic pwnc a gyfrifir.
>
> *For every one consonant there may be in the right extremity, one pause of reversion is counted.* *Dr. Roberts.*

Gorymylu, *v. a.* (gorymyl) To make a verge.

Gorymŷrawl, *a.* (ymyrawl) Self-incentive in the extreme, urging one's self to excess.

Gorymŷriad, *s. m.* (ymŷriad) A pursuing overmuch; a self-exciting overmuch.

Gorymŷru, *v. a.* (ymŷru) To pursue overmuch.

Goryn, *s. m.—pl. t.* au (gor) A pimple, a blain.

Gorynawg, *a.* (goryn) Having pimples, or blains.

Gorynu, *v. n.* (goryn) To break out in pimples.

Gorynys, *s. f.—pl. t.* oedd (ynys) A peninsula.

Gorysawl, *a.* (ysawl) Extremely consuming.

Gorysgwr, *s. m.* (ysgwr) A yoke, a pressure.

> Ni ddyly neb roddi gorysgwr ar ych ei gilydd heb ei gennad.
>
> *No one ought to place a yoke upon the ox of another without his consent.* *Welsh Laws.*

Gorysgwydd, *s. m.—pl. t.* au (ysgwydd) An extreme projection; a shouldering, or jutting over.

Gorysgwyddaw, *v.* (gorysgwydd) To project over.
Gorysgwyddawl, *a.* (gorysgwydd) Being projecting, or shouldering over.
Gorysgwyddiad, *s. m.—pl. t.* au (gorysgwydd) A projecting over, a shouldering over.
Gorysiad, *s. m.* (ysiad) A consuming extremely.
Gorysu, *v. a.* (ysu) To consume extremely.
Goryw, *v.* (*pret. of* goru) It is done; it is finished; made; he, she, or it, has done, or made.

> Serch ar ffer a'm goryw.
>
> Affection for lifer has overcome me. *D. ab Gwilym.*
>
> Galw ar Iesu, dra fu fyw,
> As ar y grog-a oryw.
>
> Call upon Jesus, and upon the cross, whilst alive, he did. *L. G. Cothi.*

Goryw, *s. m.—pl. t.* iau (rhyw) A slightly marked kind, or species; a degenerate sort.
Gorywiad, *s. m.* (goryw) A degenerating.
Gorywiaw, *v. n.* (goryw) To degenerate.
Gorywiawl, *a.* (goryw) Tending to degenerate.
Gos, *s. m.* (go—ys) That is partly the agent; that tends to, or partly is; that tends to support; that partly acts, or causes.—It is used as a prefix, whereby the force or import of the word to which it is joined becomes lowered from what it would be if standing alone.
Gosaf, *s. f.* (saf) A slight, or unsettled stand.
Gosaig, *s. m.—pl.* goseigiau (saig) A slight meal.
Gosail, *s. f.—pl.* goseiliau (sail) The under-pinning, the groundsel, or groundwork. *Gosail car*, the sole of a drag, a piece of timber put under a drag to preserve the beam from wearing out.

> Duw, cynnal ddisal seilion gobaith,
> Yn gwbl yn fy mwyfron.
>
> *God*, support the wholesome *foundations* of faith completely in my bosom. *H. D. ab Ifan.*

Gosain, *s. f.—pl.* goseiniau (sain) An indistinct sound, or noise.
Gosalw, *a.* (salw) Somewhat indisposed.
Gosalwder, *s. m.* (gosalw) A slight illness.
Gosardd, *s. m.—pl. t.* au (sardd) A slight rebuke
Gosarddawl, *a.* (gosardd) Slightly chiding.
Gosarddiad, *s. m.* (gosardd) A slightly chiding.
Gosarddu, *v. a.* (gosardd) To chide slightly.
Gosarug, *a.* (sarug) Somewhat morose.
Gosarugaw, *v. n.* (gosarug) To become rather surly or morose.
Gosarugrwydd, *s. m.* (gosarug) A little moroseness
Gosathr, *s. m.* (sathr) A gentle tread, a tread by which the foot barely touches the ground. *Gwasgwyn-feirch gosathr*, Gascogne horses of gentle tread.
Gosathrawl, *a.* (gosathr) Slightly treading.
Gosathriad, *s. m.* (gosathr) A slightly treading.
Gosathru, *v. a.* (gosathr) To tread slightly.
Gosawd, *s. m.* (sawd) A placing, or laying; a statute, or ordinance; a position; a set on, an onset.

> Gochel gosawd Ffrolo a orug Arthur.
>
> Avoid the *stroke* of Ffrolo did Arthur. *Gr. ab Arthur.*

Gosawd, *v. a.* (sawd) To place, to put, to set, to lay; to appoint, to set upon, to attack. *Gosawd tir*, to set land; *gosawd rhwyd*, to lay a net; *gosawd bwyd*, to set meat.

> Nawdd y cog yw or pan bopo y golwyth cyntaf hyd pan osoto—y diweddaf rhag bron y brenin.
>
> The protection of the cook is from the time he bakes the first joint, until *he shall set* the last before the king. *Welsh Laws.*

Gosawdd, *s. f.—pl.* gosoddion (sawdd) A slight sinking into, or blending.
Gosbaith, *s. m.—pl.* gosbeithion (paith) That is partly seen through; that is polished. *a.* Reflective; polished.

> Arddwyreaf draig o ddrud-faith awen,
> Llew llawen llawr osbaith.
>
> I will extol a dragon in boldly-aspiring muse, the joyous lion of the *polished* floor. *Cynddelw, i O. ab Madawg.*

Gosbarth, *s. m.—pl. t.* au (parth) A distinct part, or particular. *prep.* Toward.

> Gwaedlan osbarth, warth wrthryn,
> Gwych-far gwanar Gwenwynwyn.
>
> *Towards* the bloody plain, opposing shame, teeming with glorious ire the course of Gwenwynwyn. *Cynddelw.*
>
> Gwyth wyll dragon
> Gosbarth Brython,
> Gosgyman waith.
>
> Wrath is the will of the chief *towards* the Brython, a work of destruction. *Meigant.*

Gosbarthawl, *a.* (gosbarth) Particularizing.
Gosbarthedig, *a.* (gosbarth) Particularized.
Gosbarthiad, *s. m.* (gosbarth) A particularizing.
Gosbarthu, *v. a.* (gosbarth) To particularize.
Gosbeithiad, *s. m.* (gosbaith) A making to reflect.
Gosbeithiaw, *v. a.* (gosbaith) To cause to reflect.
Gosbeithiawg, *a.* (gosbaith) Having a polish.
Gosbeithiawl, *a.* (gosbaith) Tending to shine.
Gosbeithig, *a.* (gosbaith) Shining; polished.

> Gwelais i wyr gosbeithig gosbwyllad,
> A gwyar a fagai ar ddillad.
>
> I have seen men of *splendid* progress, with blood that clotted on the garments. *Taliesin.*

Gosben, *s. m.—pl. t.* au (pen) A particular.
Gosbenawl, *a.* (gosben) Particular, individual.
Gosbeniad, *s. m.* (gosben) A particularizing.
Gosbenu, *v. a.* (gosben) To particularise.
Gosborth, *s. m.* (porth) Slight support, or aid.
Gosborthawl, *a.* (gosborth) Slightly tending to support or uphold.
Gosborthi, *v. a.* (gosborth) To support slightly.
Gosborthiad, *s. m.* (gosborth) A slightly supporting
Gosbrawf, *s. m.—pl.* gosbrofion (prawf) A proof in part; a slight knowledge of.
Gosbrofawl, *a.* (gosbrawf) Tending to know a little of, slightly corroborating.
Gosbrofi, *v. a.* (gosbrawf) To know a little of; to prove slightly; to taste partly.
Gosbrofiad, *s. m.* (gosbrawf) A slightly assaying.
Gosbwyll, *s. m.* (pwyll) That is in the act of reasoning.
Gosbwyllaw, *v. n.* (gosbwyll) To decide partly.
Gosbwylliad, *s. m.* (gosbwyll) A partly deciding; a slightly reasoning.
Goseb, *s. f.—pl. t.* ion (gos—eb) A gift, or present

> Nef i'r gwr! arwr aur oseb cerddau,
> Ni ddeg cardd ei wyneb;
> Ni wn o wawd i wobeb;
> Ni wybu nacau neb.
>
> Heaven to the man! a hero of golden *gift* for songs, indignity will not approach his face; I know no panegyric by which I may honour him; he has not known how to refuse any one. *Ll. P. Moch.*

Gosebawl, *a.* (goseb) In the nature of a gift.
Gosebiad, *s. m.* (goseb) A presenting.
Gosebu, *v. a.* (goseb) To present a gift.
Gosefyll, *v. a.* (gosaf) To stand slightly.
Gosefyllian, *v. a.* (gosefyll) To stand partly.
Goseiliad, *s. m.—pl. t.* au (gosail) A founding; a laying a foundation; an underpinning.
Goseiliaw, *v. a.* (gosail) To found; to underpin; to prop. *Goseiliaw car*, to put a piece of timber under a drag.
Goseiliawg, *a.* (gosail) Having a foundation.
Goseiliedig, *a.* (gosail) Founded; under-pinned.
Goseiniad, *s. m.* (gosain) A slightly sounding.
Goseiniaw, *v. a.* (gosain) To sound slightly.
Goseiniawl, *a.* (gosain) Of a slight sound.

Gosairch, *s. pl. aggr.* (seirch) Slight harness.
Gosel, *s. m.* (sel) A beholding partly; a peep.
Goseliad, *s. m.—pl. t.* au (gosel) A peeping.
Goselu, *v. a.* (gosel) To behold slyly; to peep.
Gosen, *s. f.—pl. t.* au (sèn) A slight rebuke.
Gosènawl, *a.* (gosen) Slightly chiding.
Gosèniad, *s. m.* (gosen) A slightly chiding.
Gosènu, *v. a.* (gosen) To rebuke slightly.
Goserfyll, *a.* (serfyll) Somewhat tottering.
Goserfyllian, *v. n.* (goserfyll) To totter partly.
Gosg, *s. m.* (osg) That is partly going off.
Gosgedd, *s. f.—pl. t.* au (gosg) Figure, or form.

> Y diefl a ymrithiant y'ngosgedd engylion da i dwyllaw dynion.
>
> The devils appear in the *form* of good angels to deceive men. *Ll. O. Hergest.*

Gosgeddawg, *a.* (gosgedd) Having a shape.
Gosgeddawl, *a.* (gosgedd) Tending to shape.
Gosgeddiad, *s. m.—pl. t.* au (gosgedd) A shaping
Gosgeiddig, *a.* (gosgedd) Shapely, comely; well-shapen, well-formed.
Gosgeiddigrwydd, *s. m.* (gosgeiddig) Shapeliness.
Gosgel, *s. m.—pl. t.* ion (cel) A partial obscurity; a gloom. *a.* Rather obscure, gloomy.

> Dyre f'enwyl, dyre i fynydd,
> I le tirion glaslon glasydd,
> Lle mae'r tew-goed yn eu tegwch,
> A lle'n hawdd i gael llonyddwch.
> Ni gawn yno gilfach dawel,
> Yn y gwasgod dan y gosgel.—
>
> Come my love, come above, to a pleasant place of green inclosure, where the thick woods are in their beauty, and a place where quietness is easily obtained. There we shall have a calm retreat, in the shelter beneath the *gloom*. *E. Mathews o Forganwg.*

Gosgelawg, *a.* (gosgel) Somewhat secluded.
Gosgeliad, *s. m.—pl. t.* au (gosgel) A partly concealing, or obscuring.
Gosgelu, *v. a.* (gosgel) To conceal partly; to render somewhat obscure, or gloomy.
Gosgil, *s. m.* (cil) A slight going out of the way.
Gosgiliad, *s. m.—pl. t.* au (gosgil) A partly falling back, or retreating.
Gosgiliaw, *v. a.* (gosgil) To fall back partly.
Gosglwm, *s. m.—pl.* gosglymau (clwm) A slight, or temporary fastening; a tent-fastening.
Gosglymawl, *a.* (gosglwm) Tending to knot, or bind, slightly.
Gosglymiad, *s. m.* (gosglwm) A slightly tying.
Gosglymu, *v. a.* (gosglwm) To tie slightly.
Gosgo, *s. m.* (co) A direction, or course from, or aside; a particular direction; obliquity.—*Myned ar osgo*, to go obliquely.
Gosgöad, *s. m.* (gosgo) A going aside: a taking a particular direction; a going obliquely.
Gosgòawl, *a.* (gosgo) Tending to go aside.
Gosgöedig, *a.* (gosgo) Being gone aside.
Gosgöi, *v. a.* (gosgo) To go aside, to go obliquely.

> Gosgöa di yngod a therch.
>
> Go thou *aside* there and hide thyself. *Llywarch Hen.*

Gosgordd, *s. f.—pl. t.* ion (cordd) A retinue, a train of attendants, clients, or followers; a guard; a clan. *Dyn gosgordd*, a person that is a client.

> Gosgordd brenin yw 36 o wyr; sef 24 swyddawg, a 12 gwestai; heblaw ei deulu, ac ei wyrda, ac ei gerddorion.
>
> A king's *retinue* consists of 36 men; that is 24 officers, and 12 sojourners, besides his family, and his gentlemen, and his minstrels. *Welsh Laws.*
>
> Tair gosgordd adwy Ynys Prydain: gosgordd Mynyddawg Eidyn yn Nghattraeth, a gosgordd Melyn mab Cynfelyn, a gosgordd Drywon mab Nudd, yn rhodwydd Arderydd.
>
> The three *guards* of the pass of the Isle of Britain; the *guard* of Mynyddawg Eidyn in Cattraeth, and the *guard* of Melyn son of Cynvelyn, and the guard of Drywon son of Nudd, on the causeway of Arderydd. *Trioedd.*

Gosgorddawg, *a.* (gosgordd) Having a retinue.
Gosgorddawl, *a.* (gosgordd) Belonging to a retinue; attendant, escorting.
Gosgorddi, *v. a.* (gosgordd) To form a retinue, a going in retinue.
Gosgorddiad, *s. m.* (gosgordd) A forming a retinue
Gosgorddwisg, *s. f.—pl. t.* oedd (gosgordd—gwisg) Dress of a retinue; livery.
Gosgorddwr, *s. m.—pl.* gosgorddwyr (gosgordd—gwr) A man in attendance.
Gosgöwr, *s. m.—pl.* gosgöwyr (gosgo—gwr) One who goes aside, or obliquely.
Gosgöydd, *s. m.—pl. t.* ion (gosgo) A goer aside.
Gosgraff, *a.* (craff) That impresses slightly.
Gosgraffiad, *s. m.* (gosgraff) A slightly impressing
Gosgraffu, *v. a.* (gosgraff) To impress faintly.
Gosgrain, *a.* (crain) Partly crawling.
Gosgred, *s. f.—pl. t.* ion (cred) A faint belief.
Gosgredawl, *a.* (gosgred) Slightly believing.
Gosgredu, *v. n.* (gosgred) To believe slightly.
Gosgreiniad, *s. m.* (gosgrain) A partly crawling.
Gosgreiniaw, *v. a.* (gosgrain) To crawl partly.
Gosgryn, *a.* (cryn) That causes agitation, apt to induce dread. *Rhyn a gosgryn*, dread and terror

> Teyrnedd osgryn, mal Gwyn Gwarther,
> Teyrnaidd, gwraidd gwr yn yngder.
>
> The dread of kings, like Gwyn Gwarther, a princely and a heroic man in difficulty. *Cynddelw, i'r argl. Rhys.*

Gosgryniad, *s. m.* (gosgryn) A causing agitation.

> Gweles i'w lys—
> Diachlud wallaw wallofiad,
> Diachor osgordd osgryniad.
>
> In his court is seen the cup-bearer of unrestrained libation, and a retinue not to be restrained, *that causes trepidation*. *Cynddelw, i O. Cyfeiliawg.*

Gosgrynu, *v. a.* (gosgryn) To cause agitation.
Gosgrynwent, *s. f.* (gosgryn—gwent) An agitated scene, or a scene of tumult.

> I ti mae—
> Gosgordd wrdd a orddyfyn preiddiaw
> Gosgrynwent cadwent ced wallaw.
>
> To thee there is a fierce train accustoming itself in pillage to the *tumultuous scene* of warfare, who pour out gifts. *Cynddelw, i M. ab Owain.*

Gosgudd, *a.* (cudd) Sculking, or lurking.

> Dan Rys—ysgwydwyrdd,
> Oes ced cyrdd cerdd osgudd.
>
> Under Rhys, with the green shield, there is the gift for the songs of the *lurking* exile. *Phylip Brydydd.*

Gosguddiad, *s. m.* (gosgudd) A partly sculking.
Gosguddiaw, *v. a.* (gosgudd) To hide slightly.
Gosguddiawl, *a.* (gosgudd) Tending to sculk.
Gosgwyn, *s. f.—pl. t.* ion (cwyn) A smothered complaint, a mutter.
Gosgwynaw, *v. n.* (gosgwyn) To complain slightly.
Gosgwynawl, *a.* (gosgwyn) Slightly plaintive.
Gosgwyniad, *s. m.* (gosgwyn) A slightly complaining; a muttering.
Gosgyfeiriad, *s. m.* (gosgyfer) A placing, or going, partly in opposition.
Gosgyfeiriaw, *v. a.* (gosgyfer) To go, or come, partly in opposition.
Gosgyfeiriawl, *a.* (gosgyfer) Tending to come partly in opposition.
Gosgyfer, *a.* (cyfer) Partly opposite, or against.
Gosgyffraw, *s. m.* (cyffraw) Slight agitation.
Gosgyffred, *s. m.—pl. t.* ion (cyffred) A slight idea
Gosgyffredawl, *a.* (gosgyffred) Slightly fancied.
Gosgyffrediad, *s. m.* (gosgyffred) A slightly comprehending.
Gosgyffredu, *v. a.* (gosgyffred) To comprehend partly.
Gosgyffröad, *s. m.* (gosgyffraw) A slightly agitating
Gosgyffröawl, *a.* (gosgyffraw) Slightly agitating.
Gosgyffröi, *v. a.* (gosgyffraw) To agitate slightly.

Gosgymiad, *s. m.—pl. t.* au (cymu) A being slightly compact.

Gosgymiau, *v. n.* (cymu) To be slightly joined.

Gosgymmon, *s. m.* (cymmon) A combustible; fuel.

> Un o naw affaith tan yw ceisiaw gosgymmon.
>
> One of the nine accessaries in a fire is to procure *combustible*. *Welsh Laws.*
>
> Wedi caffael gosgymmon o'r tan ni ddiffoddes nes llosgi y castell a Gwrtheyrn ynddo.
>
> When the fire had reached a *combustible* it did not extinguish until it had burnt the castle with Vortigern in it. *Gr. ab Arthur.*
>
> Mawr ddilyw deddyw am dirion arddyn,
> Llywelyn llyw dragon;
> Gosgymmon gwyth drwyth dradion,
> Gosbarth pybl pobl dynadon.
>
> A dire flood is come after the mild sovereign, Llywelyn the leading chief; the *fuel of wrath* is the foaming of heroes towards the faculty of mortal men. *Einion Wan.*

Goslef, *s. m.—pl. t.* oedd (llef) The organ of utterance, the throat; a tone; a note; a note in music.

> Gafael yn ffyrnig ufydd
> Ae islaw rhwng gosle'r hydd.
>
> Lay hold humbly fierce, and below the windpipe, of the *throat* of the stag. *G. ab Ieuan Hen, i filgi.*
>
> Chwibanog——
> A lef wyth oslef yw thon.
>
> A pipe that sounds eight *notes* in its tone. *E. Dafydd.*

Gosmaeth, *s. m.—pl.* gosmeithion (maeth) That tends to nourish, aliment.

Gosmeithiad, *s. m.* (gosmaeth) Alimentation.

Gosmeithiaw, *v. a.* (gosmaeth) To afford aliment.

> Rhefrau, was mwythau, a'th osmeithia.
>
> Strait guts, thou youth of dainties, do *afford nourishment* to thee. *D. ab Gwilym, i R. Meigen.*

Gosmeithiawl, *a.* (gosmaeth) Alimonious.

Gosod, *s. m.—pl. t.* au (gosawd) A placing, laying, or setting; a statute, or ordinance; a set on, a stroke, onset, or assault; a site, or position; a posture. *Gosodau dynion*, human ordinances.

> Maeloging Mwynfawr mynw gyfod y gad,
> Mygr fleiniaid fleidd osod.
>
> Maeloging the courteous is the inspiring auxiliary of the battle, the splendid leader like a wolf in the *onset*. *Cynddelw.*
>
> Torri ei phen——
> Ag isarn ar un gosod.
>
> Cutting off her head with a battle ax on one *stroke*. *D. ab Gwilym.*
>
> Un osod wyf a'r nodwydd yn y blwch.
>
> I am of the same *disposition* as the needle in the box. *L. G. Cothi.*
>
> A osodo Duw parched dyn.
>
> What God *appoints* let man revere. *Adage.*
>
> Rhys—arbenig Deheubarth, trwy ddyundeb a'i wlad a osodes werth daradwng ar bob llwdn.
>
> Rhys the sovereign of South Wales, by the consent of his country did *fix* a stated value upon every beast. *Welsh Laws.*

Gosodadwy, *a.* (gosawd) That may be placed.

Gosodawl, *a.* (gosawd) Propositional; positional; decretory; established.

Gosodedig, *a.* (gosawd) That is set, or placed.

Gosodedigaeth, *s. m.—pl. t.* au (gosodedig) The act of placing, or setting; a position; a proposition; a maxim; an ordinance; a constitution.

Gosodedigaethawl, *a.* (gosodedigaeth) Propositional.

Gosodedigaethu, *v. a.* (gosodedigaeth) To constitute; to make a proposition.

Gosodedigaethydd, *s. m.—pl. t.* ion (gosodedigaeth) One who constitutes.

Gosodedigawl, *a.* (gosodedig) Tending to be established; positive.

Gosodi, *v. a.* (gosawd) To set, to lay, to put; to establish; to ordain.

Gosodiad, *s. m.—pl. t.* au (gosawd) A placing, setting, or laying; a fixing, or establishing; a position; a proposition.

Gosodwr, *s. m.—pl.* gosodwyr (gosawd—gwr) A setter, or layer; one who fixes, or appoints; a proposer; one who sets on, or makes an onset.

Gosodydd, *s. m.—pl. t.* ion (gosawd) A setter, a layer, or fixer; a proposer.

Gosoddawl, *a.* (gosawdd) Slightly sinking.

Gosoddi, *v. n.* (gosawdd) to sink in a little.

Gosoddiad, *s. m.—pl. t.* au (gosawdd) A sinking a little.

Gosom, *s. m.* (som) A slight sham, or feint.

Gosomawl, *a.* (gosom) Slightly deceiving.

Gosomi, *v. a.* (gosom) To diappoint slightly.

Gosomiad, *s. m.—pl. t.* au (gosom) A slightly deceiving, or disappointing.

Gosomiant, *s. m.* (gosom) Slight deception.

Goson, *s. m.—pl. t.* ion (son) A gentle, or easy speaking; soft or easy discourse; a rumour. *v. a.* To speak gently; to discourse; to rumour. *a.* Gently speaking, of gentle discourse; being rumoured.

> Cynddelw wyf byd tra fwyf, traethawd gyson.
> Treithitor fy ngherdd y'nghwin oson.
>
> Cynddelw am I whilst I be, of harmonious discourse, there will be reciting of my song in fair *rumour*. *Cynddelw.*
>
> Gwelais fyrdd o feirdd yn oson
> Yn moli Rodri rwyf dragon.
>
> I have seen a myriad of bards in *gentle murmur* praising Rodri the leading prince. *Ll. P. Moch.*

Gosoniad, *s. m.* (goson) A softly-speaking; a rumouring.

Gosonial, *v. a.* (goson) To speak gently, to whisper; to rumour.

Gosoniaw, *v. a.* (goson) To speak gently.

Gosoniawl, *a.* (goson) Softly-speaking; whispering; rumouring.

Gosor, *s. m.* (sòr) A slight offence, or umbrage.

Gosòrawl, *a.* (gosor) Slightly offended.

Gosori, *v. n.* (gosor) To be slightly offended.

Gosòriad, *s. m.* (gosor) A slightly offending; a being a little angry.

Gosòriant, *s. m.* (gosor) A slight offence.

Gosran, *s. f.—pl. t.* au (rhan) That tends partly to divide.

Gosranawl, *a.* (gosran) Tending to divide.

Gosraniad, *s. m.* (gosran) A tending to divide.

Gosranu, *v. a.* (gosran) To divide partly.

Gosteg, *s. f.—pl. t.* ion (teg) That is fair, or tranquil; silence; public attention; a giving out, a publication; address or invocation, in poetry; a prelude, in music.—*Gostegion priodas*, bans of matrimony; *canu ar osteg*, to sing publicly, or after silence is proclaimed; *rhoi gosteg*, to command silence; *gosteg!* silence!

> Gosteg cerdd dafawd yw chwe englyn yn ol dull parthgymeriad.
>
> The *poem* of vocal song consists of six verses under the form of the anadiplosis. *Trach. Barddoni.*
>
> Ymadaw a wnai Locrin a Gwenddolau, ac ar osteg arddercharfael Esyllt yn frenines.
>
> Part did Locrin with Gwenddolau, and *publicly* exalt Esyllt to be queen. *Gr. ab Arthur.*

Gostegawl, *a.* (gosteg) Tending to silence; silent.

Gostegiad, *s. m.* (gosteg) A silencing; a stilling.

Gostegrwydd, *s. m.* (gosteg) Silentness; stillness.

Gostegu, *v. a.* (gosteg) To make fair; to tranquillize; to still, or calm; to silence, or to cause silence; to become fair, or calm; to become silent.—*Gostega!* Peace! Be silent!

> Aswynaf auch nawdd, na chelwch auch porth,
> Can perthyn attregwch;
> Gostegwyr llys, gostegwch:
> Gosteg, beirdd! bardd a glywch.
>
> I intreat your protection, withhold not your assistance for attention is due: *silentiaries* of the court, command silence. Silence, bards! a bard you hear. *Cynddelw, i R. ab Gruffydd.*

Gostegwr, *s. m.—pl.* gostegwyr (gosteg—gwr)

One who calms, or assuages; an officer who commands silence, a silentiary.

> Gostegwr a gaiff bedair ceiniog o bob dirwy a chamlwrw a goll er am ostegu yn y llys.
>
> The *silentiary* shall have four pence out of every fine and compensation that is lost for want of silence in the court. *Welsh Laws.*

Gostegydd, *s. m.—pl. t.* ion (gosteg) A silencer.

Gostrawd, *s. m.—pl.* gostrodion (trawd) That helps forward.

Gostrodawl, *a.* (gostrawd) Tending to help onward.

Gostrodiad, *s. m.* (gostrawd) A helping forward.

Gostrodur, *s. m.—pl. t.* iau (gostrawd) That supports a burden; a pannel.

Gostwng, *s. m.* (twng) A lowering; inclination.

Gostwng, *v. a.* (twng) To abase, humble, or bring down; to lower; to assuage; to descend, to come down; to become low; to be assuaged; to be humbled, or abased.

> A godo fe ostyngir;
> A ostyngo fe dderchefir;
> A falchio, o ddysg neu ddawn,
> Yn anghall iawn fe'i bernir.
>
> He that rises *will be abased*, that *shall become abased* he shall be exalted; he that shall pride himself for learning or talent shall be deemed very indiscreet. *H. D. ab Ifan.*

Gostyngadwy, *a.* (gostwng) That may be abased, brought down, or lowered.

Gostyngaidd, *a.* (gostwng) Of a humble, or lowering disposition. *Addefwn yn ostyngeiddiaf*, we confess most humbly.

Gostyngedig, *a.* (gostwng) Being lowered; humble; not proud or arrogant.

Gostyngedigaeth, *s. m.—pl. t.* au (gostyngedig) The act of lowering; humiliation.

Gostyngedigawl, *a.* (gostyngedig) Tending to bring down; humiliating.

Gostyngeiddiaw, *v. n.* (gostyngaidd) To become abased or humble.

Gostyngeiddiawl, *a.* (gostyngaidd) Humiliating.

Gostyngiad, *s. m.—pl. t.* au (gostwng) An abasing, a bringing down; a lowering; an assuaging; a coming down; a becoming low; a becoming humble; depression.

Gostyngiadawl, *a.* (gostyngiad) Of a lowering tendency.

Gostyngiadu, *v. a.* (gostyngiad) To render abased, or depressed; to render subservient; to become abased; to become subservient.

Gostyngrwydd, *s. m.* (gostwng) Abasedness; humbleness; depressedness.

Gostyngu, *v. a.* (gostwng) To abase, to bring down; to lower; to assuage; to become low; to humble.

Gostyngwr, *s. m.- pl.* gostyngwyr (gostwng—gwr) One who lowers, one who inclines.

Gostyngydd, *s. m —pl. t.* ion (gostwng) One who abases, inclines, or humbles.

Gosur, *a.* (sur) Somewhat sour, or sharp.

Gosuraw, *v. n.* (gosur) To become sourish.

Gosurawl, *a.* (gosur) Tending to be sourish.

Gosurder, *s. m.* (gosur) A little sourness.

Goswga, *a.* (swga) Somewhat slovenly, or foul.

Goswydd, *s f.—pl t.* au (swydd) A petty office.

Goswyddaw, *v. a.* (goswydd) Partly to officiate.

Goswyddawl, *a.* (goswydd) Partly officiating.

Goswyddiad, *s. m.* (goswydd) A partly officiating.

Goswyddwr, *s. m.—pl.* goswyddwyr (goswydd—gwr) One who executes a petty office; a petty officer.

Goswyn, *s. f.—pl. t.* ion (swyn) A slight charm.

Goswynaw, *v. a.* (goswyn) To charm slightly.

Goswynawl, *a.* (goswyn) Slightly charming.

Goswyniad, *s. m.* (goswyn) A slightly charming, or fascinating.

Gosymdaith, *s. m.* (ymdaith) Provision for traveling; provisions; maintenance.

> Ni thewais er moed o'i moli mal drud;
> Ni phair gosymud ym gosymdaith.
>
> I have not been silent through my life from praising her like a knight, she will not cause my *support* to be taken away. *Cynddelw, i Efa, f. Madawg.*
>
> Gosymdaith dyn, Duw ei rhan.
>
> The *support* of man, God will dispense. *Adage.*

Gosymdeithiad, *s. m.* (gosymdaith) A provisioning, or providing for a journey.

Gosymdeithiaw, *v. a.* (gosymdaith) To provide sustenance; to procure maintenance.

> Hithau hunan a fu fodlawn ar Gerny w o'i gosymdeithiaw hyd tra fu fyw.
>
> She herself also was contented with Cornwall *to support her* as long as she lived. *Gr. ab Arthur.*

Gosymdeithiawg, *a.* (gosymdaith) Having support, or maintenance.

Gosymdeithiawl, *a.* (gosymdaith) Tending to support, or maintain.

Gosymdeithig, *a.* (gosymdaith) Yielding, or bringing sustenance.

> Neud hyabra ei lys—
> A thrydar meibion,
> A thro cerddorion,
> A thrabludd gweision
> Gosymdeithig.
>
> Surely his court is conspicuous, with cheerful noise of youths, and the round of minstrels, and bustle of servants *burdened with provisions.* *D. ab Ieuan Ddu.*

Gosymdeithiwr, *s. m.—pl.* gosymdeithwyr (gosymdaith—gwr) A purveyor.

Gosymdeithydd, *s. m.—pl. t.* ion (gosymdaith) A provider of sustenance; a purveyor.

Gosymerth, *s. m.* (symerth) That seems to dart itself; the gossamer, also called *gwawn*.

> Castell Gwys cyatyngaist yn glau,
> Ac Arberth gosymerth golau.
>
> The castle of Gwys thou didst humble anon, and Arberth of the light *gossamer.* *Ll. P. Moch, i R. Gryg.*

Gosymerthawl, *a.* (gosymerth) Gently darting.

Gosymerthu, *v. a.* (gosymerth) To dart, or puff out gently.

Gosymmaith, *s. m.—pl.* gosymmeithion (ymmaith) Travelling sustenance.

> Somnyd fi am osymmaith.
>
> I have been disappointed of *food.* *D. ab Gwilym.*

Gosymmeithiad, *s. m.* (gosymmaith) A provisioning for travelling.

Gosymmeithiaw, *v. a.* (gosymmaith) To provision for travelling.

Gosymmeithiwr, *s. m.—pl.* gosymmeithwyr (gosymmaith—gwr) A purveyor.

Gosymmeithydd, *s. m.—pl. t.* ion (gosymmaith) A purveyor of provisions.

Gosymu, *v. a.* (symu) To jet, or throw backwards and forwards; to warble.

Gosymud, *s. m.* (symud) A slight move.

> Gwae fi' gleddyf glan gloewddrud, yth arwain,
> O'th arwedd gosymud!
> Medel crwn a dryloywfud:
> Mesurig brif fesur oedd!
>
> Alas! thou brightly-glittering daring sword,
> That from thy *jingling* scabbard thou art borne!
> A fatal reap with outrage hast thou cut
> The spirited Metric owned thee heretofore!
> *Cynddelw, m. T. O. Gwynedd.*

Gosymudaw, *v. a.* (gosymud) To move partly.

Gosymudawl, *a.* (gosymud) Partly moving.

Gosymudiad, *s. m.—pl. t.* au (gosymud) A partly moving.

Gosymwy, *a.* (symwy) Warbling, trilling.

Cyfan weetlawg dwfr dydd neud gawy
Cathl o ar adar awdl osymwy.

Accordant the twirling of the water the day when I obtain a carol from the birds of *gently trilling* song. *Gwalchmai.*

Gosyn, *a.* (syn) Being partly in a maze; having the senses confounded.
Gosyndawd, *s. m.* (gosyn) Slight amazement.
Gosyndra, *s. m.* (gosyn) Slight astonishment.
Gosyniad, *s. m.—pl. t.* au (gosyn) A slightly amazing.
Gosyniaw, *v. n.* (gosyn) To draw the attention partly; to consider slightly.
Gosyniawl, *a.* (gosyn) Tending to draw the mind; slightly considering.
Gosynied, *v. a.* (gosyn) To intend partly.
Gosynu, *v. n.* (gosyn) To become a little astonished, or confounded.
Gosyrth, *s. m.* (syrth) A slight lapse, or fall.
Gosyrthiad, *s. m.* (gosyrth) A slightly falling.
Gosyrthiaw, *v. n.* (gosyrth) To fall slightly.
Gosyrthiawl, *a.* (gosyrth) Slightly falling.
Gosyrthni, *s. m.* (gosyrth) A slight aptness to fall.
Gosyth, *a.* (syth) Somewhat erect, or stiff.
Gosythawl, *a.* (gosyth) Tending to make somewhat erect.
Gosythder, *s. m.* (gosyth) Erectness in a degree.
Gosythiad, *s. m.* (gosyth) A making somewhat erect; a becoming somewhat erect.
Gosythu, *v. a.* (gosyth) To make somewhat erect; to become somewhat erect.
Got, *s. m.* (god) That stimulates, or drives out; incontinence; adultery.

Gwell cynnwys got nag un lleidr.

It is better to bear with an adulterer than any thief. *Adage.*

Neud gwell ot na'r lleidr?

Is not the *adulterer* better than the thief? *Adage.*

Tyngedfen gwraig ot.

The fate of an *adulterous* woman. *Adage.*

Got gyda got a boenir.

The *adulterer* with the *adulterer* will be tormented. *Brenad. Pawl.*

Gwae ot o'i drafod yn y dyddiau.

Woe to the *adulterer* because of his actions in those days. *Gruffydd Llwyd.*

Gotiad, *s. m.—pl. t.* au (got) A stimulating, a driving out.
Gotian, *v. a.* (got) To stimulate; to drive out.
Gotianawl, *a.* (gotian) Stimulating; goading.
Gotianu, *v. a.* (gotian) To stimulate.
Gotiaw, *v. a.* (got) To stimulate; to act incontinently; to commit adultery.
Gotiawl, *a.* (got) Stimulating; adulterous.
Gotoew, *s. f.—pl. t.* on (got—hoew) A spur.

Tra fum i yn oed y gwas draw,
A wisg o aur ei otoew,
Byddai re y rhythrwn i waew.

Whilst I was of the age of yonder youth, that wears of gold his *spur*, I was wont to push ardently the spear. *Llywarch Hen.*

Aro eto aur otoew.

Stay yet, thou with the golden *spur*. *Iolo Goch.*

Gotoew aur a gait ti.

A golden *spur* thou shouldest have. *O. ab Ll. Moel.*

Gotwr, *s. m.—pl.* gotwyr (got—gwr) An incontinent person, an adulterer.

Nid gwell yr otwr na'r lleidr.

The *adulterer* is not better than the thief. *Llywarch Hen.*

Goth, *s. m.* (go) A push off, a repulse; pride.
Gothawl, *a.* (goth) Tending to push away; haughty.
Gothi, *v. a.* (goth) To push from, to scorn, to act proudly; to become proud.
Gothiad, *s. m.* (goth) A pushing from; a scouring.
Gothus, *a.* (goth) Apt to push away; proud.
Gothusrwydd, *s. m.* (gothus) Haughtiness.
Gowaered, *s. m.* (gwaered) A down-hill.
Gowaith, *s. m.* (gwaith) That is somewhat of a work; exercise, recreation.
Gowan, *a.* (gwan) Partly opening, or gashing.

Celnlad yn nghad gowan.

A minstrel in the *gashing* battle. *Aneurin.*

Gowaniad, *s. m.* (gowan) A gashing, or opening.
Gowanu, *v. a.* (gowan) To divide, or separate nearly; to gash; to transfix.

Saith gwaew gowanon
Saith lonaid afon
O waed cynreinion
A ddylanwan.

Seven spears *that shall pierce*, seven rivers full of the blood of leading heroes they will fill. *Taliesin, ymdd. a Myrddin.*

Gowatwor, *s. m.* (gwatwor) A slight mockery.
Gowatwor, *v. a.* (gwatwor) To scoff lightly.
Gowatworiad, *s. m.* (gowatwor) A slightly scoffing.
Gowatworu, *v. a.* (gowatwor) To mock partly.
Gowatworus, *a.* (gowatwor) Apt partly to scoff, scorn, or taunt.
Goweithiad, *s. m.* (gowaith) A slightly working.
Goweithiaw, *v. a.* (gowaith) To work slightly.
Goweithiawl, *a.* (gowaith) Slightly working.
Gowel, *a.* (gwel) Partly visible; transparent.

Yfai win gowel,
Aerfaidd yn arfel.

He would drink *clear* wine, accustomed to dare the battle. *Aneurin.*

Goweled, *v. n.* (gowel) To see indistinctly.
Gowelediad, *s. m.* (goweled) A partly seeing.
Goweliad, *s. m.* (gowel) A partly seeing.
Gowelw, *a.* (gwelw) Somewhat pale, or wan.
Gowelwad, *s. m.* (gowelw) A rendering, or becoming, somewhat pale.
Gowelwawg, *a.* (gowelw) Having a slight paleness.
Gowelwi, *v. n.* (gowelw) To be somewhat pale.
Gowen, *s. f.—pl. t.* oedd (gwên) A half smile.
Gowenawl, *a.* (gowen) Slightly smiling.
Goweniad, *s. m.* (gowen) A slightly smiling.
Gowenu, *v. a.* (gowen) To smile slightly.
Gower, *s. m.* (gwêr) A small field, or close.
Gowineu, *a.* (gwineu) Partly of a bay colour.
Gowladaidd, *a.* (gwladaidd) Somewhat rustic.
Gowladeiddiad, *s. m.* (gowladaidd) A becoming somewhat rusticated.
Gowladeiddiaw, *v. n.* (gowladaidd) To become rather rustic.
Gowladeiddrwydd, *s. m.* (gowladaidd) A little rusticity.
Gowneyd, *v. a.* (gwneyd) To do slightly.
Gowni, *s. m.—pl. t.* au (gwni) A basting stitch.
Gowniad, *s. m.* (gowni) A sewing loosely.
Gowniaw, *v. a.* (gowni) To sew loosely; to baste.
Gowniedig, *a.* (gowni) Loosely sewed, basted.
Gowregysawl, *a.* (gwregysawl) Slightly girded.
Gowregysiad, *s. m.* (gwregysiad) A girding slightly.
Gowregysu, *v. a.* (gwregysu) To gird slackly.
Gowrid, *s. m.* (gwrid) A slight blush, or redness in the cheek.
Gowridaw, *v. n.* (gowrid) To blush slightly.
Gowridawg, *a.* (gowrid) Having a slight blush.
Gowridiad, *s. m.* (gowrid) A slightly blushing.
Gowrthawd, *s. m.* (gwrthawd) A slight rejection.
Gowrthawd, *v. a.* (gowrthawd) To reject slightly.
Gowrthodawl, *a.* (gowrthawd) Slightly rejecting.
Gowrthodi, *v. a.* (gowrthawd) To reject slightly, partly to refuse.
Gowrthodiad, *s. m.* (gowrthawd) A slightly rejecting, or refusing.
Gowrydd, *s. m.* (gwrydd) A slight strain.
Gowybod, *s. m.* (gwybod) Slight knowledge.

Gowybod, *v. n.* (gwybod) To know partly.

> Gogwn gogau haf
> A fyddant y gauaf.
>
> *I partly know of the summer cuckoos where they be the winter.* *Taliesin.*

Gowybodawl, *a.* (gowybod) Partly knowing.
Gowybodus, *a.* (gowybod) Somewhat knowing.
Gowych, *a.* (gwych) Somewhat brave, or gay.
Gowychiad, *s. m.* (gowych) A setting out gaily.
Gowychu, *v. a.* (gowych) To set out gaily.
Gowydn, *a.* (gwydn) Somewhat tough.
Gowydniad, *s. m.* (gowydn) A becoming rather tough, or tenacious.
Gowydnu, *v. n.* (gwydn) To become rather tough, or tenacious.
Gowyl, *a.* (gŵyl) Somewhat bashful.
Gowylder, *s. m.* (gowŷl) Slight bashfulness.
Gowyledd, *s. m.* (gowŷl) Slight bashfulness.
Gowyn, *a.* (gwyn) Rather white, whitish.
Gowynder, *s. m.* (gowyn) Whitishness.
Gowyniad, *s. m.* (gowyn) A rendering whitish.
Gowynu, *v. a.* (gowyn) To make rather white; to become whitish.
Gowyr, *a.* (gŵyr) Somewhat oblique, or aslant.
Gowyraw, *v. a.* (gowŷr) To make a little oblique.
Gowyrawl, *a.* (gowŷr) Tending rather to obliquity.
Gowyriad, *s. m.* (gowŷr) A making rather oblique.
Göyfed, *s. m.* (yfed) A slight drinking; a sipping.
Goyfed, *v. a.* (yfed) To drink slightly; to sip.
Göysiad, *s. m.* (ysiad) A slightly consuming.
Göysu, *v. a.* (ysu) To consume partly, to consume, or devour, gradually.
Gra, *s. m.* (rha) What shoots, or rises up; the down, nap, or frieze of cloth; also cloth with nap upon it.

> Ei wely oedd wiw i'r amherawdr Arthur gysgu ynddo, o ysgarlad, a gra, a phali, a sindal, a bliant.
>
> *His bed was meet for the emperor Arthur to sleep in, of scarlet, and fur, and satin, and lawn, and cambric.* *H. O. ab Urien—Mabinogion.*
>
> Gwraig wych yn arwain gra gwyn.
>
> *A fine woman trailing a white fur.* *D. ab Gwilym.*

Graawg, *a.* (gra) Downy, nappy, or friezed.

> I barthu alam berthedd goludawg,
> A gwisgoedd graawg da eu gosgedd.
>
> *To distribute towards us rich finery, and downy garments of goodly shape.* *Befnyn.*

Gráawl, *a.* (gra) Tending to rise up, as down.
Grab, *s. m.—pl. t.* oedd (gra) A cluster; what grows together in a cluster; plenty, exuberance; grape.
Grabaidd, *a.* (grab) Of a clustering tendency.
Graban, *s. f.—pl. t.* au (grab) That has clusters; that is in clusters; a cluster, a vineyard:—Many plants with clustered fruits are called Graban. *Eirin graban*, grapes; *graban yr ŷd*, corn marigold:—*Gallt Graban*, the Vineyard, a place so called in Glamorgan.
Grabawg, *a.* (grab) Having clusters, clustered.
Grabawl, *a.* (grab) Tending to cluster, clustering.
Grabiad, *s. m.* (grab) A clustering, a gathering into clusters.
Grabin, *a.* (grab) Closing, or clasping; grasping.
Grabiniad, *s. m.* (grabin) A scrambling.
Grabiniaw, *v. a.* (grabin) To grapple; to scramble
Grabiniawl, *a.* (grabin) Grappling, scrambling.
Gradd, *s. f.—pl. t.* au (rhadd) A step, a progressive act; a degree; rank.

> Dysgu gradd i hen farch.
>
> *To teach a pace to an old horse.* *Adage.*
>
> Gradd oedd, o gorddiweddir,
> Yn uwch i hwn no Chai Hir.
>
> *A rank to him belonged, if it may be conceived, more elevated than to Cai Hir.* *D. Epynt.*

> Mae' gorff mewn bedd,
> Gwyn, yn gorwedd;
> Mae enaid e
> 'N rhodio'r graddau.
>
> *His fair corpse is lying in the grave; his soul is perambulating the gradations.* *T. ab I. ab Rhys.*

Graddawd, *s. m.* (gradd) A graduation.
Graddawg, *a.* (gradd) Having steps, or degrees, graduated. *s. f.* A scale.
Graddawl, *a.* (gradd) Progressive; gradient, graduate. *s. m.—pl.* graddolion. A graduate.
Graddawr, *s. c.—pl.* graddorion (gradd) A graduate.
Graddeb, *s. f.—pl. t.* ion (gradd) A climax.
Graddedig, *a.* (grâdd) Graduated, gradated.
Graddedigaeth, *s. m.—pl. t.* au (graddedig) Graduation, the act of graduating.
Graddedigawl, *a.* (graddedig) Progressive.
Graddfa, *s. f.—pl. t.* oa (gradd) That is graduate, or divided into degrees.
Graddiad, *s. m.—pl. t.* au (gradd) A gradation.
Graddiaith, *s. f.—pl.* graddieithoedd (gradd—iaith) A climax.
Graddiannawl, *a.* (graddiant) Progressional.
Graddianniad, *s. m.* (graddiant) A graduation; a progression.
Graddiannu, *v. a.* (graddiant) To graduate.
Graddiant, *s. m.—pl.* graddiannau (gradd) Gradation; rank.
Graddiaw, *v. a.* (gradd) To graduate, to divide into degrees; to confer rank.
Graddineb, *s. m.* (gradd) Graduality.
Graddogi, *v. a.* (graddawg) To graduate.
Graddoldeb, *s. m.* (graddawl) Progressiveness.
Graddoli, *v. a.* (graddawl) To graduate.
Graddorawl, *a.* (graddawr) Graduated.
Graddori, *v. a.* (graddawr) To divide into degrees.
Graddu, *v. a.* (gradd) To graduate; to confer rank.
Graddwr, *s. m.—pl.* graddwyr (gradd—gwr) A man of degree. *Graddwr eglwys*, a church graduate.
Grae, *s. m.* (gra) That is asperous, or angulated.
Graean, *s. m. aggr.* (grae) Gravel, coarse sand.
Graeanawg, *a.* (graean) Calculous; gritty.
Graeanawl, *a.* (graean) Granulous, calculous.
Graeander, *s. m.* (graean) Granulosity.
Graeandir, *s. m.—pl. t.* oedd (graean—tir) Gravelly land.
Graeandde, *a.* (graean) Granulous, calculose.

> Bedd Ceri gleddyf hir yn ngodir Hen Eglwys,
> Yn y diffwys graeandde:
> Tarw Torment yn mynwent Corbre.
>
> *The grave of Ceri with the long sword in the confine of Old Church, in the gravelly cliff, the Bull of Conflict in the cemetery of Corbre.* *Engl. Beddau Milwyr.*

Graeanen, *s. f.* (graean) A granum, a grain.
Graeanllyd, *a.* (graean) Gravelly; gritty.
Graeanllydrwydd, *s. m.* (graeanllyd) Gravelinees.
Graeanllys, *s. m. aggr.* (graean—llys) The gritty berries. *Graeanllys y dwfr*, water speedwell.
Graeanu, *v. a.* (graean) To granulate.
Graen, *s. m.* (gra—en) Pungency, asperity, grief, dolor. *a.* Pungent, severe; grievous.

> Eiddionydd dorf cerf cariad oedd Hywel,
> Grym ergyd gryd:!
> Anhirion yn'ei feirdd, o'i fod
> Y'ngraen fedd y'ngro yn fud.
>
> *The center of love with the multitude of Eiddionydd was Hywel, the energy of the shaft of tumult, departed are the bards from his being in the mournful grave, dumb in the ground.* *Rhisierdyn, i H. ab Gruffydd.*
>
> Er dy graen waed, er dy rinwedd—
> Gwared fi'
>
> *Through thy poignant blood, through thy merit deliver me.* *Gr. Gryg.*

Graenawl, *a.* (graen) Asperous; poignant.

Graeander, *s. m.* (graen) Poignancy; grief.

Gwrando'm graender,
Oes-dawl ddwyder.

Listen to my grief, a life-wearing sadness. *D. Ll. Mathew.*

Graendde, *a.* (graen) Pervaded with asperities.

A draig Mon, mor ddrud i esillydd yn aer,
Y bu terfysg taer, a haer holi;
A rhagddo rhewys dwys dyfysgi,
A rhewin, a thrin, a thranc cymmri;
Ar gad gad greudde
Ar gryd gryd graendde
Ac am dal Moelfre
Mil fanieri.

With the dragon of Mon, in war whose progeny is bold, there were harsh tumult and insulting claim; and before him ran dire confusion, ruin, toil, and an end of preeminence; in conflict upon conflict pervaded with gore, in shriek after shriek *of fierce anguish*, and round the front of Moelfre a thousand banders waving. *Gwalchmai.*

Graenedd, *s. m.* (graen) Pungency, poignancy.
Graeniad, *s. m.* (graen) A making asperous.
Graenon, *s. pl. aggr.* (graen) Gravel, coarse sand.
Graenu, *v. a.* (graen) Asperous; pungent.
Graenus, *a.* (graen) To asperate, to roughen.
Graenwyn, *a.* (graen—gwyn) Having white asperities, or points.

Baglawg byddin, bagwy on
Hwyaid yn llyn graenwyn ton:
Trech no chant cystudd calon.

Entangling is the snare, clustered the ash; the ducks in the pond *white bristled* is the wave: more powerful than a hundred the affliction of the heart. *Llywarch Hen.*

Graenyn, *s. m.* (graen) A grain of sand, or gravel.
Graf, *s. m.* (gra) The garlick. *Sil.*
Gravel, *s. m.—pl.* grefyl (graf) One that is rough; a rawboned one; a lubber; a ruffian.

Urien Reged, greidiawl grafel,
Eryr Gal Yshwch, glew hael.

Urien Reged, a vehement *ruffian*; the eagle of the Gal of Ystwch, brave and generous. *Llywarch Hen.*

Grafel i blith gwyr ieuainc.

A *lubber* amongst young men. *D. ab Gwilym, i Gr. Gryg.*

Grai, *s. m.—pl.* greioedd (gra) A blight or blast.
Graiad, *s. m.—pl. t.* au (grai) A blighting.
Graid, *s. m.—pl.* greidiau (gra) That shoots out in points, or rays; sun-heat, sunshine; heat, ardency.

Gwyr yn afrdwyth gwyth er gwaith Meigen;
Gwyr yn amwyn graid, greddf ychain y'ngwedd;
Gwyr y'nghywryaedd; gwyr gwledd gwlyddien.

Men inflaming wrath since the battle of Meigen; men cherishing *heat*, of the disposition of oxen under the yoke are the men in conflict, the placid men of the banquet. *Cynddelw.*

Edmygaf radau rhiau rhadlawn;
Rhadwehyn granwyn graid anogawn.

I will honour the virtues of generous chieftains; the white-fronted one of unfailing *ardency* scatters blessings. *Cynddelw, i Gadwallon.*

Graid, *a.* (gra) Hot, ardent, vehement. *Graid eryr*, a vehement eagle; *graid wron*, a fierce hero; *fleimiaid graid*, fierce conflagrators; *graid gwriawr*, ardent manhood.

Ceidwad graid Grugynan lys.

The *fierce* guardian of Grugynan hall. *Cynddelw.*

Monwysion——
Haid myr graid greddf.

The men of Mon, a swarm in *ardent* disposition of mind. *Ein. Wan, i Lywelyn I.*

Mab Llywelyn hael, hawl gyfa eirchiaid,
Erchwyn graid grym tyrfa
Wyd rwyf cad, ceiwyr ddifa;
Wyd roddiad rhuddaur Afia.

Son of generous Llywelyn, the entire claim of suitors, the *ardent* bulwark and energy of the host, thou art the director of the battle and destruction of warriors, thou art the giver of the gold of Avia. *Ein. Wan, i R. ab Llywelyn.*

Grain, *s. f.—pl.* greinion (rhain) A socket; a ring

Greidell—
A'i grain yn ymyl ei grudd.

A griddle with its *ring* in the edge of its cheek. *R. ab D. Llwyd.*

Greidell——
A llafn o droed llyfn hyd rain.

A griddle with a long handle smooth to the *socket*. *R. ab D. Llwyd.*

Gran, *s. m.—pl. t.* au (gra) A sharp projection, or ledge; the ledge formed by the cheekbone from the nose to the temples; the upper part of the cheek.

Gnawd man ar ran cynnifiad.

A scar upon the *cheekbone* of a combatant is natural. *Adage.*

Llawer llef druan,
Mal pan fu Gamlan;
Llawer deigr dros ran
Gwedy groniaw!

Many a piteous cry like as there was for Camlan: many a tear over the *cheek* has fallen. *Gr. ab yr Ynad Goch.*

Tros fy ngran——
Try deigr am wr tra digrif!

Over my *cheek* rolls the tear after a man the most pleasing! *D. ab Gwilym.*

Gran, *a.* (gra) Precipitous, shelvy; sharp.

Bid gran cau gen wrth awr.

In the shout be the closing of the mouth *precipitate.* *Llywarch Hen.*

Granawl, *a.* (gran) Precipitous, shelving.
Granwawr, *s. f.* (gran—gwawr) The projecting appearance of the cheekbone.

Eidol addoer grau granwawr gwyn.

Eidol's blood is cold, whose *complexion* is white. *Aneurin.*

Granwen, *a.* (*f. of* granwyn) Having the upper part of the cheek white, or fair.

Llaw yn nghroes, gryd yn ngro granwynion.

A hand on the cross, shrieking among the gravel the *fair fronted ones.* *Taliesin.*

Granwg, *s. m.* (gran) A shelving appearance; the fall of the cheekbone.
Granwyn, *a.* (gran—gwyn) White-edged; having the upper part of the cheek white.

Bu gosgordd, a bu cerdd yn ail mehyn,
Ac eryr uch wybr, a llwybr granwyn
Rhag udd feiaig.——

There was a train, and there was a course in the second place, and an eagle above in the sky, and a *white-edged* path before the wary chief. *Taliesin.*

Granygre, *s. m.* (granwg) The course of the prominence of the cheekbone; the visage.

Gwyrth arall, gwerthfawr ei dedfryd,
Granygre dybu dybryd.

Hallowed the other, precious would be her return: the *countenance* is become dismal. *Cynddelw.*

Grawn, *s. m. aggr.* (gra) Berries; grain; the hard roe of fish.—*Grawn eiddew*, or *crawel yr eiddew*, ivy-berries; *grawn ysgaw*, or *crawel yr ysgaw*, elder-berries; *grawn yr ysbyddad*, haws; *grawn y perthi*, briony; *grawn paris*, grains of paradise; *grawn gwin*, grapes; *grawn yr haul*, common gromwell. *grawn y llew*, corn gromwell; *gronyn o ŷd*, a grain of corn.
Grawnafal, *s. m.—pl. t.* au (grawn—afal) A pomegranate.
Grawnfaeth, *s. m.* (grawn—maeth) Grain food. *a.* Being fed with grain. *Grawnfaeth grewys*, grain-fed studs.
Grawnwin, *s. m.—pl. t.* oedd (grawn—gwin) Grape wine, or wine made of grapes.
Grawth, *s. m.—pl. t.* au (rhawth) A plunge.

Mal ydd oedd yn farw lewyg rhag maint y dolur a gawsai, ydd ymchwelai ei farch, a thuth garw ganddo a grawth.

As he was in a dead fit from the intenseness of the hurt he had got, his horse returned with quick trot and a *plunge.* *H. Peredur—Mabinogion.*

Grawthawl, *a.* (grawth) Headlong, plunging.
Grawthedd, *s. m.* (grawth) Plungingness.

Grawthfrys, *s. m.* (grawth -brŷs) A plunging or headlong haste. *a.* Plungingly hasty.

> Yenym aur ac ariant, nid fod
> Ac emys grawthfrys grawn fyged.
>
> To me belong gold and silver not a little, and stallions of *headlong haste* pampered with grain. *Ll. P. Moch.*

Grawthiad, *s. m.—pl. t.* au (grawth) A running headlong, a plunging.

Grawthu, *v. a.* (grawth) To plunge headlong.

Grawys, *s. m.—pl. t.* au (gra—gwys) Lent. *Grawys Mair*, the festival of Mary; *Grawys ebystyl*, the festival of the apostles.

Grawysawl, *a.* (grawys) Lenten, of lent.

Gre, *s. f.—pl. t.* on (rhe) Several together; a flock, a herd; a stud. *Caseg re*, a brood mare; *gre fyngawg*, the maned herd.

> Gre gyfreithiawl, deg caseg a deugaint ac ystalwyn.
>
> A lawful *stud*, fifty mares and a stallion. *Welsh Laws.*
>
> Bum amws ar re.
>
> I have been a stallion over a *stud*. *Taliesin.*
>
> Diammeu anfon graenyniou gre.
>
> Doubtless the sending a *stud* of white fronted ones. *Ll. P. Moch.*
>
> Gre sy iddo,—
> A meirch, pam na rydd i'm un!
>
> A *stud* to him belongs, and steeds, why does he not give one to me! *Iolo Goch.*

Grëad, *s. m.—pl. t.* au (gre) An aggregating; a herding, a flocking; a making up a stud.

Grëal, *s. m.—pl. t.* on (gre - al) An aggregate of principles; a code; a collection; a magazine. It was the name of a celebrated book of Welsh stories, long since lost, highly extolled by different writers. *Gwlad y greal*, the elementary world, or the world of spirits, the same as *Annwn*.

> Rhodiais i'th geisio iaith ddigasog,
> Mal y greal myn y grog.
>
> I have travelled to find thee as if for the *Greal*, sincere is the speech by the cross. *D. ab Gwilym.*
>
> Gwyr o wlad y greal ydym.
>
> We are persons from the world of *intelligence*. *L. G. Cothi.*
>
> Ni chaid le i holl chwedlau hwn;
> Bain Greal yn fal i'n oedd.
>
> There was no place for all the stories of this person; he was a second *Sound Greal* to us in lal. *L. Mon, i E. ab O. ab Einion.*
>
> Am un llyfr i mae'n llefain,
> A gar mwy nag aur a main,
> Y greal teg i'r wlad hon—
> Llyfr o sawng farchogion;
> Llyfr a grefft yr holl ford gron.
>
> For one book he is complaining, which he loves more than gold and precious stones, the fair *Greal* of this country, a book of the famed knights; a book of the mystery of all the Round Table. *Gutto'r Glyn.*

Grëalu, *v. n.* (grëal) To aggregate principles.

Grëant, *s. m.* (gre) An aggregation; a code.

Grëawd, *s. m.* (gre) An aggregation; a code.

Grëawl, *s. m.* (gre) That aggregates; an aggregate. *Y grëawl*, the briony.

Grëawr, *s. m.—pl.* gréorion (gre) A flock, a herd. *Cylch greorion*, the circuit of the herds, being a tribute exacted yearly from vassals, or tenants, for supporting the herds of the chief.

> Llenwyd dwy rewr i fawr frasydd;
> Dodid meirch tanlw, a hiw eilfydd.
>
> May two kind of herds fill his ample fields; may there come the motley-coloured steeds and likewise kine. *Meilyr.*

Gredd, *s. f.—pl. t.* au (rhedd) That is implanted, or imbibed.

Greddf, *s. f.—pl.* greddfau (gredd) Nature, disposition; habit; instinct.

Greddfawd, *s. m.* (greddf) A grounding in a habit, or quality.

Greddfawg, *a.* (greddf) Having a habit, or quality

Greddfawl, *a.* (greddf) Constitutional, natural, habitual, complexional, congenial.

> Engiriawl, arwyrawl udd,
> Angerddawl greddfawl Gruffudd.
>
> Awful and wrathful chief, *naturally* vehement is Gruffudd. *Ll. P. Moch, i G. ab Llywelyn.*

Greddfedig, *a.* (greddf) Naturalized, habituated, congenial.

Greddfiad, *s. m.* (greddf) A rendering natural; a habituating; a becoming congenial.

Greddfu, *v. a.* (greddf) To render natural, or habitual, to habituate, to become natural, or habitual; to be congenial, or inbred.

Greff, *s. f.—pl. t.* ion (rheff) A sneer, irony.

> Mae'n rhoi greff i'm yn rhy gryf;
> Maint i awgrym.
>
> He is giving me a sneer too powerfully how great his dexterity. *S. ab Hywel Gwyn.*

Greffiad, *s. m.—pl. t.* au (greff) A sneering.

Greffiaw, *v. a.* (greff) To sneer, to speak irony.

Greffiawl, *a.* (greff) Sneering, ironical.

Greg, *s. m.* (rheg) A cackle, or cackling.

Gregar, *s. m.* (greg) A cackling.

Gregar, *v. a.* (greg) To cackle.

Greiad, *s. m.—pl. t.* au (grai) A singeing; a blasting.

Greiaeth, *s. m.* (grai) The act of diffusing heat; a scorching, or singeing.

Greian, *s. f.—pl. t.* au (grai) That diffuses heat; the sun.

Greiaw, *v. a.* (grai) To singe, to blast, to blight.

Greiawd, *s. m.* (grai) A singeing; a blighting.

Greiawl, *a.* (grai) Singeing, blighting, blasting.

Greidell, *s. f.—pl. t.* i (graid) A circular plate of cast iron used for baking cakes upon; a bakestone; a griddle.

> Mal yr iar dan y reidell.
>
> Like the hen beneath the griddle. *Adage.*

Greiden, *s. f.—pl. t.* au (graid) What darts light, or sparkles; what is burning, or ardent; a star.

Greidiad, *s. m.—pl. t.* au (graid) A heating; a scorching; the scorching of the sun.

Greidiaw, *v. a.* (graid) To heat, to make ardent; to scorch, to singe, to parch; to become heated, or ardent; to be scorched by the sun. *Mae'r haul yn greidio*, the sun is scorching, or the sun scorches. *Sil.*

> Wedi, ni waeth Duw ddyddanwydd ym yn myd;
> Ni gaffai llew gryd greidiaw awydd.
>
> Afterwards, God afforded me no happiness through my life; since the lion of the shout was not suffered to *heat* desire. *D. Benfras.*
>
> Fe alw y ferch hon yn liw tirion y tes,
> A gwilied ag wylaw mae'n greidiaw mewn gwres.
>
> He calls this nymph the pleasant hue of the sunshine, and watching and weeping, he is scorching in the heat. *D. Williams, o Bendiles.*

Greidiawg, *a.* (graid) Having heat or ardency; being scorched, singed, or parched.

Greidiawl, *a.* (graid) Hot, ardent; singeing, scorching, or parching.

> Argae gryd, greidiawl wrhydri.
>
> The bulwark against fear, of *ardent* manhood. *Llygad Gwr.*
>
> Greidiawl, arwyrawl arwyrhedd glyw,
> Glyw eryr teyrnedd;
> Clwyf dygyn, Deau, Gogledd,
> Clywed ei fyned i fedd!
>
> *Parched* and obnoxious the surface that covers the chief, the splendid eagle of royalty. It is a severe wound to the South and the North to hear of his going to his grave! *Ll. P. Moch, i M. ab Cynan.*

Greidiwr, *s. m.—pl.* greidwyr (graid—gwr) One who heats or makes ardent; a scorcher, a burner.

Greidur, *s. m.—pl. t.* on (graid—ur) A scorcher; a conflagrator.

Rhyfyg angerddawl, greddfawl greidur;
Rhybu gamweddawg Madawg modur ffaw;
Rhybudd fu iddaw dileu dolur.

Vehement presumption, a *conflagrator* by nature; Madawg the splendid chief has been faulty: notice has been given to him to do away a wound. *Cynddelw.*

Greidyll, *s. m.—pl. t.* au (graid) A griddle.

Greiedd, *s. m.* (grai) A singed or blighted state.

Greienyn, *s. m. dim.* (graian) A single grain of gravel; a pebble.

Greinfys, *s. m.—pl. t.* edd (grain—bys) The ring-finger.

Greiniad, *s. m.* (grain) A forming a ring.

Greiniaw, *v. a.* (grain) To form into a ring.

Greiniawg, *a.* (grain) Having a ring, ringed.

Greiniawl, *a.* (grain) In the form of a ring.

Greinyn, *s. m. dim.* (grain) A small ring; a pendant, an ear-ring.

Tywynaid greinyn i ran.

The pendant was made to shine to the side of the face. *Adagr.*

Grelyn, *s. m.—pl. t.* au (gre—llyn) A standing pool; a horsepond.

Grem, *s. m.—pl. t.* iau (rhem) A crashing noise; a gnash; a snarl; the crash of the teeth, which a beast makes in chewing the cud; a murmur.

Gremiad, *s. m.* (grem) A crashing, a gnashing.

Gremial, *v. a.* (grem) To crash, to gnash, to snarl.

Gremiaw, *v. a.* (grem) To crash, to gnash.

Gremiawl, *a.* (grem) Crashing, gnashing.

Gren, *s. f.—pl. t.* i (rhen) A large earthen vessel.

Meigred—pedair tunell o fel; pedair mu yn mhob tunell, dwy renaid yn mhob mu, a llwyth deuwr ar drosol yn mhob gren.

Honey tax—is four tons of honey; four casks in every ton, two *gren*-fulls in every cask, and the load of two men upon a bar in every *gren*. *Welsh Laws.*

Grenaid, *s. f.—pl.* greneidiau (gren) The quantity that fills the *gren*.

Grenu, *v. a.* (gren) To fill the gren, the vessel so called.

Grëolen, *s. f.* (grëawl) That is clustered together, the briony; also called *grëawl* and *bloneg y ddaiar*.

Gres, *s. m.* (rhes) That is warm, or cherishing.

Gresaw, *s. m.—pl. t.* on (gres) A welcome.

Gresaw anaw anghudd yn Mhrydain
I'm prydfawr ddadenhudd.

The public welcome of the minstrelsy in Britain to my magnificent heir apparent. *Ll. P. Moch, i R. ab Llywelyn.*

Gresawiad, *s. m.—pl. t.* au (gresaw) A welcoming.

Gresawl, *a.* (gres) Ardent, cherishing; warm.

Gresawu, *v. a.* (gresaw) To shew kindness, to welcome, to receive hospitably; to be hospitable. *Glas resawu*, to give a cold welcome.

Gresawus, *a.* (gresaw) Hospitable, kind to strangers.

Gresawwr, *s. m.—pl.* gresawwyr (gresaw—gwr) One who receives hospitably, or treats kindly.

Gresawydd, *s. m.—pl. t.* ion (gresaw) A welcomer.

Gresi, *s. m.* (gres) Pity, or compassion.

Gresiad, *s. m.* (gres) A commiseration, a pitying.

Gresin, *a.* (gres) Pitying, compassionate, piteous.

Mor gresin frenin.

So compassionate a king. *Ll. P. Moch.*

Gresyn, *s. m.* (gres) Pity, misery, calamity.

Gresynawl, *a.* (gresyn) Piteous, miserable, deplorable, lamentable, wretched.

Gresyndawd, *s. m.* (gresyn) Compassion; pitifulness.

Gresyndra, *s. m.* (gresyn) Piteousness; misery.

Gresyngar, *a.* (gresyn) Compassionate, pitiful.

Gresyngarwch, *s. m.* (gresyngar) Deplorableness.

Gresyni, *s. m.* (gresyn) Piteousness; wretchedness.

Gwelais, o'r cwr bwygilydd
Cyni a gresyni sydd.

I have seen, from one end to the other affliction and *misery* prevail. *Gro. Owain.*

Gresyniad, *s. m.* (gresyn) A commiserating.

Gresynoldeb, *s. m.* (gresynawl) Pitifulness.

Gresynolrwydd, *s. m.* (gresynawl) Miserableness.

Gresynu, *v. a.* (gresyn) To pity, to compassionate, to take pity, to be sorry for, to deplore.

Gresynus, *a.* (gresyn) Miserable, deplorable.

Grëu, *v. a.* (gre) To aggregate, to collect.

Beirdd llafar llug de,
Eu gwawd ni'm gre,
Ar ystrawd, ar ystre,
Ystryw mawr mire.

The fluent bards arrayed in light, their praise *will not bring me to associate*, nor on foot, nor on horseback, with aspect of great cunning. *Taliesin.*

Greulys, *s. m.* (greu—llys) Groundsel.

Grew, *s. m.* (rhew) That is spread, or laid even.

Owain yd elwir
Argiwydd hywydd hir;
Ef am dir yn wir
Yn wyth gybudd;
Ef y' ngraid y'ngrew yn llew llofrudd;
Ef y' ngryd y' ngryn yn ryn rybudd.

Owain he is named, a tall and slightly prince; he for land is truly accused of wrath; he in the heat, in the *plain* is a red-slaughtering lion; he in the shout in the conflict is the signal of terror. *Gwalchmai, i O. Gwynedd.*

Grëwr, *s. m.—pl.* grewyr (gre—gwr) A herdsman.

Grewys, *s. m.* (gre—gwys) A herd; a stud.

Grëydd, *s. m.—pl. t.* ion (gre) A herdsman.

Grif, *s. m.* (rhif) An aggregated mass; frog-spawn.

Griffyll, *s. pl. aggr.* (griff) Frog-spawn. *Mor oer â griffyll*, as cold as frog-spawn.

Grifft, *s. m.—pl. t.* oedd (griff) The spawn of frogs.

Grifftiaw, *v. n.* (grifft) To produce frog-spawn.

Grifftiawg, *a.* (grifft) Having frog-spawn.

Grig, *s. m.* (rhig) A low rustle, or rattle.

Grigwd, *s. m.* (grig) A rustling noise. *v. a.* To make a low rattle, or rustling noise.

Grill, *s. m.—pl. t.* iau (rhill) A crash, a crack, a gnash; a chirp or sharp noise. *a.* Creaking; chirping.

Pan ddel yn ol rhyfel rhew
Hill doldir a'i ball deil-dew,
Gleision fydd, mai, grefydd grill,
Llwybr obry lle bu'r Ebrill.

When, after the war of frost, the tree of the vale shall spread its thick-leaved mantle green, will be, in May, of *chirping* devotion, the path where April ranged. *D. ab Gwilym.*

Grillgnaw, *s. m.* (grill—gnaw) A scranch.

Grillgnöad, *s. m.* (grillgnaw) A scranching.

Grillgnöi, *v. a.* (grillgnaw) To scranch.

Grilliad, *s. m.—pl. t.* au (grill) A crashing, or creaking; a gnashing; a chirping.

Grillian, *v. a.* (grill) To make a crash, creak, or crack; to chirp, to creak.

Grilliaw, *v. a.* (grill) To crash, to creak, to chirp

Grilliedydd, *s. m.—pl. t.* ion (grilliad) A creaker, a chirper, a cricket.

Gro, *s. pl. aggr.* (rho) Pebbles, coarse gravel.—*s. f.* An aggregate of pebbles, formed by the water on the shore; a beach. *Y ro fawr*, the great ridge of pebbles, one so called near Abermaw, and another at Aberystwyth.

Ni tha fy mhen am Weno
Mwy na'r aig yn min y ro.

My lips will no more be silent about Gweno than the wave on the edge of the *beach*. *L. G. Cothi.*

Gröaidd, *a.* (gro) Pebbly, like pebbles.
Grodir, *s. m.* (gro—tir) Land full of pebbles.
GROEG, *s. f.* Greece.—*Groeg Fawr*, Græcia Magna; the part of Italy so called.
Groegaidd, *a.* (groeg) Greekish, like Greek.
Groegeiddiaw, *v. a.* (groegaidd) To make like the Greek; to become Greekish.
Groegiawl, *a.* (groeg) Grecian, or of Greece.
Groegwr, *s. m.—pl.* groegwyr (groeg—gwr) A Grecian, or a man of Greece.
Groegydd, *s. m.—pl. t.* ion (groeg) A Grecian, or one well versed in Greek.
Gronell, *s. f.—pl. t.* au (grawn) Hard roe of fish.
Gronellawg, *a.* (gronell) Abounding with roe.
Gronelliad, *s. m.* (gronell) A forming a roe.
Gronellu, *v. n.* (gronell) To generate a roe.
Gronyn, *s. m. dim.* (grawn) A single grain, or particle, a grain. *Ni byddi ronyn gwell er hyny*, thou wilt not be a *bit* the better for that.

Nid â gwaew yn ngronyn.

Pole (a dart) cannot penetrate a *particle*. *Adage.*

Gronynaidd, *a.* (gronyn) Granulous, like little particles.
Gronynawg, *a.* (gronyn) Abounding with grains, or detached particles.
Gronynawl, *a.* (gronyn) Granulary.
Gronyniad, *s. m.* (gronyn) Granulation.
Gronynu, *v. a.* (gronyn) To granulate; to become granulous.
Gröyn, *s. m. dim.* (gro) A single pebble, a pebble.
Gru, *s. m.* (rhu) That pervades, that breaks through.
Grual, *s. m.—pl. t.* au (gru—gal) Gruel. *Grual trwy laeth*, gruel made with milk; *grual trwy ddwfr*, gruel made with water; *grual peilliad*, thick milk, or milk thickened with flour; *grual llaeth*, milk gruel; *grual dwfr*, water-gruel.
Grualaidd, *a.* (grual) Like gruel, gruelly.
Grualu, *v. a.* (grual) To make into gruel.
Grud, *s. m.* (rhud) Coarse hard particles, grit.
Grudd, *s. c.—pl. t.* iau (gru) The cheek. *Deurudd*, *masc.* the two cheeks; *dwyrudd*, *fem.* the two cheeks.

Ni chel grudd gystudd calon.

The *cheek* will not conceal the affliction of the heart. *Adage.*

Y galon er a gelai,
Y grudd a'i mynegi i rai.

Whatever the heart might conceal, the *cheek* will declare it to some. *H. Hellyn.*

Gruddfan, *s. m.* (grudd—man) A groan, a moan.
Gruddfanu, *v. a.* (gruddfan) To groan, to moan.
Gruddfuddig, *a.* (grudd—buddig) Causing the cheek to be abashed, or to blush.

Gruddfuddig wledig wlad oesu,
Gregynan rwyfan rudd oeru.

The *cheek abashing* sovereign of an ancient country, the lord of Gregynan with a crimson pike. *Cynddelw, i H. ab Owain.*

Gruff, *s. m.—pl. t.* ion (rhuff) That is fierce or bold; a griffon.

Gruffudd gruff gwaewrudd gwiwryw.

Gruffudd the ruddy speared *griffon* of noble race. *Ll. Brydydd Hoddnant.*

Grufft, *s. m.—pl. t.* ion (gruff) A griffon.

Fithyd oddorh gwynt
Rhwng dau grufft ar hynt.

A course above the wind was made between two *griffins* on full wing. *Taliesin.*

Grug, *s. m.—pl. t.* oedd (rhug) Heath, or ling. *Coch y grug*, the red game.
Grugaw, *v. a.* (grug) To gather heath or ling.
Grugawg, *a.* (grug) Abounding with heath.
Grugbren, *s. m.—pl. t.* i (grug—pren) French tamarisk.
Grugeilyn, *s. m.* (grug—ail) Sea heath.
Grugiad, *s. m.—pl.* grugiaid (grug) An emmet.
Grugiar, *s. f.—pl.* grugieir (grug—iâr) A heath-hen, or heath fowl; the moor hen, grouse. *Grugieir cochion*, the red game.
Grugion, *s. pl. aggr.* (grug) Emmets or ants.
Grugionyn, *s. m. dim.* (grugion) An emmet.
Gruglwyn, *s. m.—pl. t.* i (grug—llwyn) The sweet-broom.
Grut, *s. m.* (gru) Grit, a kind of fossil so called, consisting of rough hard particles; coarse sand.

Grut oer yw gweryd tir âr.

A cold grit it is that covers the ploughed land. *D. ab Gwilym, i'r eira.*

Grutiaw, *v. a.* (grut) to cover with grit.
Grutiawg, *a.* (grut) Abounding with grit.
Grutiawl, *a.* (grut) Of the nature of grit.
Grw, *s. m.* (rhw) That is uttered imperfectly.
Grwg, *s. m.* (grw) A broken rumbling noise.
Grwgach, *s. m.* (grwg) A murmuring. *v. n.* To murmur.
Grwgachawl, *a.* (grwgach) Murmuring, grumbling.
Grwgachiad, *s. m.* (grwgach) A murmuring.
Grwgachlyd, *a.* (grwgach) Apt to grumble.
Grwgachu, *v. n.* (grwgach) To murmur, to grumble.
Grwgn, *s. m. dim.* (grwg) An indistinct rumbling.
Grwgnach, *s. m.* (grwgn) A murmur, a grumbling. *v. n.* To murmur, to grumble.
Grwgnachawl, *a.* (grwgnach) Murmuring, grumbling.
Grwgnachiad, *s. m.* (grwgnach) A murmuring.
Grwgnachlyd, *a.* (grwgnach) Apt to grumble.
Grwgnachu, *v. n.* (grwgnach) To murmur, to grumble.
Grwm, *s. m.—pl.* grymiau (grw) A murmur, a grumble. *a.* Growling; surly.
Grwn, *s. m.—pl.* gryniau (rhwn) A ridge, a lay, or land, in a field.

Mil o ryniau a wna filltir.

A thousand *ridges* make a mile. *Welsh Laws.*

Grwn, *s. m.* (grw) A broken, or trembling noise, a hallow murmur; a groan; a hum, or drone; the groaning, or cooing, of a dove.
Grwnach, *s. m.* (grwn) A murmur, a grumble.
Grwnachu, *v. a.* (grwnach) To murmur, to grumble.
Grwnan, *s. m.* (grwn) A low noise or murmur; a hum, or drone; a purring. *Canu grwnan*, to sing a murmur, to make a purring.
Grwnan, *v. n.* (grwn) To make a droning noise.
Grwnawl, *a.* (grwn) Rumbling; groaning; droning.
Grwniad, *s. m.* (grwn) A murmuring, a rumbling; a groaning; a droning, a humming.
Grwng, *s. m.* (grw) A rumbling noise; a grunt.
Grwys, *s. pl. aggr.* (rhwys) Wild gooseberries.
Grwysen, *s. f. dim.* (grwys) A wild gooseberry.
Grwyswydd, *s. pl. aggr.* (grwys—gwydd) Gooseberry-trees.
Grwyswydden, *s f.* (grwyswydd) A gooseberry-tree.
Grwyth, *s. m.—pl. t.* au (rhwyth) A murmur.
Grwythaw, *v. a.* (grwyth) To murmur, to rumble; to groan.

Hiraethaf i'm oer-hef, grwythaf i'm hir-hoen,
A mwyned ei chariad, ne manod a cheirios.

In cold accent I will regret, *I will groan* from my lasting pain, so tender was her love, with a complexion of driven snow and cherries. *D. Williams, o Benllin.*

Grwythawl, *a.* (grwyth) Murmuring, rumbling.
Grwythiad, *s. m.* (grwyth) A murmuring, a rumbling, a groaning.

Gryd, *s. m.—pl. t.* iau (rhyd) Vehement utterance; a scream; a shout, a war-hoop.

Adar dwfr dyar eu gryd.

The water-birds, tumultuous is their *scream.* *Myrddin.*

Llym fy mhar llachar yn ngryd.

Sharp-pointed is my spear, gleaming in the *shout.* *Llywarch Hen.*

Rhydd fydd gryd grym aer,
Ysgor glyw glewdaer
Ysgwyd glaer glod-ariwy.

Unrestrained will be the shout of the energy of battle, the defence of the leader obstinately brave is a bright shield provident of fame. *Cynddelw, i O. Cyfeiliawg.*

Grydiad, *s. m.—pl. t.* au (gryd) A screaming; a shouting, a whooping.

Grydian, *v. a.* (gryd) To make a rough noise; to scream; to whoop.

Gryd osbyd oesbell warchae,
Gruffudd y' maen-gudd y mae!

Guests of long-lived watching *do wail,* for Gruffudd is in the tomb. *Bleddyn Fardd.*

Grydiannawl, *a.* (grydiant) Screaming.
Grydiannu, *v. a.* (grydiant) To utter screams.
Grydiant, *s. m.* (gryd) A screaming; a shouting.
Grydiaw, *v. a.* (gryd) To utter a rough sound; to scream, to shriek; to whoop.
Grydiawl, *a.* (gryd) Screaming; whooping.
Grydwst, *s. m.* (gryd—gwst) A murmur.
Grydwst, *v. a.* (gryd—gwst) To murmur; to mutter.

Mewn ffydd dda lonydd ddewiol union gred,
Heb grydwst gwangoelion
Duw—a'm sefydla.

In a good and quiet faith, a divine and just belief, without *muttering* foolish notions, may God establish me. *H. D. ab Ieuan.*

Grydystiad, *s. m.* (grydwst) A murmuring.
Grydystiawl, *a.* (grydwst) Murmuring, muttering
Grydystu, *v. a.* (grydwst) To utter a low indistinct murmur.
Gryg, *s. m.—pl. t.* oedd (rhyg) Harshness.
Gryglys, *s. pl. aggr.* (gryg—llys) Heath-berries. They are also called *llys y brain, llys y llau,* and *grygon.*
Grygnad, *s. m.* (grygyn) A making harsh.
Grygnant, *s. m.* (grygyn) Harshness, asperity.
Grygon, *s. pl. aggr.* (gryg) Small black berries full of hard seeds, growing upon mountains.
Grygwellt, *s. m.* (gryg—gwellt) Cock's foot grass
Grygyn, *s. m.* (gryg) That is rough or harsh.
Grym, *s. m.—pl. t.* oedd (rhym) Force, energy, power, strength. *a.* Energetic, potent, mighty. —*Mewn grym,* in force;—*geiriau grym,* important words; *y gyfraith rym,* the common law.
Grymder, *s. m.* (grym) Potency; nervousness.
Grymfyw, *a.* (grym—byw) Powerfully alive.

Pawl yn rhoi goganiaeth rhwng y grymfyw, y nerthawg, a'r gwir Grist a'r geuawg.

Paul giving a distinction between the *essentially-living,* the powerful, and the true Christ, and the false one. *W. Salisbury.*

Grymeg, *s. f.—pl. t.* au (grwm) An enigma.
Grymiad, *s. m.* (grwm) A droning, a grunting.
Grymiad, *s. m.* (grym) An enduing with power.
Grymial, *v. a.* (grwm) To murmur, to mutter.

A grymial o'm gwal a'm gwas.

And from my bed *grumbling* with my servant. *Syp. Cyfeiliawg.*

Grymiala, *v. a.* (grymial) To murmur, to grumble.

Y delyn——
Y nos ei chym'ryd a wna'
Ar 'y mol i grymiala.

The harp, at night I shall take it upon my belly *to make a grumbling.* *Sir D. Trevor.*

Grymialawg, *a.* (grymial) Murmuring, muttering.

Tri pheth ni bydd eu heil-ryw,
Grymialawg, serchawg a syw.

There are three sorts which have not their equals, the *grumbling,* the amorous, and the pert. *D. ab Gwilym.*

Grymialedd, *s. m.* (grymial) A state of murmuring
Grymialu, *v. a.* (grymial) To murmur, to grumble.
Grymialus, *a.* (grymial) Grumbling.
Grymialwr, *s. m.—pl.* grymialwyr (grymial—gwr) A murmurer, a grumbler.
Grymialydd, *s. m.—pl. t.* ion (grymial) A murmurer, a mutterer, a grumbler.
Grymian, *v. a.* (grwm) To drone; to grunt.
Grymiannawl, *a.* (grymiant) Tending to give potency; to make efficacious.
Grymiannu, *v. a.* (grymiant) To endue with potency or power; efficacious.
Grymiant, *s. m.* (grym) Energy, potency, might.
Grymiaw, *v. a.* (grym) To endue with force, or energy; to strengthen; to attain force; to be able; to be of force; to avail.

O derfydd i ddyn, yn nydd coll neu gaffael, geisiaw oed, o fod ei arwaessaf, neu ei dystion, yn gleifion, neu yn anghenus ereill, y gyfraith a ddywed na rymia iddo hyny.

Should a person, on the day of determining a cause, apply for delay, on account of his voucher, or his witnesses being sick, or in other necessities, the law says that that *shall not be of effect* to him. *Welsh Laws.*

Grymiawl, *a.* (grym) Potent, tending to give force, or energy; nervous.
Grymu, *v. a.* (grym) To make potent; to endue with force, to make nervous.
Grymus, *a.* (grym) Powerful; nervous.
Grymusaw, *v. a.* (grymus) To make strong, or powerful; to become strong or nervous.
Grymusawl, *a.* (grymus) Tending to make strong.
Grymusder, *s. m.* (grymus) Potency, efficacy, mightiness, strength, nervousness.
Grymusdra, *s. m.* (grymus) Potency; nervousness.
Grymusrwydd, *s. m.* (grymus) Powerfulness; nervousness; potency.
Gryniad, *s. m.* (grwn) A laying in ridges.
Gryniaw, *v. a.* (grwn) To ridge, to lay in ridges.
Gryniawg, *a.* (grwn) Having ridges, ridgy.
Gryniawl, *a.* (grwn) Consisting of ridges, ridged.
Gryngiad, *s. m.* (grwng) A muttering; a grumbling; a purring.
Gryngian, *s. m.* (grwng) To mutter; to grunt, to grumble; to growl; to pur; to chowter.

Gryngian y bydd gwreugyn bach.

The little urchin always keeps *purring.* *L. Mon, i'r Ddylluan.*

Gryngiaw, *v. a.* (grwng) To mutter; to grunt; to grumble; to pur.
Gryngiawl, *a.* (grwng) Grumbling; grunting.
Gryw, *s. f.* The Greek tongue, Greek.

Gwir fu 'Ngryw ac Ebryw gael.

True that in *Greek* and Hebrew it was found. *L. G. Cothi.*

Gubain, *v. a.* (ubain) To howl, to moan.
GW, *s. m. r.* That inceptively denotes approach, or tendency to. It is a prefix in composition.
Gwa, *s. f.* (gw) That is inceptive as to motion, or direction; that throws from, or that is the base, or origin; the ground. It is used as a prefix to some words, denoting a beginning or tendency.
Gwach, *s. f.* (gwa) A hole, a cavity, a cell.
Gwachel, *s. m.* (cêl) A partly concealing; an avoidance, or shunning. *v. a.* To avoid.
Gwachelyd, *v. a.* (gwachel) To avoid, to eschew.
Gwachell, *s. f.—pl.* gwechyll (gwach) A needle, skewer, or broach; a knitting needle.
Gwachellu, *v. a.* (gwachell) To broach, to skewer.

Gwachul, *a.* (cul) Of a lean or lank state of body; feeble; indisposed.

Gwad, *s. m.* (gwa) A denial, or a disowning.

Gwadadwy, *a.* (gwad) That may be rejected or disowned, deniable.

Gwadaeth, *s. m.—pl.* gwadeithi (gwad) A spout; a cock; a spout that throws the flour from the mill into the trough.

Gwadal, *s. m.* (gwad) That rejects; that is fixed, grounded, stanch or firm; a stanchion.

Gwadaliad, *s. m.* (gwadal) A stanching; a rendering or becoming firm.

Gwadalrwydd, *s. m.* (gwadal) Stanchness.

Gwadalu, *v. a.* (gwadal) To render stanch, or firm; to become stanch.

Gwadalwch, *s. m.* (gwadal) Stanchness, fixedness.

Gwadawl, *a.* (gwad) Denying, negative.

Gwadedig, *a.* (gwad) Denied, disowned.

Gwadiad, *s. m.—pl. t.* au (gwad) A denying; a rejecting; a negation.

Gwadn, *s. m.—pl.* gwadnau (gwad) A base, or foundation; a pedestal, a sole. *Gwadn car*, the sole of a drag; *gwadn troed*, the sole of the foot; *gwadn aradr*, the chip of a plough.—*Ar y gwadnau*, upon the soles, or standing.

Lladd y gwadn fal y bo y troed.

To cut the sole according to the foot. *Adage.*

Gwadnawg, *a.* (gwadn) Having a base, or pedestal; having a sole, or soled.

Gwadniad, *s. m.* (gwadn) A laying a base; a soling; a footing or tripping it.

Gwadnu, *v. a.* (gwadn) To lay a base, or foundation; to sole; in familiar speech, to trip it, to foot it.—*Gwadnu esgidiau*, to sole shoes.

Gwadnwr, *s. m.—pl.* gwadnwyr (gwadn—gwr) One who soles.

Gwadu, *v. a.* (gwad) To deny; also to disown.

Ni lwydd golud a wader.

Wealth that is denied will not prosper. *Adage.*

Nid eiddo Duw a wader.

It is not the property of God that is disowned. *Adage.*

Gwadwr, *s. m.—pl.* gwadwyr (gwad—gwr) A denier, a disowner.

Gwadd, *s. f.—pl. t.* au (gwa) That is down, settled, or grounded; a mole, or want. *Pridd y wadd*, earth thrown up by the mole, or a mole-hill.

Gwaddawd, *s. m.—pl.* gwaddodion (gwadd) Sediment, grounds, dregs, or lees.

Gwaddawg, *a.* (gwadd) Being grounded; feculent.

Gwaddawl, *a.* (gwadd) That is put down, or settled. *s. m.* A portion, dower, or what is given with a wife upon marriage. *A roddes efe waddawl iddi?* Did he give her any portion? *Dyfed.*

Gwaddedig, *a.* (gwadd) Grounded; settled.

Gwaddeg, *s. f.—pl. t.* au (gwadd) What serves as a passage; a spout. *Gwaddeg melin*, the scuttle of a mill, through which the meal falls out.

Gwaddn, *s. m.—pl.* gwaddnau (gwadd) A basement, a sole.

Gwaddodawg, *a.* (gwaddawd) Feculent, dreggy.

Gwaddodi, *v. a.* (gwaddawd) To make a sediment.

Gwaddodiad, *s. m.* (gwaddawd) A settling, or casting a sediment.

Gwaddodlestr, *s. m.—pl. t.* i (gwaddawd—llestr) A vessel used in brewing.

Gwaddodlyd, *a.* (gwaddawd) Feculent, dreggy.

Gwaddolawg, *a.* (gwaddawl) Dowered, portioned.

Gwaddoledig, *a.* (gwaddawl) Settled as a portion.

Gwaddoli, *v. a.* (gwaddawl) To dower, to portion.

Gwaddoliad, *s. m.* (gwaddawl) A dowering.

Gwaddolwr, *s. m.—pl.* gwaddolwyr (gwaddawl—gwr) One who gives a dower.

Gwaddotwr, *s. m.—pl.* gwaddotwyr (gwadd—gwr) A catcher of moles.

Gwaddwr, *s. m.—pl.* gwaddwyr (gwadd—gwr) A mole-catcher; he is also called *tyrchwr*.

Gwae, *s. f.—pl. t.* oedd (gwa) That is piercing! a woe.

Awn i gwynaw ein geni;
I gwne och a gwae ni,
I fwrw dagrau am Ieuan!

Let us go to mourn that we were born; to utter sighs and woe to us; to shed tears for Ieuan. *L. G. Cothi.*

Gwae, *interj.* (gwa) Woe! Alas! *Llwyr gwae fi!* Utter woe is me! *Gwae fy nghalon!* Woe my heart! *Gwae finnau byth!* Ever woe is to me!

Arglwydd gwan gwae ei was.

Woe to the servant of a feeble lord. *Adage.*

Gwae a gâr ni garant.

Woe! that loves those who love not. *Adage.*

Gwaean, *s. m.* (gwae) That issues, or flows.

Gwaeued, *s. f.* (gwaen) That is issued, or produced.

Ys deubo gwaeuaed gwerth na pherhed.

If it should come to an issue it were well not to have sinned. *Aneurin.*

Gwaeanwyn, *s. m.* (gwaean—gwyn) The issuing, or rising of the sap; spring. It is otherwise called *Gwaenwyn*.

Gwaed, *s. m.—pl. t.* au (gwa—ed) Blood.—*Gwaed cyn delwad*, blood before the formation, or the embryo before its parts are formed. *Gwaed-ddillad*, blood-clothes; *Gwaed y gwyr*, and *ysgaw y ddaiar*, dwarf elder:—*Gwaed dyn! Gwaed dyn byw! Gwaed dyn a'i gilydd! Gwaed dy galon! Gwaed drwg! Gwaed y gwr drwg! Gwaed diawl! Gwaed y cythraul!* Interjections of swearing, analogous to—*Blood* and wounds!

Odid archoll heb waed.

There is seldom a wound without blood. *Adage.*

Gwaedast, *s. f.—pl.* gwaedeist (gwaed—gast) A blood bitch.

Gwaedawg, *a.* (gwaed) Sanguine, full of blood.

Gwaedawl, *a.* (gwaed) Of blood; sanguineous.

Gwaedboer, *s. m.* (gwaed—poer) Blood-spitting.

Gwaedboeri, *v. a.* (gwaedboer) To spit blood.

Gwaedboeriad, *s. m.* (gwaedboer) A spitting of blood.

Gwaedfaen, *s. m.—pl.* gwaedfeini (gwaed—maen) Blood-stone, used to be worn round the neck to prevent bleeding at the nose.

Gwaedffrau, *s. f.* (gwaed—ffrau) A blood-spilling.

Ni ddiengis namyn tri o wrhydri ffosawd—
A minnau o'm gwaedffrau gwerth fy ngwenwawd.

There escaped but three by the prowess of the sword, and from the spilling of my blood I also my hallowed muse did save. *Aneurin.*

Gwaedgael, *a.* (gwaed—cael) Bloodsucking.

Gwaedgi, *s. m.—pl.* gwaedgwn (gwaed—ci) A bloodhound; a mastiff.

Gwaedglais, *s. m.—pl.* gwaedgleisiau (gwaed—clais) A blood-stripe, a bloodshot.

Gwaedlys, *s. m.* (gwaed—llys) The knot-grass. *Gwaedlys mawr*, purple grasspoly; *gwaedlys bychan*, or *goradd*, red bartsia; *gwaedlys gwyn*, or *briw y march*, common vervain.

Gwaedgnud, *s. f.—pl. t.* oedd (gwaed—cnud) A bloody pack.

Gwaedgoll, *s. m.* (gwaed—coll) Bloodshed.

Gwaedgolli, *v. a.* (gwaedgoll) To shed blood.

Gwaedhuad, *s.m.—pl.* gwaedhuaid (gwaed—huad) A bloodhound.

Gwaedlad, *s. m.* (gwaed) A letting of blood.

Gwaedlain, *s. m.* (gwaed—llain) A bloody blade. *a.* Having a blade drenched in blood.

Oedd gwaedlain Gwyalfain fab Eilydd.

Reeking with blood was the *blade* of Gwyalfain son of Eilydd. *Aneurin.*

Gwaedlan, *s. f.—pl. t.* au (gwaed—llan) A bloody plain.

Llawn pelidrau gwaedled gwaedlan;
Llawn aerwyr briw breuawl sidan.

Thick the flight of darts, reeking was the *plain of blood*; thick were the wounded men of slaughter in tattered silk. *Myrddin.*

Gwaedled, *a.* (gwaed) Bloodstained, bloody.

Gwaedlen, *s. f.—pl. t.* i (gwaed—llen) A blood veil; a bloody veil.

Ef a weled——
A gwaedlen am ben yn beithiawg,
A gwaed, a bwyd brain,
A bran ar gelain,
A galon adfuddiawg.

He was seen with a *veil of blood*, conspicuous round the head, and blood and food for crows, and the raven on the corpse, and foes of hope bereft. *Ll. P. Moch, i Lywelyn I.*

Gwaedlif, *s. m.—pl. t.* oedd (gwaed—llif) An issue of blood; a bloody-flux.

Gwaedlifaw, *v. n.* (gwaedlif) To run with blood.

Gwaedlifawl, *a.* (gwaedlif) Sanguifluous.

Gwaedlin, *s. m.* (gwaed—llin) A flux, or issue of blood; a running of blood; a bloody-flux.

Mal pan ddel medel ar freith-hin
Y gwnai Marchlew waedlin.

As in the cloud-dispersing season when the reaping comes, would Marchlew cause the *stream of blood*. *Aneurin.*

Gwaedling, *s. m.* (gwaedlin) A running of blood.

Gwaedliw, *s.m.—pl.t.* iau (gwaed—lliw) A blood-colour. *a.* Of a blood colour.

Gwaedliwiad, *s. m.* (gwaedliw) A making of a blood colour; a colouring with blood.

Gwaedliwiaw, *v. a.* (gwaedliw) To colour with blood; to make of a blood colour.

Gwaedlwrw, *s.m.* (gwaed—llwrw) A blood stream.

Gwaedlyd, *a.* (gwaed) Bloodstained, bloody, cruel.

Gwaedlyd wrth faint dy drachywedd.

Cruel through the excess of thy affection. *Adage.*

Gwaedlydiad, *s. m.* (gwaedlyd) A making bloody.

Gwaedlydiaw, *v. a.* (gwaedlyd) To make bloody. to imbrue or stain with blood.

Gwaedlydrwydd, *s. m.* (gwaedlyd) Sanguinariness, bloodiness; bloodthirstiness.

Gwaedlydu, *v. a.* (gwaedlyd) To stain with blood.

Gwaed a redo hyd lawr, can ni chwyner am dano, yr argiwydd à ddyly ymyre, wrth waedlydu ei dir.

Blood that runs upon the ground, though no complaint shall be made for it, the prince should prosecute from his land being *stained with blood*. *Welsh Laws.*

Gwaedlys, *s. f.* (gwaed—llys) Bloodwort, or centinody. It is also called *Canclwm*, and *Llysiau y milwr*.

Gwaednerth, *s. m.* (gwaed—nerth) That strengthens the blood, that gives courage.

Gwinfaeth oedd waednerth lyfri.

Feasting on wine was the coward's *spur to courage*. *Aneurin.*

Gwaedneu, *s. m.* (gwaed—neu) A blood issue.

Dadgweinyd gwaedneu
Dydd cerydd caerau.

Let the *blood stream* flow again the day that walls are assailed. *Taliesin.*

Gwaedogaeth, *s. m.* (gwaedawg) Sanguinity.

Gwaedogawl, *a.* (gwaedawg) Sanguiferous.

Gwaedogen, *s. f.—pl. t.* au (gwaedawg) A blood-pudding, blackpudding.

Gwaedogi, *v. a.* (gwaedawg) To sanguify.

Gwaedogiad, *s. m.* (gwaedawg) Sanguification.

Gwaedoli, *v. a.* (gwaedawl) To sanguify.

Gwaedoliad, *s. m.* (gwaedawl) Sanguification.

Gwaedoliaeth, *s. m.* (gwaedawl) The state of being of blood; kindred by blood.

Gwaedraidd, *a.* (gwaed—rhaidd) Running with blood.

Gwaedraidd fy nghleddyf a godrudd yn nghâd;
Yn nghyfranc a Lloegr llawr neud ymgudd!

Blood-stained is my sword and vehement in battle; in the conflict with Lloegria the ground will it not hide itself! *Gwalchmai.*

Gwaedrawd, *s. m.* (gwaed—rhawd) Course of blood, circulation of the blood.

Y gwenith yw'r cnawd,
A'r gwin yw'r gwaedrawd.

The wheat is the flesh, and the wine is the *blood course*. *Taliesin.*

Gwaedreiddiad, *s. m.* (gwaedraidd) A drenching with blood.

Gwaedreiddiaw, *v. a.* (gwaedraidd) To drench with blood.

Gwaedrudd, *s. m.* (gwaed—rhudd) Blood-red. *a.* Reddened with blood.

Oedd ongyr oedd engir eu bar;
Oedd anghudd gwodrudd gwaedryar.

There were spears, dreadful was their wrath; conspicuous was the *crimson-stained* blood-rippling. *Ll. P. Moch, i Lywelyn I.*

Gwaedruddaw, *v. a.* (gwaedrudd) To blood redden, to redden with blood.

Gwaedruddiad, *s. m.* (gwaedrudd) A reddening with blood.

Gwaedruddiawl, *a.* (gwaedrudd) Blood-reddening.

Gwaedryar, *s. m.* (gwaed—rhyar) The rippling noise of blood.

Oedd Menai heb drai o drallanw gwaedryar
A lliw gwyar gwyr yn heli.

Menai was without an ebb from an overflow *of rippling blood*, and the brine was tinged with the gore of men. *Gwalchmai.*

Gwaedu, *v. a.* (gwaed) To bleed; to let blood.

Gwaedwrf, *s. m.* (gwae—twrf) A tumult of woe.

Gwaedwyllt, *a.* (gwaed—gwyllt) Of wild blood.

Gwaedd, *s. f.—pl. t.* au (gwae) A cry, a shout. *Gwaedd gwlad*, the cry of a country; a common crier.

Hydr waedd gwaeth wrth fro.

The *shout* of confidence is the worse to a country. *Adage.*

Peithiawg dy alon, dy elyn gwae ef;
Gwaedd a gwlad neu'th ganlyn!

Exposed are thy foes, woe to thy antagonist; the *shout* and the country do they not follow thee! *Ll. P. Moch, i Lywelyn I.*

Gwaeddan, *s.m.* (gwaedd) A squeaker, a squealer.

Gwiw ddyn wyd, gwaeddan ydwyf.

Thou art a meritorious person, I am a *driveller*. *D. ab Gwilym*

Gwaeddawl, *a.* (gwaedd) Crying, or shouting.

Gwaeddfan, *a.* (gwaedd—ban) Of a loud cry, loud-shouting, loud-sounding.

Diasbad fan gwynt gwaeddfan,
Oedd ban gawr am ben garthan.

The echoing point of the *high-sounding* wind was the loud shout over the camp. *Elidyr Sais.*

Gwaeddgreg, *a.* (gwaedd—creg) Of a hoarse cry, rough shouting; hoarse-voiced.

Mennwd molawd gwawd gne ton waeddgreg
Wanar wisg lafar aear ofeg.

Let praise make an impression on her whose skin is of the hue of the *rough-sounding* wave, in an azure vest, with pensive mind in her course. *Cynddelw, i Wenllian.*

Gwaeddi, *v. a.* (gwaedd) To cry, to shout, to bawl.

Gwaeddiad, *s. m.* (gwaedd) A crying, a shouting.

Gwaeddiwr, *s.m.—pl.* gwaeddwyr (gwaedd—gwr) A crier, a shouter.

Gwaeddolef, *s. f.* (gwae—dolef) A cry of woe.

Gwaeddolef, *v. a.* (gwae—dolef) To make a woeful outcry.

> ——— Dyn, gwae ef!
> Gwiw ei ddelw yn gwaeddolef!

> Alas, poor man! singular his figure *uttering a cry of woe!* — *D. ab Gwilym.*

Gwaeddreg, *a.* (gwaedd—rheg) Copious with cries.

> Neud gwaeddreg gwaaer gwynt yn adail.

> Is not the course of the wind *tumultuous* in stripping the leaves. — *Ein. ab Gwalchmai.*

Gwaefyd, *s. m.* (gwae—byd) State of woe.

Gwaeg, *s. f.—pl. t.* au (gwa) A fibula; a clasp, a buckle; the tongue of a buckle.

Gwaegawl, *a.* (gwäeg) Made to buckle, or clasp.

Gwaegiad, *s. m.* (gwäeg) A clasping; a buckling.

Gwäegu, *v. a.* (gwaeg) To clasp; to buckle.

Gwael, *a.* (gwa) Low, base, vile; ignoble. *Mae yn wael iawn arno*, it is very miserable with him, *peth gwael yw hwna*, that is a poor thing; *Gwaelion*, vile ones; *gwaelonion*, most vile ones.

> Dymunais marchogeth o amgylch y llys; nid mewn buried ymadael a'm gwael fuchedd, ond er mwyn fy rhanchoddiaeth.

> I desired to ride round about the palace, not with the intention of parting with my *vile course of life*, but for the sake of my amusement. — *Marchawg Crwydrad.*

Gwaelaidd, *a.* (gwael) Of a low or vile tendency.

Gwaelaw, *v. a.* (gwael) To make low or base; to become low, or vile.

> Duw a ddug attaw bydd gwaelaw byd,
> Deddfawl frenin, dewin diwyd.

> God has taken to him a treasure *to make wretched a country*, a king honouring the laws, and diligently pious. — *Bleddyn Fardd.*

Gwaelawd, *s. m.—pl.* gwaelodau (gwael) A bottom; also a sediment or settlement of liquor. *Dyn da ei waelawd*, a man of good bottom; *gwaelodion y ddaiar*, the bottoms, or low parts of the earth; *gwaelodion*, sediments.

> Nawf maen hyd waelawd.

> A stone swims as far as the *bottom*. — *Adage.*

Gwaelbeth, *s. m.—pl. t.* au (gwael—peth) A trifling thing, a trifle.

Gwaelder, *s. m.* (gwael) Lowness; vileness.

Gwaeldra, *s. m.* (gwael) Lowness; wretchedness.

Gwaelddyn, *s. m.—pl. t.* ion (gwael—dyn) A low, mean, or ignoble person; a wretch.

Gwaeledig, *a.* (gwael) Rendered low, or vile.

Gwaeledd, *s. m.* (gwael) Lowness; wretchedness.

Gwaeleddawg, *a.* (gwaeledd) In a low, or miserable plight.

> Yn ngwlad nef boed ef yn dreftadawg;
> Nad ei enaid hael yn waeleddawg.

> In the kingdom of heaven let him be an inheritor; suffer not his generous soul to be *miserable*. — *Meilyr, m. G. ab Cynan.*

Gwaeleddiad, *s. m.* (gwaeledd) A reducing to a a state of lowness, or wretchedness.

Gwaeleddu, *v. a.* (gwaeledd) To reduce to a low, or wretched state; to become wretched.

Gwaeleddus, *a.* (gwaeledd) Tending to make wretched.

Gwaeliad, *s. m.* (gwael) A making low, a debasing; a becoming debased.

Gwaelineb, *s. m.* (gwael) Lowliness; misery.

Gwaelni, *s. m.* (gwael) Lowness; wretchedness.

Gwaelodi, *v. a.* (gwaelawd) To bottom; to go, or sink, to the bottom; to cast a sediment.

Gwaelodiad, *s. m.* (gwaelawd) A bottoming.

Gwaelu, *v. n.* (gwael) To grow low, or poor; to become faint; to become wretched.

Gwaelwan, *a.* (gwael—gwan) Miserably feeble.

> Y truan gwael wan, lle nis gwelir tal,
> Y sy gam ymlad, a'ngymunir.

> The poor man *miserably weak*, where no payment is seen, which is a [illegible] wrong, will be excommunicated. — *E. Tudur.*

Gwaelwr, *s. m.—pl.* gwaelwyr (gwael—gwr) A low, or wretched man.

Gwaelyd, *a.* (gwae) Woeful, piteous, wretched.

> Mae braw's addiliw'r meddylion f'm bryd,
> A gwaelyd yw'r galon.

> Regret doth palsy the thoughts in my mind, and *woeful* is the heart. — *Llywelyn o Langewydd.*

Gwaell, *s. f.—pl.* gwëyll (gwa—ell) A needle, bodkin, skewer, or broach; a knitting needle. *Gwaell ysgwydd*, a shoulder-blade; *gwäell y goes*, the spindle-bone of the leg; *gwaell neidr*, is the bull-chafer most generally, also called *chwilen gorniawg*, *chwil derw*, and *carr-chwilen*, but in Anglesey it is the horsefly, and in Caermarthenshire it is the water spider.

Gwaelliad, *s. m.* (gwaell) A broaching with a skewer, a putting upon a knitting needle.

Gwaellu, *v. a.* (gwaell) To broach, to skewer; to put upon a knitting needle.

Gwaen, *s. f.—pl.* gweunydd (gwa—en) A plain, or level course; a meadow.

> Angor dewr daen,
> Sarff saffwy graen,
> Anysgogud waen
> Blaen bydin.

> An anchor-holder of gallant range, a dragon of the spear of woe, of immoveable course of the front of battle. — *Taliesin.*

Gwaenad, *s. m.* (gwaen) A stretching out even; a straight forward course; a going head-long.

Gwaenadu, *v. a.* (gwaenad) To go straight forwards, or headlong. *Eidion yn gwaenadu*, a bullock running away from the flies. *Sil.*

Gwaenawg, *a.* (gwaen) Having a straight, or even course; of a headlong tendency.

> Trichant eurdorchawg,
> Cyfeddgar gwaenawg.

> Three hundred wearing the golden torques, convivial and of *headlong course*. — *Taliesin.*

Gwaenawl, *a.* (gwaen) Of a straight, or even course; of a headlong course.

Gwaenawr, *s. m.—pl.* gwaenorion (gwaen) That is headlong; a furious one.

Gwaened, *a.* (gwaen) Headlong; furious.

Gwaengrawn, *s. m.* (gwaen—crawn) A meadow crop.

Gwaent, *s. m.* (gwaen) A plain, or full view.

Gwaentu, *v. a.* (gwaent) To appear in front.

> Ef gwaint Adam dwrch trahawg.

> He *came forward*, Adam the furious boar. — *Aneurin.*

Gwaenu, *v. a.* (gwaen) To put in full view.

> Ef gwaenid Adan fab Erfai.

> Adan the son of Ervai was *placed conspicuously*. — *Aneurin.*

Gwaenwr, *s. m.—pl.* gwaenwyr (gwaen—gwr) One who goes forward, or headlong.

Gwaenyd, *v. a.* (gwaen) To put, or go forward; to run headlong.

Gwaer, *s.m.* (gwa—er) A downward aspect; simplicity; a clownish simplicity. *a.* Simple; rustic. It is also used as an aggregate plural. *Gwaer y fàn a'r fàn*, the rustics of such place.

Gwaeraidd, *a.* (gwaer) Simple; rusticated.

Gwaerawl, *a.* (gwaer) Tending downward; of a simple or bashful look; rustic.

Gwaered, *s.m.—pl. t.* ydd (gwaer) The bottom of a descent or declivity. *I waered*, *ar i waered*, and *ar waered*, downward; *fordd hyd y gwaered*, a road along the declivity,

> Ni bydd allt heb waered.

> There is no cliff without a bottom. — *Adage.*

> [illegible]

> Through walls leaping the *declivity*. — *[illegible]*

Gwaeredawg, *s. m.* (gwaered) A flat or bottom at the foot of high ground.

Gwaeredawl, *a.* (gwaered) Tending downward.

Gwaerediad, *s. m.* (gwaered) A tending downward.

Gwaeredu, *v. n.* (gwaered) To tend downward.

Gwaes, *s. m.—pl. t.* ydd (gwa—es) That is put down, fixed or placed; a tent; a pledge, or deposit; earnest.

Oina, y parchellan, y parchellgarwy,
Na chladd dy redgyr, nag yn di fyawy,
Na char wasn na char warwy.

Attend, little pig, the rude little pig, bury not thy snout: but if thou wilt refuse, love no *pledge*, love no play. *Myrddin.*

Gwaesaf, *s. m.—pl. t.* oedd (gwaes) That may be relied upon; that is pledged, a pledge, a deposit, an earnest, a warrant; that is asserted, a deposition; an answer. *Duw—ceingadr waesaf*, God the gloriously powerful pledge.

Nid oes wad troe waesaf.

There is no denial for a *pledge*. *Adage.*

Tri gwaesaf y sydd: arddelw, neu warrant, neu amddiffyn heb warrant.

There are three *pleas*: a voucher, or a warrant, or defence without warrant. *Welsh Laws.*

Gwaesafawl, *a.* (gwaesaf) Relating to a pledge, or deposit; deponent; responsible.

Gwaesafiad, *s. m.* (gwaesaf) A laying down a pledge, or deposit: a giving earnest; a warranting; a deposition.

Gwaesafu, *v. a.* (gwaesaf) To insure, to pledge, to deposit; to warrant; to assert, to make a deposition, to depose; to make responsible.

Gwaesafwr, *s. m.—pl.* gwaesafwyr (gwaesaf—gwr) One who lays down a pledge, or deposit, one who warrants, a deponent. *Gwaesafwr brenin*, a king's protegee, a vavasour: *Cledren gwaesafwr*, a pale of protection.

Od a gwaesafwr oddiwrth ei waesaf chweugaint a dal.

If a *pledged man* shall depart from his pledge he shall pay six score pence. *Welsh Laws.*

Nawddwr brenin chweugaint fydd ei ebediw: a hwnw a elwir gwaesafwr.

A king's protegee his heriot is six score pence: and that one is called a *pledged man*. *Welsh Laws.*

Gwaesawg, *a.* (gwaes) Having a pledge, or deposit; having earnest, warranted, responsary.

Gwaesawl, *a.* (gwaes) Relating to a pledge; earnest; warranting, warranted; responsive.

Gwaesiad, *s. m.* (gwaes) A laying down, a pledging or depositing, a warranting, a making a deposition, responsion.

Gwaesu, *v. a.* (gwaes) To pledge, to deposit, to give earnest, to warrant, to response.

Gwaeswr, *s. m.—pl.* gwaeswyr (gwaes—gwr) A pledger, a depositer; a deponent.

Gwaettir, *s. m.* (gwaed—tir) Land of blood, land alienated to make compensation for murder.

Gwaeth, *s. m.* (gwa) The worse, that is less good.

Dewisaist y gwaeth yn lle y gwell.

Thou hast chosen the *worse* instead of the better one. *Adage.*

Myned ar y gwell o'r gwaeth.

To become of the best from the *worse*. *Adage.*

Gwaeth, *a.* (gwa) Worse, bad in a greater degree. *Gwaeth-waeth*, worse and worse: *Gwaeth yr oedd*, the more was the pity! Alas! *Ni waeth i ti*, it is nothing to thee.

Ai rhaid i'r haul draul drawwy
Lle mae, i geisio lliw mwy?
Nid gwaeth gwèn mewn pais wen wiw,
Nog iarlles mewn gwisg euriliw.

Is it necessary that the sun should take an additional range in his orb, to obtain greater splendour! From this, the fair one, in a goodly white flannel coat is not *worse* than if it were a lady in a gold-laced robe. *D. ab Gwilym.*

Gwiriais i'i heb un gair sen,
Gaethiwed a gwaeth awen.

I have divined to thee, without one word of reproach, restraint and a *worse* muse. *Edm. Prys.*

Gwaethâad, *s. m.* (gwaeth) A making worse; an impairing; a becoming worse.

Gwaethach, *a.* (gwaeth) Bad in a greater degree.

Gwaethaf, *s. m.* (gwaeth) The worst, or that is bad in the highest degree.

Gwaethaf, *a.* (gwaeth) Worst, most bad. *Gwaetha' gallo*, the agnail, or witlow.

Drwg yw y drwg, a gwaeth yw y gwaethaf.

Bad is the bad, and worse is the *worst*. *Adage.*

Gwaethafed, *a.* (gwaethaf) Degenerated. *Gwrgd gwaethafed*, degenerated manhood.

Gwaethâu, *v. n.* (gwaeth) To become damaged, or impaired; to become worse; to impair, or to make worse.

Gwaetherwydd, *interj.* (gwaeth—herwydd) Worse for it! Alas!

Gwaetherwydd, Dduw, na's lladded!

Alas! God, that he was not slain. *H. Bown—Mabinogion.*

Gwaethineb, *s. m.* (gwaeth) An impaired state.

Gwaethl, *s. m.—pl.* gwaethlion (gwae—tyl) Outrage; strife, contention.

Gwaethlawg, *a.* (gwaethl) Outrageous, warring.

Gwaethlfan, *a.* (gwaethl—ban) Loudly outrageous; loudly-warring.

Gwythlawn yw fy anwn yn nyfygl:
Gwaethlfan yn nghyman, yn nghymhelri.

Wrathful is my nature in the tumult; *loudly-warring* in the rencounter in the conflict. *Ll. P. Moch.*

Canaf, can caraf, can wyf gwaethlfan;
Canu cerdd am borth am byrth clodfan:
Cyfodwch! canwch! canyf o'm ban,
A mi, feirdd, y mewn, a chwi allan!

I sing, since I love, since I am *loudly contentious*; singing a song for assistance round the high-famed gates; arise! sing! I have my flowing bowl, ye bards and I am within, and you without; *Cynddelw.*

Gwaethliad, *s. m.* (gwaethl) A being outrageous, a warring, a contending.

Gwaethlu, *v. a.* (gwaethl) To act outrageously.

Gwaethl edlid o'm bron pan brofer cyfrain
I'r cyfran y doter.

Wrath *rages* from my breast when the foremost ranks are tried, from the lot which befalls. *Cynddelw, m. E. ab M. ab Iddon.*

Gwaethlus, *a.* (gwaethl) Outrageous, warring.

Gwaethu, *v. a.* (gwaeth) To make worse; to impair, to damage.

Meddylai pawb, yn ddiwall,
Na waethai un ar y llall.

Every body ought, without fail, to refrain and not to *depreciate* one another *T. Ll. D. ab Hywel.*

Gwaethwaeth, *a.* (gwaeth *repeated*) Worse and worse.

Gwaethwaeth fasnaer, gwellwell brenaer.

Worse and worse the stone-mason, better and better the carpenter. *Adage.*

Gwaethwaeth, mal mab gafr.

Worse and worse, like the goat's brat. *Adage.*

Gwaethwg, *s. m.* (gwaeth) An impaired state.

Gwaethygadwy, *a.* (gwaethwg) Damageable.

Gwaethygaidd, *a.* (gwaethwg) Tending to impair.

Gwaethygedig, *a.* (gwaethwg) Damaged.

Gwaethygiad, *s. m.* (gwaethwg) A rendering, or becoming worse; a damaging, or impairing.

Gwaethygu, *v. a.* (gwaethwg) To make worse, to impair, or to damage; to become worse.

Gwaethygus, *a.* (gwaethwg) Tending to impair.

Gwaethygwr, *s. m.—pl.* gwaethygwyr (gwaethwg—gwr) One who makes worse; a damager.

Gwaew, *s. m.—pl.* gweywyr (gwae) Pang, pain, or agony, a stitch, spasm, or gripe; a lance, a spear.——*Gwewyr esgor*, pangs of travail.—*Gwaew y brenin*, the asphodel.

> Addfwyn yw gware gwaew ac arwydd;
> Addfwyn lydd ysgwyd ar ddewr ysgwydd.
>
> Well-seeming to me the play of the lance and bearing; well-seeming the shield on the gallant shoulder. *Ein ab Gwalchmai.*

Gwaewawr, *s. m.* (gwaew) A darting of a lance.

> Esgyll gwawr oedd gwaewawr Dunawg.
>
> The *radiations of the lance* of Dunawg were like the wings of the dawn. *Llywarch Hen.*

Gwaewdwn, *a.* (gwaew—twn) Broken-lanced.

Gwaewffon, *s. f.*—*pl.* gwaewffyn (gwaew—ffon) A javelin.

Gwaewgrwydr, *s.m.* (gwaew—crwydr) The wandering of pain, the wandering of darts.

Gwaewlorf, *s. f.*—*pl.* gwaewlyrf (gwaew—llorf) The staff or shaft of a lance.

> Rhys, orau mab rhysswr Mon,
> Rhuthr waewlorf, rhyw Llywelyn.
>
> Rhys, the best son of the champion of Mon, with the hasty *spear-shaft*, of Llywelyn's race. *T. Aled.*

Gwaewrudd, *a.* (gwaew—rhudd) Ruddy-speared.

> Tri gwaewrudd feirdd Ynys Prydain: Elinog fab Cadair, bardd Urien; Cynhafal fab Argad, bardd Owain; a Afaon, bardd Cadwallawn.
>
> The three *ruddy-speared* bards of the Isle of Britain, Elinog son of Cadair, the bard of Urien; Cynhafal son of Argad, the bard of Owain, and Afaon, the bard of Cadwallon. *Trioedd.*

Gwaewsaeth, *s. m.*—*pl. t.* au (gwaew—saeth) A dart, or javelin.

Gwag, *s. m.* (gwa) A void, a vacuum. *a.* Void, empty, vacant; vain, frivolous.

> Gwag ty heb fab.
>
> *Empty* is a house without a son. *Adage.*
>
> Gwell bychod y'nghod na chod wag.
>
> A little in a bag is better than an *empty* one. *Adage.*

Gwagiad, *s. m.* (gwag) An emptying; a becoming void, or empty.

Gwagaidd, *a.* (gwag) Somewhat void, or empty.

Gwagâu, *v. a.* (gwag) To render empty, or void, to become empty, or void.

Gwagbren, *s. m.*—*pl. t.* iau (gwag—pren) A hollow, or decayed timber.

Gwagchwedl, *s. m.*—*pl.* gwagchwedlau (gwag—chwedl) An empty expression.

Gwagchwedlu, *v. a.* (gwagchwedl) To utter void, or unmeaning expressions.

Gwagder, *s. m.* (gwag) Emptiness, voidness.

Gwagdraul, *s. f.* (gwag—traul) Vain waste.

Gwagdreuliaw, *v. a.* (gwagdraul) To consume vainly. *Gwagdreuliaw amser*, to waste time frivolously.

Gwagdy, *s. m.*—*pl. t.* au (gwag—ty) An empty house.

Gwagedd, *s. m.* (gwag) Emptiness, vanity; frivolity.

> Gwagedd, cywilydd, a gogan:
> Cedwch a gwadwch y gân.
>
> *Vanity*, shame, and scandal,—hide and deny the song. *L. Morris.*

Gwageddawl, *a.* (gwagedd) Of a vain tendency.

Gwageddiad, *s. m.* (gwagedd) An acting vainly.

Gwageddu, *v. a.* (gwagedd) To act vainly.

> Bum hir yn gwageddu, a chredu'n ochrydus.
>
> I have been long *trifling*, and believing fearfully. *D. W. Dafydd.*

Gwageddus, *a.* (gwagedd) Tending to vanity.

Gwageddwr, *s. m.*—*pl.* gwageddwyr (gwagedd—gwr) A man of vanity; a trifler.

Gwagelawg, *a.* (celawg) Circumspect, cautious, heedful, wary.

> Bid wagelawg lleidr.
>
> Let the thief be cautious. *Adage.*

Gwageliad, *s. m.* (celiad) An acting cautiously.

Gwagelogrwydd, *s. m.* (gwagelawg) Wariness.

Gwagelu, *v. a.* (celu) To act cautiously, to shun.

Gwagelyd, *v. a.* (celyd) To shun, to eschew.

Gwagfalch, *a.* (gwag—balch) Vainglorious.

Gwagfalchedd, *s.* (gwag—balch) Vaingloriousness.

Gwagfalchïad, *s. m.* (gwagfalch) A rendering, or becoming vainglorious.

Gwagfalchïaw, *v. a.* (gwagfalch) To render vainglorious; to become vainglorious.

Gwagfolach, *s.m.* (gwag—molach) Vain-boasting.

Gwagfolachiad, *s. m.* (gwagfolach) A behaving ostentatiously, or in a boasting manner.

Gwagfolachu, *v. a.* (gwagfolach) To act ostentatiously, or swaggeringly.

Gwagfolachus, *a.* (gwagfolach) Ostentatious.

Gwagfoly, *s. m.*—*pl. t.* au (gwag—boly) Empty belly, *a.* Empty-bellied.

> Ni chwsg gwagfoly.
>
> The *empty-bellied* will not sleep. *Adage.*

Gwaggoned, *s. m.* (gwag—coned) Vain glory.

Gwaggonedd, *s. m.* (gwag—conedd) Vain glory.

Gwagher, *s. f.* (gwag—her) A vain bravado.

Gwagheriad, *s. m.* (gwagher) A making an empty threat, or vaunting.

Gwagheriant, *s.m.* (gwagher) An empty vaunting.

Gwagheriwr, *s. m.*—*pl.* gwagherwyr (gwagher—gwr) One who makes a vain bravado.

Gwaghoffedd, *s.* (gwag—hoffedd) Vain affection.

Gwaghoffi, *v. a.* (gwag—hoffi) To cherish a vain affection, or partiality.

Gwaghoffiant, *s. m.* (gwag—hoffi) Vain affection.

Gwagiad, *s. m.* (gwag) An emptying out.

Gwagiaith, *s. f.* (gwag—iaith) Empty tattle.

Gwaglais, *s. m.*—*pl.* gwagleisiau (gwag—llais) An empty or hollow voice. *a.* Of a hollow voice.

> Chwerw iawn yw chwarae ern
> Gydgerdd rhwng cloch ac udgorn;
> Galargyrn mychdeyrn Mon,
> Goglaisiaw beirdd gwagleision.
>
> Very bitter is to ring a peal, in concert between a bell and organ; the horns of lamentation for the sovereign of Mon are grating to the bards of *empty sounds.* *Iolo Goch.*

Gwaglwyf, *s. f.*—*pl. t.* au (gwag—llwyf) The linden, lime tree, or teil tree.

Gwaglwyfen, *s. f.* (gwaglwyf) A linden tree.

Gwagogonedd, *s.* (gwag—gogonedd) Ostentation.

Gwagogoneddgar, *a.* (gwagogonedd) Vainglorious.

Gwagogoneddiad, *s. m.* (gwagogonedd) An acting vaingloriously, or ostentatiously.

Gwagogoneddu, *v. a.* (gwagogonedd) A behaving ostentatiously.

Gwagogoneddus, *a.* (gwagogonedd) Vainglorious.

Gwagogoni, *v. a.* (gwag—gogoni) To exalt vainly.

Gwagogoniant, *s.m.* (gwag—gogoniant) Vain glory.

Gwagorchest, *s. f.*—*pl. t.* ion (gwag—gorchest) An ostentatious exploit.

> Er barn beirdd a gwagorchest, nid da gormodd arfer cynghanedd a cyfochrodli ar bennillion cyfain.
>
> Notwithstanding the opinion of the bards of *ostentatious skill*, the excessive use of consonancy and parallel rhyming is not good in whole stanzas. *Barddas.*

Gwagorchestawl, *a.* (gwagorchest) Apt to act an ostentatious exploit; vainly emulous.

Gwagorchestiad, *s. m.* (gwagorchest) A doing feats out of ostentation.

Gwagorchestu, *v. a.* (gwagorchest) To do an ostentatious feat; to be vainly emulous.

Gwagorfoledd, *s. m.* (gwag—gorfoledd) Vain exaltation, empty triumph.

> Diffrwyth fan flodau'r dyffryn
> A dawl wag orfoledd dyn.
>
> The feeble small flowers of the valley derogate from the empty boast of man. *Gro. Owain.*

Gwagorfoleddawl, *a.* (gwagorfoledd) Apt to exult vainly; vainly triumphing.

Gwagorfoleddiad, *s. m.* (gwagorfoledd) A vainly-triumphing.

Gwagorfoleddu, *v. a.* (gwagorfoledd) To rejoice, or exult, vainly

Gwagorfoleddus, *a.* (gwagorfoledd) Vainly-joyous

Gwagr, *s. m.—pl. t.* au (gogr) A sieve, or searce.

Gwagsaw, *a.* (gwag—saw) Capricious, fluttering; trifling, light; wanton.

Gwagsawrwydd, *s. m.* (gwagsaw) Capriciousness, flutteringness, levity; wantonness.

Gwagymffrost, *s. m.* (gwag—ymffrost) A vain exultation, or boasting; a rodomontade.

Gwagymffrostiad, *s. m.* (gwagymffrost) A vainly blustering; vain exultation.

Gwagymffrostiaw, *v. a.* (gwagymffrost) To rodomontade, to make an empty blustering.

Gwagymffrostiawl, *a.* (gwagymffrost) Vainly blustering, vainly exulting.

Gwagymffrostiwr, *s. m.—pl.* gwagymffrostwyr (gwagymffrost—gwr) An empty blusterer.

Gwagymgais, *s. m.* (gwag—ymgais) A vain attempt; an abortive feat.

Gwagymgeisiad, *s.* (gwagymgais) A making a vain attempt.

Gwagymgeisiaw, *v. a.* (gwagymgais) To make a vain, or fruitless attempt.

Gwahan, *s. m.* (gwa—han) A separation; diversity, difference, distinction. *Ar wahan*, apart.

Gwahan, *a.* (gwa—han) Separate, distinct, distinguished, particular.

> Hirlas yn llawen yn llaw Forgant,
> Gwr a ddyly gwawd gwahan foliant.
>
> The Hirlas seems joyous in the hand of Morgant, a man who deserves to be the theme of *peculiar* praise. *O. Cyfeiliawg.*

Gwahanadwy, *a.* (gwahan) Separable, divisible; distinguishable, discriminable.

Gwahanai, *s. m.—pl.* gwahaneion (gwahan) The genitive case, in grammar.

Gwahanator, *ger.* (gwahan) Being separating.

Gwahanawl, *a.* gwahan) Separating, disjunctive.

Gwahanblyg, *s. m.—pl. t.* ion (gwahan—plyg) The diaphora, a term in rhetoric.

Gwahanedig, *a.* (gwahan) Separated; diversified.

Gwahanedigaeth, *s. m.—pl. t.* au (gwahanedig) Separation: discrimination.

Gwahanedigaethydd, *s. m.—pl. t.* ion (gwahanedigaeth) That which denotes a proceeding from; the genitive case.

Gwahanedigawl, *a.* (gwahanedig) Implying a separation, or distinction.

Gwahanedigrwydd, *s. m.* (gwahanedig) Separability; discriminateness.

Gwahanfod, *s. m.—pl. t.* au (gwahan—bod) Diversity of existence.

> Tri pheth angen yn abred: y lleiaf o bob byw, ac o hyny dechre; defnydd pob peth, ac o hyny cynnydd, yr hynn is gellir mewn cyflwr angen; a lluniaw pob peth o'r marw, ac o hyny gwahanfod.
>
> The three things of necessity in the inchoative progression: the least of all life, and thence a beginning; the matter of all things, and thence increase, which should not take place in another state; and the forming of all things from the dead, and thence *variety of existence*. *Barddas.*

Gwahanfodawl, *a.* (gwahanfod) Of a distinct mode of existence.

Gwahanglaf, *a.* (gwahan—claf) Ill of the leprosy.

Gwahanglefyd, *s. m.—pl. t.* on (gwahanglaf) The leprosy, or separation disease.

Gwahanglwyf, *s. m.—pl. t.* au (gwahan—clwyf) A leprosy.

Gwahanglwyfawl, *a.* (gwahanglwyf) Leprous.

Gwahaniad, *s. m.—pl. t.* au (gwahan) A separatin, or dividing; separation.

Gwahaniaeth, *s. m.—pl. t.* au (gwahan) A separating, partition; discrimination, distinction.

> Tri gwahaniaeth angenorfod rhwng dyn, a pheb byw arall, a Duw: bag ar ddyn, ac nis gellir ar Dduw; dechre ar ddyn, ac nis gellir ar Dduw; ac angen newid cyflwr olynol yn nghylch y gwynfyd ar ddyn, o anodde bythoedd y ceugant, ac nis gellir ar Dduw, gan allu pob dyoddef, a hyny gan wynfyd.
>
> The three unavoidable *distinctions* between man, with every other living thing, and God; finitude as to man, which cannot be with God; a beginning as to man, which cannot be with God, and a necessity of a rotatory change of his mode of existence in the circle of felicity as to man, being from unable to bear the tedium of eternity, which cannot be with God, from his being able to endure all things, and that consistent with felicity. *Barddas.*

Gwahaniaethawl, *a.* (gwahaniaeth) Discriminative; disjunctive.

Gwahaniaethu, *v. a.* (gwahaniaeth) To make a separation; to discriminate, to distinguish.

Gwahanitor, *sup.* (gwahan) To be in separating.

Gwahanlen, *s. f.—pl. t.* i (gwahan—llen) A separation veil.

Gwahannod, *s. m.—pl. t.* au (gwahan—nod) A point of division; a colon.

Gwahannodawl, *a.* (gwahannod) Having a point of separation; characteristical.

Gwahannodi, *v. a.* (gwahannod) To put points of separation; to characterise, to punctuate.

Gwahannodiad, *s. m.* (gwahannod) A distinction by points; interpunction.

Gwahanoldeb, *s. m.* (gwahanawl) Separateness.

Gwahanoli, *v. a.* (gwahanawl) To render separate.

Gwahanolrwydd, *s. m.* (gwahanawl) Separateness.

Gwahanran, *s. f.—pl. t.* au (gwahan—rhan) A separate part; a paragraph.

Gwahanranawl, *a.* (gwahanran) Tending to separate into parts; particularizing.

Gwahanrannu, *v. a.* (gwahanran) To separate into pars; to divide into paragraphs.

Gwahanred, *s. f.—pl. t.* ion (gwahan) Discrimination; peculiarity; a characteristic.

> Nid oes i wybodaeth dynawl ond dau ran arbenig; sef yn gyntaf gwahanred rhwng y naill beth a'r llall; yn nesaf ymadrawdd fraeth.
>
> There are to human knowledge but two principal parts: that is, in the first place, a *discrimination* between one thing and another; and next readiness of speech. *H. Perri.*

Gwahanredadwy, *a.* (gwahanred) That may be separated into parts; discriminable.

Gwahanredawl, *a.* (gwahanred) Discriminating.

Gwahanredoldeb, *s. m.* (gwahanredawl) Discriminateness, distinctness.

Gwahanredoli, *v. a.* (gwahanredawl) To discriminate; to characterise.

Gwahanredoliad, *s. m.* (gwahanredawl) A discriminating, a separating into parts.

Gwahanredoliaeth, *s. m.* (gwahanredawl) The state of being separated; discrimination.

Gwahanredolrwydd, *s. m.* (gwahanredawl) Discriminateness, distinctness of character.

Gwahanredu, *v. a.* (gwahanred) To discriminate.

Gwahanrwydd, *s. m.* (gwahan) Separateness.

Gwahansang, *s. f.—pl. t.* au (gwahan—sang) An interposition; a parenthesis.

Gwahansangawl, *a.* (gwahansang) Interposing; parenthetical.

Gwahansangiad, *s. m.* (gwahansang) An interposing

Gwahansangu, *v. a.* (gwahansang) To interpose; to put in a parenthesis.

Gwahanu, *v. a.* (gwahan) To separate, to part, to divide, to sever, to put asunder; to distinguish, to discriminate.

> A wahanodd gnawd gwahanodd ddolur.
>
> He that *has parted* with flesh *has parted* with pain. *Adage.*

Gwahanwr, *s. m.—pl.* gwahanwyr (gwahan—gwr) One who separates, or divides.

Gwahanydd, *s. m.—pl. t.* ion (gwahan) A separater

Gwahardd, *s. m.—pl. t.* oedd (hardd) A prohibition; a check. *Heb wahardd, heb erbynwedyd*, without prohibition, without contradiction.

Gwahardd, *v. a.* (hardd) To prohibit, to forbid.

> Tri pheth a waherddir i fardd: dwyn anfawl, dwyn anfoes, a dwyn arfau.
>
> Three things *are forbidden* to a bard: to practise dispraise, to practise immorality, and to bear arms. *Barddas.*

> ——Earf ni'th wahardd
> Cyfaillt a mab aillt y beirdd.
>
> Arms will not *interdict* thee, thou friend and foster son of bards. *D. ab Gwilym.*

Gwaharddadwy, *a.* (gwahardd) That may be forbidden, or prohibited.

Gwaharddator, *ger.* (gwahardd) Being forbidding.

Gwaharddawl, *a.* (gwahardd) Prohibitory.

Gwaharddedig, *a.* (gwahardd) Prohibited, forbidden; under an interdiction, contraband.

Gwaharddedigaeth, *s. m.—pl. t.* au (gwaharddedig) A prohibition, or interdiction.

Gwaharddedigawl, *a.* (gwaharddedig) Prohibitory

Gwaharddiad, *s. m.—pl. t.* au (gwahardd) A prohibiting; a prohibition, or interdiction.

Gwaharddiaeth, *s. m.—pl. t.* au (gwahardd) Prohibition, interdiction.

Gwahardditor, *sup.* (gwahardd) To be forbidding.

Gwaharddu, *v. a.* (gwahardd) To prohibit, to forbid

Gwaharddwr, *s. m.—pl.* gwaharddwyr (gwahardd—gwr) One who prohibits.

Gwahawdd, *s. m.—pl.* gwahoddion (gwa—hawdd) A bidding, or invitation.

Gwahawdd, *v. a.* (gwa—hawdd) To bid to come, to invite.

> Ewch gan hyny allan i'r prif-ffyrdd; a chynnifer a gaffoch gwahoddwch i'r briodas.
>
> Go therefore out into the high-ways; and as many as ye shall find do you *invite* to the marriage. *W. Salisbury.*

> Drwg llys ni ater ond a wahodder.
>
> Poor is the court where only *such as be invited* are admitted. *Adage.*

Gwahen, *s. m.* (gwa—hen) An exhaustion.

Gwahenawl, *a.* (gwahen) Tending to empty.

Gwaheniad, *s. m.* (gwahen) A pouring out.

Gwahenu, *v. a.* (gwahen) To pour out, to empty

> Bas pan wahener hyny.
>
> Shallow when that *shall be emptied.* *Adage.*

Gwahenwr, *s. m.—pl.* gwahenwyr (gwahen—gwr) A pourer, an emptier.

Gwahenydd, *s. m.—pl. t.* ion (gwahen) One who pours out; one who empties.

Gwahoddadwy, *a.* (gwahawdd) That may be invited.

Gwahoddai, *s. m.* (gwahawdd) An inviter.

Gwahoddiator, *ger.* (gwahawdd) Being inviting.

Gwahoddawl, *a.* (gwahawdd) Inviting, bidding.

Gwahoddedig, *a.* (gwahawdd) Invited, or that is bidden. *Gwahoddedigion*, those who are invited.

Gwahoddedigaeth, *s. m.* (gwahoddedig) Invitation

Gwahoddedigawl, *a.* (gwahoddedig) Invitatory.

Gwahoddgar, *a.* (gwahawdd) Fond of inviting.

Gwahoddiad, *s. m.—pl. t.* au (gwahawdd) An invitation, or a bidding to come.

Gwahoddiaeth, *s. m.* (gwahawdd) An invitation.

> A heddyw heb wahoddiaeth,
> 'Y moethau i ymaith aeth!
>
> And to-day without an *invitation*, my cheering treatments are all gone! *S. ab Hywel Gwyn.*

Gwahodditor, *sup.* (gwahawdd) To be inviting.

Gwahoddwr, *s. m.—pl.* gwahoddwyr (gwahawdd—gwr) An inviter.

Gwai, *s. m.* (gwa) That is in motion or action.

Gwail, *s. m.—pl.* gweilion (gwa—il) That is over, spare, at hand, or attendant.

Gwailg, *s. m.* (gwail) That is over, or upon.

Gwain, *s. f.—pl.* gweiniau (gwa—in) That serves; that supports; a carriage, a wain, a waggon; a scabbard, a sheath.

> Hawdd yw tynu cleddyf byr o wain.
>
> A short sword is easily drawn from the scabbard. *Adage.*

Gwain, *a.* (gwa—in) Smart, neat; brisk, lively.

> Gwelais——
> A dan draed adar gwyr gwanar gwain.
>
> I saw under the feet of the birds of prey men of *brisk* career. *Cynddelw.*

Gwaint, *s. m.* (gwain) That is smart, or neat; that is lively, or chearful; smartness.

Gwaint, *a.* (gwain) Smart, or neat; brisk; lively.

> Er lles gwledig Mon, gwaint yn mhlymnwyd.
>
> For the good of the sovereign of Mon, *ardent* in the conflict. *Gwalchmai.*

> Neb ni wyr——
> Ganmawl tegwch fy'm dyn gwaint,
> Y a liwyr, er maint a fedr.
>
> No one is adequate justly to praise the beauty of my *smart* girl, whatever he may know. *Gofiden.*

Gwair, *s. m.—pl.* gweiriau (gwa—ir) That shoots out lively; that is brisk, or luxuriant; hay.—*Gwair rhos*, meadow hay; *gwair gwyndwn*, hay off dry land, or where corn is also grown; *gwair bras*, coarse, or rushy hay; *brag-wair*, and *rhos-wair*, hay off moist mountain-ground; *ton-wair*, common meadow hay; *gwair hallt*, hay off marshes overflowed by the sea; *gwair merllyn*, guilliwort.

Gwair, *a.* (gwa—ir) Of a fresh, or lively nature; apt to shoot, or to sprout; ardent; wanton.

> Tarianawg, rhwysawg rhwair, anghynnwys
> Argoedwys Bowys bair,
> A dyr cangyr angerdd wair,
> Ac ni dyr i deyrn-air.
>
> The shield-bearing famed ravager, the unsubduable ruler of the men of Powysian Argoed, is wont to break the sprouts of *brisk* vehemency, but does not break his royal word. *Cynddelw, i Wenwynwyn.*

Gwaisg, *s. m.* (gwa—isg) A brisk motion; briskness; vigour, energy.

Gwaisg, *a.* (gwa—isg) Of a quick motion; apt to run; brisk, sprightly; volatile. *adv.* Briskly, actively, alertly.

> Gwaisg i'm clwyfodd cawdd.
>
> *Smartly* did affliction wound me. *D. ab Gwilym.*

> Gwewais gowydd gwaisg awen,
> Gan gainc i Forganwg wen.
>
> I formed a song of the *lively* muse, a vocal strain to fair Morganwg. *Llawdden.*

Gwaith, *s. m.—pl.* gweithiodd (gwai) Act, or action; work, labour; workmanship; an action, or battle. *Gwaith y gwenyn*, chequer-work; *gwaith y pryf*, the barbles.

> Dwyparth gwaith ei ddechreu.
>
> Two parts *of a work* is to begin it. *Adage.*

> Ni cheffir gwaith gwr gan was.
>
> A man's *work* cannot be had from a boy. *Adage.*

> Ef molir pawb wrth ei waith:
> Ni char Dofydd diobaith.
>
> Every body will be praised according to his *work*: the Lord loves not the hopeless. *Llyfrau.*

> Gwae hwynt yr ynfydion
> Pan fu waith Faddon.
>
> Woe to them the foolish ones when the *battle* of Badon was. *Taliesin.*

Gwaith, *s. f.—pl.* gweithiau (gwai) Course, turn or time. *Unwaith*, one time, or once; *tair* *gwaith*, three times, or thrice; *ambell waith*, sometimes, or now and then; *weithiau*, sometimes; *llawer gwaith*, many times; *ar ddyddgwaith*, upon a certain day; *y waith hon*, this time.

Gwaith, *adv.* (gwai) Because that, since. *Gwaith goddef*, purposely; *nid eis yno waith nad allwn*, I did not go there because that I could not. *Sil.*

Gwal, *s. f.—pl. t.* au (gwa—al) A place shut in, fenced or sheltered; a place of repose; a shelter; a bed, or couch; a place where animals lie; a bed in a garden; a piece of cultivated ground; a fallow; an inhabited country.—*Gwal ceinach*, a hare's form: *gwal cwsg*, and *cysgwal*, a dormitory, a place where people at harvest retire to sleep. *Sil.* The *Cymmry* appropriated this name to regions that were cultivated and had a fixed inhabitancy, as opposed to the wilds, or the unsettled residences of the *Celtiaid*, *Celyddon*, *Gwyddyl*, *Gwyddelod*, *Ysgotiaid*, and *Ysgodogion*; which are terms descriptive of such tribes as lived by hunting and tending their flocks. In late periods *Gwal* has been a name used in a loose acceptation for *Gaul*.

Gwnaed ar Wal ysgien drwch,
Gwr a chan-fflam gwreichion-fflwch.

Let him make over *Gaul* a broken blade, the hero with a hundred flames of ardent sparks. *T. Aled, i Sir R. ab Thomas.*

——Rhag clwyf ynial,
Rhag arf a gwaed, rhag rhwyf Gwal,
Rhag gwn llaw rhaco'n y llwyn
Rhag gwaew anap, rhag gwenwyn,
Dewi a'th weddi ni thau,
Derfel a'th geid yn d'arfau.

Against dire disease, against weapon and blood, against the sovereign of *Gaul*, against a hand-gun from the opposite wood, against eventual pain, against poison, Dewi to thy prayer will not be silent, Dervel will preserve thee in thy arms. *Ll. Morganwg, i R. Mansel.*

———Curasant
Yspaen, Portyngal,—a hyd Wal.

They did beat Spain, Portugal, and as far as *Gaul*. *Meir. Dafydd, i fllwyr Elizabeth.*

I'th weled, wr, i'th wal da——
Hoff yw.

To see thee, good fellow, in thy snug *shelter* is pleasing. *D. ab Gwilym, i'r cyffylog.*

Yn lle sindal yn nghylch ei wal,
Gweled carpiau.

Instead of fine linen round his *couch*, rags were seen. *Y Brawd Mad. ab Gwallter, i Grist.*

Crêd i Dduw——
A'n rhoddes, dyfiau,
Gwen-wlad, gwal olau.

Believe in God, who, on a Thursday, prepared for us the region of bliss, a splendid *place of rest*. *Taliesin.*

Cellwair dy wal, call air da,
Uwch y wledd, na chywilyddia.

Joke thy *native spot*, in a good witty expression, over the feast, but shame it not. *Adage.*

Gwàl, *s. f.—pl. t.* iau (gwa) A fence, a rampart, or wall. *Gwàl Sefer*, the wall of Severus; *Pen y wàl*, head of the wall; *pen gwàl*, wall head.

Gwala, *s. m.* (gwal) Fullness, sufficiency, enough.

Ac odid mor ddrwg ydwyd,
Gael fyth un gwala o fwyd.

And hardly, so bad thou art, wilt thou ever get one *fill* of victuals. *W Cynwal.*

Gwalabr, *s. f.—pl. t.* au (llabr) That is spread out even; a pathway.

Gwalabr haul gloew wybr yw hi.

The sun's *pathway* is the clear ether. *D. ab Gwilym.*

Gwalabriad, *s. m.* (gwalabr) A making a path.

Gwalabru, *v. a.* (gwalabr) To make a path.

Gwalad, *s. m.* (gwal) Arrangement, order.

Gwaladr, *s. m.—pl.* gwelydr (gwalad) A disposer, or arranger; a leader or head of a tribe; a sovereign, or supreme ruler.

Pan fai welydr hydr hydwyll,
Y beirdd a ddywawd o bwyll.

When bold *rulers* are liable to deception, the bards speak discreetly. *Ll. ab O. ab Cynfrig*

Gwaladriad, *s. m.* (gwaladr) A disposing or arranging.

Gwaladru, *v. a.* (gwaladr) To dispose, to arrange, to put in order or trim.

Gwalaed, *s. m.* (gwala) A making full, or replete.

Gwalaeth, *s. m.—pl. t.* au (gw—alaeth) That grieves, a cause of sorrow.

Gwalaethiad, *s. m.* (gwalaeth) A causing grief.

Gwalaethu, *v. a.* (gwalaeth) To cause grief.

Gweirfyl deg, fy rheg, fy rhin—
Rhym gwalaeth.

Fair Gweirfyl, my bliss, my love, she *causes me grief* extreme. *H. ab Owain.*

Hiraeth a'm gwalaeth gweled arnaw fwng
Gynhebrwng echwng; och o'r cuddiaw!

Longing *makes me to mourn* to see upon him the sad attendance to the narrow space; alas, the covering over! *Bleddyn Fardd, m. O. Goch.*

Gwalaru, *v. a.* (alaru) To satiate, to surfeit.

Gwalas, *s. f.—pl. t.* au (gwal) A couch, a bed; low land, a plain or level.

Gweli canol gweilgi cain,
Gwalas morfeirch, a gwylain.

The veins across the fair ocean, the *couch* of the sea horses and the gulls. *Gr. Gryg, i'r don.*

Gwalbant, *s. f.—pl. t.* au (gwal—pant) The top of a wall of a building where the beams rest.

Gwalc, *s. f.—pl. t.* iau (gwal) Fence-work; a fender; a palisade; a battlement; a parapet; a rail; a cock of a hat; the hair of the head turned up. *Gwalc castell*, battlement of a castle; *gwalc pont*, battlement of a bridge; *gwalc car*, the frame of a drag that holds the load.

Y goludog——
Uwchlaw ei walc uchel wen,
Gofyn a wna gwaetha'r gwan.

The wealthy, over his *battlement* high and white, will ask the weak to do his worst. *W. Middleton.*

Gwalciad, *s. m.* (gwalc) A turning up; a making a fence, or parapet; a cocking.

Gwalciaw, *v. a.* (gwalc) To turn up; to make a fence-work, to make a parapet; to cock.

Gwalciawg, *a.* (gwalc) Having a fence, a battlement, parapet, or rail, cocked. *Het walciawg*, a cocked hat.

Pan fo gwyr yn walciawg
A'r gwreigedd yn gribawg,
Meibion yn asgellawg
Ac ysgawn sangau—y bydd hyn.

When the men shall be *with cocked hats*, and the women high-crested, and the youths with flaunting wings, and light steps, will all this be. *Gronw Ddu.*

Gwalciedig, *a.* (gwalc) Turned up; fenced; having a parapet; cocked.

Gwalcu, *v. a.* (gwalc) To turn up; to fence; to make a parapet; to cock.

Gwalch, *s. m.—pl.* gweilch (gwal) That rises, or towers up; a crested one; a hero; a falcon, a hawk. *Yr wyt yn walch rhyfedd*, thou art a wonderful fine fellow; *O'r gwalch!* O you sly one! *gwalch y weilgi*, the osprey; *gwalch y penwaig*, the razorbill; also called *cas gan longwr*, or the seaman's foe.

Mal adain i walch.

Like wings to the *hawk*. *Adage.*

Cynan——
Eryr tymyr gwyr, gweilch disaesneg.

Cynan, the eagle of the land of men, who are *heroes* with no English. *Casnodyn.*

Gwalchaidd, *a.* (gwalch) Apt to rise up; like a hawk; full of spirit; chearful; arch.

Gwalches, *s. f.*—*pl. t.* au (gwalch) A female hawk; a sprightly female.

Gwalchiad, *s. m.* (gwalch) A rising, or soaring.

Gwalchlys, *s. f.* (gwalch—llys) Hawk's beard; otherwise called *Llysiau yr hebawg*.

Gwalchu, *v. a.* (gwalch) To soar, or to tower up.

Gwalchwr, *s. m.*—*pl.* gwalchwyr (gwalch—gwr) A hawker, or a falconer.

Gwalchwriaeth, *s. m.* (gwalchwr) Falconry.

> Yn iach—
> Na gwalch i'w harwain na gwalchwriaeth.
>
> Adieu, no more of hawks to be carried, nor of *hawking*. *T. Aled.*

Gwalchydd, *s. m.*—*pl. t.* ion (gwalch) A falconer.

Gwalchyddiaeth, *s. m.* (gwalchydd) Falconry.

Gwald, *s. f.*—*pl. t.* iau (gwal) A hem; a welt. *Gwald esgid*, the welt of a shoe.

Gwaldas, *s. m.*—*pl. t.* au (gwal—tas) A strengthening welt, hem or border; a shoe welt.

Gwaldiad, *s. m.* (gwald) A welting; a hemming.

Gwaldon, *s. f.*—*pl. t.* au (gwal—ton) The raised bank of a river, or dike.

Gwaldu, *v. a.* (gwald) To welt, or to hem.

Gwales, *s. f.*—*pl. t.* au (gwal) A couch, a bed.

> Na fydd debyg i hwch yn dy wales.
>
> Be not like a sow in thy *couch*. *Adage.*
>
> Gwnaethost—
> Lloegr wales yn waen war.
>
> Thou didst make the country of Lloegria a tame desert. *Ll. P. Moch, i Lywelyn I.*
>
> Cyn gweled gwales nychedig,
> Caffwyf Grist, fy rhwyf, fy rhyfig!
>
> Before I see the couch of pining, may I find Christ, my lord, my glory! *Gr. ab M. ab Dafydd.*

Gwalfa, *s. f.*—*pl. t.* au (gwal) A stratum.

> Gwelwn—y llawr yn walfa o bob cigyddiaeth.
>
> I could see the floor a continued *stratum* of every kind of butchery. *Elis Wyn, Bardd Cwsg.*

Gwalfawr, *a.* (gwal—mawr) Of large extent.

> Cyfirwth y gur gwalfawr hwn.
>
> Wide is the swallow of this *huge bellied* man.

Gwaliad, *s. m.* (gwâl) An enclosing, a walling.

Gwaliaw, *v. a.* (gwâl) To enclose, to wall.

Gwaliawg, *a.* (gwâl) Enclosed with a wall.

Gwaling, *s. m.*—*pl. t.* au (gwal) A litter.

> Y'nghwr bwth anghywair
> A'i gwaling yn ei gwylion.
>
> In one corner of an untidy hut with her *litter* keeping her vigils. *Iolo Goch.*

Gwaltes, *s. m.*—*pl.* gwalteisiau (gwald) A welt.

Gwalteisiad, *s. m.* (gwaltes) A welting.

Gwalteisiaw, *v. a.* (gwaltes) To welt, as a shoe.

Gwaltysiad, *s. m.* (gwaltes) A welting.

Gwaltysu, *v. a.* (gwaltes) To welt; to hem.

Gwalu, *v. a.* (gwal) To form a bed or couch; to take to a couch; to wallow.

Gwalwys, *s. pl. aggr.*—*pl. t.* on (gwal—gwys) Gauls, or the people of France.

Gwaly, *s. m.*—*pl. t.* on (gwal) What contains, capacity, or the inside.

> Gwell wyneb na gwaly.
>
> The surface is better than the *inside*. *Adage.*
>
> Angel a'i rhif y'ngwaly rhad.
>
> An angel will count him in the *fullness* of grace. *L. G. Cothi.*

Gwalyaid, *s. m.*—*pl.* gwalyeidiau (gwaly) What is contained, the fill, or contents.

> Dyro i'm un gwalyaid o fwyd.
>
> Give me one *fill* of victuals. *H. Bown—Mabinogion.*

Gwalyaw, *v. a.* (gwaly) To fill, to make full.

Gwalyawd, *s. m.* (gwaly) A filling: a satiating.

Gwalyawg, *a.* (gwaly) Having the fill; satiated.

Gwalystawd, *s. m.* (gwal—ystawd) Peculiar location, or arrangement.

> Pob dihareb yn ngwalystawd ei llythyren gysefin.
>
> Every proverb to be under the *peculiar arrangement* of its primitive letter. *T. ab Ifan.*

Gwall, *s. m.*—*pl. t.* au (gw—all) That is effused; that is out, void, or empty; a lapse; a failing, or defect; need, want; neglect, heedlessness.—*Gwall ymgeledd*, want of cherishing; *gwall synwyr*, defect of sense; *gwall tan*, neglect of looking after fire.

> Mae diawl gwedi cael gwall arno.
>
> The devil has found a *failing* upon him. *Adage.*
>
> Mynych heb raid bod ar wall.
>
> Frequently without occasion one is upon the wrong. *Adage.*

Gwallaw, *v. a.* (gwall) To draw, or pour out; to empty; to exhaust; to let go. *Na'm gwallaw o'th law*, do not *let* me *go* out of thy hand.

> Mynaf—gorn Culgawd Gododin i wallaw arnam y nos hono; nis rhodda ef o'i fodd; ni elli dithau ei dreisiaw.
>
> I will have the horn of Culgawd of Gododin *to draw* in waiting upon us that night; he will not give it of his own accord; neither canst thou force him. *H. Culhwch—Mabinogion.*

Gwallawd, *s. m.*—*pl.* gwallodion (gwall) A failure; a mistake.

> Gellyd fod mewn gwallawd fer,
> Llym-whilch, mor ddall a Homer.
>
> Thou mightest be in one short *slip*, my acute friend, as blind as Homer. *W. Cynwal, i E. Prys.*

Gwallawf, *s. m.*—*pl.* gwallofion (gwall) An exhaustion; an out-pouring.

Gwallawg, *a.* (gwall) Defective, or faulty.

> Nid gwallawg fradawg fradwriaeth
> Mab Duw er mab dyn diriperaeth.
>
> The deceitful treachery to the Son of God is not *defective* with respect to the salvation of the sons of men. *Cynddelw.*

Gwallawgair, *s. m.* (gwallawg—gair) A false expression; an error in pleading. *a.* Faulty in pleading.

> Ni chyll neb ei dir yn ngwallawgair, oni ddygwyddo dair gwaith.
>
> No one shall lose his land in *false pleading* except it shall happen three times. *Welsh Laws.*
>
> Gwallawgair yw yr hawlwr a gollo ei hawl o wall.
>
> *Faulty in pleading* is the claimant that shall lose his claim by a defect. *Welsh Laws.*

Gwallawiad, *s. m.* (gwallaw) A pouring out.

Gwallawwr, *s. m.*—*pl.* gwallawwyr (gwallaw—gwr) A pourer out, or emptier.

> Dau lygad owrth yn gwrthgrif,
> Diystyr wallawwyr llif.
>
> Two sad eyes against each other weeping, unpitied *pourers out* of streams. *D. ab Gwilym.*

Gwallawydd, *s. m.*—*pl. t.* ion (gwallaw) A pourer.

Gwallbwyll, *s. m.* (gwall—pwyll) Defective, or fallible reason; irrationality.

Gwallbwyllaw, *v. n.* (gwallbwyll) To become defective in reason; to lose the reason.

Gwallbwyllawg, *a.* (gwallbwyll) Having a defective reason; halfwitted.

Gwalldan, *s. m.*—*pl. t.* au (gwall—tan) A consuming fire.

> Gwalldan yw'n ddofi rhai gwylltion dirtaid,
> Aur yw ac ennill i rai gweiniaid.
>
> He is like a *wildfire*, taming the mischievous bad ones; his coal is gold to those who are weak. *L. G. Cothi.*

Gwalldefnydd, *s. m.* (gwall—defnydd) A wrong use, or purpose.

Gwalldefnyddiad, *s. m.* (gwalldefnydd) A putting to a wrong use.

Gwallddefnyddiaw, *v. a.* (gwallddefnydd) To put to wrong purpose, to misuse.

Gwallddefnyddiawl, *a.* (gwallddefnydd) Tending to a wrong purpose.

Gwallfarn, *s. f.* (gwall—barn) Faulty judgment.

Gwallfarnu, *v. a.* (gwallfarn) To misjudge.

Gwallgam, *s. m.* (gwall—cam) A false step.

Gwallgamu, *v.a.* (gwallgam) To take a false step.

Gwallgof, *s. m.* (gwall—cof) Distraction.

Gwallgofi, *v. n.* (gwallgof) To fail in memory; to become distracted, or disordered in mind.

Gwallgofiad, *s. m.* (gwallgof) A distracting; a becoming distracted, or disordered in mind.

Gwallgoll, *s. m.* (gwall—coll) Loss by neglect.

Gwallgolli, *v. n.* (gwallgoll) To lose by neglect.

Gwallgyfraith, *s. f.—pl.* gwallgyfreithiau (gwall—cyfraith) A faulty, or defective law.

> O derfydd i hawlwr holi yn y llys ddygynnull, a gwr y brenin yn eistedd ar y llys hono, nid oes oed iddo i ateb: y dydd hwnw y derfydd y gwallgyfreithiau, ac y camddefodau.
>
> If a claimant should pursue a claim in the court of assembly, and the king's deputy presiding over that court, there is no delay for him to answer: on that day the *defective laws* and the wrong customs shall be at an end. *Welsh Laws.*

Gwalliad, *s. m.—pl. t.* au (gwall) A failing, a being defective; a neglecting.

Gwalling, *s. m.—pl. t.* au (gwall) A loose gown.

Gwallocâad, *s. m.* (gwallawg) Defection; a neglecting; a becoming defective.

Gwallocâu, *v.a.* (gwallawg) To render defective; to neglect; to become defective.

> Ni chyll amser y gyfraith o'i hammheu, onid gan wallocâu canlyn gwedy caniatâer.
>
> The time in law will not be lost from being dubious of it, but by *neglecting* to go on after permission is granted. *Welsh Laws.*

Gwallofain, *v. n.* (gwallawf) To become defective or fallacious.

Gwallofaint, *s. m.* (gwallawf) A defection, or failing; indigence.

> Gwell Efa wrth bawb rhag gwallofain'.
>
> Eva is better to every one against *indigence*. *L. G. Cothi.*

Gwallofawd, *s. m.* (gwallawf) An exhausting.

Gwallofi, *v. a.* (gwallawf) To pour; to exhaust.

Gwallofiad, *s. m.—pl.* gwallofiaid (gwallawf) A drawer, tapster, or butler.

Gwallofiaw, *v. a.* (gwallawf) To pour out.

Gwallofiawd, *s. m.* (gwallawf) A pouring out.

Gwallofiawdr, *s. m.—pl.* gwallofiodron (gwallof—iawd) A pourer; a drawer of liquor.

Gwallofwr, *s.m.—pl.* gwallofwyr (gwallawf—gwr)

Gwallofydd, *s. m.—pl. t.* ion (gwallawf) A pourer out; an exhauster; a drawer of liquor.

Gwallon, *s. m.* (gwall) A pourer, or scatterer.

Gwallt, *s. m. aggr.—pl. t.* au (gwall) The hair of the head. *Gwallt y ddaiar*, or *eurwallt y forwyn*, common hair-moss; *gwallt y forwyn*, common maidenhair; *gwallt gwener*, or *diwlydd*, true maidenhair.

> Nid moel gwr yn araws gwallt.
>
> A person waiting for *hair* is not bald. *Adage.*

Gwalltaidd, *a.* (gwallt) Hair-like, capillary.

Gwalltawg, *a.* (gwallt) Having hair; long-haired. *Seren walltawg*, a blazing star.

Gwalltfelen, *a.* (*f. of* gwalltfelyn) Yellow-haired.

Gwalltfelyn, *a.* (gwallt—melyn) Yellow-haired.

Gwalltgoch, *a.* (gwallt—coch) Red-haired.

Gwalltgrych, *a.* (gwallt—crych) Curly-haired.

Gwallthir, *a.* (gwallt—hir) Long-haired.

> Mawr erch anudon
> Gwenhwys gwallthirion.
>
> Greatly fearful the perjury of the people of Gwent the *long haired ones*. *Taliesin.*

Gwalltiad, *s. m.* (gwallt) A growing of hair.

Gwalltu, *v. n.* (gwallt) To grow hair.

Gwalltwen, *a.* (gwalltwyn) White-haired.

Gwalltwyn, *a.* (gwallt—gwyn) White-haired.

Gwalltwëydd, *s. m.—pl. t.* ion (gwallt—gwëydd) A peruke-maker.

Gwalltwr, *s. m.—pl.* gwalltwyr (gwallt—gwr) A dealer in hair, a hair merchant.

Gwallus, *a.* (gwall) Apt to be defective; negligent, heedless.

Gwallusaw, *v. n.* (gwallus) To become faulty; to become negligent, or heedless.

> Am na chredaist di hi, ac am it' wallusaw i chyngbor, yr wyd yn gorwedd yn yr anhapusrwydd yna.
>
> Because thou didst not believe her, and because thou didst *neglect* her counsel, thou art lying in that unhappy state. *Marchawg Crwydrad.*

Gwallusder, *s. m.* (gwallus) Default; negligence.

Gwallusdra, *s. m.* (gwallus) A neglectfulness.

Gwallusiad, *s. m.* (gwallus) A making faulty; a becoming faulty; a defection; a neglecting.

Gwallusrwydd, *s. m.* (gwallus) Defectiveness; neglectfulness; omission.

Gwallwg, *s. pl.* gwallygion (gwall) Defection.

Gwallygfa, *s. f.—pl.* gwallygfëydd (gwallwg) A failing, a blemish, an imperfection.

> Brwyng ofalon dall ein gwallygfa.
>
> Heavy and blind cares our *failing*. *Ior. ab y Cyriog.*

Gwallygiad, *s. m.—pl. t.* au (gwallwg) A rendering defective; a becoming defective.

Gwallygiadu, *v. a.* (gwallygiad) A causing a defection, or imperfection.

Gwallygiaeth, *s. m.* (gwallwg) Defection.

Gwallygiaw, *v. a.* (gwallwg) To render defective. to become fallible, or imperfect.

Gwallygiawl, *a.* (gwallwg) Tending to defection.

Gwallygus, *a.* (gwallwg) Defective; fallible.

Gwallymbwyll, *s. m.* (gwall—ymbwyll) A falsely reasoning with one's self.

Gwallymnawdd, *s. m.* (gwall—ymnawdd) A neglect of affording protection.

Gwam, *s. m.* (gw—am) That goes partly round; that partly encloses; a tilt, a vamp.

Gwammal, *a.* (gwam—bal) Wavering, fickle, capricious, inconstant, unstable, unsteady.

> Cerdd wammal fu'r mwngial mau.
>
> A *capricious* song was that muttering of mine. *D. ab Gwilym.*

Gwammalder, *s. m.* (gwammal) Waveringness, fickleness, capriciousness, instability.

Gwammaldra, *s. m.* (gwammal) Waveringness.

Gwammalddyn, *s. m.—pl. t.* ion (gwammal—dyn) A capricious, or flighty person.

Gwammaliad, *s. m.* (gwammal) A wavering.

Gwammaliaeth, *s. m.* (gwammal) The act, or state of wavering.

Gwammalrwydd, *s. m.* (gwammal) Fickleness.

Gwammalu, *v. a.* (gwammal) To waver, to act capriciously; to wamble, to become fickle.

Gwan, *s. f.—pl. t.* au (gwa—an) A going through, a dividing; a course; permeation; a thrust, stab, or prick.

> Hael ei wan, hil Owain Gwynedd,
> Hil Madawg, hydr fyuawg fonedd,
> Mwynlant cerdd, nid cerdd ei ddiwedd.
>
> Generous his *course*, offspring of Owain Gwynedd, of Madog's race, a bold and courteous stock, the theme of song, his end was not disgraceful. *Gr. ab Gwrgenau, m. Gr. ab Cynan.*

Gwan, *s. c.—pl.* gweinion (gwa) That is bereft; a weakling. *a.* Weak, feeble; faint, infirm; poor. *Ai pur wan wyd ti?* What, art thou very weak? *Byd gwan iawn sydd yno*, he is in very poor circumstances: *Aeth yn wan arni*, it is gone low with her.

> Ni bydd gwan heb ei gadarn.
>
> There is no *weak thing* without its potency. *Adage.*

> Tydi'r gwan, taw di a'r gair;
> Arian da a wrandewir.
>
> Thou *poor one*, be silent respecting the truth; it is the precious money that will be listened to. *Ior. Fynglwyd.*

Gwanâad, *s. m.* (gwan) A weakening, or enfeebling, a becoming infirm.

Gwanaf, *s. f.—pl. t.* au (gwan) A layer, or row; a stratum. *Gwanaf o yd*, a layer of corn, spread out from the reaper's hand; *gwanaf o wair*, a layer of hay, as left by the scythe.

Gwanafawg, *a.* (gwanaf) Having layers, rows, or flakes, flaky.

Gwanafawl, *a.* (gwanaf) Placed in layers.

Gwanafiad, *s. m.* (gwanaf) A placing in layers.

Gwanafu, *v. a.* (gwanaf) To place in layers.

Gwanaidd, *a.* (gwan) Tending to be weak, or feeble; evanid.

Gwanar, *s. m.* (gwan) That leads through; a pass; a guidance, a leader.

> Gwyr a aeth Ododin chwerthin wanar
>
> Heroes went the Gododin, a laughing *course*.

> Nid gwnaeddirog gwanar gwynt yn udwl.
>
> Does not the *course* of the desolating wind storm with howling? *Rin. ab Gwalchmai.*

> Peblwch, gwybyddwch mai fi yw
> Eich unig Dduw, a'ch gwanar.
>
> Desist ye, know ye that I am your only God, and your *leader*. *Edm. Prys.*

Gwanar, *a.* (gwan) Tending forward; forward; leading.

> Gwyr gwanar gwawr trydar trais.
>
> The *forward* men of the dawn of the din of violence. *Seisyll Bryffwrch.*

> Gwr a'm gwnaeth hiraeth hir ysgar ag ef
> Yni ddel llu nef, a llu daiar;
> Gwr gweithnud yn nghad, gwr gwanar yn ing —
>
> A man who has caused me regret, by long parting with him, until there shall come the host of heaven, and the host of earth; the man of thrusting in the conflict, the man *of expedient* in the difficulty. *Cynddelw, m. R. Plaidd.*

Gwanâu, *v. a.* (gwan) To weaken, to enfeeble, to enervate; to become weak, or feeble.

Gwanas, *s. f.- pl. t.* au (gwan) That runs through, or is fixed in, a jut, a prop; a shank; a tongue of a buckle; a clasp; a wooden hook, for hanging clothes upon; a tenter hook.

> Dabreda gennyf i'r ddinas;
> Athwyd medd a ryfullias,
> Ac aur coeth ar dy wanas.
>
> Come along with me to the city; thou shalt have mead, which I have prepared, thou with pure gold on thy *brooch*. *Ug. ab Mydno.*

> Cynnelwais i ddraig dragon wanas.
>
> I have aided a dragon, a glorious *bulwark*. *Gwalchmai.*

> Tôn y galon hon, hoed a gafas,
> Er twf main riain, ruddaur wanas.
>
> Broken is this poor heart, grief have I found from the growth of a slender lady, with ruddy golden *clasp*. *H. ab Owain.*

> Y bwa — —
> Ar y wanas ar uniawn,
> Ac ar y maes yn gwm iawn.
>
> The bow upon the *hook* seems straight enough, and in the field greatly bent. *Edm. Prys.*

> — — O bydd trwm yr on,
> Mae gwanas i'm gwayw union.
>
> If the ash should be heavy, there is a *rest* for my straight spear. *T. Aled.*

Gwanasawl, *a.* (gwanas) Running through; propping, tending to support.

Gwanasiad, *s. m.—pl.* gwanasiaid (gwanas) A demoniac, or one possessed.

Gwanasu, *v. a.* (gwanas) To run through, to stick, or thrust in; to prop; to clasp.

Gwanawl, *a.* (gwan) Permeant, thrusting; stabbing, pricking.

Gwanbwyll, *s. m.* (gwan—pwyll) A weak understanding. *a.* Of a feeble mind.

Gwanc, *s. f. - pl. t.* iau (gwang) That takes in amply; a hand-basket, made of matting; voracity, greediness. *Ponc y wanc*, the impulse of the appetite; *y wanc*, the adephagia.

Gwanciad, *s. m.* (gwanc) A gorging, a glutting, a swallowing greedily.

Gwanciaw, *v. a.* (gwanc) To swallow greedily, to englut, to devour.

Gwanciwr, *s. m.- pl.* gwanciwyr (gwanc—gwr) One who gorges or devours greedily.

Gwancus, *a.* (gwanc) Voracious, ravenous.

Gwancusrwydd, *s. m.* (gwancus) Voraciousness.

Gwander, *s. m.—pl. t.* oedd (gwan) Weakness.

> A phlant Eingl y'ngwander
> Dychynna fflam drais y dan fflam dai Lloegr.
>
> With the sons of the Angles in *distress*, kindle the flame of violence in the combustible houses of Lloegria. *Cynddelw.*

Gwandra, *s. m.* (gwan) Weakness, infirmity.

Gwandwf, *s. m.* (gwan—twf) A weak growth. *a.* Of a weak, or tender growth.

Gwanedig, *a.* (gwan) Being run through; separated, divided, transfixed.

Gwanedigaeth, *s. m.* (gwanedig) Permeation; a running through; a partition.

Gwaneg, *s. f.—pl. t.* au (gwan) Course, bent, gait, a drift; a surge, or billow; a haunch of venison. *Gwenyg y mor*, the billows of the sea.

> Lliw gwaneg ton am gareg.
>
> Of the hue of the *course* of the wave round a stone. *Einion Offeiriad.*

> Y llwynog———
> Dy waneg a adwaenwn;
> Croesaw'n wir i'r rhandir hwn.
>
> Reinard, thy *gait* I know; thou art truly welcome to this district. *H. Llwyd Cynfel.*

> Mae yn— — —
> Rhedeg fal gwaneg gwynt.
>
> He is running like the *course* of the wind. *H. Dafi.*

> Amrant —
> Fal gwennol ar fol gwaneg.
>
> An eyelid like the swallow on the bosom of the *wave*. *D. ab Gwilym.*

> Y fun———
> Ar wyneb fal eiry waneg.
>
> The nymph with the countenance like the *drift* of snow. *H. Reinallt.*

Gwanegawl, *a.* (gwaneg) Relating to a course, gait, or drift; driving.

Gwanegfa, *s. f.—pl.* gwanegfëydd (gwaneg) A drive forward; a drifting.

Gwanegiad, *s. m.* (gwaneg) A driving forward; a drifting; a rising in surges.

Gwanegu, *v. a.* (gwaneg) To proceed, or go; to issue; to pour out, to drift; to rise in waves.

> Tew, tra thew dra thro, o dra thrythu trin,
> A gwaedlin am ddeulin yn gwanegu.
>
> Thick, doubly thick the overthrow, from the extreme rushing of conflict, and the blood stream *flowing* round the knees. *Gw. Brycheiniawg.*

> Gwelid—man ddagrau careidd-serch yn gwanegu o'i lygaid.
>
> There were seen small tears of affectionate love running from his eyes. *Marchawg Crwydrad.*

Gwanffydd, *s. f.* (gwan—ffydd) Weak faith.

Gwanffyddiad, *s. m.* (gwanffydd) A mistrusting.

Gwanffyddiaw, *v. n.* (gwanffydd) To become hopeless; to become weak of faith.

Gwanffyddiawg, *a.* (gwanffydd) Having slight hope

Gwanffyddiawl, *a.* (gwanffydd) Distrustful.

Gwangalon, *s. f.* (gwan—calon) A weak heart. *a.* Weakhearted, fainthearted, dispirited.

Gwangalonawg, *a.* (gwangalon) Weakhearted.

Gwangalondid, *s. m.* (gwangalon) Faint-heartedness; timidity.

Gwangaloni, *v. n.* (gwangalon) To become faint-hearted, fearful, or timid.

Gwangaloniad, *s. m.* (gwangalon) A disheartening.

Gwangalonrwydd, *s. m.* (gwangalon) Faintheartedness, or want of courage.

Gwangalonus, *a.* (gwangalon) Fainthearted.

Gwangoel, *s. f.—pl. t.* ion (gwan—coel) A weak belief; a distrust; superstition.

Gwangoeliaw, *v. n.* (gwangoel) To have slight reliance; to distrust.

Gwangoelus, *a.* (gwangoel) Distrustful.

Gwangred, *s. f.* (gwan—cred) A faint belief.

Gwangredawl, *a.* (gwangred) Faintly believing.

Gwangredu, *v. n.* (gwangred) To distrust.

Gwanlleddf, *a.* (gwan—lleddf) Feebly-bending.

> Gwanlleddf deddf didawl ei hieithydd,
> Gwen-lloer Fawrth addoer addwyr wesgrydd.
>
> *Faintly-drooping* is the constant passion of her panegyrist; she that is like the cold fair moon of March of declining course. *Ior. Fychan.*

Gwanlleddfu, *v. n.* (gwanlleddf) To bend feebly, to incline through weakness.

Gwanobaith, *s. f.* (gwan—gobaith) Despondence.

Gwanobeithiad, *s. m.* (gwanobaith) A desponding.

Gwanobeithiaw, *v. n.* (gwanobaith) To have feeble hope; to despond.

> Addefais ger bron Duw, fy mod i yn awr yn gwybod nad allwn i roddi ufydddawd perffaith i'w gyfraith ef, ac etto na wanobeithiwn.
>
> I acknowledged in the presence of God, that I was now sensible that I could not give perfect submission to his law, and yet that I *would* not *despair*. *S. Trefredyn.*

Gwanobeithiawl, *a.* (gwanobaith) Desponding.

Gwant, *s. m.—pl. t.* au (gwan) That opens, or divides; a butt.

> Rhag cant ef gwant cysefin.
>
> In the presence of a hundred he is the *foremost butt*. *Aneurin.*

Gwantan, *s. m.* (gwant) That is apt to separate, or run off. *a.* Variable; fickle; wanton.

> Bu———
> Cymylau'n awr, mawr a man,
> A rhuthrau gwyntau gwantan.
>
> Now there have been light and heavy clouds, and the gusts of *wanton* winds. *Y Cudyll.*

Gwantawl, *a.* (gwant) Tending to sever.

Gwantiad, *s. m.* (gwant) A severing.

Gwantu, *v. a.* (gwant) To sever; to thrust.

> Mad yr ymddugost waew; mad y'th want arall.
>
> Well didst thou bear the spear; well did another *thrust* thee. *Ll. P. Moch.*

Gwantwy, *a.* (gwant) Apt to move away; fickle.

> Rhudd-bres cad beiddiad beirdd wantwy.
>
> The red bustle of conflict lot the fickle bards but dare. *Cynddelw.*

Gwanu, *v. a.* (gwan) To push forward, to thrust. to penetrate, to pierce, to stick, to prick; to stab. *I'm gwanpwyd â gwaew*, I have been ran through with a spear.

> Y neb a wanai nid adweinid.
>
> Whomsoever he *should send away* would not be recognized again. *Aneurin.*
>
> Can gochel dyrnawd Ffrollo, Arthur a'i gwant y'mhen ei fron, ac yn herwydd ei nerth ef a'i bwrw hyd y ddaiar.—cyfodes Ffrollo yn gyflym, ac esgynu ei gleddyf, a gwan ddyrnawd angeuawl ar ddwyfron march Arthur.
>
> Whilst avoiding the blow of Frollo, Arthur *thrust* a blow upon his breast, and by means of his strength he threw him upon the ground; Frollo rose up nimbly and lifted his sword, *thrusting* a deadly wound upon the breast of Arthur's horse. *Gr. ab Arthur.*

Gwanwch, *s. m.* (gwan) Weakness, debility.

Gwanwdan, *s. f.* (gwàn—gwdan) Perriwinkle; also called *llawrig* and *erllusg*.

Gwanwr, *s. m.—pl.* gwanwyr (gwan—gwr) One who thrusts, or sticks; a piercer.

Gwànwr, *s. m.—pl.* gwànwyr (gwàn—gwr) A feeble person; a weakling.

> Af finnau, cyd bwyf wanwr,
> Yn fardd gwin i fwrdd y gwr.
>
> I will then go, though I be a *weakling*, to be the festive bard to the hero's table. *Ieuan Tew.*

Gwanwyn, *s. m.* (gwan—gwyn) The spring.

> Gwanwyn, ar dwyn ir do,
> Dien, yw yn blodeuo.
>
> The *spring*, upon the fresh mantled bush, doth, surely, bloom. *D. Edward.*

Gwanwynar, *s. m.* (gwanwyn—ar) Spring tillage.

Gwanwyndymp, *s. m.* (gwanwyn—tymp) The spring season.

Gwanwynwynt, *s. m.—pl. t.* oedd (gwanwyn—gwynt) Vernal wind.

Gwanŵyr, *a.* (gwan—gŵyr) Feebly inclining.

Gwanychawl, *a.* (gwanwch) Weakening.

Gwanychedig, *a.* (gwanwch) Weakened.

Gwanychiad, *s. m.* (gwanwch) A weakening.

Gwanychu, *v. a.* (gwanwch) To enfeeble, to enervate; to become disabled.

Gwang, *s. f.* (gw—ang) Greediness, voracity.

Gwangen, *s. f. dim.* (gwang) The shad, a fish.

Gwangiad, *s. m.—pl.* gwangiaid (gwang) A suin.

Gwangod, *s. pl. aggr.* (gwang) The shads.

Gwar, *s. m.* (gwa—ar) That is secure; that is even or smooth, or placid.

Gwar, *a.* (gwa—ar) Placid, gentle, mild or tame.

> Neud gwar-wedd menedd mynwent fraenar.
>
> Of *tame* appearance is the store of the churchyard fallow. *Cynddelw.*
>
> Antenor, gwr hir addfain oedd, a chorff eirïawl a oedd iddo, a chyflawn a gwar oedd.
>
> Antenor was a tall slender man, and he had a comely form, and he was just and *mild*. *H. Dared.*

Gwàr, *s. f.—pl. t.* au (gw—ar) That is over, or upon; the upper region of the back, or next to the neck, the nape of the neck.

Gwara, *s. m.—pl.* gwareon (gwar) A sending, or guarding; exercise of defence; fencing; play.

Gwara, *v. a* (gwar) To fend; to fence; to play.

Gwarâad, *s. m.* (gwar) A rendering docile, gentle, or mild; a taming; a civilizing.

Gwarâawl, *a* (gwar) Tending to make tame.

Gwarad, *s. m.* (gwar) A covering over.

Gwaradrig, *s. m.* (gwara—trig) Delay, loitering.

Gwaradrigiad, *s. m.* (gwaradrig) A delaying.

Gwaradrigiant, *s. m.* (gwaradrig) Delay.

> Gwedy dawed pawb, heb waradrigiant, amryfeillion aberthau a orugynt, ac i laddedigaeth yr anifeiliaid yr ymroddynt.
>
> When every body was come, without *delay*, they offered divers sacrifices; and they gave themselves up to the killing of the animals. *Gr. ab Arthur.*

Gwaradrigiaw, *v. a.* (gwaradrig) To delay.

Gwaradrigiawl, *a.* (gwaradrig) Dilatory.

Gwaradwydd, *s. m.—pl. t.* au (gwarad—gwydd) Reproach, disparagement, dishonour, disgrace.

Gwaradwyddaw, *v. a.* (gwaradwydd) To disparage, to discredit, to disgrace, to scandalize, to pollute, to defile.

Gwaradwyddawg, *a.* (gwaradwydd) Having reproach; disgraced, scandalized.

Gwaradwyddawl, *a.* (gwaradwydd) Reproaching.

Gwaradwyddiad, *s. m.* (gwaradwydd) A reproaching; a disgracing; a scandalizing.

Gwaradwyddus, *a.* (gwaradwydd) Scandalous.

Gwaradwyddwr, *s. m.—pl.* gwaradwyddwyr (gwaradwydd—gwr) A scandalizer, a reproacher.

Gwara, *s. m.—pl.* gwareuon (gwara) Play.

Gwarafun, *s. m.—pl. t.* ion (gwa—rhafun) A restriction, a hinderance; a grudge.

Gwarafun, *v. a.* (gwa—rhafun) To prohibit, to hinder; to forbid; to begrudge.

Gwarafunaw, *v. a.* (gwarafun) To prohibit; to forbid; to begrudge.

Gwarafunawl, *a.* (gwarafun) Prohibitory; grudging, reluctant.

Gwarafunedig, *a.* (gwarafun) Prohibited; begrudged.

Gwarafunedigaeth, *s. m.—pl. t.* au (gwarafunedig) A prohibition; a grudging.

Gwarafunedigawl, *a.* (gwarafunedig) Prohibitory.

Gwarafuniad, *s. m.* (gwarafun) A prohibiting, a forbidding; prohibition; a begrudging.

Gwarafuniaeth, *s. m.* (gwarafun) Prohibition; a reluctance, or unwillingness.

Gwarafunwr, *s. m.—pl.* gwarafunwyr (gwarafun—gwr) A prohibitor; a grudger.

Gwaraidd, *a.* (gwar) Gentle; placid; benign.

Gwarandaw, *s. m.* (gwar—andaw) A listening, or attention to hearing.

Gwarandaw, *v. a.* (gwar—andaw) To listen.

Gwarandawgar, *a.* (gwarandaw) Apt to listen, or to give attention; attentive in hearing.

Gwarandawgarwch, *s. m.* (gwarandawgar) Attentiveness in hearing.

Gwarandawiad, *s. m.* (gwarandaw) A listening.

Gwarandawus, *a.* (gwarandaw) Apt to listen, attentive in hearing.

Gwarandawwr, *s. m.—pl.* gwarandawwyr (gwarandaw—gwr) A listener, a hearer.

Gwarandawydd, *s. m.—pl. t.* ion (gwarandaw) A listener, a hearer.

Gwaranred, *s. f.—pl. t.* ion (gwarant) Stability; a guarantee; a warranty; authority.

> Yno mae gweled gwaranred gwir.
>
> There is to be seen the *stability* of truth. *O. Cyfeiliawg.*

Gwaranredawl, *a.* (gwaranred) Tending to guarantee; authoritative.

Gwaranrediad, *s. m.* (gwaranred) A guaranteeing.

Gwaranredu, *v. a.* (gwaranred) To guarantee.

Gwaranrwy, *s. m.—pl. t.* on (gwarant—rhwy) A warranted pledge; a guarantee.

> Cymmry——
> Cedfain eu gwared
> Gwirawd ceudawd ged,
> Gwaranrwy Rheged
> Rhan gan ogoned.
>
> The Welsh, the signal of their deliverance is the truth-producing beverage, the treasure of the bosom, the *secured pledge* of Rheged a portion with glory. *Taliesin.*

Gwarant, *s. f.—pl. t.* au (gwar) Attestation, warrant; security; authority.

> Cyswno llu, yn llew i'th welsant:
> Cadr eryr, i'th wyr yn warant.
>
> Foremost of the host, a lion have they seen thee; a mighty eagle to thy men a *security*. *Ll. P. Moch.*
>
> Llywelyn——
> Cymmry wawr warant.
>
> Llywelyn, the Welsh's luminary of security. *Einion Wan.*
>
> O bai air heb ei warant,
> Gorau dim ei gau â'r dant.
>
> Should there be a word without its *authority*, the best thing is to close the teeth upon it. *Ieu. Llwdwyn.*
>
> Rhag methiant gwarant y gwir
> Gwared ni——
>
> Against the failure of the authority of the truth, deliver us. *H. D. ab Ifan.*

Gwarantawl, *a.* (gwarant) Authoritative, supporting, warranting.

Gwarantiad, *s. m.—pl. t.* au (gwarant) A guaranteeing, securing, or supporting.

Gwarantrwydd, *s. m.* (gwarant) A warrantise, or warranty, an avouchment.

> Cod gyflwydd gwarantrwydd gwir.
>
> A treasure completely prosperous is the *security* of truth. *Ll. B. Hiraddug.*

Gwarantu, *v. a.* (gwarant) To warrant, to avouch.

Gwarantwr, *s. m.—pl.* gwarantwyr (gwarant—gwr) A warranter, or an avoucher.

Gwarantydd, *s. m.—pl. t.* ion (gwarant) A warranter; one who attests.

Gwarau, *s. m.—pl.* gwareuon (gwara) A play, or game; amusement, pastime; a dramatic representation.—*Gwarau gwyddbwyll*, game of chess; *gwarau tawlbwrdd*, game of backgammon; *gwarau ffristial*, game of draughts, *gwarau mindda manddel*, a kind of play with the fingers; *gwarau broch yn nghod*, the game of the badger in the bag, which is acted by people's endeavouring to put each other in a bag; *gwarau argae coed*, and *gwarau gwyr Troia*, a playing at tilts and tournaments; *gwarau rhafu*, and *siglen donen*, the swinging; *gwarau ffon ddwybig*, play of two-pointed cudgel; *gwarau mi trech*, game of I conquer

> Gorau yw y gwarau tra stor.
>
> The *play* is best when left off. *Adage.*
>
> Tri gwarau ymdrech oedd gan y Cymmry gynt: gwarau ymaflyd, ac ymdaflu ag afalau dur, ac ymdynu ar draws tanau.
>
> Three *games* of contention had the Welsh of old: the game of wrestling, and throwing of iron balls, and hauling one another across fires. *Welsh Laws.*

Gwarau, *v. a.* (gwara) To play, to perform at games, feats, or exploits; to game.

> Gwarau cadr frwydr argae coed
> A phelydr.——
>
> To *play* the powerful conflict of tournament with shafts. *R. G. Eryri.*

Gwarau, *v. a.* (gwar) To make gentle, tame, or docile; to become gentle, or mild.

Gwarâus, *a.* (gwar) Tending to make gentle, or mild; softening, humanizing.

Gwârawg, *a.* (gwar) That crosses over the nape of the neck; a bow for tying cattle.

Gwarâwr, *s. m.—pl.* gwarâwyr (gwar) One who tames. *Gwarawyr meirch*, a breaker in of horses.

Gwarbin, *s. m.—pl. t.* au (gwar—pin) A bow-pin, which keeps the bow from slipping out.

Gwarchen, *s. f. dim* (gwar) The upper part of the back and shoulders.

Gwarch, *s. m.—pl. t.* au (gwar) What encloses, or shuts up; a cover or a lid.

Gwarchad, *s. m.* (gwarch) A covering over; a guarding, securing, or protecting.

Gwarchadw, *s. m.* (gwar—cadw) A preserving, securing, keeping, guarding, or looking after.

Gwarchadw, *v. a.* (gwar—cadw) To keep, to ward, to watch, to guard, or to look after.

> Pwy y tri cynwsyniaid,
> A warchadwis gwlad?
> Pwy y tri cyfarwydd
> A gadwis arwydd?
>
> Who the three foreign guests, that protected a country? Who the three historians that preserved a record? *Taliesin.*

Gwarchae, *s. m.—pl. t.* oedd (gwar—cae) A hemming in, or securing, a blocking up; a league; a siege; a place secured, or blocked up; a prison; a pound.

> Gwchwedl i'm ei warchae;
> Gorwedd y'mouenfedd y mae!
>
> Sad news to me *his imprisonment*, he lies in the stony tomb! *D. ab Gwilym.*

Gwarchae, *v. a.* (gwar—cae) To hem in, to secure, to shut, or block up; to league; to besiege; to imprison; to pound.

Gwae fi fod arch a'th warchae,
A llawr maes rh'of a'r lle mae!

Woe is me that there should be a shrine *to confine* thee, and the surface of the ground between me and where it is!
Ll. Goch ab M. Hen, m. Lleicu.

Gwarchaead, *s. m.* (gwarchae) A covering in, or blocking up; a besieging.

Gwarchaeawl, *a*, (gwarchae) Tending to hem in, or to block up; besieging.

Gwarchaëedig, *a.* (gwarchae) Hemmed in, secured; confined; besieged.

Gwarchaëedigaeth, *s. m.—pl. t.* au (gwarchaëedig) The act of shutting in, or confining.

Gwarchaëedigawl, *a.* (gwarchaëedig) Having a tendency to close up, or to confine.

Gwarchan, *s. f.—pl. t.* au (gwarch) What secures; an irresistible influence; talisman, an enchantment, an incantation.

A'n maglas blaen derw,
O warchan Maelderw.

We are ensnared by oak branches, from the *incantation* of Maelderw.
Taliesin.

Gnawd gwarchan a gan eu hawenydd:
Yn arfod adwy wy a orfydd.

What their muse shall sing will be an *enchantment*; in the stroke of the breach they will overcome.
Meilyr.

O'u carchar, y cai warchan
Duw rhag diawl a draig o dan.

From their prison, I shall have the *protection* of God, against the devil with the bolt of fire.
T. Derllysg.

Gwarchanawl, *a.* (gwarchan) Enchanting, talismanic.

Gwarchaniad, *s. m.* (gwarchan) A protecting by some covering virtue; an enchanting.

Gwarchanu, *v. a.* (gwarchan) To protect, as by a talisman, or charm.

Gwarchator, *ger* (gwarchad) In covering.

Gwrachau, *s. m.—pl.* gwarchenoedd (gwar—cau) A shutting in, or enclosing; confinement.

Gwarchau, *v. a.* (gwar—cau) To shut in, to enclose, to confine, to block up; to imprison.

Os Dwy-Went, is y Deau,
A gyrch hon, rhag ei gwarchau—]
Ni'm dawr.

If the two Gwents, below the South, shall come in quest of her, lest she *should be secured*, it affects me not.
Ieuan Dyfi, i Anni.

Gwarchauad, *s. m.* (gwarchau) A shutting in; a confining, or imprisoning.

Gwarchauawl, *a.* (gwarchau) Tending to shut in, or to enclose; confining.

Gwarchauedig, *a.* (gwarchau) Enclosed, confined, environed, encircled.

Gwarchauedigaeth, *s. m.—pl. t.* au (gwarchauedig) The act of shutting in.

Gwarchawd, *s. m.—pl.* gwarchodau (gwarch) What covers up, or secures; a cover; a looking after, or guarding. *v. a.* To look after, or to guard.

Yr wyf yn ewyllysio gan hyny i'r rhai ieuainc briodi, planta, gwarchawd y ty, heb roi dim achlysur i'r gwrthwynebwr waradwyddo.

I am desiring, therefore, for the young ones to marry, to beget children, *to take care* of the house without giving any cause for the adversary to reproach.
1 *Tim.* v. 14.

Gwarchawdwr, *s. m.—pl.* gwarchawdwyr (gwarchawd—gwr) One who guards; a warden.

Gwarchawdyr, *s. m.—pl.* gwarchodron (gwarch) A warden, a conservator.

Gwarchawr, *s. m.—pl.* gwarchorion (gwarch) A coverer, or one that encloses.

Gwarchdwr, *s. m.—pl.* gwarchdyrau (gwarch—twr) A tower that confines, or guards.

Gwarchaeaf i'th erbyn mewn gwarchdwr.

I will encamp against thee in a *watch-tower*. *Isaiah* xxix. 3.

Gwarched, *v. a.* (gwarch) To ward; to watch, to look after. *Gwarched y ty*, look after the house; *Duw a'n gwarched!* God preserve us!

Y ferch, ni chwsg a'i gwarchyd,
A garaf yr haf ar hyd.

The fair one, that *is watched* by him that sleeps not, I will love all the summer long.
D. ab Gwilym.

Gwarcheidiad, *s. m.* (gwarched) A warding, or watching.

Gwarcheidiawl, *a.* (gwarched) Conservatory.

Gwarcheidioldeb, *s. m.* (gwarcheidiawl) A state of warding, or conservation.

Gwarcheidiwr, *s. m.—pl.* gwarcheidiwyr (gwarched—gwr) A man who guards.

Gwarcheidydd, *s. m.—pl. t.* ion (gwarched) A guardian, a warder, a watcher.

Gwarcheidwad, *s. m.—pl.* gwarcheidwaid (gwarchadw) A guarder, one who keeps in; a guardian, a warden, a conservator.

Tri gwarcheidwad tir: arglwydd y disgyno y tir iddo wrth farwolaeth y perchenawg, hyd oni ddelo yr etifeddion i ofyn eu dylyed; cydetifedd hyd oni ddelo ei gydetifeddion i ofyn eu dylyed; y neb y rhodder tir atto hyd oni ddeler i'w ofyn.

The three *conservators* of land: a lord, to whom land shall descend by the death of the proprietor, until the heir shall come to demand his right; a coheir until his coheirs shall come to demand their right; he to whom land shall be given in trust, until there shall be a demand made of it.
Welsh Laws.

Gwarcheidwadaeth, *s. m.* (gwarcheidwad) Guardianship, wardenship. *Estyn gwarcheidwadaeth*, to invest with a conservatory trust.

Gwarcheidwadawl, *a.* (gwarcheidwad) Relating to guardianship, conservatory.

Gwarcheidwades, *s. f.—pl. t.* au (gwarcheidwad) A female guardian, or trustee.

Gwarcheidwadu, *v. a.* (gwarcheidwad) To act as a guardian, trustee, or conservator.

Gwarchen, *s. f.—pl. t.* au (gwarch) A cover; a surface.

Gwarchglawdd, *s. m.—pl.* gwarchgloddiau (gwarch—clawdd) An entrenchment; a fort.

Gwarchgloddiad, *s. m.—pl. t.* au (gwarchglawdd) An entrenching, to confine.

Gwarchgloddiaw, *v.* (gwarchglawdd) To entrench

Gwarchiad, *s. m.—pl. t.* au (gwarch) A covering.

Gwarchitor, *sup.* (gwarch) To be covering.

Gwarchlys, *s. m.* (gwarch—llys) Chaste-tree; also called *gwarchwydd.*

Gwarchodadwy, *a.* (gwarchawd) That may be guarded or protected.

Gwarchodaeth, *s. m.* (gwarchawd) Wardship.

Gwarchodawl, *a.* (gwarchawd) Conservative.

Gwarchodedig, *a.* (gwarchawd) Guarded; warded

Gwarchodfa, *s. f.—pl. t.* oedd (gwarchawd) A sentry.

Gwarchodi, *v. a.* (gwarchawd) To guard, to secure; to ward, to look after, or to oversee.

Gwarchodiad, *s. m.* (gwarchawd) A guarding, securing, or proctecting; conservation.

Gwarchodwr, *s. m.—pl.* gwarchodwyr (gwarchawd—gwr) A protector; a conservator.

Gwarchodydd, *s. m.—pl. t.* ion (gwarchawd) A guardian, or protector; a conservator.

Gward, *s. m.—pl. t.* au (gwar) What guards.

Gwarder, *s. m.* (gwar) Placidness; benignity.

Gwardra, *s. m.* (gwar) Tameness, docility.

Gwardwydd, *s. m.—pl. t.* au (gward—gwydd) A reproachful aspersion, scandal.

Gwardwyddaw, *v. a.* (gwardwydd) To scandalise.

Gwardwyddawl, *a.* (gwardwydd) Scandalizing.

Gwardwyddiad, *s. m.* (gwardwydd) A defaming, reproaching, or scandalizing.

Gwardwyddus, *a.* (gwardwydd) Scandalous.

Gwardwyddwr, *s. m.—pl.* gwardwyddwyr (gwardwydd—gwr) One who scandalizes.

Gwardd, *s. m.—pl. t.* ion (gw—ardd) Forbiddance or prohibition.

Gwarddawl, *a.* (gwardd) Forbidding; interdictory

Gwarddedig, *a.* (gwardd) Interdicted, forbidden.

Gwarddiad, *s. m.—pl. t.* au (gwardd) A prohibition

Gwarddrws, *s. m.—pl.* gwarddrysau (gwàr—drws) The lintel of a door.

Gwarddu, *v. a.* (gwardd) To prohibit, to forbid.

Gwarddwr, *s. m.—pl.* gwarddwyr (gwardd—gwr) An interdicter, or forbidder.

Gware, *s. m.—pl. t.* on (gwar) A play, a game.

Ni annodaf â fy ngware os myn y brenin.

I will not leave off my *play*, if it is the king's pleasure *H. Cer. Mag.—Mabinogion.*

Gware, *v. a.* (gwar) To play; to act in games.

A gware pelre â phen Saeson.

And *to play* at hurling with Saxons' heads. *Taliesin.*

Ar leithig cyfarwyneb ag ef, y gwelai ddau fachwy lennior wineuon, yn gware gwyddbwyll.

Upon a form, opposite to him, he saw two young youths with auburn hair, *playing* at chess. *Br. Max. Wledig—Mabinogion.*

Gwarëad, *s. m.* (gware) A playing, a gaming.

Gwarëawl, *a.* (gware) Playsome, sportive.

Gwared, *s. m.—pl. t.* ion (gwar) A guarding against, a saving from; a riddance, release, or deliverance; redemption; remedy; the membrane round the embryo in the matrix, the afterbirth, or secundine.

Ni ŵyr gwrach gwared i'w phen.

An old woman knows no *remedy* for her head. *Adage.*

Gwared, *v. a.* (gwar) To guard, to fence against; to save, to preserve from danger; to rid, to release, to remit; to deliver; to redeem; to rescue; to free. *Ni waredai iddo*, it would not avail him.

Rhag anwyd ni weryd cannwyll.

A candle *will not guard* against cold. *Adage.*

Hiraeth am farw ni weryd.

Regret for the dead *it will not avail.* *Adage.*

Gwaredadwy, *a.* (gwared) That may be protected; salvable, that may be released, or delivered

Gwaredator, *ger.* (gwared) In delivering.

Gwaredawg, *a.* (gwared) Having protection, being saved; having deliverance.

Gwaredawl, *a.* (gwared) Tending to protect, or to save; tending to release or to ransom.

Gwaredëdig, *a.* (gwared) Protected, preserved, saved; released, delivered, or ransomed.

Y gwaredigion canant fawl
I Ddew, gerdd nodawl gyson.

The *ransomed* race will sing praise to God, a harmonious and appropriate song *Edm. Prys.*

Gwaredëdigaeth, *s. m.—pl. t.* au (gwaredëdig) The act of protecting; preservation; deliverance, redemption, or ransoming.

Gwaredëdigawl, *a.* (gwaredëdig) Preventative, preservative, salvatory; redemptory.

Gwarediad, *s. m.—pl. t.* au (gwared) A saving; a delivering, or ransoming.

Gwarediant, *s. m.* (gwared) Salvation; deliverance, redemption, ransom,

Gwaredig, *a.* (gwar) Being made tame or docile.

Gwaredigain, *a.* (gwaredig) Having docility.

Gwaredigeiniad, *s. m.* (gwaredigain) A rendering, or becoming, gentle or mild.

Gwaredigeiniaw, *v. a.* (gwaredigain) To render of a gentle nature; to civilize.

Gwaredigeiniawl, *a.* (gwaredigain) Tending to be of a mild disposition.

Gwaredigeinus, *a.* (gwaredigain) Of a mild, or placid disposition.

Gwareditor, *sup.* (gwared) To be saving, or keeping safe, to be releasing, or delivering.

Gwaredoldeb, *s. m.* (gwaredawl) A state of safety

Gwaredoli, *v. a.* (gwaredawl) To render salvable; to become redemptory.

Gwaredolrwydd, *s. m.* (gwaredawl) A state of being saved; salvableness.

Gwaredogrwydd, *s. m.* (gwaredawg) A disposition to deliver or to save.

Duw, o'i waredogrwydd, a'i gwisgwys ef o wisg a elwir pertsonna, sef yw hono rhyw bilis o ddail.

God, out of his *delivering disposition*, clothed him with a garment called pertsonna, and that is a sort of cloak of leaves. *Hanes Addaf.*

Gwaredred, *s. c.* (gwared) A seeking of protection, a running for safety; refuge. *a.* Being under protection; ransomed.

Nifer a fraint yn anghyfred
Uffern, oer waredred,
Hyd i pumoes byd,
Hyd pan ddillyngwys
Crist gaethiwed.

Many there were in the confused course of hell, a cold *refuge* during the five periods of the world, until Christ loosened the bondage. *Taliesin.*

Yni mae gware gwaredred.

In there there is the exultation of the *ransomed.* *Cynddelw.*

Gwerthefin ddewin Duw a'm gwared:
Gwerthfawr briodawr gwawr gwaredred.

The supremely divine one of God will deliver me, the precious sovereign of the dawn of the *ransomed.* *Llywelyn Fardd.*

Gwaredu, *v. a.* (gwared) To afford protection, to save; to deliver, to release, to ransom.

Gwaredwr, *s. m.—pl.* gwaredwyr (gwared—gwr) A preserver, a saviour; a deliverer, a redeemer

Gwaredydd, *s. m.—pl. t.* ion (gwared) A preserver, a saviour; a deliverer.

Gwaredd, *s. m.* (gwar) Placidness, gentleness.

Gwareddawg, *a.* (gwaredd) Abounding with meekness, or mildness, benign.

Gwareddawl, *a.* (gwaredd) Of a gentle, mild, or softening tendency; humanizing.

Gwareddogi, *v. a.* (gwareddawg) To render of a gentle nature; to become gentle or civilized.

Gwareddogrwydd, *s. m.* (gwareddawg) Benignity

Gwareddoldeb, *s. m.* (gwareddawl) Gentleness.

Gwareddoli, *v. a.* (gwareddawl) To render of a gentle nature; to become of a mild quality.

Gwareiddiad, *s. m.* (gwaraidd) A rendering, or becoming, docile; a humanizing.

Gwareiddiaw, *v. a.* (gwaraidd) To render mild, or gentle; to humanize; to become mild.

Gwareiddiawl, *a.* (gwaraidd) Tending to make, or to become, docile; humanizing.

Gwareu, *s. m.—pl. t.* on (gware) A play.

Gwareu, *v. a.* (gware) To play; to act in games.

Gwareuad, *s. m.* (gwareu) A playing, a sporting; an acting in games, or exploits.

Gwareuawl, *a.* (gwareu) Playing, playful.

Gwareufrith, *a.* (gwareu—brith) Playfully variegated. *Gorwydd gwareufrith*, a steed playfully spotted over.

Gwarëus, *a.* (gware) Sportive, or playful.

Gwareüus, *a.* (gwareu) Sportive, playful.

Gwareüwr, *s. m.—pl.* gwareüwyr (gwareu—gwr) A player, an actor in games.

Gwareüydd, *s. m.—pl. t.* ion (gwareu) A player.

Gwarewr, *s. m.—pl.* gwarëwyr (gware—gwr) A player, one who acts in games.

Gwarëydd, *s. m.—pl. t.* ion (gware) A player.

Gwarffon, *s. f.—pl.* gwarffyn (gwàr—ffon) A stroke with a stick over the back.

Gwarffoni, *v. a.* (gwarffon) To ply a stick over the back; to trounce with a staff.

Gwarffòniad, *s. m.* (gwarffon) A trouncing.

Gwarffòniaw, *v. a.* (gwarffon) To beat with a stick over the back.

Gwargaled, *a.* (gwàr—caled) Stiffnecked.

Gwargalediad, *s. m.* (gwargaled) A making stiff-necked, or stubborn; a becoming stiffnecked.

Gwargaledrwydd, *s. m.* (gwargaled) Stiffneckedness; stubbornness.

Gwargaledu, *v. a.* (gwargaled) To render stiff-necked; to become stubborn.

Gwargam, *a.* (gwàr—cam) Stooping in the shoulders; having a bend of the neck.

Gwargemi, *s. m.* (gwargam) A stoop in the shoulders; a twist or bend of the neck.

Gwarged, *s. f.—pl. t.* ion (gwar—ced) A surplus, a relick, or remainder; orts, leavings.

Gwargrom, *a.* (*f. of* gwargrwm) Round-shouldered

Gwargrwm, *a.* (gwar—crwm) Round-shouldered.

Gwargrwth, *s. m.—pl.* gwargrythau (gwàr—crwth) A hunch on the back. *a.* Hunchbacked.

Gwargrymawl, *a.* (gwargrwm) Tending to be round-shouldered.

Gwargrymedd, *s. m.* (gwargrwm) Stoopingness.

Gwargrymi, *s. m.* (gwargrwm) Stoopingness.

Gwargrymiad, *s. m.* (gwargrwm) A becoming round-shouldered.

Gwargrymu, *v. a.* (gwargrwm) To bend the upper part of the back forward; to become round-shouldered.

Gwariad, *s. m.* (gwar) A spending, or expending.

Gwariaw, *v. a.* (gwar) To spend, to expend.

> Pan fal lawen frain, pan frydai waed
> Pan wyar warial,
> ——Ni noddai.
>
> When ravens should be joyous, when blood should hasten, when gore *should issue out*, he would give no refuge. *H. ab Owain.*
>
> Pa ham y gweriwch arian am yr hyn nid ydyw fara.
>
> Why *do you spend* money for what is not bread. *Isaiah* xl. 2.

Gwariawl, *a.* (gwar) Spending, expending.

Gwariedig, *a.* (gwar) Being expended.

Gwarineb, *s. m.* (gwar) Gentleness; mildness.

> Prif ragoriaeth merch yw gwarineb, a mwynder, a serch.
>
> The chief excellence of a female is her *gentleness*, kindness, and love. *Barddas.*

Gwariwr, *s. m.—pl.* gwariwyr (gwariaw—gwr) One who lays out or expends.

Gwarllost, *s. f.—pl. t.* an (gwàr—llost) A bar, to which the bow is fixed, to keep it round the neck of the animal; also called *Gwarog.*

Gwarog, *s. f.—pl. t.* au (gwàr) A yoke; a bar to which the bow is fastened, which goes round the neck of cattle, in fastening them to the crib; also a stroke over the shoulders.

Gwarogaeth, *s. f.—pl. t.* au (gwarawg) Subjection; homage; surrendry.

> Tri rhyw gwarogaeth y sydd cledren gwaesafwr, ac aswynwr, ac adlamwr.
>
> There are three kinds of *homages*, that of the refugee's pale, and the absentee, and sojourner. *Welsh Laws.*

Gwarogaethawl, *a.* (gwarogaeth) Subject to homage, homageable.

Gwarogaethiad, *s. m.* (gwarogaeth) A yielding homage or submission.

Gwarogaethu, *v. n.* (gwarogaeth) To cause submission; to do homage.

Gwarogawl, *a.* (gwarawg) Tending to subjection.

Gwarogi, *v. a.* (gwarawg) To subjugate; to yield homage, or submission.

Gwarogiad, *s. m.* (gwarawg) A subjugating; a doing homage, or submission.

Gwarogwr, *s. m.—pl.* gwarogwyr (gwarawg—gwr) One who does homage.

Gwarsang, *s. f.—pl. t.* au (gwàr—sang) A trampling upon the neck.

Gwarsangawl, *a.* (gwarsang) Neck-trampling.

Gwarsangiad, *s. m.—pl. t.* au (gwarsang) A trampling upon, a vanquishing.

Gwarsangu, *v. a.* (gwarsang) To trample upon.

Gwarsangwr, *s. m.—pl.* gwarsangwyr (gwarsang—gwr) A trampler upon.

Gwarsyth, *a.* (gwàr—syth) Stiffnecked; stubborn

Gwarsythawl, *a.* (gwarsyth) Apt to be stubborn.

Gwarsythdra, *s. m.* (gwarsyth) Stiffneckedness.

Gwarsythiad, *s. m.* (gwarsyth) A rendering, or becoming, stiffnecked.

Gwarsythni, *s. m.* (gwarsyth) Stiffneckedness.

Gwart, *s. f.—pl. t.* au (gward) That guards.

Gwartawl, *a.* (gwart) Guarding, fending.

Gwartiad, *s. m.—pl. t.* au (gwart) A guarding.

Gwartu, *v. a.* (gwart) To guard, or to defend.

Gwarth, *s. m.—pl. t.* au (gwar) That is upon, or over; that forms a brow or ledge over; a shore; a covering; also reproach: scandal, dishonour; shame. *Dawed i warth*, to come ashore. *Sil.*

> Fy marddair i'th barth nid gwarth, nid gwan.
>
> My bardic lore in the precinct is not a *disgrace*, is not feeble. *Cynddelw.*
>
> Bid wastad wraig o'i mynych warth.
>
> From the frequency of her *shame* let a woman be brazen. *Adage.*

Gwartha, *v. a.* (gwarth) To put or throw upon, to asperse, to scandalize.

Gwarthâad, *s. m.* (gwarth) A casting upon; a disparaging; opprobrium, contumely; injury.

Gwarthâawl, *a.* (gwartha) Tending to asperse, or to reproach; opprobrious.

Gwarthadwy, *a.* (gwarth) Reproachable.

Gwarthaed, *s. m.* (gwartha) Aspersion, infamy.

> Heb gyngbor y daetham i ddechreu ymladd â gwyr Rhufain. rhaid yw i'n ymogiyd rhag an dygwyddaw yn rhan gywilyddus o'r ymladd; canys o dygwyddwn, colled a gwarthaed a gaffwn.
>
> Without advice we have come to begin to fight with the men of Rome. we must guard against our falling into the disgraceful part of the fight; for if we shall so happen, we shall experience loss and *infamy*. *Gr. ab Arthur.*

Gwarthaf, *s. m.—pl. t.* ion (gwarth) The upper part, the summit; the surface. *Bod ar warthaf*, to be close upon, or hard by.

> Samson——
> E dynai yn oed unawr,
> Ei lys ar ei warthaf i lawr.
>
> Samson, he in an instant pulled down his hall upon his *back*. *Bedo Aerdrem.*

Gwarthafawl, *a.* (gwarthaf) Relating to the top.

Gwarthafdy, *s. m.—pl. t.* au (gwarthaf—ty) A building that is upon, abutting, or leading to.

> Pan y myno y brenin gerdd i'w gwrandaw, caned y pencerdd ddau ganu yn modd Duw, ac y trydydd o benaethau, yn y gwarthafdy.
>
> When the king would have a song to listen to, let the chief of song recite two songs addressed to God, and the third to princes, in the *antichamber*. *Welsh Laws.*

Gwarthafiad, *s. m.* (gwarthaf) A covering over; a riding.

Gwarthafl, *s. f.—pl. t.* au (gwarthaf) A stirrup.

Gwarthafliad, *s. m.* (gwarthafl) A stirruping.

Gwarthaflu, *v. a.* (gwarthafl) To stirrup.

Gwarthafu, *v. a.* (gwarthaf) To cover over; to be upon, to ride.

Gwarthair, *s. m.—pl.* gwartheiriau (gwarth—gair) A word of reproach.

Gwarthal, *s. m.* (gwar—tal) What is given in exchanging, or bartering, things, that they may be equal in value; what is given to boot.

> Ni chynghain gwarthal gan ddewis.
>
> A *settled thing* does not accord with choice. *Adage.*

Gwarthan, *s. f.* (gwarth) A covert, a shelter.

> Bum ysbwng yn aban,
> Bum gwydd y'ngwarthan.
>
> I have been spunge in the fire, I have been wood in the *covert*. *Taliesin.*

Gwarthâu, *v. a.* (gwarth) To throw upon; to reflect upon; to disparage, to disgrace, to decry.

Gwarthawl, *a.* (gwarth) Being placed over, or upon; aspersing, reproaching.

Gwarthawr, *s. m.*—*pl.* gwarthorion (gwarth) A quadrate; a quadrature.

Gwarthedig, *a.* (gwarth) Degraded, disgraced.

Gwarthedigaeth, *s. m.*—*pl. t.* au (gwarthedig) The act of reproaching, or scandalizing.

Gwarthedigaw, *v. a.* (gwarthedig) To render reproachful; to become shameful.

Gwarthedigawl, *a.* (gwarthedig) Tending to make, or to become, opprobrious.

Gwarthedd, *s. m.* (gwarth) Reproachfulness.

Gwartheg, *s. pl. aggr.* (gwarth) That serves to cover, or to make equivalent; a medium of exchange, or traffick; and cattle being that medium, amongst the Britons, the term came to imply the animals themselves in the aggregate.

> Ei wartheg oedd——
> Mil fry'n amliwio y fron,
> Teirmil o ddeutu Armon.
>
> His *cattle* were a thousand variegating the hill above, and three thousand round Saint Garmon. *L. G. Cothi.*

Gwarthegawg, *a.* (gwartheg) Having an equivalence, or indemnity; abounding with cattle.

> Cyd daeth, nid aeth yn warthegawg—
> Ni yn Eryri yn rhelawg
> Ni thorres ei lawr a fu praiddiawg.
>
> Though he came, he did not go *enriched with booty*: we in Eryri being arrayed, no interruption was given to the pasturing of such as tended the herds. *Meilyr.*

Gwarthegawl, *a.* (gwartheg) Serving to cover, or to render equivalent.

Gwarthegiad, *s. m.* (gwartheg) A settling or equalizing a value; a trafficking.

Gwarthegu, *v. a.* (gwartheg) To lay upon; to equalize transactions of dealing; to traffick.

Gwarthegydd, *s. m.*—*pl. t.* ion (gwartheg) A chapman, a dealer in cattle.

> Edwyn warth gwarthegydd;
> Gwerth gwyl a negydd;
> Ar a ddyfo dragwarth a'i deubydd.
>
> He is acquainted with the reproach of the *chapman*, the price of the bashful he will refuse; such as is past shame will obtain it. *Llywarch Hen.*

> Cynan a Chadwaladr, cadr yn llwydd,
> Edmyccawr hyd frawd, ffawd a'u deubydd;
> Dau unben dengyn, dwys eu cyngor;
> Dau a orfegyn Saeson o blaid Dofydd;
> Dau hael; dau gedawl gwlad warthegydd.
>
> Cynan and Cadwaladr, mighty in the battle, they will be honoured to the day of doom, fortune will attend them; two tenacious chiefs, profound their counsel; two that will overcome the Saxons by the aid of the Lord; two generous ones; two treasurers of a country of the merchant. *Taliesin.*

Gwartheiriad, *s. m.* (gwarthair) A using reproachful language; a libelling.

Gwartheiriaw, *v. a.* (gwarthair) To use reproachful words; to scandalize, to libel.

Gwartheiriawg, *a.* (gwarthair) Using reproachful words; opprobrious.

Gwarther, *s. m.*—*pl. t.* au (gwarth) That is used to be upon, or riding; a cavalier.

> Gwaew hydwn ysgwn, ysgwyd amdrai,
> Gwarther fab Madawg arfawg erfai.
>
> A spear ready to be broken, a shield battered round, with them the *cavalier* son of Madog used to be armed. *Cynddelw, m. Cadwallon.*

Gwarthfa, *s. f.*—*pl. t.* oedd (gwarth—ma) The private part, or privity.

Gwarthfael, *s. f.* (gwarth—mael) Gain, or advantage of reproach, mean advantage.

> Eryr cad, gwrthodiad gwarthfael,
> Esgwyn gwald, circhiaid archafael.
>
> The eagle of battle, the rejecter of a *mean advantage*, the whole most bulwark lifting up the petitioners. *Cynddelw, i O. Cyfeiliawg.*

Gwarthflawdd, *s. f.*—*pl.* gwarthfloddau (gwarth—blawdd) The tumult of the shore, or surf; the activity, or briskness, of calumny.

Gwarthfloedd, *s. f.*—*pl. t.* au (gwarth—bloedd) A cry of reproach; opprobrium.

Gwarthfor, *s. m.* (gwarth—mor) The covering sea, the sea that beats upon the shore, the surf. *adv.* Over, upon, or along the sea.

> Dyddoent gwarthfor.
>
> They would come *by sea*. *Taliesin.*

Gwarthfre, *s. f.*—*pl. t.* on (gwarth—bre) An over-topping hill; an abutting hill.

Gwarthiad, *s. m.*—*pl. t.* au (gwarth) A putting upon, or covering; aspersion.

Gwarthiant, *s. m.* (gwarth) Aspersion, calumny.

Gwarthlawn, *a.* (gwarth) Infamous; reproachful.

Gwarthle, *s. m.*—*pl. t.* oedd (gwarth—lle) The privity.

Gwarthlef, *s. m.* (gwarth—llef) A cry of reproach. *a.* Opprobrious, contumelious.

> Ni bu warthlef cerdd cynferching.
> O ben Taliesin.——
>
> Void of *calumny* has been the song devoted to Cynfarch from the mouth of Taliesin. *Cynddelw.*

Gwarthlonedd, *s. m.* (gwarthlawn) Reproachfulness; infamousness.

Gwarthol, *s. f.*—*pl. t.* ion (gwarth) A stirrup.

Gwarthred, *s. m.*—*pl. t.* ion (gwarth—rhed) Reproach, disgrace.

Gwarthredus, *a.* (gwarthred) Reproachful.

> Ysgeulusaw yw dywedyd geiriau gwarthredus o neben wrth arall.
>
> Scolding is the speaking of *reproachful* words by any body to another. *Welsh Laws.*

Gwarthrudd, *s. m.*—*pl. t.* iau (gwarth—grudd) Ignominy, disgrace, opprobrium, shame; reproach, disparagement, contumely.

> O ddiffryd Gwyndyd rhag gwander;
> O warthrudd gorthryn Gwyn Gwarther—
> Ef molir.
>
> From defending Gwyndyd against feebleness; from the *shame* of the opposition of Gwyn Gwarther, he will be praised. *Cynddelw, m. O. Gwynedd.*

Gwarthruddadwy, *a.* (gwarthrudd) Liable to opprobrium, or disgrace; reproachable.

Gwarthruddedig, *a.* (gwarthrudd) Scandalized.

Gwarthruddiad, *s. m.* (gwarthrudd) A rendering ignominious; a reproaching.

Gwarthruddiaeth, *s. m.* (gwarthrudd) The act of shaming, or disparaging.

Gwarthruddiaw, *v. a.* (gwarthrudd) To disgrace, to shame, to disparage, to reproach.

Gwarthruddiawg, *a.* (gwarthrudd) Reproachful.

Gwarthruddiawl, *a.* (gwarthrudd) Ignominious.

Gwarthruddiwr, *s. m.*—*pl.* gwarthruddwyr (gwarthrudd—gwr) One who disgraces.

Gwarthruddus, *a.* (gwarthrudd) Ignominious.

Gwarthu, *v. a.* (gwarth) To cover, or throw upon; to asperse; to scandalize.

Gwarthus, *a.* (gwarth) Aspersive; shameful.

Gwarthusrwydd, *s. m.* (gwarthus) Shamefulness.

Gwaru, *v. a.* (gwar) To render gentle, or mild.

> Mil-feirdd mawrfrydig ryddanfones Duw,
> Dyn i'm wyd a'u gwarwys.
>
> A thousand high-minded bards God heretofore has sent, thou art a person for me who *has made them docile*. *Ll. P. Moch.*

Gwarwch, *s. m.* (gwar) Gentleness, mildness.

Gwarweiniaw, *v. a.* (gwar—gweiniaw) To assume a gentle carriage; to behave gently.

Gwarweiniawg, *a.* (gwar—gweiniawg) Of a gentle, or mild demeanour.

> Deuynt——
> Pob pamp, pob pedwar yn warweiniawg.
>
> They came by fives and by fours *of gentle demeanour.* — *Meilyr.*

Gwarwg, *s. m.—pl.* gwarygau (gwar) A stoop.

> Y gwr cul a'r gwarwg hen,
> A giniawodd ar gneuen.
>
> The slender man with the aged *stoop* dined upon a nut. — *Rhis, ab Rhys Brydydd.*

Gwarwy, *s. m.—pl. t.* on (gwar) That makes mild; that soothes, or pleases.

> Ni'm gogawn gwarwy, ni'm gofwy gordderch.
>
> No *pleasure* allures me, no mistress visits me. — *Myrddin.*

Gwarwyfa, *s. f.—pl. t.* oedd (gwarwy—ma) Pleasure, delight.

> Duryn fflam y daran ffwch
> Dug warwyfa'n digrifwch.
>
> The abrupt thunder's dart of flame took away the *pleasure* of our amusement. — *D. ab Gwilym.*

Gwary, *s. m.—pl. t.* au (gwar) The bow of a yoke.

> A garo yr iau cared ei waryau.
>
> He that loves the yoke let him love his *bows.* — *Adage.*

Gwas, *s. m.—pl.* gweision (gwa—as) That is of smooth or even quality, a smooth plat; a youth, a lad, a young man; a page; a servant; *Gwas gwych*, a hero, a valiant youth; *gwyr a gweision*, men and youths, or men of all ages; *da 'ngwas i*, that's my good fellow.—*Gwas y dryw, sywidw*, or *penloyn*, the titmouse; *gwas y seiri*, jackniccol; *gwas y gog, gwichell y gog, gwigyn y gog*, and *cethlydd cog*, a little bird that follows the cuckoo, and in whose nest she lays her egg; *gwas y neidr*, and *gwaell neidr*, the adder-bolt, or dragon-fly.

> Am gwymp hen chwerddin gwen gwas.
>
> At the stumbling of the aged the smile of the *youth* is apt to break out. — *Adage.*
>
> Gwas ystafell a ddyly wallaw ar y brenin yn wastad, eithr y tair gwyl arbenig.
>
> The *page* of the chamber should wait upon the king continually except on the three principal festivals. — *Welsh Laws.*

Gwasaeth, *s. m.* (gwas) Attendance, service.

Gwasaidd, *a.* (gwas) Belonging to a servant.

Gwasan, *s. c. dim.* (gwas) A youth; a page.

Gwasanaeth, *s. m.* (gwasan) Attendance, service.

Gwasaneuthawl, *a.* (gwasanaeth) Ministering.

Gwasaneuthddyn, *s. m.—pl. t.* ion (gwasanaeth—dyn) A man-servant.

Gwasaneuthgar, *a.* (gwasanaeth) Serviceable.

Gwasaneuthgarwch, *s. m.* (gwasaneuthgar) Serviceableness; conduciveness.

Gwasaneuthiad, *s. m.* (gwasanaeth) A serving, a ministering; a conducing.

Gwasant, *s. m.* (gwas) A ministration.

> Diberch gladdu a gwasant.
>
> An irreverent burial and *ministering.* — *Taliesin.*

Gwasaneuthnyn, *s. c.—pl. t.* ion (gwasanaeth—dyn) A person who is a servant.

> Cas gwasaneuthnyn heb ofn.
>
> Odious is a *servant* void of fear. — *Adage.*

Gwasaneuthu, *v. a.* (gwasanaeth) To serve, to do service; to be of service; to minister.

> Cas ni bo ganddo a'i gwasaneutha, ac ni's gwasaneutho ei hun.
>
> Odious is he who has no one to serve him, and serves not himself. — *Adage.*
>
> E wnaeth i'w wasanaethu
> Y sydd, a fydd, ac a fu.
>
> He made to serve him that is, that will be, and that has been. — *Rhys Penarth.*

Gwasaneuthwr, *s. m.—pl.* gwasaneuthwyr (gwasanaeth—gwr) A server; a minister.

Gwasaneuthydd, *s. m.—pl. t.* ion (gwasanaeth) A server; a minister.

Gwasaneuthyddes, *s. f.—pl. t.* au (gwasaneuthydd) A female servant.

Gwasarn, *s. m.—pl. t.* au (gwa—sarn) What is strewed on the ground, or that is trodden upon; straw laid under any thing; litter; booty. *Gwasarn odyn*, straw laid on a kiln, under the grain that is to be dried.

> Ni yrir y gwir o'l garn;
> Nid a'n us dan ei wasarn.
>
> The truth will not be driven itsoff stem; it will not go to chaff beneath its *straw.* — *Lewis Mon.*

Gwasarnawl, *u.* (gwasarn) Strewed as a litter.

Gwasarniad, *s. m.* (gwasarn) A strewing on the ground; a treading under feet; a littering.

Gwasarnu, *v. a.* (gwasarn) To strew on the ground, to tread under feet; to litter, to lay a litter.

Gwasarnwr, *s. m.—pl.* gwasarnwyr (gwasarn—gwr) One who strews, or lays as litter; one who treads under foot.

Gwasâu, *v. a.* (gwas) To minister, to serve; to humble; to become humble.

> Bwyf unfod wosod wasâu,
> O weision wasanaethu;
> A'm dyfyno Duw, yn dyfynu nef
> Ar ei nawdd.——
>
> May I be coexistent and placed *to be humble*, in serving of servants; may God summon me, when he summons heaven to his protection. — *Elidr Sais.*

Gwasawd, *s. m.* (gwas) The disposition of a cow to take the bull. *a.* Being in such a state. *Buwch wasawd*, a tufty cow. It is also called *Terfenydd.*

Gwasawg, *a.* (gwas) Being serving, or minstering. *s. m.* A servant.

> Mi ni'm car Gwenddydd, ac ni'm hannerch;
> Wyf cas gan wasawg gwaesaf Rhydderch.
>
> Me Gwenddydd does not love, and she will not greet me; I am hated by the *minister* of the authority of Rhydderch. — *Myrddin.*

Gwasawl, *a.* (gwas) Ministering, serving.

Gwaseiddrwydd, *s. m.* (gwasaidd) A state of ministering, serviceableness.

Gwasel, *s. m.—pl. t.* au (gwa—sel) A glance, a view, or sight, as that taken in shooting.

Gwaseuthawl, *a.* (gwasaeth) Ministering.

Gwaseuthgar, *a.* (gwasaeth) Serviceable.

Gwaseuthiad, *s. m.* (gwasaeth) A ministering.

Gwaseuthnyn, *s. c.—pl. t.* ion (gwasaeth—dyn) A ministering person; a servant.

Gwaseuthu, *v. a.* (gwasaeth) To minister.

Gwasg, *s. f.—pl. t.* oedd (gwa) A pressure, a squeeze; a compression; a press; the waist, or where the girdle is tied. *Gwasg caws*, a cheese press.

> Ei wisg oedd, o'i wasg eiddil,
> O flodau fan-gangau fil;
> A'i gasul debygesynt
> O esgyll gwrdd fentyll gwynt.
>
> His robe, from his slender *waist*, was of a thousand tiny branching flowers; and his mantle,they compared as of the wings of the ardent flapping wind. — *D. ab Gwilym, i'r Fronfraith.*

Gwasgar, *s. m.—pl. t.* ion (gwasg—ar) A scattering, or dispersion. *a.* Scattered, dispersed.

> Glas ferau heiyrn hêasant,
> Glas lafar gwasgar gwisgasant.
>
> Blue blades of steel they strewed, blue armour scattered they did put on. — *Cynddelw.*

Gwasgaradwy, *a.* (gwasgar) Dissipatable.

Gwasgarawd, *s. m.* (gwasgar) Dispersion.

> Gwasgarawd alaf, braint uchaf bri;
> Gwasgawd cyrdd i fyrdd o farddoni.
>
> The *scattering* of riches, the highest degree of honour; and the refuge of song to a myriad of bards. — *Gr. ab M. ab Dafydd.*

Gwasgarawg, *a.* (gwasgar) Being scattered about.

> Gwr fu Llywelyn gor terfyn Taf,
> Gwawr cyhoedd wagswdd wasgarocaf.
>
> A man was Llywelyn on the confines of the Taf, the splendour of public liveries most scattered. *Bleddyn Fardd.*

Gwasgarawl, *a.* (gwasgar) Dispersive, scattering.

Gwasgarawr, *v. a.* (gwasgar) To scatter about.

> Berthedan thlws rhy wasgarawr.
>
> Princely jewels he *will scatter* most profusely. *Ll. P. Moch.*

Gwasgaredig, *a.* (gwasgar) Scattered, dispersed. *Gwasgaredigion*, scattered ones.

Gwasgaredigaeth, *s. m.* *pl. t.* au (gwasgaredig) A being scattered; dispersion.

Gwasgaredigawl, *a.* (gwasgaredig) Dispersive.

Gwasgaredigrwydd, *s. m.* (gwasgaredig) Dispersedness, diffusedness.

Gwasgaredd, *s. m.* (gwasgar) Dispersedness.

Gwasgarfa, *s. f.—pl. t.* oedd (gwasgar) A scene of scattering; dispersion.

Gwasgargerdd, *s. f.* (gwasgar—cerdd) A song of scattering; a song of prediction.

> Gorchwnn gwgnodd gwasgawd caichdoed,
> Gwasgargerdd gwingwgwein.
>
> A retinue will celebrate the shelter of enamelled covering, a scattering song of habiliment. *Cynddelw, i'r. Cyfeiliawg.*

Gwasgariad, *s. m.* (gwasgar) A scattering, a dispersing, or strewing about.

Gwasgaroldeb, *s. m.* (gwasgar) Dispersedness.

Gwasgarolrwydd, *s. m.* (gwasgar) Dispersedness.

Gwasgaru, *v. a.* (gwasgar) To scatter, to disperse.

> Gorwyn blaen derw, chwerw brig on,
> Khag hwyaid gwasgerid ton;
> Pybyr twyll pell ofal i'm calon.
>
> Glittering the tops of the oaks, harsh the branches of the ash, before the ducks the wave is made to *disperse*: audacious is deceit, very far in my heart is care. *Llywarch Hen.*

Gwasgarwr, *s. m.—pl.* gwasgarwyr (gwasgar—gwr) A scatterer, a disperser.

Gwasgawd, *s. f.—pl.* gwasgodion (gwa—ysgawd) A shelter, or shade; a covert; a waistcoat; *Gwasgawd lythyr*, a term in grammar, for two consonants together, one sheltering the other.

Gwasgawl, *a.* (gwasg) Pressing, or squeezing.

Gwasgedig, *a.* (gwasg) Pressed, compressed.

Gwasgedigaeth, *s. m.* (gwasgedig) A pression.

Gwasgfa, *s. f.—pl.* gwasgfëydd (gwasg) A pressure; a depression; a fainting fit. *Gwasgfaon angeu*, the pangs of death.

Gwasgfwrdd, *s. m.—pl.* gwasgfyrddau (gwasg—bwrdd) A pressing board; a platen.

Gwasgiad, *s. m.—pl. t.* au (gwasg) A pressing.

Gwasgodawg, *a.* (gwasgawd) Affording shelter.

Gwasgodawl, *a.* (gwasgawd) Sheltering, shading.

Gwasgodfa, *s. f.—pl. t.* on (gwasgawd) A bower.

Gwasgodedig, *a.* (gwasgawd) Sheltered, shaded.

Gwasgodi, *v. a.* (gwasgawd) To shelter, to cover with a shade, to overshadow.

Gwasgodiad, *s. m.* (gwasgawd) A sheltering.

Gwasgodle, *s. m.—pl. t.* oedd (gwasgawd—lle) A sheltered place.

Gwasgodlen, *s. f.—pl. t.* i (gwasgawd—llen) A sheltering veil.

Gwasgawdlwyn, *s. m.—pl. t.* i (gwasgawd—llwyn) A sheltering grove.

Gwasgodwydd, *s. m.* (gwasgawd—gwydd) A sheltering wood; a bower, or arbour.

> Pob pren a blaner yn wasgodwydd 24 a dal i'w berchenawg; nar yn ngarddau, nar yn ngwastawd i'w dy y plano.
>
> Every tree that shall be planted as a *sheltering bower* 24 pence is the value to its owner, whether in gardens, or whether as a shelter to his house he shall plant it. *Welsh Laws.*

Gwasgotty, *s. m.—pl. t.* au (gwasgawd—ty) A hovel, an outhouse.

Gwasgrwym, *s. m.—pl. t.* au (gwasg—rhwym) A bandage, a girdle.

Gwasgrwymyn, *s. m.—pl. t.* au (gwasg—rhwymyn) A band round the waist, a girdle.

Gwasgu, *v. a.* (gwasg) To press, to squeeze.

Gwasgwyn, *s. m.—pl.* gweisgwyn (gwa—ysgwyn) A gentle rising; a smooth hill; the hinder thigh of a horse, or a gascoin: also a managed horse, or steed; the country of Gascony. *Gweisgwyn gennymdaith*, a retinue of steeds.

> Hin falch dymhor hoen-fwyn,
> Yn wych ymlewych am lwyn,
> Gwisg-wyrdd yn dol a gwasgwyn.
>
> Kindly-smiling season of fine weather, gaily it glitters round the grove and green-robed are the dale and *gently swelling hill*. *D. ab Gwilym.*

Gwasgwynes, *s. f.—pl. t.* au (gwasgwyn) That rises, or swells gently; an epithet for a trained mare.

> Gwasgwynes y main gannwl.
>
> The *gently swelling* one with the alert body. *D. ab Gwilym, i'r Ileng.*

Gwasgwynfarch, *s. m.—pl.* gwasgwynfeirch (gwasgwyn—march) A managed horse, or steed.

> Gwasgwynfeirch, gosairch, goathr.
>
> *Gently pacing steeds* slightly harnessed, slightly trending. *Ll. P. Moch.*

Gwasodi, *v. n.* (gwasawd) To become wanting the bull, to become tufty.

Gwasodiad, *s. m.* (gwasawd) A becoming tufty.

Gwasodrwydd, *s. m.* (gwasawd) Tuftiness, or the want of a bull by a cow.

Gwast, *s. m.—pl. t.* au (gwas) A spread, a plat.

Gwastad, *s. m.—pl. t.* oedd (gwastad) That is even, smooth, steady, or continued; a plane, or level; a plain.

> Rhetid maen yn i gaffo wastad.
>
> Let the stone roll until it gets a *level*. *Adage.*
>
> Ni cheffir gwastad i bel.
>
> No *level* will be got for a ball. *Adage.*

Gwastad, *a.* (gwast) Even, smooth, level; steady; continued; constant; demure. *Mae o'n lladd arni yn wastad*, he is running her down continually; *Yn wastad teg*, continually.

> Bid wastad gwraig ni erchir.
>
> Let the woman who is never asked appear *composed*. *Llefoed.*
>
> Angen y gyhydedd wastad yw bod wythsill, a hyd y pennill o bedwar i unarbymtheg o fannau.
>
> The essential of the *smooth* co-extension is a verse of eight syllables, and the length of the stanza from four to sixteen verses. *Barddas.*

Gwastadawl, *a.* (gwastad) Of an even tendency; continued, constant, uniform.

Gwastadedd, *s. m.* (gwastad) Evenness, continuity, a level, or plain country.

Gwastadfa, *s. f.* (gwastad) A level space, a level.

Gwastadfan, *s. f.—pl. t.* au (gwastad—man) A level place, a level.

Gwastadfod, *s. f.* (gwastad—bod) A constant habitation; an even, or constant state.

Gwastadiad, *s. m.* (gwastad) A levelling, a making even or smooth.

Gwastadle, *s. m.—pl. t.* oedd (gwastad—lle) A level place, a plain.

Gwastadoldeb, *s. m.* (gwastadawl) Evenness; continuity; perennity.

Gwastadolrwydd, *s. m.* (gwastadawl) Levelness.

Gwastadrwydd, *s. m.* (gwastad) Evenness; continuity; constancy.

Cadwyn cyfrian, cyfrwydd yn rhoddi
Cod wedi wastadrwydd.

The binding chain of contemporary chiefs, habitually free in giving costly entertainments of *constancy*.
Cynddelw, i Wenwynwyn.

Gwastadu, *v. a.* (gwastad) To make level.
Gwastata, *v. a.* (gwastad) To make even; to become even; to become quiet, or tranquil.
Gwastatâad, *s. m.* (gwastata) A making even.
Gwastatâawl, *a.* (gwastata) Tending to make even; tranquillizing.
Gwastatâu, *v. a.* (gwastata) To make even, plain, or level; to smooth; to continue; to rest.
Gwastatâwr, *s. m.—pl.* gwastatawyr (gwastata—gwr) One who makes even; a calmer.
Gwastatëydd, *s. m.—pl. t.* ion (gwastata) One who makes even; one who calms.
Gwastatu, *v. a.* (gwastad) To make even; to still, to become still, or tranquil.
Gwastraff, *s. m.—pl. t.* ion (gwa—ystraff) Prodigality; waste; lavish expenditure.
Gwastraffawl, *a.* (gwastraff) Squandering.
Gwastraffedd, *s. m.* (gwastraff) Prodigality.
Gwastraffiad, *s. m.* (gwastraff) A squandering.
Gwastraffu, *v. a.* (gwastraff) To squander.
Gwastraffwr, *s. m.—pl.* gwastraffwyr (gwastraff—gwr) A prodigal, or wasteful man.
Gwastrawd, *s. m.—pl.* gwastrodion (gwas—trawd) A groom of the stable, or equerry. *Gwastrodion afwyn*, the grooms of the reign.

Gwastrawd afwyn a ddyly ddal gwarthafl y brenin pan esgyno, a phan ddisgyno, a dwyn ei farch i'w letty.

The *groom* of the reign is obliged to hold the stirrup of the king when he mounts, and when he dismounts, and take his horse to his lodging.
Welsh Laws.

Gwastrin, *s.—pl. t.* ion (gwas—trin) Servitude.
Gwastriniad, *s. m.—pl. t.* au (gwastrin) A performing the duty of a servant.
Gwastriniaw, *v. a.* (gwastrin) To minister.
Gwastrodawl, *a.* (gwastrawd) Relating to a groom.
Gwastrodedd, *s. m.* (gwastrawd) A groom's office.
Gwastrodi, *v. a.* (gwastrawd) To serve as groom.
Gwastrodiad, *s. m.* (gwastrawd) A serving as a groom, or page.
Gwastrodyn, *s. m. dim.* (gwastrawd) A page.
Gwasu, *v. a.* (gwas) To reduce to the state of a servant; to make as a slave.
Gwatwar, *s. m.—pl. t.* oedd (gwad—gwar) A mockery, derision, or jest; scorn, contempt.

Ar watwar cynnar y cad.

He was early found in *mockery*. *D. ab Gwilym.*

Gwatwar, *v. a.* (gwad—gwar) To mock, to deride, to make a jest of; to laugh, to scorn.

Gwatwar y dydd am waith nos.

To scoff the day for the work of the night. *Adage.*

Gwatwarawl, *a.* (gwatwar) Sarcastic, ironical.
Gwatwaredig, *a.* (gwatwar) Derided, contemned.
Gwatwaredigaeth, *s. f.—pl. t.* au (gwatwaredig) The act of deriding, or mocking; derision.

Nid ae un dydd heibio heb goffau buddygoliaeth y Prydeiniaid, a ffoedigaeth Iwl Celsar, a hyny gan ei watwaredigaeth.

No person was wont to pass without remembering the victory of the Britons, and the retreat of Julius Cæsar, and that with the *deriding* of him. *Gr. ab Arthur.*

Gwatwareg, *s. f.* (gwatwar) Irony, sarcasm.
Gwatwarfawl, *s. f.* (gwatwar—mawl) Satirical praise; irony.
Gwatwargar, *a.* (gwatwar) Derisive; flouting.
Gwatwargerdd, *s. f.* (gwatwar—cerdd) Irony.
Gwatwariad, *s. m.* (gwatwar) A mocking, a playing upon, a jesting; a scoffing; derision.
Gwatwaru, *v. a.* (gwatwar) To mock; to scoff.
Gwatwarus, *a.* (gwatwar) Mocking; sarcastic.
Gwatwarusrwydd, *s. m.* (gwatwarus) Sarcasticalness.
Gwatwarwr, *s. m.—pl.* gwatwarwyr (gwatwar—gwr) A mocker, a scoffer; a satirist.
Gwatwarydd, *s. m.—pl. t.* ion (gwatwar) Satirist.
Gwathred, *s. m.—pl. t.* ion (gwa—tred) Intent or purport, design.

Gwathred y llyfr hwn—y disgybl yn gofyn, ac yr athraw yn ateb.

The *purport* of this book—the disciple asking, and the master answering. *Elucidarius.*

Gwau, *s. m.—pl.* gweuoedd (gwa) A weaving, a knitting; a web.
Gwau, *v. a.* (gwa) To weave; to knit. *Mal y mae y dynion yn gwau trwy eu gilydd*, how the people are running through one another. *Coll.* *Gwau hosanau*, to knit stockings.
Gwaudd, *s. f.—pl. t.* au (gwa—udd) A daughter in law, or a son's wife.

Ni ddaw cof i chwegr ei bod yn waudd.

It will not recur to the step-mother that she has been a daughter-in-law. *Adage.*

Gwawch, *s. f.* (gwa—wch) A loud scream, or cry; a sea bird so called.
Gwawd, *s. m.* (gw—awd) A song of praise, a panegyric, or encomium; praise; also irony, sarcasm, or mockery.

Tyfed it' ar bob tafawd
Annerchion gwychion, a gwawd.

To thee from every tongue may spring fair gratulations and *praise*. *Hywel Aerdrem, i ferch.*

O Ddaw!——
Canaf it', a dadganaf wawd
O fawl fy nhafawd ffyddlawn.

O God! I will sing to thee, and I will recite an *encomium* from the praise of a faithful tongue. *Edm. Prys.*

Gwawdawd, *s. m.* (gwawd) The act of praising.
Gwawdeb, *s. f.—pl. t.* ion (gwawd) An encomiastic.
Gwawdebu, *v. a.* (gwawdeb) To compose an encomiastic, or panegyric.
Gwawdfaeth, *s. m.* (gwawd—maeth) Nurture of praise. *a.* Praise-nurtured.
Gwawdferw, *s. m.* (gwawd—berw) Ebullition of praise. *a.* Effervescent with praise.
Gwawdgan, *s. f.* (gwawd—can) An encomiastic song, or panegyric.

Mal gwawdgan Afan, ufyddfryd ffrwythlawn
O gof Cadwallawn brenin-ddawn bryd.

Like the *panegyric* of Avan, of gentle mind and fruitful, in memory of Cadwallon, of royal gifted countenance.
G. Ddu, o Arfon, m. Sir G. Llwyd.

Gwawdgar, *a.* (gwawd) Fond of praise; also sarcastic, or apt to jeer.
Gwawdiad, *s. m.—pl. t.* au (gwawd) A bestowing encomium; also a jeering.
Gwawdiaw, *v. a.* (gwawd) To bestow encomium; also to jeer, or to use sarcasm.
Gwawdiawl, *a.* (gwawd) Encomiastical.
Gwawdodyn, *s. m.* (gwawdawd) An encomiastic. *Gwawdodyn hir*, and *gwawdodyn byr*, the long encomiastic and the short encomiastic, are metres in the Welsh prosody.
Gwawdus, *a.* (gwawd) Encomiastic, panegyric.
Gwawdwr, *s. m.—pl.* gwawdwyr (gwawd—gwr) A man who makes an encomium.
Gwawdwyn, *s. m.* (gwawd—gwyn) A passion for praise. *a.* Ambitious of fame.

Ysef a'i herly, arlwy garthan dyn,
Llywelyn gwawdwyn, gwan
Gwyr.——

He that will pursue her, a prelude to a severe conflict, is Llywelyn, *ardent after praise*, that runs men through.
Llywarch Hoelly.

Gwawdydd, *s. m.—pl. t.* ion (gwawd) An encomiast, a panegyrist.

A goldw Duw, medd gwawdydd
Da gwr fodd, diogel fydd.

What God keeps, says an encomiast in a manner worthy of credit, will be safe. *H. D. ab Ifan.*

Gwawl, *s. m.* (gwa—awl) Light; radiancy.

Llys glwys barddwys———
Lle mae llewych gwych y gwawl
Hyfryd-wedd ein Naf rhadawl.

The hallowed court of paradise, where there is glorious the reflection of the *light* of the happy countenance of our gracious Lord. *Perch. Ewen Bonws.*

Gwawl, *s. f.* (gwa—wl) A wall, a rampart.

Gorug Seferus gwaith cain,
Yn draws eros Ynys Prydain:
Rhag gwerin gythrawl gwawl fain.

Severus formed a fair structure, across over the isle of Britain: against a forward throng a *wall* of stones.

Gwawlidde, *s. m.* (gwawl—de) Phosphorous.

Gwawliddëain, *a.* (gwawl—de) Phosphoric.

Gwawn, *s. m. aggr.* (gwa—awn) A quick darting of rays; the gossamer.

Gwenllian gwawn y lleuad.

Gwenllian like the *rays* of the moon. *Ieu. Llawdden.*

Gwawr dydd Meirionydd mawr aniwedd ym nwyf,
Gwynebryd nyf cyn dadddwedd;
Gwyd a gofal a'm talawdd
Gwawn liw, och, heddiw o'i chawdd!

The dawn of the day of Meirionydd, a great severity to my passion with the fair visage of the snow before it melts; mischief and anxiety has she given me, she of *gossamer* hue, woe me this day from her cruelty. *Ior. ab y Cyriog.*

E bery ei glod——
Tra fo haul arnal, ac yn eruyn gwawn;
Tra fo yr eigiawn yn llawn llynwys.

His fame will last whilst the glorious sun shall be, and the *gossamer* of glittering white; whilst the ocean is in full flow. *L. G. Cothi.*

Gwawr, *s. f.—pl. t.* oedd (gwa—awr) A breaking out of light; that radiates; the dawn, the aurora, the break of day; a hue; or cast; also a hero. *Gwawr felen*, a yellowish hue; *gwawr angeu*, a lightening before death.

Gliwynt engyll gwawr
Engorynt yn worwawr.

They tinged with blue the wings of the dawn when they sent the ashen messengers of pain. *Taliesin.*

Mawr yw cost gwawr, myn delw Garon!
Ac nid mawr yw hynt gwawr gwirion.

Great is the *hero's* expence by Caron's image! But not great the boast of the innocent *hero*. *L. G. Cothi.*

Gwawraidd, *a.* (gwawr) Like the dawn; dawning.

Gwawriad, *s. m.* (gwawr) A dawning, a breaking out of light, a glimmering.

Gwawriaw, *v. a.* (gwawr) To dawn, to begin to brighten; to glimmer.

Gwaws, *s. m.* (aws) Ruth, tenderness, pity.

Gwb, *s. m.* (wb) A moan, a doleful cry.

Gwd, *s. m.* (gw) A twist, a wind, or turn.

Gwden, *s. f.—pl. t.* i (gwd) A withe; a coil, a ring. *Gwdyn car*, drag withes, used as substitutes for iron links: *Gwden y coed, cloffrwym y moci*, the great bindweed.

Anhawdd gwahawdd gwynt y'ngwden.

It is difficult to invite the wind into a ring. *Ll. P. Moch.*

Gwdenawl, *a.* (gwden) In the form of a withe.

Gwdeniad, *s. m.* (gwden) A withing, a forming into a withe; a binding with a withe.

Gwdenu, *v. a.* (gwden) To form into a withe; to fasten with a withe.

Gwdd, *s. m.* (gw) That twists or turns round.

Gwddi, *s. m.—pl. t.* od (gwdd) A hedging bill.

Gwddw, *s. m.* (gwdd) The neck, the crag.

Ei wddw eilwaith oedd olwyn.

His neck again was like a wheel. *T. Aled, i farch.*

Gwddwf, *s. m.—pl.* gyddfau (gwddw) The neck, the crag. *Gwddwf gryg*, the common heron.

Awydd a dyr ei wddwf.

Ambition will break his neck. *Adage.*

Gwddwg, *s. m.—pl.* gyddygau (gwdd) A neck.

Gwddwgen, *s. f.* (gwddwg) A neckcloth, a cravat.

Gwddor, *s. f.—pl. t.* i (gwdd) A wooden bridge, or boards laid across a rivulet.

Gwe, *s. f.—pl. t.* oedd (gw) What is drawn, or sent out; web, a web of cloth. *Gwe copyn*, a cobweb; *gwe felen*, lesser yellow trefoil.

Gwe, *a prefix in composition* (gw) It has an inceptive import, or denotes a beginning, and a tendency.

Gwëad, *s. m.* (gwe) A weaving; a knitting.

Gwëadur, *s. m.—pl. t.* on (gwead) A weaver.

Gwëawd, *s. m.* (gwe) A weaving; a knitting.

Gwëawdr, *s. m.—pl.* gwëodron (gwëawd) A weaver. *Gwëawdr copyn*, a spider.

Gwëawl, *a.* (gwe) Relating to weaving; textile.

Gweb, *s. f.* (gw—eb) A phiz; a smirk; a smack of the lips.

———Enid
A gwen web, lawen heb lid.

Enid with a fair *countenance*, merry and free from anger. *D. ab Gwilym.*

Gwecry, *a.* (gwegr) Vapid feeble, weak, flimsy.

A phawb a heno fal brethyn gwecry.

And every one will grow old like an ancient *flimsy* garment. *Dafydd Ddu.*

Oni i yr Arglwydd a adeilado y ty, ofer fydd llafur ei adeiladwyr a gwecry.

If the Lord doth not build the house, vain is the labour of the builders and *feeble*. *Dafydd Ddu.*

Gwech, *a.* (*f. of* gwych) Brave; fine, gay. *Y gwas gwech-don*, the bold-voiced fellow.

Gwed, *s. m.* (gw—ed) An utterance, a saying.

Gwedawl, *a.* (gwed) Relating to speech; speaking.

Gwedi, *prep.* (gwed) After, later than. *Gwedi gwaith*, after work. *adv.* After, when, after the time that; afterwards. *Gwedi iddo roddi*, after he had given; *gwedi ateb o honi*, when she had answered; *a ddoi di yno wedi?* wilt thou come there afterwards? *wedi darfod*, having finished.

Bedd mab Osfran y'Nghamlan,
Gwedi lawer cyflafan,
Bedd Bedwyr yn Allt Tryfan.

The grave of the son of Osvran in Camlan, *after* many a slaughter; the grave of Bedwyr in the cliff of Tryfan. *Engl. Beddau Milwyr.*

Gwediad, *s. m.* (gwed) A speaking or saying.

Gwedn, *a.* (*f. of* gwydn) Tenacious, tough.

Gwedresi, *s. f.* (gwe—tresi) A lizard.

Gwedwr, *s. m.—pl.* gwedwyr (gwed—gwr) A speaker; one who says, or speaks.

Gwedwst, *s. m.* (gwed—gwst) A silent and listening disposition. *Dyfed.*

Gwedy, *prep.* (gwed) After. *adv.* After, when, afterwards. The same as *Gwedi.*

Gwedyd, *s. m.* (gwed) A saying, a speaking.

Tri chelwydd sydd: celwydd gwedyd, celwydd tau, a chelwydd ymddwyn, a phob un a hair credu na's dylid.

There are three falsehoods: falsehood of *speaking*, falsehood of silence, and a falsehood of conduct, and every one will induce belief that should not be. *Barddas.*

Gwedyd, *v. a.* (gwed) To say, or to speak. *Ni wedai air*, he would not say a word.

Yr awen o ddiawl—yw yr awen a wed gelwydd mewn cerdd, ac a fwyaa bechodau a gwydiau.

The muse from the devil is the muse that *speaks* falsehood in a song, and multiplies sins and vices. *Barddas.*

Gwedydd, *s. m.—pl. t.* ion (gwed) A speaker.

Gwedd, *s. f.* (gwe—edd) General connexion, contour, form, order; shape; fashion; the look, or aspect; complexion; a team; a yoke. *Drwg yw y wedd arni*, bad is her appearance: *Gwedd o feirch*, a team of horses; *gwedd o ychain*, a yoke of oxen; *Ymostwng tan wedd Crist*, to submit one's self under the yoke of Christ.

Tair gwreigedd, a'u gwedd fal gwawn,
A gafas yn gwbl gyfiawn
Pryd ein pan fu'r damwain da.

Three women, with their *complexion* like the gossamer, obtained, altogether justly a beauteous form when good fortune reigned. *D. ab Gwilym.*

Gweddaidd, *a.* (gwedd) Orderly, well-connected, well-shaped; well-behaved; civil.

A'm dewis synwyr synlaw arwreigaidd
Ban ddywed o fraidd weddaidd wofeg.

And my choicest sentiment is to contemplate female excellence, when she but scarcely utters the *appropriate* thought. *H. ab Owain.*

Gweddawd, *s. m.* (gwedd) The act of connecting.

Gweddawg, *a.* (gwedd) Connected, or having connection; seemly, coupled; yoked; wedded; conjugal. *Newydd weddawg*, newly married.

Gweddawl, *a.* (gwedd) Disposed in order; well-connected; orderly; accustomed to subjection; used to the yoke; moderate; reasonable, tolerable. *Dyn gweddawl*, a good sort of a person: *Mae hwna yn o weddawl*, that there is pretty reasonable.

Gweddeidd-dra, *s. m.* (gweddaidd) Orderliness; connectedness; moderation; decency.

Gweddeiddgar, *a.* (gweddaidd) Decent, or seemly.

Gweddeiddiad, *s. m.* (gweddaidd) A rendering, or becoming, connected; a becoming decent.

Gweddeiddiaw, *v. a.* (gweddaidd) To render orderly; to dispose; to moderate.

Gwaith cymmen o fedwen fad;
Gweddeiddiaw gwydd a wyddiad.

An elegant work of the goodly birch; she knew how *to dispose* the wood. *D. ab Gwilym.*

Gweddeiddiawl, *a.* (gweddaidd) Tending to render orderly or well-connected; of a decent tendency.

Gweddi, *s. f.—pl. t.* au (gwedd) Submission; supplication; prayer; adoration.

A fo hen arched weddi.

He that is old let him ask a *prayer*. *Adage.*

Gweddi Talhaiarn—Duw dy nawdd, ac yn nawdd nerth, ac yn nerth pwyll, yn mhwyll cyfiawnder, ac yn nghyfiawnder cariad, ac yn nghariad caru Duw, ac yn ngharu Duw, caru pob peth.

The *prayer* of Talhaiarn: God, grant thy protection, and in thy protection strength, and in strength discretion, and in discretion justice, and in justice love, in love to love God, and in loving God to love all things. *Barddas.*

Gweddïad, *s. m.* (gweddi) A supplicating, a praying.

Gweddiad, *s. m.* (gwedd) A conforming; a submitting; a subjugation.

Gweddiadur, *s. m.* (gweddiad) One who submits.

Gweddiannawl, *a.* (gweddiant) Submissive orderly.

Gweddiannu, *v. a.* (gweddiant) To bring to order or to render submissive; to become orderly.

Gweddiant, *s. m.* (gwedd) Submission to order.

Gweddïaw, *v. a.* (gweddi) To supplicate, to pray.

Ni lafur, ni weddïa,
Nid teilwng iddo ei fara.

He that works not, that *prays* not, deserves not his bread. *Adage.*

Gweddïawl, *a.* (gweddi) Praying, supplicatory.

Gweddig, *a.* (gwedd) Seemly, decent; orderly.

Gwedig argywedd ddeigr-gawad a'm gwlych.

The *decent* depression of the shower of tears bedews me. *D. ab Gwilym.*

Gweddill, *s. m.—pl. t.* ion (gwedd) A remainder, remnant, relick; orts, leavings.

Gweddill mab iach.

The *leavings* of a healthy youth. *Adage.*

Nid digon heb weddill.

It is not a sufficiency without *leavings*. *Adage.*

Gweddilliad, *s. m.* (gweddill) A leaving as remnant

Gweddilliaw, *v. a.* (gweddill) To make a remainder, to leave as a remnant; to leave orts.

Gweddillwyd ni hyd oni ddaeth sorod yr amserau oll, pan yw anwiredd yn amlâu, a chariad llaweroedd yn oeri.

We *have been left* until the refuse of all the times is come, when iniquity increases, and when the love of many becomes cold. *Jer. Owain.*

Gweddilliedig, *a.* (gweddill) Left as a remnant.

Gwedditor, *sup.* (gwedd) To be submitting.

Nid amdlawd na'm gwawd, na'm gwedditor
I'th fyw, Faelgwn ryw, ran gyfeisor.

Not despicable my panegyric, nor my *being submitted* whilst thou livest, of the race of Maelgwn, and of coequal portion. *Cynddelw.*

Gweddïwr, *s. m.—pl.* gweddïwyr (gweddi—gwr) One who prays, a supplicator, a petitioner.

Gweddlys, *s. f.* (gwedd—llys) Woad. It is also called *Melsugn*, *glas*, *glaslys*, and *glasddu*.

Gweddoli, *v. a.* (gweddawl) To render orderly, or moderate; to moderate.

Gweddu, *v. a.* (gwedd) To render orderly, or connected; to submit; to do homage; to yoke; to wed; to become orderly; to become; to befit. *Fe weddai*, it would seem; *mae'n rhaid gweddu*, it is necessary to submit.

Da gweddai y ber i'r golwyth.

The spit *would suit* well for the joint of meat. *Adage.*

Por eisor, un eisiau ni'm gwedd.

Like a prince, *he will* not *submit* me to one want. *Ll. P. Moch.*

Gronw——
Dy gywyddau da gweddynt
I'r oes oedd ar gyhoedd gynt.

Gronw, thy poems well *they might be classed* as of the age that was famed of old. *H. Huws, Bardd Coch.*

Eisteddwys yr amherawdr yn ei gader, ac y gwedddwys pawb o wyr Rhufain iddo.

The emperor sat in his chair, and all the people of Rome *did homage* unto him. *Br. Max. Wledig—Mabinogion.*

Gweddus, *a.* (gwedd) Orderly, well-befitting, well-digested; well-shaped; handsome; seemly; well-behaved; fitting, beseeming. *Ymddygiad gweddus*, a decent behaviour.

Gweddusaw, *v. a.* (gweddus) To render orderly, or connected; to become conformable, to become well-shaped, to become decent.

Gweddusdra, *s. m.* (gweddus) Orderliness, decency

Gweddusiad, *s. m.* (gweddus) A rendering orderly, or decent; a becoming orderly, or decent.

Gweddusrwydd, *s. m.* (gweddus) Orderliness.

Gweddw, *a.* (gwedd) Being passed beyond connexion or order; being unyoked; widowed; solitary.—*Dyn gweddw*, a widowed person; *dynes weddw*, a widow woman; *gwr gweddw*, a widower; *gwraig weddw*, a widow; *eidion gweddw*, an ox deprived of a fellow.

Gweddw pwyll heb amynedd.

Reason is *destitute* without perseverance. *Adage.*

Sarâad gwraig weddw cyn gwra o honi hanner sarâad ei brawd yw.

An insult-fine to a single woman before she gets a husband is half the insult-fine to her brother. *Welsh Laws.*

Gweddwad, *s. m.* (gweddw) A rendering solitary, a bereaving, a becoming widowed.

Gweddwar, *a.* (gwedd—gwar) Of a mild aspect.

Gweddwawl, *a.* (gweddw) Bereaving; widowing.

Gweddwdawd, *s. m.* (gweddw) Widowhood.

Gwell hir weddwdawd
Na drwg briawd.

A long *remaining single* is better than a bad marriage. *Adage.*

Tamar—a ddiosgodd ddillad ei gweddwdawd oddi am dani, ac a guddiodd ei hun â gorchudd.

Tamar—put away the garments of her widowhood from off her, and covered herself with a veil. *Gen. xxxviii. 14.*

Gweddwedig, *a.* (gweddw) Being widowed.
Gweddwi, *v. a.* (gweddw) To bereave; to make one a widow; to become widowed.
Gweddyg, *s. m.—pl. t.* au (gwedd) A shoe-last.
Gwef, *s. m.* (gwe—ef) That is clear, or fair.
Gwefl, *s. f.—pl. t.* au (gwef) A chop, a lip. *Gwefl* is mostly applied to mean the lips of beasts, and *Gwefus* the human lip.—*Gweflau ceimion,* wry chops.
Gweflaid, *s. f.—pl* gwefleidiau (gwefl) A chop-full
Gweflaidd, *a.* (gwefl) Like a lip, labiated.
Gweflawd, *s. m.* (gwefl) A dash on the chops.
Gweflawg, *a.* (gwefl) Blubber-lipped.
Gwefldew, *a.* (gwefl—tew) Thick-lipped.
Gweflfawr, *a.* (gwefl—mawr) Large lipped.
Gweflgrwn, *a.* (gwefl—crwn) Having the rim, or margin turned round; dog-eared.
Gweflodiad, *s. m.* (gweflawd) A dashing on the chops, a stroke on the mouth.
Gweflodiaw, *v. a.* (gweflawd) To slap the chops.
Gweflyn, *s. m.* (gwefl) One with blubber lips.
Gwefr, *s. m.—pl.* gwefrau (gwef) Amber.

Gwallt dyn befr o liw gwefr gwych.

The hair of the smart maid is of the colour of the fine *amber.* *D. ab Edmund.*

Nid muwchwdd ammwydd i'm yw,
Na gwefr; ni wn ei gyfryw.

It is to me not fine grained jet, nor *amber*, I know nothing to compare with it *Guto'r Glyn, i'r paderau.*

Gwefraidd, *a.* (gwefr) Of the nature of amber.
Gwefrawg, *a.* (gwefr) Having amber; consisting of amber.
Gwefrawl, *a.* (gwefr) Being like amber.
Gwefreiddiad, *s. m.* (gwefraidd) A making, or becoming, like amber.
Gwefreiddiaw, *v. a.* (gwefraidd) To make, or to become, of the nature of amber.
Gwefriad, *s. m.* (gwefr) A doing with amber.
Gwefriaw, *v. a.* (gwefr) To do with amber.
Gwefroli, *v. a.* (gwefrawl) To make of the quality of amber; to become like amber.
Gwefru, *v. a.* (gwefr) To do with amber.
Gwefus, *s. f.—pl. t.* au (gwe—bus) The human lip.

Ar dy wefus a'th gusan
Y mae oes.——

In thy *lip* and thy kiss there is life. *Gut. Owain.*

Gwefusaidd, *a.* (gwefus) Like a lip; labiated.
Gwefusaw, *v. a.* (gwefus) To touch with the lip; to form or make a lip.
Gwefusawg, *a.* (gwefus) Labiated, having lips.
Gwefusawl, *a.* (gwefus) Labial, relating to the lips. *Gwefusolion,* labials.
Gwefusdew, *a.* (gwefus—tew) Thick-lipped.
Gwefusglec, *s. f.—pl. t.* iau (gwefus—clec) A smack of the lip.
Gwefusglecian, *v.* (gwefusglec) To smack the lips
Gwefusiad, *s. m.* (gwefus) A doing with the lip, a touching with the lip.
Gweg, *s. m.* (gw—eg) A tottering, or shake as if ready to fall.
Gwegi, *s. m.* (gwag) Vanity emptiness, levity. *Mae hi yn llawn o wegi,* she is full of levity; *paid a'r gwegi yna,* have done with that trifling.
Gwegiad, *s. m.—pl. t.* au (gweg) A tottering.
Gwegian, *v. a.* (gweg) To shake, to totter.
Gwegiaw, *v. a.* (gweg) To totter, or to shake.
Gwegiawg, *a.* (gweg) Tottering, or unsteady.
Gwegiawl, *a.* (gweg) Tottering, or unsteady.

Gwegil, *s. m.—pl. t.* au (gwe—cil) The hinder part of the head, the bottom of the back part of the skull, the back.

Gwell gwegil car na gwyneb estrawn.

The *back* of a friend is better than a stranger's face. *Adage.*

Gwelaf ar ddigrif brif-fardd
Gwegil byd.——

I perceive the *back* of the world turned upon a pleasing poet. *Bedo Phylip Bach.*

Gwegilaw, *v. a.* (gwegil) To turn the back of the head; to turn the back.
Gwegiliad, *s. m.* (gwegil) A turning from.
Gwegilsyth, *a.* (gwegil—syth) Stiffnecked.
Gweglyd, *a.* (gweg) Tottering, feeble, weak.

Dymgolych Gogledd gweglyd luoedd.

I am praised by the North of *feeble* hosts. *Gwalchmai.*

Gwegriad, *s. m.* (gwagr) A searcing, a sifting.
Gwegru, *v. a.* (gwegr) To turn in a sieve, to sift.
Gwegrwr, *s. m.—pl.* gwegrwyr (gwagr—gwr) One who searces, a searcer, or sifter.
Gwegryn, *s. m.* (gwagr) A searcing, or sifting.
Gwegrynawl, *a.* (gwegryn) Searcing, or sifting.
Gwegryniad, *s. m.* (gwegryn) Searcing, a sifting.
Gwegrynu, *v. a.* (gwegryn) To searce, or to sift.
Gwegyd, *s. m.* (gwag) Vanity, emptiness, levity.
Gwehelyth, *s. f.—pl. t.* au (helyth) Extraction, lineage; the stock of a tribe, a tribe.

Gwae, o hilion gwehelyth,
A roddo serch ar ferch fyth!

Woe to the remains of any ancient *stock* that shall ever fix his love on woman! *Sypyn Cyfeiliawg.*

Ba ryw hael bur wehelyth;
Ba rai beilch a bery byth!

What generous one of *lineage* pure; what proud ones are there who shall ever last! *Ior. Fynglwyd.*

Gwehil, *s. f.* (gwe—hil) That is imperfectly produced, or fructified.
Gwehiliad, *s. m.* (gwehil) A producing imperfectly; to yield trash, or refuse.
Gwehiliaw, *v. a.* (gwehil) To produce imperfectly; a yielding trash, or refuse.
Gwehilion, *s. m. aggr.* (gwehil) The refuse, trash, or riffraff; the refuse or winnowing of corn.

Mae gwehilion i'r gwenith.

There is a *refuse* to the wheat. *Adage.*

Gwehilioni, *v. a.* (gwehilion) To produce trash, to leave a refuse.
Gwehyn, *s. m.—pl. t.* ion (gwe—hyn) Exhaustion.
Gwehyn, *a.* (gwe—hyn) Pouring, or shedding. *Rhad-wehyn,* grace-diffusing, *cig-wehyn,* flesh-dispensing.
Gwehyn, *v. a.* (gwe—hyn) To empty, to pour, to shed, to evacuate, to exhaust.
Gwehynadwy, *a.* (gwehyn) That may be poured out, or diffused; exhaustible;
Gwehynai, *s. c.—pl.* gwehyneion (gwehyn) That pours, or effuses, an exhauster.
Gwehynawl, *a.* (gwehyn) Effusive; pouring.
Gwehyniad, *s. m.—pl. t.* au (gwehyn) Effusion.
Gwehynu, *v. a.* (gwehyn) To pour out, to empty, to exhaust, to shed, to diffuse, to effuse.
Gwehynwr, *s. m.—pl.* gwehynwyr (gwehyn—gwr) A pourer out; a drawer.
Gwehynydd, *s. m.—pl. t.* ion (gwehyn) A pourer out, a drawer.

Yr wyd ti heddyw yn sefyll ger bron yr Arglwydd, o gymynydd dy goed hyd wehynydd dy ddwfr.

Thou art this day standing before the Lord, from thy hewer of wood to thy *drawer* of water. *Deut. xxix. 11.*

Gweiddi, *v. a.* (gwaedd) To cry out, to bawl.
Gweiddiad, *s. m.* (gwaedd) A crying out, a bawling.

Gweiddiwr, *s. m.*—*pl.* **gweiddwyr** (gwaedd—gwr) One who cries out, a bawler.

Gweifriad, *s. m.* (gwefr) A making clear like amber.

Gweifriaith, *s. f.* (gwefr—iaith) Luminous speech, perspicuous language.

Nid wyf dylawd o'm gwawd, o'm gweifriaith,
Gweifryd bryd brysiaw i ymdaith.

I am not stinted with respect to my praise, my *luminous speech*, lighting the mind to hasten to range. *Cynddelw.*

Gweilchydd, *s. m.*—*pl. t.* ion (gwalch) A falconer.

Gweilgi, *s. m.*—*pl. t.* oedd (gwailg) A torrent, a flood, a land-flood; a tide; the ocean. *Tywawd y weilgi*, the sand of the sea.

Cell argiwydd y weilgi.

The buttery of the lord of the *torrent*. *Adage.*

Dywedyd a orug—ei fod yn cylchynu, ac yn crwydraw moroedd, yn ceisiaw lle i breswyliaw ynddo: ac erchi a orug i Gwrgant ran o Ynys Prydain i breswyliaw yndi, rhag yn dyoddef tymhestl a mordwy gweilgioedd a fai fwy.

He said that he was encompassing, and wandering the seas, seeking for a place to dwell in: and he asked of Gwrgant a portion of the Isle of Britain to dwell therein, lest he should be suffering the tempest and traversing the *floods* any longer. *Gr. ab Arthur.*

Gweilging, *s. m.*—*pl. t.* oedd (gwailg) A beam, or bar; a perch; a bar lying horizontally.

Yr oedd gweilging arian ar y ddwy-fforch, ac ar y weilging llemysten.

There was a silver *perch* upon the two forks, and upon the *perch* a sparrow-hawk. *Mabinogion.*

Gweili, *s. m.* (gwail) The state of being over, or besides; surplusage.

Ni chronai na seirch na meirch gweili.

He would not collect together trappings, nor *spare* horses. *Meilyr.*

Gweilig, *a.* (gwail) Being over, or spare. *Pwys di weilig*, weight without any thing over.

Gweiling, *s. m.* (gwail) Pale brass; brass.

Gweilw, *s. m.* (gwail) The state of being used.

Gweilgordd Lleisiawn llysoedd gweddawl,
Lluoedd arwoloedd ar weilw didawl.

The tribe of Lleision of beautiful halls, hosts with riches of inexhaustible *store*. *Ein. ab Gwgan, i Lywelyn* I.

Gweilydd, *s. m.* (gwail) A sparer; an absolver.

Llw gweilydd, yw dawed o'r colledig at y dyn a dypio, a chrair ganddo, a dywedyd: tyng i Dduw a'r crair, na ddygaist y peth a'r peth o'm da.

The oath of an *absolver* is the coming of the one who is robbed to the person whom he suspects, bringing a relick with him, and saying swear before God and the relick, that thou hast not stolen such and such thing of my goods. *Welsh Laws.*

Gweini, *v. a.* (gwain) To minister, or to serve.

Gweini, *s. m.* (gwain) Service, servitude.

Gweini ffawd hyd frawd yn dir.

The *service* of prosperity, will be sure till doomsday. *Adage.*

Gweiniad, *s. m.* (gwain) An attending, or ministering; a sheathing.

Diachar llachar lluchiad i lasbar,
Llachau far llaw weiniad.

Terribly gleaming the darting of his blue shaft, the wrath of Llachau was the *dealing* of his hand. *Cynddelw, i O. Cyfeiliawg.*

Gweiniant, *s. m.* (gwain) A ministration, service.

Gweiniaw, *v. a.* (gwain) To put in a sheath.

Cyrch a chymhell yr Ellmyn
Na weinia gledd, Owain y Glyn.

Attack and chase the Germans, Owain of the Glyn, *sheath* not the sword. *I. ab R. ab Ieuan Llwyd.*

Gweiniawg, *a.* (gwain) Ministrant; having a sheath, or sheathed.

Yfais, gan deyrn, o gyrn eurawg,
Arfod faedd feiddiad angad weiniawg.

With a prince I drank out of horns adorned with gold, with a stroke daring the boar was his *ministering* hand. *Meilyr.*

Gweiniawl, *a.* (gwain) Ministrant; sheathing.

Gweinid, *s. m.* (gwain) Attendance; service.

Ni chynnydd gweinid arall.

Attendance upon another yields no increase. *Adage.*

Gweinidator, *ger.* (gweinid) In ministering.

Arwedd Gwynedd gweinidator.

In ministering the gallantry of Gwynedd. *Cynddelw.*

Gweinidawg, *s. m.*—*pl.* **gweinidogion** (gweinid) A minister, a servant.

Tri gweinidogion awen; cof, awyf, a dysg.

The three *ministers* of the muse: memory, ardour, and learning. *Barddas.*

Gweinidfarch, *s. m.*—*pl.* **gweinidfeirch** (gweinid—march) A serving horse; a working horse.

Gweiniditor, *sup.* (gweinid) To be serving.

Gweinidoca, *v. a.* (gweinidawg) To perform the function of a servant, to do service.

Gweinidogaeth, *s. f.*—*pl. t.* au (gweinidawg) A ministration, ministry, or service.

Gweinidogaethawl, *a.* (gweinidogaeth) Administrative; ministering.

Gweinidogaethiad, *s. m.* (gweinidogaeth) A ministering.

Gweinidogaethu, *v. a.* (gweinidogaeth) To perform the function of a ministry.

Gweinidogawl, *a.* (gweinidawg) Ministrant.

Gweinidoges, *s. f.*—*pl. t.* au (gweinidawg) A woman-servant, a maid-servant.

Gweinidogi, *v. a.* (gweinidawg) To perform the function of a servant; to minister.

Teg ion, os gweinidawg-wyf,
Digwl y gweinidog wyf.

Glorious supreme, if I am a servant, without blame *may I do my duty*. *Gro. Owain.*

Gweinidogiad, *s. m.* (gweinidawg) A ministering.

Gweinif, *s. m.* (gweini) Service, ministration.

Gweinifarch, *s. m.*—*pl.* **gweinifeirch** (gweini—march) A horse in attendance.

Gweinifiad, *s. m.*—*pl.* **gweinifiaid** (gweinif) An administrator.

Por elsor sesawr weinifiad.

Like a chieftain the *bearer* of a shield. *Ll. P. Moch.*

Gweinig, *a.* (gwain) Ministrant; serving.

Gweinigiad, *s. m.* (gweinig) A ministering.

Gweinigiaw, *v. a.* (gweinig) To minister, to serve.

Gweinigiawl, *a.* (gweinig) Ministrant; serving.

Sarhad gwraig gaeth deuddeg ceiniawg; os gweinigiawl fydd, nid ei nag yn rhaw nag yn mreuan, pedair arugaint fydd ei sarhad. sef yw hono gwraig wrth ei nodwydd.

The fine for insult to a bond-woman is twelve pence; should she be *attendant*, neither going to the spade, nor to the mill, her fine for injury shall be twenty-four pence. such a one is a woman at her needle. *Welsh Laws.*

Gweinydd, *s. m.*—*pl. t.* ion (gwain) An attendant, a waiter, a servitor; a servant; an administrator. *Gweinyddion ymadrawdd*, organs of speech.

Gweinyddawg, *a.* (gweinydd) Ministerial.

Gweinyddawl, *a.* (gweinydd) Ministering.

Pedair arugaint yw sarhad gweinyddawl gaeth, nid ei nag yn rhaw nag yn mreuan; sef yw hono gwraig wrth ei nodwydd.

Twenty four-pence is the fine for injury to a female *attendant* slave who goes neither to the spade nor to the mill: such a one is a woman at her needle. *Welsh Laws.*

Gweinyddes, *s. f.*—*pl. t.* au (gweinydd) A female attendant, or server; an administratrix.

Gweinyddfarch, *s. m.*—*pl.* **gweinyddfeirch** (gweinydd—march) A horse that is in use, or serving.

Gweinyddferch, *s. f.*—*pl. t.* ed (gweinydd—merch) A serving-woman, or a maid servant.

Gweinyddiad, *s. m.*—*pl. t.* au (gweinydd) A ministering, serving, or attending upon.

Gweinyddiadawl, *a.* (gweinyddiad) Ministering.

Gweinyddiadu, *v. a.* (gweinyddiad) To minister.

Gweinyddiaeth, *s. m.—pl. t.* au (gweinydd) Ministry

Gweinyddiaw, *v. a.* (gweinydd) To minister.

Gweinyddiawg, *a.* (gweinydd) Ministering.

Gweinyddiawl, *a.* (gweinydd) Ministering.

Gweinyddu, *v. a.* (gweinydd) To minister.

> Addas i bawb ei gweinyddde.
>
> Meet for every one is what serves *him*. *Adage.*
>
> Och' ddydd yn gweinydd gwanwyn.
>
> Ah ' a day *ministering* prison. *Gryff. Gwrfyn.*

Gweirdir, *s. m.—pl. t.* oedd (gwair—tir) Hay-land

Gweirdy, *s. m.—pl. t.* au (gwair—ty) A hay house.

Gweirglawdd, *s. f.—pl.* gweirgloddiau (gwair—clawdd) A hay-field; a meadow.

> Sef yw gweirglawdd, tir difwynant namyn ei wair, a chlawdd yn ei gylch.
>
> A *hay-enclosure* is land from which nothing is got except its hay, with an enclosure round it. *Welsh Laws.*

Gweiriad, *s. m.* (gwair) A becoming hay; a making into hay.

Gweiriaw, *v. a.* (gwair) To become hay; to make into hay; to become, or to wither, into hay, to make hay.

Gweiriawg, *a.* (gwair) Abounding with hay.

Gweiriedig, *a.* (gwair) Laid out into hay.

Gweirlawd, *s. f.—pl.* gweirlodau (gwair—llawd) A meadow.

> Gweirlawd a thân frig ir twyn
> Yw' nghartref, coll ysgref llwyn.
>
> My home's the *meadow* and under the green boughs, the shade of the hazel grove. *D. ab Gwilym.*

Gweiryn, *s. m. dim.* (gwair) A blade of hay.

Gweisgen, *s. f.—pl. t.* au (gwasg) A press.

Gweisgi, *a.* (gwaisg) Alert, brisk, active, lively, gay. *Y' gangen weisgi*, the lively girl; *mae hi yn weisgi ar ei throed*, she is very brisk upon her foot; *cnau gweisgi*, slip-shelled nuts, or that are ready to drop out of the husks.

Gweisgiad, *s. m.* (gweisgi) A rendering alert; a becoming brisk; a slipping out of the husk.

Gweisgïaw, *v. a.* (gweisgi) To render brisk; to slip out of the shell; to become brisk.

Gweisgion, *s. pl. aggr.* (gwaisg) Husks, or shells; the refuse of grain, or fruit, that has been squeezed out.

Gweisgioni, *v. a.* (gweisgion) To husk, to press grain out of the husks; to branch. *Gweisgioni caws*, to crumble the cheese through the hands in preparing it for the vat.

Gweisgionllyd, *a.* (gweisgion) Abounding with refuse or husks.

Gweision, *s. pl. aggr.* (gwas) Youths; servants.

Gweisionain, *s. pl. dim.* (gweision) Tiny youngsters

> Pedwar meib arugain a'm bwyn',
> Eurdorchawg tywysawg cadwyn;
> I wrth Wen gweisionain oeddyn'.
>
> Twenty four sons to me there have been, leading chiefs wearing the golden torque; compared with Gwen they were *tiny stripling*s. *Llywarch Hen.*

Gweithau, *s. pl. aggr.* (gwaith) Times. *adv.* Sometimes, now and then.

Gweithdy, *s. m.—pl. t.* au (gwaith—ty) A workshop, a manufactory.

Gweithfa, *s. f.—pl.* gweithfeydd (gwaith) A factory, a manufactory.

Gweithfuddig, *a.* (gwaith—buddig) Victorious.

> Ior clod gweithfuddig.
>
> Lord of *victorious* fame. *Rys'l Brddes Mhlarpr.*

Gweithgar, *a.* (gwaith) Well-worked: laborious.

Gweithgarwch, *s. m.* (gweithgar) Laboriousness.

Gweithiad, *s. m.—pl. t.* au (gwaith) A working; workmanship; facture, manufacture.

Gweithiau, *s. pl. aggr.* (gwaith) Times, or turns. *adv.* Sometimes, now and then.

Gweithiaw, *v. a.* (gwaith) To work, to labour.

> Ffydd a chariad gwych ara',
> Byth, a dawn, gyda gobaith da,
> Dyna 'r deiliad safadwy,
> Na 'i mwyd nid rhaid gweithio mwy.
> Duw a wnel, o'i hafel hi,
> Dan oddef, yn dwyn iddi'
>
> Faith and love, ever gentle and fair, and grace accompanied with good hope, behold that is a firm structure of goodly form. It is needless *to work* any more. God grant, from its similitude, under suffering, that we be brought into it. *Dr. S. Cent.*

Gweithiawl, *a.* (gwaith) Effective; working.

Gweithiedig, *a.* (gwaith) Being worked, or wrought.

Gweithiedigawl, *a.* (gweithiedig) Operative.

Gweithiedydd, *s. m.—pl. t.* ion (gweithiad) An operator; a manufacturer.

Gweithien, *s. f.* (gwaith) An action, a battle.

> Eilwaith gwelais, gwedy gweithien,
> Aur ysgwyd ar ysgwydd Urien;
> Be ail yno Elgno hen.
>
> A second time I saw, after *conflict*, a golden shield on the shoulder of Urien: he was there like Elgno of ancient time. *Llywarch Hen.*

Gweithiwr, *s. m.—pl.* gweithwyr (gwaith—gwr) A workman, a worker.

> Ciliwch, 'mogelwch, mae gwyliaid weithion;
> Ymaith, weithwyr direidi!
>
> Fall back, beware, there are watchmen at length; avaunt, ye evil *doers'* *W. Middleton.*

Gweithle, *s. m.—pl. t.* oedd (gwaith—lle) A work place; a manufactory.

Gweithon, *s. f.* (gwaith) The present instant. *adv.* At present, now, at this time.

Gweithred, *s. f.—pl. t.* oedd (gwaith) Action, act, deed, fact, work.

> Cas doeth heb weithredoedd da.
>
> Odious is the wise without good *works*. *Adage.*
>
> Oedd gwr gwrawl ei weithred,
> Oedd gwalch balch, bwlch ei galled.
>
> He was a man of manly *deed*, he was a soaring hawk, his loss has caused a gap. *Cynddelw.*
>
> Megis i bo y galon
> Felly bydd y gweithredoedd.
>
> As the heart may be so will be the *actions*! *T. Ll. D. ab Hywel.*

Gweithredadwy, *a.* (gweithred) Operable.

Gweithredai, *s. c.—pl.* gweithredion (gweithred) An operator.

Gweithredator, *ger.* (gweithred) In operating.

Gweithredawl, *a.* (gweithred) Operative.

Gweithrediad, *s. m.—pl. t.* au (gweithred) A working, or acting; agency; operation; transaction.

Gweithrediadawl, *a.* (gweithrediad) Relating to an operation, or manufacture.

Gweithrediadu, *v. a.* (gweithrediad) To operate.

Gweithrediannawl, *a.* (gweithrediant) Tending to operate, operative.

Gweithrediannu, *v. a.* (gweithrediant) To operate.

Gweithrediant, *s. m.* (gweithred) Operation.

Gweithredig, *a.* (gweithred) Operative, efficient.

Gweithreditor, *sup.* (gweithred) To be working.

Gweithredoldeb, *s. m.* (gweithredawl) Operativeness; practicableness.

Gweithredoli, *v. a.* (gweithredawl) To render operative, or efficient.

Gweithredu, *v. a.* (gweithred) To operate, to effect, to act, to make; to transact.

> Y cas———
> Athrodwyr gweithredodd;
> O bai chwi'n un, bychan oedd.
>
> The odious backbiters *effected* it, if ye were united, it were of no great moment. *Rhos. Iorwerth.*

Gweithredwr, *s. m.—pl.* gweithredwyr (gweithred—gwr) A worker, an operator.

Gweithredwraig, *s. f.—pl.* gweithredwreigedd (gweithred—gwraig) A working-woman.

Gweithredydd, *s. m.—pl. t.* ion (gweithred) An efficient cause; an operator.

Gweithredyddes, *s. f.—pl. t.* au (gweithredydd) A work-woman.

Gwel, *s. m.* (gwe—el) The sight, or vision.

Gwelad, *s. m.* (gwel) A seeing, or beholding.

Gweladur, *s. m.—pl. t.* on (gwelad) A beholder.

Gweladwy, *a.* (gwelad) That may be seen, visible.

Gwelameg, *s. f.* (gwel—ameg) A haw, an excrescence in the eye, so called. It is also named, *goresgwrn*, and *sychilen*.

Gwelator, *ger.* (gwelad) In seeking or looking.

Gwelator arwyddion.

In beholding signs. *Taliesin.*

Gwelawd, *s. m.* (gwel) The act of looking.

Gwelawg, *a.* (gwel) Having vision, or sight.

Gwelchyn, *s. m. dim.* (gwalch) A laneret; a little pert fellow. *Y gwelchyn!* the pert sprig.

Gweled, *s. m.* (gwel) Sight, vision, or seeing.

Gweled, clywed, a chelu.

Seeing, hearing, and concealing. *Barddas.*

Gweled, *v. a.* (gwel) To see, to behold, to look upon. *Nis gweli moni*, thou wilt not see her: *ni welir eto pa beth a ddaw*, it will not yet be seen what will come: *pan welo yn dda*, when he sees good: *os na weli mono*, if thou shalt not see him: *gwel-y-chwi*, *gwelw-chwi*, *gwelwch* and *gwelwch chwi*, behold you: *Wela*, behold.

Gwel, a chêl, a chlyw.

See, and conceal, and hear. *Barddas.*

Gwelch Cymmru yn cym'ryd arfau,
Yn Lloegr yn llosgi ei thyrau,
A'i gwelai, eiliau yn olau;
A'i gweles gwelynt ryfeddau.

The heroes of Wales taking up arms, in Lloegria burning her towers, whoever *should see it*, with buildings in a blaze: whoever *has seen it, they saw* wonders. *D. Llenfras.*

Gwelediad, *s. m.—pl. t.* au (gweled) A seeing, or descrying; perception, vision, sight.

Hydref oes hyd ar fy lad
A lwyda fy ngwelediad.

The autumn of life coming over my visage dims my *sight*. *Ll. ab H. ab I. ab Gronwy.*

Gwelediannawl, *a.* (gwelediant) Perceptive.

Gwelediannu, *v. a.* (gwelediant) To endue with vision or sight.

Gwelediant, *s. m.* (gweled) Vision, perception.

Gweledig, *a.* (gweled) Visible, being seen.

Gweledigaeth, *s. f.—pl. t.* au (gweledig) A vision, apparition, or appearance. *Gweledigaeth nos*, a vision of the night.

Gweledigawl, *a.* (gweledig) Tending to be visible.

Gweledwr, *s. m.—pl.* gweledwyr (gweled—gwr) A seer, a beholder, a spectator.

Gweledydd, *s. m.—pl. t.* ion (gweled) Spectator.

Gwelgin, *s. m.* (gwalc) A tong of a buckle.

Gwelgin torch twrch trwyd,
Cyrchesid yn fou
Cyn noi geinion.

The *tong* of the ring of the burrowing pig, it was brought, as a stem, before his jewels. *Taliesin.*

Gweli, *s. m.—pl. t.* au (gwal) That is laid open; a wound; an exposure; abusive language; contumely. *Gweli tafawd*, the wound of the tongue, or scandal, also the fine for slander.

Gware gweli ir.

The play of a green *wound*. *Adage.*

Ni thelir gweli tafawd namyn i arglwydd.

Fine for slander shall not be paid but to a lord. *Adage.*

Gweliad, *s. m.* (gweli) A laying open, or exposing; a wounding.

Gweliaw, *v. a.* (gweli) To lay open, to wound.

Gweliawg, *a.* (gweli) Having gashes; wounded.

Gwelidydd, *s. m.—pl. t.* ion (gweled) Spectator.

Gweling, *s. m.* (gwal) A clear space, a lawn.

A dan forddwyd haelion,
Cyfred cerdd wyllion
Ar weling dirion.

Under the thigh of the generous ones, in equal pace the dun ones walk, on a pleasant *lawn*. *Taliesin.*

Gwelitor, *sup.* (gweled) To be seeing.

Gweliüs, *a.* (gweli) Full of gashes, or wounds.

Gweliüs nid diddolur.

The *wounded* is not void of pain. *Adage.*

Gweliïwr, *s. m.—pl.* gweliïwyr (gweli—gwr) A wounder.

Gwelw, *s. m.* (gwel) A pale hue. *a.* Pale.

Marchogion meirch gwelwon gwelch.

The riders of the *pale* horses of heroes. *Cynddelw.*

Neud amser gauaf gwelwaf gweilgi!

In winter time is not the ocean *most pale?* *Bleddyn Fardd.*

Gwelwad, *s. m.* (gwelw) A growing pale.

Gwelwder, *s. m.* (gwelw) Paleness, or faintness.

Gwelwddu, *s. m.* (gwelw—du) Pale black. *a.* Of a light black.

Gwelwedd, *s. m.* (gwelw) Paleness, or faintness.

Gwelwgaen, *s. f.* (gwelw—caen) A pale surface.

Oedd boen blaen gwelwgaen gweilging saffir;
Diwair oedd, a doeth, deddf-goeth gywir.

She was fair as the top of the *pale surface* of the sapphire wave, she was chaste, and wise, of pure conduct, and sincere. *Gr. ab M. ab Dafydd.*

Gwelwgan, *s. m.* (gwelw—can) Pale white. *a.* Of a pale white appearance.

Gwelwgan gweilgi, heli hallt.

Of a pale white the torrent, salt the sea. *Llywarch Hen.*

Gwelwgoch, *s. m.* (gwelw—coch) A pale red. *a.* Of a pale red colour.

Gwelwi, *v. n.* (gwelw) To grow pale, or wan.

Gwelwlas, *s. m.* (gwelw—glas) A pale blue. *a.* Of a pale blue appearance.

Gwelwlym, *a.* (gwelw—llym) Of a pale sharpness of appearance.

Gwelwr, *s. m.—pl.* gwelwyr (gwel—gwr) A seer.

Gwely, *s. m.—pl. t.* au (gwal) A bed, or couch; also a family; or tribe; a family district; an inheritance; also a plot, or bed, in a garden.—*Gwely pren*, a bedstead; *gwely plu*, a feather-bed; *gwely casnach*, or *gwely casnod*, a flock-bed; *gwely gwellt*, a straw-bed:—*Gwely wyrion Cynan*, the heritage of the grandchildren of Cynan, a name given to *Eifionydd*, in Carnarvonshire: *Gwely cenedl*, a family heritage.

Nid gwely heb wraig.

It is no *bed* without a wife. *Adage.*

Hawdd yf a wŷl ei wely.

He will freely drink who sees his *bed*. *Adage.*

Gwelyaw, *v. a.* (gwely) To bed, to put in bed.

Gwelyawd, *s. m.* (gwely) A bedding; a lying in.

Gwelyawg, *a.* (gwely) Having a bed; bedded; belonging to a family; hereditary.—*Tir gwelyawg*, hereditary land: *cenedl welyawg*, a family having a heritage.

Gwelyd, *s. m.—pl. t.* on (gwal) An opening, a wound or gash.

Ni thraidd pysgod yn ebyr.
Gelwid gwelyd o waed gwyr.

The fishes will not make their way through in the mouths of rivers; there would be crying out a *wound* by the blood of men. *Llywarch Hen.*

Edewid ei ron, gan goflon galar,
A gwaed rudd y' ngwelyddon.

His shaft was left, with memorials of woe, with crimson flood in wounds. *Cynddelw, m. Cadwallon.*

Gwelydd, *s. m.—pl. t.* on (gwal) A place of repose; a bed; a stock of a family.

Anfon Ifor i fab, ac Ynyr i nai, a orug Alan, i Ynys Prydain, i geisiaw cynnal o waed, ac o wir ddylyed, rhag myned gwelyddion ar y Prydeiniaid.

Alan sent Ivor his son, and Ynyr his nephew, to the isle of Britain, to endeavour to maintain it under the blood and true title, lest that the Britons should be under rulers. *Gr. ab Arthur.*

Gwelyddain, *a.* (gwelydd) Having a place of rest.

Gwelyddaint, *s. m.* (gwelyddain) A state of rest.

Gwelyddawg, *a.* (gwelydd) Having place of rest.

Gwelyddu, *v. a.* (gwelydd) To make a place of repose, to take repose.

Cwdd a nos rhag dydd
Pan ddaw, nas gwelydd?

Where flies the night from the day, when he comes, that *he does not rest?* *Taliesin.*

Gwelyddyn, *s. m. dim.* (gwelydd) A small place of repose; the narrow house, the grave.

Gwelyddyn teyrn, tud Cynan a'i cedw;
A'i cedwis bob calan!

The *narrow house* of the prince, it is the ground of Cynan that keeps him, that kept him every festive day!
Ll. P. Moch, m. M. ab Cynan.

Gwelyf, *s. m.—pl. t.* au (gwely) A couch.

Gwelyfan, *s. f.* (gwely—man) A bed place; a bedchamber; a lodging.

Gwelyfawd, *s. m.* (gwelyf) A lying in, the time of lying in. *Amser gwelyfawd*, the month of lying in.

Gwelyfiad, *s. m.* (gwelyf) A putting in bed.

Gwelyfodi, *v. a.* (gwelyfawd) To lie in, to be in childbed.

Gwelyfu, *v. a.* (gwelyf) To bed, or to put to bed.

Gwelyg, *s. m.—pl. t.* au (gwal) A wine press.

Gwelygordd, *s. m.—pl. t.* au (gwely—cordd) That surrounds the bed; the tribe-stock, or the train of a heritage; offspring, lineage, kindred, race, or tribe.—*Gwelygordd o gydgeraint*, a race of correlatives.

A bed un o'r welygordd, efe, a'i dad, a'i hendad, a'i orhendad, y mae o'r wlad.

If one is of a *tribe*, himself, or his father, or his grandfather, or his great grandfather, he is of the country. *Welsh Laws.*

Os gofyn dyn dir, o ach ac edryd, ni ddylyir ei warandaw, oni dyngo henuriaid gwlad ei hanfod o'r welygordd a gynnalio y tir.

If a person should claim land under stock and kindred, he ought not to be heard, until the elders of the country shall swear his being descended from the *tribe-stock* that holds the land.
Welsh Laws.

Gwelyodi, *v. a.* (gwelyawd) To lie in; to be in childbed.

Gwell, *s. m.* (gw—ell) The better. *a.* Better, good in a greater degree. *A wyd ti yn well?* Art thou better? *yn well*, in a better manner; —*gwell nag aur*, great wild valerian.

Nid gwell dim no digon.

Nothing is *better* than enough. *Adage.*

Dyddaw drwg, hanfyddir gwell

Evil will come, *better* will be expected. *Adage.*

Gwell cariad y ci no'i gas.

A dog's affection is *preferable* to his hate. *Adage.*

Gnawd gwraig gwell genddi a fo gwaeth iddi.

Preferable generally with a woman what is the worse for her.
Adage.

Gwella, *v. a.* (gwell) To better, to mend, to improve.

Gwellâad, *s. m.* (gwella) A bettering, a mending; amendment, improvement.

Gwellâawl, *a.* (gwella) Tending to get better.

Gwelladwy, *a.* (gwell) That may be bettered.

Gwellaif, *s. m.—pl.* gwelleifiau (gwe—llaif) A pair of shears, or scissors.

A'r gwellaif y lladd y weirglodd.

With the *shears* he mowed the meadow. *Adage.*

Gwellâu, *v. a.* (gwella) To better, to make better, to meliorate, to become better.

Nid gwaradwydd gwellâu.

It is no disgrace to *improve*. *Adage.*

Tri chynnud lles celfyddyd: ei hoffi gan y byd; ei rhinwedd yn gwellau y byd; a'i champ yn cynnal ei hun.

The three primary signs of the benefit of an art: its reception by the world, its virtue in *improving* the world, and its sufficiency in maintaining itself. *Barddas.*

Gwelleifiad, *s. m.* (gwellaif) A cutting with shears, or scissors, a shearing.

Gwelleifiaw, *v. a.* (gwellaif) To cut with shears.

Gwelleifiedydd, *s. m.—pl. t.* ion (gwelleifiad) One who uses the shears, or scissors.

Gwelleifiwr, *s. m.—pl.* gwelleifwyr (gwellaif—gwr) A shearer, or one who uses a scissors.

Gwelleifyn, *s. m. dim.* (gwellaif) A pair of scissors.

Gwelliad, *s. m.* (gwell) A bettering, a mending.

Gwelliannawl, *a.* (gwelliant) Convalescent.

Gwelliannu, *v. a.* (gwelliant) To convalesce.

Gwelliant, *s. m.* (gwell) Amendment, improvement; convalescence.

Gwellig, *a.* (gwell) Improving, or mending.

Ffrwyth wellig, well-faeth ffrwyth ffrawdd-wyn.

The *bettering* fruit, supremely nourishing the eloquent of lively passion. *Cynddelw.*

Gwellin, *a.* (gwell) Tending to improve or mend.

Gwellineb, *s. m.* (gwellin) Improvement; culture, effect of melioration.

Gwelling, *s. m.—pl. t.* au (gwell) A blessing.

Talu ebediw a gwelling.

To pay heriot and *benediction*. *Welsh Laws.*

Ail welygordd fawr, feirdd welling, a'm pearch
Ar lygr feirch, ar lygr fing.
Bleiddion torf trefyng dierchlang,
Blaenaid, cantaid Cadelling.

The second great family, the *blessing* of bards, honours me with splendid steeds, on a fair course, wolves of the throng, of unrestrained tumult; foremost ones, of Cadellian race beloved.
Cynddelw.

Gwellt, *s. m. aggr.* (gw—ellt) Grass; straw, sward. *Gwellt y ddaear*, the grass of the field; *gwellt glas*, or *glaswellt*, green grass, *yd ar ei wellt*, corn upon its straw: *Ych gwellt*, and *ych tyw-arch*, or *gwelltawr*, and *rhychawr*, the sward ox, and furrow ox, terms used in ploughing for the beasts in both sides of the team:—*Gwellt y cwn*, or *llygad y ci*, couch-grass, *gwellt y gamlas*, grass wrack.—*Llosgi gwellt gwely*, the burning of the bed-straw of a dead person.

Bid fyw march a gnith gwellt Mai.

Let the steed live that nibbles the *grass* of May. *Adage.*

Gwelltaidd, *a.* (gwellt) Like grass, like straw.

Gwelltawg, *a.* (gwellt) Abounding with grass, or straw; grassy, swardy.

Gwelltawr, *s. m.* (gwellt) That is on the grass. *Gwelltawr a rhychawr*, the one on the sward and the one in the furrow, terms in ploughing for the two oxen abreast.

Gwelltiad, *s. m.* (gwellt) A turning to straw.

Gwelltiaw, *v. a.* (gwellt) To turn to straw; to turn off the straw, or to give the last thrash to the corn under the flail.

Gwelltoriad, *s. m.* (gwelltawr) A covering with grass; a covering with straw.

Gwelltoriaw, *v. a.* (gwelltawr) To cover with grass; to cover with straw.

Gwelltyn, *s. m.* (gwellt) A blade of grass; a straw.

Oni 'mddyddan ychwaneg,
Tor y gwelltyn a'm dyn deg.

If she discourses no more, break the *straw* with my fair one.
S. ab R. ab Morys, i latai.

Gwellwell, *a.* (gwell *repeated*) Better and better. *adv.* In a better and better manner.

Gwellwell hyd farf, gwaethwaeth hyd farw.

Better and better until poberty, worse and worse until death.
Adage.

Gwellyn, *s. m.—pl. t.* ion (gwell) What is better.
Gwellyniad, *s. m.* (gwellyn) An improving.
Gwellyniadwy, *a.* (gwellyniad) Improvable.
Gwellyniaw, *v. a.* (gwellyn) To improve.
Gwellyniawg, *a.* (gwellyn) Having a tendency to improvement; cultured.

Gwellyniawg deyrn, gedyrn gospi,
Gwallaw ym anaw enw dy foli.

A prince *bounteous of blessings*, punishing the mighty ones, pour out to my muse a theme to praise thee.
Ll. P. Moch, i D. ab Owain.

Gwellynrwydd, *s. m.* (gwellyn) Improvedness.
Gwemp, *a.* (*f. of* gwymp) Fair, or splendid.
Gwempl, *s. f.—pl. t.* au (gwemp) A wimple.
Gwen, *s. f.—pl. t.* au (gwe—en) A state of bliss or extasy; a smile.
Gwen, *s.* (*f. of* gwyn) A fair one, a beauty.

Nid hawdd cadw cymmen wen wych
Rhag lleidr yn rhy gall edrych.

It is not easy to keep the pert and gay *nymph* against a thief prying with excess of cunning.
D. ab Gwilym.

Gwen, *a.* (*f. of* gwyn) White; fair; beautiful. *Y ddyn wen*, the fair maid.

Angen y gybydedd wen yw bon degsill, a hyd y pennill o bedwar i un ban ar bymtheg.

The essential of the *fair* co-extension is a verse of ten syllables, and the length of the stanza from four to sixteen verses.
Barddas.

Gwenan, *s. f.* (gwen) A blister under the skin.
Gwenawg, *a.* (gwen) Having a smile, smiling.
Gwenawl, *a.* (gwen) Smiling, pleasing; bland.
Gwenci, *s. f.—pl. t.* od (gwanc) A stoat.
Gwendal, *a.* (gwen—tal) Having a white forehead; fair-fronted.

Teg yw dy dwf——
O bai deg Indeg wendal.

Fair is thy growth, if *white-fronted* Indeg should be deemed fair.
D. ab Gwilym.

Gwendid, *s. m.* (gwan) Weakness, or frailty.
Gwendon, *s. f.* (gwen—ton) A white skin. *a.* Of a white, or fair skin: the herb bedstraw.
Gwenddydd, *s. f.* (gwen—dydd) The morning star.
Gwener, *s. f.* (gwen) That confers happiness; Venus, *Seren Wener*, the morning star; *Dydd Gwener*, Friday; *Gwallt Gwener*, maidenhair.

Y'nghylch seren y Gwener
Y bydd swrn bob ddwy o ser.

Around the star *Venus* there be constellations of stars in pairs.
L. G. Cothi.

Gwenerawl, *a.* (gwener) Tending to diffuse happiness; relating to Venus; belonging to Friday.

Cymmry gwenerawl hyd frawd gorfydd.

The *venerable* Cymbrians until doomsday shall be supreme.
Taliesin.

Donlawg didrist Grist, groes rinweddawl,
Didlawd yn gwarawd dydd gwenerawl.

The gracious and placid Christ, whose efficacious cross was rich, in salvation on the day *of Venus.*
Gwalchmai.

Gwenfa, *s. f.* (gwen) A curb of a bridle.

Y meirch——
Ffrwynau i'w genau a gad a gwenfa,
Gydag anfodd glymiad.

The horses, bridles in their mouths were put, and a *curb* with unpleasant bandage.
W. Middleton.

Gwenfro, *s. f.—pl. t.* ydd (gwen—bro) The region of bliss.
Gwengaen, *s. f.* (gwen—caen) A white surface. *a.* Of a white surface.
Gwengan, *a.* (gwen—can) Of a bright white.
Gwenglaer, *a.* (gwen—claer) White and clear.
Gwengraith, *s. f.* (gwen—craith) Sanicle.
Gwenhaul, *s. f.* (gwen—haul) The fair sun.
Gwenhudiw, *s. m.* (gwen—hudiw) That allures with a smile; the name of a celebrated dwarf, of a character similar to Esop.

All yw Rhys, yn ael y rhiw,
Wan hudawl, i wenhudiw.

Like Gwenhudiw, is Rhys, the feeble deceiver, on the brow of the hill.
T. Prys.

Gwenhwys, *s. pl. aggr.* (gwent) Men of Gwent.
Gwenhwysaidd, *a.* (gwenhwys) After the manner of the Gwentians.
Gwenhwysawl, *a.* (gwenhwys) Relating to the Gwentians or people of Gwent.
Gwenhwyseg, *s. f.* (gwenhwys) The language of Gwent.

Mawr ddidlawd fy ngwawd y'Ngwenhwyseg.

Greatly eloquent is my muse in the *Gwentian tongue.*
Cynddelw.

Gwenhwyson, *s. pl. aggr.* (gwenhwys) The people of Gwent, or Gwentians.

Caradawg o Went a'i Wenhwysion.

Caradoc of Gwent with his *Gwentians.*

Gweniaith, *s. f.* (gwen—iaith) Bland, or soothing language; flattery.

Ni charodd——
Na Merddin weniaith-fin iach,
Na Thaliesin ei thlysach.

Nor Merddin, with *fair and flattering tongue*, nor Taliesin loved not her superior.
D. ab Gwilym, i Forfudd.

Gwenieithgar, *a.* (gweniaith) Adulatory.
Gwenieithiad, *s. m.* (gweniaith) A flattering.
Gwenieithiaw, *v. a.* (gweniaith) To use bland words; to flatter, to sooth with fair words.
Gwenieithiawl, *a.* (gweniaith) Flattering.
Gwenieithus, *a.* (gweniaith) Apt to flatter.

Nid gwenieithus ond merch.

Woman is the most *apt to flatter.*
Adage.

Gwenieithwr, *s. m.—pl.* gwenieithwyr (gweniaith—gwr) A flatterer.
Gwenith, *s. m.—pl. t.* oedd (gwen—ith) Wheat *Gwenith ysgyfarnog*, common quaking grass; *gwenith y brch, gwenith yr hydd*, buckwheat; *gwenith y gog, gwenith y ddaiar*, and *llysiau y bronau*, pilewort; *gwenith y brain*, English stonecrop.
Gwenithawg, *a.* (gwenith) Having wheat.
Gwenithdir, *s. m.* (gwenith—tir) Wheat-land.
Gwenithen, *s. f. dim.* (gwenith) Grain of wheat.
Gwenithfaen, *s. m.* (gwenith—maen) Granite.
Gwenithwellt, *s. m.* (gwenith—gwellt) Wheat-straw. *Gwenithwellt ymdaen*, creeping wheat grass.
Gwenithyd, *s. m.* (gwenith—yd) Wheat corn.
Gweno, *s. f.* (gwen) The evening star; also a woman's name, the diminutive of *Gwen.*
Gwennol, *s. f.—pl. t.* iaid (gwen—dol) A swallow, a martin. *Gwennol y dwfr*, the water swallow, or swift; *gwennol y mor*, or *ysgraean*, the sea-swallow, or scraye; *gwennol y glenydd*, the sand martin:—*Gwennol y gwëydd*, a weaver's shuttle.

Rhed i eigion afonydd,
'Rhyd maenol, mal gwennol gwëydd.

Run to the midst of rivers, along the vale, like a weaver's *shuttle.*
T. Prys, i'r gleisiaid.

Gwenonwy, *s. m.* (gwen) Lily of the valley.

Gwenrod, *s. f.* (gwen—rhod) Circle of felicity.

> Gwledig gwlad [illegible],
> Gorucbel wenrod,
> Gwrda, gwna gymmod
> Rhyngod a mi!
>
> Sovereign of the region of [illegible], the exalted *circle of felicity*, thou benign Being, make a reconciliation between thee and me. *Meilyr.*

Gwent, *s. f.—pl. t.* oedd (gwen) A fair, or open region, a champaign. It is a name now confined to nearly all Monmouthshire, but which anciently comprehended also parts of the counties of Gloucester and Hereford, being the district of which *Caer went*, or the *Venta silurum* of the Romans, was the capital.

Gwentas, *s. f.—pl. t.* au (gwent) A high shoe, a baskin.

> Yr oedd dwy wentas o gordwal du am ei draed, a gwaegau aur ar fyngau y traed yn eu cau.
>
> There were two *shoes* of black leather on his feet, and golden clasps on the insteps to fasten them. *H. Mabinogi—Mabinogion.*

Gwenu, *v. a.* (gwen) To smile, to look pleasantly.

Gwenwelw, *a.* (*f. of* gwynwelw) Of a white paleness, of wan complexion.

Gwenwialen, *s. f.* (gwen—gwialen) Common maple tree; also called *gwiniolen*, and *gwiniolwydd*.

Gwenwisg, *s. f.—pl. t.* oedd (gwen—gwisg) A surplice.

Gwenwyn, *s. m.* (gwen—gwyn) Venom, poison.

Gwenwynad, *s. m.* (gwenwyn) A poisoning.

Gwenwynaw, *v. a.* (gwenwyn) To poison; to fret.

Gwenwynawl, *a.* (gwenwyn) Poisonous; fretful.

Gwenwynder, *s. m.* (gwenwyn) Poisonousness.

Gwenwyndra, *s. m.* (gwenwyn) Poisonousness.

Gwenwynig, *a.* (gwenwyn) Poisonous, fretting.

Gwenwynigrwydd, *s. m.* (gwenwynig) Poisonousness.

Gwenwynllyd, *a.* (gwenwyn) Poisonous, or venomous; inflamed; fretful, vexatious.

Gwenwynllydrwydd, *s. m.* (gwenwynllyd) Venomousness, inflamedness.

Gwenwynwr, *s. m.—pl.* gwenwynwyr (gwenwyn—gwr) One who poisons; one who frets.

Gwenyd, *s. m.* (gwen) Felicity, bliss, happiness.

Gwenydfa, *s. f.* (gwenyd) The place of felicity, the seat of bliss; paradise.

> Coronawg faban yn y cynta'
> A gant ganon yn y gwenydfa,
> Ag awen gogoniant o'r uchelfa,
> Gan darddu bydoedd byw Adda.
>
> The crowned infant, in the beginning, sang a hymn of principles in the *region of felicity*, with the muse of glory from the highest, at which worlds burst into existence, and Adam lived. *H. Nanmor.*

Gwenydiad, *s. m.* (gwenyd) A felicitation.

Gwenydu, *v. a.* (gwenyd) To render blissful.

Gwenydd, *s. m.* (gwen) That makes happy; that diverts or amuses.

Gwenyddawl, *a.* (gwenydd) Felicitous; amusing.

Gwenyddiad, *s. m.* (gwenydd) A yielding bliss.

Gwenyddu, *v. a.* (gwenydd) To yield happiness.

Gwenyn, *s. pl. aggr.* (gwen) Bees, *Gwenyn y meirch*, gad bees, wasps.

> Bonedd gwenyn o baradwys pan yw; ac o achaws pechawd dyn y daethynt oddyno ac y dodes Duw rad arnynt.
>
> The origin of the *bees* is from paradise, and on account of the sin of man did they come from thence; and God gave his blessing upon them. *Welsh Laws.*

Gwenynawg, *a.* (gwenyn) Having bees. *s. m.* An alveary: bastard baulm; also called *llysiau y gwenyn*.

Gwenyndro, *s. m.—pl. t.* ion (gwenyn—tro) The turn, or circular range of bees.

Gwenynddail, *s. pl. aggr.* (gwenyn—dail) Baulm. also called *gwenynllys*.

Gwenynen, *s. f. dim.* (gwenyn) A bee, one bee, *Gwenynen ormes*, a drone.

> Er heddwch nag er rhyfel
> Gwenynen farw ni chasgl fel.
>
> For peace, or for war, a dead *bee* will not collect honey. *Adage.*

Gwenynlle, *s. m.* (gwenyn—lle) A place for bees.

Gwenynllestr, *s. m.—pl. t.* i (gwenyn—llestr) A bee-hive. It is also called *Cwch gwenyn*.

Gwengyn, *s. m. dim. pl.— t.* od (gwang) A sain.

Gwep, *s. m.—pl. t.* au (gweb) A visage, a phiz. *Gwneud gwep*, to make a face.

> Golwg ffrom, darfo ei siomi,
> A gwep cath a gipia ci.
>
> Pert in his look, may he be deceived, with his *grinning face* of a cat snarled by a dog. *T. Prys.*

Gwepa, *s. m.* (gwep) The visage, the phiz.

Gwepia, *s. m.* (gwep) The visage, the front.

> Pwy 'n ei fyw [illegible]
> Prydydd y' ngwepia [illegible]?
>
> Who in his life [illegible] heaven, like a poet in the *top of a building*? *Gut. Owain.*

Gwepiaw, *v. a.* (gwep) To make a wry face; to grin; to mock.

Gwepiwr, *s. m.* gwepwyr (gwep—gwr) A grinner; a mocker.

Gwer, *s. m.* (gwe—er) That is thrown to the surface; that shades; a shade. *Dyfed.* Tallow; suet. *Gwer manllwyn*, mutton suet.

Gwera, *v. a.* (gwer) To collect tallow, or suet.

Gweraidd, *a.* (gwer) Of the nature of tallow.

Gwerawg, *a.* (gwer) Abounding with tallow, or suet. *Y werawg, bara càn y defaid, men y don, llysiau y defaid, llyriad y mor*, sea plantain.

Gwerawl, *a.* (gwer) Tending to be tallowy.

Gwerchyr, *s. m.—pl. t.* iau (gwarch) A cover.

Gwerchyriad, *s. m.* (gwerchyr) A covering over.

Gwerchyriaw, *v. a.* (gwerchyr) To cover over.

> Gwyddfa a'i gwerchyr, gorchudd gwythlawn!
>
> The wild earth covers her, a wrathful hiding! *Cynddelw.*

Gwerdd, *a.* (*f. of* gwyrdd) Green, verdant.

Gwerdden, *s. f.—pl. t.* i (gwerdd) An emerald.

Gwerddig, *s. f.* (gwerdd) Chickweed, winter green

Gwerddon, *s. f.—pl. t.* au (gwerdd) A green spot, a green; a mead.

> Ehediaid———
> Rhiou, prydyddion dail
> Mwyn' cerdd yn min gwerddon.
>
> The winged ones, lords and minstrels of the leaves, most soothing in their song on the edge of the *green*. *D. ab Gwilym.*

> Treigla 'i glyn, tra gloew a glas,
> Ac irllif ei dwfr gloywlas;
> Coed bron, pob gwerddon o gylch,
> Er ymgynnull pawb i'r amgylch.
>
> Wander over its vale, most clear and verdant, and the fresh stream of its pellucid water; the wood of the hill; every green around, to allure every one to the assembly. *Meurig Dafydd.*

> Pencerdd adar y werddon,
> Ar on ewydd 'n yr ynys hon.
>
> Chief of song of the birds of the *green glade*, particularly in this isle. *W. Gr. ab Ieuan.*

Gwerddonell, *s. f.* (gwerddon) English clary.

Gwerddonig, *a.* (gwerddon) Greenish, verdant.

Gwerddyr, *s. f.* (gwardd) The sharebone. It is also called, *cylch yr arfed*.

Gweren, *s. f.—pl. t.* i. (gwer) A cake of tallow; also the cawl of the entrails. *Y weren fol, y weren fawr*, the cawl of the stomach.

Gwerganwyll, *s. f.—pl. t.* au (gwer—canwyll) A tallow candle.

Gwerganwyllydd, *s. m.—pl. t.* ion (gwerganwyll) A tallow-chandler.

Gweri, *v. a.* (gwer) To seek the shade. *Mae y da yn gweri*, the cattle are seeking the shade; the same as cysgota.

Gwerin, *s. f. pl. aggr.* (gwar) A civil society, the common people, the vulgar, the multitude; a body of men. *Gwerin y wyddbwyll*, the tablemen at chess.

Pan fo cwyn cynllwyn bro gwerthefin,
A galar gwaegar y gilbant werin,
Gwynfyd y gennau yn gyfrwys gyfrin
A lefair tri gair or hen-iaith gynsefin.

When there shall be a complaint of besetting the *supreme* country, and the grief of the dispersion of gilbant *multitude*, blessed the lips, which, fluently and privately, shall speak three words of the old primitive language. *Myrddin.*

Gwerin, *a.* (gwer) Docile; civil, common, vulgar.

Y penillion cynnrych, a ddangoswyd, a gymmerais, lawer iawn o honynt, o ben gwlad gwerin.

The specimen verses, which have been brought forward, I have taken, a great many of them, from the mouth of the *vulgar* country. *E. Dafydd.*

Gwerinad, *s. m.* (gwerin) A civilizing; a becoming prevalent, or common.

Gwerinaw, *v. a.* (gwerin) To render tame; to render prevalent, or common; to render vulgar; to become common; to civilise.

Nid yw hawdd gwerinaw anwar.

It is not easy *to civilize* the ungentle. *Adage.*

Eithin ni fu fad
Er hyny gwerinad.

The furze did not do well, nevertheless *let it overspread.* *Taliesin.*

Gwerinawg, *a.* (gwerin) Prevalent, vulgar. *Iaith werinawg*, the common tongue.

Gwerinawl, *a.* (gwerin) Civil; plebian, or rustic.

Argiwydd nef a llawr, gwawr gwerinawl,
Arddelwaf o'th nawdd rhag tawdd tanawl.

Lord of heaven and earth, the *universal* light, I beseech thy protection against the fiery dissolution. *Gwalchmai.*

Gwerindawd, *s. m.* (gwerin) Civilization.

Gwerindota, *v. a.* (gwerindawd) To practise civility, or sociality.

Gweriniad, *s. m.* (gwerin) A civilizing.

Gweriniaeth, *s. f.—pl. t.* au (gwerin) Democracy.

Gweriniaethawl, *a.* (gweriniaeth) Democratical.

Gwerinos, *s. pl. aggr.* (gwerin) The common people, the multitude; a rabble, a mob. *Tewdwr o'r gwerinos*, a great gathering of the mob; *Eilun y gwerinos*, the idol of the multitude.

Gwerinwladwriaeth, *s. f.* (gwerin—gwladwriaeth) A republican government.

Gwerlas, *s. f.* (gwer—glas) A green meadow.

Gwerlid, *s. m.* (gwer—llid) A flowing wrath.

Gwerlin, *s. m.* (gwer—llin) That is of pure, or noble race.

Gwerlin a'i lin o lan deithi.

A *nobleman* with his descent of unblemished qualities. *Dan. Ll. Mew.*

Gwern, *s. f.—pl. t.* ydd (gwer) That is inundated; a swamp, a bog, a meadow; also alder trees; which are also called *coed gwern*, or the swamp trees; also an epithet for hell.

Gwern blaen blin,
A wnant gyssefin—
Aerfa.

The alders, of restless tops, will make a general slaughter. *Taliesin.*

A'r tir ysial, dywal-wern—
A dreiddia.

And the wild land, a terrible *swamp*, he will pass through. *Prydydd Bychan.*

Gwernawg, *a.* (gwern) Abounding with alders.

Gwernen, *s. f.—pl. t.* i (gwern) An alder tree; also a mast of a ship.

Dwg y wernen deg arnad;
Dyro dy lu i dir dy wlad.

Bear the fair *mast* over thee; give thy multitude to the land of thy country. *H. Dafi.*

Gwernin, *a.* (gwern) Of a swampy nature; of, or relating to, alder.

Sengi waenawr,
Yn nydd cadwynawr,
Y'nghlawdd gwernin.

Thou wilt tread the ranks, in the day of binding in chains, in the trench *of the plain.* *Aneurin.*

Gwernlle, *s. m.* (gwern—lle) An alder grove.

Gwers, *s. f.—pl. t.* i (gwer) A space; a while; a lesson; a verse. *Dysgu gwers*, to learn a lesson; *yn mhen gwers*, in a while; *arosais wers fawr*, I stayed a great while. *adv.* For a while.

Wylaf wers, tawaf wedy.

I will weep a *while*, I will then be silent. *Llywarch Hen.*

Mi af——
I dreiglo wers draw i glud.

I will go to range *for a while* yonder to the assembly. *L. G. Cothi.*

Gwersa, *v. a.* (gwers) To spend time idly; to tattle, to gossip.

Gwersig, *s. f. dim.* (gwers) A short lesson; a versicle.

Gwersu, *v. a.* (gwers) To lecture; to repeat lessons; to recite verses.

Gwersyll, *s. m.—pl. t.* oedd (gwer—syll) A camp, an encampment.

Gwersyllawg, *a.* (gwersyll) Having a camp.

Gwersylledig, *a.* (gwersyll) Encamped; tented.

Gwersyllfa, *s. f.—pl. t.* oedd (gwersyll) The site or place, of encamping, an encampment.

Gwersylliad, *s. m.* (gwersyll) An encamping, a making a camp; a pitching of tents.

Gwersyllig, *s. m. dim.* (gwersyll) A small encampment.

Gwersyllt, *s. m.—pl. t.* au (gwersyll) A camp.

Gwersylltiad, *s. m.* (gwersyllt) An encamping.

Gwersylltu, *v. a.* (gwersyllt) To encamp.

Gwersyllu, *v. a.* (gwersyll) To encamp.

Gwersyllwr, *s. m.—pl.* gwersyllwyr (gwersyll—gwr) One who encamps.

Gwersyllydd, *s. m.—pl. t.* ion (gwersyll) One who encamps; or forms a camp.

Gwerth, *s. m.* (gwêr) Value, worth, price; sale. *Ar werth*, on sale; *pa faint yw gwerth hwn?* How much is the price of this? *Gwerth tafawd*, the worth of the tongue, a fine paid for false judgement, or testimony.

Ni ddiengai namyn tri——
A minnau o'm gwaedffrau gwerth fy ngwenwawd.

None could escape save three, besides me, who was saved from the spilling of my blood through the *merit* of my holy muse. *Aneurin.*

Dywed air cywair yn ol cawad awyf,
Can gorwyf cwyn girad;
Ai er gwerth, cannerth cenad,
Ai o'th fodd, enw rhodd yn rhad.

Speak a faithful word after the shower of love, as I am oppressed by dismal grief, or out of good will, gratuitously under the name of gift. *Gr. ab D. ab Tudur.*

Gwerthadwy, *a.* (gwerth) Saleable, vendable.

Gwerthawl, *a.* (gwerth) Relating to valuation.

Gwerthedig, *a.* (gwerth) Being sold, or vended.

Gwerthedigaeth, *s. m.* (gwerthedig) Vendition.

Gwerthedd, *s. m.* (gwerth) Value, or price.

Gwerthefin, *s. m.* (gwarthaf) That is sovereign, or supreme. *a.* Sovereign, or supreme.

Lluest Cadwallawn fy mrawd,
Y'ngwerthefin bro Dunawd;
Ei far anwar yn ffosawd.

The encampment of Cadwallon, my brother, in the *upper part* of the country of Dunod: his wrath is violent in the carnage. *Llywarch Hen.*

Wrth Dduw ydd wylaf hyny,
Werthefin Frenin fry.

To God I will weep on that account, the *supreme* King above. *Ll. P. Moch.*

> Gwerthefin frenin, frains benadur byd,
> Gwrthleddod o'm bryd pyd pechadur!

The *sovereign* King, the mighty Ruler of the world, may he drive from my intention the danger of the sinner! *Ll. P. Moch.*

> Cyfarchaf i'r dewin gwerthefin,
> Gwerthfawr wrth ei fod yn frenin,
> Cerdd foliant, mal y canl Myrddin.

I will greet the *supreme* Divinity, precious from being king, a song of praise as Merddin erst did sing. *M. ab Owain.*

Gwerthfawr, *a.* (gwerth) Precious, valuable.

Yn yr amser yd oedd Cynfelyn, fab Tenefan, yn frenin yn yr ynys hon, y ganed Iesu Grist an Arglwydd ni, y gwr er i werthfawr waed ef a brynws cenedl dyn o gaethiwed.

In the time when Cynfelyn, the son of Tenefan, was king in this island, Jesus Christ our Lord was born, the person, who, by his *precious* blood, redeemed the generation of man from bondage. *Gr. ab Arthur.*

Gwerthfawrawg, *a.* (gwerthfawr) Of a precious nature, greatly valuable, of great worth.

Tri pheth gwerthfawrocaf i ddyn: iechyd, a rhyddid, a rhinwedd.

There are three *most precious* things for man: health, liberty, and virtue. *Trioedd.*

Gwerthfawredd, *s. m.* (gwerthfawr) Preciousness.

Gwerthfawrogrwydd, *s. m.* (gwerthfawrawg) Preciousness, the state of being precious.

Gwerthfawrus, *a.* (gwerthfawr) Of a precious nature; very valuable.

Gwerthiad, *s. m.* (gwerth) A selling; vendition.

Gwerthiant, *s. m.* (gwerth) Vendition; price.

Gwerthiawg, *a.* (gwerth) Precious; valuable.

Gwerthu, *v. a.* (gwerth) To sell; to vend; to traffic, to bargain.

Angen a bryn ac a werth.

Necessity will buy and will *sell*. *Adage.*

> Cyfoethawg i werthu,
> Tylawd i brynu.

The wealthy *to sell*, the indigent to buy. *Adage.*

Gwerthwr, *s. m.—pl.* gwerthwyr (gwerth—gwr) A seller, or vender.

Gwerthyd, *s. f.—pl. t.* oedd (gwarth) Axis; spindle. *Gwerthyd melin*, the axle which passes through the stones of a mill; *gwerthyd troell*, the spindle of a spinning wheel; *gwerthyd ysgol*, a round of a ladder.

Gwerthydaid, *s. f.—pl.* gwerthydeidiau (gwerthyd) What is upon a spindle, a spindle-full.

Gwerthydu, *v. a.* (gwerthyd) To put on a spindle.

Gwerthydwr, *s. m.—pl.* gwerthydwyr (gwerthyd—gwr) One who makes spindles.

Gwerthydd, *s. m.—pl. t.* ion (gwerth) A seller.

Gwerthyr, *s. m.—pl. t.* oedd (gwarth) A fortification.

Gweru, *v. n.* (gwer) To be spreading round; to become tallow; to generate tallow.

Gwery, *a.* (gwer) Tending to spread, or grow out.

Gweryd, *s. m.—pl. t.* au (gwer) An excretion; the sward, or covering of the earth; manure. *Gweryd y dorfr*, the conferva: the lower part of the belly.

> Y gelain feinwen a oloir heddyw,
> Dan weryd ar arwydd
> Gwae fy llaw, lladd fy arglwydd!

The fair white corpse is interred this day, under *earth* and monument. woe my hand, that my lord is slain! *Lywarch Hen.*

> Mal gwyr llwyd yr wyd ar iâ,
> Ffwrn canol a fâ'n cawna;
> Garan yn burw ei gweryd;
> Garne'r wyll, ar gwr yr yd.

Thou seemest, on the ice, like a gray heron, that in the ditch picks the reeds, or a stork casting up the *contents* of her *stomach*; or with goblin limbs on the border of the field. *D. ab Gwilym, am ei gogoned.*

Gwerydiad, *s. m.* (gweryd) A swarding, or growing through the surface; a becoming mossy.

Gwerydre, *s. m.* (gweryd—rhe) Cultivated land, an inhabited region; a country.

> Safwch allan, forwynion, a syllwch werydre
> Cynddylan; llys Pengwern neud tandde!

Stand out, ye virgins, and behold the *patrimony* of Cynddylan. the court of Pengwern is it not devoured by flames! *Llywarch Hen.*

Ef a'i dwg o'i deg werydre.

He will bring him out of his fair *country*. *Ll. P. Moch.*

Gwerydu, *v. a.* (gweryd) To sward; to generate moss; to till the ground, to manure. *Dyfed.*

Gwerydwedd, *s. f.* (gweryd—gwedd) The face of the earth; the sward.

> Neud adwyth——
> A Thudyr ben gwyr is gwerydwedd!

Is it not a calamity, when Tudur, the chief of men, is beneath the *surface of the ground*. *G. ab M. ab Dafydd.*

Gwerydd, *s. m.—pl. t.* on (gwer) That springs up; a springal, or a youth.

> Credaf i awen, a'm rhoen a'm rhydd,
> Mad gynnull mawr werydd.

I trust to the muse, with which my Lord will endow me, for a fair collection of teeming *spring*. *Cynddelw.*

> Deiw ydd ym——
> Yn undawd undad frodorion,
> Can drugar, can war werydddon;
> Can terfyn, can torf engylion—
> Y byddom.

Thus we are in unity, as brothers from a common father, with compassionate, with gentle *youths*; in the end, with a host of angels may we be! *Cynddelw.*

Gweryddawg, *a.* (gwerydd) Full of vigour.

Gweryddawl, *a.* (gwerydd) Tending to spring out; apt to be wanton.

Gweryddiad, *s. m.* (gwerydd) A springing out; an acting wantonly.

Gweryddu, *v. a.* (gwerydd) To spring out.

Pan oedd yn hen gleirach, ef a weryddai megis gwr ieuanc.

When he was a decrepid old man, he would *wanton* like a young man. *Gr. Roberts.*

Gwerylym, *a.* (gwery—llym) Greatly spreading.

Ungymun, gwerylym, gwerlid gofain.

A disgusting, an *intensely spreading*, flowing wrath, of memory. *Ein. ab Gwgawn.*

Gweryn, *s. m.—pl. t.* od (gwer) A worm, or bot, that breeds in the backs of cattle.

Gweryrawl, *a.* (gwer—gyrawl) Neighing.

Gweryriad, *s. m.—pl. t.* au (gwer—gyriad) A neighing.

Gweryru, *v. a.* (gwer—gyru) To utter the voice, as a horse; to neigh.

Gwes, *s. m.—pl.* gwys (gw—es) That is moving.

Gwesawd, *s. m.* (gwes) Departure; a straying.

Gwesawl, *a.* (gwes) A departing; straying.

Gwesgrydd, *s. m.* (gwes—crydd) A course, or going round, a circumrotation.

> Gwrelliwr Fawrth addoer, addwyr wesgrydd;
> Gwan-lien wawr anhun Feirionydd y daeth.

The chilling fair moon of March, of boldly declining *orbit*, its sleep-bereaving ray came upon a feeble frame in Meirion. *Ior. Fychan.*

Gwesgryn, *s. m.* (gwes—cryn) Agitation, trepidity

Gwesgrynawl, *a.* (gwesgryn) Tending to agitate.

Gwesgryniad, *s. m.* (gwesgryn) A causing to move with agitation.

Gwesgrynu, *v. a.* (gwesgryn) To cause agitation.

> Nid yn wyry, yn war,
> Yd wesgryn esgar.

Not chastely, not mildly will the foe *agitate*. *Gwalchmai.*

> Pan wesgryn cammawn camp eulr;
> Pan lladd yn llachiad, pan llochir,
> Yn llym, yn llachar yd fernir.

When with dazzling exploit he *agitates* the conflict; when he slays in destroying wrath, when he is soothed, severe and gleaming he is all owed to be. *Cynddelw, i M. ab Owain.*

Gwesiad, *s. m.* (gwes) A departing, a going out.

Gwest, *s. f.—pl. t.* i (gwes) A going out; a visit;

an entertainment; a place of entertainment; an inn; a lodging.

Gwrthawd gwahawdd a myn'd i west.

Refusing an invitation and yet going to an entertainment. *Adage.*

Gwest, *v. a.* (gwes) To go about; to visit; to partake of entertainment; to be as a guest. *Heb orfod gwest ar le arall,* without being obliged to put up in another place.

Mi sydd——
Yn dawed i west atat.

I am coming *to be a guest* to thee. *D. ab Gwilym.*

Gwesta, *v. a.* (gwest) To go a visiting; to partake of entertainment, to go as a guest.

Gwestach, *s. m.* (gwest) The state of being as a guest, or visitant.

Gwestai, *s. c.—pl.* gwesteion (gwest) A visitor; a guest; one who partakes of entertainment, a lodger.

Y nos y dylir cadw gwestai, ac nid y dydd:—Mal hyn y dylir cadw gwestai: llw yr amddiffynwr, a deuddyn gydag ef o ddynion y tŷ y cysgodd ynddo; a thyngu o honynt eu bod yn geidwaid arno o bryd gorchyfarwy hyd y bore dranoeth.

A *lodger* should be kept during the night, and not the day:—thus ought a *lodger* to be kept: the oath of the defendant, and two persons with him, of the men of the house, wherein he slept: and they swearing of their being guardians over him from the time of twilight until the next morning. *Welsh Laws.*

Gwestawl, *a.* (gwest) Being roving; visiting.

Gwesteiad, *s. m.* (gwestai) A being a guest; a visiting, a partaking of entertainment.

Gwesteiaeth, *s. m.* (gwestai) The act of going as a guest; a frequenting of entertainments.

Gwestfa, *s. f.—pl. t.* au (gwest) A place of entertainment; entertainment; or hospitable reception; a lodging; a periodical obligation upon a vassal to contribute for the reception of the prince in his circuit.

Swydd y dystain yw rhanu arian y gwestfau.

It is the steward's office to divide the money of the *entertainments.* *Welsh Laws.*

Rheidus a gerddo dair tref, a naw tŷ yn mhob tref, heb gael na chardawd, na gwestfa, er ei ddal a'i ledrad ymborth ganddo ni chrogir.

The necessitous who shall walk three townships, and nine houses in every township, without obtaining neither alms, or *lodging,* though he be caught with theft of sustenance upon him, he shall not be hung. *Welsh Laws.*

Gwestfil, *s. m.—pl. t.* od (gwest—mil) A prowling animal; a wild beast.

Gwestiad, *s. m.* (gwest) A going above; a visiting; a being as a guest.

Gwestifiant, *s. m.—pl.* gwestifiaint (gwest) A goer about; a visitor; a guest.

Dinas gwestifiaint gostyngwy, mal gwr,
Gwestun dwr dorndwy.

The strong hold of *guests,* be humbled, like a hero, the shattered tower of Gweston. *Cynddelw, i O. Cyfeiliawg.*

Gwestl, *s. m.——pl. t.* au (gwest) A hurly-burly, or a state of confusion.

Treisiaist goed am eu trysor,
Tymhestl, a mawr-westl y mor.

Thou hast rifled the trees for their treasure, thou tempest, and great *tumult* of the sea. *M. ab Rhys.*

Gwestlawg, *a.* (gwestl) Riotous, tumultuous.

Cyfun westlawg dwfr dydd neud gawy
Cathl o ar adar, awdl oeymwy.

Accordantly *murmuring* the waters by day, when I am treated with a carol from the birds, well versed in melody. *Gwalchmai.*

Gwestle, *s. m.—pl. t.* oedd (gwest—lle) A place of entertainment; a lodging.

Gwestledd, *s. m.* (gwestl) A hurly-burly state.

Nid o westledd y ceir prestledd.

It is not from *riotousness* that witticism is to be obtained. *Catwg.*

Gwestlfan, *s. f.* (gwestl—man) A scene of riot.

Gwestliad, *s. m.* (gwestl) A making a riot.

Gwestlu, *v. a.* (gwestl) To riot, to make a riot.

Gwestr, *s. f.—pl. t.* au (gwest) A hitch.

Gwestu, *v. a.* (gwest) To entertain, or to exercise hospitality; to be as a guest; to lodge.

Gwestwng, *s. m.* (gw—estwng) A decline, or going down. *v. n.* To decline; to lower.

Gwestwr, *s. m.—pl.* gwestwyr (gwest—gwr) One who goes about; a visitor; a man who is a guest.

——Achwyn wrthi
Rhag gwestwr, brigiwydwr braint,
Yr hwn a elwir henaint.

Complain to her against a *visitor,* a painter with hoary hues of our glory, who is called old age. *Morg. ab Hywel.*

Gwestyngawl, *a.* (gwestwng) Declinatory.

Gwestyngiad, *s. m.* (gwestwng) A declining, or tending downwards.

Gwestyngu, *v. a.* (gwestwng) To decline.

Gwesu, *v. a.* (gwes) To depart, to go out.

Gwesyn, *s. m. dim.* (gwas) A little fellow; a little boy, or page; a little servant.

Gwesynaidd, *a.* (gwesyn) Like a boy, or boyish; like a servant; servile.

Gwesyndawd, *s. m.* (gwesyn) A boyish state; the office of a page; servility.

Nid oes iddo gynnyg, er dim, elwa trwy druth a gweniaith ufuddgar, neu trwy wesyndawd a chyduawseiddiad pechadurus.

He is not to attempt by any means to get riches by fawning and abject flattery, or through *servility* and sinful conformity. *Ier. Owain.*

Gwethl, *s. m.—pl. t.* au (gw—eth) A start, or sudden spring.

Gwethliad, *s. m.* (gwethl) A springing off.

Gwethlu, *v. a.* (gwethl) To make a spring.

Gwethlus, *a.* (gwethl) Apt to start, or spring.

Gwëu, *v. a.* (gwe) To weave; to knit.

Gweuad, *s. m.* (gwëu) A weaving; a knitting. *Gweuad caerawg,* that is woven like kersey.

Gweuadrestr, *s. f.—pl. t.* i (gweuad—rhestr) A woven range, or row.

Aeth——
Fal haul wybr, byw lwybr balladr,
Drwy ffenestr weuadrestr wydr.

It went, like the sun of the firmament, a beam of living course, through the glass window of *woven frame-work.* *I. ab R. ab Ieuan Llwyd.*

Gweuawl, *a.* (gwëu) Textile; weaving; knitting.

Gweuedig, *a.* (gweu) Being woven, or textile.

Gweuedigaeth, *s. m.* (gweuedig) Act of weaving.

Gweunaidd, *a.* (gwaen) Meadowy, meadow-like.

Gweunblu, *s. pl. aggr.* (gwaen—plu) Cotton grass

Gweundir, *s. m.* (gwaen—tir) Meadow-land.

Gweunwellt, *s. m.* (gwaen—gwellt) Meadow grass

Gweurydd, *s. m.—pl. t.* on (gwaer) A slave.

Euthym, a'm fi yn wr ieuangc, gydag ef i wlad Capua, yn weurydd, a'r bummed flwyddyn ynol yn drysorydd.

I went, and I being a young man, with him to the country of Capua, as a *slave,* and the fifth year following as treasurer. *Gr. Roberts, o Cicero.*

Gwëus, *s. f.—pl. t.* au (gwe) The human lip.

Dwys oedd dwy wëus heddyw.

Incessant were two *lips* this day. *D. ab Gwilym.*

Dwywes aur dwy-wëus arian.

A splendid goddess with two silver *lips.* *H. Dafi.*

Gweuwr, *s. m.—pl.* gweuwyr (gwëu—gwr) A weaver; a knitter.

Gweuwraig, *s. f.—pl.* gweuwreigedd (gwëu—gwraig) A weaving-woman; a knitting-woman.

Gweuwres, *s. f.—pl. t.* au (gweuwr) A female weaver, a female knitter.

Gweuydd, *s. m.—pl. t.* on (gwëu) A weaver.

Gweuyddes, *s. f.* (gweuydd) A female weaver.

Gwenyddiaeth, *s. m.* (gweuydd) A weaver's trade.
Gwew, *s. m.* (gw—ew) Pungency; a smart.
Gwewwr, *s. m.—pl.* gwewwyr (gwew—gwr) One who causes a smart.
Gwewyr, *s. m.* (gwew) That is pungent, that causes a smart; pain, anguish.

> Yr hin ag anian yr haf,
> A ddyr gwewyr y gauaf.
>
> The weather, with the nature of the summer, will dispel the *pain* of winter. *Guto y Glyn.*

Gwewyrlys, *s. m. aggr.* (gwewyr—llys) Dill.
Gweyd, *v. a.* (gwa) To stay, to express, to speak.
Gweydiad, *s. m.* (gweyd) A saying, a speaking.
Gwëydd, *s. m.—pl. t.* ion (gwe) A weaver.
Gwëyddes, *s. f.—pl. t.* au (gwëydd) A female weaver.
Gwëyddiaeth, *s. m.* (gwëydd) A weaver's trade.
Gweywr, *s. m.—pl.* gweywyr (gwaew—gwr) A spearman, a pikeman.
Gwg, *s. m.—pl.* gygon (wg) A piercing look, a stern look; a frown; a frowning aspect; a glance; a look. *Dal gwg*, to bear anger, or to have a pique against one.

> Dyro nawdd yn dirion wg;
> Dibdin oll dy lidwg.
>
> Give protection, with look benign, assuage all thy frown. *T. Prys.*

> Llonai'r ael allan o'r wg;
> Lladdai fil a'i lleddf olwg.
>
> The brow, when free from the *frown*, would diffuse joy; she would kill a thousand with her glancing eye. *S. Cent.*

> Gwnaed—
> Rhyw ruymedi, fal i gwyr,
> Y rhiain fwyr synwyrus;
> Ac onis gwna teg ei gwg,
> Mi af rhag drwg o'r ynys.
>
> Let her make some promise in the way she knows best, the nymph most discreet; and if she of pleasant *look* should refuse, for fear of ill, I will depart the isle. *Gofinius.*

Gwi, *s. f.* (gw) A sudden emotion. It is used as an interjection. *Wi! Ha!*
Gwiail, *s. pl. aggr.* (gwial) Rods, or saplings.

> Dysg ddedwydd â gair, dysg ddiriad â gwiail.
>
> Teach the diligent with a word, teach the mischievous with rods. *Adage.*

Gwial, *s. pl. aggr.* (gw—ial) Rods, or twigs.
Gwiala, *v. a.* (gwial) To gather rods, or twigs.
Gwialawg, *a.* (gwial) Abounding with twigs.
Gwialen, *s. f.—pl. t.* i (gwial) A rod, a perch, a yard, a measuring rod, a sceptre.

> Deunaw troedfedd a fydd yn hyd gwialen Hywel Dda.
>
> Eighteen feet are to be in the length of the *perch* of Hywel the Good. *Welsh Laws.*

> Yr hwn dir a gynnelir y dan wialen yr awdd hon.
>
> The which land is held under the *sceptre* of this court. *Welsh Laws.*

Gwialenaid, *s. f.—pl.* gwialeneidiau (gwialen) The length, or measure of a meting rod; also a stroke with a rod.
Gwialenawd, *s. f.—pl.* gwialenodiau (gwialen) The length of a measuring rod; a stroke with a rod.
Gwialenffust, *s. f.* (gwialen—ffust) The swipple part of a flail, a flail yard.
Gwialenig, *s. f. dim.* (gwialen) A small rod.
Gwialenodiad, *s. m.* (gwialenawd) A scourging, or striking with a rod.
Gwialenodiaw, *v. a.* (gwialenawd) To scourge.
Gwialffust, *s. f.* (gwial—ffust) A flail swipple.
Gwib, *s. f.—pl. t.* iau (gwi—ib) A quick course, range, or drive; a serpentine motion; the motion of a fly in its progress; a wandering, or strolling. *Cymeryd gwib o redeg*, to take a heat of running; *seren wib*, wandering star.

Gwibad, *s. m.* (gwib) A ranging about, a traversing, a turning backwards.
Gwiban, *s. c.—pl. t.* od (gwib) A fly.
Gwibdde, *s. f.* (gwib) A darting, or flying about.

> Dolau dwr abyr am gaer,
> Gwibdde adderw adwy aer.
>
> The dales where the streams come round a rampart, chilling the *passing and repassing* of the breach of battle. *Taliesin.*

Gwibddyn, *s. m.—pl. t.* ion (gwib—dyn) Stroller.
Gwibed, *s. pl.* (gwib) Flies. *Gwibed bach*, gnats.
Gwibedog, *s. m.* (gwibed) A fly-catcher.
Gwibedyn, *s. m. dim.* (gwibed) A fly, one fly.
Gwiber, *s. f.—pl. t.* od (gwib) A serpent, a viper, a flying serpent, a dragon. *Gwiber a neidr*, adder and snake. *Sil.*
Gwiberaidd, *a.* (gwiber) Serpentine; viperous.
Gwiberawg, *a.* (gwiber) Abounding with vipers.
Gwiberlys, *s. m.* (gwiber—llys) Vipers' bugloss.
Gwibfa, *s. f.—pl. t.* au (gwib) An irregular, or wandering course.
Gwibhwyliad, *s. m.* (gwib—hwyliad) A wandering course; a cruising.
Gwibhwyliaw, *v. a.* (gwib—hwyliaw) To make a wandering course; to cruise.
Gwibiad, *s. m.—pl.* gwibiaid (gwib) That flies about; a stroller, a vagabond.
Gwibiaw, *v. a.* (gwib) To range in a circular, or serpentine direction; to wander, to stroll, to rove, to gad.
Gwibiawd, *s. m.* (gwib) A ranging, a strolling.
Gwibiawdr, *s. m.—pl.* gwibiodron (gwibiawd) A wanderer, a stroller.
Gwibiawg, *a.* (gwib) Running to and fro, erratic, wandering; discursive.
Gwibiawl, *a.* (gwib) Ranging, or darting about; erratic, wandering; discursive.
Gwibiedig, *a.* (gwib) Erratic, wandering.
Gwibiwr, *s. m.—pl.* gwibwyr (gwib—gwr) A wanderer, or stroller.
Gwibl, *s. m.* (gwib) An abrupt turn, an eccentric course, a quirk.
Gwibliad, *s. m.* (gwibl) A flying, or gadding about.
Gwiblaw, *v. a.* (gwibl) To fly, or gad, about.
Gwibli, *s. m.* (gwibl) A state of wandering, or gadding. *Castell gwibli*, the castle of vagrancy, an appellation for such houses as keep beds to receive strollers of various descriptions, who would not be admitted into houses in general. *Sil.*
Gwiblong, *s. f.—pl. t.* au (gwib—llong) A cruising ship, a cruiser.
Gwiblu, *s. m.—pl. t.* oedd (gwib—llu) A band of vagrants, a strolling company.
Gwibredynen, *s. f.* (gwib—rhedyn) Rough spleenwort.
Gwibwrn, *s. m.* (gwib—gwrn) A whirling eddy. *Y bendro wibwrn*, the head turning giddiness, or a cracked brain.
Gwica, *v. a.* (gwig) To hawk about the town.
Gwicawr, *s. m.—pl.* gwicorion (gwig) A hawker, a pedlar.
Gwiced, *s. f.—pl. t.* au (gwig) A wicket.
Gwicwr, *s. m.—pl.* gwicwyr (gwig—gwr) A hawker, a pedlar.
Gwich, *s. f.* (gwi) A shrill noise, a crack, or crash; a squeak, or squeal; the weazand.

> Ni ddyd wich, ni ddyweid air
>
> He will not give a *squeal*, he will not say a word. *O. ab Ll. Moel.*

> Rhoe chwiban —
> Ac a'i wich agorai ben
> Ac a'i enau beguaned.
>
> He would give a whistle, and with his *squeak* he would open one's head, and bellowing with his lips. *Llawdden, i dorm.*

Gwichad, *s. m.* (gwich) A creaking; a squeaking.

Gwichell, *s. f.—pl. t.* od (gwich) A squeaker, a squealer. *Gwichell y gog*, the cuckoo chatter, a little bird that attends the cuckoo. It is also called *gwas y gog*, and *sethlydd y gog*.

Gwichiad, *s. m.—pl.* gwichiaid (gwich) A perriwinkle.

Gwichian, *v. a.* (gwich) To creak; to squeak, to squeal, to cry with a shrill acute tone.

Gwichiaw, *v. a.* (gwich) To creak, to crash; to squeak, to squeal.

> Cyd gwichio y fen hi a ddwg ei llwyth.
>
> Though the waggon *creaks* it will carry its load. *Adage.*

> Gwell gwichio'r coluddd
> Na chochi'r ddeurudd.
>
> It is better that the guts *should squeak*, than that the cheeks should redden. *Adage.*

Gwichiawg, *a.* (gwich) Creaking, crashing, grating; squeaking, squealing.

Gwichiedyn, *s. m. dim.* (gwichiad) A perriwinkle.

Gwichiwr, *s. m.—pl.* gwichwyr (gwich—gwr) A squeaking person, a squeaker, a squealer.

Gwichlais, *s. m.—pl.* gwichleisiau (gwich—llais) A squeaking voice.

Gwichlef, *s. m.* (gwich—llef) A squeaking cry.

Gwichlefain, *v. a.* (gwichlef) To cry squeakingly.

Gwichleisiad, *s. m.* (gwichlais) A squealing.

Gwichleisiaw, *v. a.* (gwichlais) To utter in a squeaking voice, to squeal.

Gwichleisiawg, *a.* (gwichlais) Having a squeaking voice; shrill-voiced.

Gwichlyd, *a.* (gwich) Apt to creak; or squeak.

Gwichydd, *s. m.—pl. t.* ion (gwich) A fitchet.

Gwichyll, *s. m.—pl. t.* od (gwich) A fitchet.

Gwichyn, *s. m.—pl. t.* od (gwich) A fitchet.

Gwid, *s. f.* (gw—id) A quick whirl, or twirl.

> Gwyr a'n cydberchid uch gwid gwenea;
> Gwr a'n cydberchai o'i barch angen.
>
> We are men who have been mutually honoured over the *whirl* of the white stream; a man was wont to respect us all from his peculiar regard. *Cynddelw, m. Riryd.*

Gwidd, *s. m.* (gw—idd) That is dried, or withered. *a.* Dried, or withered.

Gwiddan, *s. f.—pl. t.* od (gwidd) A hag; a witch; a sorceress, a giantess.

Gwiddanes, *s. f.—pl. t.* au (gwiddan) A witch.

> Y drwg——
> Hi aeth yn anferth gawres;
> Gwae ddynion faint gwiddanes
> I ddiwyno'r cyfan!
>
> Evil—a monstrous giantess is become; woe to men the magnitude *of such a hag*, to pollute the whole! *Elis Wyn, B. Cwsg.*

Gwiddiant, *s. m.* (gwidd) A drying, or withering.

Gwiddon, *s. pl. aggr.* (gwidd) The small particles of what is dried, or rotted; mites.

Gwiddonaidd, *a.* (gwiddon) Withered like mites.

Gwiddonawg, *a.* (gwiddon) Having a dry rot; mity, or full of mites.

Gwiddonawl, *a.* (gwiddon) Tending to dry up.

Gwiddoni, *v. n.* (gwiddon) To dry up, to wither; to dry-rot. *Mae y caws yn gwyddoni*, the cheese breeds mites.

> Rwy'n darfod bob dydd o'i phlaid,
> Bob pryd wrth synaid arni,
> Fal llysieuyn dan des Mai
> O'r pryd i bai'n gwiddoni!
>
> I am daily wasting away on her account; whenever I think of her, I am like a tender plant under the heat of May from the time it *begins to wither*. *Gafolus.*

Gwieiliawg, *a* (gwiail) Viminous; having twigs.

Gwielyn, *s. m. dim.* (gwiail) A rod; a perch.

Gwif, *s. m.—pl. t.* ion (gwi) A lever, a crow.

Gwifrwym, *s. m.—pl. t.* au (gwif—rhwym) A fulcrum, or what gives power to a lever.

Gwifwrnwydd, *s. m.* (gwif—gwydd) Mealy guelder rose. *Gwifwrnwydd y gors*, guelder rose; also called *corswigen*.

Gwig, *s. f.—pl. t.* oedd (gw—ig) A strait place; a corner, nook, or angle; a cove; a little retreat, or opening in a wood, being such a situation as the Britons, who lived by hunting and tending their flocks, generally built their hamlets in; hence in after times it denoted a fortress, a place of security, a town. *Y Gellewig Newydd*, the new Forest, so called by *Curadog*.

Gwigfa, *s. f.—pl. t.* oedd (gwig) A corner, or angle; a cove; a small opening in a wood; the site of a hamlet.

Gwigyn, *s. m.—pl. t.* od (gwig) One that lives in recesses. *Gwigyn y gog*, or *gwas y gog*, the bird called the cuckoo's servant.

Gwil, *s. m.* (gw—il) A partly turning off, or receding; the act of taking care, or avoiding.

Gwilawg, *a.* (gwil) Full of starts. *s. f.* One that starts, or plunges; an epithet for a mare.

> Dodwch—ai—march——
> Ai gwiliawg orddiawg dda.
>
> Give me, be it a horse, or a good *mare* somewhat lazy. *G. ab Ll. Pychan.*

Gwilfrai, *s. m.* (gwil—brai) Yarrow; also a brock, or badger; otherwise called *pryf llwyd*, *daiarfochyn*, *byrhwch*, *daiarhwch*, *pryf penfrith*, and *broch*.

Gwilff, *s. f.—pl. t.* od (gwil) The starter; an epithet for a mare; also a lewd woman.

> Gweryriad gwyllt, rhuad gan
> Gwilff felen am geffylau.
>
> A wild neighing, the hollow utterance of a bay *mare* after horses. *D. ab Gwilym, i'r delyn ledr.*

Gwilhersi, *s. m.* (gwil—hersi) A romping.

Gwilhersiad, *s. m.* (gwilhersi) A romping.

Gwilhersu, *v. a.* (gwil—hersu) To romp.

Gwilhobain, *v. a.* (gwil—hobain) To gallop.

Gwili, *s. m.* (gwil) That is full of turns, or starts

Gwiliad, *s. m.* (gwil) A taking care, or avoiding.

Gwiliadwr, *s. m.—pl.* gwiliadwyr (gwiliad—gwr) One who takes care, or avoids.

Gwiliadwraeth, *s. m.* (gwiliadwr) The act of taking care, shunning, or avoiding.

Gwiliaw, *v. a.* (gwil) To take care, to beware.

Gwiliawd, *s. m.* (gwil) The act of taking care.

Gwiliawdr, *s. m.—pl.* gwiliodron (gwiliawd) One who takes care, or that is upon his guard.

Gwilied, *v. a.* (gwil) To take care, to beware.

> Gwilied o gysgawd gwaliau
> Yr un dyn i'r ym ni'n dau.
>
> *Shunning*, behind the walls, the same person we are both. *D. ab Edmwnt, i eiddig.*

Gwiliedig, *a.* (gwiliad) Being taken care of.

Gwiliwr, *s. m.—pl.* gwilwyr (gwil—gwr) One who takes care, or is upon his guard.

Gwilri, *s. m.* (gwil—rhi) A wanton squeal.

Gwilrin, *s. m.* (gwil—rhin) A squeak, or squeal. uttered from pleasure, or ecstasy.

Gwilrin, *v. a.* (gwil—rhin) To squeal with ecstasy; to make a wanton noise, or squeal

Gwilwst, *s. f.* (gwil—gwst) That is troubled with starts; an epithet for a mare.

> Gwilwst aruthr o gul—
> Yw'r wrach.
>
> A *plunger* woefully lean is the hag. *D. ab Gwilym.*

> Ni wna'r gwilwst er gwialen,
> Soeglen ffol, ond siglo'i phen.
>
> The *plunger*, a stupid lump, notwithstanding the rod will only toss about her head. *R. ab Dafydd Llwyd.*

Gwilydd, *s. m.—pl. t.* ion (gwil) One who takes care, or guards.

Gwill, *s. m.—pl. t.* ion (gw—ill) A strayer; a stranger; an interloper; a vagabond. *Gwill myr*, a sea rover, a pirate.

Gwill, *a.* (gw—ill) Being fickle, or apt to stray.

Gwilliad, *s. m.—pl.* gwilliaid (gwill) One that strays about; a vagabond; a lurker.

Gwilliadaidd, *a.* (gwilliad) Like a vagabond.

Gwilliades, *s. f.—pl. t.* au (gwilliad) A female stroller or vagrant.

Gwillon, *s. m.* (gwill) Asparagus.

Gwin, *s. m.—pl. t.* oedd (gw—in) Wine.

> Dyddwg i Ruffudd, waewrudd elyn,
> Gwin a gwydr goleu yn ei gylchyn.

> Dear to Gruffudd, the foe with ruddy spear, the wine with clear glass encompassing it. *O. Cyfeiliawg.*

> Mathew Goch, mab maeth y gwin,
> Baeh'r gair yn bwrw gwerin.

> Mathew the Red, foster son of wine, has the fame of overthrowing a multitude. *Gutto'r Glyn.*

> Da fo'r gwin——
> Da iawn yw hwyl dyn a'i hyf.

> Good was the wine, very good the condition of the person that drinks it. *S. Phylip.*

Gwina, *v. a.* (gwin) To tipple wine.

Gwinaeth, *s. m.* (gwin) A making of wine.

Gwinaethiad, *s. m.* (gwinaeth) A gathering a vintage.

Gwinaethu, *v. a.* (gwinaeth) To gather vintage.

Gwinaidd, *a.* (gwin) Having the nature of wine.

Gwinau, *s. m.* (gwin) A bay, reddish brown, or auburn colour.

Gwinau, *a.* (gwin) Of a bay, or auburn colour; of a reddish brown. *Caseg wineu*, a bay mare; *meirch gwineuon*, bay horses.

Gwinaw, *v. n.* (gwin) To produce, or yield wine.

Gwinawl, *a.* (gwin) Relating to wine, vineous.

> Miaia——
> Iaith faith forthawl,
> Wiw awyf winawl.

> Articulate a speech, comprehensive and pleasing, full of love and like wine. *D. Ll. Mathew.*

Gwinc, *s. f.* (gwing) A bird called a chaffinch.

Gwinegr, *s. m.* (gwin—egr) Vinegar, sour wine.

Gwinegraidd, *a.* (gwinegr) Like vinegar.

Gwineuad, *s. m.* (gwinau) A making of a bay, or reddish brown; a turning bay.

Gwineuaw, *v. n.* (gwinau) To turn to a bay.

> Ac yn wy i gwineua
> Ac o'r wy yn gyw yr â.

> And in an egg it turns brown, and from the egg it becomes a chick. *S. Phylip, of the Phenix.*

Gwineuder, *s. m.* (gwinau) The state of being bay, or of a red brown.

Gwineuddu, *s. m.* (gwinau—du) A brown black. *a.* Of a brownish black.

Gwineuedd, *s. m.* (gwinau) The state of being bay, or of reddish brown colour.

Gwineugoch, *s. m.* (gwinau—coch) A red with a cast of brown; a brownish red. *a.* Of a brown red.

Gwineulas, *s. m.* (gwinau—glas) A blue with a cast of brown colour. *a.* Of a brownish blue.

Gwineurudd, *s. m.* (gwinau—rhudd) A crimson with a cast of bay. *a.* Of a brownish crimson.

> Canaid oeuraid a'r ael wineurudd.

> The golden luminary with the brow of ruddy brown. *Gwil. Hen.*

Gwineurwydd, *s. m.* (gwinau) The state of being of a reddish brown, or bay colour.

Gwinfaeth, *s. m.* (gwin—maeth) The nourishment of wine. *a.* Nourished with wine.

> Dragon y'ngwyar gwedy gwinfaeth
> Gwenabwy fab Gwen.

> A dragon in the stream of blood, after the *feast of wine*, was Gwenabwy son of Gwen. *Aneurin.*

> Goran torf, twrf achre ar draeth,
> Gormes draws gwenwyn-faws gwinfaeth.

> The murmur of a host, the tumult of a wave on the beach, the froward oppression of the poisonously sweet *feast of wine*. *Cynddelw, i O. Cyfeiliawg.*

Gwingafn, *s. m.—pl. t.* au (gwin—cafn) A wine-press.

Gwingar, *a.* (gwin) Loving wine; full of wine.

Gwingarwch, *s. m.* (gwingar) Fondness for wine.

Gwinien, *s. f.* (gwin) A vine tree, a vine.

Gwiniolen, *s. f.* (gwinawl) Common maple tree.

Gwiniolwydd, *s. pl. aggr.* (gwinawl—gwydd) The common maple trees.

Gwinllan, *s. f.—pl. t.* oedd (gwin—llan) A vineyard. The Britons were used to extract wine from various trees; hence, in some places, *Gwinllan helyg*, a plantation of sallows; and, in Anglesey, *gwinllan faip*, is a common expression for a field of turnips.

> Un llwybr â gwaith y winllan
> Ydyw'r llu yn myn'd i'r llan.
> Dynion ieuainc diamby,
> Yn fore aat i nef fry;
> A rhai am hanner eu hoes.—

> A road like that to the work of the vineyard has the multitude going to the churchyard. Young men void of timidity, they go early to heaven above; and some in the middle of their lives. *Gutto'r Glyn.*

Gwinllanwr, *s. m.—pl.* gwinllanwyr (gwinllan—gwr) A dresser of a vineyard.

Gwinllanydd, *s. m.—pl. t.* ion (gwinllan) A dresser of a vineyard.

Gwinllyd, *a.* (gwin) Vineous; addicted to wine.

Gwinrawn, *s. pl. aggr.* (gwin—grawn) Wine grapes; grapes.

Gwinsang, *s. f.* (gwin—sang) A wine-press.

Gwinwasg, *s. f.* (gwin—gwasg) A wine-press.

Gwinwr, *s. m.* (gwin—gwr) A vintner.

> Rhodded gwinwr cyffredin,
> O'r ciddiaw gwyr arwydd gwin.

> Let the public vintner, for the sake of drawing in men, set up the sign of wine. *L. G. Cothi.*

Gwinwryf, *s. m.—pl. t.* au (gwin—gwryf) A wine-press.

Gwinwydr, *s. m.—pl. t.* au (gwin—gwydr) A wine glass.

Gwinwydryn, *s. m.* (gwinwydr) A wine glass.

Gwinwydd, *s. pl. aggr.* (gwin—gwydd) Vines.

Gwinwyddawl, *a.* (gwinwydd) Relating to vines.

Gwinwydden, *s. f.* (gwinwydd) A vine tree, a vine. *Gwinwydden wyllt*, briony; *gwinwydden wen*, a white vine; *gwinwydden ddu*, a black vine.

Gwinydd, *s. m.—pl. t.* ion (gwin) A vintner.

Gwing, *s. f.* (gw—ing) A motion, turn, or shake made with a spring; a struggle; a wriggle; a sudden motion, as a wince, or wink of the eye; wantonness.

> Gwaeiddyn—
> Ar dybiau lleng yn rogor;
> Un a gwing yn ei gyngher;
> A'i ruth geg yn ymegor,
> E wnai ddedwrdd yn ddidor.

> An object weight in labour with weak conceits; one with lechery in his mind; with his wide mouth opening, he would mutter continually. *E. Dafydd.*

Gwingaw, *v. a.* (gwing) To struggle; to wriggle, to wince; to move as if impatient of restraint, to be wanton.

Gwingawg, *a.* (gwing) Full of struggling, wriggling, or wincing.

Gwingawl, *a.* (gwing) Struggling; wriggling.

Gwingdin, *s. f.* (gwing—tin) Wriggle-tail. *a.* Wriggle-tailed. *Gweni wingdin*, the wagtail fair one.

> Gwingdin y llwyn, yr aderyn serchoga'n fyw.

> The wagtail of the grove, the most wanton bird alive. *Adage.*

Gwinged, *s. m.* (gwing) A wriggling; wantonness.

Gwingedig, *a.* (gwinged) Struggling, wriggling.

Gwingiad, *s. m.* (gwing) A struggling; a wriggling; a wincing; a writhing.

Gwingwr, *s. m.—pl.* gwingwyr (gwing—gwr) A struggler; a wriggler; a wincer.

Gwion, *s. m.* (gwi) An elf, a fairy, a proper name of men.

Gwipai, *s. f.* (gwib) A sparrow-hawk.

Gwir, *s. m.—pl. t.* oedd (gw—ir) The pure fluid, the ether, the principle of life; purity; truth, right; legislature.—*Dywed y gwir*, tell the truth; *yn wir*, in truth; *ïe yn wir*, yes indeed; *ai ie yn wir?* is it so indeed?

Chwedlau a'm gwyddir o wir hyd lawr.

Sayings are imparted to me from *heaven* to earth. *Taliesin.*

Megitor o'u gwir hwy hir alanas.

From their *justice* there is a long animosity generated. *Myrddin.*

Peris Ros. Mortimer dala Syr Ed. de Woodstock, a lladd ei ben, heb wir, heb frawd yn y byd.

Roger Mortimer caused Sir Edm. de Woodstock to be seized, and his head to be cut off, without *justice*, without judgment of any kind. *Chronicle.*

Cyfamug ei wir a mil farchawg.

He will protect his *right* with a thousand horsemen. *Meilyr, i G. ab Cynan.*

Trech ammod no gwir.

A covenant is stronger than *right*. *Adage.*

Llew Llawgyffes—
Gwr oedd hwnw gwir i neb ni roddes.

Llew Llawgyffes, he was a man who never rendered to any one his *right*. *Taliesin.*

Perchen gwir, a thir, a thynged.

Proprietor of *legislative authority*, and land, and fealty. *L. G. Cothi.*

Gwir, *a.* (gw—ir) Of an ethereal nature; pure; true; right, just. *Ai gwir yw hyn?* Is this true? *Gan wiried a dy fod yna*, as true as thou art there; *yn wir*, indeed; *yn wir ionedd*, indeed truth; *O wir gwaith oddef*, on purpose.

Gwiraw, *v. a.* (gwir) To verify; to assert.

Gwirawd, *s. f.—pl.* gwirodau (gwir) Spirituous liquor; drink served at feasts; wassail.

Y dystain biau ardystu y gwirodau yn y llys.

To the *steward* of the household belongs the approving of the *liquors* in the palace. *Welsh Laws.*

Da yw'r gwr am dair gwirawd.

The man is excellent for three *liquors*. *L. G. Cothi.*

Gwirawd Owain—mor fynych ei harfoll!
O win cyfrgain, nid cyfrgoll,
O fedd; o fuelin oll.

The *liquor* of Owain—how incessantly it goes round! Of clear sparkling wine without lacking, and of the mead; all out of the buffalo's horn. *Cynddelw.*

Gwiredd, *s. m.—pl. t.* au (gwir) Verity, truth.

Gwireddawl, *a.* (gwiredd) Veritable, agreeable to truth, or fact.

Gwireddu, *v. a.* (gwiredd) To make true.

Gwirf, *s. m.—pl. t.* ion (gwir) Alcohol.

Gwirfodd, *s. m.* (gwir—bodd) True content, good will, or full content. *Dos o'th wirfodd*, go of thy good will, go willingly.

Gwirfoddawl, *a.* (gwirfodd) Voluntary, wilful.

Gwirfoddoldeb, *s. m.* (gwirfodd) Voluntariness.

Gwirfoddoledd, *s. m.* (gwirfoddawl) Voluntariness.

Gwirfoddolrwydd, *s. m.* (gwirfoddawl) Voluntariness, spontaneity.

Gwirgar, *a.* (gwir) Loving the truth.

Gwiriad, *s. m.—pl. t.* au (gwir) Allegation.

Gwiriadwy, *a.* (gwir) Avouchable, verifiable.

Gwiriant, *s. m.* (gwir) A verification.

Gwiriaw, *v.* (gwir) To verify, to assert as truth.

Gwiriawg, *a.* (gwir) Tending to verify.

Gwiriawl, *a.* (gwir) Tending to verify; positive.

Gwiriawn, *a.* (gwir—iawn) Truly right; innocent; ignorant. *s. m.* An innocent; an idiot.

Gwiriedig, *a.* (gwir) Verified, asserted as true.

Gwiriedigaeth, *s. m.* (gwiriedig) Verification.

Gwiriedigaethawl, *a.* (gwiriedigaeth) Tending to verificate.

Gwiriedigaethiad, *s. m.* (gwiriedigaeth) A verificating; a verification.

Gwiriedigaethu, *v.* (gwiriedigaeth) To verificate.

Gwiriedigawl, *a.* (gwiriedig) Tending to verificate.

Gwiriedigolrwydd, *s. m.* (gwiriedigawl) The state of being verificated.

Gwirin, *a.* (gwir) Of a pure, or true, nature.

Creawdr a'm crewys a'm cynnwys yn mhlith
Plwyf gwirin gwerin Enlli.

The Creator who formed me will receive me amongst the *pure* society of the multitude of Enlli. *Meilyr.*

Gwirineb, *s. m.* (gwirin) Verity, truth.

Gwirion, *a.* (gwiriawn) Truly right: innocent; ignorant. *s. m.* An innocent; an idiot.

Mal yr â i'r mor bob afon,
Yr â i'r nef bob gwirion.

As every river flows into the sea, so every *innocent one* goes to heaven. *M. ab Llywarch.*

Gwirion pawb ar ei air ei hun.

Every one is *innocent* according to his own word. *Adage.*

Gwiriondeb, *s. m.* (gwiriawn) Innocency; ignorance; stupidity.

Gwirionedd, *s. m.* (gwiriawn) Verity, truth. *Ar fy ngwirionedd*, upon my verity; *ïe yn wirionedd*, yes in truth.

Cas yw y gwirionedd lle nis carer.

The *truth* is disagreeable where it is not liked. *Adage.*

Gwirioneddawl, *a.* (gwirionedd) Tending to verify according to truth.

Gwirioneddiad, *s. m.* (gwirionedd) A verification.

Gwirioneddu, *v. a.* (gwirionedd) To verify.

Yr hwn ydoedd ef yn gwirioneddu bod yr awdurdawd ac y gallu ganto.

Whom he was *asserting* to be possessed of the authority and the power. *Marchawg Crwydrad.*

Gwirioneddus, *a.* (gwirionedd) Tending to verify.

Gwirioni, *v. n.* (gwiriawn) To become an innocent; to become simple, or foolish. *Paid a gwirioni*, do not be foolish.

Gwirioniad, *s. m.—pl.* gwirioniaid (gwiriawn) An innocent; an ignorant one; an idiot.

Gwirionllyd, *a.* (gwiriawn) Full of ignorance; simple, foolish.

Gwirionyn, *s. m. dim.* (gwiriawn) An innocent; an ignoramus; a simpleton.

Gwirionyni, *s. m.* (gwirionyn) Pure simplicity.

Gwiriwr, *s. m.—pl.* gwirwyr (gwir—gwr) A verifier, a voucher.

Gwirlafar, *s. m.* (gwir—llafar) Truth speaking.

Gwirlefariad, *s.* (gwirlafar) A speaking truth.

Gwirlefaru, *v. a.* (gwirlafar) To speak truth.

Gwirodawl, *a.* (gwirawd) To speak truth.

Gwirodi, *v. a.* (gwirawd) To serve liquor.

Gwirodwr, *s. m.—pl.* gwirodwyr (gwirawd—gwr) A server of liquor.

Gwirota, *v. a.* (gwirawd) To tipple liquors.

Gwirotai, *s. c.—pl.* gwiroteion (gwirawd) One who hunts after liquor; a dram-drinker.

Gwirotyn, *s. m. dim.* (gwirawd) A dram-drinker.

Gwisg, *s. f.—pl. t.* oedd (gw—isg) A garment.

Gwisgad, *s. m.—pl. t.* au (gwisg) An apparelling, a dressing; a wearing; habiliment.

Gwisgadwy, *a.* (gwisgad) That may be worn; that may be apparelled.

Gwisgaw, *v. a.* (gwisg) To apparel, to put on, to dress; to wear.

> Cynddylan wyn fab Cyndrwyn,
> Ni mad wisg barf am i drwyn,
> Gwr ni bo gwell no morwyn.
>
> Fair Cynddylan son of Cyndrwyn, the man does not fitly wear a beard round his nose who has been no better than a maiden. *Llywarch Hen.*

Gwisgawg, *a.* (gwisg) Apparelled, arrayed.

Gwisggloer, *s. f.—pl. t.* oedd (gwisg—cloer) A clothes-press.

Gwisgiad, *s. m.* (gwisg) An apparelling, a dressing.

Gwisgiadu, *v. a.* (gwisgiad) To apparel, to dress.

Gwisgiedig, *a.* (gwisgiad) Apparelled, clothed.

Gwisgiedydd, *s. m.—pl. t.* ion (gwisgiad) One who dresses, or clothes.

Gwisgogaeth, *s. m.* (gwisgawg) Apparelment.

Gwisgwr, *s. m.—pl.* gwisgwyr (gwisg—gwr) One who puts on dress, a clother; a wearer.

Gwiw, *a.* (gwi) Excellent; proper, fit, fitting; worthy. *Dyn gwiw iawn*, a very excellent man; *ni wiw ceisiaw*, it is of no use to attempt; *ni wiw honce pen*, it is useless to shake the head; *mae gwaith gwiw arno*, there is excellent work upon it.

> Gwiw aur i a'i dirper.
>
> Gold is proper to such as deserves it. *Adage.*

Gwiwbarch, *a.* (gwiw—parch) Worthy of respect.

Gwiwdawd, *s. m.* (gwiw) Propriety; worthiness.

Gwiwdeb, *s. m.* (gwiw) Propriety, fitness; worthiness; excellence.

Gwiwell, *s. f.—pl. t.* od (gwiw) A widgeon; the female salmon, an epithet for a lively girl.

Gwiwer, *s. f.—pl. t.* od (gwiw) A squirrel.

> Nid bywiawg ond gwiwer.
>
> Nothing so lively but a squirrel. *Adage.*

Gwiwfawl, *s. f.* (gwiw—mawl) Deserved praise. *a.* Deserving of praise.

Gwiwfoledd, *s. m.* (gwiwfawl) Merited praise.

Gwiwgais, *a.* (gwiw—cais) Worthy to be sought.

Gwiwgamp, *s. f.—pl. t.* au (gwiw—camp) A great exploit.

Gwiwglod, *s. f.* (gwiw—clod) Deserving fame. *a.* Worthy of fame.

Gwiwgoel, *s f.* (gwiw—coel) Deserved credit. *a.* Deserving of credit.

Gwiwgoeledd, *s. m.* (gwiwgoel) Credibleness.

Gwiwgof, *s. m.* (gwiw—cof) Deserved remembrance. *a.* Worthy to be remembered.

Gwiwgred, *s. f.* (gwiw—cred) Deserved belief. *a.* Worthy of belief.

Gwiwlwydd, *a.* (gwiw—llwydd) Deservedly prosperous, or fortunate.

Gwiwnod, *s m.* (gwiw—nod) A superior mark. *a.* Of distinguished mark, deservedly noted.

Gwiwryw, *a.* (gwiw—rhyw) Well descended.

Gwiwsain, *s. f.—pl.* gwiwseiniau (gwiw—sain) Euphony. *a.* Of fine sound.

Gwiwydd, *s. m. aggr.* (gwiw—gwydd) Poplar trees.

> Gwiwydd gorthorod;
> Gortheryaid y'nghad.
>
> The aspen wood has been lopt; it was lopt in battle. *Taliesin, Cad goddeu.*

Gwl, *s. m.* (gw—wl) The quality of being wet.

Gwlad, *s. f.—pl.* gwledydd (gw—llad) A country. *Codi y wlad*, to raise a hue and cry; *rhaith gwlad*, jury of the country, or the oath of fifty men, which the laws required to establish a man's character, in some cases.

> Hael Hywel o god y gwlad.
>
> Hywel is generous out of the public purse. *Adage.*

> Ni roddir gwlad i fud.
>
> A country will not be given to the dumb. *Adage.*

Gwladaidd, *a.* (gwlad) Country-like, rustic.

Gwladan, *s. f. dim.* (gwlad) A country, in familiar language.

> Gwag aelwyd heb fwg, a gwaeth fydd heb dan;
> Gwag gwladan lydan heb ddeiliadaeth.
>
> Empty is a hearth without smoke, and it is worse without fire; empty is an extensive country without inhabitancy. *L. G. Cothi.*

Gwladawg, *a.* (gwlad) Having a country.

Gwladawl, *a.* (gwlad) Belonging to a country.

Gwladeidd-dra, *s. m.* (gwladaidd) Rusticity.

Gwladeiddgan, *s. f.* (gwladaidd—cân) A rustic song.

Gwladeiddgerdd, *s. f.—pl. t.* i (gwladaidd—cerdd) A rustic song; a pastoral.

Gwladeiddiad, *s. m.* (gwladaidd) A rustication.

Gwladeiddiaw, *v. a.* (gwladaidd) To rusticate; to become rusticated; to be abashed, or confused.

Gwladeiddiawl, *a.* (gwladaidd) Apt to rusticate.

Gwladeiddrwydd, *s. m.* (gwladaidd) Rusticity, clownishness, boorishness; bashfulness.

Gwladgar, *a.* (gwlad) Patriotic, loving a country.

Gwladgarwch, *s. m.* (gwladgar) A patriotism.

Gwladlawch, *s. m.* (gwlad—llawch) A protection of a country. *a.* Being a defence of a country.

> Gwedi gwalch gwladlawch, gwladlwydd,
> Neud elrydd cerddawr, neud afrwydd cerdded,
> Cerdd am ged, am gerthrwydd,
> Can ethyw llawr llyw llawn awydd.
>
> After the hero *yielding safety to a country*, that makes a country prosper, is not the minstrel feeble and his course impeded, the song for gifts is it not for sorrow, since the chief full of ambition is gone to the ground. *Cynddelw, m. O. Gwynedd.*

Gwladlwydd, *s. m.* (gwlad—llwydd) The prosperity to a country. *a.* Being the means of prosperity to a country.

> Gwladlwydd glolf bylwydd, hil teyrnedd;
> Gwledych Rhys, glyw brys, brwysgedd Brython,
> Gwlad Fon, ac Arfon, arfod Wynedd.
>
> The *prosperity of a country* with fortunate blade, the offspring of princes; Rhys, of splendid course, let him reign over the energy of Britons, the country of Mon and Arfon, the liberality of Gwynedd. *Einion Offeiriad.*

> Ni bu gwladlwydd y dano.
>
> There was no *prosperity of country* under him. *Myrddin.*

Gwladogi, *v. a.* (gwladawg) To rusticate; to become rustic.

Gwladogrwydd, *s. m.* (gwladawg) Ruralness.

Gwladoldeb, *s. m.* (gwladawl) Social state.

> Tair colofn gwladoldeb Ynys Prydain: rhaith gwlad, teyrnedd, ac ynadaeth.
>
> The three pillars of *polity* of the Isle of Britain; jury of the country, royalty, and jurisprudence. *Triawdd.*

Gwladoli, *v. a.* (gwladawl) To rusticate; to become rural.

Gwladoliaeth, *s. m.* (gwladawl) civil constitution.

Gwladolrwydd, *s. m.* (gwladawl) Rurality, rusticity.

Gwladwch, *s. m.* (gwlad) A common weal.

Gwladwr, *s. m.—pl.* gwladwyr (gwlad—gwr) A countryman; one who is in the country; a patriot.

> Pa wladwr, arwr ar wledd?
> Pa wledig a wledych arnaf?
>
> What *patriot*, hero of the taverns; what sovereign shall reign over me? *Cynddelw.*

Gwladwriaeth, *s. f.—pl. t.* au (gwladwr) A commonwealth, a commonweal; a government.

> Aethost! —
> Aeth pob gwladwriaeth ar d'ol.
>
> Thou art gone, every government is gone after thee. *T. Prys.*

Gwladwriaethawl, *a.* (gwladwriaeth) Relating to a commonwealth, or government.

Gwladwriaethu, *v. a.* (gwladwriaeth) To conduct a commonweal, or government.

Gwladychawl, *a.* (gwladwch) Having the rule of a country; reigning.

Gwladychiad, *s. m.* (gwladwch) A ruling a country.

Gwladychu, *v. a.* (gwladwch) To rule a country.

> Gwedi marw Cunedda y daeth Rhiwallawn ei fab yntau gwedi ef; gwas ieuanc tangnefeddus a thyngedfenawl oedd hwnw; ac ef a wladychws drwy gariad.
>
> After the death of Cunedda there came Rhiwallon his son after him; he was a peaceable and fortunate young man; and *he reigned* in love. *Gr. ab Arthur.*

Gwladychwr, *s. m.—pl.* gwladychwyr (gwladwch—gwr) One who reigns over a country.

Gwladydd, *s. m.—pl. t.* ion (gwlad) A man of the country; a patriot.

Gwladyddawl, *a.* (gwladydd) Like a patriot.

Gwladyddiad, *s. m.* (gwladydd) The act of a patriot; a patriotical action.

Gwladyddu, *v. a.* (gwladydd) To act patriotically.

Gwlaidd, *s. m.—pl.* gwleiddion (gwl—aidd) That flows gently; that is mild. *a.* Abounding with moisture; mild.

> Pan alwer ynys Fon tirion fles,
> Gwyn eu byd hwy gwleiddion, Saeson ardres.
>
> When the Isle of Mon shall be called a pleasant field, happy they the *mild ones*, the affliction of the Saxons. *Taliesin, i frwdwn Llyr.*

Gwlan, *s. m.—pl. t.* oedd (gw—llan) Wool. *Cnu o wlan*, a fleece of wool; *gwlan bras*, coarse wool; *gwlan man*, or *gwlan rhywiawg*, fine wool.

> Ni chair gwlan rhywiawg ar gnaw gafr.
>
> No fine *wool* can be had on the goat's haunch. *Adage.*

Gwlana, *v. a.* (gwlan) To gather, or pick wool.

> Nid hawdd gwlana ar yr afr.
>
> It is not easy *to gather wool* upon the goat. *Adage.*

Gwlanaidd, *a.* (gwlan) Woolly, like wool.

Gwlanawg, *a.* (gwlan) Bearing wool; woolly.

Gwlanblu, *s. pl. aggr.* (gwlan—plu) Downy hairs.

Gwlanbren, *s. m.* (gwlan—pren) The cotton-tree.

Gwlanen, *s. f.—pl. t.* i (gwlan) A flannel.

Gwlaniach, *s. pl. aggr.* (gwlan) Downy hair.

Gwlanwr, *s. m.—pl.* gwlanwyr (gwlan—gwr) A wool-man, a wool-gatherer; a dealer in wool.

> Gwyr gwlanwr lle bo gwlan ar werth.
>
> A *wool-gatherer* knows where there is wool on sale. *Adage.*

Gwlaw, *s. m.—pl. t.* ion (gwl—aw) Rain.

> O bob ffordd o'r awyr ydd ymchwelo y gwynt y daw gwlaw.
>
> From every quarter of the sky where the wind returns there will come *rain*. *Adage.*
>
> Y fun—
> A'i gwyneb fel yr alaw,
> A'i mwnwgl oll fal main gwlaw,
> A'i min bach yn ei thwyn ben,
> Un anadl a'r wenynen.
>
> The nymph with her face like the lilly, and her neck altogether like the *rain* stone, and her little mouth in her goodly head with breath like the bee. *Bedo Aurdrem.*

Gwlawawg, *a.* (gwlaw) Abounding with rain.

Gwlawfydrai, *s. m.* (gwlaw—mydrai) A pluviometer, or rain gage.

Gwlawiad, *s. m.* (gwlaw) A raining, a fall of rain.

Gwlawiaw, *v. a.* (gwlaw) To rain. *Mae hi yn gwlawiaw yn ddwys*, or, *mae yn bwrw gwlaw yn ddwys*, it is raining incessant.

Gwlawiawg, *a.* (gwlaw) Abounding with rain.

Gwlawiawl, *a.* (gwlaw) Pluvial, relating to rain.

Gwlawlyd, *a.* (gwlaw) Pluvious, apt to rain.

Gwlawiogrwydd, *s. m.* (gwlawiawg) Raininess.

Gwleb, *a.* (*f. of* gwlyb) Wet, humid, or moist.

Gwledig, *a.* (gwlad) Of a country; having a country; sovereign. *s. m.* A sovereign. It was anciently an epithet given to the Lloegrian princes, as a mark of supreme authority.

> Gnawd gwin yn llaw wledig.
>
> Wine is congenial to a *princely* hand. *Adage.*
>
> Gwledig nef a phob tud,
> Ni wyddem pwy oeddyd.
>
> *Sovereign* of heaven and all regions, we knew not who thou wert. *Taliesin.*

Gwledigaeth, *s. m.* (gwledig) Social state.

> Y Fêl Ynys—gwedi gyru gwledigaeth arni, y gan Prydain ab Aedd Mawr y doded arni Ynys Prydain.
>
> The Honey Island—after it had been brought into a *social state*, by Prydain the son of Aedd the Great, the name of the Isle of Prydain was imposed thereon. *Trioedd.*

Gwledigaw, *a.* (gwledig) To rusticate; to become rusticated; to rule a country.

Gwledigiad, *s. m.* (gwledig) A rustication; a ruling a country; a reigning.

Gwledigrwydd, *s. m.* (gwledig) The state relating to a country; the rule of a country; sovereignty.

Gwledwch, *s. f.* (gwlad) A reign; government. *Ni bydd terfyn ar ei wledwch*, of his kingdom there shall be no end.

Gwledychawd, *s. f.* (gwledwch) The act, or state of reigning over a country.

> Gwledychws, ar wlad, ar wleddolion medd,
> A meddiant ar dirion;
> Gwledychawd, molawd mil feirddion
> I foli teithi teyrnon.
>
> He reigned over a country, over the carousing sons of mead, with pleasure in possession, the *reign*, the work of praise of a thousand bards, should be to celebrate the qualities of the prince. *Cynddelw.*

Gwledychawl, *a.* (gwledwch) Relating to commonweal; reigning.

Gwledychiad, *s.* (gwledwch) A ruling a country.

Gwledychu, *v. a.* (gwledwch) To exercise supreme authority, or dominion; to reign. *Gwledychu hawl*, to institute a suit. *Welsh Laws.*

> Cyhwan corf rhag torf twrf elyfle,
> Cynrabad cynnud wlad wledycha.
>
> He will be the foremost to pierce a body before the host of the tumult of oppression, the happiness of the front of battle *governing* a country. *G. Brycheiniawg, i'r argl. Rhys.*

Gwledd, *s. f.—pl. t.* au (gw—lledd) A banquet.

Gwledda, *v. a.* (gwledd) To carouse, to feast.

Gwleddawg, *a.* (gwledd) Having banquets.

> Madawg Mon, mal cynnifiwr,
> Bu gwleddawg o'i nerthawg ner.
>
> Madog of Mon, like a conqueror, he was *rich in feasts* from his powerful supreme. *Prydydd Bychan.*

Gwleddawl, *a.* (gwledd) Festival, festive, feasting

> Delw ydd ym yn ddiamrysson,
> Am lugyrn, am gyrn, am geinion,
> Yn untref, yn untraul wleddolion,
> Yn undawd undad frodorion.
>
> The way we are without contention, round the lamps, round dainties, in one abode, *feasting ones* on one expense, in unity the brothers of a common father. *Cynddelw.*

Gwledd-dy, *s. m.—pl. t.* au (gwledd—tŷ) A banqueting house.

> Yn yr amser hoffaidd mis Mai, pan oedd chwant a chariad fwyaf yn eu grym yno, y cydunwyd ar i ni gwynoffa mewn gerddau, ac nid mewn gwledd-dyau.
>
> In the charming season of the month of May, when desire and love were in their greatest vigour there, it was agreed that we should sup in gardens, and not in *banqueting houses*. *Marchawg Crwydrad.*

Gwleddfa, *s. f.—pl. t.* on (gwledd) A place of carousing, or feasting; a banqueting house.

Gwleddgar, *a.* (gwledd) Loving of feasting.

Gwleddgarwch, *s.* (gwleddgar) Love of festivity.

Gwleddgell, *s. f.—pl. t.* oedd (gwledd—cell) A banqueting room.

Gwleddiad, *s. m.* (gwledd) A carousing, a feasting.

Gwleddoca, *v. a.* (gwleddawg) To hunt after feasts

Gwleddu, *v. a.* (gwledd) To feast, or to carouse.

Gwleddwch, *s. m.* (gwledd) A carousal, a feast.
Gwleddwr, *s. m.—pl.* gwleddwyr (gwledd—gwr) A feaster, a carouser.
Gwleddychu, *v. a.* (gwleddwch) To carouse.
Gwleidiad, *s. m.—pl. t.* on (gwlad) One of a country; a citizen.

> Rhyddyly dilain gwleidiadon;
> Rhydd-lif cyniaw cadnaon,
> Cyd erfyll rhwyf draig rhodolion eirchiaid,
> Rhydalant eu rhoddion.
>
> He claims the service of *citizens*, profusely he makes to flow, from the toil of depredating foxes whilst the leading chieftain receives the wayfaring minstrels they will amply repay their gifts. *Cynddelw, i H. ab Owain.*
>
> Llywelyn llywiawdr gwleidiadon,
> Llary gyngheus drwy gyngher doethion.
>
> Llywelyn the governor of *citizens*, a gentle advocate through the advice of the sons of wisdom. *D. Benfras.*

Gwleiddiad, *s. m.—pl. t.* on (gwledd) A feaster.
Gwleiddydd, *s. m.* (gwlaidd) That is mild, or tender. *a.* Of a mild quality.

> Adwen yn Ninbych, gorwen gwylan,
> Cyweithydd wleiddydd udd Erllysan.
>
> I knew in Dinbych, the resort of the white sea-mew, the *mild* society of the lord of Erllysan. *Mic Dinbych.*

Gwlf, *s. m.—pl.* gylfon (gwl) A channel: a notch. *Gwlf bwa*, the notch on the end of a bow, where the string rests; *gwlf saeth*, the cock of an arrow.

> Dan ddau wlf y daw'n ddolen.
>
> Under the two *notches* it will become a circle. *T. Aled, i fwa.*

Gwlith, *s. m.—pl. t.* oedd (gwl—ith) Dew; the dew fall; the morning.

> Ni *saif* gwlith ar geiliogwydd.
>
> No *dew* will rest upon a gander. *Adage.*
>
> Y neb a werthe farch dilysed rhag y ddera dri gwlith.
>
> He who sells a horse shall warrant him free from the staggers for three *mornings*. *Welsh Laws.*

Gwlithaw, *v. a.* (gwlith) To cast a dew, to bedew.
Gwlithawg, *a.* (gwlith) Abounding with dew, dewy

> Adwaenwn y mab wrth ei anadlau trwm, a'i gudynau gwlithawg a'i lygaid mol-glafaidd, mai—cwsg ydoedd.
>
> I knew the youth by his heavy breathings, his dewy locks, and his drowsy waxen eyes, that he was asleep. *Elis Wyn, B. Cwsg.*

Gwlithen, *s. f.—pl. t.* i (gwlith) A small collection of humours; also a dew snail. *Gwlithen ar fys*, or *bystwn*, a whitlow on the finger; *gwlithen ar lygad*, or *llefrithen*, a stye on the eye.
Gwlithfalwen, *s. f.* (gwlith—malwen) Dew snail.
Gwlithfalwod, *s. pl. aggr.* (gwlith—malwod) Dew snails.
Gwlithiad, *s. m.* (gwlith) A falling of dew; a bedewing.
Gwlithiedig, *a.* (gwlith) Being bedewed.
Gwlithlys, *s. m.* (gwlith—llys) The sun dew.
Gwlithwlaw, *s. m.* (gwlith—gwlaw) Small rain.
Gwlithwlawiaw, *v. a.* (gwlithwlaw) To rain small rain; to drizzle.
Gwlithwlawiawg, *a.* (gwlithwlaw) Abounding with drizzling rain.
Gwlithyn, *s. m. dim.* (gwlith) A dew drop.
Gwlw, *s. m.—pl. t.* on (gwl) A channel; a notch.

> Gwelw yw'r llin o'r gwlw i'r llall.
>
> Pale is the flax from one notch to the other. *E. Cyrt, i fwa.*

Gwlyb, *s. m.—pl. t.* ion (gwl) A liquid; a wet: liquid food, or spoon victuals. *Mae fe yn hoff gwlybion*, he is fond of liquors.

> Oer pob gwlyb.
>
> Cold is every *liquid*. *Adage.*

Gwlyb, *a.* (gwl) Liquid, wet, moist. *Tywydd gwlyb*, wet weather; *mor wlyb yw hwn*, how wet this is; *dillad gwlybion*, wet clothes.

Gwlybâad, *s. m.* (gwlyb) Humefaction; a wetting
Gwlybâawl, *a.* (gwlyb) That wets, or drenches.
Gwlybaniaeth, *s. m.* (gwlyban) Humidity, wetness; a liquid.
Gwlybâu, *v. a.* (gwlyb) To humectate, to madefy.
Gwlybiad, *s. m.* (gwlyb) Humectation; a wetting.
Gwlybiannawl, *a.* (gwlybiant) Humiferous.
Gwlybiannu, *v. a.* (gwlybiant) To humectate.
Gwlybiant, *s. m.* (gwlyb) Humectation, madefaction, humidity, moisture.
Gwlybiaw, *v. a.* (gwlyb) To humectate, to wet.
Gwlybrwydd, *s. m.* (gwlyb) Wetness, humidity.
Gwlybu, *v. a.* (gwlyb) To humectate, to madefy.
Gwlybwr, *s. m.—pl.* gwlybyrau (gwlyb) A liquid.
Gwlybyrawg, *a.* (gwlybwr) Abounding with humidity; humid, wet, moist; rainy.
Gwlych, *s. m.* (gwl—ych) Moisture, or wet.
Gwlychedig, *a.* (gwlych) Wetted, moistened.
Gwlychiad, *s. m.* (gwlych) A wetting, a soaking.
Gwlychu, *v. a.* (gwlych) To wet, to moisten; to become wet, or moist; to rain. *Mae yn gwlychu yn ddwys*, it is wetting incessantly, or, it rains apace.

> Ti a gefi y cyfarws a noto dy ben a'th dafawd, hyd y sych gwynt, hyd y gwlych gwlaw, hyd y treigl haul, a hyd ydd amgyffred mor.
>
> Thou shalt have the reward which thy head and tongue shall fix, as far as the wind doth dry, as far as the rain *doth wet*, as far as the sun revolves, and as far as the sea comprehends. *H. Culhwch—Mabinogion.*

Gwlŷdd, *s. m.—pl. t.* ion (llydd) What is soft, or mild; that contains moisture; the stalk, or stem, of some plants, as the potatoe, and the like.—*Gwlydd y geifr*, the goat's weed; *gwlydd mair*, or *llysiau y cryman*, the burnet.
Gwlydd, *a.* (llydd) Of a soft, or mild, quality; tender, mild, flexible, gentle.

> Gwlydd wrth wlydd wrth wlad gyfannedd,
> Garw wrth arw wrawr gymmhwedd.
>
> *Gentle* to the *gentle* in the social country; rough to the rough the hero of combat. *Cynddelw.*
>
> Gwrhydri Beuli, ban llecher yn gwlydd.
>
> With the manly ardency of Beuli, when used he to mild. *Ll. P. Moch.*

Gwlyddâad, *s. m.* (gwlydd) A mollifying, a softening; a becoming tender or soft.
Gwlyddâawl, *a.* (gwlydd) Tending to mollify.
Gwlyddaidd, *a.* (gwlydd) Emollient; soothing.
Gwlyddâu, *v. a.* (gwlydd) To mollify; to become mild, soft, or tender.
Gwlyddedd, *s. m.* (gwlydd) Mildness; tenderness
Gwlyddeiddiad, *s. m.* (gwlyddaidd) A mollifying.
Gwlyddeiddiaw, *v. a.* (gwlyddaidd) To mollify.
Gwlyddiad, *s. m.* (gwlydd) A mollifying; a becoming mild, or gentle.
Gwlyddien, *s. m.* (gwlydd) A mild disposition.

> Gwyr y'nghynhwrynedd gwyr gwledd gwlyddien.
>
> Men in contention the men of the feast of *gentle flow*. *Cynddelw.*

Gwlyddwin, *s. m.* (gwlydd—gwin) Mild wine.

> A'i breiddin, a'i wlyddwin, a'i wledd.
>
> With his prey, with his *delicious wine*, and his feast. *Ll. P. Moch.*

Gwlyddyn, *s. m.* (gwlydd) A soft stalk. *Gwlyddyn y perthi*, goose-grass; *gwlyddyn blewawg*, mouse-ear, chickweed; also called *clust llygoden*; *gwlyddyn y cywion*, common chickweed; *gwlyddyn y dwfr*, water chickweed; *gwlyddyn y geifr*, sea campion; *gwlyddyn garw*, cleavers; *gwlyddyn gronynawg*, berry-bearing chickweed; *gwlyddyn llydanfrig*, umbelliferous chickweed; *gwlyddyn mair gwryw*, scarlet pimpernel; *gwlyddyn mair benyw*, blue pimpernel.

Gwn, *s. m.* (gy—wn) That is made to proceed; that is begun to be made apparent; a charger, a large bowl; a gun. *v. n.* To be made to proceed, or to go; to be made apparent. It is used anomalously, instead of *gwybwyf*, in answering affirmatively of knowing: as, *A wyddost di hyn?* Dost thou know this? *Gwn*, I do know. It is also used as an affix to form the terminations of the imperfect, and conditional present tenses of verbs of the first person singular, and the future tense of the first person plural: as, *carwn hi*, I loved her; *carwn hi*, I would love her; *carwn hi*, we will love her. In these verbs the determinate person and time are to be expressed by the context, otherwise they are formed thus—*Oeddwn yn ei charu, mi ei carwn, ni ei carwn*, and the like.

Gwn, *s. m.—pl.* gynau (gw—wn) A gown, a robe.

> Y gwn a rodd i gannwr,
> Ac nid â'r gwn o dŷ'r gwr.

> The *gown* was given to a hundred persons, and the *gown* goes not out of the man's house. *Adage.*

Gwna, *v. a.* (gwn) Make, do, or execute, in the second person of the future tense of the indicative mood. *Gwna, da dithau*, do, that is a good creature.

> Hen bechawd a wna gywilydd newydd.

> An old *sin will make* new shame. *Adage.*

Gwnaeth, *v.* (*pret of* gwn) Has made, has done. *Pwy a wnaeth hyn?* Who has done this?

> Duw a wnaeth eithafion
> Daiar, nef, ac eigion.

> God *did make* the extremities of earth, heaven, and sea. *W. Middleton.*

Gwnedd, *s. m.* (gwn) The act or state, of toiling; strenuousness.

> Ni chawsan' droedfedd,
> Heb wân, heb wnedd,
> O derfyn Gwynedd,
> Yn eu gweini.

> They obtained not a foot, without wounding, without *toiling*, of the boundary of Gwynedd to serve them. *Ll. P. Moch, i Lywelyn I.*

Gwneddawl, *a.* (gwnedd) Laborious, strenuous.

Gwneddiad, *s. m.* (gwnedd) An acting strenuously

Gwneddyd, *v. a.* (gwnedd) To do, to make, to perform. *Gwneddwyf oed â thi*, I made an appointment with thee; *pa ddaioni a wnaddodd?* what good has he done?

> Prydu i'th wedd a wneddwys.

> An eulogy to thy countenance *was made.* *D. ab Gwilym.*

> Diammynedd i'm gwneddyw;
> Diried ym, diweirfed yw!

> Impatient *she has made* me; mischief take me, how chaste she is! *D. ab Gwilym.*

> Dyddan gyfedd i'm gwneddwynt,
> Deuddyn, na bwyf hŷn no hwynt.

> To me *they made* pleasant festivity, the two men, may I live no longer than they shall. *Llywelyn Goch.*

Gwnelyd, *v. a.* (gwna) To make, to do. The conditional and future tenses only generally take this form. *A oes a wnelo ti â hwn?* is there any thing that thou hast to do with this?

> A wnel dyn Duw a'i barn.

> What man *will do* God will judge. *Adage.*

> Gair gwraig gwneler.

> A woman's word *let it be done.* *Adage.*

> A wnel dwyll ef a dwyllir.

> He *who makes* deception shall be deceived. *Adage.*

Gwneuthur, *v. a.* (gwnaeth) To make, to execute, to do; to commit. *Gwneuthur cyfraith*, to join issue in law: *Gwneuthur gwaed ar un*, to make one's blood to run, to wound one: *Gwneuthur y gwely, taena y gwely*, and *cyweirio y gwely*, to make the bed.

> Tri pheth nis gall Duw lai no'u gwneuthur y mwyaf ei les, y mwyaf ei eisiau, ac y mwyaf er harddwch o bob peth.

> Three things which God cannot do less than *accomplish* them that is most beneficial, that is most necessary, and the most conducive to beauty in every thing. *Barddas.*

Gwneuthuradwy, *a.* (gwneuthur) Feasible.

Gwneuthuraw, *v. a.* (gwneuthur) To do, to make, to execute, to perform; to commit.

Gwneuthurawl, *a.* (gwneuthur) Executive; doing

Gwneuthurdeb, *s. m.* (gwneuthur) Accomplishment, fulfilment.

Gwneuthuredig, *a.* (gwneuthur) Being made, done, or performed.

Gwneuthuriad, *s. m.—pl. t.* au (gwneuthur) A making, doing, or executing; workmanship.

Gwneuthuroldeb, *s. m.* (gwneuthurawl) Practicableness, feasibleness.

Gwneuthurwr, *s. m.—pl.* gwneuthurwyr (gwneuthur—gwr) One who makes, an executer.

Gwneuthyd, *v. a.* (gwnaeth) To do, to perform, to work, to execute; to commit.

> Persidia a gafas ei henw y gan Perseus frenin; ac ynddi y bu gwneuthyd cyfarfyddion gyntaf.

> Persidia had its name from king Perseus; and in it was the first *making* of histories. *Delw y Byd.*

Gwnëyd, *v. a.* (gwna) To do, to perform, to work, to execute; to commit. *Cei wnëyd yn fawr o honot*, thou shalt be made much of.

> Tri thystion Duw am a wnaeth, ac a wna; gallu anfeidrawl, gwybodaeth anfeidrawl, a chariad anfeidrawl: gan nad oes nas dichon, nas gwyr, ac nas myn y rhai hyn.

> The three testimonies of God for what he *has done*, and what he *will do*, infinite power, infinite knowledge, and infinite love: for there is nothing but what these can affect, can know, and can will. *Barddas.*

> Gwrÿd Cynan faranfo lan Teifi;
> Gwnäawd am Ddyfed ddygyfygi
> Bid iddo yn aelaw eilon yndi.

> Ardent the presence of Cynan from the banks of Teivi; a tumult *was made* round Dyved; be there for him to mourn music in it. *Myrddin.*

Gwni, *s. m.* (gwn) A stitch, or sewing; a seam.

Gwnïad, *s. m.—pl. t.* au (gwni) A stitching, a sewing; a seam.

Gwnïadur, *s. f.—pl. t.* au (gwnïad) A thimble.

Gwnïadwr, *s. m.—pl.* gwnïadwyr (gwnïad—gwr) A stitcher, a sewer.

Gwnïadwraig, *s. f.—pl.* gwnïadwreigedd (gwnïad—gwraig) A seamstress.

Gwnïadydd, *s. m.—pl. t.* ion (gwnïad) A sewer.

Gwnïadyddes, *s. f.—pl. t.* au (gwnïadydd) A seamstress, or a needle-woman.

Gwnïaw, *v. a.* (gwni) To sew, or to stitch.

Gwnïedydd, *s. m.—pl. t.* ion (gwnïad) A stitcher

Gwnïedyddes, *s. f.* (gwnïedydd) A seamstress.

Gwnïedyddiaeth, *s. m.* (gwnïedydd) The business of a stitcher; seamstressy.

Gwniferch, *s. f.* (gwni—merch) A seamstress.

Gwnïwr, *s. m.—pl.* gwnïwyr (gwni—gwr) A man who sews, a sewer.

Gwnïwraig, *s. f.—pl.* gwnïwreigedd (gwni—gwraig) A seamstress, a sewing woman.

Gwnïydd, *s. m.—pl. t.* ion (gwni) A sewer.

Gwnïyddiaeth, *s. m.* (gwnïydd) The business of sewing; the work of a sewer.

Gwo, *s. m.* (gw) A progress towards; that is gone or going; approach. It is used only as an inceptive preposition, in common with Go, and of the same import.

Gwobaith, *s. f.* (gwo—paith) Indistinct sight; hope; expectation.

Gwobeithiad, *s. m.* (gwobaith) A hoping.

Gwobeithiaw, *v. a.* (gwobaith) To hope, to expect

Gwobeithiawl, *a.* (gwobaith) Hoping, hopeful.

Gwobeithiwr, *s. m.—pl.* gwobeithwyr (gwobaith—gwr) One who hopes.

Gwobr, *s. m.—pl. t.* au (gobr) A recompense, or reward; wages, or fee; a bribe.

> Nid ammod bod ebedtw,
> Yn ahir y gwr anrheg yw,
> Nag arddelw gam, na goddwy,
> Na gwobr merch: nid gwiw bwrw mwy.
>
> There is no agreement for any heriot, in the domain of this person it is a gift, nor claim for wrong, or trespass, nor a maiden fee it is needless to mention more. *D. Ll. ab Ll. ab Gruffudd, i Dydecho.*

Gwobru, *v. a.* (gwobr) To compensate; to fee.

Gwobrwy, *s. m.—pl. t.* on (prwy) Recompense.

Gwobrwyad, *s. m.* (gwobrwy) A recompensing.

Gwobrwyaw, *v. a.* (gwobrwy) To recompense.

Gwobrwyawg, *a.* (gwobrwy) Having recompense.

Gwobrwyawl, *a.* (gwobrwy) Recompensed.

Gwobrwyedig, *a.* (gwobrwy) Recompensed.

Gwobrwywr, *s. m.—pl.* gwobrwywyr (gwobrwy—gwr) A recompenser, a requiter.

Gwobrwyydd, *s. m.—pl. t.* ion (gwobrwy) A recompenser, or requiter.

Gwobryn, *s. m.—pl. t.* ion (pryn) Desert, merit.

> Gorbo hael herlonarth wobryn,
> Hawl Medrudd hil mawr-fedd Merfyn.
>
> May the generous receive the *recompense* of generosity, the claim of Medrudd of Merfyn's line, teeming with blessing. *Cynddelw, i'r argl. Rhys.*

Gwobrynawd, *s. m.* (gwobryn) Remuneration.

Gwobrynawg, *a.* (gwobryn) Having merit.

Gwobrynawl, *a.* (gwobryn) Meriting, deserving.

Gwobryniad, *s. m.* (gwobryn) A meriting.

Gwobrynu, *v.* (gwobryn) To deserve, to merit.

Gwobrynydd, *s. m.—pl. t.* ion (gwobryn) One who merits, or deserves.

Gwodrudd, *a.* (trudd) Somewhat agitated.

> Hoed hydr am heodl wydr wodrudd.
>
> Overwhelming regret for an *agitated* life like glass. *Cynddelw.*

Gwodd, *s. m.* (gwo) That begins to break out.

Gwoddeb, *s. f.—pl. t.* ion (gwodd—eb) A purpose

> Ni rydd fy nhad, ar woddeb,
> Ei ferch yn orddereh i neb.
>
> My father will not, on *purpose*, give his daughter to be a concubine to any one. *Syr. H. Robert.*

Gwoddebawl, *a.* (gwoddeb) Intentional, designed.

Gwoddebiad, *s. m.* (gwoddeb) An intending.

Gwoddebu, *v. a.* (gwoddeb) To purpose, to intend.

Gwoddef, *s. m.—pl. t.* ion (def) Sufferance.

Gwoddefawd, *s. m.* (gwoddef) A suffering.

Gwoddefawl, *a.* (gwoddef) Suffering, passive.

Gwoddefiad, *s. m.* (gwoddef) A suffering, or bearing with; toleration; permission.

Gwoddefu, *v. n.* (gwoddef) To acquiesce.

Gwoddefus, *a.* (gwoddef) Patient; forbearing.

Gwoddew, *s. m.* (gwodd) Purpose, or design.

> Y dan llafnawr llaith woddew;
> Y dan llasar glas llas llew.
>
> Beneath the blade with the *design* of slaughter; beneath the blue armour was the lion slain. *Cynddelw, m. Bleddyn Fardd.*

> Rhudd fedd a'i cedw, wedi cain woddew,
> Artlwybr llew Lloegr ddinin.
>
> The red grave keeps him, after the great *design*, the path of the lion was Lloegria in dismay. *Cynddelw.*

Gwöen, *s. m.* (en) Influence, or tendency.

> Nid oedd dylaw drwig dragon wöen.
>
> It was not the duty of the dragon of leading *influence*. *Cynddelw.*

Gwofeg, *s. m.—pl. t.* au (meg) The mind; the will; thought; affection.

Gwofrwy, *s. m.—pl. t.* oedd (brwy) What pervades. *a.* Pervading, universal.

> Llewais wirawd gwin, a bragawd gan frawd ...
> ... wofrwy difoddi pob rhwy, rhwyf rhewiniawr!
>
> I have drunk a beverage of wine and bragget, from a departed brother, the *universal* tyrant ends every energy: sovereign of destruction! *Taliesin.*

Gwofrwyad, *s. m.* (gwofrwy) A pervading.

Gwofrwyaw, *v. a.* (gwofrwy) To pervade; to become universal.

Gwofrwyawl, *a.* (gwofrwy) Tending to pervade.

Gwolaeth, *s. m.* (gwawl) Adoration, worship.

Gwolch, *s. m.* (golch) A wash; a washing.

Gwolchi, *v. a.* (gwolch) To wash away; to belabour.

> Y'nghreulawn ymwrthryn
> Gwychr y gwylch gwolch amddiffyn.
>
> In the bloody contest, bravely *he belabours* the barons of defence. *Cynddelw.*

Gwoleu, *s. m.* (gwawl) A light. *a.* Light, clear.

Gwoleuad, *s. m.—pl. t.* on (gwoleu) A lighting.

Gwoleuaw, *v. a.* (gwoleu) To light, to illume.

Gwolwch, *s. m.* (gwawl) The act of illuminating; the bardic worship; adoration.

> Na'm gwrthryn, gwenwyn gwaid wolwch;
> Na'm gwrthod, cirl draiod arfdrwch;
> Ni wrthyd mab Duw dadolwch.
>
> Reject me not, thou white fronted one, fervent in *prayer*; refuse me not, who art inured to frequent tumults of brandishing weapons; the Son of God will not refuse reconciliation. *Cynddelw, i'r argl. Rhys.*

Gwolychawd, *s. m.* (gwolwch) Act of worshipping

Gwolychiad, *s. m.* (gwolwch) A worshipping.

Gwolychu, *v. a.* (gwolwch) To worship, to adore.

> Gwolychaf fy nhad,
> Fy Nuw, fy nerthiad,
> A ddodes trwy fy iad
> Enaid i'm pwyllad.
>
> *I will adore* my Father, my God, my strengthener, who infused through my temples a soul to direct me. *Taliesin.*

Gwor, *s. m.* (or) What is superior, uppermost, or extreme; an origin. It is used as a prefix, like Gor, and of the same import.

Gwores, *s. f.—pl. t.* au (es) What lies open, or waste. *a.* Open, or exposed; waste.

Gworgrawd, *s. m.* (crawd) A supercrescence.

Gworllwydd, *s. m.* (gwor—llwydd) Prosperity.

Gwortho, *s. m.* (to) The upper covering; roof.

Gworymda, *v. a.* (gwor—ymda) To ambulate.

> Llawer mawrair a fethia
> Ceudawd cyd worymdaw,
> O frys ni wys cwdd a.
>
> Many a boastful word will cause difficulty to the breast, whilst it *goes about*, from haste it cannot be known where it will go. *Llyfrol.*

Gworymdäad, *s. m.* (gworymda) Ambulation.

Gworymdaawl, *a.* (gworymda) Ambulatory.

Gworymdäwr, *s. m.—pl.* gworymdawyr (gworymda—gwr) One who walks over; an ambulator.

Gworymdäydd, *s. m.—pl. t.* ion (gworymda) An ambulator, a stroller.

Gwos, *s. m.* (gwo—ys) That partly is; that tends to. A prefix, like Gos, and of the same import.

Gwosbaith, *s. m.—pl.* gwosbeithion (paith) That is partly seen through; that is polished. *a.* Reflective; polished.

> Hael udd rhuddyfrodd clod faith, na'm gwrthod
> Mawr wrthyd fy nghwaith;
> Anaw drellliaw drin w wbaith
> Ewe bell, henbych gwell ganwaith.
>
> Generous chieftain with the ruddy sword of ample fame, refuse me not, great is my dependence upon thee; standing round the song, of *polished* art and far of name, be thou hailed with a hundred blessings. *Gw. Ryfel, i Ll. ab Gwain.*

Gwosbarth, *s. m.—pl. t.* au (parth) A distinct part, or particular.

Gwosbarthawl, *a.* (gwosbarth) Particularizing.

Gwosbarthiad, *s.* (gwosbarth) A particularizing.

Gwosbarthu, *v. a.* (gwosbarth) To particularize.

Gwosbeithiad, *s. m.* (gwosbaith) Illumination.

Gwosbeithiaw, *v. a.* (gwosbaith) To illume.
Gwosbeithiawl, *a.* (gwosbaith) Tending to shine.
Gwosbeithig, *a.* (gwosbaith) Shining; polished.
Gwoseb, *s. f.—pl. t.* ion (gwaws—eb) A gift.

Cyrchais eryr trais trin oheb, heb gudd
Cad wosudd, cad wöseb,
Arwr ar wir ei wyneb,
Ar wyrdd wawr wrach no neb.

I approached the eagle of violence ready for the conflict, without disguise, the leader of the onset, whose *gift* is treasure; a hero with his countenance fixed on truth, and with the green dawn more manly than any one. *Cynddelw.*

Gwosebu, *v. a.* (gwoseb) To present a gift.
Gwosgo, *s. m.* (osgo) Tangent, obliquity.
Gwosgryn, *a.* (cryn) Tending to agitate.
Gwosgryniad, *s. m.* (gwosgryn) A causing a shake.
Gwosgrynu, *v. a.* (gwosgryn) To cause agitation.
Gwosgudd, *a.* (cudd) Sculking, or lurking.
Gwosol, *s. m.* (gwos—ol) A faint trace, a vestige

Diffid Caen——
Fal nad oes, fanon di wosol,
Un o'i ryw yn wir i'w ol.

Caen was blotted out, so that there is not truly (a beginning without a *vestige*) one of his race behind him. *W. Cynwal.*

Gwosudd, *s. m.* (gwos—udd) That gives an origin.

Ni'm didawl——
Ac ai lludd cad wosudd ced.

He will not reject me; and the *genius* of battle will not debar me of treasure. *Prydydd Bychan.*

Gwyr wosudd, llofrudd Lloegr ddillyn;
Gŵyr wosgo wosgordd diergryn.

The wild *genius*, the slayer pursuing Lloegria; he knows the bent of the battalion that knows no fear. *Cynddelw, i'r argl. Rhys.*

Gwp, *s. m.—pl. t.* iau (wp) A bird's head and neck. *Gwnëyd gwp cam*, to make a wry neck.
Gwr, *s. m.—pl.* gwyr (gw—wr) A being endowed with power, will, or liberty; a man; a person, a husband.—*Gwr hen*, or *hen wr*, an old man; *gwr ieuanc*, a young man, a bachelor; *gwr wrth gerdd*, a musician; *gwr y gyfraith*, a lawyer; *gwr priawd*, a married man; *gwr a gwraig*, a man and wife; *gwr gweddw*, a widower; *gwr gwellt*, a man of straw; *gwr nod*, a man of repute, also a marked man, or slave; *gwr dinod*, or *gwr addwyn*, a man not marked; *gwr pwys*, a bridegroom; *gwr rhif*, an enlisted man; *gwr ar deulu*, a household officer; *gwr ar gylch*, a wanderer; *gwr y god*, the bag bearer; *y gwr drwg*, the evil one.

Penaf gwr o'r penau 'gyd
Goruwch byd, yw'r gwr uwch ben.

The chiefest *person* of all the chiefs over the world, is the *person* over head. *L. G. Cothi.*

Gwr eres wyd, garw ei sain,
Drud byd, heb droed, heb adain.

Thou art a terrible *being*, rough of voice, the world's bold tyrant, having neither foot nor wing. *D. ab Gwilym, i'r gwynt.*

Teithi gwr yw gallu cyd a gwraig, a bod yn gyfan ei holl aelodau.

The required qualities of a *man* is to be able to join with a woman, and to be perfect in all his members. *Welsh Laws.*

Sef yw gwr dawed, gwr a ddel trwyddo ei hun ar dir, ac ni bo neb o'i genedl cyn nog ef ar y tir.

What is implied by an advenient *man* is a *man* who shall come through himself upon land, and of whose kindred no one shall have been before him upon the land. *Welsh Laws.*

Gwyr a wnant gwr yn wrol;
Gwr a wnaw gwyr yn ei ol.

Men will make a *man* manly; a *man* will make *men* after him. *M. ab Rhys.*

Gwr, *a.* (gw—wr) Having power, or will; of manly superiority; male, masculine, man. It is prefixed in composition.
Gwra, *v. a.* (gwr) To get a husband, to wed.

O dygir trais i ar wraig wriawg, ni ddylyir talu amobrwy drosto: canys hi a'i talws pan wraws.

If a rape shall be committed upon a married woman, the guardian fee shall not be paid for it; for she has paid it when she was married. *Welsh Laws.*

Gwrâad, *s. m.* (gwr) Tending to make manly.
Gwrâawl, *a.* (gwr) Tending to make manly.
Gwrab, *s. m.—pl. t.* iod (gwr—ab) A monkey.
Gwrabaidd, *a.* (gwrab) Apish, monkeyish.
Gwrabeiddrwydd, *s. m.* (gwrabaidd) Apishness.
Gwrach, *s. f.—pl. t.* od (gwr) A withered old woman, a hag; also the ague. *Gwrachod telyn*, the pegs of a harp; *gwrachod tan yd yn ei ddas*, faggots under corn in the rick; *gwrachod mewn to*, certain bundles used to form the skirts of thatching: *Y wrach*, the wrasse, a fish so called; *y wrach*, the ague; *gwrach y cae*, the hedge-sparrow; *gwrach y lludw*, *gwrach y twca*, and *gwrach y coed*, the woodlouse.

O Sul i Sul ydd â'r forwyn yn wrach.

From Sunday to Sunday the damsel will become an *old woman*. *Adage.*

Eled y wrach i'r felin
Er ei genau ei hunan.

Let the *old woman* go to the mill for the sake of her own mouth. *Adage.*

Gwrach, *a.* (*comparative of* gwr) More masculine.
Gwrachaidd, *a.* (gwrach) Like a hag, hag-like.
Gwrachan, *s. c. dim.—pl. t.* od (gwrach) A withered little creature; a pigmy.

Haws twyllaw maban
Na thwyllaw gwrachan.

It is easier to deceive a child than to deceive a *pigmy*. *Adage.*

Gwrachanaidd, *a.* (gwrachan) Like a shrivelled dwarf.
Gwrachandawd, *s. m.* (gwrachan) Dwarfishness.
Gwrachanes, *s. f. dim.* (gwrachan) A little old woman; a female dwarf.

O chwant ennill plant pa les,
A chynnal y gwrachanes.

From desire, what good will it be to beget children, and support the *tiny wrinkled woman*. *Ieuan Brydydd Hir.*

Gwrachanu, *v. n.* (gwrachan) To become a withered little creature.
Gwrachastell, *s. f.—pl. t.* od (gwrach—astell) The mould-board of a plough.
Gwracheiddiad, *s. m.* (gwrachaidd) A becoming like a withered hag.
Gwracheiddiaw, *v. n.* (gwrachaidd) To become a hag.
Gwracheiddrwydd, *s. m.* (gwrachaidd) Anility.
Gwrachell, *s. f.—pl. t.* od (gwrach) A withered little dwarf. *Gwrachell y cae*, *gwrach y cae*, *brych y cae*, and *llwyd y gwrych*, the hedge-sparrow.
Gwrachen, *s. f.—pl. t.* od (gwrach) A crabbed little person. *Gwrachen*, and *ysgretan*, the tench; *gwrachen y mor*, the sea tench, or wrasse; *gwrachen fuir*, a yellow kind of wrasse; *gwrachen fraith*, or *cleriach gwimon*, a spotted wrasse; *gwrachen*, *penbwla*, and *adar y bili*, the miller's thumb.
Gwrachi, *s. f.—pl. t.* od (gwrach) Anility.

Rhyddaroedd i Gruffydd, ar êang, cynnullaw holl wrachiod mantach, crwm, cloff, unllygeidiawg, gormesawl, diallu, ac eu cynnyg idd y Daenysiaid, yn dwyth eu bradwriaeth.

What Gruffydd accomplished, at length, was to collect all the *aged people*, such as were toothless, bent, lame, one eyed, oppressed, and disabled, and offered them to the Danes, as a reward for their treachery. *Buch. Gr. ab Cynan.*

Gwrachïaidd, *a.* (gwrachi) Like a hag, haggish.
Gwrachïaw, *v. n.* (gwrachi) To become haglike.
Gwradwydd, *s. m.* (gwaradwydd) Reproach, scandal; opprobrious censure; infamy.
Gwradwyddaw, *v. n.* (gwradwydd) To scandalize.
Gwradwyddawl, *a.* (gwradwydd) Scandalizing.
Gwradwyddiad, *s. m.* (gwradwydd) A scandalizing
Gwradwyddus, *a.* (gwradwydd) Scandalous.

Gwradwyddwr, *s. m.—pl.* gwradwyddwyr (gwradwydd—gwr) A scandaliser.

Gwradd, *s. m.—pl. t.* au (rhadd) An aggregate. *Gwradd o ddynion*, a multitude of people; *gwradd o ddlyn*, a quantity of provision.

Gwraddawl, *a.* (gwradd) Aggregate, collective.

Gwraddiad, *s. m.* (gwradd) An aggregation.

Gwraddu, *v. a.* (gwradd) To aggregate, to collect. *Na wradd arni*, throw no contumacy on her.

Gwraf, *a.* (*superlative of* gwr) Most masculine.

> Arglwydd gwraf gwryd Echdor.
>
> A *most manly* chief having the bravery of Hector. *Cynddelw.*

Gwrag, *s. f.* (rhag) That curves against, or in contact with; that braces.

Gwragen, *s. f.—pl. t.* i (gwrag) The rib of any circular work, as of a tilt, or basket; the curved handle of a vessel, as a pail, or of a basket.

Gwrageniad, *s. m.* (gwragen) A ribbing.

Gwragenu, *v. a.* (gwragen) To rib; to furnish with a curved handle.

Gwragenus, *a.* (gwragen) Serving as a rib, or strength of any work, serving as a handle.

Gwraich, *s. m.—pl.* gwreichion (gwr—aich) A spark.

Gwraid, *s. m.* (rhaid) That is impulsive, that forces through; that is ardent; a flush.

> Ef a borea, gwres a gwraid,
> Yr un erw a'r aur euraid.
>
> He graces, during the heat and the *[illegible]*, on the same plat as the golden lamb. *Iev. Llewddeu.*

Gwraidd, *s. m. aggr.—pl.* gwreiddion (rhaidd) A root, or a radix; roots.

Gwraidd, *a.* (gwr) Manly, manlike; valiant.

> Gwas gwraidd cyn no'i gerdded.
>
> A *manly* hero before he is able to walk. *Adage.*

Gwraig, *s. f.—pl.* gwreigedd (gwr—aig) A woman, a female; a wife. *Gwraig wysg*, a bride: *gwraig wriawg*, and *gwraig briawd*, a married woman; *gwraig weddw*, a widow; *gwraig etifeddawg*, a child-bed woman; *gwraig gwely*, a concubine; *gwraig llwyn a pherth*, a woman of the grove and brake, a harlot; *gwreigedd annwyl*, and *plant y gwreigedd annwyl*, fairies.

> Nerth gwraig yn ei thafawd.
>
> The strength of a woman in her tongue. *Adage.*

> Ni thorrs Arthur nawdd gwraig.
>
> Arthur did not break a *woman's* protection. *Adage.*

Gwrain, *a.* (gwr) Masculine, virile, male.

Gwraint, *s. pl. aggr.* (rhaint) Slender worms that insinuate through a body; worms under the skin; also the ringworm, or tetters.

Gwrandaw, *s. m.* (gwr—andaw) A listening.

Gwrandaw, *v. a.* (gwr—andaw) To listen, to hearken, to hear.

> Ni wyr ni ddysg, ni ddysg ni wrendy.
>
> He does not know that does not learn, he will not learn that will not *listen*. *Adage.*

> Gwae a ddywedo lawer, ac ni wrandawo ar neb.
>
> Woe to be that says much, and will not *listen* to any one. *Adage.*

Gwrandawgar, *a.* (gwrandaw) Attentive, wistful.

Gwrandawgarwch, *s. m.* (gwrandawgar) Attentiveness, heedfulness, wistfulness.

Gwrandawiad, *s. m.* (gwrandaw) A listening, or hearkening; attention.

Gwrandawus, *a.* (gwrandaw) Attentive, heedful.

Gwrandawwr, *s. m.—pl.* gwrandawwyr (gwrandaw—gwr) A listener, a hearkener.

Gwrandawydd, *s. m.—pl. t.* ion (gwrandaw) A listener, a hearer.

Gwrâu, *v. a.* (gwr) To render manly; to be manly.

Gwrawl, *a.* (gwr) Manly; stout, valiant.

Gwrcath, *s. m.—pl. t.* od (gwr—cath) A he cat.

Gwrcatha, *v. a.* (gwrcath) To caterwaul.

Gwrcathain, *a.* (gwrcath) Caterwauling.

Gwrcathaint, *s. m.* (gwrcathain) A caterwauling.

Gwrch, *s. m.* (gwr) That is upon, or over.

Gwrda, *s. m.—pl.* gwyrda (gwr—da) A man of quality, a gentleman; a person of renown, a famous one. *Dyn a fod yn wrda*, that is being a hero, *Gwrda*! Bravo! Excellent!

> Dywed ti, pam nad wyd da!
> Dy ddewr-dad ti oedd wrda.
>
> Say thou, why art thou not good!
> Thy brave sire was a *notable* man. *Guto y Glyn.*

Gwrdäaeth, *s. m.* (gwrda) A manly quality; manliness, gallantry.

> Mwyaf y gyfarwys a roddom, mwyfwy fydd ein gwrdäaeth ninnau.
>
> The greater the prize which we should give, more and more will be our *gallantry* also. *H. Cułhwch—Mabinogion.*

Gwrdäaidd, *a.* (gwrda) Manly; gallant, heroic.

> Yn wraf ydd wyd——
> Yn ardwyaw cler yn wrdäaidd;
> Yn ardemlu beirdd yn garuaidd.
>
> Greatly dost thou regulate the minstrels in a *manly* way, rebuking the bards affectionately. *L. G. Cothi.*

Gwrdäeiddrwydd, *s. m.* (gwrdäaidd) Manliness.

> Mawr yw haelder——
> A gwrdäeiddrwydd y gwrda diddrwg.
>
> Great is the generosity, and the *gallantry* of the gentleman void of mischief. *Iolo Goch.*

Gwrdd, *a.* (wrdd) Stout, ardent, vehement.

Gwrddain, *a.* (gwrdd) Abounding with ardency.

Gwrdd-dorch, *s. f.—pl.* gwrdd-dyrch (gwrdd—torch) A strong collar.

> Yr oedd gwrdd-dorch ruddaur am fwnwgl pob un o'r cwn.
>
> There was a *strong collar* of ruddy gold round the neck of each of the dogs. *H. Geraint—Mabinogion.*

Gwrddfalch, *a.* (gwrdd—balch) Vehemently-proud.

Gwrddfar, *s. m.* (gwrdd—bar) Ardent wrath.

Gwrddiad, *s. m.* (gwrdd) A rendering vehement; a becoming vehement, or ardent.

Gwrddlam, *s. m.* (gwrdd—llam) An ardent stride.

Gwrddlaw, *s. f.* (gwrdd—llaw) A mighty hand.

Gwrddlew, *a.* (gwrdd—glew) Vehemently-brave.

> Och ar fyned gwr gwrddlew rhyfel!
>
> Woe is me, that the man *ardently-brave* in war is gone! *Llygad Gwr.*

Gwrddu, *v. a.* (gwrdd) To render ardent; to become strong, vehement, or ardent.

Gwrddwaew, *s. f.* (gwrdd—gwaew) A javelin.

Gwrddwan, *s. f.* (gwrdd—gwan) An ardent thrust.

Gwrddwawr, *s. f.* (gwrdd—gwawr) A darting ray.

Gwrddyn, *s. m.* (gwrdd) A dart; a javelin.

> Daeth Braint Hir y'mhlith torf o'r cardotion, yn y parth yd oedd y dewin yn eu rhoi; a heb un gobir, pan gafas ef fyd ar ei gyflafan, ef a ddercheфis wrddyn, ac a wanai y dewin.
>
> Braint Hir came amongst a group of the mendicants, in the part where the diviner was haranguing them! and without any hesitation, when he got an opportunity for his aim, he lifted a *javelin*, and wounded the diviner. *Gr. ab Arthur.*

Gwrechyn, *s. m.* (gwrach) A crabbed fellow.

Gwregys, *s. m.—pl. t.* au (gwrag) A girdle.

> Ni ad y mor hyd ei wregys.
>
> He will not let the sea come to his *girdle*. *Adage.*

Gwregysawg, *a.* (gwregys) Having a girdle.

Gwregysawl, *a.* (gwregys) Serving to gird.

Gwregysedig, *a.* (gwregys) Being girdled; girded.

Gwregysfa, *s. f.* (gwregys) A girding place.

Gwregysiad, *s. m.* (gwregys) A girding, a belting.

Gwregysu, *v. a.* (gwregys) To girdle, to gird.

Gwregyswr, *s. m.—pl.* gwregyswyr (gwregys—gwr) One who girdles, a girder.

Gwreica, *s. f.* (gwraig) A marriage of a wife.

> Gwedi nad oedd gwreigedd iddynt, erchi a wnaynt i'r Prydeiniaid i eu merched, ac eu carenau yn wreica iddynt.
>
> Since there were no women with them, they asked of the Britons to have their daughters and their female relatives in *marriage* for them. *Gr. ab Arthur.*
>
> Rhoddid yn wreica i Custenyn wraig a hanodd o ddyledogion Rhufain.
>
> There was given in *marriage* to Constantine a woman descended from the nobility of Rome. *Gr. ab Arthur.*
>
> Ni a wyddom wreica da it a weddai, sef yw hono gwraig Doged frenin.
>
> We know a *match* for thee which will suit, and that is the wife of king Doged. *H. Culhwch—Mabinogion.*

Gwreica, *v. a.* (gwraig) To take a wife.

Gwreicdra, *s. m.* (gwraig) Muliebrity; fondness for women; adultery.

Gwreichion, *s. pl. aggr.* (gwraich) Emanations; sparks, or sparkles.

Gwreichionawg, *a.* (gwreichion) Abounding with sparks, full of sparks; sparkling.

Gwreichionawl, *a.* (gwreichion) Sparkling.

Gwreichionen, *s. f.* (gwreichion) A spark, a sparkle.

Gwreichioni, *v. a.* (gwreichion) To produce sparks; to emit sparks, to sparkle, to scintillate.

Gwreichioniad, *s. m.* (gwreichion) Scintillation.

Gwreidd-don, *s. f.* (gwraidd—ton) The devil's bit; otherwise called *Cas gan gythraul.*

Gwreiddfalch, *a.* (gwraidd—balch) Proud.

Gwreiddiad, *s. m.* (gwraidd) A taking root.

Gŵreiddiad, *s. m.* (gŵraidd) A becoming manly.

Gwreiddiaw, *v. a.* (gwraidd) To take root; to be rooted, to originate.

Gŵreiddiaw, *v. n.* (gŵraidd) To become masculine.

Gwreiddiawg, *a.* (gwraidd) Having root, rooted.

Gwreiddiawl, *a.* (gwraidd) Radical, rooted.

Gŵreiddiawl, *a.* (gŵraidd) Masculine, manly.

Gwreiddiedig, *a.* (gwreiddiad) Rooted, radicated.

Gwreiddioldeb, *s. m.* (gwreiddiawl) Radicalness.

Gwreiddiolrwydd, *s. m.* (gwreiddiawl) Radicalness.

Gwreiddiriawg, *s. f.* (gwraidd—ir) Burnet saxifrage.

Gwreiddrudd, *s. f.* (gwraidd—rhudd) Wild madder.

Gŵreiddrwydd, *s. m.* (gŵraidd) Manliness.

Gwreiddyn, *s. m.* (gwraidd) A root; a radix.

> Hysbys y dengys y dyn
> O ba radd y bo ei wreiddyn.
>
> The man will plainly shew from what he takes his *root.* *T. Aled.*

Gwreigâad, *s. m.* (gwraig) A becoming a woman.

Gwreigâu, *v. n.* (gwraig) To grow a woman.

Gwreigdda, *s. f.* (gwraig—da) A good woman, a term in familiar language.

> Dyddgwaith yd aeth y wreigdda allan i orymdaith, y daeth hi i dŷ hen wrach.
>
> On a certain day when the *good lady* came out to take a walk, she came to the house of an old witch. *H. Culhwch—Mabinogion.*

Gwreigen, *s. f. dim.* (gwraig) A little woman.

Gwreigeddgar, *s.* (gwraig—car) Love of women.

Gwreigeddos, *s. pl. aggr.* (gwraig) A number of women; gossips.

Gwreigeddwr, *s. m.—pl.* gwreigeddwyr (gwreigedd—gwr) One addicted to women, A wencher.

Gwreigiaidd, *a.* (gwraig) Female; matronly.

Gwreigiawg, *a.* (gwraig) Having a wife.

Gwreigiawl, *a.* (gwraig) Feminine; effeminate.

> Byddinaw a wnai Brutus ei gydymdeithion yntau, nid yn wreigiawl hagen, namyn yn wrawl; ac yn ddoeth dysgu iddynt pa wedd y dylent gyrchu, neu gilliaw, neu ymladd.
>
> Brutus also set his companions in battle array, not in an *effeminate* way neither, but in a manly way; and with prudence instructed them in what manner they ought to attack, or to retreat or to fight. *Gr. ab Arthur.*

Gwreigieiddiad, *s. m.* (gwreigiaidd) Effemination.

Gwreigieiddiaw, *v. n.* (gwreigiaidd) To effeminate.

Gwreigieiddiawl, *a.* (gwreigiaidd) Of an effeminate disposition; uxorious.

Gwreigieiddrwydd, *s. m.* (gwreigiaidd) Effeminacy; muliebrity.

Gwreigiolrwydd, *s.* (gwreigiawl) Effeminateness.

Gwreignith, *s. f.—pl. t.* od (gwraig—nith) A little woman; a little doll of a wife.

Gwreinawd, *s. m.* (gwrain) Manhood, virility.

Gwreindawd, *s. m.* (gwrain) Virility, manhood.

Gwreinen, *s. f. dim.* (gwraint) A ringworm.

Gwreinyn, *s. m. dim.* (gwraint) A ringworm, a tetter. *Dwfr-wreinyn*, a watery tetter; *march-wreinyn*, a ringworm.

Gwreng, *s. m.—pl. t.* od (gwr—eng) A plebian.

> Mi wyf—gwreng i Dudyr ab Gronwy.
>
> I am a *husbandman* to Tudyr the son of Gronwy. *Goronwy Ddu.*

Gwrengaidd, *a.* (gwreng) Plebeian, boorish.

Gwrengaidd, *a.* (gwreng) Boorish, clownish.

Gwrengeiddrwydd, *s. m.* (gwrengaidd) Boorishness.

Gwrengyn, *s. m. dim.* (gwreng) A surly clown.

Gwres, *s. m.* (es) Heat; warmth. *Yr haint gwres, y twymyn*, an inflammatory fever. *Mae arnat ti ryw wres garw*, thou art troubled with some odd frolick. *Nid oes arnaf mór gwres*, I am troubled with no frolick.

Gwres, *s. f—pl. t.* au (gwr) A female.

Gwresawg, *a.* (gwres) Abounding with heat, fervid, fervent, warm.

Gwresawl, *a.* (gwres) Of a heating quality.

Gwresedd, *s. m.* (gwres) Fervidness, fervency.

Gwresiad, *s. m.* (gwres) A rendering fervid; a becoming fervid.

Gwresogi, *v. a.* (gwresawg) To make hot, or fervid; to become warm, or fervent.

Gwresogiad, *s. m.* (gwresawg) A rendering fervent; a becoming fervent.

Gwresogrwydd, *s. m.* (gwresawg) Fervidness, effervescence, fervency.

Gwresu, *v. a.* (gwres) To fill with heat.

Gwrfalch, *a.* (gwr—balch) Greatly proud.

> Ar law Owain hael, hawl dilin gwrfalch,
> Y mae gorllwch eurin.
>
> On the hand of Owain the generous, the *magnanimous*, and of fair title, there is the golden tankard. *Cynddelw.*

Gwrfalchedd, *s. m.* (gwrfalch) Towering pride.

Gwrfan, *a.* (gwr—ban) Extremely loud.

> Gorfaran gwrfan gosfyddai;
> Gwr yn aer yn araws gwaedd fai.
>
> The *tumultuous* front of battle he would vanquish; a man waiting for the shout in the slaughter he would be. *Cynddelw, m. O. Gwynedd.*

Gwrfawr, *a.* (gwr—mawr) Supremely grand.

Gwrferch, *s. f.—pl. t.* ed (gwr—merch) A virago.

Gwrforedd, *s. m.* (gwrfawr) Magnificence.

Gwrforwyn, *s. f.—pl. t.* ion (gwr—morwyn) A virago; an amazon.

> Tair gwrforwyn Ynys Prydain: Lleweg ferch Seithwedd, a Rhore ferch Usber, a Mederai Badell-fawr.
>
> The three *viragoes* of Britain: Lleweg daughter of Seithwedd, and Rhore daughter of Usber, and Mederai Broad bottom. *Trioedd.*

Gwrhewcri, *s. m.* (gwrhewgr) Jocularity. *Chwareu gwrhewcri ag un*, to play jokes upon one, or to make game of one.

Gwrhewcrus, *a.* (gwrhewgr) Full of tricks. *Dyn gwrhewcrus*, a jocose person.

Gwrhëwg, *a.* (hewg) Extremely playful.

Gwrhewgr, *s. m.* (gwrhewg) Aptness to play tricks, or to be jocular.

Gwrhyd, *s. m.—pl. t.* oedd (gwr—hyd) A man's length, a fathom, or two yards. *Gwrhyd Aberystwyth*, the Aberystwyth fathom, or five feet six inches.

Gwrhydr, *s. m.* (gwr—hydr) Extreme boldness.

Gwrhydri, *s. m.* (gwrhydr) Heroism; valour.

Gwrhydu, *v. a.* (gwrhyd) To fathom.

Gwriaeth, *s. m.* (gwr) A man's estate, or life.

> Bid byw gwr heb ddrwg wriaeth.
>
> Let a man live without evil *conduct*. — *Llefoed.*

Gwriaf, *a.* (*superl. of* gwr) Most manlike.

> Py fydd cad wriaf rhag cadwr lawn:
> Py fydd ced wallaw fal Cadwallawn?
>
> Who will be in battle *most manly* opposed to the perfect warrior, who will be the distributor of treasure like Cadwallon. — *Cynddelw.*

Gwrial, *s. m.* (gwr) A heroic act; a combat.

Gwrial, *v. a.* (gwr) To act heroically.

Gwriawg, *a.* (gwr) Having a chief; owning a chief; having a husband. *Gwraig wriawg*, a married woman.

> Dyddaw dwy rian,
> Gweddw a gwriawg fain,
> Hedeiru eu hadain,
> Ar wyr yn gorlain.
>
> There will come two ladies, a widow and a slender *wedded one*, tron their wings, brooding over men. — *Taliesin.*

Gwriawr, *s. m.* (gwr) Manhood; gallantry.

> Digabl wawr gwriawr fal Gwron.
>
> The immaculate dawn of *manhood* like Gwron. — *H. Foel ab Griffri.*
>
> Wyd ysgwyd gryd, graid gwriawr,
> Ac wyd ysgwyd rwydd, rhwyf llawr.
>
> Thou art the terror of the conflict, the ardency of *manhood*, and thou art the safe shield, the ruler of the earth. — *Ll. P. Moch, i R. ab H. ab Owain.*

Gwrid, *s. m.* (gwr id) Reddishness, or redness of the cheeks; a blush; a flush.

Gwridaw, *v. n.* (gwrid) To redden, or to blush.

Gwridawg, *a.* (gwrid) Having a colour, or blush, of a ruddy complexion; ruddy.

Gwridgoch, *a.* (gwrid—coch) Of a blushing red.

Gwridgochder, *s. m.* (gwridgoch) A blushing red.

Gwridgochedd, *s. m.* (gwridgoch) Ruddiness, floridness, rosiness.

Gwridgochi, *v. n.* (gwridgoch) To become florid.

Gwridgochni, *s. m.* (gwridgoch) Floridness.

Gwridiad, *s.m.* (gwrid) A blushing; a reddening.

Gwridliw, *s. m.* (gwrid—lliw) A blush colour; a ruddy colour, rose-colour.

Gwridogi, *v. n.* (gwridawg) To become ruddy.

Gwridogiad, *s. m.* (gwridawg) A becoming ruddy.

Gwring, *s. m.—pl. t.* oedd (rhing) A snap, a sharp noise, a crack, or crackle.

Gwringain, *v. a.* (gwring) To snap, to crackle.

Gwringell, *s. f.—pl. t.* au (gwring) A sudden, or sharp motion; a chip, or slice. *Gwringell o gaws*, a slice of cheese.

Gwringellawg, *s. m.* (gwringell) Having a sharp motion; being brandished; cracking.

Gwringelliad, *s. m.* (gwringell) A brandishing; a snapping, or cracking; a slicing.

Gwringellu, *v. a.* (gwringell) To brandish.

> *Na wringella dy fysedd wrth ymddyddan.*
>
> *Snap not thy fingers in discoursing.*

Gwriogaeth, *s. m.—pl. t.* au (gwriawg) Homage.

> Ar y rhai hyny y cyfododd Solomon dreth *wriogaeth* hyd y dydd hwn.
>
> Upon those *ones* Solomon raised a tribute of *homage* unto this day. — *1 Kings, 9. 21.*

Gwriogaethawl, *a.* (gwriogaeth) Feudatory.

Gwriogaethiad, *s.m.* (gwriogaeth) A doing homage

Gwriogaethu, *v. a.* (gwriogaeth) To do homage.

Gwriogi, *v. a.* (gwriawg) To do homage.

Gwrith, *s. m.* (rhith) That is apparent.

> *Ef gwrith, ef ddatwrith, ef gwrith ieithoedd.*
>
> *He will make plain, he will make indistinct, he will explain languages.* — *Taliesin.*

Gwrithiad, *s. m.* (gwrith) A making apparent.

Gwrithiaw, *v. a.* (gwrith) To make apparent.

Gwrlys, *s. m.* (gwr—llys) A bordering, or border, the orle, in heraldry; also a whitlow.

> O bob anrhaith y brenin a ddyly draean ei aur, a'i ariant, a'i eilit, a'i gyrn buelin, a'i fain gwerthfawr, a'i ysginau y bo wrlys wrthynt.
>
> Out of every spoil the king is entitled to a third of his gold, and his silver, and his treasure, and his buffalo horns, and his precious stones, and his robes to which there shall be *fringe*. — *Welsh Laws.*

Gwrm, *s. m.* (gwr) A dun, dusky, or brown colour; a dark brown. *a.* Dun, dusky, of a dark brown hue. *Gwrm ei hael*, dark brown her eye-brow.

> Bid gwrm biw, bid llwyd blaidd.
>
> Let the kine be brown, let the wolf be grey. — *Llywarch Hen.*

Gwrmawd, *s. m.* (gwrm) A rendering dusky, or dun; a becoming dusky, or dun.

Gwrmder, *s. m.* (gwrm) Duskiness, murkiness.

Gwrmdde, *a.* (gwrm) Of a dusky quality.

Gwrmlas, *s. m.* (gwrm—glas) A dusky green, a sea-green. *a.* Of a sea-green colour.

Gwrmlasu, *v. n.* (gwrmlas) To become of dusky green, or of a brownish green.

Gwrmlesni, *s. m.* (gwrmlas) A dusky greenness.

Gwrmsaid, *s. m.* (gwrm—said) A brown handle. *Cleddyf gwrmsaid*, a brown handled sword.

Gwrmu, *v. a.* (gwrm) To make dusky, to grow dusky, to become murky.

Gwrmwn, *a.* (gwrm) Of a dusky appearance.

> E am lafnawr coch gorfawr gwrmwn,
> Dwys dengyn ydd ymleddyn' aergwn.
>
> Round the blades, red, tremendous and *murky*, incessantly and with obstinacy the dogs of war would fight. — *Aneurin.*

Gwrn, *s. m.—pl.* gyrnau (gwr) That tops, or goes over; a narrow mouthed vessel; an urn; a kind of wooden vessel, or pail, tapering towards the top, like a churn.

> Mae bateloe'n ymhob talwrn!
> Mae Owain aeth mewn ei wrn?
>
> Where are the battles which were in every border? Where is Owain who is gone to his urn? — *Rh. ab Rh. Brydydd.*

Gwrnerth, *s. m.* (gwr—nerth) The male speedwell; otherwise called *Llysiau Llywelyn*.

Gwroeth, *s. m.* (oeth) Common tansy.

Gwrolaeth, *s. m.* (gwrawl) Virility; manhood.

Gwroldeb, *s. m.* (gwrawl) Manliness; bravery.

Gwroledd, *s. m.* (gwrawl) Manhood, bravery.

Gwrolfryd, *s. m.* (gwrawl—bryd) Magnanimity.

Gwrolgamp, *s. f.—pl. t.* au (gwrawl—camp) A manly feat; an heroic exploit.

> Y deg gwrolgamp yw chwech o rym corff: cryfder, rhedeg, neidiaw, nofiaw, ymafael, marchogaeth: a phedair o rym arfau: saethu, chwarae cleddyf a bwcled, chwarae cleddyf deuddwrn, a chwarae ffon ddwybig.
>
> Of the ten *manly games* six are of bodily exertion: strength, running, leaping, swimming, wrestling, and riding: four are feat of arms, shooting, playing with a sword and buckler, playing at a two-handed sword, and playing at a two-pointed staff. — *Welsh Customs.*

Gwroli, *v. n.* (gwrawl) To become manly; to take courage.

> Rhai yn hen Mab Duw a'u myn,
> Rhai'n ieuainc cyn gwroli.
>
> Some in old age the Son of God doth take, some that are young before *growing up to manhood*. — *T. ab Ieu. Madawg.*

Gwrolineth, *s. m.* (gwrawl) Manliness, heroism.

Gwron, *s. m.—pl. t.* ion (gwr—on) A worthy.

> *Ef goreu un gwron y'mhlaid.*
>
> He is the best *hero* in a party. — *Ll. P. Moch.*

Trinsi on gwron gorfawr.

He would wield a *hero's* mighty ashen shaft. *Einion Wan.*

Nid gair gau, ef goreu gwron,
O for add hyd for Iwerddon.

It is no false word, he is the best *hero*, from the English Channel to the Irish Sea. *Cynddelw, i O. Gwynedd.*

Gwronawd, *s. m.* (gwron) An heroic exploit.

Gwroni, *v. n.* (gwron) To become a hero.

Gwronwas, *s. m.* (gwron—gwas) A heroic youth.

Gwroriaeth, *s. m.* (gwrawr) Heroicalness.

Gwrtaeth, *s. m.—pl.* gwrteithion (gwr—taeth) Improvement of quality; improvement, what meliorates. *Gwrtaeth tir*, manure for land; *gwrtaeth bwyd*, sauce with meat; *gwrtaeth ceirch*, the dressing of oats, or making oatmeal.

Gwrtaethu, *v. a.* (gwrtaeth) To improve, to meliorate; to temper; to manure.

Gwrteithiad, *s. m.—pl. t.* au (gwrtaeth) An improving, or meliorating, a manuring of land.

Gwrteithiadwy, *a.* (gwrtaeth) That may be meliorated; manurable.

Gwrteithiaw, *v. a.* (gwrtaeth) To improve the quality, to meliorate; to temper; to manure. *Gwrteithiaw bwyd*, to improve meat with sauce; *gwrteithiaw cworanau*, to oil, or soften boots.

Nid oes crib na gwellaif yn y byd, y galler gwrteithiaw fy ngwallt ag wynt.

There is neither comb nor scissors in the world with which my hair can be *put in order*. *H. Culhwch—Mabinogion.*

Gwrteithiawg, *a.* (gwrtaeth) Being meliorated, tempered, dressed, or manured.

Gwrteithiawl, *a.* (gwrtaeth) Meliorating.

Gwrteithiedig, *a.* (gwrteithiad) Meliorated.

Gwrteithiwr, *s. m.—pl.* gwrteithwyr (gwrtaeth—gwr) One who meliorates. *Gwrteithiwr tir*, a dresser of land.

Gwrteithus, *a.* (gwrtaeth) Meliorating.

Gwrteithydd, *s. m.—pl. t.* ion (gwrtaeth) One who meliorates, a manurer of land.

Gwrth, *s. m.—pl. t.* oedd (gwr) A state of equiponderance, contact, apposition, opposition. *Dyre yn fy ngwrth*, come to meet me: *yr wyd ti yn y gwrth*, thou art in the opposition.

Nis gellir gwrth ond ar y drwg;
Nid gwrth ar y drwg ond Duw.

No *opposition* can avail but against the evil: there is no *opposition* against the evil but God. *Catwg.*

Tri pheth sydd yn ymwanâu beunydd gan faint penaf yr ymgais yn eu gwrth: cas, camwedd, ac anwybodaeth.

Three things become more and more enfeebled daily, from there being a majority of desires in *opposition* to them: hatred, injustice, and ignorance. *Barddas.*

Gwrth, *prep.* (gwr) Against, opposite to; by, close to. It is a very common prefix in composition.

Gwrthachaws, *s. m.—pl.* gwrthachosion (gwrth—achaws) A contrary effect, or cause.

Gwrthachwyn, *s. m.—pl. t.* ion (gwrth—achwyn) A counter-complaint.

Gwrthachwyn, *v. a.* (gwrth—achwyn) To recriminate, to complain in opposition to.

Gwrthachwyniad, *s. m.—pl. t.* au (gwrthachwyn) Recrimination.

Gwrthachwynwr, *s. m.—pl.* gwrthachwynwyr (gwrthachwyn—gwr) A recriminator.

Gwrthadrawdd, *s. m.—pl.* gwrthadroddion (gwrth—adrawdd) A contrary recital.

Gwrthadrawdd, *v. a.* (gwrth—adrawdd) To make a contrary recital, or declaration.

Gwrthadroddawl, *a.* (gwrthadrawdd) Being related, or declared, in a contrary manner.

Gwrthadroddiad, *s. m.—pl. t.* au (gwrthadrawdd) A relating adversely.

Gwrthaddysg, *s. f.* (gwrth—addysg) An adverse doctrine: heresy.

Gwrthagwedd, *s. f.* (gwrth—agwedd) A contrary form, or appearance.

Gwrthagweddiad, *s. m.* (gwrthagwedd) A rendering of a contrary appearance.

Gwrthagweddu, *v. a.* (gwrthagwedd) To render of a contrary appearance.

Gwrthaing, *s. m.* (gwrth—gaing) A wedge.

Gwrthair, *s. m.—pl.* gwrtheiriau (gwrth—gair) An antiphrasis; a protest.

Gwrthalw, *s. m.* (gwrth—galw) A recal.

Gwrthalw, *v. a.* (gwrth—galw) To recal.

Gwrthalwad, *s. m.* (gwrthalw) A recalling, repealing, or revoking; a revocation.

Gwrthalwadwy, *a.* (gwrthalwad) Revokable.

Gwrthalwedig, *a.* (gwrthalw) Revoked.

Gwrthalwedigaeth, *s. f.* (gwrthalwedig) A revocation, the act of recalling.

Gwrthall, *s. m.* (gwrth—gall) An opposing power

Gwrthallt, *s. f.—pl.* gwrthelltydd (gwrth—gallt) A cliff running contrary to another.

Gwrthallu, *s. m.—pl. t.* oedd (gwrthall) A contrary, or opposing power.

Gwrthallu, *v. n.* (gwrthall) To be effectual in opposition to; to have an opposing power.

Gwrthallüad, *s. m.* (gwrthallu) A counter-effectuation.

Gwrthallüaw, *v. n.* (gwrthallu) To be effectual in opposition to.

Gwrthallüawg, *a.* (gwrthallu) Counter-potent.

Gwrthallüedd, *s. m.* (gwrthallu) Counter-power.

Gwrthamcan, *s. m.—pl. t.* ion (gwrth—amcan) A counter-project.

Gwrthanfon, *s. m.* (gwrth—anfon) A sending in a contrary way; a sending back.

Gwrthanfon, *v. a.* (gwrth—anfon) To send adversely; to send back, to remit.

Gwrthanfonawl, *a.* (gwrthanfon) Being sent adversely; being sent back.

Gwrthanfoniad, *s. m.* (gwrthanfon) A sending or conducting adversely.

Gwrthanian, *s. f.* (gwrth—anian) A contrary nature, or quality.

Gwrthanianawl, *a.* (gwrthanian) Counter-natural

Gwrthannog, *s. m.* (gwrth—annog) Dehortation.

Gwrthannogaeth, *s. f.* (gwrthannog) A counter excitement, or exhortation.

Gwrthannogawl, *a.* (gwrthannog) Tending to excite adversely.

Gwrthannogiad, *s. m.* (gwrthannog) An exciting adversely; a counter excitation.

Gwrthansawdd, *s. f.—pl.* gwrthansoddion (gwrth—ansawdd) A contrary quality.

Gwrthansoddawl, *a.* (gwrthansawdd) Of a contrary quality; uncongenial.

Gwrthansoddi, *v. a.* (gwrthansawdd) To render of contrary quality; to make uncongenial.

Gwrthansoddiad, *s. m.* (gwrthansawdd) A rendering of a contrary quality.

Gwrtharall, *a.* (arall) Being opposed to another.

Tri gwahanfod pob byw gwrtharall: awen, cof, a chanfod; sef y bydd cyflawn ar bob un, ac nis gellir cyfun y rhai hyn ar un byw arall, a phob un yn gyflawn; ac nis gellir dau gyflawn ar ddim.

The three discriminations of every animated being *opposed to another*; genius, memory, and perception; that is, each in its plenitude, and so that these cannot be united in any other being, and each in plenitude: for two plenitudes of any thing is not possible. *Barddas.*

Gwrtharddangaws, *s. m.* (gwrth—arddangaws) A counter-demonstration.

Gwrtharddangaws, *v. a.* (gwrth—arddangaws) To counter-demonstrate.

Gwrtharddangosiad, *s. m.* (gwrtharddangaws) A demonstrating contrary to.

Gwrtharddelw, *v. a.* (arddelw) To counter-claim

Gwrtharddelwad, *s. m.* (gwrtharddelw) A counter-claiming.

Gwrtharf, *s. f.—pl.* gwrtheirf (gwrth—arf) An opposing weapon.

Gwrtharfawd, *s. f.* (gwrtharf) A counter-stroke.

Gwrtharwain, *s. m.* (gwrth—arwain) A counter-leading; a leading back.

Gwrtharwain, *v. a.* (gwrth—arwain) To lead back, to bring adversely.

Gwrtharweiniad, *s. m.* (gwrth-arwain) A leading adversely; a leading back.

Gwrthattal, *s. m.—pl. t.* ion (gwrth—attal) A counter-check; a counter-stop.

Gwrthattal, *v. a.* (gwrth—attal) To counter-check

Gwrthattalgar, *a.* (gwrthattal) Apt to counter-check, or to counter-stay

Gwrthattaliad, *s. m.—pl. t.* au (gwrthattal) A counter-checking; a counter-staying.

Gwrthatteb, *s. m.—pl. t.* ion (gwrth—atteb) A counter answer; a replication.

Gwrthattebawl, *a.* (gwrthatteb) Replicatory.

Gwrthattebiad, *s. m.* (gwrthatteb) A replying.

Gwrthattebwr, *s. m.—pl.* gwrthattebwyr (gwrth-atteb—gwr) One who replies, a respondent.

Gwrthaw, *v. a.* (gwrth) To oppose, to withstand.

> Duw [illegible] a'i gwared,
> Gwr gwrthaw, gwrthrych yn [illegible].
>
> May God of heaven deliver him, he is a man of opposition, an objection to his law. *Cynddelw, i'r argl. Rhys.*

Gwrthawd, *s. m.* (gwrth) A refusal, a rejection.

> Afrad yw gwrthawd.
>
> A refusal is waste. *Adage.*

Gwrthawd, *v. a.* (gwrth) To refuse, or to reject.

> Na wrthawd dy barch pan y cynnycier.
>
> Refuse not honour when it is offered to thee. *Adage.*

Gwrthawel, *s. f.* (gwrth—awel) An adverse gale.

Gwrthawl, *a.* (gwrth) Adverse; adversative.

Gwrthban, *s. m.—pl. t.* au (gwrth—pau) That is double-milled; a blanket.

> Ynfyd a gabl ei wrthban,
>
> The simpleton will despise his blanket. *Adage.*

Gwrthbannu, *v. a.* (gwrthban) To double-mill.

Gwrthben, *s. m.—pl. t.* au (gwrth—pen) A counter head; a rivet.

Gwrthbeniad, *s. m.* (gwrthben) A rivetting.

Gwrthbenu, *v. a.* (gwrthben) To rivet.

Gwrthblaid, *s. f.—pl.* gwrthbleidiau (gwrth—plaid) An opposite party; a faction.

Gwrthbleidgar, *a.* (gwrthblaid) Factious.

Gwrthbleidgarwch, *s. m.* (gwrthbleidgar) Factiousness; inclination to public dissention.

Gwrthbleidiad, *s. m.—pl. t.* au (gwrthblaid) An acting in opposition; an acting factiously.

Gwrthbleidiaw, *v.* (gwrthblaid) To act factiously

Gwrthbleidiawg, *a.* (gwrthblaid) Factious.

Gwrthbleidiawl, *a.* (gwrthblaid) Of an adverse party, adversary.

Gwrthblyg, *s. m.—pl. t.* ion (gwrth—plyg) Duplicate; a counter fold.

Gwrthblygawl, *a.* (gwrthblyg) Recurvous.

Gwrthblygedd, *s. m.* (gwrthblyg) Reflexibility.

Gwrthblygiad, *s. m.—pl. t.* au (gwrthblyg) A reduplication; a recurvation.

Gwrthblygiadwy, *a.* (gwrthblygiad) Reflexible.

Gwrthblygiedig, *a.* (gwrthblyg) Doubled back.

Gwrthblygu, *v. a.* (gwrthblyg) To double back.

Gwrthbrawf, *s. m.—pl.* gwrthbrofion (gwrth—prawf) A confutation, a refutation.

Gwrthbrid, *s. m.* (gwrth—prid) Redemption price

> Dodi gwrthbrid yn llaw ynad.
>
> To place a redemption price in the hand of a judge. *Trioedd Gwladoldeb.*

Gwrthbridiaw, *v. a.* (gwrthbrid) To fix a redeeming price.

> [illegible] yw gwrthrifiad, etifedd cynefin a wrthbrido dir ei genedl.
>
> A counter-party is a primary inheritor who gives a redeeming price for the land of his family. *Trioedd Gwladoldeb.*

Gwrthbrofadwy, *a.* (gwrthbrawf) Confutable.

Gwrthbrofedig, *a.* (gwrthbrawf) Being confuted.

Gwrthbrofi, *v. a.* (gwrthbrawf) To confute.

Gwrthbrofiad, *s. m.—pl. t.* au (gwrthbrawf) A confuting, a proving to the contrary.

Gwrthbrofwr, *s. m.—pl.* gwrthbrofwyr (gwrth-prawf—gwr) One who confutes.

Gwrthbryn, *s. m.* (gwrth—pryn) A counter-purchase; that is bought in opposition.

Gwrthbryniad, *s. m.* (gwrthbryn) A buying in opposition to; an outbidding.

Gwrthbrynu, *v. a.* (gwrthbryn) To buy contrary.

Gwrthbwys, *s. m.—pl. t.* au (pwys) A counter-balance, a counterpoise: the palm-tree.

Gwrthbwysaw, *v. a.* (gwrthbwys) To counter-balance, to counterpoise.

Gwrthbwysawl, *a.* (gwrthbwys) Counterbalanced

Gwrthbwysiad, *s. m.* (gwrthbwys) A counterbalancing, or counterpoising.

Gwrthbwyth, *s. m.—pl. t.* au (pwyth) Retaliation *a.* Apt to retaliate; obstinate.

> Gwrthbwythach a glewach fuant y gwyr o fewn, canys [illegible] Galien a Phoranus a [illegible] atteddynt, a [illegible] [illegible] hwynthau draenoeth i wrth [illegible].
>
> More resolute and more brave were the men within, for the messengers of Galien and Poranus had come to them, telling them that they themselves should come the next morning to their assistance. *[illegible] ab Arthur.*

Gwrthbwythaw, *v. a.* (gwrthbwyth) To contravene; to retaliate.

Gwrthbwythawl, *a.* (gwrthbwyth) Contravening.

Gwrthbwythiad, *s. m.* (gwrthbwyth) A contravening; retaliation.

Gwrthchwel, *s. m.—pl. t.* ion (gwrth—chwel) That is refracted; refraction.

Gwrthchweliad, *s. m.—pl. t.* au (gwrthchwel) A refracting; refraction.

Gwrthchweliant, *s. m.* (gwrthchwel) Refraction; reflected light.

Gwrthchwyl, *s. f.—pl. t.* ion (chwyl) A counter-course; a contrary turn.

Gwrthchwyth, *s. m.* (chwyth) A counter-blast.

Gwrthchwythiad, *s. m.* (gwrthchwyth) A blowing adversely.

Gwrthchwythu, *v. a.* (gwrthchwyth) To blow adversely.

Gwrthdafl, *s. m.* (tafl) A counter-throw.

Gwrthdafliad, *s. m.—pl. t.* au (gwrthdafl) A throwing adversely; a throwing back.

Gwrthdaflu, *v. a.* (gwrthdafl) To throw adversely.

Gwrthdaith, *s. f.—pl.* gwrthdeithiau (gwrth—taith) A counter-march, a retreat.

Gwrthdal, *s. m.* (tâl) A counter-payment.

Gwrthdaliad, *s. m.—pl. t.* au (gwrthdal) A counter-paying; a counter-payment.

Gwrthdalu, *v. a.* (gwrthdal) To counter-pay.

Gwrthdaraw, *s. m.* (taraw) A striking adversely.

Gwrthdaraw, *v. a.* (gwrth—taraw) To repel.

Gwrthdarawedig, *a.* (gwrthdaraw) Repellant, repercussive, reverberatory.

Gwrthdarawiad, *s. m.—pl. t.* au (gwrthdaraw) A striking adversely, or repelling; repercussion.

Gwrthdeithiad, *s. m.—pl. t.* au (gwrthdaith) A travelling in a contrary direction.

Gwrthdeithiaw, *v. a.* (gwrthdaith) To travel in a contrary direction to; to countermarch.

Gwrthdir, *s. m.—pl. t.* oedd (tir) Abutting land, or boundary land; the upland; the wild, or desert. *Maenawr wrthdir*, the hilly or wild division of a country; *bro a gwrthdir*, the cultivated country and the wild.

Gwrthdor, *s. m.* (tor) A contrary break.

Gwrthdòrawl, *a.* (gwrthdor) Refractive.

Gwrthdòredig, *a.* (gwrthdor) Refracted.

Gwrthdòri, *v. a.* (gwrthdor) To break adversely.

Gwrthdòriad, *s. m.—pl. t.* au (gwrthdor) Refraction; a breaking adversely.

Gwrthdra, *s. m.* (gwrth) Opposedness.

Gwrthdradwy, *s. m.* (tradwy) The fourth day past. *adv.* On the fourth day past, four days ago.

Gwrthdraddawd, *s. m.* (traddawd) A counter transmission; a transit back.

Gwrthdraddodawl, *a.* (gwrthdraddawd) Being transmitted adversely.

Gwrthdraddodi, *v. a.* (gwrthdraddawd) To transmit adversely; to transmit back.

Gwrthdraddodiad, *s. m.* (gwrthdraddawd) A transmitting adversely; a sending back.

Gwrthdrafod, *s. f.—pl. t.* au (trafod) A contravention; a toiling against.

Gyda ni oni bai ei fod,
Pan ddaeth gwrthdrafod dynion—
Llyncasynt ni.

With us if he had not been, when the *adverse bustle* of men did come, they would have swallowed us up. *E. Prys.*

Gwrthdrafodawl, *a.* (gwrthdrafod) Tending to contravene.

Gwrthdrafodi, *v. a.* (gwrthdrafod) To counterbuff; to counteract.

Gwrthdrafodiad, *s. m.—pl. t.* au (gwrthdrafod) A contravening.

Gwrthdraigl, *s. f.—pl.* gwrthdreiglion (traigl) A counter-course.

Gwrthdramwy, *s. m.—pl. t.* on (tramwy) A contrary journeying, or walking.

Gwrthdramwy, *v. a.* (tramwy) To retrograde.

Gwrthdramwyad, *s. m.* (gwrthdramwy) A journeying adversely; retrogradation.

Gwrthdramwyaw, *v. a.* (gwrthdramwy) To travel adversely; to retrograde.

Gwrthdramwyawl, *a.* (gwrthdramwy) Retrogradatory, travelling adversely.

Gwrthdreiglaw, *v. a.* (gwrthdraigl) To revolve adversely; to counter-turn.

Gwrthdreigliad, *s. m.* (gwrthdraigl) A revolving, or turning adversely.

Gwrthdrem, *s. f.* (trem) An adverse look.

Gwrthdremiad, *s. m.—pl. t.* au (gwrthdrem) A looking contrary; a looking back.

Gwrthdremiaw, *v. a.* (gwrthdrem) To look adversely; to look back.

Gwrthdremiawl, *a.* (gwrthdrem) Looking back.

Gwrthdremu, *v. a.* (gwrthdrem) To look back.

Gwrthdrennydd, *s. m.* (trennydd) The third day past. *adv.* On the third day past.

Gwrthdrig, *a.* (trig) Oppositely resident.

Gwrthdrigaw, *v. a.* (gwrthdrig) To dwell opposite.

Gwrthdrigawl, *a.* (gwrthdrig) Dwelling opposite. *Gwrthdrigolion*, the antoeci.

Gwrthdrigiad, *s. m.* (gwrthdrig) A dwelling opposite.

Gwrthdrigiant, *s. m.* (gwrthdrig) An opposite residence; a counter dwelling

Gwrthdrin, *s. m.* (trin) A contravention.

Gwrthdrin, *v. a.* (trin) To contravene.

Gwrthdrindodawl, *a.* (trindodawl) Antitrinitarian

Gwrthdrindodaeth, *s. m.* (trindodaeth) Antitrinitarianism.

Gwrthdriniad, *s. m.* (gwrthdrin) A contravening.

Gwrthdriniawl, *a.* (gwrthdrin) Controversial.

Gwrthdro, *s. m.—pl. t.* ion (tro) An adverse turn, a turn back; an apostrophe.

Gwrthdröad, *s. m.* (gwrthdro) A turning adversely, a turning back; retortion, inversion.

Gwrthdröadwy, *a.* (gwrthdröad) Invertible.

Gwrthdroed, *s. m.—pl. t.* ion (troed) Antipode.

Gwrthdroedawl, *a.* (gwrthdroed) Antipodal.

Gwrthdroediad, *s. m.—pl.* gwrthdroediaid (gwrthdroed) The antipode.

Gwrthdroedig, *a.* (gwrthdro) Inverted.

Gwrthdroi, *v. a.* (gwrthdro) To turn adversely, to turn back, to retort, to invert.

Gwrthdröwr, *s. m.—pl.* gwrthdrowyr (gwrthdro—gwr) One who turns adversely.

Gwrthdwng, *s. f.* (twng) A controverting oath.

Gwrthdwr, *s. m.—pl.* gwrthdyrau, (twr) A tower raised to command a besieged place.

Gwrthdwyth, *s. m.* (twyth) A spring back; reaction; elasticity.

Gwrthdwythaw, *v. a.* (gwrthdwyth) To spring back; to spring adversely.

Gwrthdwythawl, *a.* (gwrthdwyth) Springing back

Gwrthdwythiad, *s. m.* (gwrthdwyth) A springing back; contranitency.

Gwrthdyn, *s. m.* (tŷn) An adverse pull.

Gwrthdŷnawl, *a.* (gwrthdyn) Pulling adversely.

Gwrthdŷniad, *s. m.—pl. t.* au (gwrthdyn) A drawing adversely; reluctation; reluctance.

Gwrthdŷnu, *v. a.* (gwrthdyn) To pull adversely.

Gwrthdyngiad, *s. m.* (gwrthdwng) A counter-swearing.

Gwrthdyngu, *v. a.* (gwrthdwng) To counter-swear

Pa fach bynag yntau ni wrthdyngo ar y cynnogn, taled el hun y ddylyed ac yr hawl.

Whatsoever surety *who shall* not *swear in opposition* as to the original debtor, let him pay the debt and cost himself. *Welsh Laws.*

Gwrthdyst, *s. m.—pl. t.* ion (tyst) A contrary witness, a counter-evidence.

Gwrthdystiad, *s. m.* (gwrthdyst) A giving counter-evidence, a testifying adversely.

Gwrthdystiaw, *v. a.* (gwrthdyst) To give counter-evidence.

Gwrthdystiolaeth, *s. f.—pl. t.* au (gwrthdystiawl) A counter-evidence, a contrary testimony.

Gwrthdystiolaethiad, *s. m.* (gwrthdystiolaeth) A giving counter evidence.

Gwrthdystiolaethu, *v. a.* (gwrthdystiolaeth) To give counter-evidence.

Gwrthdystioli, *v. a.* (gwrthdystiawl) To testify contrarily or in opposition.

Gwrthdystiwr, *s. m.—pl.* gwrthdystwyr (gwrthdyst—gwr) One who gives counter-evidence.

Gwrthdywyn, *s. m.* (tywyn) Reflection of light.

Gwrthdywynawl, *a.* (gwrthdywyn) Tending to reflect light.

Gwrthdywyniad, *s. m.* (gwrthdywyn) A reflecting of light.

Gwrthdywynu, *v. a.* (gwrthdywyn) To reflect light, to shine back.

Gwrthddadl, *s. f.—pl. t.* au (dadl) A counter-argument; a controversy.

Gwrthddadlawl, *a.* (gwrthddadl) Contradictious.

Gwrthddadleu, *v. a.* (gwrthddadl) To counterplead, to contradict.

Gwrthddadleuad, *s. m.* (gwrthddadleu) A counter pleading; a controverting, or contradicting.
Gwrthddadleuaw, *v. a.* (gwrthddadleu) To counter-plead, to plead in opposition.
Gwrthddadleugar, *a.* (gwrthddadleu) Apt to oppose in discourse; disputatious.
Gwrthddadleugarwch, *s. m.* (gwrthddadleugar) Aptness to oppose in discourse, or to cavil.
Gwrthddadleuwr, *s. m.—pl.* gwrthddadleuwyr (gwrthddadl—gwr) A controvertist.
Gwrthddadleuydd, *s. m.—pl. t.* ion (gwrthddadleu) An opponent in discourse, a controvertist.
Gwrthddadlgar, *a.* (gwrthddadl) Contradictious.
Gwrthddadliad, *s. m.* (gwrthddadl) A contradicting.
Gwrthddadlu, *v. a.* (gwrthddadlu) To counterplead, to controvert.
Gwrthddadlwr, *s. m.—pl.* gwrthddadlwyr (gwrthddadl—gwr) A counter pleader; a controvertist
Gwrthddadlydd, *s. m.—pl. t.* ion (gwrthddadl) A controvertist, an opponent in dispute.
Gwrthddal, *s. m.* (dal) An opposite hold.
Gwrthddaliad, *s. m.—pl. t.* au (gwrthddal) A holding against; a withholding.
Gwrthddangaws, *s. m.* (dangaws) Contra-indication. *v. a.* To contra-indicate.
Gwrthddangosawl, *a.* (gwrthddangaws) Contra-indicatory.
Gwrthddangosiad, *s. m.* (gwrthddangaws) A shewing to the contrary, a remonstrating.
Gwrthddeddf, *s. f.—pl.* gwrthddeddfau (deddf) A contrary maxim, or law; opposition to law.
Gwrthddeddfawl, *a.* (gwrthddeddf) Antinomian.
Gwrthddeddfiad, *s. m.—pl.* gwrthddeddfiaid (gwrthddeddf) An antinomian.
Gwrthddeddfiaeth, *s. m.* (deddf) Antinomianism.
Gwrthddrych, *s. m.—pl. t.* ion (drych) That is opposed to view, an object; an heir apparent.

> Tir yr Iuddewon sydd yn parhau mewn galar; eu ty a adawid iddynt yn anghyfanedd; gwrthddrychion gwawd a [illegible] ydynt yn mhob tir.
>
> The land of the Jews does continue in mourning; their house has been left desolate to them: they are objects of ridicule and contempt in every land. *Jer. Owain.*

Gwrthddrychawl, *a.* (gwrthddrych) Objective.
Gwrthddrychiad, *s. m.—pl.* gwrthddrychiaid (gwrthddrych) One that is in view, or apparent; one that is an object; an heir.
Gwrthddrychiaw, *v. a.* (gwrthddrych) To render, or to place in view; to render objective.
Gwrthddrycholdeb, *s. m.* (gwrthddrychawl) Objectiveness.
Gwrthddrycholder, *s. m.* (gwrthddrychawl) Objectiveness.
Gwrthddrycholi, *v. a.* (gwrthddrychawl) To render objective; to become objective.
Gwrthddrycholrwydd, *s. m.* (gwrthddrychawl) Objectiveness.
Gwrthddrychu, *v. a.* (gwrthddrych) To place in view, to render an object; to design.
Gwrthddull, *s. f.* (dull) That is opposite to form, a catachresis.
Gwrthddulliad, *s. m.* (gwrthddull) A making informal, a making a catachresis.
Gwrthddulliaw, *v. a.* (gwrthddull) To render informal; to make a catachresis.
Gwrthddyled, *s. f.—pl. t.* ion (dyled) A counter obligation, debt, or due.
Gwrthddylyed, *s. f.* (dylyed) A counter obligation
Gwrthddysg, *s. m.* (dysg) A contrary doctrine.
Gwrthddysgawl, *a.* (gwrthddysg) Heretical.
Gwrthddysgiad, *s. m.* (gwrthddysg) A teaching in opposition; a teaching heresy.
Gwrthddysgu, *v. a.* (gwrthddysg) To teach heresy
Gwrthddywedawl, *a.* (dywedawl) Contradictory.
Gwrthddywededig, *a.* (dywededig) Being contradicted, or being gainsayed.
Gwrthddywedgar, *a.* (dywedgar) Contradictious.
Gwrthddywedyd, *v. a.* (dywedyd) To contradict.
Gwrtheb, *s. m.—pl. t.* ion (eb) A response, an objective answer; an exception; an objection.

> Mae i'm fuidd a'm car o'm cafael wrthaw,
> I wrtheb [illegible];
> Nid bleidd coed coll ei afael,
> Namwyn blaidd maes moesawg hael.
>
> I am blest with a wolf that loves me, in having me with him to raise an argument; not a wolf of the woods, of feeble grasp, but a wolf of the field, courteous and liberal. *Cynddelw, i [illegible].*

Gwrtheb, *v. a.* (eb) To response, to make answer.
Gwrthebadwy, *a.* (gwrtheb) That may be answered, answerable.
Gwrthebawl, *a.* (gwrtheb) Responsive, exceptive
Gwrthebedig, *a.* (gwrtheb) Being answered.
Gwrthebedigaeth, *s. m.* (gwrthebedig) Responsion
Gwrthebedigawl, *a.* (gwrthebedig) Tending to be objective, having the quality of an objection.
Gwrthebiad, *s. m.—pl. t.* au (gwrtheb) An answering; a responsion.
Gwrthebwr, *s. m.—pl.* gwrthebwyr (gwrtheb—gwr) One who makes answer; an objector.
Gwrthebydd, *s. m.—pl. t.* ion (gwrtheb) Replyer.
Gwrthedrych, *s. m.* (edrych) A look back.
Gwrthedrych, *v. a.* (edrych) To look adversely.
Gwrthedrychawl, *a.* (gwrthedrych) Retrospective
Gwrthedrychiad, *s. m.—pl. t.* au (gwrthedrych) A looking adversely; retrospection.
Gwrthedd, *s. m.* (gwrth) Contrariety, opposition.
Gwrthegni, *s. m.—pl. t.* on (egni) Repulsive power.
Gwrthegnïad, *s. m.* (gwrthegni) A making a contrary effort; reaction.
Gwrthegnïaw, *v. a.* (gwrthegni) To make a counter exertion, or effort; to re-act.
Gwrthegnïawl, *a.* (gwrthegni) Tending to repel.
Gwrthegor, *v. a.* (egor) To open contrarily.
Gwrthegorawl, *a.* (gwrthegor) Opening back.
Gwrthegori, *v. a.* (gwrthegor) To open adversely.
Gwrthegoriad, *s. m.* (gwrthegor) Opening back.
Gwrtheirgar, *a.* (gwrthair) Antiphrastical.
Gwrtheiriad, *s. m.* (gwrthair) Antiphrasis.
Gwrtheiriaw, *v. a.* (gwrthair) To use antiphrasis.
Gwrtheiriawg, *a.* (gwrthair) Antiphrastical.
Gwrthenwad, *s. m.* (enwad) Antonomasia.
Gwrthergyd, *s. m.—pl. t.* ion (ergyd) A repulse.
Gwrthergydiad, *s. m.* (gwrthergyd) A repelling.
Gwrthergydiaw, *v. a.* (gwrthergyd) To repulse.
Gwrthergydiawl, *a.* (gwrthergyd) Repulsive.
Gwrthern, *s. m.—pl. t.* i (gern) A relation in the seventh degree of consanguinity. See *Tras.*
Gwrthfach, *s. m.—pl.* gwrthfeichiau (mach) A counter surety.
Gwrthfach, *s. m.—pl. t.* au (bach) A counter-hook, the beard or returning point of a weapon.
Gwrthfachawg, *a.* (gwrthfach) Barbed, or bearded. *Picellau geirwon gwrthfachawg,* terrible bearded darts.
Gwrthfachu, *v. a.* (gwrthfach) To barb, to beard.
Gwrthfai, *s. m.—pl.* gwrthfeiau (bai) A contrary crime; an opposite fault or crime.
Gwrthfarn, *s. f.* (barn) A contrary judgment.
Gwrthfarnawl, *a.* (gwrthfarn) Being judged contrarily; of opposite judgement.

Gwrthfarniad, *s. m.* (gwrthfarn) A judging adversely; an opposition in judgement.
Gwrthfarnu, *v. a.* (gwrthfarn) To judge adversely.
Gwrthfechni, *s. m.—pl. t.* on (gwrthfach) A counter-security.
Gwrthfechniad, *s. m.* (gwrthfechni) A giving a counter-security.
Gwrthfechnïaw, *v. a.* (gwrthfechni) To give counter-security.
Gwrthfeiad, *s. m.* (gwrthfai) A recrimination.
Gwrthfeiaw, *v. a.* (gwrthfai) To recriminate.
Gwrthfelydd, *s.* (melydd) Counter-representation.
Gwrthfelyddiad, *s. m.* (gwrthfelydd) A representing contrarily; a contrary description.
Gwrthfelyddu, *v. a.* (gwrthfelydd) To represent adversely; to make a contrary representation.

Edrychad bod gwir y mawl; ac nas gellir ei wrthebriaw, nac ei wrthwynebu, nac ei wrthfelyddu o berwydd pwyll.

Let him observe that the praise is just; and that it cannot be gainsayed, nor opposed, nor *adversely represented* according to reason. *Barddas.*

Gwrthfer, *v. a.* (mer) To deliver back.
Gwrthferawl, *a.* (gwrthfer) Being given back.
Gwrthferiad, *s. m.* (gwrthfer) A restoring back.
Gwrthferu, *v. a.* (gwrthfer) To deliver back.
Gwrthfin, *s. m.* (min) Opposite edge; turned edge.
Gwrthfiniad, *s. m.* (gwrthfin) A counter edging.
Gwrthfiniaw, *v. a.* (gwrthfin) To counter edge.
Gwrthfiniawg, *a.* (gwrthfin) Counter-edged.
Gwrthflin, *a.* (blin) Vexatious, troublesome.
Gwrthflinaw, *v. a.* (gwrthflin) To vex; to irritate.
Gwrthflinder, *s. m.* (gwrthflin) Vexatiousness.

Cofia Dafydd, fy Nêr mer,
A'i holl wrthflinder hefyd.

Remember David, my God Almighty, and also all his *tribulation.* *E. Prys.*

Gwrthfloedd, *s. f.—pl. t.* au (bloedd) A cry against.
Gwrthfloeddgar, *a.* (gwrthfloedd) Obstreperous.
Gwrthfloeddiad, *s. m.* (gwrthfloedd) An exclaiming against; a counter-shouting.
Gwrthfodd, *s. m.—pl. t.* ion (bodd) Displeasure.

Gwr a wnaeth gwrthawd gwrthfodd Dewi,
Gwrthwyneb Lloegr, heb eu llochi.

A person who did reject the *displeasure* of Dewi, the opponent of the English, giving them no quarters.
Cynddelw, m. Cadwallon.

Gwrthfoddawg, *a.* (gwrthfodd) Being displeased.
Gwrthfoddawl, *a.* (gwrthfodd) Displeasing.
Gwrthfoddiad, *s. m.* (gwrthfodd) A displeasing.
Gwrthfoddiaw, *v. a.* (gwrthfodd) To displease.
Gwrthfrad, *s. m.—pl. t.* au (brad) A counter-plot.
Gwrthfradiad, *s. m.* (gwrthfrad) A counter-plotting; a counter-treachery.
Gwrthfradu, *v. a.* (gwrthfrad) To counter-plot.
Gwrthfrawd, *s. f.* (brawd) An adverse sentence.
Gwrthfrodawl, *a.* (gwrthfrawd) Prejudicial.
Gwrthfrodi, *a. a.* (gwrthfrawd) To prejudice.

Na'm gwrthfrawd o'm gwawd, o'm gwarweb.

Do not *prejudice* me with respect to my muse, nor my forbearance. *Cynddelw.*

Gwrthfrwydr, *s. f.—pl. t.* au (brwydr) A counter-buff.
Gwrthfrwydraw, *v. a.* (gwrthfrwydr) To battle in opposition.
Gwrthfrwydriad, *s. m.* (gwrthfrwydr) A battling against; a counterbuffing.
Gwrthfur, *s. m.—pl. t.* iau (mur) A contramure.
Gwrthfwriad, *s. m.—pl. t.* au (bwriad) A contrary casting; a contrary design.
Gwrthfwrw, *v. a.* (bwrw) To cast contrarily.

Gwrthfyn, *v. a.* (myn) To take back; to receive.

Can ni bei ammod dy fod i'm herbyn,
A Duw gwyn yn gwybod,
Oedd iawnach i fynach fod
I'm gwrthfyn nog i'm gwrthod.

Since there should be no covenant for thy being against me, and the blessed Deity knowing that, it were more just for the monk to be *to receive* me than to reject me.
Cynddelw, i fynach Ystradmarchell.

Duw, gwrthfyn f'enaid ban el o'm cnawd.

God, *receive* my soul when it goes from my flesh.
Ein ab Gwalchmai.

Gwrthfynag, *s. f.* (mynag) A counter recital.
Gwrthfynawl, *a.* (gwrthfyn) Being received.
Gwrthfynegi, *v. a.* (gwrthfynag) To recite contrarily; to counter declare.
Gwrthfynegiad, *s. m.* (gwrthfynag) A reciting, or relating contrarily.
Gwrthfyniad, *s. m.* (gwrthfyn) A taking back.

Cerddawr gwerthfawr gwrthfyniad.

A minstrel of precious *reception.* *Cynddelw.*

Gwrthfynu, *v. a.* (gwrthfyn) To receive back.

All yrth gyrth ein gwrthfynasant.

Like the push of an onset *they snatched us back.* *Ll. P. Moch.*

Gwrthgais, *s. f.* (cais) A counter-attempt.
Gwrthgam, *s. m.* (cam) A recurve; a retort.
Gwrthgamawl, *a.* (gwrthgam) Recurvous.
Gwrthgamiad, *s. m.—pl. t.* au (gwrthgam) Recurvation; a bending adversely.
Gwrthgamu, *v. a.* (gwrthgam) To recurve.
Gwrthgan, *s. f.—pl. t.* au (can) A counter song.
Gwrthganiad, *s. m.—pl. t.* au (gwrthgan) A counter singing, a repeating a song; recantation.
Gwrthganu, *v. a.* (gwrthgan) To sing against, or in opposition to; to repeat a song.

Cowydd——
Un a'i cais, arall a'i cant;
Eraw gwrthgan, na a'i gwrthgant.

A poem, one gets it, another sings it; perverse is the name, another *sings* it *again.* *D. ab Gwilym.*

Gwrthgas, *a.* (cas) Perverse, froward, obstinate.
Gwrthgasawl, *a.* (gwrthgas) Of a perverse nature.
Gwrthgasedd, *s. m.* (gwrthgas) Perverseness.

Llawenâu yn fawr a oruc holl ieuenctid llys Arthur o debygu caffael brwydr â gwyr Rhufain; ac annog a orugant i Walchmai wneuthur gwrthgasedd yn llys yr ymherawdr.

All the young men of the court of Arthur rejoiced greatly in thinking to have a battle with the men of Rome; and they exhorted Gwalchmai to commit some *perverseness* in the court of the emperor. *Gr. ab Arthur.*

Gwrthgasiad, *s. m.* (gwrthgas) An acting perversely; a becoming perverse.
Gwrthgasrwydd, *s. m.* (gwrthgas) Perverseness.
Gwrthgau, *v. a.* (cau) To shut adversely.
Gwrthgauedig, *a.* (gwrthgau) Closed adversely.
Gwrthgauedigaeth, *s. m.—pl. t.* au (gwrthgauedig) The act of shutting contrarily.
Gwrthgefn, *s. m.* (cefn) A counter-support; a support. *Mae iddo wrthgefn da*, he has got a good support.
Gwrthgefnawl, *a.* (gwrthgefn) Supporting.
Gwrthgefniad, *s. m.* (gwrthgefn) Supportation.
Gwrthgefnu, *v. a.* (gwrthgefn) To support.
Gwrthgeisiad, *s. m.* (gwrthgais) An attempting in opposition to.
Gwrthgeisiaw, *v. a.* (gwrthgais) To attempt an opposition to, to make a counter effort.
Gwrthgemi, *s. m.* (gwrthgam) Recurvousness.
Gwrthgerdd, *s. m.* (cerdd) A retrograde course.
Gwrthgerddawl, *a.* (gwrthgerdd) Retrograde.
Gwrthgerdded, *s. m.* (gwrthgerdd) A walking in a contrary direction; a retrogradation.
Gwrthgerdded, *v. a.* (gwrthgerdd) To walk adversely, or in a contrary direction.

Gwrthgerddediad, *s. m.* (gwrthgerdded) Retrogradation; a walking back.
Gwrthgerydd, *s. m.* (cerydd) Recrimination.
Gwrthgeryddawl, *a.* (gwrthgerydd) Recriminating.
Gwrthgeryddiad, *s. m.—pl. t.* au (gwrthgerydd) A counter-chiding; recrimination.
Gwrthgeryddu, *v. a.* (gwrthgerydd) To countercheck; to recriminate.
Gwrthgil, *s. m.—pl. t.* ion (cil) A revolt.
Gwrthgiliad, *s. m.* (gwrthgil) A receding, or going back; a backsliding; a revolting.
Gwrthgiliaw, *v. a.* (gwrthgil) To recede; to revolt: to apostatize.
Gwrthgiliedig, *a.* (gwrthgiliad) Being revolted.
Gwrthgiliedydd, *s. m.—pl. t.* ion (gwrthgiliad) One who revolts, a backslider, an apostate.
Gwrthgiliwr, *s. m.—pl.* gwrthgilwyr (gwrthgil—gwr) A seceder; a revolter; an apostate.
Gwrthgilydd, *s. m.—pl. t.* ion (gwrthgil) Apostate.
Gwrthgis, *s. m.—pl. t.* ion (cis) A counter-buff; a retort courteous.
Gwrthgisiad, *s. m.* (gwrthgis) A retorting upon.
Gwrthgisiaw, *v. a.* (gwrthgis) To counter-buff.
Gwrthglawdd, *s. m.—pl.* gwrthgloddiau (clawdd) Contravallation, or a counter dyke.
Gwrthgloch, *s. f.* (cloch) Echo, or reverberation.

> Llary Madawg brif cwnwg brwydr,
> Llew gwrthgloch bar-goch baladr.
>
> *The gentle Madawg the most famed in battle, a lion with a resounding shaft most red.* — *Prydydd Bychan.*

Gwrthglochedd, *s. m.* (gwrthgloch) Resonancy.

> Ni ddywedai y wrach wrthynt namyn gwrthglochedd.
>
> *The hag would not speak to them save a repetition.* — *Br. Rhonabwy—Mabinogion.*

Gwrthglochi, *v. a.* (gwrthgloch) To reverberate.
Gwrthgloddiad, *s. m.* (gwrthglawdd) A making a counter-trench, or contravallation.

> Handid o meinaid gwrthgloddiad byd
> Pryd Prydain bwysgain yn amlwyliad.
>
> *If of stone-work the world's opposing wall, may the countenance of Britain be boldly gleaming in bursting through.* — *Taliesin.*

Gwrthgloddiaw, *v. a.* (gwrthglawdd) To make a counter-trench, or dike; to countermine.
Gwrthgloddiedig, *a.* (gwrthglawdd) Counter-trenched.
Gwrthgred, *s. f.* (cred) A counter-belief; opposition to faith.
Gwrthgredawl, *a.* (gwrthgred) Of divine faith.
Gwrthgrediad, *s. m.* (gwrthgred) A holding a contrary belief.
Gwrthgredydd, *s. m.—pl. t.* ion (gwrthgred) An opposer of revelation, or who derives his religion from nature; a freethinker.
Gwrthgri, *s. f.* (cri) A counter crying.
Gwrthgrïad, *s. m.* (gwrthgri) A clamoring against.
Gwrthgrïawl, *a.* (gwrthgri) Clamorous against.
Gwrthgrif, *s. f.* (crif) A counter cry; clamour.
Gwrthgrifiad, *s. m.—pl.* gwrthgrifiaid (gwrthgrif) One who clamours against.

> Traethawd ber i buraw enaid
> Rhag gorddrud cythrawdd cythreuliaid,
> Cythreul-gas gwrthgas gwrthgrifiaid.
>
> *A sweet discourse to purify a soul from the over daring assaults of demons, repugnantly hateful, the perverse, the clamorous ones.* — *Cynddelw.*

Gwrthgrifiaw, *v. a.* (gwrthgrif) To clamour.

> Hir yn llygad a wrthgrif
>
> *Long in the eye of him who clamours* — *Adage.*

Gwrthgrist, *s. m.* (Crist) Antichrist, a false Crist.
Gwrthgristiawl, *a.* (gwrthgrist) Antichristian.
Gwrthgristiolaeth, *s. m.* (gwrthgristiawl) Antichristianism.

Gwrthgrwydr, *s. m.* (crwydr) A counter-stray.
Gwrthgrwydraw, *v. a.* (gwrthgrwydr) To wander adversely, to stray in a contrary direction.
Gwrthgrwydrawl, *a.* (gwrthgrwydr) Adversely straying; wandering back.
Gwrthgrwydriad, *s. m.* (gwrthgrwydr) Retrogradation; a wandering adversely.
Gwrthgrych, *a.* (crych) Adversely rough.

> Gwalchmai, atebion gwrthgrych,
> Gorwlychid cawod can rhych,
> Minnau af i'r lle mynych.
>
> *Gwalchmai of cross-grained answers, let the shower drench a hundred trenches, I will also go to wherever thou shouldest desire.* — *Ymdd. Trystan a Gwalchmai.*

Gwrthgrychiad, *s. m.* (gwrthgrych) A being rough in a contrary direction.
Gwrthgrychu, *v. a.* (gwrthgrych) To roughen in a contrary direction; to become cross-grained.
Gwrthgur, *s. m.* (cur) A counter-stroke.
Gwrthguraw, *v. a.* (gwrthgur) To beat adversely, to beat back; to reverberate; to repulse.
Gwrthgurawl, *a.* (gwrthgur) Repercussive.
Gwrthgurediguaeth, *s.* (gwrthgur) Repercussion.
Gwrthguredigawl, *a.* (gwrthgur) Repercussive.
Gwrthguriad, *s. m.* (gwrthgur) Repercussion; a beating against.
Gwrthgwymp, *s. m.* (cwymp) An apostacy.
Gwrthgwympai, *s. c.—pl.* gwrthgwympeion (gwrthgwymp) An apostate.
Gwrthgwympaw, *v. a.* (gwrthgwymp) To apostatize, or to fall adversely.
Gwrthgwympawl, *a.* (gwrthgwymp) Apostate.
Gwrthgwympiad, *s. m.—pl. t.* au (gwrthgwymp) An apostatizing, a falling off.
Gwrthgwyn, *s. f.* (cwyn) Counter complaint.
Gwrthgwynaw, *v. a.* (gwrthgwyn) To make a counter complaint.
Gwrthgwyniad, *s. m.* (gwrthgwyn) A complaining in opposition to; a making a counter plaint.
Gwrthgyfarch, *s. m.* (cyfarch) A rencounter.
Gwrthgyfarch, *v. a.* (cyfarch) To rencounter.

> A'm gwrthgyfarch yn glauar,
> Ei gynneddfau nwd ais!
> Wedi Cadwaladr Idwal.
>
> *He that comes before me mildly, his principles are they not worthless! After Cadwaladr comes Idwal.* — *Cyfoesi Myrddin.*

Gwrthgyfarchawl, *a.* (gwrthgyfarch) Tending to come in opposition to.
Gwrthgyfarchiad, *s. m.* (gwrthgyfarch) A meeting, or coming in opposition to.
Gwrthgyfeiriad, *s. m.* (gwrthgyfer) A contrasting.
Gwrthgyfeiriaw, *v. a.* (gwrthgyfer) To contrast.
Gwrthgyfeiriawl, *a.* (gwrthgyfer) Contrasted.
Gwrthgyfer, *s. m.* (cyfer) A contrast.
Gwrthgyfle, *s. m.* (cyfle) A counter-position.
Gwrthgyflëad, *s. m.* (gwrthgyfle) A placing in opposition, a contrasting; anteposition.
Gwrthgyflëawl, *a.* (gwrthgyfle) Counter-positional; placed adversely.
Gwrthgyflëu, *v. a.* (gwrthgyfle) To put in opposition; to contrast.
Gwrthgyfnewid, *s. m.—pl. t.* ion (cyfnewid) A counterchange.
Gwrthgyfnewid, *v. a.* (cyfnewid) To make a counterchange.
Gwrthgyfnewidiad, *s. m.* (gwrthgyfnewid) A counterchanging.
Gwrthgyfnewidiawl, *a.* (gwrthgyfnewid) Relating to counterchange.
Gwrthgyfraith, *s. f.—pl.* gwrthgyfreithiau (cyfraith) A contradictory law.
Gwrthgyhuddaw, *v.* (cyhuddaw) To recriminate.

Gwrthgyhuddawl, *a.* (cyhuddawl) Recriminatory.
Gwrthgyhudded, *s. f.* (cyhudded) A counter-accusation, or counter charge; recrimination.
Gwrthgyhuddiad, *s.* (cyhuddiad) A recriminating.
Gwrthgyhuddwr, *s. m.—pl.* gwrthgyhuddwyr (cyhuddwr) One who recriminates.
Gwrthgylch, *s. m.—pl. t.* au (cylch) A counter-circle.
Gwrthgylchawl, *a.* (gwrthgylch) Circling adversely.
Gwrthgylchiad, *s. m.* (gwrthgylch) A forming an adverse circle, or a counter circle.
Gwrthgylchsaf, *s. f.* (gwrthgylch—saf) The antiperistasis.
Gwrthgylchu, *v. a.* (gwrthgylch) To form an adverse or counter circle.
Gwrthgynllwyn, *s. m.* (cynllwyn) A counter-plot.
Gwrthgynnal, *v. a.* (cynnal) To counter-support.
Gwrthgynnaliad, *s. m.* (gwrthgynnal) A giving a counter-support.
Gwrthgynneiliad, *s. m.—pl.* gwrthgynneiliaid (gwrthgynnal) One who supports against.
Gwrthgynghor, *s. m.* (cynghor) Dehortation.
Gwrthgynghorawl, *a.* (cynghor) Dehortatory.
Gwrthgynghori, *v. a.* (gwrthgynghor) To advise to the contrary.
Gwrthgynghoriad, *s. m.* (gwrthgynghor) An advising to the contrary: dehortation.
Gwrthgyrch, *s. m.* (cyrch) An adverse, or hostile approach. *a.* Hostile.

> Dywetai lawer o'r gwrthgyrch blaid
> Yn drwm am f'enaid eisoes,
> Nid oes——waredydd iddo.
>
> Many of the *hostile* throng would say sadly now of my soul, there is no deliverer for him. *E. Prys.*

Gwrthgyrchawl, *a.* (cyrch) Adversely coming.
Gwrthgyrchiad, *s. m.—pl. t.* au (gwrthgyrch) A making a counter attack.
Gwrthgyrchu, *v. a.* (gwrthgyrch) To make a counter attack; to approach in opposition to.
Gwrthheintus, *a.* (heintus) Antipestilential.
Gwrthhawl, *s. f.—pl.* gwrthholion (hawl) A counter-claim; a counterplea.
Gwrthhoel, *s. f.—pl. t.* ion (hoel) A plug; rivet.
Gwrthhoeliad, *s. m.* (gwrthhoel) A rivetting.
Gwrthhoeliaw, *v. a.* (gwrthhoel) To rivet.
Gwrthhoeliedig, *a.* (gwrthhoeliad) Rivetted.
Gwrthholi, *v. a.* (gwrthhawl) To examine in opposition to; to lay counter-claim.
Gwrthholiad, *s. m.* (gwrthhawl) A counter-examination; a claiming in opposition.
Gwrthhwrdd, *s. m.* (hwrdd) Repulse, repulsion.
Gwrthhyrddawl, *a.* (gwrthhwrdd) Repulsive.
Gwrthhyrddiad, *s. m.* (gwrthhwrdd) A repelling.
Gwrthhyrddu, *v. a.* (gwrthhwrdd) To repulse.
Gwrthiad, *s. m.* (gwrth) An opposing; opposition.
Gwrthiaith, *s. f.* (iaith) A contradiction.

> Na chymmydd â hi o hir obaith;
> Na chymer wrtheb a dan wrthiaith.
>
> Be not reconciled to her account of long expectation; accept not an answer under *contradiction.*
> *Cynddelw, i Efa f. Madawg.*

Gwrthias, *s. f.—pl. t.* au (ias) What pervades, or gives a shock contrarily.
Gwrthiasawl, *a.* (gwrthias) Tending to give a counter-shock.
Gwrthiasiad, *s. m.* (gwrthias) A pervading in opposition to; a giving a counter-shock.
Gwrthiasu, *v. a.* (gwrthias) To give a counter-shock; to return a shock.
Gwrthiaw, *v. a.* (gwrth) To oppose, to resist.
Gwrthiawl, *a.* (gwrth) Opposing, resisting.
Gwrthieithedd, *s. m.* (gwrthiaith) A gainsaying; opposition.

Gwrthielthu, *v. a.* (gwrthiaith) To gainsay.
Gwrthladd, *s. m.* (lladd) Oppugnancy, resistance.

> Yn lladd dy wrthladd wrth lys Rheidiawl.
>
> Cutting off thy *resistance* from the court of Rheidiol.
> *Ein. ab Gwgan.*

Gwrthladd, *v. a.* (lladd) To oppugn, to oppose, to resist; to prevent; to drive off. *Gwrthladd cywilydd*, to ward off disgrace.

> Gwrthefin frenin, fraisg benadur byd,
> Gwrthladded o'm bryd pyd pechadur!
> Gorthywys nefoedd nyfed eglur,
> Gwrthyf ni bo trist Crist creadur!
>
> Supreme king, the mighty governor of the world, *may he drive away* from my mind the danger of being a sinner! The regulator of the heavens of clear ether, to me let not Christ the created one seem to be sad! *Ll. P. Moch.*

Gwrthladdawl, *a.* (gwrthladd) Tending to oppose.
Gwrthladdedig, *a.* (gwrthladd) Being opposed.
Gwrthladdiad, *s. m.* (gwrthladd) An oppugning, opposing, or resisting; a driving off.

> Oni bair cerdd annogiad ar ddaioni, a dedwyddyd, a gwynfyd; a gwrthladdiad ar ddrygioni ac anwybodaeth, a gofid, ni ddylid ei goddef ar fod a chof.
>
> If a poem does not cause an excitement to goodness, and discretion, and happiness; and a *repugnancy* to wickedness, and ignorance and misery, it ought not to be suffered to be in existence and remembrance. *Bardddas.*

Gwrthladdwr, *s. m.—pl.* gwrthladdwyr (gwrthladd—gwr) One who resists, or opposes.
Gwrthlais, *s. m.—pl.* gwrthleisiau (llais) A counter voice, an opposition voice.
Gwrthlam, *s. m.* (llam) A rebound.
Gwrthlamawl, *a.* (gwrthlam) Rebounding.
Gwrthlamiad, *s. m.* (gwrthlam) A rebounding.
Gwrthlamu, *v. a.* (gwrthlam) To rebound.
Gwrthlef, *s. m.* (llef) An exclaiming against.
Gwrthlefain, *v. a.* (gwrthlef) To exclaim against.
Gwrthlefawl, *a.* (gwrthlef) Adversely vociferous.
Gwrthlefiad, *s. m.* (gwrthlef) A calling, or crying against; an exclaiming against.
Gwrthleisiad, *s. m.* (gwrthlais) An uttering a voice in opposition to.
Gwrthleisiaw, *v. a.* (gwrthlais) To utter a counter voice; to make a counter cry.
Gwrthlewych, *s. m.* (llewych) Reflection of light.
Gwrthlewychawl, *a.* (gwrthlewych) Reflective.
Gwrthlewychiad, *s. m.* (gwrthlewych) A reflecting.
Gwrthlewychu, *v.* (gwrthlewych) To reflect light.
Gwrthlid, *s. m.* (llid) Anger in return.
Gwrthlidiad, *s. m.* (gwrthlid) A being angry, or wrathful in opposition to.
Gwrthlidiaw, *v. a.* (gwrthlid) To return anger.
Gwrthlif, *s. m.—pl. t.* oedd (llif) A counter current.
Gwrthlifaw, *v. a.* (gwrthlif) To reflow; to ebb.
Gwrthlifawl, *a.* (gwrthlif) Refluent; ebbing.
Gwrthlifiad, *s. m.* (gwrthlif) A reflowing.
Gwrthlifiant, *s. m.* (gwrthlif) A refluency.
Gwrthlithr, *s. m.* (llithr) A counter slide.
Gwrthlithraw, *v. a.* (gwrthlithr) To slide back.
Gwrthlithrawl, *a.* (gwrthlithr) Backsliding.
Gwrthlithriad, *s. m.—pl. t.* au (gwrthlithr) A backsliding.
Gwrthlun, *s. m.—pl. t.* iau (llun) Antitype.
Gwrthluniad, *s. m.* (gwrthlun) A reflecting an object; a forming a counter image.
Gwrthluniaw, *v. a.* (gwrthlun) To represent the image of an object.
Gwrthluniawl, *a.* (gwrthlun) Tending to reflect, or to represent an object.
Gwrthlys, *s. m.* (llys) That refuses a contact. *a.* Forbidding; also the herb colt's foot; otherwise called *Llun carn yr ebawl*, *pesychlys*, and *alan bychan.*

Dwyn meddiant Cynan cyn bu llwyd yr un
Arwyddawl yn mhlymnwyd!
Engyrth gyrdd gwrthlys annwyd,
Angeu! anghyfartal wyd!

Taking the estate of Cynan before one was become gray, wrathfully in the conflict! With ardent strides and *forbidding* disposition, death! thou art without an equal! *Ll. P. Moch.*

Gwrthlysawl, *a.* (gwrthlys) Tending to reject.

Gwrthlysu, *v. a.* (gwrthlys) To shew repugnance.

Gwrthlyw, *s. m.* (llyw) A counter guide.

Gwrthlywiad, *s. m.* (gwrthlyw) A guiding adversely or in opposition.

Gwrthlywiaw, *v.a.* (gwrthlyw) To guide adversely.

Gwrthlywiawl, *a.* (gwrthlyw) Tending to guide, or to direct adversely.

Gwrthnaid, *s. f.* (naid) A leap backward.

Gwrthnaws, *s. f.* (naws) An antipathy; dislike.

Gwrthneidiaw, *v. a.* (gwrthnaid) To leap back.

Gwrthneidiawl, *a.* (gwrthnaid) Resilient.

Gwrthneidiolder, *s.m.* (gwrthneidiawl) Resiliency.

Gwrthneidiolrwydd, *s.* (gwrthneidiawl) Resiliency.

Gwrthnerth, *s. m.—pl. t.* oedd (nerth) An opposing, or contrary power.

Gwrthnerthawl, *a.* (gwrthnerth) Tending to strengthen in opposition to.

Gwrthnerthiad, *s. m.* (gwrthnerth) A strengthening in opposition to.

Gwrthnerthu, *v. a.* (gwrthnerth) To strengthen in opposition to, to strengthen against.

Gwrthneu, *v. a.* (neu) To reject, to disallow; to object; to protest against.

Ni wrthneuai hi ar y brenin yr hyn a ddywedai.

She did not *object* to the king as to what he said. *H. Peredur—Mabinogion.*

Gwrthneuad, *s. m.* (gwrthneu) An objecting against; a protestation.

Gwrthneuawl, *a.* (gwrthneu) Being rejected, or disallowed; abhorent, repugnant.

Gwrthneugar, *a.* (gwrthneu) Apt to reject; apt to loath, or abhor.

Gwrthneugarwch, *s. m.* (gwrthneugar) Aptness to reject; aptness to loath.

Gwrthneuwr, *s. m.—pl.* gwrthneuwyr (gwrthneu—gwr) One who rejects, a protester.

Gwrthneuydd, *s. m.—pl. t.* ion (gwrthneu) One who rejects; a protestant.

Gwrthnewid, *s. m.—pl. t.* ion (newid) A counterchange; the antiparastasis, in rhetorick.

Gwrthnewid, *v. a.* (newid) To counterchange.

Gwrthnewidiad, *s. m.—pl. t.* au (gwrthnewid) A counterchanging.

Gwrthnewidiawl, *a.* (gwrthnewid) Counter-changing; apt to change adversely.

Gwrthnod, *s. m.—pl. t.* au (nod) A counter-mark, a check.

Gwrthnodawl, *a.* (gwrthnod) Serving as a check.

Gwrthnodi, *v. a.* (gwrthnod) To counter-mark.

Gwrthnodiad, *s. m.* (gwrthnod) A counter-marking; a checking.

Gwrthnysig, *a.* (gwrthnaws) Refractory, obstinate, stubborn, contumacious.

Gwrthnysigrwydd, *s.* (gwrthnysig) Refractoriness.

Gwrthod, *s. m.* (gwrthawd) A refusal, a rejection.

Gwrthod, *v. a.* (gwrthawd) To refuse, to reject.

Gwrthodadwy, *a.* (gwrthod) Rejectable, repudiable; that may be refused.

Gwrthodai, *s. m.* (gwrthod) The ablative case.

Gwrthodawl, *a.* (gwrthod) Tending to rejection.

Gwrthodedig, *a.* (gwrthod) Being refused.

Gwrthodedigaeth, *s. m.* (gwrthodedig) Rejection.

Gwrthodedigaethydd, *s. m.* (gwrthodedigaeth) One who causes a rejection; the ablative case.

Gwrthodedigawl, *a.* (gwrthodedig) Of a rejecting tendency; apt to reject.

Gwrthodedigrwydd, *s. m.* (gwrthodedig) Rejectedness, a rejected state.

Gwrthodi, *v. a.* (gwrthod) To refuse, to reject.

Gwrthodiad, *s. m.—pl. t.* au (gwrthod) A rejecting; a disowning, or disclaiming; rejection.

Gwrthodiaeth, *s. m.* (gwrthod) A rejection.

Gwrthodaist f'annwyl wyl oedd.

He was the *cast off* of my dear bashful one. *D. ab Gwilym.*

Gwrthodiant, *s. m.* (gwrthod) A rejection.

Gwrthodig, *a.* (gwrthod) Being rejected.

Gwrthodigaeth, *s. m.* (gwrthodig) Rejection.

Gwrthodwr, *s. m.—pl.* gwrthodwyr (gwrthod—gwr) One who refuses, or rejects.

Gwrthodwrdd, *s. m.* (godwrdd) Counter-clamour.

Gwrthodwrdd, *v.a.* (godwrdd) To clamour against.

Gwrthodyrddiad, *s. m.* (gwrthodwrdd) A clamouring in opposition.

Gwrthodyrddu, *v. a.* (gwrthodwrdd) To clamour in opposition.

Gwrthodyrddus, *a.* (gwrthodwrdd) Being adversely clamorous.

Gwrthol, *s. m.* (ol) A posterior part, or place; a rear. *prep.* Behind.

Neidiais yn sorth i'm gwrthol
I'r drws, a'r ci mws i'm ol.

I leaped hastily to my *rear* out of doors, the dingy dog following me. *D. ab Gwilym.*

Gwrtholdeb, *s. m.* (gwrthawl) Contrariety.

Gwrtholi, *v. a.* (gwrthawl) To make adversely.

Gwrtholiad, *s. m.* (gwrthawl) A making contrary.

Gwrtholwg, *s. m.* (golwg) A retrospect.

Gwrtholygawl, *a.* (gwrtholwg) Retrospective.

Gwrtholygiad, *s. m.—pl. t.* au (gwrtholwg) A retrospection.

Gwrtholygu, *v. a.* (gwrtholwg) To take a retrospect, to look back; to look contrarily.

Gwrthorwedd, *s. m.* (gorwedd) A lying in a contrary way; a lying adversely.

Gwrthorwedd, *v. a.* (gorwedd) To lie contrarily.

Gwrthorweddawl, *a.* (gwrthorwedd) Being lying adversely.

Gwrthorweddiad, *s. m.* (gwrthorwedd) A lying contrarily, or opposite.

Gwrthosawd, *s. m.* (gosawd) To put in opposition.

Gwrthosawd, *v. a.* (gosawd) To place in opposition, to set opposite, to contrast.

Gwrthosodadwy, *a.* (gwrthosawd) That may be put in opposition, or contrasted.

Gwrthosodawl, *a.* (gwrthosawd) Being in opposition; counter-positional.

Gwrthosodiad, *s. m.—pl. t.* au (gwrthosawd) A placing in opposition; a contra position; opposition; antithesis.

Gwrthosodiaeth, *s.* (gwrthosawd) Contraposition.

Gwrthosodiant, *s. m.* (gwrthosawd) A putting in opposition.

Gwrthosodwr, *s. m.—pl.* gwrthosodwyr (gwrthosawd—gwr) One who puts in opposition.

Gwrthraith, *s. f.—pl.* gwrthreithiau (rhaith) A contrary law or rule.

Gwrthran, *s. f.—pl. t.* au (rhan) Counter-part; a counter-share.

Gwrthrânawl, *a.* (gwrthran) Being counter-shared.

Gwrthrâniad, *s. m.* (gwrthran) A sharing against.

Gwrthrânu, *v. a.* (gwrthran) To share against.

Gwrthrawd, *s. f.—pl.* gwrthrodion (rhawd) An adverse, or hostile troop; an enemy's army.

Gwrthred, *s. f.—pl. t.* ion (rhed) A contrary course, a run backwards; a recurrence.

Er maint y gwrthred arnaf mi a arhoaf.

Notwithstanding the *hoste back* which I am under I will stay.
H. O. Urien—Mabinogion.

Gwrthredawl, *a.* (gwrthred) Apt to run contrarily; apt to run back; recurrent.

Gwrthredeg, *v. a.* (gwrthred) To run counter.

Gwrthrediad, *s. m.* (gwrthred) A running contrarily; a running back.

Gwrthreithiad, *s. m.—pl.* gwrthreithiaid (gwrthraith) An antinomian.

Gwrthreithiaw, *v. a.* (gwrthraith) To set up a contrary law.

Gwrthreithiawl, *a.* (gwrthraith) Antinomian. *Gwrthreithiolion*, antinomians.

Gwrthres, *s. f.—pl. t.* i (rhes) An adverse row.

Gwrthresawl, *a.* (gwrthres) Adversely ranged.

Gwrthresiad, *s. m.* (gwrthres) A placing in contrary rows; a making an opposite row.

Gwrthresu, *v. a.* (gwrthres) To range against.

Gwrthrif, *s. m.* (rhif) A counter-reckoning.

Gwrthrifad, *s. m.* (gwrthrif) A counting against.

Gwrthrifaw, *v. a.* (gwrthrif) To count against.

Gwrthrifawl, *a.* (gwrthrif) Being counter-reckoned, adversely counting.

Gwrthrifiad, *s. m.—pl.* gwrthrifiaid (gwrthrif) One who counts in opposition; one who is reckoned in contrast.

Sef yw gwrthrifiad etifedd cyssefin i gaffael dadanhudd.

A *counter-party* is a principal inheritor for obtaining an investigation of a claim. *Welsh Laws.*

Gwrthrimyn, *s. m.—pl. t.* au (rhimyn) Pincers.

Beth yw polioni neu lifio dynion yn fyw; tynu y cnawd yn damaddiau â gwrthrimynod heiairn—wrth un o'r rhai hyn!

What is the impaling, or sawing of men alive; the tearing of the flesh in pieces with iron *pincers*, compared with one of these!
Elis Wyn, B. Cwsg.

Gwrthrin, *s. m.—pl. t.* ion (trin) Contest opposed to contest; a counter-ferment.

Tored Caerfyrddin y'ngwrthrin gwyr.

Caerfyrddin was broken in the *hostile contest* of men.
Gwalchmai.

Gwrthrinaw, *v. a.* (gwrthrin) To contravene.

Gwrthrinawl, *a.* (gwrthrin) Contravening.

Gwrthringar, *a.* (gwrthrin) Apt to contravene.

Gwrthringarwch, *s. m.* (gwrthringar) Aptness to contravene, or fight against.

Gwrthriniad, *s. m.* (gwrthrin) A contravening.

Gwrthrinwr, *s. m.—pl.* gwrthrinwyr (gwrthrin—gwr) A contravener.

Gwrthrith, *s. m.—pl. t.* ion (rhith) A counter appearance; a reflected object.

Gwrthrithiad, *s. m.—pl. t.* au (gwrthrith) A reflecting an appearance, or object.

Gwrthrithiai, *s. m.—pl.* gwrthrithieion (gwrthrith) That gives a counter-appearance; a reflector.

Gwrthrithiaw, *v. a.* (gwrthrith) To make an appearance in opposition.

Gwrthrithiawl, *a.* (gwrthrith) Tending to reflect an object.

Gwrthroch, *a.* (rhoch) Adversely harsh.

Gwenhwyfar olwg wrthroch,
Doedwch imi, os gwyddoch,
Y'mha le cyn hyn i'm gwelsoch!

Gwenhwyvar of *forbidding eye*, relate to me, if you know, where before this you have seen me! *Ymdd. Arthur a Gwenhwyfar.*

Gwrthrochi, *v.* (gwrthroch) To act adversely harsh

Gwrthrod, *s. f.—pl. t.* au (rhod) A counter-wheel; a counter turn.

Gwrthrodiad, *s. m.* (gwrthrawd) A retrocession.

Gwrthrodiaw, *v. a.* (gwrthrawd) To retrocede.

Iulian, er yn ymherodr, a wrthrodies o'r ffydd yn Nghrist.

Julian, though being emperor, *apostatized* from the faith in Christ. *Ll. G. Hergest.*

Gwrthrodiawl, *a.* (gwrthrawd) Retroceding.

Gwrthrodiwr, *s. m.—pl.* gwrthrodwyr (gwrthrawd—gwr) One who walks back.

Gwrthrodd, *s. f.—pl. t.* ion (rhodd) Counter-gift.

Gwrthroddi, *v.* (gwrthrodd) To give in opposition.

Gwrthroddiad, *s. m.* (gwrthrodd) A giving in opposition.

Gwrthrus, *a.* (gwrth—rhus) Repulsive.

Gwrthrwyf, *s. m.—pl. t.* au (rhwyf) A counter impulsion or direction.

Gwrthrwyfaw, *v. a.* (gwrthrwyf) To impel in a contrary direction; to row by back strokes.

Gwrthrwyfiad, *s. m.* (gwrthrwyf) A rowing in a contrary direction.

Gwrthrwym, *s. m.* (rhwym) A counterbond.

Gwrthryd, *s. m.* (rhyd) A counter-passage. *a.* Of an adverse course.

Adfeilaw gwyn gorechyr cyd mynaf Eingl, eddyl gwrthryd.

To destroy supreme felicity is the aim of the Angles, a *hostile* crew. *Taliesin.*

Gwrthryfel, *s. m.—pl. t.* oedd (rhyfel) Rebellion

Gwrthryfela, *v. a.* (gwrthryfel) To rebel.

Gwrthryfelaidd, *a.* (gwrthryfel) Rebellious.

Gwrthryfelawg, *a.* (gwrthryfel) Rebellious.

Gwrthryfelgarwch, *s. m.* (gwrthryfelgar) Rebelliousness.

Gwrthryfeliad, *s. m.* (gwrthryfel) A rebelling.

Gwrthryfelu, *v. a.* (gwrthryfel) To rebel.

Gwrthryfelus, *a.* (gwrthryfel) Rebellious.

Gwrthryfelusrwydd, *s. m.* (gwrthryfelus) Rebelliousness.

Gwrthryfelwr, *s. m.—pl.* gwrthryfelwyr (gwrthryfel—gwr) A rebeller.

Gwrthryfus, *a.* (rhyfus) Controverting.

Gwrthryfusedd, *s. m.* (gwrthryfus) A controversy.

Gwrthrym, *s. m.—pl. t.* iau (grym) A contrary energy, or power; a disabling effect.

Tri gwrthrym defawd: bonedd anghowgant, ei gorthrymder, ac anghraifft ddrwg.

The three disabling effects in a custom: uncertain origin, its oppressiveness, and bad example. *Trioedd Dyvnwal.*

Gwrthrymiad, *s. m.* (gwrthrym) A strengthening in opposition; a counteracting.

Gwrthrymu, *v. a.* (gwrthrym) To give a contrary energy, or power; to counteract.

Gwrthrymus, *a.* (gwrthrym) Having adverse energy; having a counter power.

Gwrthryn, *s. m.—pl. t.* ion (rhyn) Oppugnancy; resistance; dispute.

Llewelyn———
Law orthrech wrth rwyfan mordwy,
Lloegr wrthryn tra llyn Llymynawy.

Llywelyn with vanquishing hand in traversing the sea, Lloegria's *opposition* beyond the lake of Llymynawy. *Ll. P. Moch.*

Gwrthryn, *v. a.* (rhyn) To oppugn, to impugn; to resist, to oppose, to repugn.

Gwrthrynawl, *a.* (gwrthryn) Resisting.

Gwrthrynder, *s. m.* (gwrthryn) Resistency.

Gwrthrynedig, *a.* (gwrthryn) Being resisted.

Gwrthrynedigaeth, *s. m.—pl. t.* au (gwrthrynedig) The act of resisting, or opposing.

Gwrthrynedigawl, *a.* (gwrthrynedig) Of a resisting tendency.

Gwrthrynedd, *s. m.* (gwrthryn) Resistence.

Gwrthryngar, *a.* (gwrthryn) Apt to resist.

Gwrthryngarwch, *a.* (gwrthryngar) Aptness to resist or to contravene.

Gwrthryniad, *s. m.* (gwrthryn) A resisting.

Gwrthrynoldeb, *s. m.* (gwrthrynawl) Resistibility, the state or quality of resisting.

Gwrthrynolder, *s. m.* (gwrthrynawl) Resistibility.

Gwrthrynelrwydd, *s. m.* (gwrthrynawl) Resistibleness, resistibility, oppugnancy.
Gwrthrynrwydd, *s. m.* (gwrthryn) Resistibility.
Gwrthrynu, *v. a.* (gwrthryn) To oppugn.
Gwrthrynwr, *s. m.*—*pl.* gwrthrynwyr (gwrthryn—gwr) One who resists.
Gwrthrynydd, *s. m.*—*pl. t.* ion (gwrthryn) One who resists, a resister.
Gwrthryw, *s. m.*—*pl. t.* iau (rhyw) A contrary kind, a contrary nature.
Gwrthrywiad, *s. m.* (gwrthryw) A rendering heterogeneous.
Gwrthrywiaeth, *s. m.* (gwrthryw) Heterogeneity.
Gwrthrywiaw, *v. a.* (gwrthryw) To render heterogeneous, to debase a kind.
Gwrthrywiawl, *a.* (gwrthryw) Heterogeneal.
Gwrthsaf, *s. f.* (saf) A counter-position.
Gwrthsafadwy, *a.* (gwrthsaf) That may be withstood, or opposed.
Gwrthsafawl, *a.* (gwrthsaf) Withstanding.
Gwrthsafiad, *s. m.*—*pl. t.* au (gwrthsaf) A standing against, or opposing; opposition.
Gwrthsafwr, *s. m.*—*pl.* gwrthsafwyr (gwrthsaf—gwr) An opposer, an antagonist.
Gwrthsafydd, *s. m.*—*pl. t.* ion (gwrthsaf) An opponent, or antagonist.
Gwrthsain, *s. f.*—*pl.* gwrthseiniau (sain) A counter-sound; a reverberated sound.
Gwrthsefyll, *s. m.* (gwrthsaf) A withstanding.
Gwrthsefyll, *v. a.* (gwrthsaf) To withstand.
Gwrthseiniad, *s. m.* (gwrthsain) A making a contrary sound; a resounding.
Gwrthseiniaw, *v. a.* (gwrthsain) To make a sound in opposition; to oppose sound to sound; to reverberate.
Gwrthseiniawl, *a.* (gwrthsain) Reverberating.
Gwrthsen, *s. f.*—*pl. t.* au (sen) A rebuke returned.
Gwrthsènawl, *a.* (gwrthsen) Recriminating.
Gwrthseniad, *s. m.* (gwrthsen) A giving a counter rebuke; recrimination.
Gwrthsènu, *v. a.* (gwrthsen) To oppose rebuke to rebuke, to retort a chide.
Gwrthsyniad, *s. m.* (syniad) A counter purpose.
Gwrthsyniaw, *v. a.* (syniaw) To maintain a contrary purpose, or design.
Gwrthsyniawl, *a.* (syniawl) Of a contrary design.
Gwrthsynied, *v. a.* (synied) To design adversely.
Gwrthsyrthiad, *s. m.* (syrthiad) A falling in a contrary direction.
Gwrthsyrthiaw, *v. a.* (syrthiaw) To fall adversely.
Gwrthsyrthiawl, *a.* (syrthiawl) Adversely falling.
Gwrthun, *a.* (gwrth—un) Unseemly, illfavoured.
Gwrthunaw, *v. a.* (gwrthun) To disfigure.
Gwrthunawl, *a.* (gwrthun) Tending to deform.
Gwrthuni, *s. m.* (gwrthun) Deformity, ugliness.
Gwrthuniad, *s. m.* (gwrthun) A disfiguring.
Gwrthus, *a.* (gwrth) Repugnant, repulsive.
Gwrthwad, *s. m.* (gwad) A counter denial.
Gwrthwadawl, *a.* (gwrthwad) Controversial.
Gwrthwadiad, *s. m.* (gwrthwad) A making a counter denial.
Gwrthwadu, *v. a.* (gwrthwad) To make a counter denial; to controvert.
Gwrthwahan, *s. m.* (gwahan) A counter separation, or division.
Gwrthwahaniad, *s. m.* (gwrthwahan) A contradistinguishing.
Gwrthwahaniaeth, *s. m.*—*pl. t.* au (gwrthwahan) A contradistinction.
Gwrthwahanred, *s. m.* (gwrthwahan) A contradistinction.
Gwrthwahanredawl, *a.* (gwrthwahanred) Tending to contradistinguish.
Gwrthwahanredoldeb, *s. m.* (gwrthwahanredawl) The state or quality of contradistinction.
Gwrthwahanredoli, *v. a.* (gwrthwahanredawl) To contradistinguish.
Gwrthwahanu, *v. a.* (gwrthwahan) To contradistinguish; to separate contrarily.
Gwrthwaith, *s. m.* (gwaith) Retroaction.
Gwrthwal, *s. f.*—*pl. t.* iau (gwàl) A contramure.
Gwrthwan, *s. f.* (gwan) A contravention.
Gwrthwanawl, *a.* (gwrthwan) Contravening.
Gwrthwaneg, *s. f.*—*pl. t.* au (gwrthwan) A counter-course; an adverse wave.
Gwrthwanu, *v. a.* (gwrthwan) To contravene.
Gwrthwe, *s. f.*—*pl. t.* oedd (gwe) A lining.
Gwrthwëad, *s. m.* (gwrthwe) A counter-weaving.
Gwrthwëawl, *a.* (gwrthwe) Being counter-woven.
Gwrthwedawl, *a.* (gwedawl) Contradictious.
Gwrthwediad, *s. m.*—*pl. t.* au (gwediad) A contradicting; contradiction.
Gwrthwedyd, *v. a.* (gwedyd) To gainsay; to unsay.

> Ni ddylid amgen noc un ansawdd, nac un amcan, nag un ymgais ar gerdd—can y byddant y pethau hyn fal gwedyd a gwrthwedyd yr un peth.
>
> There oughtto be but one form, but one design, and but one tendency, in a composition, since such things would be like saying and unsaying the same thing. *Barddas.*

Gwrthwedd, *s. f.* (gwedd) An opposing aspect.
Gwrthweddawl, *a.* (gwrthwedd) Contrasting.
Gwrthweddiad, *s. m.* (gwrthwedd) A contrasting.
Gwrthweddu, *v. a.* (gwrthwedd) To contrast.
Gwrthweithiad, *s. m.* (gwrthwaith) A retroacting.
Gwrthweithiaw, *v. a.* (gwrthwaith) To retroact.
Gwrthweithiawl, *a.* (gwrthwaith) Retroactive.
Gwrthweithred, *s. f.*—*pl. t.* ion (gwrthwaith) An adverse action; retroaction.
Gwrthweithredawl, *a.* (gwrthweithred) Tending to counteract.
Gwrthweithrediad, *s. m.* (gwrthweithred) A counteracting; a working adversely.
Gwrthweithredoldeb, *s. m.* (gwrthweithredawl) the state of counteracting.
Gwrthweithredoli, *v. a.* (gwrthweithredawl) To render retroactive.
Gwrthweithredu, *v. a.* (gwrthweithred) To counteract; to work adversely.
Gwrthwel, *s. m.* (gwel) A retrospect.
Gwrthweled, *v. a.* (gwrthwel) To see contrarily; to take a retrospect.
Gwrthwelediad, *s. m.* (gwrthweled) A seeing contrarily; a retrospection.
Gwrthweledig, *a.* (gwrthwel) Retrospective.
Gwrthwenwyn, *s. m.* (gwenwyn) Counter poison.
Gwrthŵydd, *s. m.* (gwrth—gŵydd) Absence.

> Tri dyn a gadwant fraint llys yn ngwrthŵydd y brenin:—ynad llys, gwlychwydwr llys, a rhaglaw.
>
> Three persons who maintain the privilege of a court in the absence of the king: the judge of the court, the priest, and the steward. *Trioedd Dyfnwal.*

Gwrthwyneb, *s. m.*—*pl. t.* ion (gwyneb) A contrary face, front, or side; contrariety; a wrong side; a nausea, or vomiting. *a.* Contrary, adverse. *Yn ngwrthwyneb*, in opposition, or against; *tu gwrthwyneb*, wrong side.

> Gorau gwrthwyneb gwrthwyneb cwys.
>
> The best inversion is the inversion of the furrow. *Adage.*

Gwrthwynebadwy, *a.* (gwrthwyneb) That may be opposed, oppugnable, resistible.
Gwrthwynebawl, *a.* (gwrthwyneb) That may be opposed; oppugnable, resistible.

Gwrthwynebawl, *a.* (gwrthwyneb) Tending to be adverse, or contrary; repugnant.

Gwrthwynebedig, *a.* (gwrthwyneb) Opposed.

> Mal yd oeddynt y gwrthwynebedigion fyddinoedd yn cymmysgu, e a ddamweiniwys trwy y dyngedfen cyfarfod Nynlaw ag Afarwy fab Lludd.
>
> As the *hostile* ranks were mixing together, it happened through the decree of fate that Nynio met with Afarwy the son of Lludd. *Gr. ab Arthur.*

Gwrthwynebedd, *s. m.* (gwrthwyneb) Contrariety; oppugnancy, resistance: repugnance.

Gwrthwynebiad, *s. m.* (gwrthwyneb) A presenting a contrary side; a rendering, or becoming adverse; a resisting, or oppugning: opposition.

Gwrthwyneblyd, *a.* (gwrthwyneb) Nauseous.

Gwrthwynebrwydd, *s. m.* (gwrthwyneb) Opposedness.

Gwrthwynebu, *v. a.* (gwrthwyneb) To make contrary; to become adverse; to resist; to confront.

Gwrthwynebus, *a.* (gwrthwyneb) Tending to turn against; disgustful, nauseous.

Gwrthwynebusrwydd, *s. m.* (gwrthwynebus) Repugnancy; nauseousness.

Gwrthwynebwr, *s. m.*——*pl.* gwrthwynebwyr (gwrthwyneb—gwr) An opposer.

Gwrthwynt, *s. m.* (gwynt) Adverse wind.

Gwrthydd, *s. m.*—*pl. t.* ion (gwrth) An opposite.

> Tri pheth nis gallant fod heb eu gwrthyddion: gwynfyd, gwirionedd, a gwybodaeth.
>
> Three things, which cannot exist without their *opposites:* happiness, truth, and knowledge. *Trioedd.*

Gwrthyf, *pronomial preposition* (gwrth) To me; by me, or close to me. *Gwrthyd*, to thee, by thee: *gwrtho*, to him, by him; *Gwrthym*, to us, *gwrthych*, to you; *gwrthynt*, to them; by them.

> Gwrthyf ni bo trist Crist creawdr.
>
> *To me* let not Christ the created one be sad. *Ll. P. Moch.*

Gwrthymchwel, *s. m.*—*pl. t.* ion (ymchwel) A turn to the contrary.

Gwrthymchwel, *v. a.* (ymchwel) To revert.

Gwrthymchweliad, *s. m.*—*pl. t.* au (gwrthymchwel) A returning to the contrary; a returning back; a discontinning an apostrophe.

Gwrthymchwelu, *v. a.* (gwrthymchwel) To return to the contrary; to revert.

Gwrthymchwelyd, *v. a.* (gwrthymchwel) To return to the contrary; to resume a counter-position; to return back; to apostrophize from the third to the second person.

Gwrthymdrech, *s. f.* (ymdrech) Oppugnancy.

Gwrthymdrech, *v. a.* (ymdrech) To strive in opposition; to counteract.

Gwrthymdrechawl, *a.* (gwrthymdrech) Of a counteracting tendency.

Gwrthymdrechiad, *s. m.* (gwrthymdrech) A striving in opposition; a counteracting.

Gwrthymdrin, *s. m.* (ymdrin) Oppugnancy.

Gwrthymdrin, *v. a.* (ymdrin) To toil against.

Gwrthymdriniad, *s. m.* (gwrthymdrin) A toiling in opposition.

Gwrthymdriniawl, *a.* (gwrthymdrin) Having a tendency to toil against.

Gwrthymdro, *s. m.*—*pl. t.* ion (ymdro) A self-inversion; a turning one's self against.

Gwrthymdröad, *s. m.* (gwrthymdro) A turning one's self contrarily; a becoming inverted.

Gwrthymdröawl, *a.* (gwrthymdro) Apt to become inverted, or to turn one's self back.

Gwrthymdroi, *v. a.* (gwrthymdro) To turn one's self contrarily; to become inverted.

Gwrthymdynawl, *a.* (ymdynawl) Apt to be contending in opposition.

Gwrthymdyniad, *s. m.* (ymdyniad) A being pulling adversely; a contending against.

Gwrthymdynu, *v. a.* (ymdynu) To be pulling adversely; to contend against.

Gwrthymddadl, *s. f.*—*pl.* gwrthymddadlau (ymddadl) An adverse disputation.

Gwrthymddadlawl, *a.* (gwrthymddadl) Apt to be disputing against.

Gwrthymddadliad, *s. m.* (gwrthymddadl) A being disputing in opposition.

Gwrthymddadlu, *v. a.* (gwrthymddadl) To be disputing against.

Gwrthymddangaws, *v. a.* (ymddangaws) To shew one's self against; to appear in opposition.

Gwrthymddangosawl, *a.* (gwrthymddangaws) Apt to appear in opposition.

Gwrthymddangosiad, *s. m.* (gwrthymddangaws) A shewing one's self contrarily; an appearing in opposition.

Gwrthymddwyn, *s. m.* (ymddwyn) A contrary illation, or inference; the antihypophora, in rhetoric.

Gwrthymddwyn, *v. a.* (ymddwyn) To demean one's self contrarily; to advert back.

Gwrthymddygawl, *a.* (ymddygawl) Bringing one's self contrarily; adversely inferring.

Gwrthymddygiad, *s. m.*—*pl. t.* au (ymddygiad) A conducting one's self adversely; a being of a contrary demeanour.

Gwrthymegnïad, *s. m.* (ymegnïad) A counter exertion of one's self.

Gwrthymegnïaw, *v. a.* (ymegnïaw) To exert one's self contrarily.

Gwrthymegnïawl, *a.* (ymegnïawl) Tending to counter exertion of one's self.

Gwrthymgyrch, *s. m.* (ymgyrch) A counter repetition; the antaclasis, in rhetoric.

Gwrthymgyrchawl, *a.* (gwrthymgyrch) Apt to recur contrarily; apt to recur back.

Gwrthymgyrchiad, *s. m.* (gwrthymgyrch) A recurring contrarily; a recurring back.

Gwrthymgyrchu, *v. a.* (gwrthymgyrch) To recur contrarily, to recur back.

Gwrthymladd, *s. m.* (ymladd) Oppugnancy.

Gwrthymladd, *v. a.* (ymladd) To fight against.

Gwrthymladdgar, *a.* (gwrthymladd) Apt to fight in opposition.

Gwrthymladdiad, *s.* (gwrthymladd) Oppugnancy.

Gwrthymluniad, *s. m.* (ymluniad) A being reflected as to form or figure.

Gwrthymluniaw, *v. a.* (ymluniaw) To cause one's self to be reflected as in a mirror.

Gwrthymluniawl, *a.* (ymluniawl) Tending to be reflected, or delineated in a mirror.

Gwrthymosawd, *v. a.* (ymosawd) To set one's self in opposition; to become set in opposition.

Gwrthymosodawl, *a.* (gwrthymosawd) Tending to be adversely placed.

Gwrthymosodiad, *s. m.* (gwrthymosawd) A setting one's self in opposition.

Gwrthymranawl, *a.* (ymranawl) Tending to become adversely separated.

Gwrthymraniad, *s. m.* (ymraniad) A separating one's self contrarily.

Gwrthymranu, *v. a.* (ymranu) To separate one's self contrarily; to be divided contrarily.

Gwrthymrithiad, *s. m.*—*pl. t.* au (ymrithiad) A shewing one's self in opposition.

Gwrthymrithiaw, *v. a.* (ymrithiaw) To make one's self appear in opposition.

Gwrthymrithiawl, *a.* (ymrithiawl) Of a tendency to appear adversely.

Gwrthymröad, *s. m.* (ymröad) A resigning one's self contrarily.

Gwrthymroawl, *a.* (ymröawl) Adversely resigned

Gwrthymröi, *v. a.* (ymröi) To resign one's self contrarily.

Gwrthymrwymaw, *v. a.* (ymrwymaw) To bind one's self contrarily; to be bound contrarily.

Gwrthymrwymawl, *a.* (ymrwymawl) Of a tendency to be adversely bound.

Gwrthymrwymiad, *s. m.* (ymrwymiad) A binding one's self contrarily: a being bound contrarily.

Gwrthymwthiad, *s. m.* (ymwthiad) A pushing one's self adversely; reluctation.

Gwrthymwthiaw, *v. a.* (ymwthiaw) To reluct.

Gwrthymwthiawl, *a.* (ymwthiawl) Apt to push one's self contrarily.

Gwrthyni, *s. m.* (yni) A counter energy.

Gwrthyniad, *s. m.* (yniad) Counter exertion.

> Y tri gwrthyniad farchawg: Morfran ab Tegid, hagr; Sandde Bryd Angel, teg; Glewlwyd Gafaelfawr, cryf ac erchyll.
>
> The three knights of repugnance: Morfran son of Tegid, ugly; Sandde with an Angel's form, fair; Glewlwyd with the mighty grasp, strong and fierce. *Trioedd.*

Gwrthyniawl, *a.* (yniawl) Adversely energetic.

Gwrthyrawl, *a.* (gyrawl) A driving contrarily; a repelling; a repulsion.

Gwrthyru, *v. a.* (gyru) To drive contrarily.

Gwrthysgafael, *s. m.* (ysgafael) A reprisal.

Gwrthysgafaeliad, *s. m.* (gwrthysgafael) A making reprisal.

Gwrthysgafaelu, *v. a.* (gwrthysgafael) To make reprisal.

Gwrthysgrif, *s. f.—pl. t.* ion (ysgrif) A rescript.

Gwrwgawn, *s. m.* (gwg) Tall fescue grass.

Gwrwraig, *s. f.—pl.* gwrwreigedd (gwr—gwraig) A hermaphrodite.

Gwrwreigiawl, *a.* (gwrwraig) Hermaphroditical.

Gwrwst, *s. m.* (gwst) The cramp. It is also called *cwlwm gwythi*, and *clymau gwythi*.

Gwrych, *s. m. aggr.—pl. t.* oedd (rhych) A hedge-row, a quickset hedge; the bristles on the neck of swine; bristles. *Codi gwrych*, to bristle. *Dafad rhwng gwrych a bref.*

> Gwr—
> Garwach ei drem no'r gwrych drain.
>
> A man with a visage more rough than the *hedge* of thorns. *T. Aled.*

Gwrychawg, *a.* (gwrych) Having a ridge, or row; having bristles, bristled.

Gwrychawl, *a.* (gwrych) Being ridged; bristly.

Gwrychell, *s. f.—pl. t.* oedd (gwrych) A thicket, a bush; the hedge-sparrow.

Gwrychiad, *s. m.* (gwrych) A making a hedge-row; a bristling, or setting up bristles.

Gwrychiaw, *v. a.* (gwrych) To bristle, to set up the bristles. *Gwrychiaw edaf crydd*, to bristle a shoe-maker's thread.

Gwrychu, *v. a.* (gwrych) To make a ridge, or hedge-row; to bristle.

Gwrychyn, *s. m.* (gwrych) A hedge-row, a bristle.

Gwrẏd, *s. m.* (gwr) Manliness, or manhood.

Gwryd, *s. f.—pl. t.* ion (rhyd) A chain. *Crogi wrth wrydion aur*, to hang by golden chains.

Gwrydd, *s. m.—pl. t.* au (rhydd) A wreathe.

> Gwisg angel o wallt melyn,
> Yn wrydd aur am war y ddyn.
>
> An angel's covering of yellow hair, in a *wreath* of gold round the maid's shoulder. *D. ab Gwilym.*

Gwrẏddawg, *a.* (gwrẏdd) Having a wreath.

Gwryddawl, *a.* (gwrẏdd) Like a wreath; wreathed

Gwrẏddiad, *s. m.* (gwrẏdd) A wreathing.

Gwrẏddu, *v. a.* (gwrẏdd) To wreath, to twine.

Gwrẏf, *s. m.—pl. t.* iau (rhyf) What keeps tight, or compact; a spring; a press. *Gwryfiau cwch*, the tofts of a boat; *gwrẏf basged*, the spring, or handle of a basket; *gwryf caws*, or *gwasg caws*, a cheese-press.

Gwrẏfiad, *s. m.* (gwrẏf) A pressing with a mechanical power, or press, a squeezing.

Gwrẏfiaw, *v. a.* (gwryf) To squeeze with a press.

Gwrẏfiawl, *a.* (gwrẏf) Tending to press.

Gwrẏfiedig, *a.* (gwryfiad) Being pressed.

Gwryfiwr, *s. m.—pl.* gwryfwyr (gwrẏf—gwr) One who presses, a pressman.

Gwrẏg, *s. m.—pl. t.* ion (rhyg) Energy, vigour.

Gwrygiad, *s. m.* (gwrẏg) An envigorating.

Gwrygiannawl, *a.* (gwrygiant) Envigorating.

Gwrygianniad, *s. m.* (gwrygiant) An envigorating

Gwrygiannu, *v. n.* (gwrygiant) To be envigorated.

Gwrygiannus, *a.* (gwrygiant) Envigorating.

Gwrygiant, *s. m.* (gwryg) Vigour, briskness.

Gwrygiaw, *v. n.* (gwrẏg) To become vigorous, brisk, or lively; to gather strength; to become hale; to make vigorous. *Mae efe yn dechreu gwrygiaw*, he begins to get strength.

> A mab gwraig gwrygwys y pwyllad.
>
> And a woman's son made *efficacious* the design. *Ll. P. Moch.*

Gwrygiawg, *a.* (gwryg) Full of energy, vigorous.

> Pan yw y corff yn isel, isel arno, yr ydym ni weithiau yn clywed yr ysbryd anfarwawl, a'i alluoedd, a'i weithredoedd yn gryfion, yn wrygiawg, ac yn fywiawg dros ben.
>
> When the body is in a low, low condition, we sometimes feel the immortal spirit with its powers and workings strong, and vigorous, and animated beyond measure. *Ier. Owain.*

Gwrygiawl, *a.* (gwryg) Envigorating.

Gwrygioldeb, *s. m.* (gwrygiawl) Vigorousness.

Gwrym, *s. m.—pl. t.* iau (rhym) Strength, effect, a seam; a weal, or raised mark of a stripe.

Gwrymder, *s. m.* (gwrym) Firmness, vigorousness.

> Trech trachwres trechiad ei wrymder,
> Prain Prydain, preiddwyr hyder.
>
> His *strength* is immersed in conquering ambition, the bliss of Britain, the confidence of depredators. *Cynddelw, i O. Gwynedd.*

Gwrymiad, *s. m.* (gwrym) A making a seam.

Gwrymiaw, *v. a.* (gwrym) To strengthen; to make seams; to raise weals.

Gwrymiawg, *a.* (gwrym) Having seams or weals.

Gwrymiawl, *a.* (gwrym) Tending to strengthen; relating to seams.

Gwrymiedig, *a.* (gwrymiad) Seamed: wealed.

Gwrymseirch, *s. pl.* (gwrym—seirch) Harness.

Gwrys, *s. m.—pl. t.* oedd (gwr—ys) Extreme ardency: violence. *a.* Fervent, violent, zealous.

> Teithiawl yn rhaid, yn rhin gwrys,
> Fu Bleddynt fyrg-ddrud negus.
>
> Gallant in the time of necessity, in the *violent* council, was Bleddynt of abruptly-bold career. *Prydydd Bychan.*

Gwrysedd, *s. m.* (gwrẏs) Fervidity, violence.

Gwrẏsg, *s. pl. aggr.* (gwr—ysg) Boughs, branches

Gwrysgen, *s. f.—pl. t.* i (gwrysg) A bough.

Gwrysgeniad, *s. m.* (gwrysgen) A shooting out a branch: a becoming a branch.

Gwrysgenu, *v. n.* (gwrysgen) To shoot out a branch, to form a branch.

Gwrysgiad, *s. m.* (gwrẏsg) A shooting of branches

Gwrysgiaw, *v. a.* (gwrẏsg) To shoot out branches.

Gwrysgiawg, *a.* (gwrẏsg) Having boughs.

Gwrysgryn, *s. m.* (gwrẏs—cryn) Much trembling.

Gwrysiad, *s. m.* (gwrŷs) A being fervid, or ardent.

Rhys wrys wrysiad,
Rhyw lyw luchiad,
Gad gyfaugor.

Rhys of ardent *emulation*, Rhys the leader of tumult in the completely circling battle. *Seisyll Bryf-fwrch.*

Gwrysiaw, *v. a.* (gwrŷs) To act violently, or with ardour; to be ardent, or fervid.

A llys afraid gwrys nw gwrysiaw o'i phlaid,
A llawe enaid yn direidiaw.

With a court of profuse fervency they *act with zeal* on its part, whilst a host of souls become mischievous. *D. Benfras, i uffern.*

Teulu Rhys! teilwng gwrys, gwrysiwch;
Gwrys arloes eirioes eirlolwch:
Chwi genyf gynnifiaid, sefwch:
Mi Gynddelw a gynnelw genwch.

You family of Rhys! zeal is meritorious, *be zealous*, zeal for the flowing muse do you invoke: you opponents to me, stand forward: I Cynddelw will oppose myself to you. *Cynddelw, Dadol. yr argl. Rhys.*

Gwrysiawl, *a.* (gwrys) Of a fervid tendency.

Gwrysiwr, *s. m.—pl.* gwryswyr (gwrys—gwr) One who acts with ardour; an emulator.

Gwryw, *s. m.* (gwr) A male. *a.* Male, masculine.

Gwrywgyd, *s. m.* (gwryw—cyd) Pederasty.

Gwrywgydiaw, *v. a.* (gwrywgyd) To commit sodomy

Gwrywiaidd, *a.* (gwryw) Of a male nature.

Gwrywiawl, *a.* (gwryw) Masculine, or male.

Gwst, *s. f.—pl.* gystion (wst) An humour; a distemper, disease, or malady; any humoral pain.

Can gwst gan henaint.

Old age has a hundred *disorders*. *Adage.*

Gwst, *a.* (wst) Humid, moist, fluid.

Gwstawg, *a.* (gwst) Distempered, diseased.

Gwstawl, *a.* (gwst) Tending to distemper.

Gwstiad, *s. m.* (gwst) A becoming diseased.

Gwstu, *v. n.* (gwst) To become distempered.

Gwth, *s. m.* (wth) A push, or thrust. *Mae efe mewn gwth o oedran,* he is stricken in years.

Gwneuthym â gwth gwaew gwaith anrhydeddedd,
Y rhwng glyw Powys a glwys Wynedd.

I achieved with a *push* of a spear the task of honour, between the chief of Powys and fair Gwynedd. *H. ab Owain.*

Gwthgar, *a.* (gwth) Apt to push, press, or impel.

Gwthiad, *s. m.—pl. t.* au (gwth) A pushing.

Gwthiaw, *v. a.* (gwth) To push, to thrust, to press, or to squeeze forwards; to obtrude. *Na wthia moni,* do not push her.

Gwthiawl, *a.* (gwth) Pushing, pressing, impelling.

Gwthiedig, *a.* (gwthiad) Pushed, or obtruded.

Gwthiwr, *s. m.—pl.* gwthwyr (gwth—gwr) One who impels, a pusher, a thruster.

Gwthr, *s. m.* (gwth) That pushes or drives off.

Gwthrus, *a.* (gwthr) Repulsive, or offensive. *Gair gwthrus,* an offensive word.

Gwthrym, *s. m.* (gwth—grym) Impulsive force.

Gwthwynt, *s. m.—pl. t.* oedd (gwth—gwynt) A squall of wind.

Gwull, *s. m.—pl. t.* ion (ull) Flowerets; flowers.

Casglaf y rhos o'r closydd,
Gwull dolau, a blodau gwydd——
Ar fedd Ifor.

I will collect the roses from the lawns, and the *flowerets* of the meads, and the blossoms of the wood, and lay them on the grave of Ifor. *D. ab Gwilym.*

Gwulliad, *s. m.* (gwull) A bearing flowers.

Gwulliaw, *v. n.* (gwull) To bear flowers.

Gwulliawg, *a.* (gwull) Florigerous, floriferous.

Gwy, *s. m.—pl. t.* on (gw) A fluid, or liquid; water. This word, and *Aw,* are in the composition of a great number of terms, which relate to fluidity; and especially the names of rivers; as *Dyfrdonwy, Edwy, Efyrnwy, Elwy, Llugwy, Mawddwy, Mynwy,* and *Trydonwy.*

Gwyach, *s. f.—pl. t.* od (gwy) A water-fowl, the grebe. *Gwyach gorniawg,* or *tindroed,* the great crested grebe; *gwyach glustiawg,* the lesser crested grebe; *gwyach leiaf,* the white, or dusky grebe.

Gwyach rudd gorfudd goralwal;
Ar donlar gwyar gonofal.

The blood-stained *grebe* called aloud for a glut of food; on a swelling wave of gore she swam with toil. *Cynddelw.*

A gwyach hylef, hylith,
A gwyddfa blaidd yn ei blith.

And a ready-voiced *grebe*, acutely scenting the prey, surrounded by the haunt of a wolf. *Cynddelw.*

Gwyad, *s. m.* (gwy) A yielding a fluid; liquifying.

Gwyal, *s. f.—pl. t.* au (gwy—al) A goal, or mark; also the temple of the head.

Hwyl taer-dan tra wan trwy wyal,
Hwrdd afwyfr mal hir-ddwfr hoewal.

Of the course of ardent fire when piercing through a *mark*, an impulsion free from feebleness like the long whirling water. *Cynddelw, i H. ab Owain.*

Gwyalen, *s. f. dim.* (gwyal) A goal, or mark.

Gyda pherchen bwa balch
Annelu'r un wyalen,
A saethu iwrch â saeth wên.

With the owner of a proud bow, aiming at the same *mark*, and shooting the roe with a white arrow. *L. G. Cothi.*

Gwyalfan, *s. f.—pl. t.* au (gwyal—man) A place that is marked as a goal.

Mal gwr cadwal wyalfan.

Like a man he would guard a *goal*. *Aneurin.*

Pan ddyfu Dudfwlch, dud nerthydd,
Oedd gwaedlan gwyalfan fab Eilydd.

When Tudfwlch came, the supporter of the land, the *marked station* of the son of Eilydd was a plain of blood. *Aneurin.*

Gwyalu, *v. n.* (gwyal) To set a goal, or mark.

Gwyar, *s. m.* (gwy) Gore, congealed blood.

wyarawg, *a.* (gwyar) Abounding with gore.

wyarlled, *a.* (gwyar) Drenched in gore.

Gwyarllyd, *a.* (gwyar) Drenched in gore.

Gwyarlys, *s. m.* (gwyar—llys) Grasspoly.

Gwyaru, *v. n.* (gwyar) To drench in gore.

Gwyaw, *v. n.* (gwy) To produce a fluid.

Gwyawl, *a.* (gwy) Tending to liquify.

Gwyb, *s. m.* (gwy) That is thought, or known.

Gwybad, *s. m.* (gwyb) A perceiving, or knowing.

Gwybedig, *a.* (gwybad) That is known.

Gwybedydd, *s. m.—pl. t.* ion (gwybad) One who knows, one that is initiated. *Gwybedyddion,* Gnostics.

Gwybedydd gwybodaeth y goruchaf.

One initiated in the knowledge of the Most High. *Numbers 24. 16.*

Gwybod, *s. m.—pl. t.* au (gwyb) Knowledge.

Tri pheth nis gellir amgen no'u bod ar bob byw, gan gyfiawnder Duw: cydymoddef yn abred, can heb hynny ni cheilai neb gyflawn wybod ar ddim; cydran cydfraint yng nghariad Duw; a chyd-ddiwedd, gan allu Duw wrth a fo cyfiawn a thrugar.

Three things cannot but exist towards every animated being, by the justice of God: co-sufferance in the circle of inchoation, because without that none could attain to the perfect *knowledge* of any thing; co-participation in the love of God; and co-ultimity through the power of God, as being just and merciful. *Barddas.*

Mae Ieuan, myn fy mywyd!
Llaw ddëau gwybodau'r byd.

Ieuan is, upon my life! the right hand of the *sciences* of the world. *L. G. Cothi.*

Gwybod, *v. n.* (gwyb) To know, to have perception. *Dyn yn gwybod ei dda,* a man knowing his interest; *Bu yno heb yn wybod iti,* he has been there without its being known to thee.

Nid cyfarwydd ond a wypo.

No one is intelligent but who *knows*. *Adage.*

Cas nis gwypo ac nis dysgo.

Despicable is he *who does not know* and who would not learn. *Adage.*

Ni bu gan Ddaw, eu cyfoed,
Caner wir, amcan erioed,
Dyn egwan a amcanai;
Duw net cubl wybod a wnai.

God, coeval with himself, let the truth be sung, never had a design; frail man it is that designs; the eternal God would know perfectly. *Edm. Prys.*

Gwybodadwy, *a.* (gwybod) That may be known.

Gwybodaeth, *s. f.* (gwybod) Knowledge.

Tri chadernyd gwybodaeth: darfod treiglaw pob cyflwr bywyd; cofiaw treiglaw pob cyflwr, a'i ddamwain; a gallu treiglaw pob cyflwr fal y myner, er prawf a barn: a hyn a geir yn nghylch y gwynfyd.

The three stabilities of *knowledge*: to have traversed every state of animated existence; to remember every state and its incidents; and to be able to traverse every state that can be desired, for the sake of experience and judgment: and this will be obtained in the circle of felicity. *Barddas.*

Gwybodaethawl, *a.* (gwybodaeth) Cognoscitive.

Gwybodawl, *a.* (gwybod) Cognitive, knowing.

Gwybodedig, *a.* (gwybod) Being known.

Gwybodoldeb, *s. m.* (gwybodawl) Knowingness.

Gwybodus, *a.* (gwybod) Knowing, well-informed.

Gwybodydd, *s. m.—pl. t.* ion (gwybod) One who knows, or is acquainted with.

Gwybr, *s. f.* (gwyb) That is of a subtile nature.

Gwybraidd, *a.* (gwybr) Somewhat subtile.

Gwybraw, *v. n.* (gwybr) To become subtile.

Gwybrawl, *a.* (gwybr) Of a subtile nature.

Gwybren, *s. f.—pl. t.* au (gwybr) A subtile principle; ether; sky.

Gwybybyr, *s. m.* (gwy—pybyr) Small waterwort.

Gwybydd, *s. m.* (gwyb) That is recognized.

Gwybyddawl, *a.* (gwybydd) Conscious; knowing.

Gwybyddiad, *s. m.* (gwybydd) One who knows from the evidence of his own senses.

Gwybyddiaid yw y rhai à welo yn eu gwydd yr hyn a dystiont.

Direct evidencers are those who see in their presence what they testify of. *Welsh Laws.*

Gwybyddiaeth, *s. m.* (gwybydd) Consciousness.

Nid yw engylawl wybyddiaeth, ac yn llai o lawer synwyr dyn, yn alluawg i ddamgyffred y fath orucheladdrwydd.

Angelical *knowledge*, and much less human intellect, is not capable of comprehending such a superior state of exaltation. *Marchawg Crwydrad.*

Gwybyddu, *v. n.* (gwybydd) To be conscious.

Gwybyddus, *a.* (gwybydd) Conscious, knowing.

Rhaid yw bod genym ymddiried diogel, gwybyddus yn ein cadwraeth.

It is necessary that we should have sure, *conscious*, trust in our salvation. *Marchawg Crwydrad.*

Gwybyddwr, *s. m.—pl.* gwybyddwyr (gwybydd—gwr) One who knows, or is conscious.

Gwych, *a.* (gwy) Gallant, brave; gaudy, gay. *Pa sut yr wyd ti?* How dost thou do? *Yr wyf yn wych iawn*, I am very bravely.

Gwychain, *a.* (gwych) Abounding with gaudiness; gallant; heroic.

Gwychaw, *v. a.* (gwych) To adorn; to be brave.

A thithau yn gwychaw pan grched dy bar
Ni chael dy engyr engyr lludded.

And thou *glowing with ardour* when thy spear was reddened, thy foe would not obtain relief from trouble. *Llygad Gwr.*

Gwychawd, *s. m.* (gwych) A being pompous.

Oeddynt gwychawd gwedi medd-dawd.

They were in a *pompous mood* after inebriation. *Aneurin.*

Gwychawg, *a.* (gwych) Pompous, or gorgeous.

Gorsedd teyrnedd gwersyll wychawg.

The throne of princes in the *gorgeous* camp. *Gwalchmai.*

Gwychder, *s. m.* (gwych) Gallantry, bravery; gaudiness, finery, pomp; gaiety, smartness.

Tâl Duw i chwi am y gorchwyl elusengar yma, pan i bo y byd hwn, a'i holl fawredd a'i wychder wedi llwyr ddiflanu.

God will reward you for this charitable action, when this world, with all its *splendour*, shall have utterly vanished away. *Parch. L. Evans*

Gwychedd, *s. m.* (gwych) Gorgeousness.

Gwychfawr, *a.* (gwych) Splendidly great.

Gwychi, *s. m.* (gwych) The waxy scum of honey.

Mel a fo chweccach naw gwaith no mel cynhaid, heb wychi, ac heb wenyn ynddo, a fynaf i fragodi y wledd.

Honey that shall be nine times sweeter than the honey of the virgin swarm, without *scum*, and without bees in it, I must have to make bragget for the banquet. *H. Culhwch—Mabinogion.*

Gwychlith, *s. m.* (gwych—llith) A fine lure.

Meredudd aes-drom rudd drwch,
Par awchlym wychlith gwyach.

Meredudd with the red heavy shield battered, and the keenly pointed spear the *fine lure* of the grebe. *Prydydd Bychan.*

Gwychnaws, *s. f.* (gwych—naws) A brave disposition.

Gwychr, *a.* (gwych) Valiant, resolute, bold.

Gwychraw, *v. n.* (gwychr) To become heroic.

Gwychrawl, *a.* (gwychr) Tending to gallantry.

Oeddynt——
Llyrou gwychrolion pan godeid.

They were *fierce of disposition*, as serpents, when irritated. *Aneurin.*

Gwychrfalch, *a.* (gwychr—balch) Heroically proud

Gwychrlym, *a.* (gwychr—llym) Bravely-active.

Gwychruthr, *s. m.* (gwych—rhuthr) A gallant onset, a grant assault.

Gwychu, *v. a.* (gwych) To adorn; to make gallant; to become gallant.

Gwychydd, *s. m.* (gwych) A hero, a brave man.

Rhag byddin Ododin, pan fu ddydd,
Neus gorau dan bwyllfad nerthiad gwychydd.

Before the host of Gododin, when the day of conflict raged, next to the penetrating mind was not the strength of a *hero* best! *Aneurin.*

Gwŷd, *s. m.—pl. t.* iau (gwy) Quality; disposition; passion; a prevailing bent, or inclination; sloth, laziness; vice. *Y saith brif-wyd*, the seven deadly sins.

Gwae offeiriad byd,
Ni's angreifftia gwyd,
Ac ni's areithia!

Woe to the priest of the world, who shall not rebuke sin, and who shall not perform his office! *Awdl Fraith.*

Gwydiad, *s. m.* (gwŷd) A giving a bent, or inclination; a becoming vicious.

Gwydiaw, *v. a.* (gwŷd) To follow the inclination; to lust; to be vicious.

Gwydiawg, *a.* (gwŷd) Full of vice, vicious.

Gwydiawl, *a.* (gwŷd) Of a vicious tendency.

Gwydien, *s. m.* (gwyd) A spirit supposed to preside in the air. *Gwydion* is another synonymous appellation for the same being.

I am awyr eryr Gwydien.

The eagle of *Gwydien* hovers round the sky. *Aneurin.*

Mor debyg fy mod megis Gwydien.

So likely am I to be as *Gwydien*. *Cynddelw.*

Gwydion, *s. m.* (gwyd) A mythological personage, the son of *Don*, whose history is but little known; a spirit supposed to preside in the air, or rather in the starry regions. *Caer gwydion*, an epithet often used for the galaxy. Probably he is the same as the Teutonic *Woden*.

Gwydn, *a.* (gwyd) Tough, tenacious; viscid.

Addaw teg ym ydd wyt ti,
Gwydn, a'm gomedd gwedi!

A fair promise thou dost make to me, how *tenacious*, and afterwards refusing me! *D. ab Gwilym.*

Gwydnâad, *s. m.* (gwydn) A rendering tough, or viscid; a becoming tough.

Gwydnaidd, *a.* (gwydn) Somewhat tough.

Gwydnâu, *v. n.* (gwydn) To become tough.

Gwydnaw, *v. n.* (gwydn) To become tough.

Gwydnawl, *a.* (gwydn) Of a tough quality.

Gwydnder, *s. m.* (gwydn) Toughness, viscidity.
Gwydnedd, *s. m.* (gwydn) Toughness, tenacity; viscidity, glutinousness.
Gwydr, *s. m.—pl. t.* au (gwŷd) Glass; a glass vessel, or drinking glass; a greenish blue colour

> Merddin aeth, mawr ddawn ei wedd,
> Mewn gwydr er mwyn ei gydweddd.
>
> Merddin, great the grace of his countenance, went into *glass* for the sake of his mate. *Ieuan Dyfi.*
>
> I Dre'r Twr, lliw gwydr y to,
> I cair wrth fodd a'i caro.
>
> In Tre'r Twr, of *glass* coloured roof, will be found contented all who love him. *Sir Philip Emlyn.*

Gwydr, *a.* (gwyd) Of glass; of a glas colour, of a greenish blue colour.

> Gardd Laned, gwraidd haelonion,
> Gwe drwy haf, a gwydr yw hon.
>
> The garden of Laned, the root of generous ones, a carpet through the summer, and this is *green*. *W. Egwad.*

Gwydradwy, *a.* (gwydr) That may be vitrified.
Gwydraid, *s. m.* (gwydr) A glass-full.
Gwydraidd, *a.* (gwydr) Vitreous, like glass.

> March———
> Llygadrwth a lliw gwydraidd.
>
> A full-eyed steed of a *glassy* colour. *G. ab D. Fychan.*

Gwydraw, *v. a.* (gwydr) To do with glass.
Gwydrawg, *a.* (gwydr) Abounding with glass.
Gwydrawl, *a.* (gwydr) Vitreous, or glassy.

> Arferid gynt galw y lle hwnw Ynys Wydrin, o achaws afonydd yn ei hamgylchu, a lliw glas gwydrawl a oedd ar y dwfr.
>
> It was usual formerly to call that place the *Glassy Island*, on account of being surrounded by rivers, the water of which was of a blue *vitreous* colour. *Han. Diwedd Arthur.*

Gwydredig, *a.* (gwydr) Glazed; vitrified.
Gwydredd, *s. m.* (gwydr) Vitreousness.
Gwydrin, *a.* (gwydr) Vitrean, vitreous, glassy.

> Gogyfarch feirdd tras—
> A gwaddawl tra merin,
> A chorwg gwydrin
> Ar law pererin.
>
> Greet native bards with transmarine treasure, and a *glass* goblet put into a pilgrim's hand. *Taliesin.*

Gwydro, *s. m.* (gwy—tro) Common melilot.
Gwydrogi, *v. a.* (gwydrawg) To vitrify; to become vitreous, or to vitrify.
Gwydrogiad, *s. m.* (gwydrawg) Vitrification.
Gwydroli, *v. a.* (gwydrawl) To vitrify.
Gwydroliad, *s. m.* (gwydrawl) Vitrification.
Gwydrwr, *s. m.—pl.* gwydrwyr (gwydr—gwr) A glazier.
Gwydryn, *s. m.—pl. t.* au (gwydr) A glass.
Gwydrynaid, *s. m.* (gwydryn) A glass-full.
Gwydus, *a.* (gwŷd) Of a stubborn bent; vicious.
Gwydusrwydd, *s. m.* (gwydus) Viciousness.
Gwydd, *s. m.—pl. t.* on (gw—ydd) A state of recognition, or knowledge; presence. *Dos o'm gwydd!* go from my presence!

> Dywed weithian, dad ieithydd,
> Dy feddwl ym, da foddawl wydd,
> Ai amcanu canu'r cor,
> A gwydd rhugl gywydd rhagor!
>
> Declare then now, father of languages, thy mind to me, if of well-cultured *knowledge* thou dost intend to sing in turn, on recording wood, another poem! *W. Cynwal.*
>
> Dithau, William, daith hylwydd,
> Dewr wyd ar air, dyr'd ar wydd.
>
> Thou also, William, of prosperous course, thou art bold in word, come in *presence*. *Edm. Prys.*
>
> Beirdd a'u gwawd beraidd yw gwydd,
> Berw llawn, a bair llawenydd.
>
> Bards with grateful praise in their *presence*, with fancy flowing will create mirth. *Edm. Prys.*

Gwŷdd, *s. pl. aggr.* (gwy—ydd) Trees; shrubs; a frame of wood; a loom; wood for writing on, also called *Peithynen*. *Gwŷdd arad*, a plough; which is more generally called *aradr*.

> Llais y gôg mewn llawes gwŷdd,
> Llyna ein holl lawenydd.
>
> The voice of the cuckoo in the skirt of a *wood*, behold it is our complete happiness. *T. Prys.*
>
> Llawer arfer a orfydd
> Llun ei gorff wrth ddarllain gwydd.
>
> Many an attitude does the form of his body make in reading the *wood*. *Gw. Tew.*

Gŵydd, *s. f.—pl. t.* au (gwy) A goose. *Diadell o wyddau*, a flock of geese; *gŵydd ddof*, a tame goose; *gŵydd wyllt*, a wild goose; *mam-wydd*, a mother goose; *glas-wydd*, a green goose; *sofl-ŵydd*, a stubble goose.

> Nid ynfyd ond gŵydd.
>
> Nothing so silly as a *goose*. *Adage.*

Gwŷdd, *a.* (gwy—ydd) Woody, overgrown, wild, uncultivated. *Tir gwydd, a thir ffaeth*, lay land, and tilled land.
Gwŷddad, *s. m.* (gwŷdd) Attaining of knowledge.
Gwŷddafr, *s. f.—pl.* gwŷddeifr (gwŷdd—gafr) A wild goat.
Gwyddai, *s. m.* (gwŷdd) A scientific person.
Gwyddain, *a.* (gwŷdd) Sciential, scientific.
Gwyddallt, *s. f.—pl.* gwyddelltydd (gwydd—gallt) A woody cliff.
Gwyddan, *s. c.—pl. t.* od (gwŷdd) A sylvan.
Gwyddanes, *s. f.—pl. t.* au (gwyddan) A sylvan goddess, or wood nymph.
Gwyddaw, *v. n.* (gwydd) To become perceptible.
Gwyddaw, *v. a.* (gwydd) To give knowledge; to inform; to serve as a guide.
Gwyddaw, *v. n.* (gwŷdd) To grow woody, to run wild, to be overgrown. *Tir yn gwyddaw*, land running wild, as with thistles, and brambles.
Gwyddawd, *s. m.* (gwŷdd) A state of knowledge.
Gwŷddawg, *a.* (gwŷdd) Abounding with wood.
Gwŷddawl, *a.* (gwydd) Sciential; rudimental.
Gwyddawr, *s. f.—pl.* gwyddorion (gwydd) A rudiment.
Gwyddbwyll, *s. f.* (gwydd—pwyll) Scientific reason; eduction of knowledge; also the game of chess. *Clawr y wyddbwyll*, the chess-board; *gwerin y wyddbwyll*, the table-men.

> Clogyrnach a chyngawg à fernir yn isaf eu bonedd o'r holl golofnau, am nid hawdd trefn a dosbarth arnynt herwydd rheol a gwyddbwyll.
>
> The rugose and complicate metres are considered as lowest in dignity of all canons, by reason that it is not easy to reduce them to order and arrangement according to rule and *science*. *Barddas.*

Gwydded, *s. m.* (gwŷdd) Growth, or foliation of trees.

> Gwydded coed cain eu syllu
> Hyd yd fuant, a hyd yd fu.
>
> The *foliage* of trees made them fair to behold whilst they were, and whilst it was. *Taliesin.*

Gwyddedig, *a.* (gwydd) Recognised, or known.
Gwyddedigaeth, *s. m.* (gwyddedig) State of knowledge.
Gwŷddednaint, *s. pl. aggr.* (gwŷdd—ednaint) Pheasants.
Gwyddednen, *s. f.* (gwyddednaint) A hen pheasant.
Gwyddednyn, *s. m.* (gwyddednaint) A cock pheasant.
Gwyddel, *s. m.—pl. t.* od (gwydd) That is of the woods, that is in a sylvan state; a savage. It is an appellative, synonymous with *Celt*, and *Ysgotiad*, for an individual of such tribes as lead a venatic life in woods, in contradistinction to the *Gâl*, living by cultivating the ground. Whichever of these two primary classes of mankind had the ascendency gave its name to the whole country: Hence *Gwyddel* is the general

term in Welsh for a native of Ireland, because the tribes, of which the name is descriptive, appeared predominant to those who imposed it. There is a tradition of Wales's being once inhabited by the *Gwythelians*; or, more properly, its first inhabitants were so called; and the common people in speaking of it, ascribe some ruins about the country, under the name of *Cytiau y Gwyddelod*, to them; and the foxes are said to have been their dogs; and the polecats their domestic cats, and the like.

Gwyddelaidd, *a.* (gwyddel) Gwythelian-like.

Gwyddelain, *a.* (gwyddel) Abounding with brakes

Gwyddelawg, *a.* (gwyddel) Abounding with bushes, or brakes. *Tir gwyddelawg*, land overrun with brambles. *Sil.*

Gwyddeleg, *s. f.* (gwyddel) The Irish tongue.

Gwyddeles, *s. f.* (gwyddel) An Irish-woman.

Gwyddeli, *s. pl. aggr.* (gwyddel) Brakes, bushes.

> Pam yr wyd——
> Dan y dirgel wyddeli
> Heb fod neb yn d'ateb di!

> Why art thou beneath the solitary *brakes* without any one being answering thee! *D. ab Gwilym, i'r Bi.*

Gwyddeliaith, *s. f.* (gwyddel—iaith) The Irish language.

Gwyddelig, *a.* (gwyddel) Sylvan, savage. Gwythelian, or Irish. *Llysiau gwyddelig*, parsnips.

Gwythelin, *a.* (gwyddel) Gwythelian, Irish.

> Pan ddel y cyrn gwythelin
> O'r tir draw, a'r tarw i'r drin——
> Rhyfel anwar yndarw
> A fydd.

> When the *gwythelian* horns shall come from yonder land, and the bull to the conflict, war of furious toil shall rage. *Hustyn.*

Gwyddelrwydd, *s. m.* (gwyddel) An extent of thickets, or brakes.

Gwyddelwern, *a.* (gwyddel—gwern) A moor or meadow overgrown with bushes.

Gwyddelyn, *s. m. dim.* (gwyddel) A Gwythelian.

Gwydden, *s. f.—pl. t.* i (gwydd) A standing tree.

Gwyddenig, *s. f. dim.* (gwydden) A shrub.

Gwŷdderbyn, *prep.* (gwydd—erbyn) In presence of, in front of, before.

Gwyddfa, *s. f.—pl. t.* au (gwydd) A place of presence; an eminence where bardic meetings were held; an artificial mound, or tumulus, which served to teach the people from, and also as a sepulchre. All places appropriated for those uses were comprehended in the term *Gwyddfa*; but those constructed of earth were likewise called *Bal* and *Beili*, as were the heaps of stones called *Carn* and *Carnedd*. *Yr Wyddfa*, the place of presence, is the name of the mountain, which in English is called Snowdon.

> Arthur, wyddfa llawenydd,
> A'th lu buost lwyr gynnydd.

> Arthur, the *centre* of gladness, with the army thou hast been completely prosperous. *Ymdd. Arthur ac Eliwlod.*

> Y radd a gefais ar rod
> Ounst wyddfa'n eisteddfod.

> The degree I obtained by rotation of an honest *publicity* in congress. *W. Cynwal.*

Gwyddfaawg, *a.* (gwyddfa) Having a conspicuous seat, or eminence.

Gwyddfâwl, *a.* (gwyddfa) Monumental.

Gwyddfan, *s. f.—pl. t.* au (gwydd) A place of presence; a meeting place.

Gwyddfarch, *s. m.—pl.* gwyddfeirch (gwydd—march) A wooden support; a wooden horse; an epithet for a ship.

> Gwyddfeirch ton twyni yn ertrai,
> Gwythur awen fal trane a'u trechai.

> The wooden *steeds* of the wave; he that is so fierce as Gwythur like a fury would overthrow them. *Cynddelw, i O. Gwynedd.*

Gwyddfedd, *s. f.—pl. t.* i (gwydd—bedd) A sepulchral monument.

> Gwyddfedd eu gwyddfa, gwddfid estrawn;
> Gwyddwn a'm rhoddes bedd las buddlawn!

> The tomb their place of meeting, the woodbine of strangers; I knew him who freely gave me profitable good! *Cynddelw, m. Rhyd.*

Gwyddfid, *s. m.* (gwydd—bid) The woodbine, the honeysuckle, which is also called *Gwyddwydd*, *gwynwydd*, *llaeth y geifr*, and *tethau y gaseg*.

> Ni llas blaidd uch blaenwel gwyddfid.

> The wolf was not slain above the woodbine hedge. *Ll. P. Moch.*

Gwyddfil, *s. m.* (gwydd—mil) A wild beast.

Gwyddfoch, *s. pl.* (gwydd—moch) Wild swine.

> Aml yw'ch feirdd yw fudd;
> Ewyn llys nyw lludd;
> Ewyn rhydd rhuthr gwyddfoch.

> Frequent to you bards his bounty; courtly steeds he does not withhold; bay steeds also with the *wild boars'* onset. *Cynddelw, i O. Cyfeiliawg.*

Gwyddfochyn, *s. m.* (gwyddfoch) A wild boar.

Gwyddgi, *s. m.* (gwydd—ci) A wild dog.

> Gwyddfid Eingl y'nghladd a'i trychai;
> Gwyddgwn coed, colled a'u porthai;
> Gwyddwal dyfnwal dyfnaai fy modd,
> Fy meddiant a gaffai!

> The Angles feeble as the woodbine, he that was wont to cut them is in the grave, the *wild dogs* of the wood, he that was wont to feed them is lost; he that had been laid in the wooden bed, he had made my mind tractable to himself, my all was at his disposal! *Cynddelw, m. O. Gwynedd.*

Gwyddgrug, *s. m.* (gwydd—crug) A mound of presence; a monumental mound, a tumulus.

Gwyddhwch, *s. f.—pl.* gwyddhychod (gwydd——hwch) A wild sow; otherwise called *hwch coed*, or the sow of the wood.

Gwyddi, *s. m.* (gwydd) A quickset row, or hedge.

Gwyddiad, *s. m.—pl. t.* au (gŵydd) Cognition.

Gwyddiad, *s. m.—pl.* gwyddiaid (gwydd) Knower

Gwyddiadawl, *a.* (gwyddîad) Sciential, cognitive.

Gwyddiadu, *v. n.* (gwyddiad) To know, to be versed in, or acquainted with.

> Yn ol Seisyllt y doai Blegywryd, a hwnw ni bu yn yr oesoedd, na chynt nog ef na gwedi, cerddor cystal ag ef; a rhag dlad y canu, ac y gwyddiad celfyddyd, y gelwid ef duw y gwawd.

> Next to Seisyllt came Blegywryd, than whom there has not been in the ages, neither before him nor after, a musician equal to him; and from his performing so well, and his *knowing* the science, he was called the god of music. *Gr. ab Arthur.*

> Gormes a wyddiad garwdo,
> Carn et fewyn a fyn fo——
> Mawr fwch.

> A trespasser that *knows how* to raise an abrasion one rough of hair he will have, a great buck. *W. Cynwal.*

Gwyddiannawl, *a.* (gwyddiant) Relating to knowledge, or science.

Gwyddiannawr, *v. n.* (gwyddiant) To be acquainted; to possess knowledge.

> Mynaich dychnud fal bleiddiawr,
> O gyfranc addysg a'u gwyddiannawr.

> Monks herd together like wolves, from an identity of pursuit to them they *become instructed*. *Taliesin.*

Gwyddiannu, *v. n.* (gwyddiant) To become possessed of knowledge or science.

Gwyddiant, *s. m.* (gwydd) Science, knowledge.

Gwyddiawg, *a.* (gwydd) Having knowledge.

Gwŷddif, *s. m.* (gwydd—if) A hedging-bill.

> Bwrw gwyddif ar ol yr hwyaid.

> To throw the *hedging-bill* after the ducks. *Adage.*

Gwyddin, *a.* (gwydd) Being of wood, wooden.

> Dy grog croes wyddin, frenin freinolion,
> Dygorth chweoes hyd rhag pyd poenau.

> Thy crucifixion on the wooden cross, king of privileges, is well bear the six ages of the world against the dread of punishments. *Ein. ab Gwalchmai.*

Gwydding, *s. f.—pl. t.* od (gwŷdd) A quickset hedge.

Gwŷddlan, *s. f.—pl. t.* an (gwŷdd—llan) A plantation of trees.

Gwyddle, *s. m.—pl. t.* oedd (gwydd—lle) A place covered with wood.

Gwyddlen, *s. f.—pl. t.* i (gwydd—llen) A veil of wood; a wooden covering.

Nid llawen fy mryd yn mro Gynghen,
Ar llary llaw hygad gweled gwyddlen,
Gwyddlen a'i gortho, gorthaw dristlawn;
Gwyddlan a'i gwerchyr, gorchudd gwythlawn!

My mind is not happy in the country of Cynghen, upon the mild one of liberal hand to see a *veil of wood*; a *veil of wood* does cover him, mournful the covering; a woody plain secludes him, a wrathful shroud. *Cynddelw, m. Riryd.*

Gwyddlwdn, *s. m.—pl.* gwyddlydnod (gwydd—llwdn) A wild beast.

Gwyddlwyn, *s. m.* (gwydd—llwyn) Common burnet, or pimpernel; also called *gwlydd mair*, and *llysiau y cryman*.

Gwyddon, *s. m.—pl. t.* au (gwydd) One possessed of knowledge; a philosopher, a man of science, or learning. *Gorsedd bryn gwyddon*, or *Abury*, was one of three primary places of meeting of the bards of the isle of Britain.

Pan ydoedd ein Rhen,
Hyd dros ei ddwyen,
Yn nwfr Urddonen,
Yn nirwestfa,
Pedwar engylion,
A deuddeg gwyddon,
Danfones Lesion
I lys Efa.

When our Lord was immersed over his lips in the water of Jordan, during his fasting, four of the angels, and twelve *witnesses*, the Eternal sent to the mansion of Eve. *Ion. Mynyw.*

Gwyddonawl, *a.* (gwyddon) Philosophical.

Gwyddoni, *v. a.* (gwyddon) To gather knowledge

Gwyddor, *s. f.—pl. t.* (gwydd—or) A gate.

Gwyddorawl, *a.* (gwyddawr) Rudimental.

Gwyddori, *v. a.* (gwyddawr) To investigate principles of knowledge; to form a rudiment.

Gwyddorig, *s. f. dim.* (gwyddawr) A rudiment of knowledge. *a.* Rudimental.

Neud adwen ar fy awen
Yn hanfod cun achen
Tri gwyddorig elwig wen!

Do I not recognize in my muse, proceeding from a sublime source, three *rudiments* of fair delineation' *Llywarch Hen.*

Rhaid yw gwybod dosbarth wyddorig ar yr iaith.

It is necessary to know the *rudimental* analysis of the language. *Barddas.*

Gwyddrun, *a.* (gwydd—rhun) Of awful presence.

Gwyddwal, *s. f.—pl.* gwyddwell (gwŷdd—gwal) A woody fastness; a thicket.

Ef caned rhag ei ofn, a'i arswyd, oer-gerdd;
Cyn bu daiar dogn ei ddiwedd,
Haid hafal am wyddwal gwn ebrwydd.

For fear of him, and his dread, a dismal song was sung; before his end was his measure of earth, like a swarm were the swift dogs round the *thicket couch*. *Marwnad Cynedda.*

Amsathr dynion nac anifeiliaid nis gwelai, namyn gwyddwell a llysiau.

Neither the footsteps of men nor of deer could he perceive, but *thickets* and herbs. *H. Peredur—Mabinogion.*

Gwyddwalch, *s. m.—pl.* gwyddweilch (gwydd—gwalch) A wild falcon.

Gwyddwaledd, *s. f.* (gwyddwal) The state of being surrounded with wilds; a place full of thickets; a wooded boundary; a limitation; a limit.

Nid a hawl yn llwrw gwyddwaledd yn erbyn dylyedawg nes terfynu yr achwysion uchod.

A claim shall not go under *limitation* against one who is entitled, until the above mentioned causes are ended. *Welsh Laws.*

Dwy wyddwaledd y sydd, yn nghyfraith Hywel—gwyddwaledd cywlad, ac un anghywlad.—Gelwir hi yn wyddwaledd, am fod gwyddweh rhwng dyn ac ei hawl.

There are two interventions in the law of Hywel:—an intervention of a border-country, and one not of a border-country.—It is called an intervention on account of there being *thicket interventions* between the person and his right. *Welsh Laws.*

Gwyddwalu, *v. a.* (gwyddwal) To form a woody fastness or intervention.

Gwyddweli, *s. pl. aggr.* (gwyddwal) Thicket.

Gwyddwg, *s. m.* (gwydd) Knowledge, perception.

Gwyddwig, *s. f.* (gwydd—gwig) An angle, or fastness in a wood; wit's end; embarrassment.

Gwae fi fy mod yn achaws yr wyddwig hon o wyr Ynys y Cedeirn!

Woe to me, that I should be the cause of this *embarrassment* to the men of the Isle of the Mighty! *H. Culhwch—Mabinogion.*

Gwyddwydd, *s. m.* (gwydd—gwŷdd) The honeysuckle.

Gwyddyd, *s. m.* (gwydd) Knowledge.

Gwyedig, *a.* (gwy) Liquified, being made to flow.

Gwyedigaeth, *s. m.* (gwyedig) Liquefaction.

Gwyf, *s. m.—pl. t.* on (gwy) That yields, that runs out, that draws out; that is smooth.

Gwyfaw, *v. n.* (gwyf) To run out; to become smooth, or flat.

Gwyfawl, *a.* (gwyf) Of a yielding tendency.

Gwyfen, *s. f. dim.* (gwyf) A moth, an insect that destroys woollen cloth.

Gwyfenawg, *a.* (gwyfen) Abounding with moths.

Ei gledd a'i faner wr gwyfenawg,
Gwrach hen-gest aren, a gwas torawg.

His sword, and his banner, the *moth-breeding* fellow, were a shrivel-breasted hag, and a tun-bellied chap. *D. ab Ieu. Ddu.*

Gwyfon, *s. pl. aggr.* (gwyf) The gooseberries. *Gwyfon barfawg*, rough gooseberries.

Gwyfyn, *s. m. dim.—pl. t.* od (gwyf) A moth.

Gwyfynawg, *a.* (gwyfyn) Having moths, mothy. *Gwyfynog*, moth mullein.

Gwyfynu, *v. n.* (gwyfyn) To generate moths.

Gwyfr, *s. m.—pl. t.* au (gwyfr) Wire.

Gwŷg, *s. m.* (gwy) That is flaccid, flabby; vetch. *Gwyg y mor*, sea weed, wrack.

Gwygawl, *a.* (gwyg) Of a flaccid tendency.

Gwygbys, *s. pl. aggr.* (gwyg—pys) Tufted vetch; otherwise called *Pys y llygod*.

Gwyglyd, *a.* (gwyg) Flaccid; void of energy.

Gwyglyd im' rhoi goglyd mawr,
Gwarthfodd, ar seintiau gwyrthfawr.

A *futile* thing to me to place great dependence upon wonder working saints, and scandalous. *M. ab H. Lewys.*

Gwygydd, *s. m.—pl. t.* ion (gwŷg) A flabby one.

Gwygyl, *a.* (gwŷg) Tending to flaccidity; sultry.

Gwyl, *s. f.—pl. t.* iau (gwel) A sight; a show; a holiday, or festival. *Gwyl arbenig*, a high festival; *gwyl y milfeibion*, or *gwyl y gwirioniaid*, childermas-day; *gwyl y meirw*, or *gwyl yr eneidiau*, all soul's day; *gwyliau gwyl bentan*, the keeping of the fireside vigil.

Nid oes gwyl rhag elusen.

There is no *holiday* from almsgiving. *Adage.*

Gwyl, *a.* (gwel) Modest, or bashful, diffident.

Gwyl yw hanes.

A narrative is *modest*. *Adage.*

Gwylad, *s. m.* (gwyl) A beholding; a keeping a festival.

Gwylaeth, *s. m.* (gwyl—llaeth) Lettuce. *Gwylaeth yr yd*, *gwylaeth yr oen*, *gwylaeth gwyllt*, corn-salad; *gwylaeth chwerw*, bristly ox-tongue, *gwylaeth y fagwyr*, ivy-leaved lettuce; *gwylaeth y moch*, swine's succory.

Gwylan, *s. f.—pl. t.* od (gwyl) A gull, or sea mew, *Gwylan ddu a gwyn*, the great black and white gull; *gwylan rudd a gwyn*, the brown and white gull; *gwylan frech*, the brown spotted gull *gwylan y gwenwydd*, the winter gull; *gwylan y penwaig*, the herring gull; *gwylan lwyd*, or *bolan*, the cob, or great gray gull; *gwylan gernyw*, the tarrock; *gwylan y graig*, the fulmar; *gwylan benddu*, or *bran y mor*, the pewit gull; *gwylan fechan*, the small brown gull.

> Pan dreiddiwn yno ynyd oeddynt;
> Trwy ffenestri gwydr ydd ym gwelynt;
> Trybelid wylain a wylynt arnai;
> Trael atteb attaf a ddanfonynt.
>
> When I insinuated myself there they were together in a group; through glass windows they saw me the splendid sea-mews gazed upon me, a short answer they would send to me. *Cynddelw.*

Gwylar, *s. m.* (gwy—llar) Coral, a marine plant.

Gwylaw, *v. a.* (gwyl) To act bashfully; to weep.

Gwylawd, *s. m.* (gwyl) A being bashful; a weeping

Gwylawg, *a.* (gwyl) A guillemot. *Gwylawg du*, the black guillemot.

Gwylch, *s. m.* (gwyl) A seeming, a semblance.

Gwylchiad, *s.* (gwylch) A seeming, or appearing.

Gwylchu, *v. a.* (gwylch) To seem, to appear.

> Y'nghreulawn ymwrthryn
> Gwychr y gwylch gwelch amddiffyn.
>
> In the cruel conflict heroically *seem* the guardian heroes. *Cynddelw.*

Gwylder, *s. m.* (gwyl) Bashfulness; modesty.

> Nid gwiw gwylder rhag eisiau.
>
> *Bashfulness* is of no avail against want. *Adage.*

Gwyldy, *s. m.—pl. t.* au (gwyl—ty) A watch-house.

Gwyled, *v. a.* (gwyl) To behold, or to see.

> Ni wyl wr ai weles Wallawg.
>
> He has not seen a hero who has not seen Gwallog. *Taliesin.*

> Ni wyl dyn a'i pyrth.
>
> Man *sees* not who supports him. *Adage.*

Gwyledd, *s. m.* (gwyl) Bashfulness, timidity.

> Rhag newyn nid oes gwyledd.
>
> Against hunger there is no *bashfulness.* *Adage.*

> A mi ddysgogawl, cyn diwedd byd
> Gwreigedd heb wyledd a gwyr heb wryd.
>
> And I will foretell, before the end of the world women without *modesty* and men without courage. *Myrddin.*

> Crist cyflawn awwyd, bwyd trugarawg,
> Wrth Ruffudd, Gwynedd gwyledd foddawg.
>
> May Christ, who is perfect in compassion, be merciful to Gruffudd, who yields content to the *bashfulness* of Gwynedd. *Meilyr.*

Gwyleddawg, *a.* (gwyledd) Full of bashfulness.

Gwylfa, *s. f.—pl.* gwylfëydd (gwyl) A watching place, a place of observation, or exploratory mound; a watch, or watching.

Gwylfain, *s. m.—pl.* gwylfain (gwyl—maen) A watching-stone.

Gwylfalch, *a.* (gwyl—balch) Bashfully proud. *Gwylfalch wrth gerddawr*, bashfully proud with the minstrel.

Gwylfan, *s. f.—pl. t.* au (gwyl—man) A station of a sentinel.

Gwylfawr, *a.* (gwyl) Watchful, or vigilant.

Gwylforedd, *s. m.* (gwylfawr) Watchfulness.

Gwylfryn, *s. m.—pl. t.* iau (gwyl—bryn) A watching eminence.

Gwyliad, *s. m.* (gwyl) A vision; a watching.

> Gorwyn blaen yspyddad; hydr wyliad gorwydd,
> Gnawd serchawg erlyniad;
> Gwnelid da diwyd gwnad.
>
> Glittering the top of the hawthorn: bold the *look* of the steed; the amorous is used to be a pursuer, let the quick messenger do good. *Llywarch Hen.*

Gwyliadur, *s. m.—pl. t.* on (gwyliad) A sentinel.

> Trigaint canwr a safi ar ei mur;
> Oedd anhawdd ymadrawdd a'i gwyliadur.
>
> Three score hundred men stand upon its walls, it was difficult to converse with its *watchmen.* *Taliesin.*

> Amlwg golwg gwyliadur;
> Gwnelyd sybarwyd segur
> Cruel fy mryd, clefyd a'm cur!
>
> Clear is the sight of a *sentinel*; let the idle exercise generosity; cruel is my mind, fever oppresses me. *Llywarch Hen.*

Gwyliadwr, *s. m.—pl.* gwyliadwyr (gwyliad—gwr) A watchman.

Gwyliadwriaeth, *s. m.* (gwyliadwr) The office, or duty of a watchman.

Gwyliadwrus, *a.* (gwyliadwr) Watchful, vigilant.

Gwyliaw, *v. a.* (gwyl) To watch; to be vigilant; to look for, or to expect.

> Hawdd yf a wyl ei wely.
>
> He will drink freely who *loves* his bed. *Adage.*

Gwyliawd, *s. m.* (gwyl) The act of watching.

Gwyliawdr, *s. m.—pl.* gwyliodron (gwyliawd) One who watches, a watchman.

Gwyliawl, *a.* (gwyl) Relating to a holiday.

> Caswallawn—a ddanfones gwys tros bob lle yn Ynys Prydain, i erchi o'i holl wyrda ddawed hyd yn Llundain, ac eu gwreigedd y gyd a hwynt, i dalu gwyliawl enrhydedd dyledus i eu duwiau ddwywau, trwy yr rhai'r i cawynt buddygoliaeth.
>
> Caswallon sent a summons over every place in the Isle of Britain, to desire that all his men of rank would come to London, and their wives with them, to pay due *festival* honour to their tutelary divinities, through whom they had obtained victory. *Gr. ab Arthur.*

Gwylied, *v. a.* (gwyl) To watch: to be vigilant.

Gwyliedig, *a.* (gwyliad) Being watched.

Gwyliedydd, *s. m.—pl. t.* ion (gwyliad) One who keeps watch, a sentinel.

Gwylig, *a.* (gwyl) Full of watchfulness.

Gwylion, *s. pl. aggr.* (gwyl) Seers; watchmen. *A'm dywawd gwylion*, to me seers declare.

Gwyliwr, *s. m.—pl.* gwylwyr (gwyl—gwr) A watchman.

> Rhaid yw bod y gwiliwr yn fonheddig gwlad, canys iddo ydd ymddiriedir y brenin.
>
> It is necessary that the *watchman* should be a noble of the country, for to him is entrusted the king. *Welsh Laws.*

Gwylmabsant, *s. m.—pl. t.* au (gwyl—mabsant) The feast of a patron saint; a wake.

Gwylmabsanta, *v. a.* (gwylmabsant) To keep a wake, to commemorate a saint's day.

Gwylmabsantaeth, *s. m.* (gwylmabsant) A keeping a wake, or dedication festival.

Gwylnos, *s. f.—pl. t.* au (gwyl—nos) A night of watching with the dead.

Gwylnosawl, *a.* (gwylnos) Relating to a watching night with the dead.

Gwylnosdy, *s. m.—pl. t.* au (gwylnos—ty) A night watching house. *Gwylnosdy gwrach*, an old woman's watching house, a gossip's meeting house.

Gwylwar, *a.* (gwyl—gwar) Bashfully gentle.

> Gwenhwyfar wylwar a elwir
> I drugaredd Duw, draw a gerir.
>
> The *bashfully gentle* Gwenhwyfar, who is called, to the mercy of God, is beloved in yonder region. *Gr. ab M. ab Dafydd.*

Gwylwlydd, *a.* (gwyl—gwlydd) Bashfully mild.

Gwylydd, *s. m.—pl. t.* ion (gwyl) A watchman.

Gwylys, *s. m.* (gwy—llys) The licorice plant; licorice.

Gwyll, *s. f.—pl. t.* ion (gw—yll) Gloom, darkness. *Yn ngwyll y nos*, in the dark of the evening; a shade; a fairy, a goblin; a hag, or witch; the nightmare.

> Dysgawdr mawl rhwng gwawl a gwyll
> Diegyn, nawdd Duw ar d'angyll.
>
> Teacher of praise between the light and the gloom, doomed, may heaven guard thy wings. *D. ab Gwilym, i'r cheiliog.*

> Cad wyllion Dafydd da gyrchiad,
> Cad wallaw Cadwallawn ambad.
>
> Dafydd is a successful combatant of the *goblins* of battle, the scatterer of treasure, of the race of Cadwallon. *Ll. P. Moch, i D. ab Owain.*

Garan yn bwrw ei gweryd;
Garan'r wyll ar gwr yr yd.

A crane vomiting up her crop; the shanks of a *goblin* on the border of the field. *D. ab Gwilym, i'w gygawd.*

Gŵyll, *s. m.* (gwy—yll) An inclination, or bias; the bias of the mind; will, desire.

Gwyll, *a.* (gw—yll) Gloomy, dusky, or dark.

Rhywogaeth wyll a dwyll dyn.

A *darkling* breed misleading man. *M. ab Rhys.*

Cyll cauad gwyll yw coed Gwen.

Close *darksome* hazels are the trees of the fair. *D. ab Edmwnt.*

Gwyllaidd, *a.* (gwyll) Somewhat gloomy, or dark.

Gwyllawg, *a.* (gwyll) Of a gloomy appearance.

Gwylledd, *s. m.* (gwyll) Gloominess, duskiness.

Gwyllgi *s. m.*—*pl. t.* on (gwyll—ci) Dog of darkness; one that prowls about at night.

Gwyllin, *a.* (gwyll) Having impulse, or bias; trained; cultured.

Gwyllineb, *s. m.* (gwyllin) Culture, cultivation.

Gwyllion, *s. pl. aggr.* (gwyll) Shades, ghosts; hobgoblins; night-walkers.

Gwyllon, *s. pl. aggr.* (gwyll) Shades, phantoms.

Saith ugain haelon a aethant yn wyllon,
Y'nghoed Celyddon y darfuant.

Seven score generous ones became *shades*, in the wood of Caledonia they came to an end. *Myrddin.*

Ef mal——
Echdor gadarn gad wyllon.

He is like the mighty Hector of the combat of *spirits*. *Ll. P. Moch.*

Diffrwythws daiar
O'i fod y'ngharchar;
Aed a'i car gan wyllon!

The earth is become unfruitful from his being in prison; may such as love him go with the *powers of the gloom!* *H. Foel ab Grifri.*

Gwyllt, *s. m.*—*pl. t.* oedd (gwyll) A wild, a wilderness, a place covered with brakes.

Gwyllt, *a.* (gwyll) Wild, savage; rabid, mad.

Gwylltbwyll, *s. m.* (gwyllt—pwyll) A wild, or uncultivated reason.

Gwylltbwyllaw, *v. n.* (gwylltbwyll) To become of a wild disposition.

Gwylltbwyllawg, *a.* (gwylltbwyll) Being of a wild reason, giddy-headed.

Gwylltfil, *s. m.*—*pl. t.* od (mil) A wild beast.

Gwylltfilaidd, *a.* (gwylltfil) Like a wild beast.

Gwylltgeirch, *s. m.* (gwyllt—ceirch) Wild oats.

Gwylltiad, *s. m.* (gwyllt) A making wild; a scaring

Gwylltiaw, *v. a.* (gwyllt) To make wild; to become wild; to become furious; to rage.

Gwylltiawg, *a.* (gwyllt) Of a wild disposition.

O'r awr y cöellis beichiogi ydd aeth hithau y'ngwylltiawg, heb ddygredu annedd.

From the time she understood being pregnant she became *wild*, without so much as seeking a habitation. *H. Culhwch—Mabinogion.*

Gwylltiawl, *a.* (gwyllt) Tending to wildness.

Gwylltin, *a.* (gwyllt) Of a wild disposition.

Gwylltineb, *s. m.* (gwŷlltin) Wildness, savageness

Gwylltiwr, *s. m.*—*pl.* gwylltwyr (gwyllt) One who scares or frightens; one who becomes wild.

Gwylltred, *s. f.* (gwyllt—rhed) A wild run, *a.* Rapid, or of a wild course.

Gwyllyn, *s. m.*—*pl. t.* ion (gwyll) A culture.

Gwyllyniad, *s. m.* (gwyllyn) A giving a tendency to; a culturing.

Gwyllyniaw, *v. a.* (gwyllyn) To give a tendency to; to culture.

Gwyllyniawg, *a.* (gwyllyn) Being cultured.

Gwyllys, *s. m.*—*pl. t.* ion (gŵyll) The will.

Af ato, ymwrando'r wyf,
Cant gwyllys, cynta' gallwyf:
Pond oedd lan a chyfannedd
I'r byd cyn myned i'r bedd!

I will go to him, (I am looking for it with a hundredfold *desire*) as soon as I can: was he not fair and sociable to the world before he went to the grave! *Ll. Meirig, a Forgannwg.*

Gwyllysgar, *a.* (gwyllys) Willing, or tractable.

Gwyllysgarwch, *s. m.* (gwyllysgar) Willingness.

Gwyllysiad, *s. m.* (gwyllys) A willing; volition.

Gwyllysiaw, *v. a.* (gwyllys) To will; to desire.

Gwyllysiawl, *a.* (gwyllys) Willing, or desirous.

Gwyllysu, *v. a.* (gwyllys) To will, to desire.

Rhinwedd sydd yn parodda yr wyllys i wyllysu yn ddaioni.

Virtue does prepare the will *to will* in the way that is good. *Merchawg Crwydrad.*

Gwym, *s. m.* (gwy) That is sleek, or glossy.

Gwymon, *s. m. aggr.* (gwym) Sea-weed, or wrack; any water-weed. *Rhyd Wymon*, the Weedy Ford, on the Severn, near Caer Hywel.

Gwŷmp, *a.* (gwym) Smart, trim, gairish, fair.

Os ei phryd hi a fernid yn wympaf—eto y llall oedd mwy tirion.

If her countenance was judged the *fairest*, yet the other was more pleasing. *H. Const. Mag.—Mabinogion.*

Caraf ei morfa a'i mynyddedd,—
A'i gwylain gwynion, a'i gwymp wreigedd.

I love its sea shore and its mountains, and its white sea-mews, and its *beauteous* woman. *H. ab Owain.*

Gwympaidd, *a.* (gwymp) Somewhat fair.

Gwympedd, *s.* (gwymp) Smartness, gairishness.

Gwympiad, *s. m.* (gwymp) A rendering fair.

Gwyn, *s. m.* (gwy) White; what is fair, or pleasant; what is desirable, or affords happiness. *Gwyn llygad*, the white of the eye; *gwyn wy*, white of an egg.

Gwŷn, *a.* (gwŷ) White; fair, pleasant; blessed. *Yr eira gwyn*, the white snow; *dillad gwynion*, white garments: *Tad gwyn*, a stepfather; *gwyn ei fyd*, happy his state, or blessed is he. *Gwyn y dillad*, sweet cicely.

Gwyn ei fyd, prdyw y rhoddir
Carennydd Duw, a hoedl hir.

Blessed is he, to whom is allotted the favour of God, and long life. *Llefoed.*

Gwyn, *s. m.* (gwy—yn) Ecstasy, bliss; a violent impulse of the mind; rage; throb, a smart; lust. *Mae o yn ei wyn*, he is in his fit of lust; *pa beth ywe y gwyniau yna sydd arnat?* what are those mad fits with which thou art troubled? *ni welafi ddim o'm gwyn arni*, I see in her nothing to my desire; *wrth wyn a'i caro y del adref*, may he come home agreeable to the wish of such as love him.—*Gwyn y merched*, or *torllwyd*, wild tansy.

Hir wyniau i ddireidi.

Lasting *smarts* to wickedness. *Adage.*

Ni bu'n ei oes i Foesen,
Na gwyn bys, na gwaew'n ei ben.

There were not, in all his life to Moses nor ache of the finger, nor pain in the head. *L. Mon.*

Lle bu rhyw gam llwybr a gaid:
Gwnewch iawn er gwyn i'ch enaid.

Where there has been some error a path has been obtained; make amends for the *happiness* of your soul. *T. Aled.*

Gwladwyr hy a wŷr hiraeth;
Gwyn gwen o Forganwg aeth!

Bold patriots experience regret; the smile's *happiness* is departed from Morganwg! *Ieu. Dwlwyn.*

Gwynâad, *s. m.* (gwyn) A whitening, a blanching

Gwynad, *s. m.* (gwyn) A smarting, a throbbing a lusting. *Caseg wynad*, a proud mare.

Gwynaeth, *s. m.*—*pl. t.* au (gwyn) Felicity; bliss.

Gwynaf, *s. m.* (gwyn) A fretful disposition.

Gwynafawg, *a.* (gwynaf) Vicious, peevish.

Gwynafawl, *a.* (gwynaf) Of a vicious nature.

Gwynafiad, *s. m.* (gwynaf) A becoming vicious.

Gwynafu, *v. a.* (gwynaf) To be vicious; to act peevishly; to be peevish, or froward.

Gwynain, *a.* (gwyn) Teeming with whiteness.

Gwynaint, *s. m.* (gwyn) The empyrean.

> Hwl Rodri, rwydrw ... ,
> Hawl greddfawl tra gwawl, tra gwynaint.
>
> The generous R... , enterprising as the feathered host, his congenially pursues beyond the sphere of light, beyond the *empyrean*. *Ll. P. Moch.*

Gwynâu, *v. n.* (gwyn) To become white, to whiten

Gwynawd, *s. m.* (gwŷn) Milk porridge.

Gwynawg, *a.* (gwyn) Full of rage; froward.

> A march trust Morial
> Rhuth gar rhualle gwynawg.
>
> And Morial's steed of tumult shall appear before the *fiercely impassioned* host. *Taliesin.*

Gwynawn, *s. pl. aggr.* (gwŷn) White dry sticks.

Gwynblwm, *s. m.* (gwŷn—plwm) White lead.

Gwyndawd, *s. m.* (gwyn) Felicity; blessing; a state of happiness; also an appellation for *Gwynedd*, or the greatest part of North Wales.

> A'm gwnel—
> I fod gwyndawd gwynded werin
> Gwynedd bendefig fonedig ... .
>
> May he incline me to praise the *felicity* of the people of a happy land, the Venedocian chieftain of prosperous boundary. *D. Benfras, i Lywelyn I.*

Gwŷndeb, *s. m.* (gwŷn) Whiteness, brilliancy.

Gwŷnder, *s. m.* (gwŷn) Whiteness; brightness.

Gwyndodeg, *s. f.* (gwyndawd) The Venedocian dialect.

> Mau geirias golau gwyl Wyndodeg;
> Mi a wyr moli hil rhi hael reg.
>
> Mine the perspicuous words of the modest *Venedocian tongue*; I know how to celebrate the progeny of a chief of bounteous gift. *Cosnodyn.*

Gwyndodes, *s. f.—pl. t.* au (gwyndawd) A Venedocian woman, a North Wales woman.

> Mogel ... , fy ngwyndodes,
> Dy liw yn erbyn dy les.
>
> Beware, my *Venedocian fair*, lest thy complexion should be against thy advantage. *R. Ddu.*

Gwyndodiaith, *s. f.* (gwyndawd—iaith) The Venedocian language, the North Wales dialect.

> —Dywedwn Wyndodiaith;
> Yno awn ni yn un iaith.
>
> We will speak the *Venedocian tongue*, then we shall become of one speech. *D. Llwyd.*

Gwyndodig, *a.* (gwyndawd) Venedocian, belonging to North Wales.

> Danger——
> Lle deheuaf budd, lle dehouig giwys,
> Lle a gwin da dwys lle gwyndodig.
>
> Danger, the most convenient place of profit, a rightly situated solemn place, a place with good wine without failure by the *Venedocian host*. *Gro. Gyrnawg.*

Gwyndodydd, *s. m.* (gwyndawd) A Venedocian.

Gwŷndodyn, *s. m.* (gwyndawd) A Venedocian.

Gwŷndra, *s. m.* (gwyn) Whiteness; brightness.

Gwyndraw, *s.* (gwyn—traw) Stupor; numbness.

Gwyndud, *s. m.* (gwyn—tud) An epithet for *Gwynedd*, or Venedocia.

Gwŷndwn, *s. m.* (gwŷn—twn) A white surface; lay land; lay hay. *a.* Of a white surface. *Gwair gwŷndwn*, lay hay.

Gwyndy, *s. m.—pl.* gwyndai (gwyn—tŷ) A blessed house, an episcopal residence.

> Yn amser Garmon ... y cedwrthaid gwyndai gyntaf idd yr esgobion.
>
> In the time of Saint Garmon were *episcopal houses* first allotted to the bishops. *Achau y Saint.*

Gwynddas, *s. m.* (gwyn—das) That is peevish, or fretful. *a.* Of a peevish disposition.

> Hawg a fu i'm gredu——
> Brawd fydd am wynddydd wynddas.
>
> It was hasty in me to have believed the friar respecting the *fretful Gwynddydd*. *Llewddon.*

Gwynddasawg, *a.* (gwynddas) That is peevish.

Gwynddasiad, *s. m.* (gwynddas) A rendering peevish, a becoming fretful; an acting peevishly

Gwynddasu, *v. a.* (gwynddas) To make peevish; to become peevish.

Gwynddig, *a.* (gwyn—dig) Peevishly angry.

Gwyneb, *s. m.—pl. t.* au (gwyn) A face, aspect, or a countenance.

> Dyn ni wna ddaioni i neb
> Ydyw un a dau wyneb.
>
> A person that will do good to nobody is one with two *faces*. *O. Gwynedd.*

Gwynebawg, *a.* (gwyneb) Having a face.

Gwynebawl, *a.* (gwyneb) Facing, fronting.

Gwynebedig, *a.* (gwyneb) Being faced, or fronted

Gwynebedd, *s. m.* (gwyneb) A superficies.

Gwynebiad, *s. m.* (gwyneb) A facing, a fronting.

Gwyneblas, *a.* (gwyneb—glas) Pale-faced.

Gwyneblasu, *v. n.* (gwyneblas) To become pale-faced; to turn pale.

Gwynebu, *v. a.* (gwyneb) To face, or to front.

Gwynebwarth, *s. m.* (gwyneb—gwarth) Shame of face; It is also called *gwynebwerth*.

Gwynedd, *s. m.* (gwyn) A throbbing, smarting, or aching state; a lasting impulse; the being proud, or in heat.

Gwynedd, *s. f.* (gwyn) Venedocia; North Wales, exclusive of Powys; also all North Wales, in a lax sense. *Gwynedd uch Conwy*, Gwynedd above Conwy; *Gwynedd is Conwy*, Gwynedd below Conwy. The name is on a Roman-British altar of A. D. 154.

> Hael yw ef——
> A'i ddau win i ddwy Wynedd.
>
> He is liberal, with his two sorts of wine for each *Gwynedd*. *Guto y Glyn.*

Gwyneddig, *a.* (gwynedd) Venedocian, North-Wallian. *Gwyneddigion*, Venedocians.

Gwyneg, *s. f.—pl. t.* au (gwyn) A throb; a spasm, a stitch; rheumatism. *Dyfed.*

Gwynegawl, *a.* (gwyneg) Throbbing; spasmodick

Gwynegiad, *s. m.* (gwyneg) A throbbing, or inflammatory pain; a pricking pain.

Gwynegrwydd, *s. m.* (gwyneg) A throbbing state.

Gwynegu, *v. n.* (gwyneg) To throb, to ache.

Gwyneithaid, *s. m.* (gwynaeth) That is blessed.

> Dyly yr yngnad llys dyngu ar y crair, ac ar yr allawr, ac i gyne ... a ... ar yr allawr, na farno gam farn byth hyd y gwypo.
>
> The judge of the palace is bound to swear by the relick, and by the altar, and to the *consecrated things* which shall be set on the altar, that he shall never judge a false sentence, as far as he shall know. *Welsh Laws.*

Gwyneithiad, *s. m.* (gwynaeth) A rendering blessed; a consecrating.

Gwyneithiawl, *a.* (gwynaeth) Beatifical, happy.

Gwyneithu, *v. a.* (gwynaeth) To beatify; to consecrate; to administer a sacrament.

Gwynfa, *s. f.* (gwyn) Paradise, or a place of happiness; also an appellation for a part of the ancient principality of Powys.

> Llawenydd llu nef, llawenu fy meryd
> I'th wynfyd, i'th wynfa;
> Mab Duw ... , fy llys a'm ...
> ... lle drwg ... dyddiwg i'm da.
>
> The joy of the host of heaven, gladden my mind from thy beatific state, from thy seat of bliss ... of the living God, thy ... , which doth ... me a place, from my place of evil for ... bring me to my good. *Cynddelw.*

Gwynfardd, *s. m.—pl.* gwynfeirdd (gwyn—bardd) A white bard, or one of the druidic order.

Gwynfryd, *s. m.* (gwyn—bryd) A happy mind.

Gwynfryn, *s. m.* (gwyn—bryn) The hill of felicity, the eminence of bliss.

> A'i rhoddo of gwenfro gwynfryn uch ser.
>
> May he give him the fair region of the *eminence of bliss* above the stars. *Ein. ab Gwgan.*

Gwynfyd, *s. m.* (gwyn—byd) The world of beatitude, a happy state; felicity, happiness, bliss.

Tair colofn gwynfyd: goddef o foddlonrwydd, gobaith y daw, a chred y bydd.

The three foundations of *felicity*: suffering with resignation, hope of its coming, and belief that it will be. *Barddas.*

Tri adfer cylch y gwynfyd: awen gysefin; a gared gysefin; a chof cysefin; am na's gellir gwynfyd hebddynt.

The three restorations of the circle of *felicity*; restoration of original genius and character; of all that was primevally beloved; of remembrance from the origin of existence, as without these perfect *felicity* cannot subsist. *Barddas.*

Gwynfydawl, *a.* (gwynfyd) Felicitous, happy.

Gwynfydedig, *a.* (gwynfyd) Beatified; blessed.

Gwynfydedigrwydd, *s. m.* (gwynfydedig) Felicitousness, blessedness.

Gwynfydiad, *s. m.* (gwynfyd) A becoming enthusiastical, or fanatic.

Gwynfydig, *a.* (gwynfyd) Enthusiastic, fanatic.

Gwynfydoldeb, *s. m.* (gwynfydawl) Felicitousness, blessedness.

Gwynfydu, *v. n.* (gwynfyd) To become enthusiastical; to act fanatically.

Gwynfydwr, *s. m.—pl.* gwynfydwyr (gwynfyd—gwr) An enthusiastic man, an enthusiast.

Gwell i wraig y pysgodwr
Nog i wraig y gwynfydwr.

It is better for the wife of the fisherman than for the wife of the *fanatic man*. *Adage.*

Gwyngalch, *a.* (gwyn—calch) White-washed.

Gwyngalchaid, *a.* (gwyngalch) White-washed.

Gwyngalchawg, *a.* (gwyngalch) Whitewashed.

Gwyngalchiad, *s. m.* (gwyngalch) A white-washing.

Gwyngalchu, *v. a.* (gwyngalch) To white-wash.

Gwyngoch, *s. m.* (gwyn—coch) A whitish red, a pale red. *a.* Of a whitish, or pale red.

Gwyniad, *s. m.—pl.* gwyniaid (gwyn) A whiting, the name of various fishes; a mearling. *Gwyniad y mor*, the sea whiting; *gwyniad y gwg*, a salmon trout; *gwyniad pendew*, a quab.

Gwyniaeth, *s. m.* (gwyn) The act of blessing; the state of being blessed.

Deuai pob un or a allai gerdded parth a'r eglwys, i edrych ar y gwyniaeth, a ddaroedd i Dduw wneuthur ar ei was.

Every one that could walk came towards the church, to behold the *blessed act*, which God had performed upon his servant. *Cydym. Emlyn ac Amic.*

Gwyniaeth, *s. m.* (gwyn) A smarting, a throbbing; vehemency. *v. a.* To act with ardour.

Mab Bodgad, gwnaeth gwyniaeth gwraith ei law.

The son of Bodgad, the energy of his hand did cause a *throbbing*. *Aneurin.*

Goreu gwaith gwyniaeth a'i gyweithydd.

The best act *to strive* with its auxiliary. *Meilyr.*

Gwyniain, *a.* (gwyn) Abounding with white, splendid.

Cas aegen ysgwn ysgwyd Fell;
Ced ysgain gwyniain, gwn ei golli!

Frightful the blow from the rising of the shield of Beli: he that showered *splendid* gifts, I know his loss! *Cynddelw, m. Cadwallon.*

Gwynias, *a.* (gwyn—tas) Of a glowing heat.

Gwyniasedd, *s. m.* (gwynias) The state of being red hot; a glowing heat.

Gwyniasiad, *s. m.* (gwynias) A heating red hot; a becoming red hot.

Gwyniasu, *v. a.* (gwynias) To make red hot; to become red hot.

Gwyniaw, *v. n.* (gwyn) To throb, to have a tormenting pain; to burn with desire; to lust.

Gwyniawg, *a.* (gwyn) Full of throbbing, or convulsive motion; having incitement to lust.

Gwyniedyn, *s. m. dim.* (gwyniad) A whiting; a salmon trout.

Gwynieuthedd, *s. m.* (gwyniaeth) Blessedness; hallowedness, sanctitude.

Gwynieuthiad, *s. m.* (gwyniaeth) A rendering blessed; a hallowing; consecration; sanctification.

Cryd a gymyrth
Rhag odyn mawrwyrth,
Mer gwynieuthiad.

He was seized with trembling with dread at the wonderfulness of the rock of *sanctification*. *Cosnodyn.*

Gwynieuthu, *v. a.* (gwyniaeth) To render happy, or blessed; to consecrate; to administer a sacrament; to sanctify.

Gwynig, *a.* (gwyn) Of a white or fair appearance.

Gwynin, *a.* (gwyn) Of a white, or sappy nature.

Gwyning, *s. m.* (gwyn) The outside, or sappy part of timber.

Gwynlas, *s. m.* (gwyn—glas) Pale blue. *a.* Of a whitish blue, of a light blue.

Ac ym hai arwydd, er yn was edlwyg,
Y lliw oedd debyg gwanyg gwynlas.

And on me it has been a sign, no longer being the beautified youth, the complexion is like the *pale blue waves*. *H. ab Owain.*

Gwynlasu, *v. n.* (gwynlas) To become of pale blue.

Gwynlesni, *s. m.* (gwynlas) Pale blueness.

Gwynllad, *s. m.* (gwyn—llad) A blessed gift; a blessing.

Gwynllwyd, *a.* (gwyn—llwyd) Of a white gray.

Gwelai wr gwynllwyd teledyw yn eistedd ar ystlys y neuadd.

He could see a venerable *hoary* person sitting on the side of the hall. *H. Peredur—Mabinogion.*

Gwynnaeth, *s. m.* (gwynt) Flatulency.

Gwynnawg, *a.* (gwynt) Flatulent, or windy.

Gwynniar, *s. m.* (gwynt) A gust of wind.

Gwynnod, *s. m.* (gwyn—nod) A mark, or butt.

Gwynnogrwydd, *s. m.* (gwynnawg) Windiness.

Gwynon, *s. m. aggr.* (gwyn) Dry sticks.

Ni thangnef gwynon â goddaith.

Dry sticks will not be at peace with the flame. *Adage.*

Yd lysg fy nghalon y'nghof gwaith,
Mal y llysg gwynon gan oddaith!

My heart burns with painful memory, as *dry sticks* burn in the flame! *D. Llwyd. Mtw.*

Gwynrew, *s. m.* (gwyn—rhew) Numbness from the cold, or the being frost-bitten.

Gwynt, *s. m.—pl. t.* oedd (gwyn) Wind; also odour or scent. *Diffyg gwynt*, a being out of breath; *mae e'n gwneyd gwaed o'r gwynt*, he is drawing blood out of the wind, or he is building castles in the air.

Mal rhwymaw gwynt y'ngwden.

Like binding the wind in a wyth. *Adage.*

Gwynt a lyf da gwraig weddw.

The wind will lick up the widow's goods. *Adage.*

Gwyntawg, *a.* (gwynt) Full of wind, windy.

Gwyntawl, *a.* (gwynt) Relating to the wind.

Gwyntell, *s. f.—pl. t.* i (gwynt) A basket. *Dyfed.*

Gwynthollt, *s. m.—pl. t.* au (gwynt—hollt) A wind crack.

Gwyntholltawg, *a.* (gwyntholIt) Having wind-cracks.

Gwyntholti, *v. a.* (gwyntholIt) To cause wind-cracks; also to break one's wind.

Gwyntiad, *s. m.—pl. t.* au (gwynt) Ventilation.

Gwyntiaw, *v. a.* (gwynt) To wind, or to blast.

Gwyntiedig, *a.* (gwyntiad) Being winded.

Gwyntogrwydd, *s. m.* (gwyntawg) Windiness.

Gwyntyll, *s. m.—pl. t.* au (gwynt) A ventilator, a van for winnowing.

Gwyntylliad, *s. m.* (gwyntyll) A ventilating.

Gwyntylliaw, *v. a.* (gwyntyll) To ventilate.

Gwyntylliwr, *s. m.—pl.* gwyntyllwyr (gwyntyll—gwr) One who ventilates.

Gwŷnu, *v. a.* (gwŷn) To whiten, to bleach; to blanch; to become white.

Gwynwelw, *s. m.* (gwyn—gwelw) A whitish paleness, pale blue. *a.* Of a white paleness.

Gwynwelwi, *v. n.* (gwynwelw) To become of a

Gwynwg, *s. m.* (gwyn) Whiteness; splendour.

Gwynwlydd, *s. m.* (gwyn—gwlydd) Bedstraw.

Gwynwy, *s. m.* (gwyn—wy) White of an egg.

Gwynwydd, *s. pl. aggr.* (gwyn) Woodbine.

> Pa ddrychiolaeth garth geithiw
> Y sydd yn y gwinwydd gwiw!
>
> What phantom inthralled in chains is there in the tender woodbine? *D. ab Gwilym.*

Gwynygawd, *s. m.* (gwynwg) A radiency, or glare.

Gwynygawl, *a.* (gwynwg) Glittering, shining.

Gwynygiad, *s. m.* (gwynwg) A causing to glitter, a glittering, a shining.

Gwynygiaw, *v. a.* (gwynwg) To cause to glitter; to glitter, to shine, to glare.

> [illegible] Cadwallon ar Daiâ,
> [illegible]
> [illegible] Gwynedd gwynygiat.
>
> The camp of Cadwallon upon Teiâ, blood would be commixed with brine; the vehemency of Gwynedd would gleam. *Llywarch Hen.*

Gwynygu, *v. n.* (gwynwg) To glitter. *Gwynygodd dy glod*, thy fame has thrown a radiency.

> Brodawg waith gwyn-arth gwynygal.
>
> The destructive work of vehemency would shine forth. *Cyndelw.*

Gwyr, *s. m.* (gwy—yr) A pure element a pure state; ether freshness, a green tinge.

Gwyr, *a.* (gwy—yr) That is pure; fresh; lively, vigorous; luxuriant, verdant. *Gwyr glawr*, a verdant covering.

> Iddo fo mae——
> [illegible] a gwinwydd gwyr;
> Derw ieuainc hyd awyr.
>
> To him belong orchard trees and luxuriant vines; young oaks also towering to the sky. *L. G. Cothi.*

Gŵyr, *v.* (*third person pres. of* gwyraw) He turns, he doth bias; also, anomalously used for the verb *Gwybod*, he knows.

> E ŵyr dyn pan el
> Ac ni wyr pan ddel.
>
> A person knows when he goes, and he knows not when he comes. *Adage.*

Gŵyr, *a.* (gw—wyr) Oblique, slant, slanting, bending. *Yn wyr*, obliquely, askew, awry.

Gwyra, *a.* (gwyr) That is pure; fresh; lively. *Dwfr gwyra*, fresh water.

Gŵyrad, *s. m.* (gŵyr) A making oblique, or awry; a becoming oblique; deviation.

Gŵyrag, *s. m.* (gŵyr) That bends; a bow.

Gŵyraidd, *a.* (gŵyr) Somewhat oblique, or slant.

Gwyrain, *s. pl. aggr.* (gwyran) Barnacles.

> Adar gwar [illegible] gwyrain
> A dyf o'r gwŷdd a'r gwŷr cain.
>
> The barnacles are gentle birds that grow out of the wood and the fair water. *Guto y Glyn.*

Gwyrain, *v. a* (gwyr) To sublimate; to exalt; to elevate; to become elevated.

Gwyrain, *a.* (gwyr) Sublime, elevated; rising.

Gwyraint, *s. m.* (gwyrain) That is sublimated, exalted, or elevated.

Gwyraeth, *s. m.* (gwyr) The art of sublimating.

Gwyran, *s. m. aggr.* (gwyr) That rises, or towers; a stoloniferous grass.

> Yno mae——
> Dolydd glan gwyran a gwair.
>
> There are the fair dales of pasture and hay. *Iolo Goch.*

Gŵyraw, *v. a.* (gwyr) To make crooked, or oblique, to bend; to turn, to turn aside; to become oblique; to swerve, to deviate; to bias. *Gwyraw oddiwrth y gwir*, to swerve from the truth, *gwyraw barn*, to pervert judgement.

> ——Cyrchaist [illegible] gwrdd,
> Yn gaddaw [illegible];
> [illegible] gwyr gwyrynt y'ngwydd [illegible]
> [illegible]
>
> Thou didst repair to the fierce conflict, to opposing [illegible]; the spears of warriors, they did bend in contact with the [illegible] shaft in the presence of kings. *Ll. P. Moch, i [illegible] ab H. ab Owain.*

Gŵyrawg, *a.* (gŵyr) Having obliquity devious.

> Y genedlaeth ŵyrawg a throfâus ymlygrodd yn ei erbyn.
>
> The perverse and crooked generation has corrupted itself in opposition to him. *Deut. 32. 5.*

Gŵyrawl, *a.* (gŵyr) Of an oblique tendency; slanting; bending; devious.

Gwyraws, *s. m. aggr.* (gwyr) The privet; otherwise called *ysgwydd*.

> Gwyraws, gwyn ei fyd,
> Tarw trin, teyrn byd.
>
> The privet, happy its state, the bull of conflict, the lord of the world. *Taliesin, Cad Goddeu.*

> Nid unnaws gwyraws a gwern.
>
> *Privet* and alders are not of the same nature. *Adage.*

Gwyrblyg, *s. m.—pl. t.* au (gwyr—plyg) An oblique fold or double. *a.* Being obliquely folded.

Gwyrblygawl, *a.* (gwyrblyg) Obliquely folding.

Gwyrblygiad, *s. m.* (gwyrblyg) A doubling obliquely; a folding awry.

Gwyrblygu, *v. a.* (gwyrblyg) To fold obliquely.

Gwyrda, *s. pl. aggr.* (gwrda) Gentlefolks.

Gwyrch, *s. m.* (gwyr) A rising over. *a.* Overtopping.

> Haerwyd fy mod (a[illegible] ac)
> Wyrch [illegible] fal merch [illegible].
>
> It was asserted that I was (poor and sick in the frame of an overtopping brag) like a skittish horse. *W. Cynwal.*

Gwyrdra, *s. m.* (gwyr) Freshness; greenness.

Gwyrdraws, *a.* (gwyr—traws) Obliquely athwart.

Gwyrdro, *s. m.—pl. t.* ion (gwyr—tro) An oblique turn; contortion, perversion.

Gwyrdröad, *s. m.* (gwyrdro) A contortion.

Gwyrdröadwy, *a.* (gwyrdröad) Pervertible.

Gwyrdröawl, *a.* (gwyrdro) Tending to pervert.

Gwyrdröedig, *a.* (gwyrdröad) Being perverted.

Gwyrdroi, *v. a.* (gwyrdro) To contort, to pervert.

Gwyrdröwr, *s. m.—pl.* gwyrdrowyr (gwyrdro—gwr) A perverter.

Gwyrdröydd, *s. m.—pl. t.* ion (gwyrdro) A perverter.

Gwyrdyn, *s. m.* (gwyr—tyn) An oblique tention, *a.* Having a slanting tention.

Gwyrdynawl, *a.* (gwyrdyn) Apt to draw awry.

Gwyrdyniad, *s. m.* (gwyrdyn) A drawing aslant.

Gwyrdynu, *v. a.* (gwyrdyn) To draw obliquely.

Gwyrdd, *s. m.* (gwyr) A green colour. *a.* Green, verdant. *Gwyrdd-lysiau*, green plants; *coedwyrdd* or *gwyrdd y coed*, *gwyrdd y gauaf*, winter-green.

Gwyrddain, *a.* gwyrdd) Abounding with green.

Gwyrddedd, *s. m.* (gwyrdd) Greenness, verdancy.

Gwyrddfaen, *s. m.—pl.* gwyrddfeini (gwyrdd—maen) An emerald.

Gwyrddiad, *s. m.* (gwyrdd) A making green.

Gwyrddin, *a.* (gwyrdd) Of a green colour.

Gwyrddlas, *s. m.* (gwyrdd—glas) A greenish blue. *a.* Of a greenish blue.

Gwyrddlasaidd, *a.* (gwyrddlas) Of a greenish blue.

Gwyrddlaswg, *a.* (gwyrddlas) Verdurous.

Gwyrddlasu, *v. n.* (gwyrddlas) To become of a greenish blue, to become verdant.

Gwyrddlesni, *s. m.* (gwyrddlas) Blueness with a green cast of colour.
Gwyrddliw, *s. m.* (gwyrdd—lliw) A green colour. *a.* Of a green colour.
Gwyrddon, *s. m.—pl. t.* (gwyrdd) A green spot.
Gwyrddonig, *a.* (gwyrddon) Of a greenish or verdant hue; greenish with a cast of blue.

Twyllai wyr tywyll o wedd,
Toren gwyrddonig tiredd.

It would deceive men, being dark of aspect, the *cerulean* mantle of the plains. *D. ab Gwilym, i'r niwl.*

Gwyrddu, *v. a.* (gwyrdd) To make green; to become green; to become verdant.
Gwyrddwisg *s. f.—pl. t.* oedd (gwyrdd—gwisg) A green covering, a green garment.
Gwyrddyn, *s. m.* (gwyrdd) One arrayed in green
Gwyredig, *a.* (gwyr) Being made oblique; biassed
Gwyredd, *s. m.* (gwyr) Obliquity; a bias.
Gwyreindardd, *s. m.* (gwyran—tardd) A luxuriant growth. *a.* Of vigorous growth.
Gwyreiniad, *s. m.* (gwyran) A sublimating, or elevating; sublimation, exaltation.
Gwyreiniaw, *v. a.* (gwyran) To sublimate; to become elevated; to become vigorous.
Gwyreiniawl, *a.* (gwyrain) Tending to sublimate; elevating; envigorating.
Gwyrenig, *a.* (gwyran) Of a vigorous growth; of a stately growth.

Fy nyn wyrenig ddigawn.

My fair one tolerably *stately.* *Ll. Goch.*

Teg yw'r pren, a gwyrenig
Y tyf yr aur tew o'i frig.

Fair is the tree, and *luxuriantly* grows the thick load of gold from its branches. *D. ab Gwilym, i'r bedol.*

Gywrenigrwydd, *s. m.* (gwyrenig) Exaltedness; stateliness; freshness; luxuriancy.
Gwyryf, *a.* (gwyr) Pure, fresh, void of saltness.

Morwyn wyrf, mirain ffyrf ffydd.

A *pure* virgin, the splendid pattern of faith. *D. ab Gwilym.*

Dwr gwyrf ar dir a garwn;
Dwr hallt ni'm dawr i o hwn.

Fresh water on land I should love; as to salt water I care not about it. *D. Lafi.*

Gwyrfaidd, *a.* (gwyrf) Somewhat fresh.
Gwyrfawl, *a.* (gwyrf) Tending to make fresh.
Gwyrfedd, *s. m.* (gwyrf) Pureness, freshness.
Gwyrfiad, *s. m.* (gwyrf) A making fresh or pure.
Gwyrfiaw, *v. a.* (gwyrf) To purify; to freshen.
Gwyrgam, *a.* (gŵyr—cam) Obliquely crooked.

Mi a af o'th flaen di ac a unionaf y gwyrgeimion.

I will go before thee and I will make straight the *crooked places* *Isaiah* 45. 2.

Gwyrgamder, *s. m.* (gwyrgam) An oblique crookedness; wryness.
Gwyrgamdra, *s. m.* (gwyrgam) Wryness.
Gwyrgamedd, *s. m.* (gwyrgam) Distortedness.
Gwyrgamiad, *s. m.* (gwyrgam) A turning awry.
Gwyrgamu, *v. a.* (gwyrgam) To turn awry.
Gwyrgemi, *s. m.* (gwyrgam) Wryness, crookedness
Gwyriaws, *s. m. aggr.* (gwyraws) The privet.

Caraf yn ëaws ar wyriaws wydd,
Y'Nghymmer Deuddwyfyr, dyffrynt loiudd.

I love the nightingale upon the *privet* wood, in Cymmer Deuddwfr a celebrated vale. *H. ab Owain.*

Gwyrin, *a.* (gwyr) Of a pure nature, chaste.

Creawdr a'm crewys a'm cynnwys y'mblith
Plwyf gwyrin gwerin Enlli.

The Creator, who formed me, will give me room amongst the *pure* community of the inhabitants of Enlli. *Meilyr.*

Gwyrios, *s. pl. aggr.* (gwr) Ignoble persons.
Gwyrlawd, *s. f.* (gwyr—llawd) A meadow, or grass land; also called *porfeldir.* *Gwent.*
Gwyrlen, *s. f.—pl. t.* i (gwyr—llen) A garland.
Gwŷrling, *s. m.* (gwyr) Sweet gale, also called *helyg mair.*
Gwyrlawd, *s. f.* (gwŷr—llawd) A meadow, or grass land: also called *porfeldir.* *Gwent.*
Gwyrn, *s. pl. aggr.* (gweryn) Bots, or wornils; a kind of maggots which breed under the skin on the back of a cow.
Gwyrni, *s. m.* (gŵyr) Obliquity, wryness.
Gwyrogrwydd, *s. m.* (gŵyrawg) Obliqueness.
Gwyros, *s. m. aggr.* The privet.
Gwyrth, *s. m.—pl. t.* iau (gwyr) A pure essence, or quality; virtue; that is essentially new, or fresh; a wonder, a miracle.

Ac o wyrth Duw yn graith deg
—Yr aeth y briw.

And by the grace of God a fair scar the wound became. *L. G. Cothi.*

Gwyrth, *a.* (gwyr) Essentially pure, or fresh; precious, virtuous, gracious; miraculous.

Gwilia ef yr uchelion,
Mor, a thir, am wyrth Ion.

He contemplates the heavens, sea, and land for the *wonderful work* of the Supreme. *Gro. Owain, i W. Morris.*

Gwyrthfawr, *a.* (gwyrth) Greatly pure, precious. gracious; miraculous.

Gwyrthfawr yw'r gwr mawr i mi,
Gwyrthiau alarch Gwrthell.

Gracious is the great Supreme to me, as in the miracles of the swan of Gwrthell. *D. ab Ieuan Ddu.*

Gwyrthfawredd, *s. m.* (gwyrthfawr) Essential purity, virtuousness; graciousness, miraculousness.
Gwyrthiad, *s. m.* (gwyrth) A conferring a virtue, or grace; a rendering miraculous; a working a miracle.
Gwyrthiannawl, *a.* (gwyrthiant) Of, or tending to some peculiar virtue, miraculous.
Gwyrthiannu, *v. a.* (gwyrthiant) To endue with a peculiar virtue, to render miraculous.
Gwyrthiannus, *a.* (gwyrthiant) Of a peculiar virtue, of a miraculous quality.
Gwyrthiannusaw, *v. a.* (gwyrthiannus) To render of peculiar virtue, to render miraculous, or wonderful; to become miraculous.
Gwyrthiant, *s. m.* (gwyrth) The endowment of a peculiar virtue, or grace; a miraculous work.
Gwyrthiaw, *v. a.* (gwyrth) To endue with a virtue; to confer a grace; to render miraculous; to work a miracle; to become virtuous, or gracious, to become miraculous.
Gwyrthiawg, *a.* (gwyrth) Abounding with virtue, or grace; miraculous.
Gwyrthiawl, *a.* (gwyrth) Of a virtuous nature; of a gracious nature; miraculous.

Daeth y'nghyflawnder yr amser rhagderfenedig, ac a gysylltodd ei hunan mewn modd gwyrthiawl wrth ein banian ni.

He came in the fulness of the time predetermined, and united himself in a *miraculous* manner with our nature. *Ier. Owain.*

Gwyrthioldeb, *s. m.* (gwyrthiawl) Miraculousness
Gwyrthiolder, *s. m.* (gwyrthiawl) Miraculousness
Gwyrthioledd, *s. m.* (gwyrthiawl) Miraculousness
Gwyrthioli, *v. a.* (gwyrthiawl) To render miraculous, to become miraculous.
Gwyrthiolrwydd, *s. m.* (gwyrthiawl) Miraculousness, wonderfulness.
Gwyrthiolus, *a.* (gwyrthiawl) Of a miraculous nature or tendency.
Gwyryd, *s. m.* (gwyr) Purity, freshness, chastity
Gwyrydd, *s. f.—pl. t.* on (gwyr) That is pure, or chaste, that is fresh.

Gwedi eni o Fair fwyn,
Yr hon oedd forwyn wyrydd.

Being born of the gentle Mary, who was a *chaste* maid *H. T. Phylip.*

Gwyryf, *s. f.—pl. t.* on (gwyr) A virgin, a maid.

Gwyryf, *a.* (gwyr) Fresh, pure, untainted. *Ymenyn gwyryf*, fresh butter.

Gwyryfaidd, *a.* (gwyryf) Of a pure, or chaste nature; virginal.

Gwyryfawl, *a.* (gwyryf) Virgin, virginal, maiden.

Gwyryfdawd, *s. m.* (gwyryf) Virginity, chastity.

Gwyryfiad, *s. m.* (gwyryf) A purifying; a rendering chaste; a rendering fresh.

Gwyryfu, *v. a.* (gwyryf) To purify, to make chaste, to make fresh; to become pure, or fresh

Gwyryn, *s. pl. aggr.* (gweryn) Wornils; a kind of maggots bred under the skin on the backs of cows.

Gwys, *s. pl. aggr.* (gwes) Inhabitancy; a people; a peopled region; a country.

> Ei ladd a oruc Meirig—a gwedy hynny dyrchafael maen mawr a wnaeth yn arwydd budugoliaeth yn y wlad a elwir gwedy hynny, o'i enw ef Gwys Meirig.
>
> The slaying of him was what Meirig did, and after that he raised a great stone as a token of victory, in the country, which is called in consequence, from his name, the *Country of Meirig*. *Gr. ab Arthur.*

Gwys, *s. m.* (gwy) A bottom; a profundity. *a.* Low, deep, or profound.

Gwys, *s. f.—pl. t.* ion (gw—ys) Knowledge; notice; a citation, or summons; an invitation. *Tremygu gwys*, to neglect a summons.

> Agwnigaw a anfones wys dros deyrnas Ffrainc i gynnullaw eu farchogion arfawg.
>
> Aguisiquus sent a *summons* over the kingdom of France, to assemble his armed knights. *Gr. ab Arthur.*

Gwysaw, *v. a.* (gwys) To summon, or to cite.

Gwysedig, *a.* (gwys) Being cited, or summoned.

Gwysfil, *s. m.—pl. t.* ed (gwys—mil) A gregarious animal, a gregarious wild beast.

Gwysg, *s. m.—pl. t.* oedd (gwys) A tendency downwards, or to a level, as of a fluid; gravity, a stream, or current.

> O bes prydydd wydd ddiwyg,
> O Gymro heb ddigmarwyg,
> Atteped fi.—
>
> If there is a poet, possessed of knowledge without bias, an old Welshman free from perverseness, let him answer me. *Dr. S. Cent.*

Gwysg, *a.* (gwys) Tending towards a level; falling, precipitate, headlong. *adv.* Headlong, foreward. *Dyna fo yn syrthiaw wysg ei ben*, there he is falling head foremost.

Gwysgawd, *s. m.—pl.* gwysgodion (gwysg) A tendency downwards, precipitation.

Gwysgi, *s. m.* (gwysg) A tendency downwards, or to a level, precipitantness.

Gwysgiad, *s. m.* (gwysg) A precipitation.

Gwysgiaw, *v. a.* (gwysg) To precipitate.

Gwysgiawl, *a.* (gwysg) Precipitant, headlong.

Gwysgion, *s. m. aggr.* (gwysg) Pottage, porridge. *Gwysgion llaeth*, milk porridge.

Gwysglys, *s. m.* (gwysg—llys) Mistletoe; also called *uchelfar*, *uchelawg*, *heonllys*, and *holliach*.

Gwysiad, *s. m.—pl. t.* au (gwys) A summoning, a citation, a summons, an invitation.

Gwysiaw, *v. a.* (gwys) To summon, to invite.

Gwysiawl, *a.* (gwys) Citatory, summoning.

Gwysig, *a.* (gwys) Apt to collect into blisters.

Gwysigen, *s. f.—pl. t.* au (gwysig) A blister.

Gwyslythyr, *s. m.—pl. t.* au (gwys—llythyr) A breve, or writ of citation.

Gwyst, *s. m.—pl. t.* ion (gwys) That is flat; that is shrunk, or low.

Gwystl, *s. m.—pl. t.* on (gwyst) A pledge, gage, or pawn; surety; hostage. *Gwystl cyfreithiawl*, a lawful pledge, being the third above the value of the thing due.

> Hil Rodri gwrolli gwystl feran,
> Gwrthlad gryd gwystlon byd hoed tan.
>
> The progeny of Rodri having guests with spears in pledge of incessant warfare, be thine the *hostages* of the world. *Cynddelw, i'r argl. Rhys.*

Gwystlad, *s. m.* (gwystl) A pledging, a pawning.

Gwystlair, *s. m.* (gwystl—gair) A parole.

Gwystlaw, *v. a.* (gwystl) to pledge, to gage, to pawn, to mortgage. *Gwystlaw swydd i un*, to deliver an office to one. *Welsh Laws.*

Gwystlawr, *s. m.—pl.* gwystlorion (gwystl) One who gives a pledge, or pawn.

Gwystledig, *a.* (gwystl) Being pledged or pawned

Gwystledigaeth, *s. m.* (gwystledig) The act of pledging or pawning, a mortgaging.

Gwystleidiaeth, *s. m.* (gwystlad) The act of pledging, or pawning; a mortgaging.

Gwystleiriaeth, *s. m.* (gwystlair) The act of pledging one's word; a parole.

Gwystliad, *s. m.* (gwystl) A pledging, a pawning

Gwystloriaeth, *s. m.* (gwystlawr) The act, or state of one who deposits a pledge.

Gwystlwr, *s. m.—pl.* (gwystl—gwr) A pledger.

Gwystnaw, *v. a.* (gwystyn) To become dry, to wither.

Gwystyn, *a* (gwyst) Flaccid, flabby, withered.

Gwyth, *s. m.—pl. t.* i (gwy) A channel, a drain, a gutter; a vein. *Gwyth melin*, a mill-stream; *yr wyth fawr*, the main channel, a term in draining; *gwythi gwaed*, blood vessels, or veins

Gwyth, *s. m.* (gw—wyth) Wrath, indignation.

> Cyd gorphwyso, gyffro gwyth,
> Y lu dalm ef i i dylwyth
> Cyfodi a wna.—
>
> He whose motion is *wrath*, though resting for a while with his family, he will yet arise. *Meredd. Lloyd, i O. Glyndŵr.*
>
> Torri y trefi, trwy wyth ac archoll,
> Tyrhau y tyrau oll, fal y Twrch Trwyth—
> A wnai.
>
> Demolish the towns through *wrath* and wound; break down all the towers, like the Twrch Trwyth, he would do. *L. G. Cothi.*

Gwythad, *s. m* (gwyth) A making wroth, or irritating, a growing angry; irritation.

Gwythain, *a.* (gwyth) Abounding with wrath.

Gwythaint, *s. m.* (gwythain) That abounds with wrath; an epithet for some feigned winged creature; the bird of wrath.

> Gwelais ymladd taer yn Nant Ffrangcon,
> Dydd Sul pryd plygaint, rhwng gwythaint a Gwydion.
>
> I saw a fierce conflict in Nant Francon, on Sunday at matin time, between the *bird of wrath* and Gwydion. *Taliesin.*
>
> Porthed gan frain, ac eryr, a gwythaint,
> Afagddu a'i dwalw ei gymmaint.
>
> May he be possessed by the ravens, and eagle, and the *bird of wrath*, Avagddu brought to him his equal. *Taliesin.*

Gwythaw, *v. a.* (gwyth) To irritate; to be wroth, or angry; to chafe.

> Mal y mae y cenfigenus yn gwythaw am fod gair da i un arall, felly y mae ef yn llawenau am ddyfod colled, neu ddrygair iddo.
>
> Like as the envious is *irritated* on account of another person's having a good word, so he rejoices at any loss or ill report coming to him. *Marchawg Crwydrad.*

Gwythawd, *s. m.* (gwyth) The act of irritating; a growing angry, a chafing.

Gwythawg, *a.* (gwyth) Full of rage, wrathful.

Gwythawl, *a.* (gwyth) Wrathful, outrageous.

Gwythfadd, *s. m.* (gwyth—fadd) Water violet.

Gwythen, *s. f.—pl. t.* au (gwyth) A channel, a vein. *Gwythen yr afu*, the axillary vein.

Gwythenawg, *a.* (gwythen) Having veins, veiny.

Gwythenawl, *a.* (gwythen) Belonging to the veins

Gwythenogrwydd, *s. m.* (gwythenawg) Veininess

Gwythfar, *s. m.* (gwyth—bar) Wrathful indignation. *a.* Wrathfully indignant.

Yd wosgryn esgar
Yn wythlar, yn weithfuddig.

He opposes the foe with wrathful fury, and victoriously. *Gwalchmai.*

Gwythi, *s. pl. aggr.* (gwyth) Channels, ducts: veins. *Clymau gwythi*, the cramp.
Gwythïen, *s. f. dim.* (gwythi) A vein, a blood-vessel.
Gwythig, *a.* (gŵyth) Infuriate, or wrathful.
Gwythlawn, *a.* (gwyth) Wrathful, or furious.

Garwyn blaen cawn; gwythlawn eiddig,
Ys odid a'i digawn:
Gwithred call yw caru yn iawn.

Glittering the top of straw; the jealous one is *wrathful*, there is scarcely any with whom he would be satisfied. To love truly is the act of the prudent. *Llywarch Hen.*

Gwythlid, *s. m.* (gŵyth—llid) Wrathful anger. *a.* Wrathfully angry.
Gwythloes, *s. f.—pl. t.* au (gŵyth—lloes) The pang of wrath.
Gwythlondeb, *s. m.* (gwythlawn) Wrathfulness.
Gwythlonedd, *s. m.* (gwythlawn) Indignation.
Gwythloni, *v. n.* (gwythlawn) To become wroth, or angry; to become indignant; to irritate.
Gwythlongar, *a.* (gwythlawn) Apt to be wrathful, or angry; irritable.
Gwythlwrw, *s. m.* (gŵyth—llwrw) A wrathful course. *a.* Of a wrathful course.
Gwythred, *s. f.* (gŵyth—rhed) The course, or channel of a current.
Gwythreden, *s. f.* (gwythred) A rivulet, a brook.
Gwythruthr, *s. m.—pl. t.* au (gŵyth—rhuthr) A furious onset.

Bu aruthr gwythruthr yn nydd gweithred trin
Tywys hael-fab Ednyfed.

Terrible was the *wrathful onset* of the generous son of Ednyfed in the day of the toil of conflict. *Llywelyn Fardd.*

Gwythruthraw, *v. a.* (gwythruthr) To fall upon wrathfully.
Gwythruthrawl, *a.* (gwythruthr) Of a wrathful onset; furiously rushing.
Gwythrydd, *a.* (gŵyth—rhydd) With wrath let loose

Gruffudd a orfu rhag llu gwythrydd.

Gruffudd vanquished before a host *unrestrained in wrath.* *Meilyr.*

Gwythwr, *s. m.—pl.* gwythwyr (gŵyth—gwr) An angry man.
Gwythwyn, *a.* (gŵyth—gwyn) A furious passion.
Gwyw, *a.* (gwy) Being withered, or faded.

Ydym——
Yn farwawl drange difancoll,
Yn wyw iawn, ac yn ia oll.

We are devoted to deadly destruction, very *feeble*, and altogether cold as ice. *D. ab Gwilym.*

Os marw yw hon——
Gwywon yw'r bedw a'r gwiall,
Ac weithian ni ddygan ddail!

If she is dead, the birch and the willows are withered things, and now they bear no leaves! *D. Nanmor.*

Gwywaw, *v. a.* (gwyw) To wither, to fade, to become flaccid; or flabby; to grow languid.
Gwywawl, *a.* (gwyw) Tending to wither; fading.
Gwywder, *s. m.* (gwyw) Witheredness.
Gwywedig, *a.* (gwyw) Withered, faded; palsied. *Gwywedigion*, withered ones.
Gwywel, *s. m.* (gwyw) What is withered; withered vegetation, withered leaves.
Gwywgoch, *s. m.* (gwyw—coch) Russet colour.
Gwywiad, *s. m.* (gwyw) A withering; a fading.
Gwywliw, *s. m.* (gwyw—lliw) Russet colour.
Gwywwydd, *s. m. aggr.* (gwyw—gwŷdd) Withered wood.
Gybain, *v. a.* (gwb) To wail, or to moan.

Anfon i'm ffydd, gynnydd gain,
A gobaith, lle'r wy'n gybain.

Send me faith of fair increase, and hope, where I now am wailing. *T. Gruffudd, o Forgannwg.*

Gybawl, *a.* (gwb) Wailing, or moaning.
Gyda, *prep.* (*mutation of* cyda) With, in company with; in contact with. *adv.* Along. *Pwy sy gyda ni?* who is with us? *Doi gyda mi*, thou wilt come with me; *ymlusga gyda'r ddaiar*, creep thou along the ground.
Gyddfgam, *a.* (gwddf—cam) Wry-necked.
Gygawl, *a.* (gwg) Glancing, lowering, frowning.
Gygiad, *s. m.* (gwg) A glancing; a lowering.
Gygu, *v. a.* (gwg) To glance, to look glancingly; to lower, to frown; to look grimly.
Gygus, *a.* (gwg) Glancing, lowering, frowning.

A gogam wyd, a gygus.

And awkward art thou, and *frowning.* *D. ab Gwilym.*

Agos ing ygus angof.

Near is the distress of *frowning* oblivion. *Rhys Brydydd.*

Gyl, *s. m.—pl. t.* on (yl) That is edged or sharp.
Gylf, *s. m.—pl. t.* au (gyl) A bill or a beak.

Edn a'i gylf o'r lled yn gau—
Yw'r gwalch.

A bird with his *beak* closely shut from the head is the hawk. *T. Aled.*

Gylfach, *s. m.* (gylf) That has a beak.

Tyllai ylfach
Gwryd gofurthiach.

The *beaked one* would burst through *feebly telling* manhood. *Taliesin.*

Gylfant, *s. m.* (gylf) A bill, or beak.
Gylfawg, *a.* (gylf) Having a beak, beaked.
Gylfgragen, *s. f.* (gylf—cragen) A scallop-shell.
Gylfhir, *a.* (gylf—hir) Long-beaked; a curlew.
Gylfin, *s. m.* (gylf) A beak or bill.

Ys drwg y deg ewin
Ni bortho i'r un gylfin.

Worthless are the ten claws that will not bring food to the one *mouth.* *Adage.*

Gylfinawg, *a.* (gylfin) Beaked; having a long beak. The curlew.
Gylfinbraff, *a.* (gylfin—praff) Thick-beaked. The gross beak; a bird so called.
Gylfingam, *a.* (gylfin—cam) Hook-beaked.
Gylfingroes, *a.* (gylfin—croes) Cross-beaked. The cross-beak, the name of a bird.
Gylfinhir, *a.* (gylfin—hir) Long-beaked. The curlew; *Coeg-ylfinhir*, the whimbrel.
Gylfinog, *s. f.* (gylfin) The Daffodil.
Gylu, *v. a.* (gyl) To make an edge, or rim.
Gylyf, *s. m.—pl. t.* au (gyl) A sickle, a reaping-hook.

Gylyf ceiniawg a dâl.

A *sickle* is worth a penny. *Welsh Laws.*

Gyllwng, *s. m.* (llwng) A lapse, a letting go.
Gyllyngawl, *a.* (gyllwng) Tending to let go.
Gyllyngdawd, *s. m.* (gyllwng) Relaxation, remission; a setting at liberty.
Gyllyngiad, *s. m.* (gyllwng) A loosening.
Gyllyngu, *v. a.* (gyllwng) To loosen, or to relax.
Gynaid, *s. m.—pl.* gyneidiau (gwn) A cupful.
Gynawg, *a.* (gwn) Wearing a gown, gowned.
Gynell, *s. f. dim* (gwn) A close gown.
Gynnau, *adv.* (gynt) A little while ago, just now. *Pwy oedd yma gynnau?* Who was here a little while ago?
Gynt, *adv.* (*mutation* of cynt) Primarily; formerly, heretofore, of yore, in time past.
Gyr, *s. m.—pl. t.* oedd (yr) A drive; an impulse, a thrust, a course, an onset, or attack; a drove, a herd of beasts driven together. *Gyr cyfreithiawl*, a legal process; *gyr o wartheg*, a drove of cattle.
Gyrawd, *s. m.* (gyr) A driving; impulsion.
Gyrawl, *a.* (gyr) Driving, or impulsive.

Gyrddawl, *a.* (gwrdd) Vehement, or ardent.

Gyrdd-der, *s. m.* (gwrdd) Vehemency, hardihood

Ni allai y Saeson ddyoddef gyrdd-der y Prydeiniaid.

The Saxons could not withstand the *ardour* of the Britons. *Gr. ab Arthur.*

Gyrddiad, *s. m.* (gwrdd) An acting vehemently.

Gyrddu, *v. a.* (gwrdd) To act vehemently.

Gyrddwynt, *s. m.—pl. t.* oedd (gwrdd—gwynt) A violent gust of wind; a hurricane.

Gyrfa, *s. f.—pl.* gyrfëydd (gyr) A drive, a race, or course; a running.

Gyrfarch, *s. m.—pl.* gyrfeirch (gyr—march) A race-horse.

Gyrferth, *s. f.—pl. t.* au (gyr--merth) Utterance; the sending out the breath; expiration.

Gyrferthawl, *a.* (gyrferth) Expiring, exhaling.

Gyrferthiad, *s. m.* (gyrferth) A breathing out.

Gyrferthu, *v. a.* (gyrferth) To expire, to exhale.

Gyrfëydd, *s. m.—pl. t.* ion (gyrfa) A driver.

Gyrfeydd goreu fuost.

The best racer hast thou been. *Iolo Goch, i farch.*

Gyriad, *s. m.* (gyr) A driving; a forcing, or impelling, a making an attack; a racing

Gyriedydd, *s. m.—pl. t.* ion (gyriad) A driver.

Gyrn, *s. m.—pl. t.* oedd (gyr) That is imperious; that is imperial, or supreme.

Gyrn, *a.* (gyr) Imperious, imperial; supreme.

Od ei'n uwch mab y dyn, wyd
Iör gyrn o Ddofyr i Gernyw.

If thou shouldest go higher, son of man, thou art lord *supreme* from Dover to Cornwall. *Gut. Owain, i Edward IV.*

Gyrth, *s. m.—pl. t.* iau (gyr) A contact; a touch; a dash; a hit, a push, a thrust, a combat.

Twr cynfael yn cwyddaw—
A gwyr gyrth am byrth yn borthiaw gorwlad,
A bragad yn briwaw.

The tower of Cynfael falling, and men *of conflict* round the gates repelling the marches, and the front of the battle dealing wounds. *Cynddelw, i H. ab Owain.*

Gyrthiad, *s. m.—pl. t.* au (gyrth) A touching; a dashing against, a hitting, a pushing.

— —Gadrawn ei anwyd,
Creulawr gawr gyrthiad;
Garw gymmwyd gymlad,
Yn cyfledd yn achlymmawyd.

Stubborn his disposition, with a gory path in the shout *of combat*, dreadful the social sea of a common country, destroying in the ghastly toil. *Cynddelw, i H. ab Owain.*

Gyrthiaw, *v. a.* (gyrth) To come in contact, to touch, to dash, to hit, to push, or to thrust; to run against; to fall upon; to combat.

Ni chaiff llaw yrthiaw wrthi,
Nac ymafael a'i hael hi.

A hand shall not *touch* against it, nor meddle with her brow. *D. ab Gwilym.*

Gyrthiawl, *a.* (gyrth) Tending to come in contact, touching; dashing, pushing.

Gyrthiedig, *a.* (gyrth) Being touched; dashed.

Gyru, *v. a.* (gyr) To drive, to impel, to thrust; to race; to run, to ride; to drive forward; to enforce, to press; to prosecute, to carry on; to send. *Gyr arni*, drive on, or go on; *gyr arno*, go on with it; *mae yn gyru yn arw*, he drives furiously; *gyru ar*, to run down, to detract.

Bedyddiaw y mab a wnaethpwyd a gyru Culhwch arno.

The baptising of the infant was accomplished, by imposing Culhwch upon him. *H. Culhwch—Mabinogion.*

Gyr Meirion yn Mhinion mor
Uch'eneidion trymion trwmor.

Meirion on the skirts of the ocean *sends* heavy sighs across the sea. *D. Wyn.*

Gyrwr, *s. m.—pl.* gyrwyr (gyr—gwr) A driver; a racer, a rider; one who enforces, or presses; one who carries on; a sender.

Gyrwynt, *s. m.—pl. t.* oedd (gyr—gwynt) A tornado, a hurricane.

Gyrynt, *s. m.—pl. t.* iau (gyr) A current.

Gysp, *s. m.* (ysp) The staggers, a disease incident to horses; also a long black beetle.

Gysplys, *s. m.* (gysp—llys) Hemlock water dropwort.

Gyst, *a.* (yst) Humid, moist, or damp.

Gystlys, *s. m.* (gwst—llys) Common tansy.

Gystawg, *a.* (gwst) Abounding with humidity.

Gystawl, *a.* (gwst) Of a humid nature.

Gystig, *a.* (gwst) Of a humid tendency.

Gystwng, *s. m.* (twng) The act of lowering.

Gystwng, *v. a.* (twng) To lower, to bring down, to take, or put down, to abase, to subject; to become low; to submit.

Gystyngadwy, *a.* (gystwng) That may be lowered, abased, or subjected.

Gystyngawl, *a.* (gystwng) Tending to lower.

Gystyngedig, *a.* (gystwng) Lowered; abased.

Gystyngedigaeth, *s. m.* (gystyngedig) The act of lowering, humbling, or abasing; subjection.

Gystyngiad, *s. m.* (gystwng) A lowering; an abasement, subjection.

Gystyngu, *v. a.* (gystwng) To lower; to humble, to abase, to subject, to become low.

Gystyngwr, *s. m.—pl.* gystyngwyr (gystwng—gwr) One who brings down, a subjecter.

Gyth, *s. m.—pl. t.* ion (yth) A murmur, a grumble.

Gythawl, *a.* (gyth) Murmuring, or grumbling.

Gythiad, *s. m.—pl. t.* au (gyth) A murmuring, grumbling, or repining.

Gythu, *v. a.* (gyth) To murmur, or to repine.

Gythus, *v. a.* (gyth) Apt to be grumbling.

Gythwr, *s. m.—pl* gythwyr (gyth—gwr) A murmurer, a grumbler.

H.

HA, *s. m. r.* Aptness to rise; scorn, haughtiness, disdain, hate.

Elen—
Yr hon a herlo yr ha
A thrin rhwng Groeg a Throia.

Helen the which caused the *hate* and the war between Greece and Troy. *D. ab Gwilym.*

Ha, *a.* (ha, *s.*) Haughty, proud, arrogant.

Pan gaffer fi hi ni chaffer fi ha.

When I shall be found like her I shall not be found *scornful*. *Id. gr.*

Ni bydd im un farn arna'
O beiddiwyf hyn ni bwyf ha.

There shall not be one remark on me, if I venture this may I not be *scornful*. *D. ab Gwilym.*

Ha, *interj.* (ha, *s.*) It is mostly used to denote exultation: Ha! heyday! welldone! hey.

Ha' Mab, py liwy di! Py ddrwg y sydd arnat?

Heyday! Young man, why dost thou blush? What is there amiss with thee? *H. Culhwch—Mabinogion.*

Hab, *s. m.* (hy—ab) That comes, or passes abruptly; chance, luck, fortune, good fortune.

Hab, *interj. denoting surprise.* (hy—ab) Ha!

Hac, *s. m.* –*pl. t.* iau (hag) A notch, a hack.
Haciad, *s. m.*—*pl. t.* au (hac) A hacking.
Haciaw, *v. a.* (hac) To cut, to hack, to notch.
Hacrâad, *s. m.* (hagr) A making ugly, or unsightly; a disfiguring; a becoming unsightly.
Hacrâawl, *a.* (hagr) Tending to disfigure.
Hacrâu, *v. a.* (hagr) To render ugly, or unsightly; to disfigure.

> Traethws Gildas yn eglur o'r terfysg hwnw; wrth hyny ei peidies innau rhag barrâu, o'm tylawd athrylith i, ymadrawdd gwr mor gyfrwys hyawdl a hwnw.
>
> Gildas has treated perspicuously of that commotion; I have on that account desisted, for fear of *disfiguring*, by my poor talent, the discourse of a man so skilful and eloquent as he was. *Gr. ab Arthur.*

Hacriad, *s. m.* (hagr) A making ugly or unsightly; a disfiguring; a becoming ugly.
Hacrwydd, *s. m.* (hagr) Ugliness; unsightliness.
Hacru, *v. a.* (hagr) To make ugly; to disfigure; to become ugly; to become disfigured.
Had, *s. m. aggr.*—*pl. t.* au (hy—ad) That is apt to produce or to renovate; seed. *Disgyn i'r hadau*, to fall to the state of living atoms, or to fall to the lowest point of existence. *Bardism.*
Had, *a.* (hy—ad) Easily yielding, or producing; yielding, pliant, complying.
Hadadfer, *s. m.* (had—adfer) Restoration of seed, an epithet for harvest.
Hadaidd, *a.* (had) Like seed; running to seed.
Hadawg, *a.* (had) Abounding with seed, seedy.
Hadawl, *a* (had) Seminal, pertaining to seed.
Hadedig, *a.* (had) Being run to seed, seminific.
Haden, *s. f. dim.* (had) A single seed; a small seed or a seedling.

> Coel can-haden.
>
> A hundred *seeds* are a sign. *Adage.*

Hadfa, *s. f.*—*pl.* hadfëydd (had) A seed-place.
Hadiad, *s. m.* (had) A seeding; semination.
Hadl, *a.* (had) In a state of change; decayed; rotten, corrupt.

> Gwnaethost gestyll twn tud cynnadl; cynnygn Cynnygaist, ni bu hadl.
>
> Thou hast made shattered castles in the land of contention; the adversary thou didst dare, and it did not prove *abortive*. *Ll. P. Moch.*

Hadlaidd, *a.* (hadl) Tending to a state of change; somewhat decayed, or corrupt.
Hadlan, *s. f.*—*pl. t.* au (had—llan) Seed-plot.
Hadlawg, *a.* (hadl) Having a tendency to change; abounding with decay; corrupted.
Hadle, *s. m.*—*pl t.* oedd (had—lle) A seed-place.
Hadled, *a.* (*f. of* hadlyd) Full of decay; ruinous; rotten; corrupted; corruptible.
Hadledig, *a.* (hadl) Decayed: ruined; corrupted.
Hadledd, *s. m.* (hadl) Decayedness; rottenness.

> A'm bu, udd cedawl, cydfod â thi;
> A'th fo hwyr hadledd, a hirhoedl.
>
> I have experienced, bounteous chief, concord with thee; late may thy *state of change* take place, and be length of days to thee. *Ll. P. Moch.*

Hadlestr, *s. m.*—*pl. t.* i (had—llestr) A seed-vessel, a seedlip.
Hadliad, *s. m.* (hadl) A tending to a change, or renovation; a decaying; corruption.
Hadlif, *s. m.* (had—llif) A seminal gleet.
Hadlifaidd, *a.* (hadlif) Like a seminal gleet.
Hadlifaw, *v. n.* (hadlif) To run as a gleet.
Hadlifiad, *s. m.* (hadlif) A running as a gleet.
Hadlu, *v. n.* (hadl) To decay; to corrupt, to putrify, to become rotten.

> Maenan——
> Doe yr ydoedd yn drydoll,
> Hyd lawr wedi hadlu oll.
>
> Maenan yesterday became a shattered heap, being all ruined to the ground. *I. Llwyd Brydydd.*

Hadlyd, *a.* (hadl) Full of decay; ruinous; rotten, corrupted; corruptible.

> Y drych——
> Hadlyd liw, hudawl o dlws;
> Hudolion a'i hadeilws.
>
> The mirror of *decayed* colour, is a deceiving toy; deceivers have invented it. *D. ab Gwilym.*

Hadlydedd, *s. m.* (hadlyd) Decayedness; corruptedness, rottenness.
Hadogawl, *a.* (hadawg) Seminific, seminifical.
Hadogi, *v. a.* (hadawg) To produce seed.
Hadolaeth, *s. m.* (hadawl) Seminality.
Hados, *s. pl dim.* (had) Small seeds; atoms of life; seedlings.
Hadred, *s. m.* (had—rhed) A gonorrhea.
Hadrediad, *s. m.* (hadred) A semial running.
Hadredu, *v. n.* (hadred) To run in a seminal gleet
Hadu, *v. n.* (had) To seed; to run to seed; to produce seed.
Hadwr, *s. m.*—*pl.* hadwyr (had—gwyr) A seedsman, or a dealer in seeds.
Hadyd, *s. m.* (had—yd) Seed-corn.
Hadd, *s. m.*—*pl. t.* au (hy—add) A centre of motion, or impulse; a source; a focus.
Haddef, *s. f.*—*pl. t.* au (hadd) An abode, a dwelling; a home *Gwedi ydd el yr haul yn ei haddef*, after the sun is gone down.

> Symudaw haddef rhag drwg.
>
> To remove a *dwelling* for fear of evil. *Adage.*

> Goreu tridyn y dan nef,
> A warchetwys eu haddef,
> Pyll, Selyf, a Sanddef.
>
> The best three persons under heaven, who defended their *dwelling*, were Pyll, Selyf, and Sanddef. *Llywarch Hen.*

Haddefiad, *s. m.* (haddef) An inhabiting.
Haddefu, *v. a.* (haddef) To inhabit, to dwell.
Haddfa, *s. f.*—*pl.* haddfëydd (hadd) A dwelling.

> Gorug dau fynawn cyflawn eu da;
> Ffynawn gwres yn awyr, a haul yn ei haddfa.
>
> He created two fountains, complete in blessing; the fountain of heat in the air, and the sun in its *orbit*. *Taliesin.*

Haearn, *s. m.*—*pl.* heieirn (haiarn) Iron.
Haech, *s. f.*—*pl. t.* ydd (ha—ech) A skirt; a hem.
Haedd, *s. f.*—*pl. t.* ion (ha—edd) A reach; an attainment; a hold; merit, desert.

> Hynaf fydd dyn pan aner,
> A iau iau bob amser,
> Ydd o pryderer
> O'r bresen haedd!
>
> Man is oldest when he is born, and is younger and younger continually what is there to be anxious about of the present *attainment*! *Taliesin.*

Haeddad, *s. m.* (haedd) A reaching, or attaining, a laying hold of; a meriting, or deserving.
Haeddadwy, *a.* (haeddad) That may be reached; attainable, or obtainable.
Haeddawl, *a.* (haedd) Tending to reach, or lay hold of; meritorious, deserving.
Haeddbarch, *a.* (haedd—parch) Deserving honour
Haeddedig, *a.* (haedd) Being reached, or attained; merited, deserved.
Haeddedigaeth, *s. m.*—*pl. t.* au (haeddedig) Desert
Haeddedigawl, *a.* (haeddedig) Meritorious.
Haeddel, *s. f.*—*pl. t.* i (haedd) A plough handle. *Haeddel fawr*, or *corn gwydd arad*, the ploughtail; *haeddel fach*, or *haeddel gam*, the smaller plough handle, also called *llawlyw*.
Haeddglod, *a.* (haedd—clod) Deserving applause.
Haeddgoel, *a.* (haedd—coel) Desreving credit.
Haeddiad, *s. m.* (haedd) A reaching, or attaining; a laying hold of; a meriting.
Haeddiannawl, *a.* (haeddiant) Meritorious.
Haeddiannoldeb, *s. m.* (haeddiannawl) Meritoriousness, deservedness, condignness.

Haeddiannoli, *v. n.* (haeddiannawl) To become meritorious; to render deserving.
Haeddiannu, *v. n.* (haeddiant) To become a merit.
Haeddiannus, *a.* (haeddiant) Meritorious.
Haeddiannusaw, *v. n.* (haeddiannus) To become meritorious; to become deserving.
Haeddiant, *s. m.* (haedd) Attainment; merit.
Haeddu, *v. a.* (haedd) To reach, to attain; to lay hold of; to merit, to deserve. *Haeddit dy grogi*, thou deservest to be hanged.

> [illegible]
> *To [illegible] of a wasp's nest.* — *Adage.*
> [illegible]
> *Like reaching the sky with a hook.* — *Taliesin.*
> [illegible]
> *To deserve a salutation is to [illegible].* — *Adage.*
> [illegible]
> *A blessing [illegible] is not deserved will not prosper.* — *Adage.*

Hael, *s. m.*—*pl. t.* ion (hy—ael) A bounteous, or liberal person. *Hael byrllaw[illegible]*, a prodigal without means.

> [illegible]
> *He cannot be a liberal one who has nothing.* — *Adage.*
> [illegible]
> *[illegible] the liberal until he becomes a dog.* — *Adage.*
> [illegible]
>
> The *liberal one*, [illegible] the true attribute of the Supreme, [illegible] — *[illegible]*

Hael, *a.* (hy—ael) Bounteous, generous, liberal. *Dyna fod yn ddynion haelion*, that is being generous people: *Dyn hael!* Gracious me!

> [illegible]
>
> [illegible] — *[illegible]*

Haelder, *s. m.* (hael) Bounty, liberality.
Haeledig, *a.* (hael) Endued with liberality.
Haeledd, *s. m.* (hael) Liberality, munificence.
Haelfalch, *a.* (hael—balch) Generously proud.
Haelfron, *s. f.* (hael—bron) That is of a generous breast. *a.* Generous-hearted.
Haelfudd, *s. f.* (hael—budd) A liberal profit, or advantage. *a.* Of liberal advantage.
Haelgar, *a.* (hael) Disposed to be generous.
Haelgarwch, *s. m.* (haelgar) Bountifulness.
Haelged, *s. f.* (hael—ced) A liberal treasure.
Haeliad, *s. m.* (hael) A becoming liberal.
Haelion, *s. pl. aggr.* (hael) Liberal ones.
Haelioni, *s. m.* (haelion) Generosity, liberality.

> [illegible]
>
> *There is no [illegible] in our land, because of the [illegible].* — *T. Prys.*

Haelionu, *v. n.* (haelion) To become generous; to act liberally; to practice generosity.

> [illegible]
>
> [illegible] — *[illegible]*

Haelionus, *a.* (haelion) Disposed to liberality.
Haelionusaw, *v. n.* (haelionus) To become bounteous, or generous.
Haelionusrwydd, *s. m.* (haelionus) Bountifulness.
Haelon, *s. pl. aggr.* (hael) Generous, or free ones.

> [illegible]
>
> The three sons of Cadwallon, three with opposing weapons to prevent defeat, in the front of the host of *generous men*. — *Cynddelw.*

Haelonaeth, *s. m.* (haelon) A generous act.

> [illegible]
> *The [illegible] claim of the liberality of the [illegible].* — *Cynddelw*

Haelonedd, *s. m.* (haelon) Generosity, liberality.
Haeloniaeth, *s. m.* (haelon) A generous act.

> [illegible]
> *No one will be [illegible] from its cruelty.* — *Myrddin.*

Haelryw, *s. m.*—*pl. t.* ian (hael—rhyw) A generous kind. *a.* Of a generous sort.
Haelu, *v. n.* (hael) To become liberal, or bounteous; to act generously.
Haelus, *a.* (hael) Of a liberal disposition.
Haelusaw, *v. n.* (haelus) To become bounteous.
Haelusrwydd, *s. m.* (haelus) Bounteousness.
Haelwych, *a.* (hael—gwych) Liberally splendid.
Haen, *s. f.*—*pl. t.* ydd (ha—en) A stratum; a thin sprinkling; a lay, or row; a plait, or fold.

> [illegible]
>
> *One covering is but [illegible] of [illegible], without [illegible] of [illegible] like arrow [illegible].* — *[illegible]*

Haenawl, *a.* (haen) Disposed in layers, sprinkled.
Haeniad, *s. m.* (haen) A laying a stratum; a disposing in layers, or rows; a sprinkling over.
Haenu, *v. a.* (haen) To lay a stratum; to place in layers, or rows; to sprinkle over.
Haer, *s. f.*—*pl. t.* au (ha—er) A stubbornness of opinion, positiveness. *Mae efe ar eih aer yn fawr*, he is very positive. *Sil.*
Haer, *a.* (ha—er) Stubborn; positive; urgent.

> [illegible]
>
> Against the [illegible] of M[illegible], whose progeny is to be held in the [illegible], there were [illegible] and *urgent* claims. — *[illegible], i O. Gwynedd.*

Haerawl, *a.* (haer) Affirmative, assertive.
Haeredig, *a.* (haer) Being asserted, or affirmed.
Haeredigaeth, *s. m.*—*pl. t.* au (haeredig) Assertion; affirmation; avouchment.
Haeredigawl, *a.* (haeredig) Affirmative.
Haeredd, *s. m.* (haer) Stubbornness of opinion.
Haerla, *s. f.* (haer) An affirmation: an assertion.
Haeriad, *s. m.* (haer) A being positive; allegation
Haeriannawl, *a.* (haeriant) Affirmative.
Haeriannu, *v. a.* (haeriant) To make an assertion.
Haeriant, *s. m.* (haer) An avouchment; assertion.
Haeriator, *ger.* (haer) In asserting positively.
Haeritor, *sup.* (haer) To be asserting positively.
Haerllug, *a.* (haer—llug) Positively urgent; importunate, malapert, impudent, saucy.
Haerllugaw, *v. n.* (haerllug) To urge stubbornly.
Haerllugawl, *a.* (haerllug) Disposed to be saucy.
Haerllugedd, *s. m.* (haerllug) Stubbornness.
Haerllugrwydd, *s. m.* (haerllug) Importunity; impudence, sauciness.
Haerllugyn, *s. m. dim.* (haerllug) A saucy one.
Haerllyd, *a.* (haer) Importunate, stubborn.
Haerllydrwydd, *s. m.* (haerllyd) Importunity.
Haeru, *v. a.* (haer) To assert positively, to affirm, to avouch, to assert; to be positive, to insist.
Haerwr, *s. m.*—*pl.* haerwyr (haer—gwr) One who asserts stubbornly; an assertor.
Haerydd, *s. m.*—*pl. t.* ion (haer) One who insists.
Haf, *s. m.*—*pl. t.* au (ha) That is apt to overspread, or to spread out; fullness; the summer.

> [illegible]
>
> I will go, for girls to see the dress and summer, arrayed in gladness, shall show me with her finger from afar, like [illegible] yonder whence the day does come. — *Ieu. Ddu y Bulrg, i'r gwn cach*

Hafad, *s. m.* (haf) A summering; estivation.

Hafaidd, *a.* (haf) Summer-like, summer.

Hafal, *a.* (ha—mal) Semblable, resembling, like.

Teuluoedd, a thiroedd, ai ydd neml hafal?
Nawdd hyfaeth dy wledd.

Regions and lands, are they not *like* thee? Do not thy feasts need genius! *Cynddelw.*

Rodri hael, ei hafal ni wnaid.

Rodri the generous, his *equal* has not been formed.
Ll. P. Moch.

Hafar, *s. m.* (haf—ar) A summer tillage.

Hafarch, *s. m.* (haf—arch) That overwhelms. *a.* Listless, dispirited; restive.

Hafarchawl, *a.* (hafarch) Tending to make listless, or dispirited; apt to be restive.

Hafarchedd, *s. m.* (hafarch) Listlessness; restiveness.

Hafarchiad, *s. m.* (hafarch) A rendering listless; a becoming dispirited; a becoming restive.

Hafarchu, *v. a.* (hafarch) To cause listlessness; to make restive; to become listless.

Hafawg, *a.* (haf) Abundant, luxuriant; beauteous; universal, common. *Yr hafawg i bawb*, a common strumpet; *hifyn hafawg*, a hermaphrodite; *tir hafawg*, common land; *gwneyd yn bur hafawg*, to act very bountifully.

Hafawl, *a.* (haf) Appertaining to summer.

Hafdy, *s. m.—pl. t.* au (haf—ty) A summer-house.

Hafgan, *s. m.* (haf—can) Summer sunshine.

Hafgan, *s. f.* (haf—can) Summer song, May song.

Hafiad, *s. m.* (haf) Estivation; a summering.

Hafin, *s. m.* (haf) Summer time, or days.

Un yw'r fun a fydd cynefin,
Gwenllian lliw hafin.

One is the maid that shall be pre-eminent, Gwenllian of the hue of the *summer day*. *H. ab Owain.*

Hafinaw, *v. n.* (hafin) To become like summer.

Hafinder, *s. m.* (hafin) Summer calmness.

Hafindra, *s. m.* (hafin) Summer calmness.

Hafineb, *s. m.* (hafin) Summer calmness.

Hafling, *s. m.* (haf—llig) Abundance, plenty. *a.* Uberous, abundant.

Maith y rhydd yr hyn nî'm ddug;
Meirch breiog-hir uch bragerch hafling,
Mwth, myn—gan, hir llam lawrllog.

Largely he gives what he will not deprive me of: steeds fat and long, over the *abundant* large oats, swift, white-maned, long-paced, and saucy. *Ll. P. Moch, i D. ab Owain.*

Haflingaw, *v. a.* (hafling) To uberate; to render abundant; to become plenteous, to abound.

Haflingder, *s. m.* (hafling) Uberosity.

Haflingiad, *s. m.* (hafling) A rendering uberous.

Haflingrwydd, *s. m.* (hafling) Uberosity.

Hafn, *s. m.—pl.* hafnau (hy—afn) That extends out, or that is flat, a still place; a haven.

Hafnai, *s. f.—pl.* hafneiod (hafn) A slattern.

Hafnawl, *a.* (hafn) Tending to extend out; tending to sluggishness; slatternly.

Hafnen, *s. f. dim.* (hafn) A trollop, a slattern.

Hafniad, *s. m.* (hafn) An extending out; a becoming sluggish.

Hafnos, *s. f.* (haf—nos) A summer night.

Hafnu, *v. a.* (hafn) To extend out; to become extended; to become sluggish.

Hafod, *s. f.—pl. t.* au (haf—bod) A summer dwelling; a dairy. *Hafod unnos*, a cot raised on a common in one night, wherein a family were to sleep forty nights, which, according to ancient usage, gave a free title to it, with a certain quantity of land round it, which was to be marked out with a plough.

Nid ai o'i gylch fal gwneyd hafod unnos.

Thou wilt not go about it like making the one night's summer cot. *Adage.*

Pan fytych o'th fyd hardd gydfod
O'r byd hwn ni'm hebwn hebod;
Boed yn nef a'th hendre, a'th hafod, teyrn
Teyrnas Duw uchod.

When thou shalt have run through thy life of fair converse in this world, of which I would not have concern without thee, in heaven may thy permanent mansion be, and thy *summer dwelling*, a prince of the kingdom of God above. *Ll. P. Moch.*

Hafodaidd, *a.* (hafod) Relating to summer dwelling; after the manner of a dairy; somewhat rustic.

A gasten ffraeth, gwtawg gwta ffrom,
A buwch bygddu lom, a bwch bagiawg,
Cerdd hafodaidd drwsd yw cerdd Fadawg,
A choeliaw i achau iar a cheiliawg.

With a noisy little bitch, a pert one, dock-tailed and surly, a bare pitch coloured cow, and a waddling buck, a rustic and clumsy song is the song of Madog, and giving credit to the ascent of a hen and cock. *D. ab Ieuan Ddu.*

Hafodawg, *a.* (hafod) Having a summer dwelling.

Hafodawl, *a.* (hafod) Relating to a summer dwelling; belonging to a dairy.

Hafodi, *v. a.* (hafod) To live in a summer dwelling; to attend the dairy.

Hafodwr, *s. m.—pl.* hafodwyr (hafod—gwr) One who lives in a summer dwelling; a dairyman.

Hafodydd, *s. m.—pl. t.* ion (hafod) One who lives in a summer dwelling, or a dairy.

Hafog, *s. m.* (haf) A spreading about; waste; devastation, havock. *Hai hafog*, hollo havock; a cry used by the Cardiganshire peasants on seeing their neighbour's cattle in the corn-fields.

O gwneir hafog na rhyfel—
Ef yw y blaen.

If *devastation* or war be made, he is the foremost. *D. Benf.*

Hafogawl, *a.* (hafog) Devastating, wasting.

Hafogi, *v. a.* (hafog) To commit havock.

Hafoli, *v. a.* (hafawl) To summerize.

Hafota, *v. n.* (hafod) To abide in the summer dwelling; to summer.

Gwell i'r gath nad elid i hafota.

Better for the cat if there were no going to *abide in the summer-house*. *Adage.*

Hafotty, *s. m.—pl. t.* au (hafod—ty) A summer dwelling-house; a dairy-house.

Casbeth Owain Cyfeiliawg: Saesoneg mewn hafotty.

The hated thing of Owain Cyfeiliog: English in a *dairy-house*.

Hafr, *s. f.—pl.* hafrod (haf) One that is lank, or sluggish; one that is waste, or worthless; a slattern; a gelt goat.

Hafraidd, *a.* (hafr) Apt to spread out; of a sluggish disposition; sluttish, slatternly.

Hafrawg, *a.* (hafr) Apt to be sluggish; slatternly. *s. f.* A trollop.

Hafrawl, *a.* (hafr) Tending to make lank; of a sluggish nature.

Hafren, *s. f.* (hafr) One that is lank, or sluggish; A loose woman, a strollop; a strumpet.

Hafriad, *s. m.* (hafr) A rendering lank; a rendering sluggish.

Hafru, *v. a.* (hafr) To make lank; to render sluggish; to become sluggish.

Hafu, *v. n.* (haf) To become summer; to summer.

Haff, *s. m.—pl. t.* iau (ha) A snatch, or catch.

Haffiad, *s. m.—pl. t.* au (haff) A snatching.

Haffiaw, *v. a.* (haff) To snatch, to seize hastily.

Haffiawl, *a.* (haff) Snatching, apt to snatch.

Haffiwr, *s. m.—pl.* haffwyr (haff—gwr) Snatcher.

Hag, *s. m.—pl. t.* ion (hy—ag) A gash, a cut.

Hagen, *conj.* (ha—cen) Yet, nevertheless, notwithstanding, however.

Hagen, *adv.* (ha—cen) Yet, after all, still.

Tra fu fy nghyfoeth, a gallu rodd i ddi o honof, pawb a'm carai; ar nad mi hagen a geryn, namyn fy rhoddion, a'm doniau; a phan giliwys y rhai hyny y ciliasant hwythau.

While my wealth remained, and I was able to bestow benefits, every one loved me, and not me after all were they wont to love, but my gifts, and my bounties, and when these disappeared, they also disappeared. *[illegible] ab Arthur.*

Hagr, *a* (hag) Ugly, rough, unseemly, deformed.

Llawer teg drwg ei ddefnydd;
Llawer hagr, hygar fydd.

Many a fair thing is of bad materials, many an *ugly* thing is amiable. *Adage.*

Y neb a ddywedo yn syberw wrth y brenin, neu yn hagr, taled dri buyn camlwrw yn ddeuddyblyg am hyny.

Whoever that shall speak haughtily to the king, or *roughly*, let him pay three kine of compensation fine doubled for that. *Welsh Laws.*

Hagraidd, *a.* (hagr) Somewhat ugly, or unseemly, somewhat deformed.

Hagrau, *v. a.* (hagr) To make ugly; to disfigure; to become ugly; to become disfigured.

Hagrawl, *a.* (hagr) Tending to make ugly; disfiguring.

Hagredd, *s. m.* (hagr) Ugliness, unseemliness.

Hagriad, *s. m.* (hagr) A making ugly, or unseemly, a disfiguring.

Hagru, *v. a.* (hagr) To make ugly, or unseemly; to disfigure; to become ugly.

Hagrwch, *s. m.* (hagr) Ugliness; deformity.

Haha, *s. m.* (ha, *repeated*) A boggle. *a.* Boggling.

Bid haha byddar.

Let the deaf be *apt to boggle.* *Adage.*

Haha, *interj.* (ha, *repeated*) It is expressive of hesitation, of surprize, and of mirth.

Hai, *s. m.* (ha) A sudden impulse; excitation; haste.

Yr hai a laddodd yr hwch.

The *hurry* has killed the sow. *Adage.*

Aeth [illegible]
Powys yn hai heb Sion hir.

Powys is become a scene of *confusion* without tall John. *L. Mon.*

Hi a aeth yn hai weithiau.

It is become all *confusion* now. *I. G. Cath.*

Hai, *v. a.* (*imper. of* heiaw) Hie, quick, make haste. *interj.* Expressive of excitation or setting on. *Hai how heno!* Heigho lack-a-day.

Hai how! hiraeth, ow! ni thyr.

Heigho! regret, ah! it will not subside.

Hylaw helaf haul hai hon
Hai! hai! hai! ai hi yw hon!

Dexterously I will hunt the luminary of generous ones hey! hey! hey! Is this her? *D. ab Edmwnt.*

Haiach, *s. m.* (hai) An instant; a point of time, a moment. *Ni byddwn haiach yn gwneyd hyn,* I would not be a moment doing this; *ni byddi haiach yn myned yno,* thou wilt not be an instant going there.

Haiach, *adv.* (hai) Instantly, almost, most.

Uwch wyd na haiach o wyr.

Thou art more exalted than *most* of men. *G. ab Llywelyn Moel.*

Haiachen, *s. f. dim.* (haiach) A small instant, or moment.

Haiachen, *adv* (haiach) Instantaneously; almost.

Haiarn, *s. m.* —*pl.* heieirn (hai—arn) Iron.

Gwynwas [illegible] yn y ynys a orugyt [illegible] pwygilydd o dan a haiarn.

Gwynwas and Melwas, the devastating [illegible] was what they did from one end to the other with fire and sword. *[illegible]*

Haiarnaidd, *a.* (haiarn) Ferrean, ferreous.

Haiarnawch, *s.* (haiarn—awch) Sharpness of iron.

Haiarnawg, *a.* (haiarn) Ferruginous.

Haiarnawl, *a.* (haiarn) Partaking of iron, irony.

I rwymaw eu bre[illegible] cyd[illegible] clymau,
A'u b[illegible] haiarnaidd [illegible]

To bind their kings in hard fetters, and their nobles [illegible] *Ps. 149.*

Haiarnblu, *s. pl. aggr.* (haiarn—plu) The iron scales, such as were used in armour.

Haiarndde, *a.* (haiarn) Impregnated with iron.

Haiarnddu, *s. m.* (haiarn—du) Iron-black. *a.* Of an iron-black, or iron gray.

Haiarnddur, *s. m.* (haiarn—dur) Iron steel.

Haiarngaen, *s. f.* (haiarn—caen) A covering of iron; iron armour.

Haiarniad, *s. m.* (haiarn) A doing with iron.

Haiarnliw, *s. m.* (haiarn—lliw) Iron colour. *a.* Of an iron colour.

Haiarnllyd, *a.* (haiarn) Ferruginous, irony.

Haiarnu, *v. a.* (haiarn) To do with iron.

Haiarnwedd, *s. f.* (haiarn—gwedd) An iron hue.

Haiarnwr, *s. m.*—*pl.* haiarnwyr (haiarn—gwr) An ironmonger, or a dealer in iron.

Haiarnydd, *s. m.*—*pl. t.* ion (haiarn) Ironmonger.

Haib, *s. f.* (hy—aib) That is excessive, superabundant in the extreme. *Ti a weli haib o ryfeddawd yno,* Thou wilt see an immensity of a wonder there. *Sil.*

Haid, *s. f.*—*pl.* heidiau (hy—aid) A swarm. *Haid o wenyn,* a swarm of bees; *y gynthaid,* the virgin swarm; *y ddewr-haid,* the bold swarm; *y wan-haid,* the weak swarm; *y ddyrn-haid,* the hand-swarm; *y syp-haid,* the bundle-swarm; *asgell-haid,* a wing swarm.

O englyn ni ddaliaf haid

I shall not catch a swarm by a verse. *Adage.*

Gwelais- fyddinawr bedydd
Fal haid heb fedrydaf.

I have seen the christian legions like a swarm without a hive. *Llywarch Hen.*

Haidd, *s. m. aggr.*—*pl.* heiddiau (hy—aidd) Barley.

Haiddwellt, *s. m.* (haidd—gwellt) Barley-grass.

Haif, *s. f.*—*pl.* heifion (hy—aif) A drift. *Haif o ddail,* a drift of leaves; *haif o fa,* a drift of chaff; *haif o lwch,* a cloud of dust.

Haig, *s. f.*—*pl.* heigiau (hy—aig) A shoal; a multitude. *Haig o bysgod,* a shoal of fishes.

Haihow, *s. m.* (hai—how) A heigho, a cry of alas.

Haihow, *interj.* (hai—how) Heigho! alas!

Haihwchw, *s. m.* (hai—wchw) A cry for help in extreme danger; a cry of murder.

Haihwchw, *interj.* (hai—wchw) Hollo, murder!

Hail, *s. f.*—*pl.* heiliau (hy—ail) A quantity, profusion, abundance, bounty, service, or what is served at table. *Hail o fwyd,* a service of meat; *hail o ddiawd,* a service of drink; *hail o ffrwythau,* a desert of fruits; *heilion o seigiau,* courses of victuals.

Hain, *s. f.*—*pl.* heinion (hy—ain) That is apt to pervade, or spread through. *Hain o bryfed,* a swarm of vermin.

Dim gwenith wethian,
Nid mel yn dan,
Ond dar[illegible] gan
Hain a drygedd

No longer is there now no honey is there spread, but a prevalence of plague and evil. *L. G. Cothi.*

Haint, *s. m.*—*pl.* heintiau (hain) That is profuse-full, or prevalent; a complaint, disease, or sickness. *Haint gwres,* a burning fever; *haint y galon,* heart ache; *haint chwys,* sweating sickness; *haint y nodau,* the plague; *haint y fam,* hysterical affection; *haint y ddüeg,* hypochondriac affection; *haint y marchogion* or *lledewigwst,* the hæmorrhoides; *haint dygwydd,* falling sickness; *haint y trythyllwch,* venereal disorder; *haint llyn,* epidemical disease.

Nid cyd[illegible] hen haint

[illegible] *Adage.*

Hair, *a.* (hy—air) Apt to be tedious, or long.

Tost yw trigo mewn tywyllwch,
Lle ni chaffer dim dyddanwch;
Tostach trigo yn rhy hair,
Lle ni chaffer gwrandaw'r gair.

It is severe to dwell in darkness, where no comfort is to be obtained; it is more severe to dwell too *long* where the word cannot be heard. *Parch. R. Prisiart.*

Hais, *s. m.* (hy—ais) That is full of asperites, points, or prickles.

Haith, *s. m.* (hy—aith) That is apt to reach, touch, or come in contact.

Haiwchw, *s. m.* (hai—wchw) A cry of murder.

Haiwchw, *interj.* (hai—wchw) Hollo, murder!

Hal, *s. m.—pl. t.* oedd (hy—al) A pervading element, essential salt, alkali, a salt marsh.

Hal, *a.* (hy—al) Saline, alkaline. *Tir hal*, salt land, or a salt marsh.

Halad, *s. m.* (hal) An impregnating with salt.

Haladwy, *a.* (halad) That may be impregnated.

Halaeth, *s. m.* (hal) Saturation, saturity, the state of being pervaded, or saturated, fulness.

Halant, *s. m.* (hal) A plenum, saturation.

Halar, *a.* (ha—llar) Apt to incite mirth.

Halawg, *a.* (hal) Being essentially pervaded, abounding with salt, contaminated, polluted, defiled. *Lle halawg*, an unclean place. *Pwll Halawg*, *Rhyd Halawg*, and *Penardd Halawg*, places so called in Flintshire, on the borders of the marsh of the Dee.

Ci chwyrnawg halawg ei bais.

The coat of a grinning dog is *covered with flavour*. *Adage.*

Halawgdy, *s. m.—pl. t.* au (halawg—ty) A polluted house, a devoted, or forfeited house, on account of its inhabitant being accessory to a felony. *Welsh Laws.*

Halawglw, *s. m.* (halawg—llw) A profane oath.

Haledig, *a.* (hal) Impregnated, saturated.

Haledd, *s. m.* (hal) An impregnated state.

Halen, *s. m.* (hal) Salt. *Crwth halen*, a salt-box.

Halenai, *s. m.* (halen) That produces salt: a salt-celler.

Halenaidd, *a.* (halen) Somewhat salt, or brackish.

Halenawg, *a.* (halen) Abounding with salt.

Haleniad, *s. m.* (halen) A turning to salt.

Halenu, *v. a.* (halen) To turn to salt; to salt.

Halenwr, *s. m.—pl.* halenwyr (halen—gwr) A salt-merchant, or dealer in salt.

Halenwyn, *s. m.* (halen—gwyn) A sharp, penetrating, or acrid principle.

Gogwn attrefnawr
Rhwng nef a llawr,
Pan yw brith iyrchwyn,
Pan yw hallt halenwyn.

I know who the regulator between heaven and earth; whence the deer is spotted, whence the *acrid principle* is salt. *Taliesin.*

Halenydd, *s. m.—pl. t.* ion (halen) Salt-merchant.

Haliad, *s. m.* (hal) Impregnation, saturation.

Haliw, *s. m.* (hal) The saliva, or spittle.

Ti elli wybod fod chwant bwyd arnad, pan fo gormodd haliw yn dygwyddaw i'th enau.

Thou mayest know that thou art in want of victuals, when an excess of *saliva* falls from thy lips. *Ll Meddyg.*

Yn ei wyneb rhadlawn y poerasant haliw gwenwynig.

In his gracious countenance they spat venemous *spittle*. *Brcudd. Sibli.*

Haliwiad, *s. m.—pl. t.* au (haliw) Salivation.

Haliwiaw, *v. a.* (haliw) To salivate, to produce saliva, or spittle.

Halogawl, *a.* (halawg) Tending to contaminate.

Halogedig, *a.* (halawg) Contaminated, defiled.

Halogedigaeth, *s. m.* (halogedig) Contamination, pollution, defilement, profanation.

Halogedigrwydd, *s. m.* (halogedig) Pollutedness.

Halogi, *v. a.* (halawg) To contaminate, to pollute, to defile, to corrupt, to profane.

Halogiad, *s. m.* (halawg) A contaminating, polluting, or defiling, contamination, profanation.

Halogrwydd, *s. m.* (halawg) Pollutedness.

Halogwr, *s. m.—pl.* halogwyr (halawg—gwr) A polluter, a defiler, a profaner.

Halu, *v. a.* (hal) To pervade universally; to impregnate, to saturate; to yean.

Halus, *a.* (hal) Tending to impregnate.

Halwyn, *s. m.* (hal) Brine, salt water.

Pan yw hallt halwyn.

Why the *brine* is salt. *Taliesin.*

Hall, *a.* (hal) Saline, salt, or brackish, briny.

Hallaidd, *a.* (hall) Somewhat salt, brackish.

Hallfor, *s. m.* (hall—mor) The salt sea.

Tu goror hallfor holles ysgwydawr
Ar ysgwyddau——

Towards the coast of the *briny sea* shields were split upon shoulders. *D. P. Mech.*

Hallt, *a.* (hall) Salt, saline, briny. *Cei dalu yn hallt am dano*, thou shalt pay severely for it: *Dagrau heilltion*, salt tears.

Halltaidd, *a.* (hallt) Somewhat salt, saltish.

Halltawg, *a.* (hallt) Abounding with saltness.

Halltawl, *a.* (hallt) Of a saline tendency.

Halltedig, *a.* (hallt) Saltness, salineness.

Halltiad, *s. m.* (hallt) A salting; a making salt, or briny; a becoming salt.

Halltin, *a.* (hallt) Saline, impregnated with salt.

Halltineb, *s. m.* (halltin) Saltness, salineness.

Halltni, *s. m.* (hallt) Saltness, salineness.

Halltrwydd, *s. m.* (hallt) Saltness, salineness.

Halltu, *v. a.* (hallt) To salt, to season with salt; to make salt; to become salt.

Halltwr, *s. m.—pl.* halltwyr (hallt—gwr) A salter.

Halltydd, *s. m.—pl. t.* ion (hallt) A salter.

Hallu, *v. a.* (hall) To salt; to make salt, or briny; to become salt.

Ham, *s. m.* (hy—am) A cause; a circumstance. *Nid am ei ham y daeth hyn iddo*, not without cause did this come to him; *gwneyd peth o ham i ham*, to do a thing at a venture; *ceiff beth am ei ham*, he will get a thing for a trifle; *elai am ei ham*, he went because he would go.

Adolwyn, dywed——
Heb air o hûd, ba ryw ham——
A'th nad'

I pray, tell, without a word of delusion, what *circumstance* will obstruct thee' *Edm. Prys.*

Hambwyll, *s. m.* (ham—pwyll) Reflection, or recurrence of thought.

Hambwyllaw, *v. a.* (hambwyll) To reflect, to call to mind, to consider.

Hambwylliad, *s. m.* (hambwyll) A contemplating, a considering; a calling to mind, contemplation.

Hamdden, *s. m.* (ham—dan) Leisure, spare time, respite; freedom from business; intermission; deliberation.

Hamddenawl, *a.* (hamdden) Being at leisure, or at ease. *Mae hi yn hamddenawl iawn*, she is very contented.

Hamddeniad, *s. m.* (hamdden) A taking recreation, amusement, or respite from toil.

Hamddenu, *v. n.* (hamdden) To take amusement.

Ni hamddenws Arthur yna peri claddu ei wyr, namyn myned yn ol Medrawd parth a Chernyw.

Arthur *made* no *delay* than causing his men to be buried, but went after Medrod towards Cornwall. *Gr. ab Arthur.*

Han, *s. m.* (hy—an) That proceeds from, that is

separated, or parted from. *a.* Produced; separated, or parted.

> Hywel ddihegl ddiogan dayra,
> Duw o'r nef ni'th wyl han
> A'i seredd lariaidd lyron;
> A'i saint glwys ardderchawg glan.

Hywel the secure, the unblemished prince, God of heaven will not behold thee parted from his summit, mild and comely, from his saints of glory bright and pure. — *Ll. P. Moch.*

Han, *prep.* (han, s.) From, or out of. *Hanof,* out of me; *hanot,* out of thee; *hano,* out of him, or it; *hani* and *heni,* out of her; *hanom* and *honom,* out of us; *hanoch,* out of you; *hanynt,* out of them.

Hanaeth, *s. f.* (han) A procedure, a proceed.

Hanawd, *s. m.* (han) A proceeding from, a derivation, a descent.

Hanbwyll, *s. m.* (han—bwyll) Considerance.

> Crist Fab Duw ddiwyll, hanbwyll hona.

Of Christ, the unblemished son of God, I will assert an unfeigned considerance. — *Bleddyn Fardd.*

Hanbwyllaw, *v. a.* (hanbwyll) To have consideration of, to reflect upon; to call to mind.

> Hanbwyllais Gemais gymhell;
> Hanbwyll o honaf, hanbych gwell.

I had in contemplation the trying of Cemais: a consideration with me is to give you gratulation. — *Gw. Bryhl, i D. ab Owain.*

Hanbwyllawg, *a.* (hanbwyll) Considerate.

Hanbwylliad, *s. m.* (hanbwyll) A having consideration, or reflection.

Hanbwyllus, *a.* (hanbwyll) Considerate.

Handden, *s. m.* (han—dan) The being attractive.

Handdenawl, *a.* (handden) Having an attractive source, alluring, enticing.

Handdeniad, *s. m.* (handden) A deriving an attraction, or allurement.

Handdenu, *v. a.* (handden) To derive attraction, or allurement.

> Tragwyddawl Ddaw, tra gyfansyf
> Trwyddawl, o honawd a handdenwyf!

Eternal God whilst I am composing a treatise, of thee may I derive my theme! — *Gwalchmai.*

Handdyfod, *v. n.* (han—dyfod) To be become, to be existing: *handerddwn,* I was become: *handoeddit,* thou wert become: *handoedd,* he, she, or it was become: *handwyf,* I am become: *handwyd,* thou art become: *handyw,* he, she, or it is become: *handym,* we are become: *handawaf,* I shall become: *handaw,* thou wilt become: *handaw,* he will become: *handyfwy,* I shall be become: *handyfyddi,* thou wilt be become: *handyfydd,* he, she, or it will be become: *handoed,* let it become: *handid,* let it be become.

> Handid fy Arglwydd, cyfrwydd, gyfrwys,
> O ryw dianryw, diarysfus;
> Handoed ny ariod o ucheluwys
> Handoeddiad o'r llwyth llyth cwyn.

May my lord be become prosperous, and cautious, being of renowned, and sincere stem, may the pedigree be become of high origin; thou wert derived from the family with the sleek stallions. — *Llywelyn Fardd.*

Hanad, *s. f.* (han) A procedure, a derivative.

Hanedig, *a.* (haned) Being derived or descended.

Hanedigaeth, *s. f.—pl. t.* au (hanedig) A proceeding from; a derivation.

Hanes, *s. m.—pl. t.* ion (han—es) An account, or relation; history.

> Gwyl yw hanes.

History is modest. — *Adage.*

Hanesawl, *s. m.—pl.* hanesolion (hanes) A historiographer, a chronicler.

Hanesawl, *a.* (hanes) Historical, narrative.

Hanesgerdd, *s. f.* (hanes—cerdd) An epic poem.

> Hanesgerdd yw can yn son am ddynion, a phethau anghyffredin, er hyfrydwch a lles y byd.

An epic poem is a composition making mention of men and uncommon things, for the pleasure and benefit of the world. — *Barddas.*

Hanesiad, *s. m.* (hanes) A narrating, or a giving an account; a narration.

Hanesiaeth, *s. m.* (hanes) History, a narration of an event; a description.

Hanesu, *v. a.* (hanes) To historify; to narrate, to relate; to give a description.

> Nid rhaid ond bwrw trem ar un peth o'r byd, ac yna ei gyflawn nodi wrth ei hanesu.

It is but necessary to throw a glance upon any one thing in the world, and then fully to characterise it, and to give it an appellative, and to give an account of it. — *Barddas.*

Haneswr, *s. m.—pl.* haneswyr (hanes—gwr) One who narrates, or relates; a historian.

Hanesydd, *s. m.—pl. t.* ion (hanes) Historian.

Hanesyddiaeth, *s. m.* (hanesydd) Historiography.

Hanesyn, *s. m. dim.* (hanes) A piece of history; an anecdote.

Hanfod, *s. m.—pl. t.* au (han—bod) Existence, being, essence.

> Tri chadernyd hanfod: ais gellir amgen, nid rhaid amgen, ac nis gellir gwell, gan feddwl; ac yn hyn y derfydd pob peth.

The three stabilities of existence: what cannot be otherwise, what need not be otherwise, and what cannot be conceived better; and in these will all things end. — *Barddas.*

> Tri chylch hanfod y sydd: cylch y ceugant, lle nid oes namyn Duw, na byw na marw, ac nid oes namyn Duw a ell ei dramwy; cylch yr abred, lle mae pob hanfod o'r marw, a dyn a'i tramwy; cylch y gwynfyd, lle pob hanfod o'r byw, a dyn a'i tramwy yn y nef.

There are three circles of existence: the circle of infinity, where there is nothing but God, of living or dead, and none but God can traverse it; the circle of inchoation, where all things by nature are derived from death, and man hath traversed it; and the circle of felicity, where all things spring from life, and man shall traverse it in heaven. — *Barddas.*

Hanfod, *v. n.* (han—bod) To become existent; to proceed from, or descend; to exist, to be; to subsist. *Ef a hanfydd gwaeth,* he will become worse: *Hanffych gwell!* All hail! *Hanfwyf, hanbwyf,* may I exist, or may I be; *hanfych,* or *henffych,* may you be: *hanfo,* may he be; *hanbord,* or *hanbid,* let him exist, let him be: *hanbydd,* he will be existing: *Mal yr hanfom goreuon,* so that we may be become the better ones.

> Hanbid gwell y ci o farw y llall.

Let the dog be the better from the death of another. — *Adage.*

> Hanbwyf well o honawd, wawd obryn;
> Hanbych well o Ddiaw, ac o ddyn.

May I be greeted of thee, a recompence for praise! mayest thou be welcome of God, and of man! — *Ll. P. Moch.*

Hanfodawg, *a.* (hanfod) Having existence.

> Tri rhyw hanfodogion y sydd: Duw, bywedigion, a meirwolion.

There are three kinds of existings. God, animals, and dead things. — *Barddas.*

Hanfodawl, *a.* (hanfod) Of a tendency to be, or to exist; existent, essential. *Yr undawd hanfodawl,* the hypostatical union.

Hanfodiad, *s. m.—pl. t.* au (hanfod) A becoming existent, an existing, a proceeding from.

> Duw a fedr yn ei briodoliaethau: sef ei hanfodiad er tragywyddoldeb, ac hefyd yn cynal tragywyddoldeb.

God is worshipped in his attributes: as his existing from eternity, and to the end of eternity. — *Barddas.*

Hanfodoldeb, *s. m.* (hanfodawl) A peculiar state of existence, a hypostasis.

Hanfodolder, *s. m.* (hanfodawl) Hypostasis.

Hanfodoledd, *s. m.* (hanfodawl) Hypostasis.

Hanfodoli, *v. a.* (hanfodawl) To render existent, to become existent.

Hanfodolrwydd, *s. m.* (hanfodawl) Hypostaticalness, a state of existence.

Haniad, *s. m.* (hân) A proceeding from, or origination, a being descended, derivation.

Haniator, *ger.* (haniad) In originating.

Hanitor, *imp.* (han) To be proceeding from.

Hanner, *s. m.—pl. t.* au (han—der) A half, a moiety. *a.* Half. *Hanner nos*, midnight: *hanner dydd*, midday: *hanner marw*, half dead.

Gwell hanner hai na hanner haf.

The *half* of seed is better than *half* of summer. *Adage.*

Hannerawg, *a.* (hanner) Having half, being half. *Bod yn hannerawg*, to be valued at half price.

Hannerawl, *a.* (hanner) Relating to a half.

Hannereg, *s. f.—pl. t.* au (hanner) A moiety, a half part, a half share, a half measure: a flitch of bacon.

Hannerèg yn y gegin!
Hannereg arall yn nhy'r gwin.

A *moiety* in the kitchen: another *moiety* in the wine house. *Ieu. Dewlwyn.*

Hannergrwn, *s. m.—pl.* hannergrynion (hanner—crwn) A hemisphere.

Hannergrynawl, *a.* (hannergrwn) Hemispherical.

Hannergylch, *s. m.—pl. t.* au (hanner—cylch) A semicircle.

Hannergylchawl, *a.* (hannergylch) Semicircular.

Hannergyswllt, *s. m.—pl.* hannergysylltiau (hanner—cyswllt) A half connection.

Hanneriad, *s. m.* (hanner) A dividing into halves.

Hannerob, *s. f.* (hanner—ob) A flitch of bacon.

Hannersain, *s. f.—pl.* hannerseiniau (hanner—sain) A semitone.

Hanneru, *v. a.* (hanner) To halve, to part in two.

Hannerwerth, *s. m.* (hanner—gwerth) Half price.

Hannerwybr, *s. f.* (hanner—gwybr) Hemisphere.

Hano, *pronomial prep.* (han) From, or out of him, from, or out of it.

Fe ddaw gofyn ar bob rhyw ddyn
Am a roes e yn ei enau
Ac a ddelo eilwaith hano.

There will be a demand made of every man respecting what he has put in his mouth, and what again shall come *from thence*. *T. ab Ieu. ab Rhys.*

Hanodawl, *a.* (hanawd) Having a proceeding.

Hanodi, *v. a.* (hanawd) To have proceeding.

Hanon, *pronomial prep.* (han) From us, out of us.

Ffrwyth i'n mysg ni ddichon fod:
Nid oes ond pechod hanon.

Good fruit amongst us there cannot be: there is nought but sin *from us.* *S. Dafydd.*

Hanota, *v. a.* (hanawd) To have proceeding.

Gan fod yr achwynwr yn chwenych hanota yn fore, efe a borthodd ei gyfreithiwr yn mlaenllaw.

Since the complainant was desirous *to have proceeding* early, he fed his lawyer before hand. *Adage.*

Hanred, *s. m.—pl. t.* ion (han—rhed) A parting off, or separation; recession.

Hanredawl, *a.* (hanred) Tending to part off.

Hanrediad, *s. m.* (hanred) Separation, secession.

Hanredoli, *v. a.* (hanredawl) To render separate, to become separate, or distinct.

Hanredoliaeth, *s. m.—pl. t.* au (hanredawl) A state of separation.

Hanredu, *v. a.* (hanred) To separate, to secede.

Hanu, *v. n.* (han) To proceed from, to be derived, to be descended. *O freninoedd i'th hanwyd*, from kings thou art descended: *a henyw o hono*, which proceeds from it.

Mor athrist ydyw, ein bod ni wedi bychanu, a dwyn mor isel ein heneidiau, y rhai a hanasant o'r nefoedd.

How deplorable is it, that we should have depreciated, and brought so low our souls, which *have originated* from heaven. *Ior. Owain.*

Hap, *s. f.—pl. t.* iau (hab) Luck, chance, fortune, good luck, good fortune.

Diles ydoedd ei dilyn;
Del i'n hap dala am hyn!

It was fruitless for me to follow her; may the *luck* come to me of being paid for this. *T. Prys.*

Hapiad, *s. m.—pl. t.* au (hap) A happening; a having luck, a having good fortune.

Hapiaw, *v. n.* (hap) To happen; to have luck, or chance; to have good fortune.

Hapiawl, *a.* (hap) Tending to luck, eventual.

Hapiedig, *a.* (hapiad) Being made to happen.

Hapus, *a.* (hap) Fortunate, happy, blessed.

Hapusaw, *v. a.* (hapus) To render fortunate; to make happy; to become fortunate.

Hapusawl, *a.* (hapus) Of a fortunate tendency, of a happy tendency.

Hapusiad, *s. m.* (hapus) A rendering, or becoming fortunate; a rendering, or becoming happy.

Hapusrwydd, *s. m.* (hapus) A fortunate state, happiness, felicity.

Har, *s. m.* (hy—ar) That is apt to rise over, to over-top, or to cover.

Hardd, *a.* (har) Towering, of fine growth; comely, graceful, handsome, neat.

Hardd pob newydd.

Every new thing is *handsome.* *Adage.*

Hyrddia haw, hardd oleuni,
Haul yr ellyllon yw hi.

She impels the tide, the *fair* luminary, the sun of the goblins is she. *D. ab Gwilym, i'r Lleuad.*

Harddawl, *a.* (hardd) Tending to render handsome, or trim; ornamental; beautifying.

Harddedig, *a.* (hardd) Being made handsome.

Harddedd, *s. m.* (hardd) Comeliness.

Harddiad, *s. m.—pl. t.* au (hardd) A rendering comely or handsome, an ornamenting, a becoming handsome.

Harddiant, *s. m.* (hardd) A rendering handsome; an ornamenting; a becoming handsome.

Harddineb, *s. m.* (hardd) Comeliness, trimness.

Harddu, *v. a.* (hardd) To tower, to grow finely.

Harddus, *a.* (hardd) Tending to render comely, or handsome, ornamental.

Harddwch, *s. m.* (hardd) Comeliness, handsomeness, beauty, ornament.

Tri harddwch synwyr: eglurdeb, cywirdeb, a newyddiadeb.

The three *ornaments* of good sense: perspicuity, accuracy, and novelty. *Barddas.*

Harddwr, *s. m.—pl.* harddwyr (hardd—gwr) One who makes handsome; one who ornaments.

Harddymddwyn, *s. m.* (hardd—ymddwyn) A handsome demeanour.

Harddymddygawl, *a.* (harddymddwyn) Of a handsome demeanour or bearing.

Harddymddygiad, *s. m.* (harddymddwyn) A behaving handsomely; genteel demeanour.

Haredd, *s. m.* (har) Calmness, the state of being appeased, or tranquillized.

Cei wawd haredd,
Heb waith caredd,
I'th drugaredd,
O'th dro goreu.

Thou shalt have panegyric of *peace* without any work of mischief, for thy mercy, on account of thy best work. *Ieu. Brydydd Hir.*

Hariad, *s. m.* (har) A covering over; an appeasing, or quieting.

Hariannawl, *a.* (hariant) Tending to appease.

Hariannu, *v. a.* (hariant) To appease, to quiet.

Hariant, *s. m.* (har) Appeasement, quietness.

Harl, *s. m.* (har) A jangle, a jingle.

Harn, *s. m.* (hy—arn) That aptly closes upon.

Harnais, *s. m.—pl.* harneisiau (harn—ais) Harness.

Chwyrnu, a chochi ei harnais—
A wna'r ci.

Snarl, and redden his *harness* would the dog do. *Llywelyn ab Owain.*

Harneisiad, *s. m.* (harnais) A harnessing.

Harneisiaw, *v. a.* (harnais) To harness.

Harneisiawl, *a.* (harnais) Harnessing, a dressing.

Harneisiwr, *s. m.* — *pl.* harneiswyr (harnais — gwr) A harnesser.

Haro, *interj.* (har) Used to slight, or contempt.

> [illegible]
>
> [illegible] *Iolo Wyn, B. Cwrg.*

Haru, *v. a.* (har) To raise over, to smother over; to appease, to tranquillize.

Hatr, *s. m.* (had) That enwraps, or covers.

Hatrawl, *a.* (hatr) Tending to cover over.

Hatriad, *s. m.* (hatr) A covering or dressing.

Hatru, *v. a.* (hatr) To cover over, to dress.

Hau, *v. a.* (ha) To strew over, to sow.

Haul, *s. m.* — *pl.* heuloedd (ha — ul) The sun.

Haw, *s. m.* — *pl. t.* od (ha) That is at the full, that is ripe; that is sluggish, an ass.

Haw, *a.* (ha) Being at the full, being fixt, sluggish, ripe.

Hawcaid, *s. f.* — *pl.* haweeidiau (hawg) A hod full.

Hawcwr, *s. m.* (hawg — gwr) A hod-man.

Hawd, *s. m.* (hy — awd) A whisk, or quick motion, as the course or sweep of a fly. *Hawd clyr y gelwid cleddyf Olifer*, the whisk of the hornets was the name of the sword of Oliver: *Mae yr yd yn ei hawd*, the corn is in its time of curing. *Sil.*

> [illegible]
>
> [illegible] *Guto y Glyn.*

Hawdd, *a.* (hy — awdd) Feasible, easy, free from difficulty.

> Hawdd cymmod lle bo cariad.
>
> *It is easy to reconcile where there is affection.* *Adage.*
>
> [illegible]
>
> [illegible] *Adage.*

Hawddammawr, *s. m.* (hawdd — ammawr) A gratulation; a welcome, good speed. *Hawddammawr iti*, a welcome to thee.

Hawddammawr, *v. a.* (hawdd — ammawr) To give gratulation, to welcome.

> [illegible]
>
> Welcome the month of May! let it come with its green mansions, the friend of love, and the winged tribe — the cuckoo and the amorous ones adore it. *D. ab Gwilym.*

Hawddammoredd, *s. m.* (hawddammawr) Welcomeness; gratulation.

Hawddammori, *v. a.* (hawdd — ammawr) To give gratulation; to welcome.

> [illegible]
>
> [illegible]

Hawddammoriad, *s. m.* (hawddammawr) A giving gratulation; a welcoming.

Hawddfaidd, *a.* (hawdd — baidd) Of a promptly daring disposition, venturesome.

Hawddfeiddiad, *s. m.* (hawddfaidd) A venturing easily, a daring without hesitation.

Hawddfeiddiaw, *v. a.* (hawddfaidd) To venture easily, or with alacrity.

> [illegible]
>
> [illegible] *Adage.*

Hawddfeiddiawl, *a.* (hawddfaidd) Apt to venture easily; apt to be intrepid.

Hawddfod, *s. m.* (hawdd — bod) Easy being; happiness; quietude.

Hawddfryd, *s. m.* (hawdd — bryd) Ease of mind, a pleasurable state of mind.

Hawddfyd, *s. m.* (hawdd — byd) Pleasure, or bliss.

> [illegible]
>
> [illegible] *Iolo Wyn, B. Cwrg.*

Hawddgar, *a.* (hawdd — car) Amiable, or lovely.

> [illegible]
>
> [illegible] *Adage.*

Hawddgarwch, *s. m.* (hawddgar) Amiableness.

Hawddged, *a.* (hawdd — ced) Free of treasure.

Hawddineb, *s. m.* (hawdd) Facility, easiness.

Hawddwaith, *s. m.* (hawdd — gwaith) Easy work.

> [illegible]
>
> [illegible] *Adage.*

Hawes, *s. f.* — *pl. t.* od (haw) A she ass.

Hawg, *s. m.* — *pl.* hogion (hy — awg) Completeness, fulness, perfection, a space of time; a good while; an age; also a box, shuttle, or hod, also a hawk. *Ni ddoi yma yr hawg*, thou wilt not come here for a good while; *Nid ei yno yr hawg hyd*, thou wilt not go there this great while: *Hawg glo*, a coal skuttle; *hawg gardd*, a garden box.

> [illegible]
>
> [illegible] *T. Aled.*
>
> [illegible]
>
> [illegible] *H. Cowyn.*

Hawg, *adv.* (hy — awg) Awhile, for some time.

> [illegible]
>
> [illegible] *D. ab Gwilym.*
>
> [illegible]
>
> [illegible] *T. Aled.*
>
> [illegible]
>
> [illegible] *T. Aled.*

Hawiad, *s. m.* (haw) A becoming full, a ripening; a becoming fixed, or sluggish.

Hawiaw, *v. a.* (haw) To render full, or mature; to fix upon, to become fixed. *Hawiaw ar beth*, to be intent upon a thing.

Hawl, *s. f.* — *pl.* holion (hy — awl) A claim, a suit, process, or cause. *Colli hawl*, to lose a suit; *hawl ddefnyddiawl*, a real action; *hawl lw*, a pending action; *hawl wyredig*, a cause that lies dormant; *hawl drablwyddyn*, a cause beyond the year, or after the time limited; *gyru hawl*, to carry on a suit, *mae y llog gymmaint a'r hawl*, the interest is as much as the claim.

> [illegible]
>
> [illegible] *Welsh Laws.*

Hawlblaid, *s. f.* — *pl.* hawlbleidiau (hawl — plaid) A plaintiff, a claiming party.

Hawlfainc, *s. f.* — *pl.* hawlfeinciau (hawl — mainc) A tribunal, a seat of justice.

Hawlwr, *s. m.* — *pl.* hawlwyr (hawl — gwr) A claimant, an enquirer after, a plaintiff.

Hawn, *a.* (hy — awn) Eager, brisk, full of activity.

Hawni, *s. m.* (hawn) Eagerness; briskness, alacrity; slight work; loose threads, or ravelines, flue, or down.

Hawni, *v. a.* (hawn) To run over, to stitch slightly. *Nid ydyw ond wedi ei hawni*, it is only slightly stitched.

Hawniad, *s. m.* (hawn) A doing over slightly; a basting, or stitching together slightly.

Hawnid, *s. m.* (hawn) Eagerness, briskness, hasty. *Gwaith hawnid*, hasty or careless work.

> Meingan weddeidd-wen, hoen hawnid,
> Mynygl-wen yn lien yn lle rhenid gwyrdd.
>
> The slender fair one of delicate air, the luminary of *vivacity*, with a white neck under a veil, where green is distributed. *Iorw. Fychan.*

Hawnt, *s. m.—pl. t.* iau (hawn) Alacrity, eagerness; briskness, vivacity, liveliness.

Hawntiad, *s. m.* (hawnt) An encouraging, or animating; a becoming brisk, or lively; encouragement.

Hawntiaw, *v. a.* (hawnt) To encourage, to animate; to become eager; to become animated.

Hawntiawg, *a.* (hawnt) Full of alacrity, brisk.

Hawntiawl, *a.* (hawnt) Tending to make brisk.

Hawntrwydd, *s. m.* (hawnt) Briskness, vivacity.

Hawntus, *a.* (hawnt) Full of alacrity, animated, brisk. *Nid wyf hawntus*, I am not hearty.

Hawr, *s. m.—pl.* horion (hy—awr) A spread out.

Hawr, *a.* (hy—awr) Tending to spread, or distend

Hawriad, *s. m.* (hawr) A spreading out.

Hawru, *v. a.* (hawr) To spread out; to dilate.

Haws, *s. m.* (hy—aws) Ease. It is also used for the *comparative* hawddach. More feasible, easier

> Haws cadw nog cirhain.
>
> It is *easier* to keep than to hunt after. *Adage.*
>
> Haws dadleu o goed nog o gastell.
>
> It is *easier* to argue from a wood than from a castle. *Adage.*

Hawsâad, *s. m.* (haws) A making easy, an easing.

Hawsach, *a.* (*comparative of* haws) More easy.

Hawsaf, *a.* (*superlative of* haws) Most easy.

Hawsâu, *v. a.* (haws) To facilitate; to give ease.

> A saith awr o rere hithau,
> O'm boew, o serch, i'm hawsau.
>
> And seven hours she also gave (the sprightly jewel) of love, *to give me ease.* *Bedo Aerdrem.*

Hawsder, *s. m.* (haws) Feasibleness, easiness.

Hawsdra, *s. m.* (haws) What is practicable.

Hawsedd, *s. m.* (haws) Freedom from difficulty.

Hawsineb, *s. m.* (haws) Practicability.

HE, *s. f. r.* Aptness for motion, a going.

He, *a.* (*f. of* hy) Bold, daring, adventurous. *Arf he*, a daring weapon.

Hëad, *s. m.* (he) A sowing; dissemination.

Hear, *a.* (he—ar) Apt to produce a sound, noisy.

> Araf haf, hear gweilgi.
>
> Calm is the summer, the torrent is *noisy*. *Gwalchmai.*

Hëawd, *s. m.—pl.* hëodydd (he) A drifting.

> Aderwr o rew dwyrain,
> No heawd eiry, gawawd gain.
>
> A fowler from the eastern frost, of the hue of the *drift* of snow, a fair shower. *D. ab Gwilym.*

Heb, *s. m.—pl. t.* ion (hy—eb) A pass, or utterance; speech.

Heb, *prep.* (hy—eb) Without, void of, destitute of, in a state of absence from. *Heb arian, ac heb werth*, without money, and without price: *heb ado un*, without leaving one: *heb ohir*, without delay:—*Hebwyf, hebddwyf, hebof*, and *hebddof*, without me: *hebod, hebot, hebddod, hebddot*, without thee: *hebo, hebddo*, without him, without it: *hebi, hebddi*, without her: *hebom*, or *hebddom*, without us: *heboch, hebddoch*, without you: *hebynt, hebddynt*, without them.

> Achaws heb achaws o bono.
>
> A cause *without* a cause of it. *Adage.*
>
> Ethyw corn heb ysgyfarn.
>
> The horn is become *without* an ear. *Adage.*
>
> Heb Dduw heb ddim, a Duw a digon.
>
> *Without* God *without* any thing, with God with (having) enough *Adage.*
>
> Drwg yw dryg-was, gwaeth yw bod hebddo.
>
> Bad is a bad servant, worse to be *without him*. *Adage.*

Heb, *adv.* (hy—eb) Without; by, beside.

> Mal ydd oeddynt yn myned heb gastell a elwid Espartenum, eu cyrchu a orug Brutus.
>
> As they were going *by* a castle that was called Espartenum, Brutus attacked them. *Gr. ab Arthur.*

Hebawl, *a.* (heb) Uttering, relating to utterance.

Heber, *s. m.—pl.* hebyr (heb) That serves for locomotion; a foot.

Hebgor, *s. m.* (heb—cor) The dispensing with.

Hebgor, *v. a.* (heb—cor) To put aside, to omit, to leave as unnecessary, to spare, to dispense with, or to be able to do without.

> Na fydd ry fwythus lle galler dy hebgor.
>
> Be not over nice where thou mayest be dispensed with. *Adage.*

Hebgoradwy, *a.* (hebgor) Dispensable.

Hebgorawl, *a.* (hebgor) Being dispensed with.

Hebgoredig, *a.* (hebgor) Being dispensed with.

Hebgori, *v. a.* (hebgor) To dispense with.

Hebgoriad, *s. m.* (hebgor) A dispensing with.

Hebiad, *s. m.* (heb) An uttering, utterance.

Heblaw, *prep.* (heb—llaw) Beside; over and above. *adv.* Besides, moreover.

Heboca, *v. a.* (hebog) To hunt with a hawk.

> Heboca, a hela bydd,
> A phryf gwyllt, friwiau gelltydd.
>
> He is wont to be *hawking* and hunting the sides of the cliffs after the wild beast. *R. Cyffin.*

Hebog, *s. f.—pl. t.* au (heb) A hawk. *Hebog chwyldro*, a gerfalcon: *hebog dramor*, a peregrine falcon: *hebog wlanawg*, a lanner: *hebog marthin*, a goshawk: *hebog yr ehedydd*, a hobby hawk.

> Y penhebogydd a ddyly ei anrhydeddu o dair anrheg, y dydd y laddo ei hebog un o dri aderyn; ai bwn, ai creyr, ai garan.
>
> The chief falconer ought to be honoured with three presents, the day whereon his *hawk* shall kill one of three birds: either a bittern, or a heron, or a stork. *Welsh Laws.*
>
> Haws gwneuthur hebog o'r barcutan no gwneuthur talawg yn ddysgedig.
>
> It is easier to make a *hawk* of a kite than to make a learned man of a bumkin. *Gr. ab Arthur.*

Hebogaidd, *a.* (hebog) Being hawk-like.

Heboglys, *s. m.* (hebawg—llys) Hawkweed.

Hebogydd, *s. m.—pl. t.* ion (hebog) A hawker.

> Nid yf yr hebogydd namyn tri chornaid yn y neuadd, rhag bod gwall ar ei hebogau drwy feddwd: lestri hagen a erfyll ei wirawd yn y llys.
>
> The *falconer* drinks no more than three hornfulls in the hall, lest his hawks should be neglected through drunkenness: nevertheless vessels shall hold his liquor in the court. *Welsh Laws.*

Hebogyddiaeth, *s. m.* (hebogydd) Hawking.

Hebogyn, *s. m. dim.* (hebog) A laneret.

Hebred, *s. f.* (heb—rhed) An external course; a state of evil, in the system of transmigration; it is otherwise called *Abred*. *a.* Being in an evil state.

> A gwae ni o'r naid i'n rhyddoded,
> Yn rhygnawd pechawd, pall gymyred!
> Rhag an twyllaw byth o beth hebred,
> I golli teithi tanc afneued.
>
> And woe to us the step wherein we have been placed, under the impulse of sin, an untoward course! lest we be deceived for ever by a *devious* thing, to lose the virtues of a wished-for peace. *Gwalchmai.*

Hebredawl, *a.* (hebred) Of the circle of evil.

Hebrediad, *s. m.* (hebred) A going the circle of inchoation or the state of evil.
Hebredu, *v. a.* (hebred) To go in the course of evil, to traverse the circle of evil.
Hebrwng, *s. m.* (heb—rhwng) A mission.
Hebrwng, *v. a.* (heb—rhwng) To go with, to conduct, to accompany, to send onward, to carry, or to convey. *Hebrwng hawl*, to carry on a suit; *hebrwng iawn*, to give satisfaction; *hebrwng lledrad i wrtho*, to get clear of theft.
Hebryngad, *s. m.* (hebrwng) A sending.
Hebryngadwy, *a.* (hebrwng) That may be sent, or conducted; that may be conveyed.
Hebryngawl, *a.* (hebrwng) Missive, sending.
Hebryngedig, *a.* (hebrwng) Being conducted.
Hebryngiad, *s. c.*—*pl.* hebryngiaid (hebrwng) A conductor, an accompanier, a sender.

> Ni ros y dim [illegible] d'elych i'm cyfoeth, a mydi a fyddaf hebryngiad arnat.
>
> Nothing shall start before thee until thou comest into my dominion, and I will be a conductor to thee.
> *H. P. P. Dyfed—Mabinogion.*

Hebryngu, *v. a.* (hebrwng) To go with, to conduct, to accompany, to convey.
Hebryngwr, *s. m.*—*pl.* hebryngwyr (hebrwng—gwr) A conductor, an accompanier.
Hebryngydd, *s. m.*—*pl. t.* ion (hebrwng) A sender; a conductor, a conveyer.
Hebryngyddes, *s. f.*—*pl. t.* au (hebryngydd) A female sender; a female conductor.
Hebu, *v. a.* (heb) To utter, to speak, to say. *Hebai efe*, quoth he; *heba Meilyr*, says Meilyr; *ni heb a ohybych*, none will utter what thou shalt utter.

> Dy [illegible],
> [illegible],
> [illegible] hebu [illegible],
> [illegible] hebaf [illegible].
>
> [illegible] without thee, I do not speak [illegible]. *[illegible] engl. Hâv.*

Hebus, *a.* (heb) Tending to utter; dicacious.
Hebwr, *s. m.*—*pl.* hebwyr (heb—gwr) One who utters; a sayer.
Hebydd, *s. m.*—*pl. t.* ion (heb) An utterer.
Heciad, *s. m.*—*pl. t.* au (heg) A hopping.
Hecian, *v. a.* (heg) To halt, to hop, to limp.
Heciwr, *s. m.*—*pl.* hecwyr (heg—gwr) One who hops, or goes haltingly.
Hecyn, *s. m. dim.* (hac) A little notch, or cut.
Hecynu, *v. a.* (hecyn) To make a notch.
Hed, *s. m.*—*pl. t.* oedd (hy—ed) A flight; or the act of flying, also a hat.
Hedawg, *a.* (hed) Having power to fly; flying.
Hedawl, *a.* (hed) Volant; apt to fly; flying.
Hedeg, *s. m.* (hed) A flight, or a flying.
Hedeg, *v. a.* (hed) To fly; also to shoot out, or to ear, as corn.
Hedegawg, *a.* (hedeg) Flying, or that flies.
Hedegawl, *a.* (hedeg) Volant, flying.
Hedegu, *v. a.* (hedeg) To fly, to move by wings.
Hedhynt, *s. f.* (hed—hynt) A flying course.
Hediad, *s. m.*—*pl. t.* au (hed) A flying, a flight.
Hedin, *a.* (hed) Volatic, volant, volatile.
Hedinaw, *v. a.* (hedin) To volatilize.
Hediniad, *s. m.* (hedin) A volatilization.
Hedion, *s. pl. aggr.* (hed) Things that fly, what fly with the wind, light corn, chaff.
Hedlam, *s. m.*—*pl. t.* au (hed—llam) A flying leap.
Hedlamu, *v. a.* (hedlam) To take a flying leap.
Hednaid, *s. f.* (hed—naid) A flying leap.
Hedwr, *s. m.*—*pl.* hedwyr (hed—gwr) A flier.
Hedydd, *s. m.*—*pl. t.* ion (hed) A flier, the lark, otherwise called *ehedydd*, *uchedydd*, *meilierydd*. *Hedydd cribawg*, *hedydd copawg*, a crested lark; *cor-hedydd*, a titlark; *hedydd*, sea rocket.
Hedyn, *s. m. dim.* (hâd) One seed, a grain of seed
Hedd, *s. m.* (hy—edd) That glides onward; peace, calm, tranquillity.
Heddaberth, *s. m.*—*pl. t.* au (hedd—aberth) A peace-offering.
Heddawg, *a.* (hedd) Having peace, tranquil.
Heddawl, *a.* (hedd) Tranquil, peaceable.
Heddi, *s. m.* (hedd) The present day, this day. *adv.* To day, on this day.
Heddiad, *s. m.* (hedd) A making peace, a calming
Heddswyddawg, *s. m.*—*pl.* heddswyddogion (hedd—swyddawg) A peace-officer.
Heddu, *v. a.* (hedd) To make peace, to tranquillize, to pacify.
Heddus, *a.* (hedd) Pacific, quiet, or tranquil.
Heddusaw, *v. a.* (heddus) To make peaceful, to become pacific.
Heddusiad, *s. m.* (heddus) A making pacific.
Heddusrwydd, *s. m.* (heddus) Peaceableness.
Heddwch, *s. m.*—*pl.* heddychau (hedd) Peace, quietness; tranquillity.

> Ni ddichon, mewn heddychau,
> Na bo doeth y neb a dau.
>
> In *peace makings*, he that shall be silent cannot be less than wise. *H. Cae Llwyd.*
>
> Tri angenrheidiol beirdd Ynys Prydain [illegible], a'i ddosbarth [illegible], a gyru heddwch ar ddifrawd [illegible].
>
> The three necessary duties of the bards of the isle of Britain: to manifest the truth, and to declare it, to maintain a memorial of praise for what shall be good and excellent, and to make peace prevail over anarchy and devastation. *Barddas.*

Heddwg, *s. m.* (hedd) Tranquillity, peace.
Heddy, *s. m.* (hedd) This day. *adv.* To day.
Heddychawd, *s. m.* (heddwch) The act of making peace, pacification; tranquillization.
Heddychawl, *a.* (heddwch) Peaceable, tranquil.
Heddychiad, *s. m.* (heddwch) A pacifying; a calming, a tranquillizing, pacification.
Heddychiadawl, *a.* (heddychiad) Pacificatory.
Heddychiadu, *v. a.* (heddychiad) To pacify.
Heddychlawn, *a.* (heddwch) Peaceful, peaceable.
Heddychlondeb, *s. m.* (heddychlawn) Peacefulness, tranquillity.
Heddychlonedd, *s. m.* (heddychlawn) Quietness.
Heddychloni, *v. a.* (heddychlawn) To make quiet.
Heddychlonrwydd, *s. m.* (heddychlawn) Peacefulness, quietness.
Heddycholdeb, *s. m.* (heddychawl) Peaceableness
Heddychu, *v. a.* (heddwch) To make peace, to pacify, to appease, to tranquillize.

> [illegible], heddychu ei feddwl [illegible] Pryderi [illegible].
>
> After she had made an end, through sighing, Pryderi removed [illegible], and with his mother he came towards his brother. *[illegible].*

Heddychus, *a.* (heddwch) Peaceable, or pacific.
Heddychusaw, *v. a.* (heddychus) To render pacific; to become peaceable.
Heddychusawl, *a.* (heddychus) Of pacific tendency
Heddychwr, *s. m.*—*pl.* heddychwyr (heddwch—gwr) A peacemaker; also a liberated person.
Heddygawl, *a.* (heddwg) Tending to tranquillize.
Heddygedig, *a.* (heddwg) Being tranquillized.
Heddygedigawl, *a.* (heddygedig) Pacificatory.
Heddygiad, *s. m.* (heddwg) A tranquillizing.
Heddygu, *v. a.* (heddwg) To tranquillize.
Heddyngnad, *s. m.*—*pl.* heddyngnaid (hedd— yngnad) A justice of the peace

Heddyngneidiaeth, *s. m.* (heddyngnad) The office of a justice of the peace.

Heddyw, *s. m.* (hedd) The day present, this day. *adv.* To day, on this day.

Sy ddrwg sy heddyw ar wir;
Ar un da ni wrandewir.

That is evil is *to day* in the right; the one that is good will not be listened to. *T. Aled.*

Heddyw nid ydyw y dydd!

To day that day is not! *D. ab Gwilym.*

Hefal, *a.* (he—mal) Apt to be like; semblable.

Hefeliad, *s. m.* (hefal) A making similar.

Hefelig, *a.* (hefal) Having a similitude.

Lluniaf gant molliant, mawl hefelig,
I Fangor rhagor rhag Celliwig.

I will form a hundred panegyrics, of *similar* praise, to Bangor more excellent than Celliwig. *Gronwy Gyriawg.*

Hefelwch, *s. m.* (hefal) Similitude, semblance.

Hefelychadwy, *a.* (hefelwch) That may be made like, or similar.

Hefelychawl, *a.* (hefelwch) Tending to resemble.

Hefelychedig, *a.* (hefelwch) Being likened.

Hefelychedigaeth, *s. m.* (hefelychedig) The act of making similar, a making a resemblance.

Hefelychiad, *s. m.* (hefelwch) A likening.

Hefelychu, *v. a.* (hefelwch) To imitate, to do in like manner; to liken, to compare.

Hefelydd, *s. m.—pl. t.* ion (hefal) That is like, or similar; an equal.

Nid maeth mam mab ei hefelydd.

A mother will not nurse a boy his *equal*. *D. Ll. Mew.*

Am gano, ni fu, ni fydd,
Hoew ei fawl, ei hefelydd.

For singing, there has not been, there will not be of brisk fame, his *equal*. *Gronwy Owain.*

Hefelydd, *a.* (hefal) Similar, like, semblable.

Mordaf hefelydd, rhydd ym rhoddai.

Like Mordav, freely he would give to me. *Cynddelw.*

Hefelyddawl, *a.* (hefelydd) Imitative; likening.

Hefelyddiad, *s. m.* (hefelydd) An imitating.

Hefelyddu, *v. a.* (hefelydd) To imitate, to liken.

Hefin, *a.* (haf) Estival, summer. *Alban hefin*, summer solstice; *Alban arthan*, the winter solstice.

Hefrin, *a.* (hafr) That is spread out, or incompact.

Tri chaled byd. maen callestr, corn hydd hefrin, a chalon mab y crinwas.

The three hardest things in the world: a flint stone, the horn of a *gelt* stag, and the heart of the miser. *Trioedd.*

Hefyd, *adv.* (haf) Additionally; also, likewise, too. *conj.* In addition; also, likewise, moreover, too.

Rhaid imi gynllyfan o farf y gwr a weli di rhaco; ac ni mwynaa hefyd onid yn fyw y tynir a chyllellbrennau.

A leash is necessary for me from the beard of the person whom thou seest yonder, and it will not serve *likewise* without being plucked with wooden tweezers when he is alive.
H. Culhwch—Mabinogion.

Hefys, *s. m.* (haf) A smock, or a shift.

Heg, *s. f.* (hy—eg) That has aptness to expand.

Hegab, *s. f.* (heg—ab) A grasshopper.

Hegl, *s. f.—pl.* heglau (heg) A leg, a shank. *Hegl gam*, the plough-staff.

Heglawg, *a.* (hegl) Having limbs; large limbed.

Hegr, *s. m.* (heg) That conduces to quickness.

Heiad, *s. m.* (hai) An impelling, or egging.

Heiaw, *v. a.* (hai) To impel, to egg onward.

Heiawg, *a.* (hai) Tending to egg onward.

Heibio, *adv.* (heb) By. beside, aside, to one side. *Dyna fo yn myned heibio*, there he is going by; *bwrw heibio*, to throw aside. *Dowf yn ol heibio chwi*, I shall come back by you. *Dyfed.*

Y pethau a ddelont rhagllaw, ni wyr yr engylion ddim o honynt eithr a gynnullont o'r pethau a aethant heibio, a chymaint a gan attaw Duw iddynt wybod.

The things that shall come in future, the angels know nothing of them except what they shall collect from the things that are gone *by*, and as much as God shall permit for them to know. *Elucidarius.*

Llawer gair yn wynt a â heibio.

Many a word passes *away* like the wind. *Adage.*

Heidiad, *s. m.* (haid) A swarming, a going in swarms; a flocking together.

Heidiaw, *v. a.* (haid) To swarm, to flock together; to be full of.

Heidiasant i dy y butain

They have flocked to the house of the harlot *Jeremiah* 5. 7.

Heidiawg, *a.* (haid) Abounding with swarms.

Heidiawl, *a.* (haid) Tending to swarm, swarming.

Heidda, *v. a.* (haidd) To collect or to beg barley.

Gwelais ddyn gotaes o dda,
Dannedd-hir, doe yn heidda.

I saw a person scanty of good, with long teeth, yesterday *begging barley*. *Ieu. Du'r Bilwg.*

Heiddaw, *s. m.* (haedd) Attainment; merit.

E gyrhaedd fawl, gwraidd fodd,
A'r heiddaw a'i cyrhaeddodd.

He will obtain fame in a manly way; and the *merit* has reached him. *Sim. Fychan.*

Hir bod heb——
Heliwr hydd, hael o'r heiddaw.

It is tedious to be without the pursuer of the stag, liberal of his *acquisition*. *Sim. Fychan.*

Heidden, *s. f. dim.* (haidd) A grain of barley.

Heiddiad, *s. m.* (haedd) An attaining; acquisition

Heiddiaw, *v. a.* (haedd) To obtain; to merit.

Heiddiawl, *a.* (haedd) Meritorious.

Heiddwch, *s. m.* (haedd) Attainment, acquisition.

Heiddyd, *s. m.* (haedd) Attainment; merit.

Heiedig, *a.* (hai) Tending to egg on; encouraging.

Heiernin, *a.* (haiarn) Ferrean, like iron.

Cadwyn heiernin
Am ben fy neulin.

An *iron* chain around my knees. *Aneurin.*

Heigiad, *s. m.* (haig) A producing in shoals.

Heigiaw, *v. a.* (haig) To bring forth in shoals; to produce abundantly; to shoal.

Heigied y dyfroedd.

Let the waters *bring forth abundantly*. *Genesis* i. 20.

Yr afon a heigia o lyffaint.

The river shall *teem* with frogs. *Exodus* viii. 3.

Heigiawg, *a.* (haig) Abounding with shoals.

Heigiawl, *a.* (haig) Apt to produce in shoals.

Heilgorn, *s. m.—pl.* heilgyrn (hail—corn) A drinking horn.

Heiliad, *s. m.* (hail) An acting bounteously; a ministring, or attending; a serving of liquor.

Heiliaw, *v. a.* (hail) To give abundantly, or bountifully, to minister, to serve at a feast; to serve or wait upon guests; to pour liquor. *Heiliaw gwin*, to serve wine; *heiliaw ar y brenin*, to wait upon the king.

Gwell toliaw no heiliaw.

It is better to retrench than *to lavish*. *Adage.*

Llary llawroddiad llad a llwyr ler;
Llonydd yw gantaw heiliaw haelder.

The mild munificent one of grace and perfection, pleased is he *to deal generously*. *Cynddelw. I'r argl. Rhys.*

Heiliawd, *s. m.* (hail) The act of conferring a bounty; a service at a feast.

Heiliawg, *a.* (hail) Having service; waited on.

Heiliedig, *a.* (heiliad) Being served, or attended,

Heilin, *a.* (hail) Bounteous, generous, free.

Heiliog, *s. f.—pl. t.* au (hail) A capital of a column.

Heilydd, *s. m.—pl. t.* ion (hail) A servitor.

Heilyddiaeth, *s. m.* (heilydd) Office of a servitor.

Heilyn, *s. m.—pl. t.* ion (hail) A servitor; a cupbearer, a butler, a waiter.

> Heilyn achubiad pob bro.
>
> A *cupbearer* is the saviour of every country. *Aneurin.*

Heilyniaeth, *s. m.* (heilyn) The vocation of a cupbearer or butler.

Heini, *s. m.* (hain) Fulness of motion, or life; briskness. *a.* Being brisk, or lively.

Heiniad, *s. m.* (hain) A pervading with volatility, a making full of life; a swarming with vermin.

Heiniar, *s. m.* (hain) A crop, or produce of the year.

> Hoen eiry cain heiniar coll.
>
> Of the hue of the fair snow is the *crop* of the hazels. *D. ab Gwilym.*

> A rhan a gaiff o'r heiniar,
> A'r ŷd a dyfodd o'r ar.
>
> And a share he shall have of the *produce*, and the corn that has grown from the soil. *Guto y Glyn.*

Heiniardy, *s. m.—pl. t.* au (heiniar—ty) Granary.

Heiniaw, *v. a.* (hain) To act with volatility, to pervade; to swarm, or to be full of. *Mae dy wely yn heiniaw o chwain*, thy bed is swarming with fleas. *Sil.*

Heiniawg, *a.* (hain) Teeming with, pervaded.

Heiniaw, *a.* (hain) Volatile, pervasive.

Heiniedig, *a.* (hain) Being pervaded; swarming.

Heinif, *a.* (hain) Full of vivacity, lively, cheerful, brisk.

> Teithi cerddorion cyneddfu o haelon:
> Rhan rhwy rad gorddien gwaith heinif.
>
> The talents of the minstrels are for the portraying of generous ones, the Lord will dispense supreme grace over the *cheerful* task. *Meugant.*

> Estyn lliain heinif
> Ar hyd bwrdd, lle ymwrdd llif.
>
> Spread the cloth *briskly* over the table, where the flowing liquor makes a tumult. *T. Prys.*

Heinifdra, *s. m.* (heinif) Vivacity, briskness.

Heinniad, *s. m.* (haint) A causing a contagion.

Heinniaw, *v. a.* (haint) To cause a contagion.

Heinniawg, *a.* (haint) Having a contagion.

> Da fu Rhun, ei hun fu heinniawg o serch;
> Da fu Rhydderch, gwr urddedig.
>
> Good was Rhun, who was himself *diseased* from love; good was Rhydderch, a dignified man. *Iolo Goch.*

Heintddwyn, *a.* (haint—dwyn) Pestiferous.

Heintfan, *s. f.—pl. t.* au (haint—man) Petechim.

Heintfanawl, *a.* (heintfan) Petechial.

Heintiad, *s. m.* (haint) A causing a contagion.

Heintiaw, *v. a.* (haint) To cause a contagion.

Heintiawg, *a.* (haint) Contagious; pestiferous.

Heintiawl, *a.* (haint) Contagious, epidemic.

Heintiedig, *a.* (haint) Being made contagious.

Heintnod, *s. m.* (haint—nod) Pestilence.

Heintnodawl, *a.* (heintnod) Pestilential.

Heintty, *s. m.—pl. t.* au (haint—ty) A pesthouse, or a lazaretto.

Heintus, *a.* (haint) Contagious, epidemic.

Heintusrwydd, *s. m.* (heintus) Contagiousness.

Heinydd, *s. m.* (hain) That is the seat of life.

> I'r nef gwnaed hefyd
> Tragywyddol heinydd ei hoed.
>
> In heaven was likewise established the eternal *abode* of his soul. *W. Middleton.*

Heislan, *s. f.—pl. t.* od (hais—llan) A hatchel.

> Pigau heislan o uffern
>
> The points of a *hatchel* from hell. *Syr. R. Offeiriad.*

Heislanawg, *a.* (heislan) Being hatchelled.

Heislaniad, *s. m.* (heislan) A hatchelling.

Heislanu, *v. a.* (heislan) To hatchel, to dress flax.

Heislanwr, *s. m.—pl.* heislanwyr (heislan—gwr) A hatcheller.

Heislanydd, *s. m.—pl. t.* ion (heislan) Hatcheller.

Heistain, *s. f.* (hais—tain) An utensil for whetting scythes; otherwise called *hogalen pladur*, *rhip* i *ripo pladur*, and *pren grut*.

Heisyllt, *s. f.—pl. t.* au (hais) A hatchell.

Heisylltiad, *s. m.* (heisyllt) A hatchelling.

Heisylltu, *v. a.* (heisyllt) To hatchel flax.

Heisylltydd, *s. m.* (heisyllt) A hatcheller.

Hel, *s. f.—pl. t.* oedd (hy—el) A gathering, collection, or aggregate; a haugh, or holme, a dale or a low rich meadow by a river, and collected by the water, which is sometimes overflowed; *hel-lys*, prickly saltwort. The gradation of the different sorts of land begins with *hel*; the next is *ton*; then *twyn*; then *glan*; then *bryn*; and lastly *mynydd*.

Hel, *v. a.* (hy—el) To gather, to collect; to hunt. *Hel ynghyd*, to gather together; *hel cerrig*, to gather stones; *hel gwartheg*, to collect the cattle together; *hel llwynog*, to hunt a fox; *hel bwyd*, to gather victuals, or to go a begging; *hel blew ceimion*, to gather crooked hairs, that is to stray about; *mae hi yn hel ei bywyd*, she goes a begging for subsistence.

> Brochfael ac Iddon, brodorion Hywel,
> A helynt gerddorion,
> Rhyllas a llafnau rhuddion,
> Ar lles draig yn llys dragon.
>
> Brochfael and Iddon, the comrades of Hywel, that would *collect together* the minstrels, they have been slain with ruddy blades on the part of the dragon, in the court of the chief. *Peryf ab Cedifor.*

Hela, *s. m.* (hel) A gathering, a collecting; a hunt. *Cwn hela*, hunting dogs.

Hela, *v. a.* (hel) To gather, to collect; to hunt. *Fe a heliodd lawer o bethau*, he has amassed a deal of wealth.

> Ni ellir hela Twrch Trwyth heb ueu cyffael Bwlch, a Chyfwlch, a Syfwlch, meibion Cilydd Cyfwlch,—a Glas, Glesig, a Gleisiawg, eu tri chi.
>
> The Boar of the Foam can never be *hunted* without having Bwlch, Cyfwlch, and Syfwlch, the sons of Cilydd Cyfwlch, with Glas, Glesig, and Gleisiawg, their three dogs. *H. Cilydd—Mabinogion.*

Helaeth, *a.* (hel) Spacious, extensive, wide, large, abundant, plentiful.

Helaethawl, *a.* (helaeth) Tending to make ample, spacious, or large.

Helaethder, *s. m.* (helaeth) Spaciousness, ampleness, enlargement.

Helaethdra, *s. m.* (helaeth) Spaciousness.

Helaethedig, *a.* (helaeth) Extended, amplified; diffused, enlarged, expanded.

Helaethiad, *s. m.—pl. t.* au (helaeth) A making spacious, or extensive; extension, ampliation, amplification, enlargement.

Helaethiadawl, *a.* (helaethiad) Amplifying.

Helaethiadu, *v. a.* (helaethiad) To make spacious.

Helaethiannawl, *a.* (helaethiant) Tending to amplification, or extension.

Helaethiannu, *v. a.* (helaethiant) To render amplified, to become amplified.

Helaethiant, *s. m.* (helaeth) Amplitude.

Helaethrwydd, *s. m.* (helaeth) Spaciousness, extensiveness, ampleness, wideness; abundance.

> Nid helaethrwydd heb ddigon.
>
> There is no *abundance* without enough. *Adage.*

Helaethu, *v. a.* (helaeth) To make spacious, to extend, to widen, to enlarge, to amplify.

Helaethwr, *s. m.—pl.* helaethwyr (helaeth—gwr) One who makes spacious, an amplifier.

Helaethydd, *s. m.—pl. t.* ion (helaeth) Amplifier.

Helas, *s. f.* (hal) Black saltwort.

Helbul, *s. m.—pl. t.* on (hel—pul) Anxiety, care, trouble, perplexity, solicitude.

Helbulaw, *v. a.* (helbul) To act with anxiety; to be full of care, or anxiety.

Helbulus, *a.* (helbul) Full of anxiety; anxious, perplexed, solicitous; disquieted, distressed.

Helbulusaw, *v. a.* (helbulus) To act with perplexity, to be perplexed, to be anxious.

Helbulusrwydd, *s. m.* (helbulus) An anxiousness.

Helciad, *s. m.* (helg) A prying about carefully.

Helcu, *v. a.* (helg) To pry about carefully.

Heldir, *s. m.* (hel—tir) A hunting-ground.

Heldrin, *s. m.—pl. t.* oedd (hel—trin) Business.

Heldrin, *v. a.* (hel—trin) To bustle greatly.

Heldrinedd, *s. m.* (heldrin) A bustling state.

Heledd, *s. f.—pl. t.* au (hal) A place where salt is made, a salt-pit, a salt-pan. *Heledd Wen*, Nantwich; *Heledd-Ddu*, Northwich; *Erch a Heledd*, the Orkney and some other island on the coast of Scotland.

Hwch o bob heledd.

A sow from every *salt-pit*. *Adage.*

Oer y cald——
Er pan dynwyd, wynllwyd wedd,
Yr hoel o fron yr heledd.

Cold has it been found, and pale the complexion, since the peg has been drawn from the side of the *salt pan*.
Ll. Goch ab Meurig Hen, i'r Eiry.

Helfa, *s. f.—pl.* helfëydd (hel) An aggregate, or collected heap; a hunt.

O'r naw helwriaeth, tair helfa gyffredin sydd, a thair helfa gyfarthfa, a thair helfa ddolef.

Of the nine venations, there are three common *hunts*, and three baiting *hunts*, and three cry *hunts*. *Hunting Laws.*

Helfarch, *s. m.—pl.* helfeirch (hel—march) A hunting-horse, a hunter.

Helffon, *s. f.—pl.* helffyn (hel—ffon) Hunting-pole.

Helg, *s. m.* (hel) A careful hunting about.

Helgaeth, *s. m.* (helg) What gathers round; soot.

Helgi, *s. m.—pl. t.* on (hel—ci) A hunting-dog.

Helgig, *s. m.—pl. t.* au (hel—cig) The flesh of any beast of the chace, venison.

Helgorn, *s. m.* (hel—corn) A hunting horn.

Helgyd, *v. a.* (hel) To pry about carefully; to pursue continually; to dangle after.

Helhesg, *s. m.* (hal—hesg) Stinking iris.

Helhynt, *s. f.—pl. t.* iau (hel—hynt) A course for gathering; a hunting course; course, condition, or state of being; business.

Heli, *s. m.* (hal) Brine, a salt liquor, a pickle. *Heli y mor*, sea water: *mor heli*, the briny sea: *Pwll heli*, a brine pit.

Bwrw heli yn y mor.

To throw *brine* into the sea. *Adage.*

Heliad, *s. m.* (hel) A gathering; a hunting.

Helïad, *s. m.* (heli) A seasoning with brine; a turning to brine.

Helïaidd, *a.* (heli) Of a briny quality; saline.

Helïaw, *v. a.* (heli) To season with brine.

Helïawg, *a.* (heli) Abounding with brine, briny.

Heliedig, *a.* (heliad) Gathered, hunted.

Helig, *a.* (hel) Willow, made of willows.

Ni chaf, i ble'dd af o ddig!
Un tal ond gariawnt helig;
O chaf finnau wych feinwen,
Bagl goll a geiff bygel gwen.

Where will my anger lead me? I shall not obtain one reward but *willow* garland, but should I then obtain the splendid nymph, a hazel crook shall come to the lot of the fair one's swain.
T. Aled.

Helion, *s. pl. aggr.* (hel) Gatherings; gleanings.

Heliwr, *s. m.—pl.* helwyr (hel—gwr) A gatherer, or collector; a huntsman, a hunter.

Gair heliwr am ei gi.

A *huntsman's* word of his dog. *Adage.*

Yr anifel a helier fydd ar arddelw yr heliwr cyntaf, hyd oni ymchwelo, ei wyneb parth a'i gartref, a'i gefn ar yr hely.

The animal that is to be hunted shall belong to the first *huntsman*, until he turns his face towards his home, and his back upon the hunt. *Welsh Laws.*

Helm, *s. f.—pl. t.* ydd (hel) A stack, or rick.

Helmawg, *a.* (helm) Being stacked, or ricked.

Helmiad, *s. m.* (helm) A forming into stacks.

Helmu, *v. a.* (helm) To make a stack, to stack.

Helogan, *s. f.* (hal) Wild celery, smallage.

Help, *s. m.—pl. t.* au (hel) Help, assistance.

Helpiad, *s. m.* (help) A helping, or aiding.

Helpu, *v. a.* (help) To help, to aid, to assist.

Helpwr, *s. m.—pl.* helpwyr (help—gwr) A helper.

Helw, *s. m.* (hel) Possession, ownership.

Helwi, *v. a.* (helw) To have possession, to own.

Helwriaeth, *s. m.* (heliwr) Huntsmanship.

O'r naw helwriaeth, tair helfa gyffredin sydd; carw, haid wenyn, a gleisiad.

Of the nine *venations* three are common hunts: a stag, a swarm of bees, and the salmon. *Welsh Laws.*

Hely, *s. m.* (hel) A gathering, a collection; a hunt, a chase.

Tair hely rydd, haid wenyn ar wrysgen, a llwynog, a dyfrgi, can nid oes adlam iddynt.

The three free *hunts*, a swarm of bees upon a bough, and a fox, and an otter, for to them there is no retreat. *Welsh Laws.*

Hely, *v. a.* (hel) To gather, to collect; to hunt.

Os a neb i hely, a gillwng ar anifel, a chyfarfod o gwn segur ag ef a'i ladd, y cwn cyntaf bieufydd, onid cwn y brenin fydd y rhai segur.

If any body should go *to hunt*, and should start after an animal, and should fresh dogs meet with it, and kill it, the first dogs are entitled to it, except the fresh ones are the king's dogs.
Welsh Laws.

Helyaidd, *a.* (hely) Venatic, relating to hunting.

Helydd, *s. m.—pl. t.* ion (hel) A hunter, venator.

Helyddes, *s. f.—pl. t.* au (helydd) A female hunter.

Helyddiaeth, *s. m.* (helydd) The vocation of a hunter; hunting, venation.

Helÿedig, *a.* (hely) Being hunted as game.

Helyg, *s. pl. aggr.* (hal) Willows; the salix. The varieties are, *helyg llwydion*, *helyg duon*, *helyg ffreinig*, *helyg y cwn*, and *merhelyg*. *Gwinllan helyg*, a plantation of sallows. *Mon.* Lovers were accustomed to make garlands of the willows, and of the birch; but one forsaken was presented with a *ffon gollen*, or hazel stick, instead of the other; probably punning upon the words *coll*, hazel, and *coll*, a loss.

Tra fu'r prif-feirdd heirdd, hardd weision cerddiawn,
Cyflawn o dri-ddawn ymadroddion,
Nid ef a berchid berchyll son debyg,
Grwth helyg terig tor goluddion.

In the time of the high primary bards, the elegant ministers of song, full of the three talents of eloquence, no honour was given to what is like the pigs in tone, the dirty gut-breaking fiddle of *willows*. *Ior. Goch.*

Helygbren, *s. m.* (helyg—pren) A willow tree.

Helygen, *s. f.* (helyg) A willow, a willow tree.

Helyglwyn, *s. m.—pl. t.* i (helyg—llwyn) A grove of willows.

Helyglys, *s. m.* (helyg—llys) Willow herb.

Helynt, *s. f.—pl. t.* iau (hel—ynt) A gathering course; a hunting expedition, business, affair, concern, condition of life. *Mae yn ddrwg dy helynt*, thou art in a bad plight.

Fy holl helynt i a fynega Tychicus i chwi.

All my *concern* Tychicus will declare unto you.
Colossians, iv. 7.

Helyntiad, *s. m.* (helynt) A transacting business.
Helyntiaw, *v. a.* (helynt) To engage in business.
Helyntiawg, *a.* (helynt) Having a concern, or business in hand.
Helyntiwr, *s. m.—pl.* helyntwyr (helynt—gwr) One who is engaged in a concern.
Helyth, *s. m.—pl. t.* au (hel) A stock of a family

[illegible]

The most [illegible], of pure race, will for ever [illegible] to every [illegible]. *[illegible]*

Hell, *a.* (*f. of* hyll) Ugly, unsightly, frightful.
Hellgre, *s. f.* (hell—cre) An ugly hag, a witch.
Helltni, *s. m.* (hallt) Saltness, brinishness.
Hem, *s. f.—pl. t.* iau (hy—em) A hem, a border.
Hemiad, *s. m.* (hem) A hemming, a bordering.
Hemiant, *s. m.* (hem) A hemming, a border.

[illegible]

[illegible] by the side of the streams. [illegible]

Hemiaw, *v. a.* (hem) To hem, or to border.
Hemiawl, *a.* (hem) Hemming or bordering.
Hen, *s. m.—pl. t.* ion (hy—en) Age, antiquity, oldness. *Hen* is old, in the Armenian and Burmese languages.

[illegible]

[illegible] through agedness [illegible] over the stream. *[illegible]*

Hen, *a.* (hy—en) Far advanced; old; aged. *adv.* Quite, fully. *Dyna hen ddigon*, that is quite enough.

[illegible]

Death is mature for the *aged*. *Adage*

[illegible]

It is better to [illegible] the *old* than to beat him *Adage.*

Henad, *s. m.* (hen) A becoming old, or aged.
Henadur, *s. m.—pl. t.* on (henad) An elder.
Henaduriad, *s. m.—pl.* henaduriaid (henadur) An elder; a presbyter.
Henaduriaeth, *s. m.* (henadur) Eldership.
Henaf, *a.* (*superlative* of hen) Most ancient.
Henafaidd, *a.* (hen) Somewhat old, oldish, elderly.
Henafgwr, *s. m.—pl.* henafgwyr (henaf—gwr) The eldest man; the chief man.
Henafiad, *s. m.—pl.* henafiaid (henaf) Ancestor.
Henafiaeth, *s. m.—pl. t* au (henaf) Ancestry.
Henain, *a.* (hen) Full of age, aged, ancient.
Henaint, *s. m.* (henain) Old age, agedness, age.

A glywaist ti gant Cywryd Caint,
A [illegible] lawer haint
[illegible]

Didst thou hear what Cywryd Caint hath sung, who suffered many a disease [illegible] *Engl. y Clywed.*

Hendad, *s. m.—pl. t.* au (hen—tad) A grand-father; otherwise called *taid*, and *tad cu*.
Hendaid, *s. m—pl.* hendeidiau (hen—taid) A great grandfather.
Hendeb, *s. m.* (hen) Oldness, or agedness.
Hender, *s. m.* (hen) Agedness, antiquity.
Hendra, *s. m.* (hen) Agedness, antiquity.
Hendref, *s. f.—pl. t.* ydd (hen—tref) An old or established habitation, the same as a *gaeafdy*, or winter house, being opposed to the *hafotty*, or the temporary residence in the mountains, to attend the flocks, during the summer months; also the inhabited country as distinguished from the high grounds, or mountains. It forms the name of many old mansions, as, *Hendref Gadog*, *Hendref Hywel*, *Hendref Urien*, *Hendref Forion*, *Hendre'r Mur*, *Hendre'r Coed*.
Hendrefa, *v. a.* (hendref) To make an abode.

[illegible] hendrefa.

Let us go to heaven to *fix an abode*.

Hendrefiad, *s. m.* (hendref) A fixing an abode.
Hendrwm, *a.* (hen—trwm) Heavy with age.
Henddyn, *s. m.—pl. t.* ion (hen—dyn) An old or aged person.
Henddynaidd, *a.* (henddyn) Old mannish.

[illegible]

Bent in its form, and straight, youthful, and very *old mannish*. *T. [illegible]*

Henefydd, *s. m.—pl. t.* ion (henaf) A senator.

[illegible]

And the *elder* shall be placed on the left side. *Welsh Laws*

[illegible]

[illegible] the ready hand; [illegible] *elder*! *Cyn. [illegible]*

Henefyddiaeth, *s. m.* (henefydd) Eldership.
Heneidd-dra, *s. m.* (henaidd) Oldness, agedness
Heneiddiad, *s. m.* (henaidd) A growing old.
Heneiddiaw, *v. n.* (henaidd) To grow old.

[illegible]

I grow old, it withers like the foliage of the [illegible], from day to day, my life daily draws to an end, without knowing [illegible] away. *[illegible]*

Heneiddiawl, *a.* (henaidd) Tending to grow old.
Heneiddrwydd, *s. m.* (henaidd) Agedness, oldness
Henfab, *s. m.—pl.* henfeibion (hen—mab) An old bachelor.

[illegible]

A toy in the hand of an *old bachelor*. *Adage.*

Henfam, *s. f.—pl. t.* au (hen—mam) A grandmother; otherwise called *nain* and *mam gu*.
Henferch, *s. f.—pl. t.* ed (hen—merch) An old maid
Henfon, *s. f.* (han—mon) An epithet for a cow, in the bardic theology.

Newydd bennyg yn henfon.

New guts in a *cow of renovation*. *Adage.*

Pawb yn llosgwrn ei henfon.

Every one at the tail of his *cow of renovation*. *Adage.*

Henfonfa, *s. f.* (henfon) The stall of the cow of transmigration. *Henfon*, and *Henfonfa*, seem to have been terms used in the simple state of society, when each habitation had one cow.

[illegible]

Without a monkey, without a *milch cow stall*, without a [illegible]. *Taliesin.*

Henfri, *s. m.—pl. t.* au (hen—bri) An ancient prerogative or privilege.
Hengan, *s. f.* (hen—can) An old song, an adage.
Hengaw, *s. m.—pl. t.* on (hen—caw) A great great great grandfather, an ancestor in the fifth degree.
Hengof, *s. m.—pl. t.* ion (hen—cof) Tradition.
Heni, *s. m.* (hen) Antiquity, agedness.
Henlladd, *a.* (hen—lladd) Being of an old cut. *Cynud henlladd*, fuel of an old cut, or that is quite dry.
Henlleu, *s. m.* (hen—lleu) An old beehive.
Henllydan, *s. m.* (hen—llydan) Round birthwort *henllydan y ffordd*, greater plantain.
Hennain, *s. f.* (hen—nain) A great grandmother.

Heno, *s. f.* (han) The night present. *adv.* To night, on this night.

> Ystafell Cynddylan, ys digariad heno,
> Gwedy'r neb pieu fad:
> Wi o angeu, by'r a'm gad!

The hall of Cynddylan, it is deserted *to-night*, after him that was its goodly possessor: ah death, why does he suffer me to remain! *Llywarch Hen.*

Henoed, *s. m.* (hen—oed) Decline of age.

Henoeth, *s. m.* (han—oeth) The present night. *adv.* to night, on this night.

> Handid Barddyl aflawen,
> Henoeth, a llihoeydd amgen;
> Yn Aber Lleu lladd Urien.

Let Barddyl be disconsolate *to-night*, being without the leader of armies: in Aber Lleu was Urien slain. *Llywarch Hen.*

Henu, *v. n.* (hen) To grow old, or antiquated.

> Ni hena ceudawd.

The bosom *will* not *grow old*. *Adage.*

> Ni hena eiddigedd.

Jealousy *will* not *grow old*. *Adage.*

Henur, *s. m.* (hen—ur) An elder, an ancient.

> Neus dug o Gawrnur
> Meirch gwelw gostrodur
> Teyrnon henur.

Will not Cawrnur bring pale steeds, prancing, of the sovereign *elder*. *Taliesin.*

Henuriad, *s. m.—pl.* henuriaid (henur) An elder.

Henw, *s. m.—pl. t.* au (enw) A name.

Henwad, *s. m.* (henw) A naming, a nomination.

Henwadawl, *a.* (henwad) Nominative.

Henwaith, *s. m.* (hen—gwaith) Old work.

Henwawl, *a.* (henw) Nominal, or titular.

Henwedig, *a.* (henw) Being named, nominated.

Henwedigaeth, *s. m.* (henwedig) Nomination.

Henwedigawl, *a.* (henwedig) Nominative.

Henwi, *v. a.* (henw) To name, to nominate.

Henwr, *s. m.* (hen—gwr) An old man.

Henwrach, *s. f.—pl. t.* od (hen—gwrach) An old woman, a decrepid hag.

Henwredd, *s. m.* (henwr) The state of an old man

> Pen a borthaf ar fy nghledd;
> Gwel ei fyw nog yn ei fedd;
> Oedd dinas i henwredd.

I bear a head upon my sword; better his being alive than in his grave: he was a bulwark for *old age*. *Llywarch Hen.*

Henwri, *s. m.* (henwr) Condition of an old man.

Henwriaeth, *s. m.* (henwr) State of an old man.

Henydd, *s. m.* (han) An origin, original, source.

> Dybi o Lydaw prydaw gyweithydd,
> Cedwyr ar gadfeirch ni pheirch eu henydd.

There will come from Llydaw a seasonable aid, men of conflict on war steeds who will not respect their *origin*. *Golyddan Armes Prydain.*

> Allmyn ar gychwyn i alltudydd,
> Ol wrth ol attor ar eu henydd.

The Germans are removing to a foreign land, retreating on each other's steps to their *native place*. *Golyddan, Armes Prydain.*

> Atchwelwynt Wyddyl at eu henydd;
> Rhydderchwynt Cymmry cadyr gyweithydd.

Let the Gwyddelians return to their *country*; let the Welsh exalt the mighty auxiliaries. *Golyddan, Armes Prydain.*

Henydd, *s. m.* (hen). An old beehive, or stock. See *Henlle.*

Henyddiaeth, *s. m.* (henydd) Origination.

Heng, *s. f.* (hy—eng) A push, or thrust. *Mi a roddaf heng iddo*, I will give him a push off.

Heng, *v. imp.* (hy—eng) Avaunt, be gone, away.

Hengu, *v. a.* (heng) To push, to squabble.

Heol, *s. f.—pl. t.* ydd (he—ol) A course, or path; a street; a road, or lane. *Dyfed. Heol y gwynt*, an epithet for the galaxy.

> Llymion yw'r dynion ar d'ol;
> Llewod yn ellio heol.

Fierce are the men after thee; lions cutting through a *way*. *D. ab Sieneyn.*

Heolan, *s. f. dim.* (heol) A lane, an alley.

Heon, *s. m.* (he) A bardic term for the Deity.

Heonllys, *s. m.* (heon—llys) Mistletoe.

Heor, *s. f.—pl. t.* au (he—gor) An anchor.

Heori, *v. a.* (heor) To anchor, to cast anchor.

Hephun, *s. f.* (heb—hun) A slumber, or a doze.

Hephunaw, *v. a.* (hephun) To slumber, to doze.

Hephunawl, *a.* (hephun) Slumbering, dozing.

Hephuniad, *s. m.* (hephun) A slumbering.

Hephynt, *s. m.—pl. t.* iau (heb—hynt) A whim, or reverie. *Pan dery hephynt yn dy ben doi yma eto*, when a whim takes thee in the head thou wilt come here again.

Hepiad, *s. m.—pl. t.* au (heb) A nodding.

Hepian, *s. m.* (heb) A nod; a slumber, a doze.

> Damunwn ar bob gwir Gymro, na roddai hun i'w lygaid, na hepian i'w amrantau, nes gweled gogoniant yr Arglwydd.

I would desire of every true Welshman, that he should not give sleep to his eyes, nor *slumber* to his eyelids, without first seeing the glory of the Lord. *E. Cyffie.*

Hepian, *v. a.* (heb) To nod, to slumber.

> Pan hapiodd i ddiawl hepian
> I'r drws i ddaeth ar draws ei dan.

When the devil happened *to nod*, out of doors he came across his fire. *Richard Hughes.*

Hepiaw, *v. a.* (heb) To nod; to slumber.

Hepiawl, *a.* (heb) Nodding; slumbering.

Heples, *s. m.* (eples) A fermentation, a brooding; a leaven. *Rhoi yn heples*, to set in fermentation, an expression used for the process of first mixing the meal, water, and yeast, in making bread: *Mae y dyn wedi myned yn heples*, the man is become in a ferment; said of a giddy person, who does not mind his business.

Hepwedd, *s. f.* (heb—gwedd) That is appropriate, or necessary; an attribute.

Her, *s. f.—pl. t.* iau (hy—er) A push or motion of defiance; a challenge. *Moes drwy her iddo*, give in spite of him.

> Heddyw i cefais hoew-ddawn;
> Her i ddoe; hwr yw ei ddawn.

To-day I obtained a splendid gift; *defiance* to yesterday; tardy is its reward. *D. ab Gwilym.*

Herawd, *s. m.* (her) A defying; a challenge.

Herc, *s. f.—pl. t.* iau (her) A jerk forward.

Herciad, *s. m.* (herc) A reaching, or extending.

Hercian, *v. a.* (herc) To reach forward quickly.

Herciannawl, *a.* (herciant) Tending to reach forward, or to catch suddenly.

Herciannu, *v. a.* (herciant) To make a quick reach, catch, or effort; to jerk.

Herciant, *s. m.* (herc) A quick reach or jerk.

Herciawl, *a.* (herc) Tending to reach quickly.

Hercu, *v. a.* (herc) To reach, to extend; to fetch.

> Cymaint ag a hercai groen yr ych.

As far as the skin of the ox *would extend*. *Gr. ab Arthur.*

Hercyd, *v. a.* (herc) To reach, to extend, to fetch.

Hercyn, *s. m.* (herc) A quick reach, or thrust.

Hergar, *a.* (her) Provocative, irritating.

Hergarwch, *s. m.* (hergar) Provocativeness.

Hergawd, *s. m.* (herc) A pushing, a push, thrust.

Hergloff, *s. m.* (her—cloff) Limping, halting.

Hergod, *s. m.* (her—cod) A stretched paunch; an unwieldy body.

Hergorn, *s. m.* (her—corn) A butting horn.

Hergorniaw, *v. a.* (hergorn) To butt with horns.

Hergwd, *s. m.* (herc) A push, a shove, a jerk.

Hergyd, *s. m.—pl. t.* ion (herc) A quick shove.

Hergydiad, *s. m.* (hergyd) A shoving away.

Hergydiaw, *v. a.* (hergyd) To push away,

Hergydiawl, *a.* (hergyd) Sharply pushing.

Heri, *s. m.* (her) A jerk, a limp; a lame leg.

Heriad, *s. m.* (her) A throwing out, a provocation; a challenge, a defiance.
Herial, *s. m.* (her) A stimulant; a goad.
Heriannawl, *a.* (heriant) Brandishing.
Heriannu, *v. a.* (heriant) To brandish.
Heriant, *s. m.* (her) A throwing out, a brandishing: a provocation; a defiance.
Heriaw, *v. a.* (her) To brandish, to make a threatening motion, to provoke, to challenge.

> Dos, trwy glod, rhaged, er hyn,
> Heria bob coeg ddihiryn.
>
> Proceeding forward, famously, notwithstanding this, and *defy* every blustering rascal. *Gro. Owain.*

Heriawg, *a.* (her) Being brandished, or shaken.
Heriawl, *a.* (her) Brandishing; irritating.
Heriwr, *s. m.—pl.* heriwyr (heriaw—gwr) A brandisher; one who makes signs of defiance.
Herlach, *s. m.* (harl) A jangle, a wrangle.
Herlawd, *s. m.—pl.* herlodau (her—llawd) A stripling, or a springal.

> Yn herlawd salw y'm galwed.
>
> A poor *stripling* thou didst call me. *D. ab Gwilym.*

Herlodes, *s. f.—pl. t.* i (herlawd) A hoeden.
Herlodesaidd, *a.* (herlodes) Like a hoeden.
Herlotiad, *s. m.—pl.* herlotiaid (herlawd) A stripling; a tall gawky.

> Herlotiaid yw'r hil sanch.
>
> *Striplings* are the race to you. *Rhys Nanmor*

Herlotyn, *s. m. dim.* (herlawd) A stripling.
Herlu, *v. a.* (harl) To jangle; to jaw.
Herlotyn, *s. m. dim.* (herlawd) A stripling.
Herodr, *s. m.—pl.* herodron (herawd) An embassador, a herald.
Herodraeth, *s. m.* (herodr) Embassy.
Herodri, *v. a.* (herodr) To go on an embassy.
Hers, *s. m.* (her) A sharp push; a contemptuous thrusting away; a flout.
Hersdin, *s. f.* (hers—tin) A frisky tail.
Hersedd, *s. m.* (hers) The act of scouting away.
Hersi, *s. m.* (hers) The act of scouting away.
Hersiad, *s. m.* (hers) A sending away in a hurry, a packing off.
Hersiaw, *v. a.* (hers) A sending away in a hurry, a packing off.
Hersiaw, *v. a.* (hers) To scout, to pack away.
Herw, *s. m.* (her) A flight; a scouting, a going about for pillage.

> Myned ar herw hyd yn Lloegr— a orug.
>
> Go on a *ramble* as far as into England was what he did. *Dr. Rhenallt— Mabinogion.*

Herwa, *v. a.* (herw) To range about, to fly from place to place; to wander; to scout, to hunt for spoil; to harry.
Herwad, *s. m.* (herw) A ranging, a flying from place to place; a scouting; a hunting for spoil.
Herwawl, *a.* (herw) Ranging, prowling.
Herwlong, *s. f.—pl. t.* au (llong) A privateer.
Herwlongwr, *s. m.—pl.* herwlongwyr (herwlong—gwr) A privateer man.
Herwm, *s. m.* (her) The gloss of dressed leather.
Herwr, *s. m.—pl.* herwyr (herw—gwr) One who fleeth; a scout; a fugitive; a depredator. *Herwr mor*, a sea rover. *Porthiant herwr*, subsistence of the fugitive; a contribution levied by the lords marchers in certain districts, towards the support of vagrants, with a view to preserve the country from their depredations.
Herwriad, *s. m.* (herwr) The act, or condition of a fugitive; a pillaging, or depredation.
Herwriaeth, *s. m.* (herwr) Vagrancy; a roving.
Herwriaw, *v. a.* (herwr) To lead a roving life.
Herwth, *s. f.* (he—rhwth) The strait gut.
Herwydd, *prep.* (her—gwydd) Because, for, with respect to, on account of; after, according to; by, with, the agency. *Herwydd hyn*, because of this; *herwydd cyfraith*, according to law.

> Yn wir ni ymladdai neb
> Yn union yn ei wyneb;
> O herwydd fel ddihirwaith,
> Ei gefn a droe at y gwaith.
>
> Indeed no body would fight him directly face to face; *because*, like a thing disliked, his back he would turn to that work. *T. Prys, i Elis Prys.*

Hesb, *a.* (*f.* of hysb) Dry, dried up, barren.

> Ni char buwch hesp lo.
>
> A *barren* cow does not like a calf. *Adage.*

Hesbin, *s. f.—pl. t.* od (hesb) A ewe of a year old.
Hesbinhwch, *s. f.* (hesbin—hwch) A young sow.
Hesbwrn, *s. m.—pl.* hesbyrnlaid (hesb—gwrn) A hoggerel, a young sheep.
Hesg, *s. pl. aggr.* (hy—asg) Sedges, sedge, rushes. *Mor-hesg*, the sea rushes, or mat rushes.
Hesgen, *s. f.* (hesg) A single sedge, or rush.
Hesglif, *s. f.* (hesg—llif) A two-handled saw, a whipsaw.
Hesglwyn, *s. m.—pl. t.* i (hesg—llwyn) A sedge-bed; a grove of reeds.
Hesgyn, *s. m.—pl. t.* au (hesg) A sieve, or riddle.

> Hesgyn, dwy geiniawg a dal,
> Hesgyn helyg un geiniawg.
>
> A *sieve*, its value is two pence: a willow *riddle*, one penny. *Welsh Laws.*

Hesor, *s. f.—pl. t.* au (he—sor) A hassock.
Hestawr, *s. f.—pl.* hestoran (hy—estawr) A measure equal to two bushels.
Hestoraid, *s. f.—pl.* hestoreidiau (hestawr) As much as a two bushel measure contains.
Het, *s. f.—pl. t.* iau (hed) A hat. *Het helyg*, a crown of willows.
Hetiad, *s. f.—pl.* hetieidiau (het) A hatful.
Hetiwr, *s. m.—pl.* hetwyr (het—gwr) A hatter.
Hetys, *s. m.* (hed) A small space, short space.
Heu, *v. a.* (he) To sow, to scatter about.

> Oni heuir ni fedir.
>
> If there should be no sowing there will be no reaping. *Adage.*

Heuad, *s. m.* (heu) A sowing, semination.
Heuawl, *a.* (heu) Relating to sowing.
Heuddadwy, *a.* (haedd) That may be reached; attainable; that may be deserved.
Heuddedig, *a.* (haedd) Being reached, or attained; deserved, merited.
Heuddiad, *s. m.* (haedd) A reaching; a meriting.
Heuddu, *v. a.* (haedd) To reach, to attain.
Heuedydd, *s. m.—pl. t.* ion (heuad) A sower.
Heulaw, *v. a.* (haul) To shine as the sun; to sun, to solate. *Mae hi yn heulaw*, the sun is shining, or it shines; *pan heulo*, when the sun shines.
Heulaidd, *a.* (haul) Sunlike; solar; solary.
Heulawd, *s. m.* (haul) The shining of the sun.
Heulawg, *a.* (haul) Sunny, sunshiny; solary.
Heuledd, *s. m.* (haul) Sunniness; sunshine.
Heulen, *s. f. dim.* (haul) A gleam of sunshine through fleeting clouds.
Heulenu, *v.* (heulen) To throw gleams of sunshine.
Heulfa, *s. f.—pl. t.* on (haul) A solary.
Heulfre, *s. f.* (haul—bre) A sunning hill.
Heulgi, *s. m.—pl. t.* on (haul—ci) A mock sun; also called *ci haul*, and *mab haul*.
Heuliad, *s. m.* (haul) A sunning; insolation.
Heuliadu, *v. a.* (heuliad) To give a sunning.
Heulor, *s. m.—pl. t.* ydd (haul) A half door.

Heulorsaf, *s. f.—pl. t.* ion (haul—gorsaf) A solstice. ***Heulorsaf haf***, or ***alban hefin***, summer solstice; ***heulorsaf gauaf***, or ***alban arthan***, winter solstice.

Heulorsafawl, *a.* (heulorsaf) Solstitial.

Heulrawd, *s. f.* (haul—rhawd) The ecliptic.

Heulrod, *s. f.—pl. t.* au (haul—rhod) A sun cap, a cap to keep off the sun; a glory, or circle of rays surrounding the head.

> Heulrod y sydd imi o groen pysg; a hono am fy mhen, mi a safaf rhag bron Hu, pan fo yn ciniawa; a mi a fwytâaf gydag ef, ac a yfaf, heb gyngoraf arnaf.
>
> I have a *cap* of the skin of a fish; with that on my head, I will stand before Hu, when he is dining; and I will eat with him, and I will drink, without any notice being taken of me. *H. Cor. Meg.—Mabinogion.*

Heulwen, *s. f.* (haul—gwen) The sunshine.

Heulyd, *s. m.* (haul) Sunshine; sun-heat.

> Heulyd fodd, hael wyd o farn,
> Hywel deg.——
>
> Like the *sunshine*, thou art liberal in opinion, fair Hywel. *Iolo Goch.*

Heuraw, *v. a.* (haer) To assert, to vindicate.

> Pan yrer y Gwyddel allan ynfyd ydd heurir ei fod.
>
> When the Irishman is turned out *it will be asserted* that he is a simpleton. *Adage.*

Heurawl, *a.* (haer) Assertive, or positive.

Heuredig, *a.* (haer) Asserted, or affirmed.

Heuredigaeth, *s. m.—pl. t.* au (heuredig) The act of asserting, or vindicating; an assertion.

Heuredd, *s. m.* (haer) Positiveness; vindication.

Heurgar, *a.* (haer) Apt to assert, or to affirm.

Heurgarwch, *s. m.* (heurgar) Aptness to assert.

Heuriad, *s. m.* (haer) An asserting; an assertion.

Heuriannawl, *a.* (heuriant) Vindicatory.

Heuriannu, *v. a.* (heuriant) To vindicate.

Heuriant, *s. m.* (haer) An assertion; vindication.

Heus, *a.* (he—us) Apt to surround.

Heusaw, *v. a.* (heus) To protect, to keep.

Heusawr, *s. m.—pl.* heusorion (heus) Herdsman.

> Wedi rhyddhau Gwrtheyrn, lladd a orugant y Prydeiniaid, megis bleiddiau yn lladd defaid mewn cail, wedi ydd adawai eu heusawr hwynt.
>
> After liberating Vortigern, they slew the Britons, like wolves killing sheep in a fold, after being left by their *shepherd*. *Gr. ab Arthur.*

Heuslau, *s. pl. aggr.* (heus—llau) Sheep-lice.

Heusleuen, *s. f. dim.* (heuslau) A sheep-louse.

Heusori, *v. a.* (heusawr) To act as a herdsman.

Heuwr, *s. m.—pl.* heuwyr (heu—gwr) A sower.

Heuydd, *s. m.—pl. t* ion (heu) A sower.

Hew, *s. m.* (he) A call of defiance. ***Hew iti***, defiance to thee, or I defy thee; ***hew gwaethaf iti***, I defy thee thy worse.

Hewcri, *s. m.* (hewgr) Pertness, sauciness.

Hewgr, *a.* (hew) Pert, insolent, hectoring.

Hewgrach, *s. m.* (hewgr) Pertness, insolence.

Hewiad, *s. m.* (hew) A defying, a hectoring.

Hewian, *v. a.* (hew) To defy continually, or often.

Hewrach, *s. m.* (hew) A wrangling, a squabble.

Hewyd, *s. m.—pl. t.* on (he—gwyd) Passion, zeal.

> ——Hwyr ydd a hiraeth
> Hewyd yn y fron-giwyd frau.
>
> Long will regret remain a *passion* in the frail bosom. *D. ab Ieuan Ddu.*

Hewydus, *a* (hewyd) Passionate, zealous.

Hewydusaw, *v. n.* (hewydus) To become passionate; to become zealous, or ardent.

Hewydusrwydd, *s. m.* (hewydus) Passionateness; the state of being impassioned; zealousness.

Hewydd, *s. m.* (haw) Maturity, ripeness.

Hewyn, *s. m.* (haw) That is ripe, or mature.

HI, *s. f. r.* A female, a she; a woman.

Hi, *pron. f.* (hi, *s.*) She, a female spoken of.

> Ni ad ymi, hyn a wn,
> Hi ai fyn hyn a fynwn.
>
> *She* will not suffer me to have, this I know; *she* will not have that which I would wish. *D. ab Ivan Wenl.*

Hic, *s. f.—pl. t.* ion (hy—ic) A snap, or quick noise; a trick.

> Nid oes ynddo na hic na hoc.
>
> There is in him nor *trick* nor deceit. *Adage.*

Hiced, *s. f.—pl. t.* ion (hic) Trick; cheat. ***Nid oes ond yr hiced a'r hoced rhyngddynt***, there is nothing but sharp give and sharp take between them.

> Hiced a ladd hoced.
>
> *Trick* will murder deceit. *Adage.*

Hicell, *s. f.—pl. t.* i (hic) A bill with a long handle used in cutting briers.

Hiciad, *s. m.* (hic) A tricking; a cheating.

Hiciaw, *v. a.* (hic) To snap, to catch suddenly.

Hid, *s. m.* (hy—id) Aptness to run; continuity.

> Mab Madawg, llaw-ddeawg lleuddid,
> I fawr fyw i fawr-feirdd pob hid.
>
> The son of Madoc of the dexterous hand of splendour is greatly to live to the eminent bards of every *connexion*. *Ll. P. Moch, i Gr. ab Cynan.*

Hidl, *s. m.* (hid) A strainer, a colander, a sieve.

Hidl, *a.* (hid) Distilling, dropping abundantly; flowing; dropping as out of a sieve. ***Wylaw yn hidl***, to shed tears abundantly.

Hidlaid, *a.* (hidl) Distilling, dropping; being run through a strainer.

> Dywallaw di, fenestr, fedd hidlaid melus;
> Ergyrwaew gwrys goch ays yn rhaid,
> O gyrn buelin balch oreuraid.
>
> Pour thou, cupbearer, the *distilled* mead delicious; the spear impelling spirit causing sweat in the toil, out of the buffalo horns proudly ornamented with gold. *O. Cyfeiliawg.*

Hidlaidd, *a.* (hidl) Tending to distil, or to drop.

Hidlaw, *v. a.* (hidl) To distil; to run, or strain through a strainer.

> Amlaf cwrw tra hidler.
>
> Most abundant is the ale whilst *it runs through a sieve.* *Adage.*

Hidlddeigr, *a.* (hidl—daigr) Tear-distilling.

Hidledig, *a.* (hidl) Distilled, strained in a sieve.

Hidliad, *s. m.* (hidl) A distilling, a dropping.

Hidlion, *s. pl. aggr.* (hidl) Strainings, droppings.

Hidlus, *a.* (hidl) Apt to distil, or to drop. ***Wylaw yn hidlus***, to shed tears abundantly. *Sil.*

Hidlwr, *s. m.—pl.* hidlwyr (hidl—gwr) A distiller; one who strains liquid.

Hif, *s. m.—pl. t.* ion (hy—if) A skin, or surface.

Hifiad, *s. m.* (hif) A peeling off the skin; a plucking off wool.

Hifiaw, *v. a.* (hif) To pluck off the skin; to pluck off wool, or hair, to strip.

Hifiawg, *a.* (hif) Being peeled, or stripped.

Hifiawl, *a.* (hif) Peeling, stripping, plucking.

Hifiedig, *a* (hifiad) Peeled, stripped, plucked.

Hifiwr, *s. m.—pl.* hifwyr (hif—gwr) One who peels, strips, or plucks off.

Hifyn, *s. m. dim.* (hif) A skin, a piece of skin. ***Hifyn hafog***, an hermaphrodite.

Hiff, *s. m.—pl. t.* ian (hy—iff) A flake; a drift. ***Hiff o eira***, a flake of snow.

> Ei dwy fraich——
> Pe cawn gan ddyn eu dodi
> Am fy nghorff, lliw hiff ar don
> Ni rwystrai f'm calon dori.
>
> Her two arms, if I could prevail on the fair to extend round my bosom, she that is of the hue of the *foam* on the wave, would prevent my heart from breaking. *G. Iolo.*

Hiffiad, *s. m.* (hiff) A throwing in flakes; a drifting, or flaking.

Hiffiant, *s. m.*—*pl.* hiffiant (hiff) A flaking.

> Y mae fy mron yn don am dani,
> Un wen liw'r hiffiant, o'i llwyr hoffi.
>
> My heart is broken on her account, she that is fair like the *foam*, from loving her to excess. *Gr. Morgn.*

Hiffiaw, *v. a.* (hiff) To cast in flakes; to drift.

Hiffiawg, *a.* (hiff) Being flaked, flaky; drifted.

Hiffiawl, *a.* (hiff) Tending to flake, flaky; drifting.

Hiffl, *s. m.*—*pl. t.* au (hiff) A gush through.

Hifflaid, *v. a.* (hiffl) To gush through the surface. *Gwaed yn hifflaid*, blood gushing out.

Hifflaw, *v. a.* (hiffl) To gush through the skin.

Hiffliad, *s. m.* (hiffl) A gushing, a running out.

Hiffyn, *s. m. dim.* (hiff) A flake; what is drifted.

Hil, *s. f.*—*pl. t.* ion (hy—il) A particle, piece or fragment: an emanation; issue, produce, progeny. *Tori yn hilion*, to break in pieces. *Sil.*

Hilen, *s. f.* (hil) A bearing female.

Hilgeirch, *s. pl. aggr.* (hil—ceirch) Tail oats.

Hiliad, *s. m.* (hil) An emanation; a producing, or generating.

Hiliadaeth, *s. m.* (hiliad) A production.

> Goreu hiliadaeth, gre o greyg.
>
> The best for production is a stud of mares. *Adage.*

Hiliant, *s. m.* (hil) Offspring, issue, or progeny.

> Am ei roi yn gymmhar ewig,
> Cewch, yn y parc a furciwn,
> Ladd cant o hiliant hwn.
>
> For giving him as a mate for the doe, you shall, in the park that I would m ke, kill a hundred of his *progeny*. *T. Prys i efyn corw.*

Hiliaw, *v. n.* (hil) To emanate; to yield, to produce; to bring forth.

> Da hil ceirch gan ddrwg gynnog.
>
> The oats *yield* well from the bad tub. *Adage.*

Hiliawd, *s. m.* (hil) Production; a getting issue.

Hiliawg, *a.* (hil) Having increase, having issue.

Hilig, *a.* (hil) Productive, procreative. *s. m. dim.* One that is produced or begotten.

> Gwystl bedydd byd eilig,
> Yn muchedd baeloni hilig.
>
> The pledge of baptism of the transient world, in the productive state of generosity. *Cynddelw, i O. Gwynedd.*
>
> Canaf cathl gwynfyd gwenleufer,
> Golochaf glew hael hilig Naf Ner.
>
> Singing the hymn of the happiness of the splendid light, I will adore the gracious intrepid *one begotten* of the supreme Cause. *Meigant, i Gadwallawn.*

Hiliogaeth, *s. f.*—*pl. t.* au (hiliawg) Offspring.

Hiliogaethawl, *a.* (hiliogaeth) Contributing to propagation, apt to propagate.

Hiliogi, *v. a.* (hiliawg) To render prolific; to have issue; to procure issue.

Hilion, *s. pl. aggr.* (hil) Small particles, pieces, or fragments; emanations.

Hiliwr, *s. m.* (hil—gwr) One who gets issue.

Hilus, *a.* (hil) Being in small particles, or pieces; being broken in pieces. *Sil.*

Hilyn, *s. m. dim.* (hil) A small particle, or part; an emanation.

Hill, *s. m.*—*pl. t.* ion (hy—ill) An augmentation.

Hilliaw, *v. a.* (hill) To augment, or to add.

Hin, *s. f.* (hy—in) The weather, the temperature of the air.

> Bwa'r hin heb un llinyn,
> Y sydd bedwar defnydd dyn.
>
> The bow of the sky, without a string, is of the four elements of man. *L. G. Cothi.*
>
> I ochel awel auaf
> I ufel annufn uddufn yr af.—
> Yn iach fromin yr hinon
> Yn iach em llywiadr a'n ion,
> Yn iach y cogau [illegible]
> Yn iach hin hinfinlaw haf,
> Yn iach yr haul [illegible]
>
> To avoid the winter gale, I will go to the lower world profound: then farewell thou sovereign of *serene skies*, farewell our director and our ruler; farewell the cuckoo's [illegible]. farewell the *shining* weather, the early summer; farewell thou sun! *D. ab Gwilym.*

Hinaw, *v. n.* (hin) To alter the weather.

Hinawg, *a.* (hin) Being affected by the weather.

Hinawl, *a.* (hin) Relating to the weather.

Hindda, *s. f.* (hin—da) Fair or calm weather.

> Gwedi drycin hindda.
>
> After a storm comes *fair weather*. *Adage.*

Hinedd, *s. m.* (hin) The state of the weather.

Hiniog, *s. f.*—*pl. t.* au (hin) A door frame.

> Aeth—
> Dros hiniog y drws unwaith.
>
> He went once over the threshold of the door. *T. Aled.*

Hinon, *s. f.* (hin) Serene, or fair weather, a clear atmosphere; halcyon days. *Hinon haf*, the serene season of summer.

> Pan yw dirn gwlith,
> A gorwy hinon,
> A meil, a meillion,
> A meddgyrn meddwon,
> Addwyn i ddragon
> Ddawn y Derwyddon.
>
> When the dew is fallen, and *serenity* reigns, and honey, and trefoils abound, and the mead-horns fall, pleasing to the sovereign the lore of the Druids. *Taliesin.*

Hinonaidd, *a.* (hinon) Apt to be fair weather.

Hinonawl, *a.* (hinon) Tending to fair weather.

Hinoneiddrwydd, *s. m.* (hinonaidd) Tendency to fair weather.

Hinoni, *v. n.* (hinon) To become serene, or calm; also to bask in the sun.

Hinoniad, *s. m.* (hinon) A clearing up of the weather; a becoming fine weather.

Hinonrwydd, *s. m.* (hinon) Serenity of the weather.

Hip, *s. m.*—*pl. t.* iau (hy—ip) A sudden tap.

Hipiad, *s. m.* (hip) A sudden tap, or tipping.

Hipiaw, *v. a.* (hip) To cast, or dash suddenly.

> Hap yw'r hwl hipio'r bel,
> Fe lab Ieuan ab Hywel.
>
> It is a chance for the hand *to tap* the ball, as the son of Ieuan ab Hywel was wont to do. *S. Cent.*

Hir, *a.* (hy—ir) Long; prolix, tedious; dilatory. *Hir ei hoedl*, American cudweed.

> Gwell hir bwyll no thrais.
>
> *Long consideration* is better than violence. *Adage.*
>
> Angen y gyhydedd hir yw bod deuddegsill, a hyd pennill o bedwar bann i unarbymtheg, deunaw, ac ugain.
>
> The requisite of the *long metricity* is a verse of twelve syllables, and the length of the stanza from four verses to sixteen, eighteen, and twenty. *Barddas.*

Hiraeth, *s. m.*—*pl. t.* au (hir—aeth) Longing; an earnest desire, or expectation; grief at parting, regret.

> Gwyw calon gan hiraeth.
>
> The heart is pained by regret. *Adage.*

Hiraethawg, *a.* (hiraeth) Subject to longing.

> Cethlydd cathlfoddawg, hiraethawg ei lef,
> Taith oddef, tuth hebawg,
> Cog freuer yn Aber Cuawg.
>
> A songster of contented song, with *grief-exciting* voice, subject to wander, with the flight of a hawk, the loud cuckoo in Aber Cuog. *Llywarch Hen.*

Hiraethawl, *a.* (hiraeth) Longing, regretting.

Hiraethiad, *s. m.* (hiraeth) A longing after, a regretting for absence.

Hiraethloni, *v. n.* (hiraethlawn) To become subject to longing, or regret, on account of absence.

Hiraethlawn, *a.* (hiraeth) Full of regret after.

> Hir yw byth, hebddo bod hebddaw;
> Hiraethlawn gymmraw gymmrwyn guddiel!
>
> Eternity is long, and how tedious it is to be without him; a *sorrowful* consternation, and alarm altogether grievous reign! *Llygad Gwr. m. H. ab Madawg.*

Hiraethlondeb, *s. m.* (hiraethlawn) Sorrow, regret, or longing, on account of absence.

Hiraethlonder, *s. m.* (hiraethlawn) A state of longing on account of absence.

Hiraethlonedd, *s. m.* (hiraethlawn) A state of longing, or grief on account of absence.

Hiraethloni, *v. n.* (hiraethlawn) To become subject to longing, or regret, on account of absence

Hiraethu, *v. a.* (hiraeth) To long; to desire, or to expect earnestly; to grieve after parting; to regret.

Hiraethaf am fab Dafydd
Mal y dall am oleu dydd.

I will grieve for the son of Dafydd like the blind for the light of day. — *L. G. Cothi.*

Hiraethus, *a.* (hiraeth) Subject to longing.

Hiraethusaw, *v. n.* (hiraethus) To become subject to longing on account of absence.

Hiraethusrwydd, *s. m.* (hiraethus) A state of longing on account of absence.

Hirais, *s. pl. aggr.* (hir—ais) The long ribs.

Hiramynedd, *s. m.* (hir—amynedd) Long suffering, patience.

Hiranadl, *s. f.* (hir—anadl) A long breath.

Hiranadlawg, *a.* (hir—anadlawg) Long-winded.

Hiranadliad, *s. m.* (hiranadl) A taking long respiration, a drawing the breath long.

Hiranadlu, *v. a.* (hiranadl) To take long respiration.

Hirbell, *a.* hir—pell) Very far, distant.

Hirbellder, *s. m.* (hirbell) Long distance.

Hirbelledd, *s. m.* (hirbell) Long distance.

Hirbwyll, *s. m.* (hir—pwyll) Deliberate caution.

Hirbwyllaw, *v. a.* (hirbwyll) To act cautiously.

Hirbwyllawg, *a.* (hirbwyll) Very cautious.

Hirbwyllus, *a.* (hirbwyll) Of great caution.

Hirchwedl, *s. m.—pl.* hirchwedlau (hir—chwedl) A long story, a prolix discourse.

Hirchwedlawg, *a.* (hirchwedl) Being prolix.

Hirchwedledd, *s. m.* (hirchwedl) Macrology.

Hirchwedlu, *v. a.* (hirchwedl) To talk tediously.

Hirchwedlus, *a.* (hirchwedl) Tedious in discourse

Hirder, *s. m.* (hir) Length, longitude.

Hirdra, *s. m.* (hir) Length, or longitude.

Hirdrig, *s. m.* (hir—trig) A long delay, a lingering. *a.* Long-tarrying.

Hirdrigaw, *v. a.* (hirdrig) To tarry long.

Hirdrigawl, *a.* (hirdrig) Long tarrying.

Hirdrigedd, *s. m.* (hirdrig) Long abidance.

Hirdrigiad, *s. m.* (hirdrig) A long tarrying.

Hirdrigiannawl, *a.* (hirdrigiant) Being of long residence, abidance or dwelling.

Hirdrigiannu, *v. a.* (hirdrigiant) To make a long residence or abidance.

Hirdrigiant, *s. m.* (hirdrig) Long residence.

Hirddydd, *s. m.—pl. t.* iau (hir—dydd) Long day.

Gwelais, pan gerddais gorddwyfr afon Rin,
Gwyl riain ued ai fon;
Gwir ddiwenol, a gwar dison,
Gwawr hirddydd, mawr harddedd Mon.

I saw, when I walked the borders of the water of the river Rhine, a bashful lady unattended; she was truly simple, and mildly silent, the ray of the *long day*, the great ornament of Mon. — *Gr. ab M. ab Dafydd.*

Hireinioes, *s. f.* (hir—einioes) Longevity.

Ni chain ymddiried i hireinioes.

To trust *to long life* will not do. — *Adage.*

Hirell, *s. m.* (hir—ell) A gleam, a beam of light; a ray of glory; an angel.

Fiamychodd hirell in uch Hafren.
Byddawd Cymry cynnull yn ddiwgywen.

The *flash* flamed over the region of Hafren, let the Welsh be splendidly collected. — *Taliesin.*

Hirfod, *s. m.* (hir—bod) Long abidance.

Hirfraich, *s. f.—pl.* hirfreichiau (hir—braich) A long arm. *a.* Long armed; long-handed.

Hirfryd, *s. m.* (hir—bryd) An even mind.

Hirfrydig, *a.* (hirfryd) Of even mind, of long bearing mind; magnanimous.

Hirfrydig a yfo ei holldda.

Magnanimous is he that will drink his whole wealth. — *Adage.*

Hirfrydigrwydd, *s. m.* (hirfrydig) Magnanimity.

Hirgadw, *v. a.* (hir—cadw) To keep long.

Hirglust, *s. f.—pl. t.* iau (hir—clust) A long ear. *a.* Long-eared.

Hirglwyf, *s. m.* (hir—clwyf) Long sickness.

Hirglyw, *a.* (hir—clyw) Being long eared.

Hirgrwn, *s. m.* (hir—crwn) A cylinder. *a.* Cylindrical, of the form of a roller.

Hirgrynawl, *a.* (hirgrwn) Cylindrical.

Hirgrynedd, *s. m.* (hirgrwn) Cylindricalness.

Hirgul, *a.* (hir—cul) Long and narrow.

Hirgwyn, *s. f.—pl. t.* ion (hir—cwyn) Long complaint. *a.* Long-complaining.

Hirgwynaw, *v. a.* (hirgwyn) To complain incessantly, to moan continually.

Hirgwynfan, *v. a.* (hirgwyn) To moan incessantly

Hirgylch, *s. m.—pl. t.* au (hir—cylch) Ellipsis.

Hirgylchaidd, *a.* (hirgylch) Elliptic, or oval.

Hirgylchawl, *a.* (hirgylch) Elliptical, oval.

Hirgylchiad, *s. m.* (hirgylch) A forming an ellipsis.

Hirgylchu, *v. a.* (hirgylch) To form an ellipsis.

Hirhegl, *s. f.—pl.* hirheglau (hir—hegl) A long shank, or long legged.

Hirheglawg, *a.* (hirhegl) Having long shanks.

Hirheglyn, *s. m.* (hirhegl) Long-legged spider.

Hirhoedl, *s. f.* (hir—hoedl) A long life.

Hirhoedlawg, *a.* (hirhoedl) Long-lived.

Hirhoedledd, *s. m.* (hirhoedl) Longevity.

Hirhoedli, *v. n.* (hirhoedl) To live a long life.

Hiriad, *s. m.* (hir) A lengthening; a prolongation.

Hiriain, *a.* (hir) Having length; far-extending.

Cadell hirell hiriain.

Cadell of the *long-extending* gleam. — *Cynddelw.*

Hirian, *s. m. dim.* (hir) A tall lank person, a gangrel. The same as *Climach*, *llabwst*, and *lleban*.

Hiriannawl, *a.* (hiriant) Tending to prolong.

Hiriannu, *v. a.* (hiriant) To prolong; to delay.

Hiriant, *s. m.* (hir) Length, continuity; distance, remoteness; delay, or putting off.

Hiriau, *s. f.—pl.* hirieuau (hir—iau) A long yoke, which went with eight oxen.

Hiriaw, *v. a.* (hir) To lengthen, to prolong.

Hiriell, *s. m.* (hirell) A gleam, or beam of light; a ray of glory; an angel.

Dymgwallofied i win———
Yn arfmig gaer, ger hiriell ban.

I have been cherished with wine in the Arvonian city, near the region of the *beam of glory*. — *Gwalchmai.*

Carwyr hyriawg o hiriell,
Gwenwyn y byd a'i gwnai'n bell.

Lovers of the gentle *angel*, the envy of the world removes him far. — *Deio Ddu o Ben Adeiniol.*

Hirlas, *s. m.* (hir—glas) An epithet for a drinking-horn; also the name of a celebrated ode by *Owain Cyfeiliawg*, prince of *Powys*.

Menestr, a'm gwithaw na'm adawed!
Estyn y corn, er cyd yfed,
Hiraethlawn am lyn lliw ton nawfed,
Hirlas ei arwydd aur ei dudded.

Cupbearer, who soothes me to silence let it not leave me; reach the horn for the sake of conviviality, impatiently longing for the liquor of the hue of the ninth wave, Hirlas its characteristic, its cover gold. — *O. Cyfeiliawg.*

Hirlid, *s. m.* (hir—llid) Continued anger.

Hirlidiad, *s. m.* (hirlid) A bearing long anger.
Hirlidiaw, *v. n.* (hirlid) To bear long anger.
Hirlidiawg, *a.* (hirlid) Of long continued anger.

> [illegible] —
> [illegible] hirlidiawg.
>
> [illegible] of heroic virtue in the career of the *unforgiving* course.
> *Llygad Gwr.*

Hirnos, *s. f.* (hir—nos) A long night.

> Eidduned [illegible] hirnos.
>
> The desire of the fugitive in a *long night*. *Adage.*

Hirnych, *s. m.* (hir—nych) A long affliction.
Hirnychawl, *a.* (hirnych) Tediously afflictive.
Hirnychdawd, *s. m.* (hirnych) Tedious affliction.

> Pob hirnychdawd i angeu
>
> Every *tedious affliction* leads to death. *Adage.*

Hirnychiad, *s. m.* (hirnych) A long affliction.
Hirnychu, *v. n.* (hirnych) To suffer long affliction
Hiroddef, *s. m.* (hir—goddef) Long suffering.
Hiroed, *s. m.* (hir—oed) Long abidance.
Hiroedi, *v. n.* (hiroed) To abide long; to make a long delay or putting off.
Hiroediad, *s. m.* (hiroed) A long-abiding; a delaying for a long time.
Hiroediawg, *a.* (hiroed) Of long abidance.
Hirwlych, *a.* (hir—gwlych) Incessantly wet.
Hirwlychu, *v. a.* (hirwlych) To wet continually. *A'm hirwlych dagrau*, I am continually bathed in tears.
Hirwlydd, *s. m. aggr.* (hir—gwlydd) Common hair-moss
Hirwlydd, *a.* (hir—gwlydd) Of continual mildness.

> — —Y fun, [illegible] ddefnydd,
> Ag ym [illegible] o dra newydd,
> Am [illegible] a grudd hirwlydd.
>
> The nymph, of celestial [illegible] her frame, has fixed me to consume from excess of surprise, on account of the long circling eyelash and cheek ever *mild*. *Gwalchmai.*

Hirwron, *a.* (hir—gwron) Long-circling.
Hirwst, *s. m.* (hir—gwst) Persevering anxiety.
Hirwyl, *s. f.* (hir—gwyl) A long watch.
Hirwylaw, *v. a.* (hir—wylaw) To weep incessantly, to keep weeping continually.
Hirwyliad, *s. m.* (hirwyl) A long watching.
Hirwyliaw, *v. a.* (hirwyl) To watch patiently.
Hitr, *s. m.* (hid) That is loose, or flaccid.
Hitrwm, *s. m. dim.* (hitr) One with broken testicles; a fribble.
Hityn, *s. m. dim.* (hid) A sorry fellow, ragamuffin
Hithau, *pronom. preposition.* (hi—tau) She also, she likewise, and she.
HO, *s. m. r.* Aptness to utter; an exclamation; a call upon, a prayer. *Interjection* of calling, or exclamation. *Ho, ho, ai felly mae!* Oh, oh, is that the way it is!
Hob, *s. m.—pl. t.* au (hy—ob) Any thing having an aptness to rise, throw, or swell out; a swine; a measure of various capacities, in different parts of Wales; it is a peck, in Glamorganshire; four bushels, in Caermarthen; and a third of a quarter, in Denbigh.

> [illegible]
>
> [illegible] were they called heretofore, and now they are called swine.
> *H. Culhwch — Mabinogion.*

Hobaid, *s. f.—pl.* hobeidiau (hob) The contents or capacity of a *hob*.
Hobel, *s. m.—pl. t.* au (hob) What hops, or starts suddenly; a bird, or fowl.

> [illegible]
> A [illegible]
>
> [illegible]
> [illegible]

> Trech [illegible], tro [illegible],
> [illegible].
>
> [illegible] his wrath, hover above him, whilst his *arrow is going* [illegible]
> *[illegible] i'r chedydd.*

Hobeliad, *s. m.* (hobel) A hopping, a hobbling.
Hobelu, *v. a.* (hobel) To hop, to caper.
Hobyn, *s. m.—pl. t.* au (hob) A deal at cards. It is otherwise called *gyr*.
Hoc, *s. f.* (hy—oc) A scythe for cutting brambles
Hoced, *s. f.—pl. t.* ion (hoc) Cheat, deceit, juggle

> [illegible] gwan, o fewn ei garn,
> Ryw hocedion i'r cadarn.
>
> The weak, within his retreat, will play some *tricks* to the strong.
> *T. Ald*

Hocedaidd, *a.* (hoced) Apt to cheat, tricking.
Hocedawl, *a.* (hoced) Cheating, tricking.
Hocediaeth, *s. m.* (hoced) The act of cheating.
Hocedlaes, *a.* (hoced—llaes) Slily cheating.
Hocedu, *v. a.* (hoced) To cheat, to deceive.
Hocedus, *a.* (hoced) Cheating, deceitful, juggling
Hocedwr, *s. m.—pl.* hocedwyr (hoced—gwr) A cheater, or one who plays tricks.
Hocedydd, *s. m.—pl. t.* ion (hoced) A cheater; a cheating knave.
Hocr, *s. m.* (hawg) That goes on, or increases.
Hocrell, *s. f.—pl. t.* od (hocr) A girl, a wench.

> Hocrell [illegible].
>
> A kind unblemished *girl* delicate and good. *D. ab Gwilym.*

Hocrellaidd, *a.* (hocrell) Like a girl, girlish.
Hocrellwr, *s. m.—pl.* hocrellwyr (hocrell—gwr) A wencher.
*Hocys, *s. pl. aggr.* (hoc) The mallow, otherwise called *meddalai*, or assnager. *Hocys cyffredin*, common mallows; *hocys bendigaid*, hollyhock; *hocys y gors*, *hocys y morfa*, marsh mallows; *hocysen wyllt*, musk mallow; *hocysen y mor*, or *mor-hocysen*, a tree mallow.
Hoch, *s. f.* (hy—och) An effort to cast up phlegm.
Hochi, *v. a.* (hoch) To hawk, to throw up phlegm
Hochiad, *s. m.* (hoch) A hawking up phlegm.
Hod, *s. f.—pl.* hotiau (od) A hood, or cap.
Hodi, *s. m. aggr.* (hawd) Wild shrubs, or brakes.
Hodi, *v. n.* (hawd) To shoot out; to ear; the same as *hedeg* and *hedu*.
Hodiad, *s. m.* (hawd) A shooting out, or earing.
Hodn, *s. m. dim.* (hawd) That breaks out, or shoots.
Hodni, *s. m.* (hodn) The state of breaking, or shooting out; devastation, or ravage.
Hoddawl, *a.* (hawdd) Of a flexible, or easy nature
Hoddiad, *s. m.* (hawdd) A rendering facile, or flexible; a yielding facility.

> Yn [illegible], yn heddwch, yn hedd,
> Yn hoddiad, yn hawdd [illegible].
>
> In rejoicing, in peace, in tranquillity, in *invitation*, in the ease of the [illegible]. *Cynddelw.*

Hoddiaw, *v. a.* (hawdd) To render facile, to make flexible, or easy; to become easy, or accessible

> Cyfred [illegible], a hawdd [illegible] Creawdr,
> A llwyr gredydd [illegible],
> A llafur, a [illegible],
> A chyfiaw, hoddiaw, hwyliaw hedd.
>
> Experience a burden, and with praise adore the Creator, and in perfect faith to [illegible], with [illegible], and anxiety, and [illegible] of the body, to have dealings, *to facilitate*, to traverse the [illegible].
> *Gwalchmai.*
>
> Dyro Dad, yn [illegible], [illegible] difraw,
> Dwrodd [illegible], [illegible], a hodd ew [illegible].
>
> Father, to him of placid countenance, freely grant honour free from dread, and *to enjoy* peace. *Seisyll.*

Hoe, *s. f.* (ho) Respite, quiet, rest.

> Pump rhinwedd offeren Sul [illegible] yn hoe dy bwrdd
>
> The five virtues of the Sunday mass; one is that thy *table* will be quiet. *Barddas Cymru.*

Hoean, *s. f.*—*pl. t.* au (hoe) Respite; ease.
Hoeana, *v. a.* (hoean) To take respite, to rest.
Hoed, *s. m.* (hy—oed) A stay, a delay; grief on account of absence.

> Cywrain cadwyr cyfarfuant
> Y'nghyd, yn unfryd yd gyrchasant
> Byr eu hoedl, hir eu hoed ar eu carant!

Well trained warriors met together, with one mind they made the assault, short their lives, long their *regret* to their friends! *Aneurin.*

> Hiraethawg fy nghof y'nghywelthas,
> Hoed erddi, a mi geodi yn gas!

Oppressed with longing is my memory in society, *regret* on her account, and I hated by her! *H. ab Owain.*

Hoeden, *s. f.*—*pl. t.* od (hoed) A coquette.
Hoedena, *v. a.* (hoeden) To flirt, to hoiden.
Hoedenaidd, *a.* (hoeden) Somewhat hoidenly.
Hoedenawl, *a.* (hoeden) Flirting, wanton.
Hoedenedd, *s.* (hoeden) Wantonness of a hoiden.
Hoedl, *s. f.*—*pl. t.* au (hoed) Life, the duration of life, or term of existence.

> Yr hoedl, er hy I fo'i haros,
> A dderfydd yn nydd a nos.

Life, however long its duration may be, will end in a day and night. *Adage.*

Hoedlawg, *a.* (hoedl) Having life, or lived.
Hoedledd, *s. m.* (hoedl) The state of living.
Hoedlfyr, *a.* (hoedl—byr) Short-lived, mortal.

> Gwyr a gryssiasant, buant gydnaid,
> Hoedlfyrion meddwon uch medd hidlaid.

Men hastened to arms, they were of one pace, *short-lived ones*, drunk over distilled mead. *Aneurin.*

Hoedli, *v. n.* (hoedl) To live, to lead a life, to pass through life.

> Cynnysgaeth Dofydd i gynnif Dafydd,
> I gynnal ei delthi,
> Gan glod, a gorfod gofri.
> Gwyr, a thir, a hir hoedli!

May the grace of the Supreme be to the prowess of Dafydd, to maintain his prerogatives, with fame and splendid victory, men, and land, and *to live long!* *Gwalchmai.*

Hoedd, *s. m.* (hy—oedd) That is forward, or exposed. *a.* Exposed, public.
Hoeddawl, *a.* (hoedd) Tending to expose.
Hoeddi, *v.* (hoedd) To bring forward, to expose.
Hoeddiad, *s. m.* (hoedd) Exposition, a publishing.
Hoeddus, *a.* (hoedd) Exposed, or notorious.
Hoeddusaw, *v. a.* (hoeddus) To render notorious.
Hoeddwr, *s. m.*—*pl.* hoeddwyr (hoedd—gwr) An exposer, a publisher.
Hoeg, *s. f.* (ho—eg) That is pervasive; green.
Hoel, *s. f.*—*pl. t.* ion (haw—el) A nail, spike.

Pentrulu a ddyly——pedair pedol unwaith yn y flwyddyn i gan y gof llys, ac eu to o hoelion.

The patron of the family is entitled to four horse shoes once in the year from the smith of the palace, and their sets of *nails*. *Welsh Laws.*

Hoelen, *s. f. dim.* (hoel) A small nail, a nail.
Hoeliad, *s. m.* (hoel) A fastening with nails.
Hoeliaw, *v. a.* (hoel) To nail, to fasten with nails.
Hoeliawg, *a.* (hoel) Having nails, fastened by nails
Hoeliedig, *a.* (hoel) Nailed, fastened with nails.
Hoeliwr, *s. m.*—*pl.* hoelwyr (hoel—gwr) A nailer.
Hoen, *s. f.* (ho—en) Complexion; good appearance, good plight; a joyful countenance, gladness; liveliness. *Hoen ewyn llyn*, the hue of the foam of the lake; *hoen blodau haf*, the colour of the summer flowers.

> Rhoes awen im' dros enyd
> A hoen o fewn hyn o fyd.

He gave me for a while the muse, and the *bloom of health* in this transient world. *Parch. D. Llwyd.*

> Hael ddidaer wen-glaer haul i win-glawr Mon,
> Hoew-liw manod Ionawr,
> Hun a'm lludd deurudd dyrawr
> Hoen ton ogledd Wynedd wawr

Bounteous and mild brightly shining and to the wide region of Mon, of the glittering hue of January's drifted snow, my bathed cheeks are debarred of sleep, thou who art of the *complexion* of the northern wave, the luminary of Gwynedd. *G. ab M. ab Dafydd.*

Hoenaidd, *a.* (hoen) Somewhat blithesome.
Hoeni, *v. n.* (hoen) To become complexional; to grow blithe, or merry.
Hoenus, *a.* (hoen) Complexional: of good plight; having a joyful countenance; blithesome.

> Hoenus wyf heno o'i serch.

I am *blithesome* to night with the love of her. *D. ab Gwilym.*

Hoenusrwydd, *s. m.* (hoenus) Blithesomeness.
Hoenwawr, *s. f.* (hoen—gwawr) A gairish light. *a.* Of a gaily playful light.
Hoenyn, *s. m.*—*pl. t.* au (hoen) A single hair; a springe, or gin; a slip, or leash. *Hoenynau gweithredwyr anwiredd*, the snares of the workers of iniquity.

> O hoenyn i hoenyn ydd â'r march yn gwta.

Hair after hair the horse loses his tail. *Adage.*

Hoenynu, *v. a.* (hoenyn) To set a springe.
Hoer, *s. f.*—*pl. t.* au (hoe) A hair cloth.
Hoetian, *v. a.* (hoed) To suspend; to hang in suspense; to dally, to dandle.
Hoeth, *a.* (hy—oeth) Notorious, or naked.

> Rhyfelwr——
> Was horth ei fodd a'i saeth fain.

The warrior, a *notorious* fellow with his subtile dart. *T. W. Hywel i'r angau.*

Hoew, *a.* (hoe) Alert; sprightly, lively; spruce.

> Aderyn Mai——
> Arian farchawg donlawg don,
> Urddawl air ar ddail irion,
> Hoew erddygan a ganai.

The bird of May, like a silver-coloured knight, of great note, and of high authority on the verdant leaves, a *sprightly* air would he sing. *D. ab Gwilym.*

Hoewad, *s. m.* (hoew) A rendering alert, or brisk; a becoming brisk, or sprightly.
Hoewaidd, *a.* (hoew) Somewhat alert, or brisk.
Hoewal, *s. m.* (hoew—al) Agitation of water; the whirling of a stream; an eddy; the waves formed by any thing thrown into the water. *Hoewal y maen* and *lleisiad*, the eddy formed by a rock in the stream.

> Hely'r wyf hoewal yr afon.

I am hunting the *current* of the river. *M. ab Rhys.*

> Cynt wyf at Ieuan, lle'r a gan-nyn,
> Nag awel o wynt i'r gwiail yn,——
> Ac no hoewal llif drwy ganol llyn.

I am quicker to Ieuan, where a hundred persons go, than a gale of wind to the branches of the ash, and than the *whirling* of the flood through the middle of the pool. *L. G. Cothi.*

Hoewal, *a.* (hoew—al) Whirling, eddying.

> Ef a wnai——
> Hwrdd afiwfr mal hir-ddwfr hoewal.

He would make an assault void of timidity, like the *eddying* torrent. *Cynddelw.*

Hoewaliad, *s. m.* (hoewal) A forming eddies.
Hoewalu, *v. n.* (hoewal) To whirl in eddies.
Hoewan, *a.* (hoew) Sprightly; volatile.

> Yr annuwiawl——
> Hwn o fab hoewan a fydd
> Fal manus ar fol mynydd.

The ungodly one thus so *sprightly* will be like the light chaff on the side of the hill. *W. Middleton.*

Hoewdaith, *s. f.* (hoew—taith) A brisk journey.
Hoewdeb, *s. m.* (hoew) Alertness, sprightliness.
Hoewdeg, *a.* (hoew—teg) Sprightly and fair.

> Hoen Creirwy hoewdeg a'm hudodd mal Garwy.

The complexion of Creirwy *sprightly and fair* has fascinated me like Garwy. *H. ab E. Llygliw.*

Hoewder, *s. m.* (hoew) Alertness, sprightliness.

> Nid hoewder ond cleddyf.

The only *sprightliness* is a sword. *Adage.*

Tri hoewder cerdd; hoew iaith, hoew fyfyrdawd, a hoew drefn ar y gyfansoddiad.

The three *animations of song*: spirited language, spirited thought, and a spirited arrangement of the composition. *Barddas.*

Hoewedd, *s. m.* (hoew) Alertness, sprightliness.
Hoewfalch, *a.* (hoew—balch) Briskly proud.
Hoewfalchedd, *s. m.* (hoewfalch) Sprightly pride.
Hoewfrys, *a.* (hoew—brys) Sprightly haste.
Hoewgall, *a.* (hoew—call) Quickwitted.

O'i harows bum yn oeri;
Aeth arall, hoewgall a hi.

From staying for her I have been getting cold, another *sharp-witted* is gone with her. *D. ab Gwilym.*

Hoewgalledd, *s.* (hoew—call) Quickness of wit.
Hoewgred, *s. f.* (hoew—cred) Of ready belief.
Hoewi, *v. a.* (hoew) To render alert, or sprightly; to become alert, or sprightly.
Hoewrym, *a.* (hoew—grym) Of quick energy.
Hoewserch, *s. m.* (hoew—serch) Lively affection.
Hoewwych, *a.* (hoewgwych) Of spirited bravery.
Hoewwychder, *s. m.* (hoewwych) Gay bravery.
Hof, *s. f.* (hy—of) That hangs; that hovers.
Hofiad, *s. m.* (hof) A suspending, a hanging over, a hovering; a fluctuation.
Hofian, *v. a.* (hof) To suspend, to hang over, to hover, to fluctuate, to be hanging.
Hofiaw, *v. a.* (hof) To suspend, to hang over; to hover; to fluctnate.
Hofn, *a.* (hy—ofn) Apt to intimidate, bold.
Hofni, *v. n.* (hofn) To become intimidating; to exert courage, or boldness.
Hoff, *a* (hy—off) Loved, beloved, dear, lovely.

Hoff i'w min yw iaith doethineb—
A mel dinacter dewiniaeth a'i pyrth,
A llawn-wyrth callineb.

Lovely in her lips is the language of wisdom, and the unadulterated honey of godliness supports her, and the altogether virtuous discretion. *D. Williams.*

Hoffaidd, *a.* (hoff) Tending to love; lovely.
Hoffain, *a.* (hoff) Lovely, amiable; loving.
Hoffaint, *s. m.* (hoff) Fondness, affection; love. *Rheg hoffaint*, a gift of love.
Hoffder, *s. m.* (hoff) Fondness, affection, delight
Hoffdyn, *s. m.* (hoff—tyn) A cuckold, a cornuto.
Hoffedd, *s. m.* (hoff) Fondness, affection, delight.

Hanner y wledd hoffedd yw.

Fondness is half the banquet. *Adage.*

Hoffi, *v. n.* (hoff) To delight in, or to love.
Hoffain, *v. n.* (hoff) To be about loving.

Fagwyn,—
A'r llinyn ar dyn ar dy ddeheu,
A llinon rhag bron rhag bro Eurgain,
Tyrfa clawdd Offa cled yn hoffain.

Descending, with the string on the stretch towards the ... ... and the other shaft by the breast before the region of Eurgain, the host of Offa's dyke, *seeking after fame*. *E. ab Gwgawn, i Lywelyn I.*

Hog, *s. m.* (og) The act of sharpening; a whet.
Hogal, *s. f.* (hog—gal) What gives an edge; a whetstone.
Hogalen, *s. f.* (hogal) A sharpener; a whetstone.
Hogen, *s. f.—pl. t.* od (hawg) A girl nearly full grown, a young woman.
Hogenaidd, *a.* (hogen) Like a girl, girlish.
Hogenig, *s. f. dim.* (hogen) A little young woman.
Hogi, *v. a.* (hog) To sharpen, to whet, to give an edge; to irritate, to egg on. *Careg hogi*, a whetstone.

Ni bom cyhuddgar,
Ni bom athrodgar
Ni bom anhygar
I hogi angeu.

May we not be apt to accuse, may we not be detractive, may we be not void of love, *to accelerate* death. *G. ab Rhydd. Goch.*

Hogiad, *s. m.* (hog) A whetting, a sharpening.

Hoglanc, *s. m.—pl. t.* iau (hawg—llanc) A half-grown youth, a stripling.
Hogl, *s. m.—pl. t.* oedd (hawg) A hovel.
Hogldy, *s. m.—pl. t.* au (hogl—ty) A hovel.
Hogyn, *s. m.—pl. t.* od (hawg) A stripling.
Hoi, *s. m.—pl. t.* au (oi) A call of attention.
Hoiad, *s. m.* (hoi) A calling of attention.
Hoian, *s. f.—pl. t.* au (hoi) A call of attention.
Hoian, *v. a.* (hoi) To call attention; to implore. It is also used imperatively, like hark, or hear.

Oian y parchellan, hoian hoian;
Hel achwynog, Duw gwna ymchwelan.

Attend, little pig *hear thou the calls*; for the crime of the unrighteous God would make restitution. *Merddin.*

Hol, *s. m.* (hy—ol) A fetch, a bringing to. *v. a.* To fetch. *Dos i hol peth*, go to fetch some. *Sil Nol* is used for it in *North Wales*.
Holadwy, *a.* (hawl) Claimable, actionable.
Holawd, *s. m.* (hawl) Cognisance, examen.
Holedig, *a.* (hawl) Questioned, investigated.
Holedigaeth, *s. m.—pl. t.* au (holedig) Cognisance, interrogation, examination.
Holedigawl, *a.* (holedig) Interrogative.
Holfainc, *s. f.* (hawl—mainc) A tribunal.
Holgar, *a.* (hawl) Apt to question; inquisitive.
Holi, *v. a.* (hawl) To question, to demand, to interrogate; to enquire, to investigate, to sue.

A hwnw a hawl yr hen holion.

And that one will *investigate* the old questions. *L. G. Cothi.*

Holiad, *s. m.—pl. t.* au (hawl) A questioning, or demanding; an interrogation, an investigation.
Holiadawl, *a.* (holiad) Catechetic, catechetical.

Tri holiadolion addwynder: pennaeth, benyw, a dyeithr cydmarawd.

The three *claimants* of civility; a chieftain, a female, and a coequal stranger. *Kibbined Triads.*

Holiadu, *v. a.* (holiad) To put as a question.
Holiant, *s. m.* (hawl) Cognisance; examen.
Holiaw, *v. a.* (holi) To examine minutely; to separate, or to put apart.

Holiwch i mi Barnabas a Saul.

Separate for me Barnabas and Saul. *W. Salisbury, Acts xiii. 2.*

Holiedydd, *s. m.—pl. t.* ion (holiad) A questioner, an interrogator, an investigator, a claimant.
Holiedyddes, *s. m.—pl. t.* au (holiedydd) A female questioner; a female claimant.
Holwr, *s. m.—pl.* holwyr (hawl—gwr) A claimant; one who questions, an interrogator; an investigator; a plaintiff.
Holydd, *s. m.—pl. t.* ion (hawl) A questioner.
Holl, *a.* (oll) All, the whole of, every one of.
Hollallu, *s. m.* (holl—gallu) All power.
Hollalluawg, *a.* (hollallu) Almighty, omnipotent.
Hollalluogaeth, *s. m.* (hollalluawg) Omnipotence.
Hollalluogi, *v. a.* (hollalluawg) To render omnipotent or almighty.
Hollalluogrwydd, *s. m.* (hollalluawg) Almightiness, omnipotence.
Hollawl, *a.* (holl) Total, whole, entire, complete. *Yn hollawl*, altogether, or completely.
Hollbar, *a.* (holl—par) Omnific, causing all.
Hollboeth, *s. m.—pl. t.* ion (holl—poeth) A holocaust, or a burnt sacrifice.
Hollddoeth, *a.* (holl—doeth) All-wise, possessed of supreme wisdom.
Hollfath, *a.* (holl—math) Omnifarious, comprising all sorts, or varieties.
Hollfyd, *s. m.* (holl—byd) The whole world.
Hollgyfoethawg, *a.* (holl—cyfoethawg) All-powerful, possessing all things.

Hollgyfoethogrwydd, *s. m.* (hollgyfoethawg) All-powerfulness; the state of possessing all things.
Holli, *v. a.* (hollt) To slit, to split, to cleave.
Holliach, *s. m.* (holl—iach) The herb allheal.
Holliach, *a.* (holl—iach) Perfectly well: mistletoe
Hollryw, *a.* (holl—rhyw) Omnigenous.
Hollt, *s. m.—pl. t.* au (ollt) A slit, cleft, rift.
Holltawg, *a.* (hollt) Full of slits, clefts, or rifts.
Holltedig, *a.* (hollt) Being slit, cleft, or split.
Holti, *v. a.* (hollt) To slit, to cleave, to rift, to split. *Hollti y gwynt*, to cut the wind.

Dy mron—
Braidd na hyllt o'i gorwyllt gur.

My breast it nearly *splits* from its raging pain. *D. ab Gwilym.*

Holltiad, *s. m.—pl. t.* au (hollt) A slitting, a cleaving, a rifting, a splitting.
Holltwr, *s. m.—pl.* holltwyr (hollt—gwr) A slitter, a cleaver, a rifter, a splitter.
Hollus, *a.* (holl) Whole, complete, or entire.
Hollwybod, *s. m.* (holl—gwybod) Omniscience.
Hollwybodaeth, *s. m.* (hollwybod) Omniscience.
Hollwybodawl, *a.* (hollwybod) Omniscient.
Hollwybodus, *a.* (hollwybod) Omniscient.
Hollwydd, *s. m.* (holl—gwydd) Omnipresence.
Hollwyddawl, *a.* (hollwydd) Omnipresent.
Hollwyddoldeb, *s.* (hollwyddawl) Omnipresence.
Hon, *s. m.* (hy—on) That is manifest, or present to the sight.

Wynt cenynt nas cêynt, pa hon
Y ceblynt, o'r cwbl o'n dofon.

They would sing that they obtained not, (what a *manifest thing* they scandalize) the whole of our dues. *Ll. P. Moch.*

Hòn, *pron.* (*f. of* hwn) This one, this female. *Hon a hon*, such and such a female.

Gwedi bod yn honedig dyfodedigaeth Gloew Cesar i'r ynys hon, Gwydyr yn ddiannod a gynnullws holl farchogion Ynys Prydain i'w erbyn.

When the arrival of Claudius Cæsar in *this* island was become evident, Gwydyr immediately collected together all the chieftains of the Isle of Britain against him. *Gr. ab Arthur.*

Hòna, *pron.* (*f. of* hwna) That female present.
Honacw, *pron. f.* (hon—acw) That female yonder.
Hònaid, *a.* (hon) Being insisted upon; evident, well known; famous.

Bid honaid weithian, ac amlwg i bawb, pan yw ynys y gelwir Glesynfre, canys ffrydiau ac afonydd o eigion mor Hafren y sydd yn ei chylch, cyd bai priodolach ei galw cyffinydd afonydd.

Be it *known* then, and evident to every one, that it is an island which is called Glastonbury, for streams and rivers from the body of the Severn sea surround it, so that it would be more proper to call it the confines of rivers. *H. Diwedd Arthur.*

Honaw, *pron. posses.* (hon) It; him. *Dyma beth o honaw*, here is some of it. The same as *hono.*
Hònawd, *s. m.* (hon) An insisting; affirmance.
Hònawl, *a.* (hon) Positive; dogmatical, affirmative
Honc, *s. f.—pl. t.* iau (onc) A shake, a wagging.
Honcaw, *v. a.* (honc) To shake, to wag: to stagger. *Ni wiw honco pen*, it is useless to shake the head.
Honcen, *s. f.—pl. t.* od (honc) A waddling girl.
Honciad, *s. m.—pl. t.* au (honc) A wagging.
Honcian, *v. a.* (honc) To move backwards and forwards, to stagger, to waggle, to waddle.
Honciaw, *v. a.* (honc) To shake, to stagger.
Hònedig, *a.* (hòni) Being manifested; evident.
Honei, *pron. posses.* (hon) Her; it is the same as *honi.*

Dywawd Cai, dy wain di a lygrwys y cleddyf; dyro di imi i ddiod y cyllellbrennau o honei.

Saith Cai, thy sheath hath spoiled the sword; let me pull the wood splints *out of it.* *H. Culhwch—Mabinogion.*

Honeidrwydd, *s. m.* (honaid) Manifestness.
Honfas, *s. f.* (hawn—mas) A chopping knife.
Honffest, *s. f.—pl. t.* i (hawn—ffest) A tunic.

Honffest pedair ar ugaint a dal.

A *doublet* is of the value of twenty-four pence. *Welsh Laws.*

Hòni, *v. a.* (hon) To make manifest; to proclaim; to manifest; to object, to insist. *Honi cyfreithiau*, to publish laws.
Hòniad, *s. m.—pl. t.* au (hon) A making manifest, a manifestation; an insisting upon; an objecting; an asseveration, or allegation.
Hòniannawl, *a.* (honiant) Affirmative, positive.
Hònniannu, *v. a.* (hòniant) To make manifest.
Hòniant, *s. m.* (hon) Affirmance, asseveration.
Hòno, *pron.* (*f. of* hwnw) That one female at a distance, either of time or place. *Pa un a fyni ai hon, neu hòna, neu hòno?* which one wilt thou have, is it this, or that there, or such a female absent? *Y flwyddyn hòno*, that year.
Honof, *pron.* (hon) Me, following the preposition *o*, of. *Honot*, thee; *o honaw, o hono*, from him; *o honi*, out of her; *o honom*, from, of, or out of us; *o honoch*, from you; *o honynt*, from or out of them; *o hono tithau*, out of thee also; *o hono yntau*, out of him also; *o hono ninnau*, from or out of us also; *o hono chwithau*, out of you also; *o hono nhwythau*, from or out of them also.
Honos, *s. m. dim.* (hawn—os) A tall slim fellow; the ling, a sea fish so called.

——Mil ai gweiant
O fewn y plwy'n ofni plant,
Honos o wr anhunawg
Wrth raff.

A thousand in the district will see him frightening the children, the *scarecrow* of a man, never at rest, hanging by a rope. *T. Prys.*

Honsel, *s. f.—pl. t.* au (hon—sel) A handsel.
Honw, *s. m.* (hawn) That is void of motion.
Honyma, *pron. f.* (hon—yma) This female here.
Honyman, *pron. f.* (hon—yman) This female.
Honyna, *pron. f.* (hon—yna) That female there.
Hong, *s. f.* (honc) A hang; a dangling.
Hongian, *v. a.* (hong) To put to hang; to place in a wavering way; to hang, to be suspended in a loose manner, to hang danglingly.
Hongl, *s. f.—pl. t.* au (hong) That holds suspended; that displays.
Hopr, *s. m.* (hob) That swallows, that gulps.
Hopran, *s. f.—pl. t.* au (hopr) A hopper.

Dyna, ebai yr angel a'm dygasai yno, walch a gels i y'nghanol tir ango, a ddaeth mor ysgafndroed nas profodd eich mawrhydi damaid o hono erioed. Pa fodd y gall hyny fod! ebai y brenin, ac a ledai ei hopran cyfled a daiar gryn i'm llyncu.

Saith the angel who had carried me to the place, there is a wight whom I found in the middle of the land of oblivion, who came so light footed, that your highness has never tasted a morsel of him. How can that be? saith the king, and opened his *jaw* wide as an earthquake to swallow me. *Elis Wyn, B. Cwsg.*

Hopraniad, *s. m.* (hopran) A putting in the hopper; a gormandizing, a guzzler.
Hoprann, *v. a.* (hopran) To put in a hopper; to gormandize, to guzzle.
Hor, *s. f.—pl. t.* od (hy—or) That is of a bulky rotundity; swine lice.

Addfwyn gaer y sydd yn arddwyrain,
Gochawn ei meddud, ei molud gywrain;
Addfwyn ar ei hor ragor gyurain.

A pleasant fort is there towering up, I was wont to obtain its beverage of mead, its elegant praise, pleasant on its *mound*, the progeny of a primary stock. *Mic Dinbych.*

Horator, *ger.* (hawr) In spreading, or dilating.
Horen, *s. f. dim.* (hor) A fat lazy woman. *Yr horen front!* the dirty baggage!
Horgest, *s. f.* (hawr—cest) A fat paunch.
Horitor, *sup.* (hawr) To be spread about.

Horitor ei glod o gyflawnder cyrdd
Cerddorion a'i dadfer.

His fame, *to be spread abroad* from the plenitude of songs, the minstrels will be recompensed. *Cynddelw, i O. Cyfeiliawg.*

Hort, *s. m.—pl. t.* iau (hawr) Calumny, reproach.

Hortiad, *s. m.—pl. t.* au (hort) Defamation.

Hortiaw, *v. a.* (hort) To slander, to detract.

Hortiawg, *a.* (hort) Abounding with calumny.

Hortiawl, *a.* (hort) Tending to calumniate.

Hortiedig, *a.* (hortiad) Calumniated, traduced.

Hortiedigawl, *a.* (hortiedig) Calumnious.

Hortiwr, *s. m.—pl.* hortwyr (hort—gwr) A calumniator, a slanderer, a traducer.

Hortr, *s. m.—pl. t.* au (hort) A stick, or billet. *Hortrau*, billets laid upon a drying kiln; also called *preniau duon*.

Horth, *s. m.* (hawr) That is apt to spread over.

Horyn, *s. m. dim.* (hor) An unwieldy lump; a person that indulges himself. *Y fath horyn yw y dyn oco!* what a lump yonder person is! *Dyma fol-horyn*, here is a guzzle-gut.

Hos, *s. f.* (hws) A hose, or a stocking; a boot.

Hosan, *s. f.—pl. t.* au (hos) A stocking, or hose. *Hosanau botymawg*, or *hosanau lledr*, spatterdashes; *Hosanau y gog*, blue bells: also called *blodau y gog*, *esgidiau y gog*, and *blodau cranc y brain*:—*Yd yn ei hosan*, corn in its cover, or before the ears burst out.

Hosanenawg, *a.* (hosan) Wearing stockings.

Hosaneuwr, *s. m.—pl.* hosaneuwyr (hosan—gwr) A hosier.

Hosanlawdr, *s. m.—pl.* hosanlodrau (hosan—llawdr) A pair of pantaloons.

Hosanwr, *s. m.—pl.* hosanwyr (hosan—gwr) A hosier, one who sells stockings.

Hotan, *s. f. dim.* (hod) A hood or a cap.

Hotyn, *s. m. dim.* (hod) What closes round; a cap. *Hotyn esgid*, the part of a shoe closing over the instep.

How, *interj.* (ow) It expresses languor. *Hai how heno!* Heigh ho! this night!

Hoyw, *a.* (hoew) Alert; sprightly, lively, spruce, gay, jolly. It is the same as *hoew*.

HU, *s. m. r.* That is apt to pervade, or to spread over. An epithet of the Deity, in the bardic theology, descriptive of his omniscience. *Huon* is another appellation of the same import, and derived from *Hu*. The *hound*, on account of his acute scent, was adopted as the common emblem of this attribute, and which, if we may rely upon the accounts of some authors, became an object of idolatrous worship; for he is unquestionably identified in the *Heus* of *Gaul*, and the *Anubis* of Egypt.

> Dwy ryw awen, dieir, ewyby,
> Y sy'n y byd, [illegible] lwybr
> Awen gan Grist, dinhrist [illegible],
> O iawn dro, awen drwsiadl,
> Awen arall, nid [illegible] cant,
> Ar gelwydd, fodr argoeliant,
> Yr hon a gafas, gwyr HU,
> Camrwysg prydyddion Cymru.

Truly two sorts of active geniuses are there in the world, of manifest path, a genius from Christ, pleasing the assertion, of right tendency a sprightly genius, another genius, though not discreet the song, the [illegible] of falsehood, have the sun [illegible], the which, HU [illegible], the disorderly poets of Wales obtained. *Dr. S. Cent.*

> HU gadarn, [illegible] gedwadd,
> Brenin [illegible] gwin, a'r gwawd,
> Ymherawdr tir a moroedd,
> A [illegible] oll o'r byd oedd;
> A [illegible], gwedy [illegible],
> Arw [illegible] orwedd-gadr, gwiw,
> Yr dangnws [illegible],
> I'r dyn bach, a'r [illegible],
> [illegible] gan gair,
> [illegible] gan y tad iawn grair

The mighty HU is a sovereign who is a ready protector, a king [illegible] the wine, and the praise, the emperor of the land and [illegible] all of life in the world was he, after the deluge he held the strong [illegible], active [illegible], that [illegible] to man, the [illegible] and the humble wise, [illegible] it was his choice with the faithful father, the word [illegible] *Iolo Goch.*

> Ys ein
> HU gadarn, a [illegible],
> Yn [illegible] angel a [illegible],
> A [illegible] aur [illegible]

They are the oxen of the mighty HU, with a piece of his [illegible], and his fine angels, you see, and a golden harness of active [illegible] fame. *Llywelyn Moel, [illegible].*

Hu, *a.* (hu *s.*) Apt to pervade; apt; bold.

Huad, *s. m.—pl.* huaid (hu) One that traces by scent; a hound.

Huadgi, *s. m.—pl.* huadgwn (huad—ci) A hound dog, a beagle.

Huador, *s. m.—pl. t.* ion (huad) One who hunts with a hound.

Huail, *s. m.* (hu—ail) A vicegerent, a regent.

> Huail Hywel ab Meilir,
> [illegible] a [illegible].

The lieutenant of Hywel son of Meilir, will win land wherever he [illegible]. *L. G. Cothi.*

> Huail cwmwd Cyfeiliawg,
> Hyn fu no dyn, hyd Lan Dawg.

The governor of the province of Cyfeiliog was older than any man as far as Llan Dawg. *L. G. Cothi, i O. Fychan.*

Hual, *s. m.—pl. t.* au (hu—gal) A fetter.

Hualawg, *a.* (hual) Having fetters, fettered. Also a disease to which swine are subject.

Hualedig, *a.* (hual) Being fettered, or shackled.

Hualiad, *s. m.* (hual) A fettering, a shackling.

Hualu, *v. a.* (hual) To fetter, to shackle.

Hualwr, *s. m.—pl.* hualwyr (hual—gwr) A fetterer.

Hualydd, *s. m.—pl. t.* ion (hual) A fetterer.

Huan, *s. f.* (hu—an) That has aptitude to comprehend, or compass; Phœbus, the sun.

> Ni wyr neb pan
> Rudd ir bryd huan;
> Pan yw per cwnain;
> Pan yw gwyrdd brain.

Nobody knows whence the presence of the sun is made ruddy, whence the goat's beard plant is sweet; whence the crows are of [illegible] hue. *Taliesin.*

> [illegible] mor morfawd
> Pan [illegible] huan ar fan fynydd.

The bays of the sea reflect a light upon the shore when the sun shines upon a lofty mountain. *Ier. Fychan.*

> [illegible] huan haf [illegible]
> [illegible] ar adar, mygr hwyr hin.

Early rising sun of the summer, hasten thou the melodious symphony of birds, and the pleasant season of music. *Gwalchmai.*

Huanaw, *s. m.* (hu—anaw) Aptitude for harmony; that is gifted with the muse. *a.* Gifted with the muse; having a flow of harmony.

> Cerddawr huanawl [illegible] mawl,
> Cerdd heb dawl, heb dwyllaw,
> Cerdd [illegible], anhawel, anaban;
> Nid [illegible] Tyssilaw.

A minstrel that is a poetical animator praises you, with a song without cessation, without deceit; a song that is loud, not calm, not [illegible], not the hated song of the train of Tysilio. *Cynddelw.*

Huanawl, *a.* (huan) Relating to the sun, solar.

Huanred, *s. f.* (huan) The course of the sun.

Huanu, *v. a.* (huan) To diffuse sunshine.

Huarwaes, *a.* (hy—arwaes) Ready to assist.

> Huarwaes gwas,
> [illegible] drbiau,
> Pell wyr pell gorisen.

The youth willing to assist, from earth he sprang, whether he be knowing, whether he be simple. *Taliesin.*

Huarwar, *a.* (hu—arwar) Apt to assuage.

> Galofs hi [illegible] huarwar.

An herald of the tranquil fight. *Gwalchmai.*

Huawdl, *a.* (hu—awdl) Of a ready flow of verse; eloquent.

> [illegible] huawdl [illegible],
> [illegible] Lleifeiys.

May I [illegible] an eloquent song that shall be [illegible] to the court, [illegible] Lludd and Llefelys. *[illegible] Tew.*

Huawdlder, *s. m.* (huawdl) Eloquence.

Huawdledd, *s. m.* (huawdl) Eloquence.

Huawdr, *s. m.—pl.* huodron (hu—awdr) One that has aptitude to energize; one who is effable; a guider.

> Trefnawdr, llwyr huawdr lloer a huan,
> Trefnaint, a furfaint, o ffyrf amcan,
> Trefnu ammhrylen genau a gan.
> Trual gyfaddef nef, nef pob adfan.
>
> Disposer and perfect *director* of moon and sun, thou hast disposed, and hast formed, through a grand design, the rules of utterance of the lips that sing, with acknowledged exertion, of heaven, the supreme of every secondary place. *Casnodyn.*

Hucan, *s. f.—pl. t.* od (hug) The cob, a sea fowl, also called *gwylan lwyd*, or grey sea-mew. *Hucan y pysgod*, the fisherling.

Huch, *s. f.—pl. t.* ion (hy—uch) A thin cover.

Huchaw, *v. a.* (huch) To cover thinly; to film.

Huchen, *s. f.—pl. t.* au (huch) A film, a pellicle.

Huchiad, *s. m.* (huch) A generating a film.

Hud, *s. m.—pl. t.* ion (hu) Allurement, enticement, illusion, delusion, fascination, charm; juggle, or legerdemain.

> Elgyr oedd a gwr iddi,
> A thrwy hud, Uthr ai a hi;
> Gwae finnau, o gof union,
> Am ryw hud ym roi i hon!
>
> Elgyr was possessed of a husband, and through *enchantment*, Uthr ran away with her; oh, that a happy fancy would suggest some *charm* to give this fair one to me! *Ieu. Deulwyn.*
>
> Y lleidr, o hud a lledryd,
> Aeth a hon i eithaf byd.
>
> The thief, by *enticement* and craft, has taken the fair one to the extremity of the world. *D. ab Edmwnt.*

Hudadwy, *a.* (hud) That may be allured.

Hudaw, *v. a.* (hud) To allure, to entice; to delude, to fascinate; to charm; to juggle; to deceive, to beguile.

> Y fun——
> A'm hudodd i o'm hoewder.
>
> The fair one *has deceived* me out of my cheerfulness. *D. ab Gwilym.*

Hudawg, *a.* (hud) Alluring, enticing, illusive.

Hudawl, *a.* (hud) That is apt to allure, entice, delude, fascinate, or charm. *s. m.—pl.* Hudolion. An enticer, a deluder; a juggler.

> Iesu! ai hud yw'r oes hon,
> A adeilodd hudolion!
> Dail a ddygwydd bob blwyddyn;
> Dis a'i dwyll yw einioes dyn!
>
> Jesus! is this age all delusion, made up by *deceiving ones!* The leaves do every year fall; a dice with its deceit is the life of man! *L. G. Cothi.*

Hudedig, *a.* (hud) Being allured or enticed.

Hudedd, *s. m.* (hud) Allurement, enticement.

Hudgyllaeth, *s. m.* (hud—cyllaeth) Hypochondria.

Hudhwyad, *s. m.* (hud—hwyad) A decoy duck.

Hudiad, *s. m.* (hud) An alluring; fascination.

Hudiw, *s. m.* (hud) An enticing, or deluding one.

Hudlath, *s. f.—pl. t.* au (hud—llath) A magic wand; also a lubberly fellow.

> Odid ai gwypwy
> Hudlath Mathonwy,
> Yn nghoed pan dyfwy
> Ffrwythau mwy cymhrwy
> Ar lau Gwyllionwy.
>
> Perhaps it may be known, through the *magic wand* of Mathonwy, in the wood when there should more profitable fruits grow on the banks of Gwyllionwy. *Taliesin.*

Hudle, *s. m.—pl. t.* oedd (hud—lle) A decoy place.

Hudledrad, *s. m.* (hud—lledrad) A swindling.

Hudledrata, *v. a.* (hudledrad) To swindle.

Hudleidr, *s. m.—pl.* hudladron (hud—lleidr) A swindler; one who thieves by tricking.

Hudlewyn, *s. m.—pl. t.* au (hud—llewyn) An ignis fatuus, or Will with a whisp.

> Mae llawer un no wyr well na dilyn yr hudlewyn a darddodd o'r drefn a wnaed yn Nghaerfyrddin
>
> There are many who know better than to follow the *ignis fatuus*, which had sprung out of the system formed in Caermarthen. *E. Dafydd.*

Hudnwy, *s. m.* (hud—nwy) A decoy duck.

> Golwyth hudnwy, gwlith hed-naid gwyllt,
> Nad y gwellt i'th lygaid.
>
> Thou meal of the *decoy duck*, thou of wild flying leap in the dew, hinder the grass from going into thy eyes. *D. ab Gwilym, i'r llyffant.*

Hudolaidd, *a.* (hudawl) Illusive, deceptive.

Hudoldeb, *s. m.* (hudawl) Alluringness, illusiveness; deceivableness.

Hudoles, *s. f.—pl. t.* au (hudawl) A female deceiver, a siren.

> Nesewch yma meibion yr hudoles.
>
> Draw near here, children of the *enticing woman*. *Isaiah 57. 3.*
>
> Hudoles, a dawies deg,
> Hud imi ei hadameg.
>
> A *siren*, and a goddess fair, her discourse is fascination to me. *D. ab Gwilym.*

Hudolesaidd, *a.* (hudoles) Like the siren.

Hudoli, *v. a.* (hudawl) To render illusive, to render enticing, or alluring; to become delusive.

Hudoliad, *s. m.* (hudawl) A rendering illusive, or delusive; a rendering seducive.

Hudoliaeth, *s. m.—pl. t.* au (hudawl) Allurement; illusion; fascination; deception.

> Nid hudoliaeth ond ieuenctid;
> Nid ieuenctid ond ennyd awr.
>
> The only *allurement* is youth; and youth is only for the space of an hour. *Adage.*

Hudoliaethawl, *a.* (hudoliaeth) Of an alluring, or seducive tendency.

Hudoliaethiad, *s. m.* (hudoliaeth) A practising of allurement; a seducing; a deluding.

Hudoliaethu, *v. a.* (hudoliaeth) To practise seduction, allurement, or delusion.

> Rhaid ydyw bod dy ffydd yn ddiannwadal—er casedd y neb a fo yn ceisiaw dy swynogi di, a'th hudoliaethu drwy ofer-bolder y byd hwn.
>
> It is necessary that thy faith should be without wavering, notwithstanding the dislike of such as shall be attempting to inveigle thee, and *to allure* thee with the vain pursuit of this world. *Marchawg Crwydrad.*

Hudoliaethus, *a.* (hudoliaeth) Of a seducing tendency; illusive, deceivable.

Hudwalch, *s. m.—pl.* hudweilch (hud—gwalch) A bird of the lure.

Hudwg, *s. m.* (hud—gwg) A bugbear, a scarecrow; a racket for ball playing.

> A i cyflog sydd, was gafl-hir.
> I ti, y drwg hudwg hir,
> Am f'ysbiaw?
>
> Are there wages paid to thee, thou long-forked chap, thou tall and evil *elf*, for watching me! *D. ab Gwilym, i'w gysgawd.*

Hudwr, *s. m.——pl.* hudwyr (hud—gwr) An enticer, an allurer; a deceiver.

Hudwy, *s. m.* (hud) A phantom, a delusive vision.

Hudd, *s. m.--pl. t.* ion (hy--udd) A covert, a shade, a gloom; a dusk. *a.* Dusky, dark, gloomy. *Lliw hudd*, a dusky colour, that is neither black nor brown, or that cannot be distinguished; *Lle hudd iawn*, a very gloomy place; *yn yr hudd*, in the dusk. *Sil.*

Hudladwy, *a.* (hudd) That may be covered.

Huddaw, *v. a.* (hudd) To cover, to shade, to make gloomy, to darken, to become dusky.

Huddawg, *a.* (hudd) Having a shade, or cover.

Huddawl, *a.* (hudd) Covering, shading; tending to obscure, or to make gloomy; darkening.

Huddedig, *a* (hudd) Covered, shaded, darkened.

Huddedigaeth, *s. m.—pl. t.* au (huddedig) The act of covering over, a shading over.

Huddgwyr, *s. m.* (hudd—cwyr) The black cherry

Huddiad, *s. m.* (hudd) A covering or shading over; a darkening; a becoming gloomy.

Huddiannawl, *a.* (huddiant) Tending to obscure.

Huddiannu, *v. a.* (huddiant) To render obscure, or overcast, to overspread.
Huddiant, *s. m.* (hudd) A shading over; obscurity
Huddig, *a.* (hudd) Tending to be dusky, or gloomy
Huddwg, *s. m.* (hudd) That is dusky, or gloomy.
Huddygl, *s. m.* (huddwg) Condensed smoke, soot.
Huddyglyd, *a.* (huddygl) Fuliginous, sooty, reeky; abounding with soot.
Hued, *s. m.* (hu) That follows the scent.
Huelfeiddiad, *s. m.* *pl.* huelfeiddiaid (hual—beiddiad) One that dares bonds, or fetters.

> [illegible]

> There is to me a chief of the flow of gifts *that braves chains*, on [illegible] without dispute. *Hw. ab Gwgawn.*

Huelydd, *s. m.—pl. t.* ion (hual) One who fetters.
Huenig, *a.* (huan) Apt to encircle; apt to embrace, or to comprehend.

> [illegible]

> May I obtain the refuge of the splendid power of the lord of protecting generosity. *Cynddelw.*

Huenydd, *s. m.* (huan) That has aptitude to comprehend, or to contain.

> [illegible]

> A [illegible] a splendid host, the [illegible] of hell, [illegible] of a sanctuary, in the harmony of heaven [illegible] *Cynddelw.*

> [illegible]

> White-hued [illegible] the *enveloper* of the branches [illegible] over the bounds of the dales. *Ior. Fychan.*

Huenyg, *s. m.* (huan) A state of being encircled.
Huf, *s. m.* (hu—uf) That mantles, or covers over.
Hufen, *s. m.* (huf) The mantling, or top of any liquid; cream, or the top of milk.
Hufeneidd, *a.* (hufen) Resembling cream.
Hufenawg, *a.* (hufen) Having cream, creamy.
Hufenawl, *a.* (hufen) Of the nature of cream.
Hufeniad, *s. m.* (hufen) A gathering cream.
Hufenllyd, *a.* (hufen) Apt to gather cream.
Hufenu, *v. n.* (hufen) To cream, to form cream.
Hufiad, *s. m.* (huf) A mantling, a topping.
Hufiaw, *v. a.* (huf) To mantle, to overtop.
Hufiawl, *a.* (huf) Tending to mantle, mantling.
Hufyll, *a.* (huf) Humble, or submissive.
Hufylldawd, *s. m.* (hufyll) Humility, submission.

> [illegible]

> For the sake of God, let us give meat and drink, as commanded by Christ, the balm of heaven [illegible] *[illegible]*

Hug, *s. f.—pl. t.* au (hu—ug) A coat; a gown.

> [illegible]

> Retreat, I pray thee, stop the [illegible], and tear a corner of the golden coat. *[illegible]*

Hugan, *s. f. dim.* (hug) A loose coat, or cloak.
Hugawg, (hug) Wearing a coat, or cloak.
Hugawl, *a.* (hug) Belonging to a coat or cloak.
Hugwd, *s. m.* (hug) A spectre, or a phantom.
Hugyn, *s. m. dim.* (hug) A loose coat, or cloak
Hul, *s. m.—pl. t.* oedd (hu—ul) A cover; a coverlet; a mat.
Huliad, *s. m.* (hul) A covering, or decking.
Huliaw, *v. a.* (hul) To cover, to spread over.

> [illegible]

> He gave orders to deck a table for her out of his own victuals. *Judith 12. 1.*

Huliawg, *a.* (hul) Having a cover; being spread over, or decked.
Huliawr, *s. m.—pl.* huliorion (hul) A coverer, or decker; a slater.
Huliedig, *a.* (huliad) Covered over; decked.
Huliedigaeth, *s. m.* (huliedig) The act of covering, spreading over, or decking.
Hulier, *s. m.—pl. t.* au (hul) A cover, or a lid.
Huling, *s. m.—pl. t.* au (hul) A coverlet, a rug.
Hulwr, *s. m.—pl.* hulwyr (hul—gwr) A coverer, or decker; a slater.
Hult, *s. m.* (hul) A dolt, a moping fellow.
Hultan, *s. m. dim.* (hult) A stupid fellow. *Hultan y mor*, a sea-fowl called the turnstone.
Hulyn, *s. m. dim.* (hul) A coverlet, a bed-quilt.
Hum, *s. f.—pl. t.* iau (hy—um) A bat, a racket.
Human, *s. f.—pl. t.* au (hum) A racket for playing at ball.
Humanydd, *s. m.—pl. t.* ion (human) A tennis player, a ball player.
Humawg, *a.* (hum) Having a bat or racket.
Humig, *s. f. dim.* (hum) A bat, or racket.
Humog, *s. f.—pl. t.* au (hum) A bat, a racket.

> [illegible]

> No more than the ball under the *bat.* *Adage.*

Hun, *s. f.* (hu—un) A fit of sleep; a slumber.

> [illegible]

> You will believe your enemy; if he were in the grave, he would beat you, through his *sleep*, with the ladles. *L. Mon.*

Hun, *s. m.* (hy—un) Self, one's own person; regard to one's own self, or a selfish principle. It is used as a prefix in composition.
Hun, *pron.* (hy—un) Self, the same person, the same thing, self alone. *Mi fy hun*, I myself; *dy hun*, thyself; *ei hun*, he, she, or itself; *hi ei hun*, she herself. *ni*, or *nyni*, *ein hunain*, we ourselves; *eich hunain*, yourselves; *eu hunain*, themselves.

> [illegible]

> It is right for every one to save his *self.* *Adage.*

Hunan, *s. m.—pl.* hunain (hun) Self, one's own person; regard to one's self, a selfish principle. It is used as a prefix in composition.

> [illegible]

> God has conferred three things upon every being [illegible] namely, plenitude of his kind, individuality differing from that of all others, and an original [illegible] and genius, which is that of no other being; hence every being is a perfect *self*, differing from all others. *Barddas.*

Hunan, *pron.* (hun) Self, the same person.

> [illegible]

> Who is the man that shall condemn another for the fault of which he is guilty *himself.* *Adage.*

Hunanaeth, *s. m.* (hunan) Selfishness; egotism.
Hunanaidd, *a.* (hunan) Somewhat selfish.
Hunanamcan, *s. m.—pl. t.* ion (hunan—amcan) Self-purpose.
Hunanannog, *v. a.* (annog) To excite one's self.
Hunanannogawl, *a.* (hunanannog) Self-exciting.
Hunanannogiad, *s. m.* (hunanannog) Self-excitation, or a self-encouraging.
Hunanawl, *a.* (hunan) Selfish, relating to self.
Hunanbethau, *s. pl. aggr.* (peth) Self-affairs.
Hunander, *s. m.* (hunan) Selfishness, egotism.

> [illegible]

> The three evidences of godliness: a refraining from selfishness, a liberal deportment, and encouragement of every good. *Barddas.*

Hunandwyll, *s. m.* (twyll) Self-deception.
Hunandyb, *s. m.—pl. t.* ion (tyb) Self-conceit.

Hunandybiad, *s. m.* (hunandyb) Self-opinion.
Hunandybiaw, *v. a.* (hunandyb) To cherish self-conceit, to cherish self-opinion.
Hunandybiawg, *a.* (hunandyb) Self-conceited.
Hunandybiawl, *a.* (hunandyb) Self-conceited.
Hunandybied, *v. a.* (hunandyb) To cherish self-opinion, or self-conceit.
Hunandybiolrwydd, *s. m.* (hunandybiawl) Self-conceitedness.
Hunandyst, *s. m.* (tyst) Self-evidence.
Hunandystiawl, *a.* (hunandyst) Self-evident.
Hunanddoeth, *a.* (doeth) Self-wise, self-conceited.
Hunanedd, *s. m.* (hunan) Selfishness, egotism.
Hunaneiddrwydd, *s. m.* (hunanaidd) Selfishness.
Hunanfarn, *s. f.* (barn) Self-condemnation.
Hunanfarnedig, *a.* (hunanfarn) Self-condemned.
Hunanfawl, *a.* (mawl) Self-applause.
Hunanfod, *s. m* (bod) Self-existence.
Hunanfodawl, *a.* (hunanfod) Self-existent.
Hunanfodd, *s. m.* (bodd) Self-will, self-pleasure.
Hunanfoddawg, *a.* (hunanfodd) Self-pleasing.
Hunanfudd, *s. f.* (budd) Self-interest, regard to self, profit appertaining to self.
Hunanfuddiawg, *a.* (hunanfudd) Self-interested.
Hunanfwriad, *s. m.* (bwriad) Self-determination.
Hunangadwraeth, *s. m.* (hunan—cadwraeth) Self-preservation.
Hunangar, *a.* (car) Selfish, attentive to self.
Hunangariad, *s. m.* (hunangar) Self-love.
Hunangarwch, *s. m.* (hunangar) Selfishness.
Hunangeidwad, *s. m.* (ceidwad) A self-preserver.
Hunangyfiawn, *a.* (cyfiawn) Self-righteous.
Hunangyfiawnad, *s. m.* (hunangyfiawn) Self-justification.
Hunangyfiawnder, *s. m.* (hunangyfiawn) Self-righteousness.
Hunangymhariaeth, *s. m.—pl. t.* au (cymhariaeth) Self-comparison.
Hunanhanfod, *s. m.* (hanfod) Self-existence.
Hunanhawl, *s. f.* (hawl) Self-examination.
Hunanholiad, *s.* (hunanhawl) Self-examination.
Hunanhud, *s. m.* (hud) Self-delusion.
Hunanhyder, *s. m.* (hyder) Self-confidence.
Hunanhyderus, *a.* (hunanhyder) Self-confident.
Hunaniad, *s. m.* (hunan) A becoming selfish.
Hunaniaeth, *s. m.* (hunan) Identity.
Hunaniseledd, *s. m.* (iseledd) Self-abasement.
Hunanladd, *s. m.* (lladd) Self-murder, suicide.
Hunanladdiad, *s. m.* (hunanladd) A committing suicide, a killing one's self.
Hunanleiddiad, *s. m.—pl.* hunanleiddiaid (hunanladd) One who commits suicide.
Hunanles, *s. m.* (lles) Self-interest, self-benefit.
Hunanlesawg, *a.* (hunanles) Self-interested.
Hunanlesawl, *a.* (hunanles) Self-interested.
Hunanlesrwydd, *s. m.* (hunanles) Self-interestedness, the state of being beneficial to self.
Hunanoldeb, *s. m.* (hunanawl) Selfishness.
Hunanolrwydd, *s. m.* (hunanawl) Selfishness.
Hunanred, *s. f.* (rhed) A running alone. *a.* Having the power of running alone.
Hunanrediad, *s. m.* (hunanred) Self-motion.
Hunanrith, *s. m.* (rhith) Self-evidence.
Hunanryw, *s. m.—pl. t.* iau (rhyw) Homogeny.

> Hanfawdd angen, yn bennaf ac ddim, a-bair i bob peth ragddaniant, neillduolder, a pharth a chyntefin hunanryw.
>
> Essentiality, first of all, gives to every thing pre-eminence, individuality, and a primary and original *homogeny*. *Barddas.*

Hunanryw, *a.* (rhyw) Being homogeneous.
Hunanrywiawl, *a.* (hunanryw) Homogeneal.
Hunanrywioledd, *s. m.* (hunanrywiawl) Homogeneness, homogeneousness.
Hunansaf, *s. f.* (saf) A standing alone. *a.* Having the power of standing alone.
Hunansafawl, *a.* (hunansaf) Self-standing.
Hunansafiad, *s. m.* (hunansaf) A standing alone.
Hunansymud, *s. m.* (symud) Self-motion.
Hunansymudawl, *a.* (hunansymud) Self-movement.
Hunansymudiad, *s. m.* (hunansymud) A self-moving, a moving by self-power.
Hunanu, *v. a.* (hunan) To have respect to self.
Hunanwrtheb, *s. m.—pl. t.* ion (gwrtheb) Self-contradiction.
Hunanwrthebiad, *s. m.* (hunanwrtheb) Self-contradiction, a self-contradicting.
Hunanwrthebus, *a.* (hunanwrtheb) Self-contradictory, tending to self-contradiction.
Hunanymwad, *s. m.* (ymwad) A self-denial.
Hunanymwadiad, *s. m.* (hunanymwad) A self-denying, a restraining one's self.
Hunanymmod, *s. m.* (ymmod) Self-motion.
Hunanymmodrwydd, *s. m.* (hunanymmod) Self-motivity, a state of self-motion.
Hunanysawl, *a.* (ysawl) Self-devouring.
Hunaw, *v. a.* (hun) To sleep, to slumber.
Hunawg, *a.* (hun) Having sleep, sleepy, drowsy.

> Ni bydd hunawg serchawg byth.
>
> The amorous will never be *sleepy*. *Adage.*

Hunawl, *a.* (hun) Relating to one's self.
Hundwyll, *s. m.* (twyll) Self-deception.
Hundy, *s. m.—pl. t.* au (hun—ty) A dormitory.
Hundyst, *s. m.—pl. t.* ion (tyst) That is a self-evidence, self-testimony.
Hundystiawg, *a.* (hundyst) Being self-evident.
Hundystiawl, *a.* (hundyst) Being self-evident.
Hunddenawl, *a.* (denawl) Self-delusive, self-deceiving; self-enticing.
Hunddiffyn, *s. m.* (diffyn) Self-defence, care of self, self-protection.
Hunddiffyniad, *s. m.* (hunddiffyn) Self-defence.
Hunddiogeliad, *s. m.* (diogeliad) Self-preservation.
Hunddwyn, *a.* (hun—dwyn) Depriving of sleep.
Hunddygnawl, *a.* (dygnawl) Apt to exert one's self, of self-exerting tendency.
Hunddygniad, *s. m.* (dygniad) A self-exertion.
Hunddygnu, *v. a.* (dygnu) To exert one's self.
Hunddysg, *s. m.* (dysg) Self-instruction.
Hunddysgawl, *a.* (hunddysg) Self-instructed.
Hunddysgu, *v. a.* (hunddysg) To teach one's self.
Hunedd, *s. m.* (hun) A state of sleep, somnolence
Hunell, *s. f. dim* (hun) A short sleep, a nap.

> Heno ni chwsg hi hunell;
> ——ymdrechai gwell.
>
> To-night she will not sleep the *smallest nap*, she would rather strive. *Edm. Prys.*

Hunfa, *s. f.—pl.* hunfeydd (hun) A dormitory.
Hunfawl, *s. f.* (mawl) Self-praise, self-applause.
Hunfod, *s. m.—pl. t.* au (bod) A self-existence.
Hunfodawl, *a.* (hunfod) Being self-existing.
Hunfoledd, *s. f.* (hunfawl) Self-applause.
Hunfoli, *v. a.* (hunfawl) To praise one's self.
Hungadw, *s. m.* (cadw) A self-preservation.
Hungar, *a.* (car) Having self love; selfish.
Hungariad, *s. m.* (hungar) Self-love.
Hungaru, *v. a.* (hungar) To love one's self.
Hungell, *s. f.—pl. t.* oedd (hun—cell) A dormitory
Hunglwyf, *s. m.* (hun—clwyf) A lethargy.
Hunglwyfaw, *v. n.* (hunglwyf) To be lethargic.
Hunglwyfawl, *a.* (hunglwyf) Lethargic.

Hunglwyfiad, *s.* m. (hunglwyf) A becoming lethargic, or drowsy.
Hunglwyfus, *a.* (hunglwyf) Subject to lethargy.
Hungos, *s. f.* (hun—cos) A scratching of one's self in sleep.
Hungymhariad, *s. m.* (cymhariad) Self-comparison.
Hunhaint, *s. m.* (hun—haint) A lethargy.
Hunhanfod, *s. m.* (hanfod) Self-existence.
Hunheintus, *a.* (hunhaint) Being lethargic.
Hunleiddiad, *s. c.*—*pl.* hunleiddiaid (hun—lladd) One who commits suicide.
Hunllef, *s. f.* (hun—llef) The nightmare.
Hunoli, *v. n.* (hunawl) To become selfish.
Hunolrwydd, *s. m.* (hunawl) Selfishness.
Hunred, *s. f.* (rhed) Self-motion; self-activity.
Hunredawl, *a.* (hunred) Self-movement.
Hunredeg, *v.* (hunred) To run, or move alone.
Hunrediad, *s. m.* (hunred) A running by a self-power, self-motion.
Hunryw, *s. m.*—*pl. t.* iau (rhyw) Homogeny.
Hunrywiad, *s. m.* (hunryw) A rendering homogeneous; a becoming homogeneous.
Hunrywiaw, *v. a.* (hunryw) To render or become homogeneous.
Hunrywiawl, *a.* (hunryw) Homogeneous.
Hunwr, *s. m.*—*pl.* hunwyr (hun—gwr) A sleeper.
Hunydd, *s. m.*—*pl. t.* ion (hun) A sleeper.
Hunymwad, *s. m.* (ymwad) Self-denial.
Hunymwadawl, *a.* (hunymwad) Self-denying.
Hunymwadiad, *s. m.* (hunymwad) A self-denying.
Hunymwadu, *v. a.* (hunymwad) To make a self-denial.
Hunyn, *s. m. dim.* (hun) A nap, a short sleep.

> Deuthym, heb huno hunyn,
> Gwawr dydd, i lys gorau ddyn.
>
> I came, without sleeping a *wink of sleep*, with the dawn of day, to the mansion of the best of women. *D. ab Gwilym.*

Huon, *s. m.* (hu) A pervading or subtile being; an epithet for the Deity, the same as *Hu*, in the bardic theology.

> Mi ddygais Huon
> I isar glyn Ebron.
>
> I conveyed *Huon* to the bottom of the vale of Hebron. *Ion. Mynyw.*
>
> Gwae wyntddydd brawd ger bron Huon.
>
> Woe to them, on the day of doom, in the presence of *Huon*. *Urwaint Y. Glas.*

Hupynt, *s. m.* (hwb) A brunt, a shock; a sudden effort; a push; a kind of metre, combining great varieties in the verse and in the rhyme.
Hur, *s. m.* (hy—ur) That is laid down, or fixed; hire, wages.

> Hwn a wnaeth neuadd ar hur, newydd
> Wrth neuadd Arthur.
>
> This one made a hall upon *hire*, a new one after the hall of Arthur. *L. G. Cothi.*

Huran, *s. m. dim.* (hur) A prostitute; a slattern.
Huredig, *a.* (hur) Being hired, or let for use.
Huren, *s. f. dim.* (hur) A prostitute, a whore.
Huriad, *s. m.* (hur) A hiring; a taking hire.
Huriaw, *v. a.* (hur) To hire; to take hire.
Huriawl, *a.* (hur) Relating to hire, hiring.
Huriwr, *s. m.*—*pl.* hurwyr (hur—gwr) A hirer.
Hurt, *s. m.* (hur) A base, or block. *a.* Stupid, dull, crazy, blockish.
Hurtan, *s. c. dim.* (hurt) A stupid one, an oaf, a blockhead.
Hurtiad, *s. m.* (hurt) A stupifying, stupefaction.
Hurtiaw, *v. a.* (hurt) To stupify; to stun; to become stupid; to lose the senses.
Hurtiawl, *a.* (hurt) Stupefactive, stupifying.
Hurtiedig, *a.* (hurtiad) Being stupified.
Hurtr, *s. m.*—*pl.* hurtrau (hurt) A boarded floor.
Hurtrwydd, *s. m.* (hurt) Stupidity; craziness.
Hurtyn, *s. m. dim.* (hurt) A stupid blockhead.
Hurth, *s. m.* (hur) A block; a dolt. *a.* Stupid, dull, blockish.
Hurthgen, *s. m.* (hurth—cen) A blockhead.
Hurthgenaidd, *a.* (hurthgen) Like a blockhead.
Hurthgeneiddrwydd, *s. m.* (hurthgenaidd) Oafishness, a stupified state.
Hurthiad, *s. m.*—*pl. t.* au (hurth) A stupifying.
Hurthiaw, *v. a.* (hurth) To stupify, to make dull.
Hurthiawl, *a.* (hurth) Stupifying, stupefactive.
Hust, *s. m.* (hy—ust) A low, or buzzing noise.
Hustiad, *s. m.* (hust) A making a buzzing noise.
Husting, *s. m.* (hust—ing) A whisper, a mutter.
Husting, *v. a.* (hust—ing) To whisper, to mutter

> Dwynwen——
> Ni'th wyl murwyn eleni
> Yn husting yn ing a mi.
>
> Dwynwen, through this whole year not a prude shall spy thee *whispering* with me in a corner. *D. ab Gwilym.*
>
> Mynwn dy fod——
> I'm deau glust yn husting.
>
> I would have thee to be to my right ear *whispering.* *E. Morlas.*

Hustingawl, *a.* (husting) Whispering, muttering.
Hustingiad, *s. m.* (husting) A whispering.
Hustingwr, *s. m.*—*pl.* hustingwyr (husting—gwr) A whisperer; a tale-bearer.
Hutan, *s. m. dim.* (hud) An oaf; a bird called a dotterel. *Hutan y mor*, the turnstone; *hutan lwyd*, or *llwyd y tywod*, the sanderling, sea-fowls so named.
Hutanaidd, *a.* (hutan) Oafish, like a dunce.
Hutyn, *s. m. dim.* (hud) A stupid fellow.
Hüw, *s. m.* (hu) A lullaby, a lulla.

> Heno ni chysgaf un-hun
> Be canai Ddew huw ei hun.
>
> To night I will not sleep one wink if Jove himself sings a *lullaby.* *D. ab Gwilym.*

Hüysgain, *a.* (hu—ysgain) Apt to spread out.
Hüysgwn, *a.* (hu—ysgwn) Apt to ascend.
Hüysgwr, *a.* (hu—ysgwr) Tending to be energetic

> Hydr udd cleddyf-rudd clodfras,
> Hüysgwr yn oed gwas.
>
> A bold chieftain with a ruddy sword of high renown, having the *energy* of a man in the time of youth. *Ll. P. Moch, m. H. ab G. ab Cynan.*

Hüysgwthr, *s. m.* (hu—ysgwthr) That is apt to tear forcibly.

> Yw ef Rodri hir, hüysgwr deyrn,
> Hüysgwthr cedeirn y cadwgunoedd.
>
> He is the towering Rodri, an *energetic* prince, the *swift destruction* of the mighty ones of conflicts. *Gwalchmai.*

HW, *s. m. r.* A forcible utterance; a hoot. It is also an interjection used in setting a dog on to run.

> Cayn bydd, annedwydd nad,
> Hw ddy hw hwrw ddyhead.
>
> She sings, with unhappy squeal, *hoot after hoot* to quick breathing. *D. ab Gwilym, i'r ddylluan.*
>
> Annos cwn y nos wna ef:
> Hw leidr! fy hel adref!
>
> Set on the dogs at night would he: *hoot thief!* what, drive me home! *D. ab Gwilym.*

Hwa, *v. a.* (hw) To holloo; to loo; to hoot.
Hwala, *s. f.* (hwa—la) The huntsman's halloo.

> Hwala hir fal hely hydd.
>
> A long *halloo*, like in hunting the stag. D. ab Gwilym.

Hwan, *s. f.* (hw) A hooter, an owl.
Hwb, *s. m.* (hw) A push forward, an effort; a rising up, a standing up; a lift.
Hwbach, *s. m.* (hwb) A sudden push, or spring. *Hwbach am y naid*, a hop, skip, and jump.

Hwbiad, *s. m.* (hwb) A pushing forward.

Hwbian, *v. a.* (hwb) To make a sudden push.

Hwca, *s. m.* (hwg) That is hooked, *a.* hooked. *Talcen hwca*, a frowning forehead, or hanging eyebrows.

Hwced, *a.* (hwg) Being turned, or hooked. *Talcen hwced*, a frowning forehead.

Hwch, *s. f.—pl.* hychod (hw—wch) A push forward, a thrust; a swine, a sow. *Cig hwch, cig moch*, and *cig twrch*, swine's flesh, or pork. It has been also used as an epithet for a ship, for the same reason as *banw* is applied to a pig, and to a coffer, the abstract meaning of the word being characteristic of the form of both. There is a tradition in Monmouthshire, that the first corn sown in Wales was at *Maes Gwenith*, in that county, and was brought there by a ship; which, in a triad alluding to the same event, is called *Hwch*.

> Gwr hoedlwydr, gwr bydr yn ei hwch, a'i far,
> Cyn noi fawr attregwch.

> A man whose life was brittle, like glass, a daring man in his *thrust* and his wrath, before his awful stoppage. *Ll. P. Moch i D. ab Owain.*

> Ni laddodd namyn un parchell o foch y Twrch Trwyth. Gofynwys y gwyr i Arthur, pa oedd ystyr yr hwch hwnw: y dywawd yntau, brenin fu.

> He killed only one pig of the *swine* of the laving boar. The men asked Arthur, what was the signification of that *swine*: he then said he had been a king. *H. Culhwch—Mabinogion.*

Hwchw, *s. m.* (hw—cw) A cry of hollo; a scream. *Hai hwchw!* Oh murder!

Hwd, *s. m.* (hy—wd) A take off; a taking away.

Hwda, *s. m.* (hwd) A taking off; a taking. *Byddi ar dy lawn hwda*, thou wilt be upon thy full stretch, or thou wilt be at a nonplus.

> Gwell un hwda na dau addaw.

> Better is one *take* than two promises. *Adage.*

Hwda, *v. imper.* (hwd) Take, here take.

> Hwda fawl didawl, da dyllu dy rad;
> Hwda rwydd erfyniau.

> *Accept* incessant praise, thy grace well deserves it; *accept* ready supplications. *H. D. ab Ifan.*

Hwdan, *s. m.* (hwd) A reach to lay hold of. *Llawn hwdan*, a nonplus.

Hwdwg, *s. m.* (hwd—wg) A bugbear, a bug.

Hwdwl, *s. m.* (hwd—wl) That is stark mad. *Ef aeth yn hwdwl*, he is become quite silly.

Hŵen, *s. f.* (hw) A hooting one, an owl.

Hwf, *s. m.—pl. t.* od (hy—wf) That rises over; a hood, or cowl.

> Dwyn hwf yn Llundain hefyd.

> Wearing a *hood* in London likewise. *Guto y Glyn.*

Hwfan, *s. m.* (hwf) A rising up, or over

Hwfanawl, *a.* (hwfan) Tending to rise over.

Hwfanu, *v. n.* (hwfan) To rise over.

Hwff, *s. m.—pl.* hyffion (hy—wff) Any thing precipitated, or cast off; a lump. *Hwff o eiry*, a drift of snow; *hwff o ddyn*, a clown of a man; *hwff y gydwff*, one who talks any nonsense.

Hwg, *s. m.* (hy—wg) A hook, or bend. *Heb na hwg na dwg*, without either hook or crook.

Hwgwd, *s. m.* (hwg) A dunce, a silly clown.

Hwhw, *s. m.* (hw) The hooting of an owl.

Hwi, *v. a.* (hw) To set up a holloo, to loo.

Hwm, *s. m.* (hy—wm) That is apt to sink.

Hwman, *s. m.* (hwm) A wavering motion.

Hwn, *pron. m.* (hy—wn) This here, this, this one: this one masculine present. *Hwn a hwn*, such and such a one, a certain person.

> Cas yr hwn y delo iddo lawer, ac ni roddo ddim.

> Detestable is *he* to whom much comes, and that gives nothing. *Adage.*

> Pwy y bedd hwn, bedd hwn, a hwn?
> Gofyn imi! mi a'i gwn:
> Bedd Ew, bedd Eidef oedd hwn,
> A bedd Eidal tal ysgwn.

> To whom belongs *this* grave, *this* grave, and *this*? Askest thou of me? I know: the grave of Ew, the grave of Eidef was *this*, and the grave of Eidal with uplifted front. *Engl. Beddau Milwyr.*

Hwna, *pron. m.* (hwn) That there, that, that one; that one present.

Hwnacw, *pron. m.* (hwn—acw) That one yonder.

Hwnt, *a.* (hwn) Outward, external, far off.

Hwnt, *pron.* (hwn) Other, contrary, next. *adv.* At a distance, yonder; beyond; away. *Y tu hwnt i*, the other side of.

> Yr oerfel oddi hwnt, a'r gwres oddi yma.

> The cold from *yonder*, and the heat from here. *Taliesin.*

> Trowch hwnt rhag tywarch o'i ol.

> Turn *aside* for fear of the clods thrown behind him. *T. Aled, i farch.*

Hwntian, *v. a.* (hwnt) To vibrate; to waggle; to stagger; to go backwards and forwards.

> Gwirodau, gwleddau, a gwlad ar hwntian,

> Liquors, feasts, and a whole country staggering. *Llywelyn Ddu.*

Hwnw, *pron. m.* (hwn) That, that one; that one absent, speaking of the past and future. It is also used as an interjection: *Hwnw!* That is it!

Hwnyma, *pron. m.* (hwn—yma) This one here.

Hwnyman, *pron. m.* (hwn—yman) This one here.

Hwnyna, *pron. m.* (hwn—yna) That one there.

Hwp, *s. m.* (hwb) A sudden effort, or push; a pull. *Hwp yr ychain*, the rest-harrow.

> Trwy fawr hwp, treiai for hallt.

> Through a great *effort*, he would exhaust the salt sea. *T. Prys, i Elis Pychan.*

Hwpiad, *s. m.* (hwp) A making a sudden effort; a pushing; a tugging, a lugging, a pulling.

Hwpiaw, *v. a.* (hwp) To make a sudden effort; to push; to tug, to pull.

> Pa wyr a geis hwpio'r gwynt!
> Peidien' mi wn pwy ydynt.

> What men are they who attempt to *push away* the wind? Let them desist, I know who they are. *L. Mon.*

Hwpiawl, *a.* (hwp) Pushing; tugging, lugging.

Hwpiwr, *s. m.—pl.* hwpwyr (hwp—gwr) A tugger.

Hwr, *s. m.* (hy—wr) A taking, a taking off.

> Dyrna, gwna ddydd brawd arnyn';
> A dod rys i'r Dêau draw,
> Hwr ruthr i'w hanreithiaw.

> Thresh away, bring a day of doom upon them; give a range yonder to the south, *take* a run to ruin them. *Ll. ab Gutyn, i glerwr.*

Hwra, *v. a.* (hwr) To take, to take away.

> Hwra don galon, a gwaelawd hiraeth;
> Hwra gorff llawn pechawd!

> *Accept* a broken heart, and the abasement of regret; *accept* a body full of sin! *H. D. ab Ifan.*

Hwrdd, *s. f.—pl.* hyrddau (hwr) A push forward, a thrust, or butt; an onset; a ram, plural *hyrddod*, and diminutive plural *hyrddiach*.

> Bu agwrdd ei hwrdd y'nghadau,
> Afagddu fy mab innau.

> Ardent was his *push* in combats, Afagddu my son was he. *Taliesin.*

> Y don——
> Rhois hwrdd i'm llong, rhois floeg floedd.

> The wave, it gave my ship a *push*, a hoarse scream it gave. *Gr. Gryg.*

> Nerth hwrdd yn ei ben.

> The strength of a *ram* is in his head. *Adage.*

Hwrwg, *s. m.* (hwr—wg) A lump, a bunch.

Hws, *s. m.* (hy—ws) A covering; a horsecloth.

Hwsan, *s. m. dim.* (hws) A little covering; a hood.

Hwsiad, *s. m.* (hws) A putting on a covering.

Hwstr, *a.* (hwst) Froward, or morose.

Hwstredd, *s. m.* (hwstr) Frowardness, moroseness.

Hwstriad, *s. m.* (hwstr) A doing a froward act.

Hwt, *s. m.* (hwd) A take off; a taking away. *v. imper.* Off, off with it, away! Hoot!

> Hwt! hwt! [illegible] ysgwt [illegible].
>
> Off! Off! [illegible] quickly, and go behind. *Rh. Nanmor.*

> I ddiawl y gyrell [illegible]!
> Hwt yntwy, [illegible] Owain!
>
> To the devil the tribe would go! away with them, let them! Owain! *Iolo Goch.*

Hwta, *s. m.* (hwda) A taking off; a taking. *Llawn hwta*, a nonplus.

Hwtiad, *s. m.* (hwt) A taking off; a hooting.

Hwtiaw, *v. a.* (hwt) To take off; to push away;

Hwy, *a.* (hw) Long; tedious. It is more generally used for *hwyach*, longer; more tedious, more prolix. *Hwy hwy*, longer and longer.

> Hwy pery [illegible] no golud.
>
> *Longer* will anger last than wealth. *Adage.*

Hwyâad, *s. m.* (hwyâu) A making longer.

Hwyâu, *v. a.* (hwy) To make longer; to lengthen.

Hwy, *pron.* (hy—wy) They; them. *Aent hwy yno*, they would go there.

> Y ser—
> Cylch y [illegible],
> Canwyllion hinon ynt hwy.
>
> The stars that in due order surround the moon, the lamps of serene weather are *they*. *D. ab Gwilym.*

Hwyad, *s. c. pl.* hwyaid (hy—gwyad) A duck: *ceiliawg hwyad*, a drake; *hwyad llygad aur* golden-eyed duck; *hwyad gopawg*, tufted duck; cor-hwyad, *crach-hwyad*, or *chwiwiaid*, teal; *hwyad ddanheddawg*, goosander; *hwyad fwythblu*, eider duck; *mor-hwyad ddu*, scoter; *hwyad yr eithin*, or *hwyad fraith*, sheldrake; *garan hwyad*, or *cors-hwyad*, the mallard; *hwyad lydanbig*, the shoveller; *hwyad lostfain*, or *hwyad gynffonfain*, pintail duck; *hwyad lost gwennol*, or *hwyad gynffon gwennol*, swallow-tail duck; *hwyad bengoch*, the pockard; *cors-hwyad lwyd*, the gadwal; *hwyad addfain*, the gargany; *hwyaid gwylltion*, wild ducks; *hwyaid dofion*, tame ducks.

> Nid [illegible] oni hwyad.
>
> Nothing so filthy as a *duck*. *Adage.*

Hwyadaidd, *a.* (hwyad) Like a duck, duck-like.

Hwyadawg, *a.* (hwyad) Abounding with ducks.

Hwyaden, *s. f.* (hwyad) A duck. *Hwyaden wyllt*, a wild duck; *hwyaden ddof*, a tame duck

Hwyddell, *s. f.* (hwy—dell) A female salmon.

Hwyed, *s. m.* (hwy) That is long, or lank.

Hwyedig, *a.* (hwyed) Being lengthening, or growing. *s. m.* A male hawk.

> Heledd hwyedig i'm gelwir,
>
> I am called a *filling* brine pit. *Llywarch Hen.*

> Y [illegible] a ddyly hwyedig [illegible] y penhebogydd bob gwyl [illegible]: pedair ar ugaint yw gwerth hwyedig.
>
> The steward of the household is entitled to a male hawk from the head falconer every Michaelmas: Twenty-four pence is the value of a *male hawk*. *Welsh Laws.*

Hwyedigaeth, *s. m.* (hwyedig) The act of lengthening, a prolongation.

Hwyedydd, *s. m.—pl. t.* ion (hwyed) A male hawk

> Hebogydd biau hwyedydd [illegible] of bwn nyth [illegible] a gaffer ar dir y llys.
>
> The falconer is entitled to the *male hawk*: he owns the nest of a sparrow-hawk which shall be found on the demesne of the court. *Welsh Laws.*

Hwyf, *s. m.* (hwy) That moves or plays about.

Hwyfaw, *v. a.* (hwyf) To move about; to flicker

Hwyfiad, *s. m.* (hwyf) A flickering, a fluttering.

Hwyfell, *s. f.—pl. t.* od (hwyf) A female salmon, a spawner. It is also called *hwyddell*, and *chwiwell*.

Hwyfyd, *s. m.* (hwy—byd) A long existence. *Hwyfyd i Brydain!* Britain for ever!

> Wedi profi pob lle hwyfyd i gartref.
>
> After trying every place a welcome to home. *Adage.*

Hwyl, *s. f.—pl. t.* iau (hwy) A course, a regimen, or order; plight, state, condition; a progress, journey, or voyage; a sail. *Wyt mewn purion hwyl*, thou art in tolerable order; *mae hi o'i hwyl*, she is out of her wits;—*Dwyn hwyl*, to make an onset:—*Hwyliau blaen*, fore sails; *hwylion ol*, aft sails; *hwyliau croesion*, cross or square sails.

> Dy glod a fydd—
> Hyd yd [illegible] hwyl haul Mehefin.
>
> Thy *fame* will be as far as the Midsummer sun takes up his *course*. *Gwalchmai.*

> Pwy fu fforch hwyl o ddaiar hyd nwyf?
>
> Who has born a *sail fork* reaching from the earth to the sky? *Taliesin.*

> Gochel di, ebai Merddin, dan meibion Cystennyn, canys y maent y awr hon yn lledu hwyliau ar draeth Llydaw yn dyfod i Ynys Prydain.
>
> Beware thou, said Merddin, of the fire of the sons of Constantine, for they are at this hour spreading *sails* on the shore of Llydaw, coming to the Isle of Britain. *Gr. ab Arthur.*

> Y meddydd a ddyly yr hwyl a fo ar y gerwyn fedd, neu bedwar ceiniawg, a hyny yn newis y neb bieufo y wledd.
>
> The mead-brewer is entitled to the *covering* that shall be on the mead tub, or four-pence, and that at the option of him to whom the feast shall belong. *Welsh Laws.*

Hwylbren, *s. m.—pl. t.* i (hwyl—pren) A mast.

Hwylbrenwyll, *s. f.* (hwylbren—gwyll) A demon imagined to hover about the masts of ships.

> Hwylbrenwyll hell [illegible].
>
> The *sailyard goblin* of the white [illegible]. *D. ab Gwilym.*

Hwylfa, *s. f.—pl.* hwylfëydd (hwyl—ma) A place of progression, a course; a lane.

> Haul yn ei hwylfa.
>
> The sun in its *orbit*. *Taliesin.*

Hwylfawr, *a.* (hwyl—mawr) Of ample course.

> Aur ysgwn aur ysgwyd [illegible]:
> Oedd [illegible] arf [illegible]; [illegible],
> Oedd hwylfawr glod uchel.
>
> With a golden shield he was the urger of the battle; he was the terrible blade-rushing weapon of war: he was [illegible], he was of high and *far-extending* fame. *Bleddyn Fardd*, i *R. ab Gruffudd.*

Hwyliad, *s. m.* (hwyl) A getting in a course, train, or order; a directing; a preparing; a progression; a sailing; a driving at, or a butting.

Hwyliaw, *v. a.* (hwyl) To set in a course, train, or order; to direct; to prepare; to progress; to sail; to make an attack; to butt.

> Dywed fy mod—
> Yn hwyliaw buan helynt,
> With y gwynt a roddo gwynt.
>
> Say that I am *sailing* a quick course, on [illegible] the wind may give. *T. Prys.*

> Da gweith [illegible] cyn hyrion i'r fawrh a hwyliaw [illegible].
>
> It was a good thing to give short [illegible] to the [illegible] *Adage.*

Hwyliawd, *s. m.* (hwyl) The act of putting in train; a direction, or ordering; progression, a sailing; a making an attack.

Hwyliawg, *a.* (hwyl) Having a course; under sail.

Hwyliedig, *a.* (hwyliad) Being put in train; directed, ordered; being sailed.

Hwyliedigaeth, *s. m.* (hwyliedig) The act of putting in train; a directing, or ordering; progression; the act of sailing.

Hwyliwr, *s. m.*—*pl.* hwylwyr (hwyl—gwr.) One who sets in a course, or train; one who directs; a progressor; one who sails.

> Hwyliwr pob golygnedawd,
> Hwyl ddiwad iach, hael Dduw dawd
> Help i ochel hawl pechawd.

> The regulator of every [illegible] of undoubted safe course, gracious God, grant thy aid to avoid the power of sin. *H. D. ab Ifan.*

Hwylus, *a.* (hwyl) Being in course, or regimen, orderly; going on freely, or without obstruction; prosperous; ready, dexterous. *Dos yn hwylus*, go without delay.

Hwylusaw, *v. a.* (hwylus) To render free, or uninterrupted; to render prosperous; to facilitate.

Hwylusdawd, *s. m.* (hwylus) Facility, readiness.

Hwylusder, *s. m.* (hwylus) Facileness, freedom from impediments.

> Onid rhyw i gyw yr hwyad
> Hwylusder nofio 'r ol dull ei dad?

> Is it not congenial for the duckling to have the *facility* of swimming after the manner of his father? *Adage.*

Hwylusrwydd, *s. m.* (hwylus) Facility, readiness.

Hwyluswynt, *s. m.* (hwylus—gwynt) A prosperous gale, a favourable wind.

Hwyn, *s. m.*—*pl. t.* don (hwy) A long hair.

Hwynaw, *v. a.* (hwyn) To lay a springe, or gin.

Hwynt, *pron.* (hwy) They; them. *Tynir hwynt*, they will be drawn.

> Y dynion taerion [illegible], gwaedwyllt,
> A godant dorfrwysg;
> Duw Tad, nad eu hanwydau;
> Ymwel â hwynt, rhag amlâu.

> The men of froward enterprises and furious will raise tumults; God the Father, frustrate their passions, visit *them* lest they increase. *H. D. ab Ifan.*

Hwyntau, *pron.* (hwynt) They likewise, them also; and they; and them; the others.

Hwynthwy, *pron.* (hwynt—hwy) They themselves, they.

Hwynyn, *s. m.*—*pl. t.* au (hwyn) A long slip, a hair; a springe, or gin; a feigned malignant spirit of the sea. *Hwynyn o dir*, a slang of land

> O'r sawl angeu-fagl y sydd,
> Hwynyn fo ei ddibenydd.

> Of the various death-traps that are, may *Hwynyn* be his end. *D. ab Gwilym, i'r Bwa Bach.*

Hwyr, *s. m.* (hwy) Lateness; the evening.

Hwyr, *a.* (hwy) Slow, tedious, long; late. *Milgi hwyr*, a slow hound.

> A esgyno yn hwyr ebrwydd y disgyn.

> That shall ascend *late* will soon descend. *Adage.*

> Hawsach cân hwyr no chan fore.

> Easier is the *evening* song than a morning song. *Adage.*

> Hwyraf dial dial Duw;
> Llwyraf dial dial Duw.

> The *latest* vengeance is the vengeance of God; the completest vengeance is the vengeance of God. *Adage.*

Hwyrâad, *s. m.* (hwyr) A becoming late.

Hwyrach, *a.* (*compar. of* hwyr) Slower, later. *adv.* Perhaps, peradventure.

> Hwyrach y mynwn e fo yna no chynt.

> *More tardy* was I for having him then than formerly. *H. Peredur—Mabinogion.*

Hwyraidd, *a.* (hwyr) Somewhat tardy; latish.

Hwyran, *s. c.* (hwyr) A slow one; a lame one.

Hwyrâu, *v. n.* (hwyr) To become late.

Hwyrawl, *a.* (hwyr) Relating to the evening.

Hwyrbaid, *a.* (hwyr—paid) Lately ceasing.

> Traethawd bur i boraw enaid
> Rhag trawl boen yn hir boen yn hwyrbaid.

> A divine discourse to purify a soul from the consuming of health in long and *incessant* pain. *Cynddelw.*

Hwyrbeidiaw, *v. n.* (hwyrbaid) To cease tardily.

Hwyrdawl, *a.* (hwyr—tawl) Slowly-ceasing.

Hwyrder, *s. m.* (hwyr) Tardiness, lateness.

Hwyrdrom, *a.* (*f. of* hwyrdrwm) Tardily heavy.

Hwyrdrwm, *a.* (hwyr—trwm) Tardily heavy.

Hwyrdrymder, *s.* (hwyrdrwm) Drowsy heaviness

Hwyrdrymedd, *s. m.* (hwyrdrwm) Slow heaviness.

Hwyrdrymu, *v.* (hwyrdrwm) To become sluggish.

Hwyrddig, *a.* (hwyr—dig) Long-suffering.

Hwyrddigder, *s. m.* (hwyrddig) Slowness to anger.

Hwyrddysg, *a.* (hwyr—dysg) Slow in learning.

Hwyrddysgiad, *s. m.* (hwyrddysg) A learning slowly.

Hwyrddysgu, *v. a.* (hwyrddysg) To learn tardily.

Hwyredd, *s. m.* (hwyr) Tediousness; lateness.

Hwyrfryd, *s. m.* (hwyr—bryd) A slow disposition. *a.* Of slow disposition.

Hwyrfrydig, *a.* (hwyrfryd) Of slow disposition.

Hwyrfrydigrwydd, *s. m.* (hwyrfrydig) Slowness of disposition; sluggishness of mind.

Hwyrfrydu, *v. n.* (hwyrfryd) To become inert in mind, to be of sluggish mind.

Hwyrgar, *a.* (hwyr—car) Slow or cold in love.

Hwyrgaru, *v. a.* (hwyrgar) To love tardily.

Hwyrgoel, *a.* (hwyr—coel) Tardy in believing.

Hwyrgoeledd, *s. f.* (hwyr—coel) Tardiness of belief; a tardily crediting.

Hwyrgoeliad, *s. m.* (hwyrgoel) A tardily crediting

Hwyrgoeliaw, *v. a.* (hwyrgoel) To believe tardily.

Hwyrgwyn, *a.* (hwyr—cwyn) Backward or slow in complaining.

Hwyrgyrch, *s. m.* (cyrch) A tardy approach, or attack. *a.* Of slow approach; of slow attack.

Hwyrgyrchawl, *a.* (hwyrgyrch) Slowly approaching

Hwyrgyrchedd, *s. m.* (hwyrgyrch) Slowness of approach; slowness of resorting.

Hwyrgyrchiad, *s. m.* (hwyrgyrch) A slowly approaching or resorting.

Hwyrgyrchu, *v.* (hwyrgyrch) To approach slowly.

Hwyrlid, *a.* (hwyr—llid) Slow to anger.

Hwyrnaws, *s. f.* (hwyr—naws) A slow disposition. *a.* Of a slow disposition.

Hwyrnawsedd, *s. m.* (hwyrnaws) Slowness of disposition; a sluggish nature.

Hwyrwaith, *s. m.* (hwyr—gwaith) A late course.

> Hwyrwaith i anffyniedig.

> A *late turn* to the unprosperous. *Adage.*

Hwyrwan, *a.* (hwyr—gwan) Slow and languid.

Hwyrwar, *a.* (hwyr—gwar) Slow and gentle.

Hwyrweddawg, *a.* (hwyr—gweddawg) Of a forbearing disposition.

> Hwyrweddawg Gwallawg ardebed;
> Ni ofyn i neb a wnaethodd.

> *Of a forbearing aspect* is the countenance of Gwallawg; he does not enquire of any one what he has done. *Taliesin.*

Hwys, *s. f.* (hy—wys) A draught, a load.

> Coed a losgynt a hwys fawn o fynydd Briwnant.

> Woods they would burn with a *load* of turf from the mountain of Briwnant. *Mengydion.*

Hwysaw, *v. a.* (hwys) To heap together.

Hwysg, *s. m.*—*pl. t.* an (hy—wysg) A sweep; a sudden whisk, a ravage.

Hwysgaw, *v. a.* (hwysg) To sweep or brush away

Hwysgynt, *s. f.* (hwysg—hynt) Sweeping course.

> Llywelyn llaw-ddifeirch arfawg,
> A chlod a gorfod am Geiriawg ddyfrynt,
> Gwrawl hawl hwysgynt, hynt hiriddawg.

> Llywelyn with armed war-[illegible], attended by fame and conquest round the vale of Ceiriog, [illegible] he carries on devastation, a course of lasting wrath. *Llygad Gwr.*

Hwyst, *s. m.* (hwys) A dart, or sudden glance.

Hwystin, *s. m.* (hwyst) A darting forward.

> Ef iolen' odduch lawr,
> Tân tan hwystin gwawr.

> Him they adore above the earth, the fire under the *radiation* of the dawn. *Taliesin, Can y meirch.*

Hwythau, *pron.* (hwy- tau) They likewise.

Hwywys, *a.* (hwy--gwys) Of extended reach.

> Nid er da i Hwfa hen,
> Namyn er mawr i my hun,
> Y moliaf i Bleddyn dadl trin,
> Hwywys hwyr [illegible] y'ngarthan.
>
> Not for any benefit to old Hwfa, but as an enjoyment for myself, do I praise Bleddyn, wolf of conflict, *of extended reach* to the fight. *Ll. P. Moch.*

HY, *s. m. r.* Aptitude to proceed, or to go through. It is used as a prefix in composition, and expresses aptness, disposition, or feasibility, answering to the English termination *able*; as *hygar*, amiable; *hygof*, memorable, or that may be called to mind.

Hy, *a.* (hy, *s.*) Apt; bold, daring; audacious.

> Hy pawb ar ei fabsant.
>
> Every one is *bold* to his tutelar saint. *Adage.*
>
> Artal hy at ffy, at ffoes.
>
> *Bold* vigour will not flee, it has not fled. *Ll. P. Moch.*

Hyadlais, *s. m.* (adlais) A clear resonance. *a.* Apt to resound, apt to echo.

Hyall, *a.* (gall) Possible, effectible, practicable.

> Teithi yr iaith Gymraeg—yw adrawdd yn hyfedr a hyall.
>
> The property of the Welsh language is to describe readily and *effectually*. *Barddas.*

Hyalledd, *s.* (hyall) Possibility; practicableness.

Hyallu, *v. n.* (hyall) To be possible, or practicable

Hyalluedd, *s. m.* (hyallu) Possibleness.

Hyar, *a.* (ar) Apt to resound, sonorous; vocal.

Hyaredd, *s. m.* (hyar) Aptness to resound.

Hyawdl, *a.* (awdl) Eloquent, fluent in speech.

Hyawdledd, *s. m.* (hyawdl) Eloquence, fluency.

Hyb, *s. m.* (hy—yb) A passing or getting forward; a getting foremost; a recovery.

Hyball, *a.* (pall) Fallible, apt to fail; defectible.

Hyballedd, *s. m.* (hyball) Fallibility, aptness or a tendency to fail.

Hybar, *a.* (par) Apt to get, or to provide.

Hybarch, *a.* (parch) Venerable, worthy of respect

Hybarchedd, *s. m.* (hybarch) Venerableness.

Hybaredd, *s. m.* (hybar) Aptness to provide.

Hybarth, *a.* (parth) Easily parted; divisible.

Hybarthedd, *s. m.* (hybarth) Divisibility.

Hybarthiant, *s. m.* (hybarth) A making divisible.

Hybarthrwydd, *s. m.* (hybarth) Divisibility.

Hybawl, *a.* (hyb) Tending to get foremost; recovering, convalescent.

Hybech, *a.* (pech) Apt or ready to sin; peccable.

Hybechedd, *s. m.* (hybech) Peccability.

Hybechrwydd, *s. m.* (hybech) Aptness to sin.

Hybell, *a.* (pell) Having a facility to get far.

> Cwympent yr —
> Adar hybell asgellawg.
>
> The *far-ranging* winged birds would fall. *H. Middleton.*

Hyber, *a.* (per) Apt to produce sweetness.

Hybiad, *s. m.* (hyb) A passing onward, a getting foremost; a recovering.

Hyblaid, *a.* (plaid) Apt to take a part; factious.

Hybleidrwydd, *s. m.* (hyblaid) Aptness to join a party, factiousness.

Hybleth, *a.* (pleth) Easy to weave or to twine.

Hyblethedd, *s. m.* (hybleth) Aptness to entwine.

Hyblith, *a.* (plith) Easily mixing, or blending.

Hyblithedd, *s. m.* (hyblith) Aptness to blend.

Hyblyg, *a.* (plyg) Flexible; easily doubled.

Hyblygedd, *s. m.* (hyblyg) Flexibility, pliancy.

Hyblygrwydd, *s. m.* (hyblyg) Flexibleness.

Hyblygu, *v. a.* (hyblyg) To double easily.

Hyboen, *a.* (poen) Susceptible of pain, passible.

> Neud wyf heen hyboen heb arglwyddi'
>
> Am I not of men *passible* the deprived of the lains' *Lladdyn Fardd.*

Hyboenedd, *s. m.* (hyboen) A state susceptible of pain; a tendency to suffer.

Hyboeni, *v. a.* (hyboen) To make passible.

Hyboeth, *a.* (poeth) Easily heated; apt to heat.

Hyboethedd, *s. m.* (hyboeth) Aptness to heat.

Hyborth, *a.* (porth) Easily borne, or carried. portable; that is easily sustained, or fed.

Hyborthedd, *s. m.* (hyborth) A sustaining easily.

Hybrawf, *a.* (prawf) Demonstrable, provable.

Hybred, *a.* (pred) Wanting to be divestigated, liable to transmigration in the circle of evil.

> Pan gyhyrddodd nawdd nodded hyged,
> Duw mawr nef a llawr, llarf eiddunced,
> Y daeth brenin coeth rhag caethiwed
> O uchelder ner, nef amgyffred,
> I'r ddaear, fal car i ymwared
> A dyn oedd mewn glyn o giwyf hybred.
>
> On touching a refuge of the bountiful hand of the God of heaven and earth, the wished for support, the immaculate king, to redeem from thraldom, came from the high place of the supreme, quitting heaven, to the earth, like a friend, to deliver man, that was in the dark vale, from the evil influence. *D. Llwyd.*

Hybrededd, *s. m.* (hybred) A state liable to transmigration in the circle of evil.

Hybryn, *a.* (pryn) Marketable, easily bought.

Hybrynedd, *s. m.* (hybryn) A marketable state.

Hybu, *v. a.* (hyb) To pass, to get onward; to recover; to get before, to obstruct. *Hybu y blaen*, to get foremost; *hybaist yn fuan iawn*, thou didst recover very fast.

Hybwyll, *a.* (pwyll) Sensible; discreet, prudent.

Hybwylledd, *s. m.* (hybwyll) Sensibleness; sensibility; rationality; deliberation.

Hybwys, *a.* (pwys) Ponderable; easily weighed.

Hybwysedd, *s. m.* (hybwys) Aptness to weigh down; ponderousness.

Hychaidd, *a.* (hwch) Swinish, like a sow.

Hychan, *s. f. dim.* (hwch) A little young sow.

Hycheiddrwydd, *s. m* (hychaidd) Swinishness.

Hychfryd, *s. m.* (hwch—bryd) A stubborn mind.

Hychfrydedd, *s.* (hychfryd) Stubbornness of mind

Hychgryg, *s. m.* (hwch—cryg) A quinsey.

Hychiad, *s.* (hwch) A pushing, a forcing forward.

Hychian, *v. a.* (hwch) To grunt like a sow.

Hychiaw, *v. a.* (hwch) To push, to force forward.

Hychig, *s. f.* (hwch) A little sow, a young sow.

Hychwaew, *s. f.* (hwch—gwaew) A pushing spear

> Pan dywyllwyd ei olwg llidiaw a oreg yr anghenfil; ac fal y rhed yr baedd coed yr hwch ar hyd hychwaew, y rhuthrodd yntau ar hyd cledd ar dor y cleddyf.
>
> When his sight was darkened the monster became furious, and as the wild boar rushes upon the *spear* of the huntsman, so did he rush at Arthur full upon the point of the sword. *Gr. ab Arthur.*

Hychwal, *a.* (chwal) Dissipatable, easily scattered

Hychwaledd, *s. m.* (hychwal) Aptness to dissipate

Hychwaliad, *s.* (hychwal) A dissipating readily.

Hychwalu, *v. a.* (hychwal) To dissipate readily.

Hychwant, *a.* (chwant) Apt to lust, or to desire.

Hychwantach, *s. m.* (hychwant) Aptness to lust.

Hychwardd, *a.* (chwardd) Easily laughing; risible

Hychwarddedd, *s. m.* (hychwardd) Aptness to laugh, a tendency to mirth.

Hychwil, *a.* (chwil) Apt to pry, apt to look about

Hychwydd, *a.* (chwydd) Apt to swell.

Hychwyth, *a.* (chwyth) Easily blown, apt to blow.

Hyd, *s. m.—pl. t.* oedd (hy yd) Length; continuity, duration; a while. *Hyd gyd*, full length; *hyd o hydoedd*, all places; *ar fy hyd*, at my length; *ar hyd lawr*, along the ground, *a raid i mi aros yma o hyd?* Must I stay here all the while?

> [illegible] a hyd a hedy,
> [illegible] heb [illegible]
>
> The *lengths* of the world thou wilt fly [illegible] of the hill, to high [illegible] [illegible]

Hyd, *prep.* (hyd, *s.*) To, unto, as far as. *Hyd y diwedd*, to the end; *hyd pan y delo*, to the end that he should come; *hyd yma*, as far as here; *hyd adref*, towards home; *ti ei hyd ar ddim*, thou wilt go to nothing.

Hyd, *adv.* (hyd, *s.*) Until, till, to the time that; to the place that; while, whilst; along, over. *Arows hyd y delo hi yma*, stay until she comes here; *taena hwna hyd y bwrdd*, spread that over the table.

Dalis da yn hyd fu.

He stuck to the good *whilst* it lasted. *Adage.*

Ni bu galed y Bedo;
Ni bwyf ond yr hyd y bo.

Bedo has never been hard; may I be but *whilst* he is. *L. G. Cothi.*

Hydaen, *a.* (taen) Expansible, easily spread.

Hydaenedd, *s. m.* (hydaen) Expansibleness.

Hydafl, *a.* (tafl) Missible, easily thrown.

Hydag, *a.* (tag) Apt to choak; easily choaked.

Hydaith, *a.* (taith) Apt to travel; easily going.

Delw ym peirch a meirch mygr hydaith,
Mynw ellon, mal gwyllon.

In such wise does he honour me with splendid steeds, *eager for the course*, with the bodies of deer, like sprites of the gloom. *Cynddelw.*

Hydal, *a.* (tal) Easily paid, payable; apt to pay.

Hydalm, *a.* (talm) Apt to break off, or to make transitions; apt to conjoin parts.

Pwy a fedr ddeall ystorïeuwyr hydalm, heb gydnabod â throeïlau ymadrawdd?

Who can understand *synthetical* dramatists, without being acquainted with the tropes of speech? *H. Perri.*

Hydalmedd, *s. m.* (hydalm) Aptness to make transitions; aptness to comprize.

Hydan, *a.* (tan) Apt to ignite, ignitible.

Hydardd, *a.* (tardd) Apt to break out, or to effuse.

Hydarf, *a.* (tarf) Easily scared, or driven off.

Hydarth, *a.* (tarth) Apt to exhale; easily exhaling.

Hydaw, *a.* (taw) Easily silenced, apt to be silent.

Hydawdd, *a.* (tawdd) Easily melted, dissolvable.

Hydawl, *a.* (hyd) Longitudinal; relating to length; lengthwise.

Hyd-ddof, *pronom. prep.* (hyd—dy—o—mi) Along me, over me, covering me.

Hydeb, *s. m.* (hy) Boldness; assurance.

Dy hydeb, a gwyneb gwych,
Yn gawr a wna a gerych.

Thy *frankness*, with a gay countenance, will make one thou regardest strong as a giant. *H. Swrdwal.*

Hydedd, *s. m.* (hyd) Longitude, or length.

Hydeg, *a.* (teg) Tending or apt to be fair. *Gwydd hydeg*, a presence interestingly fair.

Hydeiml, *a.* (teiml) Easily touched; tangible; susceptible of feeling.

Hydeimlad, *s. m.* (hydeiml) A being apt to feel.

Hydeimledd, *s. m.* (hydeiml) Palpability; tangibility; susceptibleness of feeling.

Hyder, *s. m.* (hy) Confidence, assurance, trust.

Deuparth bonedd yw dysg;
Deuparth dysg yw hyder.

The half of nobility is education; the half of education is *assurance*. *Adage.*

Hyderiad, *s. m.* (hyder) A confiding, a trusting.

Hyderu, *v. n.* (hyder) To confide, to have assurance, to trust, to depend, to rely.

Hyderus, *a.* (hyder) Confident, having assurance, trust, or reliance.

Hydfod, *s. m.* (hyd—bod) A continuance.

Deuddeg ebostol—
Credwn eu hydfod, ac nid ailfydd,
Yn undawd drindawd yn dragywydd.

The twelve apostles, let us believe their *continuance*, and without being reversed in the unity of the trinity to eternity. *Gwalchmai.*

Hydgyllen, *s. f.* (hyd—cyllen) A brisket.

Hydiad, *s. m.* (hyd) A lengthening; elongation

Hydoddrwydd, *s. m.* (hydawdd) Aptness to melt.

Hydo, *a.* (to) Apt to cover, easily sheltering.

Hydöedd, *s. m.* (hydo) Aptness to cover, or shelter

Prydain hydr hydöedd ymddifad.

British bravery is the *ready shelter* of the destitute. *Ll. P. Moch.*

Hydof, *pronom. prep.* (hyd—o—mi) Along me, over me, all over me, or covering me.

Hydor, *a.* (tor) Easily broken, or fractured.

Hydorf, *a.* (torf) Apt to be thronged about.

Hydorf cylch ei gorf gwrymseirch ar led.

Thronging round his person they displayed trappings of war. *Llygad Gwr.*

Hydr, *a.* (hyd) Being apt to proceed; bold, confident, daring.

Hydr gwr o'i gymydogaeth.

A man is *familiar* in his neighbourhood. *Adage.*

Hydr fydd dwfr ar dal glan.

The water will be bold in the front of the shore. *Adage.*

Hydrach, *a.* (hydr) More forward. *Yn hydrach*, more confidently, rather.

Hydraeth, *a.* (traeth) Effable; easily recited.

Hydraidd, *a.* (traidd) Penetrable, easily pierced

Hydrais, *a.* (trais) Apt to oppress, or to sway.

Mi fum hoew-drum, a hydrais,
A serth with Gymmro, a Sais.

I have been of active gait, and *over-bearing* and saucy to Welsh man as well as Englishman. *G. ab Sefnyn.*

Hydranc, *a.* (tranc) Apt to perish; perishable.

Hydras, *a.* (tras) Of notable kindred, or birth.

Hydraul, *a.* (traul) Easily consumed; digestible.

Hydraw, *a.* (traw) Apt to instruct; instructive.

Hydrawd, *a.* (trawd) Of a free course, or way.

Hydred, *s. f.—pl. t.* ion (hyd—rhed) Longitude.

Hydredawl, *a.* (hydred) Longitudinal; lengthwise

Hydref, *s. m.* (tref) The in-gathering, or harvest season; autumn, October.

O bob parth y syrthiant y celanedd yn feirw, megis y syrthynt y dail i ar y gwydd, mis Hydref, pan fai fawr y gwynt.

On every side the wounded bodies will fall down dead, as the leaves fall off the trees, in the month of *October*, when the wind is high. *Gr. ab Arthur.*

Hydrefaidd, *a.* (hydref) Like autumn; autumnal.

Hydrefawl, *a.* (hydref) Autumnal; October.

Hydrefiad, *s. m.* (hydref) A gathering together; heaping; a becoming autumn.

Hydrefn, *a.* (trefn) Well ordered, orderly.

Hydrefnedd, *s. m.* (hydrefn) Orderliness; trim.

Hydrefniad, *s. m.* (hydrefn) A well ordering.

Hydrefnid, *s. m.* (hydrefn) Orderliness.

Hydrefnu, *v. a.* (hydrefn) To render orderly.

Hydrefu, *v. a.* (hydref) To collect together with facility; to become autumn.

Cedwyr—
Talasant eu medd, mal gwyr Belyn gynt,
Teg i hydrefynt tra fu undyn.

Warriors who repaid their mead, like Belyn's men of yore, fairly *they collected together* whilst one person remained. *O. Cyfeiliawg.*

Hydreiddedd, *s. m.* (hydraidd) Penetrability.

Hydreiddiad, *s.* (hydraidd) A readily penetrating.

Magwyr mur-wydr, hydr hydreiddiad lwysle,
Hygrwedd haul fore eurne aruad.

A structure of polished wall, an enchanting place where there is a confident *entering readily*, beauteous on thee the aspect of the golden-hued sun of the morning. *H. ab Ein. Lygliw.*

Hydreiddrwydd, *s. m.* (hydraidd) Penetrability.

Hydreigl, *a.* (treigl) Apt to roll; declinable.

Hydreigledd, *s. m.* (hydreigl) Aptness to roll.

Hydreigliad, *s. m.* (hydreigl) A turning aptly.

Hydreiglrwydd, *s. m.* (hydreigl) Aptness to turn.

Hydrem, *a.* (trem) Apt to take a view.
Hydremiant, *s. m.* (hydrem) Aptitude of sight.
Hydres, *a.* (tres) Apt to strain, or to exert.
Hydreth, *a.* (treth) Easily taxed, or taxable.
Hydreuledd, *s. m.* (hydraul) Aptness to consume
Hydreuliaw, *v. a.* (hydraul) To consume readily.
Hydrfaith, *a.* (hydr—maith) Of ample extent.

> Niddodesty ngherdd y'nghyfraith erioed
> Draig Argoed, hoed hydrfaith,
> Hirwawr lorf, cerf cyfarwaith,
> Hir-falch gwalch, gwae fi o'i laith!

Never was the law consulted in recording my song by the leader of Argoed, after whom there is *far-spreading* regret; the long-reflecting beam, the centre of combination, and highly towering hawk, his death is woe to me. *Cynddelw.*

Hydrfer, *a.* (hydr—mer) Freely dropping.

> Llawer deigr hydrfer ar hynt
> Hidl am Rys, rydh anymwedt!

Many a *freely-flowing* tear on its course falling for Rhys, who has taken the church yard way! *Prydydd Bychan.*

Hydrfoled, *s. f.* (hydr—moled) Adventurous praise or commendation.
Hydriad, *s. m.* (hydr) A being bold, or daring.
Hydrig, *a.* (trig) Habitable, easily inhabited.
Hydrin, *a.* (trin) Manageable, or docile.
Hydro, *a.* (tro) Pliable, convertible, changeable.
Hydroedd, *s. m.* (hydro) A facility of turning.
Hydru, *v. n.* (hydr) To become confident.
Hydrum, *a.* (trum) Of unobstructed sway.

> Gwr ni fo hydrum iddo ei wlad.

A man whose country is not *free of access* to him. *Welsh Laws.*

Hydruth, *a.* (truth) Easily flattering, apt to flatter
Hydrwch, *a.* (trwch) Easily broken, or cut.
Hydrwm, *a.* (trwm) Apt to be heavy, or sluggish
Hydrwst, *a.* (trwst) Apt to be noisy, or blustering.
Hydrychedd, *s. m.* (hydrwch) Frangibleness.
Hydrychni, *s. m.* (hydrwch) Frangibility.
Hydrymedd, *s. m.* (hydrwm) A drowsiness.
Hydwedd, *s. m.* (hyd—gwedd) A longitudinal aspect.
Hydwf, *a.* (twf) Apt to grow; luxuriant: the cuckoo flower.

> A hydwf mae'n chedeg
> Y cnwd hwn yn y cnawd teg.

And *luxuriantly* this crop shoots forth in the fair complexion. *D. ab Gwilym.*

Hydwg, *a.* (twg) Tending to prosperity; lucky.
Hydwn, *a.* (twn) Easily broken, apt to break.

> Gwalch hyder glewder, glewdraws, difal,
> Gwaew hydwn yngwn, yngwyd amdral.

A hawk of the confidence of bravery, heroically froward, fearless, with the uplifted spear, *ever apt to be shivered*, and a shield battered round. *Cynddelw, i Gadwallon.*

Hydwrf, *a.* (twrf) Apt to be tumultuous.
Hydwyll, *a.* (twyll) Easily deceived, deceivable.

> Cadw y mae eiddig, hydwyll,
> I'i hoew-ddyn bach, hyddawn bwyll.

The jealous churl, *easily deceived*, guards his little sprightly fair one of ready-gifted wit. *D. ab Gwilym.*

Hydwylledd, *s. m.* (hydwyll) Deceivableness.
Hydwyth, *a.* (twyth) Elastic, supple; nimble.

> Cenawon Goronwy gwrdd gynnyrfed gwyth;
> Cenawon hydwyth, hydr eu gorfhwed;
> Gwyr a oferyn tal yn mhob caled.

The whelps of Goronwy ardent in the career of wrath; *nimble* whelps, bold their feat; men who deserve a reward in every difficulty. *O. Cyfeiliawg.*

> Neud ethol walch weilch hydwyth;
> Neud athyn a'm draig, neud aeth?

Did not the hero select *nimble* hawk-like youths; did he but go with my leader, is he not gone? *Prydydd Bychan, i R. Gryg.*

Hydwythaw, *v. a.* (hydwyth) To render elastic.
Hydwythedd, *s. m.* (hydwyth) Elasticity; agility.
Hydwythiad, *s. m.* (hydwyth) A rendering elastic.
Hydyb, *a.* (tyb) Easily fancying, or imagining.

Hydybedd, *s. m.* (hydyb) Aptness to surmise.
Hydyciant, *s. m.* (hydwg) Facility of prospering.
Hydyfiant, *s. m.* (hydwf) Aptness of growth.
Hydyn, *a.* (tyn) Tractable, easily drawn.

> Morgaseg hoew-deg, hydyn,
> A dreidia'i llwyth dros y llyn.

A sea-mare sprightly fair, and *tractable*, that walks her load over the lake. *G. ab H. Tudyr, i gwalad.*

Hydynrwydd, *s. m.* (hydyn) Tractableness.
Hydd, *s. m.—pl. t.* od (hy—ydd) A hart, or stag.

> Nid boneddig ond hydd.

There is nothing so noble as the *hart*. *Adage.*

> Addas yr hydd i'r llyn.

The *stag* aptly makes to the pool. *Adage.*

> Mal yr hydd a'r blaidd.

Like the *stag* and the wolf. *Adage.*

Hydda, *a.* (da) Aptly good; goodly; welcome.

Mi a ddeuaf gyda thi, os caniedi, heb y gwr crimmog-coch: os caniedi dyred yn hydda, heb Llywelyn.

I will come with thee, if thou wilt grant leave, said the long-shanked man: come and *welcome*, if thou thinkest fit, said Llywelyn. *H. Ll. ab Iorwerth.*

Hyddadl, *a.* (dadl) Disputable, controvertible.
Hyddadledd, *s. m.* (hyddadl) Aptness to dispute.
Hyddaif, *a.* (daif) Easily singed, easily blasted.
Hyddail, *a.* (dail) Apt to bear leaves; being of luxuriant foliage.

> Mis Mai—
> Hyddail coed, hyfryd anllad.

The month of May, *full of leaves* the trees, happy the amorous. *Anturia.*

Hyddal, *a.* (dal) Easily held; easily caught.
Hyddalrwydd, *s. m.* (hyddal) Facility for holding
Hyddallt, *a.* (dallt) Apt to understand; comprehensible.
Hyddalltrwydd, *s. m.* (hyddallt) Aptness to understand.
Hyddawn, *a.* (dawn) Apt to give; liberal; free.
Hyddeifiad, *s. m.* (hyddaif) A singeing easily.
Hyddeifrwydd, *s. m.* (hyddaif) Aptness to singe.
Hyddeigr, *a.* (deigr) Apt to produce tears.
Hyddeigredd, *s.* (hyddeigr) Aptness to shed tears
Hyddellt, *a.* (dellt) Apt to shiver, or shatter.

> Trystan, gynneddfau eglur,
> Hyddellt paladr o'th lafur:
> Mi yw Gwalchmai, nai Arthur.

Trystan of conspicuous talents, *apt to shiver* the shaft from thy toil: I am Gwalchmai, the nephew of Arthur. *Ymdd. Trystan a Gwalchmai.*

Hyddelltedd, *s. m.* (hyddellt) Aptness to shiver,
Hyddes, *s. f.—pl. t.* od (hydd) A hind, the female of the red deer.
Hyddestl, *a.* (destl) Apt to be neat, or trim.
Hyddestledd, *s. m.* (hyddestl) Aptness to be neat.
Hyddestlu, *v. a.* (hyddestl) To put in trim.
Hyddewis, *a.* (dewis) Easily choosing, or selecting.
Hyddewr, *a.* (dewr) Apt to be bold, or brave.
Hyddfref, *s. m.* (hydd—bref) The rutting of deer; rutting season; October.

> Calan hyddfref cain cymmwyre;
> Cyfarwydd dwfr yn ei ddyfrlle.

In the beginning of *October* fair the season; the water is well used to its course. *Gwalchmai.*

Hyddgae, *s. m.—pl. t.* au (hydd—cae) Deer park
Hyddgant, *s. m.* (hydd—cant) A herd of deer.

Efe a ddaeth yr hyddgant y rhyngddynt ill dau, ac y bwriodd y mab un o naddynt â saeth.

The *herd of deer* came between them two, and the youth shot one of them with an arrow. *Brut y Breninoedd.*

Hyddgen, *s. m.* (hydd—cen) The skin of a stag.

> Gwisgaf —
> Hyddgen y gwr gwahoddgar.

I will wear the *stag's skin* of the man who invites to the feasts. *D. ab Gwilym.*

Hyddgi, *s. m.—pl. t.* on (hydd—ci) Buck-hound.
Hyddgoed, *s. pl. aggr.* (hydd—coed) Deer park.
Hyddgorn, *s. m.—pl.* hyddgyrn (hydd—corn) A stag's horn, or hart's horn.
Hyddgroen, *s. m.* (hydd—croen) The stag's skin.
Hyddgylla, *s. m.* (hydd—cylla) A stag's stomach.
Hyddgyllen, *s. f.* (hyddgylla) A griskin, one of the twelve lawful pieces of a stag.
Hyddig, *a.* (dig) Irritable, choleric, passionate.
Hyddigder, *s. m.* (hyddig) Irritableness, irascibleness.
Hyddigrwydd, *s.m.*(hyddig) Aptness to be angry.
Hyddoeth, *a.* (doeth) Apt to be wise, easily wise
Hyddoethedd, *s.m.*(hyddoeth) Aptness to be wise
Hyddof, *a.* (dof) Easily tamed, tameable.
Hyddofrwydd, *s. m.* (hyddof) Facility of taming.
Hyddol, *a.* (dol) Apt to be wreathed or circled.
Hyddolawg, *a.* (hyddol) Being apt to be encircled

Boed dy wir ar dir——
Can mlynedd yn hedd, yn hyddolawg.

May thy sway be over the land for a hundred years in peace, in *magnificence.* *Ll. P. Moch, i Lywelyn* I.

Hyddyn Lywelyn; hyddolawg i feirdd,
A'i fyrddoedd llosog.

Affable is Llywelyn, *magnificent* are his bards, and his richly covered boards. *Ll. P. Moch.*

Hyddring, *a.* (dring) Easily climbed; apt to climb
Hyddrwg, *a.* (drwg) Apt to be bad; mischievous.
Hyddrygedd, *s. m.*(hyddrwg) Aptness to be bad.
Hyddwyn, *a.* (dwyn) Easily borne, or conveyed.
Hyddyn, *a.* (dyn) Much frequented by man; accessible to man; populous.

Lle hyddyn yw'r tyddyn tau.

Thy demesne is a *populous* place. *T. Aled.*

Milwr gwlydd, uffwyr gryd gryn,
Mal ydd wyt heddyw hyddyn.

A mild warrior, the terror of froward warriors, as thou art to-day *accessible.* *Ll. P. Moch, i Lywelyn* I.

Hyddysg, *a.* (dysg) Docible; well versed.
Hyddysgawl, *a.* (hyddysg) Of a docible nature.
Hyddysgedd, *s. m.* (hyddysg) Aptness to learn.
Hyddysgrwydd, *s. m.*(hyddysg) Aptness to learn.
Hyddysgu, *v. a.* (hyddysg) To learn readily; to render well versed; to become well versed.
Hyedd, *s. m.* (hy) Boldness; confidence.
Hyeithr, *a.* (eithr) Easily put off; exceptionable
Hyf, *a.* (hy) Bold, daring; confident; familiar.
Hyfâad, *s. m.* (hyf) A becoming confident.
Hyfach, *a.* (bach) Apt to hook, or to entangle.
Hyfad, *a.* (mad) Apt to be good; goodly.
Hyfael, *a.* (mael) Profitable; apt to gain.
Hyfaes, *a.* (maes) Apt to appear in the fields.

A Hensynyw deg o du glenydd Aeron,
Hyfaes y meillion, hyfes gorllydd.

And old fair Myvyw on the confine of the shores of Aeron, with *field-covering* trefoile, and wood prolific in acorns. *Gw. Brycheiniawg.*

Hyfaeth, *a.* (maeth) Nourishable, easily reared.
Hyfaethedd, *s. m.* (hyfaeth) Aptness to nourish.
Hyfaethu, *v. a.* (hyfaeth) To nourish easily.
Hyfagl, *a.* (magl) Apt to entangle; intricate.

Bid wen gwylan; bid fan ton;
Bid hyfagl gwyar ar on;
Bid lwyd rew, bid lew calon.

White be the sea-mew; loud be the wave; let the gore be *apt to clog* on the spear, let the frost be gray; let the heart be bold. *Llywarch Hen.*

Hyfagledd, *s. m.* (hyfagl) Aptness to entangle.
Hyfaglu, *v. a.* (hyfagl) To entangle easily.
Hyfai, *a.* (bai) Culpable; apt to criminate.
Hyfaidd, *a.* (baidd) Audacious; dauntless.
Hyfal, *a.* (mal) Apt to be like, or similar.
Hyfarn, *a.* (barn) Judicable; censorious.
Hyfarnedd, *s. m.* (hyfarn) Aptness to condemn
Hyfarnu, *v. a.* (hyfarn) To condemn readily.
Hyfath, *a.* (math) Easily paired, or assorted.
Hyfâu, *v. n.* (hyf) To become bold, or audacious.
Hyfawl, *a.* (mawl) Laudable, deserving praise.
Hyfder, *s. m.* (hyf) Boldness; audaciousness.
Hyfdra, *s. m.* (hyf) Boldness; audaciousness.
Hyfed, *a.*(med) Easily reaped; ready for reaping
Hyfedr, *a.* (medr) Expert, skilful, clever.
Hyfedredd, *s. m.* (hyfedr) Expertness, dexterity.
Hyfedrrwydd, *s. m.* (hyfedr) Expertness, skilfulness, cleverness.
Hyfedru, *v. n.* (hyfedr) To effect expertly.
Hyfedrus, *a.* (hyfedr) Apt to be expert.
Hyfeidrawl, *a.* (hyfedr) Comprehensible.
Hyfeiddiad, *s. m.* (hyfaidd) A daring easily.
Hyfeiddiawl, *a.* (hyfaidd) Easily venturing.
Hyfeiddrwydd, *s. m.* (hyfaidd) Audaciousness, intrepidity, daringness.
Hyfeiedd, *s. m.*(hyfai) Culpableness, censoriousness, aptness to find fault.
Hyfeiwr, *s. m.—pl.* hyfeiwyr (hyfai—gwr) A censorious person.
Hyfeleb, *a.* (hyfal) Apt to be similar.
Hyferw, *a.* (berw) Easily boiled, coctible.
Hyferwi, *v. a.* (hyferw) To boil easily, or aptly.
Hyfes, *a.* (mes) Abounding with acorns.
Hyfeth, *a.*(meth) Fallible; perishable, apt to fail
Hyfethiad, *s. m.* (hyfeth) A failing easily.
Hyfethrwydd, *s. m.* (hyfeth) Aptness to fail.
Hyfethu, *v. n.* (hyfeth) To fail easily.
Hyfiad, *s. m.* (hyf) A rendering bold, a growing bold or confident.
Hyflawdd, *a.* (blawdd) Apt to be tumultuous.
Hyfloedd, *a.* (bloedd) Apt to shout, shouting.
Hyflwng, *a.* (blwng) Apt to be morose, or glum.
Hyfodd, *a.* (bodd) Placable, easily pleased.
Hyfoddiad, *s. m.* (hyfodd) A rendering placable.
Hyfoddrwydd, *s. m.* (hyfodd) Aptness to please.
Hyfoes, *a.* (moes) Of easy manners, or polite.
Hyfoesedd, *s. m.* (hyfoes) Ease of manners.
Hyfolawd, *s. f.* (hyfawl) A merited praise.
Hyfolawg, *a.* (hyfawl) Having merited praise.

Hyfolawg hael, mynawg hawdd bo.

Worthy of praise the generous, may the placid one be at ease. *Ph. Brydydd, i Rys Gryg.*

Hyfoledd, *s. m.* (hyfawl) Laudableness.
Hyfoli, *v. a.* (hyfawl) To praise aptly, or easily.
Hyfoliant, *s. m.* (hyfawl) A merited praise.
Hyfrad, *a.* (brad) Apt to be treacherous or false.
Hyfradwch, *s.m.* (hyfrad) Aptness for treachery.
Hyfraw, *a.* (braw) Apt to awe; apt to be awed.
Hyfrawd, *a.* (brawd) Of apt judgment. *Barnu yn hyfrawd*, to pass a judicious sentence.
Hyfrawedd, *s. m.* (hyfraw) Aptness to be awed.
Hyfrawn, *v. n.* (hyfraw) To overawe easily.
Hyfreg, *a.* (breg) Apt to be fragile, or fractious.
Hyfregedd, *s.* (hyfreg) Aptness to be fractious.
Hyfregu, *v. a.* (hyfreg) To make fractious easily.
Hyfriw, *a.* (briw) Apt to be broken, or shattered *Hyfriw ei waew*, apt to be shivered is his spear.
Hyfro, *a.* (bro) Having access to a country.
Hyfröedd, *s. m.* (hyfro) Easy access to a country
Hyfrwd, *a.* (brwd) Easily heated, or warmed.
Hyfrwth, *a.* (brwth) Apt to be tumultuous.
Hyfrwyn, *a.* (brwyn) Easily affected, or made sensible of pain.
Hyfrwysg, *a.* (brwysg) Easily inebriated.
Hyfrwysgaw, *v. n.* (hyfrwysg) To become easily intoxicated; aptly to get drunk.
Hyfrwysgedd, *s.*(hyfrwysg) Aptness to inebriate.

Hyfryd, *a.* (bryd) Having the mind at liberty, or unimpeded; happy, cheerful; delightful, pleasant. *Mae arnat fyd hyfryd iawn*, thou leadest a very happy life.
Hyfrydaidd, *a.* (hyfryd) Pleasant in a degree.
Hyfrydedd, *s. m.* (hyfryd) Delightfulness.
Hyfrydiad, *s. m.* (hyfryd) A making happy, or pleasant; a cheering, a delighting.
Hyfrydiant, *s. m.* (hyfryd) The act of making happy, cheerful, or pleasant.
Hyfrydrwydd, *s. m.* (hyfryd) Delightfulness.
Hyfrydu, *v. a.* (hyfryd) To make cheerful.
Hyfrydwch, *s. m.* (hyfryd) Delightfulness.

Nid hyfrydwch ond gyda Duw.

There is no *happiness* but with God. *Adage.*

Hyfrys, *a.* (brys) Apt to be hasty, or quick.

Hyfrys emys ywnan darpar,
Hyfryd, cyfryd, [illegible] adar.

Impatient steeds prepared for combat, *happy* of one mind, of one course with the winged tribe. *Einion Offeiriad.*

Hyfrysedd, *s. m.* (hyfrys) Aptness to be hasty.
Hyfwyn, *a.* (mwyn) Apt to be kind, or pleased.
Hyfr, *s. m.*—*pl.* hyfrod (hyf) A gelt goat.
Hyff, *s. m.*—*pl. t.* ion (hy) A drive forward; a drift. *Hyff o eira*, a drift of snow.
Hyffagl, *a.* (ffagl) Easily made into a flame.
Hyffagledd, *s. m.* (hyffagl) Aptness to flame.
Hyffawd, *a.* (ffawd) Being apt to have success.
Hyffer, *a.* (ffer) Easily hardened; congealable.
Hyfferu, *v. a.* (hyffer) To fix or congeal easily.
Hyffiad, *s. m.* (hyff) A forcing on; a drifting.
Hyffiant, *s. m.* (hyff) An impulse forward; a drift
Hyffiaw, *v. a.* (hyff) To force forward; to drift. *Hyffiaw eira*, to drift snow.
Hyffiawl, *a.* (hyff) Apt to force forward, drifting.
Hyffi, *s. m.* (hyff) That is thrown off; a particle.
Hyfflam, *a.* (fflam) Apt to flame; inflammable.
Hyfflamedd, *s. m.* (hyfflam) Aptness to flame.
Hyfflamiad, *s.* (hyfflam) A causing to flame aptly
Hyfflamiaw, *v.* (hyfflam) To render inflammable.
Hyfflyn, *s. m. dim.* (hyffi) A particle. *Nid oes hyfflyn o hono gydai gilydd*, there is not a particle of it together. *Sil.*
Hyffo, *a.* (ffo) Apt to retreat; capable of retreat.
Hyffodiant, *s. m.* (hyffawd) Aptness to be lucky.
Hyffoedd, *s. m.* (hyffo) Aptness to fly, or retreat.
Hyffordd, *a.* (ffordd) Apt to make way; easily passing; passable: *Taith hyffordd*, an easy journey.
Hyfforddi, *v. a.* (hyffordd) To direct, to shew the way; to instruct, to train up.

Hyfforddia blentyn y'mhen ei ffordd.

Train up a child in the way he should go. *Proverbs* 22. 6.

Hyfforddiad, *s. m.* (hyffordd) A directing, a forwarding, a showing the way.
Hyfforddiadawl, *a.* (hyfforddiad) Apt to forward.
Hyfforddiannawl, *a.* (hyfforddiant) Tending to be a guidance; directory.
Hyfforddiant, *s. m.* (hyffordd) Direction, guidance
Hyfforddiaw, *v. a.* (hyffordd) To set on the way, to shew the way, to direct, to forward.
Hyfforddus, *a.* (hyffordd) Well-directed, well-conducted, being shewn the way, directed, or forwarded, well-instructed.
Hyfforddusaw, *v.* (hyfforddus) To render directory
Hyffraeth, *a.* (ffraeth) Apt to be eloquent or fluent
Hyffraethedd, *s.* (hyffraeth) Aptness to be fluent
Hyffraw, *a.* (ffraw) Easily put in agitation.
Hyffroen, *a.* (ffroen) Apt to snort, snorting.
Hyffrost, *a.* (ffrost) Apt to vaunt, or to swagger.
Hyffrwd, *a.* (ffrwd) Apt to stream, apt to flow.
Hyffrwyn, *a.* (ffrwyn) Being used to the bridle.
Hyffrydedd, *s. m.* (hyffrwd) Aptness to stream.
Hygabl, *a.* (cabl) Apt to deride; censorious.
Hygabledd, *s. m.* (hygabl) Aptness to censure.
Hygablrwydd, *s. m.* (hygabl) Censoriousness.
Hygad, *a.* (cad) Ready for battle; warlike.

Hygad ariad arial can car.

A *warlike* chief surrounded by hundred relatives. *Llywarch Hen (Offerenau).*

Hygadr, *a.* (cadr) Aptly puissant, apt to be strong
Hygadredd, *s. m.* (hygadr) Aptness to be strong.
Hygadw, *a.* (cadw) Easily kept, or guarded.
Hygael, *a.* (cael) Attainable, or obtainable.
Hygaeledd, *s. m.* (hygael) Attainableness, aptness to get or to obtain.
Hygais, *a.* (cais) Aptly attempting; easily tried.
Hygall, *a.* (call) Apt to be discreet, or cunning.
Hygalledd, *s. m.* (hygall) Aptness to be discreet.
Hygant, *s. m.* (cant) A surrounding circle.

Yn hygant y tri, yn llaw mor adaf,
Neud [illegible] ath gynnal.

In the communion of the three, in a hand so fair have I [illegible] thy support. *Ll. P. Moch*

Hygar, *a.* (car) Amiable, lovely; pleasing.

Hygar pawb wrth a garo.

Every one is *pleasing* to the one he loves. *Adage.*

Hygarad, *s. m.* (hygar) A being apt to love.

Heb ymgel hygar hygarad;
Heb yngar ysgwyd o'i angad.

Without an accessible motive of warm *affection*, without parting with the shield from his hand. *Ll. P. Moch, i G. ab Owain*

Hygardd, *a.* (cardd) Liable to disgrace.
Hygaredd, *s. m.* (hygar) Amiableness, loveliness, fondness, natural affection.
Hygarth, *a.* (carth) Easily cleansed out.
Hygarthu, *v. a.* (hygarth) To cleanse readily.
Hygarwch, *s. m.* (hygar) Amiableness, loveliness.
Hygas, *a.* (cas) Detestable, execrable, hateful.
Hygasedd, *s. m.* (hygas) Detestableness, odiousness, hatefulness.
Hygasgl, *a.* (casgl) Easily gathered together, convenable.
Hygasgledd, *s. m.* (hygasgl) Aptness to collect.
Hygasglu, *v. a.* (hygasgl) To collect readily.
Hygasrwydd, *s. m.* (hygas) Obnoxiousness.
Hygaul, *a.* (caul) Easily curdled, congealable.
Hygawdd, *a.* (cawdd) Easily provoked, irascible.

Rhyd——
Gwr ni oedd hygawdd, a oedd hygar.

Rhyd, a man that was not *apt to be provoked*, was amiable. *Cynddelw.*

Hyged, *a.* (ced) Ready of gift; bounteous. *Llaw hyged*, a liberal hand.
Hygedrwydd, *s. m.* (hyged) Bountifulness.
Hygel, *a.* (cel) Easily concealed, concealable.
Hygelu, *v. a.* (hygel) To conceal readily.
Hygelwch, *s. m.* (hygel) Aptness to conceal.
Hygeuledd, *s. m.* (hygaul) Aptness to coagulate.
Hygil, *a.* (cil) Easily receding, or retreating.
Hygladd, *a.* (cladd) Easily buried, that may be buried, easily dug open or trenched.
Hyglaf, *a.* (claf) Apt to be sick, or ill.
Hyglaer, *a.* (claer) Apt to be clear, or bright.
Hyglau, *a.* (clau) Apt to be uniform, sincere

Hael hyglau frydau, fryd eryr yn aer
Yn aros cyfergyr,
Hirgwyn brwyn [illegible] diechyr
Hirfraw am daw a'm lludyr.

Bountiful with *frank* designs, of eagle mind in slaughter waiting to attack; a deep lamenting pang unflinching [illegible] did break, as Tudyr fell [illegible] lasting woe. *Cynddelw, marw T. ab Gwynedd*

Hyglod, *a.* (clod) Deserving praise; renowned.

Hyglodedd, *s. m.* (hyglod) Laudableness; renownedness, famousness.

Hyglud, *a.* (clûd) Easily carried, or portable.

> Mis Gorphenaf hyglud gwair.
>
> The month of July the hay is apt to be carried. *Aneurin.*

Hygludedd, *s. m.* (hyglud) Portableness.

Hyglust, *a.* (clust) Of a ready ear; apt to hear.

Hyglustrwydd, *s. m.* (hyglust) Attentiveness.

Hyglwm, *a.* (clwm) Easily knotted, easily tied.

Hyglwyf, *a.* (clwyf) Easily wounded; vulnerable.

Hyglwyfaw, *v. a.* (hyglwyf) To wound easily.

Hyglyw, *a.* (clyw) Audible; apt to hear.

Hygnaif, *a.* (cnaif) Easily sheared, or clipped.

Hygnaw, *a.* (cnaw) Apt to gnaw, or bite.

Hygnöedd, *s. m.* (hygnaw) Aptness to gnaw.

Hygoddi, *v.* (hygawdd) To afflict or grieve easily.

Hygoddiant, *s. m.* (hygawdd) Aptness to afflict.

Hygoddrwydd, *s.* (hygawdd) Aptness to afflict.

Hygoel, *a.* (coel) Credible; easily believed; ready of belief, credulous.

Hygoeledd, *s. m.* (hygoel) Credibleness; readiness of belief, credulity.

> Gall fod iddo lawenydd mawr, fal pe cipied ef i fyny i'r trydydd nef: ac hygoeledd cadarn o fod ei gyflwr ef yn dda ddigon.
>
> He may be possessed of extreme joy, as if he were caught up into the third heaven; and a strong *credulity* of supposing his condition to be very well. *S. Trefredyn.*

Hygoeliad, *s. m.* (hygoel) A believing readily.

Hygoeliant, *s. m.* (hygoel) Aptness to believe.

Hygoeliaw, *v. n.* (hygoel) To believe readily.

Hygoelrwydd, *s. m.* (hygoel) Credulousness.

Hygof, *a.* (cof) Memorable; easily remembered.

Hygofiaw, *v. a.* (hygof) To remember readily.

Hygoll, *a.* (coll) Easily lost; apt to lose.

Hygolli, *v. a.* (hygoll) To lose or spill easily.

Hygor, *a.* (cor) Apt to enter a circle; accessible.

Hygosb, *a.* (cosb) Punishable, corrigible.

Hygosbedd, *s. m.* (hygosb) Aptness to punish.

Hygosbi, *v. a.* (hygosb) To punish readily.

Hygrawn, *a.* (crawn) Being easily collected.

Hygre, *s. m.* (hy—cre) Aptly sounding or roaring. The bore of the Severn, also called *tonrawg*, or wave-tearing.

Hygred, *a.* (cred) Apt to believe; credible.

Hygrededd, *s.* (hygred) Credibility, credibleness.

Hygrin, *a.* (crin) Apt to be brittle, or dry.

Hygrinaw, *v. n.* (hygrin) To grow brittle easily.

Hygrinedd, *s. m.* (hygrin) Aptness to be brittle.

Hygronedd, *s. m.* (hygrawn) Aptness to collect.

Hygroni, *v. a.* (hygrawn) To collect readily.

Hygrwydr, *a.* (crwydr) Apt to rove, or to stroll.

Hygrwydredd, *s. m.* (hygrwydr) Aptness to rove.

Hygryn, *a.* (cryn) Apt to shake, or quake.

> Hygryn helm, hoew lathr aer-ddar,
> Glaif cythrudd, anhygudd anhygur.
>
> An *aptly shaking* plume, an active polished oaken shaft of slaughter, a blade of tribulation, unavoidable, and not to be appeased. *Einion Len.*

Hygrynder, *s. m.* (hygryn) Aptness to tremble.

Hygryndra, *s. m.* (hygryn) Aptness to shake.

Hygrynedd, *s. m.* (hygryn) Aptness to quake.

Hygudd, *a.* (cudd) Apt to hide; easily hiding.

Hygur, *a.* (cur) Apt to throb, apt to beat.

Hygwl, *a.* (cwl) Culpable; exceptionable.

Hygwsg, *a.* (cwsg) Apt to sleep, easily sleeping.

Hygwydd, *a.* (cwydd) Apt to fall, or to tumble.

Hygwyddaw, *v. n.* (hygwydd) To tumble easily.

Hygwymp, *a.* (cwymp) Easily falling, apt to drop

Hygwympaw, *v. n.* (hygwymp) To fall easily.

Hygwympedd, *s. m.* (hygwymp) Aptness to fall.

Hygwyn, *a.* (cwyn) Apt to complain or grieve.

Hygyd, *a.* (cyd) Apt to join, apt to unite.

Hygydedd, *s.* (hygyd) Aptness to join or unite.

Hygylch, *a.* (cylch) Apt to surround, or to fold.

Hygylchedd, *s. m.* (hygylch) Aptness to surround

Hygylchu, *v. a.* (hygylch) To surround easily.

Hygyledd, *s. m.* (hygwl) Culpableness, culpability

Hygyrch, *a.* (cyrch) Easily approached, easily come at; approachable; much resorted.

> Hygyrchaf lle yn ei gyfoeth oedd Caer Lllon ar Wysg.
>
> The *most resorted* place in his dominions was Caer Llion upon Uske. *Gr. ab Arthur.*

Hygyrchedd, *s. m.* (hygyrch) Aptness to approach

Hygysgedd, *s. m.* (hygwsg) Aptness to sleep.

Hygysgu, *v. a.* (hygwsg) To sleep readily.

Hyhael, *a.* (hael) Apt to be generous or free.

Hyhaeledd, *s.* (hyhael) Aptness to be generous.

Hyhollt, *a.* (hollt) Easily split, or rifted.

Hyhud, *a.* (hud) Easily allured, or deceived.

Hyhudrwydd, *s. m.* (hyhud) Deceivableness.

Hyiach, *a.* (iach) Easily made well, or recovered.

Hyladd, *a.* (lladd) Apt to kill, easily killing.

Hylafar, *a.* (llafar) Ready of speech, fluent.

Hylaib, *a.* (llaib) Apt to lick, or lambative.

Hylais, *a.* (llais) Of a free or ready voice.

Hylaith, *a.* (llaith) Apt to be moist; apt to produce moisture; apt to dissolve.

Hylam, *a.* (llam) Of an apt or nimble step.

Hylamu, *v. a.* (hylam) To step readily.

Hylanw, *a.* (llanw) Apt to fill; easily filling.

Hylar, *a.* (llar) Easily satiated, or satisfied.

Hylaredd, *s. m.* (hylar) Aptness to satiate.

Hylaru, *v. a.* (hylar) To satiate readily.

Hylas, *a.* (hy—glas) Aptly producing verdancy.

Hylasu, *v. a.* (hylas) Aptly to become green.

Hylathr, *a.* (llathr) Of apt glare; highly polished.

> Hylathr ei ysgwyd, esgud barau gwrdd.
>
> *Highly polished* his shield, swift his vehement spears. *Llygad Gwr.*

Hylathraidd, *a.* (hylathr) Of a high polish.

Hylathru, *v. a.* (hylathr) To polish highly.

Hylaw, *a.* (llaw) Dexterous, ready-handed.

Hylawch, *a.* (llawch) Apt to protect, or guard.

Hylawd, *a.* (llawd) Apt to be wanton.

Hylawn, *v.* (llawn) Apt to be full; ample.

Hylawnedd, *s. m.* (hylawn) Aptness to fill.

Hylawrwydd, *s. m.* (hylaw) Dexterousness.

Hylech, *a.* (llech) Apt to lie flat, apt to sculk.

Hylechu, *v. a.* (hylech) To sculk readily.

Hyled, *a.* (lled) Easily expansive, expansible.

Hyledu, *v. a.* (hyled) To expand or spread easily.

Hyledd, *a.* (lledd) Tending to flatten.

Hylef, *a.* (llef) Of ready or free voice.

Hyleibiaw, *v. a.* (hylaib) To lick up readily.

Hyleisiaw, *v. a.* (hylais) To exert a voice readily.

Hyleithedd, *s. m.* (hylaith) Aptness to dissolve.

Hyleithiaw, *v. a.* (hylaith) To moisten readily.

Hylenwi, *v. n.* (hylanw) To become easily full.

Hyles, *a.* (lles) Aptly benefitting; beneficial.

Hylesrwydd, *s. m.* (hyles) Aptness to benefit.

Hylid, *a.* (llid) Apt to be angry; irritable.

Hylidiaw, *v. n.* (hylid) To grow angry easily.

Hylif, *a.* (llif) Apt to flow, or stream; voluble.

Hylifaw, *v. n.* (hylif) To flow or glide readily.

Hylifedd, *s. m.* (hylif) Aptness to flow, or glide.

Hylifrwydd, *s. m.* (hylif) Aptness to flow.

Hylith, *a.* (llith) Apt to allure; aptly allured.

> Cyglyu beleidr briw britho gyfergyr;
> A gwaed gwyr i ar wlith;
> A gwyach, hylef, hylith;
> A gwyddfa blaidd yn y blith.
>
> There were heard the shivered shafts rise in the conflict; and a dew of the blood of men; and the full-voiced grebe *aptly allured*, and in the midst the station of the wolf. *Cynddelw.*

Hylithedd, *s. m.* (hylith) Aptness to allure.
Hylithiad, *s. m.* (hylith) A readily alluring.
Hylithiaw, *v. a.* (hylith) To allure easily.
Hylithr, *s. f.* (llithr) Stinking hellebore; also called *hylyf* and *llegeyg y llyngyr*.
Hylithr, *a.* (llithr) Apt to slip, or to glide; easily slipping; slippery.
Hylithraw, *v. n.* (hylithr) To slip or glide easily.
Hylithredd, *s. m.* (hylithr) Aptness to slip.
Hylochi, *v. a.* (hylawch) To yield a ready refuge.
Hyloew, *a.* (gloew) Apt to clear; transparent.
Hylog, *a.* (llog) Easily hired, that may be hired.
Hylon, *a.* (llon) Apt to be cheerful, or merry.
Hylonedd, *s. m.* (hylon) Aptness to be cheerful.
Hyloni, *v. a.* (hylon) To cheer easily; to be easily cheered.
Hylosg, *a.* (llosg) Apt to take fire, easily burnt, easily kindled; combustible.
Hylosgedd, *s. m.* (hylosg) Aptness to burn.
Hylosgi, *v. n.* (hylosg) To burn or fire readily.
Hylosgrwydd, *s. m.* (hylosg) Aptness to burn.
Hylud, *a.* (glud) Apt to stick, easily adhering.
Hyludrwydd, *s. m.* (hylud) Aptness to adhere.
Hyludd, *a.* (lludd) Apt to obstruct; easily stopped.
Hyluddiaw, *v. a.* (hyludd) To obstruct readily.
Hylun, *a.* (llun) Figurable; easily formed.
Hylunder, *s. m.* (hylun) Aptness to figure.
Hylundra, *s. m.* (hylun) Aptness to figure.
Hylunedd, *s. m.* (hylun) Figurability.
Hylwgr, *a.* (llwgr) Easily defiled; corruptible.
Hylwrch, *a.* (llwrch) Of apt or high polish.

> Llaw hyladd a'r llafn hylwrch,
> Hynod glod gl[illegible] d[illegible].
>
> The ready slaying hand with the *highly polished* blade, it would acquire heroic and eminent fame.
> *Cynddelw m. Rhael ab Gruffudd.*

Hylwybr, *a.* (llwybr) Easily passed, or travelled, having facility of way; passable.
Hylwybr, *s. m.*—*pl.* hylwybrau (llwybr) A ready path, a direct road.

> Mae efe yn gwneuthur pob gwaith, ac y mae yn myned allan o'r hylwybr, a'r ffordd gyffredin.
>
> He executes every work; and he goes away out of the ready road and the common way.
> *Ier. Owain.*

Hylwybraw, *v. a.* (hylwybr) To open a ready path; to facilitate; to forward; to direct.
Hylwybredd, *s. m.* (hylwybr) Aptness to proceed.
Hylwydd, *a.* (llwydd) Apt to prosper, prosperous, successful, fortunate.

> Addfwyn medd a gulrdd gwledig hylwydd;
> Addfwyn haf hir-hyn, cain llwyn cun llwydd.
>
> Pleasant the mead, and the feast of the *fortunate* prince; pleasant the long fair summer, splendid the grove when it prospers.
> *Rhs. ab Gwalchmai.*

Hylwyddaw, *v. a.* (hylwydd) To render prosperous; to promote; to prosper, to be fortunate.
Hylwyddedd, *s. m.* (hylwydd) Prosperousness.
Hylyf, *s. m.* (llyf) The stinking hellebore.
Hylygredd, *s. m.* (hylwgr) Corruptibility.
Hylym, *a.* (llym) Apt to be sharp, or severe.
Hylyn, *a.* (glyn) Apt to cling, or to adhere.
Hylys, *a.* (llys) Easily rejected, or discarded.
Hylysrwydd, *s. m.* (hylys) Aptness to reject.
Hylyw, *a.* (llyw) Easily directed, or guided.
Hylywiaw, *v. a.* (hylyw) To direct with facility.
Hyll, *a.* (hy—yll) Dismal, gloomy, hideous, horrid, ghastly; savage, wild; fierce. *Golwg hyll*, a horrid spectacle; *paid a bod mor hyll*, cease to be so wild; *tywydd hyll iawn yw hwn*, this is very dismal weather.

> Chwaen hyll, ni roarch—
> Damaid, en chwedl [illegible].
>
> *Dismal* the event, nor [illegible], nor aught of [illegible] give ye to me
> *Bywyn Cyfeiliawg*
>
> Gwalch—hyll
> Crafangawg cryf ei esgyll.
>
> A *furious* hawk with great talons and strong of wing
> *T. Aled.*

Hylldawd, *s. m.* (hyll) Dismalness; gloominess; hideousness; savageness, fierceness.
Hyllder, *s. m.* (hyll) Hideousness, fierceness.
Hylldra, *s. m.* (hyll) Direfulness; hideousness.
Hylldraw, *s. m.* (hyll—traw) Dismay; terror.
Hylldrawiad, *s. m.* (hylldraw) A dismaying.
Hylldrawu, *v. a.* (hylldraw) To strike with terror, to dismay, to affright.
Hylldrem, *s. f.* (hyll—trem) A grim aspect.
Hylldremiad, *s. m.* (hylldrem) A looking wildly.
Hylldremiaw, *v. a.* (hylldrem) To look wildly.
Hylldremiawl, *a.* (hylldrem) Wildly looking.
Hylldremu, *v. a.* (hylldrem) To look wildly.
Hyllgryg, *s. m.* (hyll—cryg) A frightful hoarseness. *Enw math o elestron*, the stinking iris; also called *helheag*. *a.* Frightfully hoarse.

> Clywn—yma fil can mil o ffeiddiadau ac ocheidiau hyllgryg, ac ochenaidiau cryfion.
>
> I could hear in this place a thousand times a hundred thousand shrieks and frightfully hoarse groanings, and strong sighs.
> *Elis Wyn, B. Cwsg.*

Hylliad, *s. m.* (hyll) A rendering hideous; a scaring; a being frightened; a growing furious.
Hyllrwydd, *s. m.* (hyll) Ghastliness; savageness.
Hyllu, *v. a.* (hyll) To make hideous, or ugly; to scare, to frighten; to be terrified; to become wild, or furious; to look hideous, or ghastly.
Hyn, *pron. n.* (hwn) This, this thing; this much, this quantity. *Telir hyn a hyn am dano*, a certain sum will be paid for it. *Hyn a hyn*, such and such matter, thing, or quantity.

> Mwared Gymined, a weli di hyn!
> Yd lysg fy nghalon fal etewyn!
>
> Gently-gliding Cyminod, seest thou this? My heart burns like a brand!
> *Hwlgwasl m. Cynddylan.*

Hyn, *s. pl. aggr.* (hen) Ancestry, forefathers.

> Goleu-ddyn a'i hyn o had bonedd-faith
> Yw Angharad.
>
> A splendid one whose *ancestry* are of the seed of high nobility is Angharad.
> *Br. ab Gwilym.*
>
> Awn i gyd, yr hyn ac ieu,
> O'r ddwyradd, i'r ffordd orau.
>
> Let us all go, the *old* and young, of the two ranks, to the better road.
> *W. Cynwal.*

Hyn, *a.* (hen) Elder, senior. It is generally used instead of *hynach*, for the comparative degree; older, elder, or more old.

> Peth o'th oed aeth yd wy derfyn:
> Pymtheng-waith pymthengmlwydd hych hyn.
>
> Part of thy age is come to an end; fifteen times fifteen years be thou elder.
> *Ll. P. Moch, i Lywelyn I.*

Hyna, *pron. n.* (hyn) That there, that much, that quantity there, that quantity.
Hynacw, *pronoun prep.* (hyn—acw) That much yonder.
Hynaf, *a.* (*superl. of* hyn) Oldest, most ancient.

> Bo hynaf fo y dyn gwaethaf fydd ei hwyll.
>
> The *elder* a person is the worse is his disposition.
> *Adage.*

Hynaf, *s. m.*—*pl.* hynaif (hyn) Ancestor, forefather; an elder, a senator. *Pen hynaif*, chief of senators, a lieutenant general.
Hynafanedig, *a.* (hynaf—ganedig) Eldest born.
Hynafedd, *s. m.* (hynaf) Seniority, eldership
Hynafiad, *s. m.*—*pl.* hynafiaid (hynaf) An ancestor; an elder. *Hynafiaid cantref*, the elders of a *cantref*, usually called upon to give evidence respecting boundaries and local customs.
Hynafiaeth, *s. m.* (hynaf) Antiquity, old time.
Hynafiaethawl, *a.* (hynafiaeth) Antiquarian.
Hynafiaethydd, *s. m.* (hynafiaeth) An antiquary.

Hynaint, *s. m.* (hyn) Seniority, or eldership.
Hynawdd, *a.* (nawdd) Apt to give protection.
Hynawf, *a.* (nawf) Easily swimming, buoyant.
Hynaws, *a.* (naws) Good-natured, indulgent, kind, humane; gentle, mild, placid.

> A rano i lawer rhaned yn hynaws.
>
> He that distributes to the multitude let him distribute *kindly*. *Adage.*

Hynawsedd, *s. m.* (hynaws) Kindness of disposition, good-nature; gentleness, mildness.
Hynawsiad, *s. m.* (hynaws) A becoming kind.
Hynawsu, *v. n.* (hynaws) To become kind.
Hynedd, *s. m.* (hyn) Agedness, oldness, old age.
Hynefedd, *s. m.* (hynaf) Seniority, eldership.
Hynefydd, *s. m.*—*pl. t.* ion (hynaf) A senior.

> Hynefydd Powys, parth fygedd hir.
>
> The *elder* of Powys, a region fair and extensive. *Llygad Gwr.*

Hynerth, *a.* (nerth) Endued with strength.
Hyni, *adv.* (hy—ni) Until. See *oni*.

> Hyni ei dwr yn haul deg.
>
> Until water is changed to a fair sun. *L. G. Cothi.*

Hynod, *a.* (nod) Notable, remarkable, notorious.

> Nog un cythraul——
> Yn hau anadon mae'n hynodach.
>
> Than any devil, scattering blasphemies, he is more *notorious*. *T. Prys.*

> E bery dychan anhael
> Cyd a chlod hynod i hael.
>
> The dispraise of the miser will endure as long as the *illustrious* fame of the liberal. *T. Prys.*

Hynodawl, *a.* (hynod) Tending to be notable.
Hynodi, *v. a.* (hynod) To make notable, or remarkable; to become noted.
Hynodiad, *s. m.* (hynod) A rendering notable.
Hynodiaeth, *s. m.* (hynod) A notable action.
Hynodiant, *s. m.* (hynod) A notable affair.
Hynodrwydd, *s. m.* (hynod) Notableness; notoriousness, notoriety.
Hynodded, *s. f.* (hynawdd) Aptness to protect.
Hynoddi, *v. a.* (hynawdd) To give free refuge.
Hynoeth, *a.* (noeth) Apt to make naked.
Hynoethedd, *s. m.* (hynoeth) Aptness to denude.
Hynoethi, *v. a.* (hynoeth) To denude easily.
Hynofedd, *s. m.* (hynawf) Aptness to swim.
Hynofiaw, *v. a.* (hynawf) To swim easily.
Hynt, *s. f.*—*pl. t.* iau (hwnt) A way, a course, a career, a journey; a freak, whim, or humour. *Dwyn hynt*, to take a journey; *ar hynt*, straightway, or directly; *pa hynt?* how goes it? *Pa hyntiau drwg sydd yn dy ben?* what wicked freaks are in thy head.

> Hoedl——
> Fal yr awel ei helynt;
> Anhawdd dal hoewal ei hynt!
>
> Life, like the gale is its fate; it is difficult to catch the drift of its course! *M. ab H. Lewys.*

Hyntiad, *s. m.* (hynt) A going off abruptly.
Hyntiaw, *v. a.* (hynt) To take a course; to go away, to travel; to set off abruptly; to take a freak, or whim.
Hyntiawl, *a.* (hynt) Apt to set off abruptly.
Hyntiwr, *s. m.*—*pl.* hyntwyr (hynt—gwr) One who goes off abruptly; or takes a freak.
Hynwyf, *a.* (nwyf) Amorous, buxom, lively.
Hynwyfaw, *v. n.* (hynwyf) To become amorous.
Hynwyfawl, *a.* (hynwyf) Of amorous nature.
Hyny, *pron. n.* (hyn) That, that be, in speaking of what is not present. *Da oedd hyny*, that was well; *gan bwy mae hyny?* who has got that? *cei hyny*, thou shalt have that, thou shalt have that much; *y pethau hyny*, those things.

> Llawer un a ddwg newyn, ac er hyny gwnaiff a fyn.
>
> Many a one endures hunger, and yet for *that* he will get a wife. *Adage.*

> O'r rhai hyny arwynaw y forwyn decaf a oreg.
>
> Of *those* ones he claimed the fairest maid. *Mabinogion.*

Hynyma, *pron. n.* (hyn—yma) This here.
Hynyna, *pron. n.* (hyn—yna) That there.
Hyodlaidd, *a.* (hyawdl) Apt to be eloquent.
Hyodledd, *s. m.* (hyawdl) Eloquence; fluency.
Hyodli, *v. a.* (hyawdl) To speak eloquently.
Hypynt, *s. m.* (hwp) A brunt, a shock, a sudden effort; a push; a kind of metre, otherwise called *Colofn fraith*, *awdl losgyrnawg*, *lostodyn*, and *hypynt*.

> Hypynt yw un o'r mesurau goreu, a mwyaf caniadaidd yn yr iaith Gymraeg; ac yn amlach ei rywiau no neb mesur o fesur.
>
> The *brunt* is one of the best metres, and the most harmonious in the Welsh language; and it is more numerous in its variations than any other metre. *Barddas.*

Hyr, *s. m.*—*pl. t.* iau (her) A shock, or sharp push, a pushing, or egging on; also the gnar, or snarl of a dog.

> Pell nad huenwg gwen! gogwn pa hyr,
> Pan ddyfrigdrawd blawd blaen afallgyr.
>
> I wish it farther, that the fair was not asleep! I know whence the *shock*, when the blossoms flew about the tops of the apple-tree branches. *Gwalchmai.*

Hyraeth, *s. m.* (hyr) Shocking; concussion.
Hyran, *a.* (rhan) Easily divided, divisible.
Hyranawl, *a.* (hyran) Being shared easily.
Hyranedd, *s. m.* (hyran) Divisibility, the state of being easily shared, or divided.
Hyraniad, *s. m.* (hyran) A dividing easily.
Hyranrwydd, *s. m.* (hyran) Divisibleness.
Hyranu, *v. a.* (hyran) To divide or share, easily.
Hyrdd, *s. m.* (hwrdd) A sudden shock. *a.* Eager.
Hyrddaidd, *a.* (hwrdd) Apt to impel; like a ram
Hyrddawd, *s. m.* (hwrdd) Impulsion, a push.
Hyrddawl, *a.* (hwrdd) Impulsive, pushing.
Hyrddblaid, *s. f.*—*pl.* hyrddbleidiau (hwrdd—plaid) An impelling party; an aggressor.
Hyrddedig, *a.* (hwrdd) Being pushed, or impelled.
Hyrddeiddrwydd, *s. m.* (hyrddaidd) Rammishness
Hyrddfa, *s. f.* (hwrdd) The seat of impulsion.
Hyrddglawdd, *s. m.* (hwrdd—clawdd) A battery.
Hyrddhynt, *s. f.*—*pl. t.* iau (hwrdd—hynt) An impelled course; a course of assault.
Hyrddiad, *s. m.* (hwrdd) A violently impelling, a pushing; arictation, a ramming.
Hyrddiad, *s. c.*—*pl.* hyrddiaid (hwrdd) A mullet, is also called *mingrwn*.
Hyrddiannawl, *a.* (hyrddiant) Apt to be impulsive
Hyrddiannu, *v. a.* (hyrddiant) To make impulsive.
Hyrddiant, *s. m.* (hwrdd) Impulsation. *Chwyf hyrddiant*, motion of impulsation.
Hyrddiaw, *v. a.* (hwrdd) To impel, to push, to thrust, to drive; to butt; to make an assault, or onset; to arictate, to ram.

> Hyrddiai lanw, hardd oleuni,
> Haul yr ellyllon yw hi.
>
> *It would impel* the tide, the fair luminary: it is the sun of the goblins. *D. ab Gwilym, I'r lleur.*

Hyrddiedydd, *s. m.*—*pl. t.* ion (hyrddiad) An impeller.
Hyrddin, *a.* (hwrdd) Of an impulsive nature.
Hyrddiwr, *s. m.*—*pl.* hyrddwyr (hwrdd—gwr) A pusher, or impeller; one who assaults.
Hyrddu, *v. a.* (hwrdd) To push, to impel, to thrust, to butt; to make an assault.
Hyrddwynt, *s. m.*—*pl. t.* oedd (hwrdd—gwynt) A hurricane.
Hyrddyn, *s. m. dim.* (hwrdd) A mullet. *Hyrddyn coch*, a red mullet.

Hyred, *a.* (rhed) Apt to run, easily running.
Hyreg, *a.* (rheg) Having many gifts.
Hyrew, *a.* (rhew) Apt to freeze easily.
Hyriad, *s. m.* (hyr) A giving a shock, or push.
Hyrif, *a.* (rhif) Easily numbered, computable.
Hyrifedd, *s. m.* (hyrif) A computable state.
Hyrith, *a.* (rhith) Apt to appear or seem.
Hyrithedd, *s. m.* (hyrith) Aptness to appear.
Hyrithiad, *s. m.* (hyrith) An appearing easily.
Hyrithiaw, *v. n.* (hyrith) To appear aptly.
Hyrmer, *s. m.* (hyr—mer) A jolt-head.
Hyrn, *s. f.*—*pl. t.* oedd (yrn) A smooth round mass; a haugh, holme, or meadow formed by the water of a river.

> Nid af i, nid wyf ynnorth,
> I'm haiarn wing, a'm hyrn noeth.
>
> I will not go (I am not silly) into my iron drum, with my bald pole. *Gwalchmai y Glyn.*

Hyrodd, *a.* (rhodd) Apt to give, bountiful, liberal
Hyroddi, *v. a.* (hyrodd) To give liberally.
Hyrus, *a.* (rhus) Apt to start; hesitating.
Hyrusaw, *v. a.* (hyrus) To start aside easily.
Hyrusedd, *s. m.* (hyrus) Aptness to start.
Hyrusiad, *s. m.* (hyrus) A starting easily.
Hyrusrwydd, *s. m.* (hyrus) Aptness to start.
Hyrwydd, *a.* (rhwydd) Apt to be unimpeded.
Hyrwyddaw, *v. a.* (hyrwydd) To facilitate, to expedite; to make free of obstacles.
Hyrwyddedd, *s. m.* (hyrwydd) Aptness to facilitate
Hyrwyddiad, *s.* (hyrwydd) A facilitating aptly.
Hyrwym, *a.* (rhwym) Easily bound; apt to bind
Hyrwymawl, *a.* (hyrwym) Aptly astringent.
Hyrwymedd, *s. m.* (hyrwym) Aptness to bind.
Hyrwysg, *a.* (rhwysg) Aptly tending forward.
Hyrwysgaw, *v. a.* (hyrwysg) To tend forward aptly, to go headlong.
Hyrygawg, *a.* (hwrwg) Having hunches.
Hyrym, *a.* (grym) Apt to effect; forcible.
Hyrymedd, *s. m.* (hyrym) Effectibility; forcibleness; aptness to produce power.
Hyrymu, *v. a.* (hyrym) To render effectible.
Hyryn, *a.* (rhyn) Apt to shake, or to shiver.
Hyrynedd, *s. m.* (hyryn) Aptness to shiver.
Hyrynu, *v. a.* (hyryn) To shake or shiver easily.
Hyryw, *a.* (rhyw) Of a perfect kind or sort.
Hys, *s. f.*—*pl. t.* iau (hy—ys) A snarl; also the imperative of *Hysiaw*, used in setting on a dog
Hysaf, *a.* (saf) Apt to stand; steady, or firm.
Hysaidd, *a.* (hys) Snarlish, apt to be surly.
Hysaig, *a.* (saig) Readily having a meal.
Hysail, *a.* (sail) Having a ready foundation.
Hysain, *a.* (sain) Aptly or easily sounding.
Hysar, *a.* (sar) Apt to appear angry.
Hysardd, *a.* (sardd) Apt to chide; easily chided.
Hysarddedd, *s. m.* (hysardd) Aptness to chide.
Hysathr, *a.* (sathr) Aptly or easily trodden.
Hysawdd, *a.* (sawdd) Aptly or easily sinking.
Hysawl, *a.* (hys) Apt to snarl; being urged on.
Hysbys, *a.* (ysbys) Manifest, evident, well-known, certain. *Gwr hysbys*, a cunning man, or conjurer.
Hysbysai, *s. m.* (hysbys) That points out; an index; a concordance.
Hysbysawl, *a.* (hysbys) Tending to make manifest.
Hysbysedig, *a.* (hysbys) Being made manifest, certified, acquainted.
Hysbysedigawl, *a.* (hysbysedig) Tending to render manifest; significative.
Hysbysiad, *s. m.*—*pl. t.* au (hysbys) A manifesting, a making evident; an acquainting; an advertisement; a certificate.
Hysbysrwydd, *s. m.* (hysbys) Information, advertisement, notice, or intelligence.
Hysbysu, *v. a.* (hysbys) To render manifest; to acquaint; to certify, to advertise, to give notice, to inform, to publish.
Hysbyswr, *s. m.*—*pl.* hysbyswyr (hysbys—gwr) One who makes evident, a certifier.
Hysbysydd, *s. m.*—*pl. t.* ion (hysbys) Manifester
Hysedd, *s. m.* (hys) The state of being snarling.
Hysefyll, *v. a.* (hysaf) To stand easily. *a.* Surefooted, or aptly standing.
Hysefylliad, *s. m.*—*pl. t.* au (hysefyll) An aptly standing; the state of aptly being, or existing.

> Megys y mae yr holl eneidiau yn eiddo ef, [illegible] am eu dechreuad, a'u hysefylliad, felly yr eiddo ef [illegible] a'u gorsefylliad.
>
> In the same manner as all souls are his, with respect to their beginning, and their existence, so they are his [illegible] on account of their supportation and their situation. *Ezr. Dewis.*

Hyseiddiawg, *a.* (hysaidd) Of a snarling nature.
Hyseiliaw, *v. a.* (hysail) To make a foundation aptly; to found firmly.
Hyseiniaw, *v. n.* (hysain) To sound readily.
Hysel, *a.* (sel) Aptly perceiving, readily seeing.
Hysen, *a.* (sen) Aptly chiding; reprehensible.
Hysènu, *v. a.* (hysen) To chide aptly or freely.
Hyserch, *a.* (serch) Disposed to love; amiable.
Hysgw, *s. m.* (ysgw) A backing, or abetting.
Hysgwaeth, *s. m.* (hysgw) Encouragement, countenance, protection.
Hysgwaw, *v. a.* (hysgw) To encourage, to abet.
Hysgwawl, *a.* (hysgw) Tending to urge on.
Hysgwedd, *s. m.* (hysgw) The act of urging on.
Hysgwydd *s. m.*—*pl. t.* ion (hysgw) An abettor.
Hysgyr, *s. m.*—*pl. t.* ion (ysgyr) A split piece of wood; a stave; a splinter.

> Dy Gwrych bion,
> [illegible] dynaion,
> Wy cynnal eu hysgyron
> Yn ddwylaw eu gaion.
>
> The royal sons, [illegible] of men, their shivering shafts with [illegible] in the hands of their foes. *Taliesin, i Urien.*

Hysiad, *s. m.* (hys) A snarling; a making to snarl; a setting on a dog.
Hysian, *v. a.* (hys) To cause to snarl; to set on.
Hysiaw, *v. a.* (hys) To cause to snarl; to urge.
Hysigl, *a.* (sigl) Apt to shake, easily shaking.
Hysiglaw, *v. a.* (hysigl) To shake easily.
Hysigledd, *s. m.* (hysigl) Aptness to shake.
Hysoddawl, *a.* (hysawdd) Being apt to sink.
Hysoddi, *v. n.* (hysawdd) To sink easily.
Hysoddrwydd, *s. m.* (hysawdd) Aptness to sink.
Hysom, *a.* (som) Apt to disappoint, or balk.
Hysomedd, *s. m.* (hysom) Aptness to disappoint.
Hysomi, *v. a.* (hysom) To disappoint easily.
Hyson, *a.* (son) Apt to make a noise; noisy.

> [illegible]
> [illegible]
>
> [illegible] suffer to pass through [illegible] fair [illegible] of splendid fame. *[illegible] Gwalchmai.*

Hysonedd, *s. m.* (hyson) Aptness to yield sound.
Hysoniaw, *v. a.* (hyson) To produce a sound aptly
Hysp, *a.* (ysp) Dry, dried up; barren.

> [illegible] groth yn erthylu, a bronnau hyspion.
>
> [illegible] them a miscarrying womb, and dry breasts. *Hosea* 9, 14.

Hyspaidd, *a.* (hysp) Of a drying tendency.
Hyspedd, *s. m.* (hysp) A dry state; barrenness.
Hyspiad, *s. m.* (hysp) A drying, a making barren.
Hyspu, *v. a.* (hysp) To render dry; to become dry, to become without milk.
Hyspydd, *s.* (hysp) The state of being exhausted.
Hyspyddadwy, *a.* (hyspydd) Exhaustible, drainable

Hyspyddedig, *a.* (hyspydd) Being exhausted.
Hyspyddiad, *s. m.* (hyspydd) An exhausting.
Hyspyddu, *v. a.* (hyspydd) To dry, to exhaust.
Hyswn, *a.* (swn) Apt to be noisy, or loud.
Hyswydd, *a.* (swydd) Ready or apt in an office.
Hysyn, *a.* (syn) Apt to fix the mind.
Hysynedd, *s. m.* (synedd) Aptness to conceive, or design; perceptibility.
Hysyniad, *s. m.* (hysyn) A conceiving aptly.
Hysyniaw, *v. a.* (hysyn) To conceive aptly.
Hytrach, *a.* (hydrach) More forward, rather. *Yn hytrach*, rather.

Nid oes genyt na ffydd na gobaith mewn Duw, ond yn hytrach mewn grym cyfoeth, anrhydedd, a thrasegddrwydd dy genedl.

Thou hast neither faith nor hope in God; but *rather* in the power of wealth, honour, and connection of thy family. *Marchawg Crwydrad.*

Hytynt, *s. m.* (hyd—hynt) A course, a journey. *Hytynt y dwfr*, the course of the water.
Hywad, *a.* (gwad) Deniable; easily disowned.
Hywadu, *v. a.* (hywad) To deny or disown readily
Hywaedd, *a.* (gwaedd) Apt to cry out, or shout.
Hywain, *a.* (gwain) Aptly ministering.
Hywaith, *a.* (gwaith) Ready at work; dexterous.
Hywall, *a.* (gwall) Apt to be faulty; fallible.
Hywalledd, *s. m.* (hywall) Aptness to fail.
Hywallu, *v. n.* (hywall) To fail easily.
Hywan, *a.* (gwan) Easily passing through; penetrable; easily divided.
Hywanedd, *s. m.* (hywan) Penetrability.
Hywanu, *v. a.* (hywan) To penetrate easily.
Hywar, *a.* (gwar) Easily tamed, manageable.

Glaif hywan, ac nid glaif hywar:
Ac glod Gwair a'i air i ar y trihael.

A *freely stabbing* blade, and not a blade easily made quiet: Gwair in fame and word, would surpass the three generous ones. *Cynddelw.*

Hywaredd, *s. m.* (hywar) Tameableness.
Hywaru, *v. a.* (hywar) To tame readily.
Hywedd, *a.* (gwedd) Apt to be orderly, or ranged; conformable, tractable, easy to be tamed; accustomed to the yoke.
Hyweddawl, *a.* (hywedd) Conformable, tractable.
Hyweddedig, *a.* (hywedd) Rendered orderly.
Hyweddfalch, *a.* (hywedd—balch) Tractably proud. *March hyweddfalch*, a high-mettled tractable steed.
Hyweddfrys, *a.* (hywedd—brys) Of tractable haste

Rhys Gryg——
A'i aur rhudd, a'i fudd a'i fawredd,
A'i emys hyweddfrys, hywedd.

Rhys Gryg, with his ruddy gold, and his good fortune, and his wealth, and his sleek stallion, the *well-trained restlessness*. *Ll. P. Moch.*

Hyweddiad, *s. m.* (hywedd) A rendering conformable, or tractable, a breaking in, a taming, a conforming or becoming tractable.
Hyweddiant, *s. m.* (hywedd) Tractableness; aptitude.

Tair cainc hyweddiant iaith; a ddeellir, a hoffir, ac a gredir.

The three traits of the aptitude of language, what is understood, what is liked, and what is believed. *Berudas.*

Hyweddrwydd, *s. m.* (hywedd) Tractableness.
Hyweddu, *v. a.* (hywedd) To render tractable, to break in, to tame; to accustom to the yoke; to conform, to become tractable.

Rhag maint dy far, y car cu,
Nid yw hawdd dy hyweddu.

On account of thy wrath, thou amiable friend, it is not *easy to make thee tractable*. *Rhys Wyn, i T. Prys.*

Hyweddus, *a.* (hywedd) Of a tractable disposition
Hyweddwr, *s. m.—pl.* hyweddwyr (hywedd—gwr) A person who is tractable.

Hyweiniad, *s. m.—pl.* hyweiniaid (hywain) One who aptly serves.
Hyweithgar, *a.* (hywaith) Of dexterous habit.
Hyweithgarwch, *s. m.* (hyweithgar) Aptitude for work or labour.
Hyweithiaw, *v. a.* (hywaith) To work readily.
Hyweithus, *a.* (hywaith) Of a dexterous habit.
Hywel, *a.* (gwel) Easily seen; visible, perceptible; conspicuous.
Hyweledd, *s. m.* (hywel) Perceptibility; conspicuousness; visibleness.
Hywell, *a.* (gwell) Easily mended; remediable.
Hywelliant, *s. m.* (hywell) Improvableness.
Hywellus, *a.* (hywell) Of a bettering tendency.
Hywen, *a.* (gwen) Apt to smile, easily smiling.

Udd addien, hywen Hywel, neud adneu!
Nid adwna Duw a wnel.

The faultless chief, the *easily smiling* Hywel, is he not laid to rest! God will not undo what he has done. *Ll. P. Moch.*

Hywenu, *v. a.* (hywen) To smile easily or aptly.
Hywerth, *a.* (gwerth) Vendible, saleable.

Gorwyn blaen perth; hywerth gorwydd:
Yn da pwyll gyda nerth;
Gwnelid anghelfydd anferth.

Glittering the top of the bush; *valuable* the trained steed: it is good to have judgement with strength: the inaccurate will make an unsightly job. *Llywarch Hen.*

Hywerthedd, *s. m.* (hywerth) Saleableness.
Hywerthrwydd, *s. m.* (hywerth) Saleableness.
Hywest, *a.* (gwest) Easily visited; much frequented by guests; hospitable.

Ceir——Medd meddlyn
Gan Hyfaidd hywr hywest ddilyn.

There shall be had mead, the intoxicating liquor, from the heroic Hyfaidd, of *hospitable* course. *Taliesin.*

Hywestedd, *s. m.* (hywest) The state of frequent visiting; frequency of guests; hospitality.
Hywestl, *a.* (gwestl) Apt to be riotous, or noisy.

Ef——
Yn hywestl yn hywen.

He is *full of vivacity*, and wearing a constant smile. *Cynddelw.*

Hywestledd, *s. m.* (hywestl) Aptness to be riotous
Hywestu, *v. a.* (hywest) To visit freely; to have much visiting.
Hywir, *a.* (gwir) Ready for or to tell truth; truth.

A fo hyborth hywir fydd.

That is general in circulation is *apt to be true*. *Adage.*

Hywiriaw, *v. a.* (hywir) To declare truth readily.
Hywiw, *a.* (gwiw) Apt to be excellent.
Hywiwdeb, *s. m.* (hywiw) Aptness to excel.
Hywledd, *a.* (gwledd) Easily feasting; luxurious.
Hywlydd, *a.* (gwlydd) Apt to be mild, or gentle.

Hael hywlydd, lawrydd Llywelyn.

The generous, *aptly mild*, and open-handed Llywelyn. *Ll. P. Moch.*

Hywnedd, *a.* (gwnedd) Easily accomplished.
Hywneddrwydd, *s. m.* (hywnedd) Feasibleness.
Hywnel, *a.* (gwnel) Feasible, easily performed.
Hywneledd, *s.* (hywnel) Feasibility, feasibleness.
Hywr, *a.* (gwr) Aptly like a man; manly.
Hywraig, *a.* (gwraig) Aptly like a woman.
Hywredd, *s. m.* (hywr) Manliness, or heroism.

Brycheiniawg, bro hywredd.

Brycheiniog the country of *heroism*. *Gw. Brycheiniawg.*

Hywst, *a.* (gwst) Aptly disordered; easily broken

Oedd hywst gwregawn enguriawr
Yn nechreu ynganiad y geirawr.

Frangible was the awful arch at the first uttering of the word. *Taliesin.*

Hywstedd, *s. m.* (hywst) Fragility, fragileness.

Hywydd, *a.* (gwydd) Easily perceived; of apt perception. *Dyn hywydd*, an intelligent person; *haelion hywydd*, intelligent liberal ones.

> Gwen, wrth Lawen yd wylwys neithwyr,
> A'r ysgwyd ar ei ysgwydd
> [illegible] bu mab i'm bu hywydd.

> Gwen watched by the side of Llawen last night, with the shield on his shoulder; [illegible] he was my son, he was very observant. *Llywarch Hen.*

Hywyddiant, *s. m.* (hywydd) Apt perception.

Hywyl, *a.* (gwyl) Easily perceived, perceivable.

Hywyliaw, *v. a.* (hywyl) To perceive easily.

Hywys, *a.* (gwys) Easily convened, conveenable.

Hywystl, *s. m.* (gwystl) A sure pledge. *a.* Easily pledged, or pawned.

> Ef ydoedd Owain hir, hywystl hedydd.

> He was Owain the stately, the *sure pledge of* [illegible]. *Gwalchmai.*

Hyŷs, *a.* (ŷs) Easily devoured, or eaten; eatable. *Pryf y bo hyŷs ei gig*, an animal whose flesh is eatable. *Welsh Laws.*

I.

I, *prep.* To; into; toward; for. *I mi*, to me; *i fy*, i'm, to my, unto my; *i'r dref*, to the town, *tyngaf i Dduw*, I swear to God; *brysia i ganu*, make haste for to sing.—It is also used in common with *O* and *Y*, for, of, and in respect to; as, *i lawr*, downward, *i fyny*, upward; *dos i fyny*, go upward, or go up; *car i mi*, a relation of mine; *cei beth i gan y dyn hwn*, thou shalt have some from this person; *dos i ar y ffordd*, go out of the way; *i-gam o-gam*, a zig-zag; *i am ei law*, *i ach ei law*, close at his hand.

> Bwrw caeth i gythraul.

> To devote a slave *to* the devil. *Adage.*

> Gwae a ddyco ei henwas i lys.

> Woe to him who shall take his old servant *to* court. *Adage.*

> Llundain i Sais lle nad oes eisiau son
> Am wychder dynion, Mon i minnau.

> London *for* an Englishman, where there is never the want of talk about the finery of people, but Anglesey *for* me. *Gr. Owain.*

> Coffewch eich rhyddid, yr hon y mae yr hanner gwyr hyn yn chwennych ei ddwyn i arnoch.

> Remember your liberty, the which these half men are desirous of taking away *from* you. *Gr. ab Arthur.*

> Tryw i fab iar ddadogan.

> It is natural *for* a cock to proclaim. *Adage.*

I, *pron.* I, me. It is used, when a stress, or emphasis, is required, upon the possessive, my or mine, whether expressed or implied, in the common order; as, *cerais*, or *cerais i*, I have loved; *rhai a'm carasant*, or *rhai a'm carasant i*, some have loved me; *fy mam*, or *fy mam i*, my mother.

IA, *s. m. r.* That is slippery, or glib, ice.

Ia, *adv.* Yes, aye. *Dyma yd da*, here is good corn; *ai e ia?* is it so aye?

Iaeth, *s. m.* (iâ) Iciness, the state of being icy.

Iaidd, *a.* (iâ) Of an icy nature, like ice.

Iain, *a.* (iâ) Abounding with ice, like ice.

Iach, *s. f.*—*pl. t.* au (ach) A stem; a pedigree.

> A iach Wenwys i'ch wyneb.

> With the *race* of the Gwenwys in your countenance. *S. Cent.*

Iach, *a.* (ia—ach) Sane, sound, whole, well, healthy, wholesome; unhurt, undamaged. *Dyn iach*, a man in health; *nid wyf yn iawn iach*, I am not very well; *canu yn iach*, to bid adieu.

> Nid iach ond a fo marw.

> No one is *well* but who is dead. *Adage.*

> Yn iach feibion wych fobyd,
> A yn iach, bellach i'r byd!

> Farewell, ye men who glory in your youth, and farewell, at length, to the world! *R. Tudur.*

Iachâad, *s. m.* (iach) A healing; a becoming well.

Iachâawl, *a.* (iach) Of a healing quality.

Iachad, *s. m.* (iach) A healing; a becoming well.

Iachäedig, *a.* (iachad) Being healed, made well.

Iachäedigaeth, *s. m.* (iachäedig) Act of healing.

Iachäedigawl, *a.* (iachäedig) Sanative, curative.

Iachaidd, *a.* (iach) Of a healthy condition.

Iachâu, *v. a.* (iach) To render sane, sound, whole, or well; to cure, to heal; to become well.

Iachâus, *a.* (iach) Of a healing quality, sanative.

Iachawd, *s. m.* (iach) The act of healing; a becoming well, or being restored to health.

Iachawdwr, *s. m.*—*pl.* iachawdwyr (iachawd—gwr) A healer; a saviour.

Iachawdwriaeth, *s. m.* (iachawdwr) Saviourship.

Iachedig, *a.* (iach) Being made well or cured.

Iachus, *a.* (iach) Wholesome, sound in health.

Iachusaw, *v. a.* (iachus) To render healthy; to become healthy.

Iachusawl, *a.* (iachus) Of a healthy condition.

Iachusrwydd, *s. m.* (iachus) Healthiness, sanity.

Iachwy, *s. m.* (iach) A healthy state; health.

Iachwyawl, *a.* (iach) Salutary, healthful.

> O. C. 1120—y bu farw Maredudd ab Bleddyn, tegwch a diogelwch holl Bowys, ac ei hamddiffyn, gwedi cymeryd iachwyawl benyd ar ei gorff, a gleiniaid edifarwch yn ei ysbryd.

> A. D. 1120—died Meredydd son of Bleddyn, the ornament and safety of all Powys, and its defence, after undergoing *salutary* penance of his body, and sanctity of repentance in his spirit. *B. y Tywysogion.*

Iachwydd, *s. m.* (iach—gwydd) Saving knowledge

Iachwyddawl, *a.* (iachwydd) Of saving knowledge

> Y gwyrthiau a'r rhyfeddodau—ar led y bydoedd rhyddarwedd iddynt egluraw, a goleuo ei galon yntau wrth gredu i Grist iachwyddawl.

> The miracles and the wonders spread over the universe, these did open and enlighten his heart, by believing in Christ *of saving knowledge.* *Gr. ab Arthur.*

Iad, *s. m.*—*pl. t.* au (ia—ad) The side of the face from the temples upward; the fore part of the head, the pate, the skull.

> Gwallt melyn—
> Arwyan teg ar iad dyn.

> The yellow hair in beauteous ringlets over the fair one's *temples.* *D. ab Gwilym.*

> O mynnir amser mewn ir iad,
> Yr ail oes, aros Iriaid.

> If time should be wished for in thy moist *temples*, to a second age, stay and listen, thou unlearn. *H. ab D. ab I. ab Rhys.*

Iadfoel, *a.* (iad—moel) Having a bald pate.

Iadlwm, *a.* (iad—llwm) Having a bare pate.

Iaedd, *s. m.* (iâ) The state of being icy, iciness.

Iäeiddrwydd, *s. m.* (iaidd) Iciness, icy state.

Iäen, *s. f.*—*pl. t.* au (iâ) A sheet of ice. *Maen dros iaen yw arlwydd*, a chieftain is like a stone over the ice.

> Maen dros iaen.

> A stone over the ice. *Adage.*

Gwrth berw dydd oswydd; oes o iâen,
Dillyngws Celi, fal cwlwm dolen!

The exile pushes away the day of the slaughtered ones; a life of ice, the mysterious One has dissolved, like a bow knot. *Ll. P. Moch.*

Mi awn at ddeuwr o'm iaith
Drwy'r aweddwr, drwy'r oddaith,
Drwy'r ias ficn.—

I would go to two of my countrymen through the eddying stream, through the conflagration, through the blue *ice*. *L. G. Cothi.*

Iain, *a.* (iâ) Abounding with ice; very cold.

Iaith, *s. f.—pl.* ieithiau and ieithoedd (aith) A language, or speech.

Tri anhebgor iaith: purdeb, amledd, ac hyweddiant.

The three indispensables of *language*: purity, copiousness, and aptitude. *Barddas.*

Tri pheth a ddylai bardd eu cynnal: yr iaith Gymmraeg, y brifarddoniaeth, a chof am bob daionus a rhagor.

Three things which a bard ought to support: the Welsh *language*, the primitive bardism, and a memorial of every thing good and excellent. *Barddas.*

Ial, *s. f.—pl. t.* au (al) A clear, or open, space, a fair or open region.

Ial, *a.* (al) Clear, fair, or open. *Tir ial*, open land; *tir anial*, overgrown land, or a wilderness.

Ialaidd, *a.* (ial) Tending to be clear, or fair.

Ialain, *a.* (ial) Of a clear or fair quality.

Ialant, *s. m.* (ial) Clearness, fineness, lustre.

Ialawg, *a.* (ial) Abounding with clearness.

Ialedd, *s. m.* (ial) The state of being clear.

Ialen, *s. f. dim.* (ial) That is fair, or even; a rod.

Dwyn yr wy, dan arafwch,
Dy ialen drom, dy law'n drwch.

I am bearing, with patience, thy heavy *rod*, in thy severe hand. *H. R. Llywelyn.*

Ialu, *v. a.* (ial) To render clear; open, or fair.

Ialus, *a.* (ial) Of a clear nature; fine, or smooth.

Ialwch, *s. m.* (ial) Clearness, fairness; lucidness.

Ialyd, *a.* (iâ) Tending to be icy; like ice.

Ialydrwydd, *s. m.* (ialyd) The state of being icy.

Iang, *a.* (ang) At large, unrestrained; blunt.

Iangaidd, *a.* (iang) Apt to be without restraint; somewhat uncivilized; boorish, clownish.

Yn iangaidd, ni wyr waeddi
Ac yn ei grwm y gwnai gri.

When *loose*, it is not capable of calling out, but in it's bending form it would make a cry. *T. Derllys, i fwa.*

Iangawl, *a.* (iang) Of a loose, or unrestrained state; of an uncivil disposition.

Iangedig, *a.* (iang) Being rendered, or become void of restraint; being become rude.

Iangedd, *s. m.* (iang) A loose, or wild state; rudeness, boorishness.

Iangiad, *s. m.* (iang) A rendering loose, or wild; a becoming void of restraint, or rude.

Iangrwydd, *s. m.* (iang) Rudeness, boorishness.

Iangu, *v. a.* (iang) To render loose, or void of restraint; to become rude, or boorish.

Iangwr, *s. m.—pl.* iangwyr (iang—gwr) A man void of restraint; a rude man; a boor.

Nid afrywiawg ond iangwr; nid iangwr ond o arferau

No one is so ill-natured as a *clown*, no one is a *clown* but from habits. *Adage.*

Nid iangwr neb ar Ferwyn

No one is deemed a *clown* upon Berwyn mountain. *Adage.*

Iar, *s. f.—pl.* ieir (i—ar) That extends over, or stretches out, the shoulder, being one of the twelve prime parts of a royal stag; also the female of birds; a hen. *Iar orllydd, iar ddêor, iar ffegan*, a brood hen; *iar wynt*, bird of paradise; *iar wŷld, iar goed*, pheasant hen; *iar dinwen*, bald buzzard hen; *iar fynydd, iar y mynydd, grugiar*, a moor hen; *iar for*, sea hen, a fish so called.

Ni chwyn yr iar fod y gwalch yn glaf.

The *hen* will not complain for the hawk's being sick. *Adage.*

Nid afradlawn ond iar.

Nothing so prodigal as a *hen*. *Adage.*

Nis pryn efe iar ar y gwlaw.

He will not buy a *hen* in the rain. *Adage.*

Iar, *prep.* (i—ar) From off, off the top; off.

Iarc, *s. f.* (iar) That stretches out, or over.

Iarcw, *s. m.* (iarc) That points, or directs, a pilot.

Iardy, *s. m.—pl. t.* au (iar—ty) A barton.

Iarhyd, *s. f.* (iar—hyd) The chine piece, being one of the twelve prime parts of a royal stag; otherwise called *Iar*.

Iarll, *s. m.—pl.* ieirll (iar) An earl; a noble.

Gortheyrn Gorthenau, iarll oedd bwuw ar Went, ac Erging, ac Euas.

Gortheyrn Gorthenac, he was *earl* over Gwent, and Erging, and Euas. *Gr. ab Arthur.*

Iarllaeth, *s. m.* (iarll) An earldom, the dignity, or authority, of an earl.

Iarlles, *s. f.—pl. t.* au (iarll) A lady of an earl.

Iarn, *prep.* (iar) From off, off, from.

Iarnad, *pronom. prep.* (iarn) From off thee; off thee; from thee.

Iarnadd, *adv* (iarn) From off, or from the top.

Iarth, *s. f.—pl.* ierthi (iar) A long rod; a goad.

Ias, *s. f.—pl. t.* au (as) What pervades or strikes through; a shock; a shock of heat, or cold; a heat; warmth; a shivering; disposition; nature. *Berwa un ias arno*, boil one boiling on that: *Iasau drwg*, wicked impulses.

Ni thyn na gwin na thân gof
Ias Ionawr y sy ynnof.

Nor wine nor the fire of a furnace, will draw out the *chill* of January, which is in me. *T. Aled.*

Difeth oedd ar gerdd dafawd;
Tawel iasau Taliesin,
Wir o fodd, cadd ar ei fin.

He was infallible in vocal song; the gentle *strains* of a Taliesin, in perfection, from his lips were heard. *W. ab Hywel, m. T. W. Hywel.*

——Awen gu.
Trwy'r dolydd, taro'r delyn,
Oni bo'r ias yn y bryn,
O gywair dant; a gyr di
Awr orhoen i Eryri!

Lovely muse, strike, through the dales, the harp, so that the *strain* may pervade the hill, from the tuneful string; and send thou an hour of ecstasy amid Snowdonian hills! *Gro. Owain.*

Iasaidd, *a.* (ias) Of a pervading tendency.

Iasawg, *a.* (ias) Having a shock, being pervaded with any impulse, quality, or passion.

Iasawl, *a.* (ias) Tending to give a shock, tending to pervade with any quality.

Iasedig, *a.* (ias) Being pervaded with some impulse, quality, or passion.

Iasedd, *s. m.* (ias) A pervading tendency.

Iaseiddrwydd, *s. m.* (iasaidd) The state of being of a pervading quality.

Iasiad, *s. m.—pl. t.* au (ias) A pervading with any quality; a giving a shock, or impulse; a giving a heat, a giving a chill.

Iasu, *v. a.* (ias) To pervade with any quality; to give a shock; to give a heat; to chill.

Iau, *s. f.—pl.* ieuoedd (au) That is going, progressive, or in motion; *Jove*, also called *Iou*; the lungs, also, called *au* and *afu*; a junior, or the younger; a team or yoke of oxen, a yoke. The *Welsh* used four sorts of yokes, until as late as about the year 1600: the *beriau*, or short yoke, with two oxen; the *meiiau*, or field yoke, with four oxen; the *ceseiliau*, or lateral yoke, with six oxen; and the *hiriau*, or long yoke, with eight oxen, a breast.

Crempogau a bara mwd ddydd Iau fawr.

Pancakes and buns, on great Jove's day, or the Thursday before Lent. *Adage.*

A garo yr Iau cared ei warteu.

Let him who loves the *younger* also love his plays. *Adage.*

Dewis ai yr iau ai y fwyall.

Choose either the *yoke*, or the axe. *Adage.*

Iau, *a.* (au) Inceptive of progress; junior, younger. It is generally used for *Ieuach*, more young, which is the regular comparative degree. It is affixed as a plural termination.

Iaw, *s. m.* (aw) That proceeds forward; that forwards. It is affixed as a termination to form the infinitive of verbs that imply, to make, cause, or effect.

Iawd, *s. m.* (awd) That proceeds onward; season

Iawed, *s. f.* (iaw) That proceeds, or matures.

Iawg, *s. f.* (awg) That is keen, or ardent.

Iawl, *s. m.—pl.* iolau (awl) The act of glorifying.

Iawlwen, *s. f.* (iawl—gwen) Adorable fair one.

Nid yngh w dyn byw o'r byd fal mi;
Ni chymmerch amgen iawlwen ioli
I'r neb rybarther i ryborthi.

Not a living person in the world feels himself as I do: fate will not demand that the *adorable nymph* should be worshipped by him that is appointed to bear its hard decree.
Ein. ab Gwalchmai, i Nest.

Iawn, *s. m.—pl. t.* au (awn) Right, equity, atonement, satisfaction. *Iawn a dylyad*, equity and justice: *Iawn a chyfraith*, equity and law: *Iawn anianawl*, natural right: *Gosodi iawn i arall yn lle cyfraith*, to decree equity to another instead of law. *Welsh Laws.*

Duw ca'arn a farn pob iawn.

The mighty God will judge every *right*. *Adage.*

Yn iawn, rhoes Cynan, a'i wyr,
Iddo Arthbeibio bybyr.

As a *satisfaction*, Cynan, and his men, gave him the secure Garthbeibio. *D. Llwyd.*

Efe yw yr iawn dros ein pechodau.

He is the *propitiation* for our sins. *1 John ii. 2.*

Iawn, *a.* (awn) Right, equitable; just, meet; well. It is used as a prefix in composition.

Aeth y beirdd doeth heb urddas;
Aeth iawn gerdd weithian yn gas.

The intelligent bards are become without honour; just poetry is at length become despised. *Parch. E. Evans.*

Iawnach i gybydd anwir
Garu Duw nag erw o dir.

It is more proper for a wicked miser to love God than a spot of ground. *M. ab Rhys.*

Iawn, *adv.* (awn) Rightly, or very. *Da iawn*, very good, or very proper.

Iawnawl, *a.* (iawn) Of a right tendency.

Iawnbwyll, *s. m.* (iawn—pwyll) Right reason.

Iawnder, *s. m.* (iawn) Rightness; equity, justice.

Tri iawnder cerdd: iawn gyfrbwyll, iawn drefn, ac iawn fydr.

The three *justnesses* of song: just fancy, just arrangement, and just metre. *Barddas.*

Cadarn a gwastad iawnder, a gwirionedd, a osodes Elidir, ac a orchymynws eu cadw trwy y deyrnas.

A powerful and unbiassed *equity*, and truth, did Elidr establish; and he commanded them to be observed throughout the kingdom. *Gr. ab Arthur.*

Iawndda, *a.* (da) Rightly good, truly good.

Iawnedd, *s. m.* (iawn) Rectitude, rightness.

Iawnegwyddawr, *s. f.—pl.* iawnegwyddorion (egwyddawr) Right principle.

Iawnegwyddorawl, *a.* (iawnegwyddawr) Of a right principle, having right principles.

Iawnegwyddori, *v. a.* (iawnegwyddawr) To induce right principles.

Iawnfarn, *s. f.* (barn) Right or just judgement.

Iawnffydd, *s. f.* (ffydd) Right faith; true belief. *a.* Of a right faith.

Iawnffyddiaw, *v. n.* (iawnffydd) To have true faith

Iawnffyddiawg, *a.* (iawnffydd) Having true faith.

Iawnffyddiawl, *a.* (iawnffydd) Of a true faith.

Iawngred, *s. f.* (cred) Right or true belief. *a.* Of a right belief.

Iawngrededd, *s.* (iawngred) Rightness of belief.

Iawngredu, *v. n.* (iawngred) To believe rightly.

Iawni, *v. a.* (iawn) To render right or exact.

Iawniad, *s. m.* (iawn) A righting, a rectifying.

Iawnles, *s. m.* (lles) Just benefit, or advantage.

Iawnobrwy, *s. m.—pl. t.* on (gobrwy) A just reward, a right recompense.

Iawnran, *s. f.—pl. t.* au (rhan) A right share.

Iawnred, *s. f.* (rhed) A right course. *a.* Of a right course, tendency or direction.

Iawnrith, *s. m.—pl. t.* iau (rhith) A right appearance. *a.* Of a right appearance.

Iawnryw, *s. m.—pl. t.* iau (rhyw) A right kind. *a.* Of a right kind.

Iawnwaith, *s. m.* (gwaith) A right work or act.

Iawnwedd, *s. f.* (gwedd) A right aspect; a right conformity. *a.* Of a right aspect or form.

Iawnweddawg, *a.* (iawnwedd) Having a just uniformity or manner.

Iawnweddrwydd, *s. m.* (iawnwedd) Justness of manner, or propriety of conduct.

Iawnweddu, *v. n.* (iawnwedd) To render of just form or manner.

Iawnwerth, *s. m.* (gwerth) A just value or price. *a.* Of just value, of just worth.

Iawnwir, *s. m.* (gwir) A right or just truth.

Iawnwydd, *s. m.* (gwydd) A right cognizance.

Iawnwyddawr, *s. f.—pl.* iawnwyddorion (gwyddawr) That rightly informs, or gives cognizance.

Iawnwyddiad, *s.* (iawnwydd) A rightly knowing.

Iawnwyddorawl, *a.* (iawnwyddawr) Rightly informing, or of right principle.

Iawnwyddori, *v. a.* (iawnwyddawr) To endue with right cognizance.

Iawnymgais, *s. m.* (ymgais) A right pursuit.

Iawnysgrif, *s. f.* (ysgrif) Orthography.

Iawnysgrifen, *s. f.* (iawnysgrif) Orthography.

Iawnysgrifenu, *v. a.* (iawnysgrif) To write rightly, or orthographically.

Iawnysgrifiad, *s. m.* (iawnysgrif) A writing rightly.

Iawnysgrifiaeth, *s. f.* (iawnysgrif) A correct way or manner of writing.

IB, *s. m. r.* That runs forward, or extends out.

IC, *s. m. r.* That is pointed, sharp, or acute.

Icwr, *s. m.* (ic—wr) A sharp watery humour.

Pedwar, icwr
Am sefyr cwr
Edynogion.

The fourth, *ichor* in the manner of partition turning to winged ones. *Taliesin.*

ICH, *s. f. r.* A shrill noise, a screak; a squeal.

Ni ddyd ich, ni ddywed air,
Nid ysgyg ei dwy esgair.

She will not give a squeal; she will say not a word; she will not budge her two shanks. *Syr Hywel o Fuellt.*

Ichiad, *s. m.* (ich) A screaking; a squeaking.

Ichian, *v. a.* (ich) To screak; to squeal, to squeak

Ichiaw, *v. a.* (ich) To screak; to squeal, to squeak

ID, *s. m. r.* That is drawn, or stretched out; that is sharp, or penetrating; a point.

Id, *pron.* That is spoken of, indeterminately, whether a person, or thing; it.

Y sy id ar bawb ei bryder.

There is to every one his care. *Adage.*

Idiaw, *v. a.* (id) To draw, or stretch out small; to render acute; to acuminate.

IDD, *s. m. r.* That is sharp, acute, or subtile.

Idd, *prep.* (i—ydd) To, towards; for; into.

Iddas, *a.* (idd) Acute, pungent; subtile.

> Dau frodyr, dau iddas am dir.
>
> Two brothers, two *subtile* ones for land. *Myrddin.*

Iddei, *pronom. prep.* (idd—ei) To a person, or thing; to his; to her; to its.

> Iestyn a aeth adref, a gwyr Gwladforgan a aynt bob un idd ei le.
>
> Iestyn went home, and the men of Glamorgan went every one *to his place.* *Cerad. o Langarfan.*

Iddi, *pronom. prep.* (idd) To her; for her; into her.

> O gwr y drain, gywir dro,
> Elusen iddi leisio.
>
> From the skirt of the bush, happy the turn, it is charity *for her* to chaunt her strains. *T. Prys.*

Iddo, *pronom. prep.* (idd) To it; to him; for him; unto it; into him. It is also used imperatively as a verb; to it; to him; or go to it; set to, fall to, at him.

> A achwyno heb achaws gwneler achaws iddo.
>
> He that complains without a cause, let a cause be made *to him.* *Adage.*
>
> Ni bydd chwedl heb ystlys iddo.
>
> There will be no expression without a parallel *to it.* *Adage.*

Iddwf, *s. m.* (idd—wf) The herpes, or Saint Anthony's fire; also called *tan iddwf.*

Iddynt, *pronom. prep.* (idd) To them; for them.

> Y'ngharchar gwedy 'nghyrchu,
> Ac am sydd gelwydd golau,
> Ac anudon friw-don frau,
> Hyn a ddaw yn hen ddial
> Iddyn' dwyll ryw ddydd yn dal,
> Pan fo cyfrif difrifawl,
> A Duw yn rhannu a diawl.
>
> After being dragged into prison, for what is a manifest falsehood, and rank perjury in broken tone, this will come as a treasured vengeance deceitfully *to them,* some day, in retaliation, when there shall be serious reckoning, and God dividing with the devil. *T. Prys.*

Iĕ, *adv.* (i—e) Yes, yea. It is used in answering to a discriminating question. *Ai ti sydd yna?* Is it thou that is there? *Iĕ*, yes.

> D'ymadrodd a adroddir,
> Iĕ, nage, yn y gwir.
>
> Thy discourse shall be delivered, *yes,* and nay, in the truth. *Ed. Morus.*

Iechin, *a.* (iach) Salutary, healing, saving.

Iechineb, *s. m.* (iechin) A healed state; salvation.

Iechyd, *s. m.* (iach) Soundness, sanity, health.

> A fyno iechyd bid lawen.
>
> He that would have *health* let him be cheerful. *Adage.*
>
> Nid cyfoeth ond iechyd.
>
> There is no treasure like *health.* *Adage.*

Iechydawl, *a.* (iechyd) Salutary, saving, healthy.

> Terwynawl, iechydawl, iachâ
> Bardd a'th lawl, a'th fawl, a'th fawrhâ!
>
> Essential and saving one, heal a bard who adores thee, who magnifies thee! *Cynddelw.*

Iechydwr, *s. m.—pl.* iechydwyr (iechyd—gwr) One who gives health.

Iechydwriaeth, *s. m.* (iechydwr) A salvation.

Ieinder, *s. m.* (iain) Coolness, or freshness.

Ieithad, *s. m.* (iaith) A putting into language.

Ieithadur, *s. m.* (ieithad) A grammar, or the system of language.

Ieithawg, *a.* (iaith) Having language.

Ieithefyg, *s. m.* (iaith) That is of superior speech.

> Llywelyn, llew glwys Lloegrwys llugyrn;
> Llary gryg ieithefyg, llosg ei thefyrn.
>
> Llywelyn, the splendid lion surrounding the Lloegrians with torches; gentle rough voiced *most eloquent one,* burn her mansions. *Ein. ab Gwalchmai.*

Ieithgar, *a.* (iaith) Apt to cultivate a language.

Ieithgarwch, *s. m.* (ieithgar) Philology, cultivation of language.

Ieithiad, *s. m.* (iaith) A construction of speech.

Ieithiai, *s. c.* (iaith) That constructs language; a grammatist.

Ieithiaw, *v. a.* (iaith) To construct language.

Ieithiawg, *a.* (iaith) Languaged, having language.

> Pan fo teir-ieithiawg taiawg yn Mon,
> A'i fab yn gycachawg,
> Rhygel wawr Gwynedd goludawg.
>
> When a churl in Anglesey shall be *conversant in three languages,* and his son the head of a family, the splendor of wealthy Gwynedd will be hidden. *Cyf. Myrddin.*

Ieithiawl, *a.* (iaith) Relating to language.

Ieithiogi, *v. a.* (ieithiawg) To construct words.

> Dylai y bardd eglur ieithiogi y pwnc, a'i gywrain fyfyriaw.
>
> A bard ought explicitly *to construct the language of the subject,* and to study it profoundly. *Barddas.*

Ieithrym, *s. m.* (iaith—grym) Energy of speech.

Ieithus, *a.* (iaith) Of apt language; eloquent.

Ieithydd, *s. m.—pl. t.* ion (iaith) A linguist.

> Gofyn i'r mab, trwy ieithydd, o ba le pan hanoedd.
>
> Ask the youth, through an *interpreter,* from what place he comes. *Hanes Bown—Mabinogion.*

Ieithyddawl, *a.* (ieithydd) Philological, belonging to a philologist.

Ieithyddiaeth, *s. f.* (ieithydd) Philology, study, or construction of language.

Ieithyddu, *v. a.* (ieithydd) To construct language, *s. m.* A construction of speech.

> Tri pheth a bair iawn ddyfalu: iawn ddewis ar air, iawn ieithyddu, ac iawn gyffelybu.
>
> Three things which produce just description: just selection of a word, just *construction of language,* and just comparison. *Barddas.*

Ierf, *a.* (iar) That stretches or closes round.

> Edyn ierf, wyd yn aros,
> A'r aerwy rhudd euro rhos.
>
> With wings *closing round,* thou dost tarry, and with the ruddy ring thou dost gild the mead. *Gutyn Owain.*

Ierthi, *s. m.* (iarth) A rod used in driving oxen.

> Ni chyngain i'r ych wingaw
> Wrth y fraen a'r ierthi draw.
>
> It will not avail for the ox to turn about near the prickle and the impelling *rod.* *L. Morganwg.*

Iesin, *a.* (ias) Of a pervading nature; radient; glorious: fair, beautiful, gairish.

> Gorlas gwellt didryf; dwfr neud iesin;
> Gorddyar eaws awdl gynnefin.
>
> Supremely green the untrodden grass; the water how *limpid,* very noisy the nightingale well-versed in song. *Gwalchmai.*
>
> Gwr a wnaeth llewych o'r gorllewin,
> Haul, a lloer addoer, addef iesin,
> A'm gwnel——cyflawn awen!
>
> Who made to radiate from the west, the sun, and chilling moon, in a *glorious* dwelling, may he fill me with the muse! *D. Benfras.*

Iesinaidd, *a.* (iesin) Somewhat pervading; tending to radiate: somewhat fair.

Iesinaw, *v. a.* (iesin) To cast a radience, or glory. to make fair; to become radient or fair.

Iesinder, *s. m.* (iesin) Radiency; gairishness.

Iesu, *s. m.* Jesus. It is mostly preceded by the article *yr*, the; as *Doai yr Iesu*, Jesus came.

Ieuad, *s. m.* (iau) A putting in a team; a yoking

Ieuaeth, *s. m.* (iau) A progressive or yoked state.

Ieuaf, *a.* (*superlative of* iau) Youngest.

Ieuanc, *s. m.—pl.* ieuainc (ieu—anc) A youth.

> Un fath â llong ar gefnfor,
> Heb raff, heb hwyl, heb angor,
> Yw yr ieuanc heb gynghor.
>
> Like to a ship upon the open sea, without rope, without sail, without anchor, is the *youth* without counsel. *Llywarch Hen.*

Ieuanc, *a.* (iau—anc) Young, or youthful.

> Y bi——
> Buan dy hynt uwch pynt perth—
> Cyfaill dynionau ieuainc,
> Er na bych mawr, cerddawr cainc.
>
> Thou magpie, quick is thy course above the arches of the brake; the companion of *young* people, though thou art not great, sweet hopper of the bough. *D. ab Gwilym.*

Ieuant, *s. m.*—*pl.* ieuaint (ieuan) A youth.

> A'r [illegible] a gar yr ieuaint.
>
> And the piercing eye which the *young ones* love. *Llywarch Hen.*

Ieuangaidd, *a.* (ieuanc) Somewhat young.
Ieuangeiddiad, *s. m.* (ieuangaidd) A becoming rather young.
Ieuangeiddiaw, *v.* (ieuangaidd) To be youngish.
Ieuangeiddrwydd, *s. m.* (ieuangaidd) Juniority.
Ieuaw, *v. a.* (iau) To put in a team: to yoke.
Ieuawl, *a.* (iau) Bearing a yoke, or yoked.
Ieuawr, *s. m.* (iau) That connects, that yokes.
Iendawdd, *s. m.* (iau—tawdd) Male speedwell.
Ieuenctid, *s. m.* (ieuanc) The state of youth, minority, childhood, youth. *Ieuenctid y dydd,* the dawning of the day.
Ieugen, *s. f.*—*pl. t.* od (iau—cen) A ferret.
Iewan, *s. m.* (iaw) A forcible cry: a scream.

> Eryr Pengwern, pengarn llwyd,
> Aruchel ei iewan,
> Eiddig am gig Cynddylan.
>
> The eagle of Pengwern, with the grey horny head, very loud his *scream*, jealous of the flesh of Cynddylan. *Llywarch Hen.*

Iewan, *v. a.* (iaw) To utter a loud cry or scream.
Iewin, *a.* (iaw) Clamorous, or tumultuous.

> Tan [illegible] eithyd,
> I [illegible];
> O [illegible],
> [illegible].
>
> Under the sea he went, to obtain science; from obtaining science let him be of *clamorous* mind. *Taliesin.*

Iewydd, *s. m.*—*pl. t.* on (iau—gwydd) A yoke for the neck of an ox.

> Y geilwad a ddyle ddiwallu [illegible] yr iewyddon o wdyn.
>
> The driver ought to furnish the shanks of the bows for the yokes and *collars* with wythes. *Welsh Laws.*

IF, *s. m. r.* That is impelled, or cast forth.
IFF, *s. m. r.* That is thrown or sent forcibly.
IG, *s. f. r.*—*pl. t.* ion. What is sharp or pungent; an emotion; a yexing, a hickup; a sob.

> Egori dras garw drwy ig,
> A chradawd ddor [illegible].
>
> Opening the rough passage with a *puff*, and the squeaking door of the belly. *R. Nanmor, i dorr.*

> [illegible] ei bronau a wnai Eawllt, a dywedyd wrtho yn y wedd hon, ac igion yn llesteiriaw ei hymadrawdd.—Coffa fru dy fam, yn y lle i'th gwnaeth di [illegible] yr awnydan yn ddyn, ac wrth hyny, o'r anghyfnerthau a'r doluriau a ddyoddefais i erotl, coffa di heddyw, a dyro faddeuant i'th frawd.
>
> [illegible] laid her bosom bare, speaking to him in this manner, with *sighs* obstructing her discourse; Remember thy mother's womb, where in the supreme architect of nature formed thee a man; and therefore, on account of the infirmities and the pains which I suffered for thy sake, remember thou this day and grant a pardon to thy brother. *Gr. ab Arthur.*

Igi, *s. m.* (ig) A burst, or eruption.
Igiad, *s. m.*—*pl. t.* au (ig) A sighing; a sobbing.
Igian, *v. a.* (ig) To sigh, to utter sighs; to sob.

> Igian ac wylaw a wnai fam Beli a Bran.
>
> The mother of Beli and Bran, gave her herself *to sigh* and weep. *Gr. ab Arthur.*

Igiaw, *v. a.* (ig) To sigh, or to utter sighs.

> Lladd'ei feirdd, a'i wyr llys fo
> Llan Egwestl oll yn igio
>
> His bards have been slain, and the men of his court, all the village of Egwestl doth sigh. *Gutyn Owain.*

Igiawl, *a.* (ig) Sighing, giving sighs; sobbing.
Igiwr, *s. m.*—*pl.* igwyr (ig—gwr) A sigher.
IL, *s. f.*—*pl. t.* ion. That is in motion, progression, or state of producing; a ferment. *Cwrw yn yr il,* ale in the fermentation.
Iliad, *s. m.* (il) A fermenting, fermentation.
Iliaw, *v. a.* (il) To put in motion, to ferment. *Llestr iliaw,* a fermenting vessel.
Iliawg, *a.* (il) Being fermenting, fermented

Ilir, *s. m.*—*pl. t.* ion (il—ir) A butterfly. Or as it is otherwise called, *eilir,* and *gloyn.*
ILL, *s. m. r.* That is over, or beside; that is an augment; a separate particle.
Ill, *pron.* (used only for the dual, or two, and for three) Their. *Ill dau,* their two; but which is equivalent to they two: *Aut ill dau yno,* they two will go there; *ill tri,* or *triaedd,* they three. So, speaking in the first person, we say, *awn ein dau,* we two will go, *awn ein tri,* we three will go: in the second person, *ewch eich dau,* you two will go; *ewch eich tri,* you three will go.
IM, *s. m. r.* That is extreme, or ultimate.
I'm, *pronom. prep.* (i—ym) To my; into my; for my; to me.

> Och am Ferddin ddewinion,
> I fwrw i'm hud fry am hon!
>
> Oh, for Merddin's magicians, to cast *for me* a charm above for her. *Ieu. Dyfi.*

Imi, *pronom. prep* (i—mi) To me: for me.
Imp, *s. m.*—*pl. t.* iau (im) A scion, or shoot.
Impiad, *s. m.*—*pl. t.* au (imp) A shooting, a germinating; a grafting, or innoculating.
Impiaw, *v. a.* (imp) To graff, to ingraft, to innoculate; to shoot out, to germinate.
Impiawg, *a.* (imp) Having shoots, or scions.
Impiawl, *a.* (imp) Shooting or germinating.
Impiedig, *a.* (impiad) Being sprouted out.
Impog, *s. m.* (imp) Osculation, or kiss.
Impyn, *s. m. dim.* (imp) A scion, or germ.
IN, *s. m. r.* That is penetrating, or pervading.
I'n, *pronom. prep.* (i—yn) To our; for our; to us.
Indeg, *a.* (in—teg) Of subtile fairness, or fineness, sublimate; raving mad.

> Rhoed pob indeg ei dal,
> Ufudd i Dduw ei ofal.
>
> Let every one with *distracted* head humbly leave his care to God. *D. ab Gwilym.*

Iniawn, *s. m* (in—iawn) That is straight.
Iniawn, *a.* (in—iawn) Straight, direct, even.
Inionad, *s. m.* (iniawn) A straightening, a righting
Inioni, *v. a.* (iniawn) To straighten, to right.
Insel, *s. f.*—*pl.* inseiliau (in—sel) A mark, a seal. *Insel agored,* open seal, letters patent.

> Offeiriad teulu a ddyly bedair ceiniog o bob insel agored, a roddo y brenin am dir a daiar, neu am negesau mawr ereill.
>
> The family priest is entitled to have four-pence for every *open seal,* which the king shall give for land, or other weighty concerns. *Welsh Laws.*

Inseiliad, *s. m.* (insel) A marking, a sealing.
Inseiliaw, *v. a.* (insel) To impress a mark.
Inseiliawg, *a.* (insel) Having a seal; sealed.
Inseiliedig, *a.* (inseiliad) Being sealed; sealed.
Ing, *s. m.* (in) A strait; straitness; distress.

> Car cywir, yn yr ing y gwelir.
>
> In *distress* will the faithful friend be seen. *Adage.*

Ing, *a.* (in) Strait, narrow, close, or confined.

> Po ingaf gan ddyn cyngaf fydd gan Dduw.
>
> The most *difficult* it is to man, the most comprehensive it is with God. *Adage.*

> Ni fu angau fal ingach.
>
> There has not been a death that were more *distressing.* *B. Dyf.*

> O, angau du, inged wyd!
>
> Ah, gloomy death, *how distressing* art thou! *L. G. Cothi.*

Ingaidd, *a.* (ing) Somewhat strait, or narrow.
Ingawl, *a* (ing) Tending to straiten, confining.
Io, *inter.* (*expressive of concern*) Well-a-day.

> O io! ddyn byw i ddwyn byd,
> A fu lawn-falch fal ynfyd!
>
> *Lack-a-day,* what a living wight has in the world to bear! was there any completely proud like the fool! *Ieu. Brydydd.*

Ioed, *s. m.* (oed) Time past; eternity, speaking of the past; the beginning. *Erioed ni welaist moni*, never hast thou seen her.

Iogawl, *a.* (iawg) Ardent, or vehement.

Torid anfynudawl
Tuthiawl dan iogawl.

It broke out, the instantaneously moving *ardent fire*.
Taliesin, c. y meirch.

Iolad, *s. m.* (iawl) A worshipping or adoring.

Iolaeth, *s. m.* (iawl) Adoration, worship; respect

Iolaethu, *v. a.* (iolaeth) To worship.

Menestr mawr y gwaith yd iolaithir.

The cupbearer, great the work with which he *is honoured*.
O. Cyfeiliawg.

Iolawd, *s. m.* (iawl) A celebration; a praising.

Iolawg, *a.* (iawl) Being celebrated; adored.

Iolawr, *s. m.* (iawl) An adorer; a worshipper.

Iolch, *s. m.* (iawl) Act of devotion, or gratitude.

Iolchad, *s. m.* (iolch) An acting gratefully.

Iolchi, *v. a.* (iolch) To act devoutly, or gratefully.

Iolchus, *a.* (iolch) Of a grateful disposition.

Ioli, *v. a.* (iawl) To praise; to adore; to worship; to revere, to respect; to act submissively, or reverently; to implore.

Wrth Ddaw ydd iolaf hyny.

Of God *I will implore* that. *Ll. P. Moch.*

Cedawl Dduw ei ddawn a iolir.

The gracious God, his goodness *will be praised*. *D. Benfras.*

Caraf, iolaf dri; drwy ddrudaniaeth ced,
Canred o'm gwared er awch gwrdäaeth.

I will love, *I will adore* three; through the preciousness of the gift, there shall follow my deliverance for the sake of your virtue.
Ll. P. Moch.

Iolig, *a.* (iawl) Of a disposition to give praise.

Iolus, *a.* (iawl) Deserving of worship, or respect.

Iolwch, *s. m.* (iawl) Gratitude, thankfulness.

Iolwg, *s. m.* (iawl) Grateful praise; eulogy.

Iolychiad, *s. m.* (iolwch) The act of praising, or worshipping; adoration; reverence.

Iolydd, *s. m.* (iawl) An act of worship; glorification; fame, honour.

Pedestrig iolydd a'm bydd i eilwydd!
Pa hyd yth iolaf! saf rhag dy swydd.

May the bearer of *fame* accompany me to the musical grove! How long shall I worship thee! pause in thy course.
H. ab Owain.

Gorphell ym cymhell camre iolydd cain,
Gorffyag dadwyrain, gwawr ddwyrein dydd.

Very far she drives me, she with the steps of fair *fame* suddenly rising like the increasing dawn of day. *Ior. Fychan.*

Iôn, *s. m.* (on) A source, or beginning; a first cause; a name of the Deity; the Lord.

Yn iach frenin yr hinion!
Yn iach ein llywiawdr a'n Ion!
Yn iach y cogau ieuanc;
Yn iach hin fyhefin fauc!

Farewell, sovereign of serenity! farewell, our leader, and our lord! Farewell, the young cuckoos; farewell the pleasant seat in the summer season! *D. ab Gwilym, i'r haul.*

Ionawl, *a.* (ion) Belonging to a first cause.

Ionawr, *s. m.* (ion) That originates; that commences; the month of January, which, amongst ths ancient Britons, began at the winter solstice

Ior, *s. m.—pl. t.* au (or) That is extreme, that is without beginning, or continual; the Eternal; the Lord; the Ancient of Days, or the One of *Yore*.

Duw Ior y duwiaw ereill;
Dofydd a llywydd y lleill.

God the *supreme* of the other gods; the creator and governor of them. *Iolo Goch.*

Iorn, *s. m.—pl. t.* au (orn) A burst, a thrust.

Iornad, *s. m.* (iorn) A bursting; a thrusting.

Iornawl, *a.* (iorn) Tending to pierce, or thrust.

Iorni, *v. a.* (iorn) To burst through; to pierce.

Iorth, *s. m.* (ior) That is continual, or incessant. *a.* Continual, perpetual.

Iorthawl, *a.* (iorth) Incessant, continual; diligent.

Anghenan——
I nerthu dyn yn iorthawl,
Rhag bachell a dichell diawl.

Extreme unction to strengthen a man *continually* against the snare and wile of the devil. *Gw. y Tew.*

Iorthi, *v. a.* (iorth) To extend, or continue; to be incessant, or continual.

Iorthiad, *s. m.* (iorth) A going on incessantly.

Iorthiant, *s. m.* (iorth) Continuity; diligence.

Iorthrwydd, *s. m.* (iorth) The state of standing against, the being close to, or resting against.

Iorthryn, *s. m.* (iorth—rhyn) Assiduity, diligence

IR, *s. m. r.—pl. t.* ion. That is pure, subtile, pungent, or penetrating; that is oily, unctuous, or fat; that is fresh. *a.* Fresh, florid, green, juicy, or full of sap; raw. *Pren ir*, a green tree; *cig ir*, fresh meat; *hawl ir*, an unprosecuted claim.

Dyborthai y ddaiar lysau irion a gleision, ac yn dwyn eu had herwydd eu rhywogaeth.

The earth brought forth herbs *fresh* and green, and bearing their seed according to their generation. *Ll. G. Hergest.*

O'r dwr ef a gai'r pysgod irion!
Acw o'r irwydd y cair aeron.

Out of the water shall be obtained *fresh slippery* fishes; yonder out of the green wood fruits shall be got. *L. G. Cothi.*

I'r, *prep.* (i—yr) To the; into the. *I'r dyn*, to the man; *i'r fan*, to the place; *neidia i'r afon*, jump into the river.

Dedwydd i'r a'i gwyl a'i car.

Happy *for the* one that sees him if he loves him. *Adage.*

Iràad, *s. m.* (ir) A rendering, or becoming juicy. a becoming fresh or green.

Iràawl, *a.* (ir) Tending to make juicy; tending to be fresh, luxuriant, or green.

Irad, *s. m.* (ir) Pungency; passion, rage; affliction. *a.* Pungent, grievous, afflicting, rueful, terrible.

Cwymp irad, cafad, cofion i'r lleuad,
Gwenllian hil haelion!

Rueful was the fall producing painful thoughts, to the luminary Gwenllian of the race of generous ones. *R. Llyn.*

Iradedd, *s. m.* (irad) Ruefulness, grievousness.

Iradiad, *s. m.* (irad) A rendering, or becoming, afflicting; a grieving, a rueing.

Iradrwydd, *s. m.* (irad) Ruefulness, grievousness

Iradu, *v. a.* (irad) To render afflicting; to grieve.

Iradus, *a.* (irad) Rueful, woeful, afflicting.

Pa wyneb iradus, pa galon echrydus
Y fydd y pryd hyny!

What woeful countenance, what trembling heart will be at that time. *Parch R. Pritchard.*

Irai, *s. c.* (ir) A sharp point; a goad.

Samgar—a darawai o'r Philistiaid chwe chant o wyr ag irai ychain.

Samgar—smote of the Philistines six hundred men with an ox *goad*. *Judges iii. 31.*

Iraid, *s. m.* (ir) Any unctuous or oily matter, any fat liquor; grease.

Iraidd, *a.* (ir) Of an oily or unctuous nature; full of juice; sappy, succulent; fresh.

Irain, *a.* (ir) Of a pure or subtile nature; teeming with juice; luxuriant.

Irâu, *v. a.* (ir) To render pure or subtile; to render oily, or juicy; to become subtile; to grow oily; to grow juicy; to luxuriate; to become fresh. *Mae y ddaiar yn irâu*, the earth is becoming green.

Iraw, *v. a.* (ir) To do with any oily or fat substance; to annoint, to grease.

Iraw blonegen.

To *grease* a lump of lard. *Adage.*

Irawl, *a.* (ir) Of a juicy nature, luxuriant, green.
Irdanc, *s. m.* (ir—tanc) The being pervaded with stillness; stupor, amazement.
Irdant, *s. m.* (ir—tant) Amazement, wonder.

> Ar lawr [illegible] fawr gwelais irdant.
> Upon the ground of great [illegible] I saw a wonder.
> *O. Cyfeiliawg.*

Irdang, *s. m.* (irdanc) The being pervaded with stillness; stupor, astonishment.
Irdangawl, *a.* (irdang) Stupifying, astonishing.
Irdangiad, *s. m.* (irdang) A stupifying, a scaring.
Irdangu, *v. a.* (irdang) To stupify; to amaze, to astonish, to surprize.
Irdawd, *s. m.* (ir) Freshness, or greenness.
Irdeb, *s. m.* (ir) Succulency; freshness.
Irder, *s. m.* (ir) Juiciness; freshness, greenness.
Irdra, *s. m.* (ir) Juiciness, sappiness, freshness.
Irdrwnc, *s. m.* (ir—trwnc) Fresh urine.
Ireidd-dra, *s. m.* (iraidd) Succulency; freshness.
Iredig, *a.* (ir) Being made juicy, sappy, or fresh.
Iredd, *s. m.* (ir) Juiciness, freshness, greenness.
Ireidedig, *a.* (iraid) Being smeared with fat.
Ireidiad, *s. m.* (iraid) A greasing, a doing over with fat, or oily matter; an annointing.
Ireidlyd, *a.* (iraid) Of a greasy or fat quality.
Ireidlydrwydd, *s. m.* (ireidlyd) Unctuousness.
Ireidd-deb, *s. m.* (iraidd) Succulency, sappiness.
Ireidd-dra, *s. m.* (iraidd) Succulency, sappiness, juiciness; greenness, freshness.
Ireiddedig, *a.* (iraidd) Being made succulent.
Ireiddedd, *s. m.* (iraidd) Succulency, sappiness.
Ireiddiad, *s. m.* (iraidd) A rendering succulent.
Ireiddiant, *s. m.* (iraidd) Succulency; luxuriance; a vigorous state of growth; refreshment.
Ireiddiaw, *v. a.* (iraidd) To render oily or full of juice; to render fresh, or green; to become juicy, fresh, or green; to refresh.
Ireiddiawl, *a.* (iraidd) Of a juicy, or fresh nature.
Ireiddlyd, *a.* (iraidd) Of a juicy, or fresh quality.
Ireiddlydrwydd, *s. m.* (ireiddlyd) The state of being juicy, raw, fresh, or green; greenishness.
Ireiddrwydd, *s. m.* (iraidd) Succulency; freshness
Irfa, *s. f.—pl.* irfëydd (ir—ma) Anointing place.
Irfriw, *s. m.—pl. t.* iau (ir—briw) A green wound.
Irgoed, *s. pl. aggr.* (ir—coed) Sappy or green trees
Irgrau, *s. m.* (ir—crau) Fresh gore or blood.
Iriad, *s. m.* (ir) A rendering, or becoming juicy; or becoming fresh, or green.
Iriannawl, *a.* (iriant) Of a luxuriant quality.
Iriannu, *v. a.* (iriant) To render luxuriant, fresh, or green; to luxuriate.
Iriant, *s. m.* (ir) Luxuriance, verdancy.
Irlas, *a.* (ir—glas) Of a fresh, or lively verdancy.
Irlasaidd, *a.* (irlas) Of a fresh, or lively verdancy
Irlasawl, *a.* (irlas) Tending to render of a fresh verdancy.
Irlasiad, *s. m.* (irlas) A becoming of a fresh green.
Irlasrwydd, *s. m.* (irlas) Freshness of verdure.
Irlasu, *v. n.* (irlas) To become of fresh verdancy.
Irlesni, *s. m.* (irlas) A fresh or juicy verdancy.
Irllawn, *a.* (ir—llawn) Ireful, or wrathful.

> [illegible]
> [illegible]
> The [illegible] *ireful* breast with alarm
> *L. G. Cothi.*

Irllonedd, *s. m.* (irllawn) Irefulness, wrathfulness

> [illegible]
> [illegible] to moderate the wrath of the king. [illegible]

Irwedd, *s. f.* (ir—gwedd) A fresh appearance.
Irwellt, *s. m.* (ir—gwellt) Fresh or green herbage.
Irwr, *s. m.—pl.* irwyr (iraw—gwr) One who greases, or rubs over with fat; an annointer.
Irwydd, *s. pl. aggr.* (ir—gwydd) Green trees.
IS, *s. m. r.* The state of being down, prone, close upon, or in contact with.
Is, *a.* (is. *s.*) Low, under, inferior, nether. It is generally used for the comparative *isach*, lower.

> Edward fal Alfryd—[illegible] calfyddyd, a[illegible]
> Edward compared with Alfred: *lower* was he than his father with respect to [illegible], and higher than his father with respect to power and dominion. *Brut y Saeson.*

Is, *prep.* (is, *s.*) Below, under; inferior to. *adv.* Below, down, in a lower place.

> A [illegible] is gwynt, ai uwch gwynt?
> Wilt thou go *below* wind, or above wind?
> *Elis Wyn B. Cwsg.*

Isâad, *s. m.* (is) A making low, a becoming low.
Isâawl, *a.* (is) Tending to make low, abasing.
Isach, *a.* (*comparative of* is) Lower, more low.
Isaf, *a.* (*superlative of* is) Lowest, humblest.
Isafiad, *s. m.—pl.* isafiaid (isaf) An inferior.
Isathraw, *s. m.—pl. t.* on (is—athraw) An under master; an usher.
Isau, *v. a.* (is) To lower, to abase, to humble.
Isder, *s. m.—pl. t.* au (is) Lowness, inferiority; meanness, depression, humility.
Isel, *a.* (is) Low, inferior, base, mean, humble, depressed.
Iselâad, *s. m.* (isel) A making low; a becoming low, humble, or abased.
Iselâawl, *a.* (isel) Tending to lower; abasing.
Iselaidd, *a.* (isel) Somewhat low, or humble.
Iselâu, *v. a.* (isel) To make or become low.
Iseldawd, *s. m.* (isel) Lowliness, humility.
Iselder, *s. m.—pl. t.* au (isel) Lowness. *Iselderau y ddaiar*, the lowermost parts of the earth.
Iseldrem, *s. f.—pl. t.* iau (isel—trem) A low look, a sly glance.
Iseldremiad, *s. m.* (iseldrem) A casting a low look.
Iseldremiaw, *v. a.* (iseldrem) To cast a sly glance.
Iseldd, *s. m.* (isel) Lowness, lowliness.
Iselfryd, *a.* (isel—bryd) Humble-minded, condescending, complacent.
Iselfrydedd, *s. m.* (iselfryd) The state of being humble-minded, or unaspiring; humility.
Iselgreg, *a.* (isel—creg) Softly murmuring.
Iselgynglan, *v. a.* (isel—cynglan) To make a low murmuring noise.
Iseliad, *s. m.* (isel) A lowering, or depressing, a making low, or humble, a becoming low.
Iselni, *s. m.* (isel) Lowness, abjectness.
Iselradd, *s. f.—pl. t.* au (isel—gradd) A low degree
Iselraith, *s. f.* (isel—rhaith) A petty jury.
Iselreithiwr, *s. m.—pl.* iselreithwyr (iselraith—gwr) A petty juryman.
Iselrwydd, *s. m.* (isel) Lowness, humbleness.
Iselsaf, *s. f.* (isel—saf) A low position or station.
Iselu, *v. a.* (isel) To bring down, to depress, to abase, to humble.
Iselwaed, *s. m.* (isel—gwaed) Ignoble blood.
Iselwr, *s. m.—pl.* iselwyr (isel—gwr) A low man.
Isg, *s. m.* (is) That is upon the surface.
Isgal, *s. m.* (is) Froth, or scum, foam.
Isgalaidd, *a.* (isgal) Like froth, or scum: foam.
Isgalawg, *a.* (isgal) Having froth, or scum.
Isgell, *s. m.* (isg) Broth, soup, or pottage.

> Oer yw isgell yr [illegible].
> Cold is the *liquid* of the slaughter. *Adage.*

> Mwy [illegible] y blaidd, nid da ei isgell.
> As much as the wolf is not good, his *broth* is not good. *Adage.*

Isgwympawl, *a.* (is—cwympawl) Sublapsary.
Islaw, *prep.* (is—llaw) Under the hand, below.
Islinelliad, *s. m.* (is—llinelliad) Under-scoring.
Islinellu, *v. a.* (is—llinellu) To underscore.
Isloerawl, *a.* (is—lloerawl) Sublunary.
Iso, *prep.* (is) Below, beneath, underneath, down. *adv.* Below, in a lower place.

Tywyll iso, Mair! fro frad.

O Mary! dark *below* is the region of perdition.
G. ab Ieuan Hen.

Dafydd i Ifor oedd fardd dyfyn;
Iolo i Rydderch: a hen, fal hyn,
Minnau i Ieuan fardd mein-wyn araf,
Iso a brydaf armes Brydyn.

Dafydd was to Ifor a summoned bard; Iolo to Rhydderch; and aged, in this manner, I also to Ieuan am a bard, slender, hoary and gentle, who sings here *below* the fate of Britain.
L. G. Cothi, i I. ab Ll. Fychan.

Isod, *prep.* (is) Below, beneath, under. *adv.* Below, in a lower place.
Isradd, *s. f.—pl. t.* au (is—gradd) Lower degree.
Israddawl, *a.* (isradd) Of an inferior degree.
Israddiad, *s. m.—pl. t.* au (isradd) Subordination.
Israddu, *v.* (isradd) To render of inferior degree.
Iswaith, *s. m.* (is—gwaith) An under-work.
Iswas, *s. m.—pl.* isweision (is—gwas) A menial.
Isweithiad, *s. m.* (iswaith) An underworking.
Isweithiaw, *v. a.* (iswaith) To underwork.
Iswerth, *s. m.* (is—gwerth) An undersale.
Iswerthiad, *s. m.* (iswerth) An underselling.
Iswerthu, *v. a.* (iswerth) To undersell.
It, *pron.* (*mutation of* id) That is spoken of indeterminately, whether a person, or thing.
Iti, *pronom. prep.* (i—ti) To thee; for thee.

Ha unben! ebai Hafgan, pa ddyled oedd iti ar fy angau i?

A prince! said Summershine, what right hadst thou to my death?
P. P. Dyfed—Mabinogion.

ITH, *s. m. r.—pl. t.* ion, A particle, a grain; an aggregate of particles; what is a nutriment; grain, corn in its natural state, or wild corn.

Cain cynnwyre cynwal brith:
Yd gyrchynt buain braenar ith.

Splendid the uprising of the variegated first-sown crop; the oxen repair to the *corn* fallow.
Englynion Cain Cynnwyre.

Ithfaen, *s. m.—pl.* ithfeini (ith—maen) Granite.
Ithfeinin, *a.* (ithfaen) Granitic, of granite.
IUDDEW, *s. m.—pl. t.* on. A Jew, one of Judea.
Iuddewaidd, *a.* (iuddew) Judaical, like a Jew.
Iuddeweiddiad, *s. m.* (iuddewaidd) A rendering Jewish; a becoming Jewish, or Jew-like.
Iuddeweiddiaeth, *s. m.* (iuddewaidd) The act of turning to Judaism.
Iuddeweiddiaw, *v. a.* (iuddewaidd) To Judaize.
Iuddewes, *s. f.—pl. t.* au (iuddew) A Jewess.
Iuddewiaeth, *s.* (iuddew) Judaism, Jewish rites.
Iuddewig, *a.* (iuddew) Pertaining to the Jews.
IW, *s. m. r.* That is extreme; that is outward, or upon the surface.
I'w, *pronom. prep.* (i—ew) To the third person, to his, her, its, for his, her, its; into him, into her, into its.
Iwbwb, *s. m.* (i—wbwb) A cry of alarm: Hollo. There are several places of this name, which, probably were alarm posts. *Tref Iwbwb*, near *Caerdyf*, the *Iupupania* of Ptolemy.
I'wch, *pronom. prep.* (i—awch) To you; for you

A chan oes, chwenychwn i,
I'wch ei, yn eich haelioni.

And a hundred lives, I should wish, may *to you* arrive in your liberality.
Gr. Phylip.

Iwerddon, *s. f.* (gwerddon) A green spot; Ireland.
Iwerddoneg, *s. f.* (iwerddon) The Irish tongue.
Iwerddonig, *a.* (iwerddon) Relating to Ireland.
Iwin, *s. m.* (iw—in) That is outrageous, a frantic one. *a.* Outrageous, mad.

Pan farner—
Yn iwin aed yn annwg,
Yr annuwiawl.

When condemned, *outrageous* and false let the ungodly seem.
W. Middleton.

Iwrch, *s. m.—pl.* iyrchod, iyrch, and iyrchwys (wrch) A roebuck. Many places in *Wales* bear the name of this animal, where it was common in ancient times, but which is now extinct; as *Bryn yr iwrch*, *Ffynon yr iwrch*, and the like.

Mi adwen iwrch er nas daliwyf.

I know a *roebuck*, though I may not catch him. *Adage.*

Gwell blaen yr iyrchod,
Nog ol yr hyddod.

Better the foremost of roebucks, than the rear of the stags.
Adage.

Iwrth, *prep.* (i—wrth) By; in opposition.
Iyrchaidd, *a.* (iwrch) Like the roebuck.
Iyrchawg, *a.* (iwrch) Abounding with roebucks.
Iyrchawl, *a.* (iwrch) Relating to a roebuck.
Iyrchell, *s. f.—pl. t.* od (iwrch) A young roe.
Iyrches, *s. f.—pl. t.* od (iwrch) A roe.
Iyrchgi, *s. f.—pl.* iyrchgwn (iwrch—ci) A dog for hunting the roebuck.

O myni fod yn iyrchgi ti a fwri naid a fo mwy.

If thou wouldest be a *roebuck hound* thou wilt take a greater leap.
Adage.

Iyrchw, *s. m.—pl. t.* on (iwrch) A roebuck.
Iyrchwyn, *s. m. dim.* (iyrchw) A little roebuck.
Iyrchyn, *s. m. dim.* (iwrch) A little roebuck.

LL.

LLA, *s. m. r.* A principle of expansion; that expands, opens, or breaks out; that is light, or clear.
Llab, *s. m.—pl. t.* iau (lly—ab) A flag, or thin strip; a stripe; a whipping; a stroke, a rap or a slap.

Llab y deri.

A *lubberly* fellow. *Adage.*

Llabed, *s. f.—pl. t.* au (llab) A label; a flap; an appendix.
Llabi, *s. m.—pl. t.* od (llab) A tall lank person, a stripling, a lubber, a big clumsy fellow, a looby.

Lle bo un llabi—o fardd,
Ei fin, a'i farf, a'i wyneb,
Ni chel ei foes.

Where one *gawky* of a bard happens to be, his mouth, his beard and his visage conceal not his manners.
Edm. Prys.

Llabiad, *s. m.—pl. t.* au (llab) A slapping.
Llabïaidd, *a.* (llabi) Somewhat lank; like a looby.
Llabiaw, *v. a* (llab) To slap, to strap, to rap.
Llabiedig, *a.* (llabiad) Being slapped, or strapped.
Llabïen, *s. f.* (llabi) A strapping wench.
Llabïes, *s. f.—pl. t.* od (llabi) A strapping wench.

Llabr, *s. m.—pl. t.* od (llab) What stripes.

Llabwst, *s. m.—pl.* llabystiau (llab—gwst) A lank, clumsy fellow, a lubber.

Llac, *s. m.—pl. t.* ian (llag) What is slack, or loose; a quicksand.

Llac, *a.* (llag) Slack, loose; remiss; not firm, or tight, lax, out of order, sickly.

Llaca, *s. m.* (llac) Slop, mire, mud, or dirt.

Llacâad, *s. m.* (llac) A slackening, a loosening; a relaxation; a becoming slack; a drooping.

Llacâawl, *a.* (llac) Tending to slacken, or loosen.

Llacâu, *v. a.* (llac) To slacken, to loosen; to relax, to become slack, or loose, to droop.

Llacawd, *s. m.* (llac) A slack or loose state.

Llacellyd, *a.* (llaca) Abounding with puddles.

Llaciad, *s. m.* (llac) A slackening; a drooping.

Llaciaw, *v. a.* (llac) To slacken; to relax; to become relaxed, to droop.

Llaciedig, *a.* (llaciad) Being slackened; relaxed.

Llacrwydd, *s. m.* (llac) Slackness; relaxedness.

Llacw, *adv.* (lly—acw) There, yonder, at a distance, in that place.

> Yn llawn brig,
> Llacw hen-wraidd llew Cynwrig.
>
> *Full of branches, lo there the ancient stock of the lion of Cynwrig.* — *L. Mon.*

Llach, *s. m.—pl. t.* iau (lly—ach) A ray; a blade; a lick, a slap. *Llach o ddyn*, a blade of a man; *maent yn llachiau o ddynion*, they are blades of men; *a raid i mi roi iti lach?* Must I give thee a stroke?

Llachaidd, *a.* (llach) Like a blade or spire.

Llachain, *a.* (llach) Abounding with blades.

Llachar, *s. m.* (llach—ar) A gleaming, gleam, or sudden shooting of light. *a.* Gleaming, gleamy.

> Rhag eu bar gwaled—tan llachar yn ehedeg o'r arfau.
>
> Because of their fierceness, the *gleaming* fire was seen flying out of the weapons. — *H. Lludd—Mabinogion.*

> Hygyrch ei neuadd cyn lladd llachar.
>
> Much resorted was his hall before the *gleaming* slaughter. — *Cynddelw.*

Llachau, *s. pl. aggr.* (llach) Gleams, lightnings.

> Dachar llachar llachiad ei las-bar;
> Llachau far llaw-ueisiad.
>
> Tremendous the gleam of the throwing of his blue shaft; his hand dealing the wrath of *lightnings.* — *Cynddelw, i O. Cyfeiliawg.*

> Ermoed a'm clwyf am y—
> Mawr-gor gar llachar llachau gyfred!
>
> Anguish wounds me after the friend of stately frame, whose ire was swift as the *lightning.*

Llachawd, *s. m.* (llach) A blading; a slapping.

Llachawl, *a.* (llach) Blading, slapping.

Llachbren, *s. m.—pl. t.* au (llach—pren) A cudgel

Llachdwm, *s. m.* (llach—twm) A large tub.

Llachffon, *s. f.—pl.* llachffyn (llach—ffon) Cudgel

Llachiad, *s. m.—pl. t.* au (llach) A wielding a weapon, a cudgelling, a spreading out.

Llachiaw, *v. a.* (llach) To shoot out smartly; to lick; to throw or lay about, to cudgel.

Llachiedig, *a.* (llachiad) Thumped, or banged.

Llachiwr, *s. m.—pl.* llachwyr (llach—gwr) A cudgeller. Cudgelling is the common diversion amongst the people of Caermarthenshire, hence they are nicknamed *Llachwyr*, or cudgellers.

Llad, *s. m.—pl. t.* au (lla—ad) What is conferred or given; a favour, or gift; good things in general; a blessing; also a measure of about the capacity of a quarter. *Pen llad*, the chief good, or summum bonum.

> Rhaid atteb am bob defnyn o'r llyn a'r llados.
>
> An account must be given for every particle of the liquor and the *good things.* — *Bardd Glas.*

> Llawen gwyr wrth ben llad.
>
> Men are merry over the *banquet.* — *Llywarch Hen.*

> Yn llaw llew rad cyrn llad llawn.
>
> In the hand of the lion of battle there are the full horns of *enjoyment.* — *Cynddelw.*

> Deuddeg mwysel o geirch yn y llad, ac wyth o ryg, a gwenith.
>
> Twelve bushels of oats in the *quarter*, and eight of rye and wheat. — *Welsh Laws.*

Lladaeth, *s. m.—pl. t.* au (llad) The act of conferring favour; a blessing, or benediction.

Lladaethawl, *a.* (lladaeth) Benevolent, beneficent

Lladaethiad, *s. m.* (lladaeth) A rendering, or becoming benevolent.

Lladaethu, *v. a.* (lladaeth) To practise benevolence, to confer a blessing.

Lladai, *s. c.—pl.* lladeion (llad) One that does a favour; a love messenger.

> Dos craf——
> Y ddiledieith ddu ladai.
>
> *Go for me, thou good messenger of pure language.* — *H. ab Gwilym.*

Lladaidd, *a.* (llad) Of the nature of a favour.

Lladawl, *a.* (llad) Gracious, or beneficent.

Lladgawd, *s. m.* (llad—cawd) A kind of shallow vessel, used formerly for holding liquor.

Lladiad, *s. m.* (llad) A conferring a gift, blessing, or benediction.

LLADIN, *s. m.* Latin, or the Roman tongue.

Lladinaidd, *a.* (lladin) Like Latin, of Latin.

Lladineiddiaw, *v. a.* (lladinaidd) To make Latin.

Lladiniaeth, *s. m.* (lladin) Latinity; latinism.

Lladiniaw, *v. a.* (lladin) To turn into Latin.

Lladinydd, *s. m.—pl. t.* ion (lladin) A latinist.

Lladr, *s. m.—pl. t.* on (llad) What is had without value; theft. *a.* Being had without value.

Lladrad, *s. m.—pl. t.* au (lladr) Theft, stealth.

> Affeithwyr lladrad, os addefant, dirwy a dalant; ac onis gallant dalu dirwy, yr arglwydd a ddichon eu dienyddu; ac os talant, ni ddylyant fod yn ddrwyr, nag yn [illegible], nag yn [illegible].
>
> The abettors of *theft*, if they confess, they shall pay a fine; and if they cannot pay a fine, the lord can banish them; and if they do pay, they ought not to be chiles, nor to suffer death, nor be liable to execution. — *Welsh Laws.*

Lladradaidd, *a.* (lladrad) Somewhat like theft; thievish; stolen, done by stealth; private, close, secret.

Lladraeth, *s. m.* (lladr) Thievery, or stealing.

Lladraidd, *a.* (lladr) Thievish, apt to steal; sly.

> Llun twr ar wr ond ei wyneb;
> A lle i edrych yn lladraidd.
>
> The form of a tower upon a man, except his face; and a place to look *slyly* through. — *Gwilym y Glyn, [illegible].*

Lladrata, *v. a.* (lladrad) To steal, rob, or thieve.

> Nid hawdd lladrata oddiar leidr.
>
> It is not easy *to steal* from a thief. — *Adage.*

> Na ladrata.
>
> *Steal not.* — *Commandments.*

Lladrataeth, *s. m.* (lladrad) Practice of thieving.

Lladratiad, *s. m.* (lladrad) A thieving, a stealing.

Lladratwr, *s. m.* (lladrad—gwr) A stealer.

Lladrates, *s. f.—pl. t.* au (lladrad) Female thief.

Lladron, *s. pl. aggr.* (lladr) Thieves, robbers.

Lladronaidd, *a.* (lladron) Thievishly inclined.

Lladroneiddiad, *s. m.* (lladronaidd) A rendering, or becoming thievish.

Lladroneiddiaw, *v. a.* (lladronaidd) To render of a thievish disposition; to become thievish.

Lladroneiddiawl, *a.* (lladronaidd) Apt to be thievish, of a thievish disposition.

Lladroneiddrwydd, *s. m.* (lladronaidd) Pilferingness, thievishness.

Lladrones, *s. f.* (lladron) A female thief.

Lladroni, *v. a.* (lladron) To make thieves of; to become thieves.
Lladronig, *a.* (lladron) Addicted to pilfering.
Lladroniarwydd, *s. m.* (lladron) Pilferingness.
Lladronus, *a.* (lladron) Of a pilfering disposition.
Lladu, *v. a.* (llad) To confer a gift, or blessing.
Lladd, *s. m.* (lly—add) A cut, a cutting off; a killing. *v. a.* To cut, to cut off, to strike off, or do away; to slay, to kill. *Lladd gwair*, to cut down hay, or to mow; *lladd mawn*, to cut turfs; *lladd â llif*, to cut with a saw, to saw; *lladd pen*, to behead; *lladd tan*, to strike fire; *lladd dyeithr*, to kill a stranger, that is, to pretend to be a stranger.

O derfydd i ddyn ladd pren, a dygwyddo o'r pren a lladd dyn—taled werth gwaed.

If a man shall *cut* a tree, and the tree should fall down and *kill* a person, let him pay the price of blood. *Welsh Laws.*

Mis Ionawr na ladd waed.

In the month of January *do* not *let* blood. *Meddygon Myddfai.*

Ni leddir cennad.

A messenger *will* not *be slain.* *Adage.*

Crefydd a ladd y drwg, ond yw moes ond ei guddiaw.

Religion *destroys* evil, morality only hides it. *Adage.*

Lladdadwy, *a.* (lladd) That may be cut off, or killed.
Lladdawl, *a.* (lladd) Tending to cut off, or to kill
Lladdedig, *a.* (lladd) Being cut off, or slaughtered

Lladdid y fath nifer o bob ochr nes oedd y mor agos yn wridawg gan waed y lladdedigion.

Such a number was slain on each side so that the sea was almost blushing with the blood of the *slaughtered* ones. *Theo. Evans.*

Lladdedigaeth, *s. m.—pl. t.* au (lladdedig) The state of being cut off, or killed.
Lladdfa, *s. f.—pl.* lladdfëydd (lladd) Slaughter.
Lladdfre, *s. m.* (lladd—bre) A field of battle.
Lladdgar, *a.* (lladd) Apt to slaughter, or kill.
Lladdgarwch, *s. m.* (lladdgar) A slaughtering.

Bu ryfela a lladdgarwch mawr rhwng pendefigion Gwynedd a Phowys.

A warring and great *slaughtering* took place between Gwynedd and Powys. *Ieuan Brechfa.*

Lladdiad, *s. m.—pl. t.* au (lladd) A cutting off.
Lladdwr, *s. m.—pl.* lladdwyr (lladd—gwr) One who cuts off; a killer, a slayer.
Lladdwriaeth, *s. m.* (lladdwr) The act of a killer.
Llae, *s. m.* (lla) An expanse, or a spread.
Llaer, *s. m.* (lly—aer) A rippling; a reflux.

Pwy enw y teir-caer
Rhwng lliant a llaer?

What the name of the three forts between the flood and *ebb?* *Taliesin.*

Llaerawl, *a.* (llaer) Tending to ripple.
Llaered, *s. f.—pl. t.* au (llaer) A clear shallow place in a river, a ford.
Llaeriad, *s. m.* (llaer) Clearing or ebbing tide.
Llaeru, *v. a.* (llaer) To grow shallow; to ebb.
Llaes, *a.* (lly—aes) Loose, incompact; trailing.

Angen y gyhydedd laes yw bau un-sill-ar-ddeg, a phennill o bedwar bas i unarbymtheg, neu o hyny i ugain.

The requisite of the *trailing* metricity is, a verse of eleven syllables, with a stanza having from four verses to sixteen, or from that to twenty. *Barddas.*

Llaesawd, *s. m.* (llaes) That is loose, trailing, or down, a litter.
Llaesawl, *a.* (llaes) Tending to slacken or droop.
Llaesbais, *s. f.—pl.* llaesbeisiau (llaes—pais) A loose trailing coat.
Llaesder, *s. m.* (llaes) Slackness, laxness; a state of trailing, or hanging down loosely.
Llaesedig, *a.* (llaes) Being slackened, or relaxed.
Llaesedigawl, *a.* (llaesedig) Of a slackening, or drooping tendency.
Llaesedd, *s. m.* (llaes) Slackness; droopingness.
Llaesfwng, *s. m.* (llaes—mwng) Long mane. *a.* Long-maned.
Llaesglust, *s. f.—pl. t.* iau (llaes—clust) A long hanging ear. *a.* Flap-eared.
Llaesglustiawg, *a.* (llaesglust) Having long ears.
Llaesiad, *s. m.* (llaes) A rendering loose, lax, or incompact; a trailing, a dropping.
Llaesodr, *s. m.—pl. t.* au (llaesawd) A place of relaxation; litter laid under cattle in a stall.
Llaesodbren, *s. m.* (llaesawd—pren) A bar to keep in the litter of a cattle stall.
Llaesu, *v. a.* (llaes) To slacken, to bring down; to relax, to hang down, or become lax, to trail, to flag, to grow faint.

Lleision lyw——
Llaesa dy far, dy fardd wyf.

Leader of Lleision, *slacken* thy wrath, for I am thy bard. *Cynddelw, i R. ab Gruffydd.*

Llaeth, *s. m.—pl. t.* au (lly—aeth) Milk. *Llaeth llefrith, llafrith*, sweet or fresh milk; *llaeth enwyn, enwyn*, buttermilk; *llaeth cri, llaeth cadw, llaeth sur*, milk set for churning; *llaeth brith, llaeth mysg, llaeth tor*, and *llaeth melyn*, beestings.—*Llaeth y cythraul*, devil's milk, a kind of spurge; *llaeth y geifr, gwyddfid*, honey-suckle; *llaeth ysgyfarnog, llysiau y cyfog*, sun spurge; *llaeth bron mair*, common lungwort.

Llaeth ac yd, goreuon byd.

Milk and corn the best things of the world. *Adage.*

Llaetha, *v. a.* (llaeth) To collect or beg milk.

A fo aml ei fara,
Tua gans aed i laetha.

He that abounds with bread, merrily let him go *to seek for milk.* *Adage.*

Llaeth i blentyn, cig i wr, cwrw i hen.

Milk for a child, flesh for a man, ale for the aged. *Adage.*

Llaethai, *s. c.—pl.* llaetheion (llaeth) A dealer in milk; a beggar of milk.
Llaethaidd, *a.* (llaeth) Like milk, rather milky.
Llaethawg, *a.* (llaeth) Abounding with milk.
Llaethawl, *a.* (llaeth) Relating to milk, lacteal.
Llaethdwn, *s. m.* (llaeth—twn) Lay land, pasture.
Llaethedd, *s. m.* (llaeth) Milkiness; lactescence.
Llaetheiddrwydd, *s. m.* (llaethaidd) Milkiness.
Llaethfwyd, *s. m.* (llaeth—bwyd) Milk diet.
Llaethiad, *s. m.* (llaeth) A turning to milk; a yielding milk
Llaethlo, *s. m.—pl. t.* iau (llaeth—llo) A sucking calf; a milksop, otherwise named *llaethlo yr hafod.*
Llaethlyd, *a.* (llaeth) Milky, apt to be milky.
Llaethlydrwydd, *s. m.* (llaethlyd) Lactescence.
Llaethlys, *s. m.* (llaeth—llys) Milkwort; also called *amlaethai.*
Llaethogi, *v. a.* (llaethawg) To fill with milk; to become full of milk, to abound with milk.
Llaethogrwydd, *s. m.* (llaethawg) Milkiness.
Llaethon, *s. m.* (llaeth) That is milky. *Llaethon pysg*, the soft row of fish.
Llaethu, *v. a.* (llaeth) To turn to milk; to yield milk; to become milky.
Llaethwyg, *s. m.* (llaeth—gwyg) Milk-vetch.
Llaethygen, *s. f.* (llaeth) Lettuce.
Llaethysgall, *s. pl. aggr.* (llaeth—ysgall) The sow thistle; also called *ysgall y moch.*
Llaf, *s. f.* (lla) That extends, or goes round.

Llafan, *s. m.—pl. t.* au (lla—man) That is susceptible of impression, or instrumental in conveying; evil, mischief, also a strand. *Bara llafan*, and *bara lawr*, laver bread.

Llafanad, *s. m.—pl.* llafanaid (llafan) Intellection; intellect, intelligence, a faculty of the mind, sense.

> Gwdichaf fy Nhad—
> A'm gorug, 'ym gwyliad,
> Fy naith llafanad.
>
> I will adore my Father, who has formed, for my perception, my seven faculties. *Taliesin.*

Llafanog, *s. f.* (llaf) The hairweed, or crow-silk.

Llafanawl, *a.* (llafan) Intellectual, intellective.

Llafanddrwg, *s. m.* (llafan—drwg) Evil of sense, or perception; false impression.

> Gwnauthur eu tybian neillduawl eu hunain yn rheol wrth ba un i [illegible] cariad tuagat ereill; hyn, ysywaeth yr oedd, a wnaeth fwy o lafanddrwg yn y byd cristionawg na peth arall.
>
> They make their own particular notions a rule, by which they measure their love towards others; this, the more the pity, has done more mischief in the christian world than any other thing. *Ier. Owain.*

Llafanedd, *s. m.* (llafan) The state, or power of intellect, perceptivity.

Llafaniad, *s. m.* (llafan) Intellection; a figuring in the mind.

Llafanu, *v. a.* (llafan) To endue with intellect, or sense; to figure in the mind.

Llafar, *s. m.—pl. t.* au (llaf—ar) Utterance, voice, or speech; one that is loquacious.

> Llafar oen a chalon blaidd.
>
> The voice of a lamb with the heart of a wolf. *Adage.*
>
> Tri chof beirdd Ynys Prydain: cof cân, cof llafar gorsedd, a [illegible] defawd.
>
> The three memorials of the bards of the isle of Britain: memorial of song, the memorial of the voice of the convention, and the memorial of custom. *Barddas.*
>
> Llafar grwth fal llafar gro,
> Mwy no llafar maen llifo.
>
> A sound upon the Crwth, like the noise of the pebbles on the shore, louder than the noise of the grindstone. *G. ab I. ab Ll. Fychan.*

Llafar, *a.* (llaf—ar) Vocal, well-tuned, well-sounded; loud, loquacious, prating.

> Nag addef rin i lafar.
>
> Disclose not a secret to the loquacious. *Llywarch Hen.*

Llafarai, *s. c.—pl.* llafareion (llafar) A vowel.

Llafarawd, *s. m.* (llafar) The act of uttering, or pronouncing; pronunciation.

Llafarawg, *a.* (llafar) Abounding with sound, that is vocal. *s. f.—pl.* llafarogion. Vowels.

> Nid tor gymeriad yw bod un llafarawg yn ateb i lafarawg arall.
>
> It is no break of concatenation when one vowel answers to another vowel. *W. Middleton.*

Llafarawl, *a.* (llafar) Sounding, enunciative.

Llafaredig, *a.* (llafar) Uttered, or pronounced.

Llafaredigaeth, *s. m.—pl. t.* au (llafaredig) Pronunciation, or enunciation.

Llafaredigawl, *a.* (llafaredig) Enunciative.

Llafaredd, *s. m.* (llafar) The faculty of speaking.

Llafarfas, *a.* (llafar—bas) Low-speaking, murmuring, muttering.

> Y fra— —
> Breu[illegible] buil dwfr llafarfas.
>
> [illegible] swifter than the whirl of the murmuring water. *D. ab Gwilym.*

Llafariad, *s. m.—pl. t.* au (llafar) Pronunciation; also a vowel; *llafariaid*, vowels.

Llafarlais, *s. m.* (llafar—llais) A clear sound.

Llafaru, *v. a.* (llafar) To enunciate, to pronounce, to hold forth, to speak.

> [illegible]
> [illegible]
> [illegible]
>
> I may have credit for what I say: the breaking of spears on [illegible] where I be: I will not say that I shall not retreat. *Llywarch Hen.*

Llafarus, *a.* (llafar) Apt to be vocal; loquacious.

Llafarusaidd, *a.* (llafarus) Rather loquacious.

Llafarusaw, *v. a.* (llafarus) To render vocal; to become loquacious.

Llafarwch, *s. m.* (llafar) The state, or cause of speaking; loquacity.

> Tri llafarwch serchog: haf dy, cog, a lleian.
>
> The three themes of loquacity of the amorous: a summer house, a cuckoo, and a love messenger. *Trioedd.*

Llafarwedd, *s. f.* (llafar—gwedd) Character of pronunciation; a dialect.

> Tair llafarwedd y sydd ar y Gymraeg: y Wenhwyseg, y Ddeheubartheg, a'r y Wyndodeg; a chyfiawn ar gerdd ymarfer o bob un o'r tair, yn gymysg blith draphlith, yn ol barn ac awdurdawd y prifeirdd.
>
> There are three modes of speaking belonging to the Welsh: the dialect of the men of Gwent, the dialect of the Southern district, and the dialect of the men of Gwynedd, and it is just in poetry to use every one of the three blended together, according to the judgement and authority of the primary bards. *Barddas.*

Llafarwr, *s. m.—pl.* llafarwyr (llafar—gwr) A speaker: a preacher, a declaimer.

Llafarydd, *s. m.—pl. t.* ion (llafar) An enunciator; a speaker; also a vowel.

Llafas, *s. m.* (lla—mas) The act of daring.

Llafasawl, *a.* (llafas) Daring, adventurous.

Llafasedig, *a.* (llafas) Being presumed.

Llafasiad, *s. m.* (llafas) A daring, a presuming.

Llafasu, *v. a.* (llafas) To venture, to dare.

> Trais ni lafasa, na lledrad.
>
> Violence he will not dare, nor theft. *D. Benfras.*

Llafasus, *a.* (llafas) Daring, or presuming.

Llafaswr, *s. m.—pl.* llafaswyr (llafas—gwr) One who dares, one who has assurance, a presumer.

Llaferydd, *s. m.* (llafar) Utterance of speech.

Llafn, *s. m.—pl. t.* au (llaf) A blade, a thin slice, a flake. *Dyna lafn o ddyn teg*, there is a fine blade of a man.

> Yn rhith llafn anwar, llachar llain;
> Yn rhith cleddyf claer,
> Clod ysgain yn aer,
> Yn ar[illegible] cyngrain;
> Yn rhith draig rhag dragon Prydain;
> Yn rhith blaidd blaengar fu Owain.
>
> In the form of a violent blade, a gleaming ray; in the form of a shining sword, radiated with glory in the slaughter, under the cover of spears in contact; in the form of a dragon before the sovereign of Britain; in the form of a daring wolf was Owain. *Cynddelw, i O. Cyfeiliawg.*

Llafnaid, *s. m.* (llafn) A blading, that is on a blade.

Llafnaidd, *a.* (llafn) Like a blade, or lamina.

Llafnawl, *a.* (llafn) Relating to a blade.

Llafnawr, *s. pl. aggr.* (llafn) The blades weapons, spears, used by the Britons, about seven feet long, nearly three of which length was a blade, like that of a sword, and about two inches broad. Copper ones of this kind were used in Wales until as late as the time of *Owain Glyndwr;* as several of them have been found in places where he fought his battles.

> Gwelais drais trydar, ac afar, ac angen,
> Yd lethrynt lafnawr ar benwar diogywen.
>
> I saw the oppression of tumult, and mourning, and tribulation, the blade weapons glittering upon the polished helmets. *Taliesin.*

Llafndrochi, *v. a.* (llafn—trochi) To bathe a blade.

Llafndrochiad, *s. m.* (trochiad) A blade bather.

> Cad gyrchiad, llafndrochiad, llew
> Fu Rhys— —
>
> A hastener to the conflict, a bather of the blade, a lion was Rhys. *Prydydd Bychan.*

Llafndrwch, *s. m.* (llafn—trwch) A blade breaking.

Llafnedig, *a.* (llafn) Made into a blade, bladed.

Llafnedig, *a.* (llafn) Made into a blade; bladed.
Llafnes, *s. f.—pl. t.* od (llafn) A bouncing woman. *Mae hi yn llafnes o ddynes hardd*, she is a fine bouncer of a woman.
Llafniad, *s. m.* (llafn) A making a blade.
Llafnu, *v. a.* (llafn) To blade; to beat out into thin plates; to shoot out into blades.
Llafon, *s. m.* (llaf) That spreads out; lamina.
Llafr, *s. m.—pl. t.* au (llaf) A spread; the spreading out of the body; the breech. *a.* Spreading.

Llafr pob newydd.

Every thing new is *spreading*. *Adage.*

Llafraidd, *a.* (llafr) Somewhat spreading out.
Llafrawg, *a.* (llafr) Having a rotundity; having a breech; having large buttocks. *s. f.—pl.* llafrogod. The lower part; the breech.
Llafrawl, *a.* (llafr) Belonging to the breech.
Llafren, *s. f.* (llafr) A large breeched female.
Llafriad, *s. m.* (llafr) A forming a breech.
Llafru, *v. a.* (llafr) To spread out, to breech.
Llafrwyn, *s. pl. aggr.* (lla—brwyn) Bulrushes; also called *cerfrwyn*.
Llafrwynawg, *a.* (llafrwyn) Having bulrushes.
Llafur, *s. m.* (llaf) Agricultural labour, agriculture, or husbandry; toil, or labour; also the produce of tillage, all sorts of corn.

Tair meddyginiaeth Meddygon Myddfai, dwfr, mel, a llafur.

The three remedies of the Myddfai Doctors, water, honey, and *labour*. *Adage.*

Llafurgar, *a.* (llafur) Fond of labour, laborious.
Llafuriad, *s. m.* (llafur) A labouring, a toiling; a doing husbandry work.
Llafuriaeth, *s. m.—pl. t.* au (llafur) The act of labouring, or toiling; husbandry work.

Dim ond cur o'n llafuriaeth,
Dan haul gu; dyna bwyl gaeth!

Nothing but pain from our *toiling*, beneath the lovely sun: that is a distressed condition. *D. Thomas, o Geredigion.*

Llafuriant, *s. m.* (llafur) Labour or toiling.
Llafuriaw, *v. a.* (llafur) To till the ground, to do husbandry work; to toil, to labour.

Ni lafuria, ni weddia,
Nid teilwng iddo ei fara.

That *will* not *toil*, that will not pray, to him his bread is not deserved. *Adage.*

Llafuriawl, *a.* (llafur) Relating to labour; relating to husbandry.
Llafurus, *a.* (llafur) Laborious, or toilsome.

Nid llafurus llaw gywraint.

An accurate hand is not *laborious*. *Adage.*

Llafurusrwydd, *s. m.* (llafurus) Laboriousness.
Llafurwr, *s. m.—pl.* llafurwyr (llafur—gwr) A tiller of the ground, a husbandman.
Llafurwriaeth, *s. m.* (llafurwr) Agriculture.
Llag, *s. m.* (lly—ag) That is slack, or loose. *a.* Slack, loose; sluggish.
Llagad, *s. m.—pl. t.* au (llag) A shallow lake, or plash, overgrown with rushes.
Llai, *s. m.—pl.* lleion (lla) Mud; also a darkish blue colour; a gloom. It is a name given to rivers, in common with *Dulas*, whose waters are of that hue. *Coed y Llai*, Lees-wood, a place so called. *March llai*, a dark grey horse; *gwydd lai*, a goose of dusky plumage.

Ni bu ddryghin heb hinon,
Na thrai blaen Llai heb lanw llon.

There has been no tempest without fine weather, nor an ebb on the extremity of the *gully* without a smiling flood. *Ieuan Ddu.*

Llai, *a.* (lly—ai) That is small, or little. It is mostly used comparatively for *lleiach*, less or smaller. *adv.* In a smaller degree.

A wyr leiaf a wed fwyaf

He that knows the *least* will talk the most. *Adage.*

Nid llai gwerth mefl no gwerth ffawd.

Not *less* the price of disgrace than the price of good luck. *Adage.*

Llaib, *s. m.—pl.* lleibiau (lla—ib) A sup, or lap.
Llaid, *s. m.—pl.* lleidiau (llai) Clay; mud; also a disease incident to the feet of cattle, caused by clay adhering to the hoof.

Dano fo——
Di osodid, dwys hyder,
Ychain a lafuriain' laid
Yno, a defaid, nid ofer.

Under his care thou didst place, with true confidence, oxen that work there the *glebe*, and sheep; nought was waste. *W. Middleton.*

Llaidd, *s. m.* (lla—idd) That is mild, or soft, *a.* Mild; smooth; delicate.
Llaif, *s. m.—pl.* lleifion (lla—if) A shear, or shave.
Llaig, *s. m.—pl.* lleigion (lla—ig) A bubble on the water; also a quicksand.

Lluest oedd i'm fal y llaig,
Ar lun cranc ar fola craig.

I had a tent like the *bubble*, in the form of a crab upon the bosom of the rock. *I. G. ab I. ab Lleision.*

Llain, *s. m.—pl.* lleiniau (lla—in) A blade; a slip, or long narrow piece, a long patch. *Llain o dir*, a slip of land.

Ni wisg cain ni wisg lain.

He will not wear a lustre that will not wear a *blade*. *Adage.*

Glew oddef, gloes lef, a glas lain ar glun,
A glywir yn Mhrydain.

Heroic suffering, the voice of pain, and a blue *blade* on the thigh, will be heard of in Britain. *Cynddelw.*

Oedd balch gwalch gob-hlad ei lain;
Oedd balch gwallch gweled ei werin.

Proud was the hero of the laving of his *blade*; proud were the aspiring ones on seeing his host. *D. Benfras.*

Llaing, *s. m.* (lla—ing) That doubles; a clasp.
Llair, *s. m.* (llair) That is prone; that is satiated.
Llais, *s. m.—pl.* lleisiau (lly—ais) The voice.

Digrif gan bob aderyn ei lais.

Every bird is fond of his own *note*. *Adage.*

Llawenais——
Gan glywed digrifed ton
Y gog las ddigoeg leison.

I was gladdened in hearing how pleasing the note of the blue cuckoo of faultless *tones*. *D. ab Gwilym.*

Llaith, *s. m.* (llai) That is run out; a dissolved state, the being divested of energy; a dank, or a humid state; dissolution; death; slaughter.

Nid llai y cyrch dyn ei laith no'i gyfarwys.

Not less will a man draw to his *dissolution* than his entertainment. *Adage.*

Llaith, *a.* (llai) Dank, humid, moist; soft; not rigid, pliant. *Hin laith*, moist weather; *tir llaith*, wet ground; *dyn llaith*, a soft man; also a tippler; *arf laith*, a soft tempered tool.

E'm gada heb ddim——
Ond yr awen lawen laith.

He left me without any thing, but the merry *flippant* muse. *D. ab Gwilym.*

Llall, *s. c.—pl.* lleill (lly—all) The other; or other one. *O'r naill i'r llall*, from the one to the other. *Y naill bellach yn gyru y llall*, the one extreme urging on the other. *Dyfed.*

A wnelo ddrwg arhoed y llall.

He that does mischief let him expect the *other*. *Adage.*

Ni lwgr da ar y llall.

One good will not spoil upon the *other*. *Adage.*

Llallas, *s. m.* (llall) A blue colour.
Llallawg, *a.* (llall) Being other; being fellow, or accompanying part. *s. c.—pl.* llallogau. Another that accompanies; a twin.

Llallawg ceu a'm hatebydd—
Truan o chwedl a ddywedyd.

Brother, since thou hast answered me, a piteous report hast thou spoken! — *Cyfoesi Myrddin.*

Ysgydd Llanfor tra bonawg,
Ydd ân Clwyd i Glywedawg
Ac ni wn ai hi llallawg.

It is in Llanfor most tumultuous, that Clwyd goes into Clywedawg, and I do not know if she is a twin sister. — *Llywarch Hen.*

Llalliad, *s. m.—pl. t.* au (llall) Alternation.

Llallogan, *s. c.* (llallawg) Another that accompanies, a fellow, or comrade; a twin.

Cyfarchaf i'm llallogan Fyrddin,
Gwr doeth, darogenydd.

I will greet my twin brother Myrddin, a wise man, a reporter of futurity. — *Cyfoesi Myrddin.*

Llallogen, *s. f.* (llallawg) A female other one; a twin sister.

Llallu, *v. a.* (llall) To alternate, or to vary.

Llam, *s. m.—pl. t.* au (lly—am) A stride, a skip, a frisk, a bound; a step; chance, accident. *Llamau afon*, stepping stones in a river.

Gwae fy llaw, llam rymtyngid!

Woe my hand, the step that has been destined for me! — *Llywarch Hen.*

Ys trist Eurddyl o'r drallawd heno,
Ac o'r llam a'm darwedd.
Yn Aber Lliw lladd ei brawd!

Mournful is Eurddyl from the affliction of this night, and for the step that is fixed for me. In Aber Lliw her brother slain! — *Llywarch Hen.*

Llamai, *s. c.* (llam) That steps, strides, or bounds.

Llamawd, *s. m.* (llam) The act of striding over.

Llamawg, *a.* (llam) Having a stride, or step. *s. f.—pl.* llamogau. A stile. *Dim.*

Llamawl, *a.* (llam) Stepping, striding, bounding.

Llamdwy, *s. m.* (llam—twy) A course of stepping.

Llamdwyad, *s. m.* (llamdwy) A conveying.

Llamdwyaw, *v. a.* (llamdwy) To carry from place to place.

Llamddelw, *s. f.—pl. t.* au (llam—delw) A puppet.

Llamedig, *a.* (llam) Being paced, or stepped.

Llamfa, *s. f.—pl.* llamfeydd (llam—ma) A stile.

Llamfforch, *s. f.—pl.* llamffyrch (llam—fforch) Stile

Llamiad, *s. m.* (llam) A stepping, or striding.

Llamid, *s. m.—pl. t.* au (llam) A leap, or jump.

Llamidydd, *s. m.—pl. t.* ion (llamid) A vaulter; a tumbler; a porpoise.

Y llamidydd llym bew-deg,
Llamu'n frau y tonau teg.

Thou porpoise, swift and briskly fair, vault freely the swelling waves. — *T. Prys.*

Llamidyddawl, *a.* (llamidydd) Vaulting, leaping.

Llamidyddiaeth, *s. m.* (llamidydd) The act of vaulting, or tumbling, feats of activity.

Llamre, *s. f.* (llam—rhe) A skipping, or bouncing pace. *a.* Of a bounding pace, curvetting. The name of the mare of Arthur.

Llamsach, *s. m.* (llam—sach) A caper, or prance; a skipping, or prancing about. *v. a.* To caper.

Llamsachiad, *s. m.* (llamsach) A capering about.

Llamsachus, *a.* (llamsach) Full of capering, or frisking. *March llamsachus*, a capering horse.

Llàmu, *v. a.* (llam) To stride; to skip, to frisk, to bound; to step.

Am dano—
Llym y llam fy nagrau.

For him, violently start my tears. — *D. Benfras.*

Llamwr, *s. m.—pl.* llamwyr (llam—gwr) One who steps, or strides.

Llamwyr, *s. m.* (llam—gwyr) An oblique course.

Llan, *s. f.—pl. t.* au (lly—an) A clear place, area, or spot of ground to deposit any thing in; a yard, or a small enclosure; a place of gathering together, a church village; a church, or place of meeting. *Perllan*, an orchard; *gwinllan*, a vineyard; *ydlan*, a corn-yard; *corfflan*, a burying ground; *corlan*, a sheepfold.

Llànaidd, *a.* (llàn) Being clear and open.

Per-lawr parlas meura glas glog,
Yn llanaidd, a meillionog.

A sweet spot of luxuriant growth in a green mantle, that is open and even, and abounding with trefoil. — *D. ab Gwilym.*

Llanast, *s. m.* (llan) That is spread out.

Llanastr, *s. m.—pl.* llanastrau (llanast) That is thrown, or laid together confusedly, that is strewed about; a lumber place; dispersion, confusion. *Ar lanastr, yn llanastr*, in confusion, or confusedly.

Llanastrawl, *a.* (llanastr) Strewing, scattering.

Llanastredig, *a.* (llanastr) Being strewed about.

Llanastriad, *s. m.* (llanastr) A strewing about.

Llanastru, *v. a.* (llanastr) To strew about.

Llanc, *s. m.—pl. t.* iau (lly—anc) A youth. *Hen lanc*, an old bachelor; *hen lancesi*, old spinsters.

Llancaidd, *a.* (llanc) Like a youth; youthful.

Llances, *s. f.—pl. t.* i (llanc) A young woman.

Llancesig, *s. f. dim.* (llances) A tiny female.

Llanciaw, *v. n.* (llanc) To become a youth.

Llandref, *s. f.—pl. t.* i (llàn—tref) A church village

Llaned, *a.* (llan) Of a level and open surface. *Llawr llaned*, ground of smooth surface.

Llanedd, *s. m.* (llàn) Smoothness of surface.

Llanerch, *s. m.—pl. t.* i, au, ydd (llan—erch) A smooth sheltered area or place enclosed in woods; a glade; a paddock; also a term used in bay-making, when the hay is raked together into thick patches. It is the name of several places in Wales.

Och! weled y lle oeddi yn llanerch.

Ah! to see the wood place a clear plain. — *D. ab Gwilym.*

Llanerchawl, *a.* (llanerch) Being in open patches.

Llanerchiad, *s. m.* (llanerch) A laying out in patches.

Llanerchu, *v. a.* (llanerch) To lay in patches.

Llant, *s. m.—pl. t.* au (llan) An enclosed plat, raised up a foot or more, and wattled round, or otherwise, as a cockpit and the like. *Sil.*

Llanw, *s. m.* (llan) That fills up; fullness, copiousness; the flowing in of the tide; the tide of influx. *Gor llanw*, high water.

Po mwyaf y llanw mwyaf fydd y trai.

The greatest the flood greatest will be the ebb. — *Adage.*

Llanwed, *s. m.* (llanw) An influx; a tide.

Tair allawr gwyrthfawr, gwyrthau gwyned,
Y sy rwng mor a gorwydd a gorddlanwed.

Three precious altars, bearing miracles, there are between the sea and upland and a mighty influx. — *Llywelyn Fardd, i Beuno.*

Llar, *s. m.* (lly—ar) That spreads out; that drops down; that is easy, or soft.

Llarach, *v. a.* (llar) To coax, to wheedle.

Llarach, *s. m.* (llar) A coaxing, a wheedling.

Llariaidd, *a.* (llar) Of a mild nature, meek.

Llariain, *a.* (llar) Abounding with mildness.

Carafi yr adarain a'u llariain lais.

I love the winged choiristers with their soft voice. — *Gwalchmai.*

Llarieidd-dra, *s. m.* (llariaidd) Mildness, gentleness.

Llarieiddiad, *s. m.* (llariaidd) A rendering mild; a becoming mild, or gentle.

Llarieiddiaw, *v. a.* (llariaidd) To render mild; to meliorate; to become mild.

Llarieiddiawl, *a.* (llariaidd) Of a mild tendency.

Llarp, *s. m.—pl. t.* iau (llar) A shred, a torn piece, a rag, a clout.

Llarpiad, *s. m.* (llarp) A tearing into shreds.
Llarpiaw, *v. a.* (llarp) To rend, tear, or pull in pieces; to mangle.
Llarpiawg, *a.* (llarp) Having shreds; tattered.
Llarpiedig, *a.* (llarp) Being torn, or tattered.
Llarpiogrwydd, *s. m.* (llarpiawg) Raggedness.
Llarpiwr, *s. m.—pl.* llarpwyr (llarp—gwr) One who tears into shreds.
Llaru, *v. a.* (llar) To render satisfied, to satiate; to cloy; to be satisfied; to be satiated.
Llarwch, *s. m.* (llar) A state of satisfaction, or ease; mildness, softness, suavity.
Llary, *s. m.* (llar) One that is at ease, or serene; a mild or placid one.

Cwyn cyrrh cyfaened na walar,
Cwyddaw llary ar llaw fardd breuder.

Mourned in songs is a connection that shall not be denied, the falling of a *placid one* on the hand of a bard of frailty. *Cynddelw.*

Llary, *a.* (llar) Being satisfied, or at ease; mild, placid, gentle, meek. *Y dyn llaryaf o'r byd*, the mildest person in the world.

Llary deyrn cadeirn cad wasgo yn ngher;
Ys fy ngher a orfo.

The mild chief of mighty ones driving the battle in the difficulty; it is my friend that shall triumph. *Ll. P. Moch.*

Llaryad, *s. m.* (llary) A rendering mild, a softening, or assuaging; a growing mild.
Llarŷaidd, *a.* (llary) Of a mild disposition.
Llarŷaw, *v. a.* (llary) To render mild, or gentle; to become mild, gentle, or placid.
Llarychu, *v. a.* (llarwch) To assuage; to be mild.
Llarŷedd, *s. m.* (llary) Mildness, or gentleness.

Dedwydd rwyf, aer-giwyfeur-gledd ardderchawg,
Archaf it' yth llarŷedd!

Happy chief, with a noble golden sword hewing the battle, I crave of thee thy *gentleness*. *Einion Wan, i D. ab Llywelyn.*

Llarŷeiddiad, *s. m.* (llarŷaidd) A rendering of a mild disposition; a becoming mild.
Llarŷeiddiaw, *v. a.* (llarŷaidd) To render of a gentle disposition; to become gentle.
Larŷeiddrwydd, *s. m.* (llarŷaidd) Mildness of nature, or a gentleness of disposition.
Llas, *s. m.* (lly—as) That spreads over, or out; a crust or incrustation; a blue colour.
Llas, *v. a.* (*preter. of* lläu) Was slain, were slain; often used for *lladdwyd*.

E las a gafas rybudd, ac ni las a'i cymerodd.

He that got notice *was slain*, and he who took it *was* not *slain*. *Adage.*

Gan y tri hyn y llas traian y dynion.

By these three *was slain* the third part of the people.

Rev. 9. 18.

Llasar, *s. m.* (llas) A blue colour, or azure.

Dewr o was ban llas yn llasar arfau,
Mal y llas Llachau uch Llechysgar.

He was a gallant youth when slain in *blue* arms, as Llachau was slain above Llechysgar. *Bleddyn Fardd.*

Llinon belydr briw,
Llasar ysgwydliw,
Llurygawg, yn rhiw,
Cywiw cywir.

With broken ashen shafts, *blue* coloured shield, wearing a hauberk, on the ascent, excellent and just. *Einion Len.*

Cylch llys dan liw calch llasar.

Surrounding the court under the hue of *azure* enamel. *R. Goch Eryri.*

Llasaraidd, *a.* (llasar) Partly of a blue colour.
Llasariad, *s. m.* (llasar) A making of blue colour.
Llasarn, *s. m.—pl. t.* au (llas—arn) A pavement; a flooring made of pieces of stones, rammed dry, or without mortar. *Sil.*
Llasarnawg, *a.* (llasarn) Having a pavement.
Llasarniad, *s. m.* (llasarn) A paving; a flooring.
Llasarnu, *v. a.* (llasarn) To pave; to make a kind of floor, by ramming together the refuse of limestone, or the like.
Llasarnwr, *s. m.—pl.* llasarnwyr (llasarn—gwr) A pavior; a layer of floors.
Llasarnydd, *s. m.—pl. t.* ion (llasarn) A pavior.
Llasawg, *a.* (llas) Being spread over; of a blue tint. *s. f.* A streamer.
Llast, *s. m.* (llas) That surrounds, or hems in, a vessel of capacity; a measure.
Llasu, *v. a.* (llas) To spread round; to cover with a blue tint.
Llaswy, *s. m.* (llas) A bluish fluid or tint.
Llaswyr, *s. m.—pl. t.* au (llas—gwyr) An aërial freshness; a verdant freshness. *Dôaf ynô yn llaswyr y bore*, I will come there in the freshness of the morning. *Sil.*
Llaswyra, *v. a.* (llaswyr) To take the fresh air; to walk, or ramble for pleasure, or refreshment, in the pure air; to follow a scent.
Llaswyrawl, *a.* (llaswyr) Of sky-colour freshness.
Llaswyredd, *s. m.* (llaswyr) Freshness of the air.
Llatai, *s. c.—pl.* llateion (llad) A dispenser of blessings, one who does good offices; a messenger between lovers.

I'r byd fy mywyd yw Mai;
Lle glas gofron, llon llatai!

In the world my life is May, when the lawn is green, the *messenger of love* joyous. *D. ab Gwilym.*

Beiddiwr aer, bydd yr awron
Latai i'm at eiliw tôn.

Hero of the slaughter, be thou at this time a *messenger* for me to her of the hue of the wave. *D. ab Gwilym, i'r Ceiliog du.*

Llatcawd, *s. m.* (lladgawd) A sort of vessel, with marks for drinking thereto.

O derfydd bod dyn yn dywedyd ni ddylai yfed llatcawd; a bod amryson am lonaid llatcawd: sef yw maint y llestr cybyd a chygwn ewin hirfys.

If it should happen that a person is saying that he ought not to drink a *bowl*; and there should be a dispute about the fulness of the *bowl*: be it known that the size of the vessel is the length of the nail joint of the middle finger. *Welsh Laws.*

Llateiaeth, *s. m.* (llatai) The office of a love messenger.

Fe ym gelwir i Rhywun; ac nid oes llateiaeth, nac athrawd, na chelwyddau i yru rhai benben, nad arnaf fi y bwrir.

I am called Somebody; and there are not a *love message*, nor scandal, nor lies to drive people together by the ears, but they are laid upon me. *Elis Wyn, B. Cwsg.*

Llateies, *s. f.—pl. t.* au (llatai) A female love messenger.
Llateirwydd, *s. m.* (llatai) The office of carrying love messages.
Llatwm, *s. m.* (llad) Latten; a kind of brass.

Bwa llatwm didrwm droed.

A *latten* hued bow with no sluggish feet.
D. *ab Gwilym, i'r Bwyneg.*

Llath, *s. f.—pl. t.* au (lla—ath) A rod, or staff; a measuring rod; a yard; the length of a yard. *Llath Moesen*, the rod of Moses; *hanner llath*, half a yard. *Llath Bleddyn*, the yard of Bleddyn, a measure of four feet, used in the hundred of Meisgyn.
Llathaid, *s. f.—pl.* llatheidiau (llath) A yard length.

Y cleddyf— —
Llathaid o ddur llifaid llwyth.

The sword, a *yard* of ground steel, a load. *L. G. Cothi.*

Llatheg, *a.* (teg) Fair, or fine.
Llathen, *s. f.—pl. t.* i (llath) A yard; a yard in length. *Llathen o dir*, a yard of land, a measure in Anglesey, containing 30 perches of 5 ½ to an acre.
Llathenaid, *s. f.—pl.* llatheneidiau (llathen) The measure of a yard, a yard length.
Llatheniad, *s. m.* (llathen) A measuring a yard.

Llathenu, *v. a.* (llathen) To measure a yard.

Llathiad, *s. m.* (llath) A making a yard; a measuring a yard.

Llathlud, *s. m.* (llath—glud) Allurement, seduction, fascination.

Dwyn merch i lathlud heb rodd cenedl.

To carry a woman by *seduction* without the consent of her family. *Welsh Laws.*

Llathludaw, *v. a.* (llathlud) To fascinate, to allure, to inveigle, to seduce.

I ba le ffoaf rhag dy wydd,
Trwy gael fordd rwydd i lathlud.

To what place shall I fly from thy presence, so as to get an easy way *to hide.* *Edm. Prys.*

Llathludiad, *s. m.* (llathlud) Fascination, an alluring, or enticing.

Llathr, *a.* (llath) Glossy, polished; glittering.

Eryf———
I llathr ewrwrith, llathr ei bnawyd,
Llonan yn neriig llanw mor wyd.

Glide for ours, thou of *polished* passion, thou who art a sun on the top of the flood of the sea. *D. ab Gwilym, i'r Wylan.*

Llathraid, *a.* (llathr) Glittering. *Llathreid-rudd lafnawr*, glitteringly ruddy blades.

Llathraidd, *a.* (llathr) Somewhat glittering.

Gwefusau mel———
A llathraidd gorff gweddaidd gwyn.

Lips of honey, and a *delicate* frame handsome and fair. *H. ab R. ab Gwilym.*

Llathrair, *s. m.* (llathr—gair) A bland word.

Llathrawd, *s. m.* (llathr) A glittering, or glare.

Cymaint cerdd ciwdawd
A ddeuta eich tafawd!
Py'r na thrwethwch drwethawd
Llad uch llyn llathrawd,
Penodlliaeth pawb.

So much of national song your tongue has given! Why will you not recite an oration of blessing over the liquor of *brightness*, the theme of every body's rhapsody. *Taliesin.*

Llathrawl, *a.* (llathr) Of a glittering polish.

Llathred, *a.* (llathr) Glittering, gleaming.

Llathredig, *a.* (llathr) Being made to glitter.

Llathreiddiad, *s.* (llathraidd) A rendering or becoming of a glittering tendency; a polishing.

Llathreiddiaw, *v. a.* (llathraidd) To render, or to become somewhat glittering; to polish.

Llathreiddiawl, *a.* (llathraidd) Of a glittering, or a gleaming tendency.

Llathreiddrwydd, *s. m.* (llathraidd) Glitteringness. *Llathreiddrwydd ymadroddion*, splendour of expressions.

Llathriad, *s. m.—pl. t.* au (llathr) A rendering smooth, or glossy, a polishing; a causing to glitter; coruscation.

Llathrloew, *a.* (llathr—gloew) Of glittering clearness, glitteringly lucid.

Llathru, *v. a.* (llathr) To make smooth, or glossy; to calendar; to polish; to cast a splendour, to coruscate, to glitter. *Haul yn llathru*, the sun casting a splendour.

Yn llew glew, yn llyw rhag Llewlawn,
Lladdai llafn gwanar,
Llathrai gaien llasar;
Mal llachar llaw ddigrawn.

As a courageous lion, as a leader before Llewlawn, the wrathful blade would kill, the blue armour *would gleam*, like lightning would be the liberal hand. *Cynddelw, i O. Cyfeiliawg.*

Llathrudd, *s. m.* (lla—trudd) Stupration, deflourment; violation.

Llathruddaw, *v. a.* (llathrudd) To stuprate, or to deflour.

[illegible]

I greet thee, hag! Wilt thou declare to me the thing which I shall ask of thee, for the sake of God? — Where are the children of the man who hath stolen me away by violence? *H. Culhwch—Mabinogion.*

Llathruddawl, *a.* (llathrudd) Deflouring; violating, stuprating.

Llathruddiad, *s. m.—pl. t.* au (llathrudd) A stuprating, a deflouring; stupration, violation.

Llathruddiaeth, *s. m.—pl. t.* au (llathrudd) Stupration; defloration; violation.

Llathruddiaethu, *v. a.* (llathruddiaeth) To commit stupration; to do violation.

Llathruddwr, *s. m.—pl.* llathruddwyr (llathrudd—gwr) A deflourer.

Llathrwr, *s. m.—pl.* llathrwyr (llathr—gwr) A glosser, a polisher; a calenderer.

Llathryd, *s. m.* (lla—tryd) Violence, or force.

Llathrydaw, *v. a.* (llathryd) To force, to violate.

Llathrydiad, *s. m.—pl. t.* au (llathryd) A forcing, or violating.

Llathrydd, *s. m.—pl. t.* ion (llathr) One who makes a gloss; a polisher; a calenderer.

Lläu, *v. a.* (lla) To open, to lay open; to open out; to make to run or flow out; to slay.

Gedrudd far, aawar, aawan, ysgwyd-wyrdd;
Arwar cyrdd cyn lläu.

Of tumultuous rage, ruthless and not a stripling, with a green shield: about him the songs resounded ere he was slain. *Cynddelw, i E. Bryf Cragen.*

Llau, *s. pl. aggr.* (lly—au) Creepers, lice.

Llaw, *s. f.—pl. t.* iau (lly—aw) A hand. The dual *dwylaw* is mostly used for the plural. *Llaw uchaf, llaw drechaf*, the upper hand; *dan law*, under hand; *talaf iti os daw ar fy llaw*, I will pay thee if it comes in my power; *talu yn mlaen llaw*, to pay before-hand.

O sarha caeth ddyn rhydd, lladder y llaw ddëau iddo, onis prynu ei arglwydd; cymaint yw gwerth llaw y caeth a gwerth llaw y brenin.

If a slave shall insult a free man, let his right *hand* be cut off, unless his master shall redeem it. the *hand* of a slave is of equal value with the value of the *hand* of the king. *Welsh Laws.*

Y gelain feinwen a gladdwyd heddyw
Ymhlith pridd a derw:
Gwae fy llaw, lladd fy nghefnderw!

The fair delicate corpse is interred this day, in the midst of earth and oak: Woe my *hand*, the slaying of my cousin! *Llywarch Hen.*

Llawaeth, *s. m.* (llaw) The act of handling; that is brought up by hand. *Lleds llawaeth*, an animal that is reared by hand.

Llawagawr, *s. m.* (llaw—agawr) Calerage; otherwise called *Elinawg*.

Llawagawr, *a.* (llaw—agawr) Open-handed.

Llawaid, *s. f.—pl.* llaweidiau (llaw) A handful.

Llawaidd, *a.* (llaw) Handy, or dexterous.

Llawaidd pob cynnefin.

Every one accustomed is *handy*. *Adage.*

Llawarian, *a.* (llaw—arian) Silver-handed, an epithet for one lavish of gifts.

Aur Angharad lawarian,
A'i gwin gyat a gai on gwna.

The gold of the *liberal-handed* Angharad, and her wine, a few bits one once would get. *L. G. Cothi.*

Llawarwain, *s. m.* (llaw—arwain) To lead by the hand.

Llawarweiniwr, *s. m.—pl.* llawarweinwyr (llawarwain—gwr) One who leads by the hand.

Llawban, *s. m.* (llaw—pan) Felt. *Brethyn llawban*, felt cloth.

Llawbanu, *v. a.* (llawban) To work with the hand, to felt.

Llawborth, *s. m.* (llaw—porth) A feeding by hand; a supporting by hand.

Llawborthiad, *s. m.—pl.* llawborthiaid (llawborth) One whose hand provides.

Llawch eirchiad, llawborthiad adar.

The caresser of petitioners, and one whose *hand feeds* the birds. *Gwalchmai.*

Llawctad, *s. m.* (llawg) A swallowing greedily.
Llawclaw, *v. a.* (llawg) To swallow greedily.
Llawciwr, *s. m.—pl.* llawcwyr (llawg—gwr) A gulper, a greedy eater.
Llawch, *s. m.* (lly—awch) Encouragement.

Duw mawr ymherawdr dyniadon!
Dillwng dy walch trwyn-falch tirion,
Dewr Dewin, dewredd-lin fflos,
Dur-goch bar lluchar llawch deon.

Great God, sovereign ruler of mortal men! set free thy hero, indignantly proud and kind, with cheeks of crimson blush, whose red steel shaft is the protection of strangers. *H. F. ab Griffri.*

Llawchlu, *s. m.—pl. t.* oedd (llawch—llu) A guardian host.

Rhuddwaywyrion deuiu
Rhyddaw i'w nerthu,
Rhialu llawchlu,
Llychlyn ydd aiu'.

Ruddy speared ones, on either side shall come to strengthen him a myriad, a protecting host, to Lochlyn they would go. *G. ab M. ab Dafydd.*

Llawchwith, *a.* (llaw—chwith) Left-handed.
Llawd, *s. m.* (lly—awd) That is going onward, that is craving, that is empty; a gangrel; a lad. *Llawd ar hwch*, the same as *hwch lodig*. *Ynys Lawd*, an islet so called near Holyhead. *a.* Tending forward; craving; lewd.

Nid a cynnyg arglwydd i lawd.

The offer of a lord will not go to the *empty*. *Adage.*

Llawdaraw, *s. m.* (llaw—taraw) The play of Hot-cockles.
Llawdlws, *a.* (llaw—tlws) Neat-handed.
Llawdlysni, *s. m.* (llawdlws) Neat-handedness.
Llawdryfer, *s. f.—pl. t.* au (llaw—tryfer) A hand dart, or a hand harpoon.

Ewyn a'th gaidw———
Rhag llawdryfer lleidr afon.

The foam will guard thee against the *hand harpoon* of a river thief. *D. ab Gwilym, Yr Iawrg.*

Llawdwn, *a.* (llaw—twn) Maimed in the hand.
Llawdr, *s. m.—pl.* llodrau (llawd) Trouse, trowsers, or pantaloons; breeches. *Llawdr yr arth*, acanthus.

Ewyllys y gwyrgam am ei lawdr.

The desire of the deformed about his *breeches*. *Adage.*

Llawdywys, *v.* (llaw—tywys) To lead by hand.
Llawdywysiad, *s. m.* (llawdywys) Manaduction.
Llawdd, *s. m.* (lly—awdd) Pleasure, delight, solace. *a.* Pleasant, delectable; solacing.

Afraid ym cyfraid i'm cyffroi
Cyfred a lludded, a llawdd toll Creawdr
A llwyr grefydd i gynnói.

Needless my want to instigate me to feel dejection, or the *pleasant* worship of the Creator, and perfect devotion to increase. *Meilyr ab Gwalchmai.*

Llawddawg, *a.* (llawdd) Abounding with pleasure; yielding pleasure, or delight.
Llawddëau, *s. f.* (llaw—dëau) A right hand.
Llawddëawg, *a.* (llawddëau) Right-handed.
Llawddewin, *s. m.—pl. t.* ion (llaw—dewin) A chiromancer, or palmister.
Llawddewines, *s. f.—pl. t.* au (llawddewin) A female who follows chiromancy.
Llawddewiniaeth, *s. m.* (llawddewin) Chiromancy, palmistry.
Llawddewiniaw, *v. a.* (llawddewin) To practise chiromancy, or palmistry.
Llawddioli, *v. a.* (llawdd—ioli) To celebrate.
Llawddu, *v. a.* (llawdd) To delight; to soothe.

A'th lawddaf i'th lawn urddas;
A'th lawdd pawb, pennaeth gwlad.

Thee *I will strive to please* in thy full dignity; thee all will please, chief of a kingdom. *Meilyr.*

Rhyfedd———
Fy myw; am fy llyw ni'm llawdd!

I wonder it is I live; after my chief I *shall not be soothed*. *Gw. Ryfel.*

Llawed, *a.* (lla—gwed) Tending to break out.
Llawedr, *s. m.* (llawed) That breaks out.
Llawedrawg, *a.* (llawedr) Having breaks.

Sef yw llawedrawg, yn hen Gymraeg, torrawg; ac wrth hyny y gelwir carllawedrawg yn gartorawg.

Llawedrawg implies, in old Welsh, *shattered*; and therefore it is usual to call one with a *shattered car* one with a *broken car*. *Welsh Laws.*

Llawedrawr, *a.* (llawedr) Shattered, in ruins.

Llawer ci gwilig, a hebawg wyrenig
A llithwyd ar ei llawr,
Cyn bu Erlleon llawedrawr.

Many a dog that scented well the prey, and aerial hawk, have been trained on its floor, before Erlleon became *broken down*. *Llywarch Hen.*

Llawegawr, *s. m.* (llaw—egawr) Creeping thistle.
Llawegen, *s. f.—pl. t.* au (llaw) A gauntlet.
Llawen, *a.* (lla—gwen) Merry, joyful, glad, gay. *Noswaith lawen*, a merry night; *gwna yn llawen*, go on cheerfully; or much good may it do thee. *Llawenion galonau*, joyful hearts.

Bid lawen iach.

Let the healthy be *merry*. *Adage.*

Y gwr hwnw a arfollai Eneas yn llawen.

That person received Eneas *joyfully*. *Gr. ab Arthur.*

Llawenhad, *s. m.* (llawen) A gladdening.
Llawenhawl, *a.* (llawen) Tending to gladden.
Llawenhau, *v. a.* (llawen) To gladden; to be glad, or merry; to rejoice.
Llawenchwedl, *s. m.—pl. t.* au (llawen—chwedl) A glad tiding, joyful news.
Llawenedig, *a.* (llawen) Being made joyful.
Llawenedigaeth, *s. m.—pl. t.* au (llawenedig) The state of being made joyful.
Llawenu, *v. a.* (llawen) To make glad, to cause to rejoice, to gladden; to rejoice, to be glad, merry, or cheerful.
Llawenwch, *s. m.* (llawen) Merriment, gladness.
Llawenychaidd, *a.* (llawenwch) Mirth-inciting.

Ha wraig! dy bechodau a faddeuwyd iti. O, leferydd llawenychaidd!

Ha woman! thy sins have been forgiven thee. Oh, *joy-inciting expression*! *Marchawg Crwydrad.*

Llawenychawl, *a.* (llawenwch) Apt to gladden.
Llawenychiad, *s. m.* (llawenwch) A rejoicing.
Llawenychu, *v. a.* (llawenwch) To rejoice.
Llawenydd, *s. m.* (llawen) Gladness, joy; mirth, merriment; pleasure, happiness.

Nid llawenydd ond nef;
Nid anhyfryd ond uffern.

There is no *happiness* but in heaven; there is nothing melancholy but hell. *Adage.*

Tri llawenydd beirdd Ynys Prydain: llwydd gwybodaeth; gwellhad moes; a gorfod heddwch ar ddifrawd ac anrhaith.

The three causes of *gladness* of the bards of the isle of Britain; the increase of knowledge; improvement of morals; and the triumph of peace over devastation and anarchy. *Barddas.*

Llawenyddedig, *a.* (llawenydd) Being gladdened.
Llawenyddigaeth, *s. m.—pl. t.* au (llawenyddedig) The state of being gladdened.

Ni mynai Curig orwagion bethau y byd hwn; namyn bod iddo ef ryddid llawenyddigaethau paradwys.

Curig did not covet the vain things of this world; but sought to enjoy the liberty of the *pleasures* of paradise. *Ll. G. Hergest.*

Llawer, *s. m.—pl. t.* oedd (lla—gwer) A great many, a great number, a great quantity, a great deal; a diversity. *Llawer iawn, llawer byd*, a vast many, a vast quantity.

Llawer am hawl, un ei dyly.

Many after a claim, it is only due to one. *Adage.*

Llawer, *a.* (lla—gwer) Many, much; several; various. *Llawer tro*, many a time; *llawer mwy*, much more; *llawer un*, many a one.

> Llawer mab heb dad gwedy ei adaw;
> Llawer bendref faith gwedy llwybr goddaith;
> A llawer diffaith drwy anrhaith draw!

> Many a child without a father left; many a spacious habitation marked with the path of conflagration; and many a desert by devastation there be made. *G. ab yr Ynad Coch.*

Llawerawg, *a.* (llawer) Having much or many.

Llaweredd, *s. m.* (llawer) The state of being much; numerosity; multitude.

> Pan oeddem o fewn ergyd bwa croes i'r llys, Gwaeddwr—a alwad; ac ar hyny y dôynt allan laweredd o arlwyddesi mewn gwychdrwsiadau.

> When we were within the shot of a cross bow to the court, Frailty called out; and upon that there came out a *multitude* of ladies in showy dresses. *Marchawg Crwydrad.*

Llawes, *s. f.—pl.* llewys (llaw) That extends out; an outskirt, a skirt, or corner; a slieve. *Llawes rhwyd*, the bosom of a draw-net.

> Tair llawes Gwent uwch coed: Euas,
> Erging, ac Ystrad Yw.

> The three *outskirts* of Gwent above the wood: Euas, Erging, and Ystrad Yw. *Trioedd.*

> Yn ymaros â morwyn,
> Ar lawes maes, irlas mwyn.

> Waiting for a maid, on the *outskirt* of a field, luxuriantly green and pleasant. *D. ab Gwilym.*

> Llawes haul ydyw llys Sion;
> Llys rhydd a llawes rhoddion.

> A sunny *corner* is the hall of John; an open hall with a variety of gifts. *S. Tudur.*

> ——Maent oreul,
> Llysau'r haf, llawes yr haul.

> They are pleasant, the vegetations of summer, the *offspring* of the sun. *R. Ddu, ab S. Bledrydd.*

Llawesan, *s. f. dim.* (llawes) A kind of play.

> ——Eryr aer deragan;
> Gwr yn gware llawesan.

> Eagle of the predicted slaughter; a man playing the *Llawesan*. *Llywarch Llaety.*

Llawesawg, *a.* (llawes) Having outskirts, extremities or corners; having slieves.

Llawesgud, *a.* (llaw—esgud) Nimble-handed, ready-handed.

> Oni fydd cywir y cynnogn, y myn yr hawlwr i gan y mach fod yn gywir: ac am hyny y dywed cyfraith, na fydd lawesgud yn mhyrfa, ac na chymmer ddylyed arall arnat, heb ddylyed dim iti.

> If the original debtor shall not be punctual, the plaintiff will compel the surety to be punctual; and therefore the law says, be not *ready-handed* in a multitude, and do not take the obligation of another upon thee, without any thing being due to thee. *Welsh Laws.*

Llaweth, *s. f.—pl. t.* au (llaw) A handful.

Llawf, *s. f.—pl.* llofau (llaw) A palm of the hand.

Llawfaeth, *s. m.* (llaw—maeth) A feeding by hand. *a.* Brought up by hand.

> Yn llyfn fal yr oen llawfaeth.

> Smooth like the *hand-fed* lamb. *Gutto y Glyn.*

Llawfaethawl, *a.* (llawfaeth) Hand-feeding.

Llawfaethedig, *a* (llawfaeth) Nourished by hand

Llawfaethiad, *s. m.* (llawfaeth) A hand-feeding.

Llawfaethu, *v. a.* (llawfaeth) To nourish by hand, to rear by hand.

Llawfeddyg, *s. m.—pl. t.* on (llaw—meddyg) A chirurgeon, or surgeon.

Llawfeddygawl, *a.* (llawfeddyg) Chirurgical.

Llawfeddygin, *a.* (llawfeddyg) Chirurgical.

Llawfeddyginiaeth, *s. m.* (llawfeddyg) Chirurgery

Llawfeddyginiaethawl, *a.* (llawfeddyginiaeth) Relating to chirurgery.

Llawfeddyginiaw, *v.* (llawfeddyg) To do surgery.

Llawfeddygu, *v. a.* (llawfeddyg) To perform surgery, to act as a surgeon.

Llawfoled, *s. f.—pl. t.* au (llaw—moled) A handkerchief.

Llawforwyn, *s. f.—pl. t.* ion (llaw—morwyn) A handmaid.

> Llawforwyn y frenines, ei thir a gaiff yn rhydd; hi a ddyly ei march pressswyl; a hen ddillad y frenines.

> The *handmaid* of the queen, her land she shall have freely; she is entitled to her horse in ordinary; and the old garments of the queen. *Welsh Laws.*

> Llawen y carwn, cen ni'm carynt:
> Llawforwynion gwery, gwirion oeddynt!

> Joyfully I could love, though they would not love me: chaste *handmaids*, they were innocent! *Cynddelw.*

Llawfrenin, *s. m.* (llaw—brenin) The play of questions and commands.

Llawfwyall, *s. f.—pl.* llawfwyeill (llaw—bwyall) A hand-hatchet, a small hatchet.

> Llawfwyall, ceiniawg a dal.

> A *hand-hatchet*, a penny is its value. *Welsh Laws.*

Llawfyddag, *a.* (llaw—byddag) Close-handed.

> Gwyn gwaedlawedd aerfawdd aerfaidd ethol ion,
> Arf trylew trais alhed;
> Llawrodded llaw-rodd gaffaed,
> Nid llawfyddag fyddai hael.

> In slaughter strife, to blood was Gwyn inured,
> With active glave, a wolf of keen gripe,
> In scath effective; free of hand, and not
> With niggard-hand the generous one would act.
> *Cynddelw, m. i. O. Gwynedd.*

Llawffer, *a.* (llaw—ffer) Strong-handed.

Llawffon, *s. f.—pl.* llawffyn (ffon) A hand-stick.

> Gwr diawg llawffon y diawl.

> A lazy man is the devil's *walking-stick*. *Adage.*

Llawg, *s. m.—pl. t.* iau (lly—awg) That is eager, or that has a craving, appetite, or longing; the swallow; a gulp.

Llawgaead, *a.* (llaw—caead) Close-fisted, stingy.

> Cybyddiaeth yw—wedi caffel ddyn dda bydawl ei garu yn ormodd, neu fod yn llawgaead am dano.

> Cupidity is, after a person hath obtained worldly wealth the loving it to excess, or to be *close-fisted* with it. *Ll. G. Hergest.*

Llawgaeth, *a.* (llaw—caeth) Having a restrained hand.

Llawgair, *s. m.* (llawg—gair) An earnest word, a plighted troth, an oath. *Dywedai ar ei lawgair, sef gan roddi ei law ger ei ddwyfron*, he spoke upon his honour, that is, by putting his hand upon his breast.

Llawgaled, *a.* (llaw—caled) Hard-handed, close-handed; stingy.

Llawgallawr, *s. m.—pl.* llawgalleran (llaw—callawr) A hand-boiler; a saucepan.

> Llawgallawr, deg-ar-ugaint a dal.

> A *hand-boiler*, thirty pence is its value. *Welsh Laws.*

Llawgar, *a.* (llaw—car) Friendly-handed; charitable, hospitable.

> Ystum llawgar yn rhanu.

> In the manner of the *liberal-handed* distributing. *Adage.*

> Hir hynt a chyrchu llawgar.

> A long journey and then resorting to the *hospitable*. *Adage.*

Llawgelfydd, *a.* (llaw—celfydd) Of an ingenious hand.

Llawgelfyddyd, *s. f.—pl. t.* au (llawgelfydd) A handicraft, a mechanical art.

Llawgell, *s. f.—pl. t.* au (llaw—cell) A pocket.

Llawgist, *s. f.* (llaw—cist) A hand-chest.

Llawhir, *a.* (llaw—hir) Long-handed; profuse.

> Gwir lawhir lyw mor a thiredd gwoddiaf.

> The just and *bountiful* ruler of sea and lands I will invoke. *G. ab M. ab Dafydd.*

Llawhual, *s. m.—pl. t.* au (llaw—hual) Manacle.

Llawhualu, *v. a.* (llawhual) To manacle.

Llawiad, *s. m.* (llaw) A handing, a handling.

Llawiaw, *v. a.* (llaw) To hand, or to handle.

Llawiawg, *a.* (llaw) Handed, having hands.

Llawlaw, *adv.* (llaw, *repeated*) Hand to hand.

> Ymladdynt ill dau yngbyd lawlaw; ac Owain a gafas y maes, ac a laddes Oswyn.
>
> They two fought together *hand to hand*, and Owain got the field, and he killed Oswyn. *T. Pryç, H. Prydain.*

Llawliain, *s. m.—pl.* llawlieiniau (llaw—lliain) A hand towel, a napkin.

Llawlif, *s. f.—pl. t.* oedd (llaw—llif) A hand-saw.

Llawlosg, *s. m.* (llaw—llosg) A burn in the hand.

Llawlosgi, *v. a.* (llawlosg) To burn in the hand.

Llawlyw, *s. m.* (llaw—llyw) The plough handle.

Llawn, *a.* (lly—awn) Full; complete, replete.

> Alwar llawn dysg a dawn.
>
> Learning and talent make a *full* purse. *Adage.*

> Ni thyr llestr ni bo llawn.
>
> A vessel that is not *full* will not break. *Adage.*

> Ni dyr yr hwch lawn yn wich y wag.
>
> The *full* sow knows not the squeak of the empty one. *Adage.*

> Yn llys—Llelstawn,
> Yn llaw llew cad cyrn llad llawn.
>
> In the court of Lleision, in the hand of the lion of conflict there are the *full* horns of generous liquor. *Cynddelw, i O. Cyfeiliawg.*

Llawnad, *s. m.* (llawn) A filling, a making full.

Llawnaeth, *s. m.* (llawn) Impletion; plenitude.

> Yn hyn y mae y gwahaniaeth rhyngom ni a Christ; sef bod y Tad wedi tywallt arno ef anfeidrawl lawnaeth o'r Ysbryd:
>
> It is in this that the distinction is between us and Christ, namely, that the Father has poured upon him infinite *plenitude* of the Spirit. *S. Trefredyn.*

Llawnall, *s. m.* (llawn—gall) Plenipotence.

Llawnallu, *s. m.* (llawnall) Plenipotence.

Llawnalluaw, *v. a.* (llawnallu) To endue with full power, to render plenipotent.

Llawnalluawg, *a.* (llawnallu) Plenipotent.

Llawnalluawl, *a.* (llawnallu) Plenipotent.

Llawnalluedd, *s. m.* (llawnallu) Plenipotency.

Llawnalluoddawg, *a.* (llawnalluedd) Plenipotentiary.

Llawnallueddawl, *a.* (llawnalluedd) Plenipotential

Llawnalluogwr, *s. m.—pl.* llawnalluogwyr (llawnalluawg—gwr) A plenipotentiary.

Llawnawd, *s. m.* (llawn) What is full, or complete, the whole.

Llawnder, *s. m.* (llawn) Fullness; abundance.

Llawndid, *s. m.* (llawn) Fullness, plenitude, plenty

Llawndra, *s. m.* (llawn) Fullness; abundance.

Llawnddwys, *a.* (llawn—dwys) Full and general.

Llawnfryd, *s. m.* (llawn—bryd) Full purpose.

Llawnhwda, *s. m.* (llawn—hwda) A full taking; a nonplus, a dilemma.

Llawnhwde, *s. m.* (llawn—hwde) A nonplus.

Llawnlleuad, *s. f.* (llawn—lleuad) A full moon.

Llawnlleuadawl, *a.* (llawnlleuad) Plenilunary.

Llawnlloer, *s. f.* (llawn—lloer) A full moon.

Llawnlloerawl, *a.* (llawnlloer) Plenilunary.

Llawnllaned, *s. f.* (llawn—llaned) Full moon.

Llawnt, *s. f.—pl. t.* au (llawn) A smooth rising hill, a lawn.

> Fy mharadwys ar lwys lawnt.
>
> My paradise upon a pleasant *lawn*. *Ieu. Dyfi.*

Llawnwedd, *s. m.* (llawn—gwedd) A full form.

> Gwr a gynnall y lloer yn ei llawnwedd
> A gwelyw pob tro trwyddi berfedd;
> O'i ganiad, o'i rad, a'i rinwedd yn llawch,
> Llewychedig haul yn ei gyntedd.
>
> He that supports the moon in her *full form*, beholds every turn through her centre; by his permission, by his grace, and his protecting attribute, radiant is the sun in his orbit. *Llygad Gwr.*

Llawober, *s. m.* (llaw—gober) Manufacture.

Llawr, *s. m.—pl.* lloriau (lly—awr) A floor, a ground plot, or area; the ground, the earth. *Nef a llawr*, heaven and earth; *ar lawr*, upon the ground, down; *i lawr*, downwards; *dyro hwna i lawr*, put that down; *hyd lawr*, along the ground; *llawr ty*, a house floor; *llawr dyrnu*, a threshing floor; *gwr llawr*, an ignoble or base man.

Llawrfaes, *s. m.* (maes) A bare plat of ground.

Llawrfardd, *s. m.* (llawr—bardd) A poetaster.

Llawrgerdd, *s. f.* (llawr—cerdd) A base song.

> Nis dwg lleidr fy llawrgerdd odid.
>
> A thief will not steal my *rude song* hardly. *Ll. P. Moch.*

Llawrig, *s. m.* (llawr) The greater periwinkle.

Llawrodd, *s. f.—pl. t.* ion (llaw—rhodd) What is presented by the hand, a hand gift.

Llawroddiad, *s. m.—pl.* llawroddiaid (llawrodd) A liberal-handed person.

> Pennoeth, oedd pennaf, gwedy pyner cad,
> Can llary llawroddiad llad a llwyrder.
>
> Every night, most of all, after the toil of battle, had the mild *open-handed one* of enjoyment and plenty. *Cynddelw, i'r argl. Rhys.*

Llawroddiawg, *a.* (llawrodd) Liberal-handed.

Llawrudd, *s. m.* (llaw—rhudd) A red, or bloody hand; a murderer. *a.* Having a red hand.

Llawruddiad, *s. m.* (llawrudd) Hand-reddening

Llawruddiaeth, *s. m.* (llawrudd) A shedding of blood.

Llawruddiaw, *v. a.* (llawrudd) To redden a hand.

Llawruddiawg, *a.* (llawrudd) Having a red hand; bloody-handed; having shed blood.

Llawrwedd, *s. m.* (llawr—gwedd) Groundſcene.

> Triugain mlynedd
> Yd berthais lawrwedd.
>
> Three score years I have supported an *earthly scene*. *Taliesin.*

Llawrwr, *s. m.—pl.* llawrwyr (llawr—gwr) A base, low or ignoble man.

> Llawrwyr am eryr yn ymsirianwl;
> Llywelyn Lleyn lyw ardderchawl.
>
> *Low men* round the eagle are seen craving; round Llywelyn the honourable leader of Lleyn. *Ein. ab Gwgawn, i Lywelyn II.*

Llawrwydd, *s. m.* (llawr—gwydd) The laurel wood; also called *pren y gerwin* and *diodwydd*.

Llawrwyddawg, *a.* (llawrwydd) Having laurels.

Llawrwydden, *s. f.* (llawrwydd) A laurel tree.

Llawryd, *s. m.* (llawr) A tendency downwards.

Llawrydedd, *s. m.* (llawryd) Dejectedness.

> Dygawn llawrydedd cywestwch a bedd.
>
> Enough of *sadness* the visitation of the grave. *Taliesin.*

> Llawrydedd frydau,
> Er Madawg yn mau!
>
> *Pensiveness* of thoughts after Madog belongs to me! *Gwalchmai.*

Llawrydd, *s. m.—pl. t.* ion (llaw—rhydd) A hand at liberty, or unchecked; one with an ungoverned hand, that has an unrestrained hand

> Mwy yd gar llawrydd no llawgaeth.
>
> More does he love the *open-handed* than the close-handed. *Cynddelw.*

Llawryddawg, *a.* (llawrydd) Having liberal hand.

Llaws, *a.* (lly—aws) Alert, quick, brisk, ready.

> Llaw llaws ar waith.
>
> The *alert* hand at work. *Adage.*

Llawwaith, *s. m.* (llaw—gwaith) A manufacture.

Llawwst, *s. m.* (llaw—gwst) A gout in the hand.

Llawwstawl, *a.* (llawwst) Chiragrical.

Llawyniawg, *a.* (llaw—yniawg) Of energetic hand.

LLE, *s. m. r.—pl. t.* oedd. A place, space, spot, or situation; where; stead, room: It is also a prefix in composition: *Dyro bob peth yn ei le*, put every thing in its place; *af yno yn dy le di*,

I will go there in thy stead; *cymer hyn yn ei le*, take this much in lieu of it; *yn y lle*, presently.

Lle, *adv.* (lle, *s.*) Where, at the place in which.

> Lle bhenn balchder y canlyn cywilydd
>
> *Where pride precedes, shame follows.* *Adage.*
>
> Gwell cybydd lle bo na hael lle ni bo.
>
> Better a miser where he is than the liberal where he is not. *Adage.*
>
> Lle caffo Cymmro cais.
>
> The Welshman will take where he can. *Adage.*

Lleäad, *s. m.* (lleäu) A placing, a location.

Llead, *s. m.* (lle) A placing, a fixing a place.

Lleäd, *s. m.* (lla) A reading, or lecturing.

Lleädur, *s. m.—pl. t.* on (lleäd) A lecturer.

Lleädurïaeth, *s. m.* (lleädur) Literature; reading

Lleadwy, *a.* (llead) That may be placed.

Lleain, *v. a.* (lla) To read, or to lecture.

Lleäu, *v. a.* (lle) To make a place, to fix a place: to place, to set, or lay.

> Llea fi gan llu bedyddiawl,
> Na'm llea yn lle engiriawl.
>
> *Place me with the christian host, place me not in the dreadful spot.* *Eadr Duw.*

Lleäw, *v. a.* (lla) To read, or to lecture.

Lleäwd, *s. m.* (lla) A reading, a lecturing.

Lleäwdr, *s. m.—pl.* lleödron (lleäwd) A lecturer.

Lleawg, *a.* (lla) Splendid, bright, shining.

> Cleddyf llachar lleawg [illegible];
> Ac yn llaw Lleminawg [illegible]
>
> A *bright* gleaming sword to him had been brought, and in the hand of Lleminawg it was left. *Taliesin.*

Lleawl, *a.* (lle) Local, belonging to place.

> [illegible] *lleawl* i'r enaid yn y corff, [illegible] ysbrydawl ynddo ei hunan.
>
> Though he may have given a *local* existence to the soul in the body, yet he has given her a spiritual course in herself. *S. Trefredyn.*

Lleäwr, *s. m.—pl.* lleörion (lla) A lecturer.

Lleb, *s. m.* (lly—eb) A pale yellow hue.

Lleban, *s. m.—pl. t.* od (lleb) A lank figure.

Llebanaidd, *a.* (lleban) Somewhat lank or ghastly

Llebaneiddrwydd, *s. m.* (llebanaidd) Lank ghastliness.

Llebanes, *s. f.* (lleban) A pale lank woman.

Llebliw, *s. m.* (lleb—lliw) A pale yellow colour.

> [illegible]
> [illegible] *llebliw.*
>
> Very profitable and bounteous, to day a benefit to be followed in the sun over the dales of *yellow hue*. [illegible]

Llecawd, *s. m.* (lleg) A flagging or sluggish state.

Llecin, *s. m.* (lleg) The second wort, in brewing.

Llecïad, *s. m.* (lleg) A lagging, a moving slowly.

Llecyn, *s. m. dim* (llac) A small quicksand.

Llech, *s. f.—pl. t.* i, au (lly—ech) What lies flat, horizontal, or depressed; a covert, or hiding place; a being flat, or sculking; adhesion of the liver; a tablet, a flat stone, slate stone, slate rock, slate: also lightning. *Llech llafar, llech lefair, careg lefair*, a sounding stone, an echo; *llech bobi, llech grasu*, a bake stone; *bara llech*, bread baked on a stone; *bydd yna yn llech*, be thou there secretly. It gives name to many places.

> [illegible]
> [illegible]
>
> There shall arise one out of six that have been [illegible] in concealment. [illegible]
>
> [illegible]
> [illegible]
> [illegible]
> [illegible]
>
> Like the tumult of the fire of the gleaming front of lightning is the conflict of the red blue shafts; completely am I armed by a leader of ruddy blades in the [illegible], the abundant torment of the foremost rank of battle. [illegible]

Llechad, *s. m.* (llech) A flattening, a slating.

Llechaidd, *a.* (llech) Somewhat flat, of a flat form.

Llechawg, *a.* (llech) Having a horizontal position, apt to be lying down, or sculking; abounding with slate; flagged.

Llecheira, *s. m.* (llech—eira) The chilblains.

Llechen, *s. f. dim.* (llech) A flat piece; a slate.

Llechenawg, *a.* (llechen) Having any thing lying flat; having an adhesion of the liver.

Llechfa, *s. f.—pl.* llechfeydd (llech—ma) A place to lie down in, a lurking place, or covert.

> Mal yd oeddynt [illegible], [illegible] Afarwy fab Lludd, a'i fyddin [illegible], yn cyfodi o'i *lechfa*, [illegible] byddin Caswallawn.
>
> As they were in that manner fighting, behold Afarwy the son of Lludd, and his body of troops with him, rising out of his *ambuscade*, and in their rear attacking the army of Caswallon. *Gr. ab Arthur.*

Llechfaen, *s. m.—pl.* llechfeini (llech—maen) A flat stone, a slate stone. *Bara llechfaen*, bread baked on a flat stone.

Llechfan, *s. f.—pl. t.* au (llech—man) A place to lie down in; a hiding place, a lurking hole.

Llechfod, *s. m.* (llech—bod) A lurking abidance.

> Amser ym caru, ei carwn, Dafydd,
> Y [illegible] n'm llochi;
> Ni [illegible] fy llechfod heb hi.
>
> As long as thou didst love me, I loved, Dafydd, the regulation, which cherished me: without it my *lurking stay* will not succeed. *Gwalchmai, i D. ab Gwilym.*

Llechgi, *s. m.* (llech—ci) A sculking dog.

Llechgïaidd, *a.* (llechgi) Like a sculking dog.

Llechïad, *s. m.* (llech) A lying flat, a sculking; that sculks.

> Nid llechiad ond cyffylog.
>
> There is no such a *sculker* as a woodcock. *Adage.*

Llechid, *s. f.* (llech) A slate rock.

Llechlawr, *s. m.* (llech—llawr) A flag-floor.

Llechres, *s. f.—pl. t.* i (llech—rhes) Pedigree.

> Un o saith gynneddf gwr dewisawl yw bod yn fardd ar ei lechres.
>
> One of the seven accomplishments of a select man is to be a bard upon his *pedigree roll*. *Bleddau.*

Llechu, *v. a.* (llech) To lie along; also to lurk.

> Nid llwfr ond a lecho.
>
> No one is a coward but he that *sculks*. *Adage.*

Llechwedd, *s. m.—pl. t.* i (llech—gwedd) A flat, horizontal, or inclined aspect; the steep or shelving of a hill; the side of the face from the cheek-bone upward. It gives name to a great many places in *Wales*.

Llechweddawl, *a.* (llechwedd) Of an inclined appearance: pensile.

Llechweddiad, *s. m.* (llechwedd) A sloping of a hill.

Llechweddu, *v. n.* (llechwedd) To slope, to slant.

Llechwen, *s. f.* (llech—gwen) An inclining gesture. *Gwna lechwen i daro*, make a posture for striking. *Sil.*

Llechwr, *s. m.—pl.* llechwyr (llech—gwr) Sculker.

Llechwraig, *s. f.—pl.* llechwreigedd (llech—gwraig) A woman that sculks, or hides herself.

Llechwrus, *a.* (llechwr) Of a sculking disposition.

> Lle y mae y duwies [illegible] dynion llechwrus [illegible] gan mwyaf.
>
> Where the godless Lucre dwelt, *sculking* low-looking men were here for the most part. *Elis Wynn, B. Cwsg.*

Lled, *s. m.—pl. t.* au (lly—ed) Breadth, width. *Ar led*, abroad: *lled llaw*, a hand-breadth.

Lled, *adv.* (lly—ed) In the breadth; in the mean, in part, half, almost, partly. It is used as a compositive prefix.

Lled, *a.* (*used for the comparative* lledach, *and* lletach. *Sil.*) Broader, wider.

Y mae'n lled i'm na llaw.
It is *broader* than my hand. *L. G. Cothi.*

Ef a ddaw, od wyf ddewin,
Eidion lled saf'r dynell win.

There will come, if I am a prophet, a bread *broader* than the tun of wine. *Llewddon, i derw.*

Lledach, *s. f.* (ach) A mean descent or origin.
Lledachawg, *a.* (lledach) Of a mean descent.
Lledachub, *s. m.* (achub) A half saving or securing
Lledachub, *v. a.* (achub) Partly to save, or keep.
Lledachubawl, *a.* (lledachub) Partly tending to save.
Lledachubiad, *s. m.* (lledachub) A partly saving.
Lledachwyn, *s. m.—pl. t.* ion (achwyn) Half complaint.
Lledachwyn, *v. a.* (achwyn) Partly to complain.
Lledachwyniad, *s. m.* (lledachwyn) A partly complaining.
Lledadnabod, *s. m.* (adnabod) Half cognizance.
Lledadnabod, *v. a.* (adnabod) Partly to know.
Lledadrawdd, *s. m.—pl.* lledadroddion (adrawdd) A half or imperfect recital.
Lledadrawdd, *v. a.* (adrawdd) Partly to relate.
Lledadwy, *a.* (lled) Dilatable, or expansible.
Lledaddaw, *v. a.* (addaw) Partly to promise.
Lledaddewid, *s. f.* (lledaddaw) A half promise.
Lledaddfed, *a.* (addfed) Partly ripe, half ripe.
Lledaddfediad, *s. m.* (lledaddfed) A half ripening.
Lledaddfedu, *v. n.* (lledaddfed) Partly to ripen.
Lledagawr, *v. a.* (agawr) Partly to open.
Lledagored, *a.* (lledagawr) Partly open, half open.
Lledagwedd, *s. f.* (agwedd) An imperfect manner
Lledagweddiad, *s. m.* (lledagwedd) Half fashioning
Lledagweddu, *v. a.* (lledagwedd) Partly to fashion.
Lledallu, *v. a.* (gallu) Partly to effect; to be half able.
Lledamgrain, *s. m.* (amgrain) A half crawling.
Lledamgreiniad, *s. m.* (lledamgrain) A partly crawling; a partly wallowing.
Lledamgreiniaw, *v. a.* (lledamgrain) Partly to crawl; to be partly wallowing.
Lledammhau, *v. n.* (ammhau) Partly to suspect.
Lledammheuaeth, *s. m.* (lledammhau) A slight suspicion.
Lledammhëus, *a.* (ammhau) Slightly suspicious.
Lledammod, *s. f.—pl. t.* au (ammod) That is partly a covenant.
Lledammodi, *v.* (lledammod) Partly to agree.
Lledan, *s. m.* (lled) Breadth; also a flounder.
Lledanaf, *s. m.—pl. t.* au (anaf) Partly a blemish.
Lledanafu, *v. a.* (lledanaf) Partly to maim.
Lledander, *s. m.* (lledan) Latitude, or breadth.
Lledanferth, *a.* (anferth) Somewhat illfavoured.
Lledanfodd, *s. m.—pl. t.* ion (anfodd) That is partly against the will.
Lledanfoddiad, *s. m.* (lledanfodd) A partly displeasing.
Lledanfoddiaw, *v.* (lledanfodd) Partly to displease
Lledanfon, *v. a.* (anfon) Partly to send, or emit.
Lledanhawdd, *a.* (anhawdd) Somewhat difficult.
Lledaniad, *s. m.* (lledan) An expanding, expansion
Lledanial, *a.* (anial) Somewhat woody or wild.
Lledanian, *s. f.* (anian) That is partly nature.
Lledannog, *s. m.* (annog) A half incitement.
Lledannogi, *v. a.* (lledannog) Partly to incite.
Lledannogiad, *s. m.* (lledannog) A partly inciting
Lledanmrwd, *a.* (anmrwd) Being half raw.

Yr oedd yr anghenfil hwnw â berweidiau o gig moch coed ganddaw, wedi bwyta peth onaddynt yn lledanmrwd.

That monster had barrow-fulls of the flesh of wild boars with him, after having eaten some of them *half raw. Gr. ab Arthur.*

Lledanu, *v. a.* (lledan) To expand, to make broad
Lledangen, *s. f.—pl. t.* ion (angen) A little necessity, a slight state of want.
Lledaraf, *a.* (araf) Somewhat slow, slowish.
Lledarafaidd, *a.* (lledaraf) Somewhat slowish.
Lledarafu, *v. n.* (lledaraf) To be a little slow.
Lledarafwch, *s. m.* (lledaraf) A little slowness.
Lledaros, *v. n.* (aros) Partly to stay; to linger.
Lledarchwaeth, *s. m.* (archwaeth) Imperfect taste
Lledarchwaethiad, *s. m.* (lledarchwaeth) A partly or slightly tasting.
Lledarchwaethu, *v.* (lledarchwaeth) Partly to taste
Lledarddelw, *s. m.* (arddelw) A slight claim.
Lledarddelwad, *s. m.* (lledarddelw) Partly claiming
Lledarddelwi, *v. a.* (lledarddelw) Partly to claim.
Lledarofyn, *s. m.* (arofyn) A half intention.
Lledarofyn, *v. a.* (arofyn) Partly to intend.
Lledarw, *a.* (garw) Somewhat rough or harsh.
Lledarwain, *s. m.* (arwain) A partly leading.
Lledarwain, *v. a.* (arwain) Partly to lead.
Lledathraw, *s. m.—pl. t.* on (athraw) Half master.
Lledathrawiaeth, *s. f.* (athraw) Half instruction.
Lledathrawu, *v. a.* (athraw) To half instruct.
Lledau, *s. pl. aggr.* (lled) Flat-fish; flounders.
Lledawg, *a.* (lled) Having breadth or latitude.
Lledawl, *a.* (lled) Relating to breadth or latitude.
Lledbai, *a.* (lled—pai) Inclining, askew, awry; ready to fall, unstable, unsteady.
Lledban, *s. m.* (pan) Half beaten, half milled.
Lledbaniad, *s. m.* (lledban) Half beating of cloth.
Lledbanu, *v. a.* (lledban) To half beat cloth.
Lledbeiad, *s. m.* (lledbai) An inclining awry.
Lledbeiaw, *v. a.* (lledbai) To give an inclination, to bend downward; to become inclined, askew, or awry.
Lledbeiawl, *a.* (lledbai) Tending to incline.
Lledbeiedd, *s. m.* (lledbai) Deflexure, declension.
Lledbeirwydd, *s. m.* (lledbai) A deflexure; a steepness, or shelving downwards; a slope.
Lledben, *s. m.* (pen) One side of the head; a flathead, a numskull.

Eiddig gyw sarug go sur;
Lledben——

The jealous one, a harsh and surly chap, a numskull.
D. ab Gwilym.

Lledbobi, *v. a.* (pobi) To half bake, partly to bake
Lledborthi, *v. a.* (porthi) Partly to support.
Lledborthiad, *s. m.* (porthiad) Partly supporting.
Lledbrofi, *v. a.* (profi) Partly to taste.
Lledbwyll, *s. m.—pl. t.* on (pwyll) Half reason.

Gochel lediaith, a lledtyb, a lledbwyll, a lledryw, herwydd meddwl, ac ystyr, a chrebwyll.

Avoid impure language, and irrevalent fancy, and *slight reasoning*, and incongruity, with respect to thought, and sense, and invention. *Barddas.*

Lledbwylliaw, *v. a.* (lledbwyll) To half reason.
Lledbwys, *s. m.* (pwys) That is rather weighty.
Lledbwysaw, *v. a.* (lledbwys) Partly to press.
Lledbwysiad, *s. m.* (lledbwys) A partly pressing.
Lledchwaeth, *s. m.* (chwaeth) An imperfect taste.
Lledchwal, *a.* (chwal) Partly spreading, or parting
Lledchwaliad, *s. m.* (lledchwal) A partly spreading
Lledchwalu, *v. a.* (lledchwal) To half disperse.
Lledchwannawg, *a.* (lledchwant) Rather greedy.
Lledchwant, *s. m.—pl. t.* au (chwant) A slight craving.
Lledchwanta, *v. a.* (lledchwant) To lust slightly.
Lledchwara, *v. a.* (chwara) To play partly; to play between jest and earnest.
Lledchwardd, *s. m.* (chwardd) A half laugh, or grin.
Lledchwareu, *v. a.* (lledchwara) To play partly.
Lledchwelan, *s.* (lledchwal) That is partly divided

Tros fy ngrudd, llwybrau'n llif,
Try deigr am wr tra digrif!

Over my cheek, *that is furrowed* with stream, the tear doth roll after a most pleasant man' *D. ab Gwilym, m. G. Gryg.*

Lledchwennych, *s. m.* (lledchwant) A half wish.
Lledchwennych, *v. a.* (lledchwant) Partly to wish
Lledchwerthin, *s. m.* (chwerthin) A half laugh.
Lledchwerthin, *v. a.* (chwerthin) To laugh partly
Lledchwerthiniad, *s. m.* (lledchwerthin) A laughing partly, a half laughing; a cold grinning.
Lledchwerw, *a.* (chwerw) Somewhat bitter.
Lledchwibl, *a* (chwibl) Somewhat sharp, sourish.
Lledchwibiad, *s. m.* (lledchwibl) A partly souring
Lledchwibiaw, *v. a.* (lledchwibl) To make sourish, or tartish; to become somewhat sour.
Lledchwidr, *a.* (chwidr) Somewhat giddy, or wild
Lledchwidraw, *v. a.* (lledchwidr) To make a little giddy; to become somewhat giddy.
Lledchwiliaw, *v. a.* (chwiliaw) To partly seek.
Lledchwimiad, *s. m.* (chwimiad) Slightly moving.
Lledchwimiaw, *v. a.* (chwimiaw) To move slightly.
Lledchwith, *a.* (chwith) Somewhat awkward.
Lledchwithrwydd, *s. m.* (lledchwith) Slight awkwardness.
Lledchwyl, *s. f.—pl. t.* ion (chwyl) A half turn.
Lled-ddal, *s. m.* (dàl) A half hold, a slight hold.
Lled-ddal, *v. a.* (dàl) To hold slightly.
Lled-ddaliad, *s. m.* (lled-ddal) A slightly holding.
Lled-ddall, *a.* (dall) Half-blind, nearly blind.
Lled-ddalliad, *s. m.* (lled-ddall) A half-blinding.
Lled-ddallu, *v. a.* (lled-ddall) To half blind.
Lled-ddannod, *s. m.* (dannod) A half reproach.
Lled-ddannod, *v.* (dannod) To reproach slightly.
Lled-ddannodiad, *s. m.* (lled-ddannod) A partly reproaching.
Lled-ddeiliaw, *v. n.* (deiliaw) Partly to foliate.
Lled-ddenu, *v. a.* (denu) Partly to entice or allure
Lled-ddirnad, *s. m.* (dirnad) A half surmise.
Lled-ddirnad, *v. a.* (dirnad) To half surmise.
Lled-ddof, *a.* (dof) Somewhat tame, half tame.
Lled-ddofi, *v. a.* (lled-ddof) Partly to tame.
Lled-ddofiad, *s. m.* (lled-ddof) A half taming.
Lled-ddwys, *a.* (dwys) Somewhat dense, or close.
Lled-ddwysaw, *v. a.* (lled-ddwys) To make rather dense.
Lled-ddwysiad, *s. m.* (lled-ddwys) A making rather dense, or heavy; to become rather dense.
Lled-ddymunaw, *v. a.* (dymunaw) Partly to wish.
Lled-ddymunawl, *a.* (dymunawl) Partly desirable.
Lled-ddymuniad, *s. m.* (dymuniad) Half wishing.
Lled-ddynwared, *s. m.* (dynwared) Half mimick.
Lled-ddynwared, *v. a.* (dynwared) Partly to mock
Lled-ddysg, *s. m.* (dysg) Half instruction.
Lled-ddysgiad, *s. m.* (lled-ddysg) A half learning.
Lled-ddysgu, *v. a.* (lled-ddysg) To half instruct; to learn superficially.
Lledechwyrth, *a.* (echwyrth) Half-stupified.
Llededrych, *s. m.* (edrych) A slight looking.
Llededrych, *v. a.* (edrych) To look slightly.
Llededrychiad, *s. m.* (llededrych) A half looking.
Lledeithaf, *a.* (eithaf) Nearly the utmost.
Lleden, *s. f. dim.* (lledan) A flat fish, a flounder. *Lleden goch, lleden frech*, a plaice; *lleden ddu*, a flounder; *lleden gennawg*, a dab; *lleden tafawd yr hydd*, or *tafawd yr ych*, a sole; *lleden chwith*, a turbot.

Mal genau lleden chwith.
Like the mouth of a *turbot*. *Adage.*

Llledenaidd, *a.* (lleden) Flat as a flounder.
Lledenig, *s. f. dim.* (lleden) A little flounder.
Lledenw, *s. m.—pl. t.* au (enw) The antonomasia, in rhetoric.
Lledenwad, *s. m.* (lledenw) A partly naming.
Llederw, *s. m.* (lled—erw) Overgrowth of the liver, a disease in sheep.

Y neb a wertho ddefaid bid y dannod rhag tri haint clafr, a llederw, a dwfr rhudd.

Whoever sells sheep let him warrant them against the three diseases: the scab, and *spreading of the liver*, and the rot. *Welsh Laws.*

Lledewig, *a.* (ew—ig) Partly gliding or oozing.
Lledewigwst, *s. f.* (lledewig—gwst) The hemorrhoids, or piles.
Lledfag, *s. m.* (mâg) That is half nurtured.
Lledfagu, *v. a.* (lledfag) Partly to rear.
Lledfan, *s. m.* (man) That is sprawling. *a.* Sprawling, flat on the ground.
Lledfanyw, *a.* (banyw) Half feminine.
Lledfarn, *s. f.* (barn) A slight judgement.
Lledfarnu, *v. a.* (lledfarn) To judge slightly.
Lledfarw, *a.* (marw) Half dead, partly dead.
Lledfarw, *v. n.* (marw) To become half dead.
Lledfasw, *a.* (masw) Somewhat wanton.
Lledfeddal, *a.* (meddal) Somewhat soft, softish.
Lledfeddalu, *v. a.* (lledfeddal) Partly to soften.
Lledfeddawd, *a.* (meddawd) Fatuous, or stupid.
Lledfeddededd, *s. m.* (lledfeddawd) Stupidity.
Lledfeddodrwydd, *s. m.* (lledfeddawd) Fatuity.
Lledfeddw, *a.* (meddw) Half-drunk, tipsy, boosy.
Lledfeddwi, *v. a.* (lledfeddw) Partly to intoxicate
Lledfegin, *a.* (lledfag) Partly reared, or nurtured; half tame, half domesticated.
Lledfeginaw, *v. a.* (lledfegin) Partly to rear; to half tame, to domesticate partly.
Lledfeginiaw, *a.* (lledfegin) Half domesticated.
Lledfeginiad, *s. m.* (lledfegin) A partly rearing, or feeding in a domestic way.
Lledfegyn, *s. m.—pl. t.* od (lledfag) A beast that is partly reared in a domestic way.

Ni ddyly neb dalu galanas na gweithred lledfegyn; sef yw lledfegyn, hu, neu beth a ddofer yn [illegible]; sef ynnghylch elain, neu iwrch, neu wyddlwdn cyffelyb i'r rhai hyny.

No one ought to pay for the mischief, nor the act of a *half tame animal*: this *half tame animal* is a hind, or what shall be tamed in a house; namely, such as a fawn, or a fox, or a wild brute similar to those. *Welsh Laws.*

Lledfeiddiad, *s. m.* (beiddiad) A partly daring.
Lledfeiddiaw, *v. a.* (beiddiaw) Partly to venture.
Lledfelys, *a.* (melys) Somewhat sweet, sweetish.
Lledfenawl, *a.* (lledfan) Procumbent, sprawling.
Lledferw, *s. m.* (berw) A slight boiling, parboil.
Lledferwedig, *a.* (lledferw) Half-boiled.
Lledferwi, *v. a.* (lledferw) To parboil, to simmer.
Lledflawd, *s. m.—pl.* lledflodau (blawd) A semifloret, a semiflosculus.
Lledflodeuad, *s. m.* (blodeuad) A flowering imperfectly, a half-blossoming.
Lledflodeuaw, *v. n.* (blodeuaw) To flower imperfectly, to half-blossom.
Lledflodeuawg, *a.* (blodeuawg) Semiflosculous.
Lledflodeuawl, *a.* (blodeuawl) Semiflosculur.
Lledfoddi, *v. a.* (boddi) Partly to drown.
Lledfrith, *a.* (brith) Somewhat variegated.
Lledfrwysg, *a.* (brwysg) Somewhat top-heavy; half-drunk, maudlin.
Lledfrwysgaw, *v.* (lledfrwysg) To get top-heavy.
Lledfrwysgiad, *s. m.* (lledfrwysg) A making half-drunk; a becoming somewhat top-heavy.
Lledfryd, *s. m.—pl. t.* au (bryd) Listlessness.

Cyglyw don drom ei thwrf,
Fan, y rhwng graian a gro:
Crai fy mryd rhag lledfryd heno.

Hear the wave of heavy fall and loud, between the gravel and the beach: oppressed is my mind from *listlessness* to-night. *Llywarch Hen.*

Lledfrydawg, *a.* (lledfryd) Having listlessness.
Lledfrydedd, *s. m.* (lledfryd) Listlessness.

Gnawd wedi llyn lledfrydedd.

After liquor *depression of spirits* is common. *Llywarch Hen.*

Lledfrydiad, *s. m.* (lledfryd) A rendering listless; a becoming listless.
Lledfrydig, *a.* (lledfryd) Disposed to be listless.
Lledfrydu, *v. a.* (lledfryd) To make listless; to grow listless; to be half-minded; to be void of passion.
Lledfud, *a.* (mud) Somewhat dumb, half dumb.
Lledfychan, *a.* (bychan) Rather little, smallish.
Lledfychanu, *v. a.* (lledfychan) Partly to slight.
Lledfyddar, *a.* (byddar) Rather deaf, half deaf.
Lledfyddaru, *v. a.* (lledfyddar) Partly to deafen.
Lledfyfyr, *a.* (myfyr) Half contemplative.
Lledfyfyriaw, *v.* (lledfyfyr) Partly to muse.
Lledfyr, *a.* (byr) Somewhat short, or brief.
Lledfyru, *v. a.* (lledfyr) Partly to curtail.
Lledfyw, *a.* (byw) Half-alive, half-animated.
Lledffel, *a.* (ffel) Somewhat cunning, or sly.
Lledffer, *a.* (ffer) Half-strong; feeble, weak.

Ni deddyat tros for etwaeth—
Gwyddyl, diefl duon,
Ysgodogion dynion lledffer.

They will not come over sea again, the Gwyddelians, sable devils, and the Scots, *enervated men.* *Meilyr.*

Lledffol, *a.* (ffol) Somewhat silly, half foolish.
Lledffrom, *a.* (ffrom) Somewhat pettish or peevish

Pham y cablant hwy wir Ddew,
Yr anwir annuw lledffrom!

Why will they provoke the true God, the *fretful* liars that are without God! *Edm. Prys.*

Lledffromi, *v. a.* (lledffrom) To act fretfully.
Lledffydd, *s. f.* (ffydd) Slight faith, slight reliance
Lledffyddiaw, *v.* (lledffydd) To have slight faith.
Lledgaead, *a.* (caead) Half shut, half closed.
Lledgais, *s. m.* (cais) A slight attempt, or essay.
Lledgaled, *a.* (caled) Somewhat hard, hardish.
Lledgall, *a.* (call) Somewhat discreet; half witted
Lledgalledd, *s. m.* (lledgall) Half discretion.
Lledgam, *a.* (cam) Somewhat crooked or awry.
Lledgamu, *v. a.* (lledgam) Partly to bend.
Lledgariad, *s. m.* (cariad) A cold affection.
Lledgarthu, *v. a.* (carthu) Partly to clear out.
Lledgaru, *v. a.* (caru) Partly to love.
Lledgas, *a.* (cas) Somewhat hateful or odious.
Lledgasau, *v. a.* (lledgas) Partly to dislike.
Lledgau, *v. a.* (cau) To half shut, or close.
Lledgawd, *s. m.* (lled—cawd) A drinking vessel with pegs to determine each draught; stinted draught.
Lledgawdd, *s. m.* (cawdd) A slight indignity.

Nad ef daw ar eu llaw lledgawdd.

May there not come upon their hand any *indignity.* *Cynddelw.*

Lledgeisiaw, *v. a.* (lledgais) Partly to attempt.
Lledgelfydd, *a.* (celfydd) Somewhat ingenious.
Lledgeliad, *s. m.* (celiad) A partly concealing.
Lledgelu, *v. a.* (celu) Partly to conceal or hide.
Lledgellwair, *s. m.* (cellwair) A half joke and earnest, a half banter.
Lledgellweiriad, *s. m.* (lledgellwair) A joking partly; a partly bantering.
Lledgenfigen, *s. f.* (cenfigen) A little envy.
Lledgerdded, *s. m.* (cerdded) An imperfect walk.
Lledgerdded, *v. a.* (cerdded) To walk imperfectly.
Lledgerddediad, *s.* (lledgerdded) A partly walking
Lledgerydd, *s. m.* (cerydd) Slight chastisement.
Lledgeryddiad, *s.* (lledgerydd) A half chastising.
Lledgeryddu, *v. a.* (lledgerydd) To chastise slightly.

Lledgil, *s. m.* (cil) A half retreat; a slight recess.
Lledgiliad, *s. m.* (lledgil) A partly receding.
Lledgiliaw, *v. a.* (ciliaw) Partly to recede.
Lledgipiaw, *v. a.* (cipiaw) Partly to snatch.
Lledglaer, *a.* (claer) Semipellucid, half transparent
Lledglaerder, *s. m.* (lledglaer) Semidiaphaneity.
Lledglaf, *a.* (claf) Slightly diseased, half sick.
Lledglau, *a.* (clau) Somewhat persevering.
Lledglauar, *a.* (clauar) Somewhat mild or warm.
Lledglauaredd, *s. m.* (lledglauar) A medium temperature.
Lledglauaru, *v. a.* (lledglauar) To render temperately mild, or warm.
Lledgloff, *a.* (cloff) Somewhat lame, half lame.
Lledgloffi, *v. a.* (lledgloff) Partly to lame.
Lledgloffiad, *s. m.* (lledgloff) A slightly laming.
Lledglol, *s. f.* (clol) The one side of a skull.
Lledglyw, *s. m.* (clyw) An indistinct hearing.
Lledglywed, *v. n.* (lledglyw) Partly to hear.
Lledgoch, *a.* (coch) Somewhat red, half red.
Lledgochi, *v. a.* (lledgoch) Partly to redden.
Lledgochiad, *s. m.* (lledgoch) A slightly reddening
Lledgodi, *v. a.* (codi) Partly to raise, or to rise.
Lledgodiad, *s. m.* (codiad) A partly raising; a partly rising or ascending.
Lledgoddawl, *a.* (lledgawdd) Slightly insulting.
Lledgoddi, *v. a.* (lledgawdd) Partly to insult.
Lledgoddiad, *s. m.* (lledgawdd) A slightly insulting
Lledgoel, *s. f.—pl. t.* ion (coel) A slightly believing
Lledgoeliaw, *v. a.* (lledgoel) To believe slightly.
Lledgof, *s. m.* (cof) Slight remembrance.
Lledgofiad, *s. m.* (lledgof) A slightly remembering.
Lledgofiaw, *v.* (lledgof) Partly to remember.
Lledgoffa, *s. m.* (coffa) A slight remembrance.
Lledgoffa, *v. a.* (coffa) To remember slightly.
Lledgoffaad, *s. m.* (lledgoffa) A slightly remembering.
Lledgoll, *s. f.* (coll) A half or incomplete loss.
Lledgolli, *v. n.* (lledgoll) Partly to lose.
Lledgrafiad, *s. m.* (crafiad) A slightly scratching.
Lledgrafu, *v. a.* (crafu) To scratch slightly.
Lledgraff, *a.* (craff) Slightly impressive, somewhat keen or sharp.
Lledgraffiad, *s. m.* (lledgraff) A slightly impressing; a slightly kenning, or perceiving.
Lledgraffu, *v. a.* (lledgraff) To make a slight impression; partly to ken.
Lledgras, *a.* (crâs) Somewhat crisp, or dried.
Lledgrasu, *v. a.* (lledgras) Partly to crisp.
Lledgrefydd, *s. f.* (crefydd) Cold devotion.
Lledgrin, *a.* (crin) Somewhat brittle, or dry.
Lledgrinaw, *v. n.* (lledgrin) Partly to dry, or wither.
Lledgriniad, *s. m.* (lledgrin) A half withering.
Lledgroes, *a.* (croes) Somewhat transverse.
Lledgroesi, *v. a.* (lledgroes) Partly to cross.
Lledgroesiad, *s. m.* (lledgroes) A partly thwarting
Lledgronawl, *a.* (cronawl) Partly aggregating.
Lledgroni, *v. a.* (croni) Partly to collect.
Lledgroniad, *s. m.* (croniad) A partly collecting.
Lledgryno, *a.* (cryno) Somewhat compact.

Ar y dinod mewn hanesgerdd, bydded yr iaith yn fer a lledgryno.

As to what is of little note in historical poetry, let the language be brief and *rather compact.* *Barddas.*

Lledgrynôad, *s. m.* (lledgryno) A making rather compact or tidy.
Lledgrynôi, *v. a.* (lledgryno) To make somewhat compact; to become partly tidy.
Lledgudd, *a.* (cudd) Rather hidden, or obscure.
Lledguddiad, *s. m.* (lledgudd) A half obscuring.
Lledguddiaw, *v. a.* (lledgudd) Partly to hide.

Lledgul, *a.* (cul) Somewhat narrow or strait.
Lledgulaw, *v. a.* (lledgul) To make rather narrow
Lledguliad, *s. m.* (lledgul) A rendering rather narrow, a becoming rather slender.
Lledgwin, *a.* (cwin) Somewhat debilitated.
Lledgwydd, *s. m.* (cwydd) A half tumble.
Lledgwyddaw, *v.* (lledgwydd) Partly to tumble.
Lledgwyddiad, *s. m.* (lledgwydd) A partly tumbling.
Lledgwynaw, *v. a.* (cwynaw) To complain a little.
Lledgyfa, *a.* (cyfa) Being half whole, or perfect.
Lledgyfan, *a.* (cyfan) Half whole, or perfect.
Lledgyfaniad, *s. m.* (lledgyfan) A making nearly whole, or entire.
Lledgyfanu, *v. a.* (lledgyfan) To make nearly whole, to render almost entire.
Lledgyfiawn, *a.* (cyfiawn) Half righteous.
Lledgyfiawnâad, *s. m.* (lledgyfiawn) A half justifying, a becoming half righteous.
Lledgyfiawnâu, *v.* (lledgyfiawn) To half justify.
Lledgylch, *s. m.*—*pl. t.* au (cylch) A semicircle.
Lledgylchawl, *a.* (lledgylch) Half-circling.
Lledgylchiad, *s. m.* (lledgylch) A half-circling.
Lledgylchu, *v. a.* (lledgylch) To half encompass.
Lledgymmod, *s. m.* (cymmod) Half-reconcilement
Lledgymmodawl, *a.* (lledgymmod) Half-reconciling, or agreement.
Lledgymmodi, *v. a.* (lledgymmod) To half reconcile; to become partly reconciled.
Lledgynhes, *a.* (cynhes) Somewhat warm.
Lledgynnal, *v. a.* (cynnal) Partly to support.
Lledgynnaliad, *s. m.* (lledgynnal) A partly supporting; a slight supportation.
Lledgynnil, *a.* (cynnil) Rather exact, or saving.
Lledgynnilaw, *v. a.* (lledgynnil) To act rather with exactness; to become rather saving.
Lledgynt, *s. m.* (llad—cynt) A report.

Gwrandëydd, gwrandaw ledgynt.
Gwrandëydd, listen to a rumour. *Cyfoesi Merddin.*

Tenau awel, tew ledgynt.
Thin the gale, thick the rumour. *Llywarch Hen.*

Ewyllys id Meruydd, mawr o ledgynt yw
Nad oes fyw fygyo ennt!
Llas llary frwlyr, gwyr gorfynt;
A chyd lleddyd lladdesynt!

The clan of Meruydd gone, how sad the *tale*
That they are not alive as erst they were!
Mild brothers have been slain, aspiring men;
And though thus slain, they often too had slain.
Cynddelw, m. t. O. Gwynedd.

Lledgyrch, *s. m.* (cyrch) A little approach.
Lledgyrchawl, *a.* (lledgyrch) Partly approaching
Lledgyrchiad, *s. m.* (lledgyrch) A partly approaching.
Lledgyrchu, *v. a.* (lledgyrch) Partly to approach
Lledgyson, *a.* (cyson) Somewhat consonant.
Lledgysondeb, *s. m.* (cyson) Slight consonance.
Lledgysoni, *v. a.* (cyson) Partly to harmonize.
Lledgyswllt, *s. m.* (cyswllt) A half junction.
Lledgysylltiad, *s. m.* (cyswllt) A partly joining.
Lledgysylltu, *v. a.* (cyswllt) To conjoin partly.
Lledgywrain, *a.* (cywrain) Rather ingenious.
Lledhoew, *a.* (hoew) Somewhat brisk, or alert.
Lledhoewi, *v.* (lledhoew) To be a little brisk.
Lledholi, *v. a.* (holi) To examine slightly.
Lledholiad, *s. m.* (holiad) A slightly examining.
Lledhoni, *v. a.* (honi) Partly to assert, or affirm.
Lledhoniad, *s. m.* (honiad) A slightly asserting.
Lledhuddaw, *v. a.* (huddaw) Partly to cover over
Lledhuddiad, *s. m.* (huddiad) A partly covering.
Lledhunaw, *v. a.* (hunaw) To sleep partly.
Lledhurt, *a.* (hurt) Half mad, half frantic.
Lledhurtiad, *s. m.* (lledhurt) A half distracting.
Lledhurtiaw, *v. a.* (lledhurt) To make half mad, to become somewhat distracted.
Lledhynt, *s. f.*—*pl. t.* iau (hynt) Intent, purpose.
Llediad, *s. m.* (lled) A making broad, dilatation.
Llediaeth, *s. m.* (lled) Dilatation, dispansion.
Llediaith, *s. f.*—*pl.* lledieithoedd (iaith) A half-language; an unknown speech.
Lledieithiawg, *a.* (llediaith) Having a corrupt speech; being of unknown speech.
Lledir, *a.* (ir) Somewhat fresh, half raw.
Lledirdeb, *s. m.* (lledir) The state of being partly fresh, green, or raw.
Lledlaith, *a.* (llaith) Somewhat moist, dampish.
Lledlâs, *a.* (glâs) Somewhat blue, bluish.
Lledlasu, *v. n.* (lledlas) To become bluish.
Lledled, *a.* (lled, *repeated*) Widely spreading.

Lledled rydau.
Fords widely spreading. *Aneur.*

Llyw dyfalawg llidiawg, lledled fydd ei blas.
The chief of flowing wrath, widely spreading will be his mansion. *Llygad Gwr*

Lledlef, *s. m.* (llef) An imperfect utterance.
Lledlefawg, *a.* (lledlef) Of imperfect utterance.
Lledleithder, *s. m.* (lledlaith) Degree of dampness.
Lledleithiaw, *v. a.* (lledlaith) To make rather damp; to become somewhat damp.
Lledlenwad, *s. m.* (llenwad) A partly filling.
Lledlenwi, *v. a.* (llenwi) To fill in a degree.
Lledlesg, *a.* (llesg) Somewhat feeble.
Lledlesgiad, *s. m.* (lledlesg) A slightly enfeebling
Lledlesgu, *v. a.* (lledlesg) To enfeeble slightly; to become somewhat feeble, or debilitated.
Lledlipa, *a.* (llipa) Somewhat flabby or drooping
Lledlithraw, *v. a.* (llithraw) Partly to slip.
Lledlithriad, *s. m.* (llithriad) A partly slipping.
Lledlithrig, *a.* (llithrig) Somewhat slippery.
Lledloew, *a.* (gloew) Partly clear, semipellucid.
Lledloewder, *s. m.* (lledloew) Imperfect clearness
Lledloewi, *v. a.* (lledloew) To make somewhat clear; to become rather clear, or pellucid.
Lledlosg, *s. m.* (llosg) A half-burnt state.
Lledlosgi, *v. a.* (lledlosg) To burn slightly.
Lledlosgiad, *s. m.* (lledlosg) A slightly burning.
Lledludd, *s. m.* (lludd) A slight obstruction.
Lledluddiad, *s. m.* (lledludd) A slightly hindering
Lledluddiaw, *v. a.* (lledludd) To obstruct slightly
Lledlun, *s. m.*—*pl. t.* iau (llun) A semiform. *a.* Semiform, half formed.
Lledluniaw, *v. a.* (lledlun) To half form.
Lledlw, *s. m.*—*pl.* lledlyon (llw) A vain oath.

Ti Dduw, maddau—
Ein lledlyon
A'n llidfradau,
A'n lledfrydedd.

Thou God, forgive our vain oaths, and our angry weaknesses, and our apathy. *Gr. Gryg.*

Lledlwm, *a.* (llwm) Half bare, somewhat bare.
Lledlwyd, *a.* (llwyd) Somewhat grey, greyish.
Lledlwydaw, *v. n.* (lledlwyd) To grow greyish.
Lledlwydedd, *s. m.* (lledlwyd) A slight greyness.
Lledlwyddaw, *v. n.* (llwyddaw) Partly to prosper
Lledlwyr, *a.* (llwyr) Nearly entire, nearly all.
Lledlymder, *s. m.* (lledlwm) Half bareness.
Lledlymu, *v. a.* (lledlwm) To make half bare.
Lledlynawl, *a.* (glynawl) Half adhering.
Lledlyniad, *s. m.* (glyniad) A slightly adhering.
Lledlynu, *v. a.* (glynu) To adhere slightly.
Lledlyth, *a.* (llyth) Somewhat enervated.
Lledlythiad, *s. m.* (lledlyth) A slightly growing feeble, a slightly enervating.
Lledlythu, *v.* (lledlyth) To be rather feeble.

Llednacâad, *s. m.* (nacâad) A partly refusing.

Lednacâawl, *a.* (nacâawl) Partly refusing.

Lednacau, *v. a.* (nacâu) Partly to refuse.

Lednais, *a.* (nais) Elegant, neat, nice.

> Efe a dderchafai ei ledneision ar iechyd.
>
> He raised the *delicate ones* into health. *D. Ddu Ps.* 149.

Lledneisiaw, *v. a.* (llednais) To render elegant.

Lledneisrwydd, *s. m.* (llednais) Elegance.

Llednerthiad, *s. m.* (nerthiad) A slightly strengthening or supporting.

Llednerthu, *v. a.* (nerthu) Partly to strengthen.

Llednoeth, *a.* (noeth) Half-naked, somewhat bare

> Gwae berchen cyfoeth,
> A welo lednoeth
> Oni chuddia!
>
> Woe to the possessor of wealth, who sees the *half-naked*, if he does not cover him! *Ieu. Mynyw.*

Llednoethedd, *s. m.* (llednoeth) Half-nakedness.

Llednoethi, *v. a.* (llednoeth) To make half-naked.

Llednofiad, *s. m.* (nofiad) A partly swimming.

Llednofiaw, *v. a.* (nofiaw) Partly to swim.

Llednyddawl, *a.* (nyddawl) Slightly twisting.

Llednyddiad, *s. m.* (nyddiad) A slightly twisting.

Llednyddu, *v. a.* (nyddu) To twist slightly.

Lledochr, *s. m.—pl. t.* au (ochr) A half lateral position; a slanting; slight bias.

Lledochri, *v. a.* (lledochr) To edge a little sideways; to be somewhat biassed.

Lledochriad, *s. m.* (lledochr) An edging a little sideways; a being slightly biassed.

Lledoddef, *v. n.* (goddef) Partly to endure.

Lledoddefawl, *a.* (lledoddef) Somewhat patient.

Lledoddefiad, *s. m.* (lledoddef) A slightly enduring

Lledoer, *a.* (oer) Half cold, rather lukewarm.

Lledoeredd, *s. m.* (lledoer) A half coldness.

Lledoeri, *v. a.* (lledoer) To render somewhat cold; to become nearly cold.

Lledofal, *s. m.—pl. t.* on (gofal) Slight precaution.

Lledofaledd, *s. m.* (lledofal) Slight precaution.

Lledofaliad, *s. m.* (lledofal) A slightly caring.

Lledofalu, *v. n.* (lledofal) To have a little care.

Lledofer, *a.* (ofer) Rather futile, or useless.

Lledofera, *v. a.* (lledofer) Partly to trifle.

Lledoferedd, *s. m.* (lledofer) Half triflingness.

Lledofid, *s. m.—pl. t.* ion (gofid) Slight anguish.

Lledofidiaw, *v. a.* (lledofid) To cause a little anguish, or affliction; to be slightly afflicted.

Lledofn, *s. m.* (ofn) A little fear or dread.

Lledofnawg, *a.* (lledofn) Rather fearful.

Lledofni, *v. a.* (lledofn) Partly to fear or dread.

Lledofnus, *a.* (lledofn) Somewhat timid.

Lledol, *s. m.* (ol) A rearward, a hind part, a rear.

Lledoleu, *a.* (goleu) Half-lighted, half-illumed.

Lledoleuad, *s. m.* (lledoleu) A half illuming.

Lledoleuaw, *v. a.* (lledoleu) To light partly.

Lledoli, *v. a.* (lledol) To place in the rearward.

Lledolrhain, *s. m.* (olrhain) A slight tracing.

Lledolrhain, *v. a.* (olrhain) Partly to trace.

Lledolrheiniad, *s. m.* (lledolrhain) A slightly tracing

Lledollwng, *v. a.* (gollwng) Partly to drop.

Lledollyngiad, *s. m.* (lledollwng) A partly dropping

Lledommedd, *s. m.* (gommedd) Slight refusal.

Lledommedd, *v. a.* (gommedd) To refuse slightly.

Lledommeddiad, *s. m.* (lledommedd) A slightly refusing, or rejecting an offer.

Lledorchudd, *s. m.—pl. t.* ion (gorchudd) A slight cover.

Lledorchuddiad, *s. m.* (lledorchudd) A slightly covering.

Lledorchuddiaw, *v. a.* (lledorchudd) Partly to cover

Lledorfod, *v. a.* (gorfod) Partly to overcome.

Lledormes, *s. f.—pl. t.* ion (gormes) Slight trespass

Lledormesawl, *a.* (lledormes) Slightly trespassing.

Lledormesiad, *s. m.* (lledormes) A slightly trespassing, or molesting.

Lledormesu, *v. a.* (lledormes) To trespass slightly.

Lledorphen, *v. a.* (gorphen) To half finish.

Lledorphwyll, *s. m.* (gorphwyll) Slight disorder of mind.

Lledorphwyllaw, *v. n.* (lledorphwyll) To become slightly disordered in mind, to be half mad.

Lledorphwylliad, *s. m.* (lledorphwyll) A becoming half mad, a becoming half distracted.

Lledorphwys, *s. m.* (gorphwys) A slight respite.

Lledorphwysaw, *v.* (lledorphwys) To rest partly.

Lledorphwysiad, *s. m.* (lledorphwys) A slightly resting.

Lledorthrech, *s. m.* (gorthrech) Slight oppression.

Lledorthrechiad, *s. m.* (lledorthrech) A slightly oppressing, or tyrannizing.

Lledorthrechu, *v.* (lledorthrech) Partly to oppress

Lledorthrwm, *a.* (gorthrwm) Slightly oppressive.

Lledorthrymder, *s. m.* (lledorthrwm) Slight oppression or severity.

Lledorthrymiad, *s. m.* (lledorthrwm) A slightly oppressing, a partly tyrannizing.

Lledorthrymu, *v. a.* (lledorthrwm) Partly to oppress.

Lledorwedd, *s. m.* (gorwedd) Discumbency.

Lledorwedd, *v. a.* (gorwedd) Partly to lie down.

Lledorweddiad, *s. m.* (lledorwedd) A half lying down, a partly reclining; discumbency.

Lledr, *s. m.* (lled) Leather. *Côd ledr*, leather bag.

Lledrad, *s. m.* (lled—rhad) Stealth, or theft.

> Celedig fy hun yn hir ofwy lle,
> Yn lledrad fore, gan afarwy.
>
> Secretly myself long visiting a spot, by *stealth* in the morning, with grief. *Cynddelw, i Efa f. Madawg.*

Lledradaidd, *a.* (lledrad) Apt to be thievish.

Lledradawl, *a.* (lledrad) Stealing, thieving.

Lledraidd, *a.* (lledr) Like leather; leathery.

Lledran, *s. f.—pl. t.* au (rhan) A half part.

> Heb anhawdd o angen mewn rhan, neu ledran, ni fydd i ddim gyselin a neillduawl anawdd.
>
> Without a character essential in part, or *half part*, nothing can have a primary and peculiar character. *Barddas.*

Lledranawg, *a.* (lledran) Partly participating.

Lledraniad, *s. m.* (lledran) A partly sharing.

Lledranu, *v. a.* (lledran) To divide or share partly

Lledrata, *v. a.* (lledrad) To steal, or to thieve.

Lledrawg, *s. f.* (lledr) A small enclosure, a close.

Lledred, *s. f.—pl. t.* ion (lled) Latitude, broadness

Lledriad, *s. m.* (lledr) A doing with leather.

Lledrin, *a.* (lledr) Of leather, leathern.

> Addwyn eddystr yn nghebystr lledrin,
> Arall addwyn cyweithas brenin.
>
> Splendid is the steed in a *leathern* rein; again more splendid the retinue of a king. *Taliesin.*

Lledrith, *s. m.—pl. t.* ion (rhith) A half or imperfect appearance; an illusion, a disguise; a phantom; a juggle, or deception.

> Lledrith blawd gwenith a gad.
>
> The *semblance* of wheaten flour was found. *D. ab Gwilym, i'r cwr.*

> Mae'n taeru, man y tariwyf,
> Mai lledrith y'Malldraeth wyf.
>
> He asserts, where I land, that I am a *phantom* upon Malldraeth. *Guto y Glyn.*

Lledrithiad, *s. m.* (lledrith) A partly appearing, an appearing illusively, or in disguise.

Lledrithiant, *s. m.* (lledrith) Imperfect appearance; illusion; disguise.

Lledrithiaw, *v. a.* (lledrith) To half-appear; to appear illusively; to appear in disguise.

Lledrithiawg, *a.* (lledrith) Of indistinct appearance, or that is half visible; having the power of illusion; disguised; magical.

> Tri phrif lledrithiawg Ynys Prydain: Coll mab Collfrewi, Menw mab Teirgwaedd, a Drych ail Cibddar.
>
> The three chief *persons having the power of illusion* of the Isle of Britain. Coll the son of Collfrewi, Menw the son of Teirgwaedd, and Drych the son of Cibddar. *Trioedd.*
>
> Y draenllwyn glas urddasawl,
> Llety mwyn lle tyfai mawl,
> Mab lledrithiawg arfawg wyd.
>
> The dignified green thorn bush, the lovely cell whence praise doth spring, a *phantastic* armed youth art thou. *D. ab Gwilym.*

Lledrithiawl, *a.* (lledrith) Illusory, or illusive.

Lledrithiwr, *s. m.—pl.* lledrithwyr (lledrith—gwr) One who appears in disguise.

Lledrudd, *a.* (rhudd) Half ruddy, of a reddish hue

> Gwelid——
> Y llafnawr lledrudd ech grudd a gràn.
>
> The *ruddy stained* blades over the cheek and brow were seen. *Ll. P. Moch.*

Lledruddaw, *v. a.* (lledrudd) To half-redden; to tinge with red.

Lledruddiad, *s. m.* (lledrudd) Giving a ruddy tinge

Lledrwr, *s. m.—pl.* lledrwyr (lledr—gwr) A manufacturer of leather; a leather-seller.

Lledrybudd, *s. m.* (rhybudd) A slight notice.

Lledrybuddiad, *s. m.* (lledrybudd) A giving slight notice, a slightly forewarning.

Lledrybuddiaw, *v.* (lledrybudd) To warn slightly.

Lledryfedd, *a.* (rhyfedd) Somewhat wonderful.

Lledryfeddu, *v. a.* (lledryfedd) To wonder a little.

Lledryn, *s. m.—pl. t.* au (lledr) A slip of leather.

Lledryw, *s. m.—pl. t.* iau (rhyw) An imperfect or degenerate kind; a mongrel race; a mean birth. *a.* Of a degenerate kind.

> Blodau'r swydd, heb lledryw Sais.
>
> The flower of the shire, untainted by a Saxon's *mongrel kind.* *T. Aled.*

Lledrywiad, *s.* (lledryw) A partly degenerating.

Lledrywiaeth, *s. m.* (lledryw) Degeneration.

Lledrywiaw, *v. a.* (lledryw) To degenerate.

Lledrywiawg, *a.* (lledryw) Of a degenerate kind.

Lledrywiawl, *a.* (lledryw) Tending to degenerate

Lledrywiogaeth, *s. m.* (lledrywiawg) Degeneracy.

Lledrywiogedd, *s. m.* (lledryw) Degenerateness.

Lledrywiogi, *v. a.* (lledrywiawg) To render of a degenerate sort; to become of mixed kind.

Lledrywiogrwydd, *s.* (lledryw) Degenerateness.

Lledsain, *s. f.—pl.* lledseiniau (sain) A semitone.

Lledsarug, *a.* (sarug) Somewhat surly, or harsh.

Lledsarugaw, *v.* (lledsarug) To be rather surly.

Lledsel, *s. m.* (sel) A half glance, a half look.

Lledseliad, *s. m.* (lledsel) A slightly glancing.

Lledselu, *v. a.* (lledsel) To glance slightly.

Lledsèniad, *s. m.* (sèniad) A slightly taunting.

Lledsènu, *v. a.* (sènu) To taunt slightly.

Lledserth, *a.* (serth) Somewhat declivous.

Lledserthiad, *s. m.* (lledserth) A slightly precipitating: a becoming rather steep.

Lledserthu, *v. a.* (lledserth) To half precipitate; to become rather precipitous.

Lledsoddi, *v. n.* (soddi) To sink in partly.

Lledsoddiad, *s. m.* (soddiad) A slightly sinking.

Lledsom, *s. m.* (som) Slight disappointment.

Lledsomi, *v. a.* (lledsom) To half-disappoint.

Lledsomiad, *s. m.* (lledsom) A half-disappointing.

Lledsomiant, *s. m.* (lledsom) Slight disappointment

Lledson, *s. m.* (son) Slight report, slight rumour.

Lledsoniad, *s. m.* (lledson) A slightly reporting.

Lledsoniaw, *v. a.* (lledson) To report slightly.

Lledsòri, *v. n.* (sòri) To be slightly affronted.

Lledsòriad, *s. m.* (sòriad) A slightly sulking.

Lledsòriant, *s. m.* (sòriant) Slight sulkiness.

Lledsuddaw, *v. n.* (suddaw) Partly to sink down.

Lledsuddiad, *s. m.* (suddiad) A slightly sinking.

Lledsur, *a.* (sur) Half-sour, partly sour, sourish.

Lledsuraw, *v. n.* (lledsur) To grow half-sour.

Lledsuriad, *s. m.* (lledsur) A partly souring.

Lledsych, *a.* (sych) Somewhat dry, half dry.

Lledsychiad, *s. m.* (lledsych) A partly drying.

Lledsychu, *v. a.* (lledsych) To dry partly.

Lledsylw, *s. m.* (sylw) Slight observation.

Lledsylwad, *s. m.* (lledsylw) A slightly observing.

Lledsylwi, *v. a.* (lledsylw) To observe slightly.

Lledsyniad, *s. m.* (syniad) A partly proposing.

Lledsyniaw, *v. a.* (syniaw) Partly to propose.

Lledsynied, *v. a.* (synied) Partly to propose.

Lledsyrthiad, *s. m.* (syrthiad) A partly falling.

Lledsyrthiaw, *v. n.* (syrthiaw) To fall partly.

Lledsyth, *a.* (syth) Somewhat stiff, or erect.

Lledsythiad, *s. m.* (lledsyth) A partly stiffening.

Lledsythu, *v. n.* (lledsyth) To grow rather stiff.

Lledu, *v. a.* (lled) To make broad, to widen, to make wider, to expand, to enlarge; to spread, to stretch out; to become wide, to be enlarged; to be spread, or stretched out.

Ledunaw, *v. n.* (unaw) Partly to agree or accord

Lledunawl, *a.* (unawl) Partly according, half according; tending to union.

Ledundeb, *s. m.* (undeb) A slight accordance.

Lledw, *s. m.* (lled) That is heaped or closed.

> Llwyd-gun hael lledw gynnilied.
>
> A generous hoary chief, the supporter of *economy.* *D. ab Gwilym.*
>
> Lle da gwyr o'i lledw a'i gwin.
>
> Where men are happy from her rare *dainties* and her wine. *D. Llwyd.*
>
> Rhys—llin Syr Gruffudd
> (Lledw anant) Llwyd o Wynedd.
>
> Rhys, of the line of Sir Gruffudd (the minstrels' *rarity*) Llwyd of Gwynedd. *D. ab Edmund.*

Lledw, *a.* (lled) Contracted, narrow, rare.

Lledwad, *s. f.* (lledw) A ladle, a vessel to serve any liquids.

Lledwag, *a.* (gwag) Partly empty, half empty.

Lledwahan, *s. m.* (gwahan) That partly divides; a comma, in grammar.

Lledwahaniad, *s. m.* (lledwahan) A partly separating or dividing.

Lledwahanu, *v. a.* (lledwahan) Partly to separate

Lledwar, *a.* (gwar) Somewhat tame, half tame.

Lledwarâad, *s. m.* (lledwar) A partly taming.

Lledwarâu, *v. a.* (lledwar) To half tame.

Lledwasgiad, *s. m.* (gwasgiad) A slightly pressing.

Lledwasgu, *v. a.* (gwasgu) To press slightly.

Lledwedd, *s. f.* (lled—gwedd) A broadside.

Lledwenawl, *a.* (gwenawl) Half smiling.

Lledweniaith, *s. m.* (gweniaith) Half flattery.

Lledweniaithiad, *s. m.* (lledweniaith) A partly flattering.

Lledwenieithu, *v. a.* (lledweniaith) To flatter slightly, to speak smoothly.

Lledwenu, *v. a.* (gwenu) To smile partly.

Lledwg, *s. m.* (gwg) A slight frown, slight anger.

> Na anghofia, o daw dig,
> Dylodion yn dy ledwg.
>
> If anger should arise, forget not the poor in thy *displeasure.* *W. Middleton.*

Lledwig, *a.* (lledw) Of a free, or easy nature; of a soft or mild quality.

Lledwigain, *a.* (lledwig) Of a mild easy temper, easily imposed upon.

Lledwigen, *s. f.* (lledwig) A creeping thing.

Lledwigyn, *s. m.—pl. t.* od (lledwig) A worm, or creeping thing.

> Dyged y dyfredd ledwigyn ag enaid byw ynddo; a bid ehediaid ar y ddaiar dan y nef:—dyged y ddaiar enaid byw herwydd ei genedlaeth, ysgrubl a lledwigynod, a bwystfiloedd, herwydd eu rhywogaeth.
>
> Let the water bring forth every *creeping thing* with a living soul in it: and let there be winged creatures over the earth under heaven: Let the earth bring forth every living soul according to its kind, beast and *creeping things*, and wild animals, according to their kind. *Ll. G. Hergest.*

Lledwirion, *a.* (gwirion) Being half an innocent; being half an idiot.
Lledwiriondeb, *s. m.* (lledwirion) Half idiotism.
Lledwlyb, *a.* (gwlyb) Somewhat wet, slightly wet.
Lledwr, *s. m.—pl.* lledwyr (lled—gwr) Spreader.
Lledwryw, *s. m.* (gwryw) Half masculine.
Lledwydd, *s. pl. aggr.* (gwýdd) Imperfect timber, or trees that are not good in their kind.
Lledwyl, *a.* (gŵyl) Somewhat bashful or shy.
Lledwyllt, *a.* (gwyllt) Half wild, rather wild.
Lledwyn, *a.* (gwyn) Somewhat white, whitish.
Lledwyneb, *s. m.—pl. t.* au (gwyneb) The superfices; a page.

> Pryderais troi ac ymchwelyd y llyfr Cymraeg hwnw yn Lladin; canys pe llanwn y lledwynebau o amgylchion geiriau, magu blinder a wnai hwny mwy no digrifwch, neu grynodeb i'r ei darllëai.
>
> I have thought of turning and translating that Welsh book into Latin; but if I were to fill the *pages* with amplifications of words, that would produce more vexation than amusement, or information, to such as should read it. *Gr. ab Arthur.*

Lledwynebawl, *a.* (lledwyneb) Superficial.
Lledwynebiad, *s. m.* (lledwyneb) A forming of superfices, a spreading over a surface.
Lledwynebu, *v. a.* (lledwyneb) To spread a face.
Lledwynu, *v. a.* (lledwyn) To whiten a little, to make pale; to become pale.
Lledŵyr, *a.* (gŵyr) Somewhat oblique or awry.
Lledwyrad, *s. m.* (lledŵyr) A going slightly awry.
Lledwyraw, *v. a.* (lledŵyr) To turn partly awry; to become slightly oblique.
Lledwyrdd, *a.* (gwyrdd) Somewhat green.
Lledwyredd, *s. m.* (lledŵyr) A slight obliquity.
Lledymadael, *v. a.* (ymadael) Partly to leave off.
Lledymadaw, *v. a.* (ymadaw) Partly to forsake.
Lledymadawiad, *s. m.* (lledymadaw) A partly separating one's self, a partly forsaking.
Lledymannog, *v. a.* (ymannog) To excite one's self a little.
Lledymarbed, *v. a.* (ymarbed) Partly to save one's self; partly to refrain.
Lledymbleidiaw, *v. a.* (ymbleidiaw) Partly to join a faction, or a sect.
Lledymchwal, *s. m.* (ymchwal) A half spreading one's self, a becoming partly spread.
Lledymchwalu, *v. a.* (lledymchwal) Partly to spread; to become partly spread.
Lledymdynu, *v. a.* (ymdýnu) Partly to contend.
Lledymddangaws, *v. n.* (ymddangaws) To half appear, partly to appear.
Lledymddwyn, *s. m.* (ymddwyn) The hypophora, a rhetorical figure producing the objection.
Lledymddwyn, *v.* (ymddwyn) Partly to comport
Lledymddygiad, *s. m.* (ymddygiad) A slightly comporting or behaving.
Lledymlusgaw, *v. a.* (ymlusgaw) Partly to drag one's self, partly to crawl.
Lledymlusgiad, *s. m.* (ymlusgiad) A half crawling
Lledymnoethi, *v. a.* (ymnoethi) To half expose one's self; to make one's self half naked.
Lledymnoethiad, *s. m.* (ymnoethiad) A making one's self half naked.
Lledymoddef, *v. n.* (ymoddef) Partly to bear.
Lledymoddefiad, *s. m.* (lledymoddef) A partly suffering one's self; a partly bearing.
Lledymollwng, *v. n.* (ymollwng) Partly to let one's self drop; to drop one's self partly.
Lledymraniad, *s. m.* (ymraniad) A partly dividing or separating one's self.
Lledymranu, *v. a.* (ymranu) Partly to separate one's self; to become half separated.
Lledymrwystraw, *v. n.* (ymrwystraw) To hinder one's self a little; to linger partly.
Lledymrwystriad, *s. m.* (ymrwystriad) A partly hindering one's self, a partly lingering.
Lledymsèniad, *s. m.* (ymsèniad) A partly chiding or taunting one another.
Lledymsènu, *v. a.* (ymsènu) To chide or taunt one another slightly.
Lledymsythiad, *s. m.* (ymsythiad) A becoming half erect or straight.
Lledymsythu, *v. a* (ymsythu) Partly to straighten one's self: to become half erect.
Lledymunaw, *v. n.* (ymunaw) Partly to accord.
Lledymwadiad, *s. m.* (ymwadiad) A half denying one's self.
Lledymwadu, *v. a.* (ymwadu) To half deny one's self, to deny one's self partly.
Lledymweled, *v. a.* (ymweled) Partly to visit.
Lledymweliad, *s. m.* (ymweliad) A partly visiting
Lledymwylltiaw, *s. m.* (ymwylltiaw) A becoming half wild, or frantic.
Lledymyl, *s. m.—pl. t.* au (ymyl) That is partly the edge, or rim; a border near the edge.
Lledynfyd, *a.* (ynfyd) Half foolish, or silly.
Lledynfydu, *v. n.* (lledynfyd) To grow half silly.
Lledynwst, *a.* (ynwst) Somewhat dank, or moist.
Lledysawl, *a.* (ysawl) Half consuming.
Lledysgythriad, *s. m.* (ysgythriad) A half lopping
Lledysgythru, *v. a.* (ysgythru) To half lop.
Lledysiad, *s. m.* (ysiad) A half consuming.
Lledystum, *s. m.—pl. t.* iau (ystum) A half bend.
Lledystumiad, *s. m.* (lledystum) A half forming, a half fashioning, or figuring.
Lledystumiaw, *v. a.* (lledystum) To half form.
Lledysu, *v. a.* (ysu) To half consume, or devour.
Lledd, *s. m.—pl. t.* au (lly—edd) A flat, or plain.

> Yr haf——
> Pan oeddych yn wych dy wedd,
> Por glwys-liw'n porio glas ledd!
>
> The summer, wert thou not, with splendid countenance, lord of beauteous colour, covering with herbage the verdant *plain!* *D. ab Gwilym.*

Lleddf, *a.* (lledd) Having a declination, or inclined position, oblique, inclined, flat; also placid, calm; soft, tender. *Lleddf gywair*, A flat key in music.

> Tri lleddf unben Ynys Prydain: Manawydan mab Llyr Llediaith; Llywarch Hen mab Elidyr Lydanwyn; a Gwgon Gwron mab Peredur: Ac sef achaws y gelwid hwynt yn lleddf unben, wrth na cheisynt gyfoeth, ac na allai neb ei luddias iddynt.
>
> The three *disinterested* princes of the Isle of Britain; Manawydan the son of Llyr Llediaith: Llywarch Hen son of Elidyr Lydanwyn; and Gwgon Gwron son of Peredur: And the reason they were called *disinterested* princes was that they sought not for power, and no one was able to debar them of it. *Trioedd.*
>
> Y fun ail Enid——
> Lladdai fil a'i lleddf olwg.
>
> The fair one like to Enid, she would kill a thousand with her *soft* look. *N. Gerh.*

Lleddfad, *s. m.* (lleddf) A warping; a flattening; an inclining, a drooping, a softening.
Lleddfawl, *s. m.* (lleddf) An inclining state; the act of flattening, or reclining; assuagement.

> Oedd ef fy neddfawd i nos galan,
> Lleddfawd ei gan, ri rhyfel eirian.
>
> He was my law on the eve of the festival, his song was *solace*, the lord of splendid war. *Mr. Dinbych.*

Lleddfawg, *a.* (lleddf) Having an oblique, or flat direction; of a soft, or assuaging quality.
Lleddfawl, *a.* (lleddf) Warping, flattening.
Lleddfbetrual, *s. m.—pl. t.* au (lleddf—petrual) A figure called a rhomboid.
Lleddfedig, *a.* (lleddf) Warped; assuaged.
Lleddfiad, *s. m.* (lleddf) A warping; a flattening; a softening, or assuaging.
Lleddflafariad, *s. m.—pl.* lleddflafariaid (lleddf—llafariad) A dipthong.
Lleddfu, *v. a.* (lleddf) To warp, to put in an oblique position; to flatten, to become warped, or oblique; to become flat, to come down; to soften; to be assuaged. *Mae y chwydd yn lleddfu*, the swelling is coming down; *mae y mor wedi lleddfu*, the sea is become calm.
Lleddy, *a.* (lledd) Inclining, drooping; of a pliant, or mild nature; soothing.
Llëen, *s. m.* (lla—en) Literature, scholarship.

Offeiriad addwyn ei fuchedd, heb ganddo hwiach o lëen.

A minister of holy life, not having a lack of *scholarship*. *Ll. G. Hergest.*

Lleen, *a.* (llaen) Literate, scholastic, erudite; clerical. *Gwyr llëen*, literary men; *gwyr llëen a gwyr llëyg*, the clergy and the laity.

Yr etholedigion offeiriaid, a meibion lleen, a'r Cristionogion adunaddynt a las yn can amled ag ehededdynt yn fyddinoedd ar gwlad nef.

The select ministers, and the *scholastics*, and the christians under them, he slew in such numbers that they flew in hosts to the kingdom of heaven. *Gr. ab Arthur.*

Llëenaeth, *s. m.* (llëen) Literature, scholarship.
Llëenaidd, *a.* (llëen) Of a literary nature.
Llëenawg, *a.* (llëen) Literate, having scholarship learned. *Llëenogion*, literati.
Lleenawl, *a.* (llëen) Literary, scholastic.
Llëenogaeth, *s. m.* (llëenawg) Literature.
Lleenu, *v. a.* (llëen) To pursue literature.
Lleenydd, *s. m.—pl. t.* ion (llëen) A literary man
Llëenyddawl, *a.* (llëenydd) Literary, scholastic.
Llëenyddiaeth, *s. m.* (llëenydd) Scholarship.

Nis gellir cydawn fyfyrdawd heb ddysg a lleenyddiaeth.

There can be no perfect ratiocination without learning and *scholarship*. *Barddas.*

Llef, *s. f.—pl. t.* au (lly—ef) A voice, a cry.

Pan fyno y frenines gerdd o'i gwrandaw yn ei hystafell, caned y bardd teulu iddi dri chwiwm o gerdd trwy lef gymedrawl, megys na rwystro ar y llys.

When the queen would have to listen to a song in her chamber, let the domestic bard recite to her three stanzas of a composition, with a moderate voice, so that the court may not be incommoded. *Welsh Laws.*

Ban llef cwn yn niffaith.

Loud the *cry* of dogs in a desert. *Llywarch Hen.*

Llefad, *s. m.* (llef) A crying out or uttering.
Llefadwy, *a.* (llefad) Utterable, expressible.
Llefain, *v. a.* (llef) To cry aloud, to cry out, to shout; to weep, to cry.

Bum gall unwaith, hyny oedd llefain pan ym ganed.

I was wise once, that was in crying when I was born. *Adage.*

Llefain, *s. m.* (llef) A loud cry, a shout: a weeping. *Careg lefain*, an echo stone, *craig lefain*, an echo rock, an echo.
Llefaint, *s. m.* (llefain) A loud utterance, or cry.
Llefair, *s. m.* (llef) A speaking; a prate, a babble.
Llefal, *s. m.* (mal) What is figured or fancied.
Llefan, *s. m.* (llef) Utterance, cry, or shout.
Llefar, *s. m.* (llef) Utterance, voice, or speech.
Llefarawg, *a.* (llefar) Having utterance.
Llefariad, *s. m.* (llefar) A speaking, a saying.
Llefaru, *v. a.* (llefar) To utter to speak, to say.
Llefarwr, *s. m.—pl.* llefarwyr (llefar—gwr) A speaker; a preacher.

Llefawg, *a.* (llef) Shouting, squalling. *Coryn llefawg*, a squalling imp.
Llefawl, *a.* (llef) Crying, shouting, exclaiming.
Llefawr, *a.* (llef) Clamorous, talkative.

Llidiogach no neb lle y dygiai.
Lleforion Ffrancod oll a fwriai.

More wrathful than any one where he should be offended the *talkative* French he would overthrow. *Gutyn Owain.*

Llefeliad, *s. m.* (llefal) A devising or inventing.
Llefelu, *v. a.* (llefal) To devise, to invent.
Llefelyn, *s. m.* (llefal) A stye on the eye.
Llefeni, *v. a.* (llefan) To exclaim exultingly.

Pan ytoedd y fran yn addercbawg o bob cyfryw bluf, dechreu a orug gellweiriaw, a grëu, a llefeni ar yr adar oll.

When the crow was adorned with every kind of feathers, she began to jest, and to croak, and *to exult over* all the birds. *Damegion.*

Llefer, *s. m.* (llef) Utterance, a cry, or noise.

Daeth i ferch Morus wylofus lefer;
Du yw gwisg Annes diwag yngyner.
S. Brwynawg.

Lleferawg, *a.* (llefer) Having utterance, vocal.
Lleferydd, *s. m.* (llefer) Utterance, voice, expression; a vocable. *Dysgu ar dafawd leferydd*, to learn by the expression of the tongue, to learn by heart; *lleferydd nag*, a refusal; *lleferydd y llygad*, the expression of the eye.

Dyngwallofwy Duw—
Yn awdur llafur lleferydd tawn,
I gano marwnad i Gadwallawn.

May God perfect me a laborious author of just *expression*, to compose an elegy to Cadwallon! *Cynddelw.*

Llefiad, *s. m.* (llef) Enunciation; a vocative.
Llefiadawl, *a.* (llefiad) Enunciative; vocative.
Llefn, *a.* (*f. of* llyfn) Even, smooth, sleek. *Y llefnau*, the reins.

Anawdd angen y gyhydedd lefn yw hon seithsill; a rhif hono a fyner, eithr o barth amrylaf cantadaeth ei gwethe o bedwar i ddeuddeg, rhag blinaw clust.

The essential quality of the *smooth* metricity is a verse of seven syllables; and the number of the verses to be at pleasure, so that for the sake of variety of harmony, it be confined to from four to twelve, to prevent tiring the ear. *Barddas.*

Llefnyn, *s. m. dim.* (llafn) A blade, a slab.
Llefod, *s. m.—pl. t.* au (lle—bod) A situation.

Dyn a folir—yn ol ei gamp, herwydd ei lefod yn y byd.

A man shall be praised, according to what he excels in, with respect to his *situation* in the world. *Barddas.*

Llefr, *a.* (*f. of* llwfr) Coward, timid, or faint.

Aed i ddiawl, dragwyddawl dro,
Y galon lefr a gilio!

To the devil go, for everlasting, the *faint* heart that would retreat. *Gr. Grug.*

Llefrin, *a.* (llafr) That is of a spreading nature; that is fresh.

Llafr pob llefrin.

Every thing *that is fresh* will spread. *Adage.*

Llefrith, *s. m.* (llafr—ith) New milk, sweet milk.

Edwyn hen gath lefrith.

An old cat knows the *sweet milk*. *Adage.*

Nid urfaeth caffael llefrith i bawb, nes caffael bothau Rhinon Rin Barnawd, ni sura byth llyn ynddynt.

It is not possible to obtain *milk* for every body, until the bottles of Rhinon Rin Barnawd are gotten, in which liquor will never turn sour. *H. Culhwch—Mabinogion.*

Llefrithawg, *a.* (llefrith) Having sweet milk.
Llefrithen, *s. f. dim.* (lle—brith) Stye on the eye
Lleg, *s. f.—pl. t.* au (lly—eg) That whips round, or binds; that clasps.

——Rhowch weithian chwithau,
Mae'r moes, ym aur a gwin,
Mae'r lleg, wyd am iarll Godwin.

Do you also now bestow gold and wine, it is customary; it is an *obligation*, thou art for Earl Godwin. *Iu. Tew Ieuan*

Llega, *s. m.* (llag) One that lags, or flags.

Legach, *s. m.—pl. t.* od (llag) A sluggish one.
Llegach, *a.* (llag) Sluggish; lazy; feeble; weak.

Coelled hen-wrach legach lorf
Chwedlau hen-wrach ehud-lorf.

Let the old hag with *sluggish* shank believe the tales of the old hag with nimble shank. *Gro. Owain.*

Llegai, *s. c.* (llag) A sluggish one, a lagger.
Llegest, *s. m.—pl. t.* au (cest) That is all body, or belly, a gorbellied one; a lobster, otherwise called *ceimwch*, and *geifr y mor*.
Llegiad, *s. m.* (lleg) A whipping round.
Llegr, *s. m.—pl.* llegrau (lleg) That braces, or clasps
Llegu, *v. n.* (llag) To flag; to be sluggish, to lag.
Llegus, *a.* (llag) Apt to flag, sluggish. *Dyn llegus*, a lazy man; *yn llegus*, by and by, presently; in the evening.
Llegynt, *s. m.* (lleg—hynt) A constrained course
Llegyrn, *s. m.—pl. t.* edd (lleg—gyrn) A dwarf.
Lleiach, *a.* (*comparative of* llai) Lesser, or less.
Lleiad, *s. m.* (llai) A lessening, a diminution.
Lleiadawg, *a.* (lleiad) Lessening, diminutive.
Lleiadu, *v. a.* (lleiad) To diminish, to lessen.
Lleiaf, *s. m.* (*superlative of* llai) The least. *a.* least, smallest. *O'r lleiaf*, at the least; *o'r hyn lleiaf*, of the least that can be, at the leastwise.

O'r deu-ddrwg goreu y lleiaf.

Of the two evils the best is the *least*. *Adage.*

Lleian, *a.* (llai) Of a dark gloomy hue.
Lleian, *s. f.—pl. t.* od (llai) A grey one; a nun. *Y lleian*, the titmouse; *y lleian gynffon hir*, the long tailed titmouse; *y lleian wen*, the smew; *y lleian bengoch*, the red-headed smew.

Na fydd leian y gwanwyn.
Gwaeth yw lleianaeth no llwyn.

Be not a *nun* in the spring. The state of a *nun* is worse than the grove. *D. ab Gwilym.*

Lleianaeth, *s. m.* (lleian) The life of a nun.

Er dy eirian leianaeth,
Eiriol rol——ymwared.

By thy glorious *reclusion*, intercede that deliverance may be granted. *D. ab Gwilym, i Ddwynwen.*

Lleianaidd, *a.* (lleian) Like a nun; belonging to a nun. *Buchedd leianaidd*, the life of a nun.
Lleianawl, *a.* (lleian) Belonging to a nun.
Lleiandy, *s. m.—pl. t.* au (lleian—ty) A nunnery.
Lleianu, *v. a.* (lleian) To lead the life of a nun; to enter into a nunnery, to take the veil.
Lleianyn, *s. m. dim.* (lleian) A wren.
Lleiâu, *v. a.* (llai) To lessen, to diminish; to be lessened, or diminished.

Nid anhawz i'm o'l donian
Llenwi llaw hael no'i lleiâu.

It is not for me more difficult out of her gifts to fill the liberal hand than *to diminish*. D. *Epynt.*

Lleiaw, *v. a.* (llai) To make of a greyish brown, or dun; to become of a dun colour.
Lleiawg, *a.* (llai) That is of a greyish brown, or dun. *s. m.—pl.* lleiogion. A gray friar.
Lleibiad, *s. m.* (llaib) A licking, or lapping.
Lleibiadwy, *a.* (lleibiad) That may be licked.
Lleibiaw, *v. a.* (llaib) To lick, or to lap.
Lleibiawl, *a.* (llaib) Lambent, lapping.
Lleibiwr, *s. m.—pl.* lleibwyr (llaib—gwr) Lapper.
Lleibus, *a.* (llaib) Lambent, lapping, licking.
Lleidawd, *s. m.* (llaid) A turning into clay.
Lleidfa, *s. f.* (llaid—ma) A clayey place.
Lleidiad, *s. m.* (llaid) A turning into clay or mud.
Lleidiaw, *v. a.* (llaid) To turn into clay or mud.
Lleidiawg, *a.* (llaid) Lutulent, miry, muddy.
Lleidiawl, *a.* (llaid) Of a clayey nature.
Lleidiogi, *v. a.* (lleidiawg) To turn clayey.
Lleidiogrwydd, *s. m.* (lleidiawg) Muddiness.
Lleidle, *s. m.—pl. t.* oedd (llaid—lle) Muddy place.
Lleidlyd, *a.* (llaid) Clayey; muddy, lutulent.
Lleidlydedd, *s. m.* (lleidlyd) Muddiness, lutulence.
Lleidlydiaw, *v. n.* (lleidlyd) To become lutulent.
Lleidlydrwydd, *s. m.* (lleidlyd) Muddiness.
Lleidlys, *s. m.* (lleid—llys) Mudwort.
Lleidryn, *s. m. dim.* (lleidr) A petty thief.
Lleidr, *s. m.—pl.* lladron (llad) A thief. *Lleidr cyfaddef*, an arrant thief; *lleidr crogadwy*, a thief that deserves hanging; *lleidr gwerth*, a thief liable to be sold; *lleidr camlyrus*, a thief that may be cleared by a compensation fine; *lleidr dirwyus*, a thief that may be freed by a common fine. *Welsh Laws:—Lleidr pen ffordd*, a highwayman; *carn lleidr*, an accessor to a thief, or the receiver of what is stolen.

Cyntaf yn lleidr, cyntaf yn frenin.

The first that will be a *thief*, first that will be a king *Adage*

Ni bu haid ddiawliaid ddelach yn gwahodd,
Na thir fwy ladron, na thref leidrach.

There never was a more clownish swarm of devils in inviting, nor land more full of thieves, nor a town *more full of pilferers*. *L. G. Cothi, i Gaerlleon.*

Lleiddawd, *s. m.* (llaidd) A sluggish state.
Lleiddiad, *s. m.—pl.* lleiddiaid (lladd) A slayer.

Angeu goleu pob gelyn
Angad leiddiad Lywelyn.

The manifest death of every foe, the *slaughtering* hand of Llywelyn. *Gwgon.*

Lleied, *a.* (llai) So little, or equally little.
Lleiedig, *a.* (llai) Diminished, or lessened.
Lleiedigawl, *a.* (lleiedig) Tending to lessen.
Lleieingant, *s. m.* (lleian—cant) The circle of bluish gloom; an epithet for the sea.

Dygorfu Cymmru i beri cad;
A llwyth lliaws gwlad a gynnuliant,
A lluman glan Dewi a ddyrchafant,
I dywysaw Gwyddyl drwy leieingant.

The Welsh were obliged to cause a battle; and the tribes of many a region they will collect together; and the holy banner of Dewi they will lift up, to lead the Gwyddelians through the *circle of the blue gloom*. *Golyddan, Arm. Prydain.*

Lleifiad, *s. m.* (llaif) A cutting off, a reaping.
Lleifiaw, *v. a.* (llaif) To cut, or to reap.

O dir i dir, drwy y dydd,
Ac o olud ei gilydd,
Huw a'i llaif yn holl Llifon,
Heiniar y mab hanner Mon.

From region to region, through the day, and from the wealth of each, Hugh *will reap* it in all Llivon, the crop of the youth is half Anglesey. *Ieu. Deulwyn.*

Lleigiad, *s. m.—pl.* lleigiaid (llag) One who flags, or droops, a sculker.
Lleigiaw, *v. a.* (llag) To flag; to lag; to sculk.

Os i Loegr y cais leigiaw,
Mi wn dyb o'r man y daw.

If to England he shall attempt *to sculk*, I know a guess from where he will come. *Ieu. Dyfi.*

Lleigiawg, *a.* (llaig) Abounding with bubbles.
Lleigiawl, *a.* (llaig) Producing bubbles, bubbling.
Lleigiwr, *s. m.—pl.* lleigwyr (llag—gwr) A lagger; a sculker.
Lleigus, *a.* (llag) Flagging, drooping; sluggish, slow, creeping, gradual. *Yn lleigus*, presently, by and by; in the evening.
Lleilai, *a.* (llai *repeated*) Less and less.

Lleilai lymaid gaeaf.

Less and less the draught of winter. *Adage.*

Lleill, *s. pl.* (llall) The others; the rest.
Lleilldu, *s. m.* (llall—tu) A contrary side.
Lleinell, *s. f.—pl. t.* au (llain) A narrow slip.
Lleiniad, *s. m.—pl. t.* au (llain) A blading.
Lleiniaw, *v. a.* (llain) To blade; to make into long strips, or slips.

Lleion, *s. m. aggr.* (llai) A kind of marble, of a dark blue and black colour in the polish, which burns into good lime, and is like that of Kilkenny and the Giant's Causeway, in Ireland.

Lleipiaw, *v. a.* (llaib) To lick, or to lap up.

Lleipr, *a.* (llaib) Flaccid, flabby, drooping, hanging, lolling; withered; feeble.

Lleipraw, *v. a.* (lleipr) To make flabby; to droop.

> Madyn—
> Cinyn noeth lipryn, e'th leipra madredd.

Reynard, thou bare skin clout, corruption *shall make thee flabby*. *R. Goch Eryri.*

Lleiprawg, *a.* (lleipr) Having a flaccid quality.

Lleipriad, *s. m.* (lleipr) A turning flabby.

Lleiprog, *s. f.—pl. t.* od (lleipr) The lamprey.

Lleirfryd, *s. m.* (llaer—bryd) Lively mind.

> Nad wyr pawb yn llwyr, lleirfryd gynnal,
> Nad hylithr aur mal mal oddiwrthyd?

Does not every one perfectly know, keeping up a *lively imagination*, that the fine gold does not pass so currently, as from thee? *Gw. Ddu o Arfon, m. Sir Gr. Llwyd.*

Lleirwyd, *s. m.* (llaer—gwyd) Lecherwite, a fine for adultery or fornication.

Lleisiad, *s. m.—pl. t.* au (llais) The uttering of the voice, a sounding, a tonation; a counter tide

Lleisiaw, *v. a.* (llais) To utter a voice, or cry; to sound; to make a noise; to ring; to be made vocal.

> Aed i offrwm—
> Llun ei gen yn Llangynin,
> Llysiau Mair, er lleisiaw ei min.

Let her go to offer the form of her lip to Llangynin, of the herbs of Mary, for her mouth *to be made vocal*. *D. ab Edmwnd, i Fudes.*

Lleisiawg, *a.* (llais) Having voice or utterance.

Lleisiawl, *a.* (llais) Belonging to the voice, vocal.

Lleisiwr, *s. m.—pl.* lleiswyr (llais—gwr) A bawler, a squaller.

Lleisw, *s. m.* (llas) A lixivium, or lye. *Lleisw coed*, a lixivium of wood ashes; *lleisw corff*, stale urine

Rhag gwendid emenydd, cymera Griban saint Ffraid a gwna leisw, a golcha dy ben.

For a weakness of the brain, take the sawwort and make a *decoction*, and wash thy head. *Ll. Meddyg.*

Lleiswaidd, *a.* (lleisw) Lixivial, of the nature of lye

Lleiswaw, *v. a.* (lleisw) To make a lixivium.

Lleiswawg, *a.* (lleisw) Impregnated with lye.

Lleiswawl, *a.* (lleisw) Lixivious, lixiviated.

Lleithad, *s. m.* (llaith) A dissolving; a turning dank, moist, or humid.

Lleithawd, *s. m.* (llaith) A dissolution; a damping, or a moistening.

Lleithban, *s. m.* (llaith—pan) The soft row of fish.

Lleithder, *s. m.* (llaith) Humidity, moisture.

Lleithdra, *s. m.* (llaith) Moisture, dampness.

Lleithedig, *a.* (llaith) Moistened, or damped.

Lleithgar, *a.* (llaith) Apt to cause a dissolution; slaying; of a dank tendency.

Lleithgarwch, *s. m.* (lleithgar) Aptness to cause dissolution; a tendency to humidity.

Lleithiad, *s. m.—pl.* lleithiaid (llaith) That causes dissolution; a slaughterer.

> Lleithiawg, Owain llwyth ogawn;
> Lleithgar llyw gryw gryd,
> Lleithiad cad cerdd glyd,
> Cadernyd Caswallawn.

Possessed of a throne is Owain, of a mighty race; the slaughtering and fierce energy of conflict; the *slaughterer* of battle and theme of song with the strength of Caswallon. *Cynddelw, i O. Cyfeiliawg.*

Lleithiannawl, *a.* (lleithiant) Apt to dissolve.

Lleithiannu, *v. a.* (lleithiant) To cause dissolution; to turn to a dank state.

Lleithiant, *s. m.* (llaith) Dissolution; dank state.

Lleithiar, *a.* (llaith) Of dissolving tendency.

> Oedd tag, oedd angau anghymar;
> Oedd amheu i'r byd bod achar o honom
> O henaint Bebhiar!

There was trouble, there was a matchless scene of death; it was a doubt to the world if there was a remnant left of us for *decaying* old age. *Ll. P. Moch.*

Lleithiaw, *v. a.* (llaith) To moisten, to damp; to dissolve; to become moist, or damp.

Lleithiawg, *a.* (llaith) Having the power of dissolving; having a damp or humid quality.

Lleithiawl, *a.* (llaith) Dissolvent; tending to humidity or moisture.

Lleithig, *s. f. dim.* (llaith) A platform, a form, bench, or seat; a throne; a couch. *Lleithig neuadd*, a piece of timber crossing the hall, dividing it into upper and lower, and which formed a step to the upper part, which was the place of rank: *lleithig troed*, a footstool.

Tri lleithig lwyth Ynys Prydain: Arthur yn bennteyrnedd yn Nghaerlleon ar Wysg, a Dewi yn ben esgyb, a Maelgwn Gwynedd yn ben hynaif; Arthur yn bennteyrnedd yn Nghelliwig yn Nghernyw, a Bedwini yn ben esgyb, a Charadawg Freichfras yn ben hynaif, Arthur yn benteyrnedd yn Mhenryn Rhionydd yn y Gogledd, a Chyndeyrn Garthwys yn ben esgyb, a Gwrthmwl Wledig yn ben hynaif.

The three tribes *of the throne* of the Isle of Britain: Arthur the supreme king in Caerlleon upon Usk, and Dewi the primate bishop, and Maelgwn Gwynedd the first elder; Arthur the supreme king at Celliwig in Cornwall, and Bedwini the primate bishop, and Caradoc Freichfras the first elder; Arthur the supreme king at Penryn Rhionydd in the North, and Cyndeyrn Garthwys the primate bishop, and Gwrthmwl Wledig the first elder. *Trioedd.*

Gwelai dair morwyn yn eistedd ar leithig: ac ef a ai atynt i'r lleithig.

He observed three damsels sitting upon a *seat*: and he went to them to the *seat*. *H. Peredur—Mabinogion.*

Yn y neuadd yr oedd—dau facwy yn gwarea gwyddbwyll ar y lleithig aur.

In the hall there were two youths playing at chess upon the golden *seat*. *Br. Max. Wledig—Mabinogion.*

> Yr oedd y gwrda da dig,
> A'r ael uthr, ar ei leithig;
> A'i wreigdda, gul ful foel-drist,
> Wrth y tan.——

The good and irritable gentleman, with the frowning brow, was upon his *couch*, and the good woman, lean, modest and with bare dejected head, by the fire. *Ieu. Powlys, i gybydd.*

Lleithigawg, *a.* (llath) Having a seat, enthroned.

> Yfais gan deyrn o gyrn eurawg—
> Yn llys Aberffraw, er ffaw ffodiawg,
> Bum o du gwledig yn lleithigawg.

I drank with a prince out of horns adorned with gold, in the court of Aberffraw, for the glory of the prosperous; I have been by the side of the sovereign *enthroned*. *Meilyr.*

Lleithin, *s. f.* (llaith—hin) Humid weather.

Lleithineb, *s. m.* (lleithin) Humidity, moisture.

Lleithion, *s. pl. aggr.* (llaith) Moistures, liquids.

Lleithlyd, *a.* (llaith) Apt to be damp or wet.

Lleithlydrwydd, *s. m.* (lleithlyd) Dampishness.

Lleithlydu, *v. a.* (lleithlyd) To render damp; to become of a damp quality.

Lleithon, *s. m. aggr.* (llaith) The soft roe, or spawn of fish; otherwise called *lleithban*, and *bol meddal*. *Lleithon a grawell*, the soft roe and hard roe.

Lleithrid, *s. m.* (llathr) A flash of lightning.

Lleithrwydd, *s. m.* (llaith) Dampness, moistness.

Llelo, *s. m.* (llo) A dolt, a blockhead. *Taw, y llelo gwirion!* Hold thy tongue, thou foolish blockhead! It is used, in South Wales, as the diminutive of the name of *Llywelyn*.

Llem, *a.* (*f.* of llym) Sharp, pungent, severe.

Cenaw yn ei wal a gast lem.

A puppy in his kennel and a *fierce* bitch. *Adage*

Llemain, *v. a.* (llam) To hop, or dance about.

Llemeinig, *a.* (llemain) Of a roving state.

> Bu Llywarch yn ddibarch ddig;
> Bu lwm iawn, bu lemeinig.

Llywarch was without respect and irritated; he was very naked he was in a *wandering state*. *Sir Gr. Fychan.*

Llawer gorwydd blawr yn Llanfawr llogawd,
Llemenig yn Ionawr.

Many a grey steed in the stable of Llanvor, *prancing* in January. *Cynddelw.*

Llemidydd, *s. m.—pl. t.* ion (llamid) One that bounds, leaps, or springs; the porpoise.
Lleminawg, *a.* (llamu) Apt to bound or leap.
Llemitor, *sup.* (llam) To be trodden, to be treading.

Pob llwyfr llemitor arno.

Every coward *will be trodden* upon. *Llefoed.*

Llemwst, *s. m.* (llem—gwst) Sharp perception.
Llemyg, *s. f.* (llem) Sea lavender.
Llemysten, *s. f.—pl. t.* od (llemwst) A sparrowhawk; otherwise called *llymysten, gwalches, gwipia, cudyll,* and *pilan.*
Llen, *s. m.* (lleen) Literature, or scholarship.

Gwell y gwyr llen no henaint.

The *learned* knows better than old age. *Adage.*

Gwell no llen pwyll cynhenid.

Better than *learning* is natural talent. *Adage.*

Llèn, *s. f.—pl. t.* i (lly—en) A veil; a curtain, or hangings. *Llen yr ymysgar,* the caul, or omentum.
Llenawg, *a.* (llèn) Having a veil, veiled.
Llenawg, *a.* (llèn) Literate, having scholarship.

Oed Crist 959, y torres Owain ab Hywel Dda, gôr Llan Illtud yn Ngorwennydd, achaws cael ynddi lenogion pendefig o Saeson.

The *year* of Christ 959, Owain son of Hywel the Good, destroyed the *choir* of Saint Illtud in Gorwennydd, on account of finding in it learned men, of the Saxon nobility. *Carad. Llangarfan.*

Llenawl, *a.* (llèn) Tending to veil, veiling.
Llenawr, *s. m.—pl.* llenorion (llèn) A scholar.

Cyn bum llenawr.

Before I was a *scholar.* *Taliesin.*

Llencyn, *s. m. dim.* (llanc) A stripling, a lad.
Llengel, *s. f.* (llèn—cel) A veil hiding; a veil.

Llwyr drist esgar!
Llengel dawel do
A gudd grudd agro!

Altogether sad the separation! a silent covering *veil* hides the pensive cheek. *Gr. ab M. ab Dafydd.*

Llengudd, *s. f.* (llèn—cudd) A veil covering.
Llenguddiaw, *v. a.* (llengudd) To cover with a veil
Lleniad, *s. m.* (llèn) A veiling, a covering over
Lleniedig, *a.* (lleniad) Veiled, having a veil.
Lleniedydd, *s. m.—pl. t.* ion (lleniad) A veiler.
Llenig, *s. f. dim.* (llèn) A small veil, a veil.
Llenlath, *s. f.* (llèn—llath) A curtain-rod.
Llenlian, *s. m.* (llèn—llian) Sheet-cloth, sheeting

Ei lenlian a gaiff yr yngnad llys i gan y frenines yn wastad.

His *sheets* the judge of the palace shall have from the queen always. *Welsh Laws.*

Llenoriaeth, *s. m.* (llenawr) Literature.
Llenu, *v. a.* (llèn) To veil, or to envelop.

Daeth mai odiaeth mwyn,
Ir dyfiant ar dwyn,
A dail yn glas-ddardda sy'n llenu pob llwyn.

The supremely charming May is come, fresh vegetation on the brake, and the verdantly springing leaves are *veiling* every grove *D. Williams.*

Llenwad, *s. m.* (llanw) A filling, a replenishing.
Llenwedig, *a.* (llanw) Filled, or replenished.
Llenwedigaeth, *s. m.* (llenwedig) The act of filling
Llenwi, *v. n.* (llanw) To fill, to replenish; to become full; to flow in; to flow, as the tide.

Ni lenwir uffern eithr ag addewidion da.

Hell *will* not *be filled* except with fair promises. *Adage.*

Gwedi ei lenwi o Wrgant Farf Twrch dieiodd ei fuchedd ygyd a thangnefedd a heddwch ef a gladdid yn Nghaer Llëon ar Wysg.

After Gwrgant Farf Twrch *had filled* the days of his life with tranquillity and peace, he was buried in Caer Llëon upon Uske. *Gr. ab Arthur.*

Llenwiail, *s. pl. aggr.* (llèn—gwiail) Curtain rods
Llenwialen, *s. f.* (llenwiail) A curtain rod.
Llenwr, *s. m.—pl.* llenwyr (llèn—gwr) A learned

Tair lleng a ddaethant llant lestri,
Tair praff peff lyngeu wy bren brod.

Three *legions* came by the vessels of the flood, three ample and chief of sects hastily to assail him. *Gwalchmai.*

Llengawl, *a.* (lleng) Of a legion, legionary.
Llengig, *s. f.* (llèn—cig) The midriff, the diaphragma. *Toriad llengig,* a rupture.
Llëoldeb, *s. m.* (llëawl) Locality, being local.
Llëolder, *s. m.* (llëawl) Locality, being local.
Llëolrwydd, *s. m.* (llëawl) Locality, localness.
Llëoriaeth, *s. m.* (llëawr) Literature, scholarship.
Llepiad, *s. m.* (lleb) A lapping, or licking.
Llepian, *v. a.* (lleb) To lap, or to lick.
Llepiaw, *v. a.* (lleb) To lap, or to lick up.

Pob un lepio a'i dafawd, fal y llepio ci.

Every one that *shall lap* with his tongue, as a dog *laps.* *Judges* 7. 5.

Llepiawl, *a.* (lleb) Lambative; lapping, licking.
Llepiwr, *s. m.—pl.* llepwyr (lleb—gwr) Lapper.
Ller, *s. m.* (lly—er) That is stretched or drawn out; that is sharp, or crisp; the smooth rye brome; the grass. *Mae clefyd y ller arnaf,* I am oppressed with languor, or I am tired. *Sil.*

Bedd Gwrgi gwychydd, a Gwyndodydd ler;
A bedd Llawr llu odd,
Yn ngwarthaf Gwanas, gwir yaid.

The grave of Gwrgi the hero, and the *sharp* Gwyndodian; and the grave of Llawr the affliction of armies, are on the summit of Gwanas, this is troth. *Eng. B. Milwyr.*

Llerch, *s. f.—pl. t.* ias (ller) A frisk; a fit of loitering, or larking.
Llercian, *s. m.* (llerc) A frisking backwards and forwards; a loitering; a larking.
Llercian, *v. a.* (llerc) To loiter about; to lark.
Llerciannawl, *a.* (llercian) Loitering; larking.
Llerciaw, *v. a.* (llerc) To loiter about; to lurk.
Llerciwr, *s. m.—pl.* llercwyr (llerc—gwr) One who frisks about; a saunterer; one who lingers about; a lurker.
Llercyn, *s. m. dim.* (llerc) A loiterer; a lurker.
Llercyna, *v. a.* (llercyn) To frisk about; to loiter.
Llercynawl, *a.* (llercyn) Loitering; larking.
Llercynwr, *s. m.—pl.* llercynwyr (llercyn—gwr) A loiterer, a saunterer; a lurker.
Lleren, *s. f. dim.* (ller) A cockle, or darnel.

Gwenith tyner heb leren,
Gwyn had tywysogion hen.

Delicate wheat without *one darnel,* the fair seed of ancient princes. *Sim. Fychan.*

Llerf, *a.* (ller) Crisp; subtile; sharp, acerb.
Llerpyn, *s. m.—pl. t.* au (llarp) A shred, a rag.
Llerpyna, *v. a.* (llerpyn) To tear to rags.
Llerpyniad, *s. m.* (llerpyn) A tearing to rags.
Llerpynu, *v. a.* (llerpyn) To rent into shreds.
Llerth, *s. m.* (ller) Extreme fineness or subtility; an extreme agitation, or frenzy. *a.* Frantic.

Sef yw llerth cyndeirtawg.

A being *frantic* is being mad. *Ll. Meddyg.*

Llerthawl, *a.* (llerth) Tending to a frenzy.
Llerthiad, *s. m.* (llerth) A turning frantic.
Llerthrwydd, *s. m.* (llerth) A frantic state.
Llerthu, *v. a.* (llerth) To turn frantic or mad.
Llerthus, *a.* (llerth) Tending to be frantic.
Llerthusaw, *v. n.* (llerthus) To turn frantic.
Lleru, *v. a.* (ller) To make crisp or sharp; to be nice; to become subtile.

Llerw, *s. m.* (ller) That is nice, soft, delicate, or smooth. *Malwen yn gadel ei llerw ar ei hol,* a snail leaving her track behind her.

Llerw, *a.* (ller) Soft, smooth, delicate; squeamish, easily disgusted.

> Dy gusan— —
> Calenig lerw ddierwin.
>
> Thy kiss, a nice present, in no wise harsh. *D. ab Gwilym.*
>
> Dwf llerw dan defyll irwydd.
>
> A *delicate* growth beneath the green-wood glades.
> *D. ab Gwilym.*

Llerwchwimp, *a.* (llerw—chwimp) Of soft turn, of smooth gait.

Llerwddyn, *s. c.—pl. t.* ion (llerw—dyn) A nice or delicate person; a gentle person.

> Llerwddyn dan fantell orddu.
>
> A *delicate fair one* under a sable bordered mantle.
> *D. ab Gwilym.*

Llerwfalch, *a.* (balch) Nicely-proud. *Llerwfalch farchawg,* a punctiliously-proud knight.

Lles, *s. m* (lly—es) Benefit, advantage, good, profit; interest; service; use.

> Lles dibrwch yn ddiflannawl, lles cywirdeb yn dragywyddawl.
>
> The *gain* of iniquity is evanescent, the *gain* of probity is eternal.
> *Adage.*
>
> Cas a gollo ei les er afles i'w gymmydawg.
>
> Odious is he who foregoes his own *advantage* for the sake of disadvantage to his neighbour. *Adage.*

Llesawl, *a.* (lles) Beneficial, advantageous.

Llesg, *a.* (lly—esg) Feeble, faint, lax, sluggish, slothful. *Cenad lesg,* a feeble messenger.

Llesgâad, *s. m.* (llesg) A weakening; a becoming weak, or debilitated.

Llesgaidd, *a.* (llesg) Somewhat weak, or faint.

Llesgar, *a.* (llesg) Feeble, or debilitated.

Llesgarwch, *s. m.* (llesgar) Feebleness, debility.

Llesgâu, *v. n.* (llesg) To become feeble, faint, or sluggish; to debilitate.

Llesgdrwm, *a.* (llesg—trwm) Feebly heavy.

Llesgdrymedd, *s.* (llesgdrwm) Feeble heaviness.

Llesgedd, *s. m.* (llesg) Feebleness, laxity, debility; sluggishness; slothfulness; listlessness.

> Sef yw llesgedd peth a goller o wall.
>
> *Sluggishness* consists in losing a thing from neglect.
> *Welsh Laws.*
>
> Llesgedd, ceingau y pechawd hwnw ynt esgeuluso gwasanaethu Duw yn yr amser y dylyo, torri gobddunedd, anobeithio am drugaredd, tristau er colli da bydawl, neu ddynion, a'r cyffelybed iglon weithredoedd hwny.
>
> *Slothfulness,* the branches of that sin are, the neglecting the service of God in the proper time, the breaking a vow, despairing of mercy, sorrowing for the loss of worldly good, or friends, and similar acts to those. *Ll. G. Hergest.*

Llesgeddain, *a.* (llesgedd) Having a weariness.

Llesgen, *s. f.* (llesg) A sluggish, or slothful fit.

Llesgenaidd, *a.* (llesgen) Of a sluggish or inactive disposition.

Llesgeneiddrwydd, *s. m.* (llesgenaidd) Sluggishness; slothfulness.

Llesgiad, *s. m.* (llesg) A weakening, a debilitating

Llesgrwydd, *s. m.* (llesg) Feebleness, or debility.

Llesgu, *v. a.* (llesg) To weaken, to debilitate, to become weak, feeble, or debilitated.

> Gwedi llawer o amser, a dechreu o Lyr llesgu o henaint, y dau engddywedawg deboun a gyfodant yn [illegible] y [illegible] yr holl deyrnas.
>
> After a length of time, and when Llyr had begun *to grow feeble* with age, the two before mentioned sons in law rose up in opposition to him, and they subdued the whole kingdom.
> *Gr. ab Arthur.*

Llesgyn, *s. m.* (llesg) A weakling, a feeble one.

Llesiad, *s. m.* (lles) A benefiting, a doing good.

Llesiannawl, *a.* (llesiant) Advantageous.

Llesiannu, *v. a.* (llesiant) To make beneficial.

Llesiant, *s. m.—pl.* llesiannau (lles) Benefaction.

Llesin, *a.* (lles) Utile; beneficial.

Llesineb, *s. m.* (llesin) Utility; benefit.

Llesinebawl, *a.* (llesineb) Beneficial.

Llesmar, *s. f.—pl.* llesmeiriau (lles—mar) Swoon.

Llesmeiriad, *s. m.* (llesmar) A swooning, a fainting

Llesmeiriaw, *v. n.* (llesmar) To swoon, to faint.

Llesmeiriawl, *a.* (llesmar) Swooning, fainting.

Llest, *s. m.* (lly—est) That keeps from separating

Llestair, *s. m.—pl.* llesteiriau (llest) An obstruction, let, or hinderance.

> Ni bydd llesteiriach y fordd er gwrandaw offeren.
>
> The way will not be the more *obstructed* for hearing mass.
> *Adage.*

Llesteiriad, *s. m.* (llestair) A retarding, an obstructing, or hindering; a retardment.

Llesteiriaw, *v. a.* (llestair) To obstruct, to hinder

Llesteiriawg, *a.* (llestair) Having obstruction.

Llesteiriawl, *a.* (llestair) Obstructing, retarding.

Llesteiriwr, *s. m.—pl.* llesteirwyr (llestair—gwr) An obstructer, a hinderer.

Llestr, *s. m.—pl.* llestri (llest) A vessel. *Llestr ymenyn,* a butter pot; *llestr pridd,* an earthen vessel; *llestr tân hwyl,* a vessel under sail; *buwch yn bwrw y llestr,* a cow dropping the matrix.

> Llestr a erfyll wirawd y penhebogydd yn y llys, can ni ddyly efe namyn torri ei syched, sef achaws yw hyny, rhag godoed gwala ar ei adar.
>
> A *vessel* shall receive the liquor of the head falconer in the hall, as he ought only to quench his thirst; the reason of that is, lest he should leave his birds in want. *Welsh Laws.*

Llestraid, *s. m.—pl.* llestreidiau (llestr) A vessel-full; a measure containing two bushels and a half, used in *Glamorgan.*

Llestriad, *s. m.* (llestr) A putting in a vessel.

Llestru, *v. a.* (llestr) To put into a vessel.

Llestrwr, *s. m.—pl.* llestrwyr (llestr—gwr) One who puts into a vessel.

Llestryn, *s. m. dim.* (llestr) A small vessel.

Llesu, *v. a.* (lles) To benefit, to advantage.

Lleswyr, *s. m.* (llaswyr) Aërial freshness.

Lleswyra, *v. a.* (lleswyr) To gather freshness, to take the air; to follow a scent.

Lletbai, *a.* (lled—pai) Oblique, bending, pliant.

Lletbeiad, *s. m.* (lletbai) A turning oblique.

Lletbeiaw, *v. a.* (lletbai) To render oblique; to become oblique, or awry.

Lletbeirwydd, *s. m.* (lletbai) Obliqueness, wryness

Lletrawg, *s. f.—pl.* lletrogau (lledr) A cake.

Llettaeniad, *s. m.* (taeniad) A partly spreading.

Llettaenu, *v. a.* (taenu) To spread partly.

Llettaliad, *s. m.* (taliad) A partly paying.

Llettalu, *v. a.* (talu) Partly to pay, or reward.

Llettanawl, *a.* (tanawl) Partly spreading.

Llettaeniad, *s. m.* (taeniad) A partly spreading.

Llettaenu, *v. a.* (taenu) Partly to spread.

Llettardd, *s. m.* (tardd) A slight breaking out.

Llettarddawl, *a.* (llettardd) Slightly eruptive.

Llettarddiad, *s. m.* (llettardd) Slight eruption.

Llettarddu, *v. n.* (llettardd) To break out slightly, to appear through slightly, to erupt slightly.

Llettawel, *a.* (tawel) Somewhat calm.

Llettawelu, *v. n.* (llettawel) To calm a little.

Llettebyg, *a.* (tebyg) Somewhat similar, or like.

Llettebygiad, *s. m.* (llettebyg) A partly likening, a partly surmising; a being a little like.

Llettebygu, *v. a.* (llettebyg) Partly to liken; partly to guess; to be somewhat like.

Llettoddi, *v. a.* (toddi) To half dissolve.

Llettoddiad, *s. m.* (toddiad) A partly dissolving.

Llettrem, *s. f.* (trem) A half look, or glance.

Llettremiad, *s. m.* (llettrem) A slightly looking.

Llettremiaw, *v. a.* (llettrem) To look slightly.
Llettremiawl, *a.* (llettrem) Slightly looking.
Llettremiwr, *s. m.—pl.* llettremwyr (llettrem—gwr) One who slightly glances at.
Llettring, *s. f.—pl. t.* au (dring) A ladder.
Llettro, *s. m.—pl. t.* ion (tro) A half turn.
Llettröad, *s. m.* (llettro) A partly turning.
Llettroi, *v. a.* (llettro) To turn round a little.
Llettrwm, *a.* (trwm) Somewhat heavy; a little sad
Llettrymu, *v. a.* (llettrwm) To make a little heavy; to become rather heavy.
Llettwyll, *s. m.* (twyll) A slight deceit or fraud.
Llettwyllaw, *v.* (llettwyll) To deceive slightly.
Llettwymnaw, *v. a.* (llettwymyn) To warm slightly; to render lukewarm.
Llettwymyn, *a.* (twymyn) Somewhat lukewarm.
Llettyb, *s. m.* (tyb) A slight fancy or opinion.
Llettybiad, *s. m.* (llettyb) A partly fancying.
Llettybiaw, *v. a.* (llettyb) To half suspect.
Llettyniad, *s. m.* (tyniad) A partly pulling.
Llettynu, *v. a.* (tynu) Partly to draw or pull.
Llettywyll, *a.* (tywyll) Somewhat dark, darkish.
Llettywyllu, *v. a.* (llettywyll) To darken a little; to become rather dark.
Llettrawd, *s. m.* (lled—trawd) A traverse. *a.* Traversing.

> Lliwelydd llettrawd dy foliant;
> Llywelyn a Llywarch a'i cant.
>
> Over Lliwelydd *widely spreading* thy praise;
> Llywelyn and Llywarch sing it. *Ll. P. Moch, i Lywelyn II.*

Llettrodawl, *a.* (llettrawd) Wandering abroad.
Llettrodi, *v. a.* (llettrawd) To wander abroad.
Lletty, *s. m.—pl. t.* au (lled—ty) A lodging.

> Y dyn a wertho ei dy, yn mha wlad y ceiff letty!
>
> The person who sells his house, in what country will he obtain a *lodging!* *Adage.*
>
> Y pennaeth, ei letty yw ty mwyaf yn dref, a chymhesuraf.
>
> The head of the family, his *lodging* is the largest house in the town, and the most central. *Welsh Laws.*

Llettya, *v. a.* (lletty) To lodge, to take lodging.

> Gwyr y cadno yn ddigawn da
> Pa le mae 'r gwyddau yn llettya.
>
> The fox knows well enough where the geese *do lodge*. *Adage.*

Llettyad, *s. m.* (lletty) A lodging, a quartering.
Llettyaeth, *s. m.* (lletty) The practice of lodging.
Llettyawg, *a.* (lletty) Having a lodging.
Llettyawl, *a.* (lletty) Relating to lodging.
Llettyedig, *a.* (llettyad) Lodged or quartered.
Llettyu, *v. a.* (lletty) To lodge; to quarter.
Llettyua, *v. a.* (llettyu) To lodge, to take lodging.
Llettyugar, *a.* (llettyu) Apt to lodge; hospitable.
Llettyugarwch, *s. m.* (llettyugar) Hospitality.
Llettywr, *s. m.—pl.* llettywyr (lletty—gwr) A man-lodger, a lodger.
Llettywraig, *s. f.—pl.* llettywreigedd (lletty—gwraig) A woman lodger.
Llettywriaeth, *s. m.* (llettywr) The practice of lodging.
Lletwad, *s. f.* (lledwad) A ladle, or large spoon.
Llety, *s. m.—pl. t.* au (lle—ty) House room.
Lletya, *v. a.* (llety) To lodge, to take lodging.
Lletyad, *s. m.* (llety) A lodging, a quartering.
Lletyaeth, *s. m.* (llety) The practice of lodging.
Lletyawl, *a.* (llety) Relating to lodging.
Lletyedig, *a.* (llety) Lodged, or quartered.
Lletynt, *s. m.—pl. t.* iau (lled—hynt) Intent.
Lletyu, *v. a.* (llety) To lodge, to take a lodger.
Lletyugar, *a.* (lletyu) Apt to lodge; hospitable.
Lletyugarwch, *s. m.* (lletyugar) Hospitality.
Lletywr, *s. m.—pl.* lletywyr (llety—gwr) Lodger.
Lletywraig, *s. f.* (llety—gwraig) A woman lodger.

Lletywriaeth, *s.* (llettywr) The practice of lodging
Lletyydd, *s. m.—pl. t.* ion (llety) A lodger.
Lleth, *a.* (*f. of* llyth) Flabby; drooping, feeble.
Llethadwy, *a.* (lleth) That may be flattened; that may be overlayed.
Llethawl, *a.* (lleth) Flattening; overlaying.
Llethbegwn, *s. m.* (lleth—pegwn) A flattened pole
Llethbegynawl, *a.* (llethbegwn) Having a flattened pole; oblate.
Llethedig, *a.* (lleth) Flattened; overlayed.
Llethgrwn, *a.* (lleth—crwn) Spheroidal, oblate.
Llethiad, *s. m.* (lleth) A flattening, an overlaying.
Llethr, *s. f.—pl.* llethrod (lleth) A slope, a declivity, a steep; a cliff, or steep side of a hill. *Llethr grudd*, the fall of the cheek bone.

> "Pian y bedd yn llethr y bryn!"
> Llawer nis gwyr ei gofyn:
> Bedd Coel mab Cynfelyn.
>
> "Whose is the grave in *the declivity* of the hill!" many who know not do ask: it is the grave of Coel, son of Cynvelyn.
> *Englynion Beddau Milwyr.*

Llethrawd, *s. m.* (llethr) That slopes; a heap.
Llethrawg, *a.* (llethr) Having a declivity.
Llethrawl, *a.* (llethr) Declivous, pensile.
Llethredig, *a.* (llethr) Being made declivous.
Llethredd, *s. m.* (llethr) A sloping state.
Llethriad, *s. m.* (llethr) A making declivous; a sloping, or sloping down.
Llethrid, *s. f.—pl. t.* ion (llathr) A gleam, a flash of lightning, coruscation.
Llethridaw, *v. a.* (llethrid) To render gleaming.
Llethridawg, *a.* (llethrid) Gleaming, coruscant.
Llethridfawr, *a.* (llethrid) Greatly gleaming. *Ysgwydawr llethridfawr llathraid*, shields of brightly gleaming polish.
Llethridiad, *s. m.* (llethrid) A gleaming, coruscation
Llethridiannawl, *a.* (llethridiant) Productive of coruscation.
Llethridiannu, *v. a.* (llethridiant) To render coruscant, to produce coruscation.
Llethridiant, *s. m.* (llethrid) A coruscation.
Llethru, *v. n.* (llethr) To slope down steeply.
Llethu, *v. a.* (lleth) To press flat; to overlay.
Llethwr, *s. m.—pl.* llethwyr (lleth—gwr) One who presses down; an overlayer.
Llêu, *v. a.* (lla) To explain, to read, to lecture.

> Fy ngherddau, fy llyfrau llëer.
>
> My songs, my books *will be read*. *Taliesin.*
>
> "Chwi a lëwch y ddeddf, ac nis deellwch," medd Elen wrth yr Iuddewon. "Ni a llewn ac ni a deallwn," eb hwyntau.
>
> You do *read* the law, and you do not understand it," said Helen to the Jews. "*We do read it*, and we do understand it," they replied. *Ll. G. Hergest.*

Llëu, *v. a.* (lle) To place, to set, or to lay.
Lleua, *v. a.* (llau) To louse, or to hunt for lice.
Lleuad, *s. f.—pl. t.* au (llêu) The moon. *Cynydd y lleuad*, the increase of the moon; *cil y lleuad*, the wane of the moon. *See* Lloer.

> Nid gwresawg ond yr haul; nid oer ond y lleuad.
>
> Nothing is so hot as the sun; nothing is so cold as the moon. *Adage.*
>
> Tri pheth a newidiant yn fynych: lleuad, gwynt, a meddwl gwraig.
>
> Three things often change; the *moon*, the wind, and a woman's mind. *Adage.*

Lleuadawl, *a.* (lleuad) Belonging to the moon.
Lleuadglaf, *a.* (lleuad—claf) Moon-sick, lunatic.
Lleuadiad, *s. m.* (lleuad) A lunation, or an ecliptic revolution of the moon.
Ll
Ll
Ll
Ll

Lleuer, *s. m.—pl. t.* au (lleu—er) Light; splendour. *Lleuer y llygad*, the light of the eye; *lleuer dar*, a little bird of the size of a wren, with short legs.

> Astrus fu'r ffenestr——
> Lle rhoed i ddwyn lleuer haul!
>
> Vexatious was the window, where it was placed to conduct the *light of the sun*! *D. ab Gwilym.*

Lleuerad, *s. m.* (lleuer) A shedding of light.
Lleuerawd, *s. m.* (lleuer) A shedding a light.
Lleuerawg, *a.* (lleuer) Luminous; glittering.
Lleuerawl, *a.* (lleuer) Illuminating; shining.
Lleuerog, *s. f.—pl. t.* ion (lleuer) A luminary.
Lleueru, *v. n.* (lleuer) To shine, to shed light.
Lleuerwch, *s. m.* (lleuer) A luminous state.
Lleuerwg, *s. m.* (lleuer) A luminous state.
Lleuerydd, *s. m.—pl. t.* ion (lleuer) One that sheds light, one that illumes; a luminary.
Lleufer, *s. m.—pl. t.* au (lleu—mer) Splendour.

> Llywiawdr, amerawdyr mor a lleufer,
> I ddylif cynnulf cynhebycer.
>
> The governor and the sovereign of the sea and *of light*, to the conflicting torrent he is compared. *Ein. ab Gwgawn.*
>
> Eilwaith yr euthym yn negeswg,
> O leufer llyw cammawn, lawn dywysawg.
>
> A second time I have gone a messenger, from the *splendour* of the chief of conflict, the righteous prince. *Meilyr, m. Gr. ab Cynan.*
>
> Tale dylyed i'r anian a orug Gorfynilawn; ac o'r lleufer hon yd aeth, ac yn Nghaer Lundain y claddwyd.
>
> The debt of nature was paid by Gorfynion; and he passed from the *state of light*, and in the City of London he was buried. *Gr. ab Arthur.*

Lleuferâad, *s. m.* (lleufer) An enlightening.
Lleuferâawl, *a.* (lleufer) Illuminative.
Lleuferad, *s. m.* (lleufer) An illuminating.
Lleuferâu, *v. a.* (lleufer) To enlighten, to illume.
Lleuferawd, *s. m.* (lleufer) An illumination.
Lleuferawg, *a.* (lleufer) Luminous, splendid.
Lleuferawl, *a.* (lleufer) Illuminating; shining.
Lleuferiad, *s. m.* (lleufer) An illumination.
Lleuferogrwydd, *s. m.* (lleufer) Lightsomeness.
Lleuferu, *v. n.* (lleufer) To illumine; to shine.

> Pennydd cylch elfydd haul a hwylia;
> Yn uchel oddiachom lloer lleufera.
>
> Daily around the elements the sun revolves; high above us the moon *reflects a light*. *Ieuan Mynyw.*

Lleuferydd, *s. m.* (lleufer) An illuminator.
Lleulys, *s. m.* (llau—llys) The staves-acre; also called *llewyg y llau*.
Lleuogrwydd, *s.* (lleuawg) Lousiness, lousy state.
Lleurwydd, *s. m.* (llêu) Brightness, resplendency
Llew, *s. m.—pl. t.* od (lly—ew) That swallows, that takes in, or devours; a lion. *Y llew gwŷn gwyllt*, the wild orach; *Y llew gwŷn dof*, the garden orach; also called *llewyn* and *llygwyn*

> Glew a fydd llew hyd yn llwyd.
>
> The *lion* will be brave until he is grey. *Adage.*
>
> I Lywarch y bu lewod;
> A gwae wyr byw Lloegr eu bod.
>
> To Llywarch there were *lions*, and woe to the men of England that they were. *L. G. Cothi.*

Llewa, *v. a.* (llew) To swallow, to devour, to take food, to eat.

> Llewid bwyd ni bo beichiawg.
>
> She that is not pregnant *let her swallow* victuals. *Adage.*
>
> Llewais wirawd
> Gwin a bragawd.
>
> I swallowed of beverage wine and bragget. *Taliesin.*
>
> Eryr Eli ban ei lef;
> I lewsai gwyr lyn.
> Crau calon Cyndylan wyn;
>
> The eagle of Eli loud his scream; *he had devoured fresh beverage*—the heart's blood of fair Cyndylan! *Llywarch Hen.*

Llewad, *s. m.* (llew) A swallowing, a devouring.
Llewadwy, *a.* (llewad) That may be devoured.
Llewaidd, *a.* (llew) Like a lion, leonine.
Llewawd, *s. m.* (llew) The act of devouring.
Llewawl, *a.* (llew) Swallowing, or devouring.
Llewedig, *a.* (llewad) Being devoured.
Llewen, *s. m.* (llew) A point that takes in, or to which any thing verges; a focus.
Llewenydd, *s. m.* (llewen) A verging point; the occident. *Llewenydd haul*, sun set. *Sil.*
Llewes, *s. f.—pl. t.* od (llew) A lioness, a she lion.
Llewi, *v. a.* (llew) To swallow, to take in.
Llewig, *a.* (llew) Having the nature of a lion.
Llewin, *a.* (llew) Tending down, or into; occident
Llewinaw, *v. a.* (llewin) To verge; to go westward
Llewinawl, *a.* (llewin) Occiduous, occident.
Llewiniad, *s. m.* (llewin) A verging, a falling to the extreme point; a westing.
Llewych, *s. m.—pl. t.* au (lla—gwych) Light, brightness, splendour; hue, colour; aspect, appearance. *Mae dy lewych yn wiw*, thy look is excellent.

> Ef gwnaeth haul hwylfawr lewychu;
> Ef gwnaeth lloer, a llewych arddu;
> Ef gwnaeth trai a llanw; a llwyr [illegible] byd,
> A bydoedd wledychu.
>
> He made the sun *to light* a mighty round; he made the moon, and the sable-hued *aspect*; he made the ebb and flood; the universe he owns, and governs worlds. *Elidr Sais.*

Llewychad, *s. m.* (llewych) A reflecting a light.
Llewychadwy, *a.* (llewychad) Capable of reflecting light, of a glittering quality.
Llewychator, *ger.* (llewychad) In illuminating.
Llewychawd, *s. m.* (llewych) Reflection of light.
Llewychawl, *a.* (llewych) Tending to reflect light.
Llewychedig, *a.* (llewych) Shining, or glittering.
Llewychedigaeth, *s. m.* (llewychedig) A shining.
Llewychedigawl, *a.* (llewychedig) Illuminative.
Llewychfawr, *a.* (llewych) Resplendent; glorious
Llewychiad, *s. m.—pl. t.* au (llewych) A shining, a glittering.
Llewychiannawl, *a.* (llewychiant) Illuminative.
Llewychiannu, *v. a.* (llewychiant) To illuminate.
Llewychiant, *s. m.* (llewych) Illumination.
Llewychitor, *sup.* (llewych) To be illuminated.
Llewycholdeb, *s. m.* (llewychawl) Lightsomeness.
Llewycholder, *s. m.* (llewychawl) Lightsomeness.
Llewycholi, *v. a.* (llewychawl) To make luminous.
Llewychu, *v. a.* (llewych) To give light, to illumine; to shine; to glitter.

> Am a rygarad, cyn ni'm carwy——
> Nevd llawer ym llw llef ennarwy the
> Ban llewych ei bron gar ei breichrwy.
>
> For the object that I love to excess, since she will not love me, doth she not greatly consume me, who is of the hue of the foam-border of the wave, when her breast *glitters* by her bracelet. *Cynddelw, i Efa f. Madawg.*

Llewychus, *a.* (llewych) Lightsome, luminous.
Llewychusaw, *v. a.* (llewychus) To make lightsome; to become lightsome.
Llewydd, *s. m.* (llew) A point to which any thing verges; a radiating point.
Llewyddawl, *a.* (llewydd) Verging to a focus.
Llewyddiad, *s. m.* (llewydd) A radiating to a focus
Llewyddu, *v. a.* (llewydd) To verge to a focus; to tend westward.
Llewyg, *s. f.—pl. t.* on (llew) A swoon, a trance, or fainting fit. *Llewyg y blaidd*, hops; *llewyg yr iar*, henbane, also called *ffa y bugel*, *crys y brenin*, *ffa y moch*, *perfyg*, and *bela*.
Llewygawl, *a.* (llewyg) Swooning, or fainting.
Llewygiad, *s. m.* (llewyg) A swooning, a fainting.

Llewygu, *v. n.* (llewyg) To swoon or to faint.

> Bydd—dynion yn llewygu gan ofn, a dysgwyl am y pethau sydd yn dawed ar y ddaiar.
>
> There shall be men *dying* with fear, and looking for the things that are coming upon the earth. *Luke* 21. 26.

Llewygus, *a.* (llewyg) Tending to swoon or faint.

Llewyn, *s. m.—pl. t.* au (llew) A point to which any thing verges; a radiating point; a meteor; also the herb orach.

> Arf eryr gwyr llewyr llewyn
> Aer gymhl——
>
> The weapon of the eagle of men is the splendour of the *gloom* of the darting of slaughter. *Ll. P. Moch, i Lywelyn* II.

Llewynad, *s. m.* (llewyn) A verging to a focus; a reflection of rays.

Llewynawl, *a.* (llewyn) Verging to a focus.

Llewyniad, *s. m.* (llewyn) A radiating to a focus.

Llewynu, *v. a.* (llewyn) To verge to a focus; to tend westward.

Llewynydd, *s. m.—pl. t.* ion (llewyn) A verging point; the occident.

Llewyr, *s. m.—pl. t.* oedd (lla—gwyr) Radiance.

Llewyraw, *v. n.* (llewyr) To radiate, to sparkle.

Llewyrawl, *a.* (llewyr) Radiant; sparkling.

Llewyrch, *s. m.—pl. t.* au (llewyr) Reflection of light, a shining; complexion, aspect. *Wyt yn burion dy lewyrch*, thy look is very well.

Llewyrchad, *s. m.* (llewyrch) A reflecting a light.

Llewyrchawl, *a.* (llewyrch) Reflecting light.

Llewyrchedig, *a.* (llewyrchad) Illumed.

Llewyrchiad, *s. m.* (llewyrch) A reflecting a light.

Llewyrchiannawl, *a.* (llewyrchiant) Illuminative.

Llewyrchiannu, *v. a.* (llewyrchiant) To cause a light, to illuminate.

Llewyrchiant, *s. m.* (llewyrch) An illumination.

Llewyrchu, *v. a.* (llewyrch) To reflect, to shine.

Llewyrchus, *a.* (llewyrch) Lightsome, luminous.

Llewyrchusaw, *v. a.* (llewyrchus) To make lightsome; to become lightsome.

Llewyrdeb, *s. m.* (llewyr) Radiantness; a glitter.

Llewyriad, *s. m.* (llewyr) Radiation; a sparkling.

Llewyriannawl, *a.* (llewyriant) Apt to radiate.

Llewyriannu, *v. a.* (llewyriant) To cast a splendour

Llewyriant, *s. m.* (llewyr) Radiation, a sparkling.

Llewyrn, *s. m.—pl. t.* au (llewyr) A fiery exhalation, or meteor, an ignis fatuus; also called *tan llwyneg*.

> Rhys Meigen——
> Esawg, drym lleuawg, drem llewyrn.
>
> Rhys Meigen, guilty, lousy-backed, having the aspect of a *will with a whisp*. *D. ab Gwilym.*

Llewyrnaidd, *a.* (llewyrn) Like a meteor.

Llewyrnawg, *a.* (llewyrn) Having meteors.

Llewyrnawl, *a.* (llewyrn) Meteorous, having the quality of a meteor; producing meteors.

Llewyrnu, *v. a.* (llewyrn) To produce meteors.

Llêydd, *s. m.—pl. t.* ion (lla) A reader, a lecturer.

Llêyddawl, *a.* (llêydd) Belonging to reading.

Llêyddiad, *s. m.* (llêydd) A reading, a lecturing.

Llêyddiaeth, *s. m.* (llêydd) Literature, scholarship

Lleyg, *s. m.—pl. t.* ion (lle) That is local, or stationary; a layman.

Lleygiawl, *a.* (lleyg) Laical, laic, or lay.

Lleyn, *s. m.—pl. t.* oedd (lla) A long slip, or stripe; a stripe or tongue of land.

Lleynlys, *s. m.* (lleyn—llys) The scurvy-grass; also called *lliwlys*.

LLI, *s. m. r.—pl. t.* on. A flux, a flood, a stream.

Lliad, *s. m.* (lli) A fluxing, a flowing; a streaming

Llian, *s. m.—pl.* llieiniau (lli) A web; linen-cloth, linen; a towel, or napkin. *Llian cri*, unbleached cloth; *llian bras*, coarse cloth; *llian main*, fine linen; *llian brith*, check cloth; *llian hwyl*, sail cloth; *llian bwrdd*, or *llian bwyd*, table cloth, *llian amdo*, a shroud cloth.

Lliant, *s. m.* (lli) A fluxion, a flux; a torrent; flood, or stream; also the sea beach.

> Gwylain yn gware ar wely lliant,
> Lleithrion eu pluawr, pleidiau eddrin.
>
> The sea-mews playing on a bed of *flood*, glittering their plumage, in love united groups. *Gwalchmai.*
>
> Rhwng Mynyw a'r mor, mawr o drôau
> A fydd ar eu llu wy lliw dydd golau;
> Collant a'r llygaid, a'r eneidiau;
> Ni welant na lliant, nac eu llongau.
>
> Between Mynyw and the sea, great the events, which shall come upon them by the clear light of day; they shall fail in their eyes, and in their souls; they shall behold nor the *flood*, nor their ships. *Gw. Brycheiniawg.*

Lliant, *a.* (lli) Fluent, fluid, or flowing.

> Cyfarfu ysgwn ag esgarant aer,
> Llas maer, llosged caer ger mor lliant.
>
> The exalted one met with the scattered runaways from slaughter, the leader was slain, a town was burnt near the *flowing* sea. *O. Cyfeiliawg.*

Llias, *s. m.* (lli—as) A state of proceeding from, or flowing from, a parted state, a dispute.

> ——O llias
> Dewr egin dwyrëodd yn ddas.
>
> From the *parting of* the vigorous seed it rose up a stack. *Ll. P. Moch.*

Lliasawg, *a.* (llias) Being in a state of proceeding from; being separated, or put away.

Lliasawl, *a.* (llias) Tending to separate from.

Lliasiad, *s. m.* (llias) A causing to proceed or flow from; putting away; privation.

Lliasu, *v. a.* (llias) To proceed from; to part off, to separate; to become separated.

> Lloegr al am aur mal melyn,
> Er llias Dew, ai llas dyn.
>
> The goal of England for fine yellow gold, though God *put him away*, yet man slew him not. *Cynddelw, m. O. ab Madawg.*

Lliaswr, *s. m.* (llias—gwr) One who separates.

Lliaw, *v. a.* (lli) To cause to flow, or proceed from. *Dos i liaw yr wyn*, go to part the lambs away. *N. Wales.*

Lliaws, *s. f.—pl.* lliosydd (lli—aws) A multitude, a great many; a great quantity.

> Agaws yw'r lliaws i'r llall.
>
> Near is the one *multitude* to the other. *H. Dafi.*

Lliaws, *a.* (lli—aws) Many, frequent, much.

> Cefais liaws awr aur a phall
> Gan freuawl riau er eu hoffi.
>
> I obtained *many* a time gold and velvet, from frail chiefs, for loving them. *Meilyr.*
>
> Anhysbwllt ei lys o liaws eirchiaid
> Pan archant emys.
>
> Inexhaustible his court of the *multitude* of suitors, when they ask for steeds. *Cynddelw, i Ll. ab Owain.*

Llib, *s. m.* (lly—ib) A flaccid, soft or limber state.

Llibin, *a.* (llib) Flaccid, soft; limber, pliant.

Llibinaidd, *a.* (llibin) Somewhat flaccid or lank.

Llibiniad, *s. m.* (llibin) A turning flabby or lank.

Llibiniaw, *v. a.* (llibin) To make flabby and lank; to become flabby, or loose; to drag loosely.

Llibinrwydd, *s. m.* (llibin) Flabbiness, lankness.

Llibinwr, *s. m.—pl.* llibinwyr (llibin—gwr) A lank slender man; a fribble.

Llibyn, *s. m. dim.* (llib) A lank one; a fribble.

Llid, *s. m.* (lly—id) A violent effusion or gush; what is pungent; wrath, indignation; anger.

> Llid ac ynfydrwydd dau enw i'r un diawl.
>
> Wrath and foolishness are two names for the same devil. *Adage.*
>
> Ys drwg mitawr o bei llidiawr.
>
> It is bad playing if there be *shewing of anger.* *Adage*
>
> Gwedi gweled o Arthur ei luryg, a'i darian, a'i arfau yn cochi can ei waed, ennynu o lid, a gwychr frilowedd, a orug.
>
> When Arthur beheld his corselet, and his shield, and his weapons reddening with his blood, he kindled with *anger*, and heroic indignation. *Gr. ab Arthur.*

Llidfrawd, *s. f.—pl.* llidfrodau (llid—brawd) An angry judgement, an angry sentence.
Llidi, *s. m.* (llid) That is sharp or pointed.
Llidiad, *s. m.* (llid) A raising indignation; a becoming angry.
Llidiannawl, *a.* (llidiant) Of an irritating nature.
Llidiannu, *v. a.* (llidiant) To render irritating; to become irritating.
Llidiant, *s. m.* (llid) The state of being angry.

> Llidiawg fu gennt
> (Llidiant rwyddiert fu)
> Breiddiaw ei henwi
> Pan ei henwais.
>
> She was affected with wrath, (anger a power at command) that I should dare to name her, when I called her.
> *Gr. ab D. ab Tudyr.*

Llidiaw, *v. a.* (llid) To raise anger, to inflame. to be angry, to be enraged; to be inflamed.
Llidiawg, *a.* (llid) Wrathful, enraged, inclined to anger, angry. inflamed.
Llidiawl, *a.* (llid) Tending to anger, wrathful.
Llidiogi, *v. a.* (llidiawg) To become angry, to become enraged; to become inflamed.
Llidiogrwydd, *s. m.* (llidiawg) Wrathfulness.
Llidiwr, *s. m.* (llid—gwr) An angry one.
Llidus, *a.* (llid) Inclined to anger, wrathful.
Llieingig, *s. f.* (lliain—cig) The midriff.
Llieiniad, *s. m.* (llian) A putting on of linen.
Llieiniawg, *a.* (llian) Having linen, wearing linen.
Llieinrwd, *s. m.* (llian—rhwd) Lint; also called *nadd llian.*
Llieinwe, *s. f.* (llian—gwe) A piece of linen.
Llieinwerthwr, *s. m.—pl.* llieinwerthwyr (lliain—gwerthwr) A linen draper.
Llieinwisg, *s. f.* (lliain—gwisg) A linen garment.
Llieinwr, *s. m.—pl.* llieinwyr (llian—gwr) A dealer in linen, a linen draper.
Llieinydd, *s. m.—pl. t.* ion (llian) A linen draper.
Llif, *s. m.—pl. t.* au (lli) A flood, a deluge.

> Llif yn afon hinon fydd.
>
> A *flood* in the river shews that fair weather will come.
> *Adage.*
>
> Dewisais fy ngherdd yn nghynfaran cynnif
> O du llanw a llif, a llef dylan.
>
> I have chosen my course in the foremost rank of tumult, by the side of the tide, and the *flood*, and the noise of the shore.
> *Bleddyn Fardd.*

Llif, *s. f.—pl. t.* iau (lly—if) A saw. *Llif unllaw*, a hand saw; *llif draws*, a cross-cut saw; *llif hir*, a whip saw.
Llifad, *s. m.* (llif) A fluxion, a flowing, a streaming
Llifaid, *a.* (llif) Ground, sharpened, whetted. *Cleddyfawr llifaid*, sharpened swords.
Llifaw, *v. a.* (llif) To cause to flow, or run out; to flow; to overflow, to deluge.
Llifaw, *v. a.* (llif) To grind; to whet; to file.
Llifawg, *a.* (llif) Having fluidity; streaming.
Llifawl, *a.* (llif) Fluent, flowing, fluid; streaming.
Llifbysg, *s. pl. aggr.* (llif—pysg) The sawfish.
Llifddwfr, *s. m.—pl.* llifddyfroedd (llif—dwfr) A stream of water, a torrent.
Llifed, *s. m.* (llif) That is edged by grinding.

> Hil Ednyfed llifed llafn.
>
> The offspring of Ednyved with the blade of *sharpness*
> *Iolo Goch.*

Llifedig, *a.* (llifed) Being sharpened by grinding
Llifedigaeth, *s. m.* (llifedig) The act of grinding.

> Gwenwyn awch—
> Nis gwnug gof ei gurlaw;
> Nis gwnaeth llifedigaeth llaw.
>
> A poisonous edge, which was not moulded by a smith; it has not been made by the *art of grinding* by hand.
> *D. ab Gwilym, i'r Cortod.*

Llifeidrwydd, *s. m.* (llifaid) Edge by grinding.
Llifeiriad, *s. m.* (llifer) Defluxion, an overflowing
Llifeiriaidd, *a.* (llifer) Flowing in a torrent.
Llifeiriant, *s. m.* (llifer) A torrent, an inundation.
Llifeiriaw, *v. n.* (llifer) To flow; to overflow. *Gwlad yn llifeiriaw o laeth a mel*, a country flowing with milk and honey.
Llifeiriawl, *a.* (llifer) Flowing, or streaming.
Llifer, *s. m.* (lli—mer) A flux, flow, or confluence.
Llifiad, *s. m.—pl. t.* au (llif) A sawing, a cutting with a saw.
Llifiannad, *s. m.* (llifiant) A flowing; a defluxion.
Llifiannaidd, *a.* (llifiant) Defluous, fluid.
Llifiannawl, *a.* (llifiant) Apt to flow, defluous.
Llifianneiddrwydd, *s. m.* (llifiannaidd) The state of flowing away; consumptiveness.
Llifiannu, *v. a.* (llifiant) To wear away, to grind.

> Awen maen llifiannu.
>
> The grains of a grinding stone. *Adage.*

Llifiannus, *a.* (llifiant) Having a flowing tendency; defluous; consumptive.
Llifiant, *s. m.* (llif) Defluxion; a wearing away.

> Llifiant o'i chyfoeth a ddaeth atan.
>
> An *overflow* of her wealth has come to us. *H. ab Owain.*

Llifiaw, *v. a.* (llif) To saw; to file.
Llifiedig, *a.* (llifiad) Being sawed; being filed.
Llifion, *s. pl. aggr.* (llif) Saw-dust; filings.
Llifiwr, *s. m.—pl.* llifiwyr (llifiaw—gwr) Sawyer.
Lliflys, *s. m.* (llif—llys) Saw-wort; also called *dant y pysgodyn.*
Llifwell, *s. f.—pl. t.* au (llif—gwell) An issue.
Llifwydd, *s. pl. aggr.* (llif—gwydd) Boards, planks
Llifwydden, *s. f.* (llifwydd) Sawed plank, a board.
Llig, *s. m.* (lly—ig) That shoots or glides through.
Llill, *s. f.—pl. t.* od (lly—ill) Epithet for a goat.
Llillen, *s. f.* (llill) A young goat; a goat.

> Pam i rhoed y pymwyr hen
> Wrth holl allu'n werth llillen!
>
> Why were the five old men put, with all that could be done, to of the value of a *goat*? *R. ab Rhys Brydydd.*

Llim, *s. m.* (lli) That is smooth and gliding.
Llimp, *a.* (llim) Sleek, smooth, glossy, polished.

> Tagell aur teg yw a llimp,
> Alarch balch dylyn.——
>
> The double chin, fair it is and *soft*, the swan-like fair one.
> *Syppyn Cyfeiliawg.*

Llimpr, *s. m.* (llimp) That is smooth and soft.
Llimpraeth, *s. m.* (llimpr) Spoon-meat. *Sil.*
Llimpraw, *v. a.* (llimpr) To sap spoon-meat.

> Llimpraw fal hwch yn llimpraw hufen.
>
> *To sup* like a sow supping cream. *Adage.*

Llimprin, *s. m.* (llimpr) Spoon-meat.
Llin, *s. m.* (lly—in) Fine thread or fibre; a line; the grain of wood; flax. *Llin y forwyn*, or *llin y llyffant*, common toad-flax; *llin y tylwyth teg*, purging flax.

> Mal y llin ar y maen.
>
> Like the *line* on the stone. *Adage.*
>
> Arglwyddi llin o llin yat.
>
> They are lords from *line* to *line*. *L. G. Cothi.*

Llinaidd, *a.* (llin) Like thread; fibrous; flaxen.
Llinar, *a.* (llin—ar) Of a smooth, even, or free nature; genial, soothing, mild.

> I mae i chwi gar, llinar lwyth,
> Iach coed tal, o'ch cyd tylwyth.
>
> To you there is a friend, of a *mild* tribe, tall healthy trees, of the same family with you. *Edm. Prys, i F. Llwyd.*

Llinariad, *s. m.* (llinar) A making smooth, or free; a rendering genial; a softening.
Llinaru, *v. a.* (llinar) To render smooth, or free; to soften, to assuage, to mitigate.
Llindag, *s. m.* (llin—tag) A strangle, a throttle: *dodder*; also called, *llindro* and *llinglwm.*

Llindagiad, *s. m.* (llindag) A strangling, a throttling
Llindagu, *v. a.* (llindag) To strangle, to throttle.
Llindagwr, *s. m.—pl.* llindagwyr (llindag—gwr) A strangler, a throttler.
Llindro, *s. m.* (llin—tro) The plant called dodder
Llindys, *s. pl. aggr.* (llin—tys) Caterpillar; also called *pryf y dail, pryf cadachawg, pryf y gwinwydd. Llindys yr yd, pryf y gwellt*, the locust.
Llinell, *s. f.—pl. t.* au (llin) A line; a streak.
Llinellawg, *a.* (llinell) Abounding with lines.
Llinellawl, *a.* (llinell) Lineal, linear, lined.
Llinelledig, *a.* (llinell) Being lined, or ruled.
Llinelliad, *s. m.* (llinell) A making lines, a lining.
Llinellu, *v. a.* (llinell) To draw lines, to line.
Llinen, *s. f.* (llin) A stick, or piece of wood split with the grain.
Llinhad, *s. pl. aggr.* (llin—had) Linseed, flaxseed. *Llinhad y dwfr, llinos y dwfr, bwyd yr hwyaid*, and *cyflafan*, duckweed.
Llinhesg, *s. pl. aggr.* (llin—hesg) Water starwort.
Llinin, *a.* (llin) Consisting of flax, flaxen.
Llinon, *s. f.* (llin—on) The grain of ash; the grain of wood; a straight line, or rule; a shaft. *Ffon linon*, a staff of split ash.

Llawenydd i'r braich, a'r llinon caled;
Lladded; gostegred frith gostogion.

Joy to the arm, and the hard *ashen shaft*; let him kill; let him silence the motley rabble. *T. Penllyn, i wyr Caer.*

Llinos, *s. f.—pl. t.* od (llin) A linnet, otherwise called *aderyn y llin*; also an epithet for a fine woman. *Llinos felen, melynog*, and *peneurin*, the yellow-hammer; *llinos werdd, y gegid*, the greenfinch; *llinos bengoch*, red-headed linnet; *llinos fynydd*, mountain linnet:—*Llinos y dwfr*, the duckweed.
Llinosaidd, *a.* (llinos) Like a linnet; as a linnet.
Llinosen, *s. f. dim.* (llinos) A little linnet.
Llinwr, *s. m.—pl.* llinwyr (llin—gwr) A flax-dresser.
Llinwydd, *s. m. aggr.* (llin—gwydd) Hair-weed, or crow-silk; also called *llinwisg*.
Llinyn, *s. m.—pl. t.* au (llin) A line; a string. *Llinyn cyhydedd*, equatorial line; *llinyn gewnuir, llinyn pysgota*, a fishing line; *llinyn clytiaw*, cobbling thread.

Mal y saeth o'r llinyn.

Like the arrow from the *string*. *Adage.*

Attal saeth, nid dilys hyn
A el unwaith o linyn.

To stop an arrow is no feasible matter, when once it is gone from the *string*. *T. Aled.*

Llinynawg, *a.* (llinyn) Having strings; stringy.
Llinyniad, *s. m.* (llinyn) A stringing, a cording.
Llinyniaw, *v. a.* (llinyn) To draw lines, to line.
Llinynogi, *v. n.* (llinynawg) To become stringy.
Llinynogrwydd, *s. m.* (llinynawg) Stringiness.
Llinynu, *v. a.* (llinyn) To tie with a string.
Llinynwr, *s. m.* (llinyn—gwr) A stringer.
Llinynyn, *s. m. dim.* (llinyn) A small string.
Llinys, *s. m.* (llin) A line of descent, a lineage.

Tri santaidd llinys Ynys Prydain · llinys Ioseph o Arimathea, a llinys Cunedda Wledig, a llinys Brychan Brycheiniawg.

The three holy *lineages* of the Isle of Britain; the *lineage* of Joseph of Arimathea, the *lineage* of Cunedda Wledig, and the *lineage* of Brychan Brycheiniog. *Trioedd.*

Lling, *s. m.—pl. t.* od (lly—ing) A skin or coating; the fish called *ling*.
Llion, *s. pl. aggr.* (lli) A multitudinous flux; an aggregate of floods. *Llyn llion*, the lake of streams, an inexhaustible collection of waters, popularly supposed to be in the earth, and the source of the sea, rivers, and springs. *Toriad llyn llion*, the irruption of the lake of streams, a traditionary allusion of the bards, to some ancient catastrophe, by a deluge. *Llyn llion*, a small pool at Chepstow, which ebbs and flows contrary to the tides.

Un o dair engir ddichwain Ynys Prydain, tòriad Llyn Llion, a myned bawdd hyd wyneb yr holl diroedd, oni foddes yr holl ddynion, namyn Dwyfan a Dwyfach, a ddiangynt mewn llong foel, ac o honynt hwy ydd adepilied Ynys Prydain.

One of the three awful events, the breaking out of the *Lake of Streams*, and all the lands becoming inundated, so that all the people were drowned, except Dwyvan and Dwyvach, who escaped in a bare ship, and from whom the isle of Britain was repeopled. *Trioedd.*

Lle'r gwin, mal lloer ar gynnydd,
Llawn byth fal llyn llion bydd.

The store for wine, like a moon upon the increase, ever full like the lake of *multitudinous streams* it will be. *Ior. Fynglwyd.*

Eingl ar gychwyn rhag llion Llychlyn.

The Angles on their departure before the floods of Llochlyn. *Taliesin.*

Lliosadwy, *a.* (lliaws) Multipliable, that may be augmented in number.
Lliosator, *ger.* (lliaws) In multiplying.
Lliosawg, *a.* (lliaws) Multitudinous, manifold. *Canu yn lliosawg*, to sing in full harmony.

Lluest Cadwallawn ar Daf,
Ys lliosawg y gwelaf;
Cyfreulu fraisg naf.

The camp of Cadwallon upon Taf, *multitudinous* it seems to me; the quota of a powerful chief. *Llywarch Hen.*

Lliosbaladr, *a.* (paladr) Of many blades, or of a multitude of spires.
Lliosbaladrawg, *a.* (lliosbaladr) Consisting of many blades, or spires.
Lliosbaladru, *v. n.* (lliosbaladr) To shoot out, or grow, in many blades.
Lliosbarth, *a.* (parth) Consisting of many parts.
Lliosbarthiad, *s. m.* (lliosbarth) A dividing into many parts.
Lliosbarthu, *v. a.* (lliosbarth) To render multipartite, or of many parts.
Lliosben, *a.* (pen) Consisting of many heads.
Lliosbenu, *v. a.* (lliosben) To make of many heads.
Lliosbig, *a.* (pig) Consisting of many points.
Lliosbigawg, *a.* (lliosbig) Having many points.
Lliosbleth, *a.* (pleth) Of many plaits, or wreaths.
Lliosblethiad, *s. m.* (lliosbleth) A making of many plaits, wreaths, or doubles.
Lliosblethu, *v. a.* (lliosbleth) To make of many wreaths or plaits.
Lliosblyg, *a.* (plyg) Of many folds, or doubles.
Lliosblygiad, *s. m.* (lliosblyg) A making of many folds or doubles.
Lliosblygu, *v. a.* (lliosblyg) To make many folds.
Lliosbraidd, *a.* (praidd) Having many herds.
Lliosbrawf, *a.* (prawf) Having many proofs.
Lliosgchwyl, *a.* (chwyl) Multivagant, multivagous.
Lliosdaith, *a.* (taith) Multivious, multivagous.
Lliosdrem, *a.* (trem) Of many sights, multocular.
Lliosdroed, *s. m.* (troed) A multipede. *a.* Having many feet, many-footed.
Lliosddarn, *a.* (darn) Consisting of many pieces
Lliosedig, *a.* (lliaws) Multiplied, or increased.
Lliosedd, *s. m.* (lliaws) Multiplicity; multitude.
Lliosenw, *a.* (enw) Multinomial, multinominal.
Lliosged, *a.* (ced) Of many gifts, many gifted.
Lliosgeg, *a.* (ceg) Having many mouths.
Lliosgell, *a.* (cell) Consisting of many cells.
Lliosgib, *a.* (cib) Multicapsular, having many seed vessels.
Llioshil, *a.* (hil) Multiparous, yielding many.
Llioshiliad, *s. m.* (llioshil) A producing many.
Llioshynt, *a.* (hynt) Multivious, multivagous.

Lliosi, *v. a.* (lliaws) To multiply, to increase.

Llaw Iesu a'i llioso.

May the hand of Jesus increase her. *D. ab Gwilym.*

Lliosiad, *s. m.* (lliaws) A multiplying, an increasing, an increment.
Lliositor, *sup.* (lliaws) To be multiplying.
Lliosiad, *a.* (llad) Of many gifts, many-gifted.
Llioslliw, *a.* (lliw) Having many colours.
Llioslun, *a.* (llun) Multiform, of many forms.
Llioslunedd, *s. m.* (llioslun) Multiformity.
Lliosluniad, *s. m.* (llioslun) A making multiform.
Llioslunaw, *v. a.* (llioslun) To make multiform.
Lliosochr, *a.* (ochr) Multilateral; many-sided.
Lliosogadwy, *a.* (lliosawg) Multiplicable.
Lliosogal, *s. m.—pl.* lliosogeion (lliosawg) A multiplicand, or multiplicator.
Lliosogawl, *a.* (lliosawg) Tending to multiply.
Lliosogedig, *a.* (lliosawg) Being multiplied.
Lliosogedd, *s. m.* (lliosawg) A multiplicity.
Lliosogi, *v. a.* (lliosawg) To multiply, to increase.
Lliosogiad, *s. m.* (lliosawg) A multiplying.
Lliosogrwydd, *s. m.* (lliosawg) A multitude.
Lliosogwr, *s. m.* (lliosawg—gwr) A multiplier.
Lliosogydd, *s. m.—pl. t.* ion (lliosawg) One who augments, or multiplies.
Lliosradd, *a.* (gradd) Of many degrees, or kinds.
Lliosran, *a.* (rhan) Multipartite, of many parts.
Lliosranawg, *a.* (lliosran) Having many parts.
Lliosranawl, *a.* (lliosran) Of many parts.
Lliosraniad, *s. m.* (lliosran) A making of many parts or shares.
Lliosranu, *v. a.* (lliosran) To make of many parts or shares.
Lliosred, *a.* (rhed) Of many courses or ways.
Lliosrith, *a.* (rhith) Of many appearances.
Lliosryw, *a.* (rhyw) Of many sorts or kinds.
Lliosseiniad, *s. f.* (seiniad) A dipthong.
Liossill, *a.* (sill) Polysyllabic, of many syllables.
Lliossillawg, *a.* (llossill) Of many syllables.
Llioswr, *a.* (lliaws—gwr) Having many husbands
Llioswraig, *a.* (gwraig) Having many wives.
Llioswreica, *v. a.* (gwraig) To marry many wives
Llioswreigedda, *v.* (gwraig) To have many wives.

Mae Iuddewon a chenedloedd wedi dodi eu bryd ar y ddrygarfer o lioswreigedda yn dra chyffredin.

The Jews and Gentiles have given themselves up to the bad custom of *having many wives very frequently.* *Ier. Owain.*

Llipa, *a.* (llib) Flaccid, flagging, flapping.
Llipâad, *s. m.* (llipa) A turning, flaccid, or limp.
Llipaidd, *a.* (llib) Of a flaccid or flabby quality.
Lliban, *s. c.* (llib) One that is limp, or glib.
Llipaniad, *s. m.* (llipan) A rendering smooth.
Llipanu, *v. a.* (llipan) To make glib, or smooth.
Llipâu, *v. n.* (llipa) To grow flabby, to flag, to droop, to hang down, to grow lank.
Llipr, *s. m.* (llib) That is limp, glib, or soft.
Llipryn, *s. m.—pl. t.* od (llipr) Any thing flabby, flagging, hanging, or drooping; a fribble.
Llliprynaidd, *a.* (llipryn) Of flabby tendency.
Llipryneiddiad, *s. m.* (llliprynaidd) A turning flabby, a becoming of a drooping quality.
Llipryneiddiaw, *v. n.* (lliprynaidd) To become flabby, or drooping.
Llipryneiddrwydd, *s. m.* (lliprynaidd) A flabby state.
Lliprynìad, *s. m.* (llipryn) A turning flaccid.
Lliprynrwydd, *s. m.* (llipryn) Flabbiness.
Lliprynu, *v. a.* (llipryn) To render flabby, or limp; to become flabby, to droop.
Llith, *s. m.—pl. t.* iau (lly—ith) What attracts, what serves to draw to, or allure; a lesson, a lecture; a lure; a bait; meal soaked in water, or mash.

Llaith Owain llith brain bruddd frys ei faran,
Afarwy, Aedd fab Clyn.

The slaughtering of Owain was the *lure of ravens*, whose front ranks hasten the prey, like Afarwy, and Aedd son of Clyn.
Cynddelw, m. O. ab Madawg.

Tyngu trwy llith neb.

Swearing through the *enticement* of any one. *Welsh Laws.*

Cerdd ddichwith bob llith o'r lien.

A song free from blemish every *lesson* of the lore.
M. ab Gron. Gutkin.

Llithiad, *s. m.—pl. t.* au (llith) An alluring, or enticing; allectation, allurement; persuasion, a lecturing; a baiting, or alluring with food.
Llithiaeth, *s. m.* (llith) Allectation; lectureship.
Llithiannawl, *a.* (llithiant) Allective; attractive.
Llithiannu, *v. a.* (llithiant) To make an enticement, to make attraction; to make alluring.
Llithiant, *s. m.* (llith) Allectation, enticement.
Llithiaw, *v. a.* (llith) To draw to, to attract; to entice, or to allure; to lecture; to bait, to allure with food.

Teulu Madawg, mur Prydain,
Yn lluythawg, yn llithiaw brain.

The family of Madog, the bulwark of Britain, fully burthened *alluring* the ravens. *Cynddelw, i F. ab Maredudd.*

Llithiawd, *s. m.* (llith) Allectation, allurement.
Llithiawg, *a.* (llith) Attractive, allective, full of allurements; being enticed, or allured; baited, or having a bait.
Llithiawl, *a.* (llith) Allective, attractive.
Llithiedig, *a.* (llithiad) Being allured, enticed, or attracted; persuaded; lectured.
Llithiogi, *v. a.* (llithiawg) To render alluring.
Llithiogrwydd, *s. m.* (llithiawg) Alluringness.
Llithiwr, *s. m.—pl.* llithwyr (llith—gwr) One who allures, or attracts; a baiter, or one who allures with food.
Llithle, *s. m.—pl. t.* oedd (llith—lle) A lure.
Llithlyfr, *s. m.—pl. t.* au (llith—llyfr) A legend book; a missal.
Llithlyn, *s. m.—pl. t.* au (llith—llyn) A lure pond
Llithr, *s. m.* (llith) A glide; a slip; a lapse.
Llithraw, *v. n.* (llithr) To glide along, to slip.

Pan yd oedd Llyr yn llithraw parth a heneint, meddyliaw a orug pa wedd yd adawai ei gyfoeth o'i ferched gwedi ef.

When Llyr was *gliding onward* towards old age, he began to think in what manner he should leave his dominions to his daughters after him. *Gr. ab Arthur.*

A wnelo hyn ni llithra byth;
Fe gaiff y ddilyth goron.

He that shall do this *shall* never *slip*; he shall obtain the neverfading crown. *Edm. Prys.*

Llithrawl, *a.* (llithr) Gliding; slipping, sliding.
Llithred, *s. f.—pl. t.* au (llithr) A glide; a slip.
Llithredawr, *s. m.* (llithred) That is full of glides

Alaf, yn ail meal am lad
Llithredawr llyry, llon cawad,
A dwfn ryd; berwyd bryd brad!

Wealth, like a bowl round the cheering beverage, the *gliding* snake, the refreshing shower, and the deep ford, it stirs the mind to treachery. *Llywarch Hen.*

Llithrediad, *s. m.* (llithred) A gliding, a slipping.
Llithredig, *a.* (llithred) Being strayed, or elapsed
Llithredigaeth, *s. m.* (llithredig) Act of slipping.
Llithredigrwydd, *s. m.* (llithredig) Slipperiness.
Llithredydd, *s. m.—pl. t.* ion (llithred) One who slips, or slides.
Llithrfa, *s. f.—pl. t.* oedd (llithr—ma) A slide.
Llithriad, *s. m.* (llithr) A gliding; a slipping.
Llithriannawl, *a.* (llithriant) Lubricous.
Llithriannu, *v. a.* (llithriant) To lubricate.

Llithriant, *s. m.* (llithr) Lubricity; flippancy.
Llithriciad, *s. m.* (llithrig) Lubrification.
Llithricaw, *v. a.* (llithrig) To lubricate, to make slippery; to become slippery.
Llithrig, *a.* (llithr) Sliding, gliding; slippery.

> Annoeth llithrig ei dafawd.
>
> Unwise the one with *slippery* tongue. *Adage.*

Llithrigaw, *v. a.* (llithrig) To lubricitate, to lubricate, to make slippery.
Llithrigawl, *a.* (llithrig) Lubricous, tending to make slippery, tending to become slippery.
Llithrigder, *s. m.* (llithrig) Lubricity; flippancy
Llithrigdra, *s. m.* (llithrig) Lubriciousness.
Llithrigedd, *s. m.* (llithrig) Slipperiness.
Llithrigfa, *s. f.* (llithrig) A slippery place.
Llithrigiad, *s. m.* (llithrig) Lubrifaction.
Llithrigrwydd, *s. m.* (llithrig) Slipperiness.
Llithrlath, *s. f.—pl. t.* au (llithr—llath) A sliding rule.
Llithrwr, *s. m.—pl.* llithrwyr (llithr—gwr) One who slips, or slides.
Llithrydd, *s. m.—pl. t.* ion (llithr) One who slips
Llithwalch, *s. m.—pl.* llithweilch (llith—gwalch) A bird of the lure.
Llithwr, *s. m.—pl.* llithwyr (llith—gwr) Lecturer
Lliw, *s. m.—pl. t.* iau (lli) That glides through, that pervades; a stain, a hue, a colour; a figure, form, or manner.

> Golau freuddwyd a welir liw dydd.
>
> It is a manifest dream that is seen by day light. *Adage.*
>
> Nid gorthaw a wnaf wrth a garwyf,
> Celadwy lyn y, liw ton am rwyf.
>
> I will not be silent with the one I love, the secluded fair one, of the *hue* of the wave round the oar. *Cynddelw.*
>
> Tri lliw y sydd yn ymadrawdd, i wahanu iawn ymadrawdd, ac i esgusaw droe gamymadrawdd.
>
> There are three *forms* in discourse, for distinguishing just expression, and for excusing a faulty expression. *Edeyrn Dafawd Aur.*

Lliwad, *s. m.* (lliw) That gives a colour; that exposes; an evidence, a witness.

> Dyly yr hawlwr ddwyn y lliwad rhag bron yr yngnad, cymeryd crair, a gofyn iddo, 'ai ti y sy liwad?'
>
> The prosecutor ought to bring the *evidence* before the judge, take a relick, and ask him, 'art thou an *evidence*?' *Welsh Laws.*

Lliwadwy, *a* (lliwad) Colourable, that may be coloured.
Lliwaw, *v. a.* (lliw) To give a hue, or colour; to stain; to stigmatize; to give evidence.

> Mae genyf a'i gweles, ac a'i lliwa llygad yn llygad, yn y wedd y barno cyfraith oreu.
>
> I have one who saw it, and that *will make it apparent* eye to eye, in the manner, which the law shall judge best. *Welsh Laws.*

Lliwdy, *s. m.—pl. t.* au (lliw—ty) A dying house
Lliwed, *s. f.—pl. t.* ydd (lliw) That pervades; that covers the surface; a multitude, a nation.

> Ac o rodriawg rwyf lliwedydd
> Rodri rad gymryd.——
>
> And from a Rodrian leader of *hosts* Rodri obtains the blessing. *Gwalchmai.*
>
> Boed ef——
> Can lleng engylion, cain lliwed.
>
> Let him be with a host of angels, a *splendid throng.* *Ll. P. Moch.*

Lliwedawr, *s. m.* (lliwed) Multitudes, throngs.

> Cyn noc argyfrain ei waed i lawr,
> Gwerth medd yn neuadd gan lliwedawr,
> Hynaidd Hir ermygir tra fo cerddawr.
>
> Before his blood was sprinkled upon the ground, the price of mead in the hall amongst the *multitudes*, Hynaidd Hir will be celebrated, as long as there shall be a minstrel. *Aneurin.*

Lliwedig, *a.* (lliwed) Being coloured, or dyed.
Lliwedigaeth, *s. m.* (lliwedig) A colouring.

Lliwedd, *s. m.* (lliw) The state of being coloured.
Lliwen, *s. f.—pl. t.* od (lliw) An epithet for a goat
Lliwgar, *a.* (lliw) Having a good colour.
Lliwgarwch, *s. m.* (lliwgar) Goodness of colour.
Lliwiad, *s. m.—pl. t.* au (lliw) A colouring.

> O'i mynediad——
> Gwelir ar lawer galar liwiad.
>
> For her departure, there will be seen upon many the *colour* of mourning. *D. ab Gwilym, m. Angharad.*

Lliwiannawl, *a.* (lliwiant) Staining; stigmatising
Lliwiannu, *v. a.* (lliwiant) To make a stain, to give a colour; to stigmatize.
Lliwiant, *s. m.* (lliw) A stain; a reproach.
Lliwiaw, *v. a.* (lliw) To colour, to give a tint, or hue, to dye; to blush. *Lliwiaw lledrad*, to describe a thing stolen.

> Y lliwydd a'm gwnai'n llawen;
> Lliwyd Duw fi'n wr llwyd hen!
>
> The colourist would make me glad; *may God colour* me a grey old man! *I. Ddu, i'r Gwn Coch.*

Lliwiawg, *a.* (lliw) Having a colour, coloured.
Lliwiawl, *a.* (lliw) Tending to colour, or stain.
Lliwied, *v. a.* (lliw) To stain, to cast a slur, to reproach, to upbraid, to twit.

> Na liwia i neb ei dynged;
> Heb fai nid neb a aned.
>
> Stigmatize no one with his destiny; without a fault no one was born. *Llywarch Hen.*

Lliwiedig, *a.* (lliwiad) Being coloured or stained.
Lliwiog, *s. f.* (lliw) A stainer. *Y lliwiog las*, woad.
Lliwiogi, *v. a.* (lliwiawg) To make to abound with colour; to become coloured, or full of colour.
Lliwion, *s. pl. aggr.* (lliw) A collection of hues.
Lliwionen, *s. f. dim.* (lliwion) A delicately tinted surface; a film.

> Ni bu is coed heb wisg wen;
> Ni bu lwyn heb lliwionen.
>
> Nothing below the wood was without a white robe; there was not a grove without a *finely tinted veil.* *D. ab Gwilym, i'r eira.*

Lliwiwr, *s. m.—pl.* lliwiwyr (lliw—gwr) A colourist, one who colours; a dyer.
Lliwlas, *a.* (lliw—glas) Of a blue colour.
Lliwlasu, *v. a.* (lliwlas) To make of a blue tint.

> Felly——i lyfasu
> Fy'm lliwlasu,
> A'm lliasu,
> Em lliosydd!
>
> Thus to dare to *make me pale*, and to discard me, the jewel o the multitudes! *Ior. ab y Cyriog.*

Lliwlys, *s. m.* (lliw—llys) Woad: *lliwiog las.*
Lliwus, *a.* (lliw) Coloured; of good complexion.
Lliwusaw, *v. a.* (lliwus) To make well coloured.
Lliwusrwydd, *s. m.* (lliwus) Goodness of colour.
Lliwydd, *s. m.—pl. t.* ion (lliw) A colourer, a dyer.
Lliwyddiaeth, *s. m.* (lliwydd) The art of dying.
LLO, *s. m. r.—pl. t.* i. That is thrown out, or ejected, an ejected mass; a calf. *Llo llenad*, a moon calf, or false conception: *Llo meddaf, llew meddi*, I talk of chalk, you talk of cheese. *Colloq.*

> Dangaws y llo, ac na ddangaws y llaeth.
>
> Shew the *calf*, and do not shew the milk. *Adage.*

Llòb, *s. m.—pl. t.* au (llo) An unwieldy lump; a dull fellow, a blockhead.
Llobiad, *s. m.* (llòb) An acting impertinently.
Llobiaw, *v. a.* (llòb) To tease; to be impertinent.
Lloc, *s. f.—pl. t.* iau (lly—oc) A mound; a goal, or mark; a dam, a confined place, a fold.

> Balch y lloc rhag y llifeiriant.
>
> Towering is the dam against the flood. *Cynddelw.*
>
> Breiniawg loc loedir cyfanedd
> Meifod wen; nid meiwyr a'i medd.
>
> Privileged the fold of the common clear land of fair Meivod; it is not possessed by boors. *Cynddelw.*

> Os bwyf yn addef,
> Yn araws y llef,
> Y lloc a arbef,
> Achaswrthl.
>
> If I should be in my dwelling, waiting for the call, the fold will secure a proximity to it. *Meilyr.*

Llociad, *s. m.* (lloc) A making a mound, or dam; a confining, or penting up; a folding.
Llociaw, *v. a.* (lloc) To make a mound, to dam; to pent up; to fold.
Llociawg, *a.* (lloc) Having a mound, or dam; having a fold.
Llociedig, *a.* (lloc) Being mounded, or dammed.
Llociwr, *s. m.—pl.* llociwyr (lloc—gwr) One who makes a mound; one who folds.
Lloches, *s. f.—pl. t.* au (llawch) A covert, a place of safety, a hiding place, a refuge.
Llochesawg, *a.* (lloches) Having a covert or refuge
Llochi, *v. a.* (llawch) To encourage; to protect; to make much of, to fondle.

> Fe a edwyn mab a'i llawch,
> Ac nid edwyn mab a'i car.
>
> A child knows who *fondles* him, and he does not know who loves him. *Adage.*
>
> Bardd Llywelyn hael, byd vm gelwir,
> Anwar fy llachfar oni'm llochir.
>
> The bard of the generous Llywelyn, since I am called, my gleaming wrath is not still if I am not *protected*. *Cynddelw.*

Llochiad, *s. m.—pl.* llochiaid (llawch) One that encourages, a protector, one who makes much of; a fondler.

> Oni ddaw i mewn o'r medd gorau oll,
> Gwirawd o ban, dy ben faddau,
> Ar llaw Foreiddig llochiad cerddau.
>
> If there does not come in of the best of all the mead, a beverage from the goblet, thy head shall answer; let it come to the hand of Moreiddig the *encourager* of songs. *O. Cyfeiliawg.*

Llochiator, *ger.* (llochiad) In encouraging.
Llochitor, *sup.* (llawch) To be encouraging.
Llochle, *s. m.—pl. t.* oedd (llawch—lle) A place of refuge.
Llochwes, *s. f.—pl. t.* au (llawch—gwes) A covert
Llochwyd, *s. m.* (llawch—gwyd) A secret covert.
Llochwydaw, *v. a.* (llochwyd) To seek a covert; to take refuge; to sculk, or lurk about.
Llochwydgi, *s. m.* (llochwyd—ci) A lurking dog.
Llochwydd, *s. m.* (llawch—gwydd) A protecting presence.
Llochwyta, *v. a.* (llochwyd) To lie in a covert, to seek a covert; to lurk, or to hide one's self.
Llod, *s. m.—pl. t.* au (lly—od) That is inert.
Llodedd, *s. m.* (llawd) A state of growing, or shooting out; a state of craving, or want.
Llodes, *s. f.—pl. t.* i (llawd) A girl, a damsel.
Llodi, *v. a.* (llawd) To reach out, to crave.
Llodiad, *s. m.* (llawd) An extending out; a craving, brimming.
Llodig, *a.* (llawd) Having a craving; brimming. *Hwch lodig*, a brimming sow.
Llodigaw, *v. n.* (llodig) To be in a brimming, or craving state.
Llodigiad, *s. m.* (llodig) A being brimming.
Llodigrwydd, *s. m.* (llodig) A brimming state.
Llodineb, *s. m.* (llawd) Lewdness, lechery.
Llodinebus, *a.* (llodineb) Tending to be lewd.
Llodraw, *v. a.* (llawdr) To cover the breech; to bedaggle.
Llodrawg, *a.* (llawdr) Having trowsers, breeched.
Llodreuawg, *a.* (llawdr) Having trowsers.
Llodri, *v. a.* (llawdr) To put on trowsers.
Llodriad, *s. m.* (llawdr) A putting on trowsers.
Llodrwr, *s. m.—pl.* llodrwyr (llawdr—gwr) One who breeches; a breeches-maker.
Llodrydd, *s. m.—pl. t.* ion (llawdr) A breecher.
Llodryn, *s. m. dim.* (llawdr) A little breeches.
Llodw, *a.* (llod) Spirting, or squirting.
Llodwedd, *s. f.—pl. t.* i (llawd—gwedd) A mite.

> Un a bryn, er na bai'r wedd,
> Delw o wydr er dwy lodwedd.
>
> One does buy, though there should be no form, an image of glass for two *mites*. *L. G. Cothi, i'r sygnarbed.*

Llodwy, *s. m.* (llodw) A spirt, or a squirt.

> Herwlong lwyd, nwyd neidr
> Haint glas lodwy, hynt ysgwyeiddr.
>
> A dusky roving ship, having the nature of a snake with the pestilence of the blue *spirt* and the course of a sacrilegious thief. *Rhys Nanmor.*

Lloddawd, *s. m.* (llawdd) The act of soothing, solace
Lloddawg, *a.* (llawdd) Abounding with comfort.
Lloddedig, *a.* (llawdd) Solaced, comforted.
Lloddi, *v. a.* (llawdd) To solace, to comfort, to soothe; to amuse, to please, to delight.

> Cadwallawn, cyn noi golli,
> Nid oedd a lladw y lloddai fi.
>
> Cadwallawn, before he was lost, it was not with ashes that *he would greet* me. *Gwalchmai.*

Lloddiad, *s. m.* (llawdd) A solacing, a soothing.
Lloddiannawl, *a.* (lloddiant) Of a solacing nature.
Lloddiannu, *v. a.* (lloddiant) To render solacing.
Lloddiant, *s. m.* (llawdd) Solace, comfort, cheer.
Lloddwr, *s. m.—pl.* lloddwyr (llawdd—gwr) A solacer, a soother.
Lloedd, *s. m.—pl. t.* ion (lly—oedd) Abundance.
Lloeddawg, *a.* (lloedd) Abundant; rich.
Lloeddi, *v. a.* (lloedd) To make abundant.
Lloeddiant, *s. m.* (lloedd) Abundance, plenty.
Lloeg, *a.* (llo—eg) Having a tendency to open.
Lloegr, *s. f.* (lloeg) That opens or breaks out; that part of ancient Britain, which was inhabited by the *Belgians*, properly speaking; also England, south of the Humber, exclusive of Wales, Cornwall, and Devon; but now it is the popular name for England in general.
Lloegraidd, *a.* (lloegr) After the way of Lloegr.
Lloegrwr, *s. m.—pl.* lloegrwyr (lloegr—gwr) A man of Lloegr, a Lloegrian.
Lloegrwys, *s. pl. aggr.* (lloegr—gwys) The ancient inhabitants of *Lloegr*; the *Lloegrians*: The English, or the inhabitants of modern *Lloegr*, are always called *Saeson*, and never *Lloegrwys* after the name of the country.
Lloer, *s. f.—pl. t.* au (lly—oer) The moon. *Llawn lloer, llawn llaned, llawn lleuad*, the full moon; *hanner lloer*, half moon; *tair lloer*, three moons, or three months; *lloer gànaid*, the shining moon; *fy lloer wèn*, my fair Cynthia; *un a rhyw loeriau arno*, one troubled with some mad fits.

> Y lleuad, pan fo leiaf,
> A1 llai y rhed na lloer haf?
>
> The moon, when it is the least, will it run the less, than the moon of summer? *Ior. Fynglwyd.*

Lloeraidd, *a.* (lloer) Of the nature of the moon.
Lloeran, *s. f.* (lloer) A lunette; a round spot.
Lloerawg, *a.* (lloer) Having the moon's influence.
Lloerawl, *a.* (lloer) Lunar, belonging to the moon.
Lloercen, *s. f.* (lloer—cen) A moon-calf; a dolt: the green and yellow wood-pecker. *Lloercen o ddyn*, a simpleton of a man.
Lloeren, *s. f. dim.—pl. t.* au (lloer) A lunette; a round spot; or circular space.
Lloerenawg, *a.* (lloeren) Having round spots.
Lloerenu, *v. a.* (lloeren) To form round spots; to become covered with ronnd spots.
Lloergan, *s. m.* (lloer—càn) Moonshine, moonlight

> I'w fynnwn a ddiwg
> Uch argel tywyllwg,
> Pan yw calaf can,
> Pan yw nos lloergan?

What fountain breaks out above the covert of darkness when the reed is white, when it is the *moonlight* night! *Taliesin.*

Lloergant, *s. m.* (lloer—cant) The orb of the moon

Cyd archwyf ym llyw y lloergant yn rhodd,
Ef a'm rhydd yn geugant.

Though I should ask of my chief the *lunar orb* as a gift, he will certainly give it me. *Ll. P. Moch, i Lywelyn II.*

Lloergynnydd, *s. m.* (lloer—cynnydd) The moon's increase.
Lloeriad, *s. m.* (lloer) A lunation, a complete revolution of the moon.
Lloerig, *a.* (lloer) Lunatic, influenced by the moon; crack-brained.
Lloerigaw, *v. n.* (lloerig) To become lunatic.
Lloerigiad, *s. m.* (lloerig) A becoming lunatic.
Lloerigen, *s. f. dim.* (lloerig) A female lunatic.
Lloerigrwydd, *s. m.* (lloerig) Lunacy, the state of being influenced by the moon.
Lloerigyn, *s. m. dim.* (lloerig) A male lunatic.
Lloerni, *s. m.* (lloer) The influence of the moon.
Lloes, *s. f.—pl. t.* au (llo—es) That is ejected, or uttered; a sigh, a groan; anguish, pang.
Lloesawg, *a.* (lloes) Having a throwing out; having sighs; having pangs.
Lloesedd, *s. m.* (lloes) A state of throwing out; a state of groaning; languishment.
Lloesi, *v. a.* (lloes) To eject, to throw out, to exhaust; pour out, to utter groans. *Dos i loesi y dwfr hwn*, go and empty this water out.
Lloesiad, *s. m.* (lloes) A throwing out, emptying, or exhausting; exhaustion; a suffering anguish.
Llof, *s. m.—pl. t.* au (llo) A polypus; a kind of excrescence, or disorder, in the cleft of the hoofs of cattle.
Llofan, *s. m.* (llof) That branches or shoots out.
Llofel, *s. m.* (llawf) A coax with the hand.
Llofeliad, *s. m.* (llofel) A stroking, a coaxing.
Llofelu, *v. a.* (llofel) To coax with the hand.

Llofeluch gi chwerw.

You must stroke a surly dog. *Adage.*

Llofen, *s. f.—pl. t.* au (llof) A burbot, a sort of fish; it is also called *Llofenan*.
Llofenan, *s.* (llofen) A fish called a burbot.
Llofi, *v. a.* (llawf) To handle; to reach with the hand; to bestow.

Rodri mawr! rhwym llawr rym llofes!

Great Rodri! the ground binds him *who extended bounty* to me! *Ll. P. Moch.*

Llofiad, *s. m.* (llawf) A handling; a reaching with the hand; a bestowing.
Llofion, *s. pl. aggr.* (llawf) Things picked out by hands.
Lloflen, *s. f.—pl. t.* au (llawf—llen) The grasp.

Lladdai——
Rhudd onen o'i loflen law.

The ruddy ash would kill from his *grasping* hand
Cynddelw, m. I. ab Cedifor.

Gwystlid rhad, llithrid llathreid-rudd lafnawr
O loflen mab Gruffudd.

Grace was pledged, the ruddy glittering blades were glided from the *grasp* of the son of Gruffudd. *Ll. P. Moch.*

Lloflenan, *s. f. dim.* (lloflen) A weasel.
Llofres, *s. f.—pl. t.* au (llawf—rhes) The branching out of the ribs from the breast; the region under the arm.

A'i lyfrau yn ei lofres.

With his books under his *arm*. *Gw. Tew.*

Llofrudd, *a.* (llawf—rhudd) Red-handed; bloody-handed. *s. m.—pl. t.* ion. One who imbrues his hand in blood, a slayer; a murderer.

Dyfrydedd i feirdd farw achludd Einiawn
Dor bredag-lawn, brwysg lofrudd!——
Un llofrudd Prydain, pryderwn ei gerdd;
Pryderus y canwn!

A mournful thing for bards the death covering of Einion, the full and massy bulwark, the overwhelming *slaughterer!* The one *slaughterer* of Britain, we will sadly muse his song; pensively we will sing! *Cynddelw, m. E. ab M. ab Iddon.*

Llofruddiad, *s. m.* (llofrudd) An imbruing the hand in blood; a slaying; a murdering.
Llofruddiaeth, *s. m.* (llofrudd) Homicide; murder
Llofruddiaidd, *a.* (llofrudd) Homicidal, murderous
Llofruddiaw, *v. a.* (llofrudd) To redden the hand, to imbrue the hand in blood; to murder.
Llofruddiawg, *a.* (llofrudd) Homicidal, murderous
Llofruddiedig, *a.* (llofruddiad) Being slaughtered
Llofruddiwr, *s. m.—pl.* llofruddiwyr (llofrudd—gwr) One who reddens his hand; a murderer.
Llofrydd, *a.* (llawf—rhydd) Of unrestrained hand. *s. m.—pl. t.* ion. One of unrestrained hand; a criminal; a felon.
Llofryddiad, *s. m.* (llofrydd) A committing a crime; a committing felony.
Llofryddiaeth, *s. m.* (llofrydd) A felonious act.
Llofryddiaw, *v. a.* (llofrydd) To commit felony.
Llofryddiawg, *a.* (llofrydd) Guilty of felony.
Llofyn, *s. m.—pl. t.* au (llawf) A wisp; a lock, or braid of hair.

Duw a lifodd dy lofyn.

God made thy *braid* to shoot out.
D. ab Gwilym, i walit merch.

Llofynawg, *a.* (llofyn) Having a wisp; having locks of hair.
Lloff, *s. m.—pl. t.* ion (llo) That is strewed.
Lloffa, *s. m.* (lloff) A gleaning, or leaving.
Lloffa, *v. a.* (lloff) To glean, to pick up leavings.
Lloffiad, *s. m.* (lloff) A gleaning, a picking up leavings.
Lloffwr, *s. m.—pl.* lloffwyr (lloff—gwr) A gleaner.
Lloffwraig, *s. f.* (lloff—gwraig) A woman gleaner.
Lloffydd, *s. m.—pl. t.* ion (lloff) A gleaner, leaser.
Lloffyn, *s. m.—pl. t.* au (lloff) Bundle of gleanings
Llog, *s. m.—pl. t.* au (lly—og) That is attached to, an augment; a compact; benefit, service, interest; hire. *Maen llog*, the stone of covenant, or the altar of a bardic circle; also called, *maen cynghrair, maen gorsedd*, and *maen aberth*:—*Llog arian*, interest of money; *llog o dir*, twenty yards of land, or nearly four acres.

Rhag myned un llog o'r ty.

Lest there should one *loan* go out of the house. *Adage.*

Llwm ych llog.

Bare is the ox of *hire*. *Adage.*

Llogail, *s. m.—pl.* llogeillau (llog—ail) The wattled work of the round houses among the ancients, which was also called *cant* and *pared*; a crib, a pen; a fence, wattled with rods to keep the corn floor, in a barn; a wattled partition. *L'ogail y bargod*, the eaves beam, or the beam that receives the rafters.
Llogawd, *s. f.—pl.* llogodau (llog) A space parted off, or a partition; a closet, a private room; a buttery; a pantry; a cupboard; a drawer. *Llogawd eglwys*, a chancel of a church.

Mon——
Llogawd gwin, llygad Gwynedd.

Anglesey, the *repository* for wine, the eye of North Wales.
I. Mon Hen.

Llogawl, *a.* (llog) Relating to a compact; relating to hiring; relating to interest.
Llogedig, *a.* (llog) Being covenanted; hired; borrowed, or lent at interest.

Llogeilwydd, *s. m. aggr.* (llogail—gwydd) The timberwork, or beams that support the eaves of a building.

Llogell, *s. f.—pl. t.* au (llog) An attached receptacle, a depository, or place for holding any thing; a closet; a drawer; a partition in a cabinet; a pocket.

> Llygad y wlad, a'i llogell,
> Llygad y berfedd-wlad hell.
>
> The eye of the country, and its *depository*, the eye of the extensive central country. *Iolo Goch.*

Llogellaid, *s. f.—pl.* llogelleidiau (llogell) The contents of an attached receptacle; a pocket-full

Llogellawg, *a.* (llogell) Having a partitioned receptacle, closet, or drawer; having partitions; having pockets.

Llogellu, *v. a.* (llogell) To closet; to pocket.

Llogi, *v. a.* (llog) To make a compact; to hire, to borrow, or lend, at interest.

Llogiad, *s. m.* (llog) A making a compact; a hiring; a borrowing, or lending, at interest.

Llogwr, *s. m.—pl.* llogwyr (llog—gwr) A covenanter; a hirer; a borrower, or lender.

Llogwrn, *s. m.—pl.* llogyrnod (llog—gwrn) A pigmy; a listless body.

> Dawed a wnaeth——
> Llogwrn lleda-fferth, errth sall,
> O begor, yn rhith bugail.
>
> There came a *squat pigmy*, rather of unsightly form, a chap tottering on his base, in a shepherd's guise. *D. ab Gwilym.*

Llogwydd, *s. m. aggr.* (llog—gwydd) A chancel.

Llogyrnaidd, *a.* (llogwrn) Of a squat pigmy form.

Llòl, *s. f.* (llo) Foolish idle talk, tattle, or prattle.

> Llol oer o fol lwli'r fall;
> Llol sur wrth loew lais arall.
>
> A chilling *peal* from the belly of the lullaby singer of old nick; a sour *peal* another clear voice rejoins.
> *Gr. Hiraethawg, i goth.*

Llolied, *s. m.* (llòl) A babbling, a prattling.

Llolian, *v. a.* (llòl) To babble, to tattle, to prate.

Lloliaw, *v. a.* (llòl) To babble, to talk nonsense.

Lloliwr, *s. m.—pl.* lloliwyr (llòl—gwr) A babbler.

Llolyn, *s. m. dim.* (llòl) A foolish babbler.

Llòm, *a.* (*f. of* llwm) Bare, naked, or exposed.

Llomen, *s. f. dim.* (llòm) A naked female.

Llomi, *v. a.* (llòm) To make bare, or naked.

Llòn, *a.* (lly—on) Expressive of inward satisfaction and pleasure; tranquil; inwardly glad; wistfully pleased: cheerful. *Llygad llòn*, an eye expressive of inward pleasure: *Llòned dy olygon!* how expressive of pleasure thy eyes!

> Nend llòn eos lle troai
> Llafar yw man adar mai'
>
> How *wistfully pleasing* the nightingale where she roves; vocal the small feathered choir of May! *D. ab Gwilym.*

Llonaid, *s. m.* (llawn) The full of any thing, fullness.

> Ni cing mewn llestr onid ei lonaid.
>
> A vessel will contain no more than its *fill*. *Adage.*

Llònaidd, *a.* (llòn) Of a cheerful tendency.

Llònawl, *a.* (llòn) Tending to solace, comfortable

Llònc, *s. f.* (lly—onc) That draws, or sucks in; a gulp, or swallow.

Llonc, *a.* (lly—onc) Tending to draw, or suck in; of a soft nature; mild.

Llòndeb, *s. m.* (llòn) Inward pleasure, or joy.

Llònder, *s. m.* (llòn) Inward joy, cheerfulness.

Llòndra, *s. m.* (llòn) Cheerfulness, ease of mind, placid cheerfulness.

Llònedig, *a.* (llòn) Solaced, comforted, cheered.

Llònedigawl, *a.* (llònedig) Of a cheering tendency

Llònedd, *s. m.* (llòn) Cheerfulness; softness.

Llòneiddiad, *s. m.* (llònaidd) A rendering of a pleasing, or cheerful tendency.

Llòneiddiaw, *v. a.* (llònaidd) To render of a pleasing tendency, to become cheerful.

Llòneiddrwydd, *s. m.* (llònaidd) Cheerfulness, gladness.

Llòni, *v. a.* (llòn) To give inward pleasure; to cheer, to make cheerful; to be wistfully pleased, to feel satisfaction; to be cheerful.

> Fy ngelynion sy'n llòni,
> A chas wedd, o'm herwydd i.
>
> My enemies are *feeling a secret pleasure*, with a hateful countenance, upon my account *W. Middleton.*

Llòniad, *s. m.* (llòn) A giving secret pleasure; a making cheerful; a becoming cheerful.

Llòniannawl, *a.* (llòniant) Of a cheerful tendency

Llòniannu, *v. a.* (llòniant) To turn to an inward satisfaction; to become a secret pleasure.

Llòniant, *s. m.* (llòn) Comfort, solace, heartfelt pleasure; refreshment.

Llòniar, *a.* (llòn) Of a soothing tendency.

Llòniarawl, *a.* (llòniar) Tranquillizing; assuasive.

Lloniariad, *s. m.* (lloniar) A tranquillizing, a solacing, a soothing; a mitigating, or assuaging.

Lloniaru, *v. a.* (lloniar) To tranquillize, to solace, to soothe; to assuage, to mitigate.

Llonw, *s. m.* (llawn) That is made past full.

Llonwaith, *s. m.* (llawn—gwaith) Full work.

Llonweithus, *a.* (llonwaith) Full of work, busy.

Llonwi, *v. a.* (llonw) To render past full.

Llonwch, *s. m.* (llon) Satisfaction, or pleasure.

Llonychawl, *a.* (llonwch) Of a cheering tendency.

Llonychdawd, *s. m.* (llonwch) Placid cheerfulness.

Llonychiad, *s. m.* (llonwch) A yielding inward joy.

Llonychu, *v. a.* (llonwch) To make cheerful; to become cheerful.

Llonydd, *a.* (llawn) At ease, at rest, tranquil, calm.

> O bob ymryson y bydd
> Derfyn llawn drwy fyw'n llonydd.
>
> Of every dispute there will be a complete end by living *quietly*.
> *Ed. Morus.*

Llonyddawg, *a.* (llonydd) Having a quiet nature.

Llonyddawl, *a.* (llonydd) Of a quieting tendency

Llonyddedig, *a.* (llonydd) Being eased, or quieted.

Llonyddedigawl, *a.* (llonyddedig) Tending to quietude; tranquillizing, sedative.

Llonyddiad, *s. m.* (llonydd) A causing to be at ease, a tranquillizing, a calming, a quieting; a becoming quiet.

Llonyddrwydd, *s. m.* (llonydd) A state of quietness

Llonyddu, *v. a.* (llonydd) To tranquillize, to appease, to calm, to quiet; to become quiet.

Llonyddus, *a.* (llonydd) Of a quiet disposition.

Llonydduaw, *v. a.* (llonyddus) To render of a quiet nature; to become of a quiet disposition.

Llonyddwch, *s.* (llonydd) Tranquillity, quietness

> A fynno lonyddwch gofynned genad ei dafawd.
>
> He that would wish for *quietness* let him get permission of his tongue. *Adage.*

Llonyddwr, *s. m.—pl.* llonyddwyr (llonydd—gwr) One who makes quiet, or still; a tranquillizer.

Llong, *s. f.—pl. t.* au (*f. of* llwng) A ship.

> Un o dri maelgyfiawn'd Ynys Prydain. Corfinwr bardd Ceri Hir Lyngwyn, a wnaeth long hwyl a llyw gyntaf i genedl y Cymry.
>
> One of the three good inventors of the isle of Britain: Corfinwr the bard of Ceri of the Long Lake, who first made a ship with sail and rudder, for the nation of the Cymry. *Triads.*
>
> Ceisied pawb ddwfr i'w long
>
> Let every one seek water for his ship. *Adage*

Llong, *a.* (*f. of* llwng) Opening a passage; yawning, swallowing.

Pawb a ddaw i'r ddaear lwng;
Pobl fychain dreuia a drwing!

Every one will come to the *swallowing* earth; men low and miserable will perish! *D. Benfras.*

Llongaid, *s. f.—pl.* llongeidiau (llong) A ship-full.

Llongan, *s. f. dim.* (llong) A small ship, a vessel.

Llongawg, *a.* (llong) Abounding with ships.

Llongawl, *a.* (llong) Pertaining to a ship, naval.

Mwyaf gwraig a garai Gwythlach oedd y forwyn ar fynasai Bran; ac wrth hyny y dorthoedd ef i'w erlid ef; ac yn ddiannod ymladd a wnelynt o longawl frwydr.

The woman most beloved by Gwythlach was the damsel, whom Bran had taken away; and therefore he came to pursue him; and without delay they fought a *naval* battle. *Gr. ab Arthur.*

Llongborth, *s. f.—pl. t.* au (llong—porth) A harbour for ships.

Llongdor, *s. m.* (llong—tor) A shipwreck.

Llongdori, *v. n.* (llongdor) To shipwreck.

Llongdoriad, *s. m.* (llongdor) A shipwrecking.

Llongddrylliad, *s. m.—pl. t.* au (llong—drylliad) A shipwrecking.

Llongddrylliaw, *v. n.* (drylliaw) To shipwreck.

Llongen, *s. f. dim.* (llong) A small ship, a vessel.

Llonggoll, *s. f.* (llong—coll) A loss of ship.

Llonggolli, *v. n.* (llonggoll) To lose a ship.

Llonggolliad, *s. m.* (llonggoll) A losing a ship.

Llongi, *v. a.* (llong) To ship; to go on board a ship.

Wrth longi o honom, i'n llwythesynt a phethau angenrheidiawl.

As we were *going on board the ship,* they loaded us with necessary things. *W. Salisbury, Acts 21.*

Llongiad, *s. m.* (llong) A shipping: a going on board a ship.

Llongiadaeth, *s. m.* (llongiad) Navigation.

Llongiadawl, *a.* (llongiad) Navigating, naval.

Llongiadu, *v. a.* (llongiad) To navigate.

Llongiadwy, *a.* (llongiad) That may be navigated.

Llongig, *s. f. dim.* (llong) A small ship, a vessel.

Llonglwyth, *s. m.—pl. t.* i (llong—llwyth) A ship's cargo, a ship's load.

Llongsaer, *s. m.—pl.* llongseiri (llong—saer) A shipwright, a ship carpenter.

Llongsaeriaeth, *s. m.* (llongsaer) A ship-building.

Llongseirniaeth, *s. m.* (llongsaer) Naval architecture, or ship-building.

Llongwr, *s. m.—pl.* llongwyr (llong—gwr) A shipman; a sailor, a mariner.

Llongwriad, *s. m.* (llongwr) A working a ship.

Llongwriaeth, *s. m.—pl. t.* au (llongwr) Navigation, sailing; seamanship.

Hir longwriaeth i fawdd.

Long *sailing* to him that is to be drowned. *Adage.*

Llongwriaw, *v. a.* (llongwr) To work a ship.

Llongwriawl, *a.* (llongwr) Belonging to a seaman

Llongwystl, *s. m.—pl. t.* on (llong—gwystl) Bottomry.

Llongwystlad, *s. m.* (llongwystl) A charging bottomry upon a ship.

Llongwystlaw, *v. a.* (llongwystl) To charge bottomry upon a ship.

Llop, *s. f.—pl. t.* au (llo) A buskin; a boot.

Llopan, *s. f.—pl. t.* au (llop) A sort of high shoe, a sock.

Llopanau mawr am ei draed.

Great *buskins* on his feet. *H. Pwyll—Mabinogion.*

Lludw hen lopanau sy dda rhag y cig drwg.

The ashes of old *shoes* are good against proud flesh. *Ll. Meddyg.*

Llopanawg, *a.* (llopan) Having buskins.

Llopandrwm, *a.* (llopan—trwm) Heavy-footed.

Llopaniad, *s. m.* (llopan) A wearing buskins.

Llopanu, *v. a.* (llopan) To wear buskins.

Llopanwr, *s. m.—pl.* llopanwyr (llopan—gwr) A buskin maker.

Llopanydd, *s.—pl. t.* ion (llopan) Buskin maker.

Llopawg, *a.* (llop) Having buskins; buskined.

Llor, *s. m.* (lly—or) That stretches out; a bulb.

Lloraid, *s. m.—pl.* lloreidiau (llawr) A floor-full.

Llorf, *s. f.—pl.* llorfau (llor) A pillar, post, or prop; a shank; the shin-bone. *Llorf eneidiau.*

Goronwy—
Ced lorf corf cymmhrain.
Cain Cyfiawnaf.

Goronwy the *pillar* of magnificence to the body of society, splendid and most just. *Gr. ab M. ab Dafydd.*

Llorf, *a.* (*f. of* llwrf) Yielding, falling headlong, timid; a gelding.

Llorfawg, *a.* (llorf) Having a pillar, or shank.

Llorfdant, *s. m.—pl.* llorfdannau (llorf—tant) A string of the octave next to the post, in a harp, a base string.

Llorfedig, *a.* (llorf) Being propped, shanked.

Llorfiad, *s. m.* (llorf) A furnishing with a shank.

Lloriad, *s. m.* (llawr) A flooring, a laying a floor.

Lloriaw, *v. a.* (llawr) To floor, to lay a floor; to fall to the floor, to sink down.

Lloriawg, *a.* (llawr) Having a floor, floored; on the floor, grovelling. *Dyn lloriawg,* a low designing fellow.

Dechreuaf, gweuaf gywydd
It' gnaf lloriawg, wingawg wydd.

I will begin, I will combine a song to thee, thou *grovelling* knave, thou wriggling goose. *Huw Dafydd.*

Lloriedig, *a.* (llawr) Being floored, laid as a floor.

Llorion, *s. pl. aggr.* (llawr) Sweepings; bottoms.

Llorlen, *s. f.—pl. t.* i (llawr—llen) A floor-cloth.

Llorp, *s. f.—pl. t.* au (llor) A shank, or leg. *Llorp car,* the side beam of a drag.

Llorpau gwrach ar ddudfach du.

The *shanks* of a hag on a black crutch. *D. ab Gwilym.*

Llorpawg, *a.* (llorp) Having a shank, shanked.

Llorpiad, *s. m.* (llorp) A furnishing with shanks.

Llorpyn, *s. m. dim.* (llorp) A small shank, or leg.

Llorwydd, *s. pl.* (llawr—gwydd) Laurel-wood.

Llorwydden, *s. f. dim.* (llorwydd) A laurel tree.

Llos, *s. m.* (lly—os) That has a tendency to do or take away; that tends to consume.

Llosg, *s. m.* (llos) A burning, a heat, an inflammation. *Llosg eira, malaith, malerth,* and *penddiged gosi,* the chilblains.

Llosgaberth, *s. m.—pl. t.* au (llosg—aberth) Burnt sacrifice.

Llosgaberthiad, *s. m.* (llosgaberth) An offering burnt sacrifice, a burning sacrifice.

Llosgaberthu, *v. a.* (llosgaberth) To offer burnt sacrifice, to burn sacrifice.

Llosgaberthwr, *s. m.—pl.* llosgaberthwyr (llosgaberth—gwr) One who offers burnt sacrifice.

Llosgach, *s. m.* (llosg) Unnatural lust; incest.

Llosgadwy, *a.* (llosg) That may be burnt or ignited, combustible.

Llosgawg, *a.* (llosg) Abounding with combustion.

Llosgawl, *a.* (llosg) Of a burning quality.

Llosged, *s. m.* (llosg) That is burnt, or calcined.

Llosgedig, *a.* (llosged) Being burnt, scorched.

Llosgedigrwydd, *s. m.* (llosgedig) A burnt state.

Llosgedd, *s. m.* (llosg) A state of combustion.

Llosgen, *s. f.—pl. t.* au (llosg) That inflames; a blister, in pharmacy.

Llosgfa, *s. f.—pl. t.* oedd (llosg) A burnt place.

Llosgfaen, *s. m.* (llosg—maen) Brimstone, sulphur

Llosgfal, *s. f.—pl. t.* oedd (llosg—bal) A volcano.

Llosgfalus, *a.* (llosgfal) Relating to a volcano.

Llosgfeinin, *a.* (llosgfaen) Brimstony, sulphurous.

Llosgi, *v. a.* (llosg) To burn to be burning.

> Gwell y llysg dau etewyn nag un.
>
> Two brands will burn better than one. *Adage.*
>
> Llwyth byd llosgetawr,
> Cyn bỳ [illegible] matwywr.
>
> All that be in the world *will be burning*, though they may not be ashes. *Taliesin, cyrmes dyddbrawd.*

Llosgiad, *s. m.—pl. t.* au (llosg) A burning; combustion, adustion.

Llosgni, *s. m.* (llosg) A burnt state, a burn.

Llosgrach, *s. pl.* (llos—crach) Scabs of the itch.

Llosgwr, *s. m.—pl.* llosgwyr (llosg—gwr) Burner.

Llosgwrn, *s. m.—pl.* llosgyrnau (llos—cwrn) Tail.

> Cuaymdaith ci ei losgwrn.
>
> A dog's companion is his *tail.* *Adage.*
>
> Bilngo y gath hyd ei llosgwrn.
>
> To flay a cat as far as her *tail.* *Adage.*

Llosgwydr, *s. m.—pl. t.* au (llosg—gwydr) A burning-glass.

Llosgwydryn, *s. m.—pl. t.* au (llosg—gwydr) A burning-glass.

Llosgwynt, *s. m.—pl. t.* oedd (llosg—gwynt) A singeing blast.

Llosgyrnawg, *a.* (llosgwrn) Having a tail.

Llost, *s. f.—pl. t.* au (lly—ost) What projects out, a dart, a javelin, a lance; a sting, a tail; the genitals.

Llostawd, *s. m.* (llost) The state of projecting from, the being as a tail or sting.

Llostawdl, *s. f.—pl.* llostodlau (llost—awdl) A kind of metre ending with a verse of different rhyme from what proceeds it. It is also called *Llostodyn.*

Llostawg, *a.* (llost) Having a tail, or trail; also an epithet for a fox.

Llostchwydd, *s. m.* (llost—chwydd) A priapism.

Llosten, *s. f.—pl. t.* i (llost) A tail; the genitals.

Llostfawr, *s. m.* (llost—mawr) A priapus.

Llostgyfod, *s. m.* (llost—cyfod) The satyriasis.

Llostiad, *s. m.—pl.* llostiaid (llost) A forming a tail, a growing into a tail.

Llostiaw, *v. a.* (llost) To form a tail; to tail.

Llostlydan, *s. m.* (llost—llydan) The beaver.

> Tri pheth y dyly y brenin eu gwerth, py dud bynag y lladder: llostlydan, a bela, a charlwm; canys o'u crwyn y gwneir amserwyau i ddillad y brenin:—Gwerth llostlydan chweugaint yw.
>
> Three animals for which the king claims their value, in whatever regions they may be killed: the beaver, and the marten, and the ermine; for of their skins are made edgings for the garments of the king;—the value of a beaver is six-score pence. *Welsh Laws.*

Llostodyn, *s. m.—pl. t.* au (llostawd) One of the fifteen secondary canons of metres, the principle of which consists in having two or more verses rhyming together, with another of different rhyme following them. It is also called, *llostawdl, awdl losgyrniawg, colofn fraith*, and *hypynt.*

Llostrudd, *s. m.* (llost—rhudd) A priapism.

Llostruddyn, *s. m.* (llostrudd) The red tail; the name of a bird.

Llosttrwm, *a.* llost—trwm Heavy-tailed. It is also an epithet for a debilitated person.

LLU, *s. m. r.—pl. t.* oedd. That is all in motion; that darkens that is gloomy; a throng; a multitude, an army, a host. *Llu o adar* a flock of birds *y llu du*, the black host, a name given to some of the northern rovers, who anciently infested the coast of Britain.

> Gwell Duw yn gar no llu y ddaiar.
>
> It is better to have God for a friend than the *host* of the earth. *Adage.*

Lluad, *s. m.* (llu) A being all in motion, a thronging together, a flocking.

Lluadawl, *a.* (llnad) Tending to throng together.

Lluadu, *v. a.* (llnad) To throng, to flock together.

Lluadwn, *s. m.* (llnad) The state of being all in motion a press forward a throng.

> Nid oedd neb a gynhebwn
> A llew trais] pan y treiddiwn,
> Nid oedd llary mor llary mor lluadawn bynt,
> llaodd cyat y cwynwn.
>
> There was nobody that I could compare with the lion of violence, when I might make my way through, there was not a mild one so mild, with such a course of commotion, or then it might be I should have sooner complained. *Cynddelw, m. E. ab M. ab Iddon.*

Lluan, *s. f.* (llu) That glitters or reflects light.

Lluannawl, *a.* (lluant) Tending to reflect light.

Lluannu, *v. a.* (lluant) To reflect light.

Lluant, *s. m.* (llu) A body that reflects light.

Lluarth, *s. f.—pl. t.* au (llu—garth) A camp.

> Bid las llua.th.
>
> Let a *camp* be green. *Llywarch Hen.*

Lluarthiad, *s. m.* (lluarth) A forming a camp.

Lluarthu, *v. a.* (lluarth) To form a camp.

Lluaw, *v. a.* (llu) To throng, to flock together.

Lluawd, *s. m.* (llu) The act of thronging together

Lluawg, *a.* (llu) Thronged; multitudinous.

Lluawl, *a.* (llu) Thronging, or flocking.

Lluaws, *s. f.* (llu—aws) A throng, a multitude.

Lluch, *s. m.—pl. t.* ion (llu) A dart, or sudden throw, a glance; a flash.

Lluch, *a.* (llu) Darting, flizzing, glancing, flashing; of ardent motion.

> Lluchar fy nghleddyf, lluch ei aesawr yn nghad;
> Lleuychedig aur ar fy ysgwyd.
>
> Gleaming my sword, *ardent* of temper in conflict; glittering the gold on my shield. *Gwalchmai.*
>
> ——Uchel fab Owain,
> Echrys par lluchar lluch gyfwyrein gawr
> Lluoedd gawr mawr maddain.
>
> The exalted son of Owain, terribly he bids the gleaming shedder of the combined rising shout of the hosts of the great legions dispensing good. *Cynddelw, i H. ab Owain.*

Lluchdor, *s. m.* (lluch—tor) A glittering surface.

Lluchddawn, *a.* (lluch—dawn) Bounty-scattering

> Llary Elidawn lluchddawn, llochodd feirddion
> Fab Cynon, clod fenwyd.
>
> The mild and bounty-scattering Eluion, bards were cherished by the son of Cynon, of smiling fame. *Cynddelw, m. [illegible] O. Gwynedd.*

Lluched, *s. f.—pl. t.* au (lluch) A gleam lightning. *Ceryg y lluched*, thunder stones; also called *ceryg y cythraul*, and *ceryg y gythreuliec*

> Myned a orug y mab—a chleddyf eurddwrn ar ei glun, a rhagtafa aur iddo, a chroes eurgrwydr arno, a lliw lluched nef ynddi.
>
> The youth departed, with a gold-hilted sword upon his thigh, which had the first part of its blade of gold, and a gold-chased cross upon it, and which glittered with the *lightnings* of heaven. *H. Culhwch—Mabinogion.*

Lluchedawg, *a.* (lluched) Full of lightning.

Lluchedawl, *a.* (lluched) Gleaming like lightning.

Llucheden, *s. f.—pl. t.* au (lluched) A flash of lightning; a fit of fever.

Lluchedenawl, *a.* (llucheden) Like lightning; gleaming, coruscant, glittering, brilliant.

> Bendigwch Ddaw, eich llyw, y llucheden,
> Tywyllwch, llewfer, wybr, ac wybrenau.
>
> Praise ye God, your Lord, ye *lightnings*, darkness, light, air, and firmaments. *D. [illegible]*

Lluchedeniad, *s. m.* (llucheden) The flashing of lightning; a gleaming, coruscation.

Lluchedenu, *v.* (llucheden) To produce flashes.

Lluchediad, *s. m.* (lluched) A gleaming.

Lluchedig, *a.* (lluched) Being made to dart.

Lluchedu, *v. a.* (lluched) To gleam, to lighten.

Llachedyn, *s. m. dim.*(lluched) A gleam, or flash

Lluchfa, *s. f.—pl.* lluchfëydd (lluch) A drift. *Lluchfëydd o eira*, drifts of snow.

Lluchfar, *s. m.* (lluch—bar) Raging wrath.

Anwar fy llachfar oni'm llochir,

My *burning ire* is not still if I am not deprecated. *Cynddelw.*

Lluchfryd, *s. m.—pl. t.* au (lluch—bryd) Ardent passion; a fiery disposition.

Lluchfrys, *s. m.* (lluch—brys) Ardent haste.

Lluchiad, *s. m.—pl. t.* au (lluch) A throwing, flinging, or casting; a pelting; a drifting.

Godwrf llu lluchiad gwrys.

The tumult of a host in the *dealing* of violence. *Cynddelw.*

Detholais fy rhwyf yn rhwydd rad wasgar,
Yn llachar yn lluchiad.

I have chosen my leader freely scattering bounty, a gleaming *darting one*. *Cynddelw, i Wenwynwyn.*

Lluchiaw, *v. a.* (lluch) To throw, to fling, or cast about; to pelt; to drift. *Lluchiaw ceryg*, to throw stones.

Lluchiawl, *a.* (lluch) Throwing, flinging; darting.

Lluchiedig, *a.* (lluchiad) Being thrown, or flung.

Lluchiwr, *s. m.—pl.* lluchwyr (lluch—gwr) A thrower, a flinger; a darter.

Lluchladd, *v. a.* (lluch—lladd) Hastily to cut off.

Ffiam lachlam i luchladd estrawn.

A fiery flame *hastily to cut off* the invader. *Cynddelw.*

Lluchlam, *a.* (lluch—llam) A darting stride.

Lluchlwyd, *a.*(lluch—llwyd) Sprinkled with grey. *Gorwydd penlluchlwyd*, a steed with a head sprinkled with grey.

Lluchochr, *s. m.* (lluch—ochr) The coral.

Lluchryfyg, *s.* (lluch—rhyfyg) Ardent boldness.

Owain——
Cymraith gar llachar, lluchryfyg Arthur.

Owain the social friend, of Arthur's *ardent courage*. *Seifyll Bryf-fwrch.*

Lluchwaew, *s. m.* (lluch—gwaew) A missive dart, a javelin.

Ymafael a orug Ysbaddadan Bencawr yn un o'r tri llachwaew gwenwynig, oedd ach ei law, a'i odif ar eu hol.

Ysbaddaden the Giant leader laid hold of one of the three poisoned *javelins*, which were at his hand, and he cast it after them. *H. Culhwch—Mabinogion.*

Lluchwres, *s. m.* (lluch—gwres) Ardent heat; violent passion.

Llew llachar lluchwres.

A lion of gleaming *violence*. *Ll. P. Moch.*

Lluchynt, *s. m.* (lluch—hynt) A violent onset.

Nycha hen famwydd, drwyn-bant,
Yn dwyn lluchynt i'm hymlid,
Yn greulawn, ac yn llawn llid.

Behold an old mother-goose, with a distorted snout, taking a run, to pursue me, furiously, and full of anger. *D. ab Gwilym.*

Llud, *s. m.—pl. t.* ion (llu—ud) What is essential; pure ore; wealth.

Trengid lud,
Ni threing moliad.

Let *wealth* perish, fame will not perish. *Adage.*

Llud, *a.* (llu—ud) Close, compact, essential.

Cwynaw yn lutaf yn y byd rhag Arianrod.

Complaining *most incessantly* against Arianrod. *H. Math. ab Mathonwy.*

Da Gaepyn warthryn, o Werthrynionwe dud,
Oedd gerdd angod lud Ladin, gyfiawn.

Laudable was the shame-opposing Caepyn, of Gwerthrynion land, who was ready in the accurate song of compact Latin. *Gw. Ddu o Arfon.*

Lludw, *s. m.* (llud) Ashes, or the remains of any thing burnt. *Lludw gwimon*, kelp; *gwrachod lludw*, wood-lice.

Ef gwnaai gwyr lludw, a gwragedd gweddw
Cyn noi angeu.

He would make men in *ashes*, and widowed wives before his death. *Taliesin.*

Lludwad, *s. m.* (lludw) A reducing to ashes.

Lludwaw, *v. a.* (lludw) To reduce to ashes.

A chan llaw lludwaw Llanhuadain.

And with his hand *reducing to ashes* Llanhuadain. *Bin. ab Gwgawn.*

Lludwawg, *a.* (lludw) Abounding with ashes.

Cyfoethawg, lludwawg, nid colledig,
Cadr-lyw yw anlawn dawn diunig.

Wealthy and *having remains* unperishable, the mighty leader he is of just disposition and not selfish. *Meir. ab Iorwerth.*

Lludwawl, *a.* (lludw) Tending to reduce to ashes.

Lludwlyd, *a.* (lludw) Of the nature of ashes.

Lludwlys, *s. m.—pl. t.* iau (lludw—llys) Fleawort.

Lludd, *s. m.—pl. t.* ion (lly—udd) An obstacle, hinderance, obstruction, or let. *Heb ludd, heb wahardd*, without let, without forbiddance.

Lluddadwy, *a.* (lludd) Capable of obstruction.

Lludded, *s. f.—pl. t.* ion (lludd) What is an obstruction; what oppresses; fatigue.

Truan o dynged a dyngid i Lywarch
Ar y nos y ganed:
Hir gnif heb esgor lludded.

A miserable destiny was fated for Llywarch on the night that he was born: a long affliction without a riddance of his *burthen*. *Llywarch Hen.*

Lluddediad, *s. m.* (lludded) Defatigation, a tiring

Lluddedig, *a.* (lludded) Oppressed, fatigued.

Lluddedigaeth, *s. m.* (lluddedig) Defatigation.

Hai how! A oes yma le i luddedig farch fwrw lluddedigaeth oddiwrtho!

Heigh ho! Is there a place here for a tired horse to cast his *burthen* from him! *Areith Gwgon.*

Lluddedigaw, *v. a.* (lluddedig) To fatigue, to tire

Lluddedigawl, *a.* (lluddedig) Fatiguing, tiring.

Lluddedigrwydd, *s. m.* (lluddedig) Weariness.

Lluddedu, *v. a.* (lludded) To cause fatigue; to be fatigued, tired, or wearied. *Ci yn lluddedu*, a dog putting out his tongue, or panting for breath.

Lluddedus, *a.* (lludded) Of a fatiguing tendency.

Lluddfryd, *s. m.* (lludd—bryd) An obstructing mind. *a.* Of an opposing mind.

Doethion lléygion lluddfryd oedd anhawdd.

Wise are the lay people, *with a mind keeping off* a life of pain. *Ein. Wan.*

Lluddiad, *s. m.* (lludd) An obstructing, or hindering; obstruction; prevention, hinderance.

Lluddiannawl, *a.* (lluddiant) Preventional.

Lluddiannu, *v. a.*(lluddiant) To form an obstacle

Lluddiant, *s. m.* (lludd) Obstruction, prevention.

Lluddias, *v. a.* (lludd) To obstruct, to hinder.

A laddo ddyn a'i loew-ddur,
I luddias hoedl, a leddir.

He that kills a man with his shining steel, to *obstruct* the course of life, will be killed. *D. ab Gwilym.*

Lluddiaw, *v. a.* (lludd) To obstruct, to hinder.

Ni ludd anniweirdeb ffawd.

Incontinence *will not obstruct* prosperity. *Adage.*

Y budd a ludd y lludded.

The profit *prevents* the fatigue. *Adage.*

Lluddiawd, *s. m.* (lludd) Obstruction, prevention

Lluddiawl, *a.* (lludd) Intercipient, obstructive.

Lluddiedig, *a.* (lludd) Obstructed, or hindered.

Lluddiwr, *s. m.—pl.* lluddiwyr (lludd—gwr) A hinderer, obstructer, or preventer.

Lluedd, *s. m.* (llu) Warfare, the being in arms.

Lluedda, *v. a.* (lluedd) To wage war.

Yn llew 'ddoedd, berchen llaw dda,
Yn lladd, ac yn lluedda.

A lion was he, possessed of unerring hand, killing and waging war. *Hywel Cilan.*

Llueddawg, *a.* (lluedd) Having a host, bellicose.
Llueddiad, *s. m.* (lluedd) A waging war.
Llueddiaw, *v. a.* (lluedd) To wage war, to war.

> *Gwedi gwybod o Durnus hyny, llueiddiaw a orug am ben cyfoeth Latinus.*
>
> When Turnus was acquainted with that, what he did was *to lead an army* against the dominion of Latinus. *Gr. ab Arthur.*

Llueddwr, *s. m.—pl.* llueddwyr (lluedd—gwr) One who assembles, or arrays an army.
Llueiddiad, *s. m.—pl.* llueiddiaid (lluedd) One who is in warfare.

> Llwyddid Duw'r llueiddiaid tau!
>
> May God prosper thy *warring ones*. *Llywelyn Moel.*

Lluest, *s. m.—pl. t.* au (llu—est) An encampment

> Lluest Cadwallawn ar Dawy;
> Lleiddiad [illegible] yn adwy
> Clodrydd, cresydydd cyfatwy.
>
> The *camp* of Cadwallon on Tawy; he had the hand of slaughter in the breach; spreading was his fame, eagerly seeking the conflict. *Llywarch Hen.*

Lluestai, *s. c.—pl.* lluesteion (lluest) One who is in camp, a campaigner.
Lluestawg, *a.* (lluest) Abounding with camps.
Lluestfa, *s. f.—pl.* lluestfeydd (lluest—ma) A place of encampment.
Lluestiad, *s. m.* (lluest) An encamping, a tenting.
Lluestu, *v. a.* (lluest) To encamp, to pitch tents.

> Pei byw llary Lleision,
> Ni lluestai Wyndid yn mherfedd Edeyrnion.
>
> If the mild one of Lleision were alive, Venedocia *would not encamp* in the midst of Edeyrnion. *Cynddelw, F. ab Maredudd.*

Lluestwr, *s. m.—pl.* lluestwyr (lluest—gwr) One who encamps, a pitcher of tents.
Lluestydd, *s. m.—pl. t.* ion (lluest) Pitcher of tents.
Lluestyn, *s. m. dim.* (lluest) A small encampment
Llug, *s. m.—pl. t.* ion (llu) That breaks, or begins to open; a gleam, an indistinct light a focus, or source of light; a breaking out in blotches, the plague. *Llug y dydd*, the day spring.
Llug, *a.* (llu) Tending to break out, or to open; tending to shoot out, tending to gleam; dawning; partly seeming. *adv.* Partly, in part, half. *Llugoer*, half cold, or lukewarm; *llug feddw*, half drunk.

> Dadolwch teyrn tarw caddug prydfawr,
> Gwyr Prydain rwy gorug,
> O fro Echeidant uchel-grug
> Hyd Wyndryn Llundain, lle clod llug.
>
> The doing homage to the prince, the lotion bull of awful front, the men of Britain will be compelled to, from the region of Echeidant, of lofty peaks, to the White Hill of London, a place of splendid fame. *Ll. P. Moch, i D. ab Owain.*

Llugad, *s. m.* (llug) A breaking out, opening, or dawning; a shooting out, a gleaming.
Llugai, *s. c.—pl.* llugeion (llug) That breaks out, that shoots out, that dawns.
Llugain, *a.* (llug) Teeming with light.
Llugaint, *s. m.* (llug) Plenitude of light; splendour
Llugan, *s. c.* (llug) What glitters, or glares.
Lluganawl, *a.* (llugan) Tending to glitter.
Lluganedd, *s. m.* (llugan) Glitteringness.
Lluganiad, *s. m.* (llugan) A causing to glitter; a polishing; a glittering.
Llugant, *s. m.* (llug) A reflection of light.
Lluganu, *v. a.* (llugan) To cause to reflect light; to cause to glitter; to polish; to glitter, to sparkle. *Lluganu arfau*, to polish arms.
Lluganwr, *s. m.—pl.* lluganwyr (llugan—gwr) A polisher, a furbisher.
Llugas, *s. f.* (llug) A dawning of light.
Llugdwym, *s. m.* (llug—twym) Lukewarmness.
Llugdwymnaw, *v.* (llugdwym) To make lukewarm
Llugdwymyn, *a.* (llugdwym) Lukewarm.

> Os cariad yw'r gorchymyn pena',
> Gwae lugdwymnion y wlad yma!
>
> If love is the chief commandment, woe to the *lukewarm souls* of this country. *Elis Wyn.*

Llugeiniad, *s. m.* (llugain) A glittering.
Llugeiniaw, *v. a.* (llugain) To glitter; to polish.
Llugenydd, *s. m.—pl. t.* ion (llugan) A polisher, a furbisher, or one who makes bright.
Llugfryd, *s. m.—pl. t.* au (llug—bryd) A lukewarm disposition. *a.* Of a lukewarm mind.
Llugfrydedd, *s. m.* (llugfryd) Lukewarmness of mind; inertness of disposition.
Llugiad, *s. m.—pl. t.* au (llug) A breaking out, a shooting out; a gleaming; a dawning.
Llugiannawl, *a.* (llugiant) Glittering, glaring.
Llugiannu, *v. a.* (llugiant) To cause to glitter.
Llugiannus, *a.* (llugiant) Tending to glitter.
Llugiant, *s. m.* (llug) A glittering, a glare.
Lluglawn, *a.* (llug—llawn) Full of light, splendid

> Tywyna'n falch ar galch gaer,
> Yn luglawn, yn oleu-glaer.
>
> Shine proudly on the white wall, *splendidly*, and clearly bright. *D. ab Gwilym, i'r haul.*

Lluglonder, *s. m.* (lluglawn) Fulness of light.
Lluglonedd, *s. m.* (lluglawn) Fulness of light.
Lluglys, *s. m.* (llug—llys) Campion.
Llugorn, *s. m.—pl.* llugyrn (llu—corn) The horn of host; the horn of battle, the clarion of war.
Llugyn, *s. m. dim.* (llug) A beam of light; a gleam
Llugynor, *s. m.* (llu—cynor) The van of an army.

> Corn llugynor Llywelyn;
> Corn gwyd, Gwydyr ai can.
>
> Llywelyn's horn of the *front of battle*; the horn of mischief Gwydyr blows it. *Cynddelw.*

Llum, *s. m.* (lly—um) That shoots up, or ends in a point.
Llumman, *s. m.—pl. t.* au (llum—ban) A banner.

> Meibion Israel a wersyllasant bob un wrth ei lumman ei hun.
>
> The children of Israel encamped every man by his own standard. *Numbers, 2. 2.*
>
> Llumman bryn gwrthwr min bryn.
>
> The *rallying point* of crowd by the edge of the hill. *D. ab Gwilym, i'r Ehedydd.*

Llummanawg, *a.* (llumman) Having a banner.
Llummanbren, *s. m.* (llumman—pren) The staff of a banner, or of a standard.
Llummaniad, *s. m.* (llumman) Rearing a standard
Llummanig, *s. f. dim.* (llumman) A banderol.
Llummanu, *v. a.* (llumman) To rear a standard.
Llummanwr, *s. m.—pl.* llummanwyr (llumman—gwr) A standard-bearer.
Llummanydd, *s. m.—pl. t.* ion (llumman) A standard-bearer.
Llumon, *s. m.—pl. t.* au (llum) A chimney.

> Fy newis ar fy meibion,
> Pan gyrchai [illegible] at elyn,
> Pyll wyn, pwyll mal [illegible] llumon.
>
> My choice of all my sons, when such should attack his foes, is fair Pyll, whose course is like the fire through a *chimney*. *Llywarch Hen.*

Llun, *s. m.—pl. t.* iau (llu—un) A form, shape figure, effigy, image, or picture; the moon *Llun y llong*, the constellation called the great bear. *Pa sut sydd arnat ti?* how is it with you? *Nid oes arnaf fawr o lun.* I am in no great plight, or I am but so so. *Nid oes arnat ti lun yn y byd*, thou hast not the least method in the world. *Deu-lun o feirch*, two heads of horses.

> Ofn ar lwfr ofn ei lun.
>
> The coward is afraid of his *shadow*. *Adag.*

Llundain, *s. f.* (llun—tain) The form or bend of the *Tain*. *Caer Lundain*, or more properly, perhaps, *Llyndain*, the spread of the river *Tain*, the Welsh name for London. It was so called on account of its being situated on a large expanse of the river Thames, or Tain, beginning about Battersea, and including all the present low grounds, on both sides, to Erith; by which place the water ran in a narrow channel, made by its own force through a chain of hills, lying in a transverse direction to the stream: and, it would seem that a memorial of such an event is preserved in the name of the place; for *Erth*, implies a bursting through, or a ruption, and from which *Erith*, the present name differs scarcely nothing in sound. *Caer Ludd*, or the city of Lud, is another name for London; but not often made use of, except in the works of the poets.

Llunedig, *a.* (llun) Being formed, or shaped.

Yn synwyr yn llwyr yn llunedig.

In sense completely *formed*. *Gwalchmai.*

Lluniad, *s. m.—pl. t.* au (llun) A forming.

Lluniadaeth, *s. m.* (lluniad) The art of forming.

Lluniadawl, *a.* (lluniad) Formative.

Lluniadu, *v. a.* (lluniad) To form, to fashion.

Lluniadwy, *a.* (lluniad) Figurable, formable.

Lluniaeth, *s. m.—pl. t.* au (llun) A formation, a form, or figure; imagination; design; providence; regulation, rule, authority.

Dyn yn benaf—
A wnaeth o'r holl luniaethoedd.

Man he made the chief of all *beings of form*. *Dr. S. Cent.*

Trwy luniaeth Duw, ef a ddygwyddodd o olud i dylodi.

Through the *providence* of God, he fell from wealth into poverty. *Ll. G. Hergest.*

Lluniaethad, *s. m.* (lluniaeth) A giving a formation, or construction; a putting in a form.

Lluniaethawl, *a.* (lluniaeth) Of a forming tendency, contributory to form, order or design.

Lluniaethedig, *a.* (lluniaeth) Being made formative; being made to contribute to order.

Lluniaethedd, *s. m.* (lluniaeth) A state of form, order, or design.

Lluniaethiad, *s. m.* (lluniaeth) A giving a formation, a contributing to order, or regulation.

Lluniaethu, *v. a.* (lluniaeth) To put into form.

Gwedi lluniaethu y byddinoedd o bob parth, y Saeson, herwydd eu defawd, yn lew cyrchu a wnaynt, ac ar hyd y dydd yn wrawl gwrthwynebu y Prydeiniaid.

After the *putting in order* of the armies on every side, the Saxons, according to their usual mode, bravely made an attack, and during the whole day manfully opposed the Britons. *Gr. ab Arthur.*

Lluniaethus, *a.* (lluniaeth) Of a forming tendency having an aptitude to form, or order.

Lluniaethwr, *s. m.—pl.* lluniaethwyr (lluniaeth—gwr) One who puts in form, a regulator.

Lluniaidd, *a.* (llun) Of a shape, well-formed, of a good shape, or figure.

Lluniannawl, *a.* (lluniant) Modifying.

Lluniannu, *v. a.* (lluniant) To modify; to model.

Lluniant, *s. m.* (llun) Formation; modulation.

Lluniaw, *v. a.* (llun) To form, to figure, to picture, to fashion, to cut out, or into form; to make the shape of a thing.

Lluniaf wawd yn tyfu yn myd,
Lluniaeth diheuwyd bryd o bryda.

I will compose an eulogy that shall be spreading in the world, the serious design of the mind inspired by the muse. *G. ab M. ab Dafydd.*

Pob modd a luniodd Duw lwyd;
Pob glan i lan a luniwyd.

Every mode of being *was formed* by the adorable God; every fair one for a fair *was formed*. *G. ab I. ab Ll. Fychan.*

Lluniawd, *s. m.* (llun) The act of forming.

Lluniawdr, *s. m.—pl.* lluniodron (lluniawd) One that forms, a constructor.

Lluniawl, *a.* (llun) Formative; forming.

Lluniedig, *a.* (lluniad) Formed, figured, fashioned

Lluniedigaeth, *s. m.—pl. t.* au (lluniedig) Formation, construction.

Lluniedydd, *s. m.—pl. t.* ion (lluniad) A former, a framer, or fashioner; one who puts in form, or order, a delineator, a portrayer.

Lluniedyddawl, *a.* (lluniedydd) Plastic, forming.

Lluniodraeth, *s. m.* (lluniawdr) Organization.

Lluniodru, *v. a.* (lluniawdr) To organize.

Lluniwr, *s. m.—pl.* lluniwyr (llun—gwr) A former, framer, or fashioner; a delineator.

Gwae a ymryson a'i luniwr! Ymryson priddell â phriddellau y ddaiar.

Woe to him who contends with his *maker*! Let the potsherd contend with the potsherds of the earth. *Isaiah* 45. 9.

Lluosawg, *a.* (lluaws) Multitudinous; abundant.

Lluosgar, *a.* (lluaws) Philanthropic; humane.

Gwr gorddig, na's byw llyw lluosgar;
Gwr bwlch ei darian daer-lid y'nghynnl.

A fretful wight, because the chief *loving the multitude* is not alive; a hero with a battered shield of ardent wrath in the conflict. *Bleddyn Fardd, m. D. ab Gruffudd.*

Draig wobyn, aerwyn, arwar,
Drud llaw esgud, lluosgar.

Supreme of princes, panting for conflict, patient, bold with an active hand, and *humane*. *Prydydd Bychan, i M. ab Owain.*

Lluosydd, *s. pl. aggr.* (lluaws) Multitudes, hosts.

Y beddau yn Hirfynydd,
Yn llwyr y gwyr lluosydd:
Bedd Gwrien gwryd y'ngwawd, a Llwyddawg
Fab Lliwelydd.

The graves on the Long Mountain, the multitudes perfectly know: the grave of Gwrien, the hero in song, and Llwyddawg son of Lliwelydd. *Engl. Beddau Milwyr.*

Creded pawb y pair lluosydd
Lluosawg ei ddawn i ddedwydd.

Let all believe that the *multitude* will cause abundant of good to the prudent. *Cynddelw.*

Llur, *s. m.—pl. t.* ion (lly—ur) That is stretched, or extended; a pale livid hue; a gloom.

Llur, *a.* (lly—ur) Being on the stretch, or extended; of a black and blue colour, livid.

Llurgun, *s. m.—pl. t.* oedd (llur—cun) A carcase.

Llurguniad, *s. m.* (llurgun) A mangling.

Llurguniaw, *v. a.* (llurgun) To mangle, to tear.

Llurguniawl, *a.* (llurgun) Making as a carcase; mangling, or tearing.

Llurguniwr, *s. m.—pl.* llurgunwyr (llurgun—gwr) One who tears to pieces, a mangler.

Lluriad, *s. m.—pl. t.* au (llur) A making livid.

Lluriaw, *v. a.* (llur) To make pale, or livid.

Llurs, *s. f.—pl. t.* od (llur) The razor-bill, a sea bird, also called *aderyn du*, and *gwalch y penwaig*.

Llursen, *s. f.—pl.* od (llurs) The razor-bill.

Lluryg, *s. f.—pl. t.* au (llur) A lorica, a coat of mail

Llurygaw, *v. a.* (lluryg) To put on a lorica.

Llurygawg, *a.* (lluryg) Wearing a coat of mail.

O fiafaeth a meddfaeth ydd aethynt
I gynhen llurygogion: nis gwn laith ladgynt.

From the enjoyment of wine and mead they went to the conflict *of those clad in armour*: I know of no slaughter so sudden. *Aneurin.*

Llus, *s. pl. aggr.* (lly—us) Bilberries, bleaberries; *llus y brain*, *llus duon y mynydd*, or *craiglys*, crake-berry.

Cefais un addewid cofus;
Cynnil wen oedd can ael llus.

I obtained one memorable promise; sparing of smiles was she with the eyebrow of *bilberry* hue. *Bedo Brwynllys.*

deer; *llwdn gafr*, a goat; *llwdn gwydd*, a gosling; *llwdn hwch*, a swine; *llwdn dafad*, a sheep, or a beast of the sheep kind; *llwdn y gloch*, a belwether:—*Bwriant eu llydnod*, they bring forth their young ones.

Mal y bo y dyn y bydd ei lwdn.

As a man may be so will be his *offspring*. *Adage.*

Ni adawodd Arthur na dyn na llwdn yn fyw yn y cantref.

Arthur did not leave nor man nor *beast* alive in the district. *Trioedd.*

Llwf, *s. m.—pl.* llyfon (llw) That has aptitude of motion; that may be moved, or sent off; an exclamation; an oath, or solemn attestation.

Llwfr, *s. m.—pl.* llyfrion (llwf) That is apt to run; a timid one, a coward.

Nid ai'n llwfr dan holl ofal.

Thou wilt not become a *timid one* under all the cares. *T. Aled.*

Llwfr, *a.* (llwf) Timid, fearful, cowardly; sottish; spiritless.

Llwff, *s. m.—pl.* llyffiau (lly—wff) A sudden jerk, a leap, a hop; a hobble. *Awn o lwff i lwff*, I went step by step; *dyro un llwff eto*, come, give one step more.

Llwg, *s. m.—pl.* llygon (llw) That is apt to break out, that is bright; that is of a livid hue; any gathering, tumor, botch, or irruption; the scurvy; the rot, in sheep.

Llwg, *a.* (llw) Apt to break or run out; bright; livid; irruptive; scurvy, botchy.

Owain llwg a'i un llygad.

Scurvy Owen with his one eye. *Llawddeu.*

Llwgr, *s. m.—pl.* llygrion (llwg) A diseased part, a corrupt part; a gall, or fret; what is corrupt, spoiled, or damaged; damage; lucre.

O'r pan hêer ŷd, cyfreithlawn yw ei gadw rhag llwgr ysgrubl yni elo i ysgubawr.

From the time that corn is sown it is lawful to keep it from the *damage* of beasts until it goes into the barn. *Welsh Laws.*

Llwm, *a.* (lly—wm) Bare, naked, exposed; destitute; poor.

Llwm o fan a tham o dorth,
Ni cheidw ei wyneb yr gwna gwarth.

Destitute of a place and a bit of bread, such will not keep his countenance if he does what is scandalous. *Adage.*

Llwmbren, *s. m.—pl. t.* au (llwm—pren) Bare timber. *Llwmbrenau odyn*, or *prenau duon*, poles laid over a drying kiln to support the corn.

Llwmglwm, *s. m.—pl.* llwmglymau (llwm—clwm) A hard knot.

A phob un, fal llun llwmglwm,
Sydd yn eu gilydd yn glwm.

And every one, like the form of a *hard knot*, is tied to the other. *Iolo Goch.*

Llwn, *s. m.* (lly—wn) That forms a part.

Llwnc, *s. m.* (lly—wnc) A gulp, a swallow; the gullet.

Llwng, *s. m.* (lly—wng) A gulp, a swallow; the gullet.

Llwpai, *s. f.—pl.* llwpeiod (llwb) A sow. *Sil.*

Llwr, *s. m.* (lly—wr) That tends forward.

Llwrf, *a.* (llwr) Tending forward; tending to go off; timid, easily frightened.

Gnawd i lwrf ei ladd yn ffo.

The fate of the *timid* is to be killed in flight. *Adage.*

Di lwrf y daw i Arfon.

Without being *timorous* may he come to Arvon. *L. Mon.*

Llwrw, *s. m.* (llwr) A direction forwards, a tendency towards; object, respect, or account of a thing. *Cwympi yn llwrw dy ben*, thou wilt fall in the direction of thy head, or, thou wilt fall head foremost: *Yn llwrw ewynau*, on account of actions; *yn llwrw yr amddiffynblaid*, on the part of the defendant: *Ar llwrw*, directly.

Yn llwrw llwyth Dofydd a'n dyd;
Yn llawr, lliwed cawdd, anglawdd anghlyd!

In a *course towards* the elementary mass the Renovator will place us; into the ground, a captive throng, a cold lodging! *Ll. P. Moch.*

Dos heb argywrw ar llwrw o'r lle.

Go without dread on a *forward course* from the place. *Ll. P. Moch.*

Llwrw, *a.* (llwr) Precipitant; forward, towards.

Llwrw, *prep.* (llwr) Forwards, toward, in a direction, with respect to. *adv.* Towards, straight.

Llary Einiawn, llyw llwyrddawn llwrw Nêr;
Llew doeth-lyw, dothyw ei amser.

The mild Einion, a chief completely gifted *from the Lord*; a lion of discreet career, his time is come! *Cynddelw.*

Gwr llwrw llu Lloegrwys dygyfwyn,
Gwr gwrddfau am addfan addwyn.

A man *towards* the host of Loegrians apt to cause its contest; a man ardently loud round the pleasant retreat. *Cynddelw, i'r argl. Rhys.*

Crist Creawdr, llywiawdr llwrw saint,
Cred crefydd cellydd cywrain!

Christ the Creator, the director *towards* the saints, believe my devotion in scientific song. *Bleddyn.*

Llwrw na allawdd gymhell ei fechniaeth.

In respect that he could not compel his suretiship. *Welsh Laws.*

Llwrwg, *s. m.* (llwr) What is precipitated; dross, dregs, or sediment.

Llwry, *s. m.* (llwr) That is towards; provision.

Pan elai dy dad ti i helya,
Llath ar ysgwydd, llwry yn ei law,
Ef gelwy gwn gogyng.

When thy father would go for to hunt, with staff on shoulder, *provisions* in his hand, he would call the well-trained dogs. *Aneurin.*

Llwry, *a.* (llwr) Precipitant; forward, towards. *prep.* Forwards, toward, in a direction, with respect to. *adv.* Towards, straight.

Gan gredu pen llu llwry cyfodi;
Gan holl ddifryd byd o'i boen well,
Pam na faddau brawd!

With believing in the Lord of Hosts *concerning* the resurrection; with the complete redemption of the world by his five wounds; why will not a brother relent! *H. Pedr ab Griffri.*

Llws, *s. m.—pl.* llyson (llw) That separates, or parts from; that shoots off; that is separate, or apart; that is parted off, left, or rejected; what runs from.

Llws mynwr menestr anhefig.

The peat dust *track* of a servitor who has no attendance to do. *Hywel Ystorym, i Addaf Euryeh.*

Llwst, *s. m.* (llws) That is parted off; that runs out as an extremity, or tail; a kennel.

Llwt, *s. m.* (llwd) That is thrown, or ejected.

Llwtra, *s. m.* (llwtr) Slime, or mud.

Llwtrach, *s. m.* (llwtr) Any gelly-like or slippery matter; any slimy stuff.

Llwtr, *s. m.* (llwt) That runs or slips.

Llwth, *s. m.—pl.* llythion (llw—wth) That is glib, or slippery; a gulp, or swallow; greed, greediness. *Llwth yr hufain*, a selfish glutton, who eats up his junkets without sharing them amongst those about him.

Llwth, *a.* (lly—wth) Of a slippery nature; apt to swallow; greedy.

Llwy, *s. f.—pl. t.* au (llw) That serves to reach out; a spoon; a spattle.

Rhaid llwy hir i fwyta gyd a'r diawl.

It is necessary to have a long spoon to eat with the devil. *Adage.*

Llwyaid, *s. f.—pl.* llwyeidiau (llwy) A spoonful.

Llwyar, *s. f.—pl.* llwyerau (llwy) A shovel, a spoon. *Llwyerau olwyn*, the spoons of a water wheel.
Llwyaraid, *s. f.* (llwyar) A shovel-full.
Llwyarn, *s. f.—pl.* llwyerni (llwyar) A spattle; also a trowel.
Llwyarnaid, *s. f.—pl.* llwyarneidiau (llwyarn) As much as stands on a spattle, or trowel.
Llwyarnaid, *s. m.* (llwyarn) A spattling; a trowelling; the using a trowel.
Llwyarnu, *v. a.* (llwyarn) To use a spattle, or to use a trowel.
Llwyarnydd, *s. m.—pl. t.* ion (llwyarn) One who uses a spattle, or trowel.
Llwyaru, *v. a.* (llwyar) To shovel; to spoon.
Llwyaw, *v. a.* (llwy) To spoon, to use a spoon.
Llwyawg, *a.* (llwy) Having a spoon, spooned.
Llwyb, *s. m.* (llw—yb) That tends forward.
Llwybr, *s. m.—pl. t.* au (llwyb) A track, or path. *Llwybr troed*, a foot-path; *cerdded llwybrau ceimion*, to loiter up and down:—*Llwybr Caer Gwdion*, or *Llwybr y mab afradlawn*, popular epithets for the galaxy.

Eled rhyw ei lwybr.
Let kind go its path. — *Adagr.*

Llwyddawdd ei fudd i feirddion, llwybr awen,
Awen prydyddion;
Llwyr ym trallod tromaid gofalon,
Troeigadw hoed hoedlfyr gyfeillion!

His bounty prospered to the bards, *of the course of song*, the poets tuned the lay; I am all oppressed by severe cares, harbouring consuming regret for short-lived companions!
Cynddelw, m. E. ab M. ab Iddon.

Llwybraidd, *a.* (llwybr) Tending to be passable.
Llwybraw, *v. a.* (llwybr) To go a course.

Llawer uchenaid ym rhaid yd re;
Llwybrant, o'm nwyfiant, uch no'r nwyfre;
Neur aread dyfredd yn eu dyfrile.

Many a sigh I have been fated to utter; *they take their course*, from my passion, above the firmament; they proceed as the waters in their course. — *Ll. P. Moch.*

Llwybrawd, *s. m.* (llwybr) Peregrination.

Car llwybrawd anailys.
A road friend is not to be relied upon. — *Catwg.*

Llwybrawg, *a.* (llwbr) Having a path.
Llwybrawl, *a.* (llwybr) Belonging to a path.
Llwybrawr, *s. m.* (llwybr) That forms a path.
Llwybrdir, *s. m.* (llwybr—tir) Travelled ground.
Llwybredd, *s. m.* (llwybr) The state of being passable, passableness.
Llwybreiddiad, *s. m.* (llwybraidd) A making passable; a conducting onward, or expediting.
Llwybreiddiaeth, *s. m.* (llwybraidd) The act of sending onward, a directing onward.

Llwybreiddiaeth ac athrawiaeth ar farddoniaeth.
Direction and instruction for poetry. — *Barddas.*

Llwybreiddiaw, *v. a.* (llwybraidd) To render of an easy passage, to make passable; to expedite, to forward; to direct in the way.
Llwybreiddiawl, *a.* (llwybraidd) Tending to expedite; directory, expediting.
Llwybreiddiwr, *s. m.—pl.* llwybreiddwyr (llwybraidd—gwr) One who puts in the way, or directs.
Llwybriad, *s. m.* (llwybr) A making out a path.
Llwybrwr, *s. m.—pl.* llwybrwyr (llwybr—gwr) One who goes a path; a wayfaring man.
Llwyd, *s. m.—pl. t.* ion (llw—yd) That is diffusive, or universal; an universal hue; a grey colour: a hoary tint. *Llwyd y cwn*, *morddanadl gwyn*, white horehound; *llwyd y ffordd*, common cudweed; *llwyd boneddig*, sea cotton-weed; *llwyd yr eithin*, wood sage; *llwyd y dim*, or *gwyn y merched*, wild tansy; *llwyd y tywod*, the bird called a sanderling.

Llwyd ac ynfyd ni ddygymmydd.
The *hoary one* and the giddy will not agree. — *Adage.*

Llwyd, *a.* (llw—yd) Universally diffused; hoary; grey; pale, wan. *Gwallt llwyd*, grey hair; *caseg llwyd*, a grey mare; *pryf llwyd*, a badger; *papur llwyd*, brown paper; *bara llwyd*, mouldy bread; *gwedd lwyd*, a pale complexion; *gwibed llwydion*, horse flies; *brawd llwyd*, a grey friar.

Llwyd pob hen.
Every old one is *hoary*. — *Adage.*

Llwydaidd, *a.* (llwyd) Somewhat grey, or hoary; of a brownish hue; somewhat pale.
Llwydaw, *v. a.* (llwyd) To make hoary, grey, brown, or pale; to become hoary, or grey; to become brown, to grow pale, to grow mouldy.
Llwydawg, *a.* (llwyd) Having a grey hue.
Llwyd-ddu, *s. m.* (llwyd—du) A greyish black, a raven grey. *a.* Of a greyish black.
Llwyd-dduaw, *v. a.* (llwyd-ddu) To make of a grey black colour.
Llwyd-dduedd, *s. m.* (llwyd-ddu) A greyish blackness.
Llwydedd, *s. m.* (llwyd) Hoariness, greyness, paleness; mouldiness.
Llwydgoch, *s. m.* (llwyd—coch) A russet colour, a greyish red. *a.* Of a russet colour.
Llwydgochedd, *s. m.* (llwydgoch) A redness with a cast of grey, or brown.
Llwydgochi, *v. a.* (llwydgoch) To make of a russet colour, to become of a russet, or a greyish red.
Llwydgochni, *s. m.* (llwydgoch) A greyish redness
Llwydiad, *s. m.* (llwyd) A making grey, brown, or pale, a becoming hoa[illegible], [illegible]y, or brown.
Llwydlas, *s. m.* (llwyd—glas) A greyish blue; the horned poppy.
Llwydlasedd, *s. m.* (llwydlas) A greyish blueness
Llwydlasu, *v. a.* (llwydlas) To make of a greyish blue, to become of a greyish blue.
Llwydlesni, *s. m.* (llwydlas) A greyish blueness.
Llwydlos, *a.* (llwyd—llos) Of a faded grey hue.
Llwydlys, *s. m.* (llwyd—llys) Mugwort.
Llwydni, *s. m.* (llwyd) Hoariness, greyness, paleness; mouldiness, mould.
Llwydrew, *s. m.* (llwyd—rhew) A hoarfrost.
Llwydrewawg, *a.* (llwydrew) Covered with hoar.
Llwydrewi, *v. n.* (llwydrew) To cast a hoarfrost.
Llwydrewiad, *s. m.* (llwydrew) A casting a hoar.
Llwydrewlyd, *a.* (llwydrew) Tending to be rimy.
Llwydwyn, *s. m.* (llwyd—gwyn) A greyish white. *a.* Of a greyish white, drab-coloured.
Llwydwynedd, *s.* (llwydwyn) A grey-whiteness.
Llwydwynu, *v. a.* (llwydwyn) To render of a greyish white, to become of a greyish white.
Llwydyn, *s. m. dim.* (llwyd) That is of a hoary hue. *Llwydyn y ffordd*, the cudweed.
Llwydd, *s. m.* (llw—ydd) Success, prosperity.

Ein hanmorth ei'n ei phorthi;
A'n llwydd yw ei hadwyd hi.

Our want of support is what supports her, and *our good fortune* is her misfortune. — *Gro. Owain.*

Llwyddadwy, *a.* (llwydd) That may be prospered.
Llwyddaw, *v. a.* (llwydd) To cause success, or prosperity, to prosper, to be fortunate.

Ni fyno Duw ni lwydd
What is not pleasing to God *will not prosper*. — *Adage.*

Llwyddid ei gweryd, a'i had
Llwyddid gwir, a thir yn ei threfed;
Llwyddid gwledd, a medd, a meuedd mad!

Her soil *has been prospered*, her corn, and her seed; the law, and the land *have been made to prosper* in her community; the banquet, and the mead, and splendid wealth *have been made to prosper*. *Llywelyn Fardd, i Dewyn.*

Llwyddawd, *s. m.* (llwydd) A prospering.
Llwyddawg, *a.* (llwydd) Having prosperity.
Llwyddawl, *a.* (llwydd) Prosperous, prospering.
Llwyddedig, *a.* (llwydd) Being made prosperous
Llwyddedigaeth, *s. m.*—*pl. t.* au (llwyddedig) The act of prospering; the becoming prosperous.
Llwyddedigaw, *v. a.* (llwyddedig) To render prosperous; to cause to be lucky.
Llwyddedigawl, *a.* (llwyddedig) Of a prospering or fortunate tendency.
Llwyddfawr, *a.* (llwydd—mawr) Of great luck.
Llwyddgar, *a.* (llwydd) Prosperous, successful.
Llwyddgarwch, *s. m.* (llwyddgar) Prosperousness
Llwyddged, *s. f.*—*pl. t.* ion (llwydd—ced) A prospering treasure.
Llwyddiad, *s. m.* (llwydd) A prospering.
Llwyddiannad, *s. m.* (llwyddiant) A prospering.
Llwyddiannaeth, *s. m.* (llwyddiant) The state or act of prospering.
Llwyddiannaidd, *a.* (llwyddiant) Of a prospering tendency, apt to be lucky.
Llwyddiannawg, *a.* (llwyddiant) Prosperous.
Llwyddiannawl, *a.* (llwyddiant) Prospering.
Llwyddiannedd, *s. m.* (llwyddiant) Prosperousness.
Llwyddiannrwydd, *s. m.* (llwyddiant) Prosperousness.
Llwyddiannu, *v. a.* (llwyddiant) To render prosperous, or fortunate; to prosper, to succeed.

Ac oll a wnel gwella 'n wir;
Allaw ddyn a llwyddiennir.

And all that he does will certainly improve; the man of no account *will be made to prosper*. *W. Middleton.*

Llwyddiannus, *a.* (llwyddiant) Prosperous, successful, fortunate, lucky.
Llwyddiannusaidd, *a.* (llwyddiannus) Tending to be prosperous; somewhat fortunate.
Llwyddiannusaw, *v. a.* (llwyddiannus) To render prosperous, or successful.
Llwyddiannusiad, *s. m.* (llwyddiannus) A rendering prosperous; a becoming prosperous.
Llwyddiannusrwydd, *s. m.* (llwyddiannus) A tendency to prosperity; prosperousness.
Llwyddiant, *s. m.*—*pl.* llwyddiannau (llwydd) Prosperity, success, good fortune.

Gwynfydu bydd ganfod bai;
Llwyddiant dyddrwg a'i lladdai.

She is enchanted at finding a fault; the *prosperity* of the innocent would kill her. *Gro. Owain.*

Llwyddiator, *ger.* (llwyddiad) In prospering.
Llwyddineb, *s. m.* (llwydd) Prosperity, success.
Llwydditor, *sup.* (llwydd) To be prospering.
Llwyddus, *a.* (llwydd) Prospering, fortunate.
Llwyddwr, *s. m.*—*pl.* llwyddwyr (llwydd—gwr) One who gives prosperity; one who prospers.
Llwyeidiad, *s. m.* (llwyaid) A taking a spoonful.
Llwyeidiaw, *v. a.* (llwyaid) To take a spoonful.
Llwyf, *s. f.*—*pl. t.* ydd (llwy) A form, a frame; a platform; a loft; the elm.

Pan fo llwyf yn ei blodau, blwyddyn y saith ffrwythlondeb.

When the *elm* is in its blossoms, then is the year of the seven sorts of fruitfulness. *Adage.*

Llwyf, ar ei faranedd,
Nid osgoes troedfedd;
Ef laddai a pherfedd,
A'r eithaf a diwedd.

The *elm*, with his retinue, did not go aside one foot; he would fight with the centre and the flanks, and the rear. *Taliesin.*

Llwyfan, *s. f.*—*pl. t.* au (llwyf) A frame, a platform, a loft; an elm tree. *Llwyfan melin*, the platform or loft of a mill; *llwyfan men*, the frame or body of a cart.
Llwyfanen, *s. f. dim.* (llwyfan) An elm tree.
Llwyfaw, *v. a.* (llwyf) To make a platform.

Llywelyn, ef llosges dy fro;
Llas dy wyr tra llyr tra llwyfo.

Llewelyn, thy country has been consumed with fire; thy men have been slain beyond the tide whilst *it forms a strand*. *Ll. P. Moch.*

Llwyfawg, *a.* (llwyf) Abounding with elms.
Llwyfen, *s. f.*—*pl. t.* au (llwyf) An elm tree.
Llwyfenin, *a.* (llwyfen) Made of elm, of elm.
Llwyfin, *a.* (llwyf) Of elm, belonging to the elm.
Llwyg, *s. m.*—*pl. t.* au (llw—yg) That is turning round, a turn off, a turning aside; the restiveness of a horse; a mite in cheese.
Llwygaw, *v. a.* (llwyg) To move, or turn round; to become restive; to be in a maze.

Gwnaeth Dewi roddi ar hynt
I lygaid fal na lwygynt.

Dewi straightway did cause his eyes to be so that *they should not turn round*. *I. ab R. ab I. Llwyd.*

Llugorn fuost yn llwygaw;
Llygad glas maen cawad gwlaw.

Thou hast been a lamp *going round*; or the blue eye of the rain stone. *Gr. Gryg, i'r lleuer.*

O ddystaw lwygaw, a'th lygad eilwaith
Di a weli bob afrad.

From silently *revolving*, with his eye again he sees every iniquity *W. Middleton, Ps. 11.*

Llwygawl, *a.* (llwyg) Turning round; restive.
Llwygedig, *a.* (llwyg) Being turned; being in a maze; being grown restive.

Crefft ddigrif oedd, myn y crair!
Gusanu dyn gynghanedd—
A lleddfu fy ngwedd heddiw,
Llygad glas llwygedig liw.

It was a pleasant business, by the mass! to kiss the nymph of harmonious speech: and to lengthen my visage to-day, with my blue eye of a changed colour. *D. ab Gwilym.*

Llwygedd, *s. m.* (llwyg) A state of turning round; the state of being in a maze; restiveness.
Llwygiad, *s. m.* (llwyg) A turning round; a being in a maze; a growing restive.
Llwygiannawl, *a.* (llwygiant) Of a turning or changeable tendency; mazy.
Llwygiannu, *v. a.* (llwygiant) To render mazy.
Llwygiant, *s. m.* (llwyg) A turning round.
Llwyglys, *s. m.* (llwyg—llys) Elecampane.
Llwylys, *s. m.* (llwy—llys) The scurvy-grass.
Llwyn, *s. m.*—*pl. t.* i (llw—yn) That is of spontaneous motion; that is quick; that is sudden, or abrupt; a quick turn; a quirk; an encompassing; the loin; a grove, a wood, a bush; *Llwyn y tewlaeth*, great mullein; *llwyn y gyfagwy*, yellow stone crop; *byddarlys*, houseleek: —*Gwraig llwyn a fferth*, a woman of the bush and brake, a harlot; *mab llwyn a fferth*, a bastard: *Llwyn cardotwyr*, *llwyn rheidusion*, beggar's bush.

Goreu llwyn un a'm cysgodo.

The best *bush* is the one that will shelter me. *Adage.*

Llwynaidd, *a.* (llwyn) Of a quick tendency; like a grove.

Ei gwelir fyth, deg lawr fau,
Yn llwynaidd gan berllanau.

It will be ever seen, that fair spot of mine, *seeming like a grove* with orchards. *D. ab Gwilym, i Forgannwg.*

Llwynaw, *v. a.* (llwyn) To endue with apt motion; to quicken; to become a grove.
Llwynawg, *a.* (llwyn) Having a grove; of the grove. *s. m.*—*pl.* Llwynogod. One of the

bush; a fox. ***Tan llwynawg***, **ignis fatuus.**

Ni cheir gan y llwynawg ond ei groen.

There can be had from the *fox* only his skin. *Adage.*

Eisiau llew ydd â llwynawg i'r orsedd.

In the absence of the lion the *fox* will ascend the throne. *Adage.*

Llwynawl, *a.* (llwyn) That is of a quick nature; belonging to a grove.

Llwynhidl, *s. m.* (llwyn—hidl) The three ribbed plantain, also called *ysgelyn-lys, penau y gwyr, dail llwyn y neidr, astyllenlys, ystlynes, llydan y ffordd, llyriad*, and *erllyriad*.

Llwynhidydd, *s. m.* (llwyn—hid) Ribwort plantain.

Llwyniad, *s. m.* (llwyn) A rendering, or becoming of quick turn; a becoming sudden, or abrupt; a producing a grove.

Llwynin, *a.* (llwyn) Of a quick motion; of a sudden nature; tending to turn round, or to encompass; of the grove. *Llai llwynin*, the gloom of the grove.

Llwynogaidd, *a.* (llwynawg) Like a fox, vulpine.

Y llên egwan llwynogaidd,
Cul yn ei blwyf, calon blaidd.

The feeble clerical *like a fox*, that in his parish seems so slim with the heart of a wolf. *Huw Dwn.*

Llwynoges, *s. f.—pl. t.* au (llwynawg) Fox bitch.

Llwynogwydd, *s. f.* (llwynawg—gŵydd) A bergander.

Llwynogyn, *s. m. dim.* (llwynawg) A young fox.

Llwyprad, *s. m.* (llwybr) A making out a path; a taking a course; a direction, or course.

Argoedwys argleidriad—
Diachris carddwys cerdd Forad;
Diechrys llwry llwyrwys llwyprad.

Thou protector of the men of Argoed, naked the song of Morad and banished; void of harm, towards the general assembly is the course. *Cynddelw, i O. Cyfeiliawg.*

Llwypraw, *v. a.* (llwybr) To peregrinate.

Llwyprawd, *s. m.* (llwybr) A forming a path; a peregrination, a going a course; a giving a course or direction.

Per awen, parhau hyd frawd,
Er lles llawr llyw llafnawr llwyprawd.

Sweet muse, permanent till the day of doom, for the benefit of the country, of the leader of the *path* of blades. *Cynddelw, i'r argl. Rhys.*

Llwyr, *a.* (llw—yr) Comprehending or including all; utter, universal, quite, clean, complete. *Yn llwyr*, utterly, wholly altogether, or completely; *Llwyr a chwbl*, wholly and altogether It is used as a prefix in composition.

Gnawd llwyr dal gwedy llwyr dwng.

There is a custom of *complete* satisfaction after *complete* swearing. *Adage.*

Llwyr, *adv.* (llw—yr) By, in following.

Llwyrad, *s. m.* (llwyr) A rendering, or becoming universal, a being complete or whole.

Llwyrallu, *s. m.* (gallu) All power, omnipotence.

Llwyraw, *v. a.* (llwyr) To render universal.

Llwyrawd, *s. m.* (llwyr) A rendering entire.

Llwyrbryn, *s. m.* (pryn) A complete purchase; a complete redemption.

Llwyrbryniad, *s. m.* (llwyrbryn) A fully buying off; a completely redeeming.

Llwyrbrynu, *v. a.* (llwyrbryn) To buy off fully.

Llwyrdeb, *s. m.* (llwyr) Totality, completeness, universality, or entireness.

Llwyrder, *s. m.* (llwyr) Completeness, entireness

Llwyrdranc, *s. m.* (tranc) Complete mortality.

Llwyrdrengu, *v.* (llwyrdranc) To perish quite.

Llwyrdda, *a.* (da) Altogether good.

Llwyrddarfod, *v. n.* (darfod) To finish fully.

Llwyrddawn, *s. m.—pl.* llwyrddoniau (dawn) A perfect gift, or endowment.

Llwyrddifa, *v. n.* (difa) To annihilate entirely.

Llwyrddoniad, *s. m.* (llwyrddawn) A completely gifting; a fully endowing.

Llwyrddoniaw, *v. a.* (llwyrddawn) To gift fully.

Llwyrddrwg, *a.* (drwg) Completely bad, or evil.

Llwyrddull, *s. m.* (dull) A complete manner.

Llwyredd, *s. m.* (llwyr) The state of being totally, entirely, or wholly; totality, universality.

Llwyrfanwl, *a.* (manwl) Perfectly exact.

Llwyrfarw, *v. n.* (marw) To die completely.

Llwyrgael, *v. n.* (cael) To obtain completely.

Llwyrglod, *s. f.* (clod) Universal fame.

Llwyrgof, *s. m.* (cof) A perfect memory.

Llwyrgoll, *s. f.* (coll) A total loss, or privation.

Llwyrgolli, *v. n.* (llwyrgoll) To lose entirely.

Llwyrgred, *s. f.* (crêd) A complete belief.

Llwyrgrededd, *s. m.* (llwyrgred) Implicit belief.

Llwyrgredu, *v.* (llwyrgred) To believe fully.

Llwyrgyrch, *s. m.* (cyrch) A complete meeting.

Llwyrgyrchu, *v. a.* (llwyrgyrch) To meet fully.

Llwyriad, *s. m.* (llwyr) A rendering, or becoming universal, a being complete.

Llwyrles, *s. m.* (llês) Universal benefit.

Llwyrlosg, *s. m.* (llosg) A complete burning.

Llwyrlosgiad, *s. m.* (llwyrlosg) A burning fully.

Llwyrlosgi, *v. a.* (llwyrlosg) To burn fully.

Llwyrnoeth, *a.* (noeth) Perfectly naked.

Llwyrnoethi, *v. a.* (llwyrnoeth) To make quite bare, or naked.

Llwyrnoethiad, *s. m.* (llwyrnoeth) A fully denuding, a making quite naked.

Llwyroddef, *v. n.* (goddef) Wholly to suffer.

Llwyroddef, *s. m.* (goddef) A full sufferance.

Llwyroddefiad, *s. m.* (llwyroddef) A wholly suffering, or permitting.

Llwyrollwng, *v. a.* (gollwng) To loosen fully.

Llwyrollwng, *s. m.* (gollwng) Complete liberation

Llwyrommedd, *v.* (gommedd) Wholly to refuse.

Llwyrommedd, *s. m.* (gommedd) A full refusal.

Llwyrommeddiad, *s. m.* (llwyrommedd) A wholly refusing, or denying.

Llwyrunaw, *v. a.* (unaw) To agree entirely.

Llwyrundeb, *s. m.* (undeb) Perfect unanimity.

Llwyrwad, *s. m.* (gwad) A complete denial.

Llwyrwadiad, *s. m.* (llwyrwad) A fully denying.

Llwyrwadu, *v. a.* (llwyrwad) To deny fully.

Llwyrwael, *a.* (gwael) Completely low, or base.

Llwyrwaeledd, *s. m.* (llwyrwael) Perfect misery.

Llwyrwaith, *s. m.* (gwaith) Complete work.

Llwyrwaith, *adv.* (gwaith) Completely, fully.

Rhwysg goddaith pan llwyrwaith losgo.

Like the progress of a conflagration when it *entirely* consumes. *Llygad Gwr.*

Llwyrwall, *s. m.* (gwall) A complete defect.

Llwyrwalliad, *s. m.* (llwyrwall) A wholly failing.

Llwyrwallu, *v. a.* (llwyrwall) To fail wholly.

Llwyrwan, *a.* (gwan) Completely feeble.

Llwyrwander, *s. m.* (llwyrwan) Perfect weakness.

Llwyrwarth, *s. m.* (gwarth) Complete disgrace.

Llwyrwarthu, *v. a.* (llwyrwarth) To shame or to disgrace completely.

Llwyrwedd, *s. f.* (gwedd) A full appearance.

Llwyrwerth, *s. m.* (gwerth) A full value.

Llwyrwerthu, *v.* (llwyrwerth) To sell entirely.

Llwyrwir, *s. m.* (gwir) The complete truth.

Llwyrwiriaw, *v. a.* (llwyrwir) Wholly to certify.

Llwyrwiw, *a.* (gwiw) Completely excellent.

Llwyrwys, *s. f.—pl. t.* ion (llwyr—gwys) A general convocation; a general invitation; a general summons. *Llwyrwys y deyrnas*, a general assembly or convention of the nation.

> Ambell air, yn mhob llwyrwys,
> Yiyw'r hwn a dd'weto Rhys.

A word now and then of weight, in every *assembly*, is that which Rhys may utter. *L. G. Cothi.*

Llwyrwysaw, *v. a.* (llwyrwys) To cite generally.

Llwyrwysawl, *a.* (llwyrwys) Conventional.

Llwyrwysiad, *s. m.* (llwyrwys) A citing generally, a giving a general summons.

Llwyrwysiaw, *v. a.* (llwyrwys) To cite generally.

Llwyrymarbed, *v. n.* (ymarbed) To refrain entirely, to keep one's self wholly.

Llwyrymarbed, *s. m.* (ymarbed) A wholly abstaining; to keep one's self quite aloof.

Llwyrymattal, *v.* (ymattal) To abstain wholly.

Llwyrymattal, *s. m.* (ymattal) A wholly abstaining

Llwyrymgadw, *v. n.* (ymgadw) Fully to keep one's self, wholly to refrain.

Llwyrymgadw, *s. m.* (ymgadw) A wholly keeping one's self, a wholly abstaining.

Llwyrymgolli, *v. n.* (ymgolli) To lose one's self entirely; to lose mutually all.

Llwyrymgolliad, *s. m.* (ymgolliad) A wholly losing one's self; a mutually losing all.

Llwyrymgrediad, *s. m.* (ymgrediad) A wholly relying mutually.

Llwyrymgredu, *v. n.* (ymgredu) To have perfect reliance mutually.

Llwyrymgroesi, *v. n.* (ymgroesi) Wholly to beware, to be quite careful of avoiding.

Llwyrymguddiaw, *v. a.* (ymguddiaw) To hide one's self entirely.

Llwyrymnoethi, *v. a.* (ymnoethi) To make one's self quite naked; to become quite naked.

Llwyrymollwng, *v. a.* (ymollwng) To disengage one's self entirely.

Llwyrymrannu, *v. n.* (ymrannu) To separate one's self totally; mutually to part fully.

Llwyrymrithiad, *s. m.* (ymrithiad) A completely shewing one's self; an appearing fully.

Llwyrymrithiaw, *v. a.* (ymrithiaw) To make one's self fully apparent.

Llwyrymroddi, *v. n.* (ymroddi) To resign one's self entirely; to become quite resigned.

Llwyrymroddiad, *s. m.* (ymroddiad) Complete self resignation; a giving up one's self entirely.

Llwyrymunaw, *v. n.* (ymunaw) Perfectly to join one's self; to become quite conformable.

Llwyrymwad, *s. m.* (ymwad) Complete self denial

Llwyrymwadu, *v. n.* (llwyrymwad) To deny one's self completely.

Llwys, *a.* (llw—ys) That is cleared, that is cleansed; that is purified; clean, pure, holy.

> ——Ei drwyddaw
> Yn llwys a gym'ral yn llaw.

His borer he would *neatly* take in hand. *Wat. ab Hywel.*

Llwysaidd, *a.* (llwys) Of a clean nature; of a hallowed or sanctified nature.

Llwysaw, *v. a.* (llwys) To make clear, or clean; to purify; to hallow, to sanctify.

Llwysawg, *a.* (llwys) Of a clear or clean nature; cleanly; hallowed.

> Tprue lo!! lo leuawg ei gyffon;
> *Pryf* cloff-droed, 'ym rhoed rhad llwysawg mirain;
> Tenau-goeg elain un gagalawg.

Hie my calves! there is a calf with a lousy tail; a lame-footed animal, that is given me as a present *cleanly* and fair; an empty lean doe with a backside bedaggled. *Madawg Dwygraig.*

Llwysedd, *s. m.* (llwys) A state of cleanness, purity

Llwysiad, *s. m.* (llwys) A making clear, clean, or pure; a hallowing, or sanctifying.

Llwyth, *s. m.—pl. t.* au (llwy) That is sustained, or borne; the inhabitancy of a region, a tribe, or nation; a burthen, or load. *Llwyth llong*, a ship load; *llwyth mèn*, a cart load:—*Pump brenin-llwyth Cymmru*, the five royal tribes of Wales; *pymtheg llwyth Gwynedd*, the fifteen tribes of Gwynedd.

> Llwyth Maen Ceti: neu,
> Llwyth Maen Bryn Ceti.

The *load* of the stone of Ceti. *Adage.*

> Dydd brawd yn aethr yn—
> Llwyth byd yn griddfan.

On the day of doom frightfully the *inhabitancy* of the world will be groaning. *Taliesin.*

Llwythadwy, *a.* (llwyth) That may be loaded.

Llwythaw, *v. a.* (llwyth) To burthen, to load.

Llwythawg, *a.* (llwyth) Having a burthen, loaded.

Llwythawl, *a.* (llwyth) Burthening, loading.

Llwythedig, *a.* (llwyth) Loaded, or burthened.

Llwythfil, *s. m.—pl. t.* od (llwyth—mil) A beast burthen.

Llwythiad, *s. m.* (llwyth) A burthening, a loading.

Llwythwr, *s. m.—pl.* llwythwyr (llwyth—gwr) A burthener, a loader.

Llwythydd, *s. m.—pl. t.* ion (llwyth) A burthener.

Llwywr, *s. m.—pl.* llwywyr (llwy—gwr) Spooner.

LLY, *s. m. r.* That has aptitude to proceed; that extends out; that is multitudinous, various, or manifold; that is manifest. It is used as a prepositive; and in numerous instances it suffers an elision of the *y* when followed by another vowel.

Llyad, *s. m.* (lly) A stretching out; a licking; a lick; a slap, or blow.

Llyarth, *s. f.—pl. t.* au (garth) A gentle rising hill, a smooth slope.

Llyar, *a.* (lly—ar) Of a soft or mild quality.

Llyaru, *v. a.* (llyar) To assuage, to soften.

Llyaw, *v. a.* (lly) To stretch out; to lick.

Llyawl, *a.* (lly) Stretching out; imbative.

Llych, *s. m.* (lly) That is extended, or flat; a lying flat, a covering, a squat; a sudden falling; a place to squat in; a hiding place.

> Gwawl hawl mawl milcant gwych, llych llaweh anant,
> Gwarant glud ffyniant oer-glod ffynnon.

A luminary that claims the praise of a hundred thousand, the *refuge* that receives minstrels, the security of growing prosperity of a fair famed fountain. *Dafydd y Coed, i R. ab I. ab Llywelyn.*

Llychadwy, *a.* (llwch) That may be made dust.

Llychawg, *a.* (llych) Apt to fall flat, or to squat.

Llychawl, *a.* (llych) Lying flat, squatting.

Gwnaeth ef ddyn o ddefnydd dielw—er gwaradwydd i'r cythraul, ac er cythrudd iddo, fod peth priddlyd a thomlyd, *llychawl* megys hwnw, yn meddu y gogoniant y dygwyddai ef o hono.

He formed man out of base material, to the confusion of the devil, and for his affliction, that an earthy and miry thing so *humble* as that, should be possessing the glory, out of which he had fallen. *Elucidarius.*

Llychedig, *a.* (llych) Being extended flat.

Llychedd, *s. m.* (llwch) The state of being dust,

Llychgen, *s. m.* (llwch—cèn) Powdery liverwort.

Llychiad, *s. m.—pl. t.* au (llwch) A dusting, a pulverization, a powdering.

Llychiannawl, *a.* (llychiant) Pulverulent.

Llychiannu, *v. a.* (llychiant) To pulverise.

Llychiannus, *a.* (llychiant) Pulverulent.

Llychiannusaw, *v. a.* (llychiannus) To render pulverulent; to become pulverulent.

Llychiant, *s. m.* (llwch) Pulverulence.

Llychiaw, *v. a.* (llwch) To dust, to reduce to dust.

Llychiawg, *a.* (llwch) Abounding with dust.

Llychiawl, *a.* (llwch) Tending to produce dust.

Llychiedig, *a.* (llychiad) Being dusted, or powdered; being reduced to dust.

Llychineb, *s. m.* (llwch) Dustiness, a dusty state.

Llychlyd, *a.* (llwch) Full of dust, dusty, powdery.

Llychlydaw, *v. a.* (llychlyd) To render dusty; to become dusty.

Llychlydiad, *s. m.* (llychlyd) A making dusty, a growing dusty.

Llychlydrwydd, *s. m.* (llychlyd) Dustiness, a dusty state.

Llychlyn, *s. m.* (llwch—llyn) A gulf; the Baltic sea, also called *Lledlyn*, whence the nations bordering thereon, or the Scandinavians, were called *Llychlynigion*. *Llychlyn y dwfr*, brooklime, also called *y grealys fenyw*, *y glaiarlys*.

> Beth os daw heibiaw, hebom,
> I'r Traeth Coch lynges droch drom—
> Llychlyn a'u bwyeill awchlym?
>
> What if there should come by, on the outside of us, to the Red Wharf, a destructive heavy fleet of the men of Lochlin, with their keen-edged axes! *G. ab I. ab Dafydd.*

Llycho, *v. a.* (llych) To squat, to fall flat, to cover.

> Ffoes yn derwyn——
> Ffoes yn iyrchwyn,
> Mewn llwyn llychwys.
>
> He fled nimbly, he fled as a roebuck, in a grove *he covered*. *Taliesin.*

Llychw, *a.* (llwch) Tending to become mouldy.

Llychwin, *a.* (llychw) Covered with mould; blotted, spotted. *Lliw llychwin*, a mouldy colour.

> A'r holl achau rhy lychwin——
> Ar frys arfau a roesom:
> Arfau ei dad fu raw dom.
>
> And all the pedigrees were too much *covered with mould*, In a hurry arms we gave: the arms of his father were a muck shovel. *S. Tudyr.*

Llychwinad, *s. m.* (llychwin) A rendering, or becoming of a mouldy appearance.

Llychwinaw, *v. a.* (llychwin) To make mouldy; to defile; to make of a brown, or dusky hue; to become mouldy, or covered with mould; to become of a dusky hue.

Llychwinawg, *a.* (llychwin) Of a mouldy state.

Llychwinawl, *a.* (llychwin) Tending to be mouldy.

Llychwinedig, *a.* (llychwin) Become mouldy.

Llychwr, *s. m.* (llych—wr) That spreads along, declines, or flattens; that is overspread, or flat, the twilight.

> O lychwr i lychwr lwthfin.
>
> From *twilight* to *twilight* a craving mouth. *Aneurin.*

Llychwyr, *s. m.—pl. t.* on (llwch—gwyr) The fall or decline of light; the twilight.

Llychydd, *s. m.—pl. t.* ion (llwch) A duster.

Llychyn, *s. m. dim.* (llwch) A particle of dust.

Llyd, *s. m.—pl. t.* oedd (lly—yd) Breadth, extent,

> Tros yr ugeinfed,
> O Alun drefred,
> Llyd waelawd Dyfed
> Ydd eheta.
>
> Over the twentieth, from the region of Alun, the *breadth* of the low land of Dyfed he will fly. *D. Benfras, i Lywelyn II.*

Llydai, *s. m.* (llyd) That widens, or dilates.

Llydaidd, *a.* (llyd) Somewhat broad, or wide.

Llydan, *a.* (lly—tan) Broad, wide, spacious. *Llydan y ffordd*, the broad, or five ribbed plantain.

Llydander, *s. m.* (llydan) Broadness, breadth.

Llydandra, *s. m.* (llydan) Latitude, breadth.

Llydandrem, *s. f.* (llydantrem) Broad-visaged.

Llydandroed, *s. m.* (llydan—troed) A broad foot. *a.* Broad-footed.

Llydanddail, *s. pl.* (llydan—dail) Broad leaves. *a.* Broad-leaved.

Llydanedd, *s. m.* (llydan) Latitude; broadness.

Llydaniad, *s. m.* (llydan) A making broad, dilatation, dispansion, expansion.

Llydanu, *v. a.* (llydan) To expand, or to dilate.

Llydaw, *s. f.* (llyd—aw) That extends along the water; the name of the province of Brittany, or Armorica, in France.

> Cadfan —
> Pan ddaeth o Lydaw, a'r lydu bedydd.
>
> Cadvan—when he arrived from Llydaw, in spreading the faith. *Llywelyn Fardd.*

Llydawg, *a.* (llyd) Having breadth or extent.

Llydawl, *a.* (llyd) Relating to breadth; tending to widen, or to expand.

Llydiad, *s. m.* (llyd) A widening, or expanding.

Llydnaidd, *a.* (llwdn) Animal-like, brutish.

Llydnawg, *a.* (llwdn) Having a young animal.

Llydnawl, *a.* (llwdn) Producing a young animal.

Llydneg, *s. f. dim.* (llwdn) A little female animal.

Llydniad, *s. m.* (llwdn) A casting the young.

Llydnig, *s. f. dim.* (llwdn) A young female animal.

Llydnu, *v. a.* (llwdn) To bring forth young; to cast a foal, to foal.

> A wyddost ti yr amser i eifr gwylltion y creigiau lydnu?
>
> Dost thou know the season for the wild goats of the rocks to *bring forth the young*? *Job 39. 1.*

Llydnyn, *s. m. dim.* (llwdn) A little male animal.

Llydu, *v. a.* (llyd) To make broad, to widen.

Llydw, *s. m.* (llyd) That is contracted.

> Llydw ysgor, ysgwyd byddinau,
> Llid ysgwn asgwn yn gorau
> Li gymryd a'u cyd cyn barau.
>
> *Contracted* the mansion of the shield of armies, the anger that is raised had been better to be depressed, in order to take what will come before the spears. *Cynddelw, dadolwch yr Argl. Rhys.*

> Caffaf cor mawr-naf mawr-nerth, achos llydw
> Handid lled fy marchwe;
> Caffant fyrdd o feirddion eu lles
> O foli Rodri ryodres.
>
> I shall obtain the circle of my great chief of mighty power, a plain of *abundance* let my row yard be spread out; a myriad of bards shall find their benefit from praising Rodri, impatient of restraint. *Ll. P. Moch.*

> Llyma anrheg dda ddeon ei gwyrthiau,
> O lyn allorau efyll seron——
> Llydwawg, gwareddawg, llydw gwerydden.
>
> Behold a goodly gift possessed of miracles divine, of living altars of the fruits of apple-trees, spreading out, of nature mild, the bloom of youths. *G. ab M. ab Dafydd, i'r Grog.*

Llydwad, *s. m.* (llydw) A contracting out; a straitening.

Llydwaidd, *a.* (llydw) Apt to be contracted.

Llydwaw, *v. a.* (llydw) To contract, to straiten.

Llydwawd, *s. m.* (llydw) The act of contracting.

Llydwawg, *a.* (llydw) Having profusion.

> Ner fer, glewder glyw,
> Nerthawg, lydwawg lyw.
>
> A potent lord, a chief of bravery, a leader powerful and curbing. *G. ab M. ab Dafydd, i D. ab Gormwy.*

Llydwawl, *a.* (llydw) Tending to contract.

Llydwedd, *s. m.* (llydw) A contracted state.

Llydd, *s. m.* (lly—ydd) That is spread, diffused, expanded, or poured out.

Llyddad, *s. m.* (llydd) A diffusing, or pouring out.

Llyddaidd, *a.* (llydd) Somewhat spreading.

Llyddain, *a.* (llydd) Of a diffusive tendency.

Llyddaw, *v. a.* (llydd) To spread, to diffuse, to expand, to pour out.

Llyddiad, *s. m.* (llydd) A diffusing, a pouring out.

Llyddiant, *s. m.* (llydd) A diffusion, a pouring out

Llyddu, *v. a.* (llydd) To spread, diffuse or pour.

Llyddus, *a.* (llydd) Diffusive, apt to pour out.

Llyddusaw, *v. a.* (llyddus) To render diffusive.

Llyddusrwydd, *s. m.* (llyddus) Diffusiveness.

Llyer, *s. m.* (lly—er) That is sharp or crisp.

Llyerw, *a.* (llyer) Subtile, fine, nice, delicate.

> Llywelyn lyerw frelenin,
> Llary ddefawd, llyw gwyrddrawd gwydrin.
>
> Llewelyn a king *of delicate conduct*, of manners mild, the ruler of the green tumult of glasses. *Elidr Sais.*

Llyest, *s. m.—pl. t.* oedd (lly—est) A polypus.

Llyf, *s. m.—pl. t.* ion (lly) A stretching out; a lick with the tongue, a lap.

Llyfadwy, *a.* (llyf) That may be licked.

Llyfal, *s. m.* (mal) That tends to an uniformity.

Llyfan, *s. f.—pl. t.* au (llyf) A string, a rope.

Llyfanawg, *a.* (llyfan) Full of strings; stringy. *s. f.* The hairweed, or crowsilk; also called *llinwydd.*

Llyfandafawd, *s. m.* (llyfan—tafawd) A disorder in cattle, wherein the stomach is inflated; also called *llyfanwst, clwyf y llyfant,* and *gwaith y pryf.*

Llyfanen, *s. f. dim.* (llyfan) A small cord.

Llyfaniad, *s. m.* (llyfan) A binding, a cording.

Llyfant, *s. m.* (llyfan) A binding, or stricture. *Clwyf y llyfant,* the hide-bound disease.

Llyfantws, *s. m.* (llyfant) The burst-cow, a small scarlet-coloured fly.

Llyfanu, *v. a.* (llyfan) To bind, or to whip round.

Llyfanwst, *s. m.* (llyfan—gwst) The hide-bound disease in cattle.

Llyfas, *s. m.* (mas) A venture, or an attempt.

Llyfasawl, *a.* (llyfas) Venturesome, daring.

Llyfasedd, *s. m.* (llyfas) Venturesomeness.

Llyfasiad, *s. m.* (llyfas) A venturing, a daring.

Llyfasu, *v. a.* (llyfas) To dare, or to attempt.

> Oians, parchellan, oedd raid myned
> Rhag cynyddion Mordal, pei llyfased,
> Rhag dyfod erlid arnamni, a'n gweled;
> Ac or diangwn, ni chwynwn ein lludded;
> A mi ddysgoganaf rhag ton nawfed.
>
> Listen, little pig, it were necessary to go, for fear of the huntsmen of Mordal, if it *could be ventured,* lest a pursuit should come upon us, and that we should be seen: and if we escape, I should not complain of our fatigue; And I shall predict standing before the ninth wave. *Myrddin.*

Llyfasus, *a.* (llyfas) Venturing, adventurous.

Llyfasusaw, *v. a.* (llyfasus) To render daring, venturesome, or presuming; to become daring

Llyfaswr, *s. m.—pl.* llyfaswyr (llyfas—gwr) One who dares, or attempts; an adventurer.

Llyfawl, *a.* (llyf) Stretching out in a stripe; licking; lambative.

Llyfeb, *s. f.—pl. t.* ion (llwf) The act of swearing, or affirming, juration.

Llyfedig, *a.* (llyf) Being licked, or lapped.

Llyfelawg, *a.* (llyfal) Having a conformity.

Llyfeliad, *s. m.—pl. t.* au (llyfal) A contriving, a reducing to a conformity, a levelling.

Llyfelu, *v. a.* (llyfal) To devise, to invent, to contrive; to guess; to render of a mean uniformity; to reduce to a level. *Llyfelu tîr,* to make land all alike, or level.

> Mewn dyfalgerdd y dylid cyflawn gyffelybu, nodweddu, llyfelu, cyfleaw, ac amseru pob peth, herwydd hanfod ac anianwdd.
>
> In a descriptive piece, it is necessary with exactness to compare, to allude, *to make uniform,* to place, and to time every thing, according to circumstance and nature. *Beraddas.*

Llyfelus, *a.* (llyfal) Being made uniform.

Llyfelusaw, *v. a.* (llyfelus) To make uniform.

Llyfelusiad, *s. m.* (llyfelus) A making level.

Llyfelusrwydd, *s. m.* (llyfelus) Uniformness.

Llyfelwr, *s. m.—pl.* llyfelwyr (llyfal—gwr) One who contrives; a leveller.

Llyfelydd, *s. m.—pl. t.* ion (llyfal) One who makes uniform; one who levels.

Llyfen, *s. f.—pl. t.* au (llyf) The loin.

Llyfenawg, *a.* (llyfen) Belonging to the loins.

Llyfenawl, *a.* (llyfen) Belonging to the loins.

Llyfenwy, *s. m.* (llyfan) Saxifrage.

Llyferth, *s. m.—pl. t.* ion (merth) That is stretched out; an exhausted state; weariness.

Llyferthaidd, *a.* (llyferth) Somewhat exhausted.

Llyferthawg, *a.* (llyferth) Having weariness.

Llyferthawl, *a.* (llyferth) Wearisome tiring.

Llyferthedd, *s. m.* (llyferth) Wearisomeness.

Llyferthiad, *s. m.* (llyferth) A fatiguing, wearying, or tiring; a becoming wearied.

Llyferthiant, *s. m.* (llyferth) Defatigation.

Llyferthin, *a.* (llyferth) Being exhausted, tired.

> Dychyferfydd trwch â thrin;
> Bogid a fo llyferthin.
>
> The forward will be falling in with squabbles; let him that is *worn down* escape. *Llefoed.*

Llyferthineb, *s. m.* (llyferthin) Wearisomeness.

Llyferthrwydd, *s. m.* (llyferth) Tiredness.

Llyferthu, *v. a.* (llyferth) To bring down with fatigue; to be fatigued, or wearied; to loll out the tongue, as a dog, in panting for breath.

Llyferthus, *a.* (llyferth) Wearisome, tiresome.

Llyferthusaw, *v. a.* (llyferthus) To render wearisome, or fatiguing; to become tiresome.

Llyferthusrwydd, *s. m.* (llyferthus) Weariness.

Llyferthwr, *s. m.—pl.* llyferthwyr (llyferth—gwr) One who wearies, or exhausts with fatigue.

Llyferthydd, *s. m.—pl. t.* ion (llyferth) A wearier.

Llyfesig, *a.* (llyfas) Being grown adventurous.

> Trymfryd byd bod tan Saeson,
> Wedi treisyat gynt ar y goron:
> Trydeydd rhyfedd llwfr llyfasigion.
>
> It is a lamentable state to be under the Saxons, after they should have formerly taken the crown by violence: It is a third wonder to see the dastardly *daring ones.* *D. Benfras.*

Llyfi, *s. m.* (llyf) That is slimy; snivel.

Llyfiad, *s. m.—pl. t.* au (llyf) A licking.

Llyfiaidd, *a.* (llyfi) Snivelly, or snivelling.

Llyfiaw, *v. a.* (llyfi) To produce snivel.

Llyfiawl, *a.* (llyfi) Snivelling; slovenly.

Llyfieiddiad, *s. m.* (llyfiaidd) A rendering snivelly

Llyfieiddiaw, *v. a.* (llyfiaidd) To render snivelly; to produce snivel; to become snivelly.

Llyfieiddrwydd, *s. m.* (llyfiaidd) Snivelliness.

Llyfn, *a.* (llyfn) Smooth, even, level; sleek.

> Ni bydd neb llyfn heb ei anaf.
>
> There is nothing *smooth* without its blemish. *Adage.*

Llyfnâad, *s. m.* (llyfn) A smoothing, a making sleek, glossy, or slippery.

Llyfnâawl, *a.* (llyfn) Tending to make smooth.

Llyfnâu, *v. a.* (llyfn) To make smooth, or sleek, to smooth; to plane; to polish.

Llyfnâwr, *s. m.—pl.* llyfnâwyr (llyfnâu—gwr) One who makes smooth, or sleek.

Llyfnder, *s. m.* (llyfn) Smoothness, sleekness.

Llyfndra, *s. m.* (llyfn) Smoothness, sleekness.

Llyfnedig, *a.* (llyfn) Being made smooth.

Llyfnedigaeth, *s. m.* (llyfnedig) A smoothing.

Llyfnedd, *s. m.* (llyfn) Smoothness, sleekness.

Llyfnèydd, *s. m.—pl. t.* ion (llyfnâu) A smoother

Llyfniad, *s. m.—pl. t.* au (llyfn) A making smooth, even, or level; a harrowing.

Llyfniedydd, *s. m.—pl. t.* ion (llyfniad) One who makes smooth, even, or of level surface; a harrower.

Llyfnu, *v. a.* (llyfn) To make smooth, or level; to harrow.

Llyfnwr, *s. m.—pl.* llyfnwyr (llyfn—gwr) One who makes smooth; a harrower.

Llyfnydd, *s. m.—pl. t.* ion (llyfn) One who makes smooth, or of even surface, a harrower.

Llyfr, *s. m.—pl.* llyfrau (llwf) A book.

> Goreu cof, cof llyfr.
>
> The best record is the record of *book.* *Adage.*

Llyfr mawr [illegible] [illegible].

A great book is a great dunghill. *Adage.*

Mawr yw rhinlad llyfrau llên;
[illegible] Duw [illegible] [illegible] [illegible].

[illegible] are the treasures of the learned books; by God's will, not less the muse's store. *G. Ll. ab D. ab Einion.*

Llyfr, *s. m.* (llyf) What is dragged along. *Llyfr car, the car*, that part of a drag, which is on the ground.

Llyfrâad, *s. m.* (llwfr) A rendering timorous, dejected, or spiritless; a becoming heartless.

Llyfrâawl, *a.* (llwfr) Tending to make timid.

Llyfrai, *s. c.—pl.* llyfreion (llyfr) A booker.

Llyfraidd, *a.* (llwfr) Somewhat timorous.

Llyfran, *s. m. dim.* (llyfr) A little book.

Llyfrâu, *v. a.* (llwfr) To render timid, dejected, or spiritless, to become timorous.

Llyfrawg, *a.* (llyfr) Abounding with books.

Llyfrawl, *a.* (llyfr) Belonging to books.

Llyfrbryf, *s. m.—pl. t.* od (llyfr—pryf) A book-worm.

Llyfrdeb, *s. m.* (llwfr) Timidity, cowardliness.

Llyfrder, *s. m.* (llwfr) Faint-heartedness, timidity, cowardliness.

Ni [illegible] [illegible] llyfrder [illegible] lleith;
Engid [illegible] o'i gyfarwaith.

The escape of cowardice will not protect from death; let the brave escape by his boldness of action. *Llyford.*

Llyfrdra, *s. m.* (llwfr) Aptness to run off, timidity, cowardice.

Llyfrdy, *s. m.—pl. t.* au (llyfr—tŷ) A library.

Llyfredd, *s. m.* (llwfr) Timidness, cowardice.

Llyfrgell, *s. f.—pl. t.* oedd (llyfr—cell) A library.

Llyfrgloer, *s. m.—pl. t.* au (llyfr—cloer) A bookcase.

Llyfriad, *s. m.* (llyfr) A booking, a putting in a book.

Llyfrith, *a.* (brith) Eruptive, pimpled.

Llyfrithaw, *v.* (llyfrith) To break out as a rash.

Llyfrithawg, *a.* (llyfrith) Having an eruption.

Llyfrithawl, *a.* (llyfrith) Erupturient.

Llyfrithen, *s. f. dim.* (llyfrith) A pimple.

Llyfrithiad, *s. m.* (llyfrith) A breaking out as a rash, an eruption of pimples.

Llyfrithiant, *s. m.* (llyfrith) Eruption, a rash.

Llyfrothen, *s. f.—pl. t.* od (brothen) A water-snake, a gudgeon.

Gwell yw dal llyfrothen na cholli bach.

It is better to catch a water-snake than to lose a book. *Adage.*

Llyfru, *v. a.* (llyfr) To put in a book, to book.

Llyfrwerthwr, *s. m.—pl.* llyfrwerthwyr (llyfr—gwerthwr) A bookseller.

Llyfrwerthydd, *s. m.—pl. t.* ion (llyfr—gwerthydd) A bookseller.

Llyfrwr, *s. m.—pl.* llyfrwyr (llyfr—gwr) A bookman, a booker, a librarian.

Llyfrydd, *s. m.—pl. t.* ion (llyfr) A booker.

Llyfryn, *s. m. dim.* (llyfr) A little book.

Llyfu, *v. a.* (llyf) To lick with the tongue.

Llyfid y ci y [illegible] [illegible] ag [illegible]: neu,
Y ci a lyfa yr arf y brather ag e.

The dog is wont *to lick* the spear with which he shall be wounded: or,

The dog *will lick* the weapon with which he is wounded. *Adage.*

[illegible] wyr [illegible] pa [illegible] [illegible].

The cat knows what [illegible] she *licks.* *Adage.*

Llyfwr, *s. m.—pl.* llyfwyr (llyf—gwr) One who licks, a licker.

Llyfwraig, *s. f.—pl.* llyfwreigedd (llyf—gwraig) One who licks, a licker.

Llyffan, *s. m.—pl. t.* od (llwff) A hopper; the frog species; also called *llyffant*. *Llyffan melyn*, the common frog; *llyffan du*, and *llyffan dafadenawg*, the toad.

Llyffan du gafaw,
Cant ewin arnaw.

A black sprawling *toad*, with a hundred warts upon it. *Taliesin.*

Mal llyffan y [illegible] [illegible] cor.

Like a *toad* he clogs in a chair. *Ph. Brydydd.*

Llyffanaidd, *a.* (llyffan) Hopping like a frog.

Llyffanawg, *a.* (llyffan) Full of hopping.

Llyffaniad, *s. m.* (llyffan) A hopping as a frog.

Llyffant, *s. m.—pl.* llyffaint (llyffan) The act of hopping; the frog species; also called *llyffan*. *Llyffant y mor*, and *morlyffant*, a frog-fish; *llyffant aradr*, a part of a plough so called; *llyffant carn march*, the frog in a horse's hoof.

Diffaith llyffant dan iâ.

The confinement of a *frog* under ice. *Adage.*

Llyffantaidd, *a.* (llyffant) Hopping like a frog.

Llyffantu, *v. a.* (llyffant) To hop like a frog.

Llyffanu, *v. a.* (llyffan) To hop as a frog.

Llyffeth, *s. f.* (llwff) A springing up, or hopping.

Llyffethar, *s. f.—pl.* llyffetheiriau (llyffeth) The fetlock-joint; also a clog put on the fetlock.

Llyffetheiriad, *s. m.* (llyffethar) A putting a clog or shackle on the leg of a horse.

Llyffetheiriaw, *v. a.* (llyffethar) To clog, or to tie the fetlock, to shackle.

Llyffetheiriawg, *a.* (llyffethar) Having a clog or shackle on the fetlock.

Llyffetheiriawl, *a.* (llyffethar) Clogging the fetlock.

Llyffetheiriedig, *a.* (llyffetheiriad) Being clogged by the fetlock.

Llyffetheiriwr, *s. m.—pl.* llyffetheirwyr (llyffethar—gwr) One who clogs the fetlock.

Llyffethr, *s. f.* (llyffeth) The fetlock-joint.

[illegible] o [illegible] ei [illegible] [illegible]
A [illegible] y o'r llyffethr.

From the fall of his short back a span and a yard of length the *fetlock joint* begins. *Iorwerth Teu, i farch.*

Llyg, *s. m.—pl. t.* od (lly—yg) A mouse; the shrew, or field mouse.

Llygad, *s. m.—pl.* llygaid (llwg) The eyesight, the eye. *Llygad yn llygad*, face to face; *llygad drwg*, an evil eye; *llygad y goleuni*, the eye of the light; *llygad yr haul*, the full sunshine; *llygad y tan*, the middle of the fire; *llygad y ffynnon*, the issue of a spring; *llygad y berw*, the middle of the boiling: *Dyn yn llygad ei amser*, a person in the prime of his life:—*Llygad yr ych*, the purr, or sea lark; *llygad myharen*, a limpet:—*Llygad y dydd*, or *swynfri*, a daisy; *llygad Ebrill*, *llygad dyniawed*, and *bronwst*, pilewort; *llygad yr ych*, ox-eye; *llygad y gyg-arnog*, marsh cinquefoil; *llygad y cythraul*, common red poppy, *llygad y ci*, couch grass, also called *llygad y cythraul*.

Llygad Duw ar adnau.

The *eye* of God is upon a pledge. *Adage.*

Llygadawg, *a.* (llygad) Abounding with eyes; being goggle-eyed.

Llygadawl, *a.* (llygad) Belonging to the eyes.

Llygadball, *s. m.* (llygad—pall) Failure of sight. *a.* Having a failure of sight.

Llygadbwl, *a.* (llygad—pwl) Dull of sight.

Llygad-draws, *a.* (llygad—traws) Squint-eyed.

Llygad-dyn, *s. m.* (llygad—tyn) A bewitching.

Llygad-dynawl, *a.* (llygad-tyn) Bewitching.

Llygad-dyniad, *s. m.* (llygad-dyn) A bewitching.

Llygad-dynu, *v. a.* (llygad-dyn) To fascinate.

Pwy a'ch llygad-dynodd chwi.

Who has *bewitched* you. *Galat.* 3. 1.

Llygad-ddu, *a.* (llygad—du) Of black eye.

Llygaden, *s. f. dim.* (llygad) A glance of light.

Llygadfrith, *a.* (llygad—brith) Wall-eyed.

Llygadgall, *a.* (llygad—call) Having the eye turned outward, a squinting outwardly.

Llygadgam, *a.* (llygad—cam) Of a winking eye.

Llygadgamiad, *s. m.* (llygadgam) A winking.

Llygadgamu, *v. a.* (llygadgam) To wink the eye.

Llygadglaf, *a.* (llygad—claf) Having a sore eye.

Llygadgoch, *a.* (llygad—coch) Red-eyed.

Llygadgochni, *s. m.* (llygadgoch) Blear-eyedness.

Llygadgoll, *a.* (llygad—coll) Having lost an eye.

Llygadgraff, *a.* (llygad—craff) Keen-eyed.

Llygadgraffedd, *s.* (llygadgraff) Sharp-sightedness

Llygadlaith, *a.* (llygad—llaith) Having a wet eye.

Llygadlas, *a.* (llygad—glas) Having a blue eye.

Llygadlon, *a.* (llygad—llon) Having a merry eye.

Llygadloni, *v. n.* (llygadlon) To be merry-eyed.

Llygadlwyd, *a.* (llygad—llwyd) Grey-eyed.

Llygadlym, *a.* (llygad—llym) Keen-eyed: the celandine; also called *llygadlys*, and *llym y llygad*.

Llygadlys, *s. m.* (llygad—llys) Celandine.

Llygadronc, *a.* (llygad—rhonc) Of a hollow eye.

Llygadronca, *a.* (llygadronc) Hollow-eyed.

Llygadroth, *a.* (llygad—rhoth) Wide-eyed.

Llygadrudd, *a.* (llygad—rhudd) Having a red eye.

Llygadrwth, *a.* (llygad—rhwth) Wide-eyed.

Llygadrydd, *a.* (llygad—rhydd) Of unrestrained eye; felonious.

Llygadrydd, cylus am ladd, neu losg, neu ledrad.

Felonious, that is guilty of murder, or arson, or theft. *Welsh Laws.*

Llygadryddiad, *s. m.* (llygadrydd) A leaving the eye at liberty; a committing felony.

Llygadryddiaeth, *s. m.* (llygadrydd) The act of giving liberty to the eye; a felonious act.

Llygadrythiad, *s. m.* (llygadrwth) A staring.

Llygadrythu, *v. a.* (llygadrwth) To stare, to gaze.

Gwae finnau a'm baddo! pa fodd y diangant, a hwythau yn llygadrythu byth ar y peth sydd yn eu dallu fwyfwy.

Ah, woe is me and mine! how sh ll they escape, and they continually *gazing* upon what is blinding them more and more. *Ellis Wynn, B. Cwsg.*

Llygadrythus, *a.* (llygadrwth) Staring, gazing.

Efe a ddaeth, nid mewn rhodres oddi allan i dynu llygaid y gwerinos llygadrythus ar ei ol—Mab y dyn a ddaeth, nid i'w wasanaethu, ond i wasanaethu ereill.

He came, not in outward pomp to draw the eyes of the *staring* multitude after him: The Son of Man came, not to be ministered unto, but to minister unto others. *Ier. Owain.*

Llygadrythwr, *s. m.—pl.* llygadrythwyr (llygadrwth—gwr) A starer, a gazer.

Llygadrythyn, *s. m. dim.* (llygadrwth) A starer.

Llygadwib, *s. f.* (llygad—gwib) The roving or turning about of the eye. *a.* Having a roving eye.

Llygadwibiaw, *v. a.* (llygadwib) To turn the eye about; to roll the eye.

Llygadwlyb, *a.* (llygad—gwlyb) Of a moist eye.

Llygadwyr, *a.* (llygad—gwyr) Squint eyed.

Llygadwyrni, *s. m.* (llygadwyr) Squint-eyedness.

Llygaeron, *s. pl. aggr.* (llyg—aeron) Cranberries; also called *llyged eirian*, *llygeirin*, and *ceirioes y waen*.

Llygas, *s. m.* (llwg) Splendour, light, shining.

Llygaw, *v. a.* (llwg) To cast a splendour.

Llygawl, *a.* (llwg) Tending to break out, or to brighten; having bright or livid spots; scurvical

that is full of puddles; a bog. *Llyged aeron*, bogberries.

Llyged, *s. f.* (llwg) That breaks out in spots;

Llygedig, *a.* (llwg) Being made bright, or livid.

Llygedyn, *s. m. dim.* (llygad) A glance of light. *Llygedyn haul*, the partial appearance of the sun in cloudy weather.

Llygeid-ddu, *a.* (llygad—du) Having black eyes.

Llygeidiawg, *a.* (llygad) Having eyes; full of eyes

Llygeidyn, *s. m. dim.* (llygad) A glance of light.

Llygeirin, *s. pl. aggr.* (llwg—eirin) Bogberries.

Llygliw, *s. m.* (llyg—lliw) A dusky hue, a mouse colour. *a.* Of a mouse colour.

Llygod, *s. pl. aggr.* (llyg) Mice. *Llygod bach*, mice; *llygod ffreinig*, rats.

Llygoden, *s. f. dim.* (llygod) The mouse species; a mouse. *Llygoden ffreinig*, *llygoden ffrengig*, a rat; *llygoden y dwfr*, the water rat; *llygoden goch*, the field mouse; *llygoden y derw*, *lleian*, or *penloyn*, the blue titmouse.

Dadleu mawr mynych, ac engi ar lygoden.

Great and frequent disputes, and lo, a *mouse* brought forth. *Adage.*

Llygorn, *s. m.—pl.* llygyrn (llwg—orn) A lamp, a lanthorn. *Dau lygorn nef*, *haul a lleuad*, the two lamps of heaven, the sun and moon.

Delw ydd ym, yn ddiwnwrysen
Am lygyrn, am gyrn, am gelnion!

How we are, void of contention, round *lamps*, round horns, and round delicacies! *Cynddelw.*

Llygota, *v. a.* (llygod) To catch mice, to mouse.

Llygotai, *s. c.—pl.* llygoteion (llygota) A mouser.

Llygotwr, *s. m.—pl.* llygotwyr (llygod—gwr) A mouse-catcher, a mouser.

Llygotwraig, *s. f.—pl.* llygotwreigedd (llygod—gwraig) A mouse-catcher, a mouser.

Llygrad, *s. m.* (llwgr) A corrupting; a spoiling.

Llygradwy, *a.* (llygrad) Corruptible; damageable.

Llygrair, *s. m.—pl.* llygreiriau (llwgr—gair) A corrupt word, a barbarism.

Llygrawd, *s. m.* (llwgr) A dissolution of parts; corruption; spoliation; adulteration.

Llygrawg, *a.* (llwgr) Abounding with corruption.

Llygrawl, *a.* (llwgr) Corruptive, corrupting.

Llygrawr, *s. m.* (llwgr) That causes corruption.

Llygredig, *a.* (llygrad) Corrupted, depraved.

Llygredigaeth, *s. m.—pl. t.* au (llygredig) A dissolution of parts; corruption.

Llygredigaethu, *v. a.* (llygredigaeth) To turn to corruption, to cause corruption.

Llygredigaw, *v. a.* (llygredig) To render corrupted

Llygredigawl, *a.* (llygredig) Dissolvent, corruptive, of a corrupting tendency.

Llygredigrwydd, *s. m.* (llygredig) Corruptedness.

Llygredd, *s. m.* (llwgr) Corruptedness; depravity.

Llygriad, *s. m.* (llwgr) A dissolving of parts; a corrupting; corruption, depravation; adulteration; contagion.

Nid ecina——
Y grawn ni llygru unwaith;
Ac un llygriad â hadyd
Yw dynion balchion y byd.

The grain will not shoot out unless it once becomes corrupted; and of similar *corruption* with seed corn are the proud men of the world. *T. Aled.*

Llygriaith, *s. f.—pl.* llygrieithoedd (llwgr—iaith) Corrupt speech, a barbarism.

Llygroldeb, *s. m.* (llygrawl) Corruptibility.

Llygrolder, *s. m.* (llygrawl) Corruptedness.

Llygrolrwydd, *s. m.* (llygrawl) Corruptibleness.

Llygru, *v. a.* (llwgr) To corrupt, to pollute, to mar, to spoil; to gall, to fret.

A lygrwys Ddaw a lygrwys ddyn.

He that *has profaned* God *has profaned* man. *Adage.*

Tair cenedl a lygrasant a fu ganddynt ar ddysg o farddoniaeth beirdd Ynys Prydain, drwy gymysg olerbwyll, ac o hyny ai collasant: y Gwyddelod, Cymry Llydaw, ac yr Ellmyn.

Three nations *corrupted* what they had been taught of the *bardism* of the bards of the Isle of Britain, by the mixture of idle notions, and therefore they lost it: the Gwyddelian tribe, the Cymbri of Llydaw, and the Germans. *Barddas.*

Llygrwr, *s. m.—pl.* llygrwyr (llwgr—gwr) A corrupter, a polluter, a spoiler.

Llygu, *v. a.* (llwg) To make bright, to clear; to break on : to appear in spots.

Llygwyn, *s. m.* (llwg—gwyn) The orache: *llygwyn drewlyd*, stinking goose-foot.

Llym, *s. m.—pl. t.* ion (lly—ym) What is sharp, keen, or quick. *Llym y llygad, y ddilwydd felen*, celandine.

Llym, *a.* (lly—ym) Penetrating, subtile, quick, keen, sharp, rigorous, severe, rigid. It is used as a prefix in composition.

Gauaf gyd llyry llym llywid llongau.

When winter *overspreads sharp* the steering of ships. *Adage.*

Hardd blodau eithin, eithr yn mhlith drain llymion y tyfant.

Beautiful the blossoms of furze, but they grow amongst *sharp* prickles. *Adage.*

Llyma, *v. imper.* (lly—ma) Lo here, behold.

Ammodais a thydi ddarostwng Caswallawn, a goresgyn Ynys Prydain wrth dy gynghor di. Llyma hyny gwedy rygwneuthur: Llyma Gaswallawn yn ddarostyngedig: Llyma Ynys Prydain, o'm cynorthwy i gwedy i goresgyn.

I covenanted with thee subdue Caswallon, and to bring the Isle of Britain subject to thy control. *Behold* that fully accomplished: *Behold* the Isle of Britain, through my assistance, subjugated. *Gr. ab Arthur.*

Llymâad, *s. m.* (llym) A rendering keen, sharp, or pungent; a becoming sharp; a making, or becoming bare.

Llymâawl, *a.* (llym) Tending to sharpen; tending to make bare.

Llymaid, *s. m.—pl.* llymeidiau (llym) That is taken up sharply; as much liquid as is taken at one supping; a sup.

Llymaidd, *a.* (llwm) Somewhat bare, or naked.

Llymain, *a.* (llym) Of a keen quality.

Llyman *s. c.—pl.* od (llym) One that is sharp, or severe one that is stark, or quite. *Llyman noeth*, a stark naked one.

Llyman, *v. imper.* (lly—man) Lo here, behold.

Llymant, *s. m.* (llyman) The act of prying.

Llymanta, *v. a.* (llymant) To pry about; to perform magic tricks and charms for bringing spirits to an interview; to practise any branch of the occult science.

Llymarch, *s. f.—pl.* llymeirch (llym—arch) Oyster

Llymast, *s. f.* (llym—gast) A naked bitch.

Llymâu, *v. a.* (llym) To make penetrating, keen, or severe; to sharpen, to whet; to quicken.

Llymarchen, *s. f. dim.* (llymarch) An oyster.

Llymawg, *a.* (llwm) Being bare, or naked.

Llymawl, *a.* (llwm) Tending to make bare.

Llymbren, *s. m.—pl. t.* au (llwm—pren) Bare wood. *Llymbrenau odyn*, kiln spars.

Llymbwyll, *s. m.* (llym—pwyll) Acute sense.

Llymder, *s. m.* (llym) Keenness, sharpness, severity, acuteness.

Llymder, *s. m.* (llwm) Bareness, nakedness.

Llymdost, *a.* (llym—tost) Acrimonious.

Llymdostedd, *s. m.* (llymdost) Acrimony; severity

Llymdostrwydd, *s. m.* (llymdost) Acrimoniousness

Llymdra, *s. m.* (llym) Sharpness, or keenness.

Llymdra, *s. m.* (llwm) Bareness, nakedness.

Llymddoeth, *a.* (llym—doeth) Keenly-wise.

Llymddreiniog, *s.* (llym—drain) Prickly bog-rush

Llymddyn, *a.* (llym—dyn) A sharper, a sharp one

Llymedig, *a.* (llym) Being made sharp, or keen.

Llymedr, *s. m.* (llym) That tends to sharpen.

Llymedras, *s. f.* (llymedr) A whetstone; a hone.

Llymedd, *s. m.* (llym) Keenness, sharpness.

Llymeidfwyd, *s. m.* (llymaid—bwyd) Spoonmeat; the sow-thistle.

Llymeidiad, *s. m.* (llymaid) A supping, or sipping.

Llymeidiaw, *v. a.* (llymaid) To sip, to sup.

Llymeidiawl, *a.* (llymaid) That may be supped.

Llymeidyn, *s. m. dim.* (llymaid) A single sup.

Llymeiddiad, *s. m.* (llymaidd) A rendering, or becoming somewhat bare.

Llymeiddiaw, *v. a.* (llymaidd) To render somewhat bare; to become rather bare.

Llymeitai, *s. c.—pl.* llymeiteion (llymaid) One that sips often; a bibber, a tippler.

Llymeitia, *v. a.* (llymaid) To be sipping often.

Llymeitian, *v. a.* (llymaid) To sip often.

Llymeitiaw, *v. a.* (llymaid) To take sips.

Llymeitiwr, *s. m.—pl.* llymeitwyr (llymaid—gwr) One who sips continually; a tippler.

Llymes, *s. f.* (llom) One that is bare, or naked.

Llymesg, *s. c.* (llwm) That is not covered. *a.* Having no cover; unsaddled.

Llymest, *s. c.* (llwm) That has nothing on. *a.* Having nothing on. *Ceffyl llymest*, a horse without a saddle.

Llymfrwyn, *s. pl. aggr.* (llym—brwyn) Great sharp sea-rush.

Llymgi, *s. m.—pl.* llymgwn (llwm—ci) A naked dog, a poor dog; a sorry fellow.

Llymgïaidd, *a.* (llymgi) Like a sorry dog.

Llymgoes, *s. f.—pl. t.* au (llom—coes) A bare leg. *a.* Bare legged.

Llymgoesawg, *a.* (llymgoes) Having bare legs.

Llymhun, *s. f.* (llym—hun) A fainting fit.

Llymhunaw, *v. a.* (llymhun) To faint away.

Llymhunig, *a.* (llymhun) Tending to faint.

Llymhurt, *a.* (llym—hurt) Stark mad, distracted.

Llymhurtiad, *s. m.* (llymhurt) A distracting, a driving stark mad; a becoming distracted.

Llymhurtiaw, *v. a.* (llymhurt) To render stark mad, to distract, to stupify; to become distracted, or stupified.

Llymhurtiawl, *a.* (llymhurt) Distracting.

Llymiad, *s. m.* (llwm) A making bare, or naked.

Llymiaw, *v. a.* (llwm) To make bare; to become bare; to become destitute.

Llymin, *a.* (llym) Of a sharp or keen quality.

Llyminawd, *s. m.* (llymin) The act of making keen, sharp, or intense.

Llyminawg, *a.* (llymin) Very keen, sharp, or intense. *Bwyta yn llyminawg*, to eat with a keen appetite; *gwna fe yn llyminawg*, do it with spirit.

Cleddyf llech fflawg iddaw rhoddyrid;
Ac yn llaw llyminawg ydd edewid.

A brightly *gleaming* sword to him was brought, and in a *violent* hand it left. *Taliesin.*

Llymlais, *s. m.—pl.* llymleisiau (llym—llais) A shrill or sharp voice.

Llymleisiad *s. m.* (llymlais) The uttering a shrill or sharp voice.

Llymleisiaw, *v.* (llymlais) To utter a shrill voice.

Llymleisiawg, *a.* (llymlais) Having a shrill voice.

Llymnoeth, *a.* (llym—noeth) Stark naked.

Llymongl, *s. f.—pl. t.* au (llym—ongl) Acute angle

Llymonglaidd, *a.* (llymongl) Of an acute angular form.

Llymonglawg, *a.* (llymongl) Having acute angles

Llymongli, *v. a.* (llymongl) To form an acute angle.
Llymongliad, *s. m.* (llymongl) A forming an acute angle.
Llymr, *s. m.* (llym) That is of a harsh, raw, or crude quality.
Llymri, *s. m.* (llymr) A sharp, or quick quality.
Llymrïad, *s. m.—pl.* llymrïaid (llymri) Sand-fish, or sand-eel.
Llymrïaden, *s. f. dim.* (llymrïad) A sand-eel.
Llymrïeitia, *v. a.* (llymrïad) To catch sand-eels.
Llymrien, *s. f.* (llymri) A sand-fish, a sand-eel.
Llymrïod, *s. pl.* (llymri) Sand-fish, sand-eels.
Llymrig, *a.* (llymr) Crude, raw, or harsh.
Llymrigedd, *s. m.* (llymrig) Crudity, rawness.
Llymrigrwydd, *s. m.* (llymrig) Crudeness.
Llymrawd, *s. m.* (llymr—awd) Washbrew.
Llymrwydd, *s. m.* (llym) Sharpness, or keenness.
Llymry, *s. m.* (llymr) Washbrew, sings, or flummery; a kind of food made of oatmeal steeped in water until it has turned sour, which is then strained and boiled, to a proper thickness, to be eaten with milk, or other liquid.
Llymsain, *s. f.—pl.* llymseiniau (llym—sain) An acute accent, an acute tone.
Llymseiniad, *s. m.* (llymsain) A sounding acutely
Llymseiniaw, *v. a.* (llymsain) To sound acutely.
Llymsi, *s. m.* (llym) A sharp fickle motion. *a.* Of a sharp fickle motion; random; clumsy.

> Lle bo'r gamfa fwya fach,
> Llymsi fyddaf yn llamsach.
>
> Where there is the lowest and smallest stile, I shall be *clumsy* in hobbling over. *I. Brydydd Hir.*

Llymu, *v. a.* (llym) To make keen, sharp, or quick; to render subtile, or pungent; to become sharp, quick, or subtile.
Llymun, *s. m.* (llym) One that is sharp. *Noeth lymun*, a stark naked one.
Llymus, *a.* (llym) Of a keen, sharp, quick, or subtile quality.

> Y bore, pan ddelont i'r maes, a gwelad eu gelynion yn arfawg, a'r gwaewyr yn llymus—ofnant.
>
> In the morning, when they come into the field, and see their enemies in arms, and the spears *sharply pointed*, they shall tremble. *Damegion.*

Llymusaw, *v. a.* (llymus) To render of a sharp, or quick quality; to become sharp, or pungent
Llymusrwydd, *s. m.* (llymus) Keenness, sharpness, or subtileness of quality.
Llymwas, *s. m.* (llym—gwas) A sharper.
Llymwydd, *s. pl. aggr.* (llwm—gwydd) Kiln spars, or kiln ribs; also called *prenau odyn*, and *prenïau duon*.
Llymwydd, *s. pl. aggr.* (llwm—gwŷdd) Sharp wood, or spars; wooden spears.
Llymwydden, *s. f.* (llymwydd) A pointed spar of wood; a wooden spear.
Llymwst, *s. m.* (llym) A quick or violent drive.
Llymyn, *s. m. dim.* (llym) One that is sharp, keen, quick, or subtile.
Llymysten, *s. f.—pl. t.* od (llymwst) A sparrow-hawk; otherwise called *gwalches*, *gwepia*, *cudyll*, *cudyll coch*, *ciryll*, *ciryll y gwynt*, *pilan*, and *llemysten*.

> Y llymysten, freithwen frig,
> A llwyth adain llithiedig.
>
> The *sparrow-hawk*, of white variegated crest, with the load of a wing well trained to the lure. *T. Prys.*

Llymystr, *s. m.* (llymwst) That is of sharp, or subtile nature.
Llymystryn, *s. m.* (llymystr) A tough strip of any thing; a grim lank figure.

Llyn, *s. m.—pl. t.* oedd (lly) That proceeds, that is in motion, or that flows; liquor, juice, or humour; a lake, pool, or pond. *Llyn afalau*, the juice of apples, or cyder; *llyn y llygad*, the humour of the eye; *llyn y bustl*, bile; *llyn y cymalau*, the mucilage of the joints.

> Dyro lyn i ddoeth ef fydd ddoethach.
>
> Give *liquor* to the wise and he will be wiser. *Adage.*
>
> Goreu un llyn gwin; goreu un diawd dwfr.
>
> The best of any one *liquor* is wine; the best of any one drink is water. *Cadw Ddoeth.*

Llyn, *s. m.* (lly—yn) A proceeding, or going on, a passing from. *Yn llyn*, thus.

> Gwedi rhàna Cymmru yn llyn.
>
> After dividing Wales *thus*. *B. Tywysogion Dyfed.*

Llyn, *a.* (lly—yn) Proceeding, or going on. *Haint llyn*, a contagious distemper, or pestilence. *Yn llyn*, in such a manner, in this manner; *dywedyd yn llyn*, to speak thus; *ei osod allan yn llyn*, to set it forth in this manner. *Sil.*
Llyna, *v. a.* (llyn) To tipple, to boose, to guzzle.
Llyna, *v. imper.* (llŷn) Lo there, behold there, there; behold.
Llynaidd, *a.* (llyn) Of the quality of liquid.
Llynan, *s. f.* (llwn) A part, or particle; a proceed
Llynawl, *a.* (llŷn) Belonging to liquid; humoral.
Llynawr, *a.* (llŷn) Generating liquid; generating humours; abounding with humour.
Llyncawl, *a.* (llwnc) Tending to swallow.
Llyncfawr, *a.* (llwnc) Of a great swallow.
Llynciad, *s. m.* (llwnc) A swallowing, a devouring
Llynclyn, *s. m.—pl. t.* oedd (llwnc—llyn) Vortex
Llynclynawg, *a.* (llynclyn) Abounding with vortexes, or whirlpools.
Llyncoes, *s. m.* (llŷn—coes) The spavin.
Llyncu, *v. a.* (llwnc) To swallow; to devour.
Llyncwr, *s. m.—pl.* llyncwyr (llwnc—gwr) A swallower; a devourer.
Llynddail, *s. pl. aggr.* (llyn—dail) Pondweed; also called *llynwlydd*.
Llynedig, *a.* (llŷn) Being formed into a liquid; generated as an humour; filled with liquor.
Llynedigaeth, *s. m.* (llynedig) The formation of liquid; a generation of humour; a filling with liquor.
Llynedd, *s. m.* (llyn) A state or period that has proceeded; a complete course, or period; the preceding year. *Er y llynedd*, since the last year.
Llyneiddiad, *s. m.* (llynaidd) A rendering of a liquid quality; a becoming like liquid.
Llyneiddiaw, *v. a.* (llynaidd) To render like liquid; to liquify; to become as a liquid.
Llyneiddrwydd, *s. m.* (llynaidd) A liquid quality.
Llyngranc, *s. m.—pl. t.* od (llyn—cranc) A wen.
Llyniad, *s. m.* (llŷn) A producing a liquid; a producing humour; a giving liquor; a forming a pool; stagnation of any fluid.
Llyniaw, *v. a.* (llŷn) To produce a fluid, or humour; to form a pool, or body of water; to dam; to stagnate as water.
Llyniawg, *a.* (llŷn) Abounding with fluid; full of humours; abounding with pools.
Llynmeirch, *s. m.* (llŷn—march) The glanders; it is otherwise called *Llyn y meirch*. See *Ysgyfaint*.
Llynorawg, *a.* (llynawr) Full of humours.

> Bydd ar ddyn ac ar anifail yn gornwyd llynorawg.
>
> It shall be upon man, and upon beast a boil *breaking forth with* blains. *Exodus* 9. 9.

Llynori, *v. a.* (llynawr) To imposthumate.
Llynoriad, *s. m.* (llynawr) An imposthumation.
Llynorlys, *s. m.* (llynor—llys) Common chickweed.
Llynoryn, *s. m. dim.* (llynawr) A pustule, a pimple; a blister.
Llynu, *v. a.* (llyn) To proceed; to spread as a contagion, or to infect.
Llynw, *s. m.* (llyn) A collection of liquid.
Llynwlydd, *s. m.* (llyn—gwlydd) Pondweed. *Llynwlyddyn corniawg*, horned pondweed.
Llynwyn, *s. m. dim.* (llynw) A little pool, a puddle, a plash. *Llynwyn yr afon.*

Ni butra lynwyn.

A *stagnant pool* will not become dirty. *Adage.*

Pery ei glod——
Tra fo yr eigiawn yn llawn llynwyn.

His fame shall last whilst the ocean is a full *body of water*. *L. G. Cothi.*

Llynwynawg, *a.* (llynwyn) Full of pools.
Llynwyniad, *s. m.* (llynwyn) A forming pools.
Llynwynu, *v. a.* (llynwyn) To form pools or plashes, to become plashy.
Llynwys, *s. m.* (llyn) A falling or settling of humours; a plague.
Llyngawl, *a.* (llwng) Swallowing; ingulfing.
Llyngedig, *a.* (llwng) Swallowed; ingulfed.
Llynges, *s. f.—pl. t.* au (llong) A fleet, a navy.

A chwedlau cyhoedd a ddywedid yn mhob lle, bod y môr yn gyflawn o lynges Caswallawn yn erlid Iwl Cesar.

Public reports were spread in every place, that the sea was covered with the *fleet* of Caswallon pursuing Julius Cæsar. *Gr. ab Arthur.*

Llyngesawg, *a.* (llynges) Having a fleet. *s. m.—pl.* llyngesogion. That has a fleet; an admiral.

Tri llyngesawg Ynys Prydain: Geraint mab Erbin, Gwenwynwyn mab Naf, a March mab Meirchion.

The three *possessing a navy* of the isle of Britain: Geraint the son of Erbin, Gwenwynwyn the son of Naf, and March the son of Meirchion. *Trioedd.*

Toreid gormes yn llyngesawg.

The invasion was destroyed being *collected in a fleet*. *Meilyr.*

Llyngesawl, *a.* (llynges) Relating to a fleet.
Llyngesawr, *s. m.—pl.* llyngesorion (llynges) The head of a fleet, an admiral.

Nid fydd, am nid fo llyngesawr à fo.

He will not be on account that he shall not be an *admiral*. *Taliesin.*

Llyngesu, *v. a.* (llynges) To form a fleet.

Pan glybu Cadwaladr ddarfod i'r Saeson oresgyn y deyrnas, yna i lyngesai Cadwaladr i ddawed i'w gwrthwynebu.

When Cadwaladr heard of the Saxons having subdued the kingdom, then Cadwaladr *collected a navy* to come to oppose them. *Elis Gruffudd.*

Llyngeswr, *s. m.—pl.* llyngeswyr (llynges—gwr) A navigator.
Llyngeswriaeth, *s. m.* (llyngeswr) The state or condition of a navigator.

Hir lyngeswriaeth i fawdd.

Long *navigation* to him that shall be drowned. *Adage.*

Llyngesydd, *s. m.—pl. t.* ion (llynges) Admiral.
Llyngesyddawl, *a.* (llyngesydd) Belonging to an admiral.
Llyngfawr, *a.* (llwng—mawr) Of a great swallow; voracious; yawning.

Llyngfawr ddaiarawr derfyn a garaf;
A gerais i chanlyn;
Neud eddwyf yn oer dyddyn!
Nid oes dim einioes i ddyn!

The *swallowing* earth has the remains of her I love; whom I loved to follow; is she not gone to a cold mansion! the life of man, alas, is nothing! *D. Benfras.*

Llyngiad, *s. m.* (llwng) A swallowing; a gulping.
Llyngu, *v. a.* (llwng) To swallow; to devour.

A faco trael gyffro trang,
Yn unawr y llawr a'i llwng.

He that cherishes the consuming dread of dissolution, in one hour the ground *swallows* him *up*. *D. Benfras.*

Llyngyr, *s. pl. aggr.* (llwng) Maw-worms, belly-worms. *Llyngyr y ddaiar*, earth-worms.
Llyngyrawg, *a.* (llyngyr) Having worms.
Llyngyren, *s. f.* (llyngyr) A maw-worm.
Llyr, *s. m.—pl. t.* ion (lly—yr) That upon which any thing proceeds, or flows; a course; a water course, an udder; a channel, margin, or shore; the sea-side.

Gwelais ar forwyn——
Lliw golau tonau taenferw gwenyg
Llanw ebyr, ar llyr, lle ni mawr-drig.

I beheld on a maiden the bright hue of the spreading ebullition of the breakers of the waves of the flood of the effluxes of rivers, on the *strand*, where it tarries not long. *Cynddelw.*

Oedd ei far——
Megys twrf ebyr yn llyr llawn.

His rage was like the tumult of the mouths of rivers with a full *margin*. *Cynddelw.*

Calan hyddfref, tymp dydd yn edwi,
Cynhwrf yn ebyr, llyr yn llenwi.

The beginning of September, the period of the falling off of day, there is tumult in the mouths of rivers filling up the *shore*. *Ll. P. Moch.*

Rhuthr a ddug fy llyw; aeth tra llyr ei glod;
Ei glybod bu mysyr.

An assault my chief did make; his fame went beyond the *shore*. *Gwgan Brydydd.*

Llyre, *a.* (llyr) Gliding or streaming round.

Un llogawd ysydd herwydd heli,
Lleuddad a Chadfan ynt cheidwi;
Llyre werydre, wrhydri llawn,
llydraws, hydraidd, maws a mynogi.

One cloister there is beyond the brine, Lleuddad and Cadfan it protecting; a *stream girt* region whose multitude are heroes; it is traversible, accessible, and genial with hospitality. *Llywelyn Fardd, i Enlli.*

Llyren, *s. f.* (llyr) That which lies on the stream; water plantain.
Llyriad, *s. m.—pl.* llyriaid (llyr) That stretches out, that extends; that creeps; the plantain: also *erllyriad*; *llyriaid llymion*, *llyriaid y llynau*, the greater water plantain; *llyriaid y dwfr*, water plantain; *llyriaid y môr*, sea plantain; *llyriaid llwydion*, hoary plantain.
Llyrlys, *s. m.* (llyr—llys) Marsh samphire.
Llyry, *s. f.—pl. t.* on (llwr) That glides, stretches out, or extends; that proceeds, or flows; a stream, or current; also a tortoise.

Uch gwaedd gwynt, golau hynt gwylain;
Uch gwaed llyry gwaed-lanw gwaeddai gigfrain.

Above the howling of the wind, fair the course of the sea-mews; over the crimson *winding* of the tide blood, the ravens were wont to scream. *Cynddelw, m. O. Gwynedd.*

Alaf yn all mall am lad,
Llithredawr llyry llon cawad,
A dwfn ryd berwyd bryd brad.

Wealth is like the bowl that holds the cheering beverage, it glides away like the *stream*, and the refreshing shower, or deceives like the deep ford. It stirs the mind to treachery. *Llywarch Hen.*

Mal toi neuadd â dail;
Mal lladd llyry â gwiail.

Like covering a hall with leaves; like killing a *tortoise* with rods. *Taliesin.*

Ef yn fawr yn llawr, yn llyryon angerdd
Yn amgudd i roddion.

He greatly on the plain, or on the raging *streams*, concealing his bounties. *Ll. P. Moch, i R. ab Owain.*

A llyry tra llyry, a llwrw tra llwrw,
Aer fwrw furthiaw.

A *stream* after *stream*, and a fall after fall, of the death-dealing conflict. *S. Bryf-fwrch.*

Daeth delw fyw fy llyw llyryon, prif obaith,
Praff adeilad iaith prophwydolion.

The living image of my Lord passed the *streams*, the supreme of expectation, amply raised in the language of prophetic ones. *G. ab M. ab Dafydd, i'r grog.*

Llyryad, *s. m.—pl.* llyryaid (llyry) What stretches out, glides, or creeps along.

Llyryaidd, *a.* (llyry) Having a tendency to stretch out or to glide along; gliding, or creeping.

> Llyryaidd fawl trethawl tracthaf o naw fân;
> Llwyddian ellyllwgan a genydaf.
>
> With a tribute of *far-extending* praise I will rehearse from the nine principles; the prospering part of the soul-enchanting song I will sing. *Ll. P. Moch.*

Llyryaw, *v. a.* (llyry) To go on the stream.

> Llyryed, tremyned tra mor dylan,
> Rhag llaith anolaith anolo llan.
>
> *Let him launch into the stream;* let him take a view beyond the flooding sea, to avoid the irremeable dissolution of the frail tomb. *Ll. P. Moch, i Lywelyn II.*

Llys, *s. m.—pl. t.* oedd (lly—ys) That separates; that parts off; that serves to discriminate; a court of justice, a court; a hall, a palace. *Llys y brenin*, the king's court; *llys breyr, llys freyrawl*, a court baron; *llys cymwd*, the court of a comot; *llys benadur, llys bennyddiawl*, the principal or high court; *llys ddygynnull*, an extraordinary court; *llys ail goffa*, a court of adjournment:—*Gwr llys*, a courtier.

> Bonedd mawr yw y peth lleiaf o'r byd yn llys doethineb.
>
> A noble pedigree is the smallest thing in the world in the *court of wisdom.* *Adage.*
>
> Gwell car yn llys
> Nog aur ar fys.
>
> "A friend at *Court* is better than penny in purse." *Adage.*
>
> Tair uchel lys y sydd yn Nghymru; nid amgen, llys Aberffraw, a llys Dinefwr, a llys Mathrafal.
>
> Three high *courts* are there in Wales; that is to say, the *court* of Aberffraw, and the *court* of Dinefwr, and the *court* of Mathraval. *Welsh Laws.*

Llysadwy, *a.* (llysiad) That may be put aside; exceptionable.

Llysai, *s. c.—pl.* llyseion (llws) One who separates, or puts aside; one who objects.

Llysaidd, *a.* (llys) Court-like, courtly, courteous.

> Gwr dig ei ddistryw; llyw llysaiddiaf;
> Gwr dygn ei alar; car cywiraf!
>
> A man who wrathfully ravaged; a chief *most courtly;* a man who is severely mourned; a most faithful friend! *Bleddyn Fardd, m. Llywelyn II.*
>
> Py fydd llary llysaidd llysoedd byddawn?
>
> Who shall be the *courteous* mild one of the hospitable courts? *Cynddelw.*

Llysaidd, *a.* (llws) Of a nature not to be touched.

> Llew llysoedd, llysaidd ei derfyn.
>
> The lion of courts, his boundary is *sacred.* *Cynddelw.*

Llysau, *s. pl. aggr.* (llws) Herbs, or plants.

Llysawg, *a.* (llys) Having courts, or palaces.

> Llary llysawg lluosgar.
>
> The humane and gentle one *possessed of palaces.* *Gwalchmai.*

Llysawl, *a.* (llys) Belonging to a court.

Llysblant, *s. pl. aggr.* (llys—plant) Step-children

Llysblentyn, *s. m. dim.* (llysblant) A step-child.

Llyschwaer, *s. f.--pl.* llyschweirydd (llys--chwaer) A step-sister, a sister-in-law.

Llysdad, *s. m.—pl. t.* au (llys—tad) A father-in-law: also called *tad gwyn.*

Llysdy, *s. m.—pl. t.* au (llys—ty) A court-house.

Llysedig, *a.* (llysiad) Being put off, or separated; objected, or demurred against.

Llysedd, *s. m.* (llws) The state of being put off, separated, or rejected.

Llyseiddiad, *s. m.* (llysaidd) A rendering courtly.

Llyseiddiaw, *v. a.* (llysaidd) To become courtly.

Llysenw, *s. m.—pl. t.* au (llys—enw) A court name, or additional name of honour, a cognomen, or surname; a nickname.

Llysenwad, *s. m.* (llysenw) A giving a cognomen, cognomination; a nicknaming.

Llysenwi, *v. a.* (llysenw) To give a surname; to nickname.

> Llysenwa gadarn yn gall rhag ei ofn.
>
> Cunningly *give epithets* to the mighty for fear of him. *Adage.*

Llysena, *v. a.* (llysau) To collect plants, or herbs.

Llyseuad, *s. m.* (llysau) A producing of plants.

Llyseuaw, *v. a.* (llysau) To produce plants.

Llyseuawg, *a.* (llysau) Abounding with plants.

Llyseuawl, *a.* (llysau) Producing plants.

Llyseuedd, *s. m.* (llysau) Herbaceousness.

Llyseuwr, *s. m.—pl.* llyseuwyr (llysau—gwr) A collector of plants; a botanist.

Llyseuwraig, *s. f.—pl.* llyseuwreigedd (llysau—gwraig) A female botanist.

> Nid llyseuwraig ond gafr.
>
> There is no such a *botanist* as a goat. *Adage.*

Llyseuwydd, *s. pl. aggr.* (llysau—gwŷdd) Shrubs.

Llyseuydd, *s. m.—pl. t.* ion (llysau) A herbalist.

Llyseuyn, *s. m. dim.* (llysau) A single plant.

Llysfab, *s. m.—pl.* llysfeibion (llys—mab) A son-in-law.

Llysfam, *s. f.—pl. t.* au (llys—mam) A mother-in-law.

> Ni charo ei fam, cared ei lysfam.
>
> He that shall not love his mother, let him love his *mother-in-law.* *Adage.*
>
> Ni wnel gynghor ei fam, gwnaed gynghor ei lysfam.
>
> He that will not follow his mother's advice, let him follow the advice of his *mother-in-law.* *Adage.*

Llysferch, *s. f.—pl. t.* ed (llys—merch) A daughter-in-law.

Llysfrawd, *s. m.—pl.* llysfrodyr (llys—brawd) A brother-in-law.

Llysfwyd, *s. m.* (llysu—bwyd) A loathing of food.

> Cylagwst a mynych lysfwyd.
>
> A pain of the stomach and frequent *loathing of food.* *H. Culhwch—Mabinogion.*

Llysg, *s. m.—pl. t.* on (lly—ysg) A rod, a wand, a stick. *Tafu llysgon ato*, to throw sticks at him.

> Rhy hawdd ym llosgawdd o'i llysg,
> Rhod ymliw rhuad ymlysg.
>
> Too easily she burnt me with her *sticks*, the straining wheel of dragging noise. *Rhys Llwyd.*
>
> Llysgon——
> O gyll oedd, nid o'm gwall i.
>
> *Sticks* of hazel there were, but not from my neglect. *D. ab Gwilym.*

Llysgbren, *s. m.—pl. t.* au (llysg—pren) A billet.

Llysgiad, *s. m.—pl. t.* au (llws) A putting off, a setting aside, a separating, or excepting; a rejection; an exception.

Llysiannawl, *a.* (llysiant) Inducing a rejection.

Llysiannu, *v. a.* (llysiant) To cause a separation, rejection, refusal, or objection.

Llysiant, *s. m.* (llws) A separation from; a rejection, a refusal, an exception.

Llysiau, *s. pl. aggr.* (llws) Herbs, plants. *Llysiau sychon, llysiau marchnad, llysiau siopau*, dry plants, spices:—

Llysiau yr afu, livergreen.
Llysiau yr ais, ribwort plantain.
Llysiau fy anwylyd, common avens.
Llysiau yr archoll, bastard pimpernel.
Llysiau y bara, coriander.
Llysiau y blaidd, wolfbane.
Llysiau y bronau, pilewort.
Llysiau Cadwgan, great wild valerian.
Llysiau y clefyd melyn, celandine.
Llysiau y coludd, pennyroyal.
Llysiau y cribau, fuller's teasel.
Llysiau y cryman, scarlet pimpernel.

Llysiau y cwlwm, tuberous-rooted comfrey
Llysiau y cwn, pasture lousewort.
Llysiau y cwsg, white poppy.
Llysiau y cyfog, asarabacca.
Llysiau y cyrff, southernwood.
Llysiau y cywer, cheese rennet.
Llysiau y defaid, sea plantain.
Llysiau y din, biting arsemart.
Llysiau y dom, pale-flowered persicaria.
Llysiau y dryw, agrimony.
Llysiau Dwyfawg, betony.
Llysiau y dyfrglwyf, asparagus.
Llysiau y ddannodd, masterwort.
Llysiau y ddidol, sowbread.
Llysiau y ddraig, dragons.
Llysiau y ddueg, scaly spleenwort.
Llysiau efa, buck's horn plantain.
Llysiau yr echryshaint, rue.
Llysiau yr eiddigedd, globe amaranth.
Llysiau yr eryr, woodroof.
Llysiau yr eagyrn, ground ivy.
Llysiau yr ewinor, whitlow grass.
Llysiau y fagwyr, yellow stonecrop.
Llysiau y fam, motherwort.
Llysiau y fammaeth, sea spurge.
Llysiau y forwyn, meadow sweet.
Llysiau y fuddai, agrimony.
Llysiau y galon, motherwort.
Llysiau y geiniog, marsh pennywort.
Llysiau gerwyn, ground ivy.
Llysiau gias, butcher's broom.
Llysiau gingroen, common ragwort.
Llysiau y groes, mugweed.
Llysiau y gwaed, pennyroyal.
Llysiau y gwaedlin, yarrow.
Llysiau y gwaew, houseleeks.
Llysiau y gwalch, hawk's beard.
Llysiau y gwenyn, baulm.
Llysiau y gwewyr, dill.
Llysiau y gwrda, mercury goose-foot.
Llysiau y gwrid, alkanet.
Llysiau gwyddelig, parsnips.
Llysiau y gwynt, windflower.
Llysiau y gymalwst, goutweed.
Llysiau y gynddaredd, common cudweed
Llysiau yr hebog, hawkweed.
Llysiau yr hedydd, lark's spur.
Llysiau yr hidl, cleavers.
Llysiau yr hudawl, vervain.
Llysiau yr hychgryg stinking iris.
Llysiau y llau, stavesacre.
Llysiau y llaw, wild wallflower.
Llysiau y lliw, woad.
Llysiau y lludw, fleawort.
Llysiau y llwy, scurvy-grass.
Llysiau llwyd, mugwort.
Llysiau y llwynog, stinking cranebill.
Llysiau y llygaid, celandine.
Llysiau Llywelyn, speedwell.
Llysiau Mair, common bugle.
Llysiau y mel, honeywort.
Llysiau melyn, dyer's greenweed.
Llysiau y meddyglyn, wild carrot.
Llysiau y mendwy, mercury goose-foot.
Llysiau y milwr, purple grass-poly.
Llysiau y moch, common nightshade.
Llysiau y mur, pellitory of the wall.
Llysiau y muroedd, stonecrop.
Llysiau y myheryn, heart medick.
Llysiau y neidr, bistort, or snakeweed.
Llysiau yr oen, lamb's lettuce.
Llysiau y pannwr, fuller's teasel.
Llysiau y pared, pellitory of the wall.
Llysiau paris, oneberry.
Llysiau pen tai, houseleek.
Llysiau perfigedd, tutsan, park leaves.
Llysiau y poer, bladder catchfly.
Llysiau Taliesin, orpine, or livelong.
Llysiau y tarw, bull weed.
Llysiau y tenewyn, sea starwort.
Llysiau tormaen, saxifrage.
Llysiau y tryfal, shepherd's purse.
Llysiau y twrch, black-berried briony.
Llysiau ungronyn, oneberry.
Llysiau y wenol, celandine.
Llysiau yr ychain, wild campion.
Llysiau yr ysgyfaint, common lungwort.
Llysiau yr ysgyfarnog, frog satyrion.

Llysiawg, *a.* (llws) Being separated or rejected.
Llysiawl, *a.* (llws) Tending to separate or reject.
Llysiedig, *a.* (llysiad) Being put off, or rejected.
Llysieua, *v. a.* (llysiau) To simple for plants.
Llysieuad, *s. m.* (llysiau) A producing of plants; a botanizing; a simpling.
Llysieuaidd, *a.* (llysiau) Herbaceous, like plants.
Llysieuawg, *a.* (llysiau) Herbous, full of plants.
Llysieuawl, *a.* (llysiau) Producing plants, herbaceous; belonging to plants.
Llysieuedd, *s. m.* (llysiau) Herbaceousness.
Llysieufag, *s. f.* (llysiau—mag) Nursery of plants.

> Da yw bendith bardd——
> Ar orddiwes gaer, a'r ardd ddiwag,
> A'r llys shang-wen, a'r llysieufag.
>
> The blessing of bard is good to the mansion where he enters, and the garden that is not empty, and the spacious white hall, and the *plantation*. *Iolo Goch.*

Llysieulyd, *a.* (llysiau) Of the quality of plants.
Llysieulyfr, *s. m.—pl. t.* au (llysiau—llyfr) A herbal; a book of plants.
Llysieuwr, *s. m.—pl.* llysieuwyr (llysiau—gwr) One who collects plants; a botanist.
Llysieuwriaeth, *s. m.* (llysieuwr) Herbalism.
Llysieuydd, *s. m.—pl. t.* ion (llysiau) A botanist.
Llysienyn, *s. m. dim.* (llysiau) A single plant.
Llysin, *a.* (llys) Belonging to a court.
Llyslyd, *a.* (llws) Of a slimy quality.
Llyslydiaw, *v. n.* (llyslyd) To become slimy.
Llyslydrwydd, *s. m.* (llyslyd) Sliminess.
Llyslyn, *s. m.—pl. t.* oedd (llws—llyn) Mucilage.
Llyslynaidd, *a.* (llyslyn) Mucilaginous.
Llysnaf, *s. m.* (llws—naf) A running of snivel.
Llysnafaidd, *a.* (llysnaf) Running like snivel.
Llysnafawl, *a.* (llysnaf) Snivelly, snotty.
Llysnafedd, *s. m.* (llysnaf) A mucus, or viscous matter; snivel, or snot.
Llysnafeddawg, *a.* (llysnafedd) Mucilaginous.
Llysnafiad, *s. m.* (llysnaf) A running of snivel.
Llysnafu, *v. n.* (llysnaf) To snivel.
Llysoli, *v. a.* (llysawl) To render courtly.
Llysolrwydd, *s. m.* (llysawl) Courtliness.
Llyst, *s. m.* (llest) A vessel for holding liquor.
Llystyn, *s. m.* (llwst) A recess, or lodgement.

> A'r llys fraith yn arilwa fry;
> A'r llystyn yn arilwrdy.
>
> And the gay court above all empty; and the *lodge* a lumber house. *D. ab Gwilym.*

Llysu, *v. a.* (llws) To separate from, to part off; to loath, to reject, to refuse, to disallow. *Llysu tyston*, to reject witnesses.

> Gwr oedd llaidd llysedd, llwydd ei far;
> Gwr oedd rudd ei lafn a lli gwyar.
>
> A man that was a courtly wolf, his wrath was *deprecated*, a man whose blade was red with the stream of gore. *Cynddelw, m. Rhwyd*

Llysaog, *s. f.* (llysu) Great burnet; also called *llysyrawd*, and *llysyrlys*.

Llysur, *s. m.—pl. t.* on (llws) That proceeds from.

Llysw, *s. m.* (llws) Slime, glutinous matter.

Llyswen, *s. f.—pl. t.* od (llysw) An eel. *Llyswen bendoll*, a conger eel.

Llyswen mewn dwrn yw arian.

Like an *eel* in hand is money. *Adage.*

Llun neidr oedd mewn llwyn odech,
Llysauw sarff, llyswen sech.

The form of a snake I saw in a sculking brake, nicknamed a serpent, but a dry *eel* it was. *Rhys Llwyd.*

Llyswena, *v. a.* (llyswen) To sniggle, to catch eels.

Llyswenig, *s. f. dim.* (llyswen) A small eel.

Llyswenu, *v. a.* (llyswen) To produce eels.

Llyswod, *s. pl. aggr.* (llysw) Eels; so called for their slimy nature.

Llysyn, *s. m. dim.* (llys) A small court.

Llysyrawd, *s. m.* (llysu) Great burnet; also called *llysyrlys*.

Llytrod, *s. m. aggr.* (llwtr) Filths, or garbage.

Llytroda, *v. a.* (llytrod) To collect filth.

Llytrodaidd, *a.* (llytrod) Of the nature of garbage

Llytrodawg, *a.* (llytrod) Abounding with filth.

Llytrodawl, *a.* (llytrod) Breeding filth, or dirt.

Llytrodedd, *s. m.* (llytrod) Filthiness; garbage.

Llytrodi, *v. a.* (llytrod) To make filth, or dirt.

Llytrodiad, *s. m.* (llytrod) A breeding filth, or dirt

Llytrodrwydd, *s. m.* (llytrod) Filthiness, nastiness

Llyth, *s. m.—pl. t.* ion (lly) That tends to spread out, or to flatten; that is flaccid, soft, tender, or feeble.

A chadw wyneb arebydd,
A chyda llyth byth ni bydd.

And preserving the countenance of the humorist, with the *low ones* be never will be. *Syp. Cyfeiliawg.*

Llyth, *a.* (lly) Flaccid, soft, tender; feeble, weak, frail, low, or base.

Ni sangai weheiyth
—Ar nyth Cynddylan;
Ni thechai droedfedd fyth;
Ni fages ei fam fab llyth.

No brood would tread on the nest of Cynddylan; he never would flinch a foot; his mother reared no *feeble* son. *Llywarch Hen.*

Darfyddant hwy; parêi di byth,
Treuliaut fal llyth drwsiadau.

They shall end; thou shalt endure for ever; they shall wear away like *frail* garments. *Edm. Prys.*

Llythaidd, *a.* (llyth) Somewhat flat, flaccid, tender, or feeble; of a frail, or low nature.

Llythawl, *a.* (llyth) Of a flat, flaccid, tender, or feeble quality.

Llythi, *s. pl. aggr.* (llwth) Flounders, or flat fish.

Iachaf pysgod môr yw llythi.

The wholesomest sea fishes are *flounders*. *Ll. Meddyg.*

Llythiad, *s. m.* (llyth) A rendering flat, flaccid, soft, tender, or feeble.

Llythiant, *s. m.* (llyth) Flaccidity, debility.

Llythïen, *s. f. dim.* (llythi) A single flounder.

Llythrwydd, *s. m.* (llyth) Flaccidness; debility.

Llythu, *v. a.* (llyth) To render flat, flaccid, soft, or feeble; to enervate; to become flaccid.

Llythus, *a.* (llyth) Of a flaccid tendency.

Llythusaw, *v. a.* (llythus) To render of a flaccid or tender quality.

Llythusrwydd, *s. m.* (llythus) Flaccidness, debility

Llythwr, *s. m.—pl.* llythwyr (llyth—gwr) A feeble, weak, or debilitated person; a man that is imbecile.

Ni ystyr llythwyr fy llethrid ym cerdd:
Gyr di y cerdd i wrthid;
Ac onis gyri di, gyraf wrid
I'th deurudd, a'th dewrwarth ganlid.

Base men will not consider the polish of my song; send thou the stave from thee; and if thou dost not send, I will send a blush into thy cheeks for thy pert and shameful inveteracy. *Ll. P. Moch, i G. ab C. ab Owain.*

Llythyn, *s. m. dim.* (llyth) A weakling.

Llythyr, *s. m.—pl. t.* au (llyth—yr) A cut or engraved character; a letter of the alphabet, a type; a letter, epistle, or written message; an instrument in writing. *Llythyr cymyn*, a testament; *llythyr ysgar*, a bill of divorce; *llythyr ymrwym*, a bond.

Tri gweinyddion gwybodaeth: can, arwydd, a llythyr.

The three agents of knowledge: song, hieroglyphic, and *letter*. *Barddas.*

Llythyrad, *s. m.* (llythyr) A lettering.

Llythyraidd, *a.* (llythyr) Being like a letter.

Llythyrawg, *a.* (llythyr) Literary, of letters.

Ef a ddywed Crist i hun,
Gynt wrth y dyn llythyrawg,
Pan ofynai iddo ef
Y ffordd i'r nef ardderchawg—
"Gwerth sydd genyt."

It was said by Christ himself, formerly to a *literary person*, when he asked of him the way to the exalted heaven, "sell what thou hast." *H. T. Phylip.*

Llythyrawl, *a.* (llythyr) Literal, literate, literary.

Abadau Teilaw, a Theulydawg, ac Ismael, a Degeman a ddylyant fod yn llythyrawl urddolion.

The abbots of Teilo, and Teulydog, and Ismael, and Degeman ought to be persons of *literary* degrees. *Welsh Laws.*

Ac yr Alfryd hwnw a fagesid gan Lew Bab, a gwr llythyrawl oedd.

And that Alfred had been brought up by Pope Leo, and he was a man *of letters*. *Brut y Saeson.*

Llythyrdy, *s. m.—pl. t.* au (llythyr—ty) A post house, a post office.

Llythyrddysg, *s. m.* (llythyr——dysg) Grammar learning.

Llythyredig, *a.* (llythyr) Being lettered.

Llythyredigaeth, *s. m.* (llythyredig) A lettering.

Llythyreg, *s. f.* (llythyr) Grammar science.

Llythyregai, *s. c.* (llythyreg) A grammatist.

Llythyregawl, *a.* (llythyreg) Grammatical.

Llythyregydd, *s. m.* (llythyreg) A grammarian.

Llythyren, *s. f.—pl. t.* au (llythyr) A letter of the alphabet, a type, or character. *Llythyren Sul*, a Sunday letter.

Llythyrenawg, *a.* (llythyren) Literate, lettered.

Llythyrenawl, *a.* (llythyren) Literal; elementary

Llythyrenawr, *s. m.—pl.* llythyrenorion (llythyren) One who cuts letters.

Llythyreniad, *s. m.* (llythyren) A lettering.

Llythyrenu, *v. a.* (llythyren) To letter; to spell.

Llythyrenwr, *s. m.—pl.* llythyrenwyr (llythyren—gwr) A letterer; a speller.

Llythyrenydd, *s. m.—pl. t.* ion (llythyren) A letterer; a letter founder.

Llythyrfa, *s. f.* (llythyr—ma) A letter-case.

Llythyrgloer, *s. f.* (llythyr—cloer) A letter-case.

Llythyrgod, *s. f.—pl. t.* au (llythyr—cod) A letter-bag.

Llythyriad, *s. m.* (llythyr) A lettering; a spelling

Llythyriannawl, *a.* (llythyriant) Literary.

Llythyriannu, *v. a.* (llythyriant) To follow the science of grammar; to follow literature.

Llythyriant, *s. m.* (llythyr) Literature.

Llythyru, *v. a.* (llythyr) To letter; to scribe; to spell.

Peri i ddeuddengwyr rhydd cyfreithiawl edrych y borfa, a llythyru eu henwau.

To command twelve free and lawful men to view the pasture, and *to write* their names. *Stat. of Rhuddlan.*

Llythyrwr, *s. m.—pl.* llythyrwyr (llythyr—gwr) A letter-man; a letter-writer.

Llythyrydd, *s. m.—pl. t.* ion (llythyr) A letterer; a scribe; a letter-writer.

Llythyryddiaeth, *s. m.* (llythyrydd) Grammar learning, philology.

Llythyryn, *s. m. dim.* (llythyr) A billet.

Llyu, *v. a.* (lly) To lick with the tongue.

Llyw, *s. m.—pl. t.* iau (lly—yw) That guides, directs, or steers; the rudder, or the helm of a ship; the tail of a bird; the train of a gown; a guide, leader, or ruler; that sustains, or carries on; sustenance, provision.

> Dala llysfien erbyn ei llyw.
>
> To catch an eel by the *tail*. *Adage.*
>
> Da i bob merch, od umberchur,
> Dwyn llyw ei gwn dan lle gwir.
>
> It is meet for every woman, if regard for decency is preserved, to carry the *tail* of her gown in an honest place. *L. Mon.*
>
> Pen a borthaf ar fy nhu;
> Pen Urien llary llyw ei lu;
> Ac ar ei fron wen fran ddu!
>
> A head I bear by my side; the head of Urien the mild *leader* of his host; and on his white bosom the sable raven stands! *Llywarch Hen.*

Llywadur, *s. m.* (llyw) One who rules, or governs; a governor, a director.

> Bu Alexander byd lywadur.
>
> Alexander has been the *ruler* of the world. *Ll. P. Moch.*

Llywadures, *s. f.—pl. t.* au (llywadur) A governess

Llywadwy, *a.* (llyw) That may be guided.

Llywaeth, *s. m.* (llyw) Guidance; a bringing on. *Lloda llywaeth*, a reared animal; *Oen llywaeth*, a lamb brought by hand.

Llywawd, *s. m.* (llyw) Guidance, governance.

Llywawdwr, *s. m.—pl.* llywawdwyr (llywawd—gwr) A guider, or director; a governor.

Llywawdr, *s. m.—pl.* llywodron (llywawd) A governor, or director.

Llywawdydd, *s. m.—pl. t.* ion (llywawd) A guider.

Llywed, *v. a.* (llyw) To guide, to lead, to direct.

> Gwas graid a wrthyd godrwd,
> Ail eichiawg Gwaliawg yn llywed.
>
> A violent youth that rejects the milky food, like the herald of Gwallog *guiding on.* *Taliesin.*

Llywedawg, *a.* (llywed) Having a guidance.

Llywediad, *s. m.* (llywed) A guiding; a steering.

Llywedu, *v. a.* (llywed) To direct; to steer.

Llywedydd, *s. m.—pl. t.* ion (llywed) A guider, director; a pilot.

Llywedyddes, *s. f.* (llywedydd) A governess.

Llywedyddiaeth, *s. m.* (llywedydd) The act or occupation of a guide; pilotage; directorship; government, dominion.

> Cyfryw saint yn llywydyddiaeth
> Cyfoethau fy nhuw nis rhydraeth tafawd.
>
> The number of saints in the *direction* of the powers of my Lord, the tongue cannot express. *Ll. ap Sais.*

Llywel, *s. m.* (lly—gwel) The extreme boundary of vision; the horizon. *A weli di rywbeth yn y llywel?* Seest thou something in the horizon?

Llywelaidd, *a.* (llywel) Horizontal, belonging to the boundary of vision.

Llyweli, *s. m.* (llywel) The limit of vision.

Llyweliad, *s. m.* (llywel) A forming a horizon.

Llywelig, *a.* (llywel) Influenced by the horizon.

Llywelin, *a.* (llywel) Belonging to the horizon.

Llywelu, *v. a.* (llywel) To form a horizon.

Llywen, *s. m.* (lly-gwen) The extreme of the light; the west.

Llywenydd, *s. m.* (llywen) The western horizon.

> Gwedy myned yr haul i lywenydd.
>
> After the going of the sun into the *western sky.* *W. Salisbury.*

Llyweth, *s. f.—pl. t.* au (llyw) A muscle.

Llywethan, *s. f. dim.* (llyweth) A muscle: greek valerian.

> Mis Rhagfyr—
> Llwm tir, llonydd llywethan.
>
> The month of December, bare is the land, still is the *muscle.* *Aneurin.*

Llywethawg, *a.* (llyweth) Muscular, brawny.

Llywethawl, *a.* (llyweth) Muscular, musculous.

Llywethogrwydd, *s. m.* (llywethawg) Brawniness.

Llywethu, *v. n.* (llyweth) To grow muscular.

Llywiad, *s. m.* (llyw) A guiding, a steering.

Llywiadaeth, *s. m.* (llywiad) Guidance, direction.

Llywiadawl, *a.* (llywiad) Directive, directing.

Llywiadu, *v. a.* (llywiad) To direct, to manage.

Llywiadur, *s. m.—pl. t.* au (llywiad) That directs, or governs; a governor. Also the name of a part of a plough, otherwise called *Llyw*.

Llywiaduraeth, *s. m.* (llywiadur) Directorship.

Llywiadures, *s. f.—pl. t.* au (llywiadur) Governess

Llywiaeth, *s. m.* (llyw) Guidance, management.

> Ei rhol'n llaw, o ran llywiaeth
> Beuno, a'i wnlo a wnaeth.
>
> The putting it in hand, for the sake of Beuno's *management*, was what he did, and he sewed it. *H. Rhinallt, i'r hele dan.*

Llywiannawl, *a.* (llywiant) Directive, guiding.

Llywiannu, *v. a.* (llywiant) To manage.

Llywiannus, *a.* (llywiant) Tending to direct.

Llywiant, *s. m.* (llyw) Guidance, governance.

Llywiator, *ger.* (llywiad) Being governing.

Llywiaw, *v. a.* (llyw) To guide, direct, or steer; to rule, to govern.

> Gwedy bod Elidr yn llywiaw y deyrnas trwy bum mlynedd, digwydd o ddamwain yd oedd yn hely yn llwyn y Calatyr, ef a gyfarfu ag ef Arthal ei frawd, yr hwn a ddiholasid o'r frenhiniaeth.
>
> After Elidr had been *governing* the kingdom for five years, on a certain day by chance he was hunting in the forest of Calatyr, and he was met by Arthal his brother, who had been excluded from the kingly office. *Gr. ab Arthur.*
>
> Mor wrawl y maer'r eryr
> A llew gwyllt yn llywiaw gwyr.
>
> The eagle as powerfully as a wild lion *doth manage* the multitude. *L. G. Cothi.*

Llywiawd, *s. m.* (llyw) A directing; governance.

Llywiawdwr, *s. m.—pl.* llywiawdwyr (llywiawd—gwr) One who directs; a director, a governor.

Llywiawdwraeth, *s. m.* (llywiawdwr) Directorship

Llywiawdydd, *s. m.—pl. t.* on (llywiawd) One who directs, or rules, a manager.

Llywiawdr, *s. m.—pl.* llywiodron (llywiawd) A guider, director, or manager.

> Nid llywiawdr namyn Duw.
>
> There is no *governor* but God. *Adage.*

Llywiawg, *a.* (llyw) Having guidance, guiding.

> Llwyn fon, fy hun a'th aeth o'i hebryd;
> Llywiawg law euraawg, liw eiry browydd.
>
> The splen of fair one, my sleep is gone since her departure, she with her *guiding* hand, ... of the hue of the snow of the hills. *Ier. Fychan.*

Llywiawl, *a.* (llyw) Guiding, or directing.

Llywied, *v. a.* (llyw) To guide, to lead; to steer.

Llywiedig, *a.* (llywiad) Being directed, or steered.

Llywiedigaeth, *s. m.* (llywiedig) Governance.

Llywiedigawl, *a.* (llywiedig) Directive, guiding.

Llywiedydd, *s. m.—pl. t.* ion (llywiad) Director.

Llywiedyddawl, *a.* (llywiedydd) Directorial.

Llywiedyddes, *s. f.—pl. t.* au (llywiedydd) A female that guides, or directs; a governess.

Llywiedyddiaeth, *s. m.* (llywiedydd) Directorship

Llywiodraeth, *s. m.—pl. t.* au (llywiawdr) Governance, or directorship.

Llywiodraethawl, *a.* (llywiodraeth) Governing.

Llywiodraethiad, *s. m.* (llywiodraeth) A doing the office of government.

Llywiodraethu, *v. a.* (llywiodraeth) To govern.

Llywiodres, *s. f.—pl. t.* au (llywiawdr) A governess.
Llywiodri, *s. m.* (llywiawdr) The act of a director.
Llywiodru, *v. a.* (llywiawdr) To act as a director, or manager.
Llywiodu, *v.* (llywiawd) To act a directing part.
Llywiodwr, *s. m.—pl.* llywiodwyr (llywiawd—gwr) A director, or manager.
Llywiodwraeth, *s. m.* (llywiodwr) Directorship.
Llywiodydd, *s. m.—pl. t.* ion (llywiawd) One who guides, or directs.
Llywiodyddawl, *a.* (llywiodydd) Belonging to a guide; directive.
Llywiodyddes, *s. f.—pl. t.* au (llywiodydd) A female guider, a conductress.
Llywiodyddiaeth, *s. m.* (llywiodydd) The office of a conductor or director.
Llywion, *s. pl. aggr.* (llyw) Flying particles.
Llywitor, *sup.* (llyw) To be guiding, or directing.
Llywiwr, *s. m.—pl.* llywiwyr (llywiaw—gwr) A guider; a steerer, a steersman.
Llywodraeth, *s. f.* (llywawdr) Government.
Llywodraethai, *s.* (llywodraeth) That governs.
Llywodraethaidd, *a.* (llywodraeth) Of a governing or directing nature.
Llywodraethawl, *a* (llywodraeth) Governing.
Llywodraethiad, *s. m.—pl. t.* au (llywodraeth) A governing, or conducting.
Llywodraethu, *v. a.* (llywodraeth) To govern.
Llywodraethus, *a.* (llywodraeth) Governing.
Llywodraethwr, *s. m.—pl.* llywodraethwyr (llywodraeth—gwr) A governor.
Llywodraethwraig, *s. f.—pl.* llywodraethwreigedd (llywodraeth—gwraig) A governess.
Llywodraethydd, *s. m.—pl. t.* ion (llywodraeth) A governor, one who rules, or conducts.
Llywodrawg, *a.* (llywawdr) Having government.
Llywodrawl, *a.* (llywawdr) Tending to govern.
Llywodres, *s. f.* (llywawdr) A governant.
Llywodri, *s. m.* (llywawdr) Governance.
Llywodru, *v. a.* (llywawdr) To act as governor.
Llywodu, *v. a.* (llywawd) To conduct or carry on.
Llywodwr, *s. m.—pl.* llywodwyr (llywawd—gwr) One who directs, or conducts; a manager.
Llywodwraeth, *s. m.—pl. t.* au (llywodwr) Governorship, the office of a governor.
Llywodwraig, *s. f.—pl.* llywodwreigedd (llywawd—gwraig) A governing woman.
Llywodydd, *s. m—pl. t.* ion (llywawd) Governor.
Llywodyddawl, *a.* (llywodydd) Belonging to a director, or manager.
Llywodyddes, *s. f.—pl. t.* au (llywodydd) A governant, a directress.
Llywodyddiaeth, *s.* (llywodydd) Governorship.
Llywy, *s. f.—pl. t.* on (llyw) That is superior, a paragon. *a.* Of passing beauty.

> Caru bun weddaidd, luniaidd lywy.
>
> Loving the modest nymph, the shapely *paragon*. *Ll. P. Moch.*
>
> Mal eiry unlliw, lliw llywy
> Wyneb bun; mi a wn pwy.
>
> Like the unicoloured snow of *superior* hue, is the countenance of a nymph; I know who. *D. ab Gwilym.*
>
> Ac er bodd llywy lliw eiry ar goed,
> Pan fu aer rhag caer cyforiais waed.
>
> And to please the *passing fair one*, of the hue of the snow on the trees, when there was the assault of a fort, I waded in blood. *Gwalchmai.*

Llywych, *s. m.—pl. t.* ion (lly—gwych) Reflection of light, a shining; complexion, hue, or colour.
Llywychadwy, *a.* (llywych) Capable of shining.
Llywychawl, *a.* (llywych) Reflecting light.
Llywychedig, *a.* (llywych) Reflected as light, shining; glittering.
Llywychiad, *s. m.—pl. t.* au (llywych) A shining.
Llywychu, *v. n.* (llywych) To cast a light.
Llywyd, *s. m.* (llyw) Guidance, management.
Llywydd, *s. m.—pl. t.* ion (llyw) A president.
Llywyddaidd, *a.* (llywydd) Like a president.
Llywyddawl, *a.* (llywydd) Belonging to a president
Llywyddes, *s. f.—pl. t.* au (llywydd) A female president; a female guider or director.
Llywyddiad, *s. m.* (llywydd) A presiding.
Llywyddiadaeth, *s. m.* (llywyddiad) Presidentship
Llywyddiadawl, *a.* (llywyddiad) Belonging to the act of presiding.
Llywyddiadu, *v. a.* (llywyddiad) To act as a president, to fill a presidency.
Llywyddiaeth, *s. m.* (llywydd) The act, or office of a governor; presidency.
Llywyddiaethawl, *a.* (llywyddiaeth) Belonging to a presidency.
Llywyddiaethu, *v. a.* (llywyddiaeth) To fill the office of a president.
Llywyddu, *v. a* (llywydd) To act as a president.
Llywyn, *s. m.* (lly—gwyn) The extreme of light; the western horizon, the west.
Llywynawl, *a* (llywyn) Occidental, occiduous.
Llywynydd, *s. m.* (llywyn) The occident, the western horizon, the west. *Sil.*
Llŷyn, *a.* (lly—yn) Poisonous, baleful.
Llŷys, *s. m.* (lly—ys) That parts off, leaves, or rejects, a rejection; what is put off; what runs from. A mucilage, or slime. *Llyys malwen*, the track of a snail. *Llyys y barth*, the scrapings of an earthen floor, mixed with spittle, used to cure the ringworm.

M.

MA, *s. f. r.—pl. t.* oedd. What is identified as being produced, existing, or filling a space; what has space, what yields space; a place, space, or spot; a where; a state. It is used very generally as an affix, in the compostion of words, changing the initial to its secondary power, as *Camfa*, a stepping-place, or stile; *Rhedfa*, a running place, and running state, or a course, and the like.

> Goruchel Dduw golychir yn mhob ma;
> Goruchel ei enw yn Ebrew.
>
> The most high God will be adored in every *place*, the Most High is his name in Hebrew. *Taliesin.*

Mab, *s. m.—pl.* meibion (ma—ab) A male; a male child, a boy; a son. *Mab a merch*, a son and daughter; *mab maeth*, a foster son; *mab llwyn a pherth*, an epithet for a bastard; *mab aillt*, the son of an alien, in progress of naturalization by maternity, *mab uchelwr*, a gentleman, or freeholder; *mab anwar*, and *mab drud*, epithets for a son who seeks to annul a father's will; *mab yn nghyfraith*, or *llysfab*, a son-in-law; *mab bedydd*, a godson; *mab cyd bo mad*, a boy whilst he is innocent, an epithet for a minor under fourteen years of age:—*Meibion y wledd*, the sons of festivity.

> Moch dysg nawf mab hwyad.
>
> Quick is the swimming instruction of the duck's *young*. *Adage.*

> Da yw cof mab.
>
> The memory of a child is good. *Adage.*

Mabaidd, *a.* (mab) Like a boy, boyish, childish.

> Nid un bryn mebyn mabaidd a hynaif.
>
> Not the same the bargain of a *boyish* youth and an elder. *D. ab Gwilym.*

Maban, *s. m. dim.*—*pl. t.* od (mab) A babe, baby.

> Hwiban i faban, aradr i wr.
>
> A whistle for a *child*, a plough for a man. *Adage.*

Mabanaidd, *a.* (maban) Babyish, childish.
Mabandawd, *s. m.* (maban) Babyship, infancy.
Mabaneidd-dra, *s. m.* (mabanaidd) Childishness.
Mabaneiddiad, *s. m.* (mabanaidd) A making like a baby; a becoming babyish, or childish.
Mabaneiddiaw, *v. a.* (mabanaidd) To render childish; to become like a baby.
Mabaneiddiawl, *a.* (mabanaidd) Of a childish tendency or disposition.
Mabaneiddrwydd, *s. m.* (mabanaidd) Childishness
Mabaniad, *s. m.* (maban) A rendering as a child.
Mabanoed, *s. m.* (maban—oed) Childhood.
Mabanu, *v. a.* (maban) To make as a baby; to become a baby.
Mabawl, *a.* (mab) Like a child; filial, like a son.
Mabdawd, *s. m.* (mab) Childhood, babyship.
Mabddall, *a.* (mab—dall) Blind from the birth.
Mabddysg, *s. m.* (mab—dysg) What is learnt in childhood; rudiments for children.

> Ni chryn llaw ar fabddysg.
>
> The hand will not shake during *infantile instruction*. *Adage.*

> Mabddysg it dreuliaw trath.
>
> It is a *childhood instruction* for thee to spend a revenue. *Ll. P. Moch.*

> Mabinaidd, lamiaidd, lawn gwedddeiddrwydd,
> Mabddysg oedd iddi roddi yn rhwydd.
>
> Juvenile, shapely, and full of modesty, it was her *first rudiment* freely to bestow. *H. ab Owain.*

Mabgainc, *s. f.*—*pl.* mabgeinciau (mab—cainc) A shoot or sucker of a tree.
Mabgar, *a.* (mab—car) Loving children.

> Nid mabgar ond diflain.
>
> No one is *fond of children* but the unbrutal. *Adage.*

Mabgarwch, *s. m.* (mabgar) Love of children.
Mabgath, *s. c.*—*pl. t.* od (mab—cath) A kitling.
Mabgoll, *s. f.* (mab—coll) The avens. *Mabgoll bendigaid*, common avens.
Mabgorn, *s. m.*—*pl.* mebgyrn (mab—corn) The core in the horn of a beast.
Mabgynnwys, *s. m.* (mab—cynnwys) The choice or taking of one for a son; an adoption.
Mabgynnwysaw, *v. a.* (mabgynnwys) To adopt a son, to take as one's child.
Mabgynnwysiad, *s. m.* (mabgynnwys) The taking as a son, the adoption of a son.
Mabiaeth, *s. m.* (mab) Childhood; filiality.
Mabiaethiad, *s. m.* (mabiaeth) The having the state of childhood; a filiation.
Mabiaethu, *v. a.* (mabiaeth) To treat as a child.
Mabiaith, *s. f.* (mab—iaith) A prattling, or fond words used to children; the fondling speech of nurses to children; fond flattering words.

> Y frowfraith hoew fabiaith haf.
>
> The thrush of sprightly *prattling* in summer. *D. ab Gwilym.*

Mabin, *a.* (mab) Juvenile, youthful, boyish.
Mabinaidd, *a.* (mabin) Of a juvenile tendency.

> Mab ni mad aned
> Mabinaidd dynged.
>
> It were not good that a child should be born who is *of youthful* fate. *Taliesin.*

Mabinawg, *a.* (mabin) Having youth; juvenile.
Mabineiddiad, *s. m.* (mabinaidd) A rendering, or becoming of a youthful disposition.
Mabineiddiaw, *v. a.* (mabinaidd) To make childish; to become childish.
Mabineiddiawl, *a.* (mabinaidd) Of a childish tendency.
Mabineiddrwydd, *s. m.* (mabinaidd) Childishness
Mabinogai, *s.* (mabinawg) Instructor of youth.
Mabinogi, *s. m.*—*pl. t.* ion (mabinawg) Juvenility; juvenile instruction; the amusement of youth; the title of some ancient tales. *Mabinogi Iesu Grist*, The infancy of Jesus Christ, the title of one of the spurious gospels.
Mablan, *s. f.* (mab—llan) A burying place.

> Llywelyn llachar, llach farn gyfodd,
> Ni gyfyd o'i fablan!
>
> The violent Llywelyn, of animated countenance in the fight, will not rise out of his *tomb*! *Cynddelw, m. i. O. Gwynedd.*

Mabliw, *s. m.*—*pl. t.* iau (mab—lliw) A reflected hue or colour.
Mablygad, *s. m.*—*pl.* mablygaid (mab—llygad) The pupil of the eye.
Mabmaeth, *s. m.* (mab—maeth) A foster son.
Maboed, *s. m.* (mab—oed) Childhood, infancy.
Mabolaeth, *s. m.* (mabawl) Childhood, infancy.
Mabolaidd, *a.* (mabawl) Having the disposition of a child; of a filial disposition.
Mabolgamp, *s. f.*—*pl. t.* au (mabawl—camp) A juvenile game; a youthful feat.

> Deg mabolgamp y sydd: hely a milgi, hely pysg, hely adar, barddoniaeth, canu telyn, darllain Cymraeg, canu cywydd gan dant, canu cywydd pedwar ac accen, tynu arfau, herodraeth.
>
> There are ten *juvenile games*: coursing with a hound, fishing, fowling, poetry, playing the harp, reading Welsh, singing an ode with music, singing an ode of four parts with accentuation, blazoning of arms, and a going on embassy. *Welsh Laws.*

Maboli, *v. n.* (mabawl) To become as a child.
Mabollaeth, *s. m.* (mabawl) Childhood, infancy.
Mabolrwydd, *s. m.* (mabawl) A state of childhood
Mabon, *s. m.*—*pl. t.* oedd (mab) A fine youth; a young hero.

> Pa fynych gymhwyll Fabon,
> Mabon caredig yn nghywethas;
> Goruchel awen ar weilgi las,
> Mabonodd Brython pan ddelon' i'w braint.
>
> How often soever thou shalt have communion with a *youthful hero*, the *hero* is amiable in society; supremely high the voice of fame along the azure current when the *youths* of Britain come to their privilege. *Golyddan.*

Mabsant, *s. m.*—*pl. t.* au (mab—sant) A patron saint, or tutelar saint of a church.
Mabsanta, *v. a.* (mabsant) To canonize.
Mabsantaeth, *s. m.* (mabsant) A canonization.
Mabryddiaeth, *s. m.* (mab—rhyddiaeth) Payment on admission of a son to his father's estate.
Mabwraig, *s. f.* (mab—gwraig) A virago.
Mabwys, *s. m.* (mab—gwys) The taking of one for a son, an adoption of a child.
Mabwysiad, *s. m.*—*pl. t.* au (mabwys) The adopting a child; an affiliation.
Mabwysiadawl, *a.* (mabwysiad) Relating to the adoption of a child, adoptive.
Mabwysiaidd, *a.* (mabwys) Relating to the adoption of a child.

Mabwysiaw, *v. a.* (mabwys) To adopt as a son.
Mabwysiawl, *a.* (mabwys) Relating to the adoption of a child.
Mabwysiedig, *a.* (mabwysiad) Adopted as a son.
Macai, *s. c.—pl.* maceiod (mag) That breeds, or that is generated; a maggot, or grub; a caterpillar.
Maceiad, *s. m.—pl.* maceiaid (macai) A maggot of any kind; a grub; a caterpillar.
Maceied, *s. pl. aggr.* (macai) Maggots, or grubs.
Macrell, *s. m.—pl.* mecryll (magr) A mackerel.

Mae'n ei gawell facrelliaid.

There be in his basket *mackerels*. *D. ab Edmwnt.*

Macrellyn, *s. m. dim.* (macrell) A small mackerel.
Macwy, *s. m.—pl. t.* aid (mag) A youth; a page.

Myned a wnai i'r maes a dau facwy gyd ag ef.

He went into the field with two *youths* along with him. *H. O. ab Urien—Mabinogion.*

Can diffyrth Trindawd tri macwy o dan,
Trimeib glan glain ofwy—
Credwn iddo.

As the Trinity protected three *youths* from fire, three angel-visited children fair, let us trust to him. *Cynddelw.*

Mach, *s. m.—pl.* meichiau (ma—ach) A bail, a surety. *Mach ar gyfraith, mach gorfodawg*, bail to appear in court; *mach cynnogn, mach talu*, a surety for debt; *mach diebrydig*, a surety that proves nugatory.

Dau fach y sydd: mach diebrydig, a mach cynnogn. Mach cynnogn yw yr hwn a el yn fach dros ddyn ni allo sefyll wrth gyfraith; mach diebrydig yw yr hwn ni allo teithiaw ei fechniaeth gyda yr hawlwr.

There are two sorts of *surety*; a frustrative *surety*, and a *surety* of credit. A *surety* of credit is he who shall go as *surety* for a person that can not abide by law; a frustrative *surety* is he who cannot fulfil his suretiship to the prosecutor. *Welsh Laws.*

Machdaith, *s. f.—pl.* machdeithiau (mach—taith) A course of security; a dam, or embankment.

Poed emendigaid y fachdaith;
A'i gollyngodd, gwyd y gwaith!
Ffynnwn fenestr mor ddiffaith!

Accursed be the *embankment*; that opened it, evil the act! what a devastating server of a spring! *Canu C. Gwaelawd.*

Machiad, *s. m.* (mach) A making sure; a securing
Machlud, *s. m.* (mach—llud) A setting, or going down. *Machlud haul*, sun-set.
Machludaw, *v. n.* (machlud) To set, or to become obscured, as the sun.
Machludawl, *a.* (machlud) Setting as the sun.
Machludiad, *s. m.* (machlud) An occultation.
Machludiaeth, *s. m.* (machlud) The state of being covered over, or in occultation.
Machludiant, *s. m.* (machlud) An occultation.
Machraith, *s. f.—pl.* machreithiau (mach—rhaith) The law of suretiship.
Machydr, *a.* (mach) That is a pledge, or surety.

Twn ni wnaeth Mab Duw, da yw mydr, heb gam
Ar ddinam fam fachydr.

There has not been made imperfect by the Son of God, fair the theme, without wrong, upon a faultless mother a *surety*. *Anon. 1360.*

Mad, *s. m.—pl. t.* ioedd (ma—ad) What proceeds, advances, or goes forward; a term for the reptile class of animals; what is good, or beneficial; a good, a benefit; a good turn. *Heb rad na mad*, without grace or goodness. *Y fad felen*, a creature of a yellow colour and very beautiful, which is often mentioned by the poets; and some have supposed it to be the basilisk. It is frequently used in the same sense with *Y fall felen*, or the yellow plague; and it is said to have killed *Maelgwn Gwynedd*, king of the Britons.

A wnel mad mad a ddyly.

He that doth *good* to him *good* is due. *Adage.*

Mataf gil gwired.

The *most beneficial* expedient is truth. *Adage.*

Y fad felen oedd bena'
Yn deg, heb un arwydd da.

The *yellow serpent* was principally fair, without one good token. *R. Ddu.*

Os hardd heb gel fad felen,
Harddach a gwynach yw gwen.

If beautiful without disguise the *yellow serpent*, more beautiful and fairer is my love. *T. Prys.*

Mad, *a.* (ma—ad) Proceeding, or advancing; progressive; good, beneficial.

Nid mad un ni bu Gymmro.

No one is *good* who has not been a Welshman. *Adage.*

Dyro ran i'th wan, wynfyd wrthddrych hawl,
O'th wlad fad feidriawl, er mawl mynych.

Give a portion to thy supplicant, of the expected claim of happiness, thy *good and comprehensive* kingdom, for constant praise. *Casnodyn.*

Madaidd, *a.* (mad) Of a progressive tendency; of a beneficial tendency; goodly.
Madalch, *s. m.* (mad—alch) The agaric.
Madalchaidd, *a.* (madalch) Like agaric; of a tough, or leathery quality.
Madarch, *s. m. aggr.* (mad—arch) The toadstool.
Madarchaidd, *a.* (madarch) Like the toadstool.
Madarchen, *s. f. dim.* (madarch) Porous toadstool
Madarchu, *v. n.* (madarch) To generate toadstool
Madawg, *a.* (mad) Tending forward; having benefit, or advantage; goodly. *s. m.—pl.* madogod. An epithet for a fox, equivalent to the word reynard. It is also a very common name of men.

Llwyd dy glog, fy llatai glan,
Madawg was bywiawg buan.

Brown is thy cloak, my neat messenger of love, *reynard*, thou swift and lively chap. *I. ab Rhys ab Maredudd.*

Madawl, *a.* (mad) Tending to advance; benefiting
Mad-ddall, *s. f.—pl. t.* od (dall) The blindworm.
Madedd, *s. m.* (mad) Bounteousness; goodness.
Maden, *s. f. dim.* (mad) A little she fox, a vixen.
Madfall, *s. f.—pl. t.* od (mad—mall) A newt.
Madfanawg, *s. m.* (mad—banawg) Eminently beneficial.

Tri madfanogion byd: bardd, fferyllt, ac ammaeth.

The three beneficent ones of the world: a bard, a metallurgist; and a husbandman. *Trioedd.*

Madfelen, *s. f.* (mad—melen) The knapweed; also called *pengaled*.
Madgall, *s. f.—pl. t.* od (mad—call) The lizard; also called *Genau goeg*.
Madgyffinydd, *s. m.—pl. t.* ion (corf) One who puts together well, a good inventor.
Madgyflafan, *s. f.* (mad—cyflafan) A violent deed, or outrage, committed with a good intention; also violence that is productive of good; or the deed of a Scævola.
Madiad, *s. m.* (mad) An advancing onward; a being productive; a benefiting; a being good.
Madiain, *a.* (mad) Productive of good, apt to do good, beneficent, bounteous. *Creawdr madiain*, a bounteous Creator.

Arwyrain madiain modur, aur anaw,
Goronwy fab Tudur,
Arfod air pair Peredur,
Arf yn ing, aer dirfing dur.

Celebrate the *beneficent* leader, thou golden muse, Goronwy the son of Tudur, with a word meet for the occasion of the lore of Peredur, the weapon in the difficulty, the vehement toil of steel. *G. ab M. ab Dafydd.*

Echrys par llachar, llech gyfwyrain gawr
Lluoedd gwawr mawr madiain;
Gryd orddwy, grym fwyfwy frain;
Glyw llywiaw llewenydd cyngrain.

Terrible the gleaming spear, spreading the shout of acclamation of the hosts of the splendid one great and *bounteous*; the dread of a tyrant, of increasing energy and glorious; a general directing the joy of the united band. *Cynddelw, i H. ab Owain.*

Madlywydd, *s. m.* (mad—llywydd) Patriot prince.

> Nid oes [illegible] madlywydd.
>
> There is no *good governor* but God. *Adage.*

Madolaeth, *s. m.* (madawl) A benefiting state.

Madoreilid, *s. f.* (goreilid) A praiseworthy molestation. *v. a.* To disturb worthily.

Madoreilitiwr, *s. m.—pl.* madoreilitwyr (madoreilid—gwr) One who worthily disturbs.

> [illegible] Prydain ab Aedd Mawr [illegible] Prydain.
>
> One of the three *praiseworthy opposers* of the Isle of Britain: Prydain the son of Aedd the great disturbing the tyrannical grievance that was anarchy and devastation generated in the Isle of Britain. *Trioedd.*

Madr, *a.* (mad) That is become pus.

Madraidd, *a.* (madr) Tending to dissolve; tending to fester.

Madrawg, *a.* (madr) Having a tendency to dissolve, of a watery nature; full of pus.

Madrawl, *a.* (madr) Tending to dissolve.

Madredd, *s. m.—pl. t.* ion (madr) Matter that is dissolved; what is generated by putrefaction, pus, or purulent matter; also a quitter.

Madreddawg, *a.* (madredd) Abounding with pus, or matter; putrescent; sanious. *Wy madreddawg*, an addle egg.

Madreddawl, *a.* (madredd) Putrefactive.

Madreddiad, *s. m.* (madredd) A putrifying.

Madreddu, *v. n.* (madredd) To generate pus or matter; to fester; to putrify, to rot.

Madriad, *s. m.* (madr) A turning to a dissolved state; a producing matter; a festering.

Madroedd, *s. pl. aggr.* (madr) Dissolved bodies; putrid bodies, a charnel-house. *Mal y fadroedd*, like a charnel-house.

Madrogi, *v. n.* (madrawg) To become full of matter or pus.

Madron, *s. pl. aggr.* (madr) Humours; watery matter.

Madrondawd, *s. m.* (madron) A watery humour; swimming of the head; dizziness, giddiness, stupefaction; astonishment.

Madronedd, *s. m.* (madron) A dissolved state.

Madroni, *v. a.* (madron) To form a watery humour; to make dizzy, or giddy; to stupify; to become dizzy.

Madroniad, *s. m.* (madron) A generating humours; a forming water in the head; a causing a swimming in the head.

Madru, *v. n.* (madr) To dissolve; to become matter or pus; to putrify, to rot; to generate matter, to fester.

Madrudd, *s. m.—pl. t.* ion (madr) Marrow.

> Rhag Geraint gwel [illegible]
> [illegible]
>
> Before Geraint I saw confusion, and a chieftain's brow, covered with *marrow*. *Llywarch Hen.*

Madruddaidd, *a.* (madrudd) Like marrow.

Madruddaw, *v. n.* (madrudd) To form marrow.

Madruddawg, *a.* (madrudd) Having marrow.

Madruddawl, *a.* (madrudd) Of the nature of marrow.

Madruddiad, *s. m.* (madrudd) A marrowing.

Madruddyn, *s. m. dim.* (madrudd) A marrow, or a separate body of marrow. *Madruddyn y cefn*, the spinal marrow.

Madrwy, *s. f.—pl. t.* od (madr—rhwy) A newt.

> [illegible]
>
> [illegible] filthy and corrupt [illegible] snakes, vipers, and venomous insects. *Marchawg Crwydrad.*

Madryn, *s. m. dim.* (madr) An epithet for a fox. *Madryn dusw*, a fox's tail.

Madu, *v. a.* (mad) To cause to proceed; to send; to suffer to go off; to render productive, or beneficial; to become beneficial.

Madus, *a.* (mad) Beneficent; beneficial, good.

Madusaw, *v. a.* (madus) To render beneficial; to become beneficent.

Madw, *a.* (mad) Tending to inertness.

Madwr, *s. m.—pl.* madwyr (mad—gwr) A beneficent person.

Madws, *s. m.* (mad—ws) Full time, fullness of time; season, or opportunity. *adv.* It is time. *Madws yw*, it is time, it is opportune.

> Diwedd-fyd nid oedd fadws;
> Och i'r cref, na chauai'r drws!
>
> The end of the world was not *opportune*, for upon the *town*, that it would not shut the gate! *I. ab H. Sawdwal.*

> Madws iti ymadael
> O'r byd hwn, a'r bywyd hael,
> A myn'd i'r nef, gartref gwyn,
> Ne i [illegible] uffern.
>
> *It is time* for thee to depart out of this world, and the generous living, and to go to heaven, the home of spirits, or to feed the fire of hell. *T. Prys.*

Madyn, *s. m. dim.* (mad) An epithet for a fox.

Madywydd, *s. m. aggr.* (madw—gwydd) The sweetgale.

Madd, *s. m.* (my—add) That is of a divestigating tendency.

Madda, *v. a.* (madd) To be about divestigating.

Maddau, *s. m.* (madda) A setting at large, a liberating; a dismissal; a quittal; pardon.

Maddau, *v. a.* (madda) To let go, to set at large, to loosen; to liberate; to dismiss; to quit, to leave, to forsake; to forgive, to pardon, or to remit. *Enaid faddau*, that is about to let the soul depart, or one whose life is forfeited.

> Y dyn a laddo arall â gwenwyn, galanas dauddyblyg a dâl, canys ffyrnig yw; a bid enaid faddau am y naill, a'r llall ar ei genedl; a'i ddihenydd fydd yn ewyllys yr arglwydd, ai ei losgi, ai ei grogi a fyno.
>
> The person who shall kill another with poison, a twofold fine for felony shall be paid, for he is outrageous; and let him *be divestigating* of soul with respect to one, and the other upon his family; and his death shall be at the will of the sovereign, whether he will have him burnt, or will have him hanged. *Welsh Laws.*

> Llefawdd yr Iesu drachefn â llef uchel, ac efe a faddeuodd yr ysbryd.
>
> Jesus cried again with a loud voice, and *he gave up* the spirit. *W. Salisbury.*

> Mad'euasant eu rhwydau.
>
> *They left* their nets. *W. Salisbury.*

Madden, *s. m.* (madda) A dismissal; a quittal; a pardon, or forgiveness.

Maddeu, *v. a.* (madda) To let go, to liberate; to dismiss; to quit, to leave, to forgive.

Maddeuad, *s. m.* (maddeu) A letting go, a setting at large, a loosening, a liberating; a dismissing; a quitting, or leaving; a forgiving, remitting, or pardoning.

Maddeuadwy, *a.* (maddeuad) That may be set at large, or liberated; dismissible; remissible, pardonable.

Maddeuain, *a.* (maddeu) Full of a liberal or forgiving disposition.

Maddeuannawl, *a.* (maddeuant) Of a liberal or forgiving disposition.

Maddeuanniad, *s. m.* (maddeuant) A causing a remission, or pardon.

Maddeuannu, *v. n.* (maddeuant) To cause a remission, or forgiveness.

Maddeuannus, *a.* (maddeuant) Of a liberal or forgiving disposition.

Maddeuannusaw, *v. a.* (maddeuannus) To render of a liberal natnre; to become of a liberal or forgiving disposition.

Maddeuant, *s. m.* (maddeu) The act of letting go; liberation; dismission; remission.

Lle bo pur gyfeillach rhaid bod aml faddeuant o bobtu.

Where true friendship subsists there must be great *forgiveness* on both sides. *Maxim.*

Maddeuaw, *v. a.* (maddeu) To set at large, to re-mit; to dismiss; to leave; to forgive.

Ni maddeuaf di, Ddafydd,
Er naw o Ifor a Nudd.

I will not *leave thee*, David, for nine of the Ivors and the Nudds. *L. G. Cothi.*

Maddeuawd, *s. m.* (maddeu) Dismission.

Maddeuawg, *a.* (maddeu) Having a dismissal; having remission, or pardon.

Maddeuawl, *a.* (maddeu) Tending to set at large; tending to quit, forgiving.

Maddeuedig, *a.* (maddeuad) Being liberated; pardoned, or forgiven.

Maddeuedigaeth, *s. m.* (maddeuedig) The act of setting at large; a quitting; a remission.

Maddeuedigaw, *v. a.* (maddeuedig) To render at large; to render forsaken; to be pardoned.

Maddeuedigawl, *a.* (maddeuedig) Of a liberating tendency; tending to forgive.

Maddeugar, *a.* (maddeu) Apt to let go or to set at large; disposed to remit, forgiving.

Maddeugarwch, *s. m.* (maddeugar) Forgiveness.

Maddeuwr, *s. m.—pl.* maddeuwyr (maddeu—gwr) One who sets at large; one who leaves; a pardoner.

Maddeuydd, *s. m.—pl. t.* ion (maddeu) A liberator; a dismisser; a forsaker; a forgiver.

Mae, *v. n.* (ma) Be; is; are. *Mae dyn yn ddrwg*, man is wicked; *mae y fuwch wrth ben ei hal*, the cow is just about calving. *Dyfed.*

Mae wedi myned yn abred gwyllt.

It is become a wild chaos. *Adage.*

Mae, *adv.* (ma) There be; there is; it is; he is; she is; also for *pa le mae*, where is. *Mae dyn yma*, there is a man here; *mae nhw, mae nhwy, maent, maent hwy*, they are.

Yn mhob dyn y mae enaid;
Yn mhob enaid y mae deall.

In every living being *there is* a soul; in every soul *there is* understanding. *Adage.*

Mae Abel dy frawd?

Where is Abel thy brother? *Gen.* 4. 9.

Mae fy ngweision drwg a'm direidwyr! dyrchefwch y ffyrch y dan fy dwy ael a ddygwyddawdd ar fy llygaid, hyd pan welwy defnydd fy'n daw

Where are my lazy servants and my mischievous chaps? Set up the props under my two brows which have fallen over my eyes, so that I may see the form of my son-in-law. *H. Culhwch—Mabinogion.*

Maedd, *s. m.* (my—aedd) A buffet, a beating.

Maeddawd, *s. m.* (maedd) The act of buffeting.

Maeddawl, *a.* (maedd) Buffeting, or banging.

Maeddedig, *a.* (maedd) Beaten, or thumped.

Maeddedigaeth, *s. m.* (maeddedig) The act of beating about, buffeting, or banging.

Maeddgen, *s. f.—pl. t.* ion (maedd—cen) A buffet on the head.

Cadw Brydain, Arglwydd hael,
Rhag iddi gael maeddgenon.

Preserve Britain, gracious Lord, lest it should have *buffetings*. *Herri William.*

Maeddgeniad, *s. m.* (maeddgen) A buffeting, or beating about the head.

Maeddgenu, *v. a.* (maeddgen) To buffet about the head; to box the ears.

Maeddiad, *s. m.* (maedd) A beating, a thumping.

Maeddu, *v. a.* (maedd) To beat, to strike, to thump, to bang, to buffet about. *Maeddu poer*, and *malu ewyn*, to foam at the mouth.

Diwydiach fil y dywedynt,
Fydd gwas wedi faeddu gynt.

More diligent, as they say, will a servant be after he has been formerly *beaten*. *G. ab Ll. Moel.*

Maeddwr, *s. m.—pl.* maeddwyr (maedd—gwr) One who buffets about or bangs; a beater.

Mael, *s. f.—pl.* meilion (ma—el) What is produced, obtained, or got by working; gain, profit, advantage; what is worked, work; what is extracted as metal; iron, which was the only metal known when the word was first used in that sense. *Mae hyn yn fael iddo*, this is an advantage to him; *Gwyr mael*, the men on duty, the domestic, or body guards of the prince; also a farthing. *Mael* forms many proper names of men, as *Maeldaf*, *Maelderw*, or *Derfael*, *Maelgad*, or *Cadfael*, *Maelgwn*, or *Cynfael*, *Maelog*, *Maelwg*, and *Maelyrus*.

Yn Elfael, dir mael y medd,
Am daro y mae dewredd.

In Elfael, the land of *profit* and of mead, there is bravery for the conflict. *L. G. Cothi.*

Dur a mael oedd drwy 'mylau—
Ei lafn.

Steel and *iron* were through the edges of the blade. *I. Tew.*

Maela, *v. a.* (mael) To get advantage, to gain.

Maelawd, *s. m.* (mael) The act of turning to profit, advantage, or gain.

Maelawg, *a.* (mael) Abounding with produce. *s. f.* A place of traffick, a market; a mart. It is also the name of men, and of places.

Maelawr, *s. f.—pl.* maelorau (mael) A place of traffick, a mart, or market. There are districts so called in the marches of Wales, which were neutral grounds, where trade was carried on.

Cas maelawr heb goedydd.

Odious is a *district* without woods. *Catwg.*

Maeldref, *s. f.—pl. t.* i (mael—tref) A market town. There are places so called.

Maeldy, *s. m.—pl. t.* au (mael—ty) A house of trade, commerce, or traffick.

Maeledig, *a.* (mael) Produced by work.

Maeler, *s. m.—pl. t.* ion (mael) That gets.

Maelera, *v. a.* (maeler) To traffick, to trade.

Maelerfa, *s. f.—pl. t.* oedd (maeler) A place of traffick, a mart, or market.

Maeleri, *s. m.* (maeler) Traffick, or trade.

Maeleriad, *s. m.* (maeler) A merchandizing.

Maeleriaeth, *s. f.* (maeler) The business of a merchant, or chapman.

Maelerlai, *s. c.* (maeler) A trafficker, a trader.

Maeleriaw, *v. a.* (maeler) To traffick, to trade.

Maeleriwr, *s. m.—pl.* maelerwyr (maeler—gwr) A trafficker, a trader.

Maeleru, *v. a.* (maeler) To traffick, to trade.

Maelfa, *s. f.—pl. t.* oedd (mael) A market, a mart.

Maelged, *s. f.—pl. t.* ion (mael—ced) A tribute.

Maelgi, *s. m.—pl. t.* on (mael—ci) The angel-fish.

Maeliad, *s. m.* (mael) A toiling for gain; a profiting, or gaining.

Maeliannawl, *a.* (maeliant) Tending to profit, of an advantageous tendency.

Maeliannu, *v. a.* (maeliant) To get profit.

Maeliannwr, *s. m.—pl.* maeliannwyr (maeliant—gwr) One who profits.

Maeliant, *s. m.* (mael) Advantage, or gain.

Maeliaw, *v. a.* (mael) To obtain a produce; to get by work or labour: to get advantage, to gain, to profit, to get a profit.

> Gwn fod twelawyr——
> Gwynedd i'w moli; gwn, iddi maelant.

I know that the courteous men of Gwynedd do praise her; I know, to her *they procure benefit.* *D. ab Edmwnt.*

Maelier, *s. m.—pl. t.* on (mael) That obtains, that profits; a gainer, a profiter; a merchant; a chapman.

> Maelier y gerdd, a'i molawd,
> Yw Iorwerth, a werth ei wawd.

A *trafficker* in song, and its praise, is Iorwerth, who sells his muse. *D. ab Gwilym.*

Maeliera, *v. a.* (maelier) To traffick, to trade.
Maelierad, *s. m.* (maelier) A trafficking, a trading
Maelieraeth, *s. f.* (maelier) A trafficking.
Maelierai, *s. c.* (maelier) One who trafficks.
Maelierawd, *s. f.* (maelier) An act of traffick.
Maeliereg, *s. f.* (maelier) That relates to traffick. *Cyllell faeliereg*, a chopping knife.
Maelieres, *s. f.—pl. t.* au (maelier) A female merchant; a chap-woman.
Maelierfa, *s. f.—pl. t.* on (maelier) A mart.
Maelieru, *v. a.* (maelier) To traffick, to trade.
Maelierydd, *s. m.—pl. t.* ion (maelier) A trafficker
Maelieryn, *s. m. dim.* (maelier) A petty trader.
Maeliwr, *s. m.—pl.* maelwyr (mael—gwr) A regrater; or badger.
Maelota, *v. a.* (maelawd) To gain by traffick, to gain, or make a profit. *Sil.*
Maelotai, *s. c.—pl.* maeloteion (maelota) A regrater, a chapman.
Maeloteiaeth, *s. m.* (maelotai) The practice of a regrater, the occupation of a trafficker.
Maelotyn, *s. m. dim.* (maelawd) A petty trader.
Maelwg, *s. m.* (mael) Traffick, or trade.
Maelwr, *s. m.—pl.* maelwyr (mael—gwr) A regrater; a badger.
Maelydd, *s. m.—pl. t.* ion (mael) A regrater.
Maen, *s. m.—pl.* meini (ma—en) A fixt principle, or substance; a stone; a block of stone. *Maen cellt*, a flint stone; *maen clais*, or *maen mynor*, marble; *maen ehed*, *maen tynu*, or *ehedfaen*, a loadstone; *maen melin*, a millstone; *maen breuan*, a quern-stone; *maen gwn*, a bullet; *maen glain*, or *maen magl*, the adder-stone; *maen llifaw*, or *maen addwyn*, a grindstone; *maen clo*, a key stone; *maen ffin*, a boundary stone; *maen taran*, a thunderbolt; *maen tostedd*, a stone in the bladder; *maen sigl*, *maen ysgwyd*, or *maen chwyfain*, a rocking stone; *maen gwerthfawr*, a precious stone; *maen cawad*, a shower stone, and *maen gwlaw*, a rain stone, names for the crystal, which used to be rolled for procuring rain; and hence, probably, the *manalis lapis* of the Romans.

> Mal gwaith Maen Ceti.

Like the labour of the *Stone* of Ceti. *Adage.*

> Mal eiry Mawrth ar ben maen.

Like the snow of March on the top of a *stone*. *Adage.*

> Y fun——
> A'i mwnwgl oll fal maen gwlaw.

The nymph with her neck altogether like the *rain stone*. *B. Brwynllys.*

Maenad, *s. m.* (maen) A stoning; petrifaction.
Maenaidd, *a.* (maen) Like a stone; stony.
Maenan, *s. f. dim.* (maen) Any imperfect kind of stone; the cob, a substance lying upon coal; a kind of marl; also the slaty stone of which slate pencils are made; also a term for a district bound by stone mears, or a manor, which is otherwise called *maenawr*, and *maenawl*.
Maenawg, *a.* (maen) Having stone; stony.
Maenawl, *a.* (maen) Of stone, belonging to a stone
Maenawr, *s. f.—pl.* maenoran (maen) A district marked by a stone boundary, a manor.

> Saith dref sydd yn y faenawr fro, tair tref ar ddeg yn maenawr wrthdir.

There are seven townships in a *manor* of a cultivated region, and thirteen townships in an upland *manor*. *Welsh Laws.*

> Goreu maenawr gwlad fawr Fon.

The best *manor* in the ample country of Mona. *L. G. Cothi.*

Maendo, *s. m.* (maen—to) A stone covering; a sepulchre.
Maendöad, *s. m.* (maendo) A covering with stone
Maendöi, *v. a.* (maendo) To cover with stone.
Maendöwr, *s. m.—pl.* maendowyr (maendo—gwr) A coverer with stone, a slater.
Maendöydd, *s. m.—pl. t.* ion (maendo) A slater.
Maendrwch, *s. m.* (maen—trwch) Lithotomy.
Maendrychiad, *s. m.* (maendrwch) A cutting for the stone, or lithotomy.
Maendrychu, *v. a.* (maendrwch) To cut for the stone; to practise lithotomy.
Maenddeota, *s. m.* (maen—deawd) Lithotomy.
Maenddeoti, *v. a.* (maenddeota) To practise lithotomy, to cut for the stone.
Maeneiddiad, *s. m.* (maenaidd) Lapidification.
Maeneiddiaw, *v. a.* (maenaidd) To turn to a stone, to make like a stone; to petrify.
Maeneiddiawl, *a.* (maenaidd) Lapidescent.
Maenfan, *s. f.* (maen—man) The beasil of a ring.
Maenfedd, *s. f.—pl. t.* i (maen—bedd) A stone sepulchre.
Maenfur, *s. m.* (maen—mur) A stone wall.
Maengaer, *s. f.* (maen—caer) A rampart of stone.
Maenglawdd, *s. m.—pl.* maengloddiau (maen—clawdd) A stone-quarry.
Maenhad, *s. m.* maen—had) The gromwell.
Maeniad, *s. m.* (maen) A stoning; a petrifying.
Maenol, *s. f.—pl. t.* ydd (maenawl) A dale.
Maensaer, *s. m.—pl.* maenseiri (maen—saer) A stone-mason.
Maenu, *v. a.* (maen) To produce a stone; to turn to stone, to petrify; to stone, or to beat with stones. *Gwnaed ei faenu yn irad*, he was terribly mangled. *Sil.*
Maenwr, *s. m.—pl.* maenwyr (maen—gwr) A stoner; a lapidary.
Maenydd, *s. m.—pl. t.* ion (maen) A lapidary.
Maer, *s. m.—pl.* meiri (ma—er) That is stationed; one that looks after, or tends; that keeps, or guards; a provost, or mayor; a bailiff. *Maer y biswal*, the keeper of the cow lare, the land steward.

> Cosbi y maer yn mhen y dref.

Punishing the *mayor* at the head of the town. *Adage.*

> Myfi yw——
> Maer dy dda, mawr yw dy ddawn.

I am the *looker after* thy chattels; great is thy store. *D. ab Gwilym.*

> Maer y biswal a biau baratoi holl gyfreidiau y llys.

The land *steward* has to prepare all the necessaries of the palace. *Welsh Laws.*

Maerdref, *s. f.—pl. t.* i (maer—tref) A tending town, or a district that is under a bailiff; the royal domain, under the care of the *maer y biswal*. There are several places of this name.
Maerdy, *s. m.—pl. t.* au (maer—ty) The house of a mayor, or land steward. There are some houses bearing this name.

Maeres, *s. f.—pl. t.* au (maer) A female who tends, or looks after; a dairy-woman.

Maeron, *s. m.—pl. t.* ydd (maer) One who tends, keeps or looks after; one who has custody; also a dairy-farmer. *Sil.*

Maeronaeth, *s. m.* (maeron) A place, or office of custody; a prefecture; a government; also the occupation of the dairy.

Maerones, *s. f.—pl. t.* au (maeron) A female who superintends, or has custody; an epithet for a godmother in the Armoric dialect; also a dairy-woman.

Maeroni, *s. m.* (maeron) A superintendency; the office of a keeper, or one who has custody; a mayoralty; also the occupation of a farmer.

Nid mynachtid maeroni.

Husbandry is no monkery. *Adage.*

Maeroniaeth, *s. m.* (maeroni) Superintendency; dairy-work.

Maeronwr, *s. m.—pl.* maeronwyr (maeron—gwr) A man who tends, or is stationed to look after; a dairy-man.

Cell maeronwr ei fuarth.

The *dairyman's* parlour is his fold. *Adage.*

Maeronydd, *s. m.—pl. t.* ion (maeron) One stationed to tend, or to look after; a dairy-man.

Maerwr, *s. m.—pl.* maerwyr (maer—gwr) A tender, or looker after; a dairy-man.

Maerwraig, *s. f.—pl.* maerwreigedd (maer—gwraig) A woman who tends; a dairy-woman.

Maerwri, *s. m.* (maerwr) The office of a looker after, or keeper; a dairy farm.

Maerwriaeth, *s. m.* (maerwr) The occupation of a tender of cattle, or of a dairy-man.

Maerydd, *s. m.—pl. t.* ion (maer) A tender, or keeper a dairy-farmer.

Maes, *s. m.—pl.* meusydd (ma—es) That is spacious, clear, or open an open region; a plain, an open field. *Cad ar faes*, a pitched battle; *colli y maes*, to lose the field, or to lose the battle.

Achub maes mawr a dryg-farch.

To win a great *field* with a bad horse. *Adage.*

Ac ef digones
Budd coed a maes.

And he caused the produce of wood and *field*. *Taliesin.*

Maes, *prep.* (ma—es) Out without, or outward; outside. *adv.* Out, or outward; from within, in a state of disclosure, in an outward state *Mae y dyn faes ei gof*, the man is out of his wits; *awn i faes*, let us go out; *maes o law*, out of hand. *Maes* is most prevalent in the South Wales dialects, and *Allan*, in those of North Wales.

Maesa, *v. a.* (maes) To turn out; to take the field; to evacuate.

Tra bo y ci yn maesa ydd â y geinach i'r coed.

Whilst the dog *evacuates* the hare will get into the wood. *Adage.*

Maesai, *s. c.—pl.* maeseion (maes) One of the field; a campaigner.

Maesaidd, *a.* (maes) Like a field or plain.

Maesawl, *a.* (maes) Belonging to the field.

Maesdref, *s. f.—pl. t.* i (maes—tref) A villa.

Maesdir, *s. m.* (maes—tir) Champaign land.

Tri phren a ddyly pob adeiliwr maesdir eu caffael i gan y neb y bieuffo y coed, mynno y coedwr [illegible] myno, nid amgen, nenbren, a dwy nenfforch.

Three pieces of timber ought every builder on *open land* to have from him who owns the wood, whether the woodman is agreeable or not agreeable; namely, a roof beam, and two roof supporters. *Welsh Laws.*

Maesfil, *s. m.* (maes—mil) A beast of the field.

Maesiad, *s. m.* (maes) A going to the field.

Maessyng, *v. a.* (maes—sang) To trample about.

Maeswellt, *s. m.* (maes—gwellt) Bent-grass.

Maeswr *s. m.—pl.* maeswyr (maes—gwr) A field-man, or a man of the field.

Maeth, *s. m.—pl. t.* ion (my—aeth) Cherishment, nurture, nourishment; fosterage. *Tad maeth*, a foster-father; *mam faeth*, a foster-mother.

Aeth anwir ar faeth ennyd:
Aeth y gwir ar fath i gyd.

Falsehood is taken in *fosterage* awhile; the truth is altogether gone to nought. *Ior. Fynglwyd.*

Y cerddwyr ar benceirddiaeth
I'r haelion fydd meibion maeth.

The minstrels who are chief of song will be *foster sons* of the generous. *L. G. Cothi.*

Maetha, *v. a.* (maeth) To gather nourishment.

Maethai, *s. c.—pl.* maetheion (maeth) One who cherishes, or fosters.

Maethaidd, *a.* (maeth) Tending to nourish.

Maethawd, *s. m.* (maeth) Cherishment, nurture.

Drwg yw——
Am wybod o'r maethawd maith,
Euraid dymhor, yr aid ymaith!

It is a misfortune, after experiencing such ample *comfort*, that thou shouldest go away, thou golden season!
D. ab Gwilym, i'r haf.

Maethawg, *a.* (maeth) Having nourishment.

Maethawl, *a.* (maeth) Cherishment, nutritive.

Maethdad, *s. m.* (maeth—tad) A foster-father.

Maethdy, *s. m.—pl. t.* au (maeth—ty) A nursing-house, or nursery.

Maethedig, *a.* (maeth) Nourished, fostered.

Maethedigaeth, *s. m.* (maethedig) Nutrication.

Maethedigawl, *a.* (maethedig) Nutritive.

Maethen, *s. f.* (maeth) A pampered female.

Ymaith ing, famaeth angau!
Maethen front, ymaith yn frau!

Directly be gone, thou *foster-mother* of death! Thou filthy *pampered one*, abruptly avaunt! *Sils ab Sion.*

Maethfa, *s. f.—pl. t.* oedd (maeth) A nursery.

Maethfab, *s. m.—pl.* maethfeibion (maeth—mab) A nursed child a foster-son.

Maethfam, *s. f.—pl. t.* au (maeth—mam) A foster-mother; a nurse.

Maethferch, *s. f.—pl. t.* ed (maeth—merch) A foster-daughter.

Maethgar, *a.* (maeth) Apt to cherish; fostering.

Maethgarwch, *s. m.* (maethgar) Nutritiousness.

Maethiad, *s. m.* (maeth) A cherishing, a nourishing; a fostering; nutrition.

Maethiadawl, *a.* (maethiad) That is nourishing.

Maethiadu, *v. a.* (maethiad) To render nourishing; to become nutritive.

Maethiadus, *a.* (maethiad) That is nutritive.

Maethiannaidd, *a.* (maethiant) Tending to feed.

Maethiannawl, *a.* (maethiant) Nutrimental.

Maethianniad, *s. m.* (maethiant) Nutrication.

Maethiannu, *v. a.* (maethiant) To cause nutriment; to become a nutrition.

Maethiannus, *a.* (maethiant) Nutrimental.

Maethiannusaw, *v. a.* (maethiannus) To render nutrimental; to become nutritious.

Maethiannusrwydd, *s. m.* (maethiannus) Nutritiousness; a state of nourishment.

Maethiannwr, *s. m.—pl.* maethiannwyr (maethiant—gwr) One who gives nourishment.

Maethiant, *s. m.—pl.* maethiannau (maeth) Nutrition, nourishment.

Maethiator, *ger.* (maethiad) In nourishing.

Maethid, *s. m.* (maeth) Nurture; feeding.

Maethidiawl, *a.* (maethid) Nutrimental.

Maethiedydd, *s. m.*—*pl. t.* ion (maethiad) A cherisher, a nourisher, a fosterer.

Maethiedyn, *s. m. dim.* (maethiad) One who is nourished, or pampered up.

Maethineb, *s. m.* (maeth) Nourishment.

Maethitor, *sup.* (maeth) To be nourishing.

Maethle, *s. m.*—*pl. t.* oedd (maeth—lle) A nursing place, a nursery.

Maethlyd, *a.* (maeth) Being much nursed or fed.

Maetholedd, *s. m.* (maethawl) Nutritiousness.

Maetholrwydd, *s. m.* (maethawl) Nutritiousness.

Maethran, *s. f.* (maeth—rhan) A company of people who live or mess together.

Maethu, *v. a.* (maeth) To cherish, to nourish, to nurse, to foster; to feed.

Maethus, *a.* (maeth) Alimentary, nutritious.

Maethusaw, *v. a.* (maethus) To render nutritive.

Maethusrwydd, *s. m.* (maethus) Nutritiousness.

Maf, *s. m.* (ma) That breaks out; that forms into a cluster.

Mafon, *s. pl. aggr.* (maf) Raspberries.

Mafonen, *s. f. dim.* (mafon) A raspberry.

Mafonllwyn, *s. m.* (llwyn) A raspberry bush.

Mafonwydd, *s. pl. aggr.* (mafon—gwydd) Raspberry trees.

Mafonwydden, *s. f. dim.* (mafonwydd) A raspberry tree; also called *mafon llwyn*.

Mag, *s. f.* (ma—ag) The act of rearing, bringing up, or educating; rearing, education; nurture

Magad, *s. m.* (mag) A quantity; a multitude.

> Gwrwas, cyn lleas, yn llysoedd enwawg,
> Mygedawg magadoedd.
>
> The gay youth, before his death, in the magnificent courts was the idol of multitudes. *Cynddelw, m. Pyll.*

Magaden, *s. f. dim.* (magad) A nursling.

Magadwr, *s. m.*—*pl.* magadwyr (magad—gwr) One who nurses, rears, or breeds.

Magadwriaeth, *s. m.* (magadwr) The act or office of one who nurses, rears, or brings up.

Magadwy, *a.* (magad) That may be nourished.

Magai, *s. c.* (mag) One that rears, or breeds.

Magator, *ger.* (magad) In rearing, or breeding.

Magawd, *s. m.* (mag) The act of rearing, bringing up, breeding, or educating.

> Mal myn magawd.
>
> Like a kid *that is reared by hand.* *Adage.*

Magawl, *a.* (mag) Tending to rear, or to bring up; breeding; nursing.

Magdan, *s. m.* (mag—tan) What generates fire, a combustible; tinder. *a.* Combustible.

> Aeth— —
> Yn fagdan olwyn fygdarth.
>
> He went off like a *combustible* globe of smoky vapour. *Ed. Morris, i'r diawl.*

Magddu, *s. f.* (mag—du) The fountain of blackness; or the seat of darkness; hell.

> Yn y fagddu yr ydym yn rhodiaw.
>
> In *darkness* we are walking. *Isaiah 59. 9.*

Magedig, *a.* (magad) Being reared, brought up.

Magfa, *s. f.*—*pl.* magfeydd (mag) A nursery.

Magi, *s. m.* (mag) A principle of generation.

Magiad, *s. m.* (mag) A bringing up, rearing, or nursing, a breeding.

Magiad, *s. f.*—*pl.* magïaid (magi) A worm, or grub; a glow-worm.

Magien, *s. f. dim.* (magi) A worm; a glow-worm.

Magiod, *s. pl. aggr.* (magi) Worms, or grubs; glow-worms, maggots.

Magl, *s. f.*—*pl. t.* au (mag) What intricately connects, or constructs; a knot, a knot in knitting; a mesh; what entangles; a gin, or springe; a web on the eye; an issue in surgery; a portion of land.

> Sef yw magl deuddeg erw.
>
> That is to say, a *knot* is twelve acres. *Welsh Laws.*
>
> Mal gwlaw y daw drew, drwy air, y maglau,
> Tân mygiyd, a chesair— —
> Arnynt.
>
> Like the rain yonder there will come, at his word, snares, smoking fire, and hail upon them. *W. Middleton.*

Maglai, *s. c.*—*pl.* magleion (magl) A snare.

Maglawg, *a.* (magl) Tending to entangle; having knots, or meshes; having snares.

Maglawl, *a.* (magl) Tending to entangle.

Maglawr, *a.* (magl) Tending to entangle.

> Medd yfynt, melyn, melys, maglawr.
>
> Mead they were drinking, yellow, sweet, and *ensnaring.* *Aneurin.*

Magledig, *a.* (magl) Being knitted, or meshed; entangled; ensnared.

Magledigaeth, *s. m.* (magledig) The act of knitting or meshing; an entangling.

Maglen, *s. f. dim.* (magl) A springe, or gin.

Magliad, *s. m.* (magl) A knitting, or meshing; an entangling; an ensnaring.

Maglu, *v. a.* (magl) To connect intricately together; to knit, or to mesh; to entangle; to entrap, to ensnare.

Maglwr, *s. m.*—*pl.* maglwyr (magl—gwr) One who knits, or meshes; an ensnarer.

Maglys, *s. m.* (mag—llysiau) The medick.

Magodorth, *s. m.* (magawd—gorth) Generated stoppage or suppression.

> Tafawd yr hydd, gwresawg yw; a'r diodau a wneler o hwn, drwy frag, a wna drwnc—ac esmwyth magodorth y perfedd oll.
>
> The hart's tongue is of a heating quality; and the drinks which may be made of this, with malt, will produce urine; and will assuage any *suppression* in the bowels. *Meddygon Myddfai.*

Magon, *s. pl. aggr.* (mag) Berries, or baccæ.

Magu, *v. a.* (mag) To bring forward, to bring up, to rear; to instruct; to nurse; to breed. *Magu plant*, to bring up children; *magu dannedd*, to breed teeth.

> Neu'r fagaist a'th dirprwy?
>
> *Hast* thou not *reared* him that will supply thy place? *Adage.*
>
> Yn mhob gwlad y megir glew.
>
> In every country *there will be* a hero *bred.* *Adage.*

Magwr, *s. m.*—*pl.* magwyr (mag—gwr) One who brings up, rears, or instructs; one who nurses.

Magwres, *s. f.*—*pl. t.* au (magwr) A female who brings up, rears, or educates.

Magwriaeth, *s. m.* (magwr) The act of one who rears or brings up; a rearing, or instructing; nurture, nourishment.

> Ni bydd wyw gwr heb fagwraeth.
>
> A man must be feeble without *nourishment.* *Adage.*

Magwriaethawl, *a.* (magwriaeth) Relating to the act or office of one who brings up.

Magwriaethiad, *s. m.* (magwriaeth) A doing the act or duty of an educator.

Magwriaethu, *v. a.* (magwriaeth) To do the act of a rearer, bringer up, or educator.

Magwriaethus, *a.* (magwriaeth) Conducive to the act or office of rearing; nutrimental.

Magwy, *s. m.*—*pl. t.* on (mag) A cluster, a bunch.

> Gorwyn blaen a fall blodau fagwy.
>
> Splendidly white the top of the apple tree's *cluster of flowers.* *Gwalchmai.*

Magwyad, *s. m.* (magwy) A forming a cluster.

Magwyr, *s. f.*—*pl. t.* ydd (mag—gwyr) What is raised up; a structure, a wall, a building; a house, in the dialect of *Gwent*; also an enclosure, an enclosed plot of ground, or field. *Hen fagwyr*, an old building, ruin, or toft of a house: *Y fagwyr wen*, the white water-lily, otherwise called *Alaw*.

Gwelais beleidr gwyr am fagwyr fain;
Gwelais parau rhudd rhag rhuthr Owain.

I saw the shafts of heroes round a *wall* of stones; I saw crimson spears from the assault of Owain. *Cynddelw.*

Magwyrad, *s. m.* (magwyr) The act of raising a structure; a piling up, a building.

Magwyraw, *v. a.* (magwyr) To raise a structure, to pile up, to build; to raise a wall.

Magwyd, bewyd yn hawdd;
Mi gerais a'u magwyrawdd.

They have been formed, they have been spread with ease; I loved the one who *constructed* them. *Ieu. Rudd, i'r paderau.*

Magwyren, *s. f.* (magwyr) The wall or shell of a building. *Hen fagwyren*, an old ruin.

Magwyriad, *s. m.* (magwyr) A raising a structure; a piling up, a building; a raising a wall.

Magyr, *s. m.* (mag) That rears, breeds, or brings to maturity.

Mai, *s. m.—pl.* meion (ma) That stretches out; that is extended; a plain, or open field; also the month of May. *Gware y Fai*, the play of prison bars, of which there are two sorts, the other is called *Y Fai garchar*; *meirch Mai*, the steeds of the field, or war-horses; *mis Mai*, the field month, or the month of May. This word forms the names of several places, as *Pen y Fai*, *Cilfai*, *Mai Silly*, *Myddfai*, and the like.

Gwelais lyw Cattraeth tra meion:
Bid fy nar nwy llachar Cymmryon.

I saw the chief of Cattraeth beyond the *plains*: Be my prince the thunderbolt of the Cymbrians. *Taliesin.*

Yn lladd heb un ai lluddiai
Mwyalch morwyn falch ar fai.

Killing without one that should oppose her, the ousle, a proud nymph on the *field*. *D. ab Gwilym, i Easyllt.*

Mai, *conj.* (my—ai) That; that it. *Mae hi yn honi mai dall wyf*, she is asserting that I am blind; *am mai*, because that. *Taw* is used for it in *Dyfed*.

Maid, *s. m.* (ma—id) That separates, or limits.

Maidd, *s. m.* (my—aidd) Whey; curds and whey.

Maig, *s. m.—pl.* meigion (my—aig) A sudden turn, or course; an event, or hap; a fall.

Hweddl mwyfwy, garw dramwy drumain;
I faig ni bu ddadwyrain.

More and more the rumour, and the resort to the borne; for the *fall*, there was no recovery. *Seis. Bryf-furch.*

—Draig fu Ruffudd,
Udd anghudd, angerdd faig.

A dragon was Gruffudd, the chief not concealed, of violent *course*. *Ll. P. Moch.*

Mail, *s. f.—pl.* meiliau (my—ail) That is raised up, that rises round, or that is hollow; a hollow vessel of a cup form; a bowl, or bason.

Y dystain, ac y gwallofiaid oll y gyd ag ef, yn y tair gwyl arbenig, a ofwyant y dryssawr, o ddodi gwirawd yn ei lestr, o'r cyrn a'r meiliau.

The steward of the household, and all the servitors with him, in the three principal festivals, shall greet the porter, by putting liquor in his vessel, out of the horns and the *bowls*. *Welsh Laws.*

Y fol euraid ful arian,
Mal mor wrth y meiliau mân.

The golden bellied silver *bowl*, like a sea by the side of the tiny *bowls*. *W. Wynne.*

Main, *a.* (my—ain) Slender, fine, thin, or small, with respect to roundness. *Edaf fain*, fine thread; *llian main*, fine linen; *pren main*, a slender piece of timber; *dyn main*, a slim man; *diawd fain*, small beer; *dwfr yn rhedeg yn fain*, water running in a small current; *ymguddiaw yn fain*, to hide one's self closely.

Gnawd bean o fain.

That is *slender* is commonly quick. *Adage.*

Mainc, *s. f.—pl.* meincian (my—ainc) A bench.

Mainsuren, *s. f.* (main—sur) Common sorrel.

Maint, *s. m.* (main) Magnitude, size, bigness, greatness; quantity; *Dau o'r un faint*, two of the same size; *pa faint sydd yna?* how much is there? *y maint lleiaf*, the least quantity; *pa faint a dal hyna?* how much is that worth?

Ni wyl ynfydrwydd ei faint.

Folly doth not perceive her own *magnitude*. *Adage.*

Na ddos â gwr wrth ei faint.

Take not a man by his *size*. *Adage.*

Maip, *s. pl. aggr.* (ma—ib) Turnips; otherwise called *Erfin*. *Maip bendiged*, briony root.

Mais, *s. f.—pl.* meisiau (my—ais) That does away want; a device, invention, or contrivance.

Mais llaw i'm os y lluniwyd;
A mais llawn mab Tomas Llwyd.

A *device*, which will fill to me if it be formed; and the full *device* of the son of Thomas Llwyd. *H. ab D. ab I. ab Rhys.*

Maist, *s. m.* (mais) That is designed or invented.

Maith, *a.* (my—aith) Ample, large; long, tedious. *Maith ym rhoddai*, amply he would give me; *ffordd faith*, a tedious road.

Maiw, *a.* (mai) Abounding with hillocks.

Màl, *s. m.* (my—al) That is a separate particle. *a.* Trivial, trifling, small, light, or of no weight; light, vain, fond, or doating; having a semblance; like.

Màl, *conj.* (my—al) Like, similar to; as; so. *adv.* Like, so; as if; in the manner of. *Màl pe bai*, as if it were; *màl hyn*, in this manner.

Nid fàl aur da ydd â y dyn.

Not *like* the precious gold does man go onward. *Adage.*

Da gwyr, màl pawb.

He knows well, *like* every body. *Adage.*

Gair gwraig màl gwynt y cychwyn.

A woman's word sets off *like* the wind. *Adage.*

Byglymu fàl gwenyn.

Becoming knotted together *like* bees. *Adage.*

Mal gwaith Emrys.

Like the work of Emrys (Stonehenge). *Adage.*

Mal, *s. m.* (ma—al) That extends, that throws out, or produces, that is thrown out, extended, or produced; a contribution, what is reduced into small particles, or ground, a grinding.

Un yn darwedd
Gwin, a mal, a medd.

One that is generous of wine, and *bounty*, and mead. *Taliesin.*

Ff a roddes ei drefad Clynog i Dduw a Beuno yn dragywydd, heb na mal nac ardreth.

He gave his domain of Clynog to God and to Beuno for ever, without either *contribution* or tax. *Buch. Beuno.*

Nid oes na mal na threth a ddylom ei thalu.

There is neither *contribution* nor tax which we ought to pay. *H. Car. Mag.—Mabinogion.*

Mal, *a.* (ma—al) Tending to extend, throw out, or produce; extended, produced; capable of extension, smooth, glib.

Y blaenaf o bobl Wynedd,
A dal im' aur mal a medd.

The foremost of the men of Gwynedd, who bestows on me *ductile* gold and mead. *D. Nanmor.*

Malàad, *s. m.* (mal) A making or becoming like.

Malaen, *s. m.* (mal) An epithet for a snail.

Malaen a ddyly ei daith.

The *snail* deserves the end of its journey. *Adage.*

Malaith, *s. m.—pl.* maleithion (ma—llaith) Chilblains: also called *llosg eira*.

Malàn, *v. n.* (mal) To make similar, to liken.

Malawg, *a.* (mal) Full of trifling or vanity. *s. c.* One who trifles, or that is wanton.

Dangaws dy fys i falawg
Y stan a'i heirch yn gwbl.

Shew thy finger to a *trifler* and he will ask it altogether. *Adage.*

Maldawd, *s. m.* (màl) A trifling, or levity; dalliance, fondness, dotage.

Maldodi, *v. a.* (maldawd) To dally, to fondle.

Maldodus, *a.* (maldawd) Apt to dally, to fondle.

Maldodwr, *s. m.—pl.* maldodwyr (maldawd—gwr) A dallyer, a fondler, a dotard.

Maledig, *a.* (mal) Bruised, broken, ground, or pulverized. *Yd maledig*, ground corn.

Maledd, *s. m.* (màl) An over-fondness, dotage.

O rhyfedd yw'r ffoledd a'r maledd mewn merch!
Er hacred y mab, lle bo'n gadarn ei serch,
A'i fod yn llin elyn i'w thad ac i'w mam,
Hi ai dilyn hyd angau, bid cymhwys, bid cam.

How wonderful the folly and *dotage* of a woman! Be the man ever so ugly, where her love is ardent, and though he should be an inveterate foe to her father and her mother, she will follow him till death, be it right, be it wrong. *Pennill.*

Maledd, *s. m.* (mal) A state of extension.

Maleithr, *s. m.* (malaith) A blain; a kibe.

Maleithrawg, *a.* (maleithr) Having blains.

Malen, *s. f.* (mal) One that is of metal, or iron; one who uses or carries iron, one that is used to war, or violence; Bellona, Andrasta; also an epithet for a shield. *Gormes march malen*, the intrusion of the iron horse, an epithet for a tribe of depredators in ancient Britain.

A gasgler ar farch malen dan ei dor ydd â.

What is got upon the horse of Bellona, will go under his belly: or—
What is got on the devil's back is spent under his belly. *Adage.*

Afal mael ar fôl malen,
Ac yna pig yn y pen.

A golden apple on the convex of the *shield*, and then a spike on the top. *T. Aled, i farch.*

Malerth, *s. m.* (ma—llerth) Chilblains, or kibes.

Maliad, *s. m.—pl. t.* au (mal) A breaking into small pieces; a bruising, a grinding.

Maliaw, *v. a.* (màl) To think of, to care. *Nid yw yn maliaw dim amdanat*, he cares nothing about thee.

Malpai, *adv.* (màl—pai) As if it were to be, as if it were; in such a way.

Malsai, *s. f.—pl.* malseiod (màl) An eel.

Màlu, *v. a.* (màl) To imagine, to guess, to devise.

Malu, *v. a.* (mal) To reduce small, to grind.

Mal baedd yn malu ewyn.

Like a boar *grinding* foam. *Adage.*

Y felin a fal a fyn ddwfr.

The mill that *grinds* must have water. *Adage.*

Cyntaf i'r felin biau malu.

The first to the mill has a right to *grind*. *Adage.*

Malur, *s. m.* (mal) What is reduced fine, earth thrown up by a mole, or a mole-hill.

Maluria, *s. m.* (malur) That is small, or fine; that is mouldered.

Pan fo melusydd ar ben maluria,
Y bydd cagul i asgell gwalch.

When a lark is on the top of a *molehill*, the wing of the hawk is short. *Adage.*

Maluriad, *s. m.—pl. t.* au (malur) A reducing to small particles; a reducing to powder; a mouldering.

Maluriaw, *v. a.* (malur) To reduce to small particles, to bruise, to break, or to pound, to become broken, or bruised small, to moulder.

Maluriawl, *a.* (malur) Tending to break into small pieces; mouldering.

Maluriedig, *a.* (maluriad) Broken, or bruised small; being mouldered.

Malurion, *s. pl. aggr.* (malur) Broken particles. *Malurion yd*, broken, or bruised corn.

Malw, *a.* (mal) That is entire, that has no parts or joints; a snail.

Malwen, *s. f.* (malw) A snail. *Malwen ddu*, a black snail; *Malwen wen*, a white snail; *llwybr malwen*, the track of a snail.

Malwod, *s. pl. aggr.* (malw) Snails. *Cregyn malwod*, snail shells.

Malwoden, *s. f. dim.* (malwod) One of the snails.

Malwr, *s. m.—pl.* malwyr (mal—gwr) One who bruises small, or grinds, a pulverizer.

Mall, *s. f.* (my—all) A want of energy, want of compactness; a breaking out, a running out of form; softness, debility, any thing soddened: a malady: an evil. *Y fall*, the evil principle; *plant y fall*, the devil's imps. *Y fall felen*, the yellow plague, which raged over a great part of the world in the sixth and seventh centuries, as described by Procopius, book the fourth.

Gryched yw fy ngrudd—
Pa ryw fall a'i pair felly?

How wrinkled is my cheek! what is the *evil* that causes it to be so! *E. Brwynllys.*

Mall, *a.* (my—all) Void of energy, or compactness: tending to break out, or to run out of form: soft, melting: soddened: insipid: sottish; absurd; blasted; evil. *Llygad mall*, a wanton eye.

O galon dynion y deillia meddyliau mall.

Out of the hearts of men proceed *evil* thoughts.
W. Salesbury, Mark 7.

Mallaidd, *a.* (mall) Somewhat soft, lax, or loose; rather insipid; apt to be wanton.

Mallain, *a.* (mall) Abounding with softness.

Mallaint, *s. m.* (mallain) Malaxation, moisture.

Mallawd, *s. m.* (mall) A malaxation, a soddening.

Malldan, *s. m.—pl. t.* au (mall—tan) A soft or slow fire; an ignis fatuus.

Malldan dan uwd a mellten dan lymry.

A *slow fire* under porridge and lightning under flummery. *Adage.*

Malldawd, *s. m.* (mall) Softness, laxity of manners, wantonness; a soddened state, a blast.

Mallder, *s. m.* (mall) Softness, laxity, looseness of manners, wantonness; a soddened state; insipidity; a blast; sottishness.

Malldorch, *s. f.—pl.* melldyrch (mall—torch) Kibe

Malldra, *s. m.* (mall) Softness, laxity, looseness of behaviour; wantonness; a soddened state; a blasted state; insipidity.

Malldraul, *s. m.* (mall—traul) A bad digestion.

Malldreuliad, *s. m.* (malldraul) A badly digesting.

Malldreuliaw, *v. a.* (malldraul) To digest badly.

Malledig, *a.* (mall) Malaxated; softened; faded.

Malledigaeth, *s. m.* (malledig) Malaxation.

Malledigaw, *v. a.* (malledig) To malaxate.

Malledd, *s. m.* (mall) Softness; levity, wantonness, want of sharpness; insipidity; a blasted state.

Mallgaru, *v.* (mall—caru) To love wantonly.

Mallgno, *s. m.* (mall—cno) A gnawing pain.

Mallgnöad, *s. m.* (mallgno) A painfully gnawing.

Mallgnoï, *v. a.* (mallgno) To gnaw painfully.

Mallgorn, *s. m.—pl.* mallgyrn (mall—corn) The inside part of a horn.

Mallgorni, *v. n.* (mallgorn) To become an imperfect horn.

Mallgyrch, *a.* (mall—cyrch) A resort of evil beings. *Y fallgyrch eirias*, the devil-resorting fire.

Malliad, *s. m.* (mall) A divesting of energy; a softening; a becoming loose, or wanton.
Malliannawl, *a.* (malliant) Tending to softness.
Malliannu, *v. a.* (malliant) To tend to softness; to be divested of energy.
Malliannus, *a.* (malliant) Of softening tendency.
Malliant, *s. m.* (mall) A soft or lax quality, a degenerate state.
Mallineb, *s. m.* (mall) A soft or lax state.
Mallon, *s. m.* (mall) An evil principle.
Malloni, *v. n.* (mallon) To become evil.
Mallred, *s. f.* (mall—rhed) An evil course.
Mallrwydd, *s. m.* (mall) Softness; levity, wantonness; want of energy, insipidity.
Mallt, *s. m.* (mall) An evil principle; a fiend.
Mallt, *a.* (mall) Void of energy; evil. *Myn y mwci mallt!* By the evil sooty one! *Paid a galw ar y mwci mallt fal hyn*, do not call on the evil spirit in this manner. *Sil.* This *mwci mallt* is a term made use of to mince matters, instead of calling on the devil plainly.
Mallu, *v. a.* (mall) To divest of energy; to make soft, or flaccid; to sodden; to make insipid; to blast: to make evil; to become soft, or tender; to become sodden; to become insipid; to be blasted; to become evil.

Mae anadl y diogi yn mallu pob peth y cwympo arno.

The breath of idleness *blasts* every thing it falls on. *Adage.*

Mae'n glaerwyn mwnwgl eryr;
Mae lliw gwen yn mallu gwyr.

Of a splendid white is the neck of the eagle; the complexion of the fair one *blasts* the men. *S. Ceri.*

Mallus, *a.* (mall) Of a soft or lax quality, of a wanton disposition.
Mallusaw, *v. a.* (mallus) To render of a lax quality; to become blasted.
Mallusrwydd, *s.* (mallus) Flaccidity, blastedness.
Mallwaew, *s. m.* (mall—gwaew) A dull pain.
Mallwcywyr, *s. m.* (mallwaew) A dull pain.
Mam, *s. f.—pl. t.* au (ma—am) That contains, or bears; a mother, a dam. *Mam gu*, or *nain*, a grandmother; *mam wèn*, a stepmother; *mam y drwg*, the mother of mischief:—*Y fam eni*, the falling of the uterus; *gwaith y fam*, *y fam*, the mother fits; *y fam*, the matrix.

Nid gweddi ond mam.

She is no wife but who is a *mother*. *Adage.*

Ceisied asgre ei fam a gollo.

Let him seek his *mother's* bosom that loses. *Adage.*

Gwell mam godawg no thad rhieddawg.

A rich *mother* is better than a father of noble descent. *Adage.*

Mamaeth, *s. f.* (mam) Motherhood, maternity.
Mamai, *s. f.* (mam) The birth wort.
Mamaidd, *a.* (mam) Like a mother, motherly.
Mamawg, *a.* (mam) Having a mother's quality. *Y famawg ddrewllyd*, stinking goose-foot.
Mamawl, *a.* (mam) Maternal, or motherly.
Mamdref, *s. f.—pl. t.* i (mam—tref) A chief town
Mamddinas, *s. f.—pl. t.* au (mam—dinas) A metropolis, or chief city.
Mamddinasawl, *a.* (mamddinas) Metropolitical.
Mamedd, *s. f.* (mam) Motherhood, maternity.
Mameglwys, *s. f.—pl. t.* i (mam—eglwys) A mother church; a cathedral.
Mameglwysawl, *a.* (mameglwys) Belonging to a mother church.
Mameiddiad, *s. m.* (mamaidd) A becoming motherly, a rendering motherly.
Mameiddiaw, *v. n.* (mamaidd) To become motherly, to render motherly.
Mameiddrwydd, *s. m.* (mamaidd) Motherliness.
Mamen, *s. f. dim.* (mam) A little mother.
Mames, *s. f.—pl. t.* od (mam) A mother or dam with her first young.
Mamiad, *s. f.—pl. t.* au (mam) A becoming a mother.
Mamladd, *s. m.* (mam—lladd) Matricide.
Mamladdiad, *s. m.* (mamladd) A matricideal act.
Mamleiddiad, *s. m.—pl.* mamleiddiaid (mamladd) A matricide, or one who kills a mother.
Mamleiddiadawl, *a.* (mamleiddiad) Matricideal.
Mamlys, *s. m.* (mam—llys) The motherwort.
Mammaeth, *s. f.—pl. t.* od (mam—maeth) A fostering or nursing mother; a nurse.

Rhuthr mammaeth.

The attack of a *nursing mother*. *Adage.*

Afeithus pob mammaeth.

Every *nurse* is affectionate. *Adage.*

O achaws y fammaeth y cusenir y mab.

For the sake of the *nurse* the child is kissed. *Adage.*

Mammeuthaidd, *a.* (mammaeth) Of a fostering tendency; motherly.
Mammeuthiad, *s. m.* (mammaeth) The acting as a nurse, a nursing.
Mammeuthu, *v. a.* (mammaeth) To nurse.

Maethus yw mammeuthu serch.

It is tender *to cherish* love. *B. Aerdrem.*

Mammeuthus, *a.* (mammaeth) Of a motherly disposition.
Mamog, *s. f.—pl. t.* au (mam) That is with young, that is a mother or dam; an ewe with young; the womb or matrix; the hysterical passion, otherwise called *y fam*, and *clwyf y fam*; also the collapsion of the womb.
Mamogaeth, *s. f.—pl. t.* au (mamawg) Maternity.
Mamogaethu, *v. a.* (mamogaeth) To claim maternal affinity.
Mamogi, *v. a.* (mamawg) To render as a mother, to become as a mother.
Mamogiad, *s. f.—pl.* mamogiaid (mamog) That is with young; an ewe with young, also called *dafad gyfebr*.
Mamolrwydd, *s. m.* (mamawl) Motherliness.
Mamu, *v. n.* (mam) To become a mother.
Mamwch, *s. m.* (mam) A mother's fondness.
Mamwraig, *s. f.—pl.* mamwreigedd (mam—gwraig) A woman that is a mother.
Mamwydd, *s. f.—pl. t.* au (mam—gwydd) A mother goose, or a brood goose.
Mamwys, *s. f.* (mam—gwys) Maternity; a matrix; a relationship by the mother's side.

Holl tir o famwys.—Nid oes un wraig yntau a ymroddo ei hun i ail tud a ddylyo ei meibion famwys.

Claiming of land by *maternal affinity*.—There is no woman then who shall give herself to a foreigner, whose children have a right of *maternal affinity*. *Welsh Laws.*

Mamwysawl, *a.* (mamwys) Relating to maternity, or of kin by the mother.
Mamwythen, *s. f.—pl. t.* au (mam—gwythen) The crural vein, or saphœna.
Mamwythi, *s. pl. aggr.* (mam—gwythi) The main or leading channels; the main arteries.
Mamychiad, *s.* (mamwch) A fondling as a mother.
Mamychu, *v. a.* (mamwch) To fondle as a mother.
Màn, *s. f.—pl. t.* au (my—an) A space, a place, a spot, or mark; a where; a state: what holds, or contains; a hand. *Y fàn a'r fàn*, such and such a place; *y fàn dywyllaf*, the darkest period, or when the twilight is past; *yn y màn*, presently, or by and by: *màn geni*, or *màn cyncnid*, a mark from the birth, as a mole and the like: *màn y dèn*, sea plantain.

Man, *a.* (ma—an) Small, little, petty, fine. *Ceryg man*, small stones; *yd man*, small corn; *tywod man*, fine sand; *edafedd man*, fine yarn.

Nid wyf hen midd, nag eiddil,
Na gwr man, fal y gwyr mil.

I am not elderly, nor slender, nor a *small* person, as it is known to a thousand. *D. ab Gwilym.*

Manâad, *s. m.* (man) A making small, or fine; a becoming small, or fine.

Mânad, *s. f.* (màn) A mass, or lump.

Manad o ymenyn cyfled a'r ddysgl letaf yn y dref:—Sef yw manad ymenyn naw dyrnfedd led, a dyrnfedd dewedd a'r fawd yn ei sefyll.

A *mass* of butter as broad as the widest dish in the township: A *mass* of butter is so much, nine hands in breadth, and a hand in thickness, having the thumb erect. *Welsh Laws.*

Manaid, *s. f.—pl.* maneidiau (man) The contents of a mould, a print, as of butter and the like. *Manaid o ymenyn*, a print of butter; otherwise called *seigen*, and *rhisgen*.

Manarfau, *s. pl. aggr.* (man—arfau) Small arms.

Manau, *v. a.* (man) To render small, little, or fine; to become small, or fine.

Manaw, *s. f.* (man) That extends out; that forms a space, spot, or mark; the Welsh name of the Isle of Man.

Manawd, *s. m.* (man) The act of placing, a making a space, a location, a spotting.

Manawg, *a.* (man) Having a place, or space; having a spot, or mark; spotted, marked. There are a variety of tales about the *ychain banawg*, or large horned oxen, all over Wales, which probably were the moose deer; and they were also called *ychain manawg*, *ychain manodd*, and *ychain manwedd*, or the spotted oxen.

Manawl, *a.* (man) Local; relating to spots, tending to produce a spot, or mark.

Manawl, *a.* (man) Fine, nice, delicate; accurate. *Y ddyn fanawl*, the delicate fair one.

Cynnyg aur—
A main, a thlysau manawl.

Offering gold, and stones, and *curious* jewels. *Hyp. Cyfeiliawg.*

Manawyd, *s. m.—pl. t.* ydd (manaw) The staff of a banner, or standard.

Rhag byddin Ododin—
Hyder gymhell ar fresthell fanawyd.

Before the host of Gododin there was a confident impelling forward of the *shaft* of the variegated *standard*. *Aneurin.*

Manbaill, *s. m.* (man—paill) Fine flour. *a.* Of fine flour. *Bara gwyn manbaill*, white bread of fine flour.

Manbethau, *s. pl. aggr.* (man—pethau) Small things; trifling things, small matters.

Manblu, *s. pl. aggr.* (man—plu) Down-feathers.

Manbluaidd, *a.* (manblu) Like down-feathers.

Manbluawg, *a.* (manblu) Having down-feathers.

Manbysg, *s. pl. aggr.* (man—pysg) Small fish.

Manbysgod, *s. pl. aggr.* (manbysg) Small fishes.

Mando, *s. m.* (man—tô) A fine slated, or fine tiled roof.

Mandöedd, *s. m.* (mando) A covering of fine texture. *Clyd fandöedd*, a warm fine-worked roof.

Mandöi, *v. a.* (mando) To roof with fine work.

Mandon, *s. f.* (man—tôn) The dandruff, also the woodroof; otherwise called *llysiau yr eryr*.

Mandonawg, *a.* (mandon) Having a dandruff.

Mandwyn, *s. m.* (màn—twyn) The scrophula.

Mandwynawg, *a.* (mandwyn) Strumous.

Mandwynawl, *a.* (mandwyn) Strumatic.

Manddail, *s. pl. aggr.* (man—dail) Small leaves.

Manddarlun, *s. m.—pl. t.* ion (man—darlun) A miniature delineation.

Manddarluniad, *s. m.* (manddarlun) A delineating in miniature.

Manddarluniaw, *v. a.* (manddarlun) To draw in miniature.

Manddarnau, *s. pl.* (man—darnau) Small pieces.

Manddarnu, *v. a.* (man—darnu) To break into small pieces.

Manddeiliaw, *v.* (manddail) To shoot first leaves.

Manddeiliawg, *a.* (manddail) Having first leaves.

Manddel, *s. m.* (man—del) A quick whisk or send

Manddelu, *v. a.* (manddel) To whisk about.

Manddellt, *s. pl. aggr.* (man—dellt) Fine split-wood or rods, such as are used in basket work.

Manddos, *s. pl. aggr.* (man—dos) Small drops.

Manddosawg, *a.* (manddos) Having small drops.

Manddosi, *v.* (manddos) To fall in small drops.

Manddrain, *s. pl. aggr.* (man—drain) Small thorns

Manddreiniach, *s. pl.* (manddrain) Small thorns.

Manddreiniawg, *a.* (manddrain) Having small thorns, having little prickles.

Manddryllian, *s. pl. aggr.* (man—dryllian) Small fragments, small pieces.

Manddrylliaw, *v. a.* (man—dryiliaw) To break into small fragments or pieces.

Manddrylliawg, *a.* (man—drylliawg) Having small fragments or pieces.

Manddyluniad, *s. m.* (man—dyluniad) A drawing in miniature.

Manddyluniaw, *v. a.* (man—dyluniaw) To draw in miniature.

Maned, *s. f.—pl. t.* i (man) Hand basket, maund.

Manedig, *a.* (man) Spotted, marked, flecked.

Maneg, *s. f.—pl.* menyg (man) A glove.

Maneiliad, *s. m.* (man—eiliad) A platting or constructing a fine work.

Maneiliaw, *v. a.* (man—eiliaw) To plat or build up a nice piece of work.

Maneiliawg, *a.* (man—eiliawg) Of nice structure.

Maneirian, *s. pl. aggr.* (man—geirian) Little words

Manfrith, *a.* (man—brith) Of a small, nice, or fine variegation, finely striped.

Eppiliant fanfrithion.

They shall bring forth *finely striped ones*. *Genesis* 31. 8.

Manfrithad, *s. m.* (manfrith) A finely variegating.

Manfrithaw, *v.* (manfrith) To variegate finely.

Manfrithawg, *a.* (manfrith) Finely variegated.

Manfrithedd, *s. m.* (manfrith) The state of being finely variegated, small check pattern.

Manfriw, *a.* (man—briw) Finely crumbled.

Manfriwaw, *v. a.* (manfriw) To crumble small.

Manfriwiad, *s. m.* (manfriw) A braying small, a crumbling small.

Mangaled, *a.* (man—caled) Of a hard grasp.

Meiri mangaled am ben ceiniawg.

Husbandmen that are *close-fisted* after the penny. *Myrddin.*

Mangan, *s. m.* (man—can) Fine flour.

Manganu, *v. a.* (mangant) To bolt fine flour.

Mangant, *s. m.* (mangan) Fine bolted flour.

A meingorff o liw mangant.

A slender form of the hue of *fine flour*. *D. Llwyd.*

Mangaw, *s. m.* (màn—caw) A fine whipping round, or binding, nice work.

Mangawiad, *s. m.* (mangaw) A whipping or binding with fine work.

Mangawiau, *s. pl. aggr.* (mangaw) Small shreds; trifles, or toys.

Mangawiaw, *v. a.* (mangaw) To whip round, or bind, with fine work.

Mangeinion, *s. pl. aggr.* (man—ceinion) Delicate or fine jewels.

Mangerdded, *v. a.* (man—cerdded) To walk with short steps; to walk delicately.
Mangibau, *s. pl. aggr.* (man—cibau) Fine cups.
Mangoed, *s. pl. aggr.* (man—coed) Brushwood.
Mangor, *s. m.* (man—cor) A fine membrane.
Mangre, *s. f.* (man—cre) An intricate place.

> Addwyn march myngfras mangre.
>
> Beautiful is the horse with a thick mane in a *tangle*. — *Taliesin.*
>
> Y teir-bro dano a dyf;
> Tair mangre y tarw mein-gryf.
>
> The three countries under him increase; the three *strong holds* of the bull slender and vigorous. — *Gutto y Glyn.*

Mangylchau, *s. pl.* (man—cylch) Small hoops.
Mangylchawg, *a.* (man—cylchawg) Having small or fine hoops.
Mangylchu, *v. a.* (man—cylchu) To bind with fine or small hoops.
Manhedion, *s. pl. aggr.* (man—hedion) Small flying motes, or flue.
Maniad, *s. m.* (man) A placing; a spotting.
Maniadawl, *a.* (maniad) Positional; local.
Manion, *s. pl. aggr.* (man) The smaller particles of any thing; small or empty grains of corn.
Manladron, *s. pl.* (man—lladron) Petty thieves.
Manlo, *s. m. aggr.* (man—glo) Small coal.
Manllwdn, *s. m.—pl.* manllydnod (man—llwdn) A small animal, a small beast.
Manllwyn, *s. m.* (man—llwyn) Mutton. *Cig manllwyn*, mutton flesh, *gwer manllwyn*, mutton suet.
Mannodd, *s. f.* (mant) An aching of the jaw.
Mannwst, *s. f.* (mant—gwst) A soreness of the jaw; the tooth ache.
Mannwyfau, *s. pl. aggr.* (man—nwyfau) Small wares.
Manod, *s. m. aggr.* (man—od) Small or fine snow. *Lliw manod*, the hue of the driven snow, an epithet for a fair woman.
Manodi, *v. n.* (manod) To snow small snow.
Manogedig, *a.* (manawg) Bespeckled, bespotted.
Manogen, *s. f. dim.* (manawg) A speckled one.
Manogi, *v. a.* (manawg) To bespeckle.
Manogiad, *s. m.* (manawg) A bespeckling.
Manol, *a.* (man) Delicate, nice; accurate.

> Manol pob rhan, hardd y cyfan.
>
> Every part *accurate*, makes the whole handsome. — *Adage.*

Manoli, *v. a.* (manol) To make nice or accurate.

> Gwna reol a'i manoli,
> A gwardd y tair, gwrdd wyd ti.
>
> Make a rule, *rendering it accurate*, and forbid the three, for thou art powerful. — *T. Llen.*

Manoliad, *s. m.* (manol) A rendering delicate, nice, or curious; a making accurate.
Manolosg, *s. m. aggr.* (man—golosg) Small coal.
Manon, *s. f.* (man) A paragon of beauty.

> Myned er gweled gwened gwaneg
> Manon wawr Arfon, gofion gofeg.
>
> Going for the sake of beholding how fair the course of a *goddess* the luminary of Arfon, recalling thoughts of love. — *Casnodyn.*

Manred, *a.* (man—rhed) Of small step or pace.

> Manred gymined, a feddyliais
> Myned i Fenai cyn ni'm bai fais?
> Carafi a'm heneirch o dir Cemais,
> Gwerling Dogfeiling, cadelling trais.
>
> *Short-paced* traveller, did I think of going to Menai ere it was shallow for me? I love such as greet me of the land of Cemais, the chieftain of the race of Dogfael, the antagonist of oppression. — *Melgani, m. Cynddylan.*

Manrinion, *s. pl.* (man—rhin) Trifling charms.
Manro, *s. m. aggr.* (man—gro) Small pebbles.

> Mor wael myned hael hwyl gyffro galar
> Yn rhwym gwely manro!
>
> How miserable that the generous one who causes the agitation of woe, should be gone into the bands of the bed of *gravel!* — *Bleddyn Fardd.*

Manson, *s. m.* (man—son) A small talk; a low murmuring, muttering, or grumbling.
Manson, *v. a.* (man—son) To mutter, to grumble.
Mansoniwr, *s. m.—pl.* mansonwyr (manson—gwr) A mutterer, a grumbler.
Manswyddau, *s. pl.* (man—swydd) Petty offices.
Mant, *s. m.—pl. t.* au (man) That closes together, or shuts close; the jaw; the jawbone, or mandible; the mouth.
Mantach, *s. m.* (mant) An exposed jaw, produced by old age; a toothless jaw.
Mantachaidd, *a.* (mantach) Tending to close the jaws, as is done from the loss of teeth.
Mantachawg, *a.* (mantach) Of a toothless jaw.
Mantachedd, *s. m.* (mantach) The hollowness of the jaws; toothlessness.
Mantachiad, *s. m.* (mantach) A closing the mouth, as if done by a toothless person.
Mantachlyd, *a.* (mantach) Apt to close the jaws, as a toothless person does.
Mantachu, *v. a.* (mantach) To shew the jaws; to mumble; to become toothless.
Mantachwr, *s. m.—pl.* mantachwyr (mantach—gwr) One who has a toothless jaw; a mumbler.
Mantai, *s. c.—pl.* manteion (mant) A mumbler.
Mantaidd, *a.* (mant) Like the closing of the jaw.
Mantais, *s. f.—pl.* manteision (man—tais) An advantage.
Mantawl, *s. f.—pl.* mantolion (mantawl) An even weight, poise, or balance; the beam of a balance; a balance. *Arwydd y fantawl*, the sign of the balance.
Manteisiad, *s. m.* (mantais) A taking advantage.
Manteisiaw, *v. a.* (mantais) To take advantage.
Manteisiawg, *a.* (mantais) Having advantage.
Manteisiawl, *a.* (mantais) Advantageous.

> Para ansoddau manteisiawl; para foddion, a chyneddfau a sydd gan gyrff cristianogion da, yn yr adgyfodiad!
>
> What *advantageous* qualities; wh[illegible] and principles do the bodies of good christians possess, at [illegible] resurrection! — *W. Williams, T. a Kempis.*

Manteisiwr, *s. m.—pl.* manteiswyr (mantais—gwr) One who seeks advantage.
Mantell, *s. f.—pl.* mentyll (mant) A mantle, or cloak. *Mantell werddonig*, *mantell gedenawg*, an Irish mantle, a shaggy cloak.

> Gorea un todded mantell.
>
> The best covering of any is a *mantle*. — *Adage.*
>
> Y penhebogydd a ddyly y fantell y marchoco y brenin ynddi, yn y tair gwyl arbenig.
>
> The chief falconer claims the *mantle*, in which the king rides, on the three principal festivals. — *Welsh Laws.*

Mantellawg, *a.* (mantell) Having a mantle.
Mantelliad, *s. m.* (mantell) A mantling over.
Mantellu, *v. a.* (mantell) To mantle, to cloak.
Mantellwr, *s. m.—pl.* mantellwyr (mantell—gwr) One who mantles, or cloaks.
Mantoledig, *a.* (mantawl) Being balanced.
Mantoli, *v. a.* (mantawl) To balance.
Mantoliad, *s. m.* (mantawl) A balancing.
Mantolwr, *s. m.* (mantawl—gwr) A balancer.
Manu, *v. a.* (man) To make a space, or place; to make a spot, or mark, to dot, or to point, to make an impression, to impress, to imprint a mark; to be of effect. *Bendith Duw a fáno it!* may the blessing of God be of effect to thee!

Bychan fudd ei fedydd a fain.

Small the benefit, which his baptism will impress. *Seis. Bryf-fwrch.*

Yn ail gerdd 'ym rhwyf yn rhwydd yd fain.

In the next song to my chief easily it *will make an impression.* *Cynddelw.*

——Gwaedled y llafn,
A gwaedliw ar giwed;
A gwaedlen am fen a fuaed,
A gwaedian a gran yn grwaied.

Reeking the blade, and a hue of blood on the throng; and a bloody veil over the spot *that was marked*, and a plain of blood and the gory brow. *H. ab Owain.*

Manu, *v. a.* (man) To make small; to pound; to become small, to crumble.

Manus, *s. m. aggr.* (man—us) The thin or out coat of corn; chaff.

Manw, *a.* (man) Of a fine or subtile quality.

Manwaidd, *a.* (manw) Of a subtile quality.

Manwedd, *s. m.* (man—gwedd) A subtile texture

Manweddaidd, *a.* (manwedd) Of a fine texture.

Y cythraul——o natur angel, ef a wybydd lawer; ni wybydd ef hagen bob peth; ac megys i mae manweddaiddiach natur angel noc un dyn, felly i mae cyfarwyddach noc ef.

The devil, having the nature of an angel, knows a great deal; he doth not, however, know every thing; and as the angelic nature is *more subtile* than that of man, so is he more informed than man. *Elucidarius.*

Manweddiad, *s. m.* (manwedd) A rendering or becoming of a subtile texture.

Manweddu, *v. a.* (manwedd) To render of subtile texture; to become of subtile texture.

Manwerthiad, *s. m.* (gwerthiad) A retailing.

Manwerthu, *v. a.* (man—gwerthu) To retail.

Manwerthwr, *s. m.—pl.* manwerthwyr (man—gwerthwr) A retailer.

Manwg, *s. m.* (man) Spottedness; freckles.

Manwgl, *s. m.* (manwg) That is in small spots.

Manwl, *a.* (man) Accurate, exact, curious, exquisite, nice; careful, diligent.

Siwan ni byd ry fanwl.

Siwan will not be over nice. *L. G. Cothi.*

Manwlaw, *s. m.* (man—gwlaw) Small rain.

Manwlawiaw, *v. n.* (manwlaw) To rain small.

Manwr, *s. m.—pl.* manwyr (man—gwr) One who makes a mark, or impression.

Manwy, *a.* (man) Fine, rare, or subtile.

Manwyaidd, *a.* (manwy) Of a subtile texture.

Manwyaw, *v. a.* (manwy) To refine, to subtilize.

Manwydd, *s. pl. aggr.* (man—gwydd) Brushwood

Manwyddawg, *a.* (manwydd) Abounding with brushwood, or shrubs.

Manwydden, *s. f. dim.* (manwydd) A shrub.

Manwyedd, *s. m.* (manwy) Exility, fineness.

Manwyn, *s. m.—pl. t.* au (man—gwyn) A glandulous swelling, the king's-evil.

Manwŷnau, *s. pl. aggr.* (manwyn) The strumæ.

Manwŷnawg, *a.* (manwyn) Strumous.

Manwŷnion, *s. pl. aggr.* (manwyn) Strumæ.

Manwythau, *s. pl.* (man—gwyth) Capillary veins

Manwythenau, *s. pl.* (man—gwythen) Small veins

Manwythi, *s. pl.* (man—gwyth) Capillary veins.

Manyd, *s. m. aggr.* (man—yd) The smaller grain amongst corn, small corn.

Manyglawg, *a.* (manwgl) Abounding with small parts, or spots. *s. f.* The woody nightshade.

Manyglion, *s. pl. aggr.* (manwgl) The small particles, or parts, amongst corn, or other things; the small or empty grains of corn; also called *hedion*, *gwehilion*, and *manion*.

Manylai, *s. c.—pl.* manyleion (manwl) Exact one.

Manylaidd, *a.* (manwl) Somewhat exact, or nice.

Manyledd, *s. m.* (manwl) Exactness, nicety.

Manyliad, *s. m.* (manwl) A rendering accurate, correct, or nice; a becoming exact or careful.

Manyliannawl, *a.* (manyliant) Punctilious.

Manyliannu, *v. a.* (manyliant) To render exact, to be exact, or punctilious.

Manyliannus, *a.* (manyliant) Punctilious.

Manyliant, *s. m.* (manwl) Refinement.

Manylrwydd, *s. m.* (manwl) Exactness, nicety.

Manylu, *v. a.* (manwl) To render accurate, correct, or nice; to be accurate, nice, or careful.

Manylu am a wnelwyf.

To be careful about what I do. *Edm. Prys.*

Manylus, *a.* (manwl) Of a curious or nice nature.

Manylwaith, *s. m.* (manwl—gwaith) Curious or nice work; a nice operation.

Manylwch, *s. m.* (manwl) Accuracy, or nicety.

Manylweithiaw, *v. a.* (manylwaith) To make curious or nice work.

Manysgrabl, *s. pl. aggr.* (man—ysgrabl) The smaller kind of animals.

Y dystain a'r cog bieu grwyn y manysgrabl: sef yw y rhai hyny y defaid, a'r wyn, a'r mynau, a'r iyrch, a'r elanedd, a phob man llwdn y del ei groen i'r gegin amdano.

The house steward and the cook own the skins of the *small beasts* that is to say those are the sheep, and the lambs, and the kids, and the roes, and the deers, and every small animal whose skin shall come into the kitchen upon it. *Welsh Laws.*

Mäon, *s. pl. aggr.* (ma) Those who fill a space, or compose a state; the people, the multitude, or inhabitants; subjects of the realm.

Afallen beren bren——
Ymenthr yn ei bon, mäon yn ei chylch.

The apple-tree, of fragrant growth, there is the *much of* ... ing at its stem, the *multitude* surround it. *Myrddin.*

Rhwyfant mäon meddlyn.

The *multitude* will pass about the mead liquor. *Llefoed.*

Delis Gruffudd mawr, a mäon Prydain.
Nid prydferth i'w alon,
Lle teg, teyrnwaith udd Mon,
Llys er lles i feddygon.

Gruffudd the great did hold, with the *people* of Britain, not pleasant to his foes, a fair place, the princely work of the chief of Mon, a court for the benefit of those who cure themselves with mead. *Ll. P. Moch, i R. ab Hywel.*

Clyr y clner wyndiredd,
Nid Saeson y mäon a'i medd.

The minstrelsy of the clear happy regions, the Saxons are not the *people* who possess it. *Ll. P. Moch.*

Balch ei fenwyd, balch ei fäon.

Elate his joy, and elate his *people.* *Gwalchmai.*

Digardd bardd ei fardd a'i fäon.

Without restraint and splendid his bard and his *people.* *M. Pool ab Griffri.*

Ef yw'r naf mwyaf, a fag mäon byd;
Bid awdwr y Brython!

He is the greatest prince, which the *inhabitants* of the world support; may he be the maker of the Britons! *D. y Coed, i Hop. ab Thomas.*

Mapwl, *s. m.* (ma—pwl) A knob on the middle of any thing; a mop.

Mar, *s. m.* (my—ar) That is active, or flitting. *a.* Flitting about.

Maran, *s. f.—pl. t.* au (mar) A holme of moving pebbles; shifting ground; a strand, also a spawner; a spawning salmon.

Llyfn mor, llawen maranedd.

Smooth the sea, sportive the *spawners.* *Aneurin.*

Mi a wnaf——
It well no thrichan maran.

I will do for thee better than three hundred *spawners.* *Taliesin.*

Maranawg, *a.* (maran) Abounding with holmes.

Maranedd, *s. m.* (maran) A holme, or flat piece of ground formed by water; a multitude.

Maranedd gwedy mordwy,
A ddylyned cad cylchwy.

The *strand*, after sailing, was followed to surround the fight. *Llywarch Hen.*

Am dano gwyledd,
A lliaws maranedd
Eardeyrn Gogledd,
Arbenig teyrnedd.

Around him a modest demeanour, and the varied *multitude*: the splendid prince of the North, the choicest of princes. *Taliesin, i Urien.*

Rhys, ail Walchmai, ddifai, ddifeiì fonedd
Peredur, llafn-ddur, mur maranedd.

Rhys, like Gwalchmai, faultless, of unspotted lineage of Peredur, with steely blade, the bulwark of the *people*. *Einion Len.*

Caraf ei brôedd——
A'i diffaith mawr-faith, a'i maranedd.

I love its cultivated vales, and its far-extending wilds, and its *strand*. *Hywel ab Owain.*

Maraneddawg, *a.* (maranedd) Having holmes.
Maraneddiad, *s. m.* (maranedd) A forming a holme
Maraneddu, *v. a.* (maranedd) To form a holme; to become a holme.
Maraniad, *s. m.* (maran) A forming a holme.
Maranu, *v. a.* (maran) To form holmes, or flats.
Marc, *s. m.—pl. t.* iau (mar) An impression upon any thing; a mark.
Marciad, *s. m.* (marc) A marking, an observing.
Marciaw, *v. a.* (marc) To mark; to observe.
Marciwr, *s. m.—pl.* marcwyr (marc—gwr) A marker; an observer.
March, *s. m.—pl.* meirch (my—arch) A horse, a steed. *March dyre*, a stallion; *march cad*, *cadfarch*, and *march mai*, a war-horse; *march malen*, the steed of Bellona; *march tom*, a drudge horse; *march tynu*, a draught horse; *march cynnud*, a horse for carrying fuel; *march cynfas*, a stalking horse.

Nid rhywiawg ond march.

Nought tractable but a *horse*. *Adage.*

Gores march ex a'm dyco.

The best *horse* is the one that will carry me. *Adage.*

March ab Meirchion, pa beth bynag a gyffyrddai a droai yn aur; a chlustiau march oedd iddo.

March the son of Meirchion, whatsoever he touched he would turn to gold; and he had the ears of a *horse*. *Hen-chwedlau.*

March, *a.* (my—arch) Towering, rearing; of luxuriant growth. *March wreinnyn*, a ringworm; *march fiaren*, a white brier; *march redyn*, the oak-fern; *march ddyrnawd*, a great thump.
Marchai, *s. c.—pl.* marcheion (march) A rider.
Marchaidd, *a.* (march) Like a horse, horse-like.
Marchalan, *s. m.* (march—alan) Elecampane.
Marchasyn, *s. m.—pl. t.* od (march—asyn) A male ass, a jackass.
Marchau, *v. a.* (march) To ride a horse.
Marchawg, *a.* (march) Having a horse, horsed. *s. m.—pl.* marchogion. That has a horse; a cavalier, a horseman; a knight; also a jug, in *Dyfed*.

Cais farchawg da dan draed ei farch.

Seek for a good *rider* under the feet of his horse. *Adage.*

Marchawglu, *s. m.—pl. t.* oedd (marchawg—llu) A body or squadron of horse; cavalry.

Achel a gyweiriws ei farchawglu, ac ai hanfones yn barawd i Agamemnon.
Achilles put in order his *cavalry*, and sent it in readiness to Agamemnon. *H. Dared.*

Marchawgwisg, *s. f.—pl. t.* oedd (marchawg—gwisg) A riding-habit, a riding-dress.

Gwared ei marchawgwisg hi amdanei a oruc.

Pull off her *riding-habit* from her was what she did. *H. Geraint—Mabinogion.*

Marchawl, *a.* (march) Belonging to a horse.
Marchawr, *s. m.—pl.* marchorion (march) A horseman, a cavalier.
Marchbren, *s. m.—pl. t.* au (march—pren) A supporting timber, or main beam. *Marchbren meun odyn faes yn cynnal y cledr crasu*, a main timber in a field kiln supporting the drying frame.
Marchdaran, *s. f.—pl. t.* au (march—taran) A loud thunder.

Ant——
I blith y gethern
I waelawd uffern,
Lle mae migawern
Wedi migwaw,
A phob marchdaran yn ymdaraw.

They will go amongst the fiends, to the bottom of hell, where there is a quaggy bog covered over, and every *harsh thunder* re-echoing. *Gr. Ynad Goch.*

Marchdy, *s. m.—pl. t.* au (march—ty) A stable.
Marchddyrnawd, *s. m.* (march—dyrnawd) A great blow, or stroke.
Marchfaen, *s. m.—pl.* marchfeini (march—maen) A horseblock.

Addwyn ewynawg am farchfain.

It is pleasant to see *horseblocks* sprayed over with foam. *Taliesin.*

Marchfeillion, *s. pl. aggr.* (march—meillion) Clover
Marchfiaren, *s. f.* (march—miaren) A white brier
Marchfieri, *s. pl.* (march—mieri) White briers.
Marchforgrugyn, *s. m.* (march—morgrugyn) A large kind of ant; otherwise called *morgrugyn asgellawg*, or winged ant.
Marchforion, *s. pl. aggr.* (march—morion) The large winged ants.
Marchgau, *v. a.* (march—cau) To ride. *A efe i farchgau yn fore iawn*, he goes to ride very early. *Dyfed.*
Marchgen, *s. m.—pl. t.* au (march—cen) A horse's skin; also a thong of a horse's skin.
Marchgod, *s. f.—pl. t.* au (march—cod) A saddle-bag
Marchgorn, *s. m.—pl.* marchgyrn (march—corn) The outer part or shell of a horn.
Marchiad, *s. m.* (march) A lifting; a horsing.
Marchlan, *s. f.—pl. t.* au (march—llan) A stable.
Marchleidr, *s. m.—pl.* marchleidron (march—lleidr) An arrant thief.

Marchleidr a grog y corleidr.

The great thief will hang the petty thief. *Adage.*

Marchlu, *s. m.—pl. t.* oedd (march—llu) Cavalry.
Marchnad, *s. f.—pl. t.* oedd (marchyn) A lifting up, or exposing; a market.

Can ebrwydded yn y farchnad
Groen yr oen a chroen y ddafad.

As frequent in the *market* the skin of the lamb as the skin of the sheep. *Adage.*

Marchnadawl, *a.* (marchnad) As to a market.
Marchnadiad, *s. m.* (marchnad) A marketting.
Marchnadu, *v. a.* (marchnad) To market.
Marchnadwr, *s. m.—pl.* marchnadwyr (marchnad—gwr) A market-man; a chapman.
Marchnadwraig, *s. f.—pl.* marchnadwreigedd (marchnad—gwraig) A market-woman.
Marchnadwriaeth, *s. m.* (marchnadwr) The business of a market-man.
Marchnadydd, *s. m.—pl. t.* ion (marchnad) A market-man, a chapman.
Marchnadyddes, *s. f.—pl. t.* au (marchnadydd) A market-woman.
Marchnata, *v. a.* (marchnad) To market.
Marchnatâad, *s. m.* (marchnata) A marketting.
Marchnatâawl, *a.* (marchnata) As to marketting.
Marchnatâwr, *s. m.—pl.* marchnatâwyr (marchnata—gwr) A market-man.
Marchnatiad, *s. m.* (marchnad) A marketting.
Marchnatty, *s. m.—pl. t.* au (marchnad—ty) A market house.
Marchnatwr, *s. m.—pl.* marchnatwyr (marchnad—gwr) A market-man; a chapman.

Marchnatwraig, *s. f.*—*pl.* marchnatwreigedd (marchnad—gwraig) A market woman.

Marchocâad, *s. m.* (marchawg) A riding on horseback.

Marchocâawl, *a.* (marchawg) Relating to horsemanship.

Marchocâu, *v. a.* (marchawg) To ride on horseback, to ride. This is mostly used in the SILURIAN, and *marchogaeth* in the NORTHWALIAN dialect.

Marchocâwr, *s. m.*—*pl.* marchocâwyr (marchawg—gwr) A horseman, a rider.

Marchogaeth, *s. m.* (marchawg) Horsemanship, riding; chivalry, knighthood.

> Gwalchmai a rodded—i ddysgu moes, a marchogaeth, a lladd a chleddyf.
>
> Gwalchmai was placed to learn manners, and *horsemanship*, and the use of the sword. *Gr. ab Arthur.*

Marchogaeth, *v. a.* (marchawg) To practise horsemanship, or riding; to ride.

Marchogaethiad, *s. m.* (marchogaeth) The practising of horsemanhip.

Marchogaethu, *v. a.* (marchogaeth) To practise horsemanship.

Marchogaid, *s. m.*—*pl.* marchogeidiau (marchawg) A jug-full.

Marchogawl, *a.* (marchawg) Equestrian.

Marchoges, *s. f.*—*pl. t.* au (marchawg) A horsewoman, a riding-woman; a female chevalier.

> Dyma farchoges fawr, yn taro wrth y brenin yn ngwrthol ar ei hynt—Ho! modryb a'r clos, ebai rhyw ddiawl croch, nosda iwch!
>
> Here comes a *bouncing lady*, falling against the king's back in her course.—Ha! Madam with the breeches, cried some hoarse fiend, good night to you! *Ellis Wynn, B. Cwsg.*

Marchogiaeth, *s. m.* (marchawg) Knighthood.

Marchogwr, *s. m.*—*pl.* marchogwyr (marchawg—gwr) A rider, a horseman.

Marchogwraig, *s. f.*—*pl.* marchogwreigedd (marchawg—gwraig) A horse-woman.

Marchon, *s. f.* march—on) The male ash.

Marchonen, *s. f.* (marchon) A male ash-tree.

Marchrawd, *s. f.*—*pl.* marchrodion (march—rhawd) A troop or army of horse; cavalry.

Marchredyn, *s. pl. aggr.* (march—rhedyn) The oak fern, or polypody; also called *rhedyn y derw*.

Marchredynen, *s. f.* (marchredyn) Shield-fern; *marchredynen wryw*, male-fern.

Marchridyll, *s. m.*—*pl. t.* iau (march—rhidyll) A sifter, or skreen.

Marchruddygl, *s. m.* (march—rhuddygl) Horseradish; also called *rhuddygl Mawrth*.

Marchwas, *s. m.*—*pl.* marchweision (march—gwas) A horseman, a cavalier.

Marchwiail, *s. pl. aggr.* (march—gwiail) Saplings.

> Marchwiail, bedw briglas
> A dyn fy nhroed o wanas:
> Nac addef rin i was.
>
> The *saplings* of the green-topt birch will get my foot out of the shackle: disclose no secret to a youth. *Llywarch Hen.*

Marchwialen, *s. f.* (marchwiail) A sapling.

Marchwr, *s. m.*—*pl.* marchwyr (march—gwr) A horseman; a jockey, a groom; a horse-breaker.

> Gwell marchwr gwerthu nog en prynu.
>
> A selling *jockey* is superior to a buying one. *Adage.*

Marchwraig, *s. f.*—*pl.* marchwreigedd (march—gwraig) A horse-woman.

Marchwraint, *s. pl. aggr.* (march—gwraint) Tetters.

Marchwreinnyn, *s. m.* (marchwraint) A ringworm.

Marchwriad, *s. m.* (marchwr) Acting as a jockey.

Marchwriaeth, *s. m.* (marchwr) The art of managing horses, horsemanship, jockeyship.

Marchwriaw, *v. a.* (marchwr) To act as a jockey.

Marchwys, *s. pl. aggr.* (march—gwys) Horsemen.

Marchysgall, *s. pl. aggr.* (march—ysgall) The spear thistle. *Marchysgall dôf*, *marchysgall y gerddi*, artichokes.

Marchysgallen, *s. f.* (marchysgall) A spear thistle.

Mared, *s. m.* (mar) That is active or lively.

Maredawg, *a.* (mared) Active, agile, quick, nimble

> Maner foddawg,
> Maer anwerthawg,
> Maredawg doeth.
>
> A willing distributer, a house occupied steward, active, and wise.

Maredw, *a.* (mared) Devoid of action.

> Dalar, un cywar, a'n cudd,
> Deon dêrw maredw Maredudd.
>
> Earth, one small space, hides us, the separating oak plank from the *lifeless Meredudd.* *Ll. P. Moch.*

Margan, *s. f.* (mar—can) A feigned being, or goddess, to whom was assigned to conduct souls, on their departure from the bodies at death.

> Panyw Margan dwywes o annwn.
>
> *Margan* which is a goddess of the inanimate state. *Mabinogion.*

Marian, *s. m.*—*pl. t.* au (mar) A flat, or holme, such factitious ground as is deposited by water, a strand; also called *maran*.

Marianawg, *a.* (marian) Abounding with holmes.

Mariandir, *s. m.*—*pl. t.* oedd (marian—tir) Holmeland, formed of pebbles moved about.

Marianedd, *s. m.* (marian) A holme, a haugh.

Marianfa, *s. m.*—*pl. t.* oedd (marian) A place consisting of holmes or pebbles.

Marianiad, *s. m.* (marian) A forming a holme.

Mariannu, *v. n.* (marian) To form a holme.

Marl, *s. m.* (mar) Earth deposited by water; a rich kind of clay, marl.

Marlaidd, *a.* (marl) Of a marly quality.

Marlawg, *a.* (marl) Abounding with marl.

Marlbridd, *s. m.* (marl—pridd) A marly soil.

> Nid erddir marlbridd iddi.
>
> No *marly earth* will be ploughed for her. *D. ab Gwilym, i'r furyalch.*

Marledig, *a.* (marl) Being marled; turned to marl

Marliad, *s. m.* (marl) The act of marling.

Marliaw, *v. a.* (marl) To marl, to manure with marl; to become marl.

> Mae'r wlad wedi marliaw ym.
>
> The country is finished *marling* for me. *I. Deulwyn.*

Marm, *s. m.* (mar) Dead earth; chalk.

Marmawr, *s. m.* (marm) That consists of chalky earth; marble; also called *myner*.

Marmoraidd, *a.* (marmawr) Like marble.

Marmorawg, *a.* (marmawr) Having marble.

Marmori, *v. n.* (marmawr) To become marble.

Marth, *s. m.*—*pl. t.* au (mar) That is plain or open; that is evident.

> Marth marw eurdeyrn Gogledd;
> Gwynfryn ei sydd ym ery!
>
> *Evident* the death of the splendid prince of the North, the white hill is his lasting abode! *Myrddin.*

> Ystrym chwerw—
> A i marth mawr mor de;
> Ail yrth ail syrth se—
> Yw lladd Llywelyn!
>
> A bitter idea like the great *swell* of the sea of the south, like a torrent, like the fall of light, is the slaying of Llywelyn. *Gwalchmai.*

Marth, *a.* (mar) Of evident or open quality; certain, swelling, heavy.

Er Madawg ys mau
Marth gollau gyfeugar '

For Madawg *sad* memorials of regret afflict me' *Gwalchmai.*

Marthaw, *v. n.* (marth) To become swollen.

Marthawl, *a.* (marth) Tending to swell out, or to make plain.

Marthlad, *s. m.* (marth) A making evident.

Marthig, *a.* (marth) Apt to be unwieldy; heavy.

Lle rhewydd haul Mawrth ddydd marthig;
Lle rhewydd cethlydd cathl-ddig heryth-lom,
Hiraethlawn ddifwydig.

Where wantons the sun of March on a *heavy day*; where wantons the chorister of angry song, with her bare body, wistful and without food. *Hywel Ystoryn.*

Marthöedd, *s. m.* (marthaw) Unwieldiness.

Tysilaw——
Mad goreu madden marthöedd.

Tysilio, well did he put away *heaviness.* *Cynddelw.*

Marthrwydd, *s. m.* (marth) Unwieldiness.

Marthu, *v. a.* (marth) To make cumbrous.

Marthus, *a.* (marth) Cumbersome, bulky.

Marw, *s. m.—pl.* meirw (mar) That is dead, a dead one, the dead; mortality. *Marw mawr*, a great mortality; *y meirw*, the dead ones, or the dead.

Pob peth a ddaw trwy'r ddaiar,
Ond y marw—mawr ei garchar.

Every thing comes through the earth, but the *dead*, whose confinement is great. *Adage.*

O ddeall tripheth y bydd difant a gortrech ar bob drwg a marw: amwyd, achaws, a phedriant; a hyn a geir yn y gwynfyd.

By knowing three things there will be a divestigation and overcoming of every evil and mortality: effect, cause, and agent; and this will be obtained in the circle of felicity. *Barddas.*

Marw, *v. a.* (mar) To die, to become dead.

A fo marw ni ymogelir.

He that *dies* will not be run away from. *Adage.*

A naw cant maer marwawd.

And nine hundred commanders *did become dead.* *Taliesin.*

Marw, *a.* (mar) Dead; mortal, deceased. *Mae efe yn farw syth*, he is stone dead.

Marwâad, *s. m.* (marw) A mortifying; a deadening

Marwâawl, *a.* (marw) Of a deadening quality.

Marwaidd, *a.* (marw) Deadish, somewhat dead.

Marwanedig, *a.* (marw—ganedig) Stillborn.

Marwar, *s. pl. aggr.* (marw—ar) Embers. *a.* Dying like embers. *Glo marwar*, dying coal.

Marwâu, *v. n.* (marw) To mortify; to deaden.

Marwawd, *s. m.* (marw) A dying, a deadening.

Marwawl, *a.* (marw) Deadly, mortal. *s. pl.* *marwolion*, mortals.

Marwawr, *s. pl. aggr.* (marw) Hot embers.

Marwdon, *s. f.* (marw—ton) Scurf on the skin.

Marwdy, *s. m.—pl. t.* au (marw—ty) A dead house; an escheat by death.

Un dyn ni ddyly ei dy fod yn farwdy, cyd boed marw heb gymmun yngnad llys.

There is one man whose house ought not to be an *escheat*, although he should die without the sacrament the judge of the palace. *Welsh Laws.*

Marwdyst, *s. m.* (marw—tyst) A dead evidence.

Marwdystiawl, *a.* (marwdyst) Relating to dead evidence.

Marwdystiolaeth, *s. f.* (marwdystiawl) A dead evidence.

Tair marwdystiolaeth y sydd am dir, ac a safant yn nghyfraith a barn.

There are three *dead evidences* with respect to land, and which shall stand in law and judgment. *Welsh Laws.*

Marwdywarchen, *s. f.* (marw—tywarchen) A death clod, the spot where a person dies.

Pan fo marw dyn gorwlad ar dir dyn arall, unarbymtheg a delir i berchenawg y tir, dros ei farwdywarchen; a'i ebediw oll, namyn hyny, i'r brenin.

When a person of a foreign country dies on the land of another person, sixteen pence shall be paid to the owner of the land, on account of his *death clod*, and all his herriot, except that, to the king. *Welsh Laws.*

Nid hysbys gan neb ei farwdywarchen.

No body is acquainted with his *death clod.* *Taliesin.*

Marwddanadl, *s. m.* (marw—danadl) Black or stinking horehound: *marwddanadlen ber*, white horehound; *marwddanadlen felen*, yellow deadnettle; *marwddanadlen goch*, red dead-nettle; *marwddanadlen wen*, white dead-nettle.

Marwddwfr, *s. m.—pl. t.* oedd (marw—dwfr) A dead water.

Marwddydd, *s. m.—pl. t.* iau (marw—dydd) A mortal day; a critical day, or the time when physicians observe the turn of a disorder.

Marwedig, *a.* (marw) Deadened, being dead.

Marwedigawl, *a.* (marwedig) Of mortal tendency.

Marweidd-dra, *s. m.* (marwaidd) The state of being deadened, or benumbed.

Marweiddiad, *s. m.* (marwaidd) A deadening.

Marweiddiaw, *v. n.* (marwaidd) To become deadened, or benumbed; to benumb, to deaden.

Marweiddiawl, *a.* (marwaidd) Deadening.

Marweiddiedig, *a.* (marweiddiad) Deadened.

Marwerydd, *s. m.* (marwar) Delirium, distraction

Marwfis, *s. m.—pl. t.* oedd (marw—mis) The dead month, or when vegetation is dormant.

Marwgoel, *s. f.—pl. t.* ion (marw—coel) A death omen; a yellow spot on the skin; vulgarly deemed the sign of a friend's death.

Fo weles, drud fu'r loes draw,
Furgiwyddes farwgoel iddaw.

There was seen by my lady a *death omen* of him, and severe was the pang. *L. Mon.*

Marwgwsg, *s. m.* (marw—cwsg) A dead sleep, a lethargy; also an epithet for the dormouse.

Marwhaint, *s. m.—pl.* marwheintiau (marw—haint) A mortality.

Marwhun, *s. f.—pl. t.* au (marw—hun) A death sleep, a trance.

Marwi, *v.* (marw) To die. *E farwodd y fuwch wrth alu*, the cow died in calving. *Dyfed.*

Marwlas, *s. m.* (marw—glas) A pale blue. *a.* Of a dead greenish blue. *Eithyn marwlas*, a species of furze.

Marwlanw, *s. m* (marw—llanw) The dead water, or turn of the tide.

Marwnad, *s. f.—pl. t.* au (marw—nad) A death cry; a funeral song, an elegy.

Marwnadawl, *a.* (marwnad) Relating to a funeral song; elegiac.

Marwnadu, *v. a.* (marwnad) To mourn the dead.

Marwolâad, *s m.* (marwolâu) A deadening.

Marwolaeth, *s. f.—pl. t.* au (marwawl) Death, or the act of dying; mortality. *Angau* is another term, and always the one used for death personified. *Plant marwolaeth*, the children of mortality.

Marwolaethiad, *s. m.* (marwolaeth) A putting to death; a becoming dead.

Marwolaethu, *v. a.* (marwolaeth) To put to death.

Plant a gyfodant yn erbyn eu rhieni, ac eu marwolaethant wy.

Children shall rise up against their parents, and *shall put them to death.* *W. Salisbury.*

Morwolâu, *v. a.* (marwawl) To become dead.

Pan fo dirfawr ofn gwedy marwolâu drygewyllys dyn, a'i arwain hagachen i uffern, ar ol hyny y daw sain llariaidd rhad Duw.

When extreme fear shall have *deadened* the evil disposition of man, and conducted him almost to hell; after that there shall come the gentle voice of the grace of God. *Marchawg Crwydrad.*

Marwoldeb, *s. m.* (marwawl) Mortality.

Marwolder, *s. m.* (marwawl) Mortality.

Marwoli, *v. a.* (marwawl) To become dead.

Marwolrwydd, *s. m.* (marwawl) Mortalness.

Marwolus, *a.* (marwawl) Of a dead nature.

Ni ad y mor marwolus ynddo.

The sea will not let *what is dead* remain in it. *Adage.*

Marwor, *s. pl. aggr.* (marwawr) Embers, burning cinders.
Marworaidd, *a.* (marwawr) Like burning cinders.
Marworyn, *s. m. dim.* (marwawr) An ember.
Marwwystl, *s. m.—pl.* marwwystlon (marw—gwystl) A mortgage.
Marwwystlaw, *v. a.* (marwwystl) To mortgage.
Marwyd, *s. m.* (marw) A dying, or extinction.
Marwydos, *s. pl. aggr.* (marwyd) Embers.
Marwysgafn, *s. f.* (ysgafn) A death-bed song.
Marwysgar, *s. m.* (marw—ysgar) A death parting.
Mas, *s. f.—pl. t.* oedd (my—as) A going forward, a departure; swoon, a qualm, a fainting fit; ecstacy.

Sain Niclas, wedi'r fy fau,
A fo'n dwyn f'enaid innau.

May Saint Nicolas, after the *death* of me, be bearing hence my soul. *L. G. Cothi.*

Masaidd, *a.* (màs) Tending to faint, qualmish.
Masarn, *s. m.—pl. t.* au (más) The sycamore.

Mawr masarn cedarn.

Sweet the mighty *sycamore.* *Cynddelw.*

Masarnaidd, *a.* (masarn) Like sycamore.
Masarnen, *s. f. dim.* (masarn) Greater maple, or sycamore.
Masarnwydd, *s. m.* (masarn—gwydd) Sycamore.
Masawd, *s. m.* (mas) A swooning, a fainting.
Masawl, *a.* (màs) Swooning, or fainting.
Masg, *s. f.—pl. t.* au (my—asg) That is interwoven, or plaited; any reticulated work; lattice-work, wire-work, mesh-work, a mesh. *Masgau rhwyd*, the meshes of a net.
Masgawl, *a.* (masg) Interwoven, reticulated.
Masgiad, *s. m.* (masg) A plaiting, reticulation; a meshing, a making lattice work.
Masgl, *s. f.—pl.* masglau (masg) That covers; a mesh, a pod, or shell.
Masglawg, *a.* (masgl) Having mesh-work; having pods, or shells.
Masgliad, *s. m.* (masgl) A forming a mesh-work, a reticulating, a podding.
Masglu, *v. a.* (masgl) To reticulate, to shell.
Masgn, *s. m.* (masg) What is obligatory.
Masgnach, *s. m.* (masgn) Concern, affair, business.
Masgnachawl, *a.* (masgnach) Relating to business.
Masgnachu, *v. a.* (masgnach) To transact business.

Cas a fasgnacho bob peth ac heb brynu dim.

Hateful is he *who cheapens* every thing and without buying any thing. *Adage.*

Masgnachwr, *s. m.—pl.* masgnachwyr (masgnach—gwr) A chapman; a man of business.
Masgnachydd, *s. m.—pl. t.* ion (masgnach) Trader.
Masgu, *v. a.* (masg) To interweave; to reticulate, to form mesh-work, to lattice.
Masu, *v. n.* (mas) To proceed, to depart, to swoon, to faint; to die away.

Wyt goreu un gwron o'r fas,
A wnaeth Duw y dydd yn creas.

Thou art the best of any hero that *ventures*, which God made the day he created. *Ll. P. Moch, i Lywelyn II.*

Masw, *a.* (mas) Wanton, sportive, fluttering, light; languishing, soft.

Masw imi bron brif draethiad a wnewn,
Lle ni'm rhoddi iawn, ne gwawn, na gwal!

It is *trifling* for me to essay the oration, which I could make, where she gives me no amends, nor yet desires, who is of gossamer hue! *H. ab Einion, Llygliw.*

Serchawg fydd masw dan laswydd.

Amorous will be the *gay* beneath the verdant wood. *D. ab Gwilym.*

Mae syched, masw ei hachen,
Meddwdod i'th orfod i'th en.

Thirst oppresses thy utterance, thou of *wanton* breed. *D. ab Gwilym, i'r Bi.*

Maswedd, *s. m.* (masw) A fluttering state; languish, tenderness, softness.
Masweddawl, *a.* (maswedd) Fluttering, wanton.
Masweddiad, *s. m.* (maswedd) A wantoning.
Masweddu, *v. a.* (maswedd) To wanton, to frolic.
Masweddwr, *s. m.—pl.* masweddwyr (maswedd—gwr) A light flutterer; soft effeminate man.
Maswy, *a.* (masw) Soft, wanton, sportive, light.

Fy swydd, nid yw faswy hyn,
Eu harail a'u mybcryn.

My office, this is not *trifling*, is to look after them and their rams. *Ll. ab M. ab I. ab Gronwy.*

Mat, *s. m.—pl. t.* ian (my—at) A mat.
Mater, *s. m.—pl. t.* ion (mad) What is produced; exigency, occasion, affair, matter.
Matog, *s. f.—pl. t.* au (mad) A mattock, a hoe.
Matras, *s. m.—pl. t.* au (mat—rhas) A mattress.

Cawn orwedd——
Ar fatras o goed glas glyn.

We shall lie upon a *mattress* of the green woods of the dale. *D. ab Gwilym.*

Matrasu, *v. a.* (matras) To form a mattress.
Matteyrn, *s. m.—pl. t.* edd (teyrn) A patriot prince

Tri matteyrn Ynys Prydain. Prydain ab Aedd Mawr—Dyfnwal Moel Mud—a Hywel Dda.

The three *patriot kings* of the Isle of Britain: Prydain son of Aedd the Great, Dyfnwal Moel Mud, and Hywel the Good. *Trioedd.*

Màth, *s. m.* (my—ath) That is flat, spread out.
Mathr, *s. m.* (math) A strewing; a spread.
Mathrach, *s. m.* (mathr) A spreading down, or laying flat; a trampling down.
Mathrawl, *a.* (mathr) Trampling, treading.
Mathriad, *s. m.* (mathr) A trampling.
Mathru, *v. a.* (mathr) To trample, to tread.
Mathrwr, *s. m.* (mathr—gwr) A trampler.
Mau, *s. m.* (my—au) What is possessed by me.

Myfi y sydd wir briodawr o ach edryd; ac yn sef ydd wyf yn gwarchadw fy mau, a'm priodolder, fal y mae goreu y dylwyf eu gwarchadw.

I am a true proprietor with respect to lineage and kindred; and therefore I do protect my *property*, and my original right, in the best manner it behoves me to protect them. *Welsh Laws.*

Mau, *pron.* (my—au) My, mine. The article Y, *the*, is mostly put before it in construction; as, *y mau*, the mine, *m. y fau*, the mine, *f. y tàd mau*, the father of mine; *y fam fau*, the mother of mine. See *My*, *einwyf*, and *einof*.
Maufi, *pron.* (mau—mi) Mine own.
Maw, *s. m.* (my—aw) That opens, or expands; the involution, or grasp of both hands. *a.* Expanding; indulgent.

Rhagddaw yn ngbywawd maw gyfagar.

Before him in the banquet the *expanding* fumes. *Taliesin.*

Oedd maw ei rhydau.

Broad were its fords. *Taliesin.*

Maw hid mawl, taw hid tawl,
Ac o'r ddau diwedd pob hawl.

Be concession praised, be silence regulated, and from the two will every suit be ended. *Adage.*

Addfwyn gaer y sydd ar glawr gweilgi,
Bid lawen yn nghalan eirian ei rhi!
Ac amser pan wna y mor maw wrhydri,
Yn gnawd gorun beirdd uch meddlestri.

A pleasant town there is above the face of the torrent, in the splendid feast may its chief be glad! and the time when the sea works its *expanding* energy, let the bards enjoy their accustomed revel over the mead vessels. *Taliesin, Mic Dinbych.*

Ef maw wrth wirion a mwyn,
Os ynfyd wrth was anfwyn——

To the simple be *indulgent* and kind, if violent to the froward youth. *Wat. ab Hywel.*

Mawaid, *s. f.—pl.* maweidiau (maw) As much as may be held between both hands.

Gair gwraig fal gwynt yn faweidiau.

A woman's word like wind by *handfuls*. *Adage.*

Mawd, *s. m.* (maw) That is open, expanding.

Mawdd, *s. m.* (maw) That opens or spreads out.
Maweidiad, *s. m.* (mawaid) A filling both hands.
Maweidiaw, *v. a.* (mawaid) To hold as much as may be taken up between both hands.
Mawl, *s. f.* (my—awl) A tribute of gratitude; worship; praise.

Mal y ceryeh dy fawl.

As thou regardest thy *praise*. *Adage.*

Mawlâad, *s. m.* (mawl) A praising; a worshipping.
Mawlâu, *v. a.* (mawl) To praise, or to extol.

Iawnach, heb gel, gan delva,
Moli Duw no mawlâu dyn.

More appropriate, without disguise, with the harp *to praise* God than *to extol* man. *D. ab Gwilym.*

Mawn, *s. pl. aggr.* (my—awn) Peat, or turf.
Mawnawg, *a.* (mawn Abounding with peat.
Mawnbwll, *s. m.—pl.* mawnbyllau (mawn—pwll) A peat pit, a turf pit.
Mawndir, *s. m.* (mawn—tir Peat land.
Mawneg, *s. f.* (mawn) A place where peat is dug
Mawnen, *s. f.* (mawn) A single peat, or turf.
Mawnog, *s. f.—pl. t.* ydd (mawn) A place where peat is dug, a peat pit.
Mawr *a.* (my—awr) Great, large, big. *Tra mawr*, extremely large; *mawr iawn, pur fawr, mawr byd*, very great, vastly big, or huge; *mawr dda i ti*, much good be to thee, or thou art welcome; *y mor mawr*, the main sea. It is used, prefixed, and postfixed in composition.

Nid mawr ond cyfiawn.

The only one *great* is the just. *Adage.*

Bach pob dyn a dybio ei hun yn fawr.

Little is every person that thinks himself *great*. *Adage.*

Mawr, *adv.* (my—awr) Greatly also used with a verb to express a wish, or longing. *Mawr na ddelit yma!* Would heavens thou wert but coming here!

Ni fawr ddiolchir rhodd gymhell.

No *great thanks will be given* for a profered gift. *Adage.*

Mawr i doi'r mor i Dawy;
Ar ruddiau Mawd i'r oedd mwy!

Into Tawy the sea *greatly* flows; on the cheeks of Mawd there was more! *Ieu. Deulwyn.*

Mawrâad, *s. m.* (mawrâu) A magnifying.
Mawrâawl, *a.* (mawrâu) Tending to magnify.
Mawraidd, *a.* (mawr) Tending to enlarge.
Mawrair, *s. m.* (gair) A boastful word.

Llawer mawrair a fethla.

Many a *boast* is foiled. *Llyford.*

Mawrâu, *v. a.* (mawr) To magnify, to enlarge.

Ni fawrâa neges ni ragwyl ei les.

He will not *magnify* an errand who does not anticipate his advantage. *Adage.*

Rhieingerdd Efa a fawrêynt.

The panegyric on Eve's beauty *they would magnify*. *Cynddelw.*

Mawrâus, *a.* (mawrâu) Tending to magnify.
Mawrâwr, *s. m.—pl.* mawrâwyr (mawrâu—gwr) A magnifier, one who exalts.
Mawrboen, *s. f.—pl. t.* au (poen) Great pain.
Mawrbwyll, *s. m.* (pwyll) Magnanimity. *a.* Of great power of mind.
Mawrdeg, *a.* teg) Greatly fair; magnificent.
Mawrdra, *s. m.* (mawr) Greatness, or grandeur.
Mawrdrafn, *s. m.* (trafn) Great arrangement.
Mawrdrafferth, *s. f.* (trafferth) Great bustle.
Mawrdres, *s. f.* (tres) A great bustle or hurry.
Mawrdrig, *a.* (trig) Of long continuance.
Mawrdrigaw, *v. a.* (mawrdrig) To tarry long.
Mawrdrin, *s. m.* (trin) Great bustle; turmoil.
Mawrdrosi, *v. a.* (trosi) To drive about much.
Mawrdrwm, *a.* (trwm) Greatly heavy.
Mawrdrwst, *s. m.* (trwst) Great noise, or tumult.
Mawrdwyll, *s. m.* (twyll) Great fraud, or deceit.
Mawrdda, *s. m.* (mawr—da) Great good, much good. *Mawrdda i ti*, thou art welcome.
Mawrddarbod, *s. m.* (darbod) Great providence.
Mawrddawn, *s. m.—pl.* mawrddoniau (dawn) A great gift, or talent. *a.* Greatly gifted.
Mawrddoeth, *a.* (doeth) Greatly wise, very wise.
Mawrddrwg, *s. m.—pl.* mawrddrygau (drwg) A great evil; a misfortune.
Mawrddrygu, *v. a.* (mawrddrwg) To hurt greatly
Mawrddyrchaif, *a.* (dyrchaif) Greatly exalted.
Mawrddyrchafaidd, *a.* (mawrddyrchaif) Magnificent.

Gwaelder a'm harweiniai i neuadd fawrddyrchafaidd; yno nwyfiant a'm diarfa.

Frailty conducted me to a *magnificent* saloon; there wantonness took off my armour. *Marchawg Crwydrad.*

Mawrddyrchafawl, *a.* (mawrddyrchaif) Magnificent.
Mawrddyrchafiad, *s. m.* (mawrddyrchaif) A greatly exalting, great exaltation.
Mawrddyrchafu, *v.* (mawrddyrchaif) Greatly to exalt.
Mawredig, *a.* (mawr) Magnified or exalted.

Mawredig pendefig castell.

Exalted is the commandant of a castle. *Adage.*

Mawredigaeth, *s. m.* (mawredig) A being exalted.
Mawredigaw, *v. a.* (mawredig) To magnify.
Mawredigawl, *a.* (mawredig) Tending to magnify
Mawredigrwydd, *s. m.* (mawredig) Magnanimity
Mawredd, *s. m.* (mawr) Greatness, or grandeur.

Bach hedyn pob mawredd.

Small is the seed of every *greatness*. *Adage.*

Er ergryd angeu, rhag anghenwyr Lloegr,
Ni lygraf fy mawredd.

For the dread of death, before the necessitous men of Lloegr, I will not dishonour my *renown*. *Llywarch Hen.*

. (mawredd) Magnificent, grand.
(mawredd) Tending to magnify.
m. (mawredd) A magnifying.
mawredd) Magnificent, grand.

Mawreddusrwydd, *s. m.* (mawreddus) Magnificence
Mawreiddiannu, *v. a.* (mawreiddiant) To render or to become of an enlarging tendency.
Mawreiddiant, *s. m.* (mawraidd) A tendency to enlarge or to magnify.
Mawreiriawg, *a.* (mawrair) Of pompous words.
Mawrfaith, *a.* (maith) Greatly-extending.

Cafid Feifod o fraint ingawd,
Lloch fawrfaith am feddfaith feddrawd

Meifod was found of splendid endowment, cloister *greatly* ample for the revels of the sons of mead. *Cynddelw.*

Mawrfalch, *a.* (balch) Greatly proud ostentatious
Mawrfryd, *s. m.* (bryd) A great mind; magnanimity.
Mawrfrydig, *a.* (mawrfryd) Magnanimous.
Mawrfrydigrwydd, *s. m.* (mawrfrydig) Magnanimousness, magnanimity.
Mawrfrydu, *v. n.* (mawrfryd) To become magnanimous; to render great of mind.

Mawrfrydus, *a.* (mawrfryd) Magnanimous.
Mawrfrydusaw, *v. n.* (mawrfrydus) To become magnanimous.
Mawrfrys, *s. m.* (brys) Great haste, or hurry.
Mawrfudd, *s. f.* (budd) Great advantage, or gain
Mawrgais, *s. m.* (cais) A great essay, or attempt.
Mawrgall, *a.* (call) Greatly discreet, or prudent.
Mawrgas, *s. m.* (cas) Great hatred. *a.* Greatly odious, having great enmity.
Mawrgeisiaw, *v. a.* (mawrgais) To try greatly.
Mawrgerth, *a.* (certh) Greatly imminent.
Mawrglau, *a.* (clau) Greatly persevering.
Mawrgoeth, *a.* (coeth) Greatly precious.
Mawrgwydd, *s. m.* (cwydd) A great fall or lapse.
Mawrhydr, *s. m.* (hydr) Great confidence.
Mawrhydri, *s. m.* (mawrhydr) Great confidence.
Mawriad, *s. m.* (mawr) A magnifying.
Mawriaw, *v. a.* (mawr) To magnify, to enlarge.

Rhi doeth dedwydd, Duw a'i mawr.

Let the happy be wise, God *will enlarge* him. *Adage.*

Mawrlles, *s. m.* (lles) Great benefit or good.
Mawrllw, *s. m.* (llw) A great oath; perjury.

A wnel mawrddrwg a rydd mawrllw.

He that commits a great crime will swear a *great oath.* *Adage.*

Mawrth, *s. m.* (mawr) Mars. *Mis Mawrth*, the month of March; *Dyw Mawrth, Dydd Mawrth*, Dies Martis, Tuesday.
Mawrthaidd, *a.* (mawrth) Like Mars; like March
Mawrthawl, *a.* (mawrth) Belonging to March.
Mawrthig, *a.* (mawrth) Having the nature of Mars; martial, of the month of March.

Ar wyrdd wawr ar feirch mawr mawrthig.

At the green dawn on great *martial* steeds. *Cynddelw.*

Mawrwae, *s. f.* (gwae) Great woe, or tribulation
Mawrwaith, *s. m.* (gwaith) A great work.
Mawrwall, *s. m.* (gwall) A great fault; great oversight, great carelessness.
Mawrwerth, *s. m.* (gwerth) Great value; preciousness. *a.* Of great value.

Mawrwerth pob newid, bychanwerth pob prid.

Dear is every thing exchanged, cheap is every thing sold. *Adage.*

Mawrwerthiawg, *a.* (mawrwerth) Of great value.
Mawrwg, *s. m.* (mawr) Greatness, or grandeur.
Mawrwr, *s. m.* (mawr—gwr) A great man.
Mawrwraidd, *a.* (mawrwr) Magnanimous.
Mawrwri, *s. m.* (mawrwr) Magnanimity, heroism
Mawrwriaeth, *s. m.* (mawrwr) Magnanimity.
Mawrwych, *a.* (gwych) Magnificently splendid.
Mawrwychder, *s. m.* (mawrwych) Magnificence.
Mawrwychedd, *s. m.* (mawrwych) Magnificence.
Mawrwyrth, *s. m.—pl. t.* iau (gwyrth) Great virtue.
Mawryd, *s. m.* (mawr) The state of being great.
Mawrydi, *s. m.* (mawryd) Majesty, grandeur.
Mawrydig, *a.* (mawryd) Magnificent, grand.

Dygychwyn, genad, gan fawrydig dorf.

Be setting off, messenger, from a *magnificent* company. *T. O. Cyfeiliawg.*

Mawrydigrwydd, *s.* (mawrydig) Magnificence.
Mawrygawl, *a.* (mawrwg) Magnificent, extolling.
Mawrygedig, *a.* (mawrygiad) Magnified, extolled.
Mawrygiad, *s. m.* (mawrwg) A magnifying.
Mawrygu, *v. a.* (mawrwg) To magnify, to extol.
Mawrygus, *a.* (mawrwg) Tending to magnify.
Mawrygwr, *s. m.—pl.* mawrygwyr (mawrwg—gŵr) A magnifier, or one who extols.
Maws, *s. m.* (my—aws) That is gliding; delight; a sweet sensation; melody.

Nid er da i Hufa hen,
Namyn er maws i mi fy hun—
Y canaf.

Not for any good to old Hufa, but for *gratification* to myself do I sing.

Maws, *a.* (my—aws) Smoothly gliding; pleasant, delightful; sweet, grateful; melodious. *Meddgyrn maws*, grateful mead horns; *cynghor maws*, sweet counsel; *cadarnwch maws*, grateful strength; *lliw maws*, an agreeable colour; *tad maws*, an amiable father.

Mochddwyreawg haul haf dyfrestin
Maws llafar adar, mygr hear hin.

Early rising sun of summer, hasten thou the *melodious* song of birds and pleasant tide of serenity. *Gwalchmai.*

Mawsaidd, *a.* (maws) Of a grateful tendency.
Mawsain, *a.* (maws) Abounding with delight.
Mawsawl, *a.* (maws) Of a delectable tendency.
Mawsedig, *a.* (maws) Being pleased or delighted
Mawsedd, *s. m.* (maws) A state of pleasure.
Mawsi, *v. a.* (maws) To give pleasure, or delight; to be sweet, or melodious.
Mawsiad, *s. m.* (maws) A rendering pleasant, or delectable; a becoming delectable.
Mawsiannawl, *a.* (mawsiant) Pleasurable.
Mawsiannu, *v. a.* (mawsiant) To gratify, to render delectable; to be delectable.
Mawsiant, *s. m.* (maws) Delectation; delight.
ME, *s. m. r.* An agent; the agent in the third person of verbs. *pron.* He, him: Also an adverbial sign of the agency of an action. *Me fu yno rai dynion*, there were there some men; *me goflai lais y truan*, he would remember the cry of the wretched; *me wnaeth y cleddyf ddifrawd*, the sword made havoc.
Mebai, *s. c.* (mab) Infant, youth. *a.* Infant.

Nid eisteddai febai fab.

The *infant* child would not sit down. *D. ab Gwilym.*

Mebain, *a.* (mab) Youthful, or juvenile.
Mebaint, *s. m.* (mebain) Youthfulness, juvenility

E fagwyd i'n gwlad bendefigion;
O febaint fe dyg Duw hwy'n wrthion.

There have been nurtured nobles in our country; from *infancy* God has given them the growth of men. *T. ab I. Rhys.*

Mebin, *a.* (mab) Relating to infancy or youth.
Mebyd, *s. m.* (mab) Infancy, childhood.

Ef a wybu o'i febyd,
Dysg i bawb, dull y byd.

He knew from his *infancy* the way of the world, which is a lesson for every body. *L. G. Cothi.*

Mebydawl, *a.* (mebyd) Relating to childhood.
Mebydd, *s. m.—pl. t.* ion (mab) A bachelor.

Tri gwyn febydd Ynys Prydain: Cadawg ab Gwynllïw, yn Llangarfan; Madawg Morfryn, yn nghor Illtud; a Deiniol Wyn, yn Ngwynedd.

The three holy *bachelors* of the isle of Britain: Cadog the son of Gwynlliw, at Llangarfan, Madog Morfryn, in the choir of Illtud, and Deiniol the blessed, in Gwynedd. *Trioedd.*

Mebyn, *s. m. dim.* (mab) A male infant.
Mechdeyrn, *s. m.—pl. t.* edd (mach—teyrn) A tributary prince; a viceroy; a lord. *Mechdeyrn Byd*, the vicegerent of the world.

Tri mechdeyrn dyledawg a ddylai wledychu Cymmru oll dan ei therfynau, brenin Aberffraw, arglwydd Dinefwr, a hwn Mathrafal.

The three lawful *princes* who ought to govern all Wales under its boundaries: the king of Aberfraw, the lord of Dinever, and that of Mathraval. *Triodd.*

Ni allynt ronyn,
Heb gyfoeth mechdeyrn.

They could not perform a tittle, without the power of the *Lord.* *Taliesin.*

Gwelais ——
Rhag Madawg mechdeyrn Tegeingl,
Llawer twr twnlelw,
A gwaed fflau ar ffriw.

I have seen, before Madog the *lord* of Tegeingl, many a round tower, and trickling blood on the countenance. *Gwalchmai.*

Mechdeyrnaidd, *a.* (mechdeyrn) Princely.

Mechdeyrnawl, *a.* (mechdeyrn) Princely; royal.

Mechdeyrnddyled, *s. m.—pl. t.* ion (mechdeyrn—dyled) The tribute due from an inferior prince to his sovereign. Thus, according to the ancient constitution of Britain, we find in a particular period, that the kings of Scotland, Wales, and Cornwall, paid such a tribute to the crown of London; and they claimed the like homage from their respective tributaries.

Mechdeyrnddylyed, *s. f.—pl. t.* ion (mechdeyrn—dylyed) The tribute due from an inferior prince to his sovereign.

Mechdeyrnged, *s. f.* (mechdeyrn—ced) What is due from a prince to his sovereign.

Mechni, *s. m.—pl. t.* on (mach) Surety, or bail.

Mechnïad, *s. m.* (mechni) A giving surety, or bail

Mechnïadwy, *a.* (mechnïad) Capable of security.

Mechnïaeth, *s. m.* (mechni) Suretiship. *Mechnïaeth undyddiawg*, suretiship for one day.

Mechnïaethiad, *s. m.* (mechnïaeth) A performing the obligation of a surety.

Mechnïaethu, *v. a.* (mechnïaeth) To perform the obligation of a surety.

Mechnïaw, *v. a.* (mechni) To bail, to undertake, or to give surety; to become a surety.

> Barn arnat dy hun yn gyfiawn, a Duw a'th fechnïa.
>
> Pass sentence on thyself equitably, and God *will become thy surety*. *Adage.*

Mechnïawl, *a.* (mechni) Relating to suretiship.

Mechnïwr, *s. m.—pl.* mechnïwyr (mechni—gwr) A man who is a surety, or who bails.

Mechnïydd, *s. m.—pl. t.* ion (mechni) A surety.

Med, *s. f.* (me—ed) That is compact, a centre; that is made complete, full, perfect, or mature.

Med, *prep.* (me—ed) To, unto, as far as to the full; it is also an affix, forming the ordinals of numbers. *Dos fed yno*, go as far as there; *fed y leni*, until this year; *I ba le yr ei di?* to what place art thou going? *Med y fàn a'r fàn*, to such and such a place. *Med* is a South Wales idiom, for which *Hyd* is used in North Wales.

> Ei gorlliw——
> Yn waed o'i thraed fed ei thrwyn.
>
> Her colour of blood from her feet *to* her nose. *W. Llryn.*

Mededig, *a.* (med) Being reaped. *Yd mededig*, reaped corn.

Medel, *s. f.—pl. t.* au (med) A reaping; a company of reapers. *Blaenor y fedel*, the harvest lord. *Cri y fedel*, the harvest shout; also called *Tori pen y wrach*, and *Boddi y cynhauaf*; a ceremony answering to the English harvest home: When the last field is cut, some ears of corn are tied together and placed at a distance, at which each reaper throws his sickle; and he that hits it gains the honour; whereupon three huzzas are given, and a feast ends the day.

> Mybefin heulawg a wna medel mochddwyreawg.
>
> A sunny June will make an early *reaping*. *Adage.*

Medelwas, *s. m.* (medel—gwas) A reaper.

Medelwr, *s. m.* (medel—gwr) A reaper.

Medi, *s. m.* (mêd) A reaping. *Mis Medi*, September. The different methods of reaping are called, *Bawdfedi, traws-fedi, dyrneitio, gwanafu, ysgripiana, tori tan law.*

Medi, *v. a.* (med) To reap. *Meda di yr yd*, do thou reap the corn.

> Hawdd medi erw anghenawg.
>
> It is easy *to reap* the acre of the needy. *Adage.*

Mediad, *s. m.* (med) A reaping, the act of reaping.

Mediw, *s. m.* (med) Competent, or adequate.

Medlys, *s. pl.* (med—llys) Mature vegetation.

> Na ddwg i'n gwlad fad fedlys,
> Anghlod.——
>
> Bring not into our country, of teeming *mature vegetation*, any scandal. *Ieu. Du Uaf. ab Owain.*

Medr, *s. m.* (med) Skill to accomplish, knowledge how to perform; skill.

> Nid hael hael ar fedr cael ced;
> Nid call call wedi colled;
> Nid dim dim diddym od aeth:
> Nid byd byd heb wybodaeth.
>
> Not liberal the liberal with an *intent* to get a profit; not discreet the discreet after suffering a loss; not any thing the thing if it is gone to nothing; a world is no world without knowledge. *W. Lleyn.*

Medraeth, *s. m.* (medr) Skill to accomplish.

> Nid wyf fi yn cymeryd arnaf, na medraeth, nac hysbysrwydd yn y Gymmraeg.
>
> I do not take upon myself either *skill*, or knowledge in the Welsh. *S. Trefredyn.*

Medrai, *s. c.—pl.* medreion (medr) An expert one

Medraidd, *a.* (medr) Somewhat skilful or adroit.

Medrawd, *s. m.* (medr) Accomplishment.

Medrawl, *a.* (medr) Tending to accomplish.

Medredig, *a.* (medr) Accomplished, skilled.

Medredydd, *s. m.—pl. t.* ion (medr) One who can effect; a marksman.

Medredd, *s. m.* (medr) Capability of accomplishing; expertness, skill, knowledge.

Medriad, *s. m.* (medr) An accomplishing, an effecting; a being able.

Medriannawl, *a.* (medriant) Accomplishing.

Mediannu, *v. a.* (medriant) To render capable.

Medriant, *s. m.* (medr) Accomplishment.

Medroldeb, *s. m.* (medrawl) Capableness.

Medrolder, *s. m.* (medrawl) Capableness.

Medroledd, *s. m.* (medrawl) Capableness.

Medroli, *v. a.* (medrawl) To render competent.

Medru, *v. a.* (medr) To accomplish, to effect, to do; to exert skill; to be able; to know how; to take aim, to aim at; to hit, to shoot the mark; *A fedri di osodi hwn?* Canst thou place this? *Medraf*, I can.

> Ni wyr ni welodd, ni feidr ni ddysg.
>
> He does not know who has not seen, *he can not accomplish* who does not learn. *Adage.*

> Ni fedraf——
> Beth yw gwawd ond bath y gwr.
>
> *I can not comprehend* what is ridicule but the picture of that man. *Ieu Du y Bwlwg.*

> Y blaidd——
> Heb fedru preiddiaw
> Yn un a drig a'r oen draw.
>
> The wolf, without *being able* to depredate, shall dwell together with yonder lamb. *E. Evans, P. Hir.*

> Ceisio medru, cais Modron,
> Y gaer fry ar gwr y fron.
>
> Trying *to hit*, like the attempt of Modron, the towering fortress on the skirt of the hill. *D. ab Gwilym.*

> Sef a wna y mab ei fwrw, a'i fedru i rhwng gïewyn yr esgair ac yr asgwrn.
>
> What the youth did was to shoot at him, and *hit* him between the sinew of the thigh and the bone. *H. Pwyll—Mabinogion.*

Medrus, *a.* (medr) Able to effect, hit, or accomplish; expert, skilful; accomplished.

Medrusaidd, *a.* (medrus) Somewhat expert.

Medrusaw, *v. a.* (medrus) To render expert; to become expert, or skilful.

Medrusder, *s. m.* (medrus) Expertness, skill.

Medrusedd, *s. m.* (medrus) Expertness, skill.

Medruswydd, *s. m.* (medrus) Capability of effecting, or accomplishing; expertness.

Medrwr, *s. m.—pl.* medrwyr (medr—gwr) One who can effect, perform, hit, or accomplish; a marksman.

Ni fedrai fil o fedrwyr
Rane 'gamp ar un o'r gwyr.

Not a thousand *marksmen* would be able to take the share of the feat of one of the men. *Ieu. Llwyddēn.*

Medryd, *v. a.* (medr) To aim; to hit a mark; to effect, to do; to exert skill. to be able.

Medrydd, *s. m.—pl. t.* ion (medr) One who effects; one skilled, able, or capable; one who takes aim, one who hits, or shoots a mark.

Medw, *s. m.* (med) That is beyond skill or art.

Mae dy ddwyael, medw ddien,
Un rhyw a'th wallt, Cauthaith wen'

Thy eyebrows, thou gentle *peerless one*, are like thy hair, my fair tormentor! *Ed. Rhys, o Farlawr.*

Medwr, *s. m.—pl.* medwyr (med—gwr) A reaper.

Medwraig, *s. f.* (med—gwraig) Reaping woman.

Medd, *s. m.* (me—edd) The origin of motion; a centre, or middle point of motion; utterance; that is possessed, or enjoyed; that causes a turning; that causes intoxication; mead.

Cornaid medd a ddaw i'r penteulu, yn mhob cyfeddach ydd bello y dystain arni, y gan y frenines.

A hornful of *mead* shall come to the patron of the family, in every banquet in which the steward of the household shall serve, from the queen. *Welsh Laws.*

Mesur gwirawd gyfreithlawl, llonaid y llestri y gwallofer yndynt o'r cwrw, a'r hanner o'r bragawd, a'r trian o'r medd.

The measure of a lawful wassail, is the fill of the vessels used in serving of the ale, and the half of the bragget, and the third of the *mead*. *Welsh Laws.*

Meddal, *a.* (medd—al) Soft, mollient, tender.

Meddalâad, *s. m.* (meddal) A softening.

Meddalâawl, *a.* (meddal) Tending to soften.

Meddalai, *s. c.* (meddal) What softens, or meliorates; the mallow. *Meddalai y gerddi*, garden mallow; *meddalai y gors, meddalai y morfa*, marsh mallow; *meddalai gwyllt*, wild mallow.

Meddalaidd, *a.* (meddal) Somewhat soft, softish.

Meddalâu, *v. a.* (meddal) To make soft, to soften.

Meddalder, *s. m.* (meddal) Softness; mildness.

Meddaledig, *a.* (meddal) Softness, mildness.

Meddaliad, *s. m.* (meddal) A softening, a mollifying

Meddalrwydd, *s. m.* (meddal) Softness; mildness.

Meddalu, *v. a.* (meddal) To soften; to be softened

Meddalus, *a.* (meddal) Softening, mollient.

Meddalwch, *s. m.* (meddal) Softness, mildness.

Meddalwr, *s. m.—pl.* meddalwyr (meddal—gwr) A softener, one who mollifies.

Meddawl, *a.* (medd) Relating to possession.

Meddedig, *a.* (medd) Being possessed, or enjoyed

Meddedigaeth, *s. m.* (meddedig) Possession.

Meddedigaethawl, *a.* (meddedigaeth) Possessory.

Meddedigawl, *a.* (meddedig) Possessory, possessive, having possession.

Meddf, *a.* (medd) Soft, mild, or mollient.

Meddfaeth, *a.* (medd—maeth) Mead-nourished.

Meddgell, *s. f.—pl. t.* oedd (medd—cell) A mead cellar.

Y trulliad a ddyly wrth hadw y feddgell, a chadw y cloau.

The butler is bound to take care of the *mead cellar*, and to keep the keys. *Welsh Laws.*

Meddgorn, *s. m.* (medd—corn) A mead-horn.

Arbenig benaeth, mabmaeth meddgyrn.

The excellent chieftain, fostered son of *mead horns*. *Ein. ab Gwalchmai, i Lywelyn II.*

Meddiad, *s. m.* (medd) A commanding: a possessing, an owning.

Meddiannawl, *a.* (meddiant) Commanding, possessing, owning.

Meddiannedig, *a.* (meddiant) Being possessed.

Meddiannedigaeth, *s. m.* (meddiannedig) A rendering possessed; a becoming possessed.

Meddiannedigaethawl, *a.* (meddiannedigaeth) Appertaining to possession.

Meddiannedigawl, *a.* (meddiannedig) Possessory,

Meddiannu, *v. a.* (meddiant) To possess, to take possession; to become possessed.

Meddiannus, *a.* (meddiant) Belonging to possession. *Meddiannusion*, those who enjoy.

Meddiannwr, *s. m.—pl.* meddiannwyr (meddiant—gwr) A possessor, a proprietor.

Meddiannydd, *s. m.—pl. t.* ion (meddiant) A possessor, an owner.

Meddiannyddawl, *a.* (meddiannydd) Belonging to a possessor, being proprietary.

Meddiant, *s. m.—pl.* meddiannau (medd) Possession, authority, power.

Meddlad, *s. m.* (medd—llad) Gratuity of mead.

Meddlys, *s. pl. aggr.* (medd—llys) Intoxicating herbs; the meadow sweet.

Meddrawd, *s. f.* (medd—rhawd) A revel rout.

Meddu, *v. n.* (medd) To have in power, to have command of; to be able; to possess.

Canys Duw a fedd a fynwy.

For God doth *possess* what I would wish. *Cynddelw.*

Yn mywyd Madawg ni meddai undyn
Dwyn terfyn tra hyfryd;
Nid meddwl meddu hefyd,
Namyn o Dduw, ddim o'r byd.

In the life time of Madog no one *can have power* to encroach on the most happy boundary; he thinks not also *of possessing*, but from God, any portion of the world. *Cynddelw.*

Ni fedd, namyn Duw, ddigyfoethi dyn.

No one, except God, *has* to deprive man of his power. *H. Foel ab Griffri.*

Meddw, *a.* (medd) Being made to turn round; circling, turning round; causing to turn; intoxicating; intoxicated, being besides one's self. *Meddw hen-hob*, crop sick.

Meddw pob balch ar waddawd ei annorthineb.

Every proud one is intoxicated with the dregs of his ignorance. *Adage.*

Gogwn altrefnawr
Rhwng nef a llawr——
Pan yw meddw olwyn;
Pan yw lledol orddwyn.

I know who upholds order between heaven and earth; why a wheel is *revolving*, and why a mallet is flat. *Taliesin.*

Yr yfasamni feddw fedd y Drefwen.

We have drank the *intoxicating* mead of the Whitetown. *Cynddelw.*

Tyfu cas yn lle cariad;
Felly gwna y rhai meddwon;
Digio Duw a digio dynion.

Cherishing hate instead of love; so the *drunken ones* do; offending God and offending men. *T. Ll. D. Powel.*

Meddwad, *s. m.* (meddw) A causing to turn round, an intoxicating; a getting drunk.

Meddwain, *a.* (meddw) Abounding with circular motion; inebriated, drunken.

Meddwaint, *s. m.* (meddwain) Intoxication.

Fy nyn, ni hunwn ninnau,
Er maint oedd y meddwaint mau.

My dear, I would not slumber neither, notwithstanding how great was my *intoxication*. *D. ab Gwilym.*

Meddwawd, *s. m.* (medd) A turning round; intoxication, drunkenness.

Nid yf yr hebogydd namyn tri chornaid yn y neuadd, rhag bod gwall ar ei hebogau drwy feddwdawd.

The falconer drinks no more than three hornfuls in the hall lest his hawks should be neglected through *drunkenness*. *Welsh Laws.*

Meddwawl, *a.* (meddw) Tending to turn round; intoxicating, inebriating.

Meddwdawd, *s. m.* (meddw) Drunkenness.

Nid meddw y dyn a allo
Codi ei hun a rhodio,
Ac yfed rhagor diawd;
Nid yw hyny yn feddwdawd.

Not drunk the man who can get up himself, walk about, and can drink more liquor, that is not *drunkenness*. *T. Ll. D. Powel.*

Meddwedig, *a.* (meddwad) Intoxicated, drunk.

Meddwedigaeth, *s. m.* (meddwedig) Intoxication.

Meddwi, *v. a.* (meddw) To cause to turn round; to turn round; to intoxicate, to get drunk.

> A fyno nef i'w enaid,
> Medd syr Rhys, meddwi sy raid.
>
> He that would obtain heaven for his soul, as Sir Rhys says, it is necessary *to get drunk*. *Guto y Glyn.*

Meddwl, *s. m.*——*pl.* meddyliau (medd——wl) Thought, mind; intention.

> Rhydd i bawb ei feddwl; a rhydd i bob meddwl ei lafar.
>
> Free to every one his *thought*: and free to every *thought* its utterance. *Adage.*
>
> Allan o olwg allan o feddwl.
>
> Out of sight out of *mind*. *Adage.*
>
> Llawer o weddill o feddwl chwannawg.
>
> Much of waste from an ambitious *mind*. *Adage.*
>
> Ni hena meddwl.
>
> The *mind* will not grow old. *Adage.*

Meddwl, *v. a.* (medd—wl) To think, to mind; to intend; to suppose, or to imagine.

> Ni feddwl ni adfeddwl.
>
> He *will not think* who will not reflect. *Adage.*

Meddwr, *s. m.—pl.* meddwyr (meddu—gwr) A man who commands; a possessor.

Meddwwr, *s. m.—pl.* meddwwyr (meddw—gwr) A man who intoxicates; a man who gets drunk.

Meddwyn, *s. m. dim.* (meddw) A drunkard.

Meddyd, *v. a.* (medd) To express, to speak.

> Ni ellir derwydd, medd derwydd.
>
> It is impossible to make a druid, *says* a druid. *Adage.*
>
> A mi ddysgoganaf, cyn fy nygnedd,
> Brython dros Saeson; Brithwyr a'i medd.
>
> And I will foretel, before my affliction, the Britons over the Saxons; the Variegated Men *say* it. *Myrddin.*
>
> Meddai'r gwyr a ommeddwyd,
> Mab y Criawns Enns wyd.
>
> *Quoth* the men who were refused, the miser's son of Enns art thou. *Guto y Glyn, i H. Ddu.*

Meddydd, *s. m.—pl. t.* ion (medd) A mead-brewer

> Meddydd, ei nawdd yw, o'r pan ddechreuo efe wneuthur cerwyn fedd oni rwymo ei hwyl am ei phen, dwyn y dyn a wnel y cam.
>
> The *mead-brewer*, his protection is, from the time when he begins to make a tub of mead until he ties its covering over the top of it, conducting away the person that does the wrong. *Welsh Laws.*

Meddyg, *s. m.—pl. t.* on (medd) A physician, a doctor, a surgeon. *Meddyg y bugel*, or *meddyg mair*, ploughman's spikenard.

> Nid meddyg ond amser.
>
> There is no *physician* like time. *Adage.*
>
> Goreu meddyg meddyg enaid.
>
> The best *physician* is the *physician* of the soul. *Adage.*
>
> Meddyg a ddyly wneuthur meddyginiaeth rad i'r a fo yn y llys, ac i'r teulu.
>
> The *doctor* ought to perform a gratuitous cure to such as shall be at court, and to the family. *Welsh Laws.*

Meddygadwy, *a.* (meddyg) Curable, remediable.

Meddygai, *s. c.* (meddyg) That cures, or heals.

Meddygawl, *a.* (meddyg) Curative, medicinal.

> Fod e'n hawl feddygawl fyd
> A gynnwys i'm fod genyd!
>
> As it is a portion of a *healing* world, may it be suffered for me to have thee! *D. ab Gwilym.*

Meddyges, *s. f.—pl. t.* au (meddyg) A doctress; the violet; *meddyges ddu*, common figwort; *meddyges felen*, saffron crocus; *meddyges las*, selfheal; *meddyges lwyd*, betony.

Meddygfys, *s. m.* (meddyg—bys) The ring finger

Meddygiad, *s. m.* (meddyg) A making a cure.

Meddygiaeth, *s. m.* (meddyg) Medicine; the applying a remedy.

Meddygin, *a.* (meddyg) Curative, medicinal.

Meddyginiaeth, *s. m.—pl. t.* au (meddygin) Physic, medicine, remedy, or cure.

> Meddyginiaeth ynfyd ffonawd dda.
>
> The *remedy* for a fool is a good stroke. *Adage.*
>
> Meddyginiaeth rhuddell, deuddeg ceiniawg; meddyginiaeth llysiau wrth chwydd pedair ceiniawg.
>
> A *remedy* of red salve is twelve pence; a *remedy* of herbs applied to a swelling is four pence. *Welsh Laws.*

Meddyginiaethad, *s. m.* (meddyginiaeth) A making a cure; the applying a remedy.

Meddyginiaethawl, *a.* (meddyginiaeth) Belonging to the healing art; medicinal.

Meddyginiaethu, *v. a.* (meddyginiaeth) To perform a cure; to apply a remedy.

Meddygiad, *s. m.* (meddyg) A making a cure.

Meddyglyn, *s. m.—pl. t.* oedd (meddyg—llyn) Hydromel, a kind of medicinal drink: the wild carrot; also called *moron y maes*.

Meddyglys, *s. m.* (meddyg—llys) Woundwort.

Meddygu, *v. a.* (meddyg) To make a cure; to apply a remedy.

> Lles pawb pan feddyger.
>
> It is the benefit of all when *a cure shall be made*. *Adage.*

Meddygyn, *s. m. dim.* (meddyg) That heals: also the violet, otherwise called *y grinllys*, *craith unnos*, and *y feddyges*: *meddygyn menyw*, common feverfew.

Meddylfryd, *s. m —pl. t.* au (meddwl—bryd) The affection, or bent of the mind.

Meddylgar, *a.* (meddwl) Mindful, thoughtful; thinking, musing, contemplative.

> Nid meddylgar ond serchawg;
> Nid serchawg ond ceruddgar.
>
> None is *thoughtful* but the lover; none is a lover but who is fond of music. *Adage.*

Meddylgarwch, *s. m.* (meddylgar) Thoughtfulness

Meddyliad, *s. m.* (meddwl) A thinking, a supposing

Meddyliaw, *v. a.* (meddwl) To think, to mind; to intend, to purpose; to imagine, to suppose.

> Anynwyrus yw gwr a feddylio cael medi llafur y cynhauaf ar ei dir, oni bydd ef gwedy hau.
>
> Irrational is the man *who thinks* to have to reap the produce of the harvest upon his land, if he shall not have sown. *Marchawg Crwydrad.*
>
> Hudawl yw'r byd——
> Mal mai ddail, o meddyliwn.
>
> Transitory is the world, like the leaves of May, *did we but think*. *Mer. ab Rhys.*

Meddyliawg, *a.* (meddwl) Thoughtful, musing.

Meddylied, *v.* (meddwl) To think; to suppose.

Meddyliwr, *s. m.—pl.* meddylwyr (meddwl—gwr) A thinker; a supposer.

Meddysg, *s. m.* (medd—ysg) A transformed state, that is transformed. *a.* Transformed.

Mef, *s. m.* (me—ef) That is puffed out, smooth, or lubricous.

Mefl, *s. m.—pl.* meflau (mef) A filthy breaking out; nastiness; a polluted state; disgrace, scandal.

> Ni ddylir maeddu gwraig, namyn o dri achaws; sef, am roddi peth ni ddylyo; am gaffel gwr arall genddi; ac am ddymuno mefl ar farf ei gwr.
>
> A wife ought not to be beaten but for three causes: that is, for giving away what she should not; for finding another man with her; and for wishing *disgrace* on the beard of her husband. *Welsh Laws.*
>
> Gwell gochel mefl na'i ddial.
>
> Better to avoid *disgrace* than to revenge it. *Adage.*
>
> Hir weddwdawd i fefl.
>
> Long widowhood to *disgrace*. *Adage.*
>
> Anghwanegid mefl mawrair.
>
> The *disgrace* that is boasted is augmented. *Adage.*
>
> Mefl i'r llygoden un-twll.
>
> *Bad luck* to the mouse with one hole. *Adage.*

Meflâad, *s. m.* (mefl) A rendering polluted; a disgracing, a scandalizing; a becoming disgraceful.

Ni wnant eu dwyn, cyd trwy feflâad;
Nid ef eu defawd bod yn galed.

They will not take them, if it be through *disgrace*; it is not in their nature to be hard. *Taliesin, Mic. Dinbych.*

Meflâawl, *a.* (mefl) Tending to pollute; of a disgraceful nature.

Meflaidd, *a.* (mefl) Somewhat disgraceful.

Meflâu, *v. a.* (mefl) To render polluted; to render or become disgraceful.

Yn drwg y geiniawg a feflâo ei pherchen.

Bad is the penny that *disgraces* its possessor. *Adage.*

Mefledig, *a.* (mefl) Polluted; disgraced.

Meflethiant, *s. m.* (mefl—methiant) A disgraceful defect.

Tri meflfethiant gwr, bod yn argiwydd drwg, a bod yn ddryggarwr, a bod yn lilidiwr yn nadlau.

The three *shameful defects* of a man, to be a bad master, and to be a bad lover, and to be a driveller in debates. *Welsh Laws.*

Mefliad, *s. m.* (mefl) A polluting; a disgracing; a becoming disgraceful.

Meflu, *v. a.* (mefl) To pollute; to disgrace; to be polluted; to be disgraced. *Mae y plentyn gwedi meflu ei hun*, the child has befouled himself

Yn mi a feflawr o'r gynghenedd,
Gweryd i'r gwag-feirdd eu gwaghoffedd.

If I am *disgraced* from the disputation, the poetasters will be relieved by their empty boast. *Ph. Brydydd.*

Meflwr, *s. m.—pl.* meflwyr (mefl—gwr) A disgracer; a disgraceful man.

Meflwriaeth, *s. m.* (meflwr) A disgraceful act.

Tri meflwriaeth mach y sydd; gwadu ei fechni, ac ef yn fach; ac addef ei fechni, ac na allo ei chymhell; a diebryd mach gwedi rhodder.

There are three *disgraceful acts* of a bail: denying his suretiship, and be a bail; and giving his suretiship without being able to perform it; and the frustration of bail after it is given. *Welsh Laws.*

Mefus, *s. pl. aggr.* (mef) Strawberries.

Fy nyn——
A'i gwefus mal mefus mair.

My nymph with her lip like the scarlet *strawberries*. *Bedo Aeddren.*

Mefusen, *s. f. dim.* (mefus) A strawberry.

Mefuswydd, *s. pl. aggr.* (mefus—gwydd) Strawberry plants.

Meg, *s. f.* (my—eg) That takes in or contains; a fetter. *Y Feg fawr*, a large old fetter, kept at *Dinas Mawddwy*.

Megai, *s. c.—pl.* megeion(mag) The glow-worm.

Megawl, *a.* (meg) Relating to the utterance.

Megiad, *s. m.* (meg) An uttering, or expressing.

Megidydd, *s. m.* (mag) One who nourishes.

Megin, *s. f.—pl. t.* au (meg) A pair of bellows.

Mae o anadl mwy ynnof
Nog yn nghlau meginau gof.

There is within me of breath more than in the hollow of the bellows of a smith. *D. ab Gwilym.*

Meginaw, *v. a.* (megin) To work bellows.

A'i anadl diadlam dwfn
Yn megino mwg annwfn.

And his deep unreturning breath *blowing* the infernal fume. *H. Wyn.*

Meginiad, *s. m.* (megin) A working of bellows.

Meginwr, *s. m.—pl.* meginwyr (megin—gwr) One who works, or blows bellows.

Megitor, *sup.* (magu) To be nourishing.

Megitor eu gwir hwy hir alanas.

Their sincerity *nourished* a lasting feud. *Myrddin.*

Megyn, *s. m.* (mag) A nurseling; a rearling.

Megys, *conj.* (meg—ys) As, in the manner, in the state; in the same manner, like as, so as. *Megys cynt*, as formerly.

Mehefin, *s. m.* (me—hefin) The month of June.

Mehin, *s. m.* (me—hin) Fat, grease, lard.

Mehinaidd, *a.* (mehin) Like lard, fat, or grease.

Mehinaw, *v. n.* (mehin) To become fat or greasy.

Mehinawg, *a.* (mehin) Abounding with lard.

Mehinawr, *a.* (mehin) Abounding with lard.

Mehinen, *s. f. dim.* (mehin) The leaf of fat.

Meia, *v. a.* (mai) To take the field; to go out to war; also to go a maying.

Meiad, *s. m.* (mai) A taking the field; or a going out to war; a maying.

Meiaeth, *s. m.* (mai) A making a campaign.

Meiaw, *v. a.* (mai) To make a campaign.

Meiawd, *s. m.* (mai) A making a campaign.

Meiawg, *a.* (mai) Of the field; champain.

Tri thri nodded,
Atgor ar bened,
A march meiawg,
Cymbrwy teithiawg.

Thrice three protections, recurring to the native country, with a steed *used to the field*, perfect for travelling. *Taliesin.*

Meiawl, *a.* (mai) Belonging to open country.

Meibionain, *s. pl. dim.* (mab) Little children.

Meibionos, *s. pl. dim.* (mab) Little children.

Meichai, *s. c.—pl.* meicheion (mach) A surety.

Goreu meichai diniweidrwydd.

The best *surety* is innocence. *Adage.*

Meichiad, *s. m.* (mach) A bailing; a being surety

Meichiau, *s. pl. aggr.* (mach) Sureties, or bails.

Meichiaw, *v. a.* (mach) To give bail; to become a bail, or surety.

Gorug ei waith,
A fach y fechdaith.

He has completed his work, that bails the journey of a surety. *Adage.*

Meichiawg, *a.* (mach) Having surety, or bail.

Meichiawl, *a.* (mach) Relating to suretiship.

Meidr, *s. m.—pl.* meidron(maid) A measure, rule, or limit; also a lane, or road. *Dyfed.*

Mae ar weinidogion gymmodi anghyfodau, a chytuno ysbrydoedd, ag sydd wedi myned tu hwnt i bob meidr a medr.

It is incumbent upon ministers to reconcile differences, and to unite spirits, which are gone beyond every *rule* and order. *Ier. Owain.*

Meidrad, *s. m.* (meidr) A comprehending, a bringing within limit; a meting.

Meidradur, *s. m.—pl. t.* on (meidrad) A meter.

Meidradydd, *s. m.—pl. t.* on (meidrad) A meter.

Meidraeth, *s. m.* (meidr) Measurement.

Meidraw, *v. a.* (meidr) To reduce to measure, rule, or limit; to mete.

Meidrawl, *a.* (meidr) Belonging to measure; being within measure, or comprehended; limited.

Meidredig, *a.* (meidr) Comprehended; limited.

Meidriad, *s. m.—pl.* meidriaid (medr) One who is able to effect, or to accomplish.

Meidroldeb, *s. m.* (meidrawl) The state of being within measure, or comprehension; finiteness.

Meidroldeb, *s. m.* (meidrawl) Finiteness.

Meidroledd, *s. m.* (meidrawl) Comprehensiveness, comprehension, capacity.

Meidroli, *v. a.* (meidrawl) To bring under measure; to bring within comprehension; to limit.

Meidrolrwydd, *s. m.* (meidrawl) Finiteness.

Meidwy, *s. m.—pl. t.* on (maid) That is separate, or solitary; a hermit.

Meidwyfod, *s. f.* (meidwy—bod) A hermitage.

Meidyn, *s. m. dim.* (maid) A point of separation; a small space; a point of time; a moment.

Meidda, *v. a.* (maidd) To collect or go a begging for cards and whey.

> Byddi yn——
> Cawsa, yta, gwlana'n glir,
> Ciga, a meidda, meiddir.
>
> Thou wilt be collecting cheese, collecting corn, and fairly begging wool; collecting flesh, and *collecting curds and whey*, it is said. *S. Mowddwy.*

Meiddaidd, *a.* (maidd) Curdled like whey; serous

Meiddawg, *a.* (maidd) Abounding with whey.

Meiddeiddrwydd, *s. m.* (meiddaidd) A curdled state.

Meiddiad, *s. m.* (maidd) A breaking or curdling; a forming a cliff.

Meiddion, *s. pl. aggr.* (maidd) Cards and whey.

Meiddioni, *v.* (meiddion) To turn cards and whey

Meiddlyd, *a.* (maidd) Wheyish; curdled.

Meiddlydrwydd, *s. m.* (meiddlyd) A curded state.

Meiddlydu, *v. n.* (meiddlyd) To become curded.

Meiddlyn, *s. m.* (maidd—llyn) Whey drink.

Meiddogrwydd, *s. m.* (meiddawg) A curdled state

Meiddyn, *s. f.* (maidd) The limit of a plain; a cliff; a range of mountains.

Meiedd, *s. m.* (mai) The state of being plain.

Meifod, *s. f.—pl. t.* au (mai—bod) A champaign dwelling; a summer habitation.

Meifon, *s. pl. aggr.* (maf) Berries that grow in cluster; raspberries; also called *gwyfon*, *afan*, and *mafon*.

Meigen, *s. f.—pl. t.* au (maig) A sudden turn; a recess, or nook.

Meigiad, *s. m.* (maig) A turning suddenly; a happening, or befalling.

Meigiaw, *v. a.* (maig) To turn suddenly, to happen

Meigiawl, *a.* (maig) Of a sudden turn.

Meigr, *s. m.* (maig) A sudden start; terror.

Meigrad, *s. m.* (meigr) A starting suddenly.

Meigraw, *v. a.* (meigr) To start out suddenly.

Meigryn, *s. m.* (meigr) A sudden start, terror; also the megrim, or vertigo.

Meiian, *s. f.* (mai—iau) A field yoke, or a yoke with four oxen.

Meiliad, *s. m.* (mail) A holding together; a putting in a bowl; a filling with a bowl.

Meiliaid, *s. f.—pl.* meilieidiau (mail) A dishful, the fill of a platter; a bowlful.

Meiliannawl, *a.* (meiliant) Tending to uphold.

Meiliannu, *v. a.* (meiliant) To uphold.

Meiliant, *s. m.* (mail) An upholding.

Meiliar, *s. m.* (mail) That makes a bound or start.

Meiliaw, *v. a.* (mail) To hold up, to sustain; to put in a bowl; to raise liquids with a bowl.

Meiliawg, *a.* (mail) Having a structure.

Meiliawr, *s. f.* (mail) A habitation, a dwelling.

> Cyrchid dedwydd ei feiliawr.
>
> Let the prudent resort to his *dwelling*. *Adage.*

Meiliedig, *a.* (meiliad) Being put together, constructed, or built up.

Meiliedyn, *s. m. dim.* (meiliad) A small bowl.

Meilierydd, *s. m.* (meiliar) The sky-lark.

Meiliorn, *s. m.* (mêl—orn) A transgression.

Meiliornad, *s. m.* (meiliorn) A transgressing.

Meiliorni, *v. a.* (meiliorn) To transgress.

Meiliornus, *a.* (meiliorn) Transgressing.

Meiliwr, *s. m.—pl.* meilwyr (mêl—gwr) A transgressor.

Meilon, *s. pl. aggr.* (màl) Powder, dust; flour. *Meilon gwydd*, *blawd gwydd*, wood dust.

Meiloni, *v. a.* (meilon) To reduce to powder; to become dust, or powder.

Meilwn, *s. m.—pl.* meilynau (mèl) The small of the leg; also called *Deilw*.

Meilyn, *s. m. dim.* (mèl) A loop, or eye. *Crwcyn a meilyn*, *bach a dolen*, crook and eye.

Meilyndorch, *s. f.—pl.* meilyndyrch (meilwn—torch) A sashoon.

Meilynwisg, *s. f.—pl. t.* oedd (meilwn—gwisg) A sashoon, also called *arfeilyn*.

Meillion, *s. pl. aggr.* (maill) Clover; trefoil. *Meillion gwynion*, *maill gwynion*, *meillion Olwen*, the white-flowered meadow trefoil; *meillion corniawg*, Spanish trefoil; *meillion tair-dalen*, mellicot; *meillion y gors*, buckbeans; *meillion codenawg*, *traed yr ysgyfarnog*, hare's cummin; *meillion cochion*, red trefoil, or purple-wort; *march-feillion*, cultivated clover.

Meillionaidd, *a.* (meillion) Like trefoils.

Meillionawg, *a.* (meillion) Having trefoils.

Meillionawl, *a.* (meillion) Like the trefoils.

Meillionen, *s. f.* (meillion) A trefoil. *Meillionen felen*, kidney vetch, or ladies' finger; *meillionen gorniawg*, yellow medick; *meillionen y gors*, marsh-trefoil; *meillionen grogenawg*, heart medick; *meillionen Olwen*, Dutch clover; *meillionen y ceirw*, common meillot.

> Pedair meillionen wen a fyddai yn ei hol, pa ffordd bynag y delai, ac am hyny y gelwid hi Olwen.
>
> Four white *trefoils* would spring up in her track, which ever way she might come, and therefore she was called Olwen. *H. Culwch—Mabinogion.*

Meillioni, *v. n.* (meillion) To produce trefoils.

Meillyn, *s. m.—pl.* meillod (maill) A lean old ruin.

Meinâad, *s. m.* (meinâu) A making slender, exile, fine, or delicate.

Meinâawl, *a.* (meinâu) Tending to make slender.

Meinâu, *v. a.* (main) To make slender, or fine.

Meinawl, *a.* (main) Of a fine or slender make.

Meinciad, *s. m.* (mainc) A placing benches.

Meinciaw, *v. a.* (mainc) To fix benches.

Meincwely, *s. m.—pl. t.* au (mainc—gwely) A settle-bed; a sofa.

Meindeg, *a.* (main—teg) Delicately fair.

Meinder, *s. m.* (main) Exility, slenderness.

Meindlos, *a.* (main—tlos) Delicately pretty.

Meindlws, *a.* (main—tlws) Delicately pretty.

Meindra, *s. m.* (main) Exility, slenderness.

Meindwf, *s. m.* (main—twf) A slender growth. *a.* Of a slender growth.

Meinddydd, *s. m.* (main—dydd) A fine day.

Meinedd, *s. m.* (main) Exility, slenderness.

Meingan, *s. f.* (main—can) That is delicate and fair; an epithet for a beauty.

> Tra gweno meingan, cipia gusan.
>
> Whilst the *fair one* smiles, snatch a kiss. *Adage.*

Meingil, *s. m.* (main—cil) A close corner.

Meinholi, *v. a.* (main—holi) To examine narrowly, to scrutinize.

Meinholiad, *s. m.* (main—holiad) A narrowly examining; a strict examination.

Meiniad, *s. m.* (maen) A stoning; a petrifying.

Meiniawg, *a.* (maen) Of stone, or stony.

> A gelo cer manro meiniawg
> Gelynion Saeson ddanawg.
>
> And bury close to the *stony* beach the Saxon foes clad in mail. *Ll. P. Moch, i Lywelyn II.*

Meiniles, *s. f. dim.* (main) A little delicate animal.

Meinin, *a.* (maen) Of stone, stony. *Ty meinin*, *ty maen*, *ty cerrig*, a stone house.

> Gwelaf finnau gwel fein
> Baradwys Gwent.——
>
> And I perceive the *stone* wall of the paradise of Gwent. *Guto y Glyn.*

Meinir, *s. f.* (main—ir) That is of delicate growth, an epithet for a handsome woman.

Meinllais, *s. m.* (main—llais) A shrill voice.
Meinoeth, *s. f.* (main—oeth) A fine night.
Meinoledd, *s. m.* (meinawl) Exility, slenderness.

Bychodedd meinoledd.

Slenderness is littleness. *Adage.*

Meinoles, *s. f. dim.* (meinawl) An epithet for any delicate young animal, such as a heifer.
Meinus, *a.* (main) Slender, delicate; tiny.

Mawrwlus, feinus, fin yd fernid craif,
Mor wen ei hesgair uch ei hesgid!

Magnificent and *delicate*, deemed a precious relick, so white her leg above her shoe! *Ior. Fychan.*

Gogoneddus Fair' wâr, weddus, feinus farnon!

Glorious Mary! gentle, virtuous, and delicate queen!
D. Ddu o Hiraddu.

Meinusaw, *v. a.* (meinus) To render fine, or delicate; to become slender, fine, delicate.
Meinwaith, *s. m.* (main—gwaith) Nice work.
Meinwar, *a* (main—gwar) Delicate and gentle, delicate and meek; delicately mild. *s. f.* That is delicately mild.

Dy far, feinwar Fyfanwy,
Ar a'th gar: ni fu far fwy.

Thy ire, Myvanwy, delicately mild, is on him who loves thee: never was there ire more severe. *H. ab Einion Llygliw.*

Meinwedd, *s. f.* (main—gwedd) A delicate aspect
Meinweddaidd, *a.* (meinwedd) Of a delicate aspect
Meinweddawg, *a.* (meinwedd) Of a fine aspect.
Meinwen, *a.* (main—gwen) Delicately fair. *s. f.* That is delicately fair.
Meinwyn, *a.* (main—gwyn) Delicately white.
Meinwyr, *a.* (main—gwyr) Delicately chaste. *Pefr feinwyr*, the fair one delicately chaste.
Meinyn, *s. m. dim.* (maen) A lump of stone.
Meipen, *s. f. dim* (maip) A single turnip.
Meiriawl, *a.* (mer) Thawing, dissolving.
Meiriolad, *s. m.* (meiriawl) A thawing.
Meirioli, *v. n.* (meiriawl) To thaw, to dissolve; the same as *dadmeru* and *dadleithiaw*.
Meiriolus, *a.* (meiriawl) Tending to thaw.
Meirion, *s. m.* (mar) That moves about; a looker; a dairyman; tops of hemp.
Meiriones, *s. f.—pl. t.* au (meirion) A female who superintends; a house-wife; a dairy-woman; also, an epithet for a woman, or matron; and sometimes used, in a bad sense, for a concubine.

A morwyn eto a meiriones,

And a virgin yet and a *matron.* *Iolo Goch, i Fair.*

Offeiriaid—
Pob un, heb na lles na lles,
Ofer iawn, a'i feirionês.

The parsons, every one, without form or benefit, very worthless, in company with his *girl.* *Dr. S. Cent.*

Meirioni, *s. m.* (meirion) A superintendency; the office of a keeper, or one who has custody.
Meirionig, *a.* (meirion) Tending to guard, or to watch. *Drych meirionig*, a scarecrow.

Mal drych, o gwn edrych neb,
Meirionig ym yw'r wyneb

Like a *scaring* phiz to me, if I know the appearance of any one, is the face. *Gutto y Glyn*

Meirwys, *s. f.—pl. t.* od (merwys) The ousel.

Aeliau mawr, fel y meirwys,
A phenau baglau 'r un bwys.

Large eyebrows, like the ousel, of the same form as the heads of crooks. *Llewelyn, i aloriâ.*

Meirydd, *s. m.—pl. t.* ion (maer) A mayor.

Meiryddion a chynghellorion a ddylyant gyweiriaw y wlad, a gwneuthur ei deddfau.

Mayors and chancellors are bound to establish order in the country, and to administer its laws. *Welsh Laws.*

Meisgyn, *s. m. dim.* (masg) A moth; otherwise called *gwyfyn*.
Meisiad, *s. m.* (mais) A devising, an invention.

Meisiaw, *v. a.* (mais) To invent, to device.

Ceisio meisio mewn miwsig,
Casau dawn, ymgyrru dig.

Attempting *to invent* in music; hating genius, breathing up auger. *Edm. Prys.*

Meisiawd, *s. m.* (mais) An invention, a device.
Meisiawg, *a.* (mais) Full of invention.
Meisiawl, *a.* (mais) Inventive, devising.
Meisiedig, *a.* (mais) Invented, devised.
Meisiwr, *s. m.—pl.* meiswyr (mais—gwr) A deviser, or inventer.
Meistr, *s. m.—pl.* iaid (maist) A master.

Ni wnaf estron yn feistri;
Ni wnae chwech ym a wnaech chwi.

I will not make *masters* of strangers; half a dozen would not do for me what you would do. *B. Dafi.*

Meistrad, *s. m.—pl. t.* oedd (meistr) A master.
Meistrawl, *a.* (meistr) Masterly; master.
Meistres, *s. m.—pl. t.* au (meistr) A mistress.
Meistrolaeth, *s. m.* (meistrawl) Mastership, mastery; authority, dominion.
Meistrolaethu, *v. a.* (meistrolaeth) To exercise mastership; to domineer.
Meistrolaethus, *a.* (meistrolaeth) Magisterious.
Meistroledd, *s. m.* (meistrawl) Mastery.
Meistroli, *v. a.* (meistrawl) To act magisterially, to bear sway, to domineer; to be master.
Meistrolrwydd, *s. m.* (meistrawl) Mastery.
Meistrolus, *a.* (meistrawl) Having mastery.
Meityn, *s. m.* (meidyn) A point of separation; a small space; a space of time. *Wyf yma er ys meityn*, I have been here a good while.
Meithder, *s. m.* (maith) Extensiveness; distance.
Meithdra, *s. m.* (maith) Extensiveness; distance.
Meithedig, *a.* (maith) Being rendered tedious.
Meithiad, *s. m.* (maith) A rendering tedious.
Meithiaw, *v. a.* (maith) To render tedious.
Meithiw, *a.* (maith) Extensive; tedious.
Meithni, *s. m.* (maith) Extensiveness, tediousness.

Duw yw'r Drindawd—
Un Duw a thri, meithni mawr.

God is the Trinity, one God and three, great the *comprehension.* *G. Hiraethawg.*

Meithrin, *s. m.—pl. t.* ion (maeth—trin) Nurture.

Meithrinwr, trinwr, at raid mwy athraw,
Meithrin creaduriaid;
Meithrin y corff o'th rad caid;
Meithrinia, maetha 'r enaid!

A fosterer, a manager, in time of need the greatest teacher, who nourishes his creatures; the *nourishment* of the body from thy bounty would be had; nourish, and feed the soul. *H. D. ab Ifan.*

Meithrin, *v. a.* (maeth—trin) To nourish, to rear, to bring up, to educate.

Gnawd o egin meithrin dâr.

From the small shoots a rick is reared. *Adage.*

Pwy wyr tranc mab wrth feithrin!

Who knows the fate of a child when *rearing* him! *Llywarch Hen.*

Meithrinaeth, *s. m.* (meithrin) The act or office of nurturing.
Meithrinaw, *v. a.* (meithrin) To nourish, to rear, to bring up, to educate.
Meithrinawl, *a* (meithrin) Nurturing.
Meithrinedig, *a.* (meithrin) Nurtured, educated.
Meithrines, *s. f.—pl. t.* au (meithrin) A female who nurtures, or brings up.
Meithrinfa, *s. f.* (meithrin) A seminary.
Meithringar, *a.* (meithrin) Nurturing, fostering.
Meithriniad, *s. m.* (meithrin) A nurturing.
Meithrinwr, *s. m.—pl.* meithrinwyr (meithrin—gwr) A man who nurtures, or brings up.
Meithrinwraig, *s. f.—pl.* meithrinwreigedd (meithrin—gwraig) A woman who nurtures.

Meithrinydd, *s. m.—pl. t.* ion (meithrin) Nurturer.
Meithrinyddes, *s. f.—pl. t* au (meithrinydd) A woman who nurtures, or brings up.
Meithyn, *s. m. dim.* (maeth) A nurseling, a darling

—Gruffudd,
Mab meithyn Llywelyn llafnrudd.

Gruffudd, the *darling* son of Llywelyn with the ruddy blade. *D. Benfras.*

Meiwr, *s. m.—pl.* meiwyr (mai—gwr) A man of the field; a warrior.

Cas meiwyr heb ryddid.

Odious are *men of the field* without liberty. *Cetwg.*

Meiwyn, *s. m.* (mai—gwyn) Thorn-apple.
Mel, *s. m.* (me—el) Honey. *Mel y cwn*, **melsugn**, *mel y ceirw*, woad; *mel y gwenynydd*, **marsh** lousewort; also called *melawg y waen.*

Doethineb, mal goreuon'y mel, fydd yn laaf.

Wisdom, like the best of the *honey*, will be at the bottom. *Adage.*

Mêl, *s. m.* (my—el) That bounds, starts, or jets.
Mela, *v. a.* (mel) To gather honey.

Adar a hedant, gwenyn a fe/ant,
Pysgod a nofiant, pryfed a'mlusgant;
Pob peth a ymdaith i gynnull ei borthiant,
Ond cler, ac ofer, a lladron difwyniant.

The birds do fly, the bees *collect honey*, the fishes swim, reptiles creep; every thing doth travel to procure its sustenance, except the minstrels, and loiterers, and worthless thieves. *Bustl Beirdd.*

Melaid, *a.* (mel) Abounding with honey.
Melaidd, *a.* (mel) Of the nature of honey.
Melain, *a.* (mel) Abounding with honey.
Melaint, *s. m.* (melain) A being full of honey.
Melawd, *s. m.* (mel) A collecting of honey; the state of being like honey; sweetness.
Melawg, *a.* (mel) Having honey. *Y felawg*, the honey-suckle; *melawg y borfa*, pasture lousewort
Meldardd, *a.* (mel—tardd) Mellifluous, mellifluent
Melddwyn, *a.* (mel—dwyn) Melliferous.
Melen, *a.* (*f. of* melyn) Yellow; tawny.
Melengu, *s. f.* (melen—cu) The dyer's weed.
Melenog, *s. f.—pl. t.* od (melen) A linnet.
Melenydd, *s. f.* (melen) Hawk-weed; also called *gwalchlys*, and *llysiau yr hebawg.*
Melfoch, *s. pl. aggr.* (mel—moch) Honey swine.

Golwython o giz melfoch.

Stakes of the flesh of *bears*. *Peredur—Mabinogion.*

Melgan, *s f.* (mel—can) A honey song.
Melgawod, *s. f.—pl.* ydd. mel—cawod) Honeydew
Melged, *s. f.—pl. t.* ion (mel—ced) A honey tribute: the sea beet.

O Ddinefwr melged a gafal; pedair tunell o fel, pedair mu yn mhob tunell, dwy grenaid yn mhob mu, llwyth deuwr ar drosol yn mhob gren.

From Dinevor he obtained a *tribute of honey*: four tuns of honey, four tubs in every tun, two platterfuls in each tub, and the load of two men on a pole in every platter. *Welsh Laws.*

Melgorn, *s. m.—pl.* melgyrn (mel—corn) A cell of a honeycomb; a honeycomb; also an abscess containing matter like honey

Elffin gyda chyffin chwyrn
Maelgwn yn gwasgu'r melgyrn.

Elfin along the bustling boundary of Maelgon squeezing the *honey-combs*. *Ll. ab Gutyn, i H. Idu.*

Melgranc, *s. m.* (mel—cranc) An abscess containing thick honey-like matter; also called *melgorn.*
Melin, *s. f.—pl. t.* au (mal) A grinding mill.

Un o dri madgyrfinydd Ynys Prydain: Coel ab Cyllin ab Caradawg ab Bran, a wnaethai melin rhod ac olwyn gyntaf i genedl y Cymmry.

One of the three useful inventors of the isle of Britain: Coel ab Cyllin ab Caradog ab Bran, who made a *mill* turning by wheel first for the nation of the Cymry. *Trioedd.*

Melinau gwynt, yn mlaen gwyl
Dy gyrch a'u dug i'w gorchwyl.

The *windmills*, at the approach of a festival thy assembly will bring them into work. *M. ab Rhys.*

Melina, *s. m.* (melin) A going to mill.

Melina tlawd ei gwynos.

His supper is the beggar's *going to mill.* *Adage.*

Melina, *v. a.* (melin) To go to mill.

Dodwch un a'i march—
At gwilog urddiog dda,
Fal lonydd, i felina.

Give me either a horse, or a mare very lazy and good, that is quiet, for *to go to mill.* *G. ab Ll. Fychan.*

Melinaw, *v. a.* (melin) To grind in a mill.
Melinwr, *s. m.* (melin—gwr) A miller.
Melinydd, *s. m.—pl. t.* ion (melin) A miller.
Melinyddes, *s. f.* (melinydd) A female miller
Melodi, *s. m.* (melawd) A dulcified state.
Melota, *v. a.* (melawd) Honey-gathering.
Melotai, *s. f.* (melawd) The mallow, or honeyer.
Melred, *s. m.—pl. t.* ion (mel—rhed) Mellifluence
Melrediad, *s. m.* (melred) A flowing of honey.
Melsaig, *s. m.* (mel—saig) A sweet repast.

Gwell meusaig yn rhad no melsaig yn echwyn.

Better a free repast on acorns than *honey-feast* on trust. *Adage.*

Melsugn, *s. m.* (mel—sugn) The lousewort.
Melu, *v. a.* (mel) To make honey; to honey.
Melus, *a.* (mel) Of the nature of honey; sweet.
Melusaw, *v. a.* (melus) To honey; to sweeten.
Melusder, *s. m.* (melus) Sweetness, lusciousness.
Melwaith, *s. m.* (mel—gwaith) Mellification.
Melwawd, *s. m.* (mel—gwawd) Honeyed sauce; sweet praise; melody.
Melwi, *v. a.* (malw) To extend out glibly.
Melwïawg, *a.* (melwi) Of a gliding nature
Melwin, *s. m.* (mel—gwin) Honey wine.
Melwïoges, *s. f.* (melwïawg) A snail; but called *malwen*, and *malwoden.*
Melwlith, *s. m.* (mel—gwlith) Honey-dew.
Melwr, *s. m.—pl.* melwyr (mel—gwr) A man who collects honey, a dealer in honey.
Melwraidd, *s. m.* (mel—gwraidd) Liquorice.
Melŷen, *s. f. dim.* (malw) A snail; also called *malaen*, *melwioges*, and mostly *malwen.*
Melyn, *s. m.—pl. t.* ion (mel) Yellow. *Melyn yr eithin*, the gold-hammer, a bird so called; *Melyn y gauaf*, winter gillyflower; *melyn y gwanwyn*, the pilewort: also called *Milfyw.*
Melyn, *a.* (mel) Yellow, of a yellow hue; tawny. *Cŵyr melyn*, bees wax; *march melyn*, a light bay horse; *Ar y melyned*, of a yellowish hue; *melyn yr eithin*, or *melyn y twynau*, common tormentil; *melyn y gauaf*, wild wall-flower; *melyn y gwanwyn*, pilewort.

Iraw llaw ag eli melyn.

To grease a hand with *yellow* salve. *Adage.*

Melynach oedd pen Olwen no blodau y banadl; gwynach oedd ei chnawd no dystrych tòn.

The head of Olwen was *yellower* than the blossoms of the broom; whiter was her skin than the spray of the wave. *H. Culhwch—Mabinogion.*

Melynaidd, *a.* (melyn) Somewhat yellow.
Melynawg, *a.* (melyn) Abounding with yellow. *Melynawg y waen*, dyer's greenweed.
Melynder, *s. m.* (melyn) Yellowness.
Melyndra, *s. m.* (melyn) Yellowness.
Melynddu, *s. m.* (melyn—du) A yellowish black, a tawny colour. *a.* Tawny, reeky.
Melyndduaw, *v. a.* (melynddu) To make tawny.
Melynedd, *s. m.* (melyn) A yellowness.

Melynell, *s. m.* (melyn) A yellow hue.

> Chwe march melynell,
> Canwaith y sydd well
> Fy march melyngan
> Cyfred â gwylan.
>
> Six steeds of *yellow hue*, than those a hundred times better is my cream coloured steed, swift as the sea mew. *Taliesin.*

Melyneuraid, *s. m.* (melyn—euraid) Golden-rod.
Melynfaen, *s. m.* (melyn—maen) Brimstone.
Melyngan, *s. m.* (melyn—can) A yellow white. *a.* Of yellowish white; cream-coloured.
Melyngoch, *s. m.* (melyn—coch) A yellow red, orange red. *a.* Of an orange red.
Melyni, *s. m.* (melyn) Yellowness; jaundice.
Melyniad, *s. m.* (melyn) A making yellow.
Melynlas, *s. m.* (melyn—glas) A yellowish blue. *a.* Of a yellowish blue.

> Melynlas march Caswallawn ab Beli.
>
> *Yellow-grey* the steed of Caswallon son of Beli. *Trioedd.*

Melynllai, *s. m.* (melyn—llai) A yellowish dun colour. *a.* Of a yellowish dun.
Melynllwyd, *s. m.* (melyn—llwyd) A yellowish brown. *a.* Of a yellowish brown.
Melynllys, *s. f.* (melyn—llys) Celandine.
Melynog, *s. m.* (melyn) That is of a yellow colour; a mulatto; the linnet; also called *llinos felen*, and *meleneg*.
Melynu, *v. a.* (melyn) To make yellow, to grow yellow.
Melynus, *a.* (melyn) Tending to be yellow.
Melynwellt, *s. m.* (melyn—gwellt) Sweet scented vernal grass.
Melynwy, *s. m.* (melyn—wy) The yolk of an egg
Melynwyn, *s. m.* (melyn—gwyn) A yellowish white, a straw-colour. *a.* Of a yellow white.
Melynydd, *s. m.* (melyn) Long-rooted cat's ear.
Melys, *s. m.* (mel) A sweet. *a.* Sweet, dulcet.

> Gwerthu mel i brynu peth melys.
>
> Selling honey to buy a sweet thing. *Adage.*

Melysai, *s. c.* (melys) That has sweetness.
Melysaidd, *a.* (melys) Somewhat sweet.
Melysawg, *a.* (melys) Abounding with sweet.
Melysawl, *a.* (melys) Of a sweetening quality.
Melysder, *s. m.* (melys) Sweetness; gratefulness
Melysdra, *s. m.* (melys) Sweetness, lusciousness.
Melysedd, *s. m.* (melys) Sweetness, lusciousness.
Melysi, *s. m.* (melys) Sweetness, lusciousness.
Melysiad, *s. m.* (melys) A sweetening, dulcification
Melysiannawl, *a.* (melysiant) Delicious.
Melysiannu, *v. a.* (melysiant) To dulcify.
Melysiant, *s. m.* (melys) Dulcification.
Melysig, *a.* (melys) Fond of sweet things.

> Gwae fardd, o ddyn gwiw, a fai
> Felysig am fel gwin.
>
> Woe to the bard, an excellent wight, who should be *voluptuous* with respect to the honey wine. *H. ab D. ab I. ab Rhys.*

Melysigrwydd, *s. m.* (melysig) Fondness of sweets

> Yr arglwyddes Gwaeldder a'm gosodai yn y lle goruchaf; ac ar fy naill ystlys ydd oedd Melysigrwydd a Meddwdawd yn eistedd.
>
> The lady Frailty placed me in the most eminent seat; and on each side of me *Voluptuousness* and Drunkenness were sitting. *Marchawg Crwydrad.*

Melysrwydd, *s. m.* (melys) Sweetness, sweet taste
Melysu, *v. a.* (melys) To sweeten; to grow sweet
Melyswedd, *s. f.* (melys—gwedd) A sweet aspect
Mell, *s. m.* (my—ell) That shoots out, that is sharp.
Melldith, *s. f.—pl. t.* ion (mall—tith) A curse. *Rhoddaf iddo felldith ei fam*, I will give him his mother's curse; *melldith eu mamau*, cursed of their mothers, reprobates.
Melldithiad, *s. m.* (melldith) A malediction.
Melldithiaw, *v. a.* (melldith) To curse; to blaspheme, to swear.
Melldithiawg, *a.* (melldith) Full of cursing.
Melldithiawl, *a.* (melldith) Cursing; blasphemous
Melldithiedig, *a.* (melldithiad) Being cursed.
Melldithiwr, *s. m.—pl.* melldithwyr (melldith—gwr) A curser; a blasphemer.
Melldithrwydd, *s. m.* (melldith) Cursedness.
Melli, *s. m.* (mall) Softness, insipidity; a blight.
Mellni, *s. m.* (mall) Softness; insipidity; a blast.
Mellt, *s. pl. aggr.* (mell) That be darting, or bolting; lightning. *Cynneu mellt, goleuaw mellt, tafly mellt, cynneu dreigiau, cynneu gwibiau*, to lighten, or to shoot lightning.
Melltaidd, *a.* (mellt) Of the nature of lightning.
Melltawg, *a.* (mellt) Abounding with lightning.
Melltawl, *a.* (mellt) Belonging to lightning.
Mellten, *s. f. dim.* (mellt) A lightning, a thunderbolt.
Melltenaidd, *a.* (mellten) Like a thunderbolt.
Melltenawl, *a.* (mellten) Flashing as lightning.
Melltenìad, *s. m.* (mellten) A flashing of lightning
Melltenu, *v. a.* (mellten) To lighten, to flash.
Melltiad, *s. m.* (mellt) A flashing of lightning.
Melltiaw, *v. a.* (mellt) To dart lightning.
Melltig, *a.* (mellt) Struck by lightning, blasted.
Melltigaid, *a.* (melltig) Accursed, cursed. *Melltigaid lydnod*, cursed beasts.
Melltigaw, *v. a.* (melltig) To curse; to make accursed, to blaspheme.
Melltigawl, *a.* (melltig) Cursing; blaspheming.
Melltigedig, *a.* (melltig) Cursed, blasted.
Melltigedigawl, *a.* (melltigedig) Tending to blast.
Melltigedigrwydd, *s. m.* (melltigedig) Accursedness.
Men, *s. m.* (me—en) An active principle.
Men, *s. f.* (*mutation of* man) A space, a place; a where. *adv.* Where, at what place.

> Men yd las Trahaiarn yn Ngharnfynydd.
>
> *Where* was killed Trahaiarn on the mountain of Carn. *Meilyr.*
>
> O chlywi yn iach leuen
> Uchod ei fod yn ei fen.
>
> If in health and spirits thou shouldest hear of his being above in his *place*. *G. ab Ieuan.*
>
> Mae yw maes, men yw man.
>
> An enclosure is a field, a *place* is a spot. *D. Ionas.*

Men, *s. f.—pl. t.* i (my—en) A wain, a cart.

> Cyd gwichio y fen hi a ddwg ei llwyth.
>
> Though the cart creaks it carries its load. *Adage.*

Menai, *s. f.* (men) An open box; a tumbrel.

> Celwrn a menai, ceiniawg a dal pob un: Menai, ceiniawg a dal, heb ardderchafael, sef achaws yw, wrth nad oes glawr iddi.
>
> A tub and a box, a penny is the value of each; a box is worth a penny without advancement, and that is by reason that it has no cover. *Welsh Laws.*

Menaid, *s. f.—pl.* meneidiau (menaid) Cart-load.
Mendy, *s. m.—pl. t.* au (men—ty) A cart house.
Mened, *s. f.* (men) That is intellectual.
Menedig, *a.* (men) Being made intelligent.
Menediw, *a.* (mened) Of an intellectual nature; happy, or blessed.

> Caraf Gaerwys fun, fenediw deithi.
>
> I love the nymph of Caerwys, of *blessed* accomplishments. *Gwalchmai.*

Menest, *s. f.* (men—est) The act of serving.
Menestr, *s. m.—pl. t.* i (menest) One who serves or waits upon; a servitor; a cupbearer.

> Gorwyn blaen eirstr; bid fenestr pob drud;
> Gair teulu yn ygwn;
> Gnawd gan angbywir air twn.
>
> Glittering the top of the lily; let the *servitor* be bold; the word of a tribe prevails; familiar to the faithless a broken word. *Llywarch Hen.*
>
> Dywallaw di, fenestr, na fyn angeu,
> Corn can anrhydedd yn nghynteddau.
>
> Replenish thou, *cupbearer*, seek not thy death, the horn with honour in the banquets. *O. Cyfeiliawg.*

Menestrawl, *a.* (menestr) Serving, waiting.

Menestriad, *s. m.* (menestr) A serving, attending, or waiting upon.

Menestru, *v. a.* (menestr) To serve, or to wait.

Am byrth Ysgewin yn goresgyne;
Am borth Wygyr yn Mon yn menestru.

Around the gates of Ysgewin conquering; around the gate of Gwygyr in Mon *performing attendance*. *Gw. Brycheiniog.*

Meni, *s. m.* (men) A carting, a carrying in a cart.

Meniad, *s. m.* (men) A carrying in a cart.

Mensaer, *s. m.* (men—saer) A cart-wright.

Mentyn, *s. m. dim.* (mant) A thin small lip.

Mènu, *v. a.* (man) To make an impression, to imprint, to work upon, to effect.

Gwired ys dir yd fên.

Truth is certain *to have effect*. *Adage.*

Rhodd Duw yw awen—yn iawnau barn, ac ystyriaeth; ac yn mènu, ac yn tueddu ar y galon, yn gyfiawn ddibech feddwl.

The gift of God is genius, correcting the judgment and the imagination; and *working upon* and inclining the heart to a just and a pure thought. *Barddas.*

Menw, *s. m.* (men) The seat of intellect, or soul.

Menwad, *s. m.* (menw) Intellection; a rendering happy or blessed; a becoming happy.

Menwawl, *a.* (menw) Intelligential, intellectual, tending to happiness or bliss.

Menwedig, *a.* (menw) Being rendered intellectual, blessed.

Un o dri menwedigion teyrnedd ynys Prydain, Bran Fendigaid ab Llyr Llediaith, a ddygwys gyntaf ffydd yn Nghrist i genedl y Cymmry o Rufain, lle y bu efe saith mlynedd yn ngwystl ei fab Caradawg.

One of the three sovereigns of the isle of Britain *who conferred blessings*, Bran the blessed son of Llyr of barbarous speech, who first brought the faith in Christ to the nation of the Cymmry, from Rome, where he had been seven years an hostage for his son Caradog. *Trioedd.*

Menwi, *v. a.* (menw) To render intellectual.

Menwin, *a.* (menw) Intelligential, intellectual, of a happy or blessed nature.

Menwr, *s. m.—pl.* menwyr (men—gwr) A carter.

Menwyd, *s. m.—pl. t.* au (menw) Source of intelligence, intellect, happiness, blessedness.

Dafydd fab Owain, bwyf un-fryd a thi;
Yth dewr-fawr anwylyd
Cas cerdd cerddorion fenwyd;
O'n trydar trydydd hael byd.

David the son of Owain, may I be of the same mind with thee; to thy highly aspiring mind odious is a restraint on the *intellect* of minstrels; in our song thou art the third generous one of the world. *Gw. Bryfel.*

——Dafydd
Fab Madawg fynawg fenwyd diorchudd,
Fab Meredudd fedd falch ei ddedfryd.

David the son of Madog, of benign *intellect* unobscured, the son of Meredudd, of superb benefit his restoration. *Bleddyn Fardd.*

Ethyw dy ergryd
Yn eithafoedd byd,
Arthur gadernyd,
Menwyd Medrawd.

Thy dread is gone to the ends of the world, with the might of Arthur, the *talent* of Medrod. *Gwalchmai, i F. ab Meredudd.*

Liary Einiawn lluchddawn, llochwyd feirddion fab Cynon, clod fenwyd.

Gentle Einion of splendid gift, thou wouldest cherish bards, thou son of Cynon, famed for *intellect*. *Cynddelw.*

Diwahardd i fardd ei fenwyd.

Unrestricted to the bard his *talent*. *Cynddelw.*

Menwydaidd, *a.* (menwyd) Of intellectual tendency; tending to happiness.

Menwydaw, *v. a.* (menwyd) To render intellectual; to cause happiness, or bliss; to gladden.

Menwydawg, *a.* (menwyd) Abounding with intellect; full of happiness, or bliss.

Menwydawl, *a.* (menwyd) Intelligential; tending to happiness, joy, or bliss; gladdening.

Menwydedd, *s. m.* (menwyd) A state of happiness.

Menwydiad, *s. m.* (menwyd) A causing happiness, the enjoying of happiness.

Menwydig, *a.* (menwyd) Enjoying happiness.

Tri menwydigion Duw, gwar, heddgar, a thrugar.

The three *blessed ones* of God, the meek, the peaceful, and the humane. *Barddas.*

Menwydus, *a.* (menwyd) Intelligential, intellectual; of a happy or blessed nature.

Menwydusaw, *v. a.* (menwydus) To render intelligential, or intellectual; to become intelligential; to render happy; to become happy.

Menwyn, *s. m.* (menw) Gift of the mind; talent.

Gwrad fan gawr, gwrddfar, fawr fenwyn,
Ef gorau, fal gwr, yn addwyn.

Of ardent loud shout, ardently wrathful, of great *talent*, he executes, like a man, bravely. *Cynddelw, i'r argl. Rhys.*

Ban yd ran ei rad i rodolion byd,
Balch ei fenwyn, balch ei fion.

When he distributes his bounty to the sojourners of the world, proud his *talent*, proud his attendants. *Gwalchmai, i Rodri.*

Menyd, *adv.* (man—yd) To the place where.

Menyg, *s. pl.* (maneg) Gloves. *Menyg ellyllon*, or *menyg y llwynog*, and *menyg mair*, purple fox-glove; *menyg y gog*, bladder campion.

Menygawg, *a.* (menyg) Having gloves, gloved.

Menygwr, *s. m.* (menyg—gwr) A glover.

Mènyn, *s. m. dim.* (màn) A mark, or spot.

Menyniad, *s. m.* (mènyn) An imprinting.

Menynu, *v. a.* (mènyn) To imprint; to dot.

Mèr, *s. m.—pl. t.* au (my—er) That is dropped off or parted; a particle; that is received.

Mer, *s. m.—pl. t.* ion (me—er) The marrow.

Merai, *s. f.—pl.* mereion (mer) A gutter, a drain.

Meraidd, *a.* (mer) Like marrow; marrowy.

Merasgwrn, *s. m.* (mer—asgwrn) A marrowbone.

Merawg, *a.* (mer) Abounding with marrow.

Merawl, *a.* (mèr) Falling, dropping, or distilling.

Merawr, *s. m.* (mer) That drops, or falls down.

Merch, *s. f.—pl. t.* ed (my—erch) A woman, a young woman; a daughter.

Ymwan am orchest, er mwyn merched;
Nid aeth o'i flaen saeth, er ei sythed;
Mewn oror arall, na maen ar wared;
Na helynt y gwynt nid cas gynted.

Striving in a feat, for the sake of *women*; before him no arrow flew, however strait; nor, in another quarter, the stone down the steep; nor the course of the wind not so swift. *Gw. Tew.*

Merchaidd, *a.* (merch) Feminine, womanlike.

Merchan, *s. f. dim.* (merch) A little woman.

Merched, *s. pl.* (merch) Women, daughters.

Merchedaidd, *a.* (merched) Somewhat effeminate.

Merchedd, *s. m.* (merch) Feminality, womanhood.

Mercheta, *v. a.* (merched) To go after girls.

Merchetwr, *s. m.* (merched—gwr) A wencher.

Merchin, *a.* (march) Rising, or towering.

Merching, *a.* (merchin) Rising, or towering.

Merchyn, *s. m. dim.* (march) A little horse; a nag.

Merchyr, *s. m.* (march) Mercury. *Dydd Merchyr*, *Dyw Merchyr*, Wednesday.

Merddrain, *s. pl. aggr.* (mèr—drain) Dog-briars.

Merddwfr, *s. m.—pl.* merddyfroedd (mer—dwfr) Stagnant water.

Mered, *s. m.* (mer) A particle, or a drop.

Meredig, *a.* (mered) Being dropped; stupified.

Pian y gaer rhaco! Meredig, a wyr, ywch! Dros y byd y gwyr, pan yw Caer Yspyddaden Bencawr yw.

Whose the castle yonder? *Stupid* are ye, O men! Over the world is it known, for that it is the castle of Yspyddaden Bencawr. *H. Culhwch—Mabinogion.*

Meredigaeth, *s. m.* (meredig) A flattening, a deadening; a making dull, or stupid.

Mereiddiad, *s. m.* (mèraidd) A becoming marrow.

Mereiddiaw, *v. n.* (mèraidd) To become marrow.

Merf, *a.* (mèr) Insipid, flat, tasteless.

Merfaidd, *a.* (merf) Somewhat flat, or insipid.

Merfdra, *s. m.* (merf) Insipidity, flatness.

Merfedig, *a.* (merf) Being made flat or insipid.
Merfedd, *s. m.* (merf) Insipidness, flatness.
Merfiad, *s. m.* (merf) A making flat or insipid.
Merfu, *v. n.* (merf) To become insipid or flat.
Merhelyg, *s. m.* (mer—helyg) Yellow willow.
Meriad, *s. m.* (mèr) A rendering flat, a stilling; a becoming flat, or dull; a dropping, a distilling.
Merin, *s. m.—pl. t.* iau (mèr) That drops, trickles, or effuses.

Llafar meriniau gwyniau gwreigedd.

Loud the *effusions* of the passions of women. *Phylip Brydydd.*

Merinaw, *v. n.* (merin) To drop, to fall in drops.
Merinawl, *a.* (merin) Falling in drops, dropping.
Meriniad, *s. m.* (merin) A falling in drops.
Merion, *s. pl. aggr.* (mer) Drops; drippings.
Merl, *s. m.—pl. t.* od (mer) A little horse, a pony.
Merlen, *s. f. dim.* (merl) A mare of stunted growth
Merlyn, *s. m. dim.—pl. t.* od (merl) A horse of the small mountain breed, a pony.
Merlynaidd, *a.* (merlyn) Like a mountain horse.
Merlys, *s. m.—pl. t.* iau (mèr- llys) Asparagus.
Merllyd, *a.* (mer) Insipid, dull, flat, tasteless.
Merllydrwydd, *s. m.* (merllyd) Flatness, insipidity
Merllyn, *s. m.—pl. t.* au (mèr—llyn) A pool.
Merolaeth, *s. m.* (merawl) Flatness, insipidity; moisture, humidity; mustiness.
Meroli, *v. n.* (merawl) To be falling, or dropping; to become flat, soft, or humid.
Meroren, *s. f. dim.* (merawr) That trails; a tail.
Merth, *s. m.—pl. t.* au (my—erth) An exhausted state; a necessitous state.

Ni bydd rwydd yd na bo merth.

There will be no prosperity but there will be *adversity*. *Adage.*

Merthadwy, *a.* (merth) Capable of being exhausted, or racked with pain.
Merthawl, *a.* (merth) Exhausting, racking.
Merthedd, *s. m.* (merth) An exhausted state.
Merthi, *s. m.* (merth) A state of exhaustion.
Merthiad, *s. m.* (merth) An exhausting; a racking
Merthin, *a.* (merth) Tending to wear out.
Merthrwydd, *s. m.* (merth) An exhausted state.
Merthu, *v. a.* (merth) To exhaust, to wear out.
Merthus, *a.* (merth) Tending to exhaust; racking.
Merthyr, *s. m.—pl. t.* on (marth) That is made plain or laid open; a plain or clear spot; a martyr. *Dyn wedi dyoddef merthyr creulawn*, a person who has suffered a cruel wound.
Merthyraeth, *s. m.* (merthyr) A martyrology.
Merthyrai, *s. c.* (merthyr) One who martyrs.
Merthyrawd, *s. m.* (merthyr) A martyrizing.
Merthyrawl, *a.* (merthyr) Relating to martyrdom.
Merthyrdawd, *s. m.* (merthyr) Martyrdom.
Merthyredig, *a.* (merthyr) Being martyred.
Merthyriad, *s. m.* (merthyr) A martyring.
Merthyrolaeth, *s. m.* (merthyrawl) Martyrdom.
Merthyru, *v. a.* (merthyr) To martyr. *Darfu y ci ei ferthyru yn erchyll*, the dog did tear him terribly. *Mon.*
Merthyrwr, *s. m.—pl.* merthyrwyr (merthyr—gwr) One who martyrizes.
Meru, *v. n.* (mèr) To drop, or to distil.

Ni chiliai o gammawn yn i ferai waed.

He would not retreat from conflict until blood *should drop*. *Aneurin.*

Merw, *a.* (mer) Tingling, or pricking.
Merwaidd, *a.* (merw) Somewhat tingling.
Merwin, *s. m.* (merw) A tingling, a pricking, occasioned by a cold.
Merwinad, *s. m.* (merwin) A tingling
Merwinaw, *v. a.* (merwin) To tingle, or to prick.

Pentyrrant iddynt eu hunain athrawon, gan fod eu clustiau yn merwinaw.

They shall collect together to themselves teachers, for that their ears shall be *tingling*. 2 Timothy, 4. 3.

Merwinawd, *s. m.* (merwin) A tingling.
Merwinawl, *a.* (merwin) Tending to tingle.
Merwindawd, *s. m.* (merwin) A tingling.
Merwindeb, *s. m.* (merwin) A tingle, a pricking.
Merwinedig, *a.* (merwinad) Being tingled.
Merwinedd, *s. m.* (merwin) A tingling state.
Merwydd, *s. pl.* (mer—gwydd) Mulberry trees.
Merwydden, *s. f.* (merwydd) A mulberry tree.
Merwys, *s. m.—pl. t.* od (mer—gwys) The ousel, or the blackbird.

Lliw merwys yn lloi mawrion.

Of the colour of the *blackbird* being large calves. *T. Aled, i ychain dwn.*

Mor fad a'r merwys ydwyd.

So goodly as the *ousel* art thou. *T. Aled.*

Nid un ymryson don merwysod.

Not one will contend with the note of the *blackbird*. *D. Nanmor.*

Meryd, *v. a.* (mèr) To drop, or to distil.
Merydd, *s. m.* (mèr) That is flat, or low; that is flaccid, drooping, or sluggish; a wet place; a plash; a slug; a sluggard; a larder; also the sea matweed; otherwise called *morhesg*, and *merydd y mor*.

Tro wedd ein buchedd o bechawd merydd.

Turn the course of our life from *slothful* sin. *D. Ddu, Ast Hiraethog.*

Gnawd merydd yn mro.

A *plash* is usual in the plain. *Adage.*

Mis Tachwedd tachau merydd.

In the month of November the *sluggard* grunts. *Aneurin.*

Merydd, *a.* (mèr) Being flat, or low; being flaccid, or sluggish; humid, moist. *Pechawd merydd*, a slothful sin; *cwd merydd*, a rupture. *dwfr merydd*, stagnant water. *Rhufain ferydd*, sluggard Rome.

Cad yn Iwerddon, dirion drefydd,
Can a'i canfu ni fu feryd.

A battle in Ireland, of pleasant towns, each as beheld it could not be *sluggish*. *Meilyr.*

Breferad yr wybr ferydd
A wnaeth fal dori dydd.

The braying of the *humid* sky made as to break up the day. *D. ab Gwilym.*

Nid un gost ei fwrdd; nid un gist ferydd——a'r cybydd.

Not of the same cost his table; not of the same *musty* chest as the miser. *T. Aled.*

Meryddawl, *a.* (merydd) Of a humid nature.
Meryn, *s. m. dim.* (mer) A drop, or a particle.
Meryswydden, *s. f.* (mer—gwŷdd) The medlar tree.
Meryw, *s. pl. aggr.* (mer—yw) Juniper wood; also called *eithinfyw*.

Mal marwor, neu ragor yw
Ym, o eirias o'r meryw.

Like the embers, or more it is to me, of the fire of the juniper. *W. Middleton, Ps. 120.*

Geiriau, fal llymion saethau cawr,
Yngllyd a marwawr meryw.

Words like the sharp arrows of a giant warrior, joined to the embers of *juniper*. *Edm. Prys, Ps. 120.*

Merywen, *s. f.* (meryw) Common juniper.

Efe yn gorwedd, ac yn cysgu dan y ferywen, wele angel a gyffyrddai ag ef.

He lying down, and sleeping under a *juniper tree*, behold an angel stood before him. 1 Kings, 19. 5.

Mes, *s. pl. aggr.* (my—es) A portion, a meal, mast, or acorns. It is a common tradition that this fruit, as well as fern roots, was a substitute for bread, amongst the Britons.

Mesa, *v. a.* (mes) To gather acorns or mast.
Mesawg, *a.* (mes) Abounding with acorns.
Mesawl, *a.* (mes) Of the nature of acorns.
Mesbren, *s. m.—pl. t.* au (mes—pren) An acorn tree, or the acorn bearing oak.

> Mynw traglew, llew llawr mwynfawr,
> Maangan wedi mein-gain feirch mesbren.

A person brave to excess, the courteous lion of the plain, in the white sepulchre after the fine sleek steeds of the *acorn tree*. *Cynddelw, m. I. ab Cedifor.*

Mesen, *s. f. dim.* (mes) An acorn, one acorn.
Mesenig, *s. f. dim.* (mesen) A small acorn.
Mesfraint, *s. m.—pl.* mesfreintiau (mes—braint) The privilege of acorns, or pannage.
Mesglyn, *s. m. dim.* (masgl) a shell, or a hull.

> Rhaid tori y mesglyn cyn cael y cnewyllyn.

It is necessary to crack the *shell* to get the kernel. *Adage.*

Mesig, *a.* (mes) That may be chewed, or eaten.
Mesigaw, *v. a.* (mesig) To masticate; to eat.

> Afallen beren biborig
> Melyn ei harron, nid maon a'i mesig.

Sweet apple-tree full of shoots, yellow its fruit, which the multitude *shall not chew*. *Merddin.*

Mesobr, *s. m.* (mes—gobr) A pannage due.

Sef yw mesobr, o caiff gwr foch yn ei goed, o'r pummed dydd cyn gwyl Fihangel hyd y pummed dydd wedi calan gauaf, lladded y degfed o honynt.

A *pannage* means this, if a man finds swine in his wood, from the fifth day before the feast of Saint Michael until the fifth after the calend of winter, let him kill the tenth of them. *Welsh Laws.*

Mesaig, *s. m.* (mês—saig) A meal of acorns.

> Gwell mesaig o'm cell fy hun, no melsaig o gell arall.

Sweeter an *acorn meal* from my own parlour, than an honey repast from the parlour of another. *Adage.*

Mest, *s. m.* (mes) A portion of food or a meal.
Mestyg, *s. m.* (mest) What is chewed.

> Mygr ddragon gwron gwyrensg,
> Meddw meddlyn meiau eu mestyg,
> Meirian angau, angheinmyg ei farw!
> Ei ferwaad ni ddiffyg.

The splendid leader of vigorous heroes, whose *masticatory* was the sweet intoxicating mead-plant, ministers of death, unhallowed was it that he should die! his death cry shall not be wanting. *Cynddelw, m. O. Gwynedd.*

Mesur, *s. m.—pl. t.* au (mes—ur) A measure; a rule; a metre; a tune. *Mesur hawl*, the setting forth a cause, in law; *o fesur cam a cham*, step by step: *Mal y mae yr adar man yn tôri mesurau!* how the little birds are pouring out strains!

Nid oes un mesur yn gofyn cynnilach amryfeiliant ar yr acenion, ac yr erddygan, no'r banau ar y gyhydedd lefn.

There is no *measure* that demands a more accurate diversity of the accents, and the pauses, than the verses on the smooth metricity. *Barddas.*

Mesur, *v. a.* (mes—ur) To allot a share; to mete.
Mesuradwy, *a.* (mesur) Measurable, mensurable.
Mesuraw, *v. a.* (mesur) To allot a measure.
Mesurawl, *a.* (mesur) Relating to measure.
Mesuredig, *a.* (mesur) Being measured.
Mesuredigaeth, *s. m.* (mesuredig) Measurement.
Mesureg, *s. f.* (mesur) The science of mensuration; geometry.
Mesuregawl, *a.* (mesureg) Geometrical.
Mesuren, *s. f.* (mesur) A canon of measure.

> Serion awdur mesuren,
> Bardd Brytys——

Serion the author of *prosody*, the bard of Brutus. *D. Benwyn.*

Mesuriad, *s. m.* (mesur) Measuring; marjorum.
Mesuriaeth, *s. m.* (mesur) Mensuration.
Mesuriant, *s. m.* (mesur) Admeasurement.
Mesurwr, *s. m.* (mesur—gwr) A measurer.
Mesurydd, *s. m.—pl. t.* ion (mesur) A measurer.
Mesuryddawl, *a.* (mesurydd) Mensural.
Mesuryddiaeth, *s. m.* (mesurydd) Mensuration.

Mesyr, *s. m.* (mes) That is a portion or meal.
Mesyryd, *s. m.* (mesyr) Pannage food; the last quarter, or autumn.

> Ystryw per i fyw, porfeydd ynghyd,
> Yd, brawn mesyryd, mes irwydd;
> A'r pysg irion o'r afonydd.

A fair scheme to live, pastures together, corn, the fruit of autumn, the *mast* of luxuriant woods, and the fresh fishes out of the rivers. *T. Aled.*

Mettel, *s. m.—pl. t.* oedd (med—tel) Metal.

> Glew eidell gloew osodau
> Rhyfel wyt, y mettel mau.

The brave wheel of the bright assaults of war art thou, my trusty *metal*. *D. ab Gwilym, i'w gleddyf.*

Mettelaidd, *a.* (mettel) Like metal, metallic.
Mettelawg, *a.* (mettel) Abounding with metal.
Metteleiddiad, *s. m.* (mettelaidd) A turning like metal, a becoming as metal.
Metteleiddiaw, *v. a.* (mettelaidd) To turn to metal
Metteliad, *s. m.* (mettel) A turning to metal.
Mettelu, *v. a.* (mettel) To turn to metal.
Mettelus, *a.* (mettel) Of the nature of metal.
Mettelwr, *s. m.—pl.* mettelwyr (mettel—gwr) A metallurgist, a worker of metals.
Mettelwriaeth, *s. m.* (mettelwr) Metallurgy.
Mettelydd, *s. m.—pl. t.* ion (mettel) Metallurgist.
Mettelyddiaeth, *s. m.* (mettelydd) Metallurgy.
Mettelyn, *s. m. dim.* (mettel) A piece of metal.
Meth, *s. m.—pl. t.* ion (my—eth) A fail; a miss.

> Pam y gwnaeth a'th faeth fethion buwch ddiffaith;
> Pa waith ddiwydiaith addaw eidion?

Why made he that reared thee the *abortions* of a barren cow; what a turn of the truth of language to promise a beast? *M. Dwygraig.*

Methadwy, *a.* (meth) Fallible; perishable.
Methawl, *a.* (meth) Failing, abortive, missing.
Methdaith, *s. f.—pl.* methdeithiau (meth—taith) A fruitless journey.

> Gnawd mynych awn i fethdaith.

There will be a frequent let us go to a *fruitless journey*. *Adage.*

Methdal, *s. m. pl. t.*—ion (meth—tal) Nonpayment
Methdaliad, *s. m.* (methdal) A nonpayment.
Methdaniaw, *v. n.* (taniaw) To miss fire.
Methdriniad, *s. m.* (triniad) A mismanagement.
Methedig, *a.* (meth) Being fallible; infirm; decayed, decrepid, invalid, unsuccessful. *Methedigion*, invalids.
Methedigaeth, *s. m.* (methedig) A state of failing.

> A hwynt a'i air tynu a wnaeth
> O'u methedigaeth allan.

And them by his word he drew out of their *error*. *Edm. Prys, Ps. 107.*

Methenw, *s. m.—pl. t.* au (meth—enw) A misnomer
Methenwi, *v. a.* (methenw) To misname.
Methfasnach, *s m —pl. t.* oedd (meth—masgnach) A bankruptcy.
Methfrawd, *s. f.—pl.* methfrodau (meth—brawd) A fallacious judgment or sentence.
Methgais, *s. m.* (meth—cais) A failing attempt.
Methgoel, *s. f.* (meth—coel) A misbelief.
Methgyflawniad, *s. m.* (cyflawniad) A nonperformance; a nonfulfilment.
Methiad, *s. m.* (meth) A failing, a missing.
Methiannawl, *a.* (methiant) Tending to fail.
Methiannu, *v. n.* (methiant) To become failing.
Methiannus, *a.* (methiant) Of fallible nature.
Methiannusaw, *v. n.* (methiannus) To become fallible; to prove abortive; to become perishable
Methiannusrwydd, *s. m.* (methiannus) A state of failing; abortiveness; perishableness.
Methiant, *s. m.* (meth) A failure, a defect; decay

> Ig ar blentyn cryfhant, ar henddyn methiant.

A hiccup on a child is a strengthening, on an old man *debility*. *Adage.*

Methiantus, *a.* (methiant) Of a fallible nature.
Methineb, *s. m.* (meth) A failure, a missing.
Methl, *s. m.—pl.* methlion (methl) A foil, or defeat; an embarrassment, or perplexity.

> Eurdorchawg ddeifniawg o Ddyfnaint ragor
> Rhag ygor angurant,
> Ni bu frithl, ni bu fethiant,
> Ni bu fagawd meirch Morgant.

> Who wore the golden wreath more seemly than
> Did he of Devon, at the hostile camp,
> With steeds not pampered as for vain parade
> Was Morgant, never foiled, nor apt to *fail*.
> *Cynddelw, i deulu O. Gwynedd.*

Methledd, *s. m.* (methl) Embarrassment.
Methliad, *s. m.* (methl) An embarrassing, a deceiving; an entangling.
Methlig, *a.* (methl) Tending to embarrass.
Methlu, *v. a.* (methl) To embarrass, to entangle.

> Or gwrthwynepa neb farn yr ynguad llys, rhoddent eu dau wystl yn llaw y brenin; ac or methlir yr ynguad llys, diffrwydig fydd ei air; a thaled werth ei dafawd i'r brenin.

> If any one shall controvert the sentence of the judge of the palace, let the two give a pledge in the hand of the king; and if the judge of the palace *shall be foiled*, his word shall be of no force; and let him pay the price of his tongue to the king.
> *Welsh Laws.*

Methlus, *a.* (methl) Embarrassing, entangling.
Methlwr, *s. m.—pl.* methlwyr (methl—gwr) An embarrasser; one who ensnares.
Methoed, *s. m.* (meth—oed) Decline of life.
Methoedran, *s. m.* (methoed) Decline of age.
Methu, *v. n.* (meth) To fail; to miss; to become abortive; to miscarry; to decay. *Methu beichiogi*, to miscarry of a child.
Methwr, *s. m.—pl.* methwyr (meth—gwr) A failer, a misser, a miscarrier.
Meuad, *s. m.* (mau) A taking to one's self.
Meudwy, *s. m.—pl. t.* od (mau—twy) That is self-governed, or self-corrected: a hermit.
Meudwyad, *s. m.* (meudwy) A recluse life.
Meudwyaeth, *s. m.* (meudwy) A life of a hermit.

> Gwrthawd coron frwythlon fraeth,
> A dewis y feudwyaeth.

> Refusing a crown prosperous and elegant, and choosing the *hermit life*.
> *H. Duf, i Gynog.*

Meudwyaidd, *a.* (meudwy) Like a hermit.

> Bwyd y macwy meudwyaidd
> Berwr hallt, bara o'r haidd;
> Ei ddiawd, gonaid ddewin,
> Y dwr gwyn.——

> The food of the *self correcting* youth the rock samphire, bread of the barley; his drink, fair divine, the crystal water.
> *L. G. Cothi, i I. Fedyddiwr.*

Meudwyaw, *v. n.* (meudwy) To live as a hermit.
Meudwyawl, *a.* (meudwy) Hermitical.
Meudwyes, *s. f.—pl. t.* au (meudwy) A hermitess.
Meudwyfan, *s. f.* (meudwy—man) A hermitage.
Meudwyfod, *s. f.* (meudwy—bôd) A hermitage.
Meuedig, *a.* (meuad) Being taken to one's self; being possessed; possessed; rich.

> Rhag Prydain wledig——
> Llyngesoedd meuedig.

> Before the sovereign of Britain were fleets *enriched*. *Taliesin.*

Meuedd, *s. m.* (mau) Possession, or inheritance.

> Nid meuedd ond somyn Duw.

> There is no *wealth* like the blessing of God. *Adage.*

> Bardd bardd ehelaeth, bardd ai meith faeth medd,
> A meuedd marchogaeth.

> A bard handsome and comprehensive, a bard greatly nourished by mead, and the *talent* of chivalry.
> *Cynddelw, m. Bleddyn Fardd.*

> Llwyddid gwir, a thir, yn ei threfad,
> Llwyddid gwledd, a medd, a meuedd mad.

> May air and earth give prosperity in its habitation, prosperous be the feast, and the mead, and the goodly *possession*.
> *Llywelyn Fardd, i Dowyn.*

> E'm anrhegai ——
> A'i aur rhudd, a'i fudd, a'i feuedd.

> He would present me with his ruddy gold, and his benefit, and his *possession*.
> *Ll. P. Moch.*

> Can digones Duw an difan ferses,
> Yn eirian, yn eirian,
> Ow'r a'n gwnaeth a'i gwnel am danaw
> Trugaredd, cyn meuedd mablan.

> Since God has accomplished our fleeting short life in beauty, in splendor, may he that made us cause it to be for us in mercy, before the *inheritance* of the tomb.
> *Cynddelw.*

Meufedd, *s. m.* (mau—medd) Self-possession.
Mew, *s. m.* (my—ew) A mew, a cat's cry.
Mewiad, *s. m.* (mew) A mewing, a crying as a cat
Mewian, *v. a.* (mew) To mew, to cry as a cat.
Mewn, *prep.* (me—wn) Within, in; *adv.* Within, in. *Dos mewn pryd*, go in time. *Pwy sy mewn?* who is within? *Aed i mewn*, let him go in.

> Dy ffydd a'th gadwodd; ac am hyny ymado mewn hedduch, a mwynhaa gyflawn lonyddwch.

> Thy faith hath preserved thee; and therefore depart in peace, and enjoy perfect tranquillity. *Marchawg Crwydrad.*

Mewnawl, *a.* (mewn) Inward, internal.
Mewnoldeb, *s. m.* (mewnawl) Internalness.
Mewyd, *s. m.* (me—gwyd) Idleness, laziness.

> Ni weryd mewyd milwriaeth:
> Gwr a'n gwyl ni a gwriedigaeth,
> Gweled fi, gwelitor ymaeth.

> *Idleness* will not excuse warfare: He that beholds us with providence, may he behold, then I shall be beholden. *Cynddelw.*

Mewyda, *v. a.* (mewyd) To idle, or to lounge.
Mewydaidd, *a.* (mewyd) Somewhat idle, or lazy.
Mewydaw, *v. a.* (mewyd) To act idly: to be idle.
Mewydawl, *a.* (mewyd) Of an idle tendency.
Mewydedd, *s. m.* (mewyd) Idleness, laziness.
Mewydrwydd, *s. m.* (mewyd) Idleness, laziness.
Mewydus, *a.* (mewyd) Of an idle disposition.
Mewydusaw, *v.* (mewydus) To become lazy.
MI, *s. m. r.* That is in or identic. *pron.* Me. It is also used adverbially, as the agent in the first person of verbs. *Mi wn*, for *gwn*, I know.

> Gware mi trech.

> The game of *I* conquer. *Adage.*

> Gwell mi giliais nach efe a laddwyd.

> Better is *I* fled than he has been slain. *Adage.*

> Ennill mi hw a chollI mi ha.

> To gain the honour of saying *I* flinched, and lose *I* triumphed. *Adage.*

> Mi, ym drehif, wyf diamwyson
> O'r prif feirdd, ym prif gyfeillion.

> *I*, in my principle, am without strife with the chief bards, my chief of friends.
> *Ll. P. Moch.*

Miar, *s. f.—pl.* mieri (my—iar) A bramble.
Miaren, *s. f.* (miar) A briar; a bramble; *miaren y Berwyn*, or *miaren Dwywen*, mountain bramble.

> Cynt y cwymp dar no miaren o flaen y gwynt.

> Sooner will the oak fall than the *bramble* before the wind.
> *Adage.*

Mic, *s. f.—pl. t.* ion (mig) A hoot; spite, or pique. *Dra fic*, out of spite; *o fic i un*, out of spite to one: *Gware mic ymguddiawg*, the play of hide and seek.

> Cael oedd raid——
> Cyffes, er mic i uffern.

> I was necessary to have confession, in *spite* to hell.
> *Ll. ab H. ab I. ab Gr. ab Owain*

Micas, *s. m.* (mic) Bread steeped in any liquid.
Miciad, *s. m.* (mic) A hooting; a spiting.
Miciaw, *v. a.* (mic) To hoot; to spite; to be piqued
Micws, *s. m. dim.* (mic) That shoots out; spray. *Micws diawd*, the froth of liquor.
Mich, *s. f.* (my—ich) A squeal, or a squeak.
Michian, *v. a.* (mich) To squeal, or to squeak.
Mid, *s. m.—pl.* mitiau (my—id) An enclosure, or a hem round; a list, or place of combat; also

a shallow vessel, a muid. *Llonaid mid o gwrw*, a muid-full of ale. *a.* Champaign.

> Yn addef tangnef colliid
> Addef, yd buost lew yn dydd mid.

> In the habitation of peace thou wouldest lose a habitation, though thou hast been brave in the day of the *field*. *Taliesin.*

> Claf wyd——
> Call araf walch, colli'r fid.

> Thou art hurt, thou discreet and gentle hawk, for losing the *field*. *D. Ll. Mathew.*

Midedd, *s. m.* (mid) The state of being enclosed, hemmed in, or surrounded.
Midiad, *s. m.* (mid) An enclosing, or hemming in.
Midin, *a.* (mid) Belonging to the field or list.
Midlan, *s. f.—pl. t.* au (mid—llan) An enclosed plain, or area; a list for tournaments.

> Gnawd redawg rhag marchawg midlan.

> Meet is the car before the knight of the *field*. *Cynddelw.*

Midd, *s. m.—pl. t.* au (my—idd) An enclosed place
Middi, *s. m.* (midd) A pit or pool in a river, where fish resort to. *Llinyn middi, llinyn enweirio, llinyn pysgota*, a fishing-line.
Mierawg, *a.* (miar) Abounding with brambles.
Mieri, *s. pl. aggr.* (miar) Brambles, briers.

> Cas myharen mieri.

> The rams dislike the *briers*. *Adage.*

Mierïawg, *a.* (mieri) Abounding with briers.
Mierïeinllwyn, *s. m.—pl. t.* i (mierïen—llwyn) A bramble bush.
Mierïen, *s. f.* (mieri) A bramble, a brier.
Mierin, *a.* (miar) Of the bramble; brier.
Mierinllwyn, *s. m.—pl. t.* i (mierin—llwyn) A bramble bush.
Mig, *s. f.—pl. t.* ion (my—ig) A hoot; spite; pique; animosity. *Mig ymguddiaw*, the play of hide and seek, the seeker being hoodwinked, and the other crying out *mig*, or hoop.

> Idd ydwyf yn guddiedig
> I'w chare, mal chwareu mig.

> I am privately courting her, like *playing at bo-peep*. *G. ab I. ab Ll. Fychan.*

Mig, *a.* (my—ig) Hooting, hooping. *Dylluan fig*, a hooting owl.
Migedd, *s. m.* (mig) A hooting; spitefulness.
Migen, *s. f.—pl. t.* au (mig) That oozes; a boggy place; also a bad ulcer, with holes or cavities.
Migiad, *s. m.* (mig) A hooting; a spiting.
Migiain, *v. a.* (mig) To make a hooting.

> Gwychr gwynt gwydd migiain.

> Impetuous the wind *rustling* the woods. *Llywarch Hen.*

Migiaw, *v. a.* (mig) To hoot; to spite.

> Mae'n y bryd gyd ogyfarch,
> Dy furnaw, a migiaw'r march.

> It is intended when a meeting takes place, to waylay thee, and *to hoot* the horse. *I. Du. Def. ab Owain.*

Migiawl, *a.* (mig) Hooting; spiteful.
Migiwr, *s. m.—pl.* migwyr (mig—gwr) A hooter.
Mign, *s. c.—pl.* mignoedd (mig) A bog, a quag.

> Lle ni bydd mign e fydd maen.

> Where there shall not be a *quag* there will be a stone. *Llywarch Hen.*

Mignad, *s. m.* (mign) A turning to a bog.
Mignaw, *v. n.* (mign) To become a bog.
Mignawg, *a.* (mign) Abounding with bogs.
Mignawl, *a.* (mign) Boggy, or quaggy.
Mignedd, *s. m.* (mign) Bogginess, quagginess.
Mignen, *s. f. dim.* (mign) A bog, a quag.
Migniad, *s. m.* (mign) A becoming boggy.
Mignwern, *s. f.—pl. t.* ydd (mign—gwern) A boggy meadow.
Migus, *a.* (mig) Hooting; full of spite, despiteful, malicious.

Migusaw, *v. a.* (migus) To act spitefully; to become spiteful, or malicious.
Migusedd, *s. m.* (migus) Spitefulness; malice.
Migusrwydd, *s. m.* (migus) Spitefulness.
Migwern, *s. f.* (mig—gwern) A boggy meadow.
Migwrn, *s. m.—pl.* migyrnau (mig—gwrn) A joint, or knuckle; the ankle joint, the ankle.

> Gwell migwrn o wr no mynydd o wraig.

> Better a *sprig* of a man than a mountain of a woman. *Adage.*

Migwyn, *s. m.* (mig—gwyn) White bog-moss.
Migymguddiaw, *v. a.* (mig—ymguddiaw) To play at hide and seek.
Migyrnawg, *a.* (migwrn) Having knuckles; large-knuckled; having large ankle joints.
Migyrniad, *s. m.* (migwrn) The growing out of a knuckle, or ankle.
Migyrnu, *v. n.* (migwrn) To grow out as a knuckle, or ankle.
Mil, *s. m.—pl. t.* od (mi—il) A living agent; an animal, a beast.

> Goreu un mil march.

> The best of any one *animal* a horse. *Adage.*

> Goreu un anifail buwch; goreu un ysgrubl dafad.

> The best of any *animal* is a cow; the best of any beast is a sheep. *Adage.*

> Gwae y mil ni wyl ei berchen.

> Miserable the *animal* that perceives not its owner. *Adage.*

> Yr eawg——
> Glanaf un mil a luniwyd.

> The salmon, the cleanest *animal* that was formed. *D. ab Gwilym.*

> Mil ebrwydd yw mal wybrwynt.

> A *beast* quick as the wind of heaven. *I. Tew Hen, i farch.*

Mil, *s. f.—pl. t.* oedd (my—il) A thousand. *Degcan-mil o filoedd*, ten hundred thousand of thousands.
Milaid, *a.* (mil) Of an animal nature.

> Cenedlaeth filaid y sydd gynt a rithwys mo mi: mi af yn gyfarwydd rhagoch yno.

> There is an *animal* species which has appeared before me: I will go as a guide before you there. *H. Culhwch—Mabinogion.*

Milaidd, *a.* (mil) Like an animal, brutish.
Milain, *s. m.* (mil) That is of the nature of an animal; a brute, a villain.

> Gnawd mab taer yn filain.

> The son of the hard-dealer is generally *brutish*. *Adage.*

> Os gwrthodi, liw'r ewyn,
> Was a'i felyn gwdynau,
> Cai it' filain aradrgarth,
> A fo gwaeth ei gynneddfau.

> The hue of the foam, shouldest thou refuse a youth with his yellow locks, thou shalt have a *villain* bound to the plough, who may be of worse qualities. *Gu. Tew.*

Milain, *a.* (mil) Full of the nature of an animal or beast; brutish; cruel; froward, sullen, stubborn.

> Gwynt o'r dwyrain, gelyn milain.

> Wind from the East is an *inveterate* foe. *Adage.*

> Ni bu fwy lladron——
> No gwreigedd Llundain garabuteiniach,
> No gwyr un foneg garafileiniach
> No gwyr Caer.

> Never were there greater thieves; nor the women of London more whorish; nor men of the same kidney *more stubbornly brutish* than the men of Chester. *L. G. Cothi.*

Milan, *s. m.* (mil) A brutish or stubborn one.
Milast, *s. f.—pl.* mileist (mil—gast) A greyhound bitch.
Milawg, *a.* (mil) Having the nature of a beast.
Milawr, *s. m.* (mil) That is relating to; one who is military, a warrior.
Milcanmil, *s. m.—pl.* milorion (milcant—mil) A hundred millions.
Milcanfed, *s. m.* (milcant) A hundred thousandth part. *a.* Hundred thousandth part.
Milcant, *s. m.* (mil—cant) One hundred thousand

Milcerdd, *s. m.* (mil-cerdd) A millepede.

Mildraethawd, *s. m.* (mil—traethawd) Zoology.

Mildraethodydd, *s. m.—pl. t.* ion (mildraethawd) A zoologist, or one who describes animals.

Mildraethodyn, *s. m.* (mildraethawd) A treatise on zoology.

Milddail, *s. f.* (mil—dail) Common, or milford yarrow; also called *llysiau y gwaedlin*, *milfyd*, *milfydd*, and *minfel*.

Miled, *s. m.* (mil) An animal of the chace.

> Nid wyf enhyed, miled ni chadwaf,
> Ni allaf ddarymred;
> Tra fo da gan gog caned!
>
> I am no hunter, I keep no *animal of the chace*, I cannot move about, as long as it seemeth good to the cuckoo let her sing.
> *Llywarch Hen.*

Miledawr, *s. m.—pl.* miledorion (miled) One who chases an animal; one who is military.

Miledd, *s. m.* (mil) Brutishness; animal nature.

Mileiddiaw, *v. n.* (milaidd) To become brutalized.

Mileindref, *s. f.—pl. t.* i (milain—tref) A township, under villain soccage tenure.

Mileingar, *a.* (milain) Of a ferocious nature.

Mileingarwch, *s. m.* (mileingar) Ferociousness.

Mileiniad, *s. m.* (milain) A brutalizing.

Mileiniaw, *v. n.* (milain) To become brutish, or cruel; to be obstinate; to persist firmly.

Mileinig, *a.* (milain) Brutish; ferocious.

Milfed, *s. f.* (mil) A thousandth. *a.* Thousandth.

Milfedawl, *a.* (milfed) Millesimal.

Milfedran, *s. f.* (milfed—rhan) Thousandth part.

Milfil, *s. f.* (mil *repeated*) A thousand thousands, or a million.

Milflwydd, *a.* (mil—blwydd) Millennial.

Milflwyddawl, *a.* (milflwydd) Millennial.

Milflwyddiant, *s. m.* (milflwydd) Millennium.

Milfyd, *s. f.* (mil—byd) The figwort.

Milfyw, *s. f.* (mil—byw) Pilewort; also called *y fronwys*, *melyn y gwaenwyn*, *gwenith y ddaiar*, *llygad Ebrill*, *llygad y ddyniawed*.

Milgi, *s. m.—pl.* milgwn (mil—ci) A greyhound.

> Cenau milgi a morwyn ni cheiff eu mwyn a'u maco.
>
> A *greyhound* cub and a maid shall not be enjoyed by those who rear them. *Adage.*
>
> Gwnlach nad milgwn ydynt,
> Ond gweilch, neu genadau gwynt.
>
> Probably they are not *greyhounds*, but hawks, or messengers of the wind. *Guto y Glyn.*

Milgïaidd, *a.* (milgi) Like a greyhound.

> Ardal dwfn boenal Dinmilwy—
> Milgïaidd ei gwyr yn mhob tramwy.
>
> The deep tranquil region of Dinmilwy, *like the greyhound* its men in every course. *Ll. P. Moch.*

Milhanes, *s. m.*—(mil—hanes) Zoology.

Milhanesydd, *s. m.—pl. t.* ion (milhanes) Zoologist

Miliast, *s. f.—pl.* milieist (mil—gast) A greyhound bitch.

> Ni cheiff miliast groen er ei ennill, oni bydd hi yn dorawg o filgi a ennilloedd groen
>
> A *greyhound bitch* shall not obtain a skin though she should win it, unless she is with pups from a greyhound, which has won a skin. *Cyfraith Hely.*

Milplyg, *s. m.* (mil—plyg) A thousand-fold.

Milred, *s. f.—pl. t.* ion (mil—rhed) A millepede.

Milrith, *s. m.—pl. t.* ion (mil—rhith) A fœtus.

Milrym, *s. m.* (mil—grym) The woodsage.

Miltir, *s. f.—pl. t.* oedd (mil—tir) A mile.

Miltroed, *s. m.—pl. t.* ion (mil—troed) Millepede.

Miltroediawg, *a.* (miltroed) Of a thousand feet.

Milus, *a.* (mil) Of an animal nature, brutal.

Milwaith, *s. m.* (mil—gwaith) A thousand times.

Milwr, *s. m.—pl.* milwyr (mil—gwr) A warrior.

> Goreu heation milwyr drygu aw y goreu.
>
> [illegible] of *warriors* are, who can cause the greatest evil. *Adage.*

Milŵraidd, *a.* (milwr) Warrior-like; warlike.

Milŵri, *s. m.* (milwr) A warrior's life; warfare.

Milŵriad, *s. m.—pl.* milŵriaid (milwr) One who commands a thousand men; a colonel.

Milŵriadaeth, *s. m.* (milŵriad) A coloneiship.

Milŵriaeth, *s. m.* (milwr) Warfare, or war.

> Cymerai cynghor ygyd a'i wyrda, pa wedd yd ymladdynt ag eu gelynion; a pha amcawdd i luddynt i gaffael y tir; ac yna y daethoedd Beli, penteulu Caswallawn, a thywysawg ei lluoedd, a thrwy gynghor y gwr hwnw y gwnaed pob peth yn y deyrnas.
>
> He took counsel with his select men, in what manner they should fight with their enemies; and by what means they should hinder their having a landing; and thereupon came Beli, the head of the family of Caswallon, and the leader of his army, and through the advice of that person every thing was conducted in the kingdom. *Gr. ab Arthur.*

Milŵriaethawl, *a.* (milŵriaeth) Relating to a military life; relating to warfare.

Milŵriaethiad, *s. m.* (milŵriaeth) The acting a military character.

Milwriaethu, *v. a.* (milwriaeth) To act a military character.

Milwriaethus, *a.* (milŵriaeth) Respecting a military character.

Milŵriaw, *v. a.* (milwr) To carry on warfare.

Milŵrus, *a.* (milwr) Warrior-like; militant.

Milwydd, *s. m.* (mil—gwŷdd) Camomile.

Milyn, *s. m. dim.* (mil) A little animal.

Mill, *s. f.—pl. t.* ion (my—ill) The violet.

> Mor beraidd a'r mill.
>
> As fragrant as the violet. *Adage.*

Millfeillion, *s. pl.* (mill—meillion) White trefoil.

Milltir, *s. f.—pl. t.* odd (miltir) A mile. *Milltir Ffreinig*, a French mile.

> Mesurau Dyfnwal wrth hyd gronyn haidd: tri hyd y gronyn haidd yn y fodfedd; tair modfedd yn lled y llaw; tri lled y llaw yn y droedfedd; tair troedfedd yn y cam, tri cham yn y naid; tair naid yn y tir; a mil o dir, nen o rynnau a wna filltir.
>
> Dyfnwal measured by the length of a barley corn: the three lengths of a grain of a barley in a thumb breadth; three inches in the breadth of the palm; the three breadths of the palm in a foot; three feet in a pace, three paces in a leap; three leaps in a land; and a thousand lands or ridges make a mile. *Welsh Laws.*

Millyn, *s. m. dim.—pl. t.* ion (mill) A violet.

Min, *s. m.—pl. t.* ion (mi—in) A margin, a brink, or edge; a sharp edge; the lip, or mouth, in poetical language. *Min nos*, the edge of night, the evening twilight; *min y ffordd*, the way side; *yn min*, hard by.

> Byw wrth fin y cleddyf.
>
> Living by the edge of the sword. *Adage.*

Minawd, *s. m.* (min) A making an edge.

Mincoca, *v. a.* (mincog) To pop with the lips.

Mincocaeth, *s. m.* (mincog) A popping of the lips.

Mincog, *s. m.* (min—cog) A pop with the lips.

Mindag, *s. f.* (min—tâg) The lampas.

Minddu, *s. m.* (min—du) A black edge. *a.* Black-edged; black-lipped. *Minddu manddel*, children's play, wherein one turns his face away from another, who lifts up one or two fingers, and the first guesses at the number.

Mined, *s. m.* (min) An edging, or an edge.

Minedd, *s. m.* (min) Edginess, the edge part.

Minfel, *s. m.* (min—mêl) The honey of the lip; the yarrow.

Minfelys, *a.* (minfel) Sweet-mouthed; dainty.

Minfin, *a.* (min *repeated*) Edge to edge; lip to lip; kissing.

> Oedd beilch gweilch gweled ei werin.
> Oedd clywed cleddyfau fanfin.
>
> Heroes were elate at seeing his host; swords *edge to edge* were heard. *D. Benfras, i Lywelyn II.*

Minflys, *s. m.* (min—blys) Daintiness of mouth.

Minflysig, *a.* (minflys) Dainty-mouthed.

Minflysigrwydd, *s. m.* (minflysig) Epicureanism.

Minfwlch, *s. m.* (min—bwlch) A hare lip.

Minfylchawg, *a.* (minfwlch) Having a hare lip.

Minffug, *a.* (min—ffug) Of a deceitful lip.

> A'u genau ahwythau gwenieithiant, minffug
> ——y dywedant.
>
> And their lips also flattered, *with a deceitful lip* they speak. *W. Middleton.*

Mingam, *a.* (min—cam) Wry-mouthed.

> Lle'r ydoedd yn mhob gobant
> Ellyllon mingeimion gant.
>
> Where in every little hollow were a hundred *wry-mouthed* sprites. *D. ab Gwilym.*

Mingamiad, *s. m.* (mingam) A making a wry mouth, a making a grimace.

Mingamu, *v. n.* (mingam) To make a wry mouth, to make grimaces; to mock.

Mingamwr, *s. m.—pl.* mingamwyr (mingam—gwr) One who makes grimaces.

Mingeimiad, *s. m.—pl.* mingeimiaid (mingam) One who makes grimaces.

Mingrach, *a.* (min—crach) Scabby-mouthed.

Mingras, *a.* (min—cras) Having parched lips; saucy-mouthed.

Mingrased, *s. m.* (mingras) The parchedness of the lips; pertness.

Mingrechi, *s. m.* (mingrach) Scabbiness of lips.

Mingrwn, *s. m.—pl.* mingrynion (min—crwn) A mullet, a fish so called. *a.* Having a round mouth.

Mingrych, *a.* (min—crych) A puckering the lips.

Mingrychu, *v. a.* (mingrych) To pouch the lips.

Mingryniad, *s. m.—pl.* mingryniaid (mingrwn) A mullet; also called *mingrych*, and *hyrddyn*.

Mingrynu, *v. a.* (mingrwn) To draw or pouch the mouth together.

> Gwelwn dyrfa o ferenod yn ymwisgo; rhai yn mingrynu; rhai a heiyrn yn tynu eu haeliau; rhai yn ymiro; rhai yn clytio eu hwynebau.
>
> I could see a party of coquettes primming themselves up; some *screwing up the mouth*; some with irons pulling their eyebrows; some anointing themselves; some patching their faces. *Ellis Wyn, B. Cwsg.*

Miniad, *s. m.* (min) An edging; a sharpening.

Minial, *v. a.* (min) To move the lips, to osculate.

Minialedd, *s. m.* (minial) The motion of the lips; osculation.

Minialu, *v. a.* (minial) To move the lips.

Miniawg, *v. a.* (min) To make an edge, or margin; to sharpen; to make an impression; to utter from the lips.

> Rhy eglur ydyw nad oedd fymryn o ddaioni yn minio arnynt.
>
> It is too evident that there is not a particle of good *having effect* on them. *Ier. Owain.*

Miniawg, *a.* (min) Having an edge, or margin; sharp-edged, sharp. *Cleddyf dau-finiawg*, a two-edged sword.

Miniedig, *a.* (miniad) Being made into an edge.

Minllym, *a.* (min—llym) Sharp-edged; keen.

Minnau, *comp. pron.* (mi—tau) Me also, I also; and me, and I; me then, I then.

> Dywedasant wrtho;—Berth ydd wyt heusawr. Ni bo berthach byth y bych chwi no minnau!
>
> They said to him . herdsman, thou art rich. Never may you be richer than *I then!* *H. Culhwch—Mabinogion.*

Mintag, *s. f.* (min—tag) The lampas.

Minws, *s. m. dim.* (min) The lip or mouth, in fond language.

> ——Per einau tlws:
> Pond mwyn peunod ei minws.
>
> The sweet pretty mouth; how kind the discourse from her *lip* *D. ab Edmwnt.*

Miod, *s. pl. aggr.* (mi) Fritters, little cakes. *Bara miod*, manchet bread.

Mir, *s. m.* (my—ir) That is fair or bright; the aspect, look, or visage.

Mir, *a.* (my—ir) Of a fair aspect; comely; fair. *Mir arglwyddes*, a handsome lady.

Mirach, *s. m.* (mir) A good quality, a virtue.

Miraidd, *a.* (mir) Somewhat comely or fair.

Mirain, *a.* (mir) Of a fair aspect; comely; fair.

> Llas arth yn y gyfarthfa;
> Llas nerth gwyr, eryr aerfa;
> Llas Hywel wyn fab Owain;
> Llas gwr mirain uch morfa!
>
> A bear was slain in the toil; the strength of men, the eagle of slaughter was cut off: slain was fair Hywel the son of Owain. a *handsome* man has been slain above the strand. *Peryf ab Cedifor.*

Miraint, *s. m.* (mir) Pleasantness of aspect.

Mire, *s. m.* (mir) The aspect, the visage.

Mireinber, *a.* (mirain—per) Pleasantly sweet.

Mireinbryd, *s. m.* (mirain—pryd) A beauteous aspect, or of a fair countenance.

Mireindawd, *s. m.* (mirain) Handsomeness.

Mireindeb, *s. m.* (mirain) Comeliness, beauty.

Mireinder, *s. m.* (mirain) Comeliness, beauty.

Mireindra, *s. m.* (mirain) Comeliness, beauty.

Mireinedd, *s. m.* (mirain) Comeliness, beauty.

Mireiniad, *s. m.* (mirain) A rendering comely or handsome; a growing handsome.

Mireiniaidd, *a.* (mirain) Rather handsome.

Mireiniannawl, *a.* (mireiniant) Tending to make comely or beautiful.

Mireiniannu, *v. a.* (mireiniant) To make comely or beautiful; to become comely.

Mireiniannus, *a.* (mireiniant) Of a comely or beautiful nature.

Mireiniant, *s. m.* (mirain) A making comely or beautiful; a becoming comely.

Mireinrwydd, *s. m.* (mirain) Comeliness, beauty.

Mireinwch, *s. m.* (mirain) Comeliness, beauty.

> Drwg yw yn dryced an buchedd,
> Am galed amgeledd am aur,
> A mireinwch byd a'i earbydedd.
>
> It is miserable to us how evil our condition, in hard toiling for gold, and the *glory* of the world and its honour. *G. ab Gwrgenau.*

Miriad, *s. m.* (mir) A rendering comely.

Miriannawl, *a.* (miriant) Relating to the aspect.

Miriannu, *v. a.* (miriant) To render comely, or of a fine aspect; to become comely.

Miriannus, *a.* (miriant) Of a comely aspect.

Miriannusaw, *v. a.* (miriannus) To render of a comely aspect; to become handsome.

Miriant, *s. m.* (mir) Beauty of countenance.

Mis, *s. m.—pl. t.* oedd (my—is) The catamenia; also the length of that period; a month.

Misawl, *a.* (mis) Monthly, menstrual.

Misawr, *s. m.* (mis) That is of the month.

Misglwyf, *s. m.* (mis—clwyf) The menses.

Misglwyfedd, *s. m.* (misglwyf) Menstruousness.

Misglwyfus, *a.* (misglwyf) Menstruous.

Misgwaith, *s. m.* (mis—gwaith) A month's space.

Misi, *a.* (mis) Nice, delicate, dainty.

Misyriad, *s. m.—pl.* misyriaid (misawr) That is of the age of one month.

> O fab misyriad.
>
> Of a child *that is of a month old.* *Numbers* 18 61.

Mit, *s. m.—pl. t.* iau (mid) A shallow vessel, or cooler, to hold liquor in.

Miw, *s. m.* (mi) The shedding of feathers, or mewing of birds.

> Penyd dros ennyd y sydd;
> Am ei benyd miw beunydd.
>
> Penance there is for a while; for his penance daily it a *mew*. *Ieu. Deulwyn ,i hebog.*

Miwail, *a.* (miw) Smooth, sleek, or glossy.

> Ceiliog mwyalch clog miwail.
>
> The cock ousel with the *glossy* cloak. *D. ab Gwilym.*

MO, *s. m. r.* That is forward or advanced; present; that tends to enlarge; that is more.

Mo, *pron.* (mo, *s.*) It; him, or he, idiomatically applied to persons. *Dyna fo*, there it is; *fo honid fy marw*, it was asserted that I had died.

> Dyn ieuanc oedd raid yno;
> Gwae hi nad fyfi fu fo!
>
> A young man were necessary to be there: woe to her, that I am not *him!* — *D. ab Gwilym.*

Mo, *prep.* (mo, *s.*) Of concerning, more of; from. It is used to give emphasis to negatives; as *Ni chei mo ym, mo yth, mo ei;* or *ni chei mo'm, mo'th, mo'i*, thou shalt not have that of mine, or my, thy, his, her, or it; *mo yn, mo ych, mo eu;* or *mo'n, mo'ch, mo'u*, that of ours, or our, your, their:--*Ni chei mo hwn*, thou shalt not have this.

Moc, *s. m.* (my—oc) A mock, or mimic.

Mociad, *s. m.* (moc) A mocking, or mimicking.

Mociaw, *v. a.* (moc) To mock, to imitate.

Mociwr, *s. m.—pl.* mocwyr (moc—gwr) Mocker.

Moch, *s. pl. aggr.* (mo—och) Swine, or pigs.

> Y nawfed dydd calan gauaf y mae iawn i'r pencynydd fyned i hely moch coed; ac o hyny hyd galan mis Tachwedd y dyly efe fod yn eu hely hwy.
>
> The ninth day of winter it is right for the chief huntsman to go to hunt the wood *swine;* and from thence to the first of December he shall continue hunting them. — *Welsh Laws.*

Mòch, *a.* (my—och) Ready, quick, apt; early.

> Mòch dysg nawf mab hwyad.
>
> The young of the duck soon learns to swim. — *Adage.*
>
> Ni mòch ddial mefl merydd.
>
> A sluggard will not soon revenge a disgrace. — *Adage.*

Mocha, *v. a.* (moch) To litter pigs. *Hwch focha*, a sow with pigs.

Mochaidd, *a.* (moch) Like swine, hog-like.

Mochawr, *s. m.* (moch) That is like a swine.

Mochddwyre, *s. m.* (moch—dwyre) A quick rise or elevation; an early rise.

Mochddwyrëain, *v. a.* (mochddwyre) To rise up quickly; to be rising early.

Mochddwyrëawg, *a.* (mochddwyre) Quickly-rising

> Mochddwyrëawg haon haf dyffestin
> Maws llafar adar, mygr hwar hin.
>
> Thou *early-rising* summer sun, hasten the melodious song of birds, the happy season of joy. — *Gwalchmai.*
>
> Am Fochnin yn fochddwyrëawg.
>
> Around Mochnin *early-rising.*

Mocheidd-dra, *s. m.* (mochaidd) Swinishness.

Mocheiddiad, *s. m.* (mochaidd) A becoming swinish

Mocheiddiaw, *v. a.* (mochaidd) To act swinishly, to become swinish.

Mocheiddrwydd, *s. m.* (mochaidd) Swinishness.

Mochi, *v. a.* (moch) To wallow as swine, to commit sodomy.

Mochiad, *s. m.* (moch) To wallow like swine.

Mochian, *v. a.* (moch) To be as a pig, to grunt.

Mochlys, *s. m.* (moch—llys) Common nightshade.

Mochnant, *s. m.—pl.* mochnentydd (mòch—nant) A swift brook, or torrent.

Mochriw, *s. f.—pl. t.* au (mòch—rhiw) A steep shelving ascent.

Mochwraidd, *s. m. dim.* (moch--gwraidd) Sowbread

Mochysgall, *s. m.* (moch—ysgall) Common sow-thistle.

Mochyn, *s. m. dim.* (moch) A pig. *O, y mochyn brwnt!* Oh, thou dirty pig! *Mochyn bychan*, the badger; otherwise called *broch*, and *pryf llwyd.*

> Pen llyffan, cynffon mochyn, a chi wedi ei grogi, a wnant gystal pab ag a welwyd erioed yn uffern.
>
> A frog's head, a pig's tail, and a dog that has been hung, will make as good a pope as was ever seen in hell. — *Adage.*

Mochynaidd, *a.* (mochyn) Like a pig, or piggish.

Mochyneidd-dra, *s. m.* (mochynaidd) Pigritude.

Mochyneiddrwydd, *s.* (mochynaidd) Hoggishness.

Mochyria, *v. a.* (mochawr) To grunt like a boar after the sow; also to brim, or to go to boar.

> Nid iawn dala baedd an amser yn mochyria.
>
> It is not proper to catch the boars at any time in *going after the swine.* — *Welsh Laws.*

Mochyriad, *s. m.* (mochawr) A grunting.

Mochyriaw, *v. a.* (mochawr) To grunt like a boar; to procreate as the swine.

Mod, *s. m.—pl. t.* au (my—od) A circle, a turn; a motion; an enclosure.

> A'r myllt a gyrchais i'r mod,
> A thri ychain.——
>
> And the wethers I gathered into the *fold*, besides three oxen. — *Ilyr Lowarch Hen.*

Modbren, *s. m.—pl. t.* au (mod—pren) A stirrer, a stick used in stirring any thing boiled.

Modfedd, *s. f.—pl. t.* i (bodfedd) The space of the thumb; an inch.

> Cystal modfedd a milltir o ddianc.
>
> An inch is as good as a mile of escape. — *Adage.*

Modfeddig, *s. f. dim.* (modfedd) A single inch.

Modfeddu, *v. a.* (modfedd) To measure inches.

Modrwy, *s. f.—pl. t.* au (mod—rhwy) A ring. *Modrwy eiddig*, the jealous one's ring, an epithet in droll language; *bys y fodrwy*, the ring finger.

Modrwyad, *s. m.* (modrwy) A forming into a ring; a circling; a putting on a ring.

Modrwyaidd, *a.* (modrwy) Like a ring; curly.

Mordwyaw, *v. a.* (modrwy) To form into a ring; to form ringlets, or to curl.

Modrwyawg, *a.* (modrwy) Having rings; in ringlets; circling.

> O lewfer llyw cammawn, lawn dyrysawg,
> Bu lafn aur gylchwy yn fodrwyawg.
>
> From the splendour of the leader of conflict, the equitable guider, there was the gold-encompassed sword *circling.* — *Elidyr, m. G. ab Cynan.*

Modrwyawl, *a.* (modrwy) Annulary; curly.

Modrwyedig, *a.* (modrwyad) In ringlets, curled.

Modrwyen, *s. f. dim.* (modrwy) A little ring.

Modrwyfil, *s. m.—pl. t.* od (modrwy—mil) A lizard, an eft; also called *modrwyen*, *genau goeg.*

Modrwyig, *s. f. dim.* (modrwy) An annulet.

Modrwyogrwydd, *s. m.* (modrwyawg) Curliness.

Modrwywr, *s. m.—pl.* modrwywyr (modrwy—gwr) A dealer in rings.

Modrwyydd, *s. m.* (modrwy) A dealer in rings.

Modryb, *s. f.—pl.* modrybedd (mod—rhyb) An aunt; also an epithet for a matron, equivalent to dame and mistress in English. The diminutives of it, in fond language, are *Boda*, *Boda*, and *Bodo*. *Ewythr a Modryb*, terms of respect, used in some parts, equivalent to Master and Mistress.

> Ail-fam modryb dda.
>
> A good *aunt* is a second mother. — *Adage.*

Modrydaf, *s. m.—pl. t.* au (mod—rhydaf) A centre to range round; a rallying point; a standard; a stock of bees.

> Mis Awst molwynawg morfa,
> Llon gwenyn, llawn modrydaf.
>
> The month of August white with foam is the sea shore, lively the bees, full the *stock hive.* — *Aneurin.*
>
> Cymhwyllaf fy naf,
> Cymmry fodrydaf,
> Cymmro cellydaf,
> Ry wnaeth Celi.
>
> I will make mention of my chief, the *rallying point* of the Welsh, the best informed Welshman whom the Mysterious One has made. — *Ll. P. Moch, i Lywelyn II.*
>
> Milwr, milwyr fodrydaf,
> Madawg law ddenawg, llary naf.
>
> A warrior, the *rallying point* of warriors, the ready-handed Madog, the mild chief. — *L. P. Moch.*

Pa geisit fi, fodrydaf creugar!

Why soughtest thou me, thou blood-stained rallying-point! *Ph. Brydydd.*

Mal medru modrydaf ar hald.

Like shooting at the *hive* in swarming. *Ll. P. Mech.*

Modur, *s. m.* (mod—ur) That encompasses; a defence; a protecter; a sovereign.

Mur moder, llywiadur rhag llaw,
Mae ym meddwl dy geisiaw.

The rampart of *defence*, the ruler in time to come, it is in my mind to seek thee. *D. Benfras.*

Neud gwan Wynedd fan fen vd ergyd cur;
Neud gwael am fodur eglur ogiyd.

Is not lofty Gwynedd palsied, where affliction assails; is it not brought low by the loss of a protector, of manifest security. *G. Ddu o Arfon, m. Syr G. Llwyd.*

Egin Madog, ein modur,
Ni chilieadd dim a chledd dur

The offspring of Madog, our *protector*, no power has put to flight with the blade of steel. *Guto y Glyn.*

Modd, *s. m.—pl. t.* ion (my—odd) A mode, mean, or way to do a thing; a manner, form, or fashion. *Pa fodd y gwnei hyny?* how wilt thou do that? *Nid oes genyt ddim modd i'w wneyd*, thou hast no means at all to do it; *mae ganddo ddigon o foddion*, he has a sufficiency of riches.

Tri modd a ddysg beirdd Ynys Prydain: addysg llafar, can, a defawd, wrth fraint gorsedd.

The three *means* of instruction of the bards of the isle of Britain: oral instruction, song, and custom, according to the privilege of a convention. *Barddas.*

Moddaidd, *a.* (modd) Modish, formal, mannerly.
Moddawl, *a.* (modd) After a mode, means, or manner; agreeable to form; formal.
Moddedig, *a.* (modd) Being reduced to form.
Moddedigaeth, *s. m.* (moddedig) Conformation.
Moddgar, *a.* (modd) Agreeable to form.
Moddgarwch, *s. m.* (moddgar) Mannerliness.
Moddiannawl, *a.* (moddiant) Conducive.
Moddiannu, *v. a.* (moddiant) To render as a means
Moddiannus, *a.* (moddiant) Conducive.
Moddiannusaw, *v. a.* (moddiannus) To render as a means, to become conducive.
Moddiant, *s. m.—pl.* moddiannau (modd) A mean
Moddiaw, *v. a.* (modd) To bring to a form, manner, or mean; to conduce.
Moddus, *a.* (modd) After a form, or manner; formal; mannerly; decent.
Moddusrwydd, *s. m.* (moddus) Mannerliness.
Moedd, *s. m.—pl. t.* ion (my—oedd) Height.
Moeddawg, *a.* (moedd) Highly raised. *s. f.* An eminence. A hill in Caereinion is so called.
Moeddyn, *s. m.* (moedd) A high projection. A hill in Ceredigion is so called.
Moel, *s. f.—pl. t.* ydd (my—oel) A heap, or pile, a conical hill, a towering hill with its top smooth, or void of rocks and woods. *Mesur moel*, a measure that is heaped; *mesur heb foel*, a measure without a heap, or a strike:—*Moel Elian, Moel y Mwnd, Moel y Famau, Moel Hedog, Moel Siabod, Moel Wynion, Moel y Golomen, Moel Llwydiarth, y Foel Goch, y Foel Las,* mountains so called in Wales.

Ni choelir y moel oni weilr ei emenydd.

The *bald* will not be believed unless his brains be perceived. *Adage.*

Moel, *a.* (my—oel) Towering, or piled up; bare, bald; bald-headed. *Gwr moel*, a bald man; *eidion moel*, a beast without horns.

Pe bai cyrn ar ben pob ffol, fe geit arian yn dda am ddangaws gwr moel.

If there were horns on the head of every fool, thou wouldest get a good sum of money for shewing a *bald head*. *Adage.*

Moelaidd, *a.* (moel) Tending to rise up, or to appear bald; somewhat bald.
Moelcen, *s. f.—pl. t.* au (moel—cen) A bald pate
Moelder, *s. m.* (moel) Bareness, baldness.
Moeldes, *s. m.* (moel—tês) The clear sunshine.
Moeldesawd, *s. m.* (moeldes) The being in the clear sunshine.
Moeldesota, *v. a.* (moeldesawd) To frisk about, as cattle do, owing to hot weather.
Moeldra, *s. m.* (moel) Bareness, baldness.
Moelddwrn, *s. m.—pl.* moelddyrnau (moel—dwrn) A naked fist, a closed fist.
Moelddyrnfedd, *s. m.* (moel—dyrnfedd) The measure of the naked fist; a hand breadth.
Moeledd, *s. m.* (moel) Bareness, baldness.
Moelffon, *s. f.—pl.* moelffyn (moel—ffon) Spatula
Moelhwntian, *v. a.* (moel—hwntian) To drive to and fro upon the water, without sails or rudder
Moeli, *v. a.* (moel) To heap, to pile; to make bald, or bare; to grow bald, to be bared. *Moeli clustiau*, to draw the ears close to the head.
Moeliad, *s. m.* (moel) A making bald, or bare.
Moelni, *s. m.* (moel) Bareness, or baldness.
Moelron, *s. m.—pl. t.* iaid (moel—rhon) A seal, or sea-calf.
Moelyn, *s. m. dim.* (moel) A bald pate. *Dos i fyny y moelyn*, go up thou bald head.
Moelystawd, *s. f.* (ystawd) A bare elevated space.
Moelystota, *v. a.* (moelystawd) To seek the exposed places, as cattle do in hot weather; to leap, or frisk, as cattle do, owing to the heat.
Moes, *s. f.—pl. t.* au (my—oes) Civility; conduct, behaviour, manner. *Dyn da ei foes*, a man of good conduct; *moesau da*, good morals.

Moes, yna cyfraith.

Manners, then law. *Adage.*

Moes mab yn ol ei macer.

The *behaviour* of a child is as he is educated. *Adage.*

A glywaisti a gant Idloes;
Gwr gwar hygar ei einioes;
Goreu cynneddf cadw moes!

Hast thou heard what Idloes sang; a mild man of amiable life: the best quality is to preserve *morals*? *Engl. y Clywed.*

Moesa, *v. a.* (moes) To give, or to confer; the imperative of which is only used: *Moes glywed*, let me hear; *moeswch i ni fyned*, come let us go

Gwell, "moes law," na "moes fam."

Better, "give hand," than "give mother." *Adage.*

Melys! moes eto.

Sweet! *give* me some more. *Adage.*

Moesaddysg, *s. f.* (moes—addysg) The doctrine of morality; ethics.
Moesaidd, *a.* (moes) Of a moral tendency.
Moesawg, *a.* (moes) Mannerly, complaisant.

Mae ym flaidd a'm car, o'm caffael wrthaw
I'w wrtheb archafael;
Nid blaidd coed, coll ei afael,
Namwyn blaidd maes moesawg hael.

To me there is a wolf that loves me, from having me by him to take a part in his dignified discourse; not a wolf of the woods, of feeble grasp, but a wolf of the field *courteous* and liberal. *Cynddelw, i. Rhryd.*

Moesawl, *a.* (moes) Ethical, moral; civil.

A fo moesawl a fydd oesawl.

He that is *moral* will be aged. *Adage.*

Moesddysg, *s. m.* (moes—dysg) Doctrine of ethics
Moesi, *v. a.* (moes) To practise morality.
Moesogaeth, *s. m.* (moesawg) Ethology.
Moesolaeth, *s. m.* (moesawl) Morality.
Moesoldeb, *s. m.* (moesawl) Morality.
Moesolder, *s. m.* (moesawl) Morality.
Moesoledd, *s. m.* (moesawl) Mannerliness.
Moesoli, *v. n.* (moesawl) To become moral.
Moesolrwydd, *s. m.* (moesawl) Mannerliness.

Moeswymp, *a.* (moes—gwymp) Of fair deportment. *Moeswymp deulu*, a family of splendid manners.
Moeth, *s. m.—pl. t.* au (my—oeth) That is soft, nice; blandishment; a delicacy, a dainty.
Moethawl, *a.* (moeth) Yielding blandishment.
Moethedig, *a.* (moeth) Being used tenderly.
Moethen, *s. f. dim.* (moeth) A dainty one.
Moethi, *v. a.* (moeth) To treat kindly or nicely.
Moethiad, *s. m.* (moeth) An using blandishment.
Moethineb, *s. m.* (moeth) That yields pleasure.

Tri moethineb cristion: darpar Duw; a ellir gan a fo cyfiawn i bawb; ac a allo cariad at bawb ei harfer.

The three *pleasures* of a christian: the providence of God; what may be done consistent with justice to every body; and what love to all can permit to be used. *Barddas.*

Moethus, *a.* (moeth) Delicate; nice; dainty.

Nid moethus ond bela.

There is nothing so *nice* as the marten. *Adage.*

Moethusach mewn maeth iso,
Wy' ar ei fwrdd, a'i aur fo,
No'r pysg yn mysg heli'r mor;
No Dafydd ar ford Ifor;
No mab mam ar ei fammaeth:
No merch ar ei dynion maeth.

More dainty, down there, in my food I am, at his table, and of his gold, than the fish amidst the brine of the sea; than Dafydd at the board of Ifor; than a mother's child at his nursing breast; than a maid with her cherished suitors. *L. G. Cothi.*

Moethusaidd, *a.* (moethus) Somewhat nice.
Moethusaw, *v. n.* (moethus) To become nice.
Moethusder, *s. m.* (moethus) Blandishment; luxury, delicacy of living.
Moethusdra, *s. m.* (moethus) Blandishment; luxury, delicacy of living.
Moethusrwydd, *s. m.* (moethus) Luxuriousness.
Moethyn, *s. m. dim.—pl. t.* ion (moeth) A luxurious person.
Mohonof, *pronom. prep.* (mo—honof) From me, or from out of me. *Mohonof, mohonot, mohono, mohoni*, from out of me, thee, him and it, from out of her; *mohonom, mohonoch, mohonynt*, from out of us, you, them.
Moi, *v. n.* (mo) To throw out; or to cast; to foal

Mol o'r gaseg ar ebawl mawr teledîw.

The mare *foaling* of a large beautiful colt. *Mabinogi.*

Mol, *s. m.* (mo—ol) What is concreted; the congealed humour, gum, or thick matter collected in the eyes.
Molach, *s. f.* (mawl) Slight or faint praise.
Molachiad, *s. m.* (molach) A praising slightly.
Molachu, *v. a.* (molach) To praise slightly.
Molachus, *a.* (molach) Apt to praise; flattering.
Molad, *s. m.* (mawl) Commendation, praise.
Moladwy, *a.* (mawl) Commendable, praiseworthy
Molafon, *s. m.* (mol—afon) River concretion; an epithet amongst the miners, for porphyry; also called *Mwlafon.*
Molaid, *a.* (mol) Full of concretions; full of particles, or spots; dappled.

Meirch——
Yn mhob lliw ceinwiw can rylygaid dyn;
Yn felyn, yn folaid.

Steeds of every fair excelling colour, which a man can wish, some yellow, and *dappled.* *Ll. P. Moch.*

Molawd, *s. m.* (mawl) Commendation, praise.

Ef o'i barth nend gwarth gwaredwyd;
Gwawd folawd fal y derllyddwyd.

From his territory was not disgrace kept away; the song of praise as it was poured out. *Cynddelw, m. E. ab M. ab Iddon.*

Molawg, *a.* (mol) Abounding with concrete matter; gummy. *Y frech folawg, y frech wen*, the small pox.
Mold, *s. f.—pl. t.* ian (mol) A mould.
Moldiad, *s. m.* (mold) A moulding; a kneading.
Moldiaw, *v. a.* (mold) To mould, to knead. *Moldiaw toes, tylinaw toes*, to knead dough.
Moldiedig, *a.* (moldiad) Moulded; kneaded.
Moldiwr, *s. m.—pl.* moldwyr (mold—gwr) One who moulds; one who works, or kneads.
Moled, *s. f.—pl. t.* au (mo—lled) A piece of cloth, forming a part of a woman's dress, to cover the head and shoulders; a muffler; a kerchief. *Moled Olwen*, great bindweed.
Moledig, *a.* (molad) Praised; commendable.

Balch pob moledig.

The *commended* is proud. *Adage.*

Llawer o'r dydd a dreuliid yn ymladd, canys y gwyr dewraf a moledicaf a ddaugrynynt eu dehewedd pob o'u gilydd.

Much of the day was spent in fighting, for the men who were the most brave and *most famous* were vieing in their dexterity with one another. *Gr. ab Arthur.*

Molediw, *a.* (molad) Laudable, praiseworthy.
Molediwrwydd, *s. m.* (molediw) Laudableness.
Moledd, *s. m.* (mawl) Praise, eulogy; worship.
Moleddiad, *s. m.* (moledd) Commendation.
Moleddu, *v. a.* (moledd) To commend, to praise.
Moleddus, *a.* (moledd) Commendable, laudable.
Moli, *v. a.* (mawl) To praise; to adore.

Neu ni orug Duw, wryd Beuli Gawr,
Ban llef beirdd i'th foli,
Trin eirn, tranc argiwyddi,
Traul meddgyrn, teyrn fal ti!

Shall these not be formed of God; soul of Beuli Gawr, loud the voice of bards to *praise* thee, the foe of conflict, death of kings, the waste of meadhorns; a prince like thee! *G. Ryfel.*

Y ddaear——
Derchafed, moled moliannusaf.

Let the earth exalt, let it praise the *most worthy of adoration.* *D. Ddu, Hiraddug.*

Mi ei mawl â melyn eithin.

I will worship her with the yellow-blossomed furze. *H. ab Owain.*

Moli, *v. n.* (mol) To concrete, to generate gum. *s. m.* Concrete matter; gum. *Moli yn y llygad*, gum in the eye.
Molïad, *s. m.* (mol) A concretion; a yielding gum
Moliannawl, *a.* (moliant) Panegyrical.
Moliannawr, *s. m.—pl.* moliannorion (moliant) A panegyrist; a praiser.
Moliannedig, *a.* (moliant) Made an object of praise
Moliannedigaeth, *s. m.* (moliannedig) The act of praising; commendation.
Moliannu, *v. a.* (moliant) To praise, to adore.
Moliannus, *a.* (moliant) Commendable.

Nid moliannus ond cydundeb.

There is nothing so *laudable* as concord. *Adage.*

Moliannusaw, *v. a.* (moliannus) To render praiseworthy; to become an object of praise.
Moliannusrwydd, *s. m.* (moliannus) The state of being praiseworthy; adorableness.
Moliannwr, *s. m.—pl.* moliannwyr (moliant—gwr) A praiser.
Moliannydd, *s. m.—pl. t.* ion (moliant) A praiser.
Moliant, *s. m.* (mawl) Praise; adoration.

Moliant gwedi marw.

Praise after death. *Adage.*

Moliator, *ger.* (moliad) In praising, in lauding.

Odid traethator,
Mawr moliator.

Seldom making recital, great in *praising.* *Taliesin.*

Molitor, *sup.* (moli) To be praised or lauded.

Ysyni Rydderch, roddiad aur melyn,
Molitor yn mhob gwlad.

To me there is Rhydderch, the bestower of ruddy gold, *to be praised* in every country. *Ein. ab Gwgawn, i Lywelyn II.*

Moloch, *s. m.* (mol—och) Tumult, uproar. *Gwr egniol foloch*, a man of vehement roar; *moloch ddragon*, the tumultuous leader.

Trwst yn Mhrydyn,
Ac amyl ar gychwyn,
Rhag llion Llychlyn
A llynges drom droch,
A Brython ar foloch.

A rumour in Scotland, and sails on the way before the floods of the Baltic, and a fleet, heavy and terrifying, and Britons in a *tumult*. *Taliesin.*

Molochain, *a.* (moloch) Full of uproar, or riot.
Molochi, *v. a.* (moloch) To raise a tumult; to disquiet, to molest; to be tumultuous, or riotous.

Gwawr clod-red, llawged, Lloegr folochi;
Gwar wrth war, hygar, hoew-gerdd hoffi.

The *fame-spread* luminary, of bounteous hand, *disquieting* Lloegr; mild to the mild, amiable, fond of the sprightly song. *G. ab M. ab Dafydd, i Ddwywery.*

Molochiad, *s. m.* (moloch) A causing an outrage, riot, or tumult; a disquieting, a molesting; a becoming outrageous.
Molud, *s. m.* (mawl) Panegyric, or eulogy.

Trengid golud, ni threing molud.

Wealth may perish, *fame* will not perish. *Adage.*

Addfwyn gaer y sydd a'i gwna cyman
Meddud, a molud, ac adar ban.

A pleasant town there is, which is made social, by mead-drinking, and *praise*, and loud birds. *Taliesin, M. Dinbych.*

Ni weles folud am gud.

He saw no *eulogy* for treasure. *Bleddyn Fardd.*

Molwr, *s. m.—pl.* molwyr (mawl—gwr) A praiser
Molwyn, *s. m.* (mol—gwyn) That breaks out; that foams.
Molwynad, *s. m.* (molwyn) A foaming, a spraying
Molwynaw, *v. a.* (molwyn) To foam, to spray.
Molwynawg, *a.* (molwyn) Abounding with foam. It has been used as a cognomen; as *Rhodri, Molwynawg*, and *Meilyr Molwynawg*.

Mis Awst molwynawg morfa.

The month of August *foamy* the *sea shore*. *Aneurin.*

Moll, *s. f.* (my—oll) That surrounds, closes upon, or includes; that extends round.
Moll, *a.* (my—oll) Surrounding, closing upon, or extending round; close, or sultry. *March ffroen-foll*, a horse with a distended nostril, or a snorting horse; *hin foll*, close weather.
Mollaid, *a.* (moll) Tending to close round.
Mollawg, *a.* (moll) Stretching or closing round.
Molledig, *a.* (moll) Being included or closed in.
Molledigaeth, *s. m.* (molledig) The act of including, or taking in.
Molli, *v. a.* (moll) To include, to take in.
Molliad, *s. m.* (moll) A stretching round.
Mollt, *s. m.—pl.* myllt (moll) A mutton; a wether. *Mollt o babwyr*, *corn o babwyr*, a handful of stript rushes, such as are used for candles.
Mollwyn, *s. m.—pl. t.* od (moll) Mutton. *Cig mollwyn*, mutton flesh; *gwer mollwyn*, suet.
Mon, *s. f.* (mo—on) That is a separate body, or individual; an isolated one, or that is separate; a point; a centre. It is an epithet sometimes used for a cow; it is also the name by which the Isle of Anglesea is called in Welsh; and for the sake of distinguishing it from *Mon Aw*, the Mon of the Water, or the Isle of Man, it is sometimes called *Mon Fynydd*, or Mon of the Mountain: And, from that idea the small islet near the Isle of Man, came to be called the Calf of Man.

Mon mam Cymmru.

Mon the mother of Wales. *Adage.*

Cerddorion hyd Fon Fynydd
Dros hwn yn pryderu sydd.

As far as *Mon of the Mountain*, the minstrels are regretting him. *L. G. Cothi.*

Y sawl a biau yr henfon ymaeled yn ei chynffon.

He that owns the *cow of progression* let him take hold of her tail. *Adage.*

Monad, *s. m.* (mon) A rendering a separate body, an isolating; a becoming isolated.
Mones, *s. f.—pl. t.* od (mon) A sulky female.
Moni, *v. a.* (mon) To swell out, to fill; to render sulky, sullen, or displeased; to become sulky, or somewhat displeased. *Mae efe yn moni wrth ei fwyd*, he quarrels with his victuals.
Moniad, *s. m.* (mon) A sulking; a growing sullen
Monig, *a.* (mon) Sulky, sullen, ill-natured.
Monoch, *s. pl. aggr.* (mon) Entrails, guts.
Monochen, *s. f. dim.* (monoch) A small gut, or entrail; a pudding; a sausage.
Monof, *pronom. prep.* (mon—of) Of me. *Monot*, of thee; *mono*, of it or him; *moni*, of her; *monom*, of us; *monoch*, of you; *monynt*, of them
Monw, *a.* (mon) That is identified or joined with
Monwent, *s. f.—pl. t.* oedd (mon—gwent) A sepulchre, or burying place; a church yard.
Monwes, *s. f.—pl. t.* au (monw) The bosom.
Monwesawl, *a.* (monwes) Belonging to the breast
Monwesiad, *s. m.* (monwes) A bosoming.
Monwesu, *v. a.* (monwes) To put to the bosom.
Monwys, *s. pl. aggr.* (mon—gwys) Anglesea people.
Monwysion, *s. pl.* (monwys) Anglesea people.
Monyn, *s. m. dim.* (mon) One who is sulky.

Efe a wnaeth o fammaethod
Llawer un unlliw a'r od;
Minnau sydd fal monyn,
Neu fal brawd moel, heb yr un.

He made mothers of many a one of the same hue as the snow; and I am like a *sulky chap*, or like a bald friar, without obtaining one. *Syr D. Trevor.*

Mop, *s. m.—pl. t.* iau (my—op) A maukin.
Mopa, *s. m.* (mop) A maukin; a mop.
Moppren, *s. m.—pl. t.* i (mop—pren) A baker's maukin; also called *mopa*.
Mor, *s. m.—pl. t.* oedd (mo—or) That is infinite, or boundless; that is in motion, flowing, or fluctuating; the sea. *Y Mor Heli*, the briny sea; *y Mor Tawch*, the hazy sea, the German Sea; *y Mor Marw*, the Dead Sea; *Mor Udd*, the British sea.

Mor ansefydlawg a'r mor.

As full of motion as the *sea*. *Adage.*

Y don——
Caer Gwdion myr, longwyr lid.

The wave, galaxy of the *seas*, the hatred of mariners. *Gr. Gryg.*

Hil Bardam——
O For Tawch, gwnaethant ferw tost.

Offspring of Bardam, from the Hazy *sea*, thou hast raised a severe turmoil. *Dr. S. Cent.*

Mor, *s. m.—pl. t.* au (mo—or) That is incessantly moving, or fluctuating; time; also an ant, or emmet.
Mòr, *adv.* (my—or) How, so, as; how much, so much; how greatly. *Mòr à sonied am dani*, what a deal has been said about her; *mòr lawen*, as merry; *mòr dda*, so good.

Mòr hylithr a dwr hyd anbent.

As gliding as water along a trough. *Adage.*

Mòr oedd gyfrin ffyrdd cyrdd Cyridwen;
Mòr oisiau eu dwyn yn ei dyrwen.

How mysterious were the ways of the songs of Cyridwen; *how great* the necessity of producing them in her smiling mood. *Cynddelw.*

Aur ac ariant
Mòr a'u difant
Eu dibenydd.

Gold and silver *how* those who squander them do perish. *Taliesin.*

Cenadau a'm doddynt, mor ynt anfonawg.

Messengers resort to me, *how much they are sent.* *Taliesin.*

Mora, *s. m.* (môr) The motion of the sea.

Morach, *s. m.* (mor—ach) Emotion, joy, jollity.

A Dewi biau balch-lan Gyfelach,
Lle mae morach a mawr grefydd.

And Dewi owns the proud choir of Cyfelach, where there is *happiness* and great devotion. *Gw. Brycheiniawg.*

Enw'r ferch ddioganair,
A garaf fi yw'r gwyry Fair,
Merch nef, nid mwy morach neb.

The name of the woman void of reproach, whom I love, is Mary the virgin, the daughter of heaven, not greater the *joy* of any one. *H. ab D. ab I. ab Rhys.*

Moradar, *s. pl. aggr.* (môr—adar) Sea fowls.

Neud amser gauaf gweiwaf gwelgi;
Gweilging moradar hwylfar helli;
Neud arfau arian Eryri weithion;
Neud uchel gwen-don gwyndir Enlli!

Is not in winter time the torrent most pale; the perch of the *sea-birds* the brine of raging course! Does not the bright hore veil Eryri now; hark, how loud the white wave of Enlli's blessed land! *Bleddyn Fardd.*

Moran, *s. m.—pl. t.* edd (mor) An epithet for a large sea fish, a whale; also called *morfil,* and *morfarch.*

Morawd, *s. m.* (môr) A going to sea; a going by sea, or a sailing.

I edfyn terwyn torf ei forawd
Nid adfarn cerddau.——

To the severe loss of the host of his *sea voyage* songs shall not bring reproach. *Meilyr.*

Morawel, *s. f.—pl. t.* au (mor—awel) Sea breeze.

Morawg, *a.* (mor) That belongs to the sea; naval. *s. f.* That is of the sea, or a sea conveyance.

Morawl, *a.* (mor) Marine, belonging to the sea. *Morolion,* marine productions.

Morben, *s. m.—pl. t.* au (mor—pen) A promontory, or headland.

Morbryf, *s. m.—pl. t.* ed (mor—pryf) A sea animal.

Blwyddyn llawn i'm rhyddoded
Yn Mangor ar hawl cored;
Edrych di poen a'm gan morbryfed.

For a full year I was placed, at Bangor, on the post of a wear: see thou the pain I bare from *sea animals.* *Ysgolan.*

Morbysg, *s. pl. aggr.* (mor—pysg) Sea-fish.

Morbysgod, *s. pl. aggr.* (morbysg) Sea-fishes.

Morbysgodyn, *s. m.* (morbysgod) A sea-fish.

Morchwain, *s. pl. aggr.* (mor—chwain) Small insects, which jump about the sea shore; also called *chwain y mor.*

Morchwydd, *s. m.* (mor—chwydd) Swell of the sea

Mordai, *s. pl. aggr.* (mor—tai) The sea shore, the sea coast; a maritime region.

Nis adrawdd Gododin ar lawr mordai
Rhag pebyll Madawg pan adgorai,
Namyn un o gant yn y delai.

There shall not be told of Gododin on the *sea coast,* the door of the tents of Madog when opened, of but one in a hundred who should enter. *Aneurin.*

Oian, parchellan, oedd raid myned
Rhag cynyddion mordai.——

Listen, little pig, it were necessary to go for fear of the hunters of the *sea coast.* *Myrddin.*

Trengynt, trydedd o Fai, trichanllong
Yn llynges fordai,
A decrant cymaint a'u ciliai cyfarf,
Heb un farf ar Fenai'.

They perished, on the third day of May, three hundred ships, a fleet of the *strand;* and ten hundred times the number the patriotic weapon would cause to recede, leaving not a single beard on Menai. *H. ab Owain.*

Mordaith, *s. f.* (mor—taith) A sea voyage.

Mordir, *s. m.* (mor—tir) Maritime land.

Mordon, *s. f.—pl. t.* au (mor—ton) Sea breaker.

Dewisbethau—lleferydd adar, a lleihau llef mordon.

Choicest of things, the singing of birds, and the lessening of noise of the *sea wave.* *D. Mollenydd.*

Mordrai, *s. m.* (mor—trai) The ebbing of the sea.

Mordwy, *s. m.—pl. t.* on (mor—twy) A sea course, the raging of the sea; a storm at sea; a having to do with the sea.

Gobaith heb gais mordwy heb long.

Hope without exertion is like a *voyage* without a ship. *Adage.*

Oedd Dyfrdwy——
Yn llawn o fordwy a lli.

Dyvrdwy was full of the *tide of the sea* and of flood. *H. ab G. Gethin.*

Mordwyad, *s. m.—pl.* mordwyaid (mordwy) One who goes by sea.

Aches frwyfolio
Mordwyaid morio.

The briskly-moving plain of the water *voyagers.* *Taliesin.*

Mordwyaeth, *s. m.* (mordwy) A seafaring life.

Mordwyaw, *v. a.* (mordwy) To go by sea; to sail.

Mordwyawl, *a.* (mordwy) Seafaring; sailing.

Mordwyedig, *a.* (mordwy) Being gone by sea.

Mordwyn, *s. m.* (mor—twyn) An ant hill.

Mordwys, *s. m.* (mor—twys) The waving ears of corn, as caused by wind.

Mordwywr, *s. m.—pl.* mordwywyr (mordwy—gwr) A mariner.

Mordywydd, *s. m.* (mor—tywydd) The sweet-gale, or Dutch myrtle; also called *gwyrling.*

Mordywys, *s. m. aggr.* (mor—tywys) The hart's tongue, sea-weed.

Mordd, *s. m.* (mor) That is full of motion.

Morddanad, *s. pl.* (mor—danad) Horehound.

Morddanadl, *s. pl. aggr.* (morddanad) Horehound. *Morddanadl gwynion, lleryd y cwn,* and *cyngaw y gath; morddanadl duon,* stinking horehound; *morddanadl cochion,* red-mint.

Morddarlun, *s. m.—pl. t.* iau (mor—darlun) A chart of a sea; hydrography.

Morddarluniad, *s. m.* (morddarlun) Hydrography

Morddraenog, *s. m.* (mor—draenog) Button-fish.

Morddwr, *s. m.* (mor—dwr) A gulf of the sea.

Einion ab Owain ab Hywel Dda——a ddygas
Ysbail fawr o'r gwledydd yn nglan morddwr Llychwr.

Einion son of Owain son of Hywel the Good, took great spoil from the districts on the shores of the *estuary* of Llychwr. *Cronic. Ystrad-fflur.*

Morddwyd, *s. f.—pl. t.* ydd (mordd—gwyd) A thigh.

Morddyluniad, *s. m.* (mor—dyluniad) A describing of seas; hydrography.

Moreb, *s. m.* (mor—eb) The ebb tide of the sea.

Mur moreb dan wyneb Dyfnant.

The bulwark against the *ebbing sea* below the front of Dyvnant. *Cynddelw.*

Neum be arall-ddydd, ym rhyd rwy
Cer moreb cain wyneb Conwy.

Found I not a different day, when in prosperity by the *ebbing sea* of the fair front of Conwy. *Ll. P. Moch.*

Ym ni chad, yn rhad rhaid atab elwydd
Eiliw gwendon moreb,
Nag er gwerth, nag er nerth neb,
Y gan hon eto'n atab.

For me there was not obtained (freely it is necessary to answer the love assignation of her who is fair as the white wave of the *ebbing sea*) not for price, nor by the power of any one, for me any answer as yet. *G. ab Ll. ab Tudur.*

Morebiad, *s. m.* (moreb) The ebbing of the sea.

Morebu, *v. n.* (moreb) To ebb as the sea.

Moredafeddog, *s. f.* (mor—edaf) Sea cotton-weed

Moreryr, *s. m.—pl. t.* od (mor—eryr) An osprey.

Morfa, *s. m.—pl.* morfeydd (mor—ma) A sea brink; a sea marsh. *Morfa hallt,* a salt marsh

Hir nos, gorddyar morfa;
Gnawd terfysg yn nghymanfa;
Ni chyfyd diriad a da.

Long the night, noisy the *sea coast;* a tumult is common in an assembly; the mischievous agrees not with the good. *Llywarch Hen.*

Morfalwen, *s. f.* (mor—malwen) A sea snail.

Morfalwod, *s. pl. aggr.* (mor—malwod) Sea snails.

Morfan, *s. m.—pl. t.* au (mor—man) A sea shore.

Morfar, *s. m.* (mor—bar) The rage of the sea.

Morfarch, *s. m.* (mor—march) A sea horse.

> Ymarfer a wna morfeirch
> O foli hwn.——
>
> The *sea horses* do accustom themselves in praising him.
> *G. Ll. ab D. ab E. Llygliw.*

Morfil, *s. m.—pl. t.* od (mor—mil) A sea animal; a sea fish of the larger kind; a whale.

> Esyllt,—gwynach oedd ei chnawd nog echdywynedig asgwrn morfil.
>
> Esylit, whiter was her skin than the polished bone of the *sea-horse.* *Gr. ab Arthur.*

Morfin, *s. m.—pl. t.* ion (mor—min) Sea brink.

> Pood emendiged y morfin!
> A'i bellyngodd gwedi gwin,
> Ffynnon fenestr mor teiwin.
>
> Be accursed the *sea brink!* after wine, the attendant of the spring let in the spreading sea. *Gwyddno, i G. Gwaelawd.*

Morflaidd, *s. m.—pl.* morfleiddiau (mor—blaidd) A sea wolf, the base.

Morfoch, *s. pl. aggr.* (mor—moch) Grampuses.

Morfochyn, *s. m.* (morfoch) The grampus.

Morforwyn, *s. f.—pl. t.* ion (mor—morwyn) A mermaid, a siren. *Esgid morforwyn*, a mermaid's shoe, a kind of a pod of a sea plant, of a square form. In British tales, the mermaid is fancied to carry a glass in one hand, and in the other a comb, with which she combs her beantiful hair; and that she weeps during the summer, for fear of the frost of winter.

> Mae rhian ar y mor hallt
> A chrib, a drych, gwych ei gwallt,
> A wyl yr haf ar sel rhos
> Rhag ofn y rhew gaeafnos.
>
> There is a maid on the briny sea with a comb and a glass, splendid is her hair, who weeps away the summer, on the verge of the marsh, in dread of the frost of a winter night.
> *Bedo Aerdrem.*
>
> Mae o'r un wallt am war Non
> Ar fronau 'r morforwynion.
>
> There is of the same hair as round the shoulders of Non on the bosoms of the *mermaids.* *D. Nanmor.*

Morfran, *s. f.—pl.* morfranod (mor—bran) A cormorant; also called *mulfran.*

Morfrwydr, *s. f.—pl.* morfrwydrau (mor——brwydr) A sea-fight.

Morfrwyn, *s. pl. aggr.* (mor—brwyn) Rushes that grow on sea marshes; also called *tostfrwyn*, and *barf-frwyn.*

Morfrwynen, *s. f.* (morfrwyn) The sea rush.

Morfnwch, *s. f.—pl. t.* od (mor—bnwch) Sea cow.

Morfwyd. *s. m.* (mor—bwyd) Marine food, or substance in the sea serving fish for food.

> Morfwyd fydd eu cnawd,
> Hyd pan yw meidrer,
> Pan yw ganawg pysg.
>
> Their flesh shall be *marine food*, until it is transformed, when fishes shall contain it. *Taliesin.*

Morgad, *s. f.—pl. t.* oedd (mor—cad) A sea-fight.

Morgamlas, *s. f.—pl. t.* au (mor—camlas) An estuary..

Morgant, *s. m.* (mor—cant) A sea brink. It is a very common proper name of men, of which Pelagius has been given as a translation.

Morgannwg, *s. f.* (morgant) Glamorganshire.

Morgareiau, *s. pl.* (mor—carai) Sea-laces.

Morgaseg. *s. f.—pl.* morgesyg (mor—caseg) A sea breaker.

Morgath, *s. f.—pl t.* od (mor—cath) A skate, a ray; also a hollow roaring of the sea, denoting foul weather. *Morgath arw, cath arw, cath bigawg*, the thornback; *morgath lefn*, the smooth skate.

Morgeintach, *s. m.* (mor—ceintach) A sea-fight.

Morgelyn, *s. m.* (mor—celyn) Sea-holly, eryngo.

> I wellhau y clybawd: cymer sudd y morgelyn, a dod yn dwym yn y glust.
>
> To improve the hearing; take the juice of the *sea-holly*, and put warm in the ear. *Medd. Myddfai.*

Morgerwyn, *s. f.—pl. t.* i (mor—cerwyn) A gulf.

Morgi, *s. m.—pl.* morgwn (mor—ci) A sea dog; the dog fish; the shark. The varieties are *Morgi gwyn, ci brych, ci coeg*, the shark; *penci, morgi glas*, the lesser rough hound.

Morgranc, *s. m.—pl. t.* od (mor—cranc) The crab-fish; otherwise called *cranc.*

Morgrug, *s. pl. aggr.* (mor—crug) A hill of ants, or ant hillock; ants.

Morgrugyn, *s. m. dim.* (morgrug) A pismire.

Morgrwydr, *s. m.* (mor—crwydr) A roving by sea.

Morgrwydrad, *s. m.* (morgrwydr) A roving by sea

Morgrwydrwr, *s. m.—pl.* morgrwydrwyr (mor-grwydr—gwr) A sea-rover.

Morgudyn, *s. m.* (mor—cudyn) A polypus.

Morgyllell, *s. f.—pl.* morgyllyll (mor—cyllell) The calamary, or razor-fish.

Morgymmlawdd, *s. m.* (mor—cymmlawdd) The boisterousness of the sea, the raging of the sea.

> Pa beth bynag a fwrio morgymmlawdd i dir, megis tor llong, neu feirw bysgod, y brenin bieufydd.
>
> Whatever shall be cast by a *sea tempest* to land, such as a ship-wreck, or dead fishes, the king shall claim. *Welsh Laws.*

Morgynhwrf, *s. m.* (mor—cynhwrf) The agitation or tumult of the sea.

Morgynnull, *s. m.* (mor—cynnull) The flow tide of the sea.

Morhaig, *s. f.—pl.* morheigiau (mor—haig) A shoal of living things in the sea.

> Morhaig mad gynnydd cyhoedd.
>
> A conspicuous *sea shoal* of goodly increase. *Taliesin.*

Morhedydd, *s. m.* (mor—hedydd) The sea-lark.

Morherw, *s. m.* (mor—herw) A sea-roving.

Morherwa, *v. a.* (morherw) To rove by sea.

Morherwad, *s. m.* (morherw) A roving by sea.

Morherwr, *s. m.* (mor—herwr) A sea-rover.

Morherwriaeth, *s. m.* (morherwr) The life of a sea-rover.

Morhesg, *s. pl. aggr.* (môr—hesg) The sea-rushes, or mat-rushes; also called *merydd.*

Morhocys, *s pl. aggr.* (mor—hocys) The sea tree; marshmallows.

Morhwch, *s. f.—pl.* morhychod (mor—hwch) The dolphin; a grampus.

Moriad, *s. m.* (mor) A going by sea; a sailing.

Moriaw, *v. a.* (mor) To lead a sea-faring life.

Morion, *s. pl. aggr.* (mor) Ants or emmets.

Morionen, *s. f. dim.* (morion) An emmet, an ant.

Moriwr, *s. m.—pl.* morwyr (mor—gwr) A seaman.

Morladrad, *s. m.* (mor—lladrad) Piracy.

Morladradaidd, *a.* (morladrad) Piratical.

Morladradawl, *a.* (morladrad) Piratical.

Morladrata, *v. a.* (morladrad) To commit piracy.

Morlan, *s. f.—pl. t.* au (mor—glàn) A sea brink.

> Cedwyr o du myr, o du morlan,
> Uchel yn cadw eu rhyfel, nid ymgelan'.
>
> Warriors by the side of waters, by the side of the *sea shore*, highly supporting their war, they will not conceal themselves.
> *Llywelyn Fardd.*

Morlas, *s. m.* (mor—glas) Sea-green colour.

Morleidr, *s. m.—pl.* morladron (mor—lleidr) A pirate.

Morleisiad, *s. m.—pl.* morleisiaid (mor—gleisiad) The whiting pollack.

Morlo, *s. m.—pl. t.* i (mor—llo) A sea-calf, a seal.

Moriwch, *s. m.* (mor—llwch) The spray of the sea; vapour rising from the sea.

Morlwyan, *s. pl.* (mor—llwy) Scurvy-grass.

Morlyffant, *s. m.—pl.* morlyffaint (mor—llyffant) The devil-fish; also called *llyffant y mor*.

Morlyswen, *s. f.* (mor—llyswen) A conger eel.

Morlyswod, *s. pl.* (mor—llyswod) Conger eels.

Mornant, *s. m.—pl.* mornentydd (mor—nant) A sea brook, a small channel on a flat shore into which the tide runs; a small estuary; also called *moryd*, *morgamlas*, and *camlas*.

Morneidr, *s. f.—pl.* mornadroedd (mor—neidr) A sea snake.

Mornodwydd, *s. f.—pl. t.* au (mor—nodwydd) The needle-fish, or girrock.

Moron, *s. pl. aggr.* (mo—rhon) Such plants as have a single tapering root; carrots. *Moron cochion*, *llysiau cochion*, carrots; *moron gwynion*, *llysiau gwyddelig*, *pannas*, parsneps; *moron me lynion*, *moron yr allman*, *moron ffrainc*, skirrets; *moron y maes*, wild carrots; *moron y moch*, *pannas y moch*, wild parsneps; *moron y meirch*, or *efwr*, cow-parsnep.

Moronen, *s. f. dim.* (moron) A single one of the *moron* plants. *Moronen felen*, a skirret; *moronen wen*, *pannasen*, a parsnep; *moronen bigawg*, prickly samphire; *moronen y dwfr*, water parsnep.

Moronyn, *s. m. dim.* (moron) A single one of the *moron* plants.

Mortais, *s. f.—pl.* morteisiau (mor—tais) A mortise

Morteisiad, *s. m.* (mortais) A mortising.

Morteisiaw, *v. a.* (mortais) To make a mortise.

Morwaneg, *s. f.—pl. t.* au (mor—gwaneg) A wave of the sea. *Rhysgyr morwaneg*, the violence of the sea wave.

> Dug morwaneg deg o du gauaf
> Llys llawr Lleon Gawr, lliw gwawr gwympaf.
>
> A fair *sea wave* from the region of winter took the floor plot of Lleon the Worthy, image of brightest dawn.
> *G. ab M. ab Dafydd.*

Morwennol, *s. f.—pl.* morwennoliaid (mor—gwennol) The sea swallow, the sand-martin.

Morwerydd, *s. m.* (mor—gwerydd) A beach where the sea breaks; a sea-shore.

Morwiail, *s. pl. aggr.* (mor—gwiail) Grass-wreck.

> Yn y lle y gweles dylong a morwiail.
>
> In the place he saw drift and *sea-wreck*.

Morwialen, *s. f.* (mor—gwialen) Sea-girdle and hangers.

> Crynu mal y forwialen.
>
> Trembling like the *sea girdle*. *Adage.*

Morwiber, *s. f.—pl. t.* od (mor—gwiber) The sea-dragon, or viver.

Morwr, *s. m.—pl.* morwyr (mor—gwr) A seaman.

Morwregys, *s. m.* (mor—gwregys) Sea-belts.

Morwriaeth, *s. m.* (morwr) Seamanship.

Morwyf, *s. m.—pl. t.* ion (mor—gwyf) A bubble.

Morwyfiad, *s. m.—pl.* morwyfiaid (morwyf) A bubbling of water.

Morwyn, *s. f.—pl. t.* ion (mòr—gwyn) A virgin, a maid; a damsel; also a clothes-horse. *Morwyn ystafell*, a chambermaid; *llawforwyn*, a handmaid.

Morwynaidd, *a.* (morwyn) Virginlike, maidenly.

Morwynain, *a.* (morwyn) Maidenly virgin.

> Lle drwg, y'nghelfiau drain
> Y mae'r enaid morwynain.
>
> An evil place, in the recesses of thorns the *pure* soul is confined.
> *Meryn ab Rhys.*

Morwynaw, *v. n.* (morwyn) To become a virgin.

Morwynawl, *a.* (morwyn) Belonging to a virgin.

Morwyndawd, *s. m.* (morwyn) Virginity.

Morwynig, *s. f. dim.* (morwyn) A little maid.

Morwynwraig, *s. f.—pl.* morwynwreigedd (morwyn—gwraig) A virgin wife, a married virgin, a betrothed maid.

> Sef yw morwynwraig, gwraig gwedi ei rhoddi i wr, a hithau heb gyrgu gyda efe, ac yn forwyn.
>
> A *virgin-woman* is a woman after she has been given to a husband, and she without being yet slept with, and being a maid.
> *Welsh Laws.*

Morwyrdd, *s. m.* (mor—gwyrdd) Sea green colour.

Morwys, *s. pl. aggr.* (mor—gwys) Bubbles, bubblings.

Morwysiad, *s. m.—pl.* morwysiaid (morwys) A bubbling.

Morwysiaw, *v. a.* (morwys) To bubble up.

Mory, *s. m.* (mor) The time or day coming, the morrow, to-morrow. *adv.* To-morrow. It is mostly used with the article, as *y fory*, the morrow, or with a prefix, as *efory*, to-morrow.

> Arwyl o fedw irion
> Y fory a gaf dan frig on;
> Amdo wenwisg amdanaf,
> A llian bocw feillion haf!
>
> Obsequies with green birches *to-morrow* I shall receive, beneath the branches of the ash; a white covering shroud around me, and a veil of the lively trefoils of summer! *D. ab Gwilym.*

Moryd, *s. f.* (mor) A small channel of sea water running into a marsh.

Morymdaith, *s. m.* (mor—ymdaith) A voyage or travel by sea.

Morymdeithiaw, *v. a.* (morymdaith) To travel by sea, to go a voyage by sea.

Morymdeithydd, *s. m.—pl. t.* ion (morymdaith) A traveller by sea.

Moryn, *s. m. dim.* (mor) A sea or wave that breaks over any thing.

Morysbail, *s. f.* (mor—ysbail) Spoliation by sea

Morysbeiliaw, *v. a.* (morysbail) To spoil by sea.

Morysbeiliwr, *s. m.—pl.* morysbeilwyr (morysbail—gwr) A spoiler by sea; a bucaneer.

Morysgyfaint, *s. m.* (mor—ysgyfaint) The halipneumon.

MU, *s. f. r.—pl. t.* on. A bulk, or mass; a measure of capacity; a muid.

> Tunell yw pedwar mu; ac yn mhob mu y bydd dwy rownid.
>
> A tun consists of four *muids*; and in every *muid* there shall be two tubs. *Welsh Laws.*

Much, *s. m.* (mu—uch) A black, or gloom.

Muchiad, *s. m.* (much) A blackening, a lowering.

Muchiain, *a.* (much) Of a black hue; gloomy; frowning, lowering.

> Ban ymwanawdd gwyr gwedd muchiain cad;
> Nid ef diengis ysgwyd Owain.
>
> At the encountering of men with the *frowning* aspect of battle, there was no receding of the shield of Owain. *Taliesin.*

Muchiaint, *s. m.* (muchiain) Blackness of hue; gloominess; a frowning; a lowering.

Muchiant, *s. m.* (much) A blackening, a rendering of a jetty black; a frowning, a lowering.

Muchudd, *s. m.* (much) A jet black; jet.

> Ynghaer Pedryfan ynys pybyrddor,
> Echwydd a muchudd cymmysgetor.
>
> In the city of the Quadrangle of the strongly guarded isle, the twilight and the *gloomy jet* mix together. *Taliesin.*
>
> Ei gwallt hithau a'i dwy ael duach oeddynt no'r muchudd.
>
> Her hair also and her eyebrows blacker were they than the *jet*.
> *H. Peredur—Mabinogion.*

Muchuddaidd, *a.* (muchudd) Like jet, black as jet.

Muchuddawl, *a.* (muchudd) Of a jetty black.

Mud, *s. m.* (my—ud) A removal, a pass, a move, a change of residence; what is moved, as goods, or furniture; also a mew, a term in falconry.

Y penhebogydd, o'r pan ddoto yr hebog yn mud yn i dyno allan, ni ddyly ateb i neb o hawl, namyn i un o'i gydswyddogion.

The chief falconer, from the time when he shall put the hawk in a *mew* until he shall take it out, shall not be obliged to answer to any one as to a suit at law, except to one of his brother officers. *Welsh Laws.*

Mud, *a.* (my—ud) Expressing by motion, or signs; mute, dumb.

Hir y bydd y mud yn mhorth y byddar.

Long will the *dumb* be at the gate of the deaf. *Adage.*

Cenad fud drud ei cretwy.

Forward is he that believes a *dumb* messenger. *Adage.*

Eiry mynydd, gwyn blaen dar:
Mud arynaig y llafar.

Snowy mountain, white the top of the oak: *mute* is the fear of the talkative. *Tysilio.*

Mudadwy, *a.* (mud) That may be moved, movable

Mudai, *s. c.—pl.* mudeion (mud) A remover.

Mudair, *a.* (mud) Transmuted, changed.

Hweugaint yw gwerth hebog cyn mud, a thra bo yn y mud: gwedi bo mudair, a gwyn, o bydd brenin bieufydd, punt a dal.

Six-score pence is the value of a hawk before mewing, and whilst it is in the mew; when it shall have become *changed* and white, if belonging to a king, a pound is its value. *Welsh Laws.*

Mudan, *s. m.—pl. t.* od (mud) A mute.

Mudanaeth, *s. m.* (mudan) A mute state.

Udo 'r wyf——
Am y dyn o'i mudanaeth.

I am wailing for the fair one on account of her *dumbness*. *D. ab Edmwnt.*

Mudanaidd, *a.* (mudan) Like a mute, dumb.

Mudanes, *s. f.—pl. t.* od (mudan) A female mute.

Mudanu, *v. n.* (mudan) To become a mute.

Mudaw, *v. a.* (mud) To remove, to change an abode, to move; to carry to another place.

Por eisor, un eisiau ni'm gwedd,
Pen elyf! pan elwyf Wynedd:
Un llysenw a Rhun, nid rhyfedd fy mod
Yn mudaw am renfedd.

The congenial chief, he will not let me appear to have a single want, source of bounty! when I repair to Gwynedd, of the same epithet as Rhun, it is no wonder I should be *removing* to obtain wealth. *Ll. P. Moch, i R. Gryg.*

Mudawl, *a.* (mud) Belonging to a removal, or change of place; movable.

Mudedig, *a.* (mud) Being moved, or removed.

Mudes, *s. f.—pl. t.* od (mud) A female mute.

Dyro——
Dy fudes yn dafodiog.

Grant thy *dumb female* to be possessed of tongue. *D. ab Edmwnt.*

Mudfa, *s. f.* (mud) A remove, a removal.

Mudfa oedd dda ddyw calan,
Lle bai llanw ei dai o dan.

A *removal* was good on new year's day, where his houses were fully stored with fire. *Tra. Brydydd Mawr.*

Mudiad, *s. m.—pl. t.* au (mud) A removing, a changing place; a conveying; conveyance.

Mudiant, *s. m.* (mud) A removal; a moving.

Muding, *s. f.* (mud) A seat of changing; a mew.

Mudliw, *s. m.—pl. t.* iau (mud—lliw) A changing colour, a motley colour.

Mudsain, *s. f.—pl.* mudseiniau (mud—sain) A mute sound; a mute letter.

Mudseiniad, *s. f.—pl.* mudseiniaid (mud—sain) That is mute of sound, a mute letter. The mutes, the *llythyrenau mud*, or *mudion*, are these—*b, f, p, ff, c, ch, g, ng, d, dd, t, th*.

Mudw, *s. m.* (mud) That is moving or wandering.

Mudwg, *s. m.* (mud) A state of removing or changing.

Mudygfawr, *a.* (mudwg) Greatly transforming.

O blith ei blu bloedd fawr a ddodai,
A ddodwed yn Ionawr;
Edling muling mudygfawr,
Edn can adain, cain cerddawr.

From amidst his feather cloak a great outcry he would give, he that was laid in January; heir of the *greatly transforming* mew, a bird chief of a hundred wings, a beautiful songster. *Cynddelw, i'r ceiliog.*

Mul, *s. m.—pl. t.* od (my—ul) An ass. *Bastardd mul*, a bastard ass, or a mule.

Mul, *a.* (my—ul) Bashful, or modest; simple.

O'r meibion, gwyr doethion gynt
Y mulaf a ganmolynt.

Of youths, the wise of yore did the *most modest* praise. *H. Cae Llwyd.*

Mab ni char gormodd siarad,
Mul yw a doeth, mal ei dad.

A child who loves not excess of talk, *modest* he is and wise like his sire. *H. Cae Llwyd.*

Mulaidd, *a.* (mul) Of a bashful disposition.

Mulaw, *v. n.* (mul) To become bashful; to be abashed, ashamed or timid.

Muldra, *s. m.* (mul) Bashfulness, or modesty.

Muleiddiaw, *v. n.* (mulaidd) To become bashful.

Mules, *s. f.—pl. t.* od (mul) A she ass.

Parasynt iddo farchogaeth ar fules y brenin.

They caused him to ride upon the *she ass* of the king. 1 *Kings*, 1. 44.

Mulfran, *s. f.—pl. t.* od (mul—bran) A cormorant; also called *morfran*.

Nid glwth ond mulfran.

Nothing greedy but a *cormorant*. *Adage.*

Mulwirion, *a.* (mul—gwirion) Bashfully innocent, simply innocent; stupid.

Mulyn, *s. m. dim.* (mul) A little or young ass.

Mun, *s. f.—pl. t.* au (mu—un) That is capable of forming; an epithet for a hand.

Mwnai a ranai, wrth raid, i bob un;
A mwy o'i ddwyfun i ymddifaid.

Money he would distribute, when necessary, to every one; and more out of his *two hands* to the destitute. *L. G. Cothi.*

Munaid, *s. f.—pl.* muneidiau (mun) A handful.

Muned, *s. f.* (mun) That helps, or extends aid, an epithet for a hand.

Na fyned aur funed fain,
Gwawr nefolwe, garuflain.

Let not the golden *handed* slender maid, of heavenly aspect, take a perfect churl. *D. ab Edmwnt.*

Muneidiaw, *v. a.* (munaid) To deal out a handful

Muner, *s. m.—pl. t.* oedd (mun) One that conducts; a ruler, or director. *Muner Nef*, the ruler of heaven.

Ardwy cadernyd menwyd muner.

The support of prowess is the pleasure of the *sovereign*. *Gwalchmai.*

Genilles, a'm lliw ced, a'm lleddwy ar air;
Fy muner, nid mawr imi fy ngofwy.

Genilles, my fancied treasure, kills me at a word; my *Lord*, not much were for me to have my visit! *Gwalchmai.*

Neud rer muner maen
Glas gwas gwisg durgaen.

Is not the blue stone the lodging of the *leading chief*; the youth clad in a plate of steel. *G. ab M. ab Dafydd.*

Munerawd, *s. m.* (muner) A maintenance; a conducting, or regulating.

Munerawd y marw fy mwyniant,
Mal yn mhyw Lleisiawn ryw Run blant;
Nid gormod fy ngair it'.

The *bounty* of the dead is my enjoyment, as in the life of the race of Lleision, the sons of Rhun; not too much my word for thee. *Ll. P. Moch, i Lywelyn II.*

Munerawl, *a.* (muner) Maintaining, upholding.

Muneru, *v. a.* (muner) To maintain, to uphold; to conduct, to rule, to regulate.

Nis muner na fler, na ffynedig;
Nis difeirw cadeirn cad arglodig.

Him, nor the mighty, nor the fortunate *shall rule*; the mighty ones shall not condemn the famed in battle. *Gwalchmai.*

Munud, *s. m.—pl. t.* iau (mun—ud) A gesture, or motion of the body; a nod, or beck; imitation; an antick trick. *Torri munudiau ar bren*, to cut figures upon wood; *mae hi yn llawn munudiau*, she is full of anticks.

Meinir a wyr y munud.

The fair one knows the *trick*. *D. ab Gwilym.*

Munudiad, *s. m.—pl. t.* au (munud) A making a gesture, a beckoning; a mimicking; a playing antick tricks.

Munudiaw, *v. a.* (munud) To make a gesture; to beckon; to mimick; to play antick tricks.

Munudiwr, *s. m.—pl.* munudwyr (munud—gwr) One who makes gestures; a beckoner.

Munudyn, *s. m. dim.* (munud) A gesture; a beck

Mur, *s. m.—pl. t.* iau (mu—ur) That is firm, fixed, or established; a wall, a rampart.

Madawg mur menwyd;
Madawg, cyn bu bedd,
Bu ddinas edrywedd,
O gamp, a chymwedd.

Madog the *bulwark* of happiness, Madog, before he was in the grave, was the tower of strength of games and of courtesy. *Taliesin.*

Mor tawch a dyr mariau'r tir,
A'r mellt a lysg yr elltydd.

The spreading sea will break the *fences* of the land, and the lightnings will burn up the towering cliffs. *Dr. S. Cent.*

Mur, *a.* (mu—ur) Firm, fixed, or established.

Murdd, *s. m.* (mur) A foundation, or base.

Murddyn, *s. m.—pl. t.* od (murdd) The ruins of a building; a toft.

Murddynaidd, *a.* (murddyn) Like a toft; ruinous

Murddynu, *v. a.* (murddyn) To make a toft; to reduce to a ruin.

Murganllaw, *s. f.—pl. t.* iau (mur—canllaw) The battlement of a wall.

Murgraid, *s. m.* (mur—craid) A powerful and ardent principle; a firm violence, or ardency.

Seinleisid ei gleddyf yn mhen mamau;
Murgraid oedd; molid ef mab Gwyddnec.

His sword sounded on the tongue of mothers; he was *mighty violence*, let the son of Gwyddnes extol him. *Aneurin.*

Trindawd tragywydd
A oreu ellydd,
A gwedi ellydd
Addaf yn gelfydd;
A gwedi Adda,
Y goreu Efa;
Yr Israel bendigaid
A oreu murgraid.

The eternal Trinity made the element; and after the element, Adam wonderfully, and after the goodly Adam, he made Eve; the blessed Israel the *mighty spirit* made. *Taliesin.*

Muriad, *s. m.* (mur) A fixing, establishing, or determining; a walling, a building a wall.

Muriaw, *v. a.* (mur) To fix, to establish, to determine; to wall, to build a wall.

Muriawg, *a.* (mur) Having a limit, or fence; walled, having a wall.

Muriawl, *a.* (mur) Tending to establish, or to determine; belonging to a wall, mural.

Muriedig, *a.* (muriad) Fixed, determined; having a wall, or rampart; walled.

Muriwr, *s. m.—pl.* murwyr (mur—gwr) One who fixes, or establishes; one who builds a wall.

Murlysiau, *s. pl. aggr.* (mur—llysiau) Pelitory of the wall; also called *murlwyn*, and *murlys*.

Murn, *s. m.—pl. t.* au (mur) A stoppage, obstruction; a foul deed; murder.

Murniad, *s. m.—pl. t.* au (murn) A stopping, or obstructing; a harming; a murdering.

Gwyn ei fyd i gyd yn gall a farno
Furniad truan anghall.

All blessed is he who shall discreetly judge the *oppression* of the simple wretch. *W. Middleton.*

Murniaw, *v. a.* (murn) To stop, to obstruct; to harm; to murder.

Y fieren——
Murniai fi, mae arnaf ol.

The bramble, *it did harm* to me, I bear the mark. *D. ab Gwilym.*

Murniaw pen ffyrdd fal lladron.

Stopping on the high ways like thieves. *I. D. Rhys.*

Murniawl, *a.* (murn) Tending to obstruct; tending to harm; murdering.

Murniedig, *a.* (murniad) Being waylayed.

Murniwr, *s. m.—pl.* murnwyr (murn—gwr) One who stops, or obstructs; an assassin.

Ni ellir fy ngalw yn dad i'ch, namyn yn furniwr creulawn.

I can not be called a father to you, but a *cruel oppressor*. *Cyd. Emlyn ac Amis.*

Murs, *s. m.* (mur) That is stiff, nice, or prim.

Mursawg, *a.* (murs) Being trimmed up.

Mursen, *s. f.—pl. t.* od (murs) A coquette.

Mursen fydd o wr fal o wraig.

There may be a *coquette* of a man as well as of a woman. *Adage.*

Teirgwaith y dywed mursen, bendith
Dduw yn y ty.

Three times will a *coquette* say, be God's blessing in the house. *Adage.*

Pan fydd gwlan gan fursen,
Y byed gwn i bob cawnen.

When the *coquette* is possessed of wool, there will be a gown for every stalk. *Adage.*

Mursenaidd, *a.* (mursen) Somewhat affected, or over-nice; coquettish, effeminate.

Mursendawd, *s. m.* (mursen) Affectation, coyness; quaintness; coquettry.

Murseneidd-dra, *s. m.* (mursenaidd) Coquettry.

Murseneiddiad, *s. m.* (mursenaidd) A rendering, or becoming coquettish; effemination.

Murseneiddiaw, *v. n.* (mursenaidd) To become affected, coy, or coquettish.

Murseneiddrwydd, *s. m.* (mursenaidd) Coquettry

Murseniad, *s. m.* (mursen) A becoming coquettish

Mursenu, *v.* (mursen) To behave affectedly, coyly, or coquettishly; to be coy, or coquettish

Mursogen, *s. f. dim.* (mursawg) One that is trimmed up; one who is coquettish.

Tywyll ben mursogen Mai,
Tew o'r ben, rhad Duw arnei:

The *darkly* covered *doll* of May, thick from the top, heaven's blessing be upon it. *D. ab Gwilym, i fedwen.*

Mursyn, *s. m. dim.* (murs) A slighty one; a fop.

Murwyll, *s. m.* (mur—gwyll) Wild wall-flower.

Mus, *s. m.* (my—us) Constrained motion, or jerk

Musg, *s. m.* (mus) A difficulty of motion.

Musgr, *s. m.* (musg) That is sluggish, or slow.

Musgrell, *s. m.* (musgr) That moves with labour; that is helpless. *a.* Having a difficulty of action; slow, sluggish, drawling, hobbling.

Duw a byrth i fusgrell.

God will provide for the *helpless one*. *Adage.*

Mal cogel gwraig fusgrell.

Like the distaff of a *hobbling* woman. *Adage.*

Musgrelledd, *s. m.* (musgrell) Laborious motion; sluggishness; helplessness.

Musgrelli, *s. m.* (musgrell) Laborious motion; sluggishness, helplessness.

Nid nerthiant oed musgrelli.

It is not a defect short of *helplessness*. *Adage.*

Musgrelliad, *s. m.* (musgrell) A rendering slow, sluggish, or helpless; a becoming helpless.

Musgrellni, *s. m.* (musgrell) A laborious motion; a halting, or hobbling; helplessness.

Musgrellu, *v. a.* (musgrell) To render of laborious motion; to become helpless.

Musgrellyn, *s. m. dim.* (musgrell) One that moves with labour; a hobbling person; a hobbler.

MW, *s. m. r.* That is forward, upon, or about.

Mwcan, *s. f. dim.* (mwg) A cloud of fog.

Mwci, *s. m.* (mwg) Fog; a sprite, or goblin.

Mwcog, *s. pl.* (mwg) Hips; also called *egroes*.

Mwcwg, *s. m.* (mwg) Burnet rose.

Mwch, *a.* (my—wch) Hasty, swift, or quick.

> Mwch barn pob ehud.
>
> Hasty the judgement of every fool. *Adage.*

Mwchiad, *s. m.* (mwch) A hastening onward.

Mwchiaw, *v. a.* (mwch) To hasten; to be quick.

Mwchlaw, *v. a.* (mwchwl) To jumble, to mix; to daub with a variety of things.

Mwchliad, *s. m.* (mwchwl) A jumbling, a mixing.

Mwchnaw, *v. a.* (mwchwn) To jumble together.

Mwchwl, *s. m.* (mwch) A jumble, a mixture; that is full of transitions, a term for a kind of musical composition.

Mwchwn, *s. m.* (mwch) A jumble, or a mixture.

Mwd, *s. m.—pl.* mydau (mw—wd) An arch, a vaulted roof; a roof, a ceiling.

Mwdr, *s. m.* (mwd) That rises or springs up.

Mwdran, *s. m.* (mwdr) Washbrew, a sort of food, made by boiling water thickened with a soured infusion of oatmeal, and sweetened to the taste: it is also called *brithdwym*.

Mwdwl, *s. m.—pl.* mydylau (mwd—wl) A round stack, cock, or heap.

Mwdd, *s. m.—pl.* myddi (mw—wdd) An arch; a spring; a cove; also luck, or fortune.

> Cerddediad carw——
> Cryno fel mwdd, carnwelw main.
>
> Of the pace of a stag, compact like an *arch*; the pale-hoofed slender one. *T. Aled, i farch.*

Mwg, *s. m.* (mw—wg) Smoke, fume. *Mwg y ddaiar*, fumitory; *mwg y perthi*, hedge-fumitory: *Myg-fag*, confusedly, in a huddle.

> Arwydd drwg mwg yn niffaith.
>
> Smoke in a wilderness is a sign of mischief. *Adage.*

Mwgan, *s. c.* (mwg) A puff or cloud of smoke.

Mwgsychiad, *s. m.* (mwg—sychiad) A smoke-drying.

Mwgsychu, *v. a.* (mwg—sychu) To smoke-dry.

Mwgwd, *s. m.* (mwg—wd) A blind, a mask. *Gwara mwgwd y dall, chwara mwgwd yr ieir*, the play of blind-man's buff.

> Medd a ddiosg y mwgwd.
>
> Mead will pull off the *mask*. *Adage.*

Mwl, *s. m.—pl. t.* od (mw—wl) A concrete; a mass, a lump. *Mwlod a cheryg llathraidd*, lumps and well-shaped stones, say, the mason's.

Mwlwch, *s. m. aggr.* (mwl) Refuse; sweepings.

Mwlwg, *s. m. aggr.* (mwl) Refuse; sweepings. *Mwlwg mawn*, the small or refuse of peat.

> Cais yn y mwlwg.
>
> Seek in the *sweepings*. *Adage.*

Mwlyn, *s. m. dim.* (mwl) A concrete; a mass.

Mwll, *a.* (mw—wll) Close, warm, or sultry. *Tywydd mwll, hin foll*, sultry weather.

Mwn, *s. m.—pl.* mynau (mw) That rises up as a spire; that stretches out, the upper part of the shaft of a weapon next to the head; a neck.

> Gwaew anfeidrawl ei faint, a thair ffrwd o waed yn rhedeg o'r mwn hyd y llawr.
>
> A spear of immense size, and three streams of blood running from the *neck* to the ground. *H. Peredur—Mabinogion.*

Mwn, *s. m. aggr.* (mw—wn) Separate body, mass, or particle; mine, ore of metal. *Mwn aur*, gold mine; *mwn arian*, silver mine; *mwn efydd*, copper mine; *mwn plwm*, lead mine; *gwaith mwn*, mine work; *twll mwn*, a mine shaft.

Mwnai, *s. m. aggr.* (mwn) Money, or coin.

Mwnaidd, *a.* (mwn) Like mine, like ore.

Mwnawg, *a.* (mwn) Abounding with ore.

Mwnawl, *a.* (mwn) Belonging to mine or ore.

Mwndill, *s. f.* (mwn—dill) A spattle, a stirrer; a ladle; also called *modbren*.

Mwndir, *s. m.—pl. t.* oedd (mwn—tir) Land abounding with mine.

Mwndlws, *s. m.—pl.* myndlysau (mwn—tlws) A neck ornament; a necklace.

Mwndorch, *s. f.—pl.* myndyrch (mwn—torch) A collar, a wreath for the neck.

Mwnglawdd, *s. m.—pl.* mwngloddiau (mwn—clawdd) A mine pit or shaft.

Mwngloddfa, *s. f.—pl. t.* oedd (mwnglawdd) A mine pit, a mine shaft.

Mwngloddiad, *s. m.* (mwnglawdd) A mining.

Mwngloddiaw, *v. a.* (mwnglawdd) To make a mine pit or shaft; to mine.

Mwngloddiwr, *s. m.—pl.* mwngloddwyr (mwnglawdd—gwr) A miner.

Mwnt, *s. m.—pl.* mynnau (mwn) That rises up; a heap, or mound; a mount, a mountain; one hundred thousand. *Ar y mynnau*, on the hills. *Brecon.*

> Deg myrdd yn y mwnt.
>
> Ten myriads in the *hundred thousand*.

Mwnwg, *s. m.* (mwn) That shoots out as a spire; a neck. *Pen-dra-mwnwg*, headlong.

Mwnwgl, *s. m.—pl.* mynyglau (mwnwg) The neck. *Mwnwgl y troed*, the instep of the foot.

> Cyd ag y gweles Elidyr ef rhedeg a orug, a myned ddwylaw mwnwgl iddaw, a rhoddi llawer o gusanau iddaw.
>
> As soon as Elidyr saw him he ran, and went with his hands round his *neck*, and gave him many kisses. *Gr. ab Arthur.*

Mwnws, *s. pl. dim.* (mwn) Small particles; dross, refuse, dust, pelf, riches.

Mwng, *s. m.—pl.* myngoedd (mwn) A mane.

Mwngial, *v. a.* (mwng) To speak from the throat; to mutter, to speak indistinctly.

Mwngial, *s. m.* (mwng) A speaking from the throat; a muttering, a murmuring.

> Cerdd wammal fu'r mwngial mau.
>
> A flighty song was that *muttering* of mine. *D. ab Gwilym.*

Mwr, *s. m.* (mw—wr) That tends to fall, or hap.

Mwrl, *s. m.* (mwr) A crumbling freestone.

Mwrl, *a.* (mwr) Crumbling, friable. *Tir mwrl*, a loose crumbling soil.

Mwrllwch, *s. m.* (mwr—llwch) A thick vapour.

> Dyred yn nes atynt, ebai yr angel, ac a'm cipiai drwy lawer o fwrllwch difaith, oedd yn codi o'r ddinas.
>
> Come nearer to them, said the angel; and he snatched me through many a noxious *exhalation*, which were rising out of the city. *Elis Wyn, B. Cwsg.*

Mwrn, *s. m.* (mwr) Sultry or close weather.

Mwrn, *a.* (mwr) Sultry, close, or warm.

Murnaw, *v. n.* (mwrn) To become sultry.

Mwrnder, *s. m.* (mwrn) Sultriness, closeness.

Mwrndra, *s. m.* (mwrn) Sultry heat, sultriness.

Mwrnedd, *s. m.* (mwrn) Sultriness, closeness.

Mwrth, *s. m.* (mwr) That tends forward.

Mwrthwyl, *s. m.—pl. t.* ion (morth—wyl) A hammer: the same also in Coromandel.

> Gwell un dyrnawd a'r ordd no dau a'r mwrthwyl.
>
> Better one stroke with the mallet than two with the *hammer*. *Adage.*

Mwrthwyliad, *s. m.*—*pl. t.* au (mwrthwyl) A hammering; using a hammer.
Mwrthwyliaw, *v. a.* (mwrthwyl) To hammer.
Mwrthwyliedig, *a.* (mwrthwyl) Being hammered
Mwrthwyliwr, *s. m.*—*pl.* mwrthwylwyr (mwrthwyl—gŵr) A hammerer; a hammer-man.
Mws, *s. m.* (mw—ws) That shoots out; an effluvia
Mws, *a.* (mw—ws) Of a strong scent, rank.

Ciliais yn wrth i'm gwrthol,
I'r drws, a'r ci mws i'm ol.

I suddenly retreated back out of door, and the *stinking* dog after me. *D. ab Gwilym.*

Mwsg, *s. m.* (mws) The moscus, or musk.
Mwstardd, *s. m.* (mws—tardd) The mustard.
Mwswg, *s. m.* (mws) Moss. *Mwswg gwyn*, white moss; also called *migwyn*.
Mwswgl, *s. m.* (mwswg) Moss, under all its varieties, except the lichen and the sorts growing upon stones which are called *cèn*.
Mwswn, *s. m.* (mws) Moss; same as *mwswg*.
Mwth, *s. m.* (mw—wth) That has velocity.
Mwth, *a.* (mw—wth) Rapid, fleet, quick, nimble. *Nant mwth*, a rapid brook; *meirch mythion*, fleet horses.

Gochawn marchawg mwth, moled Gwrion,
O ddraig ddylan addaw, doethaw Don.

We shall have a *nimble* horseman, of Gwrion's fame, a leader of fair promise, wise as Don. *Taliesin.*

Mwy, *s. m.*—*pl. t.* on (mw) That is vast or large; that is dark or black.
Mwy, *a.* (mw) Additional; also used for the comparative *mwyach*, more, greater, larger. *adv.* More; again; henceforward. *Mwy dymunawl nog aur*, more desirable than gold.

Gwan y gormes mwyaf gerbron y glewder lleiaf.

Feeble is the *greatest* tyranny in the presence of the smallest courage. *Adage.*

Dy far, feinwar Fyfanwy,
Ar a'th gar; ni fu far fwy.

Thy ire, Myvanwy delicate and slender, is on him who loves thee; there never was *greater* ire. *H. ab Einion Llygliw.*

Cyd ddal cariad celadwy,
Cywir, nis mynegir mwy.

Mutually cherishing a concealed love, sincere, *more*, shall not be told. *D. ab Gwilym.*

Mwyâad, *s. m.* (mwyâu) An augmenting.
Mwyâawl, *a.* (mwyâu) Augmenting, increasing.
Mwyach, *a.* (mwy) More, greater, bigger. *adv.* More, again, henceforward.

Mwyach ni elwir dy enw di Jacob.

More thy name shall not be called Jacob. *Genesis 32. 28.*

Mwyad, *s. m.*—*pl. t.* au (mwy) An increasing.
Mwyadawl, *a.* (mwyad) Tending to increase.
Mwyadu, *v. a.* (mwyad) To augment, to increase.
Mwyaf, *a.* (mwy) Greatest, biggest, largest; most. *Yn fwyaf*, *gan mwyaf*, mostly, in the greatest degree.

Tri lle y bydd y mwyaf o Dduw: lle mwyaf bo a'i cais; y mwyaf a'i car; a lleiaf o'r hunan.

The three instances where there will be the *most* of God: where he is the *most* sought, where he is *most* loved; and where there is the least of self. *Barddas.*

Mwyaid, *s. pl.* (mwyad) Consecrated wafers.

Ni chenir mwyaid ar fo.

The mass will not be sung on a retreat. *Llyfoed.*

Pader a mwyaid bendigaid.

The paternoster and blessed *wafers*. *Ymdd. Arthur a Liwlod.*

Mwyalch, *s. f.*—*pl. t.* od (mwy—alch) An ousel. It is called *gwyalch*, and *aderyn du*.

Genau mwyalch ac arch blaidd.

The mouth of a *blackbird* with the request of a wolf. *Adage.*

Mwyalchen, *s. f. dim.* (mwyalch) The ousel. *Mwyalchen y dwfr*, *y fronwen*, *bronwen y dwfr*, the water ousel; *mwyalchen y graig*, the rock ousel.
Mwyar, *s. pl. aggr.* (mwy) The class of berries, growing in clusters, called acini; so called from their dark hue. *Mwyar y perthi*, or *mwyar duon*, blackberries; *mwyar berwyn*, *mwyar dwywon*, *mwyar gwenith*, *mwyar y ddaiar*, cloud-berries, *mwyar ffreinig*, *mwyar Mair*, mulberries; *mwyar y brain*, bilberries.
Mwyara, *v. a.* (mwyar) To gather berries.
Mwyarawl, *a.* (mwyar) Of the nature of berries.

Y fun fwyarawl olwg,
Feinwaidd lawn o fwyniaidd wg.

The maid of *berry* hue, very delicate, and of tender look. *Gutyn Owain.*

Mwyaren, *s f.* (mwyar) A single berry.
Mwyariad, *s. m.*—*pl.* mwyariaid (mwyar) A negro; a moor.
Mwyâu, *v. a.* (mwy) To augment, to enhance, to increase; to be increased, to grow bigger.

Hynaf mab wyt ti, ebai Gwrtheyrn, o blant Custennyn; ac ni ellir frenin o yr un o'th frodyr, mor yni ieuainc; a mi a'th wnaf di yn frenin; a mwyâa dithau finnau.

The eldest son art thou, said Gwrtheyrn, of the children of Custenyn; and not one of thy brothers can be king, for they are so young; so I will make thee king; then *do thou exalt* me likewise. *Gr. ab Arthur.*

Mwyâwr, *s. m.* (mwyâu—gwr) An augmenter.
Mwyd, *s. m.* (mwy) That is swelled or puffed up; that is moistened, soaked, or steeped.
Mwydaidd, *a.* (mwyd) Somewhat moistened.
Mwydaw, *v. a.* (mwyd) To moisten, to soak, or to steep; to become moist, or damp.
Mwydawl, *a.* (mwyd) Tending to moisten.
Mwydedig, *a.* (mwyd) Macerated, imbrued.
Mwydedd, *s. m.* (mwyd) A moist state, humidity.
Mwydiad, *s. m.* (mwyd) A moistening, a soaking.
Mwydion, *s. pl. aggr.* (mwyd) The soft parts, crumbs, or pith, of any thing. *Mwydion bara*, the crumb of bread; *mwydion y ddaiar*, puff-ball
wydionaidd, *a.* (mwydion) Like soft pith, pithy
wydionawg, *a.* (mwydion) Abounding with pith
wydioni, *v. a.* (mwydion) To become pithy.
wydionllyd, *a.* (mwydion) Full of pith.
wydionyn, *s. m. dim.* (mwydion) The pith.
wydle, *s. m.*—*pl. t.* oedd (mwyd—lle) A fetlock.
wydwr, *s. m.* (mwyd—gwr) A soaker.
wydydd, *s. m.*—*pl. t.* ion (mwyd) A soaker.
wydyn, *s. m. dim.* (mwyd) A pith, a crumb.
wyedig, *a.* (mwyad) Augmented, enhanced.
wyedigaeth, *s. m.* (mwyedig) Augmentation.
wyedigaw, *v. a.* (mwyedig) To augment.
wyeri, *s. pl. aggr.* (mwyar) Briers, brambles.
wyfwy, *a.* (mwy *repeated*) More and more.
Mwyg, *s. m.* (mwy) That is soft or puffed.
Mwygl, *a.* (mwyg) Tepid, sultry, warm; the same as *mwll*, *mwrn*, *gwygl*.

Meigen Rys——
'Mogel di, mwygl yw dy fost.

Rhys of Meigen, take thou care, thy boast is warm. *D. ab Gwilym.*

Mwyglad, *s. m.* (mwygl) A growing sultry.
Mwyglaw, *v. a.* (mwygl) To make warm, or mild, to become warm, or sultry; to grow lukewarm.
Mwygledd, *s. m.* (mwygl) Tepidity; sultriness.
Mwyglen, *s. f. dim.* (mwygl) A wanton wench.
Mwygliad, *s. m.* (mwygl) A growing sultry.
Mwyll, *a.* (mwy) Soft; tender, emollient.

Mwyn, *s. m.* (mwy) Enjoyment, fruition, use, or benefit; profit, advantage.

Nid mwyn ond mwyn ariant.

There is no *mine* except *mine* that is gold. *Adage.*

Ni bydd i feddyg mwyn or a wnêant.

The doctor shall have no *advantage* from what they do. *Taliesin.*

Mwyn, *a.* (mwy) Tender, kind, mild, gentle, courteous, affable. *Dynion mwynion*, fairies.

Gair mwyn a wna y ddadl yn gadarn.

A *mild* word will make the argument strong. *Adage.*

Cant mwyn mab y ty.

A hundred times *kind* the son of the house. *Adage.*

Main fain riain, gain Gymmraeg;
Mwyn forwyn hun-ddwyn, hoen ddygn gysteg!

A slender elegant lady, whose Welsh is polished; a kind maid stealing sleep away; the severe torment of health! *Casnodyn.*

Mwynâad, *s. m.* (mwyn) An enjoying; fruition.

Mwynâawl, *a.* (mwynâu) Tending to enjoyment.

Mwynaidd, *a.* (mwyn) Of a tender or kind nature

Mwynair, *a.* (mwyn—gair) A kind word.

Mwynas, *s. f.—pl. t.* au (mwyn) Kindness.

Mwynasiad, *s. m.* (mwynas) A doing a kindness.

Mwynasu, *v. a.* (mwynas) To do kindness.

Mwynâu, *v. a.* (mwyn) To enjoy, to make use of; to take the benefit of.

Yn lle gofal a dialedd,
Duw, i'w fwynâu danfon hedd!

Instead of anxiety and vengeance, God, send peace to be *enjoyed.* *H. D. ab Ifan.*

Mwynawl, *a.* (mwyn) Tending to enjoyment.

Mynawg, gwareddawg y gwir raddau;
Mwynawl hawl nefawl, ceffir mawl mau.

The courteous, the gentle one of the exalted ranks; the *inviting* heavenly title, my praise shall be obtained. *D. y Coed.*

Mwynâwr, *s. m.—pl.* mwynâwyr (mwynâu—gwr) One who enjoys, an enjoyer.

Mwynbell, *a.* (mwyn—pell) Extendedly enjoyed

Cynan, darogan derwyddon dy ddaw;
Ef dyddyw o Frython,
Anaw cwynaw cerddorion,
Un oedd well, udd mwynbell Mon!

Cynan, the druids foretell he shall be coming; there has come of the Britons the complaining lay of minstrels for one more excellent, the *far-enjoyed* chief of Mona! *Ll. P. Moch.*

Mwynder, *s. m.—pl. t.* au (mwyn) Tenderness, kindness; gentleness; affability; enjoyment.

Nid mwynder ond merch.

There is no tenderness but in a woman. *Adage.*

Cymer trwy fwynder, tra fych;
Dod ran o'r da a drinych.

Accept, through *enjoyment*, whilst thou art; give a part of the possession that thou dost manage. *S. Tudur.*

Mwyndra, *s. m.* (mwyn) Tenderness, kindness; gentleness; affability, enjoyment.

Mwynddyn, *s. c.—pl. t.* ion (mwyn—dyn) A tender, kind, or courteous person.

Mwynedig, *a.* (mwyn) Being enjoyed, or used.

Mwynedd, *s. m.* (mwyn) Kindness, courtesy.

Mwyneddus, *a.* (mwynedd) Full of tenderness.

Mwyneidd-dra, *s. m.* (mwynaidd) Tenderness.

Mwyneiddiad, *s. m.* (mwynaidd) A becoming of a kind or tender nature.

Mwyneiddiaw, *v. n.* (mwynaidd) To become pleasing, kind, tender, or affable.

Mwynen, *s. f. dim.* (mwyn) A pleasing one.

Mwynfawr, *a.* (mwyn—mawr) Greatly kind.

Mwynfawr garcharawr a gyrchasant,
Meurig fab Gruffudd, grym ddarogant.

A *greatly courteous* prisoner they brought away, Meurig the son of Grufudd, the object of prediction. *O. Cyfeiliawg.*

Mwyniannawl, *a.* (mwyniant) Tending to enjoyment, or fruition.

Mwyniannu, *v. a.* (mwyniant) To render an enjoyment; to enjoy.

Y rhai nad ynt yn cyfrif y bywyd yma—ond fal alltudaeth, ac yn wyllyagar i ymado ag ef i fyned i lys y brenin nefawl, y gaffant mwyniannu cyflawnder o lawenydd.

Those who do not count this life more than like a state of exile and willing to come out of it to go into the court of the heavenly king, shall get to *enjoy* fulness of pleasure. *Marchawg Crwydrad.*

Mwyniannus, *a.* (mwyniant) Tending to enjoyment; tending to please.

Mwyniannusaw, *v. a.* (mwyniannus) To render of a tendency to enjoyment.

Mwyniant, *s. m.—pl.* mwyniannau (mwyn) Benefit, use, or profit derived; enjoyment.

Cymer fwyniant y peth sy genyt, tra bo y cybydd yn blingaw y diawl am lai no chroen chweinen.

Take the *enjoyment* of what thou hast, whilst the miser is flaying the devil for less than the skin of a flea. *Adage.*

Mwynlan, *a.* (mwyn—glan) Courteously fair.

Mwynwr, *s. m.—pl.* mwynwyr (mwyn—gwr) A kind or affable man.

Mwynyn, *s. m. dim.* (mwyn) A kind one.

Mwys, *s. f.—pl. t.* au (mwy) That has capacity, or that comprehends; that has latitude of import, a pun; also a kind of covered basket, pannier or hamper; also the quantity contained in such vessel. *Mwys o ysgadain*, a mease, or five-score of herrings.

Un o'r tri thlws ar ddeg—Mwys Gwyddno Garan Hir; bwyd i ungwr a roid ynddi, a bwyd i gannwr a gaid ynddi pan egorid.

One of the thirteen rarities: the *basket* of Gwyddno Longshank; the victuals for one man being put in it, victuals for a hundred men would be found in it when opened. *Chwedlau.*

Mwys, *a.* (mwy) Comprehensive; enveloped; mysterious; ambiguous; ingenious, witty; elegant: also, of the nature of a pun, or of a double meaning. But the last sense arose from mistaking false for true wit; and hence *gair mwys*, in popular language, is a pun; of which the following part of an *englyn*, where *An*, a woman's name, and a negative particle, is the *gair mwys*, may serve as an example.—

An-fwyn, an-ddwyn, an-nych, an-lanlaidd,
An lana' lle delych.

Mwysai, *s. c.—pl.* mwyseion (mwys) A punster.

Mwysaidd, *a.* (mwys) Of a latitude of import; of the nature of a pun; ambiguous, oracular.

Mwysair, *s. m.—pl.* mwyseiriau (mwys—gair) A word of double meaning; a pun.

Mwysaw, *v. n.* (mwys) To be of capacity; to have latitude of import, to pun.

Mwysawg, *a.* (mwys) Having capacity; having latitude of import; of a double meaning.

Mwysder, *s. m.—pl. t.* au (mwys) That is comprehensive; an ambiguity, a mystery.

Mwysdro, *s. m.—pl. t.* ion (mwys—tro) A quibble

Mwysdröad, *s. m.* (mwysdro) A punning.

Mwysdroi, *v. a.* (mwysdro) To quibble, to pun.

Mwyseiriawg, *a.* (mwysair) Full of punning.

Mwyth, *s. m.—pl. t.* au (mwy) That is smooth, soft and puffed up; a fulness of humours; a fever. *Y cryd a mwyth*, the ague and fever, or intermitting fever: *y mwyth brith*, *brith y gwanwyn*, the military fever.

Cadw fi——
Rhag poenau clwyfau, rhag clefyd a mwyth,
Rhag methiant ac adfyd!

Keep me from the pains of wounds, from disease and *fever*, from debility, and from adversity! *H. D. ab Ifan.*

Mwyth, *a.* (mwy) Puffed up, soft, sleek; tender.

> Castell Mathrafal, mwyth werin wythawg,
> Du prithiawg poeth ethrin
> O'th gynnygn, gymmogn beddin:
> Nid uch wyneb neb no'i lin.
>
> The castle of Mathrafal, of a *pampered* furious multitude, is black and cleanly burnt from thy attack, thou dependance of a host: no one's face is higher than his knee.
> *Ll. P. Moch, i G. ab H. ab Owain.*

Mwythach, *s. m.* (mwyth) The state of being puffed up, or pampered.

Mwythan, *s. c. dim.* (mwyth) Any foft tender substance, a tender shoot, a cartilage, a gristle.

Mwythaw, *v. a.* (mwyth) To puff up, to make smooth; to mollify, to soften; to become puffed up; to grow soft; to have a fever.

Mwythawg, *a.* (mwyth) Puffed up, pampered.

Mwythawl, *a.* (mwyth) Emollient, softening.

Mwythedig, *a.* (mwyth) Being mollified.

Mwythedd, *s. m.* (mwyth) Emolliency, softness.

Mwythiad, *s. m.* (mwyth) A mollifying.

Mwythiant, *s. m.* (mwyth) Softness, blandishment

Mwythig, *a.* (mwyth) Puffed up, bloated.

Mwythigaw, *v. a.* (mwythig) To become puffed up or bloated; to swell with humours.

Mwythl, *s. m.* (mwyth) That has a tendency to puff up or to make sleek.

Mwythlan, *s. c. dim.* (mwythl) One that is puffed up, or pampered.

Mwythlawn, *a.* (mwyth) Puffed up, pampered.

Mwythlen, *s. f. dim* (mwythl) A soft pampered female, one that is plump.

Mwythus, *a.* (mwyth) Puffed up, sleek, pampered, delicate, nice.

> Nid mwythus ond bela.
>
> None *delicate* but the marten. *Adage.*

Mwythusaw, *v. n.* (mwythus) To become delicate, or nice, to pamper.

Mwythusder, *s. m.* (mwythus) Delicateness.

Mwythusdra, *s. m.* (mwythus) Delicateness, softness, effeminacy, a pampered state.

Mwythusiad, *s. m.* (mwythus) A rendering puffed up, sleek, or soft, a pampering.

Mwythusrwydd, *s. m.* (mwythus) Pamperedness.

MY, *s. m. r.* That is, that is present; that is in agency. It is a prefix in composition.

My, *pron.* (my, *s.*) It is mutable into *fy*, in which form it most frequently occurs. *My hun, my hunan*, myself; *mi fy hun*, I myself.

> Pan gefais fy maeddu gan adfyd, mi wybum fod fy neall yn goleuaw ychydig.
>
> When I got buffeted by adversity, I knew that my understanding was becoming a little enlightened. *Marchawg Crwydrad.*

Myanafu, *v. a.* (anafu) To maim, or to hurt.

Mychawl, *a.* (mwch) Of a rapid or quick motion.

Mychedyn, *s. m. dim.* (mwch) A sun beam.

Mychiad, *s. m.—pl.* mychiaid (moch) Swineherd.

> Cawawg mychiad o'i foch.
>
> A *swineherd* is proud of his swine. *Adage.*
>
> Llawen mychiad pan fo gwynt.
>
> Glad the *swineherd* when there is wind. *Adage.*

Mychw, *s. m.* (mwch) Motion stopped or reflected

Mychweg, *a.* (chweg) Luscious, very sweet.

Mychwegrwydd, *s. m.* (mychweg) Lusciousness.

Mychwin, *a.* (mychw) Reflected as to motion.

Myd, *s. m* (my—yd) A circular enclosure.

> Hael Arthur, myd anghuddl am rodd;
> Hael Rhydderch am aur fuld;
> Hael Mordaf, hael mawr ag Nudd;
> Haelach, greddfau hi Grufudd.
>
> Generous was Arthur, of unconcealed *enclosure* in giving; generous was Rhydderch as to the good treasure, generous was Mordaf; generous the magnificent Nudd; more generous, more good-natured is Grufudd. *Ll. P. Moch.*

Mydadwy, *a.* (mwd) That may be arched.

Mydaidd, *a.* (mwd) Like an arch, archwise.

Mydawl, *a.* (mwd) Belonging to an arch.

Mydedig, *a.* (mwd) Camerated, arched over.

Mydedd, *s. m.* (mwd) The state of being arched.

Myde**ddawg**, *a.* (mydedd) Having curvatures.

Mydeyrn, *s. m.—pl. t.* on (teyrn) A sovereign.

Mydiad, *s. m.—pl. t.* au (mwd) Cameration.

Mydiant, *s. m.* (mwd) Cameration, an arch.

Mydr, *s. m.—pl. t.* au (myd) A metre. *Mydr anghyfawdl*, blank verse.

Mydraeth, *s. m.* (mydr) Versification.

Mydraethawl, *a.* (mydraeth) Versifying.

Mydraethiad, *s. m.* (mydraeth) Versification.

Mydraethu, *v. a.* (mydraeth) To compose verse.

> Daeth y cyfryw drywyllt ac oferwagffydraethu, a dall brydydiaeth.
>
> There be come in use such perfectly wild and unconnected versifying, and such blind poetizing. *Ed. Dafydd.*

Mydraethydd, *s. m.—pl. t.* ion (mydraeth) A versificator, a maker of metres.

Mydrawl, *a.* (mydr) Metrical; rhythmical.

Mydriad, *s. m.—pl. t.* au (mydr) A versifying.

Mydrin, *a.* (mydr) Composed in metre.

Mydrwr, *s. m.—pl.* mydrwyr (mydr—gwr) A versifier, a maker of verses.

Mydrydd, *s. m.—pl. t.* ion (mydr) A versifier.

Mydryddiad, *s. m.* (mydrydd) A versifying.

Mydryddiaeth, *s. m.* (mydrydd) Versification.

> Tri anhebgor mydryddiaeth: colofn, cynghanedd, ac odl.
>
> The three indispensables of *versification*: feet, consonancy, and rhyme. *Barddas.*

Mydryddu, *v. a.* (mydrydd) To versificate.

> With fydryddu cerdd—edryched y bardd na roddo yn gyplydig y cyfryw fesur ag a font yn annhebyg ac anwastad, ac anghydbwys herwydd cyhydedd.
>
> In *versifying* a piece, let the poet see that he do not couple together such verses as shall be too dissimilar, and unequal, and incompetent, with respect to length. *Barddas.*

Mydu, *v. a.* (mwd) To arch, to vault, to make an arched roof, or ceiling.

Mydum, *s. m.—pl. t.* iau (tum) A gesture; mimicry. *Gwneud mydumiau*, to make wry faces.

Mydw, *s. m.* (myd) Aptitude; fluency.

> Gwyr ennd gwr gorfod gorfyn,
> Gwedi mydw a medd gorewyn.
>
> He knows the attack of the overbearing malicious man, after the *fluency of discourse*, and the hi, bly-foaming mead.
> *Cynddelw, i'r argl. Rhys.*

Mydwal, *a.* (mydw) Of aptitude to proceed.

Mydwaledd, *s. m.* (mydwal) Flow of expression.

> Mygr fydwaledd hawddgar.
>
> Fair is the amiable *speech*. *Hyw. Cyfeiliawg.*
>
> Dewredd mydwaledd a dawn,
> Fu rhyw fu ouid rhoi ei feirch,
> A chwn, gwelwa, ac eleirch.
>
> The spirit of *eloquence* and talent, his nature was to give away his steeds and dogs, as we perceive, and his swans.
> *B. Brwynllys.*

Mydwr, *s. m.—pl.* mydwyr (mwd—gwr) One who forms an arch, or ceiling.

Mydwrdd, *s. m.* (my—dwrdd) A tumult.

Mydylan, *s. c. dim.* (mwdwl) A small stack.

Mydylawg, *a.* (mwdwl) In the stack, cocked.

Mydyliad, *s. m.* (mwdwl) A making stacks.

Mydylu, *v. a.* (mwdwl) To make stacks, to cock.

Mydylwr, *s. m.—pl.* mydylwyr (mwdwl—gwr) One who makes stacks, or mows.

Mydylyn, *s. m. dim.* (mwdwl) A small stack.

Myddi, *s. f. pl. t.* au (mwdd) A hogshead.

Myfi, *pron.* (my—mi) I, me, myself.

Myfiaeth, *s. m.* (myfi) Egotism, a talking of self.

Myfiaw, *v. a.* (myfi) To egotize, to talk of self.

Myfinnau, *pron.* (minnau) I also, I likewise.

Myfiwr, *s. m.—pl.* myfiwyr (myfiaw—gwr) An egotist, or one who talks of himself.
Myfiydd, *s. m.—pl. t.* ion (myfi) An egotist.
Myfyr, *s. m.—pl. t.* oedd (myr) The action of the mind; muse, study. *Myfyr Elian*, the study of Elian, in Mona; *Glyn y Myfyr*, a vale in Denbighshire.
Myfyr, *a.* (myr) Contemplative, thoughtful.
Myfyrawd, *s. m.* (myfyr) Contemplation.
Myfyrbwyll, *s. m.* (myfyr—pwyll) A contemplative mind. *a.* Of a thoughtful turn of mind.

> Cynddylan fyfyrbwyll o fri
> Cadwynawg, cyndynawg llu.

Cynddylan *with a mind regardful* of honour, the one of chains, the froward one of war. *Llywarch Hen.*

Myfyrdawd, *s. m.—pl.* myfyrdodau (myfyr) Meditation, or contemplation.

Tair cynneddf cyflawn fyfyrdawd: a ddichon'fod, a ddylai fod, ac sydd hardd ei fod.

The three foundations of just *thinking*: that is possible to be, that ought to be, and that is beautiful it should be. *Barddas.*

Myfyrdodawl, *a.* (myfyrdawd) Contemplative.
Myfyrgar, *a.* (myfyr) Contemplative, cogitative.
Myfyrgarwch, *s. m.* (myfyrgar) Studiousness.
Myfyriad, *s. m.—pl. t.* au (myfyr) Cogitation, contemplation; a contemplating.
Myfyriadawl, *a.* (myfyriad) Contemplative.
Myfyriaeth, *s. m.* (myfyr) Cogitation.

Nid myfyriaeth ond ystyriaeth.

There is no *contemplation* without consideration. *Adage.*

Myfyriannawl, *a.* (myfyriant) Cogitative.
Myfyriannu, *v. a.* (myfyriant) To cogitate.
Myfyriannus, *a.* (myfyriant) Cogitative.
Myfyriannusaw, *v. a.* (myfyriannus) To become contemplative or thoughtful.
Myfyriant, *s. m.* (myfyr) Cogitation.
Myfyriaw, *v. a.* (myfyr) To contemplate, to meditate, to cogitate, to muse, to study.
Myfyriawl, *a.* (myfyr) Contemplative.
Myfyriedig, *a.* (myfyriad) Contemplated.
Myfyriedigawl, *a.* (myfyriedig) Contemplative.
Myfyrioldeb, *s. m.* (myfyriawl) Studiousness.
Myfyriwr, *s. m.—pl.* myfyrwyr (myfyr—gwr) A contemplator, a speculator.
Myfyrus, *a.* (myfyr) Apt to contemplate.
Myg, *s. m.—pl. t.* ion (my—ig) That is of great space, or grand; that is solemn or holy.

> Bendigaid fyg
> Yw'r nadolyg.

A blessed *solemnity* is the nativity. *Br. Fardd.*

Myg, *a.* (my—yg) Being of great space, or grand; reverential, respectable, honoured; holy; solemn; glorious.
Mygarogl, *s. m.—pl.* mygaroglau (myg—arogl) Holy incense.
Mygaw, *v. a.* (myg) To perform a solemnity.

> Gorddyfnais, mygais magiad llwyth Cadfor
> Goror y glasfor a gar gleisiad.

I have been assiduous, I *have honoured* the education of the tribe of Cadfor, on the coast of the blue sea, which the salmon loves. *Llywelyn Ddu.*

Mygawd, *s. m.* (mwg) A rising of smoke, steam, or vapour, suffocation.
Mygawl, *a.* (mwg) Fumous, smoking, smoky.
Mygawr, *s. m.* (myg) That is reverent, or solemn.
Mygdarth, *s. m.—pl. t.* au (mwg—tarth) Vapour, exhalation, fog; fumigation.
Mygdarthiad, *s. m.* (mygdarth) A throwing out vapour; a fumigating; a burning of incense.
Mygdarthu, *v. a.* (mygdarth) To burn incense.
Myged, *s. f.* (myg) Grandeur, reverence, honour, solemnity; glory.

> Neud ethyw'——gwanar cerddgar cyrdd fyged:
> Gwae fi o'i fyned fyn nas gwelaf!

Is he not gone! the inspired regulator of the *solemnity* of songs, woe is me that he is gone to regions where I may not behold him! *Ph. Brydydd.*

Myged, *a.* (myg) Grand; respected, honoured, solemn, glorious.

> I Dduw ydd archaf, naf, eu noddi,
> Rodd-fyged ri!

I will entreat a refuge for them of God the Father, the Lord of *glorious* gift. *Bleddyn Fardd.*

Mygedawg, *a.* (myged) Respected, reverenced.

> Y digones gwychyr Gwallawg
> Ellynod Gattraeth fawr fygedawg.

The heroic Gwallog achieved exploits equal to those of Cattraeth great and *glorious*. *Melgant.*

Mygedawl, *a.* (myged) Having respect; honorary. *Gradd fygedawl*, honorary degree.
Mygedig, *a.* (myged) Respected, reverenced.
Mygedorth, *s. f.* (myged—gorth) A funeral pile.

> Yn Llongborth gwelais i fygedorth,
> A gwyr yn goddef ammorth,
> A gorfod gwedi gorborth.

In Llongborth I beheld a *solemn pile*, and men suffering privation, and in a state of subjection after excess of fruition. *Llywarch Hen.*

Cornan, march meibion Elifer Gosgorddfawr, a ddwg arnaw Gwrgi, Peredur, Dunawd Fyr, a Chynfelyn Drwsgl, i edrych ar fygedorth Gwenddolau yn Arderydd.

Cornan, the horse of the sons of Elifer with the great retinue, carried Gwrgi, Peredur, Dunod Fyr, and Cynfelyn the Stumbler, to see the *funeral pile* of Gwenddolau in Arderydd. *Trioedd.*

Mygfa, *s. f.—pl.* mygfëydd (mwg) That suffocates; a suffocation.
Mygfaen, *s. m.—pl.* mygfeini (mwg—maen) Brimstone; also called *llosgfaen*.
Mygiad, *s. m.* (mwg) A smoking; a suffocation.
Mygiedydd, *s. m.—pl. t.* ion (mygiad) A smoker.
Myglyd, *a.* (mwg) Apt to smoke, or smoky.
Myglydrwydd, *s. m.* (myglyd) Smokiness.
Myglys, *s. m.* (mwg—llys) Tobacco.
Mygod-darth, *s. m.* (mygawd—tarth) Vapour, or exhalation.

> Mygod-darth cylch Mai goedydd.

Vapour surrounding the woods of May. *D. ab Gwilym, i'r niwl.*

> Mygod-darth am ei geden
> Y gwreichion aeth gyach a'r nen.

Vapour round his shaggy coat, the sparks flew up as high as heaven. *R. Iorwerth.*

Mygodfa, *s. f.—pl. t.* oedd (mygawd) An asthma.
Mygodorth, *s. f.* (mygawd—gorth) An oppression of wind; flatulency.

Cwmin, tôri mygodorth, a gwared dolur, a llosgfan croth a wnant.

The cummin will break the *flatulency*, and relieve pain and heat in the womb. *Medd. Myddfai.*

Mygr, *a.* (myg) Majestic, grand, glorious.

> Glyw a'm rhydd——
> Meirch ar geirch yn garcharorion,
> Maith gerdded, mygr gydred gwrdrion.

A chief will present me with steeds upon oats kept prisoners, of extensive career, *splendid*, of equal pace and powerful. *Cynddelw.*

> Carafi eawe Fai forehun ludd,
> A golyg en hwyr hirwyn ei gradd;
> Caraf eilon mygr.——

I love the nightingale of May, obstructing the morning sleep, with languid eyes and aspect long and pale. *Gwalchmai.*

Mygraidd, *a.* (mygr) Of a majestic, grand, or splendid aspect.
Mygrawl, *a.* (mygr) Tending to make majestic, grand, or splendid; beauteous; glorious.
Mygredd, *s. m.* (mygr) Majesty, grandeur; glory.
Mygrfalch, *a.* (mygr—balch) Majestically proud.
Mygriad, *s. m.* (mygr) A rendering majestic, grand, or splendid; a rendering glorious.
Mygru, *v. a.* (mygr) To render majestic, grand, or splendid, to make of glorious appearance.

Mygrwawr, *s. f.* (mygr—gwawr) A splendid ray.
Mygrwedd, *s. f.* (mygr—gwedd) A majestic, or splendid aspect.
Mygu, *v. a.* (mwg) To make smoke, to smoke; to smother, to stifle, to stop the breath, to smoke, or to rise in smoke.
Mygwr, *s. m.—pl.* mygwyr (mygu—gwr) A smoker
Mygydawl, *a.* (mwgwd) Being blindfolded.
Mygydiad, *s. m.* (mwgwd) A blindfolding.
Mygydu, *v. a.* (mwgwd) To blindfold, to blind.
Myhar, *s. m.* (har) The male of sheep, a ram.
Myharan, *s. m.—pl.* myheryn (myhar) A male sheep, a ram, also called *hwrdd*. *Llygaid myheryn*, limpets.

Myharan, tair dafad a dal; un am bob caill iddo, ac un yn lle ei gorph ei hun.

A ram is of the value of three ewes; one for each of his testes, and one in lieu of his own body. *Welsh Laws.*

Myhefin, *s. m.* (hefin) The month of June.
Myher, *s. f.—pl.* myhyr (her) An attack.

Gwirawd a'n gwrthfyn gwrth ser a lloewd,
Gan rwyf rhud rhudd fyhyr.

With liquor we are filled by the light of stars and moon, by a chief of bounty, of ruddy *onset*. *Cynddelw, i O. Gwynedd.*

Myhun, *pron.* (my—hun) Myself. It is mutable into *fyhun*, in which form it mostly occurs in construction.

E ddaeth i'm cyrchaw
Gwedi fy nghrogaw;
Y'nghrog yn greuled
Myhun i'm gwared.

He came to fetch me after I was crucified, being crucified and covered with blood, *myself* to deliver me.
Arwes dyddbrawd.

Myhunan, *pron.* (myhun) Myself, me myself.
Myldardd, *s. m.* (mwl—tardd) That is pervaded with grains, or particles. *Maen myldardd*, the porphyry.
Myllaidd, *a.* (mwll) Of a sultry or hot tendency.
Mylliad, *s. m.* (mwll) A growing sultry or hot.
Myllu, *v. n.* (mwll) To become sultry or warm.
Myllyn, *s. pl. aggr.* (mwll) The violets.
Myllynen, *s. f. dim.* (myllyn) A violet.
Mym, *s. m.* (my—ym) That is incipient.
Mympwy, *s. m.—pl. t.* on (mym—pwy) Opinion, humour, good pleasure.
Mympwyaeth, *s. m.* (mympwy) Opination.
Mympwyaw, *v. a.* (mympwy) To exercise an opinion, humour, or pleasure.
Mympwyawl, *a.* (mympwy) Opinionative.
Mympwyedd, *s. m.* (mympwy) Opinability.
Mympwyoldeb, *s. m.* (mympwyawl) Opinionativeness, a state of opination.
Mymryn, *s. m.—pl. t.* au (mym—rhyn) An atom, a mite; the smallest particle, the least that may be. *Ni fyddi fymryn nes*, thou wilt not be a bit the nearer.

Bychanaf, o'r bychenyd,
Yw Hu Gadarn, fe'i barn byd;
A mwyaf, a nef i ni,
Dy coelwn, a'n Duw celi;
Ysgafn ei daith, ac esgud,
Mymryn tes gloewyn ei glud,
A mawr ar dir, a moroedd,
A mwyaf a gaf ar gyhoedd;
Mwy no 'r bydoedd, 'marbedwn
Amarch gwael i'r mawr hael hwn.

The smallest, should he be compared with small, is the Mighty Hu, the world doth judge; also the greatest, and lord over us, and our God of mystery. Light is his course and swift; a *particle* of lucid sunshine is his car: And, great on land and seas, and the greatest whom I shall manifestly find, yea greater than the worlds: let us beware of mean indignity to this greatly bounteous one.
Rhys Brydydd.

Ni wnai hi erof fi aint
Y mymryn, gwenddyn gwynddaint.

She would not do on my account the least tittle, the white teethed fair one.

Myn, *s. m.—pl. t.* oedd (my—yn) Will, desire.

Tri rhyfraid pob gwaith, nerth, medyr, a myn.

The three necessaries towards every work: power, knowledge, and will. *Adage.*

Myn, *s. m.—pl. t.* od (my) A kid, a young goat.
Myn, *adv.* (myn, *s.*) By the will of, by. *Myn dyn!* By heavens! *Myn fy llaw!* By my hand! *Myn fy ffydd!* By my faith! *Myn diawl!* Mon diable! *Myn y nos!* By the night!

Myn dyn! pan oed lon ein dau
Lawenaf, addyn ael winau!
Taro a wnaeth, trwyn oedd,
Trwst taran — — —

By heavens! when we two were fullest of joy: the nymph with brown eyebrow! the rumbling of thunder violently struck a sudden shock. *D. ab Gwilym.*

Mynach, *s. m.—pl. t.* od (mwn) A separate body, or individual; a monk; a pillar, or supporter in a building, as the post of a tent, or booth, and the four corner posts of a mill frame.

Twyllaw Duw a mynach marw.

To deceive God with a dead monk. *Adage.*

Mynachaeth, *s. m.* (mynach) Monachism.
Mynachawl, *a.* (mynach) Monachal, monastic.
Mynaches, *s. f.—pl. t.* au (mynach) A female recluse, a nun.
Mynachlog, *s. f.—pl. t.* ydd (mynach—llog) A monastery, a covenant.
Mynachlogaidd, *a.* (mynachlog) Monasterial.
Mynad, *s. m.—pl. t.* au (myn) A willing, a desiring; volition; demand.
Mynadwy, *a.* (mynad) That may be willed, desired, desirable, demandable.
Mynag, *s. f.—pl. t.* on (myn) That is uttered, declared, or spoken; a report, or recital.

Arwaesaf i leidr ei fynag.

A warrant for a thief is his own *declaration*. *Adage.*

Mynai, *s. c.* (myn) One who wills or desires.
Mynaidd, *a.* (myn) Like a young goat.
Mynan, *s. c. dim.* (myn) A young kid.
Mynas, *s. f.* (myn) A menace, a threat.
Mynasiad, *s. m.* (mynas) A menacing.
Mynasu, *v. a.* (mynas) To menace, to threaten.

Daeth Corineus, a dwy fwyall deufiniawg yn ei law,—ac yn mynasu ei gyrchu a'r fwyall; ac yna y daethodd cydymdeithion rhyngddynt.

Corineus advanced, brandishing a two-edged battle-ax in his hand, and *menacing* to strike him with the ax; and thereupon some friends came between them. *Gr. ab Arthur.*

Mynaswr, *s. m.—pl.* mynaswyr (mynas—gwr) A menacer, a threatener.
Mynasydd, *s. m.—pl. t.* ion (mynas) A menacer.
Mynaw, *v. a.* (mwn) To penetrate; to stretch or extend out.
Mynawg, *s. m.* (myn) One who exercises his will; one who has his own will.

Rhedaint gorwydd; rhwydd pob traeth;
Cymyg mynawg marchogaeth.

Fleet is the steed; clear is every strand; the fancy of the high-minded one is chivalry. *Llefoed.*

Nid wyf fynawg blin
Ni chwerddaf.——

I am no harassing *high-minded one*; I will not laugh.——
Aneurin.

Mynawg, *a.* (myn) Willing, or desirous; ready to do; courteous, civil. *Gwr mynawg*, a courteous man; *mynawg fonedd*, courteous nobility; *mynawg wedd*, a benign aspect; *mynawg fenwyd*, a benign state of bliss.
Mynawl, *a.* (myn) Relating to the will.
Mynawyd, *s. m.—pl. t.* ydd (mynaw) That penetrates, an awl. *Mynawyd y bugel, y droedrudd*, the crane-bill.

Mynawydaw, *v. a.* (mynawyd) To pierce with an awl; to make use of an awl.
Myncawg, *s. m.* (mwng) Heath, or ling; also called *grug*, and *myncoch*.
Mynci, *s. m.—pl. t.* au (mwng) A hame.
Myncyn, *s. m. dim.* (mwng) A hame.
Mynechdid, *s. f.* (mynach) A monastery.
Myned, *v. a.* (mwn—ed) To individualize; to depart; to set out, to set off, to go. *Myned â'r gamp*, to bear away the palm.

Wedi myned âr gyrn a phibau.

After *going* on horns and pipes: or, become the common talk. *Adage.*

Nid myned a ddel eilwaith.

It is no *going* as to what comes again. *Adage.*

Myned â'r maen i'r wal.

To go with the stone to the wall. *Adage.*

Gwedi myn'd, er ail Indeg,
Hyd yn dy fron, y don deg!

After *going*, for the sake of the one like Indeg, into thy bosom, thou fair wave! *D. ab Gwilym.*

Mynedawl, *a.* (myned) Relating to departure.
Mynedfa, *s. f.—pl. t.* au (myned) Departure, a setting off; a procession.
Mynediad, *s. m.—pl. t.* au (myned) A going, or proceeding; a setting out, a departing.
Mynediant, *s. m.* (myned) A going; a departure.
Mynediw, *a.* (myned) Condescending, willing.
Mynedwy, *s. m.* (myned—gwy) A running water.

Lliw ewyn—lli llyn mynedwy.

The hue of the foam of the flood of a pool of *running water*. *Br. fwyn.*

Mynegadwy, *a.* (mynag) Expressible, utterable.
Mynegai, *s. c. pl.* mynegeion (mynag) That informs, tells, or points out: an index.
Mynegawl, *a.* (mynag) Expressive, indicative.
Mynegedig, *a.* (mynag) Expressed, or declared.
Mynegfa, *s. f.* (mynag) A catalogue.
Mynegfys, *s. m.—pl. t.* edd (mynag—bys) The pointing finger, the fore-finger.
Mynegi, *v. a.* (mynag) To express, to tell, to relate, to report, to declare, to inform.

Meddyliau dynion, na'u hewyllys, nis gwyr neb ond Duw ehun, ac y neb y myno Duw ei fynegi iddo.

The thoughts of men, nor their will, none knows except God himself, and such as God would *declare* to. *Elucidarius.*

Mynegiad, *s. m.—pl. t.* au (mynag) A telling, expressing, or informing; a declaration, relation, or information.
Mynegiadawl, *a.* (mynegiad) Declaratory.
Mynegiadu, *v. a.* (mynegiad) To make a declaration or relation.
Mynegiaeth, *s. m.* (myneg) A recital, a report.

Mae Lloegr yn wag, a'm llygru a wnaeth;
Mae'n wagach Cymry o'r mynegiaeth.

England is empty, and I am spoiled; Wales is more empty from the *recital*. *L. G. Cothi, i Edmund i. Richmond.*

Mynegiannu, *v. a.* (mynegiant) To make a declaration or recital.
Mynegiannus, *a.* (mynegiant) Declaratory.
Mynegiant, *s. m.* (mynag) A declaration.
Mynegin, *a.* (mynag) Expressive, declarative.
Myneginiaeth, *s. m.* (mynegin) Expression.

Yn mhob pall—
Genyd mae myneginiaeth.

In every failure thou hast a *way to express*. *H. D. ab Ifan.*

Mynegwr, *s. m.—pl.* mynegwyr (mynag—gwr) A teller, a declarer, a reporter, a reciter.
Mynegydd, *s. m.—pl. t.* ion (mynag) A reciter.
Mynen, *s. f. dim.* (myn) A little she kid.
Myniad, *s. m.* (myn) A willing, a having, or obtaining.
Mynial, *s. m.* (mwn) A guttural speaking.
Myniant, *s. m.* (myn) Volition, willing.
Myniar, *s. f.—pl.* mynieir (mwn—iar) A snipe.
Myniator, *ger.* (myniad) In willing; in obtaining, or in having.
Myniedydd, *s. m.—pl. t.* ion (myniad) One who obtains, or procures; a procurer.
Mynig, *a.* (myn) Apt to exert the will, willing.
Mynitor, *sup.* (myn) To be exerting the will.
Myniw, *a.* (mwn) Tending to project; jutting; peninsulated.
Mynogaeth, *s. m.* (mynawg) Courtesy, benignity, gentleness; humanity.
Mynogan, *s. c. dim.* (mynawg) A courteous one.
Mynogawl, *a.* (mynawg) Of a courteous nature.
Mynogen, *s. f. dim.* (mynawg) A courteous female
Mynogi, *s. m.* (mynawg) Courtesy, benignity, gentleness; humanity; generosity.

Ni wddant fan-feirdd; ni mawr gynfydd
Pwy a ennillo, o'r do ysydd·
Edewis earwas clos cymreydd
Cenawon Mordal mynogi rhydd.

The puny poetasters know nought; there will be no looking for who shall bear the prize, of the present race, the splendid youth of the region of the mountains has left the whelps of Mordal of unrestrained *courtesy*. *Meilyr.*

Yfais o'i win
O falch fuelin,
A'i wisgoedd eurin,
A'i fynogi.

I drank of his wine out of the proud bugle horn, and his golden vests, and his *courtesy* I enjoyed. *Ll. P. Moch, i Lywelyn II.*

Gwrndeyrn Prydain, prawf fy llochi
A'th aur rhudd, a'th fudd, a'th fynogi.

Splendid prince of Britain, essay to support me with thy ruddy gold, and thy favour, and thy *courtesy*. *Ll. P. Moch, i D. ab Owain.*

Mynogiant, *s. m.* (mynawg) Courtesy, benignity
Mynogrwydd, *s. m.* (mynawg) Courteousness.

Och am naf, am ner diwydrwydd!
Och am ner nawner mynogrwydd!

Woe for the loss of the chief, for the lord of sincerity! Woe for the loss of the lord, the support of *humanity*! *D. Benfras.*

Mynor, *s. m.—pl. t.* ion (mwn) Marble. *Maen mynor*, marble stone.
Mynoraidd, *a.* (mynor) Like marble.
Mynorain, *a.* (mynor) Marmoreous.
Mynorawg, *a.* (mynor) Abounding in marble.
Mynorawl, *a.* (mynor) Of the quality of marble.
Mynoren, *s. f. dim.* (mynor) A piece of marble.
Mynori, *v. a.* (mynor) To incrust with marble; to become marble.
Mynoriad, *s. m.* (mynor) Marmoration.
Mynta, *s. f.—pl. t.* oedd (mwnt) An aggregate; a million; also called *Buna*.

Deg rhialles yn y fynta.

Ten hundred thousand in a million. *Adage.*

Myntai, *s. f.—pl.* mynteioedd (mwnt) That is aggregated; a multitude, or a host; a troop. *Mynteioedd byd*, the multitudes of the world.
Mynteiad, *s. m.* (myntai) A congregating.
Mynteiaw, *v. a.* (myntai) To congregate.
Mynteiawg, *a.* (myntai) Congregated.
Mynteiawl, *a.* (myntai) Congregating.
Mynteiwr, *s. m.—pl.* mynteiwyr (myntai—gwr) One who collects together a company.
Myntumiad, *s. m.* (tumiad) A leading on, or encouraging; a supporting, a maintaining.
Myntumiaw, *v. a.* (tumiaw) To lead on, to encourage; to support, to maintain.
Myntumiawg, *a.* (tumiawg) Having encouragement; supported, maintained.
Myntumiawl, *a.* (tumiawl) Tending to lead on.
Myntumiwr, *s. m.—pl.* myntumwyr (tumiwr) An encourager; supporter.

Mynu, *v. a.* (myn) To exercise the will; to obtain sway; to obtain, to have; to seek, to procure; to insist, to will. *A fyni di beth?* Wilt thou have some? *Mynaf*, I will have.

Ni fyn pan gaffo, ni chaiff pan fyno.

He that will not (have) when he may
When he will (have) he shall have nay. *Adage.*

Perchen tir dietifedd o'i gorff a ddichawn briodoli ei dir i'r neb a myno.

A proprietor of land without heir of his body can appropriate his land to whomsoever he *chooses*. *Welsh Laws.*

Y fun a all a fyno,
Ai byw o wan, ai na bo;
Ni ddichon meddygon mai
Yn cinioes, ond tra mynai.

The fair that can do what she *pleases*, whether a poor wight is to live, or that he shall not; the physicians of May will not be able to preserve my life, but whilst *she chooses*. *Bedo Brwynllys.*

Mynud, *s. m.—pl. t.* iau (myn) That is courteous, or social.

Guawd nyth eryr yn mlaen dar,
Ac yn nghyfyrdy gwyr llachar.
Golwg fynud ar a gar.

Common is the eagle's nest in the top of the oak, and in the assembly house violent men: the eye of the *fond one* is on whom he loves. *Llywarch Hen.*

Mynud, *a.* (myn) Courteous; social; fond.

Ef yn llafar, ef yn fud, ef yn fynud
Ef yn wrdd, ef yn ddrud, pan dremyn dros dud.

He is eloquent, he is dumb, he is *courteous*, he is ardent, he is bold when he takes a glance over the land. *Taliesin, i'r gwynt.*

Mynud wrth foled, wrth filwyr bu gwrdd,
Bu gorddwy ar Allmyr;
Cadyr wryd, bryd Bran fab Llyr,
Cedawl, arwynawl eryr.

Attentive to praise, to warriors he was violent, he was a ruler on the foreign men, mighty of body, with the mind of Bran son of Llyr, a bounteous and fierce eagle. *D. Llwgwrn Mew.*

Mynudaw, *v. a.* (mynud) To act kindly, or civilly; to become kind or civil.

Mynudawl, *a.* (mynud) Of courteous disposition.

Mynudedd, *s. m.* (mynud) Courteousness.

Mynudrwydd, *s. m.* (mynud) Courteous deportment or behaviour; civility.

Mynudwr, *s. m.—pl.* mynudwyr (mynud—gwr) A man of courteous manners.

Mynudyn, *s. m. dim.* (mynud) A gesture, a deportment, or conduct.

Mae yn dy garu fwyaf dyn
Ar ei gair a'i mynudyn.

She loves thee above all men, in her word and her *deportment*. *T. Ll. D. ab Hywel.*

Mynw, *s. m.* (mwn) That has action; a person; a body.

Mab Cedifor, cad ormail———
Mynw ton, tremid y dygyrch,
Maen garn'———

The son of Cedifor, the tyrant of the battle, with a *body* of the ... of the wave, his approach to the stone covering has been seen! *Cynddelw.*

Yn myw mynw a fu fuchiau beirddion;
Yn mucheddi gwledig gwlad orchorddion,
Gorddyfnws uddudd budd a lwrthon.

In life when a man his bosom was the refuge of bards, in the existence of the sovereign of the superior regions, he bequeathed to them profit and riches. *Cynddelw, m. Cad. ab Madawg.*

Rhy dalaf ym rhwyf———
Delw ym peirch a meirch megr hydaith
Mynw elion, mal gwyllon goddaith.

I will repay to my chief as he shall treat me with fair steeds impatient for the course, with *body* of the hind skimming like the spectres of the conflagration. *Cynddelw.*

Mynw, *a.* (mwn) Quick, active, apt.

Machograg mwyndawr, mynw gyfod i gad,
Mygr frwfnol, flaidd ood;
Anghudd uchl ordelw hynod
Angerdd flawdd anghlawdd anghlod.

Machograg greatly kind, for war was quick to rise, the splendid leader was a wolf to tear, and had his rank in bold career of will commotion, to prevent disgrace. *Cynddelw, m. t. O. Gwynedd.*

Mynwar, *s. f.—pl.* mynweir (mwn—gwar) A collar; a collar of draught harness.

Mynwawl, *a.* (mynw) Corporeous; personal.

Gweled yn myned mynwawl ddeddfau
Gwyl gylarchafael, na chwl amheuon,
Goreugynws Mab Duw.—

The *corporeal* principles were seen to be going on the festival of the ascension, doubt not the memorial, the Son of God ascended. *Ein. ab Gwalchmai.*

Mynwed, *s. f.* (mynw) Fellowship, company.

Ei eirchion i eirchiaid ar lled,
A'i aur rhudd, a'i fudd, a'i fynwed.

His favours scattered amongst suitors, with his ruddy gold, his bounty, and his *society*. *Ll. P. Moch, i R. Gryg.*

Mynwen, *s. f.—pl. t.* au (mynw) A sepulchre.

Rhaid yw weithian
Ai addef it' fal ydd wy, wen,
Ai f'anneddu ei i'r fynwen!

It is necessary at length, either to explain my condition to thee, fair maid, or the *grave* will become my dwelling! *R. Iolo.*

Mynwennawl, *a.* (mynwent) Monumental.

Mynwent, *s. f.—pl. t.* ydd (mynw) A sepulchre, a grave, a church-yard, a burial place.

Cyn plygu Rodri rwydd esgar, yn Mon,
Mynwentydd bu braenar.

Before Rodri was made to bend by the prosperous foe, in Mon, the *burial grounds* were made a fallow. *Ll. P. Moch.*

Mynwes, *s. f.—pl. t.* au (mynw) The bosom.

Gwae a fo a'i fefl yn ei fynwes.

Woe to such as carries his disgrace in his bosom. *Adage.*

Mynwesawl, *a.* (mynwes) Belonging to the bosom

Mynwesiad, *s. m.* (mynwes) A putting to or in the bosom.

Mynwesu, *v. a.* (mynwes) To put to the bosom.

Mynwor, *s. f.—pl. t.* au (mwn—gwor) A collar; a collar belonging to draught harness.

Aur melyn am ewyn mor
Tresi man tros ei mynwor.

Like yellow gold round the foam of the sea are the delicate traces over her *collar*. *D. ab Gwilym, i wallt Morfudd.*

Myny, *s. m.* (mwn) That rises or ascends. With the preposition *i*, to, it forms adverbs; as *I fyny*, upwards, up, aloft: *Awn i fyny*, we will go up. In Gwent, *mynydd* is used.

Mynych, *a.* (mwn) Frequent, often. *Yn fynych*, frequently. *adv.* Frequently, often.

Bach a mynych fwyta, bach ac anfynych ddiota.

Little and *frequent* eating, little and unfrequent drinking. *Adage.*

Atfai gell i gi mynych ydd a iddi.

Should a dog have a chamber he would *often* go into it. *Adage.*

Mynychawl, *a.* (mynych) Frequentative.

Mynychedig, *a.* (mynych) Being frequented.

Mynychedd, *s. m.* (mynych) Frequency.

Mynychiad, *s. m.—pl. t.* au (mynych) Iteration, a rendering frequent; frequentation.

Mynychrwydd, *s. m.* (mynych) Frequentness.

Mynychu, *v. a.* (mynych) To frequent; to iterate

Ac felly y bu ef yn mynychu atri drwy yspaid saith mlynedd, heb wybod o neb, eithr ei anwyliaid chun a oedd yn ei gwarchadw.

And in that manner he was *frequenting* to her during the space of seven years, without any one knowing, except his own confidential friends who were guarding her. *Gr. ab Arthur.*

Mynychwedd, *s. f.* (mynych—gwedd) A variety of forms, or appearances. *a.* Of many forms.

Mynychwedd arall
Mewn meddgyrn bual,
Meddgar hail hwyl medlaid

Variety of attendance with mead in buffalo horns, handsome the service exciting praise. *Einion Offeiriad.*

Mynychwr, *s. m.—pl.* mynychwyr (mynych—gwr) A frequenter.

Mynychydd, *s. m.—pl. t.* ion (mynych) A frequenter.

s. m. (mwn) That is a small part or par-
a minute.
, s. m.—pl. t. oedd (mwn) A mountain.
dd, upwards. See mynу.

well angheuawg mor nag angheuawg mynydd.

accustoms at sea is better than the accustoms of the
in. *Adage.*

Rhydd o'r blaen oedd y fenor,
Os rhydd y mynydd a'r mor.

therefore was the country, if free the mountain and the
G. ab I. Tew.

awg, a. (mynydd) Mountainous, hilly.
awl, a. (mynydd) Of the mountain.
-dir, s. m.—pl. t. oedd (mynydd—tir)
tain ground.
iad, s. m.—pl. mynyddiaid (mynydd) A
aineer, or inhabitant of the mountains.
ig, a. (mynydd) Mountainous, hilly.
wr, s.m.—pl.mynyddwyr(mynydd—gwr)
ntaineer, or man of the mountain.
yn, s. m. dim.(mynydd)A small mountain
wg, s. f. (mwnwgl) The quinsy; the
nightshade, or bitter-sweet.
llws, s. m.—pl. mynygldlysau (mwnwgl—
A neck ornament.
lorch, s. f.—pl. mynygldyrch (mwnwgl—
A collar or wreath for the neck.
wisg, s. f.—pl. t. oedd (mwnwgl—gwisg)
-kerchief; a neck-cloth.
s. m. dim. (myn) A little he kid.
g, a. (mwng) Having a mane; maned.

Nis crawn cod esgud rhag ygwn,
Na thalawg myngawg, na myngdwn.

the heedless, nor the proud will collect treasure; nor a
ith long mane, nor he that is cropt. *Cynddelw.*

rn, a. (mwng—twn) Having a cropt mane

E'm rhoddes o feirch—
Llawn do, a dwn, a myngdwn melyn.

ve me of steeds, some black, and dun, and mane-cropt yel-
Gwalchmai.

, s. f. dim. (mwng) The crest of a horse.
s, a. (mwng—bras) Thick-maned.

Meirch mwth myngfras
Y dan morddwyd mygrwas.

and thick-maned steeds under the thigh of the splendid
Aneurin.

, s. m. (mwng) A gutteral manner of
ing.
, v. a. (mwngial) To speak gutterally.
s, a. (myngial) Gutterally speaking.
s, a. (mwng—llaes) Having long mane.
rd, a. (mwng—llwyd) Grey-maned.
l, a. (mwng) Being of the throat. *Siarad
glyd*, to speak indistinctly, or thickly.
a. (mwng) Of the throat, gutteral. *Dyn
s*, a person who speaks indistinctly, mut-
ly, or through the nose.
n, a. (mwng—gwen) White-maned.
n, a. (mwng—gwyn) White-maned.
m. (my—yr) That is essential, or pure;
intellectual. a. Essential, pure, or holy.

Mynw cofu, colofn cyfwyrain,
Myr meddgyrn mechdeyrn Mechain.

person, a towering column, the *spirit* of meadhorns is
reign of Mechain. *Cynddelw, i O. Cyfeiliawg.*

Mair forwynaidd mor addwynaidd;
Mair gyflawnaidd myr gyflawnau.

chaste of nature so benign; Mary all complete in *holy*
es. *I. ab R. ab I. Llwyd.*

t. aggr. (mor) That is infinite, and fluc-
; an aggregate of floods, or the sea, also
r emmets.

Llifawd fy nghendawd fy nghyd oed dydd;
Llofrudd fy neurudd yn awr echwydd;
Lloufer eilyr myr morfeydd dylan,
Pan llewych huan ar fan fynydd.

My companion in my day's assignation bade my *muse* to flow;
the spoiler of my cheeks in the evening hour; she that is bright
like the light over the *gulfs* of the *sea* amidst the surrounding
shores, when the sun illumes the lofty mountain. *Ior. Fychan.*

Myraeth, s. m. (myr) Purity, or essence.
Myrdwyn, s. m.—pl. t. au (myr—twyn) An ant-
hillock.
Myrdd, s.m.—pl.t.oedd(myr) Infinity; a myriad;
or ten thousand. *Mil-can-myrdd*, a hundred
thousand myriads.

Gwell un haul no myrdd o ser.

Better is one sun than a *myriad* of stars. *Adage.*

Caffant fyrdd o feirddion eu llus
O foli Rodri ryodres.

A *myriad* of bards will find their benefit from praising Rodri
the magnificent. *Ll. P. Moch.*

Myrddfed, s. m. (myrdd) One of a myriad. a.
Belonging to one out of a myriad.
Myrddiwn, s. m.—pl. myrddlynau (myrdd) A
million.
Myrddiynfed, s. m. (myrddiwn) A millionth. a.
Millionth.
Myred, s. m. (myr) That is pure or essential.
Myredd, s. m. (myr) A pure or essential state.
Myriad, s. m. (myr) A making pure or fair.
Myriawl, a. (myr) Of essential nature.
Myrion, s. pl. aggr. (myr) Ants, or emmets.

Gwneuther mynydd o dwmpath myrion.

To make a mountain of the *ants'* hill. *Adage.*

Myrionen, s. f. dim. (myrion) An emmet.
Myrnder, s. m. (mwrn) Sultriness, closeness.
Myrndra, s. m. (mwrn) Sultriness, closeness.
Myrnedd, s. m. (mwrn) Sultriness, closeness.
Myrniad, s. m. (mwrn) A growing sultry.
Myrniaw, v. n. (mwrn) To become sultry.
Myrierid, s. pl. aggr. (myr—iar) Pearls.

It' heu fy ngherdd nag ef fd
Mal heu rhag moch myrierid.

The spreading of my songs before thee, be it not like casting
pearls before swine. *Ll. P. Moch.*

Myrieriden, s. f. dim. (myrierid) A pearl.
Myrweryd, s. m. (myr—gwerydd) A cause of
motion; distraction; delirium.

Mydwyf myrwerydd
Molawd Duw Dadfydd.

I am *agitator* of the praise of God the renovator. *Taliesin*

Nid oes yn cadw oes, a moes, a mynadydd
Llwyth Maried mawreddus eu merweryddd.

There is no one supporting life, and manners, and courtesy, of
the tribe of Maried dignified their *cause of agitation.*
Gw. Brycheiniawg i Ddewi.

Prudd fydd yn myrwerydd mor
Y llong a goilo ei hanger.

Dismal will be in the *tumult* of the sea the ship that should lose
its anchor. *W. Llyn.*

Myrydd, s. pl. aggr. (myr) The sea rushes.
Mysangu, v. a. (sangu) To trample, to tread.

Caersalem a fysangir tan draed.

Jerusalem *will be trampled* under feet. *W. Salisbury.*

Mysawr, s. m. (mws) That is of strong scent.
Mysg, s. m. (my—ysg) The midst, the middle.
Yn mysg, ar fysg, i fysg, amongst.

Trydydd Arianllu Ynys Prydain a elei gan Gaswallawn fab Beli,
a Gwenwynwyn a Gwanar, meibion Lliaf fab Nwyfre, ac Arianrod
ferch Beli eu mam; a'r gwyr hyn o Erch a Heiniad pan hanoedd-
ynt; ac a aethynt gyda Chaswallawn eu hewythr ar fysg y Cesar.
laid o'r ynys hon: Sef lle y mae y gwyr hyny yn Ngwasgwyn.

The third silver host of the isle of Britain went with Caswallon
son of Beli, and Gwenwynwyn and Gwanar, the sons of Lliaf son
of Nwyfre, and Arianrod, daughter of Beli, their mother: and
those men were natives of Erch and Heledd; and they went
with Caswallon their uncle *amongst* the Caesarians out of this
island: Where those men dwell is Gascogne. *Trioedd.*

Mysgaid, *a.* (mysg) Mixt, or compound.
Mysgawl, *a* (mysg) Tending to mix; compound.
Mysgedig, *a.* (mysg) Being mixed or blended.
Mysgedd, *s. m.* (mysg) The state of being mixed.
Mysgi, *s. m.* (mysg) A mixed state; confusion.

Gwryd arddercliawg marchawg mysgi.

The exalted manliness of the knight of *tumult*. *Aneurin.*

Mysgiad, *s. m.* (mysg) A mixing, a blending.
Mysglwyth, *s. m.* (mysg—llwyth) A mixed race.
Mysgu, *v. a.* (mysg) To mix, to mingle, to blend.
Mysorig, *a.* (mysawr) Yielding a stench. *Wy mysorig*, an addle egg.
Myswrn, *s. m.—pl.* mysyrnau (swrn) Any small edged tool, or instrument.
Myswynog, *s. f.—pl. t.* au (swynog) A farrow cow, a cow that has passed a season without calving, and has milk through the winter.
Mysygan, *s. f.* (sygan) Soft expression.
Mysygandawd, *s. m.* (mysygan) Fond language.
Mysyganu, *v. a.* (mysygan) To use soft language.
Mysyglawg, *a.* (mwswgl) Having moss, mossy.

Ni bydd maen mysyglawg o'i fynych drafod.

A stone will not be *mossy* that is frequently turned. *Adage.*

Mysygliad, *s. m.* (mwswgl) A gathering of moss.
Mysyglu, *v. n.* (mwswgl) To gather moss.

Y maen a dreigla ni fysygla.

The stone that rolls no *moss will gather*. *Adage.*

Mysyniad, *s. m.* (mwswn) A gathering of moss.
Mysynllyd, *a.* (mwswn) Apt to gather moss.
Mysynu, *v. n.* (mwswn) To gather moss.

Maen a dreigla ni fysyna.

A stone that rolls *will gather* no moss. *Adage.*

Myth, *a.* (my—yth) That pervades; that infects; a miasma.
Mythder, *s. m.* (mwth) Swiftness, velocity.
Mythdra, *s. m.* (mwth) Swiftness, velocity.
Mythiad, *s. m.* (mwth) A giving swiftness.
Mythliad, *s. m.* (mythl) A rendering torpid.
Mythlu, *v.* (mythl) To make torpid; to canker.
Mythu, *v. a.* (mwth) To give swiftness.
Mythl, *s. m.—pl. t.* ion (myth) The state of being pervaded, or infected

Llwyr gwae fi, wyf gwyst gwyd,
Mythl oerwych gael mythl grwnd!

I am quite wretched with the life of disappointment, that the coldly torturing *canker* should find a way to spoil thee!
D. ab Gwilym, i'r fedwen.

Mywyliau, *s. pl. aggr.* (gwyl) Vigils, or eves of holidays.

Pan ddaw y garawys,
Mal y daw mywyliau dwys.

When lent shall come as the incessant *vigils* come.
M. ab Rhys.

Myw, *s. m.* (my) That has activity, motion, or life; an ant, or emmet.
Mywion, *s. pl. aggr.* (myw) Ants, pismires; also called *grugiaid*, *morion*, *myr*, and *myrion*.

Pan fo'r mywion mewn clyd letty,
Heb na gwynt, na gwlaw i'w drygu,
Ceir y ceiliog rhedyn ynfyd
Gwedi rhynu a marw o annwyd.

When the *ants* are in warm lodging, with neither wind nor rain to hurt them, the silly grasshopper will be found stiff and dead in the cold. *Engl. Hawdd ei Helyw.*

Mywionyn, *s. m. dim.* (mywion) An ant, emmet.

Oni weli di'r mywionyn,
A'r segurllyd geiliog rhedyn;
Pan fo'r naill yn cywain adre—
Bydd y llall heb ofal arno.

Dost thou not see the *ant* and the idle grasshopper; when the one is carrying home, the other is void of care.
Engl. Hawdd ei Helyw.

Mywyn, *s. m.* (gwyn) Pith; also called mwydion.
Mywynaidd, *a.* (mywyn) Like pith; pithy.
Mywynawg, *a.* (mywyn) Abounding with pith.
Mywynt, *s m.* (mywyn) The pith, or core.

N.

NA, *s. m. r.* A cessation of concomitancy, or a negation of proceeding with; that implies a negative or denial; a no.

Gwell na no gau addewid.

A *no* is better than a false promise. *Llefoed.*

Fy llysfam a dyngwys im na chaffwyf wraig byth hyd na chaffwyf Olwen.

My mother in law did swear to me that I should not ever have a wife until *that* I should have Olwen
H. Culhwch—Mabinogion.

Na, *conj.* Nor, neither; either. *Dyma beth heb na dechreu na diwedd*, here is a thing without either beginning or end. It is used before a word with a consonant initial.—*Na'm*, nor my; *na'th*, nor thy; *na'i*, nor his, nor her; *na'n*, nor our; *na'ch*, nor your; *na'u*, nor their: Contractions of *na ym*, *na yth*, *na ei*, *na ein*, *na eich*, *na eu*. *Na ym caseir*, may I not be hated.

Ni fyn cariad ei wadu,
Na'i ddangaws i lu.

Love will not have itself concealed, *nor* its being shewn to a crowd of people. *D. ab Gwilym.*

Na, *adv.* No, not, with imperative verbs, and in answering interrogatories, when governed by a verb with a consonant initial. *Na ladd*, thou shalt not kill: *A fu hi yno?* Has she been there? *Na fu*, or *na ddo*, not been, not taken place, or she has not been. It is equivalent to *that*, or that not, in wishing; as, *Na buasit ti yno!* O that thou hadst been there!

Na choll dy hen-ffordd er dy ffordd newydd.

Lose *not* thy old way for the sake of thy new way. *Adage.*

A fu ei ddoethach byd Fon?
Na fu un o nef i Elnion!

Has there been one wiser than him from here to Mon? there has *not* been one from heaven to Elnion! *L. G. Cothi.*

Nabod, *s. m.—pl. t.* au (na—bod) Cognizance.
Nabod, *v. a.* (na—bod) To know, to recognise.

Celfydd tafod hawdd ei nabod.

A tongue art'ul is easily *known*. *Adage.*

Wrth eu gweithredoedd nesa'
Y mae nabod drwg a da.

By their nearest works they are *to be known*, the evil and the good. *T. Ll. D. ab Hywel.*

Nabodaeth, *s. m.* (nabod) Cognition, cognizance.
Nabodiad, *s. m.* (nabod) Cognition, a knowing.
Nabyddadwy, *a.* (nabyddu) Cognoscible.
Nabyddiad, *s. m.* (nabyddu) Cognition.
Nabyddiaeth, *s. m.* (nabyddu) Cognizance.
Nabyddu, *v. n.* (nabod) To recognise, to know.

Nabydded fined fy mro,
Wb! o'r hin o'r wybr heno!

Let her know how afflicting my condition, lo! what weather from the firmament to night! *D. ab Gwilym.*

Nid wrth faint ei leferydd
Y nebyddir dyn dedwydd.

Not by the magnitude of his discourse is the virtuous man *to be known*. *T. Ll. D. ab Hywel.*

Nabyddus, *a.* (nabyddu) Cogniscitive.

Nac, *conj.* (na) Nor, neither; either. It is used before words, with vowel initials, as *na* precedes those with consonant initials.

Nac, *adv.* No, not, in negative imperatives, and in negative answers; than, in phrases of comparison; and that, or, oh that, in expressions of wishing. It is used before words with vowel initials for NA, which precedes consonant initials. *Nac ammheu*, doubt not.

Gwell nac nog addaw ni wnëydd.

Better is a *denial* than to promise what will not be done. *Adage.*

Naca, *v. a.* (nac) To make a denial, to deny.

Nacâd, *s. m.* (naca) Abnegation, a refusal.

Nacâawl, *a.* (naca) Belonging to denial, negative.

Nacâu, *v. a.* (naca) To refuse, or to deny.

Medd yr enaid——
A dreuliais a fu fau;
A roddais a sy fau;
A gedwais a gollais;
A nacâais sydd i'm colli.

Saith the soul—what I have wasted has been mine; what I have given is mine; what I saved I have lost; what I *refused* is to consign me to perdition.

Nacäus, *a.* (naca) Apt to deny; denying.

Nacâwr, *s. m.—pl.* nacâwyr (naca—gwr) A refuser, a denyer.

Nacwy, *a.* (nac) Tending to deny; negative.

I'r Ner edmygir, oedd nacwy o serch,
Uniawn hoewdeg ferch o Nanheudwy.

To the Lord be she hallowed, that was *negative* of love, the upright and briskly fair maid of Nanheudwy. *Sefnyn.*

Nach, *s. m.—pl.* neichiau (na—ach) That is obstructive. *Brys-neichiau cad*, the sudden efforts of battle.

Nad, *s. f.—pl. t.* au (na—ad) A shrill cry, a howl; clamour, noise. *Taw a dy nadau drwg*, have done with thy ugly cries.

Nâd, *s. m.* (na) A conditional negative or no. *adv.* That, that not. It is used before words with vowel initials. *O, nad elai hi yno!* O, that she would but go there! *Pan nad oeddwn yno*, when that I was not there.

Och wyr, nad aethant yn wreigedd.

Fie on the men, *that* they are *not* become women. *Adage.*

Och Dduw Tad, o chuddiwyd hi,
Nad oeddwn amdo iddi.

Oh! God the Father, since she has been covered over, *that* I had *not* been a shroud for her. *D. Nanmor.*

Nadael, *v. a.* (nad) To hinder, to obstruct. *Nad iddi fyned*, hinder her from going; *nedais iti dalu*, I hindered thee from paying.

Nadawl, *a.* (nad) Tending to hinder, obstructive.

Nadel, *v. a.* (nad) To hinder, to obstruct.

Nadiad, *s. m.* (nad) A hindering, or obstructing.

Nadredd, *s. pl. aggr.* (nadr) Snakes, adders.

Nadreddawg, *a.* (nadredd) Abounding with snakes

Nadu, *v. a.* (nad) To utter shrill cries, to howl.

Nadwr, *s. m.—pl.* nadwyr (nad—gwr) One who utters shrill cries, a screamer.

Nadr, *s. f.—pl. t.* odd (nad) A snake.

Nadd, *s. m.—pl. t.* ion (ny—add) That is whole, complete, or entire; that is formed, wrought or worked; that is cut or chipt.

Nadd, *a.* (ny—add) That is complete or whole; wrought, or worked. *Careg nadd*, a stone that may be wrought, or a free stone.

Pa beth a wnei—
O gofyn ferw-ddyn y fost
Rhan nadd yr hyn ni wyddost?

What wilt thou do if a rattling chap of boasting should ask about the *artificial* part, the which thou dost not know? *Edm. Prys, i W. Cynwal.*

Naddadwy, *a.* (nadd) Capable of being wrought into form; capable of being hewn.

Naddawl, *a.* (nadd) Relating to a working or hewing into form; hewing; sculpturing.

Dywed imi—— hanes y beirdd;
Pa wyr fu ar gerdd gu gynt
Naddawl athrawon iddynt.

Declare to me the history of the bards: what men were, of the lovely song of yore, *instructive* teachers to them. *Edm. Prys.*

Naddedig, *a.* (nadd) Being wrought or worked into form; hewn, cut, or chipt.

Naddedigaeth, *s. m.* (naddedig) The act of working into form; the act of chipping.

Naddfaen, *s. m.—pl.* naddfeini (nadd—maen) A stone that may be worked; free stone; hewn stone.

Costau——
Ieuan ran rwydd, dŷ difeth,
Naddfain, a gwyngalch, falch fath;
Neb ni chyst y rhyw byst byth.

Ieuan, of liberal parts, bore the expence of a substantial house, of *wrought stones*, and white wash, proud the plan; no one will ever bear the cost of similar pillars. *Hillyn.*

Naddiad, *s. m.—pl. t.* au (nadd) A working into form; a cutting, hewing, or chipping.

Naddiad dy foch nadd yn rhwy.

The *cutting* of thy cheek let it be cut close. *Adage.*

Naddial, *v. a.* (nadd) To be cutting or chipping.

Naddiaeth, *s. m.* (nadd) The practice or art of hewing into form.

Naddiaeth befr ni ddaw o'th ben,
Er neb, ond mydr annyben.

No fairly *formed subject* will come out of thy lips, for the sake of any body, but a drawling verse. *Edm. Prys.*

Naddiant, *s. m.* (nadd) The act of working into form; the state of being wrought.

Naddion, *s. pl.* (nadd) Chippings, shreds, lint.

Naddo, *adv.* (na—do) Not done, not taken place.

Naddu, *v. a.* (nadd) To work or cut into form; to hew, to cut, to chip.

Awn i wersyll y Syriaid: o cadwant hwy ni yn fyw, byw fyddwn; ac os naddant ni, byddwn feirw.

Let us go into the camp of the Syrians. if they will preserve us alive, we shall live; and if they will *cut us off*, we shall die. *S. Trefredyn.*

Naddwr, *s. m.—pl.* naddwyr (nadd—gwr) One who works or cuts into form; a hewer, a chipper.

Naf, *s. m.—pl.* neifion (ny—af) That embraces or comprehends, a forming principle; one that forms, or constructs, a creator; the Lord.

Pwyll a'm cyfeiryd,
O'r creawdr, o'r cyd
O'r Mab, o'r Ysbryd,
O'r iawnfryd fri;
O'r Drindawd Undawd, un dras â mi,
Un dra dragaredd, unwedd ofri;
Undeg dair person,
Uch archengylion,
Undonion neifion,
Nerth heb drengi.

Reason informs me of the Creator, of the junction of the Son, of the Spirit, of the rightly conceived pre-eminence; of the Trine Unity, one in kindred with me, one excelling in mercy, of universal glory; three persons in one fairly joined, higher than archangels, *creators* one in attributes, of power without end. *Gwalchmai.*

Nafawl, *a.* (naf) Relating to formation; being wrought or formed.

Nafiad, *s. m.—pl. t.* au (naf) An operation.

Diwg y rhoed ar dy grair
Dyfiad heb nafiad nafair.

Fairly has been bestowed on thy jewel a growth without the *operation* of a hand. *H. ab D. ab I. ab Rhys.*

Na ddifa na nafa neb,
Gochel wneuthur creulondeb.

Destroy not, cut not any body, beware of doing a cruelty. *M.-r. Talu*.

Nag, *s. m.* (na) A negative; a denial.

Gwell nag nog addaw ai wneir.

Better a *refusal* than to promise what will not be done. *Adage.*

Gwell nag no dau eddewid.

A *denial* is better than two promises. *Adage.*

——Cair gweled
Nad da mynych nag am ged.

It shall be seen that a frequent *denial* of a boon is not good. *Llywarch Hen.*

Nag, *conj.* (na) Nor, neither; either. It is used before words with vowel initials.

Nag, *adv.* (na) No, not; that, o that. It is used before words with vowel initials. *Nag ê*, no not, not it, it not, or not so; *nag ydyw*, *nag yw*, it is not; *nag oes*, there is not; *nag af*, I will not go; *nag wyf*, I am not; *nag wyt*, thou art not; *nag yw*, he she or it is not; *nag ym*, *nag ydym*, we are not; *nag ych*, *nag ydych*, ye are not; *nag ynt*, *nag ydynt*, they are not.

Car y dyn da, ac nag anghar y dyn drwg.

Love the good man, and do *not* hate the bad man. *Adage.*

Nage, *s. m.* (nag—e) A negative, to answer particular questions. *adv.* Not that, not so, no.

Nagu, *v. a.* (nag) To refuse, to deny; to hinder.

Crist culwydd——
O 'm rhang lles neges na'm naguy.

Christ the gracious one, of my craved errand of good *do not deny* me. *Cynddelw.*

Nai, *s. m.*—*pl.* neisint (na) That separates or branches of; a nephew.

Nid dilwyd heb nai.

Not adherent without a *nephew*. *Adage.*

Naid, *s. f.*—*pl.* neidiau (na—id) A recess; a withdrawment; a refuge, or sanctuary; a leap, or jump.

Gresyn oedd na chai groes naid,
I gynnull da rhag enaid!

It was a pity that he should not have a cross of *refuge*, to accumulate good for the soul! *D. Llwyd.*

Athraw in' oll, aeth i'r naid,
Oedd Ieuan, och na ddywaid.

A teacher to us all, who is gone to the *refuge*, was Ieuan—alas, that he speaks not. *G. D. Yehain.*

Bwrw naid i'r wybr a wnai
Ar hyder yr ehedai.

He would give a *bound* towards the sky in confidence that he should fly. *T. Aled, i farch.*

Naill, *pron.* (nall) One of two, one or the other; one. *Ar y naill tu*, on one side; *naill ai hwn*, *ai hwna*, *ai hwnw*, either this person masculine, or that one present, or that one absent.

Y naill wenwyn a ladd y llall.

The *one* poison will destroy the other. *Adage.*

Naill, *conj.* (ny—aill) Either, else, or.

Naill ai llwynog ai llwyn rhedyn.

Either a fox or a tump of fern. *Adage.*

Nain, *s. f.*—*pl.* neinoedd (ny—ain) Grandmother.

Nais, *s. m.*—*pl.* neisiau (ny—ais) A band, or tie, the being trimmed, dressed, or made elegant.

Naith, *s. m.*—*pl.* neithion (na—ith) That is past or completed; that is given; troth, faith.

Nall, *pron.* (ny—all) One of two; one. *Null ac y llall*, one and the other. *Gwent.*

Nam, *s. m.*—*pl. t.* au (na) A mark, or stigma; a defect, fault, blemish, or maim; an offence, or sin; an exception.

Yn nghyweithas nam na'm bo myned.

Into the company *of iniquity* may I not be going. *Ll. P. Moch.*

Gwnaethom nam, a rhyfedd fydd.

We committed a *fault*, and wonderful it was. *Elidr Sais.*

Oni chadw Duw rhag nam,
Fe drigia'r ferch lle trigia'r fam.

If God do not keep against a *fault*, the daughter will make a slip where the mother slips. *Adage.*

Nam, *conj.* (na) Except, but, save, only.

Nam saith ni ddyrraith o Gaer Sidi.

Only seven there proceeded not from Caer Sidi. *Taliesin.*

Named, *conj.* (nam) Except, but, save. *Named un*, except one; *named fi*, except me.

Namiad, *s. m.*—*pl. t.* au (nam) A making a mark, making a defect, a blemishing, an exception.

Namu, *v. a.* (nam) To stigmatize; to render defective; to except.

Namwy, *v. a.* (nam) To make exception.

Namwyn, *conj.* (nam) Except, but, save.

Namwyn Duw nid oes dewin.

Except God there is none that knows the future. *Llywarch Hen.*

Namyn, *s. m.* (nam) An exception. *conj.* Except, but, save.

Ni thag namyn chwd.

An *objection* will not choak a messenger. *Adage.*

Nan, *s. m.* (na) Something distinct; a what. *adv.* What, what now, now. *Wela nan*, well what now, or well what do you want.

Nant, *s. m.*—*pl.* nentydd (nan) A hollow formed by water, a ravine; a mountain torrent, a brook. It enters into the composition of a great many names of places.

Ac mewn naint lliferiaint llwyd.

And in the *brooks* were muddy torrents. *D. ab Gwilym.*

Gwar yw nannau'r hyd y ddol,
A siriol yw eu gweled.

Gentle are the *brooks* along the dale, and charming is it to see them. *Gwil. Tew.*

Nar, *s. m.*—*pl. t.* edd (ny—ar) That is forward; that is abortive; a dwarf, a puny thing; an ape.

O fadredd, O nar, O erthyl, O ynfyd, O ffol trallodedig! py le yr awr hon y mae dy ystafelloedd goyched?

Oh filth, Oh thou *puny thing*, Oh thou miscarriage, Oh thou mad one, Oh distracted simpleton! where are now thy splendid apartments? *Marchawg Crwydrad.*

Naraidd, *a.* (nar) Abortive, dwarfish, or puny.

Nareiddiad, *s. m.* (naraidd) Dwarfishness.

Nareiddiaw, *v. n.* (naraidd) To become dwarfish.

Nareiddrwydd, *s. m.* (naraidd) Dwarfishness.

Naru, *v. n.* (nar) To be abortive, to become puny.

Nas, *adv.* (na—ys) That not, may not. It is of the same force with na; but when used, it preserves to the initial of the word that follows its radical power; as, *nas delo moni*, for *na ddelo moni*, *that* she come *not*.

Nid tylawd ond nas cymero.

He is not poor but *that* does not enjoy. *Adage.*

Bychan y tal cynghor gwraig, ond gwae i wr nas cymero.

A wife's advice is of little worth, but woe to the husband *that* will *not* take it. *Adage.*

Naw, *s. m.*—*pl. t.* oedd (ny—aw) That is up or ultimate; that limits; nine, or the number nine. *a.* Nine.

Tri chaled byd: maen callt, dur naw gwynias, a chalon mab y crinwas.

The three hard things of the world: a flint stone, steel nine times heated, and the heart of the son of avarice. *Trioedd.*

Y tri naw arbenig: naw ton y weilgi, naw radd y nef, a naw mis tymp.

The three peculiar *nines*: the *nine* waves of the ocean, the *nine* orders of heaven, and the *nine* months of gestation. *Trioedd.*

Nawban, *s. m.—pl. t.* au (naw—ban) That consists of nine verses, a term in prosody. *a.* Of nine parts or verses.

Nawbanawg, *a.* (nawban) Of nine syllables.

Nawd, *s. f.* (naw) What is predominant; that is efficient; nature, a character, or trait.

> Ti cymerit gnawd,
> O fru morwyndawd
> A dynawl giwdawd
> O nawd newydd.

> Thou didst become flesh, from the womb of virginity with mankind, of *nature* new. *D. Ddu o Hiraddug.*

> Yna gwelwn o'r gwaelawd
> Un o'r nant yn oer ei nawd.

> Then I could perceive from below one from the brook in dismal *plight.* *Ifan Ddu.*

Nawd, *adv.* (naw) Effectually; easily, aptly.

> Ni nawd gymmydd blaidd â drych.

> A wolf is not *easily* reconciled to a mirror. *Adage.*

> Ni nawd difenwir cywraint.

> The ingenious is not *easily* discomfited. *Adage.*

Nawdeg, *s. m.* (naw—deg) Ninety, nine tens.

Nawdd, *s. m.—pl.* noddau (naw) Refuge, protection, sanctuary, patronage; privilege.

> Goreu nawdd diniweidrwydd.

> The best *protection* is innocence. *Adage.*

> Ni thorrei Arthur nawdd gwraig.

> Arthur broke not the *protection* of a woman. *Adage.*

> Dyfnwal a roes noddau i'r ereidr.

> Dyfnwal assigned *privileges* to the ploughs. *Gr. ab Arthur.*

> Nawdd pob merch wyf o'i erchi;
> Ag o chaf nawdd gwychaf fi.
> Ni ofynna', myn f'einioes!
> Er gair mawr, nawdd gwr i'm oes.

> The *protection* of every woman I implore; and should I *protection* have, I bravely shall go on. I will not crave, upon my life! barring a boasting word, the *protection* of a man while I live. *G. ab H. ab Tudur.*

Nawddosgordd, *s. f.* (nawdd—gosgordd) A retinue of protection.

Nawed, *s. m.* (naw) A ninth. *a.* One ninth.

Nawedran, *s. f.—pl. t.* au (nawed—rhan) A ninth part. *a.* Of one ninth part.

Nawedwaith, *s. f.* (nawed—gwaith) Ninth time.

Nawf, *s. m.—pl.* nofion (naw) A swim. *Nawf pysgodyn*, the swim or wind bladder of a fish.

Nawfed, *s. m.* (naw) A ninth. *a.* Ninth.

> Nawfed tafodiawg yw ynad.

> The *ninth* speaker is a judge. *Welsh Laws.*

> A mi ddysgogaf rhag ton nawfed.

> And I will declare the future before the *ninth* wave. *Myrddin.*

> Efa—hirdwf o'i llenrdudded—
> Liw ewyn y tu rhag ton nawfed
> Nawfed rhan fy mhoen er pan aned.

> Efa, of stately growth in her golden vest, of the hue of the fair spraying foam before the *ninth* wave: the *ninth* part of my pain from the time she was born. *Cynddelw.*

Nawfed-dydd, *s. m.* (nawfed—dydd) The ninth day, a time of appearance in law.

Nawgwaith, *s. m.* (naw—gwaith) The number of nine times. *a.* Nine times.

Nawmis, *s. m.* (naw—mis) Nine months. *a.* Of nine months.

> Cyd celer naw nos, ni chelir nawmis.

> Whilst nine nights may be concealed, *nine months* will not be concealed. *Adage.*

Nawn, *s. m.—pl.* nonau (naw) That is at the summit; the meridian, or noon; a noon meal.

> Gwasanaeth Duw yw gwneuthur iawn,
> Nid gweddiaw bore a nawn.

> The service of God is to do justice, and not to pray morning and *noon.* *Hen Sofin.*

> Tud achles buddled bo'dlawn ceirddorion
> Ceirddorion am eu nawn

> The land its safety gains when minstrels are contented, of their *noon* ... secured. *Cynddelw, m. i. O. Gwynedd.*

Nawnawl, *a.* (nawn) Belonging to noon.

Nawnoldeb, *s. m* (nawnawl) Meridionality.

Nawnu, *v. a.* (nawn) To raise up; to uphold; to come to the meridian.

> Arth warth wrthodiad, a'm nad, a'm nawn,
> Tra fu.——

> A bear rejecting shame, who kept me from departing, who *upheld* me whilst he was. *Cynddelw, m. Rhiryd.*

Nawplyg, *s. m.* (naw—plyg) That consists of nine folds. *a* Nine fold.

Nawradd, *s. f.* (naw—gradd) That consists of nine degrees; the nine degrees, or the heavenly hierarchy. *a.* Of nine gradations.

Nawrhyw, *a.* (naw—rhyw) Of nine sorts. *Cawl nawrhyw*, soup made of nine sorts of herbs.

Naws, *s. f.—pl. t.* au (naw) Nature, disposition, quality, temperament; a trait, or trace. *Dyn da ei naws*, a person of good disposition; *ni wn i naws am dano*, I know not a trace of it, or I know nothing of it. *Sil.*

> Nid un naws gwyros a gwern.

> The privet and the alder are not of the same nature. *Adage.*

> Terwyn gwyn brwyn bron
> Nis cel naws calon;
> Treiglo i'w thwy hon
> Fraglew afar.

> A severe complaint of the throbbing breast the *quality* of the heart will not conceal; a journey to visit her is terribly vexatious. *G. ab M. ab Dafydd.*

> Ni chan y gog, aerchog sydd,
> Nes delifo naws y dolydd.

> The cuckoo will not sing, that is amorous, until *nature* covers the dales with leaves. *T. Prys.*

Nawsaidd, *a.* (naws) Genial, kind, tender, soft.

> Anllad rwydd a'm dygai i'm hystafell, ac a'm gosodai mewn gwely esmwyth nawsaidd.

> Sensuality conducted me to my chamber, and put me in an easy *soft* bed. *Marchawg Crwydrad.*

Nawsain, *a.* (naws) Tending to softness.

Nawsawl, *a.* (naws) Of a temperate nature.

Nawsber, *a.* (naws—per) Kindly sweet.

Nawsedig, *a.* (naws) Being made genial, or tender, tempered.

Nawsedigaeth, *s. m.* (nawsedig) The act of rendering genial or temperate; the act of becoming temperate, or genial.

Nawseidd, *s. m.* (naws) Temperature; disposition.

Nawseidd-dra, *a.* (nawsaidd) Temperateness.

Nawseiddiad, *s. m.* (nawsaidd) A rendering genial or natural; a becoming genial.

Nawseiddiaw, *v. a.* (nawsaidd) To render genial, kind, or tender; to fill with tenderness, to become genial or tender; to become soft.

> Cariad perffaith a iraa, ac a nawseiddia y galon

> Charity doth refresh, and *doth soften* the heart. *Marchawg Crwydrad.*

Nawseiddiawl, *a.* (nawsaidd) Temperamental.

Nawseiddrwydd, *s. m.* (nawsaidd) Temperateness

Nawsiad, *s. m.—pl. t.* au (naws) A forming the nature, disposition, or quality; a tempering; a pervading; a filtration.

Nawsiannawl, *a.* (nawsiant) Temperamental.

Nawsiannu, *v. a.* (nawsiant) To render temperamental; to cause a pervasion.

Nawsiant, *s. m.* (naws) Temperament; pervasion.

Nawsiaw, *v. a.* (naws) To form the nature, disposition, or quality; to temper; to pervade, to ooze, to filtrate

Nawsill, *s. f.* (naw—sill) That consists of nine syllables; nine syllables. *a.* Of nine syllables.

Nawsillawg, *a* (nawsill) Of nine syllables.

Nawsineb, *s. m.* (naws) Temperament; pervasion.

Nawsoldeb, *s. m.* (nawsawl) Temperature.

Nawsoledd, *s. m.* (nawsawl) Temperature.

Nawsoli, *v. a.* (nawsawl) To temper; to soften.
Nawsolrwydd, *s. m.* (nawsawl) Temperateness.
Nawswyllt, *a.* (naws—gwyllt) Of a wild disposition, of a furious nature; passionate.
Nawter, *s. f.* (nawd) Nature, quality; habit, or custom. *Mae ynot ryw nawter ddrwg*, thou hast got some bad habit. *Sil.*
Nawtur, *s. f.* (nawd) Efficient principle; nature.
NE, *s. m. r.* A state of going or passing, a hue.
Ne, *conj.* (ne, *s.*) Or, otherwise, else, either.

Ne i affaith tan uffern.

Or to the influence of the fire of hell. *H. Dafi.*

Nëad, *s. m.* (ne) An opening to let out.
Neb, *pron.* (ne—eb) Whatever, any, any one, none, somebody, any body, nobody. *a.* Any, some, none.—*Y neb a elo*, whosoever that goes.

Dyn ni wnai daioni i neb
Ydyw un â dau wyneb.

A man that would not do good to *any* is the one with a double face. *D. ab Gwilym.*

Ni roe neb, ac ni rown i
beren bren er ei sori.

There would not be given by *any body*, and I would not give a chip, though he were affronted. *Gr. Gryg.*

Nebawd, *s. m.* (neb) Any body, nobody.
Nebdyn, *s. m.* (neb—dyn) Any person, any one.
Neble, *s. m.* (neb—lle) Any place, no place. *adv.* No place, no where.
Nebpell, *s. m.* (neb—pell) Any distance. *adv.* At no distance, not far.
Nebrhyw, *s. m.* (neb—rhyw) Any kind. *adv.* Of any sort; not any sort.
Nebun, *s. m.* (neb—un) Any one, somebody; nobody.

Nid mor ddiarheb nebun
I'n gwlad ni a hi ei hun.

Not so famous *any one* in our country as she herself. *D. ab Gwilym.*

Hoen ffysc, da ddysg, nid oedd un,
Huan wybr, a hi nebun.

Sprightly bloom of health, of good instruction, there were not one, luminary of the sky, and she *nobody*. *D. ab Gwilym, i Angharad.*

Nedd, *s. f.—pl.* nydd (ny—edd) That forms a whirl or turn; a small dingle or hollow; a place where any thing rests; also nits on the hair.
Neddai, *s. f.* (nadd) That works into form.
Neddair, *s. f.* (nedd) The hollow of the hand, the grasp of the hand; the hand.

Pen a borthaf i'm neddair,
Eryr erchwyd, oedd ni gair!

A head I bear in my *hand* of the eagle of the country, who was and will not again be had! *Llywarch Hen.*

A'i nedd r, f'anwyl-grair fwyn
Y nyddodd fedw yn addwyn.

With her *hand* my kind dear jewel has elegantly entwined the birch. *D. ab Gwilym.*

Neddawg, *a.* (nedd) Abounding with smalls, whirls, turns, or rests; abounding with nits.
Nedden, *s. f. dim* (nêdd) A single nit.
Neddyf, *s. f.* (nadd) A tool for cutting or working into form, and adze.

Tyfiad heb naddiad neddyf,
Tŷ, ar un piler y tyf

A growth having not the operation of the *adze*, a house, upon one pillar it rises up. *D. ab Gwilym.*

Nef, *s. m.—pl. t.* oedd (ny—ef) A limit of a course, a turn, place of rest, a hollow, heaven. *Ty yn y nef*, the house in the hollow; there are places so called.

A rannodd nef a gafas.

He that has distributed has obtained *heaven*. *Adage.*

Pump tywarchen y sydd, nef, daiar, dwfr, tan, awyr, a nef; ac o'r pedair cyntaf pob defnydd difywyd; ac o'r nef Duw, a phob bywyd, a bywydawl, ac o ymgyd y pump hyn pob peth, ai bywydawl, ai anmywydawl y bo.

Five elements there are; that is to say, earth, water, fire, air, and the *heaven*; and out of the four first comes every inanimate matter; and of the *heaven* God, and all of life, and living; and from the conjunction of these five come all things, or animate, or inanimate they be. *Barddas.*

Pan ddyfo Trindawd—
Llu nef amdano,
Llwyth llydan ato,
Cyrdd a cherddorion,
A chwithau englynion,
Dyrchafant o feddau—y meirw.

When the Trinity shall come surrounded by the host of *heaven*, pressing to him an extensive throng, with the songs of minstrels, and the hymns of angels, out of the graves the dead shall rise. *Taliesin.*

Nefair, *s. f.* (nef) An epithet for the opening or grasp of the hand; a hand.
Nefawl, *a.* (nef) Heavenly, celestial.
Nefawr, *a.* (nef) Of a celestial nature.
Nefed, *s. m.* (nef) An expansion.
Nefliw, *s. m.* (nef—lliw) A cerulean. *a.* Of a cerulean hue.
Nefoedd, *s. pl. aggr.* (nef) The heavens.

Ar ffrwst mawr gawr ddigoniant
Nifer o'r nefoedd a syrthiant.

At the great force of the shout of triumph numbers from the *heavens* shall fall. *B. Noutter.*

Nefolaidd, *a.* (nefawl) Heaven-like, heavenly.
Nefoldeb, *s. m.* (nefawl) Heavenliness.
Nefolder, *s. m.* (nefawl) Heavenliness.
Nefoledd, *s. m.* (nefawl) A heavenly state.
Nefoleiddrwydd, *s. m.* (nefolaidd) Heavenliness.
Nefolfryd, *a.* (nefawl—bryd) Heavenly-minded.
Nefolfrydedd, *s. m.* (nefolfryd) Heavenly-mindedness, a heavenly state of mind.
Nefoli, *v. a.* (nefawl) To render heavenly; to canonize; to become heavenly.
Nefolineth, *s. m.* (nefawl) A heavenly state.

Archaf i ti
Dwyfawl nefolineth
A diwedd perffaith
Penrhaith pob rhad.

I crave of thee a *heavenly state* divine, and a perfect end, thou sovereign of every grace! *D. ab Gwilym.*

Nefoliannu, *v. a.* (nefoliant) To render heavenly; to celestify; to become heavenly.
Nefoliannus, *a.* (nefoliant) Of a tendency to render celestial.
Nefoliant, *s. m.* (nefawl) Celestification.
Nefolrwydd, *s. m.* (nefawl) Heavenliness.
Nefolus, *a.* (nefawl) Of a celestial nature.
Nefwy, *s. m.* (nef) A heavenly state.

Nid wy i'm noddwy
Amgylch balch nefwy;
Ysydd rin y sydd fwy,
Gwawr gwyr Goronwy.

They shall not be protecting me around the high *heaven*, there is a virtue that is more excellent, the light of the men of Goronwy. *Taliesin.*

Nefyd, *s. m.* (naf) A performance, what is wrought or formed.

Safed wrth nefyd gwrthun
Yn dy bwyll, dy farn dy hun.

Thou wouldest stand by an absurd *performance*, in thy possession, thy own judgement. *Edm. Prys.*

Neg, *s. m.—pl. t.* ion (ny—eg) That is not open; that is not possible.
Neges, *s. m.—pl. t.* au (neg—es) An errand, or message; business.

A el i lys heb neges doed a'i neges ganto.

He that goes to court without an *errand* let him return with an *errand* in his possession. *Adage.*

Cennad hwyr drwg ei neges.

A late messenger is upon a bad *errand*. *Adage.*

Negesa, *v. a.* (neges) To go on errands.
Negesai, *s. c.—pl.* negeseion (neges) One who goes on errands; a messenger.
Negesau, *s. pl. aggr.* (neges) Errands, messages.

Negesawg, *a.* (neges) Having an errand. *s. m.* One that carries a message; a messenger.

Eilwaith ydd eathym yn negesawg
O leufer llyw cammawn, iawn dywysawg.

A second time I went as an *ambassador* from the splendor of the leader of conflict, the righteous prince. *Meilyr.*

Negesawl, *a.* (neges, Missionary. *Negesolion*, missionaries.

Negesena, *v. a.* (negesau) To go on messages; to transact business; to negociate.

Negesengar, *a.* (negesan) Officious.

Negesengarwch, *s. m.* (negesengar) Officiousness.

Negesenwr, *s. m.—pl.* negesenwyr (negesau—gwr) An errand-man, a messenger.

Negesenwraig, *s. f.—pl.* negesenwreigedd (negesau—gwraig) A woman-messenger.

Negesgar, *a.* (neges) Fond of errands, officious.

Negesgarwch, *s. m.* (negesgar) Officiousness.

Negesiad, *s. m.* (neges) A carrying an errand.

Negesiaeth, *s. m.* (neges) A commission.

Negesiannawl, *a.* (negesiant) Appertaining to a commission.

Negesiannu, *v. a.* (negesiant) To commissionate.

Negesiant, *s. m.* (neges) A commission.

Negeswas, *s. m.—pl.* negesweision (neges—gwas) An errand-boy.

Negeswr, *s. m.—pl.* negeswyr (neges—gwr) An errand-man, a messenger.

Negeswraig, *s. f—pl.* negeswreigedd (neges—gwraig) An errand-woman.

Negeswriaeth, *s. m.* (negeswr) The business of a man who transacts for another.

Negesydd, *s. m.—pl. t.* ion (neges) A messenger.

Negesyddawl, *a.* (negesydd) Appertaining to a messenger, missionary, missive.

Negesyddiaeth, *s. m.—pl. t.* au (negesydd) The business of a messenger.

Negiad, *s. m.—pl. t.* au (neg) A disabling.

Negiant, *s. m.* (neg) A disabling.

Negiaw, *v. a.* (neg) To disable, to render impossible. *Mae arnaf eisieu ei nego fe*, I am in want *of disabling* him. *Sil.*

Negiawl, *a* (neg) Tending to disable.

Negiwr, *s. m.—pl.* negwyr (neg—gwr) A disabler.

Negydd, *s. m.—pl. t.* ion (nag) A denier.

Ni bu Rodri, nai Beredur,
Negydd o'i win, nag o'i ddur.

Rodri, the nephew of Peredur, has not been a *denier* of his wine, nor of his steel. *Guto y Glyn.*

Negyddawl, *a.* (negydd) Negative, refusing.

Negyddiad, *s. m.* (negydd) A denying, a refusing.

Negyddiaeth, *s. m.* (negydd) A denial, a refusal.

Negyf, *s. m.* (nag) A negation, a denial.

Negyfiaeth, *s. m.* (negyf) A refusal, a denial.

Cedawl arwynawl ar wyneb Prydain,
Prydyddion diateb;
Ni fagai fygwl ateb;
Ni faeth negyfaeth i neb

The bounteous violent one, over the face of Britain the poets are unanswerable; he would not conceive a stern answer; he will not cherish a *denial* to any one. *Ll. P. Moch.*

Nehedd, *s. m.* (ne—hedd) Entreaty, prayer.

Neidiad, *s. m.* (naid) A leaping, or springing.

Neidiaw, *v. a.* (naid) To leap, to jump; to pulse.

Neidiawl, *a.* (naid) Leaping, springing, throbbing

Neidiwr, *s. m.—pl.* neidwyr (naid—gwr) A leaper.

Neidraidd, *a.* (naidr) Snake-like, snaky.

Neidrllys, *s. m.* (neidr—llys) Snakewort.

Neidrwydd, *s. m.—pl. t.* au (naid) The temples; also called *arlais* and *arleisiau*.

Brath y lleidr drwy ei neidrwydd:
Beth ddawr ei ladd byth, gwr gwydd.

Stick the thief through his *temples* who would ever mind his death, the goose of a man. *D. ab Gwilym.*

Neidr, *s. f.—pl. t.* edd (nad) A snake. *Neidr ddu*, a viper; *neidr fraith*, *neidr y tomenydd*, the common snake, or adder.

Cyfrithed a neidr.

As variegated as an *adder*. *Adage.*

Chwefrawr chwyth neidr o'i nyth.

February will blow the *snake* out of her nest. *Adage.*

Neifion, *s. m.* (naf) The comprehending one; the creator; also the name of a person in the British mythology, probably the same with *Neptune*.

Dadwyrain i Frython
A oreu Gwdion;
Geiwraid ar Neifion:
Ar Grist o achwyson,
Hyd pan y gwarettai.

A resurrection to the Britons was accomplished by Gwdion; there was a calling upon the *Creator*; upon Christ for causes until when he should deliver. *Taliesin, Cad Goddeu.*

Ef a yr aifer i for Neifion.

He will send a number to the sea of *Neifion*. *L. G. Cothi.*

Y nofiad a wnaeth Neifion
O Droia fawr draw i Fon.

The swimming which *Neifion* performed from great Troy afar to Mona. *D. ab Gwilym.*

Neillawr, *s. f.* (naill—awr) The other hour, the next hour. *adv.* At another time.

Eu buchedd hoen-wedd buham, y neillawr,
Na wellant rhag dryglam.

Their lives of sprightly mood why, the *next hour*, they do not mend for fear of an evil step. *W. Middleton.*

Neilldu, *s. m.* (naill—tu) One of two sides, one side. *O'r neilldu*, from one side; *ar neilldu*, on one side, or aside.

Neillduad, *s. m.* (neilldu) A going aside; a putting aside; a separating; separation.

Neillduaeth, *s. m.—pl. t.* au (neilldu) A separation, dissociation. *Tir neillduaeth*, the land of reservation.

Neillduaethu, *v. a.* (neillduaeth) To make a separation; to reserve, to put aside.

Neillduaw, *v. a.* (neilldu) To go on one aside; to go aside, to retire, to recede; to dissociate; to separate, to put asunder, to set apart.

Yno ill dau ni neillduynt
I roi y gad i wyr gynt.

Then they two *would* not *separate* in giving battle to men formerly. *L. G. Cothi.*

Neillduawl, *a.* (neilldu) Separate, retired, solitary; particular, distinct; discretive.

Neillduedig, *a.* (neillduad) Separated, abstracted.

Arthal—yn myned i ofni y gwyr a fuesynt cydymdeithion neillduedig iddo gynt; ac yn cerdded trwy y coed hwnw y cyfarfu ag Elidr ei frawd yn ddiarwybod.

Arthal, going to terrify the men who formerly had been his *particular* companions; and in walking through that wood he met with Elidr his brother unexpectedly. *Gr. ab Arthur.*

Neillduedigaeth, *s. m.—pl. t.* au (neillduedig) The state of being put aside or separated; sequestration.

Neillduedigaw, *v. a.* (neillduedig) To render separated or sequestered; to become separated.

Neillduedd, *s. m.* (neilldu) Separateness, retiredness; distinctness, discriminateness.

Neillduolaeth, *s. m.* (neillduawl) The state of being separated; discrimination.

Neillduoldeb, *s. m.* (neillduawl) Separability; distinctness, discriminateness.

Neillduoli, *v. a.* (neillduawl) To render separate, or distinct; to particularize.

Neillduolrwydd, *s. m.* (neillduawl) Separateness, distinctness; particularity.

Neillduwr, *s. m.—pl.* neillduwyr (neilldu—gwr) One who goes aside; one who puts aside.

Neilliad, *s. m.* (naill) A varying, a diversifying.
Neilliaw, *v. a.* (naill) To vary, to diversify.
Neilliawg, *a.* (naill) Diversified, varied.
Neilliedig, *a.* (neilliad) Being diversified.
Neilliedigaeth, *s. m.* (neilliedig) The being diversified or varied.
Neilliogaeth, *s. m.* (neilliawg) A variation.

> Cofier cynnal y cyfryw neilliogaeth yn yr un banau yn mhob un [illegible] o'r pennillion
>
> Be it remembered that such *diversity* is to be maintained in the same verses in [illegible] of the stanzas. *Barddas.*

Neilliogi, *v. a.* (neilliawg) To diversify.

> [illegible] allan y daw y dosparth, a rhai o'r banau o hyny yn [illegible], cofier cynnal y cyfryw neilliogaeth.
>
> If the song is derived from a secondary canon, and some of those verses *varying* from others, it is to be remembered that such diversity is to be maintained. *Barddas.*

Neina, *s. f. dim.* (nain) A grandmammy.
Neirthiad, *s. m.* (nerth) A strengthener.

> Fy Nuw, fy neirthiad, fad rad rinu.
>
> My God, my *support*, freely dispensing grace.
> *Gw. Brycheiniawg.*
>
> Gwan wyf, ym nerthwy fy neirthiad.
>
> Feeble am I, may my *supporter* support me.
> *Y Bleddyn Madawg.*

Neisiad, *s. m.*—*pl. t.* an (nais) A kerchief.
Neisiaw, *v. a.* (nais) To wrap with a band; to deck, to dress up, to trim up nicely.
Neithiad, *s. m.* (naith) A passing, completing.
Neithiaw, *v. a.* (naith) To pass, to complete.
Neithiawl, *a.* (naith) Tending to perfect.
Neithiawr, *s. m.*—*pl.* neithiorau (naith) A state that is completed or confirmed; completement, a wedding; a wedding feast, in some parts, which is kept on a fixt day after the wedding, generally the following Sunday, when the guests bring presents to the newly married couple: The term *Neithiorau* has been used for the Characteristics of Theophrastus.
Neithiora, *v. a.* (neithiawr) To bring to completion; to keep a marriage festival.
Neithiorawg, *a.* (neithiawr) Having a marriage or wedding feast.
Neithiorawl, *a.* (neithiawr) Tending to complete, relating to marriage solemnity.
Neithiori, *v. a.* (neithiawr) To render complete; to consummate a marriage solemnity.
Neithiorwr, *s. m.*—*pl.* neithiorwyr (neithiawr—gwr) One who consummates.
Neithiwyr, *s. m.* (naith—hwyr) The evening past, or last night. *adv.* Last night, yesterday evening.
Neithyr, *prep.* (eithyr) Except, unless.
Nemawr, *s. m.* (nam) A few in number. *adv.* Not many, scarcely, hardly.
Nemof, *pronom. prep.* (nam) Except of me. *nemot*, except of thee; *nemo*, except of him; or it; *nemi*, except of her; *nemom*, except of us; *nemoch*, except of you; *nemont*, except of them.

> Ei [illegible] ni [illegible] nemoch.
>
> His transgression will not be [illegible] *except of you.*
> *Cynddelw.*

Nemor, *s. m.* (nam—or) An exception of extent, of quantity, or number. *adv.* Not many; scarcely.
Nen, *s. f.*—*pl. t.* oedd (ny—en) The inside top of a vault or canopy; the ceiling, roof, or top; a roof; a vault, or canopy; the heavens.

> Ystafell Cynddylan, ys tywyll ei nen,
> Gwedy [illegible] gyweithydd
> [illegible] dyfydd
>
> The hall of Cynddylan, its *roof* is dark, after [illegible] the supporter, Woe that what shall come to it will produce no good!
> *Llywarch Hen.*

Nenawl, *a.* (nen) Appertaining to a vault, roof or ceiling.
Nenawr, *s. f.*—*pl.* nenorau (nen) An upper story, or garret.
Nenbren, *s. m.*—*pl. t.* i (nen—pren) The upper roof beam in a building.
Nenfwd, *s. f.* (nen—mwd) A ceiling arch.
Nenfydu, *v. a.* (nenfwd) To make an arched ceiling.
Neniad, *s. m.* (nen) A vaulting, a ceiling.
Neniar, *s. f.*—*pl. t.* oedd (nen—iar) The upper roof beam; also, called *nenbren.*
Nenorydd, *s. m.*—*pl. t.* ion (nenawr) A garreteer.
Nenu, *v. a.* (nen) To vault, to roof, to ceil.
Nenwawl, *s. m.* (nen—gwawl) Cerulean light.

> [illegible]
> Ar [illegible]
> A [illegible]
>
> He was the stately Owain, the [illegible] of [illegible], and surrounded with a zone of *heavenly light*, was formed with [illegible] lasting union. *Gwalchmai.*

Ner, *s. m.*—*pl. t.* edd (ny—er) That is without impulse from another; that has self energy; an epithet of God, the Lord.

> Cadfan ner [illegible]
> [illegible]
> [illegible]
> [illegible] frawdd [illegible] fraw.
>
> Cadvan the sovereign of the energy of song, the [illegible] have sojourned under thy protection, the [illegible] of the [illegible] of the [illegible] counsel, the eagle of the [illegible] of a pleasant region.
> *Ll. P. Moch.*

Nerth, *s. m.*—*pl. t.* oedd (ner) Might, power, strength, force; aid, help, or succour.

> Ei nerth yw [illegible] diriad.
>
> The *strength* of the [illegible] is his debility. *Adage.*
>
> Tri achaws bywedigion: cariad Duw, gan eithaf deall cyfiawn; deall Duw, yn [illegible] eithaf moddion, a nerth Duw, gan eithaf mynu, cariad a deall.
>
> The three causes of animated beings: the love of God with a plenitude of perfect knowledge; the knowledge of God converting a plenitude of means, and the *power* of God with a plenitude of will, love, and knowledge. *Barddas.*
>
> Am bob [illegible]
> A'i nerth, a'i [illegible]
> —[illegible]!
>
> For every [illegible] blessing, and his *power*, and his [illegible] heaven to his soul. *[illegible] Thomas, o [illegible].*

Nerthai, *s. c.*—*pl.* nertheion (nerth) Strengthener
Nerthawg, *a.* (nerth) Mighty, powerful, potent.

> With [illegible] nerthawg [illegible];
> A'i [illegible] gwan [illegible].
>
> With the mighty he was *powerful*, and to the weak merciful was he. *[illegible]*

Nerthawl, *a.* (nerth) Powerful or strong.
Nerthedig, *a.* (nerth) Being strengthened.
Nerthedigaeth, *s. m.* (nerthedig) A strengthening
Nerthedd, *s. m.* (nerth) Potency, or strength.
Nerthfawr, *a.* (nerth) Of great strength, powerful
Nerthfawrawg, *a.* (nerthfawr) Of great power.
Nerthfawrogi, *v. a.* (nerthfawrawg) To endow with great strength.
Nerthfawrogiad, *s. m.* (nerthfawrawg) An endowing with great power.
Nerthfawrus, *a.* (nerthfawr) Of a potent nature.

> [illegible] nerthfawrusion.
>
> Thou must refrain from vices, and practise the [illegible] that are *strength-creating* [illegible]. *[illegible]*

Nerthfawrusaw, *v. a.* (nerthfawrus) To render strengthening; to become strengthening.
Nerthiad, *s. m.*—*pl. t.* au (nerth) A strengthening, a supporting, or assisting.
Nerthiannawl, *a.* (nerthiant) Of a strengthening quality, empowering.

Nerthiannu, *v. a.* (nerthiant) To render strengthening; to become strengthening.
Nerthiannus, *a.* (nerthiant) Of a strengthening nature; tending to empower.
Nerthiannusaw, *v. a.* (nerthiannus) To render of a strengthening nature.
Nerthiant, *s. m.* (nerth) A strengthening.
Nerthiator, *ger.* (nerthiad) In strengthening.
Nerthineb, *s. m.* (nerth) Efficaciousness, potency.
Nerthitor, *sup.* (nerth) To be strengthening.
Nerthocâad, *s. m.* (nerthawg) A rendering powerful, strong, or potent.
Nerthocâu, *v. a.* (nerthawg) To render potent.
Nerthogi, *v. a.* (nerthawg) To make powerful.
Nerthogiad, *s. m.* (nerthawg) A making potent.
Nerthogrwydd, *s. m.* (nerthawg) Powerfulness.
Nertholdeb, *s. m.* (nerthawl) Potency, ability.
Nertholedd, *s. m.* (nerthawl) Powerfulness.
Nertholi, *v. a.* (nerthawl) To render powerful.
Nertholrwydd, *s. m.* (nerthawl) Powerfulness.
Nerthrwydd, *s. m.* (nerth) Potency, energy.
Nerthu, *v. a.* (nerth) To strengthen; to help.
Nerthus, *a.* (nerth) Efficacious, potent.
Nerthusaw, *v. a.* (nerthus) To render efficacious, to become efficacious.
Nerthusedd, *s. m.* (nerthus) Efficaciousness.
Nerthusrwydd, *s. m.* (nerthus) Efficaciousness.
Nerthweh, *s. m.* (nerth) Potency, energy, strength
Nerthwr, *s. m.—pl.* nerthwyr (nerth—gwr) A strengthener; a supporter.
Nerthydd, *s. m.—pl. t.* ion (nerth) A strengthener
Nervn, *s. m. dim.* (nar) The child of old age; a child born when the father is absent.
Nes, *s. m.* (ny—es) The state of being without distance, close, or proximate. *a.* Divested of distance: It is also used for the comparative *nesach*, nearer, closer, of less distance. *Ni byddi nes er hyny*, thou wilt not be the nearer for that.

Nes na chred.

Nearer than belief. *Adage.*

Nes, *adv.* (ny—es) Until. *Ni chei glod nes marw*, thou shalt not have fame until thou art dead.
Nesâad, *s. m.* (nesâu) Approximation; approach
Nesâawl, *a.* (nesâu) Approximating.
Nesach, *a.* (nes) Nearer, or more near.
Nesaf, *a.* (nes) Nearest, next, most near. *s. m.* The next, the nearest.

Melysaf y gwellt nesaf i'r ddaiar.

Sweetest the grass *next* to the ground. *Adage.*

Nesâu, *v. a.* (nes) To draw near, to approach.
Nesâwr, *s. m.—pl.* nesâwyr (nesâu—gwr) One who draws near or approximates.
Nesedig, *a.* (nes) Being approximated.
Nesedigaeth, *s. m.* (nesedig) Approximation.
Nesefin, *s. m.—pl. t.* ion (nesaf) A neighbour.
Neseifiad, *s. m.—pl.* neseifiaid (nesaf) One who is nearest of kin; a relative.
Nesiad, *s. m.* (nes) A drawing near, or approaching, approximation.
Nesiannawl, *a.* (nesiant) Tending to approximate.
Nesiannu, *v. a.* (nesiant) To approximate.
Nesiant, *s. m.* (nes) Approximation.
Nesiator, *ger.* (nesiad) In approximating.
Nesitor, *sup.* (nes) To be approximating.
Nesnes, *a.* (nes *repeated*) Nearer and nearer.

Nesnes y llefair i'r dref.

Nearer and *nearer* the shouting to the town. *Adage.*

Nes nes yw cerdd Taliesin,
A'i fawl benceirddiawl o'i fin

Closer and closer still is Taliesin's song, and his masterly praise from his lips. *S. Cent.*

Nesrwydd, *s. m.* (nes) Nearness, proximity.
Nest, *s. m.* (nes) That is compact or close.
Nester, *s. m.—pl. t.* i (nest) A cupboard.
Nestig, *a.* (nest) Of a compact nature.

—— Nestig meidraeth
Meidradur llafur pob llawnaeth.

Compact the structure of the accomplisher of the labour of every fulness. *Bleddyn Sais.*

Nesu, *v. a.* (nes) To draw near, to approximate.
Nestu, *v. a.* (nest) To appropriate.

O rhoddir genedl wraig diawd i alltud,—ni chaiff yr un o blant hono eisteddfa arbenig hyd y drydedd ach, ac o'r this wayn ... hono y nestir gwartheg diiach i'n teulu

If a tribe betroth a poor woman to an alien, none of the children of such a one shall obtain a special station, until the third descent, and, from that sort of connexion, cattle not available as surety *shall be appropriated* to their family.

Neu, *v. a.* (ne) To pant; to wish earnestly.
Neu, *conj.* (ne) Or. *Tydi neu arall*, thou or another; *dyred neu baid*, come or let it alone.
Neu, *adv.* (ne) Truly so; will not, is there not; otherwise, else. *Neu ym, neu'm*, will not of me; *neu yth, neu'th*, will not of thee.

Breuddwydiaw er bun balchliw arien dos;
Ysolliawg nos, neu ym ... cawdd!

Dreaming about the nymph of the superb hue of the hoar drop, excellent be the night, *does it but* save me from grief! *Gwalchmai.*

Neu'm cynnwys draig Powys trwy barch;
Neu'm arwar, neu'm car, neu'm cyfarch!

Me *will not* the leader of Powys receive with respect; *will he not me* solace, *will he not* me love, *will he not* me greet! *Cynddelw.*

Neu'm bu dydd cer elfydd Elwy.

To me *truly there* was a day by the stream of Elwy. *Ll. P. Moch.*

Neuad, *s. m.* (neu) A panting; a longing.
Neuadd, *s. f.—pl. t.* au (neu—add) A hall.

Neuadd pob diddos.

Every shelter is a *hall*. *Adage.*

Wyf bardd neuadd, wyf cyff cadair;
Digonaf i feirdd llafar lluddair.

I am bard of the *hall*, I am butt of the chair; I shall be able to frustrate the talkative bards.

Neuaddawg, *a.* (neuadd) Having a hall.
Neuaddawl, *a.* (neuadd) Belonging to a hall.
Neuaddwys, *s. f.* (neuadd—gwys) A hall-full.

Addwyn enewydd yn neuaddwys.

Pleasing the minstrel in the *hall*. *Taliesin.*

Neuant, *s. m.* (neu) A panting; longing; regret.
Neuaw, *v. a.* (neu) To pant, to wish earnestly.

Eryr glyw glewaf, neuaf na ddaw!

As an eagle the most gallant chief, *I regret* that he does not come! *Cynddelw.*

Er pan llas llyw ced neud neued nes?
Neuaf nas gwelaf fal ym gweles.

Since the leader of generosity has been slain, is not regret come near? *I regret* that I see him not as he has seen me. *Cynddelw, m. Cadwallon.*

Neuawd, *s. m.* (neu) A panting; a longing.
Neuawl, *a.* (neu) Panting, longing; regretting.

I'r gwir Dduw ydd wyf yn erchi,
Er gwyr nef o'm neuawl weddi
—Torri glas gefyn..

To the true God I am praying, for heaven knows my *earnest* request, that the blue shackles may be broken. *Hywel Foel*

Neud, *adv.* (neu) Is it not, is it not that, does not; verily it is.

Neud amser gauaf gweilwaf gweilgi,
Gwelging moradar hwylfar heli;
Neud arllen arlen Eryri weithon;
Neud uchel gwendon gwyn-dir Enlli.

Is it not the time of winter the ocean is most pale, the bed of the sea fowls is the raging course of the brine; *does not* the hoar envelope Eryri now; *is not* the white wave loud round the sacred land of Enlli. *Bleddyn Fardd.*

Neued, *s. f.* (neu) A panting; longing; regret.

> Yn y mae yfed, heb neued, heb nag,
> Heb newaud eisieued.
>
> Where there is drinking, without *regret*, without refusal, without any kind of want. *Cynddelw.*

Neuedd, *s. m.* (neu) A panting, or palpitation; a panting after, or longing.

Neufedd, *s. m.* (neu—medd) Wealth, riches.

Neur, *adv.* (neu—yr) Is it not; verily so.

Neus, *adv.* (neu—ys) Is it not; verily it is.

New, *s. m.* (ne) That is proceeding or going off.

Newid, *s. m.—pl. t.* iau (new) A change; a cheap rate, small value, or cheapness.

> Nid erchis yr hen Gyrys onid a fai rhwng y newidiau.
>
> Old Cyrys asked for no more than what might be between the *bargains*. *Adage.*
>
> Angau'r newidiau fy nodi a wna
> Yn un o'r merthyri.
> Angel a ä at Eli
> A'm un Duw, a'm enaid i.
>
> The death of *changes* will mark me as one of the martyrs. may an angel go to Eli, and my only God, with my soul! *L. G. Cothi.*
>
> Clywn dyngu, a rhegi, a chablu, oni roeswn i newid ar fy nghlustiau rhag gwrandaw.
>
> I could bear swearing, cursing and blaspheming, so that I would have set a *bargain* upon my ears rather than listen. *Elis Wynn, B. Cwsg.*

Newid, *v. a.* (new) To change, to exchange.

> Newid y gwewyr.
>
> *To change* the pain. *Adage.*

Newidiad, *s. m.—pl. t.* au (newid) A changing.

Newidiadwy, *a.* (newidiad) Changeable.

Newidiannawl, *a.* (newidiant) Tending to change

Newidiannu, *v. a.* (newidiant) To produce a change or alteration; to transform.

Newidiant, *s. m.* (newid) The act or state of changing; alteration, transformation.

Newidiaw, *v. a.* (newid) To change; to transform.

> Tri pheth nis gall namyn Duw: dyoddef bythoedd y cengant; cyfanghyd a phob cyflwr heb newidiaw, a rhoi gwell a newydd ar bob peth heb ei roi ar goll.
>
> Three things which none but God can accomplish. endure the periods of eternity, coalesce with every state without *changing*: and confer improvement and renovation upon every thing without consigning it to annihilation. *Barddas.*
>
> Mae'n ei bryd fy newidiaw;
> Mawr wall oedd fy mwrw o'i llaw.
>
> It is in her mind *to change* me; great were the rashness to cast me off her hand. *Ieuan Dyfi.*

Newidiawg, *a.* (newid) Having a change.

Newidiawl, *a.* (newid) Changeable, mutable.

Newidiedig, *a.* (newidiad) Being changed.

Newidioldeb, *s. m.* (newidiawl) Changeableness.

Newidiolder, *s. m.* (newidiawl) Changeableness.

Newidioli, *v.* (newidiawl) To be changeable.

Newidiolrwydd, *s.* (newidiawl) Changeableness.

Newidiwr, *s. m.—pl.* newidwyr (newid—gwr) A changer; one who barters.

Newidrwydd, *s. m.* (newid) A changed state.

Newidwriaeth, *s. m.* (newidiwr) Exchange, commerce, or traffick, a bartering of wares.

> Gwiwddyn wyd; gwaeddian ydwyf
> Waethwaeth newidwriaeth wyf.
>
> Thou art an excellent person, a miserable wight am I. Worse and worse the *commerce* of love. *D. ab Gwilym.*

Newidwriaethawl, *a.* (newidwriaeth) Appertaining to exchange or commerce.

Newydd, *s. m.—pl. t.* ion (new) What is new. *Papur Newydd*, a news paper; *newyddion da*, good news; *dywed imi ryw newydd*, tell me some news.

> Na roi goel i newyddion oni bont yn hen.
>
> Give no credit to news until they are grown old. *Adage.*

Newydd, *a.* (new) New; fresh. *Newydd grai, newydd danllwr*, brand new.

Newyddaidd, *a.* (newydd) Somewhat new.

Newyddawl, *a.* (newydd) Of a new quality.

Newyddban, *a.* (newydd—pan) Newly dressed.

Newyddbeth, *s. m.—pl. t.* au (newydd—peth) A new thing, a novelty.

Newydd-deb, *s. m.* (newydd) Newness, novelty.

Newydd-der, *s. m.* (newydd) Newness, novelty.

Newydd-dra, *s. m.* (newydd) Newness, novelty.

Newyddedd, *s. m.* (newydd) Novelness, newness.

Newyddgrëad, *s. m.* (newydd—crëad) A new creation. *a.* Newly created.

Newyddiad, *s. m.—pl. t.* au (newydd) The act of making new; a becoming new; innovation.

Newyddian, *s. c.—pl. t.* od (newydd) A novice.

> Nid yn newyddian, rhag iddo ymchwyddaw, a syrthiaw i farnedigaeth y diafol.
>
> Not a *novice*, lest, being lifted up with pride, he fall into the condemnation of the devil. *1 Timothy* 3. 6.

Newyddianaeth, *s. m.* (newyddian) Noviciate.

Newyddiannawl, *a.* (newyddiant) Appertaining to a new state; of a new condition.

Newyddiannu, *v. a.* (newyddiant) To render of a new state; to become novel.

Newyddiannus, *a.* (newyddiant) Tending to a new state; in a state of newness.

Newyddiant, *s. m.* (newydd) A state of newness.

Newyddiaw, *v. a.* (newydd) To make new.

Newyddiedig, *a.* (newyddiad) Being made new.

Newyddrwydd, *s. m.* (newydd) Recentness.

Newyddu, *v. a.* (newydd) To make new; to modernize, to innovate, to become new.

Newyddus, *a.* (newydd) Tending to innovation.

Newyddwr, *s. m.—pl.* newyddwyr (newydd—gwr) One who makes new; an innovator.

Newyn, *s. m.* (ne—gwyn) Hunger; famine.

> Gloddest awr a newyn blwyddyn.
>
> Excess for an hour and *famine* for a year. *Adage.*
>
> Ni ddwg newyn mam weision.
>
> Boys will not bear the *hunger* of a mother. *Adage.*
>
> Pwybynag a gyfarfai ag Arthur, ag un dyrnawd y lladdai, ag ef a'i farch; ac wrth hyny pawb a ffoynt rhagddo, megys ffoynt yr anifeiliaid rhag llew dywal, pan fai newyn mawr arno.
>
> Whoever happened to meet with Arthur, with one stroke was he slain, him and his horse, and therefore every body fled from him, as the beasts might flee from a furious lion, when he might be suffering great *hunger*. *Gr. ab Arthur.*

Newynawg, *a.* (newyn) Having hunger, famished.

> Hwareuid mab noeth, ni hwery mab newynawg.
>
> A naked child may play, a *hungry* child will not play. *Adage.*

Newynawl, *a.* (newyn) Famishing; hungry.

Newyndawd, *s. m.* (newyn) Hungriness.

Newyndra, *s. m.* (newyn) A hungry state.

Newynedig, *a.* (newyn) Being famished.

Newyniad, *s. m.* (newyn) A famishing.

Newynllyd, *a.* (newyn) Hungry, half starved.

Newynllydrwydd, *s. m.* (newynllyd) Hungriness.

Newynogaeth, *s. m.* (newynawg) Famishment.

Newynu, *v. a.* (newyn) To starve one, to famish; to be starved, to be famished.

> Lladd gloddest yw newynu y meddyg.
>
> To destroy intemperance is *to starve* the doctor. *Adage.*
>
> Mal ceiliawg y rhedyn yn canu yr haf a newynu y gauaf.
>
> Like the grasshopper singing in summer and *famishing* in winter. *Adage.*

Newynwr, *s. m.—pl.* newynwyr (newyn—gwr) One who hungers; a famisher.

Nhw, *pron.* (hwy) They, or them.

Nhwy, *pron.* (nhw) They, or them.

Nhwythau, *pron.* (nhwy—tau) They also.

NI, *s. m. r.* A number separate or apart.

Ni, *pron.* (ni, *s.*) We, us. *Dyma ni*, here we are; *ni awn*, we will go; *ni sydd yma*, it is we who are here.

Gwell gwae fi na gwae ni.

Better woe me than woe us. *Adage.*

Ni, *adv.* Not; used mostly before words with consonant initials. *Ni ddeuant*, they will not come; *ni waeth er hyny*, no matter for that; *ni ym, ni yth, ni yn, ni ych*, by syncope become *ni'm, ni'th, ni'n, ni'ch.*

Ni bydd doeth ni ddarllen.

He will not be wise that will not read. *Adage.*

Ni bydd dirïad heb hawl.

The mischievous will not be without a claim. *Adage.*

Gwr ni'th gar ni'th gydfydd.

A person who loves thee not will not bear with thee. *Adage.*

Ar ni oddefo gwas bid was iddo ei hun.

He that will not bear with a servant let him be a servant to himself. *Adage.*

Enllib ni char ei enllibo.

Scandal loves not to be scandalized. *Adage.*

Diwedd ni bydd it', na dechre ni bu.

An end there will not be to thee, nor beginning has there been. *Ein. ab Gwalchmai.*

Nid, *s. m.* (ni—id) A stop of progress; that is impending or in a state of rest.

Nid, *adv.* (ni—yd) Not; used mostly before words with vowel initials. *Nid yw da*, it is not good; *nid y fi ond v fo*, not me but him; *nid oes ond er doe er pan aeth*, it is only since yesterday that he is gone; *nid amgen*, not otherwise, to wit; *nid hwyrach*, perhaps.

A Duw nid da ymdaraw.

With God it is not good to strive. *Adage.*

Nid bod ond angen, nid angen ond Duw.

There is no being but necessity, there is not a necessity but God. *Adage.*

Nidr, *s. m.* (nid) A let, impediment, or hinderance; an entanglement; a delay, or lingering.

Nidrad, *s. m.* (nidr) An entangling; perplexity.

Nidraw, *v. a.* (nidr) To entangle; to be entangled; to embarrass; to perplex.

Y fieren——
Nidrodd amgylch fy neudroed.

The bramble *it entangled* about my two feet. *D. ab Gwilym.*

Nidrawl, *a.* (nidr) Entangling; dilatory.

Nidredd, *s. m.* (nidr) Entanglement; perplexity.

Nidri, *s. m.* (nidr) Entanglement; perplexity; obstruction, hinderance.

O nidri nid ai un adref.

From *perplexity* not one would reach home. *M. ab Gethin, i'r Saeson.*

Nidriad, *s. m.—pl.* nidriaid (nidr) An entangler.

Nidrwr, *s. m.—pl.* nidrwyr (nidr—gwr) One who entangles; a delayer.

Nif, *s. m.* (ni) A specific number or tale.

Nifer, *s. m.—pl. t.* oedd (nif) A number; a number collected together, a multitude, a host, a company; a retinue.

Niferai, *s. c.—pl.* nifereion (nifer) Numerator.

Niferawg, *a.* (nifer) Consisting of many.

Beirdd neued niferawg orsedd.

The wish of bards a numerous congress. *Cynddelw.*

Niferawl, *a.* (nifer) Relating to number; numerical, numeral.

Niferedig, *a.* (nifer) Being numbered, or told.

Niferedd, *s. m.* (nifer) Numerousness.

Niferiad, *s. m.* (nifer) A numbering.

Niferiaeth, *s. m.* (nifer) Numeration.

Nifeiriannawl, *a.* (nifeiriant) Numerary.

Nifeiriannu, *v. a.* (nifeiriant) To enumerate; to make out a number.

Nifeiriant, *s. m.* (nifer) Numeration.

Niferogi, *v. a.* (niferawg) To render numerous; to become numerous or multitudinous.

Niferogrwydd, *s. m.* (niferawg) Numerousness.

Niferu, *v. a.* (nifer) To number, to count.

Niferydd, *s. m.—pl. t.* ion (nifer) A numerist.

Nifwl, *s. m.* (nif—gwl) A mist; a cloud.

Nifwlawg, *a.* (nifwl) Misty, hazy, cloudy.

Nig, *s. m.—pl. t.* ion (ny—ig) That is strait.

Nigiad, *s. m.* (nig) A straitening, a narrowing.

Nigiaw, *v. a.* (nig) To straiten, to narrow.

Nigus, *a.* (nig) Strait, narrow, confined.

Ni wisgaf fenyg nigus
O groen unolli——

I will not wear any *strait* gloves of the skin of sheep. *D. ab Gwilym.*

Nill, *s. m.—pl. t.* ion (ny—ill) What tends to gain upon or to encroach; a poppy.

***Nilla**, *v. a.* (nill) To be over-reaching, to augment

Nillai, *s. c.—pl.* nilleion (nill) A sickle.

Ninnau, *pron.* (ni—tau) We also, and us.

Ebai Arawn ab Cynfarch, cyrchwn yr hanner-gwyr; a safwn yn eu cyrchu, hyd pan orfom ni arnaddunt hwy, cen ddwyn eu anrhydedd, yd arferom ninnau o lawen fuddygoliaeth.

Said Arawn son of Cynfarch, let us fall on these half men; and let us persevere in attacking them, until we overcome them, so by taking away their honour, that *we then* may enjoy a glad triumph. *Gr. ab Arthur.*

Nis, *adv.* (ni—ys) Not. It is synonymous with *Ni*, and used before words with consonant initials, and preserving them in their radical form; as *nis doi*, for *ni ddoi*, thou wilt not come; or *nis gweli*, for *ni weli*, thou wilt not see, and the like.

Eddewid nis gwneler nid yw.

A promise that shall *not* be performed doth not exist. *Adage.*

Ni chaiff bwyll nis pryno.

He shall not obtain wit who buys it *not*. *Adage.*

Nith, *s. f.—pl. t.* oedd (ny—ith) That is pure, or clear. a niece.

Nithiad, *s. m.* (nith) A winnowing, a cleaning.

Nithiannawl, *a.* (nithiant) Tending to purify.

Nithiannu, *v. a.* (nithiant) To make clean.

Nithiant, *s. m.* (nith) A purifying: a winnowing.

Nithiaw, *v. a.* (nith) To purify; to winnow. Also *Troelli* and *dioldi*.

Nithia o'm bron greulon gredd;
Noetha yn war nyth anwiredd.

Purge from my breast a cruel disposition; gently lay open the nest of iniquity. *H. D. ab Ifan.*

Nithiawl, *a.* (nith) Tending to clear; relating to winnowing.

Nithiedig, *a.* (nithiad) Being winnowed.

Nithiwr, *s. m.—pl.* nithwyr (nith—gwr) A winnower.

Nithlen, *s. f.* (nith—llen) A winnowing sheet.

Nithlen, pedair ceiniawg a dal.

A *winnowing sheet*, its value is four pence. *Welsh Laws.*

Niw, *s. m.* (ny—iw) That is violent or sharp.

Niw, *adv.* (ni) Of what not, of that not.

Ni chyll niw dyfydd.

There will be no loss *of what* will *not* be. *Adage.*

Niwed, *s. m.—pl.* niweidiau (niw) Harm, hurt, damage, prejudice, disadvantage.

Na chwar hyd niwed,
Na chellwair hyd lwed.

Play not till *harm* comes, jest not till it becomes calumny. *Adage.*

Niwedu, *v. a.* (niwed) To hurt, or to injure.

> Nad l'r cythrel, y gelyn,
> Nodau dig niweidu dyn.

> Prevent the devil, the foe, of wrathful impulses, to injure man. *I. Gruffudd.*

Niweidiad, *s. m.* (niwaid) A hurting a damaging.
Niweidiannawl, *a.* (niweidiant) Of a noxious or hurtful quality; injurious.
Niweidiannu, *v. a.* (niweidiant) To create a hurt, or injury; to become an injury.
Niweidiant, *s. m.* (niwed) A harming, a hurting.
Niweidiaw, *v. a.* (niwed) To hurt, to harm, to injure, to damage, to annoy.
Niweidiawg, *a.* (niwaid) Hurtful, injurious.
Niweidiawl, *a.* (niwed) Nocent, mischievous.
Niweidiedig, *a.* (niwed) Hurt, or injured.
Niweidioldeb, *s. m.* (niweidiawl) Noxiousness.
Niweidioledd, *s. m.* (niweidiawl) Noxiousness.
Niweidioli, *v. a.* (niweidiawl) To render noxious; to become noxious or hurtful.
Niweidiolrwydd, *s. m.* (niweidiawl) Noxiousness.
Niweidiwr, *s. m.—pl.* niweidwyr (niwaid—gwr) One who hurts or injures.
Niweidrwydd, *s. m.* (niwed) Hurtfulness.
Niwl, *s. m.—pl. t.* oedd (ni—gwl) Mist, fog.

> Niwl y gwanwyn, gwaesarn gwynt;
> Niwl yr haf, gwaesarn tes:
> Niwl y cynhauaf, gwaesarn gwlaw:
> Niwl y gauaf, gwaesarn eira.

> Mist in spring is the source of wind;
> Mist in summer is the source of heat;
> Mist in autumn is the source of rain,
> Mist in winter is the source of snow. *Adage.*

Niwlen, *s. f. dim.* (niwl) A small mist; a small detached cloud.
Niwliach, *s. pl. aggr.* (niwl) Scattered clouds of mist; flying clouds.

> Ni welaf onid niwliach
> Nid yfaf win, nid wyf iach.

> I see nought but *misty clouds* I will not drink wine: I am not well. *D. ab Gwilym.*

Niwliad, *s. m.* (niwl) A becoming misty or cloudy.
Niwliaw, *v. n.* (niwl) To become misty or cloudy.
Niwliawg, *a.* (niwl) Covered with mist, misty.
Niwliogrwydd, *s. m.* (niwliawg) Mistiness.
NO, *s. m. r.* That stops, confines, or keeps in.
No, *adv.* (no, *s.*) Than, compared with. It is used before words, with consonant initials. *Llai no dim*, less than nothing; *mwy no dim*, more than any thing.

> Gwell ceiniog no brawd.

> A penny is better than a brother. *Adage.*

Nod, *s. m.—pl. t.* au (no—od) A characteristic, a token, a mark, a butt, a brand. *Gwr nod*, a man of note; *haint y nodau* the plague: *nod y dwfr yw gwlybaniaeth*, the characteristic of water is liquidity.

> Lias hael [illegible] tra fu'n,
> Triwyr nod [illegible] Elgan.

> Slain were men generous whilst they were, three men of note great of fame, by Elgan. [illegible]

> Ni chwynwn [illegible],
> Nod [illegible]

> I would not complain [illegible] change condition. [illegible]

Nod, *adv.* (no—od) Marking, to, even, likewise.

> Car [illegible] dy elyn.

> Love [illegible] even thy enemy. *Adage.*

Nodach, *s. pl. aggr.* (nod) Sundry articles.
Nodadwy, *a.* (nod) Remarkable, observable.
Nodai, *s. c.—pl.* nodeion (nod) A noter.
Nodawg, *a.* (nod) Having a mark or sign, noted.
Nodawl, *a.* (nod) Tending to characterize, or to mark; marked, notable, eminent, considerable.
Nodeb, *s. m.* (nod) A characteristic.
Nodedig, *a.* (nod) Characterized, noted, marked, eminent, considerable.
Noden, *s. f.—pl. t.* i (nawd) Thread, yarn.
Nodi, *v. a.* (nod) To characterize, to note, to mark, to point out; to appoint.

> Ebai Arthur yna, cán na thrigi di yma, unben, ti a geffi y nodo dy ben. [illegible]

> Thereupon Arthur said since thou wilt not tarry here, prince, thou shalt have the request, which thy tongue may mention. *H. Culhwch—Mabinogion.*

> Wedi iddynt nodi diwrnod iddo, llawer a ddaeth ato ef, i'w lety, i'r rhai y tystiolaethodd—am yr Iesu.

> After they *had appointed* a day for him, many came to him, into his lodgings, to whom he testified concerning Jesus. *Acts* xxviii. 23.

Nodiad, *s. m.—pl. t.* au (nod) A characterising; a noting, a pointing out: an appointing.
Nodiadawl, *a.* (nodiad) Characteristical.
Nodiadu, *v. a.* (nodiad) To characterise.
Nodiadur, *s. m.* (nodiad) An annotator.
Nodiannawl, *a.* (nodiant) Characteristic.
Nodiannu, *v. r.* (nodiant) To characterize.
Nodiannus, *a.* (nodiant) Characteristical.
Nodiannusrwydd, *s. m.* (nodiannus) Characteristicalness; that is of a marked condition.
Nodiant, *s. m.* (nod) A notation, a noting.
Nodiedydd, *s. m.—pl. t.* ion (nodiad) One who characterizes. one who remarks; a notary.
Nodlyfr, *s. m.—pl. t.* au (nod—llyfr) Note book.
Nodoldeb, *s. m.* (nodawl) Characteristicalness.
Nodoledd, *s. m.* (nodawl) Characteristicalness.
Nodoli, *v. a.* (nodawl) To characterize.
Nodolrwydd, *s. m.* (nodawl) Characteristicalness; notableness, notability.
Nodrwydd, *s. m.* (nôd) A notable condition.
Nodwedd, *s. m.* (nôd—gwedd) A characteristic.
Nodweddawl, *a.* (nodwedd) Characteristical.
Nodweddedig, *a.* (nodwedd) Characterized.
Nodweddiad, *s. m.* (nodwedd) A characterising.
Nodweddu, *v. a.* (nodwedd) To characterise.

> [illegible] y mae iaith yn ddigon [illegible] dychymyg ar a ddichon bryd ar [illegible] nodweddu.

> Language is adequate to describe every idea, which the mind and genius of man may be able *to characterise.* *Llyrfyn o-Lengowydd.*

Nodweddus, *a.* (nodwedd) Characteristical.
Nodweddwr, *s. m.—pl.* nodweddwyr (nodwedd—gwr) A characterizer.
Nodydd, *s. m.—pl. t.* ion (nod) A noter, a marker.
Nodyddiad, *s. m.—pl. t.* au (nodydd) A notation.
Nodyn, *s. m. dim.* (nod) A note, a mark, a sign.
Nodd, *s. m.—pl. t.* ion (ny—odd) The moisture or fluid pervading bodies; the juice, or sap of vegetation.
Noddadwy, *a.* (nawdd) Capable of affording refuge.
Noddawl, *a.* (nawdd) Tending to protect.
Nodded, *s. f.* (nawdd) Refuge, protection.
Noddfa, *s. f.—pl. t.* au (nawdd—ma) A place of refuge, a sanctuary.

> Noddfa oeddent fanst.

> New *sanctuaries* they were. *L. G. Cothi.*

> Mae hen groes mal carreg noddfa yn mynwent Diserth.

> There is an old cross, like a stone of *refuge*, in the church-yard of Diserth. *L. Lloyd.*

Noddi, *v. a.* (nawdd) To give refuge, to protect.

> A nodd o Duw rhy nodir.

> That *will be protected* by God *will be protected* completely. *Adage.*

> [illegible] Mam
> [illegible]
> [illegible] Ddi.

> [illegible] preservation of Mon: May God the Father, [illegible] part of it. *Gr. Ll. ab Ifan.*

Noddiad, *s. m.* (nawdd) A giving refuge, a protecting, a making an asylum.
Noddiannawl, *a.* (noddiant) As to protection.
Noddiannu, *v. a.* (noddiant) To make a refuge.
Noddiant, *s. m.* (nawdd) Protection, refuge.
Noddlyd, *a.* (nodd) Of a juicy nature, sappy.
Noddlydiad, *s. m.* (noddlyd) A rendering juicy; a becoming juicy or sappy.
Noddlydrwydd, *s. m.* (noddlyd) Juiciness.
Noddlydu, *v. a.* (noddlyd) To render juicy; to become juicy or sappy.
Noddus, *a.* (nawdd) Affording a refuge or asylum.
Noddusaw, *v. a.* (noddus) To render protective; to become protective.
Noddwr, *s. m.—pl.* noddwyr (nawdd—gwr) One who gives refuge; a protector.
Noddwraig, *s. f.—pl.* noddwreigedd (nawdd—gwraig) A protectress.
Noddyn, *s. m.* (nawdd) That envelopes, an abyss.

Elor y gwr a elwir Gwyn
Ab Nudd uwch ben y noddyn——
Aed ag ef.

May the bier of him who is called Gwyn ab Nudd take him above the *abyss*. *R. Nanmor, i'r llong.*

Noe, *s. f.—pl. t.* au (no) Any shallow vessel; a platter, or flat wooden dish; a tray. *Noe bobi, cafn tylinaw*, a kneading vessel or trough.

Merch—or pan aner oni fo ddeuddeg mlwydd a ddyly fod wrth noe ei thad.

A girl, from the time when she is born until she shall be twelve years old ought to be at her father's *dish*. *Welsh Laws.*

Noead, *s. m.* (noe) A putting in a platter or dish.
Noeaid, *s. f.—pl.* noeeidiau (noe) A platter-full.
Noeaw, *v. a.* (noe) To put in a platter, to dish.
Noeth, *s. m.—pl. t.* ion (ny—oeth) A naked one.

Dod fenthyg i noeth, nis cai dranoeth.

Give a loan to the *naked one*, thou wilt not have it the next day. *Adage.*

Noeth, *a.* (ny—oeth) Naked, bare, exposed.

Careiddweh arglwydd a chledd noeth ys enbyd.

The familiarity of a lord with a *naked* sword is dangerous. *Adage.*

Noethadwy, *a.* (noeth) That may be made naked.
Noethawg, *a.* (noeth) Being naked or bare.
Noethawl, *a.* (noeth) Tending to make bare.
Noethedig, *a.* (noeth) Being made bare.
Noethedd, *s. m.* (noeth) Nakedness, nudity.
Noethi, *v. a.* (noeth) To make bare, to strip.

Tri angenwrthun beirdd Ynys Prydain: cel gân orfod, er heddwch a lles; cwyn anfawl, gan raid cyflawnder; a noethi cledd ar ddifrawd ac anrhaith.

The three repulsive obligations of the bards of the Isle of Britain: secresy by compulsion, for the sake of peace and of good; the complaint of dispraise, for the sake of justice; and *to unsheath* the sword against evil and devastation. *Barddas.*

Noethiad, *s. m.* (noeth) A making naked.
Noethiadawl, *a.* (noethiad) Apt to make bare.
Noethiadu, *v. a.* (noethiad) To denudate.
Noethiannawl, *a.* (noethiant) Apt to denudate.
Noethiannu, *v. a.* (noethiant) To denudate.
Noethiant, *s. m.* (noeth) A denudation.
Noethlwm, *a.* (noeth—llwm) Nakedly bare.
Noethlyman, *s. m.—pl. t.* od (noeth—llyman) One that is stark naked. *a.* Stark naked.
Noethni, *s. m.* (noeth) Nakedness, bareness.
Nof, *s. m.* (ny—of) That is moving or flowing.
Nofant, *s. m.* (nof) A state of motion; a fluid.
Nofiant, *s. m.—pl. t.* au (nawf) A swimming.

Ac yn noethach ym gwnaethant
Na gleisiad yn nofiad nant.

And *more naked* they made me than the salmon in the *swimming course* of the brook. *L. G. Cothi, i wyr Caerlleon.*

Nofiadaeth, *s. m.* (nofiad) The art of swimming.

Nofiadawl, *a.* (nofiad) Relating to swimming.
Nofiadoldeb, *s. m.* (nofiadawl) Buoyancy.
Nofiadoledd, *s. m.* (nofiadawl) Buoyancy.
Nofiadur, *s. m.* (nofiad) That causes to swim. *Nofiadur pysgodyn, nawf pysgodyn*, the swim or wind bladder of a fish.
Nofiadwy, *a.* (nofiad) Capable of swimming.
Nofiannawl, *a.* (nofiant) Buoyant, swimming.
Nofiannu, *v. a.* (nofiant) To render buoyant; to become buoyant.
Nofiant, *s. m.* (nawf) A swimming; a swim.
Nofiaw, *v. a.* (nawf) To swim; to cause to swim. *A elli di nofiaw dros yr afon?* Canst thou swim over the river? *Dwfr a nofia long*, water that will swim a ship.

Ni nofia mewn un afon
Y doeth yn erbyn y don.

The wise *will not swim* in a river against the stream of the wave. *Adage.*

Nofiedig, *a.* (nofiad) Being swimmed.
Nofiedigaeth, *s. m.* (nofiedig) The art of swimming; a swimming condition.
Nofiedydd, *s. m.—pl. t.* ion (nofiad) A swimmer.

Niwl wybren——
Nofiedydd y nef ydwyt:
Gwasgara i'th gwng oror;
Dy loches yw monwes mor.

Vapour of the atmosphere, thou art the *swimmer* of the sky disperse to thy region of repose; thy retreat is the bosom of the sea. *D. Richard.*

Nofiwr, *s. m.—pl.* nofwyr (nawf—gwr) A swimmer
Nofle, *s. m.* (nawf—lle) A swimming place.
Nofwg, *s. m.* (nawf) Buoyancy, a swimming state
Nog, *adv.* (no) Than, compared with. It is used before words with vowel initials.

Gwell crefft nog arllwed arglwydd.

Better is a trade *than* the profusion of a prince. *Adage.*

Nag eiriach un nog arall.

Spare not one *more than* another. *H. Llwyd Cynfal, i'r llwynog.*

Nol, *v. a.* (ny—ol) To fetch, or to bring.
Noli, *v. a.* (nol) To fetch, or to bring.
Non, *s. f.—pl. t.* au (ny—on) A stream, a brook.

Dy ffynnawn lydan, dyleinw nonau;
Dyddaw, dyhebgyr, dybrys dybrau:
Marwnad Corol a'm cyffroes!

Thy ample fountain, it will replenish the *streams*, and omens come, dispensing with the path of haste: the death-cry of Corol hath agitated me! *Taliesin.*

Nos, *s. f.—pl. t.* au (ny—os) Night. *Min nos, min y nos*, the twilight of evening; *hanner nos, canol nos*, midnight; *perfeddion y nos, dyfnder y nos*, the middle of the night, or the dead of the night; *o'r nos y ganer ef*, from the night when he shall be born.

Nos yw mam y cynlwyn.

Night is the mother of plots. *Adage.*

Gwaith y nos y dydd a'i dengys.

The work of the *night* the day will *disclose*. *Adage.*

Nosawl, *a.* (nos) Relating to night, nocturnal.

Mawrhâodd yr holl-gyfoethawg Dduw ei drugaredd yn mhlith y Prydeiniaid, rhag ei tywyllaw hwynt o nosawl dywyllwg angeu.

The omnipotent God hath magnified his mercy amongst the Britons, in preventing their being darkened by the *night-like* darkness of death. *Gr. ab Arthur.*

Nosgrwydr, *s. m.—pl.* nosgrwydrau (nos—crwydr) A night ramble.
Nosgrwydrad, *s. m.* (nosgrwydr) A night ramble.
Nosgrwydrai, *s. m.—pl.* nosgrwydroion (nosgrwydr) A night rambler.
Nosgrwydrydd, *s. m.—pl.* nosgrwydryddion (nosgrwydr) A night rambler.

Nosi, *v. n.* (nos) To become night, to draw towards night, to grow late.

> Er nos dysgleirdeb eich gwedd,
> O'ch llygad dan gwmwl y'nghudd——
> Etto e wawria.
>
> Though the brightness of your countenance is *become night*, from your eye being hidden under a cloud, again it shall shine. *Ro. Edwards Offeiriad.*

Nosi, *s. f.* (nos) A night-time, darkness of night.

> Enaid dlos, ni ddaw nosi
> I adail haf y del hi.
>
> My pretty soul, *night* will not come to the summer edifice where she comes. *D. ab Gwilym.*

Nosiad, *s. m.* (nos) A becoming night.

Nosig, *s. f. dim.* (nos) A night time, a night.

> Mabon fab Modron a ddygid yn nhair nosig iwrth ei fam.
>
> Mabon the son of Modron was taken in three *nights* from his mother. *H. Culhwch—Mabinogion.*

Noson, *s. f.* (nos) A night time, a night; a certain night.

> Iacob——a lettyai y noson hono yn y gwersyll.
>
> Jacob lodged for that *night* in the camp. *Genesis 32. 21.*

Noswaith, *s. f.—pl.* nosweithiau (nos—gwaith) A certain night, a night.

Noswyl, *s. f.—pl. t.* iau (nos—gwyl) The eventide, the nightfall, the time of leaving off work at eve; a vigil.

> Noswyl iâr, gwae ai câr.
>
> The hen's night-time, woe to such as loves it. *Adage.*

Noswyliad, *s. m.* (noswyl) A leaving off work at eve; a keeping vigils.

Noswyliaw, *v. a.* (noswyl) To give over work at eve; to keep a vigil.

Noswyliawg, *a.* (noswyl) Resting for the night.

Noswyliedig, *a.* (noswyliad) Being laid by at night

Noswyliwr, *s. m.—pl.* noswylwyr (noswyl—gwr) One who leaves off for the night; one who keeps vigils.

Notur, *s. m.—pl. t.* ion (nawd) Nature.

Noturiaeth, *s. m.—pl. t.* au (notur) Nature.

Noturiawl, *a.* (notur) Natural, or genial.

Nudd, *s. m.* (ny—udd) A fog, haze, or mist.

Nug, *s. m.—pl. t.* ion (ny—ug) A shake, a quiver, a ripple. *a.* Shaking; quivering.

> Meirch——
> Mwth, myngwyn, hirllam, harlleg,
> Na bwynt gynt na rhywynt uch ryd nug.
>
> Steeds, swift, white-maned, of long stride, and impatient, may they not be more fleet than the stormy wind above the *rippling* ford. *Ll. P. Moch.*

Nugiad, *s. m.—pl. t.* au (nug) A shaking; a rippling; or broken motion.

Nugiaw, *v. a.* (nug) To shake; to quiver; to ripple; to wrinkle.

> Nugiaw gàn y cwn.
>
> *To be shaken by the dogs.* *Adage.*

Nugiawl, *a.* (nug) Tending to shake or ripple.

Nur, *s. m.—pl. t.* ion (ny—ur) A pure body or being; essence.

> Am Fadawg deifniawg dofn awen;
> Am nur pur fal pair Ceridwen——
> Y prydderaf.
>
> For the accomplished Madawg of profound genius; for a pure *essence* like the cauldron of Ceridwen I am sad. *Sefnyn.*

NW, *s. m. r.* That is of a pervading nature.

Nwd, *s. m.* (ny—wd) That is sharp or pointed.

Nwdd, *s. m.* (nw) That is pervasive or oozing.

Nwf, *s. m.* (nw) That is subtil; that is pure, or hallowed. *a.* Holy, or pure.

Nwn, *s. m.* (nw) That is of an intense nature.

Nwth, *s. m.* (nw) That draws in or pulls.

Nwy, *s. m.* (nw) That is pervasive; spirit, or vivacity; sprightliness.

Nwyd, *s. m.—pl. t.* au (nwy) Drift, or scope; bent of the mind, or passion; a whim, or trick; a way, or manner. *Nwydau drwg*, bad tricks; *anhawdd tynu nwyd o hen geffyl*, it is difficult to break an old horse of a trick.

> O bant i bant b'ont tebyg
> Hergwlong lwyd i nwyd neidr!
>
> From bottom to bottom is not the dun roving *side* of the same *course* as a snake! *R. Nanmor.*

Nwydaw, *v. n.* (nwyd) To have a particular bias of mind; to have a whim or trick.

Nwydawg, *a.* (nwyd) Having a particular passion; having a whim or trick.

Nwydawl, *a.* (nwyd) Of a peculiar bent of mind; whimsical; apt to have tricks.

Nwydedd, *s. m.* (nwyd) The state of being of a peculiar turn of mind; whimsicalness; a habit of freaks or tricks.

Nwydiad, *s. m.* (nwyd) A filling with whims or freaks; a becoming whimsical.

Nwydiant, *s. m.* (nwyd) A whimsical disposition.

Nwydus, *a.* (nwyd) Freaky, or whimsical.

Nwydusaw, *v. a.* (nwydus) To render whimsical; to become whimsical or full of freaks.

Nwydusrwydd, *s. m.* (nwydus) Whimsicalness.

Nwydwyllt, *a.* (nwyd—gwyllt) Abounding with wild freaks; hairbrained.

Nwydd, *s. m.—pl. t.* au (nwy) Essence; stuff, substance, or materials; commodity; effects; wealth, riches. *Mae nwydd da yn yr esgidiau hyn*, there is good stuff in these shoes. *Sil.*

Nwyddaw, *v. a.* (nwydd) To endue with matter or substance; a becoming substantial.

Nwyddawg, *a.* (nwydd) Material, or substantial.

Nwyddawl, *a.* (nwydd) Material, or substantial.

Nwyddiad, *s. m.* (nwydd) A rendering material or substantial; a becoming substantial.

Nwyddus, *a.* (nwydd) Material, or substantial.

Nwyf, *s. m.—pl. t.* au (nwy) A subtil pervading element; a fine ethereal fluid; animal spirits, liveliness, or vivacity; energy.

> Tri bonedd awen, nwyf, pwyll, a gwybodaeth.
>
> The three foundations of genius, vigour, judgement, and knowledge. *Barddas.*

Nwyfaw, *v. a.* (nwyf) To cheer up the spirits, to enliven; to become sprightly or wanton.

Nwyfawg, *a.* (nwyf) Full of vivacity, sprightly; wanton, amorous.

> ————Golygus wileged
> Yn serchawg nwyfawg eu naid.
>
> Sightly mares of amorous and wanton leap. *T. Prys.*

Nwyfawl, *a.* (nwyf) Full of vivacity, sprightly; wanton, amorous.

Nwyfedig, *a.* (nwyf) Being made sprightly or wanton; being become lively or wanton.

Nwyfedigaeth, *s. m.* (nwyfedig) A rendering or becoming full of spirits.

Nwyfiad, *s. m.* (nwyf) An enlivening; a becoming sprightly or lively; a becoming wanton.

Nwyfiadawl, *a.* (nwyfiad) Of an enlivening tendency; of an amorous tendency.

Nwyfiadu, *v. a.* (nwyfiad) To render sprightly or vivacious; to become sprightly or wanton.

Nwyfiadus, *a.* (nwyfiad) Enlivening, cheering.

Nwyfiannawl, *a.* (nwyfiant) Enlivening.

Nwyfiannu, *v. a.* (nwyfiant) To render sprightly or wanton; to become full of spirits.

> Ei arogl o'i lwyn yn fwyn a'm nwyfiannodd;
> Hwyliai'm cain arfaeth.
>
> His fragrance from his grove kindly *cheered me*; it guided my brilliant design. *E. Dafydd.*

Nwyfiannus, *a.* (nwyfiant) Animating.

Nwyfiannusaw, *v. a.* (nwyfiannus) To render sprightly; to become full of vivacity.

Nwyfiant, *s. m.* (nwyf) Vivacity, sprightliness; wantonness.

—Brodyr a'm bwant
Ac o bob gorwyf nwyfiant
Ni wyr Tren perchen cyngant!

Brothers to me there were, and each of these princely heirs possessed *vigour* but Tren knows no congenial owner. *Llywarch Hen.*

Nwyfiator, *ger.* (nwyfiad) In enlivening.

Nwyfitor, *sup.* (nwyf) To be enlivening.

Nwyfoed, *s. m.* (nwyf—oed) A love meeting.

Adwaen ef o'i fedw nwyfoed,
Awdur cerdd adar y coed.

I know him from his birchen *recess of love*, the author of song for the birds of the grove. *D. ab Gwilym, i'r fronfraith.*

Nwyfre, *s. f.* (nwyf—rhe) The ethereal sphere; the firmament, the atmosphere.

Addwyn heul yn ewybr yn nwyfre.

Glorious is the sun moving in the *firmament*. *Taliesin.*

Gorddyar adar, gwlyb traeth,
Eglur nwyfre, ehelaeth tôn:
Gwyw calon rhag hiraeth!

Clamorous are the birds, the strand is wet, clear is the *welkin*, ample the wave: the heart is palsied with longing! *Llywarch Hen.*

Nwyfserch, *s. m.* (nwyf—serch) Wanton love.

Nwyfus, *a.* (nwyf) Full of spirits, sprightly, lively, cheerful; wanton.

Nwyfusaw, *v. a.* (nwyfus) To render sprightly; to become lively; to become wanton.

Nwyfusedd, *s. m.* (nwyfus) Sprightliness, vivacity; wantonness.

Nwyfusrwydd, *s. m.* (nwyfus) Sprightliness, vivacity; wantonness.

Nwyth, *s. m.—pl. t.* au (nwy) A drift, a course, whim, an oddity, a prank; impertinence. *Mae nwythau rhyfedd yn y dyn yma*, there are odd freaks in that man. *Sil.*

Nwythad, *s. m.* (nwyth) A rendering eccentric; a becoming eccentric or whimsical.

Nwythas, *s. f.* (nwyth) Eccentricity, oddity.

Dygymer pob ner, pob nwythas deyrn;
Duw o nef a'th swynas;
Wyt priawd tir Prydain a'i chlas.

Be thou taking every chieftain, every prince of *arrogancy*, God of heaven hath blessed thee; to thee appertains the land of Britain and its church. *Ll. P. Moch, i Lywelyn II.*

Nwythaw, *v. a.* (nwyth) To render whimsical; to become full of freaks or whimsical.

Nwythawg, *a.* (nwyth) Having oddities.

Nwythawl, *a.* (nwyth) Eccentric, whimsical.

Nwythedig, *a.* (nwythad) Rendered eccentric; become eccentric or whimsical.

Nwythiad, *s. m.* (nwyth) A rendering eccentric; a becoming eccentric or whimsical.

Nwythig, *a.* (nwyth) Eccentric, whimsical.

Nwythus, *a.* (nwyth) Full of whims, freaks, or oddities; whimsical, freaky; impertinent. *Dyn nwythus*, a whimsical and impertinent person.

Nwythusaw, *v. a.* (nwythus) To render whimsical; to become whimsical.

Nwythusrwydd, *s. m.* (nwythus) Eccentricity.

NY, *s. m. r.* That is spreading, pervasive, or universal; that is whole or in continuity. It is used as a prefix, implying augmentation, and certitude.

Nych, *s. m.* (ny—ych) A state of pain, a languishing, a pining away.

Hir nych i angeu.

Long *pining* to death. *Adage.*

Bid nych cwyn claf.

Languishing be the complaint of the sick. *Adage.*

Nycha, *interj.* (ny—ycha) Behold! lo! see here!

Nychawl, *a.* (nych) Languishing; tormenting.

Nychdawd, *s. m.* (nych) A state of languishment or pain; a lingering disorder; a languishment.

Gwell marw no hir nychdawd.

Better is death than long *languishment*. *Adage.*

Nychedig, *a.* (nych) Tortured, or afflicted.

Nychiad, *s. m.* (nych) A languishing; a causing pain, a tormenting.

Nychial, *v. n.* (nych) To be languishing or in pain

Nychiant, *s. m.* (nych) Languishment; pain.

Nychlyd, *a.* (nych) Languishing, pining; painful

Nychlydrwydd, *s. m.* (nychlyd) A state of anguish

Nychlydu, *v. n.* (nychlyd) To become languishing

Nychu, *v. a.* (nych) To inflict pain, to torment, to consume with pain; to languish, to pine, to waste away. *Paid a'i nychu hi*, do not torture her.

Wylaf——
Nychwyd, anafwyd nifer,
Na chawn ragor-ddawn ger'dwr.

I weep, *afflicted*, wounded are many, that we shall not enjoy the minstrel of superior talent. *Sefnyn.*

Nychwaew, *s. m.* (nych—gwaew) A languishing pain.

Nychwedd, *s. f.* (nych—gwedd) A countenance of anguish.

Nydell, *s. f.—pl. t.* i (nwd) A needle.

Nydwydd, *s. f.—pl. t.* au (nwd—gwydd) A broach, or pin; a needle. *Nydwydd ddur*, a stitching needle; *cei y cwd a'r nydwydd ar ei ol*, thou shalt have the bag and the broach after him: *Nydwydd y bygel*, shepherd's needle.

Nydwyddai, *s. c.* (nydwydd) Worker at a needle.

Nydwyddaw, *v. a.* (nydwydd) To needle.

Nydwyddes, *s. f.—pl. t.* au (nydwydd) A needlewoman, a seamstress.

Nydwyddwr, *s. m.—pl.* nydwyddwyr (nydwydd—gwr) A needleman, or seamster.

Nydd, *s. m.—pl. t.* ion (ny—ydd) A spin, a turn, or twist; a perversion; equivocation, evasion.

Nyddawl, *a.* (nydd) Spinning; turning, twisting.

Nyddedig, *a.* (nydd) Being spun or twisted.

Nyddfa, *s. f.—pl.* nyddfeydd (nydd) A spinning place.

Nyddiad, *s. m.* (nydd) A spinning; a twisting.

Nyddoes, *s. m.* (nydd—oes) Spinach.

Nyddu, *v. a.* (nydd) To spin; to turn, to twist; to pervert, to equivocate, to evade.

Nyddwedd, *s. f.* (nydd—gwedd) The size of yarn in spinning.

Nyddwr, *s. m.—pl.* nyddwyr (nydd—gwr) A spinner.

Nyddwraig, *s. f.—pl.* nyddwreigedd (nydd—gwraig) A spinning-woman, a spinster.

Nyf, *s. pl. aggr.* (nwf) Snow. It is more generally called *eiry*, *eira*, and *od*.

Gwynbryd nyf cyn daddawdd.

A white countenance of *snow* before it dissolves. *Ior. Gyriawg.*

Nyfed, *s. f.* (nwf) A pure or holy nature.

Dyphorthes meinir molud nyfed.

The slender maid bore the praise for *sanctity*. *Aneurin.*

Gorthywys nefoedd nyfed eglur,
Gwrthwyf na bo trist Crist creadur!

Supreme of the heavens of splendid *purity*, at me may Christ the creator not be grieved! *Cynddelw.*

Y gwr a orëu awyrawl edniaint,
Ac aduen daearawl,
Erglyw fi, arglwydd cannwyrawl;
Erglywed gwar nyfed nefawl;
Tu y bwyf y bo dy ganmawl,
Tad yspryd, a'n Tad ysprydawl.

The Being who caused the aerial creatures of wing, and earthly abodes, hear me, thou universal Lord; let the gentle *sanctity* of heaven listen; the side I am of be thou praised there, Father of spirit, and our spiritual Father. *Elidr Sais.*

Nyfel, *s. m.* (nwf—el) A subtil element.

> Uch awen uchel;
> Uch no pob nyfel.
>
> Above the high-flowing; higher than *every subtil element*. — *Taliesin, can y Meirch.*

Nyfiad, *s. m.* (nyf) A snowing, a falling of snow.

Nyfiaw, *v. n.* (nyf) To snow: but *bwrw eiry*, *bwrw eira*, and *odi*, are the popular words.

Nyni, *pron.* (ny—ni) We all; we, us.

> Duw Tad, o'th rad a'th fawrydi mawr,
> Ymorol â nyni.
>
> God the Father, of thy grace and thy awful majesty, have regard of us. — *H. D. ab Ifan.*

Nyninnau, *pron.* (ny—ninnau) We also; us too.

Nyth, *s. m.—pl. t.* od (ny—yth) A nest. *Nyth aderyn*, or *moron y maes*, wild carrot.

> Y penhebogydd——a ddyly nythod yr hebogau, a'r llamysteinod, a fo ar dir y brenin.
>
> The head falconer ought to have the *nests of* the falcons, and the sparrow hawks, which shall be on the land of the king. — *Welsh Laws.*

Nythai, *s. c.—pl.* nytheion (nyth) A nestling.

Nythaid, *s. m.—pl.* nytheidiau (nyth) A nestful.

Nythawd, *s. m.* (nyth) The act of nestling.

Nythdrig, *s. m.* (nyth—trig) The period of staying in the nest.

Nythdrigiad, *s. m.* (nythdrig) Nidulation.

Nythdrigiant, *s. m.* (nythdrig) The time of keeping the nest, nidulation.

Nythfa, *s. f.* (nyth—ma) A nestling place.

Nythgyw, *s. m.—pl. t.* ion (nyth—cyw) A nestling.

Nythiad, *s. m.—pl. t.* au (nyth) Nidification.

Nythlwyth, *s. m.—pl. t.* i (nyth—llwyth) A nestful, the young ones in the nest.

Nythu, *v. a.* (nyth) To build a nest; to nestle.

Nythyn, *s. m. dim.* (nyth) A little nest.

Nyw, *s. m.—pl. t.* iau (ny) Sprightliness, vivacity; ardour; vigour.

Nywiad, *s. m.* (nyw) A rendering lively; a becoming sprightly or wanton.

Nywus, *a.* (nyw) Of a sprightly nature.

Nywusaw, *v. a.* (nywus) To render sprightly; to become lively, brisk, or wanton.

Nywusedd, *s. m.* (nywus) Sprightliness.

Nywusrwydd, *s. m.* (nywus) Sprightliness.

O.

O, *s. m. r.* That goes out or proceeds. It is a termination of some nouns; and of the third person future tense of the subjunctive mood.

O, *prep.* From, of, out of; by. *O'm*, from my; *o'th*, from thy; *o'i*, from his, her, or its; *o'n*, from our; *o'ch*, from your; *o'u*, from their; *o'r*, from the; being contractions of *o ym*, *o yth*, *o ei*, *o ein*, *o eich*, *o eu*, *o yr*. *O le i le*, from place to place; *o'r gorau*, of the best, very well.

> Godrittor buwch o'i phen.
>
> The milking of a cow must be *from* her head. — *Adage.*

O, *conj.* If, used before words with consonant initials, in common with *os*, except that the mutable ones suffer no change with the latter; but with *o* the change is optional, in certain cases. *O ceri fi*, *o cheri fi*, *os ceri fi*, if thou wilt love me.

> O cheffir dyn yn llosgi yn lledrad, bid eneidfaddeu.
>
> *If* a man shall be found burning privily, let him be condemned to death. — *Welsh Laws.*
>
> Bai mawr, y'Nghymmru o bydd
> Dyn bydawl ar d'enw bedydd.
>
> A great fault, in Wales *if* there shall be a mortal man of thy christian name. — *D. ab Ieuan Ddu.*

O, *pron.* The third person neuter and masculine; it, he. *Difai oedd o*, faultless was he. This pronoun is also used idiomatically for persons, like *it* in English. *O ddywedodd imi farw*, it was said by him that I had died.

O, *interj.* Oh, alas. *O druan oedd!* Oh poor thing that he was! *O dyn!* Oh dear!

> O fi! a dwywau nef a daiar, a ddaw amser y gallwyf fi dala chwyl yn y gwrthwyneb i'r gwyr hyny, y rhai ry wnaeth i minnau ddyfod yn yr angenoctyd hwn!
>
> *Oh me!* ye gods of heaven and earth, will there come a time when I shall be able to retaliate against those men, who have caused me also to be in this adversity! — *Gr. ab Arthur.*

OB, *s. m. r.* A going out, a going from.

Oblaid, *conj.* (o—plaid) Because, for this reason.

Oblegid, *conj.* (o—plegid) Because, on that account, for, on this account that.

Obobtu, *prep.* (o—pobtu) On every side, on each side; about; from every side.

Obraidd, *adv.* (o—braidd) Hardly, or scarcely.

Obry, *prep.* (o—bry) Below, beneath, under.

> Addaf rên a'i hil ddaw fry:
> Dadebrant o dud obry.
>
> Adam the sire with his offspring will come above; they will revive and rise from the region *below*. — *W. Wyn.*

Obry, *adv.* (o—bry) Beneath, in a lower place.

> O chyrhaedd fry ni ddaw obry.
>
> If he gets above he will not come below. — *Adage.*

OC, *s. m. r.* An outward or opposite position.

Oc, *prep.* (oc, *s.*) From; of; out of; at a distance from; before, in front, or opposite to. *Oc ei wyneb*, from his face; *oc eu lle*, *o'u lle*, out of their place.

> Y Troiawnwyson a wnaynt aerfa ddirfawr oc amlaf oc eu gelynion.
>
> The Trojans made a slaughter of immense magnitude *of* their enemies. — *Gr. ab Arthur.*

Oco, *adv.* (oc) Yonder, there, at a distance.

> Ci'n hynod a hardd, oco'n hoew-nwyd i'w hynt;
> Ci'n ofn i daerion, mwy cynnar na dewr-wynt.
>
> A dog notable and handsome, *yonder* with sprightly cry on his course; a dog that is the dread of importunate ones, more swift than the impetuous wind. — *E. Dafydd, i fytheiad.*
>
> Y cnewwydd oco'n hoewon,
> Irlas frig ar ael y fron.
>
> The nut trees *yonder* lively seem, with fresh-coloured branches on the brow of the hill. — *Morg. Gruffudd.*

Ocr, *s. m.—pl.* ocrau (oc—yr) Usury.

Ocraeth, *s. m.* (ocr) Usury, profit, gain.

Ocrawl, *a.* (ocr) Relating to usury.

Ocredd, *s. m.* (ocr) Usuriousness; profit.

Ocri, *s. m.* (ocr) Usury, profit, gain.

Ocriad, *s. m.* (ocr) A dealing in usury.

Ocru, *v. a.* (ocr) To practise usury.

Ocrwr, *s. m.—pl.* ocrwyr (ocr—gwr) An usurer.

Ocrydd, *s. m.—pl. t.* ion (ocr) An usurer.

Octid, *s. m.* (og) The time of youth; youth.

> Cof can octid yn dir.
>
> Memory with *youth* is certain. — *Adage.*

OCH, *s. m. r.* A forcible utterance; a moan, a groan. *Och yn dy berfedd!* May there be a grumbling in thy guts!

Och, *interj.* (och, *s.*) Oh! Alas! Woe!

Och anwyl! o'r oer esgar,
Gweli dy fod yn drydar
Gan anben dewr diarchar,
Dy olo di y dan ddaiar!

Alas thou dear one! that a sad separation should come, after thou wert joyous with a gallant ruthless chief, that thou shouldest be covered under earth! *Cyfoesi Myrddin.*

Ocha, *interj.* (och) Oh, Ah. *Ocha druan!* Ah, poor thing! *Ocha fi! ocha finnau!* Ah me!

Ochain, *s. m.* (och) A groaning often, a groaning.

Ochain, *v. a.* (och) To be uttering groans.

Ochan, *s. m.* (och) A groan, a moan; a woe.

Ochan, *interj.* (och) Oh! Alas! Woe!

Ochan! nid pell y gelli.

Alas! not much canst thou do.

Ochenaid, *s. f.—pl.* ocheneidiau (och—enaid) A sigh.

Mae dan fy mron yn croni
Ochenaid oer na chawn di.

There is within my breast collecting a heavy *sigh* that I do not have thee. *R. Ddu.*

Ocheneidiad, *s. m.* (ochenaid) A sighing.

Ocheneidiaw, *v. a.* (ochenaid) To utter sighs.

Ocheneidiawl, *a.* (ochenaid) Sighing, sobbing.

Ocheneidiwr, *s. m.* (ochenaid—gwr) A sigher.

Ochi, *s. m.* (och) A groaning, a moaning; a sighing.

A mil o eneidiau man,
Ochi anferth, a chwynfan,
——A glywed.

And a thousand of minute souls, dreadful groaning, and complaint, were heard. *Dr. S. Cent.*

Ochi, *v. a.* (och) To utter groans, to groan, to sigh.

Rhag trymfryd ochid achenawg.

Because of an oppressed mind *let* the needy *utter groans.* *Adage.*

Ochiad, *s. m.* (och) The uttering of sighs.

Ochr, *s. m.—pl. t.* an (och—yr) A side, an edge.

Ochrawg, *a.* (ochr) Having sides, lateral.

Ochrawl, *a.* (ochr) Belonging to the side, lateral.

Ochredd, *s. m.* (ochr) The state of having sides.

Ochren, *s. f. dim.* (ochr) A side or shelving region.

Ochri, *v. a.* (ochr) To make a sharp side, ledge, edge, or rim; to side, to take a side. *Mae o yn ochri am y fron*, he is turning on one side for the breast.

Ochriad, *s. m.* (ochr) A siding, a forming a side.

Ochrwr, *s. m.—pl.* ochrwyr (ochr—gwr) A sider.

OD, *s. m. r.* that is out, clear or bright; the falling snow, snow.

Od, *a.* (od, *s.*) Notable; excellent; singular, odd.

Nid edwyn; mòr od ydyw.

She does not recognise; so *odd* is she. *D. ab Gwilym.*

Od, *conj.* (o—yd) If; used before words with vowel initials. *Od awn*, if we go; *od arosi*, if thou wilt stay.

Od ydyw yn dawedog,
Is y cbwardd eos a chog.

If she is become silent, lower will the nightingale and the cuckow sing. *D. ab Edmwnd.*

Odi, *v. n.* (od) To snow; for which *bwrw eira*, is commonly used.

Otid eiry; toid ystrad;
Dyfrysynt cedwyr i gad:
Mi nid af, anaf ni'm gad!

Let there be snowing of snow; let it cover the vale, let the warriors hasten to battle. I shall not go; infirmity will not let me! *Llywarch Hen.*

Odiad, *s. m.* (od) A falling of snow, a snowing.

Odiaeth, *s. m.* (od) A peculiarity; that is notable, rare, or precious.

Haerai rai—eich myn'd yn Sais,
A gado'ch gwyr ac odiaeth,
Ar dranc, megys llong ar draeth.

Some would assert that you are become an Englishman, and leave your men and *peculiarity* to perish, like a ship on the strand. *W. Llyn, i E. Llwyd, o Ial.*

Odiaethawl, *a.* (odiaeth) Peculiar, particular.

Odiaethu, *v. a.* (odiaeth) A rendering peculiar.

Odid, *s. m.* (od) A peculiarity, a rarity. *Ond odid*, peradventure.

Odid, *adv.* (od) Perhaps, probably; rarely.

Odid nad odid yw.

It is *probably* only a probability. *Adage.*

Odid addewid a ddel.

A *rarity* is the promise that comes. *Adage.*

Odid a gatwo wyneb o eisiwed.

A *phenomenon* is he that keeps his countenance out of necessity. *Adage.*

Odidawg, *a.* (odid) Peculiar, or remarkable.

Odidawg a fo didwyll.

He is *remarkable* that is without deceit. *Adage.*

Odlaidd, *a.* (awdl) Of the nature of rhyme.

Odlawg, *a.* (awdl) Rhythmical; having rhyme.

Odledd, *s. m.* (awdl) The state of being rhythmical; the state of having rhyme.

Odli, *v. a.* (awdl) To make rhyme; to rhyme, to have terminations of the same sound.

Odliad, *s. m.* (awdl) A rhyming.

Odlig, *s. f. dim.* (awdl) A little ode.

Odlyd, *a.* (òd) Niveous, or snowy.

Odlydrwydd, *s. m.* (odlyd) Snowiness.

Odwlaw, *s. m.* (od—gwlaw) Sleet; also called *eirwlaw.*

Odwlawiad, *s. m.* (odwlaw) A sleeting.

Odwlawiaw, *v. n.* (odwlaw) To sleet.

Odwlawiawg, *a.* (odwlaw) Abounding with sleet.

Odyn, *s. f.—pl. t.* au (od) That reduces to a calx; a kiln. *Odyn galch, cylyn calch*, a lime kiln; *odyn frag*, a malt kiln; *odyn faes*, a field kiln.

Pob odyn ni bo odyn biben, traian ei gwerth a ddygwydd.

Every *kiln* that is not a pipe *kiln*, the third of its value shall fall. *Welsh Laws.*

Odynaid, *s. f.* (odyn) A kiln-full.

Odyndy, *s. m.—pl. t.* au (odyn--ty) A kiln-house.

ODD, *s. m. r.* That tends out or from.

Odd, *prep.* (o—ydd) From, of, out of; by.

Oddeutu, *prep.* (o—deutu) On both sides; about; round about. *Oddeutu y ty*, about the house; *oddeutu mil*, about a thousand. *adv.* From both sides.

Oddf, *s. m.—pl.* oddfau (odd) A knob, an excrescence; a wen; a corn; a botch.

Wyr Farchudd arfau erchyll
A ddifa caith fal oddf cyll.

The grandson of Marchudd of terrible weapons will destroy the slaves like *knobs* of hazel. *R. Ddu.*

Oddfawg, *a.* (oddf) Protuberant, bossed.

Oddfawl, *a.* (oddf) Tending to be knobbed.

Oddfi, *v. n.* (oddf) To become bossed or knobbed.

Oddfiad, *s. m.* (oddf) A becoming knobbed.

Oddfogi, *v. n.* (oddfawg) To become knobbed.

Oddfogrwydd, *s. m.* (oddfawg) Knobbiness.

Oddfu, *v. n.* (oddf) To bump out, to boss.

Oddfyn, *s. m. dim.* (oddf) A knob, a knur; a bunch; a wen; a little swelling, a botch.

Oddi, *prep.* (odd) Out of, from; off, from off.

Digrifion, dorthion fu'r do
A aned oddi yno.

Merry and wise was the generation that was born *from* thence. *L. G. Cothi.*

Oddiacw, *adv.* (oddi—acw) From yonder.
Oddiallan, *prep.* (oddi—allan) From the outside.
Oddiallan, *adv.* (oddi—allan) From without; on the outside, outwardly.
Oddiam, *prep.* (oddi—am) From the circumference, from round. *adv.* From about.
Oddiamdanaf, *pronom. prep.* (oddiam—tanaf) From about me, from off me. *Oddiamdanad*, from about thee; *oddiamdani*, from about her; *oddiamdano*, from about him; *oddiamdanom*, from about us; *oddiamdanoch*, from about you; *oddiamdanynt*, from about them.
Oddiamgylch, *adv.* (oddiam—cylch) From round about, from about; in circumference. *prep.* About.
Oddiar, *prep.* (oddi—ar) From, or off; above.

Mal llyfu mel oddiar ddrain.

Like licking honey *off* thorns. *Adage.*

Oddiar, *adv.* (oddi—ar) From off; from, off.
Oddiarffordd, *adv.* (oddiar—ffordd) From off the way.
Oddiarffordd, *a.* (oddiar—ffordd) Out of the way. *Oddiarffordd grybwyll*, an out of the way thought
Oddiarnadd, *prep.* (oddiar) From the possession of. *Oddiarnaddynt*, from the possession of them.
Oddiarnaf, *pronom. prep.* (oddi—arnaf) From me; from off me; from above me; above me. *Oddiarnad*, *oddiarnat*, from over thee; *oddiarno*, *oddiarnodd*, from off him; *oddiarni*, *oddierni*, from off her; *oddiarnom*, *oddiarnon*, from off us; *oddiarnoch*, from off you; *oddiarnynt*, from off them, above them.

Lleddaist y gwr cyn ei weled ebai Gwgan. Paham yr ae yntau â fy march cyn fy nhegyn oddiarno.

Thou hast killed the man before seeing him, said Gwgan. Why should be take away my horse before I had alighted *from off him*. *Areith Gwgan.*

Oddicartref, *adv.* (oddi—cartref) From home.
Oddidraw, *adv.* (oddi—traw) From yonder.
Oddidref, *adv.* (oddi—tref) From home.
Oddidros, *adv.* (oddi—tros) From beyond.
Oddieithr, *conj.* (oddi—eithr) Except, unless.
Oddieithr, *prep.* (oddi—eithr) On the exterior, on the outside. *adv.* From the external.

Aethant allan oddieithr y ddinas, i beri danguos amryfrillon guareau.

They went out *on the exterior* of the city, in order to show various sorts of games. *Gr. ab Arthur.*

Oddifaes, *adv.* (oddi—maes) From without.
Oddifewn, *adv.* (oddi—mewn) From within.
Oddifry, *adv.* (oddi—bry) From above.
Oddifyny, *adv.* (oddi—myny) From above.
Oddifynydd, *adv.* (oddifyny) From above.
Oddigan, *adv.* (oddi—cân) From the possession of; from being with. It is compounded thus with pronouns: *Oddigenyf*, *oddiganwyf*, *oddiganddwyf*, *oddigenyd*, *oddigenyt*, *oddiganot*, *oddiganddot*, *oddigano*, *oddiganddo*, *oddiganto*, *oddigantho*; *oddigeni*, *oddiganddi*, *oddiganti*, *oddiganthi*, *oddigenddi*, *oddigenti*, *oddigenthi*; *oddiganom*, *oddiganddom*, *oddigantom*, *oddiganthom*, *oddigenym*; *oddiganoch*, *oddiganddoch*, *oddigantoch*, *oddiganthoch*, *oddigenych*; *oddiganynt*, *oddiganddynt*, *oddigantynt*, *oddiganthynt*, *oddigenynt*.
Oddiger, *adv.* (oddi—cer) From by, from being close to.
Oddigerth, *conj.* (oddi—certh) Except, unless.
Oddigerth, *prep.* (oddi—certh) Except; beside. *adv.* From close to. *Trwy ei hun, ac oddigerth ei hun*, through herself, and besides herself.

Oddigyda, *adv.* (oddi—cyda) From along with.
Oddigylch, *prep.* (oddi—cylch) From about, of about; about. *adv.* From about.
Oddigylchen, *adv.* (oddigylch) From round about.

Golchodd Taf oddigylchen
Dan ei bais—

The Taf did wash *from round about* under his robe. *Lang Lewys.*

Oddihwnt, *adv.* (oddi—hwnt) From far, from the farther side; from beyond; from yonder.
Oddilawr, *adv.* (oddi—llawr) From below.
Oddimewn, *adv.* (oddi—mewn) From within.
Oddiobry, *adv.* (oddi—obry) From below.
Oddirhwng, *adv.* (oddi—rhwng) From between, from the intermediate space. *Oddirhyngom*, *oddirhyngddom*, *oddirhyngtom*, *oddirhyngthom*, from between us; *oddirhyngoch*, *oddirhyngddoch*, *oddirhyngtoch*, *oddirhyngthoch*, from between you; *oddirhyngynt*, *oddirhyngddynt*, *oddirhyngtynt*, *oddirhyngthynt*, from between them
Oddiso, *adv.* (odd—iso) From below, or beneath.
Oddisod, *adv.* (odd—isod) From below, from beneath.
Odditan, *adv.* (oddi—tan) From under; from below. *prep.* Below, underneath. *Odditanaf*, *odditanof*, from under me; *odditanad*, *odditanat*, *odditanot*, from under thee: *odditano*, *odditanodd*, from under him; *odditani*, from under her; *odditanom*, *odditanon*, from under us; *odditanoch*, from under you, *odditanynt*, from under them.

Gwelwn y ddaiar—megys pellen fechan gron ymbell odditanom.

I could see the earth, like a small round ball far *below us*. *Elis Wynn, B. Cwsg.*

Odditros, *adv.* (oddi—tros) From over, or beyond.
Odditrwy, *adv.* (oddi—trwy) From through.
Oddiuchod, *adv.* (oddi—uchod) From above.
Oddiuwch, *adv.* (oddi—uwch) From above.
Oddiuwchdo, *pron. prep.* (oddiuwch) From above him.
Oddiwaered, *adv.* (oddi—waered) From below.
Oddiwrth, *prep.* (oddi—wrth) From by, from. *adv.* From being in contact, from off. *Oddiwrthof*, *oddiwrthyf*, from me; *oddiwrthot*, *oddiwrthyt*, from thee; *oddiwrtho*, from him; *oddiwrthi*, from her; *oddiwrthom*, *oddiwrthym*, from us; *oddiwrthoch*, *oddiwrthych*, from you, *oddiwrthont*, *oddiwrthynt*, from them.

Ni ddeuaf oddiwrth nai Ddafydd
Oni ddel y nos yn ddydd.

I will not come *away from* the nephew of David, until the night shall become day. *L. G. Cothi.*

Oddiyma, *adv.* (oddi—yma) From here, or hence.
Oddiyman, *adv.* (oddi—yman) From hence.
Oddiyna, *adv.* (oddi—yna) From there, from thence; from thenceforth; thence; then.
Oddiynaeth, *adv.* (oddi—ynaeth) From there, from thence; from thenceforth.
Oddiyno, *adv.* (oddi—yno) From there, or from thence, speaking of a distant place or time.

Y fro maeth hon a ranwyd yn ddwy, sef Deifr a Brynaich. Deifr oedd o afon Hwmber hyd yn afon Dren, ac oddiyno hyd y mor Ysgotiaid yw Brynaich

This kingdom was divided into two, namely Deifr and Brynaich. Deifr is from the river Humber to the river Trent; and from *thence* to the Scottish sea is Brynaich. *S. ab Gr. Kabon.*

Oddobry, *adv.* (odd—obry) From beneath.
Odduch, *adv.* (odd—uch) From above, from over. *Odduchof*, from above me. *odduchot*, from above thee; *odducho*, *odduchto*, from over him; *odduchi*, *odduchti*, from over her; *odduchom*, *odduchtom*, from above us; *odduchoch*, *odduchtoch*, from above you; *odduchynt*, *odduchtynt*, from above them.

Odducho, *adv.* (odd—uch) From above.

Oddyma, *adv.* (odd—yma) From here, or hence.

Oddyman, *adv.* (odd—yman) From hence.

Pell oddyman Aber Llyw,
Pellach an dwy gywedlyw:
Talan, telais dy ddeigr heddyw.

Far *from hence* is Aber Llyw, farther our two kindred chiefs: Talan, I have repaid thy tears this day. *Llywarch Hen.*

Oddyna, *adv.* (odd—yna) From there, from thence; from thenceforth; thence; then.

Oddynaeth, *adv.* (odd—ynaeth) From there; from thence; from thenceforth.

Pwy a wledych oddynaeth!

Who will govern *from thenceforth!* *Cyfoesi Myrddin.*

Oddyno, *adv.* (odd—yno) From there, or from thence, speaking of a distant place or time.

Oed, *s. m.—pl. t.* au (o—ed) Process of time; time to come; age; a set time, appointed time, a set day to come; a day of assignation; a delay, or put off of time. *Yn oed un dydd*, in the space of one day; also, delaying or excepting one day; *oed dydd*, a day of appointment; *gwerthu ar oed*, to sell upon credit; *oed wrth borth*, time granted in the process of a suit at law; *y mae yn oed*, it is high time. *Sil.*—*Dyn mewn oed*, a person of age; *tan oed*, under age.

Pob peth a ymdaith a gynnull ei borthiant,
Ond cler, ac oedion, a lladron difwyniant.

Every thing that moves doth collect its food, except minstrels and *idlers* and worthless thieves. *Taliesin.*

Oedawg, *a.* (oed) Full of delay; dilatory.

Oedawl, *a.* (oed) Tending to delay, procrastinating.

Oedfa, *s. f.—pl. t.* on (oed—ma) A time or place of meeting; a meeting; convenient time, opportunity.

Nid oes i ni ddysgwyl ond gwradwydd a gofid oddiwrth esgeulusaw oedfäon i ddwyn i ben amcanion daionus.

We are not to expect any thing but disgrace and affliction from neglecting *opportunities* for accomplishing good designs. *Ier. Owain.*

Oedi, *v. a.* (oed) To set a time; to procrastinate, to protract, to put off time; to postpone.

Ni hena hawl er ei hoedi.

A claim will not grow obsolete though *it be delayed*. *Adage.*

Oeda'r drel, aed ar ei dro;
Y lliw eiddot ai lladdo.

Put off the clown, let him go about his business: that complexion of thine may it kill him. *Raf. ab Robert.*

Oediad, *s. m.—pl. t.* au (oed) A setting or assigning a time, a making an appointment; a delaying; procrastination; a postponing.

Oediawg, *a.* (oed) Having a long process of time, of a long time; stricken in years, aged.

Oediedig, *a.* (oediad) Being settled as of time; being procrastinated or delayed.

Oedran, *s. m.* (oed—rhan) Time of life, duration of life; full age; age. *Mae hi o oedran priodi*, she is of age for marrying; *dyn mewn oedran*, a man in years.

Oedraniad, *s. m.* (oedran) A growing in years.

Oedrann, *v. n.* (oedran) To grow in years.

Oedranus, *a.* (oedran) Of a period of life; being in years, stricken in years; aged, elderly.

Oedwr, *s. m.—pl.* oedwyr (oed—gwr) One who appoints a time; a procrastinator, a delayer.

Oedd, *v. n.* (o—edd) Was, did exist; it, he, or she was. *A oedd hi yno? Oedd.* Was she there? She was.

Oedd gwr fy mab, oedd dysgywen hawl,
Ac oedd nai i Urien;
Ar rid Forlas y llas Gwen.

A man *was* my son, *he was* of illustrious inheritance, and *he was* the nephew of Urien; at the ford of Morlas Gwen was slain. *Llywarch Hen.*

Oeg, *s. m.* (o—eg) That is opened out.

Oel, *s. m.* (o—el) Of a protruding tendency.

Oen, *s. m.—pl.* wyn (o—en) A state of motion, briskness, or agitation; a lamb.

A wnelo ei hun yn oen a lyngcir gan y blaidd.

He that will make himself a *lamb* will be swallowed by the wolf. *Adage.*

Oen tangnefedd lle gweddid,
A llew'n y drin, llawen drud.

The *lamb of* peace where it seemed meet, and a lion in the conflict, sprightly and bold. *W. Alaw.*

Oena, *v.* (oen) To lamb, to yean.

Oenaidd, *a.* (oen) Like a lamb, lamb-like.

Oenan, *s. c.* (oen) A lambkin, a little lamb.

Oenawl, *a.* (oen) Belonging to a lamb.

Oenban, *s. m.* (oen—pan) A lamb's fur.

Oenes, *s. f.* (oen) An ewe lamb, a young ewe.

Oengen, *s. m.* (oen—cen) A lamb's skin.

Oenig, *s. f. dim.* (oen) A little ewe-lamb.

Oenyn, *s. m. dim.* (oen) A little lamb, a lambkin. *Wyniach, wynos, ŵyn bach*, lambkins.

Oer, *s. m.—pl. t.* ion (o—er) That is of a repulsive quality; a frigidity, a cold nature; severity. *a.* Cold; repulsive.

Mai oer a wna ysgubawr gynhes.

A cold May will make a warm barn. *Adage.*

Oer gwely pysgod yn nghysgawd iaen.

Cold is the bed of fishes under the shelter of ice. *Adage.*

Oeraidd, *a.* (oer) Somewhat cold, inclement.

Oerawl, *a.* (oer) Tending to frigidity; cooling.

Oerchwedl, *s. m.—pl. t.* au (oer—chwedl) A sad story, bad tidings, ill news.

Oerdeb, *s. m.* (oer) Coldness, frigidness.

Oerder, *s. m.* (oer) Coldness, or frigidity.

Oerdra, *s. m.* (oer) Coldness, or frigidity.

Oeredig, *a.* (oer) Being cooled, or made frigid.

Oeredd, *s. m.* (oer) Coldness, or frigidness.

Oeren, *s. f. dim.* (oer) A cold female.

Oerfa, *s. f.—pl. t.* au (oer—ma) A cool place.

Oerfel, *s. f.—pl. t.* on (oer—bel) Cold air, cold weather.

Yr oerfel annyoddefodig—pai bwrid mynydd o dan ynddo ydd ai yn un iaen.

The insuperable *cold*, if a mountain of fire were thrown therein it would become a perfect body of ice. *Elucidarius.*

Oerfelawg, *a.* (oerfel) Of cold temperament.

O laith Llywelyn——
Oerfelawg calon dan fron o fraw.

For the death of Llywelyn, *cold* is the heart in the bosom through regret. *Gr. ab yr Ynad Coch.*

Oerferw, *a.* (oer—berw) Coldly bubbling.

Gorwyn blaen derw, oerferw dwfr;
Cyrchid biw blaen hedwerw;
Gwnelid aeth saeth y syberw.

Glittering the tops of the oak, *coldly-bubbling* the water; the kine will resort to the skirt of the birch copse; the bolt of the boaster is soon made to fly. *Llywarch Hen.*

Oergled, *a.* (oer—cled) Cool-sheltered.

Araf haf, hôar gweilgi,
Eirioes coed, oergled celli.

Gentle the summer, calm the ocean, splendid the woods, *of a cooling shade* the grove. *Gwalchmai.*

Oerglyd, *a.* (oer—clyd) Cool-sheltered.

Oergrai, *a.* (oer—crai) Harshly-cold.

Ystafell Cynddylan yn oergrai heno,
Gwedi y parch a'm bu i;
Heb wyr, heb wreigedd ai cadwai.

The hall of Cynddylan is *harshly-cold* this night, after the honour upon me bestowed; Without the men, without the women who kept it. *Llywarch Hen.*

Oergri, *s. f.* (oer—cri) A dismal cry.

Oergrïad, *s. m.* (oergri) A crying dismally.

Oergrïaw, *v. a.* (oergri) To cry dismally.

Oergwymp, *s. m.* (oer—cwymp) A dismal fall. *Oergwymp galanas*, the sad lapse of slaughter compensation. It is an ancient law term, otherwise called *Dygngoll cenedl*, and *Dygngolled cenedl*.

> Oergwymp galanas yw: pan laddo dyn ddyn arall, dodi oed dydd i wneuthur iawn drosto, a'i ladd yntau o ddyn o genedl arall nis delyo. Oergwymp galanas y gelwir hyny, rhag trymed ei golli ef, a gadaw y gyflafan a wnaethai ar ei genedl, a gorfod ei thalu.
>
> This is the *dismal event* of murder compensation: when a person kills another, appointing a day to make satisfaction for it, and he being killed by a person of another family, to whom he owes nothing. It is called the *dismal event* of murder, by reason of the grievousness of losing him, and leaving the weight of the heinous deed, committed by him, upon his family, and being obliged to make amends for it. *Welsh Laws.*

Oeri, *v. a.* (oer) To make cold, to cool; to become cold; to grow cool.

> Gwae chwaer deg, o chwerwed oedd,
> Gan hiraeth, gwn, a'i hoerodd!
>
> It is woeful to the fair sister, so bitter was it, through regret, which I know, did *make her cold!* *Ed. Dafydd.*

Oeriad, *s. m.* (oer) A cooling, or a chilling.

Oeriain, *v. a.* (oer) To keep cooling; to seek cooling shades; to cool liquids by pouring from one vessel to another.

Oerlais, *s. m.*—*pl.* oerleisiau (oer—llais) A cold voice, a repulsive or grating voice.

Oerlef, *s. m.* (oer—llef) A dismal moan.

Oerlefain, *v. a.* (oerlef) To moan dismally.

Oerleisiad, *s. m.* (oerlais) A shrieking dismally.

Oerleisiaw, *v. a.* (oerlais) To shriek dismally.

Oerllyd, *a.* (oer) Of a cold quality; chilly.

Oerllydrwydd, *s. m.* (oerllyd) Frigidness.

Oernad, *s. f.*—*pl. t.* au (oer—nâd) A dismal howl, a lamentable or doleful cry.

Oernadu, *v. a.* (oernad) To howl dolefully.

Oerni, *s. m.* (oer) Coldness, chilliness; cold weather.

Oersych, *a.* (oer—sych) Being cold and dry.

Oerwaedd, *s. f.* (oer—gwaedd) A dismal cry.

Oerwedd, *s. f.* (oer—gwedd) A chilling aspect. *a.* Of a chilling aspect.

Oerweiddi, *v. a.* (oerwaedd) To cry dismally.

Oerwern, *s. f.* (oer--gwern) A cold slough; a bardic epithet for the seat of lowest existence; and, under the christian system, often used for hell.

> Rhag oerwern gethern afflern affan,
> Affwn anoddeu, lle anoddyn,
> Llwa fi, Dofydd hueuydd hyn:
> Llawer a wna Duw er dyniadon!
>
> From the fiends of the *cold slough* of the hell of uproar, the insuperable hold, the place profound, assign me a station, thou Creator comprehending eternity. Much doth God do for mankind! *Elidr Sais.*

Oerwlyb, *a.* (oer—gwlyb) Being cold and wet.

Oerwr, *s. m.*--*pl.* oerwyr (oer—gwr) A cold man.

Oerwynt, *s. m.* (oer—gwynt) A chilling wind.

Oeryn, *s. m. dim.* (oer) A cold person.

Oes, *s. f.*—*pl. t.* oedd (o—es) A period of time; a duration of life, an age; life. *Er cyn yr oesoedd*, from before the ages, from eternity; *oes oesoedd, pyth bythoedd*, age of ages, world of worlds.

> Hwrched oes oes Iesu, a hyd frawd y para.
>
> The sixth *age* the *age* of Jesus, and till judgement it will last. *Taliesin.*
>
> Duw! y sydd ddwy oes heddyw;
> Un fry fyth, un fer i fyw.
>
> God! there are two *existences* this day, one above for ever, one short to live. *T. Aled.*

Oes, *adv.* (o—es) There is; is there. *A oes neb yn y ty?* Is there any body in the house? *Oes*, there is.

> Nid oes cywilydd rhag gofid.
>
> *There is* no shame against affliction. *Adage.*
>
> Nid oes neb heb ei fai.
>
> *There is* not any body without his fault. *Adage.*

Oesawg, *a.* (oes) Aged, in years, olden.

Oesawl, *a.* (oes) Relating to a period of existence.

> Y bryniau oesawl a grymmasant.
>
> The *everlasting* hills did bow down. *Habacuc* iii. 6.

Oesbarth, *s. m.* (oes--parth) A period of existence.

Oesbell, *a.* (oes—pell) Of extended existence. *Oesbell gariad*, long existing love.

Oesboen, *s. m.* (oes—poen) The pain of life. *a.* Life-tormenting.

> ——Oesboen ddagrau rey
> Rhyddyg lliw fy ngruddiau!
>
> Excess of *life-tormenting* tears takes away the colour of my cheeks! *Bleddyn Fardd.*

Oesbraff, *a.* (oes—praff) Of ample existence.

Oesdaith, *s. f.* (oes—taith) A course of life.

> Menawd molawd gnawd gne tòn wanddgreg
> Manar wiw lasar afar oferg.
> Mil a'i mawl, heb dawl, dileddf chweg fwyndaith,
> Mawr-ddawn ganymdaith oesdaith osteg.
>
> Impressive be the praise of her whose skin is of the hue of the hoarse-sounding wave, the nymph of the azure vest of pensive mind. A thousand praise her, without ceasing, in sweet comprehensive speech unabased, a greatly gifted society of a *life of study*. *Cynddelw.*

Oesdlawd, *a.* (oes—tlawd) Of necessitous life.

Oesdrais, *s. m.* (oes—trais) Oppression of life. *a.* Life-oppressing.

Oesdraul, *s. f.* (oes—traul) The consumption of life. *a.* Life-consuming.

Oesdrawd, *s. m.* (oes—trawd) A course of life.

Oesdru, *s. m.* (oes—tru) Misery of life.

Oesdrwch, *s. m.* (oes—trwch) A cutting off life. *a.* Life-breaking; life-destroying.

> Py fydd cerdd olwch, oesdrwch estrawn;
> Py fydd ced wallaw fal Cadwallawn.
>
> Who will be the theme of song, the *life destruction* of strangers who will be scattering gifts like Cadwallon. *Cynddelw.*

Oesdrwydden, *s. f.* (oes—trwydd) The hornbeam.

Oesfoddawg, *a.* (oes—boddawg) Having respect to life; leading a contented life.

> Ni bydd pencenedl y mab gwedy ei dad yn uniaf iddo, canys oesfoddawg y pencenedlaeth.
>
> The son shall not be the patron of the family after his father in succession, for a headship of family is *during life*. *Welsh Laws.*

Oesfriw, *s. m.* (oes—briw) A lapse of life.

> Gorllechais eisiau o'i oesfriw wrfrau;
> O'i angeu anghlaear.
>
> I have harboured regret from his bristle-shielded *lapse of life*, from his melancholy death. *Gwalchmai.*

Oesfyr, *a.* (oes—byr) Of short life, shortlived.

> Oesfyr dy alon, aesfriw Faredudd.
>
> *Shortlived* thy foes, Meredudd with the battered shield. *Ll. P. Moch.*

Oesgaeth, *a.* (oes—caeth) Leading a captive life.

Oesgawdd, *a.* (oes—cawdd) Of a vexatious life.

> Bro amnawdd, oesgawdd, oesgaith ei gynnygn
> Fi gynnal nid hawdd-waith.
>
> The protection of the country, *of vexatious existence* the confined life of his opponent, to support him is no easy work. *Cynddelw, i O. ab Madawg.*

Oesgur, *s. m.* (oes—cur) The throb of life, the anguish of life. *a.* Life-afflicting.

Oesgwyn, *s. f.* (oes—cwyn) The complaint of life. *a.* Complaining of life.

Oesi, *v. n.* (oes) To pass through life, to live; to give life. *Bid Duw i'w oesi*, be God to grant him life.

> T'wysa, er d'enw, at oesi
> Gwirion fodd.——
>
> Conduct, for the sake of thy name, towards *existing* in an innocent way. *W. Middleton.*

Y gwr a'th roes i oesi,
Gyw du doeth, a'th gadw di.

Him that placed thee *to exist* preserve thee, thou black discreet bird. *T. Prys, i'r fwyalchen.*

Oesiad, *s. m.* (oes) A passing through life.

Oesran, *s. f.* (oes—rhan) An assigned portion of existence, a duration of life.

Oesred, *s. f.* (oes—rhed) A course of existence.

Oeswr, *s. m.—pl.* oeswyr (oes—gwr) One who passes through life; a liver.

A'm bod gannoes yn oeswr.

And my being a *liver* during a hundred ages. *T. Prys.*

Oeth, *s. m.* (o—eth) That is intense, pungent or harsh. *a.* Intense, pungent, harsh.

Ac yn llys afaeoed ym eiddunir:
Fy noeth oeth dybyddaf, o dybwyf rydd.

And in the hall of hospitality I shall be wished for: if naked I shall be harsh, if I shall be free. *Gwalchmai.*

Er mawr-gwymp Madawg, modur plymnwyd;
Am bost cad, ced goeth, oeth ym athrwyd!

For the sad fall of Madog, the leader of conflict; for the pillar of battle, of precious gift, *severely* have I been dismayed! *Gwalchmai.*

Oethi, *v. a.* (oeth) To render intense, pungent, sharp, harsh, or severe.

OF, *s. m. r.* The elementary state of a thing; an atomical state; atoms; particles, motes; flue; that is uncombined or crude.

Of, *a.* (of, *s.*) Elementary, or in an uncombined state; crude; raw; frail, mouldering.

Hirewyn a Hiratrwm—pan elynt i west, nid edewynt na thew na theneu, na thwym nac oer, na sur na chroew, nac ir na hallt, na brwd nac *of*.

Long-nail and Long-trail, if they went on a visit, they would leave nor fat nor lean, nor cold nor hot, nor sour nor sweet, nor fresh nor salt, nor boiled nor *raw*. *H. Culhwch—Mabinogion.*

Byd *of* ar fardd;——
Byd tost, mae'n fyr bywyd dyn.

A *frail* world for a bard; a cruel world, the life of man is short. *D. Benwyn.*

Ofaid, *a.* (of) Elementary; of a crude or raw quality; frail; mouldering.

Molawd Duw molaf a'i dywaid;
Ac molwy, nyw molaf ofaid,
Am obrwy, am obrid fy rhaid.

I will praise such as express the praise of God; and if I praise, I shall not praise the *frail*, for a reward, for the satisfying of my necessity. *Cynddelw.*

Ofaidd, *a.* (of) Of an elementary nature; of a crude or raw tendency; crumbling, mouldering.

Ofawd, *s. m.* (of) A reducing to an elementary state; a making crude, a mouldering.

Ofawg, *a.* (of) In an elementary state; having a crude or raw quality; crumbly.

Ofawl, *a.* (of) Elementary; of a crude nature, of a raw quality; mouldering.

Ofedd, *s. m.* (of) An elementary or atomical state; rawness; a crumbling or mouldering state.

Ofer, *a.* (of—er) Waste, vain, useless, idle, frivolous. It is prefixed in composition.

Hyd tra fuch na fydd *ofer*.

As long as thou shalt exist be not *useless*. *Adage.*

Ofera, *v. a.* (ofer) To waste, to squander; to act vainly or idly; to pass time frivolously.

Oferchwedl, *s. m.—pl. t.* au (oferchwedl) A vain or empty report.

Oferdaith, *s. f.—pl.* overdeithiau (taith) A fruitless journey.

Oferdawd, *s. m.* (ofer) Vanity; frivolity.

Hwfft o'r wael awen a gais bob overdawd.

Away with the abject muse that seeks for every *frivolity*. *Adage.*

Oferdlws, *s. m.—pl.* overdlysau (ofer—tlws) A vain toy, ornament, or jewel; a jewel merely ornamental.

Y brawdwr llys a ddyly *oferdlysau*, pan wystler ei swydd iddo, nid amgen, tawlbwrdd o asgwrn morfil i gan y brenin, a modrwy aur i gan y frenines, ac arall i gan y bardd teulu, ac yr *oferdlysau* hyny, ni ddyly efe nac eu rhoddi nac eu gwerthu tra byddo byw.

The judge of the palace claims *ornamental jewels*, when his office is pledged to him; namely, a chessboard of the bone of a sea-animal from the king, and a gold ring from the queen, and another from the domestic bard: and those *ornamental jewels* he ought neither to give, nor to sell whilst he lives. *Welsh Laws.*

Oferdraul, *s. f.* (traul) Useless expenditure.

Oferdreuliad, *s. m.* (overdraul) A using needlessly, a spending uselessly.

Overdreuliaw, *v. a.* (oferdraul) To use in vain.

Overdreuliwr, *s. m.—pl.* overdreulwyr (overdraul—gwr) One who wastes uselessly.

Oferdyb, *s. f.—pl. t.* iau (over—tyb) Idle conceit.

Oferdybiaw, *v. n.* (overdyb) To have idle notion.

Overddadl, *s. f.—pl. t.* au (dadl) A vain dispute.

Oferddadlu, *v.* (oferddadl) To dispute vainly.

Oferddawn, *s. m.—pl.* oferddoniau (dawn) An useless talent, gift, or quality.

Oferddefawd, *s. f.* (defawd) An idle custom.

Oferddyn, *s. m.—pl. t.* ion (ofer—dyn) A vain idle person; a squanderer, or a dissipated man.

Oferedd, *s. m.* (ofer) Vanity, frivolity, idleness, worthlessness, dissipation.

Oferelw, *s. m.* (elw) Useless wealth or riches.

Oferelwa, *v. a.* (oferelw) To heap useless wealth.

Oferfardd, *s. m.—pl.* oferfeirdd (ofer—bardd) A person who assumes the bardic order irregularly

Tri rhyw beirdd Ynys Prydain: prif-feirdd er cyn cred; a gwedi cred beirdd bell, ac yr oferfeirdd.

The three distinctions of bards of the Isle of Britain: the primitive bards from before christianity; and after conversion the bards of warfare, and the *bards by assumption*. *Barddas.*

Tri overfardd Ynys Prydain: Arthur, Cadwallawn mab Cadfan, a Rhyawd ail Morgant.

The three *assumptive bards* of the Isle of Britain: Arthur, Cadwallon son of Cadfan, and Rhyawd son of Morgant. *Trioedd.*

Oferfawl, *s. f.* (mawl) Empty or vain praise.

Oferfoli, *v. a.* (oferfawl) To praise vainly.

Oferfost, *s. f.* (bost) An empty boasting.

Oferfostiaw, *v. a.* (oferfost) To boast vainly.

Oferfostiwr, *s. m.—pl.* oferfostwyr (oferfost—gwr) A vain boaster.

Oferfraint, *s. m.—pl.* oferfreintiau (braint) An useless privilege.

Oferfudd, *s. f.* (budd) A vain or useless benefit.

Ofergadw, *v. a.* (cadw) To keep uselessly.

Ofergais, *s. f.* (cais) A vain attempt.

Ofergall, *a.* (call) Uselessly cunning.

Oferganlyn, *v.* (canlyn) To follow uselessly.

Ofergaru, *v. a.* (caru) To love fruitlessly.

Ofergeisiaw, *v. a.* (ofergais) To make a vain attempt, to try uselessly.

Ofergoel, *s. f.—pl. t.* ion (coel) Vain belief.

Ofergoelaidd, *a.* (ofergoel) Superstitious.

Ofergoeledd, *s. m.* (ofergoel) Superstitiousness.

Ofergoeliad, *s. m.* (ofergoel) A vainly crediting.

Ofergoeliwr, *s. m.—pl.* ofergoelwyr (ofergoel—gwr) A superstitious man.

Ofergoelus, *a.* (ofergoel) Superstitious.

Ofergred, *s. f.* (cred) Vain belief; superstition.

Ofergredu, *v. n.* (ofergred) To believe vainly.

Oferhela, *s. m.* (hela) Fruitless hunting.

Gwerth geilgi y brenin yn ei oferhela chweugaint.

The value of the king's buck-hound in his *training* is six score pence. *Welsh Laws.*

Oferhela, *v. a.* (hela) To hunt fruitlessly.

Oferiaith, *s. f.* (iaith) Useless idle talk.

Oferieithus, *a.* (oferiaith) Full of idle talk.

Oferlaeth, *s. m.* (llaeth) Useless or over milk.

Tri oferlaeth y sydd: llaeth cath, llaeth gast, a llaeth caseg, can ni ddiwygir dim am danaddynt.

There are three *waste milks*: the milk of a cat, and the milk of a bitch, and the milk of a mare; for no satisfaction is made for them. *Welsh Laws.*

Oferorchest, *s. f.*—*pl. t.* ion (gorchest) A vain exploit.

Oferorchwyl, *s. f.*—*pl. t.* ion (ofer—gorchwyl) A frivolous piece of business.

Oferwaith, *s. m.* (gwaith) Useless or vain work.

Oferwas, *s. m.*—*pl.* oferweision (gwas) A worthless chap.

Oferwawd, *s. m.* (gwawd) Empty praise.

Oferweithiaw, *v. a.* (oferwaith) To work vainly.

Oferwr, *s. m.*—*pl.* oferwyr (ofer—gwr) An useless idle man; an idler.

> Gwae oferwr yn nghynauaf.
>
> Woe to the *idler* during harvest. *Adage.*

Oferymadrawdd, *s. m.*—*pl.* oferymadroddion (ymadrawdd) Vain discourse; fruitless discussion.

> Tri oferymadrawdd, a ddywedir yn llys, ac ni fynant: gwad cyn dedfryd, a llys cyn amser, a chof a chynghaws wedi brawd.
>
> The three *fruitless discussions*, which are uttered in court, and which shall not avail. a denial before restoration, and objection before the time, and record and pleading after sentence. *Welsh Laws.*

Oferymadrawdd, *v. a.* (ymadrawdd) To discourse vainly, to talk uselessly.

Oferymboeni, *v. a.* (ymboeni) To toil vainly.

Oferymgais, *s. m.* (ymgais) An idle attempt.

Oferymryson, *s. m.* (ymryson) Vain strife.

Oferymryson, *v. a.* (ymryson) To strive vainly.

Ofi, *v. a.* (of) To decompose; to become decomposed, to fall into an atomical state; to moulder, to crumble. *Mae y gareg hon yn dechreu ofi*, this stone is beginning to crumble.

Ofiad, *s. m.* (of) A reducing to an elementary state; a falling to atoms; a becoming crude; a mouldering, a decomposing.

Ofiannawl, *a.* (ofiant) Tending to decompose, tending to fall to atoms; mouldering.

Ofiannu, *v. a.* (ofiant) To reduce to an atomical state; to render friable.

Ofiannus, *a.* (ofiant) Relating to an elementary or atomical state.

Ofiannusaw, *v. a* (ofiannus) To reduce to an elementary or atomical state.

Ofiannusedd, *s. m.* (ofiannus) An elementary or atomical state.

Ofiant, *s. m.* (of) A reducing to atoms.

Oflyd, *a.* (of) Apt to decompose, apt to fall to atoms; apt to moulder.

> Difas gandlo dy oflyd
> Eirian, heb eu cuplau cyd.
>
> Disgusting to him thy *jumbled* words, without their being connected together. *E. Evan, o Aberdar.*

Oflydedd, *s. m.* (oflyd) A state of decomposition.

Oflydrwydd, *s. m.* (oflyd) A state of decomposition; a mouldering state; friableness.

Oflydu, *v. n.* (oflyd) To become decomposed; to crumble, to moulder.

Ofn, *s. m.*—*pl. t.* au (of—yn) Fear, or dread.

> Gwell rhan ofn na rhan cariad.
>
> Better the share of *fear* than the share of love. *Adage.*

Ofnâad, *s. m.* (ofnâu) A terrifying, a frightening; intimidation; a becoming frightened.

Ofnadwy, *a.* (ofn) Terrible, frightful, awful.

Ofnâu, *v. n.* (ofn) To become fearful; to render fearful or awful.

Ofnawg, *a.* (ofn) Fearful, timorous, timid.

Ofnawl, *a.* (ofn) Tending to frighten.

Ofnedig, *a.* (ofn) Being made timid.

Ofnedd, *s. m.* (ofn) Fearfulness, timidity.

Ofni, *v. n.* (ofn) To fear, to dread, to be afraid; to frighten, to terrify, to put in fear.

> Cais Dduw yn gar, ac nag ofna far.
>
> Seek God for thy friend, and *fear* no ill. *Adage.*

> A bod ei law——
> Ar gleddau, er ei gladdu,
> A'i lun gwrawl yn gorweddi,
> Ef a wnai'r beilch ofni'r bedd.
>
> Should his hand be on his sword, though he were buried, and his manly form laid down, the proud boasters would *be made to fear* the grave. *L. G. Cothi.*

Ofniad, *s. m.* (ofn) A dreading, a fearing.

Ofnid, *s. m.* (ofn) Terror, dread, or fear.

> Llun tarian pennaeth, a llun saethau,
> Llun y pen ofnid yn llawn pinnau.
>
> The figure of a chieftain's shield, and the figure of arrows, the figure, of a *gorgon* head full of pins. *L. G. Cothi, i hulling gwely.*

Ofnocâu, *a.* (ofnawg) To stand in fear or awe.

> Rhaid yw ini frodyr, caru digrifwch paradwys, ac ofnocâu poenau uffern.
>
> It is necessary for us, brethren, to love the bliss of paradise, and *fear* the pains of hell. *Breuddwyd Paul. 1300.*

Ofnogi, *v. n.* (ofnawg) To become timid.

Ofnogrwydd, *s. m.* (ofnawg) Fearfulness.

Ofnu, *v. a.* (ofn) To fear; to frighten.

Ofnus, *a.* (ofn) Fearful, timorous.

Ofnusaw, *v. n.* (ofnus) To become timid.

Ofnusedd, *s. m.* (ofnus) Timorousness.

Ofnusrwydd, *s. m.* (ofnus) Fearfulness.

Ofnwr, *s. m.*—*pl.* ofnwyr (ofn—gwr) One who dreads or fears.

Ofus, *a.* (of) Atomical; being decomposed.

Ofusedd, *s. m.* (ofus) An atomical state.

Ofydd, *s. m.*—*pl. t.* ion (of—ydd) One who is initiated into first principles or elements; a scientific person, a natural philosopher, a teacher of science, an artist; the name for a member of the scientific class, in the bardic system; an *ovate*. *Cad ofydd*, the regulator of battle; *gal ofydd*, the regulator of hostility, whose person was sacred.

> Bedd Gwrgi gwychydd——
> A bedd Llawr, llu ofydd,
> Yn ngwarthaf Gwanas.
>
> The grave of Gwrgi the hero, and the grave of Llawr, the *regulator* of the host, in the height of Gwanas. *Engl. Beddau Milwyr.*

> Hi yn wyry, heb wâd;
> Hi yn hollawl rad,
> Yn rheg ofydd.
>
> She a virgin, without denial; she of perfect grace, the blessing of the *great artificer*. *Gwaedrhaeadr, i Fair.*

> Od ych brif-feirdd fydd o waith Duw ofydd,
> Dywedwch i'ch brenin beth fydd ei drangwydd.
>
> If ye are primary bards of faith of the work of God the great *artist*, declare to your king what will be his misfortune. *Taliesin, bustl y beirdd.*

Ofyddaid, *a.* (ofydd) Ovatic, scientific.

Ofyddawl, *a.* (ofydd) Relating to the functions of an ovate; scientifical.

Ofyddeb, *s. f.* (ofydd) A discourse upon ovatism, a treatise upon science.

Ofyddes, *s. f.*—*pl. t.* au (ofydd) A female member of the scientific class of bards.

Ofyddfardd, *s. m.*—*pl.* ofyddfeirdd (ofydd—bardd) A bard of science, a bard of arts, his office was analogous to that of a lay graduate now in the universities.

Ofyddiaeth, *s. m.* (ofydd) What is taught by an ovate, ovatism, philosophy.

> Llawer o beth gwrthwyneb ysywaeth, sydd yn tramgwydd i serchogrwydd,—gwylltineb serch, a llawer ofyddiaeth, yn lluddias cysgu.
>
> Many contrary things, alas, there are unfavourable to true affection,—the frenzy of love, and the wear of *philosophy* hindering sleep. *Iorwerth Brydydd Hir.*

Ofyddiannawl, *a.* (ofyddiant) Belonging to ovatism, philosophical.

Ofyddiannu, *v. a.* (ofyddiant) To exercise ovatism; to philosophise.

Ofyddiant, *s. m.* (ofydd) Ovatism; philosophy.

Ofyddu, *v. a.* (ofydd) To exercise ovatism, to philosophise.

OFF, *s. m. r.—pl. t.* ion. That is essential or tending to a beginning.

Offeiriad, *s. m.—pl. t.* au (offer) A minister.

> Offeiriad teulu, efe a ddyly fod yn wastad ygyd a'r brenin, canys trydydd anhebgor yw.
>
> The domestic *priest*, he ought to be continually with the king, for he is the third indispensable one. *Welsh Laws.*

Offeiriadaeth, *s. m.—pl. t.* au (offeiriad) A priesthood, the function of a priest.

> Bydd eu heneiniad iddynt yn offeiriadaeth tragywyddawl drwy eu cenedlaethau.
>
> Their anointment shall be to them for an everlasting *priesthood* through their generations. *Exodus* 40. 15.

Offeiriadaidd, *a.* (offeiriad) Of a clerical quality.

Offeiriadawl, *a.* (offeiriad) Belonging to a priest.

Offeiriadu, *v. a.* (offeiriad) To perform priestly functions, to minister as a priest.

> Eneinia feibion Aaron, megys yr eneiniaist eu Tad hwynt, i offeiriadu i mi.
>
> Anoint the children of Aaron, as thou hast anointed their father, to *minister* before me. *Exodus* 40. 15.

Offeiriant, *s. m.—pl.* offeiriaint (offer) Ministration, the act of sacrificing.

> Meifod—
> A'i balch *offeiriad*, a'i hoffeiriaint,
> A pharawd *offeren* hoffaint.
>
> Meivod with its stately priest, and its *sacrifices*, and the ready mass of love. *Cynddelw.*

Offeiriedyn, *s. m. dim.* (offeiriad) A bit of a priest, in cant language.

Offer, *s. pl. aggr.* (off—er) That has power to effect; an instrument; implements; gear, traces, or harness.

> Gwell tynu, cynnyddu nerth,
> Na thor *offer* na thrafferth.
>
> Better to pull on, exerting strength, than the breaking of *gear* or bustle. *Math. ab Llywelyn Goch.*

Offerawl, *a.* (offer) Instrumental, serving.

Offeren, *s. f.—pl. t.* au (offer) Instrumentality; the service of the church of Rome, the mass.

> Offeren pawb yn ei galon.
>
> Every body's *religion* in his heart. *Adage.*

Offerena, *v. a.* (offeren) To do the duty of the church in general; to celebrate mass.

Offerenawl, *a.* (offeren) Belonging to divine service; belonging to the mass.

Offerendor, *s. f.* (offeren—tor) The vestment worn at mass; a cope.

Offereniad, *s. m.* (offeren) A performing of divine service; a saying mass.

Offerenu, *v. a.* (offeren) To perform divine service; to say mass.

> Or gwnair eglwys mewn taeogdref gan ganiad y brenin, a'i bod yn gorflan, ac offeiriad yn offerenu ynddi, rhydd fydd y dref hono o hyny allan.
>
> If a church shall be built in a villain town, with the permission of the king, and it should be a place of interment, and a priest *doing duty* in it, that town shall be free from that time forward. *Welsh Laws.*

Offerenwr, *s. m.—pl.* offerenwyr (offeren—gwr) One who celebrates mass, a mass-priest.

Offerenwisg, *s. f.—pl. t.* oedd (offeren—gwisg) A vestment worn in celebrating mass.

Offeriad, *s. m.—pl. t.* au (offer) An acting as an instrument; a becoming an agent.

Offeriannawl, *a.* (offeriant) Instrumental.

Offerianniad, *s. m.* (offeriant) A rendering instrumental; a becoming instrumental.

Offeriannu, *v. a.* (offeriant) To be instrumental.

Offeriannus, *a.* (offeriant) Instrumental.

Offeriant, *s. m.* (offer) Instrumentality.

Offeru, *v. a.* (offer) To provide implements or tools; to equip; to furnish with gear or harness

Offerwr, *s. m.—pl.* offerwyr (offer—gwr) One who equips or furnishes.

Offeryn, *s. m. dim.—pl. t.* au (offer) An instrument, or agent; a tool.

> Offeryn gwastadawl yn llaw pob dyn yw ei ddeall, er hyny nid oes neb a wyr ei arfer yn iawn.
>
> A tool which is continually in the hand of every person is his understanding, and yet no one knows how to use it rightly. *Adage.*

Offerynawl, *a.* (offeryn) Instrumental, agent.

Offerynoldeb, *s. m.* (offerynawl) Instrumentalness

Offerynu, *v. a.* (offeryn) To act as an instrument; to be instrumental.

Offr, *s. m.* (off) That has the power to effect.

Offrwm, *s. m.—pl.* offrymau (offr) An offering.

Offrwm, *v. a.* (offr) To offer, or to sacrifice.

Offrymawl, *a.* (offrwm) Offering up, sacrificial.

Offrymiad, *s. m.* (offrwm) The act of offering.

Offrymu, *v. a.* (offrwm) To offer, or to sacrifice.

Offrymwr, *s. m.—pl.* offrymwyr (offrwm—gwr) One who offers up, a sacrificer.

Offrymydd, *s. m.—pl. t.* ion (offrwm) One who offers up, a sacrificer.

OG, *s. f. r.—pl. t.* au. That is full of motion; that is apt to open or expand; that is full of life, youth; that moves or stirs; a harrow.

> Tra rhedo yr og rheded y freuan.
>
> Whilst the *harrow* moves let the mill move. *Adage.*
>
> Mal y llyffan dan yr og.
>
> Like the frog under the *harrow*. *Adage.*

Og, *a.* (og, *s.*) Having aptitude for motion; apt to move or stir; apt to open or expand; young, youthful.

> A'm gyrwys yn nghrog,
> A wyddwn yn og.
>
> That sent me to the cross, I knew when *young*. *Taliesin, arwyrain dyddbrawd.*

Ogaid, *s. f.* (og) A stroke of the harrow.

Ogan, *s. f. dim.* (og) A little harrow.

> Cael a wnewthum beth arian,
> A phrynu aradr ac ogan.
>
> I obtained some money and bought me a plough and a *harrow*. *S. Tudur.*

Oged, *s. f.—pl. t.* au (og) That stirs or opens; a harrow.

Ogedig, *a.* (oged) Being stirred or harrowed.

Ogedu, *v. a.* (oged) To stir; to use a harrow.

Ogfaen, *s. f.—pl.* ogfain (og—maen) Hip, or the fruit of the dog-rose. It is also called *crawel y moch, bwyd y moch.*

> Mal y llwynog am yr ogfaen.
>
> Like the fox after the *hips*. *Adage.*

Ogfaenawg, *a.* (ogfaen) Abounding with hips.

Ogfaenen, *s. f.* (ogfaen) A single hip.

> Ogfaenen yn ngenau hen-wch.
>
> A *hip* in the mouth of an old sow. *Adage.*

Ogfaenliw, *s. m.* (ogfaen—lliw) The colour of hips. *a.* Of the colour of the hip.

Ogfaenllwyn, *s. m.—pl. t.* i (ogfaen—llwyn) A bush of dog-rose thorns.

Ogi, *v. a.* (og) To use the harrow, to harrow. *Llyfnu*, to smooth, is popularly used.

Ogiad, *s. m.—pl. t.* au (og) A harrowing.

Ogiadwr, *s. m.* (ogiad—gwr) A harrower.

Ogl, *s. m.* (og) That is full of motion or life; expansion; growth. *a.* Full of motion or life; expanding, growing; youthful.

> Heddyw, dydd da it'! hoewddyn
> Fain ogl o gorff, fwnwgl gwyn.
>
> This morning, good day to thee! smart maid, of slender *growth* in body, and white neck. *Sir Huw Robert.*

Ogledd, *s. m.* (ogl) Fullness of activity or motion

Ognaw, *s. m.* (og—naw) Activity, ertness.

Ogof, *s. f.—pl. t.* au (og—of) A cave; a den.

Ogofawg, *a.* (ogof) Abounding with caves.

Ohan, *pronom. prep.* (o—han) Out of, from out of. *Ohanof*, out of me, of me; *ohanot*, out of thee; *ohani*, out of her; *ohano*, out of him or it; *ohanom*, out of us; *ohanoch*, out of you; *ohanynt*, out of them.

Ohon, *pronom. prep.* (o—hon) Out of, from out; of, from. *Ohonof*, out of me; *ohonot*, of thee; *ohono*, of him or it; *ohoni*, of her; *ohonom*, out of us; *ohonoch*, of you; *ohonynt*, of them.

Oi, *v. a.* (aw) To proceed to; to come forward.

Oi, *interj.* (oi, *v.*) Expressive of applause. Well.

> Oi, was da; canys buost yn ffyddlawn yn ychydigyn, cymer feddiant ar ddeg dinas.
>
> *Well*, thou good servant; as thou hast been faithful in a very little, be thou ruler over ten cities. *W. Salisbury, Luke* 19.
>
> Gyr y gwartheg o'r egin;
> Oi! Oi! tro y lloi o'r llin.
>
> Drive the cattle out of the corn; *Come! Come!* drive the calves out of the flax. *D. ab Gwilym.*

O'i, *prep. and pron.* (o—ei) Out of or from the third person; from its, from his, from her.

> Drwg pawb o'i wybod.
>
> Every one is bad *from his* being known. *Adage.*
>
> Gwell gwr o'i berchi.
>
> A man is better *from his* being respected. *Adage.*
>
> Ni chriff chwedl nid el o'i dy.
>
> He will get no news who does not go *out of his* house. *Adage.*

Oiad, *s. m.* (oi) A listening, or hearkening.

Oian, *s. m.* (oi) A listening, a hearkening.

> Oiann, parchellan! y parchell gwyn gwyn,
> Na chysgi hun fore;
> Na chladd yn mhryng, rhag dawed
> Rhydderch Hael a'i gwn cyfrwys.
> Gan gaffael ohonot y coed
> Rhedodd dy chwys.
>
> *Listen*, little porkling! thou forward little white pig, that thou dost not sleep a morning nap: do not burrow on the open ridge, lest Rhydderch the generous should come with his cunning dogs: As thou hast been able to get to the woods, thy sweat has trickled. *Myrddin.*

Oianu, *v. a.* (oian) To hearken, or to listen.

Oiaw, *v. a.* (oi) To hark, to listen, to attend. *Gwrandaw* is the expression popularly used.

> Oia di yr Arglwydd dy Dduw.
>
> *Hear* thou the Lord thy God. *Mabinogi.*
>
> Aeth ulw dros frig wyth aelwyd;
> Oia, gyagu ddu, mau'dd wyd.
>
> Embers have become spread over eight hearths; hark, sable sleep, be to me. *D. ab Gwilym, i'r anhunedd.*

Oio, *interj.* (oi) Oh! dear! well! alack!

OL, *s. m. r.—pl. t.* ion. A mark, trace, or impression; a track, course, or path; a footstep; what is in course, the future and the past; the rear, the hinder part. *Mae arnaf ei ol*, I bear his marks; *ol bwyall*, the mark of a hatchet; *ol troed*, the print of a foot: *Mae yr amser goreu yn ol eto*, the best time is yet in course (to come); *pa un sydd ar ol?* What one is on the rear? or, what one is behind? *Blaen ac ol*, foremost and hindmost; *bod yn ol*, to be wanting; *troi yn ol*, to turn back; *rhoi yn ol*, to give back; *ar ol bod yno*, after being there; *yn ol*, according to; *yr amser yn ol*, the time hereafter; *myned ar ol*, to go after.

> Elid bryd yn ol breuddwyd.
>
> Let the mind go *after* the dream. *Adage.*

Ol, *a.* (ol, *s.*) Hindmost. *Y pen ol*, the posteriors

Olaf, *adv.* (ol) Farthest back, hindmost, last. *s. m.* The last, the hindmost.

> Gadu y nos waethaf yn olaf.
>
> To leave the worst night till *last*. *Adage.*

Olafedd, *s. m.* (olaf) Posteriority, ultimity.

Olafiad, *s. m.—pl.* olafiaid (olaf) A successor.

Olafiaeth, *s. m.* (olaf) A successorship.

Olbrain, *s. m.* (ol—brain) Wart-cress, wine-cress.

Olbre, *s. f.—pl. t.* on (ol—pre) The thrums on the end of a web; also called *eddi*.

Olddyddiad, *s. m.* (dyddiad) An after-dating.

Olddyddiaw, *v. a.* (ol—dyddiaw) To post date.

Olc, *s. f.—pl. t.* oedd (ol) A ribble; a ravine, such as is formed by the current of waters.

> Cyfarfod, yn yr olc fwyn,
> A wnaiu a lodes.
>
> A meeting, in the pleasant *dingle*, I had with a maid. *Morgan Gruffudd.*

Olew, *s. m.—pl. t.* on (ol—ew) Oil. *Dodi olew*, to administer extreme unction.

Olewwydd, *s. pl. aggr.* (olew—gwydd) Olive trees

Olewwydden, *s. f.* (olewwydd) An olive tree.

Oli, *v. a.* (ôl) To proceed lastly; to be last.

Oliad, *s. m.—pl.* oliaid (ol) That is in course, or consequent; posterity; the hindmost. *Blaeniaid ac oliaid*, leaders and followers; *cael oliad ar beth*, to get a scent of a thing.

Oliannawl, *a.* (oliant) Successive; tracing.

Oliannu, *v. a.* (oliant) To form a track; to come in succession.

Oliant, *s. m.* (ol) Succession; a tracing.

Oliedydd, *s. m.* (oliad) A pricker, in hunting.

Olion, *s. pl. aggr.* (ol) Things left behind, leavings, refuse.

Oliwr, *s. m.—pl.* olwyr (ol—gwr) A pricker.

Olp, *s. m.* (ol) A puncture; an oilet-hole.

Olpai, *s. m.* (olp) A tag put into an oilet-hole.

Olrhain, *s. m.* (ol—rhain) A searching after.

Olrhain, *v. a.* (ol—rhain) To follow by the trace; to trace, to search out, to seek by the print of the feet; to search carefully.

> Gwell cadw nog olrhain.
>
> Better to keep than *to search after*. *Adage.*

Olrhe, *s. m.* (rhe) A following a track.

Olrhëad, *s. m.—pl.* olrhëaid (olrhe) A beagle.

Olrhëain, *v. a.* (olrhe) To trace after, to indagate

> Am ael rhiw i'm olrhewyd.
>
> About the brow of the hill I *have been traced*. *O. ab Ll. Moel.*

Olrhëawd, *s. m.* (olrhe) A scrutiny, a tracing out

Olrhëawl, *a.* (olrhe) Scrutinizing, searching.

Olrheiniad, *s. m.—pl. t.* au (olrhain) Indagation.

Olrheiniadu, *v. a.* (olrheiniad) To indagate.

Olrheiniadwy, *a.* (olrheiniad) Scrutable.

Olrheiniaw, *v. a.* (olrhain) To indagate, to search out, to investigate, to scrutinise.

Olrheiniedig, *a.* (olrheiniad) Being traced out.

Olrheiniedydd, *s. m.—pl. t.* ion (olrheiniad) An indagator, a scrutinizer, a tracer.

Olrheiniwr, *s. m.—pl.* olrheinwyr (olrhain—gwr) A scrutinizer, a finder out.

Olrhëwr, *s. m.—pl.* olrhewyr (olrhe—gwr) A diligent seeker, a scrutinizer.

Olw, *s. m.* (ôl) That makes track, or mark.

Olwen, *s f.* (ôl—gwen) Of a white or fair track: the Venus of the Britons, or a poetical personage, representing the prolific principle of nature: Four white trefoils sprang up wherever she trod.

Olwr, *s. m.—pl.* olwyr (ol—gwr) One who is last; a follower; a tracer.

Olwydd, *s. m.* (ol—gwydd) Knowledge by scent.

Olwyn, *s. f.—pl. t.* ion (olw) What moves or turns to form a track; a wheel. *Olwyn ow*, the beam of a sledge or drag.

Pen a borthaf fn morddwyd,
Oedd ysgwyd ar ei wlad, oedd olwyn yn nghad.

A head I bear by the side of my thigh, that was a shield over his country, that was a *wheel* in battle. *Llywarch Hen.*

Olwyn, *a.* (ol—gwyn) Having a white track.
Olwynad, *s. m.* (olwyn) A moving in a track; a wheeling, a forming a wheel.
Olwynaw, *v. a.* (olwyn) To move in a track; to wheel, to form a wheel.
Olwynawg, *a.* (olwyn) Having wheels, wheeled.
Olymadrawdd, *s. m.—pl.* olymadroddion (ymadrawdd) An after-discourse; an epilogue.
Olynol, *adv.* (ol—yn—ol) In succession, one after another.

Dinystria, llywia i'r llaid olynol
Holl elynion f'enaid.

Destroy, send to the dust *one after another* all the enemies of my soul. *H. D. ab Ifan, ps. 143.*

Olysgrif, *s. f.—pl. t.* ion (ysgrif) A postscript.
Olysgrifen, *s. f.* (olysgrif) A postscript.
OLL, *s. m. r.* That is separate, distinct, or complete in itself; a whole, or all.
Oll, *a.* (oll, *s.*) All, the whole of, every one.

Goreu oll y goreu a ellir.

The best of *all* is what is possible. *Adage.*

Ollallu, *s. m.* (gallu) All-power, omnipotence.
Ollalluawg, *a.* (ollallu) Almighty, omnipotent.
Ollalluedd, *s. m.* (ollallu) Almightiness.
Ollallueddus, *a.* (ollallu) Omnipotential.
Ollalluogi, *v. a.* (ollalluawg) To render omnipotent, to become omnipotent.
Ollalluogrwydd, *s. m.* (ollalluawg) Almightiness.
Ollarfawg, *a.* (arfawg) Completely armed.
Ollarfogaeth, *s. m.* (ollarfawg) A panoply.
Olldifaawl, *a.* (difaawl) All-consuming.
Olldigonawl, *a.* (digonawl) All-sufficient.
Olldoeth, *a.* (doeth) All-wise, all-knowing.
Ollgyfoeth, *s. m.* (cyfoeth) All-power.
Ollgyfoethawg, *a.* (ollgyfoeth) All-powerful.
Olli, *v. a.* (oll) To render distinct or complete in itself; to make up a whole or all.
Olliach, *s. m.* (olliach) An universal remedy; the herb all-heal. *a.* Perfectly well.
Ollid, *s. m.* (oll) An entireness, or a whole.
Ollnawdd, *s. m.* (nawdd) Complete protection.
Ollnerth, *s. m.* (oll—nerth) All of power.
Ollnerthawg, *a.* (ollnerth) Omnipotent.

Moliannaf——
Yn ei wyrthiau ollnerthawg.

I will praise him in his *almighty* wonders. *W. Middleton.*

Ollnerthedd, *s. m.* (ollnerth) Omnipotence.
Ollnoddawg, *a.* (ollnawdd) All-protecting.
Ollnoddawl, *a.* (ollnawdd) All-protecting.
Ollorfod, *s. m.* (gorfod) Universal conquest.
Ollorfodawg, *a.* (ollorfod) All-conquering.
Ollrad, *s. m.* (oll—rhad) All of grace.
Ollradawg, *a.* (ollrad) All-gracious.
Ollryw, *a.* (rhyw) Omnigenions, of all kinds.
Ollsylwad, *s. m.* (sylwad) Omnipercipiency.
Ollsyniad, *s. m.* (syniad) Omnipercipiency.
Ollus, *a.* (oll) Of a whole or entire form.
Ollwedd, *s. f.* (gwedd) A whole appearance. *a.* Every way, all manner.

Bod yn uddyf, deddf y Don,
Cof ollwedd, i'ch cyfeillion.

To be humble, after the maxim of Don, remembering *always*, to your friends. *Wat. ab Hywel.*

Ollweddawg, *a.* (ollwedd) Omniform, of all forms
Ollwel, *a.* (gwel) All-seeing, seeing all things.
Ollwneuthurawl, *a.* (gwneuthurawl) Omnific.
Ollwybod, *s. m.* (gwybod) Omniscience.
Ollwybodawg, *a.* (ollwybod) Omniscious.
Ollwybodawl, *a.* (ollwybod) Omniscient.
Ollwybodus, *a.* (ollwybod) Omniscious.
Ollwydd, *s. m.* (gwydd) Omnipresence, ubiquity.
Ollysawl, *a.* (oll—ysawl) All-consuming.
Om, *s. m. r.* That stretches round, extends over, or includes; that bulges or swells out.
O'm, *pronom. prep.* (o—ym) Out of my, from my. *O'm pen*, out of my head.
ON, *s. f. r.* That rises up; that is over superior, or beyond; that is in continuity; also an ash. It is also a plural termination.
O'n, *pronom. prep.* (o—yn) Out or from our.
Onaddu, *pronom. prep.* (o—yn—addu) Of them.

Pedwar meib ar ugaint a'm bu——
Oedd Gwen goreu gwr onaddu.

Four and twenty sons there were to me: Gwen was the best man *of them*. *Llywarch Hen.*

Ni chefais——
Onadden yr un erioed.

I obtained not *of them* ever a single one. *D. ab Gwilym.*

Onaddynt, *pronom. prep.* (onaddu) Of them.
Onaidd, *a.* (on) Like the ash, ash-like, ashen.
Onawl, *a.* (on) Belonging to the ash.
Onc, *s. m.—pl. t.* od (on) That stretches out, or that is headlong; an oaf. *Rads.*
Onco, *pron.* (onc) That, speaking of what is near or under observation. *Dyro imi onco*, give me that; *a fyni di onco?* Wilt thou have that. *Dyfed.*
Onco, *adv.* (onc) There, or in that place.
Ond, *conj.* (on) But, only, except, save. *Ond odid, nid hwyrach*, peradventure; *dim ond hyny*, no more than that! *ond gwell iti beidiaw*, but thou hadst better to be quiet.

Nid derwydd eithr o enwawd;
Nid derwydd ond Duw.

Only a druid from appellation; for there is no druid *but* God. *Adage.*

Ni bu Arthur ond tra fu.

Arthur was not *but* whilst he was. *Adage.*

Onen, *s. f. dim.* (on) An ash, an ash tree; also by metonymy, a spear. *Onen wyllt*, a wild ash: *Rhiryd rudd ei onen*, Riryd with his crimson spear.
Oni, *conj.* (o—ni) If not, unless, except. It is used before words with consonant initials. *Oni ddoi*, if thou dost not come; *oni'm gweli*, if thou dost not see me.

Oni byddi cyfarwydd cyfarch.

If thou art *not* acquainted enquire. *Adage.*

Oni, *adv.* (o—ni) Until, to the time that; be not; will not. *Oni ddoi di yno?* Wilt thou not come there? *Oni weli di fi?* Dost thou not see me?

Ni cheidw Cymmro oni gollo.

A Welshman will not keep *until* he loses. *Adage.*

Onid, *conj.* (o—nid) If not, unless, except. It precedes words with vowel initials. *Onid eiff hi, arosed; if* she will *not* go, let her stay; *onid ê*, if not so.
Onid, *adv.* (o—nid) Until, to the time that; be not; will not. *Onid wyf yma?* am I not here? *Onid elo hi yno*, until she goes there.
Onide, *conj.* (onid—e) Otherwise, else, or.

Rhaid i weinidawg—fod yn gadarn yn y gwirionedd, onide ni waeir ag ef ond ceiliawg gwynt.

It is necessary for a minister to be firm in the truth, *otherwise* nothing will be made of him but a weathercock. *Ier. Owain.*

Onide, *adv.* (onid—e) If not so; if not that, otherwise; is it not so? how otherwise? *Onidê yn wir?* is it not so indeed?
Onis, *conj.* (o—nis) If not, unless. It is used before words with consonant initials, preserving such as are mutable in their radical state. *Onis tali*, if thou dost not pay.

Onis, *adv.* (o—nis) Until, to the time that; be not; will not. *Onis delom*, until we come.
Onite, *conj.* (onide) Otherwise, else, or, if not.
Onite, *adv.* (onide) If not so, if not that, or else, otherwise; is it not so? how otherwise?
Onwaew, *s.f.* (on—gwaew) An ashen spear.
Onwydd, *s. pl. aggr.* (on—gwydd) Ash trees.
Onwydden, *s. f. dim.* (onwydd) An ash tree.
Onynt, *pronom. prep.* (on—ynt) Of them.

Lle delon', wehilion baid, pawb onynt,
Pwy bynag o'r ddwy-blaid,
Tria gwerin cethin y caid.

Where they should come, the outcast rabble, every one *of them*, of whichsoever of the two parties, terribly they would be found to oppress the multitude. *H. D. ab Ifan.*

Ong, *s. f.* (on) A point of divergency.
Ongl, *s. f.—pl. t.* au (ong) A corner, an angle. *Yr ongl*, the haw, a disorder in the eye so called.
Onglaidd, *a.* (ongl) Angular, angle-wise.
Onglawg, *a.* (ongl) Having angles, angular.
Ongli, *v. a.* (ongl) To make an angle; to make angular; to form a corner.
Ongliad, *s. m.* (ongl) A forming an angle.
Ongyr, *s. f. aggr.* (on—gyr) A brunt or push of spears; an aggregate or throng of spears.

Tri eryr ongyr angerddawl.

Three eagles of the vehement *throng of spears*. *Ll. P. Moch.*

Aerddrud, aeth ragud wrth ongyll ongyr,
Eryr rhodd bybyr mewn rhwydd hebyll.

Bold in slaughter, the swift one went with the gleamings of the *throng of spears*, the eagle of magnificent gift in the moving tents. *Prydydd Brouse.*

OR, *s. f. r.—pl. t.* oedd. That is outward, extreme, or bordering; a limit, a boundary; a coast, margin, brim, or edge.

Oredd—
Tres rhag llew, rhag llyw pedair or.

There was a pressure before the lion, before the ruler of four *borders*. *Cynddelw.*

Or, *conj.* (o—yr) If; but not so generally used as *o*, *od*, and *os*. *Or bydd*, if there shall be.
O'r, *prep. and art.* (o—yr) Out of the, from the.

Gwneuthur deu-ddrwg o'r un.

Making two evils *of the one*. *Adage.*

Oraw, *v. a.* (or) To utter, to send outward.
Orch, *s. f.* (or) That is an extreme; a rim; a limit, or border.
Ori, *v. a.* (awr) To make pauses; to breath at long intervals; to utter, to send out, to puff.
Oriad, *s. m.—pl. t.* au (awr) A puffing, a panting.
Oriadur, *s. m.* (oriad) What measures the hour; a watch.

Oriadur yw gofyn ei ddirwyn i fynydd bob dydd yw meddwl.

The mind of man is like a *watch*, which requires to be wound up every day. *Dafydd y Nant.*

Oriain, *v. a.* (awr) To puff out, to pant for breath. *Mal y byddai hi yn oriain ac yn methu cael ei gwynt!* how she used to be panting and failing to draw her breath.
Orian, *s. f.—pl. t.* au (awr) An utterance; a panting, or a puffing.

Os cywair fy nghadair——
Yn gwyr Manawyd; a Phryderi,
Tair orian, i am dan, a gan rhegddi:
Ac am ei banau ffrydiau gweilgi,
A'r ffynawn ffrwythlawn yseydd oddachti;
Yn chwegach no'r gwin gwyn y llyn yndi.

If my chair is in order, it is known to Manawyd; and Pryderi, three *utterances*, around the fire, will be sung before it; and about its bowls the streams of the torrent, and the fruitful spring is above it; more delicious than the white wine the liquor in it. *Taliesin.*

Oriau, *s. pl. aggr.* (awr) Hours; periods; fits. *Dyn a rhyw oriau drwg arno*, a person with some bad fits upon him.

Oriawg, *a.* (awr) Having periods, changes, or fits; fickle, inconstant, changeable.
Oriawl, *a.* (awr) Belonging to the hour, horary.
Oriawr, *s. f.—pl.* orioran (awr) A watch.
Oriel, *s. m.—pl. t.* au (or) A porch; a gallery.
Orig, *s. f. dim.* (awr) A short hour, a little while. *adv.* Now. *Awr ac orig*, continually. *Sil.*

Oer yw'r loes,——
Sy orig yn Nrenearna.

Severe is the pang, which is now in Drumearna. *R. Cyffin.*

Origyn, *s. m. dim.* (orig) A short space.
Oriogi, *v. n.* (oriawg) To become capricious.
Oriogrwydd, *s. m.* (oriawg) Capriciousness.
Orlais, *s. m.—pl.* orleisiau (awr—llais) A clock.
Orleisiwr, *s. m.* (orlais—gwr) A clockmaker.
Orleisydd, *s. m.—pl. t.* ion (orlais) A clockmaker
Orn, *s. m.—pl. t.* au (or) A start, a push, a frown, a threat, a challenge, a stray.
Ornaidd, *a.* (orn) Tending to push out; apt to start; threatening.
Ornair, *s. m.—pl.* orneirian (orn—gair) A word of challenge or threat.

Ciliais i'm corn gan ornair;
Cael ysgwyd, celais y gair.

I receded into my shell at the *threatening word*, getting a push, I concealed the expression. *D. ab Gwilym.*

Ornawl, *a.* (orn) Repulsive; starting; threatening, challenging.
Ornedig, *a.* (orn) Threatened, challenged.
Ornedigaeth, *s. m.* (ornedig) A starting, a threatening, a challenging.
Ornedd, *s. m.* (orn) A starting; a threatening state, a challenge.

Mebolaeth arfeiliaeth waraedd,
Mab Brochwel, breuhael, haul ornedd.

A picture of mildness the infancy of the son of Brochwel, of generous breast, with scorns for claims. *Cynddelw, i Dysilio.*

Ornest, *s. f.—pl. t.* au (orn) A tilting match, or tournament; a single combat, a duel.

Ni fernir ornest ar wr oni bo 21 oed; ne o dair ar hugain allan, cyfraith hidio ornest.

A man shall not be judged liable to a combat until he shall be 21 years of age; and from three and twenty outward the law is for him to combat. *Welsh Laws.*

Ornestfa, *s. f.—pl. t.* ou (ornest) A place of combat, a place for tournament.
Ornestiad, *s. m.* (ornest) The engaging in a tilting match; a fighting in single combat.
Ornestiaeth, *s. m.* (ornest) The practice of tournaments; the practice of single combat.
Ornestle, *s. m.—pl. t.* oedd (ornest—lle) A tiltyard, a place for tournaments.
Ornestu, *v. a.* (ornest) To engage in a tournament; to fight a single combat, to fight a duel.
Ornestwr, *s. m.—pl.* ornestwyr (ornest—gwr) One who engages in tournaments; a combatant.
Ornestydd, *s. m.—pl. t.* ion (ornest) Combatant.
Ornfloedd, *s. f.* (orn—bloedd) A shout of threat.
Ornfloeddiad, *s. m.* (ornfloedd) A shouting in a threatening manner.
Ornfloeddiaw, *v. a.* (ornfloedd) To shout threateningly; a shout of defiance.
Orngri, *s. f.* (orn—cri) A threatening cry.
Orngriad, *s. m.* (orngri) A making a cry of threatening, or of defiance.
Orngriaw, *v. a.* (orngri) To cry threateningly.
Orni, *v. a.* (orn) To push out or forward; to start, to threaten, to challenge.
Orniad, *s. m.—pl. t.* au (orn) A pushing out, a starting, a threatening, a challenging.

Ornu, *v. a.* (orn) To push out or forward, to start, to threaten, to intimidate, to challenge.

Gwelwn afon——
A'i ffrydiau fal tònau Taf,
Ornais, yn curo arnaf.

A pale river, with its torrents like the waves of Tav, beating upon me, *I started with fear.* *D. ab Gwilym.*

Ornwr, *s. m.—pl.* ornwyr (orn—gwr) One who pushes or starts out; a starter, a threatener.

Ornydd, *s. m.—pl. t.* ion (orn) A starter, a threatener, one who intimidates.

Oröi, *v. a.* (oraw) To utter, to be uttering.

Oroïan, *s. f.* (oröi) An exclamation, an expression of joy; jubilation, iö pæan.

Hëais, fàl oroïan,
Ei chlod yn Ngwynedd achlan.

I have spread, as a *song of triumph*, her fame entirely over Gwynedd. *D. ab Gwilym, i Forfudd.*

Oroïan, *v. a.* (oröi) To utter a shout of triumph.

OS, *s. m. r.* That tends from, out, or forward; that tends to increase; an increment. It is also a diminutive termination affixed to plural nouns, mostly used in tender language; as *plant*, children; *plantos*, dear little children.

Os, *conj.* (o—ys) If; used in common with *o*, *odd*, *od*, and *or*, with verbs of the indicative mode. *Os doi yma*, if thou wilt come here. See PE.

Os pwyll canwyll rhag cynhen,
Goreu canwyll yw pwyll pen.

If sense is a lamp to guard against contention, the best lamp is common sense. *Huw Cae Llwyd.*

Osai, *s. m.* (aws) A sweet juice; cyder.

Mynwn—diawd, mewn mali ariant, o osai wedy ei glauaru ar dri o farwor rhudderw.

I would have for drink, to a silver bason, *cyder* after it has been warmed on three reddy-glowing embers. *Araeth Gwgan.*

Pe bai gan mil, yn ddilys,
O eryd rhif ar dir Rhys;
A thrichan gwinllan a gwin;
Ac yn malu gan melin:
Pe bai'r ddaiar yn fara!
Neu flas dwr fal osai da;
Yn ei wledd rhyfedd barna
Dwr a daiar dri dia.

If there were a hundred thousand, to a certainty, of numbered ploughs on the land of Rhys, and three hundred vine-yards teeming with wine; and in grinding a hundred mills: if the earth were of bread, or the taste of water like fine *cyder*; in his feast, it would be a wonder if the water and the land were to last for three days. *D. Nanmor.*

Osb, *s. f.—pl. t.* ion (os) That is erratic, a guest.

Gnawd osb er nas gwahoddir.

A *guest* is wont to come though he may not be invited. *Adage.*

Osbawl, *a.* (osb) Belonging to a guest.

Osbi, *v. a.* (osb) To come as a guest; to be a guest or visitor.

Osg, *s. m.* (os) That tends from or out.

Osgatfydd, *adv.* (osg—atfydd) Peradventure. The same as *agatfydd* and *ysgatfydd*.

Osged, *s. f.—pl. t.* au (osg) A laver, a bason.

Osgl, *s. m.—pl. t.* au (osg) A bough or branch; a twig, a spray.

Erchis y gwr y bioedd y berllan i'r garddwr dori un neu ddau o osglau y pren mawr.

The person who owned the orchard ordered the gardener to cut down one or two of the *branches* of the large tree. *Hanes Doethion Rhufain.*

Osglawd, *s. m.* (osgl) A ramification.

Osglawg, *a.* (osgl) Having branches, branched, branching, full of branches.

Osglawg, blaen derw; chwerw chwaith on;
Hweg efwr; chwerthiniat ton
Ni chel y grudd gystudd calon.

Full of branches the top of the oak; bitter the taste of ash, luscious the cow-parsnep; breaking out the wave: the cheek will not conceal the affliction of the heart. *Llywarch Hen.*

Osgledig, *a.* (osgl) Branched, ramified.

Osgledd, *s. m.* (osgl) Fulness of branches.

Osglen, *s. f. dim.* (osgl) A branch, a twig.

Osgli, *v. n.* (osgl) To branch, to shoot out.

Osgliad, *s. m.—pl. t.* au (osgl) A branching.

Osgo, *s. m.* (osg) Obliquity, or slope; a digression. *Ar osgo*, obliquely, aside.

Osgöad, *s. m.* (osgo) A going aslant, a going aside, a digression, a starting aside.

Osgöawl, *a.* (osgo) Tending to go aside, starting.

Osgöedd, *s. m.* (osgo) Obliquity, a starting aside.

Osgoi, *v. a.* (osgo) To go aslant, to go obliquely, to digress, to start aside.

Osgoilyd, *a.* (osgoi) Apt to go aside, apt to start aside, apt to be shy or coy.

Osgoilydrwydd, *s. m.* (osgoilyd) Aptness to start aside, aptness to avoid.

Osgöwr, *s. m.—pl.* osgöwyr (osgo—gwr) A starter, one who starts aside.

Osgyd, *s. m.—pl. t.* au (osg) A laver, a basin.

Osi, *v. a.* (os) To offer to do, to attempt.

Osiad, *s. m.—pl. t.* au (os) A making an essay.

Osiaw, *v. a.* (os) To offer to do, to essay, to make an attempt, to dare.

Osiawl, *a.* (os) Tending to make an essay.

Osid, *adv.* (os—id) If it be, if so be, peradventure.

Ost, *s. m.* (os) That is out, that extends out, that is spread or displayed.

Ostid, *s. f.* (ost) That is outward; an epithet for a shield or buckler.

Ostl, *s. f.—pl. t.* oedd (ost) An open place, an inn.

Ostler, *s. m.—pl. t.* i (ostl) One who receives guests or acts at an inn, an ostler.

Ostr, *s. m.* (ost) That is spread out, or displayed.

Ostri, *s. m.* (ostr) Display of hospitality. *Cadw ostri*, to keep open house.

Ostlys, *s. m.* (ost) Openness of conduct, display of hospitality; complaisance.

Osw, *s. m.* (os) That runs onward; a steed.

Oswydd, *s. pl. aggr.* (osw) Those that run out; ravagers; an epithet for war-horses; or the cavalry.

Ni byddai diwyth i lwyth oswydd.

There would be no abatement of wrath to the tribe of *ravagers.* *Meilyr.*

Gwelai darf ar dyrfa oswydd.

He beheld affright amongst a host of *ravagers.* *D. ab Llosgwrn Mew.*

A'i cadarnâu, ced hylwydd, yn hir,
I ymddiffyn tir rhag torf oswydd.

And long to support her, a prosperous treasure, to defend the land against a host of *ravagers.* *Llygad Gwr.*

Gwenydd gwrth lawr,
Gwenydd aesawr,
Oswydd gwyddaw.

The divider of opposing ground, the divider of shields, causing the fall of *ravagers.* *Briayll Brys-ffwrch.*

Osyd, *adv.* (os—yd) If so; peradventure.

OTH, *s. m. r.* That is exterior or extreme.

O'th, *pronom. prep.* (o—yth) Out of thy.

OW, *s. m. r.* A breathing out; a moan.

Ow, *interj.* (ow, *s.*) Woe is me, alas, ah me!

Oyma, *adv.* (o—yma) From here, from hence.

Oyna, *adv.* (o—yna) From there, from thence; speaking of what is under observation.

Oyno, *adv.* (o—yno) From thence; speaking of what is distant, as to time or place.

PA, *s. m. r.* What tends to proceed; what forms a continuity.

Pa, *pron.* (pa, *s.*) What, which. *Pa le?* which place? *pa beth?* what thing? *pa un?* which one? *pa beth bynag a fo*, what thing soever it shall be; *pa ddyn bynag*, what person soever.

Pa, *adv.* (pa, *s.*) To what, whither; what, which, how. *Pa ffordd y doi?* which way wilt thou come? *I ba le yr af?* Where shall I go? *Pa fan y byddi?* Where wilt thou be? *Pa un?* Which one? *Pa rai?* Which ones? *Pa gwaith?* How often? *Pa sut sydd?* How is it with thee? *Pa beth sydd arnat?* What is the matter with thee? *Pa sawl?* How many? *Pa gan?* With what? *Pa faint?* How much? *Pa gymaint, pa dwysg?* What quantity? *Pa hyd?* How long? *Pa rag?* From what? *Pa ryw?* What kind? *Pa am?* Wherefore? *Pa ffordd, pa ddull, pa wedd, pa ddelw, pa fodd?* in what way or form? *Pa gân gymaint?* About what quantity?

> Pa anhyberwyd, unben, a weleisti arnaf?
>
> *What* indecorum, prince, didst thou perceive in me? *H. Pwyll—Mabinogion.*
>
> Abandid ba andaw.
>
> *What* hearing can be of a tumult. *Adage.*

Pab, *s. m.—pl. t.* au (pa—ab) That produces motion; that produces life; a father; the pope.

> Arglwydd Iesu Grist erglyw,
> Un Mab Duw bab wyd a byw.
>
> Lord Jesus Christ hear me, the son of God the living *Father* art thou. *R. Leiaf.*

Pabaeth, *s. m.* (pab) Paternity: the papacy.

Pabaidd, *a.* (pab) Papal, or like the pope.

Pabawg, *a.* (pab) Having a pope, papal.

Pabawl, *a.* (pab) Belonging to a father; papal.

Pabell, *s. f.—pl.* pebyll (pab—ell) A moving habitation; tent, a pavillion; a tabernacle.

> Pan ddel milgi Llywelyn,
> Pob llwyn a fydd pebyll yn.
>
> When the greyhound of Llywelyn comes, every grove will be a *haunt* for us. *Huw Cae Llwyd.*

Pabellawg, *a.* (pabell) Having a tent, tented.

Pabelliad, *s. m.* (pabell) A fixing a tent.

Pabellig, *s. f. dim.* (pabell) A little tent.

Pabellu, *v. a.* (pabell) To pitch or fix a tent.

Pabeth, *pron.* (pa—peth) What thing.

Pabi, *s. m.—pl. t.* odd (pab) That is productive of motion or life; a poppy.

Pabiaidd, *a.* (pabi) Papaverous, poppy-like.

Pabiawg, *a.* (pabi) Abounding with poppies.

Pabïawl, *a.* (pabi) Papaverous, of poppy.

Pabir, *s. pl.* (pab—ir) Rushes, rush-candles.

> Yr aelwyd hon neus cudd myr?
> Mwy gorddyfnasai babir gloew,
> A chyfeddau cywir.
>
> This hearth, is it not covered with ants? More congenial would have been the shining *rushes*, with festivals of good faith. *Llywarch Hen.*

Pabiraidd, *a.* (pabir) Like rushes, or rush-like.

Pabirawg, *a.* (pabir) Abounding with rushes.

Pabl, *s. m.—pl.* pablau (pab) Activity; vigour, energy, faculty. *Dwfn babl*, profound faculty

Pablaidd, *a.* (pabl) Active; nervous, or potent.

> Pablaidd gorff, pabloedd a gwr,
> Post oddwyn haol, pais dewddur.
>
> *Vigorous* of body, men he overcomes, a pillar stately and generous, clad in a coat of thick steel. *Iolo Goch, i O. Glandwr.*

Pabledd, *s. m.* (pabl) Activity; vigorousness.

Pabliad, *s. m.* (pabl) A rendering active; a rendering vigorous.

Pablu, *v. a.* (pabl) To render active; to render nervous or vigorous; to give a faculty.

Pablus, *a.* (pabl) Nervous, vigorous.

Pablusaw, *v. n.* (pablus) To render vigorous.

Pablusedd, *s. m.* (pablus) Vigorousness.

Pabogaeth, *s. m.* (pabawg) The papacy.

Pabwyr, *s. pl. aggr.* (pab—wyr) The large rushes; rushes used for burning; also called *brwyn*

Pabwyra, *v. a.* (pabwyr) To gather rushes.

Pabwyraidd, *a.* (pabwyr) Like rushes.

Pabwyrawg, *a.* (pabwyr) Abounding with rushes

Pabwyren, *s. f. dim.* (pabwyr) The soft rush.

Pabwyryn, *s. m. dim.* (pabwyr) A bulrush. *Yr wyt gan wlyped a'r pabwyryn*, thou art as wet as the bulrush.

Pabydd, *s. m.—pl. t.* ion (pab) A papist.

Pabyddaidd, *a.* (pabydd) Like a papist.

Pabyddawl, *a.* (pabydd) Papistical, popish.

Pabyddiaeth, *s. m.* (pabydd) Popery.

Pabynag, *pron.* (pa—bynag) Whatsoever.

Pad, *s. m.* (py—ad) That sustains, that keeps in continuity, that keeps together.

Padell, *s. f.—pl. t.* i (pad—ell) A pan. *Padell bridd*, an earthen pan; *padell efydd*, a brass pan; *padell doddion*, a dripping pan.

> Pwyll a ddyly padell.
>
> The *pan* requires attention. *Adage.*

Padellaid, *s. f.—pl.* padelleidiau (padell) A panful, or the contents of a pan.

Padellaidd, *a.* (padell) Formed like a pan.

Padellan, *s. f. dim.* (padell) A little pan.

Padellawg, *a.* (padell) Having a pan.

Padelleg, *s. f. dim.* (padell) The kneepan; also called *padell y glin.*

Padellig, *s. f. dim.* (padell) A little pan.

Padellu, *v. a.* (padell) To form a pan.

Padellwr, *s. m.—pl.* padellwyr (padell—gwr) A pan maker; a dealer in pans.

Padwysg, *adv.* (pa—twysg) What quantity.

Padyw, *adv.* (pa—yd—yw) What is it; why.

> O Dduw! padyw yth roddir gwrmseirch,
> Cynddylan, ar bedwar-deg-meirch.
>
> O God! why to thee are given the trappings of Cynddylan, on four times ten steeds. *Llywarch Hen.*

Padd, *s. m.* (py—add) That causes to proceed; that keeps in a course.

Pae, *s. m.* (pa) That causes to go onward, that forms a continuity, that surrounds; a constraint; a panting, or constrained breathing; hesitation.

Paeled, *s. f.—pl. t.* au (pae—lled) A spread, a plaister; a skullcap.

> A thrydyllu eu helmau, a briwaw eu paeledau, ac ysigaw yr arfau a orugynt
>
> And perforate their helmets, and cut their *skullcaps*, and bruise their weapons was what they did. *H. Geraint—Mabinogion.*

Paeledu, *v. a.* (paeled) To lay on, to spread over, to plaister; to put on a skullcap.

Paen, *s. m.—pl. t.* od (pa—en) That spreads; a peacock.

Nid teg onid paen.

Nothing so fine as a *peacock*. *Adage.*

Paenes, *s. f.—pl. t.* od (paen) A peahen.

Paenos, *adv.* (pae—nos) Every night, nightly.

Paenydd, *adv.* (pae—dydd) Every day, daily.

Paent, *s. m.* (paen) Any thing plaistered on.

Paentiad, *s. m.* (paent) A painting, a daubing.

Paentiaw, *v. a.* (paent) To paint; to daub.

Paentiawl, *a.* (paent) Painting, painted.

Paentiedig, *a.* (paentiad) Painted, daubed.

Paentiwr, *s. m.* (paent—gwr) A painter.

Paeol, *s. m.—pl. t.* au (pae—ol) A pail, a pot.

Paetu, *adv.* (pae—tu) On every side, round.

Paeth, *s. m.* (py—aeth) That forms a course, that keeps in a track; concurrence, agreement.

Pafan, *adv.* (pa—man) What place, to what place, whither.

Paff, *s. m.—pl. t.* iau (py—aff) A lump, a hulk.

Paffiad, *s. m.* (paff) A thumping, a buffetting.

Paffiaw, *v. a.* (paff) To thump, or to bang.

Paffiwr, *s. m.—pl.* paffwyr (paff—gwr) A thumper.

Pagan, *adv.* (pa—can) What with, with what.

Pagwaith, *adv.* (pa—gwaith) How many times.

Pagymaint, *adv.* (pa—cymaint) What quantity, how much.

Paham, *adv.* (pa—ham) What about, wherefore, for what cause, what for, why.

Bid hysbaid weithian, a hynod yw, ac amlwg, paham y gelwir y lle hwnw yn ynys, a phaham yn afallach.

Be it known therefore; and it is notable and manifest, *wherefore* that place is called an island, and *wherefore* orchard. *H. Dinodd Arthur.*

Pahyd, *adv.* (pa—hyd) How long, what length.

Pai, *s. m.* (pa) That sends out or from; that is objective.

Paid, *s. m.* (py—aid) A cessation of motion; a cessation, a state of rest, quiet. *Paid, peidia*, be quiet; used for the imperative *peidia*.

Paill, *s. m. aggr.—pl.* peillion (pall) Farina, flour.

Pain, *s. m. aggr.* (pan) Bloom, fine powder, or dust; farina; the bloom on fruits, the farina on flowers. *Gwenith wedi bwrw y pain.*

Pair, *s. f. aggr.* (par) An union of causes, instrumentalities or energies; a cause; also a boiler, a cauldron. *Pair dadeni*, the instrumentality or the alembic of regeneration; *pair ceridwen*, the energy of the smile of love, or prolific nature. *Bardism.*

Pair Prydain profwn yn nhangnef.

The *energy* of Britain we shall enjoy in tranquillity. *Cynddelw.*

Cred fy ngair, o'm pair perid ataf.

Believe my word, from my *command* he was caused to come to me. *Llywelyn Fardd.*

Iolaf bair, o bured arwar,
A beris amad ac adar.

I will praise the *cause*, from an impulse so pure, that caused the various beasts and fowls. *Llywelyn Fardd.*

Pais, *s. f.—pl.* peisiau (py—ais) A coat. *Pais arfau*, a coat of arms; *pais ddur*, a coat of mail.

Pawb a drais yn mhais ei dad.

Every one will oppress in his father's *coat*. *Adage.*

Paisg, *s. m.* (pais) That forms a coating; a pod.

Paith, *s. m.—pl.* peithion (py—aith) An opening, a strait forward course; a glance; a prospect, a scene.

Diffwys baith odwys,
Beithyniad glud giwys,
Argoedwys arglwyddrad.

Leaning over a steep *scene*, an explorator of a beauteous pile, the defender of the men of Argoed. *Cynddelw, i O. Cyfeiliawg.*

Pal, *s. f.—pl. t.* au (pa—al) A spread, a ray, a flat body, a spade; the puffin, a bird so called. *Rhaw bal, rhaw balar*, a shovel, a spade.

Palad, *s. m.—pl. t.* on (pal) A spreading or shooting out, a beaming, a radiating, a paling.

Paladr, *s. m.—pl.* pelydr (palad) A ray, a beam, a shaft, a stem, a trunk, a stalk, axis; a pole, or perch. *Paladr melin*, the shaft of a mill wheel; *paladr gwaew*, the shaft of a spear; *paladr angor*, the shank of an anchor; *cyswyn paladr*, spear charge, a payment so called: *pelydr haul*, sun-beams; *paladr englyn*, the stave of a stanza; *paladr hir*, broom-rape; *paladr trwyddo*, the herb thorow-wax.

Ceiniawg baladr yw yr hon a dalai bob gwr o'r genedl tu ac at dalu galanas:—Ni thal gwraig geiniawg baladr, am nad oes iddi ond cogel.

The *spear-penny* is that which every man of a family used to pay towards satisfying a fine for homicide:—A woman does not pay a *spear-penny*, as she has but a distaff. *Welsh Laws*

Paladrawg, *a.* (paladr) Having a stem or shaft.

Paladriad, *s. m.* (paladr) A forming a stem.

Paladru, *v. a.* (paladr) To form a beam or shaft; to shaft; to rise in a stalk, or to bole.

Paladrwym, *s. m.* (palad—rhwym) The fastening, which joins the two parts of a flail.

Paladu, *v. a.* (palad) To spread or shoot out, to beam, to radiate.

Palalwyf, *s. f.* (pal—llwyf) A lime tree; also called *gwaglwyf*.

Palar, *s. f.* (pal—ar) Delving soil or ground.

I Addaf a'i gymhar
Y rhoid rhaw balar
I dori daiar
I gael bara.

To Adam and his partner there was given a spade for *soil-delving*, to break up the ground to obtain bread. *Awdl Fraith.*

Palawr, *s. m.—pl.* palorion (pal) A delver.

Paled, *s. f.—pl. t.* au (pal) A shaft, a javelin, a dart. *Gware paled*, a tilting match.

Guedi cyflawni o honom ni pob peth, or a berthynai ar y dwywau y damweiniwys y rhwng dau neiaint cyfrysedd am fuddugoliaeth gwarae paled.

After we had completed every thing, which appertained to the Gods, there happened between two nephews a dispute about the victory at a *tilting* match. *Gr. ab Arthur.*

Paledrydd, *s. m.—pl. t.* ion (paladr) A maker of arrows, a fletcher.

Paledu, *v. a.* (paled) To throw a javelin, to tilt

Paledwr, *s. m.—pl.* paledwyr (paled—gwr) A tilter, one who uses a javelin.

Palf, *s. f.—pl. t.* au (pal) The flat part or end of a shaft: a blade, as of an oar: a paw, the palm of a hand. *Palf y gath*, the herb cat's-foot: *palf y llew*, common ladies' mantle: *palf yr arth*, stinking hellebore: *palf y blaidd*, common club-moss: *palf y gath bali*, ground pine.

Mal llygoden dan balf y gath.

Like a mouse under the cat's *paw*. *Adage.*

Palfaid, *s. f.—pl.* palfeidiau (palf) The stroke or motion of a palm.

Palfal, *s. m.* (palf) A moving the paws in all directions, a grope.

Palfaliad, *s. m.* (palfal) A groping about.

Palfalu, *v. a.* (palfal) To grope, to creep on the hands and feet.

Palfalwr, *s. m.—pl.* palfalwyr (palfalu—gwr) One who gropes, a creeper on all-fours.

Palfawd, *s. f.—pl.* palfodau (palf) A stroke with the paw, a slap with the palm of the hand.

Palfawg, *a.* (palf) Having a palm, pawed.

Palfes, *s. f.—pl.* palfeisiau (palf) A shoulder of a quadruped. *Palfes mollt, ysgwyd mollt*, a shoulder of mutton.

Palfiad, *s. m.—pl. t.* au (palf) A pawing.

Palfodiad, *s. m.* (palfawd) A slapping with the paw, a slapping with the open hand.

Palfodiaw, *v. a.* (palfawd) To slap with the paw.

Palfodiwr, *s. m.—pl.* palfodwyr (palfawd—gwr) One who slaps, a slapper.

Palfre, *s. f.—pl. t.* od (palf—rhe) A palfrey.

Palfu, *v. a.* (palf) To paw, to grope gently with the hand.

Palfwr, *s. m.—pl.* palfwyr (palf—gwr) A pawer.

Pali, *s. m.* (pal) That is of a downy glossy surface, satin, velvet. *Cath bali*, the glossy fur cat, an epithet for some ferocious animal, probably a tiger. See *Palug*.

> Pwy y rian oco,—a gwisg o bali melyn amdeni?
>
> Who is yonder lady, with a robe of yellow *satin* on her? *Hanes O. ab Urien—Mabinogion.*
>
> Neu'm rhoddes hil Rhun rudd a phali.
>
> Have I not been gifted by the race of Rhun with crimson and satin. *Cynddelw.*
>
> Rhwyf rhadau, bian beirdd i'w foli,
> A llen, a llyfrau, a llên bali.
>
> Lord of the virtues, it is incumbent upon bards to do him honor, with learning, and books, and *satin* veil. *Gw. Bry heintawg, i Ddewi.*

Paliad, *s. m.* (pâl) A throwing out, a spreading, a delving, or digging.

Paliaidd, *a.* (pali) Glossy like satin, or velvet.

Paliawg, *a.* (pali) Of satin, of velvet.

Palis, *s. m.—pl. t.* au (pal) A thin partition, as of boards, wattling, or laths: a wainscot; the steep of a rock.

> O balis llys nef, ef a gwympid, ac a fwrid i'r carchar isaf.
>
> From the *pale* of the court of heaven, he was made to fall, and was cast into the lowermost prison. *Elucidarius.*
>
> Ni saif palis a osodir yn uchel yn erbyn y gwynt.
>
> A paling that is placed on high will not stand against the wind. *Ecclesiastes* xxii. 18.

Palisaw, *v. a.* (palis) To make a partition of boards or laths, to wainscot.

Palisawg, *a.* (palis) Partitioned, wainscotted, paled, paly.

> Dy rew balisawg darian——
> Yw hon.
>
> Thy appropriate *paly* shield is this. *Gr. Hiraethawg.*

Palisiad, *s. m.* (palis) A partitioning; a wainscotting; a paling.

Palm, *s. m.* (pal) A spread; a flag.

Palmant, *s. m.—pl. t.* au (palm) A pavement.

Palmantawg, *a.* (palmant) Having a pavement.

Palmantiad, *s. m.* (palmant) A paving.

Palmantu, *v. a.* (palmant) To make a pavement.

Palmantwr, *s. m.—pl.* palmantwyr (palmant—gwr) One who makes a pavement, a pavior.

Palmid, *s. m.* (palm) That is spreading or flat.

Palmidwydd, *s. pl.* (palmid—gwydd) Palm trees.

Palmidwydden, *s. f. dim* (palmidwydd) Palm tree

Palmwydd, *s. pl. aggr.* (palm—gwydd) Palm trees.

Palmwydden, *s. f. dim.* (palmwydd) A palm tree.

Palores, *s. f.—pl. t.* au (palawr) A chough.

Palu, *v. a.* (pal) To delve, or to dig.

Palug, *s. m.* (pâl) That is of a smooth glossy surface. *Cath palug*, the glossy coated cat, some fierce animal, probably a tiger, mentioned in the historical triads to have been one of three molestations of Mona, which were reared in it.

Palwr, *s. m.—pl.* palwyr (palu—gwr) A digger

Pall, *s. m.* (py—all) Loss of power, energy, or compactness, that is incompact; a failing; neglect, omission, deficiency; a perishing state.

> Yr holl wirioneidd ar ball aeth
> O hiith hiliogaeth dynion.
>
> All righteousness is gone to *nought* from amongst the generation of men. *Edm. Prys.*

Pall, *s. m.—pl. t.* au (pa—all) That encloses, or a loose hanging, or curtain; a mantle; also a tent, a pavillion; a throne.

> Nid y mewn ty ydd oeddynt, namyn y mywn palllau.
>
> Not in houses were they, but in *tents*. *Ystori Ben. Fran—Mabinogion.*

Pall, *a.* (py—all) Of a spreading or incompact tendency; tending to fail or decay.

> Ysgwyd ball gwall Gubelyn.
>
> The *spreading* and toilsome shield of Cubelyn. *Ll. P. Moch.*

Palladwy, *a.* (pall) Fallible; perishable.

Palldawd, *s. m.* (pall) Failure; abortiveness.

Palldeg, *a.* (pall—teg) Spreadingly-fair.

> Maengaer glod bell-daer, glyd balldeg wyggrfan.
>
> A stone mansion of far-pervading fame, a warm *spreading fair* spacious place. *Cynddelw.*

Pallder, *s. m.* (pall) Fallibleness; a perished state

Palledig, *a.* (pall) Being of a failed state.

Pallen, *s. f.—pl. t.* au (pall) A coverlid.

Palliad, *s. m.* (pall) A divesting of energy or compactness; a failing, a perishing.

Palliannawl, *a.* (palliant) Tending to fallibility.

Palliannu, *v. a.* (palliant) To render fallible, to render perishable, to become fallible.

Palliant, *s. m.* (pall) A failure, neglect, omission; a perishing, or a failing.

Pallu, *v. a.* (pall) To fail, to neglect, to omit; to be deficient, to cease; to perish, to miss.

> Gnaw i eddewid gwraig ry phall.
>
> A woman's promise naturally *will fail*. *Adage.*
>
> Ys da felin a ballodd.
>
> Good is the mill which *has been worn out*. *Adage.*
>
> Pan roddai pob rhai, nid Rhys a ballai;
> Pan ballai pob rhai, fe a roddai Rhys.
>
> When every body would be giving, Rhys would not *fail*, when every body *would fail*, Rhys would give. *D. Nanmor.*

Pallus, *a.* (pall) Apt to fail, fallacious.

Pallusaw, *v. a.* (pallus) To make fallible; to become fallible.

Pallusedd, *s. m.* (pallus) Aptness to fail.

Pallusrwydd, *s. m.* (pallus) A state of failing.

Pallwr, *s. m.—pl.* pallwyr (pall—gwr) One who fails, one who neglects or omits.

Pallydd, *s. m.—pl. t.* ion (pall) One who fails.

Pam, *adv.* (pa—am) What about, wherefore, for what cause, why.

Pan, *s. m.—pl. t.* au (py—an) A vessel of capacity; a pan; a bowl, a cup.

> Gwirawd a ddygir o ddigrawn stan;
> Gwin o ban, rhan rhadlawn.
>
> Liquor will be brought in plenty to us; wine from the *pan*, a grateful portion. *Cynddelw.*
>
> Oni ddaw i mewn o'r medd goreu oll
> Gwirawd o ban, dy ben faddeu!
>
> If there does not come of the mead the best of all, liquor from the *pan*, thy head shall answer! *O. Cyfeiliawg.*

Pan, *s. m.* (pa—an) That is universal; pervasive, of spreading grain or texture; down; fur; nap; the milling, fulling, or thickening of cloth. *Gynau pan*, fur gowns.

Pan, *adv.* (pa—yn) When, at which time; whence, from whence; since; for which cause. *Pan fo*, when there shall be; *pan elo hyn heibio*, when this shall pass away; *pan yw*, that is; *hyd pan*, so that. *pan hynoeddynt?* Whence were they descended?

> Pan ddyco cyfraith anihaith o farwdy, neu o neb dadl arall—or bydd un peth a dalo bunt, brenin bieufydd.
>
> When the law takes an eu heit from a death house, or from any other claim, if there should be any one thing of the value of a pound, it shall belong to the king. *Welsh Laws.*

Pan fai lawen frain, pan frydiai waed,
Pan wyar waryal,
Pan ryfel, pan ruddid ei thai
Pan Ruddlan pan rudd lys losgai.
Pan ruddam ruddfflam fflemychai hyd nef,
Yn addef ni noddai.

When the ravens rejoice, when blood hastens, when gore bubbles, when there was war, when its houses were reddened, when Rhuddlan at the time its red court burned, when we made the ruddy flame to glow, it flamed up to heaven, no habitation would yield shelter. — *Hywel ab Owain.*

Dywedynt hwyntau wrtho: pan deui di wr? O'r gaer a welwch chwi rhaco.

They then said to him: *Whence comest thou, man?* From the castle that you see yonder. — *Hanes Culhwch—Mabinogion.*

Panan, *s. c.* (pan) That involves together.

Panas, *s. f.* (pan) A kind of straw hangings, or plaited partition of straw; also called *plaidwellt*; parsnep; *panas y dwfr*, water parsnep.

Panawg, *a.* (pan) Covered with down or nap; furred; frized; thickened by fulling, or milled. *Y dew banawg*, the great mullein.

Panc, *s. m.—pl. t.* iau (pan) A blow; a spank.

Pand, *adv.* (pa—ond) What but; is it not.

Pandy, *s. m.—pl. t.* au (pan—ty) A fulling mill.

Paned, *adv.* (pan) When, at which time.

Panedig, *a.* (pan) Covered with down or fur; thickened by fulling or milling.

Paneg, *s. f.—pl.* penyg (pan) A gut, or entrail.

Cyrfyll hyll chwedryll, chwydrefr penyg meirch.

The ugly trunk of six parts, with a tail discharging horse's *chitterlings.* — *H. Ystoryn, i Addaf Eurych.*

Panel, *s. m.—pl. t.* i (pan) What is plaited or worked together; the thick matting of straw, or the cushion of a pack-saddle; it is also called *panlle*; also the pannel, or pack-saddle, otherwise called *ystrodyr*, and *pynioreg*.

Panelawg, *a.* (panel) Involved, or blended together; consisting of plaited work; pannelled.

Panelu, *v. a.* (panel) To involve, plait, to mat.

Panfa, *s. f.—pl.* panfëydd (pan) The state of being covered with down, nap, or fur; the act of fulling; a banging.

Paniad, *s. m.—pl. t.* au (pan) A covering with down, nap, or fur; a fulling, or thickening by beating; a banging.

Pannawl, *a.* (pant) Tending to involve; or to hem in; forming a depression or hollow.

Pannedig, *a.* (pant) Hemmed in; depressed.

Pannel, *s. m.—pl. t.* au (pant) A little slope or fall, a small dingle.

Pwy, yn all y pannelau,
A gan mor ber ei genau
A'r eaws?

What one, in the recesses of the *dingles* whose mouth so sweetly sings as the nightingale? — *Meurig Dafydd.*

Pannelawg, *a.* (pannel) Abounding with small hollows, or falls in the ground.

Pannelu, *v. a.* (pannel) To form a gentle depression in a surface; to form a small hollow.

Pannoli, *v. a.* (pannawl) To form a devexity, to sink in, to slope down, to dimple.

Pannon, *s. m.* (*mutation of* panton) That comprehends universally; an epithet for the deity, the originator, the creator.

E luniai Pannon,
Ar awr glyn Ebron,
A'i ddwylaw gwynion,
Gwiwlun Adda.
A naw can mlynedd,
Heb wawr ymgeledd,
Y bu yn gorwedd,
Heb enaidfa.

The *Creator* formed, on the ground of Ebron vale, with his fair hands, the superior frame of Adam. Nine hundred years, without the dawn of self-supporting foresight he had been lieing, before he obtained a soul. — *Awdl Fraith.*

Pannu, *v. a.* (pant) To involve, to include, to hem in, to cause to sink in, to make a depression or hollow; to cause a panic.

Pannu a fydd dir rhag dewr gorflwng,
Pan fo dydd gorwlad, a chad yn wng.

A *shrinking in* will be certain before a hero sternly fierce, when there shall be a day of depredation, and a battle near. — *Ein. ab Mad. Rhahawd.*

Pannwl, *s. m.—pl.* pannylau (pant) A depression, a hollow, a sinking in; a dimple, a dinge.

Pannylawg, *a.* (pannwl) Abounding with falls, depressions, or hollows.

Pannyledd, *s. m.* (pannwl) Devexity of surface.

Pannyliad, *s. m.* (pannwl) A devexion; sinking in, a forming a hollow.

Pannylu, *v. a.* (pannwl) To form a devexity; to sink in, to slope down into a hollow.

Pant, *s. m.—pl.* pentydd (pan) That involves, circumscribes or includes; a depression, or sinking in, a hollow, a dinge, a low place, or bottom hemmed in all round.

I'r pant y rhed y dwr.

To the *hollow* will the water run. — *Adage.*

Mau gynnelw, yr eilwir alaf gan ddraig.
A dragon modrydaf;
Heb bant molant miloedd naf,
Heb bannu gan y penaf.

After my example, there will be obtained riches from the chief and the dragon of tribes; without a *sinking* thousands will praise the prince, without the sovereign's *making any fall.* — *Ll. P. Moch, i R. ab H. ab Owain.*

Pant, *a.* (pan) Involving, hemming in; involved, encompassed, included.

Mi a'i gyraf o'm gorwedd,
Mor bant a'r mur ar y bedd.

I will cause it to be by my lying down, so involving as the masonry on the grave. — *Gw. Tew, i wely plu.*

Pant, *prep.* (pan) Down. *Af bant i Lundain*, I will go down to London. *Dyfed.*

Pantawg, *a.* (pant) Having a depression, a sinking in or hollow.

Pantawl, *a.* (pant) Depressing, apt to sink in.

Pantedd, *s. m.* (pant) The state of being depressed, sunk in, or made hollow.

Pantiad, *s. m.* (pant) A depression, a sinking in, a becoming hollow, a dimpling.

Panton, *s. m.* (pant) The all-comprehending one: a bardic appellation for the deity.

Pantu, *v. a.* (pant) To involve, to compass: to depress, to bulge in: to dimple: to sink in, to become a hollow.

Panu, *v. a.* (pan) To make universal or pervasive: to form a texture or grain: to cover with down or nap, to full or to mill cloth, to thicken by beating, to bang, to beat. *Cei dy banu yn dda*, thou shalt be well beaten.

Awen gordd banu.

The genius of a *fulling* beetle. — *Adage.*

Panwaen, *s. f.—pl.* panweunydd (pan—gwaen) A wet meadow, a peat moss; also called *gwaen bon*, and *mawnog*.

Panwlan, *s. m.* (pan—gwlan) Down or fine wool.

Panwr, *s. m.—pl.* panwyr (panu—gwr) A fuller. *Cribau y panwr*, the teasel.

Panwriaeth, *s. m.* (panwr) The fuller's trade.

Panyw, *adv.* (pan—yw) Whence it is; that it is; that is.

O deifydd i'r amddiffynwr ddodi yn mheu yr arglwydd ac yr yngnaid panyw hwnw yw y dydd.

If the defendant shall have declared to the lord and the judges *that it is* that is the day. — *Welsh Laws.*

Bid ddiau i bawb, panyw yn mynwent y fynachlog yn Ynys Afallach, gwedi gweli angeuawl ar afon Gamlan yn Nghernyw y claddid Arthur.

Be it certain to every one, *that it is* in the monastery of the isle of Avallach, after mortal wounds on the river of Camlan in Cernyw, was Arthur buried. — *Hanes Diwedd Arthur.*

Pang, *s. m.* (panc) A pang; a convulsion fit.
Pangaw, *v. n.* (pang) To have a convulsion fit.
Pangawl, *a.* (pang) Convulsive, giving a pang.
Pangiad, *s. m.* (pang) A convulsing; convulsion.
Pangu, *v. a.* (pang) To be convulsed.
Papyr, *s. m.—pl. t.* au (pab) Paper. *Papyr gwyn*, white paper; *papyr llwyd*, brown paper.
Papyraidd, *a.* (papyr) Like paper, papery.
Papyrawl, *a.* (papyr) Consisting of paper.
Papyrfrwyn, *s. pl. aggr.* (papyr—brwyn) Paper-reeds.
Papyriad, *s. m.* (papyr) A papering.
Papyrwr, *s. m.—pl.* papyrwyr (papyr—gwr) A paperman, a papermaker.
Par, *s. m.* (py—ar) That is upon, or contiguous; that is in continuity; a state of readiness or preparedness; also a pair, fellow, match, or couple.

> Ac yno, yn medw Gwynedd,
> I mi ar bar y mae'r bedd.
>
> And there, in the birch groves of Gwynedd, *for me in readiness* is the grave. *D. ab Gwilym.*

Par, *s. m.—pl. t.* au (pa—ar) A cause; that is instrumental in causing or producing; the essence, germ or seed of a thing; also a spear.
Par, *a.* (pa—ar) Causing; causative; caused; in a state of energy or instrumentality.
Para, *v. n.* (par) To continue, to endure; to last; to persevere.

> Hir nis pery yr abwy lle bo llawer o frain.
>
> The carrion *will* not *last* long where there are many crows. *Adage.*
>
> Nis pery gloewder seren;
> Na's pharyd ond ennyd i wen.
>
> The splendor of a star *will* not *endure;* nor her countenance to the fair but for a while. *Bedo Brwynllys.*

Para, *adv.* (pa—rha) What sort, what kind.

> Para lesâad arbenig yr ydym ni yn ei dderbyn oddiwrth dderchafiad Crist!
>
> *What* particular benefit are we receiving from the ascension of Christ? *Tho. Williams, in T. a Kempis.*
>
> At bara ymddadleu gynt y mae y rhyfel hwn, rhwng yr angelion da a drwg, debycaf yn bwrw!
>
> To *what* former contentions does this war, between the good angels and the bad, most probably refer! *Ibid.*

Parâad, *s. m.* (parâu) Perseverance; continuance, duration.

> Diysyrrith yw dy gariad,
> Duw'r hedd, mewn rhyfedd barâad.
>
> Inexhaustible is thy love, God of peace, in wonderful *duration.* *D. Richard, Glan y Morfa.*

Parâawl, *a.* (parâu) Continuing, continual.
Parab, *s. m.* (par—ab) Aptitude for utterance.
Parabl, *s. m.* (parab) The power of speech; speech, utterance; discourse.
Parablain, *v. a.* (parabl) To talk continually.
Parabledd, *s. m.* (parabl) Readiness of discourse
Parabliad, *s. m.* (parabl) A discoursing.
Parablu, *v. a.* (parabl) To hold a discourse.
Parablusaw, *v. a.* (parablus) To render fluent in discourse; to become eloquent.
Parablusedd, *s. m.* (parablus) Readiness in discourse or speech.
Parablwr, *s. m.—pl.* parablwyr (parabl—gwr) A discourser; a preacher.
Parad, *s. m.* (par) Causation; a causing.
Paradwy, *a.* (parad) Causable, effectible.
Paradwyad, *s. m.* (paradwy) Effectuation.
Paradwyawl, *a.* (paradwy) Efficient, effective.
Paradwys, *s. m.* (para—twys) A continuity of increase or fructification; paradise.
Paradwysaidd, *a.* (paradwys) Paradisiacal.
Paradwysain, *a.* (paradwys) Paradisiacal.
Paradwysawl, *a.* (paradwys) Relating to paradise.
Paradwysoli, *v. a.* (paradwysawl) To render paradisiacal; to become like paradise.
Paraed, *s. m.* (para—ed) A partition.
Paraeth, *s. m.* (par) A causation, a cause.
Paraethu, *v. a.* (paraeth) To render causative.
Parag, *adv.* (pa—rhag) Because of what, why so
Parai, *s. c.* (par) That causes or makes to be.
Parator, *ger.* (parad) In causing or bidding.
Parâu, *v. n.* (para) To persevere, to persist; to continue, to remain, to last, to abide.

> A fyno barâu yn hir yn ieuanc, aed yn ebrwydd yn hen.
>
> He that wishes long *to continue* young, let him soon become old. *Adage.*

Parâus, *a.* (para) Of long continuance.
Parâusder, *s. m.* (parâus) Lastingness.
Parâusrwydd, *s. m.* (parâus) Lastingness.
Parawd, *s. m.* (par) That is in readiness. *a.* Ready, prompt, prepared.

> Ni chelir nâ'i wir, nâ'i wrhydri,
> Ar gynnifer gwaed,
> Amdrychion am draed,
> Ac am bob parhed
> Parawd losgi.
>
> His justice nor his prowess will be concealed, on the frequent meetings of blood, breaking round the feet, and about every wall a *ready* burning. *Ll. P. Moch, i Lywelyn II.*

Parawl, *a.* (par) Causing, effective; creative.
Parâwr, *s. m.—pl.* parâwyr (parâu—gwr) One who continues.
Parc, *s. m.—pl. t.* iau (par) An enclosure; a field; a park.
Parcawl, *a.* (parc) Belonging to enclosure.
Parciad, *s. m.* (parc) An enclosing, a shutting in.
Parciaw, *v. a.* (parc) To enclose, to hedge in.
Parciwr, *s. m.—pl.* parcwyr (parc—gwr) One who encloses, a hedger, a ditcher.
Parch, *s. m.* (py—arch) Respect, reverence.

> A fyno barch bid gadarn.
>
> Who would obtain *honour* let him be mighty. *Adage.*
>
> Mwy parch hynaws no hynod.
>
> Greater the *respect* of the good-natured than the reverenced. *Adage.*

Parchadwy, *a.* (parch) Respectable, reputable.
Parchawl, *a.* (parch) Tending to respect.
Parchedig, *a.* (parch) Respected, reverend.
Parchedigaeth, *s. m.—pl. t.* au (parchedig) A shewing respect, a reverencing or honouring.
Parchedigaw, *v. a.* (parchedig) To render reverent; to become revered or honoured.
Parchedd, *s. m.* (parch) Respectability; repute.
Parchiad, *s. m.* (parch) A respecting, honouring.
Parchlawn, *a.* (parch) Respectful, full of respect
Parchlonder, *s. m.* (parchlawn) Respectfulness.
Parchlonedd, *s. m.* (parchlawn) Respectfulness.
Parchraith, *s. f.* (parch—rhaith) A law of honour
Parchrydd, *a.* (parch—rhydd) Respectfully free
Parchu, *v. a.* (parch) To respect, or to honour.

> Morwynion moelion, gwreigedd rhewydd,
> Carant, ni pharchant eu carennydd;
> Rhwydd ni bydd gyfrwydd wrth ei gilydd,
> Esgyb anghyfiaith, diffaith, diffydd.
>
> Bare-headed virgins, wanton wives, they will love, they will not *respect* their relatives; readily they will not be mutually liberal to one another, bishops of strange language, unprofitable and void of faith. *Myrddin.*

Parchus, *a.* (parch) Respectful; respectable.
Parchusaw, *v. a.* (parchus) To render respectable; to become respectable or respected.
Parchusedd, *s. m.* (parchus) Respectability.
Parchusrwydd, *s. m.* (parchus) Respectableness.
Parchwr, *s. m.* (parch—gwr) A respecter.
Parddu, *s. m.* (par—du) The black adhering to vessels, that are set on fire: smut.

Parddüad, *s. m.* (parddu) A covering with smut.

Parddüaw, *v. a.* (parddu) To cover with smut, to smut; to become smutty.

Parddüawg, *a.* (parddu) Covered with smut.

Parddüawl, *a.* (parddu) Tending to be smutty.

Pared, *s. m.—pl. t.* au (par—ed) A partition.

Paredig, *a.* (pared) Caused, being bidden.

Paredigawl, *a.* (paredig) Causative, mandatory.

Paredlys, *s. m.* (pared—llys) Pellitory of the wall

Parf, *s. m.* (par) That is upon, or intervening.

Parfa, *s. f.—pl.* parfëydd (par—ma) That hems in, or that serves as a fender.

Parfaes, *s. f.—pl.* parfeisiau (parf—aes) A sending plane; an epithet for a shield.

Parfyg, *s. m.* (parf) The herb henbane.

Pari, *s. m.* (par) That is close, together, or in continuity; a string, drove, or flock, as sheep

> Pari o ddefaid ar lan ffrwd, a fydd ar bob un o'r dechreu mynned trosodd; eithr pan elo un o'r blaen, y lleill igyd yn ddiarswyd a ganlynant.
>
> A *flock* of sheep on the brink of the current of a river, every one will be afraid of going through; but when one proceeds before, all the others will follow without fear. *S. Trefredyn.*

Pariad, *s. m.* (par) A causation; a causing, or effecting, a commanding, a bidding.

Pariannawl, *a.* (pariant) Causative, mandatory.

Pariannu, *v. a.* (pariant) To render causative.

Pariannus, *a.* (pariant) Causative; mandatory.

Pariannusaw, *v. a.* (pariannus) To render causative, to become causative.

Pariant, *s. m.* (par) Causation; effectuation.

Pariedydd, *s. m.—pl. t.* ion (pariad) A causer.

Parl, *s. m.* (par) That is instrumental to effectuate, a vocable.

Parlas, *s. m.—pl. t.* au (par—glas) A green plat.

Parlawr, *s. m.—pl.* parloran (par—llawr) Parlour

> Parlawr o irddail parlas.
>
> A *parlour* of fresh leaves of pure green. *D. ab Gwilym.*

Parliad, *s. m.—pl. t.* au (parl) A discoursing.

Parliaw, *v. a.* (parl) To argue; to discourse.

Parliannawl, *a.* (parliant) Interlocutory.

Parliannu, *v. a.* (parliant) To dialogue.

Parliant, *s. m.* (parl) Interlocution; dialogue.

Parliwr, *s. m.* (parl—gwr) A discourser.

Parodâad, *s. m.* (parodâu) A preparation.

Parodâawl, *a.* (parodâu) Preparatory, preparing

Parodadwy, *a.* (parawd) Capable of preparing.

Parodâu, *v. a.* (parawd) To make ready; to become ready, to be prepared.

Parodawl, *a.* (parawd) Tending to prepare.

Parodedd, *s. m.* (parawd) Preparedness.

Parodi, *v. a.* (parawd) To make ready, to prepare; to become ready or prepared.

> Ni chaed brad, na'i barodi;
> Ac ni chaed yn eich had chwi.
>
> No treachery was found, nor a *preparing of it*, nor was such a thing had in your line. *Ed. Dafydd.*

Parodiad, *s. m.* (parawd) A preparing.

Parodiaeth, *s. m.* (parawd) Preparation.

Parodiannawl, *a.* (parodiant) Preparatory.

Parodiannu, *v. a.* (parodiant) To make preparation; to become prepared.

Parodiant, *s. m.* (parawd) Preparation.

Parodoldeb, *s. m.* (parodawl) Preparedness.

Parodoledd, *s. m.* (parodawl) Preparedness.

Parodoli, *v. a.* (parodawl) To render prepared.

Parodrwydd, *s. m.* (parawd) A prepared state.

Paronen, *s. f.* (par—onen) An ashen spear.

Parotaw, *v. a.* (parawd) To prepare, to get ready

Parotöad, *s. m.* (parotöi) A preparing, preparation, a getting ready.

Parotöawl, *a.* (parotöi) Preparative; preparing.

Parotöedd, *s. m.* (parotöi) Preparedness.

Parotöi, *v. a.* (parotaw) To prepare, to get ready

> Parotöi bwyllyriau, a llenwi eu llongau o honynt—a orugynt.
>
> *Prepare* provisions, and fill their ships therewith, they did. *Gr. ab Arthur.*

Parotöus, *a.* (parotaw) Preparative, preparatory

Parotöwr, *s. m.—pl.* parotöwyr (porotöi—gwr) A preparer, one who makes ready.

Parotöydd, *s. m.—pl. t.* ion (parotöi) A preparer

Parsel, *s. m.—pl. t.* au (par—sel) What is aimed at, a butt, a mark.

> Saethu'n iaet barselau
> A wnawn, teg fu'r mawr-ddawn mau.
>
> Shoot keenly at *butts* I would, fair was my great talent. *R. ab C. Goch.*
>
> Ei fwa a saethau a arwyddoca ffolineb y rhai ffoliaid, y sydd yn cynnyg eu hunain i fod yn barselau iddo, ac yn sefyll yn llonydd tra fo efe yn eu saethu.
>
> His bow and arrows denote the folly of the foolish ones, who are offering themselves to be as *butts* for him, and standing still whilst he might be shooting at them. *Marchawg Crwydrad.*

Parth, *s. m.—pl. t.* au (par) A part; a division; a region. *Parth a Chymmru*, towards Wales; *parth ag atam*, towards us.

> Nef, daiar, uffern, pan y bernych,
> Dod nod i'm gwyneb a'm hadnepych:
> Parth cledd i minnau, ni mynych fy nod,
> Parth yr oen gorfod ni'm gosodych.
>
> Heaven, earth, hell, when thou shalt judge, set a mark in my face by which thou shalt know me. Then on the left side, thou wouldest not that I should be, on the *part* of the victim lamb thou wouldest not place me. *Y Brawd Mad. ab Gwallter.*

Parthadwy, *a.* (parth) Discriminable, divisible.

Parthawd, *s. m.* (parth) A dividing, a parting.

Parthawl, *a.* (parth) Discriminate; parting.

Parthed, *s. m.—pl. t.* oedd (parth) A part; a division; a region.

Parthedig, *a.* (parthed) Divided, severed.

Parthedigaeth, *s. m.* (parthedig) Discrimination.

Parthedigawl, *a.* (parthedig) Discriminative.

Parthedd, *s. m.* (parth) A divided state.

Parthgymeriad, *s. m.—pl. t.* au (parth—cymeriad) A participle.

Parthgymeriadawl, *a.* (parthgymeriad) Participial, relating to a participle.

Parthiad, *s. m.—pl. t.* au (parth) A parting.

Parthiannawl, *a.* (parthiant) Discriminative.

Parthiannu, *v. a.* (parthiant) To discriminate.

Parthiannus, *a.* (parthiant) Discriminative.

Parthiannusaw, *v. a.* (parthiannus) To render discriminative; to become discriminative.

Parthiant, *s. m.* (parth) A division, a severing.

Parthiator, *ger.* (parthiad) In discriminating.

Parthitor, *sup.* (parth) To be discriminating.

Parthotor, *part.* (parthawd) Dividing, parting.

Parthred, *s. f.—pl. t.* ion (parth) Distinction, discrimination; a side, or party.

> Pan welai Agamemnon ladd llawer o'i barthred, efe a anfones at Briaf, i erchi cyngrair.
>
> When Agamemnon beheld the slaughter of many of his *party*, he sent to Priam to demand a parley. *Ystori Dared.*

Parthredawg, *a.* (parthred) Of a particular party

Parthredawl, *a.* (parthred) Discriminating.

Parthrededd, *s. m.* (parthred) Discriminateness.

Parthrediad, *s. m.—pl. t.* au (parthred) A discriminating; discrimination.

Parthrediannawl, *a.* (parthrediant) Belonging to discrimination; discriminative.

Parthrediannu, *v. a.* (parthrediant) To make a discrimination, to make a distinction.

Parthrediannus, *a.* (parthrediant) Tending to discrimination.

Parthrediannusaw, *v. a.* (parthrediannus) To render discriminating, to discriminate.

Parthrediannusedd, *s. m.* (parthredi annus) The state of being discriminative.

Parthrediant, *s. m.—pl.* parthrediannau (parthred) Discrimination.

Parthredu, *v. a.* (parthred) To discriminate.

Parthredus, *a.* (parthred) Discriminating.

Parthredusaw, *v. a.* (parthredus) To render discriminative, to become discriminative.

Parthredusedd, *s.m.*(parthred) Discriminateness.

Parthryd, *s. m.* (parth—rhyd) A distinct course.

Parthu, *v. a.* (parth) To part, to partition, to separate, to divide.

> I archesgobty Llundain y parthid Lloegr yn hollawl.
>
> To the archbishoprick of London was *appropriated* the whole of England. *Gr. ab Arthur.*

Parthwr, *s. m.—pl.* parthwyr (parthu—gwr) One who makes a distinction, a separater.

Parthyd, *s. m.* (parth) Distinction, characteristic. *Parthyd y peth a'r peth*, the characteristic of such and such a thing.

Paru, *v. a.* (par) To put in continuity, to put together, to couple, to join, to pair.

Parwar, *a.* (par—gwar) Silent, still, calm.

> Eglwysau Bass, ynt barwar heno;
> A minnau wyf dyar:
> Rhudd ynt bwy; rhwy fy ngalar!
>
> The churches of Bass, they are *silent* this night, and I am clamorous: red are they; excessive is my grief! *Llywarch Hen.*

Parwg, *s. m.—pl.* parygoedd (par) Enclosed field

Parwr, *s. m.—pl.* parwyr (par—gwr) A causer.

Parwyd, *s. m.—pl. t.* ydd (par—gwyd) Partition.

> A wyddosti——
> Py peris parwyd
> Rhwng dyn ac annwyd?
>
> Dost thou know who caused a *partition* between man and frigidity? *Taliesin.*

Parwydaw, *v. a.* (parwyd) To make a partition.

Parwydawg, *a.* (parwyd) Having a partition.

Parwydawl, *a.* (parwyd) Belonging to a partition.

Parwyden, *s. f. dim.—pl. t.* au (parwyd) Work that encloses, a fence, the trunk or the region of the ribs and breast of an animal; partition work in a house.

> Gofidus wyf o barwydenau fy nghalon.
>
> I am afflicted from the *sides* of my heart. *Jeremia iv. 19.*

> Y delyn ledr——
> Ni luniwyd ei pharwyden,
> Na'i chreglais ond i Sais hen.
>
> The leathern harp, its *trunk* was not formed nor its hoarse sound, but for an old Saxon. *D. ab Gwilym.*

Parwydd, *s. m.* (par—gwydd) That is cognitive of acting or causing, a verb. It is also called *peirwyddiad*.

Parwyddawl, *a.* (parwydd) Belonging to a verb.

Parwyddiad, *s. m.—pl.* parwyddiaid (parwydd) that conveys the knowledge of causing, a verb

Parydd, *s. m.—pl. t.* ion (par) A causer.

Paryddawl, *a.* (parydd) Procuratorial; causative.

Pas, *s. m.—pl. t.* au (pa—as) That is expulsive, that causes to pass, a pass, an exit, a cough, a hooping cough.

Pasawl, *a.* (pas) Expulsive, belonging to cough.

Pasawl, *adv.* (pa—sawl) What number, how many

PASC, *s. m.* Easter. *Tri gwyl arbenig, Nadolig, Pasc, a Sulgwyn*, the three principal festivals, Christmas, Easter, and Whitsuntide.

Pasg, *s. m.* (pa—asg) A feeding, or fattening. *Bod yn mhasg*, to be fed in a stall; opposed to *pori allan*, to feed out or in pasture.

Pasgadur, *s. m.—pl. t.* ion (pasg) One who feeds.

Pasgadwy, *a.* (pasg) Capable of being fattened.

Pasgawl, *a.* (pasg) Feeding, or fattening.

Pasgdwrch, *s. m.* (pasg—twrch) A fatted pig.

Pasgedig, *a.* (pasg) Fed, fatted, crammed. *Ych pasgedig*, a fatted ox.

Pasgell, *s. f.* (pasg) A pasture, a feeding place.

Pasgfarch, *s. m.—pl.* pasgfeirch (pasg—march) A pampered steed.

Pasghwch, *s. f.—pl. t.* od (pasg—hwch) Fat sow.

Pasgiad, *s. m.* (pasg) A feeding, or a fattening.

Pasgiadur, *s. m.—pl. t.* on (pasgiad) A feeder.

Pasgle, *s. m.—pl. t.* oedd (pasg—lle) A feeding place.

Pasgnawd, *s. m.* (pasg—nawd) A tendency to become fat. *Pasgfeirch pasgnawd.*

Pasiad, *s. m.* (pas) A causing an exit, expulsion, a passing.

Pasiaw, *v. a.* (pas) To cause an exit, to expulse, to make an exit, to pass.

Pasiedig, *a.* (pas) Being expulsed or passed.

Pasiwr, *s. m.—pl.* paswyr (pas) One who passes.

Pastwn, *s. m.—pl.* pastynau (pas—twn) Long staff.

> Estynid ym bastwn dig.
>
> There was reached to me an angry *staff*. *Llawddon.*

Pastynu, *v. a.* (pastwn) To beat with a staff.

Pathawr, *adv.* (pa—tawr) What concerns it, who cares, maugre, in spite of, notwithstanding.

> Cychwyn i'w therfyr, pathawr ei hogwedd,
> Hirfelyn ei gwaewawr:
> Dwyn, dyw calan Ionawr,
> Dywed an dawed Faelawr.
>
> Set off to its confined *maugre* its sprightly society, its long yellow spears make thy way, on new year's day, say that we are coming to Maelor. *O. Cyfeiliawg.*

Pathew, *s. m.—pl. t.* od (pa—tew) A dormouse.

> Nid esmwyth ond pathew.
>
> Nothing so sleek as the *dormouse*. *Adage.*

Pau, *s. f.—pl. t.* oedd (pa) That is in continuity. that extends, or extends about, that includes, or confines: a settled country, or where the tribes spread about and are stopt in their career

> Dymgwallofied ei win o'i wên adaf odd,
> Yn Arfonig gaer, ger hirtell bau.
>
> I have been cherished with his wine from his white protecting hand, in the Arvonian town, near the region of the revolution of glory. *Cynddelw.*

> Gorpwyf gan Dduw fry, gwedy gwyddau,
> Gorfod gorphowys baradwys bau!
>
> May I be caused to be with God above, divested of transgressions, enjoying the repose of the region of paradise. *Eln. ab Gwalchmai.*

Päun, *adv.* (pa—un) Which one, what one.

Päunfodd, *adv.* (päun—modd) Which way soever, what way soever, in a manner.

Paw, *s. m.* (pa) That extends round.

Pawan, *s. c.* (paw) A spreader, or extender. *Ceiliawg pawan*, a peacock, *iar bawan*, a pea-hen

Pawb, *pron.* (paw) Every body, all persons.

> Rhydd barn i bawb.
>
> Opinion is free to every *body*. *Adage.*

> Caffant bawb eu teithi, llawen fydd Brython,
> Cenitor cyrn elwch cathl heddwch a hinon.
>
> *All persons* shall obtain their rights, Britons shall be glad; the horn of triumph proclaiming the hymn of peace and of serenity. *Myrddin.*

> Y bedd yn Ystradfachau,
> Y mae pawb yn ei amau
> Bedd Gwrtheyrn Gwrthenau.
>
> The grave in Ystradfachau, *every body* suppose it to be the grave of Gwrtheyrn Gwrthenau. *Engl. Beddau y Milwyr.*

Pawb, *a.* (paw) Every body: all, applied to people. *Pawb ac un*, one and all.

Pawd, *s. f.* (paw) That stretches out, a shank.

Pawen, *s. f.—pl. t.* au (paw) A paw, a hoof.

Pawenu, *v. a.* (pawen) To gather with the paw.

Pawenaidd, *a.* (pawen) Like a paw.

Pawenawg, *a.* (pawen) Having a paw.

Paweniad, *s. m.* (pawen) A pawing.

Pawenu, *v. a.* (pawen) To use the paw.
Pawenwr, *s. m.—pl.* pawenwyr (pawen—gwr) One who uses his paw.
Pawgen, *s. f.—pl. t.* au (paw—cèn) A sock.
Pawl, *s. m.—pl.* polion (paw) A pole, a stake.

Drwg pawl ni safo flwyddyn.

Bad is the *pole* that will not stand for a year. *Adage.*

Pawr, *s. m.—pl.* porion (py—awr) Pasture, grass, a grazing, or feeding in pasture.

Ti haf——
Dod yno 'n y fro dy frisg,
Yn wyrddo bawr, yn irwisg.

Thou summer, bestow there over the country thy track, in luxuriant *pasture*, in verdant covering. *D. ab Gwilym.*

Blodau hafaidd hyd y llawr,
A gwych y pawr ei lased.

Summer flowers strew the ground, and how gay the *grass* so green. *Gw. Tew.*

Pawrwellt, *s. m.* (pawr—gwellt) Brome-grass.
PE, *s. m. r.* That is causative, that is an agent.
Pe, *conj.* (pe, *s.*) If. It is used conditionally, with verbs of the subjunctive and potential moods, before words with consonant initials. See *ped, pes, pe, o, od, os.*

Pe a bawd y gwëid gwe.

If with a thumb a web were woven. *Adage.*

Pebr, *s. m.* (py—ebr) That is uttered.
Pebra, *v. a.* (pebr) To be chattering.
Pebraeth, *s. m.* (pebr) A chattering, a tattling.
Pebre, *s. m.* (pebr) A chatter, a babble.

Pebre o'i safn pob ryw sut.

Every kind of *chattering* from her mouth.
Gr. Hiraethawg, i fronfraith.

Pebyd, *s. m.* (pab) That is of the pope, papacy.
Pebydiawg, *s. m.* (pebyd) The popedom: also a cantref so called, in Dyfed.
Pebylliad, *s. m.* (pabell) A putting up tents.
Pebylliaw, *v. a.* (pabell) To pitch tents.
Pebylliawg, *a.* (pabell) Having tents, tented.
Pebylliwr, *s. m.—pl.* pebyllwyr (pebylliaw—gwr) One who puts up tents.
Pech, *s. m.* (py—ech) A cessation, a ceasing to exert; a still state; a swerving from; the sin of inaction; sin. *Bydd di pech*, be thou quiet. *Armoric.*

Ni aned ni wyddiad bech.

There has not been born any but has known *sin*. *Adage.*

Pech, *a.* (py—ech) Void of exertion; inert.
Pechaberth, *s. m.—pl. t.* au (aberth) Sin-offering.
Pechadur, *s. m.—pl. t.* on (pech) A sinner.

Dangaws nef i bechadur.

Shew heaven to a *sinner*. *Adage.*

Pechadures, *s. f.* (pechadur) A female sinner.
Pechaduriad, *s. m.—pl.* pechaduriaid (pechadur) One who commits sin; a sinner.
Pechaduriaeth, *s. m.* (pechadur) The state of a sinner.
Pechadurus, *a.* (pechadur) Of a sinful aptitude.
Pechadurusrwydd, *s. m.* (pechadurus) Sinfulness.
Pechaduryn, *s. m. dim.* (pechadur) A sinful one.
Pechawd, *s. m.—pl.* pechodau (pech) Sin.

Pechodau athrawon ynt athrawon pechodau.

The *sins* of instructors are instructors of *sins*. *Adage.*

Saith rhyw bechawd marwawl y sydd—syberwyd, cynghorfynt, llidiogrwydd, tristyd bydawl neu lesgedd, chwant a chybyddiaeth, glythineb a meddwdawd, godineb.

There are seven kinds of deadly *sins* pride, envy, anger, dejection in worldly affairs, or inexertion, desire and sordidness, voluptuousness and drunkenness, adultery.
Ll. Gwyn Hergest.

Pechawl, *a.* (pech) Appertaining to sin; sinning.
Pechedd, *s. m.* (pech) A sinning condition.
Pechiad, *s. m.* (pech) A sinning; a transgressing.
Pechodawg, *a.* (pechawd) Abounding with sin.
Pechodawl, *a.* (pechawd) Appertaining to sin.
Pechodlawn, *a.* (pechawd) Full of sin, sinful.
Pechu, *v. a.* (pech) To sin, to commit sin.
Pechus, *a.* (pech) Apt to commit sin; sinful.
Pechusaw, *v. n.* (pechus) To become sinful.
Pechusrwydd, *s. m.* (pechus) Sinfulness.
Pechwr, *s. m.—pl.* pechwyr (pech—gwr) A sinner.
Ped, *s. m.—pl. t.* ion (py—ed) That is agent of progression, that bears onward; a foot.
Ped, *conj.* (pe—yd) If; used for *pe*, before words with vowel initials. *Ped awn*, if I were to go: *petwn*, if I were; *petit*, if thou wert; *petai*, if it, he, or she, were; *petym*, if we were; *petych*, if ye were; *petynt*, if they were.
Ped, *adv.* (pe—yd) How many, what number.
Pedair, *s. f.* (ped) The number four, speaking of the feminine gender. *a.* Four.
Pedawl, *a.* (ped) Belonging to a foot, pedal.
Pedeirael, *s. pl. aggr.* (pedair—ael) Four skirts. *a.* Having four skirts or corners.

Ei orwydd oedd a—llen pedeirael amdano, ac afal aur wrth bob ael iddi: Can mu oedd gwerth pob aval.

His steed was with a *four-cornered* cloth about him, and an apple of gold to each of its corners: A hundred kine was the value of each apple. *H. Culhwch—Mabinogion.*

Pedeirawdl, *s. pl. aggr.* (pedair—awdl) Four rhymes. *a.* Of four varieties of rhyme.
Pedeirblwydd, *s. pl. aggr.* (pedair—blwydd) Four years. *a.* Of four years old.
Pedeirblwyddawl, *a.* (pedeirblwydd) Quadriennial.
Pedeirdalen, *s. f.* (pedair—dalen) That consists of four leaves. *a.* Quadriphyllous.
Pedeirffordd, *s. f.* (pedair—ffordd) Where four roads meet. *a.* Of four roads.
Pedeirgwaith, *s. pl. aggr.* (pedair—gwaith) Four times. *a.* Of four times.
Pedeirllaw, *s. pl. aggr.* (pedair—llaw) Four hands. *a.* Quadrimanus.
Pedeiror, *s. pl. aggr.* (pedair—or) Four limits; four regions; four quarters. *a.* Of four sides.

Ef yn ddiachor;
Ef yn ddieisor;
Ef o bedeiror;
Ni bydd wrth gynghor;
Ni bydd heb gynghor.

He unconfined; he without a fellow; he from *four regions*; he will not be according to council; he will not be without council
Taliesin, i'r gwynt.

Pedeirran, *s. pl. aggr.* (pedair—rhan) Four shares or parts. *a.* Qradripartite.
Pedeirranawg, *a.* (pedeirran) Of four parts.
Pedeirranawl, *a.* (pedeirran) Of four parts.
Pedeirraniad, *s. m.—pl. t.* au (pedeirran) A quadripartition; a quartering.
Pedeirranu, *v. a.* (pedeirran) To part into four.
Pedeirsill, *s. pl. aggr.* (pedair—sill) Four syllables. *a.* Of four syllables.
Pedeirsillawg, *a.* (pedeirsill) Of four syllables.
Pedeirsillawl, *a.* (pedeirsill) Belonging to what consists of four syllables.
Pedest, *s. m.* (ped) Motion of the feet.
Pedestr, *s. m.—pl.* pedestron (pedest) That travels on foot, a pedestrian.

Yn bedestr anwybodawl.

Being a *pedestrian* uninformed. *Ein. ab Gwalchmai.*

Pedestraidd, *a.* (pedestr) Pedestrian.
Pedestrawg, *a.* (pedestr) Having a power of walking or of using the feet.
Pedestrawl, *a.* (pedestr) Of foot travelling.

Pedestres, *s. f.—pl. t.* au (pedestr) A walking female, a female pedestrian.

> Pedestres weddaidd yn hydraidd hir,
> Pedestrig tollg, pa hyd y'th folir?
>
> The handsome *female pedestrian* a long journey travelling, thou famous in walking, how long wilt thou be famed! *Cynddelw.*

Pedestriad, *s. m.* (pedestr) A travelling on foot.

Pedestrig, *s. f. dim.* (pedestr) A foot pace.

> Ef a gafas ei bedestrig.
>
> He recovered his *walking*. *H. Cor. Mag—Mabinogion.*

Pedestru, *v. a.* (pedestr) To travel on foot.

Pedestrydd, *s. m.—pl. t.* ion (pedestr) A foot traveller, a pedestrian.

Pedfed, *adv.* (ped) Of what number.

Pedi, *adv.* (ped) A round about way of asking or craving, also a guarding against a request, by anticipating a similar want. *v. a.* To ask or crave indirectly.

> Nid rhaid pedi yn llys arglwydd.
>
> There is no necessity of *begging restrainedly* in a prince's court. *Adage.*

Pediad, *s. m.* (ped) A making use of feet.

Pedol, *s. f.—pl. t.* au (ped—ol) What is under a foot, a pedal, a shoe of a horse or other animal. *Pedol y march*, tufted horse-shoe vetch. *Ceffyl yn ennill ei bedolau*, a horse gaining his shoes, a term for a horse's laying down to tumble.

Pedolawg, *a.* (pedol) Having something under the foot, pedalled: having shoes as horses.

Pedoli, *v. a.* (pedol) To put something under the feet to save them, to pedal, to shoe a horse or other animal.

> Arian pedoli yw treth, a osodwyd er ys talm o flynyddoedd, ar ddeiliaid yr arglwydd, am bedoli meirch yr arglwydd; ac yn Mrecheiniog y telir.
>
> *Shoeing money* is a tax which was laid many years ago, on the subjects of the lord, for *shoeing* the lord's horses; and in Brecknockshire it is paid. *Hen Ddefodau.*

Pedoliad, *s. m.* (pedol) A shoeing; a forming a pedol, a fixing a pedal; the using a pedal.

Pedolwr, *s. m.—pl.* pedolwyr (pedol—gwr) A shoeer; one who makes or uses a pedal.

Pedr, *s. m.* (pad) That consists of four. It is used as a prefix in composition.

Pedrain, *s. f.—pl.* pedreiniau (pedr) The buttock, breech, or crupper. *Pedrain march*, a horse's crupper.

Pedrawg, *a.* (pedr) Of a square form, square-built, complete.

Pedrawl, *a.* (pedr) Belonging to square.

Pedreindew, *a.* (pedrain—tew) Fat-buttocked.

Pedreindor, *s. m.* (pedrain—tor) A covering of cloth reaching over a horse's crupper from the saddle. *a.* Crupper-covered.

> Coch redawg pedrydawg pedror,
> Y ar orwydd pedrogl pedreindor.
>
> A red chariot moving squarely with four limits over a *crupper-covered* steed of perfect form. *Cynddelw, i O. Cyfeiliawg.*

Pedrenwawl, *a.* (pedr—enwawl) Quadrinomial.

Pedrogl, *s. m.—pl.* pedroglau (pedrawg) That consists of four sides; a square, a quadrangle. *a.* Quidrilateral, square, complete, of perfect symmetry.

> Pedrogl friw, pwy a droigl Ffrainc.
>
> Thou *square* of visage, who will turn a France. *T. Aled.*

Pedroglaidd, *a.* (pedrogl) Like a square.

Pedroglawd, *s. m.* (pedrogl) A quadrating.

Pedroglawg, *a.* (pedrogl) Of a square form.

Pedrogledd, *s. m.* (pedrogl) A quadrature.

Pedrogli, *v. a.* (pedrogl) To quadrate.

Pedrogliad, *s. m.* (pedrogl) A quadrating.

Pedroglyn, *s. m. dim.* (pedrogl) A quadrate.

Pedrongl, *s. f.—pl.* pedronglau (pedr—ongl) A quadrangle. *a.* Of four angles.

Pedronglawg, *a.* (pedrongl) Of four angles.

Pedrongledd, *s. m.* (pedrongl) The state of being quadrangular; that consists of four angles.

Pedrongli, *v. a.* (pedrongl) To form a quadrangle.

Pedrongliad, *s. m.* (pedrongl) A making to consist of four angles, a forming a quadrangle.

Pedror, *s. m.—pl. t.* oedd (pedr—or) That consists of four sides, a square. *a.* Quadrilateral, square. *Par pedror*, a four-sided spear.

Pedrorawg, *a.* (pedror) Having four extremities.

Pedrorawl, *a.* (pedrawr) Of a square form.

Pedrorddarn, *s. m.—pl. t.* au (pedror—darn) A quarter-piece.

Pedroredd, *s. m.* (pedror) A squareness.

Pedrori, *v. a.* (pedror) To quadrate, to square.

Pedroriad, *s. m.* (pedror) A quadrating.

Pedroryn, *s. m. dim.* (pedror) A quadrate.

Pedrrod, *s. f.* (pedr—rhod) That has four wheels. *a.* Four-wheeled.

Pedrrodawg, *a.* (pedrrod) Having four wheels. *s. f.* A carriage with four wheels.

Pedru, *v. a.* (pedr) To quadrate, to square.

Pedrus, *a.* (ped—rhus) Apt to start, hesitating, dubious, uncertain.

Pedrusad, *s. m.* (pedrus) A starting aside, a doubting, a hesitating.

Pedrusaeth, *s. m.* (pedrus) Hesitation, doubting.

Pedrusaw, *v. a.* (pedrus) To start aside, to hesitate, to doubt, to scruple.

> Yr wyf innau yn erchi dy drugaredd di, ac yn ceisiaw porth a nerth y gennyd ti i geisiaw fy nghyfoeth i mi trachefn, hyd pan fo trwy fy nerth innau a'm porth y gellych dithau oresgyn Ynys Prydain: Ac o hyn nas petrusa ddim; canys nid oes dim twyll na brad yn yr ymadrawdd hwn.
>
> I am likewise entreating thy mercy, and am seeking support and strength of thee towards getting my kingdom back again, so that it shall be through my power and my aid thou likewise mayest subdue the Isle of Britain: And of this do not hesitate in the least; for there is neither deceit nor treachery in this declaration. *Gr. ab Arthur.*

Pedrusawd, *s. m.* (pedrus) Hesitation, doubting.

Pedrusawg, *a.* (pedrus) Having a doubt.

Pedrusawl, *a.* (pedrus) Hesitating, doubting.

Pedrusdawd, *s. m.* (pedrus) Hesitation.

Pedrusdeb, *s. m.* (pedrus) A doubting state.

Pedrusder, *s. m.* (pedrus) Dubiousness, scrupulosity, indeterminateness.

Pedrusedd, *s. m.* (pedrus) A state of hesitation.

Pedrusgar, *s. m.* (pedrus) Apt to hesitate.

Pedrusgarwch, *s. m.* (pedrus) Aptness to doubt.

Pedrusi, *s. m.* (pedrus) Hesitation, doubt.

Pedrusiad, *s. m.* (pedrus) A hesitating.

Pedrusiannawl, *a.* (pedrusiant) Tending to hesitation, indeterminate.

Pedrusiannu, *v. a.* (pedrusiant) To make hesitation; to become indetermined.

Pedrusiannus, *a.* (pedrusiant) Of a doubtful tendency, of an uncertain state.

Pedrusiannusaw, *v. n.* (pedrusiannus) To become of a hesitating disposition.

Pedrusiant, *s. m.* (pedrus) Hesitation.

Pedrusoldeb, *s. m.* (pedrusawl) Dubiousness.

Pedrusoli, *v. n.* (pedrusawl) To become starting or hesitating; to become scrupulous.

Pedruswrwydd, *s. m.* (pedrus) Doubtfulness.

Pedruswch, *s. m.* (pedrus) Doubtfulness.

Pedruswr, *s. m.—pl.* pedruswyr (pedrus—gwr) One who hesitates, a doubter.

Pedrwg, *s. m.* (pedr) A quadrature; a perfect state, completeness of parts.

Pedrwgl, *s. m.—pl* pedryglon (pedrwg) That is quadrate; that is perfect, a model.

> Plant Tudyr——
> Pedwar eglwr pedryglon
> Angelyssor maenor Mon.
>
> The children of Tudyr—*four*, conspicuous *models*, evangelists of the community of Mona. *Iolo Goch.*

Pedry, *s. m.* (pedr) That consists of four; that belongs to four. It is used as a prefix in composition.

Pedryad, *s. m.* (pedry) A quadrating, a squaring.

Pedryael, *s. f.—pl. t.* oedd (pedry—ael) That has four skirts or borders, a square. *a.* Square.

> Fy nghyfarws onis caffaf, dwyn dy anghlod ti a wnaf hyd y bu dy glod yn mhedryael byd bellaf.
>
> My boon if I obtain not, thy infamy will I bear as far as thy fame has been in the farthest *four extremities* of the world. *H. Culhwch—Mabinogion.*

Pedryaw, *v. a.* (pedry) To make of four parts.

Pydryawg, *a.* (pedry) Having four parts.

Pedryawl, *a.* (pedry) Belonging to four.

Pedrychwal, *s. m.* (pedry—chwal) That spreads out four ways. *a.* Four ways spreading.

Pedrychwelyd, *v. a.* (pedrychwal) To spread or separate four different ways.

> Pedryfan dwfn pedrychwelyd.
>
> A deep quarry *four ways opening*. *Llefoed.*

Pedryd, *s. m.—pl. t.* on (pedr) A quadrate.

Pedrydan, *s. m.—pl. t.* au (pedry—tan) That extends or spreads out four ways, four extents, four regions. *a.* Four ways spreading; universal.

> Perging cyanlwair pair pedrydan.
>
> The grappler of depredation of *universal* sway. *Cynddelw.*
>
> Yn ngwaith Maes Carnedd, can frŷyrau
> Dyhebyr alaf glyf doniau;
> Dychlud clod Prydain bedrydanau.
>
> In the action of Maes Carnedd, with the barons wealth dispenses with the splendour of talents; the fame of Britain accumulates in the *four regions*. *Gwalchmai.*

Pedrydant, *s. m.* (pedryd) A quadrate state; a state of perfection. *Pedrydant dannau*, strings of harmony, tuneful strings.

> Cenais dy foliant, fal nas rygannant,
> Milwr pedrydant, pedrydawg ri.
>
> I have sung thy praise, as they will not be able to sin, thou warrior of *perfection*, chief of perfect form. *Ll. P. Moch, i D. ab Owain.*
>
> Arol marw mawrgoel darogant;
> Armes draig dragon pedrydant!
>
> Come, alas, is the death of the magnificent hope of the oracle; the destiny of the *paragon* chief of Britain! *Cynddelw.*

Pedrydanu, *v. a.* (pedrydan) To extend or spread out four ways.

Pedrydawg, *a.* (pedryd) Having a quadrature, completely formed, complete.

> Pan yw du troed alarch gwyn,
> Pedrydawg gwaew llym.
>
> As the foot of the white swan is black, the sharp spear is *unerring*. *Taliesin.*
>
> Milwr pedrydawg Maelawr.
>
> The *complete* warrior of Maelor. *G. F. ab G. ab Ednyfed.*

Pedrydawl, *a.* (pedryd) Of a quadrate state, of a perfect form.

Pedrydiad, *s. m.* (pedryd) A quadrating; a rendering complete or perfect.

Pedrydu, *v. a* (pedryd) To quadrate; to perfect.

Pedrydydd, *s. m.* (pedry—dydd) The fourth day of the week. *Barddas.*

Pedryddail, *a.* (pedry—dail) Quadriphyllous.

Pedryfal, *s. m.—pl. t.* au (pedry—mal) That consists of four pieces or joints.

Pedryfan, *s. f.—pl. t.* oedd (pedry—man) That consists of four parts: a quarry, a quarter; four regions. *Pedryfanoedd byd*, the four quarters of the world.

> Adarweiniddawg caeawg cynran drud
> Draig Prydain pedryfan.
>
> The birds providing one adorned with a wreath, of a brave pre-eminent race the dragon of Britain the *complete region*. *Ll. P. Moch, i Lywelyn II.*

Pedryfannawg, *a.* (pedryfan) Having four regions or parts, of four quarters.

Pedryfannawl, *a.* (pedryfan) Belonging to four regions; quarternary.

Pedryfaniad, *s. m.* (pedryfan) A making into four regions; a quartering.

Pedryfanu, *v. a.* (pedryfan) To make into four regions; to quarter.

Pedrygan, *s. m.* (pedry—can) That is contained between four, the quantity that is taken up between three fingers and the thumb.

Pedryganu, *v. a.* (pedrygan) To pinch up between the three fingers and the thumb.

Pedrygarn, *a.* (pedry—carn) Having four hoofs.

Pedryging, *s. m.* (pedrwg—ing) The space between the three fingers and thumb closed together; the grasp.

Pedrylaw, *s. m.* (pedry—llaw) A square or quadrant, such as artisans use. *a.* Dexterous.

> Parawd o'i adaf, cyn no'i adaw,
> Paran post enwair pair pedrylaw;
> Pedryliw ei lafn i ladd rhagddaw;
> Pedrylef cwynfan cyrdd amdanaw!
>
> Ready from his hand, before his departure, were the shafts of the pillar of the chace of *dexterous* energy; of perfect colour his blade to slay before him; of continued voice the lamentation of songs for him! *Cynddelw, m. R. Ffwdd.*

Pedryled, *s. m.* (pedry—lled) Complete extension, a square superfices.

Pedrylef, *s. m.* (pedry—llef) A quadrate voice; a perfect voice.

Pedryliw, *s. m.—pl. t.* iau (pedry—lliw) A quadrate colour, a perfect colour.

Pedrylun, *s. m.—pl. t.* iau (pedry—llun) A quadrate form; a perfect figure.

Pedrŷoled, *s. m.* (pedrŷawl) That consists of four divisions or intersections; the grasp.

> Hëaidd ono bedryoled ei law.
>
> Ashen shafts were scattered from the *grasp of his hand*. *Aneurin.*
>
> Pedryoled benawr.
>
> A *four-pointed* helmet. *Aneurin*

Pedrŷoledd, *s. m.* (pedrŷawl) Quadrature.

Pedrŷoli, *v. a.* (pedrŷawl) To quadrate, to square.

Pedrŷollt, *s. m.* (pedry—ollt) That is cloven or split into four parts; two splits crossing each other so as to form four parts.

> A bollt o bedryollt bren.
>
> With a bolt from the *intersecting cleft* of a piece of timber. *D. ab Gwilym.*

Pedrŷollti, *v. a.* (pedrŷollt) To split into four parts; to make an intersecting cleft.

Pedrŷor, *s. f.—pl. t.* oedd (pedry—or) That consists of four regions; a quadrate.

Pedrŷori, *v. a.* (pedryor) To quadrate.

Pedryran, *s. f.—pl. t.* au (pedry—rhan) Quadrant.

Pedryranawl, *a.* (pedryran) Quadripartite.

Pedryranu, *v. a.* (pedryran) To quadrate.

Pedrysawdd, *s. f.—pl.* pedrysoddion (pedry—sawdd) A square root.

Pedu, *v. a.* (ped) To ask or to crave in a roundabout way, also to guard against a request, by anticipating a similar want.

Pedw, *s. m.* (ped) That is made to diverge.

Pedwar, *s. m.—pl. t.* au (ped—gwar) The number four. *a.* Four, speaking of masculines.

Pedwaraid, *s. m.* (pedwar) That is included in four, that consists of four.

Pedwaran, *s. c.—pl. t.* au (pedwar) A fourth, a quarter, a quartern; a farthing.

Pedwararbymtheg, *s. m.*(pedwar—ar—pymtheg) Nineteen. *a.* Nineteen.

Pedwararddeg, *s. m.* (pedwar—ar—deg) Fourteen. *a.* Fourteen.

Pedwarawl, *a.* (pedwar) Belonging to four.

Pedwarban, *s. m.* (pedwar—ban) That consists of four parts. *a.* Of four parts.

Pedwarbanawg, *s. m.* (pedwarban) A quadrain.

Pedwarcanfed, *s. m.* (pedwarcant) The four hundredth. *a.* Four hundredth.

Pedwarcanplyg, *s. m.* (pedwarcant—plyg) Four hundred times folded.

Pedwarcant, *s. m.* (pedwar—cant) Four hundred. *a.* Consisting of four hundred.

Pedwarcanwaith, *s. f.* (pedwarcant—gwaith) Four hundred times. *adv.* At four hundred times.

Pedwarcarn, *s. pl. aggr.* (pedwar—carn) Four hoofs. *a.* Four-hoofed.

Syrthid march oddiar ei bedwarcarn.

The horse may fall off his *four hoofs*. *Adage.*

Pedwarcarnawg, *a.* (pedwarcarn) Having four hoofs; quadrupedous.

Pedwarcarnawl, *a.* (pedwarcarn) Belonging to the four hoofs, of four hoofs.

Pedwarcarniad, *s. m.* (pedwarcarn) A using the four hoofs, a galloping.

Pedwarcarnu, *v. a.* (pedwarcarn) To use the four hoofs; to gallop.

Yr oedd pethau wedi eu dadymchwelyd, a'u tafu bendramwnwgl; a ninnau oeddym yn pedwarcarnu yn ol i Rufain.

Things were become reversed, and thrown topsy-turvy; and we were *galloping* back to Rome. *Ier. Owain.*

Pedwardull, *s. f.* (pedwar—dull) A quadriform.

Pedwardyblyg, *s. m.—pl. t.* ion (pedwar—dyblyg) A quadruplicate. *a.* Quadruple.

Pedwardyblygiad, *s. m.* (pedwardyblyg) Quadruplication; a doubling four times.

Pedwardyblygu, *v. a.* (pedwardyblyg) To quadruplicate, to double four times.

Pedwaredd, *s. m.* (pedwar) A fourth. *a.* Fourth.

Pedwariad, *s. m.—pl.* pedwariaid (pedwar) A quaternity, one that is over four.

Pedwariannawl, *a.* (pedwariant) Quaternary.

Pedwariannu, *v. a.* (pedwariant) To form a quaternity, to make up of four.

Pedwariant, *s. m.* (pedwar) Quaternity.

Pedwarochr, *s. pl. aggr.* (pedwar—ochr) Four sides. *a.* Four-sided.

Pedwarochrawg, *a.* (pedwarochr) Having four sides

Pedwarochrawl, *a.* (pedwarochr) Quadrilateral.

Pedwarochredd, *s. m.* (pedwarochr) Quadrilateralness; squareness.

Pedwarochri, *v. a.* (pedwarochr) To make quadrilateral, to render four sided.

Pedwarochriad, *s. m.* (pedwarochr) A making quadrilateral.

Pedwaroli, *v. a.* (pedwarawl) To make quarterly

Pedwarparth, *s. pl. aggr.* (pedwar—parth) Four parts. *a.* Of four parts.

Pedwarpen, *s. pl. aggr.* (pedwar—pen) Four heads. *a.* Four-headed.

Pedwarplyg, *s. pl. aggr.* (pedwar—plyg) Four doubles, four folds. *a.* Fourfold, quadruple.

Pedwarplygiad, *s. m.* (pedwarplyg) Quadruplication, a making into fourfolds.

Pedwartro, *s. pl. aggr.* (pedwar—tro) Four turns, four times. *a.* Of four turns.

Pedwartroed, *s. m.—pl. t.* ion (pedwar—troed) A quadruped. *a.* Quadruped, four-footed.

Pedwartroedawg, *a.* (pedwartroed) Quadrupedal. *Pedwartroedogion*, quadrupeds.

Pedwartroedawl, *a.* (pedwartroed) Quadrupedous

Pedwartu, *s. pl. aggr.* (pedwar—tu) Four sides. *a.* Four-sided, quadrilateral.

Pedwartuawg, *a.* (pedwartu) Having four sides.

Pedwartheg, *s. m.* (pedwar—deg) Fourteen.

Pedwaru, *v. a.* (pedwar) To make into four.

Pedwarygwr, *s. m.* (pedwar—gwr) A fourth person

Pedwerydd, *s. m.—pl. t.* on (pedwar) A fourth part, a quarter; a quartern. *a.* Fourth.

Pedyd, *s. pl. aggr.* (ped) The foot, the infantry.

Pedyddawd, *s. m.* (pedydd) The infantry.

Pedd, *s. m.—pl. t.* au (py—edd) The agent of progress; a foot. See *ped* and *troed*.

Peddest, *s. m.* (pedd) Foot travelling.

Peddestr, *s. m.—pl. t.* on (peddest) A pedestrian.

Gorea peddestr yw gau.

The best *traveller* is a lie. *Adage.*

Peddestres, *s. f.—pl. t.* od (peddestr) A female pedestrian.

Peddestrig, *s. f. dim.* (peddestr) A pedestrian.

Peddiad, *s. m.* (pedd) A travelling on foot.

Peddu, *v. a.* (pedd) To use the feet, to go on foot.

Peddyd, *s. pl. aggr.* (pedd) The infantry.

Meddyliaw a orug Baldwlph dwyn nosawl gyrch am ben Arthur a'i lu; ac Arthur a wybu hyny: sef a orug Arthur yna, anfon Cador, tywysawg Cernyw, a chwechant marchawg gantho, ac a thair mil o beddyd ynghyd ag ef, a myned yn ei erbyn; ac ei ragod y nos hono.

It was purposed by Baldolph to make a night attack upon Arthur and his army; and Arthur knew that: what did Arthur then do, but he sent Cador prince of Cornwall, along with six hundred horsemen, and with three thousand *infantry*, and which should go against him, and meet him on that night. *Gr. ab Arthur.*

Pef, *s. m.* (py—ef) That radiates or beams.

Pefr, *s. m.* (pef) That is radiant, bright, or shining. *a.* Radiant, splendid, bright, smart.

Dogn o aur pefr yw'r gwallt gwych.

A wreath of *radiant* gold is the beauteous hair. *I. ab Rh. ab I. Llwyd.*

Pefraidd, *a.* (pefr) Somewhat radiant, gairish.

Pefrawl, *a.* (pefr) Radiating, brightening, full of gaiety or smartness.

Pefredd, *s. m.* (pefr) Radiancy, gairishness.

Pefren, *s. f. dim.* (pefr) A smart little woman.

Pefri, *s. m.* (pefr) Splendour, gairishness.

Pefriad, *s. m.* (pefr) A radiating, a rendering bright or gairish; a smartening.

Pefriaw, *v. a.* (pefr) To cast a splendour, to render gairish, to become gairish, to brighten.

Pefrin, *a.* (pefr) Of a radiant or splendid appearance, gairish.

Pefrineb, *s. m.* (pefrin) Gairishness, smartness.

Pefrnwyd, *s. f.* (pefr—nwyd) A gay or smart disposition.

Pefru, *v. a.* (pefr) To radiate, to brighten, to render gairish, to become gairish, to smarten.

Pefrwellt, *s. m.* (pefr—gwellt) Canary-grass.

Pefryn, *s. m. dim.* (pefr) A smart beau.

Pefrynaidd, *a.* (pefryn) Beauish, like a beau.

Pefwch, *s. m.* (pef) Dilation, effusion.

Pefwg, *s. m.* (pef) Expansion; effusion.

Pefychawl, *a.* (pefwch) Expanding, effusive.

Pefychdawd, *s. m.* (pefwch) Effusiveness.

Pefychedd, *s. m.* (pefwch) Effusiveness.

Pefychiad, *s. m.* (pefwch) An opening out, effusion, a gushing.

Pefychu, *v. a.* (pefwch) To expand, to render clear or open, to become expanded, to puff out.

Pan ddaeth o Ffrainc Ffranc, o erchi
Iechyd rhag clefyd, rhag clwyf dallu,
Wynebglawr didawr, dim ni welid;
Pefychwys, tremwys, drwy fodd Dewi.

When there came out of France a Frank, in craving for deliverance from disease, from the ill of blindness, an uniform blank image, nothing could be see; *he brightened*, he beheld, through the will of Dewi. *Gw. Brycheiniawg.*

Peg, *s. m.* (py—eg) That is an agent of expansion or opening; that expands; also a measure of capacity, equal to eight bushels.

Pegaid, *s. m.—pl.* pegeidiau (peg) The contents of an eight-bushel measure, or a quarter.

Peged, *s. m.* (peg) A measure of capacity, equal to eight bushels or a quarter.

Pegor, *s. m.—pl. t.* au (peg) That whereon any thing turns or is suspended; a centre of rotatory motion; a pivot, a pert little fellow, a dwarf. *Y pegor drwg!* The naughty little urchin!

Gogwn py begor
Y sydd y dan for.

I partly know what *base* there is beneath the sea. *Taliesin.*

Pegoraidd, *a.* (pegor) Like a pivot or axis.

Pegorawl, *a.* (pegor) Serving as a pivot.

Pegori, *v. a.* (pegor) To form a pivot.

Pegoriad, *s. m.* (pegor) A forming a pivot.

Pegoryn, *s. m. dim.* (pegor) A small pivot or axis; a pert little chap; a dwarf.

Pegwn, *s. m.—pl.* pegynau (peg) A pole or axis, an axle, a pin, or spindle, a pivot.

Mal y dur at y pegwn.

Like the steel to the *pole*. *Adage.*

Pegwr, *s. m.—pl.* pegyrion (peg) A pivot, or axis; a dwarf, a pigmy.

Pegwrn, *s. m.—pl.* pegyrnau (peg—gwrn) The axis whereon any thing revolves; a pivot.

Pegynawl, *a.* (pegwn) Belonging to an axis.

Pegyniad, *s. m.* (pegwn) A forming an axis.

Pegynu, *v. a.* (pegwn) To form a pivot or axis.

Pei, *adv.* (pe—i) If it were, if it should be.

Pei cygynted ar droed ag ar dafawd y byddai wraig, hi a ddaliai ddigon o leched i gynnu tan y bore.

If every woman were as swift of foot as of tongue, she would catch enow of lightning to kindle a fire in a morning. *Adage.*

Peiad, *s. m.* (pai) A rendering objective.

Peiaw, *v. a.* (pai) To render objective.

Peiawd, *s. m.* (pai) A being objective.

Peiawl, *a.* (pai) Objective; perceptive.

Peiawr, *s. m.* (pai) That is objective.

Peidiad, *s. m.* (paid) A ceasing, a desisting.

Peidiannawl, *a.* (peidiant) Tending to cease.

Peidiannu, *v. a.* (peidiant) To make a pause.

Peidiant, *s. m.* (paid) A cessation, a ceasing.

Peidiaw, *v. n.* (paid) To cease; to leave off, to give over, to desist. *Gwell i ti beidiaw*, thou hadst better be quiet; *paid da dithau*, be quiet, that is a good creature.

Call a dwylla, callach a baid.

The cunning will deceive, the more cunning will *desist*. *Adage.*

Peidiawl, *a.* (paid) Tending to cease or desist.

Peidiedig, *a.* (peidiad) Being left off or ended.

Peiliad, *s. m.* (pal) A displaying, a raying.

Peiliaw, *v. a.* (pal) To spread out, to radiate.

Peiliawg, *a.* (pal) Having a display, rayonnent.

Peiliedig, *a.* (peiliad) Displayed, radiated.

Peilldy, *s. m.—pl. t.* au (paill—ty) A bolting-house.

Peillged, *s. f.* (paill—ced) A tribute of flour; such used to be paid by the prince of Mathraval to the prince of Aberfraw.

Peilliad, *s. m.* (paill) A bolting or searcing.

Peilliant, *s. m.* (paill) That is made into flour.

Peilliaw, *v. a.* (paill) To searce or to bolt flour.

Peilliawd, *s. m.* (paill) A making into flour.

Peilliawg, *a.* (paill) Abounding with flour.

Peillied, *s. m.* (paill) Bolted meal, or flour.

Peilliedig, *a.* (peilliad) Reduced to flour.

Peillion, *s. pl. aggr.* (paill) Fine flour.

Peilliwr, *s. m.—pl.* peillwyr (paill—gwr) A bolter, or siercer of flour.

Peillwy, *s. m.* (paill) Fine flour, or powder.

Peillydd, *s. m.—pl. t.* ion (paill) A siercer.

Peillyddes, *s. f.* (peillydd) A female siercer.

Peiniad, *s. m.* (pain) A producing a farina.

Peiniaw, *v. a.* (pain) To yield bloom or farina.

Peiniawl, *a.* (pain) Tending to yield farina.

Peiodawl, *a.* (peiawd) Objective, perceptive.

Peiodi, *v. a.* (peiawd) To render objective.

Gwlad pres i'th ermud,
A chyd awch belodud,
Tricbanmil blwyddynedd.

The present world will be expecting thee, and with ardour *will be making thee the object*, for three hundred thousand years. *Taliesin, armes dyddbrawd.*

Peiran, *s. f.—pl. t.* oedd (pair) A necessary.

Peiriad, *s. m.* (par) A causer, causator, or effector.

Yr haf—
Peiriad hardd yn peri dail.

The summer, a glorious *cause* causing foliage. *D. ab Gwilym.*

Peiriaid, *s. f.* (pair) As much as a cauldron holds.

Peirianna, *v. a.* (peiriant) To bring together causes or instrumentalities.

Peiriannawg, *a.* (peiriant) Having a cause.

Peiriannawl, *a.* (peiriant) Causative; effective.

Peiriannawr, *s. m.—pl.* peiriannorion (peiriant) An instrumentality; what is conducive.

Peiriannedig, *a.* (peiriant) Being made instrumental or conducive.

Peiriannedd, *s. m.* (peiriant) Instrumentalness.

Peiriannolaeth, *s. m.* (peiriannawl) The act of rendering instrumental; organization.

Peiriannoldeb, *s. m.* (peiriannawl) Instrumentality; conduciveness.

Peiriannolder, *s. m.* (peiriannawl) Instrumentality; conduciveness.

Peiriannoledd, *s. m.* (peiriannawl) Instrumentality; conduciveness.

Peiriannoli, *v. a.* (peiriannawl) To render instrumental; to become instrumental.

Peiriannu, *v. a.* (peiriant) To put in a state to act; to organize, to accoutre, to harness. *Peirianna y ceffyl*, put the furniture on the horse.

Peiriannus, *a.* (peiriant) Apt to be instrumental.

Peiriannusaw, *v. a.* (peiriannus) To render instrumental; to become instrumental.

Peiriannusedd, *s. m.* (peiriannus) Instrumentality; an organized state.

Peiriannusrwydd, *s. m.* (peiriannus) Instrumentalness; a conducive state.

Peiriannwr, *s. m.—pl.* peiriannwyr (peiriant—gwr) One who puts in a state for action; an organizer; one who accoutres.

Peiriannydd, *s. m.—pl. t.* ion (peiriant) One who puts in a state to act; an organizer.

Peiriant, *s. m.—pl.* peiriannau (par) The means or agent by which any thing is accomplished, instrumentality; an instrument, or a tool.

Tri pheiriant Duw yn abred, er gorfod drwg a chythraul, a dianc oddiwrthynt at wynfyd; angen, anghof, ac angeu.

The three *means* of God in the circle of inchoation, for subduing evil and the adverse principle, and to open a way from them to happiness; necessity, loss of memory, and death. *Barddas.*

Ni all y corff wneuthur dim obono ei hun, ond a wnel yr enaid trwyddo ef, megys trwy beiriant.—Y rhai drwg sy megys peiriannau i buraw y rhai da.

The body is not able to perform any thing of itself, but what the soul performs through it, as through a *machine*.—The wicked ones are as *instruments* to purify those that are good. *Elucidarius.*

Peirwyddiad, *s. m.*—*pl.* peirwyddiaid (parwydd) That conveys the knowledge of causing; a verb

> Peirwyddiad yw pob gair; neu beth, a arwyddoco gwneuthur, neu beiriad, o ba ddyn, neu beth, neu hanfod y bo y peri bynag.
>
> A verb implies every word, or circumstance, that denotes a doing, or causing, of what person, or thing, or existence soever the agency may be. *Edeyrn.*

Peiriennyn, *s. m. dim.* (peiriant) An instrument.

Peisgwellt, *s. m.* (paisg—gwellt) Fescue-grass.

Peisgwyn, *s. m.* (paisg—gwyn) The great white poplar.

Peiswyn, *s. m. aggr.* (pais—gwyn) Chaff; also called *us*.

Peithadwy, *a.* (paith) Capable of being made clear or open; capable of being explored.

Peithas, *s. f.*—*pl. t.* au (paith) A scout, a sort of scout boat, which with the sails, used to be all of blue colour, to prevent a discovery.

Peithawd, *s. m.* (paith) The act of making clear or open, a laying waste, a scouting.

Peithdra, *s. m.* (paith) Planity; exposedness.

Peithedig, *a.* (paith) Being made plain or clear.

Peithes, *s. f.*—*pl. t.* au (paith) A female scout.

Peithfrig, *s. m.* (paith—brig) A clear top.

> Differ fi, fy ner, rhag——
> Y pair, gair garwddig, peithfrig poethfrych!
>
> Protect me, my Lord, awful the word, from the furnace of hotly-agitated *glowing surface!* *Casnodyn.*

Peithi, *s. pl. aggr.* (paith) Those that are out or exposed, the people of the open plain; the people of the waste or desert, also those who scout; those who lay waste; the PICTS.

Peithiad, *s. m.*—*pl. t.* au (paith) A making clear or open; a reducing to a desert; an exploration; a scouting, a hunting, a looking about.

Peithiannawl, *a.* (peithiant) Tending to make clear or open, exploratory.

Peithiannu, *v. a.* (peithiant) To put in a clear or open state; to make into a waste or desert.

Peithiannus, *a.* (peithiant) Of an open or exposed state; exploratory.

Peithiant, *s. m.* (paith) The act of making clear or open; a scouting.

Peithiaw, *v. a.* (paith) To make clear or open; to lay waste; to scout, to hunt, to look about, to search; to look, to seem, to appear.

> ——Aergun gedymdaith,
> Durn-dra-durn, dragygyn yd paith.
>
> The battle-upholding companion, with fist to fist, most violently *he lays open.* *Cynddelw, i O. ab Madawg.*

Peithiawg, *a.* (paith) Having open space, open, desert, waste, having an open view or prospect

> Dy gynneddf dyfod——
> A gwaedlanw gwyr arfawg,
> A gwaedlen am ben yn beithiawg.
>
> Thy custom is to come with the blood streaming of armed men dealing slaughter, and a veil of blood over the head *conspicuously* *Ll. P. Moch.*
>
> Braw cwyddam ynghyd yn nghred anghred;
> Yn uffern gethern, garth dra-frwd ermoes;
> Yn affan porthfan, peithiawg dreiddied.
>
> Fearfully we should have fallen altogether in the lot of infidelity, amongst the fiends of hell, a habitation confined and vile, in the reach of a hot place, of *devastating* course. *Ll. P. Moch.*

Peithiawl, *a.* (paith) Tending to lay open or waste, of an open or exposed state.

Peithig, *a.* (paith) That is clear, plain, or open.

Peithin, *a.* (paith) Abounding with plainness, clearness, or openness.

Peithineb, *s. m.* (peithin) Planity; openness.

Peithioledd, *s. m.* (peithiawl) The state of being out, open, or exposed.

Peithiw, *a.* (paith) That is plain, clear, or open.

Peithiwr, *s. m.*—*pl.* peithwyr (paith—gwr) One who lays open; one who explores.

Peithlong, *s. f.*—*pl. t.* au (paith—llong) A scout-boat, an advice-boat.

Peithus, *a.* (paith) Being plain, clear, or exposed

Peithw, *a.* (paith) That is obscured or closed.

Peithwg, *s. m.* (paith) That is plain, clear, open, or exposed, an open space, hunting ground.

Peithwydd, *s. pl. aggr.* (paith—gwydd) The reeds of a loom, the slay; also called *peithyn*, *peithynau*, *rhwydau*, and *brwydau*.

Peithyll, *s. m.* (paith) That opens or yawns.

Peithyn, *s. m.*—*pl. t.* au (paith) Open space; open work; that is plain, clear, or open; what clears, or the reed-work of a loom, a slay; a slate, a tile, or other plain body. *Peithynau olwyn*, the cogs of a wheel.

> Y mur a wnaethpwyd o beithynau pridd boethedig, wedi eu gorddiau o byg.
>
> The wall was made of baked earthen tiles, after being overspread with pitch. *Hanesion yr Ysgrythyr.*

Peithynawd, *s. m.* (peithyn) The act of reducing to a flat or level: a laying flat.

Peithynawl, *a.* (peithyn) Tending to reduce to a flat or level; being an open space.

Peithyndawd, *s. m.* (peithyn) The state of being a flat or plain.

Peithyndo, *s. m.* (peithyn—to) A tiled roof.

> Tan gefail trefgordd ni ddiwygir, a fo saith wrhyd y rhyngddi a'r tai, a bithen yn beithyndo.
>
> The fire of a township smithery shall not be made good, which shall have seven fathoms between it and the houses, so that it be of *tile-covering.* *Welsh Laws.*

Peithynen, *s. f. dim.* (peithyn) That is plain or clear; a plain body, as a slate, tile, a sheet of paper, and the like; the elucidator, or frame of writing, the book of the ancient bards, which consisted of a number of four-sided or three-sided sticks written upon, which were put together in a frame, so that each stick might be turned round for the facility of reading.

Peithyniad, *s. m.* (peithyn) A making a clear place; a making into a flat; a making flat.

Peithynu, *v. a.* (peithyn) To make a clear place; to make a flat or plain, to flatten; to lay flat.

> Yn aghywrysedd a Lloegr, llwydd amed,
> Naw ugain sen un a beithynad.
>
> In the contention with Lloegria, of various conflicts, nine score for one thou wouldest lay flat. *Taliesin, G. Rheged.*

Peithynwr, *s. m.*—*pl.* peithynwyr (peithyn—gwr) One who makes a level; one who lays flat, a layer of tiles.

Peithynydd, *s. m.*—*pl. t.* ion (peithyn) One who forms a flat or plain; one who flattens.

Pel, *s. f.*—*pl. t.* i (py—el) That has a principle of motion; a ball, a sphere.

> A'r bel o ryfel yr aeth,
> Ar baladr o febolaeth.
>
> With the ball from the war he went, on the shaft of youth. *Gutto y Glyn.*

Pela, *s. m.*—*pl. t.* on (pel) That moves round or hovers; the titmouse. *Y pela glas bach*, *penlöyn*, the ox-eye, a small bird so called.

> Mor bånc a'r pela.
>
> As brisk as the *titmouse.* *Adage.*

Pelaidd, *a.* (pel) Roundish, like a ball, globular.

Peled, *s. f.*—*pl. t.* au (pel) A ball, a bullet.

> Plad gwych rhag ofn peled gwn——
> Ymgylchu dur amgylch dyn.
>
> A splendid plate for fear of the *bullet* of a gun: putting circles of steel round a person *T. Prys, i arfau gwgawn.*

Peledu, *v. a.* (peled) To throw a ball.

Peleidral, *s. m.* (paladr) The pushing of spears.

Attol beleidral, dywal dillydd;
Nid arbetwy car corff ei gilydd.

Again shall come the *toil of spears*, fierce and sharp; the friend shall not spare the body of his fellow.
Golyddan, armes Prydain.

Peleidriad, *s. m.* (paladr) A darting of rays; a gleaming; a darting or pushing of spears.

Diwreiddiws Bowys peleidriad rhyfel.

The *gleaming* of war has rooted up Powys. *Gwalchmai.*

Peleidriannawl, *a.* (peleidriant) Tending to make a radiancy or gleaming.

Peleidriannu, *v. a.* (peleidriant) To produce a radiation; to make a radiancy.

Peleidriant, *s. m.* (paladr) A radiation.

Peleidriaw, *v. a.* (paladr) To radiate.

Pelen, *s. f. dim.—pl. t.* an (pel) A little ball.

Pelenawg, *a.* (pelen) Having a ball or lump.

Peleniad, *s. m.* (pelen) A forming into a ball.

Pelenu, *v. a.* (pelen) To form into a ball.

Peleu, *s. m.—pl. t.* od (pel) The greenfinch.

A glywaisti a gant y peleu,
Gyda'i adar yn chwarea!

Hast thou heard what the *greenfinch* sang, playing with his birds!
Englynion y Clywed.

Pelgib, *s. f.—pl. t.* au (pel—cib) A ball racket.

Peliad, *s. m.* (pal) A spreading out.

Peliaw, *v. a.* (pal) To spread out, to brandish.

Pelid, *s. m.* (pal) Radiancy; splendour.

Pelre, *s. m.* (pel—rhe) A beating of a ball backwards and forwards; turmoil, bustle, trouble.

Ceiniadon moch clywid eu gofalon:
Marchawglu mor daer am Gaer Lleon;
A dial Idwal ar Aranwynion
A gware pelre a phen Saeson.

Songsters, soon would their cares be heard; an army of horsemen so harassing round Caer Lleon; and the revenge of Idwal on the Aranwynians; and the playing of *ball-buffetting* with Saxon heads.
Taliesin.

Pelrëad, *s. m.* (pelre) A playing at ball; a turmoiling; a bustling.

Pelrëu, *v. a.* (pelre) To knock a ball about; to play at ball; to turmoil.

Pelu, *v. a.* (pel) To move by revolving, to throw a ball, to ball, to throw a bullet.

Pelyd, *s. pl.* (paled) The legs of stockings with the feet cut off; also called *bacsau.*

Pelydr, *s. pl. aggr.* (paladr) Pellitory. *Pelydr gwyllt*, bastard pellitory, or bertram; *pelydr dû*, black hellebore.

Pelydraidd, *a.* (pelydr) Radiate; beaming.

Pelydrawg, *a.* (pelydr) Radiant; rayonnent.

Pelydriad, *s. m.* (pelydr) A radiating.

Pelydru, *v. a.* (pelydr) To radiate, to cast rays.

Pelydryn, *s. m. dim.* (pelydr) A ray, a beam.

Pell, *s. m.* (py—ell) An extreme limit or verge; the periphery of a circle.

Goreu amddiffynfa digawn pell.

The best place of defence is a sufficient *distance.* *Adage.*

Pell, *a.* (py—ell) Being in the round, verge, or horizon; distant, remote, far. *Pell iawn, pell byd, pur bell, tra phell*, very far.

Diawg i oed pwyllawg pell.

Remiss to an appointment is the *remote* thinker of it.
Adage.

Drwg pechawd o'i bell erlid.

Bad is sin from its being *far* pursued. *Adage.*

Pell ei fysgi a'i anaw,
Gweryd Machawe arnaw;
Beidawg Rudd yw hwn ab Emyr Llydaw.

For his turmoil and his fame, the soil of Machawe is upon him; Beidiog the ruddy is this, the son of Emyr Llydaw.
Engl. Beddau Milwyr.

Pellâad, *s. m.* (pellâu) A rendering far; a removing to a distance; a becoming distant.

Pellach, *a.* (*compar. of* pell) More distant, farther. *adv.* At some point of time lately passed, at length, further, furthermore.

Pellaf, *a.* (*superlative of* pell) Farthest, utmost.

Pellan, *s. c.—pl. t.* au (pall) A form or range of seats round an area; the range of seats of an amphitheatre.

Pellâu, *v. a.* (pell) To put far of; to remove far off; to be far removed; to elongate.

Pellbell, *a.* (pell *repeated*) Far and far, very far.

Pelldaer, *a.* (pell—taer) Remotely harassing.

Pellder, *s. m.* (pell) Remoteness, or distance.

Pelldra, *s. m.* (pell) Remoteness, distance.

Pelldrem, *s. f.—pl. t.* iau (pell—trem) A far view; a sight for a distant object.

Pelldremiaeth, *s. m.* (pelldrem) Dioptrics.

Pelldremiant, *s. m.* (pelldrem) A far viewing.

Pelldremiawl, *a.* (pelldrem) Assisting to view distant objects, dioptrical.

Pelldremyn, *s. m.* (pelldrem) A look to a great distance, a far sight.

Pellddrych, *s. m.* (pell—drych) A distant view.

Pelledd, *s. m.* (pell) Remoteness, farness.

Pellen, *s. f. dim.—pl. t.* au (pell) That is made for motion; that may be aptly implied; a compact round body; a round mass; a ball of thread, yarn, or other thing; a round lump, or gland in the body of an animal.

Pellenaidd, *a.* (pellen) Like a ball, globular.

Pellenawg, *a.* (pellen) Having aptitude for moving off; having the form of a ball.

Rhyddybydd Llyminawg,
A fydd wr chwannawg;
Arall a ddyfydd,
Pellenawg ei luydd
Llewenydd i Frython.

There shall come into existence Llyminog, who will be an ambitious man: another there will be *far-extending* his host, a triumph to Britons.
Taliesin.

Pelleniad, *s. m.* (pellen) A forming into a ball.

Pellenig, *a.* (pellan) Of a remote situation, being distant, or remote. *s. m.* That is situated at a distance, that is of a far course, a stranger.

——Brynlau, molwch
Naf daiarolion a phellenigion fwch.

Ye hills, praise the Lord of earthly creatures and of rapid *far-wandering* bodies.
D. Ddu, Hiraddug.

Pellenigaeth, *s. m.* (pellenig) Any foreign affair.

Gwr cyfrwng, yn llys, ac yn llan, ac yn nghammawn, ac yn mhob pellenigaeth—yw y teisbantyle.

A mediating man, in court, and in congregation, and in combat, and in every *foreign affair*, is the representative.
Trioedd Dyfnwal.

Pellenigaw, *v. a.* (pellenig) To render remote, to remove to a distance; to become remote.

Pellenigedd, *s. m.* (pellenig) Remoteness.

Pellenigiad, *s. m.* (pellenig) To render remote.

Pellenigrwydd, *s. m.* (pellenig) Remoteness of situation; an extreme state.

Argiwydd pellenigrwydd parch,
Owain waew blin-fain blaen-farch.

Lord of the *ultimate state* of honour, Owain with the sharp pungent spear and foremost steed.
Gr. ab D. Fychan.

Pellenigwr, *s. m.—pl.* pellenigwyr (pellenig—gwr) One who is remote; a stranger.

Taladwy arlwy eurwledd gan eryr
I bellenigwyr——

Costly the preparation of the golden feast of the eagle-hero for *foreign men.*
Mad. Dwygraig.

Pellenu, *v. a.* (pellen) To form into a ball.

Pelliad, *s. m.* (pell) A rendering remote, a moving to a distance, a farthering.

Pellineb, *s. m.* (pell) Farness, remoteness.

Pellrwydd, *s. m.* (pell) Remoteness, farness.

Pellt, *s. m.* (pell) That is external, a surface.

> Aesawr dellt am bellt adawai.
>
> Splintered shields about the *ground* he would leave. *Aneurin.*

Pelltawg, *a.* (pellt) Having a surface.

Pelltiad, *s. m.* (pellt) A forming a surface.

Pelltu, *v. a.* (pellt) To form a surface or outside.

Pellu, *v. a.* (pell) To render remote or distant; to remove far off.

> Trugarawg Arglwydd, trugarha
> Wrthwyf; i wrthyd na'm pella.
>
> Merciful Lord, be merciful to me; from thee *do not remove* me *away*. *Cynddelw.*

Pellus, *a.* (pell) Tending to the exterior or verge, surrounding, compact.

> Pellynig ei glod, pellus ei galch.
>
> Far-extending his fame, *compact* his armour. *Aneurin.*

Pellyn, *s. m.* (pell) That is extreme or exterior.

Pellynawl, *a.* (pellyn) Far extending.

Pellynig, *a.* (pellyn) Far-extending, far-wandering, far-roaming.

> Pellynig fy nghof yn Nghaerwys dir;
> Pell ydd wyf!
>
> *Far-roaming* is my memory in Caerwys land; and far off am I! *Cynddelw.*
>
> Pellynig fy nghof yn nghynteftn,
> Yn ethryb caru Caerwys febin.
>
> *Far-roaming* is my memory in the beginning of summer, on account of loving the nymph of Caerwys. *Gwalchmai.*

Pellynu, *v. a.* (pellyn) To render remote, to remove far off; to become remote.

Pellynus, *a.* (pellyn) Tending to remoteness.

Pen, *s. m.—pl. t.* au (py—en) An extremity, end, or conclusion, the upper part; the head; a chief; a capital; a summit; a beginning, or foremost end; the state of being over or upon. *Pen Tir Lloegr*, the Land's End of England; *pen y bont*, the bridge end; *y pen yma*, *y pen hwn*, this end; *y pen oco*, *pen acw*, *pen draw*, yonder end; *wedi dawed i ben*, being come to an end; *pen ty*, house top; *pen y ty*, the top of the house; *pen yn erfid*, at logger-heads; *bod yn ben*, to be a pincipal; *pen y bryn*, the summit of the hill; *lladron pen ffordd*, highway robbers; *pen blaen*, the foremost end: *Dyro hyn ar ei ben ei hun*, put this by itself; *bwrw dwfr am ben y tan*, to throw water over the fire; *mae hi yn chwerthin am dy ben*, she is laughing at thee. *Pen y neidr*, dog's violet; *pennau y gwyr*, or *llwynhidydd*, ribwort plantain.

> Tafawd aur yn mhen dedwydd.
>
> A golden tongue is in the *head* of the wise. *Adage.*
>
> Dy dafawd, wr da difeth,
> Dy ben, yw pen ar bob peth.
>
> Thy tongue, thou good and infallible man, thy *head*, over every thing be chief. *Gw. ab Ieu. Hen.*
>
> Hwedlau pen gwlad, rhy wir i hwerthin am eu pennau.
>
> The common sayings of the multitude, too true to be laughed at. *Adage.*

Pen, *a.* (pen) Head, chief, supreme, principal.

Penad, *s. m.* (pen) A making chief; a becoming a head, chief, or principal.

Penadur, *s. m.—pl. t.* on (penad) One that is supreme or principal, a primate, a sovereign.

> ——Duw benadur,
> A'th dei o'th haint, a'th dolur,
> A'th dileddf auhawdd gawdd gur!
>
> God the *supreme*, bring thee out of thy illness and thy wound, and thy anointing and severely afflicting pain! *G. ab M. ab Dafydd, i Owain.*
>
> Tri meib Llywelyn:——
> Tri araf penaf penadurion.
>
> The three sons of Llywelyn three gentle ones, supreme of sovereigns. *D. Benfras.*

Penaduriaeth, *s. m.—pl. t.* au (penadur) Pre-eminence, sovereignty, supremacy.

Penaduriaethu, *v. a.* (penaduriaeth) To create a sovereignty or pre-eminency.

Penaeth, *s. m.—pl. t.* au (pen) A pre-eminence, or supremacy, a principal, a chieftain, a chief.

> Nid gair gau, ef gorau gwron,
> Hyd Gaer Llyr, a hyd Gaer Lleon,
> Hyd Ystreigl Elegl, hyd Aeron yr aeth
> Ei benaeth o Benmon.
>
> It is no false word, he is the best of heroes; to Caer Llyr, and to Caer Lleon, to the English Ystreigl to Aeron has his sovereignty extended from Penmon. *Cynddelw, i O. Gwynedd.*
>
> Ei blant a ddeuant bob ddau,
> Nythod teg o benaethau.
>
> His children come forward two by two, a fair nestful of chieftains. *Iolo Goch, i O. Glyndyfrdwy.*

Penaethawg, *a.* (penaeth) Having sovereignty.

Penaethawl, *a.* (penaeth) Belonging to sovereignty; belonging to a sovereign.

Penaethiad, *s. m.—pl.* penaethiaid (penaeth) One who is supreme or principal, a chieftain.

Penaethu, *v. a.* (penaeth) To create a supremacy, to act as a chief, or a principal.

> Pen aig yn penaethu.
>
> A chief stock *exercising pre-eminence*. *Gw. Brycheiniawg, i'r argl. Rhys.*

Pènaf, *a.* (pen) Chiefest, most eminent.

Penafedd, *s. m.* (pènaf) Pre-eminence.

Penafiaeth, *s. m.* (pènaf) Pre-eminence.

Penafrwydd, *s. m.* (pènaf) Primeness, superiority

Penafu, *v. a.* (pènaf) To render superior.

Penag, *conj.* (pe—nag) If not; unless, except.

Penagored, *a.* (pen—agored) Open at top. *Cwch penagored*, an open boat; *llestri penagored*, vessels without decks.

Penaidd, *a.* (pen) Prime, superior, or excellent.

> Ni bu neb; ie——
> Ni bu Nudd yn benaiddiach.
>
> There has been nobody; even Nudd was not *more excellent*. *Guto y Glyn.*

Penaig, *s. m.* (pen—aig) A supreme stock, a supreme, a sovereign, a chieftain.

> Oedd cadarn ddraig benaig berth;
> Oedd ced gynnydd, cad gannerth.
>
> The fair *chieftain* was a mighty leader; he was the increase of bounty, the stay of battle. *Bleddyn Fardd.*
>
> Penaeth Gwynedd ai heddyw:
> Pa ryd ai bwyll: pam as da byw!
>
> The *prime stock* of Gwynedd departs this day: why should reason depart; why is it good to live. *Gr. ab Gwrgan, i Gronwy.*

Penain, *s. pl. dim.* (pen) Petty chiefs or lords.

> Rhaccludawdd ei gleddyf o'i wain;
> Rhagllym fu yn pannu penain.
>
> He carried forward his sword out of the sheath; forwardly keen was he terrifying of *puny chieftains*. *Cynddelw, i H. ab Owain.*

Penant, *s. m.—pl.* penaint (pen) That is at top or over; supremacy, superiority; also a flag or gritty kind of stone used for paving.

> Yn nghyfoeth Dewi difeil gerraint,
> A rhydid heb ofal, heb ofn amgen,
> Heb ofal cynhen cylch i benaint.
>
> In the dominion of Dewi there are friends void of scandal, and liberty without molestation, without leaving a revenue, without anxiety of a dispute about his *prerogatives*. *Gw. Brycheiniawg.*

Penardd, *s. f.—pl.* peneirdd (pen—gardd) The point or salient angle of a bending ridge.

Penarth, *s. f.—pl.* peneirth (pen—garth) The jutting or trending of a mountain so as to form a cove; a cape or promontory. It is also called *penardd* and *peniarth*.

Penaur, *s. m.* (pen—aur) The bird called yellow-hammer. *a.* Gold-headed.

Penawd, *s. m.* (pen) A conclusion or end.

Penawg, *a.* (pen) Having superiority, or supremacy; headed. *s. m.* That is supreme; master. *Gyda'ch cènad y penawg*, by your leave, master.

Penawl, *a.* (pen) Capital, principal, supreme.

Penawr, *s. m.* (pen) Superior, supreme, a master; covering, guard for the head; a headpiece, a helmet, also a headstall, a muzzle.

Penbaladr, *a.* (pen—paladr) Especial, particular. *adv.* Particularly.

> Dodynt emelltith Duw, ac un y gynnulleidfa hòno, ac un Cymmru benbaladr ar y neb a dòrai y cyfreithiau hyny.
>
> They imprecated the course of God, and the one of that congregation, and the *particular* one of Wales, on such as should break those laws. *Welsh Laws.*

Penben, *adv.* (pen *repeated*) With heads together, in confusion, at loggerheads. *Gyru cwn yn benben*, to set dogs together to fight; *ni ddylid dodi y pethau hyny yn benben*, those things ought not to be put confusedly together.

Penbleth, *s. m.* (pen—pleth) Confusion of the head; perplexity; anxiety, distraction of mind. *Pa benbleth sydd arno?* What perplexity is he in?

Penblethiad, *s. m.* (penbleth) A distracting the head; a becoming perplexed.

Penblethu, *v. a.* (penbleth) To distract the head.

Penblydd, *a.* (pen—plydd) Soft-headed, or dull.

Penboeth, *a.* (pen—poeth) Hot-headed. *Y benboeth*, the common hemp-nettle.

Penboethni, *s. m.* (penboeth) Hot-headedness.

Penbwl, *a.* (pen—pwl) Blunt headed. *s. m.* A blunt head, a blockhead, the pilchard, a tadpole. *Y penbwl gwirion!* thou silly blockhead!

Penbwla, *s. m.* (penbwl) A blockhead, a dolt.

Penbyledd, *s. m.* (penbwl) Blockishness.

Penbyliad, *s. m.—pl.* penbyliaid (penbwl) That is blunt-headed, a tadpole.

Penbylu, *v. a.* (penbwl) To make blunt-headed.

Pencaer, *s. f.* (pen—caer) A metropolis.

Pencais, *s. m.—pl.* penceisiaid (pen—cais) A receiver general; a chief treasurer.

Pencawna, *v. a.* (pen—cawna) To gather the tops of ryegrass; to trifle away time seemingly about business. *Gwyddau yn pencawna*, geese picking the wild rye.

Penceirddiad, *s. m.—pl.* penceirddiaid (pencerdd) A chief of song, a chief singer.

Penceirddiadaeth, *s. f.* (penceirddiad) The office of a chief of song, or of a chief musician.

Penceirddiaeth, *s. f.* (pencerdd) The office or jurisdiction of a chief of song.

> Ni eill neb bardd erchi dim, heb genad pencerdd hyd y bo ei benceirddiaeth ef, onid bardd gorwlad fydd, canys rhydd fydd hwnw.
>
> No bard can ask for any thing, without the licence of a chief of song within the extent of his *jurisdiction of song*, except he should be a bard of another country, for such a one is free. *Welsh Laws.*

Penceirddiaidd, *a.* (pencerdd) Belonging to a chief of song; like a chief of song.

Penceirddiaw, *v. a.* (pencerdd) To render masterly in song; to compose according to the laws of song.

> Pa sawl beth a benceirddia cerdd dafawd?
>
> How many points *render complete according to art* the vocal song? *Sim. Vychan.*

Penceirddiawl, *a.* (pencerdd) As a chief of song.

Penceisiad, *s. m.—pl.* penceisiaid (pencais) A chief receiver, a tax-gatherer.

> Einion ab Gwilym ab Gwrwared ab Cuhelyn Fardd a laddes chwech-ar-ugain o benceisiaid Cemais.
>
> Einion son of Gwilym son of Gwrwared son of Cuhelyn the bard, slew twenty-six of the *chief-collectors* of Cemais. *Heneston.*

Pencenedl, *s. m.* (pen—cenedl) The head of a family, tribe or clan; the representative of a family.

> Ni wedd yn bencenedl ond gwr a ymladdo gyd a'i gar ac a ofner; a ddyweto gyd a'i gar ac a wrandawer; a fechnio gyd a'i gar ac a gymerer.
>
> It is not meet for any to be the *head of family* but a man who shall fight with his relation and who shall be feared; who shall speak on the part of his relation and shall be listened to; who shall be surety with his relation and shall be accepted. *Adage.*

Pencenedlaeth, *s. f.* (pencenedl) The state or prerogative of head of a family.

> Ni ddylyir pencenedlaeth o famwys.
>
> The *representation of a family* ought not to be from maternity. *Welsh Laws.*

Pencenedlawg, *a.* (pencenedl) Having a family representation, as a head of a tribe.

Pencenedlawl, *a.* (pencenedl) Belonging to the headship of a family or tribe.

Pencerdd, *s. m.—pl.* penceirddion (pen—cerdd) A master of the science of song.

> Sef fydd pencerdd bardd gwedi enillo gadair; Ni henyw y pencerdd o rif y swyddogion llys.—Y bardd teulu a gan yn ail yn y neuadd, canys y pencerdd a ddechreua.
>
> A *master of song* is a bard after he shall have obtained a chair; the *master of song* is not reckoned of the number of the officers of court.—The bard of the family shall sing the second in the hall, for the *master of song* shall begin. *Welsh Laws.*

Pencerddradd, *s. f.* (pencerdd—gradd) The degree of a chief or master of song.

Penci, *s. m.—pl. t.* on (pen—ci) The dog-fish.

Penciwdawd, *s. m.—pl.* penciwdodon (pen—ciwdawd) A chief or leader of a colony; a generalissimo.

Penclwm, *s. m.—pl.* penclymau (pen—clwm) A knob at the end of any thing; a close.

> Dawai i fod yn babydd cyhoeddus, pan dybiai efe fod pethau wedi dawed i'r fath bencìwm, mal ag yr oedd yn ddiogel iddo ef ddiosg ei orchudd.
>
> He came to be a professed papist, as soon as he thought that things was come to such a *conclusion*, that it were safe for him to put off his mask. *Ier. Owain.*

Pencnaw, *s. m.—pl. t.* iau (pen—cnaw) The receiving end of a joint; a joint, or articulation. *Pencnawiau yr esgyrn*, articulations of bones.

Pencnawiad, *s. m.* (pencnaw) The articulation of a joint, a jointing.

Pencnawiaw, *v. a.* (pencnaw) To articulate a joint, or to form a joint.

Pencnud, *s. m.* (pen—cnud) The chief of a skulk, the chief of a pack.

> Gnawd eryr ebyr abar gwedd bangaw;
> I bencnud wy gyfedd,
> A chigfrain cyfwyrain cigwledd,
> Cigyddion coelion celanedd.
>
> The eagle of the waters exults in spoiling the fair countenance; with the *leader of wolves* he revels, and with hovering ravens glutted with flesh, butchers with keen bodings for carcases. *Ll. P. Moch, i R. Gryg.*

Pencor, *s. m.* (pen—cor) The chief of a circle.

Pencun, *s. m.* (pen—cun) A chief leader.

Pencwd, *s. m.* (pen—cwd) The top of the bag.

> A fu bencwd aeth yn dincwd.
>
> That was the *top of the bag* is become the bottom of the bag. *Adage.*

Pencyfeistedd, *s. m.* (pen—cyfeistedd) The chief place of sitting, the principal seat of assize.

Pencynydd, *s. m.—pl. t.* ion (pen—cynydd) The chief huntsman, the tenth officer of the court.

> Pencynydd, pedair ceiniawg cyfraith a gaiff y gan bob cynydd milgi; ac wyth ceiniawg cyfraith y gan bob cynydd geligi, pan roddo y brenin eu swyddau iddynt.
>
> The *chief huntsman*, four-pence in law shall he have from every huntsman with greyhound; and eight-pence in law from every huntsman with buckhound, when the king grants to them their offices. *Welsh Laws.*

Pencynghor, *s. m.—pl. t.* ion (pen—cynghor) A chief of council; a chief counsellor.

Penchwareÿdd, *s. m.—pl. t.* ion (pen—chwareÿdd) A principal player.

Penchwiban, *a.* (pen—chwiban) Light-headed.

Penchwibandawd, *s. m.* (penchwiban) Light-headedness; capriciousness, freakishness.

Penchwibanrwydd, *s. m.* (penchwiban) Light-headedness; whimsicality, capriciousness.

Penchwibanu, *v. n.* (penchwiban) To become light-headed, to become hair-brained.

Pendandde, *s. m.* (pen—tandde) A scald-head.

Pendarddiad, *s. m.* (pen—tarddiad) A breaking out of the head, a scabby head; also called *pendandde*, *pengrechi*, and *crach drwg*.

Pendawd, *s. m.—pl.* pendodau (pen) That is chief; that is ultimate; decision. *Pendawd y ty*, the principal of the house.

> Tri phendawd trefn gwaith Duw er peri pob peth; dirymu y drwg, nerthu da, ac amlygu pob gwahaniaeth; mal y gwyper a ddylai oddiwrth na ddylai fod.
>
> The three *tendencies* of the order of God's operation towards causing all things; extenuation of evil, increase of good, and manifestation of every diversity; so that it might be known what should and what should not be. *Barddas.*

Pendeddig, *s. m.—pl. t.* ion (pen—teddig) A principal one, a nobleman.

Pendefig, *s. m.—pl. t.* ion (pen—tefig) One of the highest rank; a grandee, a man of quality.

> Neges pendefig yn rhad.
>
> The errand of a *nobleman* gratis. *Adage.*
>
> Trystan wyn, bendefig llu,
> Car dy genedl, cred a fu,
> A minnau yn benteulu.
>
> Fair Trystan, *chief leader of* a host, love thy nation, overlook what has been, and me the head of the family.
> *Ymdd. Gwalchmai a Thrystan.*

Pendefigaidd, *s. m.* (pendefig) Like a chieftain.

Pendefigawl, *a.* (pendefig) Belonging to the rank of nobility.

Pendefiges, *s. f.—pl. t.* au (pendefig) A woman of high rank; a lady.

Pendefigiaeth, *s. m.—pl. t.* au (pendefig) A state of the highest rank or of pre-eminence.

Pendel, *s. m.—pl. t.* i (pen—tel) A head ornament, or chaplet.

> Gwisgaw a orug Brutus, pendel o ddail y gwinwydd am ei ben.
>
> Brutus put *a chaplet* of the leaves of the vine upon his head. *Brut. y Breninoedd.*

Pendelu, *v. a.* (pendel) To put on a chaplet.

Penderfyn, *s. m.—pl. t.* au (pen—terfyn) A conclusion, a settled point, determination.

Penderfynawl, *a.* (penderfyn) Definitive.

Penderfynedd, *s. m.* (penderfyn) Determinateness, conclusiveness.

Penderfyniad, *s. m.* (penderfyn) A determining; determination, conclusion.

Penderfynrwydd, *s. m.* (penderfyn) Conclusiveness, determinableness.

Penderfynu, *v. a.* (penderfyn) To determine.

Penderfynwr, *s. m.—pl.* penderfynwyr (penderfyn—gwr) A determinator.

Pendew, *a.* (pen—tew) Thick-headed, stupid.

Pendewedd, *s. m.* (pendew) Thick-headedness.

Pendist, *s. m.—pl. t.* iau (pen—dist) A piazza.

Pendodaeth, *s. m.* (pendawd) Superiority.

> Pendodaeth gwraig, digywilydd-dra merch, ac anwybodaeth mab a drosant y byd wyneb i waered.
>
> A wife's *governing*, a girl's shamelessness, and a boy's ignorance, will turn the world upside down. *Adage.*

Pendodawl, *a.* (pendawd) Discriminative.

Pendodi, *v. a.* (pendawd) To render peculiar; to become notable; to discriminate. *Uchelwr pendodi*, a newly created nobleman; *gwr pendodi*, a man become conspicuous, or an upstart

Pendodiad, *s. m.* (pendawd) A rendering particular; a becoming particular; discrimination. *Pendodiaid teulu*, chiefs of a family.

Pendogn, *s. m.* (pen—dogn) A major part.

Pendoll, *a.* (pen—toll) Having a head full of holes. *Llysawen bendoll*, a lamprey.

Pendraphen, *a.* (pen—tra—pen) Having head beyond head; promiscuous. *adv.* Confusedly.

Pendragon, *s. m.* (pen—dragon) A chief leader.

Pentraffollach, *a.* (pen—tra—ffollach) Having the head beyond the fork; having head over heels. *adv.* With head over heels; topsy-turvy.

Pendramynwgl, *a.* (pen—tra—mynwgl) Having the head beyond the neck; headlong. *adv.* With head foremost; topsy-turvy.

Pendrawn, *a.* (pen—trawn) Giddy-headed.

Pendraigl, *a.* (pen—traigl) Having a turning of the head; giddy-headed. *Dyn pendraigl gogeler*, a reprobate hair-brained person.

Pendreigliad, *s. m.* (pendraigl) A turning of the head, a giddiness of the head.

Pendreiglaw, *v. a.* (pendraigl) To turn or roll the head about.

Pendreigledd, *s. m.* (pendraigl) The state of being giddy-headed.

Pendrist, *a.* (pen—trist) Having a drooping head.

Pendristedd, *s. m.* (pendrist) The pensive appearance of the head, pensiveness.

Pendristwch, *s. m.* (pendrist) A droopingness of the head, pensiveness.

Pendro, *s. f.* (pen—tro) A turning of the head, giddiness of the head, a vertigo, the staggers, also called *dera*.

Pendröad, *s. m.* (pendro) A turning round of the head; a becoming giddy-headed.

Pendroch, *a.* (pen—troch) Having the head broken or cut, having the end cut. *Sain bendroch*, a sound ending brokenly.

Pendröedig, *a.* (pendröad) Vertiginous, giddy-headed, hair brained.

Pendröi, *v. n.* (pendro) To become giddy-headed.

Pendröiawg, *a.* (pendröi) Giddy-headed. *Dyn hygoel pendroiawg*, a hair-brained person.

Pendrom, *a.* (*f. of* pendrwm) Heavy-headed.

Pendromi, *v. n.* (pendrom) To become top-heavy.

Pendrondawd, *s. m.* (pendrawn) The state of being giddy-head, or hair-brained. *Pendrondawd Cymmro*, the whimsicality of a Welshman.

Pendronedd, *s. m.* (pendrawn) The state of being hair-brained; whimsicalness.

Pendroni, *v. n.* (pendrawn) To have strange whims in the head, to be hair-brained.

Pendroniad, *s. m.* (pendrawn) A rendering giddy-headed; a becoming giddy or hair-brained.

Pendrwch, *a.* (pen—trwch) Broken-headed; having the end broken, divided, or shattered.

> ——Oneseth pendragon pendrychion o wyr.
>
> The supreme leader made *broken-headed* ones of men. *Cyndelw.*

Pendrwm, *a.* (pen—trwm) Being heavy-headed.

Pendrychawl, *a.* (pendrwch) Head-breaking; end-breaking, end shivering.

Pendrychiad, *s. m.* (pendrwch) A breaking or cutting of the head; a cutting of the end.

Pendrychu, *v. a.* (pendrwch) To break the head, to break, cut, or shiver the end.

Pendrymaidd, *a.* (pendrwm) Rather top-heavy.

Pendrymdawd, *s. m.* (pendrwm) Heaviness of the head, a stupified state.

Pendrymedd, *s. m.* (pendrwm) Heaviness of the head, a state of stupefaction.

Pendrymi, *s. m.* (pendrwm) Heaviness of head.

Pendrymiad, *s. m.* (pendrwm) A rendering top-heavy; a becoming top-heavy.

Pendrymu, *v. n.* (pendrwm) To become top-heavy; to drop the head; to droop.

Pendwmpian, *v. n.* (pen—twmpian) To be nodding the head.

Pendwpa, *a.* (pen—twpa) With a nodding head.

Pendwynaw, *v. n.* (pen—twynaw) To let the head fall different ways; to stagger.

Penddar, *s. f.* (pen—dar) A vertigo, a giddiness.

Penddaredd, *s. m.* (penddar) Giddiness of head.

Penddariad, *s. m.* (penddar) A rendering giddy, a distracting the head; a becoming giddy.

Penddaru, *v. a.* (penddar) To produce a vertigo; to distract the head; to become giddy-headed.

Penddiannod, *a.* (pen—diannod) Indispensable.

Penddifadawl, *a.* (pen—difadawl) Tending to distract the head, stupifying.

Penddifadiad, *s. m.* (pen—difadiad) A distracting the head, a becoming stupified.

Penddifadu, *v. a.* (pen—difadu) To distract the head, to be distracted, to be stupified.

Penddifadden, *a.* (pen—difadden) Indispensable.

Eithr yn benddifadden yr ydym ni yn clodfori dy ddawlawl Fawrydi, am ein cadw y dydd hwn yn ddiangawl.

But in *a most special manner*, we adore thy divine Majesty, for preserving us this day in security. *R. Fychan, Y Dar wisdeb.*

Penddig, *a.* (pen—dig) Having an inflamed head.

Penddiged, *s. f.* (penddig) An inflamed tumour, a phlegmon. *Dail y benddiged*, St. John's wort.

Penddu, *a.* (pen—du) Black-head. *s. c.* Black-head. *Y benddu*, the marsh cudweed: *Penddu*, blackcap, several birds so called; *penddu y brwyn*, the blackcap of the rushes.

Pendduyn, *s. m. dim.* (penddu) A botch, a bile.

Penddüynawg, *a.* (penddüyn) Covered with biles

Penelin, *s. m.—pl. t.* au (pen—elin) The top of the elbow; the elbow.

Nes penelin nog arddwrn.

Nearer is the *elbow* than the wrist. *Adage.*

Penelinad, *s. m.* (penelin) An elbowing.

Penelinaw, *v. a.* (penelin) To push with the elbow, to elbow, to rest on the elbow.

Penelinawd, *s. m.* (penelin) An elbowing.

Penenw, *s. m.—pl. t.* au (pen—enw) A surname.

Penenwad, *s. m.* (penenw) A surnaming.

Penenwawl, *a.* (penenw) Surnamed.

Penenwi, *v. a.* (penenw) To surname.

Penes, *s. f.—pl. t.* au (pen) One that is supreme or of the highest rank of females; a lady.

Penesig, *s. f. dim.* (penes) A smart little lady.

Peneuraid, *a.* (penaur) Gold-headed. *Y beneuraid*, wood crowfoot.

Peneuryn, *s.m. dim* (penaur) The yellow-hammer

Penfadden, *a.* (pen—madden) Having the head forfeited, specially forfeited.

Tri gwystl ni ddygwydd yn benfadden.

Three pledges there are which shall not become *specially forfeited.* *Welsh Laws.*

Rhoddi gwystl i fod yn benfadden yn ammodawl.

To give a pawn which may be *under condition of sale*, at a specified time. *Welsh Laws.*

Penfain, *a.* (pen—main) Having a pointed head or top, copped, tapering to the top.

Penfar, *s. m.—pl. t.* au (pen—bar) A muzzle, a muzzle to hinder a calf from sucking.

Penfas, *a.* (pen—bas) Shallow-pated, dull.

Penfasder, *s. m.* (penfas) A shallow-pated state.

Penfasedd, *s. m.* (penfas) A shallow-pated state.

Penfasu, *v. n.* (penfas) To become shallow-pated.

Penfawr, *a.* (pen—mawr) Large-headed.

Penfeddal, *a.* (pen—meddal) Soft-headed; dull.

Penfeddw, *a.* (pen—meddw) Giddy-headed.

Penfeddwdawd, *s. m* (penfeddw) Giddiness of the head, a swimming of the head.

Penfeddwi, *v. n.* (penfeddw) To become giddy-headed, moidered, or crazed.

Penfeiniaw, *v. a.* (penfain) To acuminate.

Penfelen, *a.* (*f. of* penfelyn) Yellow headed. *Y benfelen* or *greulus*, the groundsel.

Penfelyn, *a.* (pen—melyn) Yellow-headed.

Penfoel, *a.* (pen—moel) Bare-headed, bald.

Penfoelaidd, *a.* (penfoel) Bare-headed.

Penfoeldra, *s. m.* (penfoel) Bare-headed state.

Penfoeledd, *s. m.* (penfoel) A bare-headed state.

Penfoeli, *v. a.* (penfoel) To make bare-headed.

Penfoelni, *s. m.* (penfoel) A bare-headed state.

Penfrag, *s. m.* (pen—brag) A swimming in the head, also called *penddar*, and *pendro*.

Penfras, *a.* (pen—bras) Large-headed, thick-headed, fat-headed. *Y penfras*, the cod-fish.

Penfrasedd, *s. m.* (penfras) A thick-headed state.

Penfro, *s. f.—pl. t.* ydd (pen—bro) A head-land region; also the name of Pembrokeshire.

Penffestin, *s. f.—pl. t.* ion (pen—ffestin) A helmet.

Taraw Arthur yn ei dâl a wnai Frollo, a phei na rybylai y cleddyf ar fodrwyau y benffestin.

Strike Arthur on his forehead was what Frollo did, so that the sword was blunted on the rings of his *helmet*. *Gr. ab Arthur.*

Penffestiniaw, *v. a.* (penffestin) To helmet.

Penffestiniawg, *a.* (penffestin) Wearing a helmet.

Penffestr, *s. m.—pl. t.* au (pen—ffestr) A head-stall; a collar.

Penffetur, *a.* (pen—ffetur) Headstrong, obstinate

Penffeturedd, *s. m.* (penffetur) Peremptoriness.

Penffetus, *a.* (pen—ffetus) Head-strong.

Penffluwch, *a.* (pen—ffluwch) Bushy-headed.

Penffluwchedd, *s.* (penffluwch) Bushiness of head.

Penffol, *a.* (pen—ffol) Silly-headed, block-headed.

Penffoledd, *s. m.* (penffol) Blockishness, stupidity

Penffrwyn, *s. f.—pl. t.* au (pen—ffrwyn) A head-stall; a muzzle.

Penffrwynaw, *v. a.* (penffrwyn) To muzzle.

Pengadarn, *a.* (pen—cadarn) Strong-headed.

Pengadarn yw barn pob diwybod.

Obstinate is the opinion of every Ignoramus. *Adage.*

Pengaead, *a.* (pen—cead) Close-headed.

Pengaled, *a.* (pen—caled) Having a hard head; headstrong. *Y bengaled*, the knapweed; also called *clafrllys*, *cramenog*, and *penlas*.

Pengaledrwydd, *s. m.* (pen—caled) Obstinacy.

Pengaledu, *v. n.* (pengaled) To become hard-headed; to grow obstinate or headstrong.

Pengam, *a.* (pen—cam) Wry-headed.

Pengamedd, *s. m.* (pengam) The state of having the head awry; perverseness.

Pengamiad, *s. m.* (pengam) A turning the head awry, a bending the head.

Pengamleddf, *a.* (pengam—lleddf) Having the head, or end, turning aside.

Pengamrwydd, *s. m.* (pengam) Wryness of the head, the state of having the head turning aside.

Pengamu, *v. a.* (pengam) To turn the head awry, to bend down the head; to nod.

Pengamwr, *s. m.—pl.* pengamwyr (pengam—gwr) A nodder, one who bends the head.

Pengarn, *a.* (pen—carn) The hard part of the head of some animals; a beak.

Pengemi, *s. m.* (pengam) Wryness of the head.

Pengernyn, *s. m. dim.* (pengarn) A gurnard, also called *penheirnyn* and *penhaiarn*.

Penglo, *s. m.—pl. t.* au (pen—clo) A close; a stop at the end, a conclusion.

Penglöad, *s. m.* (penglo) A closing up the end.

Penglog, *s. f.—pl. t.* au (pen—clog) A skull, a noddle; a thickhead, a blockhead.

> Deuparth clod yn mhenglog.
>
> Two parts of fame in the *skull*. *Adage.*

Penglogaidd, *a.* (penglog) Blockheaded.

Penglogedd, *s. m.* (penglog) Blockishness.

Penglogeiddrwydd, *s. m.* (penglog) Blockishness.

Pengloges, *s. f.—pl. t.* au (penglog) A blockheaded female.

Penglogfa, *s. f.* (penglog) A golgotha.

Penglogi, *v. n.* (penglog) To grow blockheaded.

Penglogyn, *s. m. dim.* (penglog) A numskull.

Penglöi, *v. a.* (penglo) To close the end, to close.

Pengiwm, *s. m.—pl.* penglymau (pen—clwm) A knot at the end.

Pengoch, *a.* (pen—coch) Red-headed. *Y bengoch*, the knotgrass; also called *y benborth*, *y dinboeth*, and *clinog goch*.

Pengochedd, *s. m.* (pengoch) Redness of the head.

Pengochi, *v. n.* (pengoch) To grow red-headed.

Pengoll, *a.* (pen—coll) Having the head lost, having the end lost or hidden.

Pengollawl, *a.* (pengoll) Having the termination lost; a term in grammar.

> Unawdl union y byddo ei gyrch yn bengollawl.
>
> The antrythm direct that has its recurrence *with a lost* termination. *Gr. Robert, Dwned.*

Pengolli, *v. n.* (pengoll) To lose the termination.

Pengrach, *a.* (pen—crach) Scabby-headed.

Pengrachedd, *s. m.* (pengrach) Scabbiness of the head.

Pengrech, *a.* (*f. of* pengrych) Curly-headed; having the end rough.

Pengrechi, *s. m.* (pengrach) Scabbiness of head.

Pengrechleddf, *a.* (pengrech—lleddf) Soft with rough termination; a term in grammar.

Pengrechni, *s. m.* (pengrach) Scabbiness of the head, the state of having a scald head.

Pengrest, *a.* (pen—crest) Scurfy-headed.

Pengroes, *a.* (pen—croes) Having a cross head, having the end crossed.

Pengroesi, *v. a.* (pengroes) To cross the head.

Pengroesni, *s. m.* (pengroes) The state of having the head, or end, crossed.

Pengron, *a.* (*f. of* pengrwn) Round-headed.

Pengrwn, *a.* (pen—crwn) Round-headed.

Pengrych, *a.* (pen—crych) Rough-headed; curly-headed; frizzle-headed; having rough or curly ends.

> Telamon, gwr grymus oedd, ag ymadrawdd eglur ganthaw, a gwallt du pengrych ar ei ben: a diwal a chreulawn oedd wrth ei elynion.
>
> Telamon was an athletic man, he had a clear pronunciation, and he had black hair *with curled ends* on his head; and fierce and cruel was he to his enemies. *Ystori Dared.*

Pengrychedd, *s. m.* (pengrych) Curly-headedness.

Pengrychiad, *s. m.* (pengrych) A becoming curly-headed, or frizzle-headed.

Pengrychni, *s. m.* (pengrych) Curly-headedness.

Pengrychu, *v. a.* (pengrych) To render rough-headed or curly-headed.

Pengrynawg, *a.* (pengrwn) Round-headed.

Pengrynedd, *s. m.* (pengrwn) Roundness of head.

Pengrynen, *s. f. dim.* (pengrwn) A round-head.

Pengryniad, *s. m.—pl.* pengryniaid (pengrwn) A round-head.

Pengrynu, *v. a.* (pengrwn) To grow round-headed; to grow to a head, as a cabbage.

Pengrynyn, *s. m dim.* (pengrwn) A round head.

Penguwch, *s. m.—pl. t.* iau (pen—cuwch) The fore part or poke of any head covering, a bonnet, a cap; also the capping or the work that joins the two pieces of a flail together.

> Penguwch melyn a wisgai merch newydd-weddawg.
>
> A yellow *bonnet* used to be worn by a woman newly married. *Hen Ddefodau.*

> Penguwch, ceiniawg a dal.
>
> A *bonnet*, its value is a penny. *Welsh Laws.*

Pengwaith, *s. m.* (pen—gwaith) A chief work.

Pengwas, *s. m.—pl.* pengweision (pen—gwas) A head servant.

Pengwastrawd, *s. m.—pl.* pengwastrodion (pen—gwastrawd) A head groom, being the sixth officer in the prince's household.

> Y pengwastrawd a gaiff groen ych y gauaf, a chroen ych yr haf, i wneuthur cebystrau i feirch y brenin.
>
> The *head groom* shall have the skin of an ox in winter and the skin of an ox in summer, to make halters for the horses of the king. *Welsh Laws.*

Pengweithiwr, *s. m.—pl.* pengweithwyr (pen—gwaith—gwr) A head workman.

Pengwleddwr, *s. m.—pl.* pengwleddwyr (pen—gwleddwr) One who is chief in the carousal.

Pengyrnig, *a.* (pen—cyrnig) Having the head pointed or tapering. *Bun pengyrnig*, a maid with a tapering crown.

Penhaiarn, *s. m.—pl. t.* od (pen—haiarn) The gurnard; also called *pengernyn*, and *penheiernyn*. *Penhaiarn coch*, the red gurnard; also called *ysgyfarnog y mor*.

Penhebogydd, *s. m.—pl. t.* ion (pen—hebogydd) The chief falconer; being the fourth officer of the royal household.

> Penhebogydd a ddyly drayan dirwy yr hebogyddion, ac amobr eu merched.
>
> The *head falconer* shall claim the third of the fine of the falconers, and the maiden fee of their daughters. *Welsh Laws.*

Penhebogyddiaeth, *s. m.* (penhebogydd) The office of the chief falconer.

Penheiernyn, *s. m. dim.* (penhaiarn) A gurnard.

Penhoeden, *a.* (pen—hoeden) Giddy-headed.

Penhwntian, *v. n.* (pen—hwntian) To have the head ready to fall; to be tottering.

Penhwntiawl, *a.* (pen—hwntiawl) Top-heavy.

Penhwyad, *s. m.* (pen—hwyad) The pike, or jack.

Penhwyliar, *s. m.* (pen—hwyliar) A main mast.

Penhynaif, *s. m.—pl.* penhynefion (pen—hynaif) A chief of the elders; a title given to the tributary princes of the first rank, who did homage to the monarch.

> Caradawg Freichfras penhynaif yn Nghernyw, ac Arthur yn benteyrnedd.
>
> Caradog with the brawny arm *chief of elders* in Cornwall, and Arthur the supreme prince. *Trioedd.*

Peniadur, *s. m.—pl. t.* on (peniad) That is the head; a principal.

> Penial beirdd llawr ceinwawr ced;
> Peniadur dewr tur Dyfed.
>
> The sovereign of the bards of the *floor* gloriously shining with treasure; the *crown work* of the gay rampart of Dyfed. *Prydydd Bychan, i Gynan ab Hywel.*

Penial, *s. m.* (pen) A capital, a helmet.

> Dafydd yw——
> Penial cerdd, dyfal dafawd.
>
> Davydd is the *chief* of song, of persevering tongue. *Mad. Benfras.*

> Gnaws edyn adnabod bore;
> Gnaws am ben penial ydre.
>
> Congenial for the birds to recognise the morn: congenial round the bowl the *chief* of the mansion. *Gwalchmai.*

> Ni symudawdd Peredur ei feddwl er gweled y penial a oedd am ben Cai.
>
> Peredur did not change his mind for seeing the *helmet* that was on the head of Cai. *H. Peredur—Mabinogion.*

Penialawg, *a.* (penial) Having a capital or chief; wearing a head-piece or helmet.

Penialu, *v. a.* (penial) To surmount with a capital; to put on a head-piece.

Peniannawl, *a.* (peniant) Being a capitation.

v. a. (peniant) To make a capitation.

m. (pen) A capitation, a heading.

dim. (pen) A little head; a nipple.

a. (pen—camp) Masterly, chief of *Saer penigamp*, a masterly wright.

Penigan, *s. f.—pl. t. i* (penig) A pink. *Penigan ruddgoch*, clove pink.

Penlas, *a.* (pen—glas) Blue-headed. *Y benlas*, field scabious; also called pengaled. Varieties: *Penlas yr yd*, and *penlas wen*, corn bluebottle.

Penlasu, *v. n.* (penlas) To become blue-headed.

Penlesni, *s. m.* (penlas) Blueness of the head.

Penlin, *s. m.—pl. t.* iau (pen—glin) The head of the knee; the knee.

Penliniad, *s. m.* (penlin) A kneeling.

Penliniaw, *v. a.* (penlin) To fall on the knees, to kneel. *s. m.* The act of kneeling.

> Denai un yn rhedeg, ac a benliniai iddo, ac a fynegai iddo; Athraw, pa beth a wnaf i gael meddiannu bywyd tragywyddawl!
>
> One came running, and *he kneeled* to him, and spoke to him thus; Master, what shall I do to obtain life everlasting.
> *W. Salisbury.*
>
> Maent hwy yn cymeryd mwy o hoffder mewn penlinio, gweddïo, ac ymprydio, nog ydi y bydolion yn na y byd hwn.

Penliniwr, *s. m.* (penlin—gwr) A kneeler.

Penlöyn, *s. m. dim.* (pen—glöyn) The blackcap; the titmouse. Varieties: *Penlöyn mwyaf*, *y wine*, the chaffinch; *pela glas bach*, the ox-eye; *y lleian*, *gwas y dryw*, *yswidw*, *sywidw*, the titmouse.

> Gwell penlöyn yn llaw no hwyad yn awyr.
>
> A *titmouse* in hand is better than a duck in the air; A bird in hand is worth two in the bush. *Adage.*

Penllad, *s. m.—pl. t.* au (pen—llad) A chief good, the highest blessing. *Rhad penllad*, the grace or gift over measure.

Penlle, *s. m.* (penlle) Where the head should be; a bead stead; a numskull.

Penllian, *s. m.—pl.* penllieiniau (pen—llian) A head-cloth.

> Penllian, wyth geiniawg a dal.
>
> A *head-cloth*, eight-pence is its value. *Welsh Laws.*

Penllinyn, *s. m.* (pen—llinyn) A head-band.

Penllorcan, *s. m.* (pen—llorcan) A jolt-head.

Penlluestai, *s. c.* (pen—lluestai) The chief arranger of tents; a quartermaster-general.

Penllwyd, *a.* (pen—llwyd) Hoary-headed, grey-headed. *s. m.—pl. t.* ion. The grayling; the sewin. *Y benllwyd*, common cudweed.

Penllwydaw, *v. n.* (penllwyd) To become grey-headed or hoary-headed.

Penllwydedd, *s. m.* (penllwyd) Greyness of the head, grey-headedness.

Penllwydeg, *s. f.* (penllwyd) A net for catching graylings, young salmon so called.

> Penllwydeg, neu rwyd penllwydiaid, deuddeg ceiniawg a dal.
>
> A *grayling net*, or *net for graylings*, twelve pence is its value. *Welsh Laws.*

Penllwydi, *s. m.* (penllwyd) Greyness of head.

Penllwydiad, *s. m.—pl.* penllwydiaid (penllwyd) The grayling or sewin.

Penllwydni, *s. m.* (penllwyd) Hoariness or greyness of the head.

Penllyw, *s. m.—pl. t.* iau (pen—llyw) The head-leader; a term in building for the stone next to, or which secures, the corner stone.

Penllywawdr, *s. m.—pl.* penllywodron (penllyw) A chief director or governor.

Penllywodraeth, *s. m.* (penllywawdr) Supreme government or direction.

Penllywodraethwr, *s. m.—pl.* penllywodraethwyr (penllywodraeth—gwr) A chief governor.

Penllywodraethydd, *s. m.—pl. t.* ion (penllywodraeth) A governor general.

Penllywydd, *s. m.—pl. t.* ion (pen—llywydd) A sovereign lord.

Penllywyddiaeth, *s. m.* (penllywydd) Supreme dominion; sovereignty.

Pennill, *s. m.—pl. t.* ion (pen—dill) A prime division or part; a complete division; wattle; a pannel, a stall, a pane, a stanza, or strophe, an epigram.

> Gwell car cell no char pennill.
>
> Better the chamber friend than the *song* friend. *Adage.*
>
> Pennill yw nifer o fraichian, o'r un neu fwy o'r cyhydeddion, lle y gadw cynbariad, cynghanedd, gair cyrch, gair toddaid, a chyforhtiad, ar yr un caniad.
>
> A *stanza* is a number of verses, of one or more of the metricities, where the common initial, concatenation, word of modulation, and parallel, are preserved on the same rhythm.
> *W. Middleton.*

Pennilliach, *s. pl. dim.* (pennill) Trifling verses.

Pennilliad, *s. m.* (pennill) A forming a stanza.

Pennilliaw, *v. a.* (pennill) To form a stanza.

> Cadwynawdl—modd gorchestawl iawn a fydd hwn ar odli a phennilliaw.
>
> The catenated rhyme, this is a very masterly mode of rhyming and *of forming of stanzas*. *Barddas*

Pennilliawg, *a.* (pennill) Consisting of stanzas.

> Mewn cerdd bennilliawg, caffer bob pennill o'r gerdd yn gyfnifer banau.
>
> In a composition *divided into stanzas*, let every stanza be formed of the same number of verses. *Barddas.*

Pennod, *s. f.—pl. t.* au (pen—nod) A concluding mark; a complete period; a chapter.

Pennodawl, *a.* (pennod) Belonging to a chapter.

Pennodi, *v. a.* (pennod) To mark the end or conclusion; to divide into chapters.

Pennoeth, *s. m.* (pen—noeth) A bare head. *a.* Bare-headed.

Pennoethi, *v. a.* (pennoeth) To make bare-headed; to uncover the head.

Pennoethiad, *s. m.* (pennoeth) A making bare—the act of uncovering the head.

Penodawl, *a.* (penawd) Particular, definitive, especial. *Yn benodawl*, especially.

Penodedig, *a.* (penawd) Defined, or specified.

Penodi, *v. a.* (penawd) To particularize, to specify; to constitute, to appoint, to assign.

Penodiad, *s. m.—pl. t.* au (penawd) A particularizing, or specifying; a specification, assignation, allotment.

Penodiaeth, *s. m.* (penawd) Specification

Penodoldeb, *s. m.* (penodawl) Definitiveness, particularity, speciality.

Penodolder, *s. m.* (penodawl) Specialness.

Penodoledd, *s. m.* (penodawl) Specialness.

Penodoli, *v. a.* (penodawl) To render definitive.

Penodolrwydd, *s. m.* (penodawl) Specialness.

Penodrwydd, *s. m.* (penawd) Particularity.

Penodwr, *s. m.—pl.* penodwyr (penawd—gwr) A specifier; one who assigns.

Penodydd, *s. m.—pl. t.* ion (penawd) A specifier

Penon, *s. f.—pl. t.* au (pen) A pennant.

Penorawg, *a.* (penawr) Wearing a helmet.

Penorawl, *a.* (penawr) Principal, supreme.

> Tri haucyuyddion teyrnedd Ynys Prydain: Prydain ab Aedd Mawr, Dyfnwal Moelmud, a Bran ab Llyr Lledialth; sef gor, a trefu eu trefn hwy ar deyrnedd Ynys Prydain, hyd oedd barnu hwy yn benorawl ar bob trefnau ereill
>
> The three consolidators of the monarchy of the Isle of Britain Prydain son of Aedd the Great, Dyfnwal Moelmud, and Bran son of Llyr Lledialth; for the best regulation was their regulation of the monarchy of the Isle of Britain, so that they were deemed *superior* over every other regulation. *Trioedd.*

Penori, *v. a* (penawr) To render supreme or principal; to put on a helmet.

Penoriad, *s. m.* (penawr) A rendering supreme; a wearing a helmet; a putting on a helmet.

Penpingion, *s. m.* (pen--pinc) Branchy head; the name of a droll character in ancient tales. *Penpingion, enw un o borthorion Arthur*, Penpingion, one of Arthur's door-keepers.

> Penpingion a ymddai ar ei ben er arbed ei draed.
>
> *Penpingion* would go upon his head to save his feet. *H. Culhwch—Mabinogion.*

Penpryd, *s. m.* (pen—pryd) A visage.

Penre, *s. f.* (pen—rhe) A hair lace, a fillet.

Penrhaith, *s. m.—pl.* penrheithian (pen—rhaith) The chief of the law: that has supreme right; a supreme claimant; a principal evidence. *Brenin penrhaith Ynys Prydain*, the king of supreme authority of the Isle of Britain.

> Drag y lliw y llaw oedd benrhaith ei luoedd.
>
> Red is the colour of the hand that was the *supreme law* of his armies *D. ab Llywarch Mew.*
>
> Meibion Brychan Brycheiniawg a aethynt yn benrheithiau yn Yspaen.
>
> The sons of Brychan Brycheiniawg became as *chiefs of jurisprudence* in Spain. *Llyfr Achau.*

Penrheithiant, *s. m.* (penrhaith) Supreme jurisdiction; sovereignty of law.

Penrheithiaw, *v. a.* (penrhaith) To constitute supreme jurisdiction.

Penrheithiawg, *a.* (penrhaith) Having supreme jurisdiction or loyal supremacy.

Penrudd, *a.* (pen—rhudd) Ruddy headed. *Y benrudd*, the common marjoram.

Penrwym, *s. m—pl. t.* au (pen—rhwym) A head-band, a hair-lace, or fillet, also called *penre, ffunen*, and *ysnoden*.

Penrwymaw, *v. a.* (penrwym) To bind the head.

> Na phenrwyma yr ych a fo yn dyludo yr yd.
>
> *Thou shalt* not *muzzle* the ox that shall be carrying the corn. *W. Salisbury.*

Penrwymiad, *s. m.* (penrwym) Binding the head

Penrwymyn, *s. m. dim.* (penrwym) A head-band

Penrydd, *a.* (pen--rhydd) Loose headed; dissolute; having loose ending. *Geiriau penryddion*, unconnected words; *can benrydd*, blank verse.

Penryn, *s. m.—pl. t.* oedd (pen—rhyn) End of a point, a promontory, cape, or head-land. It forms the names of several places, as *Penryn Blathaon*, Cathness, *Penryn Rhionydd*, the point of Galloway, in Scotland, *Penryn Penwyth*, Land's End, in Cornwall.

Penrynawg, *a.* (penryn) Forming a headland.

Penrynu, *v. n.* (penryn) To form a headland.

Pensach, *s. f.* (pen - sach) The mumps.

Pensaer, *s. m.—pl.* penseiri (pen—saer) A chief architect, a chief wright.

Pensaernïaeth, *s. m.* (pensaer) Architecture.

Pensaernïaidd, *a.* (pensaer) Architective.

Pensag, *s. m.* (pen - sag) The hop-plant; hops.

Pensedd, *s. f.* (pen - sedd) A supreme seat.

> Mair, ddeddfawl ddwyfawl, ddiwael bensedd.
>
> Mary, moral and divine, whose *throne* is without frailty. *Dafydd Ddu, Hiraddug.*

Pensel, *s. m.—pl. t.* au (pen—sel) A supreme object; a grand standard.

> Gorau arwydd gan Wyddyl
> Melyn a choch yn mlaen cwyl;
> Urdda bensel Llywelyn;
> Arddel hwy a'r ddeulliw hyn.
>
> The choicest taken with the Irish are yellow and red in the front of onset; do thou consecrate the *supreme standard* of Llywelyn; do thou lead them on with these two colours. *Iolo Goch, i O. Glyndyfrdwy.*

Penseliaeth, *s. m.* (pensel) The office of bearing the grand standard.

Pensigl, *a.* (pen—sigl) Having a shake of head.

Pensiglad, *s. m.* (pensigl) A shaking of the head

Pensiglaw, *v. a.* (pensigl) To shake the head.

> Caseion—
> A'm dygtynent, tan drai tr'y,
> A thau bensiglo ataf.
>
> Enemies treat me with contempt, in passing by, and with *wagging* their *heads* at me. *Edm. Pryss.*

Pensiglwr, *s. m.—pl.* pensiglwyr (pensigl—gwr) A wagger or shaker of the head.

Penswydd, *s. f.—pl. t.* au (pen—swydd) A chief or principal office.

Penswyddawg, *s. m.—pl.* penswyddogion (penswydd) A chief of office, a chief officer.

Penswyddwr, *s. m.—pl.* penswyddwyr (penswydd—gwr) A chief officer.

Pensyfrdan, *a.* (pen—syfrdan) A giddiness.

Pensyfrdandawd, *s. m.* (pensyfrdan) Distraction

Pensyfrdaniad, *s. m.* (pensyfrdan) A distracting the head; a becoming giddy-headed.

Pensyfrdanu, *v. a.* (pensyfrdan) To distract the head; to become stupified.

Pentan, *s. m.—pl. t.* au (pen—tan) A fire back, a fire side; a chimney corner. *Cadw gwyl bentan, gwyliaw gwyl bentan*, to sit up all night

Pentanfaen, *s. m.* (pentan—maen) The stone that forms the fire-back.

Penteulu, *s. m.* (pen--teulu) The chief of the family, the president of the household, the patron of the family.

> Y penteulu a ddyly fod yn fab i'r brenin, neu yn nai, neu yn frawd, neu yn gyfuwch gwr ag y galler penteulu o hono.
>
> The *president of the household* should be a son of the king, or a nephew, or a brother, or a man of so high a rank as he may be made a *president of the household*. *Welsh Laws.*

Penteuluaeth, *s. m.* (penteulu) The office of a president, or patron of the household.

Pentewyn, *s. m.—pl. t.* ion (pen—tewyn) A fire-brand.

> Gwae y cynhennus mewn gwlad!
> Pentewynion uffern ydynt.
>
> Woe to the contentious in a country! They are the *firebrands* of hell. *Mor. Llwyd.*

Penteyrnedd, *s. m.* (pen—teyrnedd) The supreme of princes; a sovereign.

> Arthur yn benteyrnedd yn Mhenryn Rhionydd yn y Gogledd, Cyndeyrn Garthwys yn benesgob, a Gwrthmwl Wledig yn benhynaf.
>
> Arthur a *supreme of princes* at the promontory of Rhionydd in the north, and Cyndeyrn Garthwys archbishop, and Gwrthmwl Wledig chief of elders. *Trioedd.*

Pentir, *s. m.—pl. t.* edd (pen—tir) A headland, or promontory; also a term used in *Mon* for a land steward. *Pentir Ceinion*, Cape Clear, in Ireland.

Pentref, *s. m.—pl. t.* ydd (pen—tref) The head of a township, a village, or hamlet; also the outskirt or suburb of a city.

Pentrefaeth, *s. f.* (pentref) A villagery.

Pentrefaidd, *a.* (pentref) Villatic, village.

Pentrefawg, *a.* (pentref) Having a village.

Pentrefawl, *a.* (pentref) Belonging to a village.

Pentrefwr, *s. m.* (pentref—gwr) A villager.

Pentreisiad, *s. m.* (pen—treisiad) A supreme oppressor or tyrant.

Pentreisiwr, *s. m.—pl.* pentreiswyr (pen—treisiwr) A supreme tyrant or oppressor.

Pentrethwr, *s. m.—pl.* pentrethwyr (pen—trethwr) A chief tax-man or receiver of taxes.

Pentwr, *s. m.—pl.* pentyrau (pen—twr) A raised heap or pile.

Pentwynaw, *v. a.* (pen—twynaw) To drop the head in different directions.

Pentwynawl, *a.* (pen—twynawl) Head-nodding.

Pentwyniad, *s. m.* (pen—twyniad) A nodding.

Penty, *s. m.—pl. t.* au (pen—ty) A building added to the main house; penthouse, a shed: also the head house.

> Pa'nd da yw'r ty yma ym!
> Pa'nd hwn yw'r penty cinym!
>
> Why is not this house good for me! Is not this the *first house* for me! *L. G. Cothi.*

Pentyrawg, *a.* (pentwr) Having a heap or pile.

Pentyrawl, *a.* (pentwr) Accumulative.

Pentyredig, *a.* (pentwr) Accumulated, heaped.

Pentyredd, *s. m.* (pentwr) A heaped state.

Pentyriad, *s.m.—pl. t.* an (pentwr) Accumulation.

Pentyru, *v. a.* (pentwr) To heap up, to accumulate; to amass.

> Y cnwd a bentyrir yr amser hwnw, ac a osodir i gadw erbyn amser i ddawed, a'r pryd y bydd raid wrtho.
>
> The produce *will be accumulated* in that time, and will be put to be kept against the time to come, and the season when there will be a necessity for it. *Ier. Owain.*

Pentyrwr, *s. m.* (pentwr—gwr) A heaper.

Pentywysawg, *s. m.—pl.* pentywysogion (pen—tywysawg) A supreme prince.

Pentywysogaeth, *s. f.* (pentywysawg) A supreme principality.

Penn, *v. a.* (pen) To render chief or principal; to become chief, to surpass, also to specify, to fix, to apppint.

> Tri chyflawnder gwynfyd: cyfran yn mhob anianwdd ac un cyflawn yn penu; cyfymdd yn a phob awen, ac yn un rhagori; cariad at bob byw a bod, a thuag at un, sef Duw, yn benaf; ac yn y tri un yma y saif cyflawnder nef a gwynfyd.
>
> The three plenitudes of the intellectual world: participation in every nature, with a plenary one *predominating*, conformity with every cast of genius, and in one excelling; love towards every life and existence, and towards one, that is God, more especially, and in these three ones consist the plenitude of heaven and felicity. *Barddas.*

Penuchaf, *s. m.* (pen—uchaf) An upper end.

Penuchawg, *a.* (pen—uchawg) Being pre-eminent

> Tri chlau eu parau, fal Peryddon:
> Tri chlown penyn, penuchogion;
> Tri chlo ar eu bro rhag bradogion
>
> Three with persevering spears, like Peryddon; three keystones of a capital, *superior ones*, three safe-guards over their country against depredators. *D. Benfras.*

Penwag, *a.* (pen—gwag) Empty-headed. *s. m. —pl. penweig.* A herring; also called *ysgadan*. *Penweig mair*, pilchards.

Penwan, *a.* (pen—gwan) Weak-headed. *Dynionos penweinion*, weak-headed mortals.

Penwander, *s. m.* (penwan) Weakness of head.

Penwar, *s. m.—pl. t.* au (pen—gwar) A headstall, a muzzle; a barnacle, in farriery.

> Pwn âr en, fal penwar yw.
>
> A load on a chin, like a *muzzle* it seems. *Iolo Goch, i'w farf.*

Penwen, *a.* (*f. of* penwyn) White-headed.

Penwendid, *s. m.* (penwan) Weakness of the head, brain-sickness, infatuation.

Penwg, *s. m.* (pen) That is superior, that is special or peculiar.

Penwisg, *s. f.* (pen—gwisg) A head-dress.

Penwisgiad, *s. m.—pl. t.* au (penwisg) The dressing of the head; a head-dress.

Penwn, *s. m.—pl.* penynau (pen—wn) A banner.

Penwyn, *a.* (pen—gwŷn) White-headed. *Y penwyn, y bod penwyn*, the bald buzzard.

Penwŷnder, *s. m.* (penwyn) Whiteness of head.

Penwŷnedd, *s. m.* (penwyn) Whiteness of head.

Penwŷni, *s. m.* (penwyn) Whiteness of head.

Penwynu, *v.* (penwyn) To grow white-headed.

Penŵyr, *a.* (pen—gŵyr) Having the head inclined, wry-headed.

Penŵyraw, *v. a.* (penŵyr) To incline the head.

Penŵyredd, *s. m.* (penŵyr) Inclination of head.

Penyd, *s. m.* (pan) Atonement, penance.

Penydiad, *s. m.* (penyd) A doing penance.

Penydiaw, *v. a.* (penyd) To atone, to do penance.

Penydiawl, *a* (penyd) Atoning, expiatory.

Penydiwr, *s. m.—pl.* penydwyr (penyd—gwr) An atoner; one who performs penance.

Penydu, *v. a.* (penyd) To atone, to do penance.

> Cyd elwynt i llanau i benydu,
> Dadl diau angau i eu trawdda.
>
> Whilst they went to churches *to do penance*, the certain stroke of death pervaded them. *Aneurin.*

Penydd, *s. m.—pl. t.* ion (pan) An atonement.

Penyddawl, *a.* (penydd) Atoning, expiating.

> Gwaith gwynfydig dwyn—
> Daiar a nef cyn poen oddef cun penyddawl.
>
> A blessed work, to bear off earth and heaven before suffering of punishment, thou *atoning* prince. *Rhiwardyn.*

Penygawl, *a.* (penwg) Discriminative.

Penygen, *s. f. dim.* (paneg) The region of the entrails, the paunch.

> Nid llawnach yr enaid, er llenwi y benygen.
>
> The soul is not the more satisfied, though the *paunch* be filled. *Catwg.*

Penygu, *v. a.* (penwg) To render supreme, peculiar, or notable; to discriminate.

> Penygai glod penigamp,
> Pennod, a chwympod, a champ.
>
> *He would discriminate* superlative praise, in design, compass, and execution. *Gr. Gryg, i D. ab Gwilym.*

Penyn, *s. m. dim.* (pen) A capital of a pillar.

Penynad, *s. m.—pl. t.* on (pen—ynad) A chief judge, a chief justice.

Penynadaeth, *s. m.* (penynad) Chief justiceship.

Penysgafn, *a.* (pen—ysgafn) Light-headed.

Penysgafnder, *s. m.* (penysgafn) Light-headedness, giddiness of the head.

Penystafellydd, *s. m.—pl. t.* ion (pen—ystafellydd) High chamberlain.

Pepra, *v. a.* (pebr) To be chattering.

Pepraeth, *s. m.* (pebr) Chattering, babbling.

Pepriad, *s. m.* (pebr) A chattering, a chatting.

Pepru, *v. a.* (pebr) To prate to chat, to babble.

Peprwn, *s. m.* (pebr) Chattering, babbling.

> Er pan fu Elphin yn nghywrysedd
> Maelgwn, neus porthes peprwn pell dyfrydedd!
>
> Ever since Elphin has been in the dispute of Maelgwn, has not *babbling* brought extensive woe! *Ph. Brydydd.*

Pepryn, *s. m.* (pebr) A chatter-box, a chatterer.

Per, *s. f.—pl. t.* an (py—er) That pervades, that involves, that is involved; a spit; also sweet fruit; pears, pear-trees. *Cig ar y ber*, meat on the spit.

> Per goreu gormes
> Yn mhlymnwyd maes.
>
> *Pear-trees* the best of intruders in the conflict of the plain. *Taliesin, Cad Goddeu.*

Per, *a.* (py—er) Delicious, sweet. *Afalau perion, ac afalau surion*, cultivated apples, and sour apples; *eirinen ber*, a sweet plumb; *llais per*, a sweet voice.

Periad, *s. m.* (peràn) A rendering sweet or savory, a becoming sweet or delicious.

Peraidd, *a.* (per) Somewhat delicious, sweetish, sweet, pleasant.

Perain. *s. pl. aggr.* (per) Pears; also called *gellaig*, *ellaig*, *rhwnyn*, and *peranau*.

> Un flas, neu yn felysach
> A'r perain wyd o'r pren iach.

> Of the same savour, or more delicious than the *pears*, art thou, from the luxuriant tree. *S. Cent.*

Peran, *s. c. dim.*—*pl. t.* au (per) A pear.

Peranen, *s. f. dim.* (peran) A single pear.

Perarogl, *s. m.*—*pl. t.* au (per—arogl) A perfume, or aromatic.

Peraroglai, *s. c.*—*pl.* peraroglеion (perarogl) A perfumer, a dealer in sweet scents.

Peraroglaidd, *a.* (perarogl) Odoriferous.

Perarogledig, *a.* (perarogl) Perfumed.

Peraroglеdd, *s. m.* (perarogl) Perfumery, odoriferousness, fragrancy.

Perarogli, *v. a.* (perarogl) To perfume.

Peraroglіad, *s. m.* (perarogl) A perfuming.

Peraroglіant, *s. m.* (perarogl) Fragrancy.

Peraroglus, *a.* (perarogl) Odorous, fragrant.

Peraroglusaw, *v. a.* (peraroglus) To render odoriferous or aromatic; to become odoriferous.

Peraroglwr, *s. m.*—*pl.* peraroglwyr (perarogl—gwr) A perfumer, a dealer in aromatics.

Peraroglydd, *s. m.*—*pl. t.* ion (perarogl) A perfumer, a dealer in aromatics.

Perarwynt, *s. m.* (per—arwynt) A perfume.

Perâu, *v. a.* (per) To render sweet, to become sweet, delicious, or fragrant.

Perawr, *s. m.*—*pl.* perorion (per) A musician.

Perbren, *s. m.*—*pl. t.* i (per—pren) A pear-tree.

Perc, *s. m.* (per) That is close, compact, or trim; a compact spot; a perch.

> Yn isel barsel dan berc.

> Being a low mark under a *perch*. *I. ab R. ab Ieuan Llwyd.*

Perc, *a.* (per) Compact, trim, neat, perk.

Percaidd, *a.* (perc) Tending to involve, wrap, or make compact.

Percawl, *a.* (perc) Involving, wrapping; tending to be compact or trim; perching.

Perced, *s. f.*—*pl. t.* au (perc) That encloses or wraps; a bow net, a wrapper.

> Pilin rhag drycin a drig;
> Perced ddeulled Wyddelig.

> A covering against the angry storm, an Irish *wrapper* of two breadths. *D. Ll. ab Ll. ab Gruffudd, Ysfantell.*

Percediad, *s. m.* (perched) A closing, a wrapping.

Percedu, *v. a.* (perced) To involve, to close.

Percell, *s. f.*—*pl. t.* oedd (perc) A place that is compact or safe; a store place, a magazine.

> Hwnw——a wnaeth bercell o Ddinas Basing.

> That one made a *store place* of Basingwerk.
> *I. Brwch o Fawddwy, Ll. Achau.*

Perceta, *v. a.* (perced) To amass; to gain.

Percetwr, *s. m.*—*pl.* percetwyr (perced—gwr) One who makes compact or shuts in; one who heaps together.

Perciad, *s. m.* (perc) A rendering compact, close, neat, or trim.

Percin, *a.* (perc) Tending to involve, make compact, neat, tidy, or trim, a trimming.

Percini, *s. m.* (percin) The mesentery.

Percu, *v. a.* (perc) To trim, to make smart.

Percus, *a.* (perc) Tidy, smart, trim, perk.

Percusaw, *v. a.* (percus) To render tidy, trim, or smart; to become smart, or perk.

Percusedd, *s. m.* (percus) Trimness, smartness.

Percusrwydd, *s. m.* (percus) Smartness, neatness.

Perchen, *s. c.*—*pl. t.* oedd (parch) A possessor, owner, or proprietor.

> Call mi bian, angall bum berchen.

> Cunning is I own, simple is I was a *possessor*. *Adage.*

> Adnau gan berchen.

> To pawn with the *owner*. *Adage.*

Perchenawg, *a.* (perchen) Having possession. *s. m.*—*pl.* *perchenogion.* A possessor, an owner.

> Perchenawg y tir y lladder arno a ddyle ddeg a deugaint i gan y neb a'i lladdo.

> The *proprietor* of the land whereon any thing shall be cut off shall claim fifty pence from whosoever shall cut it. *Welsh Laws.*

Perchenawl, *a.* (perchen) Possessory, possessive.

Perchenogaeth, *s. m.* (perchenawg) Ownership.

> Tri rhyw berchenogaeth y sydd ar dir, barwydd cyfraith: un yw estyn heb oresgyn; ail yw goresgyn heb estyn, trydydd yw goresgyn ag estyn.

> There are three sorts of *possessions* of land, according to law: one is extent without occupation; the second is occupation without extent; the third is occupation with extent. *Welsh Laws.*

Perchenogaethawl, *a.* (perchenogaeth) Belonging to ownership, possessory.

Perchenogaethiad, *s. m.* (perchenogaeth) A making a possession; a giving possession.

Perchenogaethu, *v. a.* (perchenogaeth) A making out a possession; a giving possession.

Perchenogawl, *a.* (perchenawg) Possessive.

Perchenogi, *v. n.* (perchenawg) To be possessed of, to possess, to own.

Perchenogwr, *s. m.*—*pl.* perchenogwyr (perchenawg—gwr) A possessioner.

Perchenoldeb, *s. m.* (perchenawl) Ownership.

Perchenoli, *v. a.* (perchenawl) To render possessive, to render possessed, to become possessed.

Perchentÿaeth, *s. m.* (perchen—tÿaeth) Possession of a house; a being a householder.

> ——Eich gwelir
> Pennaeth perchentyaeth tir.

> You will be seen the chief in *house-keeping* of the land.
> *Ieuan Llafar.*

Perchenu, *v. a.* (perchen) To possess, to own.

Perchenwr, *s. m.*—*pl.* perchenwyr (perchen—gwr) A possessor, an owner.

Perchi, *v. a.* (parch) To respect, or to honour.

> Cadwaladr cerddgar,
> Cerddau cyfarwar,
> Cyfarfu a'm perchi.

> The muse-loving Cadwaladr of selecting songs, he met with me *honouring*. *Gwalchmai.*

Perchwerwyn, *s. m.* (per—chwerw) The white horehound; also called *llwyd y cwn*.

Perchydd, *s. m.*—*pl. t.* ion (parch) A respecter.

> Yn wir, dyniti leithiawg Mon,
> Penllywydd perchydd llurygogion.

> In truth, there will be one enthroned from Mon, a sovereign the *respecter* of armour wearing men. *Taliesin.*

Perdawd, *s. m.* (per) Delicacy, sweetness.

Perder, *s. m.* (per) Deliciousness, sweetness.

Perdra, *s. m.* (per) Deliciousness, sweetness.

Peredd, *s. m.* (per) Delicateness, or sweetness.

Pereiddiad, *s. m.*—*pl. t.* au (peraidd) A sweetening, dulcification.

Pereiddiant, *s. m.* (peraidd) Dulcification.

Pereiddiaw, *v. a.* (peraidd) To dulcify, to render sweet, or mellow; to become sweet.

Pereiddiawl, *a.* (peraidd) Of a sweetening quality.

Pereiddrwydd, *s. m.* (peraidd) Deliciousness.

Pereiddsain, *s. f.* (peraidd—sain) Euphony.

Peren, *s. f. dim.* (per) A pear, one pear.

Pererin, *s. m.*—*pl. t.* ion (per—er) That has a course through; a pilgrim.

> Mi, Meilyr Brydydd, bererin i Bedr,
> Porthawr a gymedr gymen deithi.

> I, Meilyr the Bard, am a *pilgrim* to Peter, the porter who will regulate appropriate qualities. *Meilyr.*

Pererinbren, *s. m.* (pererin—pren) A pine-tree.
Pererindawd, *s. m.—pl.* pererindodau (pererin) A state of pilgrimage.
Pererindota, *v. a.* (pererindawd) To peregrinate.
Pererinlad, *s. m.* (pererin) Peregrination.
Pererinlaeth, *s. m.* (pererin) A state of peregrination, or a pilgrimage.
Pereriniaw, *v. a.* (pererin) To peregrinate.
Perfagl, *s. f.* (per—magl) The herb periwinkle.
Perfarwhun, *s. f.—pl. t.* au (per—marwhun) A rapturous trance.
Perfedd, *s. m.—pl. t.* ion (per—medd) The middle region, centre, or inward part. It is also used as a plural noun: the entrails, the bowels. *Nis dei adref oni bo berfeddion y nos*, Thou wilt not come home until it shall be the middle of night.

A genyw bob tra trwyddi berfedd
O'i ganiad, o'i rad, o'i rinwedd yn llawch,
Llewychedig haul yn ei gyntedd.

He that comprehends every course through its *centre*, by his permission, by his bounty, by his virtue in protecting, splendid is the sun in its orbit. *Gr. ab Gwrgeneu.*

Perfedd, *a.* (per—medd) Middle, inward, central. *Y bys perfedd*, the middle finger; *y tri perfeddaf*, the three inmost.

Locrinus, a gymerai y rhan berfedd i'r ynys.

Locrinus, took the *middle* portion of the island. *Gr. ab Arthur.*

Perfeddawl, *a.* (perfedd) Belonging to the middle, centrical; intestinal.
Perfeddiach, *s. pl. dim.* (perfedd) Intestines.
Perfeddwlad, *s. f.* (perfedd—gwlad) A middle country; an inland country.
Perfelys, *a.* (per—melys) Delicately sweet.
Perffaith, *a.* (per—ffaith) Perfect, complete.

Y gwr mwyn-ddoeth—
Y perffaith ddyn praff o ddysg.

The man pleasingly wise; the *perfect* person great in learning. *Morgan ab Hywel.*

Perffeithdawd, *s. m.* (perffaith) Perfectness.
Perffeithder, *s. m.* (perffaith) Perfectness.
Perffeithiad, *s. m.* (perffaith) A perfecting.
Perffeithiaw, *v. a.* (perffaith) To perfect.
Perffeithiawl, *a.* (perffaith) Perfectional.
Perffeithiedig, *a.* (perffaith) Being perfected.
Perffeithioldeb, *s. m.* (perffaith) Perfectibility.
Perffeithioli, *v.* (perffeithiawl) To perfectionate.
Perffeithrwydd, *s. m.* (perffaith) Perfectness.
Perging, *s. m.* (perc) That involves, that keeps together, that shelters or defends; a skreen, or settle. *a.* Enclosing, sheltering. *Perging penaethau*, the defence of princes.

Perging brenin, chweugaint a dal:—
Perging, pedwar-ar-ugaint a dal:—
Y pentan haiarn a'r perging.

The *fire-side skreen* of the king, its value is six score pence:—A *fire-side skreen*, its value is twenty-four pence:—The iron fire-hob and the *skreen*. *Welsh Laws.*

Llew mawr-llid enwair, llydw bair berging
Llwrw trylew; llew llawr lluryg delling.

A lion great in wrath and vigorous, amply he will cause *protection* towards the brave, the lion of the ground enveloped in armour. *Cynddelw.*

Rhys—
Na'm gwrthawd yn ddurfing,
Eryr llewyr, llaw berging.

Rhys, reject me not harshly, thou eagle of glory, of *protecting* hand. *Phylip Brydydd.*

Perhon, *adv.* (pe—rhon) Be the consequence, be it so, for all that.
Peri, *s. m.* (par) A causation, a cause.
Peri, *v. a.* (par) To cause; to cause to effect, to make to do; to bid, to command. *Duw a'm peris*, God caused me to be; *pera iddi beidiaw*, bid her to cease; *perid imi dy alw*, I was commanded to call thee.

Angen a bair i henwrach duthiaw.

Necessity *will cause* the old woman to trot. *Adage.*

Peris ef, peryf nef noddfa,
Per addawd paradwys wyddfa.

He, the causer of the sanctuary of heaven, *did cause* the blest circle of the paradisiacal place of presence. *Cynddelw.*

Iolaf bair, o bured arwar,
A beris amad ac adar.

I will worship the cause, from so pure a motive, who *did cause* all things walking and those of wing. *Llywelyn Fardd.*

Periad, *s. m.—pl. t.* au (par) A causing, a making to do, a bidding, effectuation, causation.
Periadur, *s. m.—pl. t.* on (periad) A causator.

Duw a folir yn y drindawd, Tad, Mab, ac Ysbryd Glan, yn greawdwr a pheriadur pob peth.

God shall be praised as a Trinity, Father, Son, and Holy Spirit the creator and *causer* of all things. *Berddas.*

Periant, *s. m.* (par) Causation, effectuation.
Periator, *ger.* (periad) In causing, in bidding.
Perid, *s. m.—pl. t.* ydd (par) That is caused.

Golychaf peryf peridydd,
A beris deigr mab Dafydd.

I will adore the Causer of *caused things*, who caused the tears of the son of David. *Meigant, M. Cynddylan.*

Perig, *a.* (per) Extreme; perilous.
Perigl, *a.* (perig) Perilous, or dangerous.
Periglaw, *v. a.* (perigl) To make extreme or perilous; to administer extreme unction; to become extreme.

Edlid a berid o'i beriglaw.

Vexation was caused from *bringing* him *to extremity*. *Cynddelw, m. Rhirid.*

Ac a'm gwnel peryf, pan beriglwyf,
Perffaith, waith oleg a deg dalwyf!

And may the Creator, when *I go to extremity*, make me perfect, a work of the mind, which I may fairly requite! *Einion ab Gwalchmai.*

Periglawd, *s. m.* (perigl) The act of rendering urgent, extreme, or perilous.
Periglawr, *s. m.—pl.* periglorion (perigl) One who has to do with what is extreme or dangerous; one who administers extreme unction; a parish priest.

Na ddifanw dy beriglawr.

Do not contemn thy *pastor*. *Adage.*

Peritor, *sup.* (peri) To be causing or bidding.
Perlafar, *s. m.* (per—llafar) Euphony.
Perlais, *s. m.—pl.* perleisiau (per—llais) A sweet voice, a melodious voice.
Perlef, *s. m.* (per—llef) A melodious voice.
Perleisiad, *s. m.* (perlais) Producing euphony.
Perleisiaw, *v. a.* (perlais) To produce euphony.
Perlewyg, *s. f.—pl. t.* oedd (per—llewyg) Ecstasy
Perlewygawl, *a.* (perlewyg) Rapturous.
Perlewygfa, *s. f.—pl. t.* au (perlewyg) Rapture.

O ddwywawl gariad—y deuant ysbrydolion weledigaethau yn y marwhunau ac y perlewygfiau.

From divine love there will come spiritual visions in the death-like trances and the *raptures*. *Cyfergrien Pucheild.*

Perlewygiad, *s. m.* (perlewyg) A yielding a rapture, a falling into a fit of ecstasy.
Perlewygu, *v. n.* (perlewyg) To fall into rapture
Perloes, *s. f.—pl. t.* ion (per—gloes) Ecstasy.
Perloesaidd, *a.* (perloes) Extatic, rapturous.
Perloesi, *v. a.* (perloes) To enrapture.
Perlysiau, *s. pl. aggr.* (per—llysiau) Sweet herbs

Brysia, fy anwylyd—bydd debyg i iwrch, neu i elain hydd ar fynyddoedd y perlysiau.

Hasten, my love, be like the roebuck, or the young hart on the mountains of the *sweet herbs*. *Ier. Owain.*

Perlysiawg, *a.* (per—llysiawg) Abounding with aromatic herbs.

Perllan, *s. f.—pl. t.* au (per—llan) An enclosure of sweet fruit; an orchard.

> Tri thlws cenedl, melin, cored, a pherllan; a'r rhai hyny ni ddylir eu rhanu, na'u cyhwynu; namyn rhanu eu ffrwythau i'r neb a'u dylyo.
>
> The three rarities of a family: a mill, a wear, and an *orchard*, and those things ought not to be divided, nor removed, but their produce is to be divided amongst such as may have a claim. *Welsh Laws.*

Perllanaidd, *a.* (perllan) Like an orchard.

Perllanawg, *a.* (perllan) Abounding with orchards

> Pob rhan o'r adail———
> A'r barth perllanawg llanwyd,
> Heb ddwyn ond chwyn a hesg.
>
> Every part of the structure, on a region *abounding with orchards* was filled, without producing any thing but weeds and reeds. *Elis Wyn, B. Cwsg.*

Perllanwydd, *s. pl. aggr.* (perllan—gwydd) Orchard trees.

Perllys, *s. pl. aggr.* (per—llys) Parsley: *perllys yr hel*, or *perllys y morfa*, wild celery.

Peron, *s. m.* (par) That causes or bids to be; the creator; the lord.

Perores, *s. f.—pl. t.* au (perawr) A female who practises melody, a female musician.

Peroriad, *s. m.—pl. t.* au (perawr) A producing a sweet sound; a producing of melody.

Peroriaeth, *s. m.* (perawr) Melody, harmony of sound, foolish idle talk.

Peroriaethawl, *a.* (peroriaeth) Belonging to the science of music; musical.

Peroriaethu, *v. a.* (peroriaeth) To make melody, to harmonize sounds; to practise music.

Peroriaethus, *a.* (peroriaeth) Harmonical.

Peroriaethwr, *s. m.—pl.* peroriaethwyr (peroriaeth—gwr) A practiser of music.

Peroriaethydd, *s. m.—pl. t.* ion (peroriaeth) A harmonizer of sounds, one who practises harmony, or music.

Periorianawl, *a.* (peroriant) Producing music.

Perorianu, *v. a.* (peroriant) To yield melody.

Peroriant, *s. m.* (perawr) Practice of music.

Peroriaw, *v. a.* (perawr) To practise music.

Persain, *s. f.—pl.* perseiniau (per—sain) Euphony

Perseiniad, *s. m.—pl. t.* au (persain) A producing euphony.

Perseiniaw, *v. a.* (persain) To produce euphony.

Perseiniawl, *a.* (persain) Euphonical; melodious

Pert, *a.* (per) Smart, spruce, dapper, pert, nice.

> Pert pob peth bach ond diawl bach.
>
> Pretty is every thing little except a little devil. *Adage.*
>
> Menyg, pert galenig por.
>
> The gloves, the *pretty* present of a chieftain. *D. ab Gwilym.*

Pertaidd, *a.* (pert) Of a smart or pert nature.

Pertedd, *s. m.* (pert) Smartness, neatness.

Perten, *s. f. dim.* (pert) A smart little girl.

Pertrwydd, *s. m.* (pert) Smartness, prettiness.

Pertu, *v. a.* (pert) To render smart or spruce, to become smart, trim, or spruce.

Pertyn, *s. m. dim.* (pert) A smart little fellow.

Perth, *s. f.—pl. t.* i (py—erth) A thorn bush.

> Troi o bobtu y berth.
>
> To turn on each side of the *bush*. *Adage.*
>
> Trist i gr[illegible] [illegible] perthi,
> [illegible] porthai cardota;
> Trist fu ei hyder o glera;
> Tri[illegible] [illegible] y daeth yd â
>
> It is woeful for a buffoon to be gathering hips off the *brakes*, and that charity should not support him, woeful was his dependance upon the circuit of minstrelsy, three times worse than what has been to him will be come to. *Madawg Dwygraig.*

Perthawg, *a.* (perth) Abounding with bushes.

Perthen, *s. f. dim.* (perth) A thorn bush; a bush

Pertheurddrain, *s. f.* (perth—eurddrain) A gooseberry bush.

Perthgae, *s. m.* (perth—cae) A quick-set hedge.

Perthgau, *v. a.* (perth—cau) To enclose with quickset hedge.

Perthlys, *s. m.* (perth—llys) Climbing buckwheat

Perthyn, *s. m.—pl. t.* oedd (parth) What is appropriate, relating, or belonging to. *v. n.* To be appropriate, to have relation, to belong.

> A berthyn am ddyn a ddywedaf;
> A borthe gofid bid bwyllocaf.
>
> What *relates* of man I will treat of, he that bears affliction let him be the most concerned. *Llywelyn Fardd.*

Perthynad, *s. m.* (perthyn) Appertinence.

Perthynas, *s. f.—pl. t.* au (perthyn) Relation, relationship, appertinence.

Perthynasawl, *a.* (perthynas) Appropriate.

Perthynasiad, *s. m.—pl. t.* au (perthynas) An appropriating; appropriation.

Perthynasoldeb, *s. m.* (perthynasawl) Appropriateness, an appropriated state.

Perthynasolder, *s. m.* (perthynasawl) Appropriateness, pertinentness.

Perthynasoli, *v. a.* (perthynasawl) To render appropriate, to become appropriate.

Perthynasolrwydd, *s. m.* (perthynasawl) Pertinentness, appropriateness.

Perthynasu, *v. a.* (perthynas) To render appropriate, to become appropriate.

Perthynawl, *a.* (perthyn) Pertaining. *Rhagenw perthynawl*, a relative pronoun.

Perthynedig, *a.* (perthyn) Made appropriate.

Perthynedigaeth, *s. m.* (perthynedig) Appropriation, the state of being relative.

Perthynedigawl, *a.* (perthynedig) Tending to be appropriate, or pertinent.

Perthyniad, *s. m.—pl. t.* au (perthyn) Appertainment, a rendering pertinent.

Perthynoldeb, *s. m.* (perthynawl) Appropriateness, relativeness, appertinence.

Perthynoledd, *s. m.* (perthynawl) Appropriateness, relativeness, appertinence.

Perthynoli, *v. a.* (perthynawl) To render appropriate, to become appropriate.

Perthynolrwydd, *s. m.* (perthynawl) Appropriateness, relativeness.

Perthynraid, *a.* (perthyn—rhaid) Relatively necessary; suitable.

> Llywelyn Sion—a wnai drefn a dosbarth ar fesurau cerdd, a'r y peth oedd berthynawl iddynt.
>
> Llywelyn Sion reduced to *order* and method the measures of song, and what was *appropriate* to them. *Ed. Dafydd.*

Perthynu, *v. a.* (perthyn) To render appropriate, to become appropriate or pertinent, to appertain, to belong, to have relation.

> Byr ach bonedd lle nis perthyn iddi na chrog na chara putain.
>
> Short is the genealogy of nobility to which *there belongs* neither a thief nor a whore. *Adage.*

Perthynus, *a.* (perthyn) Appropriate, relative.

> Nid yw ffydd yn berthynus i bethau amlwg, o achos nid yw gwelir yn amlwg; nid rhaid iddynt ffydd, ond y gwelediad.
>
> Faith is not *appropriate* to visible things, because faith is not necessary for things seen and conspicuous, but vision. *Marchawg Crwydrad.*

Perthynusrwydd, *s. m.* (perthynus) Appropriateness, relativeness, or appertinence.

Peru, *v. a.* (par) To cause, to effect, to bid to be, to bid, to command.

> Abwy a bair weled lle bo.
>
> A carrion *will cause* it to be known where it is. *Adage.*

Perwellt, *s. m.* (per—gwellt) Sweet-scented vernal grass, also called *melyn-wellt*.

Perwg, *s. m.—pl.* perygon (per) That is of a soft

or sweet tone, a musical instrument so called; probably a hurdy-gurdy.

Wrth y drws, un a'i grwth drwg,
A baw arall a'i berwg.

By the door, one with his crazy fiddle, and another dirty chap with his *hurdy-gurdy*. *L. G. Cothi.*

Perwr, *s. m.—pl.* perwyr (peru—gwr) A causer, a bidder to be, one who orders.

Perwraidd, *s. m.* (per—gwraidd) Liquorice.

Perwrychion, *s. pl. aggr.* (per—gwrychion) Delicious emanations.

Digrifwch yn cyflawni y clywedigaeth, o'r perwrychion melysder, mal y deuant o wanegiad y gwefusau.

Happiness replenishing the hearing with the *delicious emanations of sweetness*, as they proceed from the opening of the lips. *Cysegrlan Fuchedd.*

Perwydd, *s. pl. aggr.* (per—gwydd) Wood bearing sweet fruit, fruit trees, pear trees.

Addwyn blodau ar warthaf perwydd;
Arall addwyn a Chreawdr cerennydd.

Delightful the blossoms upon the *pear trees*; again delightful is it to hold communion with the Creator. *Taliesin.*

Perwydden, *s. f. dim.* (perwydd) A pear tree.

Perwyddiad, *s. m.—pl. t.* au (par—gwyddiad) A causal faculty, a verb.

Perwyddiadawl, *a.* (perwyddiad) Relating to, or of the nature of a verb.

Perwyl, *s. m.—pl. t.* ion (par—gwyl) Occasion.

Perwylaw, *v. a.* (perwyl) To produce an occasion or event.

Perwyliad, *s. m.* (perwyl) A producing an occasion or event.

Perwylus, *a.* (perwyl) Eventual, incidental.

Perydd, *s. m.* (par) A causer, one who bids to be, a bidder, one who orders or gives command.

Peryddon, *s. f.* (perydd) A stream possessing some powerful virtue; a divine stream; it is the name of some rivers. This appellation is used by the poets for the river Dee, in common with *Dyfrdwy*, *Dyfrdonwy*, and *Aerfen*.

Mae breuddwyd am Beryddon,
Yr ai gaer hir ar gwr hon.

There is a dream respecting *Peryddon*, that a long fort would rise upon its border. *T. Aled, i Glogen.*

Peryf, *s. m.* (par) One who causes; the giver of existence, a creator; one who bids or commands; a sovereign, a king. It has been used for the appellation of Pharaoh; as, *Peryf a'i lu*, Pharaoh and his host.

Aswynaf, archaf arch fawr i beryf
A beris nef a llawr,
Nawdd rhag dy far.——

I will put myself under protection, I will ask a great petition to the *Causer* that caused heaven and earth,—a refuge from thy wrath. *Cynddelw, i R. ab Gruffudd.*

Peryf nef, pura fy ngheudawd!

Creator of heaven, make pure my breast. *Ein. ab Gwalchmai.*

Peryg, *s. m.* (per) That is extreme or perilous.

Perygl, *s. m.—pl. t.* on (peryg) Danger.

Yn mhob clwyf y mae perygl.

In every disorder there is *danger*. *Adage.*

Aethant eu llongau ar y polion heiarn——dyoddefant ddisyfyd perygl angeuawl, hyd pan foddynt ar filoedd.

Their ships went upon the iron piles, and they suffered a sudden deadly *peril*, so that they were drowned by thousands. *Brut y Brenhinoedd.*

Perygledd, *s. m.* (perygl) Dangerousness.

Perygliad, *s. m.* (perygl) An adventuring, a hazarding; a running into danger, an endangering, an exposing to danger.

Peryglu, *v. a.* (perygl) To endanger, to expose to peril; to become dangerous.

Peryglu am farnu f'oes
Pan fynych yn pen f'einioes.

Running into danger in judging of my life: when thou shalt please is the end of my existence. *T. Aled.*

Peryglus, *a.* (perygl) Dangerous, or perilous.

Peryglusaw, *v. a.* (peryglus) To render perilous or hazardous, to become perilous.

Peryglusedd, *s. m.* (peryglus) Perilousness.

Peryglusrwydd, *s. m.* (peryglus) Dangerousness.

Peryglwr, *s. m.* peryglwyr (perygl—gwr) One who endangers.

Pes, *conj.* (pe—ys) If. It is used conditionally, for *pe*, and *ped*, with verbs of the subjunctive and potential modes, preserving the initials of words following in their radical state.

Pesgi, *v. a.* (pasg) To feed, to fatten; to pamper, to cram, to become fat.

Ban beisg berion a bwystgunion coed.

Conspicuously *he feeds* the vultures and wild beasts of the wood. *Gwalchmai.*

Pesgiad, *s. m.* (pasg) A fattening, a feeding.

Pesgiator, *ger.* (pesgiad) In fattening or feeding.

Pesgitor, *sup.* (pasg) To be fattening, or feeding.

Bid disgwyl aelau; bid an byddin;
Bid besgitor dyre;
Bid drud glew; a bid rew bre.

Be querulous the ailing; be moving the army; be *getting fat* the wanton; be bold the brave, and be the hill slippery. *Llywarch Hen.*

Pesgus, *a.* (pasg) Fattening; nutritive.

Pesgwr, *s. m.—pl.* pesgwyr (pesgi—gwr) A fattener or a feeder.

Pest, *s. m.* (py—est) That is violent, pushing, or penetrating.

Pestawd, *s. m.* (pest) A forcing, a bustling.

Pestodi, *v. a.* (pestawd) To bustle about; to frisk.

Pestota, *v. a.* (pestawd) To bustle, to frisk.

Peswch, *s. m.* (pas) A cough. *Mae arnat beswch tost*, thou hast a severe cough.

Peswch sych diwedd pob nych.

A dry *cough* ends every ill. *Adage.*

Pesychawl, *a.* (peswch) Apt to cough; coughing.

Pesychiad, *s. m.—pl. t.* au (peswch) A coughing.

Pesychlyd, *a.* (peswch) Troubled with cough.

Pesychlys, *s. m.* (peswch—llys) Coltsfoot.

Pesychu, *v. a.* (peswch) To cough. *A besycher*, that is coughed; that is ejected by coughing.

Pesychwr, *s. m.* (pesych—gwr) A cougher.

Petrus, *a.* (pedrus) Apt to cause a start, apt to start, doubtful, dubious. *Y petrus*, the starters, partridges.

Petrusad, *s. m.* (petrus) A making a start, a startling; a hesitating, a doubting.

Petrusaw, *v. a.* (petrus) To startle, to hesitate.

Petrusawd, *s. m.* (petrus) A startling, hesitation.

Petrusawl, *a.* (petrus) Startling, hesitating.

Petrusdeb, *s. m.* (petrus) A state of startling, a state of hesitation, doubtfulness.

Petrusder, *s. m.* (petrus) Doubt, hesitation, ambiguity, quandary.

Petrusdra, *s. m.* (petrus) Dubiousness, quandary.

Petrusedd, *s. m.* (petrus) Dubiousness, scrupulosity, ambiguousness.

Petrusen, *s. f. dim.* (petrus) A partridge.

Petrusgar, *a.* (petrus) Apt to startle, hesitating.

Petrusgarwch, *s. m.* (petrusgar) A state of startling, hesitation, doubtfulness.

Petrusi, *s. m.* (petrus) A startling hesitancy.

Petrusrwydd, *s. m.* (petrus) Hesitancy; doubt.

Petruswr, *s. m.—pl.* petruswyr (petrus—gwr) A startler, one who hesitates, a doubter.

Petryael, *s. m.* (pedry—ael) That consists of four skirts or sides, a square. *a.* Quadrilateral.

Petryal, *s. m.—pl. t.* au (pedry—al) That has four points or sides; a square, a space hemmed in on all sides. *a.* Quadrangular, square.

Cefn y Petryal; Petryal Clwyd; places so called on *Hiraethog*, in Denbighshire. *Bedd petryal*, a grave sided with four slabs; and such was the grave of Bronwen, the aunt of Caractacus, in an islet still called after her name, in the river Alaw, in Anglesey, where an urn, containing her ashes, was found, in 1813; and which my friend Richard Llwyd, the Bard, is now possessed of. The grave was identified by this passage in the *Mabinogi* of *Bran*.

Bedd petryal a wnaid i Fronwen ferch Llyr ar lan afon Alaw.

A square grave was made for Bronwen daughter of Llyr, on the bank of the river Alaw. *Mabinogi.*

Petryalai, *s. c.* (petryal) What forms a square, a square used by artificers.

Petryalawg, *a.* (petryal) Consisting of a square.

Petryaledig, *a.* (petryal) Being squared.

Petryaledd, *s. m.* (petryal) Squareness of form.

Petryalhad, *s. m.* (petryal) A squaring.

Petryalu, *v. a.* (petryal) To square, to quadrate.

Peth, *s. m.* -*pl. t.* au (py—eth) A thing, a something, a part, share, or fragment, a portion, a quantity, a little. *Mae ganddo ddigon o bethau*, he has abundance of riches, *dyro beth i mi*, give some to me.

Amser sydd i bob peth.

Time there is for every thing. *Adage.*

Tri pheth ys ydd ni char Duw a'u caro, gweled anladd, gweled anghenfil, a gweled rhodres balchder.

Three things that God will not love such as love them: the seeing of nothing, the seeing of a monster, and the seeing the triumph of pride. *Trioedd Barddas.*

Pethan, *s. c. dim.*—*pl. t.* od (peth) A little thing, a new-born infant.

Pethbynag, *pron.* (peth—pynag) Whatsoever. *adv.* Be it as it may, however.

Pethyn, *s. m. dim.* (peth) A tiny little thing.

Peuad, *s. m.* -*pl. t.* au (pau) A taking repose; a pausing, a hesitation, a puffing, a panting.

Peuannawl, *a* (peuant) Tending to make a pause, or rest; tending to pant.

Peuannu, *v. a.* (peuant) To make a pausing or resting, to be panting.

Peuant, *s. m.* (pau) The state of pausing or taking rest, a puffing, a panting.

Peuaw, *v. a.* (pau) To spread out; to make a pause, to hesitate, to puff, to pant, to take breath; to breathe with difficulty, to be circumspect. *Tarw yn peuaw*, a bull making a sullen roar, in challenging another.

Peuawd, *s. m.* (pau) A spreading out, circumspection, hesitation, a pausing, a panting.

Peuawl, *a* (pau) Spreading out, circumspect, puffing, or panting.

Peuawr, *a* (pae—awr) Hourly, continual.

[illegible]

[illegible]

Peuedd, *s. m.* (pau) A spreading out state, a state of repose, a panting state.

Peues, *s. f.* -*pl. t.* oedd (pau) A place of rest, an inhabited place, a dwelling place; an inhabited country, a country.

[illegible]

[illegible] *Cynddelw.*

[illegible]

[illegible]

[illegible]

[illegible]

Peufer, *a.* (peu—mer) Whining, neighing.

[illegible]

[illegible] *Merddin.*

Peuferiad, *s. m.* (peufer) A making a noise of pleasure in taking repose, a whining.

Peuferu, *v. a.* (peufer) To make a cry of pleasure and repose; to whine, or yelp as a dog, to neigh.

Peunoeth, *a.* (pae—noeth) Nocturnal. *adv.* Nightly, every night.

Peunoethawl, *a.* (peunoeth) Nocturnous.

Peunos, *a* (pae—nos) Nightly, nocturnal. *adv.* Nightly, every night.

Peunosawl, *a.* (peunos) Nocturnal, nightly.

Peunydd, *a.* (pae—dydd) Daily, diurnal. *adv.* Daily, diurnally, every day.

[illegible]

Little is he religious who is daily hunting for it. *Adage.*

[illegible]

The day after to morrow, daily and for ever. *L. G. Cothi.*

[illegible]

Woe to him who is overlooked by his lord daily. *Adage.*

Peunyddiawl, *a.* (peunydd) Diurnal, daily.

Peusyth, *s. m.* (pae—syth) A dovetail, in joinery.

Peusythiad, *s. m.* (peusyth) A dovetailing.

Peusythu, *v. a.* (peusyth) To dovetail.

Peutu, *adv.* (pae—tu) On each side, on both sides, about. It is mostly used in South Wales, and *deutu* prevails in the North. *O beutu yr afon*, on each side of the river; *peutu yr eglwys*, about the church.

Adfyd a ddysg i ddyn edrych o beutu.

Adversity will teach a man to look about him. *Adage.*

[illegible]

About it [illegible] like the moth round the candle. *Adage.*

Peutuawl, *a.* (peutu) Belonging to each side.

PI, *s. f. v.* -*pl. t.* od. The state of being in, the state of being identified in; a magpie, so called from its habit of keeping to the same spot.

[illegible]

[illegible] as a magpie. *Adage.*

Pia, *s. f. dim.* (pi) A pie, or magpie.

[illegible]

As pert as the [illegible] pie on the bush. [illegible]

Piad, *s. m.* (pi) A possessing, or owning.

Piannawl, *a.* (piant) Possessory, possessive.

Piannu, *v. a.* (piant) To make out possession.

Piant, *s. m.* (pi) Possession, or ownership.

Piau, *v. n.* (pi) To own, to be owner of, to possess. *Pwy biau hwn?* who owns this? *Ti a piau*, thou dost own it; *mi biau un*, one is mine, *ti biau y llall*, thou dost own the other.

[illegible]

[illegible] *Gutyn Owain.*

[illegible]

[illegible] *S. ab Hywel.*

[illegible]

[illegible] *[illegible]*

Piau, *adv.* (pi) Who owns, whose, whose is it?

[illegible]

[illegible] *H. Cadwr—Mabinogion.*

Piaw, *v. a.* (pi) To own, to be owner of.

Piawd, *s. m.* (pi) A possessing, or owning.

> Prydydd wyf rhag Prydain ddragon,
> Piawd cerdd cadair prydyddion.
>
> I am a poet, in the presence of a leader of Britain, *possessing* the song of the chair of poets. *Cynddelw.*

Piawg, *a.* (pi) Having possession, or possessed.
Piawl, *a.* (pi) Possessing, owning; being owned.
Pib, *s. f.—pl. t.* au (py—ib) A pipe, a tube, a squirt, a lax, a musical pipe; a flute. *Piban cod*, bagpipes; *pib gorn*, a horn pipe: *Pib waed*, the bloody flux.

> Aeth hyny ar gyrn a phibau.
>
> That is gone upon horns and *pipes*, or become a common talk. *Adage.*

Pibaw, *v. a.* (pib) To make use of a pipe, to pass through a pipe, to squirt, to pipe.
Pibawg, *a.* (pib) Having a pipe, piped.
Pibawl, *a.* (pib) Belonging to a pipe, laxative.
Pibawr, *s. m.* (pib) That is like a pipe.
Pibell, *s. f. dim.—pl. t.* i (pib) A pipe, a duct, a tube, a musical pipe. *Pibell odyn*, a kiln pipe; *pibell wynt*, or *breuant*, a windpipe.
Pibellaidd, *a.* (pibell) Like a pipe or a tube.
Pibellawg, *a.* (pibell) Having pipes, piped.
Pibelliad, *s. m.* (pibell) A forming a pipe; a piping, a smoking.
Pibellu, *v. a.* (pibell) To form a pipe, to pipe.
Pibellwr, *s. m.—pl.* pibellwyr (pibell—gwr) A pipe-man, a smoker.
Pibellydd, *s. m—pl. t.* ion (pibell) A piper.
Piben, *s. f. dim.* (pib) A pipe. *Piben odyn*, the pipe of a kiln.
Pibenawg, *a. f.* (piben) Jointed pipewort.
Pibiaeth, *s. m.* (pib) The act of piping.
Pibion, *s. pl. aggr.* (pib) Squirtings.
Pibled, *a.* (*f. of* piblyd) Apt to squirt, squirting.
Piblyd, *a.* (pib) Apt to squirt, squirting.
Piblys, *s. m.* (pib—llys) The flix-weed.
Pibon, *s. pl.* (pib) Pipes, what are as pipes.
Pibonwy, *s. m. aggr.* (pibon—gwy) Sleet, isicles.
Pibori, *s. m.* (pibawr) A state of piping or shooting out, a budding. *v. a.* To pipe or shoot out, to bud.

> Yr eos loew dlos lwydliw—
> Poed ar ddor y pibori,
> Amen fyth, o mynaf fi!
>
> The nightingale of a glossy fair brown hue, be she on the canopy of *budding*, Amen, for ever I would have it so! *D. ab Gwilym.*

Piborig, *a.* (pibawr) Piping or shooting out.

> Afallen beren biborig,
> Melyn ei haeron, nid mayon eu mesig
>
> Apple-tree delicious and *growing with buds*, yellow its fruit, not to be chewed by the multitude *Myrddin.*

Pibwr, *s. m.—pl.* pibwyr (pib—gwr) A piper.
Pibydd, *s. m.—pl. t.* ion (pib) A piper. *Pibydd cod*, a bagpipe player; *pibydd y traeth*, the sandpiper; *pibydd glas*, ash coloured sandpiper; *pibydd llwyd llydandroed*, grey scollop-toed sand-piper; *pibydd du mànawg*, black-spotted sandpiper; *pibydd gwyrdd*, green sandpiper; *pibydd rhuddgoch*, the dunlin.

> Digu pawb o anadl y pibydd.
>
> Disgusting to every body the breath of the *piper*. *Adage.*

Pibyddes, *s. f.—pl. t.* au (pibydd) Female piper.
Pibyddiaeth, *s. m.* (pibydd) Pipe-playing.
Pibyddiaethu, *v. a.* (pibyddiaeth) To practise piping, or pipe-playing.
Picell, *s. f. dim.—pl. t.* au (pig) What is darted, a dart, a javelin.
Picellai, *s. c.* (picell) A dart thrower.
Picellawg, *a.* (picell) Armed with a dart.
Picelliad, *s. m.* (picell) A throwing a dart.
Picellu, *v. a.* (picell) To throw a dart.
Picellwr, *s. m—pl.* picellwyr (picell—gwr) A dart-man, a thrower of darts.
Picellydd, *s. m.—pl t.* ion (picell) A darter.
Picffon, *s. f.—pl.* picffyn (pig—ffon) A pike-staff.
Picfforch, *s. f.—pl.* picffyrch (fforch) A pitchfork.
Piciad, *s. m.—pl. t.* au (pig) A darting, a making a sudden pass, a going suddenly.
Piciaw, *v. a.* (pig) To dart, to fly suddenly. *Picia yno a brysia yn ol*, run there and make haste back.

> Gwr du i bician gair del,
> Gwr yaig â gwâr isel.
>
> A black man *to throw* a churlish word; a crazy man with a low stoop. *T. Prys.*

Piciawl, *a.* (pig) Darting, flinging.
Piciedig, *a.* (piciad) Being darted or flung.
Picwd, *s. m.—pl.* picydau (pig) The prickled dog, or houndfish; also called *ci pigau*, and *ci pigawg*.
Picwsmaln, *s. m.* (pig—maln) Oat bread crumbled into butter-milk.
Picyn, *s. m. dim.—pl. t.* au (pig) A wooden vessel hooped, used for eating out of.
Picynaid, *s. m.—pl* picyneidiau (picyn) As much as a *picyn* will hold.
Picynwr, *s. m.—pl.* picynwyr (picyn—gwr) A good man at the *picyn*.
Picynydd, *s. m.—pl. t.* ion (picyn) A *picyner*.
Pid, *s. m.* (py—id) What tapers to a point.
Pidyn, *s. m. dim.—pl. t.* od (pid) A pintle. *Pidyn y gog*, the herb wake-robin.
Pienfod, *v. n.* (piau—bod) To be possessed of, to be owner. *Gwyn ei fyd biefai!* Happy him who should enjoy it!

> Pieufo y fuwch aed yn ei llosgwrn.
>
> Who *owns* the cow let him take to her tail. *Adage.*

Piff, *s. m.—pl. t.* iau (py—iff) A puff, or blast.
Piffiad, *s. m.—pl. t.* au (piff) A puffing.
Piffiaw, *v. a.* (piff) To puff, or to whiff.
Pig, *s. f.—pl. t.* au (py—ig) What terminates in a point, a pointed end, a point, a pike; a beak, bill, or nib; the pipe, a disease amongst fowls. *Pig yr aran*, the crane-bill; also called *troed-rudd*: *pig y bwn*, shoots of river horse-tail; *pig y crëyr*, stork's-bill.

> A moes achwyn maes uchel,
> Rhag oes y dyn rhygas del
> Y mae'r byd yma ar big
> Yn tueddu at eiddig!
>
> And let me complain out aloud, against the life of a person odiously churlish this world is on a *pivot* placed, inclining to the jealous cull! *T. Prys.*

Pigaw, *v. a* (pig) To prick, to prickle; to sting; to pick; to peck. *Pigodd draen fi*, a thorn has pricked me; *piga y goreuon*, pick the best ones; *iar a biga y briwion*, a hen will pick the crumbs; *mae yn pigaw gwlaw*, it spits of rain.
Pigawd, *s. m.* (pig) The act of pricking.
Pigawg, *a.* (pig) Prickly, full of points. *Croes bigawg*, a cross fitchee.
Pigawglym, *a.* (pigawg—llym) Sharp pointed.
Pigawglymaidd, *a.* (pigawglym) Rather sharply pointed, or acuminated.
Pigawglymedd, *s. m.* (pigawglym) The state of being sharply pointed.
Pigawglys, *s. pl. aggr.* (pigawg—llys) The spinach; also called *pigoga*.
Pigedig, *a.* (pig) Pricked, prickled.
Pigfain, *a.* (pig—main) Sharp-pointed.
Pigfan, *s. m.* (pig—màn) A mark of a point.

Pigfaniad, *s. m.* (pigfan) A punctulating.

Pigfanu, *v. a.* (pigfan) To punctulate.

Pigfeiniad, *s. m.* (pigfain) Acumination.

Pigfeiniaw, *v. a.* (pigfain) To acuminate.

Pigfforch, *s. f.—pl.* pigffyrch (pig—fforch) A pitchfork.

Pigiad, *s. m.—pl. t.* au (pig) A pricking, a stinging; a picking; a culling.

Pigiedig, *a.* (pigiad) Pricked, stung; picked.

Pigin, *s. m.* (pig) A stitch, or pricking pain.

Pigion, *s. pl. aggr.* (pig) Picked things; selections; excerptions.

Pigl, *s. m.* (pig) The herb hounds-tongue.

Pigoden, *s. f. dim.—pl. t.* au (pigawd) A prickle; a sharp point; a sting; a field mouse.

Pigoga, *s. f.* (pigawg) The spinage.

Pigwlaw, *s. m.* (pig—gwlaw) A spitting rain.

Pigwlawiaw, *v. n.* (pigwlaw) To spit of rain.

Pigwn, *s. m.—pl.* pigynau (pig) A round heap or tump; a cone; a turret; a beacon.

Pigwr, *s. m.—pl.* pigwyr (pig—gwr) A pricker, a stinger; a picker.

Pigwrda, *s. m.* (pig—gwrda) A sort of play, similar to the one of "*This is the house that Jack built.*"

Pigwrn, *s. m.—pl.* pigyrnau (pig—gwrn) A pinnacle, a spire.

Pigyn, *s. m. dim.* (pig) A stitch in the side; a pleurisy. *Pigyn rhedeg*, a stitch caused by running; *pigyn astrus, morwiber*, a weaver.

Pigyrnaidd, *a.* (pigwrn) Like a pinnacle, spired.

Pigyrnawg, *a.* (pigwrn) Having points or asperites; pinnacled, turreted. *Dyn pigyrnawg*, a wrangling person.

Pigyrnawl, *a.* (pigwrn) Shooting out in a spire.

Pigyrniad, *s. m.* (pigwrn) A shooting out in a point or spire.

Pigyrnu, *v. a.* (pigwrn) To render sharp; to form a pinnacle; to wrangle; to be crabbed.

Pil, *s. m.—pl. t.* ion (pi—il) That goes round; that is round; that hovers about; a sergeant, or apparitor; a surface, that is thrown off; a peel, paring, or rind.

Pil, *s. m.—pl. t.* iau (py—il) A small inlet of the sea filled by the tide; generally called *Camlas* in North Wales.

Ni'th ddalio pil, na milwr,
Na thwrn dwys, na thir na dwr.

May neither *sergeant* nor warrior thee enthral, nor enclosing turn, nor land, nor water. *L. Morganwg.*

Pila, *s. m.—pl. t.* on (pil) A finch; also called *pinc, pincyn, ysbincyn*, and *telor*. The varieties are, *Pila pen aur*, gold-headed finch; *pila cap sidan*, silk cap finch; *pila glas*, blue finch; *pila glas bach*, small blue finch, or titmouse.

Pilai, *s. c.—pl.* pileion (pil) A moth; a butterfly; also called *eilier, cloyn*, and *cloyn byw*.

Pilai yn ei wisg, gwenynen yn ei mel.

A *butterfly* in his coat, a bee in her honey. *Adage.*

Pilaid, *a.* (pil) Transient, frail, weak, poor; mean, wretched; sickly, indisposed. *Gwael, cwla*, and *salw* are generally used for it, in North Wales. *O chwiwgi pilaid!* Oh thou sculking mean dog! *Gwaith pilaid iawn*, very indifferent work; *yd pilaid iawn*, very poor corn; *wyf yn bilaid iawn*, I am much indisposed.

Pilan, *s. f.—pl. t.* od (pil) Sparrow hawk; a spear.

Pile, *s. m.* (pil) That turns or whisks about.

Pilcod, *s. pl.* (pile) The fish called menows.

Pilcodyn, *s. m. dim.* (pilcod) A menow.

Pilcoes, *s. f.* (pil—coes) The plane tree.

Pilcota, *v. a.* (pilcod) To catch menows.

Pildin, *s. m.* (pil—tin) A galling by riding.

Pilen, *s. f. dim.—pl. t.* au (pil) A cuticle, a membrane, a thin skin, or rind; a fringe, or border. *Sych-bilen*, a web in the eye.

Pilenaidd, *a.* (pilen) Membranceous; filmy.

Pilenawg, *a.* (pilen) Having a cuticle or thin skin; covered with a film.

Pileniad, *s. m.* (pilen) A forming a cuticle; a covering with film.

Pilenllyd, *a.* (pilen) Apt to produce a thin skin.

Pilenu, *v. a.* (pilen) To form a cuticle of thin skin; to be covered with film.

Piler, *s. m.—pl. t.* au (pil) A pillar, a post.

Pilerawg, *a.* (piler) Having a pillar; columnarious; pillared.

Pileriad, *s. m.* (piler) A forming a column or pillar; a building upon pillars.

Pileru, *v. a.* (piler) To make a pillar; to build upon pillars; to set up pillars.

Pileryn, *s. m. dim.* (piler) A small column.

Piliad, *s. m.* (pil) A stripping the surface, a paring, a peeling.

Piliant, *s. m.* (pil) A taking off the surface, or rind; a paring, a stripping, a peeling.

Piliaw, *v. a.* (pil) To take off the surface, rind or skin; to peel, to pare; to pillage. *Piliaw brwyn*, to peel rushes.

Piliaw wy cyn ei bobi.

To peel an egg before it is roasted. *Adage.*

Y bol a bil y cefn.

The belly *will strip* the back. *Adage.*

Piliant a rhwygant yr yd;
Pla i'r ddera a ddetryd.

They will strip away and will tear about the corn; a plague light on that devil. *T. Prys, i gasng.*

Piliawd, *s. m.* (pil) A stripping the surface, a rinding, a peeling.

Piliawg, *a.* (pil) Having a coating, rinded.

Piliedig, *a.* (piliad) Pared, stripped, peeled.

Pilig, *s. m. dim.* (pil) That is of rind, bark, or skin; a vessel made of any rind; a laver.

Pilion, *s. pl. aggr.* (pil) Strippings, peelings.

Pilionen, *s. f. dim.* (pilion) A thin skin or film; a fine membrane; a thin peeling.

Piliwr, *s. m.—pl.* pilwyr (pil—gwr) A stripper, parer, or peeler.

Pilo, *s. m.—pl. t.* au (pil) An apparitor's rod.

Pilus, *a.* (pil) Apt to fly about; transient; frail, weak; poor, mean, wretched.

Pilwrn, *s. m.—pl.* pilyrnau (pil—gwrn) A dart.

Pilyn, *s. m. dim.—pl. t.* au (pil) A piece of skin; a clout, a rag; a tegument, a piece of any texture used as a covering or garment; also a horse cushion or pillion. *Pilyn gwddf*, a neckkerchief.

Pilyndawd, *s. m.* (pilyn) A covering; habiliment, garment, or vesture.

Nid wyt nes er dillad twym-glyd,
I guddio'r cnaw i, i attal annwyd;
Oni fag it' gael pilyndawd
I attal bai, i guddio pechawd.

Thou art not the nearer for warmly-sheltering clothes, to hide the flesh, to keep off cold; if thou shouldest not obtain a covering to keep off vice, to hide sin. *R. Pritchard o Landdyfri.*

Pilyniad, *s. m.* (pilyn) A putting on a garment; a wrapping in any covering.

Pilynu, *v. a.* (pilyn) To cover with a garment.

Pilys, *s. m.—pl. t.* au (pil) A covering or robe made of skin; a pelisse.

Rhita Gawr a wnai bilys o grwyn barfau brenhinoedd.

Rhita the Giant made a *pelisse* of the scalps of the beards of kings. *Gr. ab Arthur.*

Rhoed pilys rhwydau pali
Rhita Gawr ar hyd dau gi.

There was put the *covering* of the velvet nettings of Rhita the Giant over the two dogs. *Gutto y Glyn.*

Pilysawg, *a.* (pilys) Wearing a robe or pelisse.
Pilysyn, *s. m. dim.* (pilys) A robe, a pelisse.
Pill, *s. m.—pl. t.* ion (py—ill) That which turns round; a pivot; a shaft; a base, a stem, or stalk; a stump, or stake; a stock; a heater for ironing; a goal, or spot to retire to in playing; a strong hold, a fortress; a support, or what keeps together, a frame. *Gwr yn mhill yn gware tawlbwrdd*, a man in a secure place playing at chess: *Pill bwcl*, the tongue of a buckle; *pill clo*, the hip of a lock; *dyn yn byw ar ei bill*, a person living upon his means. *Sil.* *Pillion ac ebillion peithynen*, the supporters and staves of the bardic writing frame.

Ni thry i'w bill nes ennill sias.

He will not turn to his *hold* until the game is gained. *L. G. Cothi.*

Blawd man yw'r pan ar bob pill.

Fine flour seems the covering upon every *stem*. *D. ab Gwilym, i'r eira.*

Bwrw llèn uwchlaw pen pob pill.

Casting a veil above the top of every *stem*. *Ll. Goch ab Meirig Hen, i'r eira.*

Ei barau, ei arfau arfoloch,
Ei bebyll, ei bill, a'i bali coch.

His spears, his weapons of tumult, his tents, his *fort*, and his red throne. *Cynddelw, i O. Cyfeiliawg.*

Pillgorn, *s. m.—pl.* pillgyrn (pill—corn) The neck bones, the neck joints. *Pillgorn y gwegil*, the nape of the neck.
Pillgun, *s. m.—pl. t.* ion (pill—cun) A plug.
Pillguniad, *s. m.* (pillgun) A plugging.
Pillguniaw, *v. a.* (pillgun) To stop with a plug.
Pilliad, *s. m.* (pill) A fixing a shaft or stem; a pegging; a forming a hold or place of safety.
Pilliaw, *v. a.* (pill) To shaft, to stem, to peg, to form a hold or place of safety.
Pilliawg, *a.* (pill) Having a pivot, or shaft; pegged; having a strong hold.

Cadfarchawg pilliawg pwyll anghlaiar gwrdd
Gorddwy ei esgar.

A warrior on a steed *with a shaft* terribly fierce in vanquishing his foes. *Prydydd Bychan.*

Pilliedig, *a.* (pilliad) Shafted, stemmed; pegged.
Pillwydd, *s. pl. aggr.* (pill—gwýdd) Dried wood, dead trees left standing.
Pillyn, *s. m. dim.* (pill) A small shaft, stem, or stock; a stake; a peg.
Pin, *s. m.—pl. t.* au (py—in) A pin; a stile for writing with; a pen.
Pinbren, *s. m.—pl. t.* i (pin—pren) The pine-tree; also called *pinwydd*.
Pinc, *s. m.—pl. t.* ion (pin) A sprig, a spray; also the bird called a finch.
Pinc, *a.* (pin) Smart, brisk, gay, or fine.

Mor binc a'r peneurin.

As *brisk* as the yellow-hammer. *Adage.*

Pincedig, *a.* (pinc) Being made smart.
Pincedd, *s. m.* (pinc) Smartness, briskness.
Pinceu, *s. f. dim.* (pinc) A sprig, a spray.

Y dryw——ar hyd pincenau,
Llwyd foddus anllad feddwl.

The wren, along the *sprays*, brown, contented, of wanton thought. *T. Prys.*

Pinciad, *s. m.* (pinc) A sprigging, a spraying.
Pinciant, *s. m.* (pinc) A state of sprigging.
Pinciaw, *v. a.* (pinc) To sprig, to spray.
Pinciawl, *a.* (pinc) Tending to sprig.
Pincrwydd, *s. m.* (pinc) Smartness, briskness.
Pincyn, *s. m. dim.—pl. t.* au (pinc) What is smart or gay; a sprig, a spray; also the finch; also called *pila*, *pinc*, *ysbincyn*, and *telor*.
Piner, *s. m.* (pin) That is fastened with a pin.
Piniad, *s. m.* (pin) A fastening with a pin.
Piniaw, *v. a.* (pin) To pin, to stick a pin.
Piniawl, *a.* (pin) Being fastened with a pin.
Piniedig, *a.* (piniad) Fastened with a pin.
Piniwn, *s. m.—pl.* pinlynau (pin) A gable, or end wall of a building.
Pinwg, *s. m.* (pin) That is tapered or pointed.
Pinwydd, *s. pl. aggr.* (pin—gwydd) Pine-wood.
Pinwydden, *s. f. dim.* (pinwydd) A pine-tree.
Pinygl, *s. m.—pl.* pinyglau (pinwg) That runs into a point; a pinnacle.
Pinygliad, *s. m.* (pinygl) A forming a pinnacle.
Pinyglu, *v. a.* (pinygl) To form a pinnacle.
Pioden, *s. f. dim.* (piawd) A piannet, a magpie.
Piog, *s. f.—pl. t.* od (pi) A pie, a magpie.
Piogen, *s. f. dim.* (piog) A pie. *Piogen y coed*, *caseg y dryc-hin*, a jay; *piogen y mor*, the sea pie.
Pipgnau, *s. pl. aggr.* (pib—cnau) Chesnuts.
Pipian, *v. a.* (pib) To be piping, to pule.
Pipianaidd, *a.* (pipian) Apt to be puling.
Pipianawl, *a.* (pipian) Tending to pule.
Pipianllyd, *a.* (pipian) Apt to be puling.
Pipianu, *v. a.* (pipian) To be piping, to pule.
Pipianydd, *s. m.—pl. t.* ion (pipian) A puler.
Pipre, *s. f.* (pib—rhe) A diarrhœa, or a lax.
Pis, *s. m.—pl. t.* ion (py—is) A spout, that is spouted; a piss; urine, piss.
Pisaw, *v. a.* (pîs) To piss, to make water.

Ni phis boneddig ei hun.

A gentleman *will* not *piss* by himself. *Adage.*

Pisawd, *s. m.* (pis) The act of voiding urine.
Piser, *s. m.—pl. t.* i (pis) A jug, a pitcher.
Pisg, *s. pl. aggr.* (py—isg) Small blisters; pods.
Pisgen, *s. f. dim.—pl. t.* au (pisg) That consists of little blisters or pods; also a pimple, a wheal: the linden.
Pisgenu, *v. n.* (pisgen) To rise in little blisters; to break out in wheals; to pod.
Pisgwrn, *s. m.—pl.* pisgyrnod (pisg—gwrn) A pimple, or wheal.
Pisgwydd, *s. pl. aggr.* (pisg—gwýdd) Lime trees, linden trees; also called *Palalwyf*.
Pisgwydden, *s. f. dim.* (pisgwydd) A linden-tree.
Pisgyrnawg, *a.* (pisgwrn) Having pimples.
Pisgyrniad, *s. m.* (pisgwrn) A breaking out in pimples.
Pisgyrnu, *v. n.* (pisgwrn) To break out in pimples.
Pisgyrnyn, *s. m. dim.* (pisgwrn) A small pimple.
Pision, *s. pl. aggr.* (pis) Urines, stales.
Pislath, *s. f.—pl. t.* au (pis—llath) A bar laid to keep in the litter of a cowhouse. See *llaesodbren*
Pislyd, *a.* (pis) Apt to void urine; diabetical.
Pislydrwydd, *s. m.* (pislyd) Aptness to void urine.
Pisodyn, *s. m. dim.* (pisawd) The quantity of urine voided at one time.

Hanbydd achwaneg y mor o bisodyn y dryw.

The sea will be augmented by the *pissing* of the wren. *Adage.*

Hawdd cronni ffrwd pisodyn.

It is easy to dam the current of a *pissing*. *Adage.*

Pistyll, *s. m.—pl. t.* ion (pis—tyll) A spout. *Pistyll yr ysgyfaint*, the spout of the lungs, or lower part of the trachea; *pistyll y breuant*, the top of the windpipe.
Pistylliad, *s. m.* (pistyll) A spouting out.
Pistylliaw, *v. n.* (pistyll) To spout out.
Pistylliawg, *a.* (pistyll) Having a spout.

Piso, *s. m.* (pis) What is staled as urine; also the same as *biswal*, the draining from where cattle are kept.

Piswydd, *s. pl aggr.* (pis-gwydd) Spindle trees.

Piswydden, *s. f. dim.* (piswydd) A spindle-tree.

Pitan, *s. c. dim.* (pid) A teat, a nipple.

Pitw, *a.* (pid) Very little, minute, or petty.

Pith, *s. m.—pl. t.* ion (py—ith) That is like grains, that is granulated.

Pithell, *s. f.—pl. t.* od (pith) A shardfish.

Piw, *s. m.—pl. t.* od (pi) A dug, or udder.

Pla, *s. m.—pl. t.* äu (py—lla) That expands, opens, or breaks out; a plague.

Daeth i lwyth Hwfa y la pla [illegible].

There befel to the tribe of Hwfa a double affliction. *Bleddyn Fardd.*

Plaaidd, *a.* (pla) Like a plague, plaguy.

Plaawg, *a.* (pla) Having a plague, or pestilence.

Plaawl, *a.* (pla) Belonging to the plague.

Plad, *s. m.* (py—llad) What is driven out, what is beaten out, or flattened; any flat piece; plate

Tra bo dur na plad, tra bo dwr na [illegible].

Whilst there be steel or *plate*, whilst there be the bold or [illegible]. *H. Llwyn.*

Pladr, *s. m.* (plad) That spreads out flatly.

Pladren, *s. f. dim.* (pladr) That is spread out.

Pladres, *s. f.—pl. t.* i (pladr) A shewy woman.

Pladru, *v. a.* (pladr) To spread out, to flaunt.

Pladur, *s. f.—pl. t.* iau (plad) A scythe.

Pladuraw, *v. a.* (pladur) To use a scythe.

Pladurawd, *s. m.* (pladur) A stroke of a scythe.

Pladuriad, *s. m.* (pladur) A making use of a scythe.

Pladuriaeth, *s. m.* (pladur) The use of the scythe.

Pladurwr, *s. m.—pl.* pladurwyr (pladur—gwr) One who uses a scythe, a mower.

Placaw, *v. a.* (pla) To plague, or to torment.

Oni [illegible] mi dy nerthu, a chymeryd trugaredd arnad, tithau a [illegible] dy blacaw gyda hwynt.

If I were not to strengthen thee, and have mercy upon thee, then thou wouldest be getting thyself *to be tormented* with them. *Marchawg Crwydrad.*

Plaid, *s. f.—pl.* pleidiau (pla—id) That parts or divides off, a side; a partition; a wall; a party; a cause. *Plaid wellt*, a straw partition. *O blaid*, on the part of, because of.

Blaid wrth annhwyll pwyll parawd.

With indiscretion there is cause for ready wit. *Adage.*

D[illegible] taw, fan' [illegible] [illegible],
D[illegible] [illegible] o dan dy blaid.

Awake, [illegible] to save my soul; an afflicted person is under thy *wall*. *D. ab Edmwnt.*

Plan, *s. m.—pl. t.* oedd (pla—an) That is parted off; or that proceeds from; a ray, a scion or shoot; a plantation, or planting; also a plane.

Planad, *s. f.* (plan) A shooting off; that shoots or radiates; that is generated; a flowing element; a meteor.

Pil [illegible], ple'r [illegible].
Planad wyllt, [illegible] wyt?

Stripper of a building, where art thou, wild meteor, where art thou not? *Maredudd ab Rhys.*

Tad planad [illegible], tad [illegible] gwyn;
Tad i'r gwynt, gwaith ei law,
Tad gwenith, tad [illegible],
Tad [illegible], tad i'r gwlaw.

The father of the regular *fluid element*, father of the silent [illegible], father of the wind, the work of his hand, father of the [illegible], father of germination, father of the dew; father to the rain. *L. G. Cothi.*

Planc, *s. m.—pl. t.* iau (plan) That is driven out; that is flat; a plank, or board. *Bara planc*, a sort of hard thin bread, used in Carmarthenshire.

Heb na chaniog, na chlogan,
(Blin yw'r [illegible]) yn blanc glan.

Sometimes without a penny, or a cloke (vexations to the complainant) like a bare *board*. *Gutto ab Ifan.*

Planaidd, *a.* (plan) Tending to shoot off.

Planawd, *s. m.* (plan) A producing by shoots; the act of planting.

Planawg, *a.* (plan) Producing shoots; planted.

Planawl, *a.* (plan) Tending to shoot; belonging to planting.

Planed, *s. f.—pl. t.* au (plan) That shoots or radiates; a shooting body; a planet.

Planedawl, *a.* (planed) Planetical, planetary.

Planedig, *a.* (plan) Being produced by shoots; planted, or set.

Planedydd, *s. m.—pl. t.* ion (planed) Planetarium

Planfa, *s. f.—pl.* planfeydd (plan—ma) A plantation, or nursery of trees.

Planiad, *s. m.* (plan) A planting, a setting shoots

Planig, *a.* (plan) Being apt to produce shoots.

Planigfa, *s. f.—pl. t.* oedd (planig) A plantation.

Planigyn, *s. m. dim.* (planig) A shoot; a plant.

Plant, *s. pl. aggr.* (plan) Emanations; issue, offspring, children.

Plant gwirionedd ynt hen ddiarebion.

Old proverbs are the *children* of truth. *Adage.*

Tri nodau plant Duw: [illegible] diffalch, cydwybod lan, a dyoddef camwedd yn amynedgar.

The three characteristics of the *children* of God; comfort void of pride, a pure conscience, and the bearing of injury patiently. *Barddas.*

Planta, *v. a.* (plant) To get or to bear children.

Plantach, *s. pl. dim.* (plant) Little children.

Plantaidd, *a.* (plant) Like children; childish.

Rhaid i'r dawiolion fod mor blentaidd na ellir eu cyfrwyso.

It is necessary for pious ones to be so *like children* as not to be possible to make them crafty. *Morgan Llwyd.*

Plantawg, *a.* (plant) Having children.

Plantawl, *a.* (plant) Belonging to children.

Planteiddiad, *s. m.* (plantaidd) A becoming like children.

Planteiddiaw, *v. n.* (plantaidd) To become like children; to grow childish.

Plantos, *s. pl. dim.* (plant) Little children.

Plannu, *v. a.* (plan) To shoot off; to produce a shoot or offspring; to plant, to set shoots.

Planwr, *s. m.—pl.* planwyr (plann—gwr) One who produces shoots; a planter.

Plas, *s. m.—pl. t.* au (pla—as) An extended plat or area: an edifice; a large house, a hall.

Llyw deifiniawg llidiawg, llediad fydd ei blas:
[illegible] warth yw ei gas no'i garenydd.

The bounteous and wrathful leader, displayed with profusion his *hall*, much worse is his hate than his connection. *Llygad Gwr.*

Plasaidd, *a.* (plas) Like a hall; like a palace.

Plasawl, *a.* (plas) Belonging to a hall.

Plast, *s. m.* (plas) That is spread out.

Plastr, *s. m.—pl.* plastrion (plast) That is spread over, a plaister, a daub.

Plastrawg, *a.* (plastr) Covered with plaister.

Plastriad, *s. m.* (plastr) A plaistering.

Plastriaw, *v. a.* (plastr) To plaister, to daub.

Plastriwr, *s. m.* (plastr—gwr) A plaisterer.

Plasu, *v. a.* (plas) To form an extended area; to build a large edifice; to build a large house.

Plau, *v. a.* (pla) To expand, to break out; to infect with a plague, to plague.

Pled, *s. m.* (py—lled) A principle of extension.

Pledr, *s. m.* (pled) That stretches out.

Pledraidd, *a.* (pledr) Tending to stretch.

Pledren, *s. f. dim.* (pledr) A bladder, a bowl. *Llonaid pledren o flawd*, a bowlful of meal. *Dyf.*

Pledrig, *s. f. dim.* (pledr) A little bladder.

Pledru, *v. a.* (pledr) To stretch or extend out.

Pledryn, *s. m. dim.—pl. t.* au (pledr) A slang, or slip: waste ground by the way side.

Pleiden, *s. f. dim.—pl. t.* i (plaid) What serves for a partition; a hurdle, a wattling.

Pleidgar, *a.* (plaid) Apt to side; factious, partial

> Pybyr wanar, pleidgar blwng.
>
> A vigorous leader, *factious* and relentless.
> *Iolo Goch. i O. Glyndyfrdwy*

Pleidgarwch, *s. m.* (pleidgar) Factiousness.

Pleidiad, *s. m.* (plaid) A taking a part.

Pleidiant, *s. m.* (plaid) The act of taking a side.

Pleidiaw, *v. a.* (plaid) To take a part, to side.

Pleidiawg, *a.* (plaid) Of a side or party; factious

Pleidiawl, *a.* (plaid) Belonging to a party.

Pleidiolrwydd, *s. m.* (pleidiawl) The state of belonging to a party.

Pleidiwr, *s. m.* (plaid—gwr) A partisan.

Pleidwriaeth, *s. m.* (pleidiwr) The state of being a party-man, or a partisan.

Pleidwyn, *s. m.* (plaid—gwyn) Party rage.

Pleidydd, *s. m.—pl. t.* ion (plaid) A partisan.

> Yn y flwyddyn 965 y dygynt bleidyddion Ieuaf ab Idwal Gotffrid ab Haralit y drydy-waith i Fon.
>
> In the year 965 the *partisans* of Ieuav son of Idwal brought Gotfrid son of Haralit the third time into Mon.
> *Cwrad. Llangarfan.*

Pleiniad, *s. m.—pl. t.* au (plan) Radiation.

Pleiniaw, *v. a.* (plan) To radiate, to cast rays.

Pleiniawg, *a.* (plan) Having rays.

Pleiniawl, *a.* (plan) Radiating, casting rays.

Plenig, *a.* (plan) Radiant, splendid, glorious.

> Cirledus Arglwydd! bwyf caredig fry,
> Yn y fro ddewisig—
> Ar warant Efa blant blenig.
>
> Gracious Lord! may I be beloved on high, in the blissful region, on the covenant of the *glorious* children of Eve.
> *Gr. ab M. ab Dafydd.*

Plent, *s. f.—pl. t.* ydd (plan) That is rayed.

Plentyn, *s. m. dim.—pl. t.* od (plant) A child.

Plentynaidd, *a.* (plentyn) Childish, babyish.

Plentynawl, *a.* (plentyn) Belonging to a child.

Plentyneiddiad, *s. m.* (plentynaidd) A becoming childish, a becoming like a baby.

Plentyneiddiaw, *v. n.* (plentynaidd) To become childish; to become as a baby.

Plentyneiddrwydd, *s. m.* (plentynaidd) Childishness.

Plenydd, *s. m.* (plan) Radiance; display; light.

> Tri chyntefigion beirdd Ynys Prydain;
> Plenydd, Alawn, a Gwron
>
> The three primordials of the bards of the isle of Britain, *Light*, Harmony, and Energy.
> *Laiddas*

Pleth, *s. f.—pl. t.* i (py—lleth) A plait, a braid.

Plethadwy, *a.* (pleth) Capable of being plaited.

Plethawl, *a.* (pleth) Plaiting, or wreathing.

Plethbin, *s. m.—pl. t.* au (pleth—pin) A bobbin, a small pin used in weaving.

Plethedig, *a.* (pleth) Plaited, wreathed, braided.

Plethiad, *s. m.—pl. t.* au (pleth) A plaiting, a braiding, a wreathing; a doubling; a twirling; also a shake in music.

Plethlinyn, *s. m.—pl. t.* au (pleth—llinyn) A plaited cord, or bobbin.

Plethu, *v. a.* (pleth) To plait, to braid, to wreath

Plethwr, *s. m.—pl.* plethwyr (pleth—gwr) A plaiter, a braider, a wreather.

Pliciad, *s. m.—pl. t.* au (plig) A peeling.

Pliciaw, *v. a.* (plig) To pluck, to peel.

Plig, *s. m.* (py—llig) A pluck off, a peel.

Pling, *s. m.* (py—lling) A flay, a strip off.

Plingaw, *v. a.* (pling) To flay, to skin.

Plingiad, *s. m.* (pling) A flaying, a skinning.

Plingwr, *s. m.* (pling—gwr) A flayer.

Plisg, *s. m.—pl. t.* ion (lly—isg) Shells, husks.

Plisgaw, *v. a.* (plisg) To shell, or to husk.

Plisgawl, *a.* (plisg) Belonging to a shell.

Plisgiad, *s. m.* (plisg) A shelling, a husking.

Plisgwrn, *s. m.* (plisg—gwrn) The lime-tree; also called *gwaglwyfen*, *plisgyrnen*, and *pisgen*.

Plisgyn, *s. m. dim.* (plisg) A shell, or a husk.

> A'th wisg a fu o'r plisgyn,
> O'th febyd hefyd hyd hyn.
>
> And thy covering was of the *shell*, from thy youth, also, to this time.
> *D. Ph. Rhys Len.*

Plith, *s. m.* (py—llith) The state of being blended or amongst. *Plith-dra-phlith*, *plith-dra-chymysg*, all in confusion, helter-skelter.

> Duw a alwodd ei deulu,
> Pen cantorion, loewon lu,
> I ganu cerdd gogoniant,
> Ac yn eu plith geuau plant.
>
> God has called his family, chief of songsters, a splendid host, to sing a hymn of glory, and in their *company* were infants' lips.
> *Gro. Owain*

Plithaw, *v. a.* (plith) To blend, to be mixed.

Plithedd, *s. m.* (plith) Mixedness, blendedness.

Plithiad, *s. m.* (plith) A blending, a mixing.

Ploc, *s. m.—pl. t.* iau (py—lloc) A block.

Plociaw, *v. a.* (ploc) To block; to plug.

Plocyn, *s. m. dim.* (ploc) A small block.

Plu, *s. pl. aggr.* (py—llu) Feathers. *Plu y gweunydd*, cotton-grass, *gwely plu*, a feather bed.

> Mae llawer gwydd heblaw yr un sy'n gwisgaw plu.
>
> There be many a goose besides the one which wears *feathers*
> *Adage.*

Pluad, *s. m.* (plu) A feathering, a fledging; a pluming; deplumation.

Pluaidd, *a.* (plu) Feathery, plumous, featherlike

Pluaw, *v. n.* (plu) To feather, to fledge; to plume, to deplume; to strip of feathers. *Pluaw eira*, to snow in large flakes.

Pluawg, *a.* (plu) Covered with feathers, fledged.

Pluawl, *a.* (plu) Plumous; feathering.

Pluawr, *s. m. aggr.* (plu) A plumage, feathers.

Plucan, *s. c. dim.* (plu) Down; kidney-vetch.

Pludd, *s. m.* (py—lludd) That is flexible or soft.

Plnddaw, *v. a.* (pludd) To render flexible.

Pluen, *s. f. dim.* (plu) A feather, a plume.

Plueniad, *s. m.* (pluen) A pluming, a feathering.

Pluenu, *v. n.* (plu) To plume, to feather.

Pluf, *s. pl. aggr.* (plu) Plumage, or feathers.

> Yr alarch——
> Palfau gwydd, yn y pluf gwyn.
>
> The swan, with shanks of a goose, in the white *plumage*
> *D. ab Ieuan Ddu.*
>
> Dyged pob eden ei bluf oddigerthi, ac felly bi a ufuddeir.
>
> Let every bird take its own *feathers* away from her, and so she shall be humbled.
> *Dameg*

Plufaidd, *a.* (pluf) Feathery, or plumous.

Plufawg, *a.* (pluf) Feathered, or plumed.

Plufawl, *a.* (pluf) Plumous; pluming.

Plufen, *s. f. dim.* (pluf) A plume, or a feather.

Plufiad, *s. m.* (pluf) A pluming; plumosity.

Plufiaw, *v. a.* (pluf) To deplume, to feather.

Plüwr, *s. m.* (plu—gwr) A feather dresser.

Plw, *s. m.* (py—llw) That spreads or expands out

Plwch, *s. m.* (plw) A space; a while: a quantity. *Plwc mawr*, a great deal; *rhaid i ti aros plwc*, thou must stay a while; *mi ei gwnaf fo plwc*, I will do it instantly.

Plwca, *s. m.* (plwc) A spread; a splash; mire.

Plwm, *s. m.* (plw) Lead. *Mwn plwm*, lead ore.

> Yr eira——
> Plwm oer ei glog; p'le mae'r gwlaw?
>
> The snow, like lead of chilling cloke; where is the rain.
> *D. ab Gwilym.*

Plwng, *s. m.* (py—llwng) A plunge, or a dip.

Plwy, *s. m.* (plw) A community, a parish.

Plwydd, *s. m.—pl. t.* au (plwy) A community.

Plwyf, *s. m.—pl. t.* au (plwy) A whole mass or complete body of people; a cure, a parish.

> Rhydderchafwy Duw ar blwyf Brython
> Arwydd llewenydd lluydd o Fon!
>
> May God exalt over the *community* of Britons the sign of gladness of a host from Mona!
> *Taliesin.*

Plwyfaidd, *a.* (plwyf) Being like a parish.

Plwyfawg, *s.* (plwyf) Having a parish.

Pwyfawl, *a.* (plwyf) Belonging to a parish.

Plwyfogaeth, *s. m.* (plwyfawg) The jurisdiction of a parish; the jurisdiction of the church.

> Yr eglwys y gorddiweddwys arno gyfraith yn ei phlwyfogaeth.
>
> The church where the law overtook him within its *parochial jurisdiction*.
> *Welsh Laws.*

Plwyfogi, *v. a.* (plwyfawg) To settle in a parish; to become settled in a parish.

Plwyfoli, *v. a.* (plwyfawl) To render parochial; to become settled in a parish.

Plwyfoliaeth, *s. m.* (plwyfawl) The act of rendering parochial; the state of being parochial.

Plwyn, *s. m.—pl. t.* iau (py—llwyn) That is full or perfect. *Plwyniau*, the hairs on the breast and other parts of a full-grown person.

Plwynaw, *v. n.* (plwyn) To have signs of puberty.

Plwyniad, *s. m.—pl. t.* au (plwyn) A having signs of puberty.

Ply, *s. m.* (py—lly) That is flexible or tender.

Plydd, *a.* (ply) Soft, delicate, tender, limber, flexible, pliant.

> Mynai adar man——
> I gael plad gwelyau plydd.
>
> He would procure small birds to enjoy the spread of *soft* beds.
> *H. ab D. ab I. ab Rhys, i walch.*

Plyddâad, *s. m.* (plyddâu) A rendering soft or tender, a becoming soft, delicate, or pliant.

Plyddâawl, *a.* (plyddâu) Tending to soften, apt to become delicate or pliant.

Plyddâu, *v. a.* (plydd) To render soft, to render pliant; to become soft or pliant.

Plyddaw, *v. a.* (plydd) To soften, to make tender or delicate, to become soft or tender.

> Clwyd ysgwydd nis plydd, nis plyg,
> Clod gyhoedd caerydd cerrig.
>
> A shivered palisade that *will* not *yield*, that will not bend, the public boast of stone forts.
> *Ll. P. Moch.*

Plyddawl, *a.* (plydd) Of a soft or tender quality.

Plyddedd, *s. m.* (plydd) Softness, tenderness.

Plyddiad, *s. m.* (plydd) A softening, a making tender or flexible, a becoming soft.

Plyddu, *v. r.* (plydd) To soften; to become soft, tender, or delicate; to grow limber.

Plyg, *s. m.—pl. t.* ion (ply) A flexion, a double, a plait, a fold, a bend.

Plygain, *s. m.—pl.* plygeiniau (ply—cain) The return of light, the early morning, the dawn.

> Yn newaint, yn mhlygeiniau
> Llewychawd yn lleufeiau.
>
> In the nightfall in the *early dawns* let our lamps brightly shine.
> *Taliesin.*

Plygaint, *s. m.* (plygain) The dawn, or day-spring

Plygawl, *a.* (plyg) Doubling, or folding.

Plygddor, *s. m.* (plyg—dor) A folding door.

Plygedd, *s. m.* (plyg) A doubled or folded state.

Plygeiniawl, *a.* (plygain) Dawning, matin.

> Y bore yn blygeiniawl iawn——ei allan.
>
> In the morning very *early*——he went out.
> *Mark i. 35.*

Plygfa, *s. f.—pl. t.* oedd (plyg) A double, a fold.

Plygiad, *s. m.—pl. t.* au (plyg) A doubling, a folding, a bending back.

Plygiadawl, *a.* (plygiad) Tending to double.

Plygiant, *s. m.* (ply) A duplication, a folding.

Plygiedig, *a.* (plygiad) Doubled, or folded.

Plygiedydd, *s. m.* (plygiad) Tweezers, pliers.

Plygu, *v. a.* (plyg) To double, to plait, to fold.

> Gwell y wialen a blyco nog a doro.
>
> Better the rod that *will bend* than the one that will break.
> *Adage.*

> Nis plyg ei feddwl, mal Cydweli;
> Ni ddifanoria'n rhoi da 'n rhaid ym.
>
> His mind *will* not *give way*, like Cydweli; he will not deviate from his purpose in distributing bounty according to our wants.
> *L. G. Cothi.*

Plygwr, *s. m.* (plyg—gwr) A folder, a doubler.

Plygyd, *s. m.* (plyg) A party or side. *O blygyd*, on account of; *yn mhlygyd*, in relation to.

Plym, *s. m.* (py—llym) That is agonising.

Plymawl, *a.* (plym) Agonizing, writhing.

Plymen, *s. f. dim.—pl. t.* au (plwm) That is of lead; a leaden vessel; a plummet. *Plymen iâ*, a flake of ice.

Plymiad, *s. m.* (plwm) A leadening.

Plymiaidd, *a.* (plwm) Like lead; leaden.

Plymiaw, *v. a.* (plwm) To leaden; to lead, or to sound with a lead-line.

Plymiawl, *a.* (plwm) Of the quality of lead.

Plymiwr, *s. m.* (plwm—gwr) A plumber.

Plymliw, *s. m.* (plwm—lliw) Lead-colour.

Plymlyd, *a.* (plwm) Of the nature of lead.

Plymnwyd, *s. f.—pl. t.* ydd (plym—nwyd) A struggle, a conflict.

> Er lles gwledig Mon gwaisg yn mhlymnwyd.
>
> To the benefit of the ruler of Mon active in the *conflict*.
> *Gwalchmai.*

Plymu, *v. a.* (plwm) To lead, to cover with lead.

> Peris gwneuthur pollon—ac eu plymu, a gosod y rhai hyny a dan y dwfr.
>
> He caused stakes to be made, and *leaden them*, and to fix these under the water.
> *Gr. ab Arthur.*

Plymwriaeth, *s. m.* (plymiwr) Plumbery.

PO, *s. m. r.* That comprehends; that is comprehended, contained, or restrained.

Po, *adv.* (po, *s.*) If; by how much, by so much.

> Po amlaf y bleiddiaid gwaethaf i'r defaid.
>
> By *so much* the more frequent the wolves the worse for the sheep.
> *Adage.*

Pob, *pron.* (po) Each, every. *Pob yn wr*, man by man; *pob yn un*, one by one; *pob yn ronyn*, *pob yn dipyn*, *pob yn ychydig*, by little and little.

Pob, *a.* (po) Each, every. *Pob dyn*, every person. *pob un*, every one; *pob peth*, every thing.

> Pob peth yn ei amser.
>
> *Every* thing in its time. *Adage.*

> Aflafar pob tawedawg.
>
> Inarticulate is *every* silent one. *Adage.*

> Cyfoethawg pob diddyled.
>
> Rich is *every* one not in debt. *Adage.*

Pob, *s. m.* (py—ob) A bake, baking. *a.* Baked; roasted, toasted.

Poban, *s. f.—pl. t.* au (pob) An oven.

Pobedig, *a.* (pob) Baked; roasted, toasted.

Pobi, *v. a.* (pob) To bake; to roast, to toast.

Pobi bara, crasu bara, to bake bread; to toast bread; *pobi caws*, to toast cheese.

> Llawn i bobi golwyth.
>
> Full to *bake* a piece of flesh. *Adage.*
>
> Anhawdd pobi heb flawd.
>
> It is difficult to *bake* without flour. *Adage.*

Pobiad, *s. m.* (pob) A baking; a roasting, a toasting; the quantity baked at once.
Pobiant, *s. m.* (pob) A baking; a batch.
Pobl, *s. pl. aggr.—pl. t.* oedd (pawb) A people.

> Credwn i'n Rheen——
> Galwaf ymeiriawl ar ei weswas,
> A holl graddau nef yn eu heddas:
> A'm eirioles Pedr, per ei efrae
> Ar bobloedd gwerin gwaned trae.
>
> Let us believe in our Creator: I will invoke the intercession of his blessed servant, and all the orders of heaven in their station: May I be interceded for by Peter, of sweet influence on simple *people* of so weak dependence. *Meilyr ab Gwalchmai.*

Poblach, *s. pl. dim.* (pobl) Low people, plebeians.
Poblawg, *a.* (pobl) Having people, populous.
Pobli, *v. a.* (pobl) To people; to become peopled.
Pobliad, *s. m.* (pobl) Population, a peopling.
Poblogaeth, *s. m.* (pobl) A populous state.
Poblogaidd, *a.* (poblawg) Popular, populous.
Poblogi, *v. a.* (poblawg) To populate, to people.
Poblogiad, *s. m.* (pobl) A rendering populous; a becoming populous.
Poblogrwydd, *s. m.* (poblawg) Populousness.
Pobpeth, *s. m.* (pob—peth) Every thing.

> Bach yw pobpeth yn ei ddechreu.
>
> Small is *every thing* in its beginning. *Adage.*

Pobtu, *s. m.* (pob—tu) Every side, the compass, or circuit. *adv.* On every side, about.

> Pump gwregys——
> Y ddau o bobtu, y dyfu tymher da,
> Gwres oddihwnt, ac oerfel oddyma.
>
> Five zones, the two on *each side*, where is good temperature, heat from that side, and cold from this side. *Taliesin.*

Pobty, *s. m.—pl. t.* au (pob—ty) A bakehouse.
Pobur, *s. m.* (pob) A baker; a roaster; a toaster.
Poburies, *s. f.—pl. t.* au (pobur) A baking woman.

> Poburies a ddyly ei bwyd o'r llys; a'i dillad; a saig pan fo y brenin, a theisen diwedd pobi o bob amryw flawd a bopo; a'i gwely yn y bwytty.
>
> The *baking-woman* claims her food from the palace; and her clothes, and a dainty when the king is there, and a cake after baking of the various sorts of meal that she bakes; and her bed in the provision house. *Welsh Laws.*

Pobwr, *s. m.—pl.* pobwyr (pobi—gwr) A baker.
Pobwraig, *s. f.* (pobi—gwraig) A female baker.
Pobydd, *s. m.—pl. t.* ion (pob) A baker.

> Darfu i drulliad brenin yr Aipht, ac y pobydd, bechu yn erbyn eu harglwydd.
>
> The butler of the king of Egypt, and the *baker*, did sin against their lord. *Genesis* 40. 1.

Pobyddes, *s. f.—pl. t.* au (pobydd) A baking woman.
Pobyddiaeth, *s. m.* (pobydd) The art of baking.
Poc, *s. m.* (py—oc) A smack; a kiss.
Poca, *s. m. dim.* (poc) A smack, a kiss.
Pocan, *s. c. dim.* (poc) A smack, a kiss.
Pocyn, *s. m. dim.* (poc) A smack, a kiss.
Pod, *s. m.—pl. t.* au (po) That is taken in.
Podi, *v. a.* (pod) To take in; to comprehend.
Podr, *a.* (*f. of* pwdr) Powdery, mouldering.
Poen, *s. f.—pl. t.* au (po—en) Pain, torment, agony; punishment; pains, labour. *Cei hyn am dy boen*, thou shalt have this for thy pains.

> Rhag pobloedd poen eu cyweithas
> Boed ef fy Nuw nef bo fy ninas.
>
> Against people whose society is a *pain*, may he who is my God of heaven be my bulwark. *Meilyr ab Gwalchmai.*

Poendawd, *s. m.* (poen) An infliction of pain.

Poenedig, *a.* (poen) Pained, or tormented.
Poenedigaeth, *s. f.—pl. t.* au (poenedig) The being pained or tormented; punishment.
Poengar, *a.* (poen) Painful, or tormenting.
Poeni, *v. a.* (poen) To inflict pain, to torment; to take pains; to suffer pains, to be in torment.
Poeniad, *s. m.* (poen) A paining, a tormenting; a taking pains; a suffering pain.
Poenof, *s. m.* (poen—of) Emotion of pain.
Poenofaint, *s. m.* (poenof) The state of suffering pain, a state of punishment.

> Cyn ergryd pengyd poenofaint,
> Porthwyr Duw, boed hwynt fy ngherraint!
>
> Before the shock of the pang of *punishment*, the porters of God, may they be my friends! *Cynddelw.*

Poenus, *a.* (poen) Painful, tormenting; full of misery, laborious, toiling.
Poenusaw, *v. a.* (poenus) To render painful; to be taking pains, to be laborious.
Poenusedd, *s. m.* (poenus) Painfulness, or a state of pain; laboriousness.
Poenusrwydd, *s. m.* (poenus) Painfulness.
Poenwedd, *s. f.* (poen—gwedd) An aspect of agony.
Poenwr, *s. m.—pl.* poenwyr (poen—gwr) One who pains, a tormentor; a toiler.
Poenydd, *s. m.—pl. t.* ion (poen) A painer.
Poer, *s. m.—pl. t.* ion (py—oer) Saliva, spittle.
Poerai, *s. m.* (poer) The bastard pellitory.
Poerawl, *a.* (poer) Spitting, salivarious.
Poeredd, *s. m.* (poer) A salivous state, spitting.
Poeri, *v. a.* (poer) To spit. *Poeru yn ei enau*, spit in his mouth: *i. e.* bribe him.
Poeriad, *s. m.* (poer) A spitting; expectoration.
Poeriannawl, *a.* (poeriant) Salivous.
Poeriannu, *v. a.* (poeriant) To salivate.
Poeriant, *s. m.* (poer) A salivation, spitting.
Poerlys, *s. pl. aggr.* (poer—llys) Master-wort.
Poerllyd, *a.* (poer) Salivous; apt to spit.
Poerllydrwydd, *s. m.* (poerllyd) The salivous state
Poerllydu, *v. a.* (poerllyd) To render salivous.
Poerwr, *s. m.—pl.* poerwyr (poeri—gwr) A spitter.
Poeryn, *s. m. dim.* (poer) A spitter, one who spits; one spitted into his mouth, like a spaniel, or that is made a tool of, a sycophant.
Poes, *s. m.—pl. t.* au (py—oes) A state of being.

> Can ai wyr a'i pwyll pelled anfoes
> Anrhaid ystyriaid ysbaid eisoes
> O gadarn gadwent camp present poes:
> A fu oedawg doe heddyw nid oes;
> Yn hir ni synwys Duw dynawl einioes.
>
> Since he that regards it knows not how spreading is immorality; unnecessary then the consideration of the extent of the severe conflict of the trial of the present *state*: That was remaining yesterday to-day is not; for long hath not God kindled human life. *Meilyr ab Gwalchmai.*

Poesawl, *a.* (poes) Belonging to a state of being.
Poesi, *v. n.* (poes) To be in a state of being.
Poesiad, *s. m.* (poes) A having a state of being.
Poeth, *a.* (py—oeth) Hot, scorching, fiery, acrid.
Poethawd, *s. m.* (poeth) The act of heating.
Poethawl, *a.* (poeth) Heating, burning.
Poethder, *s. m.* (poeth) Hotness, heat; acrimony.
Poethdra, *s. m.* (poeth) Hotness; acrimony.
Poethedig, *a.* (poeth) Being heated.
Poethedd, *s. m.* (poeth) Hotness; acrimony.
Poethfa, *s f.—pl.* poethfëydd (poeth) A burning.
Poethfan, *s. f.—pl. t.* au (poeth) A hot place.

> ——Poethfan peth uffernawl,
> Yn yr hon mae cynnygyn yn cannawl celwydd.
>
> A *burning place* of infernal nature, where there is party praising of falsehood. *Bleddyn Fardd.*

Poethfrych, *a.* (brych) Bristling with heat.

Poethfflam, *s. f.* (poeth—fflam) A hot flame; the hearts-ease; also called *blaen y gwaew*.
Poethgur, *s. m.* (poeth—cur) An inflamed throb.
Poethi, *v. a.* (poeth) To make hot, to heat, to become hot, to be heated.
Poethiad, *s. m.—pl. t.* au (poeth) A heating.
Poethiannawl, *a.* (poethiant) Tending to torrefy, of a parching nature.
Poethiannu, *v. a.* (poethiant) To torrefy.
Poethiant, *s. m.* (poeth) Torrefaction.
Poethiator, *ger.* (poethiad) In heating.
Poethineb, *s. m.* (poeth) A torrid state.
Poethitor, *sup.* (poeth) To be heating.
Poethni, *s. m.* (poeth) Hotness, or heat.
Poethotor, *part.* (poeth) Having been heating.
Poethus, *a.* (poeth) Of a hot quality.
Poethwal, *s. m.* (poeth—gwal) A place where furze, heath, or the like, has been burnt standing.
Poethwg, *s. m.* (poeth) Torridity, aridity.
Poethwraidd, *s. m.* (poeth—gwraidd) Masterwort.
Poethwy, *s. m.* (poeth—wy) The razorbill.
Poethwyn, *s. m.* (poeth—gwyn) An inflammatory heat; heat of passion.
Poethygus, *v.* (poethwg) Of a torrid nature.
Pol, *s. m.* (py—ol) That is without a trace.
Pol, *a.* (*f. of* pwl) Blunt, round, obtuse.
Poliad, *s. m.* (pawl) A fixing a pole.
Poliaw, *v. a.* (pawl) To set up a pole or stake; to beat with a stake, to cudgel.

> Bid lai nawdd; bodlon oeddwn,
> Bell hael, it boliaw hwn.
>
> Be the protection done away; I were content, generous Bell, that thou shouldest *cudgel* this one. *Rhis. Iorwerth.*

Poliedig, *a.* (poliad) That is staked.
Polion, *s. pl. aggr.* (pawl) Stakes, poles.
Polioni, *v. a.* (polion) To set stakes or poles.
Pon, *s. m.* (py—on) That is puffed or blistered.
Pona, *adv.* (po—na) If not, if it should not. It precedes words with consonant initials.
Ponad, *adv.* (po—na) If not, should it not.
Ponag, *adv.* (po—nag) Unless, except.
Ponar, *s. f.* (pon) A puff; a pod. *Teisen bonar*, a puff cake: a bean.
Ponc, *s. f.—pl. t.* iau (py—onc) A hillock.
Poncen, *s. f. dim.* (ponc) A small hillock.
Ponciad, *s. m.* (ponc) A swelling up.
Ponciaw, *v. a.* (ponc) To swell up, to puff up. *Mal y poncia dy fron!* how thy breast heaves!
Ponciawl, *a.* (ponc) Tending to swell up.
Poncyn, *s. m. dim.* (ponc) A little hillock.
Pond, *adv.* (py—ond) Is it not; what else.
Poni, *adv.* (py—oni) Why is it not; why not.

> Poni welwch hynt y gwynt a'r glaw;
> Poni welwch chwi 'r deri yn ymdaraw?
>
> Why behold you not the course of the wind and the rain; why behold you not the oaks beating one against the other? *Gr. ab yr Ynad Coch.*

Poniaw, *v. a.* (pon) To puff out, to swell out, to fatten, to feed.
Ponid, *adv.* (py—onid) What not, is it not, is it not so. *Dyn wyd ti: Ponid dyn wyd tithau?* Thou art a man: Art not thou a man too?

> Ponid erlys dy gyfreu
> A lefair dy enau?
>
> Do not thy passions counteract what is uttered by thy lips? *Taliesin, Arymes Dyddbrawd.*

Pont, *s. f.—pl. t.* ydd (pon) That rises up; that rises or supports; that elevates; a bridge. *Pont ysgwydd*, a collar-bone; *pont y trwyn*, the bone of the nose; *pynt perth*, the archings of a bush; *pont faen*, a stone bridge; *pont goed*, a wooden bridge.

> A fo pen bid pont.
>
> That would be the top let him be a *bridge*. *Adage.*

> Miloedd a wnant
> Mawl ogoniant
> Ar fryn a phant
> A phynt ysbryd.
>
> Thousands will give praise of triumph, on hill and dale, with the *elevations* of the spirit. *Plygiant i Ddew.*

> Cymmrodawg swydd cymmrodw ei fri;
> Cymmroded fyned pan fo pont Dewi.
>
> Of conciliating disposition, dartling is his honour: let him be tranquillized to go when Dewi shall be *supporting agent*. *Meilyr ab Gwalchmai.*

Pontawg, *a.* (pont) Having an arch or bridge.
Pontbren, *s. m.—pl. t.* i. (pont—pren) A rustic bridge of a single piece of timber.
Pontiad, *s. m.* (pont) A bearing over; a vaulting, a rising like a vault; a forming a bridge.
Pontiaw, *v. a.* (pont) To bear over; to raise up as a vault; to raise up like a vault or bridge.
Pontydd, *s. m.* (pont) A bridge-builder.
Pontyddiaeth, *s. m.* (pontydd) Bridge-building.
Por, *s. m.—pl.* pyr (py—or) That comprehends; that is exterior, or over; that is supreme, a sovereign, a lord.

> Pur yw ei gledd, por y Glyn,
> Pwyll rwysgwr pell orwgyn.
>
> Pure is his sword, the *lord* of the Dale, a hero of forward course far conquering. *Iolo Goch, i O. Glyndwr.*

Porch, *s. m.—pl. t.* oedd (py—orch) A pig.
Porchell, *s. m.—pl. t.* od (porch) A little pig.

> Oian, porchellan, y porchell gwyn:
> Rhymdywawd chwibleian chwedl a'n dychryn.
>
> Listen, dear little pig, the white *little pig*: a wandering nymph has imparted to me an oracle, which will terrify us. *Myrddin.*

Porchellan, *s. c. dim.* (porchell) A tiny little pig.

> Oian a porchellan, llym ewinedd,
> Cywely a fynyt, pan elyt i orwedd;
> Bychan a wyr Rhydderch Hael, heno i ar ei wledd
> A borthais i neithwyr o anhunedd!
>
> Listen, *dear little pig*, of sharp claws, thou wouldest seek a bedfellow, when thou shouldest go to lie down; Little does Rhydderch the generous know to-night what I suffered last night of affliction! *Myrddin.*

Porchelles, *s. f.—pl. t.* od (porchell) A young sow.
Porchelliad, *s. m.* (porchell) A pigging.
Porchellig, *s. f. dim.* (porchell) A young sow.
Porchelln, *v. a.* (porchell) To bring forth pigs.
Porchellwr, *s. m.—pl.* porchellwyr (porchellu—gwr) One who collects pigs, a hunter of pigs.

> Ni bu di well borchellwr,
> Llwyd do gwych yn llatai gwr.
>
> Than thee no better *pig hunter* has been, in gay tawny black a love messenger for a man. *S. ab Rhys ab Morus, i'r llwynog.*

Porchellyn, *s. m. dim.* (porchell) A little pig.
Porfa, *s. f.—pl.* porféydd (pawr) Pasture.
Porfäad, *s. m.* (porfa) A pasturing, a grazing.
Porfaawg, *a.* (porfa) Having pasture or grass.
Porfäawl, *a.* (porfa) Belonging to pasture.
Porfadir, *s. m.* (porfa—tir) Pasture ground.
Porfäu, *v. a.* (porfa) To become pasture.
Porfel, *s. f.—pl. t.* oedd (pawr—mel) Pasture.
Porfela, *v. a.* (porfel) To attend to grazing; to manage a dairy farm, to practise dairy farming.
Porfelaeth, *s. m.* (porfel) The practice of grazing or dairy farming; what relates to grazing of cattle; agistment.
Porfelawg, *a.* (porfel) Abounding with pasture. *Tir porfelawg iawn*, land very abundant in grass. *Silurian.*
Porfeldir, *s. m.—pl. t.* oedd (porfel—tir) Grass-land. *Gwent.*
Porfeliad, *s. m.* (porfel) A forming a pasture.
Porfelu, *v. a.* (porfel) To depasture, to graze.

Porfelwr, *s. m.—pl.* porfelwyr (porfela—gwr) One who attends to grazing, a grazier.

Cell porfelwr ei fuarth.

A *grazier's* parlour is his cow-yard. *Adage.*

Porfelydd, *s. m.—pl. t.* ion (porfel) A pasturer.

Pori, *v. a.* (pawr) to graze, to browse, to feed upon grass; to pasture.

Llwm tir ni phoro dafad.

Bare is the land which a sheep *will* not *browse*. *Adage.*

Yr oen yn dysgu i ddafad bori.

The lamb teaching the sheep *to graze*. *Adage.*

Tryw i ych bori meillion.

It is natural for an ox *to browse* trefoile. *Adage.*

Poriad, *s. m.* (pawr) A pasturing, a grazing.

Poriadaeth, *s. m.* (poriad) Agistment.

Poriadawl, *a.* (poriad) Belonging to pasturage; belonging to agistment.

Poriadu, *v. a.* (poriad) To depasture, to agist.

Poriannawl, *a.* (poriant) Belonging to pasturage.

Poriannu, *v. a.* (poriant) To depasture.

Poriant, *s. m.* (pawr) A pasturage, grazing.

Poriaw, *v. a.* (pawr) To cause pasture or grass; to become pasture.

Pond oeddych yn wych dy wedd,
Por glwysliw'n poriaw glasledd.

Wert thou not of gay appearance, thou lord of glorious hues, *covering with pasture* the greensward. *D. ab Gwilym i'r haf.*

Poriawg, *a.* (pawr) Having pasture or grass.

Poriawl, *a.* (pawr) Relating to pasturage.

Porth, *s. m.—pl.* pyrth (por) Aid, help, support, succour, sustenance, provision; that bears, carries on, or conveys; a carrying place, a passage, a port; a porch, or a gateway; a ferrying-place. *Oed wrth borth*, delay for support, of evidence, in law; *Duw yn borth iti!* God be thy help! *porthgwlas, porth-og*, a portcullis.

Anfon a orug Llyr gennad at y brenin, ac at ei ferch—gwedi rhyddëol o'i ddau ddofion o Ynys Prydain yn ddieurhydeddus; ac yn dawed i geisiaw porth ganddynt.

What Llyr did was the sending a messenger to the king, and to his daughter, after being disgracefully driven out by his two sons-in-law from the Isle of Britain, and he being coming to obtain *assistance* from them. *Gr. ab Arthur.*

Doai Glewlwyd i'r neuadd; ac y dywawd Arthur wrtho. Hwedlau porth genyt!

There came Glewlwyd into the hall; thereupon Arthur said to him: 'Hast thou any *gate* news?' *H. Culhwch—Mabinogion.*

Trwy byrth angeu y cawn olwg ar fyd sydd well.

Through the *gates* of death we shall have a view of a better world. *Adage.*

Portha, *v. a.* (porth) To afford aid or help.

Porthai, *s. c.* (porth) That helps, aids, or supports; that bears, or carries.

Porthawd, *s. m.* (porth) The act of helping, or assisting; maintenance; conveyance.

Porthawg, *a.* (porth) Having aid or support.

Porthawl, *a.* (porth) Helping, aiding, succouring, tending to sustain, tending to bear.

Porthawr, *s. m.—pl.* porthorion (porth) A porter.

Y porthawr a ddyly, o bob anreg a ddelo trwy y porth, eiddyrnaid, nid amgen o aeron, ac wyau, a phenwaig.

The porter has a claim out of every present that may come through the gate, of having his handful, that is to say of fruits, and eggs, and herrings. *Welsh Laws.*

Porthedig, *a.* (porth) Supported, carried on.

Porthfa, *s. f.—pl.* porthfëydd (porth) A carrying place, a passage place, a ferrying-place, a port.

Badau a aent a phob da
O'r baearth for i'r borthfa.

Boats went with every commodity from the bay into the *port*. *L. G. Cothi.*

Porthi, *v. a.* (porth) To aid, to help, to support, to succour, to sustain, to provide with food, to bear, to convey, to carry on, or to bring forward. *Porthi hen chwedl*, to make use of an old saying.

Ni ddiylch angen ei borthi.

Necessity will not thank for *to be supported*. *Adage.*

A bortho ofid bid bwyllocaf.

That *bears* affliction let him be the most circumspect. *Adage.*

Ar ni phortho ei gath porthed ei lygod.

Such *as will* not *support* his cat *let him support* his mice. *Adage.*

Pen a borthaf ar fy ysgwydd,
Ni'm arfollai waradwydd:
Gwae fy llaw, llâd fy arglwydd!

A head *I bear* upon my shoulder, that would not let me receive disgrace: Woe my hand, that my lord is slain! *Llywarch Hen, m. Urien.*

Porthiad, *s. m.—pl. t.* au (porth) A helping on, a succouring, supportation, a bearing, a conveying, a bringing forward. *Prydyddion borthiad*, that is the support of poets.

Porthiadawl, *a.* (porthiad) Tending to succour.

Porthiadu, *v. a.* (porthiad) To render succouring, to become a support.

Porthianna, *v. a.* (porthiant) To provide support or sustenance, to supply with necessaries, to deal in provisions of any sort, to deal in cattle, or to act as a drover.

Porthiannawl, *a.* (porthiant) Apt to succour.

Porthianniad, *s. m.* (porthiant) A rendering a succour, supportation.

Porthiannu, *v. a.* (porthiant) To render a succour, to become a support.

Porthiannus, *a.* (porthiant) Being provided with sustenance; pampered.

Porthiannusaw, *v. a.* (porthiannus) To render succouring, to become supportative.

Porthiannwr, *s. m—pl.* porthiannwyr (porthiant—gwr) A supporter, or a succourer.

Porthiannydd, *s. m.—pl. t.* ion (porthiant) One who supports, a succourer.

Porthiant, *s. m.* (porth) Support, maintenance.

Porthiator, *ger.* (porthiad) In supporting.

Porthid, *s. m.* (porth) Assistance, sustenance.

Porthidon, *s. m.* (porthid) That aids, assists, or succours, a helper, one who sustains.

Porthidon mwyaf,
Cyraf di imi fy ngan!

Thou supreme *Supporter*, blot out for me mine iniquity! *Ysgolan.*

Porthitor, *sup.* (porthid) To be supporting.

Porthladd, *s. f.—pl. t.* au (porth—lladd) A place of export; a port, a harbour.

Porthladdawg, *a.* (porthladd) Having a place of export; having a port; abounding with ports.

Porthle, *s. m.—pl. t.* oedd (porth—lle) A place of support; a carrying place; a port, a harbour.

Arglwydd a'm porthes porthle tewdor.

A chieftain has maintained me with the thickly covered *place of support*. *Cynddelw.*

Porthlëawg, *a.* (porthle) Having a port.

Porthlëawl, *a.* (porthle) Belonging to a port.

Porthloedd, *s. m.* (porth—lloedd) Means of support or maintenance.

Prif arglwydd brolwydd braenhelyn.
Braisg anlloedd beirdd, borthloedd berthyn.

A supreme lord of generous breast the prosperity of a country, a great blessing of bards, of appropriate *maintenance*. *Cynddelw, i'r argl. Rhys.*

Porthloeddawg, *a.* (porthloedd) Having means of support or maintenance.

Porthlys, *s. m.* (porth—llys) A portmote.

Porthmon, *s. m.—pl.* porthmyn (porth—mon) A conveyer or trader; a dealer in provisions; a provision merchant; a drover. *Porthmon* *gwartheg*, a drover of cattle; *porthmon defaid*, sheep-drover; *porthmon moch*, a pig-drover.

Porthmona, *v. a.* (porthmon) To deal in provisions; to traffic; to act as a drover.

Porthmonaeth, *s. m.* (porthmon) A dealing in provisions; purveyance.

Porthog, *s. f.—pl. t.* au (porth—og) A portcullis.

Portholaeth, *s. m.* (porthawl) Supportation.

Portholdeb, *s. m.* (porthawl) The state of being a succour, or support.

Portholi, *v. a.* (porthawl) To render supportative.

Porthordy, *s. m.—pl. t.* au (porthawr—ty) A porter's lodge.

Porthorddwy, *s. m.* (porth—gorddwy) That is aiding violence; an abettor of violence.

> Seithfed affaith galanas yw cannorthwyaw y dyn a laddo y llall; a hono a elwir porthorddwy.
>
> The seventh abetment of murder is, to assist the person who kills the other: and that is called *aiding of violence*. *Welsh Laws.*

Porthores, *s. f.* (porthawr) A female door-keeper.

Porthori, *v. a.* (porthawr) To act as a door-keeper.

Porthoriaeth, *s. m.* (porthawr) The office of a door-keeper.

> Llys Owain—
> Anhawdd yn fynych yno
> Weled na chliciad, na chlo,
> Na phorthoriaeth——
>
> The court of Owain, difficult is it there to see nor latch, nor lock, nor a *porter's office*. *Iolo Goch.*

Porthotor, *part.* (porthawd) Being succoured.

Porthwas, *s. m.* (porth—gwas) A ferryman.

Porthwy, *s. m.* (porth) Assistant, or support.

> Nac ymddiried am dy borthwy i'r peth a fwrir ymmaith.
>
> Trust not for thy *support* to what is thrown away. *Adage.*

Porthwr, *s. m.—pl.* porthwyr (porth—gwr) A supporter a provisioner; a conveyer; a ferryman; a door-man.

Porthwriaeth, *s. m.* (porthwr) The calling of one who conveys; the office of a ferryman.

Porthwys, *s. m.—pl. t.* ion (porth—gwys) That attends a ferry.

> Y fferi fawr i ffair Fon
> Wrth osawd ei phorthwysion.
>
> The great ferry to the fair of Mona under the regulation of its *ferrymen*. *Gr. ab Hywel ab Tudyr.*

Porwr, *s. m.—pl.* porwyr (pori—gwr) A man who feeds on grass.

Pos, *s. m.* (py—os) An increment; growth, or increase; that is gathered, or heaped.

Posel, *s. m.* (pos—el) Curdled milk; posset.

Posfardd, *s. m.—pl.* posfeirdd (pos—bardd) A preceptive bard, a teaching bard.

> Tewch chwi bosfeirddion.
>
> Be silent ye *teaching bards*. *Buall Beirdd.*
>
> Prydydd, neu fardd caw, sydd o dri rhyw: sef, prifardd, posfardd, ac arwyddfardd.
>
> A poet, or a bard of verse, is of three branches; namely, a primary bard, a *didactic-bard*, and a herald-bard. *S. D. Rhys.*

Posiad, *s. m.—pl. t.* au (pos) A gathering together, a collecting to a heap, a questioning, or investigation; a posing.

> Y a bosfardd, ba fardd a fo,
> 'R hyd bysedd rhaid ei bosio;
> A thrwy bwys uthr o bosiad
> Graddau gynt o'u gwraidd a gad.
>
> A didactic bard, whatever bard would be, on the fingers it is necessary *to question* him; and through the weight of a solemn *interrogation* degrees from their source were given of yore. *Edm. Prys.*

Posiannawl, *a.* (posiant) Investigating, posing.

Posiannu, *v. a.* (posiant) To investigate, to pose.

Posiant, *s. m.* (pos) An investigation.

Posiar, *s. f.—pl.* posieir (pos—iar) A fat hen.

Posiaw, *v. a.* (pos) To make an increment; to gather knowledge; to investigate, to examine, to interrogate, to pose.

> Rhaid i mi, ar y rhod mwn,
> Os doeth, dy bosiaw dithau.
>
> It is necessary for me then, from the talent given me, in wisdom, *to question* thee. *Edm. Prys, i W. Cynwal.*

Posiawl, *a.* (pos) Investigating, posing.

Posiedig, *a.* (posiad) Investigated, questioned.

Posned, *s. m.—pl. t.* au (pos) A round body, or that swells out; a squat figure; a porringer; a pap saucepan. *O y posned bach!* O the little squab!

Post, *s. m.—pl.* pyst (py—ost) What projects or branches out; a post. *Pedwar post y corff, pedair aelawd y corff*, the four limbs of the body

> Pan nad rhyfedd na thyf post aur drwy nen ty yr anwir.
>
> When it is not wonderful that a *post of gold* does not grow through the house top of the unjust. *Adage.*
>
> Tri phost cad Ynys Prydain; Dunawd Fur, mab Pabo Post Prydain, Gwallawg fab Lleenawg, a Cynfelyn Drwsgl.
>
> The three *pillars* of battle of the Isle of Britain; Dunod Var son of Pabo the pillar of Britain, Gwallog son of Lleenog, and Cynvelyn the Stumbler. *Triads.*
>
> Post ediyd ardurth Elifer.
>
> The *pillar* of the wanderers leading a life like Elivor. *Cynddelw.*

Postiad, *s. m.* (post) A shooting out a stem; a putting up a post, or pillar.

Postiaw, *v. a.* (post) To shoot out a stem; to set up a post, to set up a pillar.

Postyn, *s. m. dim.* (post) A little post.

Pot, *s. m.—pl. t.* iau (po) A pot. *Pot o laeth*, a pot of milk.

Potel, *s. f.—pl. t.* i (pot) What is puffed out; a leathern bottle; a bottle.

Poteliad, *s. m.* (potel) A bottling.

Potelu, *v. a.* (potel) To bottle, to fill a bottle.

Poten, *s. f.—pl. t.* i (pot) What bulges out; a paunch; a pudding. *Y boten fawr, y boten wen, cod wen*, the large ventricle, or the stomach; *y boten fach*, the lesser ventricle; *poten pengauad*, blind-gut; *poten wen*, a batter-pudding; *poten lysau*, a fruit pudding.

> O'i mynych brofi bwytwyd y boten i gyd.
>
> By frequently tasting it the *pudding* has been all eaten up. *Adage.*

Potena, *v. a.* (poten) To gather a paunch; to swell out the belly.

Potenaidd, *a.* (poten) Like a paunch or belly.

Potenawg, *a.* (poten) Having a paunch or belly.

Potenawl, *a.* (poten) Belonging to a paunch.

Poteniad, *s. m.* (poten) A swelling out a paunch.

Potenig, *s. f. dim.* (poten) A little paunch.

Potenu, *v. a.* (poten) To form a paunch.

Potes, *s. m.* (pot) Pottage, broth, soup.

Poteswr, *s. m.* (potes—gwr) A pottage man.

Potiad, *s. m.* (pot) A potting; a potation.

Potiaid, *s. m.* (pot) A potfull, a fill of a pot.

Potiaw, *v. a.* (pot) To put in a pot, to pot; to drink, to tipple.

Poth, *s. m.* (po) That swells out, a boss.

Pothan, *s. c. dim.* (poth) A round boss, bump, or bunch; a cub. *Pothan blaidd*, a wolf's cub.

Pothell, *s. f. dim.—pl. t.* au (poth) What is puffed, or blown out; a wheal, or blister; also a disease amongst cattle, being a blister under the tongue, which is otherwise called y [illegible] or the tongue disease.

Pothellaidd, *a.* (pothell) Like a [illegible]

Pothellawg, *a.* (pothell) Puffy [illegible] wheals or blisters.

Pothelliad, *s.* — (pothell) [illegible]

Potheilu, v. a. (pothell) To puff up; to blister.
Pothon, s. m. (poth) A round lump, or boss; a cub, a whelp.
Powys, s. m. (po—gwys) The state of being at rest, stationary, or settled. It is the name of a district in North Wales, which was anciently a principality.
Powysaw, v. a. (powys) To render at rest, or to settle; to become stationary.

Powysed angeu, Powyswg a'i gwyr
O'r goreu i hamwg;
A edau rhiau rhyddrwg,
Ac a fo da ef ei dwg!

Be arrested death, Powyswg has men the best for her defence; he spares chieftains evil in the extreme, and such as are good he takes away! *Ll. P. Moch, i Fad ab Madawg.*

Powyswg, s. f. (powys) A place that is settled upon. It is used as an epithet for *Powys.*
Pra, s. m. (py—rha) That tends to the extremity; that spreads round.
Prad, s. m. (py—rhad) A gentle spread, a stroke
Praff, a. (pra) Large, ample; thick in circumference. *Coesau preiffion*, thick legs.

Cerdded yn braff a wnai.

Walk at *large* was what she did. *H. Pwyll—Mabinogion.*

Trallawd praff a barysynt i Bown.

Affliction *ample* had they caused to Bown. *H. Bown—Mabinogion.*

Mal mab i Ddyfnwal Moel Mud
Yw Phylip praff ei olud.

Like a son of Dyvnwal Moel Mud is Phylip of *ample* wealth. *L. G. Cothi.*

Praffaidd, a. (praff) Somewhat large, or ample; somewhat thick in circumference.
Praffder, s. m. (praff) Amplitude; rotundity.
Praffdra, s. m. (praff) Amplitude; thickness in girth.
Praffedd, s. m. (praff) Largeness; thickness round
Praffiad, s. m. (praff) A rendering large, or ample; a becoming thick in circumference.
Praffu, v. a. (praff) To make large; to make thick in compass, to become thick round.
Praidd, s. f.—pl. preiddiau (pra—idd) A flock, or herd; also a booty of cattle taken in war.

Praidd gyfreithlawl: pedair bu ar ugaint a tharw.

A lawful *herd*: twenty-four cows and a bull. *Welsh Laws.*

Tair rhwyd breyr yut, allwest ei feirch, ei breiddoedd gwartheg, a'i genfaint foch.

The three nets of a baron are, the pasture of his horses, his *herds* of cattle, and his breed of swine. *Welsh Laws.*

A rhag preiddiau annwn tost yd gent.

And before the *herds* of the infernal region dismally thou dost sing. *Taliesin.*

Pell ei glod o gludaw anrhaith,
Praidd wasgar, dreisfar driseith gyfarpar
Yn ngwyar, yn ngwynlaith.

For his fame, for collecting spoil, scattering the *flock*, his wrath overbearing thrice seven of spears of conflict in blood, in the violence of passion. *Cynddelw.*

Prain, s. m.—pl. preinion (pra—in) That tends to spread or swell out; that causes to spring up; a feast, or banquet.

Lleddfawd y gau ri rhyfel ei rain,
A llen lliw ehoeg, a medd prain.

Reclined has the god of war his spear, with the veil of bright green hue, and mead of the *banquet*. *Taliesin, Mic. Dinbych.*

Gwr cymmrwyn ei ddwyn; gwawr Cymmry, neud marw!
Mawr o chwedl a'm deffry:
Owain udd prain, neud pridd wely!

A man whose being taken off is universal grief; the luminary, is he not dead? an awful report awakes me: Owain lord of the *banquet*, that earth is his bed! *Prydydd Bychan, m. O. ab Madawg.*

Rhag Teifi, yn tori twr main
Teyrn glyw terwyn, tyrynt prain yn ddrud
I gwn cnud ech cnofain!

On the Teivi, destroying a stone tower of a sovereign prince, they irefully heap together a feast for the dogs of the scolk, over the voracious gnawing. *Cynddelw, i H. ab Owain.*

Praith, s. m.—pl. preithiau (py—rhaith) An act, or deed; practice.
Pranc, s. m.—pl. pranciau (py—rhanc) A prank.
Pranciad, s. m. (pranc) A frolicking.
Pranciaw, v. a. (pranc) To frolic, to play pranks.
Pranciawl, a. (pranc) Frolicksome, playful.
Pranciwr, s. m.—pl. pranciwyr (pranc—gwr) One who plays pranks.
Pratiad, s. m. (prad) A stroking, a coaxing, or fondling, by gently drawing the hand over.
Pratiaw, v. a. (prad) To stroke, to rub gently, to sooth, to fondle, to coax. *Pratia y plentyn*, fondle the child.
Pratiawl, a. (prad) Coaxing or stroking.
Pratiwr, s. m.—pl. pratiwyr (pratiaw—gwr) A stroker, a coaxer.
Praw, s. m. (pra) An essay, a trial, or a proof.

Gweilr——
Y daw gwlaw yn ol praw prudd.

It will be seen, that a shower will come after a serious *trial*. *D. ab Gwilym.*

Prawen, s. f.—pl. t. au (praw) An essay, or cast for trial, in gaming.
Prawf, s. m.—pl. profion (praw) A proof, trial, or essay; experience. *Bod ar brawf*, to be on proof: *Prawf Ynad*, and *Llyfr Prawf*, the Judge's Proof and the Book of Proof, the name of a section of laws, according to the code of *Hywel Dda.*
Prawfaen, s. m. (praw—maen) A touchstone.
Pre, s. m. (py—rhe) The origin of a course.
Pred, s. m. (pre) A stray, or migration.
Preg, s. m. (py—rheg) A greeting or address.
Pregawthen, s. f. (preg) Prattle, rigmarole.
Pregeth, s. f.—pl. t. au (preg) A sermon.
Pregethiad, s. m. (pregeth) A preaching.
Pregethu, v. a. (pregeth) To preach.
Pregethwr, s. m.—pl. pregethwyr (pregeth—gwr) A preacher.
Prediad, s. m. (pred) A migrating, a straying.
Prediaw, v. a. (pred) To migrate, to stray.
Preiddiad, s. m.—pl. t. au (praidd) A herding; a collecting a herd; a driving of cattle away as a booty in war; predation.
Preiddiaw, v. a. (praidd) To herd; to collect a herd; to drive off a booty of cattle; to predate
Preiddiawg, a. (praidd) Abounding with herds.

Ni thores ei bawr a fu breiddiawg.

His pasture has not been cut that was *teeming with herds.* *Meilyr.*

Preiddiawl, a. (praidd) Belonging to a herd; relating to the pillage of cattle; predatory.
Preiddiawr, s. pl. aggr. (praidd) Beasts of the chase; beasts taken as prey in a foray.

Huysgwn am breiddiawr, am brain.

Aptly rising for the *prey*, for the feast. *Ll. P. Moch.*

Preiddiedig, a (praidd) Herded; depredated.
Preiddyn, s. m. (praidd) That is of the herds.

Ef a'm porthes——
Ar win, ar breiddyn, ar brain.

He nourished me on wine, on venison, on *feast.* ——

Preiddin, a. (praidd) Consisting of herds; *Moch preiddin, anrhaith o foch*, a booty of swine.
Preiddiwr, s. m.—pl. preiddwyr (praidd—gwr) One who follows a herd; one who pursues herds for booty; a piliager.

Er perygl preiddwyr peri ffoawd,
Pasgadur cyfrain Prydain briawd.

To the hazard of *depredators* causing a flight, the nourisher of the true sons of Britain. *Meilyr.*

Preiddwal, *s. f.* (praidd—gwal) The resort of the herd, where a herd lies down.

Pryffwn gawr, priodawr preiddwal.

The foremost of the shout, the proprietor of the *region of herds* *Cynddelw, i H. ab Owain.*

Preiddwalch, *s. m.—pl.* preiddweilch (praidd—gwalch) Hawk of the herds; hawk of pillage.

Preiddwriaeth, *s. m.* (preiddiwr) The calling of a herdsman; the practice of a pillager.

Preiddyn, *s. m. dim.* (praidd) A beast of chase.

Preiddyn oedd ei gwyn cyn noi gwyddaw.

For the *booty* was his anxiety before his fall. *Cynddelw.*

Preiniad, *s. m.* (prain) A carousing, a feasting.

Preiniaw, *v. a.* (prain) To carouse, to feast.

Preiniawg, *a.* (prain) Abounding with feasts.

Mi a'th arwyre udd bre breiniawg,
Breiaglew, afael hael, o hil Madawg.

I will extol thee, chief of the hill *of feasting*, a mighty lion, holding bounty, of the line of Madoc. *Ll. P. Moch, i Lywelyn II.*

Dau ychen Dewi ardderchawg oeddynt;
Dau garn a gerddynt yn gyd breiniawg.

The two oxen of Dewi majestic were; two that walked hoof to hoof together *enjoying feasts.* *Gw. Brycheiniawg.*

Y melyn gwanwyn, ac ych brych, yn ddau gyd breiniawg a fynaf.

The yellow ox of spring, and the two brindled oxen, being two *feeding together*, those I will have. *H. Culhwch—Mabinogion.*

Preiniawl, *a.* (prain) Belonging to a feast.

Preinrudd, *a.* (prain—rhudd) Ruddy with feasting

Cyrchiad, tremyniad, tra mor udd dy gas,
Dy gosgordd yn breinrudd.

An assaulter, a scouter, beyond the British sea extends thy hate, thy retinue seem *rosy with festivity.* *Ll. P. Moch, i Lywelyn II.*

Preithiad, *s. m.* (praith) A practising, a using.

Preithiaw, *v. a.* (praith) To practise, to use.

Preithiawg, *a.* (praith) Having practice.

Preithiawl, *a.* (praith) Practical, operative.

Preithiedig, *a.* (preithiad) Practised, or used.

Preithig, *a.* (praith) Belonging to practice.

Pren, *s. m.—pl. t.* iau (pre) A tree, a timber, a piece of wood. *Pren troed, gweddig, bre,* a last; *pren ceri,* a medlar tree; *pren y gerwyn,* the bay tree; *pren melyn, pren y clefyd melyn,* the barberry-tree; *pren awyr,* misletoe.

Pren yn nghoed arall biau.

A *tree* in a wood another owns. *Adage.*

Prenaidd, *a.* (pren) Lignous, or like wood.

Prenfol, *s. m.—pl. t.* au (pren—bol) A wooden coffer, box or chest.

Prenial, *s. m.* (pren) A coffer or shrine of wood.

Prenial gwedden, pedair ar ugaint a dal.

A warping *trough*, its value is twenty-four pence. *Welsh Laws.*

Prenial dywal gal ysgwn
Goruc ar Loegr lu cyngrwn;
Bedd Gwen fab Llywarch Hen yw hwn.

The *shrine* of the fierce overbearing foe, that vanquished the circularly-compact army of Lloegria; the grave of Gwen the son of old Llywarch is this. *Llywarch Hen.*

Preniaw, *v. a.* (pren) To apply timber or wood to any thing; to fasten with a wooden bar.

— — — Y nos —
Na ad un drws, undwn draw
Heb ar unwaith ei breniaw.

He will not leave a single door, we may yonder note, without *barring* it at once. *G. ab I. ab Llywelyn Fychan.*

Prenol, *s. m.—pl. t.* au (pren) A busk.

Prensaer, *s. m.—pl.* prenseiri (pren—saer) A wright or worker in wood; a carpenter.

Pres, *s. m.—pl. t.* i (pre—es) That is imminent; that is quick or ready; that is sharp or smart; that overruns; brushwood, or whatever overruns the ground, as stubble, straw, and the like; fuel wood; fodder; frequency; haste; a crib, or cratch; also brass. *Pres ffwrn,* fuel for the oven: *Pres y moch,* the resort or stye of the pigs; *pres y cwn,* the kennel of the dogs.

Truan o anian lai o annhwyll,
Trachare present, pres gynnhywyll.

A miserable state is fallen to us from indiscretion, to excess loving the present, a *thicket* involved in darkness. *Meilyr ab Gwalchmai.*

Pres, *a.* (pre—es) Imminent, at hand, quick; ready; hasty; sharp; overrunning, frequent; present. *Pres gynhauaf,* a quick harvest; *llais pres,* a sharp or shrill voice. *Sil.*

Dig yw ein hwyl, dygwn helynt
Yn bres a'r tair gormes gynt.

Vexatious is our condition, we take an *abrupt* course, like the three molestations of ancient time. *Ll. ab Gwilym.*

Presai, *s. m.—pl.* preseion (pres) A pole put across a river for hindering cattle.

Presawl, *a.* (pres) Imminent; close upon; quick.

Preseb, *s. m.* (pres—eb) A crib, or a stall.

Presebu, *v. a.* (preseb) To crib, to stall.

Presedig, *a.* (pres) Rendered imminent; quickened; hastened; made a resort.

Presel, *s. f.—pl. t.* au (pres) A place overgrown, as with furze and the like, a brake. *Sil.*

Preselaidd, *a.* (presel) Tending to be braky.

Preselawg, *a.* (presel) Overgrown with shrubs.

Preseldir, *s. m.* (presel—tir) Land overgrown with bushwood, foul land.

Preseliad, *s. m.* (presel) An overrunning with brushwood; a becoming wild.

Preselu, *v. n.* (presel) To become wild or overrun. *Mae y tir yn preselu ganto,* the land grows foul under his care. *Sil.*

Preselyn, *s. m. dim.* (presel) A brake, a thicket.

Presen, *s. f.* (pres) The present, the present time or age; the present life.

Nid aeth neb i nef er benthyg y bresen.

No one went to heaven for the lending of his *present.* *Taliesin.*

Nid oes o'r presen,
O'r dechreu hyd orphen,
Un orig o ddydd,
Wrth y fuchedd dragywydd.

There is not of the *present*, from the beginning to the end, one hour of day, compared with the state of eternity. *Taliesin.*

Pwyllai Dunawd, udd presen,
Erechwydd gwneuthur cadwen
Yn erbyn cywryssedd Pasgen.

Fiercely would Dunawd rage, the chief of the *present*, with mind elate for combat, against the strife of Pasgen. *Llywarch Hen.*

Presennawl, *a.* (present) Being imminent, near, or ready; present.

Presennoldeb, *s. m.* (presennawl) The state of being at, or upon; a present state; presence.

Presennwr, *s. m.* (present) One who is present.

Priodawr Prydain prain preiddiau;
Presennwr, prynt pres oleu.

A prince of Britain with feast of spoils; a *present man,* the dweller in a splendid abode. *Cynddelw, i'r argl. Rhys.*

Present, *s. m.* (presen) The present state.

Pan fyny Duw dy ddifuriaw
O dylwst present, o bresswyl fraw,
Cyd a'th fo di golud, golud [illegible],
Na'th lyaid, eled ar ei addaw.

When God should please to annihilate thy *frame* of the universe of the *present state*, of the abode of terror, though thou mayest possess wealth, and splendid genius, let these detain thee not, but at his call depart. *Meilyr ab Gwalchmai.*

Presiad, *s. m.—pl. t.* au (pres) A hastening, a being quick or ready; a frequenting.

Prest, *s. m.* (pres) Quickness, smartness: *a.* Ready, quick; soon.

Prestl, *s. m.* (prest) Smart, talk, repartee. *a.* Smart, ready, fluent.

> Siarad yn brestl siarad yn ddestl:
> Siarad yn westl siarad annestl.
>
> A talking *smartly* is talking elegantly, a talking tumultuously is a talking inelegantly. *Adage.*

Prestlaidd, *a.* (prestl) Disposed to prattle.
Prestlawg, *a.* (prestl) Full of smart talk.
Prestledd, *s. m.* (prestl) Smartness of discourse.
Prestliad, *s. m.* (prestl) A talking smartly.
Prestlu, *v. a.* (prestl) To talk smartly or wittily; to repartee; to prattle.
Prestlus, *a.* (prestl) Of smart or witty talk.
Presu, *v. a.* (pres) To render imminent, near, or ready at hand; to hasten, to quicken; to frequent, to resort; to render present; to become present.
Preswyl, *s. m.* (pres—gwyl) The state of being present or in readiness; a tarrying; a habitation. *a.* Being present or in readiness; waiting, tarrying. *March preswyl*, a horse kept in readiness, or a horse of attendance.

> Gwastrawd afwyn a ddwg ei farch yn gywair i'r ynguad llys, i breswyl pan y mynno.
>
> The groom of the reign shall bring his horse furnished to the judge of the palace, to be in *readiness* at his will. *Welsh Laws.*

Preswyledd, *s. m.* (preswyl) A state of abiding.
Preswylfa, *s. f.—pl.* preswylfëydd (preswyl) A place taken up as an abode; a camp; a dwelling-place, a habitation.

> Yn yr amser y caethiwid Iewdn, deg preswylfa onaddynt a aynt ar goll.
>
> In the time when Juda was led into captivity, ten *tribes* of them became lost. *Old Chronicle.*

Preswylfedd, *s. m.* (preswyl—medd) That is kept in readiness.
Preswylfeddu, *v. a.* (preswylfedd) To keep in readiness, to take care of constantly.
Preswylfod, *s. m.* (preswyl—bod) A dwelling place.
Preswylfoddawg, *a.* (preswyl—boddawg) Having an habitation, or a constant abiding at will.

> Offeiriad y frenines;—Offrwm y frenines hagen a gaiff yn breswylfoddawg.
>
> The chaplain of the queen, the offering of the queen he shall have *constantly* at his will. *Welsh Laws.*

Preswylgoll, *s. m.* (preswyl—coll) Loss of dwelling. *a.* Home-lost.

> Pall arnaw, pwyllaf, y dognir,
> Preswylgoll, hwydoll englr.
>
> A failure to him, I will foretell, there will be alloted, *loss of home*, a painful privation. *Cynddelw.*

Preswyliad, *s. m.* (preswyl) A being present; a tarrying or abiding; a taking up a residence.
Preswyliaeth, *s. m.* (preswyl) The act of frequenting, or resorting; inhabitancy.
Preswyliannawl, *a.* (preswyliant) Relating to habitation, dwelling or abiding.
Preswyliannu, *v. a.* (preswyliant) To make a resort; to settle a habitation.
Preswyliant, *s. m.* (preswyl) The act of taking up a residence or a dwelling.
Preswyliaw, *v. a.* (preswyl) To fix a residence, to dwell, to inhabit; to tarry in a place.

> Plant Addaf planigion fuant;
> Yn y presen preswyliasant;
> Gan Dduw yn lleufer llewychant.
>
> The children of Adam, graftings have they been; in the present state *they have sojourned*, with God in splendor they will shine. *Meilyr ab Gwalchmai.*
>
> Duw biau——
> Y byd, pawb enyd, pob anant,
> Is beulwen, ynddo a breswyliant.
>
> To God belong the world, every one existing, all of life, beneath the radiant sun, therein *who dwell*. *W. Middleton.*

Preswyliawg, *a.* (preswyl) Having a resort; having an abode; being attended.

> Presennwr,
> Pryswr pres olen;
> Preswyliawg farchawg feirch gwinen.
>
> A present man, a dweller in a splendid place; a warrior *constantly attended* with bay steeds. *Cynddelw. i'r argl. Rhys.*

Preswyliedig, *a.* (preswyliad) Inhabited.
Preswyliedigaeth, *s. m.* (preswyliedig) The act of taking up an abode or dwelling.
Preswyliwr, *s. m.—pl.* preswylwyr (preswyl—gwr) A dweller, or an inhabitant.
Preswylydd, *s. m.—pl. t.* ion (preswyl) An inhabitant, or a dweller.
Pri, *s. m.—pl. t.* on (py—rhi) An increment; an origin, or cause; that is prime or first.
Prïad, *s. m.* (pri) A forming an increment, or source of increase; a rendering prime, a becoming prime, or original.
Priallen, *s. f.* (pri—gall) Privet; also called *priellyn* and *yswydd*.
Prïawd, *s. m.* (pri) That is appropriate, peculiar, proper, or fitting; that is possessed or owned; a married person, the same as *gwraig bwys*, or a spouse. *a.* Appropriate, peculiar, fitting; possessed; married.

> Ni ddyly gwraig na phrynu na gwerthu, o bydd priawd, heb ganiad ei gwr.
>
> A woman ought neither to buy, nor to sell, if she be *a married one*, without the consent of her husband. *Welsh Laws.*
>
> Mal cefnin cywrain Cywryd, fardd Dunawd,
> Mau i'm draig priawd gwawd, ni bo gwyd.
>
> Like the correct memorial song of Cywryd, the bard of Dunod, to my *proper* lord is my praise, which shall not be faulty. *Gw. Ddu o Arfon, m. G. Llwyd.*

Pric, *s. m.—pl. t.* iau (pri) A small piece of wood; a broach; a skewer. *Wyd sythed â phe llyncasid bric edafedd*, thou art as stiff as if thou hadst swallowed a yarn stick.
Pricaid, *s. m.—pl.* preiceidiau (pric) What is held on a stick; the quantity of yarn taken off the spindle and put upon a stick
Prid, *s. m.* (pri) That is in unison or equivalent; price, value; ransom. *a.* Valuable, precious, dear. *Pryned hwna yn brid*, that has been dearly bought. *Sil.*

> Ni cheir geirda heb brid.
>
> There will be no good word had without *desert*. *Adage.*
>
> Nid prid pryn gair teg.
>
> The purchase of a good word is not *dear*. *Adage.*
>
> Cywryseodd Prydain y sy bryder yn;
> Y sy brid i lawer
> Armes gwr gwythlawn ei ober,
> Argleidriad, fleiniad, fleidd ulfer.
>
> The contention of Britain is afflicting to us; *dear* to many is the fate of the man of wrathful achievement, the protection, the foremost one, the wolf of a host. *Cynddelw, m. E. ab M. ab Iddon.*
>
> Ancwyn Mynyddawg enwawg y gwnaeth;
> A phrid er prynu breithell Gattraeth.
>
> The dainty of Mynyddog, notably it worked; and was the *price* for purchasing the battle of Cattraeth. *Aneurin.*

Pridadwy, *a.* (prid) Capable of being equivalent.
Pridaw, *v. a.* (prid) To render equivalent; to become equivalent; to expiate.
Pridiad, *s. m.* (prid) A rendering an equivalent; a pledging; a ransoming.
Pridiannawl, *a.* (pridiant) Tending to be an equivalent; expiatory.
Pridiannu, *v. a.* (pridiant) To render an equivalent; to become an equivalent.
Pridiannus, *a.* (pridiant) Tending to be equivalent; expiatory.
Pridiannusaw, *v. a.* (pridiannus) To render of an equivalent consideration; to become equivalent; to become expiatory.

Pridiant, *s. m.—pl.* pridiannau (prid) The act of pledging a value; a ransoming; expiation.

Pridiaw, *v. a.* (prid) To give a price, value, or equivalent; to lay a pawn or pledge; to ransom, to expiate.

> Ni bu ond Crist ar y groes,
> Yn dyoddef gloes i'n pridiaw.
>
> There has been none else but Christ upon the cross, a pang to suffer, as to ransom. *Morgan Tolai.*

Pridiawg, *a.* (prid) Having a value, price, or equivalent; being an equivalent.

Pridiawl, *a.* (prid) Equivalent; redeeming.

Pridiedig, *a.* (pridiad) Made equivalent; ransomed, expiated.

Pridioldeb, *s. m.* (pridiawl) Equivalency.

Pridioli, *v. a.* (pridiawl) To render equivalent; to render deserved; to become equivalent.

Pridiwr, *s. m.—pl.* pridwyr (prid—gwr) One who gives a price; a ransomer; an expiator.

Pridwerth, *s. m.* (prid—gwerth) Value given as a ransom, the thing given as an equivalent.

> Am ei bridwerth, ni pherthyn
> Ymliw a Duw, mal a dyn;
> Rhaid fydd lle rho Duw ei far
> Dwyn eglwys yn gynnar.
>
> Concerning his *demand*, it belongs not to man to question the will of God, it will be necessary where God sends his wrath for the effect soon to appear. *T. Aled.*

Pridd, *s. m. aggr.* (pri—idd) Mould, or earth; also a delicate term used for the ordure of an animal. *Sil.* *Pridd y wadd*, a mole-hill; *llestri priddion*, earthen ware.

Priddaw, *v. a.* (pridd) To mould, to earth, to put in the mould, to cover with earth.

> Bum yn claddu hen gydymmaith
> A giliodd yn fy mhen i ganwaith;
> Ac 'r wy'n ofni er ei briddo,
> Y cyfyd yn fy mhen i eto.
>
> I have been burying an old companion, who flew to my head a hundred times; and I fear, though *he be burried*, that he will fly to my head again. *Ateb rhywun wedi hau haidd.*

Priddawl, *a.* (pridd) Of the nature of earth, or mould; earthly.

Priddawr, *s. m.—pl.* priddorion (pridd) A potter.

Priddell, *s. f.—pl. t.* i (pridd) A mass, or clod of earth; a piece of pottery; a tile.

> Cyfrewd a phriddell.
>
> As brittle as a *piece of pottery*. *Adage.*

Priddellan, *s. f. dim.* (priddell) A small mass of earth; a small tile, or piece of pottery.

Priddellawg, *a.* (priddell) consisting of masses of earth, glebous.

Priddellig, *s. f.* (priddell) A small mass of earth.

Priddellwaith, *s. m.* (priddell—gwaith) Tile-work

Priddellwr, *s. m.* (priddell—gwr) A tile-maker.

Priddellydd, *s. m.—pl. t.* ion (priddell) A tiler.

Pridden, *s. f.—pl. t.* i (pridd) An earthen vessel.

Priddenig, *s. f.* (pridden) A little earthen vessel.

Priddfaen, *s. m.—pl.* priddfeini (maen) A brick.

Priddfeinwaith, *s. m.* (priddfaen) Brick-work.

Priddgalch, *s. m.* (pridd—calch) Calcareous earth; fuller's earth; a mixture of earth and lime, a manure so prepared.

Priddgalchawg, *a.* (priddgalch) Abounding with calcareous earth, being of earth and lime.

Priddgalchiad, *s. m.* (priddgalch) A doing with calcareous earth; a manuring with a mixture of earth and lime.

Priddgalchu, *v. a.* (priddgalch) To manure with a mixture of earth and lime.

Priddgist, *s. m.* (pridd—cist) Potters' clay.

Priddiad, *s. m.* (pridd) A doing with earth; a putting in earth; a returning to earth.

Priddin, *a.* (pridd) Of the nature of earth.

Priddlestr, *s. m.—pl. t.* i (pridd—llestr) An earthen vessel, or a piece of pottery.

Priddlestrwr, *s. m.—pl.* priddlestrwyr (priddlestr—gwr) Earthenware man.

Priddlestrydd, *s. m.—pl. t.* ion (priddlestr) A dealer in earthenware.

Priddlyd, *a.* (pridd) Earthly, mixed with mould.

Priddlydrwydd, *s. m.* (priddlyd) Earthiness.

Priddlydu, *v. a.* (priddlyd) To render earthy.

Priddred, *s. m.* (pridd—rhed) An earthly course, an earthly state.

> O bridd, o bridded
> Pan ym digoned——
>
> Of earth, of an earthly course when I was formed.—— *Taliesin.*

Priddwal, *s. m.* (pridd—gwal) An earth couch.

> Minnau sy gryg, heb deg dal,
> Yma'n priddau mewn priddwal.
>
> I am also hoarse, without a fair reward, here venting in a bed of earth. *Huw Arwystl.*

Priddwr, *s. m.—pl.* priddwyr (pridd—gwr) One who puts in earth.

Priddyn, *s. m. dim.* (pridd) That is formed of earth; an earthly being.

Prif, *s. m.—pl. t.* ion (pri) That is a source; that tends to increase; that is prime, chief or principal; the first day of the new moon; the golden number. *a.* Prime, first, principal, chief.

> Tri phrif anffawd abred: angen, anghof ac angau.
>
> The three *primary* misfortunes of the circle of inchoation: necessity, loss of memory, and death. *Barddas.*

Prifachaws, *s. m.—pl.* prifachosion (prif—achaws) A primary cause, a principal cause.

Prifafon, *s. f.—pl. t.* ydd (prif—afon) A principal river; a law term for a river preserving its regular channel as a boundary of lands.

Prifalaethwr, *s. m.—pl.* prifalaethwyr (prif—alaethwr) A chief mourner.

Prifanian, *s. f.* (prif—anian) An original nature, a primary nature.

Prifansawdd, *s. m.—pl.* prifansoddion (prif—ansawdd) An original quality or element.

> Yn nosparth a rheithiadur cerdd Ceraint Fardd Glas, ni wnair eithr deg prifansawdd; sef naw gorchan a chyngyng.
>
> In the grammar and rudiment of verse of Ceraint the Blue Bard, there are only ten *primary elements*; namely, nine restrictions and a canon of combination. *Barddas.*

Prifardd, *s. m.—pl.* prifeirdd (pri—bardd) A primitive bard, a primary bard; a doctor, or professor of sciences.

> Tri rhyw prifardd y sydd; bardd braint, neu brifardd pencerdd, wrth fraint defawd a llafar gorsedd, a'i swydd yw llywodraethu; ofydd, wrth awen, ymgais a damwain, a'i swydd yw cynnyrchu; a derwydd, wrth bwyll, ansawdd, a gorfod, a'i swydd yw athrawiaethu.
>
> There are three degrees of *primary bards*, a bard of privilege, or a *primary bard* proper, according to the privilege of the custom and voice of a convention, and his office is to exercise authority; an ovate, following genius, exertion, and incident, and his office is to apply to works of genius; and a druid, according to the reason, nature, and necessity of things, and his office is to instruct. *Barddas.*

Prifarddoni, *s. m.* (prifardd) The learning of the primitive bards; the bardic philosophy.

Prifawdl, *s. f.—pl.* prifodlau (prif—awdl) A primary or leading rhyme.

Prifdeg, *a.* (prif—teg) Primarily fair.

Prifder, *s. m.* (prif) Primeness or origin.

Prifdde, *s. m.* (prif—de) Original source.

Prifddeddf, *s. f.—pl. t.* au (prif—deddf) A primary law.

Prifddinas, *s. f.—pl. t.* oedd (prif—dinas) A principal city, or a metropolis.

Prifddinasawl, *a.* (prifddinas) Metropolitan.

Prifddull, *s. f.—pl. t.* iau (prif—dull) A primary form or manner.
Prifiad, *s. m.* (prif) A thriving, a growing, or increasing; a prospering.
Prifiaw, *v. n.* (prif) To grow up, to increase in stature, to thrive; to prosper.
Prifiawl, *a.* (prif) Tending to grow.
Prifiwr, *s. m.—pl.* prifwyr (prif—gwr) One who increases, a thriver.
Prifllad, *s. m.* (prif—llad) A sovereign grace.
Priflles, *s. m.* (prif—lles) A supreme good.
Priflys, *s. m.—pl. t.* oedd (prif—llys) A principal court, a supreme court.
Prifnawd, *s. m.* (prif—nawd) An original habit.
Prifnod, *s. m.—pl. t.* au (prif—nod) A prime point or number; an epoch.
Prifoed, *s. m.* (prif—oed) A primitive age.
Prifoes, *s. f.—pl. t.* oedd (prif—oes) A first age; a primary life, a first existence.
Prifran, *s. f.—pl. t.* au (prif—rhan) A primary share; a primary division.
Prifraniad, *s. m.* (prifran) A primary division.

> Tri phrifraniad y sydd ar dir: rhan rhwng brodyr: adran rhwng cefnderyw; a chyhydedd rhwng cyfyrdyrw.
>
> There are three *primary divisions* of land: division amongst brothers; subdivision amongst cousins, and co-extension amongst second cousins. *Welsh Laws.*

Prifred, *s. f.* (prif—rhed) A primary course.
Prifrinwedd, *s. f.—pl. t.* au (prif—rhinwedd) A cardinal virtue.
Prifsymudai, *s. c.* (prif—symudai) A primum mobile; a first cause of motion.
Prifwaith, *s. m.* (prif—gwaith) A chief work.
Prifwyd, *s. m.* (prif—gwyd) A chief sin. *Y saith brifwyd*, the seven deadly sins.
Prifwydd, *s. pl.* (prif-gwydd) Primary trees.

> Rhag llwyth wyth bechawd priawd prifwydd,
> Prynasai Mab Duw mad garennydd.
>
> From the burden of the eight original sins of the *primary wood*, the Son of God had purchased a good connection. *Gwalchmai.*

Prifwynt, *s. m.—pl. t.* oedd (prif—gwynt) A principal wind.
Prifysgol, *s. f.—pl. t.* ion (prif—ysgol) A principal school, a primary school.
Priffordd, *s. f.—pl.* priffyrdd (pri—ffordd) A principal road, a high road.

> Einym mae priffordd bob unawr adref
> I odrau Sgyryd Fawr.
>
> For us there is a *high road* at all hours homewards to the skirts of the Great Ysgyryd. *L. G. Cothi.*

Prill, *s. m.—pl. t.* ion (rhill) A rill.
Prin, *s. m.* (py—rhin) That partly appears, or breaks through; that is of slight trace.
Prin, *a.* (py—rhin) Scarce, rare, scant, spare. *adv.* Scarcely, hardly; sparingly.

> Llyma waith amlder
> O brin hyd ucher
> Dywgwener———
>
> Behold the multifarious work from morn till eve of Friday. *Awdl y Creed.*

Prinâad, *s. m.* (prinâu) A rendering scarce or scanty; a becoming scarce; a diminishing.
Prinâawl, *a.* (prinâu) Tending to scarcity.
Prinâu, *v. a.* (prin) To make scarce, scanty or small; to diminish; to grow scarce; to be diminished.
Prinder, *s. m.* (prin) Scarcity; scantiness.
Prindra, *s. m.* (prin) Scarcity, scantiness.
Print, *s. m.—pl. t.* iau (py—rhint) That forms a notch, or scratch; a print.
Printiad, *s. m.* (print) A printing, a marking.
Printiaw, *v. a.* (print) To imprint, to print.
Printiedig, *a.* (printiad) Imprinted, or printed.

Prinwydd, *s. pl. aggr.* (prin—gwydd) Scarlet-oak.
Prinwydden, *s. f.* (prinwydd) The scarlet oak.
Priodadwy, *a.* (prïawd) Capable of being appropriated; marriageable.
Prïodas, *s. f.—pl. t.* au (prïawd) A marriage.

> Priodas Sais a Gwyddeles, neidiaw dros yr ysgubell.
>
> The *marriage* of an Englishman and an Irishwoman, jumping over the broom. *Adage.*
>
> Priodas a wnaethpwyd er dibechu cydgnawd y rhwng gwr a gwraig, ac er ennill plant.
>
> *Marriage* was established for divesting of sin a carnal union between man and woman, and for begetting children. *Ll. G. Hergest.*
>
> Nid er dilëu priodas, na'i thywyllu, yddym ni yn dywedyd, geni mab i forwyn; eithr neilltuaw yddym ni ei gaffaeliad ef.
>
> It is not for annihilating *marriage*, nor for obscuring it, that we are saying, a son is born to a virgin; but the setting aside his birth is what we do. *Ystori Silvester.*

Prïodasawl, *a.* (prïodas) Matrimonial.
Prïodasfab, *s. m.* (prïodas—mab) A bridegroom.
Prïodasferch, *s. f.* (prïodas—merch) A bride.
Prïodasgan, *s. f.* (prïodas—can) A bridal song.
Prïodasgerdd, *s. f.—pl. t.* i (prïodas—cerdd) An epithalamium, or a bridal song.
Prïodawl, *a.* (prïawd) Appropriate, peculiar; legitimate; belonging to marriage; married.

> Dau fab gyfreithiawl briodolion.
>
> Two sons legitimate *ones of marriage*. *Welsh Laws.*

Prïodawr, *s. m.—pl.* prïodorion (prïawd) A proprietary, a hereditary possessor of land; a prince; one who has a natural claim; a native.

> Yn bedwarygwr ydd â dyn yn briodawr.
>
> As a fourth person will a man become a *hereditary proprietor*. *Welsh Laws.*
>
> Elidr, priodawr o'r Gogledd:——Cenau ab Coel Hen, priodawr o'r Gogledd.
>
> Elidr, a *prince* from the North:—Cenau son of Coel the Aged, a *prince* from the North. *Hengsion.*

Prïodedig, *a.* (prïawd) Appropriated; wedded.
Prïodfab, *s. m.—pl.* prïodfeibion (prïawd—mab) A bridegroom.
Prïodferch, *s. f.—pl. t.* ed (merch) A bride.
Prïodi, *v. a.* (prïawd) To render appropriate; to espouse; to marry; to be married.

> Y ferch a ddel i'w phrofi,
> Hwyr y daw i'w phriodi.
>
> The woman that comes to be tried, late will she come to be *married*. *Adage.*
>
> Mor gadarn yd geidw hyd Regec
> Mab Owain Prydain; priodes gwenfud
> Gwyndeyrn Eryres.
>
> So powerfully will the son of Owain defend Britain as far as Rhegres; the blest prince of the region of Eryri has *appropriated* the happy land. *Ll. P. Moch, i Rodri.*

Prïodiad, *s. m.* (prïodi) A marrying, a wedding.
Prïodoldeb, *s. m.* (prïodawl) Appropriateness.
Prïodolder, *s. m.* (priodawl) Appropriateness, propriety; attribute; property, the right or title to a thing.

> Os y nawfed-dyn a ddaw i ofyn tir diffoddedig yn ei briodolder, a hwnw a ddyd diasbad am ei fod yn myned o briodawr yn amhriodawr, ac yna y gwrandawa y gyfraith y diaspad hono.
>
> If the ninth person shall come to demand land extinguished as to *title* and he shall give an outcry on account of his becoming from a proprietor to be one without property, thereupon the law will listen to that outcry. *Welsh Laws.*

Prïodoledig, *a.* (prïodawl) Appropriated.
Prïodoledd, *s. m.* (prïodawl) Appropriateness.
Prïodoli, *v. a.* (prïodawl) To appropriate, to make appropriate or proper; to become appropriate; to dedicate; to render peculiar.
Prïodoliad, *s. m.* (prïodawl) An appropriating, a rendering peculiar; a dedication.
Prïodoliaeth, *s. m.—pl. t.* au (priodawl) Appropriation; the state of being peculiar.
Prïodoliaethu, *v. a.* (prïodoliaeth) To make an appropriation; to assign an attribute.

Priodolrwydd, *s. m.* (priodawl) Appropriateness.

Priodolwr, *s. m.—pl.* priodolwyr (priodawl—gwr) An appropriate man.

Priodori, *v. a.* (priodawr) To render a proprietor; to become a proprietor, or inheritor.

Priodoriaeth, *s. m.—pl. t.* au (priodawr) A peculiar property; an inheritance.

Cynnrddwys mawr ar mawr freuolaeth gnif,
Yn nghyunnt ei brif briodoriaeth.

An exalted man has increased the great frailty of anxiety, in the affliction of his primary *inheritance*. *Ll. P. Moch, i Grist.*

Prion, *s. pl. aggr.* (pri) Origination; animals in a first state of life; imps.

Prionyn, *s. m. dim.* (prion) A little imp.

Pig wenwynig anianawl;
Prionyn o dyddyn diawl.

A spike of nature poisonous; an *imp* from the devil's territory. *I. Gethin ab I. ab Lleision, i'r neidr.*

Pris, *s. m.—pl. t.* iau (pri—is) That is reckoned; that is taken; rate, value, price.

Prisiad, *s. m.—pl. t.* au (pris) A valuation.

Prisiaw, *v. a.* (pris) To value, to appraise.

Prisiawl, *a.* (pris) Belonging to rate, or price.

Pro, *s. m.* (py—rho) That is counter, or against.

Probwyll, *s. m.—pl. t.* au (pro—pwyll) The stilts of a plough.

Probwyllau a rhagarnawdd, ceiniawg a dal.

The *stilts* and the beam, the value is a penny. *Welsh Laws.*

Proc, *s. m.—pl. t.* iau (pro) A thrust, a drive.

Prociad, *s. m.—pl. t.* au (proc) A thrusting.

Prociaw, *v. a.* (proc) To thrust, to stick, to stab.

Prociwr, *s. m.—pl.* procwyr (proc—gwr) A thruster, a sticker, a stabber.

Proest, *s. m.—pl. t.* iau (pro—est) A sequel in contrast with the first; a term in prosody for a counterchange of vowels; it is also called *gorchan*. *Proest Cadwynawdl*, a quadran stanza with alternate concatenated rhyme; *proest cyfnewidiawg*, alternity interchanged; *proest unawdl*, a single rhymed alternity.

Proestawdl, *s. f.—pl.* proestodlau (proest—awdl) Rhyme with vowels interchanged.

Proestiad, *s. m.* (proest) Interchanging of vowels.

Proestiaw, *v. a.* (proest) To interchange vowels.

Proestlawn, *a.* (proest) Abounding with counterchanges of vowel sounds.

A dyrydd ei fadd i feirdd proestlawn;
A dyrnu azan; ataw ydd awn.

And he will bestow his bounty to *harmonious* bards; and he will set apart shares for us; to him let us go. *Cynddelw, i O. Gwynedd.*

Proestodliaeth, *s. m.* (proestawdl) The state of having rhyme with counterchanged vowels.

Proestodli, *v. a.* (proestawdl) To form rhyme with vowels counterchanged.

Proestodliad, *s. m.* (proestawdl) A rhyming with vowels counterchanged.

Profadwy, *a.* (prawf) Provable, or essayable.

Profawl, *a.* (prawf) Belonging to proof.

Profedig, *a.* (prawf) Proved, approved.

Profedigaeth, *s. m.—pl. t.* au (profedig) The act of rendering proved; temptation.

Cariad a bair i ddyn enogau y byd, a bod yn llawen mewn trueiniau a phrofedigaethau.

Love will cause a man to contemn the world, and to be cheerful in afflictions and *temptations*. *Marchawg Crwydrad.*

Profedigawl, *a.* (profedig) Probationary.

Profi, *v. a.* (prawf) To prove, to try, to examine; to attempt; to essay; to taste. *Profi ynad*, to examine for the function of a judge.

Nid erchis bwyd ond ei brofi

Victuals only demanded *to be tasted*. *Adage.*

Tair lleng y daethant henu fordd;
Tair praff prif lynges wy bres brwd:
Un o Iwerddon,
Arall arfogion
O'r Llychlynialon,
Llurw hirion fil.

Three legions came in vessels of the flood; three ample fleets of ships hastily *to attempt* him: one from Ireland; another of armed ones of the Llochlynian men, long burden of the flood. *Gwalchmai, i O. Gwynedd.*

Profiad, *s. m.—pl. t.* au (prawf) A proving; a trying, or essaying; a probation; a tasting; an essay, or trial.

Profiadawl, *a.* (profiad) Probationary.

Profiadu, *v. a.* (profiad) To make a probation.

Profiannawl, *a.* (profiant) Probationary.

Profiannu, *v. a.* (profiant) To make probation.

Profiannus, *a.* (profiant) Probationary.

Profiannusaw, *v. a.* (profiannus) To render probationary; to become probationary.

Profiant, *s. m.* (prawf) Probation; proof.

Profiator, *ger.* (profiad) In proving.

Profiedydd, *s. m.—pl. t.* ion (profiad) A probator.

Profitor, *sup.* (prawf) To be proving.

Profwr, *s. m.—pl.* profwyr (profi—gwr) A prover, a tryer, an examiner; one who attempts; a taster.

Proffes, *s. f.—pl. t.* au (pro—ffes) A predetermination; a vow; a profession, a calling.

Crefyddwr, a doro ei broffes, nid gair ei air.

A religious man who shall break his vow, his word is of no force. *Welsh Laws.*

Proffesawr, *s. m.—pl.* proffesorion (proffes) A votary; a professor.

Proffesiad, *s. m.* (proffes) A making a vow; an entering into an obligation; a professing.

Proffesu, *v. a.* (proffes) To predetermine a course; to make a vow; to profess.

Proffeswr, *s. m.—pl.* proffeswyr (proffes—gwr) One who enters into a solemn obligation.

Proffesydd, *s. m.—pl. t.* ion (proffes) A person who predetermines; a professor.

Prophwyd, *s. m.—pl. t.* i (pro—pwyd) A prophet.

Nid prophwyd neb yn ei wlad ei hun.

No one is a *prophet* in his own country. *Adage.*

Prophwydaw, *v. a.* (prophwyd) To prophesy.

Prophwydoliaeth, *s. m.—pl. t.* au (prophwydawl) A prophecy, a prognostication.

Pru, *s. m.* (py—rhu) That tends out, or forward.

Prudd, *a.* (pru) Circumspect, prudent, discreet; serious; sad, sorrowful.

O gydgynghor tywysogion Ffrainc, y rhodded y forwyn i Lewelyn, a choron y deyrnas ygyd â hi; a gwedi hyny ef a lywiodd y cyfoeth yn brudd ac yn ddoeth ac yn ddedwydd hyd tra pwyodd ei oes.

From the common advice of the princes of France, the maid was given to Llywelyn, and the crown of the kingdom with her; and after that he governed the realm *discreetly* and wisely and happily, as long as his life lasted. *Gr. ab Arthur.*

Pruddâad, *s. m.* (pruddâu) A rendering circumspect or prudent; a rendering serious; a becoming serious or thoughtful.

Pruddâawl, *a.* (pruddâu) Of a prudent tendency; tending to become serious or thoughtful.

Pruddâu, *v. n.* (prudd) To use circumspection; to become prudent; to be serious; to become sad or sorrowful.

Prudd-deb, *s. m.* (prudd) Prudence; seriousness.

Prudd-der, *s. m.* (prudd) Seriousness; pensiveness.

Prudd-dra, *s. m.* (prudd) Discreetness.

Pruddedd, *s. m.* (prudd) Discreetness; sadness.

Prw, *s. m.* (py—rhw) Extension or a reach forward, a state of anxiety.

Prws, *s. m.* (prw) A state tending to; a state of activity, or business.

Prwst, *s. m.* (prws) Bustle; turmoil, tumult.
Prwy, *s. m.—pl. t.* on (prw) That tends onward.
Prwyaw, *v. a.* (prwy) To attain, or to reach.
Prwyawl, *a.* (prwy) Attaining, reaching.
Prwys, *s. m.* (py—rhwys) A tendency to protrude.
Prwysaw, *v. a.* (prwys) To protrude, to reach out.
Prwysawl, *a.* (prwys) Protruding, reaching out.
Prwysg, *s. m.* (prwys) That protrudes; that is over, upon, or impending.
Prwysgaw, *v. a.* (prwysg) To surmount, to get upon, to get uppermost.

Pan dybiai, prwysgai i'r brig,
Gael ancrch——

When he thought he might, *he mounted to the top*, thinking to have a treat—— *L. Mon, duchan Ll. ab Gutyn.*

Prwysgawl, *a.* (prwysg) Surmounting, getting on.
Prwysgiad, *s. m.—pl. t.* au (prwysg) A surmounting, a getting uppermost.
Prwysgl, *s. m.* (prwysg) That is impending.
Prwysgliad, *s. m.* (prwysgl) An impending.
Prwysiad, *s. m.* (prwys) A protruding, thrusting.
Prwyst, *s. m.* (prwys) That is forward, or before; an obstacle; that causes anxiety, or care.
Prwystl, *s. m.* (prwyst) Solicitude, or anxiety.

Nac ofnwch ormod prwystl,
Mwy no'r fwyalch yn ngbelll,
Nid aradd, nid erddir iddi;
Nid llawenach neb no hi.

Be not deprest with too much *anxiety*, more than the blackbird in a grove, who ploughs not, who has no ploughing done for her; there is none more cheerful than her. *Englynion Moes.*

Prwystiad, *s. m.—pl. t.* au (prwyst) A rendering full of bustle; a becoming solicitous.
Prwystiaw, *v. a.* (prwyst) To bustle; to be full of anxiety, to be solicitous.
Prwystl, *s. m.* (prwyst) That is agitated, tumultuous or bustling. *a.* Tumultuous; bustling.

Prwystl fydd ton, a tharan:
Cyd bont prwystl eu gwahan,
Yn nydd trin mi yw Trystan.

Tumultuous will be a wave, and a thunder; so long as their course may be *tumultuous*, in the day of conflict I am Trystan. *Ymdd. Trystan a Gwalchmai.*

Prwystlad, *s. m.* (prwystl) A bustling; hurry.
Prwystlaw, *v. a.* (prwystl) To bustle, to hurry.
Prwystledd, *s. m.* (prwystl) A state of bustling.
Pry, *s. m.—pl. t.* oedd (py—rhy) That is extended; that is produced; that abounds; produce; food, victuals. *Dos i hel dy bry*, go and hunt for thy food, or seek for thy grub.
Pryd, *s. m.—pl. t.* iau (py—rhyd) That is present, that is an object or under cognizance; a stated period, set time, hour, or season; time; a meal time; also, the favour of the countenance, or visage; an aspect; also comeliness, handsomeness, beauty. *O bryd bwy gilydd*, from one time to another; *pa bryd y doi yma?* what time wilt thou come here?

Un-pryd yr iar yn ysgubawr.

The hen makes but one *meal* in a barn. *Adage.*

Hwarddedig pryd wrth a garer.

The *countenance* wears a smile towards such as be loved. *Adage.*

Nid wrth bryd cerid gwreigedd.

Not by the *aspect* do the women love. *Adage.*

Yr oedd it', er a ddywetou',
Ragor bryd rhag eiry bron.

There was to thee, whatever they may say, a *countenance* surpassing the snow of the hill. *Bedo Brwynllys.*

Pryd, *adv.* (py—rhyd) Seeing that; as it happens. *Pryd nad elit*, seeing that thou wouldest not go.
Prydain, *a.* (pryd) Exhibiting presence or cognizance; exhibiting an open or fair aspect; full of beauty, well-seeming, beautiful; polished or civilized with respect to morals. Ynys Prydain, the Fair Island, the Isle of Britain.

Tri enw Ynys Prydain; cyn ei chyfanneddu y Gal Gre ei galwai Clas Merddin; gwedi ei chaffael, y Fel Ynys; a gwedi caffael o Brydyn ab Aedd Mawr hi, Ynys Prydyn.

The three names of the Isle of Britain: before it was inhabited the Hogd Gall used to call it the Water-girt Green Plat, after obtaining it, the Honey Island; and after Prydyn son of Aedd the Great had obtained it, the Isle of PRYDYN. *Trioedd.*

Trugain cantref Prydain y sydd dan Cado Hen.

The three score hundreds of BRITAIN are under Cado the Aged. *H Culhwch—Mabinogion.*

Prydawl, *a.* (pryd) Belonging to what is present or an object of cognizance: seasonable.
Prydeiniad, *s. m.—pl.* prydeiniaid (prydain) An inhabitant of Britain, a Briton.
Pryder, *s. m.* (prw) Anxiety, solicitude, care.

Ni wyr pryder nis prydero ac nis pryno.

He knows not anxiety *that does* not *consider* and that does not experience. *Adage.*

Mi nid wyf lawen o lawenydd bryd,
Am bryder yr undydd;
Am Owain, am ddwyrain dyrnhydd,
Am deyrn, am gedyrn gydlydd.

I am not cheerful from cheerfulness of mind, because of the *trouble* of that one day; for Owain, for exalted generosity, for a prince, for the companion of the mighty. *D. Llosgwrn Mew.*

Pryderawl, *a.* (pryder) Solicitous, anxious, considerate, provident, careful, thoughtful.
Pryderi, *s. m.* (pryder) Anxiety, deep thought.
Pryderiad, *s. m.* (pryder) A causing anxiety; a considering anxiously.
Pryderu, *v. n.* (pryder) To be anxious, to be solicitous; to consider; to provide.

Dihunid a brydero.

Let such as will *be anxious* be diverted of sleep. *Adage.*

Gweddus ar wraig, y naill law yn casglu, y llall yn rhannu, ac ei phen yn pryderu.

Seemly on a woman, the one hand collecting, and the other distributing, and her head *considering*. *Trioedd Moes.*

Pryderus, *a.* (pryder) Anxious, pensive.
Pryderusaw, *v. a.* (pryderus) To render anxious; to become solicitous, to become thoughtful.
Pryderusedd, *s. m.* (pryderus) Anxiousness.
Pryderusrwydd, *s. m.* (pryderus) Anxiousness, solicitousness; pensiveness; contemplativeness.
Pryderwawd, *s. m.* (pryder—gwawd) A profoundly considered eulogy.

Pryderwawd cendawd cyfoerthi ni wn.

Profound praise of the energetic mind I am not master of. *Einion ab Gwalchmai.*

Prydfalch, *a.* (pryd—balch) Of a superb aspect.
Prydfardd, *s. m.—pl.* prydfeirdd (pryd—bardd) A bard who delineates; a recording bard.

Gwaedd uchel dwyn Hywel hardd:
Gwaeth yw dwyn brawdfaeth prydfardd.

A loud outcry for the taking away of Hywel the Superb; worse is the taking the foster-brother of a *recording bard*. *Iolo Goch.*

Prydfawr, *a.* (pryd—mawr) Magnificent.

Grasaw anaw engherdd yn Mhrydain
I'm mhrydfawr ddadeubudd.

The gratulation of the public minstrelsy in Britain to my *magnificent* restorer. *Ll. P. Moch, i G. ab Llywelyn.*

Prydferth, *a.* (pryd—berth) Of fair time, seasonable; handsome, decent, or seemly.

Cymeryd alltudes heddyw yn wraig it, ni wyddost ti pa le pan henyw, a gwrthawd fy merch innau; etnebydd hagen nad prydferth it hyny, ac nad dibrid hyd tra parho nerth yn y braich deau hwn.

Taking this day a stranger for thy wife, whom thou dost not know whence descended, and refusing also my daughter; know therefore that such a thing is not *handsome* in thee, and it shall not be unrequited, whilst there is strength in this right arm. *Gr. ab Arthur.*

Prydferthedd, *s. m.* (prydferth) Becomingness.
Prydferthiad, *s. m.* (prydferth) A rendering handsome, a becoming comely or graceful.

Prydferthrwydd, *s. m.* (prydferth) Becomingness, comeliness; gracefulness.

Prydferthu, *v. a.* (prydferth) To render becoming; to beautify; to become comely.

Prydferthwch, *s. m.* (prydferth) Becomingness, handsomeness, comeliness, gracefulness.

Prydiad, *s. m.* (pryd) A delineating of nature; a composing of poetry; poetry.

Pa yw mydr, neu brydiad!

What is metre, or *poetry!* *Sim. Fychan.*

Prydiaith, *s. f.* (pryd—iaith) Poetic language.

Prydiaw, *v. a.* (pryd) To represent an object; to record an event; to render seasonable; to set apart a time; to become seasonable.

Dybi o Alclud gwyr dred diwair,
I ddeol o Brydain firain luydd:
Dybi o Lydaw prydaw gyweithydd,
Cedwyr ar gadfeirch, ni pheirch eu henydd.

There comes from Alclud bold faithful men, to drive away war from fair Britain; there comes from Llydaw an auxiliary *becoming seasonable*, heroes on steeds of war who will not respect their home. *Golyddan, Arymes Prydain.*

Prydiawl, *a.* (pryd) Objective; belonging to an event; seasonable, or of due time.

Prydlaeth, *s. m.* (pryd—llaeth) The quantity of milk milked at one time.

Prydlawn, *a.* (pryd—llawn) Seasonable, timely.

Prydlonâad, *s. m.* (prydlonâu) A rendering seasonable; a becoming timely.

Prydlonâu, *v. a.* (prydlawn) To render seasonable; to become seasonable or timely.

Prydlonder, *s. m.* (prydlawn) Seasonableness.

Prydlonedd, *s. m.* (prydlawn) Seasonableness.

Prydloni, *v. a.* (prydlawn) To render seasonable.

Prydnawn, *s. m.—pl. t.* au (pryd—nawn) The time from mid-day to the sixth hour; the afternoon.

Plygain, dwyrain dawn,
Anterth, aberth lawn,
A bore, a nawn,
A phrydnawn hwyr.

The twilight, when bounty rises, the hour of vapour, of acceptable sacrifice, and morning, and noon, and *afternoon* late. *L. G. Cothi.*

Prydnawnawl, *a.* (prydnawn) Afternoon tide.

Prydnawnbryd, *s. m.—pl. t.* iau (prydnawn—pryd) An afternoon meal; a dinner.

Prydnawnfwyd, *s. m.* (prydnawn—bwyd) Afternoon meat; a dinner.

Prydnawngwaith, *s. m.* (prydnawn—gwaith) A certain afternoon.

Prydnawni, *v. n.* (prydnawn) To grow late in the day, or in the afternoon.

Truch i ddyn o'i wyn a'i ysi na ddaw,
Cyn i'w ddydd brydnawni.—

It is simple for a man, that from his lust and his ardour he doth not come, ere his day *grows towards a close.* *Edm. Prys.*

Prydnawniad, *s. m.* (prydnawn) A becoming late in the afternoon.

Prydred, *s. m.* (pryd—rhed) Chronology.

Prydu, *v. a.* (pryd) To represent an object; to represent an event; to record time; to delineate, to form; to compose; to compose poetry.

Prydu gefiau chwareus;—Yr Arglwydd a brydodd y pader.

To invent playful words;—The Lord *composed* the paternoster. *H. Car. Mag.—Mabinogion.*

Sef a prug Hengist, erbyn y dydd hwnw, prydu twyll, nid amgen no rhoddi cyllell hir i bob gwr onaddynt.

What did Hengist, against that day, was *to contrive* treachery, nothing less than giving a long knife to every man of them. *Gr. ab Arthur.*

Dewiswn ddwrban Dafydd
Cyn prydu ym gloewrym glod
O arall——

I would rather choose the satire of David, than to *have composed* for me splendid praise by another. *Gr. Gryg.*

Prydus, *a.* (pryd) Sightly, comely; seasonable.

Prydusaw, *v. a.* (prydus) To render comely or handsome; to become comely; to become seasonable or timely.

Prydusdra, *s. m.* (prydus) Comeliness; beauty; seasonableness.

Prydusedd, *s. m.* (prydus) Comeliness, beauty; seasonableness.

Prydusrwydd, *s. m.* (prydus) Comeliness.

Prydwen, *s. f.* (pryd—gwèn) That is white.

Tarian a gymerai Arthur ar ei ysgwydd, yr hon a elwid Prydwen.

A shield did Arthur take upon his shoulder, the which was called Prydwen. *Gr. ab Arthur.*

Prydydd, *s. m.—pl. t.* ion (pryd) One who describes or represents, a recorder of events; one who forms or composes; a delineator of what is beautiful; a teacher of what is fair, in a moral sense, a civilizer; a poet.

Tri pheth a wnant brydydd; awen, gwybodaeth a chynhyrfiad.

Three things form a *poet*; genius, knowledge, and impulse. *Barddas.*

Prydyddaidd, *a.* (prydydd) Like a poet, poetic.

Prydyddawl, *a.* (prydydd) Poetic, poetical.

Prydyddes, *s. f.—pl. t.* au (prydydd) A poetess.

Prydyddiad, *s. m.* (prydydd) A poetising.

Prydyddiaeth, *s. m.* (prydydd) The composition of poetry, poetry.

Tair dyben prydyddiaeth; cynnydd daioni, cynnydd deall, a chynnydd dyddanwch.

The three intentions of *poetry*; the increase of good, the increase of understanding, and the increase of happiness. *Barddas.*

Prydyddu, *v. a.* (prydydd) To poetise, to compose poetry, to write verses, or to versify.

Prydyn, *s. m.* (pryd) A name synonymous with Prydain, or Britain, and sometimes used for it; but in general applied to Scotland.

Hon a oresgyn
Holl Loegr a Phrydyn.

She will conquer all England and *Scotland.* *Taliesin.*

Prydd, *s. m.—pl. t.* ion (pry) That is teeming with produce; a luxuriant spot.

A'r bedwerydd
Rhan mewn tir prydd,
Yn dwyn ffrwythau
Ar ei ganfed :——
A'r bryn a'r prydd
A ynt ddedwydd;
A'r dyn a fo
Tebyg iddo,
Caei ane bwnw
Y gair a'i gadw.

And the fourth part in rich land, producing fruit a hundred fold: and the hill and *dale* are happy; and the person who is similar to that, he receives the word and keeps it. *T. ab Ieu. ab Rhys.*

Prydd, *a.* (pry) Good, teeming with good; rich, or luxuriant; comfortable, happy. *Byw yn brydd*, to live well; *gwlad brydd iawn*, a country abounding with every comfort; *llaeth prydd*, rich milk: *yd prydd*, fine corn. *Sil.*

Tragywyddoldeb yw dy oes brydd;
Pawb ereill sydd i ddarfod.

Eternity is thy happy life; all other beings are to end. *Sir E. Gwynn.*

Mae ganto'r bwydydd gorau,
Ac oll o'i brydiau'n brydd.

He has the best of victuals, and all of his meals comfortable. *Dafydd o'r Nant.*

Pryddâad, *s. m.* (pryddâu) A teeming with good; a becoming luxuriant; a being comfortable.

Pryddâawl, *a.* (pryddâu) Of a luxuriant tendency; tending to be comfortable.

Pryddâu, *v. a.* (prydd) To become teeming with luxuriance; to be productive.

Pryddedd, *s. m.* (prydd) Luxuriantness, fertility.

Pryddest, *s. f.—pl. t.* au (pry—dest) A rule or law of poetry; metre; song. *Pryddest diawdl,* blank verse.

Pryddestau Cymmru, cymmrodial gyanelw,
Nawd Cynddelw a'u cynnal!

The poetics of Wales, expressive of social harmony, shall not Cynddelw maintain them! *Cynddelw.*

Pryddestawd, *s.m.* (pryddest) Poetic composition

Gorau ym o'm rhoen ragfeddu
Rhwydd eraith o brifiaith brydu,
Pryddestawd o'r Drindawd draethe
Traeth foliant teilyngawd dalu.

Best for me from my Lord to be pre-endowed with the fluent oratory of poetry in a primitive tongue, a composition speaking of the Trinity, a discourse of praise, a tribute due to be paid. *Elidr Sais.*

Pryddestawl, *a.* (pryddest) Metrical, poetical.
Pryddestiad, *s. m.* (pryddest) A forming of metre
Pryddestu, *v. a.* (pryddest) To form rules of poetry; to make metrical compositions.
Pryddestwr, *s. m.—pl.* pryddestwyr (pryddest—gwr) A versifier, a minstrel.
Pryddfawr, *a.* (prydd) Greatly teeming or rich.
Pryddiad, *s. m.* (prydd) A teeming with produce; a rendering luxuriant.
Pryddineb, *s. m.* (prydd) Luxuriantness.
Pryddus, *a.* (prydd) Of a productive nature.
Pryf, *s. m.—pl. t.* ed (pry) Any thing produced, or generated; any small animal, a vermin; a worm. *Pryf ffyrnig yw y neidr,* the snake is a noxious vermin; *pryf cyfrwys yw llwynawg,* a fox is a cunning animal; *y pryf,* the vermin; a term often used for an animal that is hunted for *prey,* but more particularly applied to the hare. *Pryf llwyd, pryf penfrith,* a badger; also called *broch* and *mochyn bychan; pryf cadachawg, pryf y gwinwydd, blewog amldroed,* a palmerworm; *pryf y dail, pryf y cawl, pryf y bresych, llindys,* a caterpillar; *pryf clust, chwilen clust,* an earwig; *pryf y ganwyll, pryf y goleuad, pryf y melinydd, pryf dillad,* a moth; *pryf copyn, adar cop,* a spider; *pryf y gwellt, pryf ysgoed,* a cadeworm; *pryf yr yd, ydys,* the calender.
Pryfad, *s.m.—pl.* pryfaid (pryf) An animal state; an animal; a vermin; a worm.
Pryfadawg, *a.* (pryfad) Full of vermin; vermiculous; mothy.
Pryfawl, *a.* (pryf) Verminous; vermicular.
Pryfed, *s. pl. aggr.* (pryf) Vermin; worms.

Trefnaist wern uffern affaith eithaf;
Trefred i bryfed, lle yd ymbrofan'.

Thou didst prepare the slough of hell suitable for Satan; the habitation for *worms,* where they will be in mutual strife. *Casnodyn.*

Pryfediad, *s. m.* (pryfed) Vermination.
Pryfedig, *a.* (pryfed) Affected by worms. *Pren pryfedig,* worm-eaten wood.
Pryfedu, *v. n.* (pryfed) To become worms; to breed worms, to verminate.
Pryfes, *s. f.—pl. t.* au (pryf) A vermin of the female kind.

Y bryfes, gynhes geinach
A'r garau a'r berau bach.

The *animal,* the warmly clad hare, with the small shanks and hams. *T. Prys.*

Pryfeta, *v. a.* (pryfed) To gather vermin, to hunt for vermin.
Pryfetai, *s. c.—pl.* pryfeteion (pryfed) A vermin-catcher.
Pryfig, *a.* (pryf) Having worms, vermiculous.
Pryfigedd, *s. f.* (pryfig) A breeding of worms.
Pryfydd, *s. m.—pl. t.* ion (pryf) A vermin-killer.
Pryfyddiaeth, *s. m.* (pryfydd) The calling of a vermin-killer.
Pryfyn, *s. m. dim.* (pryf) A small vermin; a little worm; a single vermin.

Nid gwr dewr, nid gorau dyn
Nid pur wyf, onid pryfyn.

Not a brave man, not a best person, not pure am I, but a *frail worm.* *W. Middleton.*

Pryffiau, *s. m.* (pry—ffiau) A spreading radiation
Pryffwn, *s. m.* (pry—ffwn) A source of spreading. *a.* Excellent, principal, superior.

Gogwn Dduw, pryffwn y proffwydi.

I know God, the *one set forth* of the prophets. *Ll. P. Moch.*

Gwisgoedd ym rhoddes—
O borffor, o bryffwn fliant,
O bali, ac aur ac ariant.

Garments he bestowed on me, of purple, of *superior* linen, of velvet, and gold and silver. *Ll. P. Moch.*

Pryffwnt, *s. m.* (pryffwn) A source of spreading; a centre; a principal.

Gadewais, a hyntiais hwnt
Briffordd y bobl, a'u pryffwnt.

I forsook, and I turned off the people's high road, and their *central point.* *D. ab Gwilym.*

Pryleu, *s. m.* (pry—lleu) A fluent utterance.
Pryn, *s. m.* (pry) A take, a taking to one's self; a purchase; desert, merit. *a.* Bought.

Gwell un synwyr pryn no dau synwyr parawd.

Better is one wit *bought* than two wits ready. *Adage.*

Gwell aidion gwerth nog un pryn.

Better a selling beast than a *bought* one. *Adage.*

Prynadwy, *a.* (pryn) Purchasable; buyable.
Prynator, *ger.* (pryn) In purchasing.
Prynawl, *a.* (pryn) Purchasing, buying.
Pryned, *s. f.—pl. t.* au (pryn) A holder, or that takes hold; a hand.
Prynedig, *a.* (pryn) Being purchased; redeemed
Prynedigaeth, *s. m.* (prynedig) The act of taking, buying, or purchasing; redemption.
Prynedigawl, *a.* (prynedig) Belonging to purchase; redemptory.
Pryngar, *a.* (pryn) Addicted to buying.
Pryniad, *s. m.—pl. t.* au (pryn) A buying, a purchasing; a redeeming.
Pryniadawl, *a.* (pryniad) Purchasing; redeeming
Pryniawd, *s. m.* (pryn) The act of buying.
Pryniawdwr, *s. m.—pl.* pryniawdwyr (pryniawd—gwr) A purchaser or a buyer; a redeemer.
Pryniawdr, *s. m.—pl.* pryniodron (pryniawd) A purchaser or a buyer; a redeemer.
Prynitor, *sup.* (pryn) To be purchasing.
Prynu, *v. a.* (pryn) To take, to lay hold of; to purchase, to buy; to redeem; to deserve, to merit. *Pryna hyn,* buy this much.

Gwerth dy wybodaeth i brynu synwyr.

Sell thy knowledge *to buy* sense. *Adage.*

Cas dyn a bryno bob peth ac heb ennill ar ddim.

Odious the person *who buys* every thing without gaining upon any. *Adage.*

Cred yn Nuw a yth wnaeth; car Dduw a yth brynwys; ac ofna Dduw a yth barna.

Believe in God who made thee; love God who redeemed thee; and fear God who will judge thee. *Barddas.*

Nid mau modd dawl heb hawl pwy oeddynt;
Prynasynt eu moli——

In no wise can I be mute, without asserting who they were; *they deserved* to be extolled. *Gwalchmai.*

Prynwr, *s. m.—pl.* prynwyr (pryn—gwr) Buyer
Prynydd, *s. m.—pl. t.* ion (pryn) A buyer.
Prys, *s. m.—pl. t.* oedd (pry—ys) A covert; a resort, or an abode; brushwood, underwood. It forms the names of several places: as *Bron*

y *Prys*; *Prysaddfed*, *Pryseddfod*, *Prys Iorwerth*, *Prys Gaga*, *Prystalyn*, *Prys Dolffyn*.

> Twrf gawr goruyddawr gochwys,
> Mal twrf tymhestl am brys.
>
> The din of the shout of the toiling steed-mounted warriors, like the tumult of a whirlwind over the brushwood. *Seisyll Bryffwrch.*

Prysain, *a.* (prys) Abounding with coverts; abounding with brushwood. *s. f.* A place covered with brushwood.

Prysawl, *a.* (prys) Belonging to a covert; frequented; overrun with brushwood.

Prysedd, *s. m.* (prys) State of being frequented.

Prysedda, *v. a.* (prysedd) To make a resort; to make an abode, to dwell, to inhabit.

Pryseddawl, *a* (prysedd) Belonging to a dwelling

Pryseddfa, *s. f.—pl. t.* ou (prysedd) A place of resort; a dwelling place.

Pryseddfod, *s. f.—pl. t.* au (prysedd—bod) A dwelling place, or a habitation.

Pryseddiad, *s. m.* (prysedd) A making a resort; a fixing an abode; a dwelling.

Pryseddu, *v. a.* (prysedd) To make a resort; to take up an abode; to dwell.

> Y nos hono y doai Collen adref i'w gudigl, ac y gweddiai ar Dduw am gael lle i bryseddu tra byddai byw.
>
> That night Collen came home to his hermitage, and he prayed to God for obtaining a place to *dwell* whilst he should live. *Buchedd Collen.*

Prysel, *s. m.—pl. t.* au (prys) A place overgrown with brushwood, a thicket.

Pryseliad, *s. m.* (prysel) A becoming covered with brushwood, a growing to a thicket.

Pryselu, *v. n.* (prysel) To become overgrown with brushwood, or to become a thicket.

Prysg, *s. m.—pl. t.* au (prys) That extends or stretches over; also brushwood, or underwood. There are several mountains of this name; as the *Prysg Du*, in Radnorshire, *Y Prysg*, in Glamorganshire.

Prysgawl, *a.* (prysg) Expanding over, covering.

Prysgiad, *s. m.* (prysg) A stretching over; also a becoming covered with brushwood.

Prysgl, *s. m.* (prysg) A copse; brushwood.

Prysgliach, *s. pl. aggr.* (prysgl) Stunted straggling trees.

Prysglwyn, *s. m.—pl. t.* i (prysg—llwyn) Copse.

Prysgoed, *s. pl. aggr.* (prys—coed) Brushwood.

Prysgwydd, *s. pl.* (prysg—gwydd) Brushwood.

Prysgwydden, *s. f. dim.* (prysgwydd) A coppice-tree.

Prysgyll, *s. m.* (prys—cyll) A place overgrown with small hazel wood, a hazel copse.

Prysiad, *s. m.* (prys) A forming a covert; a making a resort; a becoming overrun.

Prystell, *s. f.* (prwst) Tumult, or uproar.

Prystellach, *s. f.* (prystell) A state of uproar. *v. a.* To make an uproar or a tumult.

> Y rhai drwg—pan drengont wy y daw y cythreuliaid yn heitiau a phrystellach fawr ganthynt yn greulawn i byrth uffern.
>
> The wicked ones, when they are deceased, the devils will urge in swarms with dire uproar horribly to the gates of hell. *Elucidarius.*

Prysu, *v. a.* (prys) To form a covert; to make a resort; to overrun; to cover with brushwood.

Prysur, *a.* (prws) Assiduous, diligent, busy; making haste; serious. *Yr wyt yn brysur iawn wrth dy waith*, thou art very busy at thy work; *gweda imi yn brysur*, tell me seriously. *Dyfed.*

> Rhaid yw ymddilwng o'llwedd present,
> [illegible] prysur ei [illegible]!
>
> It is necessary to depart from the station of the present, for [illegible] is the vanity of it. *Elidir Sais.*

Prysuraw, *v. a.* (prysur) To make haste with what is in hand; to be assiduous; to hasten; to be serious or intent upon a thing.

Prysurawl, *a.* (prysur) Tending to be assiduous, tending to hasten; of a serious turn.

Prysurdeb, *s. m.* (prysur) Assiduity, diligence; business; haste; earnestness, attentiveness.

Prysuredig, *a.* (prysur) Being busied, hastened.

Prysuriad, *s. m.* (prysur) A being diligent, a busying; a hastening, a giving attention.

Prysuriaeth, *s. m.* (prysur) The state of being diligent; a state of bustle; attention.

> Och Dduw! na ddaw ef etwaeth,
> I ystwng trawsyr [illegible] cymmyg
> Yn nghynaif pryseriaeth.
>
> Would to God that he were to come again, to humble the oppressors, of the most violent oppression, in the urgency of [illegible]. *Elidir Sais.*

Prysurwch, *s. m.* (prysur) Diligence; earnestness; a state of bustle or haste.

Prysurwr, *s. m.—pl.* prysurwyr (prysur—gwr) A bustler; a hastener.

Pryswr, *s. m.—pl.* pryswyr (prys—gwr) A resorter, a frequenter; a dweller.

Puch, *s. m.—pl. t.* ion (py—uch) A sigh; earnest desire, a wish.

Puchaw, *v. a.* (puch) To sigh; to long, to wish.

> Ar eu pechodau puchaswn arwydd crog;
> Yn dwyn croes Crist ar fy ysgwydd;
> Angeu yr enaid, afraid [illegible],
> A ddaw am buchaw am bechrwydd.
>
> On their sins *I would have desired* the sign of the crucifix, that I might bear the cross of Christ on my shoulder; the death of the soul, an untoward fate, will come for longing after wickedness. *Einion ab Gwalchmai.*

Puchedig, *a.* (puch) Being longed for or desired.

Puchiad, *s. m.—pl. t.* au (puch) A sighing after; a desiring earnestly; a desiring.

Puchiannawl, *a.* (puchiant) Panting; sighing; earnestly desirous; greatly longing after.

Puchiannu, *v. a.* (puchiant) To make a sighing; to desire earnestly, to long or to pant after.

Puchiannus, *a.* (puchiant) Sighing; longing.

Puchiant, *s. m.* (puch) A sighing; earnest desire

> Duw llywiawdr—
> Dosbarth digamwedd a'm [illegible] hyd frawd;
> Defawd [illegible] ym a bucho;
> O buchiant mawrfaw ef a'm rhoddo
> Roddion ordywyll a'm dadwyllo!
>
> God the supreme ruler, with uncorrupted laws may he sustain me for judgement; a sinless habit may he wish for me; from a greatly existing anxiety may he bestow on me mysterious gifts that shall undeceive me. *Meilyr ab Gwalchmai.*

Puchiaw, *v. a.* (puch) To sigh, to desire earnestly

Puchiawl, *a.* (puch) Sighing, longing, wishing.

Puchwr, *s. m.—pl.* puchwyr (puch—gwr) One who sighs, one who longs.

Pud, *s. m.* (py—ud) That tends to allure.

Pudd, *s. m.* (py—udd) Aptness to stop.

Pul, *s. m.—pl. t.* on (py—ul) That tends to straiten.

Pum, *s. m.* (py—um) That tends to form, or to aggregate; the number five, used as a prefix, in composition.

Pumban, *s. m.—pl. t.* au (pum—ban) A term in prosody for a stanza of five verses.

Pumbanawg, *a.* (pumban) Consisting of five verses or lines.

Pumbys, *s. pl.* (pum—bys) Five fingers. *a.* Five-fingered; common cinquefoil: *pumbys yr elfen*, procumbent sibaldia.

Pumcanfed, *s. m.* (pumcant) The five hundredth part. *a.* Five hundredth.

Pumcanmil, *s. m.* (pumcant—mil) Five hundred thousand. *a.* Five hundred thousand.

Pumcanmilfed, *s. m.* (pumcanmil) Five hundred thousandth part. *a.* Five hundred thousandth.
Pumcanmyrdd, *s. m.* (pumcant—myrdd) The number of five hundred myriads, or five millions. *a.* Five hundred myriads.
Pumcant, *s. m.* (pum—cant) Five hundred.
Pumcanwaith, *s. m.* (pumcant—gwaith) Five hundred times.
Pumdalen, *s. f.* (pum—dalen) A cinquefoil. *a.* Five-leaved.
Pumdalenawg, *a.* (pumdalen) Having five leaves.
Pumdeg, *s. m.* (pum—deg) Fifty. *a.* Fifty.
Pumdegawl, *a.* (pumdeg) Belonging to fifty.
Pumdegfed, *s. m.* (pumdeg) The fiftieth part.
Pumdegmil, *s. m.* (pumdeg—mil) Fifty thousand. *a.* Fifty thousand.
Pumdryll, *s. pl.* (pum—dryll) Five pieces. *a.* Consisting of five pieces.
Pumloes, *s. pl.* (pum—gloes) The five agonies; a term in theology.
Pumlleng, *s. pl.* (pum—lleng) Five legions. *a.* Consisting of five legions.
Pumllyfr, *s. pl.* (pum—llyfr) The pentateuch.
Pummed, *s. m.* (pump) The fifth. *a.* Fifth.
Pummedban, *s. m.* (pummed—ban) A fifth line.
Pummedmis, *s.* (pummed—mis) The fifth month.
Pummednos, *s. f.* (pummed—nos) A fifth night.
Pummedran, *s. f.* (pummed—rhan) A fifth part.
Pummil, *s. m.* (pum—mil) Five thousand.
Pummilfed, *s. f.* (pummil) The five thousandth part. *a.* Five thousandth.
Pummis, *s. pl.* (pum—mis) Five months. *a.* Of five months.
Pummisyriad, *s. m.—pl.* pummisyriaid (pum—misyriad) What is five years of age.
Pummwnt, *s. m.* (pum—mwnt) Five hundred thousand.
Pumnalen, *s. f.* (pum—dalen) Cinquefoil.
Pumnalenawg, *a.* (pumnalen) Cinquefoil.
Pumochr, *s. m.* (pum—ochr) A pentagon. *a.* Of five sides.
Pumochrawg, *a.* (pumochr) Five-sided, pentagon.
Pumoed, *s. pl.* (pum—oed) Five ages; a term used sometimes for *Pumoes*.
Pumoes, *s. pl.* (pum—oes) Five lives, or five periods; a term in theology for the period before the coming of Christ.

> Achaws pumoes byd y bu lidaw,
> Ucheiwr mirain, ber drain drwyddaw.

> For the sake of the *five ages* of the world, the glorious exalted one was pierced with the point of thorns. *D. Benfras.*

Pumongl, *s. m.* (pum—ongl) That has five angles. *a.* Of five angles.
Pumonglawg, *a.* (pumongl) Pentagonal.
Pump, *s. m.* (pum) Five, used only absolutely.
Pumplyg, *s. m.* (pum—plyg) What is doubled five times. *a.* Quintuple.
Pumplygawl, *a.* (pumplyg) Quintuple.
Pumrhan, *s. pl.* (pum—rhan) Five shares.
Pumrhanawl, *a.* (pumrhan) Quinquepartite.
Pumsill, *s. pl.* (pum—sill) Five syllables. *a.* Of five syllables.
Pumsillawg, *a* (pumsill) Of five syllables.
Pumtant, *s. m.* (pum—tant) A pentachord.
Pumtro, *s. pl.* (pum—tro) Five turns. *a.* Of five turns; five times.
Pumwaith, *s. pl.* (pum—gwaith) Five times.
Pumwan, *s. pl.* (pum—gwan) Five wounds, a term in christian theology.

> Can dug pumwan Crist pumoes o gaeth—

> Since the *five wounds* of Christ bear the five ages out of bondage. *Ll. P. Moch.*

Pumwr, *s. pl.* (pum—gwr) Five men.
Pumwriad, *s. m.—pl.* pumwriaid (pumwr) One who is over five men.
Pun, *s. m.* (py—un) That is equal, even, or equivalent. *a.* Equal, equivalent.

> Pedwar pun brodyr a'm bu,
> Ac i bob un pentenlu;
> Ni wyr Tren berchen ida.

> Four *equal* brothers to me have been, and each was allotted to be the head of a family; but Tren knows to itself no owner. *Llywarch Hen.*

Punt, *s. f.—pl.* punnoedd (pun) A denomination for the sum of twenty shillings, or a pound.
Pur, *s. m.* (py—ur) That is pure or without alloy. *a.* Pure, clean; undefiled, perfect; sincere.

> Iolwd bair, o bured arwar,
> A beris amad ac adar.

> I will adore the Cause, from *so pure* a source did produce revolving things and birds. *Llywelyn Fardd.*

Pur, *adv.* (py—ur) Essentially; very. *Pur dda*, very good; *pur dost*, very severe.
Purad, *s. m.* (pur) Depuration, a purifying.
Puradwy, *a.* (purad) Capable of being pure.
Puraidd, *a.* (pur) Somewhat pure or clean.
Purain, *a.* (pur) Abounding with purity.
Puraw, *v. a.* (pur) To purify, to cleanse.
Purawd, *s. m.* (pur) Purgation, or cleansing.
Purawl, *a.* (pur) Purifying, cleansing.
Purawr, *s. m.* (pur) A purifier, a purger.
Purdan, *s. m.* (pur—tan) Purgatory.
Purdeb, *s. m.* (pur) Purity; sincerity.

> Tair cynneddf purdeb ar iaith; prif anseawdd, prif arfer, a phrifddefnydd.

> The three principles of *purity* in a language; an established idiom, an established usage, and established application. *Barddas.*

Purdra, *s. m.* (pur) Pureness, or purity.
Puredig, *a.* (purad) Purified, cleansed.
Puredigaeth, *s. m.—pl. t.* au (puredig) The being purified; a purification; a lustration.
Puredigaethawl, *a.* (puredigaeth) Purificative.
Puredigaethu, *v. a.* (puredigaeth) To make a purification, to make a lustration.
Puredigaw, *v. a.* (puredig) To render purified.
Puredigawl, *a.* (puredig) Purificatory.
Puredd, *s. m.* (pur) Purity, pureness, cleanness.
Pureidd-dra, *s. m.* (puraidd) A purified state.
Pureiddiad, *s. m.* (puraidd) A rendering purified.
Pureiddiaw, *v. a.* (puraidd) To render pure; to become of a pure nature; to lustrate.
Pureiddiedig, *a.* (pureiddiad) Being purified.
Pureiddiedigawl, *a.* (pureiddiedig) Purificative.
Pureiddrwydd, *s. m.* (puraidd) Pureness, purity.
Puren, *s. f.—pl. t.* au (pur) A purifying machine, a sifting skreen.
Puriad, *s. m.—pl. t.* au (pur) A making pure; a becoming pure; a purifying; a lustration.
Puriannawl, *a.* (puriant) Purificative.
Puriannu, *v. a.* (puriant) To depurate.
Puriannus, *a.* (puriant) Depuratory, purifying.
Puriannusaw, *v. a.* (puriannus) To render purificatory; to become purificative.
Puriant, *s. m.* (pur) Purgation, depuration.
Puriator, *ger.* (puriad) In purifying.
Puriedydd, *s. m.—pl. t.* ion (puriad) A purifier.
Purineb, *s. m.* (pur) A state of purity.
Purion, *adv.* (pur) Essentially, purely; very well.

> Wyd burion i gyrchu angeu at wr boneddig.

> Thou art *very well* to fetch death to a nobleman. *Adage, applied to a dilatory one.*

Puritor, *sup.* (pur) To be purifying.
Purlan, *a.* (pur—glan) Purely clean.

Purwr, *s. m.—pl.* purwyr (pur—gwr) One who makes pure, a purifier.

Puten, *s. f.—pl. t.* od (pud) A whore.

Puteindra, *s. m.* (puten) Putanism, whoredom.

Puteindy, *s. m.* (puten—ty) A bawdy-house.

Puteiniad, *s. f.—pl.* puteiniaid (puten) A whore.

Puteiniaw, *v. a.* (puten) To commit whoredom.

Puteiniawl, *a.* (puten) Meretricious.

Puteinig, *a.* (puten) Whorish, adulterous.

Puteinigrwydd, *s. m.* (puten) Whorishness.

Puteiniwr, *s. m.—pl.* puteinwyr (puten—gwr) A whoremonger, a fornicator.

Puteinllyd, *a.* (puten) Addicted to fornication.

PW, *s. m. r.* That tends to push, or pass off; a tendency to pass off, or to separate.

Pwca, *s. m.—pl. t.* od (pwg) A hobgoblin.

Pwci, *s. m.—pl. t.* od (pwg) A hobgoblin.

Pwd, *s. m.* (pw—wd) A rot; the rot in sheep.

Pwdr, *a.* (pwd) Rotten, corrupt, putrid.

Pwff, *s. m.—pl.* pyffiau (pw) A puff.

Pwffiaw, *v. a.* (pwff) To puff; to come in puffs.

Pwg, *s. m.* (pw—wg) That pushes or swells out.

Pwl, *s. m.* (py—wl) That is blunt, or obtuse; that is dull. *Pwl dall*, a blindworm.

Pwl, *a.* (py—wl) Blunt, obtuse; dull, stupid.

> Dyn pwl sy'n meddwl am oes;
> Duw a ran hyd yr einioes.
>
> The *simple* man is anxious about life; God ordains the length of existence. *W. Lleyn.*

Pwlongl, *s. f.—pl.* pwlonglau (pwl—ongl) An obtuse angle.

Pwlonglawg, *a.* (pwlongl) Having obtuse angles.

Pwll, *s. m.—pl.* pyllau (py—wll) A small pool, a pit. *Pwll mawn*, a peat pit; *pwll llif*, a saw pit.

Pwm, *s. m.* (py—wm) That swells out.

Pwmp, *s. m.* (pwm) A round mass. *Pwmp o ddyn*, a large heavy man.

Pwmpa, *s. m.* (pwmp) A round lump; a large kind of apple.

Pwmpiad, *s. m.* (pwmp) A forming a round mass; a thumping, a banging.

Pwmpiaw, *v. a.* (pwmp) To form a round mass; to thump, to bang.

Pwmpl, *s. m.—pl.* pwmplau (pwmp) A knob, a boss; also the drop of a drawer.

Pwmplaw, *v. a.* (pwmpl) To boss, to knob.

Pwmplawg, *a.* (pwmpl) Knobbed, or bossed.

Pwn, *s. m.—pl.* pynau (pw) An aggregate; a pack; a burden, a load.

> A chan-pyn llyn ger ei law.
>
> And a hundred pool *dams* close at hand. *Adage.*

Pwnc, *s. m.—pl.* pynciau (py—wnc) That is present or in the instant; a point of time; a point; a note in music; a subject, or what is under observation; a point or stop, in grammar.

Pwniad, *s. m.* (pwn) A laying on a burden, a loading; a beating, a banging.

Pwniaw, *v. a.* (pwn) To burden, to load; to beat, to bang, to thump.

Pwnt, *s. m.* (pwn) That is collected, or aggregated; a reservoir. *Pwnt melin*, a mill dam.

Pwng, *s. m.—pl. t.* au (py—wng) That is in contact, upon, or together; a cluster; a crop, as of a field, of a tree, or the like. *Sil.*

> Amgylch llyw——
> Gnawd yd gyrch cynnygn o'i gwnaif pwng.
>
> Around the chief foes habitually throng together from his *gathering* storm. *E. ab M. Rhoswd.*

Pwnga, *s. m.* (pwng) That is collected together; a push, a wheal, a blister.

Pwngaidd, *a.* (pwng) Tending to cluster.

Pwngaw, *v. n.* (pwng) To teem; to cluster.

Pwngawl, *a.* (pwng) Teeming; clustering.

Pwngiad, *s. m.* (pwng) A teeming; a clustering.

Pwngu, *v. a.* (pwng) To teem; to cluster.

Pwr, *s. m.* (pw—wr) That extends; a worm. *Pwr dall, pwl dall*, a blind-worm, a slow-worm.

Pws, *s. m.* (pw—ws) That is uttered, or expelled.

Pwsach, *s. m.* (pws) A forcible utterance; an outcry. *Brecon.*

Pwt, *s. m.—pl.* pytiau (py—wt) Any short thing. *Pwt o bren*, a short piece of wood; *pwt o ddyn*, a squab of a person; *pwt o gleddyf*, a short bit of a sword; *pwt y gynnen*, a mischief maker.

Pwten, *s. f. dim.* (pwt) A squat female.

Pwtiad, *s. m.* (pwt) A butting, a poking.

Pwtian, *v. a.* (pwt) To but, to poke, to thrust.

Pwtiaw, *v. a.* (pwt) To but, or to thrust against.

Pwtiedydd, *s. m.—pl. t.* ion (pwtiad) A thruster.

Pwtienydd, *s. m.* (pwtian) A thruster, a poker.

Pwtiwr, *s. m.—pl.* pwtiwyr (pwt—gwr) Thruster

Pwtog, *s. f. dim.* (pwt) A short thick woman.

Pwtwn, *s. m.* (pwd) A kind of liquor; probably the same as the poteen whisky of the Irish.

> Cwrw iach, o frig cefrch y fro,
> Yw pwtwn, mal gwin Poito.
>
> Salutary ale, from the tops of the oats of the hill, is the *Putton*, like Poictou wine. *Guto y Glyn.*

Pwtyn, *s. m. dim.* (pwt) A short round body. *Pwtyn o bren*, a short piece of wood; *pwtyn o ddyn*, a short squab of a man.

Pwy, *s. m.—pl. t.* on (pw) A beat, a knock; a but; a thrust.

> Olpai'r bais, ol pwy o'r big,
> Ar y ddwy-dorth urddedig.
>
> Like the eilet holes of a coat, the mark of a *peck* of the beak, on the two useful masses. *Gr. Hiraethawg, i fuwsi Mailn.*

Pwy, *pron.* (pw) Who, which person; what.

> Ni wyddant pan esgor dewaint a gwawr;
> Neu wynt pwy hynt; pwy ei rynawdd;
> Py fa difa; py dir a'i blawdd.
>
> They know not when the darkness and the dawn divide; or the wind of *what* course; *what* the cause of its agitation; which the place of its termination; which the region that makes it pass. *Taliesin.*
>
> Parch a'th barcho pwy bynag he.
>
> Respect him that respects thee *who* soever he be. *Adage.*
>
> A wyddant bwy pwy yw pwyll?
>
> Do they know *what* is reason? *D. ab Gwilym.*

Pwy, *adv.* (pw) In a forward or advanced position; forward, to; in a past state. *Crwydraw o le pwy gilydd*, to wander from one place to another.

> Ni welais o'r mor bwy'r mor
> Marchawg a fai waeth——
>
> I have not beheld from the sea *to* the sea a warrior that could be worse. *Taliesin.*

Pwyad, *s. m.* (pwy) A beating, a striking.

Pwyaw, *v. a.* (pwy) To beat, to bang, to batter.

> Ni thyr hefyd, mewn bryd braw,
> A bwyall, rhag ei bwyaw,
> Taiawg, na chynnutwion.
>
> It will not be cut, in a timid mind, with a hatchet, lest he may *be beaten*, by a churl, nor by fuel gatherers. *Gr. Gryg, i ywen.*

Pwyawd, *s. m.* (pwy) A beat, a stroke, a bang.

Pwyawdr, *s. m.—pl.* pwyodron (pwyawd) A pounder, a rammer, a beetle, a pavior's beetle.

Pwyawl, *a.* (pwy) Beating, striking, banging.

Pwybynag, *pron.* (pwy—pynag) Whosoever.

Pwyd, *s. m.* (pwy) The act of putting by, or passing. It is a termination forming the impersonal preterite used for *wyd*, in some verbs.

Pwyedig, *a.* (pwyad) Beaten, banged; pounded.

Pwyedigaeth, *s. m.* (pwyedig) The act of beating, striking, or banging.

Pwygilydd, *adv.* (pwy—cilydd) To another.

Pwyll, *s. m.*—*pl. t.* oedd (pwy—yll) That clears a course forward, an opening a way; impulse; reason, sense, wit, discretion, prudence, perseverance. *Pwyll certh*, sharp wit.

Athraw doeth pwyll, athraw annoeth dylith.

The instructor of the wise is *reason*, the instructor of the unwise is example. *Adage.*

Gwell pwyll nog aur.

Prudence is better than gold. *Adage.*

A fo da ei bwyll a fydd diboen.

He that will be of good *discretion* will be free from pain. *Adag.*

Pyll wyn——
Pwyll ian trwy lumon.

Fair Pyll of a *course* of fire through a chimney. *Llywarch Hen.*

Os pwyll canwyll rhag cynnen,
Goreu canwyll yw pwyll pen.

If *sense* be a lamp to avoid contention, the best lamp is common *sense*. *H. C. Llwyd.*

A'r bwyll a syrth o'r bellen,
A'r byd a ddygwydd ar ben.

And the *impulsive power* will fall out of the globe, and the world will come to an end. *Llywelyn ab Owain.*

Pwyll, *a.* (pwy—yll) Tending onward, forward; wary, discreet.

Pur yw ei gledd, por y Glyn,
Pwyll rwysgwr pell oresgyn.

Pure is his sword, the lord of the Vale, the *forward* hero far conquering. *Iolo Goch.*

Pwyllad, *s. m.*—*pl. t.* oedd (pwyll) An impelling, or guiding forward; a reasoning; a reasoning faculty.

Fy Nuw, fy nerthiad,
A ddodes trwy fy iad
Enaid i'm pwyllad.

My God, my strengthener did infuse through my temple a soul for my *guidance*. *Taliesin.*

Pwylladwy, *a.* (pwyllad) Capable of reasoning.

Pwyllai, *s. c.*—*pl.* pwylleion (pwyll) That is impulsive; one who uses discretion.

Pwyllator, *ger.* (pwyllad) In impelling, or investigating; in reasoning.

Pwyllaw, *v. a.* (pwyll) To clear a way forward, to open a course; to impel; to reason, to think, to deliberate; to act discreetly; to call to mind, to contemplate, to think of.

Pwyllai Dunawd farchawg gwain,
Er echwydd gwneuthur celain,
Yn erbyn cryssaid Owain.

Dunawd the active warrior *would impel onward*, expecting to make a corpse, against the hasty onset of Owain. *Llywarch Hen.*

Mab Duw, dylyaf dy bwyllaw.

Son of God, I ought *to think of* thee. *D. Benfras.*

Pwyllawd, *s. m.* (pwyll) Impulsion; guidance forward; exertion of the mind.

Pwyllawg, *a.* (pwyll) Having impulse; rational, prudent, discreet, considerate, well-advised; circumspect, wary.

Pedrydawg, pwyllawg pwyll goddaith,
Pell ei glod o gludaw anrhaith.

Vigorous, *impelling forward* like the impulse of a conflagration, far his fame for collecting spoil. *Cynddelw, i O. ab Madawg.*

Pwyllawr, *s. m.* (pwyll) An impulse; a motive; reasoning faculty.

Pwylldid, *s. f.*—*pl. t.* au (pwyll—tid) A loop.

Pwylledig, *a.* (pwyllad) Endued with impulse.

Pwylledd, *s. m.* (pwyll) Discreetness, wariness.

Pwyllgall, *a.* (pwyll—call) Rationally wise.

Pwylliad, *s. m.*—*pl. t.* au (pwyll) An impelling, or guiding forward; a reasoning, exertion of the mind; contemplation.

Gwelais i feirch cymmrudd o gad,
A gwedy gawr garw bwylliad.

I beheld steeds hagged with mutual toil from battle; and after the shout a frightful *impelling*. *Llywarch Hen.*

Neus goreu dan bwylliad neirthiad gwychydd.

Were not the exertion of a hero best under *discretion*. *Aneurin.*

Nis myn pwylliad.

He will not receive *direction*. *Adag.*

Pwylliad, *s. m.*—*pl.* pwylliaid (pwyll) A pilot.

Pwylliadu, *v. a.* (pwylliad) To guide as a pilot.

Pwylliawr, *s. m.* (pwyll) Impulse; motive.

Duw dewr-wir, pellir pwylliawr o'n cynhen.

God of active truth, *reason* is far driven from our contention. *Ll. P. Moch.*

Pwyllig, *a.* (pwyll) Rational; discreet, wary. *Mae yn dawed yn bwyllig iawn*, he is coming very leisurely. *Dyfed.*

Nid pwyllig y dyn a ddalia genfigen.

The person who harbours envy is not *prudent*. *Adage.*

Pwylligrwydd, *s. m.* (pwyllig) Rationality.

Pwyllineb, *s. m.* (pwyll) Rationality, prudence.

Pwyllogi, *v. a.* (pwyllawg) To endue with reason, to become rational.

Pwyllogrwydd, *s. m.* (pwyllawg) Rationality, considerateness.

Pwyllus, *a.* (pwyll) Impulsive, rational, discreet.

Pwyllusaw, *v. n.* (pwyllus) To grow rational.

Pwyllusrwydd, *s. m.* (pwyllus) Impulsiveness, rationality, discreetness.

Pwyllwr, *s. m.*—*pl.* pwyllwyr (pwyll—gwr) One who impels; a discreet man.

Pwyn, *s. m.*—*pl. t.* iau (pwy—yn) A point.

Pwyned, *s. f.*—*pl. t.* i (pwyn) A broach; a fork.

Tri pheth hoffaidd i wr ar ei giniaw: cyllell awchus; pwyned flaenllem; ac alawr glan.

Three things seemly for a person at his dinner: a keen knife; a sharp-pointed *broach*; and a clean plate. *Trioedd Moes.*

Pwyniad, *s. m.*—*pl. t.* au (pwyn) Any pointed tool; a spike; a skewer.

Tri anharddwch gwr mewn gwledd; pwyniad ry fer, cyllell finbul, ac y saig yn mhell.

Three things unseemly to a man in a banquet: a skewer too short, a blunt-edged knife, and the victuals at a distance. *Trioedd Moes.*

Pwyniaw, *v. a.* (pwyn) To spike, to skewer.

Pwynt, *s. m.*—*pl. t.* iau (pwyn) An end, or point, a state, condition, case, or plight; good case.

A wyddant hwy pwy, o'm pwynt,
O drais ym, a droes anmhwynt!

Do they know who, out of my *good condition*, out of treachery to me, has brought about indisposition. *Bedo Brwynllys.*

Pwyntel, *s. m.*—*pl. t.* i (pwynt) Any pointed tool; a pencil, a painter's brush or tool.

Un dull yw'r byd cyngyd cel
A phaenllwr delw a phwyntel.

Of the same manner is the world of hidden design as a painter of an image with a *pencil*. *Dr. S. Cent.*

Pwyntiad, *s. m.* (pwynt) A bringing to a point; a putting into good case or plight.

Pwyntiaw, *v. a.* (pwynt) To point, to bring to a point; to put in good case or plight.

Brasêaist, tewychaist, pwyntiaist.

Thou hast become large, thou hast become fat, *thou hast become of good case.* *Deut.* 32. 15.

Pwyntiawl, *a.* (pwynt) Tending to a point; tending to be of good condition.

Pwyntiedig, *a.* (pwyntiad) Pointed, being made of good condition.

Pwyntiwr, *s. m.*—*pl.* pwyntwyr (pwynt—gwr) One who points; a fattener.

Pwyntl, *s. m.*—*pl. t.* au (pwynt) A pointed end, a tag. *Pwyntl carai*, tag of a lace; a poniard.

Pwys, *s. m.*—*pl. t.* au (pwy—ys) The state of being put down or at rest; the state of being down or upon; pressure, weight; a pound weight. *Pwys cwyr, pwys bach,* a pound avoirdupoise; *pwys cyfelin, pwys y garreg,* but varying in weight: in Meirion it is two pounds avoirdupoise, and in Mon it is five. *Dos wrth dy bwys,* go at thy leisure; *cymera bwys,* take a seat. *Dyfed.*

Myned trwy yr afon a phont ar bwys.

To go through the river with a bridge on the *spot.* *Adage.*

Pwysadwy, *a.* (pwys) Ponderable, capable of being weighed.

Pwysaw, *v. a.* (pwys) To throw upon, to throw down; to press, to weigh; to incline; to lean; to be a pressure, to be a burden: to take rest. *Pwysa y bel,* serve thou the ball; *pwysaw at yr amser,* to draw near the time; *a wnei di bwysaw?* wilt thou take rest? *Dyfed.* *Gwraig bwys,* or *gwraig brïawd,* a wedded wife; *cariad-wraig,* a love wife, or concubine.

Pwysawd, *s. m.* (pwys) The act of pressing, or weighing down; a weighing.

Pwysawdr, *s. m.—pl.* pwysodron (pwysawd) Any thing to press down with; a rammer.

Pwysawg, *a.* (pwys) Having a pressure; being of weight, being heavy.

Pwysawl, *a.* (pwys) Pressing; weighing.

Pwysedig, *a.* (pwys) Being pressed, weighed.

Pwysfawr, *a.* (pwys—mawr) Ponderous, weighty, momentous, of great consequence.

Pwysgar, *a.* (pwys) Tending to press.

Pwysgarwch, *s. m.* (pwysgar) Weightiness.

Pwysi, *s. m.* (pwys) Weight, heaviness.

Pwysiad, *s. m.* (pwys) A pressing; a weighing.

Pwysiannawl, *a.* (pwysiant) Depressive.

Pwysiannu, *v. a.* (pwysiant) To cause a depression; to become depressive.

Pwysiant, *s. m.* (pwys) Depression, pressure.

Pwysig, *a.* (pwys) Pressing, ponderous, emphatic.

Pwysigrwydd, *s. m.* (pwysig) Pressingness; ponderousness, weightiness.

Pwysineb, *s. m.* (pwys) Depressiveness.

Pwyswr, *s. m.—pl.* pwyswyr (pwys—gwr) One who presses, or bears down; a weigher.

Pwysydd, *s. m.—pl. t.* ion (pwys) One who presses, one who bears down; a weigher.

Pwyth, *s. m.—pl. t.* i (pwy—yth) That runs in; a thrust; a stitch; a point, an angle, or indenting; a retaliation, a requital, a return. *Talu pwyth,* to pay a point, or to return like for like; *pwyth celwydd,* the reward of a lie; *Pwython,* requitals; certain presents given, according to old usage, to a newly married couple, by the persons invited to the wedding: *Pwyth Meinlas,* the Narrow Green Point, the name of the place where Cæsar landed in Britain.

Pwythaw, *v. a.* (pwyth) To thrust in; to stitch.

Pwythawg, *a.* (pwyth) Having stitches.

Pwythawl, *a.* (pwyth) Stitching, sewing.

Pwythedig, *a.* (pwyth) Stitched, sewed.

Pwythiad, *s. m.* (pwyth) A stitching, a sticking.

Pwythwr, *s. m.—pl.* pwythwyr (pwyth—gwr) A stitcher.

Pwythydd, *s. m.—pl. t.* ion (pwyth) A stitcher.

PY, *s. m. r.* That is inward, that is involved; that is inversed. It is a prefix in the composition of words; but generally dropping the vowel, on account of its being the shortest and giving way to all the other vowels.

Py, *pron.* (py, *s.*) What; which. It is used for *Pa. adv.* why, for what reason. *Py efelly?* why so?

Y gelynion oeddynt yn ymroddi i'w gnotaedig frad, gan geisiaw goresgyn yr ynys, a'i diddyw oe, i blith pob peth, prodi a wnaent py wedd y gellynt gweuthur brad y brenin yn gyntaf.

The enemies were giving themselves up to their usual treachery, in trying to conquer the island, and to destroy it: and, amongst every thing, they were going to devise what way they could work the ruin of the king in the first place. *Brut y Brenhinoedd.*

Nid rhaid tra dilyn pell ofyn pwy!
Py geidw'r gorddyfr rhag pob gorddwy.

There need not be too much inquisitiveness in far asking whom; *who* will keep the bordering water from every molestation. *Ll. P. Moch, i Lywelyn II.*

Pyb, *s. m.* (py—yb) That is energetic or stout.

Pybi, *s. m.* (pyb) Vigour, potency, energy.

Rhos difro Benfro penfaddeu pybi;
Pobl fedydd rwy cyglau.

The depopulated moor of Penvro whose strength is cut off; the people of Christendom have heard it. *L. P. Moch.*

Pyblaidd, *a.* (pybl) Of a vigorous nature.

Pyblu, *v. a.* (pybl) To invigorate, to animate.

Pybyr, *a.* (pyb) Strenuous, stout, vigorous.

Pybyraidd, *a.* (pybyr) Somewhat strenuous.

Pybyriad, *s. m.* (pybyr) A rendering stout, or vigorous; a becoming vigorous; invigoration.

Pybyru, *v. a.* (pybyr) To act stoutly; to exert.

Pawb ar d'ol: pybyru; dos!
Pawb a'i wawch, pe bae achos
Y sgyfarnog fywiog fach.

Every one is after thee: *cheer up; fly!* every one is ready for his shout, if there should be occasion, thou little lively hare. *T. Prys.*

Pybyrwch, *s. m.* (pybyr) Strenuousness; stoutness, vigorousness; valiantness.

Heddwch, pybyrwch y byd,
Cyfoeth a fâca hefyd.

The peace, the *vigour* of the world, and wealth also he cherisheth. *T. Aled.*

Pyd, *s. m.—pl. t.* oedd (py—yd) That sinks in a pit; a snare; danger. *a.* Dangerous.

Ar nid yw pwyll pyd yw.

If it be not prudence it is danger. *Adage.*

Ni bo iawn yn pyd.

What is not just is dangerous. *Adage.*

Pan ddoynt i'r lle yr oedd y pyd iddynt, yn ddioed y cyfodai gwyr Rhufain iddynt.

When they came to the place where the *snare* was laid for them, immediately the men of Rome rose up against them. *Brut y Brenhinoedd.*

Pydaidd, *a.* (pyd) Tending to sink; dangerous.

Pydaw, *s. m.—pl. t.* au (pyd—aw) An oozing fluid; a quag; a well, or spring.

Pydawl, *a.* (pyd) Tending to sink; dangerous.

Pydewaid, *s. m.* (pydaw) An oozing of water.

Pydewlyd, *a.* (pydaw) Apt to ooze with water.

Pydiad, *s. m.* (pyd) A sinking; a forming a snare; a creating of danger.

Pydiant, *s. m.* (pyd) A sinking in; a snaring; the act of bringing to danger.

Pydiaw, *v. a.* (pyd) To ensnare, to endanger, to expose to danger; to be in peril.

Ni bydd a Mab Duw diymadaw
A fo meuwn byd yn ei bydiaw.

He will not be without the possibility of parting from the Son of God whom the pelf of the world *ensnares.* *D. Benfras.*

Pydiedig, *a.* (pydiad) Being ensnared, endangered, exposed to peril.

Pydoldeb, *s. m.* (pydawl) Dangerousness.

Rhys mab Tewdwr a ffoes i'r Iwerddon, rhag pydoldeb y lleddid ef.

Rhys son of Tewdwr fled into Ireland for fear of the danger that he would be slain. *Brut Brenhinedd.*

Pydraidd, *a.* (pwdr) Tending to rot, carious.

Pydrawl, *a.* (pwdr) Tending to rot, corruptive.

Pydredig, *a.* (pwdr) Being rotted, corrupted.

Pydredd, *s. m.* (pwdr) Rottenness, putridity.

Pydriad, *s. m.* (pwdr) A rotting; putrefaction.

Pydrni, *s. m.* (pwdr) Rottenness, putridity.

Pydru, *v. a.* (pwdr) To rot, or to putrefy.

Pydu, *v. a.* (pyd) To sink; to cause a sinking; to form a snare; to create danger; to endanger; to become dangerous.

> ——Mab pyd, mor fe parawd,
> Hy darfu, yn neithiawr, ni bu priawd
> Gan Ddew, py amgen plwyf, pydu dalarawd.
>
> The son of snaring, so ready was he, aptly did, in the marriage which was not appropriate to God, for want of other community, *ensnare* the earthly world. *Meigant, m. Cynddylan.*

Pydus, *a.* (pyd) Tending to sink; dangerous.

Pydusaw, *v. a.* (pydus) To render sinking; to render dangerous; to become dangerous.

Pydusedd, *s. m.* (pydus) A state of sinking; a state of snaring; a state of danger.

Pydwern, *s. f.* (pyd—gwern) A quaking bog.

> Pan ddyfu y Mab Rhad oedd rhaid wrthaw—
> I affern, bydwern, heb adaw y chwaith;
> Yn un boregwaith ei hanreithiaw.
>
> When the Son of Grace came there was a necessity for him; to hell, a *quaggy bog*, leaving not chance; in one morning tide it despoiling. *D. Benfras.*

Pydwr, *s. m.—pl.* pydwyr (pyd—gwr) A snarer.

Pydd, *s. m.* (py—ydd) The state of running out.

Pyddawl, *a.* (pydd) Tending to spread out.

Pyddiad, *s. m.* (pydd) A running out.

Pyddu, *v. a.* (pydd) To run out, to spread.

Pyg, *s. m.* (py—yg) Pitch, rosin of pine.

Pygawl, *a.* (pyg) Of a pitchy quality.

Pygbren, *s. m.—pl. t.* i (pyg—pren) Pitch tree.

Pygedig, *a.* (pyg) Covered with pitch.

Pygedd, *s. m.* (pyg) Pitchiness, a pitchy quality.

Pygiad, *s. m.* (pyg) A covering with pitch.

Pyglian, *s. m.* (pyg—llian) A cere-cloth.

Pygliw, *s. m.* (pyg—lliw) Pitch colour. *a.* Of a pitch colour.

Pyglyd, *a.* (pyg) Pitchy, of a pitchy quality.

Pyglydrwydd, *s. m.* (pyglyd) Pitchiness.

Pyglys, *s. m.* (pyg—llys) Hog's fennel, ferula.

Pygu, *v. a.* (pyg) To pitch, to cover with pitch.

Pygwydd, *s. pl. aggr.* (pyg—gwydd) Common fir, or pitch-trees.

Pygwydden, *s. f. dim.* (pygwydd) A pitch-tree.

Pylaidd, *a.* (pwl) Somewhat blunt, bluntish.

Pyledig, *a.* (pwl) Being made dull, blunted.

Pyledd, *s. m.* (pwl) Bluntness, or obtuseness.

Pylgain, *s. m.—pl.* pylgeiniau (pwl—cain) An indistinct light; the morning twilight, the morning, the dawn of day.

Pylgaint, *s. m.* (pylgain) The morning twilight.

Pylgeiniawl, *a.* (pylgain) Belonging to the morning twilight; matin.

Pyli, *s. m.* (pwl) Bluntness, dullness.

Pyliad, *s. m.—pl. t.* au (pwl) A blunting.

Pylni, *s. m.* (pwl) Bluntness, or dullness.

Pylor, *s. m.* (pwl) Dust, or powder.

Pyloraidd, *a.* (pylor) Powdery, like dust.

Pylorawg, *a.* (pylor) Full of dust, powdery.

Pyloriad, *s. m.* (pylor) A reducing to powder.

Pyloru, *v. a.* (pylor) To reduce to powder.

Pyloryn, *s. m. dim.* (pylor) A grain of powder.

Pylrwydd, *s. m.* (pwl) Bluntness, dullness.

Pylu, *v. a.* (pwl) To make obtuse, to blunt; to become obtuse, blunt, or dull.

Pylus, *a.* (pwl) Tending to make blunt or dull.

Pylwr, *s. m.* (pwl—gwr) One who blunts.

Pyll, *s. m.* (py—yll) That is compact. *a.* Compact, concentrated.

Pyllaid, *s. m.—pl.* pylleidiau (pwll) The contents of a plash or puddle.

> Y llygoden gynt a oedd yn rhodiaw mewn gwindy, ac o ddrygddamwain hi a gwympai mewn pyllaid o'r gwin.
>
> The mouse once on a time was walking about in a tavern, and through evil chance she fell into a *puddle* of the wine. *Damegion.*

Pyllawg, *a.* (pwll) Full of pits, or puddles.

Pylliad, *s. m.* (pwll) A forming a pit or puddle.

Pyllogrwydd, *s. m.* (pyllawg) The state of being full of pits or puddles.

Pyllyn, *s. m. dim.* (pwll) A small puddle.

Pymtheg, *s. m.—pl. t.* au (pump—deg) Fifteen.

Pymthegfed, *s. m.* (pymtheg) A fifteenth.

Pymthegnos, *s. m.* (pymtheg—nos) The space of fifteen nights; a fortnight.

Pymthegwaith, *s. pl.* (pymtheg—gwaith) Fifteen times. *a.* Of fifteen times.

Pyn, *s. m.* (py—yn) What is upon or in contact.

Pyna, *adv.* (py—na) Otherwise, soever. It is used before words with consonant initials, and *Pynag*, before vowels.

> Argaea——
> Bebyll ein trigolion,
> A gwna pa le byna bon'
> Na'n gwyl un o'n gelynion.
>
> Encompass the tents of our inhabitants, and make what place *soever* they are in so that not one of our foes may see us. *H. D. ab Ifan.*

Pynag, *adv.* (py—nag) Soever. *Pa beth bynag, pynag pa beth*, what thing soever; *pwy bynag*, whosoever; *pwy un bynag, pynag pwy*, what one soever: "*Pe diasbedych di bynag*," if thou wert to cry out ever so.

Pynas, *s. f.—pl. t.* au (pwn) That is collected together; that forms a compact body; a tribe.

> A'm eiriolwy Mair ar y Mab cuan,
> Nad elwyf yn llwgr, yn lloc Idas!
> Na'm gado Rheen, cyn deg pynas,
> Yn rhewin Kayn can Sathanas.
>
> May I be interceded for by Mary with the gracious Son, that I go not to corruption, in the society of Judas! May I not be left by the Creator, before the ten tribes, in the destruction of Cain with the Satanic host. *Einion ab Gwalchmai.*

Pynawr, *s. m.* (pwn) That is a load or burden.

Pynciad, *s. m.—pl. t.* au (pwnc) A noting of time. *a.* Noting; pointing; a descanting; a disquisition; a disputation; a playing at ball, by the players hitting of it to one another.

Pynciadawl, *a.* (pynciad) Relating to notation of time; relating to tuning; pointing.

Pynciaw, *v. a.* (pwnc) To note or to point time; to note; to point; to descant; to make a disquisition; to play a kind of game at ball, by the players hitting of it to one another. *Mwyned y pynciant yr adar!* How sweetly do the birds trill the song!

Pynciawl, *a.* (pwnc) Noting; timing; pointing.

Pynciedig, *a.* (pynciad) Noted; pointed; tuned.

Pynciwr, *s. m.—pl.* pynciwyr (pwnc—gwr) A noter, or one who points; a tuner.

Pyner, *s. m.—pl. t.* i (pyn) That is upon or over; a covering.

> Nis canlyn o'i dda, o'i ddiffer ymdro,
> Onid ei amdo, amdlawd byner.
>
> There will not follow him of his goods, of his means of protection, but his shroud, a wretched cover. *Gr. ab yr Ynad Coch.*

Pynfarch, *s. m.—pl.* pynfeirch (pwn—march) What serves to raise up, to aggregate, or to collect; also a pack horse, or sumpter-horse; an escheat. *Pynfarch melin*, a mill dam.

> Wyth pynfarch brenin y sydd: mor; a diffaith; ac achanawg gwlad arall yn cerdded tir y brenin; a lleidr; marw yn swrth, y brenin bia ran y marw o'r da oll, ac ni chaiff ddim o ran y wraig a'r meibion; anfab y marw y caffo ebediw; camgylus y caffo ddirwy neu gamlwrw i ganthaw.
>
> There are eight holds of the king: the sea; and a wilderness; and a vagrant of another country travelling on the king's ground; and a thief; a sudden death, the king owns the defunct's share of all the chattels, but he shall not have any of the shares of the wife and the children; the infant of a defunct from whom he receives herriot; and a criminal from whom he gets fine or penalty. *Welsh Laws.*

Pyniad, *s. m.—pl. t.* au (pwn) An aggregating, a heaping, a burdening, a loading.
Pyniaw, *v. a.* (pwn) To aggregate; to load.
Pyniawg, *a.* (pwn) Burdened, loaded.
Pyniawl, *a.* (pwn) Burdening, loading.
Pyniawr, *s. m.* (pwn) That is a load.
Pyniedig, *a.* (pyniad) Burdened, loaded.
Pynioreg, *s. f.—pl. t.* au (pyniawr) What serves to bear a load; a pack-saddle.
Pyniori, *v. a.* (pyniawr) To put on a load.
Pyniwr, *s. m.—pl.* pyniwyr (pwn—gwr) A burdener, a loader.
Pynoreg, *s. f.—pl. t.* au (pynawr) A pack-saddle. It is also called *ystrodur*.
Pynoriad, *s. m.* (pynawr) A putting on a load.
Pynoriaw, *v. a.* (pynawr) To put on a load.
Pynoriawg, *a.* (pynawr) Having a load.
Pynoriedig, *a.* (pynawr) Being under a load.
Pynu, *v. a.* (pwn) To lay upon; to burden.
Pyngaid, *v. n.* (pwng) To cluster; to swarm.
Pyngawl, *a.* (pwng) Clustering; swarming.
Pyngiad, *s. m.—pl. t.* au (pwng) A clustering.
Pyngu, *v. n.* (pwng) To cluster; to swarm.

> Pren bywiol sy'n y nefoedd fawr,
> Ac hyd y llawr ei gangau,
> A'i ffrwyth yn pyngu arno'n llawn,
> Yn rhad brydnawn a bore.
>
> In the great heaven there is a living tree, its branches spreading over the ground, with its fruit *clustering* fully on it, freely had evening and morning. *W. Williams.*

Pyr, *s. m.* (py—yr) That shoots out in a point or cone; the fir tree.

> Eira mynydd, coch blaen pyr;
> Llidiawg llwyawg ongyr.
>
> Snowy mountain, red the top of the *fir*, wrathful the push of many spears. *Llywarch Hen.*

Pyr, *adv.* (py—yr) Forward, toward, onward.

> O fail pair deon pyrdawaf;
> O ddor cor coelling cynnelwaf.
>
> In praising the cause of the lord *forward* I come; after the mystery of the circle of forebodings I will conform. *Cynddelw, i O. Gwynedd.*

Pyrag, *adv.* (py—rhag) Wherefore, why.
Pyraidd, *a.* (pyr) Tending to a point; like a fir.
Pyrchwyn, *s. m.* (pyr—cwyn) A crest of a helmet.
Pyrgwyn, *s. m.* (pyr—cwyn) A crest, or plume of a helmet.
Pyrnawn, *s. m.* (pyr—nawn) The afternoon.
Pyrdwyaw, *v. a.* (pyr—twyaw) To bear a spear pointed forward.

> Pan wisgai Garanmael gatbais Cynddylan,
> A phyrdwyaw ei onen,
> Ni chaffai Ffranc tanc o'i ben.
>
> When Caranmael should put on the war-coat of Cynddylan, and *point forward* his ashen shaft, a Franc would not obtain rest for his head. *Llywarch Hen.*

Pys, *s. pl. aggr.* (py—ys) Pease, pulse. *Pys y garanod*, or *pys yr adar*, tares; *pys y llygod*, chit-pease; *pys y coed*, heath peas; *pys y wig*, vetch; *pys y fwyall*, *pedol y march*, hatchet-vetch.
Pysen, *s. f. dim.* (pys) A single pea, a pea.
Pysg, *s. m.—pl. t.* od (py—ysg) Fish. *Pysgod duon*, *llamidyddion*, porpoises; *pysgod bychain*, sand-eels.

> Mal y pysg am y dwfr.
>
> Like the *fish* for the water. *Adage.*
>
> Yn y dwfr y goruc ef y pysg; ac yr adar yn y rhan uchaf, sef yw hwnw yr awyr.
>
> In the water he created the *fish*, and the birds in the most rarified part, that is to say the air. *Elucidarius.*

Pysgaidd, *a.* (pysg) Of the nature of fish; fishy.
Pysgawl, *a.* (pysg) Piscatory, of fish, like fish.
Pysgod, *s. pl. aggr.* (pysg) Fishes. *Pysgod y mor*, *morbysg*, *morbysgod*, sea-fishes. *pysgod afon*, river fishes; *pysgod duon*, porpoises.

> Mal y gath am y pysgod.
>
> Like the cat after the *fishes*. *Adage.*

Pysgodawg, *a.* (pysgod) Having fishes.
Pysgodawl, *a.* (pysgod) Relating to fishes.
Pysgodfa, *s. f.—pl. t.* oedd (pysgod—ma) A fishery, a fishing-place; a fish-market.
Pysgodfwyd, *s. m.* (pysgod—bwyd) Fish-meat.

> Ysgafn ar don eigion wyd,
> Eryr ifalch edn bysgodfwyd.
>
> Light art thou on the ocean wave, thou swiftly-soaring bird whose *food is fish*. *D. ab Gwilym i'r ugdon.*

Pysgodlyn, *s. m.—pl. t.* oedd (pysgod—llyn) A fish-pond.
Pysgodwr, *s. m.—pl.* pysgodwyr (pysgod—gwr) A fisher, a fisherman.
Pysgodwriaeth, *s. m.* (pysgodwr) The vocation of a fisherman.

> Gwenwynwyd Taf; gwae ninnau!
> Dyrwyd y bysgodwriaeth
> Gyda ni i gyd yn waeth.
>
> The Taf has been poisoned; Woe to us! the *fishing trade* with us is altogether worse. *Lewis Morys.*

Pysgodig, *a.* (pysgod) Teeming with fishes.
Pysgodyn, *s. m.* (pysgod) A single fish, a fish.
Pysgota, *v. a.* (pysgod) To fish. *Gwialen bysgota*, *gwialen cnwair*, *genwair*, a fishing-rod.

> Pysgota yn mlaen y rhwyd.
>
> *To fish* in the front of the net. *Adage.*

Pysgotwr, *s. m.* (pysgod—gwr) A fisherman.
Pysgotty, *s. m.* (pysgod—ty) A fish-house.
Pysgydd, *s. m.—pl. t.* ion (pysg) An ichthyologist
Pysgyddiaeth, *s. m.* (pysgydd) Ichthyology.
Pystyl, *s. m.—pl. t.* au (ystyl) A restless motion; the shank of a bow that is let into the yoke to fasten it on the neck of the ox.
Pystylad, *s. m.* (pystyl) A restless activity; the being agog; the restlessness or capering of a horse under restraint. "*Gweryrad y meirch a'u pystylad*," the neighing of the steeds and their capering.

> Annogiad cad,
> Diffreidiad gwlad,
> Gwawd am danad
> Llwrf bystylad;
> Pystylad llwrwf,
> Ac yfed cwrwf.
>
> Thou incitement to battle, the protection of a country, on thy account there has been the *capering* of the coward; the capering of the coward with drinking of ale. *Taliesin.*

Pystyled, *v. a.* (pystyl) To jump about. *Mae y bachgen yn pystyled*, the boy is capering.
Pystyliad, *s. m.* (pystyl) A capering about.
Pystylu, *v. a.* (pystyl) To move about in a restless manner; to caper.
Pystylwyn, *s. m.—pl. t.* au (pystyl—gwyn) A crupper of a saddle.
Pyswydden, *s. f.* (pys—gwydd) Bean-trefoil tree
Pyth, *s. m.—pl. t.* oedd (py—yth) A space, revolution or period of time; a world; the duration of the world; ever, never.

> Tri pheth nis gall namyn Duw, dyoddef pythoedd y ceugant; cynghyd a phob cyflwr heb newidiaw; a rhoi gwell a newydd ar bob peth, heb ei rol ar goll.
>
> Three things which God only can accomplish: to endure the *revolutions* of eternity, to participate with every state without changing, and to impart amelioration and newness to every thing, without causing a loss of its originality. *Barddas.*
>
> Trennydd a phennydd a phyth.
>
> The day after to-morrow and daily and *forever*. *L. G. Cothi.*

Pythagoras, *s. f.* (pythagori) Explanation of the universe; cosmogony.
Pythagori, *v. a.* (pyth—agori) To explain the system of the universe.

Pythawd, *s. m.* (pyth) A great period or world.
Pythawl, *a.* (pyth) Eternal, everlasting, ever.
Pythawr, *v. n.* (py—tawr) To be anxious.

A'r saeth bythorud o thyr.

And the arrow thou wouldest regret were it to break. *D. ab Gwilym.*

Pythefnos, *s. m.* (pymthegnos) A fortnight.
Python, *s. m.* (pyth) A system of the universe.
Pythonas, *s. f.* (python) A system of cosmogony.
Pythones, *s. f.—pl. t.* au (python) A female cosmogonist.
Pythoni, *v. a.* (python) To treat of cosmogony.
Pythonydd, *s. m.—pl. t.* ion (python) A cosmogonist; a systemizer of worlds.
Pyw, *s. m.—pl. t.* ion (py) That is together or in unison; that is in order, or perfect; a member, a limb. *Dyna fe yn cerdded ar ei bedwar pyw, neu ar ei bedwar agor,* There he is walking upon all fours. *Sil.*
Pyw, *a.* (py) In order of unison, regular, complete, perfect. *Dyn pyw,* a well-formed man; *brethyn pyw,* cloth of good quality. *Silurian.*

R.

RHA, *s. m. r.* That forces or drives onward.
Rhäawd, *s. m.* (rha) A forcing, or impelling.
Rhab, *s. m.* (rha) Force, constraint, control.
Rhabedd, *s. m.* (rhab) Controlment, constraint.
Rhabu, *v. a.* (rhab) To constrain, to check.
Rhac, *s. m.—pl. t.* au (rha—ac) What is in advance, forward, upper, or opposite; the wrest of a cross-bow; the spine of a quadruped, also called *glain cefn.*
Rhac, *prep.* (rha—ac) Before, fore; from; for, lest. It is dialectically used for *rhag.*
Rhaca, *s. m.—pl. t.* on (rhac) What is brought before; a spectacle, or show.
Rhacai, *s. m.—pl.* rhaceion (rhac) A rake.
Rhacan, *s. m.—pl. t.* au (rhac) A rake, a scraper.
Rhacaniad, *s. m.* (rhacan) A raking, a scraping.
Rhacanu, *v. a.* (rhacan) To rake, to use a rake.
Rhacanwr, *s. m.* (rhacan—gwr) A raker.
Rhaciad, *s. m.—pl. t.* au (rhac) The fore-running, the beginning, or first appearance; a coming forward; a coming in opposition. *Rhaciad y wawr,* the first breaking of the dawn.
Rhaciannawl, *a.* (rhaciant) Tending to advance.
Rhaciannu, *v. a.* (rhaciant) To make an advancement, to take a forward position.
Rhaciant, *s. m.* (rhac) Advancement, the act of putting forward; a precursion.
Rhaciaw, *v. a.* (rhac) To advance, to move forward; to come in opposition. *Dacw y wawr yn rhaciaw,* yonder the dawn is appearing.
Rhaco, *adv.* (rhac) Yonder, in the advance, in the distant view. *Sylla di rhaco,* behold thou yonder.

Dos i gyfrwch a'r dyn rhaco.

Go to meet with *yonder man.* *H. Culhwch—Mabinogion.*

Rhacu, *v. a.* (rhac) To put before, to put forward; to advance; to take the lead.
Rhach, *s. m.* (rhac) That is forced out.
Rhad, *s. m.—pl. t.* au (rha—ad) That comes freely, that is given freely; prosperity; good luck; a blessing; grace, favour. *Nid oes rad ar a wnelo,* there is no prosperity on what he does: *Rhad Duw yma!* Be the blessing of God here! *Rhad Duw yn y ty!* Be the blessing of God in the house! *Rhad Duw ar yr adgor! Rhad Duw ar y da!* Be the blessing of God on the cattle! *Rhad Duw arnoch! Rhad Duw ar y gwaith!* God prosper the work! *Rhad pen llad,* Grace the supreme blessing: *Rhad Duw ar ei fam!* God's blessing on its mother! said to the people in milking: *Rhad Duw ar bob rhadferthwch!* The blessing of God on every gracious gift! *Rhad Duw ar bob cywir galon!* The blessing of God on every faithful heart! *Rhad Duw ar bob ymgais dda!* The blessing of God on every good undertaking! *Rhad Duw ar bob llaw ddiflin!* The blessing of God on every industrious hand! common expressions of greeting.

Dedwydd, Dofydd ei rhydd rhad.

The assiduous, the Creator will give him *grace.* *Adage.*

Argiwydd llachynt gwynt, a gwyllt frydiau mor,
Mawr dy rad, a'th wyrthau!

Lord of the course of the wind, and the wild torrents of the sea, great thy *grace,* and thy wonders. *G. ab M. ab Dafydd.*

Rhad, *a.* (rha—ad) Free, gratuitous; cheap. *Y Mab Rhad,* The Son of Grace, the Saviour.
Rhadawl, *a.* (rhad) Gracious, or beneficent.
Rhadbryn, *s. m.* (rhad—pryn) A free purchase.
Rhadbryniad, *s. m.* (rhadbryn) A cheap buying.
Rhadbrynu, *v. a.* (rhadbryn) To buy cheaply.
Rhadedd, *s. m.* (rhad) Freeness; cheapness.
Rhadfawr, *a.* (rhad—mawr) Gracious.

Tri ellldeyrn Ynys Prydain—rhodded iddynt am eu campau ac eu cynneddfau clodforion a rhadferthoedd.

The three plebeian princes of the Isle of Britain—had principalities conferred on them for their acts and principles, praiseworthy and *virtuous.* *Trioedd.*

Rhadferth, *a.* (rhad—berth) Graciously placid.
Rhadferthwch, *s. m.* (rhadferth) Beneficent.
Rhadforedd, *s. m.* (rhadfawr) Graciousness.
Rhadgar, *a.* (rhad—car) Grace-loved.
Rhadgaredig, *a.* rhadgar) Grace-beloved.

Henpych gwell, y rhadgaredig! yr Arglwydd ys y gyd a thi!

All hail, thou grace favoured one! the Lord is with thee! *W. Salisbury.*

Rhadgariad, *s. m.* (rhadgar) Free love.
Rhadgaru, *v. a.* (rhadgar) To love freely.
Rhadlawn, *a.* (rhad) Gracious; gentle; serene.
Rhadlonaeth, *s. m.* (rhadlawn) Graciousness.

Ef biau radau rhadlonaeth,
Uch naw toryf naw tywysogaeth.

He possesses the virtues of *beneficence,* over the nine multitudes of nine principalities. *Cynddelw.*

Rhadlondeb, *s. m.* (rhadlawn) Graciousness.
Rhadlonder, *s. m.* (rhadlawn) Graciousness.
Rhadlondra, *s. m.* (rhadlawn) Graciousness.
Rhadlonedd, *s. m.* (rhadlawn) Graciousness.
Rhadloni, *v. a.* (rhadlawn) To render generous; to become gracious; to be generous; to become gentle or placid.

Nid hawdd rhadloni cenfigen.

It is not easy *to render* malice *generous.* *Adage.*

Rhadrodd, *s. f.—pl. t.* ion (rhad—rhodd) A free gift
Rhadroddedigaeth, *s. m.* (rhadroddedig) The act of giving freely; the state of being freely given or conferred.

Pawb a chwennychant gael braint yn ei radroddedigaeth.

Every one is desirous of obtaining a title in his *free offering.* *Ier. Owain.*

Rhadu, *v. a.* (rhad) To render free, to bestow grace; to render cheap; to become free.
Rhadwehyn, *s. m.* (rhad—gwehyn) A pouring of grace. *a.* Grace-diffusing.
Rhadwehynawl, *a.* (rhadwehyn) Grace-diffusing.
Rhadwehyniad, *s. m.* (rhadwehyn) A shedding of grace, a pouring of grace.
Rhadwehynu, *v. a.* (rhadwehyn) To shed grace.
Rhadd, *s. m.* (rha—add) An advance, a state of progression, or going onward.
Rhae, *s. f.—pl.* rheuau (rha) A constraint, a battle; also a chain; otherwise called *tid*, *syg*, *tres*, *cadwen*, and *cadwyn*.

O nod ffrwau hynod ffrowys
Gwr a dywys y gwyr duon,
Ys da reuau wiw ystrywys
Ai drwy Bowys.

From the mark of the gushings of the noted turbulence of a man who leads the sable men, if good the *battles* excelling in craft, he would go through Powys. *T. Prys.*

Rhaeaw, *v. a.* (rhae) To put to a stand still. *Rhaeaw gwyr*, to startle people.
Rhael, *s. m.* (rha—el) Bent, or inclination.

Wrth weled y merched mor awchus eu rhael
A minnau yn fab ieuanc heb ddim iddel gael—
—-Mae yn syn!

When I see the young women of so greedy a *disposition*, and I a young man not prospering, it is grievous! *Canu.*

Rhaf, *s. m.* (rha—af) A spread, a diffusion.
Rhafu, *s. m.* (rhaf) A tendency to diffuse.
Rhafnwydd, *s. pl. aggr.* (rhafn—gwydd) Witch-elms.
Rhafnwydden, *s. f. dim.* (rhafnwydd) A witch-elm

Tri phren nid rhydd eu torri, heb ganiad gwlad ac arglwydd: mesbren, sef derwen, bedwen, a *rhafnwydden*.

Three trees not to be cut, without the permission of the country and the lord: acorn tree, or oak: the birch tree, and the witch-elm. *Trioedd Dyfnwal.*

Rhafol, *s. pl. aggr.* (rhaf—ol) The berries of the service-tree; also called *cyrafol*, and *cyrafon*.
Rhafon, *s. pl. aggr.* (rhaf) Berries growing in clusters; the fruit of the service-tree.
Rhafu, *v. a.* (rhaf) To spread out, or to diffuse.
Rhafun, *s. m.* (rhaf) That is spread or diffused.
Rhaff, *s. f.—pl. t.* au (rha—aff) A rope.
Rhaffaidd, *a.* (rhaff) Like a rope; like a cord.
Rhaffan, *s. f. dim.* (rhaff) A small rope, a cord. *Gware rhaffan* or *siglen denen*, swinging.
Rhaffawl, *a.* (rhaff) Formed like a rope.
Rhaffiad, *s. m.* (rhaff) A roping; a cording.
Rhaffiaw, *v. a.* (rhaff) To rope, to make a rope.
Rhaffwr, *s. m.—pl.* rhaffwyr (rhaff—gwr) A roper.
Rhag, *s. m.—pl. t.* ion (rha—ag) A front, a presence, a van; an entrance. It is used as a compositive prefix. *O dy rag*, *o ylh blaen*, from before thee, before thee.

Rhag pebyll Madawg, pan atgorai,
Nawyn un o gant yni delai.

The *entrance* of the tents of Madog, when he returns, only one of a hundred therein doth come. *Aneurin.*

Seren o'u rhag yn rhoi goleu.

A star *before* them giving light. *Y Brawd Madawg.*

Rhag, *prep.* (rha—ag) Before, fore; from; for, lest, lest that; because. *Dos rhag dy flaen*, go straight forward. *Rhagwyf*, *rhagddwyf*, *rhagof*, *rhagddof*, before me; *rhagot*, *rhagddot*, before thee; *rhago*, *rhagddo*, before him or it; *rhagi*, *rhagddi*, before her; *rhagom*, *rhagddom*, before us; *rhagoch*, *rhagddoch*, before you; *rhagynt*, *rhagddynt*, *rhagddudd*, before them.

Fio rhag dryg-dir, ar na fio rhag drwg arglwydd.

He will fly *from* a bad land that flies not *from* a bad lord. *Adage.*

Achwyn rhag achwyn rhagddo.

Complaining *for fear* of a complaint *against him*. *Adage.*

Torf ysgwn yn gnawd yn aghamman
Tarf rhag cad rhag Cwcullfyriawn.

An exhalted host well trained in combat flies *from* battle *before* the tribe of Short-caps. *Cynddelw, Gwrl. Powys.*

Rhagachub, *v. a.* (achub) To save the vantage; to obtain a priority; to become before.

Rhagachubwn ei wyneb—a chanwn salmau iddaw; canys Arglwydd mawr yw Duw.

Let us come before his presence; and let us sing psalms to him; for a mighty Lord is God. *D. Ddu o Hiraddug.*

Rhagachubawl, *a.* (rhagachub) Tending to obtain advantage or priority; coming before.
Rhagachubiad, *s. m.* (rhagachub) A coming before; a getting a priority.
Rhagachubiaeth, *s. m.* (rhagachub) The act of obtaining a priority, the state of having a priority; the state of coming before.
Rhagachubwr, *s. m.—pl.* rhagachubwyr (rhagachub—gwr) One who comes before.
Rhagadail, *s. f.* (adail) An out-building.
Rhagadeiladu, *v. a.* (rhagadail) To build an outwork; to make an outbuilding.
Rhagadnabod, *v. n.* (adnabod) To know beforehand, to get a previous acquaintance.
Rhagadnabodawl, *a.* (rhagadnabod) Previously acquainted; previously recognising.
Rhagadnabyddawl, *a.* (rhagadnabod) Previously acquainted; previously known.
Rhagadnabyddiaeth, *s. m.* (rhagadnabod) A previous acquaintance.
Rhagadrawdd, *s. m.—pl.* rhagadroddion (adrawdd) A preface, a preamble. *v. a.* To preface.
Rhagadroddawl, *a.* (rhagadrawdd) Prefatory, introductory.
Rhagadroddiad, *s. m.* (rhagadrawdd) A prefacing
Rhagaddas, *a.* (addas) Previously fitting.
Rhagaddasawl, *a.* (rhagaddas) Tending to adapt or to make fit beforehand.
Rhagaddasiad, *s. m.* (rhagaddas) A fitting before.
Rhagaddasu, *v. a.* (rhagaddas) To adapt or to fit beforehand.
Rhagaddaw, *v. a.* (addaw) To promise before.
Rhagaddewid, *s. f.—pl. t.* ion (rhagaddaw) A previous promise.
Rhagaddfed, *a.* (addfed) Premature, precocious.
Rhagaddfedawl, *a.* (rhagaddfed) Tending to ripen beforehand, of early maturity.
Rhagaddfediad, *s. m.* (rhagaddfed) A ripening beforehand, to become precocious.
Rhagaddfedrwydd, *s. m.* (rhagaddfed) Precocity.
Rhagaddfedu, *v. a.* (rhagaddfed) To ripen before.
Rhagafael, *s. m.* (gafael) A previous hold; a forehold or seizure.
Rhagafaeliad, *s. m.* (rhagafael) A previously holding; a taking a first hold.
Rhagafaelu, *v. a.* (rhagafael) To hold previously.
Rhagagawr, *s. m.* (agawr) An opening before. *v. n.* To open before.
Rhagagori, *v. a.* (rhagagawr) To open before.
Rhagagoriad, *s. m.* (rhagagawr) A fore-opening.
Rhagagwedd, *s. f.* (agwedd) A prior form, a prior appearance.
Rhagagweddiad, *s. m.* (rhagagwedd) Preformation
Rhagagweddu, *v. a.* (rhagagwedd) To preform.
Rhagair, *s. m.—pl.* rhageiriau (gair) A leading word, a catch-word.
Rhagalw, *v. a.* (galw) To call beforehand.
Rhagalwad, *s. m.* (rhagalw) A calling beforehand.
Rhagallu, *s. m.* (gallu) A previous power; a being able beforehand.

Rhagalluedd, *s. m.* (gallu) Ability beforehand.

Rhagamcan, *s. m.—pl. t.* ion (amcan) A prior purpose, or design; a prenotion.

Rhagamcanawl, *a.* (rhagamcan) Previously purposing, presupposing.

Rhagamcaniad, *s. m.—pl. t.* au (rhagamcan) A purposing beforehand; a pre-supposition.

Rhagamcanu, *v. a.* (rhagamcan) To form a design beforehand; to pre-suppose.

Rhagamcanus, *a.* (rhagamcan) Previously purposing; having a previous intention.

Rhagamcanwr, *s. m.—pl.* rhagamcanwyr (rhagamcan—gwr) One who designs before-hand.

Rhagamddiffyn, *v. a.* (amddiffyn) To defend before-hand, to make a previous defence.

Rhagamddiffynawl, *a.* (rhagamddiffyn) Previously defending or protecting.

Rhagamddiffyniad, *s. m.* (rhagamddiffyn) A defending or protecting before-hand.

Rhagammheu, *v. a.* (ammheu) To pre-surmise.

Rhagammod, *s. f.—pl. t.* au (ammod) A preliminary agreement or contract.

Rhagammodawl, *a.* (rhagammod) Belonging to a preliminary agreement.

Rhagammodi, *v. a.* (rhagammod) To agree before-hand; to make a previous contract.

Rhagammodiad, *s. m.* (rhagammod) A covenanting beforehand.

Rhagammodwr, *s. m.—pl.* rhagammodwyr (rhagammod—gwr) One who agrees beforehand.

Rhagamnaid, *s. f.* (amnaid) A previous signal.

Rhagamneidiad, *s. m.* (rhagamnaid) A making a previous signal.

Rhagamneidiaw, *v. a.* (rhagamnaid) To make a previous signal.

Rhagamneidiawl, *a.* (rhagamnaid) Belonging to a previous signal.

Rhagamser, *s. m.—pl. t.* oedd (amser) A previous or prior time.

Rhagamserawl, *a.* (rhagamser) Belonging to previous time, of a previous season.

Rhagamsern, *v. a.* (rhagamser) To fix a previous time, to antedate.

Rhaganfon, *v. a.* (anfon) To send beforehand.

Rhaganfonadwy, *a.* (rhaganfon) Capable of being sent beforehand.

Rhaganfonawl, *a.* (rhaganfon) Being sent beforehand, premissive.

Rhaganfonedig, *a.* (rhaganfon) Being sent beforehand; a premission.

Rhaganfonedigaeth, *s. m.* (rhaganfonedig) The act of sending before.

Rhaganfoniad, *s. m.* (rhaganfon) A sending before; a sending a previous messenger.

Rhaganfonwr, *s. m.—pl.* rhaganfonwyr (rhaganfon—gwr) One who sends beforehand.

Rhagansawdd, *s. f.—pl.* rhagansoddion (ansawdd) A prior nature or quality.

Rhagansoddadwy, *a.* (rhagansawdd) Capable of being endued with an original nature.

Rhagansoddawl, *a.* (rhagansawdd) Of an original nature or quality.

Rhagansoddi, *v. a.* (rhagansawdd) To endue with an original nature.

Ragansoddiad, *s. m.* (rhagansawdd) A forming an original nature.

Rhagangen, *s. f.* (angen) A previous necessity.

Rhagangenawl, *a.* (rhagangen) Previously necessitated.

Rhagangeniad, *s. m.* (rhagangen) An enduing with a previous necessity.

Rhagangenrhaid, *s. f.—pl.* rhagangenrheidiau (rhagangen—rhaid) A previous necessity.

Rhagangenrheidiaw, *v. a.* (rhagangenrhaid) To render previously necessary.

Rhagangenrheidiawl, *a.* (rhagangenrhaid) Previously necessary.

Rhagangenrheidrwydd, *s. m.* (rhagangenrhaid) A previous necessity.

Rhagangenu, *v. a.* (rhagangen) To endue with a prior necessity; to necessitate beforehand.

Rhagaraeth, *s. f.—pl.* rhagareithiau (araeth) A prefatory discourse.

Rhagarawd, *s. f.* (arawd) An introductory speech

Rhagarchwaeth, *s. m.—pl.* rhagarchweithion (archwaeth) A foretaste.

Rhagarchwaethawl, *a.* (archwaeth) Foretasting.

Rhagarchwaethedig, *a.* (archwaeth) Foretasted.

Rhagarchwaethiad, *s. m.* (rhagarchwaeth) A foretasting.

Rhagarchwaethu, *v. a.* (archwaeth) To foretaste.

Rhagaraethiad, *s. m.* (rhagaraeth) A making a prefatory speech.

Rhagareithiaw, *v. a.* (rhagaraeth) To make a prefatory speech.

Rhagareithiwr, *s. m.—pl.* rhagareithwyr (rhagaraeth—gwr) One who makes an exordium.

Rhagarfaeth, *s. f.* (arfaeth) Predestination.

Rhagarfaethawl, *a.* (rhagarfaeth) Predestinarian; predisposing, pre-determining.

Rhagarfaethedig, *a.* (rhagarfaeth) Predestinated, predisposed, predetermined.

Rhagarfaethiad, *s. m.* (rhagarfaeth) A predestination; a predisposition.

Rhagarfaethu, *v. a.* (rhagarfaeth) To predestinate; to predispose.

Rhagarfaethus, *a.* (rhagarfaeth) Predestinating.

Rhagarfaethydd, *s. m.—pl. t.* ion (rhagarfaeth) A predestinarian.

Rhagarfawg, *a.* (arfawg) Being forearmed.

Rhagarfogi, *v. a.* (rhagarfawg) To arm beforehand, to forearm.

Rhagarfogiad, *s. m.* (rhagarfawg) An arming beforehand.

Rhagarfu, *v. a.* (arfu) To arm beforehand.

Rhagarganfod, *s. m.* (arganfod) A foreseeing. *v. n.* To foresee, to forecast.

Rhagargoel, *s. f.—pl. t.* ion (argoel) A foretoken.

Rhagarian, *s. pl. aggr.* (arian) Earnest money.

Rhagarlwy, *s. m.—pl. t.* on (arlwy) Food that is ready beforehand.

Rhagarlwyad, *s. m.* (rhagarlwy) A getting food ready before.

Rhagarlwyaw, *v. a.* (rhagarlwy) To get food ready beforehand.

Rhagarnawdd, *s. f.* (arnawdd) A plough handle.

Rhagarswyd, *s. m.* (arswyd) A previous dread.

Rhagarswydaw, *v. a.* (rhagarswyd) To frighten beforehand, to have a previous dread.

Rhagarwain, *v. a.* (arwain) to lead before.

Rhagarweiniad, *s. m.* (rhagarwain) A conducting or leading before.

Rhagarweiniawl, *a.* (rhagarwain) Leading beforehand; a previous conducting.

Rhagarwedd, *s. f.* (arwedd) Predisposition.

Rhagarweddawl, *a.* (rhagarwedd) Predisposing.

Rhagarweddiad, *s. m.* (arwedd) A predisposing.

Rhagarweddu, *v. a.* (rhagarwedd) To predispose.

Rhagarwydd, *s. f.—pl. t.* ion (arwydd) A prognostic, a foretoken, a presage.

Rhagarwyddaw, *v. a.* (rhagarwydd) To prognosticate, to foresignify.

Rhagarwyddawg, *a.* (rhagarwydd) Foretokening.
Rhagarwyddawl, *a.* (rhagarwydd) Foretokening.
Rhagarwyddiad, *s. m.* (rhagarwydd) A prognostication.
Rhagarwyddocâad, *s. m.* (rhagarwyddocâu) A prognosticating, a foretokening.
Rhagarwyddocâawl, *a.* (rhagarwyddocâu) Prognosticating, foretokening, foresignifying.
Rhagarwyddocâu, *v. a.* (rhagarwyddawg) To prognosticate, to foresignify.
Rhagattal, *s. m.* (attal) A previous stopping.
Rhagattalgar, *a.* (rhagattal) Apt to stop before.
Rhagattaliad, *s. m.* (rhagattal) A stopping before.
Rhagatteb, *s. m.—pl. t.* ion (atteb) Prior answer.
Rhagattebawl, *a.* (rhagatteb) A first answering.
Rhagattebiad, *s. m.* (rhagatteb) An answering beforehand, a previously answering.
Rhagattebu, *v. a.* (rhagatteb) To answer before.
Rhagawd, *s. m.—pl.* rhagodion (rhag) The act of going before; the state of being before; an obstacle, let, or hinderance.

> Nawdd y frenines yw dwyn dyn dros derfyn y wlad, heb erlid, heb ragawd.
>
> The protection of the queen is to convey the person over the borders of the country, without pursuit, without *opposition*. *Welsh Laws.*

Rhagawd, *v. a.* (rhag) To go before; to go against; to stop, to hinder. *Rhagodion*, those who take the lead, or that are in advance.

> Gwell erlid arglwydd nog ei ragawd.
>
> It is better to pursue a lord than *to go against* him. *Adage.*
>
> Gwaith teg yw marchogaeth tòn
> I ragawd pysg o'r eigion.
>
> It is pleasant work to ride the wave *to encounter* the fishes of the deep. *D. ab Gwilym.*

Rhagawdl, *s. f.—pl.* rhagodlau (awdl) A first or leading rhyme, a primary rhyme.
Rhagawl, *a.* (rhag) Being against, opposite or in front; opposing.
Rhagbarawd, *a.* (parawd) Ready-beforehand.
Rhagbarodawl, *a.* (rhagbarawd) Tending to be ready or prepared beforehand.
Rhagbarodi, *v. a.* (rhagbarawd) To prepare or make ready beforehand.
Rhagbarodrwydd, *s. m.* (rhagbarawd) The state of being prepared or ready beforehand.
Rhagbarotôad, *s. m.* (rhagbarotoi) A preparing or making ready beforehand.
Rhagbarotôawl, *a.* (rhagbarotoi) Tending to be prepared or ready beforehand.
Rhagbarotôi, *v. a.* (rhagbarawd) To prepare beforehand, to get ready beforehand.
Rhagbarotôwr, *s. m.—pl.* rhagbarotowyr (rhagbarotoi—gwr) One who prepares beforehand.
Rhagbenaeth, *s. m.* (penaeth) A vice-chief.
Rhagbenawd, *s. m.* (penawd) A prior conclusion
Rhagbenodawl, *a.* (penawd) Predetermined.
Rhagbenodi, *v. a.* (penawd) To predetermine.
Rhagbenodiad, *s. m.* (rhagbenawd) A predetermination; a previous conclusion.
Rhagborth, *s. m.—pl.* rhagbyrth (porth) An outer gate; a fore porch.
Rhagbrawf, *s. m.* (prawf) A previous trial.
Rhagbrofi, *v. a.* (rhagbrawf) To try beforehand.
Rhagbrofiad, *s. m.—pl. t.* au (rhagbrawf) A trying beforehand; a foretasting.
Rhagbrofwr, *s. m.—pl.* rhagbrofwyr (rhagbrawf gwr) One who tries beforehand.
Rhagbryder, *s. m.—pl. t.* au (pryder) Precaution
Rhagbryderawl, *a.* (rhagbryder) Precautious.
Rhagbryderiad, *s. m.* (rhagbryder) A using precaution; circumspection.
Rhagbryderu, *v. a.* (pryder) To use precaution.
Rhagbryderus, *a.* (rhagbryder) Circumspective.
Rhagbryn, *s. m.* (pryn) A prior purchase.
Rhagbrynawl, *a.* (rhagbryn) Relating to a buying beforehand; a forestalling.
Rhagbryniad, *s. m.—pl. t.* au (rhagbryn) A buying beforehand; a pre-emption.
Rhagbrynu, *v. a.* (rhagbryn) To buy before-hand; to forestall.
Rhagbrynwr, *s. m.—pl.* rhagbrynwyr (rhagbryn—gwr) One who previously buys.
Rhagbwys, *s. m.* (pwys) A previous weighing.
Rhagbwysaw, *v. a.* (rhagbwys) To weigh before.
Rhagbwysawl, *a.* (rhagbwys) Being previously weighing, a fore-weighing.
Rhagbwysedig, *a.* (rhagbwys) Being weighed beforehand.
Rhagbwysiad, *s. m.* (rhagbwys) A weighing beforehand.
Rhagchwaeth, *s. m.—pl. t.* oedd (chwaeth) A foretaste.
Rhagchwaethawl, *a.* (rhagchwaeth) Foretasting.
Rhagchwaethiad, *s. m.—pl. t.* au (rhagchwaeth) A pregustation, a foretasting.
Rhagchwaethu, *v. a.* (rhagchwaeth) To foretaste.
Rhagchware, *s. m.—pl. t.* on (chware) A prelude
Rhagchwareu, *v. a.* (rhagchware) To make a prelude.
Rhagchwedl, *s. m.—pl.* rhagchwedlau (chwedl) A prior report, a preamble.
Rhagchwedledd, *s. m.* (rhagchwedl) The state of being reported beforehand.
Rhagchwedliad, *s. m.* (rhagchwedl) A reporting or rumouring beforehand.
Rhagchwedlu, *v. a.* (rhagchwedl) To make report beforehand; to make a preamble.
Rhagchwegr, *s. f.* (chwegr) A grandmother-in-law.
Rhagchwegrwn, *s. m.* (chwegrwn) A grandfather-in-law.
Rhagchwiliad, *s. m.* (chwiliad) A previously searching.
Rhagchwiliaw, *v. a.* (chwiliaw) To search before.
Rhagdaen, *s. m.* (taen) A fore-spreading.
Rhagdaeniad, *s. m.* (rhagdaen) A fore-spreading.
Rhagdaenu, *v. a.* (rhagdaen) To spread before.
Rhagdal, *s. m.—pl. t.* au (tal) What is in front; a frontlet, a frontstal, a frontpiece.
Rhagdal, *s. m.* (tâl) Payment before; earnest.
Rhagdaliad, *s. m.—pl. t.* au (rhagdal) A paying beforehand, a paying as earnest.
Rhagdalu, *v. a.* (rhagdal) To pay beforehand.
Rhagdalwr, *s. m.—pl.* rhagdalwyr (rhagdal—gwr) One who pays beforehand.
Rhagdebygiad, *s. m.* (tebygiad) A fore-deeming.
Rhagdebygu, *v. a.* (tebygu) To presuppose.
Rhagdeilyngdawd, *s. m.* (teilyngdawd) The state of being previously suitable.
Rhagdeilyngu, *v. a.* (teilyngu) To make suitable or appropriate beforehand.
Rhagdeimlad, *s. m.* (teimlad) A feeling before.
Rhagdeimlaw, *v. a.* (teimlaw) To feel beforehand
Rhagder, *s. m.* (rhag) The state of being before, leading, or against; resistance, opposition.

> Pair cadair, cewrawg yn aglewder;
> Par anwar, anwas yn rhagder.
>
> A cause of energy renowned for bravery; a spear of unkindness, not a stripling in the *advanced post*. *Cynddelw, i O. Gwynedd.*
>
> Rhagder ei osgordd, naf lledneis ei hil.
>
> The *foremost* of his host, a chief of elegant race. *Einion Wan.*

Rhagderfyn, *s. m.—pl. t.* au (terfyn) A prior conclusion, end, or determination.
Rhagderfynedig, *a.* (rhagderfyn) Predetermined

Rhagderfyniad, *s. m.—pl. t.* au (rhagderfyn) Predetermination, a prior conclusion.
Rhagderfynu, *v. a* (terfyn) To predetermine.
Rhagdestyn, *s. m.—pl. t.* au (testyn) A preliminary theme, or discourse.
Rhagdestyniad, *s. m.* (rhagdestyn) A making a preliminary theme.
Rhagdestynu, *v. a.* (rhagdestyn) To form a preliminary theme.
Rhagdor, *s. m.* (tor) A prior fracture or break.
Rhagdori, *v. a.* (rhagdor) To break before.
Rhagdoriad, *s. m.* (rhagdor) A breaking before.
Rhagdraddawd, *s. m.* (traddawd) A prior passing
Rhagdraddodawl, *a.* (rhagdraddawd) Being previously passed over, of previous tradition.
Rhagdraddodi, *v. a.* (rhagdraddawd) To pass over previously; to give a previous tradition.
Rhagdraddodiad, *s. m.—pl. t.* au (rhagdraddawd) A previously passing over; a former tradition
Rhagdraethawd, *s. f.* (traethawd) An introductory discourse.
Rhagdraethu, *v. a.* (traethu) To recite before.
Rhagdraigl, *s. m.* (traigl) A previous turn.
Rhagdrefu, *s. f.—pl.* rhagdrefnau (trefn) A preordinance; predestination.
Rhagdrefnadwy, *a.* (rhagdrefn) Capable of preordination.
Rhagdrefnawl, *a.* (rhagdrefn) Tending to preordain; fore-ordaining.
Rhagdrefnedig, *a.* (rhagdrefn) Fore-ordained.
Rhagdrefniad, *s. m.* (rhagdrefn) A preordination, a preordaining; predestination.
Rhagdrefnu, *v. a.* (rhagdrefn) To order beforehand, to preordain; to predispose.
Rhagdreigliad, *s. m.* (rhagdraigl) A revolving before; a previous revolution.
Rhagdreigliaw, *v. a.* (rhagdraigl) To revolve before; to make a previous revolution.
Rhagdremyn, *s. m.* (tremyn) A first glance.
Rhagdremynawl, *a.* (rhagdremyn) Being looked over beforehand; having foresight.
Rhagdremyniad, *s. m.* (rhagdremyn) A glancing over beforehand.
Rhagdremynt, *s. m.* (rhagdremyn) A previous glance; a foresight.
Rhagdremynu, *v. a.* (rhagdremyn) To glance over beforehand; to have foresight.
Rhagdrin, *s. m.* (trin) To put in order, or to manage beforehand.
Rhagdriniad, *s. m.* (rhagdrin) A managing or ordering beforehand.
Rhagdriniaeth, *s. m.* (rhagdrin) A previous management; a previous arrangement.
Rhagdrochi, *v. a.* (trochi) To immerse before.
Rhagdrochiad, *s. m.* (trochiad) A prior immersion
Rhagdrosi, *v. a.* (trosi) To drive before.
Rhagdrwch, *s. m.—pl.* rhagdrychion (trwch) A fore-cut; a previous cut through.
Rhagdrychiad, *s. m.* (rhagdrwch) A cutting before; a fore-cutting.
Rhagdrychu, *v. a.* (rhagdrwch) To cut before.
Rhagdy, *s. m.—pl. t.* iau (ty) An outhouse.
Rhagdyb, *s. m.—pl. t.* iau (tyb) A preconceit.
Rhagdybiad, *s. m.—pl. t.* au (rhagdyb) Presupposition, preopinion, prenotion.
Rhagdybied, *v. a.* (rhagdyb) To presuppose.
Rhagdybu, *v. a.* (rhagdyb) To presuppose.
Rhagdybus, *a.* (rhagdyb) Presuppositious.
Rhagdybusaw, *v. n.* (rhagdybus) To become presuppositious.
Rhagdybusrwydd, *s. m.* (rhagdybus) Previous suppositiousness; a preconceived state.
Rhagdyddyn, *s. m.—pl. t.* od (tyddyn) An outtenement; a bordering farm.
Rhagdyn, *s. m.* (tyn) A fore-draught.
Rhagdyneriad, *s. m.* (tyneriad) A previous softening or melioration.
Rhagdyneru, *v. a.* (tyneru) To soften beforehand
Rhagdyniad, *s. m.* (rhagdyn) A drawing before.
Rhagdynu, *v. a.* (rhagdyn) To draw before.
Rhagdyst, *s. m.—pl. t.* ion (tyst) A prior witness
Rhagdystiad, *s. m.* (rhagdyst) A previously testifying; a giving a previous testimony.
Rhagdystiaw, *v. a.* (rhagdyst) To testify beforehand; to witness beforehand.
Rhagdystiawl, *a.* (rhagdyst) First testifying.
Rhagdystiolaeth, *s. f.—pl. t.* au (rhagdystiawl) A previous testimony.
Rhagdystiolaethu, *v. a.* (rhagdystiolaeth) To give a previous testimony.
Rhagdywyll, *a.* (tywyll) Being dark before.
Rhagdywyllu, *v. a.* (rhagdywyll) To darken before
Rhagdywyn, *s. m.* (tywyn) A radience before.
Rhagdywyniad, *s. m.* (rhagdywyn) A shining before; a previously shining.
Rhagdywynu, *v.* (rhagdywyn) To shine before.
Rhagdywys, *v. a.* (tywys) To lead before.
Rhagdywysaw, *v. a.* (rhagdywys) To fore-lead.
Rhagdywysiad, *s. m.* (rhagdywys) A leading before, or a leading in advance.
Rhagddadgan, *v. a.* (dadgan) To declare before.
Rhagddadganiad, *s. m.* (rhagddadgan) A declaring beforehand; previous declaration.
Rhagddadl, *s. f.—pl. t.* au (dadl) A previous debate, or previous question.
Rhagddadliad, *s. m.* (rhagddadl) A previous argumentation.
Rhagddadlu, *v. a.* (rhagddadl) To debate before.
Rhagddal, *v. a.* (dal) To hold beforehand.
Rhagddaliad, *s. m.* (rhagddal) A first holding.
Rhagddanfon, *v. a.* (danfon) To send before.
Rhagddanfonawl, *a.* (rhagddanfon) Being sent beforehand; being of a previous mission.
Rhagddanfoniad, *s. m.* (rhagddanfon) A sending beforehand.
Rhagddant, *s. m.—pl.* rhagddannedd (dant) A foretooth, or a front tooth.
Rhagddangaws, *v. a.* (dangaws) To shew beforehand, to premonstrate.
Rhagddangosawl, *a.* (dangaws) Premonstrating
Rhagddangosiad, *s. m.—pl. t.* au (rhagddangaws) A prognostication; a premonstration.
Rhagddangoswr, *s. m.—pl.* rhagddangoswyr (rhagddangaws—gwr) A prognosticator.
Rhagddarbod, *s. m.—pl. t.* au (darbod) Provision beforehand; circumspection.
Rhagddarbodaeth, *s. m.* (rhagddarbod) A preparation beforehand; providence.
Rhagddarbodawl, *a.* (rhagddarbod) Providential.
Rhagddarbodedig, *a.* (rhagddarbod) Being provided or furnished beforehand.
Rhagddarbodi, *v. a.* (rhagddarbod) To provide or furnish beforehand.
Rhagddarbodiad, *s. m.* (rhagddarbod) A providing or furnishing beforehand.
Rhagddarbodus, *a.* (rhagddarbod) Provident.
Rhagddarbodwr, *s. m.—pl.* rhagddarbodwyr (rhagddarbod—gwr) One who provides beforehand.
Rhagddarlun, *s. m.* (darlun) Prefiguration.
Rhagddarluniad, *s. m.—pl. t.* au (rhagddarlun) A prefigurating.
Rhagddarluniaw, *v.* (rhagddarlun) To prefigurate

Rhagddarlunledig, *a.* (rhagddarlun) Prefigurated
Rhagddarmerth, *s. m.* (darmerth) Provision made beforehand; a previous preparation.
Rhagddarmerthawl, *a.* (rhagddarmerth) Provident
Rhagddarmerthu, *v. a.* (rhagddarmerth) To provide beforehand.
Rhagddarn, *s. m.—pl. t.* au (darn) A fore-piece.
Rhagddarpar, *s. m.—pl. t.* au (darpar) Previous order or disposition.
Rhagddarparawl, *a.* (rhagddarpar) Tending to furnish beforehand; providential.
Rhagddarparedig, *a.* (rhagddarpar) Being previously ordered; being previously furnished.
Rhagddarparedigaeth, *s. m.—pl. t.* au (rhagddarparedig) The being previously furnished.
Rhagddarparedigaw, *v. a.* (rhagddarparedig) To render complete beforehand.
Rhagddarparedd, *s. m.* (rhagddarpar) The state of being previously furnished.
Rhagddarpariad, *s. m.* (rhagddarpar) A providing or ordering beforehand.
Rhagddarparu, *v. a.* (darpar) To furnish before.
Rhagddarparwch, *s. m.* (rhagddarpar) Support previously given.

Na anturia fyned drwy yr hoenynau ac y cynllwynau hyn, cyn i ti weddiaw am ragddarparwch Duw.

Do not venture to go through these snares and ambuscades, before thou hast prayed for the *providential support* of God.
R. Fychan, Ym. Dawioldeb.

Rhagddawd, *s. m.—pl.* rhagddodau (dawd) A prefix.
Rhagddawn, *s. m.—pl.* rhagddoniau (dawn) A previous gift or endowment.
Rhagddëall, *s. m.* (dëall) Previous knowledge.
Rhagddëalliad, *s. m.* (rhagddëall) A pre-apprehension.
Rhagddelw, *s. f.—pl. t.* au (delw) A prototype.
Rhagddelwad, *s. m.* (rhagddelw) Prefiguration.
Rhagddelwi, *v. a.* (rhagddelw) To prefigurate.
Rhagdderbyn, *v. a.* (derbyn) To receive before.
Rhagdderbynai, *s. c.* (rhagdderbyn) A prolepsis
Rhagdderbyniad, *s. m.* (rhagdderbyn) A receiving beforehand.
Rhagdderbyniawl, *a.* (rhagdderbyn) Previously receivable.
Rhagddewis, *s. m.* (dewis) A previous choice. *v. a.* To choose before.
Rhagddewisawl, *a.* (rhagddewis) Pre-elective.
Rhagddewisedig, *a.* (rhagddewis) Fore-chosen.
Rhagddewisiad, *s. m.* (rhagddewis) Pre-election
Rhagddial, *s. m.* (dial) A previous revenge.
Rhagddialiad, *s. m.* (rhagddial) A revenging beforehand.
Rhagddialu, *v. a.* (rhagddial) To revenge before.
Rhagddiddymiad, *s. m.* (diddymiad) A previous annihilation.
Rhagddiddymu, *v. a.* (diddymu) To annihilate beforehand.
Rhagddiogeliad, *s. m.* (diogeliad) A securing beforehand; a previously making safe.
Rhagddiogelu, *v. a.* (diogelu) To secure before.
Rhagddiogelwch, *s. m.* (diogelwch) A previous security.
Rhagddirnad, *s. m.* (dirnad) Presurmise.
Rhagddirnadawl, *a.* (rhagddirnad) Presurmising.
Rhagddirnadiad, *s. m.* (dirnad) A presurmising.
Rhagddirnadu, *v. a.* (dirnad) To presurmise.
Rhagddirymawl, *a.* (dirymawl) Tending to debilitate beforehand.
Rhagddirymiad, *s. m.* (dirymiad) A previously debilitating or enervating.
Rhagddirymu, *v. a.* (dirymu) To debilitate beforehand.
Rhagddodadwy, *v. a.* (rhagddawd) Capable of being placed before.
Rhagddodawl, *a.* (rhagddawd) Prepositive.
Rhagddodedig, *a.* (rhagddawd) Being prefixed.
Rhagddodedigaeth, *s. m.* (rhagddodedig) The act of placing before, a prefixing.
Rhagddodedigawl, *a.* (rhagddodedig) Prepositive
Rhagddodi, *v. a.* (rhagddawd) To prepose.
Rhagddodiad, *s. m.—pl. t.* au (rhagddawd) Preposition.
Rhagddoniad, *s. m.* (rhagddawn) A gifting beforehand; a previously endowing.
Rhagddoniaw, *v. a.* (rhagddawn) To gift beforehand; to endow previously.
Rhagddoniawl, *a.* (rhagddawn) Tending to endow beforehand.
Rhagddor, *s. f.—pl. t.* au (dor) A fore-door; a wicket; a half-door.
Rhagddorig, *s. f. dim.* (rhagddor) A small wicket
Rhagddrws, *s. m.—pl.* rhagddrysau (drws) A fore-door, an outer door.
Rhagddryll, *s. m.—pl. t.* iau (dryll) A fore-piece.
Rhagddychweliad, *s. m.* (dychweliad) A returning beforehand.
Rhagddychwelyd, *v. a.* (dychwelyd) To return beforehand.
Rhagddychymyg, *s. f.—pl. t.* ion (dychymyg) A prior device or invention; a presupposal.
Rhagddychymygadwy, *a.* (rhagddychymyg) Capable of being devised beforehand.
Rhagddychymygawl, *a.* (rhagddychymyg) Previously devising; presuppositious.
Rhagddychymygedig, *a.* (rhagddychymyg) Devised beforehand; presupposed.
Rhagddychymygiad, *s. m.* (rhagddychymyg) A devising beforehand; a presupposing.
Rhagddychymygu, *v. a.* (rhagddychymyg) To devise beforehand: to presuppose.
Rhagddydd, *s. m.—pl. t.* iau (dydd) A prior day
Rhagddyddiad, *s. m.* (rhagddydd) An antidating.
Rhagddyddiaw, *v. a.* (rhagddydd) To antidate.
Rhagddyfaliad, *s. m.* (dyfaliad) A describing beforehand.
Rhagddyfalu, *v. a.* (dyfalu) To fore-describe.
Rhagddyled, *s. f.—pl. t.* ion (dyled) Prior debt.
Rhagddyledus, *a.* (rhagddyled) Previously due.
Rhagddymchwel, *s. m.* (dymchwel) A previous turn over. *v. a.* To turn over previously.
Rhagddymchweliad, *s. m.—pl. t.* au (rhagddymchwel) A previously turning over.
Rhagddymchwelyd, *v. a.* (rhagddymchwel) To turn over beforehand.
Rhagddysg, *s. m.* (dysg) Previous instruction.
Rhagddysgawl, *a.* (rhagddysg) Tending to instruct beforehand.
Rhagddysgiad, *s. m.* (rhagddysg) A previously instructing.
Rhagddysgu, *v. a.* (rhagddysg) To fore-learn.
Rhagddywedawl, *a.* (dywedawl) Gainsaying.
Rhagddywededig, *a.* (dywed) Beforementioned.
Rhagddywediad, *s. m.—pl. t.* au (dywediad) A gainsaying; a speaking previously.
Rhagedrych, *v. a.* (edrych) To look before.
Rhagedrychiad, *s. m.* (rhagedrych) A foreseeing.
Rhagegawr, *s. m.* (egawr) An opening before. *v. n.* To open before.
Rhagegorawl, *a.* (rhagegawr) Opening before.
Rhagegori, *v. a.* (rhagegawr) To open before.
Rhagegoriad, *s. m.* (rhagegawr) A fore-opening.

Rhageisiau, *s. m.* (eisiau) A prior want.
Rhageistedd, *v. a.* (eistedd) To be presiding.
Rhageisteddawl, *a.* (rhageistedd) Presiding.
Rhageisteddiad, *s. m.* (rhageistedd) One that sits before; a president.

> Rhageisteddiad cantref, sef amgen y troedawg, cerwynaid o fedd a dal i'r brenin bob blwyddyn.
>
> A *president* of a hundred, that is to say, the foot-holder, a hogshead of mead shall he pay to the king every year. *Welsh Laws.*

Rhagenw, *s. m.—pl. t.* au (enw) A pronoun.
Rhagenwad, *s. m.* (rhagenw) Prenomination.
Rhagenwawl, *a.* (rhagenw) Prenominal.
Rhagenwedig, *a.* (rhagenwad) Before-named, fore-mentioned. *Rhagenwedigion*, premises.
Rhagenwi, *v. a.* (rhagenw) To premise.
Rhagerchi, *v. a.* (erchi) To pre-require.
Rhagethol, *v. a.* (ethol) To pre-elect.
Rhagetholawg, *a.* (rhagethol) Pre-electing.
Rhagetholedig, *a.* (rhagethol) Fore-chosen.
Rhagetholedigaeth, *s. m.—pl. t.* au (rhagetholedig) A pre-election.
Rhagetholi, *v. a.* (rhagethol) To pre-elect.

> Duw a'i bethole ac a'i rhagetholes,
> A'i phreswyliaw a wnel.
>
> God did choose it and *did choose* it *before-hand*, and he will dwell in it. *D. Ddu o Hiraddug.*

Rhagetholiad, *s. m.* (rhagethol) A pre-election.
Rhagetholwr, *s. m.—pl.* rhagetholwyr (rhagethol—gwr) One who chooses beforehand.
Rhagfai, *s. m.—pl.* rhagfeiau (bai) A prior fault.
Rhagfarn, *s. f.—pl. t.* au (barn) Prejudice.
Rhagfarnawl, *a.* (rhagfarn) Prejudging.
Rhagfarnedig, *a.* (rhagfarn) Prejudicate.
Rhagfarnedigaeth, *s. f.* (rhagfarnedig) Prejudication; a previous adjudication.
Rhagfarnedd, *s. m.* (rhagfarn) Prejudicialness.
Rhagfarniad, *s. m.—pl. t.* au (rhagfarn) A prejudging, a prejudication.
Rhagfarnu, *v. a.* (rhagfarn) To condemn beforehand, to prejudge, to prejudicate.
Rhagfarnwr, *s. m.—pl.* rhagfarnwyr (rhagfarn—gwr) One who prejudges.
Rhagfed, *a.* (rhag) Foremost, or anterior.
Rhagfedd, *s. m.* (medd) Preoccupancy.
Rhagfeddal, *a.* (meddal) Being soft before.
Rhagfeddalâad, *s. m.* (rhagfeddal) A softening beforehand.
Rhagfeddalu, *v. a.* (rhagfeddal) To soften before.
Rhagfeddiad, *s. m.* (rhagfedd) Preoccupation.
Rhagfeddiannawl, *a* (rhagfeddiant) Preoccupying, belonging to preoccupation.
Rhagfeddiannedig, *a.* (rhagfeddiant) Preoccupied, possessed beforehand.
Rhagfeddianniad, *s. m.* (rhagfeddiant) Preoccupation, prepossession.
Rhagfeddiannu, *v. a.* (rhagfeddiant) To preoccupy
Rhagfeddiannwr, *s. m.—pl.* rhagfeddiannwyr (rhagfeddiant—gwr) A preoccupier.
Rhagfeddiannydd, *s. m.—pl. t.* ion (rhagfeddiant) A preoccupier, a prior possessor.
Rhagfeddiant, *s. m.—pl.* rhagfeddiannau (rhagfedd) Preoccupancy.
Rhagfeddu, *v. a.* (rhagfedd) To prepossess.

> Goreu ym o'm rheen ragfeddu
> Rhwydd araith o brifiaith brydu.
>
> Best for me from my Creator *to be pre-endowed* with the fluent oratory of the poetry of the primitive tongue. *Elidr Sais.*

Rhagfeddwl, *s. m.—pl.* rhagfeddyliau (meddwl) A previous thought. *v. a.* To preconceive.
Rhagfeddwr, *s. m.—pl.* rhagfeddwyr (rhagfedd—gwr) A preoccupier.

Rhagfeddyliad, *s. m.* (rhagfeddwl) Precogitation.
Rhagfeddyliaw, *v. a.* (meddwl) To precogitate.

> Yna y dywawd Arthur—Meddyliwch bawb am gyngor da grymus; ac yr awrhon, o unfryd, rhoddwch eich cyngor, ac yn ddoeth rhagfeddyliwch pa beth a fo iawn i atteb.
>
> Then said Arthur, think every one of you of a good and energetic counsel; and in this conjuncture, with one mind, give your advice, and wisely *precogitate* what may be proper to be answered. *Gr. ab Arthur.*

Rhagfeddylied, *v. a.* (meddwl) To foredeem.
Rhagfeddyliedig, *a.* (meddyliad) Precogitated.
Rhagfeddyliwr, *s. m.—pl.* rhagfeddylwyr (rhagfeddwl—gwr) One who precogitates.
Rhagfeiad, *s. m.* (rhagfai) A criminating beforehand; a blaming beforehand.
Rhagfeiaw, *v. a.* (rhagfai) To criminate before hand, to blame beforehand.
Rhagflaen, *s. m.* (blaen) A fore point, a fore end.
Rhagflaenawl, *a.* (rhagflaen) Preceding, antecedent, foregoing.
Rhagflaenawr, *s. m.—pl.* rhagflaenorion (rhagflaen) A predecessor; an anticipater.
Rhagflaenedig, *a.* (rhagflaen) Anticipated.
Rhagflaenedigaeth, *s. m.* (rhagflaenedig) The state of being anticipated.
Rhagflaenedigawl, *a.* (rhagflaenedig) Tending to anticipate; tending to take the lead.
Rhagflaeniad, *s. m.* (rhagflaen) A going forward; a going before; precession; anticipation.
Rhagflaeniadawl, *a.* (rhagflaeniad) Tending to anticipate.
Rhagflaenorawl, *a.* (rhagflaenawr) Relating to precedency; introductory.
Rhagflaenori, *v. a.* (rhagflaenawr) To take the lead or precedency.
Rhagflaenu, *v. a.* (rhagflaen) To anticipate.
Rhagflaenwr, *s. m.—pl.* rhagflaenwyr (rhagflaen—gwr) A preceder; a precursor.
Rhagflaenydd, *s. m.—pl. t.* ion (rhagflaen) A preceder; a precursor, a forerunner.
Rhagflas, *s. m.—pl. t.* au (blâs) A foretaste.
Rhagflasu, *v. a.* (rhagflas) To foretaste.
Rhagflin, *a.* (blin) Previously weary.
Rhagfliniad, *s. m.* (rhagflin) A tiring beforehand.
Rhagflinaw, *v. a.* (rhagflin) To tire beforehand.
Rhagfod, *s. m.—pl. t.* au (bod) A prior existence.
Rhagfodawl, *a.* (rhagfod) Previously existing.

> Tri rhagfodolion doethineb: deddfoldeb, tangnefeddoldeb, a dwyfoldeb.
>
> The three *pre-existent* views of wisdom: morality, peaceableness, and piety. *Catwg ab Gwynllyw Filwr.*

Rhagfodd, *s. m.* (bodd) Previous pleasure.
Rhagfoddawl, *a.* (rhagfodd) Tending to please beforehand.
Rhagfoddiad, *s. m.* (rhagfodd) A pleasing before.
Rhagfoddiaw, *v. a.* (rhagfodd) To please before.
Rhagfoel, *a.* (moel) Bald or bare before.
Rhagfraint, *s. m.—pl.* rhagfreintiau (braint) A prerogative.
Rhagfras, *a.* (bras) Of ample presence.
Rhagfrawd, *s. f.—pl.* rhagfrodau (brawd) A sentence beforehand, prejudication.
Rhagfryd, *s. m.—pl. t.* iau (bryd) A previous design or intention.
Rhagfrydiad, *s. m.* (rhagfryd) A designing beforehand; a premeditating.
Rhagfrydiaw, *v. a.* (rhagfryd) To design beforehand; to premeditate.
Rhagfuan, *a.* (buan) Quick in front; quickly moving forward.

> Rhagfaan ei felrch rhag rhyn gawr;
> Yn nydd gwyth adwyth oedd ei lafnawr
> Pan grysiai Cynon gan wyrdd wawr.
>
> *Quick in front* his steeds before the shock of the shout of war, in the day of wrath destruction were his blades, when Cynon girded himself with the green dawn. *Aneurin.*

Rhagfur, *s. m.—pl. t.* oedd (mur) A contramure.
Rhagfuriad, *s. m.* (rhagfur) A raising a contramure; a forming a counterscarp.
Rhagfuriaw, *v. a.* (rhagfur) To make a contramure, to form a counterscarp.
Rhagfwriad, *s. m.—pl. t.* au (rhagfwrw) A forecasting; predetermination.
Rhagfwriadawl, *a.* (rhagfwriad) Predetermining.
Rhagfwriadu, *v. a.* (rhagfwriad) To predetermine, to foredesign, to foredoom.
Rhagfwriadus, *a*, (rhagfwriad) Premeditating.
Rhagfwrw, *v. a.* (bwrw) To forecast, to foredeem.
Rhagfyfyr, *s. m.—pl. t.* ion (myfyr) Forecast.
Rhagfyfyrdawd, *s. m.—pl.* rhagfyfyrdodau (rhagfyfyr) Premeditation, precogitation.
Rhagfyfyriad, *s. m.* (rhagfyfyr) A premeditating, a precogitating.
Rhagfyfyriaw, *v. a.* (rhagfyfyr) To premeditate; to contemplate beforehand.
Rhagfyfyriawl, *a.* (rhagfyfyr) Premeditating.
Rhagfyfyriedig, *a.* (rhagfyfyriad) Premeditated.
Rhagfyfyriwr, *s. m.—pl.* rhagfyfyrwyr (rhagfyfyr—gwr) One who premeditates.
Rhagfygwth, *s. m.—pl.* rhagfygythion (bygwth) A previous threat.
Rhagfygythiad, *s. m.* (rhagfygwth) A previously threatening.
Rhagfygythiaw, *v. a.* (rhagfygwth) To threaten beforehand.
Rhagfygythiawl, *a.* (rhagfygwth) Threatening beforehand.
Rhagfygythiwr, *s. m.—pl.* rhagfygythwyr (rhagfygwth—gwr) One who threatens beforehand.
Rhagfynag, *s. m.* (mynag) A prior declaration.
Rhagfyned, *v. a.* (myned) To go before.
Rhagfynedawl, *a.* (rhagfyned) Preceding.
Rhagfynediad, *s. m.—pl. t.* au (rhagfyned) A precession; a going before or in advance.
Rhagfynegawl, *a.* (rhagfynag) Prenunciating.
Rhagfynegi, *v. a.* (rhagfynag) To prenunciate, to declare beforehand.
Rhagfynegiad, *s. m.* (rhagfynag) Prenunciation.
Rhagfyr, *s. m.* (byr) That is short before; the first month of the year, according to ancient calculation, beginning at the winter solstice, it is now the name for December.
Rhagfyrâad, *s. m.* (rhagfyrâu) A foreshortening.
Rhagfyrâawl, *a.* (rhagfyrâu) Foreshortening.
Rhagfyrâu, *v. a.* (rhagfyr) To foreshorten.
Rhagffer, *a.* (ffer) Strong-fronted.
Rhagffordd, *s. f.—pl.* rhagffyrdd (ffordd) A forward road, an advance way.
Rhagfforddawl, *a.* (rhagffordd) Belonging to an advance road.
Rhagffysg, *s. m.* (ffysg) A forward haste.

> Terfysg yn rhagffysg yn rhagffer a wnaeth,
> Twrf tòn fraeth Ffraw aber.
>
> A tumult in the *forward haste* in the mighty front he made, the din of the noisy wave of the efflux of Fraw.
> *Cynddelw, m. E. ab M. ab Iddon.*

Rhagffysgiad, *s. m.* (rhagffysg) A hastening before; a hastening forward.
Rhagffysgiaw, *v. a.* (rhagffysg) To hasten before.
Rhagffysgiawl, *a.* (rhagffysg) Tending to hasten forward.
Rhaggadarn, *a.* (cadarn) Strong in front.
Rhaggadarnâad, *s. m.* (rhaggadarnâu) A strengthening before; a strengthening in front.
Rhaggadarnâawl, *a.* (rhaggadarnâu) Tending to strengthen beforehand.
Rhaggadarnâu, *v. a.* (rhaggadarn) To strengthen before; to strengthen in front.
Rhaggaer, *s. f.—pl. t.* oedd (caer) Any advance-work in fortification; an outwork; the suburbs of a city.
Rhaggais, *s. m.* (cais) A prior attempt.
Rhagganfod, *s. m.* (canfod) A foresight. *v. a.* To see before; to foresee.
Rhaggau, *v. a.* (cau) To shut before.
Rhaggauad, *s. m.* (rhaggau) A shutting before.
Rhaggeiniad, *s. m.—pl.* rhaggeiniaid (ceiniad) A precentor.
Rhaggeisiad, *s. m.* (rhaggais) A previously attempting or seeking.
Rhaggeisiaw, *v. a.* (rhaggais) To attempt beforehand; to seek previously.
Rhaggeisiawl, *a.* (rhaggais) Previously trying.
Rhaggerdded, *s. m.* (cerdded) A walk before.
Rhaggerddediad, *s. m.* (rhaggerdded) A walking before, or a walking in advance.
Rhaggiliad, *s. m.* (ciliad) A previously receding.
Rhaggiliaw, *v. a.* (ciliaw) To recede previously.
Rhagglod, *s. f.* (clod) A former fame.

> Cynneddf i Bowys cynnod yn aer
> Yn aros eu rhagglod.
>
> The characteristic of Powys is the giving the advance stroke in battle, awaiting their *former fame.* *Cynddelw.*

Rhagglud, *s. f.* (clud) A heap before, or in front.
Rhaggludaw, *v. a.* (rhagglud) To heap before.

> Rhaggludawdd ei gleddyf uch gwain;
> Rhagrym fu yn pennu penaeth.
>
> The sword above the sheath *raised a heap in front*; severe its forward course dismaying chiefs. *Cynddelw, i M. ab Owain.*

Rhaggludiad, *s. m.* (rhagglud) A heaping before.
Rhagglyw, *s. m.* (clyw) A previous hearing.
Rhagglywed, *v. n.* (rhagglyw) To hear before.
Rhaggnaif, *s. m.* (cnaif) A shearing before.
Rhaggneifiad, *s. m.* (rhaggnaif) A shearing before, a shearing the front.
Rhaggneifiaw, *v. a.* (rhaggnaif) To shear before.
Rhaggnöad, *s. m.* (cnöad) A previously chewing.
Rhaggnöawl, *a.* (cnöawl) Previously chewing.
Rhaggnöi, *v. a.* (cnoi) To chew previously.
Rhaggraff, *s. m.* (craff) A previous impression. *a.* Previously impressed; having foresight.
Rhaggraffawl, *a.* (rhaggraff) Tending to impress previously; inducing foresight.
Rhaggraffiad, *s. m.* (rhaggraff) A previously impressing; a previously perceiving.
Rhaggraffu, *v. a.* (rhaggraff) To impress before.
Rhaggri, *s. f.* (cri) A cry or shout before.
Rhaggrybwyll, *s. m.* (crybwyll) A previous hint.
Rhaggrybwyllaw, *v. a.* (rhaggrybwyll) To intimate previously; to mention beforehand.
Rhaggrybwylledig, *a.* (rhaggrybwyll) Before intimated; beforementioned.
Rhaggrybwylliad, *s. m.* (rhaggrybwyll) A previously intimating; a previously mentioning.
Rhaggydunaw, *v. a.* (cydunaw) To agree before.
Rhaggymmer, *s. m.* (cymer) A previous taking, a previous receipt.
Rhaggymerawl, *a.* (rhaggymer) Previously receiving, or taking.
Rhaggymeredig, *a.* (rhaggymer) Being previously received or taken.
Rhaggymeriad, *s. m.—pl. t.* au (rhaggymer) A taking beforehand, a prolepsis.

Rhaggymeriadawl, *a.* (rhaggymeriad) Of an anticipating tendency; proleptical.

Rhaghanfod, *s. m.* (hanfod) Pre-existence.

Rhaghanfodawl, *a.* (rhaghanfod) Pre-existent.

Rhaghanfodi, *v. a.* (rhaghanfod) To pre-exist.

Rhaghanfodiad, *s. m.* (rhaghanfod) A pre-existing; a pre-existence.

Rhaghawl, *s. f.—pl.* rhagholion (hawl) A previous question or claim.

Rhagheuddawl, *a.* (heuddawl) Premeriting.

Rhagheuddu, *v. n.* (heuddu) To premerit.

Rhagholi, *v. a.* (rhaghawl) To question before.

Rhagholiad, *s. m.—pl. t.* au (rhaghawl) A questioning beforehand.

Rhagiad, *s. m.—pl. t.* au (rhag) A getting before; a coming before; a stopping.

Rhagial, *v. a.* (rhag) To controvert.

Rhagisel, *a.* (isel) Having the fore part low.

Rhagladd, *v. a.* (lladd) To cut before.

Rhagladdawl, *a.* (rhagladd) Cutting in front.

Rhagladdiad, *s. m.* (rhagladd) A cutting before.

Rhaglafar, *s. m.* (llafar) A harangue made before or in public. *a.* Prolocutory.

> Arglwydd, nid rhaid iddo fod yn rhaglafar; ac wrth hyny y gelwir yn un o dri mud gorsedd.
>
> A sovereign, it is not requisite for him to be *prolocutory*, and therefore he is called one of the three mutes of court.
>
> *Welsh Laws.*

Rhaglafarawl, *a.* (rhaglafar) Speaking before.

Rhaglafariad, *s. m.* (rhaglafar) A speaking before.

Rhaglafaru, *v. a.* (rhaglafar) To speak before.

Rhaglafarwr, *s. m.* (rhaglafar—gwr) A prolocutor.

Rhaglam, *s. m.—pl. t.* au (llam) A forward step.

Rhaglamiad, *s. m.* (rhaglam) A stepping before.

Rhaglamu, *v. a.* (rhaglam) To step forward.

Rhaglaw, *s. m.—pl. t.* iau (llaw) A deputy, a surrogate; a lieutenant; a vice-president.

Rhaglawd, *s. m.* (llawd) A first increase.

Rhaglawiaeth, *s. f.* (rhaglaw) The office, or jurisdiction of a deputy; a lieutenancy; a prefecture; a vice presidency.

Rhaglawiaethawl, *a.* (rhaglawiaeth) Belonging to the office of a deputy or lieutenant.

Rhaglawiaethu, *v. a.* (rhaglawiaeth) To perform the function of a deputy or lieutenant.

Rhaglawiaw, *v. a.* (rhaglaw) To make a deputy.

Rhaglawn, *s. m.* (llawn) A first filling or gathering in. *Cylch rhaglawn, cylch rhaglawd,* the circuit of first fruits, certain dues anciently paid by tenants to their lords.

Rhaglef, *s. m.* (llef) A proclamation.

Rhaglefain, *v. a.* (rhaglef) To proclaim.

Rhaglewych, *s. m.* (llewych) Illumination before.

Rhaglewychiad, *s. m.* (rhaglewych) A lighting first

Rhaglewychu, *v.* (rhaglewych) To illume before.

Rhaglith, *s. m.—pl. t.* oedd (llith) A preface.

Rhaglithiad, *s. m.—pl. t.* au (rhaglith) A making an introductory discourse.

Rhaglithiaw, *v. a.* (rhaglith) To preface.

Rhaglithiawl, *a.* (rhaglith) Prefatory, introductory

Rhaglithiwr, *s. m.—pl.* rhaglithwyr (rhaglith—gwr) One who makes a preface.

Rhaglofydd, *s. m.* (rhaglaw) A vicegerent.

Rhaglun, *s. m.—pl. t.* iau (llun) A prior form.

Rhagluniad, *s. m.* (rhaglun) A preforming.

Rhagluniaeth, *s. m.—pl. t.* au (rhaglun) The act of forming beforehand; providence.

Rhagluniaethawl, *a.* (rhagluniaeth) Providential.

Rhagluniaethu, *v. a.* (rhagluniaeth) To carry on the dispensation of providence.

Rhagluniaethus, *a.* (rhagluniaeth) Providential.

Rhagluniaw, *v. a.* (rhaglun) To preform; to forecast, to foresee, to provide.

> Sawl a ragluniodd ef, y rhai hyny hefyd a alwodd.
>
> Such as *he has formed before*, those also he has called.
>
> *W. Salisbury.*

Rhagluniawl, *a.* (rhaglun) Tending to form beforehand.

Rhagluniedig, *a.* (rhaglun) Performed.

Rhaglwgr, *s. m.* (llwgr) A prior corruption.

Rhaglwybr, *s. m.—pl. t.* au (llwybr) A previous path; a path in front.

Rhaglwybraw, *v. a.* (rhaglwybr) To open a path before; to clear the way in front.

Rhaglwybrawl, *a.* (rhaglwybr) Tending to open a path before.

Rhaglyd, *s. m.* (llyd) Providence, forecast.

Rhaglydaw, *v. a.* (rhaglyd) To use forecast.

Rhaglydawl, *a.* (rhaglyd) Providential.

Rhaglyfn, *a.* (llyfn) Previously smooth.

Rhaglyfnawl, *a.* (rhaglyfn) Tending to make smooth beforehand.

Rhaglyfniad, *s. m.* (rhaglyfn) A previously making smooth.

Rhaglyfnu, *v. a.* (rhaglyfn) To smooth before.

> Gwelai rhagluniaeth Duw yn dda raglyfnu peth ar y byd, drwy athrawiaeth y Groegiaid.
>
> The divine providence saw it good *previously to smooth* the word a little, through the knowledge of the Greeks.
>
> *C. Edwards, H. y Ffydd.*

Rhaglygrawl, *a.* (rhaglwgr) Tending to corrupt beforehand.

Rhaglygriad, *s. m.* (rhaglwgr) A previously corrupting.

Rhaglygru, *v. a.* (rhaglwgr) To first corrupt.

Rhaglym, *a.* (llym) Sharp before; sharp-pointed.

> Cynon lary fron—rhaglym ei waewawr.
>
> Cynon of humane breast, *sharp in front* the pushing of his spear.
>
> *Aneurin.*

Rhaglymiad, *s. m.* (rhaglym) A sharpening before; acumination.

Rhaglymu, *v. a.* (rhaglym) To sharpen before; to make sharp-pointed.

Rhaglys, *s. m.—pl. t.* oedd (llys) An inferior court; the court of a comot, a court leet.

Rhaglyw, *s. m.—pl. t.* iau (llyw) A deputy governor.

Rhaglywiad, *s. m.—pl.* raglywiaid (rhaglyw) One who governs as a deputy.

> Gosodwn fod—rhaglywiaid cymydau dros Gymmru.
>
> We appoint that there be *deputy constables* of comots over Wales.
>
> *Gosod. Rhuddlan.*

Rhaglywiaeth, *s. m.—pl. t.* au (rhaglyw) A deputy governor, a vice presidency, a prefecture.

Rhaglywiaethawl, *a.* (rhaglywiaeth) Belonging to the office of a deputy or lieutenant.

Rhaglywiaethu, *v. a.* (rhaglywiaeth) To perform the function of a deputy governor.

Rhaglywiaw, *v. a.* (rhaglyw) To rule as a deputy.

Rhaglywiawd, *s. m.* (rhaglyw) The function of a deputy governor.

Rhaglywiawdr, *s. m.—pl.* rhaglywiodron (rhaglywiawd) A deputy governor.

Rhagllaw, *adv.* (llaw) Henceforth, in future.

Rhagnaid, *s. f.* (naid) A leap before.

Rhagnawdd, *s. m.* (nawdd) A refuge or protection before; a preservative.

Rhagnedd, *s. m.* (nedd) A station before.

> Gwelir lafar lain—
> A llu rhagnedd
> Yn rhagyrwedd,
> Yn nydd gwnedd
> Yn nghywryssedd.
>
> There will be seen the noisy blade, and a host in an *opposing station* threatening, in the day of struggle in conflict. *Aneurin.*

Rhagnerthawl, *a.* (rhagnerth) Tending to strengthen beforehand.

Rhagnerthiad, *s. m.* (rhagnerth) A previously strengthening.

Rhagnerthu, *v. a.* (rhagnerth) To strengthen beforehand.

Rhagneuadd, *s. f.* (neuadd) A hall of entrance.

Rhagnod, *s. m.—pl. t.* au (nod) A mark before.

Rhagnodawl, *a.* (rhagnod) Marking before.

Rhagnodi, *v. a.* (rhagnod) To mark before.

Rhagnodiad, *s. m.* (rhagnod) A marking before.

Rhagnoddawl, *a.* (rhagnawdd) First protecting.

Rhagnoddi, *v. a.* (rhagnawdd) To protect before.

Rhagnoddiad, *s. m.* (rhagnawdd) A protecting beforehand.

Rhagnoeth, *a.* (noeth) Naked before.

Rhagnoethi, *v. a.* (rhagnoeth) To make naked before: to expose the front.

Rhagnoethiad, *s. m.* (rhagnoeth) A making naked before; an exposing of the front.

Rhagnyth, *s. m.—pl. t.* od (nyth) A prepared nest.

Rhagnythawl, *a.* (rhagnyth) Tending to nestle.

Rhagnythiad, *s. m.* (rhagnyth) A preparing a nest.

Rhagnythu, *v. a.* (rhagnyth) To prepare a nest.

Rhagnythed iar cyn dodwy.

Let the hen prepare a nest before laying. *Adage.*

Rhagnythydd, *s. m.—pl. t.* ion (rhagnyth) One who prepares a nest.

Rhagochel, *v. a.* (gochel) To avoid previously.

Rhagocheliad, *s. m.* (rhagochel) A previously avoiding.

Rhagochelyd, *v. a* (rhagochel) To avoid previously

Rhagodawl, *a.* (rhagawd) Coming before, coming against, coming in opposition.

Rhagodfa, *s. f.—pl. t.* on (rhagawd) A place for coming against; an ambuscade.

Rhagodi, *v. a.* (rhagawd) To come before, to come against; to oppose.

Rhagodiad, *s. m.—pl. t.* au (rhagawd) A coming before, a coming against.

Rhagodli, *v. n.* (rhagawdl) To form a leading rhyme.

Rhagodliad, *s. m.* (rhagawdl) A forming a leading rhyme.

Rhagodlig, *a.* (rhagawdl) Having the quality of a leading rhyme.

Pan fo y gysain ragodlig yn ddauwynebawg, ni ellir y gynghanedd fod yn groes ddymchweledig.

When the *first rhyming* consonant has a double aspect, the consonancy cannot be a reverted transition. *Gr. Roberts*

Rhagodwr, *s. m.—pl.* rhagodwyr (rhagawd—gwr) One who comes before or against.

Rhagodydd, *s. m.—pl. t.* ion (rhagawd) One who comes before or against; an opposer.

Rhagoddef, *s. m.* (goddef) A previous suffering.

Rhagoddefawl, *a.* (rhagoddef) Previously passive.

Rhagoddefiad, *s. m.—pl. t.* au (rhagoddef) A suffering beforehand.

Rhagofal, *s. m.—pl. t.* on (gofal) Precaution.

Rhagofaliad, *s. m.—pl. t.* au (rhagofal) A taking previous care, a taking precaution.

Rhagofalu, *v. a.* (rhagofal) To take precaution.

Rhagofalus, *a.* (rhagofal) Careful beforehand.

Rhagofalwr, *s. m.—pl.* rhagofalwyr (rhagofal—gwr) One who takes previous care.

Rhagofyn, *s. m.—pl. t.* ion (gofyn) A pre requisite; an adjunct requisite.

Tair swydd llys: canghellawr, canllaw, neu blaidwr, a rhingyll; sef rhagofynion llys eu gelwir, can y gellir llys hebddynt.

The three adjunct offices of a court: a chancellor, a conductor, or partisan, and an apparitor, for they are called *adjunct requisites*, as a court can be held without them. *Trioedd Dyfnwal.*

Rhagofyn, *v. a.* (gofyn) To bespeak.

Rhagofynawl, *a.* (rhagofyn) Bespeaking.

Rhagofyniad, *s. m.* (rhagofyn) A bespeaking.

Rhagolwg, *s. m.* (golwg) Prospect; foresight.

Rhagolwyn, *s. f.—pl. t.* ion (olwyn) Fore-wheel.

Rhagolygawd, *s. m.* (rhagolwg) A prospection.

Rhagolygawl, *a.* (rhagolwg) Prospective.

Rhagolygiad, *s. m.* (rhagolwg) A foreseeing.

Rhagolygu, *v. a.* (rhagolwg) To look forward.

Rhagongl, *s. f.* (ongl) A saliant angle.

Rhagonglaidd, *a.* (rhagongl) Tending to a saliant angle; of the nature of a saliant angle.

Rhagongli, *v. a.* (rhagongl) To form a saliant angle

Rhagongliad, *s. m.* (rhagongl) A forming a saliant angle.

Rhagor, *s. m.—pl. t.* au (rhag—gor) The state of being before; excellence; attribute; superiority; difference; more. *Rhagorion*, excellencies; *yn rhagor*, in a greater degree, more. *Mae rhagor mawr rhyngot ti a mi*, there is a great difference betwixt thee and me.

Tair dyben barddoniaeth; gwellâu moes a defawd; cynnal heddwch; a moli pob daionus a rhagor.

The three intentions of bardism; to improve manners and habit; to maintain peace; and to praise all the good and the excellent. *Barddas.*

> D'ofn a drig, dwfn dy ragor,
> Od ofnir mân dwfn o'r mor.

Thy dread will remain, profound thy *superiority*, if a profound part of the sea be dreaded. *Rhys Goch.*

> Ei rad——
> Archaf ar air, a chaf yr awrhon
> Er ei wir gariad, a'i ragorion,
> Ac er a wyddiad o gerydd——
> Er ei wyth allu, a'i archollion.

His grace I crave verbally, and at the present hour I shall have it, for the sake of his true love, and his *attributes*, and on account of what he has known of reproaches; for the sake of his eight energies, and his wounds. *G. ab I. ab Llywelyn Fychan.*

Rhagorawl, *a.* (rhagor) Excellent, or superior.

Rhagorbarch, *s.* (rhagor—parch) Pre-eminency.

Rhagorbryd, *s. m.* (rhagor—pryd) Superior appearance.

Rhagorbwyll, *s. m.* (pwyll) Superior discretion.

Rhagorddawn, *s. m.* (rhagor—dawn) Superior talent or endowment.

Rhagorddull, *s. f.—pl. t.* iau (rhagor—dull) A superior form.

Rhagorddwyn, *a.* (rhagor—dwyn) Bearing a superiority; excelling. *Pethau godidogion a rhagorddwyn*, eminent and superlative things.

Rhagorddysg, *s.* (rhagor—dysg) Superior learning.

Rhagoredig, *a.* (rhagor) Being made superior.

Rhagoredigaeth, *s. m.* (rhagoredig) Superiority.

Rhagoredd, *s. m.* (rhagor) Excellentness.

Rhagoresgyn, *v. a.* (goresgyn) To come upon first. *s. m.* A prior coming upon; a prior conquest.

Rhagoresgynawl, *a.* (rhagoresgyn) Belonging to prior conquest.

Rhagoresgyniad, *s. m.* (rhagoresgyn) A previously overcoming or surmounting.

Rhagorfraint, *s. m.—pl.* rhagorfreintiau (braint) A prerogative.

Rhagorgamp, *s. f.—pl. t.* au (rhagor—camp) Superior feat or exploit.

Rhagorgampus, *a.* (rhagorgamp) Pancratical.

Rhagori, *v. a.* (rhagor) To go before, to go beyond; to excel, to surpass; to cause a difference; to differ.

Rhagoriad, *s. m.* (rhagor) An excelling, a surpassing; a differing.

Rhagoriaeth, *s. m.—pl. t.* au (rhagor) A state of being beyond, or surpassing; difference.

Tri rhagoriaeth cerdd: iawn fydryddu, iawn ddyfalu, ac iawn ymddwyn.

The three *excellencies* of song: just prosody, just description, and just tendency. *Barddas.*

Rhagoriaethawl, *a.* (rhagoriaeth) Relating to excellence; differential.

Rhagoriaethu, *v. a.* (rhagoriaeth) To form a state of excellence; to make a difference.

Rhagoriannawl, *a.* (rhagoriant) Surpassing, superlative; differential.

Rhagoriannu, *v. a.* (rhagoriant) To render superlative; to create a difference.

Rhagoriant, *s. m.* (rhagor) Excellence; difference

> Pob peth anweledig, megys angel, a folir herwydd yr ansawdd, ac y rhagoriant y sydd arno.
>
> Every thing invisible, as an angel, is praised according to the nature, and *excellence* appertaining to it. *Barddas.*

Rhagoriawd, *s. m.* (rhagor) The act or state of excelling; a difference.

Rhagoriawdr, *s. m.* (rhagoriawd) One who excels.

Rhagorineb, *s. m.* (rhagor) Excellency, superiority; preference; difference.

Rhagoroldeb, *s. m.* (rhagorawl) Preference.

Rhagorolrwydd, *s. m.* (rhagorawl) Excellentness.

Rhagosawd, *v. a.* (gosawd) To set previously; to set before, to prefix.

Rhagosodawl, *a.* (rhagosawd) Prepositive.

Rhagosodedig, *a.* (rhagosawd) Being set before; fore-appointed, pre-established; prefixed.

Rhagosodedigaeth, *s. f.—pl. t.* au (rhagosodedig) Pre-establishment, pre-ordinance.

Rhagosodedigawl, *a.* (rhagosodedig) Prepositive.

Rhagosodiad, *s. m.* (rhagosawd) A setting before.

Rhagosodwr, *s. m.—pl.* rhagosodwyr (rhagosawd gwr) One who sets before.

Rhagraith, *s. f.—pl.* rhagreithiau (rhaith) A previous adjustment; a prejudication.

Rhagran, *s. f.—pl. t.* au (rhan) A prior share.

Rhagranawl, *a.* (rhagran) Of a prior sharing.

Rhagraniad, *s. m.* (rhagran) A previously sharing.

Rhagranu, *v. a.* (rhagran) To share previously.

Rhagre, *s. f.* (rhe) A first setting off, a preamble.

Rhagred, *s. f.—pl. t.* ion (rhed) A prior course.

Rhagredawl, *a.* (rhagred) Forerunning, antecedent, procatarctic.

Rhagredeg, *v. a.* (rhagred) To forerun.

Rhagrediad, *s. m.* (rhagred) A forerunning.

Rhagredwr, *s. m.—pl.* rhagredwyr (rhagred—gwr) A precursor, a forerunner, a harbinger.

Rhagreithiad, *s. m.* (rhagraith) A previously rectifying; consideration.

Rhagreithiannawl, *a.* (rhagreithiant) Tending to previous rectitude; deliberative.

Rhagreithiannu, *v. a.* (rhagreithiant) To make a previous adjustment.

Rhagreithiant, *s. m.* (rhagraith) Previous adjustment; deliberation.

Rhagreithiaw, *v. a.* (rhagraith) To adjust beforehand; to consider.

> Rhagreithia dy air cyn noi ddodi.
>
> *Consider* thy word before it is given. *Adage.*
>
> Gwedy darffo i yr henuriaid ragreithiaw eu synwyr, a chadarnau ei doll trwy dwng, yna y dylyant y brawdwyr, fyned ar neillto, a barnu herwydd yr henuriaid.
>
> When the elders shall have finished *considering* their sentiment, and supported its form by oath, then the judges ought to go aside, and pass sentence according to the elders. *Welsh Laws.*

Rhagreithiawl, *a.* (rhagraith) Previously rectified.

Rhagreithiedig, *a.* (rhagreithiad) Previously rectified; considered, deliberated.

Rhagreithiwr, *s. m.—pl* rhagreithwyr (rhagraith—gwr) One who rectifies before-hand.

Rhagreithus, *a.* (rhagraith) Considerate.

Rhagrif, *s. m.—pl. t.* ion (rhif) A prior number.

Rhagrifaw, *v. a.* (rhagrif) To reckon beforehand.

Rhagrifawl, *a.* (rhagrif) Of previous numbering.

Rhagrifiad, *s. m.* rhagrif) A reckoning before.

Rhagrith, *s. m.—pl. t.* ion (rhith) Hypocrisy.

Rhagrithiad, *s. m.* (rhagrith) A practising of hypocrisy; dissimulation.

Rhagrithiannawl, *a.* (rhagrithiant) Of an hypocritical disposition.

Rhagrithiannu, *v. a.* (rhagrithiant) To use hypocrisy; to put on appearance.

Rhagrithiannus, *a.* (rhagrithiant) Apt to practise hypocrisy or dissimulation.

Rhagrithiant, *s. m.* (rhagrith) Simulation.

Rhagrithiaw, *v. a.* (rhagrith) To use hypocrisy.

Rhagrithiawg, *a.* (rhagrith) Using hypocrisy.

Rhagrithiawl, *s.* (rhagrith) Hypocritical.

Rhagrithiwr, *s. m.—pl.* rhagrithwyr (rhagrith—gwr) A dissimulator, a hypocrite.

Rhagrithus, *a.* (rhagrith) Hypocritical.

Rhagrodd, *s. f.—pl. t.* ion (rhodd) A gift before.

Rhagroddedig, *a.* (rhagrodd) Being previously given.

Rhagroddi, *v. a.* (rhagrodd) To give beforehand.

Rhagroddiad, *s. m.* (rhagrodd) A giving before.

Rhagroddwr, *s. m—pl.* rhagroddwyr (rhagrodd—gwr) One who gives beforehand.

Rhagruthr, *s. m.—pl. t.* au (rhuthr) A rushing forward; a rushing to the front.

Rhagruthraw, *v. a.* (rhagruthr) To rush before.

> Gwaew onen rethren a ragruthrai:
> Rhag ofn gwir golofn gwyr a giliai.
>
> A goring ashen spear *he would rush forward*; for fear of a trusty pillar heroes would flee away.
> *Hellyn Fardd, neu Ll. Brydydd Hodnant.*

Rhagruthrawl, *a.* (rhagruthr) Rushing before.

Rhagruthriad, *s. m.* (rhagruthr) A rushing before; a rushing forward.

Rhagrwym, *s. m.* (rhwym) A previous bond or tie.

Rhagrwymaw, *v. a.* (rhagrwym) To bind before.

Rhagrwymawl, *a.* (rhagrwym) First binding.

Rhagrwymedig, *a.* (rhagrwym) Bound before.

Rhagrwymiad, *s. m.* (rhagrwym) A previously binding.

Rhagrwystr, *s. m.* (rhwystr) A previous hinderance or obstacle.

Rhagrwystraw, *v. a.* (rhagrwystr) To preclude.

Rhagrwystrawl, *a.* (rhagrwystr) Previously hindering; precluding.

Rhagrwystriad, *s. m.* (rhagrwystr) A previously hindering or precluding.

Rhagrybudd, *s. m.* (rhybudd) Premonishment.

Rhagrybuddiad, *s. m.* (rhagrybudd) Premonition

Rhagrybuddiaw, *v. a.* (rhagrybudd) To forewarn.

Rhagrybuddiawl, *a.* (rhagrybudd) Premonitory.

Rhagrybuddiwr, *s. m.* (rhagrybudd—gwr) A premonisher, a forewarner.

Rhagsaf, *s. f.* (saf) A stand before or in front.

Rhagsail, *s. f.* (sail) A prior foundation.

Rhagsain, *s. f.—pl.* rhagseiniau (sain) A prior or leading sound.

Rhagsathr, *s. m.* (sathr) A tread before.

Rhagsathrawl, *a.* (rhagsathr) Treading before.

Rhagsathriad, *s. m.* (rhagsathr) A treading before; a treading in front.

Rhagsathru, *v. a.* (rhagsathr) To tread before.

Rhagsefydlawg, *a.* (sefydlawg) Pre-established.

Rhagsefydliad, *s. m.* (sefydliad) A fixing or establishing beforehand, a pre-establishing.

Rhagsefydlu, *v. a.* (sefydlu) To pre-establish.

Rhagsefyll, *v. a.* (sefyll) To stand before.

Rhagseiliad, *s. m.* (rhagsail) A laying a previous foundation.

Rhagseiliaw, *v. a.* (rhagsail) To lay a previous foundation.

Rhagseiniad, *s. m.* (rhagsain) A sounding before

Rhagseiniaw, *v. a.* (rhagsain) To sound before.

Rhagseiniawl, *a.* (rhagsain) Previously sounding

Rhagsen, *s. f.—pl. t.* oedd (sen) A prior reproof.

Rhagsènawl, *a.* (rhagsen) Previously reproving.

Rhagsèniad, *s. m.* (rhagsen) A first reproving.

Rhagsènu, *v. a.* (rhagsen) To reprove before.

Rhagswydd, *s. f.—pl. t.* au (swydd) A prior office; an adjunct office.

Rhagswyddiad, *s. m.* (rhagswydd) A filling a prior office; a previously officiating.

Rhagswyn, *s. f.* (swyn) Preventive charm.

Rhagswynaw, *v. a.* (rhagswyn) To charm before

Rhagswynawl, *a.* (rhagswyn) Fore-charming.

Rhagswyniad, *s. m.* (rhagswyn) A charming beforehand; a preventive charm.

Rhagsylw, *s. m.* (sylw) A previous remark.

Rhagsylwad, *s. m.* (rhagsylw) A previously remarking or noticing.

Rhagsylwi, *v. a.* (rhagsylw) To remark before.

Rhagsyll, *s. m.* (syll) A look forward or before.

Rhagsylliad, *s. m.* (rhagsyll) A looking forward.

Rhagsyllu, *v. a.* (rhagsyll) To look forward.

Rhagsyniad, *s. m.* (syniad) Pre-apprehension.

Rhagsyniawl, *a.* (syniawl) Premeditating.

Rhagsynied, *v. a.* (synied) To premeditate.

Rhagsyniedig, *a.* (rhagsyniad) Premeditated.

Rhagsyniedigaeth, *s. m.* (rhagsyniedig) The exercise of previous thought, premeditation.

Rhagsyniedigawl, *a.* (rhagsyniedig) Inducing premeditation.

Rhagsyniwr, *s. m.—pl.* rhagsyniwyr (syniwr) One who premeditates.

Rhagu, *v. a.* (rhag) To go before, to go in front; to get before; to oppose, to withstand.

Rhagus, *a.* (rhag) Tending to go before; opposing; contrary, adverse.

Rhagwahan, *s. m.* (gwahan) A leading division.

Rhagwahanawl, *a.* (rhagwahan) Belonging to a leading division.

Rhagwahaniad, *s. m.—pl. t.* au (rhagwahan) A forming a leading division.

Rhagwahannod, *s. m.—pl. t.* au (rhagwahan—nod) A leading division point, a semicolon.

Rhagwahanu, *v. a.* (rhagwahan) To form a leading division; to use a semicolon.

Rhagwan, *s. m.* (gwan) An advance or front division.

Rhagwanawl, *a.* (rhagwan) Belonging to an advanced division.

Rhagwaniad, *s. m.* (rhagwan) A forming an advanced division.

Rhagwant, *s. m.—pl. t.* au (gwant) The advanced division, a term in prosody for the accented part of the second pause of a verse, of *Unawdl union*, or the fifth syllable, concatenating with a preceding sound.

Rhagwanu, *v. a.* (rhagwan) To make a division or opening before.

> Cyfran yn rhagwan rhag byddinawr.
>
> A party *opening a forward way* before the hosts. *Aneurin.*

Rhagwas, *s. m.—pl.* rhagweision (gwas) A preceding minister; a harbinger; a deputy servant; a term used for the *article*, by some grammarians; and by others for the *adverb*.

> Gwas i ragwas' hen, gwas i was y cwn.
>
> A servant to an *underservant*, or, a servant to the servant of the dogs. *Adage.*

Rhagwasanaeth, *s. m.* (gwasanaeth) Previous servitude; a prior ministration.

Rhagwasanaethawl, *a.* (rhagwasanaeth) Previously serving; a ministring before.

Rhagwasanaethiad, *s. m.* (rhagwasanaeth) A serving beforehand.

Rhagwasanaethu, *v. a.* (rhagwasanaeth) To serve beforehand; to minister before.

Rhagwedd, *s. f.* (gwedd) A presence; a front.

> Rhagwedd rhoddid i feirdd y byd.
>
> A countenance was given to the bards of the world. *Taliesin.*
>
> Gwyr Gogledd yn nghynteddi yn eu cylchyn
> Yn mherfedd eu rhagwedd y disgynyn.
>
> The men of the North, in the portal around them, in the midst of their *place of presence* descended. *Golyddan, Arm. Prydain.*

Rhagweini, *v. a.* (gweini) To serve before.

Rhagweinydd, *s. m.—pl. t.* iaid (rhagweini) One who ministereth before.

> Tri rhagweinyddiaid doethineb: addysg ddeddfawl, arfer wastadawl, a serch awenawl.
>
> The three *precursors* of wisdom: moral instruction, an active habit, and an implanted fondness. *Catwg Ddoeth.*

Rhagwel, *s. m.* (gwel) Foresight, or prescience.

> Da nad pell rhagwel dyn.
>
> It is happy that the *prescience* of man extends not far. *Adage.*

Rhagweladwy, *a.* (rhagwel) Capable of being foreseen.

Rhagweled, *v. a.* (rhagwel) To foresee.

> Angen a rhagwelir ni ddaw byth ar ddoeth.
>
> Need that is *foreseen* will never come upon the wise. *Adage.*
>
> Yna y dywawd Arthur—Pa beth bynag ar a rhagwelir yn dda yn y blaen ygan ddoethion, pan edeler ar y gweithred hawsa y dygoddefer.
>
> Thereupon Arthur says, whatever thing shall be *foreseen* by the wise as good in the beginning, when we come into action it will be borne with greater ease. *Gr. ab Arthur.*

Rhagwelediad, *s. m.* (rhagweled) A foreseeing.

Rhagweledig, *a.* (rhagweled) Foreseen.

> Ni thebygaf fi gallu o neb o honom ni roddi cynghor gwerthforach, na chwynberh, na doethach, no'r hwn a [illegible] rhagweledig doethineb yr arglwydd Arthur.
>
> I do not think that any of us could give a more valuable advice, or more complete, or wiser than this, which the *providing* wisdom of the lord Arthur has preconcerted. *Gr. ab Arthur.*

Rhagwelediguaeth, *s. f.—pl. t.* au (rhagweledig) The act of foreseeing.

Rhagweledigaw, *v. a.* (rhagweledig) To render foreseen.

Rhagweledigrwydd, *s. m.* (rhagweledig) The state of being foreseen.

Rhagwelgar, *a.* (rhagwel) Apt to foresee.

Rhagweliad, *s. m.* (rhagwel) A foreseeing.

Rhagweliedydd, *s. m.—pl. t.* ion (rhagweliad) One who foresees.

Rhagwelwr, *s. m.—pl.* rhagwelwyr (rhagwel—gwr) One who foresees.

Rhagwerth, *s. m.* (gwerth) A prior sale.

Rhagwerthawl, *a.* (rhagwerth) Relating to a previous selling.

Rhagwerthiad, *s. m.* (rhagwerth) A selling beforehand; a previous selling.

Rhagwerthu, *v. a.* (rhagwerth) To sell beforehand.

Rhagwerthwr, *s. m.—pl.* rhagwerthwyr (rhagwerth—gwr) One who sells beforehand.

Rhagwiriad, *s. m.* (gwiriad) A previously affirming or certifying.

Rhagwiriaw, *v. a.* (gwiriaw) To certify beforehand

Rhagwiriawl, *a.* (gwiriawl) Previously certifying.

Rhagwiriwr, *s. m.—pl.* rhagwirwyr (gwiriwr) One who certifies beforehand.

Rhagwisg, *s. f.—pl. t.* oedd (gwisg) A fore-garment; a prior dress.

Rhagwisgaw, *v. a.* (rhagwisg) To dress previously

Rhagwisgiad, *s. m.* (rhagwisg) A first dressing.

Rhagwn, *s. m.* (rhag) A scarecrow.
Rhagwybod, *v. n.* (gwybod) To foreknow.
Rhagwybodadwy, *a.* (rhagwybod) Capable of being foreknown.
Rhagwybodaeth, *s. f.* (rhagwybod) Precognition.
Rhagwybodawl, *a.* (rhagwybod) Belonging to prescience.
Rhagwybodus, *a.* (rhagwybod) Prescient.
Rhagwyl, *s. f.* (gwyl) A previous watch.
Rhagwyliad, *s. m.* (rhagwyl) A fore watching.
Rhagwylied, *v. a.* (rhagwyl) To watch before.
Rhagwyliwr, *s. m.—pl.* rhagwylwyr (rhagwyl—gwr) One who watches before.
Rhagwyneb, *prep.* (gwyneb) Before, in presence. *a.* Ensuing, forthcoming, following.

Yn y flwyddyn ragwyneb y llas Tomas archesgob.
In the year *ensuing* was slain Thomas archbishop.
Caradawg o Langarfan.

Rhagwynebawl, *a.* (rhagwyneb) Tending to come forward, forthcoming.
Rhagwynebiad, *s. m.* (rhagwyneb) A coming before, a coming forward.
Rhagwynebu, *v. a.* (rhagwyneb) To come before.
Rhagwys, *s. f.—pl. t.* iau (gwys) A previous summons; a premonition, a forewarning.

Rhyddeg——
Y rhagwys o Loegrwys lin
Y rhag bron y brenin.

He brought the *forewarning* of the Loegrian race to the king's presence. *Ll. P. Moch.*

Rhagwysiad, *s. m.—pl. t.* au (rhagwys) A previously citing; a forewarning.
Rhagwysiaw, *v. a.* (rhagwys) To cite previously.
Rhagwysiawl, *a.* (rhagwys) Premonitory.
Rhagyma, *adv.* (yma) Henceforth; hence.
Rhagymadrawdd, *s. m.—pl.* rhagymadroddion (ymadrawdd) A prolegomena, a preface.
Rhagymadroddawl, *a.* (rhagymadrawdd) Prefatory
Rhagymadroddi, *v. a.* (rhagymadrawdd) To make a preface, or introduction.
Rhagymadroddwr, *s. m.—pl.* rhagymadroddwyr (rhagymadrawdd—gwr) A prefacer.
Rhagymddwyn, *s. m.* (ymddwyn) A prolepsis.
Rhagymegnïad, *s. m.* (ymegnïad) A previous exertion of one's self.
Rhagymegnïaw, *v. a.* (ymegnïaw) To exert one's self beforehand.
Rhagymegnïawl, *a.* (ymegnïawl) Previously exerting one's self.
Rhagymgadw, *v. a.* (ymgadw) To refrain previously; to keep one's self beforehand.
Rhagymgais, *s. f.* (ymgais) A previous attempt.
Rhagymgeisiad, *s. m.* (rhagymgais) A previously attempting or trying.
Rhagymgeisiaw, *v. a.* (rhagymgais) To attempt before; to exert one's self beforehand.
Rhagymgeisiawl, *a.* (rhagymgais) Previously attempting, trying or seeking.
Rhagymgodawl, *a.* (ymgodawl) Previously rising.
Rhagymgodi, *v. a.* (ymgodi) To raise one's self beforehand.
Rhagymgodiad, *s. m.* (ymgodiad) A previously raising one's self.
Rhagymgudd, *s. m.* (ymgudd) A previous hiding of one's self.
Rhagymguddiad, *s. m.* (rhagymgudd) A previously hiding one's self.
Rhagymguddiaw, *v. a.* (rhagymgudd) To hide one's self previously.
Rhagymguddiawl, *a.* (rhagymgudd) Previously hiding one's self.
Rhagymgymeryd, *v. a.* (ymgymeryd) To take one's self beforehand.
Rhagymgyrch, *s. m.* (ymgyrch) A previous resort.
Rhagymgyrchawl, *a.* (rhagymgyrch) Previously resorting mutually.
Rhagymgyrchiad, *s. m.* (rhagymgyrch) A previously resorting mutually.
Rhagymgyrchu, *v. a.* (rhagymgyrch) To resort beforehand mutually.
Rhagymladd, *v. a.* (ymladd) To fight before.
Rhagymladdawl, *a.* (rhagymladd) Fore-fighting.
Rhagymladdiad, *s. m.* (rhagymladd) A fighting before.
Rhagymlid, *v. a.* (ymlid) To pursue before.
Rhagymlidiad, *s. m.* (rhagymlid) A previously pursuing, or following.
Rhagymlidiawl, *a.* (rhagymlid) Fore-pursuing.
Rhagymorchest, *s. f.—pl. t.* ion (ymorchest) A previous exertion of one's self.
Rhagymorchestawl, *a.* (rhagymorchest) Tending to previous exertion of one's self.
Rhagymorchestiad, *s. m.* (rhagymorchest) A previously exerting of one's self.
Rhagymorchestu, *v. a.* (rhagymorchest) To exert one's self beforehand.
Rhagymrith, *s. m.* (ymrith) A previous appearance
Rhagymrithiad, *s. m.—pl. t.* au (rhagymrith) A previously appearing.
Rhagymrithiaw, *v. a.* (rhagymrith) To appear beforehand.
Rhagymrithiawl, *a.* (rhagymrith) Tending to appear beforehand.
Rhagymroddawl, *a.* (ymroddawl) Tending to become previously resigned.
Rhagymroddi, *v. a.* (ymroddi) To resign one's self beforehand, to become previously resigned.
Rhagymroddiad, *s. m.—pl. t.* au (rhoddiad) A previously resigning one's self.
Rhagymrwymaw, *v. a.* (ymrwymaw) To become bound beforehand; to fore bind one's self.
Rhagymrwymawl, *a.* (ymrwymawl) Tending to become previously bound.
Rhagymrwymiad, *s. m.* (ymrwymiad) A becoming previously bound.
Rhagyna, *adv.* (yna) Thenceforth, thenceforward.
Rhagyno, *adv.* (yno) Thenceforth, from that point of place or time forward.
Rhagynys, *s. f.—pl. t.* oedd (ynys) An adjacent or neighbouring island.

Tair rhagynys tir Gwynedd.
The three *adjacent* isles of the land of Gwynedd.
L. G. Cothi.

Rhagyrwedd, *s. f.* (gyr—gwedd) A forbidding aspect; a threatening.

A ganwyf i'm rhwyf o'm rhagwedd,
Rhagor na'm rhad, na'm rhagyrwedd —

What I may sing to my chief from my reception, more than my favour, than my *threatening*.—— *Cynddelw.*

Rhagysbys, *a.* (ysbys) Previously known.
Rhagysbysawl, *a.* (rhagysbys) Premonstrating.
Rhagysbysiad, *s. m.* (rhagysbys) A previously shewing or declaring; a premonishing.
Rhagysbysu, *v. a.* (rhagysbys) To make known beforehand; to premonish.
Rhagysgrif, *s. f.—pl. t.* ion (ysgrif) A prior writing; a prescript.
Rhagysgrifaw, *v. a.* (rhagysgrif) To write beforehand; to write for, to prescribe.
Rhagysgrifawl, *a.* (rhagysgrif) Belonging to an original writing.
Rhagysgrifen, *s. f.* (rhagysgrif) A prior writing; an original writing.

Rhagysgrifenedig, *a.* (rhagysgrifen) Being previously written.
Rhagysgrifeniad, *s. m.* (rhagysgrifen) A writing beforehand.
Rhagysgrifenu, *v. a.* (rhagysgrifen) To write beforehand.
Rhagysgrifiad, *s. m.* (rhagysgrif) A previously writing.
Rhagysgythrawl, *a.* (ysgythrawl) Fore-lopping.
Rhagysgythriad, *s. m.* (ysgythriad) A previously lopping.
Rhagysgythru, *v. a.* (ysgythru) To lop before.
Rhagystafell, *s. f.—pl. t.* oedd (ystafell) An antechamber.
Rhagystawd, *s. f.—pl.* rhagystodion (ystawd) A prior layer; a foremost layer.
Rhagystodawl, *a.* (rhagystawd) Belonging to a foremost layer.
Rhagystodi, *v. a.* (rhagystawd) To form a prior layer; to put a forward layer.
Rhagystodiad, *s. m.* (rhagystawd) A putting a previous layer; to put a foremost layer.
Rhagystum, *s. m.—pl. t.* iau (ystum) A prior bend or form.
Rhagystumiad, *s. m.* (rhagystum) A previously bending or forming.
Rhagystumiaw, *v. a.* (rhagystum) To mould into form beforehand.
Rhagystumiawl, *a.* (rhagystum) Belonging to previous formation.
Rhagystyr, *s. m.* (ystyr) A first idea; forethought.
Rhagystyriad, *s. m.* (rhagystyr) A considering beforehand, precogitation.
Rhagystyriaw, *v. a.* (rhagystyr) To precogitate.
Rhagystyriawl, *a.* (rhagystyr) Precogitating.
Rhagystyried, *v. a.* (rhagystyr) To precogitate.
Rhagystyriedig, *a.* (rhagystyriad) Being previously considered.
Rhagystyriwr, *s. m.—pl.* rhagystyriwyr (rhagystyr—gwr) One who precogitates.
Rhai, *s. pl. aggr.* (rha) Such as be separate or standing forward; a few, some. *Dyro i mi rai*, give some to me; *rhyw rai*, some ones, some persons.

> Pe caffai pawb a fynai,
> Ni byddai hiraethawg neb rhai.

If every body could obtain what he wished, not *any* would be longing. *Adage.*

> Rhan o bob addysg, rhai 'n bibyddion,
> Weithiau rhai ereill yn grythorion,
> Ereill yn delynorion wyl uchel,
> Rhai a a lle'dd ei, ereill a ddaw'.

A little of every lore, *some* being pipers, now and then *some* others being crowders, others being harpers on the high festival, *some* go where he goes, others come. *L. G. Cothi.*

Rhaiad, *s. m.—pl. t.* au (rhai) A radiation.
Rhaiadawl, *a.* (rhaiad) Radiating, radiant.
Rhaiadr, *s. m.—pl.* rheieidr (rhaiad) A spout or stream of falling water, a cataract.

> Rhed drwy'r main rheieidr mellt.

There will pervade the rocks *cataracts* of lightning. *Gr. Owain.*

> A rhaiadr o win yn nghylch rhian
> Hydyr, mywn aur a gwydr vanner gwawdau

And a *cataract* of wine surrounding chiefs of intrepidity, in the gold and glass of the exciter of eulogies. *G. ap M. ab Dafydd.*

Rhaiadrawl, *a.* (rhaiadr) Tending to spout forward as a cataract.
Rhaiadriad, *s. m.* (rhaiadr) A spouting forward as a cataract.
Rhaiadru, *v. n.* (rhaiadr) To spout out, to flow or to stream in a cataract.
Rhaiadu, *v. n.* (rhaiad) To radiate, to gleam.
Rhaib, *s. f.—pl.* rheibiau (rha—ib) A seizing or catching in the clutches, a snatch; a greediness, or voracity; a bewitching. *Rhaib yr angeu, gwanc yr angeu, newyn y pridd*; a craving appetite sometimes attending the mortal turn of a disease.
Rhaid, *s. m.—pl.* rheidiau (rha—id) An impetus; need, necessity. *Rheidion*, necessaries.

> Gosgordd Mynyddawg, enwawg yn rhaid,
> Gwerth eu gwledd o fedd fu eu heneid.

The retinue of Mynyddog, abounding with gold in necessity, the price of their feast of mead were their souls. *Aneurin.*

> Unben ni'th elwir yn nydd rhaid:
> Och, Cynddilig, na buost wraig!

A leader, thou wilt not be called in the day of trial. Oh, Cynddilig, that thou wert not a woman! *Llywarch Hen.*

> Troi rhaid yn rheswm.

To make a virtue of necessity. *Adage.*

Rhaid, *a.* (rha—id) Needful, necessary. *Rheitiach fyddai i ti gadw dy arian*, more necessary would it be for thee to keep thy money; *mae yn rhaid i hyny fod*, it is necessary for that to be.

> Tri amser celfyddyd; pan fo iawn, pan fo hardd, a phan fo raid.

The three times of an art: when it is proper, when it is well-becoming, and when it is necessary. *Barddas.*

Rhaid, *adv.* (rha—id) It is necessary. *Rhaid imi fod yno*, I must be there: *A raid i tithau?* must thou likewise? *na raid*, it is not necessary.

> Nid rhaid i ddedwydd ond ei eni.

The prudent *has no occasion* but to be born. *Adage.*

> Nid rhaid dodi cloch am fwnwgl yr ynfyd.

It is not necessary to put a bell round the neck of a fool. *Adage.*

> Nid rhaid dangos dirfod i gwn.

It is not necessary to point the mischievous to the dogs. *Adage.*

Rhaidd, *s. f.—pl.* rheiddiau (rha—idd) A ray; what is cast forward; spear. *Rhaidd ysgyrion*, a shivered lance.
Rhaien, *s. f.—pl. t.* au (rhai) A ray, the ray-fish.
Rhall, *s. f.—pl.* rhellion (rha—ll) That divides, or parts off; that is divided; a rail; a paddle-staff, a paddle. *Cad-rall*, a war fence. There is a dike of this kind, still called the *Cat Rail*, crossing the south-east of Scotland, in a north-east direction, from the borders of Northumberland to Gala Shiels in Selkirkshire.
Rhain, *s. pl. aggr.* (rha—in) Lances, spears.

> Nid ysgafael i neb ddwyn hiw mab;
> Cyd engiriach rhag gwyr rhain rhuddion.

Is it not fair prey for any one to take a halt every support each other against them with ruddy spears. *Taliesin.*

Rhain, *a.* (rha—in) Having a tendency to run forward or to pervade.
Rhaint, *s. m.* (rhain) That runs through.
Rhaith, *s. f.—pl.* rheithiau (rha—ith) That is straight forward, right, or just; that is set right; decision, verdict; right; law; a jury. *Rhaith gwlad*, the law or voice of the country.

> Rhaith gwlad yw llw deugwyr a deugaint o wyr daliawg dan y brenin.

The *jury* of a country is the oath of fifty men, of those who hold land under the king. *Welsh Laws.*

> Pen rhaith yw Duw.

God is supreme arbiter. *Br. S. Cant.*

Rhal, *s. m.—pl. t.* oedd (rha) A particular, a specific part; a characteristic. *Dyn o ral rhyfedd wyd ti*, thou art a person of an odd disposition. *Sil.*

> Hyd yr amser, yn mhob rhal,
> Y pery'r dial creulon,
> O flynyddau ar Brydain hir,
> Yw dwy a hanner haiarn.

The length of the time, in every *particular*, that the cruel vengeance shall continue, of years over Britain fraught with sounds, are exactly two and a half. *H. Wiliam o Fferm-y-Garn.*

Rhaledd, *s. m.* (rhal) Particularity; characteristic

Rhaliad, *s. m.* (rhal) A characterizing.

Rhalu, *v. a.* (rhal) To characterize; to form a trait of disposition.

Rham, *s. m.* (rha—am) A rise over, a reach over or beyond.

Rhamant, *s. f.—pl. t.* au (rham) A rising up, an extending over, a vaulting, or springing; an omen, sign, or token of future events; a figurative expression; a romance. *a.* Rising boldly.

Mae'n rhamant fy moliant mau.

My praise is *of a tendency to exalt*. *G. Ll. ab D. ab Einion.*

Gwiw iddi rhwymais gywyddau rhamant.

Excellently have I combined *highly-aspiring* odes to her. *D. ab Edmwnt.*

Rhamantu, *v. a.* (rhamant) To rise or extend over; to reach to a distance; to dive into futurity; to divine, to observe by omens; to romance; to allegorise.

(Oer f'am yw'r barug, a'r iâ,
A'r mendyll, i ramantu.

The hoar and the ice and the mantling clouds are chilling for me *to be flowery in speech*. *D. ab Gwilym.*

Rhamantawl, *a.* (rhamant) Of a soaring tendency; hyperbolical; romantic.

Rhamantedd, *s. m.* (rhamant) A state of soaring; figurative language.

Rhamantiad, *s. m.* (rhamant) A soaring; the using figurative language; a romancing.

Rhamantu, *v. a.* (rhamant) To use high-flown language; to speak in a romantic style.

Rhamantus, *a.* (rhamant) Highly soaring; romantic; hyperbolical; portentous.

Rhamantwr, *s. m.—pl.* rhamantwyr (rhamant—gwr) One who speaks in a figurative style.

Rhamiad, *s. m.* (rham) A rising over, a reaching over or beyond; a soaring.

Rhamp, *s. m.* (rham) A running or reaching out.

Rhamu, *v. a.* (rham) To rise over, to reach over or beyond; to soar, to vault.

Rhan, *s. f.—pl. t.* au (rha) A part, share, or portion; division. *O ym rhan i*, on my part; *o ran nad elli*, because thou canst not.

Drycid pob annhwyll ei ran.

Every indiscretion spoils its *part*. *Adage.*

Drycid annhwyll ei ran.

The indiscreet doth mar his *share*. *Adage.*

Rhan, *adv.* (rha) On the part of, in respect, on account of; because. *Rhan hyny, serch hyny*, in respect of that.

Rhanadwy, *a.* (rhan) Capable of being shared.

Rhanawg, *a.* (rhan) Having a share, or participating; being divided, or parted. *s. m.* One who shares, a participator.

Rhanawl, *a.* (rhan) Sharing, parting, or dividing.

Rhanc, *s. m.* (rha—anc) Desire, craving, want; appetite; voracity. *a.* Content, satisfactory.

Dywawd y cawr, da yw y gwaith; rhanc bodd yw genyf.

The giant said, the deed is good; it is *content* of mind to me. *H. Culhwch—Mabinogion.*

Rhanc fu gan bawb cenddyat gyngher Gwrtais.

Satisfactory to all of them was the advice of Gwrtais. *Brut y Breninoedd.*

A malat rhanc y grafanc grin.

With all the *greede* of the niggard hand. *D. ab Gwilym, i'r frân.*

Rhancawl, *a.* (rhanc) Craving, or wanting.

Rhancbodd, *s. m.* (rhanc—bodd) Content, satisfaction, pleasure.

O arlwyddes ddaionus, pa bynag pwy wyd, mi adolygaf i ti yn ryddyf, os gellir fod yn rhancbodd genyd, fy helpu allan o'r gors hatawg hon!

Oh, beneficent lady, whosoever thou art, I humbly intreat thee, if it can be a *pleasure* to thee, to help me out of this noxious slough! *Marchawg Crwydrad.*

Rhancboddawl, *a.* (rhancbodd) Tending to give contentment or pleasure; satisfactory.

Rhancboddiad, *s. m.* (rhancbodd) A yielding satisfaction of mind.

Rhancboddiaeth, *s. m.* (rhancbodd) Satisfaction of mind; enjoyment, pleasure.

Yr holl rancboddiaeth hyny, myfi a'i parodiaf i ti, a miloedd rhagor hefyd, eb yr arlwyddes Gwaeidder.

The whole of that *enjoyment*, I will prepare it for thee, and thousands beside likewise, said the lady Frailty. *Marchawg Crwydrad.*

Rhancboddiaw, *v. a.* (rhancbodd) To yield satisfaction of mind or contentment; to please.

Rhanciad, *s. m.* (rhanc) A craving, a wanting.

Rhancu, *v. a.* (rhanc) To crave, or to want.

Rhandir, *s. f.—pl. t.* oedd (rhan—tir) A portion of land; an inheritance; a shareland; a certain quantity of land.

Cabla dy fro dda i'n gwydd ni,
A'th randir, a thro ynddi.

Run down thy good country in our presence, and thy *inheritance*, and turn thyself therein. *L. G. Cothi.*

Pedair rhandir yn mhob gafael; pedair gafael yn mhob tref.

Four *sharelands* in every tenement: four tenements in every hamlet. *Welsh Laws.*

Rhandwy, *s. m.—pl. t.* on (rhan—twy) A dividend, a portion, or allotment.

Rhandy, *s. m.—pl. t.* au (rhan—ty) A house-room, an apartment where a guest dwells.

Rhanedig, *a.* (rhan) Shared, parted, divided.

Rhanedigaeth, *s. m.—pl. t.* au (rhanedig) Distribution, the act of sharing or dividing.

Rhanedigaethawl, *a.* (rhanedigaeth) Distributive.

Rhanedigawl, *a.* (rhanedig) Distributive.

Rhanedd, *s. m.* (rhan) The state of participating.

Ni'm gwnel heb ranedd
Moli'th drugaredd.

It will not make me without a *share*, to praise thy mercy. *Taliesin, Arwes Dydd Brawd.*

Rhangymerawl, *a.* (rhan—cymerawl) Participial.

Rhangymeriad, *s. m.—pl. t.* au (rhan—cymeriad) A participle.

Rhangymeriadawl, *a.* (rhangymeriad) Participial.

Rhangymeryd, *v. a.* (rhan—cymeryd) To take in part, to take in allotment.

Rhaniad, *s. m.—pl. t.* au (rhan) A parting, sharing, or dividing; partition, distribution.

Rhaniator, *ger.* (rhaniad) In dividing.

Rhaniedydd, *s. m.—pl. t.* ion (rhaniad) A divisor.

Rhanitor, *sup.* (rhan) To be sharing.

Rhant, *s. m.—pl. t.* au (rhan) That separates.

Rhanu, *v. a.* (rhan) To part, to share, to divide, to distribute; to fix an allowance. *Dylid rhanu arno*, he ought to be allowanced.

Na chryned llaw a rano i roddion.

May the hand not tremble that *distributes* to the needy. *Adage.*

Duw a ranodd
Nef a gafodd.

God *did dispense*, heaven he did obtain. *Adage.*

Dyn a ran da yn ei raid;
Duw a ran da i'r enaid.

Man *distributes* a benefit according to his want; God *distributes* a benefit to the soul. *Owain y Glyn.*

Rhanwr, *s. m.—pl.* rhanwyr (rhan—gwr) A sharer, a distributer, an allotter.

Lleiaf rhan rhan rhanwr.

The least share the share of a *sharer*. *Adage.*

Rhang, *s. f.* (rha—ang) An over content.

Rhangawl, *a.* (rhang) Tending to fulfil.

Rhangiad, *s. m.* (rhang) A fulfilling, a pleasing.

Rhangu, *v. a.* (rhang) To render replete; to fulfil; to satisfy, to render content.

Y cleddyf a ddarfu ei wrtaith; a'i roddi a orug Cai yn llaw Wrnach Gawr, y malpai i edrych a rangei ei fodd.

The sword was put in order; and Cai gave it into the hand of Gwrnach the Giant, as if it were to see if it would *answer* his purpose. *H. Culhwch—Mabinogion.*

Can rhangawdd bodd yr Argiwydd ei bobl dda ddiwyd.

For the will of the Lord *was fulfilled* by his good and prudent people. *D. Ddu o Hiraddug.*

Rhangus, *a.* (rhang) Tending to fulfil.

Rhangwr, *s. m.—pl.* rhangwyr (rhang—gwr) One who makes over-full; a fulfiller.

Rhasg, *s. f.* (rhy—asg) That is forcibly shaved off.

Rhasgl, *s. f.—pl. t.* au (rhasg) A slicer; a draw-knife, a tool used by carpenters.

Rhasgliad, *s. m.* (rhasgl) A slicing, a paring.

Rhasgliaw, *v. a.* (rhasgl) To cut with a slicer.

Rhasgliwr, *s. m.—pl.* rhasglwyr (rhasgl—gwr) One who slices.

Rhath, *s. m.—pl. t.* au (rha—ath) A smooth eminence, mound, or hill.

Y fedwen hardd—a ddaeth o'r rhath,
Nid oes ei bath yn bod.

The fair birch, which came from the *hill*, its like doth not exist. *Gr. Morys.*

Rhathawl, *a.* (rhath) Stripping; rubbing.

Rhathedig, *a.* (rhath) Stripped, rubbed, rasped.

Rhathell, *s. f.—pl. t.* au (rhath) A rasp.

Rhathelliad, *s. m.* (rhathell) A rasping, a grating.

Rhathellu, *v. a.* (rhathell) To rasp, to grate.

Rhathiad, *s. m.—pl. t.* au (rhath) A making bare or plain; a stripping, a rubbing off.

Rhathu, *v. a.* (rhath) To make clear, bare, plain, or smooth; to rub off, to rub; to strip; to rasp, to grate. *Rhathu plu*, to strip feathers off; *rhathu dail*, to strip off leaves; *rhathu croen*, to strip off a skin. *Sil.*

Rhathu y croen oddiar gefn a'i dyco.

To strip the skin from the back of him that bears it. *Adage.*

Rhathwr, *s. m.—pl.* rhathwyr (rhath—gwr) One who makes bare, rubs, or strips off.

Rhau, *s. f.—pl.* rheuoedd (rha) A band, a chain. *Cethern gaeth-rau*, an infernal crew confined in chains.

Rhaw, *s. f.—pl. t.* iau (rha) That collects together; a shovel. *Rhaw dywarch*, a paring shovel; *rhaw fawn*, a peat cutter.

Rhawaid, *s. f.—pl.* rhaweidiau (rhaw) A shovel-full; as much as a spade will hold.

Rhawbal, *s. f.—pl. t.* au (rhaw—pal) A kind of spade made all of one piece of wood, having the head rounded and edged with iron.

Rhawbalar, *s. f.* (rhawbal) A delving spade.

Rhawch, *s. m.* (rha—wch) That is imminent; that is extreme or urgent.

—Teyrnfeirdd, neus gwiddwch,
Perigl ew glew a glywawch,
Pair Prydain, pryd nad oedd rawch.

Royal bards, do you not know; you heard of extreme suction administered to a hero, the chief of Britain, when it was not *seasonable*. *Ll. P. Moch, m. G. ab C. ab Owain.*

Rhawd, *s. f.—pl.* rhodion (rha—wd) A way, course, or race; a rout. *Rhawd o goed*, a float or raft of trees; *rhawd o foch*, a drove of pigs.

Can orfod cymmod o'm camweddau,
Cyn wyf rawd beddrawd ymhlith beddau,
Cyn dyfod chwerw gyfnod chwedlau,
Cyn edfaut parhiant pechodau,
Duw a'm gad cariad y mewn cerrau nef,
Duw a glyw fy llef ym llug frydiau.

By obtaining reconciliation for my iniquities, ere I am resorting my earthly course amongst the graves, ere the tide of bitter tales occur, ere the return of remorse for sins, may God in his love grant me the mansions of heaven, God will hear my voice for my lukewarm thoughts. *Einion ab Gwalchmai.*

Rhawden, *s. f. dim.* (rhawd) A footstep.

Rhawdd, *s. m.* (rha—wdd) That is clear or open.

Rhawel, *s. m.* (rhaw) That is clustered.

Rhawffon, *s. f.—pl.* rhawffyn (rhaw—ffon) A shovel-handle.

Rhawg, *adv.* (yrhawg) For a long while.

Rhwydd fydd rhawg, dyledawg lan,
Ai caffo hi mewn cyffes.

At liberty *for a long while*, a meritorious good, will he be who obtains it in confession. *I. ab R. ab I. Llwyd, i Gyffes.*

Fy wyneb, am ddyn fanwallt,
Ni bydd y rhawg heb ddwr hallt.

My face, on account of the fair one with fine hair, it will not be *for a long time* without salt tears. *Bedo Brwynllys.*

Rhawiad, *s. m.—pl. t.* au (rhaw) A shovelling.

Rhawiaw, *v. a.* (rhaw) To throw with a shovel.

Rhawiwr, *s. m.* (rhaw—gwr) A shoveller.

Rhawlech, *s. f.—pl. t.* i (rhaw—llech) A slice, or shovel.

Rhawn, *s. m. aggr.* (rhy—awn) The long or coarse hair of beasts, the hair of a horse's tail. *Telyn rawn*, a harp strung with hair; *rhaff rawn*, a hair rope; *carthen rawn*, a hair cloth; *rhawn a bogel*, a line and plummet; *rhawn yr ebawl*, colt's tail, stonewort; *rhawn y gaseg*, mare's tail; *rhawn y march*, horse-tail.

Rhawnawg, *a.* (rhawn) Having long hair.

Rhawngoch, *a.* (rhawn—coch) Having red hair. *Y rhawngoch, y rhonellgoch*, the redstart.

Rhawni, *v. n.* (rhawn) To grow into long hair.

Rhawniad, *s. m.* (rhawn) A growing of long hair.

Rhawnt, *s. m.* (rhawn) Vigour, spirit, vivacity.

Yn llawen rhull, yn llawn rhawnt.

Exuberantly merry, full *of spirit*. *B. ab Gwilym.*

Rhawnyn, *s. m. dim.* (rhawn) A coarse hair.

Rhawol, *s. m.* (rhaw) A cluster, or a bunch.

Rhawr, *s. f.—pl.* rhorau (gawr) A roar, as of the sea or a cataract.

Rhawter, *s. f.* (rhawd) A multitude in motion.

Rhawtiad, *s. m.* (rhawd) A hurrying onward.

Rhawtiaw, *v. a.* (rhawd) To proceed onward in a hurrying manner; to rout.

Rhawtiawl, *a.* (rhawd) Hurrying; routing.

Rhawtiwr, *s. m.—pl.* rhawtwyr (rhawd—gwr) One who hurries forward.

Rhawth, *s. m.* (rha—wth) Greediness. *a.* Greedy.

Yr oedd efe yn bwyta yn rhawth rhag maint ei newyn.

He was eating *greedily* from the greatness of his hunger. *Buchedd Gwenfrewi.*

RHE, *s. f.* r.—*pl. t.* on: A swift motion, a run. *a.* Fleet, speedy; active.

A'm rhoddes meirch rhe,
Rhewydd a dawel,

He bestowed on me *fleet* steeds, neighing under me. *Taliesin.*

Oedd re redeint dan fordddwyd Geraint,
Garhirion.——

There were *swift* runners under the thigh of Geraint, with long shanks. *Llywarch Hen.*

Bydded re y rhuthrwn i waew.

I was *active* in thrusting a spear. *Llywarch Hen.*

Rhëad, *s. f.* (rhe) A running, a currency.

Rhëadawl, *a.* (rhead) Running, current.

Rhëadu, *v. a.* (rhëad) To cause a running.

Rhëan, *s. f.* (rhe) That runs; a streamlet.

Rhëawd, *s. f.* (rhe) The act or faculty of running.

Rhëawdr, *s. m.—pl.* rhëodron (rhëawd) That performs a race or course.

Yn oes Rhun rhëawdr dyhedd.

In the lifetime of Rhun the *runner of a course* of peace.

Rhëawl, *a.* (rhe) Running, or current.

Rheb, *s. m.* (rhe—eb) A run by, a going off.

Rhebydd, *s. m.—pl. t.* ion (rheb) That takes away or destroys; a destroyer, a desolator.

> Dyrgeiniadd gweryg gwyn Gyngrwawdr Fynydd
> Morfa Rhianedd, Maelgwn rebydd.

> The waves have about the white Cyngrwawdyr Mountain of Morva Rhianedd, the *destruction* of Maelgwn. *Gwalchmai.*

> Ni thycia rybudd, hael rebydd, rhacdaw.

> Warning is of no avail against him, the generous *spoiler.* *Llygad Gwr.*

> Gwelais rhag Owain Eingl eu haddoed,
> Ac o du Rhibyll rebydd yn ngraid.

> I saw before Owain the Angles meet their fate, and by the side of the Rhibyll the *destroyer* arrayed in fierceness. *Gwalchmai.*

Rhecawd, *s. m.—pl.* rhecodau (rheg) That is hackneyed or over-used.
Rheciad, *s. m.* (rheg) A hackneying, or abusing.
Rhecíain, *v. a.* (rheg) To make frequent use of a thing, to overwork.
Rheciaw, *v. a.* (rheg) To use much, to hackney.
Rheciwr, *s. m.* (rheg—gwr) A hackneyer.
Rhech, *s. f.—pl. t.* ion (rhy—ech) A forcible breaking out; a report; a fart.
Rhechain, *v. a.* (rhech) To make report; to fart.
Rhechawl, *a.* (rhech) Breaking wind.
Rhechdor, *s. m.—pl.* rhechdyr (rhech—tor) That forcibly breaks out or ravages.

> Trasthaf, canmolaf cannil gwyr yngwn,
> Hawdd engyn eu heryr;
> Caichdoed saith rifed syr,
> Cylch fy rhwyf yn ei rechdyr.

> I will record, I will celebrate a hundred thousand aspiring men, whose eagle freely soars; glittering walls seven times the stars outnumbering surround my chief in his *irruptions.* *Ll. P. Moch, i L. ab Iorwerth.*

> Gwrawl hawl hwyngynt hynt hirddiawg,
> A'i rechdyr, a'i wyr, wyal waredawg.

> A manly pursuit they followed through a long wrathful course; his *irruptions* with his men they were humane. *Llygad Gwr, i L. ab G. ab Madawg.*

> Rhechdyr Croesowallt cyulesant am ddraig.

> The *devastators* of Croesowallt they have hastened round the chief. *Ll. P. Moch.*

Rhechiad, *s. m.* (rhech) A breaking wind.
Rhechlyd, *a.* (rhech) Apt to be breaking wind.
Rhechwr, *s. m.—pl.* rhechwyr (rhech—gwr) One who breaks wind.
Rhed, *s. f.—pl. t.* ion (rhe—ed) A course, a race.
Rhedadwy, *a.* (rhed) Capable of running.
Rhedain, *v. a.* (rhed) To run continually.
Rhedain, *a.* (rhed) Running; fleet, swift.

> Rhedain gorwydd, rhwydd pob traeth.

> *Swift* the steed, open every strand. *Llefoed.*

Rhedant, *s. m.—pl.* rhedaint (rhed) A courser.

> Bid fean redaint.

> Be *swift* the racers. *Llywarch Hen.*

> Oedd re redaint dan forddwyd Geraint.

> There were fleet *runners* under the thigh of Geraint. *Llywarch Hen.*

Rhedator, *ger.* (rhed) In running, in coursing.
Rhedawl, *a.* (rhed) Current; running, racing. *Rhedolion*, wanderers, or strayers.
Rhedawr, *s. m.—pl.* rhedorion (rhed) A runner.
Rhededig, *a.* (rhed) Being made to run.
Rhedeg, *s. m.* (rhed) A course, a run, a race. *a.* Running.

> Nid ar redeg y mae aredig.

> Not upon the run is ploughing to be done. *Adage.*

Rhedeg, *v. a.* (rhed) To perform a course, to run; to race, to run a race.
Rhedegai, *s. c.* (rhedeg) One that runs, a racer.
Rhedegain, *v. a.* (rhedeg) To run continually.
Rhedegal, *s. m.* (rhedeg) Running matter. *Rhedegal y derw*, *rhedegawg y derw*, tree lichen.
Rhedegawd, *s. m.* (rhedeg) The act of running.
Rhedegawg, *a.* (rhedeg) Running, current. *Rhedegawg y derw*, tree lichen, or liverwort.
Rhedegdwys, *a.* (rhedeg—twys) Being led on a running pace.
Rhedegfa, *s. f.—pl.* rhedegfëydd (rhedeg) A place of running, a course. *Haul yn ei redegfa*, the sun in his course.
Rhedegfan, *s. f.* (rhedeg—man) A race-course.
Rhedegfarch, *s. m.—pl.* rhedegfeirch (rhedeg—march) A running horse.
Rhedegfrys, *a.* (rhedeg—brys) Of quick haste.
Rhedegiad, *s. m.* (rhedeg) A running, a racing.
Rhedegwr, *s. m.—pl.* rhedegwyr (rhedeg—gwr) A man who runs, a runner.
Rhedegydd, *s. m.—pl. t.* ion (rhedeg) A runner.
Rhedfa, *s. f.—pl.* rhedfëydd (rhed) A course.
Rhedfawr, *a.* (rhed) Apt to run much.

> Rhedfawr gorwyddawr ar des.

> Steeds are *apt to run about much* in hot weather. *Tysilio.*

Rhedgun, *s. m.—pl. t.* ion (rhed—cun) A wedge.
Rhediad, *s. m.* (rhed) A running; a currency.

> Dyn rhydaer yn dwyn rhediad
> Gormes ar lawes y wlad.

> An impertinent fellow taking a range of intrusion on the skirt of the country. *Rob. ab D. Llwyd, i Ringyll.*

Rhediannawl, *a.* (rhediant) Current, running.
Rhediannu, *v. a.* (rhediant) To give currency.
Rhediant, *s. m.* (rhed) A currency, a course.
Rhediedydd, *s. m.—pl. t.* ion (rhediad) A racer.
Rheditor, *sup.* (rhed) To be running.
Rhedle, *s. m.—pl. t.* oedd (rhed—lle) A place for running, a course.

> Gar llaw (wyr lle gyrae llawn,
> Rhedle y dyfroedd rhadlawn—
> Rhodiais.

> By the purple borders that were replete, the *course* of grateful waters, I did range. *Dr. S. Cent.*

Rhedwyf, *s. m.—pl. t.* au (rhed—nwyf) A smuggled commodity.
Rhedu, *v. a.* (rhed) To run, to race, to course.

> Nid a red a geiff y budd.

> It will not be him that *runs* who will get the benefit. *Adage.*

> I bant y rhed y dwfr.

> The water *will run* to the hollow. *Adage.*

Rhedus, *a.* (rhed) Apt to run about, straying.

> Calenig beirdd byd bucheddu rheduson.

> The portion of the bards of the world is the life of *wanderers.* *Cynddelw.*

Rhedusaw, *v. a.* (rhedus) To render straying; to become vagrant; to be of strolling habit.
Rhedusiad, *s. m.—pl.* rhedusiaid (rhedus) A wanderer, a strayer, or a stroller.
Rhedwas, *s. m.—pl.* rhedweision (rhed—gwas) A running-footman.
Rhedweli, *s. f.—pl. t.* on (rhed—gweli) An artery
Rhedwelïawg, *a.* (rhedweli) Having arteries.
Rhedwelïawl, *a.* (rhedweli) Arterial.
Rhedwr, *s. m.—pl.* rhedwyr (rhed—gwr) A man who runs; a runner.
Rhedydd, *s. m.—pl. t.* ion (rhed) A runner.
Rhedyn, *s. pl. aggr.* (rhed) Fern. *Rhedyn y cadnaw*, *marchredyn gwryw*, male fern; *rhedyn benyw*, female shield-fern; *rhedyn y derw*, or *llawredynen*, and *rhedyn y fagwyr*, common polypody; *rhedyn y clogwyn*, or *rhedyn y graig*, forked spleenwort; *rhedyn cyfrdwy*, osmund royal; *rhedyn eryraidd*, or *adain redyn*, brakes; *rhedyn gwib*, rough spleenwort; *rhedyn mair*,

heath shield-fern: *rhedyn gagefau*, common scaly spleenwort; *marchredyn*, wall-fern.

> Byddai well genyf fyw ar y mynydd, a bwyta gwraidd rhedyn nog ymostwng iddynt.
>
> I would rather live on the mountain, and eat the roots of *fern*, than submit to them. *Adage.*

Rhedyna, *v. a.* (rhedyn) To gather fern.
Rhedynach, *s. m. dim.* (rhedyn) Filmy leaved fern
Rhedynaidd, *a.* (rhedyn) Of the nature of fern.
Rhedynawg, *a.* (rhedyn) Abounding with fern. *s. f.* A place where fern grows.
Rhedyndir, *s. m.—pl. t.* oedd (rhedyn—tir) Fern land; or land overgrown with fern.
Rhedyneg, *s. f.* (rhedyn) A fern brake.
Rhedynen, *s. f. dim.* (rhedyn) A single fern.
Rhedyniach, *s. pl. dim.* (rhedyn) Small fern.
Rhedynllwyn, *s. m.* (rhedyn—llwyn) A fern brake

> Ydd wyf yn debyg i'w ddwyn
> I danllwyth mewn rhedynllwyn.
>
> Carrying that round me, I am like a blaze in a *fern-brake*. *I. Du y Bilwg i'r Gwn Coch.*

Rhedynos, *s. pl. dim.* (rhedyn) A fern-brake.

> Ymchwelynt ar ffo, gan ymddirgelu ac ymguddiaw yn ogofeu, a llwynau, a rhedynosydd, ac elltydd, a diffwysau, a chorsydd, a dyrysoch, a cherryg, ac yn mhob rhyw leoedd ereill.
>
> The returned on retreat, with secreting themselves and hiding themselves in caves, and groves, and *fern-brakes*, and cliffs, and storps, and bogs, and wilds, and stones, and in every other place of the kind. *Buch. G. ab Cynan.*

Rhedd, *s. m.—pl. t.* au (rhy—edd) A joint.
Rheddawl, *a.* (rhedd) Being separated or jointed.
Rheddedig, *a.* (rhedd) Being separate or jointed.
Rheddiad, *s. m.* (rhedd) A jointing; articulation.
Rheddu, *v. a.* (rhedd) To open by a joint.
Rheen, *s. m.* (rhe—en) A pervading principle; an epithet for the supreme being; the Lord.

> Awch rheddiaf wawd orawen gyffes:
> Awch rhoddes awch rheen
> Wrth awch bodd awch bod yn llawen;
> Wrth awch bryd awch braint o Feigen.
>
> To you I dedicate an oration of ingenuous confidence: To you your *Lord* has granted with contentment of mind that you should be glad; according to your desire your privilege from Meigen. *Cynddelw, Gwel. Powys.*

Rhef, *s. f.—pl. t.* au (rhe—ef) That is collected together, or thick; a bundle. *a.* Bundled; thick. *Cyfrefed ag y myno*, as thick as he pleases.

> Yn dir lladd y llafn wrth refed y trwsd.
>
> It is certain the blade will cut from the handle being *so thick*. *Adage.*

Rhefawg, *a.* (rhef) Binding or encompassing. *s. f.* That binds or contains; a binder, a bandage

> Nyddu pedair gwialen, a gwneuthur pedair rhefawg i rwymaw Oliver a wnaethynt.
>
> The twisting of four rods, and making four *bandages* to bind Oliver was what they did. *H. Car. Mag.—Mabinogion.*

Rhefawl, *a.* (rhef) Thickening, aggregating.
Rhefder, *s. m.* (rhef) Bigness about, thickness.
Rhefdra, *s. m.* (rhef) Thickness, an aggregate.
Rhefedd, *s. m.* (rhef) Thickness.
Rhefiad, *s. m.—pl. t.* au (rhef) A thickening.
Rhefiannawl, *a.* (rhefiant) Of a tendency to thicken in compass.
Rhefiannu, *v. a.* (rhefiant) To render thick in compass.
Rhefiannus, *a.* (rhefiant) Tending to render or to become thick round.
Rhefiant, *s. m.* (rhef) Thickness or bigness.
Rhefl, *s. m.* (rhef) That tends to grow thick.
Rheflawg, *a.* (rhefl) Being grown thick or full; blubbering.
Rheflu, *v. a.* (rhefl) To grow thick or blubbering.

Rhefr, *s. f.—pl.* rhefrau (rhef) The gut of the fundament, the anus. *Rhefr medel*, the last of a company of reapers.
Rhefrawg, *a.* (rhefr) Having a large fundament.
Rhefrawl, *a.* (rhefr) Belonging to the anus.
Rhefrrwth, *a.* (rhefr—rhwth) Loose in the anus.
Rhefrrwym, *s. m.* (rhefr—rhwym) Costiveness.
Rhefrrwymaw, *v. a.* (rhefrrwym) To render costive; to become costive.
Rhefrrwymawl, *a.* (rhefrrwym) Costive.
Rhefrrwymiad, *s. m.* (rhefrrwym) A rendering costive; a becoming costive.
Rhefrrwymus, *a.* (rhefrrwym) Being costive.
Rhefu, *v. a.* (rhef) To thicken in compass.
Rheffyn, *s. m. dim.—pl. t.* au (rheff) A small rope.
Rheffynawl, *a.* (rheffyn) Relating to cording.
Rheffyniad, *s. m.* (rheffyn) A cording, a tying with a rope.
Rheffynu, *v. a.* (rheffyn) To tie with a rope.
Rheffynwr, *s. m.—pl.* rheffynwyr (rheffyn—gwr) A corder; one who uses a rope.
Rheg, *s. f.—pl. t.* ion (rhe—eg) A sending out, or utterance; a present, a gift; a giving up, or consigning; a ban, a curse, or imprecation.

> —Caraf canu canwyd,
> Can a'm rhoddes fy rheen reg ddidawl.
>
> I love to sing of the redemption, as then my God has conferred a longed-for *gift*. *Elgnedys Bardd.*
>
> Marw fyddaf o'r clefyd hwn, a gwraig arall a fyni ditheu; a rheg dofydd ynt y gwraigedd weithon.
>
> I shall be dead of this disease, and then another wife wilt thou take; and the blessing of the Lord are the women now. *H. Cullwch—Mabinogion.*
>
> Nid adwyth rheg ni haeddor.
>
> A curse that is not deserved will do no harm. *Adage.*

Rhegadwy, *a.* (rheg) Capable of being given.
Rhegain, *v. a.* (rheg) To be sending out a murmuring noise; to mutter, to whisper.

> Ni ddaw henaint hyd-haint hwn
> I regain byth i Reged.
>
> Age oppressed with heavy infirmities will never come to Rheged to make a muttering. *Gruffydd Llwyd.*

Rhegawl, *a.* (rheg) Consigning, giving; cursing.
Rheged, *s. f.* (rheg) Liberality, or bounty.

> Dyw Iau—daliwyd yn ddiwyd
> Gwir wared, lor rheged rhwydd,
> Gwawr ewrglaer, ein gwir arglwydd.
>
> On Thursday was apprehended suddenly the true ransom, the sovereign of free bounty, a glorious light, our true Lord. *Gruffudd ab yr Ynad Coch.*

Rhegedig, *a.* (rheg) Consigned, presented, cursed.
Rhegedd, *s. m.* (rheg) The state of being given up; a cursed state.
Rhegen, *s. f. dim.—pl. t.* od (rheg) A name for some birds of a screaking note. *Rhegen yr yd*, *rhegen y rhych*, *sofliar*, the crex, dakerhen, or quail; *rhegen y dwfr*, a water-ousel.

> Ni thaw mwy no rhegen yn y rhych.
>
> He will not be silent more than the quail in the furrow. *Adage.*

Rhegi, *v. a.* (rheg) To consign, to give up; to present; to curse, to imprecate.
Rhegiad, *s. m.—pl. t.* au (rheg) A consigning, a giving up; a presenting; a cursing.
Rheglyd, *a.* (rheg) Apt to curse, cursing.
Rhegofydd, *s. m.* (rheg—ofydd) The shedder of gifts.
Rhegu, *v. a.* (rheg) To consign; to give; to present; to curse, to imprecate.
Rhegwr, *s. m.—pl.* rhegwyr (rheg—gwr) One who utters, gives, or consigns; a curser.
Rhegydd, *s. m.—pl. t.* ion (rheg) One who consigns or gives up; a presenter; a curser.

Rheiad, *s. m.—pl. t.* au (rhai) A radiating.
Rheian, *s. f.—pl. t.* au (rhai) A streak. *Rheian las*, a blue streak or weal.
Rheianawg, *a.* (rheian) Having streaks or weals.
Rheianawl, *a.* (rheian) Tending to streak.
Rheianu, *v. a.* (rheian) To streak, or to stripe.
Rheiaw, *v. a.* (rhai) To radiate; to gleam.
Rheiawg, *a.* (rhai) Abounding with radiation.

> Dyfu brenin Lloegr yn lluyddawg;
> Cyd deuth ef nid aeth yn warthegawg:
> Ni yn Eryri yn rheiawg.
>
> The king of England came with a numerous host; though he came he did not return with spoil: We were *gleaming* in Eryri. *Meilyr.*

Rheiawl, *a.* (rhai) Darting, gleaming, shooting.
Rheiawr, *s. m.* (rhai) That darts or that gleams.

> Gwaed cyrchynt, cynnullynt rheiawr,
> Yn cyson mal taran twrf aesawr.
>
> Blood they sought, the *gleamers* assembled, tumultuous like thunder the din of shields. *Aneurin.*

Rheibes, *s. f.—pl. t.* au (rhaib) A witch.
Rheibiad, *s. m.* (rhaib) An overpowering; a forcing from; a fascination, a bewitching.
Rheibiadaeth, *s. m.* (rheibiad) Witchery.
Rheibiadu, *v. a.* (rheibiad) To overcome by invincible power; to fascinate.
Rheibiadus, *a.* (rheibiad) Fascinating, bewitching
Rheibiadwy, *a.* (rheibiad) Capable of being overcome or fascinated.
Rheibiaeth, *s. m.* (rhaib) Rapacity; witchery.
Rheibiannawl, *a.* (rheibiant) Fascinating.
Rheibiannu, *v. a.* (rheibiant) To fascinate.
Rheibiannus, *a.* (rheibiant) Fascinating.
Rheibiant, *s. m.* (rhaib) A forcibly possessing; fascination; a bewitching.
Rheibiator, *ger.* (rheibiad) In fascinating.
Rheibiaw, *v. a.* (rhaib) To snatch by force; to captivate, to fascinate, to bewitch.
Rheibiawg, *a.* (rhaib) Having a power; rapacious, fascinous, bewitching.
Rheibiawl, *a.* (rhaib) Forcing, overpowering; fascinating, bewitching.
Rheibiedig, *a.* (rheibiad) Being taken by force; fascinated, bewitched.
Rheibiedigaeth, *s. m.* (rheibiedig) Fascination.
Rheibiedydd, *s. m.—pl. t.* ion (rheibiad) One who forcibly captivates, a fascinator.
Rheibioldeb, *s. m.* (rheibiawl) The state of being captivated or fascinated.
Rheibioli, *v. a.* (rheibiawl) To render fascinating.
Rheibitor, *sup.* (rhaib) To be captivating.
Rheibiwr, *s. m.—pl.* rheibwyr (rhaib—gwr) A captivator, a fascinator.
Rheibog, *s. f.* (rhaib) The power of digestion.

> A cholli rheibog aeth ei chylla'n lludw.
>
> And losing a *power of digestion* her stomach became as ashes. *Madawg Dwygraig.*

Rheibus, *a.* (rhaib) Rapacious; bewitching.

> Rheipusaf un yn holl wlad Gymmru
> Yw'r un dwdroediawg a wyr lefaru.
>
> The most *rapacious* one in the whole country of Wales is the one with two legs who is wont to harangue. *Adage.*

Rheibusaw, *v. a.* (rheibus) To become rapacious.
Rheibusrwydd, *s. m.* (rheibus) Rapaciousness.
Rheidedd, *s. m.* (rhaid) Necessity, or want.

> Torri newyn tlawd bob tro,
> A syched lle bo rheidedd.
>
> Breaking the hunger of the poor at all times, and the want of drink where *necessity* exists. *Bleddyn. S. Hywel.*

Rheidgnawd, *s. m.* (rhaid—gnawd) A natural or habitual need.

> Nid gair gau, ef gorau gwron—
> Hyd warawd rheidgnawd rheidusion.
>
> It is no false word, he is the most virtuous person, for relieving the *habitual need* of necessitous ones. *Cynddelw, i O. Gwynedd.*

Rheidiad, *s. m.* (rhaid) A necessitating.
Rheidiannawl, *a.* (rheidiant) Necessitating.
Rheidiannu, *v. a.* (rheidiant) To necessitate.
Rheidiant, *s. m.* (rhaid) Necessity, or need.
Rheidiaw, *v. a.* (rhaid) To necessitate, to need.
Rheidiawg, *a.* (rhaid) Necessitous, necessary.
Rheidiawl, *a.* (rhaid) Necessary, needful.
Rheidiolaeth, *s. m.* (rheidiawl) Necessariness.
Rheidioldeb, *s. m.* (rheidiawl) Necessariness.

> Tri chyfyctyr doethineb; rheidioldeb, moddoldeb, a buddioldeb.
>
> The three considerations of wisdom; necessity, means, and benefit. *Gobaeg Ddoeth.*

Rheidiolder, *s. m.* (rheidiawl) Necessariness.
Rheidioledd, *s. m.* (rheidiawl) Requisiteness.
Rheidioli, *v. a.* (rheidiawl) To render necessary.
Rheidiolrwydd, *s. m.* (rheidiawl) Necessariness.
Rheidrwydd, *s. m.* (rhaid) Necessity, or need.
Rheidus, *a.* (rhaid) Necessitous, needy. *Rheidusion*, needy ones, beggars.

> Gwedi dyfod Brutus hir i borth Hamwnt i dir, ef a gymerai wisg rheidus amdano, ac yn rhith anghenawl [illegible]—ac ymgymysgu â rheidusion a oedd y rhai a oeddynt yn aros [illegible] yn mhorth llys y brenin.
>
> After the coming of Brutus to the port of Hamwnt to land, he put on a *beggar garb*, and under the appearance of want he proceeded, and mixed with *necessitous ones*, the which were waiting for alms in the gate of the king's palace. *Gr. ab Arthur.*

Rheidusaidd, *a.* (rheidus) Somewhat needy.
Rheidusaw, *v. a.* (rheidus) To become necessitous.
Rheidusddyn, *s. m.—pl. t.* ion (rheidus—dyn) A necessitous person.
Rheidusedd, *s. m.* (rheidus) Neediness, poverty.
Rheidusi, *s. m.* (rheidus) Neediness, poverty.
Rheidusrwydd, *s. m.* (rheidus) Necessitousness.
Rheidusyn, *s. m. dim.* (rheidus) A pauper.
Rheidwg, *s. m.* (rhaid) A necessary thing.
Rheidwy, *s. m.—pl. t.* on (rhaid) A voyage.

> Gruffudd a esgynws ei long ac a ymchwelws o'i reidwy hyd yn Aber Menai.
>
> Gruffudd ascended his ship and returned from his *expedition* unto Aber Menai. *Buch. Gr. ab Cynan.*

Rheiddiad, *s. m.* (rhaidd) A casting rays.
Rheiddiaw, *v. a.* (rhaidd) To beam, to cast rays; to lance, or to cast a lance.

> Ar bob rhai rheiddiawl yn eur-rheddiawg.
>
> Upon all *he would beam* with golden bounty. *Meilyr.*

Rheiddiawd, *s. m.* (rhaidd) A radiation; a lancing
Rheiddiawg, *a.* (rhaidd) Having rays; pervading, apt to cast forward; bearing a lance.

> Rheiddiawg achenawg ar ffo.
>
> The necessitous on flight is violently impelled. *Adage.*

> Rheiddia a'm rhoddes Hywel
> Rheiddiawg, frisiawg, fannwg fil;
> Cefais gan dreth orddethol
> Tarw teg Talgarth yn ngwarthol.
>
> *Freely* did Hywel bestow on me a *scattering*, sleek, and spotted beast; I obtained as a choice contribution the fair bull of Talgarth to the yoke. *Cynddelw, i H. ab Ieuaf.*

Rheiddiawl, *a.* (rhaidd) Radiating; lancing.
Rheiddiawr, *s. m.* (rhaidd) That beams; lancer.
Rheiddin, *a.* (rhaidd) Tending to radiate or to dart; pervading; profuse.

> Duw Dofydd dymhyddi reiddin awen ber,
> Mal o bair Cyridwen.
>
> God the supreme ruler on me bestows the *ready* melodious muse, as if from the cauldron of Cyridwen. *Ll. P. Moch.*

Rheiddlym, *a.* (rhaidd—llym) Sharp-lanced.
Rheiddrudd, *a.* (rhaidd—rhudd) Ruddy-lanced.

Rheiddun, *s. m.* (rhaidd) One who darts or throws forward; a profuse one, one who thrusts.

> Dy hil—
> O Faelgwn Gwynedd, gwinfarth reiddun.
>
> Thy descent is from Maelgwn Gwynedd, a wine-fostered *profuse* one. *Gwalchmai.*

Rheiddus, *a.* (rhaidd) Radiating, darting; pervasive; profuse, or lavish.

Rheiddwar, *a.* (rhaidd—gwar) Mildly profuse.

Rheiddyn, *s. m. dim.* (rhaidd) A dart, or glance.

Rheiniad, *s. m.—pl.* rheiniaid (rhain) A lancing.

> Bid las lluarth; bid diwarth eiriod;
> Bid reiniad yn nghyfarth:
> Bid wraig ddrwg a mynych warth.
>
> Let the camp be green; let the peacemaker be void of reproach; be there a *spearing* in the defile; be the bad woman bearing frequent shame. *Llywarch Hen.*

Rheiniaw, *v. a.* (rhain) To use a lance, to lance.

Rheiniawg, *a.* (rhain) Having a lance, lance-bearing. *s. m.* A spear-bearer.

> Er yfais i win o gawg,
> Ef a ragwan rhag rheiniawg:
> Esgyll gwawr oedd gwaewawr Dwawg.
>
> For what of wine I from a cup have drunk, he would rush forward against the *lance-bearer*: the gleamings of the spear of Dwawg were as the wings of the morning. *Llywarch Hen.*

Rheiniawl, *a.* (rhain) Lancing, or spearing.

Rheiniwr, *s. m.—pl.* rheiniwyr (rhain—gwr) A lancier; one who bears a lance.

Rheinydd, *s. m.—pl. t.* ion (rhain) A lancier.

Rheithawr, *s. m.—pl.* rheithorion (rhaith) Rector.

Rheitheg, *s. f.* (rhaith) Canon of speech.

Rheithfawr, *a.* (rhaith) Of great rectitude. *Rheithforion*, severely just ones.

> Udden ren reithfawr, gwawr gwar.
>
> The Supreme Lord *strictly just*, light benign. *Cynddelw.*

Rheithiad, *s. m.—pl. t.* au (rhaith) The act of setting right; regulation.

> Ni ddylai fod gair yn unmhur Gymmraeg, ocf yn wrthwyneb i reithiad, ac iawnbwyll, ac anian, ac amcan.
>
> There should not be a word of impure Welsh; that is, contrary to *regulation*, and just sense, and nature, and intention. *Llywelyn o Langewydd.*

Rheithiadawl, *a.* (rheithiad) Canonical.

Rheithiadu, *v. a.* (rheithiad) To establish a principle of right; to fix a canon or rule.

Rheithiadur, *s. m.—pl. t.* on (rheithiad) A principle of regulation, a canon.

Rheithiadus, *a.* (rheithiad) Canonical, regular.

Rheithiaw, *v. a.* (rhaith) To set right, to establish as law; to appoint a jury.

Rheithiawg, *a.* (rhaith) Having an established rule, law, or canon; having a jury.

Rheithiawl, *a.* (rhaith) Established as a law.

Rheithiawr, *s. m.* (rhaith) A right principle.

Rheithioli, *v. a.* (rheithiawl) To render canonical.

Rheithioreg, *s. f.* (rheithiawr) Rhetoric.

Rheithiwr, *s. m.* (rhaith) One who sets right, one who gives effect to law; one sworn to do right; a juryman, a juror.

> Llw rheithiwr yw bod yn debycaf gantho fod yn wir yr hyn a dyngo.
>
> The oath of a *juror* implies that what he swears appears most likely to him to be true. *Welsh Laws.*

Rheithleu, *s. m.* (rhaith—lleu) The light of righteousness, the luminary of justice.

> Cyd rybwyf gan fy rhwyf, rwy gwna
> Rhwyf rheithleu rian rad gyfa;
> Rhadlawn doeth rwyf cyfoeth cuffa.
>
> Whilst I shall have been with my director, amply may the Supreme Being, the *light of justice* to princes, perform a complete act of grace, may he regard the bountiful ruler of the realm.

Rheithwraig, *s. f.—pl.* rheithwreigedd (rhaith—gwraig) A jury-woman.

Rhel, *s. m.* (rhe) That is flagging or trailing.

Rhelyw, *s. m.* (rhel) What comes after; a trail; remainder; rest, or residue.

Rhem, *s. m.* (rhe—em) That is apt to run out to extreme; that projects out.

Rhemawg, *a.* (rhem) Having a protuberance.

Rhemeinniaw, *v. a.* (rhamant) To swagger.

> Mae efe yn myned i rhemeinniaw yno.
>
> He is going there *to be swaggering*. ———

Rhemiad, *s. m.* (rhem) A running out, a swelling out; a projecting.

Rhemial, *s. m.* (rham) A confused talk; a muttering, a murmuring. *v. a.* To make a muttering noise.

> Pa rhemial, ar bob talfolwc,
> A gad o'th god gyda'th gainc?
>
> What muttering on every front form, is had from thy bag along with thy song! *Sir Dafydd Trefor.*

Rhemiala, *v. a.* (rhemial) To make a muttering.

Rhemialus, *a.* (rhemial) Muttering, babbling.

Rhemmwth, *s. m.* (rhemp) A gorbelly, a paunch.

Rhemmog, *s. f.* (rhemp) A swelling paunch.

Rhemp, *s. f.* (rhem) An extreme; an excess; that is notorious. *Mae rhemp arno*, he is under an infatuation. *a.* Bewitched, infatuated. *Mae hi yn rhemp*, she is bewitched, or notoriously bad.

> Gnawd rhemp lle bo camp.
>
> Some *eccentricity* accompanies excellence. *Adage.*

Rhempiad, *s. m.* (rhemp) A running to extreme; a rendering notorious; a becoming notorious; infatuation; a bewitching.

Rhempian, *v. a.* (rhemp) To snatch up, to devour greedily. *Ei rempian a wnant i gyd*, they will snatch it all up.

Rhempiaw, *v. a.* (rhemp) To run to an extreme; to bewitch; to be infatuated.

Rhempiwr, *s. m.—pl.* rhempwyr (rhemp—gwr) One who snatches up; a gormandizer.

Rhempus, *a.* (rhemp) Notorious; infatuated.

Rhempusrwydd, *s. m.* (rhempus) Notoriousness; the state of being infatuated.

Rhen, *s. m.* (rhe—en) A pervading principle; an influence; the Eternal.

Rhenc, *s. f.—pl. t.* iau (rheng) A row, a rank.

Rhenciad, *s. m.* (rhenc) A placing in a row.

Rhenciaw, *v. a.* (rhenc) To dispose in a row.

Rhenciedig, *a.* (rhenciad) Placed in a row.

Rhenciwr, *s. m.—pl.* rhencwyr (rhenc—gwr) One who places in a row or rank.

Rhent, *s. m.—pl. t.* i (rhen) An influx; a coming in; an income: rent.

> Nid rhent ond diwydrwydd.
>
> There is no *income* like industry. *Adage.*

> Gnawd yn Ngwent rent afeglau,
> Ac ymborth, a thorth, a thir o'r goreu.
>
> The characteristic of Gwent is the *produce* of perfumes, and meat, and a loaf, and land of the best. *Sypyn Cyfeiliog.*

> Gwr ni wyr gwaul arian;
> Ond y rhent yn dair rhan;
> Un i'w lys, a'i win o'i law,
> Wrth yr aelwyd i'w threuliaw;
> Yr ail i weiniad a rydd;
> At yr adail mae'r trydydd.
>
> A man who knows not what it is to hoard money; for the *income* is in three portions; one for his hall, where the wine circulates from his hand, at the fire-side to be enjoyed; the second to the poor be given; towards the building is the third. *Guto y Glyn.*

Rhentawl, *a.* (rhent) Yielding a produce; belonging to income; belonging to rent.

Rhentiad, *s. m.* (rhent) A producing; a yielding an income; a renting.

Rhentu, *v. a.* (rhent) To produce, to get a produce; to have an income; to rent.

Rheng, *s. f.—pl. t.* oedd (rhe—eng) A row, a rank.

> Rheng ddulas rhwng y ddwyfan.
>
> A purple *streak* between the two banks. *R. Ddu, i Alun.*

Rhengiad, *s. m.* (rheng) A placing in a row.

Rhengiaw, *v. a.* (rheng) To set in a row, or rank.

Rhengiawl, *a.* (rheng) Running in rows.

Rhengiedig, *a.* (rhengiad) Being set in a row.

Rhengiwr, *s. m.—pl.* rhengiwyr (rheng—gwr) One who places in a row.

Rheodig, *a.* (rhëawd) Persevering on a course.

> Dothyw i Ddewi, ddiffreidiad teg,
> Rhys mawr, Mon wledig, rheodig reg.
>
> There came to Dewi, of fair protection, after a great career, the Sovereign of Mon, with a *continuing* gift. *Gwyn. Brycheiniawg.*

Rheol, *s. f.—pl. t.* au (rhe—ol) Rule, or order.

> Goruchel Reen, rheol ddifrydd,
> Goleudawr argiwydd goleuad byd,
> Gorpwyf, Greawdr nef, nerth y genyd,
> Gobryd gweled gwledd yn hedd ynyd!
>
> The Most High Eternal, whose *providence* is a refuge; mighty Lord the light of the world, be there to me, Creator of heaven, strength from thee, in due time to see a feast in felicity without end! *Meilyr ab Gwalchmai.*
>
> Pawb ol-yn-ol
> Gwnaent trwy reol
> Ran wyliau,
> O nos i nos
> Fal chwant aros
> Cyfarwsau.
>
> Every body in succession would according to *rule* bear a part in vigils, from night to night, as if wishfully waiting for presents. *Madawg ab Gwallter.*

Rheolaidd, *a.* (rheol) Orderly, or regular.

Rheoledig, *a.* (rheol) Ordered, or regulated.

Rheoledigaeth, *s. f.* (rheoledig) Regulation.

Rheoleiddiad, *s. m.* (rheolaidd) A rendering regular; a becoming orderly or regular.

Rheoleiddiaw, *v. a.* (rheolaidd) To render orderly.

Rheoleiddrwydd, *s. m.* (rheolaidd) Canonicalness.

Rheoli, *v. a.* (rheol) To order, to rule, to sway.

Rheoliad, *s. m.* (rheol) An ordering, a directing.

Rheolus, *a.* (rheol) Orderly; easily ruled.

Rheolusedd, *s. m.* (rheolus) Orderliness.

Rheolusrwydd, *s. m.* (rheolus) Orderliness.

Rheolwr, *s. m.—pl.* rheolwyr (rheol—gwr) One who orders; a ruler, a conductor.

Rheonllys, *s. m.* (rhe—llys) Rhubarb.

Rhes, *s. f.—pl. t.* i (rhe—es) A row, or rank.

Rhesawl, *a.* (rhes) Belonging to a row or rank.

Rhesedig, *a.* (rhes) Being ranged or set in a row.

Rhesel, *s. m.—pl. t.* i (rhes) A rack, a grate.

Rheselawg, *a.* (rhesel) Having a rack or grate.

Rheseliad, *s. m.* (rhesel) A forming into a rack.

Rheselu, *v. a.* (rhesel) To form a rack or grate.

Rhesiad, *s. m.* (rhes) A placing in a row.

Rhesiaw, *v. a.* (rhes) To place in a row or rank.

Rhest, *s. m.* (rhes) What is set in parallel rows.

Rhestl, *s. m.—pl.* rhestlau (rhest) A rack.

Rhestog, *s. f.—pl. t.* au (rhest) Plaited mat.

Rhestr, *s. f.—pl. t.* au (rhest) Array, rank.

Rhestraidd, *a.* (rhestr) Partly ranged in rows.

Rhestrawg, *a.* (rhestr) Having rows or ranges; plaited, or matted; rowed. *s. f.* A plaited target, or buckler.

Rhestrawl, *a.* (rhestr) Ordinal; arrayed. *Rhestr-olion*, ordinal numbers.

Rhestredig, *a.* (rhestr) Ranged or arrayed.

Rhestredigaeth, *s. m.* (rhestredig) Arrangement.

Rhestriad, *s. m.* (rhestr) A ranging; a marshalling.

Rhestrig, *s. f. dim.* (rhestr) A row, or range.

> Callestrig restrig yn lle rhwystrom.
>
> A flinty *ridge* where we should be impeded. *T. Prys.*

Rhestru, *v. a.* (rhestr) To range, to marshal.

Rhestrwr, *s. m.—pl.* rhestrwyr (rhestr—gwr) A man who sets in order, a marshaller.

Rhesu, *v. a.* (rhes) To set in a row, to range.

Rheswydd, *s. pl. aggr.* (rhes—gwydd) Joists.

Rheswyddaw, *v. a.* (rheswydd) To lay joists.

Rheswydden, *s. f. dim.* (rheswydd) A joist.

Rhetgyr, *s. m.* (rhed—cyr) A projecting snout.

> Oian y parchellan, y parchell dedwydd,
> Na chladd dy retgyr yn mhen mynydd.
>
> Hark, thou pigling, thou happy pig, burrow not thy *snout* on the top of the mountain. *Myrddin.*

Rheth, *s. f.* (rhe) A pervading quality.

Rhethr, *s. f.—pl.* rhethrau (rhethr) That pervades or runs into.

Rhethrawr, *s. m.* (rhethr) That thrusts a pike.

Rhethren, *s. f. dim.* (rhethr) A pike, a lance.

> ——Dy hwyl i Brydain
> With dori brwd i'th wisg wen,
> A'th ruthr i'r maes a'th rethren,
> ——Llwyddiad!
>
> Thy course to Britain, while opening a track in thy white garb, and thy onset to the field with thy *pike*, be thou prosperous! *G. Ll. ab D. ab Einion.*

Rhëu, *v. a.* (rhe) To run about; to move.

> Eiddil hen hwyr yd re.
>
> Slender the aged, slowly he *moves along*. *Llywarch Hen.*

Rheuedd, *s. m.* (rheu) Activity, agility, speed.

> Mor yw eilon mygr maint ei rheuedd.
>
> How great the *activity* of the beauteous hinds! *Hywel ab Owain.*
>
> Dynlawl bobl ni borthant iawnedd,
> Iawn i Dduw difanw eu rheuedd.
>
> Human kind who maintain not equity, it is just for God to take away their *activity*. *Cynddelw.*

Rheueddu, *v. n.* (rheuedd) To obtain activity.

Rheueddawl, *a.* (rheuedd) Of an active nature.

Rheufawl, *a.* (rhau—mawl) Of continuous praise.

> Erglyw ddig tlawd yn gnodawl erchi
> Trugaredd i ti, fy rhi rheufawl!
>
> Hear the querulous wretch habitually craving mercy of thee, my Lord, *whose praise is universal*. *Elidr Sais.*

Rheufedd, *s. m.* (rheu—medd) Moveable property; affluence, plenty.

> Rheufedd teyrnedd ti biau i drais.
>
> The *property* of princes is thine by force. *Ll. P. Moch.*
>
> Hil Iorwerth cannerth cain wasgar rheufedd.
>
> The race of Iorwerth maintains the splendid distribution of *wealth*. *Bleddyn Fardd.*

Rheufeddawg, *a.* (rheufedd) Having abundance.

> Pan fai gyfeydd o wyr gwychawg,
> Atgoryn' deyrnedd yn rheufeddawg.
>
> If there should be an assemblage of gallant men, the leaders would return *with abundance*. *Meilyr.*

Rhew, *s. m.* (rhe) That is beyond a current state, or become fixed; ice, frost.

> Lleihau rhew, lleihau glew.
>
> As the ice is diminished, activity is diminished. *Adage.*
>
> Dybydd rhew i lyffant.
>
> There will be *frost* for the frog. *Adage.*
>
> Hawdd direwi rhew no dirywio rhyw.
>
> It is easier to unfreeze *ice* than to change the nature of a thing. *Adage.*

Rhewi, *v. a.* (rhew) To produce ice; to freeze.

Rhewiad, *s. m.* (rhew) A producing ice; a becoming ice, a freezing.

Rhewiedig, *a.* (rhewiad) Become iced; frozen.

Rhewin, *s. m.—pl. t.* iau (rhew) A sudden glide, fall, or slip; a downfal, destruction, ruin. *a.* Ruinous.

> A draig Mon, mor ddrud ei eillydd yn aer,
> Y bu terfysg taer, a haer heli;
> A rhagddo rhewys dwys dyfysgi,
> A rhewin, a thrin, a tharanc cymmri.
>
> Against the dragon of Mon, so bold his kindred in the slaughter, there was a violent tumult, and insulting claims; and before him ran dire confusion, and *ruin*, with conflict, and the end of pre-eminence. *Gwalchmai.*

Rhewiniad, *s. m.* (rhewin) A slipping, or falling down; a ruining; ruination.

Rhewiniaw, *v. a.* (rhewin) To cause to slip or to fall; to destroy; to ruin.

Py ddyrchefis mynydd cyn rhewiniaw elfydd?

Who uplifted the mountains before the elements *fell*? *Taliesin.*

A rhewiniaw Gwynedd
O'i heithaf a'i pherfedd.

And *destroy* Gwynedd from its utmost bound to its centre. *Taliesin.*

Rhewiniawd, *s. m.* (rhewin) The act of falling.

Rhewiniawg, *a.* (rhewin) Ruinous, decayed.

Rhewiniawl, *a.* (rhewin) Falling, ruinous.

Rhewintor, *sup.* (rhewin) To be falling.

Diwedd pob rhwyf rhewintor.

The end of every leader *is to be falling*. *Taliesin.*

Rhewlyd, *a.* (rhew) Freezing, or frosty.

Rhewlydrwydd, *s. m.* (rhewlyd) Frostiness.

Rhewydd, *s. m.* (rhew) Instability, fickleness; wantonness, lust. *a.* Fickle; wanton, lustful.

Gnawd gan rewydd ryclwerthin.

The *wanton* is apt to laugh much. *Adage.*

Can rewydd nid pell fydd rhin.

With *wantonness* the secret will not continue long. *Adage.*

Breuddwyd a welwn neithwyr,
Ys celfydd ei dehonglo;
Rhydraithir i rewydd;
Nis gwybydd ar nis gwelo.

A dream I happened to see last night, clever he must be who can explain it; it shall be declared to the *wanton*; it will not be known to such as do not see it. *Merlin.*

Rhewyddawl, *a.* (rhewydd) Apt to be wanton.

Rhewyddiad, *s. m.* (rhewydd) A wantoning.

Rhewyddu, *v. a.* (rhewydd) To satisfy lust.

Rhewyddu, mal anifeiliaid.

To satisfy lust, like beasts. *Gr. ab Arthur.*

Rhewyn, *s. m. dim.* (rhew) A drain, a gutter.

Rhewys, *a.* (rhew) Wanton; lusting. *Caseg rewys*, a proud mare. *Welsh Laws.*

RHI, *s. m. r.—pl. t.* au. That is an origin; a source; a sire; a chief.

Gnawd rhian eu rhadau yn wasgarawg.

Characteristic for *chiefs* that their bounties are spread abroad. *Adage.*

Dwyn fy rhwyf, a dwyn fy rhiydd;
Dwyn fy ner, fy nen cywelthydd!

Take away my prince, and take my *chiefs*, take my sovereign, my supreme supporter! *Dwinioel.*

Yr haf——
Gwnai fwyalch hygarfalch gerdd,
Y glyngoed yn llawn glan-gerdd;—
A'r coe ar ir wiail:
Rhïon prydyddion dail.

The summer would make the blackbird of lovely emulating note, and woody glade to teem with song; and on the verdant sprays the nightingales, the *chiefs* of minstrels among leaves. *D. ab Gwilym, i'r Haf.*

Rhïad, *s. m.* (rhi) An originating; a rendering as a source.

Rhiadwn, *s. m.* (rhiad) That is notable or special; that is eminent or supreme.

Rhugl yn ymwrthryn rhyn rhiadwn.

Successfully withstanding the terror of the *supreme sire*. *Aneurin.*

Rhïaidd, *a.* (rhi) Relating to a source or sire.

Rhïal, *s. f.* (rhi—al) A special or original stock, a primary race or lineage.

Un o dri chyfordd Ynys Prydain, a ddywelnid gan Gaswallawn—draw for hyd yn nhir Gell Llydaw, a hanoeddynt o rial y Cymmry.

One of the three invading armies of the Isle of Britain, which was conducted by Caswallawn over the sea to the land of the Gauls of Llydaw, was descended from the *primary stock* of the Cymmry. *Trioedd.*

Rhïallu, *s. m.—pl. t.* oedd (rhi—gallu) The power of a sovereign, army of a country; also the number of one hundred thousands.

Deg myrdd yn y rhïallu, deg rhïallu yn y fyrdd, deg mynta yn y galyrfa.

Ten myriads in the *rialiu*, ten times the rialiu in the mynta, ten times the mynta in the calyrva.

Rhïan, *s. f.—pl. t.* edd (rhi) A woman in the prime of life; a dame, a lady.

Tair gwreigedd Arthur, sef oeddynt ei dair prif rian; nid amgen, Gwenhwyfar ferch Gwryd Gwent; a Gwenhwyfar ferch Gwythyr fab Greidiawl, a Gwenhwyfar ferch Ogyrfan Gawr.

The three wives of Arthur, who were his three principal ladies, namely, Gwenhwyfar daughter of Gwryd Gwent, Gwenhwyfar daughter of Gwythyr ab Greidiol, and Gwenhwyfar daughter of Ogyrfan the Great. *Gr. ab Arthur.*

Rhianaidd, *a.* (rhïan) Feminine; lady-like.

Rhianon, *s. f.* (rhïan) A paragon of the female sex; a goddess, a mythological person.

Ei phryd a guddiwyd a phridd;
Dygn gofion rianon radd!

Her countenance has been covered with earth; severe the recollections of the *goddess* given! *Gr. Gryffydd.*

Rhiant, *s. m.—pl.* rhïaint (rhi) A parent.

Nac anmharcha yth rieni, na bugelydd allawr.

Be not irreverent to thy *parents*, nor the pastor of the altar. *Coleg Ddewi.*

Cas anmharcha rhïaint.

It is hateful to be disrespectful to parents. *Adage.*

Rhiawd, *s. m.* (rhi) The being a source or origin; parental state, the state of being eminent or chief.

Sef y caiff y pencenedl ei drwyddad yn mraint ei rhiawd.

The head of a tribe shall have his maintenance under the privilege of his *parentality*. *Trioedd Dyfnwal.*

Rhïawdr, *s. m.—pl.* rhïodron (rhïawd) Chieftain.

Rhïawl, *a.* (rhi) Belonging to a chieftain.

Rhib, *s. m.—pl. t.* ion (rhi—ib) What is thinly laid in a row or streak; a dribblet.

Rhibiad, *s. m.* (rhib) A scattering in a scanty row; a streaking; a dribbling.

Rhibiaw, *v. a.* (rhib) To place in a scanty row.

Rhibiawl, *a.* (rhib) With intermissions; dribbling.

Rhibib, *s. f.—pl. t.* au (rhi—pib) A reed pipe.

Un a chrwth——
O'r lle bai arall a'i bib,
A rhyw abwy a rhibib.

One with a fiddle, where another might be with his pipe, and some dirty chap with a *hautboy*. *L. G. Cothi.*

Rhibin, *s. m.—pl. t.* iau (rhib) A narrow row, streak, or scanty dribblet.

Rhibiniad, *s. m.* (rhibin) A throwing into a narrow row or streak; a dribbling.

Rhibiniaw, *v. a.* (rhibin) To lay in a narrow row or streak, to make a dribbling row.

Rhibiniawl, *a.* (rhibin) Running in narrow streaks.

Rhibyn, *s. m.—pl. t.* au (rhib) A row, as of hay. *Dyfed.* The same as *carfanau* and *rhencau.*

Rhic, *s. m.—pl. t.* iau (rhi—ic) A notch, a groove.

Rhiciad, *s. m.* (rhic) A notching; a grooving.

Rhician, *v. a.* (rhic) To be notching, to groove.

Rhiciaw, *v. a.* (rhic) To notch; to groove.

Rhiciawg, *a.* (rhic) Having a notch, notched.

Rhiciawl, *a.* (rhic) Notching, or grooving.

Rhiciedig, *a.* (rhiciad) Being notched, grooved.

Rhicwr, *s. m.—pl.* rhicwyr (rhic—gwr) A notcher.

Rhid, *s. m.—pl. t.* ion (rhy—id) That is secreted; that oozes, or drains; semen, sperm.

Rhidiad, *s. m.* (rhid) A secretion; an oozing; a draining; impregnation; a blissoming.

Rhidiaw, *v. a.* (rhid) To secrete; to drain; to impregnate with sperm; to blissom.

Pan fo addord ar y geifr y bychod a rhidir.

When the goats have their season the bucks *will be drained*. *Adage.*

Rhidiawg, *a.* (rhid) Abounding with secretion; having an oozing or drain; having sperm.
Rhidiawl, *a.* (rhid) Secretory; oozing, draining.
Rhidiedig, *a.* (rhidiad) Secreted; impregnated.
Rhidyll, *s. m.—pl. t.* iau (rhid) A riddle, a sieve.
Rhidylliad, *s. m.* (rhidyll) A riddling; a sifting.
Rhidylliaw, *v. a.* (rhidyll) To riddle, to sift.
Rhidys, *s. m.—pl. t.* au (rhid) A very small stream or rill; a drain.

—Rhyd oesoedd:
Wrth ridysiau meinion
Profodd megys prifaion.

For ages it will run: compared with little *rills* it has proved a primary stream. *Rice Jones.*

Rhidysiad, *s. m.* (rhidys) A flowing in a rill.
Rhidysiaw, *v. n.* (rhidys) To flow in a very small quantity; to flow as a rill; to dribble.
Rhidd, *s. m.—pl. t.* iau (rhi—idd) That is centrical; that is an obstacle; that repels.
Rhiddiad, *s. m.* (rhidd) A rendering centrical; a becoming centrical; a repelling.
Rhiddiaw, *v. a.* (rhidd) To place centrical; to repel, to drive back; to recoil.
Rhïedd, *s. m.* (rhi) Paternal governance.

Duw a'm dug, ym dogn anrhydedd,
I'w wenwlad, i'w rad, i'w riedd.

God will take me, for my complete honour, to his blest kingdom, to his grace, to his *governance*. *Cynddelw.*

Rhïeddawg, *a.* (rhïedd) Having high origin.

Elrig ei rethren rieddawg.

Splendid his *commanding* spear. *Taliesin, i Wallawg.*

Bráisg rebydd, yn rhydd, yn rhwydd nawd
Y gwna Rhys rieddawg o diawd.

The mighty ravager, freely and with good nature Rhys would make the poor one *noble*. *Cynddelw.*

Rhïeddawl, *a.* (rhïedd) A paternal authority.
Rhïeddu, *v. a.* (rhïedd) To have authority.
Rhïeingader, *s. f.* (rhïan—cader) The seat or throne of a lady or queen.
Rhïeinged, *s. f.* (rhïan—ced) A female treasure.

Gwyn ei fyd padyw Duw yd rangwy
Rhieinged.——

Blessed is he on whom God may bestow a *female treasure*. *Gwalchmai.*

Reieingerdd, *s. f.—pl. t.* i (rhïan—cerdd) A song or eulogy in praise of the fair sex.

Rhïeingerdd Efa a fawrêynt;
Tremyn y treiddwn i trefn a gedwynt.

The *female eulogy* on Eva they would extol, with a glance I could observe the order they were used to keep. *Cynddelw.*

Rhïeingylch, *s. m.—pl. t.* au (rhïan—cylch) The circuit of the female, by which vassals furnished a table for the queen, in certain cases.

Unwaith yn y flwyddyn y gwedda i bawb fyned yn lluydd i orwlad, gyda'r brenin, os myn; ac yna y frenines a ddyly rhieingylch.

Once in the year it is meet for every body to go in the army, to the borders, with the king, if he requires; and then the queen is entitled to a *female circuit*. *Welsh Laws.*

Rhieiniaidd, *a.* (rhïan) Feminine.

Rhieiniaidd fun, rhanodd fodd.

Delicate maid, she has distributed a bounty.
D. ab Gwilym, i Angharad.

Rhieiniawl, *a.* (rhïan) Feminine, abounding with female softness.

Mae Gwenhwyfar——
Yn rhieiniawl,
Yn rhagorawl
Yn nhrugaredd.

Gwenhwyvar, *of feminine softness*, in mercy doth excel. *Gronw Ddu.*

Rhieni, *s. pl. aggr.* (rhïant) Parentage; forefathers, ancestry; parents.

Rhieni dyn yw ei dad, a'i hendad, a'i orhendad.

A person's *ancestry* are his father, and his grandfather, and his great grandfather. *Welsh Laws.*

Rhieniaeth, *s. m.* (rhïeni) Parentage, ancestry.
Rhieniawl, *a.* (rhieni) Relating to ancestry.
Rhïes, *s. f.—pl. t.* au (rhi) A dame, or a lady.
Rhif, *s. m.—pl. t.* on (rhi—if) That divides, or separates; a number.
Rhifadwy, *a.* (rhif) Capable of being reckoned.
Rhifaw, *v. a.* (rhif) To number, to numerate.

Lliw ewynfriw teg rhag ton nawfed,
Nawfed ran ym poen, er pan aned,
Nis rhyborthes neb na thebyced
Ni rifaf ar fun fod yn galed.

That is of the hue of the fair spraying foam before the ninth wave, the ninth share of my pain, since she was born, no one has felt or imagined. I *will not reckon* of the damsel that she is cruel. *Cynddelw, i Eva ach Madawg.*

Rhifawl, *a.* (rhif) Numeral, or numerical.
Rhifed, *s. m.* (rhif) A number, numeration.

Rhifed syr syrthiasant yn ngrau,
O'th gynnygn, o'th gynnefodau.

Of the *number* of the stars they fell in blood, from thy conflict, from thy stratagems. *Gwalchmai.*

Rhifedi, *s. m.* (rhifed) A number.
Rhifedig, *a.* (rhifed) Numbered. *Rhifedigion*, those that are numbered.
Rhifedigaeth, *s. m.* (rhifedig) Numeration.
Rhifedydd, *s. m.—pl. t.* ion (rhifed) Numerator.
Rhifedyddawl, *a.* (rhifedydd) Numerary.
Rhifedyddiaeth, *s. m.* (rhifedydd) The science or skill of numbering.
Rhifedd, *s. m.* (rhif) Numerousness; number.
Rhifgoel, *s. f.—pl. t.* ion (rhif—coel) The property of chance belonging to numbers.
Rhifgoelydd, *s. m.—pl. t.* ion (rhifgoel) Numerist.
Rhifiad, *s. m.—pl. t.* au (rhif) A numbering.
Rhifiannawl, *a.* (rhifiant) Numerary.
Rhifiannu, *v. a.* (rhifiant) To numerate.
Rhifiant, *s. m.* (rhif) Numeration.
Rhifiawg, *a.* (rhif) Having a number; numerous.

Cadarn fab Madawg rifiawg reufedd.

The mighty son of Madawg of *multitudinous* wealth.
G. ab D. ab Tudyr.

Rhifiedydd, *s. m.—pl. t.* ion (rhifiad) Numerator.
Rhifnod, *s. c.—pl. t.* au (rhif—nod) A numeral.
Rhifnodawl, *a.* (rhifnod) Numerical.
Rhifnodi, *v. a.* (rhifnod) To numerate.
Rhifnodiad, *s. m.* (rhifnod) Numeration.
Rhifnodydd, *s. m.—pl. t.* ion (rhifnod) Numerator
Rhifrill, *s. f.* (rhif—rhill) A numerical notch.
Rhifwr, *s. m.—pl.* rhifwyr (rhif—gwr) One who numbers, a reckoner.
Rhifydd, *s. m.—pl. t.* ion (rhif) A numberer.
Rhifyddeg, *s. f.* (rhifydd) Science of numbers.
Rhifyddegawl, *a.* (rhifyddeg) Arithmetical.
Rhifyddegwr, *s. m.—pl.* rhifyddegwyr (rhifydd-eg—gwr) An arithmetician.
Rhifyddes, *s. f.—pl. t.* au (rhifydd) A female accountant, or arithmetician.
Rhifyddiaeth, *s. m.* (rhifydd) Numeration.
Rhifyn, *s. m. dim.* (rhif) A single number.
Rhiff, *s. m.—pl. t.* iau (rhi—iff) That tends to divide or to separate.
Rhifft, *s. m.* (rhiff) That is divided or cleaved.
Rhiffwnt, *s. m.* (rhi—ffwnt) The jaundice.
Rhig, *s. m.—pl. t.* au (rhi—ig) A notch; a groove, also a pillory.
Rhigaw, *v. a.* (rhig) To notch; to indent.
Rhigawd, *s. m.—pl.* rhigodau (rhig) A pillory.
Rhigawl, *a.* (rhig) Notching; indenting.
Rhigiad, *s. m.* (rhig) A notching, a grooving.
Rhigyn, *s. m. dim.* (rhig) A notch; a groove.

Rhignedd, *s. m.* (rhign) A notched or furrowed part; a notch or indenting.

> Cei wrach i grafu dy gefn, a dynai y gïau a'r gwythi gyda phob bys, o gwar dy wegil i rignedd dy din.
>
> Thou shalt have a hag to scratch thy back, who would draw the muscles and the veins with every finger, from the nape of thy neck to the *partition* of thy buttock. *Araeth Gwgan.*

Rhigodi, *v. a.* (rhig) To put in a pillory.
Rhigol, *s. m.—pl. t.* ydd (rhig—ol) A grove; a trench, a furrow; a drill; a small ditch, a drain
Rhigolawg, *a.* (rhigol) Grooved; furrowed; having a trench or drain.
Rhigoli, *v. a.* (rhigol) To groove; to trench.
Rhigoliad, *s. m.* (rhigol) A grooving; a trenching
Rhigolwr, *s. m.—pl.* rhigolwyr (rhigol—gwr) One who makes a groove or trench.
Rhigolydd, *s. m.—pl. t.* ion (rhigol) What makes a groove or trench; a groove-plane.
Rhigwm, *s. m.—pl.* rhigymau (rhig) A long rote.
Rhigymiad, *s. m.* (rhigwm) A saying by rote.
Rhigymu, *v. a.* (rhigwm) To say by rote.
Rhigymwr, *s. m.—pl.* rhigymwyr (rhigwm—gwr) One who speaks by rote.
Rhil, *s. m.* (rhi—il) An interstice.
Rhill, *s. f.—pl. t.* iau (rhi—ill) A row; a small trench or furrow; a drill.
Rhilliad, *s. m.—pl. t.* au (rhill) A drilling.
Rhilliaw, *v. a.* (rhill) To trench; to drill.
Rhilliawg, *a.* (rhill) Trenched; drilled.
Rhilliedig, *a.* (rhilliad) Being drilled.
Rhilliwr, *s. m.—pl.* rhilliwyr (rhill—gwr) One who trenches; a driller.
Rhim, *s. m.—pl. t.* iau (rhi) A rim, or edge.
Rhimiad, *s. m.—pl. t.* au (rhim) An edging.
Rhimiaw, *v. a.* (rhim) To edge, or to rim.
Rhimiawl, *a.* (rhim) Edging, or rimming.
Rhimiedig, *a.* (rhimiad) Being rimmed.
Rhimp, *s. m.—pl. t.* iau (rhim) An edge, rim, or boundary; a limit, or ending.
Rhimpyn, *s. m.* (rhimp) A close; rhyme.
Rhimpyniad, *s. m.* (rhimpyn) A terminating, or ending; a rhyming.
Rhimpynu, *v. a.* (rhimpyn) To form an ending, or termination; to rhyme.
Rhimyn, *s. m. dim.—pl. t.* au (rhim) A rim.
Rhimynawl, *a.* (rhimyn) Being formed to a rim.
Rhimyniad, *s. m.* (rhimyn) A forming an edge.
Rhimynu, *v. a.* (rhimyn) To make a rim or edge.
Rhin, *s. f.—pl. t.* iau (rhi—in) That runs through or pervades; a channel which carries off lesser waters; in draining a name for the secondary dykes, which receive the small ditches, and convey the water to the *gwyth fawr*, or great channel; a furrow between lands. *Powys.* also a pervading quality, a virtue; a secret, a mystery; a charm.

> Gochel ddammegu dy rin.
>
> Beware to allegorize thy *secret*. *Adage.*
>
> Rhin deuddyn cyfrin yw,
> Rhin tridyn cannyn ai clyw.
>
> The *secret* of two persons is a mutual pledge; the *secret* of three persons a hundred persons will hear. *Adage.*
>
> Pob math rin a doethineb
> Sydd arnad yn uwch nab neb.
>
> Every kind of *virtue* and wisdom thou dost possess above any one. *T. Prys.*
>
> Y gair deddf cyntaf sydd yn gwahardd rhiniau, a swynion, a chyfareddion.
>
> The first expression of the law doth forbid *mysteries*, and charms, and incantations *Elucidarius.*

Rhiniaw, *v. a.* (rhin) To endue with a hidden quality; to be mysterious; to use spells.

> Gwasgarawd adiad am glawdd caer,
> A minnau a ddewiniaf
> Ysgwyd bydd briw cyn tecliaf.
>
> May the torrents spread about the wall of the fort, and *I will divine* that the shield will be broken ere I recede. *Llywarch Hen.*

Rhinc, *s. f.—pl. t.* iau (rhing) A creak; a gnash; a continued sharp noise; also the quail. *Rhinc y tes, rhinc y llin*, the sand-cricket; *glo rhinc*, a sort of hard coal.

> Cane rhinc o'r cenau rhonca.
>
> The tottering whelp muttering his *clack*. *T. Aled.*

Rhinciad, *s. m.—pl. t.* au (rhinc) A creaking.
Rhinciaw, *v. a.* (rhinc) To creak; to gnash.

> Cenfigen——
> Rhinciaw y bydd, yn rhonca
> A'i chern-lasu, ar ddaint ar dda.
>
> Envy, with her lantern jaw, will be *gnashing* a [illegible] tooth on what is good. *Gr. Owain.*

Rhinciaw, *v. a.* (rhinc) To creak, to gnash.
Rhinciawl, *a.* (rhinc) Creaking; gnashing.
Rhincyn, *s. m. dim.* (rhinc) A creak, a clink; a gnash, a grinding noise; a habit of scolding. *Cadw rhincyn*, to keep scolding continually.
Rhinddysg, *s. m.* (rhin—dysg) A cabala.
Rhinddysgiad, *s. m.* (rhinddysg) A following of cabalistic learning.
Rhinddysgawd, *s. m.* (rhinddysg) Cabalistic lore.
Rhinddysgawdr, *s. m.—pl.* rhinddysgodron (rhinddysg) A cabalist.
Rhinfawr, *a.* (rhin) Endowed with great virtue.

> Cai feddygon——
> Eu galw'n ddewiniaid, trwy hyd
> Wyr rhinfawr, yn yr hen fyd.
>
> Physicians had the appellation of gods, even of consequence the *greatly endowed* men, in the ancient world. *L. Morris.*

Rhiniad, *s. m.—pl. t.* au (rhin) A pervading; an enduing with some hidden quality or virtue; a using of mystery; a charming.
Rhiniaw, *v. a.* (rhin) To pervade; to endue with a quality or virtue; to use mystery, to charm, to talk secrets, to whisper.
Rhiniawg, *a.* (rhin) Having some hidden quality, or virtue; possessed of a mystery or secret.
Rhiniawl, *a.* (rhin) Relating to a secret quality or virtue; mysterious.
Rhiniedig, *a.* (rhiniad) Rendered mysterious.
Rhiniwr, *s. m.—pl.* rhinwyr (rhin—gwr) One possessed of some hidden virtue or power; one possessed of a secret; or dealer in spells.

> Maent fal y neidr fyddar, yr hon a gae ei chlustiau, na wrando ar lais y rhinwyr.
>
> They are like the deaf adder, which shuts her ears, and will not listen to the voice of the *charmers*. *Dr. Davies.*

Rhinon, *s. m.* (rhin) A pattern of virtue.
Rhint, *s. m.—pl. t.* iau (rhin) A groove, a notch.
Rhintach, *a.* (rhint) Grooved; notched; jagged.
Rhintachrwydd, *s. m.* (rhintach) Jaggedness.
Rhinwedd, *s. f.—pl. t.* au (rhin—gwedd) A virtue; a mystery; a sacrament. *Rhinweddau da*, good qualities: *Saith rinwedd eglwys*, the seven sacraments of the church.

> Os da gwaed mewn oes deg wedd,
> Er hyny gwell yw rhinwedd.
>
> If in the splendid scene of life noble blood is prized, nevertheless *virtue* is more excellent. *Elis Rowland.*

Rhinweddawg, *a.* (rhinwedd) Having virtue.
Rhinweddawl, *a.* (rhinwedd) Being virtuous.
Rhinweddiad, *s. m.* (rhinwedd) A conferring of virtue; a becoming possessed of virtue.
Rhinweddiaeth, *s. f.* (rhinwedd) The practice of virtue; virtuous conduct.

Rhinweddoldeb, *s. m.* (rhinwedd) Virtuousness.
Rhinweddolder, *s. m.* (rhinwedd) Virtuousness.
Rhinweddoli, *v. a.* (rhinweddawl) To render virtuous; to become virtuous.
Rhinweddu, *v. a.* (rhinwedd) To endue with virtue; to acquire a virtuous habit.
Rhinweddus, *a.* (rhinwedd) Virtuous.
Rhinwedduseaw, *v. a.* (rhinweddus) To render virtuous; to become virtuous.
Rhinweddusrwydd, *s.* (rhinwedd) Virtuousness.
Rhinwraig, *s. f.—pl.* rhinwreigedd (rhin—gwraig) A woman who performs mysteries or charms.
Rhing, *s. m.* (rhi—ing) A creak, or clink.
Rhingwar, *s. m.* (rhing—gwar) A clamp.
Rhingyll, *s. m.—pl. t.* au (rhing) A citer, an apparitor, a summoner, a sergeant.

Tri enw rhingyll y sydd; gwaedd gwlad, a garw gychwedl was y cyngheilwr, a rhingyll.

The three names of an *apparitor*, the cry of a country, and the chancellor's terrible talebearer, and the *apparitor*. *Welsh Laws.*

Ieuan Fedyddiwr oedd ringyll o flaen yr Iesu.

John the Baptist was a *harbinger* before Jesus. *Elucidarius.*

Rhingyllaeth, *s. m.* (rhingyll) Serjeantship.

Gwrthodes rywyr ringyllaeth.

It rejected unseasonable *serjeantship*. *Cynddelw.*

Rhingylliad, *s. m.* (rhingyll) A performing the office of an apparitor.
Rhingyllu, *v. a.* (rhingyll) To do the duty of a serjeant or an apparitor.
Rhiolawd, *s. m.* (rhiawl) Management.
Rhiolawdr, *s. m.—pl.* rhiolodron (rhiolawd) A manager, a ruler, or a director.
Rhioledd, *s. m.* (rhiawl) Management, or sway.
Rhioli, *v. a.* (rhiawl) To manage, to rule.
Rhion, *s. m.—pl. t.* ydd (rhi) A sire.
Rhip, *s. m.—pl. t.* iau (rhib) That runs with intermission; an overskip.
Rhipai, *s. c.* (rhip) A hatchel. See *heislan.*
Rhipiad, *s. m.—pl. t.* au (rhip) An over-skipping
Rhipiaw, *v. a.* (rhip) To pass over, to skip.
Rhipiawg, *a.* (rhip) Abounding with intermissions or lapses.
Rhipiawl, *a.* (rhip) Tending to skip or pass over.
Rhipiedig, *a.* (rhipiad) Being over-skipped.
Rhipiwr, *s. m.—pl.* rhipwyr (rhip—gwr) One who passes over, or skips.
Rhis, *s. m.—pl. t.* iau (rhi—is) That tends to a point; that is broken into points; mince.
Rhisellt, *s. f.—pl. t.* i (rhis) A grater, a rasp.
Rhisg, *s. m. uggr.* (rhy—isg) Bark, or rind.

Mal y rhisg am y pren.

Like the *bark* about the tree. *Adage.*

Rhisgaw, *v. n.* (rhisg) To bark; to strip off bark.
Rhisgawg, *a.* (rhisg) Having bark or rind.
Rhisgawl, *a.* (rhisg) Belonging to the bark.
Rhisgedig, *a.* (rhisg) Barked; stripped of bark.
Rhisgen, *s. f.—pl. t.* au (rhisg) A vessel made of bark; a dish, or bowl.

Rhisgen, ffyrling a dal;—Rhisgen ymenyn tair dyrnfedd o led, a thair dyrnfedd o dewedd, heb foel.

A *bark dish*, its value is a farthing;—A *bowl of* butter is three hands in breadth, and three hands in thickness, without a top. *Welsh Laws.*

Rhisgiad, *s. m.* (rhisg) A forming of bark; a barking, or a stripping of bark.
Rhisgl, *s. m.* (rhisg) Bark, rind, or peel.
Rhisglad, *s. m.* (rhisgl) A forming of bark; a stripping of bark, a barking.
Rhisglaw, *v. n.* (rhisgl) To form bark; to bark.
Rhisglawg, *a.* (rhisgl) Having bark or rind.
Rhisgledig, *a.* (rhisgl) Barked; stripped of bark.
Rhisglan, *s. f. dim.* (rhisgl) A piece of bark.
Rhisglyn, *s. m. dim.* (rhisgl) A piece of bark.
Rhisgyn, *s. m. dim.* (rhisg) A piece of bark; a vessel of bark.
Rhisgynaid, *s. m.—pl.* rhisgyneidiau (rhisgyn) The quantity contained in a bark bowl. *Rhisgynaid o ymenyn*, a bark bowlful of batter.
Rhit, *s. m.* (rhi) A tendency or move forward.
Rhith, *s. f.—pl. t.* iau (rhi—ith) That tends to break out or to appear; an outward form, shape, or figure; appearance, guise; embryo.

Blaenu cledd athrawd a rhith gwirionedd.

To point the sword of detraction with the *semblance* of truth. *Adage.*

Yn mhob rhith y daw angeu.

In every *shape* death will come. *Adage.*

Felly, 'mhob rhith felltigedig
Gwysio y dyn a gais diawl.

Therefore, in every cursed *shape* the devil doth man entice. *T. Prys.*

Rhithedd, *s. m.* (rhith) Apparentness, semblance
Rhithgwsg, *s. m.* (rhith—cwsg) Apparent sleep.
Rhithiad, *s. m.—pl. t.* au (rhith) An appearing, a seeming; a taking a shape, or form.
Rhithiadwy, *a.* (rhithiad) Capable of appearing; capable of taking a shape or form.
Rhithiannawl, *a.* (rhithiant) Being apparent.
Rhithiannu, *v. a.* (rhithiant) To make an appearance; to take a form; to become apparent.
Rhithiant, *s. m.* (rhith) Appearance; semblance.
Rhithiator, *ger.* (rhithiad) In appearing.
Rhithiaw, *v. a.* (rhith) To tend to break out; to appear; to seem; to be formed or shaped; to become an embryo; to knit, as fruit; to change from one form to another.

Angeu——
Yn mhob cyfrith y rhithi.

Death, in every combination *thou dost appear*. *Ieuan Tew.*

Rhithiawg, *a.* (rhith) Having an appearance.
Rhithiawl, *a.* (rhith) Appearing, or seeming.
Rhithiedig, *a.* (rhithiad) Having appeared.
Rhithiogaeth, *s. m.* (rhithiawg) The state or act of appearing; a particular form.

Ail rhithiogaeth y rhyw cyntaf or droell-ymadrawdd yw gwatwar gerdd.

The second *variety* of the first species of figurative expression is irony. *H. Perri.*

Rhithiogi, *v. a.* (rhithiawg) To endue with an appearance; to have an appearance.
Rhithioli, *v. a.* (rhithiawl) To make apparent.
Rhithitor, *sup.* (rhith) To be appearing.
Rhithiwr, *s. m.—pl.* rhithwyr (rhith—gwr) An appearer, a seemer; a dissembler.
Rhiw, *s. f.—pl. t.* iau (rhi) A slope, or side of a mountain. It forms the names of many places; as *Rhiwlas*, green slope; *Rhiwfelen*, yellow slope, and the like.
RHO, *s. m. r.* That is put or extended from.
Rhöad, *s. m.* (rho) A giving, or a bestowing.
Rhöawl, *a.* (rho) Giving, or bestowing.
Rhoc, *s. m.* (rhy—oc) That shoots out in different ways; a motion in different directions.
Rhocas, *s. m.* (rhoc) A stripling, or youth.
Rhocian, *v. a.* (rhoc) To be moving in contrary directions; to rock.
Rhocos, *s. pl. dim.* (rhoc) Points, or irregularities shooting out; broken particles. *Mae y llaeth wedi suraw, oni weli di o yn rhocos?* the milk is sour, dost thou not see it broken?
Rhoch, *s. f.* (rhy—och) A broken or rough utterance; a grunt, a groan.

Rhochain, *v. a.* (rhoch) To grunt like swine.
Rhochan, *s. m.* (rhoch) A grunting; a groaning.
Rhochi, *v. a.* (rhoch) To grunt; to growl.
Rhochiad, *s. m.* (rhoch) A grunting; a groaning.
Rhochus, *a.* (rhoch) Grunting, or grumbling.
Rhod, *s. f.—pl. t.* au (rho—od) An orb, a circle; a wheel; the ecliptic; the space between the solstices; a season. *Tröad y rhod*, the turning of the circle, or the solstitial change.

> Codi rhai y caed y rhod,
> A'u gostwng o frig ystod.
>
> It was found that the *wheel* exalted some, and lowered them from the summit of the station. *Edm. Prys.*

Rhodawg, *a.* (rhod) Having a wheel; wheeled; orbed. *s. f.* That is wheeled, or orbed; an epithet for a shield; that wheels; any wheeled vehicle; a chariot.

> Boddawg ei rodawg i rodiaw torfoedd.
>
> Ready is his *chariot* to range amid armies. *Cynddelw.*
>
> Piau y rhodawg rudd faran serfle;
> A'i baerfaidd gyr ei ban,
> Pwy briw uch browys-farch can;
> Pwy ei heuw, hynod gyfrau!
>
> To whom belongs the *car* of the crimson face of the field of slaughter; and who its desolating wolf on its front, who deals wounds above the white prancing steeds; what his name, whose lot is so glorious! *Llywarch Llacty.*

Rhodawl, *a.* (rhod) Of the form of a wheel; orbical; wheeling; turning; having a tendency to turn about; vagrant, wandering.

> Ban yd ran ei rad i rodolion byd;
> Balch ei fenwyn; beilch ei faon.
>
> Conspicuously he distributes his bounty to the *wandering ones* of the world; aspiring is his mind; proud are his subjects. *Gwalchmai.*

Rhodawr, *s. f.—pl.* rhodorion (rhod) That wheels, that forms an orb; an epithet for a shield; a chariot; also the goatsucker.

> Caeawg, cynhorawg men y delai;
> Diffyn yn mlaen bun, modd y delai
> Twll tal ei rodawr, yn y clywai
> Awr, ni roddai nawdd, maint dilynai.
>
> Caeawg, supreme wherever he appears; affording protection to the maid, as the front opening of his *chariot* comes where he hears a shout, no mercy would he grant, whilst he pursued. *Aneurin.*

Rhodedd, *s. m.* (rhawd) A state of going forward.
Rhodell, *s. f.* (rhod) A whirl, a spindle; the cat's tail, or reed-mace; also called *cynffon y gath.*
Rhodellen, *s. f. dim.* (rhodell) A whirl for a spindle. It is also called *chwarwen.*
Rhodellaidd, *a.* (rhodell) Apt to whirl or whisk.
Rhodellawg, *a.* (rhodell) Having whirls or turns.
Rhodelliad, *s. m.* (rhodell) A whirling, a twirling
Rhodellu, *v. a.* (rhodell) To whirl, or to twirl.
Rhoden, *s. f. dim.* (rhawd) A switch, a whip.
Rhodfa, *s. f.—pl.* rhodfëydd (rhod) A circular course, an orbit.
Rhodiad, *s. m.—pl.* rhodiaid (rhawd) A goer up and down, a wanderer, a stroller.
Rhodiad, *s. m.—pl. t.* au (rhod) A wheeling.
Rhodiadur, *s. m.—pl. t.* on (rhodiad) A perambulator, one who walks about.

> Nid diffeithwch gwenith a luddio ffordd rhodiadur.
>
> The wheat that obstructs the way of the *perambulator* is not a wilderness. *Adage.*

Rhodian, *s. m.* (rhawd) A being traversing.
Rhodiana, *v. a.* (rhodian) To be traversing; to be going about; to walk about.
Rhodianawl, *a.* (rhodian) Ambulatory, strolling.
Rhodiar, *s. f.* (rhawd) That traverses, a ranger.

> Hyglaer arf, rwlaer rodiar byddinoedd,
> I floedd ufeliar.
>
> A glittering weapon, the vehement *ranger* through armies, a consuming fire to thousands. *Einion Lecn.*

Rhodiaw, *v. a.* (rhawd) To traverse, to ambulate, to walk about, to take a walk, to range.

> Nid da rhodio yn y gwawl,
> Lle dalo diawl y ganwyll.
>
> It is not good *to walk* in the light, where the devil holds the candle. *Adage.*
>
> Rhodd fy ngwyl, rhwydd fy ngolud;
> Rhad i'r beirdd yw rhodiaw'r byd.
>
> The gift of my festival, gratuitous is my wealth; it is free for the bards *to traverse* the world. *Llywarch Brydydd.*

Rhodiawg, *a.* (rhawd) Given to strolling.
Rhodiawl, *a.* (rhawd) Ambulatory; strolling.
Rhodiedig, *a.* (rhodiad) Being walked or strolled
Rhodiena, *v. a.* (rhodian) To walk up and down.
Rhodienad, *s. m.* (rhodian) A strolling about.
Rhodienai, *s. f.* (rhodian) A gadding gossip.
Rhodienawl, *a.* (rhodian) Ambulatory; vagrant.
Rhodienwr, *s. m.—pl.* rhodienwyr (rhodian—gwr) An ambulator; a stroller.
Rhodiwr, *s. m.—pl.* rhodiwyr (rhawd—gwr) An ambulator, one who walks about.
Rhodl, *s. f.—pl. t.* au (rhawd) A paddle; a scull:
Rhodlath, *s. f.* (rhawd—llath) A walking staff.
Rhodle, *s. m.—pl. t.* oedd (rhawd—lle) A course

> Ceint yn addfwyn rodle yn mawr rhag Urien
> Yn cwydd am ein traed gwaed ar ddifa.
>
> Briskly in the glorious *course*, before Urien with the dawn, round our feet falls the blood where death prevails. *Taliesin.*
>
> Ein rhwyddau——
> Yn rhodle gwyach gwyarllyn.
>
> Our leader in the *course* of the vulture of the blood stream. *Cynddelw.*

Rhodli, *v. a.* (rhodl) To paddle, to scull.
Rhodliad, *s. m.* (rhodl) A paddling, a sculling.
Rhodlwr, *s. m.—pl.* rhodlwyr (rhodl—gwr) A paddler.
Rhodlydd, *s. m.—pl. t.* ion (rhodl) A paddler.
Rhodol, *s. f.—pl. t.* au (rhawd) A paddle, a scull.
Rhodre, *s. f.* (rhawd—rhe) A career, a course.

> Megys ei hendad, o'i rad rodre.
>
> Like his grandfather, in his bounteous *course*. *Ll. P. Moch.*

Rhodres, *s. m.* (rhyodres) Ostentation, vainglory; a flaunting, or swaggering.
Rhodresaidd, *a.* (rhodres) Apt to be ostentatious; somewhat pragmatical; flaunting.
Rhodresawl, *a.* (rhodres) Ostentatious.
Rhodresgar, *a.* (rhodres) Pragmatical; flaunting.
Rhodresgarwch, *s. m.* (rhodres) Superciliousness
Rhodresiad, *s. m.* (rhodres) A practising of ostentation; a swaggering, a flaunting.
Rhodresolrwydd, *s. m.* (rhodres) Superciliousness
Rhodresu, *v. a.* (rhodres) To act ostentatiously; to swagger, to flaunt.

> Lle rhodreser,
> Yno neser,
> Ar eu treser,
> Y rhai trawsion.
>
> Where *a great display is made*, there be the resort, in full bustle, of froward men. *T. Prys.*

Rhodresus, *a.* (rhodres) Ostentatious, flaunting.
Rhodreswr, *s. m.—pl.* rhodreswyr (rhodres—gwr) An ostentatious man; a swaggerer.
Rhodri, *s. m.* (rhod—rhi) Raddish; also called *rhuddygl.*
Rhodwedd, *s. f.—pl. t.* i (rhod—gwedd) An orbicular course; a course.

> Ni derfydd awen i ar darwedd traul,
> Tra fo lloer a haul ar eu rhodwedd.
>
> The muse will not be exhausted from excess of use, while there shall be moon and sun on their course. *Phylip Brydydd.*

Rhodwr, *s. m.* (rhod—gwr) A wheeler.
Rhodwydd, *s. m.* (rhawd—gwydd) An open course; a centry ground.

> Ar rodwydd Forlas gwyliaf.
>
> On the *course* of Morlas I will watch. *Llywarch Hen.*

Ni thelir o wir, o wreiddrwydd hrulog,
A brwysgaw yn rhodwydd,
Rhodiw gwr briw braw dygwydd,
Yn nydd brwydr, rhag bren ei argiwydd.

From truth, from great heroism, and rushing on the war course, there shall not be paid the heriot of a wounded man, falling dreadfully in the day of battle, in the presence of his lord. *Cynddelw.*

Rhodd, *s. f.—pl. t.* ion (rho) A gift, a present. *a.* Given, gratis.

Nid edrychir yn llygad march rhodd.

The eye of a *gift* horse will not be examined. *Adage.*

Rhodd gwyr Erging.

The *gift* of the men of Erging. *Adage.*

Yn rhodd, fy athraw, beth yw gobennydd cerdd, a chymeriad, a thwyll gynghanedd?

Graciously, my master, what is the pause of a song, and repetition, and false consonancy? *T. Prys.*

Rhoddadwy, *a.* (rhodd) Capable of being given.
Rhoddai, *s. c.* (rhodd) That gives; a dative case.
Rhoddawg, *a.* (rhodd) Abound with gift; giving.

Py beris ceiniawg
O ariant rhoddawg?

Who caused coin of *current* silver? *Taliesin.*

Rhoddawg braw llaw i drengi.

The *spreader* of terror is a hand to destroy. *Taliesin.*

Rhoddawl, *a.* (rhodd) Giving, or conferring.
Rhoddedig, *a.* (rhodd) Given. *Rhoddedigion*, data.

Tri phrif roddedigion Duw: awen, deall, a rhadferthwch.

The three chief *gifts* of God; genius, understanding, and virtue. *Catwg Ddoeth.*

Rhoddedigaeth, *s. f.—pl. t.* au (rhoddedig) Donation.
Rhoddedigawl, *a.* (rhoddedig) Giving; dative.
Rhoddfawl, *a.* (rhodd—mawl) Praise-bestowing.
Rhoddfawr, *a.* (rhodd) Greatly giving; sacred.
Rhoddfyged, *a.* (rhodd—myged) Of gift.
Rhoddged, *a.* (rhodd—ced) Munificent.
Rhoddgymer, *a.* (rhodd—cymer) Gift-receiving.
Rhoddgymeriad, *s. m.* (rhoddgymer) A giving.
Rhoddgymeriawd, *a.* (cymer) Gift-reception.
Rhoddgymeriawdr, *s. m.* (rhoddgymeriawd) A receiver or accepter of gifts.
Rhoddgymeryd, *v. a.* (rhodd—cymeryd) To receive or to accept gifts.
Rhoddi, *v. a* (rhodd) To give, to bestow, to confer.

Goreu gwaredred, goredwyn ffaw,
Gobrynu gobrwy gobwyll o honaw;
Gwerth ym rhoddaist, ddyn dyniawl andaw,
A'th roddaf gyssul heb gas ynddaw;
Pan fyno Duw dy ddifuriaw
O dyllest present, a phreswyl fraw,
Ced a'th fo di goiud goleu anaw.

The best deliverance, of glorious cognizance, to purchase a reward meet of consideration; for the value thou hast bestowed on me, mortal man attend, I give the council in which no hate doth lurk. When God shall please to dissolve thee from thy present state, and dwelling of disgust, be thou possessed of the treasure of the sons of glory. *Meilyr ab Gwalchmai.*

Rhoddiad, *s. m.—pl.* rhoddiaid (rhodd) A giver, a donor; also, a giving, or bestowing.

Ef yn wyl yn olud roddiad.

He is diffidently the *bestower* of wealth. *Ll. P. Moch.*

Rhoddiannawl, *a.* (rhoddiant) Donative; giving.
Rhoddiannu, *v. a.* (rhoddiant) To make donation.
Rhoddiant, *s. m.* (rhodd) A donation, a behest.
Rhoddiedydd, *s. m.—pl. t.* ion (rhoddiad) A donor.
Rhoddwr, *s. m.—pl.* rhoddwyr (rhodd—gwr) A giver.
Rhogl, *s. m.—pl.* rhoglau (rhy—ogl) The power or sense of smelling; smell, scent.
Rhoglawg, *a.* (rhogl) Having a smell, scented.
Rhogledig, *a.* (rhogl) Being smelled; scented.
Rhogledd, *s. m.* (rhogl) The state of having a smell; scentedness.
Rhogli, *v. a.* (rhogl) To smell; to scent.

O rogli rhogla ddiniweidrwydd.

In scenting have the scent of harmlessness. *Catwg ab Gwynllior.*

Rhogliad, *s. m.* (rhogl) A smelling, a scenting.
Rhogliant, *s. m.* (rhogl) A smelling; a scenting.
Rhoglus, *a.* (rhogl) Olfactory; olidous; the stinking goose-foot.
Rhoi, *v. a.* (rho) To give, to bestow, to present.

Rhaid rhoi deall i alltud.

It is necessary *to give* information to a stranger. *Adage.*

Ni rown ai garai o groen chwanen am dy gyngor.

I would not give the thong of a flea-skin for thy advice. *Adage.*

I wan trist y rhoid win trwm;
I gadarn y rhoid godwm.

To the dejected weakling *thou wouldest give* heady wine; to the mighty *thou wouldest give* a fall. *G. ab Ieuan Hen.*

Duw, trwy dan dig anian—
I roi cadarn farn ar fyd.

He will come, with consuming fire, *to give* a mighty judgement on a world. *H. D. ab Ifan.*

Rhòl, *s. m.—pl. t.* iau (rho—ol) A roll, a cylinder. *Mae fe yn rhol*, he is like a buck.
Rholaidd, *a.* (rhol) Tending to roll, rolling.
Rholbren, *s. m.* (rhòl—pren) A rolling-pin.
Rholbreniad, *s. m.* (rholbren) A working with a rolling-pin.
Rholbrenu, *v. a.* (rholbren) To use a rolling-pin.
Rhòlen, *s. f. dim.* (rhòl) A roll, a roller. *Dyna rolen o lodes*, there is a bouncing lass.
Rholiad, *s. m.* (rhòl) A rolling; a turning round.
Rholian, *v. a.* (rhòl) To be rolling about.
Rholiaw, *v. a.* (rhòl) To roll. *Rholiaw gwlan*, to card wool into rolls for spinning.
Rholiawg, *a.* (rhòl) In the form of a roll, rolled.
Rholiwr, *s. m.* (rhòl—gwr) One who rolls.
Rholyn, *s. m. dim.* (rhòl) A roll, a roller. *Rholyn o wlan*, a roller of wool: *rholyn o ddyn*, a fat hale man.
Rhon, *s. f.—pl. t.* ian (rho—on) A tail; also a pike, or lance. *Gwlan rhonian*, the wool of tails: *rhon barcud*, dovetail, in joinery.
Rhonc, *s. f.—pl. t.* iau (rhy—onc) A swag.
Rhonca, *a.* (rhonc) Sinking, falling, swagging.
Rhoncäedd, *s. m.* (rhonca) A sinking or falling state, swagginess; a hollowness.
Rhonciad, *s. m.* (rhonc) A sinking; a swagging; a becoming hollow, loose, or goggling.
Rhoncian, *v. a.* (rhonc) To swag; to goggle.
Rhonco, *a.* (rhonc) Swaggy; goggling.
Rhonell, *s. f.—pl. t.* od (rhawn) The whisk or the whole hair of a tail; a tail. *Rhonell y march*, *marchronell*, the horsetail; *rhonell y wennol*, axe-vetch; *rhonell y ci*, the dog's-tail grass; *rhonell y cadnaw*, fox-tail grass; *rhonell y gath*, cat's-tail grass.
Rhonellawg, *a.* (rhonell) Having a tail.
Rhonellgoch, *a.* (rhonell—coch) Red-tailed. *Y rhonellgoch, y rhawngoch, y dinboeth, coch y berllan*, the redstart.
Rhongymynian, *s. f.* (rhon—cymynu) A kind of battle-axe with a long handle; a poetical epithet for Arthur's battle-axe.
Rhonos, *s. pl. dim.* (rhon) Small particles.
Rhont, *s. f.—pl. t.* iau (rhon) A frisk, a skip.
Rhonta, *v. a.* (rhont) To frisk, to gambol.
Rhontai, *s. c.* (rhont) One who gambols.
Rhontèig, *a.* (rhonta) Apt to gambol; frisky.
Rhonten, *s. f. dim.* (rhont) A frisker.
Rhontiad, *s. m.* (rhont) A gamboling, a frisking.
Rhontyn, *s. m. dim.* (rhont) A frisker.

Rhonwyn, *a.* (rhon—gwyn) White-tailed.

> Madyn rhonwyn, ryenwir
> Meingi gwych, myni gig ir.
>
> White tailed reynard, surnamed the clever slender dog, thou wilt have fresh flesh. *R. Goch Eryri.*

Rhonyn, *s. m. dim.* (rhon) A small body, or particle, of a cylindrical form.

Rhos, *s. f.—pl. t.* ydd (rhy—os) That is parched; a dry meadow; a moor. *Gwair rhos*, moor-land hay. It forms the name of many places.

Rhos, *s. pl. aggr.* What is convolved; roses. *Rhos cochion*, red roses; *rhos gwynion*, white roses; *rhos y cwn*, dog-roses. See *Breila*.

Rhosaidd, *a.* (rhos) Tending to be parched.

Rhosawg, *a.* (rhos) Abounding with dry grass.

Rhosawl, *a.* (rhos) Of a parching nature.

Rhosb, *s. m.—pl. t.* au (rhy—osb) A whim, a trick. *Gware rhosbau*, to play at crambo.

> A hoffo ei rosb hoffed a'i cosb.
>
> He that loves his whim let him love him who corrects it. *Adage.*

Rhosba, *v. a.* (rhosb) To play at crambo.

Rhosbai, *s. c.* (rhosb) One who plays at crambo; a doggerel rhymster.

Rhosbawl, *a.* (rhosb) Belonging to crambo play.

Rhosbëig, *a.* (rhosba) Apt to play at crambo.

Rhosbiad, *s. m.—pl. t.* au (rhosb) A playing at crambo; a making of doggerel rhymes.

Rhosbwr, *s. m.—pl.* rhosbwyr (rhosb—gwr) One who makes doggerel rhymes.

Rhosdir, *s. m.—pl. t.* oedd (rhos—tir) Dry ground.

Rhosedd, *s. m.* (rhos) A state of extending over; superabundance, superfluity.

Rhoslyd, *a.* (rhos) Of a parched quality.

Rhoslydu, *v. n.* (rhoslyd) To become parched.

Rhost, *s. m.* (rhy—ost) That is dried or crimped; that is browned; a roast. *a.* Roast, roasted.

> Cael rhost, edd er bost, ac er y bara.
>
> Obtaining *roasted meat*, for the sake of boast, and bitterns too. *L. G. Cothi.*

Rhostawg, *s. m.* (rhost) A plover. It is also called *bronddu y twynau*. *Rhostawg coch*, the red godwit.

Rhostiad, *s. m.* (rhost) A roasting; a toasting.

Rhostiaw, *v. a.* (rhost) To roast; to toast.

Rhostiawl, *a.* (rhost) Tending to roast, roasting.

Rhostiedig, *a.* (rhostiad) Roasted; toasted.

Rhostiwr, *s. m.* (rhost—gwr) A roaster.

Rhosyn, *s. m. dim.* (rhos) A rose. It is otherwise called *breila* and *breily*. *Rhosyn y mynydd*, *blodau y brenin*, mountain rose.

Rhoth, *a.* (*f. of* rhwth) Loose, hollow, swaggy.

RHU, *s. m. r.* A forcible sending out; a loud utterance; a roar.

Rhuad, *s. m.—pl. t.* on (rhu) A roaring; a talking loudly; loquacity.

Rhuadaidd, *a.* (rhuad) Apt to roar; noisy.

Rhuadawl, *a.* (rhuad) Roaring; blustering.

Rhuadu, *v. a.* (rhuad) To make a roaring.

Rhuadus, *a.* (rhuad) Roaring; loquacious.

Rhuadusaw, *v. a.* (rhuadus) To render loquacious, to become loquacious.

Rhuadwr, *s. m.—pl.* rhuadwyr (rhuad—gwr) A roarer; a boaster, a blusterer.

Rhuadwy, *a.* (rhuad) Roaring; loquacious. *Llew rhuadwy*, a roaring lion.

Rhuain, *a.* (rhu) Roaring; blustering.

Rhuaw, *v. a.* (rhu) To roar; to talk loudly; to bluster. *Rhua tarw yna*, a bull roars there.

Rhuawd, *s. m.* (rhu) A roaring; a loud talk.

Rhuawdr, *s. m.—pl.* rhuodron (rhuawd) A roarer.

Rhuawl, *a.* (rhu) Roaring; loquacious.

Rhuch, *s. m.* (rhy—uch) A coat, a film, a husk.

Rhuchaw, *v. a.* (rhuch) To coat over, to husk.

Rhuchawl, *a.* (rhuch) Tending to coat over.

Rhuchen, *s. f. dim.* (rhuch) A coat, a skin; a leathern jerkin; a web in the eye.

> Mychiad a rhuchen o groen amdano.
>
> A swineherd with a coat of skin about him. *H. Cilhwch—Mabinogion.*

Rhuchiad, *s. m.* (rhuch) A coating, a husking.

Rhuchiaw, *v. a.* (rhuch) To coat over, to husk.

Rhuchiedig, *a.* (rhuchiad) Coated, husked.

Rhuchion, *s. pl.* (rhuch) Husks, gurgions.

Rhuchionaidd, *a.* (rhuchion) Apt to be husky.

Rhuchionawg, *a.* (rhuchion) Having husks.

Rhuchioni, *v. a.* (rhuchion) To clear of husks.

Rhuchionllyd, *a.* (rhuchion) Full of husks.

Rhuchionyn, *s. m. dim.* (rhuchion) An outside covering, or film; a thin husk.

Rhuchiwr, *s. m.—pl.* rhuchiwyr (rhuch—gwr) One who skins, one who clears of husks.

Rhud, *s. m.* (rhy—ud) A cast or drive forward: rue; also called *gorddawn*.

Rhudd, *s. m.—pl. t.* ion (rhy—udd) A ruddy or crimson colour. *a.* Ruddy, crimson; callow.

> Yn Llongborth gwelais i waedfrau,
> Ac elorawr rhag arfau,
> A gwyr rhudd rhag rhuthr angau.
>
> In Llongborth I saw a blood stream, and biers because of arms, and red men from the assault of death. *Llywarch Hen.*

Rhuddain, *a.* (rhudd) Of a crimson colour.

Rhuddaur, *s. m.* (rhudd—aur) Ruddy gold.

Rhuddaw, *v. a.* (rhudd) To make of a crimson colour; to become of a crimson hue.

Rhuddawg, *a.* (rhudd) Having a redness. *Y rhuddawg*, the redbreast.

Rhuddawl, *a.* (rhudd) Tending to redden.

Rhuddbar, *s. f.* (rhudd—par) A ruddy spear.

Rhudded, *s. m.* (rhudd) A red streak; a path.

Rhuddedig, *a.* (rhudded) Being made ruddy.

Rhuddel, *s. f.* (rhudd) A ruddy tinge; a gleam.

> Y seren——
> Yn gannaid ruddel felen.
>
> The star appearing a luminary of yellow gleam. *Iolo Goch.*

Rhuddeli, *s. m.—pl. t.* on (rhudd—eli) A red salve.

Rhuddelin, *a.* (rhuddel) Of a ruddy tinge.

Rhuddell, *s. f.* (rhudd) A crimson colour; red ochre, or ruddle, also called *nod coch*; measles.

Rhuddellen, *s. f.* (rhuddell) One of a ruddy hue.

> Y ferch hygar ruddellen.
>
> The maid that is a lovely one of rosy hue. *D. ab Gwilym.*

Rhuddelliad, *s. m.* (rhuddell) A streaking with crimson, a staining with crimson.

Rhuddellu, *v. a.* (rhuddell) To stain with crimson.

Rhuddem, *s. f.—pl. t.* au (rhudd—gem) A ruby.

> Ac y dan ruddem ruddaur fodrwy.
>
> And beneath the ruby a ring of ruddy gold. *Cynddelw.*

Rhudden, *s. f.—pl. t.* au (rhudd) What is of a crimson hue; a red streak; a ruby.

Rhuddenu, *v. a.* (rhudden) To streak with red.

Rhudderw, *a.* (rhudd—erw) Surrounded with red. *Marwor rhudderw*, red glowing embers.

Rhuddfa, *s. f.—pl.* rhuddfëydd (rhudd) A reddened spot; a spot of ground parched or made bare of grass.

Rhuddfäawg, *a.* (rhuddfa) Abounding with crimson spots: An epithet for a warrior, synonymous with *rhuddfannwg*.

> Helm-gribawg rhuddfäawg fydd.
>
> With helm high-crested stained with crimson he will be. *Adage.*

Rhuddfan, *s. f.* (rhudd—man) A crimson spot.

Rhuddfanawg, *a.* (rhuddfan) Crimson spotted.

> Tri rhuddfanogion Ynys Prydain Arthur, Morgan Mwynfawr, a Rhun fab Beli. Sef pan elynt i ryfel, ni fynai neb aros gartref rhag maint eu cariad.

> The three *crimson spotted ones* of the Isle of Britain; Arthur, Morgan the Courteous, and Rhun the son of Beli. Because, when they went to war, no body would wish to stay at home, as they were so greatly beloved. *Trioedd.*

Rhuddfanu, *v. a.* (rhuddfan) To spot with red.

Rhuddfedel, *s. f.* (rhudd—medel) A ruddy reap.

> Rhuddfedel rhyfel a eiddunt.

> The *crimson reap* of war is thy delight. *Aneurin.*

Rhuddfelyn, *s. m.* (rhudd—melyn) An orange yellow. *a.* Of an orange yellow.

Rhuddgoch, *s. m.* (rhudd—coch) A crimson red, pink, purple colour. *a.* Of a pink colour.

Rhuddgochedd, *s. m.* (rhuddgoch) The state of being of a pink colour.

Rhuddgochi, *v. a.* (rhuddgoch) To turn to a pink.

Rhuddgochni, *s. m.* (rhuddgoch) The state of being of a pink colour.

Rhuddiad, *s. m.* (rhudd) A turning to a pink.

Rhuddiant, *s. m.* (rhudd) A turning to a pink.

Rhuddin, *s. m.* (rhudd) The heart of timber.

> ——Yw'r pren gwin;
> A Rhydderch ydyw'r rhuddin.

> ——Is the vine tree; and Rhydderch is the *heart of oak* *H. Cae Llwyd.*

Rhuddinaw, *v. n.* (rhuddin) To form a core.

Rhuddinawg, *a.* (rhuddin) Having sound wood.

Rhuddinedd, *s. m.* (rhuddin) The soundness of timber.

Rhudding, *s. m.* (rhudd) The heart of timber.

Rhuddion, *s. pl. aggr.* (rhudd) Gurgions. *Rhuddion gwenith*, the husks or bran of wheat.

Rhuddionawg, *a.* (rhuddion) Having gurgions.

Rhuddioni, *v. a.* (rhuddion) To clear of gurgions.

Rhuddionllyd, *a.* (rhuddion) Full of gurgions.

Rhuddlas, *s. m.* (rhudd—glas) A crimson blue.

Rhuddlasiad, *s. m.* (rhuddlas) A turning purple.

Rhuddlasu, *v. a.* (rhuddlas) To turn purple.

Rhuddlesni, *s. m.* (rhuddlas) A purple colour.

Rhuddlwyd, *s. m.* (rhudd—llwyd) A russet colour.

Rhuddlwydaw, *v. n.* (rhuddlwyd) To turn of a russet colour; to make of russet colour.

Rhuddos, *s. pl. dim.* (rhudd) Marigold. *Rhuddos y morfa*, or *rhuddos y gors*, marsh marigold.

Rhuddwern, *s. pl. aggr.* (rhudd—gwern) The bird-cherry trees.

Rhuddwernen, *s. f.* (rhuddwern) A bird-cherry.

Rhuddyg, *s. m.* (rhudd) That is of crimson hue.

Rhuddygl, *s. m.* (rhuddyg) Raddish. *Rhuddygl Marrch*, or *rhuddygl y meirch*, *march-ruddygl*, horse-raddish.

Rhuedd, *s. m.* (rhu) A roaring; loquacity.

Rhueinell, *s. f.* (rhuain) A clarion.

> ——Gwrdyr a'i can,
> Corn rhueinell ein geilgwn.

> Gwrdyr sounds it, the *clarion* horn of our hounds. *Cynddelw.*

Rhuf, *s. m.* (rhu) That tends forward; that breaks out; that is of a reddish hue.

Rhufain, *s. f.* Rome. *Dinas Rhufain*, the city of Rome.

Rhufeiniad, *s. m.—pl.* rhufeiniaid (rhufain) A Roman, or inhabitant of Rome.

Rhufeiniaidd, *a.* (rhufain) Romanised.

Rhufeinig, *a.* (rhufain) Roman; of Rome.

Rhufell, *s. f.—pl. t.* od) (rhuf) A roach.

Rhufon, *s. m.* (rhuf) That is reddened.

Rhug, *s. m.* (rhu) That is apt to move; that abounds with breaks or points.

Rhugl, *s. f.* (rhug) Quickness; friction. *a.* Of free motion; free, ready; fluent; rife.

Rhuglaidd, *a.* (rhugl) Apt to be in motion.

Rhuglaw, *v. a.* (rhugl) To move about briskly; to use dexterity or readiness; to clear, to clear away, to smooth, to rub. *Rhugla y baw i ffordd*, shovel away the dirt.

Rhuglchwyrn, *a.* (rhugl—chwyrn) Of apt fluency.

Rhugledig, *a.* (rhugliad) Being cleared; rubbed.

Rhugledd, *s. m.* (rhugl) A brisk motion; friction; readiness; fluency. *Rhugledd ymadrawdd*, fluency of speech.

Rhuglen, *s. f. dim.—pl. t.* i (rhugl) A drum.

Rhuglfar, *s. m.* (rhugl—bar) Of ready wrath.

Rhuglfwng, *a.* (rhugl—blwng) Apt to be sullen.

Rhuglgroen, *s. f.* (rhugl—croen) A rattle made of a dry hide, with stones in it, carried on a pole, used for scaring animals away.

Rhugliad, *s. m.* (rhugl) A moving briskly; a rubbing, a friction; a clearing away.

Rhuglwr, *s. m.—pl.* rhuglwyr (rhugl—gwr) One who rubs, makes smooth, or clears away.

Rhull, *a.* (rhu) Apt to break out; luxuriant; frank, free; rash, or hasty. *Rhoddi yn rhull*, to give frankly.

> O dderfydd i'r brenin ddodi nebun rhull, anghyfrwys yn frawdwr.——

> If the king should have appointed any one *rash* and inexperienced to be a justiciary.—— *Welsh Laws.*

> Ebwir ef rull i werin.

> He will be called *frank* to the multitude. *Llefoed.*

Rhullder, *s. m.* (rhull) Luxuriance; profusion; promptness; rashness; frankness.

Rhulldra, *s. m.* (rhull) The state of being rife; frankness; rashness.

Rhulledd, *s. m.* (rhull) Rifeness; frankness.

Rhullfalch, *a.* (rhull—balch) Rashly proud.

> Lles bychan buan yw bod yn rhullfalch,
> A'r hollfyd fal fferf rhod.

> Small and transitory the benefit from being *thoughtlessly proud*, while the universe is like a wheel. *D. ab Gwilym.*

Rhulliad, *s. m.* (rhull) A being rife; a going on rashly; a frankly acting.

Rhulliant, *s. m.* (rhull) Rashness; frankness.

Rhum, *s. m.* (rhu) That tends out; that projects, that swells out.

Rhumawg, *s. m.* (rhum) Having a rotundity. *s. f.* A paunch, a rotundity of belly.

Rhumen, *s. f. dim.* (rhum) The paunch, or belly.

> Nid iachach yr enaid er llenwi y rhumen.

> The soul is not more sane for filling of the *paunch*. *Adage.*

Rhumiad, *s. m.* (rhum) A forming a paunch.

Rhumwth, *s. m.* (rhum) A greedy-gut.

Rhun, *s. m.* (rhu—un) That is grand or awful.

Rhuon, *s. m.* (rhu) A ravager; a warrior.

Rhus, *s. m.—pl. t.* oedd (rhu) A beginning of motion; that starts out; a starting off, a recoil; a start from the effect of shyness; also an epithet for a fox, like reynard in English. In Siluria, the first starter of a fox calls *hwi rhus!* for which he gets a fee from the hunters.

Rhusaeth, *s. m.* (rhus) The act of starting.

Rhusaw, *v. a.* (rhus) To start off; to flit away; to start with fear; to hesitate.

Rhusawg, *a.* (rhus) Starting; hesitating; shy.

Rhusawl, *a.* (rhus) Starting; hesitating; shy.

Rhusedig, *a.* (rhus) Being made to start.

Rhusedd, *s. m.* (rhus) A state of starting; a state of hesitation; shyness.

Rhusfa, *s. f.—pl.* rhusfeydd (rhus) A starting.

Rhusgar, *a.* (rhus) Apt to start; restive.

Rhusgarwch, *s. m.* (rhusgar) Aptness to start.
Rhusiad, *s. m.—pl. t.* au (rhus) A beginning to move; a starting; a hesitation.
Rhusiant, *s. m.* (rhus) A starting; hesitation.
Rhusoglyd, *a.* (rhusawg) Apt to start; restive.
Rhusogrwydd, *s. m.* (rhusawg) The state of being subject to starting; restiveness.
Rhuswr, *s. m.—pl.* rhuswyr (rhus—gwr) A starter.
Rhuth, *s. m.* (rhu) A break out; a rush.
Rhuthr, *s. m.—pl. t.* au (rhuth) A sudden drive, gust, or rushing; an attack, assault, or onset; a stretch; a good while.

> Yn Llongborth gwelais i wythaint,
> Ac elorawr mwy no maint,
> A gwyr rhudd rhag rhuthr Geraint.
>
> In Llongborth I beheld the desolation of wrath, and biers not to be numbered, and warriors stained with blood from the *assault* of Geraint. *Llywarch Hen.*
>
> Gwedy treuliaw rhuthr o amser, Caswallon ac Edwyn—a ymchwelasant trach eu cefn i eu gwlad.
>
> After consuming a *length* of time, Caswallon and Edwyn returned back to their country. *Gr. ab Arthur.*

Rhuthrad, *s. m.* (rhuthr) A rushing forward.
Rhuthraw, *v. a.* (rhuthr) To make an onset, to rush, to assault, to fly or run at.
Rhuthrawg, *a.* (rhuthr) Apt to rush, apt to attack. *Tarw rhuthrawg*, a vicious bull.
Rhuthrawl, *a.* (rhuthr) Rushing, assaulting.
Rhuthredig, *a.* (rhuthrad) Being rushed upon.
Rhuthredd, *s. m.* (rhuthr) A state of rushing.
Rhuthriad, *s. m.* (rhuthr) A rushing onward.
Rhuthriam, *s. m.* (rhuthr—llam) A rushing leap.
Rhuthrlym, *a.* (rhuthr—llym) Rushingly fierce or outrageous.
Rhuthrnaid, *s. f.—pl.* rhuthrneidiau (rhuthr—naid) A ramping leap.
Rhuthrwr, *s. m.—pl.* rhuthrwyr (rhuthr—gwr) One who rushes forward; an assaulter.
Rhuthrwyllt, *a.* (rhuthr—gwyllt) Rushingly wild, outrageous, or furious.
Rhuwch, *s. m.—pl. t.* ion (rhu) An exterior coat, a rug; a rough garment. *Gogr rhuwch*, a ranging sieve, a bolter.

> Rhuwch mab aillt LX a dal:
> Rhuwch taiawg XXX a dal.
>
> A free tenant's *rug* is of the value of sixty pence: a villain's *rug* is worth thirty pence. *Welsh Laws.*

Rhuwchen, *s. f. dim.* (rhuwch) An exterior coat; a rough cloak; a rug.
Rhuwr, *s. m.—pl.* rhuwyr (rhu—gwr) A roarer; a loquacious or noisy person.
RHW, *s. m. r.* What breaks or grows out.
Rhwawg, *a.* (rhw) Abounding with growth; having hair, full of hairs. *Dyn rhwawg*, a very hairy man, or one who has a thick strong beard. *Sil. Iestyn Farfrwawg*, Iestyn with the thick beard.
Rhwb, *s. m.* (rhw—wb) A rub; a chafe.
Rhwbiad, *s. m.—pl. t.* au (rhwb) A rubbing.
Rhwbiaw, *v. a.* (rhwb) To rub; to chafe.
Rhwbiawl, *a.* (rhwb) Rubbing, tending to rub.
Rhwbiwr, *s. m.* (rhwb—gwr) One who rubs.
Rhwch, *s. m.* (rhw) That is rough; a grunt.

> Rhyw i hwch ei rhwch.
>
> Genial to the sow is her *grunt*. *Adage.*

Rhwchiad, *s. m.—pl. t.* au (rhwch) A grunting.
Rhwchial, *s. m.* (rhwch) A grunting, such as a hog makes when he is shrill with it.
Rhwchiala, *v. a.* (rhwchial) To keep grunting.
Rhwchiaw, *v. a.* (rhwch) To grunt; to grumble.
Rhwchiawl, *a.* (rhwch) Grunting, grumbling.
Rhwchws, *s. m.* (rhwch) A ray, or a skate.
Rhwd, *s. m.* (rhw—wd) What generates on a surface; rust; also the smut in corn. *Rhwd haiarn*, iron mould; *rhwd lli*, the crust or sediment left by a flood; *rhwd tomydd*, the draining of dunghills.
Rhwdawg, *a.* (rhwd) Covered with rust, rusty, of a rusty colour. *Y rhwdawg*, the redbreast; also called *Y rhuddawg*, *bronrhuddyn*, and *brongoch*.
Rhwf, *s. m.* (rhw) That breaks out; that swells or puffs out; a ravager.
Rhwg, *s. m.* (rhw) That projects; a rub.
Rhwgl, *s. m.* (rhwg) That tends to reach.
Rhwgn, *s. m.* (rhwg) A rub, a friction; a place rubbed or worn away.
Rhwm, *s. m.* (rhy—wm) That tends inward.
Rhwmnai, *s. m.* (rhwmyn) That runs through; a main channel. There are several rivers so called. *Gwin rhwmnai*, rhenish wine.
Rhwmp, *s. m.* (rhwm) A borer, an auger.

> Rhwmp, dwygeiniawg a dal.
>
> *A large auger*, its value is two-pence. *Welsh Laws.*

Rhwmyn, *s. m.* (rhwm) That perforates.
Rhwn, *s. m.* (rhy—wn) That covers over.
Rhwnc, *s. m.* (rhy—wnc) A snort, a snore. *Rhwnc yn ngwddw*, a rattle in the throat.
Rhwnciad, *s. m.* (rhwnc) A snorting; a guggling.
Rhwncian, *s. m.* (rhwnc) A snorting; a guggle.
Rhwncianu, *v. a.* (rhwncian) To make a continual snorting; to make a guggling.
Rhwnciaw, *v. a.* (rhwnc) To snort; to guggle.
Rhwnciawl, *a.* (rhwnc) Snorting; guggling.
Rhwnen, *s. f.* (rhwn) A single pear.
Rhwnsi, *s. m.* (rhwn—si) A rough-coated horse.
Rhwnt, *s. m.* (rhwn) That covers over.
Rhwnyn, *s. pl. aggr.* (rhwn) Pears. They are also called *gellaig*, *eralat*, and *peran*.
Rhwnynen, *s. f. dim.* (rhwnyn) One of pears.
Rhwng, *s. m.* (rhy—wng) Intermediacy.
Rhwng, *prep.* (rhy—wng) Between. *Rhyngof*, *rhyngwyf*, *rhyngthof*, *rhyngthwyf*, between me; *rhyngot*, *rhyngthot*, between thee; *rhyngo*, *rhyngtho*, between him; *rhyngi*, *rhyngthi*, between her; *rhyngom*, *rhyngthom*, between us; *rhyngoch*, *rhyngthoch*, between you; *rhyngynt*, *rhyngthynt*, between them.

> Cant punt yn y flwyddyn yw y gwahaniaeth rhwng dos a dyro.
>
> A hundred pounds a year is the difference between go and come. *Adage.*

Rhws, *s. f.—pl. t.* oedd (rhws) A fertile country; a cultivated region, as opposed to the wilds. It is synonymous with *bro*.
Rhwsg, *s. m.* (rhws) That tends out, that is bulky; that is luxuriant. *a.* Bulky; luxuriant, fertile. *Tir rhwsg*, rank land, that is rich, or apt to overrun with fern and the like.
Rhwtiad, *s. m.* (rhwd) A corroding; a chafing.
Rhwtiaw, *v. a.* (rhwd) To corrode; to fret, to rub.
Rhwtiawg, *a.* (rhwd) Having a fret or chafe.
Rhwtiawl, *a.* (rhwd) Corroding; chafing.
Rhwtiedig, *a.* (rhwtiad) Corroded; chafed.
Rhwtion, *s. pl. aggr.* (rhwd) Particles; dregs.
Rhwtioni, *v. a.* (rhwtion) To produce dregs.
Rhwtws, *s. pl. dim.* (rhwd) Small unconnected particles; dregs, dross.
Rhwtionllyd, *a.* (rhwtion) Drossy, or dreggy.
Rhwth, *s. m.* (rhw—wth) That is open or wide. *a.* Wide, open, gaping, yawning; greedy.

Rhwy, *s. m.* (rhw) That runs out, or through; excess, superfluity.

Nid mawr i'th garid,
Os rhwy a erchid.

Not greatly wouldest thou be loved, if thou shouldest ask for *too much*. *Adage.*

Rhwy, *adv.* (rhw) Too much, to excess; utterly.

A gwyno rhwy ni ryg wynfan.

He that complains of *too much* does not complain at all. *Adage.*

Angeu cad orddwy, rhwy rhymcoddes;
Angen a'm lleddi gwen; gwae, rwy golles
——Cadwallawn!

The death of devastating war has afflicted me *to excess*; necessity refrains my smile; alas, *utterly* lost is Cadwallon! *Cynddelw.*

Rhwyad, *s. m.* (rhwy) A producing excess; the fish called a pike.
Rhwyaw, *v. a.* (rhwy) To produce an excess.
Rhwyawl, *a.* (rhwy) Excessive, superfluous.
Rhwych, *s. f.* (rhwy) That extends out.
Rhwyd, *s. f.—pl. t.* i (rhwy) That abounds with openings or holes; a net. *Rhwyd gibliad*, a hoop net; *rhwyd dyn*, a drag net; *rhwyd ëogiaid*, *rhwyd balleg*, *ballegrwyd*, a salmon net; *rhwyd ddwyffon*, a net between two staffs; *rhwyd aden*, a wing net; *rhwyd adara*, a birding net.

Detholais fy rhwyf yn rhwyd gelynion,
Gal ynial yn mhlymnwyd.

I have chosen my leader as the *snare of foes*, a wild opponent in the conflict. *Cynddelw, i Wenwynwyn.*

Rhwydadwy, *a.* (rhwyd) Capable of being netted.
Rhwydaw, *v. a.* (rhwyd) To make a net, to net; to take in a net; to entangle, to ensnare.
Rhwydawg, *a.* (rhwyd) Reticulated, netted.
Rhwydawl, *a.* (rhwyd) Reticular, ensnaring.

Rhwth frea-fol rhwydol, rhodia y creigiau,
Rhefrau, was mwythau, a'th gymeithia.

With thy loose rotten belly *entangled*, stroll about the rocks, son of dainties, entrails shall be thy food. *R. Goch Eryri, i lwynawg.*

Rhwydedig, *a.* (rhwyd) Reticulated; ensnared.
Rhwyden, *s. f. dim.* (rhwyd) A net; a caul.
Rhwydiad, *s. m.* (rhwyd) Reticulation, netting.
Rhwydronell, *s. f.—pl. t.* i (rhwyd—rhonell) A lace; a snare, a gin.
Rhwydwaith, *s. m.* (rhwyd—gwaith) A net-work, a caul.
Rhwydwëydd, *s. m.—pl. t.* ion (rhwyd—gwëydd) A net-maker.
Rhwydwr, *s. m.* (rhwyd—gwr) A net man.
Rhwydd, *a.* (rhwy) Open, clear, or free of obstruction; easy to be accomplished; easy, frank; prosperous; tolerable, pretty well. *Rhwydd ganu*, tolerable singing. *adverb*, Tolerably. *Rhwydd iach*, tolerably well; *rhwydd debyg*, tolerably like.

Rhwydd ni bo dyrys.

What is not entangled is *unobstructed*. *Adage.*

Ni welais i lam rhwydd i ewig.

I have not seen an *unobstructed* leap for a doe. *Adage.*

Rhwyddâad, *s. m.* (rhwydd) A rendering clear free, or easy; a becoming unobstructed.
Rhwyddadwy, *a.* (rhwydd) Capable of being free, easy, or unobstructed.
Rhwyddaidd, *a.* (rhwydd) Somewhat open or easy
Rhwyddâu, *v. a.* (rhwydd) To clear of obstruction; to make easy; to facilitate, to speed.
Rhwyddaw, *v. a.* (rhwydd) To free, to clear, to make easy; to become unobstructed.
Rhwyddawl, *a.* (rhwydd) Facilitating, freeing.
Rhwyddâwr, *s. m.—pl.* rhwyddâwyr (rhwyddâu—gwr) One who clears from obstruction.
Rhwydd-deb, *s. m.* (rhwydd) Clearness from obstruction; facility; success, prosperity. *Rhwydd-deb iti!* Success attend thee!
Rhwydded, *s. f.* (rhwydd) Free course; success.
Rhwyddedig, *a.* (rhwydd) Being facilitated.
Rhwyddfodd, *s. m.* (rhwydd—bodd) A free will, good pleasure. *a.* Of free will.
Rhwyddfudd, *s. f.* (rhwydd—budd) Benefit easily obtained. *a.* Liberal of benefit.
Rhwyddgadw, *v.* (rhwydd—cadw) To keep freely.

Ni'm rhwyddgeidw Rhodri.

Rhodri *will not freely support* me. *Gwalchmai.*

Rhwyddgael, *v. a.* (rhwydd—cael) To get easily.
Rhwyddged, *s. f.* (rhwydd—ced) Treasure easily obtained. *a.* Free of treasure.
Rhwyddgof, *s. m.* (rhwydd—cof) A clear memory.
Rhwyddhynt, *s. f.* (rhwydd—hynt) Free course.
Rhwyddiad, *s. m.* (rhwydd) A rendering clear, open, easy, or unobstructed; a facilitating.
Rhwyddiannawl, *a.* (rhwyddiant) Facilitating.
Rhwyddiannu, *v. a.* (rhwyddiant) To render clear, easy, or unobstructed, to make facile.
Rhwyddiant, *s. m.* (rhwydd) Facility, or easiness.
Rhwyddiator, *ger.* (rhwyddiad) In facilitating.
Rhwyddineb, *s. m.* (rhwydd) The state of being clear, easy, or unobstructed.

Tri rhagoriaeth mydr; cywreindeb, rhwyddineb, ac accan ber.

The three excellencies of metre; accuracy, *solubility*, and harmonious accent. *Barddas.*

Rhwydditor, *sup.* (rhwydd) To be facilitating.
Rhwyddles, *s. m.* (rhwydd—lles) Unobstructed benefit. *a.* Of unrestrained advantage.
Rhwyddlwyn, *s. m.* (rhwydd—llwyn) The speedwell; also called *llysiau Llywelyn*. *Rhwyddlwyn blewynawg*, germander speedwell.
Rhwyddoldeb, *s. m.* (rhwyddawl) The state of being clear, easy, or unobstructed.
Rhwyddoli, *v. a.* (rhwyddawl) To facilitate.
Rhwyddrad, *s. m.* (rhwydd—rhad) Free grace; free bounty. *a.* Of unrestrained grace.

Rhuddredd reddiad, rhwyddrad rwn.

A ruddy lanced distributer, a prodigal of *unrestrained bounty*. *Cynddelw, i Wenwynwyn.*

Rhwyddred, *s. f.* (rhwydd—rhed) A free course. *a.* Of unobstructed course.
Rhwyddrwysg, *s. m.* (rhwydd--rhwysg) Free sway *a.* Of unrestrained sway.
Rhwyddyn, *s. m.* (rhwydd) That is loose or easy.
Rhwyddyndawd, *s. m.* (rhwyddyn) Facility.
Rhwyddynedd, *s. m.* (rhwyddyn) The state of being free, easy, or unrestricted.

Yn wir dymbi——
Rhwyddynedd buddedig rhoendd rhlydd rheithau.

In truth to me there shall come the *freedom* of the advantageous abundance of the chiefs of the laws. *Taliesin.*

Rhwyddynu, *v. a.* (rhwyddyn) To facilitate.
Rhwyf, *s. m.—pl. t.* au (rhwy) That tends forward, impels, or directs; a tendency forward; ambition; a commander, a ruler; also an oar. *Llong ddwyrwyf*, *dwyrwyfen*, a ship with two oars.

Yr haf hyneuw, rhwyf hinon,
O'm serch amdanad mae'm son'
Dychwel yn ol i'r doldydd
Yn drum draw er gwisgaw gwydd.

Thou genial summer, sovereign of serenity, my theme is of my love for thee! Return to the dales again, in fair order there to deck the wood. *D. ab Gwilym.*

Balchion, trahawn, mawr yw'n rhwyf,
I'n fo'm ar nwyf yn porthi.

Proud ones, froward ones, great is our *arrogance*, whilst on our passion we are borne. *T. ab Ieuan Madawg.*

Rhwyfad, *s. m.* (rhwyf) An impelling forward; a directing; a swaying.

Rhwyfadain, *s. f.* (rhwyf—adain) A guiding wing; a guiding or impelling fin.

> Tan dy fron—
> Ddwy adain dda odiaeth;
> Ac ar dy gefn gwryd gain,
> I fado dy rwyfadain.
>
> Beneath thy breast two wings excellently good; and on thy back of fair extent, to move along, thy *directing* fins.
> *T. Prys, i'r gleisiad.*

Rhwyfadur, *s. m.—pl. t.* ion (rhwyfad) One who sways; a ruler; a guider, a director.

Rhwyfai, *s. c.* (rhwyf) That sways, dominator.

Rhwyfain, *v. a.* (rhwyf) To be swaying.

Rhwyfan, *s. m.* (rhwyf) That sends or directs forward; rule, sway, direction. "*Oer rwyfan tymhestl,*" the cold sway of the tempest.

Rhwyfan, *v. a.* (rhwyf) To guide, to direct; to bear sway, to dominate.

> Rhyarfeiddiaf uaf nerthawg ddygyrchu,
> Yn rhwyfau teulu, rhwyf teuluawg.
>
> With confidence I will venture to approach the mighty chief, *conducting* a family, a lord of a numerous race.
> *Ll. P. Moch, i Lywelyn ab Iorwerth.*
>
> Llaw orthrech wrth rwyfan Mordwy.
>
> An overpowering hand whilst *swaying* on the watery course.
> *Ll. P. Moch.*

Rhwyfanawl, *a.* (rhwyfan) Swaying; directing.

Rhwyfanes, *s. f.—pl. t.* au (rhwyfan) A female who rules, guides, or directs.

Rhwyfaniad, *s. m.* (rhwyfan) A swaying; a directing; domination.

Rhwyfaniaeth, *s. m.* (rhwyfan) Domination.

Rhwyfanu, *v. a.* (rhwyfan) To dominate.

Rhwyfanus, *a.* (rhwyfan) Dominative; ruling.

> Gwebionain fraeth bid arfaethus;
> Yd fyddant wyr rhamant ryd rwyfanus.
>
> Loquacious youths let them be full of designs; aspiring men will be of *imperious* course.
> *Myrddin.*

Rhwyfaw, *v. a.* (rhwyf) To tend forward; to guide; to impel; to rule, to sway; also to row.

Rhwyfawl, *a.* (rhwyf) Ruling, swaying; directing; rowing.

Rhwyfedig, *a.* (rhwyf) Swayed; directed; rowed

Rhwyfenydd, *s. m.—pl. t.* ion (rhwyfan) A ruler.

> Y profwy fy marddrin,
> Gyrfeu uch cynran,
> Bedd Rhufawn rwyfenydd ran.
>
> So as to prove my bardic lore, of superior lot, this is the grave of Rhuvon with the aspect of an *imperious one.*
> *Taliesin.*

Rhwyfiad, *s. m.* (rhwyf) A tending forward; a directing; a swaying; a rowing.

Rhwyfiadawl, *a.* (rhwyfiad) Dominative.

Rhwyfiadu, *v. a.* (rhwyfiad) To dominate.

Rhwyfiadur, *s. m.—pl. t.* on (rhwyfiad) One who sways, rules, or directs; a governor.

> Oian a barchellan—
> Cladd yn lle argel yn argoedydd,
> Rhag erwys Rhydderch Hael, rhwyfiadur ffydd.
>
> Listen, little pig: burrow in a secret place in the bordering woods, for fear of the chase of Rhydderch the Generous, *leader* of the faith.
> *Myrddin.*

Rhwyfiadus, *a.* (rhwyfiad) Dominative.

Rhwyfiant, *s. m.* (rhwyf) Domination.

Rhwyfiator, *ger.* (rhwyfiad) In directing.

Rhwyfineb, *s. m.* (rhwyf) Guidance; sway.

Rhwyfitor, *sup.* (rhwyf) To be swaying.

Rhwyfolaeth, *s. m.* (rhwyfawl) Dictatorship.

Rhwyfoldeb, *s. m.* (rhwyfawl) A state of sway, direction, or authority; a dictatorial state.

Rhwyfoli, *v. a.* (rhwyfawl) To render dominant; to become possessed of sway, to become dictatorial.

Rhwyfus, *a.* (rhwyf) Fond of sway; haughty.

> Gwnaa ddilyn cynghor gwyr boneddigion ieuainc rhwyfus yn gynt no dangosiad gwyr araf doethion.
>
> He would follow the advice of *proud* young men of noble rank sooner than the direction of moderate wise men.
> *Marchawg Crwydrad.*

Rhwyfusaw, *v. a.* (rhwyfus) To render imperious or haughty; to become dictatorial.

Rhwyfusedd, *s. m.* (rhwyfus) Imperiousness.

Rhwyfwr, *s. m.—pl.* rhwyfwyr (rhwyf—gwr) One who leads or impels forward; a rower.

Rhwyfydd, *s. m.—pl. t.* ion (rhwyf) One who guides or directs; a rower.

Rhwyg, *s. m.—pl. t.* ion (rhwy) A rent, a rapture

Rhwygadwy, *a.* (rhwyg) Capable of being rent.

Rhwygaw, *v. a.* (rhwyg) To rend, or to tear.

Rhwygawl, *a.* (rhwyg) Rending, lacerating.

Rhwygedig, *a.* (rhwyg) Rent, torn, lacerated.

Rhwygiad, *s. m.—pl. t.* au (rhwyg) A tearing.

> Por cynghor rager, parha rwygiad trin,
> Pann gwirodlen win, pen gwaredied.
>
> A chief of superior council who would continue the tearing of conflict, the displayer of wassail wine, supreme deliverer.
> *D. ab Gwilym.*

Rhwygiant, *s. m.* (rhwyg) A tearing, a rending.

Rhwygiator, *ger.* (rhwygiad) In tearing.

Rhwygitor, *sup.* (rhwyg) To be tearing.

Rhwygwr, *s. m.* (rhwyg—gwr) A tearer.

Rhwyl, *s. m.—pl. t.* on (rhwy) An open space; a clear enclosed spot; a ring-fence; court.

> Rhwyl Careg Hofa cafas ynddaw
> Cawdd Saeson, lladron yn eu llwfrwus.
>
> The *hall* of Careg Hova had in it the affliction of Saxons, thieves who were reduced to dust.
> *Llygad Gwr, i Gr. Maelawr.*

Rhwylaw, *v. a.* (rhwyl) To make an opening; to form a paddock, or enclosure.

Rhwylwaith, *s. m.* (rhwyl—gwaith) Open-work; a curious interlaced work.

Rhwyll, *s. f.—pl. t.* au (rhwy) A narrow aperture, a hole; a mortise; an interstice; a passage; a casement; also a fretwork, or open-work. *Rhwyllau botymau*, button-holes; *rhwyllau gwëydd, brwydau gwëydd*, a weaver's reeds.

> A rhwyll yn nghanol pob rhod.
>
> And a *fretwork* in the midst of every circle.
> *W. Llyn, i fin.*
>
> Tri llew, glas fal yr asur,
> Trwy wyllt dan, a'r tair rhwyll dur.
>
> Three lions, blue like azure sky, through vehement fire, and the three *frets* of steel.
> *Iolo Goch, i arfau Ithel Llwyd.*

Rhwyllaw, *v. a.* (rhwyll) To make narrow aperture; to make fretwork; to make lattice-work. *Rhwyllaw edafedd*, to wind thread.

Rhwyllawg, *a.* (rhwyll) Abounding with holes or interstices; fretted, consisting of lattice-work, chequered, cross-barred.

> Yr oedd hen wisg o bali rhwyllawg amdani.
>
> There was an old garment of *fretted* velvet about her.
> *H. Peredur—Mabinogion.*

Rhwylledig, *a.* (rhwyll) Perforated with crevices; fretted, grated; latticed.

Rhwylliad, *s. m.—pl. t.* au (rhwyll) A forming of narrow apertures; a fretting; a grating, a making lattice-work.

Rhwyllwaith, *s. m.* (rhwyll—gwaith) A fret-work

Rhwyllwr, *s. m.—pl.* rhwyllwyr (rhwyll—gwr) One who makes interstices, or fretwork.

Rhwym, *s. m.—pl. t.* au (rhwy) That circumscribes or contains; a bond, a tie. *a.* Bound.

> Dyga ran dy garennydd;
> Dwg ni o'n rhwym dygn yn rhydd!
>
> Take the portion of thy kindred; take us from our severe bond and set us free!
> *Iolo Goch, i O. Glendwr.*

Rhwymaw, *v. a.* (rhwym) To bind, to tie. *Rhwymaw gwartheg*, to tie or to house cattle.

Rhwymawl, *a.* (rhwym) Tending to bind; binding; restrictive; obligatory.

Rhwymbleth, *s. f.—pl. t.* i (rhwym—pleth) An entwined wreath.

Rhwymed, *s. m.* (rhwym) A bounden state.

Rhwymedi, *s. m.* (rhwym) That keeps bound; a power to bind or to restrain.

> Ymadel heb rwymedi;
> A thost ymadel a thi!
>
> To part without a *power to prevent*, and afflicting is it to part with thee! *W. Llcyn.*

Rhwymedig, *a.* (rhwym) Bounden, tied; obliged

Rhwymedigaeth, *s. m.—pl. t.* au (rhwymedig) The state of being bound; restriction.

> Dygai, o'i rwymedigaeth,
> Dau iu i nef, da elw a wnaeth.
>
> He conducted, owing to his confinement, two hosts to heaven; a good deed he then performed. *Hop. Tho. Phylip.*

Rhwymedigaw, *v. a.* (rhwymedig) To render bounden; to become bounden.

Rhwymedigawl, *a.* (rhwymedig) Obligatory.

Rhwymedydd, *s. m.—pl. t.* ion (rhwym) Obligee

Rhwymedd, *s. m.* (rhwym) A bounden state.

Rhwymiad, *s. m.—pl. t.* au (rhwym) A tying; a binding; a bandage; restriction; obligation.

Rhwymiannawl, *a.* (rhwymiant) Restrictive.

Rhwymiannu, *v. a.* (rhwymiant) To make a restriction, to make an obligation.

Rhwymiant, *s. m.* (rhwym) Restriction; bond.

Rhwymwr, *s. m.—pl.* rhwymwyr (rhwym—gwr) One who binds.

Rhwymydd, *s. m.—pl. t.* ion (rhwym) A binder.

Rhwymyn, *s. m. dim.—pl. t.* au (rhwym) A band, a bandage; a swathe, a swaddling-band. *Rhwymyn y coed*, black briony.

Rhwymynawl, *a.* (rhwymyn) Tying, binding.

Rhwymyniad, *s. m.* (rhwymyn) A tying on a bandage; a swaddling.

Rhwymynu, *v. a.* (rhwymyn) To tie on a bandage; to swaddle.

Rhwymynwr, *s. m.—pl.* rhwymynwyr (rhwymyn—gwr) One who puts on a bandage.

Rhwyn, *s. m.* (rhwy) A stretching round, a wind, or twist.

Rhwynaw, *v. a.* (rhwyn) To stretch round.

Rhwyniad, *s. m.* (rhwyn) A stretching round.

Rhwyoli, *v. a.* (rhwyawl) To render excessive or superfluous; to become prodigal.

Rhwys, *s. m.—pl. t.* au (rhwy) Vigour; wantonness; luxuriance. *a.* Vigorous, lively, wanton; luxuriant.

> Tydi yr haf, tad y rhwys,
> A'th goed frig berth gaeadfrwys,
> Cawn genyd y byd o'i ben.
>
> Thou summer, father of *vigour*, with thy fair vegetating branches thickly spreading, of thee we shall have the world all before us. *D. ab Gwilym.*

Rhwysaw, *v. a.* (rhwys) To render vigorous; to render luxuriant; to become vigorous.

Rhwysawg, *a.* (rhwys) Full of vigour; luxuriant

> Y gog——
> A thraserch i'th iaith rwysawg
> Yn minio gwawd—Clyw fi.
>
> The cuckoo, with thy *lively* language filled with fond love, expressing praise, listen to me. *D. ab Gwilym.*

Rhwysawl, *a.* (rhwys) Invigorating; enlivening.

Rhwysdawd, *s. m.* (rhwys) Vigorousness; luxuriance; liveliness, wantonness.

Rhwysdeb, *s. m.* (rhwys) Vigorousness; vivacity

Rhwysder, *s. m.* (rhwys) Vigorousness; vivacity.

Rhwysdra, *s. m.* (rhwys) Vigorousness; luxuriance, fertility; liveliness; wantonness.

Rhwysedig, *a.* (rhwys) Invigorated; enlivened.

Rhwysedd, *s. m.* (rhwys) Vigorousness; vivacity.

Rhwysfawr, *a.* (rhwys) Full of vigour; greatly luxuriant; full of vivacity.

Rhwysg, *s. m.—pl. t.* au (rhy—gwysg) A career, a course; forwardness; sway, pomp, grandeur. *Rhwysg malwen*, a snail's track; *mae efe yn fawr ei rwysg*, he takes upon himself great sway.

Rhwysgaw, *v. a.* (rhwysg) To make a career, to run a course; to go forward, to risk; to take upon one's self to sway, to be forward.

Rhwysgawd, *s. m.* (rhwysg) The act of taking a career or swaying; a taking a career.

Rhwysgawg, *a.* (rhwysg) Having an open course or career; having sway; froward.

Rhwysgawl, *a.* (rhwysg) Going an unrestrained course; risking, swaying; forward.

Rhwysgedig, *a.* (rhwysg) Being made to run headlong; unrestrained.

Rhwysgedd, *s. m.* (rhwysg) The state of having unobstructed course or sway.

Rhwysgfawr, *a.* (rhwysg) Of great sway; of pomp

Rhwysgforedd, *s. m.* (rhwysgfawr) Greatness of sway; unrestrained course; pomposity.

Rhwysgiad, *s. m.—pl. t.* au (rhwysg) A taking an unrestrained course; a swaying.

Rhwysgl, *s. m.* (rhwysg) A tendency to go headlong.

Rhwysglaw, *v. a.* (rhwysgl) To run headlong.

Rhwysgliad, *s. m.* (rhwysgl) A going headlong.

Rhwysglyd, *a.* (rhwysg) Froward, or restive.

Rhwysgus, *a.* (rhwysg) Apt to start, starting. *March rhwysgus*, a starting horse.

Rhwysgwr, *s. m.—pl.* rhwysgwyr (rhwysg—gwr) One who takes an unrestrained course.

Rhwysiad, *s. m.* (rhwys) An invigoration.

Rhwysiannawl, *a.* (rhwysiant) Invigorating.

Rhwysiannu, *v. a.* (rhwysiant) To invigorate; to become vigorous; to luxuriate.

Rhwysiant, *s. m.* (rhwys) An invigoration.

Rhwysineb, *s. m.* (rhwys) Vigorousness.

Rhwysogi, *v. a.* (rhwysawg) To render vigorous; to become vigorous; to luxuriate.

Rhwysoldeb, *s. m.* (rhwysawl) Vigorousness.

Rhwysolder, *s. m.* (rhwysawl) Vigorousness.

Rhwysoledd, *s. m.* (rhwysawl) Vigorousness.

Rhwysoli, *v. a.* (rhwysawl) To invigorate.

Rhwystr, *s. m.—pl. t.* au (rhy—gwyst) Opposition, hinderance, impediment, let, or obstacle.

> Nid trais ond tan;
> Nid rhwystr ond dwfr.
>
> There is no violence but fire; there is no *obstruction* but water. *Adage.*

Rhwystrad, *s. m.* (rhwystr) An opposing; a hindering; opposition, obstruction.

Rhwystradwy, *a.* (rhwystr) Capable of opposing, obstructing, or hindering.

Rhwystraw, *v. a.* (rhwystr) To go before; to oppose, to hinder; to become hindered.

Rhwystrawg, *a.* (rhwystr) Abounding with opposition or hinderance; restrictive.

Rhwystrawl, *a.* (rhwystr) Opposing, hindering.

Rhwystredig, *a.* (rhwystr) Opposed, hindered.

Rhwystredigaeth, *s. m.* (rhwystredig) The act of opposing, obstruction, hinderance.

Rhwystredigawl, *a.* (rhwystredig) Obstructive.

Rhwystredd, *s. m.* (rhwystr) A state of opposition

Rhwystri, *s. m.* (rhwystr) Hinderance, or let.

> Yn myned i ynys Enlli,
> Er ymwared o bob rhwystri.
>
> Going to the isle of Enlli, for deliverance from every *obstruction*. *Categ.*

Rhwystriad, *s. m.*—*pl.* rhwystriaid (rhwystr) An obstructor, a hinderer.

Rhwystriadawl, *a.* (rhwystriad) Obstructive.

Rhwystrus, *a.* (rhwystr) Having opposition or obstacle; hindering, entangled, encumbered.

Rhwystrusaw, *v. a.* (rhwystrus) To render obstructive; to become obstructive.

Rhwystrusedd, *s. m.* (rhwystrus) Obstructiveness

Rhwystrusi, *s. m.* (rhwystrus) Hinderance.

Rhwystrusrwydd, *s. m.* (rhwystrus) A state of opposition or hinderance; cumbersomeness.

Rhwystrwr, *s. m.*—*pl.* rhwystrwyr (rhwystr—gwr) A hinderer, an obstructor.

Rhwyswawd, *s. m.* (rhwys—gwawd) Vigorous flow of genius.

Rhwyth, *s. m.* (rhwy) That pervades; juice.

> Ardwyaf, profaf prifwawd, nis cyll,
> Eurged rhaith yfed, nid rhwyth efyll.
>
> I will manage, I will essay a high strain of praise, not to perish, to the golden law of drinking, not of crab-tree *juice*.
> *Prydydd Bychan.*

Rhwythaw, *v. a.* (rhwyth) To pervade.

Rhwythawl, *a.* (rhwyth) Pervasive, penetrant.

Rhwythawr, *s. m.*—*pl.* rhwythorion (rhwyth) A pervader. *Rhwythawr llawr*, the pervader of the ground.

RHY, *s. m. r.*—*pl. t.* on. The state of being beyond or over; excess. It is used very generally as a preposition of emphasis, especially with verbs. Prefixed to the preterite of a verb it forms the preterpluperfect tense; with the present tense, it implies the action done in a signal manner: and with the future it implies a time still further. *Ni ryymwelsynt*, they had not previously seen one another.

> Nid da rhy o ddim.
>
> The *excess* of any thing is not good. *Adage.*

Rhy, *adv.* (rhy, *s.*) Over, beyond, too much; very, excessively; too. It is often compounded with the first and second pronouns singular and plural: as *rhym dorai*, it would much concern me: *rhyth welid*, thou wert previously seen: *Dofydd rhy'n digones*, the Lord did abundantly provide for us.

> Rhy ddirwy, dyrawr ei bolion;
> Rhy ddylawch eirchiad ag eirchion;
> Rhy ddyladd yn ddrud ran canon cued;
> Rhy ddylus alltudion.
>
> He fines *excessively*, he impels his claims; *greatly* he encourages petitioners with gifts; *most* boldly he slays the portion of the whelps of *sculk*; he *completely* keeps off strangers.
> *Cynddelw, i H. ab Owain.*
>
> Rhanwr pob pwnc rhy uniawn:
> Rhan ar wir yn rhann'r iawn.
>
> The giver of every point *most* just; a party on the side of truth dispensing justice *L. G. Cothi.*

Rhyachub, *v. a.* (achub) Completely to save.

Rhyachubaw, *v.a.* (rhyachub) Completely to save

Rhyachubawl, *a.* (rhyachub) Fully saving.

Rhyachubiad, *s. m.* (rhyachub) A fully saving.

Rhyachwyn, *v.a.* (achwyn) To complain overmuch

Rhyachwynawl, *a.* (rhyachwyn) Too complaining

Rhyachwyniad, *s. m.* (rhyachwyn) A complaining overmuch; a greatly complaining.

Rhyadaw, *v. a.* (gadaw) To leave utterly.

Rhyadawiad, *s. m.* (rhyadaw) A leaving utterly.

Rhyadfarn, *s. f.* (adfarn) A full rejudgment.

Rhyadfarniad, *s. m.* (rhyadfarn) A rejudging.

Rhyadfarnu, *v. a.* (rhyadfarn) To rejudge entirely; to revoke a judgment.

> Os addef a wna yr amddiffynwr, adfered i'r hawlwr yr eiddo, yn herwydd rhyadfarnu y gyfraith a fo gynt.
>
> If the defendant shall make an acknowledgement, let him restore to the claimant the property, so as *to rejudge entirely* the sentence formerly given. *Welsh Laws.*

Rhyaddaw, *v. a.* (addaw) To promise greatly.

Rhyaddawiad, *s. m.* (rhyaddaw) A promising overmuch.

Rhyaddewid, *s. f.*—*pl. t.* ion (rhyaddaw) A too great a promise.

Rhyafael, *s. m.*—*pl. t.* ion (gafael) Too great a hold; an excessive grasp.

Rhyafaelgar, *a.* (rhyafael) Grasping overmuch.

Rhyafaeliad, *s. m.* (rhyafael) An over-grasping.

Rhyal, *s. m.*—*pl. t.* oedd (al) Procreation.

Rhyaledd, *s. m.* (rhyal) Procreativeness.

Rhyaliad, *s. m.* (rhyal) A procreating.

Rhyalu, *v. a.* (rhyal) To procreate, to beget.

Rhyalus, *a.* (rhyal) Procreative; procreant.

Rhyall, *s. m.* (gall) Superior power. *a.* Of superior power; invincible.

> Coronawg faban, medd bardd arall,
> Mydonwy engeb, a fydd ryall.
>
> The crowned infant, says another bard, Mydonwy the bishop, will be *invincible*. *Rhys Brenau.*

Rhyallad, *s. m.* (rhyall) Supreme power.

> Pen a borthaf yn angad fy llaw,
> Llary udd llywiai wlad
> Pen post Prydain rhyallad.
>
> A head I bear in the grasp of my hand, a mild sovereign who governed a country, the chief pillar of Britain's *supreme power*. *Llywarch Hen.*

Rhyallu, *v. a.* (rhyall) To have superior or complete power; to be fully competent.

> Aryneigiaw ac ofnaa a orug Coel ymladd yn ei erbyn; canys ei glod a gadarnaai ac rhallasai en brenin gwrthwynebu iddo.
>
> Coel became intimidated and fearful of fighting against him: for his fame had strengthened the idea that not one sovereign *could have had the power* to withstand him. *Gr. ab Arthur.*

Rhyamcan, *s. m.*—*pl. t.* ion (amcan) Too great a design.

Rhyamcanawl, *a.* (rhyamcan) Over designing.

Rhyamcaniad, *s. m.* (rhyamcan) A designing overmuch.

Rhyamcanu, *v.a.* (rhyamcan) To design overmuch.

Rhyanfodd, *s. m.* (anfodd) Over difficulty of pleasing or giving satisfaction.

Rhyanfoddawg, *a.* (rhyanfodd) Being too difficult to please; very hard to please.

> Ni cheiff rhyanfoddawg rybarch.
>
> He that is over *difficult to please* will not get much respect. *Adage.*

Rhyanfoddiad, *s. m.* (rhyanfodd) A displeasing overmuch; a satisfying with difficulty.

Rhyanfoddiaw, *v.a.* (rhyanfodd) To over-displease

Rhyanfon, *v. a.* (anfon) To send fully.

> Gwedes Duw, megys brenin cyfoethawg, llys ardderchawg iddo, a elwir teyrnas nef;—ac i'r llys hono y rhagwelai ef rhyanfon rif hynbys o etholedigion.
>
> God, like a powerful king, established for him a magnificent court, which is called the kingdom of heaven; and to that court he foresaw that he should *have to send* a certain number of chosen ones. *Elucidarius.*

Rhyanfonawl, *a.* (anfon) Completely sending.

Rhyanfoniad, *s. m.* (anfon) A sending fully.

Rhyanhael, *a.* (anhael) Illiberal to excess.

Rhyanllad, *a.* (anllad) Wanton to excess.

Rhyanlladrwydd, *s. m.* (rhyanllad) Excess of wantonness; a state of excessive lust.

Rhyanlladu, *v.* (rhyanllad) To be too wanton.

Rhyanllofi, *v. a.* (anllofi) To over-enrich.

> Cwrwf o'l yfed,
> A chain drefred,
> A chain dudded,
> Ym rhyanllofed.
>
> Ale to be drunk, and fair habitation, and splendid raiment, these *have been profusely bestowed* on me. *Taliesin.*

Rhyanllofiad, *s. m.* (anllofiad) A profusely enriching; an endowing overmuch.

Rhyannog, *s. m.* (annog) Too much excitement. *v. a.* To excite overmuch.

Rhyannogawl, *a.* (rhyannog) Over exciting.
Rhyannogi, *v. a.* (rhyannog) To excite greatly.
Rhyannogiad, *s. m.* (rhyannog) An exciting overmuch; a greatly impelling.
Rhyannosbarth, *s. m.* (annosbarth) Excess of indiscrimination.
Rhyannosbarthawl, *a.* (rhyannosbarth) Very indiscriminate.
Rhyannosbarthu, *v. a.* (rhyannosbarth) To render or become too indiscriminate.
Rhyannwyd, *s. m.* (annwyd) Excess of chilliness.
Rhyar, *s. m.* (rhy—ar) Great agitation; a torrent.
Rhyaraf, *a.* (araf) Slow overmuch.
Rhyarafedd, *s. m.* (rhyaraf) Excess of slowness.
Rhyarafu, *v. a.* (rhyaraf) To make too slow.
Rhyarfeiddiad, *s. m.* (arfeiddiad) A behaving with too much assurance.
Rhyarfeiddiaw, *v. a.* (arfeiddiaw) To dare or to presume overmuch.
Rhyarfeiddiawl, *a.* (arfeiddiawl) Too presuming, apt to take too great a liberty.
Rhyarfer, *s. f.* (arfer) Excess of use.
Rhyarferiad, *s. m.* (rhyarfer) An over-using.
Rhyarferu, *v. a.* (rhyarfer) To use overmuch.
Rhyarganfod, *v. a.* (arganfod) To perceive completely, to over-scrutinize.
Rhyarw, *a.* (garw) Very rough; very severe.
Rhyattal, *v. a.* (attal) To stop overmuch.
Rhyattaliad, *s. m.* (rhyattal) A stopping or withstanding overmuch.
Rhyathu, *v. a.* (athu) To go completely.

Gloew, wedi caffael y gaer, a'i goresgyn, a gwasgaru y muroedd, cychwyn a wnai ar ol Gwelrydd, a ryathoedd hyd yn Nghaer Wynt.

Gloew, after having obtained the city, and subdued it, and demolished the walls, what he did was to set off after Gweirydd, who *had gone as far as* Winchester. *Gr. ab Arthur.*

Rhyawd, *s. m.* (rhy) A producing an extreme.
Rhyawl, *a.* (rhy) Tending to an extreme.
Rhyb, *s. m.* (rhy—yb) Tendency forward.
Rhyball, *a.* (pall) Extremely fallible or faulty.
Rhyballiad, *s. m.* (rhyball) A failing extremely.
Rhyballu, *v. a.* (rhyball) To fail extremely.
Rhybarawd, *a.* (parawd) Extremely ready.
Rhybarch, *s. m.* (parch) Excess of respect. *a.* Overmuch of respect; extreme regard.

Ni bydd rybarch rhagynaedd.

Too much familiarity will not be *over-respected*. *Adage.*

Rhybarchu, *v. a.* (rhybarch) To respect much.
Rhybech, *s. m.* (pech) Excess of sin. *a.* Very sinful.
Rhybechu, *v. a.* (rhybech) To sin extremely.
Rhybed, *s. m.* (ped) That is fixed by clinching.
Rhybediad, *s. m.* (rhybed) A clinching.
Rhybediaw, *v. a.* (rhybed) To clinch.
Rhybenyd, *s. m.* (penyd) Extreme penitence.

Addwyn rhybenyd i bechawd.

Happy is *extreme penance* for sin. *Taliesin.*

Rhybenydiad, *s. m.* (rhybenyd) A performing extreme penance.
Rhybenydiaw, *v. a.* (rhybenyd) To perform extreme penance; to be over-penitent.
Rhybinc, *a.* (pinc) Over-affected; too smart.
Rhybinciaw, *v. a.* (rhybinc) To adorn overmuch; to be too affected.
Rhyblanu, *v. a.* (planu) To plant fully.
Rhyblyg, *a.* (plyg) Over doubled; redoubled.
Rhyblygiad, *s. m.* (rhyblyg) Reduplication.
Rhyblygu, *v. a.* (rhyblyg) To double completely.
Rhyborth, *s. m.* (porth) Complete support.
Rhyborthi, *v. a.* (rhyborth) To maintain or to support completely.

Llys Owain, ar beuild yd rhyborthed erioed.

The hall of Owain, on spoil *it has been completely supported* always. *O. Cyfeiliawg.*

Beirdd gnaheiw gnanerth berth rhyborthes.

Bards claiming a splendid portion *he greatly maintained*. *Cynddelw.*

Rhyborthiad, *s. m.* (rhyborth) A completely bearing or upholding.
Rhybrid, *a.* (prid) Fully equivalent; of full price.
Rhybridiad, *s. m.* (rhybrid) A rendering or becoming fully equivalent; full expiation.
Rhybridiaw, *v. a.* (rhybrid) To expiate fully.
Rhybrin, *a.* (prin) Extremely scarce or scanty.
Rhybrinder, *s. m.* (rhybrin) Extreme scarcity.
Rhybrudd, *a.* (prudd) Extremely pensive or sad.

A chwarddod Palestina graeth
Ei chwerthin aeth yn rhybrudd.

And let enthralled Palestina smile: her laughter is turned *extremely sad*. *Edm. Prys.*

Rhybruddiaw, *v. n.* (rhybrudd) To be very sad.
Rhybrudd-der, *s. m.* (rhybrudd) Extreme sadness.
Rhybrydu, *v. a.* (prydu) To give a full description, to sing completely.

Mydwyf Dalliesin;
Rhyphrydaf iawnllin,
Parhawd hyd ffin
Yn nghynnelw Elffin.

I am Taliesin, *I will fully sing* of the just offspring; but it continue to the end in the right of Elfin. *Taliesin.*

Rhybryn, *s. m.* (pryn) That is previously secured; that is fully purchased.
Rhybryniad, *s. m.* (rhybryn) A previously securing; a purchasing beforehand.
Rhybrynu, *v. a.* (rhybryn) To secure fully or previously; to purchase previously.

Rhybrynawdd barfawg a eirch.

A bearded one *has previously made sure of* what he may ask for. *Adage.*

Rhybrysur, *a.* (prysur) Over-bustling, over-busy.
Rhybrysuraw, *v. a.* (rhybrysur) To hasten extremely; to be in extreme bustle or hurry.
Rhybrysurdeb, *s. m.* (rhybrysur) Overhastiness.
Rhybuch, *s. m.* (puch) Earnest longing.
Rhybuchaw, *v. a.* (rhybuch) To wish earnestly.

Nid estyn llaw ni rybuch calon.

The hand will not reach what the heart *does not long for*. *Adage.*

Rhag beiau rhiau, yni reuid budd,
Dy rybydd, Ruffydd, a rybuchid.

For the faults of chieftains, if there shall be no distribution of profit, thy warning, Gruffydd, *would be earnestly sought for*. *Ll. P. Moch.*

Rhybuched, *s. f.* (rhybuch) The fulfilment of the will; a donation of a gift asked for.

Caraf a'm rhoddes rybuched medd.

I love the one who gave me the *wished-for boon* of mead. *H. ab Owain.*

Bychan iawn o rybuched
A gair genyf o ged.

Very little indeed as a *boon* will be had of treasure from me. *Gr. Gryg.*

Y neb y rhoddo y brenin dir iddo yn gyfarwys, neu yn rhybuched arall.——

To whomsoever the king shall give land as an acknowledgement for service, or any other *donation*.—— *Welsh Laws.*

Rhybuchedig, *a.* (rhybuch) Earnestly longed-for.

Gwedi caredigion gusanau a geiriau rhybuchedig, ar fyrder, megys ymadrawdd arall, hi a fynegis o'i brawd amawdd y llys; ac a ddangoses iddo y dewin, yr oedd yn ei geisiaw.

After affectionate kisses and *endearing* words, presently, turning to another discourse, she declared to her brother the condition of the court; and she showed him the wizard, whom he was seeking for. *Gr. ab Arthur.*

Rhybuchiad, *s. m.* (rhybuch) A desiring earnestly.
Rhybuchiannawl, *a.* (rhybuchiant) Inducing earnest longing or desire.

Rhybuchiannu, *v. a.* (rhybuchiant) To cause earnest longing; to be earnestly wishing.

Rhybuchiant, *s. m.* (rhybuch) Earnest longing.

Rhybuchwr, *s. m.—pl.* rhybuchwyr (rhybuch—gwr) One who desires earnestly, a craver.

Rhybudd, *s. m.—pl. t.* ion (pudd) Warning, admonishment. *Mae ef tàn ei rybudd na wnelo hyny,* he is under warning that he may not do so.

Rhybudd i ddedwydd.

A *warning* to the provident. *Adage.*

Tri pheth a ddyly pawb ei ddiolch, gwahawdd, rhybudd, ac anrheg.

Three things every body should be thankful for; invitation, *warning*, and a present. *Trioedd.*

Rhybuddiad, *s. m.—pl. t.* au (rhybudd) An admonishing, or warning; admonition.

Rhybuddiaeth, *s. m.* (rhybudd) The act of warning.

Diwrawd rhybuddiaeth a dewredd i ddyn;
Y ddwyganp fynawg yn ddigwymp foredd.

Of no avail shall *foresight* and bravery be to man; two happy virtues of firm foundation. *Befnyn.*

Rhybuddiaw, *v. a.* (rhybudd) To give warning.

Rhybuddiaw trwch ni weryd.

To warn the giddy will be of no avail. *Adage.*

Rhybuddiawl, *a.* (rhybudd) Admonitory.

Rhybuddiedig, *a.* (rhybuddiad) Being warned.

Rhybur, *a.* (pur) Extremely pure or clear.

Rhyburaw, *v. a.* (rhybur) To purify completely.

A'th iolwyf: ryburwyf cyn no'm poeni.

May I adore thee; *may I be completely purified* before I am punished. *Meilyr.*

Rhyburawl, *a.* (rhybur) Very purifying.

Rhyburiad, *s. m.* (rhybur) A purifying extremely.

Rhybwyll, *s. m.* (pwyll) First impression of idea.

Rhybwyllaw, *v. a.* (rhybwyll) To give a first idea.

Rhybwylliad, *s. m.* (rhybwyll) A producing a first thought or consideration.

Rhybwys, *s. m.* (pwys) Extreme weight.

Rhybwysaw, *v. a.* (rhybwys) To press extremely.

Rhybwysawl, *a.* (rhybwys) Superponderant.

Rhybwysiad, *s. m.* (rhybwys) A pressing extremely; superponderation.

Rhybwyth, *s. m.* (pwyth) A retort; an over-pay. *Talu rhybwyth,* To make retaliation.

Rhybwythaw, *v. a.* (rhybwyth) To retort.

Rhybwythiad, *s. m.* (rhybwyth) A retorting.

Rhych, *s. m.—pl. t.* au (rhy—ych) A trench, a furrow; the furrow in ploughed land.

Rhychawg, *a.* (rhych) Having trenches.

Rhychawl, *a.* (rhych) In the form of a trench.

Mil o erwydd o dir rhychawl i fesur gwialen Hywel Dda.

A thousand acres of *ridged* land according to the rod of Hywel the Good. *Welsh Laws.*

Rhychawr, *s. m.—pl.* rhychorion (rhych) That is in the furrow; an epithet for the ox that draws on the furrow side in a yoke.

Rhychdir, *s. m.—pl. t.* oedd (rhych—tir) Ridged land; arable land.

Rhychganwyr, *s. m.* (rhych—canwyr) A groove plane.

Rhychiad, *s. m.—pl. t.* au (rhych) A furrowing, a trenching; a chamfering.

Rhychiedig, *a.* (rhychiad) Furrowed, trenched.

Rhychu, *v. a.* (rhych) To trench; to furrow.

Rhychwai, *a.* (chwai) Over-hasty; very quick.

Rhychwal, *s. f.* (chwal) An extreme spread.

Rhychwaliad, *s. m.* (rhychwal) A scattering extremely; a spreading overmuch.

Rhychwalu, *v. a.* (rhychwal) To scatter extremely

Rhychwanegawl, *a.* (rhychwaneg) Superadding.

Rhychwanegiad, *s. m.* (chwaneg) Superaddition.

Rhychwanegu, *v. a.* (chwanegu) To superadd.

Rhychwant, *s. m.—pl. t.* au (rhy—chwant) An overreach, an utmost stretch; a span.

Meinael o wasg mewn y tant
Chwi amdrouch i'm dau rychwant.

So slender of waist within the zone; you would turn yourself in my two *spans*. *T. Aled.*

Rhychwantiad, *s. m.* (rhychwant) A spanning.

Rhychwantu, *v. a.* (rhychwant) To span.

Mae efe yn rhychwantu yr wybren.

He is *spanning* the firmament. *Morgan Llwyd.*

Rhychwardd, *s. m.* (chwardd) Excessive laughter.

Rhychwarddiad, *s. m.* (rhychwardd) A laughing excessively; a setting up a horse laugh.

Rhychwarddu, *v. a.* (rhychwardd) To laugh excessively or overmuch.

Rhychware, *s. m.* (chware) Excess of play. *v. a.* To play overmuch; to play to excess.

Rhychwarëus, *a.* (rhychware) Over-playful.

Rhychweidawd, *s. m.* (rhychwai) Over-briskness.

Rhychweidra, *s. m.* (rhychwai) Extreme briskness.

Rhychweidd, *s. m.* (rhychwai) Over-quickness.

Rhychwerthin, *s. m.* (chwerthin) Excessive laughter. *v. a.* To laugh excessively.

Rhyd, *s. m.—pl. t.* au (rhy—yd) That is full of motion; a course; a passage; a ford.

Molad pawb y rhyd fal y caffo.

Let every body praise the *ford* as he finds it. *Adage.*

Y ddau frenin a nesynfiynghyd yn nberfedd y rhyd, ac yngyrfiad; ac ar y gosawd cyntaf, y gwr a oedd yn lle Arawn a ododes ar Hafgan.

The two kings approached together in the middle of the *ford*, and encountered one another, and on the first attack, the person who was in the stead of Arawn laid upon Havgan. *H. Pwyll—Mabinogion.*

Rhydaen, *s. m.* (taen) An excessive spreading.

Rhydaeniad, *s. m.* (rhydaen) An over-spreading.

Rhydaenu, *v. a.* (rhydaen) To spread overmuch.

Rhydaer, *a.* (taer) Too violent; too importunate.

Rhydaeredd, *s. m.* (rhydaer) Over-importunity.

Rhydaf, *s. m.* (rhy—taf) An overspreading.

Rhydafl, *s. m.* (tafl) An excessive throwing.

Rhydafliad, *s. m.* (rhydafl) A throwing excessively.

Rhydaflu, *v. a.* (rhydafl) To throw extremely.

Rhydain, *s. f.* (rhyd) That is full of motion; the young of deer, a fawn. It is also called *rhydani.*

Rhaid fydd i'r hydd—
Arawe y rhydain arab.

It will be meet for the stag to stay for the gladsome *fawn*. *Llywelyn Moel.*

Rhydal, *s. m.* (tal) An over-payment.

Rhydaliad, *s. m.* (rhydal) An over-paying; a retorting; a retaliation.

Rhydalu, *v. a.* (rhydal) To over-pay; to retort.

A rhythal y Drindawd traha.

And the Trinity *will retaliate* presumption. *Llyfrai.*

Rhydarf, *s. f.* (tarf) Excessive rout or flight.

Rhydarfaidd, *a.* (rhydarf) Of a tendency to scare away extremely.

Rhydarfaidd aerfaidd eurfaen rhodawg.

The *quickly routing* wolf of slaughter with golden bossed shield. *Ll. P. Moch, i L. ab Iorwerth.*

Rhydarfiad, *s. m.* (rhydarf) An over-scaring.

Rhydarfu, *v. a.* (rhydarf) To over-scare.

Rhydasg, *s. f.* (tasg) An excessive task.

Rhydasgiad, *s. m.* (rhydasg) An overtasking.

Rhydasgu, *v. a.* (rhydasg) To fix an over-task.

Rhydaw, *s. m.* (taw) Extreme silence, taciturnity.

Rhydawg, *a.* (rhyd) Having full course or run.

Rhydawl, *a.* (rhyd) Being full of agitation or motion. It is also an epithet for a fawn.

Rhydech, *s. m.* (tech) Extreme aptness to skulk.

Rhydechiad, *s. m.* (rhydech) A skulking greatly.

Rhydechu, *v. a.* (rhydech) To skulk extremely; to become completely concealed.

Ni rydecho rhyddygir.

Who will not conceal himself greatly will be completely taken away. *Llefoed.*

Rhydechwr, *s. m.—pl.* rhydechwyr (rhydech—gwr) One who skulks overmuch; a coward.

Rhydedig, *a.* (rhyd) Being made into a ford.

Rhydedd, *s. m.* (tèdd) Presidency, or supremacy.

Rhydeddawg, *a.* (rhydedd) Having supremacy.

Rhydeddawl, *a* (rhydedd) Apt to be supreme.

Rhydeddiad, *s. m.* (rhydedd) A making supreme.

Rhydeddu, *v. a.* (rhydedd) To render supreme or exalted; to become exalted.

Rhydeddus, *a.* (rhydedd) Superior, or exalted.

Rhydeg, *a.* (rhy—teg) Extremely fair or fine.

Rhederig, *a.* (terig) Excessive or continual aptitude to copulate; a term applied to barren animals. *Buwch rhyderig*, a cow that doth not calve; *hwch rhyderig*, a barren sow.

Rhydewi, *v. n.* (rhydaw) To be very tacit.

Ni rygar trugar tra syberwyd;
Ni rydaw anaw o'i sawyfyd.

The merciful will not be over fond of extreme pride; the minstrel *will not be quite silenced* about the object of his love. *Cynddelw, i Ddew.*

Rhydgoch, *s. m.* (rhwd—coch) A rusty red; a russet colour; also called *rhuddlwyd*.

Rhydiad, *s. m.* (rhyd) A forming a ford; a fording.

Rhydiad, *s. m.* (rhwd) A rusting; a corrotion.

Rhydiaw, *v. a.* (rhyd) To form a ford; to ford.

Hawdd rhydiaw ffrwd pisodyn.

It is easy *to ford* the stream of a piddle. *Adage.*

Rhydiawg, *a.* (rhyd) Having a rippling course; having a ford.

Rhydiawl, *a.* (rhyd) Relating to a ford.

Rhydid, *s. m.* (tid) That is out of bond; liberty.

Rhydle, *s. m.—pl. t.* oedd (rhyd—lle) A passage place, a fording place; opportunity.

Rhydlyd, *a.* (rhwd) Full of rust; rusty.

Bid lyfn dy baderau; bid rydlyd dy arfau.

Be thy beads smooth, be thy weapons *rusty.* *Adage.*

Rhydlydrwydd, *s. m.* (rhydlyd) Rustiness.

Rhydlydu, *v. a.* (rhydlyd) To become rusty.

Rhydni, *s. m.* (rhwd) Rustiness, or rust.

Rhydo, *s. m.* (to) A complete covering.

Rhydöad, *s. m.* (rhydo) A covering over fully.

Rhydogaeth, *s. m.* (rhydawg) Deliverance.

O Ddaw na chaem rydogaeth
Y 'strain oddiwrth y boncaeth!
Os tebygan' idd eu rhyw
Angharuaidd yw'r genedlaeth.

Would to God we had a *deliverance* of our tribe from the whole! If they prove like their kind unamiable is the generation. *W. Davies o Lanfair Fawr.*

Rhydöi, *v. a.* (rhydo) To cover over fully; to overspread; to overwhelm.

Seithenyn, saf di allan,
Ac edrych werydre faranres:
Mor Maes Gwyddno rhydoes.

Seithenyn, do thou stand out, and behold the fertile land of thy subjects, the sea *has overspread* the plain of Gwyddno. *Gwyddno.*

Rhydollt, *s. m.* (rhwd—ollt) Saw-dust.

Rhydraeth, *s. m.* (traeth) The state of being pre-uttered.

Rhydraethawd, *s. f.* (rhydraeth) A prediction.

Rhydraethiad, *s. m.* (rhydraeth) A predicting.

Rhydraethu, *v. a.* (rhydraeth) To predict.

Dias ddarogant
I Addaf a'i blant
Y rydraethasant
Y proffwydi.

A certain prophecy with respect to Adam and his progeny the prophets *did predict.* *Meilyr.*

Rhydraidd, *s. m.* (traidd) Extreme pervation.

Rhydrais, *s. m.* (trais) Extreme violence.

Rhydraul, *s. f.* (traul) Excess of consumption; excessive waste; excess of expence.

Rhydraws, *a.* (traws) Extremely thwarting; excessively froward or perverse.

Rhydreiddiad, *s. m.* (rhydraidd) A pervading extremely; superimpregnation.

Rhydreiddiaw, *v. a.* (rhydraidd) To pervade extremely, to penetrate thoroughly.

Rhydreisiad, *s. m.* (rhydrais) A using extreme violence; a tyrannizing to excess.

Rhydreisiaw, *v. a.* (rhydrais) To use extreme violence; greatly to tyrannize.

Rhydres, *s. m.* (tres) Arrogance; pragmaticalness.

Rhydresawl, *a.* (rhydres) Pragmatical.

Rhydresgar, *a.* (rhydres) Arrogant, assuming; ostentatious, supercilious, flaunting.

Rhydresgarwch, *s. m.* (rhydres) Arrogance, assumingness, pragmaticalness; superciliousness.

Rhydreuliad, *s. m.* (rhydraul) A consuming extremely; a wasting overmuch.

Rhydreuliaw, *v. a.* (rhydraul) To consume to excess; to waste overmuch.

Rhydrig, *s. m.* (trig) Over-continuance or delay.

Rhydrigaw, *v. a.* (rhydrig) To tarry too long.

Rhydrigiad, *s. m.* (rhydrig) An over-tarrying.

Rhydrist, *a.* (trist) Extremely dejected or sad.

Rhydristwch, *s. m.* (rhydrist) Extreme sadness.

Rhydrws, *s. m.* (trws) Too much dressing.

Rhydrwsiad, *s. m.* (rhydrws) An over-dressing.

Rhydrwsiaw, *v. a.* (rhydrws) To deck extremely.

Rhydu, *v. a.* (rhwd) To generate rust, to rust.

Ni ad, mwy no'i dad, o'i dy,
Ar y frwydr, arf i rydu.

No more than his father, will he suffer, from his house, for a weapon *to rust*, in time of battle. *Gut. Owain, m. T. Llwyd.*

Rhydweli, *s. f.—pl. t.* au (rhyd—gweli) An artery.

Mae briw saeth i'm bar-ais i,
A thrwy dal wyth rhydweli.

There is an arrow wound below my rib, and through my temple a throbbing vein. *S. Tudyr.*

Rhydwf, *s. m.* (twf) Excess of growth; exuberance.

Rhydwll, *s. m.—pl.* rhydyllau (twll) A perforation.

Rhydwng, *s. m.* (twng) An anathema.

Rhydwr, *s. m.—pl.* rhydyrau (twr) An over-heap.

Rhydyddiad, *s. m.* (tyddiad) A completing an arrangement, bargain, or compact; a final settlement.

Rhydyddiaw, *v. a.* (tyddiaw) To complete an arrangement, bargain, or compact. *Dyfed.*

Rhydyfawl, *a.* (rhydwf) Tending to overgrow.

Rhydyfiad, *s. m.* (rhydwf) An overgrowing; a supercrescence, superexcrescence.

Rhydyfu, *v. n.* (rhydwf) To overgrow.

Rhydylliad, *s. m.* (rhydwll) A perforating.

Rhydyllu, *v. a.* (rhydwll) To perforate.

A'i ddwylaw ir-waed o ddolurion;
A'i draed oll lleisiad rhydyllyson'.

And his hands reeking with blood from wounds; and his feet all livid *they pierced extremely.* *G. ab Ien. ab Ll. Fychan.*

Rhydyn, *a.* (tyn) Overtight; overstress.

Rhydyniad, *s. m.* (rhydyn) A drawing overmuch, a superstraining.

Rhydynu, *v. a.* (rhydyn) To draw to excess.

Rhydyngawl, *a.* (rhydwng) Anathematical.

Rhydyngiad, *s. m.* (rhydwng) An anathematizing.

Rhydyngu, *v. a.* (rhydwng) To anathematize.

Llias pawb pan rydyngir.

Every body will be put away when there *shall be anathematizing.* *Adage.*

Rhydyriad, *s. m.* (rhydwr) An over-heaping.

Rhydyru, *v. a.* (rhydwr) To over-heap; to gather together extremely.

> Attan rhydyrau', o'i lan lluwydd;
> Rhyddyliff cynnif can fodd Dofydd.
>
> To us *they will flock extremely*, of his fair multitude; misery will be fully relieved through the will of the Supreme.
> *Llywelyn Fardd, i Gadfan.*

Rhydd, *s. m.* (rhy—ydd) The state of being open, loose, or at large; liberty, freedom.

> Tri chyntefigaeth cyflwr dyn: cynnull cyntaf ar wybodaeth, cariad, a nerth, heb angeu; ac nis gellir hyn yn mraint rhydd a dewis cyn dyndawd; ac y tri hyn a elwir y tri gortrech.
>
> The three primitial things in the state of humanity: the accumulations of knowledge, love, and power, without undergoing dissolution; and this cannot be done as of liberty and choice previous to humanity; and these three are called the three victories.
> *Barddas.*

Rhydd, *a.* (rhy—ydd) Open, loose, at large; free.

> Or tery dyn rhydd ddyn caeth, taled ddeuddeg ceiniawg iddo.
>
> If a *free* person shall strike a bondman, let him pay to such twelve pence.
> *Welsh Laws.*
>
> Nid oedd yr all a fal can ddoethed a Helen Luyddawg yn y celfyddydau rhydd.
>
> There was not another that was so wise as Helen the Warlike in the *liberal* sciences.
> *Gr. ab Arthur.*
>
> Mae rhai a'u golwg yn rhydd,
> Yn gweled beiau' gilydd.
>
> There are some with their sight *unrestrained*, perceiving the faults of each other.
> *G. ab Hywel ab Tudyr.*

Rhyddâad, *s. m.* (rhyddâu) A loosening, an enlarging, a freeing; liberation.

Rhyddâawl, *a.* (rhyddâu) Loosening, enlarging.

Rhyddadeni, *v.* (dadeni) To be fully reproduced.

Rhyddadl, *s. f.—pl.* rhyddadlau (dadl) Excess of dispute, contention, or debate.

Rhyddadliad, *s. m.* (rhyddadl) An over-disputing.

Rhyddadlu, *v. a.* (rhyddadl) To over-dispute.

Rhyddail, *s. pl. aggr.* (dail) Over-leaves; the second growth of leaves.

Rhyddal, *v. a.* (dal) An excessive holding.

Rhyddaliad, *s. m.* (rhyddal) A holding to excess.

Rhyddaly, *v. a.* (rhyddal) To hold overmuch.

Rhyddarogan, *s. f.—pl. t.* au (darogan) A superior prediction.

Rhyddaroganiad, *s. m.* (rhyddarogan) A delivering a superior oracle or prognostication.

Rhyddaroganu, *v. a.* (rhyddarogan) To deliver a superior prediction.

> Morini Brython,
> Rhyddaroganyn';
> A medi heon
> Am Hafren afon.
>
> The Morini Britons, *their fate will be fully predicted*; and the reaping of heroes about Havren river.
> *Taliesin.*

Rhyddâu, *v. a.* (rhydd) To set open, to loosen, to set at large; to free, to liberate; to deliver, to release, to acquit.

Rhyddawn, *s. m.—pl.* rhyddoniau (dawn) Superior gift, endowment, or virtue.

Rhyddawr, *s. m.* (dawr) Extreme concern.

Rhyddâwr, *s. m.—pl.* rhyddâwyr (rhyddâu—gwr) One who sets free, one who loosens.

Rhydded, *s. f.* (rhydd) A state of liberty, freedom.

Rhyddedawg, *a.* (rhydded) Having liberty; enlarged, released, exempted, dispensed with.

Rhyddedogi, *v. a.* (rhyddedawg) To set at liberty; to render exempted; to become at liberty.

Rhyddeisyf, *s. m.* (deisyf) Earnest entreaty. *v. a.* To entreat earnestly; to crave overmuch.

Rhyddeisyfawl, *a.* (rhyddeisyf) Greatly entreating.

Rhyddeisyfiad, *s. m.* (rhyddeisyf) An entreating earnestly; a craving or begging overmuch.

Rhyddeisyfu, *v. a.* (rhyddeisyf) To entreat greatly.

Rhydderchafawl, *a.* (derchafawl) Over-exalting.

Rhydderchafiad, *s. m.* (derchafiad) An exalting overmuch, a being uplifted overmuch.

Rhydderchafu, *v. a.* (derchafu) To over-exalt.

> Ryddinoedd Cadwaladr cadr y deuant;
> Rhydderchafwynt Cymmry; cad a wnânt.
>
> The hosts of Cadwaladr mightily they would come; *they would extremely exalt* the Cymmry; they would bring on a battle.
> *Golyddan.*

Rhyddiaeth, *s. m.* (rhydd) A state of freedom.

Rhyddiaith, *s. f.* (rhydd—iaith) Free language.

Rhyddiant, *s. m.* (rhydd) Relaxation; liberation.

Rhyddïawg, *a.* (dïawg) Lazy overmuch.

Rhyddid, *s. m.* (rhydd) Liberty, freedom; immunity, exemption; licence, leave.

> Tri chyflwr hanfod bywedigion; cyflwr abred yn annwn, cyflwr rhyddid yn ddyndawd, a chydwr cariad, sef gwynfyd, yn y nef.
>
> The three states of existence of living beings; the state of inchoation in the great deep, the state of *liberty* in humanity, and the state of love, that is felicity, in heaven.
> *Barddas.*

Rhyddieithaidd, *a.* (rhyddiaith) Like prose.

Rhyddieithawl, *a.* (rhyddiaith) Prosaic.

Rhyddifeichiaw, *v. a.* (difeichiaw) To exonerate bail fully; to free a surety fully.

Rhyddifoneddu, *v. a.* (difoneddu) To divest completely of nobility.

Rhyddig, *a.* (dig) Extremely wroth or angry.

Rhyddigon, *s. m.* (digon) A more than enough.

Rhyddigonedd, *s. m.* (digon) Over-sufficiency.

Rhyddigoni, *v. a.* (rhyddigon) To satiate.

Rhyddillyn, *a.* (dillyn) Smart to excess.

Rhyddillynedd, *s. m.* (rhyddillyn) Affectation.

Rhyddineb, *s. m.* (rhydd) Exemption from restraint, freedom, facility, readiness, fluency.

Rhyddïogi, *v. n.* (rhyddïawg) To become extremely lazy, or indolent.

> Ni rofn noeth yn ysgall;
> Pawb pan ryddiogwr yd fall.
>
> The naked is not bold amongst thistles; every body *when rendered very idle*, will fail.
> *Taliesin.*

Rhyddiriad, *s. m.* (diriad) Excess of iteration; a being troublesome to excess; a being very mischievous.

Rhyddiriaw, *v. a.* (diriaw) To iterate to excess.

> Un rodd orwag ni ryddiriwn o ged.
>
> One empty gift of treasure *I would not greatly importune*.
> *Gw. Gwgawn.*

Rhyddiriawl, *a.* (diriawl) Excessively iterating.

Rhyddisgyn, *s. m.* (disgyn) A bringing down fully. *v. a.* To alight completely.

Rhyddisgyniad, *s. m.* (rhyddisgyn) A completely bringing down or alighting.

Rhyddisgynu, *v. a.* (rhyddisgyn) To bring or put down completely; to alight fully.

> Gwedi dawed ohono hyd geriaw glyn, oedd yn agos i gaer Caint, ef gwelai yn y lle hono llu gwyr Rhufain ag eu pebyllau ac eu lluestau, gwedi rhyddisgynu yn y glyn.
>
> After he had come close to a valley, which was near to Canterbury, he saw in that place the army of the men of Rome, with their tents and their booths having *been quite taken down* in the valley.
> *Gr. ab Arthur.*

Rhyddodawl, *a.* (dodawl) Superinducing.

Rhyddodi, *v. a.* (dodi) To superinduce.

Rhyddodiad, *s. m.* (dodiad) Superinduction.

Rhyddoeth, *a.* (doeth) Wise overmuch.

Rhyddoethedd, *s. m.* (rhyddoeth) Over-wisdom.

Rhyddogn, *s. m.* (dogn) An over-quantity.

Rhyddognedd, *s. m.* (rhyddogn) Over-quantity.

Rhyddogni, *v. a.* (rhyddogn) To give an over-quantity; to satiate.

> Aele o'm dygnedd ydd ym dogned;
> Rhyddognais fawr gerdd am ei fawr-ged.
>
> With grievous severity I have been portioned; *I dedicated a superfluity* of exalted song for his great treasure.
> *Cynddelw, i Gadwallon.*

Rhyddogniad, *s. m.* (rhyddogn) A giving an over-quantity; a satiating.

Rhyddoniad, *s. m.* (rhyddawn) A gifting with superior talent or endowment.

Rhyddoniaeth, *s. m.* (rhyddawn) Superior gift.

> Gwn na welwn——
> Wr un faeth ryddoniaeth rym,
> Na gwaladr a wnai Gwilym.
>
> I know that we shall not see a person of like education with the energy of *superior talent*, nor such a leader as Gwilym would make. *Rhys Goch Eryri.*

Rhyddoniaw, *v. a.* (rhyddawn) To gift in a superior manner.

> Diriaidion ddynion, ni ryddonych, Tad,
> Dirydd ffydd ffoed, brad a'i bredych.
>
> Mischievous men, whom thou dost not endow with grace, Father, without a way to escape through faith, ruin will destroy them. *Casnodyn.*

Rhyddorawl, *a.* (rhyddawr) Of extreme concern.

Rhyddori, *v. a.* (rhyddawr) To give extreme concern; to be extremely concerned.

Rhyddoriad, *s. m.* (rhyddawr) A rendering or becoming of great concern.

Rhyddrent, *s. m.* (rhydd—rhent) Gavel-kind. *Sil.*

Rhyddrud, *a.* (drud) Over-bold; dear to excess.

Rhyddwyllys, *s. m.* (rhydd—gwyllys) Free will.

> Ein rhyddwyllys nid ydyw yn cyfarwyddaw rhad Duw; ond rhad Duw yn cyfarwyddaw ein rhyddwyllys.
>
> Our *free will* doth not influence the grace of God; but the grace of God doth influence our *free will*. *Marchawg Crwydrad.*

Rhyddwyn, *v. a.* (dwyn) To over-carry.

Rhyddyd, *s. m.* (rhydd) Liberty, or freedom.

Rhyddyddiad, *s. m.* (dyddiad) A making a compact

Rhyddyddiaw, *v. a.* (dyddiaw) To make a compact

Rhyddygiad, *s. m.* (dygiad) An over-carrying; superfetation, superconception.

Rhyddygn, *a.* (dygn) Being excessively severe.

Rhyddygnawl, *a.* (rhyddygn) Over-toiling.

Rhyddygnu, *v. a.* (rhyddygn) To toil to excess.

Rhyddygwydd, *v. n.* (dygwydd) To over-happen.

Rhyddygwyddawl, *a.* (rhyddygwydd) Previously happening or coming to pass.

Rhygddygwyddiad, *s. m.* (rhygddygwydd) A previously happening; superconsequence.

Rhyddygyd, *v. a.* (dygyd) To over-carry; to superferate; to take away overmuch.

Rhyddyhun, *a.* (dyhun) Previously slumbering.

Rhyddyhunaw, *v. a.* (rhyddyhun) To be taking a slumber previously.

> Rhyddyhunaf dremud.
>
> I *will previously take a nap* awhile. *Taliesin.*

Rhyddylawch, *s. m.* (dylawch) Excess of solace.

Rhyddylif, *s. m.* (dylif) A complete flowing away.

Rhyddylifaw, *v. a.* (rhyddylif) To be flowing or passing away completely.

Rhyddylochi, *v. a.* (rhyddylawch) To encourage extremely; to be cherishing greatly.

> Rhyddylawch eirchiad ag eirchion.
>
> He *will extremely cherish* the petitioner with requests. *Cynddelw.*

Rhyddylochiad, *s. m.* (rhyddylawch) A cherishing or protecting extremely.

Rhyddylud, *s. m.* (dylud) Extreme pursuit.

Rhyddyludaw, *v. a.* (rhyddylud) To follow, or to pursue excessively. *Rhyddylud alltudion*, foreigners *he persues extremely.*

Rhyddyly, *v. n.* (dyly) To be fully incumbent.

> Rhyddyly dilain gwleiddiadon,
> Rhyddylif cynnif cadfaon;
> Rhyn erwyll rwyf, draig rhodolion, eirchiaid
> Rhydalant eu rhoddion.
>
> The feasting ones *ought to be extremely* instigated fully to cause the affliction of fields of battle to pass away; a chief of gloomy course, the resort of wanderers, petitioners who will fully repay their gifts. *Cynddelw, i H. ab Owain.*

Rhyddymunaw, *v. a.* (dymunaw) To desire earnestly, to wish extremely.

Rhyddymunawl, *a.* (dymunawl) Extremely desirous; extremely wishful.

Rhyddymuniad, *s. m.* (dymuniad) A desiring earnestly; a wishing extremely.

Rhyddyoddef, *v. a.* (dyoddef) To suffer greatly.

Rhyddyoddefiad, *s. m.* (rhyddyoddef) A suffering or bearing extremely.

Rhyddyrchawl, *a.* (dyrchawl) Apt to over-exalt.

Rhyddyrchiad, *s. m.* (dyrchiad) An over-exalting.

Rhyddyrchu, *v. a.* (dyrchu) To over-exalt.

Rhyddyrllid, *v. a.* (dyrllid) To flow extremely.

> Rhyddyrllid fy ngherdd yn nghelnion o fedd
> Yn nghyntedd teyrnon.
>
> My muse *will be greatly made to flow* in carousals of mead in the hall of princes. *Cynddelw, i H. ab Owain.*

Rhyddysg, *s. m.* (dysg) Profound learning.

Rhyddysgawl, *a.* (rhyddysg) Being over-learned.

Rhyddysgiad, *s. m.* (rhyddysg) A learning greatly

Rhyddysgu, *v. a.* (rhyddysg) To instruct profoundly; to become extremely learned.

> Rhyddysgaf ddysgywen feirddion.
>
> *I will profoundly instruct* illustrious bards. *Cynddelw.*

Rhyddysgwyl, *v. a.* (dysgwyl) To be expecting extremely, or earnestly looking for.

Rhyddysgwyliad, *s. m.* (rhyddysgwyl) A being expecting extremely.

Rhyddysgwyliaw, *v. a.* (rhyddysgwyl) To be expecting extremely.

Rhyddysgyrch, *s. m.* (dysgyrch) Excess of resorting

Rhyddysgyrchawl, *a.* (rhyddysgyrch) Being resorting extremely.

Rhyddysgyrchiad, *s. m.* (rhyddysgyrch) A being resorting extremely.

Rhyddysgyrchu, *v. a.* (rhyddysgyrch) To be resorting extremely.

> Rhaith anolaith rhyddysgyrchasant:
> Yn agorphen eu trethan angeu a wddant.
>
> The maxim of devastation *they have resorted to extremely*: in the conclusion of their impositions they experienced death. *Golyddan.*

Rhyddywediad, *s. m.* (dywediad) A previously saying, a fully declaring.

Rhyddywedyd, *v. a.* (dywedyd) To say previously; to declare fully.

> Gwedi gweled o Wl Caisar y llythyr hwnw, yn ddiannod parotoi ei lynges a orug, ac aros gwynt, wrth ei lenwi o'i weithred, yr hyn a ryddywedasai Gaswallawn.
>
> After Julius Cæsar had seen that letter, immediately he prepared his fleet, and waited for wind, which should accomplish the act that *he had before intimated* to Caswallon. *Gr. ab Arthur.*

Rhyedd, *s. m.* (rhy) The state of being extreme.

Rhyeiddil, *a.* (eiddil) Extremely slender, or slim

Rhyeiddilaw, *v. a.* (rhyeiddil) To render extremely slender; to become very slender.

Rhyeiddiliad, *s. m.* (rhyeiddil) A making extremely slender, a becoming very slim.

Rhyeiddilwch, *s. m.* (rhyeiddil) Great slenderness

Rhyeistedd, *s. m.* (eistedd) A sitting before; presidency. *v. a.* To sit over; to preside.

Rhyeisteddawl, *a.* (rhyeistedd) Presiding.

Rhyeisteddiad, *s. m.* (rhyeistedd) A presiding.

Rhyeni, *v. n.* (geni) To be born previously.

> Ar glawr elfydd
> Ei gystedlydd
> Ni ryaned.
>
> On the face of the earth, his equal was not *born before*. *Taliesin.*

Rhyerchi, *v. a* (erchi) To beseech earnestly.

> Rhybrynawys a ryerchis.
>
> He has bought very dear *who has importuned much*. *Adage.*

Rhyerfyniad, *s. m.* (erfyniad) An entreating or imploring extremely.
Rhyerfyniaw, *v. a.* (erfyniaw) To entreat extremely, to implore earnestly.
Rhyerfyniawl, *a.* (erfyniawl) Extremely imploring, earnestly beseeching.
Rhyesgeulus, *a.* (esgeulus) Over-careless.
Rhyesgeulusaw, *v. a.* (rhyesgeulus) To act extremely careless; to be over-careless.
Rhyesgeulusdawd, *s. m.* (rhyesgeulus) Extreme carelessness, or negligence.
Rhyesgeulusiad, *s. m.* (rhyesgeulus) A neglecting overmuch; a being careless overmuch.
Rhyesgyn, *s. m.* (esgyn) An ascent before; an ascent over. *v. a.* To ascend before.
Rhyesgynawl, *a* (rhyesgyn) Previously ascending.
Rhyesgyniad, *s. m.* (rhyesgyn) A previously ascending; an ascending overmuch.
Rhyesgynu, *v. a.* (rhyesgyn) To ascend beyond.
Rhyf, *s. m.—pl. t.* ion (rhy) That enlarges or swells out; what is rife or abundant; a swell or puff out; arrogance, pride; also a berry; a currant.

Afraid i briddin afryn,
Rh'of fi a Duw, faint fo rhyf dyn,
Llunaw baich llawn o bechod:
Lle rhyfedd i falchedd fod!

It is needless for frail clay, between me and God, however great man's *presumption* may be, to form a full load of sin: what a place for pride to exist! *Gutt. ab Sefnyn, i bengl.g.*

Rhyfab, *s. m.—pl.* rhyfeibion (rhy—mab) A boy under age, or an infant. *Welsh Laws.*
Rhyfaeddawl, *a.* (rhyfaedd) Being much dragged.
Rhyfaeddiad, *s. m.* (rhyfaedd) A dragging much.
Rhyfaeddu, *v. a.* (rhyfaedd) To drag about extremely; to buffet extremely.
Rhyfael, *s. f.* (mael) Excessive gain or profit.
Rhyfaeliad, *s. m.* (rhyfael) A gaining excessively.
Rhyfaelu, *v. a.* (rhyfael) To gain extremely.
Rhyfaeth, *s. m.* (maeth) Much nurture.
Rhyfaethawl, *a.* (rhyfaeth) Greatly nourishing.
Rhyfaethiad, *s. m.* (rhyfaeth) A nourishing greatly; a being over-nursed.
Rhyfaethu, *v. a.* (rhyfaeth) To over-nourish.
Rhyfagawl, *a.* (magawl) Much nursed.
Rhyfagiad, *s. m.* (magiad) An over-nursing.
Rhyfagl, *s. f.—pl.* rhyfaglau (magl) A snare.
Rhyfagliad, *s. m.* (rhyfagl) An ensnaring.
Rhyfaglu, *v. a.* (rhyfagl) To ensnare fully.
Rhyfagu, *v. a.* (magu) To rear up or to nourish extremely; to be over-nursed.

Twyllid rhyfegai rhyfygu i.

Deceived has he been *who has been much nourished* with presumption. *Adage.*

Nid perthyn rhyfyg rhyfegais i'm bryd.

Not proper the presumption that *I have much nourished* in my mind. *Cynddelw.*

Rhyfagwyr, *s. f.* (magwyr) An advanced wall.

Clod wellwell c'u law allan
Coed mawr yn fagodau man;
O wartha'r rhai'n wrth yr hwyr
Arfogion a'u rhyfagwyr.

With increasing fame carrying out large trees as tiny bundles; behind these at evening came armed men having their *entrenchment.* *H. ab D. ab I. ab Rhys.*

Rhyfai, *s. m.—pl.* rhyfeiau (bai) Extreme fault.
Rhyfaidd, *s. m.* (baidd) An over-daring.
Rhyfail, *s. m.* (mail) Prepossession.
Rhyfaint, *s. m.* (maint) Excess of quantity.

Ffawd i ddiawg nid rhyfaint.

Prosperity to the idle is not an *excess.* *Adage.*

Rhyfalu, *v. a.* (malu) To grind very small.
Rhyfaniad, *s. m.* (maniad) A making an extreme impression, a making an over-effect.
Rhyfânu, *v. a.* (mânu) To make an extreme mark or impression.

Ffawd i ddrwaid ni ryfân.

Prosperity to the mischievous *will not take effect.* *Adage.*

Rhyfarn, *s. f.* (barn) An over-opinion; prejudice.
Rhyfarnawl, *a.* (rhyfarn) Prejudging.
Rhyfarniad, *s. m.* (rhyfarn) A judging overmuch; a condemning extremely.
Rhyfarnu, *v. a.* (rhyfarn) To judge overmuch; to condemn extremely; to prejudge.
Rhyfas, *a.* (bas) Extremely or very shallow.
Rhyfasiad, *s. m.* (rhyfas) A rendering very shallow; a becoming extremely shallow.
Rhyfasu, *v. a.* (rhyfas) To render very shallow; to become very shallow.
Rhyfawl, *a.* (rhyf) Assuming or arrogant.
Rhyfawl, *s. f.* (mawl) Extreme praise; flattery.
Rhyfawr, *s. m.* (rhyf) A frequent stretching about or scrambling.
Rhyfawrth, *s. m.* (mawrth) The beginning of the storms of March.
Rhyfawrthin, *s. f.* (rhyfawrth—hin) The equinoxial weather or storms of March.

Mawrth a'i ryfawrthin.

March with its *spring-forerunning weather.* *Iolo Goch.*

Rhyfedd, *a.* (medd) Being over possession or scope; wonderful, marvellous, strange.

Iach rydd rhyfedd pa gwyn.

With health at liberty *it is wonderful* what the complaint. *Adage.*

Rhyfeddawd, *s. f.—pl.* rhyfeddodau (rhyfedd) What is surprising or extraordinary, a rarity; a wonder, a miracle.

Rhewydd pob rhyfeddawd.

Every *wonder* is changeable. *Adage.*

Rhyfeddawl, *a.* (rhyfedd) Wonderful, strange.
Rhyfeddeb, *s. f.* (rhyfedd) Exclamation, admiration; a term in rhetoric.
Rhyfeddoldeb, *s. m.* (rhyfeddawl) Extraordinariness; miraculousness; marvellousness.
Rhyfeddoli, *v. a.* (rhyfeddawl) To render marvellous; to become wonderful.
Rhyfeddolrwydd, *s. m.* (rhyfedd) Wonderfulness.
Rhyfeddu, *v. a.* (rhyfedd) To wonder, to marvel.
Rhyfeddwl, *s. m.—pl.* rhyfeddyliau (meddwl) An over-thought; a previous thought.
Rhyfeddyliad, *s. m.* (rhyfeddwl) Premeditation.
Rhyfeddyliaw, *v. a* (rhyfeddwl) To premeditate.

Nid porthi penyd rhyfeddyliais.

To undergo penance *I have not premeditated.* *Cynddelw.*

Rhyfeiad, *s. m.* (rhyfai) An over-criminating.
Rhyfeiaw, *v. a.* (rhyfai) To over-criminate.
Rhyfeiddiad, *s. m.* (rhyfaidd) An over-daring.
Rhyfeiddiaw, *v. a.* (rhyfaidd) To over-dare.
Rhyfeiliad, *s. m.* (rhyfail) A prepossessing.
Rhyfeiliaw, *v. a.* (rhyfail) To prepossess.
Rhyfeilus, *a.* (rhyfail) Prepossessing.
Rhyfeius, *a.* (rhyfai) Over-faulty.
Rhyfel, *s. m.—pl. t.* oedd (bel) War, or warfare.

Grefydd diawl annog rhyfel.

The religion of the devil is to instigate war. *Adage.*

Yn mhob rhyfel mae gofal.

In every *warfare* there is anxiety. *Adage.*

Mae gobaith gwr o ryfel, nid gobaith neb o'r bedd.

There is hope for a man from war, there is no hope for any one from the grave. *Adage.*

Gwiliwch y droell—
A fo cryf a fag rhyfel;
Rhyfel a fag rhyw afar
Tlodi, byth at ei a bar;
Tylodi, trueni trwch
A fo caeth, a fag heddwch.

Beware of the wheel: that is powerful will beget *war*; war will beget some misfortune of poverty, ever disposed to anger and wrath; poverty, distressful the misery of such as be captive, will beget peace. *T. Aled.*

Rhyfela, *v. a.* (rhyfel) To war, to wage war.
Rhyfelawd, *s. m.* (rhyfel) An hostile act.
Rhyfelawg, *a.* (rhyfel) Belligerous; belligerent.
Rhyfelbeiriant, *s. m.* (peiriant) A war engine.
Rhyfeldir, *s. m.—pl. t.* oedd (rhyfel—tir) A place where war is carried on, a seat of war.

Pa ryfeldir bynag y cerddynt ynddo, ni wnelid drwg iddynt.

What *hostile land* soever they might walk in, no harm would be done to them. *Breudd. Maxen.*

Rhyfeledig, *a.* (rhyfel) Being warred. *Arfau rhyfeledig*, warlike implements.
Rhyfeledigaeth, *s. m.* (rhyfeledig) The act of carrying on war.
Rhyfelfa, *s. f.* (rhyfel) A seat of war.
Rhyfelgar, *a.* (rhyfel) Apt to war, warlike.
Rhyfelgarwch, *s. m.* (rhyfelgar) Warlikeness.
Rhyfeliad, *s. m.* (rhyfel) A waging of war.
Rhyfeloffer, *s. m.* (rhyfel—offer) A war engine.
Rhyfelogi, *v. a.* (rhyfelawg) To render warring; to become subject to wars and fightings.
Rhyfelogrwydd, *s. m.* (rhyfelawg) A state of war
Rhyfelu, *v. a.* (rhyfel) To war, to wage war.
Rhyfelus, *a.* (rhyfel) Warring, belligerent.
Rhyfelusaw, *v. a.* (rhyfelus) To render warring.
Rhyfelusrwydd, *s. m.* (rhyfelus) A state of war.
Rhyfelwr, *s. m.—pl.* rhyfelwyr (rhyfel—gwr) A warrior, or a man of war.

Cas a fo ryfelwr llesg, ac ni ddymuno heddwch o flaen rhyfel.

Odious is he who is a *feeble warrior*, and doth not desire peace rather than war. *Adage.*

Rhyfelwynt, *s. m.—pl. t.* oedd (rhyfel—gwynt) A hurricane.
Rhyfelydd, *s. m.—pl. t.* ion (rhyfel) A warrior.
Rhyfer, *a.* (mer) Over-teeming with moisture.
Rhyferad, *s. m.* (rhyfer) A drivelling.

Rhuo a wnai a rhyw nad,
A briw ferw, ab ryferad.

He would mutter with a sort of din, and grind his spittle, the *drivelling* monkey. *D. ab Gwilym, i'r tafawd.*

Rhyferig, *a.* (rhyfer) Drivelling, snivelling.
Rhyferth, *s. m.* (rhy—merth) A violent gust.
Rhyferthin, *s. m.* (rhyferth) A violent gushing.

Yna y disgynai rhyferthin o wylaw ar Amic.

Thereupon a *severe gust* of weeping fell upon Amic. *Cyd. Emlyn ac Amic.*

Rhyferthwy, *s. m.* (rhyferth—gwy) An inundation, a torrent; a tempest. *Rhyferthwy Mawrth*, the tempest of the vernal equinox; *Rhyferthwy Medi*, the tempest of the autumnal equinox

Hir argae a fag ryferthwy.

A long damming will collect a *torrent*. *Adage.*

Un o'r tri engir ddichwain—dychrys y tan rhyferthwy, pan holltes y ddaiar hyd annwn, ag y difaed y rhan fwyaf o bob byw.

One of the three awful events; the tremulation of the *torrent* fire, when the earth was rent to the great deep, so that the greatest part of every life was destroyed. *Barddas.*

Rhyferthwyad, *s. m.* (rhyferthwy) An overflowing, an over-whelming, an inundating.
Rhyferthwyaw, *v. a.* (rhyferthwy) To overspread in a torrent, to overflow.
Rhyferthwyawg, *a.* (rhyferthwy) Having an inundation; apt to overflow.
Rhyferthwyawl, *a.* (rhyferthwy) Overwhelming.
Rhyferw, *s. m.* (berw) An over-boiling.
Rhyferwad, *s. m.* (rhyferw) An over-boiling.
Rhyferwi, *v. a.* (rhyferw) To over-boil.
Rhyfeth, *s. m.* (meth) Extreme failing.
Rhyfethiant, *s. m.* (rhyfeth) Extreme debility.
Rhyfethu, *v. n.* (rhyfeth) To fail extremely.
Rhyfiad, *s. m.* (rhyf) A stretching out; an arrogating, or assuming.
Rhyfig, *a.* (rhyf) Apt to be assuming.
Rhyflin, *a.* (blin) Over-tiresome; teasing.
Rhyflinaw, *v. a.* (rhyflin) To over-tire.
Rhyflinder, *s. m.* (rhyflin) Extreme tiresomeness
Rhyfod, *v.* (bod) To be before; to be fully.

Minnau o'm rhoddion, rhyfodant
Yn rhuddaur, yn rhwydd arddeiniant.

I also from my gifts, which *were to me completely* of ruddy gold, was in ample honour. *Ll. P. Moch.*

Rhyfodd, *s. m.* (bodd) Unrestrained desire.
Rhyfoddawg, *a.* (rhyfodd) Of unconstrained will.

Rhyfoddawg rhy fawr a wyl.

The *over-indulged* casts his eye on too much. *Adage.*

Rhyfoddiaw, *v. a.* (rhyfodd) To give full will.
Rhyfoes, *s. f.—pl. t.* au (moes) Over-ceremony.
Rhyfoeth, *s. m.—pl. t.* au (moeth) Extreme daintiness; an over-pampered state.
Rhyfoethus, *a.* (rhyfoeth) Being over-dainty.
Rhyfoli, *v. a.* (rhyfawl) To praise extremely.

Rhyfoliant unant unaw cymer;
Rhyfolir ei wir, ei orober.

The minstrels of accordant melody will *greatly praise*; his justice, his exploit *will be greatly praised*. *Ein. ab Gwgawn, i L. ab Iorwerth.*

Rhagorai corff, ceryddi ni beiddai!
Rhai a'i rhyfolai, llawr hwfdydd.

The fair lover did excel, she could not merit reproach; some would *flatter her*, abject as the ground. *Bofwyn, i Wenhwyfar.*

Rhyfoliant, *s. m.* (rhyfawl) Extreme praise.
Rhyfon, *s. pl. aggr.* (rhyf) Currants.
Rhyforiad, *s. m.* (rhyfawr) A stretching about, a scrambling; a sawing the air with the hands.
Rhyforiaw, *v. a.* (rhyfawr) To stretch about; to scramble; to saw the air with the hands.

I Fangor, i ryforiaw,
Gwr cul, bob dyw Sul y daw.

To Bangor, *to scramble about*, the meagre wight will on every Sunday come. *R. ab Dafydd Llwyd.*

Rhyfrys, *s. m.* (brys) Precipitation. *a.* Precipitate; impatient, over-hurrying.

Rhys rhyfrys emys, amlged brydyddion;
Rhys hysbys ei lys ar les cerddorion.

Rhys with *impatient* steeds, and bards of many gifts; Rhys whose court is conspicuous for the benefit of minstrels. *Einion Offeiriad.*

Rhyfrysiad, *s. m.* (rhyfrys) A hurrying extremely; an acting with impatience.
Rhyfrysiaw, *v. a.* (rhyfrys) To make too much haste, to precipitate.
Rhyfrysiawl, *a.* (rhyfrys) Over-hastening.
Rhyfunaw, *v. a.* (rhyf—unaw) To unite fully.
Rhyfus, *a.* (rhyf) Apt to bear sway; presuming.
Rhyfusaw, *v. a.* (rhyfus) To render presuming; to become stubborn or froward.
Rhyfusedd, *s. m.* (rhyfus) Stubbornness.
Rhyfwydd, *s. pl.* (rhyf—gwydd) Currant trees.
Rhyfwydden, *s. f. dim.* (rhyfwydd) A currant tree
Rhyfychan, *s. m.* (bychan) Extreme littleness. *a.* Very little; too little, over-small.

Nid gwell gormodd no rhyfychan.

Excess is not better than too *little*. *Adage.*

Rhyfychawd, *s. m.* (bychawd) Extreme smallness

Rhwy fu rhyfychawd gynnen.

The very *little* contention was too much. *Adage.*

Rhyfyg, *s. m.* (rhyf) Presumption, arrogance.
Rhyfygaid, *s. m.* (rhyfyg) Presumption.
Rhyfygawl, *a.* (rhyfyg) Presuming, insolent.
Rhyfygiad, *s. m.* (rhyfyg) A presuming.
Rhyfygu, *v. a.* (rhyfyg) To presume, to dare; to act arrogantly or insolently.
Rhyfygus, *a.* (rhyfyg) Presumptuous, arrogant.
Rhyfygusaw, *v. a.* (rhyfygus) To render presumptuous; to become presuming.
Rhyfygusedd, *s. m.* (rhyfyg) Presumptuousness.
Rhyfygusrwydd, *s. m.* (rhyfyg) Presumptuousness.
Rhyfygwr, *s. m.—pl.* rhyfygwyr (rhyfyg—gwr) One who presumes, an arrogant man.
Rhyfynych, *a.* (mynych) Frequent overmuch.
Rhyfynychiad, *s. m.* (rhyfynych) A frequenting overmuch; an occurring too often.
Rhyfynychu, *v. a.* (rhyfynych) To render very frequent; to frequent overmuch.
Rhyfysg, *s. m.* (mysg) Extreme mixture; confusion. *a.* Confused.
Rhyfysgiad, *s. m.* (rhyfysg) A confusion.
Rhyfysgu, *v. a.* (rhyfysg) To confuse.
Rhyffaeth, *a.* (ffaeth) Over ripe, too mellow.
Rhyffaethiad, *s. m.* (rhyffaeth) A rendering over-mellow; a becoming over-mellow.
Rhyffaethu, *v. a.* (rhyffaeth) To render over-mellow; to become over-mellow.
Rhyffle, *s. m.* (ffle) An extreme verge or border.
Rhyffiwch, *a.* (ffiwch) Extremely apt; very rife.
Rhyffo, *s. m.* (ffo) Extreme flight or escape.
Rhyffoad, *s. m.* (rhyffo) A fleeing overmuch.
Rhyffoi, *v. a.* (rhyffo) To flee overmuch.
Rhyffrau, *s. m.* (ffrau) An extreme flow; a respiration; a violent breathing.
Rhyffreuad, *s. m.* (rhyffrau) A respiring.
Rhyffreuaw, *v. a.* (rhyffrau) To respire greatly.

> Rhyfeddaf——
> Nas gwddant yn ddiau,
> Enaid pwy ei badnau;
> Pwy bryd ei baelodau;
> Py barth pan ddyneu;
> Py wynt a ryffreu.

> I am surprised that they know not, without a doubt, concerning the soul, which is her seat; her members of what form; through what part she causes to pass out; what air she *doth respire*. *Taliesin.*

Rhyffrom, *a.* (ffrom) Extremely irritable or testy
Rhyffromi, *v. a.* (rhyffrom) To taunt or to irritate overmuch; to become very testy.
Rhyffromiad, *s. m.* (rhyffrom) A taunting overmuch, a becoming very testy.
Rhyffrost, *s. m.* (ffrost) Extreme vaunting.
Rhyffrostiad, *s. m.* (rhyffrost) A vaunting or swaggering overmuch.
Rhyffrostiaw, *v. a.* (rhyffrost) To over-vaunt.
Rhyffrostiawl, *a.* (rhyffrost) Extremely vaunting.
Rhyg, *s. m.—pl. t.* au (rhy—yg) Rye.

> Po hynaf fo y rhyg tebycaf fydd i'w dad.

> By so much older the *rye* may be the more like it will be to its father. *Adage.*

> Coll mab Collfrewi a ddoai a gwenith a hahld gyntaf i Ynys Prydain, lle nid oedd cyn no hyny namyn ceirch a rhyg.

> Coll the son of Collvrewi brought wheat and barley first into the Isle of Britain, where there were before then only oats and *rye*. *Trioedd.*

Rhyga, *v. a.* (rhyg) To gather or collect rye.
Rhygabl, *s. m.* (cabl) Extreme calumny.
Rhygablaidd, *a.* (rhygabl) Very calumnious.
Rhygabledd, *s. m.* (rhygabl) Extreme calumny.
Rhygabliad, *s. m.* (rhygabl) A calumniating extremely; a greatly scandalizing.
Rhygablu, *v. a.* (rhygabl) To shew extreme contempt; to calumniate extremely.

> A glywch chwi, ddeon, a ddywedir;
> A ddywed rhianau rygeblir?

> Do you hear, strangers, what is said; what a lady says is it not *be severely derided!* *Cynddelw.*

Rhygadw, *v. a.* (cadw) To keep extremely.
Rhygaffael, *v. a.* (caffael) To over-get; to obtain previously.

> Pencerdd a ddyly bedair ar ugaint y gan bob gwreig a gysgo gan wr, or nis rhygaffo y genti gynt.

> A chief of song is entitled to twenty-four pence from every woman who sleeps with a husband, if he has not *previously obtained* it of her. *Welsh Laws.*

Rhygaffaeliad, *s. m.* (rhygaffael) An over-obtaining; a previously getting.
Rhygais, *s. m.* (cais) An over-attempt or trial.
Rhygall, *a.* (call) Extremely discreet.

> Ni bydd cyfoethawg rhygall.

> The powerful will not be *discreet overmuch*. *Adage.*

Rhygalledd, *s. m.* (rhygall) Excess of cunning.
Rhygallineb, *s. m.* (rhygall) Excess of cunning.
Rhygam, *a.* (cam) Extremely crooked.
Rhygamiad, *s. m.* (rhygam) A bending extremely, an over-bending.
Rhygamu, *v. a.* (rhygam) To bend extremely.
Rhygant, *s. m.—pl. t.* au (cant) An extreme or outmost circle.
Rhyganu, *v. a.* (canu) To sing before.

> Cerdd newydd i'm rhebydd rhyganiad
> Cain awen, gan awel bylgaint.

> A new song to my chieftain the exalted muse *has before sung*, with the gale of the morning. *Cynddelw.*

Rhygardd, *s. m.* (cardd) A violent drive or thrust
Rhygarddiad, *s. m.* (rhygardd) A chasing or driving overmuch; a violently afflicting.
Rhygarddu, *v. a.* (rhygardd) To over-impel.

> Rhygarddwys fy mis;
> Fy nghalon, neud dores!

> My bosom *has been severely racked*, my heart, is it not broken? *Llywarch Hen.*

Rhygariad, *s. m.* (cariad) Extreme fondness.
Rhygaru, *v. a.* (caru) To love extremely.

> Ti a noddyd
> A rygeryd
> O bob carchar.

> Thou wouldest protect such as *thou shouldest dearly love* from every bondage. *Taliesin.*

Rhygas, *s. m.* (cas) Extreme hate. *a.* Very hateful.

> Rhygas rhywelir.

> That is *extremely hated* will be seen too soon. *Adage.*

> A glywaist a gant Rhydderch,
> Trydydd hael serchawg serch;
> Gnawd rhygas gwedi Rhyserch!

> Hast thou heard how Rhydderch sang, the third generous one of cordial affection; common is *extreme hate* after extreme love? *Engl. y Clywed.*

Rhygasâad, *s. m.* (rhygasâu) An over-hating.
Rhygasâu, *v. a.* (rhygas) To hate extremely.
Rhygastelliad, *s. m.* (castelliad) A completely spreading round.
Rhygastellu, *v. a.* (castellu) To raise a complete fence round about.
Rhygawdd, *s. m.* (cawdd) An extreme affront.
Rhygawg, *a.* (rhyg) Abounding with rye.
Rhygawl, *a.* (rhyg) Of the quality of rye.
Rhyged, *s. f.* (ced) Excess of treasure. *a.* Very bountiful; lavish; prodigal.
Rhygeisiad, *s. m.* (rhygais) An over-attempting.
Rhygeisiaw, *v. a.* (rhygais) To over-attempt.
Rhygel, *s. m.* (cel) A complete concealment.
Rhygeliad, *s. m.* (rhygel) A fully concealing.
Rhygelu, *v. a.* (rhygel) To conceal fully.

> Ni rygelir drygiam.

> Misfortune will not *be fully concealed*. *Adage.*

Rhygen, *s. f. dim.* (rhyg) A grain of rye.

Rhygethlig, *a.* (cethlig) Excelling in song.

Rhygethlydd, *s. m.* (cethlydd) A master in song.

Unlle rhygethlydd, rhygethlig,
Rhyddeisyfaf; rhychanaf i wledig.

The station of the *complete songster*, excellent of song, I ardently desire; *I will greatly sing* to a sovereign. *Taliesin.*

Rhygil, *s. m.* (cil) A complete recession.

Rhygiliad, *s. m.* (rhygil) A fully receding.

Rhygiliaw, *v. a.* (rhygil) To recede fully.

Rhygipiaw, *v. a.* (cipiaw) To snatch violently.

Rhygloff, *a.* (cloff) Extremely lame or halting.

Rhygloffedd, *s. m.* (rhygloff) Extreme lameness.

Rhygloffi, *v. a.* (rhygloff) To lame extremely.

Rhygloffiad, *s. m.* (rhygloff) A rendering very lame; a becoming extremely lame.

Rhyglud, *s. m.* (clud) An over-carriage.

Rhygludaw, *v. a.* (rhyglud) To over-carry.

Rhygludiad, *s. m.* (rhyglud) An over-carrying.

Rhyglydd, *s. m.—pl. t.* ion (rhwgl) Desert, merit

Myn weision, ryglyddion clod;
Mwy no neb myn ei nabod.

He will have attendants, *fame-deserving ones*; more than any body he will cause himself to be known. *Iev. Tew, i Syr E. Herbert.*

Rhyglyddaidd, *a.* (rhyglydd) Of a meritorious or a deserving tendency.

Rhyglyddawd, *s. m.* (rhyglydd) A meriting.

Rhyglyddawl, *a.* (rhyglydd) Meritorious.

Rhyglyddedig, *a.* (rhyglydd) Merited, deserved.

Rhyglyddedigaeth, *s. m.* (rhyglyddedig) Meritoriousness.

Rhyglyddiad, *s. m.* (rhyglydd) A meriting.

Rhyglyddiannawl, *a.* (rhyglyddiant) Meritorious

Rhyglyddiannu, *v. a.* (rhyglyddiant) To render meritorious; to become deserving.

Rhyglyddiannus, *a.* (rhyglyddiant) Meritorious.

Rhyglyddiannusaw, *v. a.* (rhyglyddiannus) To render meritorious; to become deserving.

Rhyglyddiant, *s. m.—pl.* rhyglyddiannau (rhyglydd) Merit, desert, worth, reward, claim.

Rhyglyddu, *v. n.* (rhyglydd) To deserve, to merit

Galwes Arthur ar bawb i un lle, i dalu eu gwasanaeth iddynt; a hyny fal y rhyglyddynt.

Arthur called every body to one place, to reward them for their service, and that according as *they might deserve*. *Gr. ab Arthur.*

Rhyglyw, *s. m.* (clyw) A full hearing; a previous hearing.

Rhyglywed, *v. a.* (rhaglyw) A fully hearing; a previously hearing.

Rhygnawg, *a.* (rhwgn) Having friction; having scores or hacks.

Rhygnawl, *a.* (rhygn) Rubbing; scoring.

Rhygnbren, *s. m.—pl. t.* au (rhygn—pren) A stick for scoring upon, a tally.

Rhygnedig, *a.* (rhwgn) Rubbed, chafed; scored.

Rhygnedd, *s. m.* (rhwgn) A state of friction; the state of being scored or hacked.

Rhygnell, *s. f.* (rhwgn) A whipsaw.

Rhygnen, *s. f.—pl. t.* au (rhwgn) A file.

Rhygniad, *s. m.* (rhwgn) A rubbing, a chafing; a scoring; a hacking.

Rhygnogrwydd, *s. m.* (rhygnawg) The state of being rubbed, chafed, or scored.

Rhygnu, *v. a.* (rhwgn) To rub, to chafe; to score; to hack.

Rhag Teifi, yn tori twr main,
Rhygnasant rif naw cant celain.

Before Teivi, demolishing a stone tower, they *scored* the number of nine hundred corpses. *H. ab Owain.*

Rhygnwr, *s. m.—pl.* rhygnwyr (rhwgn—gwr) One who rubs, a scorer.

Rhygoddawl, *a.* (rhygawdd) Very insulting.

Rhygodded, *s. f.* (rhygawdd) Extreme insult.

Rhygoddedig, *a.* (rhygodded) Extremely thwarted

Rhygoddi, *v. a.* (rhygawdd) To vex extremely.

A rygoddwy glew, gogeled rhagddaw:
Gnawd yw o'i ddygnaw ddeifnydd codded.

Who *greatly insults* the brave, let him beware; from his being irritated generally proceedes a cause of trouble. *D. Cyfeiliawg.*

Rhygoddiad, *s. m.* (rhygawdd) A thwarting extremely or overmuch.

Rhygoddiant, *s. m.* (rhygawdd) Extreme vexation; extreme insult.

Rhygoddwr, *s. m.—pl.* rhygoddwyr (rhygawdd—gwr) One who vexes extremely.

Rhygoel, *s. f.—pl. t.* ion (coel) Superstition.

Rhygoeledd, *s. m.* (rhygoel) Superstitiousness.

Rhygoeliad, *s. m.* (rhygoel) A believing overmuch

Rhygoeliaw, *v. a.* (rhygoel) To believe overmuch.

Rhygoelus, *a.* (rhygoel) Being superstitious.

Rhygoll, *s. f.* (coll) Extreme loss. *a.* Over apt to lose.

Lloegr aeth o'r llaw rygoll;
I'r llaw gref yr aeth Lloegr oll.

England is gone from the *greatly losing* hand; to the strong hand is all England gone. *D. Llwyd, i Henri VI.*

Rhygolled, *s. f.—pl. t.* ion (rhygoll) Extreme loss.

Rhygolledig, *a.* (rhygolled) Being totally lost.

Rhygolledu, *v. a.* (rhygolled) To cause extreme loss; to damage extremely.

Rhygolli, *v. a.* (rhy—goll) To lose overmuch.

Ni rygollwyf Duw o ddewredd byd:
Ni rygolles nef ni fo ynfyd.

May I not totally lose God through the gaiety of the world: *he has not completely lost* heaven who is not mad. *Ll. P. Moch.*

Rhygrëad, *s. m.* (crëad) A perfectly creating.

Rhygred, *s. f.* (cred) Over-belief; credulity.

Rhygrediad, *s. m.* (rhygred) An over-believing.

Rhygredu, *v. n.* (rhygred) To be credulous.

Rhygreu, *v. a.* (creu) To create perfectly.

Ac yn oreu dyn Duw rhygreas.

And the best man God *did perfectly create* him. *Gwalchmai.*

Rhygrin, *a.* (crin) Being extremely brittle.

Rhygrinaw, *v. n.* (rhygrin) To become extremely dry, parched, or brittle.

Rhygriniad, *s. m.* (rhygrin) An over-drying.

Rhygronawl, *a.* (cronawl) Tending to collect overmuch; very accumulating.

Rhygroni, *v. a.* (croni) To collect overmuch.

Rhygroniad, *s. m.* (croniad) An over-collecting.

Rhygu, *s. m.* (cu) Over-fondness. *a.* Over-fond.

Rhygu pob rhyfychawd.

Over-precious every thing very small. *Adage.*

Ni bu rygu na bai rygas.

There has been no *over-fondness* but there would be excess of hate. *Adage.*

Rhygudd, *s. f.* (cudd) A full hiding. *a.* Being completely concealed.

Rhyguddiad, *s. m.* (rhygudd) A fully hiding.

Rhyguddiaw, *v. a.* (rhygudd) To hide fully.

Och mor drwm yw ych marw draw:
Och roi gwedd i'ch rhyguddiaw!

Alas! how sad that you should yonder die: to put a covering so *completely to hide* you how direful! *Rhys Pyngiwyd.*

Rhygwellt, *s. m.* (rhyg—gwellt) Rye-grass.

Rhygwsg, *s. m.* (cwsg) Extreme sleep.

Rhygwydd, *s. m.* (cwydd) An extreme fall.

Rhygwyddaw, *v. n.* (rhygwydd) To fall extremely

Rhygwyddawl, *a.* (rhygwydd) Tending to fall extremely; being very apt to tumble.

Rhygwyddiad, *s. m.* (rhygwydd) An over-falling.

Rhygwyn, *s. f.* (cwyn) Extreme complaint.

Rhygwynaw, *v. a.* (rhygwyn) To complain extremely; to be very querulous.

Rhychwynant unant anhawddgoll teyrn
Teyrnedd Cymmru oll.

Minstrels *will extremely deplore* the hard-to-be-lost prince of all the princes of Wales. *D. ab Llewelyn Mew.*

Rhygwynawl, *a.* (rhygwyn) Very querulous.
Rhygwyniad, *s. m.* (rhygwyn) A complaining extremely, a being very querulous.
Rhygybydd, *s. m.* (cybydd) A complete miser.

Nid gwell ryhael, anfael fydd,
Yn rhoi ei gwbl, no rhygybydd.

Not better the over-liberal than the *greatest miser*, disadvantage will ensue in giving his all. *D. ab Edmwnd.*

Rhygybyddawl, *a.* (rhygybydd) Over-miserly.
Rhygybydd-dawd, *s. m.* (rhygybydd) Extreme niggardliness or stinginess.
Rhygybydd-dra, *s. m.* (rhygybydd) Extreme miserliness; over-stinginess.
Rhygybyddu, *v. a.* (rhygybydd) To act very niggardly, to be over miserly or stingy.
Rhygyfarch, *s. m.* (cyfarch) A presentment.
Rhygyfarchawl, *a.* (rhygyfarch) Presenting.
Rhygyfarchiad, *s. m.* (rhygyfarch) A presenting.
Rhygyfarchu, *v. a.* (rhygyfarch) To present.
Rhygyfariad, *s. m.* (cyfariad) A fully meeting.
Rhygyfarn, *v. a.* (cyfarn) To meet fully.

Anfon cennad a wnai at ei ferch, i fynegi iddi y rhyw angbyfnerth a rygyfarai ag ef.

He sent a messenger to his daughter, to inform her of the peculiar misfortune that *had completely met* with him. *Gr. ab Arthur.*

Rhygylch, *s. m.—pl. t.* oedd (cylch) A periphery.

Deg mlynedd, cymyredd cylch,
Ar hugain yw ei rhygylch.

Three times ten years, that circle of renown
Will solemn Saturn's *revolution* crown.
Ed. Richard, i Sadwrn.

Rhygylchiad, *s. m.* (rhygylch) A going round an orbit; a performing a revolution.
Rhygylchu, *v. a.* (rhygylch) To go round an orbit.
Rhygynnal, *v. a.* (cynnal) To support fully.
Rhygynnaliad, *s. m.* (rhygynnal) A fully supporting, maintaining, or upholding.
Rhygynnar, *a.* (cynnar) Over-early.
Rhygynnaredd, *s. m.* (rhygynnar) Over-earliness.
Rhygynnarwch, *s. m.* (rhygynnar) Prematureness
Rhygynnil, *a.* (cynnil) Over-exact; over-sparing.
Rhygynnilaw, *v. a.* (rhygynnil) To act too exactly; to be over-sparing.
Rhygynniledd, *s. m.* (rhygynnil) Over-exactness.
Rhygynniliad, *s. m.* (rhygynnil) A being over-exact; a being over-sparing.
Rhygynnilwch, *s. m.* (rhygynnil) Over-exactness.
Rhygynnull, *v. a.* (cynnull) To heap together overmuch, to over-collect.
Rhygynnullaw, *v. a.* (rhygynnull) To gather together overmuch, to over-collect.

Baich rhygynnullais
O bechawd annyfais;
Rhyddyergrynais
O'i gymheirt.

A load *I have over-heaped* of inconsiderate sin; I have been trembling extremely from the distress of it. *Meilyr.*

Rhygynnulliad, *s. m.* (rhygynnull) A heaping or collecting together overmuch.
Rhygynnyg, *v. a.* (cynnyg) To over-offer.
Rhygynnygiad, *s. m.* (rhygynnyg) A making an extreme offer.
Rhygyng, *s. m.—pl. t.* au (rhwg—yng) An ambling pace.
Rhygyngawd, *s. m.* (rhygyng) An ambling.
Rhygyngawg, *a.* (rhygyng) Of ambling pace.
Rhygyngedd, *s. m.* (rhygyng) An ambling pace.
Rhygyngen, *s. f.* (rhygyng) A rattle in the throat
Rhygyngfarch, *s. m.—pl.* rhygyngfeirch (rhygyng—march) An ambling horse.

Rhygynghan, *s. f.* (cynghan) Superior accordance.
Rhygynghaniad, *s. m.* (rhygynghan) An according excellently.
Rhygynghanu, *v. n.* (rhygynghan) To accord excellently.

Cred a ched a cherdd rhygynghanu i'th blaid.

Faith and treasure and song *do befit extremely* in thy company. *Cynddelw.*

Rhygyngiad, *s. m.* (rhygyng) An ambling.
Rhygyngu, *v. a.* (rhygyng) To amble, to go with an ambling pace; to stalk.
Rhygyngydd, *s. m.* (rhygyng) An ambler.
Rhygyrch, *s. m.* (cyrch) An over-resort.
Rhygyrchawl, *a.* (rhygyrch) Over-resorting.
Rhygyrchiad, *s. m.* (rhygyrch) An over-resorting.
Rhygyrchu, *v. a.* (rhygyrch) To over-resort.

Rhyliarychynt, rhygyrchynt yn nghledd dyfnu
Ariiwydr gwrid arth gwryd dearchau.

They would greatly moderate, *they would greatly* resort to the sword-conflict of the crimson track of the ruthless bear of tumult. *Taliesin.*

Rhygyrchwr, *s. m.—pl.* rhygyrchwyr (rhygyrch—gwr) One who resorts overmuch.
Rhygyrhaedd, *v. a.* (cyrhaedd) To reach over.
Rhygyrhaeddawl, *a.* (rhygyrhaedd) Tending to reach over; an over-extending.
Rhygyrhaeddiad, *s. m.* (rhygyrhaedd) A reaching or extending over.
Rhygyrhaeddyd, *v. a.* (rhygyrhaedd) To reach over, to reach beyond.
Rhygysgawl, *a.* (rhygwsg) Over sleeping.
Rhygysgiad, *s. m.* (rhygwsg) An over-sleeping.
Rhygysgu, *v. a.* (rhygwsg) To sleep overmuch.
Rhygysgwr, *s. m.—pl.* rhygysgwyr (rhygwsg—gwr) One who over-sleeps.
Rhygystlwn, *s. m.* (cystlwn) Much intercourse.
Rhygystlynawl, *a.* (rhygystlwn) Of much intercourse or connexion.
Rhygystlynedd, *s. m.* (rhygystlwn) A state of much intercourse or connexion.

Yn rhygystlynedd o bennaeth weision,
Rhyddyfydd Lyminawg,
A fydd wr chwannawg
I oresgyn Mon.

In the *close alliance* of the sovereign's servants, Llyminawg will first appear, who will be an ambitious man, to subdue Mon. *Taliesin.*

Rhygystlyniad, *s. m.* (rhygystlwn) A carrying on much intercourse; a forming close alliance.
Rhygystlynu, *v. a.* (rhygystlwn) To have much intercourse; to form close alliance.
Rhygystlynwr, *s. m.—pl.* rhygystlynwyr (rhygystlwn—gwr) One of much intercourse.
Rhygywir, *a.* (cywir) Extremely exact.
Rhygywiraw, *v. a.* (rhygywir) To make very exact; to be over exact or accurate.
Rhygywiredd, *s. m.* (rhygywir) Extreme exactness
Rhyhael, *a.* (hael) Liberal overmuch.
Rhyhaeledd, *s. m.* (rhyhael) Over liberality.
Rhyhawd, *s. m.* (hawd) An extreme shoot up.
Rhyher, *s. f.* (hèr) Excess of defiance.

Dychymmydd tristyd byd a rhyher.

The misfortune of the world will bear with much fortitude. *Golyddan.*

Rhyheriad, *s. m.* (rhyher) A brandishing about extremely; a defying greatly.
Rhyheriaw, *v. a.* (rhyher) To brandish extremely.
Rhyherw, *s. f.* (herw) Excess of roving.
Rhyherwa, *v. a.* (rhyherw) To rove about extremely; to stray overmuch.
Rhyhiraeth, *s. m.* (hiraeth) Extreme longing.
Rhyhiraethawl, *a.* (rhyhiraeth) Over-longing.

Rhyhiraethiad, *s. m.* (rhyhiraeth) A longing or wishing extremely.

Rhyhiraethu, *v. a.* (rhyhiraeth) To long or to wish extremely.

> [illegible] a'm rhyhiraeth [illegible]
>
> I have listened to a nightingale that has caused me extreme longing ever since I heard her. *Gwalchmai.*

Rhyhiraethus, *a.* (rhyhiraeth) Apt to long much.

Rhyhodi, *v. a.* (rhyawd) To soar greatly.

Rhyhodig, *a.* (rhyhawd) Extremely aspiring.

> [illegible]
>
> I came to Dygannwy to contend; I liberated my lord in the presence of strangers, and of Maelgwn, the greatest in [illegible] ... Elffin the sovereign of greatly aspiring. *Taliesin, i'r* [illegible]

Rhyhoddiad, *s. m.* (hoddiad) Over-facilitating.

Rhyhoddiaw, *v. a.* (hoddiaw) To over-facilitate.

Rhyhoff, *a.* (hoff) Extremely fond, over-fond.

Rhyhoffawl, *a.* (rhyhoff) Apt to be over-fond.

Rhyhoffi, *v. a.* (rhyhoff) To be over-fond.

Rhyhoffiad, *s. m.* (rhyhoff) An over-loving.

Rhyhwyr, *a.* (hwyr) Too late; high time; far-extending. *Mae yn rhyhwyr ini beidiaw,* it is high time for us to leave off.

> [illegible]
>
> Time will swiftly [illegible] the far extending [illegible] which the course of [illegible] *Ll. P. Moch.*

Rhyhwyrhad, *s. m.* (rhyhwyr) A rendering over late; a growing over late.

Rhyhwyrhau, *v. a.* (rhyhwyr) To become over late.

Rhyhwyredd, *s. m.* (rhyhwyr) An over-lateness.

Rhyhy, *a.* (hy) Over-bold; over-forward.

Rhyhyd, *a.* (hyd) Extremely long, over-long.

> Gwae fab dyn ——
> Cam gwy [illegible] yn rhyhyd [illegible]
>
> Woe to the son of man from loving vice for too long [illegible] *Cynddelw.*

Rhyhyder, *s. m.* (hyder) Excess of confidence.

Rhyhyderiad, *s. m.* (rhyhyder) A confiding much.

Rhyhyderu, *v. a.* (rhyhyder) To confide much.

Rhyhyderus, *a.* (rhyhyder) Over-confiding.

Rhyladd, *v. a.* (lladd) To cut off completely.

Rhyladdiad, *s. m.* (rhyladd) A fully cutting off.

Rhylaes, *a.* (llaes) Trailing or falling very low.

Rhylafur, *s. m.* (llafur) Over-labouring.

Rhylafuriaw, *v. a.* (rhylafur) To labour much.

Rhylafuriawl, *a.* (rhylafur) Very laborious.

Rhylam, *s. m.—pl. t.* au (llam) An over-step.

Rhylamawl, *a.* (rhylam) Over-stepping.

Rhylamiad, *s. m.* (rhylam) An over-stepping.

Rhylamu, *v. a.* (rhylam) To o[ve]r-step.

Rhylanw, *s. m.* (llanw) An over-fulness.

Rhylar, *a.* (llar) Very mild or soothing.

Rhylarwch, *s. m.* (rhylar) Extreme mildness.

Rhylarwchiad, *s. m.* (rhylarwch) A much assuaging.

Rhylarychu, *v. a.* (rhylarwch) To assuage greatly.

Rhylas, *a.* (glas) Very blue, very livid. *Rhylas-wedd fy nghrau!* Of very pale hue my brow!

Rhylasiad, *s. m.* (rhylas) A making very blue.

Rhylasu, *v. a.* (rhylas) To becom[e v]ery blue.

Rhylathr, *a.* (llathr) Extremely glittering.

Rhylathraidd, *a.* (rhylathr) Extremely glittering.

Rhylathrawl, *a.* (rhylathr) Very glittering.

Rhylathredd, *s. m.* (rhylathr) Extreme glitter.

Rhylathriad, *s. m.* (rhylathr) A making very glittering, a polishing extremely.

Rhylathru, *v. a.* (rhylathr) To make very glittering, to polish extremely; to glitter much.

Rhylawn, *a.* (llawn) Redundant, over-full.

Rhylawnder, *s. m.* (rhylawn) A redundance.

Rhylawnedd, *s. m.* (rhylawn) A redundance.

Rhylawni, *v.* (rhylawn) To make redundant.

Rhyle, *s. m.* (lle) An over-place; superiority.

> Ystryw [illegible], nid [illegible] rhyle.
>
> A bitter trick, but [illegible] means for superiority. *Gwalchmai.*

Rhyleâd, *s. m.* (rhyle) An over-placing; a giving a superior place.

> Prif gyfarch [illegible] rhyleâd.
>
> An artful first greeting will ensure an over-placing. *Taliesin.*

Rhyleäwl, *a.* (rhyle) Tending to over-place.

Rhylef, *s. m.* (llef) An extreme cry.

Rhylefain, *v. a.* (rhylef) To cry out much.

Rhylenwi, *v. a.* (rhylanw) To over charge, to fill over; to abound to excess.

Rhylesgu, *v. a.* (rhy—llesgu) To relax.

Rhylid, *s. m.* (llid) Extreme rage or anger.

Rhylidiad, *s. m.* (rhylid) A greatly irritating.

Rhylidiaw, *v. a.* (rhylid) To irritate greatly.

Rhylithr, *s. m.* (llithr) That is slippery overmuch; a diarrhœa. *a.* Too slippery.

Rhylithraw, *v. a.* (rhylithr) To slip extremely.

Rhylithrawl, *a.* (rhylithr) Very slippery.

Rhylithredd, *s. m.* (rhylithr) Extreme slipperiness.

Rhylithriad, *s. m.* (rhylithr) A slipping extremely.

Rhyliw, *s. m.—pl. t.* iau (lliw) A high colour.

Rhyliwiad, *s. m.* (rhyliw) A colouring highly.

Rhyliwiaw, *v. a.* (rhyliw) To colour highly.

Rhyliwiawg, *a.* (rhyliw) Of high colour.

Rhylofi, *v. a.* (llofi) To bestow greatly.

> O'r dawn rhylofaist [illegible] wyf,
>
> From the talent thou hast amply conferred [illegible] *Meilyr ab Gwalchmai.*

Rhylofiad, *s. m.* (llofiad) A greatly bestowing.

Rhylog, *s. m.—pl. t.* au (llog) Over-hire.

Rhylogawl, *a.* (rhylog) Relating to over-hire.

Rhylogi, *v. a.* (rhylog) To over-hire; to deal usuriously.

Rhylogiad, *s. m.* (rhylog) An over-hiring.

Rhylosg, *s. m.* (llosg) An extreme burning.

Rhylosgedd, *s. m.* (rhylosg) Extreme burning.

Rhylosgi, *v. a.* (rhylosg) To burn extremely.

Rhylosgiad, *s. m.* (rhylosg) Over-burning.

Rhyludd, *s. m.* (lludd) Extreme hinderance.

Rhyluddiad, *s. m.* (rhyludd) A hindering much.

Rhyluddiaw, *v. a.* (rhyludd) To hinder greatly.

Rhylun, *s. m.* (llun) A complete form; a preform.

Rhyluniad, *s. m.* (rhylun) A fully forming.

Rhyluniaeth, *s. m.* (rhylun) Complete formation.

Rhyluniaethawl, *a.* (rhyluniaeth) Tending t[o] complete formation.

Rhyluniaethiad, *s. m.* (rhyluniaeth) Preformation.

Rhyluniaethu, *v. a.* (rhyluniaeth) To form completely; to preform.

> [illegible]
>
> From my tongue [illegible] completely [illegible] the truth will be [illegible] *D. ab Gwilym.*

Rhyluniaw, *v. a.* (rhylun) To form fully.

Rhylwgr, *s. m.* (llwgr) Extreme damage or bu[rst].

Rhylwnc, *s. m.* (llwnc) An extreme swallow.

Rhylwyth, *s. m.* (llwyth) An over-load.

Rhylwythaw, *v. a.* (rhylwyth) To over-load.

Rhylwythawg, *a.* (rhylwyth) Over-loaded.

Rhylwythiad, *s. m.* (rhylwyth) Over loading.

Rhyly, *a.* (lly) Extremely apt to move.

> Yn gerdd [illegible]
>
> [illegible] an amicable song of [illegible] *Prydydd y Moch.*

Rhylygrawl, *a.* (rhylwgr) Tending to de[file] extremely; extremely defiling.

Rhylygredd, *s. m.* (rhylwgr) The state of being extremely damaged; extreme defilement.

Rhylygriad, *s. m.* (rhylwgr) A damaging extremely; a defiling extremely.

Rhylygru, *v. a.* (rhylwgr) To damage extremely; to pollute extremely.

Rhylyncawl, *a.* (rhylwnc) Fully swallowing.

Rhylynciad, *s. m.* (rhylwnc) A fully swallowing.

Rhylyncu, *v. a.* (rhylwnc) To swallow fully.

Rhyll, *s. m.* (rhy—yll) A rift, cleft, or parting.

Rhym, *s. m.* (rhy—ym) That stretches round.

Rhym, *pronom. prep.* (rhy—ym) Signally mine; me signally; me before.

Rhym a fal blw blith yr haf;
Rhym a fai eddystrod y gauaf:
Rhym a fai win gloew.——

Peculiarly mine were the milch kine of summer; *peculiarly mine* were the harnessed steeds of winter; *peculiarly mine* was the sparkling wine.—— *Taliesin.*

Rhym gelwir yn ffyrf, yn ffyng arab hwyl
Yn arabhawl derfysg.

I particularly shall be called the powerful, the quick of blithesome course in the joy-inciting tumult. *Cynddelw.*

Rhodri mawr rhwym llawr; rhym llofes,
A rydd budd i bawb ei gymhes.

Great Rodri the ground doth bind; he *before* endowed me, who gives to every one his appropriate good. *Ll. P. Moch, i R. ab Owain.*

Rhymofyn, *v. a.* (ymofyn) Peculiarly to enquire, seek, or demand.

Rhymofyn Celwydd cyreifiaint;
Ei folawd rhy bydd rhy caint.

The Fountain of love *peculiarly demands* contrition; his praise will be supremely the first of songs. *Meigant, m. Cynddylan.*

Rhymofynawl, *a.* (rhymofyn) Peculiarly enquiring or demanding.

Rhymofyniad, *s. m.* (rhymofyn) A peculiarly enquiring or demanding.

Rhyn, *s. m.—pl. t.* oedd (rhy—yn) That reaches, shoots, or extends into; that causes to run into; a principle of motion; impulse; a shiver, or shake; dread; an instant; a small space; a small quantity; a point, or cape. *s. f. Rhen*, a torrent, a brook. Hence *Aeddren* and *Onren*.

O amddifad feibion ac ereill ryn.

Of orphan children and others a *few*. *Taliesin.*

Rhyn, *a.* (rhy—yn) Pervading; agitating, shivering; terrible.

Mynaist gyfarfod yn gyfarfawg
A Gwenwynwyn, ryn rwyf lluosawg.

Thou didst seek to meet in arms with Gwenwynwyn, the *terrible* chief of many hosts. *Ll. P. Moch, i L. ab Iorwerth.*

Yn gorwyn ewyn rhyn yn rhedeg;
Yn gwrid yn Ionawr mawr morgroeg.

Supremely white is the *shivering foam* in running; in January how mighty the great surging of the sea. *D. Benfras.*

Rhyn, *pronom. prep.* (rhy—yn) Ours peculiarly; us signally; us before.

Ni'm gatwy Rheen yn rhan faddeu!
Rhoddyaid i Dduw yn an dechreu,
Rhod per paradwys parsa goleu;
Rhyn parasai Duw heb ddim eisieu.

May my Creator not leave me in the discarded party! There was given of God to us our beginning, in the blissful circle of paradise of continuing light; *us originally* God had caused void of every want. *Meilyr ab Gwalchmai.*

Rhynaidd, *a.* (rhyn) Tending to be shivering.

Rhynaig, *a.* (rhyn) Tremulous, or trembling.

Rhynawd, *s. m.* (rhyn) Pervasion, a running into; agitation; that is fleeting or passing; a moment; a while; a small space; a small quantity. *Rhynawd yn y coed*, a little way in the wood.

Digawn yw gware rhynawd.

Sufficient is the play of a *moment* *Adage.*

Rhag rhynawd tan dychyfriwy mwg.

From the *agitation* of fire smoke will be raised. *Taliesin.*

Rhynawl, *a.* (rhyn) Agitating; shivering.

Rhyndawd, *s. m.* (rhyn) A shivering, a quake.

Rhyned, *s. f.* (rhyn) That runs in; a small space. a small quantity; a moment.

Rhynedig, *a.* (rhyn) Agitated; shivered.

Rhynedd, *s. m.* (rhyn) A state of agitation.

Rhyni, *s. m.* (rhyn) An agitating, or trembling.

Otan a phorchellan, a phorchell ryni
Tenea yw fy llen, nid llonydd lmi.

Listening with a pigling, with a little pig *of trembling*, thin is my covering, for me there is no contentment. *Myrddin.*

Rhyniad, *s. m.* (rhyn) An agitation; a shivering.

Rhyniaw, *v. a.* (rhyn) To pervade; to agitate; to have instinct; to follow instinct.

O saith ienaid——
Un yw a ryniaf:
A dau y tynaf;
A thri a waeddaf;
A phedwar a fleaaf;
A phump a welaf;
A chwech a glywaf;
A saith a rogleuaf.

Of seven faculties: one is what *I know by instinct*; with the second I touch; with the third I call; with the fourth I taste, with the fifth I see; with the sixth I hear; with the seventh I smell. *Taliesin.*

Ci i dynu, march i ryniaw,
 Edion i wan, hwch i dyraw.

A dog to pull, a horse to move, a kine to gore, a sow to burrow. *Taliesin.*

Rhyniawg, *a.* (rhyn) Being pervaded; being agitated; having instinct.

Rhyniawl, *a.* (rhyn) Pervasive; apt to agitate.

Rhynion, *s. pl.* (rhyn) Oats cleared of the husks.

Rhynllyd, *a.* (rhyn) Full of shivering.

Rhynllydrwydd, *s. m.* (rhynllyd) Shiveringness.

Rhynswch, *s. m.—pl.* rhynsychau (rhyn—swch) The trunk of an elephant.

Rhynu, *v. a.* (rhyn) To cause an emotion; to extend into; to cause a shivering or quaking; to shiver, to shake with cold, to be chilled. *Wyf yn rhynu*, I am shivering with cold.

Rhyngad, *s. m.* (rhwng) Intervention.

Rhyngadwy, *a.* (rhyngad) Capable of intervening, capable of fulfilling.

Rhyngadwy fodd genym bob gwnc ohoni.

Agreeable to our will is every article of it. *Breint Bangdd y Wenn.*

Rhyngawd, *s. m.* (rhwng) An intervention.

Rhyngawg, *a.* (rhwng) Having intervention. *s. m.* That mediates.

Bid ryngawg dirlwch.

Let an elder be a *mediator*. *Llywarch Hen.*

Rhyngawl, *a.* (rhwng) Intervening; mediate.

Rhyngawr, *s. m.* (rhwng) That intervenes.

Rhyngdawd, *s. m.* (rhwng) Intervention.

Rhyngedig, *a.* (rhwng) Intervening.

Rhyngedd, *s. m.* (rhwng) Intermediateness.

Rhyngiad, *s. m.* (rhwng) An intervention.

Rhynglinell, *s. f.—pl. t.* au (rhwng—llinell) An intervening line.

Rhynglinellawl, *a.* (rhynglinell) Interlineary.

Rhynglinelliad, *s. m.* (rhynglinell) Interlineation.

Rhynglinellu, *v. a.* (rhynglinell) To interline.

Rhyngsang, *s. f.—pl. t.* au (rhwng—sang) A discope, in rhetoric.

Rhyngu, *v. a.* (rhwng) To intervene; to mediate; to bring to pass; to content. "*A rync dy fodd di hyny?*" Will that be agreeable to thy will?

Rhyodidawg, *a.* (godidawg) Superexcellent.

Rhyodres, *s. m.* (godres) Ostentation, or pomp.

Caffant fyrdd o feirddion eu lles
O foli Rodri ryodres.

A myriad of bards will find their good from praising the pomp of Rhodri. *Ll. P. Moch.*

Oedd chynghorfynt can y teyrnasoedd pell i wrtho, maint olod ei lys, a rhyodres ei deulu.

Envy filled the kingdoms far from him, for the fame of his court and the *pomp* of his family. *Gr. ab Arthur.*

Rhyoddef, *v. a.* (goddef) To bear extremely.
Rhyoddefawl, *a.* (rhyoddef) Over-patient.
Rhyoddefiad, *s. m.* (rhyoddef) A bearing much.
Rhyoddefu, *v. a.* (rhyoddef) To bear extremely.
Rhyoed, *s. m.* (oed) Over-age, extreme age.
Rhyoedran, *s. m.* (rhyoed) Extreme age.
Rhyoedranus, *a.* (rhyoedran) Superannuated.
Rhyofal, *s. m.* (gofal) Extreme care.
Rhyofalu, *v. a.* (rhyofal) To act very cautiously; to be over-anxious.
Rhyofalus, *a.* (rhyofal) Over-careful.
Rhyofn, *a.* (ofn) Extreme terror or fear.
Rhyofnawg, *a.* (rhyofn) Over-fearful.
Rhyofni, *v. a.* (rhyofn) To fear extremely.
Rhyofniad, *s. m.* (rhyofn) A fearing extremely.
Rhyogwydd, *s. m.* (gogwydd) An over-bias.
Rhyogwyddaw, *v. a.* (rhyogwydd) To over-bias.
Rhyogwyddawl, *a.* (rhyogwydd) Over-inclining.
Rhyogwyddiad, *s. m.* (rhyogwydd) An inclining extremely; an over-biassing.
Rhyorchwyl, *s. f.—pl. t.* ion (gorchwyl) An over-performance, supererogation.
Rhyorchwylaw, *v.* (rhyorchwyl) To supererogate.
Rhyorchwyliad, *s. m.* (gorchwyl) Supererogation.
Rhyorchwylus, *a.* (rhyorchwyl) Supererogatory.
Rhyoresgyn, *s. m.* (goresgyn) A full subjection.
Rhyoresgynawl, *a.* (rhyoresgyn) Fully subduing.
Rhyoresgyniad, *s. m.* (rhyoresgyn) A fully subduing; a completely overcoming.
Rhyoresgynu, *v.* (rhyoresgyn) To subdue fully.
Rhyorfod, *v. a.* (gorfod) To overcome fully; to be fully necessitated.

Gwedi gweled o Wl Caisar ryorfod arno, yngbyd ag ychydig o'i nifer vdd ai ar ffo yn ei longau, a chymeryd diogelwch y mor yn amddiffyn iddo.

After Julius Cæsar had perceived that he was *completely overcome*, with a small part of his army he retreated to his ships, and took the security of the sea for his protection. *Gr. ab Arthur.*

Rhyorfodawg, *a.* (rhyorfod) Being completely overcome; under full subjection.
Rhyorfodawl, *a.* (rhyorfod) Tending to overcome completely.
Rhyorfodiad, *s. m.* (rhyorfod) A fully over-coming, a making a complete conquest.
Rhyorugaw, *v. a.* (gorugaw) To perform, to make completely, to accomplish fully.

Rhygorez Duw dda——
Rhygorux fy awen,
I foli fy rhen:
Mydwyf Taliesin,
Araeth llif dewin.

God *originally formed* good; he *originally formed* my muse, to praise my sovereign. I am Taliesin with flowing speech of prophecy. *Taliesin.*

Rhyorugawl, *a.* (gorugawl) Tending to do fully.
Rhyorugiad, *s. m.* (gorugiad) A doing fully.
Rhyosgoew, *a.* (gosgoew) Having a very contrary direction or bearing.
Rhyran, *s. f.—pl. t.* au (rhan) Extreme part.
Rhyranawl, *a.* (rhyran) Tending to over-divide.
Rhyraniad, *s. m.* (rhyran) An over-dividing.
Rhyranu, *v. a.* (rhyran) To over-divide.
Rhyrawd, *s. f.* (rhawd) An extreme course.
Rhyred, *s. f.* (rhed) An extreme running.

Ac yn ini feddyg, a fedd gwared an gau,
A dodwn innau yn ymddiried;
Ysef arglwydd nef a nerthaed,
I ddiofryd gwyd gwedi rhyred.

And to us there is a physician, who has the power to put away our falsity, and let us then place our dependence; for it is the Lord of heaven who is endued with power, to put aside vice after an *excessive course.* *Gwalchmai.*

Rhyredawl, *a.* (rhyred) Tending to run beyond.
Rhyredeg, *v. a.* (rhyred) To run extremely.
Rhyrediad, *s. m.* (rhyred) A running extremely.
Rhyrif, *s. m.* (rhif) An over-number.
Rhyrifaw, *v. a.* (rhyrif) To over-number.
Rhyrifawl, *a.* (rhyrif) Supernumerary.
Rhyrifiad, *s. m.* (rhyrif) An over-numbering.
Rhyrith, *s. m.* (rhith) A prior appearance.
Rhyrithiad, *s. m.* (rhyrith) A previously appearing; an over-appearing.
Rhyrithiaw, *v. a.* (rhyrith) To appear before.
Rhyrithiawl, *a.* (rhyrith) Previously appearing.
Rhyrodiad, *s. m.* (rhyrawd) A rambling overmuch.
Rhyrodiaw, *v. a.* (rhyrawd) To ramble overmuch.
Rhyrodiawl, *a.* (rhyrawd) Apt to stroll much.
Rhyrodd, *s. f.—pl. t.* ion (rhodd) An over-gift.
Rhyroddawl, *a.* (rhyrodd) Over-giving.
Rhyroddi, *v. a.* (rhyrodd) To give overmuch.
Rhyroddiad, *s. m.* (rhyrodd) An over-giving.
Rhyrwym, *s. m.* (rhwym) Extreme stricture.
Rhyrwymaw, *v. a.* (rhyrwym) To bind extremely
Rhyrwymawl, *a.* (rhyrwym) Over-binding.
Rhyrwymiad, *s. m.* (rhyrwym) An over-binding.
Rhyrys, *s. m.* (rhys) Extreme strait or difficulty.

Nis deubi ryrys.

There would not come a *great difficulty.* *Taliesin.*

Rhyrysiaw, *v. a.* (rhyrys) To hesitate extremely.
Rhyrysiawl, *a.* (rhyrys) Extremely hesitating.
Rhys, *s. m.—pl. t.* oedd (rhy—ys) Extreme ardency; extreme tendency; aptitude to set off, begin, pervade, or to overrun; a rushing; a strait; a trial, a difficulty.

Dywed Myrddin y daw
Y rhys a'r aflwydd ar rai.

Myrddin said that there would come a certain *difficulty* and misfortune upon some. *Ieuan Tew.*

Rhys, *pronom. prep.* (rhy—ys) That signally; of that particularly.

Rhys gwollychwyf rwyf rhyfeddau,
Can digones Duw o'i ddefnyddiau.

That above all may I adore the Lord of wonders, since God has formed him from his materials. *Meilyr ab Gwalchmai.*

Rhysaeth, *s. m.* (rhys) The act of putting in a moving tendency; a putting in a course; a running a course; a straitening.
Rhysail, *s. f.—pl.* rhyseiliau (sail) An extreme or first foundation.
Rhysawl, *a.* (rhys) Rushing; over-running.
Rhyse, *s. m.* (se) Extreme fixedness; the state of being quite fixed or determined.

Gnawd gwedi rhyserch rysa.

Frequently after extreme fondness comes *excess of obstinacy.* *Gwalchmai.*

Rhysedd, *s. m.—pl. t.* au (rhws) Superfluity, excess, an over-abundance.

Gwell golud no rhysedd.

Better are means than *superfluity.* *Adagr.*

Rhysedd, *s. m.* (rhys) A rush, or violent course.

Pan amug Tegeingl, teg rhysedd
Rhysfa cad Cadelling fonedd
Oedd trameawr trameirw yn dyhedd.

When he defended Tegeingl, splendid the *career* on the course of battle of Cadell's progeny, innumerable those to death consigned falling to silence. *Cynddelw m. O. Gwynedd.*

Rhysedda, *v. a.* (rhysedd) To rush on; to rush into difficulty or trial.

Gwell dyhedd no rhysedda.

Better is forbearance than *to rush into contest.* *Adagr.*

Gwell rhwydd no rhysedda.

Better what is easy than *to encounter difficulties.* *Llyfred.*

Rhysoddawg, *a.* (rhysedd) Having superfluity.

Rhyseddu, *v. a.* (rhysedd) To make a superfluity.

Rhyseiliad, *s. m.* (rhysail) A laying a complete foundation.

Rhyseiliaw, *v. a.* (rhysail) To lay a complete foundation.

> Gnawd wedi rhyserch rysciliaw cas.
>
> Commonly after over-fondness hate is *completely implanted.* — *Gwyddnaint.*

Rhyseiliawg, *a.* (rhysail) Having a complete foundation; completely implanted.

Rhyseiliedig, *a.* (rhysail) Completely founded.

Rhysel, *s. m.* (sel) A stedfast look, a stare.

Rhyseliad, *s. m.* (rhysel) A viewing stedfastly.

Rhyselu, *v. a.* (rhysel) To view stedfastly.

Rhysen, *s. f.—pl. t.* au (sen) An extreme rebuke

> ——I mrys hen
> A dirysedd, pond oedd rysen
> Braich haelwen brau uwchelwyr.
>
> Old Ambrose became embarrassed, was it not an extreme check, as that was the frank and liberal arm of nobility? — *Mered. ab Roser.*

Rhysenawl, *a.* (rhysen) Severely checking.

Rhyseniad, *s. m.* (rhysen) A severely chiding.

Rhysenu, *v. a.* (rhysen) To chide extremely.

Rhyserch, *s. m.* (serch) An over-fondness.

Rhyserchawg, *a.* (rhyserch) Being over-fond.

Rhyserchawl, *a.* (rhyserch) Over-fondling.

Rhyserchiad, *s. m.* (rhyserch) A loving greatly.

Rhyserchu, *v. a.* (rhyserch) To love extremely.

Rhyseu, *v. a.* (rhyse) To remain firm, to be very stubborn.

> Dy glwfeirdd ynt beirdd i'th barwd glas,
> Dy glwdyfn ay glod rhyseas.
>
> Thy assembling bards are gay in thy sumptuous mansion; thy word *hath firmly established* thy fame. — *Ll. P. Moch, i L. ab Iorwerth.*

Rhysfa, *s. f.—pl.* rhysfeydd (rhys) A course.

Rhysgain, *a.* (rhwsg) Tending to overrun.

Rhysgawg, *a.* (rhwsg) Being covered with luxuriancy; overgrown. *Tir rhysgawg*, land overgrown or run wild.

Rhysgawl, *a.* (rhwsg) Tending to be overgrown.

Rhysgiad, *s. m.* (rhwsg) A growing luxuriantly; an overgrowing, a running wild.

Rhysgwydd, *s. m.* (rhys—cwydd) Succour; patronage, protection.

> Rhysgwydd gweddw, car dieithraid.
>
> The succour of the widow, the friend of strangers. — *R. Pritchard o Landdyfri.*

Rhysgwyddaw, *v. a.* (rhysgwydd) To succour.

Rhysgwyddawl, *a.* (rhysgwydd) Succouring.

Rhysgwyddiad, *s. m.* (rhysgwydd) A succouring.

Rhysgyr, *s. m.—pl. t.* au (rhys—gyr) Violence; a furious assault, onset, or attack.

> [illegible] rhag rhysgyr arfau
> Arfod Cai a Bedwyr.
>
> Protection was not afforded [illegible] against the violence of arms, the the stroke of Cai and Bedwyr. — *Klaer Sais, m. Edw. Tych.m.*

Rhysgyrawl, *a.* (rhysgyr) Furiously assaulting.

Rhysgyriad, *s. m.* (rhysgyr) A fiercely assaulting.

Rhysgyru, *v. a.* (rhysgyr) To assault fiercely.

Rhysiad, *s. m.* (rhys) A rushing violently; agitation; a straitening; or a putting to trial.

Rhysiannawl, *a.* (rhysiant) Fiercely rushing.

Rhysiannu, *v. a.* (rhysiant) To rush onward.

Rhysiant, *s. m.* (rhys) A rushing course.

Rhysiaw, *v. a.* (rhys) To rush violently; to straiten, to entangle.

Rhysiawg, *a.* (rhys) Full of violence, straitened.

Rhysiawl, *a.* (rhys) Violently-rushing: tending to straiten or cause obstruction.

Rhysiedig, *a.* (rhysiad) Rendered violent.

> Rhysiedig a dig, y dyrn ei ddannedd
> Rhysedd iechis [illegible].
>
> *Ardent* and angry, his teeth work a profusion of [illegible] — *D. ab Gwilym, i [illegible].*

Rhysod, *s. pl. aggr.* (rhys) Burning embers; glowing cinders; also called *marwor*.

Rhysodi, *v. n.* (rhysod) To turn to embers.

Rhysodiad, *s. m.* (rhysod) A turning to embers.

Rhysodyn, *s. m. dim.* (rhysod) A hot ember.

Rhysu, *v. a.* (rhys) To render straitened or difficult; to entangle. *Gwallt wedi rhysu*, hair become entangled.

Rhyswr, *s. m.—pl.* rhyswyr (rhys—gwr) A man inured to violence, difficulty, or trial; a champion, a combatant; a savage.

> Syll di racw dan rhyswr.
>
> See thou yonder the fire of a savage. — *H. Cyfeiliog—Hirlas.*
>
> Y mynydd hagen, y bu y frwydr ynddo, a elwir [illegible] y Mynydd Carn; sef yw hyny mynydd y garnedd; [illegible] dirfawr garnedd o fain a ddaear [illegible] yr oesoedd gynt.
>
> Now the mountain, on which the battle was, is called by the people of the country the Carn Mountain; that is to say, the mountain of the tumulus; for in that place there is an immense heap of stones, under which was buried a champion in [illegible] ages of antiquity. — *Buch. Gr. ab Cynan.*

Rhyswriaeth, *s. m.* (rhyswr) The warfare of a champion; warfare.

> Gwynedd yn rhysedd yn rhyswriaeth [illegible],
> A [illegible],
> Mal [illegible] alarth;
> Mal ton [illegible] dreath.
>
> Gwynedd in conflict in the *warfare* of the chief, they heard where he went, like a host whom grief doth not [illegible] wave, of brisk tumult, over the strand. — *Ll. P. Moch, i L. ab Iorwerth.*

Rhyswydd, *s. pl.* (rhws—gwydd) Privet wood.

> Er angelach bywyd,
> Rhyswydd a gwyddfyd.——
>
> For life's security, *privet* and woodbine.—— *Taliesin.*

Rhyswydden, *s. f. dim.* (rhyswydd) Privet tree.

Rhysyn, *s. m. dim.* (rhys) A burning ember.

Rhysyrch, *s. m.* (syrch) Extreme affection.

> Tremyn Llywelyn hyw rhysyrch Prydain,
> Prid i Loegr ei ddisyrch.
>
> Behold Llywelyn the *idolized* chief of Britain, whom Lloegria cares not to love. — *Ll. P. Moch, i [illegible].*

Rhysyrchawl, *a.* (rhysyrch) Very affectionate.

Rhysyrchiad, *s. m.* (rhysyrch) A loving greatly.

Rhysyrchu, *v. a.* (rhysyrch) To love extremely.

Rhytion, *s. pl. aggr.* (rhwd) Particles worn off by friction; scourings.

Rhyth, *pronom. prep.* (rhy—yth) Thee signally: thine extremely or signally.

> Mi [illegible], buddig Felt,
> Ab M[illegible];
> Rhys[illegible];
> [illegible];
> Teithawg oedd iddi.
>
> I will *thee* [illegible] worship, victorious Felt, son of [illegible] the chief, [illegible] reserve the rights of the [illegible] he was qualified for it. — *[illegible].*

Rhythawl, *a.* (rhwth) Tending to gape or to open widely; yawning.

Rhythedd, *s. m.* (rhwth) A state of gaping.

Rhythfol, *s. m.* (rhwth—bol) A gorbelly.

Rhythfoliawg, *a.* (rhythfol) Gorbellied.

Rhythgi, *s. m.* (rhwth—ci) A greedy dog.

Rhythgnawd, *s. m.* (rhwth—cnawd) Bloated flesh.

Rhythiad, *s. m.* (rhwth) Distention, a gaping.

Rhythni, *s. m.* (rhwth) A state of gaping.

Rhython, *s. pl. aggr.* (rhwth) Cockles. *Rhython y brain*, clams.

Rhythu, *v. a.* (rhwth) To stretch out, to make wide, open, or large. *Rhythu llygaid*, to open the eyes very wide, to stare.

Rhythwch, *s. m.* (rhwth) A gaping, a yawning.

> Bum banw, bum bauhwch,
> Bum bawr yn rhythwch
>
> I have been a boar, I have been a sow, I have been a shout in a tumult. *Taliesin.*

Rhythwr, *s. m.—pl.* rhythwyr (rhythu—gwr) One who gapes; a yawner.

Rhyw, *s. m.—pl. t.* iau (rhy—yw) A kind, a species, a sort; a sex; some.

> Eled rhyw ar bath pa yw.
>
> Let kind belong to what is meet. *Adage.*
>
> Pob byw wrth ei ryw yr aeth
>
> Every living to his *kind* is joined. *Llywarch.*

Rhyw, *a.* (rhy—yw) Some. *Rhyw rif*, some number; *rhyw rai*, some ones; *rhyw faint*, some quantity; *rhyw dro*, some time.

Rhyw, *adv.* (rhy—yw) It is genial or natural.

> Rhyw i fab iwrch lamu.
>
> *It is genial* for the young roe to skip. *Adage.*

Rhywad, *s. m.* (gwad) Extreme denial.

Rhywadawl, *a.* (rhywad) Being fully denying.

Rhywadu, *v. a.* (rhywad) To deny extremely.

Rhywan, *s. m.* (gwan) An extreme division; an extreme wound or stab.

Rhywaniad, *s. m.* (rhywan) A dividing extremely, a wounding extremely.

Rhywanu, *v. a.* (rhywan) To make an extreme division; to wound extremely.

Rhywared, *s. m.* (gwared) Full deliverance

Rhywaredawl, *a.* (rhywared) Tending to complete deliverance.

Rhywarediad, *s. m.* (rhywared) Full deliverance

Rhywaredu, *v. a.* (rhywared) To deliver fully.

Rhywasgar, *s. m.* (gwasgar) Extreme dispersion.

Rhywasgarawg, *a.* (rhywasgar) Being extremely scattered or dispersed.

Rhywasgarawl, *a.* (rhywasgar) Tending to scatter extremely; a greatly dispersing.

Rhywasgariad, *s. m.* (rhywasgar) A scattering extremely; a being greatly dispersed.

Rhywasgaru, *v. a.* (rhywasgar) To scatter much.

Rhywawg, *a.* (rhyw) Having a sexual distinction, sexual, of a particular kind.

Rhywbeth, *s. m.* (rhyw—peth) Something.

Rhywbryd, *s. m.* (rhyw—pryd) Sometime. *adv.* Sometime, once on a time; formerly.

Rhywelydd, *s. m.* (gwelydd) One that is very sparing, parsimonious, or frugal.

Rhywelyddu, *v. n.* (rhywelydd) To be very sparing, to be over parsimonious.

> [illegible]
>
> [illegible] *Ll. P. Mab, i D. ab Owain.*

Rhywel, *s. m.* (gwel) Extreme sight; foresight.

Rhyweled, *v. a.* (rhywel) To see beyond.

> [illegible]
>
> The danger of war we foresee, and what a world likewise is to us. *Dr. S. Cent.*

Rhyweledig, *a.* (rhywel) Being foreseen.

Rhywelad, *s. m.* (rhywel) A foreseeing.

Rhywfaint, *s. m.* (rhyw—maint) Some quantity.

> [illegible]
>
> [illegible] a word of every ten thou shalt hear, and thou wilt obtain [illegible] *Adage.*

Rhywerth, *s. m.* (gwerth) Extreme price.

Rhywerthiad, *s. m.* (rhywerth) An over-selling, a selling extravagantly.

Rhywerthu, *v. a.* (rhywerth) To over-sell.

Rhywesthiad, *s. m.* (gwestliad) A tormenting.

Rhywestlu, *v. a.* (gwestlu) To torment greatly.

Rhywfan, *s. f.* (rhyw—man) A particular place. *adv.* Somewhere.

Rhywiad, *s. m.* (rhyw) A giving a specific character; a partaking of a specific character.

Rhywiaeth, *s. m.* (rhyw) Distinction of species.

Rhywiaw, *v. a.* (rhyw) To endue with a specific or sexual distinction, to be specific; to partake of a sort or species.

Rhywiawg, *a.* (rhyw) Kindly, kind; genial; of good kind. *Anifel rhywiawg*, a kind animal; *tir rhywiawg*, land of good quality.

> [illegible]
>
> No fine wool can be had from a goat's shoulder. *Adage.*

Rhywiawl, *a.* (rhyw) Special; sexual.

Rhywiogaeth, *s. f.—pl. t.* au (rhywiawg) The state of being specific, or of a particular sort; distinction, sort, or species.

> [illegible] mawl, gogan, a dychan.
>
> There are three primary *distinctions* of song; eulogy, elegy, and satire. *Barddas.*

Rhywiogaethawl, *a.* (rhywiogaeth) Generical.

Rhywiogaethiad, *s.* (rhywiogaeth) Specification.

Rhywiogaethu, *v. a.* (rhywiogaeth) To endue with a specific distinction.

Rhywiogaidd, *a.* (rhywiawg) Somewhat genial.

Rhywiogedd, *s. m.* (rhywiawg) Genialness.

Rhywiogeiddiad, *s. m.* (rhywiogaidd) A rendering or becoming genial in a degree.

Rhywiogeiddiaw, *v. a.* (rhywiogaidd) To render somewhat genial; to become somewhat genial.

Rhywiogeiddrwydd, *s. m.* (rhywiogaidd) A genial or kindly disposition.

Rhywiogi, *v. a.* (rhywiawg) To render genial or kindly; to become genial.

Rhywiogrwydd, *s. m.* (rhywiawg) Genialness.

Rhywiolaeth, *s. m.* (rhywiawl) Sexual distinction; a specific difference.

Rhywioli, *v. a.* (rhywiawl) To render specifically different; to have a specific difference.

Rhywir, *s. m.* (gwir) Complete truth. *a.* Very true; too true.

> Rhygas pob rhywir.
>
> Extremely offensive is every *naked truth.* *Adage.*

Rhywiriad, *s. m.* (rhywir) A fully certifying.

Rhywiriaw, *v. a* (rhywir) To certify fully.

Rhywlaw, *s. m.* (gwlaw) Excessive rain.

Rhywlawiad, *s. m.* (rhywlaw) A raining greatly.

Rhywlawiaw, *v.* (rhywlaw) To rain excessively.

Rhywle, *s. m.* (rhyw—lle) A certain place. *adv.* Somewhere.

Rhywneuthur, *v. a.* (gwneuthur) To over-perform, to supererogate.

Rhywneuthurawl, *a.* (rhywneuthur) Supererogatory, tending to over do.

Rhywneuthuriad, *s. m.* (rhywneuthur) Supererogation; an over doing.

Rhywogaeth, *s. f.—pl. t.* au (rhywawg) The state of being specific; a kind, or species.

Rhywr, *s. m.—pl.* rhywyr (gwr) One that is more than human.

Rhywres, *s. m.* (gwres) Extreme warmth.

> Mawr Duw digones
> Haul haf a'i rywres;
> Ac ef digones
> Budd coed a maes.
>
> The great God did cause the sun of summer with its *extreme warmth*, and he did cause the abundance of the wood and field. *Taliesin.*

Rhywresawg, *a.* (rhywres) Being over warm.

Rhywresawl, *a.* (rhywres) Over-heating.

Rhywresiad, *s. m.* (rhywres) An over-heating.

Rhywresogi, *v. n.* (rhywresawg) To acquire too much warmth, to cause over-heat.

Rhywresu, *v. n.* (rhywres) To become too warm

Rhywrys, *s. m.* (gwrys) Extreme ardency or zeal. *a.* Over-ardent.

Yn mhryffwn rywrys
Yn rhwyoll gwrys
Yn Mhrydain Ynys
Gwys an gwesil.

In the height of *extreme ardency* augmenting of zeal in the British Isle he proclaims our visitations. *Ll. P. Moch, i L. ab Iorwerth.*

Rhywrysiad, *s. m.* (rhywrys) A rendering over-ardent; a becoming very ardent or zealous.
Rhywrysiaw, *v. a.* (rhywrys) To act with extreme ardency or warmth.
Rhywrysiawl, *a.* (rhywrys) Being very ardent.
Rhywun, *s. m.* (rhyw—un) Some one, somebody.
Rhywyl, *s. m.* (gwyl) A very sharp look out.
Rhywyliad, *s. m.* (rhywyl) A watching greatly.
Rhywyliaw, *v. a.* (rhywyl) To watch extremely.
Rhywyllt, *a.* (gwyllt) Extremely wild.
Rhywylltiad, *s. m.* (rhywyllt) A rendering very wild; a becoming extremely wild.
Rhywylltiaw, *v. a.* (rhywyllt) To make extremely wild; to scare extremely.
Rhywynt, *s. m.—pl. t.* oedd (gwynt) A hurricane.

Ardwyad can-cad—
Ys cynt no rhywynt uch rudd wybren.

The master of a hundred conflicts: being more active than the *violent wind* over the ruddy atmosphere. *Ll. P. Moch.*

Rhyŵyr, *a.* (gŵyr) Oblique overmuch.
Rhyŵyraw, *v. a.* (rhyŵyr) To make over-oblique.
Rhyŵyrawl, *a.* (rhyŵyr) Of extreme obliquity.
Rhyŵyriad, *s. m.* (rhyŵyr) A rendering extremely oblique; a becoming over-oblique.
Rhywystl, *s. m.—pl. t.* on (gwystl) An over-pledge; a previous pledge.
Rhywystlaw, *v. a.* (rhywystl) To give an over-pledge; to pledge previously.
Rhywystlawg, *a.* (rhywystl) Over-pledged.
Rhywystliad, *s. m.* (rhywystl) An over-pledging.
Rhywyth, *s. m.* (gwyth) Extreme violence.
Rhywythaw, *v. a.* (rhywyth) To enrage extremely; to be extremely enraged.
Rhywythawg, *a.* (rhywyth) Full of extreme rage.
Rhywythiad, *s. m.* (rhywyth) An enraging extremely; a being extremely enraged.
Rhŷymadaw, *v. a.* (ymadaw) To go away utterly; to forsake utterly.
Rhŷymadawiad, *s. m.* (rhŷymadaw) A going away utterly; a forsaking utterly.
Rhŷymgadw, *v. a.* (ymgadw) To keep or preserve one's self fully; fully to abstain.
Rhŷyrawl, *a.* (gyrawl) Extremely impulsive.
Rhŷyriad, *s. m.* (gyriad) A driving extremely.
Rhŷyru, *v. a.* (gyru) To drive on extremely.

S.

Sa, *s. m. r.* A negative of motion; a state of opposition; a fixed state; a firm, steady, or even state; a standing.
Sach, *s. f.—pl. t.* au (sa—ach) A sack, or bag. *Sach diawl*, a demoniac, or one possessed.
Sachaid, *s. f.—pl.* sacheidiau (sach) A sackful.
Sachawl, *a.* (sach) Sacking, or bagging.
Sachbwn, *s. m.* (sach—pwn) A bale.
Sachedig, *a.* (sach) Being put in a sack, sacked.
Sachell, *s. f. dim.* (sach) A small sack, or a bag.
Sachelliad, *s. m.* (sachell) A bagging; a padding, or stuffing out, as with wool or the like.
Sachellu, *v. a.* (sach) To bag; to stuff in; to pad.
Sachiad, *s. m.* (sach) A putting in a sack.
Sachlian, *s. m.* (sach—llian) Sackcloth.
Sachu, *v. a.* (sach) To put in a sack, to stuff.
Sachwisg, *s. f.* (sach—gwisg) Sackcloth covering.
Sachwr, *s. m.—pl.* sachwyr (sach—gwr) A man who sacks or puts in a bag.
Sad, *a.* (sa—ad) Permanent, firm; discreet, sober. *Merch sad*, a discreet woman.

Sai yn sad heb un gadwyn.

She will stand firmly without any chain. *R. Dafydd Llwyd.*

Sadell, *s. f.—pl. t.* i (sad) A dorser, or a pannel.
Sadelliad, *s. m.* (sadell) A putting on a packsaddle.
Sadelliaeth, *s. m.* (sadell) The use of a packsaddle.
Sadellu, *v. a.* (sadell) To put on a packsaddle.
Sadellwr, *s. m.—pl.* sadellwyr (sadell—gwr) A maker of packsaddles.
Sadiad, *s. m.* (sad) A rendering firm or steady.
Sadiaw, *v. a.* (sad) To render firm or steady.
Sadiawl, *a.* (sad) Of a firm or steady tendency.
Sadiedig, *a.* (sad) Rendered firm or steady.
Sadrwydd, *s. m.* (sad) Firmness, steadiness.
Sadwrn, *s. m.* (sad—gwrn) A fixt or firm point; a centre point: also the name of Saturn.

Sae, *s. m.* (sa) A kind of woollen stuff, say.

Gwisg a ddanfoned—
Is dail yt, o sae du.

A robe has been sent to thee, under the leaves, of black say. *D. ab Gwilym.*

Saen, *s. f.—pl. t.* i (sa—en) A vehicle, a carriage.
Saer, *s. m.—pl.* seiri (sa—er) A wright, an artificer, an artisan. *Saer coed*, *saer pren*, *prensaer*, a carpenter; *saer maen*, *maensaer*, a stonemason; *saer melin*, a millwright; *saer priddfaen*, a bricklayer; *saer cist*, a cabinet-maker; *saer llong*, a shipwright; *saer llestri gwellt*, a straw-joiner.

Pen saer pob perchenawg.

Every proprietor is the chief *artificer*. *Adage.*

Un o dri madgyrfinyddion Ynys Prydain—Morddal Gwr Gweilgi, saer Ceraint ab Greidiawl, a ddysges waith maen a chalch gyntaf i genedl y Cymmry.

One of the three beneficial inventors of the Isle of Britain; Morddal the Man of the Torrent, the *architect* of Ceraint son of Greidiol, who first taught the work of stone and lime to the nation of the Cymmry. *Triads.*

Saeraidd, *a.* saer) Wright-like, workman-like.
Saerawl, *a.* (saer) Artificial; architectural.
Saeriad, *s. m.* (saer) A forming a wright or artisan.
Saeriannawl, *a.* (saeriant) Architectonic.
Saeriannu, *v. a.* (saeriant) To practise or carry on architecture or the work of a wright.
Saeriant, *s. m.* (saer) Architecture.
Saerni, *s. m.* (saer) A wright's work.
Saerniaeth, *s. m.* (saerni) The calling of a wright or artificer; the art of building or framing; mechanism; architecture.
Saerniaethawl, *a.* (saerniaeth) Architectonic.
Saerniaethiad, *s. m.* (saerniaeth) A constructing a piece of work, or mechanism.
Saerniaethu, *v. a.* (saerniaeth) To carry on the calling of a wright; to construct a piece of work or mechanism.

Saernïaidd, *a.* (saerni) Like the work of an artist; masterly; mechanical; architectonic.
Saernïaw, *v. a.* (saerni) To work as a wright.
Saernïawl, *a.* (saerni) Architectural.
Saernïeiddiad, *s. m.* (saernïaidd) A rendering workman-like; a becoming mechanical.
Saernïeiddiaw, *v. a.* (saernïaidd) To render workman-like; to become mechanical.
Saernïeiddrwydd, *s. m.* (saernïaidd) Masterliness, as a wright, that is workman-like.
Saeru, *v. a.* (saer) To work as an artisan.
Saerwaith, *s. m.* (saer—gwaith) A wright's work.
Saesoneg, *s. f.* (saeson) The Saxon language; the English language.
Saesones, *s. f.* (saeson) An English-woman.
Saeson, *s. pl.* (sais) Saxons; Englishmen.
Saesonach, *s. pl. dim.* (saeson) Saxon hordes.
Saesonaidd, *a.* (saeson) Saxon like; English.
Saesoniad, *s. m.—pl.* saesoniaid (saeson) A Saxon.

Synwyr yr holl Saesoniaid.

The sense of all the Saxons. *Llawddon.*

Saesonig, *a.* (saeson) Saxon, or English.
Saesyn, *s. m. dim.* (sais) An Englishman.
Saeth, *s. m.—pl. t.* au (sa—aeth) An arrow.

Gwnelid aeth saeth i syberw: or
Gwnelid serch saeth syberw.

Let love make an *arrow* for the courteous. *Adage.*

Saethawd, *s. m.* (saeth) The act of shooting.
Saethawl, *a.* (saeth) Tending to shoot; ejective.
Saethbenig, *s. m.* (saeth—pen) Arrow-grass.
Saethebawl, *s. m.—pl.* saethebolion (saeth—ebawl) A cast foal, an epithet for a young colt.

Ni ddylyir daly ebawl yn ol ei fam; a hwnw a elwir saethebawl.

It is not proper to lay hold of a colt after its dam; and that is called a *cast foal.* *Welsh Laws.*

Saethedig, *a.* (saeth) Being ejected or shotten.
Saethflew, *s. m. aggr.* (saeth—blew) The hairs which rise through the fur, in some animals.
Saethiad, *s. m.* (saeth) A shooting; ejection.
Saethiant, *s. m.* (saeth) The act of shooting.
Saethlys, *s. m.* (saeth—llys) Common arrowhead.
Saethu, *v. a.* (saeth) To shoot, or to dart.

Haws barnu no saethu.

It is easier to judge than *to shoot.* *Adage.*

Nid rhydd i neb saethu anifel y bo helwriaeth arno, pan fo yn ei esmwythdra, tan boen colli ei fwa a'i saeth i arglwydd y tir.

It is not free for any body *to shoot* an animal of the chace, when it shall be in its state of rest, under pain of forfeiting his bow and his arrow to the lord of the land. *Cyfraith Hely.*

Saethwr, *s. m.—pl.* saethwyr (saeth—gwr) A shooter; an archer.
Saethwriaeth, *s. m.* (saethwr) The act of shooting; archery.
Saethwrym, *s. m.—pl. t.* iau (saeth—gwrym) The sagittal suture.
Saethyd, *s. m.* (saeth) A shooting, or a darting.
Saethydd, *s. m.* (saeth) A shooter; an archer.

——Cariad
Saethodd, briwodd fi i'm bron:
Syth euddnw y saethyddion.

——Love did shoot, did wound me in my breast: the sturdy idol of the *archers.* *S. Tudyr.*

Saethyta, *v. a.* (saethyd) To shoot, or dart about; to frolick; to banter, to jest.

Dywawd Ysbyddaden Bencawr: Na saethyta fi bellach, oni dy farw a fyni.

Said Ysbyddaden Bencawr: *banter* me no further, unless thou hast a mind to die. *H. Culhwch—Mabinogion.*

Saethytawl, *a.* (saethyd) Frolicksome.
Saethytiad, *s. m.* (saethyd) A playing of frolick.
Saf, *s. f.* (sa) A stand; the act of standing.
Safadwy, *a.* (saf) Capable of standing; permanent, lasting, durable.
Safaeth, *s. m.* (saf) A standing still, rest; a stand.
Safawl, *a.* (saf) Standing; permanent; resting.
Safdal, *s. m.* (saf—tal) Pitching money paid for stands in a fair.
Safdoll, *s. f.* (saf—toll) Pitching toll.
Safedig, *a.* (saf) Being made to stand; established, fixed, confirmed.
Safedigawl, *a.* (safedig) Having a tendency or power of standing. *Enw safedigawl,* noun substantive. *G. Roberts.*
Safedd, *s. m.* (saf) A fixed state, stationariness.
Safiad, *s. m.—pl. t.* au (saf) A remaining still, or resting; a standing; stature.

Sai yn sad heb un gadwyn;
Safiad fal dafad ar dwyn.

She will stand firmly without any chain; a *standing* like a sheep on the hill. *R. Dafydd Llwyd, i hen gaseg.*

Safiadawl, *a.* (safiad) Stationary, standing.
Safiadu, *v. a.* (safiad) To render stationary; to become stationary.
Safiannawl, *a.* (safiant) Stationary, standing.
Safiannu, *v. a.* (safiant) To render stationary; to become stationary.
Safiant, *s. m.* (saf) The act of standing; posture.
Safiator, *ger.* (safiad) In standing.
Savitor, *sup.* (saf) To be standing.
Safle, *s. m.—pl. t.* oedd (saf—lle) A station.

Syfled pob mis o'i safle
Ac aed a gwyl gyd ag e.

Removed be every month from its *place,* and let the festival go along with it. *Gro. Owain.*

Safn, *s. f.—pl. t.* au (saf) The upper region of the mouth; the mouth, the chop.

Cau dy safn, ac agor dy glust a'th lygad.

Shut thy *mouth,* and open thine ear and thine eye. *Adage.*

Safnaid, *s. f.—pl.* safneidiau (safn) A chopful, a mouthful.
Safnawg, *a.* (safn) Having a large wide mouth.
Safnawl, *a.* (safn) Relating to the palate.
Safndrom, *a.* (safn—trom) Of heavy jaw, of drawling enunciation.
Safndrwm, *a.* (safn—trwm) Drawling.
Safndrymedd, *s. m.* (trwm) Slowness of speech.
Safneidiad, *s. m.* (safnaid) A taking a mouthful.
Safneidiaw, *v.* (safnaid) To swallow by mouthfuls.
Safniad, *s. m.* (safn) A mouthing; a gaping.
Safnrwth, *a.* (safn—rhwth) Wide-mouthed.
Safnrythiad, *s. m.* (safnrwth) A stretching the mouth widely; a gaping.
Safnrythni, *s. m.* (safnrwth) Wideness of mouth.
Safnrythu, *v. a.* (safnrwth) To open the mouth widely, to gape.
Safnrythwr, *s. m.—pl.* safnrythwyr (safnrwth—gwr) One who makes a wide mouth.
Safu, *v. a.* (saf) To stand; to become fixed.

Ni saif gogan ar gadarn.

Slander will not *fix* on the mighty. *Adage.*

Safwr, *s. m.—pl.* safwyr (saf—gwr) A stander.
Safwyr, *s. m.* (saf—gwyr) Savour; odour, scent.

Safwyr hwn sy fwy'r hanner,
Fal pwn o afalau per.

The *odour* of this is greater by half, like a load of sweet apples. *D. ab Edmwnd.*

Safwyraw, *v. a.* (safwyr) To produce a savour.
Safwyrawl, *a.* (safwyr) Savoury; odorous.
Safwyrber, *a.* (safwyr—per) Sweet-savoured.
Safwyriad, *s. m.* (safwyr) A savouring.
Safwyrus, *a.* (safwyr) Savoury; odorous.
Saff, *s. m.* (sa) That stands or shoots out.

Saffar, *s. m.* (saff) A spike, a spire.

> Crynant eu bar, seirff saffar-sen.
>
> They will tremble at their rage, serpents with sting of reproof. *Cynddelw.*

Saffrwm, *s. m.* (saffr) Saffron, or crocus.
Saffrymu, *v. a.* (saffrwm) To blend with saffron.
Saffwn, *s. m.* (saff) A beam, or a shaft.

> Saffwn praff [illegible] saffar.
>
> A shaft, [illegible] to its spike. *Cynddelw.*

Saffwy, *s. f.—pl. f.* on (saff) A pike or a lance.

> [illegible]
> O [illegible]
>
> Ready are their lance, he [illegible] not his sight on wealth that he will not [illegible]. *Cynddelw.*
>
> Gwr praff with baladr saffwy.
>
> An athletic man by the shaft of a lance. *Iolo Goch.*

Saffwyad, *s. m.* (saffwy) A using a pike or lance.
Saffwyaw, *v. a.* (saffwy) To use a pike or lance.
Saffwyawg, *a.* (saffwy) Having a pike or lance.

> [illegible] Cynan [illegible]
> Yn [illegible] saffwyawg—
>
> He [illegible] make no declaration that Cynan would not see a corpse in harness bearing a lance.— [illegible]

Saffwyawl, *a.* (saffwy) Belonging to a pike.
Saffwyawr, *s. m.* (saffwy) A lancier, a pikeman.
Saffr, *s. m.* (saff) Saffron. *Meddygon Myddfai.*
Sag, *s. m.* (sa—ag) A squeeze of the gullet.
Sagfa, *s. f.—pl.* sagfeydd (sag) That is closed up; a choke; a squeeze in the gullet.
Sagiad, *s. m.* (sag) A squeezing together; a stifling.
Sagiaw, *v. a.* (sag) To close up; to choke; to stifle; to squeeze in the chops.
Sagiawl, *a.* (sag) Choking, or stifling.
Sagiedig, *a.* (sagiad) Choked, or stifled.
Sagmwrn, *s. m.* (sag—mwrn) A strangle, a choke.
Sagmwrniad, *s. m.* (sagmwrn) A strangling.
Sagmwrniaw, *v. a.* (sagmwrn) To strangle, to throttle, or to choke.
Sagmwrniawl, *a.* (sagmwrn) Strangling, choking.
Sagmwrniwr, *s. m.—pl.* sagmwrniwyr (sagmwrn—gwr) A strangler, a throttler, a choker.
Sai, *s. m.* (sa) That is still or at rest.
Saib, *s. m.* (sa—ib) The state of standing about; a state of rest or leisure; sedateness; a state of musing or study. *a.* Sedate, quiet, resting.

> Pwy [illegible] saib;
> Pwy a'i tramwy o'r [illegible]?
>
> Who is possessed of the morality of studious genius; who will travel it of the three sons? *Edm. Prys.*

Said, *s. m.—pl.* seidiau (sa—id) That is inserted; the tongue or the part of a tool that is inserted in the handle; a haft, or hilt. *Cleddyf crynsaid*, a sword with a round handle.

> A [illegible] said,
> [illegible]
>
> And I know there will not [illegible], being weak [illegible] for three hours even. *H. Middleton.*

Saig, *s. m.—pl.* seigiau (sa—ig) Mess; a meal.

> Yr ail saig [illegible] a [illegible] y [illegible] brenin.
>
> The second most honourable dish in the palace is due for the patron of the family to [illegible], and that the first after the king. *Welsh Laws.*

Sail, *s. f.—pl.* seiliau (sa—il) A base, foundation, or ground-work.

> [illegible] Duw, yngan dyn, a [illegible] bywyd.
>
> The three foundations of genius; the gift of God, the exertion of man, and the event of life. *[illegible]*
>
> Tri sail gwybodaeth [illegible], a thyst.
>
> The three bases of knowledge: reason, nature, and evidence. *Barddas.*

Saim, *s. m.—pl.* seimiau (sa—im) Grease.

Sain, *s. m.—pl.* seiniau (sa—in) A sound, a tone.

> Gwr [illegible] sain;
> Drud hyd, heb droed, heb aden.
>
> A wonderful being art thou, of [illegible] world, without foot, without wing. *D. ab Gwilym,* [illegible]

Sais, *s. m.* (sai) That is still; quiet, or [illegible].
Sais, *s. m.—pl.* saeson. A Saxon; an Englishman.
Saith, *s. m.—pl.* seithiau (sa—ith) That is [illegible]; that is separated; an essence; a [illegible]; a crucible; the number seven. *a.* Seven. *Tywyn saith*, a small sandy cove in Llansaith, Ceredigion.

> Saith [illegible] y [illegible].
>
> For seven years will blindness be prognosticated. *[illegible]*

Sal, *s. f.* (sa—al) A safety; plight; relief.

> [illegible] sal, [illegible],
> [illegible] a [illegible].
>
> Sad, ah the [illegible] of discord, it the plight [illegible] storm. *[illegible]*
>
> [illegible]
> [illegible], heb gwbl undal,
> O [illegible] y [illegible] —
>
> Woe to the soul without a relief from trouble, without complete release, if it turns as the body has turned. *D. ab Gwilym.*

Sal, *a.* (sa—al) Safe, secure; precious; [illegible].

> Aur sal [illegible] o'i law.
>
> Precious gold he gave me from his hand. *D. ab Edmwnd.*

Salaidd, *a.* (sal) Somewhat hale or firm.
Salau, *v. a.* (sal) To render sane, or safe.
Salder, *s. m.* (sal) Safety, good plight.
Salw, *a.* (sal) Vile, base, sorry, frail; poor; ill, sick. *Dillad seilwon*, poor clothes; *[illegible] seilwon*, poor cattle; *tir salw*, poor land; *dyn salw*, a sick man; *pa fyd sydd arnat? go salw*, how goes the world with thee? rather indifferent.
Salwad, *s. m.* (salwau) A rendering frail or mean; a becoming frail or despicable.
Salwawl, *a.* (salwau) Of a frail tendency.
Salwau, *v. a.* (salw) To render frail or mean; to become frail or despicable; to become ill.

> Ti a [illegible], y bore, pan [illegible] gwybodaeth, ac [illegible] Duw, [illegible] cynghor, ond salwau fy [illegible].
>
> Thou wilt be seeking for me, in the morning, when thou shalt not find me; for that thou hast hated knowledge, and because thou didst not receive the fear of God, nor follow my advice, but despise my reproof. *Marchawg Crwydrad.*

Salwder, *s. m.* (salw) Frailty, meanness; illness.

> Nid [illegible] y [illegible], nid [illegible] salwedd.
>
> He did not act [illegible], his not the action of frailty. *Cynddelw.*

Salwdra, *s. m.* (salw) Frailty, debility, illness.
Salwedd, *s. m.* (salw) Illness; sorriness.
Salwin, *a.* (salw) Of a frail nature.
Salwinaw, *v. a.* (salwin) To render frail, or ill.
Salwineb, *s. m.* (salwin) Frailty, debility.
Salwiniad, *s. m.* (salwin) A becoming debilitated.
Salwwedd, *s. f.* (salw—gwedd) A frail appearance.

> [illegible] Sulian
> [illegible] salwwedd!
>
> Setting aside the Sabbaths, meanly-seeming manners. *Iolo Goch.*

Sall, *s. m.* (sy—all) That is out, or exposed.
Sallawg, *a.* (sall) Being exposed; outcast.

> [illegible] rhag nych [illegible],
> A'r [illegible],
> [illegible] sallawg [illegible]
>
> Protect me, my Lord, from the torment of hell fiends, and the [illegible] repelled, bristled with [illegible], the [illegible] region, [illegible] bells. *[illegible]*

Salledd, *s. m.* (sall) Externalness; outwardness.
Salliad, *s. m.* (sall) A turning out; a sallying.
Sallt, *s. m.—pl.* t au (sall) An exterior estate.
Salltawg, *a.* (sallt) Having an exterior.
Salltiad, *s. m.* (sallt) A going out; a sallying.

Sailtiing, *s. m.—pl. t.* au (sallt—rhing) Snuffers; also called *Gleiniadur*.

Salltu, *v. a.* (sallt) To go out, to go off; to go away to hide, whilst the eyes of the seeker is covered, in the play of hide and seek. *Gware salltu*, the play of hide and seek. *Sil.* It is also called *Mic ymguddiaw*.

Samp, *s. m.—pl. t.* au (sy—amp) A mole, or mark on the skin.

San, *s. m.* (sa—an) The state of being out, beside, apart, or divested; a state of being wary; a gaze; a maze. *a.* Aware; wary.

Sànawl, *a.* (sàn) Gazing; amazed, stupified.

Sànedig, *a.* (sàn) Being made to gaze; amazed.

Sànedigaeth, *s. m.* (sànedig) Amazement.

Sàniad, *s. m.* (sàn) A gazing; a rendering amazed.

Sant, *s. m.—pl.* seintiau (san) A saint. *a.* Holy.

Santaidd, *a.* (sant) Sanctified, hallowed, holy.

Santawl, *a.* (sant) Saintly, hallowed, or holy.

Santeiddiad, *s. m.* (santaidd) Sanctification.

Santeiddiaeth, *s. m.* (santaidd) Sanctification.

Santeiddiaw, *v. a.* (santaidd) To sanctify.

Santeiddiawg, *a.* (santaidd) Having holiness.

Santeiddiawl, *a.* (santaidd) Sanctified, holy.

Santeiddiedig, *a.* (santeiddiad) Sanctified.

Santeiddiedigaeth, *s. m.—pl. t.* au (santeiddiedig) Sanctification.

Santeiddiedigawl, *a.* (santeiddiedig) Of a sanctifying or hallowing tendency.

Santeiddrwydd, *s. m.* (santaidd) Holiness.

Santes, *s. f.—pl. t.* au (sant) A female saint.

Santolaeth, *s. m.* (santawl) Sanctitude.

> Eglur oedd o'i santolaeth a'i fucbedd.
>
> He was conspicuous for his *sanctity* and his course of life. *Gr. ab Arthur.*

Sànu, *v. a.* (san) To gaze; to astonish, to amaze.

Sang, *s. f.—pl. t.* au (sa—ang) A tread; a trample.

Sangad, *s. f.—pl. t.* au (sang) A treading.

Sangawd, *s. m.* (sang) The act of treading.

> Breithgad gwyr,
> Brydian Llyr,
> Lloegr oddfrawd;
> Bri Brython
> Braint Saeson
> Sangawd.
>
> The confused conflict of men, like the shore swells, Lloegr's ruin; the glory of the Brython is the *trampling* of the privilege of Saxons. *Cynddelw.*

Sangawl, *a.* (sang) Treading; trampling.

Sangedig, *a.* (sang) Trodden; trampled.

Sangedigaeth, *s. m.* (sangedig) The act of treading.

Sangiad, *s. m.—pl. t.* au (sang) A treading.

Sangiar, *s. f.* (sang) A treading place; a doorway, a gateway.

Sangu, *v. a.* (sang) To tread; to trample.

> Na sang ar droed ei chwerw.
>
> *Tread* not on the foot of a surly dog. *Adage.*

Sangwr, *s. m.—pl.* sangwyr (sang—gwr) Treader.

Sar, *s. m.* (sa—ar) That is on or along; that is apt to cast down; fury, insolence; insult.

Saraad, *s. m.—pl. t.* au (sarâu) A throwing upon; a discarding; an abusing, an insulting, an affronting; an injuring; a disgracing; reproach; offence.

> [illegible] brenin [illegible] un yw, pan dorer ei [illegible] a'i ladd, ail yw, pan ddel dau [illegible] ac yn ngwydd y ddau [illegible], trydydd yw, camarferu ei [illegible].
>
> In three ways [illegible] an *insult* be given to the king: one is, when his protection is broken, from his giving protection to a person and who may be killed; the second is, when two kings [illegible] the confines of their dominions, for the sake of an interview, and in the presence of the two kings, a man belonging to one [illegible] man of the other side; the third is, to have improper [illegible] his wife. *Welsh Laws.*

Saràadu, *v. a.* (saràad) To give an insult.

Saràadus, *a.* (saràad) Insulting, affrontive.

Saràawl, *a.* (sarâu) Abusive; insulting.

Saràed, *s. f.—pl. t.* au (sarâu) Abuse; insult, affront, offence; injury; reproach.

> Mi ei tangnefeddaf ef a'r amherawdr; canys, o gwnaeth ef saràed i mi, digawn o iawn yw cenyf innau, ei fod ef yn erchi fy nhrugaredd.
>
> I will pacify him and the emperor; for, if he has done me an *injury*, enough of satisfaction is it with me then, that he doth crave my mercy. *Gr. ab Arthur.*

Sarâu, *v. a.* (sar) To throw off; to abuse; to insult; to affront; to offend; to injure.

> Pwybynag a sarâo eu gilydd, o werin—Deheubarth, Gwynedd, Powys, a Lloegr, talet bedair bu a phedwar ugaint ariant.
>
> Whosoever shall *insult* another, of the people of South Wales, North Wales, Powys, and England, let him pay four cows and four-score pieces of silver. *Welsh Laws.*

Saràus, *a.* (sarâu) Insulting, offensive; abusive.

Saraüsaw, *v. a.* (saràus) To become insulting.

Saraüsdra, *s. m.* (saràus) A disposition to insult.

Saraüsedd, *s. m.* (saràus) Offensiveness; abuse.

Saraüsrwydd, *s. m.* (saràus) Offensiveness.

Sarch, *s. m.—pl.* seirch (sar) What is upon, or covers; a piece of harness.

Sarchawl, *a.* (sarch) Covering, as a harness.

Sarchiad, *s. m.* (sarch) A harnessing; a furnishing.

Sarchu, *v. a.* (sarch) To cover, as with harness.

Sard, *s. m.—pl. t.* ian (sar) A beat down; a rebuff.

Sardiad, *s. m.* (sard) A beating down; a rebuffing; a chiding, a chastising.

Sardiaw, *v. a.* (sard) To beat down; to rebuff; to chastise, to reprove, to rebuke, to chide.

> Sardia feilch yn sorod fan;
> Od oes gwg nid ysgogan.
>
> *He would beat down* proud ones to dust; if there be a frown he will not go aside. *Iocu Drydydd.*
>
> Ar hyny mi drown at Ffolineb, ac a ddechreuais ei sardio.
>
> Upon that I turned to Folly, and I began *to rebuke* her. *Marchawg Crwydrad.*

Sardiawl, *a.* (sard) Beating down; chastising.

Sardiedig, *a.* (sardiad) Beaten down; chastised.

Sardiwr, *s. m.—pl.* sardiwyr (sard—gwr) One who beats down; a chastiser, a rebuker.

Sardd, *s. m.—pl. t.* au (sar) That is recumbent.

Sarddain, *a.* (sardd) Reptile, or creeping.

Sarddan, *s. f.—pl. t.* au (sardd) A creeping thing.

Sarddawl, *a.* (sardd) Reptilitious, reptile.

Sarddedig, *a.* (sardd) Being rendered creeping.

Sarddiad, *s. m.—pl. t.* au (sardd) A causing to creep, a creeping.

Sarddu, *v. a.* (sardd) To cast down; to creep.

Sarddus, *a.* (sardd) Causing to creep, or crawl.

Sarddusaw, *v. a.* (sarddus) To render creeping.

Sarddusdra, *s. m.* (sarddus) A creeping state.

Sarddusrwydd, *s. m.* (sarddus) A creeping state.

Sarf, *s. m.* (sar) That is prone, or on the ground.

Sarff, *s. f.—pl.* seirff (sar) A serpent; also the true service-tree.

> Gwelem wely haiarn yn dwym coch, yn yr hwn yr oedd gwraig yn gorwedd yn noeth, a sarff yn ei braichedio.
>
> We could perceive an iron bed red hot, in which there was a woman lying naked, with a *serpent* embracing her. *Marchawg Crwydrad.*
>
> Nerth sarff yn ei chloren.
>
> The strength of a *serpent* is her tail. *Adage.*

Sarffaidd, *a.* (sarff) Like a serpent; serpentine.

Sarffawl, *a.* (sarff) Of the nature of a serpent.

Sarffes, *s. f.* (sarff) A female serpent.

Sarffwydd, *s. pl. aggr.* (sarff—gwydd) Service trees

Sarffwydden, *s. f.* (sarffwydd) True service tree.

Sariad, *s. m.* (sar) A rendering haughty or arrogant; a becoming overbearing.

Seguredd, *s. m.* (segur) A state of leisure.
Seguren, *s. f. dim.* (segur) An idling female.
Seguriad, *s. m.* (segur) An enjoying of leisure.
Segurllyd, *a.* (segur) Loving leisure; idle.
Segurwas, *s. m.* (segur—gwas) An idle youth.
Segurwr, *s. m.—pl.* segurwyr (segur—gwr) One who enjoys leisure; an idler.
Seguryd, *s. m.* (segur) A state of leisure or ease.

> Tri pheth sydd yn llygru y byd: balchder, afraid, a seguryd.
>
> Three things do corrupt the world: pride, excess, and *idleness*. *Barddas.*

Seguryn, *s. m. dim.* (segur) An idler.
Seibiad, *s. m.* (saib) A standing at leisure.
Seibiannawl, *a.* (seibiant) Leisureable.
Seibiaeth, *s. m.* (saib) A state of rest; sabbath.
Seibiannu, *v. a.* (seibiant) To procure leisure.
Seibiant, *s. m.* (saib) A standing about, a resting, or stopping: a respite; leisure.
Seibiaw, *v. a.* (saib) To stand about, to take respite; to be at leisure.
Seibiawl, *a.* (saib) Leisurely; resting, at rest.
Seidiad, *s. m.* (said) An insertion; the insertion of a tong into the handle.
Seidiaw, *v. a.* (said) To insert; to insert a tool into a handle.
Seidiawg, *a.* (said) Having an insertion; tonged.
Seidyn, *s. m. dim.* (said) The part of a tool that is inserted in the hilt.
Seifiad, *s. m.—pl.* seifiaid (saf) A stander.
Seigen, *s. f. dim.* (saig) A little mess or meal.
Seigiad, *s. m.* (saig) A messing; a taking a meal.
Seigiaw, *v. a.* (saig) To mess, to partake of a meal; to serve up dishes or messes.
Seigiawl, *a.* (saig) Relating to a mess or meal.
Seigiwr, *s. m.—pl.* seigwyr (saig—gwr) A messer
Seilddar, *s. f.—pl.* seilddery (sail—dar) A main beam or pillar; a prop; a foundation pile.
Seilddarluniad, *s. m.* (darluniad) An ichnography
Seilddor, *s. f.—pl. t.* au (sail—dor) A threshold.
Seiler, *s. f.—pl. t.* i (sail) A foundation space; a ground floor; a cellar.
Seilfaen, *s. m.—pl.* seilfeini (sail—maen) A foundation stone.
Seilgam, *a.* (sail—cam) Having a wry tread.
Seilgamiad, *s. m.* (seilgam) A treading awry.
Seilgamu, *v. a.* (seilgam) To tread a sole awry.
Seiliad, *s. m.—pl. t.* au (sail) A foundation.
Seiliannawl, *a.* (seiliant) A base, or foundation.
Seiliannu, *v. a.* (seiliant) To make a foundation.
Seiliant, *s. m.* (sail) Relating to foundation.
Seiliaw, *v. a.* (sail) To found, to lay a foundation.
Seiliawd, *s. m.* (sail) A being made a foundation.
Seiliawg, *a.* (sail) Having a foundation.
Seiliedig, *a.* (seiliad) Having a foundation laid.
Seiliedigaeth, *s. m.* (seiliedig) The act of founding
Seiliwr, *s. m.* (sail—gwr) One who founds.
Seilwaith, *s. m.* (sail—gwaith) Ground-work.
Seilydd, *s. m.—pl. t.* ion (sail) A founder.
Seimiad, *s. m.* (saim) A greasing.
Seimiaw, *v. a.* (saim) To grease, to make greasy.
Seimiawg, *a.* (saim) Abounding with grease.
Seimiawl, *a.* (saim) Of a greasy quality.
Seimiedig, *a.* (saim) Greased; made greasy.
Seimiwr, *s. m.—pl.* seimiwyr (saim—gwr) Greaser
Seimlyd, *a.* (saim) Of a greasy quality.
Seindraws, *a.* (sain—traws) Transversely sounding. *Cynghanedd seindraws*, a transversely sounding consonancy.
Seindwll, *s. m.* (sain—twll) A sound-hole.
Seinfawr, *a.* (sain) Sonorous, of great sound.
Seinfwrdd, *s. m* (sain—bwrdd) A sounding-board
Seinglawr, *s. m.* (sain—clawr) A sounding-board
Seingroes, *a.* (sain—croes) Transversely sounding. *Cynghanedd seingroes*, a transversely sounding consonancy.
Seingudd, *a.* (sain—cudd) Of concealed sound.
Seinguddgyswllt, *s. m.* (seingudd—cyswllt) A junction of concealed sound.
Seinguddgysylltgroes, *a.* (seinguddgyswllt) Being of transversely conjoined concealed sound.
Seinguddhannergysylltgroes, *a.* (seingudd—hanner—cyswllt—croes) Being of half transversely conjoined concealed sound.
Seiniad, *s. m.—pl. t.* au (sain) A sounding.
Seiniannawl, *a.* (seiniant) Productive of sound.
Seiniannu, *v. a.* (seiniant) To produce a sound.
Seiniant, *s. m.* (sain) A making a sound.
Seiniaw, *v. a.* (sain) To sound, to resound.
Seiniawd, *s. m.* (sain) A resounding, a sounding.
Seiniawdr, *s. m.—pl.* seiniodron (seiniawd) That yields a sound.

> Molwch yr Arglwydd—
> Molwch ef ar seiniodron glych.
>
> Praise ye the Lord; praise him ye bells that *are high sounding*. *B. Edm. Hughes.*

Seiniawg, *a.* (sain) Having a sound or tone.
Seiniawl, *a.* (sain) Sounding; toned.
Seiniedig, *a.* (seiniad) Sounded; toned.
Seiniedigaeth, *s. m.* (seiniedig) Act of sounding.
Seiniwr, *s. m.—pl.* seiniwyr (sain—gwr) One who sounds or makes a sound.
Seintiad, *s. m.* (saint) A canonization.
Seintiaw, *v. a.* (saint) To canonise.
Seintiawl, *a.* (saint) Sanctified, saintly.
Seintiedig, *a.* (seintiad) Canonized, sainted.
Seintiolaeth, *s. m.* (seintiawl) Sanctitude.
Seintwar, *s. f.* (saint—gwar) A sanctuary.

> Seintwar i'r adar ydwyd.
>
> The *sanctuary* of the feathered tribe art thou. *[illegible]*

Seirch, *s. pl. aggr.* (sarch) Equipage, horse trappings, furniture, or harness, a set of harness.

> Gwr gwiw uch ei amliw seirch,
> A roddai feirch i eirchiad.
>
> A superior man on his many-coloured *trappings*, who would give horses to the suitor. *[illegible]*
>
> Dyphorthynt ei seirch meirch rhygyngawg.
>
> Ambling steeds conveyed his *equipage*. *[illegible]*

Seirchiad, *s. m.* (seirch) A harnessing.
Seirchiaw, *v. a.* (seirch) To harness, to equip.
Seirchiawg, *a.* (seirch) Harnessed, equipped.
Seirchiawl, *a.* (seirch) Belonging to harness.
Seirchiedig, *a.* (seirchiad) Harnessed, equipped.
Seiriad, *s. m.* (ser) A sparkling like stars.
Seirian, *s. m.—pl. t.* au (ser) A sparkling.

> Nid oes yna dy hanner,
> Na'th draian, liw seirian ser.
>
> There is not in that place thy half, nor thy third, thou so bright as the *glittering* of stars. *D. ab Gwilym.*

Seirianad, *s. m.* (seirian) A sparkling.
Seirianaidd, *a.* (seirian) Tending to sparkle.
Seirianawl, *a.* (seirian) Sparkling, glittering.
Seirianu, *v. a.* (seirian) To sparkle, to twinkle.
Seirnial, *v. a.* (sarn) To trample down.
Seisoneg, *s. f.* (saeson) The English tongue.
Seisonig, *a.* (saeson) Saxon; English.
Seisonigaw, *v. a.* (seisonig) To turn into English; to imitate the English.
Seithblyg, *s. pl. aggr.* (saith—plyg) Seven folds.
Seithdant, *s. pl. aggr.* (saith—tant) Seven strings; a heptachord. *a.* Seven-stringed.
Seithdro, *s. pl. aggr.* (saith—tro) Seven turns; seven times. *a.* Of seven turns.

Seguredd, *s. m.* (segur) A state of leisure.
Seguren, *s. f. dim.* (segur) An idling female.
Seguriad, *s. m.* (segur) An enjoying of leisure.
Segurllyd, *a.* (segur) Loving leisure; idle.
Segurwas, *s. m.* (segur—gwas) An idle youth.
Segurwr, *s. m.—pl.* segurwyr (segur—gwr) One who enjoys leisure; an idler.
Seguryd, *s. m.* (segur) A state of leisure or ease.

Tri pheth sydd yn llygru y byd: balchder, afraid, a seguryd.

Three things do corrupt the world: pride, excess, and *idleness*.
Barddas.

Seguryn, *s. m. dim.* (segur) An idler.
Seibiad, *s. m.* (saib) A standing at leisure.
Seibiannawl, *a.* (seibiant) Leisureable.
Seibiaeth, *s. m.* (saib) A state of rest; sabbath.
Seibiannu, *v. a.* (seibiant) To procure leisure.
Seibiant, *s. m.* (saib) A standing about, a resting, or stopping; a respite; leisure.
Seibiaw, *v. a.* (saib) To stand about, to take respite; to be at leisure.
Seibiawl, *a.* (saib) Leisurely; resting, at rest.
Seidiad, *s. m.* (said) An insertion; the insertion of a tong into the handle.
Seidiaw, *v. a.* (said) To insert; to insert a tool into a handle.
Seidiawg, *a.* (said) Having an insertion; tonged.
Seidyn, *s. m. dim.* (said) The part of a tool that is inserted in the hilt.
Seifiad, *s. m.—pl.* seifiaid (saf) A stander.
Seigen, *s. f. dim.* (saig) A little mess or meal.
Seigiad, *s. m.* (saig) A messing; a taking a meal.
Seigiaw, *v. a.* (saig) To mess, to partake of a meal; to serve up dishes or messes.
Seigiawl, *a.* (saig) Relating to a mess or meal.
Seigiwr, *s. m.—pl.* seigwyr (saig—gwr) A messer
Seilddar, *s. f.—pl.* seilddori (sail—dar) A main beam or pillar; a prop; a foundation pile.
Seilddarluniad, *s. m.* (darluniad) An ichnography
Seilddor, *s. f.—pl. t.* au (sail—dor) A threshold.
Seiler, *s. f.—pl. t.* i (sail) A foundation space; a ground floor; a cellar.
Seilfaen, *s. m.—pl.* seilfeini (sail—maen) A foundation stone.
Seilgam, *a.* (sail—cam) Having a wry tread.
Seilgamiad, *s. m.* (seilgam) A treading awry.
Seilgamu, *v. a.* (seilgam) To tread a sole awry.
Seiliad, *s. m.—pl. t.* au (sail) A foundation.
Seiliannawl, *a.* (seiliant) A base, or foundation.
Seiliannu, *v. a.* (seiliant) To make a foundation.
Seiliant, *s. m.* (sail) Relating to foundation.
Seiliaw, *v. a.* (sail) To found, to lay a foundation.
Seiliawd, *s. m.* (sail) A being made a foundation.
Seiliawg, *a.* (sail) Having a foundation.
Seiliedig, *a.* (seiliad) Having a foundation laid.
Seiliedigaeth, *s. m.* (seiliedig) The act of founding
Seiliwr, *s. m.* (sail—gwr) One who founds.
Seilwaith, *s. m.* (sail—gwaith) Ground-work.
Seilydd, *s. m.—pl. t.* ion (sail) A founder.
Seimiad, *s. m.* (saim) A greasing.
Seimiaw, *v. a.* (saim) To grease, to make greasy.
Seimiawg, *a.* (saim) Abounding with grease.
Seimiawl, *a.* (saim) Of a greasy quality.
Seimiedig, *a.* (saim) Greased; made greasy.
Seimiwr, *s. m.—pl.* seimiwyr (saim—gwr) Greaser
Seimlyd, *a.* (saim) Of a greasy quality.
Seindraws, *a.* (sain—traws) Transversely sounding. *Cynghanedd seindraws*, a transversely sounding consonancy.
Seindwll, *s. m.* (sain—twll) A sound-hole.
Seinfawr, *a.* (sain) Sonorous, of great sound.
Seinfwrdd, *s. m.* (sain—bwrdd) A sounding-board
Seinglawr, *s. m.* (sain—clawr) A sounding-board
Seingroes, *a.* (sain—croes) Transversely sounding. *Cynghanedd seingroes*, a transversely sounding consonancy.
Seingudd, *a.* (sain—cudd) Of concealed sound.
Seinguddgyswllt, *s. m.* (seingudd—cyswllt) A junction of concealed sound.
Seinguddgysylltgroes, *a.* (seinguddgyswllt) Being of transversely conjoined concealed sound.
Seinguddhannergysylltgroes, *a.* (seingudd—hanner—cyswllt—croes) Being of half transversely conjoined concealed sound.
Seiniad, *s. m.—pl. t.* au (sain) A sounding.
Seiniannawl, *a.* (seiniant) Productive of sound.
Seiniannu, *v. a.* (seiniant) To produce a sound.
Seiniant, *s. m.* (sain) A making a sound.
Seiniaw, *v. a.* (sain) To sound, to resound.
Seiniawd, *s. m.* (sain) A resounding, a sounding.
Seiniawdr, *s. m.—pl.* seiniodron (seiniawd) That yields a sound.

Molwch yr Arglwydd——
Molwch ef ar seiniodron glych.

Praise ye the Lord; praise him ye bells that *are high sounding*.
D. Ddu Hiraddug.

Seiniawg, *a.* (sain) Having a sound or tone.
Seiniawl, *a.* (sain) Sounding; toned.
Seiniedig, *a.* (seiniad) Sounded; toned.
Seiniedigaeth, *s. m.* (seiniedig) Act of sounding.
Seiniwr, *s. m.—pl.* seiniwyr (sain—gwr) One who sounds or makes a sound.
Seintiad, *s. m.* (saint) A canonization.
Seintiaw, *v. a.* (saint) To canonize.
Seintiawl, *a.* (saint) Sanctified, saintly.
Seintiedig, *a.* (seintiad) Canonized, sainted.
Seintiolaeth, *s. m.* (seintiawl) Sanctitude.
Seintwar, *s. f.* (saint—gwar) A sanctuary.

Seintwar i'r adar ydwyd.

The *sanctuary* of the feathered tribe art thou.
H. Machno, i y [illegible].

Seirch, *s. pl. aggr.* (sarch) Equipage, horse trappings, furniture, or harness, a set of harness.

Gwr gwiw uch ei amliw seirch,
A roddai feirch i eirchiad.

A superior man on his many-coloured *trappings*, who would give horses to the suitor. *Taliesin.*

Dyphorthynt ei seirch meirch rhygyngawg.

Ambling steeds conveyed his *equipage*. *Meilyr.*

Seirchiad, *s. m.* (seirch) A harnessing.
Seirchiaw, *v. a.* (seirch) To harness, to equip.
Seirchiawg, *a.* (seirch) Harnessed, equipped.
Seirchiawl, *a.* (seirch) Belonging to harness.
Seirchiedig, *a.* (seirchiad) Harnessed, equipped.
Seiriad, *s. m.* (ser) A sparkling like stars.
Seirian, *s. m.—pl. t.* au (ser) A sparkling.

Nid oes yna dy hanner,
Na'th draian, liw seirian ser.

There is not in that place thy half, nor thy third, thou so bright as the *glittering* of stars. *D. ab Gwilym.*

Seirianad, *s. m.* (seirian) A sparkling.
Seirianaidd, *a.* (seirian) Tending to sparkle.
Seirianawl, *a.* (seirian) Sparkling, glittering.
Seirianu, *v. a.* (seirian) To sparkle, to twinkle.
Seirnial, *v. a.* (sarn) To trample down.
Seisoneg, *s. f.* (saeson) The English tongue.
Seisonig, *a.* (saeson) Saxon; English.
Seisonigaw, *v. a.* (seisonig) To turn into English; to imitate the English.
Seithblyg, *s. pl. aggr.* (saith—plyg) Seven folds.
Seithdant, *s. pl. aggr.* (saith—tant) Seven strings; a heptachord. *a.* Seven-stringed.
Seithdro, *s. pl. aggr.* (saith—tro) Seven turns; seven times. *a.* Of seven turns.

Seithddeg, *s. m.* (saith—deg) Seventy.

Seithddegfed, *s. m.* (seithddeg) A seventieth.

Seithddegwaith, *s. pl. aggr.* (seithddeg—gwaith) Seventy times. *a.* Seventy times.

Seithfan, *s. pl. aggr.* (saith—ban) Seven verses or lines. *a.* Of seven lines.

Seithfanawg, *a.* (seithfan) Having seven verses.

Seithfed, *s. f.* (saith) A seventh. *a.* Seventh.

> Cei dy benyd ar dy seithfed.
>
> Thou shalt take thy penance on thy *seventh.* *Tysilio.*

Seithfetdydd, *s.m.* (seithfed—dydd) The seventh day, the ancient name for Sunday.

Seithganfed, *s. m.* (seithgant) A seven hundredth

Seithgant, *s. pl.* (saith—cant) Seven hundreds.

Seithganwaith, *s. pl.* (seithgant—gwaith) Seven hundred times. *a.* Seven hundred times.

Seithi, *s. m.* (sath) Frustration; disappointment.

> Cerddorion allan heb ran seithi.
>
> Minstrels abroad without a portion of *disappointment.* *Myrddin.*

Seithiawl, *a.* (saith) Septenery, of seven.

Seithmlwydd, *s. pl. aggr.* (saith—blwydd) Seven years. *a.* Septennial.

Seithnalen, *s. f.* (saith—dalen) Tormentil.

Seithnyn, *s. pl. aggr.* (saith—dyn) Seven persons. *a.* Consisting of seven persons.

Seithochr, *s. pl. aggr.* (saith—ochr) Seven sides; a heptagon. *a.* Seven sided.

> A seithochr waew ym saethawdd;
> A seith-wawd cymhendawd cawdd.
>
> With a *seven-sided* spear she shot me; with sevenfold flow of insulting eloquence. *D. ab Gwilym, i Forfudd.*

Seithochrawg, *a.* (seithochr) Heptagonal.

Seithochrawl, *a.* (seithochr) Heptagonal.

Seithochri, *v. a.* (seithochr) To be seven-sided.

Seithongl, *s. pl. aggr.* (saith—ongl) Seven angles; a septangle. *a.* Septangular.

Seithonglawg, *a.* (seithongl) Septangular.

Seithongli, *v. a.* (seithongl) To render septangular, or to render of seven angles.

Seithor, *s. pl. aggr.* (saith—gor) Seven regions or sides; a heptagon. *a.* Of seven regions.

Seithrad, *s. pl. aggr.* (saith—rhad) Seven endowments, seven virtues. *Seithrad esgob*, the seven endowments of a bishop.

Seithran, *s. pl. aggr.* (saith—rhan) Seven parts; that is of seven parts. *a.* Of seven parts.

> Saith meib Elifer, saith gwyr ban brofer,
> Saith gwaew ni ochel yn eu seithran.
>
> The seven sons of Elifer, seven men when tried by seven spears they shun not on their *seven parts.* *Taliesin.*

Seithranawl, *a.* (seithran) Of seven parts.

Seithrif, *s. pl. aggr.* (saith—rhif) Seven numbers; seven times a number. *a.* Seven times the number.

Seithrifed, *a.* (seithrif) Seven times the number.

Seithsill, *s. pl. aggr.* (saith—sill) Seven syllables; that consists of seven syllables.

Seithsillawg, *a.* (seithsill) Of seven syllables.

Seithug, *a.* (sath) Being frustrated; futile, vain.

Seithwaith, *s. pl. aggr.* (saith—gwaith) Seven times. *a.* Seven times.

Seithwedd, *s. pl. aggr.* (saith—gwedd) Seven forms; that is of seven forms. *a.* Septiform.

Seithwr, *s. pl. aggr.* (saith—gwr) Septemviri. *a.* Consisting of seven men.

Seithwriaeth, *s. m.* (seithwr) Septemvirate.

Seithygiad, *s. m.* (seithug) A frustrating, a rendering futile; a becoming futile.

Seithygiaeth, *s. m.* (seithug) A frustration.

Seithygiant, *s. m.* (seithug) A frustration.

Seithygiaw, *v. a.* (seithug) To frustrate, to render futile or vain; to disappoint.

Seithygiawl, *a.* (seithug) Frustrating.

Sel, *s. m.* (se—el) An espying, sight at a distance

Seldeb, *s. m.* (sel) Keen-sightedness.

Selder, *s. m.* (sel) Keen-sightedness.

Seldra, *s. m.* (sel) Keen-sightedness.

Seldrem, *s. f.—pl. t.* an (sel—trem) A prospect; a perspective view; a vanishing line or point; arrangement; what is placed in a straight line; a layer, as of corn after the reaper.

> Pwyll, a chrebwyll, a sylwedd, a seldrem, a barn, a dychymyg, ac ystyr, a meddwl; ac o hyn godidawg Gymmraeg a ddeilliа.
>
> Reason, idea, observation, *perspicuity*, judgement, invention, significancy, and thought; and from these the excellency of the Welsh language proceeds. *Barddas.*
>
> Ni ad fy nhrem seldrem sech.
>
> My sight leaves not a dry *prospect.* *D. ab Gwilym.*

Seldremiad, *s. m.* (seldrem) A putting in prospect

Seldremiaw, *v. a.* (seldrem) To put in prospect; to place in view; to lay in a strait line or row.

> Teilyngdawd a theithi yr iaith Gymmraeg—yw adrawdd—pob peth er a allo y meddwl a'r bryd ei ddychymmyg, a'i seldremiaw, ac ei sylweddu.
>
> The merit and characteristics of the Welsh language are, that it can express every thing, which the thought and the mind may be able to conceive, *to arrange*, and to substantiate. *Barddas.*

Seldremiawg, *a.* (seldrem) Perspicuous.

Seldremiawl, *a.* (seldrem) Perspicacious.

Seldremiwr, *s. m.—pl.* seldremwyr (seldrem—gwr) One who makes perspicuous.

Seldremu, *v. a.* (seldrem) To place perspicuously; to place in layers.

Seledig, *a.* (sel) Perceived, or observed.

Seledigaeth, *s. m.* (seledig) Observation.

Seliad, *s. m.—pl. t.* au (sel) A descrying, an espying; perception; observation. *Dyn seliad*, a person of observation, or of quick wit.

Seliadwy, *a.* (seliad) Perceivable, observable.

Seliannawl, *a.* (seliant) Perceptive.

Seliannu, *v. a.* (seliant) To render perceptive.

Seliant, *s. m.* (sel) Perception, observation.

Selsig, *s. f.—pl. t.* od (sal—sig) A sausage.

> No bela i fel, no gwraig i selsig.
>
> Than a marten to honey, than a woman to a *pudding.* *Adage.*

Selsigen, *s. f. dim.* (selsig) A pudding, a sausage.

Selu, *v. a.* (sel) To espy, to perceive, to behold; to gaze.

> Cael dirgelu
> Clwyf saethu
> Cair dy selu
> Craew des haelion.
>
> Being able to conceal the wound of the arrow shot, an opportunity can be had *to behold* thee, the warm luminary of generous ones. *W. Llyn.*
>
> Seiliaist, cryf eiliaist bob cur ofalon;
> Seliaist, a deliaist ffordd yr hudolion;
> Selu, annelu yr ael yn wiwlon,
> Synwyraidd llwyraidd lle y ceilwеirion.
>
> Thou didst found, thou didst firmly build all throbbing cares; *thou didst espy*, thou didst take the way of deluders; beholding, aiming at the brow supremely smiling love, the pending sensible scene of sportive ideas. *W. Llyn.*

Selus, *a.* (sel) Apt to espy; perspicacious.

Selusaw, *v. a.* (selus) To render perspicacious.

Selusdra, *s. m.* (selus) Perspicacity.

Selwedd, *s. m.* (sel—gwedd) Perceptivity.

Selweddawl, *a.* (selwedd) Perspicacious.

Selweddiad, *s. m.* (selwedd) A perceiving.

Selweddu, *v. a.* (selwedd) To endue with perceptivity; to exert perspicacity.

Selweddus, *a.* (selwedd) Perspicacious.

Selwr, *s. m.—pl.* selwyr (sel—gwr) An espyer.

Selydd, *s. m.—pl. t.* ion (sel) An espyer.

Sellt, *s. m.* (sallt) A limit or border.

Sellti, *s. m.* (sellt) An exploring; a seek out, the play of hide and seek.

Seilliad, *s. m.—pl. t.* au (seilt) Exploration.
Selltu, *v. a.* (sellt) To explore, to seek out.
Sèn, *s. f.—pl. t.* au (sy—en) The state of being extended; that is capable of affecting; a taunt, a scoff, a chide.
Senadwy, *a.* (sèn) Liable of being chided.
Senaidd, *a.* (sèn) Invective, reproachful.
Senawl, *a.* (sèn) Censorious; taunting, scoffing, reprehending; reproaching.
Senedig, *a.* (sèn) Scoffed, reproached, rebuked.
Senedigaeth, *s. m.* (senedig) Reprehension.
Senedigawl, *a.* (senedig) Reprehensive.
Senedd, *s. f.—pl. t.* au (sen) A synod; a senate. *Senedd wyllt*, wild senate; an epithet used for the bishop's visitation.
Senedda, *v. a.* (senedd) To resort to a synod.
Seneddawl, *a.* (senedd) Synodal; senatorial.
Seneddu, *v. a.* (senedd) To form a synod.
Seneddwr, *s. m.—pl.* seneddwyr (senedd—gwr) A member of a synod; a senator.
Seneddwriaeth, *s. m.* (seneddwr) Senatorship.
Senferw, *a.* (sèn—berw) Censure-brooding.
Sèngar, *a.* (sèn) Censorious; taunting, scoffing.
Sengarwch, *a.* (sèngar) Censoriousness, reproachfulness; aptness to chide.
Sèniad, *s. m.* (sèn) A reprehension, a chiding.
Senoldeb, *s. m.* (sènawl) Censoriousness.
Senolder, *s. m* (sènawl) Censoriousness.
Senoli, *v. a.* (sènawl) To render censorious.
Senolrwydd, *s. m.* (sènawl) Censoriousness.
Sensigl, *s. m.—pl. t.* on (sèn—sigl) The great daisy, or white ox-eye.
Sènu, *v. a.* (sèn) To censure, to chide, to reprehend; to reproach; to taunt, to scoff.
Senw, *s. m.* (sèn) That is past a chide; boldness.

> Enw heb senw.
>
> A name without *dignity*. — *Adage.*
>
> Enw heb senw oedd ei henw hi.
>
> A name without *dignity* was her name. — *Iolo Goch.*

Senwad, *s. m.* (senw) A giving boldness.
Senwawl, *a.* (senw) Tending to embolden.
Senwi, *v. a.* (senw) To give confidence.
Sènwr, *s. m.—pl.* senwyr (sen—gwr) A censurer.
Senyllt, *s. m.* (sèn) A seneschal; a constable.

> Cenea fab Llywarch ddihafarch ddrud,
> Nid ef borthi gwarth gorsedd:
> Senyllt a'i lestri llawn medd.
>
> Cenea the son of Llywarch magnanimously bold, he would not support the reproach of a convention: a *seneschal* with his vessel full of mead. — *Aneurin.*

Sengi, *s. m.* (sang) A treading; a trampling *v. a.* To tread about; to trample.
Sèr, *s. m.—pl. t.* oedd (sy—er) That tends to, that is apt to enclose; a bill, a tool so called.

> Ser, dimai a dal.
>
> A *bill-hook*, its value is a halfpenny. — *Welsh Laws.*

Ser, *s. pl. aggr.* (se—er) Stars. Poets also give them the appellations of *syr*, and in the singular *se* and *sy*. *Ser-ysgall*, common star-thistle.

> Cyffoled a'r cwn yn cyfarth y ser.
>
> As foolish as the dogs barking the *stars*. — *Adage.*
>
> Ser y bore a ddwyreynt,
> Yn llu i gydgann gynt.
>
> The *stars* of the morning were wont to rise, assembled to sing in harmony of yore. — *Gro. Owain.*

Seraidd, *a.* (ser) Like stars; sideral; starred.
Serawg, *a.* (ser) Starry, studded with stars.
Serawl, *a.* (ser) Sideral, astral, starry.
Serch, *s. m.* (ser) Appulsion; desire; affection, love. *Serch anllad*, wanton desire: *rhois fy serch arnat*, I have placed my affection on thee.

> Trafn llugyrn a'i liw lafn Lloegr elyfn;
> Treigla'm bron anserch serch dwyrchu.
>
> He leads the horns of battle with his gleaming sword the rage of England; to him my breast returns the greeting of love incessant. — *G. ab M. ab Dafydd.*
>
> Ei gasbeth a'i argoelion,
> Gwr meddw serch a gormodd son.
>
> With his odious instrument and its torments, a fellow drunk with *love* and noisy to excess. — *H. ab D. ab I. ab Rhys.*

Serch, *prep.* (ser) With respect to, because of, for. *adv.* Notwithstanding. *Ni wiw iti serch hyny*, it is no use for thee because of that; *ni waeth ganto serch hyny*, he is not sorry notwithstanding that.
Serchaidd, *a.* (serch) Tending to excite desire.
Serchawg, *a.* (serch) Having desire; amorous.

> Eiddig—
> Ni ddaw hwn oni ddaw haf;
> Rhoed ei gyfoed o'r gauaf;
> A rhan serchogion yw'r haf.
>
> The jealous one—he will not come unless summer comes: cotemporary with him was winter given; and the portion of *loving ones* is summer. — *D. ab Gwilym.*

Serchawl, *a.* (serch) Exciting love; lovely.
Serchedig, *a.* (serch) Being rendered loving.
Serchedd, *s. m.* (serch) A state of desire; fondness.
Sercheiddiad, *s. m.* (serchaidd) A disposing to love
Sercheiddiaw, *v. a.* (serchaidd) To dispose to fondness; to become disposed to fondness.
Serchfawr, *a.* (serch) Very fond or affectionate.
Serchiad, *s. m.—pl. t.* au (serch) Appulsion; a desiring; a creating love or fondness.
Serchiadaeth, *s. m.* (serchiad) A causing to love.
Serchiadawl, *a.* (serchiad) Love-exciting.
Serchiadu, *v. a.* (serchiad) To excite fondness.
Serchiant, *s. m.* (serch) Affection, fondness.
Serchiator, *ger.* (serchiad) In loving or fondling.
Serchitor, *sup.* (serch) To be loving or fondling.
Serchlawn, *a.* (serch) Amorous, full of love.
Serchlondeb, *s. m.* (serchlawn) Amorousness.
Serchlonedd, *s. m.* (serchlawn) Amorousness.
Serchloni, *v. a.* (serchlawn) To fill with love.
Serchogaeth, *s. m.* (serchawg) State of fondness.
Serchogaidd, *a.* (serchawg) Somewhat amorous.
Serchogeiddiad, *s. m.* (serchogaidd) A rendering or becoming somewhat amorous.
Serchogeiddiaw, *v. a.* (serchogaidd) To render somewhat loving; to become a little amorous.
Serchogi, *v. a.* (serchawg) To render fond or amorous; to become amorous.
Serchogiad, *s. m.* (serchawg) A rendering fond or amorous; a becoming amorous.
Serchothe deb, *s. m.* (serchawl) Amorousness.
Serchoi, *v. a.* (serchawl) To become amorous.
Serchu, *v. a.* (serch) To desire; to affect; to be affected; to have affection; to love.
Serchus, *a.* (serch) Creating fondness; agreeable.
Serchusaw, *v. a.* (serchus) To tend to fondness.
Serchusdra, *s. m.* (serchus) Fondness.
Serchusedd, *s. m.* (serchus) Lovingness, fondness.
Serchusrwydd, *s. m.* (serchus) Desirableness; agreeableness; affectionateness, fondness.
Serchwr, *s. m.—pl.* serchwyr (serch—gwr) One who fixes his desire; one who is fond or loving.
Serddewin, *s. m.—pl. t.* ion (ser—dewin) An astrologer, one who foretells by the stars.
Serddewindeb, *s. m.* (serddewin) Astrology.
Serddewiniad, *s. m.* (serddewin) A divining by the stars; a practising of astrology.
Serddewiniaeth, *s. m.* (serddewin) Astrology.
Serddewiniaw, *v. a.* (serddewin) To astrologize.
Serddewiniawl, *a.* (serddewin) Astrological.

Seren, *s. f. dim.* (ser) A star. *Seren walltawg, seren gynffonawg, seren y gynffon, seren losgyrnawg*, a blazing star, a meteor.

Mawr yw seren y morwyr;
Mwy yw no swrn o'r man syr.

Grand is the *star* of the mariners; greater than a crowd of tiny spangles. *L. G. Cothi.*

Ni roe neb, ac ni rown i
Seren bren er ei sori.

Nobody would give, and I would not give a *star* of wood for offending him. *Gr. Gryg.*

Serenawl, *a.* (seren) Sparkling like a star.
Sereniad, *s. m.* (seren) A sparkling.
Serenig, *s. f. dim.* (seren) An asterisk.
Serenllys, *s. pl.* (seren—llys) Starwort.
Serenu, *v. a.* (seren) To sparkle, to glitter.
Serenwyl, *s. f.—pl. t.* iau (seren—gwyl) Epiphany. It is also called *Ystwyll.*
Serenyn, *s. m. dim.* (seren) The vernal squill.
Serf, *a.* (sy—erf) Whirling; dizzy or giddy.
Serfan, *a.* (serf) Tending to dizzy; dizzied.
Serfanawl, *a.* (servan) Startling; staring.
Serfaniad, *s. m.* (serfan) A startling.
Serfanu, *v. a.* (servan) To start; to stare; to dizzy. *Serfanu llygaid*, to turn about the eyes wildly; to astonish.
Serfawl, *a.* (serf) Whirling; dizzying.
Serviad, *s. m.* (serf) A startling; a dizzying.
Serfu, *v. a.* (serf) To startle; to dizzy.
Serfyll, *a.* (serf) Dependent; ready to fall, unsteady, waggling: shattered; crazy.

Serfyll oer bebyll yw'r byd;
Somwr ar bob rhyw symyd.

A *crazy* cold tent is the world; a deceiver on every sort of change. *S. Tudyr.*

Serfylldra, *s. m.* (serfyll) Craziness.
Serfylliad, *s. m.* (serfyll) A crazing, a shattering.
Serfylliaw, *v. a.* (serfyll) To craze, to shatter.
Serfyllrwydd, *s. m.* (serfyll) Craziness.
Serfyllus, *s. m.* (serfyll) Tending to fall; tending to become crazy.
Seri, *s. pl. aggr.* (sar) Sullen ones, furies.

Meirw sengi, mal seri sathar.

The treading of the dead, like the trampling of *furies.* *Ll. P. Moch.*

Serig, *a.* (ser) Starred, studded with stars.
Serigl, *s. m.* (serig) That is spangled, or studded. *a.* Studded with stars. *Arfau seriglfriw*, arms with spangled surface.

Edein-feirch a seirch serigl cynwe.

Winged steeds and harness with *spangled* borders. *Ll. P. Moch.*

Seriglaw, *v. a.* (serigl) To stud with stars.
Serigliad, *s. m.* (serigl) A spangling.
Serliw, *s. m.* (ser—lliw) Starlight.

Meillion teg, mae llonaid twyn,
Man serliw mynwes irlwyn.

Fair spangles, which will fill the bush, the minute *starlight* of the bosom of the verdant grove. *Ieu. Deulwyn, i fedwen.*

Serloew, *s. m.* (ser—gloew) A star-glow. *Mae yn serloew heno*, it is a star-glow to-night, or it is very starry. *Sil.*
Serloew, *a.* (ser—gloew) Star-glowing.
Sernial, *v. a.* (sarn) To graze, to rase; to jar.
Serofydd, *s. m.—pl. t.* ion (ofydd) Astronomer.
Serofyddawl, *a.* (serofydd) Astronomical.
Serofyddiaeth, *s. m.* (serofydd) Astronomy.
Seroli, *v. a.* (serawl) To proceed as the stars.
Seroliaeth, *s. m.* (serawl) The starry system.

Rhy gron yw hon ar ei hynt,
Fwyfogaeth seroliaeth sant.

Round to excess is this one on her course, through the community of the solemn *starry system.* *D. ab Gwilym, i'r lleuad.*

Seron, *s. m.* (ser) The system of the stars.
Seronawl, *a.* (ser) Astronomical.
Seroni, *s. m.* (seron) To systemise the stars; to pursue or study the science of astronomy.
Seronydd, *s. m.—pl. t.* ion (seron) Astronomer.

Tri gwyn seronyddion Ynys Prydain: Idris Gawr, a Gwydion, mab Don, a Gwyn ab Nudd; a chan faint eu gwybodau am y ser, a'u hanianau, au hansoddau, y darogenynt a chwenychid ei wybod.

The three excelling *astronomers* of the Isle of Britain: Idris the Mighty, and Gwydion son of Don, and Gwyn son of Nudd; and from the magnitude of their discoveries, respecting the stars, their natures and their dispositions, they could foretel whatever might be desired to be known. *Trioedd.*

Serth, *s.* (ser) Inclination, tendency, bias, or fall; a steep.
Serth, *a.* (ser) Inclining, tending, falling; steep, abrupt, slippery; obscene.

Ffam danllyd ynfyd anferth
Yw tyfiad swydd tafawd serth.

The fiery flame of monstrous folly is the fruit of the office of a *foul* tongue. *Ed. Morris.*

Serthadwy, *a.* (serth) Capable of precipitancy.
Serthaidd, *a.* (serth) Somewhat inclined.
Serthair, *s. m.—pl.* sertheirian (serth—gair) An obscene word or expression.
Serthallt, *s. f.* (serth—gallt) A steep cliff.
Serthan, *s. f.* (serth) A precipice, a cliff.
Serthawl, *a.* (serth) Precipitous; obscene.
Serthedig, *a.* (serth) Inclined; precipitated.
Serthedd, *s. m.* (serth) Inclinedness; steepness; abruptness; slipperiness; obscenity.
Sertheiriawg, *a.* (serthair) Having obscene words.
Serthfrwnt, *a.* (serth--brwnt) Grovellingly filthy.
Serthfryntni, *s. m.* (serthfrwnt) Grovelling filthiness or obscenity.
Serthi, *s. m.* (serth) A falling tendency; slipperiness; obscenity.
Serthiad, *s. m.* (serth) An inclining, a tending; a rendering steep; a becoming obscene.
Serthiannawl, *a.* (serthiant) Tending to be precipitous or steep.
Serthiannu, *v. a.* (serthiant) To render steep or declivous; to become steep.
Serthiant, *s. m.* (serth) Precipitancy, steepness.
Serthrwydd, *s. m.* (serth) A precipitous state.
Serthu, *v. a.* (serth) To render precipitous; to become steep; to act obscenely.
Serthus, *a.* (serth) Precipitous; declivous; obscene, vulgar.
Serthusaw, *v. a.* (serthus) To render precipitous; to become steep; to grow vulgar.
Serthusdra, *s. m.* (serthus) A precipitous state; vulgarity.
Serthusedd, *s. m.* (serthus) Steepness; vulgarity.
Serthusrwydd, *s. m.* (serthus) Steepness.
Serthyd, *s. m.* (serth) A steep or falling tendency; vulgarity, obscenity.

Tri harddwch cerdd; mawl heb druth, nwyf heb anlladrwydd, a duchan heb serthyd.

The three ornaments of song; praise without flattery, gaiety without licentiousness, and satire without *vulgarity.* *Barddas.*

Serw, *a.* (ser) That is flat and opake or dull.
Serydd, *s. m.—pl. t.* ion (ser) An astronomer.
Seryddawl, *a.* (serydd) Astronomical.
Seryddiaeth, *s. m.* (serydd) Astronomy.

Y dyn a garaf nis digerais,
Yn seryddiaeth Don
Yn swydd Gaernarfon,
Lle bu ron dragon
Dreigan Emrais.

The man I respect, whom I have not ceased to love, studying the *astronomy* of Don in the county of Caernarvon, where the shaft of the chief of the dragons of Emrais has been. *Gr. ab D. ab Tudur.*

Seryddiannawl, *a.* (seryddiant) Astronomical.
Seryddiannu, *v. a.* (seryddiant) To follow the science of astronomy.

Seryddiant, *s. m.* (serydd) Astronomy.

Seryla, *v. a.* (ser) To gaze upon; to spare. *Er seryla yr arian hyd yr eithaf*, though sparing of the money to the utmost.

Seth, *a.* (*f.* of syth) Stiff, rigid; being set or put up; erect, upright; disdainful.

Sëu, *v. a.* (se) To render fixed, or stated.

Sew, *s. m.—pl. t.* ion (se) Gravy; jelly.

Sewed, *s. m.* (se—gwed) Discourse of the stars.

Sewedawl, *a.* (sewed) Descriptive of the stars.

Sewedydd, *s. m.—pl. t.* ion (sewed) Astronomy.

Sewedyddawl, *a.* (sewedydd) Astronomical.

Sewedyddiaeth, *s. m.* (sewedydd) Astronomy.

Sewlyd, *a.* (sew) Abounding with gravy.

Sewyd, *s. m.—pl. t.* ion (se—gwyd) A diffusion of stars. *Sewyd am loer*, a sprinkling of stars round the moon. *Taliesin.*

SI, *s. m. r.* A hiss, a whiz; a buz; a tingling noise.

Sïad, *s. m.* (si) A hissing, a whizzing; a buzzing.

Siâd, *s. f.—pl. t.* au (sy—iad) The top of the skull, the crown of the head; the cranium.

> Eiliaw troell——
> Ar ei siâd, eres ydiw.
>
> Shaving a ring on his *noddle*, strange it is. *I. B.*
>
> Duw a wyr synwyr dy siâd,
> Sori a bair dy siarad.
>
> God knows what sense thy *head* contains, anger causes thy talk. *T. Prys.*

Siadfoel, *a.* (siâd—moel) Bald-pated.

Siar, *s. m.* (si—ar) An articulate sound.

Siarad, *s. m.—pl. t.* au (siar) A talking, a talk.

> Gwaeddodd fal siarad gwyddau.
>
> He cried out like the *gabbling* of geese. *D. ab Gwilym.*

Siaradach, *s. m.* (siarad) Chitchat, babbling, garrulity, dicacity.

Siaradaidd, *a.* (siarad) Talkative, or prating.

Siaradawl, *a.* (siarad) Talking, or speaking.

Siaradfa, *s. f.—pl.* siaradfëydd (siarad) A talking place, or a gossip shop.

Siaradgar, *a.* (siarad) Querulous, prating, talkative, garrulous, fond of talking.

Siaradgarwch, *s. m.* (siaradgar) Garrulity.

Siaradu, *v. a.* (siarad) To make a talking.

Siaradus, *a.* (siarad) Talkative, loquacious.

> Tripheth nid hawdd eu rhifaw; banynau y goleu, geiriau benyw siaradus, a dichellion cybydd.
>
> Three things that are not easily numbered; the particles of light, the words of a *talkative* female, and the schemes of a miser. *Catwg Ddoeth.*

Siaradusaw, *v. a.* (siaradus) To render talkative; to become talkative.

Siaradusedd, *s. m.* (siaradus) Talkativeness.

Siaradusrwydd, *s. m.* (siaradus) Talkativeness.

Siaradwr, *s. m.—pl.* siaradwyr (siarad—gwr) A talker; a prater.

Siaradwraig, *s. f.—pl.* siaradwreigedd (siarad—gwraig) A talking woman, a gossip.

Siared, *v. a.* (siar) To talk, to chat, to discourse.

> Siared cymaint a mab Seithgudyn.
>
> To talk as much as the son of Seven locks. *Adage.*
>
> Siared cymaint a Merddin ar bawl.
>
> *To talk* as much as Merddin on a pole. *Adage.*

Sïaw, *v. a.* (si) To hiss, to whiz, to buz; to tingle

Sïawl, *a.* (si) Hissing, whizzing, buzzing.

Sib, *s. m.* (si—ib) That tends to involve or to encircle.

Sibol, *s. pl. aggr.* (sib) Young onions, scallions.

Sibolen, *s. f. dim.* (sibol) A young onion.

Sibr, *s. m.* (sib) That is imbibed or taken in.

Sibrad, *s. m.* (sibr) A dressing with sauce.

Sibraw, *v. a.* (sibr) To sauce, to do with sauce.

Sibrydawl, *a.* (sibrwd) Doing with sauce.

Sibwl, *s. pl. aggr.* (sib) Young onions, scallions.

Sibylen, *s. f. dim.* (sibwl) A small or young onion a scallion.

Siciad, *s. m.—pl. t.* au (sig) A steeping.

Siciant, *s. m.* (sig) A steeping, a seething.

Siciaw, *v. a.* (sig) To steep, to wet; to wash.

Siciawl, *a.* (sig) Steeping, or seething.

Siciedig, *a.* (siciad) Steeped, seethed, wetted.

Sicion, *s. pl. aggr.* (sig) Steepings, washings.

Sicioni, *v. a.* (sicion) To make steepings.

Sid, *s. m.* (si—id) A wind, a round, a circling.

Sidan, *s. m.—pl. t.* au (sid) Silk, satin. *Sidan y waen*, cotton-grass, *sidan y brain*, hair-weed.

Sidana, *v. a.* (sidan) To collect silk.

Sidanaidd, *a.* (sidan) Like silk, silky. *Gwallt sidanaidd*, silky hair.

Sidanawg, *a.* (sidan) Having silk; in silk.

> Gwaedlen am ben yn heiddawg,
> A gelo eur man-ro [illegible]
> Gelynion Saeson sidanawg.
>
> A veil of blood over the head conspicuous, and begging by the bunch of small stones the Saxon foes arrayed in silk. *[illegible]*

Sidanawl, *a.* (sidan) Of the quality of silk.

Sidanblu, *s. pl.* (sidan—plu) Down feathers.

> Gwelem rai ar wolyna sidanblu yn ymdrylaeddu [illegible]wch.
>
> We could perceive some on beds of *down*, [illegible] tuousness. *[illegible]*

Sidanen, *s. f. dim.* (sidan) That is silken, or made of silk. It is the name of an old tune; also an epithet for a fine woman; and has been applied particularly to queen Elizabeth.

Sidaniad, *s. m.* (sidan) A making of silk; a making silky.

Sidanion, *s. pl. aggr.* (sidan) Silken things, silkmercery.

Sidanu, *v. a.* (sidan) To make silk; to wind; to make silky, or smooth: to coax, to wheedle. *Nyddu a sidanu*, to twist and to wind.

> Mae y diawl yn dda tra y sidanner.
>
> The devil is civil so long as *he is coaxed*. *Adage.*

Sidanwe, *s. f.—pl. t.* oedd (sidan—gwe) A silk web.

Sidanwëydd, *s. m.—pl. t.* ion (sidanwe) A silkweaver.

Sidanwr, *s. m.—pl.* sidanwyr (sidan—gwr) A silkman.

Sidanydd, *s. m.—pl. t.* ion (sidan) Silk-mercer.

Sidedd, *s. m.* (sid) A state of twirling.

Sidell, *s. f.—pl. t.* i (sid) A winder; a whirl; the rim of a wheel; a fly-wheel.

Sidellawg, *a.* (sidell) Having a whirl or wheel.

Sidelliad, *s. m.* (sidell) A whirling round.

Sidellu, *v. a.* (sidell) To whirl round.

> Ys dy lafn, gwrle dan [illegible]
> Ysdylien yn sidellu.
>
> A blade that is trusty, between two hosts a gleam *whirling round*. *[illegible]*

Sidellydd, *s. m.—pl. t.* ion (sidell) A winder.

Sider, *s. m.—pl. t.* ion (sid) That winds or twirls; that is in ringlets; lace, fringe.

Sidera, *v. a.* (sider) To form into ringlets.

Sideraidd, *a.* (sider) Like twirls or ringlets.

Siderawg, *a.* (sider) That is made up of winds or ringlets; full of fringes; fringed; laced.

> Marchawg siderawg [illegible].
>
> A cavalier *decked with lace*. *D. ab [illegible], i [illegible].*

Siderawg, *a.* (sider) Formed into ringlets; fringed

Sideriad, *s. m.* (sider) A twirling into ringlets; a fringeing.

Siderogrwydd, *s. m.* (siderawg) The state of being in ringlets, or fringed.

Sideru, *v. a.* (sider) To make ringlets; to plait; to fringe; to make lace; to lace.

Siderwr, *s. m.—pl.* siderwyr (sider—gwr) A maker of fringe.

Siderydd, *s. m.—pl. t.* ion (sider) Fringe maker.

Sidi, *s. f.* (sid) A state of revolution. *Caer sidi*, a zone of revolving, the zodiac; also called *caer sidin*, and *caer sidydd*.

Sidin, *a.* (sid) Winding, or revolving.

> Mi a fum yn nghadair flin
> Uwch caer sidin;
> A hono yn troi sydd
> Rhwng tri elfydd.
>
> I have been in a toilsome seat, above the revolving zone; and that continues turning between three elements. *Taliesin.*

Sidydd, *s. m.—pl. t.* ion (sid) The agent of revolving; the zodiac. *Caer sidydd*, the circle of the zodiac, the ecliptic.

Sidyll, *s. m.—pl. t.* au (sid) A whirl, a turn round, the circumference or rim of a wheel. *Sidyll troell*, the rim of a spinning wheel; *Troi yn sidyll*, to turn in a twirl.

Siff, *s. m.* (si—iff) An intermitted noise.

Siffr, *s. m.* (siff) A rustle; a whisper.

Siffraw, *v. a.* (siffr) To rustle; to murmur.

Siffrwd, *s. m.* (siffr) A soft rustling; a murmuring; a whispering. *v. a.* To rustle; to murmur; to whisper.

Sig, *s. m.—pl. t.* ion (si—ig) A shatter; a bruise.

Sigaw, *v. a.* (sig) To shock, to craze, to shatter; to bruise.

Sigawl, *a.* (sig) Crazing, shattering; bruising.

Sigiad, *s. m.* (sig) A shattering; a bruising.

Sigl, *s. m.—pl. t.* ion (sig) A shake, a rocking; a stir. *a.* Shaking, rocking. *Sigl-din y gwys*, *sigl-din sionc*, *tinsigl y gwys*, *brith y fuches*, the wag-tail; *Sigl dyhoedan*, *siglathan*, neu *tinsiliosa*, the play of swinging.

Sigladwy, *a.* (siglad) Capable of being shaken.

Siglaeth, *s. m.* (sigl) A shaking; a swinging.

Siglaethan, *s. f. dim.* (sigl) A play of swinging.

Siglaw, *v. a.* (sigl) To shake, to rock; to stir; to be shaken. *Sigla law*, shake hand. *Dimet.*

> Agor ei law i bob ci a siglo ei gynffon arno.
>
> He opens his hand to every dog that *wags* his tail at him. *Adage.*
>
> Rhag bod y sul heb siglaw.
>
> For fear of being on Sundays without *stirring*. *Adage.*

Siglawg, *a.* (sigl) Having a shaking.

Sigledig, *a.* (sigl) Shaked, rocked; stirred.

Sigledigaeth, *s. m.* (sigledig) A shaking.

Sigledd, *s. m.* (sigl) The state of being shaken.

Siglen, *s. f. dim.—pl. t.* ydd (sigl) What shakes or rocks; a swing; a quag. *Siglen donen*, *siglen donc*, *siglen denyn*, a swing rope.

Siglenawg, *a.* (siglen) Abounding with quags.

Siglwr, *s. m.—pl.* siglwyr (sigl—gwr) A shaker, a rocker; a stirrer.

Sil, *s. m.—pl. t.* ion (si—il) That is produced, or brought forth; issue, progeny; seedling; spawn, or fry; also the cleansing or hulling of grain. *Sil pysgod*, fry of fish; *sil penwaig*, herring fry: *Eisin sil*, husks or hullings of oats.

Silen, *s. f. dim.* (sil) A single issue; a seedling; a single spawn or fry.

Sili, *s. m.* (sil) A state of teeming, a shoaling.

Siliad, *s. m.—pl. t.* au (sil) A producing; a spawning; a hulling of grain; grain that is hulled.

Siliadu, *v. a.* (siliad) To produce an issue; to produce a spawning.

Siliannawl, *a.* (siliant) Belonging to the act of producing; spawning.

Siliannu, *v. a.* (siliant) To cause an issuing; to cause a spawning.

Siliant, *s. m.* (sil) The state of being produced, or issued; a spawning; a hulling of grain.

Siliaw, *v. a.* (sil) To produce, to bring forth; to spawn; to hull grain. *Siliaw ceirch*, to hull oats.

Siliawg, *a.* (sil) Having issue; having spawn.

Silied, *s. m.* (sil) That is produced; cleared grain, as the grits of oats, and the like.

Siliedig, *a.* (siliad) Produced as young; spawned; divested or separated from the hull.

Siliedyn, *s. m. dim.* (siliad) An individual issue; a single grain divested of the hull.

Silod, *s. pl. aggr.* (sil) Seedlings, spawns, fry, or young fishes. *Silod brithion*, *brith y gro*, samlets; *silod y mor*, sea fry; *silod y dom*, *brithylliaid y dom*, *pysgod y gath*, sticklebacks.

Silodi, *v. a.* (silod) To issue seedlings, fry, or spawn; to form a fry.

Silodyn, *s. m. dim.* (silod) A single one of a fry.

Silyn, *s. m. dim.* (sil) A single issue, a single seedling, fry, or spawn.

Sill, *s. f.—pl. t.* au (si—ill) A component part, fragment, or element; a syllable; a word. *Ni chlywais i sill amdani*, I have not heard a syllable about her. *Sil.*

> Heb wybod—
> Na furf un sill ar ei phen,
> Na thoriad un llythyren.
>
> Knowing not the form of one *syllable* apart, nor the cutting of a single letter. *Iew. ab Hywel Surdwal.*

Silldrwm, *a.* (sill—trwm) Of a heavy syllable.

Silleb, *s. f.—pl. t.* au (sill—eb) An elementary part of speech: a syllable.

Sillebawl, *a.* (silleb) Elementary of speech.

Sillebiad, *s. m.* (silleb) A forming the elements of speech.

Sillebu, *v. a.* (silleb) To syllabize; to form the elements of speech.

Silliad, *s. m.—pl. t.* au (sill) A forming of syllables; a spelling.

Silliadaeth, *s. m.* (silliad) The system or formation of syllables.

> Un aball ni adnebydd——
> Yn ngeiriau'r anoddau sydd;
> Na'u bannau 'mhob gobenydd,
> A llef silliadaeth hefyd.
>
> A feeble one doth not recognise, in words, what qualities there are; nor their feet in every pause, and the accent of the *syllabic system*. *Iew. ab Hywel Surdwal.*

Silliadawl, *a.* (silliad) Syllabic, syllabical.

Silliadu, *v. a.* (silliad) To syllabize; to spell.

Silliaw, *v. a.* (sill) To arrange into elements or parts; to syllabize.

Silliawg, *a.* (sill) Consisting of elements; consisting of syllables.

Silliedig, *a.* (silliad) Formed of syllables.

Silliedigaeth, *s. m.* (silliedig) Formation of elementary parts or syllables.

Sillt, *s. f.—pl. t.* au (sill) An elementary part; a syllable.

> Deall silltau sy'n gwau'r gerdd,
> Yw cynseirgorn cywirgerdd.
>
> To understand the *syllables* which combine the song is the key of correct versification. *Iew. ab Hywel Surdwal.*

Silltaer, *s. f.—pl. t.* au (sillt—aer) A connection of links; a chain. *Silltaerau heieirn oddieithr arfau*, links of iron on the outside of the armour.

Silltaeren, *s. f.—pl. t.* au (silltaer) A link.

> Caeau silltaerau serch,
> Er gwawd y tafawd, loew-ferch,
> A rodd[illegible].——
>
> Wreaths of the *links* of love, for the praise of the tongue, lively maid, which I bestowed. *D. ab Gwilym.*

Silltiad, *s. m.* (sillt) A forming an elementary part; a forming a kindred.

Silltiaw, *v. a.* (sillt) To connect, to form a part; to be joined, to be a component part.

> O faith wylfa'r byd, af i'th elfydd;
> At Adda silltia', a'i eilltydd.
>
> From the tedious station of the world, I will go to thy element; to Adam *I will become connected*, and his progeny.
> *Ieuan Brydydd Hir.*

Silltiawg, *a.* (sillt) Consisting of parts; having syllables.

Silltiawl, *a.* (sillt) Component, kindred.

Silltiedig, *a.* (silltiad) Connected by parts; formed into syllables.

Silltydd, *s. m.* (sillt) That forms an elementary or a component part; a kindred.

Sillydd, *s. m.—pl. t.* ion (sill) A syllabary.

Sillyddiad, *s. m.* (sillydd) An arranging of syllables

Sillyddiaeth, *s. m.* (sillydd) The system of arranging syllables; prosody.

> Trefn sillyddiaeth oedd gaeth gynt,
> I bob gair bawb ei geryst.
>
> The order of *prosody* was strict of yore, to every word each his kindred one.
> *Ieuan ab Hywel Swrdwal.*

Sillyddu, *v. a.* (sillydd) To arrange syllables.

Sim, *s. m.—pl. t.* od (si—im) That is light, flippant, or full of motion.

Simach, *s. m.* (sim) A monkey, an ape.

> Cymwythach corach a simach.
>
> The mutual complacency of the pigmy and the *monkey*.
> *Adage.*

Simdde, *s. f.—pl. t.* au (sim—de) A chimney.

Simer, *s. m.* (sim) Levity, trifling; a frisk.

Simera, *v. a.* (simer) To play or frisk about; to trifle, to dally.

Simiawl, *a.* (sim) Full of motion, flippant.

Simne, *s. f.—pl. t.* iau (sim—ne) A chimney.

Simp, *s. m.* (sim) The state of being instable; a flutter.

Simpl, *a.* (simp) Tottering, ready to fall.

Simplaidd, *a.* (simpl) Seeming to fall.

Simplaw, *v. a.* (simpl) To totter.

Simpliad, *s. m.* (simpl) A tottering.

Simsan, *a.* (sim—san) Tottering, ready to fall.

Simwr, *s. m.—pl. t.* au (sim—wr) A kind of vesture; a chimmar.

Sin, *s. m.* (si—in) That is an outside or surface; donation, alms.

> Sin dynion gwelnion o gan;
> Sin i ereill sy'n arian.
>
> The *alms* of poor persons of white flour; the *alms* of others be in money.
> *L. G. Cothi.*

Sinach, *s. m.—pl. t.* au (sin) A mere or landmark; a balk, a ridge; jungle; but, in Rhos and about Conwy, it is any spot of wild land in a cultivated field.

> Terfyn dwy erw, dwy gwys, a hwnw a elwir sinach.
>
> The boundary of two acres consists of two furrows, and that is called a *ridge*.
> *Welsh Laws.*

Sinachad, *s. m.* (sinach) A cutting into dribblets. *Paid â sinachad y bara*, cease with mangling the bread. *Dyfed.*

Sinachu, *v. a.* (sinach) To cut into dribblets.

Sindal, *s. m.* (sin—tal) Sindon, fine linen; cambric

> A Dewi fab Sant sindal dudded.
>
> And Dewi son of Sant with a *fine linen* vest.
> *Gw. Brycheiniawg.*

Sindw, *s. pl. aggr.* (sin—tw) That is forced to the surface; the scoria or cinders of a forge.

Siniad, *s. m.* (sin) A burning to cinders.

Siniaw, *v. a.* (sin) To reduce to cinders; to become cinders.

Siniawg, *a.* (sin) Abounding with cinders. *s. f.* The part of a hearth which holds the cinders.

Siniawl, *a.* (sin) Of the quality of cinders.

Sinid, *s. m.* (sin) Surface, or scum.

Sinidr, *s. m.* (sinid) The scoria or dross of iron.

Sinidraw, *v. a.* (sinidr) To form dross.

Siob, *s. f.—pl. t.* au (si—ob) A tuft; a tassel.

Sioba, *s. f. dim.* (siob) A tuft; the crest of a bird.

Siobawg, *a.* (siob) Having a tuft, tufted.

Siobo, *s. m. dim.* (siob) A tuft; a sprinkle used in throwing holy water.

> Tynai Collen y siobo allan, ac a fwriai y dwfr bendigaid am eu penau; ac ar hyny y diflanynt o'i olwg.
>
> Collen pulled out the *sprinkler*, and he threw the holy water over them; and upon that they vanished out of his sight.
> *Buchedd Collen.*

Siobyn, *s. m. dim.* (siob) A small tuft.

Siobynawg, *a.* (siobyn) Tufted; crested.

Siobynu, *v. a.* (siobyn) To form a small tuft.

Sioch, *s. f.—pl. t.* au (si—och) That spreads out; bushy hair.

Siochen, *s. f. dim.* (sioch) A small tuft of hair; a bushy tuft.

Siochi, *v. a.* (sioch) To form a tuft, to make bushy.

Siol, *s. m.* (si—ol) The top of the head; the skull.

Siolyn, *s. m. dim.* (siol) A noddle.

Sionc, *a.* (si—onc) Brisk, nimble, active; flippant

Sioncaidd, *a.* (sionc) Somewhat brisk.

Sioncawl, *a.* (sionc) Tending to vivacity.

Sioncedd, *s. m.* (sionc) Briskness, nimbleness.

Sionci, *v. a.* (sionc) To make brisk; to become brisk, or lively.

Sioncrwydd, *s. m.* (sionc) Briskness, vivacity.

> Ond mawr na fedrai sioncrwydd Ffrainc
> Rygynga cainc rhag angau!
>
> How odd it is that the *briskness* of France should not devise to trip some tune to escape from death!
> *Elis Wyn, B. Cwsg.*

Siopos, *s. pl. aggr.* (siob) What is all in clutters; a mass bruised or beat together.

Sipiad, *s. m.* (sib) A sipping, a drawing with the lips, a drawing the lips together.

Sipian, *s. m.* (sib) A sipping, a smacking of lips.

Sipian, *v. a.* (sib) To keep sipping; to sip.

Sipiaw, *v. a.* (sib) To draw the lips.

Sipiawl, *a.* (sib) Sipping, drawing the lips.

Sipiedig, *a.* (sipiad) Sipped, drawn with the lips.

Sipiwr, *s. m.—pl.* sipiwyr (sib—gwr) A sipper.

Sipyn, *s. m. dim.* (sib) A single sip.

Sir, *s. m.* (si—ir) Cheer, solace, comfort.

Siriad, *s. m.* (sir) A cheering, a comforting.

Siriaw, *v. a.* (sir) To cheer, to be cheered.

Siriawl, *a.* (sir) Cheering, or cheerful.

Siriedig, *a.* (siriad) Cheered, comforted.

Sirioldeb, *s. m.* (siriawl) Cheerfulness.

Sirioledd, *s. m.* (siriawl) Cheerfulness.

Sirioli, *v. a.* (siriawl) To make cheerful; to become cheerful.

Sis, *s. m.* (si—is) A sharp low sound; a whisper.

Sisial, *s. m.* (sis) A gossip. *v. a.* To whisper.

Sisiala, *v. a.* (sisial) To keep whispering.

Sisialawg, *a.* (sisial) Full of whispering.

Sisialu, *v. a.* (sisial) To whisper, to mutter.

Sisialwr, *s. m.—pl.* sisialwyr (sisial—gwr) A whisperer; a gossiper.

Sisiw, *v. imper.* (sis) Only used to drive fowls.

Sistrain, *v. a.* (sis) To whisper, to buzz.

Sitell, *s. f.—pl. t.* i (sid) A whisk, a brush.

Sitelliad, *s. m.* (sitell) A whisking round.

Sitellu, *v. a.* (sitell) To whisk round.

Sitiad, *s. m.* (sid) A whirling, a whisking round.

Sitiaw, *v. a.* (sid) To whirl, to whisk round.

Sitiawl, *a.* (sid) Whirling, whisking round.

Sitiwr, *s. m.*—*pl.* sitiwyr (sitiaw—gwr) One who whirls, turns, or goes round.

> Saith awr y buan'
> Yn cadw'r berllan,
> Cyn cwrdd a Satan,
> Sitiwr Tartara.
>
> Seven hours had they been guarding the garden, before meeting with Satan, the *ranger* of Tartarus. *Awdl Fraith.*

Sitr, *s. m.* (sid) That jags, or that shreds.
Sitrach, *s. m.* (sitr) That is in jags or shreds, like a beaten end of a stick.
Sitrachawg, *a.* (sitrach) Jagged, or in shreds.
Sitrachiad, *s. m.* (sitrach) A jagging, a shredding
Sitrachu, *v. a.* (sitrach) To jag, or to shred.
Siw, *s. m.* (si) A hiss. *Siw!* An exclamation used in driving fowls away.

> Nid oedd na siw na miw.
>
> There was nor *hiss* nor mew. *Adage.*

Siwen, *s. m.* (siw) An epithet for the mermaid, the general name for which is *morforwyn.*
Siwr, *s. m.*—*pl.* siwyr (si—gwr) A hisser.
SO, *s. f. r.* A spread out, along, or over.
Sob, *s. m.*—*pl. t.* au (sy—ob) A tuft; a bunch, a cluster; a mass.
Soba, *s. f. dim.* (sob) A small tuft, bunch, cluster, or mass.
Soban, *s. f. dim.* (sob) A small tuft, or bunch.
Socan, *s. f. dim.* (sog) A wallower. *Socan eira, socan lwyd,* a fieldfare.
Socas, *s. f.* (sog) A wallower; the fieldfare.
Socyn, *s. m. dim.* (sog) A pig; an urchin, a boy, in droll style.
Soch, *s. f.* (so—och) A sink, or a drain.
Sodawl, *a.* (sawd) Tending to fix, implant, or settle; characteristic.
Sodi, *v. a.* (sawd) To constitute, to fix, or to set.
Sodiad, *s. m.* (sawd) A constituting, a fixing, or implanting.
Sodlawg, *a.* (sawdl) Having a heel, heeled.
Sodli, *v. a.* (sawdl) To heel; to trip the heel.
Sodliad, *s. m.* (sawdl) A heeling; a tripping.
Sodwedd, *s. f.* (sawd—gwedd) A characteristic.
Soddadwy, *a.* (sawdd) Capable of being sunk.
Soddawl, *a.* (sawdd) Sinking; plunging.
Soddedig, *a.* (sawdd) Being sunk or plunged.
Soddedigaeth, *s.m.* (soddedig) The act of sinking
Soddi, *v. a.* (sawdd) To sink, to submerge.
Soddiad, *s. m.* (sawdd) A sinking; a plunging.
Soddwr, *s.m.*—*pl.* soddwyr (soddi—gwr) A sinker
Soeg, *s. m.* (so—eg) That is puffed by seething; grains of malt; draff.

> A fegir gyda moch a ddysg fwyta soeg.
>
> That is bred with swine will learn to eat *grains.* *Adage.*
>
> Yr hwch a dau a fwyty y soeg.
>
> The silent sow eats the *draff.* *Adage.*
>
> Hwch dy gyfeillai, hi a ddysg iti fwyta soeg.
>
> Be a sow thy companion, she will teach thee to eat *grains.* *Adage.*

Soegen, *s. f. dim.* (soeg) A swaggy female.
Soegi, *v. a.* (soeg) To puff up with moisture; to steep; to slabber.
Soeglyd, *a.* (soeg) Puffed by steeping; slabbered
Soeglydrwydd, *s. m.* (soeglyd) A steeped state; slabbiness.
Sofl, *s. m.*—*pl.* soflydd (sawf) Stubble.
Soflawg, *a.* (sofl) Having stubble, stubbly.
Sofliar, *s. f.*—*pl.* soflieir (sofl—iar) A quail; also called *Rhinc.*
Soflyn, *s. m. dim.* (sofl) A single stubble.
Sog, *s. f.* (so—og) A wallow, a spread.
Soga, *a.* (sog) Wallowing; slovenly. *Geneth soga,* a slovenly girl. *Sil.*

Som, *s. f.*—*pl. t.* au (sy—om) A vacuity, a void; a balk, a disappointment.
Somawl, *a.* (som) Disappointing, balking.
Somedig, *a.* (som) Disappointed, balked.
Somedigaeth, *s. f.* (somedig) Disappointment.

> Nid somedigaeth ond gwraig.
>
> There is no *deception* equal to a woman. *Adage.*

Somedigawl, *a.* (somedig) Disappointing.
Somedd, *s. m.* (som) A disappointment.
Somgar, *a.* (som) Apt to disappoint.

> Somgar a soma ei hunan yn y diwedd.
>
> The *deceitful* will deceive himself at last. *Adage.*

Somgarwch, *s. m.* (somgar) Aptness to balk.
Somi, *v. a.* (som) To balk, to disappoint.

> Y cryf a'r doeth——
> Disymwth dau a somir.
>
> The strong and the wise, two that suddenly *will be deceived.* *E. Evan o Aber Dar.*

Somiad, *s. m.* (som) A disappointing, a balking.
Somiant, *s. m.* (som) A disappointment.
Somwr, *s. m.*—*pl.* somwyr (som—gwr) A balker; a disappointer, a deceiver.
Son, *s. m.*—*pl. t.* ion (so—on) A noise; a report; a rumour; a mention. *v. a.* To noise; to report; to mention. *Mae son amdani,* there is talk about her; *na wna son amdanad,* do not cause a talk about thee:—*Na son,* do not say so; *taw a son,* hold thy tongue.

> Son am y son amdano,
> Ni cheir son dda o hano.
>
> *To talk* of the *talk* about him, no good *talk* will be had from that. *Adage.*
>
> A fo doeth, ar fyd weithion,
> A dwys air, fe dau â son.
>
> Such as be wise, at present on the world, with a significant word, he will cease with *talking.* *T. Prys.*

Sonfawr, *a.* (son) Noisy, or rumbling.
Songryf, *a.* (son—cryf) Of powerful noise.
Soniad, *s. m.* (son) A noising, a reporting, a rumouring, a mentioning.
Sonial, *s. m.* (son) A continued noise. *v. a.* To keep a continual noise.

> O edwedd Morial
> A gwedi Rhys mawr y sonial.
>
> For the disappearing of Morial, and after Rhys great the *lamentation.* *Llywarch Hen.*

Soniaw, *v. a.* (son) To noise; to report; to rumour; to make mention; to talk. *Gostega bawb a sonio amdanad,* silence every body that shall talk about thee.

> Soniwn bellach am—ddyledswyddau teuluaidd.
>
> *We will mention* now about domestic duties. *Thos. Evans.*

Soniawl, *a.* (son) Noising, reporting, rumouring.
Soniawr, *s. m.* (son) That is noisy, or loud.

> Ein henaid a drywanesai drwy garawg soniawr ei li.
>
> Our soul had been made to pass through a brook *of noisy* flood. *D. Ddu, pa.* 194.

Soniedig, *a* (soniad) Noised, reported, rumoured, mentioned, talked.
Soniwr, *s. m.*—*pl.* soniwyr (son—gwr) A man who makes a report or rumour; a mentioner; a talker.
Sopen, *s. f.*—*pl. t.* i (sob) Any mass squeezed or trussed together, a bundle, a truss. *Sopen o gaws,* a ball of cheese curds; *sopen o flew,* a bundle of hair; *sopen o wair,* a truss of hay. *Dos, y sopen front,* Go, thou dirty baggage.
Sopenawg, *a.* (sopen) Being squeezed into a mass.
Sopeniad, *s. m.* (sopen) A squeezing into a mass, a making into a bundle.
Sopenu, *v. a.* (sopen) To bundle, to truss.

Sopiad, *s. m.* (sob) A pressing together into a mass; a bundling, a trussing.

Sopiaw, *v. a.* (sob) To press together into a mass; to bundle, to truss.

Sòr, *s. m.* (sy—or) The state of being pressed upon, chafed, or irritated; the being displeased or silently angry; sullenness. *a.* Sullen, sulky; angry; harsh, grating; sullen.

> Dial yn sòr am dori
> Da glos, Duw, dy eglwys di.

> Avenge *harshly*, for breaking a goodly sanctuary, God, thy church. *Ieu. Llwyd ab Gwilym.*

Sòriad, *s. m.* (sòr) A displeasing; a becoming displeased, sullen, or sulky.

Sòradwy, *a.* (sòrad) Capable of displeasing.

Sòrawl, *a.* (sòr) Displeasing, tending to sullenness.

Soredig, *a.* (sorad) Displeased, offended.

Soredigaeth, *s. m.* (soredig) The act of displeasing; displeasure, sullenness.

Sòri, *v. a.* (sòr) To press upon; to chafe; to displease, to offend; to render sullen or sulky; to become displeased or offended; to grow sullen or sulky. *Ystafell sòri*, a sulking room: *Na sòra wrth dy fwyd*, do not quarrel with thy victuals.

> Nid sòri yt ar dy fam.

> Be there not for thee *to be sulky* to thy mother. *Adage.*

> Ni fydd am nid fo,
> Na bryn, na thyno,
> Na rhynawd godo
> Rhag gwynt pan soro.

> There can be no where free, nor hill, nor dale, nor the least of shelter from the wind when *it shall rage*. *Taliesin.*

Sòriad, *s. m.*—*pl.* sòriaid (sòr) A grating, chafing, or irritating; a becoming offended, sullen, or sulky.

> Saer dy fawl, sòriad wyf fi.

> The author of thy praise, an *offended one* am I. *R. Ddu.*

Sòriannawl, *a.* (sòriant) Tending to displeasure, offensive; tending to sullenness.

Sòriannu, *v. a.* (soriant) To cause displeasure, offence, or sullenness.

Sòriant, *s. m.* (sòr) Displeasure, disgust, offence; sullenness.

Sòrig, *a.* (sòr) Apt to take offence; sulky.

Sòrllyd, *a.* (sòr) Apt to grow angry, or sulky.

Sorllydrwydd, *s. m.* (sorllyd) Aptness to be offended, or sulky.

Sorod, *s. pl. aggr.* (sòr) Small particles, parts, or fragments; shatters; dregs, dross, sordes; also called *sorod*.

Sorodi, *v. a.* (sorod) To yield dross or dregs.

Sorth, *s. f.* (sòr) That is sudden, imminent, or upon; chance.

Sorth, *a.* (sòr) Sudden; imminent, falling; unwieldy; slothful; rude, rough, fell.

> Ffydd dda i'n cadw'n hoff ddiwerth,
> O ffwrn a safn uffern sorth.

> Wholesome faith to keep us pleasantly without price, from the furnace and the jaw of *precipitous* hell. *S. Meredydd.*

Soth, *s. m.* (sy—oth) That is on the outside.

Sothach, *s. pl. aggr.* (soth) Refuse, dross.

> Llyw a'm dysgawdd hawdd hoddiaw gwawd berffaith,
> Nid fal sothach-iaith beirdd caeth Cacaw.

> A chief has instructed me with facility to acquire the perfect song, not like the *refuse-speech* of the slavish bards of Caco. *Cefnyn.*

Sothachlyd, *a.* (sothach) Abounding with refuse.

Sothachu, *v. a.* (sothach) To cast a refuse.

SU, *s. m. r.* That tends to pervade; a buzz.

Suad, *s. m.* (su) A buzzing; a lulling; a lullaby.

Suaw, *v. a.* (su) To hush, to lull to rest.

Suawl, *a.* (su) Hushing, lulling to rest.

Sucan, *s. m.* (sug) Any thing soothed, or steeped; washbrew, gruel, flummery; small beer. *Sucan blawd*, *cawl dwr*, water gruel; *sucan gwyn*, *bruchan*, caudle, made with soured or soothed oatmeal, and sweetened.

> Gwell sucan meddiant no gwin cardawd.

> Better is *small beer* that is one's own than wine on charity. *Adage.*

Sucanaidd, *a.* (sucan) Of a washy quality.

Sud, *s. m.* (su—ud) A first glance; an outside; appearance; condition, fashion, shape. *A wyt ti yn dda dy sud?* Art thou in a good way?

Sudd, *s. m.*—*pl. t.* ion (su—udd) That pervades or sinks in; moisture; juice, sap.

Suddadwy, *a.* (sudd) Capable of pervading; capable of containing juice.

Suddas, *s. m.* (sudd) A sinking, an immersion. *Clych suddas*, water bubbles.

Suddaw, *v. a.* (sudd) To sink in, to pervade; to sink; to become sunk. *Suddaw llong*, to sink a ship.

Suddawl, *a.* (sudd) Tending to sink in, or to pervade; sinking.

Suddedig, *a.* (sudd) Pervaded as moisture; sunk.

Suddiad, *s. m.* (sudd) A sinking, a plunging.

Suddiant, *s. m.* (sudd) Pervasion of moisture; a sinking.

Sug, *s. m.*—*pl. t.* ion (su—ug) An imbibing principle; a suck, or drawing; what is imbibed; juice, sap.

Sugaeth, *s. m.* (sug) The state of being juicy; moisture; succulence.

Sugaethan, *s. m.* (sugaeth) What is soaked; washbrew, caudle; a poultice.

Sugaw, *v. a.* (sug) To imbibe; to fill with juice; to have juice.

Sugawl, *a.* (sug) Imbibing; juicy; succulent.

Sugedig, *a.* (sug) Imbibed; filled with juice.

Suger, *s. m.* (sug) Extracted juice; cyder.

Sugiad, *s. m.* (sug) An imbibing of juice; a becoming juicy.

Sugllian, *s. m.* (sug—llian) A cerecloth, a drawing plaister.

Sugn, *s. m.* (sug) A suck: *sugn y gwyfr*, woodbine, or honey-suckle.

Sugnad, *s. m.* (sugn) A sucking, an imbibing.

Sugnai, *s. c.* (sugn) That sucks or imbibes.

Sugnaw, *v. a.* (sugn) To suck, to imbibe.

Sugnawl, *a.* (sugn) Sucking, imbibing.

Sugnbeiriant, *s. m.* (sugn—peiriant) An hydraulic machine; a pump.

Sugnbib, *s. f.*—*pl. t.* au (sugn—pib) A drawing pipe; a syringe.

Sugndraeth, *s. m.*—*pl.* sugndraethydd (sugn—traeth) A quicksand.

Sugndrec, *s. m.* (sugn—trec) A pump.

Sugnedydd, *s. m.*—*pl. t.* ion (sugnad) A sucker; a pump.

Sugneiydd, *s. m.*—*pl. t.* ion (sugnai) A pumper.

Sugnfor, *s. m.*—*pl. t.* oedd (sugn—mor) A vortex in the sea; a quicksand.

Sugngostrel, *s. m.*—*pl. t.* au (sugn—costrel) A sucking-bottle.

Sugniad, *s. m.* (sugn) A sucking, or imbibing.

Sugnwr, *s. m.*—*pl.* sugnwyr (sugn—gwr) One who sucks, or imbibes.

Sugnwydr, *s. m.*—*pl.* sugnwydrau (sugn—gwydr) A cupping-glass.

Sugnydd, *s. m.*—*pl. t.* ion (sugn) A pump.

Sugolaeth, *s. m.* (sugawl) Succulency.

Sugoli, *v. a.* (sugawl) To render juicy; to become juicy or succulent.

Sugr, *s. m.—pl.* sugron (sug) An extracted juice crystalized; sugar.

Sugraw, *v. a.* (sugr) To sugar; to sweeten.

Sugrawl, *a.* (sugr) Of the quality of sugar.

Sul, *s.m.—pl. t.* iau (su—ul) That extends round; the sun. *Dydd Sul*, Sunday; also called *Dywsul, Dydd yr Arglwydd*, and simply *Sul*. *Sul, a gwyl, a gwaith*, Sunday, holiday, and workday; *Sul y gweddïau*, rogation Sunday.

Sulgwyn, *s. m.* (sul—gwyn) Whitsunday.

Sulw, *s. m.* (sul) Observation, notice, remark. *Dal sulw*, take notice.

Sulwy, *s. m.* (sulw) A scope round; exploration.

Sum, *s. m.—pl. t.* iau (su—um) Amplitude, magnitude, bulk, size; sum. *Nid oes ynddo fawr o sum*, it is of no great bulk.

Sumiad, *s. m.* (sum) A bestowing amplitude, or magnitude; a becoming of bulk; a making observation as to size; a summing.

Sumiaw, *v. a.* (sum) To endue with amplitude, or magnitude; to sum; to deduce the size or bulk of a thing by poising it in the hand.

Sumiawl, *a.* (sum) Relating to amplitude.

Sumiedig, *a.* (sumiad) Endued with bulk; measured as to size; summed.

Sumiwr, *s. m.—pl.* sumwyr (sum—gwr) One who deduces the size of a body.

Sur, *s. m.* (su—ur) The state or quality of sourness; an acid. *a.* Sour, acid; stale. *Llaeth sur*, sour milk; *afalau surion*, crab apples; *eirin surion*, sloes.

> Ni chair afal per or bren sur.
>
> No sweet apple can be had from a sour tree. *Adage.*

Suraidd, *a.* (sur) Somewhat sour, subacid.

Suran, *s. f.—pl.* surain (sur) The sorrel. *Surain yr yd*, sheep's sorrel; *suran y maes, suran y waen*, common sorrel; *surain y fran*, sorrel; *surain hirion, tafol y dwfr*, great water dock; *surain codawg*, winter cherry; *surain y coed, surain y gog, surain tairdalen*, wood sorrel.

Suranen, *s. f. dim.* (suran) A sorrel. *Suranen godawg, dagrau addaf*, winter-cherry plant.

Suraw, *v. n.* (sur) To sour, to turn sour; to make sour.

Surawl, *a.* (sur) Of a sour tendency.

Surber, *a.* (sur—per) Of an acid sweetness.

Surfwg, *s. m.* (sur—bwg) Sillabub.

Surdeb, *s. m.* (sur) Acidity, sourness; tartness.

Surder, *s. m.* (sur) Acidity, sourness; tartness.

Surdoes, *s. m.* (sur—toes) Sour dough, leaven.

Surdoesawg, *a.* (surdoes) Having leaven.

Surdoesawl, *a.* (surdoes) Leavening.

Surdoesi, *v. a.* (surdoes) To leaven.

Surdra, *s. m.* (sur) Acidity, or sourness.

Surdrwnc, *s. m.* (sur—trwnc) Stale urine.

Suredig, *a.* (sur) Acidulated or soured.

Suredd, *s. m.* (sur) Acidness, sourness.

Surfedd, *s. m.* (sur—medd) A syrup.

Surfelys, *a.* (sur—melys) Of an acid sweetness.

Surian, *s. f.—pl.* suriain (sur) A cherry.

> Eurais wawd—
> Er hoen blodau surian.
>
> I have ornamented an eulogy for her who is of the hue of the cherry blossoms. *H. ab Ein. Lygliw.*

Surni, *s. m.* (sur) Sourness, tartness, acidity.

Surwern, *s. f.* (sur—gwern) A sour swamp; also an epithet for hell, consonant to the bardic theology.

> Affaith gaeth gethern, surwern nid sych,
> Lle mae llawer gwae weatherrych anegor
> Lla do——
>
> Hell, the receptacle of a slavish crew, a sour swamp that dries not, where there is many a woe dismally uprising without relief of the black host. *Casnodyn.*

Suryn, *s. m. dim.* (sur) Any acid thing.

Sut, *s. m.* (sud) An exterior; appearance; manner, condition, plight; shape. *Pa sut sydd?* How goes it? *Neidia yna: Pa sut?* Jump to there: which way? How?

> Wrth sut eu haraith or son
> Yr adwaenir y dynion.
>
> By the manner of their discourse in talking will the persons be known. *Iro. Brydydd Hir.*

Sutiad, *s. m.* (sut) A seeming; giving a manner, form, or shape; a suiting.

Sutiaw, *v. a.* (sut) To endue with a manner, plight, or shape; to adapt, to suit.

Sutiawl, *a.* (sut) Relating to manner, condition, or shape; adapted, suiting, befitting.

Süwr, *s. m.—pl.* süwyr (su—gwr) A husher.

SW, *s. m. r.* That remains, that is on, fixed upon, or exterior.

Swb, *s. m.* (sw) That is piled, heaped, or pressed together; a bundle.

Swba, *s. m. dim.* (swb) A small bunch.

Swbach, *s. m.* (swb) That is drawn together in a heap.

Swbachiad, *s. m.* (swbach) A shrinking up.

Swbachu, *v. a.* (swbach) To shrink up; to become shrunk up or decrepit.

Swci, *s. m.* (swg) That is soaked; steepings. *Oen swci, oen llawfaeth*, a lamb reared by hand; *llo swci*, a calf reared by hand.

Swch, *s. f.—pl.* sychod (sw—wch) A snout; a soc. *Swch aradr*, ploughshare; *swch esgid*, the point of a shoe.

> Sychu y swch i fyned i'r pridd.
>
> To wipe the share to go into the soil. *Adage.*

Swchiad, *s. m.* (swch) A snouting, a turning about with the snout.

Swchiaw, *v. a.* (swch) To snout; to search with the snout, as a pig, or a dog; also to share a plough.

Swchiawl, *a.* (swch) Belonging to the snout; belonging to a ploughshare.

Swd, *s. m.* (sw—wd) An exterior; appearance, manner, condition, plight; shape. *Sil.*

Swdd, *s. m.* (sw—dd) A frame, beams put together to support any thing; what is piled together.

Swdden, *s. f.—pl. t.* i (swdd) A beam.

Swf, *s. m.* (sw) That is on; a spot, a space.

Swg, *s. m.* (sw—wg) A soak, or imbibing.

Swga, *a.* (swg) Tending to soak; soaked; filthy. *Mor swga wyt ti!* how filthy thou art!

Swgan, *s. f.* (swg) A slut, or a slattern.

Swgawl, *a.* (swg) Tending to soak; soaking, drenching.

Swgiaw, *v. a.* (swg) To soak; to become soaked, to become flaccid; to become filthy.

Swgiad, *s. m.* (swg) A soaking, a drenching; a growing flaccid; a becoming filthy.

Swl, *s. m.* (sw—wl) A flat space, or surface, the ground; soil, dirt.

Swl, *a.* (sw—wl) Flat; grounded, soiled.

> Salw'th gais, swl-iaith gywen;
> Ilaf swch y dylodi a son.
>
> Feeble is thy attempt, with thy plain uniform speech; perch above the rafter and talk away. *D. ab Gwilym, i'r ceiliog.*

Swla, *a.* (swl) Being grounded, or covered with soil; dirty. *Sil.*

Swll, *s. m.—pl. t.* oedd (sw—wll) That is clear or open; a scene, a prospect.

Swllt, *s. m.—pl.* sylltau (swll) That has a clear surface; a shilling; money; treasure.

> Rhois ar ferch drawrch a drig,
> Esyllt wedd, a swllt eiddig.
>
> I have fixed on a fair one fondness that will remain, with the form of Esyllt, and the *treasure* of a jealous cuff. *D. ab Gwilym.*
>
> Y gaer a gymeryut, a chuddiedig swllt y ciwdodwyr a rannat.
>
> The city they got possession of, and the concealed *treasure* of the citizens they divided. *Gr. ab Arthur.*

Swm, *s. m.* (sw—wm) The state of being together.

Swmer, *s. m.—pl. t.* i (swm) That supports, or keeps together; a beam. *Swmer cȧr*, the hind part of a drag or dray, which holds up the load.

Swmerfarch, *s. m.—pl.* swmerfeirch (swmer—march) A sumpter-horse.

Swmeriad, *s. m.* (swmer) A supporting, upholding, or propping; a fixing a beam.

Swmeru, *v. a.* (swmer) To support, uphold, or prop; to fix a beam.

Swml, *s. m.—pl.* symlau (swm—yl) A goad.

Swmwl, *s. m.—pl.* symylau (swm—wl) A goad.

> Syml iawn rol swmwl ynnod.
>
> It was very simple to put a *goad* in thee. *Llywelyn Moel.*

Swn, *s. m.—pl.* syniau (sw—wn) A noise; a sound. *Swn taran*, the noise of thunder; *swn llu*, the noise of a multitude.

Swniad, *s. m.* (swn) A noising; a sounding.

Swnial, *v. a.* (swn) To make a continual noise; to make a clattering; to ring.

Swniaw, *v. a.* (swn) To noise; to sound.

Swniawl, *a.* (swn) Noisy, loud, sounding.

Swniedig, *a.* (swniad) Being noised, or sounded.

Swniwr, *s m.—pl.* swnlwyr (swn—gwr) One who makes a noise; a sounder.

Swp, *s. m.—pl.* sypiau (swb) A squeezed lump or mass; a heap; a pile; a bunch, a cluster. *Gwnaf di yn swp yn dy groen*, I will beat thee all to a mummy; *dyma fo yn un swp*, here it is all in a heap.

Swpwa, *s. pl. aggr.* (swp) A heap of things squeezed or beat together.

Swr, *s. m.* (sw) That is surly, sullen, or cross; a surly one.

Swr, *a.* (sw) Surly, sullen, sulky, cross. *Dyn swr iawn*, a very illnatured man.

Swri, *s. m.* (swr) Surliness; sullenness; a snarling, a barking. *Swri! swri!* words used to invite a dog to one.

Swrn, *s. m.—pl.* syrnau (sy—wrn) A small opening, space, or separation; a somewhat, a quantity, a little; the joint next to the foot of a quadruped; the pastern-joint or fetlock-joint.

> A swrn hyd Ddywsadwrn sydd.
>
> And a *good space* till Saturday there is. *D. ab Gwilym.*

Swrnach, *s. m.* (swrn) A snarl, or a grin.

Swrnach, *v. a.* (swrn) To grin, or to snarl.

Swrndaraw, *v. a.* (swrn—taraw) To cut or knock the pastern-joints together.

Swrth, *s. m.* (swr) That is sudden, imminent, or falling.

Swrth, *a.* (swr) Sudden; imminent, falling; drowsy; unwieldy; slothful; rude, rough, fell. *Dywedi yn swrth*, thou speakest roughly. *Sil.*

> Swrth pob diawg.
>
> Every lazy one is *clumsy*. *Adage.*
>
> Mor swrth y syrthiodd march Paen!
>
> How *suddenly* fell the steed of Paen! *Llywarch Hen.*
>
> Swrth oedd ei fyn'd, syrthiodd fo
> Drwy orfing i dir ango.
>
> *Sad* was his departing, he fell through severe affliction to the land of oblivion. *Ed. Samuel.*

Swrthdrwm, *a.* (swrth—trwm) Of a drowsy heaviness.

Swrthlyd, *a.* (swrth) Apt to be drowsy.

Swrthyn, *s. m. dim.* (swrth) A clumsy one.

Swrw, *s. m.* (swr) Surly, snarling; sullen.

Swrwd, *s. pl. aggr.* (swr) Parts, fragments; shatters; dross, sordes. *Mae e yn swrwd yn ei groen*, he is all to shatters in his skin.

Swta, *s. m.* (swd) That is volatile, flying, or sudden; also soot. *a.* Volatile, flying, sudden.

> Lle satan mewn lliw swta.
>
> Satan's host in livery of *soot*. *Iolo Goch.*

Swtan, *s. m.—pl.* swtain (swd) A whiting pout. It is called *bawd melinydd*, and *cod lwyd*.

Swtiad, *s. m.* (swt) A flying about; a being of sudden motion.

Swtiaw, *v. a.* (swt) To fly about; to be volatile or sudden.

Swtr, *s. m.* (swd) A sudden crack, or crash.

Swtrach, *s. pl. aggr.* (swtr) Dross, dregs.

Swtrws, *s. pl. aggr.* (swtr) That is bruised. *Twi yn swtrws*, to bruise to a mash.

Swth, *s. m.* (sw—wth) A frame, or what keeps together; a pile, a heap.

Swy, *s. m.* (sw) That is on, over, or exterior.

Swyd, *s. m.* (swy) That extends over; awe.

Swydaw, *v. a.* (swyd) To awe, to intimidate.

Swydawl, *a.* (swyd) Tending to awe.

Swydiad, *s. m.* (swyd) A creating an awe.

Swydus, *a.* (swyd) Tending to awe.

Swydd, *s. f.—pl. t.* au (swy) Employ, office, duty; suit; service, with respect to tenure; also a jurisdiction; a shire. *Tir a swydd arno*, land with service attached to it; *tir heb swydd*, land free of service: *Eis yno yn un swydd*, I went there on purpose.

> Drwg y swydd ni thal ei gwasanaethu.
>
> Bad is the *office* that is not worth serving. *Adage.*
>
> A gado swydd afrwyddawl
> Y gyfraith ddiffaith i ddiawl.
>
> And leave the intricate *pursuit* of the wicked law to the devil. *Sion Llwyd Ieuanc.*

Swyddawg, *a.* (swydd) Having an office. *s. m.—pl.* swyddogion. An officer. *Swyddogion y llys*, the officers of the court; *swyddogion bwyd a llyn*, parveyors of meat and drink; *swyddawg y dollfa*, an officer of the customs.

Swyddawl, *a.* (swydd) Official, of office.

Swyddfa, *s. f.—pl.* swyddfeydd (swydd) A place of business, or office.

Swyddgar, *a.* (swydd) Officious, full of business.

Swyddgarwch, *s. m.* (swyddgar) Officiousness.

Swyddogaeth, *s. f.—pl. t.* au (swyddawg) The sway or extent of any office; the jurisdiction of a county.

> Had swyddogaeth a dyfant yn mhob tir.
>
> The seeds of *office* will grow in every land. *Adage.*

Swyddogawl, *a.* (swyddawg) Belonging to office.

Swyddogedig, *a.* (swyddawg) Officered.

Swyddoges, *s. f.—pl. t.* au (swyddawg) A female officer.

Swyddogi, *v. a.* (swyddawg) To hold an office.

Swyddogiad, *s. m.* (swyddawg) A holding an office.

Swyddwial, *s. f.—pl.* swyddwiail (swydd—gwial) A rod of office.

Swyddwialen, *s. f.* (swyddwial) A rod of office.

Swyddwr, *s. m.—pl.* swyddwyr (swydd—gwr) An officer.

Swyddymgais, *s. m.* (swydd—ymgais) A seeking or looking after office.

Swyddymgeisiad, *s. m.* (swyddymgais) A seeking after an office.

Swyddymgeisiaw, *v. a.* (swyddymgais) To seek after an office.

Swyf, *s. m.—pl. t.* au (swy) That is on the surface; froth; yest; also suet. See *Ysgai.*

Maer y biswal a gaiff *swyf* a bloneg ysgrubl y llys.

The land steward shall have the *suet* and the lard of the animals of the palace. *Welsh Laws.*

Swyfaw, *v. n.* (swyf) To produce a scum or surface; to yield suet; to turn to suet.

Swyfawg, *a.* (swyf) Having a scum; having suet.

Swyfedd, *s. m.* (swyf) That becomes a surface or coating; suet.

Swyfen, *s. f.* (swyf) Scum, froth, or top.

Swyfi, *s. m.* (swyf) Scum, froth, or top.

Swyfiad, *s. m.* (swyf) A yielding scum or surface; a yielding suet.

Swyl, *s. f.—pl. t.* on (swy) A saving.

Swylaw, *v. a.* (swyl) To save, or to put by.

Swylaw ar y cilyn diweddaf.

To save when reduced to the last scrap. *Adage.*

Swyn, *s. f.—pl. t.* ion (swy) A preservative, protection, or comfort; a remedy; a charm. *Dwfr swyn*, holy water; *swyn ddrwg*, bad comfort.

Gwae fi na allaf, ha ferch!
Dy ddwyn gan wneuthur swyn serch.

Woe to me that I cannot, oh maid! bear thee away by making a love *charm.* *Ieuan Tew.*

Swyna, *v. a.* (swyn) To collect preservatives or remedies; to deal in charms.

Swynaw, *v. a.* (swyn) To apply a preservative, comfort or cure; to charm; to bless; to save harmless; to excuse.

A'm swynasai Math,
Cyn bum diaered:
A'm swynwys i Wdion,
Mawr-nur y Brython:
O Eurwys, o Euron,
O Euron, o Fedron,
O bump pummwnt celfyddon
Athrawon ail Math.

Math *had given* one *preserving means*, before that I was made immortal; I was also *made secure* by Gwdion, the mighty profound of the Brython; by Eurwys, by Euron, by Euron by Medron, by five times five hundred thousand arts of doctors equal to Math. *Taliesin.*

Duw o nef a'th swynas.

God of heaven *hath blessed* thee. *L. P. Moch.*

Swynawg, *a.* (swyn) Possessed of a preserving virtue.

Swynawl, *a.* (swyn) Preservative; tending to comfort; curative; blessing; tending to charm.

Swynedig, *a.* (swyn) Furnished with a preservative, or remedy; endued with a charm.

Dwfr a halen swynedig yn y bedydd.

Consecrated water and salt in the baptism. *Ll. Gwyn Hergest.*

Swynedigaeth, *s. f.* (swynedig) The act of preserving or remedying by some hidden virtue; a preserving by charm.

Swynedigawl, *a.* (swynedig) Tending to preserve or to remedy by any hidden virtue.

Swynfri, *s. m.* (swyn—bri) The daisy.

Swyngyfaredd, *s. f.—pl. t.* ion (swyn—cyfaredd) An amulet; witchcraft.

Swyngyfareddawg, *a.* (swyngyfaredd) Possessed of witchcraft.

Swyngyfareddawl, *a.* (swyngyfaredd) Belonging to witchcraft.

Swyngyfareddiad, *s. m.* (swyngyfaredd) A practising of witchcraft.

Swyngyfareddu, *v. a.* (swyngyfaredd) To practise or deal in witchcraft.

Swyngyfareddwr, *s. m.* (swyngyfaredd—gwr) A dealer in witchcraft.

Swyniad, *s. m.* (swyn) A preserving, a comforting; the applying of a remedy; a charming; a blessing; a saving harmless; an excusing.

Swynogl, *s. f.—pl. t.* au (swynawg) An amulet, a charm.

Yno Ffolineb a wisgai amdanaf ryw arall o barnais, yr hon a elwir oferogoniant—a'm hanogai i ofyn cynghor i wreigedd y swynoglau, yn wrthwyneb i gyfraith Duw.

Thereupon Folly arrayed me in another sort of attire, which is called vainglory—that would instigate me to ask counsel from women who deal in *charms*, contrary to the law of God *Marchawg Crwydrad.*

Swynogli, *v. a.* (swynogl) To apply a preservative; to apply a remedy; to charm; to fascinate.

Y geiriau hyny a'm swynoglai i, megys ag yr oedd hir genyf, o eisiau cael gweled y llys hafaidd hwnw.

Those words *fascinated* me, as it was tedious to me, for want of getting to see that palace of summer days. *Marchawg Crwydrad.*

Swynogliad, *s. m.* (swynogl) Fascination.

Swynoglwr, *s. m.—pl.* swynoglwyr (swynogl—gwr) A dealer in spells, a fascinator.

Swynwr, *s. m.—pl.* swynwyr (swyn—gwr) One who uses a preservative, or remedy; a comforter; a dealer in amulets, or charms; a magician. *Swynwr drwg wyt ti*, thou art a Job's comforter.

Swynwraig, *s. f.—pl.* swynwreigedd (swyn—gwraig) A woman who deals in charms.

Swynydd, *s. m.—pl. t.* ion (swyn) A wizard.

Swys, *s. m.—pl. t.* au (sy—wys) A scope round; emotion; impulse; a throb, a throw.

Cynnyddwn ninnau, heb swysau saeth,
Can an Duw fry freniniaeth.

We also shall grow up, without the arrow *throws*, in the kingdom of our God on high. *Cynddelw.*

Swysaw, *v. a.* (swys) To fill with emotion.

Swysawg, *a.* (swys) Having emotion, or impulse.

Bid swysawg ton tu porth Wygyr,
Bid swysawg serchawg, bannawg breyr.

Foamy be the wave towards the port of Gwygyr, *anxious* be the lover, exalted be the chieftain. *Gwalchmai.*

Swysawl, *a.* (swys) Tending to give impulse.

Swysiad, *s. m.—pl. t.* au (swys) A producing emotion, impulse, or feeling.

Swyson, *s. pl. aggr.* (swys) Emotions; passions.

SY, *s. m. r.* That is, existeth, or remaineth; that is fixed or stated; a star. *v. n.* Is, existeth, or hath a being. It is used as a prefix in composition.

Pwybynag sy heb wraig sy heb ymryson.

Whoever *is* without a wife *is* without contention. *Adage.*

Syber, *a.* (swb—er) Having a low tendency; of good conduct, sober, staid.

Tri hardd byd: duwfawl, celfydd, a syber.

The three ornaments of the world: the pious, the ingenious, and the one *of sober conduct.* *Catwg ab Gwynlliw.*

Syberedig, *a.* (syber) Being rendered of sober demeanour.

Syberi, *s. m.* (syber) A good demeanour; neatness; sobriety.

Syberw, *a.* (syber) Stately, magnificent, noble; courteous, generous; supercilious, haughty, highminded; elegant. *Meirch syberw*, proud steeds; *ach syberw*, a noble lineage.

Y neb a ddyweto yn syberw, neu yn hagr, wrth y brenin, taled deir bu camlwrw.

Whoever shall speak *superciliously*, or unseemly, to the king, let him pay three kine for compensation of injury. *Welsh Laws.*

A rhag syberwed Rolant ef a adewis iddo gysgu.

And from Rolant being *so magnanimous* he suffered him to sleep. *H. Car. Mag—Mabinogion.*

Pan glywer bod enw brenin iddynt, syberwach fyddant.

When it shall be heard that they possess the name of a king, more arrogant will they be. *Gr. ab Arthur.*

Syberwad, *s. m.* (syberw) A rendering stately.

Syberwaidd, *a.* (syberw) Tending to be stately.

Syberweiddrwydd, *s. m.* (syberwaidd) Stateliness

Syberwi, *v. a.* (syberw) To make stately, to become noble, high, or elated; to become elegant

Syberwyd, *s. m.* (syberw) Stateliness, magnificence, nobleness; courtesy, generosity, munificence; highmindedness; haughtiness, elegance. *Rhodd a syberwyd gorsedd*, the grant and courtesy of a convention. *Barddas.*

Gwell syberwyd no bonedd.

Better is *courtesy* than nobility. *Adage.*

Er dy syberwyd, pwyllà wrtho heno.

For thy *honour*, be considerate to him this night. *H. Peredur—Mabinogion.*

Llawer a barís Rolant eu colli o wyrda, o'i syberwyd ef.

Many did Rolant cause to perish of brave men, owing to his *highmindedness*. *H. Car. Mag—Mabinogion.*

Sybid, *s. m.* (swb) That is all in a heap.

Sybidan, *s. f. dim.* (sybid) A weakly female.

Sybidyn, *s. m. dim.* (sybid) A worthless fellow.

Sybwb, *s. m.* (swb—wb) A rumple, a pressing out of shape.

Sybwbiad, *s. m.* (sybwb) A tumbling about; a rumpling.

Sybwbiaw, *v. a.* (sybwb) To toss, to rumple.

Sybwbiwr, *s. m.* (sybwb) A tosser, a rumpler.

Sybwll, *s. m.—pl.* sybyllau (sy—pwll) A puddle, or a plash.

Sybwrn, *s. m.—pl.* sybyrnau (sy—bwrn) Bundle

Sybwydd, *s. pl. aggr.* (swb—gwydd) Pines, or fir-trees.

Sybwydden, *s. f. dim.* (sybwydd) A pine-tree.

Sybyllawg, *a.* (sybwll) Having puddles, plashy.

Sybylldir, *s. m.* (sybwll—tir) Plashy ground.

Sybyllu, *v. a.* (sybwll) To make plashy.

Sybyrnawg, *a.* (sybwrn) Bundled, trussed.

Sybyrnawl, *a.* (sybwrn) Like a bundle.

Sybyrniad, *s. m.* (sybwrn) A bundling.

Sybyrniaw, *v. a.* (sybwrn) To bundle.

Sybyrnyn, *s. m. dim.* (sybwrn) A little bundle.

Sych, *s. m.* (sy—ych) Drought. *a.* Dry. *Dillad sychion*, dry clothes.

Tri pheth anhawdd eu cael: dwfr sych, tan gwlyb, a gwraig dawgar.

Three things difficult to be obtained: *dry* water, wet fire, and a silent wife. *Adage.*

Tri pheth a gryfâant y corff: gorwedd ar wely caled, wybren oerllyd, a bwyd sych.

Three things that strengthen the body: a laying on a hard bed, a cold atmosphere, and *dry* victuals. *Adage.*

Sychadwy, *a.* (sych) Capable of drying.

Sychawl, *a.* (sych) Tending to dry, drying.

Sychbilen, *s. f.—pl. t.* au (sych—pilen) A dry film.

Sychder, *s. m.* (sych) Drought, or dryness.

Syched, *s. m.* (sych) Drought; thirst. *Gad imi dori fy syched*, let me quench my thirst.

Dymunaw ydd wyf y dydd y cyfarfyddom ni ynghyd; canys syched eu gwaed hwynt y sydd arnaf.

I am wishing for the day when we shall meet together; for a *thirst* after their blood is upon me. *Gr. ab Arthur.*

Sychedawl, *a.* (syched) Tending to cause thirst.

Sychediad, *s. m.* (syched) A thirsting; a causing thirst.

Sychedig, *a.* (syched) Being made dry; thirsty.

Sychedigaeth, *s. m.* (sychedig) A causing to be dry, or thirsty.

Sychedigawl, *a.* (sychedig) Tending to make dry

Sychedigrwydd, *s. m.* (sychedig) A dried state.

Sychedu, *v. n.* (syched) To thirst, to be thirsty.

Sychedwr, *s. m.—pl.* sychedwyr (syched—gwr) A thirster.

Sychedydd, *s. m.—pl. t.* ion (syched) A thirster.

Sychfa, *s. f.—pl.* sychfëydd (sych) A drying place

Sychgernyn, *s. m. dim.* (sych—cernyn) A dry scale, or scarf.

Sychin, *s. f.* (sych—hin) Dry weather.

Sychinawg, *a.* (sych—hin) Being dry weather.

Sychiad, *s. m.* (sych) A drying, a siccation.

Sychiadu, *v. a.* (sychiad) To desiccate, to siccate.

Sychiannawl, *a.* (sychiant) Desiccative, desiccatory

Sychiannu, *v. a.* (sychiant) To desiccate.

Sychiant, *s. m.* (sych) Desiccation, siccation.

Sychin, *s. f.* (sych) Drought, or dry weather.

Hau ar y sychin, plannu ar y gwlybin.

Sow on the *dry weather*, plant on the wet weather. *Adage.*

Sychmer, *s. m.* (sych—mer) Paroxism of a hectic

Sychnych, *s. m.* (sych—nych) A dry pining.

Sychnychdawd, *s. m.* (sychnych) Consumption.

Sychnychiad, *s. m.* (sychnych) A pining of tabes.

Sychnychu, *v. n.* (sychnych) To pine with a tabes.

Sychrwyd, *s. f.—pl. t.* au (sych—rhwyd) A dry web, or film, on the eye; also called *sychgernyn*, *sychbilen*, and *rhuchen*.

Sychu, *v. a.* (sych) To dry, to wipe dry; to become dry. *Sycha dy drwyn*, wipe thy nose.

Hyd y daw y gwlaw, ac y gwlych [illegible]
Hyd y chwyno [illegible], a hyd y sych[illegible];
Ni'm dawr o ungerdd [illegible]
Ni'm dawr o [illegible] pan orweddych.

Whilst rain shall come, and winter drowns; whilst [illegible] provoken, and whilst *it dries*; I shall not be [illegible] course but whilst thou dost sojourn; I shall care not [illegible] when thou shalt be laid down. *Ior. Fynglwyd.*

Sychwr, *s. m.—pl.* sychwyr (sych—gwr) A dryer; a wiper.

Sychwydd, *s. pl. aggr.* (sych—gwydd) Dry wood; fuel; also called *tanwydd*, and *cynnud*.

Sychydd, *s. m.—pl. t.* ion (sych) A desiccant.

Sydyn, *a.* (swd) Abrupt, quick, sudden.

Sydynrwydd, *s. m.* (sydyn) Abruptness.

Sydd, *s. m.—pl. t.* au (sy) That is, existeth, or remaineth; rest. *v. n.* Is, existeth, or hath a being. *Pwy sydd yna?* who is there?

Freuer wen, brodyr a'th fu,
Pan glywynt gywrein [illegible],
Ni ochwyddai sydd [illegible].

Fair Freuer, brothers hast thou had, when they should hear the din of army, their *abode* would not be left to [illegible]. *[illegible]*

Gwae hi y ddraig goch, canys ei hadail sydd yn brysio.

Woe to her, the red dragon, for her destruction is approaching. *Darogan yr Eryr.*

Syddawl, *a.* (sydd) Relating to being or dwelling.

Syddiad, *s. m.* (sydd) A being, a remaining.

Syddu, *v. a.* (sydd) To exist, to abide, to dwell.

Syddyn, *s. m.—pl. t.* au (sydd) A habitation; a tenement.

Cawn oedd, liw can, i'n syddyn,
Cain wiail a glasddail glyn.

We shall have a seat, thou of blossom hue, for our abode, the fair branches and the green leaves of the glen. *D. ab Gwilym.*

Syddynawl, *a.* (syddyn) Tenementary, of a farm.

Syddyniad, *s. m.* (syddyn) A holding a tenement

Syddynu, *v. a.* (syddyn) To take up a settled abode; to hold a tenement.

Syddynwr, *s. m.—pl.* syddynwyr (syddyn—gwr) A fixed inhabitant; a husbandman, a farmer.

Syfa, *s. m.—pl. t.* oedd (swf) A riddle; also called *rhidyll*.

A golir yn y syfa a gair yn y gwagr.

What is lost in the *riddle* will be found in the sieve. *Adage.*

Syfag, *s. f.—pl. t.* au (swf—ag) That is outspreading.

> Pwybynag a friwo dy, taled—am y pollon syfagau, ceiniawg.
>
> Whoever damages a house, let him pay for the poles for *outspreadings*, a penny. *Welsh Laws.*

Syfal, *a.* (sy—mal) Fickle, changeable.

Syfalâad, *s. m.* (syfal) A rendering fickle.

Syfalâu, *v. a.* (syfal) To render fickle; to become fickle or uncertain.

Syfaldawd, *s. m.* (syfal) Fickleness, uncertainty.

Syfalu, *v. a.* (syfal) To act with fickleness.

Syfi, *s. pl. aggr.* (swf) Strawberries; also called *mefus*.

> Lle aml y syfi aml y neidredd.
>
> Where the *strawberries* abound there snakes abound. *Adage.*

Syfien, *s. f. dim.* (syfi) A single strawberry.

> Syfien yn mola hwch.
>
> A *strawberry* in a sow's belly. *Adage.*

Syfi, *s. m.* (swf) A tendency to move.

Syfiad, *s. m.* (syfi) A moving, a stirring.

Syfiawg, *a.* (syfi) Having motion or stir.

Syfiiad, *s. m.* (syfi) A moving, a stirring.

Syfiwr, *s. m.—pl.* syfiwyr (syfi—gwr) A stirrer.

Syflyd, *v. a.* (syfi) To move, to stir; to be moved. *Na syfled un oddyna*, let no one stir from there; *o syfli*, if thou stirrest.

Syfn, *a.* (swf) Of a firm quality.

Syfnawl, *a.* (syfn) Of a firm quality.

Syfngnawd, *s. m.* (syfn—cnawd) Firm flesh.

> Gwisg na ddiosg saith noswaith,
> Gwasgawd mwythus syfngnawd meith.
>
> A garment that she will not put off for seven nights, the shelter of a delicate plump *firm flesh*. *D. ab Gwilym.*

Syfniad, *s. m.* (syfn) A making firm.

Syfnu, *v. a.* (syfn) To make firm or hard.

Syfr, *a.* (swf) Tending to make hard or severe.

Syfrdan, *s. m.* (syfr—tan) A state of giddiness.

> Yn mhob man syfrdan sydd,
> A blinaw heb lawenydd.
>
> In every place there is *distraction*, and weariness void of pleasure. *D. Benfras.*

Syfrdan, *a.* (syfr—tan) Giddy, dizzy; stupified; delirious.

> Col' medd y fran, syfrdan son
> Ddugan, pan gaffai ddigon;
> Felly'r gwyr a faligarant.
>
> Col' quoth the raven, slandering with *crazy* noise, when she has had enough; so the men who falsely love. *D. ab Dafydd Llwyd.*

Syfrdanaidd, *a.* (syfrdan) Tending to be giddy, dizzy, or crazy; somewhat stupified.

Syfrdanawl, *a.* (syfrdan) Stupifying.

Syfrdandawd, *s. m.* (syfrdan) Giddiness, dizziness; stupefaction; delirium; craziness.

Syfrdander, *s. m.* (syfrdan) Giddiness; craziness.

Syfrdanedd, *s. m.* (syfrdan) Giddiness, craziness.

Syfrdaniad, *s. m.* (syfrdan) A making giddy, dizzy, or crazy; a stupifying.

Syfrdanu, *v. a.* (syfrdan) To make giddy, or dizzy, to stupify; to astonish; to become giddy, dizzy, or stupified.

Syfrdanus, *a.* (syfrdan) Tending to make giddy or dizzy; stupifying.

Syfrdanwr, *s. m.—pl.* syfrdanwyr (syfrdan—gwr) One who makes giddy; a stupifier.

Syfriad, *s. m.* (syfr) A rendering severe.

Syfru, *v. a.* (syfr) To render hard or severe.

Syfyd, *s. m.* (swf) That is gradual, that forms a space.

Syg, *s. f.—pl. t.* iau (sy—yg) A chain formed of links; a trace; also called *tid*, and *rhan*. *Bonsyg*, the chain extending from the plough beam to the yoke.

Sygan, *s. m.* (sy—can) A whisper; a mutter.

Syganawl, *a.* (sygan) Whispering, muttering.

Syganiad, *s. m.* (sygan) A whispering, muttering.

Syganu, *v. a.* (sygan) To whisper, to mutter.

> Syganai'r bi cynal cwyn.
>
> The pie *would be muttering* a burden of complaint. *D. ab Gwilym.*

Sygn, *s. f.—pl.* sygnau (syg) A circle; a zodiacal sign.

> Bu Alexander, byd lywiadur;
> Hyd sygnoedd nefoedd ni bu segur.
>
> There has been Alexander, the ruler of the world; even to the *signs* of heaven he was not idle. *Cynddelw.*

Sygog, *s. f.* (sy—gog) A shove, a move.

Sygogi, *v. a.* (sygog) To move about, to fidget; to be restless or fidgetting.

Sygogiad, *s. m.* (sygog) A fidgetting, a being restless.

Syl, *s. f.* (sy—yl) A surface, ground, or foundation.

Sylch, *s. f.—pl. t.* au (syl) A furrow.

Sylchdan, *s. m.* (sylch—tan) A wheel plough.

Sylchiad, *s. m.* (sylch) The opening a surface.

Sylfa, *s. f.—pl. t.* on (syl) A foundation.

Sylfaen, *s. f.—pl.* sylfeini (syl—maen) A foundation stone.

Sylfaenedig, *a.* (sylfaen) Having a base stone.

> Rhaid i'r duwiolion fod mor sylfaenedig na ellir eu siglaw; mor blantaidd na ellir eu cyfrwyssaw.
>
> It is necessary for the godly to be so *established* that they cannot be moved; so like children that they cannot be made crafty. *Morgan Llwyd, Y Tri Aderyn.*

Sylfaeniad, *s. m.* (sylfaen) A laying a foundation stone; a foundation.

Sylfaenu, *v. a.* (sylfaen) To lay a foundation stone; to found.

Sylfaenwr, *s. m.—pl.* sylfaenwyr (sylfaen—gwr) One who lays a foundation stone.

Sylfaenydd, *s. m.—pl. t.* ion (sylfaen) A founder.

Sylfan, *s. f.—pl. t.* au (swl—man) A foundation.

Sylfanawl, *a.* (sylfan) Foundatory.

Sylfaniad, *s. m.* (sylfan) A laying a foundation.

Sylfon, *s. m.—pl. t.* au (swl—bon) A subject.

Sylgyngan, *v. a.* (swl—cyngan) To speak with a low voice, to mutter.

Syliad, *s. m.* (syl) A making a foundation.

Sylu, *v. a.* (syl) To make a foundation.

Sylw, *s. m.—pl. t.* au (swl) Observation, sight, view, regard, notice. *Dal sylw*, to take notice.

Sylwad, *s. m.* (sylw) A regarding, or observing.

Sylwaew, *s. m.* (syl—gwaew) A radical disease.

> Nid sylwaew onid salwedd.
>
> Not a *radical ailing* but indisposition. *Gr. Gryg.*

Sylwedig, *a.* (sylwad) Being observed.

Sylwedd, *s. m.—pl. t.* au (sylw) Observation.

Sylwedd, *s. m.—pl. t.* au (syl—gwedd) Substance.

> Sylwedd yw pob ysbryd; ac nid yw y byd a welir ond cysgawd o'r byd nis gwelir, yr hwn sy drwy y byd yma.
>
> Every spirit is *substance*, and the world that is seen is but a shadow of the world that is not seen, and which pervades this world. *Morgan Llwyd.*

Sylweddawg, *a.* (sylwedd) Having substance.

Sylweddawl, *a.* (sylwedd) Substantial; corporeal.

Sylweddiad, *s. m.—pl. t.* au (sylwedd) Substantiating.

Sylweddiannawl, *a.* (sylweddiant) Substantiating.

Sylweddiannu, *v. a.* (sylweddiant) To substantiate.

Sylweddiannus, *a.* (sylweddiant) Substantiating.

Sylweddiant, *s. m.* (sylwedd) Substantiality.

Sylweddogi, *v. a.* (sylweddawg) To substantiate.

Sylweddogiad, *s. m.* (sylweddawg) A rendering substantial, substantiation.

Sylweddolder, *s. m.* (sylweddawl) Substantialness, reality; corporature, materiality.
Sylweddolder, *s. m.* (sylweddawl) Substantialness.
Sylweddoldra, *s. m.* (sylweddawl) Substantialness.
Sylweddoli, *v. a.* (sylweddawl) To render substantial, to realize; to consolidate.
Sylweddoliaeth, *s. m.* (sylweddawl) Materialism.
Sylweddolrwydd, *s.* (sylweddawl) Substantialness.
Sylweddu, *v. a.* (sylwedd) To make of substance.
Sylweddus, *a.* (sylwedd) Substantial; corporeal.
Sylweddusaw, *v. a.* (sylweddus) To make substantial; to become substantial.
Sylweddusder, *s. m.* (sylweddus) Substantialness.
Sylweddusrwydd, *s.* (sylweddus) Substantialness.
Sylweddwr, *s. m.—pl.* sylweddwyr (sylwedd—gwr) One who treats of substance or matter.
Sylwi, *v. a.* (sylw) To observe, to regard, to notice.

Tri pheth a ddylid sylwi yn benaf ar bob peth: anian, agwedd, a gweithred.

Three things should be principally *regarded* as to every thing: nature, appearance, and action. *Catwg ab Gwynlliw.*

Sylwyn, *s. m.—pl. t.* ion (sylw) A pryer.

Nid sylwyn oed cybydd.

There is no one that is such a *pryer* as a miser. *Adage.*

Syll, *s. m.—pl. t.* ion (sy—yll) A gaze, a stare; the act of beholding; sight, view.
Syllbeiriannaeth, *s. m.* (syllbeiriant) The science of optics.
Syllbeiriannawl, *a.* (syllbeiriant) Relating to optics
Syllbeiriant, *s. m.—pl.* syllbeiriannau (syll—peiriant) An optical instrument.
Sylldy, *s. m.—pl. t.* au (swll—tŷ) A shop. *Brethyn sylldy*, fine woollen cloth.
Syllgar, *a.* (syll) Keen of sight; speculative.
Syllgarwch, *s. m.* (syllgar) Speculativeness.
Sylliad, *s. m.* (syll) A gazing, a staring; a looking, a beholding; observation.
Syllîannawl, *a.* (sylliant) Speculative.
Sylliannu, *v. a.* (syll) Observation, speculation.
Sylliaw, *v. a.* (syll) To gaze; to behold, to observe.
Sylliawg, *a.* (syll) Endued with observation.
Sylliedig, *a.* (sylliad) Being observed; endued with observation.
Syllt, *s. m.* (syll) That is fair or clear; a look.
Sylltiad, *s. m.* (swllt) A forming a surface.
Sylltiawg, *a.* (swllt) Having an exterior.
Sylltiawl, *a.* (swllt) Of a fair exterior.
Sylltty, *s. m.—pl. t.* au (swllt—ty) A treasury.
Sylltu, *v. a.* (syllt) To make a fair surface.
Syllu, *v. a.* (syll) To gaze, to stare; to look; to behold; to observe. *Syll di raco*, behold thou yonder.

Sefwch allan forwynion a syllwch werydre Cynddylan,
Llys Pengwern neud tandde!

Stand ye out virgins and *behold* the fair region of Cynddylan, is it not with flame pervaded! *Llywarch Hen.*

Du sy well wedi syllid.

Black is better after *it has been seen*. *L. G. Cothi.*

Syllwg, *s. f.* (syll) An open prospect.
Syllwr, *s. m.—pl.* syllwyr (syll—gwr) A spectator.
Syllwydr, *s. m.—pl.* syllwydrau (syll—gwydr) A spyglass.
Syllwydryn, *s. m. dim.* (syllwydr) A spyglass.
Syllwydrwr, *s. m.—pl.* syllwydrwyr (syllwydr—gwr) An optician.
Syllyr, *s. m.* (syll) That is open or prospective.
Sym, *s. m.—pl. t.* iau (sy—ym) That is integral; that is whole or complete.

Digrif oeddym o sym serch;
A meinir yn ymanerch.

Happy were we from the *enjoyment* of love; and the fair one fvalguing herself. *D. ab Gwilym.*

Symaeth, *s. m.* (sym) A middle or central state; a state of ease.
Symawl, *a.* (sym) Integral; middling. *Pa sut yr wyt ti? symawl:* How dost thou do? pretty well.
Symedd, *s. m.* (sym) An integral condition.
Symerth, *s. m.* (sym—erth) Integral energy; simple power.
Symiad, *s. m.* (sym) A rendering integral.
Symiannawl, *a.* (symiant) Penetrating.
Symiannu, *v. a.* (symiant) To penetrate; to apprehend, to comprehend.
Symiant, *s. m.* (sym) Penetration; apprehension.
Symiaw, *v. a.* (sym) To penetrate; to apprehend.

Ni sym twyll mo bwyll y byd.

Deceit *will* not *comprehend* the sense of the world. *Adm. Pug.*

Symiedig, *a.* (symiad) Being comprehended.
Symiwr, *s. m.—pl.* symiwyr (sym—gwr) One who enters into, penetrates, or perceives.
Syml, *s. m.* (sym) That is simple. *a.* Simple.
Symlad, *s. m.* (syml) A pointing; a simplifying.
Symlant, *s. m.* (syml) Pointedness, simplicity.
Symlawg, *a.* (syml) Of a simple nature.
Symledig, *a.* (symlad) Pointed; simplified.
Symledd, *s. m.* (syml) Simplicity, plainness.

Un o dair prif orchest bardd: [illegible] ni ellir cynnefnach o'r symledd.

One of the three chief excellencies of a bard; [illegible] prehended that nothing more known can be [illegible] *plicity*. [illegible]

Symlen, *s. f. dim.* (syml) A simple one. *Symlen ben bys*, the name of an old tune.
Symliad, *s. m.* (syml) A pointing, a simplifying.
Symliaw, *v. a.* (syml) To point, to simplify.
Symlogen, *s. f. dim.* (symlawg) A simple female, a simple yielding girl.
Symlu, *v. a.* (swml) To point; also to goad.

Symlau dur yn symlu dyn.

Like points of steel *goading* man. [illegible]

Cyngu wedi symlu sud
A wnaethant, bobl annoethion.

After *driving* on the talk the foolish people went to sleep. [illegible]

Symlwr, *s. m.—pl.* symlwyr (swml—gwr) One who points; a goader.
Symlyn, *s. m. dim.* (syml) A simpleton.
Symlynaidd, *a.* (symlyn) Like a simpleton.
Symu, *v. a.* (sym) To render integral; to become whole or complete.
Symud, *s. m.—pl. t.* ion (sy—mud) Motion. *v. a.* To move, to remove; to change place.
Symudadwy, *a.* (symud) Capable of moving.
Symudaw, *v. a.* (symud) To move, to remove.

Symudaw aelwyd rhag drwg.

To move an abode for fear of evil. *Adage.*

Tri pheth y sydd a melldigedig y neb a'u symudo; [illegible] dwfr, ac arwydd fordd ac artiwybr.

There are three things that renders accursed such as shall remove them; a land mark, a watercourse, and a finger-post. *Cyfoeg* [illegible]

Symudawg, *a.* (symud) Being moved.
Symudawl, *a.* (symud) Moving, moveable.
Symudedig, *a.* (symud) Moved, removed.
Symudedigaeth, *s. m.* (symudedig) A removal.
Symudedigawl, *a.* (symudedig) Transitive.
Symudfa, *s. f.—pl.* symudfëydd (symud) A transition.

Symudfa ar dyniadau a chyweiriadau.

A transition of the tractions and key *strings*. *Cerddoriaeth.*

Symudiad, *s. m.—pl. t.* au (symud) The act of moving, a moving; transmutation; conveyance.
Symudiedydd, *s. m.—pl. t.* ion (symudiad) One that transmutates.

Symudliw, *a.* (symud—lliw) Of various shades of colours; of changing hues; shot with divers colours.

Symudoldeb, *s. m.* (symudawl) Moveableness.

Symudolder, *s. m.* (symudawl) Mobility.

Symudoli, *v. a.* (symudawl) To render moveable; to become moveable or transitive.

Symudolrwydd, *s. m.* (symudawl) Moveableness.

Symudwr, *s. m.—pl.* symudwyr (symud—gwr) A mover, a remover.

Symudydd, *s. m.—pl. t.* ion (symud) A mover.

Symwl, *s. pl. aggr.* (sym—wl) Common primroses. These were held in great veneration amongst the Britons, on account of their many medicinal virtues.

Symwth, *a.* (sy—mwth) Of interrupted motion.

Un a braw saeth yn ei bron,
Mor symwth, am air Simon.

One became with her bosom filled with dread, so *embarrassed* because of the word of Simon. *D. ab Edmwnd, i Fair.*

Symwy, *s. m.* (sym) Ample, prominent.

Symylawg, *a.* (swmwl) Having a point or goad.

Symylen, *s. f. dim.* (symwl) A primrose.

Mor ddiwair a symylen.

As uncontaminated as a *primrose.* *Adage.*

Symyliad, *s. m.* (swmwl) A goading.

Symylu, *v. a.* (swmwl) To egg on, to goad.

Symythawl, *a.* (symwth) Interruptive.

Symythiad, *s. m.* (symwth) Interruption.

Symythu, *v. a.* (symwth) To interrupt; to embarrass.

Syn, *s. m.* (sy—yn) That is upon or with; sense, feeling, sensibility, perception. *a.* Feeling, sensible, of quick sensation; overcome with feeling, concerned; amazed; stunned; confounded. *Newydd syn iawn yw hwn*, this is very distressing news.

Gnawd syn syml anghyfiaith.

A simple stranger to a language must seem *confused.* *Adage.*

Syna, *v. imper.* (syn) Feel, be concerned; perceive; behold.

Sŷnaidd, *a.* (syn) Somewhat sensitive.

Syndawd, *s. m.* (syn) Sensation; amazement; concern; the state of being stunned.

Syndeb, *s. m.* (syn) Sensation; anxiety. *Teimlwn ryw syndeb ynof*, I felt a kind of sensation within me.

Sŷnder, *s. m.* (syn) Sensation; concern.

Sŷndra, *s. m.* (syn) Sensation; perceptivity.

Synedig, *a.* (syn) Having the sense affected; astonished, stunned.

Synedigaeth, *s. m.* (synedig) Sensation; astonishment, the act of stunning.

Synedigawl, *a.* (synedig) Sensitive; tending to stun

Synedigrwydd, *s. m.* (synedig) Sensitiveness.

Synfeddwl, *s. m.—pl.* synfeddyliau (syn—meddwl) Deep thought.

Synfeddyliad, *s.* (synfeddwl) A deeply thinking.

Synfeddyliaw, *v. a.* (synfeddwl) To think or meditate feelingly.

Syniad, *s. m.—pl. t.* au (syn) Sensation, feeling. *Syniad y cnawd*, carnal sensation.

Tri pheth a gynnull addysg; synwyr, syniad, a dichwain.

Three things accumulate instruction; reason, *feeling*, and incidence. *Barddas.*

Syniadawl, *a.* (syniad) Sensitive; sensuous.

Syniadwy, *a.* (syniad) Capable of sense; sensible.

Syniannawl, *a.* (syniant) Sensitive; sentimental.

Syniannu, *v. a.* (syniant) To give sensation; to become sensitive; to be sentimental.

Syniannus, *a.* (syniant) Sentimental.

Syniannusaw, *v. a.* (syniannus) To render sentimental; to become sentimental.

Sŷniant, *s. m.* (syn) Sensation; sentiment.

Syniaw, *v. a.* (syn) To feel, to perceive; to be sensible; to consider; to consult; to make up the mind. *Synia y tylawd*, consider the poor.

Cai fawr glod er cymmodi:
Synia, ferch: cusana fi.

Thou shalt have great praise for becoming reconciled: *think*, fair one: come kiss me. *Bedo Brwynllys.*

Duw a orug y nefoedd o ddeall. yr haul a'r lloer ei syniant, canys hwynt a gadwant eu cylch, ac a droant drachefn iddo ar eu rhoddes; y ddaiar ei synia, canys hi a ddwg ffrwythau a'u gwreiddiau yn amserawl ac yn wastad; yr afonydd ei syniant, canys hwynt a ymchwelant drachefn i'r lle y llithrant o hono; y mor a'r gwyntoedd ei syniant, canys hwynt a ufuddant iddo, ac orphwysant pan i harcho iddynt yn ddiannod.

God formed the heavens in wisdom: the sun and the moon do acknowledge him, for they preserve their course, and will return again to him who gave them; the earth doth acknowledge him, for she bears fruits with their roots in season and continually; the rivers do acknowledge him, for they recur again to the place from whence they glide; the sea and the winds acknowledge him; for they submit to him, and they rest when he commands them, without delay. *Elucidarius.*

Syniawg, *a.* (syn) Having the sense affected.

Syniawl, *a.* (syn) Sensible, perceptive, considerate

Syniedig, *a.* (syniad) Considered; perceived.

Syniedigaeth, *s. m.* (syniedig) The faculty of feeling or knowing by the sense; sensation; consideration; contemplation.

Syniedigawl, *a.* (syniedig) Cognitive, perceptive, sensitive; considerate; contemplative.

Synig, *a.* (syn) Having a sensation.

Synigl, *s. m.* (synig) That stimulates, or eggs.

Syniglaw, *v. a.* (synigl) To agitate, to stimulate.

Synigliad, *s. m.* (synigl) A stimulation.

Syniolaeth, *s. m.* (syniawl) Perceptivity.

Synioldeb, *s. m.* (syniawl) Sensibility: perceptibility; consciousness; contemplation.

Syniolder, *s. m.* (syniawl) Sensibleness.

Synioldra, *s. m.* (syniawl) Sensibleness.

Synioledd, *s. m.* (syniawl) Considerateness.

Synioli, *v. a.* (syniawl) To render sensible; to become sensible or considerate.

Syniolrwydd, *s. m.* (syniawl) Considerateness.

Sŷnu, *v. a.* (syn) To observe or to look stedfastly; to beware; to be affected; to be amazed, or surprised; to be overpowered with feeling; to be stunned. *Syni pan weli di fo*, thou wilt be astonished when thou seest it; *tarawai fi onid oeddwn yn synu*, he struck me so that I was stunned.

Sŷnwr, *s. m.—pl.* sŷnwyr (syn—gwr) One whose sense is affected or looks astonished.

Synwyr, *s. m.—pl. t.* au (syn—gwyr) Rational sense, wit; meaning. *Synwyr pen, synwyr cyffredin*, common sense.

Nid dysg heb synwyr.

There is no learning without *sense.* *Adage.*

Gwell synwyr no chyfoeth.

Wit is better than wealth. *Adage.*

Tair colofn synwyr; eglurdeb, helaethder, a chyfiawnder.

The three supports of *sense*; perspicuity, amplitude, and justness. *Barddas.*

Y llyn dyfnaf o'r afon
Lleiaf ei haf yw ei son;
Y doeth ni ddywed a ŵyr;
Nid o son y daw synwyr.

The deepest pool in the river, the least in the summer month its noise: the wise utters not all he knows; it is not from noise that *sense* proceeds. *Gw ab Ieuan Hen.*

Synwyraidd, *a.* (synwyr) Sensible, rational.

Synwyraw, *v. a.* (synwyr) To endue with sense, to make rational; to become sensible or rational; to gather sense.

Brenin nefoedd a ser a'm synwyro!

The sovereign of mobilities and stars, may he *endue* me with *sense!* *Meilyr ab Gwalchmai.*

> Trawd angeu ferau [illegible] fyddan';
> Tra hy yw pob dyn na synwyran',
> Trymder Lucifer a'i loes [illegible].

Pierced by death's flying shafts they will be; bold to excess are all men *that they will not think* of the sad state of Lucifer with his pang of conflict. *Cuwodyn.*

Synwyrawl, *a.* (synwyr) Sensible, rational.

> Nid synwyrawl ond cydwybodus;
> Nid cydwybodus ond cywir.

There is none *sensible* but the conscientious; no one is conscientious but the equitable. *Adage.*

Synwyrbell, *a.* (synwyr—pell) Of profound sense
Synwyrbwl, *a.* (synwyr—pwl) Dull-witted.
Synwyrdeb, *s. m.* (synwyr) Sensibleness.
Synwyredig, *a.* (synwyr) Being endued with sense
Synwyrddoeth, *a.* (synwyr—doeth) Sensibly wise
Synwyreb, *s. f.* (synwyr) A sentence; paragraph
Synwyredd, *s. m.* (synwyr) Rationality.
Synwyreg, *s. f.—pl. t.* au (synwyr) A complete expression of the sense, or a sentence.
Synwyrfa, *s. f.* (synwyr) A sensory.
Synwyrfas, *a.* (synwyr—bas) Shallow-witted.
Synwyrfawr, *a.* (synwyr) Pregnant with sense.
Synwyrgael, *a.* (synwyr—cael) Wit-acquiring.
Synwyrgall, *a.* (synwyr—call) Keen-witted.
Synwyrgar, *a.* (synwyr) Sententious.
Synwyrgarwch, *s. m.* (synwyr) Sententiousness.
Synwyrgoll, *a.* (synwyr—coll) Reason-losing.
Synwyriad, *s. m.* (synwyr) An enduing with sense; a becoming rational.
Synwyrlawn, *a.* (synwyr) Pregnant with sense.
Synwyrlym, *a.* (synwyr—llym) Sharp-witted.
Synwyroldeb, *s. m.* (synwyrawl) Sensibleness, the state of being endowed with good sense.
Synwyrolder, *s. m.* (synwyrawl) Sensibleness.
Synwyroledd, *s. m.* (synwyrawl) Sensibleness.
Synwyroli, *v. a.* (synwyrawl) To render sensible; to become sensible or rational.
Synwyroliad, *s. m.* (synwyrawl) Sensualization.
Synwyrolrwydd, *s. m.* (synwyrawl) Sensibleness.
Synwyrus, *a.* (synwyr) Sensible, discreet.
Synwyrusaw, *v. a.* (synwyrus) To render sensible; to become sensible.
Synwyrusdra, *s. m.* (synwyrus) Sensibleness.
Synwyrusrwydd, *s. m.* (synwyrus) Sensibleness.
Synwyrwan, *a.* (synwyr—gwan) Weak-witted.
Sypiad, *s. m.—pl. t.* au (swp) A heaping, or squeezing together; a bundling; a bunching.
Sypiaw, *v. a.* (swp) To heap or squeeze together; to bundle or lap together; to form into a bundle or heap. *Mi dy sypiaf di*, I will squeeze thee to a mummy.
Sypiawl, *a.* (swp) Tending to heap or press together; being made into a bundle.
Sypiedig, *a.* (sypiad) Being bundled together.
Sypiwr, *s. m.—pl.* sypiwyr (swp—gwr) One who heaps or bundles together.
Sypyn, *s. m. dim.—pl. t.* au (swp) A small bundle or packet; a little heap or mass.
Sypyniad, *s. m.* (sypyn) A forming a bundle.
Sypynu, *v. a.* (sypyn) To form a bundle.
Syr, *s. pl. aggr.* (*inflection of* ser) The stars.

> Trefnaist syr a myr morawl dylan;
> Trefnaist daiar fawr a'i chlawr achlan.

Thou hast regulated *stars* and fluctuations of ocean tide; thou hast regulated the ample earth, and its surface all complete. *Cuwodyn.*

Syrch, *s. m.* (serch *inflected*) Appulsion; approach; desire, affection, love.
Syrchawl, *a.* (syrch) Tending to cause desire.
Syrchiad, *s. m.* (syrch) A causing desire or love.
Syrchu, *v. a.* (syrch) To cause approach; to fill with desire; to cause love.

Syrn, *adv.* (*inflection of* swrn) Partly, half. *Syrn deg*, tolerably fair; *syrn debyg*, somewhat like; *syrn galed*, rather hard; *syrn gryf*, pretty strong.
Syrniad, *s. m.* (swrn) A forming into small shares.
Syrnu, *v. a.* (swrn) To divide into parts.
Syrnyn, *s. m. dim.* (swrn) Some quantity, a very little, ever so little.
Syrth, *s. m.—pl. t.* oedd (swrth *inflected*) A fall, a chance, a lot; a sort; inclination, propensity; also the offal, small parts, or cuttings off a carcase, as the feet, head, entrails, and the like. *a.* Falling, inclining, or steep. *Gwedi syrth*, after the fall.

> A dim syrth nid ymserthwn.

With any *propensity I would not demean myself.* *Rhys ab Rhys Brydydd.*

Tri pheth o'u deall a baraant haddwch: syrth anian, hynt cyfiawnder, a llafar gwirionedd.

Three things from being understood will produce peace: the *tendency* of nature, pursuit of equity, and the [illegible] of truth. *[illegible]*

Amcan cerdd, o bob rhyw a syrth, yw [illegible] a [illegible]; ac amlâu doethineb.

The design of poetry of every kind and tendency, is to enlarge the understanding and mind; and to increase wisdom. *[illegible]*

Syrthfa, *s. f.—pl.* syrthfeydd (syrth) Fallen state.

Cofiais hefyd y cariad, yr hwn a ddangosai ef i mi, pan y tynai ef fi allan o syrthfa pechawd.

I have remembered too the love, which he showed to me, when the drew me out from the *fallen state* of sin. *Marchawg Crwydrad.*

Syrthiad, *s. m.* (syrth) A falling, a tumbling.
Syrthiadwy, *a.* (syrthiad) Capable of falling.
Syrthiannawl, *a.* (syrthiant) Of a falling tendency
Syrthiannu, *v. a.* (syrthiant) To render of a falling tendency; to become apt to fall.
Syrthiannus, *a.* (syrthiant) Of a falling tendency.
Syrthiant, *s. m.* (syrth) A falling; propensity.
Syrthiaw, *v. a.* (syrth) To fall, or to tumble.

> Syrthid mell o gwall.

Evil wish *is made to fall* from the bosom. *Adage.*

Yna y syrthynt y gwyr brathedig yn mhlith y byddinoedd, megys y syrthiai yd y cynhauaf, pan fyddynt y medelwyr da yn [illegible]ryson.

Then the wounded men were *falling* amongst the hosts, as the corn of harvest *might fall*, when the skilled reapers [illegible] them. *Gr. ab Arthur.*

> Cydwybod lan a gan yn hoy,
> Pan syrthio'r ser i'r ddaiar.

A clear conscience will sweetly sing, when stars *shall fall* toward the earth. *[illegible]*

Syrthiawl, *a.* (syrth) Falling, or tumbling.
Syrthiedig, *a.* (syrthiad) Fallen, or tumbled.

> Pawb a'i droed ar syrthiedig.

Every one with his foot on the *fallen.* *Adage.*

Syrthineb, *s. m.* (syrth) Propensity, tendency.
Syrthiwr, *s. m.—pl.* syrthiwyr (syrth—gwr) One who falls or tumbles down.
Syrthni, *s. m.* (swrth) A heavy or unwieldy state; listlessness, torpitude.

> Nid diogi ond syrthni;
> Nid syrthni ond pechawd.

The essence of idleness is *torpitude*; the essence of torpitude is sin. *Adage.*

Syth, *s. m.* (sy—yth) The state or quality of being stiff, rigid, or erect; that has a tendency to stiffen; that is put up, set, or erect; also size, or cement, as glue, starch, or paste; a stiffening.

> Degle'n nes, dwy goes syth
> Diflas wyt, dan dafu syth.

Draw nearer, with thy two spindle shanks, disagreeably thou art throwing thy *slaver*. *Gr. Gryg, i [illegible].*

Syth, *a.* (sy—yth) Stiff, rigid; being set or put up; erect, upright; disdainful.

> Sythaf ac urddaf, mewn gorddwy, o'm iaith,
> Ail Math mab Mathonwy.

> The most *erect* and most honourable, in the post of danger, of any who speak my speech, like Math son of Mathonwy. *Gw. Tew.*

Sythadwy, *a.* (syth) Capable of being made stiff, or rigid; capable of being made erect.

Sythaw, *v. a.* (syth) To stiffen with size; to cement

Sythawl, *a.* (syth) Tending to make stiff, or rigid; tending to erectness; perpendicular.

Sythdant, *s. m.*—*pl.* sythdannau (syth—tant) A string that is of sharp discordancy.

Sythdeb, *s.* (syth) Stiffness, rigidness; erectness

Sythder, *s. m.* (syth) Stiffness, rigidity; erectness.

Sythdoes, *s. m.* (syth—toes) Putty.

Sythdra, *s. m.* (syth) Stiffness, rigidity, erectness

Sythedig, *a.* (syth) Stiffened; being made erect.

Sythedd, *s. m.* (syth) Stiffness, rigidity; erectness

Sythfalch, *a.* (syth—balch) Rigidly-proud.

Sythfalchedd, *s. m.* (sythfalch) Stiff pride.

Sythi, *s. m.*—*pl. t.* on (syth) That stiffens or keeps erect; a beam in a building.

Sythiad, *s. m.* (syth) A rendering stiff, or rigid; a setting upright; a becoming erect, or perpendicular.

Sythiannawl, *a.* (sythiant) Tending to stiffness, or rigidity; tending to erectness.

Sythiannu, *v. a.* (sythiant) To render of a stiff quality; to tend to erectness; to become of a stiff or rigid nature.

Sythiant, *s. m.* (syth) A stiffening; erection, or a setting upright.

Sytholdeb, *s. m.* (sythawl) A tendency to rigidity; a tendency to erectness.

Sytholder, *s. m.* (sythawl) A tendency to be stiff; a tendency to erectness.

Sytholdra, *s. m.* (sythawl) A tendency to stiffness; a tendency to be erect.

Sytholedd, *s. m.* (sythawl) A tendency to stiffness; a tendency to erectness.

Sytholi, *v. a.* (sythawl) To render, or to become of a stiff tendency; to tend to erectness.

Sytholrwydd, *s. m.* (sythawl) A tendency to stiffness; a tendency to erectness.

Sythrwydd, *s. m.* (syth) Stiffness, erectness.

Sythu, *v. a.* (syth) To stiffen, to make rigid or erect; to put up, or to set erect; to stiffen with size; to starch; to become erect.

Sythus, *a.* (syth) Of a stiffening quality; tending to erectness.

Sythusaw, *v. a.* (sythus) To render of a rigid quality; to tend to erectness; to become of a rigid quality.

Sythusdeb, *s. m.* (sythus) A tendency to be stiff; a tendency to erectness.

Sythusder, *s. m.* (sythus) A tendency to be rigid; a tendency to erectness.

Sythusdra, *s. m.* (sythus) Aptitude to be stiff or rigid; aptitude to erectness.

Sythusedd, *s. m.* (sythus) Aptness to be stiff; tendency to erectness.

Sythusrwydd, *s. m.* (sythus) A tendency to stiffness; a tendency to erectness.

Sythwr, *s. m.*—*pl.* sythwyr (syth—gwr) One who makes stiff, rigid, or erect; one who becomes rigid or erect.

Syw, *s. m.* (sy) That is circling, stated, or regular. *a.* Constant, stated, regular; trim, smart

> Nid syw ond y bi.

> There is nothing so *smart* as the magpie. *Adage.*

> Gorau bod——
> Morwyn yn syw.

> It is best for a maid to be *smart.* *Catwg Ddoeth.*

> Dewi mawr Mynyw syw sywedydd.

> Great Dewi of Mynyw a *constant* observer of the stars.

> Y daeth i Fynyw syw synwyrau.

> There came to Mynyw *constant* intellects.

> Mab Sant syw gormant, gormes haint ni ad.

> The son of Sant of *constant* plenitude, no affliction of pestilence will he suffer to remain. *Gw. Brycheiniawg, i Ddewi.*

> Y lloer——
> Moliannus yw ei syw swydd.

> The moon, praiseworthy is her *constant* duty. *D. ab Gwilym.*

Sywdeb, *s. m.* (syw) Constancy; statedness; regularity; trimness, smartness.

Sywder, *s. m.* (syw) Constancy; smartness.

Sywdra, *s. m.* (syw) Constancy; smartness.

Sywed, *s. m.* (sy—gwed) Astronomy.

Sywedydd, *s. m.*—*pl. t.* ion (sywed) A speaker of the stars; an astronomer; an astrologer.

> Ni chaiff sywedydd yn unfron.

> An *astronomer* will not be restricted to one breast. *Adage.*

> Talhaiarn y sydd
> Mwyaf sywedydd.

> Talhaiarn is the greatest *astronomer.* *Taliesin.*

> Selyf swynedig sywedydd,
> Mab gwledig goludawr gwrthegydd.

> Selyf the consecrated *astronomer*, the son of a sovereign the possessor of immense herds. *Meigant, m. Cynddylan.*

> Selyf ben sywedyddion.

> Selyf the chief of *astronomers.* *Ll. P. Moch.*

Sywedyddawl, *a.* (sywedydd) Astronomical.

Sywedyddiaeth, *s. m.* (sywedydd) Astronomy.

Sywiad, *s. m.* (syw) A rendering uniform; a trimming, a making smart.

Sywiaw, *v. a.* (syw) To make uniform; to trim.

> Sywiwch y llysewwair——
> Sywiwch, didrwyniwch drainwydd.

> *Trim* ye the herbaceous hay—*trim* ye, nip ye off the tops of the thorn-woods. *Edm. Prys.*

Sywiawl, *a.* (syw) Tending to render regular.

Sywidw, *s. f.* (sy—gwid) A titmouse; also called *yswidw*, and *yswigw*.

> Sywidw, iso ydwyd
> Wés y dryw, a'i mawdiwr wyd.

> The *titmouse*, there below thou art the servant of the wren, and his soldier too art thou. *Guto y Glyn.*

Sywin, *a.* (syw) Being in constant turning.

Sywinaw, *v. a.* (sywin) To use continually.

> Sywinaw yr arian yn ddim.

> *To dissipate* the money to nothing. *Adage.*

Sywiniad, *s. m.* (sywin) A continually using.

Sywydd, *s. m.*—*pl. t.* on (sy—gwydd) Star-knowledge.

> A'm swynwys sywydd
> Sywyddon.

> I have been made safe from harm by the *astrology* of astrologers. *Taliesin.*

Sywyddaw, *v. a.* (sywydd) To study star-knowledge; to astrologize.

> Sywydd sywedydd;
> Erewif sywedd.

> The astrologer *doth astrologize*; Erewif was regulated. *Taliesin.*

Sywyddawl, *a.* (sywydd) Having star-knowledge.

Sywyddiad, *s. m.* (sywydd) An astrologizing.

TA, *s. m. r.* That spreads or extends onward; a superior or supreme one. *Y ta urddawl*, the noble superior.

Tab, *s. m.* (ta—ab) A spread over; a surface.

Tabar, *s. m.—pl.* tebyr (tab—ar) A tabard.

> Tabar hir tew i barau.
>
> A long *tabard*, thick to last. *T. Aled, am wn.*
>
> Y celynllwyn—
> Tew byr-walit was tabar-wyrdd.
>
> The holly-bush, a thick short-hair'd youth in green *tabard*. *D. ab Gwilym.*

Tabwrdd, *s. m.—pl.* tabyrddau (tab—gwrdd) A tabour, a drum.

Tabyrddawl, *a.* (tabwrdd) Tabouring; drumming

Tabyrddiad, *s. m.* (tabwrdd) A tabouring.

Tabyrddu, *v. a.* (tabwrdd) To tabour; to drum.

Tabyrddwr, *s. m.—pl.* tabyrddwyr (tabwrdd—gwr) A tabourer; a drummer.

Tacl, *s. m.—pl. t.* au (tag) That combines; an instrument, or tool.

Taclau, *s. pl. aggr.* (tacl) Implements, tackling; accoutrements, equipage, furniture.

Tacledig, *a.* (tacl) Being put in repair.

Tacliad, *s. m.—pl. t.* au (tacl) A repairing.

Taclu, *v. a.* (tacl) To put in order, to accoutre; to dress, to deck, to trim. to repair, or to set right. *Taclu melin*, to repair a mill; *taclu esgidiau*, to mend shoes.

> A daclwys a gerddwys.
>
> He that *hath made ready* hath set off. *Adage.*

Taclus, *a.* (tacl) Being in order; accoutred, trim, neat, or tidy; complete. *Dynes daclus iawn yw hi*, she is a very tidy woman; *dyna i ti dro taclus*, there is for you a pretty piece of business.

Taclusaw, *v. a.* (taclus) To put in order; to set to right; to render neat or tidy.

Taclusder, *s. m.* (taclus) Orderliness; neatness.

Taclusdra, *s. m.* (taclus) Orderliness; neatness.

Taclusedd, *s. m.* (taclus) A compact state.

Taclusiad, *s. m.* (taclus) A putting in order; a repairing; a smartening up.

Taclusiant, *s. m.* (taclus) The act of putting in order, or repair.

Taclusrwydd, *s. m.* (taclus) Orderliness; neatness

Tacluswr, *s. m.—pl.* tacluswyr (taclus—gwr) One who puts in good order or repair.

Tach, *s. m.* (ta—ach) That spreads, vanishes, or is diffused.

Tachwedd, *s. m.* (tach—gwedd) A receding appearance, a tending to a conclusion; an end or annihilation; a somewhat, a little quantity, or space; a remnant; also the month of November. *Tachwedd o ariant*, a small sum of money; *tachwedd o yd*, a small quantity of corn; *amser tachwedd*, the time of receding, or latter end of the season, the time of fattening cattle; that is from midsummer to the winter solstice.

> Pan aeth Tegeingl, teg rysedd,
> [illegible]
> [illegible]
> [illegible]
>
> When he [illegible] Tegeingl, of splendid course, [illegible] beyond [illegible] appeared [illegible] there was rapidly seen the interchange of red stains from the incessant sword [illegible] of ruthless termination. *Cynddelw, i O. Gwynedd.*

> Llys lwybr y gwys, nid gwyd, eer Aeron,
> Carwraidd gymhlegyd;
> Lloegrwys dachwedd arfeddyd,
> Llafn awchlym yn ngrym, yn ngryd.
>
> A court conspicuous for resort; not of vice, by Aeron, of amiable concern; its maxim is the *extermination* of the Lloegrwys, with the ardently keen blade in energy, in the conflict. *Hoddyn.*

Tachweddawl, *a.* (tachwedd) Tending to an end.

Tachweddiad, *s. m.* (tachwedd) A causing to disappear; a bringing to an end; a determining.

Tachweddu, *v. a.* (tachwedd) To cause to disappear; to bring to an end; to terminate.

> Llyr ofn'ser frwyngeddofn, a'r freisgidu froneder;
> Llawch feiddd, lor angor Eingl dachweddu.
>
> Dreadful as Llyr in the precipitously-deep slaughter, with the black overwhelming shield; he protects the bards, the sturdy chief *exterminating* the Angles. *G. ab M. ab Dafydd.*

Tad, *s. m.—pl. t.* au (ta—ad) That spreads a continnity; a father. *Tad a mam*, father and mother; *tad cu*, a father of fondness, an epithet for *taid*, or grandfather, in some parts of Wales; but in some districts of Powys *tad da*, or good father, is a grandfather, and *tad cu*, a great grandfather, or *hendad*, and *hendad cu*, is a *gorhendad*, or great great grandfather: *Tad gwyn*, a stepfather, in North Wales, but the same as *tad cu*, in parts of the South: *Tad yn nghyfraith*, a father in law; *tad bedydd*, a godfather.

> Nid cynghor ond tad.
>
> There is no counsel like a *father*. *Adage.*
>
> Llaw mab yn llawes ei dad.
>
> The hand of a son in the skirt of his *father*. *Adage.*

Tadaeth, *s. m.* (tad) Fatherhood, paternity.

Tadaidd, *a.* (tad) Fatherly, or paternal.

Tadawg, *a.* (tad) Having a father; patronal.

Tadawl, *a.* (tad) Belonging to a father; fatherly; tutelar, patronal.

> Alectus oedd yn Llundain yn gwneuthur gwylfa i'r duwiau tadawl.
>
> Alectus was in London holding a festival to the *tutelary gods*. *Gr. ab Arthur.*

Tadenw, *s. m.—pl. t.* au (tad—enw) Patronymic.

Tadenwawg, *a.* (tadenw) Patronymical.

Tadenwawl, *a.* (tadenw) Patronymical.

Tadenwogawl, *a.* (tadenwawg) Patronymical.

Tadiad, *s. m.* (tad) A fathering; a becoming a father.

Tadladd, *s. m.* (tad—lladd) A father-killing.

Tadladdawl, *a.* (tadladd) Parricidial.

Tadladdiad, *s. m.* (tadladd) A killing a father.

Tadleiddiadawl, *a.* (tadleiddiad) Parricidial.

Tadmaeth, *s. m.* (tad—maeth) A foster-father.

Tadmaethawl, *a.* (tadmaeth) Belonging to a foster-father.

Tadmaethu, *v. a.* (tadmaeth) To act as a foster-father; to become as a foster-father.

Tadogaeth, *s. m.* (tadawg) Paternity, or fatherhood; also the origin of a word, etymology.

Tadogaethawl, *a.* (tadogaeth) Belonging to paternity; etymological.

Tadogaidd, *a.* (tadawg) Fatherly in a small degree

Tadogair, *s. m.—pl.* tadogeiriau (tadawg—gair) A radical word. or etymon.

Tadogawl, *a.* (tadawg) Patronal, patronymic.

Tadogi, *v. a.* (tadawg) To assign a father to; to have a father.

Tadolaidd, *a.* (tadawl) Somewhat fatherly.
Tadolddeb, *s. m.* (tadawl) Fatherliness, paternity.
Tadoli, *v. n.* (tadawl) To become fatherly; to become a father.
Tadoliad, *s. m.* (tadawl) A rendering fatherly or paternal; a becoming paternal.
Tadoliaeth, *s. m.* (tadawl) Fatherhood.
Tadu, *v. a.* (tad) To father; to become a father.
Tadus, *a.* (tad) Paternal, or fatherly.
Tadusaw, *v. n.* (tadus) To render fatherly; to become fatherly.
Tadusedd, *s. m.* (tadus) State of being fatherly.
Tadusrwydd, *s. m.* (tadus) Fatherliness.
Tadws, *s. m.* (tad) The sire of an animal.
Tadwy, *s. m.* (tad) Paternal; tutelar.

Mor fydd llwydd llonydd llaw dadwy;
Mor attreg pob chweg pan chwerwy.

So prosperous will be the tranquillity of the *paternal* hand; so repugnant will be every sweet when it becomes bitter. *Cynddelw.*

Tadwys, *s. m.* (tad—gwys) A fatherhood, a father's side, connexion, or kindred.

Cyn dwyn coron Llundain, ac y deyrnwialen, o'r Saeson, Dyfnwal Moelmud oedd frenin ar yr ynys hon; a mab oedd efe i Iarll Cernyw, o ferch brenin Lloegr: a gwedi diffoddi tadwys y frenhiniaeth y cafas yntau y deyrnas o gogel wrth fod yn ŵyr i frenin.

Before the crown of London, and the sceptre, were taken by the Saxons, Dyfnwal Moelmud had been king over this island; and he was son to the earl of Cornwall, by a daughter of the king of Lloegria: and after the *paternity* of the sovereign power had become extinct he then obtained the kingdom by the distaff, as being the grandson of a king. *Welsh Laws.*

Tadwysiad, *s. m.* (tadwys) The obtaining or arriving at the state of fatherhood.
Tadwysiaw, *v. a.* (tadwys) To form a fatherhood.
Tadwysiawl, *a.* (tadwys) As to a fatherhood.
Taen, *s. f.—pl. t.* ion (ta—en) A spread; a sprinkle; a layer. *Taen toniar*, the spread of a wave.
Taenadwy, *a.* (taen) Capable of spreading or diffusing; expansible.
Taenawd, *s. m.* (taen) Expansion; respersion.
Taenawl, *a.* (taen) Spreading, expansive.
Taenedig, *a.* (taen) Expanded; sprinkled.
Taenedigaeth, *s. m.* (taenedig) Expansion.
Taenell, *s. f.—pl. t.* au (taen) A small spread; a sprinkle; a small layer.
Taenellaidd, *a.* (taenell) Somewhat sprinkled.
Taenellawg, *a.* (taenell) Having a sprinkle.
Taenelledig, *a.* (taenell) Besprinkled, aspersed.
Taenelliad, *s. m.* (taenell) A sprinkling, a strewing
Taenelliedydd, *s. m.—pl. t.* ion (taenelliad) A sprinkler, one who strews.
Taenellu, *v. a.* (taenell) To sprinkle, to besprinkle, to asperse, to strew.
Taenellwr, *s. m.—pl.* taenellwyr (taenell—gwr) One who sprinkles, or strews.
Taenellydd, *s. m.—pl. t.* ion (taenell) A sprinkler.
Taenfa, *s. f.—pl.* taenfeydd (taen) A spread of hay. Dyfed. The *llanerch* of N. Wales.
Taenferw, *a* (taen—berw) Spreadingly boiling.

Golwg diserchawg, syberw, celnmyg,
Lliw golau tonau taenferw gwenyg.

An aspect void of wantonness, courteous, magnificent, like the light hue of the breakings of the *expandingly boiling* waves. *Casnodyn.*

Taeniad, *s. m.—pl. t.* au (taen) A spreading.
Taeniator, *ger.* (taeniad) In expanding.
Taenitor, *sup.* (taen) To be expanding.
Taenotor, *sup.* (taenawd) To be expanded.
Taenu, *v. a.* (taen) To spread, to expand; to sprinkle; to become spread, or scattered. *Taenu y gwely*, to make the bed; *lledu y gwely*, Gwent; and *cyweiriaw y gwely*, in N. Wales.
Taenwr, *s. m.—pl.* taenwyr (taen—gwr) A spreader; a strewer; a resperser.
Taenydd, *s. m.—pl. t.* ion (taen) A spreader.
Taer, *s. m.* (ta—er) The state of being eager, ardent, urgent, or importunate.
Taer, *a.* (ta—er) Eager, earnest, ardent, urgent, importunate.

Taer ringyll wyt ti'r angau,
Difrawd tost yw dy fryd tau!

An *urgent* messenger art thou, oh death! severely bent on ruin is thy design. *Rhys Iones.*

A draig Mon, mor ddrud ei esillydd yn aer,
Y bu terfysg taer, a haer holi.

With the dragon of Mon, so bold his kindred in the slaughter, there was *urgent* tumult and insulting claim. *Gwalchmai.*

Taeraidd, *a.* (taer) Somewhat eager or urgent.
Taerannog, *s. m.* (taer—annog) Eager excitation. *v. a.* To excite urgently.
Taerawg, *a.* (taer) Being eager; importunate.
Taerawydd, *s. f.* (taer—awydd) Ardent inclination
Taerawl, *a.* (taer) Apt to be eager, or urgent.
Taerboen, *s. f.—pl. t.* au (taer—poen) Severe pain.
Taerdeb, *s. m.* (taer) Eagerness, earnestness.
Taerder, *s. m.* (taer) Eagerness; importunity.
Taerdra, *s. m.* (taer) Eagerness; ardency.
Taerdrais, *s. m.* (taer—trais) Violent oppression.
Taerdyn, *a.* (taer—tyn) Violently straining.
Taerdyniad, *s. m.* (taerdyn) A pulling ardently.
Taerdynu, *v. a.* (taerdyn) To pull ardently.
Taerddadl, *s. f.—pl.* taerddadlau (taer—dadl) An eager or violent dispute.
Taerddadliad, *s. m.* (taerddadl) A vehemently disputing; ardent disputation.
Taerddadlu, *v. a.* (taerddadl) To dispute violently.
Taerddymunaw, *v. a.* (taer—dymunaw) To desire earnestly.
Taerddymuniad, *s. m.* (taer—dymuniad) A desiring earnestly; an ardent desire.
Taeredig, *a.* (taer) Being eagerly disposed.
Taeredd, *s. m.* (taer) Eagerness, earnestness, ardency, vehemency; importunity.
Taererchi, *v. a.* (taer—erchi) To crave earnestly.
Taerfaith, *a.* (taer—maith) Ardently continuing.
Taerfalch, *a.* (taer—balch) Ardently proud.

Taerfalch fal Gwalchmai.

Ardently proud like Gwalchmai. *Cynddelw.*

Taerfar, *s. m.* (taer—bar) Ardent wrath. *Torf taerfar*, a host of ardent wrath.
Taerferw, *a.* (taer—berw) Violently boiling.
Taerferwi, *v. a.* (taerferw) To boil violently.
Taerflin, *a.* (taer—blin) Severely tiring.
Taerflinaw, *v. a.* (taerflin) To tire severely.
Taergais, *s. m.* (taer—cais) An eager attempt.
Taergeisiad, *s. m.* (taergais) A trying eagerly.
Taergeisiaw, *v. a.* (taergais) To try eagerly.
Taergwyn, *s. f.—pl. t.* ion (taer—cwyn) An earnest or vehement complaint.
Taergwynaw, *v. a.* (taergwyn) To complain earnestly.
Taeriad, *s. m.* (taer) An acting eagerly in opposition; an insisting; a contending.
Taeriant, *s. m.* (taer) Importunity; contention.
Taerlew, *a.* (taer—glew) Ardently persevering. *Taerlew bar*, an ardently driving shaft.
Taerloes, *s. f.—pl. t.* au (taer—gloes) A severe pang
Taerni, *s. m.* (taer) Eager opposition; importunity.
Taeru, *v. a.* (taer) To act with eagerness; to aver or to affirm vehemently, to insist; to contend.
Taerwr, *s. m.—pl.* taerwyr (taer—gwr) One who importunes; a contender.
Taerwres, *s. m.* (taer—gwres) Ardent heat.

Taerwrys, *s. m.* (taer—gwrys) Fierce contention.

Taeth, *s. m.* (ta—eth) That pervades; essence.

Taethawl, *a.* (taeth) Essential; fertilizing.

Taethedig, *a.* (taeth) Rendered of a fertilizing quality.

Taethiad, *s. m.* (taeth) A rendering of a fertilizing quality.

Taethu, *v. a.* (taeth) To render fertilizing.

Taethus, *a.* (taeth) Essential; fertilizing.

Taf, *s. m.—pl.* teifion (ta—af) A spread.

Tafad, *s. m.* (taf) A spreading; extension.

Tafal, *s. f.—pl.* tafeli (taf) A balance.

> Mihangel, dirgel ei dal,
> Dyfod a wna a'r dafal.
>
> Michael, with veiled front, come he will with the *balance*.
> *Math. ab Llywelyn Goch.*

Tafar, *s. m.* (taf) That spreads or displays.

Tafarch, *s. m.* (taf—arch) A cricket bat. *Pel dafarch*, a cricket ball.

Tafarn, *s. f.—pl. t.* au (taf—arn) A tavern.

Tafarndy, *s. m.—pl. t.* au (tafarn—ty) A tavern.

Tafarnwr, *s. m.—pl.* tafarnwyr (tafarn—gwr) A tavern-keeper.

Tafarth, *s. m.* (tafar) That is spread or laminated.

Tafawd, *s. m.—pl.* tafodau (taf) A tongue. *Tafawd drwg*, a scolding; *tafawd cloch*, a bell clapper:—*Tafawd yr hydd*, the sole fish; *tafawd yr ych*, the burt fish:—Also the name of many plants—*Tafawd y bwch*, or *tafawd yr afr*, common viper's bugloss; *tafawd yr hydd*, hart's tongue; *tafawd y ci*, broad-leaved pondweed; *tafawd yr ych*, *tafawd y fuwch*, borage; *tafawd yr oen*, hoary plantain; *tafawd y llew*, bristly ox-tongue; *tafawd y march*, horse tongue; *tafawd y neidr*, adder's tongue; *tafawd yr eden*, common stitchwort, *tafawd yr hedydd*, larkspur; *tafawd yr wydd*, sneeze-wort yarrow; *tafawd yr ych anwyw*, evergreen alkanet; *tafawd yr ych culddail*, small bugloss.

> Goreu gwraig, gwraig heb dafawd.
>
> The best wife is a wife without a *tongue*. *Adage.*
>
> Da daint rhag tafawd.
>
> The teeth are good to stop the *tongue*. *Adage.*
>
> Un o dri deifnogion cerdd a chenedl cenedl y Cymmry: Gwyddon Ganhebon, a wnai gerdd dafawd gyntaf o'r byd.
>
> One of the three improvers of science and the art of composition of the nation of the Cymmry: Gwyddon Ganhebon, who was the first in the world that made *vocal* song. *Barddas.*

Tafawdlyag, *a.* (tafawd—llysg) Of slow moving tongue; plaintive.

> Yn ffyrdd cyrdd cerdd dafawdlysg,
> Yn brydydd, yn brifardd dysg.
>
> In the ways of songs of the *plaintive* muse, a poet, a primary bard of learning. *Cynddelw.*

Tafawl, *a.* (taf) Spreading, expanding; an epithet for the various kinds of the dock plant. *Dail tafawl*, dock leaves; *tafawl y mor*, golden dock, *tafawl y dwfr*, *tafawl hirion*, great water-dock; *tafawl mair*, *tafawl cochion*, tobacco; *tafawl newydd*, *gwellt newydd*, new herbage. *Welsh Laws.*

Tafell, *s. f. dim.—pl. t.* i (taf) Any flat mass, piece, or spread, a tablet; a slice. *Tafell o fara*, a slice of bread.

> Rhoi y dorth a gofyn y dafell.
>
> To give a loaf and ask for the *slice*. *Adage.*
>
> Fis Mai caf weled bun yn——
> Dyfod dan wyrddion dafyll.
>
> The month of May I shall see the maid resting under green *foliages*. *D. ab Gwilym.*

Tafellan, *s. f. dim.* (tafell) A small slice.

Tafellawg, *a.* (tafell) Being in thin masses; being in slices.

Tafelliad, *s. m.* (tafell) A spreading into a thin mass; a slicing.

Tafellu, *v. a.* (tafell) To form into a slice or flat mass; to slice; to spread as foliage.

Tafl, *s. m.—pl.* taflau (taf) A spread, a cast; a throw, a fling; a balance. *Ffon dafl*, a sling; *taflau*, a pair of scales.

Tafladwy, *a.* (tafl) Capable of being thrown down

Taflan, *s. f.—pl.* tafleni (tafl) A balance.

Taflawd, *s. f.—pl.* taflodydd (tafl) A spread, or covering: a roof; the space next to the roof in a building; a loft, a garret. *Taflawd y genau*, the roof of the mouth; *taflawd gwair*, a hay-loft; *taflawd ieir*, a hen-roost.

Taflawg, *a.* (tafl) Having a throw; projectile.

Tafled, *s. f.* (tafl) That serves for throwing.

Tafledig, *a.* (tafl) Being thrown, or flung.

Tafledigaeth, *s. m.* (tafledig) The act of throwing; projection; interjection.

Tafledigawl, *a.* (tafledig) Tending to throw.

Tafledydd, *s. m.—pl. t.* ion (tafliad) A hurler, a flinger.

> Tithau—
> Tafledydd, defnyddwydd da,
> Brath y lleidr.——
>
> Thou too, the *flinger*, with well-seasoned wood, wound the thief. *D. ab Gwilym, am Rys Goggin.*

Taflen, *s. f.—pl. t.* au (tafl) That is spread out; a tablet; a table of figures.

Taflenawl, *a.* (taflen) Tabular.

Tafleniad, *s. m.* (taflen) A tabulation.

Taflenu, *v. a.* (taflen) To tabulate.

Taflfaen, *s. m.—pl.* taflfeini (tafl—maen) A hurling stone.

Taflhual, *s. m.—pl. t.* au (tafl—hual) The jesses of a hawk.

> Y penhebogydd a ddyly groen hydd, yr hydref, ac y gwanwyn groen ewig, i wneuthur menyg wrth arwain ei adar, a thaflhualau.
>
> The chief falconer ought to have a stag skin in autumn, and in the spring the skin of a doe, to make gloves for leading his hawks, and for *jesses*. *Welsh Laws.*

Tafliad, *s. m.—pl. t.* au (tafl) A throwing.

Tafliedydd, *s. m.—pl. t.* ion (tafliad) A thrower.

Taflnerth, *s. m.—pl. t.* oedd (tafl—nerth) A projectile power.

Taflodawl, *a.* (taflawd) Interjective.

Taflodi, *v. a.* (taflawd) To interject.

Taflodiad, *s. m.—pl.* au (taflawd) Interjection.

Taflrwyd, *s. f.—pl. t.* au (tafl—rhwyd) A casting net.

Taflrym, *s. m.* (tafl—grym) Projectile force.

Taflu, *v. a.* (tafl) To throw, to cast, to fling, to hurl, to project. It is synonymous with *fwrw*, *bwrw*, *lluchiaw*, *taenu*.

> Mal dall yn taflu ei ffon.
>
> Like the blind *throwing* his staff. *Adage.*
>
> Gwell march hagr a'm dyco no march teg a'm taflo.
>
> Better is an ugly horse that will carry me than a fine horse that *will throw* me. *Adage.*

Taflwr, *s. m.—pl.* taflwyr (tafl—gwr) A thrower.

Taflydd, *s. m.—pl. t.* ion (tafl) A thrower.

Tafodaeth, *s. m.* (tafawd) Language.

Tafodawg, *a.* (tafawd) Having a tongue.

> Tri phrif dafodogion llys: arglwydd, brawdwr, a mach.
>
> The three primary speakers of a court: the lord, the justiciary, and the bail. *Trioedd Dyfnwal.*

Tafodawl, *a.* (tafawd) Belonging to the tongue.

Tafodi, *v. a.* (tafawd) To tongue; to use the tongue; to scold.

Tafodiad, *s. m.* (tafawd) A tonguing.

Tafodiaeth, *s. m.* (tafawd) The action of the tongue, articulation of the voice; enunciation.

Tafodiawg, *a.* (tafawd) Having a tongue, tongued; having a good tongue; an epithet for an advocate or pleader; also for a single verbal evidence.

Tafodlafar, *a.* (tafawd—llafar) Articulated or expressed by the tongue.

Tafodleferydd, *s. m.* (tafodlafar) Articulation of the tongue; a speaking out, or by rote; verbal evidence. *Dyweda ar dafodleferydd*, say it off by heart.

Tafodogaeth, *s. m.* (tafodawg) The use of the tongue.

Tafodrudd, *a.* (tafawd—rhudd) Red-tongued; in the laws, an accessary to murder by information of the one to be murdered.

Tafodruddiaeth, *s. m.* (tafodrudd) A red-tongued act; a felonious information.

> Cyntaf o naw affaith galanas yw tafodruddiaeth: mynegi y neb a ladder i'r neb a'i lladdo.
>
> The first of the nine abetments of felony is the *reddening of the tongue*: the informing of the one to be slain to him who shall slay him. *Welsh Laws.*

Tafodrwym, *a.* (tafawd—rhwym) Tongue-tied.

Tafodrydd, *a.* (tafawd—rhydd) Loose-tongued.

Tafodrydd-deb, *s. m.* (tafodrydd) Freedom of tongue.

Tafodrydd-der, *s.* (tafodrydd) Freedom of tongue.

Tafodrydd-dra, *s. m.* (tafodrydd) Freedom of tongue.

Tafodwr, *s. m.—pl.* tafodwyr (tafawd—gwr) One who uses his tongue.

Tafodwst, *s. m.* (tafawd—gwst) The tongue disease, incident to cattle, which swells the tongue so as to cause suffocation. It is called *y bothell*, in South Wales.

Tafodydd, *s. m.—pl. t.* ion (tafawd) One who useth his tongue; a declaimer.

Tafolawg, *a.* (tafawl) Abounding with docks.

Tafolen, *s. f. dim.* (tafawl) A dock leaf: *tafolen goch*, or *tafolen waedlyd*, bloody-veined dock; *tafolen grych*, curled dock; *tafolen mair*, or *trython*, sharp dock.

Tafoli, *v. n.* (tafawl) To grow dock leaves.

Tafu, *v. a.* (taf) To overspread, to spread.

Taffithlen, *s. f. dim.* (ta—ffithlen) A glider.

Tag, *s. m.—pl. t.* ion (ta—ag) The state of being stuffed, or clogged; a strangle. *Tag aradr*, restharrow, or cammock; also called *hwp yr ychain*, and *tegwch meinwen*.

Tagadwy, *a.* (tag) Capable of being choked.

Tagawl, *a.* (tag) Clogging; strangling.

Tagedig, *a.* (tag) Clogged; strangled, choked.

Tagedigaeth, *s. m.* (tagedig) The act of clogging; a choking.

Tagedigawl, *a.* (tagedig) Obstructive; strangling.

Tagell, *s. f. dim.—pl. t.* i (tag) A barb, any thing growing to the throat; a double chin; a dewlap; a wattle.

Tagellaidd, *a.* (tagell) Tending to form a double chin; somewhat like a dewlap.

Tagellawg, *a.* (tagell) Barbed; having a double chin; having a dewlap, or wattle.

Tagelliad, *s. m.* (tagell) A forming a double chin; a forming a dewlap, or wattle.

Tagellu, *v. a.* (tagell) To make a double chin; to grow as a double chin, dewlap, or wattle.

Tagellwag, *a.* (tagell—gwag) Having an empty or loose double chin.

Tagfa, *s. f.—pl.* tagfëydd (tag) An obstructed place; an obstruction; a stifling, a strangling, a strangle, a choke.

Tagfagl, *s. f.—pl. t.* au (tag—magl) A springe.

Tagiad, *s. m.—pl. t.* au (tag) A choking.

> Cafas tagiad ei enw o herwydd ei fod yn attal cyweirdant a thyniad ryw amser pan ddel mewn cerdd.
>
> The *clogging* had its name on account of its stopping the key note and the drawing sometimes when it occurs in music. *Cerddwriaeth.*

Tagiant, *s. m.* (tag) A clogging; a choking.

Taglys, *s. m.* (tag—llys) Small bindweed: *taglys yr yd*, black bindweed; *taglys mawr*, great bindweed; also called *tagwydd*.

Tagu, *v. a.* (tag) To obstruct, to stop or clog up; to stifle, to strangle, to choke.

> Brawd yw mygu i dagu.
>
> Suffocation is brother to *choking*. *Adage.*

Tagwr, *s. m.—pl.* tagwyr (tag—gwr) A choker.

Tagwydd, *s. m.* (tag—gwydd) Great-bindweed.

Tagwyg, *s. m. aggr.* (tag—gwyg) Tufted vetch.

Tai, *s. m.—pl.* teiau (ta) A stretch or a reach; the state of being stretched or at rest; the state of being held or possessed: also houses, used for the regular plural *tyau*.

Taiad, *s. m.* (tai) An overspreading; an enclosing.

Taiaw, *v. a.* (tai) To spread over; to close in.

Taiawg, *a.* (tai) Having an overspread; rustic, rude; having land on servile tenure. *s. m.—pl.* taiogion. A vassal, a villain, tenant in villanage; a tike, a churl, a husbandman, a peasant. *Dyn taiawg*, a clownish person.

> Taiawg y bydd taiawg cyd bo coronawg.
>
> The clown will be *clownish* though he should wear a crown. *Adage.*
>
> Traian byw y taiogau, ac eu marw, a ddaw i'r maer ac y cangellawr.
>
> The third of the live-stock of the *villains*, and of their dead-stock, shall come to the steward and the chancellor. *Welsh Laws.*

Tail, *s. m.* (ta—il) A spreading or growing principle; the surface of the earth, or soil; manure; dung, muck.

> Yn ei arch a'i dywarchen
> Dan y tail, mae'r dawned hen.
>
> In his shrine with his clod, beneath the soil, the ancient lore is put. *Ieuan Madawg, m. Llyr D. Trefor.*

Tain, *s. m.* (ta—in) That is of a spreading quality.

> O fysg dy werin tain tawch
> Dy haeddiant, Duw, dy heddwch.
>
> From amongst thy people the *dissipation* of the mist will be by thy merit, God, thy peace. *H. D. ab Ifan.*

Taiogaeth, *s. m.* (taiawg) Vassalage.

Taiogaidd, *a.* (taiawg) Somewhat rustic.

Taiogdref, *s. f.—pl. t.* i (taiawg—tref) A villain-town.

> Tair rhandir a fydd yn y daiogdref, yn mhob un o'r ddwy y bydd tri thaiawg; a'r drydedd yn borfa iddynt.
>
> There shall be three sharelands in a *villain-town*; in each one of the two there shall be three villains; and the third shall be a pasture for them. *Welsh Laws.*

Taiogawl, *a.* (taiawg) Appertaining to a villain.

Taiogeiddiad, *s. m.* (taiogaidd) A rendering rustic; a becoming rusticated.

Taiogeiddiaw, *v. a.* (taiogaidd) To render rusticated; to become rusticated.

Taiogeidd-dra, *s. m.* (taiogaidd) Rusticity.

Taiogeiddrwydd, *s. m.* (taiogaidd) Boorishness.

Taioges, *s. f.—pl. t.* au (taiawg) A rustic female.

Taiogi, *v. a.* (taiawg) To make rustic; to become rustic.

Taiogrwydd, *s. m.* (taiawg) Boorishness, rusticity.

> Gwell bonedd no thaiogrwydd.
>
> Nobility is better than *boorishness*. *Adage.*

Talogyn, *s. m. dim.* (talawg) A rude fellow.

Taid, *s. m.—pl.* teidiau (ta—id) That has spread a contingence; a grandfather. But in parts of Powys, and South Wales, *taid* is a great great grandfather; in others it is a father in the fifth degree, *hendaid* in the sixth, and *gorhendaid* in the seventh degree: See *Tad.*—*Taid a nain*, a grandfather and grandmother.

Tair, *s. f.* (ta—ir) Three of feminine gender. *a.* Three, speaking of females. *Tair merch, tair o ferched*, three women.

Tair ffynnon gwybodaeth: crebwyll, ystyriaeth, a dysgeidiaeth.

The *three* fountains of knowledge: imagination, meditation, and learning. *Barddas.*

Tairth, *s. m. aggr.—pl.* teirthion (tarth) An ague.

Tais, *s. f.—pl.* teision (ta—is) That spreads round; a cover, a daiz, a canopy; a cake.

Taith, *s. f.—pl.* teithiau (ta—ith) A journey.

Cam dros y trothwy yw hanner y daith.

A step over the threshold is half the *journey*. *Adage.*

Meian a ddyl ei daith.

Meian deserves his *journey*. *Adage.*

Taiwr, *s. m.—pl.* taiwyr (tai—gwr) A rustic man.

Brad werthu ei bryd i wr
A fwytâi fwyd taiwr.

It was deceitful to sell his meal to a man who would eat the food of a *ploughman*. *Syr Lewys Meudwy.*

Tal, *s. f.—pl. t.* ion (ta—al) A space spread out or over; that is even or clear; clearance; pay, reward, requital; an equivalent, or value. *Pa a dal hwna?* what is the value of that?

Llyma Forfudd ddiledryw,
A gaf o dal: gofid yw.

Behold, Morfudd of underbased race, what of *recompence* I get: it is grief! *D. ab Gwilym.*

Dynion sy'n cael daloni;
Dydd tal yw pob dydd i ti.

The multitudes are receiving benefit; a day of *payment* is every day to thee. *Hywel ab Reinallt.*

Tàl, *s. m.—pl. t.* oedd (ty—al) That is over, that tops, that is fronting, or upon; a front; the forehead. *a.* Towering; tall. In the names of places it answers to *end;* as *Tal-y-Bont*, Bridgend: In the names of men it denotes *front;* as *Taliesin*, Fair-front; *Talariant*, Silver-front; *Talhaiarn*, Iron-front.

Ffawd pawb yn ei dàl.

Every body's fortune is in his *forehead*. *Adage.*

Dy lewych, ddyn dàl ewyn,
Dy gorff a luniodd Duw gwyn.

'Twas heav'n thy form, thy bloom, that gave,
Thy *forehead* like the foamy wave. *S. Tudyr.*

Telynior tàl awenydd,
Trwythaw beirdd mewn truethau bydd.

The harper, blest with *lofty* muse,
The bards in briny floods imbrues. *Guto y Glyn.*

O deir-llith y gwnaf darllain clod Efa,
O dalau India hyd wal Lundain.

In three lectures I will read the praise of Efa, extending from the *frontiers* of India to the wall of London. *L. G. Cothi.*

Talâad, *s. m.* (tàl) To elevate; to grow tall.

Taladwy, *a.* (tal) Capable of being paid; payable.

Cusan cariad taladwy
Cefais, ni ddymunais mwy.

A kiss *as due* to faithful love
She gave; for that alone I strove. *S. Tudyr.*

Taladdurn, *s. m.—pl. t.* au (tal—addurn) A front ornament; a moulding.

Taladdurnaw, *v. a.* (taladdurn) To adorn the front.

Taladdurnawg, *a.* (taladdurn) Having an ornamented front.

Taladdurniad, *s. m.* (taladdurn) An adorning the front.

Talaeth, *s f.—pl.* taleithiau (tàl) A front region; a frontier; a province, or dependent territory.

Ynys Prydain a gynnelir dan un goron a thair talaeth.

The isle of Britain is held under one crown and three principalities. *Welsh Laws.*

Talaidd, *a.* (tàl) Somewhat high; tallish.

Talais, *s. f.* (tal—ais) An empannelled jury.

A deuddeg o brydyddion,
Yn dalais deg, diys don.

With twelve poets, a fair *jury*, of certain voice. *W. Cynwal.*

Talais o wyr maladaidd,
Trefn hardd, rhwng 'y mardd a mi.

A *jury* of men of property, a fair order, between my bard and me. *Ed. Prys.*

Talaith, *s. f.—pl.* taleithion (tàl—aith) A band worn round the head; a frontlet, a headband; a chaplet; a radial crown; a diadem.

Talar, *s. f.—pl.* taleri (tàl—ar) A headland in a field, at the end of ridges; a cross-ridge.

Talarawg, *a.* (talar) Having cross-ridges.

Talariad, *s. m.* (talar) A forming cross-ridges.

Talaru, *v. a.* (talar) To form cross-ridges.

Talarw, *a.* (tàl—garw) Roughly fronted.

Talarw yn nghymmwsc yn nghyfrenn brwydr, tal ysgwyd eurgrwydr torynt yn fann.

The *rough-fronted* ones in the mutual struggle of the share of the battle, the front of the gold-covered shield they would quickly break. *O. Cyfeiliawg.*

Talâu, *v. a.* (tàl) To make high; to grow tall.

Talawd, *s. m.* (tal) A payment, a requital.

Talawdr, *s. m.—pl.* talodron (talawd) A payer.

Talawg, *a.* (tàl) High-fronted; bold-faced.

Talawr, *s. m.* (tal) One who makes equable; a rewarder; a payer.

Ef tarddo talawr,
Tarddant nef i lawr.

When the remunerator shall appear let the heavens appear below. *Taliesin, armes dydbrawd.*

Talben, *s. m.—pl. t.* oedd (tal—pen) A settled price or standard value. In order to adjust transactions of barter, the law affixed to every thing a settled mean value; and if any article given in payment fell short of its standard, the deficiency was made good in money.

Talbenig, *a.* (talben) Of current value. *Talbenigion*, things of standard value.

Eidion a dalo ddeg ar ugaint yw buwch talbenig;—ac yw buwch talbenig, gwartheg heb dderchafael gydag hwynt o arian talbenig.

An ox that is worth thirty pence is a kine of standard value.—Kine of *standard value* are those with which an advance is not made of kine-qualifying money. *Welsh Laws.*

Talbenigiad, *s. m.* (talbenig) A regulating to a standard value.

Talbenigiaw, *v. a.* (talbenig) To regulate to a standard value; to become of standard value.

Talbenigrwydd, *s. m.* (talbenig) The state of being of standard value.

Talbenu, *v. a.* (talben) To set a mean price.

Talbren, *s. m.—pl. t.* i (tàl—pren) A front log, or a stock of wood placed behind the fire; the same as *talpentan*.

Talcen, *s. m.—pl. t.* i (tàl—cen) The fore part or end of anything; the forehead; the end, of a building; the head, of a barrel, and the like.

Nid edrych angau pwy decaf ei dalcen.

Death doth not regard who hath the fairest *forehead*. *Adage.*

Gradd pob un yn ei dalcen.

Every one's condition is in his *forehead*. *Adage.*

Talcenawg, *a.* (talcen) Having a fore part or end; having a forehead; ample-fronted.

Talcenawl, *a.* (talcen) Relating to the fore part or end; belonging to the forehead.

Talcenïad, *s. m.* (talcen) A forming a forepart or end; a forming a forehead.

Talcenu, *v. a.* (talcen) To form a fore part or end; to form a forehead; to butt with the forehead. *Talcenu ty*, to raise the gable end of a house; *talcenu baril*, to put in the end of a barrel.

Talch, *s. m.—pl.* teilchion (ta—alch) A piece, a fragment, any thing broken; grist, or coarse meal. *Dyna fo wedi tori yn deilchion man*, there it is broken all to shatters.

Talchaidd, *a.* (talch) Somewhat broken or brayed.

Talchawg, *a.* (talch) Consisting of broken parts.

Talchedig, *a.* (talch) Made into fragments; fracted. *Talchedigion*, broken things.

Talcheiddiad, *s. m.* (talchaidd) A rendering somewhat broken; a rendering half broken.

Talcheiddiaw, *v. a.* (talchaidd) To render somewhat broken; to become partly broken.

Talcheiddrwydd, *s. m.* (talchaidd) A half broken state or condition.

Talchiad, *s. m.—pl. t.* au (talch) A making into fragments; a shattering.

Talchu, *v. a.* (talch) To fract, to break in pieces; to make grit.

Talchwr, *s. m.—pl.* talchwyr (talch—gwr) A man who fracts; a shatterer; one who makes grit.

Talchydd, *s. m.—pl. t.* ion (talch) One who brays; a shatterer; one who makes grit.

Taldal, *a.* (tàl *repeated*) Being front to front.

> A'm dallawdd, be hawdd, bu hy,
> Daldal yn nghongl y deildy.
>
> He that caught me, if easy, was bold, *tete-a-tete* in the corner of the bower. *D. ab Gwilym.*

Talder, *s. m.* (tàl) Loftiness; tallness, stature.

Taldra, *s. m.* (tâl) Loftiness; tallness, stature.

Taldrwch, *s. m.—pl.* taldrychion (tal—trwch) bushiness, of the front; a forelock. *a.* Of front thickness; front-covered. *Gwallt taldrwch*, hair that is thick over the forehead.

Talddrws, *s. m.—pl.* talddrysau (tàl—drws) A front door.

> Penteulu a ddyly eistedd ar y tàl isaf i'r neuadd, ag ei law aswy ar y talddrws.
>
> The patron of the family ought to sit at the lower end of the hall, with his left hand towards the *front door*. *Welsh Laws.*

Taledig, *a.* (tal) Being paid; requited, rewarded.

Taledigaeth, *s. f.—pl. t.* au (taledig) Payment, remuneration.

Taledigawl, *a.* (taledig) In a course to be paid; remunerative.

Taleithiad, *s. m.* (talaeth) A forming a province.

Taleithiaw, *v. a.* (talaeth) To form a province.

> Am lunaw gwr yn mlaen, gynt,
> Iuda lwyth a daleithynt.
>
> For producing a man to lead, of yore, the tribe of Iuda *they formed into a principality.* *S. Brwynawg.*

Taleithiawg, *a.* (talaith) Wearing a diadem. *s. m.* One who wears a princely crown.

> Tri thaleithiawg cad Ynys Prydain; Trystan mab Tallwch, Huall mab Caw, a Chai mab Cynyr Ceinfarchawg; ac un oedd daleithiawg arnaddynt bwyntau ill tri, Bedwyr mab Pedrawg oedd hwnw.
>
> The three *diademed chiefs* of the isle of Britain; Trystan son of Tallwch, Huall son of Caw, and Cai son of Cynyr the Splendid Knight; and one was a *diademed chief* over them three, this was Bedwyr son of Pedrog. *Trioedd.*

Taleithiawl, *a.* (talaeth) Being provincial.

Taleithiedig, *a.* (talaith) Diademed.

Taleithig, *s. f. dim.—pl. t.* ion (talaith) A fillet, a bandlet; a bandlet, in heraldry.

Taleithydd, *s. m.—pl. t.* ion (talaeth) A provincial.

Talfa, *s. f.—pl.* talfëydd (tàl) A front place; a pediment; a projection.

Talfaawg, *a.* (talfa) Having a pediment.

Talfäedig, *a.* (talfa) Pedimented; projected in front.

Talfainc, *s. f.—pl.* talfeinciau (tàl—mainc) A front form; a throne.

> Holl Ffrainc, ei thalfainc, ei thir,
> A'i choron uwch a yrir.
>
> All France, her *throne*, her wide domain,
> And crown, will higher honour gain. *S. Tudyr.*

Talfedel, *s. f.* (tàl—medel) Garden angelica.

Talflodau, *s. pl. aggr.* (tàl—blodau) Festoons.

Talflodeuwaith, *s. m.* (talflodau—gwaith) Festoon-work.

Talflodeuyn, *s. m. dim.* (talflodau) A festoon.

Talfoel, *a.* (tàl—moel) Having a bald front.

Talfoeledig, *a.* (talfoel) Being grown bald-fronted.

Talfoeledd, *s. m.* (talfoel) A bald-fronted state.

Talfoeli, *v. a.* (talfoel) To render bald-fronted; to become bald-fronted; to expose the front.

Talfoeliad, *s. m.* (talfoel) An exposing the front.

Talfoelni, *s. m.* (talfoel) Front-baldness.

Talfrith, *s. m.—pl. t.* ion (tàl—brith) A variegated front. *a.* Of many-coloured front.

> Arwr a dwy ysgwydd y dan
> Ei dalfrith, ag all tuth Prwydan,
> Bu trydar yn aerfre, bu tan,
> Bu ebud waewawr bu baan.
>
> His *painted front* on ample shoulders soars,
> Which marks the hero, swifter in his course
> Than Prwydan, when the sound of war he hears,
> And sees the thick incessant gleams of spears. *Aneurin.*

Talfrithaw, *v. a.* (talfrith) To adorn the front.

Talfrithawg, *a.* (talfrith) Of variegated front.

Talfrithedig, *a.* (talfrith) Front-painted.

Talfrithiad, *s. m.* (talfrith) A variegating the front

Talfriw, *s. m.—pl. t.* au (tàl—briw) A front wound or cut. *a.* Having a cut or bruised front.

> Lle meithlion cein-gairawd rwydd riolle,
> O Ddindywydd yn nyfn-wydd o'n dyfne,
> Ysgwyd rygu rhag tarw trin talfriw fu.
>
> Our faithful band in martial pomp array'd
> Wean'd from Dindywydd's deep and woody glade,
> Clash'd *front-bruis'd* shields before the bull of war.
> *Aneurin.*

Talfriwaw, *v. a.* (talfriw) To cut or hurt the front.

Talfriwedig, *a.* (talfriw) Front-bruised.

Talfriwiad, *s. m.* (talfriw) A cutting the front.

Talfwrdd, *s. m.—pl.* talfyrddau (tàl—bwrdd) The front or upper table in a hall.

Talfyr, *a.* (tàl—byr) Short-fronted, short towards the front; brief, abrupt.

Talfyradwy, *a.* (talfyr) Capable of being foreshortened; recissable.

Talfyredig, *a.* (talfyr) Foreshortened; abridged.

Talfyredigaeth, *s. m.* (talfyredig) The act of foreshortening; abridgment.

Talfyredigawl, *a.* (talfyredig) Tending to foreshorten; abbreviative.

Talfyriad, *s. m.—pl. t.* au (talfyr) A foreshortening; abbreviation; recission.

Talfyru, *v. a.* (talfyr) To foreshorten; to abridge.

Talfyrwr, *s. m.—pl.* talfyrwyr (talfyr—gwr) A foreshortener; an abbreviator.

Talffrwyn, *s. f.—pl. t.* i (tàl—ffrwyn) The front-stall or fillet of a bridle.

Talgainc, *s. f.—pl.* talgeinciau (tàl—cainc) A browantler.

Talgeinciad, *s.* (talgainc) A forming browantlers.

Talgeinciaw, *v. n.* (talgainc) To form browantlers.

Talgeinciawg, *a.* (talgainc) Having browantlers.

Talgell, *s. f.—pl. t.* oedd (tàl—cell) A pantry.

Talgellawg, *a.* (talgell) Having a pantry.

Talgrib, *s. f.—pl. t.* au (tàl—crib) The frontboard that holdes the spindle of a spinning-wheel.

Talgron, *s. f.—pl.* talgrynion (tàl—cron) That is round fronted; an abrupt turn; an inflection.

a. Front-turning; inflective. *Sain dalgron*, an inflective sound, a dipthong: *Talgron gadr*, of strong inflection, as *gwasw*; *talgron ledlf*, of soft inflection, as *hoew*; *talgron fud*, mutely inflective, as *gwyw*; *talgron gota*, of short inflection, as *marw*; *talgron wib*, of transitive inflection, as *gwawd*.

Talgrwn, *s. m.—pl.* talgrynion (tàl—crwn) That is round-fronted; precipitance. *a.* Precipitate, straightway.

Oed a'm ridan——
A wnaethwn yn dalgwrn deg.

An assignation with my love I made
Straightways to meet her in the shelter'd glade.
D. ab Gwilym.

Talgrych, *s. m.—pl. t.* ion (tàl—crych) A rough front; a wrinkled front. *a.* Rough-fronted; frowning. *Dyna genawon talgrychion*, those are rough-headed whelps.

Dirhaid, nid tehaid, talgrych wythiender.

Mischievous, not comely, is *rough fronted* cruelty.
Cusnedyn.

Talgrychedd, *s. m.* (talgrych) Rough-fronted state

Talgrychiad, *s. m.* (talgrych) A ruffling the brow, a frowning.

Talgrychni, *s. m.* (talgrych) Roughness of the forehead.

Talgrychu, *v. a.* (talgrych) To knit the brow.

Talgrychwr, *s. m.* talgrychwyr (talgrych—gwr) One who knits his brows; a frowner.

Talgryf, *s. m.—pl. t.* ion (tàl—cryf) That is hard-fronted. *a.* Hard-fronted; impudent.

Talgryfion a chaled-galon ydynt hwy.

Impudent ones and hard-hearted are they. *Ezekiel* 3. 7.

Talgryfâad, *s. m.* (talgryf) A rendering impudent; a becoming impudent.

Talgryfâu, *v. a.* (talgryf) To render impudent; to have effrontery.

Talgryfder, *s. m.* (talgryf) Effrontery.

Talgrynadwy, *a.* (talgrwn) Capable of inflection; capable of abbreviation.

Talgrynedig, *a.* (talgrwn) Inflected; abridged; precipitate; without hesitation.

Talgrynawl, *a.* (talgrwn) Inflective; precipitate.

Talgryniad, *s. m.—pl. t.* au (talgrwn) A rounding the front; inflection; precipitation.

Talgrynu, *v. a.* (talgrwn) To inflect; to precipitate.

Talgrynrwydd, *s. m.* (talgrwn) Roundness of front; aptness for inflection; promptness.

Gwedi dysgu sail y ffydd—y mae yn dysgu pawb i rodiaw mewn talgrynrwydd cydwybod.

After comprehending the ground-work of faith, every body becomes instructed how to walk in *rectitude* of conscience.
W. Salisbury.

Talgrynydd, *s. m.—pl. t.* ion (talgrwn) An inflector; an abbreviator; that precipitates.

Talgudyn, *s. m.—pl. t.* au (tàl—cudyn) A forelock; a love-lock. *Hardded ei thalgudynau arian*, How beautiful her silver fore-locks.

Talgudynawg, *a.* (talgudyn) Having fore-locks.

Talgwn, *s. m.* (tal—cwn) A high front. *a.* High-fronted.

Talgynawd, *s. m.* (talgwn) Erection of the front.

Ni bu cyfergyriad, ni bu gyanwys
Talgynawd Urien y rhag Powys.

He was not an aggressor, the *uplifted front* of Urien appeared not before Powys.
Taliesin.

Talgynedig, *a.* (talgwn) Being with elated front.

Talgynu, *v. a.* (talgwn) To uplift the front.

Taliad, *s. m.—pl. t.* au (tal) A clearing, discharging, or paying: payment; remuneration.

Taliadawl, *a.* (taliad) Tending to clear, or to pay off; remunerative.

Taliadu, *v. a.* (taliad) To make a clearing or payment; to make a remuneration.

Taliant, *s. m.* (tal) A payment; requital.

Taliator, *ger.* (taliad) In paying; in requiting.

Talitor, *sup.* (tal) To be paying; to be requiting.

Talm, *s. m.—pl. t.* oedd (talym) Any thing that comes on abruptly; an impression; a short space, a while, a good while; a small quantity; a some, or somewhat; much, a surge of any thing in motion; a clap of thunder. *Pa sut yr wyt er ys talm?* How art thou since this good while? *Ni welais i moni er ys lîr dalm o amser*, I have seen nothing of her for this long space of time: *Nid oes dim o dalm arno*, there is not the least impression upon him: *Mwy o dalm*, more by much.

Saith salm i gadw talwr o'n tir.

Seven psalms to keep *scarcity* from our land.
Gr. Hiraethawg.

Nawdd y pengwastrawd yw hyd y parho talm y march cyntaf: Neu, hyd tra parho rhedeg y march buanaf.

The protection of the head groom is whilst the course of the quickest horse shall continue; Or, whilst the run of the fleetest horse continues.
Welsh Laws.

Ond talm gwedi, sef yn y chweched oes, newidiodd eglwys Rufain ei harfer.

But a *short space* after, that is in the sixth age, the church of Rome changed its practice.
C. Edwards, Ff. y Ffydd.

Talmedig, *a.* (talm) Interrupted; broken off; concluded.

Talmedd, *s. m.* (talm) Interruptedness.

Talmeithr, *s. m.* (talm—eithr) That is exempt from interruption. *a.* Uninterrupted.

Talmiad, *s. m.—pl. t.* au (talm) An affecting or coming on suddenly; a cessation.

Talmig, *a.* (talm) Having a course, having a sudden impulse; freakish. *Teuluwr talmig*, a freakish domestic.

Talmu, *v. a.* (talm) To cause to come on abruptly; to be abrupt; to make impression, to move, to work upon; to assign a course or range; to make summary or brief; to draw to a conclusion, to draw to an end; to be at an end. *Wyf yn talmu ar henaint*, I am drawing to an old age: *Wyf ar dalmu*, I am just at an end.

Nid yw yn talmu ar fy nghalon, hyd y dydd heddyw, [illegible]

It is not impressive upon my heart, to the [illegible] have sinned.
[illegible]

Talmus, *a.* (talm) Tending to break off.

Talmyrth, *s. m.* (talm—yrth) That suddenly strikes upon; an impression.

Talogi, *v. a.* (talawg) To render high-fronted; to become high-fronted or bold.

Talogiad, *s. m.* (talawg) A making haughty.

Talogrwydd, *s. m.* (talawg) Haughtiness.

Talon, *s. m.* (tàl) The protuberance of the belly.

Talp, *s. m.—pl. t.* iau (tàl) A mass, a lump, a piece. *Prynu wrth y talp, prynu wrth y llon, prynu yn y crynswth, prynu yn y cyfan*, to buy by the lump, or piece.

Talpen, *s. f. dim.* (talp) A knoll, a knob.

Talpiad, *s. m.* (talp) A making into lumps.

Talpiaw, *v. a.* (talp) To form into lumps.

Talpiawg, *a.* (talp) Being in lumps.

Talpiedig, *a.* (talp) Broken into masses.

Talpentan, *s. m.* (tal—pentan) The fire-back.

Talrwn, *s. m.—pl.* talrynion (tal—grwn) A head ridge in a field, or a headland.

Talryniad, *s. m.* (talrwn) A forming a headland.

Talryniaw, *v. a.* (talrwn) To form a headland in a field.

Talryniawg, *a.* (talrwn) Having a head ridge.

Talu, *v. a.* (tal) To make even or clear, to discharge, or to pay; to requite, to reward; to be worth; to answer a purpose. *Os pryni hwn cei dalu amdano*, if thou buyest this thou shalt pay for it: *Pa á dal hwna?* What is that worth? *Pa beth a dal son am hyny?* What is the use of talking about that?

> Gwael y peth ni thal ei ofyn.
>
> It is a poor thing that *is not worth* asking for. *Adage.*
>
> Y gwlaw a'r hinon a dalant yn gywir y naill i'r llall.
>
> The rain and the fair weather will *repay* equitably the one to the other. *Adage.*
>
> A goreiwo taled i'r crythawr.
>
> He who dances *let him pay* the fiddler. *Adage.*

Talwg, *a.* (tàl—gwg) Toweringly frowning.

> ——Ar bob ty talwg
> Simneiau lle magal mwg.
>
> On all highly-frowning houses chimneys where smoke generates.
> *Iolo Goch i lys O. Glendwr.*

Talwisg, *s. f.—pl. t.* oedd (tàl—gwisg) What is worn on the forehead, a head-dress.

Talwr, *s. m.—pl.* talwyr (tàl—gwr) A person who requites; a payer.

Talwrn, *s. m.—pl.* talyrnau (tàl—gwrn) What projects forward.

Talym, *s. m.—pl.* talmau (tàl) Any thing that comes on abruptly; an impression; a short space, a while; a good while; a small quantity; a some, or somewhat; a range of any thing in motion; a clap of thunder. *Ni buaist yma er ys talm*, thou hast not been here for this good while.

> Oedd cywir ei air erioed;
> Oedd hael talym diwael teledd.
>
> Ever equitable was his word; he was the generous one of a period undebased and splendid. *Prydydd Bychan, m. Bleddyn.*

Tall, *s. m.* (ta—all) A spread out or over.

Tallawg, *a.* (tall) Being spread out or over.

Talliad, *s. m.* (tall) A spreading out or over.

Tallu, *v. a.* (tall) To make a spread out or over.

Tallwch, *s. m.* (tall) The state of being spread.

Tam, *s. m.—pl. t.* ion (ta—am) A stretch over so as to take in; as much as can be bitten off; a morsel, a bite.

> Hoff tam mab ni charer.
>
> Sweet is the *morsel* of a child disliked. *Adage.*
>
> Nid tam o giniaw amaeth.
>
> Not a *morsel* of a ploughman's dinner. *D. ab Gwilym.*

Tama, *s. m.* (tam) Hard food, or that is to be masticated, as bread and flesh; and what is taken with it, as butter and the like, is called *enllyn*.

> Colli——
> Ei thymyr tlawd, a'i thama,
> A'i chaws, drwg yw gnaws a'i gwna.
>
> Losing her poor estate, her *bread*, and her cheese, bad is the condition that is the cause. *Madawg Dwygraig.*

Tamaid, *s. m.—pl.* tameidiau (tam) The quantity taken by a bite, a morsel, a bit, a bite, or mouthful. *Bu raid iddo hel ei damaid*, he was obliged to beg his subsistence: *Yr wyt yn braff dy damaid*, thou goest on with ample bite, or with good appetite: *Hwda damaid*, take a bite: *tamaid y cythraul*, devil's bit scabious.

> Bara ac ymenyn yw un tamaid.
>
> Bread and butter make one *morsel*. *Adage.*

Tameidiad, *s. m.* (tamaid) A forming a morsel; a breaking off a morsel.

Tameidiaw, *v. a.* (tamaid) To break into mouthfuls, to make morsels, to take bites; to bite off a morsel.

Tameidiawl, *a.* (tamaid) Like a mouthful.

Tameidiwr, *s. m.—pl.* tameidiwyr (tamaid—gwr) One who takes a mouthful.

Tameidyn, *s. m. dim.* (tamaid) A little mouthful.

Tamiad, *s. m.* (tam) A forming into bits.

Tamig, *s. m. dim.—pl. t.* ion (tam) A small morsel or bite.

Tamigaw, *v. a.* (tamig) To take a nibbling bite; to nibble; to nib.

Tamigawl, *a.* (tamig) Nibbling; nipping.

Tamigiad, *s. m.—pl. t.* au (tamig) A nibbling.

Tammborth, *s. m.* (tam—porth) Sustenance.

> Neud angeu Ffreuer a'm de heno'
> Am dammborth brodyrdde,
> Dihunaf, wylaf fore!
>
> How the death of Freuer makes me solitary to-night! For the *sustenance* of the community, I will be awake, I will early weep. *Llywarch Hen.*
>
> Neur sylliais i ddinlle Frecon?
> Ffreuer werydre
> Hiraeth am dammborth frodyrdde'
>
> Have not I gazed on the camp plot of Wrecon! The fair patrimony of Freuer regrets the lost *sustenance* of the community. *Llywarch Hen.*

Tamp, *s. m.* (tam) That is pervasive.

Tampawg, *a.* (tamp) A fit of passion or anger.

> Gochel y tampawg tros awr; gochel y gwedwst tros fywyd.
>
> Avoid a *passion fit* for an hour; avoid babbling for ever. *Adage.*

Tampr, *s. m.—pl.* tamprau (tamp) A taper.

> Maeddai hi ef a thampr cwyr, can nid oedd wialen genti, oni tetti ei enaid oheno agaws.
>
> She did beat him with a wax *taper*, not having a stick by her, so that his soul went out of him almost. *Brut. y Saeson.*

Tampriad, *s. m.* (tampr) A forming a taperlight; a burning as a torch.

Tampru, *v. a.* (tampr) To make a taper light; to burn as a torch.

Tamyn, *s. m. dim.* (tam) A small bit or morsel.

Tan, *s. m.—pl. t.* au (ta—an) An expanding principle; a cause of expansion; fire.

> Awen heb ddoethineb, tan yn llaw ffolineb.
>
> Talent without wisdom is a fire in the hand of folly. *Adage.*
>
> Tri pheth sydd ar eu cynnydd: tan, sef goleuni; deall, sef gwirionedd; ac enaid, sef bywyd: a gorfod a wnant ar bob peth, ac yna diwedd abred.
>
> Three things are on their increase: *fire*, which is light; intellect, which is truth; and soul, which is life: and they will overcome all things, and then there will be an end of the inchoative state. *Barddas.*
>
> Tri char-elyn dyn: tan, dwfr, ac arglwydd.
>
> The three cherished foes of man: *fire*, water, and a governor. *Cyfrinach Beirdd.*
>
> Tan y sy gorfforawl; ac ni allai i gyfryw hyny boeni ysbryd.
>
> The *fire* is material; and what is of such a nature could not torment a spirit. *Hanes Gwido.*

Tàn, *s. m.* (ty—an) A spread or expansion; continuity. *a.* Spreading; flat, low; continuous. *prep.* To, till, until, as far; under, beneath, below. *adv.* Along; under. *Tàn yr oes hon*, till this age; *tàn ammod*, under covenant; *y goreu tàn haul*, the best under the sun. A verb, of the infinitive mood, preceded by *tan*, forms a participle. *Dyna hi yn myned tàn ganu*, there she is going singing along.

> Pruddled ni's parodd hi
> Tan ael un tan eleni.
>
> Dejection she has not caused *beneath* one brow until this year. *W. Wyn.*
>
> Ei blwyf, yn gwbl afeg,
> Yw ei lu, dan ei law deg.
>
> His parish, with entire concern, is his host, *under* his fair hand. *L. G. Cothi, i Syr H. ab M. ab Dafydd.*

Tanaf, *pronom. prep.* (tàn) Under me. *Tanad*, under thee; *tano*, under him, or it; *tani*, under

Tangnefedd, *s. m.* (tangnef) A state of celestial expansion; heavenly tranquillity; tranquillity.

> Crist, ti—
> Oen tangnefedd a hoddwch!
>
> Christ, thou Lamb of *heavenly rest and peace*! *Gate y Glyn.*
>
> Crist creawdr—
> Crist cell, colofn tangnefedd.
>
> Christ the Creator, Christ the mysterious one, the pillar of *tranquillity*. *Ll. P. Moch.*

Tangnefeddawl, *a.* (tangnefedd) Tranquillizing.

Tangnefeddiad, *s. m.* (tangnefedd) A tranquillizing; a producing peace.

Tangnefeddu, *v. a.* (tangnefedd) To tranquillize.

Tangnefeddus, *a.* (tangnefedd) Tranquillous. *Heddwch tangnefeddus*, tranquil peace.

Tangnefeddusaw, *v. a.* (tangnefeddus) To render tranquillous; to become tranquillizing.

Tangnefeddusder, *s. m.* (tangnefeddus) Tranquillousness.

Tangnefeddusdra, *s. m.* (tangnefeddus) Tranquillousness.

Tangnefeddusedd, *s. m.* (tangnefeddus) Tranquillousness.

Tangnefeddusiad, *s. m.* (tangnefeddus) A rendering tranquillous; a becoming tranquillous.

Tangnefeddusrwydd, *s. m.* (tangnefeddus) Tranquillousness.

Tangnefeddwr, *s. m.—pl.* tangnefeddwyr (tangnefedd—gwr) A tranquillizer; a peace-maker.

Tangnefiad, *s. m.* (tangnef) A tranquillizing.

Tangnefig, *a.* (tangnef) Tranquillous.

> Gwledig pob tangnefig.
>
> Patriotic is every thing *tranquillous*. *Adage.*

Tangnefoldeb, *s. m.* (tangnefawl) Tranquillousness; a state of peace.

Tangnefolder, *s. m.* (tangnefawl) Tranquillousness; a state of peace.

Tangnefoledd, *s.* (tangnefawl) Tranquillousness.

Tangnefoli, *v. a.* (tangnefawl) To render tranquil; to become tranquil.

Tangnefolrwydd, *s. m.* (tangnefawl) Tranquillousness.

Tangnefu, *v. a.* (tangnef) To tranquillize.

> Amherawdr mor a thir,
> Caffwyf nef, lle tangnefir!
>
> Sovereign of sea and land, may I obtain heaven, where *tranquillity takes place*! *Dafydd y Coed.*

Tangnefus, *a.* (tangnef) Tranquillous.

> Hywel Dda—a lywodraethai yn gydwybodus yn mhob iawnder tangnefus.
>
> Hywel the Good was wont to govern conscientiously in every *tranquillizing* equity. *Car. Llangarfan.*

Tangnefusaw, *v. a.* (tangnefus) To render tranquillous; to become tranquillous.

Tangnefusedd, *s. m.* (tangnefus) Tranquillousness.

Tangnefusiad, *s. m.* (tangnefus) A rendering tranquillous; a becoming tranquillous.

Tangnefusrwydd, *s. m.* (tangnefus) Tranquillousness.

Tangnefwr, *s. m.—pl.* tangnefwyr (tangnef—gwr) A tranquillizer.

Tangnefydd, *s. m.—pl. t.* ion (tangnef) A tranquillizer.

Tangwedd, *s. f.* (tanc—gwedd) A tranquil aspect.

Tangweddawg, *a.* (tangwedd) Of tranquil aspect.

> Ystadl tir Penprys a Gwallawg,
> Teyrn teyrnedd tangweddawg.
>
> The support of the land of Penbrys and Gwallawg, the king of the kings *of tranquil aspect*. *Taliesin.*

Tangweddawl, *a.* (tangwedd) Tranquillous.

Tangweddiad, *s. m.* (tangwedd) A tranquillizing.

Tangweddu, *v. a.* (tangwedd) To tranquillize.

Tangweddus, *a.* (tangwedd) Tranquillous.

Tangwystl, *s. m.—pl.* tangwystlon (tanc—gwystl) A pledge of tranquillity; a hostage of peace. *Tref tangwystl*, a town delivered as a pledge of peace.

> Pan ddyhaler tangwystl yn hir o dir Gwynedd,
> Dybydd seithgantlong o wynt gan wynt gogledd.
>
> When there shall be a long waiting for a *pledge of peace* from the land of Gwynedd, there will be seven hundred ships upon sea with the northern wind. *Myrddin, Hoianau.*

Tangwystlaw, *v. a.* (tangwystl) To give a pledge of tranquillity.

Tangwystliad, *s. m.* (tangwystl) A pledging of peace or tranquillity.

Tangwystlwr, *s. m.—pl.* tangwystlwyr (tangwystl—gwr) One who pledges peace.

Tap, *s. m.—pl. t.* iau (tab) A projecting ledge or shelf; a projecting rock. *Tap esgid*, the heel of a shoe.

Tapiad, *s. m.—pl. t.* au (tap) A shelving, a ledging.

Tapiaw, *v. a.* (tap) To form a step, or ledge.

Tapiawg, *a.* (tap) Abounding with steps, shelves, or ledges; abounding with precipices.

Tapig, *s. m. dim.* (tap) A small step, or ledge.

Taplas, *s. m.—pl. t.* on (tap—llas) A gambol; a dance.

> O gwledycha meddwawg, a chariad y gwreigedd, a seguryd, a thaplas, a gwyddbwyll, colle y glewder ac y nerthoedd.
>
> If drunkenness should reign, and the love of women, and idleness, and dancing, and chessplaying, lost will be the courage and the strength. *Brut. y Breninoedd.*

Taplasa, *v. a.* (taplas) To gambol; to dance.

Taplasawl, *a.* (taplas) Skipping; dancing.

Taplasiad, *s. m.* (taplas) A skipping; a dancing.

Taplasu, *v. a.* (taplas) To gambol; to dance.

Taplaswr, *s. m.—pl.* taplaswyr (taplas—gwr) A person who gambols.

Tapyn, *s. m. dim.—pl. t.* au (tap) A small projection, ledge, or shelf. *Tapyn ffust, tapig ffust*, the capping of a flail.

Tapynu, *v. a.* (tapyn) To form a ledge or shelf.

Tar, *s. m.* (ta—ar) A pervading principle.

Tarad, *s. m.* (tar) A pervasion, a striking through; taste, flavour.

Taradr, *s. m.—pl. t.* on (tarad) That pervades; a ray; a piercer; an auger. *Taradr y coed*, the woodpecker.

> Haul haf—
> Hebrwng trwy wydr terydr tes.
>
> Sun of summer, send through the glass rays of heat. *D. ab Gwilym.*
>
> Taradr perfedd, celndawg a dal.
>
> A medium auger its value is a penny. *Welsh Laws.*

Taradriad, *s. m.* (taradr) A penetrating, a piercing, a boring.

Taradru, *v. a.* (taradr) To penetrate, to pierce; to bore with an auger.

Taradrydd, *s. m.* (taradr) One who bores.

Taran, *s. f.—pl. t.* au (tar) That pervades, impels, or gives a shock; a clap of thunder, a thunder. *Mellt a tharanau*, lightnings and thunders: *Maen taran*, a thunderstone.

> Tan a dwr yn ymwriaw
> Yw taranau dreigiau draw.
>
> Fire and water striving for mastery are the *thunders* of yonder lightnings. *D. ab Gwilym.*
>
> Y march—
> A'i wddf anwar fal taran,
> A'i ffroenau dig fal ffwrn dan.
>
> The horse with neck like *thunder*, brooking no restraint, and his nostrils ardent as a fiery furnace. *Gro. Owain.*

Taran, *a.* (tar) Of goodly size or magnitude.

> Cymerai Gwdion ei hudlath ac y tarawai Gilfaethwy yni fydd yn daran ewig.
>
> Gwdion took his wand of illusion and struck Gilfaethwy, so that he becomes a *well sized* hind. *Mabinogi Math.*

Tanlwyddiad, *s. m.*—*pl.* tanlwyddiaid (tanlwydd) A subject.

> Duw a'ch rhwyddo oll i fod—yn danlwyddiaid ffyddlawn, yn frodyr anegor.
>
> God prosper you all to be faithful *subjects*, to be inseparable brethren. *H. Perri.*

Tanllachar, *a.* (tan—llachar) Fire-gleaming.

Tanllestr, *s. m.*—*pl.* tanllestri (tan—llestr) A lanthorn.

> Rhy bell yw ym ddirprwyaw
> Llatai drud i'w llety draw—
> Na dwyn o'm blaen danllestri,
> Na physt cwyr, pan fo hwyr hi.
>
> Too far is it for me to commission an audacious messenger to her lodging yonder; nor to have born before me *lamps* nor tapers of wax, when it happens to be late. *D. ab Gwilym.*

Tanlli, *s. m.* (tan—lli) A fire glow. *a.* Ignifluous; span new.

> Cyllell—
> Tanlli galleotr dur-restr don
> Ufyl wrych efail wreichion.
>
> A knife *span new*, steel-rayed striking from the flint spirting fire like sparks of a forge. *Rhys Goch Eryri.*

Tanlliw, *s. m.* (tan—lliw) Flame-colour. *a.* Of flame-colour; bran new.

Tanllwynawg, *s. m.* (tan—llwynawg) Alopecia.

Tanllwyth, *s. m.*—*pl. t.* i (tan—llwyth) A great blazing fire.

Tanllyd, *a.* (tan) Fiery, full of fire.

Tanllydrwydd, *s. m.* (tanllyd) Fieriness.

Tanllydu, *v. a.* (tanllyd) To render fiery; to grow fiery.

Tannawg, *a.* (tant) Having sudden starts, or flights

Tanniad, *s. m.* (tant) A stretching; a starting; a causing a sudden impulse; a throbbing.

Tannorth, *s. m.* (tan—dorth) An overspreading; a substitute.

> Pan ddyfe y Mab Rhad oedd raid wrtho,
> Er porth, yn dannorth a dawn arno.
>
> When the Son of Grace did come, there was a necessity for him, as a help, as a *substitute* endowed with virtue. *D. Benfras.*

Tannu, *v. a.* (tant) To stretch; to start, to give a sudden impulse; to throb, to ache; to stretch a string.

Tano, *prep.* (tàn) Below, beneath.

Tano, *pronom. prep.* (tàn) Under it, under him.

Tanoedd, *prep.* (tàn) Under, beneath, below.

Tanogan, *s. m.*—*pl. t.* au (tan—gogan) Pyromancy.

Tanoganawl, *a.* (tanogan) Belonging to pyromancy.

Tanoganiad, *s. m.* (tanogan) A divining by fire.

Tanoganu, *v. a.* (tanogan) To divine by fire.

Tanradd, *s. f.*—*pl. t.* au (tàn—gradd) An inferior rank.

Tanre, *s. f.* (tan—rhe) A fire course. *a.* Pervaded by fire.

Tanrew, *s. m.* (tan—rhew) A nipping frost.

Tànrif, *s. m.*—*pl. t.* ion (tàn—rhif) An inferior number.

Tànryw, *s. m.*—*pl. t.* iau (tàn—rhyw) An inferior kind.

Tansang, *s. f.*—*pl. t.* au (tàn—sang) An undertread.

Tansangawl, *a.* (tansang) Subpedaneous.

Tansangiad, *s. m.*—*pl. t.* au (tansang) An undertreading.

Tansangu, *v. a.* (tansang) To under-tread.

Tansawdd, *s. m.*—*pl.* tansoddion (tàn—sawdd) Submersion.

Tansoddawl, *a.* (tansawdd) Submersing.

Tansoddi, *v. a.* (tansawdd) To submerge.

Tansoddiad, *s. m.* (tansawdd) A submersion.

Tanswydd, *s. f.*—*pl. t.* au (tàn—swydd) An inferior office.

Tanswyddawg, *a.* (tanswydd) Subaltern. *s. m.* A subaltern; a subdelegate.

Tanswyddiad, *s. m.* (tanswydd) A subdelegation.

Tant, *s. m.*—*pl.* tannau (tan) A stretch, or distension; a sudden start, or impulse; a spasm, a throb, or agony; a gust of passion, flight, or whim; what is stretched; a string; a string of a musical instrument. *Rhyfedd yw dy dannau di*, thou hast strange whims; *tannau o lawenydd*, sudden fits of joy; *tannau gwyllion*, wild fits; *tannau poethion*, violent passions; *tannau dolur*, the prickings or agonies of a sore; *tannau yr ewinrew*, the sharp pains occasioned by being frost-bitten: *Tant telyn*, a harp string; *tant rhwyd*, a net-line.

Tantawr, *s. m.*—*pl.* tantorion (tant) A player on a stringed instrument; a musician.

> Nerth tantawr yn ei fys;
> Nerth llwrf ei droed hyfrys.
>
> The power of the musician is in his finger; the power of the timid is in his nimble foot. *Catwg ab Gwynlliw.*

Tantiad, *s. m.* (tant) A stretching, or tightening; a starting; a taking a sudden fit; a throbbing; a stringing.

Tantiaw, *v. a.* (tant) To stretch, to tighten; to start, to cause a sudden impulse; to take a fit; to produce a spasm; to throb; to string.

Tanu, *v. a.* (tàn) To spread, to scatter.

Tanu, *v. a.* (tan) To fire, to set on fire.

> Hawdd tanu crinwellt.
>
> It is easy *to fire* parched grass. *Adage.*
>
> Hawdd tanu eithin crinion, nid hawdd eu diffawdd.
>
> It is easy *to fire* parched furze, it is not easy to extinguish them. *Adage.*

Tanwaith, *s. m.* (tan—gwaith) Fire-work.

Tanwr, *s. m.*—*pl.* tanwyr (tan—gwr) A fire-man; a fuel-man.

Tànwr, *s. m.*—*pl.* tànwyr (tàn—gwr) A spreader.

Tanwyd, *s. m.* (tan—gwyd) A breaking out of fire.

Tanwydyn, *s. m.* (tanwyd) A fiery meteor.

> Mal rhod tanwydyn tros elfydd,
> Mal ton teithiawg Llwyfenydd.
>
> Like an orb of kindling meteor over the humid plain, like the bursting wave is he who justly sways Llwyfenydd. *Taliesin.*

Tanwydr, *s. m.*—*pl.* tanwydrau (tan—gwydr) A burning-glass.

Tanwydd, *s. m.* (tan—gwydd) Fire-wood.

Tanysgrif, *s. f.* (tàn—ysgrif) A subscription.

Tanysgrifaw, *v. a.* (tanysgrif) To underwrite.

Tanysgrifiad, *s. m.*—*pl. t.* au (tanysgrif) An underwriting.

Tangnef, *s. m.* (tanc—nef) Celestial expansion; tranquillity, peace.

> Aed lle mae'r eang dangnef;
> Ac aed y gerdd gydag ef!
>
> May he go to where there is extensive *tranquillity*; and with him go the song! *Iolo Goch, m. D. ab Gwilym.*
>
> Tair cludawd addwyn Ynys Prydain: cyntaf oedd cenedl y Cymmry, a ddoynt gyda Hu Gadarn i Ynys Prydain, sef ni fynai efe wlad a thiroedd o ymladd ac ymlid, eithr o gyfiawnder ac yn nhangnef; ail oedd al y Lloegrwys, a ddoynt o dir Gwasgwyn, ac a hanoeddynt o brif genedl y Cymmry; trydydd oeddynt y Brython, ac o dir Llydaw y daethynt, ac on hanoe o gynefin al y Cymmry.
>
> The three beneficent tribes of the Isle of Britain: the first was the nation of the Cymmry who came with Hu the Mighty to the Isle of Britain, who would not possess nor country nor lands through fighting and persecution, but of equity and in *peace*, the second was the stock of the Lloegrians, who came from the land of Gwasgwyn, and were descended from the primitive nation of the Cymmry; the third were the Brython, and from the land of Llydaw they came, having their descent from the primary stock of the Cymmry. *Trioedd.*

Tangnefawl, *a.* (tangnef) Tranquillous.

Taranad, *s. m.* (taran) A thundering, fulmination.

Taranadu, *v. a.* (taran) To make a thundering or fulmination.

Taranawg, *a.* (taran) Charged with thunder.

Taranawl, *a.* (taran) Fulminant, thundering.

Tarandrwst, *s. m.* (taran—trwst) A thunder-rumbling. *a.* Thunder-rumbling.

> Homer—
> Daw, a'i farn darandrwst,
> I gad—
>
> Homer will repair, with his *thunder-rumbling* taste, to maintain the battle. *Gro. Owain.*

Tarandwrf, *s. m.* (taran—twrf) A thunder-tumult; a thunderstorm. *a.* Thunder-dinning.

Taraniad, *s. m.—pl. t.* au (taran) Intonation, fulmination; a thundering.

Taranoldeb, *s. m.* (taranawl) A fulminatory state.

Taranolder, *s. m.* (taranawl) A fulminant state.

Taranoli, *v. a.* (taranawl) To render fulminant; to become fulminant.

Taranolrwydd, *s. m.* (taranawl) A fulminant state.

Taranon, *s. m.* (taran) That is pervasive; that is impulsive, or apt to produce a shock; a thunderer.

Taranu, *v. a.* (taran) To fulminate; to thunder. *Ofni pan darano*, thou wilt fear when it thunders.

> Pindar—
> A'i luoedd o'i gylchoedd gant
> Hyd trinoedd y taranant.
>
> Pindar with his hosts about him in hundred bands, *they will thunder* through the wars. *Gro. Owain.*

Taranus, *a.* (taran) Fulminant, thunderous.

> Mi af—
> Lle ni wypo neb fy hynt,
> Ar agwedd gwynt taranus.
>
> I will go where no one may know my course, just like the *thundering* wind. *Gafalus.*

Taranwlaw, *s. m.* (taran—gwlaw) A thunder-shower.

Taranwr, *s. m.—pl.* taranwyr (taran—gwr) A thunderer.

> Ni threchai neb ond y Taranwr hollalluawg fy nerth.
>
> No one but the almighty *Thunderer* would overcome my power. *Elis Wyn, B. Cwsg.*

Taranydd, *s. m.—pl. t.* ion (taran) A thunderer.

Taraw, *s. m.* (tar) A shock, a collision, a stroke; an effect or impression; a hit. *Nid oes arni fawr o daraw*, she is under no great hardship: *Ti elli hyny heb daraw yn y byd*, thou canst do so without any trouble in the world.

> O dair ffordd y sarhëir pob dyn yn y byd: o daraw, a gosawd, a dwyn trais arno.
>
> By three means may every person in the world be insulted: by *striking*, and attacking, and by forcing from him. *Welsh Laws.*
>
> O bai ar Siasper daro,
> Trwy fil y tarawai fo.
>
> If any *difficulty* should be on Jasper, through a thousand would *he strike*. *L. G. Cothi.*

Taraw, *v. a.* (tar) To produce a shock, or collision; to strike, to hit; to affect. *Taraw â ffon*, to strike with a stick: *Tarewais wrthi o ddamwain*, I met her by chance: *Taraw dy glun i lawr*, seat thyself down.

> Meddyg a ddyly, pan darawer dyn ar ei ben, o bob asgwrn uch creuan bedair ceiniawg gota; asgwrn is creuan pedair ceiniawg cyfraith.
>
> A doctor should have, when a person *shall be struck* on the head, for every bone on the skull region four curtailed pence; a bone below the cranium four pence in law. *Welsh Laws.*

Tarawd, *s. m.* (tar) A pervasion; impulsion.

Tarawiad, *s. m.—pl. t.* au (taraw) A collision.

Tarawwr, *s. m.—pl.* tarawwyr (taraw—gwr) A striker, or one who gives a stroke.

Tarawydd, *s. m.—pl. t.* ion (taraw) A striker.

Tardd, *s. m.—pl. t.* ion (tar) A state of breaking through, issuing, or proceeding from; an issue, or vent, a bubbling, flow, or spring; a budding, or sprouting.

> Tri pheth tardd o'r tri un cyntefig: pob bywyd, pob daioni, a phob gallu.
>
> There are three things the *effect* of the three primeval unities: all of life, all of good, and all of power. *Barddas.*

Tarddawg, *a.* (tardd) Having an issue or spring.

Tarddawl, *a.* (tardd) Issuing; springing.

> Rhag oaran Cynan tan tarddawl;
> Cadwaladr a'i cwyn.
>
> Before the front of Cynan there was the *issuing* fire; Cadwaladr mourns it. *Taliesin.*

Tarddadwy, *a.* (tardd) Capable of breaking out, issuing, or springing.

Tarddain, *v. a.* (tardd) To break out, to ooze.

Tarddedig, *a.* (tardd) Being sprung; being made to break out, or to appear; derived.

Tarddedigaeth, *s. m.* (tarddedig) The act of breaking through, issuing, or springing.

Tarddell, *s. f. dim.—pl. t.* i (tardd) An issue, a spring

Tarddelliad, *s. m.* (tarddell) A running out, or springing. *Tarddelliad gwaed*, a hemorrhage.

Tarddellu, *v. a.* (tarddell) To issue, to spring, or to run out; to bubble out.

Tardden, *s. f.—pl. t.* i (tardd) The orifice of any efflux or issue; the mouth of a spring.

Tarddiad, *s. m.—pl. t.* au (tardd) A pervasion; a breaking out, emanation, effusion, or eruption, an issuing; a derivation; a proceeding; a springing; a spouting; a budding.

Tarddiadawl, *a.* (tarddiad) Effluent, effusive, efflorescent.

Tarddiadu, *v. a.* (tarddiad) To cause an effusion or springing; to become effusive.

Tarddiannawl, *a.* (tarddiant) Pervasive; eruptive; tending to issue; derivative.

Tarddiannu, *v. a.* (tarddiant) To render pervasive or eruptive; to become a spring.

Tarddiannus, *a.* (tarddiant) Tending to cause an effusion or breaking out.

Tarddiannusaw, *v. a.* (tarddiannus) To render effusive; to become of a springing tendency.

Tarddiannusrwydd, *s. m.* (tarddiannus) Effusiveness, a tendency to break out.

Tarddiant, *s. m.—pl.* tarddiannau (tardd) An issuing, or proceeding; an emanation.

Tarddoldeb, *s. m.* (tarddawl) Effusiveness; a state of springing or breaking out.

Tarddolder, *s. m.* (tarddawl) A state of breaking out, springing, or effusion.

Tarddoldra, *s. m.* (tarddawl) Effusiveness.

Tarddoli, *v. a.* (tarddawl) To render effusive; a breaking out; to become effusive.

Tarddu, *v. a.* (tardd) To pervade; to cause to break out; to break out, to issue, to proceed, to emanate; to spring, to bud, to sprout. *Dacw y wawr yn tarddu*, yonder see the dawn appearing.

Tarddus, *a.* (tardd) Tending to break out.

Tarddusaw, *v. a.* (tarddus) To render effusive; to become of a tendency to break out.

Tarddusedd, *s. m.* (tarddus) Aptness to break out.

Tarddwraint, *s. m.* (tardd—gwraint) A tetter.

Tarddwreinnen, *s. f. dim.* (tarddwraint) A ringworm, or tetter; also called *tarwden*, *tarwyden*, and *taroden*. *Sil.*

Tarddwreinnyn, *s. m. dim.* (tarddwraint) A tetter

Tared, *s. m.* (tar) That is uttered; noise, clamour.

> Bei cyman cain dared wedi cyffraw cad.
>
> Consonant was the joyous *clamour* after the agitation of battle. *Aneurin.*

Taredd, *s. m.* (tar) A tendency to pervade.

Tarell, *s. f. dim.* (tar) An issue, or a spring.

Taren, *s. f.—pl. t.* i (tar) What breaks through or shoots out; a spot; a tump, or knoll; a spot of wild land, overgrown with furze. *Taren o dir*, a spot of ground. *Taren hwyr*, rather late. *Dyfed.*

> Bu mewn hir garchar y gan Owain, mewn diffeithwch a thareni.
> He was in long confinement under Owain, in wilds and brakes. *Brut. W. Llyn.*

Tarenawg, *a.* (taren) Abounding with excrescences, tumps, or knolls.

Tarenawl, *a.* (taren) Tending to grow out.

Tareniad, *s. m.* (taren) A growing out; a forming a tump or knoll.

Tarenig, *s. f. dim.* (taren) A small tump.

Tarenu, *v. n.* (taren) To form a tump.

Tarf, *s. m.—pl. t.* oedd (tar) A violent throw out, or expulsion; a sudden drive; a scattering; a scaring; dispersion; flight.

> Rhys rwy anaw,
> Gwanai drwy gorf,
> A barf ar farf,
> Ac Eingl ar darf,
> Godwrf gitiaw.

> Rhys the theme of the muse, he would break through a ring, with beard on beard, and Angles on *flight*, avoiding the rising storm. *Seisyll Bryf-fwrch.*

Tarfaidd, *a.* (tarf) Tending to scatter; scaring.

Tarfawg, *a.* (tarf) Being driven; scared.

Tarfawl, *a.* (tarf) Expulsive, scaring.

Tarfedig, *a.* (tarf) Expelled, dispelled, chased, driven away, put to flight; scared.

Tarfgryd, *s. m.* (tarf—cryd) The common feverfew; also called *amranwen*.

Tarfhutan, *s. m.—pl. t.* od (tarf—hutan) A scarecrow.

Tarfiad, *s. m.* (tarf) A violently driving out, dispersing, or expelling; a scaring.

Tarfiadu, *v. a.* (tarfiad) To cause a dispersion; to cause a scaring.

Tarfle, *s. m.—pl. t.* oedd (tarf—lle) A place of flight. *Tarfle Saeson*, the Saxons' place of flight.

Tarflyd, *a.* (tarf) Easily scared; skittish.

Tarflydrwydd, *s. m.* (tarflyd) Aptness to scare.

Tarfu, *v. a.* (tarf) To expel; to chase; to put to flight; to scare. *Twrf a darf ar awen*, tumult will dismay the muse.

> Llais dalen yn y gwynt a darf gydwybod euawg.
> The rustling of a leaf in the wind scares a guilty conscience. *Adage.*

Tarfus, *a.* (tarf) Expulsive; tending to scare.

Tarfusaw, *v. a.* (tarfus) To render expulsive; to become dismayed.

Tarfusdra, *s. m.* (tarfus) A state of dismay.

Tarfwgan, *s. f.* (tarf—gwgan) Perforated St. John's wort.

Tarfwr, *s. m.—pl.* tarfwyr (tarf—gwr) A putter to flight; a scarer.

Tarfydd, *s. m.—pl. t.* ion (tarf) That puts to flight; a scarer.

Targ, *s. m.* (tar) A percussion; a clash.

Targed, *s. f.—pl. t.* i (targ) A target.

Tariad, *s. m.* (tar) A striking against, a collision; a stopping; a staying, a tarrying.

Tarian, *s. f.—pl. t.* au (tar) A clasher; a shield; defence. *Lluch a tharian*, lightning and thunder. *Casnodyn.*

> Goreu tarian cyfiawnder.
> The best *shield* is righteousness. *Adage.*
> Car dy gymydawg, ond na ro iddo na'th gledd na'th darian.
> Love thy neighbour, but give him not thy sword nor thy *shield*. *Adage.*
> Nid amddiffyn ond tarian.
> The only defence is a *shield*. *Adage.*

Tariana, *v. a.* (tarian) To clash a shield; to make use of a shield.

Tarianad, *s. m.* (tarian) The using a shield.

Tarianaidd, *a.* (tarian) Like a shield.

Tarianawg, *a.* (tarian) Having a shield.

> Asswynaf nawdd hawdd haelon Dinefwrth,
> Dinefwrth cerddorion,
> A'th dorf o'th darianogion,
> A'th dorf o'th deyrn-[illegible].

> I will secure the ready protection of the [illegible] of South Wales, the sure support of minstrels, and thy host of shield-bearing men, and thy throng of princely ones. *Cynddelw, i Rys ab Gruffudd.*

Tarianedig, *a.* (tarian) Being shielded.

Tarianedigaeth, *s. m.* (tarianedig) The act of shielding.

Tarianu, *v. a.* (tarian) To shield, to use a shield.

Tarianwr, *s. m.—pl.* tarianwyr (tarian—gwr) One who makes use of a shield.

Tarianydd, *s. m.—pl. t.* ion (tarian) A shielder.

Tariaw, *v. a.* (tar) To strike against, to come in contact; to stop; to stay, to tarry.

Tarlais, *s. m.—pl.* tarleisiau (tar—llais) A piercing noise.

Tarleisiad, *s. m.* (tarlais) A making a sharp noise.

Tarleisiaw, *v. a.* (tarlais) To make a clashing noise.

Tarleisiawg, *a.* (tarlais) Having a harsh noise.

Tarleisiawl, *a.* (tarlais) Yielding a harsh noise.

Tarleisiwr, *s. m.—pl.* tarleiswyr (tarlais—gwr) One who makes a harsh noise.

Tarlwnc, *s. m.* (tar—llwnc) An eructation.

Tarlwng, *s. m.* (tar—llwng) An eructation.

Tarlynciad, *s. m.* (tarlwnc) A belching.

Tarlyncu, *v. a.* (tarlwnc) To belch, to eructate.

Tarn, *s. m.—pl. t.* au (tar) A wipe, the act of wiping up any liquid, or absorbing.

Tarnawl, *a.* (tarn) Absorbent, drying.

Tarnedig, *a.* (tarn) Absorbed, dried up.

Tarniad, *s. m.* (tarn) An absorption.

Tarnu, *v. a.* (tarn) To absorb, to dry up.

> Peirian faban, tarn dy ddagrau.
> Commanding prince, *wipe* thy tears. *[illegible]*

> Llywarch hen, na fydd di wyl,
> Trwyddedd a gefi di aswyl:
> Tarn dy lygaid, taw nag wyl.

> Old Llywarch, be thou not abashed, [illegible] thou shalt have: wipe thine eyes, be silent and weep not. *Llywarch Hen.*

Taroden, *s. f. dim.* (tarawd) A tetter.

Tarodwll, *s. m.—pl.* tarodyllau (tarawd—twll) A punch-hole.

Tarth, *s. m.—pl. t.* oedd (tar) Vapour, exhalation.

> Golaith dy esgarant amgant dy fro,
> Mal tan twym tarth yn yd fo.

> The slaughter of the foes about the borders of thy country, [illegible] fire it heats a vapour where it happens to be. *[illegible]*

Tarthadwy, *a.* (tarth) Capable of evaporating.

Tarthain, *v. a.* (tarth) To cause a continual exhalation; to puff out the breath.

Tarthawg, *a.* (tarth) Abounding with vapour.

Tarthawl, *a.* (tarth) Vaporous; foggy.

Tarthedig, *a.* (tarth) Being evaporated.

Tarthedigaeth, *s. m.* (tarthedig) Vaporation.

Tarthiad, *s. m.* (tarth) Evaporation, exhalation.

Tarthlyd, *a.* (tarth) Apt to be vaporous; foggy.

Tarthlydrwydd, *s. m.* (tarthlyd) Fogginess.

Tarthu, *v. a.* (tarth) To exhale, to rise in vapour.

Tarthus, *a.* (tarth) Vaporiferous; hazy.

Tarthusaw, *v. a.* (tarthus) To render vaporiferous; to become vaporiferous.

Tarthusdra, *s. m.* (tarthus) Vaporiferousness.

Tarthusedd, *s. m.* (tarthus) Vaporiferousness.

Tarthusrwydd, *s. m.* (tarthus) Vaporiferousness.

Tarw, *s. m.—pl.* teirw (tar) That strikes against; a bull. *Tarw trefgordd*, a bull kept by a township; *tarw trin*, *tarw cad*, *tarw byddin*, a bull of conflict, bull of battle, bull of armies.

Nerth tarw yn ei ddwyfron.

The strength of a *bull* is in his breast. *Adage.*

Gwerth tarw trefgordd yw tarw arall, a allo lamu, a bewch o'i flaen ac arall yn ei ol.

The value of a township *bull* is another *bull*, which can leap, with a cow before him and another after him. *Welsh Laws.*

Tri tharw cad Ynys Prydain: Cynfawr Cad Cadawg mab Cynwyd Cynwydion, Gwenddolau mab Ceidiaw, ac Urien ab Cynfarch.

The three *bulls* of conflict of the Isle of Britain: Cynvawr Cad Cadawg son of Cynwyd Cynwydion, Gwenddolau son of Ceidiaw, and Urien son of Cynvarch. *Trioedd.*

Tarwain, *s. m.* (tar—gwain) A spout, a gush; a flutter. *v. a.* To spout; to be spouting, to gush; to flutter.

Gwelais i gelain fain a brain ar gnawd,
Ac arall ar darwain gwall grain cleddyfawd.

I beheld a delicate corpse with crows feeding on flesh, and another on a *flutter* from the fell wound of a sword stroke. *Golyddan, dar. Cadwaladr.*

Gwaedlaw ar darwedd, gwaed ar darwain.

A blood-hand at work, blood in a *state of spouting*. *Cynddelw.*

Tarwedd, *s. m.* (tar—gwedd) The state of being pervaded; a ferment.

Tarw y rhisg hwnw, yn ddogn rhwng dwylaw, a'i ddodi ar darwedd mewn llestr i suraw, a'i fragodi a llaeth geifr.

Put that bark in a bundle between both hands, and place it in a *steep* in a vessel to sour, then breaking it with goat's milk. *Meddygon Myddfai.*

Ac odduch gwadnau gwaed ar darwedd.

And above the soles of the feet blood on a *ferment*. *Llygad Gwr.*

Ni dderfydd awen i ar darwedd traul.

Genius will not be exhausted from the *operation* of wear. *Ph. Brydydd.*

Tarweddadwy, *a.* (tarwedd) Fermentable.
Tarweddawg, *a.* (tarwedd) Having a ferment.
Tarweddawl, *a.* (tarwedd) Fermentarious.
Tarweddedig, *a.* (tarwedd) Fermented.
Tarweddiad, *s. m.* (tarwedd) Fermentation.
Tarweddu, *v. a.* (tarwedd) To put in a state of pervasion; to ferment.
Tarweddus, *a.* (tarwedd) Fermentative.
Tarwgi, *s. m.—pl. t.* on (tarw—ci) A bull-dog.
Tarwhaid, *s. f.—pl.* tarwheidiau (tarw—haid) The bull swarm, the second swarm of bees that leaves the hive.
Tas, *s. m.—pl. t.* au (ta—as) That hems in, combines, or binds together; fascia; a band.
Tasawl, *a.* (tas) Tending to combine.
Tasedd, *s. m.* (tas) A combined state.
Tasel, *s. m.—pl. t.* i (tas) A bandage; a sash; a fringe; a tassel.
Taselawg, *a.* (tasel) Sashed; fringed; tasselled.
Taseliad, *s. m.* (tasel) A sashing; a fringing; a tasselling.
Taselu, *v. a.* (tasel) To sash; to fringe; to tassel.
Tasg, *s. f.—pl. t.* oedd (tas) That is set aside, that is fixed; a bond, a pledge; that is settled, or agreed, as to be done; a job, a piece of work; a task. *Medi ar dasg*, to reap by the piece; *gweithiaw ar dasg*, to work by the job; *a roi di dasg i mi?* wilt thou give me a job?

Haws genyd, trwy naws cynnydd,
Ar dasg, bob amser o'r dydd,
Pigaw gwenith.——

More ready art thou, with increasing avidity, on *task* every hour of the day, to pick up wheat. *D. ab Gwilym, i'r frân.*

Tasgawl, *a.* (tasg) Tending to bind, being fixed, rated, or set as a job; starting, springing.
Tasged, *s. f.* (tasg) That is tense or strict.
Tasgedig, *a.* (tasg) Bound, settled, or fixed to be done; set as a task, or job.

Tasgell, *s. f. dim.—pl. t.* i (tasg) A bandlet, a band, what fastens or confines; a bunch, a whisk; a handful; also a closet, or pantry. *tesgyll o flodau*, bunches of flowers; *tasgell o wellt*, *tusw o wellt*, a whisk of straw; *tasgell clo*, the spring of a lock.

——Tusw gwyrdd,
Tesgyll yn sefyll yn sofl.

A green whisk, *bunches* standing like stubble. *D. ab Gwilym, i Fedwen.*

Tasgellawg, *a.* (tasgell) Being in bundles.
Tasgelliad, *s. m.* (tasgell) A tying, a forming into a bunch or whisk.
Tasgellu, *v. a.* (tasgell) To tie, to form into a small bundle, to form a whisk.
Tasgiad, *s. m.* (tasg) A binding, a settling to be done, a rating; a setting a job or task.
Tasgu, *v. a.* (tasg) To set, settle, assign, or fix; to rate; to job; to task; also to spring, to rebound, to start, or to leap back; to cause to start; to urge. *Na thasga arni*, do not urge her to do much. *Tan yn tasgu o bedolau march*, fire striking from the shoes of the horse. *Dyf.*

Llew glew glaifwym, grym gryd flamychus;
Llorf corf cad, ceiniad canon dasgu.

A courageous lion with keen blade, of gleaming energy in the conflict; the pillar of the centre of battle, assigning a task to the composer of song. *G. ab M. ab Dafydd.*

Tasgwr, *s. m.—pl.* tasgwyr (tasg—gwr) One who assigns a task.
Tasgydd, *s. m.—pl. t.* ion (tasg) A tasker.
Tasiad, *s. m.* (tas) A tying or combining together.
Tasiaw, *v. a.* (tas) To tie together, to combine.
Tau, *s. m.* (ta) A stretch, a reach; the state of being at rest; the state of being held or possessed. *v. a.* To stretch out, to extend; to become still, or silent.
Tau, *pron.* (ta) Thine. It is used after a noun in the genitive case; as *y tad tau*, the father thine.

Gwartheg arall yn adnau,
Pan fo cuweccaf ni bydd tau.

The cattle of another in pledge, when it shall be most fair they will not be *thine*. *Adage.*

Taw, *s. m.* (ta) The state of being spread or extended; rest, quiet; silence. *a.* Still; silent. *Gyru taw ar un*, to urge silence upon one; *gyru daw arno*, make him to be silent; *awr daw*, a silent hour.

Teyrn tud anaw,
Yw mau i gwynaw,
Oni fwyf y dydd taw.

The sovereign of the region of harmony, it is my lot to mourn him, until I shall be at the day of *silence*. *Taliesin, Gorchan Cynfelyn.*

Beloch fydd daw.

Mischief will be *silent*. *Adage.*

Goreu taw taw tewi.

The best *silence* the *silence* of silencing. *Adage.*

Taw, *conj.* (ta) That. It is used in *Gwent* and *Dyfed*, synonymously with *mai*. *Clywais taw e oedd*, I have heard that it was him; *gwedir taw celwydd yw*, it is said that it is a falsehood.

Pan wybu taw o gyfoeth Herod yr hanoedd, ef ei danfones at Herod.

When he knew *that* of the dominion of Herod he was descended, he sent him to Herod. *W. Salesbury.*

Tawch, *s. m.—pl. t.* ion (taw) That rises, or stretches over; vapour, exhalation, steam, damp, haze, fog. *a.* Humid, hazy, foggy. *Mor tawch*, a hazy sea; also the name of the German Ocean. *Clych tawch*, bubbles.

Y llong——
Lladd bellbell y'th gymbellir
Lle mae tawch, lle amwlau tir.

Thou ship, to cut farther and farther thou wilt be impelled, where there is a *haze*, where land is imagined. *Morys ab Llywelyn.*

Cawn dywydd cain-dawel,
Nid tawch a gwynt uchel.

We shall have weather fairly-serene, not an *overcast* with high wind. *D. Williams.*

Ni wys heddyw na suddir;
Och, roi mor tawch rho'm a'r tir!

It is not known to-day but we may sink; woe that a *hazy* sea is placed between us and the land! *T. Aled.*

Dwr a wylais——
Dafnau tawch, wedi f'un tad!

Tears I have wept, *thick* drops, after my only father. *L. Morganwg.*

Tawchlyd, *a.* (tawch) Vaporous, hazy; sultry.

Tawd, *s. m.* (taw) A spread, a distension.

Tawdd, *s. m.*—*pl.* toddion (taw) What is in a dissolved state; a melting. *a.* Melted. *Toddion*, drippings, as of meat that is roasting: *Delw dawdd*, a molten image.

Tawddgyrch, *s. m.* (tawdd—cyrch) That is meltingly recurrent; a term in prosody.

Tawddleddf, *a* (tawdd—lleddf) Meltingly-pliant; a term in prosody.

Tawddlestr, *s. m.* (tawdd—llestr) A melting-pot.

Tawed, *s. m.* (taw) A state of silence.

Tawedawg, *a.* (tawed) Tacit, silent, reserved.

Tawedawg, tew ei ddrwg.

The *reserved* is full of mischief. *Adage.*

Nid tawedawg ond goddefus;
Nid goddefus ond synwyrawl.

No one is *silent* but the patient; no one is patient but the sensible. *Adage.*

Tawedig, *a.* (taw) Silenced, being hushed.

Tawedogrwydd, *s. m.* (tawedawg) Taciturnity.

Gorea o gampau doethineb tawedogrwydd.

The best of the feats of wisdom is *taciturnity*. *Adage.*

Tawedwst, *a.* (tawed—gwst) Murmuring.

Tawel, *a.* (taw—el) Calm, tranquil, serene, gentle; silent. *Dyn tawel*, a tacit person. *Taweled yw yr hin!* How serene the weather is!

Tawel awel, tu hirglyw:
Odid a fo moledyw,
Nam Urien, can nid yw!

Gently-breathing gale, wistfully art thou heard: scarcely is there one meriting fame, after Urien, since he is not! *Llywarch Hen.*

Tros y rhiw tores yr haul
Wen bore wyneb araul;
Mae'n deg min dydd,
Tawel tywydd.

Over the brow of the hill the sun has spread the morning smile of cheering countenance; fair is the verge of day, *serene* the weather. *Gro. Owain.*

Tawelaidd, *a.* (tawel) Calm in a small degree.

Tawelawg, *a.* (tawel) Abounding with calmness.

Taweldra, *s. m.* (tawel) Calmness; serenity.

Taweledig, *a.* (tawel) Calmed, tranquillized.

Taweledigaeth, *s. m.* (taweledig) The state of being made calm or serene.

Taweledd, *s. m.* (tawel) Calmness, serenity.

Taweli, *s. m.* (tawel) A calm or still state.

Taweliad, *s. m.* (tawel) A calming, a stilling.

Taweliannawl, *a.* (taweliant) Tranquillous.

Tawelianmu, *v. a.* (taweliant) To produce calmness; to become a calm.

Taweliannus, *a.* (taweliant) Tranquillous.

Taweliant, *s. m.* (tawel) A making serene.

Tawelin, *a.* (tawel) Of a calm tendency.

Oen Duw——
Brenin tawelin wyt ti!

Lamb of God, a *tranquillizing* king art thou. *H. D. ab Ifan.*

Tawelu, *v. a.* (tawel) To calm, to tranquillize, to soothe; to silence; to become calm or serene: *Pan dawelo ton y mor*, when the wave of the sea grows calm: *Ti ddyn, tawela dy far*, thou man, calm thy rage.

Tawelus, *a.* (tawel) Of a serene tendency.

Tawelusaw, *v. a.* (tawelus) To render of a serene tendency; to become tranquillous.

Tawelusder, *s. m.* (tawelus) Tranquillousness.

Tawelusdra, *s. m.* (tawelus) Tranquillousness.

Tawelusrwydd, *s. m.* (tawelus) Tranquillousness, calmness, serenity.

Tawelwch, *s. m.* (tawel) Calmness, serenity; gentleness; stillness. *Tawelwch angeu*, the stillness of death.

Tawelwr, *s. m.*—*pl.* tawelwyr (tawel—gwr) A calmer, one who makes still.

Tawf, *s. m.* (taw) A stretched or extended state.

Tawg, *s. f.* (taw) That is lengthened, or stretched out in length.

Tawgar, *a.* (taw) Disposed to be silent.

Doeth pob tawgar.

Wise is every *silent one*. *Adage.*

Tawiad, *s. m.* (taw) A quelling, a silencing.

Tawl, *s. m.*—*pl.* tolion (ta—awl) A cast off, a throw; a take off; a separation; a cut off; an interruption; a diminishing.

Goronwy rwyg greidiawl,
Caer ar aer, car arwrawl,
Cedeirn ostwng, detiwng dawl.

Goronwy of ardent course, the bulwark of battle, a heroic friend, the debaser of the mighty ones, a meritorious *throw*. *G. ab M. ab Dafydd.*

Tawlfwrdd, *s. m.*—*pl.* tawlfyrddau (tawl—bwrdd) A throw board, a certain game, seemingly like the present game of backgammon.

Tawlfwrdd chweugaint a dal; ac fal hyn y rhenir, triugaint ar y werin wynion, a thriugaint ar y brenin a'i werin.

A *throw-board* its value is six score pence; and is thus proportioned, three score on the white men, and three score on the king and his men. *Welsh Laws.*

Tawlffon, *s. f.*—*pl.* tawlffyn (tawl—ffon) A throwing staff, an engine for throwing darts.

Tawlgar, *a.* (tawl) Apt to put aside; apt to throw off; interruptive.

Tawlgarwch, *s. m.* (tawlgar) Apt to put aside, aptness to throw off.

Tawliad, *s. m.* (tawl) A casting off; a throwing; a taking off; a separating; a cutting off; a diminishing; an interrupting.

Tawlnerth, *s. m.*—*pl. t.* oedd (tawl—nerth) Projectile force.

Tawlrym, *s. m.*—*pl. t.* iau (tawl—grym) Projectile power.

Tawlu, *v. a.* (tawl) To cast off, to throw; to take off; to separate; to interrupt.

Gwell asyn a'm dyco no march a'm tawlo.

Better an ass that will carry me than a horse that will throw me. *Adage.*

Tawr, *s. m.*—*pl.* torion (taw) A covering, surface.

Awn i'r llwyni artlonaidd,
A theced tawr y llawr llaidd.

Let us go to the pleasure inciting groves, as the *covering* of the luxuriant ground is so fair. *D. ab Gwilym.*

TE, *s. m. r.* That is spread or extended.

Teb, *s. m.* (te—eb) The state of being assimilated; a type.

Tebed, *s. m.* (teb) A prospect, a spectacle.

Pell debed bw hyd o Iwerddon,
Teg ffaw dillyngiaw Cesaregion.

A far *prospect* if extending from Ireland, the splendid prominence of sending away the men of Caesar. *Ym. Lludd. Mawr.*

Gwelais, o arfawd aerfab Gruffudd,
Rhailuoedd trwch, tebed wonedd.

I have seen, from the stroke of the warlike son of Gruffudd, broken armies, a *scene* of wonder. *Gwalchmai.*

Tebedawg, *a.* (tebed) Having a prospect.

A'i lasawg tebedawg tra mordwy alon.

With his blue streamer *displayed* whilst the foes range the sea. *Aneurin.*

Tebedu, *v. a.* (tebed) To render prospective.

Tebig, *a.* (teb) Similar, like; probable.

Nid ef a byrth dyn ei debig.

A person will not bear his *like*. *Adage.*

Tebu, *v. a.* (teb) To assimilate; to typify.

Tebyg, *a.* (teb) Similar, like. *Tebyg iawn*, very likely. *Tebyced yw hwn i ti!* how like this is to thee! *Tebycaf peth*, the most likely thing.

Tri pheth tebyg y naill i'r llall: ysgubawr deg heb yd, mall deg heb ddiawd, a merch deg heb ei geirda.

Three things *similar* to one another: a fine barn without corn, a fine goblet without drink, and a fine woman without her reputation. *Catwg Ddoeth.*

Nid tebyg hyn i ddrych cenadau: ef tebycach hyn i elynion, a fynynt wneuthur trais, a goresgyn gwladoedd.

This is not *like* the appearance of messengers; *more like* is this to enemies, that would commit a trespass, and conquer countries *Gr. ab Arthur.*

Tebygadwy, *a.* (tebyg) Capable of being like; comparable; presumable.

Tebygawl, *a.* (tebyg) Tending to be like or similar; likely, probable, presumptive. *Tebygawl genyf y byddi di yno*, I presume that thou wilt be there.

Tebygedig, *a.* (tebyg) Being likened; assimilated; compared; imagined.

Tebygiad, *s. m.—pl. t.* au (tebyg) A likening, a comparing; a thinking probable.

Tebygiaeth, *s. m.* (tebyg) The act of likening or comparing; comparison; imagination.

Nid wyf fi ar fedr dannod un pechawd iddo, yn amgen no thrwy ymadrawdd o debygiaeth.

I am not upon the intention of upbraiding him with one sin, otherwise than through speaking from *comparison*. *S. Trefredyn.*

Tebygiannawl, *a.* (tebygiant) Tending to similitude; comparative; conjectural.

Tebygiannu, *v. a.* (tebygiant) To make a similitude; to make a comparison.

Tebygiant, *s. m.* (tebyg) A similitude.

Tebygoldeb, *s. m.* (tebygawl) Similarity; probableness.

Tebygoli, *v. a.* (tebygawl) To render similar; to render likely or probable; to compare.

Tebygolrwydd, *s. m.* (tebygawl) Similarity; likeliness, likelihood, probability.

Tebygrwydd, *s. m.* (tebyg) Similitude; likelihood, probableness; conjecture.

Tebygu, *v. a.* (tebyg) To render similar; to assimilate; to compare; to presume, to think probable, to deem, to conjecture; to be like.

Hen a wyr, ieuanc a debyg.

The aged knows, the young *supposes*. *Adage.*

Cas a debyco orfod o falchder.

Hateful is he *that thinks* to overcome through haughtiness. *Adage.*

Tebygaf ni wyddant hwy ddim i wrth filwriaeth, wrth eu bod yn preswyliaw eithr y byd yn mewn yr eigiawn; ac ysgafn, herwydd y tebygaf, fydd eu cymbell hwynt i dalu teyrnged.

I think it likely that they know nothing of military matters, from their being inhabiting without the world in the ocean; and easy, as *I imagine*, will it be to compel them to pay tribute. *Gr. ab Arthur.*

Tebygwr, *s. m.—pl.* tebygwyr (tebyg—gwr) One who supposes, one who compares.

Tecàad, *s. m.* (teg) A rendering fair or fine; a becoming fair or beautiful.

Tri thecàad cerdd: bardd grebwyll, bardd berthynas, a bardd gwreiingamp ar fydrau.

The three *ornaments* of song: fine conception, fine connexion, and a fine masterly skill in the metres. *Barddas.*

Tecàawl, *a.* (tecàu) Tending to make fair or fine; tending to become fair.

Tecàu, *v. a.* (teg) To make fair; to become fair.

Teclyn, *s. m. dim.* (tacl) A tool, an instrument.

Tech, *s. m.* (te—ech) A sculk, a lurk, a hide.

Techawg, *a.* (tech) Of a disposition to sculk.

Techawl, *a.* (tech) Sculking, or lurking.

Techiad, *s. m.—pl. t.* au (tech) A sculking.

Techial, *s. m.* (tech) A frequent sculking. *v. a.* To be sculking continually.

Techialu, *v. a.* (techial) To sculk continually.

Techu, *v. a.* (tech) To sculk, to lurk, to lie hidden

Cynddylan, ni thechai troedfedd byth.

Cynddylan, *he would* never *sculk* a foot. *Llywarch Hen.*

Aerwalch eirf ni theirf, ni thech.

The slaughter-hawk of arms will not recede, *will not sculk*. *Prydydd Bychan.*

Techus, *a.* (tech) Disposed to sculk or lurk.

Techusaw, *v. a.* (techus) To render sculking; to become disposed to sculk.

Techusdra, *s. m.* (techus) Aptness to sculk.

Techwr, *s. m.—pl.* techwyr (tech—gwr) A sculker, a lurker.

Techydd, *s. m.—pl. t.* ion (tech) A sculker.

Techyn, *s. m. dim.* (tech) A sculking fellow.

Ted, *s. m.* (te—ed) A stretch, a distended state.

Tedu, *v. a.* (ted) To stretch out, to distend.

Tedyn, *s. m. dim.* (ted) Anything distended.

Tedd, *s. m.* (te—edd) A spread; a display; a range, a row.

Nifer hyn, os nef ar hynt
Am ei gael, i'mozelynt,
Wedi'r cig rhost, fost feithrin,
Ar llain gwyn fain, a gwin,
A'r gwleddau, a'r gwarau gwiwreg,
A'r gwreigedd eurwedd, tedd teg.

This number, if heaven were of course to be obtained, they would keep themselves aloof; after the roasted viand, a boasted fare, and the fine white linen and wine, and the feasts, and the emulating games, and the women bedecked with gold, a fair *display*. *S. Cent.*

Teddawg, *a.* (tedd) Being spread, displayed.

Teddawl, *a.* (tedd) Spreading, displayed.

Teddiad, *s. m.* (tedd) A spreading out; a displaying; a disposing in a row.

Teddu, *v. a.* (tedd) To spread out, to display.

Teddus, *a.* (tedd) Tending to spread or display.

Teddyf, *s. m.* (tedd) A socket, a hollow for receiving a handle, or the like.

Y gof llys a ddyly—gwneuthur rheidiau y llys yn rhad, eithr tri pheth; sef ynt y rhai hyny, gwarthaf cham callawr, a chwll cwlltr, a theddyf bwyall gynnud a phen gwaew.

The smith of the palace ought to perform all the jobs of the palace gratuitously, except three things; those are particularly, the rim of a pot, the edge of a coulter, and the *socket* of a hatchet and of a spear head. *Welsh Laws.*

Tefawg, *a.* (taf) Respectable, or of repute. *Dyn tefawg*, a respectable person. *Dyfed.*

Tefig, *a.* (taf) Over-spreading; sovereign.

Pen nig o nef, pen a'n gwnaeth,
Pen defig pob pen difeth.

The supreme source of heaven, the supreme that made us, the *sovereign* head of every infallible head. *L. G. Cothi.*

Tefin, *a.* (taf) Of a spreading tendency.

Tefydd, *s. m.* (taf) That is ample or large.

Tefyddawg, *a.* (tefydd) Having possession. *Dyn tefyddawg*, a person of consequence.

Tefu, *v. a.* (taf) To spread, to become spread.

Teg, *a.* (te—eg) That opens out, that is clear or smooth; clear, fair; beautiful, pretty, bland. *Hin deg*, fair weather; *chware teg*, fair play; *gwartheg teg*, fine cattle.

A ddialo air hagr rhoed ateb teg.

He that would revenge a harsh word let him give a *gentle* reply. *Adage.*

Ni thyr pen er dywedyd yn deg.

The head will not break on account of speaking *fairly*. *Adage.*

Teg yd gan yr aderyn ar berwydd bren,
Uch pen Gwen, cyn ei olo tan dywarch;
Briwai galch Llywarch Hen.

Fair the song of the bird on the apple tree, over the head of Gwen, before he was covered under the sod; he was wont to bruise the armour of old Llywarch. *Llywarch Hen.*

Tegâad, *s. m.* (tegâu) A rendering fair or fine; an adorning; a becoming fair.

Tegâawl, *a.* (tegâu) Tending to render fair; tending to become fair; beautifying.

Tegaidd, *a.* (teg) Somewhat fair; fairish.

Tegan, *s. m. dim.—pl. t.* au (teg) A pretty thing, a toy, a bauble, a jewel.

Anwybodus a ddengys yn fuan a wyr, fal plentyn yn dangaws tegan.

The ignorant will quickly shew all he knows, like a child shewing his *toy*. *Adage.*

Teganaidd, *a.* (tegan) Like a plaything.

Teganawg, *a.* (tegan) Having a plaything.

Teganwaith, *s. m.* (tegan—gwaith) Toywork.

Teganwr, *s. m.—pl.* teganwyr (tegan—gwr) A toyman.

Tegâu, *v. a.* (teg) To render clear, smooth, or fair, to beautify; to appease; to become clear, smooth, or fair.

Tegawl, *a.* (teg) Tending to make fair.

Tegedd, *s. m.* (teg) Fairness, clearness, fineness.

Tegeirian, *s. m.* (teg—eirian) Orchis, cullions, or dog's stones, also called *baldar*, *ceillian y ci*, *eirin y ci*, *tegeirian y waen*, meadow orchis.

Tegid, *s. m.* (teg) Fairness, or beauty.

Tegrwydd, *s. m.* (teg) Fairness, fineness.

Tegu, *v. a.* (teg) To make fair, to beautify.

Tegwch, *s. m.* (teg) Clearness, fairness, fineness; beauty; fine weather. *Gwir degwch*, perfect beauty.

Tegwch a gosgedd dynlawl—cynt y derfydd ac y diflana, nog anwadalwch blodau y gwanwyn.

The *beauty* and symmetry of the human form, will sooner end and vanish, than the fleetingness of the blossoms of the spring. *Hanes Dinedd Arthur.*

Tegwedawg, *a.* (teg—gwedawg) Fair spoken.

Tegwedd, *s. f.* (teg—gwedd) A fair appearance. *a.* Of a fair appearance.

Tegwel, *s. m.* (teg—gwel) A fair countenance. *a.* Of a fair aspect.

A phan el ieuenctyd ymaith,
A'i degwel digam,
—Ni ddaw eilwaith.

So when youth shall pass away, with its *fair aspect*, it will not come a second time. *H. Morus.*

Tegychawl, *a.* (tegwch) Of a tendency to fairness; beautifying, adorning.

Tegychiad, *s. m.* (tegwch) A rendering fair or fine; an embellishing; a becoming fair.

Tegychu, *v. a.* (tegwch) To render of a clear or fair aspect; to adorn, to embellish; to become fair; to become fine weather.

Teidiawg, *a.* (taid) Having a grandfather.

Teidiawl, *a.* (taid) Belonging to a grandfather.

Teilai, *s. m.* (tel) The dipsacus, or teasel: *teilai gwyllt*, wild teasel; *teilai mawr*, fuller's teasel

Teilaw, *v. a.* (tail) To spread manure.

Teilawg, *a.* (tail) Manured, having dung.

Teilchion, *s. pl. aggr.* (talch) Fragments, pieces, shatters. *Dyna fo yn deilchion man*, there it is all in shatters.

Teilfa, *s. f.* (tail) A place for manure; a dunghill

Teilfforch, *s. f.—pl.* teilffyrch (tail—fforch) A dung-fork.

Teiliad, *s. m.* (tail) A spreading of manure.

Teiliedig, *a.* (teiliad) Covered with manure.

Teilig, *a.* (tel) Tending to cover, enveloping.

Teiling, *a.* (tel) Meet to cover, enveloping; meet. *Lluryg deiling*, an enveloping armour.

Nog y bydd cyfing gwlydd teiling gwledd.

Than there shall be scanty the covering delicacy of the banquet. *G. ab [illegible]*

Teiliwr, *s. m.—pl.* teiliwyr (teln—gwr) A maker of habits, a tailor.

Teiliwriaeth, *s. m.* (teiliwr) A tailor's trade.

Teiliwriaw, *v. a.* (teiliwr) To work as a tailor.

Teilw, *a.* (tel) Gentle, or yielding; complying.

Owain—
Gwr teiaid trwlosodd lochi;
Gwr teilw, teilwng ei foli.

Owain, a comely man protecting of families; a meek man worthy to be praised. *[illegible]*

Teilwng, *a.* (tal—wng) Worthy, meritorious; merited, deserved, genuine.

Teilwr, *s. m.—pl.* teilwyr (tail—gwr) A manurer; a dungman, a muckman.

Teilyngawl, *a.* (teilwng) Tending to render worthy; meritorious.

Teilyngdawd, *s. m.* (teilwng) Merit, desert, right, deservedness, worthiness.

Cyfodes Eudaf Iarll Erging ac Euas yn erbyn y tywysogion, a ry adawsai Cystenyn yn cynnal yr ynys wrth Rufeinawl deilyngdawd.

Eudaf the earl of Erging and Euas rose against the princes which had been left by Constantine to maintain the island under the Roman *jurisdiction*. *Gr. ab Arthur.*

Teilyngdra, *s. m.* (teilwng) Meritoriousness.

Teilyngedig, *a.* (teilwng) Being deserved.

Teilyngedd, *s. m.* (teilwng) Meritoriousness.

Teilyngiad, *s. m.* (teilwng) A rendering worthy.

Teilyngrwydd, *s. m.* (teilwng) Worthiness.

Teilyngu, *v. a.* (teilwng) To render worthy; to think worthy; to vouchsafe.

Teilyngus, *a.* (teilwng) Tending to make worthy.

Teilyngwr, *s. m.—pl.* teilyngwyr (teilwng—gwr) One who makes worthy.

Teimlad, *s. m.—pl. t.* au (teimyl) A sensation.

Teimladaidd, *a.* (teimlad) Somewhat sensible.

Teimladawl, *a.* (teimlad) Of a feeling nature.

Teimladedig, *a.* (teimlad) Endued with feeling.

Teimladedd, *s. m.* (teimlad) Feelingness.

Teimladrwydd, *s. m.* (teimlad) Feelingness.

Teimladwy, *a.* (teimlad) Capable of feeling, sensible; capable of being felt.

Teimlaw, *v. a.* (teimyl) To feel; to feel by the touch; to be sensible.

Hen y teimler ergydion a gaed yn ieuanc.

In age *will be felt* the blows that have been obtained in youth. *Adage.*

Na fyno weled ei ynfydrwydd heddyw, fe ei teimla a fory.

He that desires not to see his foolishness to-day he will feel it to-morrow. *Adage.*

Trais y cedeirn a'u hyssdrin
Ar y llafurgar werin,
Gwae a'u teimyl! gwae dyngedfawr!

The tyranny of the mighty and their treasons on the laborious multitude, woe to such *as feel* them! doomful woe! *Geraint Fardd Glas.*

Teimlawd, *s. m.* (teimyl) Feeling, sensation.

Teimledig, *a.* (teimyl) Being felt; touched.

Teimledigaeth, *s. m.* (teimledig) A being endued with feeling.

Teimlfa, *s. f.—pl. t.* oedd (teimyl) The seat of feeling.

Teimliad, *s. m.—pl.* teimliaid (teimyl) A feeling, a touching.

Teimlwr, *s. m.—pl.* teimlwyr (teimyl—gwr) A feeler.

Teimlydd, *s. m.—pl. t.* ion (teimyl) A feeler, a toucher.

> Iubal oedd dad pob teimlydd telyn ac organ.
>
> Jubal was the father of every *one who handles* the harp and organ. *Genesis* 4. 21.

Teimyl, *s. m.* (tem) The faculty of feeling.

Teirawdl, *s. pl. aggr.* (tair—awdl) Three rhymes. *a.* Consisting of three rhymes. *Englyn teirawdl, englyn milwr, triban.*

Teirawr, *s. pl. aggr.* (tair—awr) Three hours. *a.* Of three hours duration.

Teirblwydd, *s. pl. aggr.* (tair—blwydd) Three years. *a.* Of three years.

Teircaill, *s. m.* (tair—caill) The small ragwort.

Teirdalen, *s. pl. aggr.* (tair—dalen) Three leaves. *a.* Three-leaved, trefoil. *Suran teirdalen*, wood-sorrel.

Teirgwaith, *s. pl. aggr.* (tair—gwaith) Three times. *a.* Of three times.

> Doeth a dwyllir deirgwaith, ni thwyllir drud ond unwaith.
>
> The wise will be deceived *three times*, the bold will be deceived but once. *Adage.*

Teiriaith, *s. pl. aggr.* (tair—iaith) Three languages. *a.* Of three languages.

Teirieithawg, *a.* (teiriaith) Having three languages

Teirnos, *s. pl. aggr.* (tair—nos) Three nights. *a.* Of three nights.

Teirodlawg, *a.* (teirawdl) Having three rhymes.

Teirongl, *s. pl. aggr.* (tair—ongl) Three angles; that is of three angles. *a.* Of three angles.

Teironglawg, *a.* (teirongl) Triangular.

Teirongli, *v. a.* (teirongl) To form a triangle.

Teirrhan, *s. pl. aggr.* (tair—rhan) Three parts or shares. *a.* Of three shares.

Teirrhanawl, *a.* (teirrhan) Tripartite.

Teirthon, *s. f.* (tarth) An ague fit; a fever.

> Pedair teirthon y sydd.
>
> There are four sorts of *fevers*. *Meddygon Myddfai.*

Teisban, *s. f.—pl. t.* au (tais—pan) A middle space, a central point; an origin, or stock; what spreads out, an overspread; any cloth worked over; a piece of tapestry; a quilt; a hassock; a kind of seat or stool made of straw-work; otherwise called *tinpan;* also an epithet for a fat heavy wench. *Teisban y ddwyffroen*, the gristle that divides the nostrils: *Doda deisban arno yn ei wely*, put a quilt over him in his bed.

> Gwaethaf i'r yd rhyfel teisban.
>
> The worst for the corn is an *intestine* war. *Adage.*
>
> Oed Crist 777——y bu ryfel teisban rhwng y Deheuwyr a'u brenin.
>
> The year of Christ 777 there was an *intestine* war between the South Wales men and their king. *Carad. Llangarfan.*

Teisbanawg, *a.* (teisban) Having a central space; central, intestine; having a spread.

Teisbanteulu, *s. m.—pl. t.* oedd (teisban—teulu) The central place of a family; a family stock; a representative of a family.

> Galwes Hywel ato holl benceneddoedd gwlad, a'u teisbanteuluoedd, a phob doethion a dysgedigion o wyr llên a lleygion, yn ddygynnull gorsedd, hyd y Ty Gwyn.
>
> Hywel called to him all the heads of tribes of the country, with their *family representatives*, and all the wise and the learned men of the laity and the clergy, in a general convention, to the White House. *Car. Llangarfan.*

Teisbantyle, *s. m.* (teisban—tyle) A dormitory squab or couch; a centre or representative of a family; a mediator, an arbitrator.

> Teisbantyle, sef yw hwnw gwr cyfrwng, yn llys, ac yn llan, ac yn nghammawn, ac yn mhob priligniaeth; efe a fydd o ddoethion y genedl, gan raith penteuluoedd y genedl, ac yn gydgyfarall ag y pencenedl, yn mhob rhaith a dygynnull gwlad.
>
> The *representative*, who is the mediating man, in court, and in congregation, and in combat, and in every foreign affair; he is to be of the wise men of the tribe, by the vote of the heads of families of the tribe, and to be a coadjutor with the head of the tribe, in every vote and convention of a country. *Trioedd Dyfnwal.*
>
> Tri marchogaeth a ddyrchaif fraint dyn, pryd na gallo hwynt: marchogaeth i lwydd, a dadlau, a llan. Sef fydd efe yna teisbantyle; ac mwy fydd y gosb am ei ladd, no phe bai ar ei wadd ei hun.
>
> Three cavalcades extend the right of a man, at the time he can perform them: to ride to warfare, to a court of law, and to church. For he is then a *family representative;* and more will be the punishment for killing him, than if he were on his own errand. *Welsh Laws.*

Teisbanu, *v. a.* (teisban) To form a central space; to originate; to spread out; to form a hassock.

Teisen, *s. f. dim.—pl. t.* i (tais) A cake. *Teisen briodas*, a bride cake.

> Goreu rhan o'r deisen an â gafir.
>
> The best share of the cake is the one that is obtained. *Adagr.*

Teisenan, *s. f. dim.* (teisen) A little cake.

Teiseniad, *s. m.* (teisen) A caking.

Teisenig, *s. f. dim.* (teisen) A small cake.

Teisenu, *v. a.* (teisen) To form into a cake.

Teithawl, *a.* (taith) Wayfaring, itinerant.

Teithdrwydded, *s. f.—pl. t.* au (taith—trwydded) A passport.

Teithedig, *a.* (taith) Journeyed, or travelled.

Teithgynnwys, *s. m.* (taith—cynnwys) A passport.

Teithi, *s. m.* (taeth) Faculty, quality, characteristic; the peculiar trait, which distinguishes one thing from others; the peculiar state of a being, or its perfection. *Teithi gwraig*, the female catamenia. *Welsh Laws.*

> Teithi trais yw, llef, a chorn, a chwyn.
>
> The *characteristics* of trespass are, a shout, and horn, and complaint. *Welsh Laws.*
>
> O hawl dyn 24 i'r mach, a dywedyd o'r amddiffynwr nad 12 a ddyly efe, aed yr hawl yn edryd y mach: ac os yntau a ddywed mai am 6 cheiniog y rhoed efe yn fach, taled y cwbl, am na wnaeth teithi mach, am na ddywed yr un o'r ddau edryd.
>
> If a person should sue the bail for twenty-four pence, and the defendant should say that what he owes is twelve pence, let the claim be referred to the statement of the bail; but if he should say that for six-pence he was held to bail, let him pay the whole, forasmuch as he did not perform the *functions* of a surety, because he declares neither of the two statements. *Welsh Laws.*
>
> Teithi cath yw, bod yn gyfglust, gyflygad, gyfewin, gyflosgwrn, difan o dan, a lladd llygod, ac na chathrica bob lloer, ac na ysa ei chenawon: a'i gwerth yw ei theithi.
>
> The *perfections* of a cat are, that she be complete in ears, complete in eyes, complete in nails, complete in tail, not spotted with fire, and killing mice, and that she doth not go a rutting every moon, and that she devours not her young; and her value are her *perfections.* *Welsh Laws.*
>
> Mi Feilyr Brydydd, bererin i Bedr,
> Porthawr a gymmedr gymmes deithi.
>
> I Meilyr the Poet, a pilgrim to Peter, a porter who regulates appropriate *perfections.* *Meilyr.*

Teithiad, *s. m.—pl. t.* au (taith) A travelling.

> Am y fun——
> Adwythedig ei deithiadau
> A fwrw bradau drwy fawr brydiad.
>
> On account of the fair one, vexatious his *journeyings*, who forms deceptions, through great study. *Gutyn Owain.*

Teithiannawl, *a.* (teithiant) Itinerary.

Teithiannu, *v. a.* (teithiant) To make a journey.

Teithiannus, *a.* (teithiant) Itinerant.

Teithiant, *s. m.* (taith) A journeying.

Teithiator, *ger.* (teithiad) In journeying.

Teithiaw, *v. a.* (taith) To travel, to journey.

Teithïawg, *a.* (teithi) Having faculties, qualities, or traits; characteristic; perfect as to character.

Arddwyrëaf hael o hil Rodri;
Ardwyad gorwlad, gwerlin teithi;
Teithiawg Prydain,
Twyth afrdwyth Owain,
Teyrnain ni grain, ni grawn rei.

I will exalt the bountrous one of the offspring of Rodri; the curber of the country's border, endued with the characteristics of an illustrious race; *having a right* to Britain's throne, Owain the active one in the course of wrath, a prince who will not succumb, who hoards not pelf. *Gwalchmai.*

I neuadd Arthur, namyn mab brenin gwlad teithiawg, neu i gerddawr a ddyco ei gerdd, ni ater i mewn.

Into the hall of Arthur, except the son of a king of a country *of acknowledged right*, or to an artist who brings his art, none will be suffered to enter. *H. Culhwch—Mabinogion.*

Teithiawl, *a.* (taith) Journeying, travelling.

Teithïawl, *a.* (teithi) Of perfect concurrency, character, faculty, or quality; characteristic; perfect. *Anifel teithïawl*, a beast in which all natural qualities are perfect: *March teithïawl*, a sound horse.

Nawfeddydd Mai y dyly bawch fod yn deithiawl; dawed llaeth o ben pob teth iddi; ac ymdaith o'i llo naw cam yn ei hol.

The ninth day of May a cow ought to be *complete as to natural qualities*, the milk coming through the end of every dug; and that her calf walk nine paces after her. *Welsh Laws.*

Teithiedig, *a.* (teithiad) Journeyed, travelled.

Teithig, *a.* (taith) Being characteristical.

Teithigrwydd, *s. m.* (teithig) Characteristicalness.

Ych yn ei gyflawn deithigrwydd.

An ox in his complete *state of natural qualities*. *Welsh Laws.*

Teithiwr, *s. m.—pl.* teithiwyr (taith—gwr) A journeyer, a traveller.

Teithlyfr, *s. m.—pl. t.* au (taith—llyfr) A journey-book, an itinerary.

Teithwg, *s. m.* (taith) A wayfaring, a journeying.

Teithydd, *s. m.—pl. t.* ion (taith) A traveller.

Teithygawl, *a.* (teithwg) Belonging to wayfaring.

Teithygiad, *s. m.* (teithwg) A making a journey.

Teithygu, *v. a.* (teithwg) To make a journey.

Tèl, *s. m.—pl. t.* ion (ty—el) That is straight, that is drawn tight or strict, that is on a stretch, a tightness; a stricture; that keeps on a stretch, or props up; a straight line; a warp, in weaving; *telau* are also teats, as of a sow, and of a bitch; also a suppressed laugh, titter, or giggle. *a.* Tight, strict, compact, stretched, on the stretch; straight, prompt. *Dàl yn dèl ar y gwir*, to keep strictly to the truth. *Daethost yn dèl iawn y ffordd hono*, thou didst come very exactly that way.

Dos a'th dèl, was ffel; nes ffoli, rhodia
Ar hyder dy feistri.

Away with thy *titter*, thou sly fellow; until thy folly is complete, range about on the credit of thy mastery. *Huw Dof. Probert.*

Tel, *s. m.—pl. t.* au (te—el) That is even, regular, smooth, or compact; that is fair; a regulator, or standard measure of capacity, and of length; in South Wales, a corn measure, equal to 5¼ bushels, and in North Wales 4 bushels, divided into 8 parts. In some places *Tèl* is for capacity, and *Ystaca*, for long measure; but in others they are reversed. *a.* Even, regular, compact; fair.

Telai, *s. m.—pl.* teleion (tèl) That is strained or even; that is regular; a kind of thistle; the teasel. *Telai gwyllt*, *teilai gwyllt*, the common or wild teasel.

Telaid, *s. m.* (tèl) That is stretched, or tightened; that is even, smooth, or of fair appearance. *a.* Fair, beautiful, graceful. *Teleidion*, graceful ones, the graces.

Llary deleid hoenaw hael.

A mild *graceful one* famed for being generous. *Bleddyn Fardd.*

Ef mwyaf, y medd adroddiaid;
Ef haelaf, ef tecaf teleid.

He is the greatest, as minstrels declare; he the most generous, he the fairest *graceful one*. *Ll. P. Moch, i R. ab Owain.*

Gnawd tawel yn deleid.

It is genial for the silent to be *graceful*. *Adage.*

Bendigwch Ddew teleid.

Bless ye God *full of grace*. *Dafydd Ddu.*

Telaid, *s. m.—pl.* teleidiau (tel) The measure, or contents, of a *tel*, a *tel-full*.

Telaidd, *a.* (tel) Somewhat strained, tight, even, or compact; harmonious.

Telain, *v. a.* (tèl) To put on a stretch; to break out as a suppressed laugh; to titter, to giggle.

Telain, *a.* (tel) Being on the stretch; being made smooth, fair or tight.

Telan, *s. f.—pl. t.* au (tèl) A harp; but *telyn* is now the general name for it.

Telawd, *s. m.* (tèl) The act of stretching or tightening.

Telawr, *s. m.—pl.* telorion (tèl) A warbler; the goldfinch, also called *pinc*; *telawr y coed*, the woodlark.

Telc, *s. m.* (tèl) A straightened state; a shrink.

Telciad, *s. m.* (telc) A shrinking, a crimpling.

Telcu, *v. a.* (telc) To shrink up, to crimple.

Telchyn, *s. m. dim.* (talch) A small fragment.

Teled, *s. m.* (tel) That is stretched or strained.

Teledawg, *a.* (teled) Being on the stretch, or straitened. *s. m.* A jealous one.

Teledig, *a.* (tel) Handsome, or comely.

Teledigrwydd, *s. m.* (teledig) Handsomeness.

Telediw, *a.* (teled) Compact; perfect; of fair aspect, comely, handsome, beautiful. *Gwas telediw*, a handsome youth; *rhian deledïw*, a beautiful woman; *eidion telediw*, a beast that is perfect in its kind.

Telediwrwydd, *s. m.* (telediw) Compactness; comeliness, handsomeness; gracefulness.

Ych a ymadawo a'i deledïwrwydd, ni ddylid ei ddamdwng yn gymaint a 60; canys ei werth yn ei deledïwrwydd oedd 60.

An ox that shall lose his *perfectiveness*, should not be subject to a rate equal to 60 pence; for his value in his *perfectiveness* was 60 pence. *Welsh Laws.*

Helen Lüyddawg, pryd hono hagen a'i theledïwrwydd, ni chafid yn yr ynysedd yn ei chylch a'i cyffelybai.

Helen with the numerous host, as to her form then and her *gracefulness*, there should not be found in the islands round her any to compare with her. *Gr. ab Arthur.*

Teleidiad, *s. m.* (telaid) A rendering comely, beautiful, or graceful; a becoming comely, or graceful.

Teleidiaw, *v. a.* (telaid) To render comely, elegant, or graceful. to become comely or graceful.

Teleidiawg, *a.* (telaid) Abounding with comeliness, elegance, or grace.

Teleidiawl, *a.* (telaid) Tending to render comely, or graceful; tending to become elegant.

Teleidrwydd, *s. m.* (telaid) Comeliness; elegance; gracefulness.

Teleiddiad, *s. m.* (telaidd) A rendering even, consonant, or harmonious.

Teleiddiaw, *v. a.* (telaidd) To produce harmony; to practise minstrelsy.

Teleiddwr, *s. m.—pl.* teleiddwyr (telaidd—gwr) A minstrel, a songster.

Cwyned cerddorion cywall,
A theleiddwyr, mwynwyr mil.

Let correct musicians complain, and minstrels, a thousand pleasant men.
Wil. ab Hywel. m. T. W. Hywel, [illegible]

Teleiddyn, *s. m.—pl. t.* ion (telaidd) A songster.

Teleiniad, *s. m.* (telain) A playing the harp.

Teleiniaw, *v. a.* (telain) To play the harp.

Teleinlwr, *s. m.—pl.* teleinwyr (telan—gwr) A harper. *Ll. Llandaf.*

Teler, *s. m.—pl. t.* au (tèl) That keeps tight or stretched: a stretcher; a compact, or condition. *Teler llif hir*, the handle, and frame, of a long saw: *Ar y telerau hyny*, on those conditions. *Dyfed.*

Telg, *s. m.* (tel) A straitened state, a shrink, a crimple.

Telging, *a.* (telg—ing) Constricted; crimpled.

Wyt telging, enaid Talgarth.

Thou art *constricted*, thou soul of Talgarth. *D. ab Edmwnt.*

Telgorn, *s. m.—pl.* telgyrn (tel—corn) A hautboy.

Telgwn, *s. m.* (telc—wn) A rebound; a stagger.

Telgwng, *s. m.* (telg—wng) A crimpling.

Telgynawd, *s. m.* (telgwn) A resiliency.

Telgyniad, *s. m.* (telgwn) A rebounding.

Telgynu, *v. a.* (telgwn) To rebound; to stagger.

Telgyngawd, *s. m.* (telgwng) A crimpling.

Telgyngawg, *a.* (telgwng) Crimpling; staggering.

Telgyngiad, *s. m.* (telgwng) A crimpling.

Telgyngu, *v. a.* (telgwng) To crimple; to stagger, to falter. *Cei ddyrnawd a wna i ti delgyngu*, thou shalt have a blow that will cause thee *to stagger*.

Teli, *s. m.—pl. t.* au (tèl) The being compact, or tight; exactness; an art.

Teliad, *s. m.—pl. t.* au (tèl) A rendering stretched, a tightening; a making smooth or fair.

Telïad, *s. m.* (teli) A rendering compact; an acting ingeniously.

Telïaidd, *a.* (teli) Being compact, or tightly put together; ingenious. *Dyn telïaidd iawn*, a very ingenious person. *Sil.*

Chwi sydd heb——
Na bri telïaidd, na braint
Hoenus, ond a fyn henaint.

You are without any *ingenious* pre-eminence, or active quality, save what old age doth claim. *Grw. Wiliam.*

Teliaw, *v. a.* (tel) To strain, to tighten; to make accordant.

Telïaw, *v. a.* (teli) To put compactly together; to practise any ingenious art.

Al Ceraint Fardd Glas yn fardd telïaw at Aelfryd frenin Lloegr.

Ceraint the Blue Bard went as a bard of *art* to Alfred king of England. *Ed. Dafydd.*

Telid, *s. m.—pl. t.* au (tèl) That is combined tightly; a compact frame; elegance; gracefulness.

Gwnevnt eu perorion
Oferwynt heb don;
Gwneynt eu telidau
Yn oes oesau
Dydwyth dyddycawd
O ddylnwedydd gwawd.

Their musicians would produce a fruitless wind without sound; their *instruments* would ever make from the effect of vibration a profound flow of praise. *Taliesin.*

Telitor, *sup.* (tal) To be requiting; to be paying.

O's llygrir yd i neb yn ymyl trefgordd, ac na chaffo y perchenawg ddaly un llwdn arno, cymered efe grair a doed i'r dref: ac os tyngant hwy diarnabod, talent yr yd i rif y llwdn: a'r gyfraith hono a elwir telitor gwedi halawglw.

If the corn of any one shall be damaged on the border of a township, and the owner shall not be able to catch one beast upon it, let him take the relicks and then come to the town; and if they shall swear an oath of ignorance of the fact, let them pay for the corn to the number of the beast: and that law is called *paying* after a polluted oath. *Welsh Laws.*

Teliw, *a.* (tèl) Being stretched or expanded.

Telm, *s. f.—pl. t.* au (tel) A gimcrack; a toy; a springe.

Y fiaren——
Telm yw ar lethr bron talar.

The briar, a *snare* is it on the headland slope. *D. ab Gwilym.*

Telma, *v. a.* (telm) To play with toys; to trifle.

Telmaidd, *a.* (telm) Toyish; like a snare.

Telmiad, *s. m.* (telm) A toying; a laying a snare.

Telmu, *v. a.* (telm) To form a toy; to snare.

Telmyn, *s. m. dim.* (telm) A little toy; a trap.

Telori, *v. a.* (telawr) To warble, to be warbling.

Telpyn, *s. m. dim.—pl. t.* au (talp) A small lump.

Telpynawg, *a.* (telpyn) Having small lumps.

Telpyniad, *s. m.* (telpyn) A forming small lumps.

Telpynu, *v. a.* (telpyn) To form small lumps.

Telu, *v. a.* (tèl) To put on a stretch, to strain; to make compact or regular.

Telwr, *s. m.—pl.* telwyr (tèl—gwr) One who strains; one who makes compact.

Telydd, *s. m.—pl. t.* ion (tèl) One who strains or draws tight; a harmonist.

Telyn, *s. f.—pl. t.* au (tèl) What is stretched, what is compact or straight, what is in even row; a harp; also the ribs and whole side of a carcase, when divided into two. *Sil.*

Pencerdd a ddyly i gan y cerddorion ieuainc, pan ymadawont a thelyn rawn, a mynu bod yn gerddorion cyweithas, ac yn eirchiaid, pedair ar ugaint o ariant yn ei obrwy.

The master of art ought to receive from young minstrels, when they leave off the hair-strung *harp*, and desire to become associated minstrels, and suitors, the sum of twenty-four of silver for his fee. *Welsh Laws.*

Nid oes nag angel, na dyn,
Nad wyl pan gano delyn.

There is nor angel, nor man, but would weep, when the *harp* resounds. *D. ab Edmwnt.*

Telynai, *s. c.—pl.* telyneion (telyn) A harpist.

Telynaidd, *a.* (telyn) Of the form of a harp.

Telynawr, *s. m.—pl.* telynorion (telyn) A harpist.

Telyn aur telynorion,
Ti sydd yn tewi a son!

The golden harp of the *harpists*, thou are becoming silent! *D. ab Edmwnt, m. S. Ees.*

Cor o saint——
Cu eu hodlau cyhydlef,
Gwynion delynorion nef.

A choir of saints, lovely their accordant strains, the white-robed *minstrels* of heaven. *Grw. Owain.*

Telyniad, *s. m.—pl. t.* au (telyn) A harping.

Telyniawr, *s. m.* (telyn) A harp player.

Telyniwr, *s. m.—pl.* telyniwyr (telyn—gwr) A harper, a harp player.

Telynores, *s. f.—pl. t.* au (telynawr) A female harpist.

Enwawg yth wnair, gair gyrddbwyll,
Armes, telynores twyll.

Eminent art thou made, of thought profound, the word, predicting thee the *fair minstrel* of deceit. *D. ab Gwilym, i Forfudd.*

Telynoriad, *s. m.* (telynawr) A playing a harp.

Telynoriaw, *v. a.* (telyn) To play on the harp.

Telynwr, *s. m.—pl.* telynwyr (telyn—gwr) Harper

Telyr, *s. m.* (tèl) That constricts, or tightens.

Telyraw, *v. a.* (telyr) To keep on the stretch; to keep on, to persevere. *Pa le buost, er ys llawer dydd, yr hen was, yn telyraw?* Where hast thou been, for these many days, old boy, keeping it up? *Sil.*

Telyw, *s. m.* (tel) A covering, a garment.

Llem awel, llwm benyd er byw,
Pan orwisg coed telyw haf;
Terydd glaf wyf heddyw.

Sharp the gale, it is bare punishment to live, when the woods wear the robe of summer: I am severely ill this day. *Llywarch Hen.*

Tell, *s. m.* (te—ell) The state of being stretched over. *a.* Being stretched over.

Telliad, *s. m.* (tell) A stretching over; a covering.

Tellu, *v. a.* (tell) To stretch over; to cover.

Tellwedd, *s. f.* (tell—gwedd) A covered aspect; a covered state; an amnesty, or indemnity, in law.

Meddyg a ddyly gymeryd tellwedd i gan y genedl am archolledig, o bydd marw o'r feddyginiaeth a wnel efe; ac onis cymera, gwitherpyd dros ei weithred.

A doctor ought to require an *amnesty* from the family for the wounded, in case he should die under the operation he may perform; and if he doth not take it, let him answer for his act. *Welsh Laws.*

Dall fyddar cyn tellwedd!

Blind and deaf before the *grave!* *Gr. ab Gwrgenau.*

Tellweddiad, *s. m.* (tellwedd) A burying in oblivion; a giving a release.

Tellweddu, *v. a.* (tellwedd) To bury in oblivion; to grant a release; to save harmless.

Tem, *s. m.* (te—em) A round spread or space.

Temig, *s. m. dim.—pl. t.* au (tam) A particle, a small part, or portion. *Yn demigau*, by parts, by morsels, severally, or particularly. *Sil.*

Teml, *s. m.—pl. t.* au (tem) A temple, a church.

Teml, *s. m.* (tem) That is extended or expanded; that extends; a seat, a place of sitting.

Yn eistedd ar deml o irfrwyn—gwelid macwy.

Sitting on a *seat* of green rushes, a youth was seen. *H. Arthur—Mabinogion.*

Temliad, *s. m.* (teml) A forming an expanse; a forming a seat; a forming a temple.

Temlu, *v. a.* (teml) To form an expanse; to form a seat.

Ten, *a.* (*f. of* tyn) Stretched, drawn, tight.

Tenau, *a.* (tan) Thin, rare, rarefied; lean.

Teneu, *a.* (tan) Thin, rare, rarefied; lean.

Teneuâd, *s. m.* (teneuâu) Attenuation.

Teneuâawl, *a.* (teneuâu) Tending to thinness, attenuating, rarefying.

Teneuad, *s. m.* (tenau) Emaciation, attenuation; rarification; a making thin.

Teneuadwy, *a.* (teneuad) Capable of thinning.

Teneuâu, *v. a.* (tenau) To make thin, to attenuate; to rarefy; to become thin.

Teneuaw, *v. a.* (tenau) To make thin; to become thin, to emaciate.

Teneuawl, *a.* (tenau) Tending to thinness, attenuating, emaciating.

Teneudeb, *s. m.* (tenau) Thinness; tenuity.

Teneuder, *s. m.* (tenau) Thinness; leanness.

Teneudra, *s. m.* (tenau) Thinness; leanness.

Teneuedig, *a.* (teneuad) Being thinned.

Teneuedd, *s. m.* (tenau) Thinness, tenuity.

Teneuwrwydd, *s. m.* (tenau) Thinness; leanness.

Teneuwe, *s. f.* (tenau—gwe) A fine web.

Tenewyn, *s. m.* (tan—gewyn) What is extended or stretched; a flank of an animal.

Tenlli, *s. m.* (tan—lli) That is thinly wove; Linsey-woolsey; shalloon.

Ni bydd tenlli yn llawdr rhingyll

There shall be no *shalloon* in the trowse of a serjeant. *Welsh Laws.*

Tennyn, *s. m. dim.—pl. t.* od (tant) A cord, a rope, a halter. *Tennyn pen bawd*, a rope made by twisting the stuff about the thumb.

Tent, *s. m.* (ten) That is stretched, or drawn tightly; a tent. *a.* Tightly drawn.

Mewn crys gwyn, tyn mal tent,
Yr af innau i'r fynwent.

In a white shirt, tight like a *tent*, I also shall go to the grave. *Ledo Dwrgyllys.*

Y llong—Gwegilgan gweilgi,
Coedwig dent, ceidw Iago di.

The ship, with a wake foaming the torrent, with *stretched* group of timbers, Iago will thee preserve. *Rhys Nanmor, i'r llong.*

Teng, *s. m.* (te—eng) That is tough. *a.* Tough, tenacious.

Tengl, *s. f.—pl. t.* au (teng) A girth.

Tengliad, *s. m.* (tengl) A tying with a girth.

Tenglu, *v. a.* (tengl) To tie with a girth.

Tengyn, *s. m.* (teng) That is tenacious; obstinacy. *a.* Tenacious, obstinate.

Dwys dengyn ydd ymleddan' ungyn.

With persevering obstinacy the dogs of war would fight. *Anearin.*

Gan rian tyfal dengyn.

With chiefs of tenderous war. *Hywddin.*

Teon, *s. m.* (te) That overspreads or is superior.

Yn agharanal meirch marchogion;
Yn agharuedd tan teon.

In the prancing of the steeds of knights, amid the menu pile, thine the superior. *Llywelyn Fardd Cywrig.*

Tepyn, *s. m. dim.* (tap) A small ledge or step.

Tepyniad, *s. m.* (tepyn) A forming a step.

Tepynu, *v. a.* (tepyn) To form a step or ledge.

Ter, *s. m.* (te—er) That is fine, clear, or transparent. *a.* Clear, fine, transparent, pure, clarified, purified.

Tèr, *s. m.* (ty—er) A state of ardency; aptness to pervade, or to break out.

Teraidd, *a.* (ter) Somewhat clear or pure.

Terawg, *a.* (tèr) Having ardency or avidity.

Terawl, *a.* (ter) Clarifying, purifying.

Terc, *s. m.—pl. t.* iau (tèr) A jerk, a jolt.

Terciad, *s. m.* (terc) A jerking, a jolting.

Tercu, *v. a.* (terc) To jerk, or to jolt.

Terch, *s. f.—pl. t.* au (ty—erch) Any fastening by which a thing is suspended; a loop. *Terch rhwng dwy gostrel*, a fastening between two bottles.

Costrel a'i therch wrth erchwyn.

A bottle with its *loop* to the bedside. *Bedo Brwynllys.*

Terchawg, *a.* (terch) Having a loop, furnished with a string or the like, to hang by.

Terchiad, *s. m.* (terch) A looping, a furnishing with anything to hang by.

Terchu, *v. a.* (terch) To loop, to furnish with a cord, or the like, to hang by.

Terchwyn, *s. m.* (terch) That serves to suspend or to uphold.

Detholais fy rhwyf yn rhad welling mawr,
Yn llwythfawr llawr llaw derchwyn.

I have selected my leader a magnificent shedding of gifts, greatly loading the ground with *upholding* hand. *Cynddelw, i Wenwynwyn.*

Teredig, *a.* (ter), Being made clear; clarified; purified.

Teredigaeth, *s. m.* (teredig) Clarification.

Teredd, *s. m.* (ter) A pure or clarified state.

Terf, *a.* (tèr) Being extreme or outward.

Terfan, *v. a.* (terf) To render extreme; to produce a crisis; to become extreme.

Terfedig, *a.* (terf) Being rendered extreme.

Terfenydd, *s. m.* (terfan) An extremity or crisis; the time of the copulation of cattle. *Terfenydd buwch, buwch derfenydd, buwch wasawd*, the time of a cow's seeking the bull.

Terfyll, *s. m.* (terf) That is puffed out; plump.

Terfyn, *s. m.—pl. t.* au (terf) An extremity, a limit, a termination. *Mae yr amser ar derfyn*, the time is just at an end; *wyf ar derfyn*, I am just at an end.

Endewais wanerg o Wynedd dir,
I am derfyn mawr melldu Beli.
Oedd hydraidd wrthi llif yn llenwi;
Oedd hyr am dwylan gwynfan genti;
Hyd oedd ei drddf, hwyrdeddf hoti;
Hallt oedd ei dagrau digrawn heli.

I listened to a wave from Gwynedd land, round the ample border of the sons of Beli. Impetuous was its course filling upon the strand, incessantly round the shore she uttered wail; but oppressive was her law, a tardy law to one, her tears from the dishonless brine were salt. *Llw. ab Gwalchmai, m. Rud.*

Terfynadwy, *a.* (terfyn) Determinable.

Terfynal, *s. c.* (terfyn) That terminates.

Terfynawl, *a.* (terfyn) Conclusive, ending.
Terfynedig, *a.* (terfyn) Determined, ended.
Terfynedigaeth, *s. m.* (terfynedig) Determination, conclusion.
Terfynedigawl, *a.* (terfynedig) Of a limiting tendency, restrictive, determinate.
Terfynfa, *s. f.* (terfyn) A boundary spot.
Terfyniad, *s. m.* (terfyn) A terminating.
Terfynoldeb, *s. m.* (terfynawl) Finiteness.
Terfynolder, *s. m.* (terfynawl) Finiteness.
Terfynoldra, *s. m.* (terfynawl) Finitude.
Terfynoledd, *s. m.* (terfynawl) Conclusiveness.
Terfynoli, *v. a.* (terfynawl) To render conclusive; to become conclusive.
Terfynolrwydd, *s. m.* (terfynawl) Conclusiveness.
Terfynu, *v. a.* (terfyn) To fix a bound, to limit, to determine, to conclude.

> Meddwl dyn, Duw a'i terfyn.
>
> The thought of man, God doth *determine*. *Adage.*

Terfynwr, *s. m.—pl.* terfynwyr (terfyn—gwr) One who concludes or terminates.
Terfynydd, *s. m.—pl. t.* ion (terfyn) A concluder, a finisher, a determiner.
Terfysg, *s. m.—pl. t.* oedd (tèr—mysg) Confusion, commotion, tumult, disturbance.

> Pan nad oedd plant i Les, a ddylyai gyanal y deyrnas yn ei ol; wrth hyny y cyfodes ciwdodawl derfysg y rhwng y Prydeiniaid ac y Rhufeiniawl gyfoeth.
>
> Since there were no children to Lles, who had a right to govern the kingdom after him; upon that there arose a civil commotion between the Britons and the Roman dominion. *Gr. ab Arthur.*

Terfysgaidd, *a.* (terfysg) Apt to to be riotous.
Terfysgawg, *a.* (terfysg) Full of tumult.
Terfysgawl, *a.* (terfysg) Tumultuous.
Terfysgblaid, *s. f.* (terfysg—plaid) A tumultuous faction.
Terfysgedig, *a.* (terfysg) Rendered tumultuous.
Terfysgedigaeth, *s. m.* (terfysgedig) The act of raising a tumult.
Terfysgedd, *s. m.* (terfysg) Tumultuousness.
Terfysgiad, *s. m.* (terfysg) A making a tumult.
Terfysglyd, *a.* (terfysg) Apt to be tumultuous; riotous, mutinous.
Terfysglydrwydd, *s. m.* (terfysglyd) Tumultuousness, riotousness, factiousness.
Terfysgu, *v. a.* (terfysg) To raise a tumult; to become tumultuous; to be in an uproar.

> Terfysga, dalla, mal deillion mewn braw,
> Eu bryd a'u hamcanion.
>
> *Render tumultuous*, blind, like blind ones in terror, their purpose and their designs. *H. D. ab Ifan.*

Terfysgus, *a.* (terfysg) Tumultuous.
Terfysgwr, *s. m.—pl.* terfysgwyr (terfysg—gwr) One who makes a tumult.
Terfysgydd, *s. m.—pl. t.* ion (terfysg) One who makes a tumult.
Tèri, *v. n.* (tèr) To grow sullen, to sculk. *Mae ef yn tèri ar ei fwyd*, he is quarrelling with his meat.
Teriad, *s. m.* (ter) A rendering clear, a clarifying; a purifying.
Tèriad, *s. m.* (tèr) A rendering ardent; irritation.
Terica, *v. a.* (terig) To irritate; to become irritated; to rut, to go a rutting.
Terig, *a.* (tèr) Ardent, poignant; severe, harsh; also an epithet for the season of copulation of cats, and some other animals.

> Euelrel fal ---
> Lleuad aur yn llaw derig.
>
> A buckler like a golden moon in an *ardent* hand. *Rhys Nanmor*

Terigaw, *v. a.* (terig) To render ardent or severe; to become harsh or severe.
Terigiad, *s. m.* (terig) A rendering severe or harsh; a becoming fierce or severe.
Terllyd, *a.* (tèr) Outrageous; sullen.
Terllydrwydd, *s. m.* (terllyd) Outrageousness.
Terllydu, *v. a.* (terllyd) To render outrageous; to become outrageous.
Term, *s. f.—pl. t.* ydd (tèr) An extreme point, a crisis, a limited space of time, a term; a drinking bout.

> Gwell angeu o'm gollyngir
> No thori 'mhen a therm hir.
>
> "Better death that I might be released, than to distract my head with a long *term*. *T. Aled.*

Termiad, *s. m.* (term) A limiting of time, a fixing a term; a making a drinking bout.
Termiaw, *v. a.* (term) To limit a time, to fix a term; to keep up a drinking bout.
Termud, *a.* (tèr—mud) Tacit, silent.

> Rhai trallwfyr tra llafar eu sôn;
> Ac ereill taerlew termudion.
>
> Some very cowardly extremely loud in their talk; and others perseveringly brave being *silent ones*. *Ll. P. Moch.*

Termudaw, *v. a.* (termud) To render tacit or silent; to become silent.
Termudedd, *s. m.* (termud) Taciturnity.
Termudiad, *s. m.* (termud) A rendering tacit; a becoming tacit or silent.
Termudrwydd, *s. m.* (termud) Taciturnity.

> Gorea moes termudrwydd.
>
> The best behaviour is *taciturnity*. *Adage.*

Tern, *s. m.* (tèr) That is ardent or vivid, or full of motion. *a.* Of an ardent or vehement nature.
Terniad, *s. m.* (tern) A moving ardently.
Ternu, *v. a.* (tern) To move or turn ardently.
Terogen, *s. f. dim.* (tèrawg) A female miser.
Terogi, *v. a.* (terawg) To render full of avidity; to become full of avidity.
Terogyn, *s. m. dim.* (terawg) A miserly churl.
Terth, *s. m.—pl. t.* au (tèr) A bung.
Terthain, *v. n.* (tarth) To pant for breath.
Teru, *v. a.* (ter) To purify, to clear, to clarify; to render fine or smooth. *Teru mel*, to clarify honey.
Tèru, *v. a.* (tèr) To act sullenly; to grow sullen, to pout, to sulk. *Teru ar fwyd, sori ar fwyd*, to quarrel with the victuals. *Sil.*
Tèrwr, *s. m.—pl.* tèrwyr (tèr—gwr) A sullen man.
Terwr, *s. m.—pl.* terwyr (ter—gwr) A purifier, a clarifier, or one who makes clear.
Tèrwyn, *a.* (ter—gwyn) Of a violent disposition; ardent, fervent; strong.
Terwynaidd, *a.* (terwyn) Somewhat ardent.
Terwynawl, *a.* (terwyn) Of an ardent tendency.
Terwyndeb, *s. m.* (terwyn) Ardentness.
Terwynder, *s. m.* (terwyn) Ardency, vehemency.
Terwyndra, *s. m.* (terwyn) Ardency, vehemency.
Terwynddrud, *a.* (terwyn—drud) Very bold.
Terwynfalch, *a.* (terwyn—balch) Highly proud.
Terwyniad, *s. m.* (terwyn) A rendering ardent; a becoming ardent; a glowing.
Terwyniaw, *v. a.* (terwyn) To render ardent; to become ardent; to glow.
Terwynu, *v. a.* (terwyn) To render ardent; to become ardent; to glow.

> Ei gyd-dirogion yn cam-derwynu wrtho.
>
> His fellow-countrymen unjustly *becoming enflamed* against him *H. Geraint—Mabinogion.*

Terydd, *s. m.—pl. t.* ion (ter) A refiner.

Terydd, *a.* (tèr) Ardent, vehement, full of activity, volatile; swift, nimble.

— — Torfoedd terydd eu gawr, trwm eu dyar.

Hosts of *vehement* shout, heavy their din. *Taliesin.*

Teryddawl, *a.* (terydd) Tending to render ardent or vehement; apt to be volatile.

Pummed bwystnou
Ar holl wibion
Eifftion;
Gwelsid milied,
O drwm aeled
Deryddolion.

The fifth was destruction upon all the flying things of the Egyptians, the animals were seen, through severe disease, *maddened ones.* *Taliesin.*

Teryddiad, *s. m.* (terydd) A rendering ardent, vehement, or full of activity.

Teryddu, *v. a.* (terydd) To render rapid; to grow rapid.

Teryg, *s. m.* (tèr) An incrustation, a crust, or any thing clotted on the surface, incrusted dirt. *Mae teryg ar dy sodlau*, there is a crust of dirt on thy heels.

Teryll, *a.* (tèr) Ardently glancing. *Golwg teryll*, an ardently-glancing eye, a piercing eye.

Teryllaidd, *a.* (teryll) Tending to glance ardently

Terylliad, *s. m.* (teryll) A glancing ardently.

Teryllu, *v. a.* (teryll) To glance ardently; to look fiercely.

Tes, *s. m.* (te—es) A spreading of rays; sunheat, sunshine, hot weather. *Graid* is used for it in South Wales generally.

Cydwynsed a'r tes.

As warm as the *sunshine.* *Adage.*

Edrych harddwch yr haul yn ei des, ac nid yn ei fliw.

Look at the beauty of the sun in its *shining*, and not in its disk. *Adage.*

Morfudd glaer——
Mal haul ymylau hoewles,
Mamaeth tywysogaeth tes.

Bright Morfudd, like a sun with rays of active beneficence, the mother of the sovereignty of *heat.* *D. ab Gwilym.*

Dillad i noeth——
A gwely, a thy, a thes aelwyd.

Clothing for the naked, and bed, and house, and the *warmth* of a hearth. *Gwalchmai.*

Tesa, *v. a.* (tes) To gather warmth; to wanton.

Tesach, *s. m.* (tes) Fullness of heat; wantonness.

Tesain, *a.* (tes) Abounding with warmth.

Tesaint, *s. m.* (tesain) A state teeming with warmth; cheeringness, gladness.

Meifod wen——
A'i balchwyr, a'i balchwir tesaint.

Fair Meivod, with its eminent men, and its soaring truth of *gladness.* *Cynddelw.*

Tesawg, *a.* (tes) Abounding with heat; abounding with sunshine, sunny, hot.

Un o'r tri engir ddichwain—yr haf tesawg, pan aethynt y coedydd a'r llysiau ar dan, gan angerdd gwres yr haul, a cholli llawer o ddynion, ac anifeiliaid, a rhywiau adar, a phryfed, a choedydd, a llysiau, yn anesgorawl.

One of the three awful events: the *hot* summer, when the woods and the herbs took fire, from the vehemency of the heat of the sun, and many men being lost, and cattle, and species of birds, and animals, and woods, and herbs, irretrievably. *Trioedd.*

Tesawl, *a.* (tes) Affording warmth or heat.

Tesfawr, *a.* (tes) Abounding with much heat.

Tesiad, *s. m.* (tes) A dispensing warmth.

Tesiant, *s. m.* (tes) A producing warmth.

Testun, *s. m.—pl. t.* au (tes—tun) A theme, or subject of investigation.

Erioed ni welais yr un,
Euraid wystl, a roe destun.

Never have I seen one, of golden pledge, that would propose a *subject.* *D. ab Gwilym.*

Testunaw, *v. a.* (testun) To set a subject or theme

Teth, *s. f.—pl. t.* au (te—eth) A teat, a dug, or pap. *Tethau y gaseg*, honeysuckle; also called *gwyddfid.*

Tethaidd, *a.* (teth) Like a teat or dug.

Tethan, *s. f. dim.* (teth) A small teat.

Tethawg, *a.* (teth) Having teats or dugs.

Tethawl, *a.* (teth) Papillary, belonging to teats.

Tethiad, *s. m.* (teth) A forming a teat.

Tethu, *v. n.* (teth) To grow into a teat.

Teulu, *s. m.—pl. t.* oedd (tau—llu) A family, or household; a clan, or tribe. *Y teulu, y tylwyth teg, bendith eu mamau*, fairies: *Cwn teulu*, fairy dogs.

Tri diwair deulu Ynys Prydain—teulu Cadwallawn ab Beli, pan fuant huaslogion; teulu Gafran mab Aeddan, pan fu yn y difancoll; a theulu Gwenddoleu ab Ceidio, yn Arderydd, a ddaliasant yr ymladd bythefnos a mis wedi lladd eu harglwydd.

The three faithful *clans* of the Isle of Britain: the clan of Cadwallon son of Beli, when they were fettered together; the clan of Gavran son of Aeddan, when he was in the overwhelming wreck; and the clan of Gwenddoleu son of Ceidio in Arderydd, who carried on the war for a fortnight and a month after the death of their lord. *Triads.*

Teuluaeth, *s. m.* (teulu) Domestic economy; social intercourse; hospitality.

Brodyr teuluaeth: bardd, ysgolaig, a dadgeiniad.

The brothers of *social life*: a bard, a scholar, and a singer. *Adage.*

Teuluaidd, *a.* (teulu) Belonging to a family, or household; domestic, familiar.

Teuluaeth, *s. m.* (teulu) Domestic economy.

Teuluawg, *a.* (teulu) Having a family.

Teuluawl, *a.* (teulu) Belonging to a family.

Teuluedd, *s. m.* (teulu) Familiarity; concord.

Ar ol talu yr alanas, bid teuluedd tragywyddawl rhwng y ddwy genedl.

After paying the fine of homicide, let there be *eternal concord* between the two generations. *Welsh Laws.*

Teulueidd-dra, *s. m.* (teuluaidd) Domesticity.

Teulueiddiad, *s. m.* (teuluaidd) A domesticating, a familiarizing; a becoming hospitable.

Teulueiddiaw, *v. a.* (teuluaidd) To domesticate; to become hospitable.

Teulueiddrwydd, *s. m.* (teuluaidd) Domesticness; hospitality.

Ac ni char gwanar genym
Ond teulueiddrwydd rwydd ym.

And the distributor loves with us but *hospitality* of [illegible]. *E. [illegible]*

Teuluwas, *s. m.—pl.* teuluweision (teulu—gwas) A domestic servant.

Nid oes—i'th deuluwas
Awr daw, ond wylaw gwlaw glain.

There is not for thy *household servant* a silent hour, but to weep the pearly drops. *D. ab Gwilym.*

Teuluwr, *s. m.—pl.* teuluwyr (teulu—gwr) Household man, a family man; a hospitable man.

Teulüwriaeth, *s. m.* (teulüwr) Household economy, domestic order; hospitality.

Teuluwraig, *s. f.—pl.* teuluwreigedd (teulu—gwraig) A housewife.

Teulüydd, *s. m.—pl. t.* ion (teulu) One who domesticates; a family man.

Teulüyddawl, *a.* (teulüydd) Apt to familiarize.

Teulüyddes, *s. f.—pl. t.* au (teulüydd) Housewife

Teuluyddiaeth, *s. m.* (teulüydd) The act of domesticating; a domestic state.

Tew, *s. m.—pl. t.* ion (te) That is thick, or gross; fat. *a.* Thick, gross, fat, plump; frequent, or abundant. *Croen tew*, a thick skin; *dyn tew*, a fat person; *y mor sy dew o bysgod*, the sea is thick of fishes.

Tew y beiau lle teneu y cariad.

Thick are the faults where the affection is slender. *Adage.*

Tewâad, *s. m.* (tewâu) A thickening.
Tewâawl, *a.* (tewâu) Tending to thicken.
Tewaidd, *a.* (tew) Somewhat thick or gross.
Tewâu, *v. a.* (tew) To thicken; to condense; to fatten; to become thick; to grow fat.
Tewban, *s. m.* (tew—pan) That is thickened by beating, or by fulling.
Tewbanawg, *a.* (tewban) Being thickened by milling; an epithet for several thick-leaved plants. *Y dewbanawg, canwyll yr adar, y banawg, clust y fuwch*, the great mullein, or high-taper; *y dewbanawg fechan*, cowslip; *y dewbanawg wen wryw, gwynddail, menyg y merched*, rose-campion; *yr hanner-pan*, white-mullein.
Tewder, *s. m.* (tew) Thickness; denseness, density; fatness.
Tewdor, *s. m.* (tew—tor) A thick cover; a thick shelter or defence. *a.* Of a thick covering or shade. *Tarw tewdor*, a thick-breasted bull; *tewdor annedd*, a thickly covered habitation.

> Bid yth arfaeth i'r tri——
> Can dug pum-wan Crist pumoes o gaeth,
> O ing, o gyfing gymydogaeth,
> O angor tewdor tud alaeth.
>
> Be thy practice devoted to the three, as the five wounds of Christ brought the five ages out of thraldom; from a strait, from a constrained society, from the tenacity of the *thick shade* of the region of woe. *Cynddelw.*
>
> Gwrdd fyddin feiddiad yn nhewdor.
>
> One who attacks a powerful host in the *thickest part*. *Cynddelw.*
>
> Uchel-lan Gadfan ger glan glas-for,
> Ni chollir ei thir nac ei thewdor.
>
> The choir of Cadvan by the shore of a blue sea, its land will not be lost, nor its *thick crop*. *Llywelyn Fardd.*

Tewdra, *s. m.* (tew) Thickness, density.
Tewdrwch, *s. m.* (tew—trwch) Density, solidity. *a.* Thick in bulk, solid.

> Ein heneidiau nid ydynt yn tarddu o gorff, neu ddefnydd tewdrwch annhreiddiadwy.
>
> Our souls do not originate from a body, or *dense matter* not to be pervaded. *Ier. Owain.*

Tewdwr, *s. m.* (tew—twr) This is a thick heap.
Tewdws, *s. m.* (tew—tws) A thick assemblage. *a.* Thickly collected. *Y twr tewdws*, the pleiades.
Tewi, *s. m.* (taw) A keeping silent, a holding one's tongue. *v. a.* To keep silent, to hold one's tongue.

> Nid doethineb ond tewi.
>
> There is no wisdom like *holding the tongue*. *Adage.*
>
> Tawed doeth, annoeth ni thau.
>
> *Let* the wise *be silent*, the unwise *will* not *cease talking*. *Llywarch Hen.*
>
> Tawn, tawn, goreu yw tewi;
> Am hwn nid ynganwn i.
>
> *Let us silence, let us silence*, it is best *to be silent*, about this we will not utter a word. *Iolo Goch.*

Tewiad, *s. m.* (tew) A thickening, a condensing.
Tewlaeth, *s. m.* (tew—llaeth) Thick milk. *Llwyn y tewlaeth*, the bell-flower.
Tewlyd, *a.* (tew) Tending to grow thick.
Tewu, *v. a.* (tew) To thicken; to grow thick.
Tewwch, *s. m.* (tew) Thickness, denseness.
Tewychaidd, *a.* (tewwch) Partly tending to thicken, or condense.
Tewychawl, *a.* (tewwch) Of thickening tendency
Tewychedig, *a.* (tewwch) Condensed; spissated.
Tewychedd, *s. m.* (tewwch) Spissitude.
Tewychiad, *s. m.* (tewwch) A thickening.
Tewychiannawl, *a.* (tewychiant) Condensing.
Tewychiannu, *v. a.* (tewychiant) To condensate.
Tewychiant, *s. m.* (tewwch) Condensation.
Tewychu, *v.* (tewwch) To thicken, to condense.

Tewyn, *s. m.—pl. t.* ion (te—gwyn) A firebrand, or a torch; a burning coal.

> Tewyn a than yn mhob pen.
>
> A *brand* with a fire in both ends. *Adage.*

Tewynawl, *a.* (tewyn) Tending to produce light.
Tewynllyd, *a.* (tewyn) Apt to produce light.

> Callestr tanllestr tewynllyd,
> O waith gof yn boeth i gyd.
>
> A flint fire-pan *aptly striking fire*, the work of a smith altogether hot. *T. Prys, on two pistols.*

Teyrn, *s. m.—pl. t.* edd (te—gyrn) A sovereign, a king, a supreme ruler.

> Truan teyrn heb ei osgordd.
>
> A *sovereign* is miserable without his train. *Adage.*
>
> Tarw——
> Cyrn, mal yn deyrn, y dwg,
> Mawr gwynion, yn Morgannwg.
>
> The bull, like a *sovereign*, carries horns large and white, in Morganoc. *D. ab Ieuan Ddu.*

Teyrnaidd, *a.* (teyrn) Like a sovereign.
Teyrnaig, *s. f.* (teyrn—aig) A supreme origin.

> Teyrnaig arwar arfollitor gwen
> Teyrngerdd awen amgen am gor.
>
> The *sovereign source* of tranquillity receiving the smile of the peculiar royal song of the muse round the circle. *Cynddelw, i O. Gwynedd.*

Teyrnain, *a.* (teyrn) Having sovereignty.
Teyrnair, *s. m.* (teyrn—gair) A royal word.
Teyrnas, *s. f.—pl. t.* oedd (teyrn) A kingdom.

> Bwyf yn heddwch—gloew deyrnas
> Gwledig nef a llawr a llwyr ddinas,
> Llary arglwydd llawer llewyn gwanas.
>
> May I inherit the peace of the glorious *kingdom* of the Supreme of heaven and earth and the whole universe, the beneficent Lord of many central radiations. *Meilyr ab Gwalchmai.*

Teyrnasawl, *a.* (teyrnas) Having a kingdom.
Teyrnasiad, *s. m.* (teyrnas) A reigning, a reign.
Teyrnasiaeth, *s. m.* (teyrnas) The rule of a kingdom; a reign.
Teyrnasu, *v. a.* (teyrnas) To govern a kingdom, to perform the functions of a king, to reign.
Teyrnawg, *a.* (teyrn) Having a king.
Teyrnawl, *a.* (teyrn) Belonging to royalty.
Teyrndlws, *s. m.—pl.* teyrndlysau (teyrn—tlws) A jewel or part of regalia.
Teyrndreth, *s. f.—pl. t.* i (teyrn—treth) A tribute.
Teyrnddrud, *a.* (teyrn—drud) Royally bold.
Teyrnedd, *s. m.* (teyrn) Sovereignty, kingship.

> Prydain ab Aedd Mawr a wnai wladoliaeth a theyrnedd gyntaf ar Ynys Prydain; a chyn no hyny nid oedd o iawn namyn a wnelid o addwynder, na deddf namyn y trechaf treisied.
>
> Prydain son of Aedd the Great formed a body politic and *sovereignty* first in the Isle of Britain; and previously there was of justice only what might be done through kindness of disposition, nor any law but the strongest might oppress. *Trioedd.*

Teyrnes, *s. f.—pl. t.* au (teyrn) Female sovereign.
Teyrnfar, *s. m.* (teyrn—bar) A kingly wrath.
Teyrnfardd, *s. m.—pl.* teyrnfeirdd (teyrn—bardd) A royal bard.
Teyrnfoes, *s. f.* (teyrn—moes) A kingly demeanour.

> Teyrnfoes eirioes eiriachador
> Teyrnedd ai gwyl, a gwelator.
>
> A splendid *kingly demeanour* to be imploring, princes behold it, and it will be seen. *Cynddelw, i O Gwynedd.*

Teyrnfrad, *s. m.* (teyrn—brad) Treason against a sovereign; high treason.
Teyrnfradu, *v. a.* (teyrnfrad) To commit treason against a sovereign.
Teyrnfradwr, *s. m.—pl.* teyrnfradwyr (teyrnfrad—gwr) A traitor against a king.
Teyrnfradwriaeth, *s. m.* (teyrnfradwr) High treason.

Teyrnfro, *s. f.—pl. t.* ydd (teyrn—bro) A country under the rule of a king.
Teyrnfudd, *s. f.* (teyrn—budd) Benefit of the king.
Teyrnged, *s. f.—pl. t.* oedd (teyrn—ced) Tribute

> Gwedi clybod o Gloew Celsar y chwedl hwnw, yntau a anfones Fespasian, i gymbell Gweirydd ar dangnefedd â gwyr Rhufain, ac i dalu y gostsedig deyrnged.
>
> After Claudius Cæsar had heard that report, he then sent Vespasian, to prevail on Gweirydd to be on terms of peace with the men of Rome, and to pay the accustomed *tribute*. *Gr. ab Arthur.*

Teyrngerdd, *s. f.—pl. t.* i (teyrn—cerdd) Royal song.
Teyrngoron, *s. f.—pl. t.* au (teyrn—coron) A diadem.
Teyrnialen, *s. f. dim.* (teyrn—ialen) A sceptre.

> Yn yr ystafell hono yr oedd cader, yn yr hon yn fawredig yr oedd tywysawg yn eistedd—ac yn ei law deyrnialen.
>
> In that chamber there was a chair, in which majestically there was seated a prince, and holding in his hand a *sceptre*. *Marchawg Crwydrad.*

Teyrnlaw, *s. f.* (teyrn—llaw) A royal hand.
Teyrnles, *s. m.* (teyrn—lles) The good of a king.
Teyrnlid, *s. m.* (teyrn—llid) Royal wrath.
Teyrnlin, *s. m.* (teyrn—llin) Royal line.
Teyrnlw, *s. m.* (teyrn—llw) A royal oath.
Teyrnogaeth, *s. f.* (teyrnawg) A kingly office.
Teyrnogi, *v. a.* (teyrnawg) To render kingly; to become regal.
Teyrnoldeb, *s. m.* (teyrnawl) A regal state.
Teyrnolder, *s. m.* (teyrnawl) Regality.
Teyrnoledd, *s. m.* (teyrnawl) Royalty.
Teyrnoli, *v. a.* (teyrnawl) To render regal.
Teyrnolrwydd, *s. m.* (teyrnawl) Regality.
Teyrnon, *s. m.* (teyrn) A princely one.

> Selyf yngnad——
> Bu gwell nog udd
> Mab teyrnon;
> Bu gnawd berthon
> O'i gyweithydd.
>
> Selyf the judge, superior to him was the son of a *royal chief*, wealth was eventual from having his support. *Taliesin.*

Teyrnwal, *s. f.* (teyrn—gwal) A regal couch.
Teyrnwalch, *s. m.—pl.* teyrnweilch (teyrn—gwalch) An aspiring prince.
Teyrnwarth, *s. m.* (teyrn—gwarth) Royal shame.
Teyrnwas, *s. m.—pl.* teyrnweision (teyrn—gwas) A royal youth.

> Dinas teyrnas teyrnwais oben
> Teyrnwalch din Emrais:
> Bu da dethol a gefais;
> Bu doeth fal y detholais.
>
> The bulwark of the kingdom of yielding *princely youths* is the aspiring lord of the castle of Emrais, a choice good fortune I obtained; wise was the course I chose. *Cynddelw.*

Teyrnwawd, *s. m.* (teyrn—gwawd) Royal eulogy.
Teyrnwawl, *s. m.* (teyrn—gwawl) Royal splendor.
Teyrnwawr, *s. f.* (teyrn—gwawr) Dawn of royalty
Teyrnwialen, *s. f.* (teyrn—gwialen) A sceptre.
TI, *s. m. r.* That is in; that is separate; that is distinct. *pron.* Thee; thou. *I ti a mi da peidiaw*, for thee and me it is good to desist: *Ti yw y dyn*, thou art the person.

> Gwna iawn, ti a gei iawn amdano.
>
> Do justice, *thou* shalt have justice in return for it. *Adage.*
>
> Tal am dy wawd, cyn toll;
> Twyll y prydyddion wyt ti.
>
> Pay for thy praise, ere it be curtailed. the delusion of the poets art *thou*. *D. ab Gwilym, i Ierfudd.*

Tib, *s. m.—pl. t.* ion (ti—ib) A particle; a bit.
Tiboeth, *s. m.* (tib—oeth) A pure particle. It was the name of a rare book, left by Beuno in the church of Clynawg, and said to have been written by Twrog, in the beginning of the seventh century.

> Llygad fal glain cawad coeth,
> Tebyg i faen y tiboeth.
>
> An eye like the pure shower crystal, to be compared to the pure drop gem. *Egg. Cyfeiliawg.*

Tic, *s. m.—pl. t.* ion (ti—ic) A particle.
Ticiad, *s. m.—pl. t.* au (tic) A forming into small particles.
Ticial, *v. a.* (tic) To produce small particles, or drops; to drain the last drops, in milking.
Ticyn, *s. m. dim.—pl. t.* au (tic) A particle, a small bit, a little scrap.

> Mae pob ticyn yn dicyn, chwedl y dryw, pan biswys yn y mor.
>
> Every *little* is a *little*, said the wren, when he pissed in the sea. *Adage.*

Tid, *s. f.—pl. t.* au (ti—id) A draught chain. *Bwrw tidau*, to let drivel, to fall, to drivel, to tiddle.
Tidaw, *v. a.* (tid) To fasten with a chain or rope, to chain.
Tidawg, *a.* (tid) Having a chain, chained.
Tidawl, *a.* (tid) Belonging to a chain; like a chain.
Tidiad, *s. m.—pl. t.* au (tid) A chaining.
Tidiedig, *a.* (tidiad) Being fastened with a chain.
Tidmwy, *s. m.—pl t.* au (tid—mwy) A tedder.
Tidmwyad, *s. m.* (tidmwy) A teddering.
Tidmwyaw, *v. a.* (tidmwy) To tie, to tedder.

> Cymer a fo yn dy feddiant,
> A thidmwya dy fawrchwant,
> Haws no'u cadw cynnull ariant.
>
> Take of what is in thy possession, and *restrain thy cupidity*; it is easier than to keep to collect money. *Cattwg ab Gwynllyw.*

Tidraff, *s. f.—pl. t.* au (tid—rhaff) A chain-rope.
Tifar, *a.* (ti—bar) Repentant, contrite.
Tifariad, *s. m.* (tifar) A repenting; repentance.
Tifaru, *v. a.* (tifar) To repent, to be sorry.

> Tifaru fal y gwr a laddwys ei filgi.
>
> *To repent* like the man who killed his greyhound. *Adage.*
>
> Mae yn rhy hwyr tifaru,
> Yn ol i'r fagl gynnu.
>
> It is too late *to repent*, after the trap hath sprung. *Adage.*

Tifarus, *a.* (tifar) Repenting, penitent.
Tifedd, *s. m.—pl. t.* ion (ti—medd) An heir.

> Plant Tudyr—haelion peotcuin
> A thifeddion, iaith fyddyd,
> Gwynedd; pedwar cydwedd ced.
>
> The children of Tudyr, generous chiefs of tribes, and *heirs* (ominous be the words) of Gwynedd; four alike for gifts. *Iolo Goch.*

Tifeddadwy, *a.* (tifedd) Hereditable; inheritable.
Tifeddawg, *a.* (tifedd) Having inheritance.
Tifeddawl, *a.* (tifedd) Hereditary; inheriting.
Tifeddedig, *a.* (tifedd) Being inherited.
Tifeddes, *s. f.—pl. t.* au (tifedd) An inheritrix.
Tifeddiad, *s. m.* (tifedd) An inheriting.
Tifeddiaeth, *s. m.* (tifedd) Inheritance.
Tifeddiaethu, *v. a.* (tifeddiaeth) To form an inheritance.
Tifeddogi, *v. a.* (tifeddawg) To endow with an inheritance; to have an inheritance.
Tifeddogrwydd, *s. m.* (tifeddawg) The state of being inherited.
Tifeddoldeb, *s. m.* (tifeddawl) The state of being hereditary.
Tifeddoli, *v. a.* (tifeddawl) To render hereditary.
Tifeddolrwydd, *s. m.* (tifeddawl) The state of being hereditary.
Tifeddu, *v. a.* (tifedd) To inherit; to possess.
Tifeddus, *a.* (tifedd) Hereditary; possessory.
Tifeddusaw, *v. a.* (tifeddus) To render hereditary, to become hereditary.

Tifeddusrwydd, *s. m.* (tifeddus) The state of being hereditary.

Tifeddwr, *s. m.—pl.* tifeddwyr (tifedd—gwr) An inheritor.

Tifeiriad, *s. m.* (tifar) A repenting.

Tifeiriannawl, *a.* (tifeiriant) Tending to repentance, or remorse.

Tifeiriannu, *v. a.* (tifeiriant) To produce repentance, or remorse.

Tifeiriannus, *a.* (tifeiriant) Tending to repentance, or remorse.

Tifeiriant, *s. m.* (tifar) Repentance, remorse.

> Mair Fawdlen, seren y saint,
> Y dwf orea difeiriaint.
>
> Mary Magdalene, the luminary of saints, the choicest fruit of repentance. *Gutyn Ceiriawg.*

Tifeirwch, *s. m.* (tifar) Repentance, remorse.

> Tifeirwch newydd am hen bechawd.
>
> New *remorse* for an old sin. *Adage.*

Til, *s. m.—pl. t.* ion (ti—il) A minute particle.

Tiliad, *s. m.—pl.* tiliaid (til) A small fly like a gnat.

Tim, *s. m.—pl. t.* ion (ti—im) A little.

Timyn, *s. m. dim.—pl. t.* au (tim) A small particle; a little bit, a small matter.

> A ryddywedais i hyd hyn,
> I Wenddydd waesaf unbyn,
> Dyaderbid cymaint timyn.
>
> What I have predicted until now, to Gwenddydd the idol of princes, it shall come to pass to the smallest *tittle.* *Cyf. Merddin.*

Tin, *s. f.—pl. t.* au (ti—in) A tail, a bottom, a breech. *Tin y cwd*, the bottom of the bag: *Tin y nyth, bach y nyth*, the tail of the nest, or the least of the brood; *tin y gler*, the tail of the minstrels, a poetaster: *Tinion yr yd*, the light grains of corn: *Tin ab*, the ape's breech, a fault in prosody, being the full rhyme, as used in English versification.

Tinagored, *a.* (tin—agored) Open tailed. *Tinagored*, the common medlar; also called *y dindoll.*

Tinaw, *v. a.* (tin) To form a tail; to stretch out the posteriors.

Tinawg, *a.* (tin) Having a tail; having large posteriors.

Tinawl, *a.* (tin) Belonging to the posteriors.

Tinbais, *s. f.—pl.* tinbeisiau (tin—pais) A petticoat.

Tinben, *adv.* (tin—pen) Head to tail. *Tinbendrosben, tin-drosben*, topsy-turvy.

Tinbleth, *a.* (tin—pleth) Tail-twined.

Tinboeth, *a.* (tin—poeth) Hot-tailed. *Y dinboeth*, arsesmart; also called *elinawg: y tinboeth, y tingoch*, the redstart, a bird so called.

Tinbren, *s. m.—pl. t.* i (tin—pren) The bracer.

Tinc, *s. m.—pl. t.* ion (ting) A tink, a tinkle.

Tinceirddiad, *s. m.—pl.* tinceirddiaid (tincerdd) A doing tinkery work.

Tinceirddiaeth, *s. m.* (tincerdd) Tinkery.

Tinceirddiaw, *v. a.* (tincerdd) To work as a tinker.

Tinceirddiawl, *a.* (tincerdd) Belonging to a tinker's work.

Tincerdd, *s. m.—pl.* tinceirddion (tin—cerdd) The tail of a craft, a tinker.

Tincerddiaeth, *s. m.* (tincerdd) Tinkery.

Tinciad, *s. m.* (tinc) A tinking, a tinkling.

Tincial, *v. a.* (tinc) To tinkle, to tingle; to draw the last milk, in milking.

Tincian, *v. a.* (tinc) To tink, to tinkle, to tingle; to draw the last milk; to drain the last drops. *Ni waeth i ti dewi no thincian*, thou mayest as well be silent as to be dinning.

Tinciaw, *v. a.* (tinc) To tink, to tinkle; to ring.

Tincion, *s. pl. aggr.* (tinc) The last-drawn milk.

Tincwd, *s. m.* (tin—cwd) The bottom of a bag.

> A fyno fod yn bencwd, na wnaed a wedd i dincwd.
>
> He that would be the top of a bag, let him not commit what suits the *bottom of a bag.* *Adage.*

Tindafliad, *s. m.* (tin—tafliad) A throwing the tail, a shaking the tail.

Tindaflu, *v. a.* (tin—taflu) To throw the tail; to winch.

Tindew, *a.* (tin—tew) Fat-buttocked.

Tindin, *adv.* (tin *repeated*) Tail to tail.

Tindoll, *a.* (tin—toll) Having the tail sink. *Y dindoll*, the common medlar.

Tindopiaw, *v. a.* (tin—topiaw) To flounce.

Tindraphen, *adv.* (tin—tra—pen) Arse over head.

Tindraws, *a.* (tin—traws) Cross-tailed.

Tindro, *s. m.* (tin—tro) A turn of the tail.

Tindroed, *s. m.* (tin—troed) The didapper.

Tindroi, *v. a.* (tin—dro) To turn the tail.

Tindrom, *a.* (tin—trom) Heavy-tailed.

Tindrosben, *adv.* (tin—tros—pen) Arse over head.

> Dedeirawr y bu daraw
> Annyben dindrosben draw.
>
> For four hours there was yonder a tedious *topsy-turvy* contest. *Morgan Elfael.*

Tindrwm, *a.* (tin—trwm) Heavy-tailed.

Tinfoel, *a.* (tin—moel) Bare-tailed. *Brayan dinfoel*, a round-bottomed quern.

Tingloff, *a.* (tin—cloff) Lame in the hip.

Tingloffedd, *s. m.* (tingloff) Lameness of the hip.

Tingloffi, *v. a.* (tingloff) To render lame in the hip; to become lame in the hip.

Tingloffni, *s. m.* (tingloff) A limping, a halting.

Tingoch, *a.* (tin—coch) Red-tailed. *Aderyn tingoch, aderyn rhawngoch, gwas y seiri*, the bullfinch.

Tingrach, *a.* (tin—crach) Scabby-tailed.

Tingrechi, *s. m.* (tingrach) Scabbiness of the tail.

Tiniaw, *v. a.* (tin) To turn tail.

Tinlach, *a.* (tin—llach) Broad-bottomed; squabby.

Tinlethu, *v. a.* (tin—lletbu) To overlay.

Tinllachiad, *s. m.—pl.* tinllachiaid (tinlach) A broad-bottomed one.

Tinllom, *a.* (tin—llom) Bare-bottomed.

Tinllwm, *a.* (tin—llwm) Bare-bottomed.

Tinllwyd, *s. m.* (tin—llwyd) Wild-tansy.

Tinnoeth, *a.* (tin—noeth) Bare-tailed.

Tinpen, *s. f.—pl. t.* i (tin—pen) A hassock or straw stool. *Tinpen fagu*, a nursing-stool.

Tinred, *s. f.* (tin—rhed) A tail running.

Tinroth, *a.* (tin—rhoth) Open-tailed.

Tinrwth, *a.* (tin—rhwth) Open-tailed.

Tinrythiad, *s. m.* (tinrwth) A tail opening.

Tinrythu, *v. a.* (tinrwth) To open tail.

> Nycha'r fran—
> Yn dwyn rhuthr dan dinrythu.
>
> Behold the crow making an assault while *spreading out the tail.* *D. ab Gwilym.*

Tinsigl, *s. m.* (tin—sigl) A wagtail. *Tinsigl y gwys, brith y fuches*, the field wagtail; *tinsigl y dwfr*, the water wagtail or kingafisher.

Tinsiglad, *s. m.* (tinsigl) A shaking the tail.

Tinsiglaw, *v. a.* (tinsigl) To shake the tail.

Tinwyg, *a.* (tin—gwyg) Open-tailed.

Tinwygydd, *s. m.—pl. t.* ion (tinwyg) One with open tail.

> Mynaich—ynt ar eu breigig,
> Braigon dinwygyddion dig.
>
> The monks, they feast on their fat viands, the surly pampered open tailed ones. *Dr. S. Cent.*

Ting, *s. m.* (ti—ing) A crinkle; a tingle.

Tingaw, *v. a.* (ting) To draw up, or to contract; to tingle.

> Y glyw glew dywal, ni dal, ni ding.
>
> The chief brave and fierce, that will not concede, that will not *flinch*. *Cynddelw.*

Tingawl, *a.* (ting) Crinkling; tinking.

Tingiad, *s. m.* (ting) A crinkling; a tinking.

Tip, *s. m.—pl. t.* iau (tib) A particle, a bit, or small fragment. *Dyma fo wedi tori yn dipiau man*, here it is broken all to shatters.

Tipyn, *s. m.—pl. t.* au (tip) A point; a small particle, bit, or piece. *Tipynau crynion*, round particles: *Taled imi o dipyn i dipyn*, it has been paid to me by little and little: *O dipyn i beth*, from a little to some.

Tipyniad, *s. m.* (tipyn) A forming a small bit, or particle.

Tipynu, *v. a.* (tipyn) To form into a small bit, to divide into particles.

Tir, *s. m.—pl. t.* oedd (ti—ir) Land; earth, soil, ground. *Tir sych, sychdir*, dry land; *tir llan*, glebe land; *tir bwrdd y llys*, land for the table of the palace; *tir cyfrif, tir cyllidus*, land liable to a tax or rent, copyhold land; *tir swch a chwillir*, land under socage tenure; *tir diffodd-edig*, alienated land; *tir gwelyawg*, land held by gavel kind; *tir gwydd, tir gwyddwyr*, wood land turned into arable; *tir ar*, arable land; *tir y faerdref*, demesne land.

> Un o dri chyfarwyddawg Ynys Prydain: Hu Gadarn, a ddangoses y ffordd i aru tir gyntaf i genedl y Cymmry.
>
> One of the three gift-bestowers of the Isle of Britain: Hu the Mighty, who shewed the way to plough *land* first to the nation of the Cymmry. *Trioedd.*
>
> Yno y caiff Brython
> Eu tir, a'u coron;
> A'r bobl estronion
> A ddiflanna.
>
> Then the Brython shall obtain their *land*, and their crown; and the foreign people shall disappear. *Ionas Athraw o Fynyw.*

Tir, *s. m.* (ty—ir) That extends, or continues.

Tiraeth, *s. m.* (tir) Continuity, continuation.

Tiraw, *v. a.* (tir) To extend in continuity.

Tirawg, *a.* (tir) Continual; continuative.

> Truan im', wr glan rhy galonawg,
> Tori fy llygaid tirawg yn wylaw!
>
> Miserable for me, after the agreeable man courageous to excess, I burst my eyes with *continual* weeping! *L. G. Cothi.*

Tirdra, *s. m.* (tir—tra) Land detention, one of the three causes for rejecting witnesses in trials respecting land, which was when the witness had an issue undetermined upon it.

> Tirdra, neu drais am dir y sy lys ar wybyddiaid.
>
> *Land detention*, or forcible occupation of land, is a cause of rejection of cognizers. *Welsh Laws.*

Tirdriniad, *s. m.* (tir—triniad) A dressing of land.

Tirdriniaeth, *s. m.* (tir—triniaeth) Land dressing.

Tirdriniawl, *a.* (tir—triniawl) Agricultural.

Tirddiwyll, *s. m.* (tir—diwyll) Agriculture.

Tirddiwylliad, *s. m.* (tirddiwyll) A practising of agriculture.

Tirddiwylliaw, *v. a.* (tirddiwyll) To practise agriculture.

Tirddiwylliawd, *s. m.* (tirddiwyll) Agriculture.

Tirddiwylliawdr, *s. m.—pl.* tirddiwylliodron (tirddiwylliawd) An agriculturist.

> Annogai y brenin y tirddiwylliodron i ddiwylliaw y ddaiar.
>
> The king was wont to urge the *husbandmen* to cultivate the earth. *Gr. ab Arthur.*

Tirddiwylliawdwr, *s. m.—pl.* tirddiwylliawdwyr (tirddiwylliawd—gwr) An agriculturist.

Tirddiwylliodraeth, *s. m.* (tirddiwylliawdr) The practice of agriculture.

Tirf, *a.* (tir) Fresh, vigorous, luxuriant, rich, lively, fat.

> Y rhai a blanwyd yn nhy yr Arglwydd, a flodeuant yn nghynteddoedd ein Duw: Ffrwythant eto yn eu henaint; tirfion ac iraidd fyddant.
>
> Those that have been planted in the house of the Lord, will flourish in the courts of our God: They will bring forth fruit again in their old age: *fresh* and lively they will be. *Psalm* [illegible]

Tirfhad, *s. m.* (tirf) A freshening; a fattening.

Tirfhawl, *a.* (tirf) Tending to enrich.

Tirfâu, *v. a.* (tirf) To freshen; to enrich.

Tirfdra, *s. m.* (tirf) Freshness, richness.

Tiriad, *s. m.* (tir) A landing, a making land.

Tiriadu, *v. a.* (tiriad) A making a landing.

Tiriaeth, *s. m.* (tir) What has respect to land.

Tiriaethawl, *a.* (tiriaeth) Agrarian.

Tiriaw, *v. a.* (tir) To land; to turn up the ground; to come to land, to come ashore.

> Rhyw iddo dirlaw ereill diredd.
>
> It is habitual for him *to land* in other lands. *Llygad Gwr.*
>
> Wedi ein tiriaw i Syracusa y trigasom yno dridiau.
>
> After we *came to land* to Syracuse we abided there for three days. *W. Salisbury.*

Tiriawg, *a.* (tir) Having land, or landed.

Tiriawl, *a.* (tir) Terreous, or earthly.

Tiriedig, *a.* (tiriad) Being made land; landed.

Tiriogaeth, *s. m.* (tiriawg) Landed property.

> Gorpo teyrnfar teyrnogaeth brud
> Ar Brydain diriogaeth.
>
> May his royal energy obtain the predicted sovereignty over the *territory* of Britain. *Cynddelw, i O. Cyfeiliawg.*

Tiriogawl, *a.* (tiriawg) Agrarian; belonging to the possession of land.

Tiriogi, *v. a.* (tiriawg) To possess land.

Tirion, *s. m.* (tir—ion) A source of continuance; a familiar spot; a situation, or station.

> Ei threthau yw traethadurion,
> A gyfyd yn gyfoethogion:
> A hynaf henw henyw o'i thirion,
> Randid rhyd rhwng ei dwy afon.
>
> Its tributes are orators, who shall rise up possessors of wealth; and the oldest name, which proceeded from its *situation*, it used be the ford between its two rivers. *Cynddelw i Feifod.*
>
> Dwyn Dafydd o'i dud ac o'i dirion!
>
> Taking away Dafydd out of his land and out of his *familiar spot*! *Ll. P. Moch.*

Tirion, *a.* (tir—ion) Pleasant, pleasing, genial; kind, courteous; lovely, delightful. *Lle tirion*, a pleasant place; *dyn tirion*, a courteous person; *O, dirioned ydyw hi!* Oh, how lovely she is!

> Ei deurudd dirion
> A gar y gwirion,
> A llu coed irion,
> Lle cadeiriant.
>
> Her *lovely* cheeks the innocent doth love, and the haunts of verdant woods, where they spread themselves. *W. Llyn.*

Tirionaidd, *a.* (tirion) Of a tendency to delight.

Tirionawl, *a.* (tirion) Delighting, pleasing.

Tiriondeb, *s. m.* (tirion) Pleasantness; kindness, courteousness; loveliness; gentleness.

Tirionder, *s. m.* (tirion) Pleasantness; kindness.

Tiriondra, *s. m.* (tirion) Pleasantness; kindness.

Tirionedd, *s. m.* (tirion) Pleasantness; kindness.

Tirioneiddiad, *s. m.* (tirionaidd) A rendering somewhat pleasing; a becoming pleasing.

Tirioneiddiaw, *v. a.* (tirionaidd) To render somewhat pleasing; to become rather pleasing.

Tirioneiddrwydd, *s. m.* (tirionaidd) Pleasingness.

Tirioni, *v. a.* (tirion) To render pleasant or pleasing; to render kind or lovely; to become pleasant or genial; to be kind or compassionate;

to become delightful; to become gentle. *O, tiriona wrtho, da dithau!* Oh, be compassionate to him, that is a good creature!

O daw gwedi, dig ydwyf;
Trwy na ddel, tirion 'ddwyf.

If afterwards he come, I am angry grown; so he comes not, I am *becoming pleasant.* *I. ab Hywel Gwyn.*

Tirioniad, *s. m.* (tirion) A rendering pleasant, delightful, or lovely; a becoming pleasant.

Tirionus, *a.* (tirion) Pleasing; delighting.

Tirionusaw, *v. a.* (tirionus) To render pleasing, or delightful; to become pleasing.

Tirionusedd, *s. m.* (tirionus) Pleasingness.

Tirionusrwydd, *s. m.* (tirionus) Pleasingness.

Tirionwch, *s. m.* (tirion) Pleasantness, delectableness; kindness, genialness, suavity, courteousness; loveliness; gentleness.

Pan fo Mon a'i thirionwch,
O wres fflam, yn eirias fflwch.

When Mona and its *pleasantness* shall be, from the heat of destructive flame, a fervid ember. *Gro. Owain.*

Tirogedd, *s. m.* (tirawg) Continuity.

Tirwibiad, *s. m.—pl.* tirwibiaid (tir—gwibiad) A landloper; a vagrant.

Tis, *s. m.—pl. t.* ion (ti—is) A sneeze.

Tisiad, *s. m.—pl. t.* au (tis) A sneezing.

Tisian, *v. a.* (tis) To sneeze, to keep sneezing.

Tisiaw, *v. a.* (tis) To sneeze, to sternutate.

Tisiawg, *a.* (tis) Having a sneezing.

Tisiawl, *a.* (tis) Tending to sneeze, sneezing.

Tisiedig, *a.* (tisiad) Sneezed, or sternutated.

Tisiwr, *s. m.—pl.* tisiwyr (tis—gwr) A sneezer.

Titen, *s. f. dim.* (tid) That turns, or spins; the name of a small fly like a gnat.

Titiad, *s. m.—pl.* titiaid (tid) A sort of small fly, like a gnat. *Titiaid* are also called *gwibed bach*, and *tiliaid*.

Titw, *s. f.* (tid) Puss, a fond name for a cat.

Titr, *s. m.—pl. t.* au (tid) That makes a whirl, or spin. *Titr bach*, the name of one of the 24 measures in music.

Tithau, *pron.* (ti—tau) Thyself; thou also.

Car heddwch, a Duw a'th gar dithau.

Love peace, and God will love *thee then.* *Adage.*

Mi Lywarch; tithau Lywelyn
Mychdeyrn cedyrn.

I am Llywarch; *and thou* art Llywelyn sovereign of the mighty ones. *Ll. P. Moch.*

Tlawd, *s. m.—pl.* tlodion (tylawd) That is poor or needy, the poor. *a.* Poor.

Tlodaidd, *a.* (tlawd) Somewhat poor, or needy.

Tlodedig, *a.* (tlawd) Being rendered poor.

Tlodedd, *s. m.* (tlawd) Poverty, poorness.

A glywaisti a gant Heledd,
Ferch Cyndrwyn, fawr ei rheufedd
Nid rhodd da a wna dlodedd.

Hast thou heard what Heledd sung, the daughter of Cyndrwyn, of great wealth. It is not the giving of goods that causes *poverty.* *Eng. y Clywed.*

Tloden, *s. f. dim.* (tlawd) A poor female.

Tlodi, *s. m.* (tlawd) Poverty. *v. a.* To make poor, to impoverish; to become poor.

Tlodiad, *s. m.* (tlawd) A making poor, an impoverishment.

Tlodrwydd, *s. m.* (tlawd) Poverty, neediness.

Tlodus, *a.* (tlawd) Necessitous, needy.

Tlodusaw, *v. a.* (tlodus) To render necessitous; to become necessitous.

Tlodusdeb, *s. m.* (tlodus) Necessitousness

Tlodusder, *s. m.* (tlodus) Necessitousness.

Tlodusdra, *s. m.* (tlodus) Necessitousness.

Tlodusedd, *s. m.* (tlodus) Necessitousness.

Tlodusrwydd, *s. m.* (tlodus) Necessitousness.

Tlodyn, *s. m. dim.* (tlawd) A poor fellow.

Tlos, *a.* (*f. of* tlws) Pretty, or handsome.

Digio, dâl aur Degau dlos,
Ydyw bechawd, heb achos.

To be offended, thou with golden front like *beauteous* Tegau, is a sin, and without cause. *S. Tudyr.*

Tlosen, *s. f. dim.* (tlos) A pretty little female.

Tlosgain, *a.* (tlos—cain) Pretty and splendid. *Bun dlosgain*, a maid pretty and fine.

Tlws, *s. m.—pl.* tlysau (ty—llws) Any thing pretty; a jewel. *a.* Pretty, beautiful.

Gorau un tlws gwraig dda.

The best *jewel* of any is a good wife. *Adage.*

—— Geiriau dy fin,
Tlysau dy frawd Taliesin.

The words of thy lips, are the *beauties* of thy brother Taliesin. *H. ab Huw Bardd Coch.*

Tlysaidd, *a.* (tlws) Somewhat pretty.

Tlysair, *s. m.—pl.* tlyseiriau (tlws—gair) A fine word; a bon mot.

Tlysawg, *a.* (tlws) Abounding with jewels.

Tlysawl, *a.* (tlws) Of a pretty appearance.

Tlysedd, *s. m.* (tlws) Prettiness, handsomeness.

Tlysgist, *s. f.—pl. t.* iau (tlws—cist) A cabinet for jewels.

Tlysi, *s. m.* (tlws) Prettiness, handsomeness.

Tlysiad, *s. m.* (tlws) A rendering pretty.

Tlysiant, *s. m.* (tlws) A rendering pretty.

Tlysni, *s. m.* (tlws) Prettiness, handsomeness.

Tlysrwydd, *s. m.* (tlws) Prettiness, handsomeness.

Tlysu, *v. a.* (tlws) To render pretty.

Tlysyn, *s. m. dim.* (tlws) A pretty thing.

TO, *s. m. r.—pl. t.* au. That is out or over; an exterior, a surface; a covering; a layer; a generation; the covering of a house, a roof. *Tan do*, under cover: *pedol a'i tho o hoelion*, a horse shoe with its set of nails: *Am y to a elo to arall a ddaw*, for the generation that passes away another generation will come; *y to a ddel*, the generation to come: *To ar do*, stratum super stratum: *To gwellt*, a thatch roof; *to ceryg*, a slate roof: *Adar y to*, sparrows.

Ni wyddant ——
Pwy a ennillo o'r to y sydd.

They know not who would get the advantage of the *race* that is. *Meilyr.*

Nid dim gan y to yma,
Trwy lid oll ond treulio da

This *generation* thinks of nothing, altogether in a rage, but of wasting property. *T. Aled.*

Töad, *s. m.* (to) A covering, or spreading over; a roofing.

Töadwy, *a.* (töad) Capable of being covered.

Toawg, *a.* (to) Having a covering; being roofed.

Töawl, *a.* (to) Belonging to a covering, or roof.

Tob, *s. m.* (to—ob) A summit, or a top.

Tobren, *s. m.—pl. t.* i (to—pren) A thatcher's dibber or stick.

Tobyn, *s. m. dim.* (tob) A summit, or highest point. *Dibyn dobyn*, impending top, an expression used in childish play.

Toc, *s. m.* (to—oc) That is upon or over; that is instantaneous, short or abrupt; a hat, a cap, or bonnet.

Toc, *adv.* (toc, *s.*) Instantly, forthwith, presently, shortly. *Mi af yno toc*, I will go there presently; *toc a da*, presently and in good time.

Tocen, *s. f. dim.—pl. t.* au (toc) That is cut or docked.

Toci, *s. m.* (toc) That is cut into a piece; what is cut out; an allowance.

Tociad, *s. m.* (toc) A cutting off; clipping.
Tociaw, *v. a.* (toc) To curtail, to clip, to trim, to dock.

> Darfu i'r dinistriwr mawr wanhâu grym llaweroedd ar y ffordd, ac a dociodd eu hadenydd hwynt yn dost, fal na bu mo'r gallu ynddynt byth mwyach i ehedeg yn uchel.
>
> The great destroyer has enfeebled the energy of many on the way, and *has clipped* their wings dreadfully, so that there was no power in them ever after to fly on high. *Ier. Owain.*

Tociawg, *a.* (toc) Having a clipping, or docking; having a ticket, or ticketed.
Tociawl, *a.* (toc) Clipping, docking; ticketing.
Tociedig, *a.* (tociad) Being curtailed; clipped.
Tociwr, *s. m.—pl.* tociwyr (toc—gwr) A clipper, one who clips or docks.
Tocyn, *s. m. dim.—pl. t.* od (toc) A short piece or slip; a ticket. *Tynu tocyn*, to draw a lot; *dewis ai byraf docyn ai hiraf docyn*, choose whether the shortest lot or the longest lot.
Tocynawl, *a.* (tocyn) Belonging to a ticket.
Tocyniad, *s. m.* (tocyn) A ticketing.
Tocynu, *v. a.* (tocyn) To ticket, to draw lots.
Tochawl, *a.* (tawch) Moistening, soaking; hazy.
Tochi, *v. a.* (tawch) To render moist, to soak; to thicken; to become humid; to become foggy or hazy.
Tochiad, *s. m.* (tawch) A soaking; a hazing.
Todawl, *a.* (tawd) Being stretched in contact.
Todi, *v. a.* (tawd) To stretch over; to constrict.
Todiad, *s. m.* (tawd) A constriction; a junction.
Todyn, *s. m. dim.* (tawd) That stretches over.
Toddadwy, *a.* (tawdd) Capable of being melted.
Toddaid, *s. m.* (tawdd) That is in a melting state; that is of a melting nature; the name of a species of metre, consisting of nineteen syllables. *Y doddaid felen*, common butterwort; *y doddaid wèn*, or *toddedig*, the white rot, or marsh pennywort.
Toddawl, *a.* (tawdd) Dissolving, or melting.
Toddedig, *a.* (tawdd) Dissolved, melted. *Toddedigion*, liquids, in grammar: *Y doddedig rudd*, the rosasolis. *y doddedig wèn*, ladies bedstraw, a herb used instead of rennet.
Toddedigaeth, *s. m.* (toddedig) The act of melting
Toddedigawl, *a.* (toddedig) Of a tendency to melt
Toddi, *v. a.* (tawdd) To melt, to dissolve; to become melted.

> Ni thawdd dyled er ei haros.
>
> A debt *will* not *dissolve* in waiting for it. *Adage.*
>
> Gormes mawr a dawdd o flaen glewder bach.
>
> Great oppression *will melt away* before a little courage. *Adage.*

Toddiad, *s. m.* (tawdd) A melting, a dissolving.
Toddiannawl, *a.* (toddiant) Dissolvent.
Toddiannu, *v. a.* (toddiant) To make a solution.
Toddiant, *s. m.* (tawdd) A solution, a melting.
Toddion, *s. pl.* (tawdd) Meltings; dripping.
Toddwr, *s. m.—pl.* toddwyr (tawdd—gwr) A melter, or one who dissolves; a smelter.
Töed, *s. m.* (to) A covering; a roofing.

> Ystafell Cynddylan a'm gwân,
> Ei gweled heb doed, heb dân!
>
> The hall of Cynddylan wounds me, to see it without *covering*, without fire! *Llywarch Hen*

Töedig, *a.* (töed) Covered, or roofed.
Toes, *s. m.* (taw) Dough, or paste of bread.
Toesaidd, *a.* (toes) Somewhat like dough.
Toesawg, *a.* (toes) Abounding with dough.
Toesawl, *a.* (toes) Of a doughy quality.
Toeseg, *s. f.* (toes) A kneading trough.
Toesi, *v. a.* (toes) To make dough; to become dough.
Toesiad, *s. m.* (toes) A making into dough.
Toeslyd, *a.* (toes) Doughy or like dough.
Toeslydrwydd, *s. m.* (toeslyd) Doughiness.
Toesyn, *s. m. dim.* (toes) A lump of dough.
Tofi, *v. a.* (tawf) To draw out; to place in a range.
Tofiad, *s. m.* (tawf) A drawing out in a range.
Tofrwyn, *s. pl. aggr.* (to—brwyn) Thatch-rushes.
Togi, *v. a.* (tawg) To elongate, to extend.
Toi, *v. a.* (to) To cover over, to put a layer over; to cover in, or to roof, to thatch, to slate, or to tile a building.

> Toi y cyfreithwyr a doir â chrwyn y cyfreithgar.
>
> The houses of the lawyers are covered with the skins of the litigious. *Adage.*

Tol, *s. m.* (to—ol) that covers or includes; that separates; that is loud.
Tolach, *s. m.* (tol) A moan. *v. a.* To moan.
Tolc, *s. m.—pl. t.* iau (tol) An impression or hollow made by a blow; a dent, a dinge.

> Ni roed tolc yn yr hed hon.
>
> A *dent* has not been given to that head of thine. *O. ab Llywelyn Moel.*

Tolciad, *s. m.—pl. t.* au (tolc) A forming a hollow, or lapse; a punching, or driving in; a denting, a creasing, a dinging.

> Y tolciadau sydd yn gwasanaethu yn lle bylchau, ac y plethiadau yn tegan rhwng tyniadau a chyweirdannau.
>
> The *stops* serve instead of bowings: and the [illegible] between drawings and chords. [illegible]

Tolciaw, *v. a.* (tolc) To make a hollow, or impression by a blow; to dent, to crease, to dinge.
Tolciawg, *a.* (tolc) Having falls, dents, or creases.
Tolciedig, *a.* (tolciad) Being impressed, or dinged by any force; dinged.
Tolciwr, *s. m.—pl.* tolciwyr (tolc—gwr) One who makes a mark, or dent, by a blow.
Tolch, *s. f.—pl. t.* au (tol) A congulated mass, a clod.
Tolchedig, *a.* (tolch) Clotted, congulated.
Tolchen, *s. f.—pl. t.* i (tolch) A clod, a congulated mass. *Tolchen o waed*, a clotted mass of blood.
Tolchenawg, *a.* (tolchen) Full of clotted masses.
Tolcheniad, *s. m.* (tolchen) A forming a clod.
Tolchenu, *v. a.* (tolchen) To form into a clod.
Tolchi, *v. a.* (tolch) To form a congulated mass; to clod; to become clotted.
Tolchiad, *s. m.* (tolch) A clotting, a congulating.
Tolfaen, *s. m.—pl.* tolfeini (tol—maen) An open stone.
Tolgorn, *s. m.—pl.* tolgyrn (tol—corn) A trump, or a clarion.
Toli, *v. a.* (tawl) To curtail; to diminish; to put aside, to spare; to take from, to deal out.

> Hawdd toli yn helaeth o dorth gwr arall.
>
> It is easy *to deal* amply from another man's loaf. *Adage.*
>
> Gwr curiol i dlodd heb doll.
>
> A man of unrestrained gifts of gold without *sparing*. *M. Carl ab Gwyffe.*
>
> Morfudd —
> Tal am dy wawd ewn toli;
> Twynu y prydyddion wyt ti.
>
> Morvudd, pay for thy praise before a diminution takes place, the sunbeam of the poets art thou. *Dafydd ab Gwilym.*

Toliad, *s. m.—pl. t.* au (tawl) A diminishing; a privation; a sparing.
Toliannawl, *a.* (toliant) Privative, curtailing.
Toliannu, *v. a.* (toliant) To make a diminution; to cause a privation.
Toliant, *s. m.* (tawl) A diminution, a privation; a saving, a sparing.

Toliaw, *v. a.* (tawl) To diminish; to curtail; to take away, to deprive; to save, to spare.

Haws tolia[w] no harlaw.

It is easier *to spare* than to hire. *Adage.*

Ni tholles fy lies llyw rhybudd;
Ni tholiaf a ganaf heb gudd.

The portended chief *has* not *restricted* my bliss; *I will* not *restrain* what I sing without disguise. *Cynddelw.*

Toliedig, *a.* (tawl) Diminished, taken away.

Toliwr, *s. m.—pl.* toliwyr (toli—gwr) A diminisher; one who puts aside, or spares.

Tolo, *s. m.* (tol) That is overwhelming; heavy; loud; a pound weight.

Cyglyw dòn drom ei tholo.

Hear the wave of sullen *din.* *Llywarch Hen.*

Tolwr, *s. m.* (tol) That makes a roar, a roarer.

Toll, *s. f.—pl. t.* au (ty—oll) A fraction; custom, or toll.

Toll fawr a wna doll fechan.

A great *toll* will produce a small *toll.* *Adage.*

Ystafell Cynddylan neud athwyd heb fedd!
Mae yn medd dy ysgwyd,
Hyd tra fu ni bu doll glwyd.

The hall of Cynddylan art thou not gone devoid of mead! thy shield is in the grave, which whilst remaining was no *broken* shelter. *Llywarch Hen.*

Tolladwy, *a.* (toll) Capable of being tolled.

Tollawg, *a.* (toll) Having a toll, tolled.

Tolledig, *a.* (toll) Being exacted as toll.

Tollfa, *s. f.—pl.* tollfeydd (toll) A place to receive toll; a receipt of custom; a custom house.

Tolli, *v. a.* (toll) To subtract, or to take a part from; to exact toll, or custom; to toll.

Tolliad, *s. m.* (toll) A subtracting, a taking a part away; a taking custom, or toll; a tolling.

Tolliant, *s. m.* (toll) A toll, or custom.

Tollrydd, *s. m.* (toll—rhydd) Free of custom; toll-free. *Aeth y tir yn dollrydd*, the land is become free of toll.

Tollwr, *s. m.—pl.* tollwyr (toll—gwr) One who takes toll, or custom.

Brodyr cyweithas, arglwydd, tollwr, a chythraul.

Confederate brothers, a lord, a toll-gatherer, and the devil. *Adage.*

Tollydd, *s. m.—pl. t.* ion (toll) A toll-gatherer.

Tom, *s. f.—pl. t.* ydd (to—om) A mound, a heap, a tumulus; a heap of dirt; dung.

Tom Elwyddan neus gwlych gwlaw
Mae Maodyn y danaw;
Dyn ini Cynon i gwynaw!

The mound of Elwyddan how drenched by rain. Maodyn is under it, a man whom Cynon is left to mourn! *Llywarch Hen.*

Tomawd, *s. m.* (tom) A monument; a tomb.

Gwae ddyn nad ystyr
Nad â yn ebrwyr,
Cyn rhythr tymyr,
Tomawd farnfedd.

Woe to the man who will not consider that he may ruefully go, before a short space, to the stone grave with its *monument.* *D. Ddu Hiraddug.*

Tomawg, *a.* (tom) Having a heap; covered with dung; mucky.

Tomdail, *s. m.* (tom—tail) Dung manure.

Tomen, *s. f.—pl. t.* ydd (tom) A mound, a tumulus, a hillock, a dunghill.

A gaselo domen a gaiff un car cywir.

He that collects a *dunghill* will have one faithful friend. *Adage.*

Pob ci a fydd gwr ar ei domen ei hun.

Every dog will be a lord on his own *dunghill.* *Adage.*

Tomfoi, *v. a.* (tom—moi) To drop dung.

Gwerth porchell o'r nos y ganer ynd el i domfoi, ceiniawg.

The value of a pig from the night it is brought forth until it goes *to drop dung*, a penny. *Welsh Laws.*

Tomi, *v. a.* (tom) To make a heap; to dung.

Tomiad, *s. m.* (tom) A forming a heap; a dropping of dung.

Tomlyd, *s. m.* (tom) Abounding with dung.

Tomlydu, *v. a.* (tomlyd) To render mucky.

Tomwr, *s. m.—pl.* tomwyr (tom—gwr) One who heaps; a muck-man.

Tòn, *s. f.—pl. t.* iau (ty—on) A surface, an outer coating, peel, paring, or skin; also, lay land, or unploughed land; a green. *Ton las, glasdon*, a greensward.

Dar a dyfwys ar y ton:
Gwedi gwaedffrau, a briw bron,
Gwae a gar wyd amrysou!

An oak has grown on the *green* after blood-spilling, and the wounded breast, woe to him that loves the vice of contention! *Robert T. Normandi.*

Tòn, *s. f.—pl. t.* au (*f. of* twn) That breaks out, that is broken; a breaker, a surge, or wave. *a.* Shattered, broken.

Ni noda nawf un afon
Y doeth yn erbyn y don.

Not in any river will the wise swim against the *wave.* *Ed. Dafydd.*

Oedd amliw tonau, twn achar eu naid,
Nid oeddynt dilafar.
Tòn bell helaeth trwy far,
Tòn arall gwall goch gwyar.

Many-coloured were the waves, broken and of mixed did their course, they were not void of sound: a wave of brine ample in its rage, another dreadful wave red with gore. *Ll. P. Moch.*

Bid grafangawg iar; bid trydar lew;
Bid ynfyd ymladdgar;
Bid tòn calon gan alar.

A hen scratches with her claws; a lion roars: the fool is fond of brawls; the heart is *broken* oppressed with woe. *Llywarch Hen.*

Ton, *s. f.—pl. t.* au (to—on) A tone, an accent.

Un adlais a Thelabon,
Eneid-lyw teg, difrig don.

Of the same fine as Telabon, a fair superior soul, of unbroken *accent.* *D. y Coed.*

Tònawg, *a.* (tòn) Abounding with breaks, abounding with breakers or waves; turbulent, froward, stubborn.

Tònawl, *a.* (tòn) Breaking like a surge.

Tonc, *s. f.—pl. t.* iau (ty—onc) A tink, a ring. *Cei eithaf tonc*, thou shalt have extreme joy. *Dyfed.*

Tonciad, *s. m.* (tonc) A tinking, a ringing.

Tonciaw, *v. a.* (tonc) To tinkle, to ring.

Tònen, *s. f. dim.* (tòn) A surface, an outer coating, peel, or paring; a cuticle; also, a bog, or quag.

Tonfryd, *a.* (tòn—bryd) Of a rough disposition.

Tongar, *a.* (ton) Sonorous, resounding.

Tòni, *v. a.* (tòn) To form a surface; to become covered with a skin, or cuticle; to pare, to peel.

Toniad, *s. m.* (ton) A making a tone, or accent.

Tòniad, *s. m.* (tòn) A forming a surface; a forming a cuticle, a paring, a peeling.

Toniadur, *s. m.* (toniad) That forms an accent.

Tonlar, *s. f.* (tòn) A plank, a shingle.

Tònlar, *s. f.—pl.* tonieri (tòn) A breaker, a surge, or wave.

Gwirawd Owain hary, fiechar ei dery[s]g
Ar derfyn ei esgar,
Balch y daw yn llaw llachfar;
Meddw ei thorf; medd ei thonlar.

The cup of Owain the mild, whose tumult gleams on the border of his foe, proudly it comes on the wrath-dispensing hand, drunk its surrounding votaries, its wave is mead. *Cynddelw.*

Toniardy, *s. m.—pl. t.* au (toniar—ty) A house or booth made of boards.

Toniaru, *v. a.* (tòniar) To lay planks, to board.

Toniaw, *v. a.* (ton) To tone, to accent.

Tonogi, *v. a.* (tònawg) To raise breakers or billows; to rise in billows; to become boisterous or turbulent.

Tonogiad, *s. m.* (tònawg) A raising of breakers; a rising in waves, or surges; a becoming turbulent.

Tonogrwydd, *s. m.* (tònawg) The state of rising in surges; turbulence.

Tonwaed, *s. m.* (tòn—gwaed) A blood clod.

Tonwen, *a.* (tòn—gwèn) White-skinned.

Tonwryg, *a.* (tòn—gwryg) Rising in billows; turbulent.

Tonwrygiad, *s. m.* (tonwryg) A rising in billows; a becoming turbulent.

Tonwrygiaw, *v. a.* (tonwryg) To raise surges; to rise in surges; to become turbulent.

Tonwyn, *a.* (tòn—gwỳn) White-skinned.

Tonydd, *s. m.—pl. t.* ion (ton) An accenter.

Tonyddiaeth, *s.* (tonydd) A tonation, accentation.

> Tonyddiaeth helaeth hylawn,
> A gair, mewn llafair a gawn.
>
> A tonation ample and complete, and a word, in expression we obtain. *Meiryg Dafydd.*

Top, *s. m.—pl. t.* iau (tob) A top; a stopple.

Topiad, *s. m.* (top) A topping, a cresting.

Topiaw, *v. a.* (top) To top, to form a crest.

Topiawg, *a.* (top) Having a top, or crest.

Topiawl, *a.* (top) Tending to form a top.

Topiwr, *s.m.--pl.* topiwyr (top--gwr) One who tops

Topyn, *s. m. dim.—pl. t.* au (top) A top, a bunch, bush of hair; a topple; a stopple.

> Erfynied i'm rhwyf ydd wyf ei dda—
> A warawd topyn felyn fwla.
>
> I sue to my chief for his goods, that renders unnecessary a *top*, a yellow knob. *Gr. ab D. ab Tudyr.*

Topyniad, *s. m.* (topyn) A forming a top.

Topynu, *v. a.* (topyn) To form a top, or crest.

Tòr, *s. m.* (ty—or) A break, a rupture; a cut; an interruption, a cessation, a discontinuation. *Tòr calon*, a heart breaking.

Tòr, *s. f.—pl. t.* au (to—or) A swell out, a bulge, a prominence; a belly; the lower part of the belly. *Tòr y mynydd*, the swell of the mountain; *tòr y llaw*, the ball of the hand; *tòr tarian*, the convex or outside of a shield.

> Tyfid enderig o'i dòr.
>
> The steer grows from his *belly*. *Adage.*

Tòradwy, *a.* (tòr) Capable of being broken.

Toraeth, *s. f.—pl.* toreithiau (tòr) Produce, profit; fecundity, fruitfulness; abundance, store. *Nid oes dim toraeth ohono*, there is no good to be had out of him.

> Mawr yw toraeth yr aflwydd.
>
> Great is the *store* of the unfortunate. *Adage.*
>
> Mawr toraeth aflwydd ban fyno.
>
> Great is the *store* of misfortune when he commands. *Adage.*

Torammod, *s.* (tòr—ammod) Breach of covenant.

Torarfoll, *s. f.* (tòr—arfoll) Breach of faith.

Torawg, *a.* (tòr) Having a prominence; big-bellied; an epithet applied to a sow, a bitch, and a cat, when big with young.

Torawl, *a.* (tòr) Tending to spread round; prominent.

Torbwt, *s. m.—pl.* torbytiaid (tòr--pwt) A turbot.

Torcalon, *s. m.* (tòr—calon) A heart-breaking.

Torcalonus, *a.* (torcalon) Heart-breaking.

> Ystyrineth dorcalonus ydyw ein bod ni bob dydd yn myned ymaith oddiwrth ein dedwyddwch.
>
> It is a *heart breaking* consideration that we should be every day going away from our happiness. *Ios. Rhys.*

Torch, *s. f.--pl.* tyrch (tòr) A wreath; a coil; a collar; a badge of distinction, worn by the ancient Britons, which it was a point of honour for a warrior to preserve from being lost to the enemy in battle. *Tynu am y dorch*, to strive for the torques: *Mi dynaf y dorch a thi*, I will pull the torques with thee.

> Braich uwch balawgyn llemyrch;
> Brychwaith ei braich a'i thyrch.
>
> A handle above the point of the fickle; of fretwork its handle and its *wreaths*. *Rhys Trem, i fwchel.*

Torchawg, *a.* (torch) Having a wreath, coil, or turn; wreathed, coiled, twisted, turned up; wearing a torques.

Torchawl, *a.* (torch) Wreathing, twisting, coiling

Torchawr, *part.* (torch) Wreathing, entwining.

> Gwefrawr godrwyawr torchawr am rudd.
>
> Amber-beads in ringlets *entwining* round the temples. *Anonym.*

Torchedig, *a.* (torch) Wreathed, twisted; coiled

Torchi, *v. a.* (torch) To wreath, to twist, to twine; to coil, to gather into a chain; to turn up. *Torcha dy lewys*, turn up thy sleeves.

> Torchi gwraidd tywarch a gro
> I'r gwynt, ac i'r wybr, ganto.
>
> *Turning up* the roots of sods and gravel into the wind, and into the air, by him. *L. Morganwg.*

Torchiad, *s. m.—pl. t.* au (torch) A wreathing.

Torchwr, *s. m.—pl.* torchwyr (torch—gwr) A coiler, a wreather, a twister.

Tordain, *s. m.* (tor—tain) A spread out in a lolling manner. *v. a.* To loll.

Tordanawl, *a.* (tordain) Swelling out the belly.

Tordaniad, *s. m.* (tordain) A lolling on the belly.

Tordanu, *v. a.* (tordain) To spread out the belly.

Tordor, *adv.* (tor *repeated*) Belly to belly.

Tordyn, *a.* (tor—tyn) Tight stomached; full-bellied; high-stomached, proud-stomached.

> Bydd dordyn wrth elynion man,
> Fal chwythu tan mewn sorod.
>
> Be *high-stomached* to petty foes, like blowing the fire amongst dross. *Edm. Prys.*

Tordyniad, *s. m.* (tordyn) A stretching the belly.

Tordynu, *v. a.* (tordyn) To tighten the belly.

Tordd, *s. m.* (tor) A murmur, a din, a tumult.

Torddawl, *a.* (tordd) Murmuring, tumultuous.

Torddiad, *s. m.* (tordd) A murmuring, a raising a din.

Torddu, *v. a.* (tordd) To murmur, to make a din.

Torddus, *a.* (tordd) Murmuring, tumultuous.

Tored, *s. m.* (tor) That expands round. *a.* Vast.

Tòredig, *a.* (tòr) Broken, fractured, cut.

Toredlu, *s.—pl. t.* oedd (tored—llu) A vast host.

> Mynegid iddo fod yr amherawdr wedi lluestu yn agos yn y lle, a thoredlu gantho; ac yn y lle ydd oedd Arthur a lluestu ar lan afon
>
> It was told him that the emperor had encamped near to that place, having a vast *host* with him; and in the spot where he was Arthur encamped on a river side. *Gr. ab Arthur.*

Toredwynt, *s. m.—pl. t.* oedd (tored—gwynt) A whirlwind.

> Twrf toredwynt mawr uch mor diffaith.
>
> The din of a mighty *whirlwind* over a desert sea. *Llygad Gwr.*
>
> Torynt toredwynt uch teg adfan.
>
> They would burst a *whirlwind* over a fair retreat. *G. Cyfeiliawg.*

Toreithiad, *s. m.* (toraeth) A forming a store.

Toreithiannawl, *a.* (toreithiant) Of a productive tendency, tending to store.

Toreithiannu, *v. a.* (toreithiant) To cause abundance; to become abundant.

Toreithiant, *s. m.* (toraeth) Abundance; store.

Toreithiaw, *v. a.* (toraeth) To render productive, or abundant, to yield increase; to be productive.

Toreithiawg, *a.* (toraeth) Having produce, plenty, or abundance; profitable, yielding increase.

Toreithiawl, *a.* (toraeth) Productive, abundant.

Toreithiedig, *a.* (toreithiad) Made abundant.

Toreithus, *a.* (toraeth) Productive, abundant.

Toreithusaw, *v. a.* (toreithus) To render productive; to become productive.

Toreithusdra, *s. m.* (toreithus) Productiveness.

Toreithusrwydd, *s.m.* (toreithus) Productiveness

Torf, *s. f.—pl. t.* oedd (tor) A croud, a throng, a multitude; a troop; a host.

Godwrf—
Teulu Madawg, mur eglor,
Mal gawr torf teulu Arthur.

The murmur of the tribe of Madawg, a conspicuous bulwark, like the *host* shout of the tribe of Arthur. *Cynddelw.*

—Gorddrud ei lafer,
Drud rwyf torf twrf llanw yn aber.

Impetuous to extreme his blue shaft, the bold leader of a *host* tumultuous as a flood in the mouth of a river. *Cynddelw, i O. Gwynedd.*

Torfa, *s. f.—pl.* torfëydd (torf) An assembled host; also the number of one thousand millions

Deg degwaith yw cant, deg cant yn y fil, deg mil yn y myrdd, deg myrdd yn y mwnt, deg mwnt yn y thialla, deg rhialla yn y fanda, deg mwnda yn y dorfa, deg torfa yn y gattyrfa fawr: y rhif mwyaf yw hwnw.

Ten ten times is a hundred, ten hundreds in a thousand, ten thousands in a myriad, ten myriads in a hundred thousand, ten hundred thousands in a million, ten millions in the cumulus, ten cumuluses in the *aggregate multitude, ten aggregate multitudes* in the great protecting host: the greatest number is that.

Torfagl, *s. f.* (tor—magl) That breaks or dissipates a stye; the eyebright, or wild English clary, also called *gloewlys*, and *goleudrem*.

Torfawg, *a.* (torf) Having a host; multitudinous

Owain—
Diofn cad cedeirn dorfogion.

Owain dauntless in the battle of mighty *ones assembled together* *H. Poel ab Griffri.*

Torfiad, *s. m.* (torf) An assembling of a host.

Torflawdd, *s. m.* (tor—llawdd) A spreading tumult, or uproar.

Torfloddiad, *s. m.* (torflawdd) An expanding of a tumult.

Dym cyfarwyddiad Unhwch dywal,
Blwng chwerthin mor ryfel dorfloddiad
Urien —

May the furious Unhwch lead me on, like the sullen agitation of the sea is the war *expanding tumult* of Urien *Llywarch Hen.*

Torfu, *v. a.* (torf) To collect a host, to assemble in a body.

Torfynwgl, *a.* (tòr—mynwgl) Neck breaking.

Torfynygliad, *s. m.* (torfynwgl) A breaking the neck, a casting headlong; a prostration.

Torfynyglu, *v. a.* (torfynwgl) To cause a neck-breaking, to break the neck; to cast headlong.

Torgeingl, *s. f.—pl. t.* au (tor—ceingl) A girth.

Torgest, *s. f.—pl. t.* i (tor—cest) A hernia.

Torgestawg, *a.* (torgest) Having a hernia.

Torgestiad, *s. m.* (torgest) A forming a hernia.

Torgestu, *v. a.* (torgest) To form a hernia.

Torgoch, *a.* (tor—coch) Red-bellied; an epithet for the red char fish of the Alpine lakes.

Torgochiad, *s. m.—pl.* torgochiaid (torgoch) A red-bellied one; a red char fish; also called *brithyll melyn.*

Tòri, *v. a.* (tòr) To break, to make a rupture; to cut; to become broken.

Un o dri gorchestwaith Ynys Prydain: Llong Nefydd Naf Neifion a ddug ynddi wryw a benyw, pan dores llyn llion.

One of the three superior exploits of the isle of Britain: the ship of Nevydd Nav Neivion, which carried in it male and female when the aggregate of floods *broke out.* *Trioedd.*

Pei gwnelit fy nghynghor i, ni thorit gyfreithiau y llys erddo.

If thou hadst done my advice, *thou wouldest* not *break* the laws of the court on his account. *H. Culhwch—Mabinogion.*

Tòriad, *s. m.—pl. t.* au (tòr) A breaking, a making a rupture; a cutting; a becoming broken; a cessation, a breaking off, a breaking in, or taming. *Tòriad y dydd*, the break of day: *Nid oes arno dòriad yn y byd*, he is not under the least regulation in the world.

Gofyn i ddall a ydyw yn doriad gwawr.

Asking of the blind whether it is *break* of day. *Adage.*

Toriadawl, *a.* (tòriad) Fractive, fracturing.

Toriadu, *v. a.* (tòriad) To make a break.

Toriannawl, *a.* (tòriant) Fractory.

Toriannu, *v. a.* (tòriant) To make a fraction.

Tòriant, *s. m.* (tòr) A fraction, a fracture.

Toriator, *ger.* (tòriad) In breaking.

Toriedydd, *s. m.—pl. t.* ion (tòriad) A fracturer

Toritor, *sup.* (tòri) To be breaking.

Torlaith, *s. m.* (tòr—llaith) White hellebore.

Tòrlan, *s. f.—pl.* tòrlènydd (tòr—glàn) A broken bank, a bank worn away by water.

Gellir yfed yr afon, ond nid ellir bwyta y dòrlan.

The river may be drunk, but the *bank* cannot be eaten. *Adage.*

Torlla, *s. f.—pl. t.* od (tòr—lla) A slattern.

Torllengig, *s. m.* (tòr—llengig) A hernia.

Torllwyd, *a.* (tòr—llwyd) Having the prominence or belly of a grey colour. *Y dorllwyd*, the wild tansy, or silverweed; also called *torllwydig*, and *torllwydog, y dinllwyd, gwyn y merched.*

Torllwydog, *s. f.* (torllwyd) The wild tansy.

Torllwyth, *s. m.—pl. t.* i (tor—llwyth) The burden of the belly; the burden of the womb; an epithet for a litter of pigs, and for other animals that bring forth several at once.

Hwch a fwrw, o chyfeirir,
Dorllwyth o dylwyth i dir;
Yn myn'd rhwng Arfon a Mon
Y chwery freichiau hirion.

A sow that will cast, if resorted to, a *litter* of progeny on the land, visiting between Arvon and Mon she plays about her long arms. *Gr. ab Hyw. ab Tudyr, i Yagraff*

Torm, *s. f.* (tòr) That is stretched or crouded round.

Tormach, *s. m.* (tòr—mach) A forfeit of bail, contempt of court: hardship.

Tormaen, *s. m.* (tòr—maen) That breaks the stone; the saxifrage; also called *maen-had*, and *llyfnury.*

Tormaenawl, *a.* (tormaen) Lithontriptic.

Tormaenwydd, *s. m.* (tormaen—gwydd) Sassafras-tree, or stone-dissolver.

Tormennawg, *a.* (torment) Having a surrounding assemblage.

Aesgor dy far, fur tormennawg.

Unavoidable thy wrath, *host-surrounding* bulwark. *Llygad Gwr.*

Tormenniad, *s. m.* (torment) A pressing or crouding round.

Tormennu, *v. a.* (torment) To croud round; to croud together in conflict.

Mae yntau orau an tormennawg;
Tormennoedd anlloedd an llyw tiriawg.

He also is the best of any *host surrounded one*; our leader amply possessing land, caused riches *to surround.* *Gwalchmai.*

Torment, *s. m.* (torm) The state of pressing round; a conflicting host; a conflict; torment

Teyrnllyw teyrnas terfysg torment.

A supreme leader of a kingdom the tumult of *conflict.* *LL. P. Moch.*

Trylliw ei ysgwyd ysgydwir yn nhermant.

Three-coloured his shield that is made to move in *conflict*. *Cynddelw.*

Godwrf a glywaf am glawr leithon hir;
Hydyr ei wir ar Saeson:
Treis Madawg, mur gelon,
Mal twrf tormeunoedd Cynon.

A murmur I hear along the surface of the far-extending leithon; its truth is confidence to the Saxons, of the tribe of Madawg, a bulwark against foes, like the tumult of the *conflicts* of Cynon. *Cynddelw.*

Tormiad, *s. m.* (torm) A gathering round.

Tormiannawg, *a.* (tormiant) Being surrounded by retinue.

Gwr tormiannawg cyfoethawg.

A *magnificent* wealthy man. *Mabinogi.*

Tormiannu, *v. a.* (tormiant) To form a surrounding retinue.

Tormiant, *s. m.* (torm) A surrounding assemblage

Tormu, *v. a.* (torm) To assemble round.

Tormwyth, *s. m.* (tòr—mwyth) Feverfew.

Tormyn, *s. m.* (torm) A surrounding croud.

Tormynawg, *a.* (tormyn) Surrounded by retinue.

Tormynogaeth, *s. m.* (tormynawg) The state of having a surrounding retinue.

Torogen, *s. f. dim.* (tòrawg) A big-bellied one; a tike.

Torogenawg, *a.* (torogen) Full of tikes.

Torogeniad, *s. m.* (torogen) A breeding of tikes.

Torogenu, *v. a.* (torogen) To breed tikes.

Toroges, *s. f.* (torawg) A big-bellied one.

Torogi, *v. a.* (torawg) To make a big belly, to swell the belly; to cause a gestation; to become big-bellied; to become big with young.

Yn Ganga y mae llysfod a thrichant troedfedd yn eu hyd; ac yno y mae pryfed tebyg i wreigedd, a dwy fraich iddynt, chwe chufydd yn eu hyd; ac o'r rhai hyny y torogant yr eliffant, ac yn y tonau y suddant, ac yn y mor hwnw y magant; ac yn eu cibynau y dichawn dynion nofiaw.

In Ganga there are eels having three hundred feet in their lengths; and therein are animals like women, having two arms, six cubits in their lengths; and those *gestate* from the elephant, and in the waves they sink, and in the sea there they rear their young; and in their shells men might swim about. *Delw y Byd.*

Torogiad, *s. m.* (torawg) A making a big belly, a swelling the belly; a causing a gestation; a becoming big with young.

Torogwr, *s. m.—pl.* torogwyr (torawg—gwr) One who swells out the belly.

Torogyn, *s. m. dim.* (torawg) A big-bellied one.

Toron, *s. f.—pl. t.* au (tawr) That spreads over; a plot in a garden laid out in beds; a decking out of a table; a mantle, or cloak.

Toronaeth, *s. m.* (toron) The act of decking out.

Toronawg, *a.* (toron) Having a mantle.

Tarw a gaf. Pond hir y gwallt
Toronawg.—

A bull I shall get: surely the *covering* hair is long. *T. Penllyn.*

Toronawl, *a.* (toron) Mantling, cloaking.

Toroni, *v. a.* (toron) To deck out, to cover over, to spread out a table, to spread a feast, to cover with a mantle, to mantle, to cloak.

Glewlwyd Gafaelfawr a dynai y pair oddiar y tan, pan oedd yn —'Toroni tair ynys.'—

Glewlwyd with mighty grasp pulled the cauldron off the fire, when he was *feasting* three islands. *Iolo Goch.*

Toroniad, *s. m.* (toron) A spreading over, a decking, or covering; a mantling.

Torp, *s. m.* (tor) A round mass, a lump.

Torpell, *s. f. dim.—pl. t.* i (torp) A small mass or lump; any thick or coagulated matter formed into a mass; a clod; a dumpling.

Torpellawg, *a.* (torpell) Abounding with masses, or clods; formed into lumps.

Torpelliad, *s. m.* (torpell) A clotting.

Torpellu, *v. a.* (torpell) To clod, to form a lump.

Torpwth, *s. m.* (tor—pwth) A short big-bellied person; a squab.

Tors, *s. f.—pl. t.* au (tawr) A covering.

Teirtors i'r corff, tors aur cerdd.

Three lives to the person, the golden shelter of song. *H. Dyfnwal.*

Torsed, *s. f.—pl. t.* i (tors) A rug, a coverlid; also called *cadwy*.

Torsed gogyfled a'r gwydd.

A rug of equal breadth with the loom. *L. G. Cothi.*

Torsi, *v. a.* (tors) To deck, or cover over.

Torsiad, *s. m.* (tors) A decking over.

Torstain, *a.* (tors—tain) Prominent, bulging.

Y bwa—
Hirfain a thorstain ei thyr.

The bow long and slender and *bulging* out thus with red bosses. *T. Prys.*

Torsyth, *a.* (tor—syth) Swaggering out the belly stiffly, stiff-stomached.

Torsythaidd, *a.* (torsyth) Rather stiff-stomached.

Torsythawg, *a.* (torsyth) Swaggering.

Torsythawl, *a.* (torsyth) Apt to swagger.

Torsythiad, *s. m.* (torsyth) A swaggering, a swelling out the belly.

Torsythni, *s. m.* (torsyth) A swaggering.

Torsythu, *v. a.* (torsyth) To stiffen the belly.

Torth, *s. f.—pl. t.* au (ty—orth) That supports, or sustains; a loaf of bread.

Torthawl, *a.* (torth) Being like a loaf.

Torthi, *v. a.* (torth) To form into a compact mass; to harden, to settle; to cake. *Gwair wedi torthi,* hay after it is settled.

Torthiad, *s. m.* (torth) A forming a loaf.

Torwen, *a.* (tòr—gwên) White-bellied.

Torwenwyn, *s. m.* (tòr—gwenwyn) Rue.

Torwyn, *a.* (tor—gwŷn) White-bellied.

Torympryd, *s. m.—pl. t.* iau (tòr—ympryd) A breakfast; also called *borefwyd, tori ympryd*.

Pan oeddwn yn ymdrwsiaw, Meddwdod a ddoai i mewn, y rhai a barotoes i mi fy nhorymprydd.

When I was dressing myself, Voluptuousness, with her sister Drunkenness, came in, who prepared for me my breakfast. *Marchawg Crwydrad.*

Torymprydiad, *s. m.* (torympryd) A breakfasting.

Torymprydiaw, *v. a.* (torympryd) To breakfast.

Toryn, *s. m.—pl. t.* iau (tawr) An outer-covering, a mantle, a cloak; a cope, or sacerdotal vesture.

Ni byddaf ua thoryn fwyn na chwpan glaw.

I will not be a carrying *cloak* nor rain cup. *Adage.*

Torynawg, *a.* (toryn) Having a mantle.

Toryniad, *s. m.* (toryn) A cloaking, a mantling.

Torynu, *v. a.* (toryn) To cloak, to mantle.

Tos, *s. m.* (ty—os) A quick jerk; a toss; a snatch.

Tosed, *s. m.* (tos) A snatch; a rapine.

Tosiad, *s. m.* (tos) A jerking; a tossing.

Toslaw, *v. a.* (tos) To jerk; to snatch; to toss.

Tost, *a.* (to—ost) Severe, harsh; violent; painful.

Tost fydd ar ddyn pan gaffo ddewis.

It is *hard* on a person when he is put to his choice. *Adage.*

Mae yn dost ar a ddymunai farw; mae yn dostach ar ei ofno.

It is grievous on such as would wish to die; it is more grievous on such as would dread it. *Adage.*

Tostaidd, *a.* (tost) Somewhat severe or harsh.

Tostalar, *s. m.* (tost—galar) Severe grief.

Tostalariad, *s. m.* (tostalar) A severely grieving.

Tostalaru, *v. a.* (tostalar) To grieve severely.

Pa oedfaon gwerthfawr a gollwyd!—hwyrfrydig, y rhai a'u hesgeulusasant, a dostalarant am danynt yn eu canlyn.

What precious opportunities have been lost! they who have neglected them, will *deeply lament* about them for ages to come. *Ed. Samuel.*

Tostalarus, *a.* (tostalar) Severely grieving.
Tostawl, *a.* (tost) Of a severe quality.
Tostedig, *a.* (tost) Being made severe or harsh.
Tostedd, *s. m.* (tost) Severity, pungency, harshness; also the stranguary.
Tostfrwyn, *s. pl. aggr.* (tost—brwyn) Sea rushes.
Tostfrwynen, *s. f. dim.* (tostfrwyn) A sea rush.
Tosti, *v. a.* (tost) To cause violent pain, to rack, to torture; also to feel for, or to be pained.

> Mal dala gel bendoll ym tostes yr haiarn dur!
>
> Like catching an open headed leech the steely iron *pained* me! *H. Culhwch.*
>
> Tosti a thruanu wrtho a orug.
>
> *To take pity* and to commiserate with him was what he did. *Hanes No.*

Tostiad, *s. m.* (tost) A causing severity; a torturing
Tostlym, *a.* (tost—llym) Poignant, acrimonious.
Tostlymder, *s. m.* (tostlym) Acrimoniousness.
Tostlymdra, *s. m.* (tostlym) Acrimoniousness.
Tostlymrwydd, *s. m.* (tostlym) Acrimoniousness.
Tostur, *s. m.* (tost) Misery, severe plight.
Tosturâad, *s. m.* (tosturâu) A commiseration.
Tosturâawl, *a.* (tosturâu) Commiserating.
Tosturâu, *v. a.* (tostur) To commiserate, to pity.

> Nid ystyr hon dosturâu!
>
> No idea *to compassionate* hath she! *T. Aled.*

Tosturi, *s. m.* (tostur) Compassion, pity, mercy.
Tosturiad, *s. m.* (tostur) A pitying, a taking pity.
Tosturiaeth, *s. m.—pl. t.* au (tostur) Compassion.

> A aeth dy dosturiaethau
> Oll ymaith am ein gwaith gau!
>
> Are all thy *tender mercies* fled away on account of our deceitful art? *D. Richard Glan y Morfa.*

Tosturiannawl, *a.* (tosturiant) Compassionate.
Tosturiannu, *v. a.* (tosturiant) To compassionate.
Tosturiant, *s. m.* (tostur) Compassion, pity.
Tosturiaw, *v. a.* (tostur) To compassionate, to pity.
Tosturiawg, *a.* (tostur) Compassionate.
Tosturiawl, *a.* (tostur) Compassionate; piteous.

> Pan glywai Rhad Duw fy nghwynfan tosturiawl, hi o'i daioni a estynai i mi wialen aur, ac a orchmynai imi ddodi fy llaw arni.
>
> When the Grace of God heard my *pitiful* complaint, she out of her goodness extended to me a golden rod, and desired me to place my hand upon it. *Marchawg Crwydrad.*

Tosturiedig, *a.* (tosturiad) Commiserated, pitied.
Tosturioldeb, *s. m.* (tosturiawl) Compassionateness
Tosturiwr, *s. m.—pl.* tosturiwyr (tostur—gwr) One who takes compassion.
Tosturus, *a.* (tostur) Compassionate; piteous.
Tosturusaw, *v. a.* (tosturus) To soften to pity; to become compassionate; to render piteous; to become piteous.
Tosturusrwydd, *s. m.* (tosturus) Compassionateness
Töwr, *s. m.—pl* towyr (to—gwr) One who forms a covering, one who roofs; a thatcher, a tiler, a slater.
Tprue, *s. m.* A noise made in calling cattle.

> Tprue loi'! lo llwm ei gynffon,
> Prin o rodd.——
>
> Come my calves! avoid that bare-tailed calf, a niggardly gift. *Mad. Dwygraig.*

Tra, *s. m.* (ty—rha) An extreme, an extremity; an excess; a turn; whatever is, thing. It is also prefixed in composition. *Paid a gwneuthur tra*, do not be over nice.

> Gwolychaf wledig, pendefig pob fa,
> Gwr a gynnail y nef, arglwydd pob tra.
>
> I will adore the Supreme, the sovereign of every region, he that upholds the heaven, the Lord of every *thing*. *Taliesin.*
>
> As gynnull gwenyn, ac nis mwynâa,
> Medd hidlaid molaid, molud i bob tra.
>
> The bees collect, and they do not enjoy it, the distilled mead delightful, the delight of every *extremity*. *Taliesin.*

Tra, *prep.* (ty—rha) Over, above; beyond. *Tra mynydd*, over the mountain; *tra mor*, beyond sea; *tra dy gefn*, beyond thy back.
Tra, *adv.* (ty—rha) Over; very, excessively; whilst, as long as, so long as.

> Tra dichell tra dychell.
>
> *Excess of* cunning *excess of* loss. *Adage.*
>
> Amlaf y mel tra hidler.
>
> Honey is most frequent *whilst* it is put through a sieve. *Adage.*
>
> Doeth dyn tra tawo.
>
> A person is wise *whilst* he keeps silent. *Adage.*
>
> O gwyl di ddyn gael dy dda,
> A chymer tra fych yma:
> Na fydd cybydd, celfydd call,
> I ddwyn aur i ddyn arall.
>
> See, oh man! when thou obtainest thy wealth, and enjoy it *whilst* thou shalt be here: be not a miser, of cunning scheme, to hoard gold for another person. *S. Tudyr.*

Träannog, *s. m.* (annog) Extreme excitement. *v. a.* To excite beyond measure.
Träannogiad, *s. m.* (träannog) Extreme excitation
Träannos, *s. m.* (annos) A chasing extremely. *v. a.* To drive overmuch.
Träannosiad, *s. m.* (träannos) A chasing greatly.
Träarglwyddiaethiad, *s. m.* (arglwyddiaethiad) A governing tyrannically; a domineering.
Träarglwyddiaethu, *v. a.* (arglwyddiaethu) To exercise dominion to excess; to domineer.
Traberw, *s. m.* (berw) An over-boil.
Traberwad, *s. m.* (traberw) An over-boiling.
Traberwedig, *a.* (traberw) Over-boiled.
Traberwi, *v. a.* (traberw) To over-boil.
Trablawdd, *s. m.* (blawdd) Extreme activity. *Trablawdd ffossawd*, the extreme velocity of gashing.
Trablawr, *s. m.* (blawr) Extremely gloomy.
Trabloedd, *s. f.* (bloedd) A great outcry.
Trabloeddi, *v. a.* (trabloedd) To make an outcry.
Trabloeddiad, *s. m.* (trabloedd) A making an outcry.
Trabludd, *s. m.—pl. t.* ion (bludd) Trouble, toil, pains, business; turmoil, tumult.

> Ni welais i lys
> Mor lwys edwyg——
> A thrydar meibion,
> A thro cerddorion,
> A thrabludd gweision
> Gosymddeilwig.
>
> I have not beheld a court so fair and solemn, with the noise of youths, and the turn of minstrels, and the *bustle* of servants serving the feast. *D. ab Ieuan Llda.*

Trabluddiad, *s. m.* (trabludd) A troubling.
Trabluddiaw, *v. a.* (trabludd) To trouble, to tease.
Trabluddiawg, *a.* (trabludd) Full of trouble.
Trabluddiawl, *a.* (trabludd) Troublous, teasing.
Trabluddiedig, *a.* (trabludd) Troubled, teased.
Trabluddiwr, *s. m.—pl.* trabluddiwyr (trabludd—gwr) A troubler, a teaser.
Trablwng, *a.* (blwng) Extremely surly.
Trablwydd, *adv.* (blwydd) Beyond the year.
Trablwyddyn, *adv.* (trablwydd) Beyond the year.
Trabrys, *s. m.* (brys) Extreme haste, or hurry.
Trabrysgar, *a.* (trabrys) Extremely hasty.
Trabrysiad, *s. m.* (trabrys) An over-hastening.
Trabrysiaw, *v. a.* (trabrys) To over-hasten.
Trabuan, *a.* (buan) Extremely quick.
Trabychan, *a.* (bychan) Extremely small.
Trabychaniad, *s. m.* (trabychan) A making extremely little.
Trabychanu, *v. a.* (trabychan) To make extremely little; to depreciate extremely.
Trabywiawg, *a.* (bywiawg) Extremely lively.
Trach, *s. m.—pl. t.* au (tra) A hill protruded as it were into low ground. *Trach Dindyrn*, a hill over Tintern Abbey; also a hill near

Denbigh, with a farm house in front of it, called *Taldrach*.

Trach, *adv.* (tra) Beyond; beside; at; aside.

Chamawl doeth trach ei gefn, a merch o flaen ei gwyneb.

Praise the wise *behind* his back, and a woman before her face. *Adage.*

Tria dygwydd trwch trach ei lafnawr.

A dreadful fall of slaughter *beneath* the stroke of his blade. *Aneurin.*

Trachadw, *v. a.* (cadw) To keep extremely.

Trachaer, *s. f.*—*pl. t.* au (caer) Advanced wall.

A thori trachaer Rhufain.

And breaking the *advanced wall* of Rome. *Taliesin.*

Trachaled, *a.* (caled) Extremely hard.

Trachalediad, *s. m.* (trachaled) A hardening extremely.

Trachaledu, *v. a.* (trachaled) To harden extremely

Trachall, *a.* (call) Extremely cunning.

Trachallder, *s. m.* (trachall) Extreme cunning.

Trachariad, *s. m.* (cariad) Extreme love.

Tracharu, *v. a.* (caru) To love to excess.

Trachas, *s. m* (cas) Extreme hatred.

Caraf trachas Lloegr.

I love the *extreme enmity* of England. *H. ab O. Gwynedd.*

Trachasâad, *s. m.* (trachas) A hating extremely.

Trachasâu, *v. a.* (trachas) To hate extremely.

Trachawdd, *s. m.* (cawdd) Excess of vexation.

Trachefn, *adv.* (cefn) Behind the back; again.

Trachelfydd, *a.* (celfydd) Extremely skilful.

Trachgefn, *adv.* (trach—cefn) Behind the back.

Trachil, *s. m.* (cil) An extreme recess.

Trachiliad, *s. m.* (trachil) A receding extremely.

Trachiliaw, *v. a.* (trachil) To recede extremely.

Trachoddi, *v. a.* (trachawdd) To vex extremely.

Trachoddiad, *s. m.* (trachawdd) A vexing extremely.

Trachoddiant, *s. m.* (trachawdd) Extreme vexation; extreme offence.

Trachraff, *a.* (craff) Of very keen hold; of extremely keen perception.

Trachraffiad, *s. m.* (trachraff) A taking a very keen hold; extreme perception.

Trachraffu, *v. a.* (trachraff) To take very keen hold; to perceive extremely.

Trachrin, *a.* (crin) Extremely brittle or fragile.

Trachrinaw, *v. a.* (trachrin) To render extremely brittle; to become extremely brittle.

Trachryn, *s. m.* (cryn) Extreme shaking.

Trachrynawl, *a.* (trachryn) Tending to shake extremely.

Trachryniad, *s. m.* (trachryn) A shaking extremely

Trachrynu, *v. a.* (trachryn) To shake extremely.

Trachu, *a.* (cu) Extremely fond or loving.

Trachudd, *s. m.* (cudd) Extreme obscurity.

Trachuddiad, *s. m.* (trachudd) A hiding to excess.

Trachuddiaw, *v. a.* (trachudd) To hide to excess.

Trachuddiedig, *a.* (trachudd) Extremely hidden.

Trachuedd, *s. m.* (trachu) Over fondness.

Trachul, *a.* (cul) Extremely narrow.

Trachulaw, *v. a.* (trachul) To narrow extremely.

Trachuledd, *s. m.* (trachul) Extreme narrowness.

Trachur, *s. m.* (cur) Extreme beat or throb.

Trachuraw, *v. a.* (trachur) To beat extremely.

Trachwannawg, *a.* (trachwant) Extremely greedy

Trachwant, *s. m.*—*pl. t.* au (chwant) Immoderate desire: lust; covetousness; ambition.

Tri gwrthgefnyddion daioni: balchder, llid, a thrachwant.

The three contrasts of goodness: pride, wrath, and *ambition*. *Catwg ab Gwynllw Filwr.*

Hawdd tangnefedd rhwng twyll a thrachwant.

It is easy to make peace between deceit and *cupidity*. *Adage.*

Trachwant a brad a ddoynt i Ynys Prydain ar farch euraid.

Cupidity and treachery came to the Island of Britain on a golden horse. *Adage.*

Trachwanta, *v. a.* (trachwant) To lust extremely.

Trachwantaidd, *a.* (trachwant) Tending to lust.

Trachwantawl, *a.* (trachwant) Extremely coveting.

Trachwantiad, *s. m.* (trachwant) A coveting extremely, a lusting extremely.

Trachwantu, *v. a.* (trachwant) To lust extremely.

Ei olud i gyd, ar gais, a'i dwnin,
A'i dy, drwy chwant, a drachwantais.

His wealth altogether, in idea, and his family, and his house, through coveting, *I coveted extremely*. *H. D. ab Ifan.*

Trachwantus, *a.* (trachwant) Extremely covetous.

Tlawd pob trachwantus.

Every *covetous* one is poor. *Adage.*

Trachwantusaw, *v. a.* (trachwantus) To render extremely covetous; to become full of avidity.

Trachwar, *a.* (chwar) Extremely active or playful. *Trin trachwar*, a conflict *extremely active*.

Trachwennych, *v.* (trachwant) To covet extremely.

Trachwennychiad, *s. m.* (trachwennych) A coveting extremely.

Trachwennychu, *v. a.* (trachwennych) To covet extremely.

Trachwiliad, *s. m.* (chwiliad) A searching much.

Trachwiliaw, *v. a.* (chwiliaw) To search to excess.

Trachwres, *s. m.* (trach—gwres) Extreme heat; ambition.

Prenial yw i bawb ei drachwres

"The path of *glory* leads but to the grave." *Taliesin.*

Pummed yw y parfedd, neb nis cyfanneddi,
Rhag maint trachwres haul.—

The fifth is the middle, which nobody doth inhabit, because of the *extreme heat* of the sun. *Taliesin.*

Trachwsg, *s. m.* (cwsg) Excess of sleep.

Trachwydd, *s. m.* (cwydd) Extreme fall.

Trachwyddaw, *v. a.* (trachwydd) To fall greatly.

Trachwyddawl, *a.* (trachwydd) Tending to fall extremely.

Trachwyddedig, *a.* (trachwydd) Extremely fallen.

Trachwyddiad, *s. m.* (trachwydd) A falling extremely.

Trachwyl, *s. f.* (chwyl) An extreme course.

Trachwylaw, *v. a.* (trachwyl) To make an extreme course or revolution.

Trachwyliad, *s. m.* (trachwyl) A making an extreme course.

Trachwymp, *s. m.* (cwymp) An extreme fall.

Trachwympaw, *v. a.* (trachwymp) To fall greatly.

Trachwympawl, *a.* (trachwymp) Tending to fall extremely.

Trachwympiad, *s.* (trachwymp) A falling greatly.

Trachwyn, *s. f.* (cwyn) Extreme complaint.

Trachwynaw, *v. a.* (trachwyn) To complain extremely.

Trachwynawl, *a.* (trachwyn) Extremely plaintive.

Trachwyniad, *s. m.* (trachwyn) A complaining extremely; an over complaining.

Trachwys, *s. m.* (chwys) Excessive sweat.

Trachwysawl, *a.* (trachwys) Tending to sweat excessively.

Trachwysiad, *s. m.* (trachwys) A sweating much.

Trachwysu, *v. a.* (trachwys) To sweat extremely.

Trachwyth, *s. m.* (chwyth) An extreme blast.

Trachwythawl, *a.* (trachwyth) Greatly blowing.

Trachwythiad, *s.* (trachwyth) A blowing greatly.

Trachwythu, *v. a.* (trachwyth) To blow much.

Trachyflawn, *a.* (cyflawn) Over-complete.

Trachyflawnder, *s. m.* (trachyflawn) Over-completion; the state of being over-full.

Trachyflawnedig, *a.* (trachyflawn) Over-completed, preterpluperfect.
Trachyflawnedd, *s. m.* (trachyflawn) Over-completeness.
Trachyflawni, *v. a.* (trachyflawn) To render over-complete.
Trachyflawniad, *s. m.* (trachyflawn) A rendering over-complete.
Trachyfoeth, *s. m.* (cyfoeth) Excess of means.

Nef dref drachyfoeth.

Heaven a seat of *extreme enjoyment*. *Dr. S. Cent.*

Trachyfoethawg, *a.* (trachyfoeth) Having excess of means; extremely rich.
Trachyfoethi, *v. a.* (trachyfoeth) To endow with excess of means.
Trachyfoethiad, *s. m.* (trachyfoeth) An endowing with excess of means.
Trachyfoethogi, *v. a.* (trachyfoethawg) To enrich extremely.
Trachyfoethogiad, *s. m.* (trachyfoethawg) An enriching extremely.
Trachyfrif, *s. m.* (cyfrif) An over-reckoning.
Trachyfrifaw, *v. a.* (trachyfrif) To over-reckon.
Trachyfrifawl, *a.* (trachyfrif) Supernumerary.
Trachyfrifiad, *s. m.* (trachyfrif) A making an over-reckoning.
Trachyfrwys, *a.* (cyfrwys) Extremely cunning.
Trachyfrwysaw, *v. a.* (trachyfrwys) To render extremely cunning; to be very cunning.
Trachyfrwysdra, *s. m.* (trachyfrwys) Extreme cunningness.
Trachyffraw, *s. m.* (cyffraw) Extreme agitation.
Trachyffröad, *s. m.* (trachyffraw) A causing extreme agitation.
Trachyffroï, *v. a.* (trachyffraw) To agitate greatly.
Trachymhwys, *a.* (cymhwys) Extremely connected; very befitting.
Trachymhwysaw, *v. a.* (trachymhwys) To render extremely connected.
Trachymhwysdra, *s. m.* (trachymhwys) Extreme connectedness or fitness.
Trachymhwysiad, *s. m.* (trachymhwys) A rendering extremely connected or fit.
Trachymmen, *a.* (cymmen) Extremely fluent of speech.
Trachymmendawd, *s. m.* (trachymmen) Extreme fluency of speech.
Trachymmeniad, *s. m.* (trachymmen) A discoursing extremely eloquent.
Trachymmenu, *v. a.* (trachymmen) To use extreme fluency of speech.
Trachymysg, *a.* (cymysg) Over-mixed.
Trachymysgawl, *a.* (trachymysg) Tending to mix extremely.
Trachymysgedd, *s. m.* (trachymysg) The state of being extremely mixed.
Trachymysgiad, *s. m.* (trachymysg) A mixing extremely.
Trachyndyn, *a.* (cyndyn) Extremely stubborn.
Trachyndynawl, *a.* (trachyndyn) Tending to be extremely obdurate.
Trachyndyniad, *s. m.* (trachyndyn) A being extremely obstinate.
Trachyndynu, *v. a.* (trachyndyn) To act extremely stubborn, or obstinately.
Trachynhen, *s. f.* (cynhen) Extreme contention.
Trachynhenawl, *a.* (trachynhen) Extremely contentious, or quarrelsome.
Trachynheniad, *s. m.* (trachynhen) A contending or quarrelling extremely.

Trachynhenu, *v. a.* (trachynhen) To contend extremely; to be very quarrelsome.
Trachynhwrf, *s. m.* (cynhwrf) Extreme agitation, bustle, or tumult.
Trachynhyrfawl, *a.* (trachynhwrf) Extremely agitating, very tumultuous.
Trachynhyrfiad, *s. m.* (trachynhwrf) A causing extreme agitation.
Trachynhyrfu, *v. a.* (trachynhwrf) To agitate extremely, to ruffle extremely.
Trachynnil, *a.* (cynnil) Extremely exact.
Trachynnilaw, *v. a.* (trachynnil) To act with extreme exactness; to be extremely sparing.
Trachynnildeb, *s. m.* (trachynnil) Extreme exactness; extreme sparingness.
Trachynnyg, *s. m.* (cynnyg) An extreme attempt. *v. a.* To make an extreme attempt.
Trachynnygiad, *s. m.* (trachynnyg) A making an extreme attempt.
Trachynnygiaw, *v. a.* (trachynnyg) To make an extreme attempt.
Trachywed, *s. m.* (cywed) An extreme uniformity or congeniality. *a.* Very uniform.

Granwynion trychion trachywed eiddun,
Trachwyddynt ben o draed.

Pale cheeks mangled *highly congenial* to them, they fell excessively head and feet confused. *Cynddelw.*

Trachywedd, *s. m.* (cywedd) Extreme conformity. *a.* Extremely conformable.

Llew Cemais llym drais drychywedd.

The lion of Cemais of severe sway *extremely habitual*.
Llygad Gwr.

Trachyweddiad, *s. m.* (trachywedd) A conforming extremely; a becoming extremely adapted.
Trachyweddu, *v. a.* (trachywedd) To conform extremely; to be extremely adapted.

Edrywant trachwant trachywedd an cnawd.

The trace of ambition *pervades extremely* our carnal nature.
Gr. ab Gwrgenen.

Trachywir, *a.* (cywir) Extremely exact or just.
Trachywiraw, *v. a.* (trachywir) To render extremely exact; to be very exact.
Trachywirdeb, *s. m.* (trachywir) Extreme exactness; extreme justness.
Trachywiriad, *s. m.* (trachywir) A rendering extremely exact; a becoming extremely just.
Trachywrain, *a.* (cywrain) Extremely accurate; extremely ingenious.
Trachywreindeb, *s. m.* (trachywrain) Extreme accuracy; extreme ingenuity.
Trachywreiniad, *s. m.* (trachywrain) A rendering extremely accurate.
Trachywreiniaw, *v. a.* (trachywrain) To render extremely accurate.
Trad, *s. m.* (tra—ad) That runs or spreads out.
Trada, *a.* (da) Extremely good, very good.
Tradaionus, *a.* (daionus) Extremely good.
Tradedwydd, *a.* (dedwydd) Extremely happy.
Tradedwyddwch, *s. m.* (tradedwydd) Extreme happiness.
Tradestl, *a.* (destl) Extremely smart.
Tradestledd, *s. m.* (tradestl) Extreme smartness.
Tradestliad, *s. m.* (tradestl) A trimming extremely.
Tradestlu, *v. a.* (tradestl) To smarten extremely.
Tradestlus, *a.* (tradestl) Apt to be over-smart.
Tradewr, *a.* (dewr) Over-brave; foolhardy.
Tradewredd, *s. m.* (tradewr) Foolhardiness.
Tradichell, *s. f.*—*pl. t.* ion (dichell) Extreme craft.
Tradichellgar, *a.* (tradichell) Extremely crafty.

Tradichelliad, *s. m.* (tradichell) A making use of extreme craft.
Tradichellu, *v. a.* (tradichell) To use extreme craft
Tradichlyn, *a.* (dichlyn) Extremely assiduous.
Tradichlyniad, *s. m.* (tradichlyn) A using extreme assiduity.
Tradichlynu, *v. a.* (tradichlyn) To use extreme assiduity; to be extremely assiduous.
Tradiflas, *a.* (diflas) Extremely insipid.
Tradiflasdawd, *s. m.* (tradiflas) Extreme insipidity.
Tradiflasiad, *s. m.* (tradiflas) A disgusting extremely; a becoming very insipid.
Tradiflasu, *v. a.* (tradiflas) To disgust extremely.
Tradifrif, *a.* (difrif) Extremely serious.
Tradifrifaw, *v. a.* (tradifrif) To act very seriously; to be extremely serious.
Tradifrifawl, *a.* (tradifrif) Extremely serious.
Tradifrifiad, *s. m.* (tradifrif) A using extreme seriousness; a being very serious.
Tradifrifwch, *s. m.* (tradifrif) Extreme seriousness
Tradigawn, *a.* (digawn) Over-sufficient.
Tradigonawl, *a.* (tradigawn) Over-sufficing.
Tradigonedd, *s. m.* (tradigawn) Over-sufficiency.
Tradigoni, *v. a.* (tradigawn) To over-suffice.
Tradigrif, *a.* (digrif) Extremely diverting.
Tradigrifaw, *v. a.* (tradigrif) To divert extremely.
Tradigrifwch, *s. m.* (tradigrif) Extreme pleasantry
Tradilyn, *v. a.* (dilyn) To follow to excess.
Tradilyniad, *s. m.* (tradilyn) A following to excess.
Tradillyn, *a.* (dillyn) Extremely smart.
Tradillyniad, *s. m.* (tradillyn) A rendering extremely smart, a becoming very smart.
Tradillynu, *v. a.* (tradillyn) To render extremely smart; to become very smart.
Tradirgel, *a.* (dirgel) Extremely secret.
Tradirgeliad, *s. m.* (tradirgel) A rendering extremely secret; a becoming very secret.
Tradirgelu, *v. a.* (tradirgel) To render extremely secret; to become very secret.
Tradiwyd, *a.* (diwyd) Extremely industrious.
Tradiwydiad, *s. m.* (tradiwyd) A using extreme industry; a being very industrious.
Tradiwydiaw, *v. a.* (tradiwyd) To act with extreme industry; to be extremely assiduous.
Tradrwg, *a.* (drwg) Extremely bad or naughty.
Tradrygioni, *s. m.* (drygioni) Extreme badness.
Tradrygionus, *a.* (tradrygioni) Very iniquitous.
Tradwy, *s. m.* (tra—dwy) The third day to come.
Tradwy, *adv.* (tra—dwy) Three days hence.
Tradwys, *a.* (dwys) Very dense; very constant.
Tradwysaw, *v. a* (tradwys) To render extremely dense; to become extremely dense.
Tradwysiad, *s. m.* (tradwys) A rendering extremely dense; a becoming extremely dense.
Tradyfal, *a* (dyfal) Extremely persevering.
Tradyfaliad, *s. m.* (tradyfal) A persevering extremely.
Tradyfalu, *v. a.* (tradyfal) To persevere greatly.
Tradynawl, *a.* (dynawl) Superhuman.
Tradynoldeb, *s. m.* (tradynawl) A superhuman state.
Tradynoli, *v. a.* (tradynawl) To render superhuman; to become superhuman.
Tradysgedig, *a.* (dysgedig) Extremely learned.
Tradd, *s. m.—pl. t.* au (tra—add) Extreme motion. *Eidion ac y tradd arno,* a beast that has the scouring.
Traddawd, *s. m.* (dawd) A delivery over.
Traddiad, *s. m* (tradd) A moving violently.
Traddodawl, *a.* (traddawd) Tending to deliver over; surrendering.
Traddodedig, *a.* (traddawd) Delivered over, surrendered; delivered as a tradition.
Traddodi, *v. a.* (traddawd) To deliver over; to surrender, to give up; to deliver as a tradition.
Traddodiad, *s. m.—pl. t.* au (traddawd) A delivering over; a surrendering; a tradition.
Traddodiadawl, *a.* (traddodiad) Traditionary.
Traddodiadu, *v. a.* (traddodiad) To deliver over; to deliver by tradition.
Traddodiedydd, *s. m.—pl. t.* ion (traddodiad) A traditionist.
Traddodwr, *s. m.—pl.* traddodwyr (traddawd—gwr) One who delivers over.
Traddodydd, *s. m.—pl. t.* ion (traddawd) One who delivers over, one who surrenders.
Traddu, *v. a.* (tradd) To produce violent motion.
Traddygawl, *a.* (dygawl) Tending to transfer.
Traddygiad, *s. m.* (dygiad) A transferring.
Traddygyd, *v. a.* (dygyd) To carry over; to carry, or to lead, from one place to another.
Traed, *s. pl. aggr.* (tra—ed) That whereby transition is effected; feet. It is used as a plural for *Troed*, a foot, instead of the regular plural *Troedau.*

> I galon wan da traed buan.
>
> For a weak heart nimble *feet* are good. *Adage.*

Träegwan, *a.* (egwan) Extremely feeble.
Träeiddil, *a.* (eiddil) Extremely slender.
Träeiddilaw, *v. a.* (träeiddil) To make very slender; to become extremely slender.
Träeiddiliad, *s. m.* (träeiddil) A making extremely slender; a becoming extremely slender.
Träeiddilwch, *s.* (träeiddil) Extreme slenderness.
Träerchyll, *a.* (erchyll) Extremely horrible.
Träerchylldawd, *s.* (träerchyll) Extreme horror.
Träerchylliad, *s. m.* (träerchyll) A rendering extremely horrible; a becoming very horrid.
Träerchyllu, *v. a.* (träerchyll) To render extremely horrid; to become very horrible.
Träesgud, *a.* (esgud) Extremely nimble.
Träesgudaw, *v. a.* (träesgud) To render extremely nimble; to become very nimble.
Träesgudrwydd, *s.* (träesgud) Over nimbleness.
Traeth, *s. m.—pl.* traethydd (tra—eth) An extremity, or outside; that is clear, or open; a tract; the margin, shore, or sandy beach of the sea, or the sand between high and low water marks.

> Pwybynag a bieuffo dir yn ymyl traeth, efe bieufydd gyfled y tir o'r traeth; a gwnaed gored arno os myn.
>
> Whosoever owns land on the margin of a *strand*, he shall own as much in breadth as the land of the *strand*; and he may form a wear upon it if he will. *Welsh Laws.*

Traethad, *s. m.* (traeth) A spreading out; a forming a tract; a treating; a declaring, or uttering.
Traethadur, *s. m.—pl. t.* ion (traethad) One that treats or declares.

> Pan brofer traethawd traethadurion call,
> Nid colledig fy nghyfeillion.
>
> When the treatise of those who *treat* skilfully is tried, my companions will not be losers. *Cynddelw.*

Traethadwy, *a* (traethad) Utterable, effable.
Traethator, *ger.* (traethad) In reciting.
Traethawd, *s. m.—pl.* traethodau (traeth) A discourse, a treatise, a tract.

> Rhwych wych wenwawd,
> Rhad deg draethawd a draethitor.
>
> The splendid scope of fair eulogy, be the gift of polished discourse that is discoursed. *[illegible]*

Traethawdl, *s f.—pl.* traethodlau (traeth—awdl) A recitative ode; also called *traethodyn.*
Traethawl, *a.* traeth) Tending to open, expressive.

Traethawr, *s. m.* (traeth) That utters or expresses.

Traethawyr, *s. m.* (traeth—awyr) Sand sky, or clouds when they are much broken.

Traethedig, *a.* (traethad) Being spread out; being uttered, treated, or expressed.

Traetheg, *s. f.* (traeth) Science of declamation.

Traethell, *s. f. dim.*—*pl. t.* i (traeth) A sandbank.

Traethellfor, *s. m.* (traethell—mor) A sea that breaks over a sandbank.

Traethelliad, *s. m.* (traethell) A forming a sandbank.

Traethellu, *v. a.* (traethell) To form a sandbank.

Traethen, *s. f. dim.*—*pl. t.* i (traeth) A sand-drift.

Traethiad, *s. m.* (traeth) A treating; a diction.

Traethitor, *sup.* (traeth) To be reciting; to be discoursed of.

Traethodydd, *s. m.*—*pl. t.* ion (traethawd) One who makes a treatise.

Traethodyn, *s. m. dim.* (traethawd) A recitative verse, a sort of free versification.

> Traethodyn, neu draethawdl, a wneir ar yr un a fynnir o'r pumgolofn, neu y gyhydedd hwyaf, yn gyplau unawdl.
>
> A *recitative* or reciting ode, is composed upon any one that may be desired of the five fundamental metres, or the longest metricity, in unirhyme couplets. *Barddas.*

Traethoriaeth, *s. m.* (traethawr) Declamation.

Traethu, *v. a.* (traeth) To utter, to relate, to rehearse, to discourse; to treat.

> Nid rhaid tafawd i draethu serch.
>
> A tongue is not necessary for *declaring* love. *Adage.*
>
> Tenefan a draethws y deyrnas trwy heddwch a thangnefedd.
>
> Tenevan *treated* the kingdom through peace and tranquillity. *Bryt. Gwaliter o Rydychain.*

Traethwr, *s. m.*—*pl.* traethwyr (traeth—gwr) One who utters, or relates, a discourser.

Traethydd, *s. m.*—*pl. t.* ion (traeth) A treater.

Traf, *s. m.* (tra) A strain, a stir; a scour.

Trafael, *s. f.*—*pl.* trafaelion (tra—mael) Extreme effort; trouble, travail.

> Trafael a chur, gyda dolur, gwedi doliad
> Trwm gymeraist, traws yn prynaist,
> O'r pren croeliad.
>
> Trouble and affliction, with pain, after apprehension, heavily thou didst receive, opposing all thou didst redeem us, from the crucifying tree. *Cusnodyn.*

Trafaeliad, *s. m.* (trafael) A travailing.

Trafaelu, *v. a.* (trafael) To travail, to toil.

Trafaelus, *a.* (trafael) Harassing, travailing.

Trafaes, *s. m.*—*pl. t.* oedd (traf) A stir, or bustle. '*Trafaes ac amryson*,' Bustle and contention.

Trafawd, *s. f.*—*pl.* trafodau (traf) A stirring, a turning about; a bustle; an intermeddling; labour, pains, trouble.

> Po mwyaf y drafawd mwyaf fydd y gorfod.
>
> The more the *pains* may be the more will be the necessity. *Adage.*
>
> O drafodion yr ystyr y tardd y deall;
> O drafodion y deall y tardd y meddwl.
>
> From the *impulses* of the sense proceeds the understanding; from the *impulses* of the understanding proceeds the thought. *Geraint Fardd Glas.*
>
> Nead dyfod trafod trafn alltudedd hir,
> Y mor dros dir cwbl i anwedd!
>
> Does there not exist the *affliction* of a course of tedious banishment, the sea completely over a sinful land? *G. ab M. ab Dafydd.*

Trafel, *s. m.*—*pl. t.* au (traf) That stirs, or works, a press; a hatchel.

Traflwnc, *s. m.*—*pl.* traflynciau (traf—llwnc) A greedy swallow, a guzzle.

Traflwng, *s. m.* (traf—llwng) A guzzle.

Traflyncawl, *a.* (traflwnc) A guzzling.

Traflynciad, *s. m.* (traflwnc) A guzzling.

Traflyncu, *v. a.* (traflwnc) To swallow greedily.

> Ni chefais i fawr o aros, nad dyma fi yn ngolwg allawr fawr arswydus, lle gwelwn y brenin dychrynadwy yn traflyncu cig a gwaed dynion, a mil o fan angeuod o bob twll yn ei borthi.
>
> I obtained only a short stay, but here I was in sight of a large dreadful altar, where I perceived the terrible king devouring the flesh and blood of men, with a thousand tiny deaths from every corner supplying him. *Bardd Cwsg. Elis Wyn, B. Cwsg.*

Traflyncwr, *s. m.* (traflwnc) A greedy swallower.

Trafn, *s. m.*—*pl. t.* au (traf) That causes a stir, turn, or motion; a stir; a bustle; a course; a turn; an impulse. *Carw mawr-drafn*, the greatly moving stag; *dyfeis-drafn*, the invention-moving.

> Trafn gwaew eurllafn gwyarllyd.
>
> The *course* of a golden-bladed spear imbrued with gore. *H. ab O. Gwynedd.*
>
> Lle mae pen brawd Cystenyn Fendigaid,
> Llafn drafn y drin.
>
> Where is deposited the head of the brother of Constantine the Blessed, the blade of the *course* of conflict. *R. Goch Eryri.*
>
> Cartrefaf, trefnaf trafnau goleuni,
> Trwy foli fy Rhi tra fwyf innau.
>
> I will fix my home, I will prepare for the *paths* of light, by adoring my Lord whilst I exist. *G. ab M. ab Dafydd.*
>
> Angleddiad trefnad trafn bröydd gwynfyd,
> A'm try o gywyd ym tragywydd.
> Ein crair wyd, Fab Mair, morach gwynydd,
> A'n llawen amdor, a'n llunied ydd!
>
> The upholder of the system of the *course* of the regions of happiness, will turn me from a falling state to my eternity. Our hope art thou, Son of Mary, dispensing bliss, and our joyful tender, and our former! *G. ab M. ab Dafydd.*

Trafnawl, *a.* (trafn) Ranging; revolving; changing, mutable.

Trafnedig, *a.* (trafn) Ranged; being made to turn, revolve, or change.

Trafniad, *s. m.*—*pl. t.* au (trafn) A ranging, a making a turn, a revolving; a changing.

Trafnid, *s. m.* (trafn) A range, a turn; a change; exchange; commerce.

Trafnidaeth, *s. m.* (trafnid) Intercourse, commerse, exchange; business. *Pa drafnidaeth sy ganddo?* in what line of business is he?

Trafnidiad, *s. m.* (trafnid) A carrying on intercourse, or commerce; a bartering.

Trafnidiaw, *v. a.* (trafnid) To carry on intercourse, or commerce; to exchange, to barter.

> O derfydd i ddyn fynu gwerthu ych o'r cyfar a rygyfarodd ynddo, ni ddyly ei werthu, na ei drafnidiaw, yni ddarffo y cyfar.
>
> If a man should desire to sell an ox out of joint ploughing wherein he has ploughed, he ought not to sell it, nor to *exchange* it, until he completes the joint ploughing. *Welsh Laws.*

Trafnidiawg, *a.* (trafnid) Having intercourse, commerce, or exchange.

Trafnidiawl, *a.* (trafnid) Commercial.

Trafnidiwr, *s. m.*—*pl.* trafnidiwyr (trafnid—gwr) One who has intercourse; a trafficker.

Trafnidydd, *s. m.*—*pl. t.* ion (trafnid) Trafficker.

Trafnig, *a.* (trafn) Of aptitude to range, or to revolve; mutable, declinable.

> Tri o enwau nid trafnig.
>
> Three of names not *declinable.* *Llawdden.*

Trafnoldeb, *s. m.* (trafnawl) A state of ranging, or revolving; mutableness.

Trafnu, *v. a.* (trafn) To range; to revolve; to mutate.

Trafnus, *a.* (trafn) Ranging; revolving.

Trafnusaw, *v. a.* (trafnus) To render ranging, or revolving; to become mutable.

Trafnusdeb, *s. m.* (trafnus) A state of ranging, or revolving; mutableness.

Trafnusder, *s. m.* (trafnus) Mutableness.

Trafnusdra, *s. m.* (trafnus) Mutability.

Trafnusrwydd, *s. m.* (trafnus) A state of ranging, or revolving; mutableness.

Trafnwr, *s. m.—pl.* trafnwyr (trafn—gwr) A ranger, one who revolves.

Trafodadwy, *a.* (trafawd) Capable of stirring.

Trafodaeth, *s. m.* (trafawd) The act of stirring; a bustle; an intermeddling.

Trafodawl, *a.* (trafawd) Stirring; bustling.

Trafodi, *v. a.* (trafawd) To stir, to turn about; to bustle; to strive; to intermeddle.

> Bram y gant chwedl gan wawr,
> With a'i bolai'n ei battawr;
> Doeth ni thrafyd nyw ymdawr.

> A crow did sing her adage with the dawn, to such as questioned her on her onset; the wise *who doth not take pains* doth not regard himself. *Calueg ab Gwynllinv.*

> Gwyr a aeth Gattraeth gan wawr;
> Trafodynt yn hedd yn cofnawr.

> Men went the Cattraeth with the dawn; *they would strive* in peace with audacity. *Aneurin.*

Trafodiad, *s. m.* (trafawd) A stirring, a turning about; a bustling; a striving; an intermeddling

Trafodiaeth, *s. m.* (trafawd) The act of stirring; a bustling; an intermeddling; a transaction. *Trafodiaeth y byd hyn*, the transaction of this world. *Sil.*

Trafodus, *a.* (trafawd) Apt to stir; bustling.

Trafodusaw, *v. a.* (trafodus) To render bustling or striving; to become bustling.

Trafodusedd, *s. m.* (trafodus) A stirring state.

Trafodusrwydd, *s. m.* (trafodus) A stirring state, tumultuou ness.

Trafodwr, *s. m.—pl.* trafodwyr (trafawd—gwr) One who stirs; a bustler; a striver; an intermeddler.

Trafodydd, *s. m.—pl. t.* ion (trafawd) A stirrer; a bustler; an intermeddler.

Trafoliad, *s. m.* (boliad) A gormandizing.

Trafoliaw, *v. a.* (boliaw) To gorge the belly.

Trafoliwr, *s. m.—pl.* trafoliwyr (trafoliaw—gwr) A gorger, a gormandizer.

Trafu, *v.* (traf) To stir, to agitate; to scour, to purge.

Trafus, *a.* (traf) Apt to stir, or to agitate.

Trafusaw, *v. a.* (trafus) To produce a stirring.

Trafusder, *s. m.* (trafus) A stirring state.

Trafusedd, *s. m.* (trafus) A commotion.

Trafusrwydd, *s. m.* (trafus) An agitated state.

Traff, *s. m.* (tra) A spread; a scatter.

Traffaeth, *a.* (ffaeth) Over-mellow.

Traffaethiad, *s. m.* (traffaeth) A rendering over-mellow; a becoming extremely mellow or rich.

Traffaethu, *v. a.* (traffaeth) To render over-mellow; to become over-mellow.

Traffaith, *s. m.—pl.* traffeithiau (paith) A plot.

Traffeithus, *a.* (traffaith) Plotting. *Dynion traffeithus*, plotting men.

Trafferth, *s. m.—pl. t.* ion (traff—erth) Business, painstaking, toil, trouble; a great to do. *Mae arno lawer o drafferth amdani*, he is in great taking about her.

> Trafferth ych byd ei wyddi.

> The toil of the ox till the afternoon. *Adage.*

Trafferthawg, *a.* (trafferth) Full of bustle.

Trafferthawl, *a.* (trafferth) Bustling, toiling.

Trafferthedig, *a.* (trafferth) Being busied.

Trafferthiad, *s. m.* (trafferth) A toiling.

Trafferthiant, *s. m.* (trafferth) Busy toiling.

Trafferthu, *v. a.* (trafferth) To bustle, to be busy; to be busily employed; to be toiling.

Trafferthus, *a.* (trafferth) Bustling, full of business; toiling, laborious; troublous.

Trafferthusaw, *v. a.* (trafferthus) To render toiling; to become toiling or laborious.

Trafferthusder, *s. m.* (trafferthus) Laboriousness.

Trafferthusrwydd, *s. m.* (trafferth) Toilsomeness

Trafferthwr, *s. m.—pl.* trafferthwyr (trafferth—gwr) A bustler, a toiler.

Traffiad, *s. m.* (traff) A making a stir; a spreading

Traffu, *v. a.* (traff) To make a stir; to spread.

Traffull, *s. m.* (ffull) Extreme bustle, or haste.

Traffulliad, *s. m.* (traffull) A bustling greatly.

Traffulliaw, *v. a.* (traffull) To bustle greatly.

Traffun, *s. f.* (ffun) Extreme panting. *a.* Having extreme panting.

Traffunaw, *v. a.* (traffun) To pant extremely.

Traffuniad, *s. m.* (traffun) A panting extremely.

Traffwyr, *s. m.* (ffwyr) Extreme impulse, or gust; an extreme drive; an extreme assault.

> Dru'lwyr ei draffwyr ar draffun ferch
> O'i drafferth rhag Fortun.

> Altogether bold his *most violent assault* on steeds extremely panting from his exertion before Mortun.
> *Cynddelw i O. Cyfeiliawg.*

Traffwyraw, *v. a.* (traffwyr) To impel greatly.

Traffwyriad, *s. m.* (traffwyr) A greatly driving.

Traffysg, *s. m.* (ffysg) Extreme hurry or haste.

Traffysgiad, *s. m.* (traffysg) A hurrying greatly.

Traffysgiaw, *v. a.* (traffysg) To hurry greatly.

Traffysgiawl, *a.* (traffysg) Extremely bustling.

Trag, *adv.* (tra) Beyond; beside; at; aside.

Tragalar, *s. m.* (galar) Extreme grief.

Tragalariad, *s. m.* (tragalar) A grieving greatly.

Tragalaru, *v. a.* (tragalar) To grieve extremely.

Tragalarus, *a.* (tragalar) Very grievous.

Tragall, *s. m.* (gall) Extreme power or might.

Tragallu, *v. n.* (tragall) To be extremely able.

Tragalluawg, *a.* (tragallu) Having over-power.

Tragallued, *s. m.* (tragallu) Extreme power.

Tragarw, *a.* (garw) Extremely rough or harsh.

Tragerwin, *a.* (tragarw) Extremely harsh.

Tragerwinaw, *v. a.* (tragerwin) To render extremely harsh; to become extremely rough.

Tragerwindeb, *s.* (tragerwin) Over harshness.

Traglew, *a.* (glew) Extremely clever.

Traglewder, *s. m.* (traglew) Extreme cleverness, extreme bravery.

Tragloes, *s. f.* (gloes) An extreme pang.

Tragloesawl, *a.* (tragloes) Extremely painful.

Tragloesi, *v. a.* (tragloes) To pain extremely.

Tragloesiad, *s.* (tragloes) A paining extremely.

Tragloew, *a.* (gloew) Extremely clear.

Tragloewder, *s. m.* (tragloew) Extreme clearness

Tragloewi, *v. a.* (tragloew) To render extremely clear, pellucid, or transparent.

Tragoes, *s. f.* (trag—oes) An after age. *adv.* Beyond age, after age.

> I Wenddydd y dywedaf;
> O's tragoes dysgaganaf:
> Wedi Cadwaladr, Cyndaf.

> To Gwenddydd I will declare; *age after age* I will foretell. after Cadwaladr, Cyndaf. *Cyfoesi Myrddin.*

Tragoesawl, *a.* (tragoes) Relating to after age.

Tragoesi, *v. a.* (tragoes) To render of an after age; to become of an after age.

Tragoesiad, *s. m.* (tragoes) A rendering of an after age; a becoming of an after age.

Tragofal, *s. m.—pl. t.* on (gofal) Extreme care.

Tragofaliad, *s. m.* (tragofal) A taking extreme care; a being very anxious.

Tragofalu, *v. a.* (tragofal) To take extreme care, to be very careful.

Tragofalus, *a.* (tragofal) Extremely careful.

Tragolau, *a.* (golau) Extremely luminous.

Tragoleuad, *s. m.* (tragolau) A greatly enlightening, a becoming extremely enlightened.

Tragoleuaw, *v. a.* (tragolau) To illume greatly.

Tragolud, *s. m.* (golud) Extreme wealth.
Tragoludaw, *v. a.* (tragolud) To render extremely wealthy.
Tragoludawg, *a.* (tragolud) Very wealthy.
Tragor, *s. m.* (gor) Superabundance, superfluity.
Tragorawl, *a.* (tragor) Excessive; transcendental
Tragori, *v. a.* (tragor) To render transcendental; to become transcendent.
Tragoriad, *s. m.* (tragor) A transcending.
Tragoriaeth, *s. m.* (tragor) Transcendency.
Tragoriant, *s. m.* (tragor) Transcendency.
Tragoroldeb, *s. m.* (tragorawl) Superexcellence.
Tragorolder, *s. m.* (tragorawl) Superexcellence.
Tragoroldra, *s. m.* (tragorawl) Superexcellence.
Tragoroledd, *s. m.* (tragorawl) Superexcellence.
Tragoroli, *v. a.* (tragorawl) To render superexcellent; to transcend.
Tragoroliad, *s. m.* (tragorawl) A transcending.
Tragorolrwydd, *s. m.* (tragorawl) Superexcellentness; pre-eminence.
Tragorthrwm, *a.* (gorthrwm) Extremely oppressive
Tragorthrymawl, *a.* (tragorthrwm) Tending to be extremely oppressive.
Tragorthrymder, *s. m.* (tragorthrwm) Extreme oppression.
Tragorthrymiad, *s. m.* (tragorthrwm) A greatly oppressing, a tyrannising greatly.
Tragorthrymu, *v. a.* (tragorthrwm) To oppress extremely.
Tragoruch, *a.* (goruch) Most supreme.
Tragoruchder, *s. m.* (tragoruch) Superexcellence, supereminency; extreme altitude.
Tragoruchel, *a.* (tragoruch) Extremely elevated.
Tragwael, *a.* (gwael) Extremely frail.
Tragwaelder, *s. m.* (tragwael) Extreme frailty.
Tragwaelu, *v. a.* (tragwael) To render extremely frail, to become extremely frail.
Tragwall, *s. m.* (gwall) Extreme failing.
Tragwallder, *s. m.* (tragwall) Extreme fallacy.
Tragwalledd, *s. m.* (tragwall) Extreme fallacy.
Tragwallu, *v. a.* (tragwall) To fail extremely.
Tragwallus, *a.* (tragwall) Extremely fallible.
Tragwan, *a.* (gwàn) Extremely weak.
Tragwander, *s. m.* (tragwan) Extreme weakness.
Tragwaniad, *s. m.* (tragwan) A weakening extremely.
Tragwànu, *v. a.* (tragwan) To weaken greatly.
Tragwarth, *s. m.* (gwarth) Extreme disgrace.
Tragwarthiad, *s. m* (tragwarth) A disgracing extremely.
Tragwarthu, *v. a.* (tragwarth) To disgrace extremely.
Tragwarthus, *a.* (tragwarth) Very disgraceful.
Tragwelw, *a.* (gwelw) Extremely pale.
Tragwelwad, *s. m.* (tragwelw) A turning pale.
Tragwelwedd, *s. m.* (tragwelw) Extreme paleness
Tragwelwi, *v. a.* (tragwelw) To turn very pale.
Tragwerth, *s. m.* (gwerth) Over-value.
Tragwerthiad, *s. m.* (tragwerth) An over-valuing; an over-selling.
Tragwerthu, *v. a.* (tragwerth) To over-sell.
Tragwiw, *a.* (gwiw) Most excellent, most worthy
Tragwiwdeb, *s.* (tragwiw) Extreme worthiness.
Tragwr, *s. m.* (gwr) A superior man.
Tragwrawl, *a.* (tragwr) Extremely masculine.
Tragwres, *s. m* (gwres) Extreme heat.

> Daeth cysgu arno, sef a wnai ei weision ystafell castellu tarianau yn ei gylch ar bennau gwaewawr rhag y tragwres.
>
> Sleep came upon him; thereupon his chamberlains did spread a screen with shields around him on the shafts of spears against the *extreme heat*. *Breuddwyd Maxen Wledig.*

Tragwresawg, *a.* (tragwres) Extremely hot.
Tragwresawl, *a.* (tragwres) Extremely heating.
Tragwresiad, *s. m.* (tragwres) A heating greatly
Tragwresu, *v. a.* (tragwres) To heat greatly.
Tragwth, *s. m.* (gwth) An extreme push.
Tragwthiad, *s. m.* (tragwth) A pushing greatly.
Tragwthiaw, *v. a.* (tragwth) To push extremely.
Tragwydd, *a.* (gwydd) Being beyond presence or cognition; eternal.
Tragwyddawg, *a.* (tragwydd) Eternal, ever.
Tragwyddawl, *a.* (tragwydd) Being beyond cognizance, or knowledge; eternal.
Tragwyddogder, *s. m.* (tragwyddawg) Eternalness

> Pa hyd, Arglwydd!——
> A drig dig dy dragwyddogder?
>
> How long, Lord! will thy wrath endure to *eternity!*
> *M. Middleton.*

Tragwyddoldeb, *s. m.* (tragwydd) Eternity.
Tragwyddoli, *v. a.* (tragwyddawl) To eternize.
Tragwyl, *a.* (gwyl) Extremely bashful.
Tragwylaw, *v. a.* (tragwyl) To render extremely bashful; to become very bashful.
Tragwylder, *s. m.* (tragwyl) Extreme bashfulness
Tragwyn, *a.* (gwŷn) Extremely white.
Tragwyniad, *s. m.* (tragwyn) A whitening greatly
Tragwŷnu, *v. a.* (tragwyn) To whiten extremely
Tragŵyr, *a.* (gŵyr) Extremely oblique.
Tragŵyraw, *v. a.* (tragŵyr) To render extremely oblique; to become extremely oblique.
Tragŵyredd, *s. m.* (tragŵyr) Extreme obliquity.
Tragŵyriad, *s. m.* (tragŵyr) A rendering extremely oblique.
Tragyr, *s. m.* (gyr) Extreme impulse.
Tragyrawl, *a.* (tragyr) Extremely impulsive.
Tragyriad, *s. m.* (tragyr) A driving extremely.
Tragyru, *v. a.* (tragyr) To drive extremely.
Tragywydd, *a.* (cywydd) Being beyond cognition; eternal, everlasting. *adv.* Eternally.

> Dyro ran i'th wàn, wynfyd wrthddrych hawl,
> O'th wlad fad feddrinwl, er mawl mynych,
> I'th wledd, llyw buchedd, lle y bych dragywydd.
>
> Grant a share to thy supplicant, an object having claim on happiness, of thy kingdom commensurate with good, for incessant praise, in thy banquet, Lord of life, where thou art *to eternity*.
> *Casnodyn.*

Tragywyddaw, *v. a.* (tragywydd) To eternize.
Tragywyddawg, *a.* (tragywydd) Of eternal duration.
Tragywyddawl, *a.* (tragywydd) Eternal, ever.
Tragywyddogder, *s.* (tragywyddawg) Eternalness.
Tragywyddoldeb, *s. m.* (tragywyddawl) Eternity
Tragywyddolder, *s. m.* (tragywyddawl) Eternity

> Y dydd cyntaf y gwnai ef ddydd tragywyddolder, sef yw hyny lleufer ysbrydawl.
>
> The first day he made the day of *eternity*, that is to say spiritual light.
> *Eluciderius.*

Tragywyddoledd, *s. m.* (tragywyddawl) Eternalness.
Tragywyddoli, *v. a.* (tragywyddawl) To eternalize; to eternize; to perpetnate.

> Gwerthu a thragywyddoli tir.
>
> To sell and *to perpetuate* land. *Welsh Laws.*

Tragywyddoliad, *s. m.* (tragywyddawl) Eterni' zation, a making eternal; a perpetnating.
Tragywyddoliaeth, *s. m.* (tragywyddawl) Eternization.

> Nid ynt tri tragywyddawl, namyn un tragywyddawl; sef yw hyny un diwahan yw tragywyddoliaeth y tri.
>
> They are not three eternals, but one eternal; that is to say one undivisible is the *eternity* of the three.
> *Llyfr Dudrydd Llanddewi Brefi.*

Tragywyddolrwydd, *s. m.* (tragywyddawl) Everlastingness, eternalness.

Traha, *s. m.* (tra—ha) Extreme exaltation; haughtiness, arrogance, presumption.

> Gwaed wedi traha trano hir.
>
> After *presumption* a lasting perdition follows. *Adage.*
>
> Gnawd o ben drythyll draha.
>
> From the mouth of the affluent *presumption* is natural. *Adage.*
>
> Tair traha gadarn cenedl y Cymmry y gelwir y tair cyfordwy.
>
> The three mighty *presumptions* of the nation of the Cymmry the three universal expeditions were called. *Trioedd.*
>
> Gwae a godiwy Duw drwy syberwyd,
> Traha a'i syrth yn mhoen yn mhell ddeincryd.
>
> Woe to him that offends God through pride, *presumption* shall cast him down in torment in the extreme gnashing of teeth. *Meilyr ab Gwalchmai.*

Trahâad, *s. m.* (traha) A rendering arrogant; a becoming arrogant, a presuming.

Trahâawg, *a.* (traha) Arrogant, presuming.

> Tri thrahâawg Ynys Prydain; Sawyl Benuchel, Pasgen, mab Urien, a Rhun, mab Einiawn.
>
> The three *arrogant ones* of the Isle of Britain; Sawyl Benuchel, Pasgen son of Urien, and Rhun son of Einion. *Trioedd.*

Trahâawl, *a.* (traha) Presumptuous.

Trahardd, *a.* (hardd) Extremely handsome.

Traharddiad, *s. m.* (trahardd) A rendering extremely handsome; a becoming of extremely fine growth.

Traharddu, *v. a.* (trahardd) To render extremely handsome; to become very comely.

Trahâu, *v. a.* (traha) To render arrogant, to fill with presumption; to become arrogant.

Trahâus, *a.* (traha) Arrogant, haughty.

Trahausder, *s. m.* (trahâus) Haughtiness.

Trahausdra, *s. m.* (trahâus) Arrogance.

Trahausedd, *s. m.* (trahâus) Arrogance.

Trahausfalch, *a.* (trahâus—balch) Arrogantly-proud.

Trahawdd, *a.* (hawdd) Extremely easy.

Trahawl, *s. f.*—*pl.* traholion (hawl) An extreme claim.

Trahelaeth, *a.* (helaeth) Extremely ample.

Trahelaethiad, *s. m.* (trahelaeth) A rendering extremely ample.

Trahelaethu, *v. a.* (trahelaeth) To render extremely ample; to become very extended.

Traheini, *a.* (heini) Extremely brisk or lively.

Trahen, *a.* (hen) Extremely old or aged.

Trahenu, *v. a.* (trahen) To grow extremely old.

Trahir, *a.* (hir) Extremely long; very tedious.

Trahiriad, *s. m.* (trahir) A lengthening greatly.

Trahiriaw, *v. a.* (trahir) To lengthen extremely.

Trahoen, *s. f.* (hoen) Extreme vivacity.

Trahoff, *a.* (hoff) Most lovely; very engaging.

Trahoffi, *v. a.* (trahoff) To like extremely.

Trahoffiad, *s. m.* (trahoff) A liking extremely.

Traholi, *v. a.* (trahawl) To make an over claim; to question extremely.

Traholiad, *s. m.* (trahawl) A making an extreme claim; questioning extremely.

Trahòni, *v. a.* (hòni) To assert extremely.

Trahòniad, *s. m.* (hòniad) An asserting greatly.

Trahurt, *a.* (hurt) Extremely foolish.

Trahurtiad, *s. m.* (trahurt) A crazing extremely; a becoming extremely foolish.

Trahurtiaw, *v. a.* (trahurt) To render extremely crazy: to become extremely foolish.

Trahwyl, *s. f.*—*pl. t.* ion (hwyl) Extreme course.

Trahwyliad, *s. m.* (trahwyl) A making an extreme course.

Trahwyliaw, *v. a.* (trahwyl) To make an extreme course.

Trahy, *a.* (hy) Extremely bold or daring.

Trahyder, *s. m.* (hyder) Extreme confidence.

Trahyderiad, *s. m.* (trahyder) A confiding extremely; an over-confiding.

Trahyderu, *v.* (trahyder) To confide extremely.

Trahyfryd, *a.* (hyfryd) Extremely happy.

Trahyfrydawl, *a.* (trahyfryd) Greatly pleasing.

Trahyfrydiad, *s. m.* (trahyfryd) A rendering extremely happy; a becoming greatly pleased.

Trahyfrydu, *v. a.* (trahyfryd) To make extremely happy; to be extremely pleased.

Trahyll, *a.* (hyll) Extremely frightful.

Trahylliad, *s. m.* (trahyll) A scaring extremely; a becoming extremely ugly.

Trahyllu, *v. a.* (trahyll) To scare extremely; to make very ugly.

Trahynaws, *a.* (hynaws) Extremely goodnatured

Trahynawsedd, *s. m.* (trahynaws) Extreme kindness of disposition.

Trahynod, *a.* (hynod) Extremely remarkable.

Trahynodi, *v. a.* (trahynod) To render extremely remarkable.

Trahynodiad, *s. m.* (trahynod) A rendering extremely remarkable.

Trai, *s. m.* (tra) An extreme state; a decrease, diminishing, or lessening; an ebb, an ebb tide. *Distyll trai*, low water mark.

> Mydd a fyrchyg, ac a [illegible],
> Ac a gerdda yn drwm gwrthan trai;
> Mydd y gwr a ddaliai Cai.
>
> I do ride, and do stand, and pensively walk on the brink of the *ebbing tide:* I am the person who would catch Cai. *Ymddiddan Arthur a Gwenhwyfar.*
>
> Mal llyn melin ar drai.
>
> Like a mill pond on the ebb. *Adage.*

Traidd, *s. m.* (tra—idd) A passage or pervasion, a pierce through; a strait, passage, or narrow sea.

Traig, *s. m.* (tra—ig) That tends over.

Traigl, *s. m.*—*pl.* treiglion (traig) A turn over, a turn, a roll; a revolution; an accidence; a walk about, a case, in grammar.

> Traigl maen hyd wastad.
>
> The rolling of a stone to the level. *Adage.*

Traill, *s. m.*—*pl.* treillion (tra—ill) A drawing over; a trail, a drawing out; a turn; a circumstance. *Traill o bysgod*, a draught of fishes.

> Gwr yw Iesu——
> Garw ei draill a girad rhon.
>
> Iesu is a person of terrible course with a destructive spear. *[illegible]*
>
> Mewn dau beth y mae'n debyg
> I draill y ci a'r dryll cig.
>
> In two things it is similar to the *circumstance* of the dog with the piece of meat. *[illegible]*

Train, *s. m.*—*pl.* treinion (tra—in) A run out, a stroll, a stray; a scattering; a reporting of news. *Aur ar drain*, gold spread abroad.

> Gwelais eu trychni, trichant celain;
> Gwelais wedi cad coluddion ar drain.
>
> I saw their mangled state, three hundred bodies; I saw after conflict entrails on a *spread*. *Cynddelw.*
>
> Yn dda da ei ryw, yn ddi drain,
> A goreu yn Nghymmru gywrain.
>
> A property good in its kind, void of being hackneyed, and the best in fair Wales. *[illegible]*
>
> Nid ai y rhai'n ar drain draw,
> Amrwd wedd, i 'mwradwyddaw.
>
> These would not go yonder on a *stroll*, with raw countenances, to brood over mutual scandal. *W. Cynwal.*

Trais, *s. m.*—*pl.* treisiau (tra—is) A break of bound; rapine; ravishment, violence; oppression.

> Pa beth bynag a gaffer o drais, a thwyll, a chadernyd, nid a ddylid y cynnelir hwnw.
>
> Whatsoever is obtained by *violence*, and deceit, and power, such is not maintained through justice. *Gr. ab Arthur.*

Traith, *s. m.—pl.* treithion (tra—ith) An utterance, or expression; a treatise.

> A chanmawl gwaith traith, lle trig
> Bronfraith mewn coed ar fanwfrig.
>
> To commence the performance is an *expression*, wherever the thrush abides on the twig of a tree in woods. *R. Goch Eryri.*

Trallafur, *s. m.* (llafur) Excessive labour.
Trallanw, *s. m.* (llanw) An over-filled state.
Trallawd, *s. m.—pl.* trallodion (llawd) Adversity, affliction.

> Drwg trallodau, gwaeth hebddynt.
>
> Bad are *afflictions*, it is worse without them. *Adage.*
>
> Trallodion yw ffyn yr ysgol sydd yn esgyn i'r nefoedd.
>
> *Afflictions* are the staves of the ladder that ascends to heaven. *Adage.*

Trallawen, *a.* (llawen) Extremely merry.
Trallawenu, *v. a.* (trallawen) To render extremely glad; to become extremely merry.
Trallawn, *a.* (llawn) Extremely full.
Trallawnder, *s. m.* (trallawn) Extreme fulness.
Tralleddf, *a.* (lleddf) Being extremely flat.
Tralleddfawl, *a.* (tralleddf) Tending to flatten extremely.
Tralleddfiad, *s. m.* (tralleddf) A flattening extremely; an inclining extremely.
Tralleddfu, *v. a.* (tralleddf) To decline extremely.
Trallenwad, *s. m.* (trallanw) An over-filling.
Trallenwi, *v. a.* (trallanw) To over-fill.
Trallea, *s. m.* (lles) Supreme benefit.
Trallesawl, *a.* (trallea) Extremely beneficial.
Trallesiad, *s. m.* (trallea) A benefiting extremely.
Trallesu, *v. a.* (tralles) To benefit extremely.
Trallid, *s. m.* (llid) Extreme anger.
Trallidiad, *s. m.* (trallid) A greatly irritating.
Trallidiaw, *v. a.* (trallid) To irritate extremely.
Trallidiawg, *a.* (trallid) Extremely angry.
Tralliw, *s. m.* (lliw) Excess of colour.
Tralliwiad, *s. m.* (tralliw) An over-colouring.
Tralliwiaw, *v. a.* (tralliw) To over-colour.
Trallodawl, *a.* (trallawd) Afflicting, vexing.
Trallodedig, *a.* (trallawd) Being afflicted.
Trallodi, *v. a.* (trallawd) To afflict, to vex.
Trallodiad, *s. m.* (trallawd) An afflicting.
Trallodus, *a.* (trallawd) Afflicting, vexatious.
Trallodusaw, *v. a.* (trallodus) To render afflicted; to render afflicting; to become afflicting.
Trallodusedd, *s. m.* (trallodus) Afflictedness.
Trallodusrwydd, *s. m.* (trallodus) Afflictedness.
Trallodwr, *s. m.—pl.* trallodwyr (trallawd—gwr) One who afflicts.
Trallon, *a.* (llon) Extremely pleased within.
Trallonaidd, *a.* (trallon) Tending to yield extreme inward pleasure.
Trallonder, *s. m.* (trallon) Extreme inward pleasure.
Tralloni, *v. a.* (trallon) To give extreme delight or inward satisfaction; to be extremely pleased.
Tralloniad, *s. m.* (trallon) A yielding extreme inward pleasure.
Trallonydd, *a.* (llonydd) Extremely quiet.
Trallonyddiad, *s. m.* (trallonydd) A quieting extremely; a becoming very quiet.
Trallonyddu, *v. a.* (trallonydd) To render extremely quiet, to become extremely quiet.
Trallonyddwch, *s. m.* (trallonydd) Extreme quietness.
Trallosg, *s. m.* (llosg) An extreme burning.
Trallosgach, *s. m.* (trallosg) A state of extreme burning; extreme lust.
Trallosgi, *v. a.* (trallosg) To burn extremely.
Trallosgiad, *s. m.* (trallosg) A burning extremely.
Trallusg, *s. m.* (llusg) Extreme dragging.
Trallusgaw, *v. a.* (trallusg) To drag extremely.
Trallusgawl, *a.* (trallusg) Dragging extremely.
Trallusgiad, *s. m.* (trallusg) A pulling or dragging after extremely.
Trallwybr, *s. m.—pl.* trallwybrau (llwybr) An extreme path; extreme hazard.

> Nes nas trawd trallawd trallwybr eisiau;
> Archaf arch i Ddaw, a'n dodes nef,
> Nas dote Pedr gloiau
> Ym lluddias ym addas ar naw!
>
> May we not be visited by the affliction to walk the *extreme path* of poverty; I beseech of God, who dispenses heaven to us, that Peter may not lay on locks, to hinder me to my appropriate place for myself! *Ein. ab Gwalchmai.*

Trallwybraw, *v. a.* (trallwybr) To make out an extreme path; to go an extreme path.
Trallwybriad, *s. m.* (trallwybr) A going on an extreme path; a going into extreme hazard.
Trallwydd, *s. m.* (llwydd) Extreme prosperity.
Trallwyddaw, *v. a.* (trallwydd) To prosper greatly
Trallwyddiad, *s. m.* (trallwydd) A prospering extremely; a being very fortunate.
Trallwyddiannawl, *a.* (trallwyddiant) Extremely prosperous or fortunate.
Trallwyddiannu, *v. a.* (trallwyddiant) To cause extreme prosperity; to become very prosperous
Trallwyddiannus, *a.* (trallwyddiant) Extremely prosperous or fortunate.
Trallwyddiant, *s. m.* (trallwydd) Great prosperity

> Nid gelyn ond trallwyddiant.
>
> There is no enemy like *too much prosperity*. *Adage.*

Trallwyth, *s. m.—pl. t.* i (llwyth) Extreme load.
Trallwythaw, *v. a.* (trallwyth) To overload.
Trallwythawg, *a.* (trallwyth) Overloaded.
Trallwythawl, *a.* (trallwyth) Tending to overload.
Trallwythedig, *a.* (trallwyth) Overloaded.
Trallwythiad, *s. m.* (trallwyth) An overloading.
Trallydan, *a.* (llydan) Extremely broad.
Trallydander, *s. m.* (trallydan) Extreme breadth.
Trallydaniad, *s. m.* (trallydan) A rendering extremely broad; an over-expanding.
Trallydanu, *v. a.* (trallydan) To render extremely broad; to become extremely expanded.
Trallym, *a.* (llym) Extremely sharp, or acute.
Trallymder, *s. m.* (trallym) Extreme sharpness.
Trallymiad, *s. m.* (trallym) A sharpening extremely; a becoming very sharp or severe.
Trallymu, *v. a.* (trallym) To sharpen extremely.
Tram, *s. m.* (tra—am) An extreme range round.
Tramain, *a.* (main) Extremely fine or slender.
Tramaint, *s. m.* (maint) Extreme size. *a.* Immense

> Meifod—
> A'i balchradd, a'i balchrodd tramaint.
>
> Meivod with its proud degree, and its proud gift *immense*. *Cynddelw.*

Tramantawl, *s. f.* (mantawl) An over-balance.
Tramantoli, *v. a.* (tramantawl) To over-balance.
Tramanwl, *a.* (manwl) Extremely accurate, exact, or nice; very careful.
Tramanyliad, *s. m.* (tramanwl) A rendering extremely exact; a becoming very careful.
Tramanylu, *v. a.* (tramanwl) To render extremely accurate; to become very exact.
Tramanylwch, *s. m.* (tramanwl) Extreme accuracy; extreme attention.
Tramawl, *s. f.* (mawl) Extreme praise.
Tramawr, *a.* (mawr) Exremely large; immense, infinite.
Tramawriad, *s. m.* (tramawr) A magnifying extremely.
Tramawru, *v. a.* (tramawr) To magnify extremely; to become extremely large.

Tramawredd, *s. m.* (tramawr) Extreme greatness.

Trambydiaw, *v. n.* (tram—pydiaw) To become exposed to great danger.

Tramdaw, *s. m.* (tram—taw) Extreme silence.

> Ni wiw cwynaw— —
> Na cheisiaw tramdaw yn y trymder'

> It is useless to complain, or to seek an *excess of silence* in the sad event' *Llywelyn Fardd.*

Tramdawiad, *s. m.* (tramdaw) A causing a deep silence; a becoming extremely silent.

Trameinder, *s. m.* (tramain) Extreme fineness, or slenderness.

Trameddal, *a.* (meddal) Extremely soft.

Trameddalder, *s. m.* (trameddal) Extreme softness

Trameddaledd, *s. m.* (trameddal) Extreme softness

Trameddaliad, *s. m.* (trameddal) A softening extremely.

Trameddalu, *v. a.* (trameddal) To soften greatly.

Trameddw, *a.* (meddw) Extremely drunk.

Trameddwad, *s. m.* (trameddw) Over intoxication

Trameddwi, *v. a.* (trameddw) To intoxicate extremely; to get very drunk.

Tramelys, *a.* (melys) Extremely sweet.

Tramelysder, *s.* (tramelys) Extreme sweetness.

Tramelysiad, *s. m.* (tramelys) A rendering extremely sweet; a becoming very sweet.

Tramelysu, *v. a* (tramelys) To sweeten extremely.

Trameth, *s. m.* (meth) Extreme failure.

Tramethiant, *s. m.* (trameth) Extreme debility.

Tramglwydd, *s. m.* (tram—clwydd) A stumble.

Tramglwyddaw, *v. a.* (tramglwydd) To fall over, to tumble, to stumble.

> Ni lwydda ond a dramglwydda.

> No one shall prosper but who *shall tumble.* *Adage.*

Tramglwyddiad, *s. m.* (tramglwydd) A tumbling over, a stumbling.

Tramgoll, *s. f.* (tram—coll) Extreme loss.

Tramgolli, *v. a.* (tramgoll) To lose extremely.

Tramgwydd, *s. m.—pl. t.* ion (tram—cwydd) A downfal, a tumble, a stumble.

> Oznad wedi traha tramgwydd.

> After *presumption* a *fall* is a natural consequence. *Adage.*

Tramgwyddaw, *v. a.* (tramgwydd) To tumble.

> Ni lwyddodd ond a dramgwyddodd.

> No one has prospered but who *has fallen.* *Adage.*

Tramgwyddawl, *a.* (tramgwydd) Stumbling.

Tramgwyddedig, *a.* (tramgwydd) Stumbled.

Tramgwyddfa, *s. f.—pl. t.* oedd (tramgwydd) A stumbling-block.

Tramgwyddiad, *s. m.—pl. t.* au (tramgwydd) A stumbling, a falling, or tumbling down.

Tramgwyddwr, *s. m.—pl.* tramgwyddwyr (tramgwydd—gwr) A stumbler, one who falls.

Tramhwyl, *s. f.—pl. t.* ian (tram—hwyl) An extreme course.

> Mal rhod yn troi tramhwylian,
> Trallawd maith trwy ymhell trethau.

> Like the universe revolving *immense courses*, a tedious affliction is the severely compelling of taxes. *Taliesin.*

Tramhwyliad, *s. m. pl. t.* au (tramhwyl) A taking an extreme course.

Tramhwyliaw, *v. a.* (tramhwyl) To make an extreme course.

Tramodd, *s. m. pl. t.* ion (modd) Extreme means or ability.

Tramoddawl, *a.* (tramodd) Beyond possibility.

Tramoddiad, *s. m.* (tramodd) A rendering beyond means; a rendering impossible.

Tramoddiaw, *v.* (tramodd) To render impossible

Tramoed, *adv.* (tra—ym—oed) Beyond my time.

Tramolawd, *s. f.* (tramawl) Extreme praise.

Tramoli, *v. a.* (tramawl) To praise extremely.

Tramoliannu, *v. a.* (tramoliant) To praise extremely; to flatter.

Tramoliannus, *a.* (tramoliant) Extremely commendable.

Tramoliant, *s. m.* (tramawl) Extreme praise.

Tramor, *s. m.—pl. t.* oedd (mor) A place beyond sea. *a.* Transmarine; foreign.

> Nid mor heb dramor.

> There is no sea without a *transmarine region.* *Adage.*

> Y mynyddoedd ac y fforestydd a gynnalai y brenin yn ddiffaith iddo ei hun; megys y gallo dderbyn alltudion tramor yn wyr iddo; ac i aw roddi yn nghyfarwys; ac i aw briodoli yn gardotir i fynachlogydd.

> The mountains and the forests the king preserved as waste for himself; so that he might receive *transmarine exiles* to become his men; and to give it as a gratuity; and to appropriate it as eleemosynary land to monasteries. *Welsh Laws.*

Tramorawl, *a.* (tramor) Transmarine.

Tramoredig, *a.* (tramor) Being made transmarine. *Tramoredigion,* transmarine things.

Tramori, *v. a.* (tramor) To render transmarine; to pass beyond sea; to become transmarine.

Tramp, *s. m.—pl. t.* iau (tram) A ramble. *Myned ar y tramp,* to set out on the ramble.

Trampiad, *s. m.* (tramp) A rambling.

Trampiaw, *v. a.* (tramp) To ramble, to tramp.

Trampiawl, *a.* (tramp) Rambling, tramping.

Trampiwr, *s. m.—pl.* trampiwyr (tramp—gwr) A rambler, a tramper.

Tramwy, *s. m.* (tram) A transit; a going about.

Tramwy, *v. a.* (tram) To go about; to go often; to frequent, to resort; to pass over, to traverse.

> A glywaisti a gant y fronfraith:
> Pan dramwyych dros ddiffaith
> Na fid elyn dy gydymaith.

> Didst thou hear what the thrush did sing: When *thou dost traverse* the wilderness, 'be not an enemy thy companion.' *Eng. y Clywed.*

Tramwyad, *s. m.* (tramwy) A traversing.

Tramwyadwy, *a.* (tramwyad) Traversible.

Tramwyaeth, *s. m.* (tramwy) The act of going about, or traversing.

Tramwyaw, *v. a.* (tramwy) To traverse.

Tramwyawl, *a.* (tramwy) Traversing.

Tramwyedig, *a.* (tramwyad) Traversing; transitory; traversed.

> Hardd gweled y planedau,
> A'u llwybr yn y gwagllwybr gau:
> Tremiadau tramwyedig,
> A chall yn deall eu dig.

> It is magnificent to behold the planets, with their course in the empty surrounding ether, of *transitory* aspects, whose frown the cunning doth understand. *Gro. Owen*

Tramwyedigaeth, *s. m.* (tramwyedig) The act of going about or traversing.

Tramwyfa, *s. f.—pl.* tramwyfeydd (tramwy) A traversed place.

Tramwyn, *a.* (mwyn) Extremely genial or kind.

Tramwywr, *s. m.—pl.* tramwywyr (tramwy—gwr) A traverser; a traveller.

Tramwyydd, *s. m.—pl. t.* ion (tramwy) A traverser.

Tramynych, *a.* (mynych) Extremely frequent.

Tramynychiad, *s. m.* (tramynych) A frequenting extremely; a becoming very frequent.

Tramynychu, *v. a.* (tramynych) To frequent extremely; to become very frequent.

Tramynydd, *s. m.* (mynydd) That is over a mountain. *a.* Beyond the mountain; tramontane.

Tramynyddawl, *a.* (tramynydd) Tramontane.

Tran, *s. m.—pl. t.* au (tra—an) A space, a stretch; a district, or region.

Gwr heb werth ai wyr chwerthin,
Tran fain oed bed tro'n i fin.

A man without property he knows not how to laugh, with a slender *stretch* only there is a twist in his mouth. *Huw Dwn.*

Tranawf, *s. m.* (nawf) An over-swim.
Tranawl, *a.* (tran) Belonging to a region.
Tranc, *s. m.* (tra—anc) A cessation; exhaustion; end; decease; departure; dissolution, death.

Rhag draig Mon——dwys dyfysgi,
A rhewin, a thrin, a thranc cymmri
Ar gad gad greudde,
Ar gryd gryd graendde,
Ac am Dal Moelfre
Mil fanieri.

Against the dragon of Mona perpetual confusion, ruin, toil, and an end of pre-eminence ran before him; in conflict upon conflict pervaded with gore; in carnage upon carnage of horrid forms; and round the front of Moelvre a thousand banners waving. *Gwalchmai.*

Od â i'r drin, hyd awr dranc,
Drwy Dduw y gall dewr ddianc.

Should he go to the conflict, until the hour of *departure*, through God the brave may escape. *Rhys Cain.*

Trancadwy, *a.* (tranc) Perishable; exhaustible.
Trancawl, *a.* (tranc) Perishing, vanishing.
Tranced, *s. f.—pl. t.* i (tranc) An earthen vessel or cup, such a cup with a handle as is in common use.
Trancedig, *a.* (tranc) Perishing, evanescent.
Trancedigaeth, *s. m.* (trancedig) A state of perishing or vanishing.
Trancedigrwydd, *s. m.* (trancedig) Perishableness.
Trancedu, *v. a.* (tranced) To lade with a cup.
Trancell, *s. f.* (tranc) A quantity of liquor drank at once, a draught.
Tranciad, *s. m.—pl. t.* au (tranc) An exhausting; a coming to an end; dissolution.
Trancu, *v. a.* (tranc) To exhaust; to bring to an end; to perish, to pass away, to die.
Tranerth, *s. m.* (nerth) Extreme strength.
Tranerthawl, *a.* (tranerth) Extremely potent.
Tranerthu, *v. a.* (tranerth) To strengthen extremely.
Traniad, *s. m.* (tran) A stretching; a laying out a space.
Tranial, *s. m.* (tran—ial) A clear space; a field of battle.

Prydain par praff drydar draaial;
Prydyddion gadair gadr yaial.

Britain the cause of the ample tumult of the *hostile field*, the throne of poets of mighty energy. *Cynddelw, i H. ab Owain.*

Barf ar farf, ac arf yn greulyd,
Tal trathal tranial trachaled.

Beard on beard, and weapon imbrued with blood, front over front, a *field of battle* most dreadful. *Cynddelw.*

Tranoeth, *s. m.* (noeth) That is extremely naked; that is over or beyond the night; the next morning. *adv.* On the next morning, on the morrow.

Ni elwir daw hyd tranoeth.

Coming will not be so called till *the morrow*. *Adage.*

Drwg trennydd wrth dranoeth.

Bad is the third day to the *morrow*. *Adage.*

Tranoethi, *v. a.* (tranoeth) To make very bare.
Tranofiad, *s. m.* (tranawf) Transnation.
Tranofiaw, *v. a.* (tranawf) To over-swim.
Tranofiawl, *a.* (tranawf) Over-swimming.
Tranos, *s. m.* (nos) A time beyond the night; a future night. *adv.* After the night.

Tranu, *v. a.* (tran) To stretch; to lay out a space.
Tranwyd, *s. m.—pl. t.* au (nwyd) Extreme passion.
Tranwydaw, *v. a.* (tranwyd) To render extremely passionate; to become extremely passionate.
Tranwydawl, *a.* (tranwyd) Extremely passionate.
Tranwyf, *s. m.—pl. t.* au (nwyf) Extreme liveliness or vivacity.
Tranwyfaw, *v. a.* (tranwyf) To enliven extremely; to become very lively.
Tranwyfawl, *a.* (tranwyf) Extremely animating or exhilarating.
Tranwyfus, *a.* (tranwyf) Extremely brisk.
Tranydd, *s. m.* (dydd) A time beyond the day; a future day. *adv.* After the day.
Trang, *s. m.—pl. t.* au (tranc) A cessation; exhaustion; end, decease, death. *a.* Ceasing, vanishing. *Ar drang*, at the point of death.

Dar a dyfwys yn ngwynnau,
A thwrf, a thriu, a thrangau:
Gwae a wyl na bo goleu!

An oak has grown in the downs, abounding with tumult, and conflict, and deaths: woe to him that sees that it is not light! *Robert Tywysawg Normandi.*

Credwn——
Ei fyn'd ar drang gloes angau
Dros dyn, i ufydd draeau.

We believe his going on the *departure* of the pang of death, for man, humbly to sorrow. *Huw Arwystl.*

Llefwa teyrnedd lliaws dyfrydedd;
Am ddyfrys eu trangi
Trangai traaf traeni!

Princes have given room for a multitude of woes; for the hastening of their departure *most destructive*, most miserable of misery. *Gwalchmai, i D. ab Owain.*

Trangawl, *a.* (trang) Perishing, vanishing.
Trangedig, *a.* (trang) Being perished.
Trangiad, *s. m.* (trang) A perishing; dissolution.
Trangu, *v. a.* (trang) To perish, to pass away.
Traoed, *s. m.* (oed) Extreme delay.
Traoedi, *v. a.* (traoed) To delay extremely.
Traoediad, *s. m.* (traoed) A delaying extremely.
Traoer, *a.* (oer) Extremely cold or chill.
Traoeri, *v. a.* (traoer) To cool extremely; to become extremely cold.
Traoeriad, *s. m.* (traoer) A cooling extremely.
Traoes, *s. f.* (oes) Extreme age. *a.* Over-age.
Traoesawl, *a.* (traoes) Superannuated.
Traoesi, *v. n.* (traoes) To become of extreme age; to be superannuated.
Traoesiad, *s. m.* (traoes) Superannuation.
Traofn, *s. m.* (ofn) Extreme fear or dread.
Traofnawg, *a.* (traofn) Extremely timid.
Traofni, *v. a.* (traofn) To fear extremely.
Traofniad, *s. m.* (traofn) A fearing extremely; a frightening extremely.
Traphlith, *adv.* (tra—plith) In a most confused state.
Traphont, *s. f.—pl.* traphynt (tra—pont) The other side of a bridge. *adv.* On the other side of the bridge.

Nid pont heb draphont.

There is no bridge without a place *beyond bridge*. *Adage.*

Traphwyll, *s. m.* (tra—pwyll) Extreme impulse.
Traphwys, *s. m.* (tra—pwys) Extreme pressure.
Trarif, *s. m.* (rhif) An over number.
Trarifaw, *v. a.* (trarif) To over-reckon.
Trarifawl, *a.* (trarif) Supernumerary.
Tras, *s. f.—pl. t.* au (tra—as) Kindred, relationship, affinity. According to the ancient laws, a person who could prove his descent through nine degrees was a free native. Proof of collateral relationship was also required in the

ninth degree, for that determined the family of a person; and this was necessary, as the whole family was liable to be fined for the crimes of its members, rated according to proximity of kindred.

Descending kindred.

1 *Tad*, *mam*, father, mother.
2 *Mab*, *merch*, son, daughter.
3 *Wyr*, *wyres*, grandson, grand-daughter.
4 *Gorwyr*, *gorwyres*, son, daughter, in the 3d degree.
5 *Hengaw*, *hengawes*, son, daughter, in the 6th degree.
6 *Gorhengaw*, *gorhengawes*, son, daughter, in the 7th degree.

Ascending kindred.

1 *Tad*, *mam*, father, mother.
2 *Tad cu*, *mam gu*, grandfather, grandmother, or *hendad*, *henfam*.
3 *Gorhendad*, *gorhenfam*, a father, mother, in the 4th degree.
4 *Taid*, *nain*, a father, mother, in the 5th deg.
5 *Hendaid*, *hennain*, a father, mother, in the 6th degree.
6 *Gorhendaid*, *gorhennain*, a father, mother, in the 7th degree.

Collateral kindred descending.

1 *Brawd*, *chwaer*, brother, sister.
2 *Cefnderw*, *cyfnitherw*, male cousin, female cousin.
3 *Cyfyrderw*, second cousin.
4 *Ceifn*, third cousin.
5 *Gorcheifn*, fourth cousin.
6 *Ysgiwion* neu *plant cyfyrderw*, third cousins.
7 *Gwrthysgiwion*, neu *plant plant cyfyrderw*, fourth cousins.
8 *Caw*, *cawes*, son, daughter, in the 4th degree.
9 *Gorchaw*, *gorchawes*, son, daughter, in the 5th degree.
10 *Gerni*, seventh cousin.
11 *Gwrtherni*, eighth cousin.

Or thus:

1 *Cefnderw*	6 *Gwystyn*, neu *gorchudd*
2 *Cyfyrderw*	7 *Gorchwystyn* neu *gorchwant*
3 *Plant cyfyrderw*	8 *Car trig*, neu *goreiddyn*
4 *Ceifn*	9 *Car clud*.
5 *Gorcheifn*	

Collateral Kindred.

1 *Ewythr*, *modryb*, uncle, aunt.
2 *Nai*, *nith*, nephew, niece.
3 *Cyfnai*, *cyfnith*, nephew, niece, in the 2d deg.
4 *Gorchyfnai*, *gorchyfnith*, nephew, niece, in the 3d degree.
5 *Clud*, collateral relative in the 4th degree.
6 *Car clud*, *car a chlud*, a collateral relative in the 5th degree.
7 *Gwrth clud*, a collateral relative in the 6th degree.
8 *Car o waed*, a collateral relative in the 7th degree.

Trasaidd, *a*. (tras) In some degree related.
Trasail, *s. f.*—*pl.* traseilian (sail) Extreme base.

Trasain, *s. f.* (sain) An extreme sound.
Trasalw, *a*. (salw) Extremely frail or poor.
Trasalwder, *s. m.* (trasalw) Extreme frailty.

> A Duw a'm tynny o'm trasalwdef [illegible],
> I iawn obaith [illegible] a wybydher!
>
> And may God bring me out of my extreme wretchedness to him, rightly to hope for what is known. *[illegible]*

Trasawdd, *s. m.* (sawdd) Extreme sinking.
Trasawg, *a*. (tras) Having kindred.
Trasawl, *a*. (tras) Belonging to kindred.

> Tros wledydd trasawl ydwyd.
>
> Over countries thou art connected by kindred. *[illegible]*

Trasedig, *a*. (tras) Connected by kindred.
Trasedd, *s. m.* (tras) A kindred state.
Trasefyll, *v. a.* (sefyll) To over-stand; to persist; to be permanent.
Traseiddiad, *s. m.* (trasaidd) A rendering partly related; to be connected by kindred.
Traseiddiaw, *v. a.* (trasaidd) To form a slight relationship; to become slightly related.
Traseiddrwydd, *s. m.* (trasaidd) Slight relationship; common kindred.

> Cymerwn esgrafft oddiwrth Priaf, brenin Troia, yr [illegible] blodeuaw mewn traseiddrwydd, a chyfoeth, [illegible].
>
> Let us take an example from Priam, king of Troy, he who has been flourishing in extensive kindred and [illegible] and power. *[illegible]*

Trasefiad, *s. m.*—*pl.* trasefiaid (seifiad) That stands extremely firm.

> Y Ty yn y Penrhyn——
> Trasefiad trefed [illegible],
> Treth [illegible] Tidach Helig.
>
> The house in the peninsula, an extreme permanent support of society where it is, serving out a revenue on the brink of the Bed of Helig. *[illegible]*

Traseiliad, *s. m.* (trasail) A forming an extreme base or foundation.
Traseiliaw, *v. a.* (trasail) To lay an extreme base.
Traseiniad, *s. m.* (trasain) A sounding greatly.
Traseiniaw, *v. a.* (trasain) To sound extremely.
Traseiniawl, *a*. (trasain) Very sonorous.
Trasen, *s. f.* (sen) An extreme reproach.
Trasènawl, *a*. (trasen) Very reproachful.
Trasèniad, *s*. (trasen) A reproaching extremely.
Trasènu, *v. a.* (trasen) To reproach extremely.
Traserch, *s. m.* (serch) Excess of fondness, a doting, dotage.

> Nid brenhiniaeth ond serch;
> Nid ynfydrwydd ond traserch.
>
> There is no empire like that of love, there is no foolishness like dotage. *[illegible]*
>
> Morganwg——
> Lle trom ran o'm traserch;
> Lle dewr mab, lle diwair merch.
>
> Morganwg, to where a portion of my fondness is directed; where the son is bold, where the daughter is chaste. *D. ab Gwilym.*

Traserchawg, *a*. (traserch) Extremely loving.
Traserchawl, *a*. (traserch) Apt to dote.
Traserchiad, *s. m.* (traserch) A doting, a fondling.
Traserchu, *v. a.* (traserch) To love extremely.
Traserchus, *a*. (traserch) Apt to dote.
Traserth, *a*. (serth) Extremely precipitous; very steep.
Traserthiad, *s. m.* (traserth) A rendering extremely precipitous; a becoming very steep.
Traserthu, *v. a.* (traserth) To render extremely precipitous; to become very steep.
Trasg, *s. m.* (tra—asg) That is laid together.
Trasgl, *s. m.*—*pl. t.* au (trasg) A rake.
Trasiad, *s. m.* (tras) A forming a kindred; a becoming connected by kindred.
Trasoddawl, *a*. (trasawdd) Tending to sink greatly

Trasoddi, v. a. (trasawdd) To sink extremely.
Trasoddiad, s. m. (trasawdd) A sinking greatly.
Trasom, s. m. (som) Extreme deception.
Trasomawl, a. (trasom) Extremely deceiving.
Trasomgar, a. (trasom) Extremely deceiving.
Trasomi, v. a. (trasom) To deceive extremely; to disappoint extremely.
Trasomiad, s. m. (trasom) A deceiving greatly; a disappointing extremely.
Trason, s. m. (son) Excess of noise or talk.
Trasoniad, s. m. (trason) A talking extremely.
Trasoniaw, v. a. (trason) To talk extremely.
Trasoniawl, a. (trason) Extremely noisy.
Trasu, v. a. (tras) To connect by kindred; to become connected by kindred.
Trasur, a. (sur) Extremely sour or acid.
Trasuraw, v. a. (trasur) To sour extremely.
Trasuriad, s. m. (trasur) A souring extremely.
Traswydd, s. f.—pl. t. au (swydd) An over office or employment.
Traswyddawg, a. (traswydd) Having an over-office. s. m. One who fills an over-office.
Traswyddgar, a. (traswydd) Over-officious.
Traswyddgarwch, s. m. (traswyddgar) Over-officiousness.
Trasych, a. (sych) Extremely dry or parched.
Trasychiad, s. m. (trasych) A drying extremely.
Trasychu, v. a. (trasych) To dry extremely.
Trasylw, s. m. (sylw) Extreme notice or regard.
Trasylwad, s. m. (trasylw) A regarding much.
Trasylwi, v. a. (trasylw) To notice extremely.
Trasyn, a. (syn) Extremely concerned.
Trasyndawd, s. m. (trasyn) Extreme concern.
Trasyniad, s. m. (trasyn) Much consideration.
Trasyniaw, v. a. (trasyn) To feel extremely; to consider extremely.
Trasyniawl, a. (trasyn) Extremely sensible; of extreme consideration.
Trasynu, v. a. (trasyn) To concern or to amaze extremely; to be extremely concerned.
Trasyth, a. (syth) Extremely stiff or erect.

Y balchaf, trawsaf trasyth,
Lleiaf ei barch yn mhob lle byth.

The proudest, the most froward *extremely stiff*, the least his respect ever in every place. *D. ab Edmund.*

Trasythiad, s. m. (trasyth) A rendering very stiff or erect, a becoming very erect.
Trasythu, v. a. (trasyth) To render extremely erect; to become very erect.
Trathal, s. f. (tal) An over-payment.
Trathaliad, s. m. (trathal) An over-paying.
Trathalu, v. a. (trathal) To over-pay.
Trathanawl, a. (tanawl) Extremely expanding.
Trathaniad, s. m. (taniad) A spreading greatly.
Trathanu, v. a. (tanu) To expand extremely.
Trathardd, s. m. (tardd) An excess of spring, or breaking out.
Tratharddawl, a. (trathardd) Tending to spring, or break out extremely.
Tratharddiad, s. m. (trathardd) A springing, issuing, or breaking out extremely.
Tratharddu, v. a. (trathardd) To issue greatly.
Trathasg, s. f. (tasg) An extreme task.
Trathasgawl, a. (trathasg) Being an over task.
Trathasgiad, s. m. (trathasg) A tasking much.
Trathasgu, v. a. (trathasg) To task extremely.
Trathaw, s. m. (taw) Extreme silence.
Trathebyg, a. (tebyg) Extremely similar.
Trathebygiad, s. m. (trathebyg) A rendering very similar, a becoming very like.
Trathebygu, v. a. (trathebyg) To liken much.

Tratheg, a. (teg) Extremely fair or open.
Tratheilwng, a. (teilwng) Extremely worthy.
Tratheilyngiad, s. m. (tratheilwng) A rendering extremely worthy; to merit extremely.
Tratheilyngu, v. a. (tratheilwng) To render extremely worthy; to become very worthy.
Trathelaid, a. (telaid) Extremely elegant.
Tratheneu, a. (teneu) Extremely thin.
Trathenead, s. m. (tratheneu) A rendering extremely thin; a becoming very thin.
Trathaneuaw, v. a. (tratheneu) To make extremely thin; to become very thin.
Trather, a. (ter) Extremely pure or clear.
Tratheriad, s. m. (trather) A purifying greatly.
Tratheru, v. a. (trather) To purify extremely.
Tratherwyn, a. (terwyn) Extremely ardent.
Tratherwyniad, s. m. (tratherwyn) A rendering extremely ardent; a becoming very ardent.
Tratherwynu, v. a. (tratherwyn) To render extremely ardent; to become extremely ardent.
Tratheryll, a. (teryll) Extremely piercing.
Trathes, s. m. (tes) Extreme warmth; extreme sun-heat.
Trathew, a. (tew) Extremely thick.
Trathewâd, s. m. (trathew) A thickening extremely.
Trathewâu, v. a. (trathew) To over-thicken.
Trathewi, v. a. (trathaw) To render profoundly silent; to become very silent.

A Ffranc twrch trathewys.

And the wounded Frank *became profoundly silent*. *Gwalchmai.*

Trathirion, v. a. (tirion) Extremely pleasing.
Trathirionad, s. m. (trathirion) A rendering extremely pleasant or genial; a becoming very pleasing.
Trathirioni, v. a. (trathirion) To render extremely pleasant; to become very pleasing.
Trathôri, v. a. (tôri) To break extremely.
Trathôriad, s. m. (tôriad) An over-breaking.
Trathost, a. (tost) Extremely severe.
Trathostur, s. m. (trathost) Extreme pity.
Trathosturi, s. m. (trathostur) Extreme pity.
Trathosturiad, s. m. (trathostur) A pitying extremely, a commiserating much.
Trathosturiaw, v. a. (trathostur) To commiserate extremely.
Trathosturiawl, a. (trathostur) Extremely commiserating; greatly pitying.
Trathraul, s. f. (traul) Extreme consumption, wear, waste, or charge.
Trathreuliad, s. m. (trathraul) A consuming extremely; an over-wasting.
Trathreuliaw, v. a. (trathraul) To consume extremely; to over-waste.

Byd a fydd byd, heb wynt, heb wlaw,
Heb ormod eredig, heb drathreuliaw;
Tir digawn fydd un erw i naw.

The world will be a world, without wind, without rain, without too much ploughing, without *consuming to extreme*; sufficiency of land will one acre be for nine. *Gwasgar. Myrddin.*

Trathrin, s. m. (trin) Extreme striving; extreme strife or conflict.
Trathriniad, s. m. (trathrin) A busying about extremely; a striving extremely.
Trathriniaw, v. a. (trathrin) To strive extremely.
Trathriniawl, a. (trathrin) Extremely bustling.
Trathro, s. m. (tro) An extreme turn.
Trathröad, s. m. (trathro) A turning much.
Trathröawl, a. (trathro) Tending to turn much.
Trathroi, v. a. (trathro) To turn extremely.
Trathrwm, a. (trwm) Extremely heavy.
Trathrwst, s. m. (trwst) Extreme noise.

ninth degree, for that determined the family of a person; and this was necessary, as the whole family was liable to be fined for the crimes of its members, rated according to proximity of kindred.

Descending kindred.

1 *Tad*, *mam*, father, mother.
2 *Mab*, *merch*, son, daughter.
3 *Wyr*, *wyres*, grandson, grand-daughter.
4 *Gorwyr*, *gorwyres*, son, daughter, in the 3d degree.
5 *Hengaw*, *hengawes*, son, daughter, in the 6th degree.
6 *Gorhengaw*, *gorhengawes*, son, daughter, in the 7th degree.

Ascending kindred.

1 *Tad*, *mam*, father, mother.
2 *Tad cu*, *mam gu*, grandfather, grandmother, or *hendad*, *henfam*.
3 *Gorhendad*, *gorhenfam*, a father, mother, in the 4th degree.
4 *Taid*, *nain*, a father, mother, in the 5th deg.
5 *Hendaid*, *hennain*, a father, mother, in the 6th degree.
6 *Gorhendaid*, *gorhennain*, a father, mother, in the 7th degree.

Collateral kindred descending.

1 *Brawd*, *chwaer*, brother, sister.
2 *Cefnderw*, *cyfnitherw*, male cousin, female cousin.
3 *Cyfyrderw*, second cousin.
4 *Ceifn*, third cousin.
5 *Gorcheifn*, fourth cousin.
6 *Ygiwion* neu *plant cyfyrderw*, third cousins.
7 *Gwrthysgiwion*, neu *plant plant cyfyrderw*, fourth cousins.
8 *Caw*, *cawes*, son, daughter, in the 4th degree.
9 *Gorchaw*, *gorchawes*, son, daughter, in the 5th degree.
10 *Gerni*, seventh cousin.
11 *Gwrtherni*, eighth cousin.

Or thus:

1 *Cefnderw*
2 *Cyfyrderw*
3 *Plant cyfyrderw*
4 *Ceifn*
5 *Gorcheifn*
6 *Gwystyn*, neu *gorchudd*
7 *Gorchwystyn* neu *gorchwant*
8 *Car trig*, neu *goreiddyn*
9 *Car clud*.

Collateral Kindred.

1 *Ewythr*, *modryb*, uncle, aunt.
2 *Nai*, *nith*, nephew, niece.
3 *Cyfnai*, *cyfnith*, nephew, niece, in the 2d deg.
4 *Gorchyfnai*, *gorchyfnith*, nephew, niece, in the 3d degree.
5 *Clud*, collateral relative in the 4th degree.
6 *Car clud*, *car a chlud*, a collateral relative in the 5th degree.
7 *Gwrth clud*, a collateral relative in the 6th degree.
8 *Car o wacd*, a collateral relative in the 7th degree.

Trasaidd, *a.* (tras) In some degree related.
Trasail, *s. f.—pl.* traseiliau (sail) Extreme base.
Trassain, *s. f.* (sain) An extreme sound.
Trasalw, *a.* (salw) Extremely frail or poor.
Trasalwder, *s. m.* (trasalw) Extreme frailty.

> A Duw a'm trowy o'm trasalwder allaw,
> I fawn obeithiaw a wybyther!
>
> And may God bring me out of my *extreme worthlessness* to him, rightly to hope for what is known. *Llywelyn Fardd.*

Trasawdd, *s. m.* (sawdd) Extreme sinking.
Trasawg, *a.* (tras) Having kindred.
Trasawl, *a.* (tras) Belonging to kindred.

> Tros wledydd trasawl ydwyd.
>
> Over countries thou art *connected by kindred.* *Iolo Goch.*

Trasedig, *a.* (tras) Connected by kindred.
Trasedd, *s. m.* (tras) A kindred state.
Trasefyll, *v. a.* (sefyll) To over-stand; to persist; to be permanent.
Traseiddiad, *s. m.* (trasaidd) A rendering partly related; to be connected by kindred.
Traseiddiaw, *v. a.* (trasaidd) To form a slight relationship; to become slightly related.
Traseiddrwydd, *s. m.* (trasaidd) Slight relationship; common kindred.

> Cymerwn engraifft oddiwrth Priaf, brenin Troia, yr hwn a fu yn blodeuaw mewn traseiddrwydd, a chyfoeth, anrhydedd a gallu.
>
> Let us take an example from Priam, king of Troy, he who has been flourishing in *extensive kindred* and riches, honour and power. *Marchawg Crwydrad.*

Trascifiad, *s. m.—pl.* trascifiaid (seifiad) That stands extremely firm.

> Y Ty yn y Penrhyn—
> Trasefiad trefad lle trig
> Trwyth hall ar lan Traeth Helig.
>
> The house in the peninsula, an *extreme permanent* support of society where it is, serving out a revenue on the brink of the Sand of Helig. *Rhys Goch Eryri.*

Traseiliad, *s. m.* (trasail) A forming an extreme base or foundation.
Traseiliaw, *v. a.* (trasail) To lay an extreme base.
Traseiniad, *s. m.* (trasain) A sounding greatly.
Traseiniaw, *v. a.* (trasain) To sound extremely.
Traseiniawl, *a.* (trasain) Very sonorous.
Trasen, *s. f.* (sen) An extreme reproach.
Trasènawl, *a.* (trasen) Very reproachful.
Trasèniad, *s.* (trasen) A reproaching extremely.
Trasènu, *v. a.* (trasen) To reproach extremely.
Traserch, *s. m.* (serch) Excess of fondness, a doting, dotage.

> Nid breniniaeth ond serch;
> Nid ynfydrwydd ond traserch.
>
> There is no empire like that of love, there is no foolishness like *dotage.* *Adage.*

> Morganwg—
> Lle trwm rhan o'm traserch;
> Lle dewr mab, lle diwair merch.
>
> Morganwg, to where a portion of my *fondness* is dispensed; where the son is bold, where the daughter is chaste. *D. ab Gwilym.*

Traserchawg, *a.* (traserch) Extremely loving.
Traserchawl, *a.* (traserch) Apt to dote.
Traserchiad, *s. m.* (traserch) A doting, a fondling.
Traserchu, *v. a.* (traserch) To love extremely.
Traserchus, *a.* (traserch) Apt to dote.
Traserth, *a.* (serth) Extremely precipitous; very steep.
Traserthiad, *s. m.* (traserth) A rendering extremely precipitous; a becoming very steep.
Traserthu, *v. a.* (traserth) To render extremely precipitous; to become very steep.
Trasg, *s. m.* (tra—asg) That is laid together.
Trasgl, *s. m.—pl. t.* au (trasg) A rake.
Trasiad, *s. m.* (tras) A forming a kindred; a becoming connected by kindred.
Trasoddawl, *a.* (trasawdd) Tending to sink greatly

Trawed, *s. m.* (traw) Advancement; the state of being over or at the top.
Trawedig, *a.* (trawed) Being advanced, disciplined.
Trawedigaeth, *s. m.* (trawedig) Discipline.
Trawedydd, *s. m.—pl. t.* ion (trawed) A disciplinarian.
Trawen, *s. f.* (traw) That is over, or up.

> Owain——
> Dygwystlir iddo o dir Alclud Gogledd;
> Draig yw yn dyhedd drawen yn y Dehou.
>
> Owain, to him hostage will be given from the land of Alclud in the North; he is a leader stilling *insurrection* in the South. *Gwalchmai.*

Traweniad, *s. m.* (trawen) An over-passing; an over-rising; insurrection.
Trawenu, *v. a.* (trawen) To pass or rise over.
Trawf, *s. m.* (traw) An advance, pass, or turn over.
Trawiad, *s. m.—pl. t.* au (traw) An advancing, a forwarding; a rearing, educating, or maturing; a going over; a surpassing.

> Y fwyalchen——
> Tref wasrwyn yw'r tewlwyn tau,
> Twr adail y trawiadau.
>
> Thou thrush, thy thick bush is the dwelling of the spring, the tower of the edifice of *competitions*. *D. ab Gwilym.*

Trawiadawl, *a.* (trawiad) Tending to effect an advance or forwardness; instructive.
Trawiadu, *v. a.* (trawiad) To make an advance or progress; to educate; to effect a passing over.
Trawiadur, *s. m.—pl. t.* ion (trawiad) One who advances, a forwarder; one who educates; one who goes over, or beyond; one who surpasses.

> Y fwyalchen——
> Trydar syw, trawiadur serch.
>
> The thrush of smart chirping, the *master of the art* of love. *D. ab Gwilym.*

Trawial, *s. m.—pl. t.* au (traw) A sneezing.
Trawialu, *v. a.* (trawial) To sneeze.
Trawiedydd, *s. m.—pl. t.* ion (trawiad) One who causes to advance, one who perfects; an instructor.
Trawien, *s. f.—pl. t.* ydd (traw) A vale, a defile or pass, between mountains.
Trawn, *s. m.* (traw) That is over or superior.
Trawo, *adv.* (traw) On the distance; on the farther side; on the other side; over, beyond.

> Canmoled pawb y bont a'i dyco drawo.
>
> Let every body praise the bridge that brings him *over*. *Adage.*

Traws, *s. m.—pl. t.* ion (tra) A transverse direction; a traverse; a cross or refractory one. *a.* Adverse, cross. *Torasant ar eu traws gan ddig*, they burst themselves with rage.—It is prefixed in composition.

> Ni rodd hwn, wrudd hynaws,
> Erioed led ei droed i draws.
>
> He, who is manly and generous, never gave the breadth of his foot to the *froward*. *D. Nanconwy.*
>
> Angen y gyhydedd draws yw ban nawsill; a hyd pennill o bedwar i un ban ar bymtheg.
>
> The characteristic of the *cross metricity* is a verse of nine syllables, and the length of the stanza from four to sixteen verses. *Barddas.*
>
> Trawsion, ail Meirion mawredd, un ofeg,
> Traíu mawrdeg diffreg dyfr gymyredd.
>
> *Froward ones*, like Meirion of magnificence, of the same design, in the unbroken course greatly fair of combining water rolling. *G. ab M. ab Dafydd.*

Trawsachwyn, *s. m.* (achwyn) A counter complaint. *v. a.* To recriminate.
Trawsachwynawl, *a.* (trawsachwyn) Recriminating
Trawsachwyniad, *s. m.* (trawsachwyn) A recrimination; a recriminating.
Trawsaddysg, *s. m.* (addysg) A contrary doctrine
Trawsaddysgiad, *s. m.* (trawsaddysg) A teaching in opposition.
Trawsaddysgu, *v. a.* (trawsaddysg) To instruct contrarily, to teach in opposition.
Trawsagawr, *s. m.* (agawr) A transverse opening. *v. a.* To open across.
Trawsagorawl, *a.* (trawsagawr) Tending to open transversely.
Trawsagori, *v. a.* (trawsagawr) To open across; to become open across.
Trawsagoriad, *s. m.* (trawsagawr) An opening transversely.
Trawsaidd, *a.* (traws) Apt to be contrary.
Trawsair, *s. m.—pl.* trawseiriau (traws—gair) A metonymy.
Trawsdyle, *s. m.* (tyle) The cross way or upper end of a dwelling.
Trawsamcan, *s. m.—pl. t.* ion (amcan) A cross purpose; an adverse design.
Trawsamcaniad, *s. m.* (trawsamcan) A purposing or designing adversely.
Trawsamcanu, *v. a.* (trawsamcan) To pursue a cross purpose.
Trawsariad, *s. m.* (ariad) A cross-ploughing.
Trawsaru, *v. a.* (aru) To cross-plough.
Trawsbwyth, *s. m.* (pwyth) A cross-stitch.
Trawsbwythaw, *v. a.* (trawsbwyth) To cross-stitch, to overcast.
Trawsbwythiad, *s. m.—pl. t.* au (trawsbwyth) A cross-stitching or overcasting.
Trawschwedl, *s. m.—pl. t.* au (chwedl) A hyperbaton.
Trawschwedliad, *s. m.* (trawschwedl) A speaking contradictory expressions.
Trawschwedlu, *v. a.* (trawschwedl) To utter adverse expressions; to speak in contradiction.
Trawsder, *s. m.* (traws) Crossness, adverseness.
Trawsdeyrn, *s. m.—pl. t.* au (teyrn) An usurper
Trawsdeyrnedd, *s. m.* (trawsdeyrn) Usurpation.

> Gwrtheyrn Gwrthenau a wahoddes y Saeson gyntaf i'r ynys hon, yn gynllawiaid iddo yn ei drawsdeyrnedd.
>
> Gwrtheyrn Gwrthenau invited the Saxons first into this island, as auxiliaries for him in his *usurpation*. *Trioedd.*

Trawsdori, *v. a.* (tòri) To cut a cross cut.
Trawsdoriad, *s. m.* (tòriad) A cross-cutting.
Trawsdyn, *s. m.* (tyn) That is pulled cross-wise.
Trawsdyniad, *s. m.* (trawsdyn) A pulling cross-wise; a distorting.
Trawsdynu, *v. a.* (trawsdyn) To distort; to draw aside; to pull cross-wise.
Trawsddawd, *s. m.* (dawd) A transverse position.
Trawsddodawl, *a.* (trawsddawd) Transpositional.
Trawsddodi, *v. a.* (trawsddawd) To transpose.
Trawsddodiad, *s. m.* (trawsddawd) An antithesis; a metathesis; transposition.
Trawsddwyn, *s. m.* (dwyn) Transportation.
Trawsddygiad, *s. m.* (dygiad) Transportation.
Trawsedig, *a.* (traws) Being crossed.
Trawsedd, *s. m.* (traws) The state of being transverse, adverse, or cross; crossness, refractoriness, frowardness.
Trawselfen, *s. f.—pl. t.* au (elfen) A contrary element.
Trawselfeniad, *s. m.* (trawselfen) Transubstantiation, transelementation.
Trawselfenu, *v. a.* (trawselfen) To transubstantiate.
Trawselfydd, *s. m.* (elfydd) A contrary element.

Trawselfyddiad, *s. m.—pl. t.* au (trawselfydd) Transubstantiation, transelementation.
Trawselfyddu, *v. a.* (trawselfydd) To transubstantiate.
Trawsenw, *s. m.—pl. t.* au (enw) Metonymy.
Trawsenwad, *s. m.* (trawsenw) Transnomination; a forming a metonymy.
Trawsenwawl, *a.* (trawsenw) Metonymical.
Trawsenwi, *v.a.* (trawsenw) To form a metonymy
Trawsfalch, *a.* (balch) Frowardly-proud.
Trawsfalchedd, *s. m.* (trawsfalch) Froward pride
Trawsfarn, *s. f.—pl. t.* au (barn) A cross judgment, a contradictory opinion.
Trawsfarniad, *s. m.* (trawsfarn) A judging adversely; a contrary decision.
Trawsfarnu, *v. a.* (trawsfarn) To judge adversely
Trawsfedd, *s. m.* (medd) Wrong possession.
Trawsfeddiannawl, *a.* (trawsfeddiant) Having possession wrongfully.
Trawsfeddiannu, *v. a.* (trawsfeddiant) To possess wrongfully; to usurp.
Trawsfeddiant, *s. m.* (trawsfedd) Usurpation.
Trawsfeddu, *v. a.* (trawsfedd) To possess adversely, to possess wrongfully.
Trawsfiwng, *a.* (blwng) Frowardly-sullen.
Trawsfor, *a.* (mor) Being across the sea.
Trawsforawl, *a.* (trawsfor) Transmarine.
Trawsforedig, *a.* (trawsfor) Being rendered transmarine.
Trawsfraint, *s. m.—pl.* trawsfreinniau (braint) Usurpation of right.

Gwrtheyrn Gwrthenau a roddes iddei fab Gotta, o drawsfraint, unbennaeth Ynys Prydain.

Gwrtheyrn Gwrthenau gave to his son *Gotta*, by *usurpation*, the monarchy of the isle of Britain. *Trioedd.*

Trawsfreinniad, *s. m.* (trawsfraint) An usurping of right.
Trawsfreinniaw, *v. a.* (trawsfraint) To usurp a right.
Trawsfreinniawl, *a.* (trawsfraint) Relating to an usurped right.
Trawsfud, *s. m.* (mud) A transit; migration.
Trawsfudaw, *v. a.* (trawsfud) To emigrate.
Trawsfudawl, *a.* (trawsfud) Migratory.
Trawsfudiad, *s. m.* (trawsfud) Transmotion; a migrating.
Trawsgainc, *s. f.—pl.* trawsgeinciau (cainc) A cross-bough.
Trawsgan, *s. f.* (can) An adverse song; a satire.
Trawsganiad, *s. m.* (trawsgan) A satirizing.
Trawsganu, *v. a.* (trawsgan) To satirize.
Trawsgerdded, *s. m.* (cerdded) Transmigration. *v. a.* To transmigrate.
Trawsgerddediad, *s. m.* (trawsgerdded) A transmigrating.
Trawsglud, *s. m.* (clud) Transportation.
Trawsgludaw, *v. a.* (trawsglud) To transport.
Trawsgludiad, *s. m.* (trawsglud) Transportation.
Trawsglwm, *s. m.—pl.* trawsglymau (clwm) A cross-knot; a node.
Trawsglwyd, *s. f.—pl. t.* au (clwyd) Cross hurdle.
Trawsglwydd, *s. m.* (clwydd) A transportation.
Trawsglwyddaw, *v. a.* (trawsglwydd) To transport
Trawsglwyddawl, *a.* (trawsglwydd) Transporting.
Trawsglwyddiad, *s. m.* (trawsglwydd) A transporting.
Trawsgryf, *a.* (cryf) Frowardly strong.
Trawsgymeriad, *s. m.* (cymeriad) Metalepsis.
Trawsgymeryd, *v. a.* (cymeryd) To take or to accept adversely.
Trawsgynnal, *v. a.* (cynnal) To hold adversely.

Trawsgynnaliad, *s. m.* (trawsgynnal) A holding or supporting adversely.
Trawsgynghanedd, *s. f.* (cynghanedd) A contrasted consonancy.
Trawsgynghaneddiad, *s. m.* (trawsgynghanedd) A forming a contrasted consonancy.
Trawsgynghaneddu, *v. a.* (trawsgynghanedd) To form a contrasted consonancy.
Trawshediad, *s. m.* (hediad) Transvolation.
Trawsiad, *s. m.* (traws) A crossing; a putting crosswise.
Trawsineb, *s. m.* (traws) Adverseness, frowardness.

A wyr neb drawsineb serch.

Does any body know the *frowardness* of love! *Iorwerth Fynglwyd.*

Trawslath, *s. f.—pl. t.* au (llath) A bar or beam placed transversely; a toft of a boat.
Trawslathiad, *s. m.* (trawslath) A laying a transverse beam or toft.
Trawslathu, *v. a.* (trawslath) To lay a transverse beam; to fix a toft.
Trawslëad, *s. m.* (llëad) Translocation.
Trawslinell, *s. f.—pl. t.* i (llinell) A cross line.
Trawslusg, *s. m.* (llusg) Transverse trailing. *a.* Transversely-drawing. *Cynghanedd drawslusg*, a transversely trailing consonancy.
Trawslusgaw, *v. a.* (trawslusg) To drag across.
Trawslusgiad, *s. m.* (trawslusg) A dragging across.
Trawslyw, *s.* (llyw) An adverse guide or steerer.
Trawslywiad, *s. m.* (trawslyw) A guiding adversely; a misgoverning.
Trawslywiaw, *v. a.* (trawslyw) To guide contrarily; to steer across; to govern frowardly.
Trawsosawd, *s. m.* (gosawd) To transpose.
Trawsosodawl, *a.* (trawsosawd) Transposing.
Trawsosodi, *v. a.* (trawsosawd) To transpose.
Trawsosodiad, *s. m.* (trawsosawd) Metathesis; a transposition.
Trawsrwym, *s. m.—pl. t.* au (rhwym) A cross-bind
Trawsrwymaw, *v. a.* (trawsrwym) To bind across.
Trawsrwymawl, *a.* (trawsrwym) Relating to cross binding.
Trawsrwymiad, *s.* (trawsrwym) A binding across.
Trawsryw, *s. m.—pl. t.* iau (rhyw) A cross breed.
Trawsrywiad, *s. m.* (trawsryw) A transexion.
Trawsrywiaw, *v. a.* (trawsryw) To transpeciate.
Trawst, *s. m.—pl. t.* iau (traws) A rafter.
Trawstiad, *s. m.* (trawst) A laying a rafter.
Trawstiaw, *v. a.* (trawst) To lay a rafter.
Trawsu, *v. a.* (traws) To render cross or adverse.
Trawswch, *s. f.—pl.* trawsych (traw—swch) A whisker. *Gwas heb drawswch arno*, a youth without mustaches.
Trawswyr, *a.* (gŵyr) Transversely oblique.
Trawswyraw, *v. a.* (trawswyr) To render transversely oblique.
Trawswyrawl, *a.* (trawswyr) Tending to transverse obliquity.
Trawswyredd, *s. m.* (trawswyr) Transverse obliquity.
Trawswyriad, *s. m.* (trawswyr) A turning transversely oblique.
Trawsylwedd, *s. m.* (traw—sylwedd) A contrary substance.
Trawsylweddiad, *s. m.* (trawsylwedd) Transubstantiation.
Trawsylweddu, *v. a.* (trawsylwedd) To transubstantiate.
Trawsymddwyn, *s. m.* (ymddwyn) A metaphor.
Trawsymmod, *s. m.* (ymmod) A moving over; a moving adversely

Trawsymmodawl, *a.* (trawsymmod) Tending to move adversely.

Trawsymmodi, *v. a.* (trawsymmod) To move adversely.

Trawsymmodiad, *s. m.* (trawsymmod) A moving adversely; transmotion.

Trawsymud, *v. a.* (traw—symud) To transpose.

Trawsymudawl, *a.* (trawsymud) Transposing.

Trawsymudiad, *s. m.—pl. t.* au (trawsymud) A transposition.

Trawsymsymud, *s. m.* (ymsymud) A mutual moving over; a self moving over.

Trawsymsymudaw, *v. a.* (trawsymsymud) To move over mutually; to move one's self over.

Trawsymsymudawl, *a.* (trawsymsymud) Mutually moving over; self-transporting.

Trawsymsymudiad, *s. m.* (trawsymsymud) A mutually moving over; a moving one's self over.

Trawu, *v. a.* (traw) To forward, to lead onward; to mature, to perfect; to cause to excel.

> Eiriol, *trawa*, Duw tri: O Arglwydd,
> Erglyw ar fy ngweddi!
>
> Intercede, *make perfect*, Triune God; O Lord, hearken to my prayer!
> *H. D. ab Ifan.*

Trawus, *a.* (traw) Tending to bring forward.

Trawusaw, *v. a.* (trawus) To render progressive; to render instructive; to become instructive.

Trawusrwydd, *s. m.* (trawus) Instructiveness.

Traymanerch, *s. m.* (ymanerch) Excess of mutual greeting. *v. a.* Mutually to greet over-much.

Traymannos, *s. m.* (ymannos) Extreme self-excitation. *v. a.* To excite one's self extremely.

Traymaraws, *s. m.* (ymaraws) Excess of mutual forbearance. *v. a.* Mutually to forbear extremely

Traymbarotöad, *s. m.* (ymbarotöad) Extreme mutual preparation; extreme self-preparation.

Traymbarotoi, *v. a.* (ymbarotoi) Mutually to prepare over-much; to prepare one's self over-much

Traymboeni, *v. a.* (ymboeni) Mutually to afflict severely; to take extreme pains.

Traymboeniad, *s. m.* (ymboeniad) Mutually afflicting or toiling extremely.

Traymdaith, *s. f.* (ymdaith) An excess of travelling.

Traymdeithiaw, *v. a.* (traymdaith) To travel over-much.

Traymdrosi, *v. a.* (ymdrosi) Mutually to drive over-much; to over-hurry one's self.

Traymdynawl, *a.* (ymdynawl) Over-contentious.

Traymdyniad, *s. m.* (ymdyniad) Extreme contention; a contending over-much.

Traymdynu, *v. a.* (ymdynu) To contend much.

Traymddadledd, *s. m.* (ymddadledd) Extreme mutual disputation.

Traymddadliad, *s. m.* (ymddadliad) A mutually disputing extremely.

Traymddadlu, *v. a.* (ymddadlu) Mutually to dispute extremely.

Traymdderiad, *s. m.* (ymdderiad) A mutually wrangling extremely.

Traymdderu, *v. a.* (ymdderu) Mutually to wrangle extremely.

Traymddiriad, *s. m.* (ymddiriad) An over-confiding

Traymddiried, *v. a.* (ymddiried) To confide over-much.

Traymddwyn, *s. m.* (ymddwyn) An over-bearing of one's self. *v. a.* To over-bear one's self.

Traymddygiad, *s. m.* (ymddygiad) An over-carrying one's self.

Traymegnïad, *s. m.* (ymegnïad) Over-exertion.

Traymegnïaw, *v. a.* (ymegnïaw) To over-exert one's self.

Traymegnïawl, *a.* (ymegnïawl) Over-exerting.

Traymerlid, *s. m.* (ymerlid) An extreme mutual persecution. *v. a.* Mutually to persecute extremely.

Traymerlidiad, *s. m.* (traymerlid) A persecuting one another extremely.

Traymestyn, *s. m.* (ymestyn) An over-stretch of one's self. *v. a.* To over-stretch one's self.

Traymestynawl, *a.* (traymestyn) Tending to be over-stretching.

Traymestyniad, *s. m.* (traymestyn) An over-stretching or over-extending of one's self.

Traymgais, *s. m.* (ymgais) An over-attempt.

Traymgeisiad, *s. m.* (traymgais) An over-attempting, or over-exerting.

Traymgeisiaw, *v. a.* (traymgais) To over-exert.

Traymgeisiawl, *a.* (traymgais) Tending to over-attempt; apt to over-exert.

Traymlid, *s. m.* (ymlid) An over-pursuit. *v. a.* To pursue over-much.

Traymlidiad, *s. m.* (traymlid) An over-pursuing.

Traymlidiaw, *v. a.* (traymlid) To over-pursue.

Traymlidiawl, *a.* (traymlid) Apt to over-pursue.

Traymoedi, *v. a.* (ymoedi) Mutually to delay over-much; to keep one's self away over-much.

Traymoediad, *s. m.* (ymoediad) A mutually delaying over-much; a keeping one's self away over-much.

Traymorchestawl, *a.* (ymorchestawl) Tending to exult extremely in an exploit.

Traymorchestiad, *s. m.* (ymorchestiad) An exulting extremely in an exploit.

Traymorchestu, *v. a.* (ymorchestu) To exult extremely in an exploit.

Traymryson, *s. m.* (ymryson) Extreme competition or emulation.

Traymrysonawl, *a.* (traymryson) Very emulous.

Traymrysoni, *v. a.* (traymryson) To engage in extreme competition.

Traymrysoniad, *s. m.* (traymryson) Extreme competition, or emulation.

Traymsènawl, *a.* (ymsènawl) Mutually apt to reproach over-much.

Traymsèniad, *s. m.* (ymsèniad) A mutually reproaching over-much; a reproaching one's self extremely.

Traymsènu, *v. a.* (ymsènu) Mutually to reproach overmuch; to reproach one's self extremely.

Traymsoddawl, *a.* (ymsoddawl) Apt to sink one's self extremely.

Traymsoddi, *v. a.* (ymsoddi) To sink one's self extremely.

Traymsoddiad, *s. m.* (ymsoddiad) A sinking one's self extremely.

Traymsythawl, *a.* (ymsythawl) Apt to make one's self extremely erect.

Traymsythiad, *s. m.* (ymsythiad) A making one's self extremely erect.

Traymsythu, *v. a.* (ymsythu) To make one's self extremely erect.

Traymwadawl, *a.* (ymwadawl) Of extreme self-denial; mutually denying greatly.

Traymwadiad, *s. m.* (ymwadiad) A denying one's self extremely.

Traymwadu, *v. a.* (ymwadu) To deny one's self extremely.

Tre, *s. f.* (ty—rhe) A resort; a homestead; a hamlet; a town. *Treberied*, *Tredegar*, mansions so called.

Trec, *s. m.—pl. t.* iau (ty—rhec) An implement; harness geer. *Trec mên*, cart harness.

Treciad, *s. m.* (trec) A furnishing, a harnessing.
Treciaw, *v. a.* (trec) To furnish, to equip out.
Treciawl, *a.* (trec) Furnishing, harnessing.
Treciedig, *a.* (treciad) Furnished, harnessed.
Trecïwr, *s. m.*—*pl.* treciwyr (trec—gwr) A furnisher, a harnesser, a dresser out.
Trecyn, *s. m. dim.* (trec) An implement, a tool.
Trech, *a.* (tre—ech) Superior, passing; of superior power: It is generally used for *trechach*, stronger, more powerful.

> Trech gwlad nog arglwydd:
> Trech glew no gwlad.
>
> A country is *more powerful* than a prince; a great man is *more powerful* than a country. *Adage.*
>
> Trech arfer nog arfaeth.
>
> Habit is *stronger* than resolution. *Adage.*
>
> Trech angen no dewis.
>
> Necessity is *stronger* than choice. *Adage.*
>
> Trech dygwydd no deall.
>
> Chance is *more powerful* than wit. *Adage.*
>
> A fo trechaf treisied.
>
> He that is *strongest* let him oppress. *Adage.*
>
> Trech a gais nog a geidw.
>
> *Stronger* is he who obtains than who keeps. *Adage.*

Trechad, *s. m.* (trech) A getting the better.
Trechawl, *a.* (trech) Vanquishing, conquering.
Trechedig, *a.* (trech) Vanquished, conquered.
Trechedd, *s.* (trech) Superiority; stronger state.
Trechiad, *s. m.*—*pl.* trechiaid (trech) An overcoming one, a vanquisher, a victor.

> Arddwyreaf naf—
> Aerdorf gorf gwrdd derwyn ei naid
> I gynnif ar gynnygu trechiaid.
>
> I will extol a chief, the strength of the slaughtering band, whose leap is ardently fierce to depredate on the security of *conquerors*.
> *Ll. P. Moch, i Rodri.*

Trechiannawl, *a.* (trechiant) Overpowering.
Trechiannu, *v. a.* (trechiant) To obtain superiority, to obtain a conquest.
Trechiannus, *a.* (trechiant) Overpowering.
Trechiant, *s. m.* (trech) An overcoming.
Trechryni, *s. m.* (trech—rhyni) Aptitude for superiority; ambition.

> Dychyrch cyfarwydd; dychyfarwyd a mi;
> O drechryni y tri, ydd ym treulwyd.
>
> The informed will resort; I have been visited; owing to the *passion for superiority* of the three, I have been consumed.
> *Gwalchmai.*

Trechu, *v. a.* (trech) To overpower, to overcome; to conquer; to surpass; to be superior.
Trechwr, *s. m.*—*pl.* trechwyr (trech—gwr) One who overcomes, a vanquisher.
Tred, *s. f.*—*pl. t.* i (tre—ed) A course, or place of resort; a hamlet.—*Coed Andred, Caer Andred*, the Weald of Kent: *Tred Eleirch*, a district on Rumney in Monmouthshire, called by the English Swanton.
Tredd, *s. f.*—*pl. t.* au (tre—edd) That is over, that is taken off or from; a crop, or growth; corn; also the same as *treth*, contribution of corn; a tribute, or tax.
Tref, *s. f.*—*pl. t.* ydd (tre) A dwelling place; a homestead; a hamlet; a township; a town. *Pwy sydd yn nhref?* Who is at home? It forms the names of many places, as *Tref Ithel*, Ithelham; *Trefa*, Hamburg; and the like. As the name of a single house it answers to the English *Ham*.

> Nid tref ond nef.
>
> There is no *dwelling place* but heaven. *Adage.*
>
> Ni châr morwyn mab o'i thref.
>
> A damsel loves not a youth of her own *hamlet*. *Adage.*
>
> Pedair rhandir a fydd yn mhob tref; y tair yn gyfanedd, ar y bedwaredd yn borfa i'r tair.
>
> Four sharelands there are in every *hamlet*; the three inhabited, and the fourth as pasture to the three. *Welsh Laws.*

Trefa, *s. f.*—*pl.* trefëydd (tre) A place of resort, assembly, or dwelling. *Trefa y tylwyth teg*, a fairy circle: *Trefa o yd*, a thrave of corn; also a quantity of sheaves laid on the threshing-floor.
Trefad, *s. f.* (tref) A domicil, a habitation; a dwelling, or inhabiting.

> Trefad fy hendad a'i hundy.
>
> The *dwelling* of my ancestor and his dormitory.
> *D. Benfras.*
>
> Cynnyddasai llawr llwyr drefad.
>
> Over the ground had accumulated complete *inhabitancy*.
> *Gwalchmai.*

Trefan, *s. f. dim.* (tref) A small hamlet.
Trefawg, *a.* (tref) Having a home, or town.
Trefawl, *a.* (tref) Relating to a home, or town.
Trefedig, *a.* (trefad) Settled, inhabited; colonized. *Trefedigion*, settlers, or colonizers.
Trefedigaeth, *s. m.*—*pl. t.* au (trefedig) The act of settling, or colonizing; the state of being settled, a colony.
Trefgordd, *s. f.* (tref—cordd) The round or limit of a hamlet, a township; community.
Trefiad, *s. m.*—*pl.* trefiaid (tref) That maketh a home; that dwelleth; that is domestic; a sparrow.
Trefiannawl, *a.* (trefiant) Belonging to inhabitancy or habitation.
Trefiannu, *v. a.* (trefiant) To form an inhabitancy, to form a habitation.
Trefiant, *s. m.* (tref) Habitancy, habitation.
Trefig, *a.* (tref) Homely, domestic. *Gwr trefig*, a domestic man.
Treflawg, *a.* (traf) Tending to turn about. *Gweflau treflawg*, pouting lips.
Treflys, *s. m.*—*pl. t.* oedd (tref—llys) A court leet.
Trefn, *s. f.*—*pl. t.* oedd (trefn) The state of being disposed in connection; arrangement, system, order.

> Hawdd daffar o drefn.
>
> It is easy to accomplish by *good order*. *Adage.*
>
> Nid oes yn uffern ond eisieu trefn dda.
>
> There is in hell but the want of *good order*. *Adage.*

Trefnadwy, *a.* (trefn) Capable of arrangement.
Trefnau, *s. pl. aggr.* (trefn) Utensils, implements.

> Llewyssynt afonoedd
> Tai a threfnau,
> A thyllau,
> A chellau bwyd.
>
> They devoured rivers, houses and *utensils*, and couches, and provision rooms. *Taliesin, Plaau yr Aipht.*
>
> Y brawd ieuaf biau yr eisyddyn arbenig ac wyth erw, ac y trefnau oll.
>
> The youngest brother owns the principal tenement, and all the *implements*. *Welsh Laws.*

Trefnawl, *a.* (trefn) Orderly, systematic.
Trefnedig, *a.* (trefn) Ordered, systemized.
Trefnedigaeth, *s. f.*—*pl. t.* au (trefnedig) Regulation, adjustment; ordinance.
Trefnfawr, *a.* (trefn) Well-ordered.
Trefngar, *a.* (trefn) Orderly, well-ordered.
Trefngarwch, *s. m.* (trefngar) Orderliness.
Trefniad, *s. m.*—*pl. t.* au (trefn) A regulating, arranging, or ordering.
Trefniadu, *v. a.* (trefniad) To make an arrangement, order, system, or regulation.
Trefniannawl, *a.* (trefniant) Systematical.
Trefniannu, *v. a.* (trefniant) To systemize.
Trefniant, *s. m.* (trefn) System.
Trefniawd, *s. m.* (trefn) Regulation.

Trefniawdr, *s. m.—pl.* trefniodron (trefniawd) A regulator; a systemizer.

> Trefniawdr, llwyr hyswdr lloer a haul,
> Trefnaist a ffurfaist, o ffyrf amcan,
> Trefnau amhrylau genau a gân.

> Thou *regulator*, perfect organizer of moon and sun, thou didst ordain and thou didst form, by ample design, the unrestrained powers of the lips that sing. *Cannodyn.*

Trefnid, *s. m.—pl. t.* au (trefn) Arrangement; management; disposal; settlement; order.

Trefnidaeth, *s. m.* (trefnid) The act of arranging, managing, or ordering; management.

> Gwraig briawd a folir am drefnidaeth, a'i gofal dros ei theulu, a'i serch at ei gwr a'i phlant.

> A married woman is to be praised on account of *management*, and her care for her family, and her love to her husband, and her children. *Barddas.*

Trefnidaw, *v. a.* (trefnid) To make an arrangement, or disposition; to manage.

Trefnidawl, *a.* (trefnid) Economical.

Trefnidedd, *s. m.* (trefnid) Economy.

Trefnidiad, *s. m.* (trefnid) An economizing.

Trefnidwr, *s. m.—pl.* trefnidwyr (trefnid—gwr) An economist; a manager.

Trefnidydd, *s. m.—pl. t.* ion (trefnid) An economist, a manager.

Trefniedydd, *s. m.—pl. t.* ion (trefniad) One who disposes, or puts in order; a disposer.

Trefnoldeb, *s. m.* (trefnawl) Orderliness.

Trefnolder, *s. m.* (trefnawl) Orderliness.

Trefnoldra, *s. m.* (trefnawl) Orderliness.

Trefnoli, *v. a.* (trefnawl) To render orderly.

Trefnu, *v. a.* (trefn) To dispose, to arrange, to connect or to put in order; to regulate; to manage; to appoint, to settle.

> Traethawd o'th folawd filoedd gyman:
> Trefnaist syr, a myr moryawl dylan;
> Trefnaist ddaiar fawr a'i chlawr achlan;
> Trefnaist wern uffern, uffaith sathan.

> Thousands in concert declare thy praise: thou hast regulated stars, and seas of fluctuating tide; thou hast regulated the ample earth with its surface all complete; thou hast regulated the dark region of hell, with respect to Satan. *Cansodyn.*

Trefnus, *a.* (trefn) Being arranged, put in order, or disposed; orderly, methodical; well arranged, being in good order, compact, neat, decent.

Trefnusaw, *v. a.* (trefnus) To render orderly, to put in good order.

Trefnusdeb, *s. m.* (trefnus) Orderliness.

Trefnusder, *s. m.* (trefnus) Orderliness.

Trefnusdra, *s. m.* (trefnus) Orderliness.

Trefnusedd, *s. m.* (trefnus) Orderliness.

Trefnusrwydd, *s. m.* (trefnus) Orderliness.

Trefnwr, *s. m.—pl.* trefnwyr (trefn—gwr) One who regulates, or arranges, an orderer.

Trefnydd, *s. m.—pl. t.* ion (trefn) An orderer.

Trefnyddiad, *s. m.—pl. t.* au (trefnydd) The practice of an economist.

Trefnyddiaeth, *s. m.* (trefnydd) Economy.

Trefnyddiaw, *v. a.* (trefnydd) To economize.

Trefred, *s. f.* (tref—rhed) An inhabited region; a homestead, a domicil, a habitation.

> Gnawd diogelder yn nhrefred.

> Security is obtained in an *inhabited place*. *Adage.*

> Gwell bach yn nhrefred no mawr yn anialdred.

> Better the little in an *inhabited place* than the great in a wilderness. *Adage.*

Trefstad, *s. f.* (tref—tad) Patrimony, heritage.

> Caranmael oedd ddiaidd
> Ac oedd did holedig trefstad,
> A geisiwys Caranmael.—

> Caranmael was void of ambition; and clear from every claim the *patrimony*, which Caranmael did seek. *Llywarch Hen.*

Trefstadaeth, *s. f.* (trefstad) A patrimony.

Trefstadawg, *a.* (trefstad) Having a patrimony, or heritage; an inheritor. *s. m.—pl.* trefstadogion. One who has a patrimony, one in possession of a paternal estate; an heir.

> Myfi ei gwnaethof ef yn drefstadawg.

> I myself have made him *possessed of an inheritage*. *Brut y Breninoedd.*

Trefstadawl, *a.* (trefstad) Patrimonial, hereditary.

Trefstadiad, *s. m.* (trefstad) A forming a patrimony or heritage.

Trefstadoges, *s. f.—pl. t.* au (trefstadawg) A female who inherits; a heiress.

Trefstadu, *v. a.* (trefstad) To form a patrimony.

Trefstadwr, *s. m.—pl.* trefstadwyr (trefstad—gwr) One who establishes a patrimony.

Trefu, *v. a.* (tref) To form a place of resort; to make a home; to inhabit.

Treiad, *s. m.—pl. t.* au (trai) A decreasing, or abating, a diminution; an ebbing.

Treiaw, *v. a.* (trai) To decrease, to lessen; to abate; to ebb.

> Trugarawg Ddofydd,
> Treia fy ngherydd!

> Merciful Creator, *lessen* my chastisement! *Gwalchmai.*

> Treiaw Goronwy, trafn mordwy medd:
> Cof garw o'i lwyr farw!

> Goronwy *to be taken away*, the tide of mead will turn: Sad the reflection that he should be completely dead! *G. ab M. ab Dafydd.*

Treiawl, *a.* (trai) Tending to decrease, lessen, or abate; ebbing, neapy.

Treidiad, *s. m.—pl. t.* au (tred) A coursing; a resorting.

Treidiaw, *v. a.* (tred) To course, to range.

> Y cyffylawg—
> Trist big, hen goedwig a gar,
> Treidia, adwyau daiar.

> The woodcock, with drooping bill, loving an ancient woody dell, *he would range* the crannies of the ground. *D. ab Gwilym.*

Treidiawl, *a.* (tred) Ranging; resorting.

Treiddgof, *s. m.* (traidd—cof) A wounded mind.

> Pell ym traidd treiddgof o'i rygolled!

> Deeply doth *piercing memory* pierce me for his sad loss! *Cynddelw.*

Treiddiad, *s. m.—pl. t.* au (traidd) A penetrating.

Treiddiadwy, *a.* (treiddiad) Penetrable.

Treiddiaw, *v. a.* (traidd) To penetrate; to pervade.

> Colofn hawl heillew
> Cowtwin, drin dreiddiaw,
> Canu anant anaw
> Aelaw alaf.

> The pillar of the prerogative of serving costly wine, bursting the conflict, minstrels sing with melody of poetic store. *G. ab M. ab Dafydd.*

Treiddiawg, *a.* (traidd) Being penetrated.

Treiddiawl, *a.* (traidd) Penetrating; pervading.

Treiddiedig, *a.* (treiddiad) Penetrated; pervaded.

Treiddiedigawl, *a.* (treiddiedig) Penetrative.

Treiddioldeb, *s. m.* (treiddiawl) Piercingness.

Treiddiolder, *s. m.* (treiddiawl) Penetrability.

Treiddiolrwydd, *s. m.* (treiddiawl) Piercingness.

Treiddiwr, *s. m.—pl.* treiddiwyr (traidd—gwr) One who penetrates, a piercer.

Treiddle, *s. m.—pl. t.* oedd (traidd—lle) A resorting place.

Treiddyn, *s. m.—pl. t.* au (traidd) A ridge of high ground running into a vale.

Treiedig, *a.* (treiad) Decreased, abated, ebbed.

Treiedigaw, *v. a.* (treiedig) To render lessened.

Treiedigawl, *a.* (treiedig) Tending to decrease.

Treiglad, *s. m.—pl.* treigliaid (treigl) One who roves about, a wanderer.

red-necked diver; *trochydd danneddawg*, the lesser dun diver.

Trodawl, *a.* (trawd) Transitive; passing over.

Trodi, *v. a.* (trawd) To make a transit; to pass onward; to journey.

Trodiad, *s. m.* (trawd) A passing onward.

Trodwen, *s. f.* (trawd—gwen) A starling.

Troddail, *s. pl. aggr.* (tro—dail) Flowers in festoon. *Cor o droddail*, a bower of leaves.

Troddawl, *a.* (trawdd) Progressive; forwarding.

Troddedig, *a.* (trawdd) Being passed onward.

Troddi, *v. a.* (trawdd) To make a transit; to move onward, to make a progress.

> Gwen wrth Lawen ydd wylas neithwyr:
> Arthur ni thechas:
> Aodd a drawdd ar glawdd Gorlas.
>
> Gwen on Llawen he did watch last night: Arthur never retreated: the slaughter *he passed through* on the dyke of Gorlas.
> *Llywarch Hen.*

> Rhoi rhan o'th dorth gân, a'th giniaw i lu,
> Heb le i wrwgnach;
> A'th gi, cyn troddi un tro,
> A'th fran, aeth yn farw yno.
>
> Giving a share of thy white loaf and thy dinner to a multitude, without room to grumble: and thy dog, before *moving forward* one step, and thy crow, there did die.
> *D. Ll. ab Ll. ab Gruffudd.*

Troddiad, *s. m.* (trawdd) A transition, a passing over; progression.

Troed, *s. m.—pl.* traed (traw—ed) A foot. It forms the names of many plants: *Troed y ceiliawg*, cock's-foot grass; *troed y golomen*, *llysiau y colwm*, columbine; *troed yr hedydd*, lark spur, *troed ysgyfarnawg*, *meillion cedenawg*, hare's-foot trefoil; *troed yr asen*, *yr arllegawg*, garlick hedge-mustard; *troed yr arth*, bear's foot; *troed yr aderyn*, common bird's foot; *troed y tarw*, *llysiau y tarw*, bullwort; *troed yr wydd*, goose foot; *troed y cyw*, hedge parsley; *troed y gath*, mountain cat's foot, field cypress; *troed y gywen*, water purslain; *troed y dryw*, field ladies' mantle; *troed y barcud*, common meadow-rue; *troed yr ebawl*, marsh marigold; *troed yr crydd*, celery-leaved crow foot; *troed y llew*, ladies' mantle.

> Pan lithro doeth, pob ffol a dery droed arno.
>
> When the wise slips, every fool will stamp a *foot* upon him.
> *Adage.*

Troedawg, *a.* (troed) Having a foot. *s. f.* A fetlock; a fetter.

Troedawl, *a.* (troed) Belonging to the foot, pedal.

Troed-draws, *a.* (troed—traws) Splay-footed.

Troed-droed, *adv.* (troed *repeated*) Foot to foot.

Troedfedd, *s. f.—pl. t.* i (bedd) A foot measure.

Troedfeddawl, *a.* (troedfedd) Of a foot measure.

Troedfeddu, *v. a.* (troedfedd) To divide into feet.

Troedfyr, *a.* (troed—byr) Short-footed.

Troedgall, *a.* (troed—call) Having the foot turned out; club-footed.

Troedgam, *a.* (troed—cam) Wry-footed.

Troedhir, *a.* (troed—hir) Long-footed.

Troediad, *s. m.—pl. t.* au (troed) A footing.

Troediant, *s.* (troed) A setting a foot, a footing.

> Cair y gair ffres yn ngwaith yr hen feirdd, cyn cael o'r Saesoneg droediant yn Ynys Prydain.
>
> The word fresh is to be found in the works of the old bards, before the Saxons had *footing* in the isle of Britain.
> *Llywelyn Sion.*

Troediaw, *v. a.* (troed) To foot; to use the foot; to tread; to kick.

Troediawg, *a.* (troed) Having feet, footed. *s. m.* A pedifer; a foot-holder. He is also called *rhageisteddiad*.

> Troediawg a ddyly ddaly traed y brenin yn ei arffed, o'r pan ddechreuo eistedd yn ei gyfeddach [illegible] y brenin; ac yn gylyd [illegible] a ymladd gwyliaw y brenin rhag gwall.
>
> The *footman* ought to hold the *feet* of the king in his lap, from the time when he begins to sit in his conviviality to the time he goes to sleep; and he ought to scratch the king; and during such a space let him guard the king against accident. *Welsh Laws.*

Tröedig, *a.* (tröed) Turned, converted; being disposed to turn. *Tröedigion*, proselytes.

> Addaf gyta gribin, gwibiad dig;
> Addaf glaf gleiriach troedig.
>
> Adam the rotten rake, a surly branch; Adam a diseased vagabond.
> *Rhys Yaunge.*

Tröedigaeth, *s. m.—pl. t.* au (tröedig) Circulation.

Tröedigawl, *a.* (tröedig) Circulating, revolving.

Troedlas, *s. f.—pl. t.* au (troed—llas) A treadle.

Troedlath, *s. f.—pl. t.* au (troed—llath) Treadle.

Troedle, *s. m.—pl. t.* oedd (troed—lle) A trodden place; a place of resort. *Troedle hyglyw*, a well-known place of resort.

Troedlen, *s. f.—pl. t.* i (troed—llen) A footboard; a treadle.

Troedlydan, *a.* (troed—llydan) Broad-footed.

Troednoeth, *a.* (troed—noeth) Barefooted.

> A heuo ddrain na cherdded yn droednoeth.
>
> Who sows thorns let him not walk *barefooted*. *Adage.*

Troednoethi, *v. a.* (troednoeth) To make barefoot.

Troednoethiad, *s. m.* (troednoeth) Discalceation.

Troedogi, *v. a.* (troedawg) To fetter, to shackle.

Troedogiad, *s. m.* (troedawg) A fettering.

Troedraw, *s. f.* (troed—rhaw) A foot-spade.

Troedrudd, *a.* (troed—rhudd) Of a ruddy foot. *s. f.* The stinking cranebill; also called *llysiau y llwynawg*, *mynawyd y bugel*, *pig yr aran*.

Troedsych, *a.* (troed—sych) Dry-footed, dry foot.

Troedwst, *s. f.* (troed—gwst) A foot disease; gout.

Troedwstawl, *a.* (troedwst) Podagrical, gouty.

Troedyn, *s. m. dim.* (troed) A little foot.

Troedysgafn, *a.* (troed—ysgafn) Light-footed.

Troell, *s. f.—pl. t.* au (tro) That effects a turn; a whirl, a wheel for turning, spinning, or winding; a reel; a pulley; a windlass, a screw; a trope. *Troellau melin*, the pinions of mill-work; *troell nyddu*, a spinning wheel. *Aderyn y droell*, the goatsucker.

> Tori llinyn troell einioes.
>
> To break the thread of the wheel of life.
> *G. Ll. ab Ll. Fychan.*

Troellaidd, *a.* (troell) Like a wheel or whirl.

> Cryman digofaint Duw:—Amlwg yw fod y gair yn myned dan yr arwyddocaad cyffelybiaethawl troellaidd.
>
> The sickle of the wrath of God:—It is manifest that the expression comes under the denomination that is comparative *of the nature of a trope*.
> *Iør Owain.*

Troellawg, *a.* (troel) Having a turn, whirl, or wheel; of the form of a whirl, or screw, or ringlet; brocaded; having the marks called watered, on silks or stuffs; grained, as appearing on boards.

> Trillw gwych troellawg eidd—
> Y tarw.
>
> Of three gay hues in *ringlets* was the bull.
> *E. Car.*

Troelledig, *a.* (troell) Twirled; in ringlets.

Troellen, *s. f.—pl. t.* i (troell) A whirl, a twirl.

Troellenaidd, *a.* (troellen) Like a whirl.

Troellenawg, *a.* (troellen) Composed of whirls, or ringlets; formed like a cobweb; brocaded, flowered.

Troelleniad, *s. m.* (troellen) A forming into whirls, or ringlets.

Troellenu, *v. a.* (troellen) To form a whirl; to form into ringlets.

Troellgorun, *s. m.* (troell—corun) Moss rush.

Treisioli, *v. a.* (treisiawl) To render oppressive;

Treisiolrwydd, *s. m.* (treisiawl) Oppressiveness.

Treisiwr, *s. m.—pl.* treisiwyr (trais—gwr) A forcer, a ravisher; an oppressor.

Ac i'r treisiwyr, ac i'r trawsion,
Terfyn aio,
Yn lle delo
Llu dawiollon.

So to the *oppressors*, and to the froward ones, may there come an end, where comes a host of godly men. *W. Middleton.*

Treisledrad, *s. m.* (trais—lledrad) Rapine.

Treislu, *s. m.—pl. t.* oedd (trais—llu) A rapacious host.

Tremynud trwm ynof y chwant
Fremyne treisiu tros llant.

Sadly was observed in me a desire to observe an oppressing host over the stream. *Casnodyn.*

Treiswaew, *s. f.* (trais—gwaew) Spear of rapine.

Treiswg, *s. m.* (trais) A frown of oppression. *a.* Oppression-frowning.

Gwanach a digiach ym dwg
Dy olwg treiswg trosof.

More feeble and more troubled in every way thy *oppression-frowning* eye doth bring me. *Gr. ab D. ab Tudyr.*

Treiswriaeth, *s. m.* (treisiwr) The act of a forcer, ravisher, or oppressor.

Treisydd, *s. m.—pl. t.* ion (trais) A forcer.

A Dafydd, dreisydd drosedd, cyn golo,
Ni bu o Gymmro ei gymmrodedd.

And David, the *oppressor* of frowardness, before sepulture there was not a Welshman his equal in worth. *D. Benfras.*

Treithiad, *s. m.* (traith) A treating; a reciting.

Treithiaw, *v. a.* (traith) To treat, to discourse.

Tafawd a draith, buchedd a ddengys.

A tongue *recites*, but the conduct shews. *Adage.*

Treithiawl, *a.* (traith) Treating, reciting.

Treithiedig, *a.* (treithiad) Being treated.

Treithiwr, *s. m.—pl.* treithiwyr (traith—gwr) One who treats, a discourser.

Treithydd, *s. m.—pl. t.* ion (traith) A reciter.

Trem, *s. f.—pl. t.* iau (ty—rhem) Sight, look.

Trembeiriannaeth, *s. m.* (trembeiriant) An optician's trade.

Trembeiriannawl, *a.* (trembeiriant) Relating to optical instruments.

Trembeiriannu, *v. a.* (trembeiriant) To furnish optical instruments.

Trembeiriannydd, *s. m.—pl. t.* ion (trembeiriant) An optical instrument maker.

Trembeiriant, *s. m.—pl.* trembeiriannau (trem—peiriant) An optical instrument.

Tremiad, *s. m.—pl. t.* au (trem) An observing.

Tremiannawl, *a.* (tremiant) Observant.

Tremiannu, *v. a.* (tremiant) To make observation; to cast a look.

Tremiant, *s. m.—pl.* tremiannau (trem) Observation; appearance, aspect.

Diau oedd ganto na welsai dremiant erioed cho deced a hi ar arall.

Certain it was to him that he had never seen an *appearance* so fair as she on another. *H. Peredur—Mabinogion.*

Tremiator, *ger.* (tremiad) In observing.

Tremiaw, *v. a.* (trem) To look, to observe.

Tremiawl, *a.* (trem) Looking, observing.

Tremid, *s. m.* (trem) Appearance, object.

Mab Tegwared hael hawl dremid galon;
Gal ag ef ni borthid.

The son of Tegwared the generous questions the *appearance* of foes, an enemy could not subsist with him. *Cynddelw.*

Tremidydd, *s. m.—pl. t.* ion (tremid) Observer.

Tremiedig, *a.* (tremiad) Observed; eyed.

Tremitor, *sup.* (tremid) To be observing.

Tremiwr, *s. m.—pl.* tremiwyr (trem—gwr) A looker, an observer, one who eyes.

Tremrudd, *a.* (trem—rhudd) Of red aspect.

Tremwyllt, *a.* (trem—gwyllt) Of wild aspect.

Tremyd, *s. m.* (trem) The state of being seen.

Tremydiad, *s. m.* (tremyd) An apparition.

Tremydiad mynydd, manod tew ai'th fodd,
Ni'th lesgo eiry na rhew.

Thou *phantom* of the mountain, no thickly driven snow will obstruct thee, may neither snow nor frost affect thee. *Llywarch Llaety.*

Tremydiaw, *v. a.* (tremyd) To raise a phantom; to appear as a phantom.

Tremydd, *s. m.—pl. t.* ion (trem) A looker.

Tremyddiaeth, *s. m.* (tremydd) Science of optics.

Tremyg, *s. m.—pl. t.* ion (tram) Contempt; disparagement. *Tremyg barn*, contempt of judgment.

Tremyg gwys yw na ddelo dyn y dydd y galwer i'r llys.

A *contempt* of summons is that a person comes not on the day he is called to the court. *Welsh Laws.*

Tremygiad, *s. m.* (tremyg) A contemning, a slighting. *Tremygiad llys*, contempt of court.

Tremygiawl, *a.* (tremyg) Contemning.

Tremygiedig, *a.* (tremygiad) Contemned.

Tremygu, *v. a.* (tremyg) To contemn, to slight.

Tremygus, *a.* (tremyg) Contemptuous.

Tremygwr, *s. m.—pl.* tremygwyr (tremyg—gwr) A contemner, a slighter.

Tremyn, *s. m.—pl. t.* au (trem) Sight, look, aspect, view; a glance.

Dyd! was o ddu a melyn:
Wrth hir edrych dy dremyn,
Tybiais dy weled cyn hyn.

Hold! young man of black and yellow; by long observing thy *aspect*, methought I saw thee before this. *Eng. Arthur a Gwenhwyfar.*

Tremynawd, *s. m.—pl.* tremynodau (tremyn) An object.

O bydd hen, nid mwy y syniа ar y dyig,—nog ar dremynodau eraill a welo.

If he be old, no more will he look, upon learning than upon other *objects* he may see. *Welsh Laws.*

Tremynawl, *a.* (tremyn) Observant, looking.

Tremynfa, *s. f.—pl. t.* oedd (tremyn) A watch-tower.

Tremyngar, *a.* (tremyn) Observant; keen-eyed.

Tremyngarwch, *s. m.* (tremyngar) Aptness to observe or to look about.

Tremyngwag, *s. m.* (tremyn—cwag) A light sleep.

Tremyniad, *s. m.—pl. t.* au (tremyn) An apparition, a phantom; also an epithet for a boar.

Y naill yw yn enaill had
Ai tarw main, ai tremyniad.

Either of the two he is, begetting seed, of a sleek bull, or an *apparition*. *Guto y Glyn.*

Tremynt, *s. m.* (trem) Sight, look; a glance.

Tremynu, *v. a.* (tremyn) To look about, to scout.

Oedd trawsawr tremynai tachwedd.

Immense the ruin *seemed*. *Cynddelw.*

Yn Aber Taradr yn tremynu.

In Aber Taradr *observing*. *Gw. Brycheiniawg.*

Eilgwd trom y tremynasant
Udd addien uch Dygen Dyfnant.

In a second heavy conflict *they observed* the comely chief above Dygen Dyvnant. *Ll. P. Moch.*

Tremynwr, *s. m.—pl.* tremynwyr (tremyn—gwr) An explorer, or a scoret.

A glyweisti a gant Gwion,
Dremynwr, golwg unlawn:
Duw cadarn a farn pob iawn.

Hast thou heard what Gwion sang, an *observer* of steady sight: the mighty God will judge every right. *Eng. y Clywed.*

Tremynwriaeth, *s. m.* (tremynwr) The employment of an explorer.

Tremynydd, *s. m.—pl. t.* ion (tremyn) An explorer, one employed to observe; a centinel.

Tremynyddiaeth, *s. m.* (tremynydd) The employment or duty of an explorer.

Tren, *s. m.* (ty—rhen) Force; rapidity; fury.

> [illegible]
> A gnawd edduch tren [illegible].
>
> Many a Saxon, what I lamented not, has been made to complain of his head; and, from high insolence, made to bend himself. *D. Benfras.*

Tren, *a.* (ty—rhen) Impetuous, forcible, furious; powerful, strenuous. *Mae efe yn edrych yn dren iawn*, he looks very furious: *Afon dren iawn yw hon*, this is a very rapid river. *Sil.*

> [illegible]
>
> Fair approaching dawn, [illegible] the furious wave; the [illegible] repairs under the branches of the oak: misfortune [illegible] her possessor. *Ystyffan Bardd Telo.*

Trenaidd, *a.* (tren) Somewhat impetuous.

Trenawl, *a.* (tren) Impetuous; strenuous.

Treniad, *s. m.* (tren) An acting impetuously.

Trenig, *a.* (tren) Impetuous, or furious.

Trenllif, *s. m.* (tren—llif) A rapid torrent. *Sil.* It is as *Cefnllif*, is used in North Wales.

Trent, *s. m.* (tren) Force; rapidity; fury.

Trenu, *v. a.* (tren) To act impetuously.

Trenus, *a.* (tren) Impetuous; strenuous.

Trenusaw, *v. a.* (trenus) To render impetuous, or strenuous; to become impetuous.

Trenusdeb, *s. m.* (trenus) Impetuosity, rapidity.

Trenusder, *s. m.* (trenus) Impetuousness.

Trenusdra, *s. m.* (trenus) Rapidness.

Trenusedd, *s. m.* (trenus) Rapidity; quickness.

Trenusrwydd, *s. m.* (trenus) Impetuousness, rapidness; strenuousness.

Trenydd, *s. m.* (tra—dydd) The third day to come, the day after to-morrow. *adv.* Two days hence, the day after to-morrow.

Trenyddiawl, *a.* (trenydd) Relating to the third day to come.

Trengawl, *a.* (tranc) Perishing, vanishing.

Trengi, *v. n.* (tranc) To pass away, to be passing away, to expire, to be at an end; to give up the ghost. *Mae y dydd yn trengi*, the day is at an end.

> Trengid golud, ni threnc molud.
>
> Wealth passeth away, but fame will not pass away. *Adage.*

Trengidydd, *s. m.—pl. t.* ion (tranc) A destroyer.

Trengwr, *s. m.—pl.* trengwyr (tranc—gwr) One who is at an end, an expiring man.

Tres, *s. f.—pl. t.* i (ty—rhes) That is on the stretch, or in exertion, labour, pains, trouble; a trace, or chain, for drawing; a stroke, as with a rod or whip.

Tresawg, *a.* (tres) Being on the stretch.

Tresawl, *a.* (tres) Straining; exerting; bustling.

Tresg, *s. m.* (tres) That is on a stretch.

Tresgl, *s. m.* (tresg) Tormentil. It is also called *tresgl melyn, tresgl yr eithin*, or *melyn yr eithin; tresgl y moch*, the common tormentil.

Tresglen, *s. f. dim.* (tresgl) A thrush; also called *bronfraith, pen y llwyn*. *Y dresglen lwyd*, the shrite; *y dresglen goch, crecer, socen eira*, the swine-piper.

Tresglerddyn, *s. m.* (tres—clerddyn) A sturdy vagabond.

Tresiad, *s. m.* (tres) A putting on a stretch, or straining; a whipping.

Tresiaw, *v. a.* (tres) To labour; [illegible] *Cei dy dresiaw*, thou shalt be bel[illegible]

Tresiwr, *s. m.—pl.* tresiwyr (tr[illegible] who belabours or thrashes.

Trest, *s. m.* (tres) That is strained[illegible]

Trestl, *s. f.—pl.* trestlau (trest) T[illegible] stretcher, a frame; a trestle.

> Y ddau drestl, a'r holl ddodrefn.
>
> The two trestles, and all the furniture.

Trestlawg, *a.* (trestl) Having a str[illegible]

Trestliad, *s. m.* (trestl) A furni[illegible] stretcher; a framing.

Trestlu, *v. a.* (trestl) To furnish wi[illegible] trestle, or frame; to frame.

Tresu, *v. a.* (tres) To put on a tra[illegible]

Treth, *s. f.—pl. t.* i (tre—eth) Tha[illegible] is taken off or from; a crop, [illegible] duce; a crop of corn; otherwis[illegible] also an allowance, contribution, [illegible] tribute. *Y dreth fawr*, the land[illegible]

> [illegible]
>
> I saw the [illegible] of a stock [illegible]

Trethadwy, *a.* (treth) Taxable, ra[illegible]

Trethawg, *a.* (treth) Having a rat[illegible]

Trethawl, *a.* (treth) Tributary; ta[illegible]

> [illegible]
>
> Tumult and dissention amongst any [illegible] men of Rome [illegible] this island; and through it tributary.

Trethedig, *a.* (treth) Rated, or tax[illegible]

Trethiad, *s. m.* (treth) A rating, a [illegible]

Trethu, *v. a.* (treth) To rate, or to[illegible]

Trethwr, *s. m.—pl.* trethwyr ([illegible] taxer.

Treulfawr, *a.* (traul) Expensive; [illegible]

Treulfawredd, *s. m.* (treulfawr) E[illegible]

Treulgadw, *v. a.* (traul—cadw) T[illegible] consuming.

Treulgar, *a.* (traul) Profuse, or pr[illegible]

Treulgarwch, *s. m.* (treulgar) Pro[illegible]

Treuliad, *s. m.* (traul) Consum[illegible] pending; digestion.

Treuliadwy, *a.* (traul) Capable of [illegible]

Treuliaw, *v. a.* (traul) To consume[illegible] to expend; to digest; to be wa[illegible]

> [illegible]
>
> The tooth has [illegible] destroying the [illegible]

Treuliawd, *s. m.* (traul) Expence; [illegible]

Treuliedig, *a.* (treuliad) Consumed[illegible]

Treuliedydd, *s. m.—pl. t.* ion (tre[illegible] sumer; an expender.

Treuliwr, *s. m.—pl.* treulwyr ([illegible] consumer; an expender; a dig[illegible]

Trew, *s. m.* (tra) A sneeze, the act[illegible]

> [illegible]
>
> Nor one sneeze nor two will end in death.
>
> [illegible]
>
> Nor one sneeze nor two will [illegible]

Trewi, *v. n.* (trew) To sneeze, to s[illegible]

Trewiad, *s. m.* (trew) A sneezing; [illegible]

Trewlwch, *s. m.* (trew—llwch) Sne[illegible]

Trewydd, *s. m.* (traw) A push forwa[illegible] or a driving to a distance.

> [illegible]
>
> While foam-covered wave hold in [illegible] [illegible]

Trewyddiad, *s. m.* (trewydd) A pushing forward, a pushing off, a driving to a distance.

Trewyddu, *v. a.* (trewydd) To push forward, to push off, to drive to a distance.

> Y ddalen a drewydd gwynt,
> Gwae hi ei thynged
> Hen hi, eleni ganed '

> This leaf that is *driven onward* by the wind, woe to it its fate: old is it, this year born' *Llywarch Hen.*

Trewyn, *s. m.* (traw) A means of leading away; persuasion.

Trewynawl, *a.* (trewyn) Persuasive; diverting.

Trewyniad, *s. m.* (trewyn) A persuading, an averting or leading from; persuasion.

Trewynu, *v. a.* (trewyn) To persuade, to dissuade, to prevail with; to part those who fight; to pacify.

Trewynwr, *s. m.—pl.* trewynwyr (trewyn—gwr) One who leads; a persuader.

> Pob barnwr, trewynwr trin,
> Dysgwch.—

> Every judge, and *pacifier* of broils, instruct.— *W. Middleton.*

Trewynydd, *s. m.—pl. t.* ion (trewyn) Persuader

Trewynyddiaeth, *s. m.* (trewynydd) The office of a persuader or pacificator.

Trewynyn, *s. m.* (trewyn) Yellow loose-strife.

Tri, *s. m.—pl. t.* oedd (ty—rhi) That is firm, fixed, permanent, or in continuity; three. *a.* Three. The number three was adopted, by the ancient Britons, as a means of facilitating the use of oral tradition; consequently a great deal of their historical memorials, and moral maxims, have been put into the form, which from the number of articles classed together under each head, are called TRIOEDD, or *Triades.*

> Tri dyn y sydd: dyn i Dduw, a wna dda dros ddrwg; dyn i ddyn, a wna dda dros dda, a drwg dros ddrwg; a dyn i ddiawl, a wna ddrwg dros dda.

> There are *three* sorts of men: a man to God, who does good for evil; a man to man, who does good for good, and evil for evil; and a man to the devil, who does evil for good. *Barddas.*

> Tri dyn a wnant cyfanneddle bont: bardd, gof, a thelynawr.

> There are *three* persons who create society where they are: a bard, a smith, and a harper. *Trioedd.*

> Tri yw Duw Celi, colofn deon,
> Trwy rad, ar un nad, eiriaid canon:
> Trech yw ei Tad nef, naf glwlmou radau,
> No'r creaduriau gorau gwrou.

> The God of Mystery is *Three*, the support of emanated beings, through grace, and one benign, the theme of song: More powerful is one, the Father of heaven, Lord of glorious attributes, than the creatures of excelling virtue. *Casnodyn.*

Triad, *s. m.* (tri) A forming a triad.

Triadawl, *a.* (triad) Belonging to a triad.

Triadu, *v. a.* (triad) To make into three.

Triaelawd, *s. m.* (tri—aelawd) That consists of three members. *a.* Consisting of three members

Triaelodawg, *a.* (triaelawd) Of three members.

Triannawg, *a.* (triant) Having a triad.

Triannawl, *a.* (triant) Tertian; triadic.

Trianniad, *s. m.* (triant) A forming a triad.

Triannu, *v.* (triant) To tertiate; to make a triad

Triant, *s. m.* (tri) That is in three; a triad.

Triarbymtheg, *s. m.* (tri—ar—pymtheg) Eighteen. *a.* Eighteen, or consisting of eighteen.

Triarddeg, *s. m.* (tri—ar—deg) Thirteen.

Triawd, *s. m.* (tri) A forming a triad.

Triawg, *a.* (tri) Having three, of three.

Triawl, *a.* (tri) Belonging to three or triad. '*Y trawl Duw*,' the triadic God.

Triban, *s. m.—pl. t.* au (tri—ban) That consists of three parts; a triplet, or verse of three lines

> Mesurau cyn cof y bernir y gorchanau, a thriban milwr, a chyhydedd; sef oeddynt cyn oes oesoedd.

> Metres from time immemorial are primary cantos, warrior *triplet*, and recitative, judged to be; that is they were from age of ages. *Barddas.*

Tribanawg, *a.* (triban) Of three parts; triplet.

Tribanawl, *a.* (triban) Triplicate; tripled.

Tribandawd, *s. m.* (triban) Triplicity.

Tribaniad, *s. m.* (triban) Triplication.

Tribaniaeth, *s. m.* (triban) Triplicity.

> Triban Milwr—nid o gyhydedd, eithr o'i deibanlaeth, ac ei fraint o awdl a brithfan, y tyf ei enw.

> The warrior triplet, not from equal metricity, but from its *triplicity*, and its property of rhyme and varied verse arises its character. *Barddas.*

Tribanu, *v. a.* (triban) To triplicate; to triple.

Tribedd, *s. m.—pl. t.* i (tri—bedd) That has three feet; a tripod. *a.* Three-footed.

Triblaen, *s. m.* (tri—blaen) That has three points

Tribys, *s. m.* (tri—bys) That has three fingers.

Tribysig, *a.* (tribys) Of three fingers.

> Hwch trigaeaf tribysig:—Hwch dribysigyn ei hysgwydd, ac yn ei hais, ac yn ei chlun, a gaiff y brenin yn ddawnbwyd gauaf.

> A sow of three winters *three fingers in thickness*:—A sow of *three fingers* in her shoulder, and in her ribs, and in her haunch, shall the king have as a winter's provision-gift. *Welsh Laws.*

Trichanfed, *a.* (trichant) Three hundredth.

Trichanmil, *s. m.* (trichant—mil) The number of three hundred thousand. *a.* Three hundred thousand.

Trichanmilfed, *a.* (trichanmil) Three hundred thousandth.

Trichant, *s. m.* (tri—cant) Three hundred.

Trichanwaith, *s. pl.* (trichant—gwaith) Three hundred times. *a.* Three hundred times.

> Dy ysgwyd rhwygwyd rhaged trichanwaith
> Trichan-gwyth gyfarfod.

> Thy shield before thee torn has been *three hundred times* in three hundred wrathful conflicts. *Ll. P. Moch, i R. Gryg.*

Trichorn, *s. m.* (tri—corn) That has three horns.

Trichorniawg, *a.* (trichorn) Having three horns.

Tridant, *s. m.* (tri—dant) A trident. *a.* Three-toothed.

Trideg, *s. m.* (tri—deg) Three tens; thirty.

Trideintiawg, *a.* (tridant) Having three teeth.

Tridiau, *s. m.* (tri—diau) The space of three days

Tridieuawl, *a.* (tridiau) Relating to three days.

Tridincod, *s. m.* (tri—dincod) That has three pips or seeds. *a.* Having three pips.

Tridincodawg, *a.* (tridincod) Having three seeds; a medlar with three seeds.

Tridull, *s. m.* (tri—dull) That is of three forms. *a.* Triform.

Tridulliawg, *a.* (tridull) Having three forms.

Tridyblyg, *s. m.* (tri—dyblyg) That has three folds. *a.* Threefold:

> Wyf hen, wyf unig, wyf anelwig oer,
> Gwedi gwely celmyg;
> Wyf truan, wyf tridyblyg.

> I am old, I am alone, I am debilitated and cold, after the magnificent couch; I am wretched, I am *bent three times.* *Llywarch Hen.*

Tridyblygawl, *a.* (tridyblyg) Triplicate.

Tridyblygiad, *s. m.* (tridyblyg) Triplication.

Tridyblygu, *v. a.* (tridyblyg) To triplicate.

Tridyn, *s. pl.* (tri—dyn) Three persons.

> Rhin tridyn canwyn ei clyw.

> The secret of *three persons* a hundred persons will hear it. *Adage.*

Trifforch, *s. m.* (tri—fforch) That has three prongs. *a.* Three pronged.

Trifforchawg, *a.* (trifforch) Three-pronged.

Trifforchi, *v. a.* (trifforch) To trifurcate.

Trig, *s. m.* (tri—ig) A stay, a fixed state.

Triged, *s. m.* (trig) A staying, tarrying, or remaining fixed.

Trigadied, *s. m.—pl.* trigadieid (triged) A sojourner, inhabitant, or dweller.

Trigadwy, *a.* (triged) Capable of staying, dwelling or remaining.

[illegible]

He preserved [illegible], against [illegible], severely. L. G. Cothi.

Trigeaaf, *s. m.* (tri—gauaf) That is of three winters. *a.* Of three winters old.

Trigaw, *v. a.* (trig) To stay, to tarry; to be stationary; to remain; also to dwell; to starve, to perish, as with cold. *Nis gallaf yr trigiaw*, I cannot for the life of me.

[illegible]
A thrig yno.

[illegible] thy country and tarry there. Adage.

[illegible]

He stays where he is not invited. Adage.

[illegible]

After the circuit is ended, let the [illegible] of the family come upon the king, and let [illegible] abide with him until the end of the year. Welsh Laws.

[illegible]

Why should we be [illegible]; there is not a place to be [illegible] from the [illegible] of dread; there is not a place to be [illegible] away with singing. G. ab yr Ynad Coch.

Trigawl, *a.* (trig) Tarrying, abiding, dwelling. Trigolion, inhabitants.

Trigfa, *s. f.—pl.* trigfeydd (trig) An abode.

Trigfan, *s. f.—pl. t.* au (trig) A dwelling-place.

Trigfanawl, *a.* (trigfan) Belonging to a dwelling-place or a residence.

Trigfaniad, *s. m.* (trigfan) A making a dwelling-place; a fixing a residence.

Trigfanu, *v. a.* (trigfan) To make a dwelling-place; to fix a residence.

Trigiad, *s. m.* (trig) A tarrying, an abiding.

Trigiannawl, *a.* (trigiant) Residentiary.

Trigianniad, *s. m.* (trigiant) A residing.

Trigiannu, *v. a.* (trigiant) To make a residence, to reside, to dwell, to inhabit.

Trigiannus, *a.* (trigiant) Residentiary, resiant.

Trigiannydd, *s. m.—pl. t.* ion (trigiant) An inhabitant.

Cia ty heb drigiannydd.

Odious is a house without an inhabitant. Catwg.

Trigiant, *s. m.* (trig) Residence, habitation.

Trigias, *s. f.* (trig) Residence, habitation.

Trigiaw, *v. a.* (trig) To stay, to tarry, to abide. '*Cybydd ni thrigiaf*,' a miser I will not remain.

Trigiawd, *s. m.* (trig) A residing, a dwelling.

Trigiawdwr, *s. m.—pl.* trigiawdwyr (trigiawd—gwr) A resider, a dweller; an inhabitant.

Trigiawdr, *s. m.—pl. t.* on (trigiawd) A resiant, a resident, a dweller.

Trigiedig, *a.* (trigied) Being dwelled in.

Trigle, *s. f.—pl. t.* oedd (trig—lle) A dwelling-place

Trilliw, *s. m.* (tri—lliw) That is of three colours. *a.* Tri-coloured. Tansy violet, or heart's ease.

Trilliwiawg, *a.* (trilliw) Of three colours.

Trillwyf, *s. m.* (tri—llwyf) That has three stories. *a.* Of three stories.

Trillwyfan, *s. m.* (trillwyf) That is of three stories. *a.* Of three stories.

Trillwyfanawg, *a.* (trillwyfan) Of three stories.

Trimarch, *s. pl.* (tri—march) Three horses. *a.* Of three horses.

Trimarchfen, *s. f.—pl. t.* i (trimarch) A car or cart drawn by three horses.

Trimarchwyr, *s. pl. aggr.* (trimarch—gwyr) Men driving three horses.

Trimis, *s. m.* (tri—mis) [illegible] *a.* Three [illegible]

Trimisawg, *a.* (trimis) Having three [illegible]

Trimis, *s. m.* (tri—mis) A space of [illegible]

Trimisawl, *a.* (trimis) Of [illegible]

Trimisyr, *s. m.* (trimis) [illegible]

Trimisyriad, *s. c.—pl.* [illegible] is three months old.

Trin, *s. f.—pl. t.* oedd (tri—in) [illegible] or continual; that is [illegible] the act of meddling, or handling [illegible] or conducting any affair; labour, [illegible] quarrel, a battle.

[illegible]

A [illegible] grows to a quarrel.

Trin, *v. a.* (tri—in) To meddle, [illegible] manage, to conduct any business [illegible] at; to quarrel; to trim, or [illegible] to dress land: Trin [illegible] rea.

[illegible]

He [illegible] in the world, [illegible] to the end of [illegible] life.

Trinai, *s. c.—pl.* triniaion (trin) [illegible] conducts an affair; a bustler; [illegible]

[illegible]

The [illegible] away, with the [illegible]

There were mighty [illegible] of the Hebrews, the [illegible]

Trinaw, *v. a.* (trin) To meddle; [illegible] affair; to bustle; to conflict.

Trinawg, *a.* (trin) Full of bustle [illegible]

Trinawl, *a.* (trin) Bustling; [illegible]

Trindawd, *s. m.* (trin) The Trinity.

[illegible]

Attempt not to seek for the Trinity [illegible] in the Unity.

Trindodawl, *a.* (trindawd) Trinitarian [illegible]

Trindodaeth, *s. m.* (trindawd) Trinitarian [illegible]

Trindodi, *v. a.* (trindawd) To [illegible]

Trindodydd, *s. m.—pl. t.* ion (trindawd) [illegible] tarian.

Trined, *s. m.* (trin) A trinity, [illegible]

[illegible]

A [illegible] with [illegible]

[illegible]

May the Trinity God [illegible]

Tringar, *a.* (trin) Intermeddling, [illegible]

Tringarwch, *s. m.* (tringar) A [illegible]

Triniad, *s. m.* (trin) A meddling, a [illegible] managing, a dealing; an intermeddling; quarrelling.

Triniaeth, *s. m.* (trin) A meddling [illegible] ment; dealing; an undertaking, [illegible]

Triniaw, *v. a.* (trin) To persevere in [illegible] to meddle; to manage, to conduct, [illegible]

Triniawl, *a.* (trin) Managing, conducting [illegible]

Triniator, *ger.* (triniad) In managing [illegible]

Triniedig, *a.* (triniad) Managed, conducted.

Triniedigaeth, *s. m.* (triniedig) Management; cultivation.

Trinitor, *sup.* (trin) To be managing.

Triniwr, *s. m.—pl.* triniwyr (trin—gwr) A manager, or one who carries on any affair.

Trinogaeth, *s. m.* (triniawg) The act of managing, or carrying on any dealing; traffick.

Trinydd, *s. m.—pl. t.* ion (trin) A manager.

Triochr, *s. m.* (tri—ochr) That has three sides.

Triochrawg, *a.* (triochr) Having three sides.

Triochri, *v. a.* (triochr) To render trilateral.

Triochriad, *s. m.* (triochr) A rendering trilateral.

Triochryn, *s. m.* (triochr) That is trilateral.

Triodawl, *a.* (triawd) Belonging to a triad.

Triodi, *v. a.* (triawd) To form a triad.

Triogi, *v. a.* (triawg) To render of three.

Triogiad, *s. m.* (triawg) A rendering to consist of three.

Trioldeb, *s. m.* (triawl) The state of being tertiated.

Trioli, *v. a.* (triawl) To tertiate.

Trioliad, *s. m.* (triawl) A tertiation.

Trip, *s. m.—pl. t.* iau (ty—rhip) A trip.

Tripa, *s. c.* (trip) The bowels or guts.

Tripiad, *s. m.* (trip) A tripping, a falling.

Tripian, *v. a.* (trip) To be tripping.

Tripiaw, *v. a.* (trip) To trip, to stumble.

> A dreisio gwan, o'i drot is cil,
> E dripia Mab Duw'r epil.
>
> He that oppresses the weak, by turning him behind, the Son of God *will cause* his race to *fall*. *Sefnyn.*

Triphen, *s. m.* (tri—pen) That has three heads. *a.* Three headed.

Triphlyg, *s. m.* (tri—plyg) That has three folds. *a.* Triplicate.

Triphlygiad, *s. m.* (triphlyg) Triplication.

Trisill, *s. m.* (tri—sill) That consists of three elements or syllables. *a.* Of three syllables.

Trisillawg, *a.* (trisill) Having three syllables.

Trist, *a.* (ty—rhist) Pensive, sorrowful, sad.

> Trwch iawn yth farnaf, Dafydd;
> Trist a fu Dyddgu o'r dydd.
>
> Very unlucky I deem thee, David, *sorrowful* was Dyddgu of the day. *Gr. Gryg.*

Tristâad, *s. m.* (trist) A sorrowing.

Tristâawl, *a.* (tristâu) Tending to deject.

Tristau, *v. a.* (trist) To render sorrowful, to become sad or pensive.

Tristedd, *s. m.* (trist) Pensiveness, sadness, dejection.

Tristiad, *s. m.* (trist) A sorrowing, a rueing.

Tristiaw, *v. a.* (trist) To cause sorrow or sadness.

Tristlawn, *a.* (trist) Sorrowful, or rueful.

Tristlondeb, *s. m.* (tristlawn) Ruefulness.

Tristlonder, *s. m.* (tristlawn) Ruefulness.

Tristlondra, *s. m.* (tristlawn) Ruefulness.

Tristlonedd, *s. m.* (tristlawn) Sorrowfulness.

Tristloni, *v. a.* (tristlawn) To render sorrowful; to become sad or rueful.

Tristlonrwydd, *s. m.* (tristlawn) Sorrowfulness.

Tristwch, *s. m.* (trist) Pensiveness, or sadness.

> Adfyd pob hir dristwch.
>
> Every lasting sorrow is adversity. *Adage.*

Tristyd, *s. m.* (trist) Sadness, or sorrow.

Tritham, *s. m.* (tri—tam) That consists of three bites or bits.

Trithamaid, *s. m.* (tritham) An epithet for a large sort of oyster.

Trithant, *s. m.* (tri—tant) That consists of three strings, the rebeck.

Trithri, *s. m.* (tri *repeated*) Three times three.

Trithro, *s. m.* (tri—tro) That is of three turns.

Trithroed, *s. m.* (tri—troed) That consists of three feet. *a.* Three-footed.

Trithroediawg, *a.* (trithroed) Three-footed.

Trithu, *s. m.* (tri—tu) That is of three sides.

Trithuawg, *a.* (trithu) Trilateral, three-sided.

Triugain, *s. m.* (tri—ugain) Sixty. *a.* Sixty.

Triugaint, *s. m.* (triugain) Sixty. *a.* Sixty.

Triugeinfed, *s. m.* (triugain) Sixtieth. *a.* Sixtieth.

Triugeiniawl, *a.* (triugain) Sexagesimal.

> March glas teithiawl triugeiniawl.
>
> A grey horse perfect and *of the value of threescore pence.* *Welsh Laws.*

Triugeinwaith, *s. pl.* (triugain—gwaith) Threescore times. *a.* Threescore times.

Triunaw, *v. a.* (tri—unaw) To unite three in one.

Triunawd, *s. m.* (tri—unawd) A Trinity.

Triunawl, *a.* (tri—unawl) Triune.

Triundawd, *s. m.* (tri—undawd) A Trinity in unity

> Goleua'n ffydd galon ffawd,
> Trwy iawnder, Duw triundawd.
>
> Illume our faith, with a happy heart, through righteousness, thou God of *Trinity in unity.* *T. Ll. Deio Powel.*

Tro, *s. m.—pl. t.* ion (ty—rho) A turn; a while, a time; a lax. *Tro da*, a good turn; *o dro i dro*, from time to time; *tros dro*, for a while; *y tro yma*, this time; *rhai troion*, sometimes; *rhyw dro*, sometime.

Tröad, *s. m.—pl. t.* au (tro) A turning; conversion.

> ——Ar wydd tir ar,
> A glyw droadau'r glosw drydar,
> Oll o'i galon cyll y galar.
>
> On the border of the cultivated land, he who hears the *turns* of the sprightly chirping, entirely from his heart he will lose his grief. *C. Buttom.*

Tröadwy, *a.* (tröad) Capable of turning.

Tröawl, *a.* (tro) Turning, rolling, revolving.

Troch, *s. f.—pl. t.* ion (tro—och) A spray; a lave.

Troch, *a.* (*f.* of trwch) Cut, broken; maimed; unlucky, desperate, fell.

> Cymynid ar dres droch lynges lyr.
>
> Cut off was on a sudden the *fell* fleet of the torrent. *Gwalchmai.*

Trochadwy, *a.* (troch) Capable of being bathed.

Trochawl, *a.* (troch) Bathing, immersing.

Trochedig, *a.* (troch) Bathed, immersed.

Trochedigaeth, *s. f.* (trochedig) The act of bathing

Trochfa, *s. f.—pl.* trochfeydd (troch) A bathing-place; a bathing.

Trochgader, *s. f.* (troch—cader) A duckingstool.

Trochi, *v. a.* (troch) To immerse, to dip, to duck, to plunge, to bathe.

> Lluest Cadwallawn ar Feiuin,
> Llew llu lluosawg ei werin,
> Twrf mawr trochas ei orddin.
>
> The camp of Cadwalloh on Meiuin, the lion of the host of numerous train, a great tumult drenched his skirt. *Llywarch Hen.*

Trochiad, *s. m.—pl. t.* au (troch) An immersion.

> Tres trachwres trochiad ei wrymder.
>
> The bustle of ambition is the *immersion* of his energy. *Cynddelw.*

Trochiant, *s. m.* (troch) A splashing; immersion.

Trochion, *s. pl.* (troch) Splashings; suds, lather.

Trochioni, *v. a.* (trochion) To raise a lather.

Trochionllyd, *a.* (trochion) Abounding with froth.

Trochwr, *s. m.—pl.* trochwyr (troch—gwr) An immerser, a bather.

Trochydd, *s. m.—pl. t.* ion (troch) A dipper, a plunger, a diver; a bather. *Trochydd mawr*, the great northern diver; *trochydd bach*, the grey speckled diver; *trochydd gwddfgoch*, the

Troellhoel, *s. f.—pl. t.* ion (troell—hoel) A screw-nail.
Troellhoeliad, *s. m.* (troellhoel) A screwing.
Troellhoeliaw, *v. a.* (troellhoel) To screw.
Troelli, *v. a.* (troell) To put in a whirling motion; to turn as a whirl, or wheel; to turn as a screw; to screw. *Gwagr troelli*, a sieve used in cleaning corn.
Troelliad, *s. m.—pl. t.* au (troell) A whirling.
Troelliannawl, *a.* (troelliant) Of a whirling or spinning motion.
Troelliannu, *v. a.* (troelliant) To produce a whirling motion.
Troelliant, *s. m.* (troell) A whirling motion.
Troellig, *s. f.* (troell) The spurrey.
Troellrych, *s. m.—pl. t.* au (troell—rhych) The counterpart of a screw, or the groove that receives it.
Troellrychiad, *s. m.* (troellrych) A grooving or forming the concave part of a screw.
Troellrychiaw, *v. a.* (troellrych) To groove the concave part of a screw.
Troellwaith, *s. m.* (troell—gwaith) Wheel-work; the movement of a clock or watch.
Troellweithiad, *s. m.* (troellwaith) A making of wheel-work.
Troellweithiaw, *v. a.* (troellwaith) To make wheel-work.
Troellweithiwr, *s. m.—pl.* troellweithiwyr (troellwaith—gwr) One who makes wheel-work.
Troellymadrawdd, *s. m.—pl.* troellymadroddion (troell—ymadrawdd) A figurative speech, tropology.
Troellymadroddi, *v. a.* (troellymadrawdd) To express in figurative speech.
Troellymadroddiad, *s. m.* (troellymadrawdd) A making use of figurative speech.
Troen, *s. f.—pl. t.* au (tro) A turn; a twirl; a while, a good while. *Ni buaist er ys troen yma*, thou hast not been here this good while. *Powys.*
Troetys, *s. m.—pl. t.* an (troed—ys) A snare. *Sil.*
Troeth, *s. f.* (trwyth) Wash; lye; urine.
Troethai, *s. c.* (troeth) A chamber pot.
Troethbair, *a.* (troeth—pair) Diuretical.
Troethi, *v. a.* (troeth) To void urine.
Troethiad, *s. m.* (troeth) A voiding urine.
Troethlif, *s. m.* (troeth—llif) A diabetes.
Trofa, *s. f.—pl.* troféydd (tro) A place of turning or revolving; a turn; a tropic; a glance.

> Gweiais, ar drofa golwg,
> Gwen ber.——
>
> I saw, with a *glance* of the eye, a sweet smile. *Bedo Brwynllys.*

Trofaad, *s. m.* (trofâu) A turning; a revolving; a transition.
Trofâawl, *a.* (trofâu) Turning; flexuous.
Trofâedd, *s. m.* (trofa) Tortuosity, flexure.
Trofaeg, *s. f.—pl. t.* au (trofa) A trope.
Trofan, *s. f.—pl. t.* au (tro—man) A tropic.
Trofanawl, *a.* (trofan) Tropical, of the tropic.
Trofâu, *v. a.* (trofa) To make a turn.

> Mal neidr fyddar yn trofâu,
> Tan gau ei chlustiau cyndyn.
>
> Like the deaf adder *winding round*, with closing her repulsive ears. *Edm. Prys.*

Trofâus, *a.* (trofa) Flexuous; tortuous.
Trofawl, *a.* (trawf) Tending to pass over; transitive; tending forward.
Trofedig, *a.* (trawf) Being made transitive; being led forward; being instructed, disciplined. *Trofedigion neu ewenyddion*, disciples or students. *Barddas.*
Trofedigaeth, *s. f.—pl. t.* au (trofedig) The act of transition; the act or state of forwarding; a discipleship.
Trofiad, *s. m.—pl. t.* au (trawf) A transition; a passage; a clause. *Trofiadau caniadaeth*, the transitions of music.
Trofiant, *s. m.* (trawf) A pass over; transition.
Trofus, *a.* (trawf) Tending to pass over.
Trofusder, *s. m.* (trofus) A transitive state.
Trohidl, *s. m.* (tro—hidl) An instrument for the twisting of ropes.
Troi, *v. a.* (tro) To turn. *Troi tir*, to plough land: *Troi âr*, to chide; *tro arni*, chide her.

> Euawg a dry y cellwair yn wir.
>
> The guilty will *turn* the jesting to truth. *Adage.*
>
> Gwae a dro o glan i glan,
> Ac ni fedda beth ei hun.
>
> Woe to him that *turns* from side to side, and who possesses nothing for himself. *Adage.*
>
> Try allan ddynion triflu,
> A sydd, a fydd, ac a fu—
> Ger bron ynad.
>
> *There will turn out* of men three hosts, that be, that will be, and that have been, in the presence of the judge. *Grn. Owain.*
>
> Grym a gwendid, troent o'r enid.
>
> Strength and weakness, *they turn* from the birth. *Adage.*

Troiad, *s. m.* (troi) A turning, a circling.
Troiadur, *s. m.—pl. t.* on (troiad) That effects a turning or transition.
Troiadr, *s. m.—pl. t.* on (troiad) That forms a transition or turn.

> Cefais er na fedrais fydr,
> Gyfarid draw a'r gerdd droiadr.
>
> I obtained, though I knew no metre, a contact there with the song *that abounds with transition.* *I. ab R. ab Ieuan Llwyd.*

Tròl, *s. c.—pl. t.* ian (ty—rhòl) A cylinder, a roller; a roll; a small cart, otherwise called *càr tròl*; also, a round fat man. *Berfa dròl*, a wheelbarrow.
Tròlaid, *s. f.—pl.* troleidiau (tròl) A cart load.
Tròlaidd, *a.* (tròl) Cylindrical, like a roll.
Tròlen, *s. f.* (tròl) A roundlet; a fat female.
Tròliad, *s. m.* (tròl) A trolling, a rolling.
Tròlian, *v. a.* (tròl) To troll, to keep rolling.
Tròliaw, *v. a.* (tròl) To troll, to trundle.
Tròliedig, *a.* (tròliad) Trolled; trundled.
Tròliwr, *s. m.—pl.* troliwyr (tròl—gwr) A troller; one who rolls; a trundler.
Tròlyn, *s. m. dim.* (tròl) A roller; a fat one. *Tròlyn o ddyn*, a chubby person.
Tròlynaidd, *a.* (tròlyn) Of the form of a roll.
Tròlynawg, *a.* (tròlyn) Cylindrical.
Tròlyniad, *s. m.* (tròlyn) A making a roll.
Tròlynu, *v. a.* (tròlyn) To form a cylinder.
Trom, *a.* (*f.* of trwm) Heavy, weighty; sad.
Tromfron, *s. f.* (bron) A grief-oppressed breast.
Tromgad, *s. f.* (trom—cad) A main battle.
Tromleddf, *a.* (trom—lleddf) Gravely inflective, a term in prosody for syllables like *ceirw*.
Tromsain, *s. f.—pl.* tromseiniau (trom—sain) A grave accent.
Tron, *s. f.—pl. t.* au (tro—on) A circle, a round; a throne.
Trònawl, *a.* (trawn) Transcendent.
Trònawl, *a.* (tròn) Relating to a periphery.
Tròni, *v. a.* (trawn) To render superior.
Tròni, *v. a.* (tròn) To rim; to form a periphery.
Tròniad, *s. m.* (trawn) A transcending.

Trôniad, *s. m.* (trôn) A forming a circle, round.

Tros, *s. m.—pl. t.* iau (tro—os) That is over or placed across, a transverse bar; a lock.

Tros, *prep.* (tro—os) Over; for, instead of. *adv.* Over. *Teg dros ben*, supremely fair; *da dros ben*, excellently good: *Ei drosto ar redeg*, thou wilt go over it on full speed.—*Trosaf, trostof*, over or for me; *trosot, trostot*, over or for thee; *troso, trosto*, over or for him and it; *trosi, trosti*, over or for her; *trosom, trostom*, over or for us; *trosoch, trostoch*, over or for you; *trosynt, trostynt*, over or for them.

Dyclid chwant dros ben y cant.

Cupidity snatches *over* a hundred. *Adage.*

Gwna dda dros ddrwg, uffern ni'th dwg.

Do good *for* evil, hell will not have thee. *Adage.*

A ddadlo dros ei fai, a wna ddau ddiawl o un cythraul.

He that pleads *for* his fault makes two devils out of one fiend. *Adage.*

Ni doddynt dros for etwaeth,
Pobl annyfaeth Nanhyfer.

They come not over sea again, the uncivilized people of Nanhyver. *Meilyr.*

Trosadwy, *a.* (tros) Capable of being driven over.

Trosedig, *a.* (tros) Diverted, or turned aside.

Trosedd, *s. m.* (tros) Transgression, trespass.

Troseddadwy, *a.* (trosedd) Transgressible.

Troseddawg, *a.* (trosedd) Full of transgression.

Troseddawl, *a.* (trosedd) Transgressing.

Troseddedig, *a.* (trosedd) Being transgressed.

Troseddiad, *s. m.—pl. t.* au (trosedd) Transgression.

Troseddu, *v. a.* (trosedd) To transgress; to err.

Troseddwr, *s. m.—pl.* troseddwyr (trosedd—gwr) A transgressor.

Trosel, *s. m.—pl. t.* i (tros) A plashed fence.

Troselu, *v. a.* (trosel) To plash a fence.

Trosenw, *s. m.—pl. t.* au (tros—enw) A name that is put for another.

Trosenwad, *s. m.* (trosenw) Transnomination.

Trosenwawl, *a.* (trosenw) Relating to transnomination.

Trosenwi, *v. a.* (trosenw) To put one name for another.

Trosfa, *s. f.—pl.* trosfeydd (tros) A place for turning to. *Trosfa gyffredin*, a common for turning cattle to.

Trosfynediad, *s. m.* (tros—mynediad) Metabasis.

Trosglud, *s. m.* (tros—clud) A conveyance over.

Trosgludaw, *v. a.* (trosglud) To carry over.

Trosgludawl, *a.* (trosglud) Transporting.

Trosgludiad, *s. m.* (trosglud) A transportation.

Trosglwydd, *s. m.* (tros—clwydd) A carrying over; a transfer; a conveyance.

Trosglwyddadwy, *a.* (trosglwydd) Transferrable.

Trosglwyddaw, *v. a.* (trosglwydd) To transport; to carry over; to transfer; to convey.

Trosglwyddawl, *a.* (trosglwydd) Transferring.

Trosglwyddedig, *a.* (trosglwydd) Transported; transferred; conveyed over; consigned. *Trosglwyddedigion*, those that are carried over.

Trosglwyddedigaeth, *s. m.* (trosglwyddedig) The act of conveying over or transferring.

Trosglwyddiad, *s. m.—pl. t.* au (trosglwydd) A carrying over, a transporting; a transferring; a consigning.

Trosglwyddwr, *s. m.—pl.* trosglwyddwyr (trosglwydd—gwr) A transporter.

Trosgl, *a.* (*f.* of trwsgl) Clumsy, or stumbling.

Angen y gyhydedd drosgl yw [illegible]; a hyd y [illegible] o bedwar hyd i wyth bein.

The requisite of the clumsy metricity is a verse of six syllables; and the length of the stanza from four verses to eight. *[illegible].*

Trosi, *v. a.* (tros) To turn out, to send over, to convey; to move onward; to move about. *Trosi gwartheg*, to drive out cattle; *Troi a throsi*, to turn and move about: *Trosi parth a henaint*, to verge towards old age.

Eich chwerthin a drosa yn wylaw.

Your laughter will *turn* to weeping. *Cyd [illegible].*

Morganwg——
Lle trosa ran o'm hanerch.

Morganwg, where a portion of my fondness *strays*. *D. ab Gwilym.*

Trosi ei hwyliau a orug Vespasian, a disgynu yn aberth Totness a orugant; ac wedi caffael tir oandd[illegible], cyrchu a wnaeth gaer Penhwylcoed.

To hoist his sails was what Vespasian did; and descend in the port of Totness did they; and when they had reached land, they approached the castle of Penhwylcoed. *Gr. ab Arthur.*

Troso, *pronom. prep.* (tros) Over a person or thing; for or on account of a person or thing.

Trosodd, *prep.* (tros) Over; beyond. *adv.* Over.

Trosol, *s. m.—pl. t.* ion (traws—ol) A lever; a bar, or bolt, which is placed across any thing.

Mal wy ar drosol.

Like an egg on a pole. *Adage.*

Trosoli, *v. a.* (trosol) To work with a lever.

Trosoliad, *s. m.* (trosol) A working a lever.

Trosoliaw, *v. a.* (trosol) To work a lever.

Trosoliedig, *a.* (trosol) Being worked as a lever.

Trosolwaew, *s. f.* (trosol—gwaew) A lever-beam.

Trosolwydd, *s.* (trosol—gwydd) Wooden leaver.

Trosten, *s. f.—pl. t.* i (trawst) A long rod.

Trosto, *pronom. prep.* (tros) Over a person or thing; for or on account of any one.

Pawb drosto ei hunan, Duw drosom ni gyd.

Every body *for* himself, God *for* us all. *Adage.*

Haws dywedyd mynydd na myned trosto.

It is easier to say mountain than to go *over* it. *Adage.*

Trostr, *s. m.—pl. t.* au (trawst) A slider.

Gwregys y cleddyf o gordwal du, a threstrau [illegible] arno.

The girdle of the sword of black leather, with gilt *sliders* on it. *Breudd. Rhonabwy.*

Troterth, *s. m.—pl. t.* od (trawd—erth) A trotter.

Cyfrwy a roist nis caf ar warth;
Dyro eto ym drotorth.

A saddle thou didst give such as I can not have on sale; give me again a *trotter*. *T. Prys.*

Trotiad, *s.* (trawd) A trotting, a going on a trot.

Trotial, *v. a.* (trawd) To keep trotting.

Trotian, *v. a.* (trawd) To keep trotting.

Y march——
Traed tano y trotiynt.

The horse, under him feet *would continue trotting*. *Gw. Ynn Ham.*

Trotiaw, *v. a.* (trawd) To trot, to go on a trot.

Trotiawl, *a.* (trawd) Trotting, apt to trot.

Trotiwr, *s. m.—pl.* trotiwyr (trawd—gwr) One who trots, a trotter.

Troth, *s. m.* (tro—oth) That tends through.

Troth, *prep.* (tro) Through, from side to side.

Dygyrch bar carreg creg ei hadnain,
Llid y mywn lyngeel treiddiad troth main.

She assaults the top of the stone with her hoarse clamour, the wrath borne by fate let it burst *through* the rock. *Taliesin, Mic Dinbych.*

Trothi, *s. m.* (troth) A state of passing through.

Trothwy, *s. m.—pl. t.* on (troth) A threshold.

Cybydd am drothwy ty y lladron.

The miser is about the *threshold* of the house of thieves. *Adage.*

Trowynt, *s. m.—pl. t.* oedd (tro—gwynt) A whirlwind.

Tru, *s. m.* (ty—rhu) An outcast; wretchedness.

Tru, *a.* (ty—rhu) Being outcast: wretched.

Tru mòr anghall dall dell anedrian
Troseid, tray gymwedd a gymeran'.

Piteous that so indiscreetly blind the unseemly way of the transgression, which through avidity they take. *Casnodyn.*

Truad, *s. m.* (tru) A causing misery; a turning to misery or wretchedness.

Trualdd, *a.* (tru) Somewhat wretched or piteous.

Truan, *a.* (tru) Feeble, slender; poor, wretched, miserable, pitiful. *Wyt yn edrych yn druan iawn*, thou dost look very poorly. *Druan bach!* poor little thing! *Druan hwnw!* poor dear that it was! *O druan!* oh poor thing! *Truaned yw!* how miserable it is!

Gwell rhy draws no rhy druan.

Better too perverse than too *wretched*. *Adage.*

O druelnion ddagrewoedd y llithra hithau.

Of *piteous* tears she then let fall. *Dar. Merddin.*

Truanâad, *s. m.* (truanâu) A rendering miserable, a becoming miserable.

Truanaidd, *a.* (truan) Somewhat miserable.

Truanâu, *v. a.* (truan) To render wretched; to become miserable or wretched.

Truanawg, *a.* (truan) Full of wretchedness.

Trnanawl, *a.* (truan) Tending to misery.

Truander, *s. m.* (truan) Piteousness; misery.

Truanedig, *a.* (truan) Being made wretched.

Truanedd, *s. m.* (truan) Wretchedness.

Fy sylwedd, truanedd trig,
Niwl ydyw anweledig!

My substance, a *wretchedness* of existence, is only a mist invisible! *H. ab Huw Fardd Coch.*

Truaneiddiad, *s. m.* (truanaidd) A rendering miserable; a becoming wretched.

Truaneiddiaw, *v. a.* (truanaidd) To render miserable; to become miserable.

Truaneiddrwydd, *s. m.* (truanaidd) Miserableness

Truanen, *s. f. dim.* (truan) A poor little female.

Truanes, *s. f.* (truan) A wretched female.

Truaniad, *s. m.* (truan) A rendering wretched; a becoming wretched.

Truanu, *v. a.* (truan) To pity, to commiserate; to become feeble, poor, wretched, or miserable. *Truana wrtho!* have pity on him!

Truaw, *v. a.* (tru) To render piteous; to become piteous, or wretched.

Truawl, *a.* (tru) Miserable, piteous, wretched.

Truawr, *a.* (tru) Wretched, or miserable.

Gwell rhy drawe no rhy druawr.

Better is it to be too overbearing than too abject. *Catwg Ddoeth.*

Trudd, *s. m.* (tru) A break through, a burst.

Truedig, *a.* (truad) Being made wretched.

Truedd, *s. m.* (tru) Wretchedness, misery.

Trueddu, *v. a.* (truedd) To render wretched; to become miserable.

Trueddus, *a.* (truedd) Piteous, or wretched.

Trueiddiad, *s. m.* (truaidd) A rendering wretched; a becoming wretched.

Trueiddiaw, *v. a.* (trualdd) To render wretched; to become wretched.

Trueiniad, *s. m.—pl.* trueiniaid (truan) A wretched one.

Trueiniaw, *v. a.* (truan) To render miserable; to become miserable or pitiful.

Trueiniawl, *a.* (truan) Tending to misery.

Trueinig, *a.* (truan) Full of misery.

Y rhai enwir y sy drueinig ac afalwedig.

The wicked ones are *wretched* and necessitous. *Elucidarius.*

Trueinrwydd, *s. m.* (truan) Wretchedness.

Trueiniwr, *s. m.—pl.* trueinwyr (truan—gwr) A wretched man.

Trueni, *s. m.* (truan) Misery, wretchedness.

Bid lygad Duw ar drueni.

Be the eye of God on *wretchedness*. *Adage.*

Truenus, *a.* (truan) Miserable, wretched.

Truenusaw, *v. a.* (truenus) To render miserable, to become wretched.

Truenusdra, *s. m.* (truenus) Pitifulness.

Truenusedd, *s. m.* (truenus) Piteousness.

Truenusrwydd, *s. m.* (truenus) Miserableness.

Truenyn, *s. m. dim.* (truan) A poor little wretch.

Trugar, *a.* (tru—car) Compassionate, or merciful.

Tri dyn a ddylid bod yn drugar wrthynt: alltud, gweddw, ac amddifad.

Three persons that should be dealt with *mercifully*: the stranger, the widow, and the orphan. *Catwg ab Gwynlliw.*

A'th orchymynaf gàn y mawr drugar,
Pìau a gar plant Addaf.

I commend thee to the mighty *compassionate*, he that loves the children of Adam. *Cynddelw.*

Gwr a gynnail nef, gwir addef gwar,
Gwawr gwerthfawr boed trugar.

He that upholds heaven, the true mansion of peace, the precious light be he *merciful*. *Bleddyn Fardd.*

Trugarâad, *s. m.* (trugarâu) Commiseration.

Trugarâawl, *a.* (trugarâu) Commiserating.

Trugarâu, *v. a.* (trugar) Tfe commiserate.

A'm trugarawg Arglwydd, trugarâed wrthyf,
A rhi i wrtho na'm gwrthoded!

And my merciful Lord, may *he have mercy* on me; and me from him let him not reject. *Gwalchmai.*

Trugarâus, *a.* (trugarâu) Compassionate.

Trugarawg, *a.* (trugar) Merciful; pitying.

Addoli Duw yw bod yn gyfiawn, yn afydd, ac yn drugarawg.

To worship God is to be just, humble, and *merciful*. *Adage.*

Trugarawl, *a.* (trugar) Commiserating.

Trugarâwr, *s. m.—pl.* trugarâwyr (trugarâu—gwr) One who compassionates.

Trugarddawn, *s. m.* (trugar—dawn) A merciful disposition.

Glyned Duw triued yn trugarddawn â
O fawr nen Merfyniawn.

May the Trinity God continue my *gift of mercy* from the great sovereign of the tribe of Mervyn. *Ll. P. Moch.*

Trugaredig, *a.* (trugar) Compassionated.

Trugaredd, *s. m.—pl. t.* au (trugar) Compassion.

Car dy Ddew—
Athraw gwir a thrugaredd.

Love thy God, the Lord of truth and *mercy*. *Huw Dyn.*

Trugareddawg, *a.* (trugaredd) Merciful.

Trugareddawl, *a.* (trugaredd) Commiserating.

Trugareddfa, *s. f.* (trugaredd) A mercy-seat.

Trugarogrwydd, *s. m.* (trugarawg) Mercifulness.

Trul, *s. m.—pl. t.* iau (tru) A tool used for turning or trilling of holes.

Truliad, *s. m.—pl. t.* au (trul) A trilling a hole.

Truliaw, *v. a.* (trul) To trill a hole.

Trull, *s. m.* (ty—rhull) A store; a store of liquor.

Beirdd gynnull am drull, am dri llad.

Bards assembling round a *store*, round those delicacies. *Cynddelw.*

Trulliad, *s. m.—pl.* trulliaid (trull) One who serves out or draws liquor, a butler.

Y trulliad a ddyly drulliaw y llyn, a rhoddi i bawb herwydd y dylyo.

The *drawer* ought *to draw* the liquor and to give to every body according to his due. *Welsh Laws.*

Trulliadaeth, *s. m.* (trulliad) Butlership.

Trulliades, *s. f.—pl. t.* au (trulliad) A female butler.

Trulliaw, *v. a.* (trull) To serve out liquor.

Tridyn a'r trillyn yn eu trulliaw.

Three persons with the three liquors *solacing* them. *L. G. Cothi.*

Trulliedig, *a.* (trulliad) Being served with liquor

Trulliwr, *s. m.—pl.* trulliwyr (trull—gwr) A server of liquor, a butler.

Trum, *s. m.—pl. t.* iau (ty—rhum) A ridge, a back. *Trum y mynydd*, ridge of the mountain; *trum y ty*, the roof of the house; *trum grwn*, the elevated part of a ridge of land; *rhych a thrum*, furrow and ridge.

Treftad i tithau yw'r trum
Tan gastell teg ei ystum.

An inheritance for thee is the *ridge* beneath a castle of splendid aspect. *Iolo Goch.*

Trumain, *a.* (trum) Having a ridge, coped.

——Nid eiddaw o Wynedd
Namyn farn drumain fain fedd.

Of Gwynedd he owns nothing, save the *coped* heap of the narrow grave. *Einion Wan.*

Truman, *s. c.—pl.* trumain (trum) A ridge.

Gweleis drydar crain ar drumain mor.

I saw a grovelling tumult on the *ridges* of the sea. *Cynddelw.*

Trumbeithin, *s. pl.* (trum—beithin) Ridge tiles.

Trumbeithinen, *s. f.* (trumbeithin) A ridge tile.

Trumbren, *s. m.—pl. t.* i (trum—pren) A keel.

Trumiad, *s. m.—pl. t.* au (trum) A ridging.

Trumiaw, *v. a.* (trum) To ridge, to make a ridge. to cope, or to trim into a ridge. *Trumiaw grwn*, to trim or raise a ridge, in a field; *trumiaw ty*, to form the coping of a house.

Trwm yw'r plwm yn trumiaw'r plas,
To dulas tai dawiolion.

Heavy is the lead *coping* the nave, the gloomy roof of the houses of religious people. *L. Morganwg, i Fynachlog Nedd.*

Trumiawg, *a.* (trum) Having ridges; ridged.

Trumiawl, *a.* (trum) Ridging, coping.

Trumwydd, *s. m.* (trum—gwydd) A keel.

Trus, *s. m.* (ty—rhus) A ward, or a guard.

Trusi, *s. m.* (trus) That is an obstacle or guard.

Efdodes rhag tres trusi tewdor.

He put before the brunt the thickly covering *guard*. *Aneurin.*

Trusiad, *s. m.—pl.* trusiaid (trus) That wards.

Ef ysgrud, ef drud, ef drusiad.

He is of compact frame, he is daring, he is a *bulwark*. *Ll. P. Moch.*

Trusiaw, *v. a.* (trus) To ward off, to guard.

Trusiawl, *a.* (trus) Warding, or guarding.

Truth, *s. m.* (ty—rhuth) Loose unmeaning talk; flattery, fawning, wheedling.

Truthad, *s. m.* (truth) A fawning, a wheedling.

Truthadwy, *a.* (truthad) That may be wheedled.

Truthan, *s. c.—pl.* truthain (truth) A wheedler.

Y truthan a'i traethai;
Croesanaeth crocw a sonial.

The *wheedler* would declare it; sheer ribaldry would be talk. *D. ab Gwilym, i R. Meigen.*

Truthgar, *a.* (truth) Apt to fawn or to wheedle.

Truthgarwch, *s. m.* (truthgar) Aptness to fawn.

Truthiad, *s. m.—pl.* truthiaid (truth) A sycophant

Truthiaith, *s. f.* (truth—iaith) A fawning; flattering language, adulation.

Truthiaw, *v. a.* (truth) To fawn, or to wheedle.

Truthiawg, *a.* (truth) Fawning, or fondling.

Truthiawl, *a.* (truth) Apt to fawn or wheedle.

Truthiedig, *a.* (truthiad) Being wheedled.

Truthiwr, *s. m.—pl.* truthiwyr (truth—gwr) A fawner, a wheedler.

Trw, *s. m.* (ty—rhw) A turn, or whirl; a state of penetrating or pervading; that is thoroughly or quite. It is prefixed in composition.

Trw, *prep.* (ty—rhw) Through, or by.

Nid oes ini ymladd a gwyr rhaco, namyn—trw ymadroddion cleer, ceisiaw tangnefeddu ag wynt.

We have not to fight with yonder men, but, *through* open expressions, to endeavour to make peace with them. *Brut. y Brenhinedd.*

Trwb, *s. m.* (ty—rhwb) That is rubbed.

Trwc, *s. m.—pl.* trycion (trw) That is rounded; a turn; a truck.

Moes y march diawg——
Trwc lawrodd trwcwl orwch,
Trawe fal hardd, trwm fal hwch.

Give me a lazy steed, the handed truck, a truckle for your sake, a froward comely one, a lump like a sow. *Ieu. ab Rhys.*

Trwca, *s. m.—pl. t.* od (trwc) A bowl, a cup.

Trwcwl, *s. m.* (trwc) A rundle; a truckle.

Moes drwcwl—o farch——
Clustdrwm, llopandrwm, pendrist.

Give me a *truckle* of a steed, ear-drooping, heavy-footed, hanging his head. *Ieu. ab Rhys.*

Trwch, *s. m.* (ty—rhwch) A cut into, an incision; a section; a thickness or depth; a churl. *O drwch tribys*, of the depth of three fingers.

Chwannawg trwch i drin.

The *churl* is addicted to contention. *Adage.*

Trwch, *a.* (ty—rhwch) Cut; broken, maimed; unlucky; desperate, fell.

Trefnwyd hwynt f'm tra ofni;
Trwch fum gyfarfod a'r tri.

They have been ordained to frighten me extremely; I was *unlucky* to meet with the three. *D. ab Gwilym, i eiddig.*

Trwd, *s. m.* (trw) That is circulating; that pervades, or passes through.

Trwl, *s. m.—pl.* trylau (trw) A pack; a cushion; a couch. *Trwl o ddyn*, a lump of a man.

Trwli, *s. m.* (trwl) That is round and bulky. *Trwli moli*, a fat squabby woman.

Trwliad, *s. m.—pl. t.* au (trwl) A bundling up.

Trwlian, *v. a.* (trwl) To heap together; to roll together.

Trwliaw, *v. a.* (trwl) To bundle; to roll.

Trwlyn, *s. m. dim.* (trwl) A soft heap or lump. *Trwlyn o ddyn*, a fat chub of a man.

Trwm, *s. m.—pl.* trymion (ty—rhwm) That is heavy, a pressure.

O bob trwm trymaf henaint.

Of every *pressure* the most pressing is old age. *Adage.*

Trwm, *a.* (ty—rhwm) Heavy, weighty; sad.

Trymaf dial yw dirmyg.

The *heaviest* revenge is contempt. *Adage.*

Marw Morgenea, marw Cyfrenin,
Marw Morien mur trin:
Trymaf oed am dy addoed di, Ferddin!

Morgenea dead, Cyvrenin dead, Morien the bulwark of conflict dead: most *sad* the lingering that thou art left, O Merddin! *Cyfoesi Merddin.*

Trwmgalon, *s. m.* (trwm—calon) One with a heavy heart. *a.* Heavy at heart.

Afiach pob trwmgalon.

Diseased is every *heavy hearted one.* *Adage.*

Trwmorddig, *a.* (trwm—gorddig) Sullenly shy.

Trwn, *s. m.*—*pl.* trynion (trw—wn) A circle.
Trwnc, *s. m.* (ty—rhwnc) Urine; lye, or stale.
Trwncrwydd, *a.* (trwnc—rhwydd) Diuretic.
Trwncrwyddai, *s. c.* (trwncrwydd) A diuretic.
Trwodd, *prep.* (trw) Through. *adv.* Through.
Trwpa, *s. m.*—*pl. t.* od (trwb) A washing-tub; a hod; also a trollop.
Trws, *s. m.*—*pl. t.* oedd (ty—rhws) A covering garment; a trouse; dress, or habiliment.
Trwsa, *s. m.*—*pl.* trwsëydd (trws) A packet; a truss.

Ni chwery cath, ewinlew,
Dros ei blwydd, hen drwsa blew.

A cat, with nail of sure gripe, will not play beyond her year, the old *truss* of hair. *Iolo Goch.*

Trwsëyn, *s. m. dim.* (trwsa) A packet; a truss.
Trwsgl, *a.* (trwsg) Clumsy, bungling.
Trwsglaidd, *a.* (trwsgl) Somewhat clumsy.
Trwsgliaith, *s. f.* (trwsgl—iaith) Awkward speech
Trwsglyn, *s. m. dim.* (trwsgl) A bungler.
Trwsiad, *s. m.*—*pl. t.* au (trws) A dressing, a cloathing; habiliment, raiment, dress.
Trwsiadawl, *a.* (trwsiad) Relating to dress.
Trwsiadu, *v. a.* (trwsiad) To clothe, to dress.
Trwsiadus, *a.* (trwsiad) Dressed; decked out.
Trwsiaw, *v. a.* (trws) To dress; to deck, to trim, to garnish, to adorn.
Trwsiedig, *a.* (trwsiad) Dressed, or habited.
Trwsiedydd, *s. m.*—*pl. t.* ion (trwsiad) A dresser
Trwsiwr, *s. m.*—*pl.* trwsiwyr (trws—gwr) A dresser, one who prepares.
Trwst, *s. m.*—*pl.* trystiau (try—wst) A noise, a din; a sound; a rustling; a rattling.

Nid cymaint Bleddyn a'i drwst.

Bleddyn is not so great as his *noise*. *Adage.*

Trwstan, *a.* (trwst—an) Clumsy; unsteady, apt to tumble; unlucky.
Trwstanaidd, *a.* (trwstan) Somewhat clumsy.
Trwstaneiddiad, *s. m.* (trwstanaidd) A rendering rather clumsy; a becoming rather clumsy.
Trwstaneiddiaw, *v. a.* (trwstanaidd) To render somewhat clumsy; to become apt to stumble.
Trwstaneiddrwydd, *s. m.* (trwstanaidd) Clumsiness, aptness to stumble; unluckiness.
Trwstaneiddwch, *s. m.* (trwstanaidd) Clumsiness
Trwstaniad, *s. m.* (trwstan) An acting clumsily; a becoming clumsy.
Trwstanu, *v. a.* (trwstan) To act clumsily.
Trwstanwch, *s. m.* (trwstan) Clumsiness.
Trwstyll, *s. m.*—*pl. t.* on (trwst) What makes a tumult, din, or murmur.
Trwth, *s. m.*—*pl.* trythion (ty—rhwth) That is apt to expand.
Trwy, *s. m.*—*pl. t.* on (trw) A pass through.
Trwy, *prep.* (trw) Through; by, by the means of. *Trwyof*, through me; *trwyot*, through thee; *trwyo*, through him, or it; *trwyi*, through her; *trwyom*, through us; *trwyoch*, through you; *trwyynt*, through them.

Tafawd teg a â trwy y byd.

A fair tongue will go *through* the world. *Adage.*

Twyll trwy ymddiried.

Deception *through* confiding. *Adage.*

Adrawdd gwir trwy Dduw a gaf,
I'r byd, ac nis arbedaf.

Declare the truth *through* God, I shall have to do to the world, and I will not spare. *Ieuan Tew.*

Cymer drwy wychder dy ran;
Gad i ereill gadw arian.

Take *through* a nobleness of spirit thy share; leave to others to board money. *Meredydd ab Rhys.*

Mi awn at ddeuwr o'm iaith—
Trwy'r las iaen, trwy'r maen mynor,
Trwy dan maith, trwy ddonn mor.

I would resort to two persons of common speech with me, *through* the blue sheet of ice, *through* the marble stone, *through* extensive fire, *through* the waves of the sea. *L. G. Cothi.*

Trwyad, *s. m.* (trwy) Permeation, pervasion.
Trwyadl, *a.* (trwyad) Active, alert, smart, lively; playful, sportive.

Am areith drwyadl gadair gyson
Rhym gelwir gyfrwys yn llys Don.

For the *sportive* fancy of harmonious poesy, I am called skilful, in the court of Don. *Taliesin, Cadair Ceridwen.*

Trwyadledd, *s. m.* (trwyadl) Sprightliness.
Trwyadlu, *v. a.* (trwyadl) To render alert, smart, or sprightly; to become sprightly.
Trwyaw, *v. a.* (trwy) To permeate, to pervade.
Trwyawg, *a.* (trwy) Pervasive, pervading.
Trwyawl, *a.* (trwy) Tending to pervade.
Trwyd, *s. m.* (trwy) A burst, or pass through. *a.* Bursting, or passing through.

Cafid eu cetiallith, cwn cynllwyd;
Caffynt furyon forefwyd;
Caffor ymdwr am drwyd, hefelydd
Twrch terydd i ar fwyd.

Obtaining their dainty food, the grey-headed dogs; were the kites to obtain a morning meal; a gathering together will be obtained round a *pass*, like the fierce boar on his feast. *Cynddelw, i H. ab Owain.*

Y tro a aeth, i'r twrch trwyd,
I Ddafydd a addefwyd.

The fortune that befel the *bursting* boar, to David has been promised. *L. G. Cothi.*

Trwydaw, *v. a.* (trwyd) To penetrate; to burst.
Trwydawg, *a.* (trwyd) Being penetrated.
Trwydawl, *a.* (trwyd) Penetrating; bursting.
Trwydiad, *s. m.* (trwyd) A penetrating.
Trwydoll, *a.* (trwy—toll) Being burst through.
Trwydwll, *a.* (trwy—twll) Bursted through.
Trwydd, *s. m.* (trwy) A passage through; a bore
Trwydd, *prep.* (trwy) Through; by; with, or by means of. *Trwyddof*, through me; *trwyddot*, through thee; *trwyddo*, through him; *trwyddi*, through her; *trwyddy*, through it; *trwyddom*, through us; *trwyddoch*, through you; *trwyddynt*, through them.
Trwyddaw, *v. a.* (trwydd) To pass through.
Trwyddawg, *a.* (trwydd) Having a passage.
Trwyddawl, *a.* (trwydd) Tending to perforate.
Trwydded, *s. f.*—*pl. t.* au (trwydd) A passage through, a pass; a passport, freedom of passing and repassing; licence, leave; the act of passing through; reception; provision, or maintenance; fruition.

Mi a wn eu trwydded,
A'u tro a'u cerdded.

I know their *reception*, and their course and their journey. *Taliesin.*

Efrydd fydd dechreu
Dyn, dewraidd dyrfau;
A'i ddiwedd ef dian,
Angau ynged:
Ac nid oes gochel gochwerw drwydded,
Gwely anghlaear daear dudded!

Frail is the beginning of man, of gallant exploits; and his end is certain, death so closely pressing; and there is no avoiding the bitter *passage*, the uncheering bed of the earthly covering. *Meilyr ab Gwalchmai.*

Rhoddi trwydded iddo, a'i weision, o fwyd, a diawd, a dillad.

Giving a *welcome* to him, and his servants, of victuals, and drink, and clothes. *Cyd. Emlyn ac Amic.*

Trwyddedawg, *a.* (trwydded) Having a passage, or pass; having liberty of passing and repassing; having admittance as a guest. *s. c.*—*pl.* trwyddedogion. One who has leave of egress or ingress; a licentiate; a free guest. Tri *thrwyddedawg llys Arthur*, the three free guests of the court of Arthur.

Na ddal dy dŷ wrth gynghor dy drwyddedawg.

Keep not thy house according to the advice of thy *guest*. *Adage.*

Drwg a drefna wrth ei drwyddedawg.

Badly off is he who manages by the advice of his *guest*. *Adage.*

Nid trwyddedawg ond dimair.

There is no *free traveller* like a penny. *Adage.*

Trwyddedawl, *a.* (trwydded) Relating to the free passing through; licensing.

Trwyddedig, *a.* (trwydded) Freely admitted.

Trwyddedogaeth, *s. f.* (trwyddedawg) Freedom of passing through.

Tair braint beirdd Ynys Prydain: trwyddedogaeth lle yr elont, nas dycer arf noeth yn eu herbyn, a gair eu gair hwy ar bawb.

The three privileges of the bards of the Isle of Britain: *freedom of sojourning* wherever they go, that a naked weapon be not borne against them, and that their word be taken before every one. *Barddas.*

Trwyddedogi, *v. a.* (trwyddedawg) To permit a free passage.

Trwyddedogiad, *s. m.* (trwyddedawg) A rendering of free passage, permission of passing.

Trwyddedogrwydd, *s. m.* (trwyddedawg) Freedom of passing through, free admission.

Trwyddedu, *v. a.* (trwydded) To pass through; to give free reception.

Trwyddedwr, *s. m.—pl.* trwyddedwyr (trwydded—gwr) One who freely passes through.

Trwyddedwraig, *s. f.—pl.* trwyddedwreigedd (trwydded—gwraig) A free female ranger.

Trwyddedwraig llen bedweni,
Trig a dyhudd, Forfudd, fi!

The *free ranger* of the glade of birches, stay and solace me, O, Morvudd! *D. ab Gwilym.*

Trwyddew, *s. m.* (trwydd) What perforates; a piercer, a borer.

Trwyddiad, *s. m.* (trwydd) A passing through.

Trwyddyd, *s. m.—pl. t.* au (trwydd) A passage through; a pass; leave of ingress and regress; licence, admittance; fare; provision.

Trwyll, *s. f.—pl. t.* au (trwy) What turns round; a swivel, or ring, on a pivot; a ring in a swine's nose.

Dodi trwyll yn ei drwyn.

To put a *ring* in his nose. *Adage.*

Mi yn son am Wyl Fair; ti yn son am drwyll mochyn.

I talking about Lady Day; thou talking about a pig's *ring*. *Adage.*

Esgynais i fyngid mewn cerbyd, yr hon oedd a thrwyll o aur, a dau farch gwynion yn ei dynu.

I mounted up in a chariot the which had a *ring of gold*, and two white steeds drawing it. *Marchawg Crwydrad.*

Trwyllaw, *v. a.* (trwyll) To form a swivel, or ring, to turn round on a pivot; to ring a pig's nose; to trawl, or to fish by trawling.

Da trwyllaw trwyn mochyn a fo yn turiaw.

It is well *to ring* a pig's nose that turns the ground. *Adage.*

Trwyllawg, *a.* (trwyll) Having a swivel, or ring.

Trwylliad, *s. m.* (trwyll) A swivelling; a forming a ring; a forming a pivot.

Trwyn, *s. m.—pl. t.* au (trwy) A point; a snout; a nozzle; a nose. *Trwyn y llo*, snapdragon.

Sychu trwyn y swch i fyned i'r pridd.

To wipe the *point* of the share before it goes into the soil. *Adage.*

Trwynaw, *v. a.* (trwyn) To nozzle; to nose, to smell with the nose close to a thing.

Trwynawg, *a.* (trwyn) Having a snout or nose.

Trwynawl, *a.* (trwyn) Belonging to the snout; nasal.

Trwynbant, *a.* (trwyn—pant) Having the nose falling in.

Trwynbica, *a.* (trwyn—pica) Having a turned up nose; snub-nosed.

Trwynbwt, *a.* (trwyn—pwt) Snub-nosed.

Trwyndwn, *a.* (trwyn—twn) Broken-nosed.

Trwynedig, *a.* (trwyn) Snouted; nosed.

Trwynfawr, *a.* (trwyn—mawr) Large-nosed.

Trwynfyr, *a.* (trwyn—byr) Short-nosed.

Trwynffrwyn, *s. f.—pl. t.* au (trwyn—ffrwyn) A nose-band of a bridle.

Trwynffychain, *v. a.* (trwyn—ffychain) To snort, to snuffle. *s. m.* A snorting, a snuffling.

Trwynffychain ac agori ei safn a wnaeth.

Snorting and opening his jaw was what he did. *H. Bown—Ehelingtn.*

Trwyngaued, *a.* (trwyn—caued) Having the nose closed up.

Trwyngorn, *a.* (trwyn—corn) Horn-snouted.

Trwyngorniawg, *a.* (trwyngorn) Having a horned nose. *s. m.* A rhinoceros.

Trwyngrwm, *a.* (trwyn—crwm) Having an aquiline nose.

Trwyngrych, *a.* (trwyn—crych) Crinkle-nosed.

Trwyngrychiad, *s. m.* (trwyngrych) A crinkling the nose.

Trwyngrychu, *v. a.* (trwyngrych) To nose crinkle.

Trwynhir, *a.* (trwyn—hir) Long-nosed.

Trwyniad, *s. m.* (trwyn) A nosing, a snouting.

Trwynllem, *a.* (*f. of* trwynllym) Sharp-nosed.

Trwynllif, *s. m.* (llif) A running at the nose.

Trwynllifaw, *v. n.* (trwynllif) To run at the nose.

Trwynllifawg, *a.* (trwynllif) Snivelly.

Trwynllym, *a.* (trwyn—llym) Sharp-nosed.

Trwynsor, *a.* (trwyn—sor) Apt to turn the nose; apt to take a huff. *Y trwynsor*, the stinking goose-foot.

Trwynsori, *v. n.* (trwynsor) To turn up the nose; to take a huff.

Trwynsoriad, *s. m.* (trwynsor) A turning up the nose, a taking a huff.

Trwynswch, *s. m.* (trwyn—swch) Tip of the nose.

Trwyo, *prep.* (trwy) Through. *adv.* Through, to the other side.

Trwyogaeth, *s. f.—pl. t.* au (trwyawg) The act or state of passing through; pervasion.

Tair trwyogaeth cerdd: trylen, trywyrf, a thrylanw.

The three *pervasions* of song: thorough learning, thorough vigour, and thorough nature. *Barddas.*

Trwyogedd, *s. m.* (trwyawg) Pervasiveness.

Trwyogi, *v. a.* (trwyawg) To render pervading; to become pervasive.

Trwyth, *s. f.—pl. t.* i (trwy) What pervades; a solvent, dissolvent, or menstruum; lye; a decoction. *Twrch Trwyth*, the bursting boar.

Trwythadwy, *a.* (trwyth) Capable of being affected by a menstruum or lye.

Trwythaw, *v. a.* (trwyth) To make a solvent or menstruum; to steep in lye; to wash in hot suds.

Trwythawl, *a.* (trwyth) Belonging to a solvent or menstruum; steeped in lye.

Trwythedig, *a.* (trwyth) Being steeped in lye.

Trwythi, *s. m.* (trwyth) A menstruum; lye.

Trwythiad, *s. m.* (trwyth) A forming a solvent or menstruum; a steeping in lye.

Trwythwr, *s. m.—pl.* trwythwyr (trwyth—gwr) One who steeps in lye.

Try, *s. m.* (ty—rhy) Aptness to go beyond, to turn, to go to the other side, or to go through.

prep. Through. *adv.* Through.—It is used as a prefix in composition.

Didraw aeth dry, aeth o dref.

Wandering, he went *through*, he went from home. *Ieuan Rhaiadr.*

Tryad, *s. m.* (try) A passing through; pervasion.

Tryal, *s. m.*—*pl. t.* au (try—al) A homestead.

Tryarllais, *a.* (try—arllais) Of a stunning voice. *Dyn tryarllais*, a person with a stunning voice.

Tryaw, *v. a.* (try) To render thorough.

Tryawch, *s. f.* (try—awch) A pervading energy to attract; magnetism.

Tryawchiad, *s. m.* (tryawch) A magnetizing.

Tryawchu, *v. a.* (tryawch) To magnetize.

Tryb, *s. m.*—*pl. t.* oedd (ty—rhyb) The state of being connected or blended.

Trybaeddiad, *s. m.* (try—baeddiad) A daubing thoroughly; a wallowing completely.

Trybaeddu, *v. a.* (try—baeddu) To daub thoroughly

Trybawl, *a.* (tryb) Tending to blend or to mix.

Trybed, *s. f.*—*pl. t.* au (try—ped) A brandiron.

Trybedd, *s. f.*—*pl. t.* au (try—pedd) A stay, or support; a trivet, or brandiron. *Trybedd yr ysgwydd*, the collar-bone.

Trybeddawg, *a.* (trybedd) Of thorough footing.

Trybeddawl, *a.* (trybedd) Thoroughly supporting.

Trybeddiad, *s. m.* (trybedd) A making a stay.

Trybeddu, *v. a.* (trybedd) To make a stay.

Trybeddiad rhawd rhag eu dawed.

Let the band make a firm stay against their coming. *Taliesin.*

Trybelid, *a.* (try—pelid) That is thoroughly penetrating; perspicuous, luminous.

Trybelid wylain a wylynt arnaf.

The *quickly kenning* sea-mews gazed upon me. *Cynddelw.*

Morwyn a welais, mor drybelid,
Mirain gall, o bail a bail glywid.

A damsel I beheld, *so elegant*, transcendently wise, who from a throne would be far heard of. *Ior. Fychan.*

Cywod, di was Asaf eadil, orfid fawr-lawr;
Gnawd o synwyrfawr farn drybelid.

Arise, thou youth of the line of Asav, meet on the grand scene; from the greatly wise we expect a *perspicuous* sentence. *Phylip Brydydd.*

Trybelidiad, *s. m.* (trybelid) A penetrating thoroughly; a making perspicuous.

Llu Maelgwn bu ysgwn y daethan',
Aerwyr ced, trybelidiad gwaedlan.

The hosts of Maelgwn it was fortunate that they came, the warriors of liberality, the *illumination* of the gory plain. *Ym. Taliesin a Merddin.*

Trybelidiaw, *v. a.* (trybelid) To penetrate thoroughly; to become perspicuous.

Trybelidrwydd, *s. m.* (trybelid) Perspicuousness.

Trybelyd, *a.* (try—pelyd) Thoroughly radiant.

Trybelydr, *s. m.* (trybelyd) A thorough radiance.

Trybelydrawg, *a.* (trybelydr) Thoroughly radiant.

Trybelydriad, *s. m.* (trybelydr) A radiating through.

Trybelydru, *v. a.* (trybelydr) To radiate through.

Trybest, *s. m.* (tryb) Bustle, or commotion.

Trybestawd, *s. m.* (trybest) A bustling state.

Atorelwis Fflamddwyn, fawr drybestawd,
A ddodynt yn ngwystlon!——

Then replied Flamddwyn, of mighty *bustle*, would they give in as hostages! *Taliesin.*

Trybestiad, *s. m.* (trybest) A bustling.

Trybestu, *v. a.* (trybest) To bustle, to bluster.

Trybestyd, *s. m.* (trybest) Bustle; officiousness.

Tryblith, *s. m.* (try—plith) A chaos.

Tryboeth, *a.* (poeth) Being thoroughly hot.

Tryboethi, *v. a.* (tryboeth) To heat thoroughly.

Tryboethiad, *s. m.* (tryboeth) A thoroughly heating.

Trybola, *s. m.* (trybawl) A mixture; a wallowing place, a mire where swine wallow.

Tryboli, *v. a.* (trybawl) To huddle; to wallow.

Trybolied, *s. m.* (trybawl) A huddling; a wallowing

Trybwl, *a.* (try—pwl) Thoroughly dull.

Trybwyll, *s. m.* (pwyll) Thorough reason. *a.* Thoroughly rational; of a penetrating mind.

Trybwyllaw, *v. a.* (trybwyll) To endue with a penetrating mind; to exert a penetrating mind.

Trybwyllawg, *a.* (trybwyll) Of a penetrating mind.

Trybwylliad, *s. m.* (trybwyll) An endowing with a penetrating mind; penetration of mind.

Trybwyllus, *a.* (trybwyll) Of a penetrating mind.

Trybylawg, *a.* (trybwl) Being pervaded or loaded with what is thick and heavy. *Hin drybylawg*, thick gloomy weather, without rain.

Trybyliad, *s. m.* (trybwl) A pervasion of dullness.

Trybylu, *v. a.* (trybwl) To pervade with dullness.

Tryciad, *s. m.* (trwc) A dragging heavily; a failing, a flagging.

Tryciaw, *v. a.* (trwc) To cause to fail; to flag.

Draig hir, pan drycial ereill——
Nawf ei yni.

The towering leader, when others *should fail*, great his energy. *T. Aled.*

Tryciaw ardal tir Cawrdaf.

To cause to fail the region of the land of Cawrdaf. *Hywel Reinallt.*

Tryciawl, *a.* (trwc) Flagging, dragging.

Tryciedig, *a.* (tryciad) Being made to flag.

Trych, *s. m.* (ty—rhych) An opening; a scope.

Trychad, *s. m.* (trwch) A cutting off, excision.

Trychadwy, *a.* (trychad) Capable of being cut.

Trychawl, *a.* (trwch) Cutting, mangling, lopping.

Trychddawn, *a.* (trwch—dawn) Endued with a cutting quality.

Trycheb, *s. f.*—*pl. t.* au (trwch) The figure called a *tmesis*, whereby a word is divided by the interposition of another.

Trychedig, *a.* (trwch) Being cut or bisected.

Trychedd, *s. m.* (trwch) The state of being lopped

Trychfa, *s. f.*—*pl.* trychfeydd (trwch) A cut or chopping-place.

Trychgyf, *s. m.*—*pl. t.* ion (trwch—cyf) A chopping-block.

Trychiad, *s. m.*—*pl.* trychiaid (trwch) A cutter, a lopper; that makes an incision or excision.

A'i lyw cyferyw cyfwyrain a thrin,
A thrychiaid gwerin Caerfyrddin fain.

And his leader met insurrection and tumult, and the *manglers* of the people of Caerfyrddin built of stone. *Ein. ab Gwgawn, i L. ab Iorwerth.*

Trychiedig, *a.* (trwch) Being cut off; truncated.

Trychiedigaeth, *s. m.* (trychiedig) An incision.

Trychiedigawl, *a.* (trychiedig) Incisive, incisory.

Trychiedydd, *s. m.*—*pl. t.* ion (trychiad) A cutter, a lopper.

Trychineb, *s. m.* (trwch) The state of being cut off; disaster, calamity; mischief.

Ar fyrder y daw amser cynhauaf iddi; sef yw hyny amser aflwydd, trychineb, a dialedd.

Shortly there will come the time of harvest for her; that is to say, the time of misfortune, *mischief*, and vengeance. *Ior. Owain.*

Trychinebawl, *a.* (trychineb) Calamitous.

Trychinebiad, *s. m.* (trychineb) A causing a calamity or mischief; a becoming disastrous.

Trychinebu, *v. a.* (trychineb) To cause a calamity; to become calamitous.

Trychinebus, *a.* (trychineb) Disastrous, fell.

Trychion, *s. pl. aggr.* (trwch) Cuttings; shreds.

Trychionyn, *s. m. dim.* (trychion) A shred.

Trychlam, *s. m.*—*pl. t.* au (trwch—llam) A disastrous or sad step.

Trychni, *s. m.* (trwch) Disaster, calamity, mishap, misfortune.

> Trychni, nid hawdd ei ochel.
>
> *Disaster*, it is not easy to avoid it. *Adage.*

> ——Aeth fy mwa i
> Yn dri-chnap, anian drychni.
>
> My bow is gone in three pieces, a woeful *accident*. *D. ab Gwilym.*

Trycholdeb, *s. m.* (trychawl) A mangled state.
Trycholedd, *s. m.* (trychawl) A mangled state.
Trycholi, *v. a.* (trychawl) To render mangled; to become cut and mangled.
Trychu, *v. a.* (trwch) To cut, to cut into, to make an incision; to lop.

> Trychwys Eingl: trychion eu hadawal.
> I Loegrwys hwysgyst lletgynt nid llai,
> Can llas——
>
> He *mangled* the Angles: mangled ones he would leave them. To the Lloegrians the devastation of wrath not the less, though he be slain. *Cynddelw, m. Cadwallon.*

> Gwinllan sydd i ym hanwylyd—ac ef a drychodd winwryf ynddi.
>
> To my well beloved there is a vineyard: and *he cut* a wine-press in it. *Isaiah* 5. 2.

Trychwan, *s. m.* (trwch—gwan) A slit, a split.
Trychwanawg, *a.* (trychwan) Having slits. *Llenlian drychwanawg*, a veil cloth full of slits.
Trychwanu, *s. m.* (trychwan) To slit, to split.
Trychwil, *a.* (try—chwil) Thoroughly searching.
Trychwiliaw, *v. a.* (trychwil) To search keenly.
Trychwn, *s. m.* (try—cwn) That bursts or rises through. *a.* Bursting through.
Trychwr, *s. m.—pl.* trychwyr (trwch—gwr) A cutter, a lopper.
Trychwydd, *s. m.* (trych—gwydd) A glance of the present; a glance or view of knowledge.

> Cerddgar cyfarwar cyfarwydd yw Duw
> Diweddwr cyn trychwydd;
> A'm rhoddes, nid rhodd gwaradwydd,
> Trech Wynedd, haelonedd hylwydd.
>
> The calm pleasure of the love of song is cognizable with God, he that determines before the *glance of knowledge*, he who gave, not the gift of disgrace, that Gwynedd, prosperous in liberality, should prevail. *Cynddelw, m. O. Gwynedd.*

Trychwyddaw, *v. a.* (trychwydd) To obtain visual knowledge.
Trychwyddawl, *a.* (trychwydd) Visibly present.
Trychwyddiad, *s.* (trychwydd) A visibly knowing.
Trychwyl, *s. f.* (trw—chwyl) A course through.
Trychwylaw, *v.* (trychwyl) To circulate through.
Trychwyliad, *s. m.* (trychwyl) A circulating through.
Trychwys, *s. m.* (trw—chwys) A sweat through.
Trychwysawl, *a.* (trychwys) Transuding.
Trychwysiad, *s. m.* (trychwys) Transudation.
Trychwysu, *v. a.* (trychwys) To transude.
Trychwyth, *s. m.* (trw—chwyth) A blast through.
Trychwythawl, *a.* (trychwyth) Blowing through.
Trychwythiad, *s.* (trychwyth) A blowing through.
Trychwythu, *v. a.* (trychwyth) To blow through.
Trychydd, *s. m.—pl. t.* ion (trwch) A cutter, a lopper.
Trychyn, *s. m. dim.* (trwch) A small cut, a nip.
Tryd, *s. m.* (try) That tends through. *a.* Apt to penetrate, or to run through.

> Anelais rhwng fy nwylaw
> Ywa, yw dryd a fu draw.
>
> I aimed between my hands a yew bow, *pervading* was the shock. *D. ab Gwilym.*

Trydan, *s. m.* (trw—tan) A pervading principle of expansion, a pervading fire; electric fluid.
Trydanawl, *a.* (trydan) Belonging to the electric fluid.
Trydaniad, *s. m.* (trydan) An electrifying.
Trydaniaeth, *s. m.* (trydan) Electricity.
Trydanu, *v. a.* (trydan) To electrify.
Trydar, *s. f.* (tryd—ar) A pervading noise; a chirp, a chatter; a din, a tumult.

> Oedd ryn rudd ebyr o'r gwyr gwaed;
> Oedd ran feirw fwyaf o'r drydar;
> Oedd amliw tonau, iwn amar eu naid
> Rid oeddynt dilafar.
>
> There ran dreadful streams of red from the [illegible]; dead were they the greatest part of the *tumult*; motley-tinted were the waves, breaking in discordant course, they were not failing in utterance. *Ll. P. Moch.*

Trydar, *v. a.* (tryd—ar) To make a pervading noise; to chirp, to chatter; to din.
Trydarawl, *a.* (trydar) Chirping; chattering.
Trydariad, *s. m.* (trydar) A chatting; a dinning.
Trydaru, *v. a.* (trydar) To chirp, to chatter.
Trydarwr, *s. m.—pl.* trydarwyr (trydar—gwr) One who makes a chatter.
Trydarydd, *s. m.—pl. t.* ion (trydar) Chatterer.
Tryde, *s. f.* (tryd) A third. *a.* Third.
Trydedydd, *s. m.* (tryd—e—dydd) The third day; the third day of the week. *Bardism.*
Trydedd, *s. f.* (tryd—edd) A third. *a.* Third.
Trydeddwaith, *s. f.* (trydedd—gwaith) Third time.
Trydewaith, *s.* (tryde—gwaith) The third time.
Trydiad, *s. m.* (tryd) A pervasion. *Trydiad dryliad*, the pervasion of destruction.
Trydolwyn, *s. f.* (tryd—olwyn) Course of a wheel.

> Am eurfro, am eurfron terwyn,
> Torf anwar trydar trydolwyn.
>
> Round the golden region, round the golden [illegible] ruthless host makes a tumult like the *pervading wheel*. *Cynddelw, i'r argl. Rhys.*

Trydon, *s. f.* (tryd) That is pervasive. *Y drydon*, the stinking goose-foot; also called *trwyngoer*.
Trydon, *a.* (try—ton) Thoroughly toned.

> Trydon dy fân ar lannerch
> Trydar syw, trewiadur serch.
>
> *Full-toned* thy strain on the glade, with smart chirp, the [illegible] of love. *D. ab Gwilym, i [illegible].*

Trydwan, *s. m.* (tryd—gwan) Four days to come. *adv.* Four days hence.
Trydwll, *s. m.—pl.* trydyllau (trw—twll) A hole through any thing, a perforation. *a.* Perforated.
Trydy, *s. m.* (tryd) The third. *a.* Third.
Trydydyn, *s. m.* (trydy—dyn) A third person.
Trydydd, *s. m.* (tryd—ydd) A third, one out of three. *a.* Third.

> Trydydd anhebgor brenin yw ei [illegible]; y ddau [illegible] yw ei offeiriad teulu, ac ei ynad llys.
>
> The *third* indispensable of a king is his patron of the family; the other two are his domestic chaplain, and his judge of the palace. *Welsh Laws.*

> Pan weles Llyr nad oedd ganddo [illegible] [illegible] [illegible], ond ei fod ar ei drydydd, cywilyddiaw a wnaeth.
>
> When Llyr perceived that he had not many in his retinue, but that he was on his *third*, he became abashed. *Gr. ab Arthur.*

Trydyddiad, *s. m.* (trydydd) A forming a third.
Trydyddu, *v. a.* (trydydd) To tertiate.
Trydygwr, *s. m.* (trydy—gwr) A third person.
Trydylledig, *a.* (trydwll) Perforated, bored.
Trydylliad, *s. m.—pl. t.* au (trydwll) Perforation.
Trydyllu, *v. a.* (trydwll) To perforate.
Trydyllwr, *s. m.—pl.* trydyllwyr (trydwll—gwr) One who perforates.
Trydyllydd, *s. m.—pl. t.* ion (trydwll) Perforator.
Trydd, *s. m.* (try) That is thoroughly.
Trydded, *s. f.—pl. t.* au (trydd) Passage through.
Tryddedawg, *a.* (trydded) Having a free passage.
Tryddedawl, *a.* (trydded) Passing through.
Tryddediad, *s. m.* (trydded) A passing through.
Tryddedu, *v. a.* (trydded) To pass through.
Tryddedwr, *s. m.—pl.* tryddedwyr (trydded—gwr) A passenger.

Tryddedydd, *s. m.—pl. t.* ion (trydded) A passer through, a passenger.
Tryddyd, *s. m.* (trydd) A passage through.
Tryf, *s. m.* (try) That is thorough.
Tryfal, *s. m.—pl. t.* au (tryf—al) What has three corners; a triangl. *Tryfal cyfochrawg*, equilateral-triangle; *tryfal daugyfochr*, isocclestriangle; *tryfal anghyfochrawg*, a scalenous-triangle; *tryfal lleddf*, oblique-angular triangle.
Tryfaledd, *s. m.* (tryfal) The state of having three points or angles; the bottom of a fork, or where it divides.
Tryfaliad, *s. m.* (tryfal) A forming a triangle.
Tryfalu, *v. a.* (tryfal) To form a triangle.
Tryfall, *a.* (trw—mall) Thoroughly evil.

Nid mall tryfall ond diogi.

There is no evil *thoroughly evil* but idleness. *Adage.*

Tryfalledd, *s. m.* (tryfall) A state thoroughly evil.
Tryfalliad, *s. m.* (tryfall) A rendering thoroughly evil; a becoming thoroughly evil.
Tryfallu, *v. a.* (tryfall) To render thoroughly evil; to become evil thoroughly.
Tryfan, *s. m.* (try—man) That is spotted through. *Dail y tryfan*, *alan mawr*, the petasites, or butter-burr.
Tryfar, *s. m.* (trw—bar) Thorough wrath. *a.* Malignant.
Tryfarus, *a.* (tryfar) Thoroughly malignant.
Tryfawl, *a.* (tryf) Being thorough or complete.
Tryfer, *s. f.—pl. t.* i (tryf) A forked spear, or harpoon.

A thryfer brwydr a thrafod.

And the *barbed shaft* of battle and tumult. *Iolo Goch.*

Tryferawg, *a.* (tryfer) Having a bearded spear.
Tryferiad, *s. m.* (tryfer) A harpooning.
Tryferu, *v. a.* (tryfer) To spear; to harpoon. '*Tryferai alon*,' he transfixt the foes.
Tryferw, *s. m.* (trw—berw) A thorough boil. *a.* Thoroughly boiling.
Tryferwad, *s. m.* (tryferw) A boiling through.
Tryferwi, *v. a.* (tryferw) To boil through.
Tryferwr, *s. m.—pl.* tryferwyr (tryfer—gwr) A spearer; a harpooner.
Tryfesur, *s. m.—pl. t.* au (trw—mesur) A diameter
Tryfesuraw, *v. a.* (tryfesur) To form a diameter.
Tryfesurawl, *a.* (tryfesur) Diametrical.
Tryfesuriad, *s. m.* (tryfesur) A measuring a diameter.
Tryfol, *s. m.* (try—bol) That is all belly.
Tryfoliad, *s. m.* (tryfol) A gormandizing.
Tryfoliaw, *v. a.* (tryfol) To gormandize.
Tryfoliawg, *a.* (tryfol) Gormandizing.
Tryfoliwr, *s. m.—pl.* tryfoliwyr (tryfol—gwr) A gormandizer, a greedy-gut.
Tryfrad, *s. m.* (trw—brad) Thorough treachery.
Tryfrith, *a.* (trw—brith) Streaked, diversified, or spotted all through; thoroughly mixed; swarming, or teeming. *Mae y mor yn dryfrith o bysgod*, the sea is swarming with fish.
Tryfrithaw, *v. a.* (tryfrith) To variegate thoroughly; to mix all through; to be swarming.
Tryfrithiad, *s. m.* (tryfrith) A variegating thoroughly; a mixing thoroughly; a swarming.
Tryfrwyd, *s. m.* (trw—brwyd) The state of darting through and through. *a.* Interweaving.
Tryfrwydaw, *v. a.* (tryfrwyd) To run through backwards and forwards.

Yn tryfrwyd peleidr.

Javelins *darting through backwards and forwards* Aneurin.

Tryfrwydawl, *a* (tryfrwyd) Interweaving.
Tryfrwydiad, *s. m.* (tryfrwyd) An interweaving.
Tryfwg, *s. m* (try—mwg) Thorough smoke.
Tryfygawl, *a.* (tryfwg) Tending to smoke through
Tryfygiad, *s. m.* (tryfwg) A thorough fumigation
Tryfygu, *v. a.* (tryfwg) To fumigate through.
Tryfyned, *v. a.* (trw—myned) To go through.
Tryfynediad, *s. m.* (tryfyned) A going through a passing through; pervasion.
Tryfyw, *a.* (trw—byw) Thoroughly alive.
Tryfywiad, *s. m* (tryfyw) A thoroughly animating.
Tryfywiaw, *v. a.* (tryfyw) To animate thoroughly.
Tryfywiawg, *a.* (tryfyw) Thoroughly animated.
Tryffaeth, *a.* (trw—ffaeth) Thoroughly mellow
Tryffaethawl, *a.* (tryffaeth) Tending to make thoroughly mellow.
Tryffaethder, *s.* (tryffaeth) Thorough mellowness.
Tryffaethiad, *s. m.* (tryffaeth) A thoroughly mellowing.
Tryffaethu, *v. a.* (tryffaeth) To mellow thoroughly
Tryffin, *s. f.* (trw—ffin) A thorough boundary.
Tryffiniad, *s. m.* (tryffin) A making a boundary through.
Tryffiniaw, *v. a.* (tryffin) To make a boundary through.
Tryffiniawl, *a* (tryffin) Thoroughly bounding.
Tryffraw, *a.* (trw—ffraw) Thoroughly agitated.
Tryffwn, *s. m.* (try—ffwn) Thorough prosperity.

Am Drefan dryffwn rhag eiriolydd.

About Trevan *complete prosperity* before the intercessor. *Meilyr.*

Tryffwrch, *s. m.—pl.* tryffyrch (trw—ffwrch) The commencement of a forking, or ramification. *Tryffwrch pren*, the part of a tree where it becomes forked.
Trylais, *s. m.—pl.* tryleisiau (trw—llais) A thorough voice. *a.* Of thorough voice.

Cyfarchais, yn drylais, draw,
Well lüd,'n gan i'w llwyddiaw

I greeted, *distinctly of voice*, yonder, to her a better fare in song for her prospering D. ab Gwilym, i'r gog.

Trylanw, *s. m.* (trw—llanw) A thorough fulness.
Trylaw, *s. f.* (try—llaw) A complete hand. *a.* Thoroughly handy; dexterous.

Amdrynl drylaw drylen.

Encompassed with wrath, *dexterous*, of thorough training *Aneurin.*

Trylawn, *a.* (trw—llawn) Thoroughly full.
Trylawnder, *s. m.* (trylawn) Thorough fulness.
Trylawni, *v. a.* (trylawn) To fill thoroughly.
Trylawniad, *s. m.* (trylawn) A filling thoroughly.
Trylef, *s. m.* (trw—llef) A thorough utterance. *a.* Of thorough utterance, of complete voice.

Llew trylew, trylef ei geiniaid.

The lion altogether brave, *completely of voice* his minstrels. *Ll. P. Moch, i R. ab Owain.*

Trylefawl, *a.* (trylef) Of complete utterance.
Trylefiad, *s. m.* (trylef) A rendering of complete utterance.
Trylefu, *v. a.* (trylef) To render of complete utterance; to render articulate.
Tryleisiad, *s. m.* (trylais) A rendering of complete voice.
Tryleisiaw, *v. a.* (trylais) To articulate clearly.
Tryleisiawl, *a.* (trylais) Of clear articulation.
Trylen, *s. f.—pl. t.* i (trw—llen) Thorough learning. *a.* Thoroughly learned.
Trylenwad, *s. m.* (trylanw) A thoroughly filling.
Trylenwawl, *a.* (trylanw) Tending to fill thoroughly

Trylenwi, *v. a.* (trylanw) To fill thoroughly.
Tryles, *s. m.* (trw—lles) A thorough benefit.
Tryleswl, *a.* (tryles) Thoroughly beneficial.
Tryleswiad, *s. m.* (tryles) A thoroughly benefiting.
Trylesu, *v. a.* (tryles) To benefit thoroughly.
Trylew, *a.* (trw—glew) Thoroughly collected; full of capability; very brave.

> [illegible] trylew yn llaw,
> A'i [illegible] drylwyn wiw,
> A'i darian drylliw droch.
>
> He *abundant in resources* on the [illegible], with his excelling host of [illegible] movements, and his shield broken and pervaded with [illegible]. *Cynddelw.*

Trylewder, *s. m.* (trylew) The state of thorough resource or ability; thorough bravery.
Trylewdid, *s. m.* (trylew) Thorough resource of mind; thorough bravery.
Trylewych, *s. m.* (trw—llewych) Translucency.
Trylewychawl, *a.* (trylewych) Translucent.
Trylewychiad, *s.* (trylewych) A lighting through.
Trylewychu, *v. a* (trylewych) To shine through.
Trylid, *s. m.* (trw—llid) Thorough rage.
Trylidiad, *s. m.* (trylid) A thoroughly angering.
Trylidiaw, *v. a.* (trylid) To enrage thoroughly; to become thoroughly angry.
Trylidiawg, *a.* (trylid) Thoroughly wrathful.
Trylif, *s. m.* (try—llif) A thorough flow.
Trylifaw, *v. a* (trylif) To flow through.
Trylifawl, *a.* (trylif) Flowing through.
Trylifiad, *s. m.* (trylif) A flowing through.
Trylith, *s. m.* (trw—llith) A thorough training.
Trylithawr, *s. m.*—*pl.* trylithorion (trylith) That is thoroughly trained.
Trylithiad, *s. m.* (trylith) A thoroughly training.
Trylithiaw, *v. a.* (trylith) To train thoroughly.
Trylithiawl, *a.* (trylith) Tending to train thoroughly; of a thoroughly alluring tendency.
Trylithr, *a.* (trw—llithr) Thoroughly gliding.
Trylithraw, *v. a.* (trylithr) To glide through.
Trylithrawl, *a.* (trylithr) Apt to glide through.
Trylithriad, *s. m* (trylithr) A gliding through.
Tryliw, *s. m.*—*pl. t.* iau (trw—lliw) A pervading colour. *a.* Being stained through, of one pervading hue; deeply coloured. '*Tarian dryliw goch*,' a shield thoroughly stained with red.
Tryliwiad, *s. m.* (tryliw) A colouring through.
Tryliwiaw, *v. a.* (tryliw) To pervade with colour, to stain through; to make of a deep dye, to engrain.
Tryliwiawg, *a.* (tryliw) Of a thorough colour.
Tryliwiedig, *a.* (tryliw) Thoroughly coloured.
Tryloes, *s. f.*—*pl. t.* au (trw—gloes) A pang that penetrates through.
Tryloesi, *v. a.* (tryloes) To strike a pang through.
Tryloesiad, *s. m.* (tryloes) A striking a pang through
Tryloew, *a.* (trw—gloew) Diaphanous, transparent
Tryloewad, *s. m.* (tryloew) A rendering transparent.
Tryloewdeb, *s. m.* (tryloew) Transparency.
Tryloewder, *s. m.* (tryloew) Transparency.
Tryloewdra, *s. m.* (tryloew) Transparency.
Tryloewi, *v. a.* (tryloew) To render transparent.
Trylon, *a.* (trw—llon) Being thoroughly glad.
Trylonder, *s. m.* (trylon) Thorough gladness.
Tryloni, *v. a.* (trylon) To render thoroughly glad; to become pleased thoroughly.
Tryloniad, *s. m.* (trylon) A gladdening thoroughly.
Trylosg, *s. m.* (llosg) Thorough ignition. *a.* Thoroughly burnt.
Trylosgi, *v. a.* (trylosg) To burn thoroughly.
Trylosgiad, *s. m.* (trylosg) A burning thoroughly.
Trylwg, *s. m.*—*pl.* trylygon (trw—llwg) Perspective.
Trylwyn, *a.* (trw—llwyn) Very quick, ready, or dexterous; ingenious; thoroughly complete. *Gwr trylwyn*, a man of quick capacity; *ach drylwyn*, an illustrious pedigree.

> Terfysg a thrylew a thrylwyn fromder.
>
> A tumult against the thoroughly brave with a quarrelsome shield. *Cynddelw.*
>
> Dawn ganym yn lawn, yn ddyn ethrylith
> A thrylwyn [illegible].
>
> A talent I justly possess, being a person of capacity with good perceptions. *Ein. ab Gwalchmai.*

Trylwynaw, *v. a.* (trylwyn) To render thoroughly quick or expert; to become thoroughly quick.
Trylwyndeb, *s. m.* (trylwyn) Thorough dexterity.
Trylwynder, *s. m.* (trylwyn) Thorough dexterity.
Trylwyndra, *s. m.* (trylwyn) Thorough quickness.
Trylwyniad, *s.* (trylwyn) A rendering thoroughly quick; a becoming thoroughly quick or expert.
Trylwyr, *a.* (trw—llwyr) Thoroughly complete.
Trylwyraw, *v. a.* (trylwyr) To render thoroughly complete; to become thoroughly complete.
Trylwyrdeb, *s. m.* (trylwyr) Thorough completeness.
Trylwyrder, *s. m.* (trylwyr) Thorough completeness, a state quite entire.
Trylwyrdra, *s. m.* (trylwyr) Thorough completeness, or thorough entirety.
Trylwyriad, *s. m.* (trylwyr) A thoroughly completing or making entire.
Trylwys, *a.* (trw—glwys) Thoroughly hallowed.
Trylwysder, *s. m.* (trylwys) Thorough holiness.
Trylwysaw, *v. a.* (trylwys) To render thoroughly pure, holy, or delectable; to become thoroughly holy.
Trylwysiad, *s. m.* (trylwys) A hallowing thoroughly
Trylygawl, *a.* (trylwg) Relating to perfect vision; perspective.
Trylygiad, *s. m.* (trylwg) A perspectively viewing; a forming a perspective.
Trylygu, *v. a.* (trylwg) To view perspectively.
Trylym, *a.* (trw—llym) Thoroughly keen.
Trylymder, *s. m.* (trylym) Thorough keenness.
Trylymdra, *s. m.* (trylym) Thorough keenness.
Trylymiad, *s. m.* (trylym) A rendering thoroughly keen, sharp, or severe.
Trylymu, *v. a.* (trylym) To sharpen thoroughly.
Trylyn, *a.* (try—glyn) Thoroughly adherent.
Trylyniad, *s. m.* (trylyn) A thoroughly adhering.
Trylynu, *v. a.* (trylyn) To adhere thoroughly.
Trym, *s. m.* (ty—rhym) That is compact. *a.* Compact; energetic; trim.

> Nid wyf i'th [illegible]—
> [illegible] trym, ond rhag [illegible]
> Gasweith i arall geisio.
>
> I am not for putting you off, *energetic* lord, but for fear of the one disgusting turn of another making an attempt. *D. Benfras.*
>
> Mae 'n y nef yn cartrefu,
> Llew trym, a dyna lle trig.
>
> He is in heaven residing, the *energetic* lion, and there he will remain. *Tho. W. Hywel.*

Trymâad, *s. m.* (trymâu) A rendering heavy or weighty; a becoming heavy: a saddening.
Trymâawl, *a.* (tryman) Of a tendency to make heavy; saddening.
Trymaidd, *a.* (trwm) Somewhat heavy or sad.
Trymâu, *v. a.* (trwm) To make heavy, to sadden, to become heavy; to become sad or dejected.
Trymder, *s. m.* (trwm) Heaviness, weightiness, depression, sadness; dejectedness, sorrow.
Trymdra, *s. m.* (trwm) Heaviness; sadness.
Trymdrais, *s. m.* (trwm—trais) Heavy oppression.
Trymdde, *a.* (trwm—de) Pervaded with heaviness; sad; drooping.

Trymeiddiad, *s. m.* (trymaidd) A rendering somewhat heavy; a becoming rather heavy.
Trymeiddiaw, *v. a.* (trymaidd) To render somewhat heavy; to become rather heavy.
Trymeidd-dra, *s. m.* (trymaidd) A some degree of heaviness or pressure.
Trymeiddrwydd, *s. m.* (trymaidd) Some degree of heaviness or pressure.
Trymedd, *s. m.* (trwm) Heaviness; sadness.
Trymfraw, *s. m.* (trwm—braw) Heavy dread.
Trymfron, *s. f.* (trwm—bron) Sad breast.
Trymfryd, *s. m.* (trwm—bryd) Depression of mind, pensiveness; sorrow.

> Morfudd——
> Afraid it ddala trymfryd,
> Am bren, na bedwen o'r byd.
>
> Morvudd, needless is it for thee to harbour sadness, about a tree, or any birchen in the world. *D. ab Gwilym.*

Trymfrydiad, *s. m.* (trymfryd) A rendering depressed in mind, a becoming dejected.
Trymfrydig, *a.* (trymfryd) Oppressed in mind.
Trymfrydigrwydd, *s. m.* (trymfryd) Pensiveness.
Trymgur, *s. m.* (trwm—cur) A heavy throb.
Trymguraw, *v. a.* (trymgur) To beat heavily.
Trymguriad, *s. m.* (trymgur) A beating heavily.
Trymgwsg, *s. m.* (trwm—cwsg) A heavy sleep.
Trymgwyn, *s. f.—pl. t.* ion (trwm—cwyn) A heavy complaint.
Trymgwynaw, *v.* (trymgwyn) To complain sadly.
Trymgwyniad, *s. m.* (trymgwyn) A complaining heavily.
Trymgysgiad, *s. m.* (trymgwsg) A sleeping heavily.
Trymgysgu, *v. a.* (trymgwsg) To sleep heavily.
Trymhun, *s. f.* (trwm—hun) A heavy sleep.
Trymhunaw, *v. a.* (trymhun) To sleep heavily.
Trymhunawl, *a.* (trymhun) Heavily sleeping.
Trymhuniad, *s. m.* (trymhun) A sleeping heavily.
Trymhwrdd, *s. m.* (trwm—hwrdd) A heavy push.
Trymhyrddawl, *a.* (trymhwrdd) Heavily pushing.
Trymhyrddiad, *s.* (trymhwrdd) A pushing heavily.
Trymhyrddig, *a.* (trymhwrdd) Lumpish, blockish.
Trymhyrddigaw, *v. a.* (trymhyrddig) To render a blockhead, to become dull and heavy.
Trymhyrddigrwydd, *s. m.* (trymhyrddig) Lumpishness, blockishness.
Trymiad, *s. m.* (trym) A rendering energetic.
Trymiaw, *v. a.* (trym) To render energetic; to become energetic; to become trim.
Trymiawg, *a.* (trym) Having compactness; having energy; having trimness.
Trymiawl, *a.* (trym) Of a compact tendency.
Trymlwyth, *s. m.—pl. t.* i (trwm—llwyth) A heavy load.
Trymlwythaw, *v. a.* (trymlwyth) To load heavily.
Trymlwythawg, *a.* (trymlwyth) Heavily laden.
Trymly, *s. m.* (trwm—lly) A heavy look.
Trymlŷad, *s. m.* (trymly) A rendering sluggish.
Trymlŷaw, *v. a.* (trymly) To render sluggish.
Trymlyawg, *a.* (trymly) Heavily drooping; drowsy, flagging. *Hin drymlyawg*, heavily oppressing weather.
Trymlyogder, *s. m.* (trymlŷawg) Drowsiness.
Trymlyogi, *v. a.* (trymlŷawg) To render drowsy.
Trymlyogrwydd, *s.* (trymlŷawg) Drowsiness.
Trymog, *s. f.* (trym) One that is compact or trim.

> Rhoddais fy mryd ar [illegible];
> [illegible] i'm llaw.
>
> I set my mind on obtaining one: give a *trim one* with large [illegible] into my hand. *Iew ab Huw, i [illegible].*

Trymswrth, *a.* (trwm—swrth) Heavily sluggish.
Trymsyrthni, *s. m.* (trymswrth) Drowsiness.
Trymysg, *s. m.* (try—mysg) Confusion.
Trymysgawl, *a.* (trymysg) Tending to confuse.
Trymysgiad, *s. m.* (trymysg) A confusion.
Trymysgu, *v. a.* (trymysg) To blend through and through; to confuse.

> Nid hawdd trymysg ar gall.
>
> It is not easy *to bring confusion* on the cunning. *Adage.*

Tryn, *s. m.—pl. t.* i (ty—rhyn) Ardency, fierceness. *a.* Ardent, fierce, sharp, stern. *Dyn a golwg tryn iawn*, a person with a very stern look. *Sil.*
Trynaidd, *a.* (tryn) Of an ardent tendency.
Trynawf, *s. m.* (trw—nawf) A swim through.
Trynawl, *a.* (tryn) Of an ardent quality; of a fierce or stern quality.
Trynaws, *s. m.* (trw—naws) A temper or quality that pervades.
Trynawsedd, *s. m.* (trynaws) A pervading temperament or nature.
Trynawsi, *v. a.* (trynaws) To pervade with a quality or disposition.
Trynawsiad, *s. m.* (trynaws) A pervading with a quality, disposition, or nature.
Trynedd, *s. m.* (tryn) Ardency; fierceness.
Trynerth, *s. m.* (trw—nerth) Thorough strength.
Trynerthawl, *a.* (trynerth) Thoroughly strong.
Trynerthedd, *s. m.* (trynerth) Thorough strength.
Trynerthiad, *s. m.* (trynerth) A thoroughly strengthening.
Trynerthu, *v. a.* (trynerth) To strengthen thoroughly.
Trynodd, *s. m.—pl. t.* ion (trw—nodd) A pervading juice, or fluid.
Trynoddawl, *a.* (trynodd) Tending to ooze through.
Trynoddi, *v. a.* (trynodd) To ooze through.
Trynoddiad, *s. m.* (trynodd) An oozing through.
Trynoddlyd, *a.* (trynodd) Thoroughly oozing.
Trynofiad, *s. m.* (trynawf) A swimming through.
Trynofiaw, *v. a.* (trynawf) To swim through.
Trynofiawl, *a.* (trynawf) Tending to swim through.
Trynwyd, *s. m.—pl. t.* au (trw—nwyd) A pervading emotion, energy, or passion.
Trynwydaw, *v. a.* (trynwyd) To pervade with an emotion or passion.
Trynwydawg, *a.* (trynwyd) Having a pervading emotion or passion.
Trynwydawl, *a.* (trynwyd) Being thoroughly impassioned.
Trynwydiad, *s. m.* (trynwyd) A pervading with an emotion or passion.
Trynwyf, *s. m.—pl. t.* au (trw—nwyf) Thorough liveliness, thorough vivacity.
Trynwyfaw, *v. a.* (trynwyf) To render thoroughly brisk or lively; to become full of gaiety.
Trynwyfawl, *a.* (trynwyf) Thoroughly lively.
Trynwyfiad, *s. m.* (trynwyf) A rendering full of vivacity; a becoming thoroughly animated or enlivened.
Trynwyfus, *a.* (trynwyf) Full of vivacity.
Trynwyfusaw, *v. a.* (trynwyfus) To render full of vivacity, to become thoroughly animated.
Trynwyfusrwydd, *s. m.* (trynwyfus) A state of thorough liveliness.
Tryred, *s. f.* (trw—rhed) A run through.
Tryredawl, *a.* (tryred) Being running through.
Tryredeg, *v. a.* (tryred) To run through.
Tryrediad, *s. m.* (tryred) A running through.
Tryrith, *s. m.—pl. t.* ion (trw—rhith) A thorough appearance.
Tryrithiad, *s. m.* (tryrith) An appearing through.

Tryrithiaw, *v. a.* (tyrith) To appear through.
Tryrithiawl, *a.* (tyrith) Appearing through.
Tryryw, *s. m.—pl. t.* iau (try—rhyw) A perfect kind. *a.* Thorough-bred.
Tryrywiad, *s. m.* (tryryw) A rendering of a perfect kind; a becoming of perfect kind.
Tryrywiaw, *v. a.* (tryryw) To render of perfect kind; to become of a perfect kind.
Tryrywiawg, *a.* (tryryw) Being of perfect kind.
Tryrywiawl, *a.* (tryryw) Of a perfect kind.
Trysain, *s. f.—pl.* tryseiniau (trw—sain) A thorough sound. *a.* Of complete sound.
Trysawdd, *s. f.—pl.* trysoddion (trw—sawdd) A cube root.
Trysawr, *s. m.—pl.* trysorau (trws) A treasure.
Tryseiniad, *s. m.* (trysain) A thoroughly sounding
Tryseiniaw, *v. a.* (trysain) To sound perfectly.
Tryseiniawl, *a.* (trysain) Of a perfect sound.
Trysglaidd, *a.* (trwsgl) Somewhat awkward.
Trysgledd, *s. m.* (trwsgl) Awkwardness.
Trysgleidd-dra, *s. m.* (trysglaidd) Awkwardness.
Trysgleiddiad, *s. m.* (trysglaidd) A rendering clumsy or awkward; a becoming awkward.
Trysgleiddiaw, *v. a.* (trysglaidd) To render clumsy; to become clumsy or awkward.
Trysgleiddrwydd, *s. m.* (trysglaidd) Awkwardness.
Trysorawl, *a.* (trysawr) Belonging to treasure.
Trysorfa, *s. f.—pl.* trysorfëydd (trysawr) A treasury.
Trysori, *v. a.* (trysawr) To treasure, to store up.
Trysoriad, *s. m.* (trysawr) A treasuring.
Trysorwr, *s. m.—pl.* trysorwyr (trysawr—gwr) A treasurer.

> Rhys y Fel Ynys flaenawr——
> Trysorwr pob cerddawr.

> Rhys the sovereign of the Honey Island, the *treasurer* of every minstrel. *D. Nanmor.*

Trysorydd, *s. m.—pl. t.* ion (trysawr) A treasurer
Trystan, *s. c.* (trwst) A noisy one, a blusterer.
Trystfawr, *a.* (trwst) Of great tumult or din.
Trystforedd, *s. m.* (trystfawr) A blusteringness.
Trystiad, *s. m.* (trwst) A blustering, a clattering.
Trystian, *v. a.* (trwst) To keep a clattering.
Trystiaw, *v. a.* (trwst) To make a noise; to rattle; to rustle; to bluster, to bustle.

> Methu a wna cnawd—mal blodau—
> Neu ddail y gwydd, pan ddel gwynt
> I drystiaw'n arw drostynt.

> The body shall fail, like flowers, or the leaves of the wood, when wind shall come *to bluster* harshly over them. *D. Jones o Lanfair.*

Trystiawg, *a.* (trwst) Full of noise; clattering; blustering.
Trystiawl, *a.* (trwst) Blustering, clattering.
Trystiwr, *s. m.—pl.* trystiwyr (trwst—gwr) A blusterer, a clatterer.
Tryswn, *s. m.* (try—swn) A thorough noise. *a.* Thoroughly noisy.
Trysyniad, *s.* (tryswn) A making a noise through
Trysyniaw, *v. a.* (tryswn) To noise through.
Trysyniawl, *a.* (tryswn) Thoroughly noisy.
Trythain, *a.* (trwth) Expanding, swelling out.
Trythawl, *a.* (trwth) Tending to expand out.
Trythfa, *s. f.* (trwth) A stretching place.
Trythgwd, *s. m.—pl.* trythgydau (trwth—cwd) A bag or satchel that is made to draw together.

> [illegible] yw trythgwd y llawgydau ag a fo ynddynt, eithr aur neu ariant, o bydd lle cedwir hwnw.

> *A distending bag* is thus considered, the hand-bags in which [illegible] may be every thing, except gold and silver, if they be where [illegible] kept. *Welsh Laws.*

Trythiad, *s. m.* (trwth) An expanding out.
Trython, *s. m.* (try—ton) The sharp dock.

Trythu, *v. a.* (trwth) To expand or swell out.
Trythwch, *s. m.* (trwth) The state of being expanded or filled out.
Trythwr, *s. m.—pl.* trythwyr (trwth—gwr) One who expands himself out.
Trythyll, *a.* (trwth) Voluptuous; addicted to pleasure; wanton; indulgent.

> Drwg ddichwain trythyll.

> Evil is the destiny of one *addicted to pleasure.* *Adage.*

> Trythyll maen yn llaw cegud.

> *Wanton* is a stone in an expert hand. *Adage.*

> Nid oes edn——
> A'i thrwth oll ei thrythyllach.

> There is not a bird with all her dotage more *wanton.* *D. ab Gwilym, i fergeddi.*

Trythyllaidd, *a.* (trythyll) Rather voluptuous.
Trythylliad, *s. m.* (trythyll) A living voluptuously; a taking enjoyment, a taking pleasure.
Trythyllu, *v. a.* (trythyll) To live voluptuously; to take enjoyment; to follow pleasure.
Trythyllwch, *s. m.* (trythyll) A state of ease or enjoyment; voluptuousness; pleasure.

> Megys y ceiff y rhai da drythyllwch o ddirfawr ewyllys; felly y ceiff y lleill chwerwedd o ddirfawr drueni.

> In the manner that the good ones shall obtain the *enjoyment* of extreme free will; so the others shall obtain the bitterness of extreme misery. *Elucidarius.*

Trythyllwg, *s. m.* (trythyll) A state of ease, voluptuousness, or enjoyment; pleasure.

> Trythyllwg drwg ei ddichwain.

> *Pleasure* is of evil consequence. *Adage.*

> Trythyllwg a ddwg i ddyn
> Dialedd o'i hir ddilyn.

> *Pleasure* will bring to a person vengeance from long pursuing it. *Hywel Cilan.*

> Nid oedd o'r teyrnasoedd a allai ymgyffelybu o gyfoeth, a thrythyllwg, ac amlder pob da ynddi, ag Ynys Prydain.

> There was not of the kingdoms that could vie in power, and *enjoyment*, and the abundance of every blessing in it, as the Isle of Britain. *Gr. ab Arthur.*

Trythyllwr, *s. m.—pl.* trythyllwyr (trythyll—gŵr) A voluptuary, a man who takes his enjoyment.
Tryw, *s. m.* (try) That pervades, that is continual, or constant; constancy; a trace, what gives perception; knowledge, skill; truth. *a.* Universal; constant; true. *Y tryw*, the agrimony.

> Tryw i hwch dyrfu.

> It is natural for a sow to burrow. *Adage.*

Trywal, *s. m.* (try—gwal) That is spread through
Trywan, *s. f.* (trw—gwan) An opening or gash through; a thrust through; a stab. *a.* Being run through.

> Erchwynawg esgar, ysgwyd trywan,
> Yr yfais i'th lys Lleisiawn gyman
> Eurmyddeddawg lyn, erbyn eurban.

> Thou the opposer of the foe, with *perforated* shield, I have quaffed in thy elegant court of Lleision the golden-wreathing liquor received in golden cup. *Cynddelw, i F. ab Meredudd.*

Trywanawl, *a.* (trywan) Tending to open a passage through; transfixing, stabbing.
Trywanawr, *s. pl.* (trywan) Acts of stabbing.

> Gwawr trywanawr trin, Elfin ail-flawd,
> Gwisgaist amdanad gwisgawd llurig.

> Thou dawn of the *gashing* of conflict, second to Elfin in fortune, thou didst array thyself in a covering of lorica. *Ll. Goch ab Meurig Hen.*

Trywaniad, *s. m.* (trywan) An opening a passage through; a thrusting through; a stabbing.
Trywanoldeb, *s. m.* (trywanawl) A state of having a passage through; the state of being transfixed.

Trywanu, *v. a.* (trywan) To divide or open through; to pierce, thrust, or burst through; to transfix.

> Trillu aeth o Gymmru gynt;
> Trwy Wynedd y trywenynt.
>
> Three hosts went from Wales of yore; through Gwynedd *they penetrated.* *Guto y Glyn.*
>
> Dywan wan, trywan trwyddi:
> Dywed an dawed Geri.
>
> Perambulate a course, *pass through* it, say that we visit Ceri. *O. Cyfeiliawg.*

Trywanwr, *s. m.—pl.* trywanwyr (trywan—gwr) One who opens a passage through; a transfixer

Trywar, *a.* (trw—gwar) Thoroughly tame or mild

Trywedd, *s. m.* (tryw) A trace by scent.

Tryweddiad, *s. m.* (trywedd) A tracing by scent.

Tryweddu, *v. a.* (trywedd) To trace by scent.

Trywel, *s. m.* (trw—gwêl) A vision through. *a.* Perspicuous.

> Gwelant yn gyfloew a thrywel, mai hon yw y farn ac y ddosbarth gyfiawn ar gerdd.
>
> They will see clearly and *perspicuously*, that this is the just sentiment and regulation with respect to the system of verse. *Ed. Dafydd.*

Tryweled, *v. a.* (trywel) To see through.

Tryweledíad, *s. m.* (trywel) A seeing through.

Trywiad, *s. m.* (tryw) A pervading through.

Trywiaw, *v. a.* (tryw) To pervade, to run through; to become continual, or constant.

Trywydd, *s. m.—pl. t.* au (tryw) A trace, a scent; intimation. *Trywydd ceinach*, scent of a hare.

Trywyddawl, *a.* (trywydd) Having a trace.

Trywyddiad, *s. m.* (trywydd) A forming a trace; a following a scent.

Trywyddu, *v. a.* (trywydd) To trace, to follow a scent.

Trywyllt, *a.* (try—gwyllt) Thoroughly wild.

Trywyn, *a.* (try—gwyn) Thoroughly happy.

Trywynawl, *a.* (trywyn) Tending to pervade with bliss; of a conciliatory temper.

Trywyngar, *a.* (trywyn) Apt to diffuse happiness

> Gwrfan esgob Teilaw—gwr doeth haelionus ydoedd, ac a ddyddiai yn drywyngar yn mhob ymrysonau.
>
> Gwrvan the bishop of Teilo, he was a wise liberal man, and he was wont to arbitrate *with a conciliatory effect* in all disputes. *Caradawg o Langarfan.*

Trywyniad, *s. m.* (trywyn) A conciliating.

Trywyniaw, *v. a.* (trywyn) To conciliate.

Trywynwr, *s. m.—pl.* trywynwyr (trywyn—gwr) A reconciler, one who conciliates.

TU, *s. m. r.—pl. t.* oedd. That forms a side; a side, a region, a part. *Tu a thraw*, towards yonder; *tu ag yma*, towards here: *Tu yma*, this side; *tu yna*, that side; *tu acw*, yonder side; *tu hunt*, *tu draw*, the other side, beyond.

> Tu ni fyno Duw ni lwydd.
>
> The *side* that God wills not will not prosper. *Adage.*
>
> Tenen fy ysgwyd ar aswy fy nhu.
> Cu bwyf hen, as gallaf,
> Ar rodwydd Morlas gwyliaf
>
> Thin my shield on the left of my *side* though I be old, if I am able, on the course of Morlas I will watch. *Llywarch Hen.*

Tua, *adv.* (tu—à) Towards, in a direction to. It is used when a consonant follows.

> I gam o gam, mal gwr boneddig yn rhodiaw y ffordd tua nef.
>
> Zig zag like a gentleman perambulating the road towards heaven. *Adage.*

Tuag, *adv.* (tu—ag) Towards. It is used instead of *tua* when a vowel follows.

> Gwedi treiglaw pob tref,
> Teg edrych tuag adref.
>
> After rambling every town, it is pleasant to look *towards* home. *Adage.*

Tuagat, *prep.* (tuag—at) Towards. *Tuagataf*, towards me; *tuagatat*, towards thee; *tuagato*, towards him or it; *tuagati*, towards her; *tuagatom*, towards us; *tuagatoch*, towards you; *tuagatynt*, towards them.

Tuallan, *s. m.* (tu—allan) An outside. *a.* Outside. *prep.* On the outside. *adv.* Outward.

Tuaw, *v. a.* (tu) To form a side; to side.

Tuawl, *a.* (tu) Relating to a side or party.

Tuch, *s. m.* (ty—uch) A grunt, a grumble.

Tuchan, *s. m.* (tuch) A sighing; a groaning.

Tuchanawl, *a.* (tuchan) Grunting, grumbling.

Tuchaniad, *s. m.* (tuchan) A groaning.

Tuchanllyd, *a.* (tuchan) Apt to grumble.

Tuchanu, *v. a.* (tuchan) To grunt, to groan.

> Ni thuchwn ond o'th achaws.
>
> *I would not grumble* but on thy account. *D. ab Gwilym.*

Tuchanus, *a.* (tuchan) Apt to grunt; grumbling.

Tuchanwr, *s. m.—pl.* tuchanwyr (tuchan—gwr) A grunter, a grumbler, a groaner; a murmurer

Tuchaw, *v. a.* (tuch) To grunt, to grumble.

Tuchiad, *s. m.* (tuch) A grunting, a grumbling.

Tud, *s. m.—pl. t.* oedd (ty—ud) A surface; a region, a district.

> Moes pob tud yn ei dud.
>
> The custom of every *place* in its *place*. *Adage.*
>
> Penaf udd Gruffudd, graid eryr Prydain,
> Priodawr tud allmyr.
>
> A supreme lord is Grufudd, the ardent eagle of Britain, the proprietor of a transmarine *region*. *Ll. P. Moch, i R. ab Owain.*
>
> Gweled y bum a golwg
> Goludoedd drwy'r gwledydd drwg;
> Gweled na chaid eu golud;
> Ac nid hael ugain o'u tud;
> Gweled yn Elfael haelion;
> Gweled nad hael gwlad ond hon.
>
> Observing with an eye I have seen the riches in bad countries; then seeing that their wealth could not be had; and that there were not twenty liberal ones on the *surface* of them; seeing in Elvael liberal ones; and seeing that there was no liberal country but this. *L. G. Cothi.*

Tudalen, *s. m.* (tu—dalen) A side of a leaf.

Tudalenawg, *a.* (tudalen) Having a page.

Tudalenawl, *a.* (tudalen) Paginal, paged.

Tudaleniad, *s. m.* (tudalen) A paging.

Tudalenu, *v. a.* (tudalen) To form a page.

Tudaw, *v. a.* (tud) To form a surface or region.

Tudfach, *s. m.—pl. t.* au (tud—bach) A stilt.

Tudgi, *s. m.—pl. t.* on (tud—ci) A terrier.

Tudhaul, *s. m.* (tud—haul) A sunning place.

Tudlath, *s. f.—pl. t.* au (tud—llath) Meting rod.

Tudlëau, *s. pl.* (tud—lle) Brogues.

Tudwed, *s. m.* (tud—gwed) A sward, or sod.

> Llwyr losged ei thudwed a'i tho.
>
> Completely burnt was its *ground* and its roof. *Ll. P. Moch.*

Tudwedd, *s. f.* (tud—gwedd) The face of the earth; the sward, or sod.

> Mor druan——
> Ar ddeurudd Fadawg fod tudwedd!
>
> How miserable that on the cheeks of Madawg there should be the *sod!* *Gwalchmai.*

Tudd, *s. m.—pl. t.* ion (ty—udd) That is over, or that covers; an obscurity, or shade; gloom; smoke, vapour.

Tuddad, *s. m.* (tudd) A covering, or enveloping.

Tuddadwy, *a.* (tuddad) Capable of being covered

Tuddaw, *v. a.* (tudd) To cover, to envelope.

> Pian y bedd yn yr ynys,
> Ai tudd mor a goror gwrys?
> Bedd Meigen mab Rhun, rwyf llys.
>
> Who owns the grave in the island, which the sea *covers* with a border of tumult? The grave of Meigen son of Rhun, the regulator of a court. *Eng. Beddau Milwyr.*

Tuddawg, *a.* (tudd) Being covered, enveloped.

Tuddawl, *a.* (tudd) Tending to cover over.

Tuddad, *s. f.*—*pl. t.* au (tudd) A covering.

> Gwas ystafell biau ben ddillad y brenin oll, eithr ei dudded grawys.
>
> The groom of the chamber owns all the old clothes of the king, except his Lent *garment*. *Welsh Laws.*

Tuddedawg, *a.* (tudded) Having a covering.
Tuddedawl, *a.* (tudded) Belonging to a garment.
Tuddediad, *s. m.* (tudded) A putting on a garment.
Tuddedu, *v. a.* (tudded) To put on a covering.
Tuddedyn, *s. m. dim.* (tudded) A covering.

> Pob tuddedyn dinesig xxiv a dal: pob tuddedyn pentan viii.
>
> Every town-wrought *garment* twenty-four pence is its value: every homespun *garment* eight pence. *Welsh Laws.*
>
> Can ni bo i dalawdr namyn tri thuddedyn, efe a ddyly dalu y ddau.
>
> Since there should be to a debtor only three *garments*, he ought to part with two in payment. *Welsh Laws.*

Tuedd, *s. m.* (tu) The state of being on a side; a coast, a region, district; inclination, proneness, tendency.

> A oes bryd mor ysbrydawl
> A bod ar ffordd——
> Tuedd cymyredd mawr;
> Tref Rufain tyrfa ryfawr?
>
> Is there any season so spiritual as to be on the road, a course of great estimation, to the city of Rome over-teeming in population? *R. Ddu.*
>
> Mellt, gwlaw, mwg, fo eu dwg hyd ar
> Duedd eithafion daiar.
>
> Lightning, rain, smoke, it bears them to the *region* of the extremities of the earth. *W. Middleton.*

Tueddadwy, *a.* (tuedd) Capable of being rendered inclined or partial.
Tueddawg, *a.* (tuedd) Having inclination, partial.
Tueddawl, *a.* (tuedd) Tending to a side; partial, inclined; conducive.
Tueddedig, *a.* (tuedd) Being made partial.
Tueddfryd, *s. m.* (tuedd—bryd) Bent of the mind.
Tueddiad, *s. m.*—*pl. t.* au (tuedd) Inclination.
Tueddogi, *v. a.* (tueddawg) To render partial; to take a side; to become partial.
Tueddoldeb, *s. m.* (tueddawl) Tendency; partiality; inclinedness; conduciveness.
Tueddolder, *s. m.* (tueddawl) Tendency; partiality.
Tueddoli, *v. a.* (tueddawl) To render inclined or partial; to become partial.
Tueddoliad, *s. m.* (tueddawl) A rendering inclined or partial; a becoming partial.
Tueddolrwydd, *s. m.* (tueddawl) Inclinedness.
Tueddu, *v. a.* (tuedd) To incline, to bias.
Tueddus, *a.* (tuedd) Tending to make partial.
Tueddusaw, *v. a.* (tueddus) To render partial; to become inclined or partial.
Tueddusrwydd, *s. m.* (tueddus) Inclinedness.
Tueddwr, *s. m.*—*pl.* tueddwyr (tuedd—gwr) An incliner, one having partiality.
Tuell, *s. f.*—*pl. t.* i (tu) A covert, a cover.

> Y tri pheth y dyly gwr maeddu ei wraig: am roddi peth ni ddylyo ei roddi; ac am ei chaffel gan wr a dan duell; ac am uswyd ar ei farf.
>
> The three things for which a husband ought to beat his wife: for giving away what she ought not to give; for finding her with a man under a *covert*, and for wishing disgrace on his beard. *Welsh Laws.*

Tuelliad, *s. m.* (tuell) A forming a covert.
Tuellu, *v. a.* (tuell) To form a covert; to take to a covert.

> Tuellu bydd tua lle bo,
> Tir i werth tery wrtho.
>
> *Taking to a covert* he will be about where he stays, land for sale he will find out. *S. Brwynawg.*

Tufaes, *s. m.* (tu—maes) An outside. *a.* Outside. *prep.* On the outside. *adv.* Outward.

Tufewn, *s. m.* (tu—mewn) An inside. *a.* Inside. *prep.* Inside. *adv.* Inwardly.

> Gwell tufewn bwth no thufaes castell.
>
> Better *withinside* a hut than outside of a castle. *Adage.*

Tufewnawl, *a.* (tufewn) Internal, inward.
Tuhwnt, *s. m.* (tu—hwnt) The further side, the off side, the other side. *prep.* On the further side, on the other side.
Tul, *s. m.*—*pl. t.* ion (ty—ul) An envelop; a shroud.
Tuli, *s. m.* (tul) That envelopes; a shroud.
Tuliad, *s. m.* (tul) An enveloping, a shrouding.

> Gwythi aur, gwaith Eneplit;
> O'i gnawd yn gwna yn don gwyllt;
> Tuliad am [illegible] ddiys!
> Enwais ar [illegible] Rhys.
>
> Golden veins, of Eneplit's art, from his flesh shooting in wild fire; an *envelop* round a safety-guarding shield; I have [illegible] named the nephew of Sir Rhys. *[illegible]*

Tuliaw, *v. a.* (tul) To envelop; to shroud.
Tum, *s. m.*—*pl. t.* iau (tu—um) A bend, or turn.
Tumiad, *s. m.*—*pl. t.* au (tum) A forming a bend.
Tumiaw, *v. a.* (tum) To form a bend, or angle.
Tumiawg, *a.* (tum) Having a bend, or angle.
Tumiawl, *a.* (tum) Tending to form a bend.
Tumon, *s. f.* (tum) A bender, the rearer or hinder region of the back, the spine; the part of a carcase called a saddle; one of the twelve prime pieces of a stag.
Tun, *s. m.* (tu—un) That pierces or pervades.
Tunad, *s. m.* (tun) A piercing, a pervading.
Tunaw, *v. a.* (tun) To pierce, or to pervade.
Tunawl, *a.* (tun) Piercing, pervading.
Tur, *s. m.* (tu—ur) A change of side, or a reverse.
Turiad, *s. m.* (tur) A reversing, a turning out.
Turiaw, *v. a.* (tur) To reverse, to turn up.
Turiawl, *a.* (tur) Reversing, turning.
Turn, *s. m.*—*pl. t.* au (tur) A turn. *a.* Round.

> Mae'n ei gylch er mwyn eigil,
> Dwrn byr mor durn a baril.
>
> There is about it, for the sake of the one behind it, a short handle as round as a barrel. *L. G. Cothi, fo [illegible]*

Turnen, *s. f. dim.* (turn) That turns; a whirl; a turner's wheel; the wood in the centre of a wheel, or the shaft. *Turnen maen,* the wood in the centre of a millstone wherein the spindle is fastened.
Turniad, *s. m.* (turn) A turning, a whirling.
Turniaw, *v. a.* (turn) To turn round, to whirl; to do turnery work.
Turs, *s. m.*—*pl. t.* iau (tur) A snout, or chaps.
Tursiad, *s. m.* (turs) A making a snout.
Tursiaw, *v. a.* (turs) To make a snout.
Tursyn, *s. m. dim.* (turs) A snout, or chap.
Tus, *s. m.* (tu—us) That binds or wraps.
Tusiad, *s. m.* (tus) A binding or wrapping.
Tusiaw, *v. a.* (tus) To bind round; to wrap.
Tusw, *s. m.*—*pl. t.* au (tus) A whisp, a whisk, a small bundle, a bunch.
Tuswad, *s. m.* (tusw) A whisping, a whisking.
Tuswaw, *v. a.* (tusw) To form a whisp, or bundle.
Tuswawg, *a.* (tusw) Having a whisp or bundle.
Tuswy, *s. m.*—*pl. t.* on (tusw) A whisp, a bunch.
Tuth, *s. m.* (ty—uth) A trot. *Tuth bleidd,* the trudge of a wolf; *tuth march,* the trot of a horse.
Tuthfawr, *a.* (tuth) Greatly trotting.
Tuthiad, *s. m.*—*pl. t.* au (tuth) A trotting.
Tuthiaw, *v. a.* (tuth) To trot, to go on a trot.

> Daethost dan agwrdd duthiaw,
> Ar frys rhag arswn fraw.
>
> Thou didst come with mighty *driving*, in haste lest we should be in dread. *M. ab Gro. Gethin, i Ddygfryd.*

Tuthiawg, *a.* (tuth) Having a trot; trotting.

Tuthiawl, *a.* (tuth) Trotting, going on a trot.
Tuthiedig, *a.* (tuthiad) Being made to trot.
Tuthiwr, *s. m.—pl.* tuthiwyr (tuth—gwr) A man who trots, or a trotter.
Tuthwraig, *s. f.—pl.* tuthwreigedd (tuth—gwraig) A trotting-woman; a gadding gossip.
TW, *s. m. r.* A rise up or out; a drive, an urging; sway. It is also the imperative of the verb.

Tw! farch benthyg.

Gee on' hired horse. *Adage.*

Twa, *v. a.* (tw) To drive, to impel, to urge on.
Twb, *s. m.—pl. t.* iau (ty—wb) A round lump. *Twb y dail*, a chevin, a chub fish.
Twc, *s. m.—pl. t.* ion (tw) A cut, clip, or chip.
Twca, *s. m.—pl. t.* od (twc) A kind of knife.
Twciad, *s. m.* (twc) A clipping, a docking.
Twciaw, *v. a.* (twc) To clip, to dock, to trim.
Twciwr, *s. m.—pl.* twciwyr (twc—gwr) A clipper.
Twdd, *s. m.* (tw) That pokes or juts out.
Twddf, *s. m.—pl.* tyddfau (twdd) What pokes out.

Ai twddf sy yt, ai oddfyn!

Is it a hunch or an excrescence that thou hast! *D. ab Edmwnt.*

Tweg, *s. f.* (tw—eg) A shock or bush of hair.

Teg o dwf yw tweg dyn,
Tent haul, mal tannau telyn.

Fair of growth is the *hair* of the nymph, a sun's radiation like the strings of a harp. *D. ab Edmwnt, i wallt.*

Twf, *s. m.* (tw—wf) A growth; an increase.

Mall can efnin,
Mal twf tir Gwynin.

Soft the bloom of avens, like the *growth* of the soil of Guienne. *Adage.*

Gwr difai o'i gryd i'w fedd,
A yr twf ar ei ufedd.

A man faultless from his cradle to his grave, will bring *increase* on his issue. *W. Lleyn.*

Twff, *s. m.* (tw—wff) A rise, a lift; a tuft.
Twg, *s. m.* (tw—wg) That is forward; luck.

Por y tir yn peri twg
Ar y gwin yn Morganwg.

The lord of the soil causing *prosperity* on the wine in Morganwg. *D. ab Gwilym, i Ifor.*

Haf——
Yn llenwi dail f'm llanerch,
A thwg ar fan amlwg serch.

The summer filling my glade with leaves, and a *prospering* of the conspicuous fit of love. *D. ab Gwilym.*

Twl, *s. m.—pl.* tylau (ty—wl) That is rounded or smooth; a toft.

O gorfydd, un dydd na dau,
Dori'r talar drwy'r tylau.

If there should be an occasion on one day or another, to break up the headland through the *tofts.* *Ll. Goch y Dant.*

Twlc, *s. m.—pl.* tylciau (twl) A dent, a hollow; a small cot, or hovel; a stye. *Heb na thy na thwlc*, without either house or hovel. *Is Aled.*

Neidiai——
Ci coch o dwlc moch i mi.

A red dog leaped from the pig *stye* upon me. *D. ab Gwilym.*

Twlch, *s. m.—pl.* tylchau (twl) A round mass, a heap; a tump, or knoll; a pile. *Tylchau*, the Knolls, a hilly district in Glamorgan so called.

Bu bwlch, bu twlch tandde.

There was an opening, there was a pile pervaded with flame. *Aneurin.*

Twlff, *s. m.—pl.* tylffau (twl) A round lump.
Twlffen, *s. f. dim.* (twlff) A bulky female. *Dyna globen o dwlffen*, see there a load of a chubby one
Twlffyn, *s. m. dim.* (twlff) A fat bulky person.
Twli, *s. m.* (twl) Buckram, stiff cloth.
Twlo, *s. m.* (twl) A bulk; a booth, a hut.
Twll, *s. m.—pl.* tyllau (tw—wll) A hole; a pit; a cavern; a dimple. *Twll olp*, an oilet hole; *twll yn ei boch*, dimple in her cheek.
Twm, *s. m.* (ty—wm) A round heap.
Twmffed, *s. m.—pl. t.* i (twm—ffed) A funnel.
Twmffedu, *v. a.* (twmffed) To use a funnel.
Twmp, *s. m.—pl.* tympiau (twm) A tump.
Twmpan, *s. f. dim.* (twmp) A round mass; an epithet for a fat female.
Twmpath, *s. m.—pl. t.* au (twmp) A hillock, a knap, a tump; also a bush. *Twmpathau*, a sort of games.

Gwneuthur mynydd o dwmpath myrion.

Making a mountain of an ant *hill.* *Adage.*

Y twmpath lle claddid Rhys a'i wyr a elwir Bryn y Beddau.

The *tump* where Rhys and his men were buried is called the *Hill of the Graves.* *Cwrdawg o Langarfan.*

Twmpathawg, *a.* (twmpath) Abounding with tumps or knolls; covered with bushes.
Twmpathiad, *s. m.* (twmpath) A forming a tump; a forming a bush.
Twmpathu, *v. a.* (twmpath) To form a tump or knoll; to form a bush.
Twmpethyn, *s. m. dim.* (twmpath) A small hillock.
Twmpiad, *s. m.—pl. t.* au (twmp) A dropping.
Twmpian, *v. a.* (twmp) To continue dropping, or falling; to drop; to let fall suddenly; to nod, or to drop, as the head does when a person is overcome with sleep; to strike upon, to stamp, to flap, to thump.
Twmpiaw, *v. a.* (twmp) To drop, to fall.
Twmpiawl, *a.* (twmp) Dropping, falling.
Twn, *s. m.—pl. t.* ion (ty—wn) A break, or rising up of a surface; a scaling, a splint; a fracture. *a.* Having the surface broken; scaled, splintered; fractured, broken. *Esgyrn twnion*, splintered bones: *Bara twn*, broken bread.
Twnadwy, *a.* (twn) Capable of being fractured.
Twnc, *s. m.* (ty—wnc) That is brought forward or upon; a deposit; the chief rent. *Twnc y brenin*, the king's rent.
Twnedig, *a.* (twn) Being broken, fractured.
Twnfriw, *a.* (twn—briw) Broken to pieces.

Llawe twr twnfriw.

Many a tower *broken to shatters.* *Gwalchmai.*

Twniad, *s. m.* (twn) A breaking, a fracturing.
Twniaw, *v. a.* (twn) To break, to fracture.
Twnrif, *s. m.—pl. t.* ion (twn—rhif) A broken number, or fraction.
Twnrifaw, *v. a.* (twnrif) To reckon fractionally.
Twnrifawg, *a.* (twnrif) Consisting of fractions.
Twnrifawl, *a.* (twnrif) Fractional.
Twnrifedd, *s. m.* (twnrif) Fractions.
Twnrifiad, *s.* (twnrif) A reckoning fractionally.
Twnrifyn, *s. m.* (twnrif) A fractional number.
Twng, *s. m.* (ty—wng) That is brought forward, destined, fated, or assigned; that is pledged, or alledged; a lot or share; a plight, troth, or oath; a pledge of homage; a yearly acknowledgement due to the lord of the soil, according to the laws of Wales; also a certain ration of corn due from tenant to landlord.

Nid twng ond a fyno Duw.

There is no *destiny* but what God wills. *Adage.*

Mi wn eu trwydded,
Eu tro, eu cerdded,
Eu twng, a'u tynged.

I know their course, their turn, their walk, their lot, and their *destiny.* *Taliesin.*

Twr, *s. m.—pl.* tyrau (tw—wr) A heap, a pile, an aggregate; a tower.

> Yr aur, ei adel sy raid·
> Yn dwr i ryw ddyn dirlaid.

> The gold, it must needs be left a *heap* for some mischievous person. *S. Tudyr.*

> Tair tid fal y twr tewdws.

> Three chains like the *pleiades.* *D. ab Edmund.*

Twra, *s. m. dim.* (twr) An aggregate, a mass.

> Twra, bid crog a'i tyrawdd.

> The heap, hang him who heaped it! *D. ab Gwilym, i gaseg eira.*

Twrch, *s. m.—pl.* tyrchod (tw—wrch) That raises burrows, or heaps up; a hog; a splayed boar. *Twrch daiar*, a mole.—*Twrch Trwyth, mab Taredd Wledig*, The hog of the Spray, son of the monarch Taredd, a personage often introduced in ancient tales. Such brooks as sink into the ground are generally called *Twrch*, or the Burrower.

> Nid ungerdd twrch ag eaws.

> Not of the same song the *pig* and the nightingale. *Adage.*

> Nerth twrch yn ei aflach.

> The strength of a *hog* in his hind legs. *Adage.*

> Son wrth foch am orchestion twrch.

> Discourse with swine about the feats of a *hog.* *Adage.*

Twrd, *s. m.—pl.* tyrdau (twr) A shallow tub; also called *mit*, *twrnel*, and *twred*.

Twrdd, *s. m.—pl.* tyrddau (tw—wrdd) A tumult.

> Yn ebyr—
> Twrdd ac anferth ryferthwy
> Dygyfor, ni fu for fwy.

> In the mouths of rivers, *tumult* and dreadful torrent of meeting waters, there never was a greater sea. *Gronw Owain.*

Twred, *s. m.* (twr) That is raised, or piled; a pile; a turret; a tub.

> Dyred, hen dwred eira,
> Diddawn wyd——

> Come along, thou old snow *ball*, void of good art thou. *R. Goch, Eryri.*

Twrf, *s. m.—pl.* tyrfoedd (twryf) That rises; is high, or loud; a stir, a tumult; that is drawn together; or shrunk. *Twrf ac enwed*, riot and damage; *twrf cyfraith*, a tumult of law: *Twrf gïau*, contraction of sinews: *Tyrfau*, thunder claps. *Sil.*

> Arileng torf rhag twrf cammawn,
> Mal twrf ebyr yn llyr llawn.

> The foremost rank of a host before the *turmoil* of combat, like the *turmoil* of the mouths of rivers when full of flood. *Cynddelw, i O. ab Madawg.*

> Twrf yw llosgi tai neu dorri aradr.

> A tumult is the burning of houses, or breaking of a plough. *Welsh Laws.*

Twriad, *s. m.* (twr) A turning or throwing up.

Twriaw, *v. a.* (twr) To raise up, to heap; to turn up. *Moch yn twriaw tir*, swine turning up the ground.

Twriawl, *a.* (twr) Tending to turn or throw up.

Twrll, *s. m.—pl. t.* au (twr) A round mass, or lump. *Twrll torllaes*, a bulky one with a swagging belly.

Twrlla, *s. m.—pl. t.* od (twrll) A round-bellied one; a mountain mouse, a marmot.

Twrllach, *s. m.—pl. t.* au (twrll) A round lump; a bulky squab. *Rhyd y Twrllachau*, the Ford of the Lumps, a place so called.

Twrllachiad, *s. m.—pl.* twrllachiaid (twrllach) One with a bulky body.

Twrlläes, *s. f.—pl. t.* au (twrlla) A bulky one.

> Twrllësau torllaesion.

> Round bulky ones with low bellies. *T. Aled, i [illegible].*

Twrn, *s. m.—pl.* tyrnau (ty—wrn) A round; what revolves, or circulates; a turn. *Twrn da*, a good turn; *twrn drwg*, an ill turn.

> P'le bynag, diorwag dwrn
> Yr adeilais ar dalwrn,
> ——[illegible]ynodd.

> In whatever spot, not vain the *turn*, the building I have [illegible] on a bendland, it prospered. *[illegible]*

> Gwna Suddas, gwn ei oddi
> Dafara' twrn, dy frad di.

> Judas brought about treachery to thee, an *event* [illegible] repented of, I know that he sunk. *D. ab [illegible]*

> Rhai'n dda'i tyrnau, tonnau tân;
> Rhai'n ddrwg o'r hen ddaroganau.

> Some whose *turns* are good, waves of fire; some [illegible] ancient predictions. *[illegible]*

Twrnel, *s. m.—pl. t.* i (twrn) A tub; a vat.

Tws, *s. m.* (tw—ws) An extreme; an outlet.

Twsel, *s. f.—pl. t.* i (tws) A tap, a faucet.

> Can feddwed a'r dwsel.

> As drunk as the *faucet.* *Adage.*

Twselig, *s. f. dim.* (twsel) A small faucet.

Twt, *s. m.* (tw—wt) That is simple, whole, complete, or having an interval with respect to any thing else; a drive; a puff.

> Gormodd iaith yw twt ar farch.

> Too much speech is *tut* to a horse. *Adage.*

Twt, *a.* (tw—wt) Being whole or complete; having an interval; complete; neat.

Twtach, *s. m.* (twt) A dispnœa, hard breathing.

Twti, *s. m.* (twt) The state of being simple, whole, or unconnected with any thing else; an intermittent state.

Twtiad, *s. m.* (twt) A making an intermission; a making neat or trim.

Twtial, *v. a.* (twt) To make intermission; to [illegible].

Twtiaw, *v. a.* (twt) To intermit; to render a thing complete by itself; to make neat.

Twtnais, *a.* (twt—nais) Altogether neat.

Twtne, *s. m.* (twt—ne) A simple hue; dun.

Twtneisiad, *s. m.* (twtnais) A making quite neat.

Twy, *s. m.* (tw) That is extreme, that surrounds, that hems in; check, stop, restraint.

Twyad, *s. m.* (twy) A hemming in; a checking.

Twyaw, *v. a.* (twy) To hem in; to check, to restrain; to curb; to manage.

Twyawg, *a.* (twy) Hemming in; checking.

Twyawl, *a.* (twy) Hemming in; checking.

Twyg, *s. f.—pl. t.* au (twy) A garment; a toga.

> Ni chymeraf gymun gan gygymun Synnich,
> Ag eu twygau ar eu clun;
> A'm cymuno Duw ei hun.

> I will not receive a communion from accursed monks, with their cloaks on their hips; who communes with me let him be God himself. *[illegible]*

> Braidd y medd, dan bridd a main
> Dig ei ir, dwyg o liain!

> Scarcely doth he possess, under earth and stones in [illegible] plight, a *wrapper* of cloth! *L. G. Cothi.*

Twygaw, *v. a.* (twyg) To cover, to wrap over; to cover with a toga.

Twygawg, *a.* (twyg) Having a garment; wearing a toga.

Twygawl, *a.* (twyg) Belonging to a garment.

Twygiad, *s. m.* (twyg) A wrapping round with a garment: a putting on a toga.

Twyll, *s. m.—pl. t.* au (twy) That is masked: deception, illusion; deceit, fraud.

Tan enw pwyll y daw twyll.

Under the name of reason *deceit* will come. *Adage.*

Pan aned dysg daeth twyll i'n mysg;
Pan ddysger dysg daw gwir i'n mysg.

When learning was born delusion came amongst us; when learning shall become learned truth will come amongst us. *Adage.*

Gwedi myned Gortheyrn yn frenin, anfon a orug i geisiaw pawb i ddeol y Pichtiaid: necus a orug y Prydeiniaid; ac erchi iddo, o gwnathoedd dwyll iddynt, wneuthur iawn, neu ddebyn a ddelai ato.

After Gortheyrn had become king, he sent to get every body to expel the Picts: what the Britons did was to refuse him: then desiring of him, if he had committed a fraud to them, to make retribution, or to abide what might befal him. *Gr. ab Arthur.*

Twyllad, *s. m.* (twyll) A deceiving, deception.
Twylladwy, *a.* (twyllad) That can be deceived.
Twyllaw, *v. a.* (twyll) To deceive, to disappoint; to beguile, to cheat, to defraud.

Twyllaw arall twyllaw yth hunan.

To deceive another is *to deceive* thyself. *Adage.*

Twyllaw arall yn fawr twyllaw yth hun yn fwy.

To deceive another greatly is *to deceive* thyself more. *Adage.*

A wnel dwyll ef a dwyllir.

He that worketh deceit *will be deceived.* *Adage.*

Twyllawd, *s. m.* (twyll) The act of deceiving.
Twyllawdl, *s. f.* (twyll—awdl) False rhyme.
Twyllawdr, *s. m.* (twyllawd) A deceiver.
Twyllawg, *a.* (twyll) Full of deception.
Twyllawr, *s. m.—pl.* twyllorion (twyll) A deceiver.
Twyllchware, *s. m.* (twyll—chware) False play.
Twyllchwareu, *v. a.* (twyllchware) To play falsely
Twyllchwarëus, *a.* (twyllchware) Falsely playing.
Twyllchwareydd, *s. m.—pl. t.* ion (twyllchware) One who plays cheatingly.
Twylleb, *s. f.* (twyll) Sophistry, sophism.
Twylledig, *a.* (twyll) Being deceived, cheated.
Twylledigaeth, *s. m.* (twyll) The act of deceiving.
Twyllfarchnata, *v. a.* (twyll—marchnata) To practise fraud in trading.
Twyllfawr, *a.* (twyll) Full of deceit, or fraud.
Twyllforwyn, *s. f.—pl. t.* ion (twyll—morwyn) A false maid.

Os twyllforwyn a geffir, heb wad, ei chrys a dorir iu rhagddi a thra ei chefu, ac oddiyna ei gwr a ddyry iddi enderig, gwedi iraw ei losgwrn; ac o dichona hi ei attal berwydd ei losgwrn, cymered hi ef yn ei hegweddi.

If a *false maid* shall be found, without defence, her shift shall be cut on the fore side and behind her, and then her husband shall give her a steer, whose tail has been greased; so if she shall be able to stop him by his tail, let her have him for her separate settlement. *Welsh Laws.*

Twyllgam, *s. m.—pl. t.* au (twyll—cam) False step.
Twyllgar, *a.* (twyll) Deceptious, apt to cheat.
Twyllgynghanedd, *s. m.—pl. t.* ion (twyll—cynghanedd) False consonancy.
Twyllgynghaneddiad, *s. m.* (twyllgynghanedd) A forming a false consonancy.
Twyllgynghaneddu, *v. a.* (twyllgynghanedd) To form false consonancy.
Twyllodli, *v. a.* (twyllawdl) To form false rhyme.
Twyllodliad, *s. m.* (twyllawdl) A forming of false rhyme.
Twyllodrus, *a.* (twyllawdr) Deceiving, deceitful; fraudulent, false; crafty.

Tri chas Duw, a dyn. golwg ymladdgar, tafawd twyllodrus, ac anbri drygionus.

The three hated by God and man. a look denoting war, a deceitful tongue, and a mischievous disposition. *Coelog Ddoeth.*

Twyllodrusaw, *v. a.* (twyllodrus) To render deceitful; to become deceitful.

Twyllodrusedd, *s. m.* (twyllodrus) Deceitfulness.
Twyllodrusrwydd, *s. m.* (twyllodrus) Deceitfulness.
Twyllofaint, *s. m.* (twyll) Deceitful conduct, circumvention, that is unawares.
Twyllrin, *s. m.* (twyll—rhin) A false secret.

Ac os mi ai haedd berwydd twyllrin,
Ni'm bo un cyfaill namyn Cain.

And if I deserve it on account of *false secret*, may I meet with no conversing friend excepting Cain. *Gwalchmai.*

Twyllwr, *s. m.* twyllwyr (twyll—gwr) A deceiver.

Nid twyll twyllaw twyllwr.

It is no deceit to deceive a *deceiver*. *Adage.*

Twyllwriaeth, *s. m.* (twyllwr) The practice of a deceiver.
Twym, *s. m.* (twy) A heat; a flush. *Twym y mynydd*, mountain heat, a disease among cattle. *a.* Hot, warm.

Iachus arogli bara twym, afiachus ei fwyta.

It is healthy to smell *warm* bread, it is unhealthy to eat it. *Adage.*

Cydwymed a'r pathew.

As warm as the dormouse. *Adage.*

Twymad, *s. m.* (twym) Calefaction, a heating.
Twymadwy, *a.* (twymad) Capable of being heated.
Twymaw, *v. a.* (twym) To calefy, to warm.

Cynt y twyma gwaed no dwfr.

Sooner *will* blood *grow warm* than water. *Adage.*

Twymawl, *a.* (twym) Tending to make warm.
Twymdra, *s. m.* (twym) Warmth, hotness.
Twymdwyr, *a.* (twym—twyr) Lukewarm.
Twymdwyrad, *s. m.* (twyr) A making lukewarm.
Twymdwyraw, *v. a.* (twyr) To make lukewarm.
Twymedig, *a.* (twymad) Being warmed, heated.
Twymedd, *s. m.* (twym) Warmth, warmness.
Twymnaw, *v. a.* (twymyn) To warm, to heat.
Twymnawl, *a.* (twymyn) Tending to warm.
Twymnder, *s. m.* (twymyn) Warmth, hotness.
Twymndra, *s. m.* (twymyn) Warmth, heat.
Twymnedig, *a.* (twymyn) Being warmed.
Twymnedd, *s. m.* (twymyn) A warm state.
Twymniad, *s. m.* (twymyn) A warming.
Twymnwr, *s. m.—pl.* twymnwyr (twymyn—gwr) One who heats, a warmer.
Twymp, *s. m.* (twym) That is warm or cheering.

Eur-air penraith, aerwymp twymp pob taith,
Aergorf Iorf Lloegr-laith, gwaith gwythloneaf.

A golden word is the fiat of the supreme, the brightly fair *cheerer*, of every course, the war-bulwark with a shaft slaying the English, most wrathful work. *G. ab M. ab Dafydd, i Owain.*

Twymyn, *s. m.* (twym) A heat, a flush; a fever. *Y dwymyn doben*, the mumps, a disease in the head so called. *a.* Hot, warm.
Twyn, *s. m.—pl. t.* au (twy) A hillock; also a tuft; a bush. *Ar dwyn*, on an eminence, conspicuous.
Twynaw, *v. n.* (twyn) To form a tump; to tuft.
Twynawg, *a.* (twyn) Abounding with tumps.
Twyndir, *s. m.* (twyn—tir) Hilly ground.
Twynen, *s. f.—pl. t.* ydd (twyn) A sand-hill.
Twyniad, *s. m.* (twyn) A forming a tump.
Twynyn, *s. m.* (twyn) A tump; a tuft; a bush.
Twyogi, *v. a.* (twyawg) To manage, to restrain.
Twyr, *s. m.* (twy) That is agitated or heated. *a.* Agitated; freshened, parched, torrid.
Twyrad, *s. m.* (twyr) An agitation; a parching.
Twyraw, *v. a.* (twyr) To agitate; to parch, to heat.
Twys, *s. m.—pl. t.* au (twy) A top, a tuft, a head, a heap. *Twys yd*, ear of corn.
Twysaw, *v. a.* (twys) To top, to tuft; to spire.

Twysawg, *a.* (twys) Being a top; having a top, or tuft; having a spire, eared.

Twysawl, *a.* (twys) Topping; tufting, spiring.

Twysen, *s. f. dim.—pl. t.* i (twys) An ear of corn.

> Twysen lawn a ostwng ei phen; twysen wag a saif yn syth.
>
> A full *ear* lowers its head; an empty *ear* stands up straight. *Adage.*

Twysenawl, *a.* (twysen) Spiring, earing.

Twyseniad, *s. m.* (twysen) A spiring, a shooting into ears.

Twysenig, *s. f. dim.* (twysen) A single ear.

Twysenu, *v. a.* (twysen) To spire, to ear.

Twysg, *s. m.—pl. t.* au (twys) A mass, a heap; a quantity; some quantity, some part; the quantity of yarn usually contained on a spindle.

> Mae wedi dirwyn ei dwysg.
>
> He has gone his *length*. *Adage.*
>
> Teg gloew teg, twysg liw tywyn,
> A haul a ddattodai hyn.
>
> Fair clear radiancy, *some* dawn of shining, and the sun would this dissolve. *D. ab Gwilym, i'r rhew.*

Twysgaw, *v. a.* (twysg) To amass, to heap, to collect a certain quantity; to get to a head, to get on, to get to an end with any thing; to limit. *Yr wyf yn twysgaw ar fy arian yn arw*, I am getting through with my money sadly.

> All yn disgyn, alon dwysaw,
> Wrth ecr-frwysgaw Arthur fawrgedd.
>
> When descending, the foes *consuming*, like in stalking through the slaughter to the greatness of Arthur. *D. ab Edmwnt, i Rys o Fon.*
>
> Y tyntal a dwysgai ato.
>
> The multitude *gathered* to him. *W. Salisbury.*

Twysgawl, *a.* (twysg) Tending onward, proceeding; collective, aggregating.

Twysged, *s. f.—pl. t.* au (twysg) A mass; a quantity; a good deal; a certain portion, some.

> Yr wybodaeth y buom trwy ein bywydau yn ei chasglu, nid yw llawer o honi ond anwybodaeth yn unig; a thwysged o honi yn waeth.
>
> The knowledge that we have been through our lives collecting, much of it is nothing but sheer ignorance; and *some* of it is worse. *Ier. Rhys.*

Twysgen, *s. f. dim.* (twysg) A quantity; a good deal; a certain quantity or portion; some.

Twysgiad, *s. m.* (twysg) A proceeding, a going on; a getting through; a limiting; a collecting.

Twysgwr, *s. m.—pl.* twysgwyr (twysg—gwr) One who proceeds; one who goes through; a limiter.

Twysiad, *s. m.* (twys) A topping; a spiring.

Twyth, *s. m.—pl. t.* ion (twy—yth) A spring, or pliancy, aptness to proceed; celerity, dispatch. *Dyn hydwyth*, a tractable person.

> Arddwyreaf hael o hil Rodri,
> Ardwyad gorwlad, gwerlin teithi;
> Teithiawg Prydain,
> Twyth afrdwyth Owain,
> Teyrnain ni grain ni grawn rai.
>
> I will exalt the generous one of the line of Rodri, the curber of the bordering country, endued with gifts of an illustrious stock; the heir of Britain, *ambition* the passion of Owain, the princely one who submits to none, who hoards no treasures. *Gwalchmai.*

Twythad, *s. m.* (twyth) A springing, a bounding.

Twythadwy, *a.* (twythad) Capable of springing.

Twythaw, *v. a.* (twyth) To spring, to bound.

Twythawd, *s. m.* (twyth) The act of springing.

Twythawg, *a.* (twyth) Having spring, elastic.

Twythawl, *a.* (twyth) Springing, bounding.

Twythedig, *a.* (twythad) Being made elastic.

Twythedigaeth, *s. m.* (twythedig) The act of rendering elastic; a springing.

Twythfalch, *a.* (twyth—balch) Aspiringly proud.

> Nest ——
> Golwg gwalch dwythfalch o brif deithi.
>
> Nest with eye of a hawk *aspiringly proud*, of princely origin. *Gwalchmai.*

Twythfawr, *a.* (twyth) Greatly springing.

> Arglwydd teithiawg twythfawr yn arfau,
> Yn arfwaith beiddiawr,
> Argae torf rhag torf arawr,
> Arglwyddriad dewiad, daldd gawr.
>
> A rightful sovereign *greatly energetic* in arms, in the superior toil of martial feats; the bulwark of a host before the ... of shields, the overshadowing leader, the wall of the shout. *Cynddelw, i Wenwynwyn.*

Twythiad, *s. m.* (twyth) A springing, resilition.

Twythiannawl, *a.* (twythiant) Of a tendency to spring or bound; resilient; of an elastic quality.

Twythiannu, *v. a.* (twythiant) To cause a springing or resiliency; to make a rebound.

Twythiant, *s. m.* (twyth) Elasticity; resiliency.

Twythig, *a.* (twyth) Springing, elastic; rising.

Twythigrwydd, *s. m.* (twythig) Aptness to spring.

Twythus, *a.* (twyth) Apt to spring or bound.

Twythusaw, *v. a.* (twythus) To render elastic.

Twythusdra, *s. m.* (twythus) Aptness to spring.

Twythusrwydd, *s. m.* (twythus) Aptness to spring.

Twythwal, *s. m.* (twyth—gwal) Elastic couch.

> Pell o Fon fain ydwyt, dwythwal, wenfro
> Esmwyth ymydd yn aneirw gyfoeth.
>
> Far from pleasant Mon art thou, *soft place of repose*, whose inhabitancy is at ease enjoying a splendid affluence. *Gwalchmai.*

Twythwalch, *s. m.—pl.* twythweilch (twyth—gwalch) A springing hawk.

TY, *s. m. r.—pl. t.* au. A being about or going on; that is inclusive; a house. *Ty ac anifeil*, house and chattels. It is a prefix in composition, implying a state of being going on or being in.

> Athraw pawb yn ei dy.
>
> Every body is master in his *house*. *Adage.*
>
> Ni wyr dyn nad el o'i dy.
>
> A man knows nought who goes not out of his *house*. *Adage.*
>
> Gwae y ty lle nas clywer llais cerydd.
>
> Woe to the *house* where the voice of reproof is not heard. *Adage.*
>
> Nid allan o'i ffordd a grwydra i dy dewiniaid.
>
> He is not out of his way who strays to the *house* of the druid. *Adage.*

Tyad, *s. m.* (ty) A housing; a domifying.

Tyaeth, *s. m.* (ty) A house establishment; a household. *Perchen tyaeth*, the owner of a household.

> Mae Duw ei hun yn gorchymyn yn neillduol i bob perchen tyaeth athrawiaethu ei deulu.
>
> God himself doth command particularly that every owner of a *household* should instruct his family. *Rees Prichard, Yn. Dewiniaid.*

Tyaid, *s. m.—pl.* tyeidiau (ty) A houseful.

Tyaidd, *a.* (ty) Like a house; domestic.

Tyaw, *v. a.* (ty) To house, to put in a house; to domify.

Tyawg, *a.* (ty) Having a house, or housed.

Tyawl, *a.* (ty) Belonging to a house, domestic.

Tyb, *s. m.—pl. t.* iau (ty—yb) Opinion, notion, sentiment, thought; suspicion.

> Celwydd ni wna ond cilwg;
> Nid da heb droed un tyb drwg.
>
> A falsehood will only create an angry look; no bad *opinion* is commendable without a foundation. *G. ab I. ab Llywelyn Fychan.*

Tybgar, *a.* (tyb) Opinionated; suspectful.

Tybgarwch, *s. m.* (tybgar) Opinionativeness; suspectfulness, suspiciousness.

Tybiad, *s. m.—pl. t.* au (tyb) A supposing, a suspecting, an imagining, a thinking.

Tybiant, *s. m.* (tyb) Opiniation, opinion.

Tybiaw, *v.* (tyb) To opine, to suppose, to suspect.

> Cas a dybio ei fod yn well no neb ar bob peth ac yntau yn waethaf oll.
>
> Odious is he *who thinks* that he is better than any body in every thing and he being the worst of all. *Adage.*
>
> A dybiwys a gamsynwys.
>
> He that *hath suspected* hath mistaken. *Adage.*

Tybiawl, *a.* (tyb) Supposing, suspecting.
Tybied, *v. a.* (tyb) To suppose, to suspect.
Tybiedig, *a.* (tybiad) Supposed, imagined.
Tybiedigawl, *a.* (tybiedig) Putative, opiniative.
Tybiwr, *s. m.—pl.* tybiwyr (tyb—gwr) An opiniator, a supposer, a suspecter.
Tybost, *s. m.—pl.* tybyst (ty—post) A house-post.

> Y tybost, pedair ceiniawg cyfraith yw ei werth.
>
> A *house-post*, four lawful pence is its value. *Welsh Laws.*

Tybus, *a.* (tyb) Apt to suppose, suspecting.
Tybusaw, *v. a.* (tybus) To render suspecting; to become suspicious, to be suspectful.
Tybusrwydd, *s. m.* (tybus) Suspectfulness.
Tybwg, *s. m.* (tyb) The state of being supposed.
Tybygadwy, *a.* (tybwg) Supposable, imaginable.
Tybygawl, *a.* (tybwg) Suppositive; supposed.
Tybygiad, *s. m.* (tybwg) An imagining.
Tybygiedig, *a.* (tybygiad) Supposed, imagined.
Tybygoldeb, *s. m.* (tybygawl) Suppositiousness.
Tybygoli, *v. a.* (tybygawl) To render suppositious; to become suppositive.
Tybygoliaeth, *s. m.* (tybygawl) Supposition.
Tybygolrwydd, *s. m.* (tybygawl) Imaginariness.
Tybygwr, *s. m.—pl.* tybygwyr (tybwg—gwr) A supposer, one who imagines.
Tyciad, *s. m.* (twg) A prospering, a succeeding; a prevailing; a befitting.
Tyciannawl, *a.* (tyciant) Prospering; prevailing; tending to suit or to agree with.
Tyciannu, *v. a.* (tyciant) To cause prosperity, or success; to become successful.
Tyciannus, *a.* (tyciant) Prosperous; lucky.
Tyciannusaw, *v. a.* (tyciannus) To render prosperous; to become successful.
Tyciannusdra, *s. m.* (tyciannus) Prosperousness.
Tyciannusrwydd, *s. m.* (tyciannus) Prosperousness, successfulness.
Tyciant, *s. m.* (twg) Prosperity, success; meetness
Tyciaw, *v. a.* (twg) To prosper, to succeed; to prevail; to befit, to suit, to agree with.

> Yn lle y bo y da
> Y rhoir ac y tycia.
>
> Where there is property, there will be given and *it will prosper.* *Adage.*
>
> Nid oedd yn Ffrainc wr a dyciai iddo gyhydreg ag Emrais.
>
> There was not in France a man to whom *it would succeed* to contend with Emrais. *Gr. ab Arthur.*

Tyciawl, *a.* (twg) Prospering; prevailing.
Tyd, *s. m.* (ty—yd) That is continuous or whole.
Tydain, *s. m.* (ty—tain) The centre of expansion, the centre of fire; that is universally pervasive; an epithet for the sun. *Tydain Tad Awen*, or Tydain Father of the Muse, is a personage often alluded to in the Triades and in our poetry, as the founder of the bardic system; and he probably was so named on account of his superior genius; as, in such a case, the epithet was not improperly applied to him, in a metaphorical sense. It is remarkable that, in the mythology of the Greeks and Romans, *Apollo* had similar attributes with the *Tydain* of the *Cymmry*; and therefore he was probably the same person; and was feigned to be the sun from the cogency of the original epithet. I believe *Tydain* to have been a real person; yet it were easy to turn the whole into an allegory, supported by a verse, which says that his grave was in *Bron Aren*; for *Bron* means the *breast*, and the *swell of a hill*, often applied in the names of places; *Aren*, also is the appellative of several hills, descriptive of their smoothness, and it means smooth or eloquent, with respect to composition.

> Bedd Tydain Tad Awen
> Yn ngodir Bron Aren.
>
> The grave of Tydain Father of the Muse in the boundary region of Bron Aren. *Eng. Beddau Milwyr.*

Tydalaeth, *s. m.* (ty—talaeth) House-perch.
Tydi, *pron.* (ty—ti) Thou. *Tydi dyhun, tydi yth hun, tydi dy hunan, tydi yth hunan*, thou thyself.

> Tydi, Arglwydd, rwydd rinweddau bob awr,
> A rodded dan llawr, fawr fwriadau;
> Tydi, Duw, gwedi gwawdiau cof ydyw
> Cyfodaist i'th radau.
>
> *Thou*, Lord, at all times freely dispensing virtues, wert placed beneath the sod, great the designs; *thou*, God, afterwards, memorable themes of praise, didst rise in thy blessings. *G. ab M. ab Dafydd.*

Tyddfawg, *a.* (twddf) Having a jutting, hunchy.
Tyddfawl, *a.* (twddf) Tending to jut out.
Tyddfiad, *s. m.* (twddf) A jutting or projecting.
Tyddfu, *v. a.* (twddf) To poke out, to jut out.
Tyddiad, *s. m.* (twdd) A spreading or laying out.
Tyddu, *v. a.* (twdd) To spread out, to lay out.
Tyddyn, *s. m.—pl. t.* od (twdd) Land under cultivation; a farm, a tenement.

> Pedair erw yn mhob tyddyn a ddyly fod; pedwar tyddyn yn mhob rhandir: deuddeg erw a thriugaint a fydd yn y rhandir gyfreithiawl, rhwng rhwydd a dyrys, a choed a maes, a gwlyb a sych, eithr yr orfottref.
>
> There ought to be four acres in every *messuage*, four messuages in every shareland: there are to be seventy-two acres in a lawful shareland, between the open and the wild, and wood and field, and wet and dry, except the accessory township. *Welsh Laws.*
>
> Awn i aredig y tyddyn,
> Sy rhwng y ty a'r odyn.
>
> Let us go to plough the *field* that is between the house and the kiln. *D. ab Gwilym.*

Tyddynawl, *a.* (tyddyn) Relating to a tenement.
Tyddynyn, *s. f. dim.* (tyddyn) A small tenement.
Tyedig, *a.* (tyad) Being housed; domified.
Tyfadwy, *a.* (twf) Capable of growing.
Tyfawl, *a.* (twf) Growing or vegetating.
Tyfedig, *a.* (twf) Being grown or vegetated.
Tyfiad, *s. m.—pl. t.* au (twf) A growing.
Tyfiannawl, *a.* (tyfiant) Vegetative, growing.
Tyfiannu, *v. a.* (tyfiant) To produce vegetation.
Tyfiannus, *a.* (tyfiant) Tending to vegetate.
Tyfiannusaw, *v. a.* (tyfiannus) To render vegetative; to become vegetative.
Tyfiant, *s. m.* (twf) A growth, or vegetation.
Tyfu, *v. a.* (twf) To grow; to cause to grow.

> Had dyniewlaid a dyf ant yn mhob tir;
> Had synwyr braidd y tyfant yn un tir.
>
> The seed of placemen *will grow* in every land; the seed of reason scarcely *will they grow* in any land. *Adage.*
>
> Dar a dyfwys yn meillion,
> A chan a'i briw ni bu gron.
> Gwae wr wrth ei gaseion.
>
> An oak *hath grown* amidst the trefoils, and since it has been wounded it is not round; woe to a man amongst his foes. *Robert Tywysawg Normandi.*

Tyfwr, *s. m.—pl.* tyfwyr (twf—gwr) A grower.
Tygiad, *s. m.* (twg) A prospering, a succeeding,
Tygiaw, *v. a.* (twg) To prosper, to befit.

> Yn ngwlad Tegaingl y tygia,
> Am glod a wn, ym gael da.
>
> In the county of Tegaingl *it will prosper*, for the fame I collect, for me to obtain a benefit. *O. ab S. ab Rhys, ab Hy. Cortwer.*

Tyhun, *pron.* (ty—hun) Thyself. See *Tydi*.
Tyhunan, *pron.* (tyhun) Thyself, thou thyself.

Tylad, *s. m.* (twl) A making smooth; a forming a smooth toft.
Tylaith, *s. m.* (ty—llaith) That destroys.
Tylath, *s. f.—pl. t.* au (ty—llath) A house beam.
Tylawd, *a.* (ty—llawd) Poor, needy, being in want, being bereaved.

Ffawd ar ol ffawd a wnant ddyn yn dylawd.

Luck after luck will make a person *poor*. *Adage.*

Tylcyn, *s. m. dim.* (twlc) A small hovel.
Tylchawg, *a.* (twlch) Abounding with knolls.
Tylchiad, *s. m.* (twlch) A forming a knoll.
Tylchu, *v. a.* (twlch) To form a knoll or tump.
Tyle, *s. m.—pl. t.* au (twl) A gentle swell or elevation, a small bank or rising hill, a down; a toft, the site of a building; a couch. It forms the names of several places; as *Tyle Denis Powys*; *Tyle Forgan*; *Tyle Garw*; *Tyle y Gaul*; *Tyle Tref Gatwg*. *Tyle Ysgawd*, or Scottish Tyle, an old appellation for Ireland.

Treiddiant—
Tai a threfnau,
A thyliau,
A cheliau bwyd.

They will pervade houses and furniture, and *couches*, and meat closets. *Taliesin.*

Yn nghyfarfod clod cludfeirdd dyle,
Yn nghyfrwys gynnwys gan wawr y ser.

In the convention of fame on the *area* of the assembling bards, in an intellectual reception in the glory of the stars.
Ll. P. Moch.

Pan edrychynt y dyle, nid oedd arnei namyn byrwellt dystlyd chweinllyd.

When they surveyed the *couch*, there was upon it only broken straw dusty and full of fleas. *Breudd. Rhonabwy.*

Tylinad, *s. m.* (glin) A kneading of dough.
Tylinaw, *v. a.* (glin) To knead, to work dough.

Mae gwaith Gildas wedi myned trwy ddwylaw y mynaich; gwyr a fedrynt yn dda ddigawn dylinaw pob peth i'w dybenion eu hunain.

The work of Gildas hath past through the hands of the monks; men who knew well enough how *to mould* every thing to their own purposes. *Evan Evans.*

Tylinedig, *a.* (tylinad) Being kneaded.
Tylinwr, *s. m.* (tylinaw—gwr) A kneader.
Tylodaidd, *a.* (tylawd) Somewhat poor or needy.
Tylodedd, *s. m.* (tylawd) Poverty, poorness.
Tylodi, *s. m.* (tylawd) Poverty, or poorness.

Nid oes gan gyfiawnder na golud na thylodi.

Equity has neither wealth nor *poverty*. *Adage.*

Amledd cybydd yn tylodi arno.

A miser's abundance is *poverty* to him. *Adage.*

Nid tylodi ond clefyd.

There is no *poorness* like disease. *Adage.*

Tylodus, *a.* (tylawd) Tending to make poor.
Tylodusaw, *v. a.* (tylodus) To render poor.
Tylodusedd, *s. m.* (tylodus) Impoverished state.
Tylodusrwydd, *s. m.* (tylodus) State of poverty.
Tylotyn, *s. m. dim.* (tylawd) A poor person.
Tylu, *s. m.—pl. t.* oedd (ty—llu) A household.
Tylüaidd, *a.* (tylu) Familiar; sociable, domestic.
Tylüedd, *s. m.* (tylu) The state of being a household, socialness, sociableness.

Mad ganed o genedl fonedd,
Mawr wledig mawrwlad tylüedd.

Blessed was he born of a noble race, the great sovereign of the great country of *society*. *Cynddelw, i Dysilio.*

Tylüeiddiad, *s. m.* (tylüaidd) A familiarizing.
Tylüeiddiaw, *v. a.* (tylüaidd) To familiarize.
Tylüeiddrwydd, *s. m.* (tylüaidd) Familiarness.
Tylüwr, *s. m.—pl.* tylüwyr (tylu—gwr) A family man, a domestic man.
Tylwyth, *s. m.—pl. t.* au (ty—llwyth) A household, a family; kinsfolk, a tribe. *Y tylwyth teg, bendith eu mamau, gwreigedd annwyl, y teulu,* aerial beings, sylphs, gnomes, or fairies, but they are not considered of a diminutive form, as the fairies are, in English tales.

Byw ar dir y tylwyth teg.

To live on the land of the fairy *tribe*, or by unknown means. *Adage.*

Tylwythaw, *v. a.* (tylwyth) To form a family.
Tylwythawg, *a.* (tylwyth) Having a household, having a family, or kindred; having a great family; populous.

Tylwythawg dyrfa yr annuwiawl, ni bydd [illegible].

The ungodly *of extended household*, it shall not be prosperous. [illegible]

Tylwythiad, *s. m.* (tylwyth) A forming a family.
Tylwythogi, *v. a.* (tylwythawg) To form a household or family.
Tylwythogrwydd, *s. m.* (tylwythawg) The state of having a family.
Tylywodraeth, *s. m.* (ty—llywodraeth) House management, household economy.
Tyllawg, *a.* (twll) Having holes, perforated.
Tyllfras, *a.* (twll—bras) Of ample opening.

Gwen forddwyd tyllfras
A wyliai neithwyr yn ngwrwr rhyd Forlas:
A chan bu mab yn ni thechas.

Gwen with thigh *of wide opening* did watch last night on the border of the ford of Morlas: and as he was my son he fled not.
Llywarch Hen.

Tyllgrug, *s. m.* (twll—crug) The opening of the ground in dry weather.
Tylliad, *s. m.—pl. t.* au (twll) A boring.

Pan oeddwn yn sefyll ac yn rhyfeddu gyfynged y tylliad, mi welwn hen wiber yn myned i mewn, ac yn gyflawnd yn dyfod yn ei hol yn gyfnewydd ac yn ieuanc.

When I was standing, and wondering how narrow was the *perforation*, I beheld an old serpent going in, and immediately coming back renovated and young. *Marchawg Crwydrad.*

Tylliedig, *a.* (tylliad) Bored, or perforated.
Tylliedydd, *s. m.—pl. t.* ion (tylliad) A borer.
Tyllogi, *v. a.* (tyllawg) To make full of holes.
Tyllogrwydd, *s. m.* (tyllawg) The state of being full of holes, porousness.
Tyllu, *v. a.* (twll) To make a hole, to bore.

Y dafn a dyll y gareg, nid o gryfder ond o fynych syrthiaw.

The drop *will perforate* the stone, not through strength but from often falling. *Adage.*

Tyllwr, *s. m.—pl.* tyllwyr (twll—gwr) One who bores a hole, or perforates.
Tyllydd, *s. m.—pl. t.* ion (twll) A borer.
Tym, *s. m.* (ty—ym) A principle of extension, a principle of enlargement; a tendency to enlarge; space.
Tymher, *s. m.* (tymp) Temperament.
Tymheraidd, *a.* (tymher) Temperamental.
Tymherawl, *a.* (tymher) Temperamental.
Tymhereiddiad, *s. m.* (tymheraidd) A rendering temperamental; a becoming temperate.
Tymhereiddiaw, *v. a.* (tymheraidd) To render temperate; to become temperate.
Tymhereiddrwydd, *s. m.* (tymheraidd) Temperateness.
Tymheriad, *s. m.—pl. t.* au (tymher) A tempering.
Tymheriedydd, *s. m.—pl. t.* ion (tymher) One who renders temperate.
Tymheru, *v. a.* (tymher) To temper; to mollify.
Tymherus, *a.* (tymher) Temperate.
Tymherusaw, *v. a.* (tymherus) To render temperate; to become temperate.
Tymherusdra, *s. m.* (tymherus) Temperateness.
Tymherusedd, *s. m.* (tymherus) Temperateness.
Tymherusrwydd, *s. m.* (tymher) Temperateness.
Tymherwr, *s. m.* (tymher—gwr) A temperer.

Tymherydd, *s. m.—pl. t.* ion (tymhor) A seasoner

Tymhest, *s. m.* (tymp) That breaks out.

Tymhestl, *s. f.—pl.* tymhestledd (tymhest) A tempest, a storm.

Tymhestlaidd, *a.* (tymhestl) Tempestive.

Tymhestlawg, *a.* (tymhestl) Tempestuous.

Tymhestliad, *s. m.* (tymhestl) A tempesting.

Tymhestlu, *v. a.* (tymhestl) To tempest.

> Mal ydd oeddynt felly yn ymladd o bob parth, ar warthaf yr eigiawn, enycha yn ddisyfyd y gwyntoedd gwrthwyneb yn chwythu, ac yn tymhestlu y weilgi, ac yn gwasgaru y llongau i amryfeillion draethau.
>
> As they were in that manner fighting on all sides, upon the face of the ocean, behold suddenly the adverse winds blowing, and *tempesting* the torrent, and dispersing the ships to various shores. *Gr. ab Arthur.*

Tymhestlus, *a.* (tymhestl) Tempestuous.

Tymhig, *s. m.—pl. t.* ion (tymp) A prickle, a twitch, a stinging.

Tymhigaw, *v. a.* (tymhig) To twitch, to prickle.

Tymhigawl, *a.* (tymhig) Twitching, pricking.

Tymhigiad, *s. m.* (tymhig) A twitching.

> Gallai fod i ddyn, cyn y credai ef cariad Duw tuag ato yn Nghrist, mesur mawr o ymostyngiad cyfreithiawl, a thymhigiad calon.
>
> A person might have, before he believed in the love of God towards him in Christ, a great degree of obedience according to the law, and *pricking* of conscience. *S. Trefredyn.*

Tymhigiedig, *a.* (tymhigiad) Being twitched.

Tymhigwr, *s. m.—pl.* tymhigwyr (tymhig—gwr) A twitcher, a stinger.

Tymig, *a.* (tym) Ample; seasonable, timely, of full time, mature, efficient.

> Nid oes o ddyn——
> Ond tywarchen dymig briddles, domawg briddled!
>
> There is nothing of man but the clod an extending gloomy cell, miry and composed of dust! *Gr. Ddu.*

Tymmor, *s. m.—pl. t.* au (tym—mor) Season.

> Hinon heddwch a wna bob tymmor yn haf.
>
> The halcyon days of peace make every *season* like summer. *Adage.*

Tymmoraidd, *a.* (tymmor) Tending to be seasonable; seasonable; fit, befitting. *Byw yn dymmoraidd*, to live comfortably.

Tymmorawl, *a.* (tymmor) Temporal; seasonable.

Tymmordy, *s. m.—pl. t.* au (tymmor—ty) A house that is managed by the season; a house that is held by the season, or tenanted at will.

Tymmoreidd-dra, *s. m.* (tymmoraidd) Seasonableness; comfortableness.

Tymmoreiddiad, *s. m.* (tymmoraidd) A rendering seasonable; a becoming seasonable.

Tymmoreiddiaw, *v. a.* (tymmoraidd) To render or become seasonable; to render fitting.

Tymoreiddrwydd, *s. m.* (tymmoraidd) Seasonableness; comfortableness.

Tymmoreiddwch, *s. m.* (tymmoraidd) Seasonableness; comfortableness.

Tymmorgwaith, *s. m.* (tymmor—gwaith) A certain season, a certain time.

Tymmori, *v. a.* (tymmor) To make a season.

Tymmoriad, *s. m.—pl. t.* au (tymmor) A making a season; a fixing a season.

Tymmoroldeb, *s. m.* (tymmorawl) Seasonableness

Tymhyr, *s. m.—pl. t.* au (tymp) A temporality.

> Pwyllai Forgant ef a'i wyr,
> Fy neol a llosgi fy nhymhyr.
>
> Morgant and his men would rush onward, expelling me and burning my *native place*. *Llywarch Hen.*
>
> Fy mrodyr a'm tymhyr a gwynaf!
>
> My brothers and my *native land* I mourn! *Llywarch Hen.*
>
> Llüest Cadwallon heno
> Trathir yn nhymhyr Penfro.
>
> The encampment of Cadwallon to-night in the extreme of the *temporality* of Penvro. *Llywarch Hen.*

> Ni rydd rhwyng eryr
> Hyd troed o'i dymhyr,
> Er ofyn berwyr
> Yn berw ystawd.
>
> He that is of eagle course will not give the length of his foot of his *temporality*, for fear of depredators in the path of depredation. *Gwalchmai, i F. ab Meredudd.*

Tymhyraw, *v. a.* (tymhyr) To attemperate, to temper; to moderate. *Tymhyra fe yn dda*, temper it well.

Tymhyrawl, *a.* (tymhyr) Attemperate.

Tymhyriad, *s. m.* (tymhyr) A tempering.

Tymhyroldeb, *s. m.* (tymhyrawl) Temperateness

Tymp, *s. m.* (tym) Enlargement; the act or time of bringing forth; birth; season.

> Budd cyn tymp.
>
> Profit before the *birth*. *Adage.*

Tyn, *s. m.* (ty—yn) A pull, a draught; a stretch; a tendency, or inclination.

> Ni phaid Prydeiniaid a'u tyn.
>
> The Britons will not refrain from their *inclination*. *D. ab I Ddu.*

Tyn, *a.* (ty—yn) Stretched, tight, strait, tightly stuffed or pressed; stubborn, pertinacious.

> Po tynaf fo y llinyn cyntaf y tyr.
>
> The *tightest* the string may be the sooner it will break. *Adage.*
>
> Gochel 'y pechawd cyntaf, canys y mae lleng yn dyn wrth ei sawdl.
>
> Avoid the first sin, for there is a legion *close* at its heel. *Adage.*

Tynâad, *s. m.* (tynâu) A tightening, a straining.

Tynâawl, *a.* (tynâu) Tightening, straining.

Tynâu, *v. a.* (tyn) To tighten, to strain.

Tynawl, *a.* (tyn) Drawing, straining, pulling.

Tynchwydd, *s. m.—pl. t.* au (tyn—chwydd) A tumour.

Tynder, *s. m.* (tyn) Stretchedness, tightness, straitness; rigidity, rigour; austerity; stubbornness.

> Rhag balchder, tynder y tir,
> Gwared fi, Arglwydd gwirwir.
>
> From the pride, the stubbornness of the land, deliver me righteous Lord. *H. D. ab Ifan.*

Tyndir, *s. m.—pl. t.* oedd (twn—tir) A fallow.

Tyndra, *s. m.* (tyn) Tightness, or straitness.

Tyndrec, *s. m.—pl. t.* iau (trec) A draught geer.

Tyndrecyn, *s. m. dim.* (tyndrec) An elevatory, a chirurgical instrument so called.

Tynedig, *a.* (tyn) Being drawn or pulled.

Tynedigaeth, *s. m.—pl. t.* au (tynedig) Attraction

Tynedigawl, *a.* (tynedig) Attractive, drawing.

Tynedigolrwydd, *s. m.* (tynedig) Attractiveness.

Tynell, *s. f.—pl. t.* i (tyn) A barrel; a tun.

Tynellaid, *s. f.—pl.* tynelleidiau (tynell) The quantity contained in a tun.

Tynelliad, *s. m.* (tynell) A filling a tun.

Tynellu, *v. a.* (tynell) To fill a tun.

Tyner, *a.* (tyn) Tender, lenient; assuasive.

> Gair tyner dadl galed.
>
> *Tender* word hard argument. *Adage.*

Tynerâad, *s. m.* (tynerâu) A rendering tender, an assuaging; a becoming tender.

Tynerâawl, *a.* (tynerâu) Tending to soften.

Tyneraidd, *a.* (tyner) Somewhat tender.

Tynerâu, *v. n.* (tyner) To become tender.

> Y llu——
> Er gradd ei drugareddau
> Duw Ner rhoed hwy i dynerâu!
>
> The multitude, according to the degree of his mercies, may the Lord God incline them *to become gentle*. *H. D. ab Ifan.*

Tynerawl, *a.* (tyner) Of a soothing nature.

Tyneredig, *a.* (tyner) Being made tender.

Tyneredd, *s. m.* (tyner) Tenderness, leniency.

Tyneriad, *s. m.* (tyner) A making tender; emollition, mollification.

Tyneriant, *s. m.* (tyner) Emollition; leniency.

Tynerwyf, *s. m.—pl. t.* au (tyner—nwyf) A tender passion.

Tyneru, *v. a.* (tyner) To soften, to assuage, to lenify, to make tender; to become tender.

Tynerus, *a.* (tyner) Of a tender quality.

Tynerusaw, *v. a.* (tynerus) To render lenient; to become tender, or lenient.

Tynerusrwydd, *s. m.* (tynerus) Tenderness.

Tynerwch, *s. m.* (tyner) Tenderness, lenity.

Tynfa, *s. f.—pl.* tynfëydd (tyn) A draught.

> A oedd y fath rin a thynfa yn llais yr athrylyd i ennill yr hen eglwys gynt? [illegible]
>
> Was there such a charm and *attraction* in the voice of the lover to gain the old church formerly? *Ier. Owain.*

Tynfach, *s. m.—pl. t.* au (tyn—bach) A harpago, the gaffle of a cross-bow.

Tynfaen, *s. m.* (tyn—maen) A loadstone.

Tynfalch, *a.* (tyn—balch) Stubbornly proud.

Tynfalchedd, *s. m.* (tynfalch) Stubborn pride.

Tynfarch, *s. m.* (tyn—march) A draught horse.

Tynhegl, *s. f.* (tyn—hegl) A stretching limb.

> Gorewynawg [illegible], tynhegl ebrwydd.
>
> Crowned with foam the wave, *of stretching limb* the quick one. *H. ab Owain Gwynedd.*

Tynhug, *s. f.—pl. t.* au (tyn—hug) A close coat.

Tyniad, *s. m.—pl. t.* au (tyn) A pulling, a drawing, a tension; a pull, a draught; deduction. *Tyniadau a chyweirdannau*, modulations and chord-strings.

Tyniar, *s. f.—pl. t.* oedd (tyn—iar) A bubble.

Tyniedydd, *s. m.—pl. t.* ion (tyniad) A drawer.

Tynlath, *s. f.* (tyn—llath) A draught-tree.

Tyno, *s. m.* (twn) A plain area, a plat, or plot; a dale; a green. *Tyno Coch*, the old name of Ceredigion.

> Coed, maes, tyno, a bryn.
>
> Wood, field, *dale*, and hill. *Taliesin.*
>
> Nid oes dwyn, na dwys dyno,
> Yn [illegible] glyn Nant y Glo—
> Na wyddost.
>
> There is nor damp nor tedious *dale*, about the *dingle of* Nant y Glo, but thou knowest. *D. ab Gwilym.*

Tynraff, *s. f.* (tyn—rhaff) A drawing rope.

Tynrwyd, *s. f.* (tyn—rhwyd) A dragnet.

Tynrwydd, *s. m.* (tyn) Rigidity, or tightness.

Tynrwym, *s. m.* (tyn—rhwym) A tight bandage.

Tynrwymaw, *v. a.* (tynrwym) To bind tightly.

Tynrwymiad, *s. m.* (tynrwym) Astriction.

Tynu, *v. a.* (tyn) To draw, to pull, to lug. *Tyn hi gan bwyll*, draw her on gently. *Dyfed.*

> Cyfiaw a dynant at y mel.
>
> The wasps will *draw* to the honey. *Adage.*
>
> Na thyn [illegible];
> Na fydd ry hyf ar [illegible].
>
> *Draw* no play from a savage; be not over encroaching on the good-natured. *Llywarch Hen.*
>
> Hawdd tynu danneddi blaidd, ond hwyr y tynir o hono ei anian.
>
> It is easy *to draw* a wolf's teeth, but it will be long before his nature is *pulled* out of him. *Adage.*
>
> Antur[illegible], [illegible] hell a thonau,
> A thynwn tua yn rhi,
> Tad pob gwlad rhad roddi,
> Un [illegible] [illegible] a [illegible].
>
> Let us venture, let us range the brine and waves, and *let us draw* towards our Lord, the Judge of every nation, dispensing grace, one supreme of lords and three. *Cynddelw.*

Tynwr, *s. m.—pl.* tynwyr (tyn—gwr) A puller.

Tynwydd, *s. m.* (tyn—gwydd) Direction, information, intelligence.

Tynwyddaw, *v. a.* (tynwydd) To direct, to guide

Tynwyddawl, *a.* (tynwydd) Directin[g]

Tynwyddiad, *s. m.* (tynwydd) Direct[ion]

Tynwyddwr, *s. m.—pl.* tynwyddwy[r] [(tynwydd—]gwr) One who directs, or an infor[mer]

Tynwyddyd, *s. m.* (tynwydd) Directi[on], information, intelligence. *A [illegible] wyddyd i mi am danu?* canst thou [give me in]telligence about it? *Sil.*

Tyngad, *s. m.* (twng) A making a [illegible] plighting; a swearing; adjuration.

Tyngadwr, *s. m.—pl.* tyngadwyr (t[illegible]) An exorcist; an adjurer.

Tynged, *s. f.—pl. t.* ion (twng) Desti[ny], [for]tune, luck. *Tynged ddrwg iddo!* [illegible] him!

> Goreu tynged diwedd da.
>
> The best *fortune* is a good end.
>
> Nid i bob [illegible] tynged.
>
> *Fate* is not attached to every [illegible]
>
> Trech tynged nag arfaeth.
>
> *Fate* is more powerful than [illegible]
>
> Ni ellir dyn ochel tynged.
>
> A person cannot avoid *fate*.

Tyngedawl, *a.* (tynged) Belonging t[o fate]

Tyngedfen, *s. f.—pl. t.* au (tynged[illegible]) fated or sworn necessity, fate, des[tiny]

> Nid oes nawdd rhag tyngedfen.
>
> There is no refuge against *destiny*.

Tyngedfenawg, *a.* (tyngedfen) Bein[g]

Tyngedfenawl, *a.* (tyngedfen) Belon[ging] fatal; fortunate; predestined.

Tyngedfeniad, *s. m.* (tyngedfen) A [illegible] ble to fate; predestination.

Tyngedfenoldeb, *s. m.* (tyngedfenaw[l]) of being subject to destiny; fatali[ty]

Tyngedfenoli, *v. a.* (tyngedfenawl) [illegible] fate; to become destined.

Tyngedfenolrwydd, *s. m.* (tyngedfen[illegible]) subject to destiny.

Tyngedfenu, *v. a.* (tyngedfen) To pr[edestine]

Tyngedfenus, *a.* (tyngedfen) Pred[illegible]

> O ffol-dreg tyngedfenus! [illegible]
> [illegible]
>
> Oh thou foolish son *of destiny!* [illegible] than a shadow of a [illegible] belongs to a beast. [illegible]

Tyngedfenwr, *s. m.—pl.* tyngedfen[wyr] (tyngedfen—gwr) A fatalist; a predestina[rian]

Tyngediad, *s. m.—pl. t.* au (tynged) [illegible]

Tyngedig, *a.* (tynged) Being sworn. [illegible] *dyngedig*, he is rather addicted to [illegible]

Tyngedigawl, *a.* (tyngedig) Jurator[y]

Tyngediad, *s. m.* (tynged) Adjuratio[n]

Tyngedu, *v. a.* (tynged) To make [illegible] adjure. *Wyf yn dy dyngedu i fyn[d]* [I] adjure thee to go out.

> [illegible]
>
> [illegible] *Fond. Tryn*[illegible]

Tyngedwr, *s. m.* (tynged—gwr) An [adjurer]

Tyngiad, *s. m.* (twng) A swearing, a[illegible]

Tyngnaith, *s. f.* (twng—naith) A sw[illegible]

> I'w tyngnaith [illegible]
> Y gwyr eil o'i fangor el.
>
> To their *sanctuary* they will [illegible] of his high choir. [illegible]

Tyngnawdd, *s. m.* (twng—nawdd) [Pro]tection.

Tyngu, *v. a.* (twng) To render fixed or unalterable; to depose; to swear, to take an oath; to adjure. *Tyngu anudon*, to swear a false oath.

Niddawr diriad pa dyng.

The mischievous cares not what *he swears*. *Adage.*

Mal hyn y bu y dangnefedd rhyngddynt: sef amgen, talu o Henri—dirfawr swmp o ariant i Lowys, fab brenin Ffrainc, trwy dyngu ohono yntau deyrnas Lloegr yn dragywyddawl.

In this manner was there peace between them: that is to say, by Henry's paying an immense sum of money to Louis, the son of the king of France, through his *adjuring* on his part the kingdom of England for ever. *Brut y Saeson.*

Tyngwr, *s. m.—pl.* tyngwyr (twng—gwr) A swearer.

Tyrawl, *a.* (twr) Heaping, or accumulating.

Tyrch, *s. m.* (torch) That consists of circles.

Tyrchaidd, *a.* (twrch) Hoggish, or like a hog.

Tyrchawl, *a.* (twrch) Belonging to a pig, or hog.

Tyrches, *s. f.—pl. t.* od (twrch) A splayed sow. *Twrch a thyrches*, a splayed boar and splayed sow.

Tyrchiad, *s. m.* (twrch) A burrowing, as a pig.

Tyrchu, *v. a.* (twrch) To turn up; to burrow.

Tyrchwr, *s. m.* (twrch—gwr) A mole-catcher.

Tyrchyn, *s. m. dim.* (twrch) A little hog; a hoggish fellow.

Tyrddain, *v. a.* (twrdd) To be blustering, to storm.

Tyrddan, *s. m.* (twrdd) A blustering, a turmoil.

Tyrddiad, *s. m.* (twrdd) A blustering, a storming.

Tyrddu, *v. a.* (twrdd) To bluster, or to storm.

Triged yno ny fro fras,
Tyrdded mewn tai o urddas.

Let him abide there in the rich country, *let him bluster* in houses of renown. *Tho. Llywelyn.*

Tyrddwr, *s. m.* (twrdd—gwr) A blusterer.

Tyredig, *a.* (twr) Heaped, or accumulated.

Tyrfa, *s. f.—pl.* tyrfeydd (twrf) A multitude.

Un dyrfa a wna derfysg,
Rhag i'r llall gael mael i'n mysg.

One *host* raiseth a tumult, lest the other should obtain an advantage amongst us. *H. D. ab Ifan.*

Tyrfain, *v. a.* (twrf) To be blustering, to storm. *s. m.* A storm, a tumult.

Mal gwaith Arderydd gwyth ar dyrfain cad.

Like the battle of Arderydd wrath in the *storm* of conflict. *Cynddelw.*

Tyrfâu, *v. a.* (twrf) To cause a drawing together; to be contracted.

Tyrfedig, *a.* (twrf) Being heaped; being drawn together; contracted.

Tyrfiad, *s. m.* (twrf) A heaping; a turning up, as swine do the ground; a contraction, or shrinking.

Tyrfu, *v. a.* (twrf) To draw together; to rise tumultuously; to contract, to shrink.

Tòn tyrfid, todd erfid.

The wave is *boisterous*, it covers the shore. *Llywarch Hen.*

Ehon i wan, hwch i dyrfu.

An ox to spread, a sow *to turn up*. *Taliesin.*

Tyriad, *s. m.* (twr) A heaping; accumulation.

Tyriaw, *v. a.* (twr) To heap up; to turn up.

Tyru, *v. a.* (twr) To heap, to pile; to make a heap, to amass, to collect, to accumulate.

Am benaeth ydd ym, am benaf terwyn
Tyrant feirdd am alaf.

Around a chief we are, around the chiefest of the fierce bards *will gather together* after wealth.
Cynddelw, i O. ab Madawg.

Tyrwn, *s. m.—pl.* tyrynod (twr) A sand-bank; also called *tyroden* and *traethell*.

Tyrwr, *s. m.—pl.* tyrwyr (tyru—gwr) A heaper.

Tysmwy, *s. m.—pl. t.* on (tws—mwy) A throbbing, a palpitation; horror, trembling. *Tysmwy ar un wedi gweled ellyll*, horror upon one after seeing a monster.

Nid esmwyth hyn o dysmwy;
Ni bu boen ar farw-groen fwy.

Not comfortable this *fit of shivering*, there never was a benumbed skin in greater pain. *D. ab Gwilym.*

Tysmwyad, *s. m.* (tysmwy) A throbbing, a palpitating; a trembling with fear.

Tysmwyaw, *v. a.* (tysmwy) To throb; to tremble with fear.

Tysmwyawl, *a.* (tysmwy) Throbbing; shivering.

Tyst, *s. m.—pl. t.* ion (ty—yst) One who testifies.

Tystiad, *s. m.* (tyst) A testing, a witnessing.

Tystiant, *s. m.—pl.* tystiaint (tyst) A witness.

Tystiaw, *v. a.* (tyst) To testify, to bear witness.

Tystiawl, *a.* (tyst) Testifying, witnessing.

Tystiedig, *a.* (tystiad) Being testified or witnessed

Tystiolaeth, *s. f.—pl. t.* au (tystiawl) Testimony.

Tystiolaethawl, *a.* (tystiolaeth) Testimonial.

Tystiolaethiad, *s. m.* (tystiolaeth) A testifying.

Tystiolaethu, *v. a.* (tystiolaeth) To give a testimony; to bear witness.

Tystiolaethwr, *s. m.—pl.* tystiolaethwyr (tystiolaeth—gwr) One who gives testimony; testifier.

Tystiwr, *s. m.* (tystiaw—gwr) A testifier.

Tysyn, *s. m. dim.* (tws) The bottom of a ball of yarn or thread.

Tytmwy, *s. m.—pl. t.* au (twt—mwy) A loop; a clasp; a buckle.

Tytmwy ar adwy ydoedd,
Tant coed, ar nant cadarn oedd—
Y fieren.——

A *fastening* on a gap to it, the string of the wood, across a dingle strong was the brier. *D. ab Gwilym.*

Tytmwyad, *s. m.* (tytmwy) A fastening with a loop, clasp, or buckle.

Tytmwyaw, *v. a.* (tytmwy) To fasten with a loop, clasp, or buckle; to buckle.

Tytmwyawg, *a.* (tytmwy) Having a fastening loop

Tytmwyedig, *a.* (tytmwyad) Fastened by looping.

Tyw, *s. m.* (ty) That tends to over-spread.

Tywall, *s. m.* (tyw—gwall) A pour; a spill. *v. a.* To pour; to shed, to spill.

Tywalliad, *s. m.* (tywall) A pouring; a shedding.

Tywallt, *s. m.* (tywall) A pour; a spill. *v. a.* To pour; to shed, to spill.

Tywalltawg, *a.* (tywallt) Having a pouring.

Tywalltawl, *a.* (tywallt) Pouring, spilling.

Tywalltedig, *a.* (tywallt) Being poured out.

Tywalltiad, *s. m.* (tywallt) A pouring; a shedding.

Tywalltiedydd, *s. m.—pl. t.* ion (tywalltiad) One who makes a pouring; a pourer.

Tywalltu, *v. a.* (tywallt) To pour; to shed.

Tywalltwr, *s. m.—pl.* tywalltwyr (tywallt—gwr) A pourer; a shedder.

Tywalltydd, *s. m.—pl. t.* ion (tywallt) A pourer.

Tywarch, *s. m. aggr. pl.* tyweirch (tyw—arch) A spreading element; a sod, a clod, a turf.

Nid oes dim dyfnfawn, ond digon o dywarch yn y Wyddgrug.

There is no deep peat, but plenty of *turf* in the Wyddgrug. *Ed. Llwyd.*

Tywarchawg, *a.* (tywarch) Turfy, glebous; swardy

Tywarchawl, *a.* (tywarch) Turfy, or glebous.

Tywarchawr, *s. m.—pl.* tywarchorion (tywarch) That is of the sod; an epithet for the ox in a yoke on the turf side, as opposed to *rhychawr*, or the one that walks in the furrow.

Tywarchen, *s. f.—pl. t.* i (tywarch) That is over or covering, a stratum; an element, a constituent matter; a sod, a clod. *Y pum tywarchen*, the five elements. *Barddas.*

Y ddwy dywarchen yr â pawb iddynt; y nef ac y ddaiar.

The two *elements* into which every body go; the heaven and the earth. *Trioedd Athrawl.*

Syrthiynt y rhai brathedig, a'r ergydiau yn eu hymysgaroedd; a chin amled y rhedai y dywarchen o'r gwaed, a chyd bai dirfyd ddeheuwynt yn llyncu eiry i'r mor.

The wounded ones were falling, with the propelled shafts in their bowels; and so abundantly did the *sod* run with blood, as if a sudden south wind were sinking the snow into the sea. *Gr. ab Arthur.*

Tywarchiad, *s. m.* (tywarch) A forming of glebe, turf, or sod; a swarding.

Tywarchlyd, *a.* (tywarch) Turfy, swardy, glebous.

Tywarchu, *v. a.* (tywarch) To form turf or sod; to sward; to cover with turf.

Cyn gweryd gorofer digu,
Cyn annawr tywawr tywarchu
Fy nghnawd, tywarchen o bobtu,
Bwyf gwas Duw cyn bom gostegu!

Before the bed frail in the extreme and unlovely, before the ungenial spread of covering with turf my flesh, a sod on either side, may I be a servant of God ere I be silenced! *Elidir Sais.*

Tywas, *s. m.—pl.* tyweision (ty—gwas) A house servant, a domestic.

Dy gynnogn ni gynnall y tywas.

Thy debtor will not maintain the *domestic*. *Ll. P. Mach, i L. ab Iorwerth.*

Tywawd, *s. m.—pl.* tywodydd (tyw) Sand.

Tywel, *s. m.—pl. t.* i (tyw) A cloth, a towel. *Tyweli caws*, cheese cloths.

Tywell, *a.* (*f. of* tywyll) Dark, obscure, dusky.

Nos da i'r ynys dywell;
Ni wn oes un ynys well.

Good night to the *dusky* isle; I know not that there is a better isle. *Ll. Goch ab Meurig Hen.*

Tywerchyn, *s. m. dim.* (tywarch) A clod, a sod.

Tywi, *s. m.* (tyw) The state of being spread

Tywiad, *s. m.* (tyw) A spreading over.

Tywiaw, *v. a.* (tyw) To spread abont.

Tywiawl, *a.* (tyw) Tending to overspread.

Tywodaidd, *a.* (tywawd) Arenaceous; like sand.

Tywodawg, *a.* (tywawd) Having sand; sandy.

Tywodawl, *a.* (tywawd) Arenaceous; sandy.

Tywodi, *v. a.* (tywawd) To sand; to become sand.

Tywodiad, *s. m.* (tywawd) A forming of sand.

Tywodlyd, *a.* (tywawd) Sandy, full of sand.

Tywodlydrwydd, *s. m.* (tywodlyd) Sandiness.

Tywodwlydd, *s. m.* (tywawd—gwlydd) Sandwort.

Tywodyn, *s. m. dim.* (tywawd) A grain of sand.

Tywota, *v. a.* (tywawd) To gather sand.

Tywu, *v. a.* (tyw) To spread about, to dilate.

Tywydd, *s. m.* (tyw) That is of a spreading principle; the atmosphere; the weather.

Hwn ar dywydd dydd, a wnaeth deuddyn hen;
Hwynt a gad o briddyn.

He, on the *expansion* of day, did form two primitive persons, they were had from earthly substance. *L. G. Cothi.*

Am y tywydd goreu tewi.

About the *weather* it is best to be silent. *Adage.*

Tywyll, *s. m.* (ty—gwyll) Dark; dusk, gloom. *a.* Dark; dusky, gloomy.

Llewychid gwir yn nhywyll.

The truth shines in the *dark*. *Adage.*

Ystafell Cynddylan ys tywyll heno,
Heb dân, heb oleuad:
Elid amdaw am danad!

The hall of Cynddylan is *dark* this night, without fire, without light: a deadly silence goes about thee! *Llywarch Hen.*

Tywyllawd, *s. m.* (tywyll) An obscuration.

Tywyllawdr, *s. m.—pl.* tywyllodron (tywyllawd) One who makes obscure or dark.

Tywyllawr, *s. m.* (tywyll) An obscurer.

Tywylledig, *a.* (tywyll) Darkened, obscured.

Tywylliad, *s. m.* (tywyll) A darkening, an obscuring.

Tywyllu, *v. a.* (tywyll) To darken, to obscure; to grow dark, to become obscure, to grow dusky or gloomy.

Tywyllwch, *s. m.* (tywyll) Darkness, obscurity.

Tywyllwg, *s. m.* (tywyll) Darkness, obscurity.

Tywyllwr, *s. m.—pl.* tywyllwyr (tywyll—gwr) A darkener, one who renders obscure.

Tywyn, *s. m.—pl. t.* ydd (tyw) A spread; a strand; a ray, or beam of light.

Blin yw ar bob blaenawgwydd,
Blodeuyn o dywyn dydd.

Troubled is it on every change, a flower from the *light* of day. *D. ab Gwilym, i'r Rhosyn.*

Tywynawg, *a.* (tywyn) Having a splendor.

Tywynawl, *a.* (tywyn) Shining, resplendent.

Tywynedig, *a.* (tywyn) Being made shining.

Tywynedigaeth, *s. m.* (tywynedig) Resplendency

Tywynedigrwydd, *s. m.* (tywynedig) Shiningness

Tywyniad, *s. m.* (tywyn) A shining, a radiating.

Tywynu, *v. a.* (tywyn) To shine, to cast a lustre.

Tan o fron y tyno fry
Tywynodd.——

Fire from the bosom of the expanse above *did shine*. *Iolo Goch, i sarn rab.*

Tywynwg, *s. m.* (tywyn) A shiningness.

Tywynygawl, *a.* (tywynwg) Resplendent.

Tywynygiad, *s. m.* (tywynwg) Illumination.

Tywynygu, *v. a.* (tywynwg) To cast a splendor.

Y fai a wneler yn rhin nant,
Hi a dywynyg yn ngwydd cant.

The crime that is committed in the secret of the dingle, it will *reflect a light* in the presence of a hundred. *Adage.*

Tywys, *s. m.* (ty—gwys) A lead, or guidance. *v. a.* To lead, to conduct.

Lliaws gorwydd——
Lliaws gwineu fladw frowdd tywys.

Many a steed, many of dusky bay prancing in the *lead*. *Gwalchmai.*

Tywysaw, *v. a.* (tywys) To lead, or to conduct.

Tywysawg, *a.* (tywys) Having a lead. *s. m.—pl.* Tywysogion. A leader, a prince.

Mynych i'r praidd bod ar wall pan fo tywysawg yr anifeiliaid.

Frequently must the herd be astray when the steer is a *leader*. *Adage.*

Tywysawl, *a.* (tywys) Leading, conducting.

Tywysedig, *a.* (tywys) Being conducted or led.

Tywysel, *s. f.—pl. t.* i (tywys) A plug.

Tywysg, *s. m.* (ty—wysg) A procession. *v. a.* To proceed forward.

Bu, o Gadwaladr hyd at Gwilym Bastardd, ugain brenin o'r Saeson olynol, a thrichanmlynedd y buant yn tywysg.

There have been, from Cadwaladr down to William Bastard, twenty kings of the Saxons in succession, and three hundred years they continued *going on*. *Brut y Saeson.*

Tywysgaw, *v. a.* (tywysg) To proceed onward.

Tywysgawl, *a.* (tywysg) Tending to go onward.

Tywysgiad, *s. m.* (tywysg) A proceeding forward.

Tywysiad, *s. m.* (tywys) A leading, a conducting.

Tywysogaeth, *s. f.—pl. t.* au (tywysawg) Principality.

Tywysogaidd, *a.* (tywysawg) Like a leader.

Tywysogawl, *a.* (tywysawg) Like a leader.

Tywysogeiddiad, *s. m.* (tywysogaidd) A rendering princely; a becoming princely.

Tywysogeiddiaw, *v. a.* (tywysogaidd) To render princely; to become princely.

Tywysogeiddrwydd, *s. m.* (tywysogaidd) Princeliness.

Tywysoges, *s. f.—pl. t.* au (tywysawg) A princess.

Tywyswr, *s. m.—pl.* tywyswyr (tywys—gwr) A man who leads.

U.

UB, *s. m. r.* That is out, or extreme; that is high, or loud; a howl, a loud cry.

Ubain, *v. a.* (ub) To howl, to utter doleful cries. *s. m.* A howling.

> Gwae hwynt y gethern,
> A fynant uffern
> Byth gwedi yma;
> Yn y mae ubain,
> Yn y mae llefain,
> A llawer pla.

> Woe to them the fiends, who seek for hell ever after the present; where there is *howling*, where there is wailing, and many a torment. *Ioan. Athraw.*

Uban, *s. m.* (ub) A howling, a loud crying.

UCH, *s. f. r.—pl. t.* ion. That breaks out, or rises; a sigh.

> Onid uch yn nghawdd,
> Nead Urien ei biaudd?

> If there is a cry in distress, is it not Urien who drives it away? *Taliesin.*

Uch, *a.* (uch, *s.*) Being over or above; higher.

Uch, *prep.* (uch, *s.*) Above, over. *a.* Higher, used for *uchach*.

> Gnawd uch ben dedwydd diddos.

> Accordant over the head of the prudent is a shelter. *Adage.*

Uchad, *s. m.* (uch) The act of rising higher.

Uchaf, *a.* (uch) Upmost, uppermost, highest.

> A gair Duw yn uchaf.

> With the word of God *uppermost*. *Adage.*

Uchafael, *s. m.* (uchaf) A going aloft; ascension.

> Gostwng a fu'r cyfrwng cael
> A chyfod Iau'r Uchafael.

> Humiliation was the intermediate act, and a resurrection on *Ascension* Thursday. *Ieuan Deulwyn.*

Uchafed, *a.* (uchaf) Being over or above. *Lledr uchafed*, upper leather.

Uchafedu, *v. a.* (uchafed) To make a top part; to vamp.

Uchafedd, *s. m.* (uchaf) Loftiness, pre-eminence.

Uchafiad, *s. m.* (uchaf) A rising over or above.

Uchafiaeth, *s. m.* (uchaf) Supremacy, superiority.

> Llyma fal y dosparthant deyrnasau Cymmru yn dair rhan: un a bia uchafiaeth ar y ddwy, nid amgen nog Aberffraw pia y bendefigaeth.

> Behold the manner they divide the kingdoms of Wales into three parts one possesses *supremacy* over the two, that is to say, Aberffraw has the sovereignty. *Trioedd.*

Uchafiaethawl, *a.* (uchafiaeth) Appertaining to supremacy.

Uchafiaetholdeb, *s. m.* (uchafiaethawl) A state of supremacy or superiority.

Uchafiaethu, *v. a.* (uchafiaeth) To create supremacy; to exercise superiority.

Uchanedd, *s. m.* (uch—anedd) The gums. *Dodi mel ar uchanedd plentyn*, to apply honey to the gums of a child. *Dyfed.*

Uchanian, *s. f.* (uch—anian) A superior nature. *a.* Of superior nature, supernatural.

Uchanianaeth, *s. f.* (uchanian) Metaphysics.

Uchanianawl, *a.* (uchanian) Metaphysical.

Uchanianoldeb, *s. m.* (uchanianawl) A state of superior nature; supernaturalness.

Uchanianolder, *s.* (uchanianawl) Supernaturalness

Uchanianoli, *v. a.* (uchanianawl) To render of superior nature; to become of superior nature; to become supernatural.

Uchanianolrwydd, *s. m.* (uchanianawl) A state of superior nature; supernaturalness.

Uchaniannu, *v. a.* (uchanian) To render of superior nature; to become of superior nature; to become supernatural.

Ucharn, *s. m.—pl. t.* edd (uch—arn) The region of the ankle; the ankle; the same as *uffarn*.

Uchaw, *v. a.* (uch) To heighten, or to elevate.

Uchawl, *a.* (uch) Relating to height; elevating.

Uchdeb, *s. m.* (uch) Highness, loftiness, height.

Uchder, *s. m.* (uch) Highness, loftiness, height.

Uchdeyrn, *s. m.—pl. t.* oedd (uch—teyrn) A sovereign prince.

Uchdeyrnas, *s. f.—pl. t.* oedd (uchdeyrn) A superior realm or kingdom.

Uchdeyrnedd, *s. m.* (uchdeyrn) Supreme monarchy

Uchdra, *s. m.* (uch) Loftiness, altitude, height.

Uched, *a.* (uch) High, elevated, or exalted.

> Pum ucher uched pan achubed Ffrainc,
> Pan ffaraon foed.

> Five *elevated* vespers were had when France was saved, when mighty ones were put to flight. *H. ab Owain Gwynedd.*

Uchediad, *s. m.* (uched) A soaring, an elevation.

Uchedu, *v. a.* (uched) To soar; to elevate.

Uchedydd, *s. m.—pl. t.* ion (uched) A soarer.

> I gysgu gyda thrawd yr ych,
> A chodi gyda'r uchedydd.

> To sleep with the turning out of the ox, and to rise with the *lark*. *Adage.*

Uchedd, *s. m.* (uch) Highness, loftiness, altitude; grandeur; a top, or surface.

Uchel, *a.* (uch—el) High, lofty; towering, stately. It is prefixed in composition. '*Molwch ef yn yr uchelion*,' Praise him in the high-places.

> A ddringo yn rhy uchel, fe dyr y brigyn dano.

> He that climbs too *high*, the branch will break under him. *Adage.*

> Darfu'r gauaf, darfu'r oerfel,
> Darfu'r gwlaw a'r gwyntoedd uchel;
> Daeth y gwanwyn glas eginog,
> Dail i'r llwyn, a dol feillionog.

> Past is the winter, past is the cold, past is the rain and the *high* winds, the green vegetating spring is come, leaves to the grove, and the dale covered with trefoils. *Ed. Mathew, o Forgannwg.*

Uchelawg, *a.* (uchel) Having height or altitude: *yr uchelawg*, the misseltoe; also called *uchelwor*, *uchelfa*, *uchelfal*, and *uchelfar*.

Ucheldad, *s. m.* (uchel—tad) A supreme father.

Uchelder, *s. m.—pl. t.* au (uchel) Loftiness, height.

> Y Duw anfeidrawl—
> Fy llygaid i fy hun ei gwel,
> Ar dirion uchelderau.

> The incomprehensible God, my own eyes shall him behold, on pleasant *heights*. *Elis Wyn.*

Ucheldir, *s. m.—pl. t.* oedd (uchel—tir) High land

Ucheldra, *s. m.* (uchel) Highness, or elevatedness

Ucheldrem, *s. f.—pl. t.* iau (uchel—trem) A high look. *a.* Of supercilious look.

Ucheldremiad, *s.* (ucheldrem) A highly looking.

Ucheldremiaw, *v. a.* (ucheldrem) To look highly.

Ucheldremiawl, *a.* (ucheldrem) Highly looking.

Ucheldrum, *a.* (uchel—trum) A high ridge.

Ucheldrumiad, *s. m.* (trum) A forming a high ridge

Ucheldrumiaw, *v. a.* (ucheldrum) To form a high ridge.

Ucheldrumiawg, *a.* (ucheldrum) Being high ridged

Ucheldyb, *s. m.—pl. t.* iau (uchel—tyb) A high opinion. *a.* Of a high opinion.

Ucheldybiaw, *v. a.* (ucheldyb) To hold a high opinion.

Ucheledig, *a.* (uchel) Being heightened, elevated.
Ucheledd, *s. m.* (uchel) Altitude, elevatedness.
Uchelfa, *s. f.*—*pl.* uchelfëydd (uchel) High place.
Uchelfaer, *s. m.* (uchel—maer) A high constable.
Uchelfal, *s. m.* (uchel—bal) The misseltoe.
Uchelfalch, *a.* (uchel—balch) Of stately pride.
Uchelfalchedd, *s.* (uchelfalch) High-mettledness.
Uchelfan, *s. f.*—*pl. t.* au (uchel—màn) High place
Uchelfar, *s. m.* (uchel—bar) A high summit; also the misseltoe, otherwise called *uchelfa, uchelfal, uchelwydd, uchellawg, uchellawr, pren awyr*, and *gwysgonllys*.

—Cor goelfain
Uchelfar uchelfab Owain.

The circle of the oracle stone of the *high branch* of the elevated son of Owain. *Cynddelw.*

Uchelfawr, *a.* (uchel) Eminently great or grand.
Uchelfeddwl, *s. m.* (uchel—meddwl) Lofty mind.
Uchelfen, *s. f.*—*pl. t.* au (uch—elfen) A superior element.
Uchelfryd, *s. m.* (uchel—bryd) A lofty mind. *a.* High-minded, magnanimous.
Uchelgaer, *s. f.* (uchel—caer) A high rampart.
Uchelgaerawg, *a.* (uchelgaer) Of high rampart.
Uchelgais, *s. f.* (uchel—cais) A lofty attempt.
Uchelgeisiaw, *v. a.* (uchelgais) To make a lofty attempt; to be ambitious.
Uchelgrug, *s. m.* (uchel—crug) A lofty tump.

O fro Echelfaint uchelgrug.

From the region of Echelfaint *of elevated peak.* *Ll. P. Moch.*

Uchelgyllid, *s. m.* (uchel—cyllid) A chief rent; an annual tribute of corn.
Uchelhed, *s. f.* (uchel—hed) A high flight or soar.
Uchelhediad, *s. m* (uchelhed) A high-flying.
Uchelhedydd, *s. m.* (uchelhed) A high-flier.
Ucheliad, *s. m.* (uchel) A making lofty, a heightening; a becoming elevated.
Ucheliant, *s. m.* (uchel) Elevation, exaltation.
Uchelradd, *s. f.* (uchel—gradd) A high degree.
Uchelraddawg, *a.* (uchelradd) Of a high degree.
Uchelraddiad, *s. m.* (uchelradd) Of a high degree.
Uchelraddu, *v. a.* (uchelradd) To raise to a high degree.
Uchelraith, *s. f.*—*pl.* uchelreithiau (uchel—rhaith) A grand jury.
Uchelred, *s. f.* (uchel—rhed) An elevated course.
Uchelreithiad, *s. m.* (uchelraith) A forming a grand jury.
Uchelreithiaw, *v. a.* (uchelraith) To form a grand jury, to act as a grand jury.
Uchelreithiwr, *s. m.*—*pl.* uchelreithiwyr (uchel-rhaith—gwr) A grand jury man.
Uchelryw, *s. m.*—*pl. t.* iau (uchel—rhyw) A superior kind. *a.* Of superior kind; highborn.
Uchelsaf, *s. f.* (uchel—saf) High standing.
Uchelsain, *s. f.* (uchel—sain) A high note.
Uchelsant, *s. m.* (uchel—sant) A superior saint.

Eurbarch uchelsaint braint breiniawl.

The gloriously revered *superior saints* of royal privilege. *Bleddyn Fardd.*

Uchelsantaeth, *s. m.* (uchelsant) A hierarchy.
Uchelswydd, *s. f.*—*pl. t.* au (uchel—swydd) A high office.
Uchelswyddawg, *a.* (uchelswydd) Having a high office. *s. m.*—*pl.* uchelswyddogion, A high officer
Uchelsyth, *a.* (uchel—syth) Being highly erect.
Uchelsythiad, *s. m.* (uchelsyth) A rendering highly erect.
Uchelsythu, *v. a.* (uchelsyth) To be highly erect.
Uchelu, *v. a.* (uchel) To make high, to exalt.
Uchelurdd, *s. f.*—*pl. t.* au (uchel—urdd) High order
Uchelurddas, *s. f.*—*pl. t.* au (uchelurdd) High dignity.
Uchelurddaw, *v. a.* (uchelurdd) To raise to a high order, rank, or station.
Uchelurddiad, *s. m.* (uchelurdd) A raising to a high order, rank, or dignity.
Uchelward, *s. m.* (uchel—gwaed) High blood.
Uchelwr, *s. m.*—*pl.* uchelwyr (uchel—gwr) A high man; a gentleman; a freeholder.

Un lle y dyly mab fod yn arglwydd ar ei dad o gyfraith: o der-fydd i uchelwr roddi ei ferch i'w alltud ei hun, a bod meibion iddynt, a gwedi hyny marw yr uchelwr, a chaffel o feibion yr alltud famwys o dir eu hendad; y rhai hyny fyddant arglwyddi ar eu tad, o famwys, a dawed eu tad yn rhan yr alltudion: yna y bydd y mab yn arglwydd ar ei dad.

There is one case where a son ought to be lord over his father by law: if a *freeholder* should have given his daughter to his own alien, and they have children, and then the *freeholder* dies, and the children of the alien obtain maternal right to the land of their grandfather; those sons will be lord over their father, through maternity, as their father comes under the division of the aliens: so therefore the son becomes lord over his father. *Welsh Laws.*

Uchelwriaeth, *s. m.* (uchelwr) The rank or state of a gentleman, or freeholder.
Uchelwyl, *s. m.* (uchel—gwyl) A high festival.
Uchelydd, *s. m.*—*pl. t.* ion (uchel) A superior.

Lle bydd uchelydd ar ychydig.

Where there is *lord* over a little. *Hywel Tâmyn.*

Uchelyddiaeth, *s. m.* (uchelydd) The state of a superior.
Uchell, *s. f.* (uch) What is on high or aloft.
Uchellawg, *a.* (uchell) Having a lofty site.
Uchellawr, *s. m.* (uchell) What is most exalted; the misseltoe.

Caing uchellawr trigaint a dal.

A branch of *misseltoe* sixty pence is its value. *Welsh Laws.*

Uchenaid, *s. f.*—*pl.* ucheneidion (uch—enaid) The rising or groan of the soul; a sigh.

Uchenaid gwrach ar ol ei hawd.

The *sigh* of an old woman after her candle. *Adage.*

Am frig Moruddig mawr raid uwyggawdd
Ar Loegr fwrw uchenaid.

For the top of Moruddig great the necessity for the men of England to cast a *sigh*. *Rhiciart Iorwerth.*

Ucheneidiad, *s. m.*—*pl. t.* au (uchenaid) A sighing
Ucheneidiaw, *v. a.* (uchenaid) To utter sighs.
Ucheneidiawl, *a.* (uchenaid) Sighing, apt to sigh.
Ucheneidiwr, *s. m.* (uchenaid—gwr) A sigher.
Ucher, *s. m.* (uch) An overcast; the evening.

Po decaf y bore, hacraf yr ucher.

The more fine the morning, the more rough the evening. *Adage.*

Ucher a ddaw gan ddrycin.

A gloom will come with the storm. *Adage.*

Cadfan—
Bendigaid a daith o'i gyweithydd,
Pan doeth i'r cyfoeth, brennath, beunydd;
Pan dyfu chwant cylch ar ceiliydd,
Yn mhet Aber Menwenfer ucher echwydd.

Cadvan, blessed is whoever travels through his neighbourhood, when he comes into the country, by night, by day: when a desire of beholding came on a progeny, in the sweet estuary of Menwenver of tranquil *evening*. *Llywelyn Fardd.*

Ucherawl, *a.* (ucher) Being overcast; evening.
Ucherddaw, *s. m.* (ucher—daw) Evening tide.

Mor deg y gellit di gall arwyddaw
Merwerydd echwydd ar ucherddaw.

So fair canst thou discreetly delineate the tranquil scene and *evening tide*. *D. Benfras.*

Uchergyd, *s. m.* (uch—ergyd) A high shock.

Mal uchergyd gwynt wrth onwydd.

Like the *high shock* of the wind on ash trees. *Taliesin.*

Ucheriad, *s. m.* (ucher) An overcasting; a becoming evening.
Ucheru, *v. a.* (ucher) To overcast; to become evening. *Pan ucherai y dydd*, when the day drew to a close.

Ucherwyl, *s. f.—pl. t.* ian (ucher—gwyl) Evening tide watch; a vesper, or vigil.
Uchfraint, *s. m.—pl.* uchfreintiau (uch—braint) A supreme right, a prerogative.
Uchfreintlys, *s. m.* (uchfraint—llys) A court of superior privilege.
Uch-hed, *s. f.* (uch—hed) A superior flight.
Uch-hedeg, *v. a.* (uch-hed) To fly in a higher course
Uch-hedfa, *s. f.* (uch-hed) A superior flight.
Uch-hediad, *s. m.* (uch-hed) A superior flying.
Uchiad, *s. m.* (uch) A heightening; exaltation.
Ucho, *prep.* (uch) Above. *adv.* Above, over.

> Y byd go domlyd a delmlais i gyd,
> A chwaen o iechyd a chwennychais;
> Am olud y byd mi a wylais dwr byw,
> Am ucho wirddew mi a chwerddais!
>
> The world of frail tendency I have experienced all, and a state of health I have desired; after the wealth of the world I have wept living water, concerning the true God *above* I have laughed. *L. G. Cothi.*

Uchod, *prep.* (uch) Above. *adv.* Above, over head. *Nef uchod a daiar isod*, heaven above and earth beneath.
Uchuch, *prep.* (uch, *repeated*) Above and above.

> Gwynlluch eiry uchuch achaw dolydd.
>
> White driving snow *above and above* the surface of the dales. *Iorwerth Fychan.*

UD, *s. m. r.* That is high, loud, or shrill; a howl; a blast of a clarion or trumpet.
Udaw, *v. a.* (ud) To howl, to yell; to yelp.

> Aruthredd gweled y diefyl, y seirff, ac y dreigiau! a chan wreichion y tan y gwelant wy; wynt hagen a'r gormaf trueni gan-ddynt; ac yn udaw, ac yn wylaw, ac yn ymffust.
>
> Dreadful thing to behold the devils, and the serpents, and the dragons! and it is from the sparks of the fire that they see; they besides keep up the most miserable outcry, and are *howling*, and weeping, and striking one another. *Elucidarius.*

Udawg, *a.* (ud) Full of howling; yelling.
Udawl, *a.* (ud) Howling, yelling; yelping.
Udfa, *s. f.—pl.* udfëydd (ud) A howling, yelling.
Udgan, *s. f.* (ud—can) A sound of a trumpet.
Udganawl, *a.* (udgan) Sounding as a trumpet.
Udganiad, *s. m.* (udgan) A sounding a trumpet.
Udganu, *v. a.* (udgan) To sound a trumpet.
Udganwr, *s. m.—pl.* udganwyr (udgan—gwr) A trumpeter.
Udgorn, *s. m.—pl.* udgyrn (ud—corn) A trumpet

> Udgorn angau yw peswch sych.
>
> The *trumpet* of death is a dry cough. *Adage.*

Udiad, *s. m.* (ud) A making a howling, a yelling.
Udlais, *s. m.—pl.* udleisiau (ud—llais) A howling noise.

> ——Bar oedd
> Eigion udlais genedloedd.
>
> Furious was the deeply *howling cry* of nations. *W. Middleton.*

Udlef, *s.* (ud—llef) Ejaculation; howling voice.
Udlefain, *v. a.* (udlef) To make a howling cry.
Udlefawg, *a.* (udlef) Having a howling cry.
Udlefawl, *a.* (udlef) Of a howling cry.
Udlefiad, *s. m.* (udlef) A making a howling cry.
Udon, *s. m.* (ud—on) A solemn cry; an imprecation.
Udonawl, *a.* (udon) Being imprecated.
Udoni, *v. a.* (udon) To make imprecation.
Udoniad, *s. m.* (udon) An imprecating.
Udoniaeth, *s. m.* (udon) An imprecation.
Udwr, *s. m.—pl.* udwyr (ud—gwr) A howler.
UDD, *s. m. r.* That is over, above, or superior; a chief; a lord. *Mor Udd*, the name of the British Sea, or King's Channel.

> Gruffudd mynawg udd mynud;
> Mynud wrth folud, wrth filwyr bu gwidd,
> Bu gorddwy ar allmyr.
>
> Grufudd the courteous *master* of civility; civility to the song of praise, towards the warriors he was furious, he was the trouble of regions beyond the seas. *D. ab Ll. Mynyw, m. G. ab Cynan.*

Uddyf, *a.* (udd—yf) Humble, obedient, meek.

> A fynych gennyf finnau,
> Uddyf y tyf a fydd tau.
>
> What thou wouldest likewise have from me, *obsequiously* will grow up what will be thine. *H. ab D. ab I. ab Rhys.*

Uddyfiad, *s. m.* (uddyfu) Obedience.
Uddyfu, *v. a.* (uddyf) To humble; to obey.
Uddyfdawd, *s. m.* (uddyf) Obedience; humility.
UF, *s. m. r.* That is over, spread, or diffused.
Ufel, *s. m.—pl. t.* ion (uf—el) Elementary fire; a spark of fire.

> Ai un hynt gwynt, ai un dwfr mor,
> Ai un ufel tan twrf diachor!
>
> Is there but one course to the wind, is there but one to the water of the sea, is there but one to the *spark of fire* of irresistible tumult! *Taliesin.*

> Rhuthr uthr ufel,
> Rhynawd awel
> Rhyfel febin.
>
> Like the dread assault of fire, like the chilling of the gale is the war of youth. *Cuhelyn.*

> Ti angau——
> Nis llysg ufel,
> Nis lludd oerfel,
> Nis lladd arfau.
>
> Thou death, that *fire* will not burn, that cold will not obstruct, that arms will not slay. *Iolo Goch.*

Ufelai, *s. c.* (ufel) That generates fire, that is elementary of fire; oxygen.
Ufelaidd, *a.* (ufel) Of fiery tendency; sulphurous
Ufelawg, *a.* (ufel) Full of fiery particles.
Ufelfre, *s. f.* (ufel—bre) A fire hill; a volcano. The name of a hill in Pembrokeshire, giving name to a comot.
Ufeliar, *s. m.* (ufel) That generates fire; that yields sparks or flame; sulphur.

> Llywelyn, cyd lladdwy trwy far,
> Cyd llosgwy nid llosg ufeliar.
>
> Llywelyn, whilst he slays through wrath, whilst he burns not feeble the *sulphur flame*. *Ll. P. Moch.*

> Llas Asser aerllew, aerllyd ufeliar,
> Aerbair bar baedd erfid;
> Llyw glyw glewdraws yn ngofid,
> Llew torf tarian eur-gymid.
>
> The slaughter-lion Asser fell! in wrath
> As *fiery flame* the boar with scathing lance,
> In difficulty brave as guide and chief,
> With gold rim shield a lion of the host.
> *Cynddelw, m. I. O. Gwynedd.*

Ufelin, *a.* (ufel) Of a fiery nature, generating fire; oxygen.
Ufelu, *v. a.* (ufel) To generate fire; to ignify, to ignite.
Ufelydd, *s. m.* (ufel) That is on fire.

> Dwr ar fain drwy'r erw a fydd
> Dan ili yn dan ufelydd.
>
> Beneath the noble beast along the plain water to *sparkling fire* kindles upon the stones. *T. Aled, i farch.*

Ufelyddiad, *s. m.* (ufelydd) Ignition, an igniting.
Ufelyddiaeth, *s. m.* (ufelydd) Pyrotechny.
Ufelyn, *s. m.* (ufel) The element of fire.

> Saith tan ufelyn
> Saith cad cyferbyn,
> Seithfed Cynfelyn
> I bob cynfan.
>
> The seven fires of the *pervading element* are seven hosts in opposition, the seventh is Cynfelyn to every foremost station. *Ymdd. Taliesin a Merddin.*

> Rhoes hi flagl yn yr odyn
> Oni aeth yn dan ufelyn.
>
> She put a flame in the kiln so that it became a *fire of conflagration*. *D. ab Gwilym.*

Ufell, *a.* (uf—ell) Obsequious, or humble.
Ufelldawd, *s. m.* (ufell) Obsequiousness.

Ufydd, *a.* (uf—ydd) Humble, obedient, meek.

> Dy ddelw wyt, lle'r wyf rydd
> Dy eos wyt, dy was ufydd.

> Thy beautiful image, where I am at liberty thy nightingale I am, and thy *obedient* servant. *L. G. Cothi.*

Ufyddâad, *s. m.* (ufyddâu) An obeying; a becoming humble, humiliation; obedience.

Ufyddâawl, *a.* (ufyddâu) Of obedient disposition

Ufyddaidd, *a.* (ufydd) Tending to humility.

Ufyddâu, *v. a.* (ufydd) To obey; to be humble.

> Yn y faint hono y gorddyfnasam ni ei chaffael a'i meddu, hyd na wddam ni ufyddâu i gaethiwed; a hono hagen pei ceisynt y dwywiau ei dwyn i cenym, ni a lafuriem yn y faint y gallem oc yn holl nerth o'i hattal yn eu herbyn.

> In such a degree we were accustomed to obtain and enjoy it, so that we know not how *to be humbled* to servitude; and this, peradventure were the Gods to attempt to deprive us of it, we would exert ourselves to the utmost of all our power to preserve against them. *Brut y Brenhinoedd.*

Ufyddaw, *v. a.* (ufydd) To obey; to humble.

Ufyddawl, *a.* (ufydd) Obedient, or humble.

Ufyddâwr, *s. m.—pl.* ufyddâwyr (ufyddâu—gwr) One who obeys.

Ufydd-dawd, *s. m.* (ufydd) Humility, obedience.

Ufydd-dra, *s. m.* (ufydd) Humbleness, obedience

Ufyddfryd, *s. m.* (ufydd—bryd) Humble mind. *a.* Of an obsequious disposition.

Ufyddgar, *a.* (ufydd) Obsequious; dutiful.

Ufyddgarwch, *s. m.* (ufyddgar) Obsequiousness.

Ufyddiad, *s. m.* (ufydd) A humbling; an obeying

Ufyddiannawl, *a.* (ufyddiant) Of a humbling tendency; tending to obedience.

Ufyddiannu, *v. a.* (ufyddiant) To be obedient.

Ufyddiannus, *a.* (ufyddiant) Of a humiliating tendency; disposed to obedience.

Ufyddiannusaw, *v. a.* (ufyddiannus) To render obedient; to become obedient.

Ufyddiant, *s. m.* (ufydd) Obedience; humility.

Ufyddoldeb, *s. m.* (ufyddawl) Humbleness.

Ufyddolder, *s. m.* (ufyddawl) Humbleness.

Ufyddolrwydd, *s. m.* (ufyddawl) Humbleness.

Ufyddwr, *s. m.* (ufydd—gwr) An obedient man.

Ufyll, *a.* (uf—yll) Obsequious, or humble.

Ufylldawd, *s. m.* (ufyll) Obsequiousness.

Ufyllder, *s. m.* (ufyll) Humility; meekness.

> Rhag hirddilyd prid, praw ufyllder bryd,
> Rhi y byd a'm dyd dysg a chalider.

> Against over pursuing of an object, the experience of an *humility* of mind, the lord of the world will give me instruction and discretion. *G. ab M. ab Dafydd.*

UFF, *s. m. r.* That straitens, closes, or confines.

Uffarn, *s. f.—pl. t.* au (uff—arn) The ankle; also called *uchurn*, *ffer*, and *migwrn*.

> Y rhingyll a ddyly gwr-an yr ychain ac y gwartheg, a gaffer o'i gyhuddef, i wneuthur crwenau cyfuwch a'i uffarnau.

> The sergeant ought to have the legs of the oxen and the cows, which shall be obtained through his informing, for making buskins reaching up to his *ankles*. *Welsh Laws.*

Uffern, *s. f.—pl. t.* i (uff—ern) A strait or confined drift; the state of reprobation in the bardic doctrine of transmigration; the infernal region, hell.

> Nid oes ar uffern ond eisiau ei threfnu.

> There is in *hell* only the want of being put in order. *Adage.*

> Hunanoldeb yw y diawl duaf yn uffern.

> Selfishness is the blackest devil in *hell*. *Adage.*

> Y diawl ffolaf yn uffern yw hunanolyb.

> The simplest devil in *hell* is self-conceit. *Adage.*

> Yr aderyn a fager yn uffern yn uffern y myn drigaw.

> The bird that is reared in *hell*, in *hell* he will seek to dwell. *Adage.*

Uffernaidd, *a.* (uffern) Like hell, or hellish.

Uffernawl, *a.* (uffern) Infernal, or hellish.

> I ti y mae canied i gerdded trwy awyrawl ffyrdd, ac uffernawl dai, a thrwydaw dialeddion difanol: Dyweid i mi pa oesawr a fynych ei pheroedyliaw obenaid.

> For thee there is liberty to traverse through aërial paths, and *infernal* mansions, and to assign the destiny of terrestrial beings. Inform me what region thou wouldest have me to dwell therein. *Brut y Brenhinoedd.*

Uffernci, *s. m.* (uffern—ci) A hell-hound.

UG, *s. m. r.* That is over or exterior; that closes upon or envelops.

Ugain, *s. m.—pl.* ugeiniau (ug) That has a completion, or close; the close of reckoning; twenty. *a.* Twenty.

Ugaint, *s. m.—pl.* ugeiniau (ugain) Twenty.

> Ugaint, teg; deg-ar-ugaint, cryf; deugaint, gwrolwg; deg-a-deugaint, doeth; a thrwy eu hendraeth, nid gwiw son am y naill na'r llall.

> *Twenty*, fair; thirty, strong; forty, bustling about wealth; fifty, wise; and as to those in the extremes of their ages, it is not worth while to make mention of the one or the other. *Adage.*

Ugeinfed, *s. f.* (ugain) The twentieth.

Ugeiniawl, *a.* (ugain) Belonging to twenty.

Ugeinplyg, *s. m.* (ugain—plyg) That is twenty-fold. *a.* Twenty-fold.

Ugeintro, *s. m.* (ugain—tro) That consists of twenty turns. *a.* Of twenty turns.

Ugeintroed, *s. m.* (ugain—troed) That has twenty feet. *a.* Of twenty feet.

Ugeinwaith, *s. pl.* (ugain—gwaith) Twenty times.

UL, *s. m. r.* That is humid, or damp. *a.* Humid, damp, or muggy. *Mae yn ul iawn heddyw*, it is very muggy to-day: *Mae yr ud yn rhy ul iddei falu*, the corn is too damp to be ground: *Mae y gwair yn rhy ul iddei gywain*, the hay is too moist to be carried off. *Sil.*

Ulai, *s. c.* (ul) That generates humidity or moisture; hydrogen.

Ulaw, *v. a.* (ul) To render moist or humid; to smother; to become close, damp, or muggy; to heat by closeness, to generate hydrogen.

Uliad, *s. m.* (ul) A filling with humidity; a smothering; a growing close, or muggy; a heating by laying close together; a producing hydrogen.

Uliar, *s. m.* (ul) A humid nature; a phlegmatic habit.

> Un a fo a'i ardymer o'r uliar a fydd winau, o herwydd nad yw ei natur ond egwan; yn yr un cyfarwel hwy a fydd foliawg tewion y bobl a font o'r uliar—a hwy a fyddant ddifrwythach na phobl o'r cyfnwydau ereill, o herwydd eu hoerfel.

> One whose constitution is of the *phlegmatic habit* is apt to be of brown complexion, because their nature is but feeble: in a second respect they who are of a *phlegmatic habit* will be short and fat; and they will be less energetic than people of other dispositions, because of their cold nature. *Meddygon Myddfai.*

Ulw, *s. m.* (ul) That is divested of the principle of moisture; the remains of any thing burnt; ashes; cinders. *Mae fo wedi llosgi yn ulw*, it is become burnt to cinders.

Ulwaidd, *a.* (ulw) Like smothered hot ashes.

Ulwawg, *a.* (ulw) With remains of combustion.

Ulwyn, *s. m.* (ulw) The scoria or remains of any burnt matter; ashes, embers, or cinders.

ULL, *s. m. r.* That bursteth out; that is sudden, or abrupt.

Ullda, *s. m.* (ull—ta) That has sudden starts; an oaf; a dolt.

Ulldach, *s. m.* (ull—tach) An oaf, a changeling.

Ulliad, *s. m.* (ull) A bursting out; a sudden drive or impulse.

UM, *s. m. r.* That spreads out or about.

UN, *s. m. r.—pl. t.* au. That is individual, that is identified as one; one. *Yr un un*, the same one, the very same, *idem, eadem*. It is a prefix in composition.

Cared pob un ei gynhefinfel.

Let every one love his native place. *Adage.*

Tri un cyntefig y sydd; ac nis gellir amgen nog un o honynt: un Duw, un gwirionedd, ac un pwnc rhyddyd, sef y bydd lle bo cydbwys pob gwrth.

There are three primitial *ones*, and nothing otherwise than one of them can possibly be: *one* God, *one* truth, and *one* point of liberty, that is where every opposition equiponderates. *Barddas.*

Gwell mared gwr nog un gwraig.

Better is the activity of a man than *that* of a woman. *Adage.*

Un, a. (un, s.) One; identical, of the same, same. *Nid yw fal yr un un*, he is not like the same one.

Un gadernyd, un fryd fry,
Un fraint, un feddiant, un frys,
Un allu, un ewyllys—Un Duw.

Of one energy, *of one* mind above, *of one* pre-eminence, *of one* possession, *of one* impulse, *of one* power, *of one* will: *one* God. *Iolo Goch.*

Yn awr ydych un rodoedd
A'ch hael daid.——

At present you are of the *same* attributes as your generous grandsire. *S. Cain.*

Unad, s. m. (un) A making into one; union.
Unagwedd, s. m. (agwedd) One appearance. a. Of similar appearance.
Unarbymtheg, s. m. (un—ar—pymtheg) Sixteen. a. Sixteen.
Unarddeg, s. m. (un—ar—deg) Eleven. a. Eleven
Unaw, v. a. (un) To make into one; to unite; to accord, to agree.
Unawdl, s. f. (awdl) A single rhyme. a. Unirhyme.
Unawl, a. (un) Belonging to one; uniting.
Unawr, s. f. (awr) A single hour. a. Of one hour.
Unbaladr, a. (paladr) Of one shaft; of one or the same verse.
Unbaladrawg, a. (unbaladr) Of one shaft; of one or the same verse.
Unban, s. m. (ban) Being of one verse or line.
Unbanawg, a. (unban) Having one verse.
Unben, s. m.—*pl.* unbyn (pen) A one head, a one supreme, a monarch; also a complimentary appellation, like sir.

Tri unben rhaith Ynys Prydain: un, Caswallawn ab Lludd ab Beli ab Mynogan; ail, Caradawg ab Bran ab Llyr Lledialth; trydydd, Owain ab Macsen wledig: sef o raith gwlad a chenedl y doded arnynt yr unbenaeth, lle nad oeddynt hynafiaid.

The three jury *monarchs* of the Isle of Britain: the first, Caswallon son of Lludd son of Beli son of Mynogan; second, Caradog son of Bran son of Llyr of Barbarous Speech; third, Owain son of Maxen the patriot, that is to say, through the juratory election of the country and nation was the monarchy given them, when they were not elders. *Trioedd.*

Tri tharw unben Ynys Prydain: Elmur mab Cadair, Cynhafal mab Argad, Afaon mab Taliesin: Tri meib beirdd oeddynt.

The three bull *chieftains* of the Isle of Britain: Elmur son of Cadair, Cynhaval son of Argad, Avaon son of Taliesin; They were three sons of bards. *Trioedd.*

Ha unben! Duw a'ch noddo; ni ddaeth gwestai erioed o honai a'i fywyd gantho.

Oh sir! God protect you; there never escaped a guest from me with his life. *H. Culhwch—Mabinogion.*

Unbenaeth, s. m.—*pl.* t. an (unben) Sovereignty. *Unbenaeth Prydain*, the sovereignty of Britain; the name of a national hymn, now lost, which used to be sung before the armies, on the onset of battle. Probably, this was some piece of music, to which different words were adapted, agreeably to the incidents of the times; but all tending to impress an idea, consonant to the title of the piece, that the welfare of the British Monarchy was the object contended for: thus all the different chiefs of the island, in their quarrels, were impelled by a national maxim, ostensibly to be supporting the supreme government.

Y bardd teulu a gaiff eidion o bob anrhaith y bo wrth ei dwyn gyda'r teulu; a rhan gwr hefyd, mal pob teulwr arall; yntau a gan Unbenaeth Prydain rhagddynt, yn nydd cad ac ymladd.

The bard of the household shall have a beast out of every spoil he bears a part in taking with the family; and the share of a man besides, like every other individual of the family; and he then shall sing the *Monarchy of Britain* before them, in the day of battle and war. *Welsh Laws.*

Unbenaethawl, a. (unbenaeth) Monarchical.
Unbenaethiad, s. m. (unbenaeth) A forming a monarchy or sovereignty.
Unbenaethu, v. a. (unbenaeth) To establish a monarchy or sovereignty.
Unbenaidd, a. (unben) Monarchal; royal.

Bonedd hon unbenaidd had.

Her descent of royal progeny. *Meurig Dafydd.*

Unbenawl, a. (unben) Monarchal; royal.
Unbenes, s. f.—*pl.* t. au (unben) A female monarch; also a title of respect, equivalent to lady and madam.

Arglwydd, ni thycia i neb ymlid yr unbenes racco; ni wyddwn i farch cynt yn y cyfoeth no hwn; ac ni thycia i mi ei hymlid!

Lord, it will avail nobody to pursue yonder *lady*: I knew of no swifter horse in the kingdom than this; and it doth not avail me to pursue her! *H. Pwyll—Mabinogion.*

Unbenesaidd, a. (unbenes) Appertaining to a female monarch; like a queen; royal.

Gwrth y rhod trwod y treiddi,
Ynysig unbenesaidd.

The reverse of the wheel through thee will run, thou little isle *seeming like a queen.* *Gr. Owain, i Fon.*

Unbeniad, s. m.—*pl.* unbeniaid (unben) That is one head, a monarch; a sovereign.

Tri glewion unbeniaid Ynys Prydain; Cynfelyn Wledig, Caradawg ab Bran, ac Arthur: sef y gorthrechynt ar eu galon, hyd nas gellid namyn o frad a chynllwyn eu gorfod.

The three brave *sovereigns* of the Isle of Britain; Cynvelyn the Patriot, Caradog son of Bran, and Arthur; that is to say, they would obtain success over their enemies, so that it were not possible except by treachery to overcome them. *Trioedd.*

Unbenig, a. (unben) Monarchical, monarchal.
Unbenigder, s. m. (unbenig) Monarchicalness.
Unbenigdra, s. m. (unbenig) Monarchicalness.
Unbenigrwydd, s. m. (unbenig) Monarchicalness.
Unbriodas, s. f. (un—priodas) Monogamy.
Uncorn, s. m.—*pl.* uncyrn (corn) That has one horn; an unicorn.

Mi cadw——
Rhag cyrn yr uncyrn ennyd.

Me preserve awhile from the horns of the unicorns. *W. Middleton.*

Undad, s. m. (tad) A same father. a. Of the same father.
Undanc, a. (tanc) Being united in tranquillity.
Undawd, s. m. (un) A state of being one.

Boed ef y byddwyf, gwedi beddrawd,
Cyd a'r Unduw mawr yn ei undawd.

Be it that I may exist, after the course of the grave, with the great one God in his *unity.* *Einion ab Gwalchmai.*

Undeb, s. m. (un) Unity. *Undeb a brawdgarwch*, unity and brotherly love.
Undeg, s. m. (deg) Eleven. a. Eleven.
Undegawl, a. (undeg) Belonging to eleven.
Undegfed, s. m. (undeg) An eleventh. a. Eleventh

Undeg fad awen: undegfed wrydd
A weinydd fy nhynged,
O'm gwawd ran, o'm ban, o'm bardd-ged,
O walch falch, o Walchmai'n [illegible]

Eleven goodly themes; the *eleventh* wish my destiny will produce, with respect to my share of praise, of my elevation, of my bardic treasure, from a towering battlement, from the [illegible] tribe. *Cynddelw, Gwelygorddau Powys.*

Under, s. m. (un) Unity, simpleness, singleness.

Goruwch, o ran bonedd, yw y peth a saif ar under hanfod ac ansawdd, ar bob cymhlethdod hanfod ac ansawdd.

Superior, with respect to origin, is the thing which stands upon *simpleness* of existence and quality, over every complex existence and quality. *Barddas.*

Undodiad, *s. m.*—*pl.* undodiaid (undawd) Unitarian.

Undodiaeth, *s. m.* (undawd) Unitarianism.

Undon, *s. f.* (ton) That is of one tone or voice. *a.* Monotonous.

Undonydd, *s. m.* (undon) A monotonous one.

Undonyddiaeth, *s. f.* (undonydd) Monotony.

Undras, *s. f.* (tras) That is of the same kindred. *a.* Of the same kindred.

Undrwch, *a.* (trwch) Of equal thickness.

Undud, *s. m.* (tud) Sameness of region. *a.* Of the same region.

> Gogoniant—
> I'r Drindawd Undawd unded preswylydd.
>
> Glory to the Trinity of Unity the inhabitant of *the same region*. *D. Ddu o Hiraddug.*

Undull, *s. m.* (dull) Same form or manner. *a.* Of the same form.

Unduw, *s. m.* (duw) The same or one God.

Undwf, *s. m.* (twf) That is of one growth. *a.* Of the same growth.

Undydd, *s. m.* (dydd) One day; same day. *a.* Of one day. *Undydd a blwyddyn*, a year and a day.

Undyddiawg, *a.* (undydd) Of a single day.

> Ni ddyly neb gymeryd mach yn undyddiawg.
>
> No body ought to take bail as *of one day*. *Welsh Laws.*

Undyn, *s. m.* (dyn) A single person.

> Gwae undyn a wnel gant yn drist.
>
> Woe to the *one person* who makes a hundred sorrowful. *Adage.*
>
> O caf fy nghledd ar fy nghlun,
> A'm llaw ddeau i'm diffyn,
> Ai gwaeth dinasu nog undyn?
>
> If I obtain my sword by my side, and my right hand to defend me, am I then more despicable than *any person*? *Ymdd. Trystan a Gwalchmai.*

Unddalen, *s. f.* (dalen) One leaf; one page; same leaf. *a.* Of one leaf; of the same leaf.

Unddalenawg, *a.* (unddalen) Monopetalous.

Unddawn, *s. m.* (dawn) Sameness of attribute. *a.* Of one attribute; of the same endowment.

> ——Uch archengylion,
> Unddoniun neilltu nerth heb drengi—
> Undaw ynt wyntau a dau dri.
>
> Over archangels, lords *of attributes—coequal ones* with power never failing, one God are they and truly three. *Gwalchmai.*

Unddefnydd, *s. m.* (defnydd) That is of the same material. *a.* Homogenial.

Unddull, *s. f.* (dull) Unity of form. *a.* Uniform.

Uned, *s. m.* (un) Unity; accordance, concurrence; entreaty, solicitation.

> Archaf i Dduw drwy uned.
>
> I will ask of God through *entreaty*. *Llywelyn Fardd.*

Unesgar, *s. m.* (esgar) Sameness of foe. *a.* Having the same enemy, of common foe.

> Cymmodi a wnaynt, a myned ungar unesgar.
>
> They were reconciled, and became of common friend *of common foe*. *Gr. ab Arthur.*

Unfaint, *s. m.* (maint) Unity of size. *a.* Of the same size, of equal magnitude.

Unfan, *s. m.* (màn) The same place. *Safa yn ei unfan yn wastad*, he stands in his one place continually.

Unfath, *s. m.* (math) Unity of sort. *a.* Of the same sort, similar.

Unfed, *s. m.* (un) The order of one; a first. *a.* Being in the order of one; first.

Unfed-dydd, *s. m.* (unfed—dydd) The first day.

Unfin, *s. m.* (min) A one edge. *a.* One-edged.

Unfiniawg, *a.* (unfin) Having one edge.

Unfodd, *s. m.* (modd) Sameness of mode. *a.* Of the same manner; similar.

Unfraint, *s. m.* (braint) Sameness of rank, right, or privilege. *a.* Of the same rank.

> O bydd amryson rhwng deuddyn unfraint am derfyn, ac na wyper gwirionedd y rhyngddynt, tynged pob un ei derfyn, a gwedi hyny rhaner y tir amryson.
>
> If there shall be contention between two persons *of equal rank* respecting a boundary, and the truth be not manifest between them, let each one swear his boundary; and after that let the land of contention be divided. *Welsh Laws.*

Unfri, *s. m.* (bri) Sameness of privilege. *a.* Of equal privilege.

Unfryd, *s. m.* (bryd) One mind, sameness of intention. *a.* Of one mind, unanimous.

> Nid unfryd ynfyd a chall.
>
> Not *of the same mind* the simple and the cunning. *Adage.*
>
> Nid unfryd cybydd a charedyn.
>
> Not *of the same mind* the miser and the liberal. *Adage.*

Unffenud, *s. f.* (ffenud) Sameness of appearance. *a.* Of the same appearance; exactly alike.

Unffurf, *s. m.* (ffurf) Sameness of form. *a.* Of the same form; uniform.

Ungar, *s. m.* (car) Sameness of friend. *a.* Of common friend.

Unged, *s. f.* (ced) Sameness of treasure. *a.* Of one treasure, having one treasure in common.

Ungoel, *s. f.* (coel) Sameness of belief. *a.* Of one belief, of the same creed.

> Deon, unged, ungoel,
> Ys berth, yd berthir yn wyl.
>
> The supreme arbiter, of universal bounty, *of undivided belief*, that is holy, he is served with humility. *Cynddelw.*

Ungor, *s. f.* (cor) That is of one turn or twist. *a.* Of a single turn or twist. *Edaf ungor*, a single twisted thread.

> Cadarnach yw yr edaf yn gyfrodedd nag yn ungor.
>
> Stronger is the thread of double twist than *of single twist*. *Adage.*

Ungorn, *s. f.* (corn) That is of one turn. *a.* Of a single turn. *Edaf ungorn*, the same as *edaf ungor*.

Ungwaith, *s. m.* (un—gwaith) A particular turn, or purpose. The same as *unswydd*.

> Ungwaith merched y gwledydd
> Ei edrych fo fal drych fydd.
>
> The *sole work* of the girls of the countries round will be to gaze at it as at a mirror. *I. ab Hywel Swrdwal.*

Ungwr, *s. m.* (gwr) One man; any man.

Ungyfun, *a.* (cyfun) Uniformly the same.

> Tri hanogion pob byw yn nghylch y gwynfyd; swydd, braint, ac awen; ac nis gellir dau yn bod yn ungyfun yn unrhyw peth; sef y bydd cyflawn pob un yn y bo hanogion arno; ac nid oes cyflawn ar ddim, heb y maint oll a ddichon fod o hono.
>
> The three peculiar distinctions of every living being in the circle of felicity; vocation, privilege, and disposition; and it is not possible for two beings to be *uniformly the same* in every thing, for every one will have a plenitude of what is essentially peculiar to him; and there is no plenitude of any thing, without being it in a degree that comprehends the whole of it that can exist. *Barddas.*

Unhaen, *s. f.* (haen) A single layer, or spread. *a.* Of one spread or stratum.

Unhawl, *s. f.* (hawl) A sole claim. *a.* Of single claim, of common claim.

Unhwyl, *s. f.* (hwyl) A sole course. *a.* Of one course, of a common course.

Unhyd, *s. m.* (un—hyd) A single length. *a.* Of one length; of the same length, or duration.

Uniad, *s. m.* (un) A making one; a uniting.

Uniaith, *s. f.* (iaith) A single speech. *a.* Of one language, of a common speech.

Uniannawl, *a.* (uniant) Tending to unite.

Uniannu, *v. a.* (uniant) To produce union.

Uniant, *s. m.* (un) The state of being one.

Uniawn, *s. m.* (iawn) That is right, straight, or direct. *a.* Right, straight, direct; upright, perfect, just. *Rhed yno yn uniawn*, run there directly: *Mi af yn uniawn deg*, I will go immediately.

Lluniwr pob deall uniawn,
A llyfr cyfraith yr iaith iawn.

The former of every *just* idea, the law book of the perfect language. *Gr. Gryg, i D. ab Gwilym.*

A fo'n enwog fyw'n uniawn,
Fe rydd Duw fawredd a dawn.

He who nobly leads a *righteous* life, God will give him greatness and virtue. *S. Tudyr.*

Unig, *a.* (un) Sole, only, lonely, lonesome, single, solitary, singular. *O yr unig!* How singular!

Digawn Duw da i unig.

God is able to help the *solitary*. *Adage.*

Hydr unaw unig.

Confident is the song of the *solitary*. *Adage.*

Uniganedig, *a.* (unig—ganedig) Only-begotten.

Unigaw, *v. a.* (unig) To render sole; to become sole, single, or solitary.

Unigawl, *a.* (unig) Of a solitary or singular quality; ununited, independent. *Y naw unigolion*, the nine digits.

Unigder, *s. m.* (unig) Solitariness, loneliness.

Unigdra, *s. m.* (unig) Solitariness, loneness.

Unigedd, *s. m.* (unig) Solitude, or loneliness.

Unigenid, *a.* (unig—genid) Only-born.

Unigffydd, *a.* (unig—ffydd) Of singular faith.

Unigffyddiad, *s. m.—pl.* unigffyddiaid (unigffydd) A solifidian.

Unigiad, *s. m.* (unig) A rendering solitary.

Unigoldeb, *s. m.* (unigawl) Singularness.

Unigolder, *s. m.* (unigawl) Singularness.

Unigoli, *v. a.* (unigawl) To render solitary or singular; to become singular.

Unigolrwydd, *s. m.* (unigawl) Solitariness.

Unigrwydd, *s. m.* (unig) Loneliness, solitariness.

Unionad, *s. m.* (uniawn) A straightening, a righting, a making even, a rectifying.

Uniondeb, *s. m.* (uniawn) Rightness, rectitude, uprightness; straightness; evenness.

Unionder, *s. m.* (uniawn) Rightness; straightness.

Uniondra, *s. m.* (uniawn) Rightness; directness.

Unionedd, *s. m.* (uniawn) Rightness; directness.

Uniongongl, *s. f.—pl. t.* au (uniawn—congl) A right angle.

Uniongonglawg, *a.* (uniongongl) Rectangular.

Uniongred, *s. f.* (uniawn—cred) Orthodoxy. *a.* Of right belief, orthodox.

Uniongyrch, *s. m.* (uniawn—cyrch) A direct course. *a.* Of a direct course; immediate.

Yr ysbryd a henyw o Dad yr ysbrydoedd; yr hwn a elwir felly, mae yn debygawl, o herwydd eu henyw hwynt o hono ef yn uniongyrch, heb fod ailachosion yn cydgerdded, nac yn cyfryngu dim oll.

The spirit proceeded from the Father of spirits; who is so called, it is probable, because of their proceeding from him *immediately* without second causes being concurring, or contributing any thing at all. *Ier. Owain.*

Uniongyrchawl, *a.* (uniongyrch) Directly proceeding.

Uniongyrchiad, *s. m.* (uniongyrch) A directly or immediately proceeding.

Uniongyrchu, *v. a.* (uniongyrch) To proceed directly; to proceed straightly.

Unioni, *v. a.* (uniawn) To straighten, to rectify; to make even; to become straight.

Unionran, *s. f.* (uniawn—rhan) An exact portion.

Unionraniad, *s. m.* (unionran) A sharing exactly.

Unionrann, *v. a.* (unionran) To share exactly.

Unionred, *s. f.* (uniawn—rhed) A direct course. *a.* Directly recurrent.

Unionrwydd, *s. m.* (uniawn) Straightness.

Unionserth, *a.* (uniawn—serth) Straightly falling.

Unionserthawl, *a.* (unionserth) Of a perpendicular fall or dip.

Unionserthiad, *s. m.* (unionserth) A dipping or falling perpendicularly.

Unionserthu, *v. a.* (unionserth) To dip or fall perpendicularly.

Unionsyth, *a.* (uniawn—syth) Directly erect.

Unionsythawl, *a.* (unionsyth) Tending to a perpendicular erectness.

Unionsythiad, *s. m.* (unionsyth) A rendering perpendicularly erect.

Unionsythu, *v. a.* (unionsyth) To render perfectly erect or upright.

Unionwr, *s. m.* (uniawn—gwr) A straightener.

Unionydd, *s. m.—pl. t.* ion (uniawn) Straightener.

Unlef, *s. f.* (llef) Sameness of tone. *a.* Of one tone, of the same sound; monotonous.

Awdl yw sain unlef y geiriau gobenyddiawl.

Rhyme is the *unison* sound of the terminating words. *Barddas.*

Unllaw, *s. f.* (llaw) One hand. *a.* One-handed, single-handed.

Bwrw a'th unllaw, cais a'th ddwylaw.

Cast with thy *one hand*, get with thy two hands. *Adage.*

Unllawiawg, *a.* (unllaw) Having one hand.

Unllawiawg fydd mammaeth.

A nurse is *single-handed*. *Adage.*

Unlle, *s. m.* (lle) One place, same place; any place, any where. *Ni bum yn unlle*, I have not been any where.

Unlled, *s. m.* (lled) One breadth. *a.* Of one breadth, of equal breadth.

Unllef, *s. m.* (llef) Sameness of tone or voice. *a.* Of the same voice, unison.

Unlliw, *s. m.* (lliw) Sameness of colour. *a.* Of one colour.

Adar o'r unlliw a dynant i'r unlle.

Birds of a *colour* will flock together. *Adage.*

Unlliwiawg, *a.* (unlliw) Having one colour.

Unllygad, *s. m.* (llygad) One eye. *a.* One-eyed.

Unllygeidiawg, *a.* (unllygad) Monoculous.

Unllygeidiawg a ddyly cant.

The *one-eyed* ought to have a hundred. *Adage.*

Unllygeidiawg fydd brenin yn ngwlad y deillaid.

The *one-eyed* will be a king in the country of the blind ones. *Adage.*

Unman, *s. f.* (man) Same place, sameness of place; any where. *a.* Of the same place.

Gwir tros byth yn yr unman.

The truth for ever in the *same place*. *Adage.*

Nid llai y crefydd yn unman no lle bo mwyaf y dadlu am dano.

Not less the religion *any where* than in the place where there is most disputing about it. *Adage.*

Unmodd, *s. m.* (modd) Sameness of mode; any wise. *a.* Of the same mode.

Unnawd, *s. m.* (nawd) Sameness of nature. *a.* of the same nature or quality.

Unnaws, *s. f.* (naws) Sameness of disposition or temper. *a.* Of the same temper.

Unne, *s. m.* (un—gne) That is one colour. *a.* Of one hue, of the same hue. *Unne geirw*, equal in hue to the torrents.

Unnerth, *s. m.* (nerth) Sameness of power. *a.* Of one power, of equal might.

Triawdawd yn gwaredawd a'n gwarant,
Tri uniawn unnerth gogoniant:
Trwy y Tad, a Rhad yn rhoddiant,
Trwy y Mab gwnaed hawl bob grymiant.

The Trinity our deliverance and our security, three perfect of *coequal power* in glory; through the Father, with Grace concomitant, through the Son, all were made of every energy. *Cattwdyn.*

Unodlaeth, *s. f.* (unawdl) Sameness of rhyme.

> Ni ddylai gydsain fod yn nechreu y sill olaf o air yr awdl yn amgen a fo yn yr unodlaeth.
>
> The consonant ought not to be in the beginning of the last syllable of the word of the rhyme different from what may be in the unity of rhyme. *Bardism.*

Unodlawg, *a.* (unawdl) Having unity of rhyme.
Unodledd, *s. m.* (unawdl) The state of being of continued rhyme; unirhyme.
Unodli, *v. a.* (unawdl) To agree in rhyme.

> Nid unodla sillaf dalgron ond ag un dalgron arall o'r un berynadl.
>
> An inflective syllable will agree in rhyme only with another inflective syllable of the same accent with itself. *W. Middleton.*

Unodliad, *s. m.* (unawdl) A forming unirhyme.
Unoed, *s. m.* (un—oed) One age, same age, sameness of age. *a.* Of one age, of equal age; of the same time.

> Fy m pedwar prif-gas erymoed,
> Yngyd[illegible] yn unoed;
> Pas a haint, haint a hood.
>
> My four principal foes through life, they have met together in *unity of time*: cough and old age, disease and grief. *Llywarch Hen.*

Unoes, *s. f.* (un—oes) One life; same age, sameness of age. *a.* Of one age; cotemporary.
Unoldeb, *s. m.* (unawl) Unity; identicalness.
Unolder, *s. m.* (unawl) Identicalness, sameness.
Unoldra, *s. m.* (unawl) Sameness, similarity.
Unoli, *v. a.* (unawl) To render united, to accord; to become the same; to identify.
Unoliad, *s. m.* (unawl) Unition; accordance.
Unoliaeth, *s. m.* (unawl) The state of being the same or identified; accordance.

> Yn nghred ni weled, unoliaeth Gwalchmai,
> Wr well——
>
> In christendom there has not been seen, the *likeness* of Gwalchmai, a better man. *T. Aled, i T. Salsbri.*

Unoliant, *s. m.* (unawl) Unition; integration.
Unolrwydd, *s. m.* (unawl) Sameness, similarity.
Unon, *s. m.* (un—on) Particularity; doubt, question, supposition. *v. a.* To suppose. *Ni raid unon y dei di yma*, there is no need to suppose that thou wilt come here.

> Er bod dy ddyben di yn nesu o fewn ychydig ddalenau yn fy llyfr discomlant i; eto nid rhaid i ti unon soddi at Lucifer.
>
> Notwithstanding that thy end draws near within a few leaves in my unerring volume; yet thou needest not to *fear* of sinking to Lucifer. *Elis Wyn, Bardd Cwsg.*

Unparth, *s. m.* (parth) One part. *a.* Of one part.
Unpeth, *s. m.* (peth) One thing, same thing. *a.* Of one thing.
Unplyg, *s. m.* (plyg) One double or fold. *a.* Of one double or fold.
Unraith, *s. f.* (rhaith) Sameness of right or law. *a.* Of equal law, of equal right.
Unran, *s. f.* (rhan) One share. *a.* Of one share.
Unrwydd, *s. m.* (un) A state of being one.
Unrwysg, *s. m.* (rhwysg) Sameness of course or sway. *a.* Of the same sway.
Unryw, *s. m.* (rhyw) A same kind, a same sex; same. *a.* Of the same kind.
Unrywiaeth, *s. m.* (unryw) A rendering of the same kind; identity.
Unsain, *s. f.* (sain) An unison. *a.* Unison.
Unsawd, *s. f.* (sawd) A same state. *a.* Of the same state.
Unseiniad, *s. m.* (unsain) A forming an unison.
Unseiniaw, *v. a.* (unsain) To form an unison.
Unseiniawg, *a.* (unsain) Having one sound.
Unsill, *s. f.* (un—sill) One syllable. *a.* Of one syllable.
Unsillawg, *a.* (unsill) Having one syllable.
Unsud, *s. m.* (sud) Same state. *a.* Of one state.

U[illegible] *s. m.* [illegible] *a.* Of one state. [illegible] *Unsud* as unsud, so [illegible]

Unswn, *s.* [illegible] sound. *a.* Of the same sound.
Unswydd, *s. m.* (swydd) A same office or business; [illegible] purpose. *a.* Of one business or purpose. [illegible] *yno yn unswydd*, I went there on purpose.
U[illegible]lwedd, *s. m.* (sylwedd) Sameness of substance. *a.* Of one substance, or material.
U[illegible]lweddawg, *a.* (unsylwedd) Consubstantial.
U[illegible]lweddawl, *a.* (unsylwedd) Homogeneal.
U[illegible]lweddiad, *s. m.* (unsylwedd) A rendering of the same substance; a becoming homogeneal.
U[illegible]ith, *s. f.* (taith) One journey. *a.* Of the same journey.
U[illegible]ithiawg, *a.* (untaith) Having one journey.
U[illegible]ef, *s. f.* (tref) Sameness of habitation. *a.* [illegible] the same habitation or town.

> Nid untref gwalch ac eryr.
>
> Not *of one habitation* a [illegible] and an eagle. *Adage.*

Untri, *s. m.* (un—tri) Three united in one.
Untro, *s. m.* (tro) One turn. *a.* Of one turn.
Untroed, *s. m.* (troed) One foot. *a.* One-footed.
Untroedawg, *a.* (untroed) Having one foot.
Untu, *s. m.* (tu) One side. *a.* One sided.
Untuawg, *a.* (untu) One-sided; partial. *Cyfrwy untuawg*, a side-saddle.

> Taw, gwyn untuawg [illegible],
> A [illegible].
>
> Be silent, thou complainant *partial* and [illegible] fault. [illegible]
>
> Untuawg [illegible]
> Ac yn [illegible]?
>
> The *one-sided* [illegible] is it not fair, [illegible] day's [illegible]. [illegible]

Untuawl, *a.* (untu) Belonging to one side.
Untuogrwydd, *s. m.* (untuawg) The state of being on one side; partiality.
Untuolrwydd, *s. m.* (untuawl) A one-sided state.
Unwaith, *s. f.* (un—gwaith) One time. *a.* Of one time. *adv.* Once, at one time.

> A fo drwg unwaith a wyr fod yn ddrwg [illegible].
>
> He that is bad *one time* knows how to be bad [illegible]. *Adage.*
>
> Unwaith yr aeth yr arfwyddes i nofiaw [illegible].
>
> Once the lady went to swim she was drowned. *Adage.*

Unwedd, *s. f.* (un—gwedd) Sameness of appearance, similitude. *a.* Similar; [illegible], equable. *adv.* Alike.

> Y doeth a'r annoeth unwedd,
> O gyrau'r byd [illegible] bedd.
>
> The wise and the unwise alike, from the [illegible] he sends to the grave. [illegible]

Unweddawg, *a.* (unwedd) Having a fellow or partner. *s. c.* A monogamist.
Unweddawl, *a.* (unwedd) Uniform; of one aspect.
Unwr, *s. m.*—*pl.* unwyr (gwr) A man who unites, agrees, or accords.
Unwyneb, *s. m.* (gwyneb) Sameness of face. *a.* Of the same face or surface.
Unwynebawg, *a.* (unwyneb) Having one face.

> Gall cyrsain ragodlg fod [illegible] yn [illegible], ai [illegible] y [illegible], [illegible].
> 'A'm try angen a'm [illegible].'
>
> A consonant of the leading rhyme may [illegible] that is, without [illegible] the former pause, as in the above verse. [illegible]

Unyd, *s. m.* (un) The state of being one; continuity; a state of being thoroughly united; alike. *a.* Being united, continual, or uninterrupted; like. *adv.* [illegible], continually; like.

Cadr fab Gruffydd
Gwawr Eiddionydd,
Gweirydd unyd.

The mighty son of Grufydd, the luminary of Eiddionydd, *the same as* Gweirydd. *Rhisierdyn.*

Gwel, ddyn, adeilad hyfryd,
O lawr i nen yn unyd.
Daiarfyd dirfawr.

Behold, O man, a pleasant structure rise, from the bottom to the summit all *complete*, the immense terrestrial world.
Elis Wyn, Bardd Cwsg.

UR, *s. m. r.* That is extreme, over, or superior; that is essential, or pure; that is sacred, holy, or inviolable.

Urael, *s. m.* (ur) That is of pure element; amianthus, asbestos; also the cloth made of that fossil.

Urael yw llieinwisg o'r manweiddiaf, o'r maen ystinos, ac a olchid a'r tan, wedi y badreddai.

The *Urael* is a cloth garment of the finest texture, made of the asbestos stone, and which used to be cleansed with the fire, after it had been soiled. *Adrodd. Pryd Mab Duw.*

Ar dyrau gwynion, ar dai urael,
Mawr y mae ei—fryd.

On white towers, on houses of *amianthus*, great is his delight.
L. G. Cothi.

Mab addwyn o rwym urael maith,
Mab Argiwydd yr Israel.

A beatific Son out of a bandage of ample *asbestos*, the Son of the the Lord of Israel. *L. G. Cothi.*

Urdd, *s. f.—pl. t.* au (ur) A dignified order, rank, or class; a sacred order.

——Yn gweddiaw
Ar Dduw nef a'i urddau naw.

Praying to God of heaven and his *orders* nine.
I. ab Rh. ab Ieuan Llwyd.

Urddain, *a.* (urdd) Abounding with dignity.

I feirdd dwfn dyfydd a goffain';
I Gynddelw oedd arddelw urddain.

To bards profound will be preserved what they commemorate; to Cynddelw it was his *honourable* claim.
Cynddelw, m. O. Gwynedd.

Urddas, *s. f.—pl. t.* au (urdd) Dignity; a sacred order; church hierarchy, or orders.

Deuparth urddas enw da.

Two parts of *dignity* is a good name. *Adage.*

Yn mhob ennill y mae anrhydedd,
Yn mhob anrhydedd y mae urddas,
Yn mhob urddas y mae braint,
Yn mhob braint y mae dyledswydd.

In every gain there is honour, in every honour there is *respect*, in every *respect* there is privilege, in every privilege there is a duty. *Catwg ab Gwynlliw.*

Urddasoedd——
A wnaeth ef, ei iawnwaith oedd.

Hierarchies he created, his righteous work was that.
Dr. S. Cent.

Urddasaidd, *a.* (urddas) Relating to dignified or holy orders; honorary.

Urddasawg, *a.* (urddas) Having sacred orders; dignified. *s. m.—pl.* urddasogion, A dignitary.

Urddasawl, *a.* (urddas) Relating to dignified rank; relating to sacred orders; dignified; honourable.

Urddasedig, *a.* (urddas) Dignified; ordained.

Urddaseiddiad, *s. m.* (urddasaidd) A dignification.

Urddaseiddiaw, *v. a.* (urddasaidd) To render dignified, or honorary; to become dignified.

Urddaseiddrwydd, *s. m.* (urddasaidd) A dignified state.

Urddasiad, *s. m.* (urddas) A dignification; a conferring of holy orders.

Urddasoldeb, *s. m.* (urddasawl) A dignified state.

Urddasoldeb swydd yw ei chyflawni yn gyfiawn.

The *honourableness* of an office is to fulfil it justly. *Adage.*

Urddasolder, *s. m.* (urddasawl) Honourableness.

Urddasoldra, *s. m.* (urddasawl) Honourableness.

Urddasoli, *v. a.* (urddasawl) To render dignified, to become dignified.

Urddasolrwydd, *s. m.* (urddasawl) Honourableness

Urddasu, *v. n.* (urddas) To dignify, to honour; to confer orders.

Urddaswr, *s. m.—pl.* urddaswyr (urddas—gwr) A dignifier; one who confers orders.

Urddaw, *v. a.* (urdd) To confer dignity, rank, or order; to confer holy orders; to ordain.

Dyn a urdd y lle, ac nid urdd y lle y dyn.

A man *honours* the station, and the station *honours* not the man. *Adage.*

Urdd wledig llaryg lle aergrain;
Urddws Duw diwyrnawd Owain!

A patriot *dignifies* the arms of a host ranging through slaughter; *God has ordained* the day of Owain!
Cynddelw, m. O. Gwynedd.

Urddawd, *s. m.* (urdd) A dignification; an ordaining.

Urddawg, *a.* (urdd) Having dignity or orders.

Urddawl, *a.* (urdd) Relating to dignity, rank, or order; dignified; honorable.

Seiniad pob ceiniad canon cerdd eiliad,
Seiliad aur ddeiliad o waed urddolion.

Proclaimed by every songster is the regular composition of song, the subject is the golden branch from the blood *of exalted ones.* *W. Llyn.*

Urddawn, *a.* (urdd) Of dignified or exalted state.

Beirdd wogawn bardd urddawn urddwch,
Urddawl cerdd, can edifeirwch.

Ye energetic bards, do honour to an *honourable* bard, the graduated of song, through repentance. *Cynddelw.*

Urddedig, *a.* (urdd) Dignified; being ordained.

Prydai y prydyddion——
Gan rwyf Bangor, gor goron urddedig.

The poets would poetize before the chief of Bangor, the choir of a *dignified* crown. *Iorwerth Beli*

Urddedigaeth, *s. f.—pl. t.* au (urddedig) Ordination.

Urddedigaw, *v. a.* (urddedig) To render dignified; to ordinate; to become dignified.

Urddedigawl, *a.* (urddedig) Tending to dignify.

Urddedigrwydd, *s. m.* (urddedig) A dignified state

Urddeiniad, *s. m.* (urddain) Dignification.

Urddeiniaw, *v. a.* (urddain) To render dignified.

Urddeiniawl, *a.* (urddain) Dignifying; tending to honour.

Mae'r pen ffydd, Dofydd dwyfawl, gyda thi
I'th urddoni eneth urddeiniawl.

The object of the faith, the Divine Regulator, is with thee, to exalt thee, thou *honoured* virgin. *D. Ddu o Hiraddug.*

Urdden, *s. f.* (urdd—gen) A superior intelligence or genius; a sacred intelligence. *a.* Of superior genius.

Awdl urdden amgen amgall digawn.

A different song *of superior intellect* amply comprehensive
Cynddelw.

Gwanai yn nghynghor eisor Medrawd
Mal Urien urdden, a'i amgyffrawd.

He that is second to Medrod would distinguish in council, like Urien *of exalted genius*, with his comprehension. *Meilyr.*

Gwyr Powys——
Cad orllawen orllawen,
Pedair cynneddf, cadw cadyr urdden,
Ar ddeg yr dugant o Feigen.

The Men of Powys, in far-extending battle triumphant, fourteen prerogatives, the preservation of mighty *pre-eminence of genius*, they bore from Meigen. *Cynddelw.*

Urddiad, *s. m.—pl. t.* au (urdd) A dignifying, a conferring of honour; a giving of degree, rank, or order; an ordaining.

Urddiain, *a.* (urdd) Abounding with dignity.

Dywawd Derwyddon——
O wyron Owain,
Ar wyneb Prydain
Un urddiain Llundain,
O lan deithi.

Druids declare, of the descendants of Owain, over the face of Britain one shall be *supreme* of London, of sacred character.
Ll. P. Moch, i L. ab Iorwerth.

Urddiannawl, *a.* (urddiant) Dignifying.
Urddiannu, *v. a.* (urddiant) To create dignity.
Urddiannus, *a.* (urddiant) Dignifying, honouring.
Urddiannusaw, *v. a.* (urddiannus) To render dignified; to become honourable.
Urddiant, *s. m.* (urdd) Dignification; ordination.
Urddiator, *ger.* (urddiad) In dignifying.
Urddin, *a.* (urdd) Being honoured or exalted.

Cyfoethawg Dduw urddin.

The powerful God *of exalted state.* *Taliesin.*

Urddineb, *s. m.* (urddin) A dignified state.
Urddoldeb, *s. m.* (urddawl) A dignified state; the state of being ordained.
Urddolder, *s. m.* (urddawl) A dignified state.
Urddoldra, *s. m.* (urddawl) A dignified state.
Urddoledd, *s. m.* (urddawl) A dignified state.
Urddoles, *s. f.—pl. t.* au (urddawl) A female who holds dignity or rank.
Urddoli, *v. a.* (urddawl) To render dignified; to ordinate, to ordain.
Urddoliad, *s. m.* (urddawl) A dignifying, a conferring of rank, degree, or orders; ordination.
Urddolineth, *s. m.* (urddawl) Ordination.
Urddolrwydd, *s. m.* (urddawl) A dignified state.
Urddon, *s. m.* (urdd) The grass-poly.
Urddoni, *v. a.* (urddawn) To exalt, to honour.
Urddoniad, *s. m.* (urddawn) A yielding dignity.
Urddoniant, *s. m.* (urddawn) Exaltation, honour.
Urddrad, *s. m.—pl. t.* au (urdd—rhad) An exalting virtue.
Urddun, *s. m.* (urdd) An exalted state or rank.
Urddunaw, *v. a.* (urddun) To honour, to exalt.
Urddunawl, *a.* (urddun) Tending to honour.
Urdduniad, *s. m.* (urddun) A dignification.
Urdduniannu, *v. a.* (urdduniant) To endow with pre-eminence.
Urdduniannus, *a.* (urdduniant) Tending to dignity
Urdduniant, *s. m.* (urddun) Pre-eminence, honour
Urddwisg, *s. f.—pl. t.* oedd (urdd—gwisg) A robe of state, a dress of order.
Urddwr, *s. m.—pl.* urddwyr (urdd—gwr) A man who dignifies; one who confers orders.
Urddyn, *s. m.* (urdd) A dignified or exalted one.

Wyr Owain Prydain praff ddychryn galon——
Mab Iorwerth mad ganed urddyn.

The grandson of Owain of Britain, the ample terror of the foes; the son of Iorwerth, happily was the *exalted one* begotten. *Ll. P. Moch.*

Uriad, *s. m.—pl. t.* on (ur) That is pre-eminent, an exalted one; an elder.

Dug llaw ffon Aron uriad
Aeron a dail.——

The hand-stick of Aaron the *elder* bore berries and leaves *I. ab Hywel Swrdwal.*

US, *s. m. r.—pl. t.* ion. What is a peel, or connected coating; also the husks of corn, or chaff. *a.* Outside; illusive; trifling, light, frail. It is a general termination of words of quality or adjectives; as *gweddus*, covered with decency, of a decent appearance, or seemly.

Adwaen hen farch us.

An old horse knows *chaff.* *Adag.*

Yr enaid, gochel rinwedd
Y cotti us o'i fetus fedd.

My soul, avoid the nature of the *frail* [illegible] joyment. *D. ab Dafydd Llwyd.*

Usaidd, *a.* (us) Like husk, or chaff; husky.
Usawg, *a.* (us) Abounding with husks or chaff.
Usion, *s. pl. aggr.* (us) Chaff, husks of corn.
Usiongrug, *s. m.* (usion—crug) A chaff heap.
Usioni, *v. a.* (usion) To yield husks or chaff.
Uslyd, *a.* (us) Abounding with chaff, full of chaff.
Uslydrwydd, *s. m.* (uslyd) Fulness of chaff.
Ust, *s. m.* (us) A silence; a hush, or hist. It is also the imperative verb: Hush!

Y taranau——
Duw a bair: ar ei air ent
Ust ewybr a dystawent.

Thunder-claps God doth cause; at his word they become a sudden *silence* and are stilled. *[illegible]*

Ustiad, *s. m.* (ust) A silencing, a hushing.
Ustiaw, *v. a.* (ust) To silence, to quell, to hush.
Uswydd, *a.* (us—gwydd) Of peeled surface.

Llwgoch ei lafnawr, ysgwyd uswydd.

Red-stained his blade, shield *of battered front.* *Llygad Gwr.*

Gwr ourgiawr [illegible] uswydd holli.

A hero splitting the gold-covered shield *of battered front.* *H. Foel ab Griffri.*

Usyn, *s. m. dim.* (us) A single particle or chaff.

Usyn wyf, ac eisiau nerth,
Ac angeu yn egyngerth!

A *frail chaff* am I and wanting strength, with death to [illegible]! *D. ab Gwilym.*

Utgorn, *s. m.—pl.* utgyrn (udgorn) A trumpet.
UTH, *s. m. r.* That is extreme; extended.
Uthr, *s. m.* (uth) That stunneth. *a.* Awful, wonderful; astonishing; terrific; horrible.

Y cythraul acw uthr-was.

The fiend yonder a *horrid* stripling. *W. Llyn.*

Uthraidd, *a.* (uthr) Tending to astonish.
Uthraw, *v. a.* (uthr) To astonish, to amaze.
Uthrawl, *a.* (uthr) Astonishing, amazing.
Uthredig, *a.* (uthr) Astonished, terrified.
Uthredd, *s. m.* (uthr) Astonishment; horror.
Uthriad, *s. m.* (uthr) An astonishing.
Uthroldeb, *s. m.* (uthrawl) Astonishment; awfulness; horribleness.
Uthrolder, *s. m.* (uthrawl) Astonishment; awfulness; horribleness.
Uthroledd, *s. m.* (uthrawl) Astonishingness; awfulness; horribleness.
Uthroli, *v. a.* (uthrawl) To render astonishing; to render awful; to render terrified; to become awful; to become terrified.
Uthrolrwydd, *s. m.* (uthrawl) Awfulness.
Uwch, *prep.* (uch) Above, over; also used for *uchach*, higher, upper.

Uwch pen no dwy ysgwydd.

Higher a head than two shoulders. *Adag.*

Uwchder, *s. m.* (uwch) Highness, altitude.
Uwchdra, *s. m.* (uwch) Highness, altitude.
Uwchedd, *s. m.* (uwch) Highness, altitude.
Uwchel, *a.* (uwch) High, lofty; eminent.
Uwd, *s. m.* (wd) Any liquid thickened by boiling meal in it; hasty-pudding; bargoo; pap; or the like mixtures. *Uwd peilliad*, flour boiled in milk; *uwd maidd glas*, grits boiled in whey; *uwd sugaethan*, a poultice.

A fo ami ei fel rhoed ar ei uwd.

He who has abundance of honey let him put it on his *pudding.* *Adag.*

Uwdaidd, *a.* (uwd) Like hasty-pudding.
Uwdfys, *s. m.* (uwd—bys) The nursing finger, the fore-finger.

W.

W. THIS vowel's sound is an inflection of *o*; and it expresses a tendency from, out, or beyond; and when affixed to primitives, it gives them a contrary import; as in *gwedd*, that is wedded, if formed into *gweddw*, it denotes being beyond a wedded state, or a widow; so *ul*, moisture, becomes *ulw*, the remains what is deprived of moisture, as embers, or cinders: and with respect to the gender or words, the *w* denotes the masculine and *o* the feminine. It is used as an interjection expressive of alarm.

Wab, *s. m.*—*pl. t.* iau (ab) A slap, a stroke.

Wabiad, *s. m.* (wab) A slapping, a beating.

Wabiaw, *v. a.* (wab) To slap, to beat, to cuff.

Wabiwr, *s. m.*—*pl.* wabiwyr (wab—gwr) Slapper.

WB, *s. m. r.* The state of being expelled; the state of being out, over, or up. *interj.* It is expressive of anxiety: ah!

> Wb wyr! nawdd nef rhagoch; er y byd na wnewch hyny: ni ddaeth neb erioed i ercid yr arch o Olwen a elai a'i fywyd ganto.
>
> *Avaunt ye men! God's protection before you! for the world do not so: no body ever came to demand Olwen who went away with his life.* *H. Culhwch—Mabinogion.*

> Wb o'r hin, o'r wybr heno!
>
> *Out with the weather from the sky to-night!* *D. ab Gwilym.*

Wbain, *v. a.* (wb) To keep howling, to howl.

Wbwb, *interj.* (wb *repeated*) It is expressive of distress, anxiety, and revolting.

WCH, *s. m. r.* A spread out, or expansion.

Wchw, *interj.* (wch) It is expressive of calling out for assistance: Hoa.

WD, *s. m. r.* That is extreme, extended, or stretched out.

Wedi, *adv.* (gwedi) After, afterwards; then.

> Y da a el yn dy waith
> Wedi'r el y daw'r ailwaith;
> Dy ran o dir ariannau,
> Dy wlad oll a dal y da.
>
> The property expanded in the work, after it is gone the second time it will come thy portion of rent producing land, thy whole country will the property make good. *Iorwerth Fynglwyd.*

Weithian, *adv.* (gwaith) This time, now, at length. It is used for *y waith hon*, *y weithon*, and *weithion*.

Weithiau, *adv.* (gwaith) Sometimes, at times.

> Eiddig——
> Wrth glywed, tybied fod dyn,
> E glyw weithiau drwst gwlithyn.
>
> The jealous one in listening thinking there is a man, he *sometimes* hears the noise of the falling dew-drop. *T. Prys.*

Weithion, *adv.* (gwaith) This time, at length.

Weithon, *adv.* (gwaith) This time, now; at last.

Wel, *v. imp.* (gwel) Lo, behold, see, see now. *conj.* So, well. *Wel dacw fo*, lo yonder it is: *wel diso*, see now below: *wel ducho*, lo above: *wel dyma iddi beth*, well here is some for her: *wel dyna i ti*, see there now for you.

> Wel, dyna weled anhawdd!
>
> *Well, that is a difficult perception!* *D. ab Gwilym.*

Wela, *v. imp.* (wel) Lo, behold, see, see now; well. *Wela dyma fi*, see now here am I: *wela paid*, well then be quiet: *wela hai*, very well then, well then it shall be so.

WF, *s. m. r.* A flow, glide, or running out; that is liquid.

WFF, *s. m. r.* Motion from or out; expulsion.

Wfft, *s. m.* (wff) A push off; a slight, or scorn; a fie, an expression of disapprobation:

> Wfft i'r dyn a wfftio pawb heb wybod mwy am dano.
>
> *Fie upon the person whom every body cries fie upon without knowing any more about him.* *Adage.*

Wfftiad, *s. m.* (wfft) A pushing off scornfully; a shewing disapprobation with surprize; a crying fie upon.

Wfftiaw, *v. a.* (wfft) To push away with disapprobation; to cry shame; to cry fie.

WG, *s. m. r.* An overspread; an outside.

Whw, *interj.* It is expressive of calling out for assistance.

WI, *interj.* It is expressive of joy; Hey; heyday; oh.

> O wi! O Dduw! y gynnifer gwaith ydd arfaethasant ieirll Caer gwrthwynebu i Ruffydd, ac nis gallasant!
>
> O yes! O God! the number of times that the earls of Chester purposed to oppose Gruffydd, and they could not! *Bucheddd G. ab Cynan.*

> Am fy ngwddf ei breichiau——
> Wawr euraid: wi o'r amwy!
>
> Round my neck her arms, the golden luminary: oh, what a wreath! *D. ab Gwilym.*

> Wi! o'r grefft yw ar ei grys:
> Wi! o'r lliw ar y llewys!
>
> *Oh! what art there is on his vest: Oh! what a colour on the skirts!* *D. ab Gwilym, i hosan.*

Wichwach, *interj.* (gwich) It expresses frolick.

Wihi, *s. m.* (wi) The whinnying of a horse.

Wihïad, *s. m.* (wihi) A whinnying, as a horse.

Wihïaw, *v. a.* (wihi) To whinny like a horse.

Winc, *s. m.*—*pl. t.* od (gwinc) A chaffinch.

WL, *s. m. r.* That is subtile, fine, or small.

WLL, *s. m. r.*—*pl.* yllod. A fragment, a fraction.

WM, *s. m. r.* That closes about; a covert; a void, or hollow.

Wmp, *s. m.* (wm) A covert, or a shade.

> ——Mal imp coedydd,
> Wmp ar dalwrn ei fwrn fydd.
>
> Like the shoots of trees, a shade on the headland its load will be. *Llywarch Brydydd.*

WN, *s. m. r.* That is on, upon, close, or at; that is beginning or commencing; that tends to; that is of an energetic nature.

Wnc, *s. m.* (wn) The state of being close, at, or hard by; proximity. *a.* Close, near, hard by. *prep.* Near, nigh. *adv.* Here.

> Dyweddi o wnc, gelanas o bell.
>
> Espousal from a *neighbourhood*, murder from afar. *Adage.*

Wnco, *pron. m.* (wnc) That one at a distance, speaking of the masculine; the feminine is *once*. *adv.* There. *Dyfed.*

Wncw, *adv.* (wng) There; yonder.

Wng, *s. m.*—*pl.* yngon (wnc) The state of being close, at, or by. *a.* Close, near, hard by; strait. *prep.* Near, nigh. *adv.* Here. *Engyrth yngaf*, difficulty the most confined.

> Ing yn ing yngon eangedd.
>
> Strait in strait be *proximities* of amplitude. *Adage.*

> Trwy a thrwy, wng a chwng, y daethan';
> Traw a thraw, unfedd Bran a Melgan.
>
> Through and through, close and between, they came; over and over, of the same course Bran and Melgan. *Myrddin.*

WO, *s. m. r.* A motion out or ended; a call made to stop a horse. *v. imper.* Wo, stop, stand still.

Wö, *s. m.* The cry of hounds in chace.

WP, *s. m. r.* The state of being out or over.

WR, *s. m. r.* The state of being on, over, or at.

Wrch, *s. m.* (wr) That is high, or rotund.

Wrdd, *s. m.* (wr) Touch, contact; impulse.

Wrth, *s. m.* (wr) A touch, a contact, the state of being by, opposite, or against.

Wrth, *prep.* (wrth, *s.*) In contact, close to; by; with; in comparison, compared with. *adv.* While. *Pa beth yw hyny wrth hyn?* What is that compared with this? *Wrth fyned heibio*, in going by: *Wrth liw dydd*, by day light: *Nid allaf wrth hyny*, I cannot help that: *Wrth ganu*, while singing: *Taraw wrth*, to meet with: *Dos wrth dy bwys*, go taking thy time: *Cadw oddi wrth y byd*, keep from the world; *ymneilldua i wrth y byd*, separate thyself from the world: *Y byd bo wrth eich bodd!* be the world well with you! *Dyfed.* *Mae y fuwch wrth ben ei hal*, the cow is just in calving. *Dyfed.* *Wrth* is compounded with pronouns, and is declined thus—*Wrthwyf*, *wrthof*, by me; *wrthyt*, *wrthot*, by thee; *wrtho*, by him, or it; *wrthi*, by her; *wrthym*, *wrthom*, by us; *wrthych*, *wrthoch*, by you; *wrthynt*, by them. *Ni elli wrtho*, thou canst not help it: *Wrtho ei hun*, by himself.

Calon Sais wrth Gymmro.

The heart of an Englishman *towards* a Welshman. *Adage.*

Rhaid i'r fuwch wrth losgwrn.

Necessary to the cow *the being with* a tail. *Adage.*

WS, *s. m. r.* That is impulsive, that is precipitous; action, effort; ardour.

Wsg, *s. m.* (ws) That opens or separates.

Wst, *s. m.* (ws) A thrust, push, or drive; a gust; the hypochoudria, the hip.

Wsw, *s. m.—pl. t.* od (ws) That abounds with impulse, or energy; an epithet for the horse; a steed.

Os gwaywyr, ewch dros Gaer Wyat;
Os harnais wsw arnynt—
Ymgelwch.

If spears, go ye over Winchester; if on them *steed* harness be, hide yourselves. *L. Mon.*

WT, *s. m. r.* That is extreme, or outward; out.

Wtre, *s. f.—pl.* wtrëydd (wt—rhe) A lane.

Wttres, *s. f.—pl. t.* au (wt—tres) A revel, a carousal.

Carw mewn cor!—
Cyn y ffair canu 'fferen,
A myn'd i wttres a merch,
A rhoddi neges Rhydderch.

A buck in a choir! before the bargain he sings a mass, and goes to *revel* with a damsel, and presents the gift of Rhydderch.
G. ab Hywel ab Tudyr.

Wttresaidd, *a.* (wttres) Revelous, carousing.

Wttresawl, *a.* (wttres) Revelling, carousing.

Wttresgar, *a.* (wttres) Revelous, apt to feast.

Wttresgarwch, *s. m.* (wttresgar) Riotousness.

Wttresiad, *s. m.* (wttres) A revelling.

Wttreslaeth, *s. f.* (wttres) Loose festivity.

Lluniais mewn llanerch
Wttreslaeth traserch
I winfaeth wenferch.

I prepared in a glade a *carousal* of ardent love for a wine-nurtured damsel fair. *D. Edward.*

Wttresu, *v. a.* (wttres) To carouse, to revel.

Wttreswr, *s. m.—pl.* wttreswyr (wttres—gwr) A carouser, a riotous person, a spendthrift.

Wttreswyl, *s. f.—pl. t.* iau (wttres—gwyl) A carousal.

Wtr, *s. m. aggr.* (wt) The small light grain amongst corn.

Od oes wtr mewn das ifi.

If there be *empty grain* in a stack of thine. *Ieuan Tew.*

WTH, *s. m. r.* That expands or stretches out.

WY, *s. m. r.—pl. t.* au. That proceeds from; that is produced; an egg.

Mal wy ar drosol.

Like an *egg* on a lever. *Adage.*

A ddygo yr wy a ddwg yr iar.

He that steals the *egg* will steal the hen. *Adage.*

Wy, *pronom. prep.* Of or to the third person; of him, of her, of it; for which *i*, *ei*, *i'w*, *iddi*, are generally used. '*Hi yn fam wy thad*,' She being mother to her father.

Wybr, *s. f.—pl. t.* au (gwybr) Firmament, or atmosphere; the sky; ether; the least possible thing.

Nid ysgafn ond wybr.

There is nothing so light as *air*. *Adage.*

Yr haul—
Ymddangosa erof, cof certh,
Yn entrych wybr, cyn anterth.

Thou sun, shew thyself for my sake, with sure sign, in the midst of the *firmament*, before the time of noon.
G. Llwyd ab Dafydd.

Moesen fu farw o henaint;
Ni bu ar hwn wybr o haint.

Moses did die of old age; there was upon him not the *smallest sign* of disease. *L. G. Cothi.*

Wybraidd, *a.* (wybr) Like the firmament.

Mis Ebrill wybraidd gorwlir;
Lluddedig ychain; llwm tir.

The month of April *aerial* is the horizon; fatigued the oxen; bare the land. *Adage.*

Wybraw, *v. a.* (wybr) To form a firmament; to move in the air; to soar into the air; to become äerial.

Wybrawl, *a.* (wybr) Firmamental; äerial.

Y paderau—
Gwlith wybrawl gwlaw wyth Ebrill.

The beads seem as *aërial* dew of April eight times purified.
Ieuan Rhaidr.

Wybreiddiad, *s. m.* (wybraidd) A rendering like the firmament; a becoming äerial.

Wybreiddiaw, *v. a.* (wybraidd) To render firmamental; to render äerial; to become like air.

Wybren, *s. f.—pl. t.* i (wybr) A firmament.

Ardwyad cancad—
Yn cynt no rhywynt ach rhudd wybren.

The swayer through a hundred battles, he is more quick than a storm-wind over the ruddy *welkin*.
Ll. P. Moch, i Gr. ab Llywelyn.

Drwy'r wybrennydd y dydd a daen
Ei lwyrwych wely ariant.

Through the *skies* the day doth spread his silver couch supremely gay. *D. Ionawr.*

Wybrenaidd, *a.* (wybren) Firmamental; atmospheric.

Wybrenawl, *a.* (wybren) Being firmamental; atmospheric.

Wybrgoel, *s. f.* (wybr—coel) Aëromancy.

Wybriad, *s. c.—pl.* wybriaid (wybr) That is of the firmament; that exists in the air.

Llamysten—
A'i hedfad ffrwm wybriad ffwch.

The falcon with her gleaming flight a fuming *inhabitant of air*.
O. Brwnlaw.

Wybriaeth, *s. m.* (wybr) Aërology; formation of air.

Wybrig, *a.* (wybr) Firmamental; atmospheric.

Wybrliw, *s. m.* (wybr—lliw) A cerulean hue.

Wybrwr, *s. m.—pl.* wybrwyr (wybr—gwr) One of the firmament; one who soars into the air; an äerologist.

Ni fynwn, er mwyn f'enaid,
Wybrwr llon, a'm bwriai'r llaid.

I would not, for the sake of my soul, have a lively *flier* in the air, that would throw me in the dirt.
Ieu. ab Rhys, i ofyn march dimay.

Wyd, *v.* (wy) Art, thou art. It is used for *wyd ti*, when no emphasis is required.

Wyengawl, *a.* (wy—engawl) Oviparous.

Wyengi, *v. a.* (wy—engi) To propagate by eggs.

Wyf, *v.* (wy) Am, I am. When the person is emphatically discriminated *mi* is used with it: *Wyf fi yn barawd ond nid wyd ti*, *I* am ready, but *thou* art not.

> Wyf tridyblyg hen, wyf anwadal drud,
> Wyf ehud, wyf anwar:
> Y sawl a'm carodd ni'm car!
>
> *I* am old three ways bent, *I* am sickly bold, *I* am heedless, *I* am wild; the one who has loved me loves me not!
> *Llywarch Hen.*

Wyl, *s. m.* (wy—yl) A gush out; a wail.

Wylad, *s. m.* (wyl) A wailing, a weeping.

Wylaw, *v. a.* (wyl) To wail, or to weep. *Wyli ddagrau heilltion*, thou wilt weep salt tears.

> Wylid ni wyl ei berchen.
>
> *Let him weep* who sees not his owner. *Adage.*
>
> Hawdd peri i fingam wylaw.
>
> It is easy to cause the wry-mouth *to weep*. *Adage.*
>
> Myfi wylaf am Ddafydd;
> A wylwyf fi eli fydd.
>
> Myself *I will weep* for Davydd; what *I do weep* it will be a salve. *L. G. Cothi.*

Wylof, *s. m.* (wyl—of) A weep, a wailing.

Wylofaeth, *s. m.* (wyl—of) The act of wailing.

> Clywais lef clais wylofaeth,
> Cnill dros y wlad trad aeth!
>
> I heard a cry of the breaking out of *weeping*, a knell over the country woefully hath gone! *Ieu. Thomas.*

Wylofain, *v. a.* (wylof) To wail, to weep.

Wylofedd, *s. m.* (wylof) A weeping, a wailing; mourning, lamentation.

Wylofi, *v. a.* (wylof) To wail, or to weep.

Wylofus, *a.* (wylof) Wailing; doleful.

Wyn, *s. pl. aggr.* (oen) Lambs. *Wyn bach*, little lambs.

Wyna, *v. a.* (wyn) To collect lambs; to yean.

> Os gefyn a gaiff dyn da
> Yn y chwaen, yn iach wyna.
>
> If fetters be a good man's lot in the event, adieu with *collecting lambs*. *Llywelyn ab Gutyn.*

Wyneb, *s.m.—pl. t.* au (gwyneb) A face, a visage; a surface. *Wyneb uchel*, of a high look; *derbyn wyneb*, a receiving the presence, a receiving fairly; *ar y wyneb*, upon the surface.

> Wyneb trist drwg a ery.
>
> A sad *countenance* awaits mischief. *Adage.*
>
> Tri pheth sydd ar wraig, a garo weled y cyntaf nis anghar y ddau arall: wyneb ei hun mewn drych; cefn ei gwr o bell, a gorddercbwr yn ei gwely.
>
> Three things appertain to a woman, who loves to see the first she will not dislike to see the other two; her own *face* in a glass; her husband's back far off, and a paramour in her bed.
> *Trioedd.*

Wynebawg, *a.* (wyneb) Having a face; faced.

Wynebawl, *a.* (wyneb) Belonging to the face.

Wynebiad, *s. m.* (wyneb) A facing, a fronting.

Wynebpryd, *s. m.* (wyneb—pryd) A countebance

Wynebu, *v. a.* (wyneb) To face, to front.

Wynebus, *a.* (wyneb) Of countenance, of goodly visage; seemly.

Wynebwarth, *s. m.* (wyneb—gwarth) A face covering; shame of face; blush of face; an affront; also the fine in law for an affront.

> Wynebwarth pawb ei sarhed heb ddyrchafael.
>
> The *affront fine* of every one is his insult fine without advancement. *Welsh Laws.*
>
> Y drysawr, os ettali yr un o'r penswyddogion, taled iddo ei wynebwarth.
>
> The doorkeeper, if he obstruct any one of the chief officers, he must pay to him his *blush of face*. *Welsh Laws.*

Wynebwnïad, *s. m.* (wyneb—gwnïad) A fine-drawing in sewing.

Wynebwnïaw, *v. a.* (gwnïaw) To fine draw.

Wynebwr, *s. m.* (wyneb—gwr) A facer.

Wynos, *s. pl. dim.* (wyn) Lambkins.

Wyr, *s. m.—pl. t.* ion (wy—yr) That is spread, stretched, or extended; a grandson.

> Ni cherir yn llwyr
> Oni ddelo yr wyr.
>
> There will be no loving completely until the *grandchild* comes. *Adage.*
>
> Och, a Garm, a Diasbad, tair wyrion
> Bwlch, a Cyfwlch, a Sefwlch.
>
> Groan, Shout, and Scream, the three *grandchildren* of Gash, Tear, and Rent. *H. Culhwch—Mabinogion.*

Wyrain, *a.* (wyr) Spreading, extending.

> Diegymid yn drwm rhag alawfedd wyrain,
> Wyra lle llans ysgwydawr.
>
> There was a heavy falling down from the *spreading* flow of mead, the spread of a host with trailing shields. *Aneurin.*

Wyraw, *v. a.* (wyr) To distend, to reach out.

Wyre, *s. f.* (wyr) A spread, an expanse. *Yr Wyre Fawr*, *Yr Wyre Fach*, The Great Spread, The Little Spread, rivers in Cardiganshire.

Wyres, *s. f.—pl. t.* au (wyr) A grand-daughter.

Wys, *s. m.* (wy—ys) Aptitude or tendency for motion.

Wysawg, *a.* (wys) Having aptitude; abounding with currency or fluidity. *Caer Wysawg*, one of the old names of Oxford.

Wysg, *s. m.* (wys) A tendency forward, tendency, direction, bias; presence; a current, course, or stream. *Ar wysg y Cesariaid*, in pursuit of the Romans: *Llusga fe yn wysg ei draed*, drag him with his feet foremost: *Yn wysg dy drwyn*, in the direction of thy nose.

> Canaid lu crau-dwysg
> A gerddant i'th wysg,
> Yn lle aur dor-frwysg,
> Yn llwyr dorf-ryddid.
>
> A glorious blood-spilt host will come into thy *presence*, as a golden host conquering, a multitude completely free.
> *D. Ddu o Hiraddug.*
>
> Aethym——
> Yn wysg fy mhen yn esgud.
>
> I went in the *direction* of my head nimbly. *D. ab Gwilym.*

Wysg, *adv.* (wys) In a forward direction; forward. *Dos wysg dy ben*, go with thy head forwards, go headlong.

Wysgaw, *v. n.* (wysg) To move onward; to glide onward; to go headlong.

Wyt, *v.* (wyd) Art, thou art. When there is an emphasis required to distinguish the second person from any other *Ti* is added: *Wyt yma*, thou art here; *wyt ti yna, ac nid arall*, thou art there, and not another.

> Neud wyt wr aerdwr, ardwy efrwe cad
> Cedernyd Enens.
>
> Surely *thou art* a man that is the bulwark of conflict, a sturdy swayer of battle of the prowess of Eneas.
> *Ll. P. Moch, i L. ab Iorwerth.*

Wyth, *s. m.—pl. t.* au (wy—yth) The state of being extended out, or separate from an identity; the number eight, eight. *a.* Eight.

Wythaw, *v. a.* (wyth) To form into eight, to make up eight; to divide into eight parts.

Wythawl, *a.* (wyth) Belonging to eight.

Wythban, *s. m.* (wyth—ban) That is of eight parts; that is of eight verses; that is of eight syllables. *a.* Of eight parts.

Wythbanawg, *a.* (wythban) Of eight parts; of eight verses; of eight syllables.

Wythblyg, *s. m.* (wyth—plyg) That is of eight folds. *a.* Of eight folds.

Wythblygawl, *a.* (wythblyg) Of eight folds.

Wythblygiad, *s. m.* (wythblyg) A forming of eight folds.

Wythblygu, *v. a.* (wythblyg) To render eight fold.
Wythdeg, *s. m.* (wyth—deg) Eighteen.
Wythdegfed, *s. m.* (wythdeg) Eighteenth.
Wythdro, *s. m.* (wyth—tro) That is of eight turns. *a.* Of eight turns.
Wythdroed, *s. m.* (wyth—troed) That is eight-footed. *a.* Eight-footed.
Wythdroedawg, *a.* (wythdroed) Having eight feet
Wythddeg, *s. m.* (wyth—deg) Eighty. *a.* Eighty.
Wythddegfed, *s. m.* (wythddeg) Eightieth.
Wythfed, *s. m.* (wyth) An eighth. *a.* Eighth.
Wythfedwaith, *s. f.* (wythfed—gwaith) Eighth time
Wythganfed, *s. m.* (wythgant) Eight hundredth.
Wythganfedwaith, *s. f.* (wythganfed—gwaith) The eight hundredth time.
Wythganmil, *s. m.* (wythgant—mil) Eight hundred thousands.
Wythganmilfed, *s. m.* (wythganmil) An eight hundred thousandth.
Wythgant, *s. m.* (wyth—cant) Eight hundred.
Wythganwaith, *s. pl.* (wythgant—gwaith) Eight hundred times.
Wythiad, *s. m.* (wyth) A forming of eight; a dividing into eight parts.
Wythmis, *s. m.* (wyth—mis) A space of eight months. *a.* Of eight months.
Wythmlwydd, *s. m.* (wyth—blwydd) That is of eight years. *a.* Of eight years.
Wythmlwyddawl, *a.* (wythmlwydd) Octennial.
Wythmlynedd, *s. m.* (wyth—blynedd) That is of eight years. *a.* Of eight years.
Wythmlyneddawl, *a.* (wythmlynedd) Octennial.
Wythnos, *s. f.—pl. t.* au (wyth—nos) That consists of eight nights; a week. *Wythnos y gweddiau*, rogation week. Anciently the days of the week were thus named—*Unfetdydd*, first day; *deufetdydd, deuedydd, eilfetdydd*, second day; *trydedydd*, third day; *pedrydydd*, fourth day; *pummetdydd*, fifth day; *chwechetdydd*, sixth day; *seithfetdydd*, seventh day.

Wythnos y llwynawg.

The week of the fox. *Adage.*

Wythnosawl, *a.* (wythnos) Weekly.
Wythnosi, *v. a.* (wythnos) To form a week, to divide into weeks.
Wythnosiad, *s. m.* (wythnos) A forming a week, a dividing into weeks.
Wythnydd, *s. m.* (wyth—dydd) A space of eight days. *a.* Of eight days.
Wythnyddiawl, *a.* (wythnydd) Of eight days.
Wythnyn, *s. m.* (wyth—dyn) That is of eight persons. *a.* Of eight persons.
Wythnynawl, *a.* (wythnyn) Of eight persons.
Wythochr, *s. m.* (wyth—ochr) An octagon.
Wythochrawg, *a.* (wythochr) Octagonal.
Wythochrawl, *a.* (wythochr) Octagonal.
Wythochri, *v. a.* (wythochr) To form an octagon.
Wythochriad, *s.* (wythochr) A forming an octagon.
Wythongl, *s. m.* (wyth—ongl) That has eight angles. *a.* Octangular.
Wythonglawg, *a.* (wythongl) Octangular.
Wythonglawl, *a.* (wythongl) Octangular.
Wythongli, *v. a.* (wythongl) To form an octangular figure.
Wythongliad, *s. m.* (wythongl) A forming an octangular figure.
Wythor, *s. m.* (wyth—or) That has eight borders. *a.* Of eight borders.
Wythorawl, *a.* (wythor) Of eight borders.
Wythori, *v. a.* (wythor) To make to consist of eight borders.
Wythoriad, *s. m.* (wythor) A making to consist of eight borders.
Wythran, *s. f.* (wyth—rhan) That has eight shares. *a.* Of eight shares or parts.
Wythranawl, *a.* (wythran) Relating to what consists of eight parts.
Wythryw, *s. m.* (wyth—rhyw) That consists of eight sorts. *a.* Of eight sorts.

Wythryw yd a thri o wair.

Eight sorts of corn and three of hay. *D. ab Gwilym.*

Wythrywiad, *s. m.* (wythryw) A forming into eight sorts or kinds.
Wythrywiaw, *v. a.* (wythryw) To form eight sorts.
Wythrywiawg, *a.* (wythryw) Of eight sorts.
Wythrywiawl, *a.* (wythryw) Of eight sorts.
Wythsill, *s. f.* (wyth—sill) That has eight syllables. *a.* Of eight syllables.
Wythsillawg, *a.* (wythsill) Having eight syllables.
Wythwaith, *s. pl.* (wyth—gwaith) Eight times.
Wythweithfed, *s. f.* (wythwaith) The eighth time.

Y.

Y. THIS is a derivative sound, whose origin is E, being short, open, and indistinct, and having much of the character of the Hebrew *sheva*, or that transient sound, which transpires between certain consonants. It is the mutation of O and W in some forms of construction, and it particularly forms the plural of monosyllables. It is also the article *the*, preceding the words with consonant initials; but before vowels, for the sake of euphony, it takes *dd* and *r*, as affixes, to form *ydd*, *yr*. With verbs it assumes an adverbial character; and often is a mere expletive sound.

Gwyn fyd y wreig a allo fod ganei hunan.

Happy is *the* woman that can be by herself. *Adage.*

Ar ddiwedd y mae barnu.

On the conclusion is to be judging. *Adage.*

Arthur——
Yn mhen llu Camlan y llas.

Arthur, in the front of the host of Camlan was he slain. *L. G. Cothi.*

YB, *s. m. r.* A state of expulsion; the state of being out, over, or up.
Ybain, *v. a.* (yb) To make a howling; to howl.
YCH, *s. m. r.* That is out, over, or before: a neat, bullock, or ox. *Ychain*, oxen.

Ni sengis yr ych du ar dy droed.

The black ox has not trodden on thy foot. *Adage.*

Gwell oen fy hun nog ych arall.

Better a lamb of my own than the *ox* of another. *Adage.*

Tal ychain sy fyth a ddodes Maud Walderborff, o Gastell Paen yn Elfael, yn lle aredig cymhorth iddi, unwaith bob pedair blynedd.

Payment for *oxen* is a tax that was established by Maud Walde-bort, of Pain's Castle in Elvael, instead of the [illegible] ploughing to her, once every four years. [illegible]

Ych, *v.* (ych, *s.*) Ye or you are; are ye, are you.
Ycha, *v. imper.* (ych) Lo, behold, see. *Ycha acw*, lo yonder.
Ychad, *s. m.* (ych) A coming in view.
Ychadaf, *adv.* (ychad) In a most conspicuous way.

Rhedegawg tôn ar hyd traeth:
Ychadaf torid arfaeth:
Cad o acdo gnawd ffo ar ffraeth.

Full of motion the wave along the strand: *thus plainly* a purpose is broken; a battle near him the prattler takes to flight. *Llywarch Hen.*

Ychwaen, *adv.* (chwaen) Peradventure, by chance
Ychwaith, *conj.* (chwaith) Neither, not even so.
Ychwaneg, *s. m.* (chwaneg) More. *adv.* More.
Ychwanegadwy, *a.* (ychwaneg) Capable of augmentation.
Ychwanegawl, *a.* (ychwaneg) Apt to augment.
Ychwanegedig, *a.* (ychwaneg) Being augmented
Ychwanegiad, *s. m.* (ychwaneg) Augmentation.
Ychwanegu, *v. a.* (ychwaneg) To augment.
Ychwardd, *s. m.* (chwardd) Tendency to laughter.
Ychwarddawl, *a.* (ychwardd) Tending to laughter.
Ychwarddiad, *s. m.* (ychwardd) A causing laughter
Ychwarddu, *v. a.* (ychwardd) To cause laughter.

Ychwerddais yn wych irddydd;
Yn wylaw y daeth yr ail dydd.

I laughed bravely the passing day; weeping came the second day. *D. ab Ieuan Ddu.*

Ychwarian, *adv.* (chwarian) In a gentle manner.

Cyfarchaf o echlysur byd,
A'm dawed ychwarian:
Pwy wledych wedi Cynan!

I will congratulate on account of the world, as I *gently* come forward. Who will reign after Cynan! *Cyfoesi Merddin.*

Ychwerig, *adv.* (chwerig) Playfully, sportively.
Ychwinsa, *adv.* (chwinsa) At present; immediately

Pan fo yn swperu ychwinsa ddechreu nos.

When he is supping *just at* the beginning of night. *H. Bown—Mabinogion.*

Ha wraig! y neb pian y gelain, ti ei gweli yma ychwinsa.

Ha woman! he to whom the corpse belongs, thou shalt see here *immediately*. *H. Culhwch—Mabinogion.*

Ychydig, *s. m.—pl. t.* ion (cyd) A little, a small quantity; a few. *a.* Little, small as to quantity and number. *adv.* Little.

Ychydig yn aml a wna llawer.

A *little* often will make much. *Adage.*

Ychydig a wneid am y nef pei diffoddid uffern.

Little would there be done for heaven if hell were extinguished. *Adage.*

Tri ychydig a wna colli llawer: ychydig o aawydau drwg, ychydig o wall, ac ychydig o ledrad.

Three *small things* will be the means of losing much: a *little* of angry passions, a *little* carelessness, and a *little* theft. *Triordd.*

Ychydigaw, *v. a.* (ychydig) To lessen in quantity or number; to render few; to become few.
Ychydigawl, *a.* (ychydig) Tending to lessen.
Ychydigder, *s. m.* (ychydig) A littleness of quantity and number; fewness, paucity.

Goreu ar bob chware ychydigder.

The best of every play is a *little*. *Adage.*

Ychydigdra, *s. m.* (ychydig) Littleness, fewness.
Ychydigrwydd, *s. m.* (ychydig) Littleness, fewness
Ychydigyn, *s. m.—pl. t.* au (ychydig) A very little.

Y tir hwn—yr oedd rhyw ychydigynau o oleuni yn saethu i mewn iddo yn awr ac eilwaith.

This land, there were some *small particles* of light shooting into it at one time and at another. *Ier. Owain.*

YD, *s. m. r.—pl. t.* au That is; a being; corn. *Yd byw*, standing corn. It forms the termination of a class of nouns, and of some verbs in the infinitive mood. *Yd meddw*, *darnel*.

Po hynaf yr yd tebycaf fydd i'r byd.

By so much the older the *corn* more like it will be to the world. *Adage.*

Tew o frig y tyf yr on,
Tewach yw cardotwion;
Bai yd y gwellt a bwyd gwyr,
Rhy fan yw i'r Rhufeinwyr.

Thick of branches the ash doth grow, more thick are mendicants; if the grass were *corn* and food for men, too scanty it would be for the Romans. *Ieu. Du. y Bilwg.*

Yd, *adv.* (yd, *s.*) A particle idiomatically used, answering to *it*, *that*, and *doth*, in the formation of verbs; and it is often merely an expletive, used for euphony.

Trist yd gwyn pob colledig.

Sadly *doth* every condemned one complain. *Taliesin.*

Tarf cynnygn cân yd weler.

He would intimidate an opponent were he but seen. *Ll. P. Moch.*

Hir yd goffeir a goffaf.

Long will be remembered what I record. *D. Benfras.*

Yda, *v. a.* (yd) To gather corn; to go about begging for corn.
Ydaidd, *a.* (yd) Like or of the nature of corn.
Ydawg, *a.* (yd) Abounding with corn, full of corn.
Ydawl, *a.* (yd) Belonging to corn, of the quality of grain.
Ydbys, *s. pl. aggr.* (yd—pys) Vetches. *Ydbys tragwyddawl*, cichlings.
Yd-dir, *s. m.—pl. t.* oedd (yd—tir) Corn land.
Yd-dy, *s. m.—pl. t.* au (yd—ty) A granary.
Yden, *s. f. dim.* (yd) A grain of corn.
Ydfaes, *s. m.* (yd—maes) A corn field.
Ydfran, *s. f.—pl.* ydfrain (yd—bran) A rook.
Ydfwyd, *s. m.* (yd—bwyd) Food made of corn.

Ydfwyd i ddyn, cigfwyd i gwn.

Grain food for man, flesh food for dogs. *Adage.*

Tri ymborth dyn a barant iechyd, hiroes, a synwyr gloew; ydfwyd, blithfwyd, a garddfwyd.

The three sustenances of man that will cause health, long life and clear sense: *food made of corn*, milk food, and vegetable food. *Catwg ab Gwynlliw.*

Ydgeirch, *s. pl. aggr.* (yd—ceirch) Wild oats.
Ydgist, *s. f.—pl. t.* iau (yd—cist) A corn bin.
Ydgordd, *s. f.—pl. t.* au (yd—cordd) Corn-yard.
Ydi, *v.* (yd) Is; it is, he is, she is; is it, is he, is she.
Ydig, *s. m. dim.* (yd) Degenerate corn; cockle; it is also called *gith*.
Ydlan, *s. f.—pl. t.* oedd (yd—llan) A corn-yard.
Ydoedd, *v.* (yd—oedd) Was. *Ydyw*, is.
Ydwal, *s. f.—pl. t.* au (yd—gwal) A corn garth.
Ydwyd, *v.* (wyd) Art, thou art, art thou. *Pwy ydwyd?* who art thou? *Ai Meilyr ydwyd?* Art thou Meilyr?
Ydwyf, *v.* (wyf) Am; I am; am I. *Ydwyf yma*, I am here: *a ydwyf?* am I?
Ydych, *v.* (ych) Ye are, you are; are ye, are you.
Ydynt, *v.* (ynt) They are; are they. *Dynion ydynt*, they are men: *ai dynion ydynt?* are they men?

Bost a chelwydd, nid deubeth ydynt.

Boasting and lying, *they are* not two things. *Adage.*

Ydŷs, *s. m.* (yd—ŷs) The calender, or weevil.
Ydyw, *v.* (yw) Is; it is, he is, she is, when the particular person is known.

Dyn ni wna daioni neb
Ydyw un a dau wyneb.

A person who will do no good to any body *is* the one with two faces. *O. Gwynedd.*

YDD, *s. m. r.* That is moving before; that is conspicuous. *a.* Forward; conspicuous. It is the article *the*, used in common with *yr*, before nouns with vowel initials, as *y* is before those with consonants; with verbs it assumes an adverbial character; and it is frequently a mere expletive sound. It is used sometimes as a pronoun. It is also a termination of masculine nouns.

> Ffordd Llanfaglen ydd air i nef.
>
> By the way of Saint Mary Magdalen it is that we must go to heaven. *Adage.*
>
> O erw i gant yr a gwr;
> O ddwy i un ydd a nawr.
>
> From an acre to a hundred will a man proceed; from two to one it is that the fribble falls. *Ieuan Deulwyn.*
>
> Neum rhoddes i Run, rwyf iolydd, cantref,
> A chant eidionydd!
> Ac un rodd oedd well nog ydd.
>
> Have I not been gifted by Rhun, a chief of celebrity, with district and a hundred kine! but one gift was better than *them*. *Llywarch Hen.*

YF, *s. m. r.* That is of a flowing or liquid nature; a liquid; a moisture.
Yfadwy, *a.* (yf) Drinkable, capable of being drank
Yfawl, *a.* (yf) Relating to drinking.
Yfed, *v. a.* (yf) To drink. *s. m.* A drinking.

> Yf dy gawl cyn oero.
>
> *Drink* thy broth before it cools. *Adage.*
>
> Ar ol yfed syched sydd.
>
> After *drinking* there comes thirst. *Adage.*
>
> Ac os yf un gwas afiach
> I'n feddwi ef, e fydd iach.
>
> And if any youth unwell *shall drink* so as to make him drunk, he will be well. *Ieu. ab Gr. Leiaf, i'r cwrw.*

Yfedgar, *a.* (yfed) Fond of drinking, or tippling.
Yfedgarwch, *s. m.* (yfedgar) Fondness for drink.
Yfedr, *s. m.* (yfed) A drinking habit.
Yfetri, *v. a.* (yfedr) To drink often; to tipple.
Yfgar, *a.* (yf) Fond of drink, bibaceous.
Yfgarwch, *s. m.* (yfgar) Fondness for drink.
Yfiad, *s. m.* (yf) A drinking; a bibbing.
Yfory, *s. m.* (mory) To-morrow. *adv.* To-morrow.
Yfu, *v. a.* (yf) To drink; to imbibe, to suck.
Yfwr, *s. m.—pl.* yfwyr (yf—gwr) A drinker.
Yfwraig, *s. f.—pl.* yfwreigedd (yf—gwraig) A drinking woman.
YFF, *s. m. r.* A tendency out or from.
Yffi, *s. m.* (yff) A bit broken off; a particle.
Yffiaw, *v. a.* (yffi) To break off; to shiver.
Yffion, *s. pl. aggr.* (yffi) Fragments; shatters. *Dyna fo yn yffion man*, there it is all to shatters.
Yffiyn, *s. m.* (yffi) A piece, a shiver.
YG, *s. m. r.* The state of being open, or void.
YL, *s. m. r.* That is pervasive; that is apt to move; a moving agent. It is a termination of a class of words.
Yleni, *s.* (eleni) The present year. *adv.* This year.
YLL, *s. m. r.* That tends to part, or to separate.
Ylldryd, *s. m.* (yll—tryd) A vagabond, a stroller.
Ylliad, *s. m.* (yll) A ripping, or a dividing.
Yllt, *s. m.* (yll) A rip, rent, or parting.
Ylltyd, *s. m.* (yllt) A ripper; an epithet used for a plough.
Yllynedd, *s.* (llynedd) Last year. *adv.* Last year.
Yllyr, *s. m.—pl. t.* ion (yll) A mole or want.
YM, *s. m. r.* That tends to identify; that is identic. It is a particle of very general use in composition. Prefixed to verbs, and verbal nouns, it makes a reflexion of the action on the agent or agents; as, *golchi*, to wash; *ymolchi*, to wash one's self: *sènu*, to chide; *ymsènu*, to chide mutually. It is also the pronoun *my*, used for *my* or *vy* in certain forms of construction: and, it is the personal verb, we are.

> Am ŵyn, ym Crist, mwy ni'm cred!
>
> About lambs, my Christ, he will not believe me more. *Gutto y Glyn.*
>
> Cynghorwr ar wr, yr a'i mewn gwar;
> Cynghorfynt ni gar wrth ni caro.
> Caru ym myd i'm, a'm digapio;
> Cariad a'i bwylliad i'm ni ballo;
> Car an dadl ddyn, a'm dywetto;
> Carennydd Dofydd beunydd a'm bo!
>
> A counsellor to man, for such as humbly seeks him; envy he will not harbour to who loves him. The love of my country be to me that shall not contemn me; love with his guidance to me let it not fail; the friend whose intercession is sure, may he elect me. the favour of the Creator be it daily to me! *Meilyr ab Gwalchmai.*

Yma, *s. m.* (ma) Here, this place. *adv.* Here, in this place.

> Gwae'nt hwy y gethern
> A fynnant uffern
> Byth gwedi yma.
>
> Woe to them the crew, who seek for hell ever after the present. *Ioan. Ddiwan.*
>
> A orchfygo yma a goronir fry.
>
> That conquers *here* will be crowned above. *Adage.*

Ymachlud, *s. m.* (achlud) The act of enveloping. *v. a.* To obscure one's self; to obscure mutually; to become obscured.
Ymachludaw, *v. a.* (ymachlud) To be obscuring; to obscure mutually; to become obscured.

> Iosph a ymachludws gorff yr Iesu mewn llian glan.
>
> Joseph *shrouded* the body of Jesus in clean linen.

Ymachludawl, *a.* (ymachlud) Tending to be enveloped or to be obscured.
Ymachludiad, *s. m.* (ymachlud) A becoming enveloped; a mutually obscuring.
Ymachludd, *s. m.* (achludd) The act of enveloping. *v. a.* To obscure one's self; to become obscured.

> Y mae gwely i'm gelyn,
> Lle'r ymachludd deurudd dyn.
>
> To my foe there is a bed, where the cheeks of a young person are obscured. *H. ab Rhys.*

Ymachluddaw, *v. a.* (ymachludd) To obscure one's self; mutually to obscure.
Ymachluddawl, *a.* (ymachludd) Tending to become obscured.
Ymachluddiad, *s. m.* (ymachludd) A becoming obscured; a mutually obscuring.
Ymachub, *s. m.* (achub) Self-security. *v. a.* To save one's self, to deliver one's self; to save mutually.

> Cyfod, ddrygwas cas, cais hoeth hwnnw mach,
> Ymachub a'th giwyfau.
>
> Arise, thou odious wicked chap, get thee with of [illegible] *deliver thyself* of thy disorders. *Madawg Dwygraig.*

Ymachubaw, *v. a.* (ymachub) To save one's self, to deliver one's self; to save mutually.
Ymachubawl, *a.* (ymachub) Tending to self-preservation; mutually preserving.
Ymachubiad, *s. m.* (ymachub) A saving one's self; a mutually saving.
Ymachubwr, *s. m.—pl.* ymachubwyr (ymachub—gwr) One who saves himself; one who mutually saves.
Ymachwyn, *s. m.* (achwyn) A complaint of one's self; a mutual complaint. *v. a.* To complain of one's self, to complain mutually.
Ymachwyniad, *s. m.* (ymachwyn) A complaining of one's self; a mutually complaining.
Ymachwynwr, *s. m.—pl.* ymachwynwyr (ymachwyn—gwr) One who complains of himself; a mutual complainer.
Ymadael, *v. a.* (gadael) To leave, to forsake, to quit; to depart; to leave mutually.

Ymadaw, *v. a.* (gadaw) To leave, to forsake; to depart; to elope; mutually to leave.

> Llyma gynnifer ffordd yr ymedy dyn a'i dda, trwy drais, lledrad, anghyfarch, llog, adnau, benthyg.
>
> Behold the various ways that a person *will part* with his property, through oppression, theft, trover, hire, pledge, loan. *Welsh Laws.*

Ymadawiad, *s. m.* (ymadaw) A leaving, a forsaking; a departing, egression; elopement.

Ymadawwr, *s. m.—pl.* ymadawwyr (ymadaw—gwr) One who leaves or forsakes.

Ymadferth, *s. m.* (adferth) Self-exertion. *v. a.* To exert one's self; to defend or help one's self.

Ymadferthawl, *a.* (ymadferth) Self-exerting; tending to mutual aid.

Ymadferthiad, *s. m.* (ymadferth) Self-exertion; a helping one's self.

Ymadferthu, *v. a.* (ymadferth) To exert one's self, mutually to aid.

Ymadferthwch, *s. m.* (ymadferth) A state of self-exertion.

Ymadfyw, *s. m.* (adfyw) Self-revival. *a.* To revive one's self; to become revived.

Ymadfywiad, *s. m.* (ymadfyw) A reviving of one's self; a becoming revived; reviviscence.

Ymadfywiaw, *v. a.* (ymadfyw) To revive one's self; to become revived, to come to life again.

Ymadgryfâad, *s. m.* (ymadgryfâu) A self-reinvigoration; a becoming strengthened.

Ymadgryfâawl, *a.* (ymadgryfâu) Self-reinvigorating.

Ymadgryfâu, *v. a.* (adgryfâu) To strengthen one's self again; to become reinvigorated.

Ymadgyweiriad, *s. m.* (adgyweiriad) A repairing of one's self; a becoming repaired.

Ymadgyweiriaw, *v. a.* (adgyweiriaw) To restore one's self to order; to become repaired.

Ymadlenwad, *s. m.* (adlenwad) A self-replenishing; a becoming replenished.

Ymadlenwawl, *a.* (adlenwawl) Self-replenishing; tending to become replenished.

Ymadlenwi, *v. a.* (adlenwi) To replenish one's self; to become replenished.

Ymadnabod, *s. m.* (adnabod) Self-knowledge; mutual acquaintance. *v. n.* To know one's self; to become acquainted.

Ymadnewyddawl, *a.* (adnewyddawl) Self-renovating; tending to become renewed.

Ymadnewyddiad, *s. m.* (adnewyddiad) Self renovation; a becoming renewed.

Ymadnewyddu, *v. a.* (adnewyddu) To renovate one's self; to become renewed

Ymadolwyn, *v. a.* (adolwyn) To interest one's self; to entreat earnestly and often.

Ymadrawdd, *s. m.—pl.* ymadroddion (adrawdd) Discourse; a sentence or period, in discourse, speech. *v. a.* To discourse, to talk.

> Heb awen d'a — —
> Nis gwyr modd yr ymadrawdd,
> Na llwian bryd y llen.
>
> Without a great genius, he knows not the *form of sentences*, nor the characters of Lhud where they exist. *I. ab Hywel Swrdwal*
>
> Ymadrawdd yw cynnulleidfa llawer o eiriau ynghyd.
>
> A *sentence* is a collection of a number of words together. *L[illegible] Dd[illegible] Ar[illegible].*

Ymadred, *s. f.* (adred) A self-returning; a return.

Ymadredawl, *a.* (ymadred) Self-returning.

Ymadredeg, *v. a.* (ymadred) To return one's self back, mutually to return.

Ymadrediad, *s. m.* (ymadred) A returning one's self back, a mutually returning.

Ymadroddawl, *a.* (ymadrawdd) Discoursive.

Ymadroddi, *v. a.* (ymadrawdd) To discourse.

Ymadroddiad, *s. m.* (ymadrawdd) A discoursing.

Ymadroddiaeth, *s. m.* (ymadrawdd) Conversation.

Ymadroddiant, *s. m.* (ymadrawdd) Interlocution.

Ymadroddus, *a.* (ymadrawdd) Well-spoken.

Ymadroddwr, *s. m.—pl.* ymadroddwyr (ymadrawdd—gwr) A discourser, an interlocutor.

Ymadwedd, *s. m* (adwedd) A self-returning.

> I gaer ragorawl,
> Ag arfaeth gwerthfawl,
> Ammodawl ymadwedd
>
> To an excellent city, with praise worthy usage, under promise is a return. *S. Fychan.*

Ymadweddawl, *a.* (ymadwedd) Tending to bring one's self back.

Ymadweddiad, *s. m.* (ymadwedd) A bringing one's self to a former condition.

Ymadweddu, *v. a.* (ymadwedd) To bring one's self to a former state.

Ymaddasawl, *a.* (addasawl) Self-qualifying; mutually fitting.

Ymaddasiad, *s. m.* (addasiad) A qualifying one's self; a becoming qualified, meet, or proper.

Ymaddasu, *v. a.* (addasu) To qualify one's self; to qualify mutually.

Ymaddaswr, *s. m.—pl.* ymaddaswyr (addaswr) One who makes himself fit or meet.

Ymaddaw, *v. a.* (addaw) To promise mutually; to bind one's self in a promise.

> O derfydd i ddyn ymaddaw ag arall am beth, heb dystion yn y lle, nid amfod hwnw.
>
> If a person should *enter into a promise* with another for a thing without witnesses in the place, that is not a covenant. *Welsh Laws*

Ymaddawiad, *s. m.* (ymaddaw) A mutually promising; a binding one's self in a promise.

Ymaelodi, *v. a.* (aelodi) To make one's self a member; to become a member.

Ymaelodiad, *s. m.* (aelodiad) A making one's self a member; a becoming a member.

Ymaes, *prep.* (maes) Without. *adv.* Without.

Ymafael, *s. m.—pl. t.* ion (gafael) A mutual hold; a wrestle, a struggle. *v. a.* To lay hold; to wrestle.

> Nac ymafael a'i hael hi.
>
> Do not *connect thyself* with her skirt. *D. ab Gwilym*

Ymafaelgar, *a.* (ymafael) Apt to lay hold.

Ymafaelgarwch, *s. m.* (ymafaelgar) Aptness to lay hold mutually.

Ymafaeliad, *s. m.—pl. t.* au (ymafael) A laying hold mutually.

Ymafaelu, *v. a.* (ymafael) To lay hold; to lay hold mutually, to wrestle.

Ymafaelwr, *s. m.—pl.* ymafaelwyr (ymafael—gwr) One who lays hold; a wrestler.

Ymafaelydd, *s. m.—pl. t.* ion (ymafael) One who takes hold, a wrestler.

Ymaflwr, *s. m.—pl.* ymaflwyr (gaflwr) One who lays hold; a wrestler.

Ymaflyd, *s. m.* (gaflyd) A mutual laying hold; a wrestle. *v. a.* To lay mutual hold; to lay hold; to wrestle. *Ymaflyd cwymp,* to wrestle a fall.

Ymagawr, *s. m.* (agawr) A becoming open.

Ymagenawl, *a.* (agenawl) Tending to become rifted or chapped.

Ymageniad, *s. m* (ageniad) A becoming rifted.

Ymagenu, *v. n.* (agenu) To become rifted.

Ymagorawl, *a.* (ymagawr) Self-expanding; tending to become open.

Ymagori, *v. a.* (ymagawr) To become open or expanded; to open one's self

Ymagoriad, *s. m.*—*pl. t.* au (ymagawr) A becoming open; an opening of one's self.
Ymagoryd, *v. n.* (ymagawr) To become open.
Ymagwedd, *s. m.* (agwedd) Self-conformity; mutual conformity.
Ymagweddawl, *a.* (ymagwedd) Self-conforming.
Ymagweddiad, *s. m.* (ymagwedd) A conforming one's self; a mutually conforming.
Ymagweddu, *v. a.* (ymagwedd) To conform one's self; to conform mutually.
Ymagweddwr, *s. m.*—*pl.* ymagweddwyr (ymagwedd—gwr) One who conforms himself.
Ymaith, *adv.* (maith) Hence, away. *v. imp.* Hence, avaunt, away, be gone. *Dos ymaith*, go away.

> A fwrw ymaith ei fywyd yn ddiachaws, marw dros y diawl y mae.
>
> He that throws away his life without cause, dies for the devil. *Adage.*

Ymalw, *v. a.* (galw) To continue calling; to invocate; to call mutually.
Ymalwad, *s. m.* (ymalw) A mutual calling.
Ymalltudaw, *v. a.* (alltudaw) To banish one's self; to become strange.
Ymalltudawl, *a.* (alltudawl) Self-estranging.
Ymalltudiad, *s. m.* (alltudiad) A self-estranging; a banishing one's self.
Ymallu, *v. n.* (gallu) To take to one's self power; to be able. *Od ymeill, o dichawn*, if he be able.
Ymalluaw, *v. a.* (ymallu) To endue one's self with power; to become able or capable.
Ymamlâad, *s. m.* (amlâad) A self-multiplying.
Ymamlâu, *v. a.* (amlâu) To self-multiply.
Yman, *s. m.* (man) Here, this place. *adv.* Here.
Ymanafawl, *a.* (anafawl) Tending to self-harm.
Ymanafiad, *s. m.* (anafiad) A self-hurting.
Ymanafu, *v. n.* (anafu) To hurt one's self.
Ymanafyd, *v. n.* (anafyd) To hurt one's self.
Ymanaws, *s. m.* (anaws) Self-excitement; mutual excitement. *v. a.* To excite one's self; to excite mutually.
Ymandaw, *s. m.* (andaw) A keeping one's self in listening or attention; a mutual listening. *v. a.* To keep one's self listening; to listen mutually.

> Dyrd a glud, gwladoedd ymandaw,
> Doeth a choeth, cyfoeth cyfanaw.
>
> A bold one and a leader, the *admiration* of countries, wise and precious, the subject of a kingdom's united prayer. *Llygad Gwr, i Ruff. Maelawr.*

Ymandawiad, *s. m.* (ymandaw) A keeping one's self in listening; a mutually listening.
Ymanfon, *s. m.* (anfon) A mutual sending. *v. a.* To send mutually.

> Mynych ymanfon dygn golon dig
> Erof, arien ganwyll ryfyg.
>
> Frequently she *commissions* severe remembrances of anger on my account, the splendidly cold luminary of presumption. *Cynddelw.*

Ymanfoniad, *s. m.* (ymanfon) A mutually sending.
Ymanerch, *s. m.*—*pl. t.* ion (anerch) A mutual greeting; congratulation. *v. a.* To congratulate.

> Saethodd o'i glaew fron glau
> Serch ymanerch i minnau.
>
> She darted from her constant beauteous breast a love-shaft of *congratulation* to me. *D. ab Gwilym, i Forfudd.*

Ymanerchawl, *a.* (ymanerch) Mutually greeting.
Ymanerchi, *v. a.* (ymanerch) To greet mutually.
Ymanerchiad, *s. m.* (ymanerch) A mutually greeting.
Ymannog, *s. m* (annog) Mutual excitement, self-excitement. *v. a.* To excite one another; to self-excite.

Ymannos, *adv.* (yman—nos) The night past; the night before the present; the night before last; heretofore.

> Mynwn fy mod ymannos
> Yn torri pen Atropos.
>
> I could have wished to be *the other night* cutting off the head of Atropos. *Gutto y Glyn.*
>
> Lleidr, y mewn dirym dewrerch,
> Ymannos fum: mynnais ferch.
>
> A thief, in graceless dotage, *the other night* I was: I carried off a maid. *D. ab Gwilym.*

Ymanosawl, *a.* (ymanaws) Self-exciting; mutually exciting.
Ymanosiad, *s. m.* (ymanaws) A self-exciting; a mutually urging or exciting.
Ymanrheithiad, *s. m.* (anrheithiad) Self-spoliation; mutual spoliation.
Ymanrheithiaw, *v. a.* (anrheithiaw) To self-despoil; to despoil one another.
Ymanrheithiawl, *a.* (anrheithiawl) Self-despoiling; mutually despoiling.
Ymanurddaw, *v. a.* (anurddaw) To self-disfigure.
Ymanurddawl, *a.* (anurddawl) Self-disfiguring.
Ymanurddiad, *s.* (anurddiad) A self-disfiguring.
Ymangerddawl, *a.* (angerddawl) Tending to put one's self in a passion.
Ymangerddiad, *s. m.* (angerddiad) A making one's self violent.
Ymangerddu, *v. a.* (angerddu) To make one's self violent; to become impassioned.
Ymangwanegawl, *a.* (angwanegawl) Self-augmenting.
Ymangwanegiad, *s. m.* (angwanegiad) A self-augmenting.
Ymangwanegu, *v. a.* (angwanegu) To increase one's self.
Ymaraws, *s. m.* (araws) A bearing with; long-suffering. *v. a.* To bear with, to endure.
Ymarbed, *s. m.* (arbed) A self-restraint.
Ymarbedawl, *a.* (ymarbed) Self-refraining; mutually abstaining.
Ymarbediad, *s. m.* (ymarbed) A self-refraining; a mutually abstaining.
Ymarbedu, *v. a.* (ymarbed) To save one's self, to abstain; mutually to abstain.
Ymarbedus, *a.* (ymarbed) Self-restraining.
Ymarbedusaw, *v. n.* (ymarbedus) To become abstemious.
Ymarbod, *s. m.* (arbod) Self-preparation, self-introduction; self-manifestation; the state of being interested or concerned. *v. a.* To interest one's self, to be concerned. *A oes dim ymarbod amdano?* Is there no stirring about it?

> Duw a folir—yn gynnelwr a gwaredwr, ac yn briodol yn ei ymarbod o barth Mab, ac oll odd y rhinweddau, ac y priodolion [illegible].
>
> God is to be worshipped, as the upholder and saviour, and as [illegible] in his second *interesting of himself* with respect to the Son, and all of the virtues, and the appropriate attributes. *Barddas.*

Ymarbodawl, *a.* (ymarbod) Self-preparing.
Ymarbodi, *v. a.* (ymarbod) To prepare one's self, to become concerned or interested.
Ymarbodiad, *s. m.* (ymarbod) A preparing one's self, a becoming concerned about or interested.
Ymarbodus, *a.* (ymarbod) Being concerned about.
Ymarbodusaw, *v. n.* (ymarbodus) To become concerned or interested.
Ymarbodusrwydd, *s. m.* (ymarbodus) The state of being concerned, or interested.
Ymarbodwr, *s. m.*—*pl.* ymarbodwyr (ymarbod—gwr) One who prepares himself; one who interests himself.

Ymarbwyll, *s. m.—pl. t.* ion (arbwyll) A concerting. *v. a.* To be concerting.

Goreu gwaith celfydd ymarbwyll a'i amcan.

The best act of the ingenious is *to be concerting* with his invention. *Catwg Ddoeth.*

Ymarbwylliad, *s. m.* (ymarbwyll) A being concerting or considering.

Ymarddelw, *s. m.* (arddelw) A possession; a setting up a claim; a challenge. *v. a.* To make a profession; to set up a claim; to challenge.

Cael ymadrawdd hawdd a hi,
Ymarddelw serch hum erddi.

Obtaining an easy conversation with her, *making profession* of love I was for her sake. *D. ab Gwilym, i Ferfudd.*

Ymarddelwad, *s. m.* (ymarddelw) A making a claim.

Ymarddercbafael, *s. m.* (arddercbafael) A self-exalting. *v. a.* To become exalted.

Gwedi gwybod o Arthur bod ei ofn efelly ar bawb, ymarddercbafael a orug ynteu.

After it was known to Arthur that his dread was thus upon every body, he then *uplifted himself.* *Gr. ab Arthur.*

Ymardderchafiad, *s. m.* (ardderchafiad) Self-exaltation; a becoming uplifted.

Ymardderchafu, *v. a.* (ardderchafu) To uplift one's self; to be self-exalted.

Ymardderchafus, *a.* (ardderchafus) Self-exalting.

Ymardderchawl, *a.* (ardderchawl) Self-exalting.

Ymardderchiad, *s.* (ardderchiad) Self-exaltation

Ymardderchogawl, *a.* (ardderchogawl) Self-exalting.

Ymardderchogi, *v. a.* (ardderchogi) To self-exalt.

Ymardderchu, *v.* (ardderchu) To exalt one's self.

Ymarddysgwyl, *s. m* (arddysgwyl) A keeping one's self in expectation. *v. a.* To keep one's self in expectation.

Brysiaw a orugynt parth a'r mwg; a dynesu parth ag yno, dan ymarddysgwyl o bell, yny fydd Dillus Farfawg yn deifaw baedd coed.

They made haste towards the smoke; and approaching towards there, by *keeping on the watch* from a distance, behold Dillus Longbeard scorching a wild boar. *H. Culhwch—Mabinogion.*

Ymarddysgwyliad, *s. m.* (ymarddysgwyl) A keeping one's self in expectation.

Ymarddysgwyliaw, *v. a.* (ymarddysgwyl) To keep one's self in expectation.

Ymarddysgwylus, *a.* (ymarddysgwyl) Apt to keep one's self in expectation.

Ymarfaeth, *s. m.* (arfaeth) A self-exercising. *v. a.* To habituate one's self.

Bran a gant chwedl yn mlaen traeth,
Wrth nas gellynt ymarfaeth:
Nid meddiant ond gwybodaeth.

A crow did sing her adage at the head of the sand, to those who could not *habituate themselves*; there is no possession like knowledge. *Catwg Ddoeth.*

Ymarfaethiad, *s. m.* (ymarfaeth) A self-habituating or inuring.

Ymarfawd, *s. f.* (arfawd) A self-arming.

Ymarfer, *s. f.—pl. t.* ion (arfer) The using of one's self exercise, practice habit, custom. *v. a.* To use one sel ; to exercise.

Ymarferawl, *a.* (ymarfer) Self-exercising.

Ymarferiad, *s. m.* (ymarfer) A sel -exercising.

Ymarferu, *v. a.* (ymarfer) To exercise one's self, to accustom one's self.

Ymarferwr, *s. m —pl.* ymarferwyr (ymarfer—gwr) One who exercises himself.

Ymarfiad, *s. m.* (arfiad) A self-arming.

Ymarfodawl, *a.* (ymarfawd) Self arming.

Ymarfodi, *v. a.* (ymarfawd) To deal blows mutually.

Ymarfogi, *v. a.* (arfogi) To arm one's self; mutually to arm.

Ymarfogiad, *s. m.* (arfogiad) An arming of one's self; a mutually arming.

Ymarfoll, *s. m.* (arfoll) A mutual reception; a becoming confederated.

Ymarfollu, *v. a.* (ymarfoll) To receive one another to become mutually connected to connect one's self to become confederated.

Ar hyny pawb onaddynt ymarfollynt hyd ar Enea.

Upon that every one of them *collected themselves together* unto Eneas. *H. Dared.*

Ymarfolliad, *s. m.* (ymarfoll) A mutual reception; a becoming mutually connected; a becoming confederated.

Ymarfu, *v. a.* (arfu) To arm one's self.

Ymarial, *s. m.* (arial) A self-invigoration.

Ymarialiad, *s. m.* (ymarial) A self-invigorating; a becoming lively.

Ymarialu, *v. a.* (ymarial) To self-invigorate; to become full of animation.

Ymarialus, *a.* (ymarial) Self-invigorating.

Ymarlloes, *s. m.* (arlloes) A self-emptying. *v. a.* To empty one's self.

Ymarlloesi, *v. a.* (ymarlloes) To pour out one's self, to empty one's self.

Ymarlloesiad, *s. m.* (ymarlloes) A pouring out or emptying one's self.

Ymarllwys, *s. m.* (arllwys) A pouring out one's self. *v.* To empty one's self, to self-empty.

Ymarllwysawl, *a.* (ymarllwys) Self-emptying.

Ymarôad, *s. m.* (ymarôi) A keeping one's self in waiting; a bearing with; mutual forbearance.

Ymarôawl, *a.* (ymarôi) Keeping one's self in waiting; of a forbearing temper.

Ymarôi, *v. a.* (arôi) To bear with; to forbear.

Ymarosawl, *a.* (ymaraws) Apt to be waiting.

Ymarosi, *v. a.* (ymaraws) To keep one's self in waiting: to wait mutually.

Ymarosiad, *s. m.* (ymaraws) A keeping one's self in waiting; a mutually waiting.

Ymarôus, *a.* (ymarôi) Long-suffering, patient. '*Bydd ymarôus wrthyf,*' be patient with me.

Ymarôwr, *s. m.—pl.* ymarôwyr (ymarôi—gwr) One who bears with.

Ymarswyd, *s. m.* (arswyd) A self-terrifying.

Ymarswydaw, *v. a.* ymarswyd To terrify one's self, to dread mutually.

Ymarswydawl, *a.* (ymarswyd) Self-terrifying.

Ymarswydiad, *s. m.* (ymarswyd) A self-terrifying

Ymarteithiad, *s. m.* (arteithiad) A self-torturing.

Ymarteithiaw, *v. a.* (arteithiaw) To self-torture.

Ymarteithiawl, *a.* (arteithiawl) Self-torturing.

Ymarteithiwr, *s. m.—pl.* ymarteithwyr (arteithiwr) One who tortures himself.

Ymaruthraw *v. a.* (aruthraw) To astonish one's self; mutually to astonish.

Ymaruthrawl, *a.* (aruthrawl) Tending to amaze one's self.

Ymaruthriad, *s. m.* (aruthriad) A making one's self amazed; a mutually astonishing.

Ymarwain, *s. m.* (arwain) A self conducting. *v. a.* To conduct one's self.

Hafren a—
Ddirwyn afonydd mwy;
Ac f'e mot, gwyr ymarwain,
Y rhed—

Severn other rivers doth attract, and knowing how *to conduct itself*, runs to the sea. *E. Fychan.*

Ymarwar, *s. m.* (arwar) A calming one's self; a mutual assuagement. *v. a.* To calm one's self; to assuage one another.

Mal ymarwar Lludd a Llefelys.

Like the *reconciliation* of Lludd and Llevelys. *Llywelyn Fardd.*

Ymarwedd, *s. m.* (arwedd) Comportment, demeanour. *v. a.* To demean one's self, to behave.

Ymarweddawl, *a.* (ymarwedd) Self-demeaning.

Ymarweddiad, *s. m.—pl. t.* au (ymarwedd) A demeaning one's self, a behaving; behaviour. *Ymarweddiad da*, good behaviour.

Ymarweddu, *v. a.* (ymarwedd) To self-demean.

Ymarweddwr, *s. m.—pl.* ymarweddwyr (ymarwedd—gwr) One who demeans himself.

Ymarweiniad, *s. m.* (ymarwain) A conducting or leading one's self.

Ymarweiniaw, *v. a.* (ymarwain) To lead one's self; mutually to lead.

Ymarweiniawl, *a.* (ymarwain) Self-leading.

Ymarwerthu, *v. a.* (arwerthu) To offer one's self to be bought, sold, or redeemed.

Archaf arch i'm Naf,
Y dewin doethaf,
Nid ymarwerthaf,
Heb ei wyrthiau.

I will implore a favour of my Lord, the Divine Being most wise, *I will not offer to redeem myself*, without his miracles.
Gr. ab yr Ynad Coch.

Ymaswyn, *s. m.* (aswyn) A self-excusing.

Twrf twrfaith goddaith gwasanwyn
Torf a thewlu a thewlwyn waewawr
A gwyr mawr ymaswyn

Like the violently far extending tumult of the conflagration of spring the tribe with a thick multitude bearing a thick grove of spears, and the mighty men *mutually pledging*.
Cynddelw, i'r argl. Rhys.

Ymaswynaw, *v. a.* (ymaswyn) To excuse one's self; to plead for one's self.

Ymaswynawl, *a.* (ymaswyn) Self-excusing.

Ymaswyniad, *s. m.* (ymaswyn) A self-excusing.

Ymateb, *s. m.—pl. t.* ion (ateb) A mutual answer.

Ymatebawl, *a.* (ymateb) Mutually answering.

Ymatebiad, *s. m.* (ymateb) A correspondence.

Ymatebu, *v. a.* (ymateb) To answer mutually.

Ymatgno, *s. m.* (ad—cno) A rumination.

Ymatgnôad, *s. m.* (ymatgno) A ruminating.

Ymatgnôi, *v. a.* (ymatgno) To ruminate.

Ymatgof, *s. m.* (ad—cof) A self-recollection.

Ymatgofiad, *s. m.* (ymatgof) A self-recollecting.

Ymatgofiaw, *v. a.* (ymatgof) To self-recollect.

Ymatgor, *s. m.* (atgor) A self-return. *v. a.* To return one's self.

Llu Prydain yn ymatgor.

The army of Britain *returning itself back*. *Cynddelw.*

Ymatgorawl, *a.* (ymatgor) A self returning.

Ymatgudd, *s. m.* (ad—cudd) A self-revealing.

Ymatguddiad, *s. m.* (ymatgudd) A self-revealing.

Ymatguddiaw, *v. a.* (ymatgudd) To self-reveal.

Ymatguddiawl, *a.* (ymatgudd) Self-revealing.

Ymattreg, *s. f.* (attreg) A self-stopping; a mutual stop or demur.

Ymattregawl, *a.* (ymattreg) Self-stopping; mutually stopping.

Ymattregiad, *s. m.* (ymattreg) A self-stopping; a demurring with one's self; a mutually stopping.

Ymattregu, *v. a.* (ymattreg) To stop one's self; to stop one another; to demur mutually.

Ymattal, *s. m.* (attal) Self-restraint; continence. *v. a.* To restrain one's self; to live in abstinence, to contain one's self.

Ymattalgar, *a.* (ymattal) Self-restraining.

Ymattaliad, *s. m.* (ymattal) A self-restraining.

Ymattalrwydd, *s. m.* (ymattal) Abstemiousness.

Ymattalus, *a.* (ymattal) Self-restraining.

Ymawyddiad, *s. m.* (awyddiad) A filling one's self with desire.

Ymawyddu, *v. a.* (awyddu) To fill one's self with avidity or desire.

Ymbaffiad, *s. m.* (paffiad) A mutually boxing.

Ymbaffiaw, *v. a.* (paffiaw) To box mutually.

Ymbaffiwr, *s. m.—pl.* ymbaffiwyr (paffiwr) One who uses himself to boxing; a boxer.

Ymbaid, *a.* (paid) Self-refraining.

Ymbalfaliad, *s. m.* (palfaliad) A groping.

Ymbalfalu, *v. a.* (palfalu) To reach one's limbs in every direction; to grope out one's way.

Ymbalfalwr, *s. m.—pl.* ymbalfalwyr (palfalwr) One who gropes his way.

Ymbalffust, *v. a.* (ymbalf—ffust) To encounter. *Gorfod ymbalffust a gofalu*, obliged to strive and economize.

Ymball, *s. m.* (pall) A self-failure.

Ymballu, *v. a.* (ymball) To fall into error.

Ymbarchawl, *a.* (parchawl) Self-respecting.

Ymbarchiad, *s. m.* (parchiad) A self-respecting, a mutually respecting.

Ymbarchu, *v. a.* (parchu) To respect one's self, to respect mutually.

Ymbarotöad, *s. m.* (parotöad) A self-preparing.

Ymbarotöawl, *a.* (parotöawl) Self-preparing.

Ymbarotöi, *v. a.* (parotöi) To prepare one's self.

Dwyparth taith ymbarotöi.

Two parts of a journey is *to prepare one's self*. *Adage.*

Ymbarotoi i gyhwrdd adfyd yw y ffordd nesaf at hawddfyd.

To prepare one's self to meet adversity is the nearest way to happiness. *Adage.*

Ymbawr, *s. m.* (pawr) The eating of pasture.

Ymbedawl, *a.* (pedawl) Being using one's feet, being ranged in order of battle.

Ymbediad, *s. m.* (pediad) A taking to one's feet, a ranging in order of battle.

Ymbedu, *v. a.* (pedu) To take to one's feet, to make use of the feet.

Gwedi darfod i'r Brython o'r parth arall gwbl [illegible] ac ymbedu, ni [illegible] pob parth [illegible] [illegible].

After the Britons on the other part had finished arming of themselves and *putting themselves in array*, they did not refrain from every side with exchanging deadly blows. *Gr. ab Arthur.*

Ymbeidiad, *s. m.* (peidiad) A making one's self to cease; a desisting.

Ymbeidiaw, *v. n.* (peidiaw) To abstain, to desist.

Ymbeidiawl, *a.* (peidiawl) Abstaining, desisting.

Ymbellâad, *s. m.* (pellâad) A rendering one's self distant or far removed.

Ymbellâawl, *a.* (pellâawl) Tending to render one's self distant.

Ymbellâu, *v. a.* (pellâu) To render one's self distant; to be far removed.

Ymbenbleth, *s. m.* (penbleth) The distraction of one's own head.

Ymbenblethiad, *s. m.* (ymbenbleth) A distracting one's head.

Ymbenblethu, *v. a.* (ymbenbleth) To distract one's head.

Ymbennoethi, *v. a.* (pennoethi) To make one's head bare.

Ymbennoethiad, *s. m.* (pennoethiad) A making one's head bare.

Ymbesgi, *v. a.* (pesgi) To fatten one's self.

Ymbesgiad, *s. m.* (pesgiad) A fattening one's self.

Ymbil, *s. m.—pl. t.* ion (pil) An entreaty, a petition. *v. a.* To entreat, to implore, to crave.

Ymbiliad, *s. m.—pl. t.* au (ymbil) An imploring.

Ymbiliaw, *v. a.* (ymbil) To implore, to crave.

Ymbiliwr, *s. m.—pl.* ymbiliwyr (ymbil—gwr) An implorer.

Ymbinciad, *s. m.* (pinciad) A trimming or smartening one's self.

Ymbinciaw, *v. a.* (pinciaw) To trim one's self. '*Hi a ymbinciai yn wych iawn*,' she arrayed herself very finely.

Ymbinciawl, *a.* (pinciawl) Self-smartening.

Ymbinciwr, *s. m.—pl.* ymbinciwyr (pinciwr) One who smartens himself.

Ymblaid, *s. f.—pl.* ymbleidiau (plaid) A faction.

> Tyn yr oes o tàn yr iau echryswl
> A chroesion ymbleidiau.
>
> Deliver the age from beneath a horrid yoke and adverse *factions.* *D. Thomas.*

Ymbleidgar, *a.* (ymblaid) Apt to be factious.

Ymbleidgarwch, *s. m.* (ymbleidgar) Factiousness

Ymbleidiad, *s. m.* (ymblaid) An attaching one's self to a party or faction.

Ymbleidiaw, *v. a.* (ymblaid) To attach one's self to a party, to join a faction.

Ymbleidiawl, *a.* (ymblaid) Apt to join one's self to a party.

Ymbleidiwr, *s. m.* (ymblaid—gwr) One who attaches himself to a party.

Ymblethawl, *a.* (plethawl) Self-entwining.

Ymblethiad, *s. m.* (plethiad) A self-entwining.

Ymblethu, *v. a.* (plethu) To self-entwine.

Ymbluad, *s. m.* (pluad) A feathering itself.

Ymbluaw, *v. a.* (pluaw) To plume one's self.

Ymbluawl, *a.* (pluawl) Self-depluming.

Ymblufiaw, *v. a.* (plufiaw) To self-feather.

> Mynag edn, miniawg ydwyd,
> I b'le'r ai, ymblufiaw'r wyd?
>
> Say bird, for thou art endowed with utterance, where art thou going, as thou art *adjusting thy feather?* *D. Ll. ab Ll. ab Gruffudd.*

Ymblufiawl, *a.* (plufiawl) Self-feathering.

Ymblygawl, *a.* (plygawl) Self-bending.

Ymblygiad, *s. m.* (plygiad) A self-bending.

Ymblygu, *v. a.* (plygu) To bend one's self.

Ymblwyfaw, *v. a.* (plwyfaw) To attach one's self to a parish.

Ymblwyfiad, *s. m.* (plwyfiad) An attaching one's self to a parish.

Ymboenawl, *a.* (poenawl) Pains-taking.

Ymboeni, *v. a.* (poeni) To pain one's self.

Ymboerawl, *a.* (poerawl) Self-bespawling.

Ymboeri, *v. a.* (poeri) To bespawl one's self.

Ymboethawl, *a.* (poethawl) Self-heating.

Ymboethi, *v. a.* (poethi) To heat one's self.

Ymboethiad, *s. m.* (poethiad) A self heating.

Ymborth, *s. m.* (porth) Sustenance, support.

> Ymborth anwiredd yw aur ac arian.
>
> The *sustenance* of iniquity are gold and silver. *Adage.*

Ymborthawl, *a.* (ymborth) Sustaining, supporting; alimentary.

Ymborthedig, *a.* (ymborth) Self-supported.

Ymborthi, *v. a.* (ymborth) To sustain one's self, to bear or carry one's self; to feed one's self; to feed.

> Mair ni wnaeth ymborthes ei beichiogi.
>
> Mary well *did make herself to bear* her pregnancy. *Meilyr*
>
> Ar orwyddawd Iorth yd ymborthaf.
>
> On splendid cavalcade *I will be conveyed.* *Llywelyn Fardd.*
>
> A ddyco y god ymborthed o honi.
>
> Who bears the bag *let him feed himself* out of it. *Adage.*

Ymborthiad, *s. m.* (ymborth) A sustaining one's self; a bearing one's self.

Ymborthianna, *v. a.* (ymborthiant) To seek self-support; to seek mutual support; to supply one another; to traffick.

Ymborthiannawl, *a.* (ymborthiant) Tending to self-support; mutually supporting.

Ymborthiannu, *v. a.* (ymborthiant) To afford self-support, to afford mutual support.

Ymborthiannus, *a.* (ymborthiant) Tending to self-support; tending to mutual support.

Ymborthiant, *s. m.* (ymborth) Self-supportation; mutual supportation.

Ymborthwr, *s. m.—pl.* ymborthwyr (ymborth—gwr) One who supports himself; a mutual supporter.

Ymbrawf, *s. m.* (prawf) A putting one's self to trial; experience; trial, essay; contest.

> Am ddefodau a breiniau beirdd Ynys Prydain, mi a lwyr ymroddais i'r ymbrawf a allwn i rywfaint o les.
>
> With respect to the customs and privileges of the bards of the isle of Britain, I gave myself entirely to the *trial* whether I could afford some degree of benefit. *Ed. Dafydd.*

Ymbrestledd, *s. m.* (prestledd) The habit of giving mutual repartees.

Ymbrestliad, *s. m.* (prestliad) A mutually giving repartees.

Ymbrestlu, *v. a.* (prestlu) To repartee mutually.

Ymbriodawl, *a.* (priodawl) Tending mutually to marriage.

Ymbriodi, *v. a.* (priodi) To marry one's self; to become married, to intermarry.

Ymbrofawl, *a.* (ymbrawf) Self-trying.

Ymbrofedig, *a.* (ymbrawf) Being self-tried; being mutually tried.

Ymbrofi, *v. a.* (ymbrawf) To try together; to encounter; to vie; to try one's self; to experience.

> Ni chawsan'—
> Eithyr gwarth a gwrthryn wrth ymbrofi.
>
> They obtained nothing but disgrace and repulse in *contesting.* *Ll. P. Moch.*
>
> Trefred i bryfed, lle yd ymbrofan'
> Tros heol ysgol esgar boethfau.
>
> The habitation of reptiles, where *they will experience* a fell course of ascent of a divided region of heat. *Cotnodyn.*
>
> Dydd prawf yn y diffaith; yn y lle yr ymbrofynt eich tadau.
>
> The day of trial in the wilderness; in the place where your fathers *entered into temptation.* *D. Ddu o Hiraddug.*

Ymbrofiad, *s. m.—pl. t.* au (ymbrawf) A mutually trying; a contesting; a trying one's self; an experiencing.

Ymbrofwr, *s. m.—pl.* ymbrofwyr (ymbrawf—gwr) One who mutually tries; a contester; one who tries himself.

Ymbryd, *s. m.—pl. t.* iau (pryd) The using of one's self to seasons; a fast.

Ymbrydiad, *s. m.* (ymbryd) A using one's self to seasons; a fasting.

Ymbrydiaw, *v. a.* (ymbryd) To use one's self to stated times or seasons; to observe seasons; to fast.

Ymbrydiawl, *a.* (ymbryd) Apt to use one's self to seasons; fasting.

Ymbrydiwr, *s. m.—pl.* ymbrydiwyr (ymbryd—gwr) One who observeth seasons; a faster.

Ymbryn, *s. m.* (pryn) Self-redemption.

Ymbrynawl, *a.* (ymbryn) Self-redeeming.

Ymbryniad, *s. m.* (ymbryn) A self-redeeming.

Ymbrynu, *v. a.* (ymbryn) To redeem one's self.

> Os amddiffynwr a oddiweddir—carcher ef trwy garchar, neu ymbryned.
>
> If it be the defendant who is cast, let him be punished by imprisonment, or *let him redeem himself.* *Deddfau Rhaddau.*

Ymbrynwr, *s. m.—pl.* ymbrynwyr (ymbryn—gwr) One who redeems himself.

Ymbrysuraw, *v. a.* (prysuraw) To self-hasten.

Ymbrysurawl, *a.* (prysurawl) Self-hastening.

Ymbrysurdeb, *s. m.* (prysurdeb) A self-hastening.

Ymbrysuriad, *s. m.* (prysuriad) A hastening one's self.

Ymbrysurwr, *s. m.—pl.* ymbrysurwyr (prysurwr) One who hasteneth himself.

Ymburaw, *v. a.* (puraw) To purify one's self.

Ebai angeu, Tu draw i'r wal o'th ol y mae y purdan; canys yn dy fywyd y dylasit ymburaw.

Said a death, On the other side of the wall behind thee is the purgatory, for in thy life time thou shouldest *purify thyself*. *Elis Wyn, B. Cwsg.*

Ymburawl, *a.* (purawl) Self-purifying.

Ymburiad, *s. m.* (puriad) A self-purification.

Ymburwr, *s. m.—pl.* ymburwyr (purwr) One who purifies himself.

Ymbwyad, *s. m.* (pwyad) A self-buffeting.

Dy gyfoeth yn unoeth, poen ymbwyad,
A gollais, I drais, drosedu ffyngiad.

The property, the *infliction to one's self* of pain, nightly I have lost, to rapine, the stroller's crime. *Trahaiarn Brydydd Mawr.*

Ymbwyaw, *v. a.* (pwyaw) To buffet one's self.

Ymbwyawl, *a.* (pwyawl) Self-buffeting.

Ymbwyll, *s. m.—pl. t.* ion (pwyll) Consideration, concern.

Addysg ffol ei ymbrawf; addysg doeth ei ymbwyll.

The instruction of the fool his experience; the instruction of the wise his *consideration*. *Adage.*

Duw Ysbryd Glan a folir—am ein darweddi i fywyd—a ffydd ddiffuant yn mhob ymbwyll yn Nghrist Iesu.

God the Holy Spirit is to be praised, for his leading us into life and unerring faith in every *concern* in Christ Jesus. *Barddas.*

Ymbwyllaw, *v. a.* (ymbwyll) To consider with one's self; to have consideration; to be concerned.

Ymbwyllgar, *a.* (ymbwyll) Considerate, rational.

Ymbwylliad, *s. m.* (ymbwyll) A considering with one's self; a concerning one's self.

Ymbwyllus, *a.* (ymbwyll) Apt to reason with one's self; considerate.

Ymbwyllwr, *s. m.* (ymbwyll—gwr) One who considereth with himself.

Ymbwyth, *s. m.* (pwyth) Self-exertion.

Ymbwythaw, *v. a.* (ymbwyth) To exert one's self; to vie mutually.

Am bethau teg ymbwythwn;
Am gig hydd, a magu cwn.

For fair things we *will mutually strive*; for the flesh of the stag, and the rearing of dogs. *Llawdden.*

Ymbwythawl, *a.* (ymbwyth) Self-exerting; mutually vieing.

Ymbwythiad, *s. m.—pl. t.* au (ymbwyth) An exerting of one's self; a mutual competition.

Ymbwys, *s. m.* (pwys) A self-pressure.

Ymbwysaw, *v. a.* (ymbwys) To weigh one's self; to cause one's self to weigh or incline; to press mutually.

Ymbwysawl, *a.* (ymbwys) Self-pressing; mutually pressing.

Ymbwysiad, *s. m.* (ymbwys) A weighing one's self; a self-pressing; a mutually pressing.

Ymbyd, *s. m.* (pyd) A self-danger.

Ymbydiad, *s. m.* (ymbyd) A self-endangering.

Ymbydiaw, *v. a.* (ymbyd) To endanger one's self

Ymbydiawl, *a.* (ymbyd) Self-endangering.

Ymbydiwr, *s. m.—pl.* ymbydiwyr (ymbyd—gwr) One who endangers himself.

Ymbyliad, *s. m.* (pyliad) A self-blunting.

Ymbylu, *v. a.* (pylu) To become self-blunted.

Ymchwaen, *s. f.* (chwaen) A self-yielding to chance.

Ymchwaenawl, *a.* (ymchwaen) Tending to yield one's self to chance.

Ymchwaeniad, *s. m.* (ymchwaen) A consigning one's self to chance.

Ymchwaenu, *v. a.* (ymchwaen) To consign one's self to chance.

Ymchwal, *s. f.* (chwal) A spread of one's self.

Ymchwaliad, *s. m.—pl. t.* au (ymchwal) A self-spreading; a self-dispersion.

Ymchwalu, *v. a.* (ymchwal) To spread one's self.

Ymchwalwr, *s. m.—pl.* ymchwalwyr (ymchwal—gwr) One who spreads himself.

Ymchwant, *s. m.* (chwant) That yields to lust.

Ymchwanta, *v. a.* (ymchwant) To yield one's self to lust or desire.

Ymchwantiad, *s. m.* (ymchwant) A self-yielding to lust, a giving one's self to covet.

Ymchwedleua, *v.* (chwedleua) To chat together.

Ymchwedleuad, *s. m.* (chwedleua) Confabulation.

Ymchwedleuaw, *v. a.* (chwedleuaw) To chat together.

Ymchwedleuawl, *a.* (chwedleua) Confabulatory.

Ymchwedliad, *s. m.* (chwedliad) A confabulation.

Ymchwedlu, *v. a.* (chwedlu) To confabulate, to chat together.

Ymchwedlwr, *s. m.—pl.* ymchwedlwyr (chwedlwr) A confabulator.

Ymchwelliad, *s. m.—pl.* ymchwelliaid (ymchwel) One that returns or causes a return.

Daeth esgyrn gwr chwyrn ei ymchweledion;
Ymchweliad trumgad, trwm ei gofion!

The bones of a hero of rapid revertions are come: the *cause of the return* of the heavy battle, and the recollections of him! *D. Benfras, i Lywelyn III.*

Ymchwel, *s. f.* (chwel) A return; a reverse.

Ymchweladwy, *a.* (ymchwel) Reversible.

Ymchweledig, *a.* (ymchwel) Reversed.

Ymchweledigaeth, *s. m.* (ymchwel) Conversion.

Ymchweliad, *s. m.—pl. t.* au (ymchwel) Conversion

Ymchwelwr, *s. m.—pl.* ymchwelwyr (ymchwel—gwr) One who returns, a reverter; a converter

Ymchwelyd, *v. a.* (ymchwel) To return, to revert; to convert; to turn upside down, to overturn, to reverse. '*Ymchwelyd brawd*,' to reverse a judgment.

Pwybynnag a fyno yn llwyr gwybod breiniau y fyrdd hyn, ceisied ef cyfreithiau Dyfnwal Moelmud, y rhai a ymchwelodd Gildas o Gymmraeg yn Lladin.

Whosoever would completely know the privileges of these roads, let him procure the laws of Dyvnwal Moelmud, the which Gildas *translated* out of Welsh into Latin. *Gr. ab Arthur.*

Ymchwerwad, *s. m.* (chwerwad) An embittering one's self; a mutually exasperating.

Ymchwerwi, *v. a.* (chwerwi) To self-embitter; to become exasperated; mutually to exasperate.

Ymchwiliad, *s. m.* (chwiliad) A self-searching.

Ymchwiliaw, *v. a.* (chwiliaw) To search one's self.

Ymchwilied, *v. a.* (chwilied) To self-scrutinize.

Ymchwiliwr, *s. m.—pl.* ymchwiliwyr (chwiliwr) One who searches himself.

Ymchwydd, *s. m.* (chwydd) A swelling of one's self.

Tri pheth mawr o ymchwydd ymborth ar waed: gele, bytheu, a rhyfelwr.

Three things great with *self-swelling* by feeding on blood: a leech, a tike, and a warrior. *Adage.*

Ymchwyddaw, *v. a.* (ymchwydd) To self-swell.

Ymchwyddawl, *a.* (ymchwydd) Self-swelling.

Ymchwyddedig, *a.* (ymchwydd) Self-inflated.

Beth er dawed o honynt atom, ag ymchwyddedig eiriau gwagedd, a dderbyniwn ni hwynt er mwyn hwy?

What, if they should come to us, with the *pompous* words of vanity, shall we receive them in consideration of them? *[illegible]*

Ymchwyddiad, *s. m.* (ymchwydd) A self-puffing.

Ymchwyth, *s. m.* (chwyth) A self-blowing.

Ymchwythiad, *s. m.* (ymchwyth) Self-inflation.

Ymda, *v. a.* (ta) To be walking about.

Or ymdaa gwraig ei hunan.—

If a woman *perambulates* by herself. *Welsh Laws.*

Ymdacliad, *s. m.* (tacliad) A self-trimming.
Ymdaclu, *v. a.* (taclu) To trim one's self.
Ymdaclusaw, *v. a.* (taclusaw) To make one's self tidy; to trim one's self.
Ymdaclusiad, *s. m.* (taclusiad) A making one's self tidy.
Ymdacluswr, *s. m.—pl.* ymdacluswyr (tacluswr) One who makes himself tidy.
Ymdaenawl, *a.* (taenawl) Self-expanding.
Ymdaeniad, *s. m.* (taeniad) Self-expansion.
Ymdaenu, *v. a.* (taenu) To expand one's self.
Ymdaenwr, *s. m.—pl.* ymdaenwyr (taenwr) One who expands or spreads himself.
Ymdaerawl, *a.* (taerawl) Mutually disputing.
Ymdaeriad, *s. m.* (taeriad) A mutually disputing.
Ymdaeru, *v. a.* (taeru) To dispute together.

O ymdaeru i ymdaraw, o eiriau i arfau.

From mutual dispute to mutual blows, from words to arms. — *Elis Wyn, B. Cwsg.*

Ymdaerwr, *s. m.—pl.* ymdaerwyr (taerwr) One given to disputation; a disputer.
Ymdafliad, *s. m.* (tafliad) A throwing one's self; a mutually throwing.
Ymdaflu, *v. a.* (taflu) To throw one's self; to throw mutually. *Ymdaflu ag afalau dur*, to throw at one another with iron balls, a kind of ancient game.
Ymdafodi, *s. m.* (tafodi) A wrangling. *v. a.* To wrangle together.

Tafawd ni chel ei ynni,
Gwaethaf dysg ymdafodi,
Nid hwyr ile hawdd drigioni.

A tongue that doth not conceal its energy, the worst of acquirement is *contention*, it will not be long but it will easily do mischief. — *Catwg ab Gwynlliw.*

Ymdafodiad, *s. m.* (tafodiad) A wrangling together.
Ymdafodwr, *s. m.—pl.* ymdafodwyr (tafodwr) One given to wrangling.
Ymdagelliad, *s. m.* (tagelliad) A forming to one's self a double chin; a bridling up one's self.
Ymdagellu, *v. a.* (tagellu) To bridle up one's chin.
Ymdaith, *s. f.—pl.* ymdeithiau (taith) A journey. *v. a.* To journey, to travel; to go, to walk.

Y barddorion a'r gwyr wrth gerdd a aynt ar ymdaith i glera, o dy Iestyn ab Gwrgant i dy Rhys fab Tudyr, a Rhys a oedd hael wrthynt.

The bards and the musicians went on a *journey* to exercise minstrelsy, from the house of Iestyn son of Gwrgant to the house of Rhys son of Tudyr, and Rhys was liberal to them. — *Caradawg o Lan Carvan.*

Ymdalpu, *v. a.* (talpu) To clod together.
Ymdan, *s. m.* (tan) A self-spreading. *v. a.* To spread one's self; to mount a horse.
Ymdanawl, *a.* (ymdan) Self-spreading.
Ymdaniad, *s. m.* (ymdan) A self-spreading.
Ymdanu, *v. a.* (ymdan) To spread one's self.
Ymdanc, *s. m.* (tanc) Mutual peace or amity.
Ymdaraw, *v. a.* (taraw) To strike mutually; to keep striking, or warding off blows; to fight it out, or to shift for one's self. *Pa fodd yr wyt yn ymdaraw?* How dost thou battle it out: How goes it with thee? *Mi ymdarawaf yn lew*, I shall get through very well.

Poni welwch chwi'r deri yn ymdaraw?

See you not the oaks *striking together*? — *Cynddelw.*

Nid oedd farchawg, er ei gryfed, a feiddiai ymdaraw neu ymdrech ag ef.

There was not a knight, let him be ever so strong, who would dare *to combat* or to contend with him. — *G. Bown—Mabinogion.*

Ymdarawiad, *s. m.* (ymdaraw) A striking mutually; a warding off blows; a combating; a shifting for one's self.

Ymdarawus, *a.* (ymdaraw) Notable in shifting for one's self.
Ymdawdd, *s. m.* (tawdd) A self-dissolving.
Ymdaweliad, *s. m.* (taweliad) A self-assuaging.
Ymdawelu, *v. a.* (tawelu) To calm one's self; to grow calm; to recover from passion.
Ymdawr, *s. m.* (tawr) The being concerned.

Nerth penteulu ei ymdawr.

The strength of the patron of a family is his *anxious care*. — *Catwg Ddoeth.*

Ymdecâad, *s. m.* (ymdecâu) A making one's self fair; a self-beautifying.
Ymdecâawl, *a.* (ymdecâu) Tending to make one's self fair.
Ymdecâu, *v. a.* (tecâu) To self-beautify.
Ymdebygiad, *s. m.* (tebygiad) A making one's self similar.
Ymdebygu, *v. a.* (tebygu) To make one's self like.

Mewn tri pheth ydd ymdebyga dyn i Dduw: cyfiawnder, gwybodau, a thrugaredd.

In three things man *doth make himself like* God: righteousness, knowledge, and mercy. — *Catwg ab Gwynlliw.*

Ymdeg, *s. m.* (teg) A self-adorning. *a.* Of native fairness.

Mal y pelligant ymdeg.

Like the flower *of native beauty*. — *Adage.*

Ymdeimlaw, *v. a.* (teimlaw) To feel one's self.
Ymdeimliad, *s. m.* (teimliad) A self-feeling.
Ymdeithiad, *s. m.—pl. t.* au (ymdaith) A travelling
Ymdeithiaw, *v. a.* (ymdaith) To travel, to journey
Ymdeithiawg, *a.* (ymdaith) Travelling, journeying
Ymdeithiawl, *a.* (ymdaith) Travelling, journeying.
Ymdeithig, *a.* (ymdaith) Ready for travelling.

Lluddedig eu hoelion, ymdeithig eu hafwyn,
Gwlad weddyn fargodion.

Tired out their nails, *ready for journeying* their rein, the borderers of a ravaging country. — *Taliesin.*

Ymdeithigrwydd, *s. m.* (ymdeithig) Aptness for travelling.
Ymdeithiocâad, *s. m.* (ymdeithiawg) A preparing one's self for travelling; a becoming wayfaring.
Ymdeithiocâawl, *a.* (ymdeithiawg) Tending to become wayfaring.
Ymdeithiocâu, *v. a.* (ymdeithiawg) To prepare one's self for travelling; to become wayfaring.
Ymdeithiwr, *s. m.—pl.* ymdeithiwyr (ymdaith—gwr) A traveller, a sojourner.
Ymdeithwastad, *a.* (ymdaith—gwastad) Of an even pace.
Ymdeithydd, *s. m.—pl. t.* ion (ymdaith) A traveller, a sojourner.
Ymdeneuâad, *s. m.* (ymdeneuâu) A self-attenuation; a self-rarefying.
Ymdeneuâawl, *a.* (ymdeneuâu) Self-rarefying.
Ymdeneuâu, *v. a.* (teneuâu) To self-attenuate; to self-rarefy.
Ymderfyniad, *s. m.* (terfyniad) A mutually limiting; a self-limiting.
Ymderfynu, *v. a.* (terfynu) To limit mutually; to fix a limit to one's self.
Ymderfysgawl, *a.* (terfysgawl) Apt to put one's self in a tumult; mutually tumultuous.
Ymderfysgiad, *s. m.* (terfysgiad) A putting one's self in a tumult; a becoming agitated; a raising a tumult together.
Ymderfysgu, *v. a.* (terfysgu) To put one's self in a tumult, to raise a tumult together.
Ymderiad, *s. m.* (teriad) A self-purifying.
Ymderu, *v. a.* (teru) To self-purify.
Ymdesach, *s. m.* (tesach) A wanton dalliance. *v. a.* To give up one's self to wantonness.

Ymdesiad, *s. m.* (tesiad) A basking one's self in the sun.

Ymdesu, *v. a.* (tesu) To bask one's self in the sun.

Ymdewâad, *s. m.* (tewâad) A making one's self thick; a mutually thickening.

Ymdewâawl, *a.* (tewâawl) Self-thickening.

Ymdewâu, *v. a.* (tewâu) To self-thicken.

Ymdiraw, *v. a.* (tiraw) To stretch out one's self; to bask one's self; to enjoy one's self.

> Mae des-wres ym i'm diro,
> Ei goed o'r glyn gyda'r glo.
>
> There are two warmths for me *to bask myself*, his wood from the dingle with the coal. — *Guto y Glyn.*

Ymdirioni, *v. a.* (tirioni) To make one's self pleasing; to become pleasing; to become mutually pleasing.

> Wrth ym mron, drwy 'mdirioni,
> Yn fy mywyd un a mi.
>
> Close at my breast, by *becoming mutually pleasing*, through my life one with me. — *Edm. Prys.*

Ymdirioniad, *s. m.* (tirioniad) A becoming mutually pleasing.

Ymdlysiad, *s. m.* (tlysiad) A self-beautifying.

Ymdlysu, *v. a.* (tlysu) To make one's self smart or pretty; to smug one's self up.

Ymdo, *s.m.* (to) A self-covering, a self-sheltering.

Ymdöad, *s. m.* (ymdo) A covering one's self.

Ymdoddawl, *a.* (ymdawdd) Self-dissolving.

Ymdoddi, *v. a.* (ymdawdd) To self-dissolve.

Ymdoddiad, *s. m.* (ymdawdd) To self-dissolve.

Ymdoi, *v. a.* (ymdo) To cover one's self.

Ymdolciad, *s. m.* (tolciad) A self-butting, or self-punching; a mutually butting.

Ymdolciaw, *v. a.* (tolciaw) To punch one's self; to butt one another.

Ymdoliad, *s. m.* (toliad) A becoming more sparing of one's self.

Ymdoliaw, *v. a.* (toliaw) To be more sparing of one's self; to spare one's self.

> Cenawon Cymmry
> Cannaid a'i deffry
> Cenedl a'i dyly,
> Nid ymdolia.
>
> The whelps of the Welsh are leaders who will rouse him, a generation that claims him, *he will not reserve himself.* — *D. Benfras, i Lywelyn III.*

Ymdomi, *v. a.* (tomi) To bemire one's self.

Ymdomiad, *s. m.* (tomiad) A self-bemiring.

Ymdon, *s. f.* (ton) A self-breaking in waves.

> Dar a dyfwys ar dir pen gallt
> Ger ymdon mor Hafren:
> Gwae wr na bai digon hen!
>
> An oak did grow on the land on the cliff top by the *self spraying* of the Severn sea: woe to the man that he should not be old enough. — *Robert T. Normandi.*

Ymdòni, *v. n.* (ymdon) To break out in waves.

Ymdòniad, *s. m.* (ymdon) A breaking out in waves.

Ymdorchawl, *a.* (torchawl) To self-roll or coil.

Ymdorchi, *v. a.* (torchi) To roll one's self; to self-coil; to become entwined.

Ymdorchiad, *s. m.* (torchiad) A self-coiling.

Ymdordain, *s. m.* (tordain) A lolling. *v. a.* To loll, to stretch one's self along.

Ymdordynawl, *a.* (tordynawl) Self-gorging.

Ymdordyniad, *s. m.* (tordyniad) A gorging.

Ymdordynu, *v. a.* (tordynu) To self gorge.

Ymdorf, *s. f.* (torf) A thronging together.

Ymdorfawl, *a.* (ymdorf) Mutually thronging.

Ymdorfiad, *s. m.* (ymdorf) A jointly thronging.

Ymdorfu, *v. a.* (ymdorf) To throng mutually.

Ymdorfynygliad, *s. m.* (torfynygliad) A breaking one's neck; a throwing one's self headlong; a prostrating one's self.

Ymdorfynyglu, *v. a.* (torfynyglu) To break one's own neck; a throwing one's self headlong; a prostrating one's self.

> Ar y bylchau a'r pyrth ydd ymdorfynyglynt i gyfarch gwell.
>
> On the battlements and the gates *they had prostrated themselves* to make a salutation. — *H. Geraint—Mabinogion.*

Ymdòri, *v. a.* (tòri) To be cutting one's self.

> Nid ymdorir, ac nid ymfoelir drostynt.
>
> Men *shall* not *cut themselves*, and shall not make themselves bald for them. — *Jeremi 16. 6.*

Ymdòriad, *s. m.* (tòriad) To break one's self; to self-break; to become bursted; disruption.

Ymdorlwythaw, *v. a.* (torlwythaw) To self-gorge.

> Ymdorlwythant â bwyd a diawd, ac yno porthant eu trachwantau.
>
> *They glut themselves*, with victuals and drink, and then they satisfy their lusts. — *H. Vychan, Ym. Dunwiddi.*

Ymdorlwythawl, *a.* (torlwythawl) Self-gorging.

Ymdorlwythiad, *s. m.* (torlwythiad) A self-gorging.

Ymdrafael, *s. f.* (trafael) A mutual toiling.

> Gwnaeth draillif gwyar uch Trallwng Elfael,
> Pan fu ymdrafael drud ac eddirwng.
>
> He caused a vast torrent of gore above Trallwng Elvael, when the *mutual toiling* bold and imminent took place. — *E. ab M. Rhend.*

Ymdrafaeliad, *s.m.* (ymdrafael) A mutually toiling.

Ymdrafawd, *s. f.* (trafawd) A mutual stirring; a bustling of one's self.

Ymdrafodawl, *a.* (ymdrafawd) Mutually stirring or bustling; self-bustling.

Ymdrafodi, *v. a.* (ymdrafawd) To make a mutual stir; to strive together; to conflict.

> Doe'r pryd hwn yr oeddwn i
> Drwy fedw yn ymdrafodi.
>
> Yesterday at this time I was through birches *hurrying myself.* — *Llawdden.*

Ymdrafodiad, *s. m.* ymdrafawd) A making a mutual stir; a striving together, a hurrying of one's self.

Ymdrafodwr, *s. m.*—*pl.* ymdrafodwyr (ymdrafawd—gwr) A mutual stirrer; a self-hurrier.

Ymdrafferth, *s. f.*—*pl. t.* ion (trafferth) A self-bustling.

Ymdrafferthawl, *a.* (ymdrafferth) Self-bustling.

Ymdrafferthiad, *s. m.* (ymdrafferth) A busying one's self.

Ymdrafferthu, *v. a.* (ymdrafferth) To busy one's self; mutually to bustle.

Ymdrafferthus, *a.* (ymdrafferth) Self-busying.

Ymdrafferthwr, *s. m.* (ymdrafferth—gwr) One who is full of bustle.

Ymdraffull, *s. m.* (traffull) A self-bustling.

Ymdraffulliad, *s. m.* (ymdraffull) A mutually bustling, a busying one's self.

Ymdraffulliaw, *v. a.* (ymdraffull) To keep one's self in a bustle; to bustle mutually.

Ymdraffulliwr, *s. m.*—*pl.* ymdraffulliwyr (ymdraffull—gwr) One who bustles greatly.

Ymdraigl, *s. f.* (traigl) A mutual turn; a self-turning.

Ymdrallodawl, *a.* (trallodawl) Mutually afflicting, self-vexing.

Ymdrallodi, *v. a.* (trallodi) To afflict mutually; to afflict one's self.

Ymdrallodiad, *s. m.* (trallodiad) A mutually afflicting; a self-afflicting.

Ymdrallodwr, *s. m.*—*pl.* ymdrallodwyr (trallod—wr) A self-afflicter.

Ymdramwy, *s. m.* (tramwy) A mutual resorting, being using one's self to resort.

Ymdramwyad, *s. m.* (ymdramwy) A mutually resorting, a being resorting.

Ymdramwyaw, *v. a.* (ymdramwy) To resort mutually; to use one's self to resorting.

Ymdraphwyll, *s. m.* (traphwyll) A mutual impulsion; an opposing of one's self. *v. a.* To oppugn mutually; to oppose one's self.

> Dylid wrth sene y drwg ei droigiaw yn llwyr o galon ac arfer dyn, yn ymdraphwyll a diawl.
>
> In rebuking evil it were proper to expel it utterly from the heart and the habit of man, in *opposing one's self to the devil.*
> *Barddas.*

Ymdras, *s. f.* (tras) Mutual relationship.

Ymdrasawl, *a.* (ymdras) Of joint relationship.

Ymdrasiad, *s. m.* (ymdras) A forming of mutual relationship; a becoming related.

Ymdrasu, *v. a.* (ymdras) To form mutual relationship; to become related.

Ymdrech, *s. m.* (trech) A mutual struggle.

> Archasai Brutus ei gadw i weled cadwent ac ymdrech rhyngddo ef a Corineus.
>
> Brutus had commanded him to be kept in order to see a combat and *mutual striving* between him and Corineus. *Gr. ab Arthur.*

Ymdrechawl, *a.* (ymdrech) Mutually struggling.

Ymdrechfa, *s. f.* (ymdrech) A place of mutual strife; a contest.

> Nid oes [illegible] ddim i'w weled—yn anghreulondeb yr ymdrechfa.
>
> There is nothing for us to behold in the cruelty of the *contest.*
> *C. Edwards, H. y Ffydd.*

Ymdrechiad, *s. m.* (ymdrech) A jointly struggling.

Ymdrechu, *v. a.* (ymdrech) To mutually strive.

> Gorllelaw gwaed am draed a ymdrychant,
> Amdrychion pan ymdrechasant.
>
> Blood will overflow round the feet of those who strive together, they were mangled [illegible] when *they strove together.*
> *Ll. P. Moch.*

Ymdrechus, *a.* (ymdrech) Given to mutual strife.

Ymdrechwr, *s. m.—pl.* ymdrechwyr (ymdrech—gwr) A mutual striver or struggler.

Ymdrechydd, *s. m.—pl. t.* ion (ymdrech) A mutual striver or struggler.

Ymdrefn, *s. f.* (trefn) A self-ordering.

Ymdrefnawl, *a.* (ymdrefn) Self-ordering.

Ymdrefniad, *s. m.* (ymdrefn) A self-ordering.

Ymdrefnu, *v. a.* (ymdrefn) To put one's self in order.

Ymdrefnwr, *s. m.* (ymdrefn—gwr) One who puts himself in order.

Ymdreidiad, *s. m.* (treidiad) An exercising one's self in walking; perambulation.

Ymdreidiaw, *v. a.* (treidiaw) To exercise one's self in walking.

> Wedi mynych ymdreidiaw o'r niferoedd o'r eglwys pwy eilydd, i wrandaw amryfal gynyddoliaethau—daned i'r llys a crugyni.
>
> After frequently *exercising themselves in walking* of the companies from one church to another, to hear various musical compositions, they [illegible] to the court. *Gr. ab Arthur.*

Ymdreidiawl, *a.* (treidiawl) Being exercising one's self in walking; perambulatory.

Ymdreiddiad, *s. m.—pl. t.* au (treiddiad) A thrusting one's self through.

Ymdreiddiaw, *v. a.* (treiddiaw) To self-penetrate.

Ymdreiddiawl, *a.* (treiddiawl) Mutually penetrating; self-thrusting.

Ymdreiglaw, *v. a.* (treigl) To roll one's self.

Ymdreiglfa, *s. f.* (treiglfa) A place for rolling one's self in.

Ymdreigliad, *s. m.* (treigliad) A self-rolling.

Ymdreuliad, *s. m.* (treuliad) A self-consuming.

Ymdreuliaw, *v. a.* (treuliaw) To self-consume.

Ymdrin, *s. m.* (trin) Mutual striving; contention; variance; the act of busying one's self. *v. a.* To strive mutually; to busy one's self.

Ymdriniad, *s. m.* (ymdrin) A mutually striving; a busying one's self.

Ymdriniaeth, *s. m.* (ymdrin) Mutual strife; a self-busying.

Ymdro, *s. m.* (tro) A self-turning; self-course.

> Ys ymi nid [illegible], cas agro,
> Ffyddiawg, ffodiawg ei ymdro.
>
> To me belongs a chief of pleasing countenance, hating melancholy, faithful, fortunate in his *career.*
> *Phylip Brydydd, i Rys Gryg.*

Ymdröad, *s. m.* (ymdro) A turning one's self about; a delaying.

Ymdröawl, *a.* (ymdro) Self-turning about.

Ymdroch, *s. m.* (troch) A self-immersion.

Ymdrochawl, *a.* (ymdroch) Self-immersing.

Ymdrochi, *v. a.* (ymdroch) To bathe one's self; to plunge one's self in; to wallow.

Ymdrochiad, *s. m.* (ymdroch) A bathing one's self.

Ymdroi, *v. a.* (ymdro) To turn one's self; to delay; to loiter.

Ymdrws, *s. m.* (trws) A self-attiring.

Ymdrwsiad, *s. m.—pl. t.* au (ymdrws) A self-arraying; a dressing one's self.

Ymdrwsiadu, *v. a.* (ymdrwsiad) To self-trim.

Ymdrwsiaw, *v. a.* (ymdrws) To self-trim.

> Dwyparth pryd ymdrwsiaw.
>
> Two thirds of appearance is *to dress one's self.* *Adage.*

Ymdrwsiawl, *a.* (ymdrws) Self-attiring.

Ymdrwsiwr, *s. m.—pl.* ymdrwsiwyr (ymdrws—gwr) A self-arrayer.

Ymdrybaeddawl, *a.* (trybaeddawl) Self-wallowing; mutually wallowing.

Ymdrybaeddiad, *s. m.* (trybaeddiad) A self-wallowing; mutually wallowing.

Ymdrybaeddu, *v. a.* (trybaeddu) To wallow, or to welter; to wallow mutually.

Ymdryboli, *v. a.* (tryboli) To self-wallow; to wallow mutually.

Ymdryboliad, *s. m.* (tryboliad) A wallowing one's self; a mutually wallowing.

Ymdrychawl, *a.* (trychawl) Mutually cutting.

Ymdrychiad, *s. m.* (trychiad) A mutually cutting.

Ymdrychu, *v. a.* (trychu) To cut mutually.

> Moch daw rhwng Saeson rhewinol ymdrychu.
>
> Speedily will come between Saxons the [illegible] of *mutual wounding.*
> *Taliesin.*

Ymdryfoliad, *s. m.* (tryfoliad) Self-gorging.

Ymdryfoliaw, *v. a.* (tryfoliaw) To self-gorge.

Ymdryfoliwr, *s. m.—pl.* ymdryfoliwyr (tryfoliwr) One who gorges himself.

Ymdrymàad, *s. m.* (trymàad) A rendering one's self heavy; a becoming heavy.

Ymdrymàawl, *a.* (trymàawl) Tending to grow or become heavy.

Ymdrymâu, *v. a.* (trymâu) To become heavy.

> Mae pechodau dynion yn ymgynnyddu, ac yn ymdrymâu, pan ydynt yn esgeulusaw gosodedigaethau cyhoeddus Duw.
>
> The sins of men are increasing, and *becoming heavy*, when they are neglecting the public institutions of God.
> *Ier. Owain.*

Ymdrythylliad, *s. m.* (trythylliad) A mutually enjoying; a self-enjoying.

Ymdrythyllu, *v. a.* (trythyllu) To enjoy mutually; to enjoy one's self.

Ymdrythyllwch, *s. m.* (trythyllwch) Mutual enjoyment; self-enjoyment.

Ymdrythyllwr, *s. m.—pl.* ymdrythyllwyr (trythyllwr) A self-enjoyer.

Ymdudd, *s. m.* (tudd) A self-envelopement.

Ymdoddaw, *v. a.* (ymdudd) To envelope mutually; to envelop one's self, to self-envelope.

Ymduddawl, *a.* (ymdudd) Self-enveloping.

Ymdnddiad, *s. m.* (ymdudd) A self-enveloping.

Ymdueddawl, *a.* (tueddawl) Self-inclining; apt to incline mutually.

Ymdueddiad, *s. m.* (tueddiad) A self-inclining; mutual inclination.

Ymdueddoli, *v. a.* (ymdueddawl) To incline one's self; to incline mutually.

Ymdueddu, *v. a.* (tueddu) To make one's self partial; to become partial, to incline one's self; to incline mutually.

Ymdueddwr, *s. m.—pl.* ymdueddwyr (tueddwr) One who inclines himself.

Ymdum, *s. m.—pl. t.* au (tum) A mutual bend; a self-bending.

Ymdumiad, *s. m.* (ymdum) A mutually bending; a bending one's self.

Ymdumiaw, *v. a.* (ymdum) To bend mutually; to bend or to mould one's self.

Ymdumiawl, *a.* (ymdum) Mutually bending into shape; self-bending.

Ymdwng, *s. m.* (twng) Mutual swearing.

Ymdwr, *s. m.* (twr) A self-heaping.

Ymdwyll, *s. m.* (twyll) Mutual deceit; self-deception.

Ymdwyllaw, *v. a.* (ymdwyll) To deceive mutually; to deceive one's self.

Ymdwylliad, *s. m.* (ymdwyll) A mutually deceiving; self-deception.

Ymdwymaw, *v. a.* (twymaw) To warm one's self.

Ymdwymiad, *s. m.* (twymiad) A self-warming.

Ymdwymnaw, *v. a.* (twymnaw) To self-warm.

Ymdwymniad, *s. m.* (twymniad) A warming of one's self.

Ymdwysgaw, *v. a.* (twysgaw) To limit mutually; to limit one's self.

Ymdwysgawl, *a.* (twysgawl) Mutually limiting; self-limiting.

Ymdwysgiad, *s. m.* (twysgiad) A mutually determining or limiting; a self-limiting.

Ymdwyth, *s. m.* (twyth) A mutual spring, aptness, or pliancy; a self-springing.

Ymdwythaw, *v. a.* (ymdwyth) To spring mutually; to spring one's self.

Ymdwythiad, *s. m.* (ymdwyth) A springing mutually; a self-springing.

Ymdŷad, *s. m.* (tŷad) A housing one's self.

Ymdŷaw, *v. a.* (tŷaw) To house one's self.

Ymdyn, *s. m.* (tyn) A mutual pull; contention.

Ymdynawl, *a.* (ymdyn) Mutually pulling.

Ymdyniad, *s. m.* (ymdyn) A mutually pulling; a contending, a striving mutually.

Ymdynu, *v. a.* (ymdyn) To pull or drag one another; to strive together, to contend. '*Ymdynu ar draws tanau*,' to pull one another across fires.

Ymdynwr, *s. m.—pl.* ymdynwyr (ymdyn—gwr) One who pulls mutually; a contender.

Ymdyngawl, *a.* (ymdwng) Mutually swearing one's self.

Ymdynged, *s. f.* (ymdwng) A state of being mutually devoted; self-devotion.

Ymdyngedawl, *a.* (ymdynged) Mutually adjuring, self-devoting.

Ymdyngediad, *s. m.* (ymdynged) A mutually adjuring; a self-devoting.

Ymdyngedu, *v. a.* (ymdynged) To adjure mutually; to pledge one's self.

Ymdyngiad, *s. m.* (ymdwng) A mutually swearing; a swearing one's self.

Ymdyngu, *v. a.* (ymdwng) To swear mutually; to plight one's troth.

> Bran a gant o frig gwŷdd
> Yn [illegible] holl adar coedydd;
> Doeth a ymdwng a Dafydd.
>
> A crow sang from the top of the trees, in the hearing of all the birds of the woods: the wise unites himself with the Creator.
>
> [illegible]

Ymdyrawl, *a.* (ymdwr) Mutually thronging.

Ymdyriad, *s. m.* (ymdwr) A jointly thronging.

Ymdyru, *v. a.* (ymdwr) To throng together.

Ymdystiaw, *v. a.* (tystiaw) To witness mutually; to self-testify.

Ymdystiawl, *a.* (tystiawl) Mutually testifying; self-witnessing.

Ymdywylliad, *s. m.* (tywylliad) A mutually darkening; a self-obscuring.

Ymdywyllu, *v. a.* (tywyllu) To darken mutually; to self-obscure.

Ymdywyn, *s. m.* (tywyn) A mutual shining; a self-shining.

Ymdywynawl, *a.* (ymdywyn) Mutually shining; self-shining.

Ymdywyniad, *s. m.* (tywyniad) A mutually shining; a self-shining; a becoming resplendent.

Ymdywynu, *v. a.* (tywynu) To shine mutually; to become resplendent.

Ymdywynyg, *s. m.* (tywynyg) A self-shining.

Ymdywynygawl, *a.* (tywynyg) Self-shining.

Ymdywynygiad, *s. m.* (ymdywynyg) A casting a mutual splendour; a becoming resplendent.

Ymdywynygu, *v. a.* (ymdywynyg) To cast a mutual splendour; to cause one's self to shine; to become splendid.

> Rhod euraid a ymdywynygai ynghylch yr haul.
>
> A golden circle *became resplendent* about the sun.
>
> [illegible]

Ymddadchwyddaw, *v. a.* (dadchwyddaw) To divest one's self of swelling.

Ymddadchwyddiad, *s. m.* (dadchwyddiad) A divesting one's self of swelling.

Ymddadebrawl, *a.* (dadebrawl) Self-resuscitating.

Ymddadebriad, *s.* (dadebriad) Self-resuscitation.

Ymddadebru, *v. a.* (dadebru) To self-resuscitate.

Ymddadflinaw, *v. a.* (dadflinaw) To divest one's self of fatigue.

Ymddadfliniad, *s. m.* (dadfliniad) A divesting one's self of fatigue.

Ymddadgrymiad, *s. m.* (dadgrymiad) An unbending or raising one's self.

Ymddadgrymu, *v. a.* (dadgrymu) To unbend one's self from a bending posture.

Ymddadguddiad, *s. m.* (dadguddiad) A self-revealing.

Ymddadguddiaw, *v.* (dadguddiaw) To self-reveal.

Ymddadguddiawl, *a.* (dadguddiawl) Self-revealing.

Ymddadl, *s. f.* (dadl) Mutual dispute.

Ymddadlawl, *a.* (ymddadl) Controversial.

Ymddadleithiad, *s. m.* (dadleithiad) A mutually dissolving; a self-dissolving.

Ymddadleithiaw, *v. a.* (dadleithiaw) To dissolve mutually; to self-dissolve.

Ymddadleithiawl, *a.* (dadleithiawl) Mutually dissolving; self-dissolving.

Ymddadleu, *v. a.* (ymddadl) To contend in words.

Ymddadleuad, *s. m.* (ymddadleu) Mutual disputation; jointly disputing.

Ymddadleuaw, *v. a.* (ymddadleu) To dispute mutually.

Ymddadlewychawl, *a.* (dadlewychawl) Tending mutually to reflect light; self-refracting.

Ymddadlewychiad, *s. m.* (dadlewychiad) A mutually reflecting light; a self-refraction.

Ymddadlewychu, *v. a.* (dadlewychu) To reflect light mutually; to self-refract.

Ymddadliad, *s. m.—pl. t.* au (ymddadl) A mutually arguing; controversy, contention.

Ymddadlu, *v. a.* (ymddadl) To dispute mutually; to use one's self in dispute.

Ymddadlwr, *s. m.—pl.* ymddadlwyr (ymddadl—gwr) A mutual disputer.

Ymddadlwythaw, *v. a.* (dadlwythaw) To divest one's self of a load.

Ymddadlwythawl, *a.* (dadlwythawl) Tending to disburden one's self.

Ymddadlwythiad, *s. m.* (dadlwythiad) A disburdening one's self.

Ymddadlydd, *s. m.—pl. t.* ion (ymddadl) A disputant.

Ymddadwreiddiad, *s. m.* (dadwreiddiad) A self-eradicating.

Ymddadwreiddiaw, *v. a.* (dadwreiddiaw) To self-eradicate; to be plucked up by the root.

> Pe byddai gennych ffydd gellych ddywedyd wrth y sycamorwydden hon, Ymddadwreiddia.
>
> If ye had faith, ye might say unto this sycamine tree, *Be thou plucked up by the root.* *Luke* 17. 6.

Ymddadwreiddiawl, *a.* (dadwreiddiawl) Tending to be self-eradicated.

Ymddaiariad, *s. m.* (daiariad) A self-burying.

Ymddaiaru, *v. a.* (daiaru) To burrow one's self.

Ymddal, *s. m.* (dal) The act of mutual holding; perseverance. *v. a.* To persevere.

> Tri arddangaws doethineb: ymddal ar bwyll, ymddal ar awen, ac ymddal ar welliedigaeth.
>
> The three indications of wisdom: a *keeping* after reason, a *keeping* after genius, and *keeping* after improvement. *Catwg ab Gwynlliw.*

Ymddaliad, *s. m.—pl. t.* au (ymddal) A mutually holding; a self-holding; that is holden; an opinion.

> Yr Arglwydd a draethai hyny, i faeddu i'r llawr falch ymddaliad y Phariswr.
>
> The Lord declared that, to beat to the ground the proud *opinion* of the Pharisee. *Marchawg Crwydrad.*

Ymddaliwr, *s. m.—pl.* ymddalwyr (ymddal—gwr) One who mutually holds; one who holds himself.

Ymddalliad, *s. m.* (dalliad) A mutually blinding; a self-blinding.

Ymddallu, *v. a.* (dallu) To blind mutually; to blind one's self.

> Mae gormod yn ymddallu wrth y tair tywysoges obry.
>
> Too many do *blind themselves* with the three princesses below. *Elis Wyn, B. Cwsg.*

Ymddallus, *a.* (dallus) Being self-blinding.

Ymddallwr, *s. m.—pl.* ymddallwyr (dallwr) One who blinds himself.

Ymddanneddiad, *s. m.* (danneddiad) A mutually shewing the teeth, mutually snarling.

Ymddanneddu, *v. a.* (danneddu) To snarl mutually; to employ one's self in snarling.

> Gwelwn rai yn ymwthiaw ac yn ymddanneddu am eu braint.
>
> We could perceive some thrusting themselves forward and *mutually snarling* for their rank. *Elis Wyn, B. Cwsg.*

Ymddanneddwr, *s. m.—pl.* ymddanneddwyr (danneddwr) A snarler.

Ymddantiad, *s. m.* (dantiad) A shewing one's teeth.

Ymddantu, *v. a.* (dantu) To shew one's teeth.

> Megys corgi yn ymddantu a march rhygyngawg.
>
> Like a cur dog *snarling* at an ambling steed. *Theo. Evans.*

Ymddangaws, *s. m.* (dangaws) A mutual shew; a shewing of one's self. *v. a.* To appear mutually; to shew one's self.

Ymddangosawl, *a.* (ymddangaws) Mutually appearing; self-exposing.

Ymddangosgar, *a.* (ymddangaws) Ostentatious.

Ymddangosgarwch, *s. m.* (ymddangosgar) Ostentatiousness.

Ymddangosiad, *s. m.—pl. t.* au (ymddangaws) A self-shewing, an appearing; an appearance.

Ymddangosiadawl, *a.* (ymddangosiad) Relating to self-shewing.

Ymddangosiadus, *a* (ymddangosiad) Ostentatious

Ymddarostwng, *s. m.* (darostwng) Self-debasement. *v. a.* To debase one's self.

Ymddarostyngawl, *a.* (darostwng) Self-debasing.

Ymddarostyngiad, *s. m.* (darostwng) A lowering one's self, a humbling one's self; a self-debasing, condescension.

Ymddarostyngwr, *s. m.—pl.* ymddarostyngwyr (ymddarostwng—gwr) A self-debaser.

Ymddarpar, *s. m.* (darpar) Self-preparation.

Ymddarpariad, *s. m.* (darpar) A self-preparing.

Ymddarparu, *v. a.* (darpar) To self-prepare.

Ymddarparwr, *s. m.—pl.* ymddarparwyr (darpar—gwr) A self-preparer.

Ymddarwedd, *s. f.* (darwedd) A self-yielding.

> Ynghylch 1111, yr oedd Owain ab Cadwgawn yn drygu yn ddiymarwedd o'i amgylch.
>
> About the year 1111, Owain son of Cadwgan was ravaging *without remorse* all around him. *Caradawg o Lan Carfan.*

Ymddarweddawl, *a.* (darwedd) Self-conforming; of a pliant nature; mutually complying.

Ymddarweddiad, *s. m.* (darwedd) A self-conforming; a mutually complying.

Ymddarweddu, *v. a.* (darwedd) To conform one's self; to comply mutually.

Ymddattawd, *s. m.* (dattawd) A mutual loosening; a loosening of one's self.

> Clywwn lais yn peri i minnau, wrth fy enw, ymddattawd: ar y gair, mi yn clywwn yn dechreu toddi, mal caseg eira yn ngwres yr haul.
>
> I could hear a voice commanding me also, by my name, *to loosen myself*: at the word, I could feel myself beginning to melt, like a snowball in the heat of the sun. *Elis Wyn, B. Cwsg.*

Ymddattodawl, *a.* (ymddattawd) Self-loosening.

Ymddattodi, *v. a.* (ymddattawd) To loosen mutually; to loosen one's self.

Ymddattodiad, *s. m.* (ymddattawd) A mutually loosening; a loosening one's self.

Ymddefodwr, *s. m.—pl.* ymddefodwyr (defodwr) One who adheres to a custom.

Ymddeffraw, *s. m.* (deffraw) A self-waking. *v. a.* To wake one's self.

Ymddeffröad, *s. m.* (ymddeffraw) A self-waking.

Ymddeffröawl, *a.* (ymddeffraw) Self-waking.

Ymddeffröi, *v. a.* (ymddeffraw) Self-waking.

Ymddeintiad, *s. m.* (deintiad) A mutually snarling

Ymddeintiaw, *v. a.* (deintiaw) To snarl mutually.

Ymddenawl, *a.* (denawl) Mutually alluring; self-alluring.

Ymddeniad, *s. m.* (deniad) A mutually alluring; a self-alluring.

Ymddenu, *v. a.* (denu) To allure mutually; to allure one's self.

Ymddëodi, *v. a.* (deawd) To divest one's self.

> Am Fadawg manawg mynw haelioni,
> Medel glyw glewdraws mawr mynogi;
> Am Owain Prydain, Pryderi halal,
> Prenial ymddial ymddëodi.
>
> For Madawg, the distinguished centre of liberality, the bravely-froward leader whose store was sweet benignity; for Owain of Britain, equal to Pryderi, the casket of self revenge *is mutually cast off.* *Cynddelw.*

Ymddëodiad, *s. m.* (ymddëodi) A divesting one's self of garments.

Ymddëol, *s. m.* (dëol) Mutual separation; self-separation; self banishment.

Ymddëoli, *v. a.* (ymddëol) To separate mutually; to separate one's self; to banish one's self.

Ymddëoliad, *s. m.* (ymddëol) A mutually separating; a separating one's self.

Ymddëor, *s. m.* (dëor) The state of being hatched. *v. a.* To be hatched.

> Cydwybod yw y nyth lle ydd ymddëor pob daioni.
>
> Conscience is the nest where every good is *hatched*. *Adage.*

Ymddëorawl, *a.* (ymddëor) Being employed in hatching or brooding.

Ymddëori, *v. a.* (ymddëor) To be employed in hatching.

Ymddëoriad, *s. m.* (ymddëor) A being in the act of hatching.

Ymddèrawl, *a.* (dèrawl) Mutually taunting.

Ymdderbyn, *s. m.* (derbyn) Mutual reception. *v. a.* To receive mutually; to employ one's self in receiving.

Ymdderbyniad, *s. m.* (ymdderbyn) A mutually receiving; a being receiving.

Ymdderbyniaw, *v. a.* (ymdderbyn) To receive mutually; to be receiving.

Ymdderbyniawl, *a.* (ymdderbyn) Mutually receiving; being receiving.

Ymddèriad, *s. m.* (dèriad) A mutually taunting.

Ymddèru, *v. a.* (dèru) To taunt mutually.

Ymddïal, *s. m.* (dïal) A revenging one's self. *v. a.* To revenge one's self; to be revenged. *Ysbryd ymddïal*, a vindictive spirit.

> Ez beddau a'u cudd gwyddwal
> Ni lesaint heb ymddïal:
> Gwrien, Morien, a Morial.
>
> They whose graves are obscured by furze, they were not slain without *avenging themselves*: Gwrien, Morien, and Morial. *E. Beddau Milwyr.*

Ymddïalgar, *a.* (ymddïal) Revengeful, vindictive

Ymddïaliad, *s. m.* (ymddïal) A self-avenging.

Ymddïalu, *v. a.* (ymddïal) To avenge one's self.

Ymddïalydd, *s. m.—pl. t.* ion (ymddïal) A self-avenger.

Ymddïang, *s. m.* (dïang) Self-escape. *v. a.* To extricate one's self.

> Pan adnabu Grufudd ab Cynan na allai ymddïang efelly, ydd aeth yn ysgraff y canonwyr yn Aberdaron, ac yn hono a dan rwyf ydd aynt yn Iwerddon.
>
> When Grufudd son of Cynan perceived that he could not *extricate himself* so, he procured the ferry of the canons in Aberdaron, and in that, by the use of the oar, they went to Ireland. *Buch. Gr. ab Cynan.*

Ymddïangawl, *a.* (ymddïang) Self-extricating.

Ymddïangiad, *s. m.* (ymddïang) A self-escaping.

Ymddïarfiad, *s. m.* (dïarfiad) A self-disarming.

Ymddïarfogi, *v. a.* (dïarfogi) To self-disarm.

Ymddïarfogiad, *s. m.* (dïarfogi) A self-disarming.

Ymddïarfu, *v. a.* (dïarfu) To disarm one's self.

Ymddïargeliad, *s. m.* (dïargel) A divesting one's self of seclusion, a revealing one's self.

Ymddïargelu, *v. a.* (dïargelu) To divest one's self of seclusion to manifest one's self.

Ymddïarialiad, *s. m.* (dïarialiad) A divesting one's self of wantonness.

Ymddïarialu, *v. a.* (dïarialu) To divest one's self of wantonness.

Ymddïaruthraw, *v. a.* (dïaruthraw) To divest one's self of astonishment.

Ymddïaruthriad *s. m.* (dïaruthriad) A divesting one's self of astonishment.

Ymddïasgeniad, *s. m.* (dïasgeniad) A divesting one's self of blemish; a rendering one's self unpolluted.

Ymddïasgenu, *v. a.* (dïasgenu) To divest one's self of blemish or harm.

Ymddïawchiad, *s. m.* (dïawchiad) A divesting one's self of appetency or desire.

Ymddïawchu, *v. a.* (dïawchu) To divest one's self of appetency or eagerness.

Ymddibarchiad, *s. m.* (dibarchiad) A divesting one's self of respect.

Ymddibarchu, *v. a.* (dibarchu) To divest one's self of respect or reverence.

Ymddibetrusaw, *v. a.* (dibetrusaw) To divest one's self of hesitation; to cease hesitating.

Ymddibetrusiad, *s. m.* (dibetrusiad) A divesting one's self of hesitation.

Ymddiblaw, *v. a.* (diblaw) To daggle one's self.

Ymddibleidiad, *s. m.* (dibleidiad) A divesting one's self of a party.

Ymddibleidiaw, *v. a.* (dibleidiaw) To divest one's self of a party to appeal from a decision.

> Tri rhyw ymddibleidiaw y sydd [illegible] wrth y plas i'r orsedd, ail yw yn y [illegible]
>
> There are three ways of *appealing from a decision*: the first is from the hall to the high court, the second is with respect to the form, the third is in the matter. *Welsh Laws.*

Ymddibleidiawl, *a.* (dibleidiawl) Respecting the being divested of a party.

Ymddibleidiwr, *s. m.—pl.* ymddibleidiwyr (dibleidiwr) One who recedes from a party.

Ymddiblethiad, *s. m.* (diblethiad) A divesting one's self of plaits or wreathes.

Ymddiblethu, *v. a.* (dibleth u) To self-divest of plaits; to become unwreathed.

Ymddibliad, *s. m.* (dibliad) A self-daggling.

Ymddiblisgaw, *v. a.* (diblisgaw) To become divested of shell.

Ymddiblisgiad, *s. m.* (diblisgiad) A becoming divested of shell.

Ymddiboeni, *v. a.* (diboeni) To divest one's self of pain or labour.

Ymddiboeniad, *s. m.* (diboeniad) A divesting one's self of pain or labour.

Ymddiborthi, *v. a.* (diborthi) To divest one's self of support.

Ymddiborthiad, *s. m.* (diborthiad) A divesting one's self of support.

Ymddibwyllaw, *v. a.* (dibwyllaw) To divest one's self of impulse or of reason.

Ymddibwylliad, *s. m.* (dibwylliad) A divesting one's self of reason or wit.

Ymddibwysaw, *v. a.* (dibwysaw) To divest one's self of weight.

Ymddibwysiad, *s. m.* (dibwysiad) A divesting one's self of weight.

Ymddibynawl, *a.* (dibynawl) Self-suspending, self-impending; dependent.

Ymddibyniad, *s. m.* (dibyniad) A suspending one's self; a becoming dependent.

Ymddibynu, *v. a.* (dibynu) To suspend one's self; to render one's self dependent.

Ymddichelliad, *s. m.* (dichelliad) A making one's self cunning.

Ymddichellu, *v. a.* (dichellu) To furnish one's self with cunning or wiles.

> Dichell ar bob dichell ymddichellu dyn.
>
> An art above every art is *to make one's self artful* in goodness. *Adage.*

Ymddichoni, *v. a.* (dichoni) To become able.

Ymddichoniad, *s. m.* (dichoniad) A rendering one's self able or capable.

Ymddidoli, *v. a.* (didoli) To separate one's self; to separate mutually.

Ymddidoliad, *s. m.* (didoliad) A separating one's self; a mutually separating.

Ymddidresiad, *s. m.* (didresiad) A divesting one's self of bustle.

Ymddidresu, *v. a.* (didresu) To divest one's self of bustle or hurry.

Ymddidwyllaw, *v. a.* (didwyllaw) To undeceive one's self; mutually to undeceive.

Ymddidwylliad, *s. m.* (didwylliad) An undeceiving of one's self.

Ymddiddwyn, *s. m.* (diddwyn) A self-weaning. *v.* To wean one's self.

Rhaid ymddiddwyn a'r byd os eir i'r nef.

It is necessary *to wean one's self* from the world, if one is to go to heaven. *Adage.*

Ymddiddyrysiad, *s. m.* (diddyrysiad) A disentangling one's self.

Ymddiddyrysu, *v. a.* (diddyrysu) To disentangle one's self.

Ymddïeithraw, *v. a.* (dïeithraw) To render one's self unexceptionable.

Ymddïeithriad, *s. m.* (dïeithriad) A rendering one's self unexceptionable.

Ymddïenyddiad, *s. m.* (dïenyddiad) A making away with one's self.

Ymddïenyddu, *v. a.* (dïenyddu) To make away with one's self.

Ni ddyly arglwydd obedyw gwr a ymddïenyddo.

The lord is not entitled to the heriot of a man *who puts an end to his own existence.* *Welsh Laws.*

Ymddifa, *v. a.* (difa) To end one's self.

Ymddifäad, *s. m.* (ymddifa) A self-ending.

Ymddifad, *a.* (difad) Being destitute of good or comfort; fatherless or motherless. *Plant ymddifad*, orphan children.

Un wedd wyf yn ymddifad
A dyn wedi' fam a'i dad!

I am in the same manner *void of comfort* as a person after losing his father and mother! *Owain Brisriwn.*

Ymddifadiad, *s. m.* (ymddifad) A being made destitute; a becoming destitute.

Ymddifadu, *v. a.* (ymddifad) To bereave of comfort; to become destitute.

Ymddifanniad, *s. m.* (difanniad) A making one's self to vanish away.

Ymddifannu, *v. a.* (difannu) To make one's self to vanish.

Ymddifedi, *s. m.* (ymddifad) A state void of solace; the being destitute; deprivation; an orphan state.

Mwy ym cymhellir i wylaw nog i ddywedyd araeth ac ymadroddion uchel, sef achaws yw hyny truaned yw genyf i yr ymddifedi a'r gwander a ddamweiniws ini.

I am more compelled to weep than to speak an oration and high expressions, the reason of which is the *wretchedness* and the weakness that have happened to us. *Gr. ab Arthur.*

Ymddifeiad, *s. m.* (difeiad) Self-exculpation.

Ymddifeiaw, *v. a.* (difeiaw) To self-exculpate.

Ymddifeichiad, *s. m.* (difeichiad) A clearing one's self from bail.

Ymddifeichiaw, *v. a.* (difeichiaw) To clear one's self from bail.

Ymddiflaniad, *s. m.* (diflanniad) A making one's self to vanish.

Ymddiflannu, *v. a.* (diflannu) To cause one's self to vanish.

Ymddiflinaw, *v. a.* (diflinaw) To divest one's self of fatigue; to refresh one's self.

Ymddifliniad, *s. m.* (difliniad) A divesting one's self of fatigue; a refreshing one's self.

Ymddifregawl, *a.* (difregawl) Tending to be sad.

Ymddifregiad, *s. m.* (difregiad) A rendering one's self serious.

Ymddifregu, *v. a.* (difregu) To render one's self void of frailty; to become serious. *Ymddifregu a Duw*, to address one's self seriously to God.

Ymddifreinniad, *s. m.* (difreinniad) A divesting one's self of privilege or right.

Ymddifreinniaw, *v. a.* (difreinniaw) To divest one's self of privilege or right.

Ymddifrodi, *v. a.* (difrodi) To rob one's self.

Ymddifrodiad, *s. m.* (difrodiad) A self robbing.

Ymddifwynaw, *v. a.* (difwynaw) To divest one's self of enjoyment.

Ymddifwyniad, *s. m.* (difwyniad) A divesting one's self of enjoyment.

Ymddifyddinaw, *v. a.* (difyddinaw) To become disbanded as an army.

Ymddifyddiniad, *s. m.* (difyddiniad) A becoming disbanded as an army.

Ymddifyrawl, *a.* (difyrawl) Self-diverting.

Ymddifyriad, *s. m.* (difyriad) A diverting one's self: a mutually diverting.

Ymddifyru, *v. a.* (difyru) To divert one's self; to divert one another.

Ymddiffawdd, *s. m.* (diffawdd) A self-extinguishing. *v. a.* To self-extinguish.

Ymddiffer, *s. m.* (differ) Self-protection; mutual defence or protection.

Ymddifferawl, *a.* (ymddiffer) Self-protecting.

Ymddifferiad, *s. m.* (ymddiffer) A self-protecting; mutual protection.

Ymddiffern, *v. a.* (ymddiffer) To defend one's self; to protect mutually.

Aynt hyd yn Mon, ac wynt a Grufudd; ac yno ydd ymddifferynt

They went as far as Mon, them and Grufudd; and there *they defended themselves.* *Buch. Gr. ab Cynan.*

Ymddifferwr, *s. m.*—*pl.* ymddifferwyr (ymddiffer—gwr) A self-defender.

Ymddiffoddawl, *a.* (ymddiffawdd) Self-extinguishing.

Ymddiffoddi, *v. a.* (ymddiffawdd) To self-extinguish.

Ymddiffoddiad, *s. m.* (ymddiffawdd) A self-extinguishing.

Ymddiffwys, *s. m.* (diffwys) The state of being imminent or impending; eventful.

Y galon—
Hon a bair cadair ceudawd,
Henw ymddiffwys, gynnwys gwawd.

The heart: it will cause the seat of imagination, *eventful* the name, to harbour praise. *B. ab Gwilym.*

Ymddiffwysaw, *v. a.* (ymddiffwys) To render one's self impending.

Ymddiffwysawl, *a.* (ymddiffwys) Self-impending.

Ymddiffwysiad, *s. m.* (ymddiffwys) A rendering one's self impending.

Ymddiffyn, *s. m.* (diffyn) Self-defence; mutual defence. *v. a.* To defend one's self.

Ymddiffynadwy, *a.* (ymddiffyn) Defensible.

Ymddiffynawl, *a.* (ymddiffyn) Self-protecting.

Ymddiffynedig, *a.* (ymddiffyn) Self-protected.

Ymddiffynfa, *s. f.*—*pl.* ymddiffynfëydd (ymddiffyn) A place of defence.

Ymddiffyniad, *s. m.* (ymddiffyn) A defending.

Ymddiffyniaeth, *s.* (ymddiffyn) System of defence

Ymddiffynu, *v. a.* (ymddiffyn) To self-defend.

Ymddiffynus, *a.* (ymddiffyn) Self-defending.

Ymddiffynwr, *s. m.*—*pl.* ymddiffynwyr (ymddiffyn—gwr) A defender, a protector.

Ymddiffynydd, *s. m.*—*pl. t.* ion (ymddiffyn) A defender.

Ymddigaloni, *v. a.* (digaloni) To dishearten one's self; to become disheartened.

Ymddigaloniad, *s. m.* (digaloniad) A disheartening one's self.

Ymddigariad, *s. m.* (digariad) A divesting one's self of love.

Ymddigaru, *v. a.* (digaru) To divest one's self of love or affection.

Ymddigasâad, *s. m.* (digasâad) A divesting one's self of hatred or enmity.

Ymddigasâu, *v. a.* (digasâu) To divest one's self of hatred or enmity.

Ymddigeliad, *s. m.* (digeliad) A self-revealing.

Ymddigelu, *v. a.* (digelu) To reveal one's self.

Ymddigeniad, *s. m.* (digeniad) A self-exfoliation.

Ymddigenu, *v. a.* (digenu) To self-exfoliate.

Ymddigiad, *s. m.* (digiad) A making one's self angry; a becoming angry.

Ymddigiaw, *v. a.* (digiaw) To anger one's self.

Ymddigiawl, *a.* (digiawl) Tending to anger one's self; becoming angry.

Ymddigonad, *s. m.* (digonad) A self-sufficing.

Ymddigoni, *v. a.* (digoni) To self-suffice.

Ymddigrifâad, *s. m.* (digrifâad) A delighting one's self; a self-amusing.

Ymddigrifâu, *v. a.* (digrifâu) To amuse one's self; to delight one's self.

Ymddigrifaw, *v. a.* (digrifaw) To amuse one's self, to delight one's self; to make one's self happy.

Ymddigrifais yn dy gyfraith.

I have delighted in thy law. *Psalm* 119. 70.

Ymddigrifawl, *a.* (digrifawl) Tending to self-delight; becoming delighted.

Ymddigrifiad, *s. m.* (digrifiad) A self-delighting; a becoming delighted.

Ymddigrifwch, *s. m.* (digrifwch) Self-delight.

Ymddiguddiad, *s. m.* (diguddiad) A rendering one's self unhidden.

Ymddiguddiaw, *v. a.* (diguddiaw) To unhide one's self; to become unhidden.

Ymddigyfeilliad, *s. m.* (digyfeilliad) A divesting one's self of friendship.

Ymddigyfeilliaw, *v. a.* (digyfeilliaw) To deprive one's self of friendship.

Ymddigyfnerthiad, *s. m.* (digyfnerthiad) A divesting one's self of assistance.

Ymddigyfnerthu, *v. a.* (digyfnerthu) To divest one's self of assistance.

Ymddigyfoethi, *v. a.* (digyfoethi) To divest one's self of wealth or power.

Ymddigyfoethiad, *s. m.* (digyfoethiad) A divesting one's self of wealth.

Ymddigyfraniad, *s. m.* (digyfraniad) A divesting one's self of participation.

Ymddigyfranu, *v. a.* (digyfranu) To divest one's self of participation.

Ymddigyfrwyddaw, *v. a.* (digyfrwyddaw) To render one's self unpropitious.

Ymddigyfrwyddiad, *s. m.* (digyfrwyddiad) A rendering one's self unpropitious.

Ymddigyfyngiad, *s. m.* (digyfyngiad) A rendering one's self unstraitened.

Ymddigyfyngu, *v. a.* (digyfyngu) To render one's self unstraitened.

Ymddigyffröad, *s. m.* (digyffröad) A divesting one's self of agitation.

Ymddigyffröi, *v. a.* (digyffröi) To divest one's self of agitation or excitement.

Ymddigymhorthi, *v. a.* (digymhorthi) To deprive one's self of assistance.

Ymddigymhorthiad, *s. m.* (digymhorthiad) A depriving one's self of assistance.

Ymddigynheniad, *s. m.* (digynheniad) A divesting one's self of contention.

Ymddigynhenu, *v. a.* (digynhenu) To divest one's self of contention.

Ymddigysylltiad, *s. m.* (digysylltiad) A rendering one's self unconnected.

Ymddigysylltu, *v. a.* (digysylltu) To disconnect one's self.

Ymddigywilyddiad, *s. m.* (digywilyddiad) A divesting one's self of shame.

Ymddigywilyddiaw, *v. a.* (digywilyddiaw) To divest one's self of shame.

Ymddihafarchiad, *s. m.* (dihafarchiad) A divesting one's self of timidity or dread.

Ymddihafarchu, *v. a.* (dihafarchu) To divest one's self of timidity or fear.

Ymddihalogi, *v. a.* (dihalogi) To divest one's self of pollution.

Ymddihalogiad, *s. m.* (dihalogiad) A divesting one's self of pollution.

Ymddihatriad, *s. m.* (dihatriad) A divesting one's self of covering or dress.

Ymddihatru, *v. a.* (dihatru) To divest one's self of covering or dress.

Ymddiheiniad, *s. m.* (diheiniad) A divesting one's self of infection.

Ymddiheiniaw, *v. a.* (diheiniaw) To divest one's self of infection.

A'm bo gan Dduw——
Bod ar iawn, am ddawn ymddiheint[illegible]
Byd——

Please God, may I be on the right, for grace divesting myself of the infection of the world. [illegible]

Ymddiheurad, *s. m.* (diheurad) Self-vindication.

Ymddiheuraw, *v. a.* (diheuraw) To self-absolve; to vindicate one's self.

Ymddihoeni, *v. a.* (dihoeni) To self-enfeeble; to divest one's self of spirit; to pine one's self.

Ymddihoeniad, *s. m.* (dihoeniad) A divesting one's self of vivacity or spirits.

Ymddihuddaw, *v. a.* (dihuddaw) To self-uncover.

Ymddihuddiad, *s. m.* (dihuddiad) An uncovering of one's self; a becoming uncovered.

Ymddihunaw, *v. a.* (dihunaw) To self-wake.

Ymddihuniad, *s. m.* (dihuniad) A self-waking.

Ymddihwylaw, *v. a.* (dihwylaw) To disarray one's self; to disorder one's self.

Ymddihwyliad, *s. m.* (dihwyliad) A disarraying of one's self; a self-disordering.

Ymddilesiad, *s. m.* (dilesiad) A depriving one's self of benefit.

Ymddilesu, *v. a.* (dilesu) To deprive one's self of benefit or advantage.

Ymddilidiad, *s. m.* (dilidiad) A divesting one's self of wrath or anger.

Ymddilidiaw, *v. a.* (dilidiaw) To divest one's self of wrath; to become pacified.

Ymddiloni, *v. a.* (diloni) To divest one's self of cheerfulness; to make one's self sad.

Ymddiloniad, *s. m.* (diloniad) A divesting one's self of cheerfulness.

Ymddiluddaw, *v. a.* (diluddaw) To render one's self unobstructed or unrestrained.

Ymddiluddediad, *s. m.* (diluddediad) A divesting one's self of restraint; a divesting one's self of weariness.

Ymddiluddedu, *v. a.* (diluddedu) To divest one's self of restraint, or of weariness.

Ymddiluddiad, *s. m.* (diluddiad) A divesting one's self of obstruction.

Ymddilwythaw, *v. a.* (dilwythaw) To unload one's self, to unburden one's self.

Ymddilwythiad, *s. m.* (dilwythiad) A disburdening of one's self.

Ymddilygriad, *s. m.* (dilygriad) A divesting one's self of corruption.
Ymddilygru, *v. a.* (dilygru) To divest one's self of corruption.
Ymddilyn, *s. m.* (dilyn) The being in pursuit; mutual pursuit. *v. a.* To be in pursuit; to pursue mutually.
Ymddilynawl, *a.* (ymddilyn) Apt to be pursuing.
Ymddilyngar, *a.* (ymddilyn) Apt to be pursuing.
Ymddilyniad, *s. m.* (ymddilyn) Being pursuing; a mutually pursuing.
Ymddilynwr, *s. m.*—*pl.* ymddilynwyr (ymddilyn—gwr) One who uses himself to pursue.
Ymddilysiad, *s. m.* (dilysiad) A self-securing.
Ymddilysu, *v. a.* (dilysu) To secure one's self.
Ymddilladiad, *s. m.* (dilladiad) A self-clothing.
Ymddilladu, *v. a.* (dilladu) To clothe one's self.
Ymddilliad, *s. m.* (dilliad) A self-folding.
Ymddilliaw, *v. a.* (dilliaw) To self-fold.
Ymddinerthiad, *s. m.* (dinerthiad) A self-enervating, a becoming debilitated.
Ymddinerthu, *v. a.* (dinerthu) To self-debilitate.
Ymddinidraw, *v. a.* (dinidraw) To disentangle one's self, to disembarrass one's self.
Ymddinidriad, *s. m.* (dinidriad) A disentangling of one's self.
Ymddiniweidiad, *s. m.* (diniweidiad) A rendering one's self harmless.
Ymddiniweidiaw, *v. a.* (diniweidiaw) To render one's self harmless.
Ymddinwyfaw, *v. a.* (dinwyfaw) To divest one's self of vivacity or spirit.
Ymddinwyfiad, *s. m.* (dinwyfiad) A divesting one's self of vivacity, life, or vigour.
Ymddïobeithiad, *s. m.* (dïobeithiad) A divesting one's self of hope.
Ymddïobeithiaw, *v. a.* (dïobeithiaw) To render one's self hopeless.
Ymddïodi, *v. a.* (dïodi) To supply one's self with drink; to be drinking.
Ymddïodiad, *s. m.* (dïodiad) A supplying of one's self with drink.
Ymddïofaliad, *s. m.* (diofaliad) A divesting one's self of care; a becoming careless.
Ymddïofalu, *v. a.* (diofalu) To divest one's self of care; to become careless.
Ymddïofidiad, *s. m.* (diofidiad) A divesting one's self of affliction.
Ymddïofidiaw, *v. a.* (dïofidiaw) To divest one's self of affliction.
Ymddïofni, *v. a.* (dïofni) To divest one's self of fear; to become fearless.
Ymddïofniad, *s. m.* (dïofniad) A divesting one's self of fear; a becoming fearless.
Ymddïofrydiad, *s. m.* (dïofrydiad) A rendering one's self decided, determined, or devoted.
Ymddïofrydu, *v. a.* (dïofrydu) To render one's self decided, resolved, or devoted.
Ymddïoganiad, *s. m.* (dioganiad) A divesting one's self of reproach.
Ymddïoganu, *v. a.* (dioganu) To divest one's self of reproach or scandal.
Ymddïogeliad, *s. m.* (dïogeliad) A self-securing.
Ymddïogelu, *v. a.* (diogelu) To self-secure.
Ymddïogi, *v. a.* (diogi) To make one's self lazy.
Ymddïogiad, *s. m.* (diogiad) A making one's self lazy or listless.
Ymddïoli, *v. a.* (dïoli) To divest one's self of a trace or footstep.
Ymddïoliad, *s. m.* (dïoliad) A divesting one's self of a trace or track.

Ymddireidiad, *s. m.* (direidiad) An employing one's self unnecessarily.
Ymddireidiaw, *v. a.* (direidiaw) To employ one's self unnecessarily.

Gwell peidiaw nog ymddireidiaw.

Better to desist than *to employ one's self uselessly.* *Adage.*

Ymddirgeliad, *s. m.* (dirgeliad) A making one's self private or secret.
Ymddirgelu, *v. a.* (dirgelu) To self-secret.
Ymddiriad, *s. m.* (diriad) Self-instigation; mutual instigation; confidence.

Gwaethaf twyll twyll ymddiriad.

The worst deceit is deceit through *confidence.* *Adage.*

Ymddiriaw, *v. a.* (diriaw) To self-instigate; to instigate mutually.

Meflir a ymddir hamdden.

He that trusts to opportunity will be foiled. *Adage.*

Ymddiriawl, *a.* (diriawl) Being self-impelling.
Ymddiried, *s. m.* (diried) Mutual impulse; mutual dependence; confidence, trust. *v. a.* To give mutual impulse; to confide, to rely or depend upon.

Nid ymddiried ond cydymaith.

There is no *trust* like a companion. *Adage.*

Cas a ymddirieto i rodd.

Hateful is he that *trusteth* to a gift. *Adage.*

Tri pheth nid eilir ymddiried iddynt: iechyd i hen, hindda y gauaf, a diwydrwydd arglwydd.

Three things to which *no trust can be given*: health to the old, fair weather in winter, and the diligence of a lord. *Adage.*

Ymddiriedіad, *s. m.* (ymddiried) A confiding.
Ymddiriedu, *v. a.* (ymddiried) To confide, to trust.
Ymddiriedus, *a.* (ymddiried) Confiding, trusting.
Ymddirmygiad, *s. m.* (dirmygiad) A self-contemning.
Ymddirmygu, *v. a.* (dirmygu) To self-contemn.
Ymddirper, *s. m.* (dirper) The being deserving.
Ymddirperiad, *s. m.* (ymddirper) A rendering one's self deserving or meriting.
Ymddirperu, *v. a.* (ymddirper) To render one's self deserving.
Ymddirprwy, *s. m.* (dirprwy) A mutual supply.
Ymddirprwyad, *s. m.* (ymddirprwy) A self-supplying, a getting one's place filled by proxy.
Ymddirprwyaw, *v. a.* (ymddirprwy) To supply one's self; to self-accommodate.
Ymddirwest, *s. m.* (dirwest) A self-refraining. *v. a.* To refrain one's self.

Goreu pob dirwest ymddirwest rhag trachwant.

The best refraining *is to refrain one's self* from cupidity.

Cattwg Ddoeth.

Ymddirwyad, *s. m.* (dirwyad) A self-fining.
Ymddirwyaw, *v. a.* (dirwyaw) To fine one's self.
Ymddirwydaw, *v. a.* (dirwydaw) To extricate one's self, to become disentangled.
Ymddirwydiad, *s. m.* (dirwydiad) A disentangling one's self; a freeing one's self.
Ymddirwymaw, *v. a.* (dirwymaw) To unbind one's self, to liberate one's self.
Ymddirwymiad, *s. m.* (dirwymiad) A liberating or unbinding one's self.
Ymddirwystraw, *v. a.* (dirwystraw) To render one's self void of impediment or interruption.
Ymddirwystriad, *s. m.* (dirwystriad) A divesting one's self of hinderance or impediment.
Ymddirymiad, *s. m.* (dirymiad) A divesting one's self of energy or power.
Ymddirymiaw, *v. a.* (dirymiaw) To divest one's self of energy or power.
Ymddirywiad, *s.* (dirywiad) A self-degenerating.
Ymddirywiaw, *v. a.* (dirywiaw) To degenerate one's self, to become degenerate.

Ymddiscyn, *s. m.* (discyn) The act of bringing one's self down.
Ymddiscyniad, *s. m.* (ymddiscyn) A bringing one's self down; a self-dismounting.
Ymddiserchiad, *s. m.* (diserchiad) A divesting one's self of affection.
Ymddiserchu, *v. a.* (diserchu) To divest one's self of affection or fondness.
Ymddisomi, *v. a.* (disomi) To undeceive one's self; to become undeceived.
Ymddisomiad, *s. m.* (disomiad) A divesting one's self of disappointment.
Ymddiwalliad, *s. m.* (diwalliad) A self-satiating.
Ymddiwalltu, *v. a.* (diwalltu) To divest one's self of the head hair.
Ymddiwallu, *v. a.* (diwallu) To self-satisfy.
Ymddiweddu, *v. a.* (diweddu) To finish one's self.
Ymddiwreiddiad, *s. m.* (diwreiddiad) A self eradicating; a being unrooted.
Ymddiwreiddiaw, *v. a.* (diwreiddiaw) To eradicate one's self; to be plucked up by the root.
Ymddiwresiad, *s. m.* (diwresiad) A divesting one's self of heat.
Ymddiwresu, *v. a.* (diwresu) To divest one's self of heat or warmth.
Ymddiwydiad, *s. m.* (diwydiad) A rendering one's self diligent or persevering.
Ymddiwydiaw, *v. a.* (diwydiaw) To render one's self diligent or persevering.
Ymddiwygiad, *s. m.* (diwygiad) Self-reformation.
Ymddiwygiaw, *v. a.* (diwygiaw) To self-reform.
Ymddiwynaw, *v. a.* (diwynaw) To self-pollute.

Ymddiwynasant gan waed, mal na ellid cyhwrdd a'u dillad hwynt.

They have polluted themselves with blood, so that their garments could not be touched. *Galarnad* 4. 14.

Ymddiwyniad, *s. m.* (diwyniad) A self polluting.
Ymddïysgogi, *v. a.* (dïysgogi) To render one's self unshaken or inflexible.
Ymddïysgogiad, *s. m.* (dïysgogiad) A rendering one's self unshaken or firm.
Ymddodawl, *a.* (dodawl) Self depositing.
Ymddodi, *v. a.* (dodi) To deposit one's self.
Ymddodiad, *s. m.* (dodiad) A self-depositing.
Ymddofi, *v. a.* (dofi) To tame one's self.
Ymddofiad, *s. m.* (dofiad) A self-taming.
Ymddogni, *v. a.* (dogni) To self-allow.
Ymddogniad, *s. m.* (dogniad) Self-allowancing.
Ymddoleniad, *s. m.* (doleniad) A self-coiling.
Ymddolenu, *v. a.* (dolenu) To coil one's self.
Ymddoli, *v. a.* (doli) To self-curve; to become curved.
Ymddoliad, *s. m.* (doliad) A self-curving.
Ymddoniad, *s. m.* (doniad) A self-endowing.
Ymddoniaw, *v. a.* (doniaw) To self-endow.
Ymddori, *v. a.* (dori) To concern one's self.
Ymddoriad, *s. m.* (doriad) A self-concerning.
Ymddreliad, *s. m.* (dreliad) A rendering one's self churlish or boorish.
Ymddreliaw, *v. a.* (dreliaw) To render one's self churlish, froward or surly; to abuse mutually.
Ymddringaw, *v. a.* (dringaw) To use one's self to climb; to be climbing.
Ymddrychiad, *s. m.* (drychiad) A self-appearing.
Ymddrychiawl, *a.* (drychiawl) Self-apparent.
Ymddrychioli, *v. a.* (ymddrychiawl) To make one's self apparent; to become apparent.
Ymddrychioliad, *s. m.* (ymddrychiawl) A making one's self apparent; a becoming apparent.
Ymddrychu, *v. a.* (drychu) To make one's self to appear.

Ymddrygiad, *s. m.* (drygiad) A becoming bad.
Ymddrygu, *v. a.* (drygu) To become bad.
Ymddrylliad, *s. m.* (dryllied) A pulling one's self to pieces.
Ymddrylliaw, *v. a.* (dryllaw) To pull one's self to pieces; to pull to pieces mutually.
Ymdduad, *s. m.* (duad) A blackening one's self.
Ymdduaw, *v. a.* (duaw) To blacken one's self.
Ymdduchan, *s. f.* (duchan) A mutual lampoon.
Ymdduchanawl, *a.* (ymdduchan) Mutually jeering.
Ymdduchaniad, *s. m.* (ymdduchan) A mutually lampooning; a using one's self to scoff.
Ymdduchanu, *v.* (ymdduchan) To scoff mutually.

Ei swydd—
Fu ymdduchanu a chant.

His employment was *to lampoon mutually* with a hundred. [illegible]

Ymdduliad, *s. m.* (duliad) A self-beating; a mutually beating or thumping.
Ymdduliaw, *v. a.* (duliaw) To beat one's self; to beat mutually.
Ymddulliad, *s. m.* (dulliad) A self-modification; a mutually modifying.
Ymddulliaw, *v. a.* (dulliaw) To shape one's self; to modify mutually, to shape mutually.
Ymddwlw, *s. m.* (dwlw) A fancying one's self. *v. a.* To fancy in one's self.
Ymddwyn, *s. m.* (dwyn) A self comportment; gestation. *v. a.* To bear, comport, or demean one's self; to bear, or go with young.

Hwyra' tâl tâl ymddwyn.

The latest recompence is the recompence of *deportment*. *Adage.*

Ymddwyre, *s. m.* (dwyre) A self-elevation. *v. a.* To elevate one's self.
Ymddwyrëad, *s. m.* (ymddwyre) A self-elevating.
Ymddyben, *s. m.* (dyben) Mutual conclusion; self-conclusion.
Ymddybenawl, *a.* (ymddyben) Mutually conclusive; self-concluding.
Ymddybeniad, *s. m.* (ymddyben) A mutually concluding; self-concluding.
Ymddybenu, *v. a.* (ymddyben) To end mutually; to conclude with one's self.
Ymddyberi, *v. a.* (dyberi) To be self-ceasing.
Ymddybleidiad, *s. m.* (dybleidiad) A connecting one's self with a party.
Ymddybleidiaw, *v. a.* (dybleidiaw) To connect one's self with a party; to be mutually espousing a party.
Ymddybleidiawl, *a.* (dybleidiawl) Being mutually espousing a party.
Ymddyblygiad, *s. m.* (dyblygiad) A self-bending; a mutually bending or folding.
Ymddyblygu, *v. a.* (dyblygu) To be doubling one's self; to be mutually bending.
Ymddyborthi, *v. a.* (dyborthi) To self-support.
Ymddyborthiad, *s. m.* (dyborthiad) Self-supportation.
Ymddychryniad, *s. m.* (dychryniad) A frightening one's self.
Ymddychrynu, *v. a.* (dychrynu) To self-frighten.
Ymddychwedliad, *s. m.* (dychwedliad) A being in mutual discourse.
Ymddychwedlu, *v. a.* (dychwedlu) To converse mutually.
Ymddychweliad, *s. m.* (dychweliad) A self-turning; a self-conversion; a mutually returning.
Ymddychwelyd, *v. a.* (dychwelyd) To self-turn; to self-convert; to turn back mutually.

Ymddyddan, *s. m.—pl. t.* ion (dyddan) A conversation. *v. a.* To converse or to discourse together.

> Mae ymddyddanion drwg yn llygru moesau da.
>
> Evil *communications* corrupt good manners. *Adage.*

> Nid cerddgar ond ymddyddangar;
> Nid ymddyddan ond am Dduw.
>
> None so informed as the conversible person; no *conversation* like that concerning God. *Adage.*

Ymddyddanaidd, *a.* (ymddyddan) Communicative

Ymddyddanawl, *a.* (ymddyddan) Discoursing.

Ymddyddangar, *a.* (ymddyddan) Apt of discourse.

Ymddyddaniad, *s. m.* (ymddyddan) A conversing.

Ymddyddanu, *v. a.* (ymddyddan) To converse.

Ymddyddanwr, *s. m.—pl.* ymddyddanwyr (ymddyddan—gwr) A converser, a discourser.

Ymddyeithrad, *s. m.* (dyeithrad) A self-estranging; a mutually estranging.

Ymddyeithraw, *v. a.* (dyeithraw) To self-estrange, to estrange mutually.

Ymddyfaliad, *s. m.* (dyfaliad) A being guessing or figuring to one's self.

Ymddyfalu, *v. a.* (dyfalu) To be guessing or describing to one's self.

> Ymddyfalu a gwrandaw ar gierwriaeth orwag, ac ofergerdd i leiau synwyr.
>
> *To be amusing one's self* and listening to frivolous minstrelsy and vain song to weaken the understanding. *Damegion.*

> Ymddyfalu meddw folaid;
> Son yn ffraeth am gwrw Sanffraid.
>
> *To imagine in one's self* a drunken panegyric: eloquently to talk of the ale of Santffraid. *D. ab Gwilym.*

Ymddyfeisiad, *s. m.* (dyfeisiad) A being imagining; a mutually devising.

Ymddyfeisiaw, *v. a.* (dyfeisiaw) To be imagining in one's self; to devise mutually.

Ymddyfetha, *v. a.* (dyfetha) To destroy mutually; to destroy one's self.

Ymddyfethiad, *s. m.* (dyfethiad) A mutually destroying; a self-destroying.

Ymddyfniad, *s. m.* (dyfniad) A becoming used.

Ymddyfnu, *v. a.* (dyfnu) To use one's self.

Ymddyfoliad, *s. m.* (dyfoliad) A being gorging one's self; a being mutually swelling.

Ymddyfoliaw, *v. a.* (dyfoliaw) To be gorging one's self; to be mutually gorging.

Ymddyfrysiad, *s. m.* (dyfrysiad) A being hurrying one's self; a being mutually hurrying.

Ymddyfrysiaw, *v. a.* (dyfrysiaw) To be hurrying one's self; to be mutually hurrying.

Ymddyfustlaw, *v. a.* (dy—bustlaw) To be mutually throwing out gall; to deal in mutual sarcasm.

> Am ddau ystlys dwfr dofn afon
> Ymddyfustlynt gynt gymrodeion;
> Ymddyfustlai lew ar lan Aeron berth,
> Pan borthes eryron.
>
> About the two sides of the stream of a deep river, comrades formerly were *dealing gall to one another*; then a lion would be *throwing out bitterness* on the banks of fair Aeron, when he fed the eagles. *Cynddelw, i H. ab Owain.*

Ymddyfustliad, *s. m.* (bustliad) A being mutually throwing out gall or sarcasm.

Ymddyfyniad, *s. m.* (dyfyniad) A self-approximating, a self-summoning; a mutually approximating.

Ymddyfynu, *v. a.* (dyfynu) To self-approximate; to self-summon; to summon mutually.

> Ymddyfynwch fy amcanion diniwed o ogoneddu enw Duw.
>
> *Enquire within yourselves* as to my innocent intention of glorifying God. *S. Trefredyn.*

Ymddygeliad, *s. m.* (dygeliad) A being mutually concealing; a being self-concealing.

Ymddygelu, *v. a.* (dygelu) To be mutually concealing; to be self-concealing.

> Rhys wyf fi, heb ynteu, mab Tewdwr, arglwydd y cyfoeth hwn o fewn ychydig, ac yr awron yn wrthladedig, ac yn ffoedig, ac yn ddifancedig haiach ydd wyf yn ymddygelu yn y noddfa hon.
>
> I am Rhys, replied he, the son of Tewdwr, the sovereign of this country a little while ago, but now expelled, and fleeing, being almost perishing, I am *concealing myself* in this sanctuary. *Hanes Gr. ab Cynan.*

Ymddygawl, *a.* (dygawl) Self-deporting; mutually deporting.

Ymddygiad, *s. m.—pl. t.* au (dygiad) Self-deportment; behaviour, deportment, demeanour.

Ymddygiadus, *a.* (ymddygiad) Relating to self-deportment or demeanour.

Ymddygnawl, *a.* (dygnawl) Self-tormenting.

Ymddygniad, *s. m.* (dygniad) A self-tormenting; a mutually tormenting.

Ymddygnu, *v. a.* (dygnu) To torment or to harrass one's self; to toil mutually.

Ymddygoddi, *v. a.* (dygoddi) To be mutually vexing; to be vexing one's self.

Ymddygoddiad, *s. m.* (dygoddiad) A mutually vexing; a vexing one's self.

Ymddygrymiad, *s. m.* (dygrymiad) A being bowing one's self; a being mutually bowing.

Ymddygrymu, *v. a.* (dygrymu) To be self-bowing; to be mutually bowing.

Ymddygrynöad, *s. m.* (dygrynöad) A being collecting one's self; a being mutually collecting.

Ymddygrynöi, *v. a.* (dygrynöi) To be self-collecting; to be mutually collecting.

Ymddygrysiad, *s. m.* (dygrysiad) A being hastening one's self; a being mutually hastening.

Ymddygrysiaw, *v. a.* (dygrysiaw) To be self-hastening; to be mutually hastening.

Ymddyguddiad, *s. m.* (dyguddiad) A being self-hiding; a being mutually hiding.

Ymddyguddiaw, *v. a.* (dyguddiaw) To be self-hiding; to be mutually hiding.

Ymddyguraw, *v. a.* (dyguraw) To be beating mutually; to be beating one's self.

Ymddyguriad, *s. m.* (dyguriad) A being mutually beating; a being beating one's self.

Ymddygwd, *s. m.* (dygwd) A self-striving. *v. a.* To employ one's self in toil; to be toiling.

Ymddygwydd, *s. m.* (dygwydd) A mutual befalling

Ymddygwyddaw, *v. a.* (ymddygwydd) To befal mutually; to be happening.

Ymddygwyddawl, *a.* (dygwydd) Mutually falling.

Ymddygwyddiad, *s. m.* (ymddygwydd) A mutually befalling.

Ymddygwympaw, *v. a.* dygwympaw) To be mutually falling; to be self-falling.

Ymddygychwyn, *v. a.* (dygychwyn) To be mutually starting off; to be starting one's self.

Ymddygychwyniad, *s. m.* (ymddygychwyn) A being mutually starting; a being starting one's self

Ymddygyd, *s. m.* (dygyd) Deportment. *v. a.* To demean one's self, to conduct one's self; to bear or go with young.

> Mab Owain, gyfwyrain gwddwg,
> Mad ganed, mad fam a'i hymddwg.
>
> The son of Owain, of uprising tempest, fortunately was he born, fortunate the mother who bore him. *Ll. P. Moch.*

Ymddygyfeiriad, *s. m.* (dygyfeiriad) A mutually coming in opposition.

Ymddygyfeiriaw, *v. a.* (dygyfeiriaw) To be coming mutually in opposition.

Ymddygyfiad, *s. m.* (dygyfiad) A being mutually combining or becoming equal.

Ymddygyfiaw, *v. a.* (dygyfiaw) To be combining mutually.

Ymddygyfranc, *s. m.* (dygyfranc) A mutual intercourse. *v. a.* To have mutual intercourse.

Ymddygyffröad, *s. m.* (dygyffröad) A being self-agitating; a being mutually agitating.

Ymddygyffroi, *v. a.* (dygyffroi) To be self-agitating; to be mutually agitating.

Ymddygylchiad, *s. m.* (dygylchiad) A being mutually surrounding; a being surrounding one's self.

Ymddygylchu, *v. a.* (dygylchu) To be mutually surrounding; to be self-surrounding.

Ymddygymhell, *v. a.* (dygymhell) To be mutually instigating, to be self-instigating.

Ymddygymhelliad, *s. m.* (ymddygymhell) A being mutually instigating; a being putting one's self forward.

Ymddygymmod, *s. m.* (dygymmod) Self-reconciliation; a mutual reconciliation.

Ymddygymmodi, *v. a.* (ymddygymmod) To be reconciling one's self; to be mutually reconciling.

Ymddygymmodiad, *s. m.* (ymddygymmod) A being reconciling one's self; a being mutually reconciling.

Ymddygymysgiad, *s. m.* (dygymysgiad) A being mutually mixing; a being mixing one's self.

Ymddygymysgu, *v. a.* (dygymysgu) To be mutually mixing; to be mixing one's self.

Ymddygynnal, *v. a* (dygynnal) To be self-supporting; to be mutually upholding.

Ymddygynnaliad, *s. m.* (ymddygynnal) A being self-supporting; a being mutually upholding.

Ymddygynnull, *s. m.* (dygynnull) A self-collecting, a mutual collection. *v. a.* To collect one's self; to collect together.

Ymddygynnulliad, *s. m.* (ymddygynnull) A being collecting one's self; a being mutually collecting.

Ymddygynnwys, *v. a.* (dygynnwys) To be mutually receiving or containing; to be containing one's self.

Ymddygynnwysiad, *s. m.* (ymddygynnwys) A being mutually receivng or containing; a being containing one's self.

Ymddygyrchawl, *a.* (dygyrch) Mutually resorting.

Ymddygyrchiad, *s. m.* (dygyrch) A being mutually resorting; to be resorting.

Ymddygyrchu, *v. a.* (dygyrchu) To be mutually resorting; to be resorting.

Ymddygysgodi, *v. a.* (dygysgodi) To be self-sheltering; to be mutually sheltering.

Ymddygysgodiad, *s. m.* (dygysgodiad) A being sheltering one's self; a being mutually sheltering.

Ymddygystuddiad, *s. m.* (dygystuddiad) A being self-afflicting; a being mutually afflicting.

Ymddygystuddiaw, *v. a.* (dygystuddiaw) To be self-afflicting; to be mutually aggrieving.

Ymddygythruddaw, *v. a.* (dygythruddaw) To be perturbating one's self; to be mutually perturbating.

Ymddygythruddiad, *s. m.* (dygythruddiad) A being perturbating one's self; a being mutually perturbating.

Ymddyhaeriad, *s. m.* (dyhaeriad) A being mutually asserting; a being asserting one's self.

Ymddyhaeru, *v. a.* (dyhaeru) To be mutually asserting; to be asserting one's self.

Ymddyhebu, *v. a.* (dyhebu) To be self-divesting.

Tri nod cywir sydd ar ddyn i ddiawl, ac nis gall ymddyhebu ag hwynt: ei air, ei olwg, a'i ymmod.

There are three certain marks on a person who belongs to the devil, and he cannot *divest himself* of them: his word, his look, and his deportment. *Catwg ab Gwynlliw.*

Ymddyheuad, *s. m.* (dyheuad) A making one's self to pant; a mutually panting.

Ymddyheuaw, *v. a.* (dyheuaw) To make one's self to pant; to pant mutually.

Ymddyhewydiad, *s. m.* (dyhewydiad) A fixing a mutual affection or devotion; a devoting one's self; a self-resolving.

Ymddyhewydiaw, *v. a.* (dyhewydiaw) To fix a mutual affection; to devote one's self.

Ymddyhiraw, *v. a.* (dyhiraw) To use one's self to linger; to linger or to loiter mutually.

Ymddyhiriad, *s. m.* (dyhiriad) A using one's self to linger; a mutually lingering.

Ymddyholi, *v. a.* (dyholi) To be mutually questioning; to be questioning one's self.

Ymddyholiad, *s. m.* (dyholiad) A being mutually questioning; a being questioning one's self.

Ymddyhuddaw, *v. a.* (dyhuddaw) To be covering one's self; to be covering mutually; to appease one's self; to be mutually quieted.

Ymddyhuddiad, *s. m.* (dyhuddiad) A being covering one's self; a being mutually covering; a quieting one's self; a mutually appeasing.

Ymddyhysbyddiad, *s. m.* (dyhysbyddiad) A being mutually exhausting; a being self-exhausting.

Ymddyhysbyddu, *v. a.* (dyhysbyddu) To be mutually exhausting; to be self-exhausting.

Ymddylamiad, *s. m.* (dylamiad) A being self-rebounding; a being mutually rebounding.

Ymddylamu, *v. a.* (dylamu) To be self rebounding; to be mutually rebounding.

Ymddylathriad, *s. m.* (dylathriad) A being rendering one's self glittering.

Ymddylathru, *v. a.* (dylathru) To be making one's self to glitter.

Ymddylenwad, *s. m.* (dylenwad) A being filling one's self; a being mutually filling.

Ymddylenwi, *v. a.* (dylenwi) To be filling one's self; to be mutually filling or replenishing.

Ymddylifad, *s. m.* (dylifad) A being mutually flowing; a self-flowing.

Ymddylifaw, *v. a.* (dylifaw) To be mutually flowing; to be self flowing.

Ymddylochi, *v. a.* (dylochi) To protect mutually; to protect one's self.

Ymddylochiad, *s. m.* (dylochiad) A protecting mutually; a protecting one's self.

Ymddyludaw, *v. a.* (dyludaw) To employ one's self in pursuing; to adhere mutually.

Ymddyludiad, *s. m.* (dyludiad) A self adhering; a mutually adhering.

Ymddyluniad, *s. m.* (dyluniad) A self-delineation; a mutually delineating.

Ymddyluniaw, *v. a.* (dyluniaw) To delineate one's self; to delineate mutually.

Ymddylusgaw, *v. a.* (dylusgaw) To be dragging one's self; to be mutually dragging.

Ymddylusgiad, *s. m.* (dylusgiad) A being dragging one's self; a being mutually dragging.

Ymddylŷad, *s. m.* (dylŷad) A being mutually obliged; a rendering one's self obligatory.

Ymddylŷaw, *v. a.* (dylŷaw) To be mutually obligatory; to render one's self obligatory.

Ymddylyniad, *s. m.* (dylyniad) A being mutually adhering; a causing one's self to adhere.

Ymddylynu, *v. a.* (dylynu) To be mutually adhering; to cause one's self to adhere.

Ymddylliad, *s. m.* (dylliad) A mutually overshadowing; a self-overwhelming; a looking frowningly.

Ymddyllu, *v. a.* (dyllu) To overshadow mutually;

to overshadow one's self; to look frowningly; to stare with a stern look.

> Dygryswys Ffamddwys yn bedwarllu,
> Goddeu a Rheged i ymddyllu.
>
> Fflamddwys hastened with four hosts, Goddeu and Rheged to *overwhelm*. *Taliesin.*

Ymddyllyngiad, *s. m.* (dyllyngiad) A being self-loosening; a being mutually liberating.

Ymddyllyngiaw, *v. a.* (dyllyngiaw) To be self-loosening; to be mutually loosening.

Ymddynesâad, *s. m.* (dynesâad) A being self-approximating; a being mutually approximating.

Ymddynesâu, *v. a.* (dynesâu) To be self-approximating; to be mutually approximating.

Ymddynesiad, *s. m.* (dynesiad) A self-approaching; a being mutually approaching.

Ymddynesu, *v. a.* (dynesu) To be drawing one's self near; to be mutually approaching.

Ymddynoethi, *v. a.* (dynoethi) To be self-denuding; to be mutually denuding.

> Ymddynoethaist i arall heb fy llaw i.
>
> *Thou hast discovered thyself* to another besides me. *Esay lvii 8.*

Ymddynoethiad, *s. m.* (dynoethiad) A being denuding or exposing one's self; a being mutually making naked.

Ymddynwared, *s. m.* (dynwared) A being as a mimick. *v. a.* To be mimicking; to be mimicking one another.

Ymddynwarediad, *s. m.* (ymddynwared) A being employing one's self in mimickry; a being mutually mimicking.

Ymddŷoddef, *v. a.* (dŷoddef) To be self-suffering; to be mutually suffering.

Ymddŷoddefiad, *s. m.* (ymddŷoddef) A being self-suffering; a being mutually suffering.

Ymddŷodden, *v. a.* (dŷodden) To be bearing one's self; to be mutually bearing.

> Bydd gydymaith glorwaith glan;
> Ymddyodda'n well ymddyddan.
>
> Be a true companion of lucid speech; *accommodate thyself* better to discourse. *D. ab Gwilym, i'r bercud.*

Ymddŷosg, *s. m.* (dŷosg) A self-disarraying.

Ymddŷosgi, *v. a.* (dŷosg) To undress one's self.

Ymddŷosgiad, *s. m.* (ymddŷosg) An undressing or disarraying of one's self.

Ymddyrchafael, *s. m.* (dyrchafael) A self-exalting. *v. a.* To exalt one's self; to exalt mutually.

> Y mab hwnw, wedi ymddyrchafael, ymroddi a orug yn ngodineb.
>
> That youth after *exalting himself*, gave himself up to adultery. *Gr. ab Arthur.*

Ymddyrchafiad, *s. m* (dyrchafiad) A self-exalting; a mutually exalting.

Ymddyrchafiaeth, *s. m.* (dyrchafiaeth) Self-exaltation; self-advancement; mutual exaltation.

Ymddyrchafu, *v. a.* (dyrchafu) To exalt one's self; to exalt or to advance mutually.

Ymddyrchafwr, *s. m.*--*pl.* ymddyrchafwyr (dyrchafwr) One who exalts himself.

Ymddyrchawl, *a.* (dyrchawl) Raising one's self.

Ymddyrchiad, *s. m.* (dyrchiad) A self raising.

Ymddyrchu, *v. a.* (dyrchu) To uplift one's self.

Ymddyrnodiad, *s. m.* (dyrnodiad) A mutually boxing; a beating one's self.

Ymddyrnodiaw, *v. a.* (dyrnodiaw) To box one another; to thump one's self.

Ymddyröad, *s. m.* (dyröad) A being self-yielding

Ymddyröi, *v. a.* (dyröi) To be yielding one's self.

> Yn wrol i'th fabolaeth
> Ymddyro'n Gymmro, nid gwaeth.
>
> Manfully through the time of thy youth *be passing thyself* as a Welshman, and no worse will come. *I. Tew Brydydd Ieuanc.*

Ymddyrwyddaw, *v. a.* (dyrwyddaw) To be facilitating one's self.

Ymddyrwyddiad, *s. m.* (dyrwyddiad) A being facilitating one's self.

Ymddyrwyn, *s. m.* (dyrwyn) A self-winding. *v. a.* To wind one's self; to wind up mutually.

Ymddyrwyniad, *s. m.* (ymddyrwyn) A winding of one's self; a mutually winding up.

Ymddyrysiad, *s. m.* (dyrysiad) A self-entangling; a mutually entangling.

Ymddyrysu, *v. a.* (dyrysu) To entangle one's self to entangle mutually.

> Dichell a ymddyrysa yn ei chroglath ei hunan.
>
> Craft will *entangle herself* in her own snare. *Adage.*

Ymddysbwyll, *s. m.* (dysbwyll) Self-consideration. *v. a.* To examine one's self.

> Goreu gwaith synwyr ymddysbwyll diffuant.
>
> The best act of the sense is undisguised *examination of one's self.* *Catwg Ddoeth.*

Ymddysbwylliad, *s. m.*—*pl. t.* au (ymddysbwyll) A considering one's self.

Ymddysbyddiad, *s. m.* (dysbyddiad) A self-depletion.

Ymddysbyddu, *v. a.* (dysbyddu) To empty one's self.

Ymddysgleiriad, *s. m.* (dysgleiriad) A making one's self to shine; a mutually glittering.

Ymddysgleiriaw, *v. a.* (dysgleiriaw) To make one's self to glitter; to glitter mutually.

Ymddysgiad, *s. m.* (dysgiad) A self-instructing; a mutually instructing.

Ymddysgori, *v. a.* (dysgori) To clamour mutually; to be clamouring.

Ymddysgoriad, *s. m.* (dysgoriad) A clamouring mutually; a keeping a clamour.

Ymddysgu, *v. a.* (dysgu) To instruct one's self; to instruct mutually.

Ymddysgwyl, *s. m.* (dysgwyl) A keeping one's self in expectation. *v. a.* To keep one's self expecting; to expect mutually.

Ymddysgwylgar, *a.* (ymddysgwyl) Apt to keep one's self expecting; mutually looking.

Ymddysgwyliad, *s. m.* (ymddysgwyl) A keeping one's self expecting; a mutually expecting.

Ymddysgyriad, *s. m.* (dysgyriad) A keeping one's self in screaming.

Ymddysgyriaw, *v. a.* (dysgyriaw) To scream mutually; to keep one's self in screaming.

Ymddystawiad, *s. m.* (dystawiad) A mutually silencing; a making one's self silent.

Ymddystewi, *v. a.* (dystewi) To become mutually silent; to make one's self silent.

Ymddŷunaw, *v. a.* (dŷunaw) To unite one's self; to unite together, to confederate.

Ymddŷuniad, *s. m.* (dŷuniad) A connecting one's self; a mutually uniting.

Ymddywadiad, *s. m.* (dywadiad) A being mutually denying; a being denying one's self.

Ymddywadu, *v. a.* (dywadu) To be mutually denying; to be denying one's self.

Ymddywalâad, *s. m.* (dywalâad) A mutually enraging; a making one's self furious.

Ymddywalâu, *v. a.* (dywalâu) To enrage mutually; to render one's self furious.

Ymddywasgiad, *s. m.* (dywasgiad) Self-compression; a being mutually squeezing.

Ymddywasgu, *v. a.* (dywasgu) To self-compress; to be mutually squeezing.

Ymddywediad, *s. m.* (dywediad) A mutually speaking; a keeping one's self speaking.

Ymddywedyd, *v. a.* (dywedyd) To speak mutually; to employ one's self in speaking.

> Gwedi darfo eistedd yn gyfreithiawl, yna y mae iawn i'r ygnad ddywedyd wrth y ddwy blaid, Ymddywedwch o gyfraith weithon.
>
> When the court shall be lawfully sitting, then it is right for the judge to say to the two parties, *now do you mutually speak* of law. *Welsh Laws.*

Ymddyweddïad, *s. m.* (dyweddïad) A mutually espousing; a coupling one's self.

Ymddyweddïaw, *v. a.* (dyweddïaw) To espouse mutually; to become wedded or espoused; to yoke or join one's self.

> Gwrtheyrn Gwrthenau a ymddyweddïas a Rhonwen ferch Hors.
>
> Vortigern with Repulsive Lips *yoked himself* with Rhonwen the daughter of Hors. *Trioedd.*

Ymddywisgaw, *v. a.* (dywisgaw) To be dressing one's self; to be mutually arraying.

Ymddywisgiad, *s. m.* (dywisgiad) A being dressing one's self; a being mutually arraying.

Ymddywyn, *s. m.* (dywyn) A mutual blessing; a self-blessing. *v. a.* To bless mutually; to render one's self blessed.

> O treinc mab dyn heb ymddywyn a Duw.—
>
> If a son of man shall depart without *sanctifying himself* of God.— *Elaeth.*

Ymddywynaw, *v. a.* (ymddywyn) To devote, to consecrate; to pay a vow.

Ymddywyniad, *s. m.* (ymddywyn) A mutually blessing; a consecrating or blessing one's self.

Ymddywynygu, *v. a.* (dywynygu) To appear resplendent.

> Ni thâl dim lle nad ymddywynyco ynddo ryw grynodeb.
>
> What there *doth* not *appear conspicuous* in it some connection is good for nothing. *Cattwg Ddoeth.*

Ymddywystlaw, *v. a.* (dywystlaw) To be mutually pledging; to be giving one's self a hostage.

Ymddywystliad, *s. m.* (dywystliad) A being mutually pledging; a being pledging or giving one's self as a hostage.

Ymëangiad, *s. m.* (ëangiad) A self-amplifying; a mutually giving space.

Ymëangu, *v. a.* (ëangu) To self-amplify; to enlarge mutually.

Ymebrwyddaw, *v. a.* (ebrwyddaw) To accelerate one's self.

Ymebrwyddiad, *s. m.* (ebrwyddiad) A self-accelerating; a mutually hastening.

Ymechrydiad, *s. m.* (echrydiad) A causing one's self to tremble; a mutually quaking.

Ymechrydu, *v. a.* (echrydu) To cause one's self to tremble; to tremble mutually.

Ymechrysiad, *s. m.* (echrysiad) A causing a mutual shock or terror; a rendering one's self shocking.

Ymechrysu, *v. a.* (echrysu) To cause mutual horror; to be self shocked.

Ymechwyna, *v. a.* (echwyna) To borrow or to lend mutually; to lend one's self.

Ymechwyniad, *s. m.* (echwyniad) A mutually lending; a lending one's self.

Ymedfryd, *s. m.* (edfryd) Self-restoration. *v. a.* To restore one's self, to renew one's self.

Ymedliw, *s. m.* (edliw) Mutual reproach; self-reproach.

Ymedliwiad, *s. m.* (edliw) A mutually reproaching; a self-upbraiding.

Ymedliwiaw, *v. a.* (ymedliw) To reproach mutually, to upbraid one's self.

Ymedliwied, *v. a.* (ymedliw) To upbraid mutually; to upbraid one's self.

Ymedrych, *s. m.* (edrych) To look mutually; to look at one's self.

Ymedrychgar, *a.* (ymedrych) Being apt to look about warily.

Ymedrychiad, *s. m.* (ymedrych) A mutually looking; a looking at one's self.

Ymedryd, *s. m.* (edryd) Self-restoration; mutual restoration. *v. a.* To restore one's self; to restore mutually.

Ymedrydiad, *s. m.* (ymedryd) Self-restoration; mutual restoration.

Ymegluräad, *s. m.* (egluräad) Self-manifestation; mutual illustration or manifestation.

Ymegluràu, *v. a.* (egluràu) To manifest one's self; to be mutually manifest.

Ymegluraw, *v. a.* (egluraw) To explain one's self; to explain mutually.

Ymegluriad, *s. m.* (egluriad) A self-explaining; a mutually explaining.

Ymegnïad, *s. m.* (egnïad) A self-exertion; mutual exertion.

Ymegnïaw, *v. a.* (egnïaw) To exert one's self; to exert mutually.

Ymegnïawl, *a.* (egnïawl) Self-exerting; of mutual exertion.

Ymegnïwr, *s. m.*—*pl.* ymegnïwyr (egnïwr) One who exerts himself.

Ymegori, *v. a.* (egori) To open one's self; to open mutually.

Ymegoriad, *s. m.* (egoriad) A disclosing one's self; a mutually opening.

Ymegwyddori, *v. a.* (egwyddori) To furnish one's self with principles or elements; mutually to instil principles.

Ymegwyddoriad, *s. m.* (egwyddoriad) A furnishing one's self with principles; a mutually instilling principles.

Ymehedeg, *v. a.* (ehedeg) To make one's self to fly; to fly mutually.

Ymehediad, *s. m.* (ehediad) A making one's self to fly; a mutually flying.

Ymeiddilaw, *v. a.* (eiddilaw) To diminish one's self; to enervate one's self.

Ymeiddiliad, *s. m.* (eiddiliad) Self-enervation.

Ymeiddunaw, *v. a.* (eiddunaw) To employ one's self in wishing; to wish mutually.

Ymeidduniad, *s. m.* (eidduniad) An employing one's self in wishing; a mutually wishing.

Ymeilliad, *s. m.* (eilliad) A shaving one's self.

Ymeilliaw, *v. a.* (eilliaw) To shave one's self.

> Ymfoela ac ymeillia am dy blant moethus.
>
> Make thee bald and *poll thee* for thy delicate children. *Micah* i. 16.

Ymeirgar, *a.* (geirgar) Querulous; loquacious.

Ymeirgarwch, *s. m.* (ymeirgar) A cavilling disposition.

Ymeiriach, *s. m.* (eiriach) A mutual deprecation. *v. a.* To deprecate mutually; to be deprecating.

Ymeiriad, *s. m.* (geiriad) Altercation; mutual war of words.

Ymeiriaw, *v. a.* (geiriaw) To contend in words.

Ymeiriawl, *a.* (eiriawl) An employing of one's self in interceding; mutual persuasion. *v. a.* To employ one's self in interceding; mutually to intercede.

> Uffern—
> Yny mae mawrwae heb ymeiriawl.
>
> Hell: in it there is extreme of woe without *intercession*. *Bleddyn Fardd.*

Ymeiriolad, *s. m.* (ymeiriawl) A mutual intercession; a mutual persuasion.

Ymeirioli, *v. a.* (ymeiriawl) To intercede mutually; to be interceding or persuading.

Ymeiriwr, *s. m.—pl.* ymeirwyr (ymeiriaw—gwr) A talkative man.

> Nid mynych gwr mawr ymeiriwr.
>
> A *talker* is seldom a great man. *Adage.*

Ymeisiwaw, *v. a.* (eisiwaw) A making one's self destitute; mutually to make destitute.

Ymeisiwiad, *s. m.* (eisiwiad) A rendering one's self destitute; a mutually making destitute.

Ymeistedd, *s. m.* (eistedd) A mutual sitting; a seating one's self. *v. a.* To sit mutually; to seat one's self.

Ymeisteddiad, *s. m.* (ymeistedd) A mutually sitting; a seating one's self.

Ymelïad, *s. m.* (elïad) An anointing one's self.

Ymelïaw, *v. a.* (elïaw) To annoint one's self.

Ymelwa, *v. a.* (elwa) To seek self-profit; mutually to seek gain.

Ymelwad, *s. m.* (elwad) The employing one's self in seeking gain.

Ymelwain, *v. a.* (gelwain) To keep calling.

Ymen, *s. m.* (en) That is contained, pent, or dammed up. *a.* Being collected together.

> Gwnai man y delai na myn doll gwin,
> Mwy no dwfr melin ymen Deifi.
>
> He would cause where he might come that he should not lack wine, more than the water of the mill of *where there is a dam of* Teivi. *Madawg Dwygraig.*

Ymeniwed, *s. m.* (eniwed) A self-hurting; a mutual hurting.

Ymeniwaw, *v. a.* (eniwaw) To hurt one's self; to cause mutual harm.

Ymenllibiad, *s. m.* (enllibiad) A mutually detracting; a self-scandalizing.

Ymenllibiaw, *v. a.* (enllibiaw) To detract mutually; to scandalize one's self.

Ymennyliad, *s. m.* (annellad) A taking aim.

Ymennylu, *v. a.* (annelu) To employ one's self in aiming.

> Y seren——
> Minnau oedd yn ymennyl.
>
> The star, I too was *employing myself in viewing*. *Iolo Goch.*

Ymennyn, *s. m.* (ennyn) A self-kindling. *v. a.* To self-kindle, to kindle mutually.

Ymennyniad, *s. m.* (ennyniad) A self-kindling, a mutually kindling.

Ymennynu, *v. a.* (ennynu) To self-kindle; to kindle mutually.

Ymenwad, *s. m.* (enwad) Self-nomination; a mutual naming.

Ymenwaediad, *s. m.* (enwaediad) A self-circumcising.

Ymenwaedu, *v. a* (enwaedu) To self-circumcise.

Ymenwi, *v. a.* (enwi) To self nominate, to nominate mutually.

Ymenwogi, *v. a.* (enwogi) To signalize one's self

Ymenwogiad, *s. m* (enwogiad) A self-signalizing

Ymenydd, *s. m.—pl t.* au (ym—enydd) The brain.

Ymenyddawl, *a.* (ymenydd) Belonging to the brain

Ymenydd-dro, *s. m.* (ymenydd—tro) A vertigo.

Ymenyddiad, *s. m.* (ymenydd) A braining.

Ymenyddu, *v. a.* (ymennydd) To form brains.

Ymenyn, *s. m.—pl. t.* au (ymen) Butter.

> Tri enllyn iechyd mel, ymenyn, a llaeth.
>
> The three sauces of health honey, *butter*, and milk *Adage.*

Ymenynaidd, *a.* (ymenyn) Like butter.

Ymenynawl, *a.* (ymenyn) Of buttery nature.

Ymenyneiddiad, *s. m.* (ymenynaidd) A rendering like butter; a becoming like butter.

Ymenyneiddiaw, *v. a.* (ymenynaidd) To render like butter; to become like butter.

Ymenyniad, *s. m.* (ymenyn) A buttering.

Ymenynllyd, *a.* (ymenyn) Full of butter.

Ymenynu, *v. a.* (ymenyn) To form butter.

Ymëofni, *v. a.* (ëofni) To self-embolden; mutually to embolden.

Ymëofniad, *s. m.* (ymëofni) A making one's self bold; a mutually emboldening.

Ymëoni, *v. a.* (ëoni) To embolden one's self; to embolden mutually.

Ymëoniad, *s. m.* (ëoniad) A self-emboldening; a mutually emboldening.

Ymeppiliad, *s. m.* (eppiliad) A self-producing.

Ymeppiliaw, *v. a.* (eppiliaw) To self-produce.

Ymerbyn, *s. m.* (erbyn) The being in opposition or ready to receive. *v. a.* To be in opposition; to receive mutually.

> Ydd oedd ymerbyn heb ysarbed.
>
> There was a *mutual encounter* without self sparing. *Cynddelw.*
>
> Ffoes Octa—hyd i Gaer Efrawc, at Oen ei gefnderw; a rhan arall i Gaer Alclwyd, ac yno ymerbyn ag Emrys.
>
> Octa fled as far as the city of York, to Osa his cousin; and another division to the city of Alclwyd, and there *putting himself in opposition* to Emrys. *Gr. ab Arthur.*

Ymerbyniad, *s. m.* (ymerbyn) One who employs himself in receiving; one who is in opposition; one mutually in opposition.

> Cad ymerbyniaid enaid dichwant.
>
> The *mutual opponents* of battle regardless of life. *O. Cyfeiliawg.*

Ymerbyniaw, *v. a.* (ymerbyn) To put one's self to receive or in apposition; to receive mutually

Ymerbyniawl, *a.* (ymerbyn) Being in receiving.

Ymerbynied, *v. a.* (ymerbyn) To put one's self to receive or in apposition; to receive mutually

Ymerbyniwr, *s. m.—pl.* ymerbynwyr (ymerbyn—gwr) One who employs himself in receiving; one who places himself in apposition; a mutual receiver.

Ymerfyniad, *s. m.* (erfyniad) A being requesting or intreating; a mutually intreating.

Ymerfyniaw, *v. a.* (erfyniaw) To be requesting; to request mutually.

Ymergydiad, *s. m.* (ergydiad) A self-projecting; a mutually projecting or casting.

Ymergydiaw, *v. a.* (ergydiaw) To project one's self; to project mutually.

Ymerlid, *s. m.* (erlid) The employing one's self in pursuing; mutual persecution.

Ymerlidiad, *s. m.* (ymerlid) An employing one's self in pursuing or persecuting; a mutually persecuting.

Ymerlyn, *v. a.* (erlyn) To employ one's self in pursuing; to pursue mutually.

Ymerlyniad, *s. m.* (ymerlyn) An employing one's self in pursuing; a mutually pursuing.

Ymerlynwr, *s. m.—pl.* ymerlynwyr (ymerlyn—gwr) One who employs himself in pursuing; a mutual pursuer.

Ymerlynydd, *s. m.—pl. t.* ion (ymerlyn) One who employs himself in pursuing; one who pursues mutually.

Ymerthu, *v. a.* (erthu) To strive together.

Ymerwinad, *s. m* (gerwinad) A self-exasperation; a mutually ruffling.

Ymerwinaw, *v. a.* (gerwinaw) To ruffle one's self; to exasperate mutually.

Ymerwinawl, *a.* (gerwinawl) Self-ruffling, mutually exasperating.

Ymesgar, *s. m.* (esgar) A self-separation; mutual separation. *v. a.* To separate one's self; to separate mutually.

Ymesgariad, s. m. (ymesgar) A separating one's self; a mutually separating.
Ymesgaru, v. a. (ymesgar) To separate one's self; to separate mutually.
Ymesgeulusaw, v. a. (esgeulusaw) To make one's self neglectful; to neglect mutually.
Ymesgeulusiad, s. m. (esgeulusiad) A causing one's self to neglect; a self-neglecting; a mutually neglecting.
Ymesgor, s. m. (esgor) The state of being delivered or brought to bed.
Ymesgori, v. a. (ymesgor) To be delivered.
Ymesgoriad, s. m. (ymesgor) A self-delivering.
Ymesgusodi, v. a. (esgusodi) To make excuse for one's self; to make a mutual excuse.
Ymesgyn, v. a. (esgyn) To cause one's self to ascend; to ascend mutually.
Ymesgyniad, s. m. (ymesgyn) A self-ascending; a mutually ascending.
Ymesmwythaw, v. a. (esmwythaw) To ease one's self; to relieve one's self.
Ymesmwythawl, a. (esmwythawl) Self-easing; tending to mutual ease.
Ymesmwythiad, s. m. (esmwythiad) A self-easing; a making mutually easy.
Ymestyn, s. m. (estyn) A self-stretching. v. a. To stretch one's self.
Ymestynawl, a. (ymestyn) Self-extending.
Ymestyniad, s. m. (ymestyn) A self-extending.
Ymethol, s. m. (ethol) Self-election; mutual election.
Ymetholi, v. a. (ymethol) To self-elect; mutually to elect.
Ymetholiad, s. m. (ymethol) A self-electing; a mutually electing.
Ymeuocâad, s. m. (euocâad) A making one's self guilty; a becoming mutually guilty.
Ymeuocâu, v. a. (euocâu) To make one's self guilty; to become mutually guilty.
Ymeuogi, v. a. (euogi) To make one's self guilty; to become mutually guilty.
Ymeuogiad, s. m. (euogiad) A making one's self guilty; a rendering mutually guilty.
Ymewinad, s. m. (ewinad) A using one's nails.
Ymewinaw, v. a. (ewinaw) To fasten one's nails.
Ymfachiad, s. m. (bachiad) A hooking one's self.
Ymfachu, v. a. (bachu) To hook one's self.
Ymfalchïad, s. m. (balchïad) A priding one's self.
Ymfalchïaw, v. a. (balchïaw) To be self-proud.

Pa hyd——
Yr ymfalchïant yn eu drwg,
Gan fygwth amlwg ffrostus!

How long will they pride themselves in their wickedness, with manifest and scornful threat! — *Edm. Prys, Ps. 94.*

Ymfanson, s. m. (manson) A muttering. v. a. To mutter to one's self.
Ymfarweiddiad, s. m. (marweiddiad) A deadening or mortifying one's self.
Ymfarweiddiaw, v. a. (marweiddiaw) To deaden one's self.
Ymfawdd, s. m. (bawdd) A self-drowning.
Ymfawrâad, s. m. (mawrâad) A self-magnifying; a magnifying mutually.
Ymfawrâu, v. a. (mawrâu) To self-magnify; to magnify mutually.
Ymfawrygiad, s. m. (mawrygiad) A magnifying one's self; a mutually magnifying.
Ymfawrygu, v. a. (mawrygu) To magnify one's self; to magnify mutually.
Ymfeiddiad, s. m. (beiddiad) A venturing one's self; a mutually daring.
Ymfeiddiaw, v. a. (beiddiaw) To venture one's self; to adventure, or dare mutually.

[illegible]
[illegible]

It is easy for every body to look thee in the face, for a gift, to presume for an answer. — [illegible]

Ymfelltithiaw, v. a. (melltithiaw) To self-curse; to curse mutually.
Ymfenwedigaw, v. a. (menwedigaw) To bless one's self; to bless mutually.
Ymfenwedigiad, s. m. (menwedigiad) A blessing one's self; a mutually blessing.
Ymfenwydaw, v. a. (menwydaw) To make one's self happy; to yield mutual happiness.
Ymfenwydiad, s. m. (menwydiad) A making one's self happy; a mutually giving happiness.
Ymfinial, v. a. (minial) To be mutually putting lips together; to kiss one another.
Ymfiniaw, v. a. (miniaw) Mutually to touch lips.
Ymflinaw, v. a. (blinaw) To tire one's self.

Yn awr nac ymflined neb
O'th wyniau am ddoethineb.

At present let no one trouble himself about the [illegible] wisdom. — [illegible]

Ymfliniad, s. m. (bliniad) A tiring one's self.
Ymfoddâad, s. m. (boddâad) A pleasing one's self.
Ymfoddâu, v. a. (boddâu) To please one's self.
Ymfoddiad, s. m. (boddiad) A contenting one's self; a mutually contenting.
Ymfoddiaw, v. a. (boddiaw) To content one's self; to yield mutual contentment.
Ymfoddloni, v. a. (boddloni) To make one's self contented; to rest contented; to acquiesce; to content mutually.
Ymfoddloniad, s. m. (boddloniad) A self-contenting; a mutually contenting.
Ymfoeli, v. a. (moeli) To make one's self bald.
Ymfolach, s. m. (molach) Self-flattery; mutual flattery or wheedling.
Ymfolachiad, s. m. (ymfolach) A flattering one's self; a mutually flattering.
Ymfolachu, v. a. (ymfolach) To self-flatter.
Ymfolachus, a. (ymfolach) Self-flattering; apt to flatter mutually.
Ymfolachwr, s. m. (ymfolach) One who flatters himself; a mutual flatterer.
Ymfoldesiad, s. m. (boldesiad) A basking one's self in the sun.
Ymfoldesu, v. a. (boldesu) To be basking one's self in the sun.
Ymfolheulaw, v. a. (bolheulaw) To bask one's belly in the sun.
Ymfolheuliad, s. m. (bolheuliad) A basking one's belly in the sun.
Ymfoliaw, v. a. (boliaw) To gorge one's self.
Ymfolrythiad, s. m. (bolrythiad) A stretching out one's belly.
Ymfolrythu, v. a. (bolrythu) To stretch out one's belly.
Ymfonclustiad, s. m. (bonclustiad) A mutually boxing the ears.
Ymfonclustiaw, v. a. (bonclustiaw) To box the ears mutually.
Ymforiad, s. m. (moriad) An employing one's self in seafaring.
Ymforiaw, v. a. (moriaw) To employ one's self in seafaring.
Ymfrasâad, s. m. (brasâad) A self-fattening.
Ymfrasâu, v. a. (brasâu) To fatten one's self.

Mae y goludog yn ymfrasâu ar ddagrau y tylodion.

The wealthy is fattening himself on the tears of the poor. — *Adage.*

Ymfrawiad, *s. m.* (brawiad) A self-dismaying.

Ymfrawu, *v. a.* (brawu) To dismay one's self.

Ymfrawychiad, *s. m.* (brawychiad) A filling one's self with dismay.

Ymfrawychu, *v. a.* (brawychu) To fill one's self with dismay.

Ymfreicheidiad, *s. m.* (breicheidiad) A mutually embracing.

Ymfreicheidiaw, *v. a.* (breicheidiaw) To embrace mutually.

Ymfrithaw, *v. a.* (brithaw) To self-variegate.

Ymfrithiad, *s. m.* (brithiad) A self-variegating.

Ymfrochi, *v. a.* (brochi) To be in a fume.

Ymfrochiad, *s. m.* (brochiad) A putting one's self in a fume or chafe; a self-ruffling.

Ymfroni, *v. a.* (broni) To swell one's bosom.

> Mae llawer yn boewfalchion, yn ymfroni, ac yn ymosawd allan orea y galloat.
>
> There are many in sprightly pride, *swelling out their bosoms*, and shewing themselves out as well as they are able.
> *Morgan Llwyd.*

Ymfrwydraw, *v. a.* (brwydraw) To engage one's self in battle; to fight mutually.

Ymfrwydriad, *s. m.* (brwydriad) An engaging one's self in battle; a mutually battling.

Ymfrysiad, *s. m.* (brysiad) A hastening one's self; a mutually hastening.

Ymfrysiaw, *v. a.* (brysiaw) To hasten one's self; to hasten mutually.

Ymfucheddiad, *s. m.* (bucheddiad) A conducting one's self in life.

Ymfucheddu, *v. a.* (bucheddu) To conduct one's self in life; to pass a life.

> A fyno ddial yn drwm ar ei elyn ymfuchedded yn lan.
>
> He that would revenge heavily on his foe *let him conduct himself* uprightly.
> *Adage.*

Ymfustiaw, *v. a.* (bustlaw) To self-embitter; mutually to deal in sarcasms.

Ymfustliad, *s. m.* (bustliad) An employing one's self in rancorous words; a mutually shewing rancour.

Ymfwriad, *s. m.* (bwriad) A purposing with one's self; a mutually designing or purposing.

Ymfwriadu, *v. a.* (ymfwriad) To employ one's self in purposing; to purpose mutually.

Ymfwynâad, *s. m.* (mwynâad) A self enjoying; a mutually enjoying.

Ymfwynâu, *v. a.* (mwynâu) To enjoy one's self; to enjoy mutually.

Ymfychaniad, *s. m.* (bychaniad) A lessening one's self; a mutually lessening or disparaging.

Ymfychanu, *v. a.* (bychanu) To lessen one's self; to be mutually lessening or depreciating.

Ymfydiaw, *v. a.* (bydiaw) To conduct one's self in the world.

> Goreu diwydrwydd ymfydiaw yn ddarbodawl.
>
> The best assiduity *is to conduct one's self in the world* circumspectly.
> *Catwg Ddoeth.*

Ymfyddinad, *s. m.* (byddinad) A self-embattling; a mutually embattling.

Ymfyddinaw, *v. a.* (byddinaw) To embattle one's self; mutually to embattle.

> Ffoes Hingestr a'i wyr i Gaer Cynan—a'u hymlid a orug Emrys; ac yno ymfyddinaw a lladd llawer o bobta.
>
> Hingestr and his men fled to the fortress of Cynan; so Emrys pursued them, and thereupon *they mutually array*, and kill many on both sides.
> *Gr. ab Arthur.*

Ymfyfyriad, *s. m.* (myfyriad) A contemplating with one's self.

Ymfyfyriaw, *v. a.* (myfyriaw) To contemplate with one's self.

Ymfygydiad, *s. m.* (mygydiad) A self-masking.

Ymfygydu, *v. a.* (mygydu) To mask one's self.

Ymfynteiad, *s. m.* (mynteiad) A joining one's self to a throng; a mutually flocking.

Ymfynteiaw, *v. a.* (mynteiaw) To unite one's self to a multitude; to flock mutually.

Ymfyrâad, *s. m.* (byrâad) A self-curtailing; a mutually shortening.

Ymfyrâu, *v. a.* (byrâu) To self-curtail.

Ymfyriad, *s. m.* (byriad) A self-shortening.

Ymfyriaw, *v. a.* (byriaw) To self-shorten.

Ymfywâad, *s. m.* (bywâad) A self-animating; a mutually enlivening.

Ymfywâu, *v. a.* (bywâu) To enliven one's self; to animate mutually.

Ymfywiocâad, *s. m.* (bywiocâad) A self-enlivening; a mutually animating.

Ymfywiocâu, *v. a.* (bywiocâu) To enliven one's self; to animate mutually.

Ymfywiogi, *v. a.* (bywiogi) To self-enliven; to become mutually animated.

Ymfywiogiad, *s. m.* (bywiogiad) A self-enlivening; a mutually enlivening.

Ymffieiddiad, *s. m.* (ffieiddiad) A self-loathing; a mutually loathing.

Ymffieiddiaw, *v. a.* (ffieiddiaw) To loathe one's self; to loathe mutually.

Ymffonodiad, *s. m.* (ffonodiad) A mutually cudgelling or dealing blows.

Ymffrost, *s. m.* (ffrost) A self-vaunting.

Ymffrostiad, *s. m.* (ymffrost) A self-vaunting.

Ymffrostiaw, *v. a.* (ymffrost) To self-vaunt.

> Cas a ymffrostio o'i gywilydd ei hun.
>
> Odious is he *who prides himself* of his own shame. *Adage.*

Ymffrwynaw, *v. a.* (ffrwynaw) To self-bridle.

Ymffrwyniad, *s. m.* (ffrwyniad) A self-bridling.

Ymffurfiad, *s. m.* (ffurfiad) A self-conforming; a mutually forming or shaping.

Ymffurfiaw, *v. a.* (ffurfiaw) To conform one's self; to conform mutually.

Ymffust, *s. m.* (ffust) A self-threshing; a mutual beating or boxing.

Ymffustiad, *s. m.* (ymffust) A self-threshing; a mutually threshing.

Ymffustiaw, *v. a.* (ymffust) To self-thresh; to beat one another.

Ymffyddiad, *s. m.* (ffyddiad) A plighting one's self; a plighting mutual faith.

Ymffyddiaw, *v. a.* (ffyddiaw) To plight one's faith; to plight a mutual troth.

> Rhaid yw dawed tair llaw ynghyd wrth roddi dyn yn fach: llaw y mach, a llaw y neb a'i rhoddo yn fach, a llaw y neb ei cymero, ac ymffyddiaw o law i law.
>
> It is necessary for three hands to come together on producing a person for bail: the hand of the bail, and the hand of him who gives him to bail, and the hand of the one who shall have accepted him, and to *plight mutually* from hand to hand.
> *Welsh Laws.*

Ymgabliad, *s. m.* (cabliad) A self-calumniating; a mutually calumniating.

Ymgablu, *v. a.* (cablu) To calumniate one's self; to calumniate mutually.

Ymgadarnâad, *s. m.* (cadarnâad) A self-strengthening; a mutually strengthening.

Ymgadarnâu, *v. a.* (cadarnâu) To self-strengthen; to strengthen mutually.

> Cas a ymgadarnâo mewn drwg.
>
> Odious is he who *shall defend himself* in evil. *Adage.*
>
> Rhyw i ddyn bechu, ond rhyw i ddiawl yn unig ymgadarnâu yn ei bechawd.
>
> It is natural for man to sin, but it is natural for the devil alone *to defend himself* in his sin.
> *Adage.*

Ymgadw, *v. a.* (cadw) To keep one's self; to contain one's self; to refrain, to forbear; to keep or guard mutually.

> *Daeth Hors a Hingestyr at y brenin, i gaffaw caer neu gastell i ymgadw.*
>
> Hors and Hingestr came to the king, to obtain a fortress or castle to *secure themselves*. *Gr. ab Arthur.*

Ymgadwad, *s. m.* (ymgadw) A self-keeping; self-preservation; self-restraint.

Ymgadwynaw, *v. a.* (cadwynaw) To chain one's self; to chain mutually.

Ymgadwyniad, *s. m.* (cadwyniad) A self-chaining; a mutually chaining.

Ymgael, *v. a.* (cael) To obtain to one's self; to conceive; to obtain mutually; to meet together.

> *Pa fam a'i hymgaeodd?*
>
> What mother has *conceived* him? *Mabinogi.*
>
> Pa gyfarwydd a fydd imi o ymgael ag y gwr a ddywedi di?
>
> What certainty will there be for me *of finding* the person thou art speaking of? *H. Pwyll—Mabinogion.*

Ymgaethiwaw, *v. a.* (caethiwaw) To confine one's self; mutually to confine.

Ymgaffael, *s. m.* (caffael) Self-acquirement; mutual attainment. *v. a.* To be acquiring; to attain mutually.

Ymgaffaeliad, *s. m.* (ymgaffael) A self-acquiring; a mutually obtaining.

Ymgaffiad, *s. m.* (caffiad) A reaching out one's arms; a mutually catching or grasping at.

Ymgaffiaw, *v. a.* (caffiaw) To reach out one's arms to catch; to catch at mutually.

Ymgagliad, *s. m.* (cagliad) A bedaggling one's self.

Ymgaglu, *v. a.* (caglu) To bedaggle one's self.

Ymgaint, *s. f.—pl.* ymgeinniau (caint) The act of mutual bickering or scolding.

Ymgais, *s. f.—pl.* ymgeisiau (cais) An effort, an attempt; self-exertion. *v. a.* To make an effort; to attempt; to seek for; to seek mutually.

> *Galledig pethau mawrion gan ymgais.*
>
> Great things are possible with *self-exertion*. *Adage.*
>
> Tri pheth sydd yn ymgadarnâu beunydd, gan fod mwyaf yr ymgais atynt: cariad, gwybodaeth, a chyfiawnder.
>
> Three things are daily acquiring strength, since the *attraction* towards them is greater: love, knowledge, and equity. *Barddas.*
>
> *Nid ymgais drwg â da.*
>
> The mischievous will not *exert himself* towards good. *Adage.*

Ymgalediad, *s. m.* (calediad) A self-hardening; a mutually hardening.

Ymgaledu, *v. a.* (caledu) To harden one's self; to harden mutually.

Ymgaloni, *v. a.* (caloni) To hearten one's self; to encourage mutually.

Ymgaloniad, *s. m.* (caloniad) A heartening one's self; a mutually encouraging.

Ymgallâad, *s. m.* (callâad) A making one's self cunning; a becoming mutually cunning.

Ymgallâu, *v. a.* (callâu) To make one's self cunning or discreet; to be mutually cunning.

> Wrth ffo Iwl Caisar rhag y Prydeiniaid—glewach oedd y Ffreinc yn ceisiaw ei wrthladd o'u terfynau. A gwedi gweled o Iwl Caisar hyny ymgallu a oreg, ac nid ymroddes i fodruader ysladd a'r bobl greulawn hono, namyn agori ei dryser.
>
> By Julius Caesar's *retreat* from the Britons, more courageous were the French, in endeavouring to drive him from their boundaries. So when Julius Caesar had seen that, what he did was *to employ himself craftily*, and he did not give himself up to the uncertainty of war with that ferocious people, but he opened his treasure. *Gr. ab Arthur.*

Ymganlyn, *v. a.* (canlyn) To employ one's self in following; to follow mutually.

Ymganlyniad, *s. m.* (canlyniad) An employing one's self in following; a mutually following.

Ymganmawl, *s. m.* (canmawl) Self-praise; mutual praise. *v. a.* To praise one's self; to praise mutually.

Ymganmoli, *v. a.* (ymganmawl) To praise one's self; to praise mutually.

Ymganmoliad, *s. m.* (ymganmawl) A praising one's self; a mutually praising.

Ymganred, *s. f.* (canred) A mutual pursuit. *v. a.* To pursue or follow mutually.

> [illegible]
>
> There will be no mutual fellowship, there will be no [illegible] with any towards others. [illegible]

Ymgangheniad, *s. m.* (cangheniad) A self-branching; a mutual ramification.

Ymganghenu, *v. a.* (canghenu) To branch out one's self; to branch mutually.

Ymgardodi, *v. a.* (cardodi) To employ one's self in charity; to practise mutual charity.

> [illegible]
>
> The best religion is to practise mutual charity [illegible] *Adage.*

Ymgardodiad, *s. m.* (cardodiad) An employing one's self in charity; a practising mutual charity.

Ymgaredigaw, *v. a.* (caredigaw) To be caressing mutually.

Ymgaredigiad, *s. m.* (caredigiad) A being mutually caressing.

Ymgariad, *s. m.* (cariad) The using one's self to love; a mutually loving.

Ymgarthiad, *s. m.* (carthiad) A self-cleansing.

Ymgarthu, *v. a.* (carthu) To self-purge.

Ymgaru, *v. a.* (caru) To habituate one's self to love; to love mutually.

> *Nid ymgar y [illegible].*
>
> Confidants will not love one another. *Adage.*

Ymgasâad, *s. m.* (casâad) The using one's self to hating; a mutually hating.

Ymgasâu, *v. a.* (casâu) To fill one's self with hate; to become disgusted; to hate mutually.

> [illegible]
>
> The life of [illegible] *[illegible]*

Ymgasgliad, *s. m.* (casgliad) A self-collecting; a mutually aggregating or collecting.

Ymgasglu, *v. a.* (casglu) To self-collect; to collect mutually; to assemble mutually.

Ymgastelliad, *s. m.* (castelliad) A spreading one's self round; a mutually spreading round.

Ymgastellu, *v. a.* (castellu) To spread one's self round, to spread round mutually.

Ymgatâad, *s. m.* (ymgatâu) An employing one's self in battle; a mutually battling.

Ymgatâu, *v. a.* (catâu) To employ one's self in battle; to battle mutually.

Ymgathewrach, *s. m.* (cathewrach) A bickering together. *v. a.* To bicker together.

Ymgau, *v. a.* (cau) To shut one's self; to become closed; to shut mutually.

> *Y braster a ymgauai am y llafn.*
>
> The fat *closed itself* about the blade. *Barnwyr* iii. [illegible]

Ymgecraeth, *s. m.* (cecraeth) A mutual brawling.

Ymgecriad, *s. m.* (cecriad) A mutually brawling.

Ymgecru, *v. a.* (cecru) To brawl mutually.

Ymgefnogi, *v. a.* (cefnogi) To back one's self; to back mutually; to encourage one another.

Ymgefnogiad, *s. m.* (cefnogiad) A backing one's self; a mutually backing.

Ymgegiad, *s. m.* (cegiad) A mutually mouthing.

Ymgegu, *v. a.* (cegu) To mouth mutually.

Ymgegwr, *s. m.—pl.* ymgegwyr (cegwr) A mouther, a wrangler.

Ymgeingar, *a.* (ymgaint) Quarrelsome.

> Dirnad bid ymgeingar.
>
> The mischievous let him be *quarrelsome*. *Llywarch Hen.*

Ymgeinniad, *s. m.* (ymgaint) A scuffling mutually.

Ymgeinniaith, *s. m.* (ymgaint—iaith) Quarrelsome language.

> Rhys Meigen—
> Gwaith ymgeinniaith a gaal i bawb.
>
> Rhys Meigen, the work of *abusive language* he would sing to every body. *D. ab Gwilym.*

Ymgeinniaw, *v. a.* (ymgaint) To scuffle; to scold.

> Daith draws, ni wnei dithau draw
> Amgenach nog ymgeinniaw.
>
> Untoward the journey, thou wilt yonder do nothing else but *quarrel*. *D. ab Gwilym, i Gr. Gryg.*
>
> Yr oedd trwst gwreigedd yn ymgeinniaw yn eu mysg, a rhyferthwy fawr o eiriau, mal llif mewn afon.
>
> There was the din of women *quarrelling together* amongst them, and a great torrent of words, like a flood in a river. *Morgan Llwyd.*

Ymgeintach, *s. m.* (ceintach) Mutual scuffle. *v. a.* To bicker, to scuffle, or to scold mutually.

Ymgeintachiad, *s. m.* (ymgeintach) A mutually scuffling or quarrelling.

Ymgeisiad, *s. m.* (ymgais) A making an effort or attempt; self-exertion; mutual exertion; a mutual seeking.

Ymgeisiaw, *v. a.* (ymgais) To make an effort or attempt; to seek; to exert one's self; to make a mutual effort or attempt; to exert mutually.

> Yr oedd Eidol—yn ymgeisiaw â Hingestyr; ac o'r diwedd yr ymgeffynt, ac ymladd oni bu y tan o'u harfau, mal mellt lluchedawl yn mlaen taran.
>
> Eidol was *exerting himself to meet* with Hingestyr; and at length *they mutually met*, and fought so that the fire was struck from their arms, like gleaming lightening before thunder. *Gr. ab Arthur.*

Ymgeisiwr, *s. m.—pl.* ymgeisiwyr (ymgais—gwr) One who makes an effort or attempt; one who exerts himself.

Ymgel, *s. m.* (cel) Self-concealment; mutual concealment.

> Yn mhob rhwy, yn mhob rhyfel,
> A welir hawdd ei ochel,
> Nid drwg ond drwg yn ymgel.
>
> In every extremity, in every war, what is seen is easily avoided, there is no mischief like mischief in *concealment*. *Geraint.*

Ymgelciad, *s. m.* (celciad) A self-sculking.

Ymgelciaw, *v. a.* (celciaw) To hide one's self slyly; to sculk mutually.

Ymgeledig, *a.* (ymgel) Self-concealed; mutually concealed.

Ymgeledd, *s. m.* (cel) A protection, or succour; a taking care; solicitude. *Priodi er mwyn ymgeledd*, to marry for the sake of being nursed. *Nef a gadwo iddo ei ymgeledd!* Heaven preserve to him his succour!

> Ni cheffir hoedl hir er ymgeledd.
>
> Long life will not be obtained with *being careful*. *Adage.*

Ymgeleddawl, *a.* (ymgeledd) Employing one's self in cherishing; mutually cherishing.

Ymgeleddiad, *s. m.* (ymgeledd) An employing one's self in screening; a cherishing.

Ymgeleddu, *v. a.* (ymgeledd) To take care of, to look after; to succour, to cherish, to nourish. *Ymgeleddu yr iaith*, to cultivate the language.

Ymgeleddus, *a.* (ymgeledd) Apt to cherish.

Ymgeleddwr, *s. m.* (ymgeledd) A cherisher.

Ymgeliad, *s. m.* (ymgel) A hiding one's self; a mutually hiding.

Ymgelu, *v. a.* (ymgel) To hide one's self; to hide mutually.

> Y gwr gwrdd uchel,
> A'r gwaew gwaedd awel,
> Pan el yn rhyfel
> Nid ymgela.
>
> The man ardently towering, with the spear making the gale to howl, when he goes into war *he will not hide himself*. *D. Benfras, i Lywelyn III.*

Ymgellwair, *s. m.* (cellwair) The being in jest; a mutual jesting.

Ymgellweiriad, *s. m.* (ymgellwair) A being jesting; a jesting with one another.

Ymgellweiriaw, *v. a.* (ymgellwair) To employ one's self in jesting; to jest mutually.

Ymgenfigeniad, *s. m.* (cenfigeniad) A making envious; a mutually envying.

Ymgenfigenu, *v. a.* (cenfigenu) To make one's self envious; to envy mutually.

Ymgernial, *s. m.* (cernial) A wrangling. *v. a.* To wrangle; to be cheek by jowl.

Ymgernodiad, *s. m.* (cernodiad) A knocking one another about the head.

Ymgernodiaw, *v. a.* (cernodiaw) To knock one another about the head.

Ymgerydd, *s. m.* (cerydd) Self-reprehension; mutual reproof or reprimand.

Ymgeryddiad, *s. m.* (ymgerydd) A self-reprehending; a mutually reprehending.

Ymgeryddu, *v. a.* (ymgerydd) To self-rebuke; to reprehend mutually.

Ymgestiad, *s. m.* (cestiad) A self-guzzling; a mutually guzzling.

Ymgestu, *v. a.* (cestu) To guzzle one's self; to guzzle mutually.

Ymgethriad, *s. m.* (cethriad) A self-urging; a mutually driving or egging on.

Ymgethru, *v. a.* (cethru) To drive one's self; to drive, to urge, or to importune mutually.

Ymgigaw, *v. a.* (cigaw) To go after the flesh.

Ymgigiad, *s. m.* (cigiad) A seeking carnal gratification.

Ymgigweiniad, *s. m.* (cigweiniad) An employing one's self in clutching of flesh; a mutually clutching.

Ymgigweiniaw, *v. a.* (cigweiniaw) To employ one's self in clutching of flesh; to mangle flesh mutually.

Ymgil, *s. m.* (cil) A self-retreating; a mutual recession or retiring.

Ymgiliad, *s. m.* (ymgil) A being retreating, a mutually retreating or receding.

Ymgiliaw, *v. a.* (ymgil) To be retreating; to retreat or to recede mutually.

> Trystan barabl difai,
> Yn nydd [illegible] nid ymgiliai,
> Cydymaith it oedd Gwalchmai.
>
> Trystan of blameless conversation, in the day of conflict that *would not be retreating*, a comrade of thine was Gwalchmai. *Eng. Gwalch mai a Thrystan.*

Ymgiprys, *s. m.* (ciprys) A mutual brawl.

Ymgiprysiad, *s. m.* (ymgiprys) A mutually brawling, or scrambling.

Ymgiprysu, *v. a.* (ciprys) To wrangle mutually.

Ymgladdiad, *s. m.* (claddiad) A self-burrying.

Ymgladdu, *v. a.* (claddu) To bury one's self.

Ymgleddyfawd, *s. m.* (cleddyfawd) A mutual cutting with sword.

Ymgleddyfiad, *s. m.* (cleddyfiad) A mutually cutting or fencing with sword.

Ymgleddyfu, *v. a.* (cleddyfu) To use the sword mutually; to fence.

Ymglöad, *s. m.* (clöad) A locking one's self; a mutually locking.

Ymglodfori, *v. a.* (clodfori) To exalt one's self in fame; to celebrate mutually.

Y cenedloedd—ynddo ef yr ymglodforant.

The nations, in him *they shall bless themselves*. *Jerem.* 4. 2.

Ymglodforiad, *s. m.* (clodforiad) A self-exalting in fame; a mutually celebrating.
Ymglöi, *v. a.* (cloi) To lock one's self; to lock mutually.
Ymglollad, *s. m.* (cloliad) A mutually babbling.
Ymglolian, *v. a.* (clolian) To babble mutually.
Ymgludaw, *v. a.* (cludaw) To self-carry; to carry mutually; to heap mutually.
Ymgludiad, *s. m.* (cludiad) A self-carrying; a mutually carrying or heaping.
Ymglwydd, *s. m.* (clwydd) The act of bringing one's self forward.
Ymglwyddaw, *v. a.* (ymglwydd) To bring one's self forward; mutually to bring to pass.
Ymglymiad, *s. m.* (clymiad) A self-binding; a mutually binding.
Ymglymu, *v. a.* (clymu) To self-bind; to bind or tie mutually.

Ymglymynt yr hesg am fy mhen.

The sedges *have wrapped themselves* about my head. *Jonah* 2. 5.

Ymglywad, *s. m.* (clywad) A feeling one's self; a mutually feeling.
Ymglywed, *v. a.* (clywed) To feel one's self; to feel mutually.

Neum goreu angeu anghyfnerthl:
Nid ymglyw dyn byw o'r hyd fal fi'

Shall I not be overcome by death of pining grief: not a living person in the world *feels himself* like me'
Ein. ab Gwalchmai, m. Nest

Ymgnöad, *s. m.* (cnöad) A being gnawing.
Ymgnöi, *v. a.* (cnöi) To keep gnawing.
Ymgodi, *v. a.* (codi) To raise one's self.
Ymgodiad, *s. m.* (codiad) A raising one's self.
Ymgodymiad, *s. m.* (codymiad) A tumbling one's self; a mutually tumbling.
Ymgodymu, *v. a.* (codymu) To tumble one's self; to tumble mutually.
Ymgoddi, *v. a.* (coddi) To vex one's self; to vex or tease mutually.

Yn llys y Wyddgrug,
A Lloegr yn nghuddug,
Llawer a'n godding
Yn ymgoddi.

In the court of Gwyddgrug, whilst England is under a cloud, many will attract our notice *afflicting themselves*.
Ll. P. Moch.

Ymgoddiad, *s. m.* (coddiad) A vexing one's self; a mutually vexing or afflicting.
Ymgoeliad, *s. m.* (coeliad) A being believing; a mutually believing.
Ymgoeliaw, *v. a.* (coeliaw) To be believing; to believe mutually.
Ymgofiad, *s. m.* (cofiad) A self-recollecting; a mutually remembering.
Ymgofiaw, *v. a.* (cofiaw) To self-recollect; to remember mutually.
Ymgofleidiad, *s. m.* (cofleidiad) A being embracing; a mutually embracing.
Ymgofleidiaw, *v. a.* (cofleidiaw) To employ one's self in embracing; to embrace mutually.

Mae——
Adeg i ymgofleidiaw.

There is a time *to embrace one another*. *L. Hopryn.*

Ymgoffäad, *s. m.* (coffâad) A self-recollecting.
Ymgoffäu, *v. a.* (coffäu) To self-recollect; to remember mutually.
Ymgoledd, *s. m.* (coledd) A self cultivating; a mutual cultivation.
Ymgoleddiad, *s. m.* (ymgoledd) A being self-cultivating; a mutually cultivating.
Ymgoleddu, *v. a.* (ymgoledd) To self-cultivate; to cultivate mutually.
Ymgoleddwr, *s. m.* (ymgoledd—gwr) One who self-cultivates.
Ymgoll, *s. m.* (coll) A self-loss; a mutual loss.
Ymgolli, *v. a.* (ymgoll) To lose one's self; mutually to lose.
Ymgolliad, *s. m.* (ymgoll) A losing one's self; a losing one another.
Ymgomiaw, *v. a.* (comiaw) To be conversing.
Ymgorffiad, *s. m.* (corffiad) A self-embodying; a mutually embodying.
Ymgorffiaw, *v. a.* (corffiaw) To self-embody; mutually to embody.
Ymgorffolaethu, *v. a.* (corffolaethu) To self incorporate; to incorporate mutually.
Ymgorniad, *s. m.* (corniad) A mutually butting with horns.
Ymgorniaw, *v. a.* (corniaw) To butt one another with horns.
Ymgosbi, *v. a.* (cosbi) To punish one's self.
Ymgosbiad, *s. m.* (cosbiad) A punishing one's self; a mutually punishing.
Ymgosi, *v. a.* (cosi) To scratch one's self; to scratch one another.
Ymgosiad, *s. m.* (cosiad) A scratching of one's self; a mutually scratching.
Ymgrafangiad, *s. m.* (crafangiad) A self-clawing; a mutually clawing.
Ymgrafangu, *v. a.* (crafangu) To claw one's self; to claw one another.
Ymgrafiad, *s. m.* (crafiad) A scratching of one's self; a mutually scratching.
Ymgrafu, *v. a.* (crafu) To scratch one's self; to scratch mutually.

Nid oes ganddo yr ewinedd i ymgrafu.

He has not got the nails to scratch *himself*. *Adage.*

Ymgrafwr, *s. m.*—*pl.* ymgrafwyr (crafwr) One who scratches himself.
Ymgrebychiad, *s. m.* (crebychiad) A becoming crinkled; a mutually crinkling.
Ymgrebychu, *v. a.* (crebychu) To become crinkled; to crinkle mutually.
Ymgred, *s. m.* (crêd) A mutual pledge or plight; espousal; a self-pledging.
Ymarediad, *s. m.* (ymgred) A mutually pledging; a pledging one's faith.
Ymgredu, *v. a.* (ymgred) To enter into mutual belief; to give mutual pledge.
Ymgrefiad, *s. m.* (crefiad) A being craving; a mutual craving.
Ymgrefu, *v. a.* (crefu) To employ one's self in craving; to crave mutually.
Ymgreiniad, *s. m.* (creiniad) A self-crawling along the ground.
Ymgreiniaw, *v. a.* (creiniaw) To be crawling.

Lle yr ymgreinio y march y gedy beth o'i flew.

Where the horse *shall have rolled himself* he will leave some of his hair.
Adage.

Ymgreiriad, *s. m.* (creiriad) A swearing one's self on relicks; a mutually covenanting.
Ymgreiriaw, *v. a.* (creiriaw) To swear one's self; to covenant mutually.
Ymgreuloni, *v. a.* (creuloni) To become cruel; to become mutually cruel.
Ymgreuloniad, *s. m.* (creuloniad) A becoming cruel; a becoming mutually cruel.
Ymgripiad, *s. m.* (cripiad) To claw one's self; to claw or scratch one another.

Ymgripiaw, *v. a.* (cripiaw) To claw one's self; to scratch or claw one another.

Ymgroesi, *v. a.* (croesi) To cross one's self; to secure one's self; to be cautious, to be mindful, to beware. *Gwell i ti ymgroesi*, better for thee to beware.

Ymgroesiad, *s. m.* (croesiad) A securing one's self, a bewaring; a taking heed.

Ymgrogi, *v. a.* (crogi) To hang one's self.

Ymgrogiad, *s. m.* (crogi) A hanging one's self.

Ymgrothi, *v. a.* (crothi) To swell one's paunch.

Ymgrothiad, *s.* (croth) A swelling out one's paunch.

Ymgrwydrad, *s. m.* (crwydrad) A using one's self to stray; a mutually straying.

Ymgrwydraw, *v. a.* (crwydraw) To use one's self to stray; to wander mutually.

Ymgryfâad, *s. m.* (cryfâad) A self-strengthening; a mutually strengthening.

Ymgryfâu, *v. a.* (cryfân) To strengthen one's self; to strengthen mutually.

> Ymgryfâa ac ymwrola; nac arswyda ac nac ofna; canys yr Arglwydd dy Dduw sy gyda thi.
>
> *Fortify thyself* and be of good courage; be not afraid, neither be thou dismayed; for the Lord thy God is with thee. *Joshua* 1. 9.

Ymgrymawl, *a.* (crymawl) Self-prostrating; mutually prostrating.

Ymgrymiad, *s. m.* (crymiad) Self-prostration; a mutual prostration; a mutually bowing.

Ymgrymu, *v. a.* (crymu) To prostrate one's self; to prostrate mutually.

Ymgrymwr, *s. m.—pl.* ymgrymwyr (crymwr) One who prostrates himself.

Ymgrynâad, *s. m.* (crynâad) A rounding of one's self; a mutually rounding.

Ymgrynâu, *v. a.* (crynân) To round one's self; to become rounded; to round mutually.

Ymgryniad, *s. m.* (cryniad) A causing one's self to tremble; a mutually trembling.

Ymgrynöad, *s. m.* (crynöad) A gathering one's self together; a making one's self tidy; a mutually collecting together.

Ymgrynöi, *v. a.* (crynöi) To gather one's self together, a making one's self tidy; a mutually collecting together.

Ymgrynu, *v. a.* (crynu) To cause one's self to tremble; to tremble mutually.

Ymgudd, *s. m.* (cudd) A hiding one's self.

Ymguddiad, *s. m.* (ymgudd) A hiding of one's self; a mutually hiding.

Ymguddiaw, *v. a.* (ymgudd) To hide one's self; to hide mutually.

> Ymguddiaw ar gefn y gist.
>
> *To hide one's self* on the top of the chest. *Adage.*

Ymguddiwr, *s. m.—pl.* ymguddiwyr (ymgudd—gwr) One who hides himself.

Ymgulâad, *s. m.* (culâad) A making one's self slender, or narrow; a mutually narrowing.

Ymgulâu, *v. a.* (culâu) To make one's self lean or slender; mutually to narrow.

Ymguraw, *v. a.* (curaw) To beat one's self; to beat mutually.

Ymguriad, *s. m.* (curiad) A self-beating; a mutually beating.

Ymgurwr, *s. m.—pl.* ymgurwyr (curwr) One who beats himself; one who employs himself in beating; a fighter.

Ymgusaniad, *s. m.* (cusaniad) A mutually kissing.

Ymgusanu, *v. a.* (cusanu) To kiss mutually.

> Gwyr dda, lyn gyrai ddau lu
> Am gas hen i 'mgusanu.
>
> The fresh good liquor, it would send two hosts concerning an old grudge to *kiss one another*.
> *Iea ab Gruffudd Leiaf, i Gwrw Conwy.*

Ymguwg, *s. m.* (cuwg) A putting on a frown; *v. a.* To put one's self in a frown.

> Mi yn ymguwg, a'm plant yn ymgernial.
>
> *I putting on a frown*, and my children altogether by the ears. *Aneirin Gwrgon.*

Ymgwydd, *s. m.* (cwydd) A self-falling; a mutual fall.

Ymgwyddaw, *v. a.* (ymgwydd) To cause one's self to fall; to fall mutually.

Ymgwyddiad, *s. m.* (ymgwydd) A falling of one's self; a mutually falling.

Ymgwynaw, *v. a.* (cwynaw) To be complaining; to complain mutually.

Ymgwynfan, *v. a.* (cwynfan) To keep one's self in continual wailing; to wail or to complain mutually.

Ymgwyniad, *s. m.* (cwyniad) A being complaining; a complaining mutually.

Ymgwynofain, *v. a.* (cwynofain) To employ one's self in complaining, to be mutually wailing.

Ymgyd, *s. m.* (cyd) A self-connection; a mutual union or junction; communion.

> Tri pheth a gaiff dyn o gredu yn Nuw: a fo raid yn y byd, heddwch cydwybod, ac ymgyd a'r nefawl.
>
> Three things will man obtain by believing in God: what may be necessary in the world, peace of conscience, and *communion* with the heavenly. *Barddas.*

Ymgydgam, *s. m.* (cydgam) A mutual dalliance. *v. a.* To dally mutually.

> Cael——
> A wnaethom ymgydgam gynt.
>
> We obtained a *mutual dalliance* formerly. *D. ab Gwilym.*

Ymgydgori, *v. a.* (cydgor) To join one's self to a congregation; mutually to unite in a congregation.

> Gwelygordd Emyr Llydaw a ddaethoedd i'r ynys hon gyda Garmon ab Rhidigys, i adnewyddu cred a bedydd, ac ymgydgori yn Ynys Enlli a wnaynt.
>
> The family of Emyr Llydaw came into this island with Garmon son of Rhidigys, to renew the christian faith, and *unite themselves in congregation* in the Isle of Enlli was what they did. *Bonedd y Saint.*

Ymgydgyfarch, *s. m.* (cydgyfarch) A self-congratulation; a mutual congratulation. *v. a.* To congratulate one's self; to congratulate mutually

Ymgydgyfarchiad, *s. m.* (ymgydgyfarch) A self-congratulating; a mutually congratulating.

Ymgydiad, *s. m.* (ymgyd) A joining mutually; a coupling one's self.

Ymgydiaw, *v. a.* (ymgyd) To lay hold or to join mutually, to couple one's self; to grapple together.

Ymgydoesi, *v. a.* (cydoesi) To make one's self cotemporary; mutually to be cotemporary.

Ymgydoesiad, *s. m.* (cydoesiad) A making one's self cotemporary; a mutually becoming cotemporary.

Ymgydredeg, *v. a.* (cydredeg) To render one's self concurrent; a mutually concurring.

Ymgydrediad, *s. m.* (cydrediad) A being concurrent; to concur mutually.

Ymgydsyniad, *s. m.* (cydsyniad) A being consenting; a mutually consenting.

Ymgydsyniaw, *v. a.* (cydsyniaw) To be consenting; to consent mutually.

Ymgydsynied *v. a.* (cydsynied) To render one's self consenting; mutually to consent.

Ymgydwybodi, *v. a.* (cydwybod) To be mutually conscientious.

Ymgyfâad, *s. m.* (cyfâad) A making one's self whole; a becoming mutually whole.

Ymgyfadnabod, *s. m.* (cyfadnabod) A mutual acknowledgement; a self-acknowledgement.

Ymgyfadnabod, *v. a.* (cyfadnabod) To acknowledge mutually; to acknowledge one's self.

Ymgyfaddasiad, *s. m.* (cyfaddasiad) A mutually conforming; a rendering one's self mutually suitable.

Ymgyfaddasu, *v. a.* (cyfaddasu) To conform mutually; to adapt one's self.

Ymgyfaddaw, *v. a.* (cyfaddaw) To bind one's self in a mutual promise.

Ymgyfaddawiad, *s. m.* (ymgyfaddaw) A binding one's self in a mutual promise.

Ymgyfagweddiad, *s. m.* (cyfagweddiad) A self-conforming; mutual conformation.

Ymgyfagweddu, *v. a.* (cyfagweddu) To conform one's self; to conform mutually.

Ymgyfammodi, *v. a.* (cyfammodi) To covenant mutually; to self-covenant.

Ymgyfammodiad, *s. m.* (cyfammodiad) A mutually covenanting; a covenanting or agreeing for one's self.

Ymgyfaniad, *s. m.* (cyfaniad) A making one's self whole; a becoming mutually entire.

Ymgyfanu, *v. a.* (cyfanu) To make one's self whole; to become mutually entire.

Ymgyfarfod, *s. m.* (cyfarfod) A mutually meeting; a mutual contact; a mutual encounter. *v. a.* To meet mutually; to make a mutual onset.

Ar yr ymgyfarfod cyntaf, ef a las pedwar cant o wyr Bradmwnt.

On the first *encounter* there were slain four hundred of the men of Bradmont. *H. Bown—Mabinogion.*

Eb Hywel—ni a ddygwn rhagddynt hwyntau yr eiddynt, o rhydd Duw cenad i ymgyfarfod a hwynt.

Hywel said: we will take from them too what they possess, if God will give permission for *to come in mutual contact* with them. *Gr. ab Arthur.*

Ymgyfarfodiad, *s. m.* (ymgyfarfod) A being meeting; a mutually meeting.

Ymgyfartaliad, *s. m.* (cyfartaliad) A making one's self equal, a comparing one's self; a mutually vieing.

Ymgyfartalu, *v. a.* (cyfartalu) To make one's self equal; to vie mutually.

Pa dywysawg a ell ymgyfartalu i frenin Prydain, o gadernid a dewredd marchogion?

What prince can *put himself in competition* with the king of Britain, as to the fortitude and gallantry of his knights? *Gr. ab Arthur.*

Ymgyfarwyddaw, *v. a.* (cyfarwyddaw) To self-inform; mutually to direct or inform.

Ymgyfarwyddiad, *s. m.* (cyfarwyddiad) A directing one's self; a mutually directing.

Ymgyfateb, *s. m.* (cyfateb) Mutual correspondence. *v. a.* To correspond mutually.

Ymgyfatebawl, *a.* (ymgyfateb) Mutually corresponding.

Ymgyfatebiad, *s. m.* (ymgyfateb) A mutually corresponding.

Ymgyfathrach, *s. m.* (cyfathrach) A mutual connection.

Ymgyfathrachiad, *s. m.* (ymgyfathrach) A forming a mutual connection.

Ymgyfâu, *v. a.* (cyfâu) To render one's self whole; to become mutually whole.

Ymgyfeilliachu, *v. a.* (ymgyfeilliach) To join one's self in friendship; to contract a mutual friendship.

Ymgyferbynawl, *a.* (cyferbynawl) Being set in opposition; mutually opposing.

Ymgyferbyniad, *s. m.* (cyferbyniad) A coming in opposition; a mutually opposing.

Ymgyferbynied, *v. a.* (cyferbynied) To set one's self against; to counteract mutually.

Nid oedd yr ail a fai can ddewred ag ef yn y deyrnas, neu allai ymgyferbynied ag ef.

There was not another who were so brave as he in the kingdom, and who could *mutually contend* with him. *Gr. ab Arthur.*

Ymgyfethl, *s. m.* (cyfethl) A mutual struggle. *v. a.* To be striving together.

Damweiniaw dau was ieuanc arddarchawg, y naill oeddynt yn nai i'r brenin, a'r llall yn nai i Afarwy fab Lludd ymdaro yn gware paled, ac o'r diwedd llidiaw am y fuddygoliaeth: ac yssef oedd enw nai y brenin Hirlas, ac enw y llall Cuhelyn: a gwedi ymlidiaw ac ymgyfethl ygyllu cleddyf a wnai Cuhelyn a llâd pen Hirlas.

Two noble young men, the one of them a nephew to the king, and the other a nephew to Afarwy son of Lludd, happened to dispute, in playing at ball, and at last to grow angry about the winning: and to be particular, the name of the king's nephew was Hirlas, and the name of the other Cuhelyn: then, after growing mutually angry and *striving together*, Cuhelyn drew his sword and cut off the head of Hirlas. *Gr. ab Arthur.*

Ymgyfethliad, *s. m.* (ymgyfethl) A being striving; a mutually struggling.

Ymgyfethlu, *v. a.* (ymgyfethl) To be struggling; to struggle mutually.

Ymgyfhogi, *v. a.* (cyfhogi) To edge at one another mutually.

Dyrbeiliaw cleddyf a wnaeth ac ymgyfhogi.

Draw sword was what they did and *mutually cut at one another*. *H. Owain ab Urien—Mabinogion.*

Ymgyfhogiad, *s. m.* (cyfhogiad) A mutually edging at one another.

Ymgyfiad, *s. m.* (cyfiad) A making one's self equal; a mutually equalling.

Ymgyfiaw, *v. a.* (cyfiaw) To make one's self equal; to become mutually equal.

Ymgyfiawnâad, *s. m.* (cyfiawnâad) A self-justification; a mutually justifying.

Ymgyfiawnâu, *v. a.* (cyfiawnâu) To self-justify; to justify mutually.

Pa fodd yr ymgyfiawnhawn?

What way *shall we justify ourselves?* Genesis 44. 16.

Ymgyfiawniad, *s. m.* (cyfiawniad) A self-justifying; a mutually justifying.

Ymgyfiawnu, *v. a.* (cyfiawnu) To justify one's self; to justify mutually.

Ymgyflawni, *v. a.* (cyflawni) To self-complete; to become mutually complete.

Ymgyflawniad, *s. m.* (cyflawniad) A self-completing; a mutually completing.

Ymgyflëad, *s. m.* (cyflëad) A self-collocation; a mutual collocation.

Ymgyflesiad, *s. m.* (cyflesiad) A making one's self mutually beneficial.

Ymgyflesu, *v. a.* (cyflesu) To make one's self mutually beneficial.

Ymgyflëu, *v. a.* (cyflëu) To situate one's self; mutually to collocate.

Ymgyflogi, *v. a.* (cyflogi) To hire one's self; to hire mutually.

Nid esmwyth ymgyflogi.

It is not *easy to hire one's self*. *Adage.*

Ymgyflogiad, *s. m.* (cyflogiad) A hiring one's self; a mutually hiring.

Ymgyflogwr, *s. m.—pl.* ymgyflogwyr (cyflogwr) One who hires himself.

Ymgyfiwynaw, *v. a.* (cyfiwynaw) To be consociated; mutually to consociate.

Tudfyl ferch Brychan a las gan y Saeson, pan oedd yn ymgyflwyn a'i thad.

Tudfyl daughter of Brychan was killed by the Saxons, when she was *visiting* her father. *Achau y Saint.*

Ymgyfiwyniad, *s. m.* (cyfiwyniad) An associating one's self; a mutually associating.

Ymgyflychiad, *s. m.* (cyflychiad) A mutually connecting one's self.

Ymgyflychu, *v. a.* (cyflychu) To connect one's self mutually.

> Ymgyfwyn a doeth, ac nac ymgyflych ag annoeth.
>
> Consociate thyself with the wise, and *do not connect thyself* with the unwise. *Adage.*

Ymgyfnawsi, *v. a.* (cyfnawsi) To render one's self of the same temper; to become mutually of one temper.

Ymgyfnawsiad, *s. m.* (cyfnawsiad) A making one's self congenial.

Ymgyfnerthiad, *s. m.* (cyfnerthiad) A collecting one's strength together; a mutually assisting.

Ymgyfnerthu, *v. a.* (cyfnerthu) To collect together one's strength; to assist one another mutually.

Ymgyfnesiad, *s. m.* (cyfnesiad) Self-approximation; mutual approximation.

Ymgyfnesu, *v. a.* (cyfnesu) To self-approximate; mutually to approximate.

Ymgyfnewid, *s. m.* (cyfnewid) Self-transformation; a' mutual change of one's self; a mutual interchange.

Ymgyfnewidiad, *s. m.* (ymgyfnewid) A self-transforming; a mutually interchanging.

Ymgyfnewidiaw, *v. a.* (ymgyfnewid) To transform one's self; to interchange mutually.

Ymgyfnydd, *s. m.* (cyfnydd) A self-intertwining; a mutual intertwining.

> Yn ymgyfnydd ddydd neu ddau.
>
> *Intwining together* a day or two. *W. Cynwal.*

Ymgyfnyddawl, *a.* (ymgyfnydd) Self-intertwining; mutually intertwining.

Ymgyfnyddiad, *s. m.* (ymgyfnydd) A self-intertwining; a mutually intertwining.

Ymgyfnyddu, *v. a.* (ymgyfnydd) To self-intertwine; mutually to intertwine.

Ymgyfodi, *v. a.* (cyfodi) To raise one's self; a mutually rising.

> Y rhai a ymgyfodynt i ym herbyn a ddarostyngaist danaf.
>
> Them who *raised themselves* against me hast thou subdued under me. *2 Samuel* 22. 40.

Ymgyfodiad, *s. m.* (cyfodiad) A raising one's self; a mutually rising.

Ymgyfoethi, *v. a.* (cyfoethi) To enrich one's self; a mutually becoming rich.

Ymgyfoethiad, *s. m.* (cyfoethiad) A self-enriching; a mutually enriching.

Ymgyfoethogi, *v. a.* (cyfoethogi) To self-enrich; to be mutually enriched.

Ymgyfoethogiad, *s. m.* (cyfoethogiad) A self-enriching; a mutually enriching.

Ymgyfranc, *s. m.* (cyfranc) A bringing one's self into mutual contact; a mutually meeting. *v. a.* To bring one's self into mutual contact; to meet mutually.

Ymgyfraniad, *s. m.* (cyfraniad) A bringing one's self to participate; a mutually participating.

Ymgyfranogi, *v. a.* (cyfranogi) To render one's self participating; to become mutually participating.

Ymgyfranogiad, *s. m.* (cyfranogiad) A rendering one's self participating; a becoming mutually participating.

Ymgyfrannu, *v. a.* (cyfrannu) To bring one's self to divide mutually; a mutually partaking, dividing, or communicating.

Ymgyfred, *s. m.* (cyfred) Mutual concurrence.

Ymgyfredawl, *a.* (ymgyfred) Mutually concurrent

Ymgyfredeg, *v. a.* (ymgyfred) To run together mutually; to form a concourse.

Ymgyfrediad, *s. m.* (ymgyfred) A mutually running together; a mutually concurring.

Ymgyfreithgar, *a.* (cyfreithgar) Apt to be litigious; mutually litigious.

Ymgyfreithgarwch, *s. m.* (ymgyfreithgar) Aptness to be litigious; mutual litigiousness.

Ymgyfreithiad, *s. m.* (cyfreithiad) A being litigious; a mutually litigating.

Ymgyfreithiaw, *v. a.* (cyfreithiaw) To commit one's self to law; to bind one's self by law; to ligitate mutually.

> Gwell cydunaw yn ddrwg nog ymgyfreithiaw yn dda.
>
> Better to agree badly than *mutually to litigate* well. *Adage.*

Ymgyfreithiwr, *s. m.* (cyfreithiwr) One who litigates.

Ymgyfrif, *s. m.* (cyfrif) A self-reckoning; a mutual reckoning.

Ymgyfrifaw, *v. a.* (ymgyfrif) To reckon one's self, to esteem one's self; mutually to reckon.

Ymgyfrifiad, *s. m.* (ymgyfrif) A reckoning one's self; self-estimation; a mutually reckoning.

Ymgyfrin, *s. m.* (cyfrin) A confederacy. *v. a.* To join in mutual secresy.

> Gorea cyfeillach ymgyfrin a dedwydd.
>
> The best company is a communion with the happy. *Cattwg Ddoeth.*

Ymgyfrinachiad, *s. m.* (cyfrinachiad) A being communicating mutual secrets.

Ymgyfrinachu, *v. a.* (cyfrinachu) To employ one's self in mutual secrets; to talk mutual secrets.

> Ymgyfrinachasant yn ddichellgar yn erbyn dy bobl.
>
> *They have taken counsel together craftily* against thy people. *Psalm* 83. 3.

Ymgyfrinaw, *v. a.* (cyfrinaw) To render one's self mysterious; to become mutually mysterious.

Ymgyfriniad, *s. m.* (cyfriniad) A rendering one's self mysterious; a becoming mutually mysterious; a joining together.

Ymgyfrithiad, *s. m.* (cyfrithiad) A making one's self to seem or to appear; a mutually appearing.

Ymgyfrithiaw, *v. a.* (cyfrithiaw) To make one's self to appear; mutually to seem or to appear

Ymgyfroddi, *v. a.* (cyfroddi) To render one's self contributary; mutually to contribute.

Ymgyfroddiad, *s. m.* (cyfroddiad) A making one's self to contribute; a mutually contributing.

Ymgyfrwch, *s. m.* (cyfrwch) A bringing one's self in contact; a mutual meeting. *v. a.* To put one's self in contact; to meet mutually.

Ymgyfrwyddaw, *v. a.* (cyfrwyddaw) To self-expedite; to become mutually expeditious.

Ymgyfrwyddiad, *s. m.* (cyfrwyddiad) A self-expediting; a mutually expediting.

Ymgyfunaw, *v. a.* (cyfunaw) To combine one's self; to combine mutually.

> Ymgyfunaw a oreg Gwrgi Garwlwyd a'i wyr ag Edelfled brenin y Saeson.
>
> What Gwrgi Garwlwyd did was *to unite himself* with Edelfled king of the Saxons. *Trioedd.*

Ymgyfuniad, *s. m.* (cyfuniad) A self-uniting; a mutually uniting or combining.

Ymgyfwrdd, *s. m.* (cyfwrdd) A meeting together; a rencounter. *v. a.* To come into mutual contact.

Ymgyfyngiad, *s. m.* (cyfyngiad) A self-straitening, a mutually straitening.

Ymgyfyngu, *v. a.* (cyfyngu) To self-straiten, to straiten or embarrass mutually.

Ymgyffelybiad, *s. m.* (cyffelybiad) A self-comparison; a becoming mutually similar.

Ymgyffelybu, *v. a.* (cyffelybu) To compare one's self; to become mutually similar.

Ymgyffred, *s. m.* (cyffred) Self-comprehension; a mutual comprehension.

Ymgyffredawl, *a.* (ymgyffred) Self-comprehending; mutually comprehending.

Ymgyffrediad, *s. m.* (ymgyffred) A self-comprehending; a mutually comprehending.

Ymgyffredu, *v. a.* (ymgyffred) To self-comprehend; to comprehend mutually.

Ymgyffröad, *s. m.* (cyffröad) A self-agitating; a mutually agitating.

Ymgyffröawl, *a.* (cyffröawl) Self-agitating; mutually agitating or moving.

Ymgyffröi, *v. a.* (cyffröi) To agitate one's self; to become mutually agitated.

Ymgyhoeddi, *v. a.* (cyhoeddi) To announce one's self; to become mutually public.

Ymgyhoeddiad, *s. m.* (cyhoeddiad) A proclaiming or announcing one's self; a mutually proclaiming.

Ymgyhuddaw, *v. a.* (cyhuddaw) To accuse one's self; to accuse mutually.

Pan el lladron i ymgyhuddaw, y ceiff cywiriaid eu da.

When thieves go *to accuse one another*, honest people get their property. *Adage.*

Ymgyhuddiad, *s. m.* (cyhuddiad) A self-accusing; a mutually accusing.

Ymgyhwrdd, *s. m.* (cyhwrdd) A mutual contact. *v. a.* To bring one's self in contact; to meet mutually.

Ymgyhydiad, *s. m.* (cyhydiad) A rendering one's self co-extending.

Ymgyhydriad, *s. m.* (cyhydriad) A mutually vieing or emulating; a putting one's self in competition.

Ymgyhydru, *v. a.* (cyhydru) To put one's self in competition; mutually to emulate.

Ymgyhydu, *v. a.* (cyhydu) To make one's self co-equal in length; mutually to co-extend.

Mae iawn i yr amddiffynwr ddangaws ei fraint, ac ymgyhydu ei fraint ag yr hawlwr.

It is proper for the defendant to shew his right, and *to compare mutually* his right with the plaintiff. *Welsh Laws.*

Ymgyhyrddiad, *s. m.* (ymgyhwrdd) A becoming in contact; a mutually encountering.

Ymgyhyrddu, *v. a.* (ymgyhwrdd) To come in contact; mutually to come in contact.

Ymgyllaeth, *s. m.* (cyllaeth) The giving up one's self to grief; a mutual sorrow.

Ymgyllelliad, *s. m.* (cyllelliad) A cutting one's self with a knife; a mutually cutting with knives.

Ymgyllellu, *v. a.* (cyllellu) To cut one's self with a knife; to cut one another with knives.

Ymgymdeithasiad, *s. m.* (cymdeithasiad) A mutually consociating; a mutual incorporation; a connecting one's self with society.

Ymgymdeithasu, *v. a.* (cymdeithasu) To associate mutually; to associate one's self.

Ymgymedriad, *s. m.* (cymedriad) A proportioning or regulating one's self, a mutually proportioning.

Ymgymedroli, *v. a.* (cymedroli) To moderate one's self, mutually to moderate.

Ymgymedroliad, *s. m.* (cymedroliad) A self moderating, a mutually befitting.

Ymgymedru, *v. a.* (cymedru) To regulate mutually.

Ymgymeriad, *s. m.* (cymeriad) A taking one's self, a being taking, a mutually taking.

Ymgymeryd, *v. a.* (cymeryd) To take one's self, to be taking, to take mutually.

Pe baech yma [illegible] weled y tan [illegible] i ych [illegible] ymgymeryd i ych [illegible] hyd [illegible].

If you were here you should see the fire on the further side of the walls just *becoming kindled* to burn you to nothing. *Elis Wyn, B. Cwsg.*

Ymgymer ymaith a bwrw dy hun i'r mor.

Take thyself away and cast thyself into the sea. *W. Salisbury.*

Ymgymesuraw, *v. a.* (cymesuraw) To proportion one's self, mutually to adapt.

Ymgymesuriad, *s. m.* (cymesuriad) A self-adaptation, a mutually proportioning.

Ymgymhariad, *s. m.* (cymhariad) A joining one's self in fellowship; a mutually becoming connected.

Ymgymharu, *v. a.* (cymharu) To pair one's self; to associate mutually.

Gwyllt a gwar a 'mgymharant
Er [illegible]——

The wild and the tame *will couple together* to beget [illegible]. *[illegible]*

Ymgymhell, *s. m.* (cymhell) A self-urging; a mutual urging. *v. a.* To urge one's self; to urge mutually.

Ymgymhelliad, *s. m.* (ymgymhell) An urging one's self; a mutually urging.

Ymgymhwyllaw, *v. a.* (cymhwyllaw) To persuade one's self, to persuade mutually.

Ymgymhwylliad, *s. m.* (cymhwylliad) A reasoning one's self, a mutually persuading.

Ymgymhwysaw, *v. a.* (cymhwysaw) To adapt one's self, to adjust mutually.

Ymgymhwysiad, *s. m.* (cymhwysiad) A self-adapting; a mutually proportioning.

Ymgymmodi, *v. a.* (cymmodi) To make one's self agreeable; to reconcile one's self; to become mutually reconciled.

Ymgymmodiad, *s. m.* (cymmodiad) Self-reconciliation; mutual reconciliation.

Ymgymoni, *v. a.* (cymoni) To make one's self compact; to become mutually compact.

Ymgymoniad, *s. m.* (cymoniad) A rendering one's self compact; a mutually disposing.

Ymgymwynasiad, *s. m.* (cymwynasiad) A rendering one's self complacent, a becoming mutually courteous.

Ymgymwynasu, *v. a.* (cymwynasu) To render one's self complacent; to become mutually courteous.

Gorau ar bob gwynfyd ymgymwynasu.

The best of every happiness is *to be mutually complacent.* *Adage.*

Ymgymyreddiad, *s. m.* (cymyreddiad) A self-assuming, a mutually assuming.

Ymgymyreddu, *v. a.* (cymyreddu) To arrogate to one's self; to assume mutually.

Ymgymysgiad, *s. m.* (cymysgiad) A mixing one's self, a mutually mixing.

Ymgymysgu, *v. a.* (cymysgu) To mix one's self; to mix mutually.

Ymgymyniad, *s. m.* (cymyniad) A self-cutting; a mutual excision.

Ymgymynu, *v. a.* (cymynu) To cut one's self; to cut down mutually.

Mal yr oedd y byddinoedd yn ymffust ac yn ymgymynu blith draphlith, ydd ymgafas Eidol a Hengyst ynghyd, ac ymgyfhogi a'r cleddyfau.

As the hosts were mutually dealing blows and *cutting down one another* mixed helter-skelter together, Eidol found an opportunity to come in contact with Hengist, and they mutually edged with the swords. *Brut y Brenhinedd.*

Ymgyndyniad, *s. m.* (cyndyniad) A making one's self stubborn, a mutually being obstinate.

Ymgyndynu, *v. a.* (cyndynu) To be stubborn; to act with mutual obstinacy.

Ymgynddeiriogi, *v. a.* (cynddeiriogi) To madden one's self; to become mutually enraged.

Ymgynddeiriogiad, *s. m.* (cynddeiriogiad) A maddening one's self, a becoming mutually enraged.

Ymgynheniad, *s. m.* (cynheniad) A being contending, a mutually wrangling.

Ymgynhenu, *v. a.* (cynhenu) To contend, to wrangle mutually.

Goreu swydd—
Gan hwn oedd ymgynhenu.

The choicest office with this one was *to employ himself in wrangling.* *Ieuan Tew.*

Ymgynhesiad, *s. m.* (cynhesiad) A self-warming, a becoming mutually warmed.

Ymgynhesu, *v. a.* (cynhesu) To warm one's self, to become mutually warmed.

Ymgynhyrfiad, *s. m.* (cynhyrfiad) A self-agitating, a mutually disturbing.

Ymgynhyrfu, *v. a.* (cynhyrfu) To disturb one's self; to disturb mutually.

Ymgynnadl, *s. f.* (cynnadl) Mutual dispute or conversation.

Ymgynnadliad, *s. m.* (ymgynnadl) An employing one's self in conversation, a mutually conversing.

Ymgynnadlu, *v. a.* (ymgynnadl) To be conversing; to converse mutually.

Na chwenaych ymgynnadlu â dig[l]on.

Seek not *to be disputing* with an angry person. *Catwg.*

Ymgynnal, *s. m.* (cynnal) A self-support; mutual support. *v. a.* To support one's self; to contain one's self; to support one another.

Ymgynnaliad, *s. m.* (ymgynnal) Self-supportation, a mutually supporting.

Ymgynnefinaw, *v. a.* (cynnefinaw) To accustom one's self; to become mutually familiar.

Ymgynnefiniad, *s. m.* (cynnefiniad) A familiarizing one's self; a mutually habituating.

Ymgynnull, *s. m.* (cynnull) A self-collecting; a mutual gathering.

Ymgynnullaw, *v. a.* (ymgynnull) To self-collect; mutually to collect.

Gwedi ysbaid ychydig o ddyddiau enychaf Bran gwedi ymgynnullaw ei longau ac yn disgynu ar dir yr Alban.

After the space of a few days behold Bran after *having his ships collected together* making, a descent on the land of Alban. *Gr. ab Arthur.*

Ymgynnulled y dyfredd y dan y nef yn un lle.

Let the waters under the heaven *be gathered together* unto one place. *Genesis* 1. 9.

Ymgynnulliad, *s. m.* (ymgynnull) A self-collecting; a mutually assembling.

Ymgynnwys, *s. m.* (cynnwys) Self-compression; a mutual compactness; mutual admission.

Ymgynnwysaw, *v. a.* (ymgynnwys) To make one's self compact, to compress one's self; to contain one's self; mutually to compress; mutually to admit.

Ymgynnwysiad, *s. m.* (ymgynnwys) A containing one's self; a shrinking one's self; a mutually receiving or admitting.

Ymgynnyg, *s. m.* (cynnyg) A presenting one's self; a mutual offer. *v. a.* To offer one's self; to offer mutually.

Lle y mae Ysbryd Duw yn athraw, yno yr ydys wedi ein dodi ni i ddefnyddiaw yn ofalus pob rhyw oedfa a fyddo yn ymgynnyg.

Where the Spirit of God is a teacher, there we are placed carefully to make use of every kind of opportunity, which may be *offering itself.* *Ier. Owain.*

Ymgynnygiad, *s. m.* (ymgynnyg) A self-offering; a mutually offering.

Ymgynnyrch, *s. m.* (cynnyrch) Self-produce; a mutual produce or increase.

Ymgynnyrchiad, *s. m.* (ymgynnyrch) A self-increasing; a mutually increasing.

Ymgynnyrchu, *v. a.* (ymgynnyrch) To increase one's self; to increase mutually.

Ymgynghan, *s. m.* (cynghan) Self-harmony; mutual harmony.

Ymgynghaniad, *s. m.* (ymgynghan) A self-harmonizing; a mutually harmonizing.

Ymgynghori, *v. a.* (cynghori) To consult mutually; to consult one's self.

Ymgynghorasant yn erbyn dy rai dirgel di.

They have consulted together against thy hidden ones. *Psalm* 83. 3.

Ymgynghoriad, *s. m.* (cynghoriad) A mutually consulting, a consultation together, a self-counselling.

Ymgynghreiriad, *s. m.* (cynghreiriad) A giving a mutual pledge; a self-pledging.

Ymgynghreiriaw, *v. a.* (cynghreiriaw) To give a mutual pledge; to combine together; to pledge one's self.

Dyg Medrawd y goron oddiar Arthur o drais a lledrad; ac fal y cadwai efe hi ymgynghreiriai a'r Saeson.

Medrawd took the crown from Arthur through usurpation and adultery; and so that he might keep it what he did was *to enter into a mutual compact* with the Saxons. *Trioedd.*

Ymgynglyn, *s. m.* (cynglyn) Mutual adhesion; a mutual coupling; a self-coupling.

Ymgynglyniad, *s. m.* (ymgynglyn) A mutually connecting or coupling; a coupling one's self.

Ymgynglynu, *v. a.* (cynglynu) To adhere mutually; to couple mutually; to couple one's self.

Ymgyngwystlaw, *v. a.* (cyngwystlaw) To lay a mutual pledge or wager.

Ymgyngwystliad, *s. m.* (cyngwystliad) A laying a mutual pledge or wager.

Ymgyrch, *s. f.* (cyrch) A mutual approach; an encounter.

Ymgyrchawl, *a.* (ymgyrch) Congressing; encountering, mutually approaching

Ymgyrchiad, *s. m.* (ymgyrch) A mutually approaching, a mutually resorting.

Ymgyrchiant, *s. m.* (ymgyrch) A mutual approach, a mutual onset.

Ymgyrchu, *v. a.* (ymgyrch) To approach or to resort mutually; to make a mutual onset; to use one's self to resort.

Ymgyrchu a wnaynt y byddinoedd, ac elwng eu gwaed i redeg.

Mutually to attack was what the armies did, and let their blood to flow. *Gr ab Arthur.*

Ymgyrhaedd, *s. m.* (cyrhaedd) A self-reaching; a mutual reach or attainment. *v. a.* To reach one's self; to attain mutually.

Ymgyrhaeddiad, *s. m.* (ymgyrhaedd) A reaching one's self, a mutually reaching or attaining.

Ymgyrhaeddyd, *v. a.* (ymgyrhaedd) To reach one's self; to reach or to attain mutually.

Ymgysdadliad, *s. m.* (cysdadliad) A matching or comparing one's self; a mutually comparing or vieing.

Tonogi, *v. a.* (tònawg) To raise breakers or billows; to rise in billows; to become boisterous or turbulent.

Tonogiad, *s. m.* (tònawg) A raising of breakers; a rising in waves, or surges; a becoming turbulent.

Tonogrwydd, *s. m.* (tònawg) The state of rising in surges; turbulence.

Tonwaed, *s. m.* (tòn—gwaed) A blood clod.

Tonwen, *a.* (tòn—gwèn) White-skinned.

Tonwryg, *a.* (tòn—gwryg) Rising in billows; turbulent.

Tonwrygiad, *s. m.* (tonwryg) A rising in billows; a becoming turbulent.

Tonwrygiaw, *v. a.* (tonwryg) To raise surges; to rise in surges; to become turbulent.

Tonwyn, *a.* (tòn—gwỳn) White-skinned.

Tonydd. *s. m.—pl. t.* ion (ton) An accenter.

Tonyddiaeth, *s.* (tonydd) A tonation, accentation.

> Tonyddiaeth helaeth hylawn,
> A gair, mewn llafar a gawn.
>
> A tonation ample and complete, and a word, in expression we obtain. *Meuryg Dafydd.*

Top, *s. m.—pl. t.* iau (tob) A top; a stopple.

Topiad, *s. m.* (top) A topping, a cresting.

Topiaw, *v. a.* (top) To top, to form a crest.

Topiawg, *a.* (top) Having a top, or crest.

Topiawl, *a.* (top) Tending to form a top.

Topiwr, *s. m.—pl.* topiwyr (top—gwr) One who tops

Topyn, *s. m. dim.—pl. t.* au (top) A top, a bunch, bush of hair; a topple; a stopple.

> Erfynied i'm rhwyf ydd wyf ei dda—
> A warawd topyn felyn fwla.
>
> I sue to my chief for his goods, that renders unnecessary a *top*, a yellow knob. *Gr. ab D. ab Tudyr.*

Topyniad, *s. m.* (topyn) A forming a top.

Topynu, *v. a.* (topyn) To form a top, or crest.

Tòr, *s. m.* (ty—or) A break, a rupture; a cut; an interruption, a cessation, a discontinuation. *Tòr calon*, a heart breaking.

Tòr, *s. f.—pl. t.* au (to—or) A swell out, a bulge, a prominence; a belly; the lower part of the belly. *Tòr y mynydd*, the swell of the mountain; *tòr y llaw*, the ball of the hand; *tòr tarian*, the convex or outside of a shield.

> Tyfid enderig o'i dòr.
>
> The steer grows from his *belly*. *Adage.*

Tòradwy, *a.* (tòr) Capable of being broken.

Toraeth, *s. f.—pl.* toreithiau (tòr) Produce, profit; fecundity, fruitfulness; abundance, store. *Nid oes dim toraeth ohono*, there is no good to be had out of him.

> Mawr yw toraeth yr aflwydd.
>
> Great is the *store* of the unfortunate. *Adage.*
>
> Mawr toraeth aflwydd ban fyno.
>
> Great is the *store* of misfortune when be commands. *Adage.*

Torammod, *s.* (tòr—ammod) Breach of covenant.

Torarfoll, *s. f.* (tòr—arfoll) Breach of faith.

Torawg, *a.* (tòr) Having a prominence; big-bellied; an epithet applied to a sow, a bitch, and a cat, when big with young.

Torawl, *a.* (tòr) Tending to spread round; prominent.

Torbwt, *s. m.—pl.* torbytiaid (tòr—pwt) A turbot.

Torcalon, *s. m.* (tòr—calon) A heart-breaking.

Torcalonus, *a.* (torcalon) Heart-breaking.

> Ystyriaeth dorcalonus ydyw cin bod ni bob dydd yn myned ymaeth oddiwrth ein dedwyddwch.
>
> It is a *heart-breaking* consideration that we should be every day going away from our happiness. *Ios. Rhys.*

Torch, *s. f.—pl.* tyrch (tòr) A wreath; a coil; a collar; a badge of distinction, worn by the ancient Britons, which it was a point of honour for a warrior to preserve from being lost to the enemy in battle. *Tynu am y dorch*, to strive for the torques: *Mi dynaf y dorch a thi*, I will pull the torques with thee.

> Braich uwch balenaya llonyrch;
> Brychwaith ei braich a'i thyrch.
>
> A handle above the point of the fields; of fretwork its handle and its *wreaths*. *Rhys Trew, i fwckd.*

Torchawg, *a.* (torch) Having a wreath, coil, or turn; wreathed, coiled, twisted, turned up; wearing a torques.

Torchawl, *a.* (torch) Wreathing, twisting, coiling

Torchawr, *part.* (torch) Wreathing, entwining.

> Gwefrawr godrwyawr torchawr am rudd.
>
> Amber-beads in ringlets *entwining* round the temples. *Aneurin.*

Torchedig, *a.* (torch) Wreathed, twisted; coiled

Torchi, *v. a.* (torch) To wreath, to twist, to twine; to coil, to gather into a chain; to turn up. *Torcha dy lewys*, turn up thy sleeves.

> Torchi gwraidd tywarch a gro
> I'r gwynt, ac i'r wybr, ganto.
>
> *Turning up* the roots of sods and gravel into the wind, and into the air, by him. *L. Morganwg.*

Torchiad, *s. m.—pl. t.* au (torch) A wreathing.

Torchwr, *s. m.—pl.* torchwyr (torch—gwr) A coiler, a wreather, a twister.

Tordain, *s. m.* (tor—tain) A spread out in a lolling manner. *v. a.* To loll.

Tordanawl, *a.* (tordain) Swelling out the belly.

Tordaniad, *s. m.* (tordain) A lolling on the belly.

Tordanu, *v. a.* (tordain) To spread out the belly.

Tordor, *adv.* (tor *repeated*) Belly to belly.

Tordyn, *a.* (tor—tyn) Tight stomached; full-bellied; high-stomached, proud-stomached.

> Bydd dordyn wrth elynion man,
> Fal chwythu tan mewn sorod.
>
> Be *high-stomached* to petty foes, like blowing the fire amongst dross. *Edm. Prys.*

Tordyniad, *s. m.* (tordyn) A stretching the belly.

Tordynu, *v. a.* (tordyn) To tighten the belly.

Tordd, *s. m.* (tor) A murmur, a din, a tumult.

Torddawl, *a.* (tordd) Murmuring, tumultuous.

Torddiad, *s. m.* (tordd) A murmuring, a raising a din.

Torddu, *v. a.* (tordd) To murmur, to make a din.

Torddus, *a.* (tordd) Murmuring, tumultuous.

Tored, *s. m.* (tor) That expands round. *a.* Vast.

Tòredig, *a.* (tòr) Broken, fractured, cut.

Toredlu, *s.—pl. t.* oedd (tored—llu) A vast host.

> Mynegid iddo fod yr amherawdr wedi lluestu yn agos i yno, a thoredlu gantho; ac yn y lle ydd oedd Arthur a luestwa ar lan afon
>
> It was told him that the emperor had encamped near to that place, having a *vast host* with him; and in the spot where he was Arthur encamped on a river side. *Gr. ab Arthur.*

Toredwynt, *s. m.—pl. t.* oedd (tored—gwynt) A whirlwind.

> Twrf toredwynt mawr uch mor diffaith.
>
> The din of a mighty *whirlwind* over a desert sea. *Llygad Gwr.*
>
> Torynt toredwynt uch teg adfan.
>
> They would burst a *whirlwind* over a fair retreat. *G. Cyfeiliawg.*

Toreithiad, *s. m.* (toraeth) A forming a store.

Toreithiannawl, *a.* (toreithiant) Of a productive tendency, tending to store.

Toreithiannu, *v. a.* (toreithiant) To cause abundance; to become abundant.

Toreithiant, *s. m.* (toraeth) Abundance; store.

Ymhel, *v. a.* (hel) To employ one's self, to meddle; to meddle mutually. *Paid ag ymhel a hwn*, cease meddling with this.

Ymhela, *v. a.* (ymhel) To employ one's self; to meddle, to meddle mutually.

Ymhelaethawl, *a.* (helaethawl) Self-amplifying, mutually amplifying.

Ymhelaethiad, *s. m.* (helaethiad) A self-enlarging; self-elongation; a mutually amplifying.

Ymhelaethu, *v. a.* (helaethu) To amplify one's self; to amplify mutually.

Ymhell, *adv.* (pell) At a distance, far off.

Ymhellach, *adv.* (ymhell) At a greater distance.

Ymheneiddiad, *s. m.* (heneiddiad) A making one's self seem old.

Ymheneiddiaw, *v. a.* (heneiddiaw) To make one's self seem old.

Ymherawd, *s. m.* (perawd) A self-causing.

Ymherawdr, *s. m.—pl.* ymherodron (ymherawd) That is self-causing; a tyrant; an emperor. It is the same with *amherawdr* and *ymddyherawdr*. *Ymherawdr o ddyn*, a tyrant of a person. *Sil.*

Ymherawdwr, *s. m.—pl.* ymherawdwyr (ymherawd—gwr) One who causeth of himself; an emperor.

Ymhercyd, *v. a.* (hercyd) To apprehend.

Ymherodraeth, *s. m.* (ymherawdr) The sway or government of an emperor; an empire.

Ymherodraidd, *a.* (ymherawdr) Like an emperor.

Ymherodrawl, *a.* (ymherawdr) Imperial.

> Gwedi eu hymgymysgu ynghyd, yr ymherodrawl fyddin [illegible] a wasgarwyd rhag y Prydeiniaid.
>
> After the *mutually mixing* of them together, the *imperial* army presently dispersed before the Britons. *Gr. ab Arthur.*

Ymherodres, *s. f.* (ymherawdr) An empress.

> Em loewserf, am oleuni
> Ymherodres [illegible] wyt ti.
>
> Gem of the refulgent heaven, for light the *empress* of radiancy art thou. *D. ab Gwilym, i'r haul.*

Ymheriad, *s. m.* (heriad) A shewing one's self out; a putting one's self in a posture of defiance; a mutual defying.

Ymheriaw, *v. a.* (heriaw) To shew one's self out; to put one's self in a threatening posture; to threaten mutually.

Ymheulaw, *v. a.* (heulaw) To bask in the sun.

Ymheuliad, *s. m.* (heuliad) A sunning one's self.

Ymhewydiad, *s. m.* (hewyd) A self-devoting; a mutually devoting.

Ymhewydu, *v. a.* (hewydu) To devote one's self; to devote mutually.

> O ymhewydu, ymhewydu ddwyfoldeb.
>
> *In self-devoting, devote thyself* to godliness. *Adage.*

Ymhiliad, *s. m.* (hiliad) A self-generating; a mutually producing or generating.

Ymhiliaw, *v. a.* (hiliaw) To self-produce; to produce or generate mutually.

Ymhiràad, *s. m.* (hiràad) A self-lengthening; a mutually lengthening.

Ymhiràu, *v. a.* (hiràu) To self-lengthen; to lengthen or elongate mutually.

Ymhlegyd, *adv.* (plegyd) In respect of.

Ymhlith, *adv.* (plith) Amongst, in the midst.

Ymhoewi, *v. a.* (hoewi) To enliven one's self; to be mutually sprightly.

Ymhoffi, *v. a.* (hoffi) To please one's self; to take delight; to love mutually.

> Yr hwn sydd yn toi y nefoedd â chymylau—nid ymhoffa efe yn esgeiriau gwr.
>
> He who covereth the heavens with clouds: *he taketh no pleasure* in the legs of a man. *Psalm* 147. 10.

Ymhoffiad, *s. m.* (hoffiad) A pleasing one's self; a taking delight; a mutually loving.

Ymhoffwr, *s. m.—pl.* ymhoffwyr (hoffwr) One who takes delight.

Ymholi, *v. a.* (holi) To employ one's self in questioning; to be enquiring; mutually to question. *Paid ag ymholi*, adone with questioning.

Ymholiad, *s. m.* (holiad) A being questioning; a mutually questioning.

Ymholwr, *s. m.—pl.* ymholwyr (holwr) One who employs himself in questioning.

Ymholydd, *s. m.—pl. t.* ion (holydd) One who employs himself in questioning; a disputant.

> P'le mae ymholydd y byd hwn!
>
> Where is the *disputer* of this world? 1 *Corinthiaid* 1. 20.

Ymhollti, *v. a.* (hollti) To split one's self; to split mutually.

Ymholltiad, *s. m.* (holltiad) A splitting one's self; a mutually splitting.

Ymhòni, *v. a.* (hòni) To assert one's self; to avouch, to claim, to challenge for one's self; to assert mutually.

Ymhòniad, *s. m.* (hòniad) An assuming to one's self; a mutually assuming.

Ymhonwr, *s. m.—pl.* ymhonwyr (honwr) One who assumes or asserts himself.

Ymhuddaw, *v. a.* (huddaw) To cover one's self.

Ymhuddiad, *s. m.* (huddiad) A self-covering.

Ymhuliad, *s. m.* (huliad) A decking one's self over; a mutually enveloping.

Ymhuliaw, *v. a.* (huliaw) To deck or envelope one's self; to envelope mutually.

Ymhunaw, *v. a.* (hunaw) To sleep one's self; to sleep mutually.

Ymhuniad, *s. m.* (huniad) A sleeping one's self; a mutually sleeping.

Ymhunydd, *s. m.* (hunydd) Self-repose.

> Ac os Duw o nef wna ym cynydd,
> Cefnfod gan [illegible] llawr ymhunydd.
>
> And if God of heaven but prosper me, fairly placed with the splendid one there will be for me the spot of *self-repose*. *Gwalchmai.*

Ymhŵedd, *s. m.* (hŵedd) A beseeching earnestly. *v. a.* To be beseeching; to implore mutually.

Ymhwrdd, *s. m.* (hwrdd) A mutual push; a mutual assault. *v. a.* To make a mutual assault.

Ymhwyl, *s. m.* (hwyl) A putting one's self in a course; a mutual setting off.

Ymhwyliad, *s. m.* (ymhwyl) A putting one's self in order or on a course; a mutually setting off.

Ymhwyliaw, *v. a.* (ymhwyl) To take to one's self a course; mutually to set in order.

Ymhyderiad, *s. m.* (hyderiad) A self confiding; a mutually depending.

Ymhyderu, *v. a.* (hyderu) To fill one's self with confidence; a mutually confiding.

Ymhyfàad, *s. m.* (hyfaad) A self-emboldening; a mutually emboldening.

Ymhyfàu, *v. a.* (hyfàu) To self-embolden; to embolden mutually.

Ymhyfiad, *s. m.* (hyfiad) A self-emboldening; a mutually emboldening.

Ymhyfrydiad, *s. m.* (hyfrydiad) A self-delighting; a becoming mutually delighted.

Ymhyfrydu, *v. a.* (hyfrydu) To delight one's self; to be mutually delighted.

Ymhyfu, *v. a.* (hyfu) To embolden one's self; to be mutually assuming confidence.

> Ymhyfaf er argyhoeddi dyn—ei fod ef mewn cyflwr o elyniaeth yn erbyn Duw.
>
> *I will embolden myself* to admonish man, of his being in a state of enmity against God. *S. Trefredyn.*

Ymhyiliad, *s. m.* (hylliad) A scaring one's self; a mutually scaring.

Ymhyllu, *v. a.* (hyllu) To scare one's self; to scare mutually.

Ymhynodi, *v. a.* (hynodi) To signalize one's self, to signalize mutually.

Ymhynodiad, *s. m.* (hynodiad) A self-signalizing; a mutually signalizing.

Ymhyrddiad, *s. m.* (ymhwrdd) A thrusting one's self; a mutually impelling or thrusting.

Ymhyrddu, *v. a.* (ymhwrdd) To impel or thrust one's self; to thrust mutually.

Ymhyrddwr, *s. m.—pl.* ymhyrddwyr (ymhwrdd—gwr) One who thrusteth himself.

Ymhysbysiad, *s. m.* (hysbysiad) An informing one's self; a making one's self known; a mutually informing.

Ymhysbysu, *v. a.* (hysbysu) To inform one's self; to make one's self known; to inform mutually.

> Ha fab dyn, llefara wrth henaduriaid Israel—pa rai yr ymhysbysais iddynt hwy, wrth eu dwyn allan o dir yr Aipht.

> Son of man, speak unto the elders of Israel, those to whom *I have made myself known*, in bringing them forth out of the land of Egypt. *Ezekiel* 20. 9.

Ymiachâad, *s. m.* (iachâad) A self-healing; a mutually healing; a bidding mutual adieu.

Ymiachâu, *v. a.* (iachâu) To heal one's self: to heal mutually; to bid farewell to one another.

> A chwi pan ymiachawyf,
> Porfa dir y pryfaid wyf.

> With you when *I mutually bid farewell*, I am the food of worms. *Ll. ab Hywel ab Ieu. ab Gronw.*

Ymiasâad, *s. m.* (iasâad) A pervading one's self with a sudden emotion or shock; a mutually giving a shock.

Ymiasâu, *v. a.* (iasâu) To pervade one's self with a shock; to shock mutually.

Ymiasiad, *s. m.* (iasiad) A being affected; a mutually filling with quick emotion.

Ymiasu, *v. a.* (iasu) To fill one's self with emotion; mutually to shock.

Ymiawl, *s. m.* (iawl) The employ of one's self in worship; mutual worship.

Ymiolad, *s. m.* (ymiawl) A being worshipping; a mutually worshipping.

Ymioli, *v. a.* (ymiawl) To employ one's self in adoration; to worship mutually.

> Ni nawd i ddiriad ymioli â Duw,
> Yn erbyn dydd cyni;
> Ni thybyg drud y trengi.

> It is not common for the mischievous *to be employing himself* in converse with God, against the day of affliction. the bold thinks not that he shall die. *Llarth.*

Ymiraw, *v. a.* (iraw) To anoint one's self.

> Pwy bynag a ymiro â'i iawn enaint, fe wel ei friwiau.

> Whoever *anoints himself* with the true unction, he will see his wounds. *Elis Wyn, B. Cwsg.*

Ymiriad, *s. m.* (iriad) A self-anointing.

Ymiseliad, *s. m.* (iseliad) A self-lowering; a mutually lowering or humbling.

Ymiselu, *v. a.* (iselu) To humble one's self; mutually to lower or humble.

Ymlacâad, *s. m.* (llacâad) A slackening one's self; a mutually slackening.

Ymlacâu, *v. a.* (llacâu) To slacken one's self.

Ymladiad, *s. m.* (lladiad) A blessing one's self.

Ymladrata, *v. a.* (lladrata) To employ one's self in stealing; to steal mutually.

Ymladu, *v. a.* (lladu) To bless one's self.

Ymladd, *s. m.—pl. t.* au (lladd) A mutual cutting off; a battle, a fight. *v. a.* To cut off mutually, to fight.

> Sef yw ymladd, dyrchaf, a gosod, a gwaed, a gweli.

> What constitutes *fighting* is lifting up the hand, and striking, and blood, and wound. *Welsh Laws.*

> A wyrda, ebai Dyfrig, ymleddwch tros eich gwlad.

> Ah, good people, said Dyfrig, *fight* for your country. *Gr. ab Arthur.*

> Er bod yn hawdd ei charu,
> Hi a ymladd drwy orweddu.

> Though she is easy to be courted, she *will fight* through lying. *Araeth y gwreigedd.*

> Nid gwaeth yr ymladd dig no glew.

> Not worse *will* the wrathful *fight* than the brave. *Adage.*

Ymladdawl, *a.* (ymladd) Pugnacious, fighting.

Ymladdfa, *s. f.* (ymladd) A place of battle.

Ymladdgar, *a.* (ymladd) Pugnacious, fighting.

Ymladdgarwch, *s. m.* (ymladdgar) Pugnacity.

Ymladdiad, *s. m.* (ymladd) A fighting.

Ymladdwr, *s. m.—pl.* ymladdwyr (ymladd—gwr) A fighter.

Ymlaen, *adv.* (blaen) Before, forward, onward.

> Gwell un gair ymlaen no dau yn ol.

> Better one word *before* than two after. *Adage.*

Ymlaenllaw, *adv.* (ymlaen—llaw) Before-hand.

Ymlaesiad, *s. m.* (llaesiad) A self-declining; a decaying gradually or drooping.

Ymlaesu, *v. a.* (llaesu) To slacken one's self; to decline mutually; to flag; to decline; to become indifferent.

Ymlafniad, *s. m.* (llafniad) A mutually blading; a romping, or pulling about.

Ymlafniaw, *v. a.* (llafniaw) To be mutually blading; to romp.

Ymlamiad, *s. m.* (llamiad) An employing one's self in striding; a mutually striding or skipping.

Ymlamsach, *s. m.* (llamsach) An employing one's self in skipping; a mutually skipping. *v. a.* To be skipping; to skip mutually.

Ymlamu, *v. a.* (llamu) To employ one's self in striding or skipping; to stride mutually.

Ymlanâad, *s. m.* (glanâad) A cleansing one's self; a mutually purifying.

Ymlanâu, *v. a.* (glanâu) To self-cleanse; to exculpate one's self; mutually to purify.

> Taenellu arnynt ddwfr puredigaeth—a golchent eu gwisgoedd, ac felly ymlanâant.

> Sprinkle over them the water of purification: and let them wash their clothes, and so *they shall make themselves clean*. *Numbers* 8. 7

Ymlanâwr, *s. m.—pl.* ymlanâwyr (glanâwr) One who cleanseth himself.

Ymlanw, *v. a.* (llanw) To fill one's self; to fill mutually.

Ymlanwad, *s. m.* (ymlanw) A self-filling; a mutually filling.

Ymlaryeiddiad, *s. m.* (llaryeiddiad) A self-mollifying, a mutually assuaging.

Ymlaryeiddiaw, *v. a.* (llaryeiddiaw) To self-assuage, mutually to soften.

Ymlasiad, *s. m.* (glasiad) A making one's self pale; a mutually turning blue.

Ymlasu, *v. a.* (glasu) To make one's self blue, to turn blue or pale mutually.

Ymlawenâad, *s. m.* (llawenâad) A gladdening one's self, a mutually gladdening.

Ymlawenâu, *v. a.* (llawenâu) To gladden one's self; to gladden mutually.

Ymlaweniad, *s. m.* (llaweniad) A gladdening one's self; a mutually gladdening.

Ymlawenu, *v. a.* (llawenu) To gladden one's self; to become mutually glad.

Ymlawenychiad, *s. m.* (llawenychiad) A causing one's self to exult; a mutually rejoicing.

Ymlawenychu, *v. a.* (llawenychu) To fill one's self with rejoicing; to rejoice mutually.

Ymlawenychwr, *s. m.—pl.* ymlawenychwyr (llawenychwr) One who rejoices in himself.

Ymleâad, *s. m.* (lleâad) A self-placing or self-location; a mutually placing.

Ymleâu, *v. a.* (lleâu) To place one's self; to self-locate, to place mutually.

Ymlechiad, *s. m.* (llechiad) A hiding one's self; a mutually sculking.

Ymlechu, *v. a.* (llechu) To secrete one's self.

Ymlechwr, *s. m.—pl.* ymlechwyr (llechwr) One who hides himself.

Ymlediad, *s. m.* (llediad) Self-expansion.

Ymledrithiad, *s. m.* (lledrithiad) A making one's self visible and invisible at pleasure; a mutually using delusion.

Ymledrithiaw, *v. a.* (lledrithiaw) To make one's self illusive; to use illusion mutually.

Ymledu, *v. a.* (lledu) To self-expand, to spread one's self; to become diffused; to expand mutually.

Ymlefariad, *s. m.* (llefariad) A self-speaking; a mutually speaking.

Ymlefaru, *v. a.* (llefaru) To employ one's self in talking; to talk mutually.

> Nid â ar for nid ymlefair.
>
> He will not go to sea who *doth not use himself in talking.* *Adage.*

Ymleferydd, *s. m.* (lleferydd) Dotage, drivelling, deliriousness. *v. a.* To utter nonsense; to drivel, to be delirious.

> Nid yw Camden er dysgedked, diwytel, a manyled gwr ydoedd, ond ymleferydd am lawer o bethau.
>
> Camden, though he was so learned, so industrious, so accurate a man, *doth* only *drivel* with respect to many things. *E. Evans.*

Ymleflef, *s. m.* (lleflef) A quarrelling in words. *v. a.* To utter out words mutually.

Ymleiâad, *s. m.* (lleiâad) A self-lessening; a mutually diminishing.

Ymleiâu, *v. a.* (lleiâu) To lessen one's self.

Ymleiddiad, *s. m.—pl.* ymleiddiaid (ymladd) A combatant.

Ymlenwad, *s. m.* (ymlanw) A self-filling.

Ymlenwi, *v. a.* (ymlanw) To fill one's self.

> Gwychr ddysg, fal terfysg taerfor gweilgi gan,
> Gennym ni, fan am lan yn ymlenwi.
>
> Heroic the example possessed by us, like the tumult of the raging sea in a white torrent loudly round the shore *filling itself.* *Gr. ab M. ab Dafydd.*

Ymletgynt, *s. m.* (lletgynt) A mutual contact.

> Dygawn ymletgynt;
> Cennadau a'm dodynt,
> Mor ynt amlymawg.
>
> We shall have *to be mutually coming together*, messengers to me are come, so numerously are they sent. *Taliesin.*

Ymletŷa, *v. a.* (lletŷa) To lodge one's self; to lodge mutually.

Ymletŷad, *s. m.* (lletŷad) A lodging of one's self; a mutually lodging.

Ymletŷwr, *s. m.—pl.* ymletŷwyr (lletŷwr) One who lodges himself.

Ymlewaad, *s. m.* (glewâad) An aptly exerting one's self; a being mutually clever.

Ymlewâu, *v. a.* (glewâu) To exert one's self, to become mutually clever.

Ymlewychiad, *s. m.* (llewychiad) A causing one's self to shine; a mutually shining.

Ymlewychu, *v. a.* (llewychu) To make one's self to shine; to be mutually shining.

Ymlewydd, *s. m.* (llewydd) Persuasion. *v. a.* To use persuasion, to persuade.

> Yr henuriaid ymlewydd a wnaynt a'r bobl, er mwyn gofyn Barabbas, a cholli yr Iesu.
>
> The elders, what they did was *to use persuasion* with the people, for the sake of asking for Barrabas, and destroy Jesus. *W. Salisbury.*

Ymlewyddiad, *s. m.* (ymlewydd) A persuading.

Ymlewyrchiad, *s. m.* (llewyrchiad) A self-shining; a mutually shining.

Ymlewyrchu, *v. a.* (llewyrchu) To make one's self to shine; to shine mutually.

> Ymlewyrchai o fynydd Paran.
>
> *He shined forth* from mount Paran. *Deut.* 33. 2.

Ymliasiad, *s. m.* (lliasiad) A mutually wrangling; an employing one's self in wrangling.

Ymliasu, *v. a.* (lliasu) To wrangle mutually; to employ one's self in wrangling.

Ymlid, *s. m.—pl. t.* iau (llid) A pursuit; a following. *v. a.* To pursue.

> Ennyg a fy lle nas ymlidier.
>
> The guilty will flee where he *is* not *pursued.* *Adage.*

Ymlidfa, *s. f.* (ymlid) A pursuit, a chase.

Ymlidiad, *s. m.* (ymlid) A pursuing, a chasing.

Ymlidiawl, *a.* (ymlid) Pursuing, chasing.

Ymlidiwr, *s. m.—pl.* ymlidiwyr (ymlid—gwr) A pursuer, a chaser.

Ymliosogi, *v. a.* (lliosogi) To self-multiply; to multiply mutually.

Ymliosogiad, *s. m.* (lliosogiad) A self-multiplying; a mutually multiplying.

Ymlithr, *s. m.* (llithr) A sliding or slipping one's self away; a defection.

Ymlithrad, *s. m.* (ymlithr) A self-slipping; a mutually slipping or sliding.

Ymlithraw, *v. a.* (ymlithr) To slip one's self.

> Ieremia a aeth allan o Ierusalem, i fyned i wlad Benjamin, i ymlithraw oddiyno yn nghanol y bobl.
>
> Jeremiah went forth out of Jerusalem to go into the land of Benjamin, *to separate himself* thence to the midst of the people. *Ieremi* 37. 12.

Ymlithrawl, *a.* (ymlithr) Slipping one's self.

Ymliw, *s. m.* (lliw) A reproach, a finding fault. *v. a.* To reproach, to find fault, to expostulate.

> Rhaid imi——
> Ymliw a'th aden emlaes.
>
> I must *find fault* with thy studded trailing wing. *D. ab Gwilym, i'r barcud.*
>
> Anmhedwydd ym, nad yw wiw,
> A'ch amled a chwi ymliw.
>
> Unfortunate we are, that it is of no use, and you being so numerous, with you *to expostulate.* *T. Aled.*

Ymliwiad, *s. m.* (ymliw) Self-expostulation.

Ymliwiaw, *v. a.* (ymliw) To self-reproach; to expostulate.

Ymliwiawl, *a.* (ymliw) Self-accusing.

Ymliwied, *v. a.* (ymliw) To self-reproach; to expostulate.

Ymlochlach, *s. m.* (llawch—llach) Pederasty. *v. a.* To commit pederasty.

Ymlodraw, *v. a.* (llodraw) To breech one's self; to breech mutually.

Ymlodriad, *s. m.* (llodriad) A breeching one's self; a mutually breeching.

Ymloewi, *v. a.* (gloewi) To brighten one's self.

Ymlogawl, *a.* (llogawl) Hiring of one's self.

Ymlogi, *v. a.* (llogi) To hire one's self, to prostitute one's self; to hire mutually.

Ymlogiad, *s. m.* (llogiad) A hiring of one's self, self prostitution; a mutual hiring.

Ymloni, *v. a.* (llòni) To make one's self cheerful. to recreate one's self; to grow cheerful.

Ymloniad, *s. m.* (lloniad) A cheering one's self; a being mutually cheerful.

Ymlonychiad, *s. m.* (llonychiad) A self-cheering; a mutually cheering.

Ymlonychu, *v. a.* (llonychu) To cheer one's self; to become mutually cheerful.

Ymlonyddiad, *s. m.* (llonyddiad) A quieting one's self; a mutually quieting.

Ymlonyddu, *v. a.* (llonyddu) To compose one's self; mutually to quiet.

Ymlosgach, *s. m.* (llosgach) A giving one's self to incest. *v. a.* To give one's self to incest.

Ymlosgi, *v. a.* (llosgi) To burn one's self; to burn mutually.

> Nid eisteddir ar dan heb ymlosgi.
>
> There can be no sitting on a fire without *burning one's self*. *Adage.*
>
> Gwedi pechu onaddynt wy, ydd ymlosgynt pob un o chwant ei gilydd.
>
> After sinning of them *they mutually burned* every one with a desire for the other. *Elucidarius.*

Ymlosgiad, *s. m.* (llosgiad) A self-burning; a mutually burning.

Ymluchiad, *s. m.* (lluchiad) A self-flinging, an employing one's self in casting; a mutually flinging.

Ymluchiaw, *v. a.* (lluchiaw) To fling one's self; to cast mutually.

Ymluddediad, *s. m.* (lluddediad) A self-fatiguing; a mutually fatiguing.

Ymluddedigaw, *v. a.* (lluddedigaw) To self-fatigue; to become mutually fatigued.

Ymluddedigiad, *s. m.* (lluddedigiad) A self-fatiguing: a becoming mutually fatigued.

Ymluddedu, *v. a.* (lluddedu) To fatigue one's self; mutually to fatigue.

Ymluniad, *s. m.* (lluniad) A self-forming.

Ymluniaw, *v. a.* (lluniaw) To form one's self.

Ymlusgad, *s. m.* (llusgad) A dragging one's self.

Ymlusgaw, *v. a.* (llusgaw) To drag one's self along; to creep, to crawl; to slide along; to drag mutually.

> Anffawd a ddaw dan redeg, ac a â ymaith dan ymlusgaw.
>
> Misfortune will come on a run, and will go away with *dragging herself along*. *Adage.*

Ymlusgawl, *a.* (llusgawl) Self-dragging.

Ymlusgiad, *s. m.—pl.* ymlusgiaid (llusgiad) A creeping or crawling thing.

Ymlusgwr, *s. m.—pl.* ymlusgwyr (llusgwr) One who drags himself or creeps along.

Ymlutrodi, *v. a.* (llutrodi) To besmear one's self; mutually to besmear.

Ymlutrodiad, *s. m.* (llutrodiad) A besmearing one's self; a mutually besmearing.

Ymluyddu, *v. a.* (lluyddu) To prepare one's self for hostility; mutually to become hostile.

Ymlwybrau, *v. a.* (llwybrau) To be moving one's self sluggishly along.

Ymlwybraw, *v. a.* (llwybraw) To move one's self sluggishly, or to crawl along.

Ymlwybriad, *s. m.* (llwybriad) A moving one's self sluggishly along; a crawling.

Ymlwyth, *s. m.* (llwyth) A self-burdening; a mutual burden.

Ymlwythaw, *v. a.* (ymlwyth) To burden one's self; mutually to burden.

> Gwnaf Ierusalem yn faen trwm i yr holl bobloedd; pawb a ymlwytho ag ef yn ddiau a rwygir.
>
> I will make Jerusalem a burdensome stone to all the people; all that *burden themselves* with it shall be cut in pieces. *Zechariah* 12. 3.

Ymlwythiad, *s. m.* (ymlwyth) A burdening one's self; a mutually burdening.

Ymlydaniad, *s. m.* (llydaniad) A making one's self wide or broad; a mutually widening.

Ymlydanu, *v. a.* (llydanu) To make one's self broad; to expand mutually.

Ymlyfiad, *s. m.* (llyfiad) A licking one's self; a mutually licking with the tongue.

Ymlyfu, *v. a.* (llyfu) To lick one's self; to lick mutually, to lick one another.

Ymlygrawl, *a.* (llygrawl) Self-corrupting; mutually corrupting or defiling.

Ymlygriad, *s. m.* (llygriad) A self-corrupting; a mutually corrupting or defiling.

Ymlygru, *v. a.* (llygru) To corrupt one's self; to corrupt or defile mutually.

> Pan fyddai farw y barnwyr, dychwelynt ac ymlygrynt yn fwy na'u tadau.
>
> When the judges should die, they would return and *they would corrupt themselves* more than their fathers. *Barnwyr* 2. 19.

Ymlygrwr, *s. m.—pl.* ymlygrwyr (llygrwr) One who corrupts or defiles himself.

Ymlymâad, *s. m.* (llymâad) A sharpening one's self; a mutually sharpening.

Ymlymâu, *v. a.* (llymâu) To sharpen one's self; to sharpen mutually.

Ymlyn, *s. m.* (glŷn) Cohesion, or adherence.

> O dri pheth y syrth angen abred ar ddyn: [illegible] gwybodaeth, anymlyn ag y da, ac ymlyn ag y drwg; sef y [illegible] o bethau hyd ei gydryw yn abred, a [illegible] yn ei [illegible] y bu gyntaf.
>
> From three causes will the destiny of the inchoatic transmigration fall on man; a disregard of knowledge, non-adherence with the good, and *adherence* to the evil; that is, he will fall for these things to his correspondent state in the inchoatic circle, and transmigrate back, as at first. *Barddas.*

Ymlynawl, *a.* (ymlyn) Self-adherent; adherent; mutually adhering.

Ymlyngi, *s. m.—pl. t.* on (ymlyn—ci) A following dog, a dog that follows by scent.

Ymlyniad, *s. m.—pl.* ymlyniaid (ymlyn) An adherent; a follower.

> Gnawd serchawg ymlyniad.
>
> The amorous is accustomed to be a *follower*. *Adage.*
>
> Gwell un ceidwad na dau ymlyniad.
>
> One keeper is better than two *pursuers*. *Adage.*

Ymlynu, *v. a.* (ymlyn) To adhere; to follow; to adhere mutually.

> Tri chydgyfran dyn; abred a gwynfyd, angen a rhyddid, a drwg a da, ac oll yn gydbwys, a gallu gan ddyn ymlynu wrth y un a fyno.
>
> The three co-participations of man; transmigration and intellectual perfection, necessity and liberty, and good and evil; and all equiponderate, and man having the power to *adhere* to whichever he will. *Barddas.*

Ymlynwr, *s. m.—pl.* ymlynwyr (ymlyn—gwr) An adherer, or a follower.

Ymlysiad, *s. m.* (llysiad) A self-discarding; a mutually discarding.

Ymlysied, *v. a.* (ymlysiad) To divest one's self; to run wildly, as cattle do in hot weather; also called *Moelysdota.*

Ymlysu, *v. a.* (llysu) To discard one's self; to discard mutually.

Ymlythiad, *s. m.* (glythiad) A self-gorging.

Ymlythu, *v. a.* (glythu) To gorge one's self.

Ymlythwr, *s. m.—pl.* ymlythwyr (glythwr) One who gorges himself.

Ymlywiad, *s. m.* (llywiad) A conducting one's self; a shifting for one's self; a mutually managing.

Ymlywiaw, *v. a.* (llywiaw) To conduct one's self; to shift for one's self. *Ymlywiaw ag y byd,* to shift for one's self with the world.

Ymmod, *s. m.* (mod) Motion. *v. a.* To move.

Ymmod pren ni ddeil i'w ymmod.

To shake a tree that will not bear *to be shaken*. *Adage.*

Ymmodadwy, *a.* (ymmod) Moveable.

Ymmodawl, *a.* (ymmod) Moving. *Ymmodolion*, moving things.

Ymmodbren, *s. m.—pl. t.* i (ymmod—pren) A stirring stick.

Ymmodedig, *a.* (ymmod) Being moved.

Ymmodi, *v. a.* (ymmod) To move, to stir.

Ymmodiad, *s. m.* (ymmod) A moving, a stirring.

Ymmodoldeb, *s. m.* (ymmodawl) Moveableness.

Ymmodrwydd, *s. m.* (ymmod) Moveableness.

Ymmodwr, *s. m.—pl.* ymmodwyr (ymmod—gwr) A mover, a stirrer, an agitator.

Ymnabod, *s. m.* (nabod) Mutual acquaintance. *v. a.* To be acquainted.

Goreu adnabod ymnabod dy hunan.

The best acquaintance is *to be acquainted of thyself*. *Catwg Ddoeth.*

Ymnacâad, *s. m.* (nacâad) A refusing one's self; a mutually refusing.

Ymnacâu, *v. a.* (nacâu) To refuse one's self; to refuse mutually.

Ymnawdd, *s. m.* (nawdd) A being a protection.

Ymnoddi, *v. a.* (ymnawdd) To be employed in protecting.

Ymnedd, *s. m.* (nedd) Earnest entreaty. *v. a.* To beseech earnestly; to use mutual persuasion.

Ymneddawl, *a.* (ymnedd) Entreating; persuasive

Ymneddiad, *s. m.* (ymnedd) An entreating, a using persuasion; a mutually persuading.

Ymneddu, *v. a.* (ymnedd) To employ one's self in entreaty; to entreat earnestly; to persuade; to entreat mutually.

Y tylawd—pa faint mwy yr ymbellâa ei gyfeillion oddiwrtho! er maint a ymneddo, ni throant ato.

The poor, how much more do his friends go far from him! howsoever *he may pursue them with words*, they will not turn to him. *Diarhebion* 19. 7.

Ymneddwr, *s. m.—pl.* ymneddwyr (ymnedd—gwr) One who entreats.

Ymneilltuad, *s. m.* (neilltuad) A putting one's self aside; a mutually going aside.

Ymneilltuaeth, *s. m.* (neilltuaeth) Self-recession; a mutual recession.

Ymneilltuaw, *v. a.* (neilltuaw) To put one's self aside; mutually to go aside.

Ymneilltua, attolwg, oddiwrthyf.

Separate thyself, I pray thee, from me. *Genesis* 13. 9.

Ymneilltuawl, *a.* (neilltuawl) Self-separating; mutually separating.

Ymneilltuwr, *s. m.—pl.* ymneilltuwyr (neilltuwr) One who separates himself, a separatist.

Ymnerthawl, *a.* (nerthawl) Self-strengthening; mutually strengthening.

Ymnerthiad, *s. m.* (nerthiad) A self-strengthening; a mutually fortifying.

Ymnerthu, *v. a.* (nerthu) To strengthen one's self; to strengthen mutually.

Ymnerthed eich dwylaw, a byddwch feibion grymus.

Let your hands *be strengthened*, and be ye valiant men. *2 Samuel* 2. 7.

Ymnerthwr, *s. m.—pl.* ymnerthwyr (nerthwr) One who strengthens himself.

Ymnesâad, *s. m.* (nesâad) A drawing one's self near; a mutually drawing near.

Ymnesâawl, *a.* (nesâawl) Tending to draw one's self near; mutually approaching.

Ymnesâu, *v. a.* (nesâu) To draw one's self near; to draw near mutually.

Ymnesiad, *s. m.* (nesiad) A putting one's self near; a mutually moving nearer.

Ymnesu, *v. a.* (nesu) To move one's self near; to move near mutually.

Ymnewid, *s. m.* (newid) A change of one's self; a mutual change. *v. a.* To change one's self; to change mutually.

Ymnewidiad, *s. m.* (ymnewid) A changing of one's self, a mutually changing.

Ymnewidiaw, *v. a.* (ymnewid) To change one's self; to change mutually.

Ymnidraw, *v. a.* (nidraw) To entangle one's self; to entangle mutually.

Ymnidriad, *s. m.* (nidriad) A self-entangling; a mutually entangling.

Ymnifeiriad, *s. m.* (nifeiriad) A self-increasing in number, a mutually making numerous.

Ymnifeiriaw, *v. a.* (nifeiriaw) To self-increase in number; to become numerous mutually.

Sef a orug Gruffudd ab Rhys—dechreu ymlueyddu, a gwyr ei genedl oc ei carai yn ymnifeiriaw tuag ato.

What Gruffudd son of Rhys did was to begin to form an army, and the men of his nation *gathering themselves in numbers* towards him. *Ceredawg o Lan Carfan.*

Ymnoddi, *v. a.* (noddi) To self-protect, to seek refuge; to protect mutually.

Ymnoddiad, *s. m.* (noddiad) A self-protecting; a mutually protecting.

Ymnoethi, *v. a.* (noethi) To self-denude, to expose one's self, mutually to expose.

Noah—a yfai o'r gwin, ac a feddwai, ac a ymnoethai yn nghanol ei babell.

Noah drank of the wine, and was drunken, and *he uncovered himself* within his tent. *Genesis* 9. 21.

Ymnoethiad, *s. m.* (noethiad) A making one's self naked; a mutually exposing.

Ymnofiad, *s. m.* (nofiad) A swimming one's self, a mutually swimming.

Ymnofiaw, *v. a.* (nofiaw) To swim one's self, to swim mutually.

Ni waeth gandde pwy a foddo, os gall efe ymnofiaw.

He cares not who shall be drowned, if he can *swim himself*. *Adage.*

Ymnwyfaw, *v. a.* (nwyfaw) To enliven one's self, mutually to wanton.

Ymnwyfiad, *s. m.* (nwyfiad) A self-enlivening; a mutually wantoning.

Ymnyddiad, *s. m.* (nyddiad) An entwining one's self; a mutually entwining.

Ymnyddu, *v. a.* (nyddu) To entwine one's self.

Ymnythiad, *s. m.* (nythiad) A nestling one's self; a mutually nestling.

Ymnythu, *v. a.* (nythu) To nestle one's self, a mutually nestling.

Ymo, *adv.* (wm—o) Aptly forthcoming.

Breisglym orwyddawr roddion ymo.

Steeds amply swift the gifts *aptly coming forth*. *Llygad Gwr.*

Ymobeithiad, *s. m.* (gobeithiad) A filling one's self with hope, a mutually hoping.

Ymobeithiaw, *v. a.* (gobeithiaw) To fill one's self with hope, mutually to hope.

Ymobryn, *s. m.* (gobryn) A mutual bargain. *v. a.* To bargain mutually.

Ymobryn a wnai a'r wraig feithria y mab.

He entered into a bargain with the woman to nurse the boy. *Mabinogi.*

Ymobryniad, *s. m.* (ymobryn) A mutually bargaining, a self-bargaining.

Ymochel, *s. m.* (gochel) An avoidance or eschewing; a mutual avoidance.

Ymochelgar, *a.* (ymochel) Apt to take care of one's self, apt mutually to avoid.

Ymocheliad, *s. m.* (ymochel) A taking heed of one's self, a mutually avoiding.

Ymochelwr, *s. m.—pl.* ymochelwyr (ymochel—gwr) One who takes care of himself.

Ymochelyd, *v. a.* (ymochel) To take heed of one's self; mutually to avoid.

> Rhag yr hyn oll a ddywedais wrth y wraig, ymocheled hi.
>
> Of all that I have said unto the woman, *let her beware.* *Barnwyr* 13. 13.

Ymodinebu, *v. a.* (godinebu) To commit adultery

> Gwrtheyrn Gwrthenau a roddes Ynys Daned—am gael ymodinebu â Rhonwen.
>
> Vortigern of repulsive lips gave the Isle of Thanet for leave *to commit adultery* with Rowena. *Trioedd.*

Ymodwrdd, *s. m.* (godwrdd) The engaging one's self in a tumult, a mutual tumult. *v. a.* To engage one's self in a tumult, to raise a mutual tumult.

Ymoddef, *s. m.* (goddef) A self-sufferance, mutual forbearance. *v. a.* To suffer one's self; to forbear mutually.

Ymoddefawl, *a.* (ymoddef) Self-suffering, of mutual forbearance or suffering.

Ymoddefiad, *s. m.* (ymoddef) A suffering one's self, a mutually bearing.

Ymoddefu, *v. a.* (ymoddef) To suffer one's self, to forbear or to bear mutually.

Ymoddefwr, *s. m.—pl.* ymoddefwyr (ymoddef—gwr) One who suffers himself.

Ymoedi, *v. a.* (oedi) To delay one's self, to delay or linger mutually.

Ymoediad, *s. m.* (oediad) A delaying one's self; a mutually delaying.

Ymoerfela, *v. a.* (ymoeri) To seek cool retreats.

Ymoeri, *v. a.* (oeri) To cool one's self.

Ymoeriad, *s. m.* (oeriad) A cooling one's self; a mutually cooling.

Ymofaliad, *s. m.* (gofaliad) A making one's self careful; a mutually caring.

Ymofalu, *v. a.* (gofalu) To make one's self careful; to be careful; to care mutually.

> Ymofalwn am foli,
> I wneuthur arch Un a Thri.
>
> *Let us be careful* in adoring, to fulfil the command of the One and Three. *D. ab Edmund.*

Ymofalwr, *s. m.* (gofalwr) One who is careful.

Ymofeg, *s. f.* (gofeg) The having an impulse of the mind; an idea.

> I myfi daeth ymofeg
> Ymofyn pwy yw'r dyn deg.
>
> An *idea* occurred to me of enquiring who the fair person can be. *D. ab Gwilym.*

Ymofegiad, *s. m.* (gofeg) A forming an idea.

Ymofidiad, *s. m.* (gofidiad) A paining one's self; a mutually afflicting.

Ymofidiaw, *v. a.* (gofidiaw) To pain one's self; mutually to afflict.

> Ymofidia a griddfana, merch Sion!
>
> *Be thou in pain,* and do thou groan, daughter of Zion! *Micah* 4. 10.

Ymofidiwr, *s. m.—pl.* ymofidiwyr (gofidiwr) One who puts himself in pain.

Ymofni, *v. a.* (ofni) To fill one's self with fear; mutually to become fearful.

Ymofniad, *s. m.* (ofniad) A filling one's self with fear; a mutually fearing.

Ymofwyad, *s. m.* (gofwyad) A visiting one's self; an employing one's self in visiting; a mutually visiting.

Ymofwyaw, *v. a.* (gofwyaw) To visit one's self; to employ one's self in visiting; to visit mutually.

Ymofyn, *s. m.—pl. t.* ion (gofyn) The employ of one's self in asking; a mutual asking; an enquiry. *v. a.* To enquire.

> Ni wyr ond a welas;
> Nid hysbys ond a ymofyno.
>
> No one knows but who has seen; no one is informed but who *shall have enquired.* *Adage.*

Ymofynawl, *a.* (ymofyn) Enquiring.

Ymofynblaid, *s. f.* (ymofyn—plaid) The seeking party; a plaintiff.

Ymofyngar, *a.* (ymofyn) Inquisitive; prying.

Ymofyngarwch, *s. m.* (ymofyn) Inquisitiveness.

Ymofyniad, *s. m.—pl. t.* au (ymofyn) An inquiring or seeking.

Ymofyniedydd, *s. m.* (ymofyniad) An inquirer.

Ymofynwr, *s. m.* (ymofyn—gwr) An inquirer.

Ymofynyd, *v. a.* (ymofyn) To inquire.

Ymofynydd, *s. m.* (ymofyn) An inquirer.

Ymogan, *s. f.* (gogan) Self-ridicule; mutual banter

Ymoganiad, *s. m.* (ymogan) A ridiculing one's self; a mutually ridiculing.

Ymoganu, *v. a.* (ymogan) To ridicule one's self; to banter mutually.

Ymogawr, *s. m.* (gogawr) A shelter; a dwelling.

> Gwae yr hen a golle ei ymogawr.
>
> Woe to the aged who shall have lost his *dwelling.* *Taliesin.*

Ymogel, *s. m.* (gogel) Self-care; mutual wariness.

Ymogelawg, *a.* (ymogel) Apt to avoid; wary.

Ymogelgar, *a.* (ymogel) Apt to avoid; wary.

Ymogeliad, *s. m.* (ymogel) A taking care of one's self; an avoiding; a mutually avoiding.

Ymogelus, *a.* (ymogel) Apt to take care; mutually apt to avoid.

Ymogelwr, *s. m.—pl.* ymogelwyr (ymogel—gwr) One who takes care of himself; one who avoids.

Ymogelyd, *v. a.* (ymogel) To take care of one's self; to avoid; to avoid mutually.

> Gwaith ysgafn ymogelyd.
>
> It is light work *to avoid.* *Adage.*
>
> A wnel drwg ymogeled.
>
> Who doth evil *let him take care of himself.* *Adage.*
>
> A ymogelo rhag dyn ni ymogel rhag Duw.
>
> He that *shall protect himself* against man will not protect himself against God. *Adage.*

Ymogoneddiad, *s. m.* (gogoneddiad) A self-glorifying; a mutually glorifying.

Ymogoneddu, *v. a.* (gogoneddu) To glorify one's self, to glorify mutually.

> Ti fy ngwas, Israel, yr hwn yr ymogoneddaf ynnot.
>
> Thou my servant, O Israel, in whom *I will be glorified.* *Esay* 49. 3.

Ymogoni, *v. a.* (gogoni) A becoming elated or proud.

> Ymogoni a wneynt y gwyr o weled eu gwragedd.
>
> The men *become elated* from seeing their wives. *Hanes Gr. ab Arthur.*

Ymogoniannu, *v. a.* (gogoniannu) To exalt one's self in triumph.

Ymogoriad, *s. m.* (ymogawr) A sheltering.

Ymogoriaw, *v. a.* (ymogawr) To shelter one's self.

> Pob gogawr yidd ymogorio dyn ag ef, cadwed pawb ei ogawr.
>
> As to a shelter that a person *shall shelter himself* with, let every body keep his shelter. *Welsh Laws.*

Ymoguddiad, *s. m.* (goguddiad) A partly self-hiding; a mutually hiding partly.

Ymoguddiaw, *v. a.* (goguddiaw) To hide one's self partly; mutually to hide partly.

Ymogwyddaw, *v. a.* (gogwyddaw) To incline one's self; a mutually inclining.

Ymogwyddiad, *s. m.* (gogwyddiad) An inclining one's self; a mutually inclining.

Ymogyfarch, *s. m.* (gogyfarch) A partly greeting or noticing mutually.

Ymogyfartaliad, *s. m.* (gogyfartaliad) A rendering one's self partly equal; a mutually becoming partly equal.

Ymogyfartalu, *v. a.* (gogyfartalu) To make one's self partly equal.

Ymogyfuchiad, *s. m.* (gogyfuchiad) A rendering one's self equally exalted, a mutually becoming equally exalted.

Ymogyfuchiaw, *v. a.* (gogyfuchiaw) To render one's self equally exalted: mutually to become equally exalted.

> Pan weles ef ei fod yn rhagori ar holl raddau yr engylion o ogoniant a thegwch, gan dremygu pawb, ef a arfaethai ymogyfuchiaw â Duw.
>
> When he perceived that he was surpassing all the orders of angels in glory and beauty, by contemning every one, he formed the design *to exalt himself equally* with God. *Elucidarius.*

Ymogylchiad, *s. m.* (gogylchiad) A partly surrounding one's self, a mutually surrounding partly.

Ymogylchu, *v. a.* (gogylchu) To self-encircle partly, mutually to surround partly.

Ymogyniauniad, *s. m.* (gogyniauniad) A rendering one's self elated, a mutually elating.

Ymogyniannu, *v. a.* (gogyniannu) To make one's self elated, mutually to elate.

> Ymogyniannu a oruc Constans, ac addaw i Wrtheyrn gadu iddo ef lywiaw y deyrnas.
>
> What Constans did was *to elate himself*, and promise Gortheyrn to leave to him the government of the kingdom. *Gr. ab Arthur.*
>
> Ymogyniannu a oruc Uthr, ac ymdroi ehun ar yr elawr—a dywedyd—gwiwsaant i yn hanner marw: ys gwell yr hanner marw a orfo nor byw cwbl y gorfer arno.
>
> What Uthyr did was *to elate himself*, and turn himself on the litter, with saying, thou better is the half dead that conquers than the completely living who is conquered. *Gr. ab Arthur.*

Ymolöad, *s. m.* (golöad) A self-wallowing.

Ymolchfa, *s. f.—pl. t.* oedd (golchfa) A lavatory.

Ymolchi, *v. a.* (golchi) To wash one's self.

Ymolchiad, *s. m.* (golchiad) A washing one's self, a mutually washing.

Ymoleuthiaw, *v. a.* (goleuthiaw) To self-worship, mutually to flatter.

Ymoloi, *v. a.* (goloi) To lie down, to wallow.

> A fagwyd ar y domen a gar ymoloi yn y dom.
>
> That is bred upon the dunghill loves *to wallow* in the dung. *Adage.*

Ymolli, *v. a.* (olli) To grasp, to lay hold.

> Persidia—ynddi y mae pyramus, maen a lysg y llaw a'i hymollo.
>
> Persidia, in there is the pyramus, a stone that burns the hand that *shall lay hold of it.* *Delw y Byd.*

Ymolliad, *s. m.* (olliad) A grasping, a holding.

Ymollwng, *s. m.* (gollwng) To let or loosen one's self, mutually to let go.

> Troesom oddiwrth y byd bach, a thros y cyfwng ymollyngasom i'r wlad dragwydd wi, rhwng y ddau lys, i y gwagle hyll.
>
> We turned away from the little world, and over the intermediate region, *we dropped ourselves* to the eternal country, between the two courts, into the terrific void. *Elis Wyn, B. Cwsg.*

Ymollyngawl, *a.* (ymollwng) Self-loosening, mutually loosening.

Ymollyngiad, *s. m.* (ymollwng) A letting one's self off; a mutually letting go.

Ymommedd, *s. m.* (gommedd) A self-refusal; a mutual refusal. *v. a.* To refuse one's self; to refuse mutually.

> Rhen nef a'n rhoddo ni ran trugaredd,
> Teyrn-tron tanc erom heb ymommedd.
>
> The Sovereign of heaven give us a portion of the mercy of the royal throne of peace, for our sake without *inclining himself to refuse.* *Gr. ab Yr Ynad Coch.*

Ymoralw, *s. m.* (goralw) An inquiry, a seeking. *v. a.* To inquire.

Ymoralwad, *s. m.* (ymoralw) An inquiring.

Ymorbwyll, *s. m.* (gorbwyll) A self-persuading; a mutual persuasion.

> Dylid ymorbwyll â dynion drwg, a cheisiaw eu darwedd at ddaioni a doethineb.
>
> It is necessary *to use persuasion* with bad men, and endeavour to allure them to goodness and wisdom. *Barddas.*

Ymorbwyllaw, *v. a.* (ymorbwyll) To employ one's self in persuading; to persuade mutually; to persuade:

Ymorbwylliad, *s. m.* (ymorbwyll) A being persuading; a mutually persuading.

Ymorchest, *s. f.* (gorchest) Self-exertion; mutual exertion or emulation.

Ymorchestawl, *a.* (ymorchest) Self-exerting; mutually striving, mutually emulous.

Ymorchestfa, *s. f.—pl.* ymorchestfëydd (ymorchest) A place for feats or games.

Ymorchestgar, *a.* (ymorchest) Apt to exert one's self; mutually emulous.

Ymorchestiad, *s. m.* (ymorchest) A striving to excel; a mutual emulation.

Ymorchestu, *v. a.* (ymorchest) To employ one's self in excelling; to strive mutually for excellence; to struggle together; to emulate.

> Yr ydym yn ymorchestu—ein bod yn gymeradwy ganddo ef.
>
> We are *labouring* that we be acceptable with him. *2 Corinthiaid 5. 9.*

Ymorchestwr, *s. m.—pl.* ymorchestwyr (ymorchest—gwr) One who strives to excel.

Ymorchuddiad, *s. m.* (gorchuddiad) A self-covering, a mutually covering over.

Ymorchuddiaw, *v. a.* (gorchuddiaw) To cover over one's self; to cover over mutually.

> Merch weddw heb ymorchuddiaw.
>
> A single woman without *entering into coverture.* *T. Aled.*

Ymorchwydd, *s. m.* (gorchwydd) A self-swelling, a filling one's self with rage; mutual rage. *v. a.* To swell with rage; to swell with mutual rage.

> Cynwan torf terfysg ymorchwydd,
> Cynwaew gwyth gweithfuddig arglwydd.
>
> The foremost rank of a host of the tumult of *mutual outrage*, there the foremost spear of wrath a conquering chieftain bears. *Cynddelw, m. O. Gwynedd.*
>
> Llyw glyw glew yn ymorchwydd.
>
> The leader of a brave prince *swelling himself with rage.* *Prydydd Bychan.*

Ymorchwyddaw, *v. a.* (ymorchwydd) To swell one's self with rage, to grow mutually enraged.

Ymorchwyddiad, *s. m.* (ymorchwydd) A swelling one's self with rage.

Ymorchwyliad, *s. m.* (gorchwyliad) A self-occupying; a mutually working.

Ymorchwyliaw, *v. a.* (gorchwyliaw) To employ one's self; to operate mutually.

Ymorchymyniad, *s. m.* (gorchymyniad) A self-commending; a mutually desiring.

Ymorchymynu, *v. a.* (gorchymynu) To self-commend; to desire mutually.

> I Dduw a Dewi ydd ymorchymynynt.
>
> To God and Dewi they *were commending themselves.* *Golyddan, Arymes Prydain.*

Ymorddiweddiad, *s. m.* (gorweddiad) An advancing one's self to an end; a making one's self to surpass; a mutually advancing to an equality.

Ymorddiweddu, *v. a.* (gorddiweddu) To make one's self to come up, to advance one's self to an equality; mutually to advance to an end.

Megys nad ymorddiwedda un creadur â Duw, ac ef yn ymorddiwes a phob peth; felly nid oes un creadur or a weler a allo ymorddiwedd â'r enaid, canys ef a ymorddiwes a phob creadur gweledig.

As no creature *advanceth itself to be equal* with God; and he *self advancing to be present* with every thing; so there is not one creature, which is seen, that can *advance itself equal* with the soul for *it advanceth itself* to be *present* with every visible creature. *Elucidarius.*

Ymorddiwes, *s. m.* (gorddiwes) A mutual overtaking; the making one's self to overtake.

Ymorddiwesiad, *s. m.* (ymorddiwes) A making one's self to overtake.

Ymorddiwesu, *v. a.* (ymorddiwes) To overtake mutually; to make one's self to overtake.

Ymorfoleddiad, *s. m.* (gorfoleddiad) A mutually exulting; a self-exulting.

Ymorfoleddu, *v. a.* (gorfoleddu) To exult mutually; to exult in one's self.

Ymorfoleddwr, *s. m.—pl.* ymorfoleddwyr (gorfoleddwr) One who exults mutually, one who exults in himself.

Ymorfod, *s. m.* (gorfod) A self-conquest, a mutual conquest. *v. a.* To conquer one's self, to conquer mutually.

Ymorfodiad, *s. m.* (ymorfod) A self-conquering, a mutually conquering.

Ymorfoli, *v. a.* (gorfoli) To vaunt mutually, to vaunt one's self.

Ymorfawl am a orfu,
Ymwan a llain yn min llu.

He vaunts himself as to what he accomplished, thrusting with a blade in front of a host. *Iolo Goch.*

Ymorphwys, *s. m.* (gorphwys) A resting one's self, a mutual rest. *v. a.* To rest one's self, to rest mutually.

Ymorphwysaw, *v. a.* (ymorphwys) To rest one's self; to rest mutually.

Ymorheula, *v. a.* (gor—haul) To bask one's self in the sun. *s. m.* The seeking of sunshine.

Dewisbeth—Ymorheula pen mynydd.

A choice enjoyment—the *seeking of the sunshine* of a mountain top. *Adage.*

Ymorheuliad, *s. m.* (gor—heuliad) A basking one's self in the sun.

Ymorhoffi, *v. a.* (gorhoffi) To delight one's self extremely; mutually to take extreme delight or fondness.

Ymorhoffiad, *s. m.* (gorhoffiad) A delighting one's self extremely; a mutually loving extremely.

Ymorllaesiad, *s. m.* (gorllaesiad) A self-trailing.

Ymorllaesu, *v. a.* (gorllaesu) To trail one's self.

Ymorllwyn, *s. m.* (gorllwyn) A mutual escort; a self-protection.

Ymorllwyniad, *s. m.* (ymorllwyn) A mutually escorting; a self-protecting.

Ymornest, *s. f.* (gornest) A mutual combat.

Ymornestiad, *s. m.* (ymornest) A mutually combating; an employing one's self in combat.

Ymornestu, *v. a.* (ymornest) To combat mutually, to employ one's self in combat.

Ymornestwr, *s. m.—pl.* ymornestwyr (ymornest—gwr) One employed in combating.

Ymorol, *s. m.* (gorol) The act of seeking.

Ymorolgar, *s. m.* (ymorol) Inquisitive, seeking.

Ymoroli, *v. a.* (ymorol) To enquire, to seek.

Ymorsaf, *s. f.* (gorsaf) A station where one fixes himself.

Gwiw dy weled—
A'th folchlafn a'th falch ymorsaf.

Glorious to behold thee, with thy notched blade and thy exalted *station.* *Cynddelw, i H. ab Owain.*

Ymorsafiad, *s. m.* (ymorsaf) A stationing one's self, a mutually stationing.

Ymorsafu, *v. a.* (ymorsaf) To station one's self, to station mutually.

Ymortho, *s. m.* (gortho) A self-envelopement.

Ymorthöad, *s. m.* (ymortho) A self-enveloping.

Ymorthöi, *v. a.* (ymortho) To self-envelope.

Ymorthöus, *a.* (ymortho) Self-enveloping.

Ymoruchafiad, *s. m.* (goruchafiad) A self-exaltation, a mutually exalting.

Ymoruchafiaethiad, *s. m.* (goruchafiaethiad) An assuming to one's self pre-eminence, a mutually assuming pre-eminence.

Ymoruchafiaethu, *v. a.* (goruchafiaethu) To assume to one's self pre-eminence, to assume pre-eminence mutually.

Ymoruchafu, *v. a.* (goruchafu) To exalt one's self, to exalt mutually.

Ymorwyliad, *s. m.* (gorwyliad) The using one's self to watch or overlook.

Ymorwyliaw, *v. a.* (gorwyliaw) To use one's self to watch or overlook.

Ymorwyth, *s. m.* (gorwyth) An enraging. *v. a.* To put one's self in a rage.

Ymorwythaw, *v. a.* (gorwythaw) To put one's self in a rage, to enrage mutually.

Ymorwythiad, *s. m.* (gorwythiad) A putting one's self in a rage, a mutually enraging.

Ymosawd, *s. m.* (gosawd) A setting or placing one's self, a mutual onset. *v. a.* To place one's self, to set on mutually, to assault.

A'th waew rudd yn rhyn ymosawd.

With thy ruddy spear dreadfully *assaulting.* *Ll. P. Moch.*

Ymosgöad, *s. m.* (osgöad) A mutually going aside or avoiding, a withdrawing one's self aside.

Ymosgöi, *v. a.* (osgöi) To shun mutually, to withdraw one's self aside.

Ymosgorddi, *v. a.* (gosgorddi) To surround one's self with a retinue, mutually to form a retinue.

Ymosgorddiad, *s. m.* (gosgorddiad) A surrounding one's self with a retinue, a mutually forming a retinue.

Ymosgrain, *s. m.* (gosgrain) A crawling along.

Ymosgreiniad, *s. m.* (ymosgrain) A dragging one's self along, a crawling along.

Ymosgreiniaw, *v. a.* (ymosgrain) To drag one's self along, to crawl along.

Pe gwelai ddiawg y drwg a'i ery, efe a ymosgreiniai o'i fegid rhag ofn a chywilydd.

If the lazy were to see the evil that awaits him, he would *drag himself* out of his sloth for fear and shame. *Cathag Ddoeth.*

Ymosgryd, *s. m.* (gosgryd) A self-trepidation; mutual trepidation.

Ymosgrydiad, *s. m.* (ymosgryd) A mutually trembling; a making one's self to quake.

Ymosgrydiaw, *v. a.* (ymosgryd) To tremble mutually; to cause one's self to tremble.

Ymosgryn, *s. m.* (gosgryn) A mutual shock, a self-agitation.

Gosawd gosgo gosgordd yn ddian
Fal ymosgryn mawr gawr Camlan;
Gosawd canawl folian, fal Afan Ferddig,
Neu farddawwd Aronan.

The character of a host running away is like the great *mutual perturbation* of the shout of Camlan; it is characteristic for me to sing an eulogy, like Avan Verddig, or like the bardic lay of Aronan. *Cynddelw, i H. ab Owain.*

Ymosgryniad, *s. m.* (ymosgryn) A mutually concussing; a causing a self-perturbation.

Ymosgrynu, *v. a.* (ymosgryn) To concuss mutually; to agitate one's self; to give one's self a shock.

Ymosmeithiad, *s. m.* (gosmeithiad) A self-provisioning; a mutually provisioning.

Ymosmeithiaw, *v. a.* (gosmeithiaw) To furnish one's self with provision; to provide mutually.

Ymosodawl, *a.* (ymosawd) Relating to self-placing; relating to mutual onset.

Ymosodi, *v. a.* (ymosawd) To self-place; to attack mutually.

Ymosodiad, *s. m.* (ymosawd) A placing one's self; a mutually placing; a setting on mutually.

Ymosodwr, *s. m.—pl.* ymosodwyr (ymosawd—gwr) One who places himself.

Ymostegiad, *s. m.* (gostegiad) A silencing one's self; a mutually silencing.

Ymostegu, *v. a.* (gostegu) To silence one's self; to silence mutually.

Ymostwng, *s. m.* (gostwng) Self-debasement, self-humiliation, self-submission; a mutual lowering. *v. a.* To bring one's self down; to make a bow.

Ymostyngawl, *a.* (ymostwng) Self-debasing.

Ymostyngar, *a.* (ymostwng) Self-submissive.

Ymostyngiad, *s. m.* (ymostwng) A lowering of one's self; self-humiliation; self-condescension; a bowing one's self; a mutually lowering.

Ympryd, *s. m.—pl. t.* iau (pryd) A fast.

Ymprydiad, *s. m.* (ympryd) A fasting.

Ymprydiaw, *v. a.* (ympryd) To keep a fast.

Ymprydiawl, *a.* (ympryd) Relating to a fast.

Ymprydiwr, *s. m.—pl.* ymprydiwyr (ympryd—gwr) One who keeps a fast.

Ymrabin, *s. m.* (grabin) A mutual grasping. *v. a.* To clasp, close, or grapple together.

> Wrth ymrabin y mae y cathau yn ymgaru.
>
> By *clawing together* it is that the cats shew their love. *Adage.*

Ymrabiniad, *s. m.* (grabin) A mutually grasping.

Ymrabiniaw, *v. a.* (ymrabin) To grasp mutually.

Ymrafael, *s. f.—pl. t.* ion (rhy—gafael) Contention, variance, or strife. *Tòri yr ymrafael*, to break the dispute.

Ymrafaelgar, *a.* (ymrafael) Contentious.

Ymrafaelgarwch, *s. m.* (ymrafaelgar) Contentiousness, a state of mutual wrangling.

Ymrafaeliad, *s. m.* (ymrafael) A contending.

Ymrafaeliaw, *v. a.* (ymrafael) To contend.

Ymrafaeliwr, *s. m.—pl.* ymrafaeliwyr (ymrafael—gwr) One who engages in contention, a wrangler.

Ymrain, *s. m.* (rhain) A partaking in coition. *v. a.* To partake in coition.

> Tri achaws y gedy gwraig ei gwr: o bydd clafr, neu ag anadl ddrewedig iddo, neu heb allu ymrain.
>
> For three causes a wife forsakes her husband: if he be leprous, or with stinking breath, or without being able *to partake of coition.* *Welsh Laws.*

Ymraint, *adv.* (braint) Almost, at the point of.

> Gwelliad ymraint ei golli.
>
> A neglectful one *at the point of* being lost. *T. Aled.*

Ymran, *s. f.—pl. t.* au (rhan) A schism; a sect.

Ymranawl, *a.* (ymran) Schismatic, mutually separating or dividing.

Ymraniad, *s. f.—pl. t.* au (ymran) A becoming divided, a dividing into schisms. *Rhwyf ymraniad*, a leader of a sect.

Ymranu, *v. a.* (ymran) To self-separate; to become divided; to separate mutually.

> [illegible]
>
> [illegible] without [illegible] to the edge of the pre[illegible] veil, whilst [illegible] *Lla* [illegible]

Ymranwr, *s. m.—pl.* ymranwyr (ymran—gwr) One who separates himself.

Ymrathiad, *s. m.* (rhathiad) A mutually rubbing; a rubbing one's self.

Ymrathu, *v. a.* (rhathu) To rub mutually; to rub one's self.

Ymre, *s. f.* (rhe) Procreation. *v. a.* To copulate.

> Nid o'i gorff ydd ymre y gwybedyn.
>
> It is not from his body that a fly *doth procreate.* *Adage.*

Ymrëad, *s. m.* (ymre) Coition, copulation.

> Ni thal dim drwg ymrëad.
>
> No kind of bad *connection* will prosper. *Adage.*

Ymrëain, *v. a.* (ymre) To copulate, to couple.

> Tair gwaith y dyrchaif ar sarhad gwr, pan ymrëer ei wraig.
>
> Three advancements shall be made on the insult fine, to a husband when *connection shall be had* with his wife. *Welsh Laws.*

Ymredeg, *s. m.* (rhedeg) To run one's self; to run mutually.

Ymrediad, *s. m.* (rhediad) A running one's self; a mutually running.

Ymreddfiad, *s. m.* (greddfiad) A self-habituating; a mutually habituating.

Ymreddfu, *v. a.* (greddfu) To habituate one's self; to mutually habituate.

Ymrefriad, *s. m.* (rhefriad) A basking one's self; a basking mutually.

Ymrefru, *v. a.* (rhefru) To bask one's self; to bask mutually.

Ymreg, *s. f.* (rheg) A mutual ban or curse.

Ymregawl, *a.* (ymreg) Mutually cursing.

Ymregiad, *s. m.* (ymreg) A cursing mutually.

Ymregu, *v. a.* (ymreg) To curse mutually.

Ymrem, *s. f.* (rhem) A wambling, a stir; a stir in the stomach.

Ymremial, *s. m.* (ymrem) A wrangling together.

Ymrewydd, *s. m.* (rhewydd) Coition, copulation. *v. a.* To copulate.

> Ni fynai y rhai creulawn, gan y morwynion, ond ymrewydd a hwynt; ac am nas caent, eu lladd a orugynt.
>
> The cruel ones would have no less, from the virgins, than *to cohabit* with them, and forasmuch as they could not they slew them. *Gr. ab Arthur.*

Ymrewyddiad, *s. m.* (ymrewydd) A copulating.

Ymrewyddu, *v. a.* (ymrewydd) To copulate.

Ymrifaw, *v. a.* (rhifaw) To number one's self; to number mutually.

Ymrifiad, *s. m.* (rhifiad) A numbering one's self; a mutually numbering.

Ymrinciad, *s. m.* (rhinc) A mutually jarring.

Ymrincian, *v. a.* (rhincian) To jarr mutually; to employ one's self in jarring.

Ymriniad, *s. m.* (rhiniad) An employing one's self in mysteries; a talking mutual secrets.

Ymriniaw, *v. a.* (rhiniaw) To employ one's self in secrets; to talk mutual secrets.

> A fyno na wypo neb ei rin, ymrined a'i bwyll yn unig.
>
> He who would that no body should know his secret, *let him employ himself about secrets* with his mind alone. *Adage.*

Ymrithiad, *s. m.* (rhithiad) A shewing one's self; a making one's self to appear; a mutually appearing; a taking a form.

Ymrithiaw, *v. a.* (rhithiaw) To shew one's self; to make one's self to appear or to seem; to become apparent; to knit, as applied to the formation of fruit; to appear mutually.

> Ymrith y drwg ar lun da[illegible].
>
> Evil will shew itself in the form of good. *Adage.*

Ymrithiaw a oruc Menw yn rhith aderyn, a disgyn a wnai uwch ben y gwal

What Menw did was *to appear* in the semblance of a bird, and he alighted above the den. *H. Culhwch—Mabinogion.*

Ymrithiawl, *a.* (rhithiawl) Apt to make one's self seem; mutually seeming.

Ymrithiwr, *s. m.—pl.* ymrithiwyr (rhithiwr) One who appears or puts on a semblance.

Ymröad, *s. m.* (rhöad) Self-resignation; a mutually giving or resigning.

Ymröawl, *a.* (rhöawl) Self-resigning; mutually resigned.

Ymrodiad, *s. m.* (rhodiad) An employing one's self in walking about; a mutually walking about or perambulating.

Ymrodiaw, *v. a.* (rhodiaw) To employ one's self in walking about; to perambulate mutually.

Ymroddawl, *a.* (rhoddawl) Self-resigning; mutually resigning or giving up.

Ymroddedig, *a.* (rhoddedig) Self-resigned; mutually resigned or become yielding.

Ymroddi, *v. a.* (rhoddi) To resign one's self; to give up or resign mutually.

Cas dyn a ymroddo mewn anurddas er urddas i un arall.

Hateful the person who *shall give himself up* to dishonour for the honour of another. *Adage.*

Ymroddiad, *s. m.* (rhoddiad) A self-resignation; mutual resignation.

Ymroddwr, *s. m.—pl.* ymroddwyr (rhoddwr) One who resigns or yields himself.

Gwell ymroddwr no dialwr.

Better the *one who forgoes* than the retaliator. *Adage.*

Ymroi, *v. a.* (rhoi) To give one's self; to resign one's self, to become resigned, to submit; to resolve; to give up mutually. *Ymroi i farw*, to resign one's self to die; *ymroi i fyw yn dda*, to resolve to live well; *ymroi ati*, to fall to it in earnest.

Ymroliad, *s. m.* (rholiad) A rolling one's self; a mutually rolling.

Ymrolian, *v. a.* (rholian) To be rolling one's self; to be mutually rolling.

Ymroliaw, *v. a.* (rholiaw) To roll one's self; to roll mutually.

Ef oedd——
Yn ymroliaw am yr aelwyd.

He was *rolling himself* about the hearth. *Rhys. Iorwerth.*

Ymron, *adv.* (bron) Hard by; almost. *Ymron marw*, almost dying; *ymron tagu*, almost choaked.

Ymronyniad, *s. m.* (gronyniad) A becoming granulated; a self-granulating.

Ymronynu, *v. n.* (gronynu) To become granulated; to self-granulate.

Ymruglaw, *v. a.* (rhuglaw) To trail one's self; to trail mutually.

Ymrugliad, *s. m.* (rhugliad) A trailing one's self; a mutually trailing.

Ymruthraw, *v. a.* (rhuthraw) To rush one's self on; to rush on mutually.

Ymruthriad, *s. m.* (rhuthriad) A rushing one's self on; a mutually rushing.

Ymruthrwr, *s. m.—pl.* ymruthrwyr (rhuthrwr) One who rushes himself onward.

Ymrwgnach, *s. m.* (grwgnach) A using one's self to grumbling. *v. a.* To use one's self to grumbling.

Ymrwtiad, *s. m.* (rhwtiad) A self-chafing.

Ymrwtiaw, *v. a.* (rhwtiaw) To rub one's self.

Ymrwydaw, *v. a.* (rhwydaw) To entangle one's self; to entangle mutually.

Ymrwydiad, *s. m.* (rhwydiad) A self-entangling, a mutually entangling.

Ymrwyddâad, *s. m.* (rhwyddâad) A facilitating one's self, a mutually facilitating.

Ymrwyddâu, *v. a.* (rhwyddâu) To facilitate one's self, mutually to facilitate.

Ymrwyddaw, *v. a.* (rhwyddaw) To facilitate one's self, to facilitate mutually.

Ymrwyddiad, *s. m.* (rhwyddiad) A facilitating one's self; a mutually facilitating.

Ymrwyfaw, *v. a.* (rhwyfaw) To urge one's self forward, to row one's self; to row mutually.

Ymrwyfiad, *s. m.* (rhwyfiad) A working one's self onward; a rowing one's self; a mutually rowing.

Ymrwygaw, *v. a.* (rhwygaw) To tear one's self, to tear mutually.

Ymrwygiad, *s. m.* (rhwygiad) A tearing or rending one's self; a mutually rending.

Ymrwyllaw, *v. a.* (rhwyllaw) To become full of interstices; to work out through crevices.

Lle'r ymrwyllo'r mor allan,
Lle bag y mae'r llongau man.

Where the sea *through crevices works itself out*, is a close place the small ships are laid. *Lewis Mon.*

Ymrwylliad, *s. m.* (rhwylliad) A becoming full of interstices; a working through crevices.

Ymrwymaw, *v. a.* (rhwymaw) To bind one's self, to bind mutually.

Ymrwymawl, *a.* (rhwymawl) Self-binding, being mutually binding.

Ymrwymiad, *s. m.* (rhwymiad) A binding one's self; a mutually binding.

Ymrwymwr, *s. m.—pl.* ymrwymwyr (rhwymwr) One who binds himself.

Ymrwysaw, *v. a.* (rhwysaw) To self-invigorate, to invigorate mutually.

Deuparth iechyd ymrwysaw.

The two parts of health is exercise. *Adage.*

Ymrwysiad, *s. m.* (rhwysiad) A self-invigoration; a mutually invigorating.

Ymrwystraw, *v. a.* (rhwystraw) To hinder one's self, to hinder or to delay mutually.

Ymrwystriad, *s. m.* (rhwystriad) A hindering one's self, a mutually hindering.

Ymrwystrwr, *s. m.—pl.* ymrwystrwyr (rhwystrwr) One who hindereth himself.

Ymrwythaw, *v. a.* (rhwythaw) To pervade one's self, to pervade mutually.

Ymrwythiad, *s. m.* (rhwythiad) A self-pervading, a mutually pervading.

Ymrydwst, *s. m.* (grydwst) An employing one's self in twittering. *v. a.* To be twittering, to twitter mutually.

Ymryddâad, *s. m.* (rhyddâad) A liberating one's self, a mutually liberating.

Ymryddâu, *v. a.* (rhyddâu) To liberate one's self; to liberate mutually.

Ymryfeddiad, *s. m.* (rhyfeddiad) A wondering in one's self, a mutually wondering.

Ymryfeddu, *v. a.* (rhyfeddu) To wonder in one's self, to wonder mutually.

Ymryfel, *s. m.* (rhyfel) The being engaged in war; mutual warfare.

Ymryfeliad, *s. m.* (ymryfel) An engaging one's self in war; a mutually warring.

Ymryfelu, *v. a.* (rhyfelu) To engage one's self in war; to war mutually.

> Marwawl ddyn——
> Sef ymryfelu a mi bydd;
> A phoenydd ym gorthrymau.

> Mortal man: *he engages himself in war* against me; and daily he causes me affliction. *Edm. Prys, Psalm* lvi. 2.

Ymryfelwr, *s. m.—pl.* ymryfelwyr (ymryfel—gwr) One who uses himself to war.

Ymryfygawl, *a.* (rhyfygawl) Self-arrogating; mutually presuming.

Ymryfygiad, *s. m.* (rhyfygiad) To assume to one's self, a mutually presuming.

Ymryfygu, *v. a.* (rhyfygu) To assume to one's self; to presume mutually.

> Syberwyd, sef yw hyny ymryfygu o ddyn yn ei geudawd, a chebisaw ymddyrchafael yn uwch nog y dylyo.

> Haughtiness, that is for a person *to arrogate to himself* in his imagination, and seek to exalt himself higher than he ought. *Ll. O. Hergest.*

Ymryfygwr, *s. m.—pl.* ymryfygwyr (rhyfygwr) One who arrogates to himself.

Ymryfysg, *s. m.* (rhyfysg) A confused state; mutual confusion.

> Pan ddel ymrafael ac ymryfysg blin,
> Heb lonydd gan derfysg,
> Taraw i mewn.——

> When there comes contention and dire *confusion*, void of rest from tumult, do thou strike in. *H. D. ab Ifan.*

Ymryfysgiad, *s. m.* (ymryfysg) A putting one's self in confusion; a mutual confusion.

Ymryfysgu, *v. a.* (ymryfysg) To confuse one's self; to confuse mutually.

Ymrygniad, *s. m.* (rhygniad) A rubbing or galling one's self; a mutually rubbing.

Ymrygnu, *v. a.* (rhygnu) To rub or gall one's self, to rub mutually.

Ymrymiad, *s. m.* (grymiad) To strengthen one's self, to self-invigorate, to invigorate mutually.

Ymrymiaw, *v. a.* (grymiaw) To self-invigorate; mutually to invigorate.

Ymrynu, *v. a.* (rhynu) To study with one's self, inwardly to digest.

Ymryniad, *s. m.* (rhyniad) A studying to one's self, a deeply considering.

Ymryson, *s. m.—pl. t.* au (rhyson) The engaging of one's self in dispute; mutual dispute, contention, disputation. *v. a.* To contend in argument, to dispute.

> Nid gwall synwyr ond ymryson.

> There is no want of sense like *contention*. *Adage.*

> Tri pheth sy goreu eu gwneyd ar frys: dal chwain, troi o ffordd ci cynddeiriawg, a gochel ymryson.

> Three things which are best to be done in a hurry: to catch fleas, to turn out of the way of a mad dog, and to avoid *contention*. *Adage.*

Ymrysonaeth, *s. m.* (ymryson) Contention.

Ymrysonawl, *a.* (ymryson) Controversial.

Ymrysongar, *a.* (ymryson) Contentious.

Ymrysongarwch, *s. m.* (ymrysongar) Contentiousness.

Ymrysoni, *v. a.* (ymryson) To contend, to strive.

Ymrysoniad, *s. m.* (ymryson) A contending.

Ymrysonus, *a.* (ymryson) Contentious.

Ymrysonusder, *s. m.* (ymryson) Contentiousness.

Ymrysonwr, *s. m.—pl.* ymrysonwyr (ymryson—gwr) A contender, a wrangler.

Ymrythiad, *s. m.* (rhythiad) A stretching one's self widely.

Ymrythu, *v. a.* (rhythu) To stretch out one's self widely; to stretch out mutually.

Ymrywiad, *s. m.* (rhywiad) A rendering one's self of a kind; a mutually becoming of a kind.

Ymrywiaw, *v. a.* (rhywiaw) To render one's self of a kind; to become mutually of a kind.

Ymrywiogi, *v. a.* (rhywiogi) To render one's self kindly or genial, mutually to become genial.

Ymsaethiad, *s. m.* (saethiad) The employing one's self in shooting; a mutually shooting or darting.

Ymsaethu, *v. a.* (saethu) To employ one's self in shooting; to shoot or dart mutually.

> Rhyngom yr aeth ymsaethu
> A dwy drem, mi ac em gu.

> Between us a *mutual shooting* took place with two sights, me and the lovely fair one. *Bedo Aerddren.*

Ymsafniad, *s. m.* (safniad) The opening of one's jaw; a mutually jawing.

Ymsafnrythiad, *s. m.* (safnrythiad) An employing one's self in extending the jaws; a mutually gaping.

Ymsafnrythu, *v. a.* (safnrythu) To employ one's self in opening the jaws.

Ymsafnu, *v. a.* (safnu) To open one's jaw; a mutually jawing.

Ymsang, *s. f.* (sang) A mutual treading or trampling, an employing one's self in treading; a mutual struggle; a wrestling. *Ymsang torf*, the trampling of a host: *Llythyren ymsang*, epenthesis.

Ymsangawl, *a.* (ymsang) Self-treading; mutually treading or trampling.

Ymsangiad, *s. m.* (ymsang) An employing one's self in treading; a mutually treading.

Ymsangu, *v. a.* (ymsang) To employ one's self in treading, to tread mutually.

Ymsarddiad, *s. m.* (sarddiad) A self-chiding, a mutually chiding.

Ymsarddu, *v. a.* (sarddu) To chide mutually.

Ymsarllach, *s. m.* (sarllach) A behaving riotously. *v. a.* To behave riotously.

Ymsathr, *s. f.* (sathr) The employment of one's self in treading; a mutual tread.

Ymsathriad, *s. m.* (ymsathr) An employing one's self in treading; a mutually treading.

Ymsathru, *v. a.* (ymsathr) To employ one's self in treading; to tread mutually.

Ymsawdd, *s. m.* (sawdd) A sinking of one's self; a mutual sinking in.

Ymseddiad, *s. m.* (seddiad) A seating one's self; a becoming mutually seated.

Ymseddu, *v. a.* (seddu) To seat one's self; to become mutually seated.

Ymsefydliad, *s. m.* (sefydliad) A fixing one's self, a mutually fixing or establishing.

Ymsefydlu, *v. a.* (sefydlu) To fix one's self, to fix or to establish mutually.

Ymseiliad, *s. m.* (seiliad) A making a foundation for one's self; a mutually founding.

Ymseiliaw, *v. a.* (seiliaw) To lay a foundation for one's self; a mutually founding.

Ymsel, *s. m.* (sel) The state of being beholding; a mutual beholding; perception.

> Dylid cyflawn gyffelybu—herwydd hanfod, ac ansawdd, a rhyw, a phwyll, a deall, ac ymsel, ac amser.

> A simile should be justly drawn, with respect to nature, and quality, and genius, and reason, and understanding, and *perception*, and time. *Barddas.*

Ymseliad, *s. m.* (ymsel) The employing one's self in beholding; a mutually beholding.

Ymselu, *v. a.* (selu) To employ one's self in beholding; to behold mutually.

Ymsènawl, *a.* (sènawl) Self-reproaching; mutually reproaching or upbraiding.

Ymsèniad, *s. m.* (sèniad) A self-reproaching; a mutually upbraiding or reproaching.

Ymsènu, v. a. (sènu) To use one's self in reproach, to upbraid one's self; to upbraid or to reproach mutually.

> Y neb sydd hoff ganddo ymsènu, sydd hoff ganddo bechawd.
>
> He that is delighted in *engaging himself in strife*, is delighted with sin. *Diarhebion 17. 19.*

Ymsenwr, s. m.—pl. ymsènwyr (sènwr) One who uses himself to reproaching.

Ymsengi, v. a. (ymsang) To employ one's self in trampling, to be encroaching.

Ymserchiad, s. m. (serchiad) A filling one's self with fondness or love, a mutually doating.

Ymserchu, v. a. (serchu) To fill one's self with fondness; to entertain mutual fondness.

> Aholah—a ymserchai yn ei chariadau.
>
> Aholah *doated* on her lovers. *Ezekiel 23. 5.*

Ymsereniad, s. m. (sereniad) A spangling one's self with stars or sparkles.

Ymserenu, v. a. (serenu) To make one's self to sparkle with stars.

Ymserth, s. m. (serth) The giving one's self up to abuse, mutual abuse.

> Ymserth gwraig sy megys defni parâus.
>
> The *contention* of a wife is like a continual dropping. *Diarhebion 19. 13.*

Ymserthiad, s. m. (ymserth) A using one's self to abuse, a mutually abusing.

Ymserthu, v. a. (ymserth) To employ one's self in abuse or in talking obscenely; to talk abuse or obscenity mutually.

> Ymserthiant, cablant eu gwyr;
> Treiniant benau truenwyr.
>
> *They mutually abuse*, they curse their husbands; they belay the heads of wretched men. *S. Phylip.*

Ymsiarad, s. m. (siarad) An employing one's self in talking; a mutually talking.

Ymsiaradaeth, s. m. (ymsiarad) A using one's self to talking; a state of mutual talking.

> Grym y trydydd orchymyn yw barniad ar ofer addoliad Duw; a gwaharddiad o ymsiaradaeth ofer.
>
> The substance of the third commandment is a condemnation of impropriety in the worship of God; and the interdiction of vainly *being employed in talking*. *S. Trefredyn.*

Ymsiared, v. a. (siared) To employ one's self in talking; to keep talking; to talk mutually.

Ymsiglaw, v. a. (siglaw) To shake or rock one's self; to shake mutually.

> Seiliau y nefoedd a gyffroasant, ac a ymsiglasant am iddo ef ddigiaw.
>
> The foundations of the heavens have been agitated, and *they have been shaken*, because he was wroth. *2 Samuel 22. 8.*

Ymsigliad, s. m. (sigliad) A shaking or rocking one's self; a mutually shaking.

Ymsisial, s. m. (sisial) A mutual chat. v. a. To chat together; to employ one's self in chatting or whispering.

Ymsoddawl, a. (ymsawdd) A sinking of one's self; mutually sinking.

Ymsoddi, v. a. (ymsawdd) To sink one's self.

Ymsoddiad, s. m. (ymsawdd) A sinking one's self; a mutually sinking.

Ymsomi, v. a. (somi) To disappoint one's self; mutually to disappoint.

Ymsomiad, s. m. (somiad) A disappointing one's self; a mutually deceiving.

Ymson, s. m. (son) The employment of one's self in mentioning; mutual talk. v. a. To be mentioning; to talk mutually.

> Mewn cerdd hawl ac ateb—hawdd pwysaw yn dyn at y pwyll ar y deall o bethau, nag mewn un dull arall; ac yn hawdd ymson am amryfillion farnau.
>
> In a poem that is in dialogue, it is easier to press closely to the reason and the understanding of things, than in any other mode, and it is easier *to make mention* about various opinions. *Barddas.*

Ymsoniad, s. m. (ymson) An employing one's self in talking; a mutually talking.

Ymsoniaw, v. a. (ymson) To employ one's self in talking; to talk mutually.

Ymsori, v. a. (sori) To shew one's self offended, or to be sulky; to sulk mutually.

Ymsoriad, s. m. (soriad) A shewing one's self sulky; a becoming mutually offended.

Ymswrn, s. m. (swrn) The employment of one's self in snarling; a mutual snarl. v. a. To employ one's self in a snarly mood; to snarl mutually.

> Ymswrn ag ysgwr gwr gwrdd.
>
> A *snarling* with the asperity of a passionate man. *[illegible] Goch Bryt.*
>
> Amser yw hwn i ymswrn;
> Ammheu y swn y mae [illegible].
>
> A time is this *to be grumbling*, about the rumour a number do express a doubt. *Llyw. ab G. ab Cynfrig.*

Ymswyddaw, v. a. (swyddaw) To employ one's self in office; to seek for office; to officiate.

> Gwelwn nad oes gywilydd:
> Rhedeg ac ymswyddaw sydd.
>
> We see that there is no shame: to scramble and *to seek for office* is what prevails. *[illegible]*

Ymswyddiad, s. m. (swyddiad) An employing one's self in office; an officiating.

Ymswyn, s. m. (swyn) Self-security by some mysterious rite.

Ymswynaw, v. a. (ymswyn) To bless one's self; to secure one's self, as by some secret rite or charm; to cross one's self, to beware.

Ymswyniad, s. m. (ymswyn) A blessing one's self; to secure one's self by a talisman; to cross one's self.

Ymswynwr, s. m.—pl. ymswynwyr (ymswyn—gwr) One who blesses himself; one who crosses himself, or uses charms.

Ymsyfrdaniad, s. m. (syfrdaniad) A making one's self giddy; a mutually stupefying.

Ymsyfrdanu, s. m. (syfrdanu) To stupefy one's self; mutually to stupefy.

Ymsymud, s. m. (symud) Self-motion. v. a. To move one's self; to move mutually.

Ymsymudaw, v. a. (ymsymud) To move one's self; to move mutually.

Ymsymudawl, a. (ymsymud) Self-moving, self-removing; mutually moving.

Ymsymudiad, s. m. (ymsymud) A moving one's self; a mutually moving.

Ymsymudwr, s. m.—pl. ymsymudwyr (ymsymud—gwr) One who moves himself.

Ymsymudydd, s. m.—pl. t. ion (ymsymud) A self-mover.

> Pob ymsymudydd, yr hwn sy fyw, a fydd i chwi yn fwyd.
>
> Every *moving thing*, the which is alive, shall be meat for you. *Genesis 9. 3.*

Ymsyniad, s. m. (syniad) A perceiving or feeling one's self; a mutual feeling.

Ymsyniaw, v. a. (syniaw) To perceive or to feel one's self; to reflect, to contemplate; to intend mutually.

Ymsyniawl, a. (syniawl) Self-perceptive; relating to mutual feeling or impulse.

Ymsynied, *v. a.* (synied) To perceive or to feel one's self; to reflect, to feel or to be affected mutually.

Ymsynu, *v. a.* (synu) To astonish one's self; to be mutually struck or astonished.

Ymsynwyraw, *v. a.* (synwyraw) To reason with one's self; to reason mutually.

> Y rhai ydynt herwydd y cnawd, am bethau y cnawd yr ymsynwyrant.
>
> They that are after the flesh, about the things of the flesh do *they concern themselves.* *W. Salisbury.*

Ymsynwyriad, *s. m.* (synwyriad) A reasoning to one's self; a mutually reasoning.

Ymsypiad, *s. m.* (sypiad) A gathering one's self in a heap, a mutually thronging.

Ymsypiaw, *v. a.* (sypiaw) To gather one's self into a heap; to agglomerate; mutually to press together.

Ymsyrthiad, *s. m.* (syrthiad) A falling one's self; a mutually falling.

Ymsyrthiaw, *v. a.* (syrthiaw) To fall one's self; to fall mutually.

Ymsythiad, *s. m.* (sythiad) A raising one's self erect; a mutually rising up.

Ymsythu, *v. a.* (sythu) To raise one's self erect, to straighten one's self; to swagger.

Ymsythwr, *s. m.—pl.* ymsythwyr (sythwr) One who raises himself up.

Ymufyddâad, *s. m.* (ufyddâad) Self-humiliation; mutual humiliation.

Ymufyddâu, *v. a.* (ufyddâu) To humble one's self; to humble mutually.

Ymunaw, *v. a.* (unaw) To unite one's self; to join or to combine together; to incorporate mutually.

Ymundawd, *s. m.* (undawd) The act of uniting one's self; a mutual union.

Ymuniad, *s. m.* (uniad) A self-uniting; a mutually uniting or connecting.

Ymunioni, *v. a.* (unioni) To straighten one's self; to be straightened.

> Yr oedd gwraig ag yddi ysbryd gwendid—ac ni allai hi mewn modd yn y byd ymunioni.
>
> There was a woman which had a spirit of infirmity; and she could in no wise *lift up herself.* *Luc 13. 11.*

Ymunioniad, *s. m.* (unioniad) A self-straightening; a mutually straightening.

Ymwad, *s. m.* (gwad) Self-denial, mutual denial.

Ymwadawl, *a.* (ymwad) Self-denying; mutually denying or disowning.

Ymwadiad, *s. m.* (ymwad) A self-denying; a renouncing; a disavowal; abjuration.

Ymwadu, *v. a.* (ymwad) To deny one's self; to renounce, to disavow; to deny mutually.

> Os myn neb ddawed ar fy ol i, ymwaded ag ef ei hun.
>
> If any man shall come after me, *let him deny himself.* *Matthew 16. 24.*

Ymwadwr, *s. m.—pl.* ymwadwyr (ymwad—gwr) One who denieth himself.

Ymwaediad, *s. m.* (gwaediad) A self-bleeding; a mutually letting blood.

Ymwaedlydiad, *s. m.* (gwaedlydiad) An imbruing one's self in blood; a mutually imbruing in blood.

Ymwaedlydu, *v. a.* (gwaedlydu) To imbrue one's self in blood.

Ymwaedu, *v. a.* (gwaedu) To bleed one's self; to let blood mutually.

Ymwaethiad, *s. m.* (gwaethiad) A making one's self worse; a mutually growing worse.

Ymwaethu, *v. a.* (gwaethu) To make one's self worse; to become mutually worse.

> Gwaeth no phob gwaethaf ymwaethu.
>
> The worse of every bad thing is *to make one's self worse.* *Adage.*

Ymwagâad, *s. m.* (gwagâad) A self-emptying.

Ymwagâu, *v. a.* (gwagâu) To empty one's self.

Ymwahanawl, *a.* (gwahanawl) Self-separating; mutually separating.

Ymwahaniad, *s. m.* (gwahaniad) A self-separating; mutual separation.

Ymwahaniaeth, *s. m.* (gwahaniaeth) Self-separation; mutual separation.

Ymwahanu, *v. a.* (gwahanu) To separate one's self; to be divided or parted; to separate mutually.

> Elias—a darawai y dyfroedd, a hwy a ymwahanynt yma ac acw.
>
> Elijah smote the waters, and *they were divided* hither and thither. *2 Brenhinoedd 2. 8.*

Ymwahanwr, *s. m.—pl.* ymwahanwyr (gwahanwr) One who separates himself.

Ymwallâad, *s. m.* (gwallâad) A rendering one's self faulty or neglectful; a mutually neglecting.

Ymwallâu, *v. a.* (gwallâu) To render one's self faulty, to become neglectful; to neglect mutually.

Ymwallgofi, *v. a.* (gwallgofi) To distract one's self; to become mutually distracted.

Ymwallgofiad, *s. m.* (gwallgofiad) A self-distracting; a mutually distracting.

Ymwan, *s. f.* (gwan) A mutual wounding or transfixing; combat, tournament. *v. a.* To transfix mutually; to combat with lances.

> Dangos arwydd ymwan, ac felly gware paldyd a marchogion, a phob cyfryw amryfal wareu a welid yno.
>
> Exhibiting a sign of combat, and so the sport of infantry and horsemen, and every kind of the like sports was seen there. *Gr. ab Arthur.*
>
> Yna yr aeth Gwalchmai i ymwan ag y marchawg, a chwnsallt o bali amdano ac amdan ei farch.
>
> Thereupon Gwalchmai went to combat with the knight, having a covering of velvet about him and about his horse. *H. G. ab Urien—Mabinogion.*

Ymwanâad, *s. m.* (gwanâad) A weakening of one's self; a mutually weakening.

Ymwanâu, *v. a.* (gwanâu) To weaken one's self; mutually to weaken.

> Gwelwn liw y dydd golau
> Yn min hwyr yn ymwanâu.
>
> I could see the light of the splendid day on the verge of evening *growing faint.* *T. Llwyd Ieuaf.*
>
> Tri pheth sydd yn ymwanâu beunydd, gan faint gwaethaf yr ymgais yn eu gwrth: cas, camwedd, ac anwybodaeth.
>
> Three things are daily *growing weaker,* from the continual increase of their opposing impulse: enmity, injustice and ignorance. *Barddas.*

Ymwaniad, *s. m.* (ymwan) A mutually wounding; a combating with lances; a combating.

Ymwanu, *v. a.* (ymwan) To combat mutually; to be combating; to combat.

Ymwanwr, *s. m.—pl.* ymwanwyr (ymwan—gwr) One who wounds with a lance.

> Ymwanwyr gwych mewn [illegible] gynt,
> Y bedyddiwd byd iddynt.
>
> Brave *combatants* in battle of ancient time, by them the world was named. *G. ab Llywelyn Fard.*

Ymwanychiad, *s. m.* (gwanychiad) A self-debilitating; a mutually enfeebling.

Ymwanychu, *v. a.* (gwanychu) To self-debilitate; to enfeeble mutually.

Ymwarchad, *s. m.* (gwarchad) A self-guarding; a mutual care. *v. a.* To employ one's self in guarding; to take care of one's self, to have mutual care.

> Ar don, oer ei adenydd,
> Ymwarchad o'r bad y bydd.
>
> On the wave, cold his wings, *to preserve himself* from the boat is what he seeks. *T. Cclli.*

Ymwared, *s. m.* (gwared) The having in one's self the means of averting; deliverance, defence. *v. a.* To deliver one's self, to avert mutually.

> Addwyn gaer y sydd ar don nawfed;
> Addwyn ei gwerin yn ymwared.
>
> A pleasant fort stands on the brink of the ninth wave, pleasant its multitude *affording mutual defence.* *Taliesin.*

Ymwaredawl, *a.* (ymwared) Self-delivering; mutually averting.

Ymwarediad, *s. m.* (ymwared) A self-delivering, the extricating one's self; a mutually averting

Ymwaredu, *v. a.* (ymwared) To deliver one's self; to deliver or to avert mutually.

Ymwaredus, *a.* (ymwared) Self-delivering, having in one's self the means of deliverance; mutually delivering.

> Argiwydd Dad, mawr rad, ymwaredus nerth,
> Iawn wyrthiau rhyglyddus,
> Cymer fi.——
>
> O Lord the Father, abundant in grace, of power *being the means of deliverance*, whose true miracles are efficacious, receive me. *H. D. ab Ifan.*

Ymwarthiad, *s. m.* (gwarthiad) A self-disgracing, a mutually disgracing.

Ymwarthu, *v. a.* (gwarthu) To disgrace or to shame one's self, mutually to disgrace.

Ymwasgariad, *s. m.* (gwasgariad) A spreading of one's self, a mutually spreading or dispersing.

Ymwasgaru, *v. a.* (gwasgaru) To spread one's self, to disperse mutually, to become scattered

> Ymwasgerwch yn mysg y bobl.
>
> *Disperse yourselves* amongst the people. 1 *Samuel* 14. 34.

Ymwasgiad, *s. m.* (gwasgiad) To squeeze or to press one's self; to press mutually.

Ymwasgodi, *v. a.* (gwasgodi) To shelter one's self, mutually to shelter.

Ymwasgodiad, *s. m.* (gwasgodiad) A sheltering of one's self; a mutually sheltering.

Ymwasgu, *v. a.* (gwasgu) To squeeze one's self; to keep one's self close, to cleave; to press together.

Ymwastatàad, *s. m.* (gwastatàad) A rendering one's self even or level; an establishing of one's self; a mutually establishing.

Ymwastatàu, *v. a.* (gwastatàu) To make one's self even; to establish one's self; to make mutually even.

Ymwawd, *s. m.* (gwawd) Self-praise; self-flattery, mutual flattery.

Ymwawdiad, *s. m.* (ymwawd) A flattering one's self, a mutually flattering.

Ymwawdiaw, *v. a.* (ymwawd) To flatter one's self; to flatter mutually.

Ymwëad, *s. m.* (gwëad) A self-combining; a becoming interwoven; a mutually weaving.

Ymwedd, *s. f.* (gwedd) Self-demeanour; mutual conformity or fitness.

Ymweddiad, *s. m.* (ymwedd) A self-conforming; a demeaning; a mutually according.

Ymweddu, *v. a.* (ymwedd) To conform one's self; to conform mutually.

> Tri modd, pond da'r ymweddyn?
> Hudawl, a dis, a buchedd dyn!
>
> Three circumstances how aptly *they assimilate together*, that of the mountebank, and a dice, and the life of man! *T. Aled.*

Ymwehyniad, *s. m.* (gwehyniad) A pouring out or emptying one's self; a mutually pouring.

Ymwehynu, *v. a.* (gwehynu) To empty one's self; to self-exhaust; to become empty.

Ymweisiad, *s. m.* (gweisiad) A rendering one's self a servant; a mutually serving.

Ymweisiaw, *v. a.* (gweisiaw) To make one's self a servant; a mutually serving.

> Nid ymweis a fo parch.
>
> That is of honour *will not stoop to serve.* *Adage.*

Ymweithiad, *s. m.* (gweithiad) A self-working; a fermentation; a mutual operation.

Ymweithiaw, *v. a.* (gweithiaw) To work one's self, to ferment, to operate mutually.

Ymweled, *s. m.* (gweled) A mutual seeing, a visitation. *v. a.* To shew one's self, to see mutually, to visit.

Ymweledïad, *s. m.* (ymweled) A mutually visiting; a visitation.

> Os ymwelir â hwynt ag ymweliad pob dyn, nid yr Arglwydd a'm hanfonodd.
>
> If they be visited after the *visitation* of all men, it is not the Lord who hath sent me. *Numbers* 16. 29

Ymweliad, *s. m.*—*pl. t.* au (gweliad) A visitation.

Ymwelwr, *s. m.*—*pl.* ymwelwyr (gwelwr) A visitor.

Ymwellaad, *s. m.* (gwellàad) Self-improvement; a mutually mending.

Ymwellàu, *v. a.* (gwellàu) To improve one's self; to improve mutually.

> Tra ydoeddynt yn ymladd yn wychr felly, llyma y Rhufeinwyr yn wychr yn ymwellau, ac yn dwyn rhuthr i wyr Llydaw.
>
> Whilst they were bravely fighting thus, behold the Romans gallantly repairing *themselves*, and making an assault upon the men of Llydaw. *Gr. ab Arthur.*
>
> Gwyn ei fyd a ymwellao o gynghor ei bwyll ac nid o gynghor ei ofuan.
>
> Happy is he who *makes himself better* from the counsel of his reason, and not from the counsel of his fears. *Adage.*

Ymwelliannu, *v. a.* (ymwelliant) To make one's self better; to become improved or reformed.

> Nid anghlod ymwelliannu.
>
> It is no disgrace *to reform one's self.* *Adage.*

Ymwelliant, *s. m.* (gwelliant) Self-improvement.

Ymwenieithiad, *s. m.* (gwenieithiad) A flattering of one's self; a mutually flattering.

Ymwenieithiaw, *v. a.* (gwenieithiaw) To flatter one's self; to flatter mutually.

> Ymwenieithiaw y mae yr annuwiawl iddo ei hun.
>
> The ungodly *flattereth himself* in his own eyes. *Psalm* 36. 2.

Ymwenwynaw, *v. a.* (gwenwynaw) To poison one's self; to be fretting one's self; to fret mutually.

Ymwenwyniad, *s. m.* (gwenwyniad) A poisoning of one's self; a fretting one's self, a mutually fretting.

Ymwerinaw, *v. a.* (gwerinaw) To associate one's self, to become mutually associated, to become civilized.

> Tair bradormes Ynys Prydain—cydymwerinaw a'u gwaith a wnaent, yn Lloegr, ac yr Alban.
>
> The three treacherous molestations of the Isle of Britain, *mutually confederate themselves together* was what they did, in England and Scotland. *Triawd.*

Ymweriniad, *s. m.* (gweriniad) A joining one's self to society; a mutually associating, a becoming civilized.

Ymwerthiad, *s. m.* (gwerthiad) A self-selling, self-prostitution, a mutually selling.

Ymwerthu, *v. a.* (gwerthu) To sell one's self, to prostitute one's self; to sell mutually.

> Wedi ein gwneuthur yn weithredwyr rhydd, ac wedi ein gadael i ryddid ein hewyllysiau ein hunain, a ymwerthasom yn gaethweision i ddwylaw y gelyn.
>
> After we have been made free agents, and after we have been left to the freedom of our own inclinations, we *have sold ourselves* as bondmen into the hands of the enemy. *Ier. Owain.*

Ymwëu, *v. a.* (gwëu) To self-combine, to interweave, mutually to interweave.

Ymwingaw, *v. a.* (gwingaw) To writhe one's self, to writhe mutually.

Ymwingiad, *s. m.* (gwingiad) A writhing one's self, a mutually writhing.

Ymwiriad, *s. m.* (gwiriad) A self-asserting as true, a mutually asserting.

Ymwiriaw, *v. a.* (gwiriaw) To employ one's self in proving, to assert the truth mutually.

Ymwisgaw, *v. a.* (gwisgaw) To dress one's self.

Ymwisgiad, *s. m.* (gwisgiad) A self-dressing, the state of being arrayed.

> Y fronfraith——
> Ymwisgiad angel esgyll.
>
> The thrush, angel wings her *native dress* does form. *D. ab Gwilym.*

Ymwledda, *v. a.* (gwledda) To feast one's self, to be feasting mutually.

Ymwleddiad, *s. m.* (gwleddiad) A feasting one's self, a being mutually feasting.

Ymwnc, *s. m.* (wnc) The being near or immediate. *a.* Imminent, immediate.

> Duw——
> Ti yn mhob pwnc:
> Myn ry ymwnc
> Ni wyr ommedd.
>
> God, thou art in every point; the desire ardently *approaching* who doth not know how to refuse. *Gr. Gryg.*

Ymwneuthur, *s. m.* (gwneuthur) A mutual operation. *v. a.* To combine one's self, to resolve mutually.

> Ymgyngorasant yn unfryd, ac ymwneuthant i'th erbyn.
>
> They have consulted together with one consent, *they have confederated* against thee. *Psalm* 83. 5.

Ymwneyd, *v. a.* (gwneyd) To combine one's self, to combine mutually.

Ymwng, *s. m.* (wng) The being immediate. *a.* Imminent, immediate. *adv.* Instantly.

> A rhoddi yn ymwng ruddion emau.
>
> And giving *immediately* ruddy gems. *Gr. ab M. ab Dafydd.*
>
> Llosgi eu trefred,
> A dwyn eu lludded,
> Ac ymwng colled.
>
> Burning their habitation, and taking away their load, with *imminent* loss. *Taliesin.*

Ymwr, *s. m.* (gwr) The becoming superior.

Ymwradwyddaw, *v. a.* (gwradwyddaw) To scandalize one's self; mutually to scandalize.

Ymwradwyddiad, *s. m.* (gwradwyddiad) A self-scandalizing; a mutually scandalizing.

Ymwrandaw, *s. m.* (gwrandaw) To employ one's self in listening; to listen mutually.

> O nef! ymwrandaw â ni,
> I drol gwyr o'u drygioni.
>
> Oh heaven! *give an attentive ear* to us, to that men may be turned from their iniquity. *T. Llew.*

Ymwrandawiad, *s. m.* (ymwrandaw) An employing one's self in listening; a mutually listening.

Ymwrdd, *s. m.* (gwrdd) The being ardent.

> Mawr oedd wrth ymwrdd ei ddart.
>
> Great was the push of the *ardency* of his dart. *T. Aled.*

Ymwregysiad, *s. m.* (gwregysiad) A self-girding.

Ymwregysu, *v. a.* (gwregysu) To gird one's self.

Ymwresogi, *v. a.* (gwresogi) To fill one's self with warmth; to become zealous; mutually to fill with warmth.

Ymwresogiad, *s. m.* (gwresogiad) A filling one's self with warmth; a becoming zealous; a mutually filling with warmth.

Ymwriad, *s. m.* (ymwr) An acting manfully; a mutually striving.

Ymwrial, *s. m.* (ymwr) The being in continual strife. *v. a.* To strive mutually.

Ymwriaw, *v. a.* (ymwr) To act manfully; to shew courage; to strive mutually.

> Tan a dwr yn ymwriaw
> Yw'r taranau, dreigiau draw.
>
> Fire and water *mutually warring* are the thunder claps, the distant gleaming darts. *D. ab Gwilym.*

Ymwringelliad, *s. m.* (gwringelliad) A putting one's self in a flutter.

Ymwringellu, *v. a.* (gwringellu) To put one's self in a flutter; to make a fluttering.

Ymwroli, *v. a.* (gwroli) To render one's self manful; to grow courageous.

> Ymgryfha ac ymwrola, nac ofna ac na arswyda.
>
> Be strong and *be of good courage*, fear not, and be not dismayed. *1 Chronicles* 22. 13.

Ymwrthawd, *s. m.* (gwrthawd) An using one's self to reject; abdication; abjuration. *v. a.* To abdicate, to abstain.

Ymwrthfyn, *s. m.* (gwrthfyn) A self-withdrawing, a self-withholding.

Ymwrthfynu, *v. a.* (ymwrthfyn) To withdraw one's self.

Ymwrthladd, *s. m.* (gwrthladd) Self-opposition. *v. a.* To oppose one's self.

Ymwrthladdiad, *s. m.* (ymwrthladd) A self-opposing; a mutual pugnation.

Ymwrthodawl, *a.* (ymwrthawd) Self-rejecting. *Ymwrthodolion*, abstinents.

Ymwrthodi, *v. a.* (ymwrthawd) To restrain one's self; to abstain mutually.

Ymwrthodiad, *s. m.* (ymwrthawd) A self-refusing, abdication, abjuration, dereliction.

Ymwrthodwr, *s. m.—pl.* ymwrthodwyr (ymwrthawd—gwr) One who abstains.

Ymwrthodydd, *s. m.—pl. t.* ion (ymwrthawd) One who abstains or rejects.

Ymwrthryn, *s. m.* (gwrthryn) Mutual exertion to oppose; mutual resistence; mutual ejectment.

> Os o ymwrthryn y dewisa dyn ei hawl; ni ellir ymwrthryn namyn dau ddyn a fyddont yn eistedd ar yr un tir ynghyd; ac os un onaddynt a fyn wrthryn y llall, yn y dydd y goddiweddo, hawn dywedyd ei fod ef yn briodawr.
>
> If by *mutually ejecting* a person shall choose his action; there cannot be a *mutually ejecting* but by two persons who shall be seated upon the same land together; and, if one of them be minded to eject the other, in the day that he succeeds, it is right to say that he is a proprietor. *Welsh Laws.*

Ymwrthrynawl, *a.* (ymwrthryn) Mutually opposing; controversial.

Ymwrthryniad, *s. m.* (ymwrthryn) An exerting one's self in opposition, a mutually exerting in opposition.

Ymwrthrynu, *v. a.* (ymwrthryn) To exert one's self in opposition; mutually to strive in opposition; to engage in mutual controversy.

Ymwrthrywiad, *s. m.* (gwrthrywiad) A rendering one's self heterogeneous; a mutually becoming of opposite kind.

Ymwrthrywiaw, *v. a.* (gwrthrywiaw) To render one's self of opposite kind; to become heterogeneous, to become mutually of contrary kind.

Ymwrthsefyll, *s. m.* (gwrthsefyll) A placing one's self in opposition; a mutually withstanding.

Ymwrthsefyll, *v. a.* (gwrthsefyll) To place one's self against; to withstand mutually.

Ymwrthunaw, *v. a.* (gwrthunaw) To self-disfigure; to disfigure mutually.

Ymwrthuniad, *s. m.* (gwrthuniad) A self-disfiguring, a mutually disfiguring.

Ymwrthwynebiad, *s. m.* (gwrthwynebiad) A setting one's self against.

Ymwrthwynebu, *v. a.* (gwrthwynebu) To set one's self against; to oppose mutually.

Ymwrwst, *s. m.* (ymwr) A mutual struggle. *v. a.* To struggle mutually.

Ymwrys, *s.* (gwrys) A self-striving, mutual strife.

Ymwrysiad, *s. m.* (ymwrys) A striving one's self; a mutually striving.

Ymwrysiaw, *v. a.* (ymwrys) To strive one's self; to strive mutually.

Ymwrystwr, *s. m.—pl.* ymwrystwyr (ymwrwst—gwr) One who engages in strife.

Ymwth, *s. m.* (gwth) A mutual pushing.

Ymwthgar, *a.* (ymwth) Mutually pushing.

Ymwthiad, *s. m.* (ymwth) A pushing one's self, a mutually pushing.

Ymwthiaw, *v. a.* (ymwth) To push one's self, to push together, to crowd.

Ymwthiawl, *a.* (ymwth) Self-obtruding; mutually pushing or pressing.

Ymwthiwr, *s. f.—pl.* ymwthiwyr (ymwth—gwr) One who pushes himself.

Ymwybod, *s. m.* (gwybod) Self-knowledge; mutual acquaintance. *v. a.* To acquaint one's self, to get mutual knowledge.

> Myned yr wyf——
> I ymwybod a meibion
> Tudyr, ben ymwanwyr Mon.
>
> I am going to *acquaint myself* with the sons of Tudyr, the chief defenders of Mona. *Iolo Goch.*

Ymwybodi, *v. a.* (gwybodi) To employ one's self in obtaining knowledge; to become acquainted.

> Dylai ynad—ymwybodi yn gyflawn â phob hawl a dadl a ddelawr ger ei fron.
>
> A judge ought—*to employ himself* justly *in obtaining a knowledge of every* claim and dispute brought before him. *Trioedd Dyfnwal.*

Ymwychiad, *s. m.* (gwychiad) A making one's self gay or fine; a mutually decking out.

Ymwychu, *v. a.* (gwychu) To make one's self gay, mutually to deck out.

Ymwyliad, *s. m.* (gwyliad) An employing one's self in watching; a mutually watching.

Ymwyliaw, *v. a.* (gwyliaw) To employ one's self in watching; to watch mutually; to shew solicitude.

> Prydnawn——
> Ymwyl i'm emyl a mi.
>
> In the afternoon *be thou visiting* my jewel and me. *D. ab Gwilym, i'r haul.*

Ymwylltiad, *s. m.* (gwylltiad) A making one's self wild; a mutually scaring.

Ymwylltiaw, *v. a.* (gwylltiaw) To make one's self wild; to scare mutually.

Ymwyraw, *v. a.* (gwyraw) To put one's self awry; mutually to bend aside.

Ymwyriad, *s. m.* (gwyriad) A putting one's self awry; a mutually bending.

Ymwystlaw, *v. a.* (gwystlaw) To pledge one's self; to give mutual hostage

> Oed a gaiff yr yngnad llys i ymgoffâu deugain niwyrnawd, os eirch, cyn ymwystlaw.
>
> The judge of the palace shall have time to refresh his memory for forty days if he desires, before *he enters into mutual pledge*. *Welsh Laws.*

Ymwystliad, *s. m.* (gwystliad) A pledging one's self; a mutually giving hostage.

Ymwystlwr, *s. m.—pl.* ymwystlwyr (gwystlwr) One who pledges himself.

Ymwythaw, *v. a.* (gwythaw) To put one's self in a rage, to become mutually enraged.

Ymwythiad, *s. m.* (gwythiad) A self-enraging, a mutually enraging.

Ymyfed, *s. m.* (yfed) A tippling; a mutual drinking. *v. a.* To be drinking, to be tippling; to drink mutually.

Ymyl, *s. m.—pl. t.* au (byl) A side; an edge or brink. *Safa yn fy ymyl*, stand by the side of me.

> Torì, ddyn dàl, mae 'nghalon,
> Mal y tŷr ymylau tòn.
>
> Breaking, slender nymph, is my heart, as when the edge of the wave do break. *Ed. Rhys, a Baledwr.*

Ymylawg, *a.* (ymyl) Having edges, rimmed.

Ymylfwlch, *s. m.—pl.* ymylfylchau (ymyl—bwlch) A notch in an edge.

Ymylfylchiad, *s. m.* (ymylfwlch) An engrailing.

Ymylfylchu, *v. a.* (ymylfwlch) To edge-notch.

Ymylgylch, *s. m.—pl. t.* au (ymyl—cylch) A border or fringe.

> I wys ymylgylch pais Maelgwn.
>
> To touch the *border trimming* of the coat of Maelgwn. *Rees. Dyf.*

Ymylgylchiad, *s. m.* (ymylgylch) A putting a fringe or trimming round the edge.

Ymylgylchu, *v. a.* (ymylgylch) To put a fringe or trimming about the edge.

Ymyliad, *s. m.* (ymyl) A rimming or edging.

Ymylu, *v. a.* (ymyl) To rim, to edge; to strive, as in the throws of an animal.

Ymylwe, *s. f.—pl. t.* oedd (ymyl—gwe) Selvage.

Ymyr, *s. m.* (gyr) A mutual drive; a self-instigation; a tendency; an intermeddling.

Ymyraeth, *s. m.* (ymyr) A mutual driving; a making one's self busy; an intermeddling.

> Pob ffol a fyn ymyraeth.
>
> Every fool seeks for *intermeddling*. *Diarhebion xx. 3.*

Ymyrawl, *a.* (ymyr) Apt to intermeddle.

Ymyrgar, *a.* (ymyr) Apt to be intermeddling.

Ymyriad, *s. m.* (ymyr) An intermeddling.

Ymyrth, *s. m.* (gyrth) The state of being touching against or repelling; a mutual appulse.

Ymyrthawl, *a.* (ymyrth) Tending to be touching or appulsive; mutually touching.

Ymyrthiad, *s. m.* (ymyrth) A being touching; mutual appulsion.

Ymyrthu, *v. a.* (ymyrth) To be touching one's self against; mutually to touch or run against.

> Anian ni ymyrth a'i ymyr.
>
> Nature *will* not *be repulsive* to its cause. *Adage.*

Ymyrthwr, *s. m.—pl.* ymyrthwyr (ymyrth—gwr) One who touches or runs against.

Ymyru, *v. a.* (ymyr) To drive on mutually; to instigate one's self; to be pursuing; to be intermeddling.

> Cas a ymyro ar bob peth heb achaws.
>
> Hateful is he who *intermeddles* with every thing without occasion. *Adage.*
>
> Soriw Cai wrth Arthur; nid ymyrwys Cai yn rhaill gyd ag ef o hyny allan.
>
> Cai was offended with Arthur; Cai *did not concern himself* to assist with him from thence forward. *H. Culhwch—Mabinogion.*

Ymyrus, *a.* (ymyr) Apt to be intermeddling.

Ymyrwr, *s. m.—pl.* ymyrwyr (ymyr—gwr) One who pursues or concerns himself.

Ymyryd, *v. a.* (ymyr) To drive one's self on; to drive mutually, to tamper, to intermeddle.

Gad ymaith ymryson cyn ymyryd arni.

Leave off contention before *it is meddled* with. *Diarhebion* 17. 14.

Ymysgafnhad, *s. m.* (ysgafuhad) A self-lightening, a mutually lightening.

Ymysgafnau, *v. a.* (ysgafnau) To lighten one's self, to lighten mutually.

Ymysgafniad, *s. m.* (ysgafniad) A lightening one's self; a mutually lightening.

Ymysgafnu, *v. a.* (ysgafnu) To lighten one's self, to lighten mutually.

Ymysgar, *s. pl. aggr.* (ysgar) That carry on secretion; the bowels.

Ymysgargoel, *s. f.* (ysgar—coel) Haruspicium, divination by examining of entrails.

Ymysgariad, *s. m.* (ymysgar) A self-separation, a mutual separation.

Ymysgariaw, *v. a.* (ymysgar) To separate one's self; to separate mutually.

Ymysgaroedd, *s. pl. aggr.* (ymysgar) The bowels.

Ymysgethriad, *s. m.* (ysgethriad) A being instigating, a mutually goading.

Ymysgethru, *v. a.* (ysgethru) To employ one's self in instigating, to be mutually goading.

Ymysgrain, *s. m.* (ysgrain) Self-prostration; mutual state of prostration. *v. a.* To prostrate one's self; to be mutually prostrate.

Torfoedd ymosgryn tarf ymysgrain.

The hosts of terror put to flight so as *to cause a mutual prostration.* *Cynddelw.*

Ymysgreiniad, *s. m.* (ymysgrain) A prostrating one's self along; a being mutually prostrating.

Ymysgreiniaw, *v. a.* (ymysgrain) To prostrate one's self; to be mutually grovelling.

Ymysgrytiad, *s. m.* (ysgrytiad) A being wriggling one's self.

Ymysgrytian, *v. a.* (ysgrytian) To be wriggling one's self.

Ymysgrytiaw, *v. a.* (ysgrytiaw) To wriggle.

Ymysgwfl, *s. m.* (ysgwfl) The employing one's self in snatching; a mutual snatch.

Addysg mysg ymysgwfl ffyrnig;
Addurn marn yn marn crogedig.

Instruction is the confusion of the *mutual scramble* of the ferocious. felony is fair in the opinion of him who deserves a halter. *Hywel Ystoryn.*

Ymysgwyd, *s. m.* (ysgwyd) To shake one's self, to shake mutually.

Dyna y byd yr ych chwi yn ei fawrhu, ebai efe; ac attolwg cymerwch fy rhan i hono; ac ar y gair efe ymysgydwai oddiwrthynt.

Lo that is the world, which you do magnify, said he; and I beseech you take my portion of it; and on the word *he shook him self* away from them. *Elis Wyn, B. Cwsg.*

Y mynyddoedd—wele yr oeddynt yn crynu; ac yr holl fryniau a ymysgydwynt.

The mountains, behold they were trembling: and all the hills *were shaken.* *Jeremi* 4. 24.

Ymysgyfliad, *s. m.* (ymysgwfl) A being snatching, a mutually snatching.

Ymysgyflu, *v. a.* (ymysgwfl) To be snatching, to be mutually snatching.

Ymysgytiad, *s. m.* (ysgytiad) A self-concussion, a concussing mutually.

Ymysgytiaw, *v. a.* (ysgytiaw) To shake one's self, to produce a mutual concussion.

Ymyslotiad, *s. m.* (yslotiad) A being dabbling or slopping one's self in water.

Ymyslotian, *v. a.* (yslotian) To be slopping.

Ymyslotiaw, *v. a.* (yslotiaw) To employ one's self in slopping or dabbling in water.

Ymystwyraw, *v. a.* (ystwyraw) To agitate one's self; to stretch one's self, as in the act of recovering from drowsiness.

Ymystwyriad, *s. m.* (ystwyriad) Pandiculation.

YN, *s. m. r.* The state of being in, contained, or included. *prep.* In, at; in the way of; for, for the use of, into. *pron.* Our. If **yn** be put before verbs and adjectives, it forms the expressions denominated participles and adverbs. *Yn tori*, breaking; *yn fuan*, quickly: *Os gweli yn dda*, if thou seest good; *yn awr*, at present; *yn lleigus*, by and by; *yn y man, yn y lle*, presently.

Arf glew yn ei galon.

The weapon of the brave is in his heart. *Adage.*

Adfyd a ddaw a dysg yn ei law.

Adversity comes with instruction in his hand. *Adage.*

Golwg yn yd gwyl yd gar.

Sight in such as can see is lovely. *Adage.*

Gwell bwth yn gartref no llys yn alldref.

Better a cottage for a home, than a palace to resort to as a stranger. *Adage.*

Ac yn iach bellach i'r bei;
Ac yn iach gaan uchel!

And adieu at length to the triumph; and adieu the loud rejoicing. *L. G. Cothi, m. ei fab.*

Llyma yn gobaith ni, ac yn amddiffyn, ac yn llawenydd, ac yn brenin.

Behold *our* hope, and *our* defence, and *our* joy, and *our* king. *Gr. ab Arthur.*

Yna, *adv.* (yn—a) There, in that place; then, at that time: there now! lo!

Yna y mae fy enaid glan,
A'm ellyll yma allan.

In there is my pure soul, and my phantom here without. *D. ab Gwilym, i'an bared Morfudd.*

Yna o ben y geulan anseic ymollyngasem.

Then from the top of the dreadful steep we let ourselves down. *Elis Wyn, B. Cwsg.*

Ynad, *s. m.—pl. t.* on (wn—ad) That is wary or deliberate; a judge.

Pan farner tri aifer—
Bernid Duw an dwyn i wenblaid
Y nefoedd, yn nefawd ynaid.

When the three multitudes shall be judged, God will be judging our being conveyed to the blessed society of heaven, agreeably to the attributes of *judges.* *Cynddelw.*

Ynadaeth, *s. m.* (ynad) The office of a judge.

Ynaeth, *adv.* (yn—aeth) Then, thereafter.

Yndid, *s. m.* (wn) Energy, vigour, force.

Elid yndid ynao.

Let *vigour* go into him. *Adage.*

Ynddo, *pronom. prep.* (yn) In it; in him. *Ynddof*, in me; *ynddot*, in thee; *ynddi*, in her; *ynddom*, in us; *ynddoch*, in you; *ynddynt*, in them.

O bydd marw cerddedawr o alltud ar y ffordd, pa dir bynag y bo marw ynddo, efe a ddyly dalu 24 o ebediw.

If a traveller who is a foreigner shall die on the road, whatsoever land he dies *in*, he ought to pay twenty-four pence of heriot. *Welsh Laws.*

Ynedd, *s. m.* (wn) Energy, vigour, force.

Ynfer, *s. m.—pl. t.* oedd (yn—mer) An influx, a confluence, the fall of one water into another. It is generally called *Cymer* and *Aber.*

Cad yn rhyd Alclud, cad yn ynfer.

A battle in the ford of Alclud, a battle in the *confluence.* *Taliesin.*

Ynfyd, *s. m.—pl. t.* ion (yn—myd) That is furious or mad, that is foolish. *a.* Furious, frantic, mad, foolish.

Y dynion hyn, ni ddylyir credu eu tystiolaeth: caeth, mud, byddar, ac ynfyd cannwrthwy, neu rathrawg.

These persons, their testimony is not to be believed: a slave, a mute, a deaf one, and one *insane* under restraint, or that is frantic. *Welsh Laws.*

Ni chel ynfyd ei feddwl.

The *foolish* will not conceal his mind. *Adage.*

Arf doeth pwyll, arf ynfyd dur.

The weapon of the wise reason; the weapon of the *foolish* steel. *Adage.*

Po hynaf y Cymmro ynfytaf fydd.

By so much the older the Welshman the *most simple* he is. *Adage.*

Ynfydawg, *a.* (ynfyd) Abounding with folly.
Ynfydawl, *a.* (ynfyd) Tending to folly.
Ynfydedd, *s. m.* (ynfyd) Foolishness, franticness.
Ynfydiad, *s. m.* (ynfyd) Dementation; a rendering foolish or frantic, a becoming foolish.
Ynfydrwydd, *s. m.* (ynfyd) Foolishness.

Nid ynfydrwydd ond cariad.

There is no *foolishness* like love. *Adage.*

Ynfydu, *v. a.* (ynfyd) To render frantic, to make foolish, to rave, to be mad, to lose the wits.
Ynfytty, *s. m.—pl. t.* au (ynfyd—ty) A mad-house.
Yni, *s. m.—pl. t.* au (wn) Energy, vigour.

Tri athrawon yniau dyn: synwyr awenaidd o reddf ac anian; pwyll o ystyrieth a chydwybod, a damweinoldeb cylch einioes; ac hebddynt nis gellir gwybyddiaeth cyfiawn.

The three instructors of the *energies* of man: good sense from disposition and nature, reason from consideration and conscience, and the eventfulness of the course of human life; and without these no perfect knowledge is possible. *Cattwg ab Gwynllyw.*

Yni, *adv.* (yn—i) Until, until the time.

Ni ddoaf oddiwrth nai Dafydd
Yni ddel y nos yn ddydd.

I will not come away from the nephew of David *until* the night turns to day. *L. G. Cothi.*

Ynïaw, *v. a.* (yn) To energize; to invigorate.
Yniawl, *a.* (yni) Energetic or vigorous.
Ynig, *a.* (wn) Energetic, or vigorous.
Ynmhell, *adv.* (pell) In the distance; far.
Ynmhlaid, *adv.* (plaid) In respect of.
Ynmhlegyd, *adv.* (plegyd) In respect of.
Ynmhlith, *adv.* (plith) Amongst, among.
Ynmlaen, *adv.* (blaen) In the advance; before.
Ynmlaenllaw, *adv.* (blaen—llaw) Beforehand.
Ynmraint, *adv.* (braint) In right; nearly.
Ymron, *adv.* (bron) In presence; nearly, almost.
Ynmysg, *adv.* (mysg) Amongst, amidst.

Mwy no physg yn mysg mor.

More than fishes *in the midst* of the sea. *Adage.*

Ynnill, *s. m.* (yn—nill) Advantage, gain.

Bonedd ynnill bonedd o Dduw;
Bonedd geni bonedd o ddyn.

Nobility by *acquirement* is nobility from God; nobility by birth is nobility from man. *Adage.*

Ynnill, *v. a.* (yn—nill) To get advantage, to gain, to win; to profit. *Ynnill plant*, to beget children.

Cas a bryno bob peth, ac heb ynnill dim.

Hateful is he who buys every thing, and without *gaining* any thing. *Adage.*

Ynnilladwy, *a.* (ynnill) Profitable; acquirable.
Ynnillaw, *v. a.* (ynnill) To gain, to get.
Ynnilledig, *a.* (ynnill) Gained, gotten.
Ynnillfawr, *a.* (ynnill) Advantageous.
Ynnillgar, *a.* (ynnill) Profitable, gainful.
Ynnilliad, *s. m.* (ynnill) A gaining, a getting.
Ynnillwr, *s. m.—pl.* ynnillwyr (ynnill—gwr) A gainer, a winner, a getter.
Ynnof, *pronom. prep.* (ynddof) In me. *Ynnot*, in thee; *ynno*, in him; *ynni*, in her; *ynnom*, in us; *ynnoch*, in you; *ynnynt*, in them.
Yno, *adv.* (yn—o) There; then: speaking of the distant, either as to time or place. *Awn yno*, we will go there. *Yno y marwai hi*, there she died. *Dyfed*

O cheri di ni'th caro,
Colledd a geraist yno.

If thou wilt love the one who loves thee not, *then* hast thou lost the fruit of thy love. *Adage.*

Yno y denai yntau atai hi yn guddiawg.

Then he would repair to her secretly. *Gr. ab Arthur.*

Ynt, *v.* (wn) Are; they are. It is used in common with its derivative *ydynt*.

Marw Cai a Meurig—
Man wyr ynt Mon ar eu hol.

Dead are Cai and Meurig: small men *are they* of Mona after them. *Y. Mad.*

Yntau, *pron.* (wn—tau) Him also, him too, he also, him neither; the other.

Sant yw, a mabsant i'r mau,
Santaidd y gwelais yntau.

A saint is he, and a tutelar saint for mine: and sanctified I have seen *him too*. *L. G. Cothi.*

Cas na chredo neb, na neb yntau.

Odious is he who believes nobody, and nobody *him neither*. *Adage.*

Ynte, *adv.* (ynt—e) Else, then. *Ai ynte*, or otherwise.

A fyni di ffoi dri mis o flaen dy elynion, a hwy yn dy erlid? ai ynte bod haint yn y wlad dri diwrnod?

Wilt thou flee three months before thine enemies, while they pursue thee? or *that there* be pestilence for three days in the land? *2 Samuel* 24. 13.

Yntef, *adv.* (ynt—ef) Else, then, that, there.

Rhy lleFes yntef
Undanc gyfaddef
Gan engylion nef,
Neu ry urddwyd.

There was consecrated *then* an unanimous acknowledgment from the angels of heaven, that he had been ordained. *Gwalchmai.*

Ynwst, *s. m.* (yn—gwst) Humidity, dampness.
Ynwysg, *adv.* (gwysg) In a forward direction.
Ynyd, *s. m.—pl. t.* oedd (wn) A state of forming or gathering strength; a beginning; recreation: Shrove-tide. *Ynyd y grawys*, the beginning of Lent; *Sul ynyd*, Shrove-sunday; *Nos ynyd*, Shrove-tide eve; *Mawrth ynyd*, Shrove-tuesday: *Mae ef yn cael ei ynyd*, he obtains the height of his enjoyment.

Nid oes wedd na moes mawr ynyd yn'n gwlad;
Nid oes mad eithr gwad a gwyd!

There is neither order or manners, a frivolous *sport* is our country; there is no good, but infidelity and vice! *Gwil. Ddu o Arfon, m. syr Gr. Llwyd.*

Ynyfydd, *v. imp.* (yn—y—bydd) There be.

Deuthant am y fagwyr a'r carcharwr: ynyfydd corpain o griddfan a glywynt.

They came on the other side of the wall with the prisoner: *behold* they could hear lamentation and groaning. *H. Culhwch—Mabinogion.*

Ynys, *s. f.—pl. t.* oedd (wn—ys) That is upon, beginning, or forming; an island; also a rising ground or dry spot in a marshy place.

Tair rhagynys gysefin Ynys Prydain—Orc, Manaw, a Gwyth; a gwedi hyny y tores y mor y tir, onid ai Mon yn ynys; ac yn unwedd Ynys Orc a dored, onid ai yno lawer o ynysoedd; a myned yn ynysoedd a wnaynt mannau ereill o yr Alban a thir Cymmru.

The three primary adjoining *islands* of the isle of Britain—Orc, Manaw, and Gwyth; and afterwards the sea broke the land, so that Mon became an *island*, and in the same manner the isle of Orc was broken, so that many islands were formed there; and other places of Alban and the land of Cymmru became *islands*. *Triads.*

Ynysdir, *s. m.—pl. t.* oedd (ynys—tir) Low or flat land. *Gwent.*
Ynysawg, *a.* (ynys) Having islands.
Ynysawl, *a.* (ynys) Insular, belonging to an isle.
Ynysig, *s. f. dim.* (ynys) A small island, an islet.
Ynystâad, *s. m.* (ynystâu) A becoming humid.
Ynystâu, *v. a.* (ynwst) To become humid.
Ynystrwydd, *s. m.* (ynwst) Humidity, dampness.
Ynyta, *v. a.* (ynyd) To seek after recreation.

Yng, *s. m.* (yn) That is close or near upon; a bare touch or slight hint.

Yngan, *s. m.* (yng) Intimation. *v. a.* To intimate.

O gelli, rho i gall ran;
Ac i anghall nac yngan.

If thou canst, give a share to the discreet; and to the indiscreet *give* no *intimation*. *U. Gwynedd.*

Ynganawl, *a.* (yngan) Intimating, hinting.

Ynganiad, *s. m.* (yngan) A closely whispering; a hinting or intimating.

Ynganu, *v. a.* (yngan) To utter indistinctly, to whisper; to intimate, to hint.

Yngawg, *a.* (wng) Being proximate or near.

Yngawl, *a.* (wng) Being close or near upon.

Yngder, *s. m.* (wng) Closeness, or nearness.

Yngdra, *s. m.* (wng) Closeness, proximity.

Yngenyd, *v. a.* (yngan) To intimate, to hint.

Ynghyrch, *adv.* (wng—cyrch) Imminently.

Ynghyd, *adv.* (cyd) In contact, together. *Myned ynghyd*, to go in contact.

Yn Llongborth gwelais i frwydrin
Gwyr ynghyd, a gwaed hyd ddeulin,
Rhag rhuthr mawr mab Erbin.

In Llongborth I saw the turmoil of men *together*, and blood to the knees, from the great assault of the son of Erbin. *Llywarch Hen.*

A aeth ynghyd, aeth i'r byd.

That is gone *together* it is gone into the world. *Adage.*

Ynghylch, *adv.* (cylch) About, round, in compass.

Pali ni myn:
Nid urael gwyn
Ei gynhinion;
Yn lle sindal,
Ynghylch ei wyal
Gweled carpiau.

Velvet he will not have: not the white asbestos his bands; instead of fine linen, *around* his temples rags were seen. *Y Brawd Madawg ab Gwallter.*

Yngiad, *s. m.* (wng) A rendering close or near.

Ynglais, *s. m.* (wng—llais) A confined voice, a voice of distress.

Ynglef, *s. m.* (wng—llef) A cry of distress.

Oedd ddoe i Dangwystl ddodi ynglef.

It was yesterday that Tangwystl had to utter the shriek. *L. G. Cothi.*

Ynglefain, *v. a.* (ynglef) To cry confinedly.

Yngleisiad, *s. m.* (ynglais) A speaking or uttering with difficulty.

Yngleisiaw, *v. a.* (ynglais) To speak or to utter the voice with difficulty.

Yngnad, *s. m.—pl. t.* on (wng—nad) A judge.

Yngneidiad, *s. m.* (yngnad) The acting as a judge.

Yngneidiaeth, *s. m.* (yngnad) The office of a judge; legislature; judicature.

Tair colofn gwladoldeb Ynys Prydain—rhaith gwlad, teyrnedd, ac yngneidiaeth, herwydd dosparth Prydain ab Aedd Mawr.

The three foundations of government of the Isle of Britain—the voice of the country, monarchy, and *legislature*, according to the regulation of Prydain son of Aedd the Great. *Trioedd.*

Yngneidiaw, *v. a.* (yngnad) To act as a judge.

Yngneidiawl, *a.* (yngnad) Belonging to a judge.

Yngnis, *s. f.* (wng—gnis) An epithet for a shoulder.

Gwen wrth Lawen yd wylis neithwyr,
A'r ysgwyd ar yngnis;
A chan bu mab ym ni ddiengis.

Gwen by Llawen did he watch last night with the shield on his *shoulder*, and as he was my son he did not retreat. *Llywarch Hen.*

Yngo, *adv.* (wng) Hard by, or near, here.

Yngod, *adv.* (yngo) Hard by, or near, here.

Rhudd a fydd heb ludd i fod,
Rhwng with y bobl yngod.

A [illegible] will be, without any one's aid for it, severe to the people *here*. *Llywelyn ab Owain*

Ewig——
A ddiengis o'm ffridd yngod.

A hind has escaped from my park *hard by*. *Ieuan Du.*

Yngogiad, *s. m.—pl.* yngogiaid (yngawg) A neighbour, a proximate.

Goreu yngogiaid geifr;
Goreu amgyffing moch.

The best as *neighbours* are goats, the best in confinement are swine. *Adage.*

Yngreg, *a.* (wng—rhég) Of narrow gift; stingy.

Yngres, *s. m.* (wng—gres) Violence, ardency.

Yn llawn o yngres gwres.

Being full of the *ardency* of heat. *Taliesin.*

Dau ddragon yn yngres.

Two dragons in *violence*. *Gwalchmai.*

Yngu, *v. a.* (wng) To close upon, to straiten.

Yngus, *a.* (wng) Of a close or narrow quality.

Yngwrth, *adv.* (yn—gwrth) Suddenly, unexpectedly.

Yngwrth orthrechiad angau!

Unexpectedly the conquest of death! *Lewis Morris.*

Yngyrth, *s. m.* (wng—gyrth) A close push.

Anhygar ei bar, berygl brys yngyrth,
A bair angau diljo.

Unlovely his shaft, the danger of hasty *onset*, that causes certain death. *Einion Offeiriad.*

YR, *s. m. r.* That is distant, past, out or from; that is opposite or against. *prep.* For, with respect to. *art.* The, used for *y*, preceding words with vowel initials: It is also used adverbially, as—*Yr oedd gwr a'i enw Ioan*, there was a man whose name was John.

Cerid doeth yr encilion.

Let the wise love *the* remains of antiquity. *Adage.*

Mal y tan yn yr aelwyd.

Like the fire in *the* hearth. *Adage.*

Ci a ballo bob llwdn ni bydd da ar yr un.

A dog that hunts every beast will not be good for any one. *Adage.*

Pan goller yr hinon,
O'r gogledd daw eilon.

When *the* fine weather shall be lost, from *the* north it will come again. *Adage.*

Arfer anarfer yw yr arfer waethaf yn y byd.

To be in the habit of no habit is *the* worst habit in the world. *Adage.*

Yrth, *s. m.—pl. t.* ion (yr) A touch; a stop, obstacle, let, or hinderance. *a.* Impeding. *Mae efe yn siarad yn yrth*, he is speaking lispingly. *Sil.*

All marth mawr mor de;
All yrth, all syrth se.

Like the great expanse of the south sea; like the *concussion*, like the fall of stars. *Gwalchmai.*

All yrth gyrth yn gwrthfynasant;
All arwrdd ymhwrdd am hardd amgant bre,
Bron yr Erw y galwant.

A second *shock* of onset they sought against us; a second vehement conflict round the fair circumference of a hill, Bron yr Erw, which they call. *Ll. P. Moch, i Lywelyn II.*

Yrthiad, *s. m.* (yrth) A touching; a stopping.

Yrthiaw, *v. a.* (yrth) To touch; to stop.

Yrthwch, *s. m.* (yrth) An impediment, a stammer.

Gnawd gwedy rhydeg yrthwch.

After extreme smoothness generally comes a rub. *Adage.*

YS, *s. m. r.* That is, that arises or issues out; that proceeds; that is active, violent, or consuming; a combustible principle. It is a common prefix in composition.

Ys, *v.* (ys, *s.*) Is, hath, a being, existeth. *Ys id?* Is there? is it? be there?

Arfer no deddf ys trech.

Custom is mightier than law. *Adage.*

Amledd cybydd ys tlodi arno.

The abundance of the miser is poverty to him. *Adage.*

Meß ys gnawd o weddwdawd hir.

Reproach is attendant on long widowhood. *Adage.*

Bedd Elchwyth ys gwlych gwlaw,
Maes Mawedawg y danaw;
Dylyal Cynon yno ei gwynaw.

The grave of Elchwyth the rain *doth* drench, the plain of Mawedawg beneath him; him Cynon ought to mourn.
E. Beddau Milwyr.

Ys id yn y boly hwn blawd?
Ceiniaid cynniflaid, digyniaid yn ahrin
Rhag cedwyr cad barawd!

Is there in this leathern bag some meal? singers of depredators, falling ones in conflict before the warrior of ready battle.
H. Bran, Mabinogion.

Ysadwy, *a.* (ys) Consumable, or ignitible.

Ysawl, *a.* (ys) Consuming, or devouring; caustic. *Tan ysawl*, consuming fire.

Ysbach, *s. m.* (bach) A grapple, or a clawing.

Ysbachawl, *a.* (ysbach) Grappling; rumpling.

Ysbachiad, *s. m.* (ysbach) A clawing; a rumpling

Ysbachu, *v. a.* (ysbach) To claw; to rumple.

Ysbag, *s. f.—pl. t.* an (bag) A talon.

Ysbagawg, *a.* (ysbag) Having claws or talons.

Ysbagawl, *a.* (ysbag) Like a talon or claw.

Ysbagu, *v. a.* (ysbag) To claw, to clutch.

Ysbawd, *s. f.—pl.* ysbodau (pawd) A blade, a blade-bone, a shoulder-bone; a shoulder. *Ysbawd mollt, palfais mollt, palfais dafad*, a shoulder of mutton.

Ysbledd, *s. m.* (bledd) That is got by rapacity.

Ysbledda, *v. a.* (ysbledd) To gather spoil.

Ysbleddach, *s.m.* (ysbledd) Spoil, prey, or booty.

Y brenin angau: cyfarch, a goruchafiaeth, ac ysbleddach dragwyddawl!

The monarch death: I greet thee pre-eminency and eternal *spoil!*
Elis Wyn, B. Cwsg.

Ysblenyddiad, *s.—pl. t.* au (ysplenydd) A raying.

Ysbrig, *s. m.—pl. t.* ion (brig) A sprig.

Ysbrigaw, *v. a.* (ysbrig) To produce sprigs.

Ysbrigawg, *a.* (ysbrig) Full of sprigs.

Ysbrigawl, *a.* (ysbrig) Tending to yield sprigs.

Ysbrigiad, *s. m.* (ysbrig) A sprigging.

Ysbrigyn, *s. m. dim.* (ysbrig) A sprig, a twig.

Ysbril, *s. m.—pl. t.* ion (ys—bril) A bat. *Dyfed*

Ysbrychiad, *s. m.* (brychiad) A speckling.

Ysbrychu, *v. a.* (brychu) To speckle, to blur.

Ysbryd, *s. m.—pl. t.* ion (pryd) That is intelligent, that is mental; a spirit.

Gwae ai llafur lles yn ei ysbryd,
Ysbaid fyr fydawl fod yn mounyd;
Gwae a el yn nghaen yn nghymlegyd Cain
Cynrylelawg, lygriad enbyd!

Woe to him who labours not a benefit in his *spirit*, during the short worldly space being in penance; woe to him who goes into iniquity in a course similar to Cain the first rebellious, a perilous corruption!
Meilyr ab Gwalchmai.

Mae rhyw nerth yn mysg dynion, yr awr hon, nad oedd o'r blaen; mae rhyw ysbryd rhyfedd yn gweithiaw.

There is some power, at present, among men, which was not heretofore; there is some extraordinary *spirit* working.
Morgan Llwyd.

Ysbrydawg, *a.* (ysbryd) Having a spirit.

Ysbrydawl, *a.* (ysbryd) Spiritual, or ghostly.

Ysbrydiad, *s. m.—pl.* ysbrydiaid (ysbryd) An intelligence, a spiritual agent.

Ni aethon drwy deyrnas yr wybr, lle yr oedd holl ddryg ysbrydiaid yn trigaw.

We went through the kingdom of the air, where all the evil *intelligences* had their abode.
Marchawg Crwydrad.

Ysbrydiaeth, *s. m.* (ysbryd) Spirituality.

Dyben cerdd yw gwellàu y deall, dyddanu y bryd, ac yr ysbrydiaeth.

The intention of poetry is to improve the understanding, to delight the mind and the *spirit*.
Barddas.

Ysbrydlawn, *a.* (ysbryd) Spirited, full of spirit.

Ysbrydlondeb, *s. m.* (ysbrydlawn) Spiritfulness.

Ysbrydlonedd, *s. m.* (ysbrydlawn) Spiritfulness.

Ysbrydloni, *v. a.* (ysbrydlawn) To render spiritful; to become spiritful.

Ysbrydlonrwydd, *s. m.* (ysbrydlawn) Spiritfulness

Ysbrydoldeb, *s. m.* (ysbrydawl) A spiritual state

Ysbrydolder, *s. m.* (ysbrydawl) A spiritual state.

Ysbrydoledig, *a.* (ysbrydawl) Spiritualized.

Ysbrydoledd, *s. m.* (ysbrydawl) Spirituality.

Ysbrydoli, *v. a.* (ysbrydawl) To render spiritual; to spiritualize.

Ysbrydoliad, *s. m.* (ysbrydawl) Spiritualization.

Ysbrydoliaeth, *s. m.* (ysbrydawl) Inspiration, the working of the spirit.

Ysbrydoliaethu, *v.a.* (ysbrydoliaeth) To spiritualize, to render spiritual.

Ysbrydolrwydd, *s. m.* (ysbrydawl) A spiritual state.

Ysbrydus, *a.* (ysbryd) Spiritful, spiritual.

Ysbrydusaw, *v. a.* (ysbrydus) To render spirited; to become spirited.

Ysbrydusedd, *s. m.* (ysbrydus) Spiritedness.

Ysbur, *s. m.—pl. t.* ian (bur) The pedestal or base of a pillar; a short post or supporter of a shelf, in ancient houses, projecting into the floor, in the form of a skreen, and used to put by such victuals as is in present consumption.

Ysbwrial, *s. m. aggr.* (bwrw) Refuse, trash, sweepings, rubbish.

Ysbwrialu, *v. a.* (ysbwrial) To make rubbish.

Ysbyd, *s. m.—pl. t.* ion (osb) Hospitality.

Ysbydaeth, *s. m.* (ysbyd) The practice of receiving guests, hospitality.

Ysbydawl, *a.* (ysbyd) Relating to the receiving of guests.

Ysbydiad, *s. m.* (ysbyd) A receiving of guests.

Ysbydu, *v. a.* (ysbyd) To receive guests.

Ysbydwr, *s. m.—pl.* ysbydwyr (ysbyd—gwr) The master of an hospital.

Ysbys, *a.* (bys) Noticeable; manifest, evident.

Ysbysawl, *a.* (ysbys) Tending to manifest.

Ysbysiad, *s. m.* (ysbys) A specifying.

Ysbysoli, *v. a.* (ysbysawl) To render manifest; to become special or particular.

Ysbysoliad, *s. m.* (ysbysawl) Specification.

Ysbysrwydd, *s. m.* (ysbys) A specification, notice, or information.

Ysbysu, *v. a.* (ysbys) To specify, to give notice.

Ysbyswr, *s. m.—pl.* ysbyswyr (ysbys—gwr) A specifier, a declarer.

Ysbysydd, *s. m.—pl. t.* ion (ysbys) A specifier.

Ysbytty, *s. m.—pl. t.* au (ysbyd—ty) A hospital.

Ysdawr, *s. m.* (dawr) That is of concern or an object of care or anxiety.

Ysdiff, *s. m.* (diff) That forms a spout or jet.

Ysdiffiad, *s. m.* (ysdiff) A spouting out.

Ysdiffiaw, *v. a.* (ysdiff) To spout or to jet out.

Ysdiffl, *s. m.* (ysdiff) That spouts or spirts.

Ysdifflawg, *a.* (ysdiffl) Full of spouting or jettings *s. f.* The cuttle-fish.

Ysdill, *s. m.—pl. t.* ion (dill) That folds or plaits.

Ysdilliad, *s. m.* (ysdill) A making a plaiting.

Ysdilliaw, *v. a.* (ysdill) To form a fold or plait.

Ysdori, *s. f.—pl. t.* au (ysdawr) What is of concern or in mind; a matter of record.

Ysdorïad, *s. m.* (ysdori) A relating as history.

Ysdorïaw, *v. a.* (ysdori) To relate a story.

Ysdorïawl, *a.* (ysdori) Historical, historic.

Ysdragiad, *s. m.* (dragiad) A dragging about.

Ysdragiaw, *v. a.* (dragiaw) To mangle, to drag

Ysdwrdiad, *s. m.* (dwrdiad) A threatening.
Ysdwrdiaw, *v. a.* (dwrdiaw) To threaten.
Ysdwrdiwr, *s. m.—pl.* ysdwrdiwyr (dwrdiwr) A threatener.
Ysdyferiad, *s. m.* (dyferiad) A distillation.
Ysdyferion, *s. pl. aggr.* (dyferion) Distillations.
Ysdyferu, *v. a.* (dyferu) To distil, to drop.
Ysdyfnig, *a.* (dyfnig) Obstinate, stubborn.
Ysdyfnigaw, *v. a.* (ysdyfnig) To act stubbornly; to become obstinate or stubborn.
Ysdyfnigrwydd, *s. m.* (ysdyfnig) Stubbornness.
Ysedig, *a.* (ys) Corroded; consumed; oxidated.
Ysenyd, *s. m.* (enyd) A space of time, a while.

Byd efrifed dros wledydd;
Brithfyd er ysenyd sydd.

A world of numerous changes over countries; a confused world for a *good while* hath been. *Lly. ab Ber. ab Ednyfed.*

Ysfa, *s. f.—pl.* ysfeydd (ys—ma) A spot devoured or consumed; a feeding place, a sheep walk; an itching.

Dwg ysfa, lle'r wyd, goesfain,
Dan rodiaw a dringaw drain.

Bear an *itching*, where thou art, slender shank, while perambulating and climbing of thorns. *T. Prys, i'r dryw.*

Ysfan, *s. f.—pl. t.* au (ys—man) A consuming place; a biting place; an itching. *Mae yn codi ysfan*, it causes an itching.
Ysg, *s. m.* (ys) A tendency to act, or move, or to separate.
Ysgadan, *s. pl. aggr.* (cad) Herrings; also called *penwaig*, or empty heads.
Ysgadenyn, *s. m. dim.* (ysgadan) A herring.
Ysgaen, *s. f.—pl. t.* au (caen) A sprinkle.
Ysgaeniad, *s. m.* (ysgaen) A sprinkling.
Ysgaenu, *v. a.* (ysgaen) To sprinkle, to spread.
Ysgafael, *s. m.—pl. t.* au (cafael) That is taken; capture, prey.

Manred gymined, mawr ysgafael,
Y rhag Caer Lwydgord, neus dug Morial?
Pymtheccant meyn a phen Gwrial.

Briskly pacing for combat, a great *booty*, before the fortress of Grey-wood, has not Morial taken! fifteen hundred kine, and the head of Gwrial. *Meugant, m. Cynddylan.*

Ysgafaeliad, *s. m.* (ysgafael) A capturing.
Ysgafaelu, *v. a.* (ysgafael) To capture.
Ysgafaelus, *a.* (ysgafael) Predatory, rapacious.
Ysgafaeth, *s. f.—pl. t.* au (cafaeth) A booty, a hoard.
Ysgafaethawl, *a.* (ysgaeth) Rapacious.
Ysgafaethiad, *s. m.* (ysgafaeth) A making a booty; a hoarding.
Ysgafaethu, *v. a.* (ysgafaeth) To make a booty; to lap up a hoard.
Ysgafn, *s. m.* (cafn) A light heap or body; that is light or easy; a stack of corn. *Marw ysgafn*, a death-bed; a resignation to death, or a death-bed song.
Ysgafn, *a.* (cafn) Light, volatile; fickle.

Ysgafn y daeth, ysgafn yr aeth.

Lightly it came, *lightly* it went. *Adage.*

Gloewach fyddant y saint yna seithwaith no'r haul, ac ysgafnach o fuander fyddant no meddwl.

The saints will be then seven times brighter than the sun, and *lighter* of motion than thought. *Elucidarius.*

Ysgafnâad, *s. m.* (ysgafnâu) A lightening.
Ysgafnâawl, *a.* (ysgafnâu) Tending to be light.
Ysgafnaidd, *a.* (ysgafn) To render light.
Ysgafnâu, *v. a.* (ysgafn) To make light, to make easy: to become light.
Ysgafnder, *s. m.* (ysgafn) Lightness; levity.
Ysgafndra, *s. m.* (ysgafn) Lightness; levity.
Ysgafndrefn, *a.* (ysgafn—trefn) Of light order; lightly arrayed, lightly armed.

Ysgafnedd, *s. m.* (ysgafn) Lightness, levity.
Ysgafniad, *s. m.* (ysgafn) A making light.
Ysgafnleddf, *a.* (ysgafn—lleddf) Softly yielding.
Ysgafnrwydd, *s. m.* (ysgafn) Lightness, levity.
Ysgafnu, *v. a.* (ysgafn) To lighten, to make light; to make a light heap, to stack corn; to become light.
Ysgaffell, *s. f.—pl. t.* au (caffell) A ledge, edge, rim, or brow. *Dyna fe yn edrych dan ei ysgaffell*, there he is looking slyly, or under his brow.

Efe a'm cipiai i ymbell bell y tu uchaf i'r castell, ac ar ysgaffell o gymwl gwyn gorphwysem.

He snatched me far and far above the castle, and on the *edge* of a white cloud we rested. *Elis Wyn, B. Cwsg.*

Ysgaffellawg, *a.* (ysgaffell) Having a ledge.
Ysgaffelliad, *s. m.* (ysgaffell) A ledging.
Ysgaffellu, *v. a.* (ysgaffell) To form a ledge.
Ysgai, *s. m.* (ysg) Froth, foam, or scum.
Ysgain, *s. m.* (cain) A sprinkle. *a.* Sprinkling. *v. a.* To sprinkle, or to spread out.

Rhuddfoawg farchawg farch ysgain.

A red-stained knight with a *spattering* steed. *Cynddelw.*

Bradw ysgwyd bryd ysgain wrth lef.

With a frail shield his front *gleaming* at the shout. *Cynddelw.*

Yn rhith cleddyf claer,
Clod ysgain yn aer.

In the semblance of a bright sword, *spreading* fame in conflict. *Cynddelw.*

Cod ysgain cad ddiysgog.

Bounty scattering in battle unshaken. *Prydydd Bychan.*

Ysgainc, *s. f.—pl.* ysgeinciau (cainc) That branches or forms a branch.
Ysgaing, *s. f.* (caing) That forms a branch. *Ysgaing o edaf*, a skain of thread.
Ysgais, *s. m.* (cais) That is attempted or essayed.
Ysgall, *s. pl. aggr.* (call) The thistle. *Ysgall gwynion, ysgall mair, ysgall brithion*, milk thistle; *ysgall duon*, black thistle; *ysgall bendigaid* blessed thistle; *ysgall y pannwr*, the teasel; *ysgall y blaidd, ysgall gwylltion*, spear thistle; *ysgall canpen*, field eryngo; *ysgall y moch, llaeth ysgall, llymeidfwyd*, sow-thistle; *ysgall y meirch, marchysgall*, endive.

A heu ysgall ni fed wenith.

Who soweth *thistles* will not reap wheat. *Adage.*

Ysgallaidd, *a.* (ysgall) Like a thistle.
Ysgallawg, *a.* (ysgall) Abounding with thistles; of the nature of thistle. *Llysiau ysgallawg*, acanacious plants.
Ysgallen, *s. f.* (ysgall) A thistle: *ysgallen ddu*, black chameleon thistle; *ysgallen ddraenwen*, common carline thistle; *ysgallen foglynawg*, sea eryngo; *ysgallen fwyth*, melancholy thistle.
Ysgant, *s. m.* (cant) That forms a curve or whirl.
Ysgar, *s. f.—pl. t.* ion (car) A separate part, a part, portion; or share; a piece, or fragment; a separation, a divorce.
Ysgar, *v. a.* (car) To separate, to divide; to divorce; to cast off.
Ysgarant, *s. m.—pl.* ysgeraint (ysgar) One that is separated or parted; an adversary.

Pian y bedd hwn? Bedd Braint
Y rhwng llewyn a lledneint;
Bedd gwr gwae i ysgeraint.

Who owns this grave? The grave of Braint, between the horizon and a slight ravine; the grave of a man the woe of the enemies. *E. Beddau Milwyr.*

Ysgardd, *s. f.* (ysgar) A spread, a dispersion.
Ysgarddawl, *a.* (ysgardd) Dispersing, scattering.
Ysgardde, *s. m.* (ysgardd) Separation, dispersion.
Ysgaredig, *a.* (ysgar) Separated, divided.

Ysgaredigaeth, *s. m.—pl. t.* au (ysgaredig) Separation; a scattered state.

Ysgaredd, *s. m.* (ysgar) Separateness.

Ysgariad, *s. m.—pl. t.* au (ysgar) Separation.

Ysgariaeth, *s. m.* (ysgar) A separation.

Ysgariaw, *v. a.* (ysgar) To separate, to part.

Ysgarm, *s. f.—pl. t.* oedd (garm) An outcry.

Ysgarmain, *v. a.* (ysgarm) To keep up a continual outcry or shouting.

Ysgarmawl, *a.* (ysgarm) Shouting, screaming.

Ysgarmes, *s. f.—pl. t.* au (ysgarm) The being employed in an outcry or shout; the work of shouting; a skirmish.

> Maes a naw 'ysgarmes a wnan'.
>
> A battle and nine *skirmishes* they would go through. *L. G. Cothi.*

Ysgarmiad, *s. m.* (ysgarm) A shouting.

Ysgarmu, *v. a.* (ysgarm) To set up a shout.

Ysgarth, *s. m.—pl. t.* ion (carth) Offscouring.

Ysgarthawg, *a.* (ysgarth) Excrementitious.

Ysgarthawl, *a.* (ysgarth) Excremental, excretive

Ysgarthiad, *s. m.* (ysgarth) Excretion; a scouring out, or purging.

Ysgarthlyd, *a.* (ysgarth) Tending to expel or to purge.

Ysgarthu, *v. a.* (ysgarth) To purge out, to expel.

Ysgaru, *v. a.* (ysgar) To separate, to part.

> Nid ysgar newyn a diogi.
>
> Hunger *will* not *part* from idleness. *Adage.*

Ysgatfydd, *adv.* (gad—bydd) Peradventure, perhaps.

Ysgau, *s. m.* (cau) That is hollow or scooped; a scoop. *a.* Scooped.

Ysgaw, *s. m. aggr.* (caw) Elder wood, elder. *Ysgaw y ddaiar, cor-ysgaw, ysgaw Mair, gwaed y gwyr*, dwarf-elder.

> Tri pheth a gynnydd ar y gwlaw,
> Gwlydd, ac ysgall, ac ysgaw.
>
> Three things increase in the rain, grass, and thistle, and elder. *Adage.*

Ysgawd, *s. m.* (cawd) That rises over, a shade.

> Gnawd rwyf yn hell Bell wirawd,
> Gnawd ysgwyd ysgafn ar gefn ysgawd.
>
> Like the effect of the oar in the brine is the liquor of Bell, like a light shield on the back of a *shadow*. *Taliesin.*

Ysgawen, *s. f.* (ysgaw) An elder-tree. *Ysgawen y gors*, or *corswigan*, water-elder.

Ysgawl, *a.* (ysg) Abounding with activity. *Ysgawl gwyth*, wrath is active.

> Ysgawl disgynnodd ffawdd gymmre.
>
> *Vehemently* descended the tumult of the concurrency. *Taliesin.*

> Gogwn —
> Py ysgawl oddef
> Pan dderchafwyd nef;
> Pwy fu fforch hwyl
> O ddair hyd awyr.
>
> I have an idea what was the *exciting* patience when heaven was upreared; what was a sail staff from earth to sky. *Taliesin.*

Ysgawn, *s. m.* (cawn) A light body. *a.* Light.

> Ysgawn lwyth a gnud.
>
> The *light* load will accumulate. *Adage.*

> Ysgawn i mewn ysgawn i maes.
>
> *Light* in entering, *light* in egress. *Adage.*

Ysgawnâad, *s. m.* (ysgawnâu) Alleviation.

Ysgawnâawl, *a.* (ysgawnâu) Tending to lighten.

Ysgawnâu, *v. a.* (ysgawn) To lighten; to become light; to become volatile.

Ysgecran, *s. m* (cecran) A bickering, a brawling.

Ysgecrain, *v. a.* (cecrain) To be bickering.

Ysgecrawl, *a.* (cecrawl) Bickering, brawling.

Ysgecriad, *s. m.* (cecriad) A bickering, a brawling.

Ysgecru, *v. a.* (cecru) To bicker, to brawl.

Ysgedd, *s. m.* (ys—cedd) The sea kale.

Ysgegiad, *s. m.* (cegiad) A throttling; a shaking by laying hold of the throat.

Ysgegiaw, *v. a.* (cegiaw) A shaking by laying hold of the throat; a shaking roughly.

Ysgegiwr, *s. m.—pl.* ysgegiwyr (ysgegiaw—gwr) A throttler, one who shakes roughly.

Ysgeindorf, *s. f.* (ysgain—torf) A spreading host.

> Ysgeindorf [illegible] [illegible] [illegible] [illegible].
>
> The spreading host of the [illegible] by legions [illegible] [illegible]. *Ll. P. [illegible].*

Ysgeiniad, *s. m.—pl. t.* au (ysgain) A spreading out; a sprinkling; a squinting.

Ysgeiniaw, *v. a.* (ysgain) To spread abroad; to spirt, to slap; to sprinkle; to squint.

> Yna y gwelid y tan llachar yn ysgeiniaw o'r arfau.
>
> Then was seen the gleaming fire *sprinkling* from the arms. *[illegible] y [illegible].*

> Ysgeinynt yn afel
> O du yn uchel.
>
> *They would spread out* in a flame high from the [illegible]. *Taliesin.*

> Dyddeu cynrain
> O am dir Rhufain;
> Ys cerdd a gynghrain,
> Eu gwawd a ysgain.
>
> Tribes would come from about the land of Rome; [illegible] will harmonize, their praise *will spread abroad*. *Taliesin.*

Ysgeiniawl, *a.* (ysgain) Sprinkling; squinting.

Ysgeiniedig, *a.* (ysgeiniad) Scattered; speckled.

Ysgeiniedydd, *s. m.—pl. t.* ion (ysgeiniad) A scatterer; a sprinkler; a squinter.

Ysgeiniwr, *s. m.—pl.* ysgeiniwyr (ysgain—gwr) A scatterer; a sprinkler; a squinter.

Ysgeintiad, *s. m.* (ysgant) A whisking about.

Ysgeintiaw, *v. a.* (ysgant) To whisk about.

Ysgeintiawl, *a.* (ysgant) Whirling, whisking.

Ysgeintiwr, *s. m.—pl.* ysgeintiwyr (ysgant—gwr) One who whisks about.

Ysgeisiad, *s. m.* (ysgais) An endeavouring.

Ysgeisiaw, *v. a.* (ysgais) To be endeavouring.

Ysgeisiawl, *a.* (ysgais) Endeavouring.

Ysgeisiwr, *s. m.—pl.* ysgeisiwyr (ysgais—gwr) One who attempts or endeavours.

Ysgeler, *a.* (cel) Atrocious, villainous, nefarious, detestable; obscene.

Ysgelerdawd, *s. m.* (ysgeler) Atrociousness.

Ysgelerder, *s. m.* (ysgeler) Atrociousness.

Ysgelerdra, *s. m.* (ysgeler) Flagitiousness.

Ysgeleredd, *s. m.* (ysgeler) Flagitiousness.

Ysgeleriad, *s. m.* (ysgeler) A rendering flagitious; a becoming scandalous.

Ysgeleru, *v. a.* (ysgeler) To render flagitious; to become atrocious or flagitious.

Ysgelynllys, *s. m.* (celyn—llys) The ribwort. It is also called *cstyllenlys*.

Ysgellog, *s. f.* (ysgall) Wild succory.

Ysgemydd, *s. m.* (cam) A curve, the outside edge of any thing that curves.

> Tri ysgemydd aerau Ynys Prydain: Gilbert mab Cadgyffro, Morien ail Ingid, a Gugan Gleddyfrudd.
>
> The three *benders* in of battle of the Isle of Britain: Gilbert son of Cadgyffro, Morien son of Ingid, and Gugan Longsword. *Triawd.*

> Ysgemydd clodrydd culwydd a Lleyfan.
>
> A celebrated circle equally prosperous with Lleyfan. *[illegible] ab [illegible].*

> Yn grwm iawn, yn gryman[illegible],
> Yn blyg fal ewin bladd;
> Yn llym ar ei ysgemydd,
> Yn hir i gymynu bydd.
>
> Being much bent, like a sickle, turning like the claw of a [illegible] being keen on its curving edge, being long to cut up a [illegible]. *[illegible] y Glyn, [illegible].*

Ysgen, *s. m.* (cen) Morphew, or dandriff.

Ysgenedl, *s. f.* (cenedl) A generation, a tribe.

Ysgor diffreiddiad mad ysgwyddfawr
Ysgar ysgenedl gychwedl gychwyrn.

The departure of the protection of the good monarch will spread the quickly flying report of the *family*.
Ein. ab Gwalchmai, i Lywelyn II.

Ysgenedlawg, *a.* (ysgenedl) Generating.

Ysgenedliad, *s. m.* (ysgenedl) A generating.

Ysgenedlu, *v. a.* (ysgenedl) To generate.

Ysgeniad, *s. m.* (ysgen) A generating of scales; a generating of dandriff.

Ysgenllys, *s. m.* (ys—cèn—llys) Hemispheric liver-green.

Ysgentyn, *s. m. dim.* (ysgant) A caperer; a buffoon.

Ysgentynaidd, *a.* (ysgentyn) Buffoon-like.

Ysgenu, *v. a.* (ysgen) To generate scales; to generate scurf or dandriff.

Ysger, *s. f.—pl.* ysgyr (cer) A kind of stone which breaks into bars.

Ysgerbwd, *s. m.* (ysgar—pwd) A skeleton, a carcase; carrion.

Samson—a droes i edrych ysgerbwd y llew.

Samson turned to examine the *carcase* of the lion.
Barnwyr 14. 8.

Ysgeth, *s. f.—pl. t.* au (ceth) That pushes or repels; a spear.

Hyder gymhell ar freithell fanawyd,
Ni nodi nac ysgeth nac ysgwyd.

With a confident impulse towards the banner staff, thou wilt mark nor *spear* nor shield.
Aneurin.

Ysgethiad, *s. m.—pl. t.* au (ysgeth) Propulsion; repulsion.

Ysgethin, *a.* (ysgeth) Propulsive; repulsive.

Ysgethr, *s. f.—pl. t.* au (cethr) That drives.

Ysgethrawg, *a.* (ysgethr) Iterating, driving.

Ysgethrawl, *a.* (ysgethr) Iterating, driving.

Ysgethriad, *s. m.* (ysgethr) An iterating.

Ysgethrin, *a.* (ysgethr) Iterative, impulsive.

Yr oedd dreigiau mellt ysgethrin yn rhwygaw y mwg dudew oedd y safn anfeith yn ei fwrw.

There shafts of *impulsive* lightening rended the thick black smoke, which the horrid gulf threw out. *Elis Wyn, B. Cwsg.*

Ysgethru, *v. a.* (ysgethr) To iterate, to impel.

Ysgethu, *v. a.* (ysgeth) To push; to repulse.

Ysgeuad, *s. m.* (ysgau) A hollowing, a scooping.

Ysgeuaw, *v. a.* (ysgau) To hollow, to scoop.

Ysgeuawl, *a.* (ysgau) Hollowed, scooped.

Ysgeueg, *s. f.—pl. t.* au (ysgau) A scoop.

Ysgeuegiad, *s. m.* (ysgeueg) A scooping.

Ysgeuegu, *v. a.* (ysgeueg) To scoop out, to hollow.

Ysgewin, *a.* (ysgaw) Being of elder wood.

Ysgewyll, *s. pl. aggr.* (ysgaw) Oziers; twigs.

Aderyn a'i —
Lagyll blaen ysgewyll blwydd.

A bird with its wings the tops of yearling *twigs*.
H. ab D. ab Ieu. ab Rhys.

Ysgewyll yr ar gaewydd
Ac yn y gwaith egin gwydd.

Twigs form a leafy circle, and in the work the seed of woods.
D. ab Edmund, i Gae bedw.

Ysgewyllawg, *a.* (ysgewyll) Having twigs.

Ysgi, *s. m.—pl. t.* od (ysg) Exertion; a clearance, a cutting off, a parer, a clearer; a bat, either for play or to beat clods; a paring knife; an instrument for cutting up mole hills, with handles like a plough, guided by one person and drawn by another. *Cenedl ysgi*, a tribe of depredation.

Llad yn eurgyrn,
Eurgyrn, yn llaw,
Llaw yn ysgi,
Ysgi yn modrydaf.

Liquor in golden horns, golden horns in hand, hand in *labour*, labour in society.
Taliesin.

Ysgïad, *s. m.* (ysgi) A cleasing, a cutting off.

Ysgïaw, *v. a.* (ysgi) To cut away, to pare, to clear; to bat, to beat clods.

Ysgïawl, *a.* (ysgi) A paring, or a slicing.

Ysgiell, *s. f.* (ysgi) A scud of fine weather.

Ysgïen, *s. f. dim.* (ysgi) A cutter, a parer, a chopper; a scymitar; a large knife; a grafting knife; a wooden knife for cutting of butter; a turner's spring or lath; a tall awkward woman.

Nis lladd cledd nac ysgïen.

Nor sword nor *scymitar* will kill him. *D. Nanmor.*

Ysgig, *a.* (cig) Carnivorous, flesh-eating.

Ysgil, *s. m.—pl. t.* iau (cil) The state of being behind, as on horse-back; a recess.

Ysgilbren, *s. m.—pl. t.* i (ysgil—pren) The stent in the traces of a horse.

Ysgiliad, *s. m.* (ysgil) A setting behind; a going or riding behind; a recession; a throwing behind.

Ysgiliaw, *v. a.* (ysgil) To set behind; to lay or throw aside; to go behind; to ride behind on horseback.

Ysgiliwr, *s. m.—pl.* ysgiliwyr (ysgil—gwr) One who sets behind; one who takes behind on horseback.

Ysgin, *s. f.—pl. t.* au (cin) A robe made of skin with the fur on it, a pelisse.

Rhita Gawr a wnai iddo ysgin o farfau brenhinoedd.

Rhita the Giant made for him a robe of the beards of kings.
Gr. ab Arthur.

Ysginaw, *v. a.* (ysgin) To dress in a robe.

Ysginawg, *a.* (ysgin) Having a robe, gowned.

Ysginawr, *s. m.—pl.* ysginorion (ysgin) A robe.

Ysginawr porfor—
Ysgarlad, liw fflamiad flamlar.

An immense robe of scarlet, the hue of the gleaming of flames.
Ll. P. Moch.

Ysginen, *s. f. dim.* (ysgin) A robe, a gown.

Ysginiad, *s. m.* (ysgin) A dressing in a robe.

Ysginydd, *s. m.—pl. t.* ion (ysgin) A robe-maker.

Ysginyddiaeth, *s. m.* (ysgin) The trade of a robe-maker, a pelisse-maker.

Ysgip, *s. m.—pl. t.* iau (cip) A quick snatch.

Ysgipiad, *s. m.* (ysgip) A snatching away.

Ysgipiaw, *v. a.* (ysgip) To snatch away.

Ysgipiai farf—
Ysgrwydr hwyl belydr haul.

It would snatch off a beard of a wandering course like the sun beams.
R. Goch Eryri, i Gyllell.

Ysgipiawg, *a.* (ysgip) Snatching, rapacious.

Ysgipiawl, *a.* (ysgip) Snatching, rapacious.

Ysgipiedig, *a.* (ysgipiad) Being snatched.

Ysgipiolrwydd, *s. m.* (ysgipiawl) Rapaciousness.

Ysgiw, *s. m.—pl. t.* ion (ciw) A skreen or shelter; a cousin in the third degree.

Ysgiwiad, *s. m.* (ysgiw) A screening, a sheltering.

Ysgiwiaw, *v. a.* (ysgiw) To screen, to shelter.

Ysglawring, *s. m.* (clawr) Glue, cement.

Ysglawringaw, *v. a.* (ysglawring) To glue.

Ysglawringiad, *s. m.* (ysglawring) A gluing.

Ysglem, *s. f.—pl. t.* iau (clem) A slice, a slive.

Ysglem glew o'r crimprew crau.

A good *slice* of the brittle sharp ice. *D. ab Gwilym.*

Ysglemiad, *s. m.* (ysglem) A sliving, a slicing.

Ysglemiaw, *v. a.* (ysglem) To slice, to slive.

Ysglemiawl, *a.* (ysglem) Slicing, or sliving.

Ysglemiwr, *s. m.—pl.* ysglemiwyr (ysglem—gwr) One who slives.

Ysglemydd, *s. m.—pl. t.* ion (ysglem) A slicer.

> Rhiagyn o wr—
> A gen lem fal ysglemydd.
>
> A skeleton of a man, with a sharp chin like a *slicer*. *Gronw William.*

Ysglen, *s. f.—pl. t.* oedd (ysg—llen) A sex.
Ysglenawg, *a.* (ysglen) Having a sex.
Ysglenawl, *a.* (ysglen) Sexual, belonging to sex.
Ysgleniad, *s. m.* (ysglen) A forming a sex.
Ysglent, *s. f.—pl. t.* iau (ysg—llent) A slide, a slippery drift, as of ice.
Ysglentiad, *s. m.* (ysglent) A making a slide.
Ysglentiaw, *v. a.* (ysglent) To form a slide, to slide as upon the ice.
Ysglentiawl, *a.* (ysglent) Sliding, like a slide.
Ysglentiwr, *s. m.—pl.* ysglentiwyr (ysglent—gwr) A slider on the ice.
Ysglin, *s. m.—pl. t.* ion (glin) A knob, a knot.
Ysglinaw, *v. a.* (ysglin) To form a knob.
Ysglinen, *s. f. dim.* (ysglin) A knot in a tree.

> Osgl iawnwaed heb ysglinen.
>
> A branch, of true blood, without a *knot*. *S. Tudyr.*

Ysgliniad, *s. m.* (ysglin) A forming a knob.
Ysgloen, *s. f. dim.* (cloen) A maiden, a damsel.
Ysglofen, *s. m. dim.* (clofen) A slip, a spray.
Ysglofeniad, *s. m.* (ysglofen) A branching.
Ysglofenu, *v. a.* (ysglofen) To cut a slip.
Ysglyf, *s. m.—pl. t.* ion (glyf) That seeks prey.

> Yn nherfysg yn nherfyn Saeson,
> Yn nhorfoedd cyhoedd cyngreinion,
> Yn nharf ewrwrys gwrys gwron,
> Yn nhwrf llu, a llef ysglyfion,
> Cyrn cenynt, ceiddynt carn weilwion ar dir,
> Ar derfyn Caer Lleon.
>
> In a tumult on the Saxons, boundary, in the conspicuous hosts of mutual stragglers, in the violent pursuit by an ardent hero, in the turmoil of a host and scream of *birds of prey*, horns resounded, the pale-hoofed steeds scudded over the land, on the limit of Caer Lleon. *Cynddelw, m. O Gwynedd.*

Ysglyfaeth, *s. f.—pl. t.* au (ysglyf) Depredation.
Ysglyfaethawl, *a.* (ysglyfaeth) Depredating.
Ysglyfaethiad, *s. m.* (ysglyfaeth) A depredating.
Ysglyfaethu, *v. a.* (ysglyfaeth) To depredate.
Ysglyfaethus, *a.* (ysglyfaeth) Predatory.

> Mor ysglyfaethus a barcud.
>
> As *rapacious* as a kite. *Adage.*

Ysglyfiad, *s. m.—pl.* ysglyfiaid (ysglyf) A depredator, a ravager.

> Ysglyfiad bid glewddrud.
>
> Let the *depredator* be craftily bold. *Adage.*

Ysglyfiannawl, *a.* (ysglyfiant) Depredating.
Ysglyfiannu, *v. a.* (ysglyfiant) To depredate.
Ysglyfiant, *s. m.* (ysglyf) Depredation.
Ysglyfiaw, *v. a.* (ysglyf) To depredate.
Ysglyfied, *v. a.* (ysglyf) To depredate, to spoil.
Ysglyfiedydd, *s. m.—pl. t.* ion (ysglyfiad) A ravager, a depredator.
Ysglyfiwr, *s. m.—pl.* ysglyfiwyr (ysglyf—gwr) A rapacious one; a snatcher.
Ysglyfu, *v. a.* (ysglyf) To take forcibly, to snatch, to depredate.

> Cyridwen yn dawed i mewn ac yn gweled ei llafur yn golledig, ysglyfu rhodyl a tharaw y dall Mordaf ar ei ben a wnai.
>
> Cyridwen coming in and seeing her labour lost, what she did was *to snatch up* a staff and strike the blind Mordaf on his head. *Hanes Taliesin.*

Ysglymawl, *a.* (clymawl) Tending to knit.
Ysglymiad, *s. m.* (clymiad) A forming a knot.
Ysglymu, *v. a.* (clymu) To form into a knot.
Ysgnawd, *a.* (ys—cnawd) Being habitual.
Ysgnodawg, *a.* (ysgnawd) Having a habit.
Ysgnodawl, *a.* (ysgnawd) Tending to habituate.

Ysgo, *s. m.* (ysg) A going or starting aside; a winter habituation, or the *hendref*.
Ysgöad, *s. m.* (ysgo) A going or starting aside.
Ysgöawl, *a.* (ysgo) Tending to start aside.
Ysgob, *s. m.* (cob) That bears away.

> Henaint methiant ddaw i ti.
> A hyny'n ddigymfeddd;
> Hwnw arnad fyn a ysgob
> I'th droi o bob ofered.
>
> Old age of decrepitude will come to thee, and that without [illegible]; that will on thee bear a *sway* to turn thee from every vain pursuit. *Huw. S. Rys.*

Ysgobell, *s. f.—pl. t.* i (ysgob) A saddle.
Ysgodawg, *a.* (ysgawd) Sheltered, shadowed, frequenting shades. *s. m.—pl.* ysgodogion; One of the shades, one of the woods; a person in disguise; a hobgoblin; a Scot; otherwise called *Gwyddel*, *Celt*, and *Celtiad*.

> Gwyddyl, diefyl duon;
> Ysgodogion, dynion lledffer.
>
> The Gwyddelians, black devils; Scots, men void of [illegible]. *Beddyr.*

Ysgodawl, *a.* (ysgawd) Sheltering, shadowing.
Ysgodi, *v. a.* (ysgawd) To shelter, to shadow.
Ysgodig, *a.* (ysgawd) Sheltered, shaded.
Ysgodigaw, *v. a.* (ysgodig) To frighten by disguise; to be frightened.
Ysgoeg, *a.* (coeg) Empty, vain, frivolous.
Ysgoegi, *v. a.* (ysgoeg) To make empty; to become empty or frivolous.
Ysgoegiad, *s. m.* (ysgoeg) A rendering empty; a becoming empty or frivolous.
Ysgoegyn, *s. m. dim.* (ysgoeg) A coxcomb, a fop.
Ysgoel, *s. f.—pl. t.* ion (coel) That is to be credited, or relied upon.
Ysgoeliad, *s. m.* (ysgoel) An inducing a belief.
Ysgoeliaw, *v. a.* (ysgoel) To induce a belief.
Ysgoew, *a.* (ysgo) Apt to fly backwards and forwards; full of motion; wavering.
Ysgoewain, *a.* (ysgoew) Full of fickleness.
Ysgoewan, *s. f.* (ysgoew) A fickle or wavering one.
Ysgoewi, *v. a.* (ysgoew) To waver; to fly backwards and forwards.
Ysgog, *s. m.—pl. t.* ion (cog) A sudden motion, a stir. *v. a.* To stir, to start.

> Mae gallu yn yr ewyllys i ysgog; ond nid oes mor ewyllys gyda gallu i ddychwelyd.
>
> There is power in the will for *stirring*; but there is not the will with the power to return. *Morgan Llwyd.*
>
> Marw yw—
> Nid ysgyg er meddyg mwy.
>
> He is dead: *he will stir* no more for all the doctor's art. *Dr. S. Cent.*

Ysgogawl, *a.* (ysgog) Tending to stir, starting.
Ysgogedig, *a.* (ysgog) Being stirred; started.
Ysgogi, *v. a.* (ysgog) To wag, to stir, to move.
Ysgogiad, *s. m.—pl. t.* au (ysgog) A stirring.

> Mae rhai weili ymeagor erioed yn y cariad, drwy ysgogiad yr ewyllys, yr hwn sydd yn eu gwasgaru fal gwreichion allan o'hono ei hun.
>
> There are some who have ever borne themselves in that love, through the *working* of the will, which scattereth them like sparks out of itself. *Morgan Llwyd.*

Ysgogydd, *s. m.—pl. t.* ion (ysgog) A stirrer.
Ysgogyn, *s. m. dim.* (ysgog) A fickle one.

> Gwelwn lawer ysgogyn rhygyngawg, a allai rhidyllaw ffa wrth wynt ei gynffon.
>
> I could see many strutting *fops*, who might winnow beans by the wind of his train. *Ellis Wynn, B. Cwsg.*

Ysgoi, *v. a.* (ysgo) To turn or start aside; to shun; to go aslaunt; to avoid; to escape.
Ysgol, *s. f.—pl. t.* ion (col) That matures; a school.

> Tri harddwch gwlad: ysgubawr, efail, ac ysgol.
>
> The three ornaments of a country: a barn, a smithery, and a school. *Adage.*

Ysgòl, *s. f.—pl. t.* ion (cól) That rises up in a point; a peak, a pointed rock; a ladder. It is the same with *colon* and *colfa;* and it forms the names of some precipices, as *Ysgolion Duon*, in Caermarthenshire; and *Nant yr Ysgolion*, in Montgomeryshire.

> Trefnaist wern uffern—
> Trefred i bryfed, lle yd ymbrofan';
> Troch heol ysgol esgar boethfan.
>
> Thou didst prepare the slough of hell, a habitation for worms, where they struggle together; a broken path of the *precipice* of the fiery place of separation. *Cynddelw.*

Ysgolaidd, *a.* (ysgol) Appertaining to a school.

Ysgolàig, *s. m.—pl.* ysgolèigion (ysgol—aig) A scholar; a clerk, a clergyman; a parish clerk. *Ysgolaig y ddinas*, the town clerk.

Ysgolawr, *s. m.—pl.* ysgolorion (ysgol) A scholar.

Ysgoldy, *s. m.* (ysgol—ty) A school-house.

Ysgoleigdawd, *s. m.* (ysgolàig) Scholarship.

Ysgoleigdra, *s. m.* (ysgolàig) Scholarship.

Ysgoleiges, *s. f.* (ysgolàig) A female scholar.

Ysgoleigiad, *s. m.* (ysgolàig) A schooling.

Ysgoleigiaeth, *s. m.* (ysgolàig) A schooling.

Ysgoleigiaw, *v. a.* (ysgolàig) To school.

Ysgoleigiawl, *a.* (ysgolàig) Scholastical.

Ysgoleigiwr, *s. m.—pl.* ysgoleigiwyr (ysgolàig—gwr) A schoolman.

Ysgoli, *v. a.* (ysgol) To school, to give schooling.

Ysgoliad, *s. m.* (ysgol) A giving a schooling.

Ysgolp, *s. m.—pl. t.* iau (colp) A sharp pointed spar or wagget, a wooden pin. It is also called *colp*, and *aseth*.

Ysgolpen, *s. f. dim.* (ysgolp) A sharp spar.

Ysgolpiad, *s. m.* (ysgolp) A fastening with a wooden pin or wagget.

Ysgolpiaw, *v. a.* (ysgolp) To pin, or to wagget.

Ysgolydd, *s. m.—pl. t.* ion (ysgol) A schoolmaster.

Ysgor, *s. f.—pl. t.* au (cór) That encircles; a circular entrenchment; a fortification; rampart, or bulwark.

> Ysgor ymddiffyn pan ymddiffer gwlad.
>
> A *bulwark* of defence when he guards a country. *Cynddelw.*
>
> Lrais ar ysgwyd rhag ysgor Dinteirw.
>
> The shield was borne down before the *camp* of Dinteirw. *Cynddelw.*
>
> Ysgor gadw ni gedwis llyfrder.
>
> A protecting *bulwark* that protected not cowardice. *Cynddelw.*
>
> Blawdd esgar ysgor yn ddiffaith;
> Balch eryr bara i Llyr Lledieith.
>
> He will blast the *rampart* of the foe to ruins; a towering eagle with the front of Llyr Lledieith. *Cynddelw, i O. ab Madawg.*
>
> Ni lleiais neb trais tros ei *ysgor*:
> Ni thymhwyll neb twyll tylla ei ddor.
>
> No body dares any trespass over his *wall*, no body will devise a fraud to break through his door. *Llywelyn Fardd.*

Ysgorawg, *a.* (ysgor) Having a surrounding fence or rampart, an epithet for a ship.

Ysgorawl, *a.* (ysgor) Relating to fortification.

Ysgordd, *s. m.—pl. t.* ion (cordd) That encircles as a retinue.

Ysgorfa, *s. f.—pl.* ysgorfëydd (ysgor) A place of defence; protection, defence.

> Gwyr a aeth Gattraeth gan wawr,
> Wy neb nis vn' ysgorfa ysgwydawr;
> Crau cyrchynt cyn hynt treiawr,
> Yn gynlan fal taran twrf aesawr.
>
> Heroes went to Cattraeth with the dawn, to whom there was no *protection* from shields; blood they would seek before the course of the ebbing tide, loud in the front like thunder the din of shields. *Aneurin.*
>
> Awen pan ddyfrao
> Am ddedwydd ddiau
> A'm buchedd ara',
> Am oesau ysgorfa.
>
> The muse when it flows, in happy days and in my tranquil life it shall be the *protection* of ages. [illegible]

Ysgori, *v. a.* (ysgor) To form a circular camp.

Ysgoriad, *s. m.* (ysgor) An encompassing with a rampart; an entrenching or forming a circular camp.

Ysgorn, *s. m.* (ysg—orn) Scorn, contumely.

> Ai byddar wyd, fy ngharíad,
> Ai ysgorn heb geisiaw gwad?
>
> Art thou deaf, my love, or is it *scorn*, without seeking a denial. *D. ab Gwilym.*

Ysgorniad, *s. m.* (ysgorn) A scorning, a slighting.

Ysgorniaw, *v. a.* (ysgorn) To scorn, to slight.

Ysgornllyd, *a.* (ysgorn) Scornful, slighting.

Ysgort, *s. f.—pl. t.* iau (ysg—or) A harsh noise; a report; a jar; a twang; a rap.

> Ag ysgort megys y gwn.
>
> With a *report* as of the gun. *D. Nanmor.*
>
> Dwy Went a glyw hyd awyr
> Ysgort gwn yn mysg gwart gwyr.
>
> The two Gwents will hear through the air a *report of a gun* among a guard of men. *Rhys Brydydd.*

Ysgortiad, *s. m.—pl. t.* au (ysgort) A making a report, an explosion; a jarring.

Ysgortiaw, *v. a.* (ysgort) To make a report.

Ysgortiawl, *a.* (ysgort) Apt to make a report.

Ysgorwg, *s. m.* (ysgor) That forms a screen round.

Ysgorydd, *s. m.—pl. t.* ion (ysgor) One who forms a rampart or camp.

Ysgotiad, *s. m.—pl.* ysgotiaid (ysgawd) One of the shades, or of the woods; a Scot.

Ysgotiaith, *s. f.* (ysgawd—iaith) The Scottish or Gwyddelian tongue.

Ysgoth, *s. m.* (coth) A purge, or a voidance.

Ysgothawl, *a.* (ysgoth) Purging, or voiding.

Ysgothfa, *s. f.—pl.* ysgothfëydd (ysgoth) A privy.

Ysgothi, *v. a.* (ysgoth) To void by a purge, to scour.

Ysgothiad, *s. m.—pl. t.* au (ysgoth) A purging.

Ysgra, *s. m.* (cra) That is harsh or dry.

Ysgrab, *s. f.—pl.* ysgrebau (crab) What is drawn up or puckered; a scrip.

Ysgrabin, *a.* (ysgrab) Tending to pucker.

Ysgrabiniad, *s. m.* (ysgrabin) A puckering.

Ysgrabiniaw, *v. a.* (ysgrabin) To pucker.

Ysgrabiniawl, *a.* (ysgrabin) Puckering.

Ysgrabiniwr, *s. m.—pl.* ysgrabiniwyr (ysgrabin—gwr) A puckerer.

Ysgrabwth, *s. m.* (ysgrab) That is in a heap.

Ysgrad, *s. m.* (crad) That is rigid or stiff.

Ysgräell, *s. f.* (ysgra) The sea-swallow.

Ysgräen, *s. f. dim.* (ysgra) A sea-swallow; also called *morwennol*. *Ysgraen ddu*, the black tern.

Ysgraf, *s. m.* (craf) That scrapes or scratches.

Ysgrafell, *s. f.—pl. t.* i (ysgraf) A currycomb; a grater; a rasp.

Ysgrafelliad, *s. m.* (ysgrafell) A currying.

Ysgrafellu, *v. a.* (ysgrafell) To curry, to scrape.

Ysgrafellwr, *s. m.—pl.* ysgrafellwyr (ysgrafell—gwr) A currier; a scraper.

Ysgrafellydd, *s. m.—pl. t.* ion (ysgrafell) A currier, or a scraper.

Ysgrafen, *s. f.—pl. t.* au (ysgraf) A scraper.

Ysgrafena, *v. a.* (ysgrafen) To go a begging.

Ysgrafiad, *s. m.* (ysgraf) A scraping.

Ysgrafu, *v. a.* (ysgraf) To scrape; to grate.

Ysgraff, *s. f.—pl. t.* au (craff) That is sharp; that makes an impression; also a ferry.

Ysgraffin, *a.* (ysgraff) Apt to scratch or graze.

Ysgraffiniad, *s. m.* (ysgraffin) A scarification.

Ysgraffiniaw, *v. a.* (ysgraffin) To scarify.

Ysgraffiniawl, *a.* (ysgraffin) Scarifying.

Ysgraffiniwr, *s. m.—pl.* ysgraffiniwyr (ysgraffin—gwr) A scarifier.

Ysgrain, *s. m.* (crain) That is crawling.

Ysgraw, *s. f.* (craw) That forms a crust.

Ysgrawen, *s. f.*—*pl. t.* i (ysgraw) A crust.
Ysgraweniad, *s. m.* (ysgrawen) An incrustation.
Ysgrawenu, *v. n.* (ysgrawen) To incrustate.
Ysgrawiad, *s. m.* (ysgraw) An incrustation.
Ysgrawiaw, *v. a.* (ysgraw) To incrustate.
Ysgrawling, *s. m.* (ysgraw) Cement, glue.

> Y rhew——
> Ias greulon, fal ysgrawling.
>
> The ice of cruel touch, like *glue*. *D. ab Gwilym.*

Ysgrawlingaw, *v. a.* (ysgrawling) To glue.
Ysgrawlingiad, *s. m.* (ysgrawling) A gluing.
Ysgre, *s f.* (cre) That makes a crying.
Ysgrëad, *s. m.* (ysgre) A making a crying.
Ysgrëaw, *v. a.* (ysgre) To make a crying noise.
Ysgrëawl, *a.* (ysgre) Crying, or craving.
Ysgrech, *s. f.*—*pl. t.* ion (crech) A scream, a shriek. *Ysgrech y coed;* a jay; also called *ysgrechog.*
Ysgrechawg, *a.* (ysgrech) Full of screaming.
Ysgrechiad, *s. m.* (ysgrech) A screaming.
Ysgrechian, *v. a.* (ysgrech) To scream, to shriek; to chatter as a jay.
Ysgrechiaw, *v. a.* (ysgrech) To scream, to shriek.
Ysgrechiawl, *a.* (ysgrech) Screaming, shrieking.
Ysgrechiwr, *s. m.* (ysgrech—gwr) A screamer.
Ysgrechlais, *s. m.* (ysgrech—llais) A screaming voice.
Ysgrechlef, *s. m.* (ysgrech--llef) A screaming voice.
Ysgrechlefain, *v. a.* (ysgrechlef) To utter a screaming noise or chattering.
Ysgrechleisiad, *s. m.* (ysgrechlais) A making a screaming noise.
Ysgrechleisiaw, *v. a.* (ysgrechlais) To make a screaming noise.
Ysgrechleisiawl, *a.* (ysgrechlais) Of a screaming or shrieking voice.
Ysgrechleisiwr, *s. m.*—*pl.* ysgrechleisiwyr (ysgrechlais—gwr) One who screams.
Ysgrechog, *s. f.* (ysgrech) A jay or cuist.
Ysgrepan, *s. f. dim.* (ysgrab) A wallet, a scrip.
Ysgrepana, *v. a.* (ysgrepan) To collect into a bag; to go a begging; also called *cardota, hel bywyd,* and *cerdded tai.*
Ysgrepaniad, *s. m.* (ysgrepan) A scripping.
Ysgrepanu, *v. a.* (ysgrepan) To put in a bag.
Ysgretan, *s. c. dim.* (ysgrad) Any lean or lank looking animal; the sea-swallow; also called *gwrachen,* and *ysgraen.*
Ysgrew, *s. f.* (ysgre) That is full of loquacity.
Ysgri, *s. f.*—*pl. t.* on (cri) A shriek, or scream.

> Diarheb iddynt dori
> Dy eagair wen wedi ysgri.
>
> It is a proverb that they broke thy white shank after the *shriek.* *L. G. Cothi.*

Ysgrïad, *s. m.* (ysgri) A shrieking, a screaming.
Ysgrïaw, *v. a.* (ysgri) To make a screaming.
Ysgrïawl, *a.* (ysgri) Screaming or shrieking.
Ysgribiniad, *s. m.* (cribiniad) A raking together.
Ysgribiniaw, *v. a.* (cribiniaw) To rake together.
Ysgrif, *s. f.*—*pl. t.* ion (crif) A writing.
Ysgrifaw, *v. a.* (ysgrif) To notch; to write.
Ysgrifawl, *a.* (ysgrif) Relating to writing.
Ysgrifed, *s. f.* (ysgrif) A writing; a manuscript.
Ysgrifen, *s. f. dim.* (ysgrif) A piece of writing.
Ysgrifenawl, *a.* (ysgrifen) Relating to writing.
Ysgrifenedig, *a.* (ysgrifen) Being written.
Ysgrifeniad, *s. m.*—*pl. t.* au (ysgrifen) A writing.
Ysgrifenu, *v. a.* (ysgrifen) To write, to pen.

> Pei ysgrifenasai Duw wir enw pob dyn ar ei dalcen, pa le y cawsid defnydd mygwd i bawb a'i ceisiai!
>
> If God had written the true name of every man on his forehead, where could there have been found stuff for a mask for every one who should seek for it? *Adage.*

Ysgrifenwr, *s. m.*—*pl.* ysgrifenwyr (ysgrifen—gwr) A writer.
Ysgrifenydd, *s. m.*—*pl. t.* ion (ysgrifen) A scribe, a writer, a secretary.
Ysgrifenyddiaeth, *s. m.* (ysgrifenydd) The trade or profession of a writer.
Ysgrifiad, *s. m.* (ysgrif) A writing, a scribbling.
Ysgriflyfr, *s. m.*—*pl.* ysgriflyfrau (ysgrif—llyfr) A manuscript.
Ysgrifwr, *s. m.*—*pl.* ysgrifwyr (ysgrif—gwr) A writer.
Ysgrog, *s. m.* (crog) That is hung or swung.
Ysgrogell, *s. f.*—*pl. t.* i (ysgrog) A [illegible].
Ysgrogi, *v. a.* (ysgrog) To suspend, to impend.
Ysgrogiad, *s. m.* (ysgrog) A suspending.
Ysgrubl, *s. m.*—*pl. t.* od (crubl) A beast.

> Ysgrubl dirfal yn allanol.
>
> A mischievous *beast* on the outside. *Adage.*

Ysgrubleidd, *a.* (ysgrubl) Being beast-like.
Ysgrublawg, *a.* (ysgrubl) Abounding with beasts.
Ysgrubliad, *s. m.*—*pl.* ysgrublaidd (ysgrubl) A beast, a brute creature.
Ysgrud, *s. f.*—*pl. t.* ion (crud) A frame; a skeleton; a carcase.

> Ysgrud fud draig [illegible].
>
> A silent corpse is the potent leading chief. [illegible]

Ysgrudiad, *s. m.* (ysgrud) A making a frame; a making a skeleton.
Ysgrudiaw, *v. a.* (ysgrud) To make a frame, to form a skeleton; to make a carcase.

> Ysgrud glud glewyd fyd [illegible]
> Ysgryd gryd [illegible].
>
> The chief will make a skeleton of the heroism of the world's glory; he will shout a shout of the vehement shake of the [illegible]. [illegible]

Ysgrudiawl, *a.* (ysgrud) Belonging to a frame, belonging to a skeleton.
Ysgruth, *s. m.*—*pl. t.* oedd (ysg—rhuth) A full speed. *Mae ef yn myned ar ei ysgruth,* he is going on his full pace.
Ysgrwd, *s. m.*—*pl.* ysgrydion (crwd) A carcass. *Hen ysgrwd,* an old wretch.

> Pa ddull enaid——
> Ysgrwd wag is y fagwyr,
> Os gwych, nys fy ngwaed, nis gwyr.
>
> What the condition of the soul, whether happy, the empty carcase beneath the wall knows not, upon my faith. [illegible]

> Ni rodir pen un o'r cenin
> Er ei ysgrwd.——
>
> Not the head of one of the leeks would be given for his carcass. [illegible]

Ysgrwdiad, *s. m.* (ysgrwd) A carcasing.
Ysgrwdiaw, *v. a.* (ysgrwd) To make a carcass.
Ysgrwth, *s. m.* (crwth) A heap or bulk; a pile.
Ysgrwydr, *s. m.* (crwydr) A straying course.
Ysgrwydraw, *v. a.* (ysgrwydr) To make a wandering journey.
Ysgrwydrawl, *a.* (ysgrwydr) Of a wandering tendency.
Ysgrwydriad, *s. m.* (ysgrwydr) A making a straying journey.
Ysgryd, *s. m.*—*pl. t.* ion (cryd) A shiver, a quake.
Ysgrydiad, *s. m.* (ysgryd) A shivering.
Ysgrydian, *v. a.* (ysgryd) To keep shivering.
Ysgrydiannawl, *a.* (ysgrydiant) Shivering.
Ysgrydiannu, *v. a.* (ysgrydiant) To be in a constant shivering or shuddering.
Ysgrydiant, *s. m.* (ysgryd) A shivering.

> Maint fydd yn ngwasgar yr ysgrydiant.
>
> So great in the dispersion will be the *trepidation.* [illegible]

Ysgrydiaw, *v. a.* (ysgryd) To shiver, to quake.

Ysgryd gryd rhag gryd ehorthus
Ysgrud wlydd ar wledd y mellion.

The *shout will re-echo* before the vehement purveyor of the pampered carcase over the carrion feast.
Cynddelw, i O. Cyfeiliawg.

Ysgrydiawl, *a.* (ysgryd) Shivering, quaking.
Ysgrydu, *v. a.* (ysgryd) To shiver, to quake.
Ysgrydwr, *s. m.—pl.* ysgrydwyr (ysgryd—gwr) A trembler.
Ysgryn, *s. m.* (cryn) A trembling, a shiver.
Ysgrynawl, *a.* (ysgryn) Tremulous, quaking.
Ysgrynedig, *a.* (ysgryn) Trembling, quaking.
Ysgryniad, *s. m.* (ysgryn) A tremulation.
Ysgrynu, *v. a.* (ysgryn) To cause a trembling.
Ysgrytian, *v. a.* (ysgrwd) To keep wriggling, to writhe the body, as to allay an itching.
Ysgrythiad, *s. m.* (ysgrwth) A going all of a heap; a tumbling about on the ground as animals do.
Ysgrythu, *v. a.* (ysgrwth) To tumble in a heap, to tumble about as horses and other animals do.
YSGRYTHYR, *s. f.—pl. t.* au. The Scripture.
Ysgrythyrawl, *a.* (ysgrythyr) Scriptural.
Ysgrythyriad, *s. m.* (ysgrythyr) A making use of the Scripture, a quoting Scripture.
Ysgrythyru, *v. a.* (ysgrythyr) To make use of the Scripture, to quote Scripture.
Ysgrythyrydd, *s. m.—pl. t.* ion (ysgrythyr) A scripturist.
Ysguall, *a.* (cuall) Of a furious or fierce nature.

Ar eruchwydd ethyw gwall
O fraw marchawg ysguall!
A fydd wrth Urien arall!

Upon the intention there came a disappointment from the dread of a *terrific* knight; Will there be another compared with Urien!
Llywarch Hen.

Ysgub, *s. f.—pl. t.* au (cub) A sheaf; a besom.

Hawdd rhifaw yr ysgubau ar faes gwr diawg.

It is easy to reckon the *sheaves* on the field of an idle man.
Adage.

Ysgubaidd, *a.* (ysgub) Bundle-wise; like a whisp; like a sheaf; like a broom.
Ysgubaw, *v. a.* (ysgub) To whisk, to whisp; to sweep.
Ysgubawl, *a.* (ysgub) Sweeping, brushing.
Ysgubawr, *s. f.—pl.* ysguboriau (ysgub) A place for corn in the sheaf, a cornyard; a barn.

Cynt y tyrr yr odyn no'r ysgubawr.

Sooner will the kiln be burst than the *barn*.
Adage.

Ysgubedig, *a.* (ysgub) Being swept with a broom.
Ysgubell, *s. f. dim.—pl. t.* i (ysgub) A whisp, a small bundle; a besom; a brush. *Ysgubell o lysiau per*, a bunch of aromatic herbs.
Ysgubellaidd, *a.* (ysgubell) Like a whisp.
Ysgubellan, *s. f. dim.* (ysgubell) A small whisk.
Ysgubellig, *s. f. dim.* (ysgubell) A small besom.
Ysgubiad, *s. m.* (ysgub) A sweeping.
Ysgubion, *s. pl. aggr.* (ysgub) Sweepings.
Ysgubolion, *s. pl. aggr.* (ysgubawl) Sweepings.
Ysguboran, *s. f. dim.* (ysgubawr) A small barn.
Ysguboriad, *s. m.* (ysgubawr) A putting in a barn.
Ysguboriaw, *v. a.* (ysgubawr) To put in a barn.
Ysguborig, *s. f. dim.* (ysgubawr) A small barn.
Ysguborwr, *s. m.—pl.* ysguborwyr (ysgubawr—gwr) A barn-keeper.
Ysgubwr, *s. m.—pl.* ysgubwyr (ysgub—gwr) A sweeper with a besom.
Ysgubwraig, *s. f.—pl.* ysgubwreigedd (ysgub—gwraig) A female sweeper.
Ysgubydd, *s. m.—pl. t.* ion (ysgub) A sweeper.
Ysgubyddes, *s. f.* (ysgubydd) A female sweeper.

Ysgud, *s. m.* (cud) That rounds or whirls.
Ysgudaw, *v. a.* (ysgud) To scud about; to whisk.
Ysgudawl, *a.* (ysgud) Scudding, whisking.
Ysgudell, *s. f.—pl. t.* i (ysgud) A dish, a platter.
Ysgudellaid, *s. f.—pl.* ysgudelleidiau (ysgudell) A dishful.
Ysgudelliad, *s. m.* (ysgudell) A dishing.
Ysgudellu, *v. a.* (ysgudell) To put in a dish.
Ysgur, *s. m.* (cur) That is impulsive.
Ysguraw, *v. a.* (ysgur) To make an impulse.

Yn ysguraw hawl hawdd adneu,
Yn ysgur i bawb am beuea.

In *impelling* a claim easily he gave a pledge, being a foe to every body for a country.
Ll. P. Moch, i Rodri.

Ysgurawl, *a.* (ysgur) Impulsive, repulsive.
Ysguriad, *s. m.* (ysgur) An impulsion.
Ysgutyll, *s. m. dim.* (ysgud) A scudder.

Ysgutyll yn cynnull cad.

A *scudder* gathering the battle together.
D. ab Gwilym, i grilliawg du.

Ysguth, *s. m.* (cuth) A scud, a sudden whisk.
Ysguthan, *s. f.—pl. t.* od (ysguth) A woodpigeon.

Nerth ysguthan yn ei hadanedd.

The strength of a *wood-pigeon* in her wings.
Adage.

Ysguthaw, *v. a.* (ysguth) To scud, to whisk.
Ysguthell, *s. f.—pl. t.* od (ysguth) A scudder.

Doai ysguthell o ddiafyn carngam i mewn, tan ddyhead a chryno.

There came in a *scudder* of a wry-footed imp with panting and trembling.
Elis Wyn, B. Cwsg.

Ysguthiad, *s. m.* (ysguth) A scudding.
Ysgw, *s. m.* (cw) Guard, care, or safeguard; refuge. *v. imper.* Regard, take care.
Ysgwad, *s. m.* (ysgw) A guarding, a taking care.
Ysgwaeth, *s. m.* (ysgw) Guardianship; refuge.
Ysgwaetheroedd, *adv.* (gwaeth—er—oedd) The more the pity.
Ysgwaw, *v. a.* (ysgw) To guard, to take care.
Ysgwawl, *a.* (ysgw) Guarding, care-taking.
Ysgwd, *s. m.* (ysg) A thrust, a push, a jet, a drive, an impulsion; a step, a stile. *Ysgwd melin*, a mill jet.
Ysgwdawl, *a.* (ysgwd) Pushing, impulsive.
Ysgwdiad, *s. m.* (ysgwd) A pushing away.
Ysgwdu, *v. a.* (ysgwd) To make a push, to thrust.
Ysgwdwl, *s. m.* (ysgwd) That pokes or pushes.
Ysgwer, *s. f.* (ysgw) A kind of musical composition, so called.

Per, per ysgwer, oes enine mawr foliant
Mor felys gan ieuainc!

Melodious, melodious the *ysgwer*, is there a tune greatly famed so sweet to youths?
L. G. Cothi, i Ysgwer fach.

Ysgwf, *s. m.* (cwf) That closes upon or holds.
Ysgwfl, *s. m.—pl.* ysgyflon (ysgwf) A grapple, a snatch; a scuffle.
Ysgwl, *s. m.—pl.* ysgylion (cwl) An excrescence; a knob, or knur; a scab.

Ysgwl du yn mlaen ongl dar.

A black *excrescence* on the top of an oak branch.
D. ab Gwilym.

Ysgwn, *s. m.* (cwn) That rises or soars.

Nis crawn cad ysgud rhag ysgwn;
Na thaiawg mynygawg, na mynyglwn.

Treasure will not be accumulated by the hasty before the *exalted one*: nor by the boor with long hair, nor that is cropt.
Cynddelw, i O. Cyfeiliawg.

Cyfarfu ysgwn ag esgarant aer.

The *exalted one* met with the dispersed ones of slaughter.
O. Cyfeiliawg.

Ysgwn, *a.* (cwn) Rising, uplifting, raising.

Gair teulu yn ysgwn.

The word of a family *uplifting*.
Adage.

Gwaew ysgwn esgud yn mhlymnwyd.

The *uplifted* spear flitting to the livid slaughter.
Cynddelw.

Ysgwn ffleimiad yn nghadian.

The *towering* conflagrator in the battle field. *Cynddelw.*

Cad aagen ysgwn ysgwyd Beli.

The ruin of battle with the *uplifted* shield of Beli. *Cynddelw.*

Gal ysgwn ysgwyd anghyfan,
Garw esgar yn ysgor Gadfan.

A foe with uplifted shield unentire, furiously he scatters in the field of Cadvan. *Cynddelw, i H. ab Owain.*

Oedd ysgwn, oedd twn taleeth ei darian.

It was *uplifted*, it was broken, the border of his shield. *D. Llwyarch Mew.*

Deucan-waew terwyn ef tores bar dygrwn,
Pan ysgwn esgores.

Two hundred ardent spears the accumulating wrath did break, when *eminently* he escaped. *Ll. P. Moch.*

Ys gwyr hi hydr ein gormail,
Ysgwn daith dan ysgin dail.

She knows the drift of our vexation, on her *flying* journey under a covert of leaves. *D. ab Gwilym, i'r ewes.*

Ysgwr, *s. m.—pl.* ysgyr (cwr) A spike, a splinter; a bough or a branch; also violence.

Hawl bleiddiad lleiddiad lluch ar ysgyr.

The claim of the wolf the gleaming slaughtering on the *spikes.* *O. Cyfeiliawg.*

Neum gwant ysgwr o gur dy god?

Am I not wounded by a *spike* from the corner of thy bag? *Llywarch Hen.*

Ar ysgwr o'r afallen ydd oedd corn canu mawr.

On a *branch* of the apple-tree there was a large blowing horn. *H. Geraint—Mabinogion.*

Nac esgud frwydr, nac ysgwr,
Nac ysgwydd gorwydd, na gwr—

Nor the flying battle, nor *spike*, nor the shoulder of a steed, nor man, will obstruct thee. *D. ab Gwilym.*

Ysgwrlwg, *s. m.* (ysgwr—llwg) A rustle, crackle

Ysgwrlwgach, *v. a.* (ysgwrlwg) To rustle; to crackle; to rattle, to clatter, to clash.

Ysgwrn, *s. m.* (cwrn) That juts or runs out.

Ysgwt, *s. m.* (cwt) A scud, a tail, a bottom. *Ysgwt y gynhen*, a mischief maker.

Ysgwth, *s. m.—pl. t.* ion (cwth) A push, a thrust.

Ysgwthiad, *s. m.* (ysgwth) A propulsion.

Ysgwthiaw, *v. a.* (ysgwth) To push, to impel.

Ysgwthiawl, *a.* (ysgwth) Propulsive, pushing.

Ysgwthiwr, *s. m.—pl.* ysgwthiwyr (ysgwth—gwr) An impeller.

Ysgwthr, *s. m.—pl.* ysgythrion (ysgwth) A carving, engraving, or cutting into; a cut out or from; a paring.

Yn ysgwthr trydar,
Yn ysgwn darpar,
Yn llachar ny'n lloches.

In the *lopping* of tumult, in the exalted preparation, gleamingly he protected us. *Ll. P. Moch.*

Ysgwyd, *s. m.* (ysg) A shake, a flutter. *v. a.* To shake, to flutter. *Ysgwyd llaw*, a shake hand; *ysgwyd law*, shake hand; *ysgwyd aden*, to flutter a wing.

Ysgŵyd, *s. f.—pl. t.* au (ysgw) A shield, a target.

Lludw ysgor ysgwyd byddinau.

Ashes the structure that was the *shield* of hosts. *Cynddelw.*

Oedd ysgwn ysgwyd twn.

Uplifted was the broken *shield.* *Cynddelw.*

Yn rhith rhyn ysgwyd,
Rhag ysgwn blymnwyd.

In the similitude of a terrific shield in front of a *rising* tumult. *Cynddelw.*

Ei ysgwn gynnif,
Ei ysgwyd yn ngnif.

His *rising* conflict, his shield in toil. *Cynddelw.*

Grym ysgwn ysgwyd wyarlled.

The rising energy of the gory *shield.* *Llygad Gwr.*

Atr ysgwn aur ysgwyd oedd.

The stay of slaughter with a golden shield was he. *Bleddyn Fardd.*

Ysgwydadwy, *a.* (ysgwyd) That may be shaken.

Ysgwydaw, *v. a.* (ysgwyd) To use a shield.

Ysgwydawg, *a.* (ysgwyd) Having a shield.

Ysgwydawl, *a.* (ysgwyd) Belonging to a shield.

Ysgwydawr, *s. m.* (ysgwyd) A shield, a target.

Neum rhoddes i Run Rhyfeddawr
Cant haid, a chant ysgwydawr.

Have I not been gifted by Rhun the Magnificent with a hundred swarms, and a hundred *shields?* *Llywarch Hen.*

Ysgwydedig, *a.* (ysgwyd) Shaken, or agitated.

Ysgwydfa, *s. f.* (ysgwyd) A shake; a toss.

Ysgwydfolch, *a.* (ysgwyd—bolch) With notched shield.

Ysgwydfrith, *a.* (brith) With a variegated shield.

Ysgwydfriw, *a.* (briw) With a broken shield.

Ysgwydfwrw, *s. m.* (ysgwyd—bwrw) A cast of shields, an aggregate of shields.

Yn nydd gwyth gwaithfuddig ddragon
Ar llwrw ysgwydfwrw ysgyrion.

In the day of wrath a conquering leader amidst the *dissevered throng of shields.* *Cynddelw, i O. Gwynedd.*

Ysgwydiad, *s. m.—pl.* ysgwydiaid (ysgwyd) One that bears a shield.

Pan ddofes pair trachwres trwch[illegible]
Par trwy far trwy fyrdd ysgwydiad,
Por chor aeswr [illegible],
Pond rhagddaw bu ffaw bu ffyngiad!

When calmed the ardent impulse of the plunging of the spear through wrath through a myriad of *shieldsmen*, the chief equally the bearer of the buckler, before him was there not a glorious thronging! *Ll. P. Moch, i D. ab Owain.*

Ysgwydrwy, *s. f.* (rhwy) A shield border.

Rhudd em fy nghylchwy;
Aur fy ysgwydrwy.

Of ruddy gem my wreath; gold my *shield border.* *Taliesin.*

Ysgwydwas, *s. m.—pl.* ysgwydweis (ysgwyd—gwas) A shield-bearer.

Ysgwydwr, *s. m.* (ysgwyd—gwr) A shield-man.

Ysgwydwyn, *a.* (ysgwyd—gwyn) White-shielded.

Canad gwastad ysgwydwyn.

An equanimous *white-shielded* herald. *Cyfoesi Merddin.*

Ysgwydydd, *s. m.* (ysgwyd) A shield-bearer.

Ysgwydd, *s. f.—pl. t.* au (cwydd) A shoulder.

Gorwen fy ysgwyd ar fy ysgwydd i drais;
Cerais ni gefais gyfes awydd.

White topt my shield on my *shoulder* for conquest; I loved what I did not obtain, notwithstanding what there might be of avidity. *H. ab Owain.*

Ysgwyddaw, *v. a.* (ysgwydd) To shoulder.

Ysgwyddawg, *a.* (ysgwydd) Having a shoulder. *s. f.* That has the whole shoulder; a shoulder, as of mutton; a gammon.

Ysgwyddawg y derchafael a gymerais i gan feibion Israel.

The heave *shoulder* I did receive from the children of Israel. *Leviticus* 7. 34.

Ysgwyddawl, *a.* (ysgwydd) Scapulary; shoulder.

Ysgwyddiad, *s. m.* (ysgwydd) A shouldering; a jutting out; a jostling.

Ysgwyddlian, *s. m.* (ysgwydd—llian) A shoulder-scarf; an ephod.

Ysgwyddwisg, *s. f.—pl. t.* oedd (ysgwydd—gwisg) A shoulder-scarf; an ephod.

Ysgwyf, *s. m.* (cwyf) A thin covering or sprinkle; scum.

Ysgwyfan, *s. c.* (ysgwyf) A sprinkle. *Tafla ysgwyfan o la drosto*, throw a sprinkle of cash over it.

Ysgwyfawl, *a.* (ysgwyf) Generating scum.

Ysgwyfen, *s. f. dim.* (ysgwyf) A sprinkle; a thin scum.

Ysgwyfiad, *s. m.* (ysgwyf) A scumming.

Ysgydfa, *s. f.* (ysgwd) A shake; a stirring.

Ysgydiad, *s. m.* (ysgwd) A shaking; a stirring.

Ysgydiaw, *v. a.* (ysgwd) To shake; to stir.

Na ddoda dy boffder mewn cnawdawl gariad; ysgyd ymaith ei gwryd, drwy ymarfer a gorchwylion daionus.

Place not thy affection upon carnal love; *shake* off slothfulness, through the being accustomed with good occupations. *Marchawg Crwydrad.*

Ysgydiawl, *a.* (ysgwd) Shaking, agitating.
Ysgydig, *a.* (ysgwd) Apt to be shaking.
Ysgydigaw, *v. a.* (ysgydig) To cause a shake.
Ysgydiwr, *s. m.* (ysgwd—gwr) A shaker.
Ysgydw, *s. m.* (ysgwd) That is made to shake or stir. *v. a.* To be made to shake.

> Ef ysgydw am eagor ei dad
> Ysgwydawr llathridfawr llathraid.
>
> He *causes to shake* about the dwelling of his grandsire a shield glittering with high polish. *Ll. P. Moch, i Rodri.*

Ysgydwad, *s. m.* (ysgydw) Agitation.
Ysgydwawl, *a.* (ysgydw) Being agitated, shaking.
Ysgydwyd, *v. a.* (ysgydw) To cause a shake.
Ysgyfain, *a.* (ysgwf) That abounds with involutions, that is convolved; pulmonary.
Ysgyfaint, *s. f.* (ysgyfain) The lights; the lungs; also the strangles.

> Tri rhyw ysgyfaint y sydd; ysgyfeinwst, a gwyn ysgyfain, a du ysgyfain.
>
> There are three sorts of *pulmonaria*; inflammation of the lungs, white pulmonaria, and black pulmonaria. *Meddyginiaeth.*

Ysgyfala, *a.* (cyfal) Being in an uniform state; unemployed, being at ease, being at leisure; careless. *Ystafell ysgyfala.*

> Myned a wnai i le dirgel ysgyfala i ddwyn buchedd ddwywawl.
>
> He went to a private place that was secure, to lead a pious life. *Hanes G. ab Cynan.*
>
> Efe a darawodd y fyddin: canys y fyddin oedd ysgyfala.
>
> He smote the host: for the host was *secure*. *Barnwyr* 8. 11.

Ysgyfalâad, *s. m.* (ysgyfala) A rendering easy or secure; a becoming safe.
Ysgyfalâu, *v. a.* (ysgyfala) To render easy, to render secure; to become at leisure.
Ysgyfalâwch, *s. m.* (ysgyfala) A state of ease or composure; security.
Ysgyfar, *s. f.—pl. t.* au (ysgwf) An auricle, an ear.

> Ysgyfar waeddgar ylldfram.
>
> A wry-necked *flap* full of noise. *D. ab Gwilym, i delyn ledr.*

Ysgyfarllynig, *a.* (ysgyfar—llyn) Having stained ears.

> Sarhaed brenin Aber Ffraw fal hyn y telir: can muw wrth bob cantref a fo iddo, a tharw gwyn ysgyfarllynig wrth bob can muw o honddynt, a gwialen aur gyhyd ag ef ei hun, a chan fraised a'i fys bychan, a chan dewed ag ewin amaeth rhyfo a naeth naw mlynedd.
>
> The insult fine of the king of Aber Fraw in this manner shall it be paid: a hundred kine for every cantrev that belongs to him; and a white bull *with red ears* to every hundred kine of them; and a gold rod as long as himself, and equal in roundness to his little finger, and as thick as the nail of a husbandman who has been a husbandman for nine years. *Welsh Laws.*

Ysgyfarn, *s. f.—pl. t.* au (ysgyfar) An ear.

> Y gwas ystafell bian o'r gwartheg anrhaith cynnifer ag a fo cyhyd eu corn ag eu hysgyfarn.
>
> The groom of the chamber claims of the captured cattle as many as have their horn and *ear* of equal length. *Welsh Laws.*

Ysgyfarnawg, *a.* (ysgyfarn) Abounding with ears. *s. f.—pl.* ysgyfarnogod. That is large-eared, a hare; also called *ceinach*, and *cath eithin*. *Ysgyfarnawg y mor*, the gurnard.

> Rhaid pwyaw llawer llwyn cyn cael ysgyfarnawg.
>
> It is necessary to beat many a bush before a *hare* is started. *Adage.*
>
> Ysgyfarnawg sy helfa ddolef, am ei bod yn cadw ei helynt er maint fo yr ymlid arni.
>
> The *hare* is a cry chase, because that she keeps her course however great the pursuit of her may be. *Cyfraith Hela.*

Ysgyfarnogaidd, *a.* (ysgyfarnawg) Like a hare.
Ysgyfemiad, *s. m.* (ysgyfain) A forming of lungs.
Ysgyfeiniaw, *v. n.* (ysgyfain) To furnish or form lungs; to get the strangles.
Ysgyfeiniawg, *a.* (ysgyfain) Having lungs; pulmonary; having the strangles.
Ysgyfeiniawl, *a.* (ysgyfain) Pulmonical.
Ysgyfeinllyd, *a.* (ysgyfain) Pulmonarious.
Ysgyfeinwst, *s. m.* (ysgyfain—gwst) Pulmonaria.
Ysgyflaid, *v. a.* (ysgwfl) To snatch hold.
Ysgyflgar, *a.* (ysgwfl) Apt to snatch hold.
Ysgyflgarwch, *s. m.* (ysgyflgar) Rapaciousness.
Ysgyflgi, *s. m.—pl.* ysgyflgwn (ysgwfl—ci) A worrying dog.
Ysgyflin, *a.* (ysgwfl) That is laid hold of. *Bara ysgyflin*, shew-bread.
Ysgyfliad, *s. m.* (ysgwfl) A snatching hold.
Ysgyflu, *v. a.* (ysgwfl) To snatch hold.

> Pan ydoedd Achel yn mynu tynu arfau Troilws i amdano, nycha Menon yn dawed ac yn ysgyflu corff Troilws.
>
> When Achilles was about to pull the armour of Troilus from off him, lo Menon coming and *snatching away* the body of Troilus. *H. Dares.*

Ysgyflwr, *s. m.* (ysgwfl—gwr) A snatcher.
Ysgyfrang, *s. m.* (cyfrang) That comes in contact
Ysgyfrith, *a.* (cyfrith) Being of uniform aspect.
Ysgyl, *s. m.* (ysg) That is thin or edged.
Ysgylf, *s. m.—pl. t.* ion (gylf) That is taken or held by the beak; prey.
Ysgylfiad, *s. m.* (ysgylf) A beak-snatching.
Ysgylfiaw, *v. a.* (ysgylf) To snatch with the beak
Ysgylfu, *v. a.* (ysgylf) To snatch with the beak.
Ysgymmod, *s. m.* (cymmod) That is accordant.
Ysgymmodawl, *a.* (ysgymmod) Accordant.
Ysgymmodi, *v. a.* (ysgymmod) To unite together.
Ysgymmodiad, *s. m.* (ysgymmod) Accordance.
Ysgymyn, *s. m.* (cymyn) A felling or hewing.
Ysgymyngyf, *s. m.—pl. t.* ion (ysgymyn—cyf) A chopping-block.
Ysgyn, *s. m.* (cyn) An ascent, rise, or mount.
Ysgynawl, *a.* (ysgyn) Ascending, or rising.
Ysgyniad, *s. m.—pl. t.* au (ysgyn) Ascension.
Ysgynial, *v. a.* (ysgyn) To be ascending.

> Rhag bron Buddygre
> Brain-dwyre wybr ysgynial.
>
> Before the course of victory the hovering crows *ascend* in the sky. *Aneurin.*

Ysgynu, *v. a.* (ysgyn) To ascend, to mount.
Ysgynwil, *s. m.* (ysgyn) That uplifts or raises.

> Ys canaf i'r ysgynwil,
> A droes y pumoes o'r pwll.
>
> I will sing to the *uplifter*, that turned the five ages from the pit. *Herri Hir.*

Ysgynydd, *s. m.—pl. t.* ion (ysgyn) A mounter.
Ysgyrch, *s. m.* (cyrch) That tends towards.
Ysgyrchawl, *a.* (ysgyrch) Tending to, gravitating.
Ysgyrchiad, *s. m.* (ysgyrch) A tending towards.
Ysgyrchiant, *s. m.* (ysgyrch) Gravitation.
Ysgyrchlam, *s. m.—pl. t.* au (ysgyrch—llam) A leap towards.
Ysgyrchlamawl, *a.* (ysgyrchlam) Apt to leap or bound towards.
Ysgyrchlamiad, *s.* (ysgyrchlam) A leaping towards.
Ysgyrchlamu, *v. a.* (ysgyrchlam) To leap towards.

> Rhyw i fab ysgyrchlamu.
>
> It is natural for a youth *to run forwards*. *Adage.*

Ysgyrchu, *v. a.* (ysgyrch) To tend to; to gravitate.
Ysgyren, *s. f. dim.* (ysgwr) A split piece of wood, a splinter; a stave.
Ysgyrenig, *s. f. dim.* (ysgyren) A small splint.
Ysgyrion, *s. pl. aggr.* (ysgwr) Staves, splinters.

> Rhoddes Duw ym llyw y llafn waedlif, a'i ysgyr
> Ysgyrion yn ymlif.
>
> God furnished my chief with the blood-stained blade, and his shaft of *shivers* in the conflict. *Einion Wan.*

Ysgyrioni, *v. a.* (ysgyrion) To cleave into splinters, to shiver; to stave.
Ysgyrioniad, *s. m.* (ysgyrion) A splintering.
Ysgyrionyn, *s. m. dim.* (ysgyrion) A splinter.
Ysgyrnwg, *s. m.* (ysgwrn) A snarl, or a grin.

Ysgyrnygawl, *a.* (ysgyrnwg) Snarling, grinning.
Ysgyrnygiad, *s. m.* (ysgyrnwg) A snarling.
Ysgyrnygu, *v. a.* (ysgyrnwg) To snarl, to grin.
Ysgyrwydd, *s. pl. aggr.* (ysgwr—gwydd) Cleft wood. *Pont ysgyrwydd*, a bridge of split timber; *cylchau ysgyrwydd*, hoops of split wood.
Ysgyryd, *s. m.* (ysgwr) That consists of branches, spikes, or points; that is rough or harsh. *a.* Full of ruggedness.

> Dewis, wr du ysgyryd.
> Choose, thou black *rough* man. *S. Dafi.*
> Y cawr ac y widdon a gyrchynt lleoedd ysgyryd.
> The giant and the hag were resorting to *rugged* places. *Mabinogi.*

Ysgytfa, *s. f.* (ysgwd) A concussion, a shake.
Ysgytiad, *s. m.—pl. t.* au (ysgwd) A concussion.
Ysgytian, *v. a.* (ysgwd) To keep shaking violently.
Ysgytiaw, *v. a.* (ysgwd) To shake violently.
Ysgytiawl, *a.* (ysgwd) Concussive, percussive.
Ysgytiwr, *s. m.—pl.* ysgytiwyr (ysgwd—gwr) One who shakes violently.
Ysgythawl, *a.* (ysgwth) Jetting, or spouting.
Ysgythiad, *s. m.* (ysgwth) A spouting out.
Ysgythr, *s. m.—pl. t.* ion (ysgwth) A fang; a tusk.

> Gwerth pob un o'r ysgythredd, dwy fuw, a deugaint ariant; canys bugul y dannedd ynt.
> The value of every one of the *fang teeth*, two cows, and forty pence; for they are the guards of the teeth. *Welsh Laws.*
> Rhaid imi olchi fy mhen, ac eilliaw fy marf: ysgythr Ysgythrwyn Pen Baedd a fynaf i eilliaw.
> It is necessary for me to wash my head, and to shave my beard: the *tusk* of Whitetusk the Supreme Boar I will have to shave. *H. Culhwch—Mabinogion.*

Ysgythradwy, *a.* (ysgythr) That may be lopt.
Ysgythrawd, *s. m.* (ysgythr) A cut off, or gash.
Ysgythrawg, *a.* (ysgythr) Having tusks or fangs.
Ysgythrawl, *a.* (ysgythr) Cutting; lopping; carving; engraving.
Ysgythrddant, *s. m.—pl.* ysgythrddaint (ysgythr—dant; a fang tooth.
Ysgythredig, *a.* (ysgwthr) Cut out; carved.

> Penffestin euraid ysgythredig o arwydd draig.
> A golden helmet *carved* with the figure of a dragon. *Gr. ab Arthur.*

Ysgythredd, *s. m.* (ysgythr) The state of being projected or jutting out.

> Ai wrth dy orchymyn di yr ymgyfyd yr eryr—ac yr erys—ar ysgythredd y graig?
> Is it at thy command that the eagle doth rise up, and that it resteth on the *pinnacle* of the rock? *Job* 39. 28.

Ysgythriad, *s. m.—pl. t.* au (ysgwthr) A cutting; a carving; an engraving.
Ysgythru, *v. a.* (ysgwthr) To cut away, to lop, to shred; to carve; to engrave.

> Ysgythred yma gylch o naw radd yr engylion, megys y perthyno i bob gradd yn briawd.
> *Let him carve* here a circle of the nine orders of angels, as it may appertain to every order in particular. *Cysegrlan Fuchedd.*

Ysgythrwr, *s. m.—pl.* ysgythrwyr (ysgythru—gwr) A cutter; a carver; an engraver.
Ysgythrydd, *s. m.—pl. t.* ion (ysgythru) A cutter; a lopper; a carver; an engraver.
Ysgythu, *v. a.* (ysgwth) To jet or spout out.
Ysgywen, *s. m.* (cy—gwen) That is fair or bright.
Yshiliad, *s. m.* (hiliad) A spawning.
Yshiliaw, *v. a.* (hiliaw) To deposit spawn.
Yshwyliad, *s. m.* (hwyliad) A making a course.
Yshwyliaw, *v. a.* (hwyliaw) To take a course.
Ysi, *adv.* (ys—i) There is, there may be; it may be.
Ysiad, *s. m.* (ys) A consuming; a devouring.
Ysiannawl, *a.* (ysiant) Tending to consume.
Ysiannu, *v. a.* (ysiant) To make a consumption.
Ysiant, *s. m.* (ys) A consuming; a devoration.

Ysid, *adv.* (ys—id) There is; it may be.

> Ysid ar bawb ei bryder.
> There is to every one his anxiety. *Adag.*
> Hawdd yw genyf gaffael hyny. Cyd tybych hyny ysid nis delych.
> It is easy for me to obtain that. Though thou mayest think that, *it may be* thou wilt not obtain it. *H. Culhwch—Mabinogion.*

Ysig, *a.* (ys) Inflammatory, fretting.
Ysigaw, *v. a.* (ysig) To inflame; to fret.

> Hawdd ysigaw hen glwyf.
> It is easy *to fret* an old sore. *Adag.*

Ysigdawd, *s. m.* (ysig) A bruise, a contusion.
Ysigfa, *s. f.—pl.* ysigfeydd (ysig) A bruise, a crush.
Ysigiad, *s. m.* (ysig) A bruising; a contusion.
Ysigiedig, *a.* (ysigiad) Bruised, or crushed.
Ysigwr, *s. m.—pl.* ysigwyr (ysig—gwr) A bruiser, or one who makes a contusion.
Yslab, *s. m.* (llab) That is lengthened out, or distended.
Yslabi, *s. m.* (yslab) A maulkin, a slattern.
Yslabiad, *s. m.* (yslab) A forming a slab.
Yslac, *a.* (llac) Disjunct, slack, or loose.
Yslacâad, *s. m.* (yslacâu) A making slack; a slackening, a becoming slack.
Yslacâu, *v. a.* (yslac) To make slack, to slacken.
Yslacawd, *s. m.* (yslac) A slack or loose state.
Yslaciad, *s. m.* (yslac) A slacking; a loosening.
Yslaciaw, *v. a.* (yslac) To slack; to loosen.
Yslaciwr, *s. m.—pl.* yslaciwyr (yslac—gwr) A slacker; a loosener.
Yslacrwydd, *s. m.* (yslac) Slackness, looseness.
Yslafan, *s. m.* (llafan) The laverplant.
Yslaif, *s. m.* (glaif) A slash; a slice, or cut.
Yslam, *s. m.* (llam) That leaps or bounds. *a.* Skipping or leaping.

> Gwneuthur gwaith yslam ag ef.
> To make *hasty* work of it. *Adag.*

Yslamawl, *a.* (yslam) Tending to rebound.
Yslamiad, *s. m.* (yslam) A making a rebound.
Yslamu, *v. a.* (yslam) To make a bound.
Yslan, *s. m.* (glan) That is pure, clean or immaculate. *a.* Immaculate.
Yslanaidd, *a.* (yslan) Of a clean, or pure nature.
Yslaniad, *s. m.* (yslan) A rendering pure.
Yslanu, *v. a.* (yslan) To render immaculate.
Yslapiad, *s. m.* (yslab) A slapping; a flapping.
Yslapiaw, *v. a.* (yslab) To slap; to flap.
Yslath, *s. f.—pl. t.* au (llath) A rod; a perch.
Yslebawg, *a.* (yslab) Lanky, gawky. *Yslebawg o ddynes*, a slattern of a woman.
Yslebr, *s. m.* (yslab) That is lanky.
Yslebren, *s. f. dim.* (yslebr) A slattern.
Yslebyn, *s. m. dim.* (yslab) A lanky thing.
Yslecawd, *s. m.* (yslac) The state of being slack, or out of tone; a slight indisposition.
Ysled, *s. f.—pl. t.* i (lled) A drag, a dray.
Ysledfen, *s. f.—pl. t.* i (ysled—men) A drag-cart.
Ysleifiad, *s. m.* (yslaif) A slashing, a slicing.
Ysleifiaw, *v. a.* (yslaif) To slash, or to slice.
Ysleifiawl, *a.* (yslaif) Slashing, or slicing.
Ysleifiwr, *s. m.—pl.* ysleifiwyr (yslaif—gwr) A slasher, a slicer.
Ysleifyn, *s. m. dim.* (yslaif) A slash, or a slice.
Yslepan, *s. f.—pl. t.* au (yslab) A trap.
Ysletan, *s. f.—pl. t.* au (ysled) Any flat body or vessel, a flat, a flat-bottomed boat; a flat boat peculiar to some of the creeks in Wales, now growing out of use.
Yslib, *s. m.* (llib) That is glib or smooth.
Yslipan, *s. m.* (yslib) A burnish, or a polish.
Yslipaniad, *s. m.* (yslipan) A burnishing.

Yslipanu, *v. a.* (yslipan) To burnish, to polish.

> Ha wr! ai gwir a ddywedir wrthyt ti, y gwyddost yslipanu cleddyfau yn dda?
>
> Well man! is it true what is said of thee, that thou knowest how to burnish swords in a good manner? *H. Culhwch—Mabinogion.*

Yslipanwr, *s. m.—pl.* yslipanwyr (yslipan—gwr) A burnisher, a polisher.

> Yslipanwr cleddyfau goreu yn y byd wyf fi, ebai Cai.
>
> The best *burnisher* of swords in the world am I, said Cai. *H. Culhwch—Mabinogion.*

Yslod, *s. m.* (llod) A paddle; a dabble.
Yslotiad, *s. m.* (yslod) A paddling, a dabbling.
Yslotian, *v. a.* (yslod) To paddle; to dabble.

> Rhwyfau, mal rhawiau i'n rhan,
> Isel ateg i 'slotian—
> Ar hyd gwâr tonau.
>
> Oars, like shovels for our share, of low stay *to paddle* along the top of the waves. *T. Prys.*

Yslotiwr, *s. m.—pl.* yslotiwyr (yslotian—gwr) A paddler, a dabbler.
Yslwch, *s. m.—pl.* yslychau (llwch) A slough.
Ysmach, *s. m.* (mach) A buffet; a rumple.
Ysmacht, *s. m.* (ysmach) A buffet; a rumple.
Ysmachtiad, *s. m.* (ysmacht) A buffeting.
Ysmachtiaw, *v. a.* (ysmacht) To buffet, to rumple.
Ysmachtiwr, *s. m.—pl.* ysmachtiwyr (ysmacht—gwr) A buffeter, one who rumples.
Ysmal, *s. m.* (mal) That is light or fickle.
Ysmala, *a.* (ysmal) Light, fickle; droll, waggish, humorous, whimsical.
Ysmalâad, *s. m.* (ysmala) A rendering humorous or droll; a becoming droll.
Ysmalâawl, *a.* (ysmala) Of a droll tendency.
Ysmalâu, *v. a.* (ysmala) To act with humour; to become droll or humorous.
Ysmalâwch, *s. m.* (ysmala) Levity; drollery, waggery, humour.
Ysmaldawd, *s. m.* (ysmal) Drollery, humour.
Ysmalder, *s. m.* (ysmal) Drollery, waggery.
Ysmalrwydd, *s. m.* (ysmal) Waggishness, drollery.
Ysmeityn, *s. m.* (meityn) A space, a while; a good while. *Er ysmeityn*, a good while since.
Ysmiciad, *s. m.* (ysmig) A blinking, a winking.
Ysmician, *v. a.* (ysmig) To blink; to ogle.
Ysmiciaw, *v. a.* (ysmig) To blink; to wink.
Ysmiciawl, *a.* (ysmig) Blinking; winking.
Ysmiciwr, *s. m.* (ysmig—gwr) A blinker; a winker.
Ysmig, *s. f.* (mig) A blink or wink, an ogle.
Ysmigiad, *s. m.* (ysmig) A blinking; an ogling.
Ysmigiaw, *v. a.* (ysmig) To blink; to ogle.
Ysmigwst, *s. f.* (ysmig—gwst) A blinking ailment; dumps. *Mae yr ysmigwst arno, mae ef yn glaf o ysmigwst*, he is in the dumps.
Ysmot, *s. m.—pl. t.* iau (mod) A patch, a spot.
Ysmotiad, *s. m.* (ysmot) A dappling, a spotting.
Ysmotiaw, *v. a.* (ysmot) To dapple, to spot.
Ysmotyn, *s. m. dim.* (ysmot) A small spot or patch; a hare's scut; also called *cwt, cwtyn*, and *cwtawg*.
Ysmud, *s. m.* (mud) Emotion, instigation.
Ysmudai, *s. c.—pl.* ysmudeion (ysmud) That causes emotion; that instigates.
Ysmudaw, *v. a.* (ysmud) To cause emotion.
Ysmudawl, *a.* (ysmud) Instigating; motive.
Ysmudiad, *s. m.* (ysmud) Instigation, emotion.
Ysmudwr, *s. m.—pl.* ysmudwyr (ysmud—gwr) One who moves; an instigator.
Ysmwca, *v. a.* (ysmwg) To collect a little smoke, to dim, to be dimmed.
Ysmwcach, *s. m.* (ysmwg) A little puff of smoke, fog, or mist
Ysmwcan, *s. c. dim.* (ysmwg) A little volume of smoke, fog, or mist; fog.
Ysmwciad, *s. m.* (ysmwg) A dimming with smoke, mist, fog, or vapour.
Ysmwciaw, *v. a.* (ysmwg) To dim with smoke, *Mae y drych wedi ysmwciaw*, the glass is become dim.
Ysmwciawl, *a.* (ysmwg) Somewhat smoked.
Ysmwg, *s. m.* (mwg) That generates smoke.
Ysmwll, *s. m.* (mwll) That is close and damp. *a.* Sultry and damp.
Ysmwllach, *s. m.* (ysmwll) Close damp weather.
Ysmwt, *s. m.* (mwd) That is round or squabby. *a.* Squabby. *Trwyn ysmwt*, a bottle nose.
Ysmygawl, *a.* (ysmwg) Tending to smoke.
Ysmygiad, *s. m.* (ysmwg) A dimming with smoke.
Ysmygu, *v. a.* (ysmwg) To dim with smoke.
Ysnid, *s. f.—pl. t.* au (nid) A snout or beak; a drop at the nose; a snipe.
Ysniten, *s. f. dim.* (ysnid) A snout; a drop at the snout.
Ysnoden, *s. f.—pl. t.* i (noden) A fillet, band, riband or lace; a head band, a hair lace; a marilock, also called *cudyn dedwydd*. *Ysnoden gorni, rhwymyn*, a swaddling band; *ysnoden y mor*, sea-thongs; *ysnoden mair*, English galingale.

> Ysnoden aur a gwn carth.
>
> A gold *lace* with a hempen gown. *Adage.*

Ysnodenaidd, *a.* (ysnoden) Like a fillet or lace.
Ysnodenawg, *a.* (ysnoden) Having a fillet, band, or riband; filleted, laced.
Ysnodenawl, *a.* (ysnoden) Filleted, laced.
Ysnodeniad, *s. m.* (ysnoden) A filleting, a lacing.
Ysnodenig, *s. f. dim.* (ysnoden) A bandlet.
Ysnodenu, *v. a.* (ysnoden) To fillet, to bind with a lace or riband; to belace.
Ysnodenwr, *s. m.—pl.* ysnodenwyr (ysnoden—gwr) A dealer in fillets or laces.
Ysnodenydd, *s. m.—pl. t.* ion (ysnoden) A dealer in fillets, laces, and ribands.
Yso, *adv.* (ys—o) Is thence; it may be thence.
Ysoldeb, *s. m.* (ysawl) A consuming state.
Ysoli, *v. a.* (ysawl) To render consuming; to cauterize.
Yspadd, *s. m.* (padd) That is exhausted, or spent.
Yspaddawl, *a.* (yspadd) Tending to exhaust.
Yspaddiad, *s. m.* (yspadd) An exhausting.
Yspaddu, *v. a.* (yspadd) To exhaust, to empty.
Yspai, *s. m.* (pai) That is clear or visible.
Yspaid, *s. m.* (paid) A cessation, an intermission; a term or space of time. *Tros yspaid tair blynedd*, for the space of three years.
Yspaidd, *a.* (paidd) Being emptied or exhausted.
Yspail, *s. f.—pl.* yspeiliau (pail) A spoil or prey.

> Nid yspail ond gwynt.
>
> There is no *spoiling* like that of wind. *Adage.*

Yspaith, *s. m.* (paith) That is open or clear; a prospect, a scene, a view, a vision.
Yspant, *s. f.—pl.* yspeinniau (pant) That is involving or inclosing; a flake.
Ysper, *s. f.—pl.* ysperi (par) A spear, or pike.

> Llathrlaw ysb euraw, ysperi wyll.
> Llid Pyll arf drydryll, arfaeth Rhodri.
>
> A smooth 'hand giving gold to guests, with blades of *spears* wrathful as Pyll, with weapon broken in three, and design of Rhodri. *D. ab Gwilym.*

Ysperawg, *a.* (ysper) Having a spear or pike.
Yspardun, *s. f.—pl. t.* au (ysper—tun) A spur; also called *ethy*. *Ysperdunau y marchawg*, the larkspur.

Yspardunad, *s. m.* (yspardun) A spurring.
Yspardunaw, *v. a.* (yspardun) To spur.
Yspardunwr, *s. m.—pl.* yspardunwyr (yspardun—gwr) One who uses a spur.
Ysparth, *s. m.—pl. t.* au (parth) A separation.
Ysparthiad, *s. m.* (ysparth) A separating.
Ysparthu, *v. a.* (ysparth) To separate, to part.
Yspas, *s. m.* (pas) That is in the act of passing. *a.* Passing; probationary.
Yspawr, *s. m.—pl.* ysporion (pawr) That is used as fodder; the refuse of fodder.
Yspeiad, *s. m.* (yspai) An exploring, a spying.
Yspeiant, *s. m.* (yspai) An exploration.
Yspeiaw, *v. a.* (yspai) To explorate; to spy.
Yspeiawd, *s. m.* (yspai) An exploration.
Yspeiawl, *a.* (yspai) Exploratory; spying.
Yspeiawr, *s. m.* (yspai) That is visible.
Yspeidiad, *s. m.* (yspaid) An intermission.
Yspeidiaw, *v. a.* (yspaid) To make an intermission; to form a space of time; to desist.
Yspeidiawl, *a.* (yspaid) Intermittent.
Yspeienna, *v. a.* (yspeiant) To prowl about.
Yspeiliad, *s. m.* (yspail) A spoliation.
Yspeienddyn, *s. m.—pl. t.* ion (yspeiant—dyn) A person who prowls about.
Yspeiliata, *v. a.* (yspeiliad) To be pilfering.
Yspeiliatan, *v. a.* (yspeiliad) To be pilfering.
Yspeiliaw, *v. a.* (yspail) To spoil, to ravage.
Yspeiliawd, *s. m.* (yspail) A spoliation.
Yspeiliedig, *a.* (yspeiliad) Spoiled, ravaged.
Yspeiliedydd, *s. m.—pl. t.* ion (yspeiliad) Ravager.
Yspeiliota, *v. a.* (yspeiliawd) To be pilfering.
Yspeiliwr, *s. m.—pl.* yspeiliwyr (yspail—gwr) A spoiler, a ravager.
Yspeinniad, *s. m.* (yspant) An involving or enclosing; a shelling.
Yspeinniaw, *v. a.* (yspant) To involve, to enclose, to shell. *Yspeinniaw ffa*, to shell beans.

> Yspeinniaw Rhys ab Einion
> A [illegible] y [illegible] hon.

> The [illegible] of Rhys the son of Einion renders the voice of this generation dismal. *L. G. Cothi.*

Yspeinwydd, *s. m.* (ys—pan—gwydd) Box-wood.
Yspeiorad, *s. m.* (yspeiawr) Exploration.
Yspeiorawl, *a.* (yspeiawr) Exploratory.
Yspeiori, *v. a.* (yspeiawr) To explorate.
Yspeithiad, *s. m.* (yspaith) A looking about.
Yspeithiaw, *v. a.* (yspaith) To look about.
Yspeithiawl, *a.* (yspaith) Relating to a looking about; exploratory.
Yspeithig, *a.* (yspaith) Tending to look about.
Yspeithigaw, *v. a.* (yspeithig) To form an open prospect or view.
Yspel, *s. m.* (pel) An exposition; expulsion.
Yspeliad, *s. m.* (yspel) An exposing.
Yspeliaw, *v. a.* (yspel) To expose; to expel.
Yspelw, *s. m.* (yspel) A gall, a rub, or fret.
Yspelwad, *s. m.* (yspelw) Exulceration.
Yspelwi, *v. a.* (yspelw) To gall, to be galled.
Yspell, *s. m.* (pell) That is far or long.

> [illegible]

> The eagle said, I am arrived here for this long [illegible] time.
> *H. Cuthech* [illegible]

Yspelliad, *s. m.* (yspell) A rendering distant.
Yspellu, *v. a.* (yspell) To render distant.
Yspennydd, *s. m.* (yspant) That involves. *a.* Involving; overwhelming.

> [illegible]
> [illegible]

> A wild one with a spear of *overwhelming* [illegible] to the slaughter, and a [illegible] one to the [illegible]
> *Ll. P. Moch,* [illegible]

Yspergyl, *s. f.* (pergyl) A leg bone, or the tibia.

Yspicell, *s. f.—pl. t.* au (yspig) A dart.
Yspicella, *v. a.* (yspicell) To throw darts.
Yspicelliad, *s. m.* (yspicell) A darting.
Yspicellu, *v. a.* (yspicell) To throw a dart.
Yspig, *s. f.—pl. t.* au (pig) A spike, a spine.
Yspigaw, *v. a.* (yspig) To spike; to prick.
Yspigawd, *s. f.—pl.* yspigodau (yspig) A spindle, a spiggot.
Yspigawg, *a.* (yspig) Full of spikes or pricks.
Yspigawglys, *s. pl. aggr.* (yspigawg—llys) Spinage.
Yspigydd, *s. m.—pl. t.* ion (yspig) The titmouse; also called *yspigydd bach*.
Yspil, *s. m.—pl. t.* ion (pil) A dribblet.
Yspilyn, *s. m. dim.* (yspil) A little matter, a dribblet. *Mae arno ryw yspilyn bach i mi*, he owes me some small trifle.
Yspin, *s. m.—pl. t.* ion (pin) A spine, a prick.
Yspinan, *s. m. dim.* (yspin) That is spinous; a gooseberry-bush.
Yspinawg, *a.* (yspin) Abounding with prickles. *s. f.* The squincy.
Yspinc, *s. m.* (pinc) That is smart or trim.
Yspincyn, *s. m. dim.* (yspinc) A finch; it is also called *pinc*.
Yspinen, *s. f. dim.* (yspin) That is spinous; any prickly plant.
Yspinglairch, *s. m.* (yspin—clairch) Bridegroom.
Ysplan, *a.* (plan) Clear, bright, splendid.
Ysplana, *v. a.* (ysplan) To elucidate, to explain.
Ysplanawl, *a.* (ysplan) Luminous, lucid.
Ysplander, *s. m.* (ysplan) Brightness, splendour.
Ysplandra, *s. m.* (ysplan) Brightness, clearness.
Ysplanedig, *a.* (ysplan) Being brightened.
Ysplanedd, *s. m.* (ysplan) Brightness, lucidity.
Ysplaniad, *s. m.—pl. t.* au (ysplan) A brightening.
Ysplenydd, *a.* (ysplan) Lucid or luminous.
Ysplenyddu, *v. a.* (ysplenydd) To irradiate.
Ysplent, *s. f.—pl. t.* ydd (ysplan) A slippery place or slide; a sheet of ice.

> Rhaid eu gyru, am oered eu rhenyntau, i'r ysplent [illegible] ngwlad yr ia tragwyddawl.

> They must be driven, because of the coldness of their [illegible], to the great *sheet of ice* in the region of eternal frost.
> *Ellis Wynn, B. Cwsg.*

Ysplyg, *s. m.—pl. t.* ion (plyg) A splice.
Ysplygawl, *a.* (ysplyg) Spliced, infolded.
Ysplygiad, *s. m.—pl. t.* au (ysplyg) A splicing.
Ysplygu, *v. a.* (ysplyg) To splice, to infold.

> Da ni ddi ysplygu y cynghaneddion a'n hamryw [illegible].

> It serve well *to enfold* the consonants with their various sorts. *Gr. Robert.*

Yspodol, *s. f.—pl. t.* au (yspawd) A slice or spattle.
Yspodoli, *v. a.* (yspodol) To spattle; to beat with the flat side of any thing; to slap.
Yspodoliad, *s. m.* (yspodol) A spattling; a slapping.
Yspone, *s. f.—pl. t.* iau (ponc) A jerk, a jet, a spirt; a skip or quick bound.

> [illegible]
> [illegible]

> Striking, from my mischievous whims, three [illegible] the [illegible] broke. *D. ab Gwilym,* [illegible]

> [illegible]

> And the smack of the delicate lip. *Lewis* [illegible]

Ysponciad, *s. m.* (yspone) A sudden jet or bound, a twitch; a smack.
Ysponciaw, *v. a.* (yspone) To bound sharply; to smack; to jerk, to jet.
Yspori, *v. a.* (yspawr) To feed; to eat fodder.
Ysporiad, *s. m.* (yspawr) A feeding; the eating of fodder, a foddering.
Ysporiaw, *v. a.* (yspawr) To eat fodder.

Ysporion, *s. pl. aggr.* (yspawr) Refuse of fodder.

Ysporioni, *v. a.* (ysporion) To produce refuse or leavings of fodder.

Ysporth, *s. m.—pl. t.* ion (porth) Sustenance.

Ysporthawl, *a.* (ysporth) Supporting, sustaining.

Ysporthell, *s. f.—pl. t.* i (ysporth) A provision basket or pannier.

Ysporthen, *s. f. dim.—pl. t.* i (ysporth) A basket or pannier.

Ysporthi, *v. a.* (ysporth) To support or sustain.

Ysporthiad, *s. m.—pl.* ysporthiaid (ysporth) A sustainer or supporter.

Cyfarchaf——
I filwyr eryr, arf gwenwlad a gwaed
A gwyddgwn ysporthiad.

I will greet the warriors of the eagle, the weapon of a happy country with blood, and the *feeder* of the wild dogs.
Ll. P. Moch, i D. ab Owain.

Ysporthiadawl, *a.* (ysporthiad) Of a supporting or sustaining tendency.

Ysporthiannawl, *a.* (ysporthiant) Yielding sustenance or support.

Ysporthiannu, *v. a.* (ysporthiant) To produce sustenance or support.

Ysporthiant, *s. m.* (ysporth) Sustenance, food.

Ysporthion, *s. pl. aggr.* (ysporth) Refuse of fodder.

Ysporthioni, *v. a.* (ysporthion) To make leavings of fodder.

Yspred, *s. pl. aggr.* (pred) Outcasts; refuse.

Ys cail—o eifr—
Yspred o anysbrydoedd.

There was a fold of goats, *outcasts* of mere phantoms.
Gr. ab Hywel ab Tudyr.

Fe dal yr Arglwydd i'r yspred
A wnaeth y weithred dywyll.

The Lord will requite the *crew* who committed that dark deed.
Lewis Morris.

Ysprudd, *a.* (prudd) Moping, stupid, or dull.

Yspruddach, *s. m.* (ysprudd) That is of a dejected aspect, a moper, a stupid one.

Yspwng, *s. m.—pl. t.* au (pwng) A light tuft, such as the tops of reeds; sponge.

Gnawd yd gyrch cynnygn o'i gynnif pwng,
Mal pan gyrch flamdan flamdo yspwng.

Habitual for him to attack adversaries in his overwhelming rage, as when the flaming fire invades an inflammable covering *of reeds.*
E. ab Madawg ab Rhawd.

Yspwy, *s. m.* (pwy) A rebuff, or a repulse.

Yspwyad, *s. m.* (yspwy) A rebuffing, repulsion.

Yspwyaw, *v. a.* (yspwy) To rebuff, to repulse.

Yspwyll, *s. m.* (pwyll) A mental faculty.

Yspwyllaw, *v. a.* (yspwyll) To ratiocinate.

Yspwylliad, *s. m.* (yspwyll) Ratiocination.

Yspwyllus, *a.* (yspwyll) Ratiocinative.

Yspwys, *s. m.* (pwys) That is impressive or weighty. *a.* Impressive, imposing. *Gwraig yspwys*, and *gwraig bwys*, a wedded wife, or a spouse.

Moes yspwys ysbys echrys ochren.

The *imposing* conduct of the conspicuous terrific party.
Cynddelw.

Rheoli gwyllt——
Sy o yspwys i Siasber.

The ruling of the outrageous is of *weight* to Jasper.
L. G. Cothi.

Yspwysaw, *v. a.* (yspwys) To impress.

Yspwysawl, *a.* (yspwys) Impressive, imposing.

Yspwysiad, *s. m.* (yspwys) An imposing.

Yspydd, *s. m.* (pydd) A jutting, or run out.

Yspyddad, *s. m. aggr.* (yspydd) That runs out; that expels; that is projecting; a hawthorn.

Yspyddad amnad,
Haint ach ei angad.

The *hawthorn* surrounded by obstacles, with pain at his hand.
Taliesin.

Yspyddaden, *s. f. dim.* (yspyddad) One that is armed or protected; hawthorn, whitethorn.

Yspyddaid, *a.* (yspydd) Jetting; prickly; harsh, sharp, repulsive; protected. *Mae o yn dywedyd mor yspyddaid*, he is speaking so wildly. *Sil. Beirdd yspyddaid*, refugee bards.

Yspyddawd, *s. m.* (yspydd) A running out; a repelling or guarding; protection.

Parawd yspyddawd i ysbyd Prydain,
Udd prydfawr ei wryd,
Maredudd——

Of ready *protection* to the refugees of Britain, a chief of stately form, Maredudd.——
Ll. P. Moch, m. M. ab Cynan.

Yspyddiad, *s. m.* (yspydd) A jutting out.

Yspyddu, *v. a.* (yspydd) To jut, to run out.

Ysran, *s. f.—pl. t.* au (rhan) A dividend.

Ysranawl, *a.* (ysran) Forming a dividend.

Ysraniad, *s. m.* (ysran) A making a dividend.

Ysranu, *v. a.* (ysran) To make a dividend.

Ysrath, *s. m.* (rhath) That is rubbed.

Ysrathawl, *a.* (ysrath) Productive of friction.

Ysrathiad, *s. m.* (ysrath) A causing a friction.

Ysrathu, *v. a.* (ysrath) To cause a friction.

Ysrith, *s. m.—pl. t.* ion (rhith) That is apparent.

Ysrithiad, *s. m.* (ysrith) A making apparent.

Ysrithiaw, *v. a.* (ysrith) To make apparent.

Ysrwydd, *a.* (rhwydd) Tending to facilitate.

Ysrwyddaw, *v. a.* (ysrwydd) To render facile.

Ysrwyddawl, *a.* (ysrwydd) Of a clearing tendency

Ysrwyddiad, *s. m.* (ysrwydd) A rendering facile.

Yssawd, *s. m.* (sawd) That combines or forms.

Yssig, *a.* (ys—sig) Shattered, crushed, bruised.

Yssigaw, *v. a.* (yssig) To shatter, to crush, to bruise. *Yssigaw byddinoedd*, to crush armies.

Yn Saxonia—
Tyrau twn eu mur,
Terfysg eu llafur,
Torfoedd diesgur
A'u hyssigs.

In Saxony towers with their broken walls, tumult their toil, hosts void of inactivity *will crush* them.
D. Benfras.

Yssigawl, *a.* (yssig) Tending to shatter or crush.

Yssigdawd, *s. m.* (yssig) Shatteredness, bruisedness; contusion, a crushed state.

Yssigiad, *s. m.* (yssig) A shattering, a crushing, a bruising; a contusion.

Yssigwr, *s. m.—pl.* yssigwyr (yssig—gwr) A shatterer, one who bruises, or makes a contusion.

Yssodi, *v. a.* (yssawd) To render combined.

Yssy, *s. m.* (ys—sy) That has existence, or has entity. *adv.* That is, that be.

Yssydd, *s. m.* (ys—sydd) That has existence, or that has entity. *adv.* That is, that be.

Na saethyta ni bellach, namyn anaf ac addoed yssydd arnat, ag a fo mwy, os mynei: dyro iai dy ferch.

Be not shooting at us any more, for the harm and ruin *that is* upon thee, as to what more may be, if thou wilt; give us thy daughter.
H. Culhwch—Mabinogion.

Yssyddawl, *a.* (yssydd) Causing of existence.

Yssyddiad, *s. m.* (yssydd) A causing of existence.

Yssyddu, *v. a.* (yssydd) To cause to be, or exist.

Yssyddyn, *s. m. dim.—pl. t.* od (yssydd) That is occupied; a tenement.

Yssyddynawl, *a.* (yssyddyn) Under occupation.

Yssym, *adv.* (ys—sy—ym) That is to me, that is of mine.

Yssymi heddyw pen y mis,
Yn y westfa ydd edewis.

What might be mine this day ending the month, in the entertainment I have left it.
Llywarch Hen.

Yssym argiwydd gwrdd.

There is to me a powerful lord.
Cynddelw.

Yst, *s. m.* (ys) That exists; that proceeds; that is active or ardent.

Ystac, *s. m.—pl. t.* iau (tag) That is reared; a heap; a stack.

Ystac, *s. m.—pl. t.* oedd (ystac) A standard; a heap; a measure of capacity, equal to 5½ bushels, used in Glamorgan; but in the neighbouring parts it is called *Tel*; and *Ystaca* is used as a measure of length.

Ystaciad, *s. m.* (ystac) A forming a standard; a forming a heap; a stacking.

Ystaciaw, *v. a.* (ystac) To form a standard; to form a heap; to stack.

Ystad, *s. m.—pl. t.* au (tad) That is continuous or proceeding; state, condition.

Ystadawl, *a.* (ystad) Being continuous or even.

Ystaden, *s. f. dim.* (ystad) A measure of length; a stadium.

Ystadiad, *s. m.* (ystad) A forming a position.

Ystadl, *s. m.* (ystad) That is continuous, that is proceeding, or that is uninterrupted.

> Ystadl cad cynnygydd.
>
> The threatener of the *indecision* of battle. *Taliesin.*

Ystadledd, *s. m.* (ystadl) A continuous state.

Ystadliad, *s. m.* (ystadl) A rendering continuous.

Ystadu, *v. a.* (ystad) To remain, to stay.

Ystaen, *s. m.* (taen) That is spread out; that is sprinkled over; a stain; also tin. *a.* Outspreading; stained.

> Niwl——
> Rhidyll ystaen yn rhydu;
> Rhwyd adar y ddaiar ddu.
>
> The mist, an outspreading riddle diffusing rust; the net of the birds of the sable earth. *D. ab Gwilym.*

Ystaenaidd, *a.* (ystaen) Tending to overspread; of a staining quality; like tin.

Ystaenawd, *s. m.* (ystaen) The state of being spread, sprinkled, or stained.

> Rhag gwyar ar gnawd,
> Afar ystaenawd.
>
> Against gore on flesh, a dismal *staining.* *Taliesin.*

Ystaenawl, *a.* (ystaen) Tending to spread, of a staining quality; belonging to tin.

Ystaenawr, *s. m.—pl.* ystaenorion (ystaen) A tinner, or a worker of tin.

Ystaeniad, *s. m.* (ystaen) A spreading out; a staining, a working of tin; a tinning.

Ystaeniaw, *v. a.* (ystaen) To spread over; to stain; to tin.

Ystaeniwr, *s. m.—pl.* ystaeniwyr (ystaen—gwr) One who stains; a tinner.

Ystaenu, *v. a.* (ystaen) To cover with tin.

Ystaenydd, *s. m.—pl. t.* ion (ystaen) A tinner.

Ystaf, *s. f.* (taf) That is spread, extended, or laid out; that is stretched out or laminated.

Ystafell, *s. f.—pl. t.* oedd (ystaf) A chamber, an upper room; a bedchamber.

> Mi a fedraf ystafell:
> Das o wair; nid oes ei well.
>
> I can form a *chamber*: a haystack, there is not its better. *D. ab Gwilym.*

Ystafelliad, *s. f.—pl.* ystafelleidiau (ystafell) A chamber-full, a room-full.

Ystafellaidd, *a.* (ystafell) Like a chamber.

Ystafellawg, *a.* (ystafell) Having a chamber; having a room, or a cell.

> Pedair ar ugaint fydd ebediw gwr ystafellawg; deuddeg ceiniawg yw ebediw gwraig ystafellawg; ac i arglwydd y tir y bo yr ystafell arno y bydd.
>
> Twenty four pence shall be the herriot of a man *having a cell*; twelve pence is the herriot of a woman *having a cell*, and to the lord of the soil whereon the cell may be shall it be paid. *Welsh Laws.*

Ystafelliad, *s. m.* (ystafell) A chambering.

Ystafellu, *v. a.* (ystafell) To form a chamber.

Ystafellwas, *s. m.—pl.* ystafellweision (ystafell—gwas) A chamberlain.

Ystafellwr, *s. m.—pl.* ystafellwyr (ystafell—gwr) A chamber-man.

Ystafellwraig, *s. f.—pl.* ystafellwreigedd (ystafell—gwraig) A chamber-woman.

Ystafellydd, *s. m.—pl. t.* ion (ystafell) A chamberlain, a groom of the chamber.

> Pwy gyd a mi? Pwy! A dau neu dri o'r ystafellyddion a edrychynt arno.
>
> Who along with me! Who! And two or three of the *chamberlains* looked at him. *Y Breuddwyd [illegible].*

Ystafellyddes, *s. f.—pl. t.* au (ystafellydd) A chambermaid.

Ystafellyddiaeth, *s. m.* (ystafell) Chamberlainship.

Ystagiad, *s. m.* (tagiad) A causing a choking.

Ystagu, *v. a.* (tagu) To suffocate, to choak.

Ystain, *s. m.* (tain) That spreads or expands.

Ystal, *s. f.—pl. t.* au (yst—al) A stock or produce, a stall; a frame on stone pillars for corn ricks.

> Aeth i'r cor ystor ar ystal [illegible],
> Gwaed tywysawg Mathrafal.
>
> Gone to the circle is the treasure and the *stock* of [illegible], the blood of the prince of Mathraval. *W. Cynwal.*
>
> Ffynnodd, estynodd ystal;
> Fynnu'n Rhywyn a Phenal.
>
> He prospered, he extended a *stock*; prospering in Tywyn and Penal. *[illegible].*

Ystaliad, *s. m.* (ystal) A producing a stock.

Ystalm, *s. m.* (talm) A determined space; a good while, a good space.

Ystalmiad, *s. m.* (ystalm) A forming a determined space; a determining.

Ystalmu, *v. a.* (ystalm) To form a determined space; to form a conclusion; to determine.

Ystalu, *v. a.* (ystal) To form a stock; to obtain produce.

Ystalw, *a.* (ystal) Being made productive.

Ystalwyn, *s. m.—pl. t.* i (ystalw) A stallion.

> Gwerth ystalwyn gwewyr a allo [illegible], a chaseg [illegible] o'i flaen ac arall yn ei ol.
>
> The value of a *stallion* is a stud that he can carry, with a [illegible] mare before him and another behind him. *Welsh Laws.*

Ystalwynaidd, *a.* (ystalwyn) Like a stallion.

Ystan, *s. f.* (tan) That is spread or laid out.

> Eistedd 'n un ystan [illegible],
> Trin fydd cyn y [illegible].
>
> Sitting in one *spread* of coldness, a [illegible] there will be before they carve any victuals. *[illegible].*

Ystanc, *s. m.—pl. t.* iau (yst—anc) That is stuck; that confines; a pile; a holdfast; a bracket; a wooden hook nailed to a wall. *Ystanc [illegible]*, a horse block; *ystanc i [illegible] sarn*, a pile in the ground to keep up a causeway.

Ystanciad, *s. m.* (ystanc) A piling; a propping; a bracketing.

Ystanciaw, *v. a.* (ystanc) To pile; to prop; to pin; to bracket.

Ystang, *s. m.—pl. t.* au (yst—ang) That is stuck; that straitens or bounds; a stang or perch, used as a measure; in some parts of South Wales it is 18 feet; in others 21 feet; and it is also a square measure: in Cardiganshire it is 160 square rods 13½ feet each: in Pembrokeshire it is a quarter of a Welsh acre, and contains 160 yards by 16 yards.

> A'i ystang a wnaeth angau.
>
> And his *space* has death accomplished. *D. [illegible].*

Ystangiad, *s. m.* (ystang) A straitening, a fastening; a limiting; a measuring the space of an *ystang*.

Ystangu, *v. a.* (ystang) To straiten, to pin; to limit; to measure out the space of an ystang.

Ystarn, *s. m.—pl. t.* au (tarn) Saddle; a pack-saddle.

> Gweddo, mal ystarn ar gefn [illegible].
>
> Fitting, like a *saddle* on the back of a [illegible]. *[illegible].*

Ystarnawg, *a.* (ystarn) Having a saddle.

Ystarniad, *s. m.* (ystarn) A saddling.

Ystarnu, *v. a.* (ystarn) To saddle; to put on a packsaddle.

Y brawdwr llys a ddyly, y gan y pengwastrawd, ddiwallu ei farch o'r hoel gyntaf hyd y ddiweddaf; ac ei ystarnu, ac ei ddwyn iddo ac ei ystarn arno, pan farchoco.

The judge of the palace ought to have, from the chief groom, his horse made complete, from the first nail to the last; and *to have the saddle put on*, and brought to him with the saddle on, when he rides. *Welsh Laws.*

Ystarnwr, *s. m.* (ystarn—gwr) A saddler.

Ystaw, *s. m.* (taw) That is silent or calm.

Ystawd, *s. f.—pl.* ystodion (tawd) A course, a race; a layer; a swath of hay or corn, laid with a scythe. *Ystawd anian*, course of nature.

Mae efe wedi terfynu—y dygwyddiadau anghyffredin sydd yn damwain yn ystawd rhagluniaeth.

He has determined the uncommon accidents that happen in the *course* of providence. *Ier. Owain.*

Ystawf, *s. m.—pl.* ystofion (tawf) That is regulated or ranged; a warp, in weaving.

Ystawiad, *s. m.* (ystaw) A rendering silent.

Ystawl, *s. f.—pl.* ystolion (tawl) A stool. *Ystawl fair*, the lesser centory.

Ystawl, dwy geiniawg a dâl.

A *stool*, its value is two pence. *Welsh Laws.*

Ystawr, *s. f.—pl.* ystorau (tawr) What covers; any resin; rosin.

Eu gwynfyd yw cyfoeth, dyb annoeth bob awr
Hyd elawr, wan ystawr, yn wastad.——

Their happiness is wealth, a foolish notion, continually to the bier, a frail *covering*. *D. Williams.*

Ystefaig, *s. f.* (ystaf) The roof of the mouth.

Ysteiniad, *s. m.* (ystain) A causing a spread.

Ysteiniaw, *v. a.* (ystain) To cause to spread.

Ystel, *s. m.—pl. t.* ion (tel) That stretches.

Ystelc, *s. f.—pl. t.* iau (telc) That is shrinking; a lurk; a loiter.

Ystelciad, *s. m.* (ystelc) A causing a shrinking; a lurking; a loitering.

Ystelcian, *v. a.* (ystelc) To go in a shrinking manner; to lurk about; to loiter.

Ystelciaw, *v. a.* (ystelc) To go shrinkingly; to lurk; to loiter.

Ystelciwr, *s. m.—pl.* ystelciwyr (ystelc—gwr) A lurker; a loiterer.

Ystelff, *s. m.—pl. t.* od (ystel) That is rigid; a blockhead.

Ystelffiad, *s. m.* (ystelff) A rendering rigid.

Ystelffu, *v. a.* (ystelff) To render rigid or stiff.

Ysteliad, *s. m.* (ystel) A stretching, a causing a spring or elasticity.

Ysteliaw, *v. a.* (ystel) To stretch, to spring.

Yn Mynyw wên y mae'n wir;
Dros dwy-wlad yr ystelir.

In fair Mynyw it is in truth! over two countries it *will be made to extend*. *L. G. Cothi.*

Ystelyw, *s. m.* (ystel) That is stretched out.

Ystem, *s. f.* (tem) That forms a round spread; a base, a stem.

Yster, *s. m.—pl. t.* ion (ter) That is ardent.

Ysteraig, *a.* (yster) Apt to produce ardency.

Hwerthiniawg tu craig
Per nid ysteraig.

Abounding with broken sound by the side of a rock the pear tree *is not of an ardent quality*. *Taliesin, Cad Goddeu.*

Ysterc, *s. f.—pl. t.* iau (terc) That makes a jerk.

Ysterciad, *s. m.* (ysterc) A making a jerk.

Ystercian, *v. a.* (ysterc) To be jerking out.

Ysterciaw, *v. a.* (ysterc) To jerk, throw, or mount up, as a football.

Ysteriad, *s. m.* (yster) A rendering ardent.

Ysterlewyn, *s. m.* (yster—llewyn) A meteor.

Ystern, *s. m.—pl.* ystyrn (tern) That produces ardency or motion; that is sharp or active. *a.* of an active or sharp tendency.

Gogwn atreguawr
Rhwng nef a llawr——
Cwrw pan yw ysteru;
Pan yw lledradd gwern.

I know the regulation between heaven and earth . or ale why it is *of an active quality*; the alder why it is of a purplish hue. *Taliesin.*

Hwn yw yr ail praw, cinlaw cam,
Oer ei 'styrn, a roist arnam.

This is the second taste, an adverse mess of cold *impulses*, which thou hast set upon us. *Rhys Goch Eryri.*

Ysteru, *v. a.* (yster) To render ardent or vivid.

Ystid, *s. f.—pl. t.* au (tid) That forms a wreath.

Ystid goch, yn da dy gof.

A red *wreath*, thy memory is good. *D. ab Gwilym, i gelmach.*

Ystidaw, *v. a.* (ystid) To form a chain.

Ystidiad, *s. m* (ystid) A rig-ma-roll.

Ystig, *a.* (yst) Assiduous, persevering.

Ystyr, nad da yn ystig
I ddyn ei dda a'i Dduw yn ddig.

Consider that man's wealth is not *uninterruptedly* good should his God be displeased. *Dr. S. Cent.*

Ystigaw, *v. a.* (ystig) To act with assiduity, to persevere; to become assiduous.

Ystigiad, *s. m.* (ystig) A persevering; a becoming assiduous; a sticking close to work.

Ystigrwydd, *s. m.* (ystig) Perseverance, assiduity, diligence, close application.

Ystigl, *s. f.* (ystig) A stile. *Ceredigion.*

Ystin, *a.* (yst) Of a tendency to be or to act.

Ystinos, *s. m.* (ystin) The asbestos.

Yn y gwregys—aur melyn——
A gais dyn ac ystinos.

In the girdle, yellow gold will a person seek, and *asbestos*. *R. Goch, Eryri.*

Ystle, *s. m.* (ystyl) That is impulsive; that is extreme; a flight or retreat; kindred.

Caranmael, cymhwy arued,
Alwen dy ystle o gad;
Gnawd mau ar rnu cynaifad.

Caranmael, there being a constraint on thee, Alwen thy *retreat* from battle; a mark is natural on the brow of a combatant. *Llywarch Hen.*

Ail dydd brawd, brew ystawd ystle.

Like the day of judgement, terrific the course of *retreat*. *Gwalchmai.*

Ystlen, *s. f.—pl. t.* i (yst—llen) A sex, a kind.

Cyfrwng dros ofnedawl wraigiawl ystlen.

Intercede for the devout female *sex*. *Dafydd Ddu, o Hiraddug.*

Ystlenaidd, *a.* (ystlen) Sexual; kindred.

Ystlenawl, *a.* (ystlen) Sexual; kindred.

Ystlom, *s. m.* (ystyl—om) Excrement, ordure.

Ystlomi, *v. a.* (ystlom) To void excrement.

Ystlomiad, *s. m.* (ystlom) A voiding excrement.

Ystlwn, *s. m.* (yst—llwn) Connection; kindred.

Ystlwyd, *s. m.* (yst—llwyd) Grey or hoary.

Ystlwyn, *s. m.* (yst—llwyn) A luxuriant grove.

Aml yn rhial yr wyd
Tu a'r ystlwyn tir ystlwyd.

Often of superior quality thou art towards the *lively grove* of land of dusky growth. *Ieuan Tew.*

Ystlym, *s. m.—pl. t.* od (yst—llym) A bat.

Nid diffeith ond ystlym.

There is nothing so filthy as a *bat*. *Adage.*

Ystlynawl, *a.* (ystlwn) Connected; related.

Ystlyned, *s. f.* (ystlwn) That is connected, associated, or in communion.

Ac ym Rhen gwyn gwan ystlyned wyf i.——

And to my blessed Creator a feeble *communicant* am I. *Elidir ab Uwchmael.*

Ystlynedd, *s. f.* (ystlwn) Connection, kindred.

Ni bu ocsiliawd beirdd o'i ystlynedd.

Bards have not been of needy life from his *connexion*. *Gr. ab Gwrgenau.*

Ystlyniad, *s. m.* (ystlwn) A forming a society; a forming a relationship.

Ystlynu, *v. a.* (ystlwn) To associate; to form a connection, or kindred.

Ystlys, *s. f.—pl. t.* au (ystyl) A side, a flank.

> Cadarn a chreulawn oeddynt oc y ddwy ystlys; ond ar y diwedd Iestyn a gafal y fuddygoliaeth.
>
> Mighty and furious were they of the two *sides*; but at length Iestyn obtained the victory. *Caradawg o Langarfan.*

Ystlysawl, *a.* (ystlys) Lateral, or sided.

Ystlysbost, *s. m.* (ystlys—post) A side-post.

Ystlysdid, *s. f.—pl. t.* au (ystlys—tid) A side chain, the trace of draught harness.

Ystlysgam, *a.* (ystlys—cam) Lob-sided.

Ystlysgamiad, *s. m.* (ystlysgam) A bending laterally; a rendering lob-sided.

Ystlysgamu, *v. a.* (ystlysgam) To be lob-sided.

Ystlysgell, *s. f.—pl. t.* oedd (ystlys—cell) A side-chamber, a cell.

Ystlysgerdded, *v. a.* (ystlys—cerdded) To walk by the side; to walk sideways.

> Mae yn ystlysgerdded a gwirionedd.
>
> It is going *parallel* with truth. *Adage.*

Ystlysglawdd, *s. m.—pl.* ystlysgloddiau (ystlys—clawdd) A flanker, in fortification.

Ystlysiad, *s. m.* (ystlys) A forming a side; a rendering lateral; a sideling.

Ystlysu, *v. a.* (ystlys) To tend to one side.

Ystlyswaith, *s. m.* (ystlys--gwaith) A lateral work, a work that flanks.

Ystodi, *v. a.* (ystawd) To dispose a course, range, or layer; to form a swath.

Ystodiad, *s. m.* (ystawd) A disposing a course, a ranging; a forming layers or swaths.

Ystofawl, *a.* (ystawf) Tending to regulate or dispose in order; warping.

Ystofen, *s. f. dim.* (ystof) A warping tray.

Ystofi, *v. a.* (ystof) To regulate, to dispose; to warp thread or yarn for weaving; it is also called *dylifaw*. *Ystofi y gwaith*, to regulate the work.

> Aswr bar taerfar yn tori cadau,
> Cadarn frwydr ystofi.
>
> A hero with an ardently wrathful spear breaking through battles, *disposing* a mighty conflict. *Llygad Gwr, i Lywelyn III.*

Ystofiad, *s. m.—pl. t.* au (ystawf) A regulating, a disposing; a warping.

Ystofiawd, *s. m.* (ystawf) Regulation, disposition; the act of warping yarn.

Ystofiawdr, *s. m.—pl.* ystofiodron (ystofiawd) A regulator; a warper.

> Ystofiawdr gwydd yn difai.
>
> The *combiner* of wood that is faultless. *D. ab Gwilym, i hel fedw.*

Ystofwr, *s. m.—pl.* ystofwyr (ystawf—gwr) One who regulates or puts in order; a warper.

Ystol, *s. f.—pl. t.* ion (tol) That involves; that covers or includes.

Ystola, *s. f.* (ystol) A scarf, an ephod; a wrapper, a loose gown, a stole.

> Gwelsynt wr ieuanc yn eistedd ar y tu deau; wedi rhy wisgaw mewn ystola gannaid.
>
> They beheld a young man sitting on the right side, being clad in a shining *vest*. *W. Salisbury.*

Ystolc, *s. m.—pl. t.* iau (tolc) That is hollow or indented by pressure.

Ystolciad, *s. m.* (ystolc) A forming a hollow or indenting by punching; a butting.

Ystolcian, *v. a.* (ystolc) To butt repeatedly.

Ystolciaw, *v. a.* (ystolc) To make a depression or indenting by butting.

Ystor, *s. m.—pl. t.* au (tor) That forms a bulk or heap; a store.

Ystorad, *s. m.* (ystawr) A forming of resin.

Ystoraeth, *s. f.* (toraeth) That is a produce; that is productive or plentiful; a store.

Ystoraidd, *a.* (ystawr) Resinous, or like resin.

Ystorawl, *a.* (ystawr) Resinaceous, resinous.

Ystordy, *s. m.—pl. t.* au (ystor—ty) A storehouse.

Ystordyn, *s. m. dim.* (tor—tyn) A trigger in bowling; a mark to jump from.

Ystoreithiad, *s. m.* (ystoraeth) A rendering productive; a forming a store.

Ystoreithiaw, *v. a.* (ystoraeth) To render productive or yielding; to form a store.

Ystori, *v. a.* (ystawr) To cover with resin; to do with rosin.

Ystoriad, *s. m.* (ystor) A forming a store.

Ystoriaw, *v. a.* (ystor) To treasure up, to store.

> Y doethion a ystoriant wybodaeth.
>
> The wise men do *treasure up* knowledge. *Diarhebion* x. 14.

Ystorm, *s. f.—pl. t.* ydd (torm) A tempest, a storm.

> Ystorm o fynwes dwyrain.
>
> A *storm* from the bosom of the east. *D. ab Gwilym.*
>
> Bloedd a estynit—
> Ystyrmant yr ystormoedd.
>
> A shout thou wouldest give, thou trumpet of the storms. *M. ab Rhys, i'r gwynt.*

Ystormawl, *a.* (ystorm) Stormy, tempestuous.

Ystormiad, *s. m.* (ystorm) A raising a storm.

Ystormiaw, *v. a.* (ystorm) To raise a storm.

Ystormus, *a.* (ystorm) Stormy, tempestuous.

Ystorwr, *s. m.—pl.* ystorwyr (ystor—gwr) A warehouseman.

Ystrad, *s. m.—pl. t.* au (trad) A flat, a vale, a bottom, or valley, formed by the course of a river. It forms the names of many places in Wales; as *Ystrad Yw*, *Ystrad Tywi*, and the like.

> Llas dau gymynawg am gymynad Eingl,
> Am Degeingl, deg ystrad.
>
> Two hewers were slain in hewing of the Angles, about Tegeingl, a pleasant vale. *Cynddelw.*

Ystradaidd, *a.* (ystrad) Like a vale or dale.

Ystradawl, *a.* (ystrad) Belonging to a vale.

Ystraff, *s. f.* (traff) That stirs about or strews.

Ystraffawl, *a.* (ystraff) Strewing; wasteful.

Ystraffiad, *s. m.* (ystraff) A strewing; a wasting.

Ystraffu, *v. a.* (ystraff) To strew, to lavish.

Ystraffwr, *s. m.—pl.* ystraffwyr (ystraff—gwr) A strewer, a lavisher, a waster.

Ystraig, *s. m.—pl.* ystreigiau (traig) A buckle.

Ystraigl, *s. m.—pl.* ystreiglion (traigl) A turn.

Ystraill, *s. m.—pl.* ystreillion (traill) That is drawn, trailed, or turned over; a mat.

Ystrain, *s. f.* (train) A tribe; a crew, a breed. *Gochel yr ystrain*, beware of the breed.

Ystram, *s. f.—pl.* ystremydd (tram) A frame. *Ystram y drws*, the door-frame; *ystram y ffenestr*, the window-frame.

Ystranc, *s. m.—pl. t.* iau (tranc) A trick, a wile.

Ystranciad, *s. m.* (ystranc) A playing tricks.

Ystranciaw, *v. a.* (ystranc) To play tricks, to quirk. *March yn ystranciaw*, a horse shewing vicious tricks.

Ystranciawl, *a.* (ystranc) Apt to play tricks.

Ystrancus, *a.* (ystranc) Apt to play tricks.

Ystraul, *s. f.* (traul) That is diminished.

Ystraw, *s. m.—pl. t.* on (traw) That is progressive; that is advanced or matured.

> Arglwydd o'r nen pen pob ystraw;
> Arglwydd pob maendy a'i ryw y daw.
>
> The Lord from above is the head of every contingency: the lord of every house of stone his energy is to come to silence. *Llywarch Offeiriad, m. Llywelyn III.*

Ystrawd, *s. m.—pl.* ystrodion (trawd) That makes a course or transit.

> Beirdd llafar—
> Ni gwnawd ni'm gre,
> Ar ystrawd, ar ystre.
>
> The fluent bards, their praise will not bring me to a stud, nor on a *course*, nor on a station. *Taliesin.*

Ystrawiad, *s. m.* (ystraw) An advancing.

Ystrawu, *v. a.* (ystraw) To advance; to educate.

Ystre, *s. f.—pl. t.* on (yst—rhe) A course.

> Cynnif aber rhag ystre.
>
> The tumult of a conflux before the *course*. *Aneurin.*
>
> Cynneddf i Owain eogyan ar ystre.
>
> The disposition of Owain is to mount upon the course. *Aneurin.*
>
> Oedd ddinas ar ystre.
>
> He was a bulwark on the *course*. *Llywarch Hen.*
>
> Pan wisg glew yr ystre.
>
> When a hero arrays the *course*. *Llywarch Hen.*
>
> Caeroedd Gwenllian, gwyn llyne ae
> Caredwy lywy lewych ystre.
>
> The ramparts of Gwenllian, fair as the sparkling of stars, the lovely fair one the splendor of the *course*. *Ll. P. Moch.*
>
> Dy fedd a'th reuedd a ddoeth rent,
> Difeddiawg farchawg feirch ystry.
>
> Thy mead and thy wealth thou wilt wisely distribute, thou disinterested rider of the steeds of the *course*. *D. Benfras, i Lywelyn* 111.

Ystred, *s. f.—pl. t.* i (tred) A village. *Daethost trwy yr ystredi*, thou hast come through the villages, said to a drunken person. *Sil.*

Ystref, *s. f.—pl. t.* i (tref) That forms a dwelling.

Ystrefiad, *s. m.* (ystref) A forming a dwelling.

Ystrefu, *v. a.* (ystref) To form a dwelling.

Ystreiglaw, *v. a.* (ystraigl) To turn; to roll.

Ystreigliad, *s. m.* (ystraigl) A turning.

Ystreillach, *s. m.* (ystraill) A trundling along. *Mi af dinben ystreillach*, I will go topsy-turvy.

Ystreilliad, *s. m.* (ystraill) A trundling along.

Ystreilliaw, *v. a.* (ystraill) To trundle along.

Ystrem, *s. m.* (trem) That forms a scene; that is exhibited or displayed. *Geiriau ystrem*, magical words.

Ystremiad, *s. m.* (ystrem) A forming a scene.

Ystremiaw, *v. a.* (ystrem) To form a scene.

Ystremp, *s. f.—pl. t.* iau (ystrem) A dash, a stroke; a trick, a charm, witchery.

Ystrempiad, *s. m.* (ystremp) A dashing; a tricking; a charming, a bewitching.

Ystrempiaw, *v. a.* (ystremp) To dash; to stroke; to trick; to charm; to bewitch.

Ystrempiawl, *a.* (ystremp) Dashing; charming.

Ystrempiwr, *s. m.—pl* ystrempiwyr (ystremp—gwr) A tricker; a bewitcher.

Ystres, *s. f.—pl. t.* i (tres) That forms a wreath.

> Y Neidr——
> Ystres fraith astrus frathau.
>
> The snake, a variegated *chain* of afflicting bites *Ieuan Gethin.*

Ystresawl, *a.* (ystres) Forming a wreath.

Ystresiad, *s. m.* (ystres) A forming a wreath.

Ystresu, *v. a.* (ystres) To form a wreath or chain.

Ystrew, *s. m.—pl. t.* au (trew) A sneeze.

Ystrewi, *v. a.* (ystrew) To sneeze, to sternutate.

Ystrewiad, *s. m.—pl. t.* au (ystrew) A sneezing.

Ystrewlwch, *s. m.* (ystrew—llwch) Snuff.

Ystrewlys, *s. m. aggr.* (ystrew—llys) Sneezewort, tansy; water tansy.

Ystrin, *s. f.—pl. t.* oedd (trin) That causes strife or bustle. *v. a.* To cause strife.

> Gwae elynion, bitnon braid,
> Ac ystrin gwae estroniaid.
>
> Woe to foes, a vexatious crew, and *to cause a strife* woe to strangers. *T. Prys, i gleddyf.*

Ystrodur, *s. f.—pl. t.* iau (ystrawd) The framework of a saddle or of a packsaddle; a packsaddle; the saddle of draught harness.

Ystrodwm, *s. m.* (ystrawd) A roundabout.

Ystrwy, *s. m.* (trwy) That passes through.

Ystrwyad, *s. m.* (ystrwy) A forming a passage.

Ystrwyaw, *v. a.* (ystrwy) To form a pass through.

Ystrwyth, *s. m.* (trwyth) That is pervasive.

Ystrwythaw, *v. a.* (ystrwyth) To saturate.

Ystrwythiad, *s. m.* (ystrwyth) A saturation.

Ystrych, *s. m.* (trych) That forms an opening.

Ystrychawl, *a.* (ystrych) Having a scope.

Ystrychiad, *s. m.* (ystrych) A forming a scope.

Ystrychu, *v. a.* (ystrych) To form a scope.

Ystryd, *s. f.—pl. t.* oedd (tryd) That is trodden or travelled; a street.

> Ystryd anhyfryd yw hon,
> Is daiar sent weision!
>
> An unpleasant *way* is this, under ground sojourners go! *D. ab Ieuan Ddu.*

Ystrydawl, *a.* (ystryd) Belonging to a street.

Ystrydeb, *s. m.* (ys—try—teb) Stereotype.

Ystrydebu, *v. a.* (ystrydeb) To stereotype.

Ystrym, *s. m.—pl. t.* oedd (trym) A main stream, a current, a channel; also called *rhin*.

> Ystrym yw y Meistr Edmwnt,
> A yr y morwyr o'r mwnt.
>
> Master Edmund is a *stream* that will drive the sailors from the mount. *Gwilym Tew.*

Ystryw, *s. f.—pl. t.* iau (tryw) Penetration, subtility; finesse, craftiness, stratagem, devise; a trick. *Mae efe yn llawn o ystrywiau drwg*, he is full of bad tricks.

> Y sawl ni rodia dedwydd yw
> Yn ol drwg ystryw gynghor.
>
> Happy is such as walks not according to the counsel of bad device. *Edm. Prys, Psalm* 1.

Ystrywgar, *a.* (ystryw) Subtile; full of finesse, devises, or tricks; wily.

> Nid ystrywgar ond ysgyfarnawg.
>
> There is nothing so *apt to use quirks* as a hare. *Adage.*

Ystrywgarwch, *s. m.* (ystrywgar) Craftiness.

Ystrywiad, *s. m.* (ystryw) A devising schemes.

Ystrywiaeth, *s. m.* (ystryw) A using subtility; a using finesse or stratagem; a plotting; a devising or imagining.

Ystrywiaw, *v. a.* (ystryw) To act with craft or cunning; to devise, to invent.

> Yn Aber Ystwyth yn ystrywiaw gwyth,
> Gwaith Faddon ymddelliaw,
> Gwasgarai bawb rhagddaw.
>
> In Aber Ystwyth *devising* wrath, appearing as in the battle of Badon, every body would disperse before him. *Cynddelw, i H. ab Owain.*

Ystrywiawg, *a.* (ystryw) Full of craftiness.

> Y ddwybleid——
> Os drwg un, ystrywiawg wall,
> Draw o'i gyrhaedd, drwg arall.
>
> Both parties, if bad the one, *of crafty* failing, yonder out of his reach, bad is the other. *H. D. ab Ifan.*

Ystrywiawl, *a.* (ystryw) Plotting, devising.

Ystrywus, *a.* (ystryw) Crafty, wily, cunning.

Ystum, *s. m.—pl. t.* iau (tum) A shape, form, gait, or fashion; turn, bend, or curve. *Garw dy ystumiau di*, strange are thy looks; *derbyn ystum*, to receive a turn, a term in coursing.

> Ffown yn gadno,
> Cydnaid ystumiau;
> Ffown yn felau,
> Mal na thyciwys.
>
> I fled as a reynard, of even-paced *turns*: I fled a marten, so that it availed not. *Taliesin.*

Ystumgar, *a.* (ystum) Flexible; well-formed.

Ystumgarwch, *s. m.* (ystumgar) Flexibleness.

Ystumiad, *s. m.—pl. t.* au (ystum) A giving a shape, form, or fashion; sinuation.

Ystumiaw, *v. a.* (ystum) To form, to shape, to mould, to fashion; to bend.

Ystumiawg, *a.* (ystum) Having a form, shape or mould; having a bend.

Ystumiawl, *a.* (ystum) Tending to form or to fashion; pliable, sinuous.

Ystumiwr, *s. m.—pl.* ystumiwyr (ystum—gwr) One who assumes shapes.

Ystun, *s. m.* (tun) That is irritating.

Ystunad, *s. m.* (ystun) Instigation, irritation.

Ystunaw, *v. a.* (ystun) To instigate, to irritate.

Mae anadliad cythreulaidd yn ystunaw llygredigaethau meddwl dyn a chyuhyrfu angerddawl annhwyll, chwantau, a chyfeiliorni.

The breath of devils is *irritating* the corruptions of the mind of man with vehement impulses of madness, lusts, and excess. *C. Edwards, H. y Ffydd.*

Ystunawl, *a.* (ystun) Instigating, irritating.

Ystwc, *s. m.—pl.* ystyciau (twc) A shallow wooden vessel, a pail, a bucket, also a shock of corn

Ystwff, *s. m.* (twff) That forms a lift, or rise.

Ystwffwl, *s.m.—pl.* ystyffylau (ystwf) That keeps up or suspends; a log, a stock; a holdfast; a staple; the knocker of a door.

> Yr ystwffwl hwn a'r hwn draw,
> Mwy gorddyinaul am danaw
> Eiwch lla, a llwybr anaw.

The *stock* that is here, and this one there, more congenial round them would have been the triumph of a host, and the path of melody. *Llywarch Hen.*

Ystwng, *s. m.* (twng) A putting down; a depression. *v. a.* To put down; to depress.

> Yr un fab ym rhwng fy gwnaeth ystwng
> Ar ei estroniou, yn drud echwng.

The only son of my lord completely caused a *depression* on those estranged to him, an awful event. *E. ab Madawg Rhaawd.*

Ystwr, *s. m.* (twr) That makes a rising; a stir.

> Lleia' 'stwr, fal llais 'deryn,
> Awr doet, gwna flinder i'r dyn.

The least *noise*, as the note of a bird, on a painful moment, causes trouble to a man. *L. Hopcin.*

Ystwriad, *s. m.* (ystwr) A making a bustle.

Ystwriaw, *v. a.* (ystwr) To make a bustle or stir.

Ystwy, *s. m.* (twy) That causes a stop, a check.

Ystwyad, *s. m.* (ystwy) A checking, a curbing.

Ystwyal, *s. f.—pl.* ystwyail (ystwy) A cudgel.

Ystwyaliad, *s. m.* (ystwyal) A cudgelling.

Ystwyalu, *v. a.* (ystwyal) To cudgel.

Ystwyaw, *v. a.* (ystwy) To check, to restrain.

Ystwyawl, *a.* (ystwy) Checking, restraining.

Ystwyll, *s. m.—pl. t.* au (yst—gwyll) That exists in the gloom; an epithet for the star of the Epiphany; the Epiphany. *Dydd ystwyll*, twelfth day

Ystwyr, *s. m.* (twyr) That is agitated; that is stretched out.

Ystwyrain, *v. a.* (ystwyr) To cause a continual agitation; to be stretching.

Ystwyraw, *v. a.* (ystwyr) To agitate; to stretch out as to recover from lassitude.

Ystwyrawl, *a.* (ystwyr) Apt to be agitated; stretching as recovering from lassitude.

Ystwyrgam, *a.* (ystwyr—cam) Obliquely stretched

Ystwyriad, *s. m.* (ystwyr) A rendering agitated; a stretching out.

Ystwyth, *a.* (twyth) That is springing; flexible, pliant, supple, limber.

Ystwythad, *s. m.* (ystwyth) A making pliant.

Ystwythaidd, *a.* (ystwyth) Apt to be pliant.

Ystwythaw, *v. a.* (ystwyth) To render elastic; to render flexible or supple; to become elastic; to grow flexible or pliant.

Ystwythawl, *a.* (ystwyth) Of a pliant nature.

Ystwythder, *s. m.* (ystwyth) Elasticity; flexibleness, suppleness, pliancy.

Ystwythdra, *s. m.* (ystwyth) Elasticity, pliancy.

Ystwythedig, *a.* (ystwythad) Being made pliant.

Ystwythedd, *s. m.* (ystwyth) Elasticity; pliancy.

Ystwythiad, *s. m.* (ystwyth) A rendering pliant, flexible or elastic.

Ystwytholdeb, *s. m.* (ystwythawl) Pliancy.

Ystwythwr, *s. m.—pl.* ystwythwyr (ystwyth—gwr) One who makes pliant or elastic.

Ystycaid, *s. m.—pl.* ystyceidiau (ystwc) A pailful.

Ystycyll, *s. m.* (ystwc) A signal of safety.

> Y ceiliawg du—
> Ystycyll yn cynnull cad.

The black cock, a *signal* collecting a host. *D. ab Gwilym.*

Ystyffernach, *s. pl. aggr.* (ystwff—arn) Utensils.

Ystyffylawg, *a.* (ystwffwl) Having stocks; stapled. *Cist ystyffylawg*, a stock chest; a great chest with a raised lid, hutch, or bin, that has pedestals.

Ystyffylgi, *s. m.* (ystwffwl—ci) A dog with a log fastened to him.

Ystyffyliad, *s. m.* (ystwffwl) A stocking or logging; a suspending by a staple.

Ystyffylu, *v. a.* (ystwffwl) To prop with a stock or log; to fasten with a staple.

Ystyl, *s. m.* (yst—yl) A cause of activity.

Ystyr, *s. m.—pl. t.* ion (yst—yr) That gives existence, form, or figure; that gives similarity; sense, meaning. *adv.* As may be deemed.

Tri chyfeiriyniaid doethineb: awen, ystyr, ac ymgais.

The three concomitants of wisdom: genius, study, and exertion. *Catwg ab Gwynlliw.*

Ystyrbell, *a.* (ystyr—pell) Of profound import.

Tri pheth blodeuawg ar gerdd: ystyrbell iaith, a goleuder synwyr, a chywrain geilfyddyd.

Three things that are florid in song: profoundly contrived language, and sweetly lucid ideas, and accurate art. *Barddas.*

Ystyrbwyll, *a.* (ystyr—pwyll) Of important consideration or meaning.

Ystyredig, *a.* (ystyr) Being considered or studied.

> Arglwydd, gwrandaw fy ngweddi yn rhwydd,
> Bid dy glustiau yn ystyredigion!

Lord, hearken kindly to my prayer, be thine ears attentive now! *Dafydd Ddu, o Eryri.*

Ystyrgar, *a.* (ystyr) Apt to reflect, considerate.

Nid ystyrgar ond awenawl.

There is none so *apt to consider* as the ingenious. *Adage.*

Ystyriaeth, *s. m.—pl. t.* au (ystyr) Reflection.

Tri chynfodolion doethineb; deall, ystyriaeth, ac addysg.

The three originations of wisdom; understanding, reflection, and instruction. *Catwg Ddoeth.*

Tad doethineb yw cof, a'i fam yw ystyriaeth.

The father of wisdom is memory, and his mother is reflection. *Adage.*

Ystyriaethawl, *a.* (ystyriaeth) Having consideration or reflection.

Ystyriaethiad, *s. m.* (ystyriaeth) A using consideration or reflection.

Ystyriaethu, *v. a.* (ystyriaeth) To use consideration, to use reflection.

Ystyriannawl, *a.* (ystyriant) Considerate.

Ystyriannu, *v. a.* (ystyriant) To use consideration

Ystyriant, *s. m.* (ystyr) Consideration.

Ystyriaw, *v. a.* (ystyr) To consider; to regard, to take notice.

> Cyfarchaf ym Rhen,
> Ystyriaw awen,
> Py ddyddwg angen,
> Cyn no Chyridwen.

I will enquire of my Creator, musing upon intellect, who underwent the state of necessity, before Cyridwen. *Taliesin.*

Ystyriawg, *a.* (ystyr) Having consideration.

Ystyriawl, *a.* (ystyr) Considerate; sentimental.

Ystyried, *v. a.* (ystyr) To consider, to reflect.

Tri pheth a ddyly dyn ei ystyried; o ba le y daeth, yn mha le y mae, ac i ba le yr ei.

Three things ought a man *to consider*; from what place he has come, to what place he is, and to what place he goes. *Trioedd Moes.*

Ystyriedig, *a.* (ystyr) Considered, studied.

Ystyriedigaeth, *s. m.* (ystyriedig) Consideration.

Ystyrioldeb, *s. m.* (ystyriawl) Considerateness.

Ystyrioli, *v. a.* (ystyriawl) To render considerate; to become considerate.

Ystyriwr, *s. m.—pl.* ystyriwyr (ystyr—gwr) One who considers or reflects, a studier.

Ystyrmant, *s. m.—pl. t.* au (ystyr—mant) A jaws-harp.

> Y gwynt——
> Ystyrmant yr ystormydd.

The wind, the *trump* of the storms. *D. ab Gwilym.*

Ystyw, *s. m.* (tyw) That spreads out or about; a settlement.

Ystywaws, *s. f.* (ystyw) Stays, a pair of stays.

> Dwy ystywaws pedair ceiniawg a dalant.
>
> Two *stays* fourpence are they worth. *Welsh Laws.*

Ystywan, *s. m.* (ystyw) A settling, a flattening.

Ystywaniad, *s. m.* (ystywan) A settling; a slapping.

Ystywanu, *v. a.* (ystywan) To settle; to belabour.

Ystywell, *a.* (ystyw) Stedfast; manageable.

> Baglan bren, bid ystywell,
> A'm cynnelych a fo gwell.
>
> Wooden crook, be *steady* that thou mayest support me the better. *Llywarch Hen.*

Ystywelliad, *s. m.* (ystywell) A making stedfast.

Ystywellu, *v. a.* (ystywell) To make steady.

Ysu, *v. a.* (ys) To hanker, to itch: to corrode; to consume, to devour, to eat. *Mae fy nyrnau yn ysu am dy daraw*, my fists are itching for striking thee.

> Ni dylyy drwg foly namyn drwg ysu.
>
> A bad stomach ought but to *devour* badly. *Adage.*

Yswad, *s.* (gwâd) A throwing down, a falling flatly

Yswadan, *s. m.—pl. t.* au (yswad) A stroke, a slap.

Yswaetheroedd, *adv.* (ys—gwaeth—er—oedd) It is worse for what was, the more the pity.

Yswail, *s. m.—pl.* ysweilion (yswail) That ejects; that is thrown out, ejected, or wasted.

Yswain, *s. m.—pl.* ysweinoedd (gwain) An esquire; an armour-bearer.

> Yswain aur-adain ydyw.
>
> A golden-winged page is he. *Sypyn Cyfeiliawg.*
>
> A'th yswain a'th lain o'th flaen.
>
> And thy *esquire* with thy blade before thee. *Iolo Goch.*

Yswatiad, *s. m.* (yswad) A squatting down.

Yswatiaw, *v. a.* (yswad) To squat, to lie flat.

Yswatiwr, *s. m.—pl.* yswatiwyr (yswatiaw—gwr) A squatter.

Yswbwb, *s. m.* (wbwb) A tossing about; a hubbub. *interj.* Confusion!

> Yswbwb! bobl anysberw ydych;
> Mi a adwaen eich arfer.
>
> Confusion! a pack of ignoble people ye are: I know your custom. *D. ab Gwilym.*

Yswbwbiad, *s. m.* (yswbwb) A tossing about; a rumpling.

Yswbwbiaw, *v. a.* (yswbwb) To toss about, to tumble about; to rumple.

Yswbwbiwr, *s. m.—pl.* yswbwbiwyr (yswbwb—gwr) One who tosses about, a rumpler.

Ysweiliad, *s. m.* (yswail) An ejecting, or casting out; a wasting; a brawling.

Ysweiliaw, *v. a.* (yswail) To eject, to cast out; to waste; to bicker.

Ysweilydd, *s. m.—pl. t.* ion (yswail) One who ejects or casts out; a brawler.

Ysweiniad, *s. m.—pl.* ysweiniaid (yswain) An esquire, an armour-bearer; a page.

> Myned a orugyut ar eu traed, a gadaw eu meirch gan eu hysweiniaid; a gado Arthur yn eu blaen a orugyut.
>
> Go they did on their feet, and leave their horses with their *pages*; and letting Arthur to be before them was what they did. *Gr. ab Arthur.*

Yswid, *s. m.* (gwid) That makes a quick turn.

Yswidw, *s. f. dim.* (yswid) That is made to twirl or hop about; the titmouse.

Yswigw, *s. f. dim.* (gwig) A titmouse; also called *yswidw*, and *sywidw*.

> A'r yswigw ar seigiad.
>
> And the titmouse on a banquet. *Phylip Emlyn.*

Yswil, *a.* (gwil) Bashful, abashed; timid.

Yswilder, *s. m.* (yswil) Bashfulness, timidity.

Yswildra, *s. m.* (yswil) Bashfulness, timidity.

Yswiliad, *s. m.* (yswil) An abashing.

Yswiliaw, *v. a.* (yswil) To induce bashfulness; to be abashed.

Yswitiad, *s. m.—pl. t.* au (yswid) A chirping.

Yswitian, *v. a.* (yswid) To chirp, to make a small noise.

Yswitiaw, *v. a.* (yswid) To chirp, to twitter.

Yswr, *s. m.—pl.* yswyr (ysu—gwr) A consumer.

Yswydden, *s. f.* (gwydden) A privet tree.

Yswymbren, *s. m.—pl. t.* i (gwym—pren) A quiver for arrows.

Yswŷr, *s. m.* (gwŷr) That dawns; the east.

Yswŷrain, *a.* (yswŷr) Eastern or oriental.

Yswyth, *s. m.* (gwyth) That pervades; that aches.

Yswythbysg, *s. pl. aggr.* (yswyth—pysg) The cramp-ray, the torpedo.

Ysyn, *s. m. dim.* (ys) That is all in agitation.

> Mae wedi myned yn ysyn gwyllt.
>
> He is become a wild *firebrand.* *Adage.*

Ysywaeth, *adv.* (y—sy—gwaeth) That is the worse, the more the pity.

Yta, *v. a.* (yd) To collect corn; to beg for corn.

Ytoedd, *v.* (*m. of* ydoedd) That was, was, were; she, it, was or were. *Pan ytoeddwn*, when I was.

Ytyw, *v.* (*m. of* ydyw) That is, is; he is, she is, it is.

YTH, *s. m. r.* That tends to stretch out or to be continuous.

Yw, *v.* (yw, *s.*) Is; be; it is. *Pwy yw?* Who is it?

> Angen rhyw angen yw.
>
> Want of kind *is* want indeed. *Adage.*

YW, *s. m. r.—pl. t.* ydd. That exists; yew tree.

> Bangor Esgor, a Bangor Henllan,
> Ysaid ar cladfan clyd ywydd.
>
> The minster of Esgor, and the minster of Henllan, they be for celebrity for sheltering yews. *Gw. Brycheiniawg.*

Ywen, *s. f. dim.* (yw) A single yew tree.

AN

OUTLINE

OF

THE CHARACTERISTICS

OF THE

WELSH,

AND

ITS UTILITY IN CONNECTION WITH OTHER

Ancient Languages,

FOR

DEVELOPING THE PRIMITIVE SPEECH OF MANKIND.

BY

W. OWEN PUGHE, D.C.L. F.A.S.

DENBIGH:

PRINTED AND PUBLISHED BY THOMAS GEE.

1832.

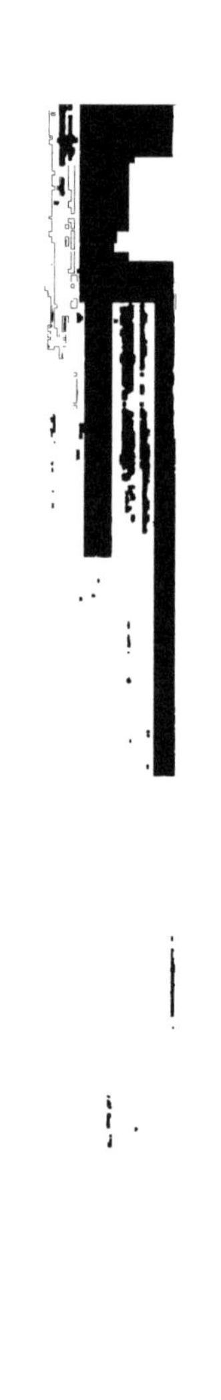

AN OUTLINE

OF

THE CHARACTERISTICS

OF THE

Welsh, &c.

THE language of the Cymmry, or Welsh, is limited, at the present time, to express the wants of a population, amounting in number to about six hundred thousand, which inhabits the mountains of Wales.* This language, in the course of the long period of its existence, extended over the most considerable part of Europe; and it still remains spoken, with more or less variety of dialect, by about four millions of the inhabitants of the western parts of France, under the name of the Breton; and also in Lusatia, and other districts of the north of Germany, under the name of Wendish,† being the connecting link between the Welsh and the various Sclavonic dialects. It has largely contributed to the formation of other tongues, which have supplanted it, through several subsequent periods, in different countries.

There are many peculiar characteristics in the Welsh language which are well deserving the attention of the learned; and from this consideration, some account of them becomes a pertinent appendage to my Dictionary: I shall therefore endeavour to convey to the reader a general idea of the subject, with as much precision as I am able, and as far as the brevity of this sketch will admit.

The investigation may be conveniently included under the five following heads:

1. The structure and character of the Welsh language, with its dialects.
2. Its alphabet, with an analysis of its literal mutations.
3. Its stability shown, by comparing its present state, with what, from proofs, it was in other periods, with examples of different evidences of the high antiquity of its formation.
4. Its three primary branches, with the extent of their difference.
5. Its affinity with other languages, as a corroborative evidence of its being spoken by the first inhabitants of Europe, and who migrated out of Asia, as is evident, from a comparison with the oriental languages.

* The population of Wales, according to the [illegible] al [illegible]

† Some interesting particulars [illegible] be s[illegible] pp 433, 477.

1. The Structure of the Welsh, or Language of the Cymmry.

This is a subject that is highly deserving the attention of the philosopher; as it abounds with some remarkable phenomena, and, perhaps, peculiar to itself, which may greatly contribute to illustrate the original formation of speech.

I consider the most prominent peculiarity of the Welsh tongue to be, that it has for its basis, nearly two-thirds of all the possible variety of simple or elementary sounds, each of them being the appropriate or fixed symbol of one simple idea. Upon these radical and indigenous principles depends the whole of its structure, regularly combined, so that, by having an accurate knowledge of the import of the ideas symbolized by those elements, we become considerably advanced towards learning the signification generally of all the compounded words in the language.

What I have here pointed out is an excellence, which can be but imperfectly appreciated by those who are acquainted only with languages that are not formed upon their own intrinsic materials: therefore, it may be necessary to enter into a particular illustration of the subject. And, in the first place, the following table of the elementary words will be useful for accomplishing the design in view.

Class 1, of elementary words.

a e i o w y
ac ai au aw—ei eu ew—ia ie io iw—oe oi ow—wi wy—yw=23.

Class 2, of elementary words.

ab ac ach ad add af aff ag ang al all am an ar as at ath—
eb ec ed edd ef eff eg eng el ell em en er es eth—
ib ic ich id idd if iff ig ing il ill im in ir is it ith—
ob oc och od odd of og ong ol oll om on or os ot oth—
ub uch ud udd uf uff ul ull um un ur us ut uth—
wb wch wd wdd wf wff wg wng wl wll wm wn wr ws wt wth—
yb ych yd ydd yf yff yg yl yll ym yn yr ys yth=109.

Class 3, of elementary words.

ba be bi bo bu bw by—ca ce ci co cu cw cy—
da de di do du dw dy—ffa ffe ffi ffo ffu ffw ffy—
ga ge gi go gu gw gy—ha he hi ho hu hw hy—
lla lle lli llo llu llw lly—ma me mi mo mu mw my—
na ne ni no nu nw ny—pa pe pi po pu pw py—
rha rhe rhi rho rhu rhw rhy—sa se si so su sw sy—
ta te ti to tu tw ty=91.

Total 23+109+91=223.

The number of elements in the foregoing table amounts to two hundred and twenty-three. Out of these, seventy-eight are words of defined and common acceptation; that is to say, they are used as names for some actions, qualities or things.

Of the remaining one hundred and forty-five elements, I do not know that any are used simply and unconnectedly as absolute names; but in their combined forms we may discover them to be signs of abstract ideas; and by which it may be inferred, in what manner they originally stood absolutely for the names of things, like the others.

Out of the last mentioned number of one hundred and forty-five, there are fifty-one which may be classed under the denomination, given them by Horne Tooke, of "little winged words;"* and which perform the various functions of pronouns, articles, conjunctions, and prepositions.

Deducting those fifty-one symbols, we have ninety-four still left to be designated; and these are not discoverable in their individual capacities, but enter into combinations, and serve as prefixes and affixes.

In the first compartment of the table are seen the vowels, standing singly, and also connected together in couples. These vowel sounds are symbols in themselves, or words having significations, of which it is important to obtain an accurate knowledge. Notwithstanding this, some philological theorists have asserted, that these vowel sounds are in themselves symbols of no ideas; and that, being of no consequence as to meaning, they may be used one for the other, promiscuously, in the analysing and comparing of languages.†

The vowels, in a general sense, are words significant of action, or of motion, either past, present, or future: and this faculty they even preserve, in various degrees, when they are combined with other powers.

Illustrations.

The word *a* implies action or motion; also what is present, or objective; and continuity, or accompaniment. Whatever functions it has to perform in speech, they originate from the attributes here detailed as belonging to it. In the structure of the Welsh tongue it performs the functions of the words *and, that, with, do, did, does*, in English.

By the word *e* is expressed that which is past, gone, or distant; and therefore it is used as the pronoun for the third person masculine.

The vocable *i* is a word that has respect to the future, and it implies *to, towards, into, unto;* and, as a pronoun, it represents the first person.

By the vocable *o* is indicated the past; and thus it implies *of, from, out of.* As a pronoun it stands for the third person neuter.

The remaining three vowels, *u, w, y* are derivatives, as being inflections of the primary vowels. It is only the last, or the *y*, that stands as a word unconnected with other powers; and it serves to point out an object; and therefore it is a definitive article, answering to *the* in English.

The important functions performed by these primary elements of speech, in the vocable class, demand some additional illustration; and this may be obtained by attending to the following examples.

* From the Homeric expression, *επεα πτεροεντα.*—

† Theorists thus forget the difficulty they would have to encounter in finding what affinity there could subsist, for instance, between the words *bed, bad, bid, bud; bit, bet, bat, but*, and others, of similar consonants.

Examples of vowel-words in construction.

A e i o—

Going is he into out of.

A e o dy i dy—

He goes from house to house.

I ba le yr ei di?—

To what place art thou going?

Af i do y ty—

I will go to the roof of the house.

A ei di o dy le?—

Going wilt thou go out of thy place?

or

Wilt thou go from thy place?

Ai da i ti à yw da i mi?—

Is it good for thee that is good for me?

Ti a ei er dy lw.

Thou--going--wilt go for the sake of thy oath

Cu yw hi i ti, a da i mi.

Dear is she to thee, and good to me.

Ni bu da i ni a fu da i ti.

It has not been good for us that has been good for thee.

A ei di yno?

Going, wilt thou go there?

A á hi i ei thy?—

Going, will she go into her house?

Pwy à á yno?

Going, who will go there?*

The vowel *w*, which is a mutation of *o*, discovers a very peculiar faculty, or power, in the termination of words, for it describes a state beyond what is expressed by the past participle.

Thus *gwedd*, connection, order or trim, when formed into *gweddw*, is a state beyond connection, or a widow.†—Again, *ul* is moisture; and *ulw* what has been divested of moisture; that is, embers, or cinders; and further, *a*, motion, by having *w* joined to it, becomes *aw*, a fluid, or water; and that is, instead of moving or flowing, it is become the element that is flowing. The same may be said of the following words:

Ban—banw	*Ca—caw*	*Gwac—gwaew*	*Llan—llanw*
Ble—blew	*Del—delw*	*Gwel—gwelw*	*Lli—lliw*
Cad—cadw	*Du—duw*	*Her—herw*	*Llud—lludw*
Car—carw	*Da—daw*	*Hel—helw*	*Rhe—rhew:*

also of several other words.

* *Yno*, there, means a place out of view, or distant; as *yna*, there, implies a place in view, pointed at, or present.

† The English words, a *wedded state* and a *widow*, are derived from one common original—the Welsh *gwedd*: for the initial of *gwedd* in many forms of construction becomes quiescent.

The remarkable discrimination of time, action, and position, in the vowel words, is retained even when they are combined with other powers, producing articulate sounds; yet this principle may be often so subtile as to elude common observation, in words composed of several elements; but in simple words it is plainly discernible.

EXAMPLES.

Ta, that spreads, or is in continuity.
Te, that is spread or extended.
Ti, that is in, that is in prospect; thou, thee
To, that is outer or over; a covering, a roof
Tu, that is lateral; a side; a region.
Tw, that rises out or up; drive: sway.
Ty, that is about or including; a house.

A clear knowledge of these elements, or seeds of language, and of their significations, opens to the mind a prospect for speculation, wherein many very curious phenomena may be discovered; and respecting which the following general hints may satisfy or amuse the cursory observer of the mechanism of language.

A radical word denoting some abstract idea becomes the name of a thing, which has its predominant characteristic described thereby: thus *to*, that is over, or as an exterior, becomes the appellation for a roof;* and *ty*, which is an inflection of *to*, signifies a house.

This principle extends also to words of the first order of compounds: thus, for instance, the word *tan*, a compound of the two elements, *ta* and *an*, abstractedly implies an expanding principle; and as the name of the greatest agent of expansion, it signifies fire. The word *dal*, compounded of the elements *da* and *al*, means abstractedly what is held out, or borne, and a bearing; it also denotes a leaf.† But, in these two, and in similar instances, in order to preserve the characteristic difference between the abstract and the appropriated significations, each class has its peculiar inflections and terminations: thus *tanu* and *taenu* are to expand, and *taniaw* is to fire; again, *dala* is to hold or bear, and *deiliaw* is to foliate, and *deila* is to accumulate leaves.

All the elementary words of the Welsh tongue are to be explained in the same manner as the foregoing examples; and, according to a few simple rules, their powers and meanings, when they enter into various combinations to form longer words, may be discovered; the component parts of which longer words must therefore be pregnant with their several primary ideas. And, as before observed, they extend to the compass of about two-thirds of

* The form of the letter T, in some ancient inscriptions, represents the gable end of a house; there being a line crossing the perpendicular from the two points of the sloping top; and indeed its general form sufficiently preserves the resemblance.

† The Hebrew letter ד is called *daleth*, which also means a leaf; and so the Welsh *dalaeth* and *deiliaeth* mean foliation: and the same letter in the Arabic alphabet was called *dal*. The form of the letter D in most alphabets represents a leaf; and in some ancient inscriptions the fibres of the leaf are delineated.

all the possible simple articulations; for that reason, no sound, or articulation can be uttered, but what is significant of some meaning in the language now under consideration, unless it may happen to be one of the number pointed out as not retained therein. This is a circumstance, which to persons who may only be acquainted with such languages as, by intermixture or other causes, have been deprived of their original simplicity of character, can scarcely be represented with due effect; such languages, for instance as the Greek, the Latin, and all the modern ones; but, on the contrary, a speaker of these mixed tongues utters many of the longest words, the component parts whereof separately convey to his mind no meaning whatever.

By having a correct knowledge of the elementary keys, briefly noticed here, many of the intricate arcana even of modern languages may be opened; not excepting those that have undergone every kind of commixion, like the French and the English, the intricacies of which are impenetrable by all other means.* The power, that has been explained as belonging to the vowel words of the Welsh language, for instance, is seen to govern in the formation of the past, the present, and the future, of the English verbs.

With the exception of the Welsh and its sister dialects of the Celtic, there is not one of the European languages that has preserved the benefits resulting from being constructed upon the significant elements which are here under consideration; and yet these elements, in a greater or lesser number, can easily be proved to pervade all languages, but destitute of any abstract import annexed to them in those languages that have suffered intermixion; and the number of elements, any way preserved in such mixed languages, is very small, as may be seen in the following table.

A table of elementary words in mixed languages.

	Nouns.	*Pronouns, Prepositions, &c.*	*Total.*
Greek	4	40	44
Latin	5	40	45
German	4	27	31
French	6	33	39
English	7	31	38

Should the same criterion be applied to the Oriental languages, which all allow to be more ancient than those that are analysed above, a very different result will appear, and that result stands in them as follows.

	Nouns.	*Pronouns, Prepositions, &c.*	*Total.*
Hebrew	35	30	65
Arabic	100	48	148
Persian	81	41	122

* The English word *love* is preseved in the Welsh, with its primary meaning, which is a *lick with the tongue*, being the way in which animals show their fondness; and the verb. *to love*, is in the Welsh to lick with the tongue. The primary import of *heaven*, *hymen*, and *cream*, is the same; and this may be thought rather strange. But let it be recollected, that *heaven*, or *himmel*, is the expanse over-head; and *hymen*, (though, in aftertimes, a little deity,) meant originally a veil, and *cream* is the top of milk: and the verb to heave is from the same root.

Two thousand years and upwards have passed away since the Hebrew was a living language, as spoken in its purity*: much of it is, therefore, undoubtedly lost; and of the portion of it preserved, with respect to a great many words, the exact and primitive significations are not known. Had it been otherwise, a critic, well versed in that tongue, would be able probably to show a greater number of simple sounds, as signs of ideas, to be preserved therein, than I have produced, as still existing in the Welsh. But, even as we have the Hebrew in ruins, it exhibits the very remarkable fact, that 33 of its elements, out of the whole number of 65, which we now discover in it, have an identity of signification and functions with those in the Welsh.

In the next place, by examining the other more ancient languages of the East, and still spoken, there are of elementary words, agreeing in like manner with the Welsh, in the Arabic 63, and in the Persian 61.

Though the several European tongues, exhibited in a foregoing table, have not preserved the elementary words, as signs of abstract ideas, or as names of things; nevertheless, such elements are distinctly discoverable as contributing largely to the structure of them all; and on that account they are deserving of very particular attention from those who investigate the principles of language. And the result, which is above brought to the view of the reader, is of itself very conclusive evidence of the descent of the several nations of the world from one common origin. It may serve, also, as an unerring index, by which may be pointed out the nature and form of the primitive language of mankind, which has ceased to exist, as entire, prior to every record of history, though we discern more or less remains of its ruin in all subsequent combinations of speech. And, aided by this index, we obtain a glance at that original language, leading to a conviction of its being in its construction far more perfect than has been hypothetically conceived, as the perfection of speech, by the profoundest philosopher of ancient or modern times†.

The structure of the Welsh language more particularly analysed.

The first form which the elementary words takes is, when any two of such words are combined together, the first with a consonant initial, and the other with a vowel; the first element is then a qualifying prefix to the other, which is the object.

Words of this first combination are either short or long monosyllables, as the vowel of the first element happens to be short or long. Thus, the *y*, being a short vowel, and dropped in the combination, forms *tdu*, which

* The Hebrew ceased to be a living language about four hundred and fifty years before our era, when the Chaldee, closely resembling it in idiom and genius, but differing in some characteristics, was substituted in its stead. Hence from that period, the Old Testament is found to be written only in the Chaldee.—H. P.

† Many learned writers, and, among the number, Grotius, are of opinion, that the primitive language was entirely lost in the confusion at Babel. It is, however, far more probable, as above intimated, that it was partially retained in all the new dialects, and most perfectly in the Hebrew. Yet it should be noticed, that this distinction has been claimed for the Syriac, the Arabic, the Cophtic, the Ethiopic, the Armenian, and others, by their respective champions.—H. P.

word is from *ty* and *an*, the first vowel disappearing by such a formation; and *a*, being a long vowel, forms *tan*, a word compounded of the elements *ta* and *an*. All similar words, or those of the first combination, claim our particular attention, as being to be depended upon in etymological researches and comparisons, like *bár*, *bar*, *câr*, *car*, *cân*, *can*, and others; and, being a class of the first formed words, they are therefore most likely to be found diffused through the various languages of the earth*. Words under the primary combinations are generally signs of ideas more precise and unequivocal than the elements themselves, when they are separately made use of; for the latter being of general import, a nice discrimination is requisite to fix upon a word in a different tongue, which shall preserve their subtile meanings.

Another class of monosyllabic words of the first combination is, that where the short vowel *y* disappears, so that two consonants come together either in the beginning or in the ending of such words. They are like the following:—

Brad, bran, bardd, barn, cras, carn,—braint, brwnt, plant, trawst,—cain, main, cwyn, mwyn, swyn, trwyn, plaid, plwyf, ffrawdd, ffrwyl.

Words of the second form of combination are dissyllables, and consist of two elements, each preserving its original form entire; and such are the following:

Adar, anaw, arad, awel, awyr—bala, bara, delw, derw, ewin, elw, isel, iwin, ogof, ofer, ufel, ulw, sylw.

The elementary words, with the above three classes of their combination, comprehend the substance of the language; as all other kinds of words are farther combinations, by prefixes of various functions, or by postfixes, for the formation of verbs, adjectives, and the several distinctions of nouns. And these are so numerous, and in so many ways connected, as to give the language a copiousness of expression beyond all others, and almost unlimited.

A primary source of the copiousness above mentioned, is the great number of qualifying prefixes in the language, and which are, unlike what we find in other languages, capable of being universally applied to qualify all nouns, adnouns, and verbs.

There are fifty-two simple prefixes; and these may be compounded, so as to make altogether about three hundred: thus any radical word, whether in the form of a noun, adnoun, or verb, should such a thing be required, may be modified in form and sense three hundred ways.

A few examples may suffice for the illustration of these prefixes: *Lled*, is breadth or expanse; *lledawl*, expanding; *lledu*, to expand.

Amledu, to expand about.
Ymledu, to expand one's self.
Goledu, partly to expand.
Gorledu, to over expand.
Dyledu, to be expanding.
Tryledu, to expand through.

* Thus the word *hen*, old, is common to the Welsh, the Armenian, and the Burman languages.

Traledu, to expand extremely.
Arledu, to expand on the surface.
Diledu, to unexpand.
Afledu, to cease expanding.
Adledu, to re-expand.
Cyfledu, to expand equally.
Amymledu, and *ymamledu*, to expand one's self about.
Goamledu, partially to expand about.
Goymledu, partly to expand one's self.
Gorymamledu, to expand one's self about extremely.
Diymledu, to cease expanding one's self.

It is in consequence of the copiousness of the language, that some peculiarities of dialect are to be found in different parts of Wales; for that variety is principally produced by the use of many synonymous modes of expression. Hence also has arisen the poetic dialect, which generally is very unlike the speech of common life; and especially, as it appears in the poetry of some of the early periods, and in none more so, than in the remains of the twelfth and thirteenth centuries. Indeed in the poetry of these eras so freely are the transcendental prefixes made use of in addition to singular modes of construction, that a person, acquainted only with the speech of common life, would almost conclude the other to be altogether a distinct language. There can scarcely be a greater dissimilarity, and at the same

express the ideas in the following expressions:—

Dychymmriw tòn amliw am lân;
The billow of many hues will be spraying itself together about the shore.

Dychymer ufeliar bar;
The sulphur fire will be taking to itself rage.

Dymgwaddoles Duw dofn awen;
I have been endowed of God with a profound genius.

Caraf drachas Lloegr;
I love the extreme enmity of England.

Rhymdoddwy ddawn;
There was given of talent to me superabundantly.

Dadlidia;
Divest thyself of wrath.

---

2. On the Alphabet, and the origin of Writing among the Cymmry.

The articulations of the Welsh language are represented by sixteen radical letters, four vowels and twelve consonants, to denote so many primary sounds; and from these are derived twenty-seven secondary letters, eight vowels, and nineteen consonants, which are mutations or modified powers of the radicals, under certain circumstances of combination, as signs of the same number of secondary sounds.

From the two classes of radical and secondary letters is derived the system of literal mutation, which is more peculiarly Welsh, and forms a prominent portion of its grammatical principles; a system that displays the aptitude which the radical letters possess of changing their sounds, as before observed, thus requiring, by a modification of their forms, as many secondary characters as equal the number of their mutations. But, since an original alphabet, of which a description will be given in the sequel, has fallen into disuse, the mutable characteristic of the letters is become more difficult of explanation than otherwise it would have been to those who are unacquainted with our language. And, though this principle of literal mutation, according to fixed rules, is now peculiar to the Welsh, yet the effects of such an aptitude in some of the letters, both consonants and vowels, to change their sounds, is observed to pervade all languages, more or less; but, in the Welsh, it regulates many of its fundamental forms of construction, as well with respect to syntax, as to the composition of words.

There are nine out of the twelve radical consonants which are susceptible of being affected by the principle of mutation, or which have their sounds changed under certain forms of construction; and, for representing such sounds, so many modifications of the primary letters are used in forming the secondary ones.

The mutable consonants are *c, p, t,—b, d, g,—ll, m, rh:* and these are reducible to three classes, each class consisting of three letters. Those of the first class are *c, p, t;* which undergo three modifications each; that is, they take a soft, an aspirate, and a light sound. The letters of the second class are, *b, d, g;* and these assume a soft and an aspirate sound. The third class consists of *ll, m, rh;* and they have each one mutation, from being aspirates, by becoming soft.

Thus the letters *c, p, t,* by being softened, sound respectively like *g, b, d;* by being aspirated, they sound as *ngh, mh, nh;* and their light sounds are like *ch, ph,* and *th.*

The letters *b, d, g,* by being softened, assume sounds like *f, dh,* and *i,* (or quiescent); and, by being aspirated, they sound as *m, n,* and *ng.*

The remaining three letters, *ll, m, rh,* by losing their inherent aspirate character, sound as *l, f,* and *r.**

* The system of literal mutation, it is certain, formerly prevailed in most tongues, and its remains are still to be traced in several. In the Welsh alone, however, is it preserved as intimately connected with the grammatical construction of the language. The following table of the mutation of initial letters, in Welsh, will perhaps be acceptable here, as reducing to a compressed form the observations above made.

Mutable Letters,	c	p	t	b	d	g	ll	m	rh
Soft Mutations,.	g	b	d	f	dd	—	l	f	r
Aspirate,······	ngh	mh	nh	m	n	ng			
Light, ········	ch	ph	th						

It would be curious to trace the ruins of this system as they are to be found in other languages, but space does not suffice in the compass of a note. A short collation of words

Some tribes of the Britons, the Cymmry more particularly, from very remote antiquity, were possessed of a characteristic alphabet, containing all the appropriate and necessary signs for representing every modification of sound in their language; and which alphabet, as implied by the method of writing it, was denominated COELBREN Y BEIRDD, or *Steve of the Bardic Symbols.* The forms of the letters consisted of straight perpendicular strokes and angles, as all curves were necessarily excluded, in consequence of their being written, or cut across the sides of squared pieces of sticks; and these sticks, or staves, after having been so written upon, were put into a frame-like form, and so inserted, as to admit of being turned round, to facilitate the reading of the inscription on all the sides; and this aggregate of staves was called a *Peithynen.*

Allusions to such a method of writing on sticks very frequently occur in the voluminous remains of the poetry of the bards of Wales of all periods; and this is an important evidence of its existence from the most early times.* To such evidence may be added another of at least an equally decided character; and which is, that the *Coelbren y Beirdd* is preserved among many other curious remains, collected under the sanction of several congresses of the bards, convened in the course of the fifteenth, sixteenth, and seventeenth centuries, by the Nevilles, the Herberts, and other noblemen and gentlemen of South Wales; and the last of these congresses was held in the year 1681, at Bewpyr Castle, in the county of Glamorgan, wherein all the prior collections were blended into one, examined, and sanctioned by the procuration of Sir Richard Bassett.† For the more complete verification of the genuineness of the bardic alphabet, a third important proof to be referred to is, the inscriptions on ancient stone monuments. Amongst those preserved in Camden's Britannia, several may be seen, having the Bardic characters occasionally intermixed with those that are generally Roman: such are the *l* in legion, the *s* in *filius* and *ejus*; also the *ff*, *p*, *f*, and the *t*.‡

The invention of the Bardic Alphabet was particularly convenient and useful in a pastoral state of society, such as the Historical Triads describe to have been that of the Cymmry;§ and, as the only necessary tool was a knife for preparing the sticks, and for cutting letters thereon, such an invention might have been, and probably was, of universal usage wherever the

in various languages, ancient and modern, that appear to have undergone this process, may be seen in the *Cambro-Briton*, vol. i. p. 407. H. P.

* Writing on sticks is alluded to in Ezekiel xxxvii. 16—20. "Son of man, take thee one stick and write upon it, For Judah, and for the children of Israel his companions: then take another stick, and write upon it, For Joseph, &c." Also, Numbers xvii. 2—"Take of every one of them a rod—write thou every man's name upon his rod."

† A more particular account of those bardic meetings is prefixed to Owen's translation of the Heroic Elegies of Llywarch Hen, prince of the Cambrian Britons, printed in 1792.

‡ See Gibson's edition of Camden, vol. ii. pages 1007, 1030, 1031, 1038, and 1458. Ancient graves were also discovered, in 1821, at Pentrev Voelas, in Denbighshire, whereon, among others, the peculiar character for the *s* (r) is to be seen, in the word *ejus*.

§ It may be doubted whether a state of society, strictly pastoral, according to the popular acceptation of the term, was ever known to the Cymmry. The *Coelbren y Beirdd*, or Bardic Alphabet, above alluded to, will be seen in the subjoined comparative table. It has also appeared in other publications. In the CAMBRO-BRITON, vol. i. p. 241, may be seen the derivative as well as the radical letters, amounting altogether to forty-four. H. P.

bardic system, or druidism, had extended its influence. But, after the introduction of Roman arts, and that of writing on parchment, among others, the ancient practice of cutting letters on staves gradually gave way to the use of the Latin characters and manner of writing, excepting so far as being traditionally preserved amongst other bardic memorials. By the adoption of the present common alphabet of Europe, the Welsh have been reduced to the expedient of using double, and even triple signs, for representing single articulate sounds. Yet the uncouthness thus produced might be easily obviated, by affixing the soft, aspirate, and light accents to those primary letters of modern formation that undergo such mutations, as may be represented by those accents: for there could exist no other difficulty than to obtain the public sanction to their being admitted into general use.

By a comparison of the various forms of the alphabets in use amongst all the nations in Europe, it at once appears evident that they are derived from one common origin; and the oldest specimen known of such a primitive character is the one commonly denominated the Pelasgic, or the Græco Phœnician. To prove the proposition thus advanced, it will only be necessary to examine the following table, wherein those ancient alphabets are collaterally exhibited.

Old Greek,	[illegible]
The same,	[illegible]
Etruscan,	[illegible]
Old Latin,	A B C D E F H I K L M N O P R S T V
Runic,	[illegible]
Bardic,	[illegible]

As the Welsh is not written in its proper orthography, there are some double letters used in this work, for representing single sounds. Such are the following:—*ch* sounds as the Hebrew ח, the Greek χ, the Spanish *j* and *x*; *dd* sound as *th*, in the words *the, this,* or *that;* the *ll* represent an aspirated *l*, which is peculiar to the Welsh; the *th* may merely be noticed as being like the Greek ϑ.

---

3. On the Stability of the Welsh Language and its Antiquity.

Those languages which are constructed upon the basis of their own regular elements, but whose origin is obscured or lost in the various revolutions that they may have undergone, are thereby necessarily involved in a state of endless fluctuation and change. On the contrary, one that is formed upon its own intrinsic materials, and those being elementary words of obvious meaning and in use, is by that circumstance secured against innovations. And this is one of the most remarkable characteristics discoverable in the Welsh tongue, and is highly deserving the attention of the philologist. It still remains the same as it was, to a certainty, thirteen hundred years past, as can be fully proved; and I have no hesitation in asserting its usage in common parlance above two thousand years since. As to its being spoken by the Cymmry in the sixth century, it will be sufficient to lay the few following extracts from the works of the bards of that period before the reader, as being the familiar speech of the present day, to obtain his assent to the first fact; and then some of the names of places in Britain, as given by the Romans, and still preserved, may, without going farther, suffice as to the other point, as corroborated by some collateral evidences in the sequel of this sketch.

Familiar Welsh Phrases from the Bards of the Sixth Century.

TALIESIN.

Gwelais wyr gorfawr,	I have seen men pre-eminent,
A ddygyrchynt awr,	who were assembling to the shout,
Gwelais waed ar lawr:	I have seen blood on the ground:
Rhag rhuthr cleddyfawr	from the rush of swords
Glesynt esgyll gwawr.	they tinged with blue the wings of the dawn.
Addwyn aeron yn amser cynhauaf;	Pleasant the fruits in the time of harvest;
Arall addwyn gwenith ar galaf.	another pleasure—wheat on stalk.
Màn y mae meillion,	Where there are trefoils,
A gwlith ar dirion;	and dew on lands;
Màn y mae cerddorion.	where there are minstrels
Yn gywair gyson—	in accordant harmony—
Cain bid eu gofalon	precious be their anxieties
Gan Wledig gorchorddion.	with the Sovereign of supreme circles.
Enaid Owain ab Urien	The soul of Owain the son of Urien
Gobwyllid ei Ren ei raid:	may his Lord compassionate his necessity;
Rheged udd ei cudd tom las,	the chief of Rheged that is hidden by the green mound,
Nid oedd fas ei gywyddaid.	not low was his panegyric.

ANEURIN.

Mal pan ddel medel ar freith-hin	As when there comes a reaping in fair weather
Y gwnai Marchleu waedlin.	would Marchleu cause a stream of blood.
Pan grysiai Caradawg i gad,	When Caradawg arrayed for conflict
Mal baedd coed trychwn trychiad.	like a boar of the woods an upturning tearer,
Tarw byddin yn nhrin gymyniad,	a bull of the host in the felling toil,
Ef lithiai wyddgwn o'i angad:	he would allure wild dogs from his hand:
Ys wy fy nhyst, Owain fab Eulad,	there be my evidence, Owain the son of Eulad,
A Gwrien, a Gwyn, a Gwriad,	and Gwrien, and Gwyn, and Gwriad.
O Gattraeth gymyniad.	from the felling of Cattraeth.

Gwyr a grysiassant, buant gydnaid,	Men have arrayed themselves, they have together leaped,
Hoedlfyrion, meddwon uch medd hidlaid;	short-lived ones, drunken ones over purified mead;
Gosgordd Mynyddawg, eurawg yn rhaid,	the retinue of Mynyddawg, adorned with gold in a strait,
Gwerth eu gwledd o fedd fu eu henaid.	the price of their feast of mead has been their soul.
Yn nydd gwyth adwyth oedd ei lafnawr,	In the day of wrath his blades were devastation,
Pan grysiai Cynon gan wyrdd wawr.	when Cynon had arrayed with the green dawn.
O gywrysedd gwragedd gwych y gwnaethant	From the contention of women gallantly they have caused
Llawer mam a deigr ar ei hamrant.	many a mother with a tear on her eyelid.

LLYWARCH HEN.

Yr aelwyd hon, neus cudd glesin?	This hearth, is it not hidden by green sward?
Yn myw Owain ac Elffin	in the life of Owain and Elfin
Berwasai ei phair breiddin.	its cauldron had boiled venison.
Tawel awel ti hirglyw:	Gentle gale, far art thou heard:
Odid a fo moledyw,	scarcely shall there be that is praiseworthy,
Nam Urien, can nad yw!	after Urien, since he is not!
Y ddeilen hon neus cynnired gwynt,	This leaf so buffeted by wind,
Gwae hi ei thynged:	woe to her her fate:
Hi hen, eleni ganed!	she is old, this year was she born.

Examples of British Names of Places in Roman Authors, and still in use.

Mona, Anglesey, in Welsh *Mon*. It is pronounced long, as if written Mone.

Aberconovium, *Aberconwy*, or the Efflux of the Conwy, in Carnarvonshire.

Aberavonium, *Aberavan*, or the Efflux of the Avan, in Glamorganshire.

Abergavennium, *Abergavèni*, the Efflux of the Gaveni, in Monmouthshire

Avona, or Auvona, the *Avon* river; one in Somersetshire, one in Wiltshire, and another in Worcestershire. *Avon* is the common term for a river in Welsh; therefore I conceive that those rivers in England, if correctly written, should be *Avan*, like the river in Glamorganshire.

Avalonia, or Glastonbury, which the Welsh call *Ynys Avallen*, or the Island of the Apple-tree.

Caledonia, the woody parts of Scotland, or the Forest of Caledonia, which the Welsh call *Coed Celyddon*, or the Wood of the Coverts. And this name is synonymous with Celtica, Scotia, and Goidheli, or *Gwyddeli*.

Ceretica, Cardiganshire, called by the Welsh *Ceredigion*.

Corinium, Cirencester, called by the Welsh *Caer Corun*.

Conovium, the river Conway, called by the Welsh *Conwy*, or the Dart Stream.

Deva, the river Dee, passing by Chester, and the Dee at Dundee, in Scotland. The Welsh name is *Dwyv*. Hence the inhabitants near the Deva or Dwyv were called Ordovices, or the dwellers on the Dwyv; or, as the Welsh would stile them, *Arddwyvigwys*.

Demetia, Pembrokeshire, called in Welsh *Dyved*.

Damnonia, Devonshire, which the Welsh call *Dyvnaint*.*

Isca, or Osca, the Esk, in Devonshire and in Scotland, and the Usk in Monmouthshire, the Welsh name for which is *Wysg*.

Menevia, the district where St. David's is situated, called *Mynyw* in Welsh.

Nidum, the Neath river in Glamorganshire, which is called *Nedd* in Welsh.

Tava, the name of several rivers, synonymous with *Tain;* therefore the Welsh call the Thames, *Tain* and *Tav;* and the Tyne in Devon and Northumberland is called *Tava*, as well as the Tay and the Esk, in Scotland. *Tav* and *Tain* mean the spreading stream.

In addition to what has been here brought forward to prove the antiquity of the Welsh language in its present state, there is another most remarkable evidence: and it is, that the people of Wales and of Britany are able at this day to converse together;† yet they must have been separated from each other for upwards of two thousand years.‡ We learn from the Triads that the Cymmry migrated to Britain over the Hazy Sea from about the Elbe, where they left a memorial of their name in the Chersonesus Cimbrica; and in that neighbourhood we find the Wendi still preserving the language of the Cymmry, though not so purely as in Wales and Britany, owing to their being in a situation more liable to produce an intermixture with strangers.

From the period, when the Romans abandoned Britain, down to the present time, the Welsh language had to withstand the effects of the intimacy and encroachments of the English, which must have been more intrusive upon its stability than any thing it had to oppose during any former period of equal duration, even including the time of its being under the

* This word implies, literally, deeps and hollows, which, it will be allowed, is descriptive enough of the country to which it is appropriated.—H. P.

† A vessel from Morlaix, in Britany, being in the Thames, in 1820, the captain was invited to come to hear the harp, by the Cymreigyddion. One of the members, after an air had been played, said to the Breton, in Welsh,—"Dyna ganu da." To this the Breton replied,—"Na: dyna chware da: *canu* à genau; a *chware* à thelyn." So that the Welshman was corrected in his own speech by the stranger, thus—"No: that is good playing: it is *singing* with the voice; and *playing* with the harp."

‡ The Historical Triads record, that the Cymmry came to Britain, and another colony of them to Llydaw, Armorica, or Brittany, from the Chersonesus Cimbrica, or Jutland. The Welsh cannot discourse with the Irish of Ireland and Scotland; therefore the latter must have separated at an earlier period from the original stock. The old name of Hamburg is Treva, and of which, as a Welsh name, the former is a literal translation.

influence of the Latin language. If therefore the English connection has produced no change in our language during a thousand years, the inference is, that it must have undergone less alteration in any other equal period.

As a collateral evidence in support of the subject before examined, the Laws of Hywel may particularly be referred to. The body of this code of ancient institutes, divested of some technical phrases and of several allusions to obsolete customs, is expressed in the familiar speech of the present time.* Names of places still left existing in England and Scotland, which are Welsh words of common use, are also good proofs, so far as they extend; for they show that portion of the language once spoken, where the names are found, was exactly the same as is now used in Wales; and by plain inference in proving a part, they prove the identity altogether. Such, for instances, are the names of *Avon* and *Aber*, which are preserved, even without a literal difference, in various parts of the island.

Again, we have manuscripts as old as the twelfth and thirteenth centuries, which prove the remarkable fact, that even the peculiarity of the dialects of the different parts of Wales then existed as we find at this day.

And lastly, next to the internal structure of the Welsh language, the primary cause of the preservation of it without a change has been probably the singular institution of bardism; and the system of poetical prosody under that institution became gradually, from the thirteenth century downwards, so very strict and mechanical as to euphony, that even the sounds and syllables intended to be expressed could not possibly be mistaken. Consequently, we know to a certainty what the ancient pronunciation of the language must have been. Besides which, its preservation unadulterated was a fundamental maxim of the Bardic system, as appears by the following triad:—

> "Tri pheth a ddylai Bardd eu cynnal: yr iaith Gymmraeg, y brif farddoniaeth, a chof am bob daionus a rhagor"

> Three things which a bard ought to maintain: the Welsh language, the primitive bardism, and the memorial of every thing good and excellent.

---

3. On the three primary divisions of the Language of the Cymmry.

The three dialects of the primitive language of a great part of Europe are—the Sclavonic; the Cymmryic, of which there are remains in Wales, and in Britany; and the Gwyddelig, originally spoken in Gaul and the south-east of Britain, and still spoken in Ireland and the Highlands of Scotland.†

The first people that penetrated Europe westward from the shores of

* The Laws of Hywel were compiled in the tenth century.—H. P.

† Perhaps the popular distinctions of Gothic and Celtic would embrace the three dialects here noticed, though the subdivisions, above adopted, must be allowed to be more accurate. Some excellent observations on this point, by the same writer, may be seen in the Cambrian Register, vol. i. p. 13—20.—H. P.

the Euxine, went under the general appellation of Celts† among the Greek historians; and the Romans recognised, in after ages, the wooded parts of Gaul under the same name, in contradistinction to the *Gal*, or open country. The generic name of Cymmry,—the Cimmerioi of the Greeks—by which the original stock was known while it remained on the sides of the Caucasus and on the Cimmerian Bosphorus, became lost among all the colonies from thence; by their assuming appellations descriptive of peculiar situations, excepting the faint traces of the Cimmerii in Italy, the Cimbri in Denmark, and the Cymmry in Britain.

Now, as the Wendi, on the Elbe, the Bretons, in France, and the Cymmry, in Wales, have so far preserved an identity of speech, as to be able to hold an intercourse one with another, whilst at the same time neither of these three nations can converse with those who speak the Irish in Ireland and Scotland, the necessary conclusion must be, that an earlier separation must have taken place between the progenitors of the Irish people of Ireland and Scotland, and the progenitors of the Wendi, the Bretons, and the Cymmry of Wales, than the separation between the three last mentioned people respectively. The inference to be drawn therefore is, that the ancestors of the Irish people, though of the same original stock as the Cymmry, who migrated towards the Elbe, in the north of Germany, must have separated themselves from their brethren by taking a rout from the shores of the Euxine, following the course of the Danube, and eventually spread colonies over Gaul and Italy.

It must be owing to the proximity of the ancestors of the Irish people to the Romans that there is a greater affinity of character between the Irish dialect and the Latin, than there is between the Welsh and the Latin: for the Romans formed no settlements in Ireland, so as to produce that affinity, which is much more evident than what can be traced between the Welsh and the Latin, though the Romans remained in Britain about five hundred years. In addition to this remarkable fact, there is another equally so, which is, that the Welsh language has a far greater resemblance to the Greek than to the Latin, in its characteristics, which leads to the conclusion of there having been an intermixture of the progenitors of the Cymmry and of the Greeks, in some period prior to all historical record, by which the manner of that intermixture can be satisfactorily explained.

At about what era that the more central mass of the Celts, or Woodmen, of Europe began to be distinguished under the appellation of Sclavonians would be difficult to determine satisfactorily; but it is pretty evident that they must have originated from that branch of the Cymmry before mentioned, as having had an intimate connection with the Greeks, before their

† The name of Celt was the most appropriate that could be applied by the first colonies to themselves; and, no doubt, it was applied by themselves, and so the Greeks got it. The meaning of *Celt* is a covert, from *Cel*, a shelter; and it is applied to woody places, as opposed to *Gal*, an open place or plain. Celt would necessarily be a name of frequent use among first colonies, as is now the case in America, where woodmen is the term applied. It is remarkable, that all the old synonymes of Celti, Celyddon, Gwyddell, and Ysgodi, or Ysgodogion, are still preserved in Welsh, being the originals of Celtica, Caledonia, Gwethelia, and Scotia.

progression into the north of Germany; and that the other branch of the Cymmry, which penetrated into Gaul and Italy, had not the appellation of Sclavonians applied to any of its colonies. Under the name of Sclavonic are comprehended the several dialects spoken in Dalmatia, Albania, Carniola, Croatia, Servia, Poland, Russia, and Lusatia, with other small districts in the neighbourhood, by the people called Wendi. And this last dialect is the connecting link between the Welsh and the Sclavonic dialects.

In the South-east part of Britain an extensive colony established itself, known to the Cymmry under the appellation of Lloegrwys, and the territory inhabited by this people was called Lloegr, which is now the name given by the Welsh to all England, notwithstanding its being brought under the sway of the Saxons and Angli. Our Triads of History record that the Lloegrwys originally came to Britain from Gascony, that is, from Celtic Gaul; where they left traces of their name on the river Liger, or the Loire, as well as in the North of Italy, which we recognise in Liguria.* Names of places in Lloegria still preserved, and of men, as given by Roman authors, warrant the inference before drawn, and the Lloegrwys of Britain, and the Ligari of Celtic Gaul and of North Italy, spoke a dialect, whereof the present Irish is the remains. So that the Lloegrwys were probably the first people that settled in Ireland, with whom subsequent colonies of Belgians from the South of Britain intermixed, as mentioned in our old chronicles.

There is reasons for supposing that the dissimilitude between the Irish and the Welsh languages has been increased by an intermixture or some other cause as affecting the former in Ireland, one third of the words of which only is recognised in the Welsh tongue, as words in common use.† It deserves to be noticed that the Irish people, owing to some cause not easily accounted for, have greatly altered the pronunciation of their language since the first use of letters among them, and arising principally from their causing a great many of the sounds in their words as written to be quiescent. Thus most Irish words preserved in the Welsh would not be understood by a Welshman, when spoken by a native of Ireland, though readily understood when committed to writing: for every word is distinctly pronounced in Welsh as written, without variation or exception.‡

Like the rendering of sounds quiescent, as above mentioned, in the Irish, what causes the dissimilitude of dialect between the Welsh and the Sclavonic, in all its varieties, is the vitiating of the letters *t*, *th*, and *d*, in the latter by a mutation, into sounds represented by *sch*, *tz*, *dz*. This mutation of *t* and *d* into *tz* and *dz* is rather common in the pronunciation of the Irish;

* The Triadic record, here alluded to, describes the Lloegrwys as one of the "three social" tribes of Britain: the other two are the Cymmry and Brython.—H. P.

† The patronymic name of the Irish, in their own tongue, as well as in the Welsh, is Gaoidhel, or Gwydhel, which the Welsh pronounce as if written Goithel, but the Irish pronounce it Gaël. And the Irish who write on their own history, in this age, take the liberty to write the name Gäel, to the discredit of their history, with a view of identifying the Irish as the descendants of the Gauls.

‡ Yet, by selecting phrases, identities such as this may be found: "O Ddia! baithidh mi mi fhein mar dhuin uasal." "O Duw! boddaf fi fy hun mâl dyn gwysawl." O God, I will drown myself like a gentleman.

and not unfrequently the Welsh use it in familiar talk. When an Irishman swears, he pronounces his *Mon diaul* as if written *Mon dxiaul*, which is the *Myn diawl* of the Welsh, and the *Mon diable* of the French. And the Welsh word *Meddyliau*, cogitations, is pronounced *Medzolie* by the Wendi; *Mezoulion* by the Bretons; but the Welsh pronounce their words as if written *Metholiæ* or *Medholiæ*. In the Albanian dialect *Vladica*, or *Wladica*, signifies a Bishop; but *Gwledig*, in Welsh, is a supreme one over a country, in a general sense, and often applied by the poets to the Deity; as *Iolaf Wledig nef*, I will adore the Supreme of heaven. Here, *Iolaf Gwledig nef* would be the phrase, independent of the literal mutation; but the *g* takes its soft sound, or becomes quiescent.

---

4. The affinity between the Welsh, or Cymmraeg, and other languages, as a corroborative evidence of its oriental origin, and of its being spoken by the first inhabitants of Europe.

This is a very important topic, and upon which the true history of the origin of nations principally depends; for, though much has been said and written upon it, the light elicited thereby has been so very faint and imperfect, that little knowledge and information has been thereby obtained. Indeed, it is what would require a perseverance in labour so intense for its accomplishment, as almost to deter any one from the undertaking, even though possessed of the requisite qualifications. The outline of such a work has been laid down, though imperfectly, by E. Lhwyd, in his Archaiologia Britannica; and it has been so far advanced by Gebelin, in his Monde Primitif, as sufficiently to discover, that the Greek and Latin, with the modern languages of Europe generally, are derived, for the most part, from a common origin, and which common origin, though improperly, is denominated the Celtic, and of which the language still spoken in Wales, owing to some fortuitous circumstances, preserves the most uncontaminated remains. If the extraordinary writer last-mentioned had had the advantage of acquainting himself with the whole compass and characteristics of the language, which he took as the basis of his superstructure, he would have accomplished every thing that could be desired; but, as such advantage did not fall to his lot, the work remains to be finished by some other Gebelin who may arise to do justice to this curious and interesting subject. All that I profess to do here, however, is merely to state the case, and, by way of estimate, to exhibit a few general observations, accompanied by some necessary examples for the illustration of it, with a view of being serviceable to future inquirers.

The following vocabularies of the affinities, existing between the Welsh and the Hebrew and Greek languages, must be considered only as specimens, and that generally with respect to their primitive words only. Connections equally close might be proved between the first-mentioned tongue and the Sanscrit; and in the next place, it might be shown, that about one half of the primary words of the French and English consist of the remains of the speech of the original population of Europe, commonly denominated Celts, blended with the Teutonic or Gothic.

Examples of Hebrew and Welsh Affinities.

The extinction of a primitive language has been asserted in a former section of this work; and we find, in Genesis xi. the scene of that event laid at Babel, and the cause assigned for it to have been the dispersion of mankind It may be pertinent to offer one or two remarks here, in support of the proposition, that the Hebrew tongue, notwithstanding all that has been said to the contrary, had its origin, like others, in the confusion of the first language.

Men had not multiplied so greatly, after the flood, as to be compelled to form themselves into separate communities, or at least to acquire national distinctions, at the era of the confusion of Babel; and, from the tenour of the history given of that confusion, we are plainly to infer the implication of the whole of the human race therein. But, towards obtaining a clearer view of the subject, we shall be aided by recurring to the subjoined table of a few leading dates, subsequent to the epoch of the flood, A. C. 2348.

EVENTS.	*Years after the flood.*
The confusion of language	101
The birth of Abraham	352
The birth of Isaac	452
The death of Shem	502
The birth of Moses	775

Or the following dates may be taken.

Shem lived until the age of Isaac was	50
Isaac lived until Levi was	60
Levi lived until Amram was	41
Amram lived until Moses was	40

Thus, it appears that Shem died only two hundred and seventy-three years before the birth of Moses, or that only four generations intervened between them. Again: by examining the above dates, we observe, that Shem lived four hundred years after the dispersion from Babel; and, Shem being the patriarch of all the families then on the earth, it cannot be well supposed, that the building of the tower could have been projected without his concurrence. Had it been otherwise, the primitive language must, undoubtedly, have been preserved by him in its purity until his death, and by his descendants, through two hundred and seventy-three years, to the time of Moses; so that, in that case, he and they must have spoken Hebrew. But there are the remains of the first language discoverable in the composition of all the ancient tongues, which collectively prove them to be formed from the ruins of an original one now lost; and this original language, as those ruins prove, was, in every respect, far more perfect than the Hebrew, or any other known language.

On a comparison being made between the Welsh and the Hebrew, we do not, at first sight, discover any great connection between the two languages; though, by a closer examination, we recognise their common origin;

and this apparent dissimilitude is, perhaps, principally to be accounted for, from that system of construction, in the Hebrew, of blending the prepositions, conjunctions, pronouns, and other particles, with the primary words, either as prefixes, or as postfixes; whereas they preserve their separate stations, in the Welsh. The affinity might also appear more manifest, if the Hebrew had remained better preserved as a living language: for, as that is not the state wherein we find it, we may suspect many niceties of pronunciation, without adverting to words and phraseology, to have been lost, notwithstanding the precautionary adoption of the masoretic points, both in respect to the vowels, as also the mutable consonants.

Hebrew	Welsh
אב, greenness, verdure; pleasantness.	*Ov*, that is elementary; crude, raw.
אח, exclamation of pleasure, or of pain.	*Och*, a forcible utterance; a moan; oh! alas!
אח, or אחי, one of the same kindred or kind; a brother.	*Ach*, a root, a stem; lineage, kindred; by, near, at.
אל, or איל, strength, power; virtue; an epithet applied to the Deity, and to any being or thing that is great.	*El*, what has in itself the power of motion; a moving principle; an intelligence; a spirit; an angel.
אל, a negation; not; nothing.	*All*, other; another; extra or outward; very, most.
אל,אלה, a plural pronoun; these.	*Eill*, they, those: *eill dau*, they twain.
אל, a ram.—אלילים, idols.	*Ell*, what is out or divided: *ellyllon*, goblins.
אל, a deer, male or female; that is, a buck or a doe.	*Al*, influence; harmony; power: *elain*, a musical being, a fawn.
איש, a being, a person, a man: יש, to be.	*Oes*, a space of existence, or being; an age.
אלה, a curse, or ban; an oath.	*Llw*, *elw*, *hylw*, a curse, an oath.
אלף, to teach; to manage, to rule.	*Alavu*, to energise, to endow, to enrich.
אלף, a kine, or one of the cattle kind; also a thousand. אלפים, or אלופים, cattle or bullocks.	*Alav*, pl. *alavoedd* and *elyn*, cattle, also chattels. Like Aleph, the Welsh use *mil* for an animal, and for a thousand.
אן, און, vigour, strength; labour.	*Yni*, vigour, energy, strength; force.
אן, און, affliction, grief, sorrow.	*Hoen*, effusion; hue; liveliness.
אן, און, virtue, or good quality.	*Han*, that proceeds from, or that is derived.
אן, און, an object of worship in Egypt, and in Canaan.	*Huan*, the sun, from *Hu*, that is pervasive. *On*, in Egypt, was called by the Greeks Heliopolis.
אן, אנה, אין, an interrogative particle as to time or place: when, where; here; there.	*Yn*, *yna*, *yno*: *yn*, in; *yna*, in there; *yno*, in such a place; there; then, at such a time or place.
אין, not; nothing, nonentity.	*An*: *na*: *an*, prefix of negation; and *na*, is no.
אנס, to press, to molest, to trouble.	*Annos*, to pursue, to drive, to molest.
אף, fie! ha! denoting dislike.	*Wft!* fie! *wft iti!* fie upon thee!
אץ, to urge, to press forward, to drive on.	*Aethu*, to point, to sharpen; to urge; to vex.
אר, a river; light, lucidity.	*Air*, brightness, splendour, lucidity.
אר, to flow, to run as a fluid.	*Aru*, to emit; to utter; to utter a sound.

אש, fire: to set on fire, to consume.	*Ys*, that consumes; *ysu*, to consume, to burn.
אש, a verbal particle, or adverb, is, there is.	*Oes*, there is. *A oes yma neb?* Is there any body here?
אתה, to come, to arrive, to reach to.	*Athu*, to proceed or to go: *dathu*, to come.
אתה, a pruning knife, or cutter.	*Aeth*, that is sharp, or pointed; a point.

ב

באר, a well, or pit. *See* בר	*Bwr*, a trench, an entrenchment; a vallum.
בית, a house, a dwelling.	*Bwth*, a hut, a cottage, or a booth.
בטן, the belly, or the stomach.	*Poten*, a paunch, a belly, a stomach.
בכה, to weep, to moan, to lament.	*Beichiaw*, to cry aloud, to roar, to scream.
בל, to mix, to blend; to confound.	*Boli; cyboli*, to mix, to commix.
בל, the idol of Babilon; Belus.	*Bal*, that breaks out, a peak; a budding.
בול, a stump of a tree, or a stem.	*Bwl*, a rotundity; a bole, or stem.
בול, decay, or withering; October.	*Pall*, ruin, decay; failure; a miss.
בלה, to decay, to waste, to wear out.	*Pallu*, to decay; to fail; to miss.
בלי, corruption, decay, waste.	*Beli*, havoc, devastation; war.
בלע, destruction, ravage ruin.	*Bela*, havoc, ravage; tumult; war.
בן, that is reared, that is built; a son	*Ban*, high, lofty; a height, a peak.
בנה, to build, to erect, to rear.	*Banu*, to elevate; to exalt; to rear.
בניה, a structure, a building.	*Banaeth*, what is raised or reared up
בנין, a structure, a building.	*Banan, dybanan*, what rears; a builder; an ant.
בר, to purify, to clean; to be clean.	*Briaw*, to render excellent; to dignify.
בר, בור, a pit, a well; a grave.	*Bwr*, a trench; an entrenchment.
בר, corn; a child, a son. ברה, corn, bread.	*Bara*, bread; *bar*, a summit, a top.
ברי, clearness, the pure matter of the heavens.	*Bri*, excellence; dignity, honour.
ברית, purification, or a cleansing.	*Briaeth*, excellency; the giving dignity.
ברא, to create. ברא אלוים, the Aleim created.	*Peru: e berai elyw*, the powers caused, or created.
ברך, to honour, as in bending the knee; to bless.	*Parchu*, to revere, to respect, to honour; to confer honour.

ג

גאות, loftiness; raging, as of the sea	*Gwyth*, a swell out; wrath, indignation.
גאל, to redeem, to buy off; to avenge	*Galu*, to render clear, open, or free.
גאל, a redeemer; an avenger.	*Gal*, a conspicuous station; that breaks out; a foe.
גדל, to greaten; to grow great or large.	*Gwyddoli*, to render cognitive, or conspicuous.
גדל, greatness; dignity, honour.	*Gwyddawl*, that is conspicuous, or present.
גדר, to fence, to enclose, to hedge.	*Godrëu*, to form a skirt, border, or rim.

גבר, a fence, or an enclosure.	*Godre*, a skirt, a border, a rim.
גוה, גו, a body, the whole person.	*Ciw*, compact; what is compact. *Ysgiwion*.
גוי, a body of people, a nation.	*Ciwed*, a multitude; a tribe; a rabble
גלה, what rolls along, up and down, or to and fro; any rotundity in form or motion; and often it is compounded into גלגל.	*Gele*, that moves or rolls along; that oozes; a leech, from its rolling motion. *Gel*, aptness to move, flow, or ooze; a leech.
גלה, to roll, to turn, or to wheel.	*Gelu*, to move with a rolling motion
גנן, גן, to defend, to fence, to protect; also a shelter, a place sheltered.	*Ganu*, to contain, to include. *Gan*, capacity; a mortise.
גר, to make strange; to sojourn.	*Gweiriaw*, to break out, to stray: *Gwair*, a stray.
גרר, a sojourner, a stranger.	*Gweirawr*, one who roves or strays.
גת, a press, as for grapes or olives.	*Gwth*, a press; a push; a thrust.

ד

דא, to fly, as birds do.	*Dawu*, to come or move towards.
דג, to be fruitful, to multiply, to increase.	*Dwgu*, to bear; to produce, to yield
דג, fish, from their great increase.	*Dwg*, that is full or perfect; a bearing
דגן, corn, or grain of any sort.	*Dwgon*, a continuity of bearing; a produce.
דגון, fertility. To this idol the Philistines attributed all their plenty.	*Dwgan*, a bearing or producing agent, a producer.
דד, plural דדים, paps; love.	*Did*, *diden*, a pap or a nipple.
דיו, ink, for writing with.	*Du*, black; a black; ink.
דחה, דח, to drive, force, urge, or expel.	*Tecku*, to cause to sculk; to sculk.
דלת, דל, a leaf; the thin part of a door; a lid, a cover: the letter ד, or D	*Dal*, *daleeth*, *deiliad*; *dal*, a leaf; *daleeth*, foliage; *deiliad*, a leafing, or foliation.
דל, poor, low, meek, humble.	*Del*, churlish, dogged: obdurate.
דלי, a bucket, or a pail.	*Dalai*, that holds; a receptacle.
דמן, dung, a heap of dung.	*Tomen*, a heap of dung, a dung-hill.
דן, to judge, to rule, to order, to govern. And with the formative א, אדן, one who has power to judge; a lord, or master; and it is also written אדון or אדני, a dispenser of virtue.	*Doniaw*, to dispense, in any way; to endow, or to enrich; *addonai*, one who has to dispense a virtue or gift; one who has a virtue or endowment. It is formed from the prefix *a* an *dawn*, a gift.
דור, דר, space, or time, a round of life; an age, a generation.	*Dor*, what overspreads, a covering; the leaf of a door.
דשן, to make fat, to become fat.	*Dwysaw*, *dwysain*, to make dense, to be dense.
דת, statute, law, or appointment.	*Dedd*, and *deddf*, statute, or rule of action.

ה

הבה, הב, to give, to bring to.	*Hybu*, to get onward; to recover; to get before.
הדה, הד, to praise, to give thanks.	*Hoddi*, *hoddiaw*, to render easy or accessible.
הוי, an exclamation expressive of grief.	*Hwi*, to set up a halloo; a halloo.
הי, heigh; alas! oh! ah! woe!	*Hai*, excitation; hurry, haste! hie!

הן, הנה, a demonstrative pronoun, and adverb.

Hon, *hwn*, *hyn*: *hon*, this female; *hwn*, this masculine; *hyn*, this thing: *hyna*, that thing.

הר, הרה, to be big, to grow big: הרת, she bigged with, she conceived.

Hori, to become round or bulky: dyhorai, she became bulky, or paunched.

הר, חור, הרר, a mountain, a hill.

Hawr, what is distended or swelled out.

חר־גבננום, a mount of several heights.

Hawr gofanynau, a swell of several heights.

הררי טרף, mountains of prey.

Horori tarf, protuberances of scaring.

הרה, חורה, one pregnant, plural חרית, הריות.

Horai, *horen*, one that is swelled out. Pl. *Horoedd*, and *horod*, tikes.

ז

זב, to flow, to gush, to bubble out.

Swyf, scum; yeast, *swyfaw*, to form scum.

זג, liquor, also a husk, or shell.

Sug, liquor, juice; what is sucked.

זה, זו, זות—compound of זא and את—a demonstrative pronoun; it; this; that; here.

Sy, and *Sydd*, is: *pwy sy glaf?* who *is* ill: *pwy sydd yma?* who *is* here. *Pa elw sydd?* What profit *is* there.

זהר, clear, bright; a clear sky; clearness.

Ser, stars, the starry system: *Serw*, sparkling.

זחל, to be afraid. A serpent.

Sychwylaw, to turn or roll aside: *Sychwyl*, a whirl off.

זל, profusion, squandering; waste.

Sil, that is produced; spawn, seedling; issue.

זם, זמם, to imagine, to think, to devise; whim, fancy—to *seem*: זמות, whim, fancy, conceit: זמזמים, Deut. ii. 20. Imaginers.

Symiaw, to consider the magnitude of a thing; to consider: *sym*, size, magnitude: *symaeth*, a state of ease, or enjoyment: *somsymisid*, illusory seemers.

זן, to feed, to provide; store, provision.

Swyn, a preservative: *swynaw*, to apply a preservative.

מזון, store, provision, victuals.

Myswyn, that is put by; that is protected.

זנה, to fornicate, to whore.

Synu, to cause sensation; to cause consternation.

זנה, זונה, a harlot: זנות, whoredoms.

Synai, that causes concern: *Synoedd*, dreads.

זע, זעה, to move, or shake, to be agitated.

Sangu, to trample; to tread, to pace.

זרא, loathsome, repulsive, offensive.

Sar, a repulse; insult, offence.

זרה, to disperse; to winnow.

Saru, to throw off, to repulse; to insult.

זר, זרה, מזר, a stranger.

Sarai, *mysar*, that is thrown or pushed off.

זר, a rim, a bandlet; a crown.

Ser, *seri*, that tends round; a bill-hook.

ח

חב, חבה, חבא, to lay up close, to hide.

Cub, a bundle; *cubaw*, to make into a heap.

חדל, to cease, to desist, to leave.

Gadel, *gadu*, to desist, to leave; to forsake.

חדל, the world, or the universe. — *Gwadal,* that is fixed, firm, or established.

חדר, a recess, a retired place; a chamber. — *Cader,* a strong hold, or fortress; a chair.

חוה, Eve, the first woman. — *Chwyfai,* that exerts motion, that has motion.

חזה, to look upon, to see: to contemplate. — *Gwyddaw,* to become perceptible or present.

חזה, חזון, חזיון, מחזה, a vision, a sight that is shown. — *Gwydd,* knowledge; presence: *gwydden,* a knowing one, a perceiver; one having presence.

חח, חוח, any hooked, prickly, or bushy stuff, briar, thorn; a clasp, a fibula; a bracelet. — *Cuwch,* that is wrinkled; a knitting of the brows, or a frown.

חט, חטה, to tie up, to bind; to restrain. — *Cadw,* to keep, to guard; to save.

חיה, to live, or to have life. — *Chwelaw,* to be volatile, brisk, or lively.

חי, life; living, lively, vivacious. — *Chwai,* ertness; alert; brisk; nimble, quick.

חיה, חית, a living creature, an animal. — *Chwaiai,* that is recipient of motion, or activity.

חך, the palate; the mouth. — *Ceg,* a mouth, an inlet, or outlet.

חל, חלל, to break in upon, to violate: wounded, smitten; slain. — *Cwll,* what separates; a stomach: *cyllu,* to separate, to divide.

חלה, to hurt, to annoy, to grieve; to be sick. — *Cwl,* a fault: *cwlau,* to hurt; to become sick.

חלי, sickness, illness, malady. — *Cwli,* a weak state, sickness.

חול, the sand or beach of the sea. — *Chwel,* a spread, a dispersion.

חלץ, the loins. Kings shall come out of thy loins. — *Caludd,* bowels, or entrails.

חמה, חומה, a wall, a mound. The waters were a wall on the right and on the left. — *Cwm,* a rounding or rising up, the sides of hills forming a hollow.

חמר, to desire, to long after; to take pleasure in: also desire. — *Cymmodi,* to be sociable; to reconcile; to covenant.

חמק, to turn aside: חמוקי, the joints of the thighs. — *Cameg,* what is bent; a felly: *camegu,* to form bends or fellies.

חמש, five, from the number of the fingers, and their use in counting: also חמשה, חמשה, five. — *Cymmys,* and *cyfys,* from *cy* and *bys,* the finger in conjunction: also *cymmysai,* and *cymmysaeth.*

חן, חנן, to be kind, gracious, or favourable. — *Cwynaw, cwynain,* to utter complaint.

חן, kindness, grace, or favour. — *Cun,* one that attracts, a chief; kind, gracious.

חנן, one that is kind, gracious, or merciful. — *Cunen,* a kind or gracious one.

חנון, kindly disposed, gracious merciful. — *Cunain,* attractive, kindly disposed.

חין, graceful, comely: חין ערכו, his comely body. — *Cain,* bright, fair: *ei gain gorff e.*

חנון, חנינה, תחנה, תחנון, supplication. — *Cwynen,* the uttering plaints, a complaint.

חנה, to pitch a tent, or to encamp. — *Chwaenu,* to come abruptly, or by chance.

חנה, תחנה, a pitching, or encamping. — *Chwaen, chwaena,* a hap, a start; a pitch.

חנית, a spear, a halbert, a pike.	*Conad, conaeth*, a point; a shaft.
חסד, a turning from; חסד הוא, it is a bad or wicked thing.	*Casedd*, hatefulness, hatred; an odious thing.
חסד, goodliness; mercy: חסדו, its goodliness, his love, or good will.	*Cysed*, what tends to assuage; a quiet state, quietude.
חסות, מחסה, shelter, refuge, safety.	*Cysaeth, mychysaeth*, security; quietude.
חפה, to cover over: חפו, they covered.	*Cyfu*, to compass, to hem in, to surround.
חוף, a sea-port, where ships are under cover.	*Cwf*, that hems in or encompasseth.
חפן, to be in a hurry, or flurried.	*Chwyfan*, to flutter; to heave; to hover.
חפץ, to delight in any thing, to fancy.	*Hoffeddu, hoffi*, to render delightful; to like.
חפץ, delight; frankness; willingness.	*Hoffedd*, delight; endearment, fondness.
חוץ, what is divided; a field; a street: על פני חוץ, upon the field.	*Cwys*, a division; a gore; a furrow; *hul pen y cwys*, the cover of the furrow head.
חר, חרה, to heat, to kindle, to incense.	*Chwerwi*, to become bitter; to embitter; to incense.
חרי, חרן, חרון, heat, anger, or ire.	*Chwerw*, that is acrid; a bitter; bitter, severe.
חרים, חורים, noble or illustrious ones: בן חורים, a son of nobles.	*Cawri*, great ones of strength, or stature; giants; *mab cawri*, son of mighty ones.
חרס, the solar fire; the sun.	*Gwres*, sun heat; ardency; fever.
חרס, some hot fiery humour.	*Gwres*, heat, inflammation; fever.
חש, חשה, to hurry, to hasten; חושה, haste, stay not. חשי, hurry, haste.	*Chwysu*, to sweat: *chwysa*, be thou in a sweat; *chwys, chwysi*, sweat.
חת, חתה, to sink down, to bring down or under; to reduce; to cast down.	*Coth*, an ejection; *cothi*, to eject, to cast out, to expel, to force out.

ט

טב, good; goodly, fair, sweet, pleasing, profitable, regular, in order.	*Tef*, that tends to spread out; an even spread; a spread, or layer.
טהר, clean, clear, pure, refined; also clearness.	*Ter*, subtile, pure, clear, refined, transparent, clarified.
טח, to overlay, to daub, to plaster; a daub, a plaster.	*Tawch*, that rises or stretches over; vapour, haze: *tochi*, to cover with haze.
טח, the inside: טחות, inward parts.	*Tech*, a hidden place; a sculk, a lurk
טיט, mud, mire, or clay.	*Tud*, ground, soil; a surface, a region
טור, טיר, טר, a row, a rank, a range.	*Tor*, a bulge, a swell out, a prominence.
טל, dew, or fallen vapour.	*Til*, a minute particle, a grain.
טלל, to cover, to envelop, to enclose.	*Telu*, to expand over: *telyw haf*, summer covering.
טף, little children, or youngsters.	*Twf*, growth, growth in the aggregate
טיר, a castle; a habitation, a town, a village.	*Twr*, a tower; *tref*, a habitation; a town.
טרף, to break in pieces, to snap a bit, to tear.	*Tori*, to break, to fracture; to cut.
טרף, that is chaced; prey, or spoil.	*Tarf*, expulsion; a scare, a drive, a flight.

יגון, to grieve, to vex, to afflict.	*Igiaw, igian*, to sob, to sigh deeply.
יגון, grief, sorrow, or affliction.	*Igian*, a sobbing, or a sighing deeply
יד, ידה, to cast, to put forward; to handle; to shoot, to throw, to cast	*Id*, that is stretched out; a point: *idiaw*, to push out; to render acute
יד, a hand, or the fore limb.	*Adaf*, a hand, what takes hold.
יד, a banner, a monument; a trophy	*Id*, that is drawn or stretched out.
יל, ילל, to cry out, to exclaim, to howl	*Wylaw*, to cry, to weep, to wail.
יונה, a dove; an emblem of love.	*Ion*, a source, or origin; the Lord.
יצר, the ׳ mutable, to form, to fashion	*Saern*, to act as a wright, joiner, or mason.
יצר, one who formeth, a fashioner.	*Saer*, a wright, a carpenter, a mason.
יש, is, or are; there is, there are.	*Oes*, there is; is there? *A oes yma neb? Oes.*
יתר, overplus, remainder; excellence; also a string, as of a bow, a cord.	*Eithr*, that is besides or over; an exception; except; but.

כבד, weight; glory, weighty: heavy	*Cyfoeth*, power, dominion; wealth, riches.
כבד, the liver, the organ so called.	*Cyfawd*, a coming or rising together.
כבש, to bring under, to keep in subjection, to subdue.	*Cyfasu*, to bring down together, to subdue together.
כד, a pitcher, a bottle, a jar, a jug.	*Ced*, a receptacle to keep any thing in
כד, destruction, ruin, ravage.	*Cid*, havoc, ravage, destruction.
כידון, supposed to be a dart: Joshua put it out as a sign to an ambuscade	*Cudyn*, a flowing lock of hair or wool, a flowing ringlet.
כה, masculine, and כי, feminine, a restrictive particle: thee; thine; there; here; so.	*Cw*, a rounding; quick motion; wherefrom, whence; at or in what place, where.
כי, restriction, used as a particle; why, wherefore, so, therefore; but; if; because.	*Cy*, a particle denoting a mutual act, or quality, or effect. *Cy gynted*, as quick.
כהן, a priest; a minister of God; also of a king.	*Cwyn*, a setting in motion, or agitating; a plaint, a complaint.
כלא, to restrain, to withhold, to confine.	*Ciliaw*, to draw back, to recede; to drive back.
כלא, כליא, confinement; a prison.	*Cilfa*, a retired place, a recess, a retreat.
כלי, any piece of work, or thing done: a tool, an instrument: כלי ביתך, the utensils of thy house.	*Celfi*, tools, instruments, or utensils: also any trifling things: *celfi dy fwth*, the utensils of thy house.
כן, some insect that settles in the skin; louse.	*Chwain*, fleas, from their nimbleness.
כן, right, fixed, stable: adverb, so.	*Can*, sight; brightness; because; for; as; with; of.
כנס, to heap, to gather, to collect together.	*Cynnwys*, to concentrate; to contain; to admit.
כס, כסה, a covering; a covered place	*Cas*, a being separated; a castle; hate, envy.
כסל, the flank, or loins, the haunches	*Cesail*, the arm-pit, the bosom; a cove
כף, a curvity, or bending over; the bottom of the foot; the hollow of the hand; a vault.	*Caf*, what curves inward; a grapple, a grasp, a rake with bent prongs; a snatch.
כפה, a stem, a stock, as of a tree.	*Cyf*, a stock, a stem, a stump, or boll

כפל, coupled or double; כפול, a couple.	*Cwpwl*, a junction, or joint; a couple
כרי, כרים, soldiers keeping guard by their going round; patroles.	*Cor*, a round, a circle; *cori*, rounds, circles: *cor*, is also a crib, or stall
כר, to dig, or to delve; to turn the ground.	*Cori*, to turn; to form rounds or circles.
כת, כתת, to break, to bruise, or to wear to pieces; to dissipate; a wearing away.	*Cothi*, to cast off, to throw off, to eject, to squirt: a throw off: a squirt.
כתן, a coat, or vesture; raiment: Χιτων.	*Coden*, what envelopes; a bag; *ceden*, a shaggy coat.

ל

לא, לוא, not; nay; nothing. לא צר, not oppressed.	*Llai*, lesser, less; it is used for *lleiach*, smaller: *llai sar*, less offence.
לאט, to cover, or to conceal: to suppress, to be silent.	*Llethu*, to press flat: to overlay or press down.
לבא, לביא, a lion, male or female.	*Lleibai* or *lleibiai*, that licks up.
להט, to burn, to set on fire.	*Llidiaw*, to inflame; to grow angry.
לז, to wrest, to turn aside, to distort; to depart: perverse.	*Llysu*, to bar out, to put aside, or to reject. *Llys* and *llysiad*, rejection.
לח, לוח, a slab, a plank, a table: לחת, tables, or slabs.	*Llech*, a flat stone, a slab: also a squat, a sculk: *llechoedd*, *llechau*, and *llechi*, slabs, flat stones.
לחי, the flat part or side of the face.	*Llechwedd* and *llechi*, the side of the face, the temple.
לט, to drop, to hang as a drop: a drop; also dropping, pendant. בלט, cautiously.	*Lledd*, that is prone or flat: a flat: *lleddu*, to make flat; to become flat
לט, some rich gum; what drops.	*Llydd*, that is diffusive: that is poured out.
ליש, a lion, from לש, to temper the chops, as a sign of greediness.	*Llwys*, that is cleared or cleaned: that clears or cleans out.
לכד, to take, to catch, to lay hold on.	*Llochiadu*, to mound, to pen up, to fold.
לכד, a taking, or catching; a trap.	*Llochiad*, a forming a mound or dam, a penning up.
לן, to lodge, to stay, to harbour at a place.	*Llen*, a cover, a veil: *llenu*, to cover, to veil.
לע, to swallow, to gulp: the swallow.	*Llyngu* or *llyncu*, to swallow: *llwng*, the swallow.
לץ, to repeat; to explain: to interpret	*Llithiaw*, to allure, to train: to read a lesson.
לץ, and לצון, a repeater; an interpreter, or explainer.	*Llith*, that is given as nurture, a lesson. *Llithion*, one who allures; a trainer, a lecturer.
לש, to temper; to knead, or work about.	*Llws*, mucilage, slime: *llwsu*, to yield mucilage, to slime.
לשד, moisture; juice of plants; fresh oil.	*Llysaid*, a slimy state, mucilage.
לשן, to tongue; to abuse; to prattle.	*Lleisoni*, to produce a voice; to form the voice.
לשן, לשון, the tongue; language; Arabic, Lisan.	*Lleison*, the organ that forms the voice.

מ

מאר, strength, might; greatness: adverb, very much: entirely.	*Med*, that is full, perfect, or mature: as far as to the full; to, unto, as far as.
מאס, to abhor, to despise: to reject, to cast off.	*Maus*, to depart; to swoon, or to faint away.
מנג, מג, to melt away, to dissipate, to dissolve.	*Mygu*, to become smoke; to smoke; to suffocate.
מגד, what is excellent, or precious: thus, pleasant things are מדי מגדים.	*Myged*, reverence, honour; grandeur; glory: *mygedion*, grand things.
מוד, מד, to mete, to measure.	*Medu*, to render extended, full, or perfect.
ממד, מדה, מד, a measure.	*Med*, *medai*, that is full or perfect.
מי, מה, how? what? who?	*Mae*, there is; is there? what is? where is?
מהר, to hasten, to speed, to be quick; also one that is hasty or rash.	*Meru*, to flit, to drop: *mer*, that is dropped off or parted; a drop.
ממט, מט, to slide, to slip aside or asunder: thus, בל מוט, is, they cannot be moved.	*Mudaw*, and *symudaw*, to flit, to move, to quit; also *ymmod*, motion; and *ymmodi*, to move.
מל, to cut, to chop, to chop off, to cut down, to bray, or to bruise.	*Malu*, to bray or break small, to grind; *malu ewyn*, to chafe, to foam at the mouth, as a horse doth.
מלל, מל, to speak, to talk: מלה, a word.	*Malu*, to liken: to joke; to utter levity.
מל, to cut off the top; to circumcise.	*Moeli*, to make bare or bald the top or head.
מול, plural. מלים, circumcised.	*Moel*, bare, bald: plural *moelion*, bald ones.
מולת, circumcision, that is a baring the top.	*Moeleeth*, the act of making bare or bald.
מול, מל, opposite to, near to, over against.	*Moll*, that surrounds, closes upon, or includes.
מלא, to fill, to fill up: to complete: fulness.	*Mola*, to concrete matter, to form gum.
מלח, to salt, to season with salt: salt, or saltness.	*Molochi*, to raise a ferment: *moloch*, ferment. *Prydain erfoloch*, Britain in a ferment.
מלחה, pervaded by salt; barren.	*Molochaw*, that has passed through a ferment.
מלאכה, work, affair to be managed; affair, business.	*Maeloca*, the act of trafficking, or a merchandising.
מלאך, an agent, a messenger; an angel.	*Maluch*, one that is light or volatile.
מלך, to have supreme power, to reign, to rule.	*Maelychu*, *maelogi*, to act as a manager, or trader.
מלך, a sovereign, a king, or a prince: also the title of an object of worship—Moloch.	*Maelawg*, *maelog* that has means of power, that has abundance; that has traffick.
מלכן, a brazen image of Moloch, so named, probably from its form of a bust.	*Maelgwn*, the summit or head of power: the name of a king of Wales, who died A. D. 542.
מלכה, the queen of heaven, the ruler of heaven; the moon.	*Maelocai*, a teeming one: that tends to increase.
מלוכה, ממלכה, מלכות, a kingdom; reign.	*Maelogaeth*, a state of teeming or abundance.
מלץ, sweet, of a sweet savour or smell	*Melys*, sweet, dulcet: a sweet.

מנה, to dispose into classes or ranges, to sort.	***Moni***, to individualize, to become a separate one.
מן, מנה, מין, מינה, a species, or kind; likeness, or appearance; a peculiar thing; a particle like hoar, which the Israelites on seeing, called out מן הוא! it is a species of itself; as they knew not what it was	***Mon***, a separate or isolated being: ***man***, a spot, a speck; a place: ***man***, what consists of small particles: ***manion***, small particles of any thing: ***man yw fo***, a speck it is, or ***yw fo man***, it is a spot.
מנה, מנים, plural, a sum or quantity of money.	***Mwnai***, that is formed of or having ore; money.
מין, מינה, kind, or species: למינו, after his kind.	***Mynw***, an individual; a person, a body.
מני, an object of idolatry: a drink offering to מיני, that number; therefore מניתי, I will number you to the sword. Isaiah lxv. 11.	***Menw***, an intellect, mind, or soul: also a mythological personage, stiled ***Menw mab teirgwaedd***, or Menw the son of three cries.
מני, to rule, to order: what is regular, rule, order.	***Mynu***, to will, to exert volition; to obtain.
מסה, מסס, to melt, to dissolve, to loosen: a soft or melting mood; voluptuousness.	***Masu***, to volatilize; to swoon, to faint. ***Maswedd***, a volatile state; voluptuousness.
מסך, to mix, or to intermingle.	***Mysgu***, to mix, to intermingle, to blend.
מץ, מצה, to squeeze, to press together, to crush, to squeeze out; also a squeezer.	***Mathu***, to render flat or even; ***mathru***, to tread or trample: that is flat, spread out, or even.
מצא, to find, to meet with, to come upon; to supply; to be present: to succeed.	***Meddu***, to possess, to own, to have, to have command of: to be able.
מריא a fatling; plural מריאים	***Merydd***, a fatling; plural ***meryddon***.
מש, משש, to feel, to handle, to take hold: משה, to take or draw out: to remove.	***Moes***, conduct, behaviour; civility: ***moesa***, to give, or to confer: to hand.
מת, מתח, to die: מתי, I die.	***Methu***, to fail; to become inert: ***methwyf***, I fail.
מת, a dead person: מתים, mortals.	***Meth***, a failure; a state of inertness.
מתק, pleasant, agreeable, sweet.	***Mwythawg***, tender; soothed; pampered; softening.

נ

ניד, comfort, or solace; joy; ease.	***Naid***, a refuge, or a sanctuary.
נהה, to make a moaning, to grieve.	***Neuaw***, to wish earnestly, to long, to pant.
נה, ני, נהי, a lament, a moan, a wail.	***Neu***, a pant, or an earnest wish.
נהר, to run as a stream, to flow; to run: a stream.	***Nar***, that tends out; that is forward: abortion.
נוה, a home, a dwelling a habitation.	***Naf***, a hollow; a place of rest; heaven.
נץ, to shoot out, to fly out or upon.	***Nwyth***, a drift; a whim: ***nwythaw***, to do a freak.
נתח, to cut in pieces; to dissect.	***Naddu***, to chip; to cut with any tool.

ס

סבך, to entangle; to perplex, to vex.	***Sybachu***, to draw in a heap, to shrink up.
סבך, a tangle; a thicket, or brake.	***Sybach***, that is drawn in a heap.

סג, סוג, סיג, scum, dross, or dregs.	*Seeg*, that is seethed; draff; grains of malt.
סגר, to enclose, to shut up; to confine.	*Segru*, to enclose; to put apart; to secrete.
סגר, what encloses; a caul; a border.	*Segr*, that keeps apart; that is enclosed.
סוד, to lay a foundation, to found; to advise: to ordain.	*Sodi*, to fix, to constitute, to implant; to limit.
	Sawd, tendency; juncture; extremity, limit.
	Sychu, to dry; to grow dry; to wipe.
	Swydaw, to intimidate, to awe: *swydfon*, intimidated or scared ones.
	Swchu, to envelope the point of a thing, as a cone: *swchu esgid*, to toe-piece a shoe.
	Swch, a snout; a soc, or share of a plough: *swch esgid*, point of a shoe.
	Swchai, that envelopes in the form of a cone.
silly.	*Siglaw*, to waver, to act with fickleness.
סכל, thoughtless, foolish, silly: a fool.	*Sigl*, a waver, a shake or rocking; a wag.
סכלות, thoughtlessness, folly, stupidity.	*Siglaeth*, a state of wavering or fickleness.
סל, סלה, to exalt, to elevate, to raise.	*Syllu*, to gaze. *Sylla*, *sela*, behold! lo!
סלם, a ladder, a gradual raise.	*Sylam*, that serves for a step or a stride.
סע, סעה, to move along, or to proceed.	*Sangu*, to tread, to trample, to tramp along.
סעד, to stay, or to prop; to strengthen: also a stay or prop.	*Sangadu*, to make a step: *sangad*, a pace, a tread, a trampling.
סר, to turn aside, to turn off; to take a huff.	*Sòri*, to offend; to become sulky, to sulk.
סר, סור, סורר, one that revolts, or turns off.	*Sor*, a sulk: *sorai*, one that sulks or revolts.
סרה, a turning away; revolt; aversion.	*Sor*, a sulk; sullenness; aversion.
סת, to stir up, to irritate; to entice: also a stirring up, or irritation; enticement.	*Sythu*, to render erect or stiff: erectness, rigidity; erect, stiff; rigid.
סתו, winter, or the cold season.	*Sytha*, that causes stiffness or rigidity

ע

עד, to set, appoint, constitute, or fix: an appointment; a set portion, or an allotment; a witness; any length of time: עד, מני, of old.	*Oedi*, to set a time, to make an appointment; to delay: *Oed*, a set time; age; an appointment; *yn oed y dydd*, during the day: *plentyn blwydd o oed*, a child of a year old.
עד, עדי, עוד, to, unto; yet; whilst: כל עוד, all the while.	*Hyd*, to, unto, until; whilst: *hyd yma*, as far as here; *o hyd*, all the while.
עדה, an assembly; a putting off; protest; testimony, evidence.	*Oedi*, a setting of time; an appointment; a putting off, or delaying.
עדי, plural עדיים, an ornament.	*Eddi*, fine; fringe: also thrums.

עדן, delight; delicacy; delicate, nice.	***Addwyn*, what is fair; delight: becoming; kind.**
עדן, the name of a country; Eden.	***Addwyn*, that is intellectual.**
על, עלה, to be up or upon; to ascend.	***Hulaw*, to cover, to deck, to spread over.**
על, above, up, over, on high.	***Hul*, a cover; a coverlet; a mat.**
על, עליון, on, upon: near by.	***Hul, hulyn*, what covers; a coverlet.**
על, עול, a yoke. לא עלה עליה על, which no yoke hath come upon.	***Hwyl*, a course; regimen, order; plight, or state; also a sail.**
עלה, עולה, what ascends; burnt offering.	***Hulai*, that tends to cover, or to overspread.**
עלה, a leaf; also a branch.	***Hulai*, that tends to cover, that forms a cover.**
ענן, to cloud: a cloud: בענני ענן, when I cloud a cloud.	***Haenen*, a stratum; a sprinkling; a covering: *pan haenwyf haenen.***
עץ, plural עצים, a tree; wood.	***Gwydd*, a shrub, a tree: a wood.**
ער, ערה, to pour out, to stir up, to rouse.	***Gweiriaw*, to shoot out; to make hay.**
ער, a stirrer up, a rouser, a mover.	***Gwair*, that shoots out, is brisk, or luxuriant; hay.**
ער, plural ערות, a juicy plant; papyrus.	***Gwyr*, that is luxuriant or verdant; verdancy.**
ערב, Arabia: Arabia is a peninsula.	***Gwyreb*, that juts out; a peninsula.**
ערב, the evening, or night-fall.	***Gwyrfa*, the place of declination.**
עשק, to press down, to oppress; also a pressure, or oppression.	***Gwasgu*, to press, to squeeze: *gwasg*, a press; pressure.**
עת, a time or season of any thing.	***Gwaith*, course, turn, or time; season**
עות, to distort, to wrest, to writhe.	***Gwaethu*, to deteriorate, to hurt.**
עתד, עתוד, an he goat; a ram; from the idea of their pushing.	***Gwthiad*, that butts, or pushes: a pusher.**

פ

פגר, a carcase, or a dead body.	***Pegor*, a pivot; a dwarf; a pert little body.**
פז, to be stiff; to be dense; to be strong.	***Pwysaw*, to weigh; to press, to weigh down.**
פז, that is dense; solid metal; solid gold.	***Pwys*, weight, pressure, moment.**
פח, to blow, to give wind; to vent.	***Puchaw*, to pant; to sigh: *puch*, a pant.**
פחד, to be amazed; to surprise, to astonish.	***Puchadu*, to make a panting: to sigh.**
פחד, amazement, surprise, dread.	***Puchad*, a producing a panting; a sighing.**
פיד, destruction, ravage, havoc, ruin	***Pyd*, that sinks or falls in; a pit, a snare.**
פלג, to divide, to sever, to share.	***Pellogi*, to render of remote state.**
פלג, a division, a distribution.	***Pellwg*, a distant or remote state.**
פלד, it is rendered torches.	***Peiliad*, a brandishing, a gleaming.**
פלת, to separate, to sever; to divide	***Pellu*, and *pellau*, to render distant.**
פנה, to turn to, to turn about.	***Penu*, to head; to come to head or end.**
פנה, a turning, a corner: the פנות, chief of the tribes of Israel: a corner stone is אבן פנחת.	***Pen*, a head, a front: an end or extremity: *penaeth*, a chief, or principal: a corner stone, *maen penaetha***
פנים, in regimen פני, the face or fore part.	***Pen*, a head: a front: an end: a fore part.**
פניאל, face of God, a place so called	***Pen-i-el*, a head or front to a spirit.**

פסח, to halt, to limp, to be lame.	*Pesychu*, to intermit; to cough.
פסח, the passover; but literally a halting at, or stopping at.	*Paswch*, and *peswch*, an intermittent effort: a cough.
פר, to break, to fracture; to cut off.	*Pori*, to graze, from *pawr*, what is grazed.
פר, a bullock: plural פרות, kine; and פרים, bulls.	*Porai*, that grazes, a grazing animal: *poreion*, grazers.
פור, a lot, destruction: plural פורים: to throw down: to break.	*Bwrw*, a cast, a throw; a woof; a tally: to cast, to throw down.
פרור, a boiling pot, or a kettle.	*Pair*, a cauldron, or a boiler.
פרד, to separate, to divide, to part off	*Paredu*, to make a partition, to partition.
פרס, a village, or open town.	*Pres* a resort: a covert: *pres y ci*, a dog-kennel.
פרך, It is rendered rigour: the Egyptians made the Israelites serve with rigour.	*Parch*, awe, respect, reverence, honour: *parchu*, to be in awe; to respect.
פרץ, to break forth, to burst, to spread abroad: a breach, a breaking forth: a destroyer: Mount Perizim.	*Preiddiaw*, to make a booty of cattle, to predate: *praidd*, a herd; a booty of cattle, to predate: *praidd*, a herd; a booty of cattle: *mynydd preiddiau*.
פריץ, one that bursts forth; a robber	*Preiddiai*, one that hunts for prey; a depredator.
פרש, to spread, stretch out, or extend	*Prwysaw*, to protrude: *presu*, to hurry
פרש, a rider, upon any animal.	*Prwysai*, one that urges or presses on.
פש, to increase, to grow big: that is great, or of weight. בפש מאר, with great extremity.	*Pwysaw*, to weigh: to press: to oppress: *pwys*, weight, pressure: *myned wrth bwys*, to go on leisurely; *peth o bwys*, a thing of moment.
פשתה, flax, the filament of the plant.	*Peisiaeth*, coating: *peiswyn*, chaff of oats.
פשע, to stride, to take a step; to march: also the stride by which we step: a step.	*Pysang* and *mysang*, a trample: *Pysangu and mysangu*, to trample.
פת, a bit, a morsel, a mouthful.	*Peth*, a thing; a small quantity, a little; some.
פת, a hinge, that part of the body on which it turns, the hip; fickle; sudden.	*Pwyth*, that runs in; a point; a turn; an angle, a stitch; a requital.
פת, to slide, to slip, or to glide.	*Pwythaw*, to thrust in; to form an angle; to stitch.
פתה, פתי, easily turned; fickle; simple.	*Pwythaidd*, having a tendency to thrust in.
פתן, it is rendered the asp, or adder.	*Python*, a period or circle of time.
פתח, to open, in a general sense; to loose; to grave, to engrave; to carve: a laying open; an engraving; a carved work: an aperture; a door.	*Peithwchu*, and *peithwgu*, to make clear or open: *peithwch*, and *peithwg*, that is open or clear; that abounds with openings, as a comb; hunting ground.
פתל, to twist, to twine together.	*Pwythyllu*, to form interstices or intertexture.
פתיל, a twist; a cord; a thread; a lace.	*Pwythell*, an interstice, an intertexture.
פתר, to open, to explain; to interpret, to expound dreams, or oracles: an opening, or expounding.	*Peithori*, to lay open, to explore. The Gauls called the priests of Apollo *pateræ*: *peitheroeu*, expounders.

צ

צד, a side; a turn; a hunt; בצדה, in the side thereof.	*Sid*, a turn; a rim; a circle; a wind, a reel.
ציד, צידה, that is aside, store, provisions; a hunting: also one that hunts.	*Sidai*, a recipient of turns or courses; one that winds about.
צדיה, a laying by, or in wait, a sculk	*Sidiaw*, to wind about: a winding about.
צדק, exact, righteous; just: righteousness: to render exact, to justify	*Sodig*, that is fixed or constituted: *sodigaw*, to render fixed or exact.
צדקה, exactness, righteousness, justice.	*Sodica*, that is fixed or implanted.
צדיק, one that is exact or just; a just man; one that can justify.	*Sodawg*, that is implanted or exact; one that is fixed or exact.
צח, to be dried up; to desiccate: such a hue as a dry wind gives: pale, white.	*Sychu*, to dry; to be dried, to desiccate; to wipe: *hin sych*, dry weather.
צח, dry; white, pale: a dry wind.	*Sych*, dry, parched: *syched*, thirst, drought.
צחצח, a drought: that is dry, dry.	*Sych-sych*, drought upon drought.
צחק, to laugh, to deride; to sport.	*Swchoca*, to make mouths, to grimace
צין, ציון, a title; a way-mark; a sign	*Senw*, a mark, sign, or stigma.
צל, צלל, a shadow: shelter: צלמות, shadow of death: the plural of צלם, an image, is צלמות.	*Sel*, a distant sight or glance: *selw*, a gaze, a beholding, a view: *selw meth*, a sight of annihilation.
צום, to be empty; to fast: צום יום, fasted a fast: צמים, robbers.	*Somi*, to produce emptiness; to balk, to disappoint.
צום, the being empty: a fasting.	*Som*, a vacuity, or a void; a balk.
צמא, to hunger; to thirst: emptiness, thirst, or hunger.	*Soma*, to gather emptiness: emptiness, a void state.
צמת, to bring to nothing; to vanish, to waste, to consume.	*Somaethu*, to produce emptiness, or a void state.
צעד, to step, to go along; to march.	*Sangu*, *sangadu*, to step; to trample.
צעד, צעדה, מצעד, a stepping; a march, a treading, a pacing.	*Sangad*, *sangiada*, *ymsangiad*, *mysangiad*, a treading, a trampling.
צעה, a throwing down, or prostrating; a travelling.	*Sangu*, to trample, to tread upon.
צעצע, tread to tread; he made two cherubims of צעצע, mutual movement.	*Sang-sang*, tread to tread, of mutual tread, or stepping together.
צר, to vex, to afflict, to straiten, to press together; to bind up.	*Sarhu*, to throw off; to abuse; to insult, to offend; to injure.
צר, צרר, צורר, צרור, that afflicts, that oppresses, an enemy: vexed: straitened, close, narrow, bound up.	*Sar*, that is on or along; that is apt to cast down; fury, rage; insolence: offence: disgrace, reproach
צר, some cutting tool; a knife: a flint	*Ser*, that tends to enclose; a bill, or bill-hook.

ק

קבל, to receive, to accept, to obtain.	*Cafael*, to get, to obtain, to have.
קבל, an engine of war; a grapple.	*Gafael*, a hold, a gripe, a grapple.
קב, to hollow out; to dent, to pierce	*Cibaw*, to form a vessel, shell, or pod
קב, a vessel of measure, as is supposed; a cob.	*Cib*, a vessel; a shell, a pod: *cibyn*, a peck measure.
קבה, the maw; the belly, or paunch.	*Cwb*, a concavity; a cote, or kennel; a hut.

קד, to bend or bow down the head.	*Cwyddaw*, to fall, to lapse; to tumble
קו, קוה, a line, a string, a cord.	*Caw*, a bine, a bind, a tie, a band, a bandage.
קל, to abate: to see if the waters חקלו, were abated; lightness, vileness; despised, vile.	*Ciliaw*, to retreat; to retire; to chase, to drive away: *cil*, a recess; a flight, a retreat.
קלט, to contract, to shrink.	*Caledu*, to harden; to grow hard or dense.
קלע, to sling; a sling; what is slung, also a slinger: a hanging.	*Gollwng*, to let go; to loosen: a departing point; a loosening.
קם, קום, what is raised or set up; a rising up; a statue: an image; also one that rises up, an insurgent; to raise up; to arise; to stand up, to fix.	*Cwm*, a rounding together; a hollow, by the rising of the sides: the sides of hills forming a dingle; a deep valley: *cwman*, a buttock; a hive.
קן, קנה, a reed; a cane; a pipe; a stalk.	*Cawn*, what is empty; cawns, reed-grass.
קן, קנה, to get, to acquire, to obtain; to purchase.	*Caun*, to have in possession or with: to be with.
קנה, קנן, to lament, or to bewail.	*Cwynaw*, *cwynain*, to complain, to lament.
קנה, קנת, one who acquires or gets; a buyer.	*Canai*, a recipient of possession.
קינה, lamentation, or complaining.	*Cwyna*, a reiteration of complaint.
קנא, zeal: envy, jealousy: one that is zealous; an envious one.	*Ceina*, a glancing cautiously: *ceiniaw ni lwydd*, it is useless to pry.
קנוא, one full of zeal; a jealous one.	*Ceinai*, one that looks suspiciously.
קיר, קריה, in regimen קרית, plural קריות, a wall: בקיר החומה, on the battlement of the wall.	*Caer*, a wall or mound; a fortified camp; a fort, a fortress; *caer sidi*, the ecliptic.
קרן, to shoot forth, to cast rays or horns; to have horns.	*Corni*, to be formed as a horn; to have a horn.
קרן, a horn; a ray, or beam; a shoot	*Corn*, any pointed projection; a horn; a roll.
קש, stubble, bits of straw, or any refuse	*Cws*, *cwswr*, refuse of corn and straw
קשה, to be rigid, hard, or stiff; to be cruel; to harden.	*Casau*, to be severe; to be at enmity, to hate.
קשי, rigidity, stiffness, stubbornness.	*Casi*, hatred; envy: *cesair*, hard snow, hail.
קשת, a bow, for shooting with.	*Cisaeth*, that is by the effect of a touch or twang.

ר

ראה, to look; to see, to perceive.	*Rheiaw*, to ray, to gleam, to radiate.
ראי, the look; a gazing-stock; מראה, mirror.	*Rhai*, a ray, a glance, or a gleam: *rheiaeth*, radiation.
ראש, the head; a chief; a point; priority: principal, head, chief.	*Rhys*, a start, effort: a beginning. *Pen Rhys*, in Wales, and Start Point, in England, are synonymous names.
ראש, to sum up: a sum total; account.	*Rhesu*, to place in a rank, or row: *rhes*, a row, a rank.
ראשית, the chief or first; a beginning.	*Rhysaeth*, the act of putting on a start.
רב, to strive, to contend; to make words.	*Rhaibiaw*, to snatch violently, to clutch.

רב, ריב, strife, contention, quarrel.	*Rhaib*, greed, voracity: a snatch, or clutch.
רבה, to increase; to multiply; to grow large.	*Rhyfu*, to enlarge, to swell out, to puff.
רב, that is large or big: great, large: much; enough.	*Rhyf*, that enlarges or swells out; a puff; pride: *rhyf*, *rhy*, too much, excess, extreme.
רב, רוב, multitude; greatness.	*Rhyf*, the state of being beyond or over: excess.
רבץ, to lie or squat down; to repose.	*Rhybwysaw*, to over-press, to preponderate.
רבץ, a reposing, a squatting down.	*Rhybwys*, over-pressure, preponderance.
רגל, to foot, to trace by the foot.	*Rhuglaw*, to move on briskly: to clear away.
רגל, a foot, a limb to move with.	*Rhugl*, that is of free motion; quick, ready.
רגן, to murmur, to mutter.	*Rhegain*, to make a murmur: to creak.
רגע, to be at ease, to settle, to rest; to pause.	*Rhygyngu*, to go leisurely, to amble.
רגע, a being easy; a pause; ease.	*Rhygyng*, an easy or ambling pace.
רדה, רד, to go down, to submit; to subdue, to have dominion.	*Rheidiaw*, to necessitate; to need, to render needful.
רדה, רד, a being down; submission: down.	*Rhaid*, need, necessity; that is unavoidable.
רוח, רח, wind; breath, breathing; spirit.	*Rhoch*, a forcible or rough utterance; a grunt.
רח, to blow; to breathe, to take breath: to wind.	*Rhochi*, to breathe forcibly: to grunt.
רח, to triturate, to grind: a mill.	*Rhwgu*, to triturate; to rub: *rhwg*, a rub.
רחת, something to fan with for blowing off chaff.	*Rhochad*, a blower, that blows roughly
רווחה, a breathing, or a blowing.	*Rhocha*, a making a rough noise: a grunting.
רוח, to wind; to smell; to stink.	*Rhechu*, to break wind forcibly; to fart.
רם, to raise, to lift up, to exalt; to be high.	*Rhamu*, to rise over; to soar; to vault.
רם, רום, high, exalted: height; exaltation; haughtiness.	*Rham*, exalted, soaring; a rise over; a reach over.
רמת, exaltation: praise, eulogy.	*Rhamaeth*, the state of being over or above.
רמה, to cast, to fling; to throw out; to report.	*Rhemiaw*, to run or thrust out, to puff out.
רע, רעה, noise, din, or clatter.	*Rhinc*, a continued sharp noise; a creak.
רעה, to be with, to accompany; to manage, to feed: a companion; a friend; a mate.	*Rhangu*, to accommodate; to render replete; to satiate: *rhang*, accommodation.
רע, רעה, רוע, a companion; a mate; also another: a shepherd; attendance; pasture.	*Rhangai*, one that fulfils or satisfies; one that renders conducive.
רץ, to run; to break, to crumble, to bruise.	*Rhedu*, to run, to perform a course, to race.
רץ, one that runs; a post; a soldier; what is made to run.	*Rhedai*, one that runs; one that produces a running.

רצה, to delight, to be pleased, to enjoy.	***Rhwyddaw***, to make easy; to become free.
רצון, רצן, delight; will, pleasure; acceptance.	***Rhwyddon***, a facilitating faculty.
רצד, to leap, to bound, or to jump.	***Rhuthadu***, to make a burst; to burst away.
רש, to drive out: to inherit: to succeed.	***Rhusaw***, to cause to start; to start; to hesitate.
רש, poor: ריש, poverty: רישון, driven out, expelled.	***Rhus***, that is started or driven out; also a fox.
רשע, to vex: to worst; to wrong: to be wrong.	***Rhysangu***, to over tread, to over trample.
רשע, worsting: vexing: wrong, injury.	***Rhysang***, an over-tread, an over-trample.

ש

שאל, שאול, the lowest state; the grave; a pit.	***Sail***, a base, a ground-work; a foundation.
שאון, משאון, noise; ostentation; pomp.	***Son***, ***ymson***, noise, report, rumour.
שאר, to remain, to be left as a residue.	***Sarau***, to throw off; to injure; to insult.
שאר, שארית, remainder, remnant.	***Sar***, ***saraeth***, a throw off; fury, insult.
שאר, שארית, ferment, leaven.	***Sur***, an acid; ***suraeth***, sourness: acid sour.
שב, שבב, to turn; to turn to and fro; to change: a turn, a change, return.	***Swbiaw***, ***sybwbiaw***, to pile or bundle together, to toss about: ***sybwb***, a rumple.
שבת, to cease, to stop, to desist, to rest.	***Seibiaw***, ***seibaethu***, to take respite, to rest.
שבת, שבתון, cessation, rest, leisure.	***Seibiaeth***, respite, leisure, rest.
שד, שדד, to harrass, to spoil, to dissipate.	***Swydaw***, to awe, to intimidate, to scare.
שד, שדד, שוד, שודד, a harrasser, a spoiler.	***Swydai***, that is a cause of intimidation.
שדי, that causes to be set forth; a maintainer, or establisher; the all-bountiful.	***Swyddai***, that has jurisdiction or office, that has service.
שדים, heathen gods, or idols: that is, heavenly bodies.	***Sidydd***, the tropics: ***sidoedd***, revolvings; and ***sidion***, revolving bodies.
השדים, a vale where now the dead sea is: if not so called from a temple to the stars of heaven, it might be from its immersion.	***Soddion***, immersions, or sinkings. If so named from a temple, the Welsh word ***sidion*** would be descriptive of it.
שד, to plaister; to bedaub; to lime.	***Suddaw***, to pervade; to moisten.
שיד, lime, burnt stone; plaister.	***Sudd***, what pervades; moisture; juice.
שט, שטה, to turn or go aside, to run aside.	***Swta***, to be volatile or sudden; to fly about.
שטן, to stand up against; an adversary: Satan.	***Swydan***, one that intimidates or scares.
של, שלל, to shed; to put off, to pull off.	***Siliaw***, to yield; to spawn; to hull grain.
שלה, to be easy, quiet, or inactive.	***Swlau***, to become flat or prone; to make flat.
שלו, שלי, שלם, tranquillity, ease, quiet.	***Swla***, the being flat, prone, or grounded.

שמט, to throw off: to dismiss, to cast out of the hand; to release. — *Symudaw*, to move, to stir, to remove; to displace.

שמטה, a throwing off; a discarding; a release. — *Symud*, motion, move, stir, or removal.

שמן, to fatten, to become fat; to make fat. — *Seimiaw*, *seimiaw*, to grease, to become greasy.

שמן, fat; rich juice; oil; ointment. — *Saim*, *seimiant*, grease, oily fat.

שנה, to hate, to dislike, to reject, to disapprove. — *Sanu*, to taunt, to scoff; to chide; to reproach.

שק, a sack, a bag, or pouch. — *Sach*, a sack, or a bag: *sachaid*, a sackful.

שקל, to weigh, or to balance. — *Siglaw*, to vibrate as a balance: to shake, to rock.

שקל, weight: a coin so called: a weigher: and thus—משקלת is a plummet. — *Sigl*, vibration; a shake, a stir; a rocking: *sigleath*, vibration.

שר, שרר, to regulate or order the voice; to sing: and שירה שיר, a song. — *Saer*, a wright, or mason: it is curious that the Welsh word *cerdd* is also a craft, and a song.

שרף, a burning; also a serpent. — *Sarff*, a serpent, or a dragon.

שרק, to hiss; to whistle, to blow. — *Sarugaw*, to be stern, surly, or austere.

שת, to set, to put; to beset; to appoint: also that is set or put. — *Sythu*, to stiffen, to make rigid or erect; to become stiff, rigid, or erect.

שת, a foundation; the buttocks. — *Sedd*, a sedate or still state; a seat.

שתי, the fixed threads in weaving; the warp. — *Sythi*, straight or stiff things, upshots.

ת

תכן, to fix the proportion or quantity of a thing: to establish. — *Dogni*, to settle a quantity, to proportion: to fix an allowance.

תכן, a settled quantity or proportion: a sum or tale, a total. — *Dogn*, a settled quantity, share, or proportion: sufficiency.

תלה, to hang up, or to suspend. — *Telu*, to put on a stretch, to strain.

תל, a heap, a pile, a mass. — *Twl*, what is rounded, also a tuft.

תלי, a quiver for holding arrows. — *Telai*, that is strained; that is suspended.

תר, to turn or go about, as a person turns to look about him. — *Troi*, to turn, to wind, to wheel, to circulate.

תר, one who pries about, a traverser. — *Tresi*, one that is made to turn or wind.

תר, a turn, order, or round: a prying — *Tro*, a turn, a round; a twist.

תר, תור, a turtle dove, from its wheeling in flight. — *Tur*, a turn, or reverse; an overturn

תם, תום, a whole: integrity: entirely. — *Twm*, a bend, a turn, a form; a round heap.

Examples of Greek and Welsh Affinities.

There are in the Welsh several characteristics, which discover it to have a greater affinity than any other language of Europe with the Greek; and, among the most prominent of those characteristics are the following.

The Welsh and the Greek agree in containing about an equal number of vowels and consonants; that is, upon an average, there are in each a hundred vowels to every hundred consonants. The language that approaches nearest to the like proportion is the Italian, the average of vowels wherein is eighty-eight to every hundred consonants; then follow in order, the Latin, the Spanish, the French, and the English.*

There is a great variety of qualifying prefixes in both the Greek and the Welsh, but in the latter tongue more particularly; for, enumerating such as are simple and compound together, it contains upwards of two hundred and fifty, and which are of universal application to all classes of words.

A considerable identity exists in respect to the conjugation of the verbs of the two languages, but more especially in each having reflective verbs, or those denominated of the middle voice; yet with this difference, that, in the Welsh, the qualifying agent is prefixed to the root of the verb, and in the Greek inserted between the root and the various terminations. Thus *ymdwywyf* is, in the Welsh, I regulate myself, and *τίομαι*, in Greek, is I honour myself: and the root of the former is *twy*, and of the latter *τί* is the, root.

The two languages are so alike in the general sound of their words, that the first impression upon strangers, from hearing the service of the church read in Welsh, is of its being the Greek which they hear.

The primitive words of the Welsh language are capable of being compounded almost infinitely, and generally upon similar principles to those of the Greek, so celebrated for this convenient quality. Thus Βοῶπις, the Homeric epithet for the queen of heaven, might be expressed in the Welsh with equal elegance, by these words—*buolwg, bulygad, budrem, budremant, budremiant* and *budremynt*; or, in a plural form thus—*buolygon, bulygaid, bylygadon, budremion, budremeinnion, budremiannion*, and *budremynnion*. This epithet of Βοῶπις discovers the poverty and inelegance of the French translation, wherein it is rendered *Junon aux yeux de bœuf*, which is scarcely better than *beef-eyed Juno;* but, in the Welsh, *Juno lygad-eidion* is not quite so bad.

Again, βυκολος, a cow-keeper, has, in the Welsh, the very ancient equivalent term of *Bygeilydd*; and from which we might use the name of *Bugeileg*, or the speech of the herdsman, for the *Bucolics* of the poets.

Independently of the above mentioned analogies, we discover in both languages a large stock of primitive words, agreeing in sound and meaning, as is exemplified in the subjoined vocabulary.

A

Ἄγγος, ἀγγεῖον, a vessel: αγγεια, Matt. xiv. 4—8.	*Angad, angen, angeian: angeiau*—a receptacle.
Ἀγκαὶ, αγκαλαι, the arms.	*Angeieu, angellau*, a fore leg, a pinion; an arm.
Ἄγκυρα, an anchor.	*Angor*, a bearing round; an anchor.
Ἀδεω, to please, to delight, to content	*Hoddiaw*, to render easy: to become easy.
Ἀεί, always, ever, continually.	*Au*, a continuity of motion: the liver

* I have not made out the average in any of the Teutonic dialects, excepting the Dutch, which has a less proportion of vowels than the English.

'Αερ, air, the element to breath in.	*Awyr*, sky; air; the firmament.
'Αηρος, vehement, eager, or earnest.	*Aethus*, pungent, acrid; grievous.
Αἰγιαλος, the shore, or the sea coast.	*Aigial*, the bound or limit of the sea.
Ἀιδης, ἅδης, hell: πῦ σν, ἅδη τὸ νυκος.	*Had*, seed; the bardic hell: *py tau, had, dy nychad?*
Αἴθω, to burn, to consume by fire.	*Aethu*, to be pungent; to smart; *godddeithiaw*, to burn.
Αικάλλω, a fawn, a young deer.	*Eigell*, a teeming or bearing animal.
Αἴξ, a she goat.	*Ewig*, the she of deer, or a hind.
Αἴω, to hear, to perceive by the ear.	*Oiaw*, to hear; to hearken, or to listen.
Αιών, αιῶνος, an age, life.	*Einioes*, life, or the duration of life.
'Ακτή, the shore, or the sea-coast.	*Aigdde*, a shoaling spread; the sea shore.
'Αλείφω, to anoint, to rub with oil.	*Eliaw*, to anoint, to rub with salve.
'Αλίσκω, to take, to seize, or to catch	*Hylusgaw*, to drag, to trail along.
'Αλίω, to roll, or to turn about.	*Oliaw*, to track, to leave a trace.
'Αλλοίω, to change, or to alter.	*Alleiaw*, *allu*, to alternate, to alter.
'Αλς, salt.	*Hal*, *halen*, *heli*, *hallt*, salt, brine.
'Αλύω, to pine, or to languish.	*Aelu*, *alaethu*, to grieve, to pine.
'Αμφι, about, in a circle, around.	*Am*, about, round; for concerning.
'Ανία, sadness, dejection.	*Annwyf*, ENNUI, want of vivacity.
'Ανώγω, to instigate, to spur; to command.	*Annogi*, to incite, to instigate; to exhort.
'Αρα', prayers; vows, or promises.	*Ar*, the faculty of speech: *area*, speeches.
Ἄρης, a title of Mars.	*Aerwas*, a youth of slaughter: a hero
Ἄρκτος, a bear, the animal so called.	*Arth*, a bear: *arthes*, a she-bear.
'Αροτῆς, a plougher, a ploughman.	*Aradawr*, a plougher: *arader*, a ploughman.
'Αρόω, to plough, or to till.	*Aru*, to plough, to till: *aru tir*, to till
'Αρτύω, to dress, to deck, to adorn.	*Ardwyaw*, to keep in trim, to keep in check.
Ασπις, a shield, or buckler.	*Aes*, a flat; a shield: *aesbaith*, a flat surface.
'Αυλή, an area; a hall, a court.	*Gal*, a clear space; *dyna dy al*, there is thy station.
Αὐλος, a pipe, or flute: αὐλα, pipes.	*Awelai*, any wind instrument.
Αυχέω, to vaunt, to boast, to brag.	*Awchiaw*, to be ardent; to sharpen.
'Αχλὺς, darkness, or obscurity.	*Achlud*, covert, concealment; darkness.
Αχλύω, to grow dark, to darken.	*Achludaw*, to cover with darkness; to conceal.

B

Βαίνω, to ascend, to mount up.	*Banu*, to elevate, to go to the top.
Βάθος, deepness, profundity, depth.	*Bawdd*, an immersion, a drowning.
Βαιος, little; small, diminutive.	*Bach*, little, small, tiny, or minute.
Βάλανος, an acorn; a bolt; a clasp.	*Balant*, a shoot, a spray; a bud.
Βάλλω, to throw, to dart, to fling.	*Balu*, to throw out, to eject; to shoot
Βήξ, a cough.	*Pas*, *peswch*, that is expulsive; a cough.
Βίος, life: age, or duration of life.	*Byw*, *bywyd*, life, duration of life.
Βιὸς, a bow, for shooting with.	*Bwa*, a bow; an arch: *bwa cyfammod*, bow of covenant, rainbow.
Βόμβος, a buzz, a humming.	*Bwmbwr*, a hollow noise, a murmur.

Βορα, food, nourishment.	*Bara*, bread; food: *bara miod*, fritters.
Βυλὴ, counsel, or advice.	*Pwyll*, *pwylla*, impulse; reason, sense, wit.
Βυλέυω, to deliberate, to counsel.	*Pwyllaw*, to clear a way; to deliberate
Βϋνὸσ, a hill, an ascent, or rise.	*Ban*, *bant*, *banad*, a height, an ascent.
Βϋυτ, an ox, kine, or cow; cattle.	*Bu*, *biw*, *buch*, *buwch*, an ox, or kine, a cow.
Βόσκω, to graze, to feed.	*Pesgi*, to feed, to fatten, to grow fat.
Βραδὺς, dull, heavy, dejected.	*Bradw*, fretting away, diminishing.
Βραχίων, an arm; force, or strength.	*Braich*, *breichiawn*, an arm; strength of arm.
Βραχιόνιον, a bracelet, or armlet.	*Breichionen*, *breichienyn*, a bracelet.
Βράχω, to resound, to bruit; to brake	*Brochi*, to wax fierce, to bluster, to chafe.
Βρύχω, to bite, to gnash the teeth; to shiver.	*Brwchu*, to make a stir, or tumult.
Βρύω, βρυσω, to bud, to sprout.	*Bruaw*, *brwysaw*, to generate; to flourish.
Βρῶμος, a stink, a bad smell.	*Brem*, *bremiad*, a breaking wind.
Βρωμέω, to stink, to smell offensively.	*Bramu*, *bremiaw*, *bremian*, to break wind.
Βρωμώδης, stinking, of ill scent.	*Bremiadus*, apt to break wind.
Βρώσκω, to eat; to browse, to graze.	*Brwysgaw*, to grow heavy, or unwieldy; to get drunk.
Βυκάνη, a trumpet.	*Bugunai*, that makes a bellowing.
Βῶλος, βῶλαξ, a lump, a clod.	*Bwl*, *bwlog*, rotundity; a round hollow body.

Γ

Γαίω, to boast, to vaunt, or to brag.	*Gawa*, *gewa*, to stretch, or extend out.
Γάλα, γαλαξ, γαλακτος, milk.	*Gal*, what is fair; milk: *galaeth*, the galaxy.
Γένεσις, Genesis, generation.	*Genidas*, the act or state of bringing forth.
Γένος, kind, race or generation.	*Genad*, *genadaeth*, a generating; a being born.
Γένυς, the chin, the mandible.	*Cen*, the chin: *car gen*, the jaw bone.
Γέρανος, a crane, the bird so called.	*Garan*, a crane, the bird so called.
Γέρων, an old man, an old fellow.	*Geryn*, a querulous, or grumbling one.
Γλαφω, to carve, to engrave, to grave.	*Gleifiaw*, to blade, to use a blade.
Γλήνη, the apple of the eye, or pupil; the eye.	*Glain*, *gleinai*, what is pure; a gem; the pupil.
Γλῶσσα, γλωττα, the tongue.	*Glwth*, *glytha*, a couch, from its form; a voluptuary.
Γνάθος, the mouth, the jaw, or chops.	*Gnawth*, *gnythawd*, voracity: *gnythai*, a devourer.
Γοάω, a sigh, a wail, a weeping.	*Gwae*, woe; a wail, a moan; grief; a curse.
Γόης, a cheat, trickster, or deceiver.	*Geuus*, *geuawg*, that is false or lying.
Γραῖα, an old woman, or a hag.	*Gerai*, *gwrach*, a querulous one, a hag.
Γράφω, to engrave, to grave, to write.	*Creifiaw*, to notch: *crafu*, to scratch.
Γύνη, γυναιξ, a woman, a female.	*Genai*, *genog*, that generates; *geneth*, a girl.

Δ

Δαὴρ, a brother-in-law, a step-brother.	***Daw**, **dawawr**, a boon; a son-in-law.*
Δάκνω, to bite, to separate with the teeth.	***Dogni**, to divide into morsels: **dygnoi**, to bite.*
Δακρυ, a tear: μετα δακρύον, with tears.	***Dagr**, **deigr**, **deigryn**, a tear: **cyda dagrion**, with tears: **meddu deigrion**, having tears.*
Δαμάω, to tame, to make gentle.	***Dofâu**, **dofi**, to tame, to grow tame.*
Δάνος, a gift: interest; usury, gain.	***Dawn**, **doniad**, a gift, or talent.*
Δεκα, ten: δέκατος, tenth.	***Deg**, ten: **degfed**, **degaid**, tenth.*
Δέρκω, to see, to look, or to behold.	***Drychu**, to make manifest; to give a look.*
Δέργμα, a look, aspect, or appearance.	***Drychfa**, **drychiad**, **drychiant**, appearance.*
Δηλέω, to deceive, to impose upon.	***Twyllaw**, to deceive, to cheat, to mislead.*
Δηρις, quarrel, strife, debate, brawl.	***Deriad**, a bickering, or a brawling.*
Διδάσκω, to teach: διδασκε, teach thou.	***Dysgu**, **dyddysgu**, to teach: **dyddysga**, do thou teach.*
Δόλος, deceit, treachery, artifice.	***Twyll**, **twyllad**, deceit, cheating, fraud.*
Δολόω, to deceive, to mislead, to cheat.	***Twyllaw**, to deceive, to cheat, to mislead.*
Δονέω, δονεύω, to shake, or to move.	***Twynaw**, to move, or wave about; to nod.*
Δοῦλος, a slave, a servant.	***Dylai**, **dylad**, that is owned or possessed.*
Δράσσω, to snatch, to lay hold.	***Treisiaw**, to do violence; to ravish.*
Δρῦς, δρυός, an oak; the oak.	***Dar**, **derw**, **derwen**, an oak; the oak.*
Δυω, two: δύο ουαι, two woes.	***Dau**, two, masculine: **dwy**, two, feminine: **dwy wae**, two woes.*
Δοω, to give: δο εμι, I give.	***Dodi**, to give, to place: **dodwyf**, I give.*
Δωρεω, to present: δῶρον, a gift.	***Dyroi**, to give, to present, to bestow.*

E

Ἔαρ, ηρ, the spring, the vernal season.	***Ir**, that is verdant; verdant, green, juicy.*
Ἐαρίζω, to send the spring season.	***Ireiddiaw**, **ireiniaw**, to render juicy, or green.*
Εγγὺς, near, contiguous, or close.	***Wng**, **yngus**, near, contiguous, or close*
Ἐγγίζω, to approach, to approximate.	***Yngu** **yngiadu**, **ynguseaw**, to become near, to near.*
Εδω, to eat, to take food, to feed.	***Eidiaw**, to enliven: **ysu**, to consume.*
Επω: ειπον: ειπε μοι, he said to me.	***Ebu**, to say: **ebwn**: **ebai imi**, said he to me.*
Εχ, from, or out of, and of.	***Ach**, off; near; by: **ach ei law**, by his hand.*
Εἰλυω, to cover, or to envelope.	***Huliaw**, to cover, or to envelope.*
Ἐμοὶ, for me, or to me.	***Imi**, to me, or for me.*
Εν, in: ἐν ἀγορᾷ in the market.	***Yn**, in: **yn agorfa**, in an open place.*
Ενθα, adverb, there, on that side.	***Yna**, there, or in that place.*
Ετι, as yet, yet: ἔρχονται ετι δύο ουαι.	***Eto**, yet, again: **erchwyna eto ddwy wae**, two woes are yet to come.*

H

῞Η, or: ἢ ειπεῖν, Ἔγειρα, or to say, arise. — *Ai*: *ai ebian*, *agora*, or to say, open.

Ἡ῀, a pronoun: ηῖ ὄνομα, her name. — *Ei*, his, her, its: *ei henw*, her name.

῞Ηλιος, and anciently, ἥλ, the sun. — *Haul*, the sun; also called *huan*.

Ἡνία, a bridle, or a head-stall. — *Hoenai*, *hwynai*, *hoenen*, *hwynyn*, a thong.

Ἠρέμος, soft, peaceable, or tranquil. — *Araf*, *arafaidd*, *arafus*, slow, soft, gentle.

Ἠρεμέω, to rest; to appease, to tranquillize. — *Arafu*, *arafeiddiaw*, *arafusaw*, to appease.

Ἡσυχοσ, ἡσυχαῖος, ease, quietude. — *Heddwch*, *heddychiad*, *hedd*, peace, tranquility.

Ἡσυχία, peace, rest, or quietude. — *Heddychiad*, an appeasing or quieting.

Ἡσυχάζω, to be at rest, to be quiet. — *Heddychusaw*, *heddychiadu*, to become at ease.

῏Ηχος, ἠχώ, sound, noise, or din. — *Aich*, *eichiad*, a loud noise; a scream, a roar.

Ἠως, ἠως, aurora, the dawn, the day-spring. — *Eaws*, *eosig*, the nightingale.

Θ

Θέμηλον, θεμέλιον, a base, or foundation. — *Teml*, *temlon*, a spread, or expanse: a seat.

Θεὸς, God, the supreme being, deity. — *Duw*, that is beyond darkness; God

Θέρω, to warm, to heat moderately. — *Twyraw*, to agitate; to parch; to heat.

Θηλὴ, the nipple, a teat, or a dug. — *Telai*, that is strained, or stretched out.

Θὴρ, θηρίον, a wild beast. — *Ter*, *terydd*, *teryn*, a furious state; that is vehement.

Θις, a bunch, a heap, a cluster. — *Twys*, a bunch; an ear of corn.

Θην, a rampart, or a wall. — *Din*, *dinas*, an intrenchment, a fort; a city.

Θολὸς, filth, dirt; mud, or mire. — *Tail*, dung, manure, soil, muck.

Θόρυβος, tumult, noise, stir, bustle. — *Twrf*, tumult, din, noise, bustle, stir.

Θορυβεω, to make a noise, to shout. — *Twrfu*, to make a tumult, or uproar.

Θράυω, to break, or to fracture. — *Trafu*, to stir; to scour: *tori*, to break.

Θρώσω, θρώχω, to jump, or to leap. — *Trosi*, *tracku*, to convey over, or beyond.

Θύελλα, a storm, or a tempest. — *Tywyllai*, that produces gloom or darkness.

Θύρα, a door, a gate, or opening. — *Trwy*, *trwya*, a passage, or a pass.

Θῶ, θάω, to nourish, to nurse. — *Toi*, to cover over, to cover in; to roof.

Θῶ, θέω, to run: to fine; to do. — *Twya*, *twyaw*, to put in order or form; to order.

I

Ἰάχω, to bawl out, to make a noise. — *Eichiaw*, to make a loud din; to scream.

῎Ιδιος, own, proper, one's own, peculiar. — *Eiddaw*, *eiddo*, one's own: *eiddof*, mine; *eiddot*, thine.

῏Ις, ινοσ, a sinew; a fibre; strength. — *Gi*, *gien*, a fine fibre or string; a nerve.

Ιστωρ, ιστορια, learning; knowledge. — *Ystyr, ystyriad*, meaning; consideration.

Ινα, preposition: *ἵνα ῥυσθῶ ἀπὸ*, that I may be delivered from. Rom. xv. 31. — *Hyna*, that: *hyna y rhyddwyf heibio*, that I be loosened past, or from.

K

Καθαιρω, to purge, or to cleanse out. — *Cothi, cothori*, to cast out, or to eject

Καινος, new, recent, or fresh. — *Cain*, that is clear, bright, or fair.

Καινω, to kill, to deprive of life. — *Ceintiaw, ceinniaw, ceintach*, to bicker

Καινις, slaughter, or a killing. — *Ceinta, ceintach*, a conflict, or a scuffle.

Καλαμος, reed, cane, or straw. — *Calaf*, reed; stalk or straw of corn.

Καλεω, to call, to implore, to crave. — *Galw*, to call; to name; to summons

Καλυπτω, to conceal, or to hide. — *Celu, celiadu*, to conceal, or to hide.

Καμηλος, a camel, a dromedary. — *Camell*, a curving or bending animal.

Καμπτω, to bend, to curve. — *Camu, camiadu*, to bend, or to curve.

Καρδια, κραδια, the heart. — *Craidd*, the centre, or middle part.

Καρηνον, κρανον, κρανιον, the head; a skull. — *Corun, corunon*, the crown of the head; a summit.

Κατα, by, of, according to; against: *κατα σῷ*, with thee, *κατα σῇ*, with thy: *καταγγέλλω*, I declare: *ὃν καταγγέλλομεν*, whom we preach. Col. i. 28. — *Cyda*, along with, with; *cyda thi*, with thee, *cyda dy*, with thy: *cydanghelwyf*, I bring out of concealment: *hwn cydanghelwn*, him we declare.

Καύχησις, boasting: *ποῦ οὖν ἡ καύχησις* — *Coegedd*, vaunting, boasting: *py yna y coegedd?*

Κελλω, to land safely, to get ashore. — *Cellu*, to make a lodgement, or recess

Κέρκος, a tail, or hinder part. — *Cwrcwd*, a squat; the posterior; a cowering.

Κεύθω, to hide, to conceal, to cover. — *Cuddiaw*, to hide, to secrete, to conceal.

Κεῦθος, κεύθεος, a lurking-place. — *Cudd, cudded*, a hide, a secret place.

Κεω, to cleave, to rend, or to rift. — *Cenaw*, to make hollow: to penetrate

Κηρὸς, wax: *ὁ κηρὸς*, the wax. — *Cwyr*, wax: *y cwyr*, the wax.

Κιβωτὸς, a coffer, a chest; an ark. — *Cib, cibawd*, any vessel; a measure.

Κίρκος, a circle, or a round. — *Cyrch*, a round place; a resort; a meeting.

Κισσα, disgust, nausea; a magpie. — *Cas, casedd*, odious; hate, loathing.

Κισσάω, to have a disgust, or hate. — *Casau*, to hate; to become disgustful

Κλειω, to shut up, to close in, to enclose. — *Cloi*, to lock: to fasten with a lock; to enclose.

Κλεις, a key; also a bolt, or bar. — *Clo*, a knob, or boss; a lock; a close

Κλίνω, to incline, to bend, to lean, to decline: *κλίνησαν*, they prostrated themselves. — *Cleiniaw*, to lie prostrate: *cleiniasant*, they have prostrated themselves.

Κλισια, κλισία, a tent. — *Clydai*, that gives shelter, that covers

Κλύω, to hear; to understand, to apprehend. — *Clywu, clywed*, to hear; to have perception.

Κλυτὸς, famous, or renowned. — *Clodus*, renowned: praiseworthy.

Κνάω, κνεω, κναιω, to gnaw; to vex. — *Cnoi, cnawu*, to gnaw, to bite: to vex

Κοιλία, the belly, the stomach. — *Cylla*, the separating organ, the stomach.

Κολλώμενος, a joining, or tying together. — *Cylymyniad*, connection, a tying together.

Κολεω, to cut off, or to sever apart. — *Cwllu*, to cut, to separate to sever.

Κολωνὸς, a hill, a mount, a bank.	*Col, colyn;* a round point; a pivot; a sting.
Κόχλω, to turn, or to wind about.	*Cwchlu, cylchu,* to circle; to round; to hoop,
Κυκλος, a circle, a cycle, a round.	*Cylch,* a circle, a round; a hoop.
Κραίνω, κραιαίνω, to perfect, to finish.	*Cywreiniaw,* to make accurate, to perfect.
Κρέκω, κρεξω, to sound, or to report.	*Creciaw, crechu,* to creak; to scream
Κρημνὸς, a precipice, a steep place.	*Crim, crimell,* crimen, a ridge, a ledge
Κρήνη, a spring, or fountain: also κρουνὸς.	*Cronei,* that collects, or generates.
Κρίζω, κρίξω, κρίχα, to make a sharp noise, or cry.	*Cregu, crecu, crechu, crechian,* to creak, to squeal.
Κρινον, κριναν, the lily.	*Crinon, crinen, crinlys,* the violet.
Κρίνα, the poor, or necessitous ones.	*Crinion,* brittle or dried ones; hunks, misers.
Κρῖνον, a kind of dance.	*Cronen,* that forms a round or circle.
Κρίνω, to choose, to judge, to decide.	*Crynöi,* to gather or put together.
Κρούω, to beat, to strike, or to bang.	*Curaw,* to beat, to strike, to throb.
Κυλλος, maimed, lame, or halt.	*Call, callus,* that is divergent: *troed-gall,* club-footed.
Κῦμα, a wave, or a billow at sea.	*Cwmai,* that rises to form a hollow.
Κύμβοσ, a concavity, or hollowness.	*Cwm, cwman,* a sinking in; a kive, a rump.
Κυμβη, a boat, or a small vessel.	*Cafn,* a trough; a boat; a ferry-boat
Κύτοσ, a cavity, or a hollow place.	*Cwt, cut,* a hovel, a shed, a sty.
Κύω, κυέω, to carry, also to kiss.	*Cuaw,* to fondle: cu, a cleaving to.
Κύων, a dog, an animal so called.	*Ci, cian,* a dog: plural, *cion* and *cwn.*
Κώθων, a crater; a cup, a rummer.	*Cwthwn, cwthyn,* what throws off, or ejects.
Κώμη, a village; also a street.	*Cyma, cymod, cymmod,* a community.
Κωμητησ, a peasant, a countryman.	*Cymydai,* one of a commune; a neighbour.
Κῶνος, a cone, a figure so called.	*Con,* that ends in a point; *coned,*
Κωναω, to cause to kindle, to kindle.	*Cynneu, cynneuaw,* to kindle, to set on fire.
Κωφοσ, a silly fool; dull; deaf; dumb	*Cyff,* a stock, a stump, a butt, a dolt.

Λ

Λᾶς, λᾶας, a stone, a stone slab.	*Llech,* a flat stone, or a slate.
Λάλεω, to speak; to chat, to talk.	*Lloliaw, llolian,* to chatter, to prate, to chat.
Λάλος, a prattler, or a chatterer.	*Llolyn,* a chatterer, a jabberer, a babbler.
Λαὸσ, λεοσ, the people, or multitude.	*Lliaws,* a multitude, a great many; a mob.
Λάπτω, to lap, or take with the tongue.	*Lleibiaw, lleipiaw, lleipian,* to lick, to lap.
Λαρινὸσ, fat and sweet, plump, agreeable.	*Llerwin,* nice, delicate, or fine.
Λαρινεύω, to fatten, to become fat.	*Llerwi, llerwinaw, llerweiniaw,* to grow nice.
Λαρὸσ, agreeable, sweet, or dulcet.	*Llerw,* nice, smart, delicate; fine; subtile.
Λάσκω, to revile, to calumniate.	*Llesgu,* to be or become weak; to enfeeble.

Λάω, to see; to enjoy, to be pleased.	*Llywu*, to guide, to direct: to steer.
Λαύω, to enjoy, or to feel pleased.	*Llywiaw*, to direct: *llywy*, a paragon.
Λέγω, to say; to enjoin, or to bid.	*Llygu*, to clear: *llug*, a gleam, a glance.
Λέχω, to lie down, to be prostrate.	*Llechu*, to lie close, to squat: to sculk.
Λέσχη, idle chat, tattle or babble.	*Llesga*, *llesgedd*, listlessness; idleness.
Λήγω, to cease, to make an end; to quit.	*Llagu*, to grow slack, loose, or sluggish.
Λήθω, λησω, to lie hid, to sculk.	*Llethu*, to press flat: *llaesu*, to trail.
Λιάζω, to divide, or to separate.	*Llysu*, *lliasu*, to part off, to separate.
Λιμην, a harbour, port, or haven.	*Llifon*, *llion*, a place of flooding.
Λίμνη, a lake, a pool, a mere.	*Llyn*, *llifon*, a lake, a pool, a mere.
Λιτή, a prayer, or a petition.	*Llith*, a lure; a lesson, or a lecture.
Λουτρόν, washings.	*Llwtron*, any liquid dirt, or dregs.
Λοχοσ, an ambush, also a troop.	*Lloches*, a covert, a hiding place.
Λοχαω, to lay an ambuscade.	*Llochi*, *llochiaw*, *lochesu*, to make a covert.
Λύθρον, blood and dust, or grime.	*Llwtron*, *llwtrach*, slimy matter, grime
Λυθροω, to wallow in blood or grime.	*Llutriaw*, to begrime; to form grime.
Λύπη, grief, sorrow, vexation: εν λύπη.	*Llipa*, that is flaccid or flagging.
Λύρα, a lyre, a stringed instrument.	*Llyre*, a tortoise: the shell formed the lyre.
Λυχνοσ, a lamp, a torch, a flambeau.	*Lluch*, *lluchyn*, *llugas*, a gleam of light.

M

Μάκαρ, happy, blessed, fortunate.	*Mygyr*, grand; splendid, glorious.
Μαλάσσω, to mollify, or to soften.	*Mallusaw*, to make soft or lax; to grow soft.
Μαλοσ, tender, soft, or delicate.	*Mall*, *mallus*, soft or lax; insipid; blasted.
Μαμμη, μαμμα, μαμμαια, a grand-mother.	*Mam*, a mother; *mammai*, a matron.
Μανός, rare, thin, fine, or slender.	*Man*, small, fine: *main*, thin, slender.
Μαραινω, to fade, to wither, to decay.	*Merwinaw*, to grow torpid; to benumb.
Μαρνάμαι, to fight, to combat, to battle.	*Murniaw*, *murnofi*, to obstruct; to murder.
Μαχομαι, to fight, to battle, to contend.	*Machu*, *machofi*, to endeavour to secure.
Μάχη, a battle, a fight, a combat.	*Mach*, *machai*, security, that secures
Μεγασ, μεγαλον, great, grand, puissant, big: Διδάσκαλε, ποία εντολὴ μεγάλη ἐν τῷ νομῳ;	*Myg*, *mygawl*, grand; solemn, glorious: *dyddysgolai*, *pa y ddylyed mygolaf yn y nam*?
Μέδω, to command: also μεδέω, μεδεύω.	*Meddu*, to possess, to have command of.
Μεθυ, μεθυοσ, wine, the juice of grapes.	*Medd*, origin of motion; centre: mead
Μεθη, drunkenness, or intoxication.	*Meddw*, drunk; *meddwad*, ebriety.
Μεθυω, to drunk: εμεθύσθησαν: μεθυσαι.	*Meddwi*, to inebriate: *ymfeddwasant*: *meddwasai*.
Μεθυσκω, to make drunk, to intoxicate	*Meddwadu*, to make drunk, to intoxicate.
Μελισσω, to sweeten; to become sweet.	*Melysu*, to sweeten, to become sweet.
Μελαινω, to become black, to blacken.	*Melynu*, to grow yellow, to grow swarthy.

Μελι, *μελιτοσ*, honey, the food of bees.	***Mel***, ***melid***, honey; ***melys***, honeyed, sweet.
Μελιηδεσ, sweet, or dulcet.	***Melaidus***, of the nature of honey.
Μέλισσα, a bee, or gatherer of sweets.	***Melysai***, a honey-bearer: a sweetener.
Μέλλω, to delay, to defer, to put off.	***Malu***, to dally, to fondle; to trifle.
Μέλοσ, melody; verse or song.	***Melawd***, that is sweet, like honey.
Μένοσ, the mind, or intelligent power.	***Menw***, intellect, mind, or soul.
Μένω, to remain; to last, to wait.	***Manu***, to set a place; to impress.
Μέσσ, the middle, or central part.	***Medd***, the origin of motion; a middle.
Μέτρον, measure, that metes things.	***Mydr***, ***mydrai***, ***mydryn***, a metre.
Μινυὸς, small, little, or slender.	***Man***, ***manu***, small, fine, tiny, petty.
Μινύθω, to diminish or to lessen.	***Manaethu***, ***manweiddiaw***, to make fine
Μόλος, battle and noise: also *μῶλος*.	***Moloch***, tumult, uproar, riot, stir.
Μολυνω, to pollute, or to defile.	***Molwynaw***, to spot; to cover with foam.
Μόνος, alone, deserted, or desolate.	***Mynaw***, that is isolated or lonely.
Μονον, one; only, single; singly.	***Mon***, ***monyn***, that is alone: a sulky one.
Μοῦσα, a muse, the power of poetry.	***Mawsai***, a recipient, of sweetness.
Μυδάω, to moulder, to wear away.	***Mwydaw***, to become damp, to sodden.
Μυδαλέοσ, mouldy, musty, stale.	***Mwydiolus***, of a soddening tendency.
Μυδαίνω, to rot, or to putrefy.	***Mwydioni***, to become pulp or pith.
Μυλη, a mill-stone, a grinder.	***Malai***, that grinds or that brays.
Μύρμοσ, *μύρμηξ*, an ant; *μυρμηδον*, an ant-hillock.	***Myr***, ***myrion***, ants: ***mor***, an ant: ***morion***, ants: ***myrfydon***, a mound of ants
Μύρω, to flow, or to run as water.	***Meru***, to drop; to dribble, to distil.
Μωροσ, silly, foolish, or simple.	***Meredig***, being drooping; stupid.

N

Ναίω, *ναίσω*, *ναω*, to dwell, to abide.	***Noddi***, ***noddau***, to harbour; to take refuge.
Ναὸσ, a temple: *ναοσ τῶ θεῶ*. 1 Cor. iii. 17.	***Neuadd***, a hall, a saloon: ***neuadd y Duw***.
Ναὺσ, a ship, or a sailing vessel.	***Nawfai***, ***nofai***, a floating agent.
Νέμω, to divide, or to separate.	***Nammu***, to stigmatize; to except.
Νέοσ, new, novel, or recent.	***Newydd***, new, novel; that is new.
Νέω, to swim, to move on water.	***Nofiaw***, to swim; also to float.
Νησοσ, an island, or an isle.	***Ynys***, an island: ***ynysig***, an islet.
Νικάω, to overcome: *νικα*, overcome.	***Nychu***, to torture; to pine: ***nychu***, cause pain.
Νίφω, to snow, to drop in snow.	***Nyfu***, ***nyfiaw***, ***odi***, ***bwrw eira***, to snow.
Νηθω, to spin, to draw out in threads	***Nyddu***, to spin; to twist, or to writhe.
Νόθοσ, illegitimate, bastard.	***Nwythus***, ***nwydus***, eccentric, freakish.
Νόοσ, the mind, intelligent power.	***Naws***, temperament, disposition.
Νύξ, night.	***Nos***, night: ***noson***, ***noswaith***, a certain night.

O

'O, the article *the*.	***Y***, and ***yr***, the article ***the***.
Oi, pronoun: *οἱ εἶπον*, they said.	***Hwy***, they: ***hwy ebynt***, they said.
Oἴγω, to open, to set open, to lay out.	***Agu***, ***agenu***, to rift; ***agori***, to open.
'Ὅλοσ, a whole, all of a thing, a total.	***Holl***, ***oll***, a whole, or all, a total.
'Ὁμίλεω, to engage.	***Ymaelu***, ***ymaelyd***, to take mutual hold
Oν, pronoun: ὃν καταγγέλλομέν. Col. i. 28.	***Hwn***, this one; whom: ***hwn cydanghelwn***.

Ὄνομα, a name: ηἶ ὄνομα, her name.	*Enw*, a name: *ei henw*, her name.
Ὀξυσ, sharp, quick, ready: sour: ὀξεῖσ οι ποδεσ αὐτων. Rom. iii. 15.	*Awchus*, keen, ardent; greedy: *awchus eu pedos hwynt.*
Οὖν, therefore: πῶ οὖν ἡ καύχησις Rom. iii. 27. Where then the boasting?	*Yna*, there; then; there now! *pa yna y coegedd?* what then the vaunting?
Οὐαι, a woe, or wailing.	*Gwae*, a woe, a wailing, a curse.

Π

Παιω, to strike, to beat, to knock.	*Pwyaw*, to beat, to pummel, to thump
Παλλω, to dart, to throw, or to fling.	*Peiliaw*, to spread out, to radiate.
Παύω, to cease; to rest, to be still.	*Peuaw*, to pause; to hesitate; to pant.
Πέδιλον, a shoe; a sock, a buskin.	*Pedol, pedolan*, a foot-trace; a horse-shoe.
Πιέζω, to press, to squeeze, to crush.	*Pwysaw*, to weigh; to press; to ponder
Πλεκω, to double, to fold, or to plait.	*Plygu*, to double, to fold; to bend.
Πνέω, to blow, to breathe, to respire.	*Peuaw*, to pause; to hesitate; to pant.
Πουσ, ποδοσ, a foot: ὀξεῖσ οἱ ποδεσ αὐτων,	*Pedd, ped*, a foot: *awchus eu pedos hwynt.*
Πρίαμαι, to purchas, to buy: ἐκπριοω, to redeem.	*Prwyaw*, to attain, or to reach: *eckbrwyaw*, to attain from.
Πρὶν, preposition; before: πριν Αβρααμ γενεσθαι, εγώ είμι: before Abraham was, I am.	*Prin*, scarce; scarcely: *prin y genid Abraham, myfi wyf*, scarcely was Abraham produced, I am.
Πρὸ, for, before, instead.	*Prwy*, a tendency forward or onward.
Πωλέω, to sell, to offer for sale.	*Peliaw*, to spread out, to brandish.
Πωλοσ, a colt, or a young horse.	*Ebawl*, a male colt; *eboles*, a she colt.

Ρ

Ῥαδιοσ, easy, facile, of free course.	*Rhwydd, rhwyddus*, facile, easy of progress.
Ῥασσω, to dash against, or to rush.	*Rhysiaw*, to move violently, to rush.
Ῥέγχω, to snore, or to breathe hard.	*Rhochi*, to make a rough noise; to grunt.
Ῥέω, to flow: to spread, to scatter.	*Rheu*, to move; to be active; to run.
Ῥέω, to speak; to tell, or to relate.	*Rhuaw*, to cry aloud, to roar; to chatter.
Ῥιζα, a root, or a radix.	*Rhadd*, that advances, or proceeds onward.
Ῥιν, a nose; as of a man or beast.	*Rhyn*, that stretches out; a point, a cape.
Ῥοδανὸσ, running, or swiftly moving.	*Rhodiannus*, coursing; *rhediannus*, running.
Ῥουσ, a stream, or a current.	*Rhawd*, a course, a way, a rout; a race.

Σ

Σὰρξ, the flesh, the body.	*Sarch*, what covers; also gear, harness
Σκόλοψ, a stake, post, or pale.	*Ysgolp*, a sharp pointed spar or stake
Σκοτοσ, darkness, obscurity.	*Ysgawd*, that rises over; a shade.
Σκοτοω, σκοτιζω, σκοταζω, to darken.	*Ysgodi, ysgodusaw, ysgodiadu*, to shade
Σκύβαλον, dung, filth, or rubbish.	*Ysgubellion*, or *ysgubion*, sweepings, refuse.
Σκυβαλιζω, to cast out filth or refuse.	*Ysgubellu, ysgubaw*, to sweep, to use a broom

Σταυρος, a cross; a gallows.	*Ystwyrai*, that writhes: a stretcher.
Στήλη, a pillar: στύλος: στηλαι.	*Ystawl*, a stem; a stool: *ystolion*, pinnacles.
Στομα, στοματος, the mouth.	*Ystumai*, the organ of shaping or turning.

T

Ταλαντον, a talent; scales; weight.	*Tawl*, *toliant*, a cast: *mantawl*, a balance.
Τασσω, to order, or to arrange.	*Tywysaw*, to lead, or to conduct.
Ταῦρος, a bull, the male of kine.	*Tarw*, that strikes or bursts through; a bull.
Ταχὺς, quick: ταχὺ, quickly.	*Toc*, that is short or quick; shortly.
Τείνω, to stretch, or to extend.	*Taenu*, to spread, to extend, or stretch out.
Τείρω, to beat; to vex, or to afflict.	*Taraw*, to strike; to hit; to affect.
Τελαμὼν, a strap, or a thong.	*Telamwyn*, a stretch-defence or band
Τέλος, the end, or termination.	*Telad*, a straining out or to a verge.
Τελέω, to finish, to terminate.	*Telu*, to put on a stretch; to extend out.
Τέμνω, to cut, to cleave, to break down	*Timynu*, to break into small bits.
Τερέω, to bore through, to perforate.	*Trwyaw*, to bore through, to pass through.
Τιτθὸς, the breast, or the nipple.	*Teth*, a teat; a nipple, a dug; a breast
Τιθὴ, τιθηνη, a nurse.	*Tethai*, *tethenai*, that has a teat.
Τερην, tender, delicate, or soft.	*Tirion*, pleasant, tender, or genial.
Τιμάω, τίω, to honour, to respect.	*Tumiaw*, to make a bend: *tywyaw*, to order.
Τραχὺς, rough, harsh, or rugged.	*Trwch*, a cut; cutting; rough, harsh
Τρεῖς, τρία, three; τρίτος, third.	*Tri*, three; *trifed*, *trydydd*, third.
Τρέχω, to run, to race, to strive in a race.	*Trechu*, to surpass, to overcome, to master.
Τρίπλαξ, τριπλακα, triple, three-fold.	*Triphlyg*, threefold, or triple.
Τρύω, to break, to tear; to push, to thrust.	*Trwyaw*, to penetrate: *tori*, to break
Τύμβος, a tomb, a tumulus.	*Tom*, *tomen*, a mound, or heap; a tumulus.
Τύπος, a type, figure, form, likeness.	*Tob*, a parallel state, a type, a like.
Τυφλὸς, blind, deprived of sight.	*Tywyll*, dark, obscure: *dall*, blind.
Τυφλόω, to blind, to deprive of sight.	*Tywyllu*, to darken: *dallu*, to blind.

Υ

Ὕδω, to sing, to make melody.	*Hudaw*, to allure, to fascinate.
Ὑμὴν, a covering, a membrane.	*Hufen*, the top formed upon liquids; cream.

Φ

Φάω, to shine, to glitter, to illume.	*Ffawu*, to render radiant or glorious
Φάνος, light; splendour; sunshine.	*Ffawdd*, radiation, splendour.
Φέρβω, to pasture, to depasture; to feed.	*Porfau*, to pasture, to depasture.
Φορβη, φορβεια, pasture, or grass.	*Porfa*, pasture, a grazing place.
Φεύγω, φύγω, to shun, or to avoid.	*Ffoi*, to flee, to run away, to retreat.
Φυγας, a fugitive; a vagrant.	*Ffoadai*, a fugitive, or a vagrant.
Φλάω, to smash, to break.	*Ffławu*, to shiver, to splinter, to flaw
Φλέγω, φλεγεθω, to burn, to blaze.	*Ffaglu*, *ffaglethu*, to flame, to blaze
Φλυω, φίω, to trifle, to act idly.	*Ffleuaw*, to radiate: *ffuaw*, to seem.

Φρέαρ, a well ; a ditch.	*Ffrewer*, a ditch : *ffrewad*, a gushing.
Φρὶξ, the roaring of the sea.	*Ffrwch*, *ffroch*, a violent gust ; a storm.
Φονὴ, voice ; report, noise or din.	*Ffwn*, respiration, breath ; a puff ; a sigh.
Φὼρ, a thief ; a spy, or a prying one.	*Ffwyr*, a violent drive or chase : assault.

X

Χαίρω, to rejoice, or to be glad.	*Chwarae*, to play, to sport ; to be merry
Χαλάω, to loosen, or to relax.	*Chwalu*, to spread, to disperse, to separate.
Χαρίσ, grace, favour ; love, kindness.	*Cariad*, love, affection, or kindness.
Χθὲσ yesterday, or the day past.	*Echdoe*, the day before yesterday ; *doe*, yesterday.
Χολὴ, choler, bile, or gall.	*Caul*, a maw ; chyle ; rennet ; curd.
Χορὸσ, a choir, a ball, a rout, or assembly.	*Cor*, a circle, a round ; a crib ; a choir.
Χρόνοσ, time, space, or season.	*Cronawd*, a state or act of revolving.

Ω

Ὠθέω, to push, to thrust, or to press	*Gwthiaw*, to push, to thrust ; to obtrude.
Ὠλένη, the elbow, or bend of the arm	*Elin*, the elbow, the bend of the arm.
Ὠμὸσ, crude, raw, undigested.	*Of*, uncombined ; crude, raw, fresh.
Ὠὸν, ὤιον, also ὤιον, an egg.	*Wy*, *wyan*, and *wyyn*, an egg.
Ὥρα, time, or age ; an hour.	*Awr*, an hour ; time or season.
Ὠρυω, to howl, to cry as a dog.	*Gawru*, to howl, to scream ; to shout

---

On the Affinities of the Latin and Welsh.

Those who form systems from general premises, without being duly acquainted with the characteristic features of their various component parts, would not hesitate to assert, that a considerable portion of the Welsh tongue must necessarily be derived from the Latin, in consequence of the dominion held by the Romans over Britain, for about five hundred years. What impression might have been produced upon the dialect of the Lloegrian Britons by such an intimate connexion with foreigners, it would be difficult, at this time, to determine, as the peculiar characteristic of that dialect cannot be traced, from its having been successively blended with the Saxon, the Danish, and the Norman, so as to have gradually formed the present English tongue. But, in respect to Wales, it might be urged as an argument of great weight, that the proportionate intercourse of the Romans there, must have been of too insignificant extent, to produce any change in the dialect of the natives, as none has been subsequently effected by the far more general intercourse of the English, holding a sovereignty there, and in every way a closer connexion, and through a much longer period of time. All the influence, that the Roman domination had upon our language, was the giving of currency to a few score words ; and the sway of the English has effected about as much : yet the strange words, whether from one nation or the other, have not been naturalized in the Welsh, as they still plainly discover their alien origin.

However, it is not by any means intended here to claim the smallest advantage from such argumentative objections, but, on the contrary, to state the important fact, that the Welsh language contains thousands of words in common with the Latin; yet these words can be satisfactorily proved not to have been borrowed by the Welsh from the Romans; neither could the latter people be indebted to the Britons for them. Therefore, the affinity, existing between the two languages, must be attributed to a common origin of such words, and preserved in each from a period anterior to the commencement of the history of either nation.

The Latin is, to a very considerable degree, a mixed language, being gradually formed by adventitious circumstances, whereby the original basis of its structure has been so obscured, that scarcely any of the words therein are regularly reducible to those primary elements, or radices, within itself, which are essentially the characteristics of the Welsh and other unmixed languages. Had not the Welsh a systematic combination of its words, yielding to an obvious and certain analysis, it would then stand only on equal terms with the Latin, with respect to words common to both languages; and in that case there would be no certain criterion, by which the claim of originality to such words could be awarded to either of them. This point may be illustrated by a few of those common words, traced to their primary elements in the Welsh, and which are not capable of being so analysed in the Latin language. The following are obvious proofs :—

Latin words.	*Welsh words.*
Catena	Cadwen, a chain
Caterva	Cattyrfa
Turba	Tyrfa
Garrio	Geiriaw
Garrulus	Geiriolus.

These words are precisely of the same signification in both languages; but it is only in the Welsh that they can be resolved to their primary elements.

The feminine noun *cadwen* is in the masculine form *cadwyn*; the *en*, in the former, and *yn*, in the latter, being general terminations for all similar nouns. Taking away these terminations, we have *cadw*, a keeping, a guarding, a preserving in safe custody; also, to keep, to guard, to have in custody; and *cadw* is derived from *cad*, a striving to take; also a conflict, or a battle; the simple elements forming *cad* being *ca* and *ad*. The plurals, most commonly used, out of several, of *cadwen* and *cadwyn*, are *cadweni* *cadwenau*, *cadwyni*, and *cadwynau*.

The *caterva* is a very remarkable word, from its being so written in the Latin; because that one of its parts, *terva*, is plainly the Welsh word *tyrva*, which used to be written *terva*, before the *y* was introduced into our alphabet; and which is precisely of the same import as *turba*. The Welsh word is nearly of the same import, whether written *catyrva* or *cattyrva*,—the first from *ca* and *tyrva*, and the other from *cad* and *tyrva*,—and implies a troop of defence and a troop of conflict: *cattyrva*, in ancient numeration, expressed 100, 000. The meaning of *cad*, a conflict, is literally an aptitude or effort to keep, having *ca* and *ad* for its elements. The word *tyrva* is partly explained already; but its structure may be farther defined. *Twr* implies a heap, a crowd, an aggregate, or accumulation; and thence comes *twrv*, a multitudinous noise, or tumult, and often used for *taran*, thunder. The *w* of all monosyllables becomes *y*, when such words are extended; and thus *twrv* becomes *tyrva*. The *a* postfixed gives the idea of continuity, accumulation, or collection; and such words are used both as nouns and verbs.

The Welsh primitive *gair*, a word, by a regular inflection forms the verb *geiriaw*, to word, to express words, to form words, to use words. From *gair*, in the same manner, is formed the adnoun *geiriawl*, wordy, verbose, belonging to a word; and from *geiriawl* is formed *geiriolus*, apt to be wordy, full of words, or garrulous.

Some thousand Latin compound words have their similitudes in the Welsh with respect to structure and signification; and all to be analyzed, like the foregoing examples, in the latter language, thus proving, that they could not have been borrowed from the former, but that such words exist in both languages from one common origin.

CONCLUSION.

Notwithstanding all that has been hitherto written, the origin and affinities of the several nations of Europe remain in great obscurity: and the principal cause for this, where we have not the light of history to guide us, must be attributed to the want of a proper examination of the languages of those nations, so as to discover the approximate relation existing between some of them, and the contrary characters of other. As a proof of how little is generally and correctly known in respect to this subject, we need only point out that there are remnants of an original population still existing in France, in Flanders, in Germany, in two parts of Britain, and in Ireland, and who speak their ancient and common language, under diversities of dialects, and which is identified with the Sclavonic; and these remnants of a primitive people are the Bretons, the Walloons, the Wendi, the Welsh, and the Gwydhelians of Scotland and Ireland. Historians have not used an appropriate and generic name for the common language of the people here mentioned; for the several appellations mostly in use, except the Sclavonic, which is not very ancient, of Gallic, and Celtic, are only relevant to circumstances of locality: such as denote a dwelling in open regions, or in woods and forests. There is one name, however, which is descriptive of a generic character, and still preserved by one remnant of those nations, and used to designate itself, and also applied to it nationally, from the remotest periods of history. This appellation is used by the Welsh, who call themselves CYMMRY; and which was written *Cimmerioi*, *Cimmerii*, and *Cimbri*, by the Greeks and Romans.

N.B. *The preceding Notes, with the Initials* H.P. *are by the late Mr. Humphreys Parry; and were added by him to an Edition of this Treatise published by the Cymmrodorion Society.*

THOMAS GEE, PRINTER, DENBIGH.

SD - #0005 - 200821 - C0 - 229/152/40 - PB - 9780282214166